BECKETT WRESTLING ALMANAC

BECKETT - THE #1 AUTHORITY ON COLLECTIBLES

THE HOBBY'S MOST RELIABLE
AND RELIED UPON SOURCE ™

Founder: Dr. James Beckett III
Edited by Matt Bible and the Price Guide Staff of Beckett Collectibles LLC

BECKETT is a registered trademark of BECKETT COLLECTIBLES LLC, PLANO, TEXAS
Manufactured in the United States of America | Published by Beckett Collectibles LLC

BECKETT

Beckett Collectibles LLC
2700 Summit Ave, Ste 100, Plano, TX 75074
(866) 287-9383 • beckett.com

First Printing
ISBN: 978-1-953801-14-2

BECKETT WRESTLING ALMANAC

NUMBER 6
BECKETT - THE #1 AUTHORITY ON COLLECTIBLES

EDITORIAL
Mike Payne - **Editorial Director**
Eric Knagg - **Lead Graphic Designer**

COLLECTIBLES DATA PUBLISHING
Brian Fleischer
Manager | Sr. Market Analyst
Daniel Moscoso - **Digital Studio**
Matt Bible, Jeff Camay, Steven Dalton, Justin Grunert, Rex Pastrana, Kristian Redulla, Chris Roberts, Adrian Saba, Angelou Talle, Bryl Trinidad, Sam Zimmer - **Price Guide Staff**

ADVERTISING
Alex Soriano - **Advertising Sales Executive**
alex@beckett.com
619.392.5299

BECKETT GRADING SALES/SHOW STAFF
Dallas Office
2700 Summit Ave, Ste 100, Plano, TX 75074
Aram Munoz - **Senior Sales Executive**
amunoz@beckett.com

Grading and Auth Customer Service
customerservice@beckett.com

New York Office
484 White Plains Rd, 2nd Floor, Eastchester, N.Y. 10709
Charles Stabile - **Northeast Regional Sales Manager**
cstabile@beckett.com
914.268.0533

Asia Office
Seoul, Korea
Dongwoon Lee - **Asia/Pacific Sales Manager**
dongwoonl@beckett.com
Cell +82.10.6826.6868

OPERATIONS
Alberto Chavez - **Sr. Logistics & Facilities Manager**

EDITORIAL, PRODUCTION & SALES OFFICE
2700 Summit Ave, Ste 100, Plano, TX 75074
972.991.6657 www.beckett.com

CUSTOMER SERVICE
Beckett Collectibles LLC
2700 Summit Ave, Ste 100, Plano, TX 75074
Subscriptions, address changes, renewals, missing or damaged copies - 866.287.9383

Foreign inquires
subscriptions@beckett.com

Price Guide Inquiries
customerservice@beckett.com
866.287.9383
Back Issues beckettmedia.com
Books, Merchandise, Reprints 496.830.3996 OPT 7
Dealer Sales 496.830.3996 OPT 7 dealers@beckett.com

BECKETT

Beckett Collectibles LLC
Kevin Isaacson - **CEO**

COVER FIGURES: PHOTOGRAPHED BY DANIEL MOSCOSO

CONTENTS

BECKETT WRESTLING ALMANAC - NUMBER 6

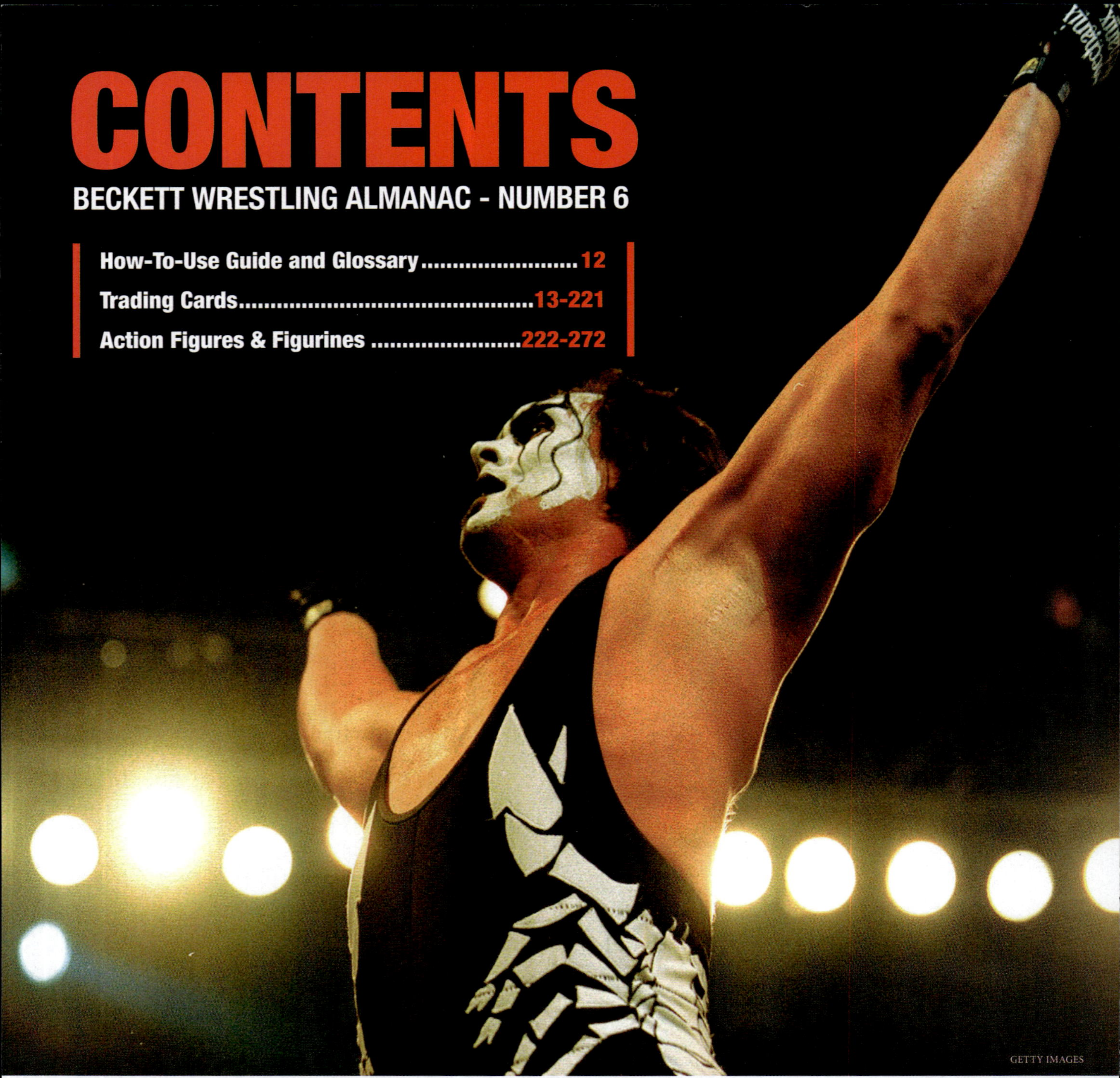

GETTY IMAGES

ABOUT THE AUTHOR

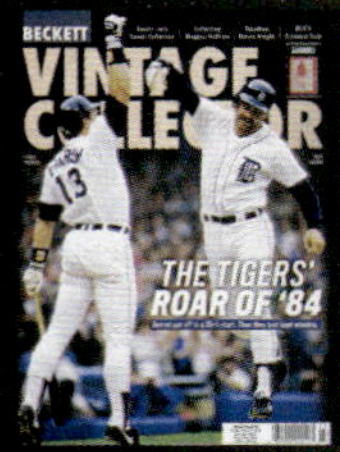

Based in Dallas, Beckett Collectibles LLC is the leading publisher of sports and specialty market collectible products in the U.S. Beckett operates Beckett.com and is the premier publisher of monthly sports and entertainment collectibles magazines.

The growth of Beckett Collectibles sports magazines, ***Beckett Baseball, Beckett Basketball, Beckett Football, Beckett Hockey*** and ***Beckett Vintage Collector,*** is another indication of the unprecedented popularity of sports cards. Founded in 1984 by Dr. James Beckett, Beckett sports magazines contain the most extensive and accepted Price Guide, collectible superstar covers, colorful feature articles, the Hot List, tips for beginners, information on errors and varieties, autograph collecting tips and profiles of the sport's hottest stars. Published 12 times a year, ***Beckett Baseball*** is the hobby's largest baseball periodical.

BECKETT WRESTLING ALMANAC

2022-23 TRADING CARD PRODUCTS

1

2023 Panini Prizm WWE

2

2023 Select WWE

3

2023 Upper Deck AEW

4

2022 Upper Deck Allure AEW

5

2023 Revolution WWE

2022-23 TOP AUTOGRAPH SIGNERS

1

MJF

2
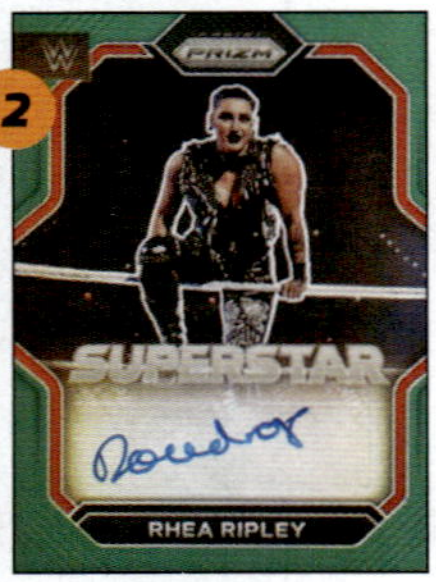

Rhea Ripley

3

Jade Cargill

4

Cody Rhodes

5

Roman Reigns

6

Becky Lynch

7

CM Punk

8

Jamie Hayter

9

Anna Jay

10
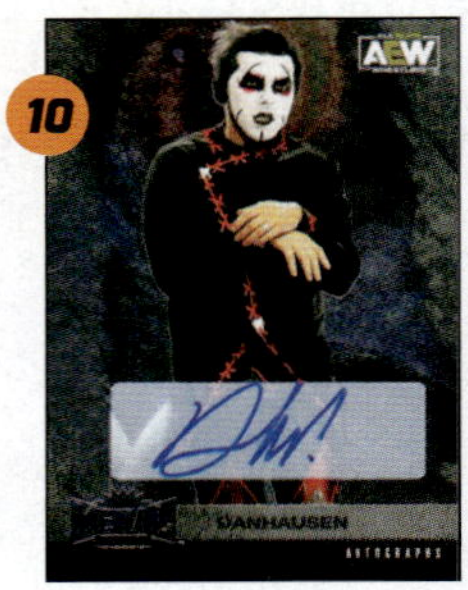

Danhausen

2022-23 INSERT SETS

1

2023 Panini Prizm WWE
Color Blast

2

2022 SkyBox Metal Universe
AEW Precious Metal Gems Red

3

2023 Select WWE
Color Wheel

4

2023 Upper Deck
AEW UD Canvas

5

2022 SkyBox Metal Universe
AEW Jambalaya

BECKETT WRESTLING ALMANAC

2022-23 ROOKIE CARDS

1

2022 Upper Deck Allure AEW #66 Skye Blue

2

2022 SkyBox Metal Universe AEW #96 Jamie Hayter

3

2023 Upper Deck AEW #64 "Switchblade" Jay White

4

2022 SkyBox Metal Universe AEW #98 HOOK

5

2022 Upper Deck Allure AEW #11 Julia Hart

6

2022 Upper Deck Allure AEW #30 Konosuke Takeshita

7

2022 SkyBox Metal Universe AEW #92 Brian Pillman Jr.

8

2023 Select WWE #335 Arianna Grace

9

2022 SkyBox Metal Universe AEW #83 Danhausen

10

2022 SkyBox Metal Universe AEW #99 Daniel Garcia

ACTION FIGURES

1

2023 Mattel WWE Defining Moments Exclusives Cody Rhodes

2

2023 Mattel WWE Defining Moments Exclusives Mankind

3

2023 Mattel WWE Elite Collection Series 102 Gunther

4

2024 Mattel WWE Elite Collection Series 105 Dominik Mysterio

5

2023 Jazwares AEW Exclusives Danhausen (Very Nice Very Evil)

6

2023 Mattel WWE Elite Collection Series 104 Solo Sikoa

7

2023 Jazwares AEW Unmatched Series 6 Ruby Soho

8

2023 Mattel WWE Ultimate Edition Series 17 Seth Rollins

9

2023 Mattel WWE Elite Collection Series 101 Mr. America

10

2024 Mattel WWE Series 141 LA Knight

TOP 5 STING CARDS

1988 Wonderama NWA #17 RC

1995 CARDZ WCW Main Event #4

2021 Upper Deck AEW #81

1998 Topps WCW/nWo Retail Stickers #S4

2016 Topps Heritage WWE #36

TOP 5 STING AUTOGRAPHS

1999 Topps WCW/nWo Nitro Authentic Signatures #NNO

2020 Topps Transcendent Bat Relic Autographs #RCST

2016 Topps WWE Undisputed Autographs #UAST

2021 Upper Deck AEW Autographs #81 B

2015 Topps WWE Sting Tribute Autographs #NNO

TOP 10 STING ACTION FIGURES

1991 Galoob WCW Superstars Series 1 Orange Tights

2015 Mattel WWE Elite Collection Defining Moments

1991 Galoob WCW Superstars UK

2016 WWE Elite Collection Exclusives Wolfpac RSC

2011 Jakks Pacific TNA Legends of the Ring RSC American Sting Exclusive

2010 Jakks Pacific TNA Deluxe Impact Exclusives (Joker)

2018 Mattel WWE Elite Collection Series 62 (Great American Bash Attire)

2019 Mattel Masters of the WWE Universe Series 1

2022 AEW Unmatched Collection Series 2/5,000 CHASE

2016 Mattel WWE Mutants

IN MEMORIAM

ADRIAN STREET

BRAY WYATT

BUSHWHACKER BUTCH

DARREN DROZDOV

IRON SHEIK

JOYCE GRABLE

KILLER KHAN

MANTAUR

SUPERSTAR BILLY GRAHAM

TERRY FUNK

2024 Beckett® Wrestling Almanac Collectibles Price Guide

The World's Most-Trusted Source in Collecting

Welcome to the Beckett® Wrestling Almanac. This 6th edition is an enhanced and expanded volume with the addition of new releases, updated prices, and changes to older listings. The Beckett® Wrestling Almanac will do what no other publication has done -- give you the most complete and comprehensive collectible listings possible. The prices were added to the checklists just prior to printing and reflect not the author's opinions or desires, but the going retail prices for each collectible, based on the marketplace such as conventions and shows, hobby shops, online trading, auction results and other first-hand reports of realized sales.

What is the best price guide available on the market today? Of course sellers will prefer the price guide with the highest prices, while buyers will naturally prefer the one with the lower prices. Accuracy, however, is the true test. Compared to other price guides, The Beckett® Wrestling Almanac may not always have the highest or lowest values, but the accuracy of both our checklists and pricing – produced with the utmost integrity – will make it the most widely used reference book in the hobby.

LISTINGS AND SECTIONS

Each collection is personal and reflects the individuality of its owner. There are no set rules on how to collect. Since collecting is a hobby or leisure pastime, what you collect, how much you collect, and how much time and money you spend collecting are entirely up to you. The funds you have available for collecting and your own personal taste should determine how you collect.

It is not possible to collect every card and action figure ever produced. Therefore, beginners, as well as intermediate and advanced collectors, usually specialize in some way. One of the reasons this hobby is popular is that individual collectors can define and tailor their collecting methods to match their own tastes.

Many collectors select complete sets from particular years or acquire only certain wrestlers/athletes, while some collectors are only interested in collecting certain figures or autographs.

WHAT'S LISTED

Products listed in the Price Guide typically:

- Are produced by licensed manufacturers
- Are widely available
- Have market activity on single items
- International releases

HOW IT'S LISTED

Unlike regular Beckett® Almanacs, the sort order of this publication is somewhat unique. Like the others, all listings are organized 1) alphabetically then 2) chronologically.

WHAT THE COLUMNS MEAN

The LO and HI columns reflect current retail selling ranges. The HI column on the right generally represents the full retail selling price. The LO column on the left generally represents the lowest price one would expect to find with extensive shopping

GRADING

All cards in the price guide are based on NrMint to Mint condition. Damaged cards are generally sold for 25 to 75 percent of Mint value. Toy prices are based on Mint condition. Toys that are loose (out-of-package) are generally sold for 50 percent of the listed price, but may list for less/more depending on market sales.

CURRENCY

This price guide is intended to reflect the entire North American market. While not all of the cards are produced in the United States, they will reflect the market value in U.S. dollars.

GLOSSARY/LEGEND

Our glossary defines terms most frequently used in the collecting hobby. Some of these terms are common to other types of collecting while others may have several meanings depending on the use and context.

7-11	7-11 Exclusive
AMZ	Amazon Exclusive
ARGO	Argo's Exclusive
BJ	BJ's Exclusive
BL	Big Lots Exclusive
CAN	Issued in Canada
CH	Chase Figure
FB	Flashback
FCE	Fall Convention Exclusive
FHQ	Funko Headquarters Exclusive
FL	Foot Locker Exclusive
FP	First Piece in an Action Figure Line
FYE	fYe Exclusive
GITD	Glow-in-the-Dark
GS	GameStop Exclusive
HILLS	Hills Exclusive
HT	Hot Topic Exclusive
KB	Kay-Bee Toys Exclusive
KM	K-Mart Exclusive
LE	Limited Edition
MA	Mail-Away
MANIA TIX	WrestleMania Ticket Mail-In Exclusive
MEI	Meijer Exclusive
NYC TF	New York City Toy Fair Exclusive
NYCC	New York Comic Con
OL	Internet/Online Exclusive
PROFIG	Profigures.com Exclusive
RTWM21 TOUR	- Road to WrestleMania 21 Tour Giveaway Exclusive
RSC	Ringside Collectibles Exclusive
RSF	Ringside Fest Exclusive
SC	Sam's Club Exclusive
SCE	Summer Convention Exclusive
SDCC	San Diego Comic Con Exclusive
SE	Special Edition
TAR	Target Exclusive
TFM	Toyfare Magazine Exclusive
TRU	Toys R Us Exclusive
UK	Issued in United Kingdom
US	Issued in the United States
V	Vaulted (applies only to Funko products)
WG	Walgreens Exclusive
WM	Walmart Exclusive
WRMS	WrestleMania Shop Exclusive
WWE SZ	WWE Shopzone Exclusive

As with any new publication, we appreciate reader feedback. If you have any questions, concerns, corrections or suggestions, please contact us at: **nonsports@beckett.com**

Trading Cards

1994 Action Packed WWF

COMPLETE SET (42)	20.00	50.00
COMPLETE FACTORY SET (42)	25.00	60.00
UNOPENED BOX (24 PACKS)		
UNOPENED PACK (6 CARDS)		
COLOSSAL CRUSHERS (30-36)		
1 Bam Bam Bigelow	1.25	3.00
2 I.R.S.	.75	2.00
3 Doink the Clown	.40	1.00
4 Diesel RC	3.00	8.00
5 Razor Ramon	.25	.60
6 Ludvig Borga RC	.20	.50
7 Shawn Michaels	.40	1.00
8 Yokozuna	1.25	3.00
9 Head Shrinkers	.20	.50
10 Bushwhackers	.20	.50
11 Bob Backlund	.20	.50
12 Undertaker	5.00	12.00
13 Macho Man Randy Savage	.50	1.25
14 Adam Bomb RC	.20	.50
15 Bret Hit Man Hart	.60	1.50
16 Luna RC	.25	.60
17 1-2-3 Kid RC	1.50	4.00
18 Owen Hart	3.00	8.00
19 Lex Luger	.60	1.50
20 Bastion Booger RC	.20	.50
21 Quebecers	.20	.50
22 Marty Jannetty	.20	.50
23 Freddie Blassie	.25	.60
24 Stenier Brothers	.25	.60
25 Smoking Gunns	.20	.50
26 Andre the Giant	2.00	5.00
27 Paul Bearer	.30	.75
28 M.O.M.	.20	.50
29 Tatanka	.20	.50
30 Yokozuna CC	2.00	5.00
31 Diesel CC	2.00	5.00
32 Adam Bomb CC	.20	.50
33 Bastion Booger CC	.20	.50
34 Earthquake CC	.20	.50
35 Mabel CC RC	.20	.50
36 Ludvig Borga CC	.20	.50
37 Razor Ramon	2.50	6.00
38 Shawn Michaels	2.00	5.00
39 Macho Man Randy Savage	2.00	5.00
40 Bret Hit Man Hart	2.00	5.00
41 Steiner Brothers	.25	.60
42 Undertaker/Paul Bearer CC	4.00	10.00

1994 Action Packed WWF 24 Kt Gold Leaf

COMPLETE SET (6)	25.00	60.00
STATED ODDS 1:24		
1G Razor Ramon	15.00	40.00
2G Shawn Michaels	8.00	20.00
3G Macho Man Randy Savage	6.00	15.00
4G Bret Hit Man Hart	6.00	15.00
5G Steiner Brothers	5.00	12.00
6G Undertaker/Paul Bearer	10.00	25.00

1994 Action Packed WWF Autographed Prototypes

1 Macho Man Randy Savage	500.00	1000.00
2 Undertaker	300.00	600.00

1994 Action Packed WWF Prototypes

COMPLETE SET (2)	3.00	8.00
1 Macho Man Randy Savage	2.00	5.00
2 Undertaker	2.50	6.00

1995 Action Packed WWF

COMPLETE SET (42)	15.00	40.00
COMPLETE FACTORY SET (42)	15.00	40.00
1 Bret Hit Man Hart	.30	.75
2 Undertaker	.75	2.00
3 Razor Ramon	.40	1.00
4 Diesel	.20	.50
5 Heavenly Bodies	.20	.50
6 Doink the Clown	.20	.50
7 Lex Luger	.25	.60
8 Alundra Blayze RC	.50	1.25
9 Yokozuna	.20	.50
10 Bam Bam Bigelow	.25	.60
11 British Bulldog	.25	.60
12 Crush	.20	.50
13 King Kong Bundy	.25	.60
14 Nikolai Volkoff	.20	.50
15 Tatanka	.20	.50
16 Paul Bearer	.30	.75
17 Head Shrinkers	.20	.50
18 Duke the Dumpster RC	.20	.50
19 Dink RC	.20	.50
20 Bushwhackers	.20	.50
21 Diesel	.20	.50
22 Mabel	.20	.50
23 Smoking Gunns	.20	.50
24 Undertaker	1.25	3.00
25 Shawn Michaels DD	.75	2.00
26 Owen Hart DD	.50	1.25
27 Jim The Anvil Neidhart DD	.25	.60
28 Mr. Fuji DD	.20	.50
29 IRS DD	.60	1.50
30 Luna DD	.40	1.00
31 Well Dunn DD	.20	.50
32 Jerry The King Lawler DD RC	.40	1.00
33 Double J Jeff Jarrett DD RC	.25	.60
34 Mr. Bob Backlund DD	.20	.50
35 Bull Nakano DD RC	.20	.50
36 Ted DiBiase DD	.30	.75
37 1-2-3 Kid HFR	.20	.50
38 Shawn Michaels HFR	.40	1.00
39 Adam Bomb HFR	.20	.50
40 Bob Spark Plugg Holly HFR RC	.25	.60
41 Bret "Hit Man" Hart HFR	.40	1.00
42 Bam Bam Bigelow HFR	.25	.60

1995 Action Packed WWF 24 Kt Gold Leaf

COMPLETE SET (12)	30.00	75.00
STATED ODDS 1:96		
G1 Shawn Michaels	6.00	15.00
G2 Owen Hart	6.00	15.00
G3 Jim The Anvil Neidhart	4.00	10.00
G4 Mr. Fuji	4.00	10.00
G5 IRS	4.00	10.00
G6 Luna	5.00	12.00
G7 Well Dunn	3.00	8.00
G8 Jerry The King Lawler	5.00	12.00
G9 Double J Jeff Jarrett	4.00	10.00
G10 Mr. Bob Backlund	4.00	10.00
G11 Bull Nakano	3.00	8.00
G12 Ted DiBiase	5.00	12.00

1995 Action Packed WWF Promos

LT1 Lawrence Taylor WMXI	15.00	40.00
MM1 Diesel	6.00	15.00
MM2 Undertaker	10.00	25.00

2018 All In Series 1

COMPLETE SET (36)	75.00	200.00
1 All In	.60	1.50
2 Cody	4.00	10.00
3 Brandi	2.00	5.00
4 Kenny Omega	8.00	20.00
5 Matt Jackson	6.00	15.00
6 Nick Jackson	6.00	15.00
7 Nick Aldis	1.25	3.00
8 Stephen Amell	2.00	5.00
9 Joey Janela	2.00	5.00
10 Penelope Ford	3.00	8.00
11 Tessa Blanchard	4.00	10.00
12 Kazuchika Okada	2.00	5.00
13 Kota Ibushi	2.00	5.00
14 Penta El Zero M	2.50	6.00
15 Rey Fenix	3.00	8.00
16 El Bandido	.60	1.50
17 Flip Gordon	.60	1.50
18 MJF	25.00	60.00
19 Adam Page	8.00	20.00
20 Joey Ryan	3.00	8.00
21 Rey Mysterio	1.50	4.00
22 Jerry Lynn	.60	1.50
23 Jay Lethal	2.00	5.00
24 Burnard	.60	1.50
25 Briscoe Brothers	5.00	12.00
26 Best Friends	2.00	5.00
27 Chelsea Green	6.00	15.00
28 Britt Baker	15.00	40.00
29 Madison Rayne	2.50	6.00
30 Marty Scurll	.60	1.50
31 SoCal Uncensored	2.00	5.00
32 BTE	.60	1.50
33 Masa	.60	1.50
34 Bury	.60	1.50
35 Cracker Barrel	.60	1.50
36 Checklist	.75	2.00

1999 Artbox WWF MotionCardz

COMPLETE SET (40)	10.00	25.00
1 The Undertaker SM	.40	1.00
2 Stone Cold Steve Austin SM	.50	1.25
3 Kane SM	.40	1.00
4 Kane SM	.40	1.00
5 Road Dogg SM	.40	1.00
6 The Rock SM	.60	1.50
7 Stone Cold Steve Austin SM	.50	1.25
8 The Undertaker SM	.75	2.00
9 The Undertaker/Kane	.40	1.00
10 The Undertaker/Kane	.40	1.00
11 The Undertaker/Kane	.40	1.00
12 The Undertaker/Kane	.40	1.00
13 The Undertaker/Kane	.40	1.00
14 The Undertaker/Kane	.40	1.00
15 The Undertaker/Kane	.40	1.00
16 The Undertaker/Kane	.40	1.00
17 D-Generation X	.40	1.00
18 D-Generation X	.40	1.00
19 D-Generation X	.40	1.00
20 D-Generation X	.40	1.00
21 D-Generation X	.40	1.00
22 D-Generation X	.40	1.00
23 D-Generation X	.40	1.00
24 D-Generation X	.40	1.00
25 The Rock	.60	1.50
26 The Rock	.60	1.50
27 The Rock	.75	2.00
28 The Rock	.75	2.00
29 The Rock	.75	2.00
30 The Rock	.60	1.50
31 The Rock	.60	1.50
32 The Rock	2.00	5.00
33 Stone Cold Steve Austin	.50	1.25
34 Stone Cold Steve Austin	.50	1.25
35 Stone Cold Steve Austin	.50	1.25
36 Stone Cold Steve Austin	.50	1.25
37 Stone Cold Steve Austin	.50	1.25
38 Stone Cold Steve Austin	.50	1.25
39 Stone Cold Steve Austin	.50	1.25
40 Stone Cold Steve Austin	.50	1.25
41 Sable Revealed	5.00	12.00

1999 Artbox WWF MotionCardz Attitudes

COMPLETE SET (4)	8.00	20.00
STATED ODDS 1:12		
AT1 Undertaker	6.00	15.00
AT2 No Holds Barred	1.50	4.00
AT3 Kane	1.25	3.00
AT4 D-Generation X	2.00	5.00

1999 Artbox WWF MotionCardz Temporary Tattooz

COMPLETE SET (8)	6.00	15.00
STATED ODDS 1:1		
WWF11 Stone Cold 3:16 Logo	1.25	3.00
WWF12 Kane	1.00	2.50
WWF13 Undertaker	1.25	3.00
WWF14 Stone Cold Skull Logo	1.25	3.00
WWF15 Stone Cold Skull Logo	1.25	3.00
WWF16 Stone Cold Skull Logo	1.25	3.00
WWF17 Raw Is War Logo	.75	2.00
WWF18 War Zone Logo	.75	2.00

1999 Artbox WWF MotionCardz Promos

P1 Val Venis/Taka Michinoku	4.00	10.00
P2 Undertaker/Road Dogg	5.00	12.00

2001 Artbox WWF Slams! MotionCardz

COMPLETE SET (45)	12.00	30.00
COMPLETE SET W/O SP (40)		
SP 41-44 STATED ODDS 1:12		
SP 45 STATED ODDS 1:240		
1 Test	.25	.60
2 Rikishi vs. Val Venis	.25	.60
3 The Undertaker vs. HHH FM	.75	2.00
4 Bradshaw vs. Edge FM	.40	1.00
5 Trish Stratus FM	6.00	15.00
6 HHH vs. Chris Jericho	.60	1.50
7 The Rock vs. Chris Benoit	1.00	2.50
8 Too Cool FM	.25	.60
9 Road Dogg vs. Chris Jericho FM	.40	1.00
10 Bradshaw vs. Edge	.40	1.00
11 The Rock FM	2.50	6.00
12 D-Von & Buh-Buh Ray vs. Edge	.30	.75
13 Buh-Buh Ray Dudley vs. Christian	.40	1.00
14 Trish vs. Lita FM	1.00	2.50
15 Rikishi vs. Val Venis	.25	.60
16 Steve Blackman	.15	.40
17 Steve Blackman vs. Crash Holly	.15	.40
18 Kurt Angle vs. The Undertaker	.75	2.00
19 The Undertaker vs. HHH	.75	2.00
20 Lita vs. Test	.75	2.00
21 Edge and Christian vs. Kane	.40	1.00
22 Bob Hardcore Holly vs. Kurt Angle	.40	1.00
23 Buh-Buh Ray vs. Road Dogg	.25	.60
24 X-Pac vs. Buh-Buh Ray Dudley	.25	.60
25 Commissioner Foley FM	.60	1.50
26 Faarooq vs. X-Pac	.25	.60
27 X-Pac vs. Faarooq	.25	.60
28 Chyna vs. Edge	.40	1.00
29 Buh-Buh Ray Dudley vs. Edge	.30	.75
30 Hardyz vs. Dudley Boyz	.40	1.00
31 Steve Austin vs. Mr. Ass #1	1.00	2.50
32 The Rock	1.00	2.50

33 Stephanie vs. Buh-Buh Ray Dudley	.75	2.00
34 The Rock vs. Shane McMahon	2.50	6.00
35 Mankind vs. Prince Albert FM	.60	1.50
36 Grandmaster Sexay vs. Test FM	.25	.60
37 Rock & Mick Foley vs. Chris Benoit	1.00	2.50
38 Chris Benoit vs. Eddie Guerrero	.40	1.00
39 Edge vs. Buh-Buh Ray Dudley	.30	.75
40 Val Venis vs. Rikishi	.25	.60
41 Kurt Angle/Hardcore Holly SP	1.00	2.50
42 Kane vs. Kurt Angle SP	1.00	2.50
43 Steve Blackman/Shano Mac SP	1.00	2.50
44 Matt Hardy SP	1.00	2.50
45 The Godfather SP		

1998 Artbox WWF Super-Size Stickers

COMPLETE SET (12)	12.00	30.00
NNO Austin 3:16	2.50	6.00
NNO D-Generation X	1.25	3.00
NNO D-Generation X LOGO	1.25	3.00
NNO Kane LOGO	1.00	2.50
NNO Ken Shamrock	1.00	2.50
NNO Stone Cold Steve Austin	2.50	6.00
NNO Stone Cold Steve Austin	2.50	6.00
NNO Stone Cold Steve Austin	2.50	6.00
NNO Stone Cold Steve Austin Skull LOGO	2.50	6.00
NNO Stone Cold University Class of 3:16	2.50	6.00
NNO Undertaker	2.00	5.00
NNO Whoop-Ass 101	2.50	6.00

2001 Authentic Images WWF 24K Gold

NNO Hunter Hearst Helmsley
NNO Kurt Angle
NNO Stone Cold Steve Austin

1999 Authentic Images WWF 24K Gold Signature Series

1 The Rock	20.00	50.00
2 Sable	12.00	30.00
3 Stone Cold Steve Austin	25.00	60.00
4 Undertaker	20.00	50.00

2011 Bondy Fiesta WWE Bubble Gum Stickers

1 Tiffany	.30	.75
2 Rosa Mendes	.50	1.25
3 Undertaker	1.50	4.00
4 Caylen Croft		
5 Rey Mysterio	.75	2.00
6 Kofi Kingston	.30	.75
7 JTG	.30	.75
8 Shad	.30	.75
9 Tyler Reks	.30	.75
10 Tyson Kidd	.30	.75
11 Triple H	1.25	3.00
12 William Regal	.50	1.25
13 Yoshi Tatsu	.30	.75
14 Sheamus	.50	1.25
15 Wade Barrett	.30	.75
16 Vladimir Kozlov	.50	1.25
17 Melina	1.25	3.00

2009 Bondy Fiesta WWE RAW Bubble Gum Stickers

1 John Cena	2.00	5.00
2 Cody Rhodes	.30	.75
3 Mark Henry	.50	1.25
4 Festus	.30	.75
5 Santino Marella	.30	.75
6 Hacksaw Jim Duggan	.40	1.00
7 Chavo Guerrero	.50	1.25
8 Beth Phoenix	1.50	4.00
9 Jack Swagger	.30	.75
10 Maryse	.75	2.00
11 Randy Orton	.75	2.00
12 Mickie James	1.50	4.00
13 Gail Kim	.75	2.00
14 Jillian	1.25	3.00
15 Kofi Kingston	.30	.75
16 Batista	1.25	3.00
17 Alicia Fox	.50	1.25
18 Primo	.30	.75
19 Hornswoggle	.50	1.25
20 Carlito	.75	2.00
21 Big Show	.75	2.00
22 Evan Bourne	.30	.75
23 Shawn Michaels	2.00	5.00
24 Kelly Kelly	1.25	3.00
25 The Miz	.50	1.25

2009 Bondy Fiesta WWE SmackDown Bubble Gum Stickers

1 Rey Mysterio	.75	2.00
2 David Hart Smith	.30	.75
3 Funaki	.30	.75
4 Edge	1.25	3.00
5 Curt Hawkins	.30	.75
6 Rey Mysterio	.75	2.00
7 Dolph Ziggler	.50	1.25
8 Charlie Haas	.30	.75
9 Tyson Kidd	.30	.75
10 Michelle McCool	1.25	3.00
11 Jimmy Wang Yang	.30	.75
12 CM Punk	.50	1.25
13 Chris Jericho	.75	2.00
14 JTG	.30	.75
15 Matt Hardy	1.25	3.00
16 Layla	.75	2.00
17 Undertaker	1.50	4.00
18 Shad	.30	.75
19 Maria	1.25	3.00
20 Melina	1.25	3.00
21 Finlay	.50	1.25
22 R-Truth	.30	.75
23 Natalya	1.25	3.00
24 Mike Knox	.30	.75
25 Randy Orton	.75	2.00
26 Big Show	.75	2.00
27 Eve	1.25	3.00
28 Beth Phoenix	1.50	4.00

1999 Bungeez WWF Medallions

1 B.A. Billy Gunn	.60	1.50
2 Chyna	.50	1.25
3 Cactus Jack	.75	2.00
4 Al Snow with Head	.40	1.00
5 D'Lo Brown	.30	.75
6 Big Boss Man	.30	.75
7 WWF LOGO	.30	.75
8 Ken Shamrock	.40	1.00
9 Edge	.75	2.00
10 Val Venis	.40	1.00
11 The Godfather	.50	1.25
12 Marc Mero	.40	1.00
13 The New Age Outlaws	.60	1.50
14 Undertaker	1.50	4.00
15 Mankind	.75	2.00
16 Brothers from the Darkside	1.50	4.00
17 Kane	.60	1.50
18 Kurrgan	.30	.75
19 The Godfather	.50	1.25
20 X-Pac	.60	1.50
21 Mark Henry	.40	1.00
22 Darren Drozdov	.30	.75
23 Paul Bearer	.40	1.00
24 Chyna	.50	1.25
25 Sable	.60	1.50
26 Sable	.60	1.50
27 The Oddities	.30	.75
28 Stone Cold Steve Austin	2.00	5.00
29 Stone Cold Steve Austin	2.00	5.00
30 Goldust	.60	1.50
31 Headbangers	.30	.75
32 Tiger Ali	.30	.75
33 Too Much	.30	.75
34 Triple H	.75	2.00
35 Kane	.60	1.50
36 The Rock	2.00	5.00
37 Christina	.60	1.50
38 The Rock	2.00	5.00
39 Jacqueline	.30	.75
40 Darren Drozdov	.30	.75
41 D-Generation X	1.00	2.50
42 X-Pac	.60	1.50
43 Gangrel	.30	.75
44 The Rock	2.00	5.00
45 Sable	.60	1.50
46 Triple H & Chyna	.75	2.00
47 Stone Cold Steve Austin	2.00	5.00
48 Triple H	.75	2.00
49 Jacqueline	.30	.75
50 Mankind	.75	2.00
51 Legion of Doom 2000	.75	2.00
52 Val Venis	.40	1.00
53 Undertaker	1.50	4.00
54 Ken Shamrock	.40	1.00

1999 Candy Planet WWF Poster Puzzle Cards

NNO Kane	.60	1.50
NNO The Rock	2.00	5.00
NNO Sable	.60	1.50
NNO Stone Cold Steve Austin	2.00	5.00
NNO The Undertaker	1.50	4.00

1997 Cardinal WWF Trivia Game Cards Series 1

COMPLETE SET (30)	200.00	400.00
1 Stone Cold Steve Austin	60.00	120.00
2 Justin Bradshaw	2.50	6.00
3 Brakus	2.00	5.00
4 British Bulldog	3.00	8.00
5 Crush	1.50	4.00
6 Diesel	2.00	5.00
7 Faarooq	1.50	4.00
8 Flash Funk	1.25	3.00
9 Doug Furnas	1.25	3.00
10 Henry Godwinn	1.25	3.00
11 Phineas Godwinn	1.25	3.00
12 The Goon	1.25	3.00
13 Bret Hit Man Hart	5.00	12.00
14 Owen Hart	3.00	8.00
15 Hunter Hearst-Helmsley	15.00	40.00
16 Bob Holly	2.00	5.00
17 Goldust	2.50	6.00
18 Ahmed Johnson	1.50	4.00
19 Philip LaFon	1.25	3.00
20 Jerry Lawler	2.00	5.00
21 Rocky Maivia	150.00	300.00
22 Mankind	4.00	10.00
23 Marc Mero	1.25	3.00
24 Shawn Michaels	3.00	8.00
25 Aldo Montoya	1.25	3.00
26 Papa Shango	1.25	3.00
27 Sycho Sid	2.00	5.00
28 The Sultan	1.25	3.00
29 Undertaker	10.00	25.00
30 Vader	2.00	5.00

2001 Cardinal WWF Trivia Game Cards Series 3

NNO Al Snow	1.50	4.00
NNO APA	1.50	4.00
NNO The Big Show	2.00	5.00
NNO Chris Benoit		
NNO Chris Jericho		
NNO Chyna	15.00	40.00
NNO Debra		
NNO Dudley Boyz	1.50	4.00
NNO Edge & Christian	1.50	4.00
NNO Hardy Boyz	3.00	8.00
NNO Kane		
NNO K-Kwik		
NNO Kurt Angle	10.00	25.00
NNO Lita	15.00	40.00
NNO Perry Saturn w/Terri		
NNO Rhyno		
NNO Rikishi		
NNO The Rock	20.00	50.00
NNO RTC		
NNO Steve Blackman	1.50	4.00
NNO Stone Cold Steve Austin	10.00	25.00
NNO Tazz		
NNO Test		
NNO Too Cool		
NNO Triple H w/Stephanie McMahon-Helmsley		
NNO Trish Stratus	25.00	60.00
NNO Undertaker	8.00	20.00
NNO Vince McMahon	4.00	10.00
NNO William Regal	1.50	4.00
NNO X-Pac	1.50	4.00

1995 CARDZ WCW Main Event

COMPLETE SET (100)	30.00	75.00
UNOPENED BOX (36 PACKS)	300.00	500.00
UNOPENED PACK (8 CARDS)	8.00	15.00
1 Wild Cat Willie	.20	.50
2 Hulk Hogan	2.00	5.00
3 Ric Flair	.30	.75
4 Sting	.25	.60
5 Macho Man Randy Savage	.20	.50
6 Frank Andersson RC	.10	.25
7 Marcus Bagwell RC	1.00	2.50
8 The Patriot RC	.10	.25
9 Paul Roma	.10	.25
10 Paul Orndorff	.12	.30
11 Blacktop Bully	.10	.25
12 Bobby Eaton	.10	.25
13 Diamond Dallas Page	.25	.60
14 Meng	.10	.25
15 Bunkhouse Buck RC	.10	.25
16 Booker T RC	8.00	20.00
17 Stevie Ray RC	.10	.25
18 Brad Armstrong	.10	.25
19 Arn Anderson	.12	.30
20 Lord Steven Regal RC	.75	2.00
21 Johnny B. Badd	.10	.25
22 Flyin Brian	.30	.75
23 Big Bubba	.10	.25
24 Dustin Rhodes	.12	.30
25 Jerry Sags	.10	.25
26 Brian Knobs	.10	.25
27 Kevin Sullivan	.10	.25
28 Vader	.12	.30
29 Stunning Steve Austin RC	10.00	25.00
30 Alex Wright RC	.10	.25
31 Avalanche	.10	.25
32 Butcher	.10	.25
33 Hacksaw Jim Duggan	.20	.50
34 Dave Sullivan RC	.10	.25
35 Nasty Boys	.10	.25
36 Harlem Heat	1.25	3.00
37 Pretty Wonderful	.10	.25
38 Stars & Stripes	.10	.25
39 Monster Maniacs	.40	1.00
40 Jimmy Hart	.20	.50
41 Sister Sherri	.12	.30
42 Harley Race	.10	.25
43 Colonel Parker RC	.10	.25
44 Gary Cappetta RC	.10	.25
45 Mean Gene Okerlund	.60	1.50
46 Bobby Heenan	.20	.50
47 Tony Schiavone	.10	.25
48 Eric Bischoff RC	1.50	4.00
49 Gordon Solie RC	.10	.25
50 Larry Zbyszko	.12	.30
51 Nick Bockwinkel RC	.10	.25
52 Diamond Doll RC	2.00	5.00
53 Das Wunderkind Alex Wright RC	.10	.25
54 Harlem Heat	1.25	3.00
55 Dave Sullivan RC	.10	.25
56 Atomic Leg Drop	.40	1.00
57 Scorpion Death Lock	.25	.60
58 Power Bomb	.12	.30
59 Bulldog	.12	.30
60 Sleeper	.10	.25
61 Sunset Flip	.10	.25
62 Hollywood & Vine	5.00	12.00
63 Vadersault	.12	.30
64 Pit Stop	.10	.25
65 Flying Elbow	.20	.50
66 Figure Four Leglock	.30	.75
67 Headlock	.40	1.00
68 Hulk Hogan/Ric Flair	2.50	6.00
69 Hulk Hogan/Ric Flair	2.50	6.00
70 Hogan/Vader	.20	.50
71 Rhodes/Anderson	.20	.50
72 Macho Man Randy Savage	.40	1.00
73 Macho Man Randy Savage	.40	1.00
74 Macho Man Randy Savage	.40	1.00
75 Macho Man Randy Savage	.40	1.00
76 Ric Flair	.30	.75

77 Ric Flair	.30	.75
78 Ric Flair	.30	.75
79 Ric Flair	.30	.75
80 Sting	.30	.75
81 Sting	.30	.75
82 Sting	.30	.75
83 Hulk Hogan	2.00	5.00
84 Hulk Hogan	2.00	5.00
85 Hulk Hogan	2.00	5.00
86 Hulk Hogan	2.00	5.00
87 Hulk Hogan	2.00	5.00
88 Hulk Hogan	2.00	5.00
89A Uncensored	.10	.25
89B Spring Stampede	.10	.25
90 Starrcade 1994	.10	.25
91 Halloween Havoc 1994	.10	.25
92 Fall Brawl	.10	.25
93 Bash at the Beach	.10	.25
94 Slamboree 1994	.10	.25
95A Superbrawl IV	.10	.25
95B Superbrawl V	.10	.25
96 Arn Anderson	.12	.30
97 Harlem Heat	1.25	3.00
98 Vader	.12	.30
99 Hulk Hogan	2.00	5.00
100 Checklist	.10	.25

1995 CARDZ WCW Main Event Promos

P1 Hulk Hogan	3.00	8.00
P2 Sting	3.00	8.00
NNO Hogan vs. Flair TEK	2.00	5.00
NNO Clash of the Champions KKLZ		

2019 Carl's Jr-Hardee's WWE Star Pals Superstar Card Game Sheets

NNO Bryan/Lynch/Balor/Cena Mysterio/Banks/Rollins (Blue)
NNO Bryan/Lynch/Balor/Cena Mysterio/Banks/Rollins (Multi-Color)
NNO Bryan/Lynch/Balor/Cena Mysterio/Banks/Rollins (Orange)
NNO Bryan/Lynch/Balor/Cena Mysterio/Banks/Rollins (Red)

2019 Carl's Jr-Hardee's WWE Star Pals Superstar Card Game Singles

NNO Becky Lynch/Blue	1.25	3.00
NNO Becky Lynch/Multi-Color	1.25	3.00
NNO Becky Lynch/Orange	1.25	3.00
NNO Becky Lynch/Red	1.25	3.00
NNO Daniel Bryan/Blue	.75	2.00
NNO Daniel Bryan/Multi-Color	.75	2.00
NNO Daniel Bryan/Orange	.75	2.00
NNO Daniel Bryan/Red	.75	2.00
NNO Finn Balor/Blue	.60	1.50
NNO Finn Balor/Multi-Color	.60	1.50
NNO Finn Balor/Orange	.60	1.50
NNO Finn Balor/Red	.60	1.50
NNO John Cena/Blue	1.50	4.00
NNO John Cena/Multi-Color	1.50	4.00
NNO John Cena/Orange	1.50	4.00
NNO John Cena/Red	1.50	4.00
NNO Rey Mysterio/Blue	.75	2.00
NNO Rey Mysterio/Multi-Color	.75	2.00
NNO Rey Mysterio/Orange	.75	2.00
NNO Rey Mysterio/Red	.75	2.00
NNO Sasha Banks/Blue	1.25	3.00
NNO Sasha Banks/Multi-Color	1.25	3.00
NNO Sasha Banks/Orange	1.25	3.00
NNO Sasha Banks/Red	1.25	3.00
NNO Seth Rollins/Blue	.75	2.00
NNO Seth Rollins/Multi-Color	.75	2.00
NNO Seth Rollins/Orange	.75	2.00
NNO Seth Rollins/Red	.75	2.00

1986 Carnation Major League Wrestling

COMPLETE SET (6)	150.00	300.00
NNO Kamala	15.00	40.00
NNO The Koloffs	20.00	50.00
NNO Ric Flair	75.00	150.00
NNO Rick Martel	15.00	40.00
NNO The Road Warriors	30.00	75.00
NNO Sergeant Slaughter	25.00	60.00

1992 Catcher Quartett WWF Series 1

COMPLETE SET (32)		
A1 Macho Man Randy Savage	2.50	6.00
A2 Ultimate Warrior	2.00	5.00
A3 Undertaker	3.00	8.00
A4 Bret Hitman Hart	1.50	4.00
B1 Big Boss Man	1.00	2.50
B2 British Bulldog	1.25	3.00
B3 Sgt. Slaughter	1.25	3.00
B4 Tatanka	.75	2.00
C1 El Matador	1.25	3.00
C2 Virgil	.60	1.50
C3 Crush	.75	2.00
C4 Natural Disasters	1.00	2.50
D1 Animal of the Legion of Doom	1.25	3.00
D2 Ric Flair	2.50	6.00
D3 Papa Shango	.75	2.00
D4 Berzerker	.60	1.50
E1 Shawn Michaels	2.50	6.00
E2 Skinner	.60	1.50
E3 Nailz	.60	1.50
E4 Repo Man	.60	1.50
F1 The Mountie	.60	1.50
F2 The Model Rick Martel	1.00	2.50
F3 Kamala	.60	1.50
F4 Ted Di Biase of Money Inc.	1.25	3.00
G1 Beverly Brothers	.60	1.50
G2 Nasty Boys	.75	2.00
G3 Bushwhackers	.75	2.00
G4 Hulk Hogan	3.00	8.00
H1 The Rocket Owen Hart of High Energy	1.50	4.00
H2 Razor Ramon	1.50	4.00
H3 Mr. Perfect	1.25	3.00
H4 Hacksaw Jim Duggan	1.00	2.50

1992 Catcher Quartett WWF Series 2

COMPLETE SET (32)		
A1 Macho Man Randy Savage	2.50	6.00
A2 Ultimate Warrior	2.00	5.00
A3 Undertaker	3.00	8.00
A4 Bret Hitman Hart	1.50	4.00
B1 Big Boss Man	1.00	2.50
B2 British Bulldog	1.25	3.00
B3 Sgt. Slaughter	1.25	3.00
B4 Tatanka	.75	2.00
C1 El Matador	1.25	3.00
C2 Virgil	.60	1.50
C3 Crush	.75	2.00
C4 Typhoon UER/Spelled Thyphoon	.75	2.00
D1 Legion of Doom	1.50	4.00
D2 Ric Flair	2.50	6.00
D3 Papa Shango	.75	2.00
D4 Berzerker	.60	1.50
E1 Shawn Michaels	2.50	6.00
E2 Skinner	.60	1.50
E3 Nailz	.60	1.50
E4 Repo Man	.60	1.50
F1 The Mountie	.60	1.50
F2 The Model Rick Martel	1.00	2.50
F3 Kamala	.60	1.50
F4 Money Inc.	1.25	3.00
G1 Beverly Brothers	.60	1.50
G2 Brian Knobbs of the Nasty Boys	.75	2.00
G3 Bushwhackers	.75	2.00
G4 Hulk Hogan	3.00	8.00
H1 High Energy	1.50	4.00
H2 Razor Ramon	1.50	4.00
H3 Mr. Perfect	1.25	3.00
H4 Hacksaw Jim Duggan	1.00	2.50

1992 Catcher Quartett WWF Series 3

COMPLETE SET (32)		
A1 Macho Man Randy Savage	2.50	6.00
A2 Ultimate Warrior	2.00	5.00
A3 Undertaker	3.00	8.00
A4 Bret Hitman Hart	1.50	4.00
B1 Big Boss Man	1.00	2.50
B2 British Bulldog	1.25	3.00
B3 Sgt. Slaughter	1.25	3.00
B4 Tatanka	.75	2.00
C1 El Matador	1.25	3.00
C2 Virgil	.60	1.50
C3 Crush	.75	2.00
C4 Natural Disasters	1.00	2.50
D1 Legion of Doom	1.50	4.00
D2 Ric Flair	2.50	6.00
D3 Papa Shango	.75	2.00
D4 Berzerker	.60	1.50
E1 Shawn Michaels	2.50	6.00
E2 Skinner	.60	1.50
E3 Nailz	.60	1.50
E4 Repo Man	.60	1.50
F1 The Mountie	.60	1.50
F2 The Model Rick Martel	1.00	2.50
F3 Kamala	.60	1.50
F4 Money Inc.	1.25	3.00
G1 Blake of the Beverly Brothers	.60	1.50
G2 Jerry Sags of the Nasty Boys	.75	2.00
G3 Bushwhackers	.75	2.00
G4 Hulk Hogan	3.00	8.00
H1 High Energy	1.50	4.00
H2 Razor Ramon	1.50	4.00
H3 Mr. Perfect	1.25	3.00
H4 Hacksaw Jim Duggan	1.00	2.50

1992 Catcher Quartett WWF Series 4

COMPLETE SET (32)		
A1 Macho Man Randy Savage	2.50	6.00
A2 Ultimate Warrior	2.00	5.00
A3 Undertaker	3.00	8.00
A4 Bret Hitman Hart	1.50	4.00
B1 Big Boss man	1.00	2.50
B2 British Bulldog	1.25	3.00
B3 Sgt. Slaughter	1.25	3.00
B4 Tatanka	.75	2.00
C1 El Matador	1.25	3.00
C2 Virgil	.60	1.50
C3 Crush	.75	2.00
C4 Natural Disasters	1.00	2.50
D1 Hawk of the Legion of Doom	1.25	3.00
D2 Ric Flair	2.50	6.00
D3 Papa Shango	.75	2.00
D4 Berzerker	.60	1.50
E1 Shawn Michaels	2.50	6.00
E2 Skinner	.60	1.50
E3 Nailz	.60	1.50
E4 Repo Man	.60	1.50
F1 The Mountie	.60	1.50
F2 The Model Rick Martel	1.00	2.50
F3 Kamala	.60	1.50
F4 Money Inc.	1.25	3.00
G1 Beverly Brothers	.60	1.50
G2 Nasty Boys	.75	2.00
G3 Bushwhackers	.75	2.00
G4 Hulk Hogan	3.00	8.00
H1 High Energy	1.50	4.00
H2 Razor Ramon	1.50	4.00
H3 Mr. Perfect	1.25	3.00
H4 Hacksaw Jim Duggan	1.00	2.50

1993 Catcher Quartett WWF Series 5

A1 Bret Hit Man Hart	1.50	4.00
A2 Undertaker	3.00	8.00
A3 Hulk Hogan	3.00	8.00
A4 Crush	.75	2.00
B1 Mr. Perfect	1.25	3.00
B2 Bam Bam Bigelow	1.25	3.00
B3 Kamala	.60	1.50
B4 Money Inc.	1.25	3.00
C1 Doink	.75	2.00
C2 Macho Man Randy Savage	2.50	6.00
C3 Big Boss Man	1.00	2.50
C4 Tatanka	.75	2.00
D1 Virgil	.60	1.50
D2 Papa Shango	.75	2.00
D3 Shawn Michaels	2.50	6.00
D4 Repo Man	.60	1.50
E1 Hacksaw Jim Duggan	1.00	2.50
E2 Razor Ramon	1.50	4.00
E3 Bushwhackers	.75	2.00
E4 Nasty Boys	.75	2.00
F1 Giant Gonzalez	.60	1.50
F2 Head Shrinkers	.75	2.00
F3 Beverly Brothers	.60	1.50
F4 Damian Demento	.60	1.50
G1 Bob Backlund	1.00	2.50
G2 Brutus The Barber Beefcake	1.00	2.50
G3 Lex Luger	1.25	3.00
G4 Steiner Brothers	1.50	4.00
H1 Yokozuna	1.50	4.00
H2 El Matador	1.25	3.00
H3 Paul Bearer	1.00	2.50
H4 Billy of the Smoking Gunns	1.00	2.50

1993 Catcher Quartett WWF Series 7

A1 Bret Hit Man Hart	1.50	4.00
A2 Undertaker	3.00	8.00
A3 Hulk Hogan	3.00	8.00
A4 Crush	.75	2.00
B1 Mr. Perfect	1.25	3.00
B2 Bam Bam Bigelow	1.25	3.00
B3 Kamala	.60	1.50
B4 Money Inc.	1.25	3.00
C1 Doink	.75	2.00
C2 Macho Man Randy Savage	2.50	6.00
C3 Big Boss Man	1.00	2.50
C4 Tatanka	.75	2.00
D1 Virgil	.60	1.50
D2 Papa Shango	.75	2.00
D3 Shawn Michaels	2.50	6.00
D4 Repo Man	.60	1.50
E1 Hacksaw Jim Duggan	1.00	2.50
E2 Razor Ramon	1.50	4.00
E3 Bushwhackers	.75	2.00
E4 Knobbs of the Nasty Boys	.75	2.00
F1 Giant Gonzalez	.60	1.50
F2 Head Shrinkers	.75	2.00
F3 Beverly Brothers	.60	1.50
F4 Damian Demento	.60	1.50
G1 Bob Backlund	1.00	2.50
G2 Brutus The Barber Beefcake	1.00	2.50
G3 Lex Luger	1.25	3.00
G4 Steiner Brothers	1.50	4.00
H1 Yokozuna	1.50	4.00
H2 El Matador	1.25	3.00
H3 Paul Bearer	1.00	2.50
H4 The Smoking Gunns	1.00	2.50

1993 Catcher Quartett WWF Series 8

A1 Bret Hit Man Hart	1.50	4.00
A2 Undertaker	3.00	8.00
A3 Hulk Hogan	3.00	8.00
A4 Crush	.75	2.00
B1 Mr. Perfect	1.25	3.00
B2 Bam Bam Bigelow	1.25	3.00
B3 Kamala	.60	1.50
B4 Money Inc.	1.25	3.00
C1 Doink	.75	2.00
C2 Macho Man Randy Savage	2.50	6.00
C3 Big Boss Man	1.00	2.50
C4 Tatanka	.75	2.00
D1 Virgil	.60	1.50
D2 Papa Shango	.75	2.00
D3 Shawn Michaels	2.50	6.00
D4 Repo Man	.60	1.50
E1 Hacksaw Jim Duggan	1.00	2.50
E2 Razor Ramon	1.50	4.00
E3 Luke of the Bushwhackers	.75	2.00
E4 Nasty Boys	.75	2.00
F1 Giant Gonzalez	.60	1.50
F2 Head Shrinkers	.75	2.00
F3 Beverly Brothers	.60	1.50
F4 Damian Demento	.60	1.50
G1 Bob Backlund	1.00	2.50
G2 Brutus The Barber Beefcake	1.00	2.50
G3 Lex Luger	1.25	3.00
G4 Steiner Brothers	1.50	4.00
H1 Yokozuna	1.50	4.00
H2 El Matador	1.25	3.00
H3 Paul Bearer	1.00	2.50
H4 Billy of the Smoking Gunns	1.00	2.50

1991 Championship Marketing WCW

COMPLETE SET (110)	12.00	30.00
1 Sting	.40	1.00
2 Arn Anderson	.15	.40
3 Michael Hayes	.12	.30

4 Rick Steiner	.15	.40
5 The Fabulous Freebirds	.15	.40
6 The Steiner Brothers	.25	.60
7 Lex Luger	.15	.40
8 Ric Flair	.50	1.25
9 Tom Zenk RC	.12	.30
10 Sid Vicious RC	.12	.30
11 Brian Pillman	.15	.40
12 Ric Flair	.50	1.25
13 Sid Vicious RC	.12	.30
14 The Four Horsemen	.50	1.25
15 Jim Ross RC	.20	.50
16 Ron Simmons	.15	.40
17 Barry Windham	.20	.50
18 Sid Vicious RC	.12	.30
19 Sid Vicious RC	.12	.30
20 Sting and Ric	.50	1.25
21 Beautiful Bobby...	.12	.30
22 New Champion/Sting	.40	1.00
23 Paul E. with Mouth Open	.20	.50
24 Michael Hayes	.12	.30
25 Scott Steiner RC	.25	.60
26 Rick Steiner	.15	.40
27 TV Champ Arn Anderson	.15	.40
28 Barry Windham with Arms Raised	.20	.50
29 Tommy Rich RC	.12	.30
30 Ricky Morton	.12	.30
31 Horsemen Press Conference	.50	1.25
32 The Freebirds	.15	.40
33 Terry Taylor	.12	.30
34 Dirty Dutch Mantell RC	.15	.40
35 Nature Boy Ric Flair	.50	1.25
36 Lex Presses Ric	.50	1.25
37 Lex and Sting	.15	.40
38 Flyin' Brian RC	.15	.40
39 Ric Flair	.50	1.25
40 Sting and Lex	.40	1.00
41 Missy Hyatt	.20	.50
42 Three Out of Four/Horsemen	.12	.30
43 Sid Vicious in Action	.12	.30
44 Terry Taylor vs. Z-Man	.12	.30
45 Southern Boys	.12	.30
46 Sting	.40	1.00
47 What Did You Say?/Ric Flair	.50	1.25
48 Arn, Paul E. and Ric Flair	.50	1.25
49 Sting	.40	1.00
50 Say Uncle/Sid Vicious	.12	.30
51 Paul E. Dangerously RC	.20	.50
52 Sting and Ric	.50	1.25
53 Sting, Jim and Lex	.40	1.00
54 What a Belt!/Sting	.40	1.00
55 Sting	.40	1.00
56 Ric All In White	.50	1.25
57 Lex Presses Ric II	.50	1.25
58 El Gigante	.15	.40
59 Arn Says My Turn	.15	.40
60 Sid Vicious RC	.12	.30
61 Brian and Ric	.50	1.25
62 Flyin Brian	.15	.40
63 The Fabulous Freebirds	.15	.40
64 No Sid This High	.12	.30
65 El Gigante RC	.12	.30
66 Ric, Jim and Sting	.50	1.25
67 No It's Mine/Flair, JR & Sting	.50	1.25
68 Golden Nature Boy	.50	1.25
69 Missy and Scott	.25	.60
70 Ron Simmons	.15	.40
71 Telephone/Paul E. Dangerously	.20	.50
72 Jimmy Jam Garvin	.15	.40
73 Ric Flair in Pink Robe	.50	1.25
74 Beautiful Bobby	.12	.30
75 Lex Luger	.15	.40
76 Z-Man RC	.12	.30
77 Where's The Door?/Ric Flair	.50	1.25
78 El Gigante RC	.12	.30
79 What Do You Think?/Ric Flair	.50	1.25
80 6 Time World Champion/Ric Flair	.50	1.25
81 Missy Hyatt	.20	.50
82 The New Champion/Sting	.40	1.00
83 Celebration/Sting	.40	1.00
84 USA Sting	.40	1.00
85 Sting Is Injured	.40	1.00
86 Let's Get Busy/Sting	.40	1.00
87 Courage of a Champion/Sting	.40	1.00
88 Paul E. Dangerously	.20	.50
89 Lex Presses Ric III	.50	1.25
90 Barry Windham	.20	.50
91 Ric Flair & Lex Luger	.50	1.25
92 US Champ/Lex Luger	.15	.40
93 Getting Ready.../Lex Luger	.15	.40
94 Lex Wins the Title	.15	.40
95 Ric Goes Too Far	.50	1.25
96 El Gigante and Sting	.40	1.00
97 Z-Man RC	.12	.30
98 Tag Team Champs Doom w/Teddy Long	.12	.30
99 Missy in Evening Gown	.20	.50
100 Missy Hyatt	.20	.50
101 Tony Schiavone	.15	.40
102 Ricky Morton	.12	.30
103 Flyin Brian	.15	.40
104 The Steiners Want Sting Revenge	.25	.60
105 Z-Man Tom Zenk RC	.12	.30
106 Southern Boys	.12	.30
107 Teddy R. Long	.12	.30
108 Arn Anderson in Action	.15	.40
109 Sting in Action	.40	1.00
110 Doom	.12	.30

1991 Championship Marketing WCW Puzzle

COMPLETE SET (110)	6.00	15.00
STATED ODDS 1:1		
1 Puzzle Card	.12	.30
2 Puzzle Card	.12	.30
3 Puzzle Card	.12	.30
4 Puzzle Card	.12	.30
5 Puzzle Card	.12	.30
6 Puzzle Card	.12	.30
7 Puzzle Card	.12	.30
8 Puzzle Card	.12	.30
9 Puzzle Card	.12	.30
10 Puzzle Card	.12	.30
11 Puzzle Card	.12	.30
12 Puzzle Card	.12	.30
13 Puzzle Card	.12	.30
14 Puzzle Card	.12	.30
15 Puzzle Card	.12	.30
16 Puzzle Card	.12	.30
17 Puzzle Card	.12	.30
18 Puzzle Card	.12	.30
19 Puzzle Card	.12	.30
20 Puzzle Card	.12	.30
21 Puzzle Card	.12	.30
22 Puzzle Card	.12	.30
23 Puzzle Card	.12	.30
24 Puzzle Card	.12	.30
25 Puzzle Card	.12	.30
26 Puzzle Card	.12	.30
27 Puzzle Card	.12	.30
28 Puzzle Card	.12	.30
29 Puzzle Card	.12	.30
30 Puzzle Card	.12	.30
31 Puzzle Card	.12	.30
32 Puzzle Card	.12	.30
33 Puzzle Card	.12	.30
34 Puzzle Card	.12	.30
35 Puzzle Card	.12	.30
36 Puzzle Card	.12	.30
37 Puzzle Card	.12	.30
38 Puzzle Card	.12	.30
39 Puzzle Card	.12	.30
40 Puzzle Card	.12	.30
41 Puzzle Card	.12	.30
42 Puzzle Card	.12	.30
43 Puzzle Card	.12	.30
44 Puzzle Card	.12	.30
45 Puzzle Card	.12	.30
46 Puzzle Card	.12	.30
47 Puzzle Card	.12	.30
48 Puzzle Card	.12	.30
49 Puzzle Card	.12	.30
50 Puzzle Card	.12	.30
51 Puzzle Card	.12	.30
52 Puzzle Card	.12	.30
53 Puzzle Card	.12	.30
54 Puzzle Card	.12	.30
55 Puzzle Card	.12	.30
56 Puzzle Card	.12	.30
57 Puzzle Card	.12	.30
58 Puzzle Card	.12	.30
59 Puzzle Card	.12	.30
60 Puzzle Card	.12	.30
61 Puzzle Card	.12	.30
62 Puzzle Card	.12	.30
63 Puzzle Card	.12	.30
64 Puzzle Card	.12	.30
65 Puzzle Card	.12	.30
66 Puzzle Card	.12	.30
67 Puzzle Card	.12	.30
68 Puzzle Card	.12	.30
69 Puzzle Card	.12	.30
70 Puzzle Card	.12	.30
71 Puzzle Card	.12	.30
72 Puzzle Card	.12	.30
73 Puzzle Card	.12	.30
74 Puzzle Card	.12	.30
75 Puzzle Card	.12	.30
76 Puzzle Card	.12	.30
77 Puzzle Card	.12	.30
78 Puzzle Card	.12	.30
79 Puzzle Card	.12	.30
80 Puzzle Card	.12	.30
81 Puzzle Card	.12	.30
82 Puzzle Card	.12	.30
83 Puzzle Card	.12	.30
84 Puzzle Card	.12	.30
85 Puzzle Card	.12	.30
86 Puzzle Card	.12	.30
87 Puzzle Card	.12	.30
88 Puzzle Card	.12	.30
89 Puzzle Card	.12	.30
90 Puzzle Card	.12	.30
91 Puzzle Card	.12	.30
92 Puzzle Card	.12	.30
93 Puzzle Card	.12	.30
94 Puzzle Card	.12	.30
95 Puzzle Card	.12	.30
96 Puzzle Card	.12	.30
97 Puzzle Card	.12	.30
98 Puzzle Card	.12	.30
99 Puzzle Card	.12	.30
100 Puzzle Card	.12	.30
101 Puzzle Card	.12	.30
102 Puzzle Card	.12	.30
103 Puzzle Card	.12	.30
104 Puzzle Card	.12	.30
105 Puzzle Card	.12	.30
106 Puzzle Card	.12	.30
107 Puzzle Card	.12	.30
108 Puzzle Card	.12	.30
109 Puzzle Card	.12	.30
110 Puzzle Card	.12	.30

1987 Circle K Coca-Cola WWF Supermatch

COMPLETE SET (20)	30.00	75.00
1 Hulk Hogan	10.00	25.00
2 Hercules and Bobby Heenan	2.00	5.00
3 The Hart Foundation	2.50	6.00
4 Randy Macho Man Savage	3.00	8.00
5 Koko B. Ware	1.25	3.00
6 George The Animal Steele	1.25	3.00
7 Ricky The Dragon Steamboat	1.50	4.00
8 The Honky Tonk Man	2.00	5.00
9 Hacksaw Jim Duggan	1.25	3.00
10 Kamala and Kimchee	2.50	6.00
11 Billy Jack Haynes	1.25	3.00
12 Junk Yard Dog	1.50	4.00
13 Jake The Snake Roberts	4.00	10.00
14 The Killer Bees	1.25	3.00
15 Tito Santana	1.25	3.00
16 The Can-Am Connection	1.25	3.00
17 Andre the Giant	6.00	15.00
18 Elizabeth	3.00	8.00
19 The British Bulldogs	2.00	5.00
20 The Iron Sheik	1.25	3.00

1989 Classic WWF

1 Hulk Hogan	2.00	5.00
2 Big Boss Man	.50	1.25
3 Ravishing Rick Rude RC	.60	1.50
4 Randy Savage	1.25	3.00
5 The Ultimate Warrior RC	1.50	4.00
6 Demolition	.60	1.50
7 Jake The Snake Roberts	.60	1.50
8 Ted DiBiase RC	.60	1.50
9 Hacksaw Jim Duggan RC	.50	1.25
10 Andre the Giant	2.00	5.00
11 Miss Elizabeth	.75	2.00
12 Brutus The Barber Beefcake	.50	1.25
13 Rowdy Roddy Piper	.75	2.00
14 Superfly Jimmy Snuka	.60	1.50
15 Bushwhackers	.40	1.00
16 Dusty Rhodes	.60	1.50
17 Hercules	.30	.75
18 Sensational Queen Sherri RC	.60	1.50
19 Mr. Perfect RC	.60	1.50
20 Rick Martel RC	.50	1.25
21 Tito Santana	.50	1.25
22 Mr. Fuji	.50	1.25
23 Jimmy Hart	.40	1.00
24 Brother Love RC	.30	.75
25 Akeem RC	.40	1.00
26 Bad News Brown RC	.30	.75
27 Honky Tonk Man	.40	1.00
28 The Rockers	.60	1.50
29 Koko B. Ware	.30	.75
30 Bobby The Brain Heenan	.60	1.50
31 Dino Bravo RC	.30	.75
32 The Genius RC	.40	1.00
33 Greg The Hammer Valentine	.50	1.25
34 Virgil RC	.30	.75
35 Haku RC	.40	1.00
36 Rugged Ronnie Garvin	.30	.75
37 Twin Towers	.50	1.25
38 Hart Foundation	.75	2.00
39 Red Rooster	.30	.75
40 Hillbilly Jim	.30	.75
41 Slick RC	.30	.75
42 The Widow Maker	.60	1.50
43 The Ultimate Warrior RC	1.50	4.00
44 Honky Tonk Man	.40	1.00
45 Bret Hitman Hart	.75	2.00
46 Jim The Anvil Neidhart	.40	1.00
47 Bushwhackers	.40	1.00
48 Paul Roma RC	.30	.75
49 Barry Horowitz RC	.30	.75
50 Brooklyn Brawler RC	.30	.75
51 Mean Gene Okerlund RC	.60	1.50
52 Gorilla Monsoon RC	.60	1.50
53 Jesse The Body Ventura		
54 Sean Mooney RC	.30	.75
55 Danny Davis RC	.30	.75
56 Jack Tunney RC	.30	.75
57 Hulk Hogan	2.00	5.00
58 Big Boss Man	.50	1.25
59 Ravishing Rick Rude RC	.60	1.50
60 Macho King Randy Savage	1.25	3.00
61 The Ultimate Warrior RC	1.50	4.00
62 Demolition	.60	1.50
63 Jake The Snake Roberts	.60	1.50
64 Ted DiBiase RC	.60	1.50
65 Hacksaw Jim Duggan RC	.50	1.25
66 Andre the Giant	2.00	5.00
67 Miss Elizabeth	.75	2.00
68 Brutus The Barber Beefcake	.50	1.25
69 Superfly Jimmy Snuka	.60	1.50
70 Bushwhackers	.40	1.00
71 Dusty Rhodes	.60	1.50
72 Hercules	.30	.75
73 Sensational Queen Sherri RC	.60	1.50
74 Mr. Perfect RC	.60	1.50
75 Jimmy Hart	.40	1.00
76 Jimmy Hart	.40	1.00
77 Brother Love RC	.30	.75
78 Akeem RC	.40	1.00
79 Bad News Brown RC	.30	.75
80 Honky Tonk Man	.40	1.00
81 The Rockers	.60	1.50
82 Koko B. Ware	.30	.75
83 Bobby The Brain Heenan	.60	1.50
84 Dino Bravo RC	.30	.75
85 The Genius RC	.40	1.00
86 Greg The Hammer Valentine	.50	1.25
87 Virgil RC	.30	.75
88 Haku RC	.40	1.00
89 Rugged Ronnie Garvin	.30	.75
90 Twin Towers	.50	1.25

91 Red Rooster .30 .75
92 Hillbilly Jim .30 .75
93 The Widow Maker .60 1.50
94 Freddie Blassie RC .50 1.25
95 Bret Hitman Hart .75 2.00
96 Jim The Anvil Neidhart .40 1.00
97 Demolition .60 1.50
98 Paul Roma RC .30 .75
99 Barry Horowitz RC .30 .75
100 Brooklyn Brawler RC .30 .75
101 Danny Davis RC .30 .75
102 Hulk Hogan 2.00 5.00
103 Big Boss Man .50 1.25
104 Ravishing Rick Rude RC .60 1.50
105 Randy Savage 1.25 3.00
106 The Ultimate Warrior RC 1.50 4.00
107 Demolition .60 1.50
108 Jake The Snake Roberts .60 1.50
109 Ted DiBiase RC .60 1.50
110 Hacksaw Jim Duggan RC .50 1.25
111 Andre the Giant 2.00 5.00
112 Miss Elizabeth .75 2.00
113 Brutus The Barber Beefcake .50 1.25
114 Superfly Jimmy Snuka .60 1.50
115 Tito Santana .50 1.25
116 Bushwhackers .40 1.00
117 Honky Tonk Man .40 1.00
118 The Rockers .60 1.50
119 Koko B. Ware .30 .75
120 Haku RC .40 1.00
121 Twin Towers .50 1.25
122 Red Rooster .30 .75
123 Bret Hitman Hart .75 2.00
124 Jim The Anvil Neidhart .40 1.00
125 Hulk Hogan 2.00 5.00
126 Randy Savage 1.25 3.00
127 The Ultimate Warrior RC 1.50 4.00
128 Demolition .60 1.50
129 Hulk Hogan 2.00 5.00
130 Andre the Giant 2.00 5.00
131 Superfly Jimmy Snuka .60 1.50
132 Bushwhackers .40 1.00
133 Honky Tonk Man .40 1.00
134 The Rockers .60 1.50
135 Haku RC .40 1.00
136 Miss Elizabeth .75 2.00
137 Hulk Hogan 2.00 5.00
138 Ultimate Warrior RC 1.50 4.00
139 Demolition .60 1.50
140 Andre the Giant 2.00 5.00
141 Bushwhackers .40 1.00
142 Honky Tonk Man .40 1.00
143 The Rockers .60 1.50
144 Hulk Hogan 2.00 5.00
145 Hulk Hogan 2.00 5.00
146 Freddie Blassie RC .50 1.25
147 The Ultimate Warrior RC 1.50 4.00
148 Bushwhackers .40 1.00
149 Brutus The Barber Beefcake .50 1.25
150 Big Boss Man .50 1.25
151 Simply Ravishing .60 1.50
152 Ted DiBiase RC .60 1.50
153 Honky Tonk Man .40 1.00
154 Ultimate Warrior RC 1.50 4.00
155 Macho Madness 1.25 3.00
156 Miss Elizabeth .75 2.00
157 Hulk Rules 2.00 5.00
158 Koko B. Ware .30 .75
159 Tito Santana .50 1.25

1990 Classic WWF

COMPLETE FACTORY SET (145) 10.00 25.00

1 Hulk Hogan 1.25 3.00
2 Big Boss Man .20 .50
3 Ravishing Rick Rude .30 .75
4 Macho Man Randy Savage .75 2.00
5 The Ultimate Warrior .50 1.25
6 Demolition .20 .50
7 Jake The Snake Roberts .50 1.25
8 Ted DiBiase .30 .75
9 Hacksaw Jim Duggan .30 .75
10 Andre the Giant .75 2.00
11 Miss Elizabeth .30 .75
12 Brutus The Barber Beefcake .30 .75
13 Rowdy Roddy Piper .75 2.00
14 Jimmy Superfly Snuka .50 1.25
15 Bushwhackers .20 .50
16 Dusty Rhodes .20 .50
17 Hercules .20 .50
18 Sensational Queen Sherri .30 .75
19 Mr. Perfect .30 .75
20 Rick Martel .60 1.50
21 Tito Santana .20 .50
22 Mr. Fuji .20 .50
23 Jimmy Hart .30 .75
24 Brother Love .20 .50
25 Akeem .20 .50
26 Bad News Brown .20 .50
27 Honky Tonk Man .30 .75
28 The Rockers .30 .75
29 Koko B. Ware .30 .75
30 Bobby The Brain Heenan .30 .75
31 Dino Bravo .20 .50
32 The Genius .20 .50
33 Greg The Hammer Valentine .30 .75
34 Virgil .20 .50
35 Haku .20 .50
36 Rugged Ronnie Garvin .20 .50
37 Bret Hit Man Hart .30 .75
38 Hart Foundation .30 .75
39 Red Rooster .20 .50
40 Hillbilly Jim .20 .50
41 Slick .25 .60
42 The Widow Maker .20 .50
43 The Ultimate Warrior .50 1.25
44 Honky Tonk Man .30 .75
45 Bret Hit Man Hart .30 .75
46 Jim Neidhart .30 .75
47 Bushwhackers .20 .50
48 Paul Roma .20 .50
49 Barry Horowitz .20 .50
50 Brooklyn Brawler .20 .50
51 Mean Gene Okerlund .20 .50
52 Gorilla Monsoon .20 .50
53 Jesse The Body Ventura .75 2.00
54 Sean Mooney .20 .50
55 Danny Davis .20 .50
56 Jack Tunney .20 .50
57 Hulk Hogan 1.25 3.00
58 Big Boss Man .20 .50
59 Ravishing Rick Rude .30 .75
60 Macho Man Randy Savage .75 2.00
61 The Ultimate Warrior .50 1.25
62 Demolition .20 .50
63 Jake The Snake Roberts .50 1.25
64 Ted DiBiase .30 .75
65 Hacksaw Jim Duggan .30 .75
66 Andre the Giant .75 2.00
67 Miss Elizabeth .30 .75
68 Brutus The Barber Beefcake .30 .75
69 Jimmy Superfly Snuka .50 1.25
70 Bushwhackers .20 .50
71 Dusty Rhodes .20 .50
72 Hercules .20 .50
73 Sensational Queen Sherri .30 .75
74 Mr. Perfect 1.00 2.50
75 Jimmy Hart .30 .75
76 Andre the Giant .75 2.00
77 Brother Love .20 .50
78 Akeem .20 .50
79 Bad News Brown .20 .50
80 Honky Tonk Man .30 .75
81 The Rockers .30 .75
82 Koko B. Ware .30 .75
83 Bobby The Brain Heenan .30 .75
84 Dino Bravo .20 .50
85 The Genius .20 .50
86 Greg The Hammer Valentine .30 .75
87 Virgil .20 .50
88 Haku .20 .50
89 Rugged Ronnie Garvin .20 .50
90 Hulk Hogan 1.25 3.00
91 Red Rooster .20 .50
92 Hillbilly Jim .20 .50
93 The Widow Maker .20 .50
94 Freddie Blassie .20 .50
95 Bret Hit Man Hart .30 .75
96 Jim Neidhart .30 .75
97 Demolition .20 .50
98 Paul Roma .20 .50
99 Barry Horowitz .20 .50
100 Brooklyn Brawler .20 .50
101 Danny Davis .20 .50
102 Hulk Hogan 1.25 3.00
103 Big Boss Man .20 .50
104 Ravishing Rick Rude .30 .75
105 Macho Man Randy Savage .75 2.00
106 The Ultimate Warrior .50 1.25
107 Demolition .20 .50
108 Jake The Snake Roberts 1.25 3.00
109 Ted DiBiase .30 .75
110 Hacksaw Jim Duggan .30 .75
111 Andre the Giant .75 2.00
112 Miss Elizabeth .30 .75
113 Brutus The Barber Beefcake .30 .75
114 Jimmy Superfly Snuka .50 1.25
115 Tito Santana .20 .50
116 Bushwhackers .20 .50
117 Honky Tonk Man .30 .75
118 The Rockers .30 .75
119 Koko B. Ware .30 .75
120 Haku .20 .50
121 The Rockers .30 .75
122 Red Rooster .20 .50
123 Bret Hit Man Hart 2.50 6.00
124 Jim Neidhart .75 2.00
125 Hulk Hogan 1.25 3.00
126 Macho Man Randy Savage 1.50 4.00
127 The Ultimate Warrior 1.50 4.00
128 Demolition 1.25 3.00
129 Hulk Hogan 3.00 8.00
130 Andre the Giant 2.00 5.00
131 Jimmy Superfly Snuka .50 1.25
132 Bushwhackers .20 .50
133 Honky Tonk Man .30 .75
134 The Rockers 1.25 3.00
135 Haku .20 .50
136 Miss Elizabeth 1.00 2.50
137 Macho Madness .75 2.00
138 Honky Tonk Man .30 .75
139 The Ultimate Warrior 1.50 4.00
140 Ted DiBiase .30 .75
141 Simply Ravishing .30 .75
142 Big Boss Man .20 .50
143 Brutus The Barber Beefcake .30 .75
144 Koko B. Ware .30 .75
145 Hulk Hogan Rules 1.25 3.00

1990 Classic WWF History of WrestleMania

COMPLETE SET (150) 10.00 25.00
COMPLETE FACTORY SET (150)
*TRADEMARK: .6X TO 1.5X BASIC CARDS

1 Greg Valentine/JYD
2 T.Santana/Executioner .10 .25
3 Hulk Hogan .50 1.25
4 Dream Team/Bulldogs .10 .25
5 Battle Royal .10 .25
6 Battle Royal .10 .25
7 Battle Royal .10 .25
8 B.Beefcake/British Bulldogs .12 .30
9 T.Santana/JYD/Funks .12 .30
10 Greg Valentine .12 .30
11 H.Hogan/K.K.Bundy .50 1.25
12 Macho Man/George Steele .20 .50
13 Macho Man/George Steele .20 .50
14 H.Hogan/K.K.Bundy .50 1.25
15 H.Hogan/K.K.Bundy .50 1.25
16 Andre the Giant .40 1.00
17 Slick/T.Santana .10 .25
18 R.Piper/A.Adonis .20 .50
19 Andre/Hogan .50 1.25
20 J.Neidhart/Dynamite Kid .10 .25
21 Davey Boy/Danny Davis .12 .30
22 Slick/T.Santana .10 .25
23 Stadium Scene .10 .25
24 Honky Tonk Man/Jake Roberts .15 .40
25 Brutus Beefcake/Adrian Adonis .12 .30
26 Hulk Hogan/Andre .50 1.25
27 Hulk Hogan/Andre .50 1.25
28 Hulk Hogan/Andre .50 1.25
29 Million Dollar Man/Macho Man .20 .50
30 Million Dollar Man/Macho Man .20 .50
31 Million Dollar Man/Macho Man .20 .50
32 Hulk Hogan/Macho Man .50 1.25
33 Hulk Hogan/Macho Man .50 1.25
34 Hulk Hogan/Andre .50 1.25
35 Hulk Hogan/Andre .50 1.25
36 Hulk Hogan/Andre .50 1.25
37 Hulk Hogan/Andre .50 1.25
38 Hulk Hogan/Andre .50 1.25
39 Hulk Hogan/Andre .50 1.25
40 Hulk Hogan .50 1.25
41 Hulk Hogan .50 1.25
42 Brutus Beefcake .12 .30
43 Brutus Beefcake/Honky Tonk Man .12 .30
44 Honky Tonk Man/Brutus Beefcake .12 .30
45 Rick Martel/Demolition .10 .25
46 Demolition/Strike Force .10 .25
47 Rick Rude/Jake Roberts .15 .40
48 Hercules/Ultimate Warrior .12 .30
49 The Hammer/Macho Man .20 .50
50 The Hammer/Macho Man .20 .50
51 Hulk Hogan .50 1.25
52 Million Dollar Man/Virgil/Andre .40 1.00
53 Hulk Hogan/Macho Man .50 1.25
54 Macho Man/Akeem .20 .50
55 Ring Scene .10 .25
56 Bobby Heenan/Koko B. Ware .10 .25
57 Battle Royal .10 .25
58 Million Dollar Man/Jim Duggan .12 .30
59 Dino Bravo/Don Muraco .10 .25
60 Jake Roberts/Rick Rude .15 .40
61 Hercules/Ultimate Warrior .12 .30
62 Jake Roberts/Rick Rude .15 .40
63 Hercules/Ultimate Warrior .12 .30
64 Hercules/Ultimate Warrior .12 .30
65 Hercules/Ultimate Warrior .12 .30
66 Mr. Fuji/Ax .10 .25
67 Demolition/Tito Santana .10 .25
68 Rick Martel/Smash .10 .25
69 Honky Tonk Man/Brutus Beefcake .12 .30
70 Bret Hart/Bad News Brown .12 .30
71 Bret Hart/Bad News Brown .12 .30
72 Bret Hart/Bad News Brown .12 .30
73 Bad News Brown .10 .25
74 Power of Pain/Demolition .10 .25
75 Million Dollar Man/Virgil .12 .30
76 Mr. Fuji/Ax .10 .25
77 Demolition .10 .25
78 Andre/Jake Roberts .40 1.00
79 Bret Hart/Honky Tonk Man .12 .30
80 Brooklyn Brawler .10 .25
81 King Haku/Hercules .10 .25
82 King Haku/Hercules .10 .25
83 Million Dollar Man/Brutus Beefcake .12 .30
84 Dino Bravo/Ronnie Garvin .10 .25
85 B.N.Brown/J.Duggan .12 .30
86 B.N.Brown/J.Duggan .12 .30
87 Bret Hart/Greg Valentine .12 .30
88 Bret Hart/Honky Tonk Man .12 .30
89 Mr. Perfect/Blue Blazer .12 .30
90 Bobby Heenan .12 .30
91 Bushwhackers/Rougeaus .10 .25
92 Bushwhackers/Rougeaus .10 .25
93 Dino Bravo/Ronnie Garvin .10 .25
94 Hulk Hogan/Macho Man .50 1.25
95 Hulk Hogan/Macho Man .50 1.25
96 Hulk Hogan/Macho Man .50 1.25
97 Akeem/HBK .15 .40
98 Rockers/Akeem .12 .30
99 Hulk Hogan/Macho Man .50 1.25
100 Hulk Hogan/Macho Man .50 1.25
101 Hulk Hogan/Macho Man .50 1.25
102 Hulk Hogan/Macho Man .50 1.25
103 Hulk Hogan/Macho Man .50 1.25
104 Rick Rude/Ultimate Warrior .12 .30
105 Rick Rude/Ultimate Warrior .12 .30
106 Ultimate Warrior .12 .30
107 Hulk Hogan/Macho Man .50 1.25
108 Marty Jannetty/Akeem .10 .25
109 Brutus Beefcake/Virgil .12 .30
110 Rick Rude/Ultimate Warrior .12 .30
111 Rick Rude/Ultimate Warrior .12 .30
112 Rick Rude/Ultimate Warrior .12 .30
113 Haku/Andre .40 1.00
114 Million Dollar Man/Jake Roberts .15 .40
115 Barbarian/Tito Santana .10 .25

116 Rick Martel/Koko B. Ware .10 .25
117 Ted DiBiase .12 .30
118 Jim Duggan/Dino Bravo .12 .30
119 Jim Duggan/Dino Bravo .12 .30
120 Jim Duggan/Dino Bravo .12 .30
121 Macho King/Dusty Rhodes .10 .25
122 Dream/Sapphire/Elizabeth .15 .40
123 Macho Man .20 .50
124 Hart Foundation .12 .30
125 Dusty Rhodes/Macho Man .20 .50
126 Dream/Sapphire/Sherri .12 .30
127 Bad News/Roddy Piper .20 .50
128 Brutus Beefcake/Genius .12 .30
129 Sato/Tanaka/Marty Jannetty .10 .25
130 Big Boss Man/Akeem .10 .25
131 Sato/Shawn Michaels .15 .40
132 Hulk Hogan/Ultimate Warrior .50 1.25
133 Hulk Hogan/Ultimate Warrior .50 1.25
134 Hulk Hogan/Ultimate Warrior .50 1.25
135 Hulk Hogan/Immortal One .50 1.25
136 The Ultimate Warrior .12 .30
137 Rhythm and Blues .10 .25
138 Rick Rude/Jimmy Snuka .15 .40
139 Rhythm and Blues/Jimmy Hart .12 .30
140 Demolition .10 .25
141 Andre/Bobby Heenan .40 1.00
142 Haku/Smash .10 .25
143 Smash/Haku/Ax .10 .25
144 Brutus Beefcake/Mr.Perfect .12 .30
145 Hulk Hogan/Ultimate Warrior .50 1.25
146 Brutus Beefcake .12 .30
147 Ultimate Warrior .12 .30
148 Bushwhackers .10 .25
149 Rockers .12 .30
150 Dusty Rhodes .10 .25

1991 Classic WWF Promos

NNO Brutus The Barber Beefcake
NNO The Bushwhackers
NNO Hulk Hogan
NNO Macho King Randy Savage
NNO Ultimate Warrior

1991 Classic WWF Superstars

COMPLETE SET (150) 50.00 100.00
COMPLETE FACTORY SET (150) 100.00 200.00
*EUROPEAN: SAME VALUE

1 Hulk Hogan .50 1.25
2 Ultimate Warrior .30 .75
3 Texas Tornado RC .12 .30
4 Jake The Snake Roberts .20 .50
5 Big Boss Man .10 .25
6 Hacksaw Jim Duggan .12 .30
7 Davey Boy Smith .12 .30
8 The Model Rick Martel .10 .25
9 Ted DiBiase .12 .30
10 Bobby Heenan .75 2.00
11 Rockers .15 .40
12 Legion of Doom .12 .30
13 Tugboat RC .10 .25
14 Power & Glory .10 .25
15 Bushwackers .10 .25
16 Macho King Randy Savage .30 .75
17 Koko B. Ware .10 .25
18 Superfly Jimmy Snuka .15 .40
19 Davey Boy Smith .12 .30
20 Sensational Queen Sherri .12 .30
21 Barbarian .10 .25
22 Virgil .10 .25
23 Nasty Boys 1.00 2.50
24 Ted DiBiase .12 .30
25 Big Boss Man .10 .25
26 Sgt. Slaughter RC .15 .40
27 Barbarian .10 .25
28 Nasty Boys .10 .25
29 Mr. Perfect .15 .40
30 Undertaker RC 6.00 15.00
31 Rowdy Roddy Piper .40 1.00
32 The Mountie RC .10 .25
33 Davey Boy Smith .12 .30
34 General Adnan RC .10 .25
35 Hulk Hogan .50 1.25
36 Ultimate Warrior .30 .75
37 Texas Tornado RC .12 .30
38 Hacksaw Jim Duggan .12 .30
39 Jake The Snake Roberts .20 .50
40 Hulk Hogan .50 1.25
41 The Model Rick Martel .10 .25
42 Earthquake RC .10 .25
43 Jimmy Hart .15 .40
44 Rockers .15 .40
45 Slick .10 .25
46 Legion of Doom .12 .30
47 Mr. Fuji .10 .25
48 Tugboat RC .10 .25
49 Power & Glory .10 .25
50 Bushwackers .10 .25
51 Macho King Randy Savage .30 .75
52 Hulk Hogan .50 1.25
53 Koko B. Ware .10 .25
54 Superfly Jimmy Snuka .15 .40
55 Haku .10 .25
56 Sensational Queen Sherri .12 .30
57 Nasty Boys .10 .25
58 Virgil .10 .25
59 Ted DiBiase .12 .30
60 Big Boss Man .10 .25
61 Sgt. Slaughter RC .15 .40
62 Barbarian .10 .25
63 Mr. Perfect .15 .40
64 Undertaker RC 20.00 50.00
65 Rowdy Roddy Piper .40 1.00
66 The Mountie RC .10 .25
67 General Adnan RC .10 .25
68 The Dragon Ricky Steamboat .12 .30
69 Hulk Hogan .50 1.25
70 Ultimate Warrior .30 .75
71 Texas Tornado RC .12 .30
72 Hacksaw Jim Duggan .12 .30
73 Jake The Snake Roberts .20 .50
74 The Model Rick Martel .10 .25
75 Earthquake RC .10 .25
76 Mr. Fuji .10 .25
77 Jimmy Hart .15 .40
78 Rockers .15 .40
79 Legion of Doom .12 .30
80 Tugboat RC .10 .25
81 Paul Roma .10 .25
82 Power & Glory .10 .25
83 Bushwackers .10 .25
84 Macho King Randy Savage .30 .75
85 General Adnan RC .10 .25
86 The Mountie RC .10 .25
87 Rowdy Roddy Piper .40 1.00
88 Undertaker RC 5.00 12.00
89 Mr. Perfect .15 .40
90 Sgt. Slaughter RC .15 .40
91 Hulk Hogan .50 1.25
92 Earthquake RC .10 .25
93 Paul Bearer RC 1.50 4.00
94 Koko B. Ware .10 .25
95 Superfly Jimmy Snuka .15 .40
96 Sensational Queen Sherri .12 .30
97 Sgt. Slaughter RC .15 .40
98 Rowdy Roddy Piper .40 1.00
99 Hulk Hogan .50 1.25
100 Ultimate Warrior .30 .75
101 Texas Tornado RC .12 .30
102 The Model Rick Martel .10 .25
103 Earthquake RC .10 .25
104 Legion of Doom .12 .30
105 Bret Hart .75 2.00
106 Undertaker RC 15.00 40.00
107 Mr. Perfect .15 .40
108 Sgt. Slaughter w/General Adnan .15 .40
109 Big Boss Man .10 .25
110 Ted DiBiase .12 .30
111 Hulk Hogan .50 1.25
112 Legion Of Doom .12 .30
113 Mr. Perfect .15 .40
114 Ultimate Warrior .30 .75
115 Big Boss Man .10 .25
116 Hacksaw Jim Duggan .12 .30
117 Power & Glory w/Slick .10 .25
118 Macho King Randy Savage .30 .75
119 Bushwackers .10 .25
120 Tugboat RC .10 .25
121 Mr. Perfect .15 .40
122 Barbarian .10 .25
123 Hulk Hogan .50 1.25
124 Ultimate Warrior 3.00 8.00
125 Big Boss Man 1.00 2.50
126 Hacksaw Jim Duggan 1.50 4.00
127 Jake The Snake Roberts 2.50 6.00
128 The Model Rick Martel .10 .25
129 The Dragon Ricky Steamboat .12 .30
130 Mr. Perfect 1.50 4.00
131 Haku .10 .25
132 Ted DiBiase .12 .30
133 Texas Tornado RC .12 .30
134 Macho King Randy Savage .30 .75
135 Macho King Randy Savage .30 .75
136 Legion of Doom .12 .30
137 Rockers .15 .40
138 Earthquake RC .10 .25
139 Superfly Jimmy Snuka .15 .40
140 Hulk Hogan 3.00 8.00
141 The Dragon Ricky Steamboat 1.50 4.00
142 Sgt. Slaughter RC 2.00 5.00
143 Texas Tornado RC .12 .30
144 Ted DiBiase .12 .30
145 Earthquake RC .10 .25
146 Legion of Doom .12 .30
147 Rockers .15 .40
148 Macho King Randy Savage 2.00 5.00
149 Earthquake RC .10 .25
150 The Model Rick Martel .10 .25

1994 Coliseum Video WWF Akklaim Strategy Tips

COMPLETE SET (4) 5.00 12.00
NNO Doink 2.00 5.00
NNO Luna Vachon 2.00 5.00
NNO Shawn Michaels 2.50 6.00
NNO Yokozuna 2.00 5.00

1994 Coliseum Video WWF Bret Hart

COMPLETE SET (5) 2.50 6.00
1 Bret Hitman Hart .75 2.00
2 Bret Hitman Hart .75 2.00
3 Bret Hitman Hart .75 2.00
4 Bret Hitman Hart .75 2.00
5 Bret Hitman Hart .75 2.00

1993 Coliseum Video WWF Collectors Cards

COMPLETE SET (9) 10.00 25.00
COLISEUM VIDEO RENTAL EXCLUSIVE
1 Hulk Hogan/Mr. T 2.50 6.00
2 King Kong Bundy/Hulk Hogan 2.50 6.00
3 Andre The Giant/Hulk Hogan 2.00 5.00
4 Macho Man/Miss Elizabeth 2.00 5.00
5 Macho Man/Hulk Hogan 4.00 10.00
6 Ultimate Warrior 1.50 4.00
7 Sgt. Slaughter/Hulk Hogan 2.00 5.00
8 Macho Man Randy Savage 1.50 4.00
9 Wrestlemania IX 1.25 3.00

1993 Coliseum Video WWF Lenticular

COMPLETE SET (5) 10.00 25.00
NNO Bret Hit Man Hart 4.00 10.00
NNO Hulk Hogan 3.00 8.00
NNO Mr. Perfect 2.50 6.00
NNO Tatanka 1.50 4.00
NNO The Undertaker 5.00 12.00

2003 Comic Images WWE Raw Deal Absolutely Raw and Ultimate Smackdown

1 Overhand Chairshot
2 Get Out of Here
3 She's Got Legs
4 This Has Gone Over By...
5 Elimination Chamber
6 Raw Deal
7 Undermine the Competition
8 Raw GM Eric Bischoff
9 Stone Cold, Triple H, or Christian?
10 Chris Jericho, Kane, or...
11 Suicide Lariat
12 Atomic Knee Drop
13 Escape to the Side
14 There Can Only Be One...
15 Caution: Dangerous Curves...
16 Banned from Ringside
17 Layin' the Smacketh Down
18 Smackdown GM...
19 Rock, Deadman, or Matt Hardy?
20 Rikishi, Chris Benoit, or...
21 You're Fired
22 Redemption
23 Divas Divas Divas
24 Vince McMahon Interferes
25 Get Off My Program
14TR Shawn Michaels
15TR Chris Nowinski
16TR Big Show
17TR Rey Mysterio
25PR Mae Young
31PR Hitting the G-Spot
32PR Stacy Keibler blank Superstar...

2004 Comic Images WWE Raw Deal Armageddon

1 Flying Head Scissors TB C .12 .25
2 Double Axe Handle TB C .12 .25
3 Leg Drop TB U .50 1.00
4 Splash TB U .50 1.00
5 Flying Clothesline TB R 2.00 4.00
6 Moonsault TB R 2.00 4.00
7 Chump Punch C .12 .25
8 Slap C .12 .25
9 Super Punch C .12 .25
10 Struck by a Kendo Stick TB C .12 .25
11 Shoulder Thrust U .50 1.00
12 Solarplex Knife Chop U .50 1.00
13 Cold-Cocked U .50 1.00
14 Ensugiri TB U .50 1.00
15 Knee Lift TB R 2.00 4.00
16 Whirling Backhand R 2.00 4.00
17 European Uppercut R 2.00 4.00
18 Flurry of Strikes R 2.00 4.00
19 Throw C .12 .25
20 Inverse Atomic Drop TB C .12 .25
21 Rib Breaker TB C .12 .25
22 Back Breaker TB C .12 .25
23 Double Leg Takedown TB U .50 1.00
24 Fireman's Carry TB U .50 1.00
25 Toss U .50 1.00
26 Leg Drag TB U .50 1.00
27 Brainbuster TB R 2.00 4.00
28 Airplane Spin TB R 2.00 4.00
29 Power Slam TB R 2.00 4.00
30 Atomic Driver R 2.00 4.00
31 Short Arm Hammerlock TB C .12 .25
32 Cranial Crunch C .12 .25
33 Chin Lock TB C .12 .25
34 Go-Behind C .12 .25
35 Grab U .50 1.00
36 Head Vise TB U .50 1.00
37 Chicken Wing TB U .50 1.00
38 Asphyxiater U .50 1.00
39 Rest Hold R 2.00 4.00
40 Abdominal Stretch TB R 2.00 4.00
41 STF TB R 2.00 4.00
42 Figure Four Leg Lock TB R 2.00 4.00
43 Anything and Hate It C .12 .25
44 I Gotta Say, Out of Play U .50 1.00
45 Raw and Ready R 2.00 4.00
46 Ask Yourself... C .12 .25
47 I Got That, Too C .12 .25
48 Hmmmm Don't Think... TB C .12 .25
49 Back in Style C .12 .25
50 From the Middle Turnbuckle C .12 .25
51 Throw Opponent Out... TB C .12 .25
52 From the Top Rope TB C .12 .25
53 I'm Desperate C .12 .25
54 J.R. Style Action U .50 1.00
55 Volley This U .50 1.00
56 Flawless Execution U .50 1.00
57 Great Power Brawl TB U .50 1.00
58 The Rub U .50 1.00
59 Egomaniacal U .50 1.00
60 It's Not Always the Charisma U .50 1.00
61 Throwback Represent U .50 1.00
62 Calculated Revenge R 2.00 4.00

63 The Show Must Go On R 2.00 4.00
64 I'm Giving You a Chance R 2.00 4.00
65 Personal Vendetta R 2.00 4.00
66 I Won't Stop R 2.00 4.00
67 Defensive Style TB R 2.00 4.00
68 Take It Back R 2.00 4.00
69 The Switch R 2.00 4.00
70 Like a Bat Out of Hell R 2.00 4.00
71 Boston, Massachusetts C .12 .25
72 I Want to Play the Game C .12 .25
73 Old School Antics C .12 .25
74 San Diego, California C .12 .25
75 Unbreakable Chain C .12 .25
76 All Alone in the Night U .50 1.00
77 Managed by William Regal U .50 1.00
78 New Orleans, Louisiana U .50 1.00
79 Buried Alive Match U .50 1.00
80 Washington, DC U .50 1.00
81 Little Rock, Arkansas R 2.00 4.00
82 Managed by the Coach R 2.00 4.00
83 Evening Gown Match R 2.00 4.00
84 Singapore City, Singapore R 2.00 4.00
85 Clear the Way C .12 .25
86 Old-Fashioned Lock-Up C .12 .25
87 Pop You One C .12 .25
88 Atomic Bear Hug C .12 .25
89 Here Comes the Coach C .12 .25
90 Out of Control U .50 1.00
91 You'll Really Be Stunned U .50 1.00
92 The Darkness Before the Dawn U .50 1.00
93 Goodnight, Everybody U .50 1.00
94 Sometimes You Need to... U .50 1.00
95 Here Comes the Headache R 2.00 4.00
96 Suicide Plancha TB R 2.00 4.00
97 I'm Making This Up As I Go Along R 2.00 4.00
98 It's All For My Fans R 2.00 4.00
99 Anybody Can Be King... R 2.00 4.00
100 Babe of the Year EX
101 Give Me a Little UR 7.50 15.00
102 Time to Catch My Breath UR 7.50 15.00
103 Babe Buster EX
104 Tyson Interferes EX
105 Keys to the City EX
106 John Bradshaw Layfield EX
107 Ten Gallon Hat UR 7.50 15.00
108 JBL's Limo UR 7.50 15.00
109 Work Harder, Work Smarter EX
110 You Forgot About Orlando... EX
111 JBL's Clothesline from Hell EX
112 The Phenom EX
113 The Urn UR 7.50 15.00
114 Takin' Care of Business UR 7.50 15.00
115 The Dead Will Rise Again EX
116 There is No Forgiveness... EX
117 The Deadman is Alive EX
118 Randy Orton EX
119 The Legend Killer UR 7.50 15.00
120 RKO UR 7.50 15.00
121 Youngest Champion in WWE... EX
122 Third Generation Superstar EX
123 Overdrive EX
124 Shane O'Mac EX
125 Mean Streets of Greenwich, CT UR 7.50 15.00
126 Coast to Coast UR 7.50 15.00
127 Mean Streets Silver Spoon EX
128 Here's Where the Buck Stops EX
129 Leap of Faith EX
130 Shelton Benjamin EX
131 World's Greatest Upset... UR 7.50 15.00
132 T-Bone Exploder Suplex UR 7.50 15.00
133 Ain't No Stopping Me Now EX
134 Shelton's Spinning Heel Kick EX
135 Shelton's Splash EX
136 Eugene PR
137 I'm Special UR 7.50 15.00
138 Eugening Up PR
139 The Jacket's Coming Off PR
140 The Pride of the Family PR
141 The Dream Lives On PR
142 Rene Dupree PR
143 Rene's Elbow Drop UR 7.50 15.00
144 Managed by Fifi PR
145 The French Tickler PR
146 Fifi Interferes PR
147 The French Neck Breaker PR
148 Cerebral Spray PR
149 Pago Pago, American Samoa PR
150 Out of the Hellfire PR
151 Don't You Wish You Were Me? PR
152 For Real PR
153 El Paso, Texas PR
154 Angle's Leg Bar PR
155 Dudleyville, USA PR
156 You're Just a Puppet PR
157 Captain Charisma Strikes PR
158 I Can Slap a Tornado PR
159 The Hog Log PR
160 A Less Traveled Road PR
161 Step Over Heel Kick PR
162 I Ain't No Minor Leaguer PR
163 People Like Us Are Just Born... PR
164 The Best Thing Going Today PR
165 Double Chop PR
166 Superhero in Training PR
167 Crossing Borders PR
168 The Legend Lives On PR
169 Throwback PR
170 Taunt the Crowd PR
171 Why Can't We Just Dance? UR 7.50 15.00
172 The Inmates Aren't Running... UR 7.50 15.00
173 It's Not a Wig UR 7.50 15.00
174 The Cena Throwback UR 7.50 15.00
175 A Welcome Distraction UR 7.50 15.00
176 Victoria's Secret UR 7.50 15.00
177 Drastic Times... UR 7.50 15.00
178 If You Want to Play... UR 7.50 15.00
179 Master Manipulator UR 7.50 15.00
180 Armageddon is Upon Us UR 7.50 15.00
181 Vinny Mac Attack UR 7.50 15.00

2004 Comic Images WWE Raw Deal Divas Overload

1 Show and Go C .12 .25
2 Diving Bulldog U .50 1.00
3 Suicide Dive R 2.00 4.00
4 Girly Punch C .12 .25
5 Boot Lace C .12 .25
6 Chop Block C .12 .25
7 Elbow Smash C .12 .25
8 Jab U .50 1.00
9 Forearm Uppercut U .50 1.00
10 Ax Kick U .50 1.00
11 Spinning Clothesline U .50 1.00
12 Chick Kick R 2.00 4.00
13 Double Clothesline Takedown R 2.00 4.00
14 Atomic Lariat R 2.00 4.00
15 Hurricane Clothesline R 2.00 4.00
16 Chest Lock Drop C .12 .25
17 Wheelbarrow Slam C .12 .25
18 Running Spinebuster U .50 1.00
19 Gut Buster On Top Rope U .50 1.00
20 Top Rope Toss R 2.00 4.00
21 Reverse Fall-away Slam R 2.00 4.00
22 Modified Clutch Onto Opponent C .12 .25
23 Arm Breaker C .12 .25
24 Unorthodox Wrist Lock U .50 1.00
25 Modified Bow and Arrow U .50 1.00
26 Front Chancery R 2.00 4.00
27 Lady's Grapevine R 2.00 4.00
28 Girl on Girl Action C .12 .25
29 Some Gals Don't Get Any Action C .12 .25
30 Overshot Your Mark U .50 1.00
31 Reach for the Ropes U .50 1.00
32 Too Many Rules... R 2.00 4.00
33 You Fight Like a Woman R 2.00 4.00
34 Let's Wrestle Already C .12 .25
35 No Matching Tights C .12 .25
36 Don't Be Shy C .12 .25
37 It's Time I Made Some Changes C .12 .25
38 Lousy Foot Work C .12 .25
39 Recover Again C .12 .25
40 Name of the Game... C .12 .25
41 I've Got a Leg Up On You C .12 .25
42 I've Got a Nice Bottom U .50 1.00
43 I'll Take a Shot U .50 1.00
44 The Hubbub Backstage U .50 1.00
45 Get a Look at These U .50 1.00
46 So Solly So Sorey U .50 1.00
47 Sump'tin' Be Started U .50 1.00
48 This Diva's Got Claws U .50 1.00
49 Shake My Hand, Boy U .50 1.00
50 My New Gimmick R 2.00 4.00
51 Puppy Love R 2.00 4.00
52 What Are You Gawking At? R 2.00 4.00
53 Where's the Payoff? R 2.00 4.00
54 Don't Cross the Boss R 2.00 4.00
55 Twisted Smile R 2.00 4.00
56 Tap Tap Tap, You Sonofa- R 2.00 4.00
57 If You're Not Cheating... R 2.00 4.00
58 Asset Retrieval C .12 .25
59 Not Today, Cupcake C .12 .25
60 I'm Always on Top C .12 .25
61 Distractingly Divalicious C .12 .25
62 You Should Cover Your Eyes C .12 .25
63 Old School Psychology C .12 .25
64 Back to Basics U .50 1.00
65 Falls Count Anywhere Match U .50 1.00
66 Skirt vs. Skirt Match U .50 1.00
67 Dare to Take a Challenge U .50 1.00
68 Perennial Fan Favorites U .50 1.00
69 Run the Gauntlet U .50 1.00
70 Backstage Interview with Terri R 2.00 4.00
71 I've Had More Championships... R 2.00 4.00
72 I'm Gonna Break You R 2.00 4.00
73 Rules Were Meant to be Broken R 2.00 4.00
74 Managed by Miss Jackie R 2.00 4.00
75 Managed by Theodore Long R 2.00 4.00
76 Took That on the Chin C .12 .25
77 Skirt the Issue C .12 .25
78 Get the Tables C .12 .25
79 Teaser Mode C .12 .25
80 Victory Roll C .12 .25
81 I'm Trying Not to Lose... U .50 1.00
82 Panic Assault U .50 1.00
83 Panic Grab U .50 1.00
84 Panic Throw U .50 1.00
85 This Is Going Nowhere Fast U .50 1.00
86 That's Gonna Leave a Mark R 2.00 4.00
87 It Doesn't Stop R 2.00 4.00
88 Divas Overload R 2.00 4.00
89 It's Over R 2.00 4.00
90 Reverse 180-Degree Chair Shot R 2.00 4.00
91 Goldberg EX
92 Gooooooollllllldddddd-berg UR 7.50 15.00
93 Goldberg's Jackhammer UR 7.50 15.00
94 Who's Next? EX
95 Believe the Hype EX
96 Goldberg's Spear EX
97 Stacy Keibler EX
98 Straddle the Ropes UR 7.50 15.00
99 Superior Leg Work UR 7.50 15.00
100 Test or Freakzilla? EX
101 Pump Me Up EX
102 I Know How to Use Them EX
103 Gail Kim and Molly Holly EX
104 Change Reality UR 7.50 15.00
105 Gail's Hurricanrana UR 7.50 15.00
106 Wake Up EX
107 Look Around EX
108 Molly-Go-Round EX
109 John Cena EX
110 Yo Kill da Beat UR 7.50 15.00
111 F-U UR 7.50 15.00
112 You Can't See Me EX
113 Word Life EX
114 I'm Gonna Teach You... EX
115 Sable EX
116 Sable-licious UR 7.50 15.00
117 And the Men that Come... UR 7.50 15.00
118 APA or A-Train? EX
119 For the Women that Want... EX
120 Sable Bomb EX
121 Torrie Wilson EX
122 WWE Centerfold of the Year UR 7.50 15.00
123 Torrie's DDT UR 7.50 15.00
124 Does This Look Good on Me? EX
125 Strike a Pose EX
126 The Boise Beauty EX
127 Victoria PR
128 Widow's Peak UR 7.50 15.00
129 Managed by Stevie Richards PR
130 All the Things She Said PR
131 Yes, I've Lost My Mind PR
132 Stevie Interferes PR
133 Nidia PR
134 The Special Kiss UR 7.50 15.00
135 Managed by Jamie Noble PR
136 Trailer Park Slap PR
137 Drop Dead Gorgeous PR
138 Jamie Noble Interferes PR
139 Do You Want a Hug? PR
140 You're Gonna Pay PR
141 The Peep's Champ PR
142 A Beating You'll Never Forget PR
143 Unmasked Vengeance PR
144 Highlight Reel PR
145 Rikishi's Superkick PR
146 Wrestling with a Broken... PR
147 Benoit's German Suplex PR
148 Gory Special PR
149 That One Thing PR
150 Beatings from Dudleyville PR
151 Side Effect PR
152 Showdown PR
153 Mr. Monday Night PR
154 Houston Hangover PR
155 The Goddess Returns PR
156 Drinking Beer - Raising Hell... PR
157 The Flair Flop PR
158 Puppy Power PR
159 Tough Enough Head Trainer PR
160 Series of Kicks PR
161 Gregory Helms, Ace Reporter PR
162 You Will Never Forget... UR 7.50 15.00
163 Brock Block UR 7.50 15.00
164 Rey Rey's Flying Body Press UR 7.50 15.00
165 Nidia, Hook Up the Double Wide UR 7.50 15.00
166 Steiner Flatliner UR 7.50 15.00
167 I'm Just a Sexy Boy UR 7.50 15.00
168 The World's Greatest Suplex UR 7.50 15.00
169 Once You Go Test... UR 7.50 15.00
170 Unstoppable UR 7.50 15.00
171 RVD or Booker T? UR 7.50 15.00
172 Edge or Big Show? UR 7.50 15.00

2006 Comic Images WWE Raw Deal Great American Bash

1 Blindside Elbow Drop C .12 .25
2 BASH Drop Kick C .12 .25
3 Technical Splash in the Corner U .50 1.00
4 BASH Aerial Clothesline U .50 1.00
5 Corkscrew Somersault R 2.00 4.00
6 Dynamic Flying Body Press R 2.00 4.00
7 BASH Punch C .12 .25
8 Straight Head Butt C .12 .25
9 Shoot Kicker Hold C .12 .25
10 Sizzling Clotheslin C .12 .25
11 Blindside Hook U .50 1.00
12 BASH Kick U .50 1.00
13 Shoot Forearm U .50 1.00
14 The Ol' Straight-Arm Shot U .50 1.00
15 Thrust Knee Lift R 2.00 4.00
16 Technical Lunging Lariat R 2.00 4.00
17 Dynamic Gut Stomp R 2.00 4.00
18 Precision Haymaker R 2.00 4.00
19 BASH Suplex C .12 .25
20 Blindside Drop Toe Hold C .12 .25
21 Leaping DDT C .12 .25
22 Technical Monkey Flip U .50 1.00
23 BASH Slam U .50 1.00
24 Quick Snap Suplex U .50 1.00
25 Precision Reverse Neck Breaker R 2.00 4.00
26 BASH Drop Over the Ropes R 2.00 4.00
27 Dynamic Back Breaker R 2.00 4.00
28 BASH Headlock C .12 .25
29 Diva Lock C .12 .25
30 Shoot Double Arm Lock C .12 .25
31 Stretch Opponent C .12 .25
32 BASH Vise U .50 1.00
33 Blindside Sleeper U .50 1.00
34 Technical Bear Hug U .50 1.00
35 Precision Figure Four U .50 1.00
36 Shoot Lock-up R 2.00 4.00
37 Neck Torque R 2.00 4.00
38 BASH Pin Hold R 2.00 4.00
39 Dynamic Torture Rack R 2.00 4.00
40 BASH Evader C .12 .25
41 Me Llamo... Armando... C .12 .25

42 Get Back in the Ring U	.50	1.00
43 The Return BASHÖ U	.50	1.00
44 Booby Trap R	2.00	4.00
45 Volleyed Beyond the Edge R	2.00	4.00
46 Takiní a BASH C	.12	.25
47 Stay Away from Daivari C	.12	.25
48 Give me an S...Give me a P... C	.12	.25
49 Hide and Seek U	.50	1.00
50 Blindsided by the... U	.50	1.00
51 Shane OíMac Delivers the BASH U	.50	1.00
52 Give & Take R	2.00	4.00
53 Jillian: Foxy Fixer R	2.00	4.00
54 Kristal: Broadcast Beauty R	2.00	4.00
55 Donít BASH the Star C	.12	.25
56 Find Out How to Fight From Finlay C	.12	.25
57 Straight-Shootiní Interview C	.12	.25
58 The Luck of the Draw C	.12	.25
59 All Together Now U	.50	1.00
60 Itís Not My Fault Being... EX	.50	1.00
61 The Best Laid PlansÖ U	.50	1.00
62 Not On My Broadcast U	.50	1.00
63 A No Show R	2.00	4.00
64 First of All R	2.00	4.00
65 For the Love of The Game R	2.00	4.00
66 Managed by Shane OíMac R	2.00	4.00
67 My Name is Matt Striker... C	.12	.25
68 Cheaters Never Win C	.12	.25
69 Throw DownóDonít Kiss Up C	.12	.25
70 Trevor Murdoch Is Gonna... U	.50	1.00
71 Backfire U	.50	1.00
72 A Phoenix Rising U	.50	1.00
73 Can U Believe the Witte Retort? R	2.00	4.00
74 This Is Between You and Me R	2.00	4.00
75 BASH: Great American Style R	2.00	4.00
76 Andre ìThe Giantî EX		
77 We Face Each Other... UR	7.50	15.00
78 The 8th Wonder of the World UR	7.50	15.00
79 Giant Head Butt EX		
80 Inspiration for a New... PR		
81 Obey EX		
82 Lashley EX		
83 The Elevator Lift UR	7.50	15.00
84 The Real Hard Dominator UR	7.50	15.00
85 Hard Hitting EX		
86 Soft Spoken EX		
87 Iím the Real Deal EX		
88 Ken Kennedy EX		
89 Mr. Kennedyís Mic UR	7.50	15.00
90 The Kenton Bomb UR	7.50	15.00
91 Say It Loud; Say It Proud: EX		
92 Mmmmmisterrrrr KennedyyyyyÖ EX		
93 ÖKENóNEóDY! EX		
94 Mickie James EX		
95 You Think Iím a Psycho? UR	7.50	15.00
96 Laree DDT UR	7.50	15.00
97 Do You Love Me Now? EX		
98 Mick Kick EX		
99 Itís Time for a Great... U		
100 Mr. Pay-Per-View EX		
101 Unscripted UR	7.50	15.00
102 The Fury of the Storm UR	7.50	15.00
103 Flying Higher Than Ever EX		
104 Still Ö One of a Kind EX		
105 Split-legged Moonsault EX		
106 The Ultimate Survivor EX		
107 You Couldnít Pay Me Enough UR	7.50	15.00
108 Stronger Than Death UR	7.50	15.00
109 The Matt Hardy Movement... EX		
110 The Shirt Is Off EX		
111 Indestructible Soul EX		
112 The Boogeyman PR		
113 The Bottomless Pit UR	7.50	15.00
114 The Tick Tock of the Clock PR		
115 Mouthful of Worms PR		
116 I Am The BoogeymanÖ PR		
117 ÖAnd Iím Coming To Getcha! PR		
118 The Spirit Squad PR		
119 Johnny PR		
120 Kenny PR		
121 Mikey PR		
122 Mitch PR		
123 Nicky PR		
124 High Spirits UR	7.50	15.00
125 S-P-I-R-I-T-S-Q-U-A-D... PR		
126 The Johnny-Go-Round Kick PR		
127 Trampoline Leap PR		
128 Air Kenny PR		
129 The Condemned PR		
130 Look Into the Eyes... PR		
131 The King of Kings PR		
132 See No Evil PR		
133 Angleís Uppercut PR		
134 20 Years: From theÖ PR		
135 The Rated R Superstar PR		
136 You Wonít See It ComingÖ PR		
137 Sharmellís Shenanigans PR		
138 The Art of Persuasion PR		
139 Regal Readying PR		
140 Hulkamania: Always in Style PR		
141 16-Time HeavyweightÖ PR		
142 Diva of the Decade PR		
143 The Size Advantage PR		
144 Grapple With Your Faith PR		
145 Billion Dollar Princess PR		
146 The Chain Gang: Hustle... PR		
147 Chloe: Best in Show PR		
148 I Ainít the Lady to Mess With PR		
149 Zero Tolerance: Kiss MyÖ PR		
150 I Am Who I Say I Am PR		
151 Fully Evolved: PR		
152 McMahon-icide PR		
153 Iíve Seen the Light PR		
154 Inspiration for a New Generation PR		
155 Blindside Spinebuster UR	7.50	15.00
156 Seen the GloryóTold the Story UR	7.50	15.00
157 Never Bet Against Me, Playa UR	7.50	15.00
158 Ground & Pound UR	7.50	15.00
159 I Wish Monsoon Was Here UR	7.50	15.00
160 JYDís Chain UR	7.50	15.00
161 Cobra Clutch UR	7.50	15.00
162 United We Stand UR	7.50	15.00
163 Divided You Fall UR	7.50	15.00
164 Whoís Under the Paint? UR	7.50	15.00
165 Carlitoís Cool Caribbean... UR	7.50	15.00
166 The Snakeline UR	7.50	15.00
167 Backed by Virgil UR	7.50	15.00
168 The Three Amigos UR	7.50	15.00
169 Funakiís Ensugiri UR	7.50	15.00
170 Size Matters UR	7.50	15.00

2003 Comic Images WWE Raw Deal Insurrextion

1 Flying Choke Hold C	.12	.25
2 Flying Takedown U	.50	1.00
3 Flying Lariat R	2.00	4.00
4 Poke C	.12	.25
5 Noggin Knocker U	.50	1.00
6 Series of Punches R	2.00	4.00
7 Shake C	.12	.25
8 Capture Suplex C	.12	.25
9 Tossed Between the Ropes C	.12	.25
10 Rolling Suplex U	.50	1.00
11 Inside Cradle U	.50	1.00
12 Inverted Snake Eyes U	.50	1.00
13 Snap Slam R	2.00	4.00
14 Hangman's Neck Breaker R	2.00	4.00
15 Faceplant R	2.00	4.00
16 Split Finger Lock C	.12	.25
17 Body Vise U	.50	1.00
18 Inverted Leg Lock R	2.00	4.00
19 Dude, Try Something Else C	.12	.25
20 Fall into the Corner U	.50	1.00
21 Don't Try This at Home R	2.00	4.00
22 Blind Tag C	.12	.25
23 The Devil's in the Detail C	.12	.25
24 Hey, Whatcha Doin'? C	.12	.25
25 Crowd Pleaser C	.12	.25
26 Pump Up the Crowd C	.12	.25
27 How Ya Like Me Now? C	.12	.25
28 Perplex Opponent C	.12	.25
29 Always U	.50	1.00
30 Add Insult to Injury U	.50	1.00
31 It's Your Own Fault U	.50	1.00
32 This is Gonna Get Ugly U	.50	1.00
33 What's Mine is Mine... U	.50	1.00
34 Beat You Raw U	.50	1.00
35 Forget the Smackdown... U	.50	1.00
36 No One Wants to Watch... R	2.00	4.00
37 I Can't Be Reading This Right R	2.00	4.00
38 Pass the Buck R	2.00	4.00
39 From the Mind of Eric Bischoff R	2.00	4.00
40 Stephanie McMahon Decrees R	2.00	4.00
41 The End Is Near R	2.00	4.00
42 Forceable Entry R	2.00	4.00
43 Give and Take C	.12	.25
44 I'm the Underdog C	.12	.25
45 Ring Psychology: Arm C	.12	.25
46 Ring Psychology: Leg C	.12	.25
47 Stun the Crowd C	.12	.25
48 Take Care of Number One C	.12	.25
49 Backstage Donnybrook U	.50	1.00
50 Dance, Coach, Dance U	.50	1.00
51 Man of 1000 Holds U	.50	1.00
52 Premiere Raw Superstar U	.50	1.00
53 Premiere Smackdown Superstar U	.50	1.00
54 Smackdown #1 Announcer Funaki U	.50	1.00
55 According to Linda and the Board of Executives R	2.00	4.00
56 Backstage Politics R	2.00	4.00
57 It's Hard Being This Original R	2.00	4.00
58 Mangled Intro by Lillian Garcia R	2.00	4.00
59 Raw Roulette Wheel R	2.00	4.00
60 Series of Stipulations R	2.00	4.00
61 The Ref Takes Control C	.12	.25
62 Power Struggle C	.12	.25
63 Chase Off Manager C	.12	.25
64 Cut the Ring in Half C	.12	.25
65 Really, That's Enough C	.12	.25
66 Mental Acumen C	.12	.25
67 Don't Cross a McMahon U	.50	1.00
68 Give You the Runaround U	.50	1.00
69 Electric Chair U	.50	1.00
70 Glad Someone Has My Back U	.50	1.00
71 You Make Me Sick U	.50	1.00
72 Do Something R	2.00	4.00
73 Show Me Something R	2.00	4.00
74 Chief Morley Says R	2.00	4.00
75 Real Predictable R	2.00	4.00
76 Outside Interference R	2.00	4.00
77 Big Poppa Pump EX		
78 Holla If Ya Hear Me UR	7.50	15.00
79 Genetic Freak Push-ups UR	7.50	15.00
80 Freakzilla Says... EX		
81 All I Care About Are My... EX		
82 The Big, Bad Booty Daddy... EX		
83 The Rattlesnake EX		
84 The Bionic Redneck UR	7.50	15.00
85 Gimme a Hell Yeah UR	7.50	15.00
86 Stomp a Mudhole EX		
87 Don't Trust Nobody EX		
88 Walk It Dry EX		
89 Shawn Michaels EX		
90 The Icon, The Showstoppa... UR	7.50	15.00
91 Sweet Chin Music UR	7.50	15.00
92 Don't Hunt What You Can't Kill EX		
93 Top Rope Elbow Drop EX		
94 The Heart Break Kid EX		
95 The Crippler EX		
96 There's No Holding Me Back UR	7.50	15.00
97 Toothless Aggression UR	7.50	15.00
98 Cripple Opponent EX		
99 Rabid Attack in the Corner EX		
100 Surprise Drop Kick EX		
101 Los Guerreros EX		
102 We Lie, We Cheat, We Steal UR	7.50	15.00
103 Chavo's Inverted Powerbomb UR	7.50	15.00
104 Cheat 2 Win EX		
105 Tu Locas, Ese You Crazy, Man EX		
106 Lasso from El Paso EX		
107 Team Angle EX		
108 Collegiate Champions UR	7.50	15.00
109 Leapfrog Stun Gun UR	7.50	15.00
110 Submit EX		
111 It's All About the Benjamins EX		
112 The Haas of Pain EX		
113 Test PR		
114 Test Drive UR	7.50	15.00
115 I Love My Testicles PR		
116 Stacy Keibler, Marketing... PR		
117 Test's Pump Handle Slam PR		
118 Test's Running Boot PR		
119 Rhyno PR		
120 GORE GORE GORE UR	7.50	15.00
121 Extreme Warfare PR		
122 Rhyno's Garbage Can PR		
123 The Manbeast PR		
124 Rhyno Stampede PR		
125 Big Evil - Red Devil PR		
126 Screw the Rules PR		
127 Get Ready... PR		
128 Big Freak'n Powerslam PR		
129 I'm the King of the World PR		
130 Makin' a Difference PR		
131 Dudleyz3 PR		
132 You're a Human Vacuum... PR		
133 I Ain't Not No Sucka Neitha PR		
134 Version 1.0 PR		
135 X-treme Sendoff PR		
136 You Can't Manhandle... PR		
137 Dude Whatever PR		
138 Yo Dawg, Respect... PR		
139 Proper Planning Prevents... PR		
140 I Live for My Hulkamaniacs UR	7.50	15.00
141 You're Going to Space Mountain UR	7.50	15.00
143 No Gimmicks Needed UR	7.50	15.00
144 Double Face Kick UR	7.50	15.00
145 Shining Wizard Kick UR	7.50	15.00
146 Electrifying UR	7.50	15.00
147 Here Comes the Pain UR	7.50	15.00
148 West Coast Bronco Buster UR	7.50	15.00
149 3 Minutes and We're Out UR	7.50	15.00
150 Nidia Interferes UR	7.50	15.00
142-A X-treme Hedonism - A Image UR	7.50	15.00
142-B X-treme Hedonism - B Image UR	7.50	15.00

2004 Comic Images WWE Raw Deal Lethal Library

1 Vince McMahon
2 Remember Who Pays Your Salary
3 Master of Promotion
4 I'm Vincent Kennedy McMahon...
5 First Family of Professional Wrestling
6 A Dynasty's Destiny
7 Shane O'Mac or Stephanie ?
8 King's Crown
9 White Wedding
10 Osaka, Japan
11 I Don't Care About the Heat
12 Change in Programming Lineup
13 The Road to Victory
14 Suicide Strike
15 Counterproductive Ambitions
16 How Important Is It?
17 Sucker Punch
18 Gut Punch Body Slam
19 Atomic Spine Buster
20 Leg Lock
21 McMahon Family Values
22 Explosion Raw Deal
23 Lethal Library
24 The Price We Pay

2006 Comic Images WWE Raw Deal No Way Out

1 Technical Stomp C	.12	.25
2 Shoot Aerial 360-Degree Kick U	.50	1.00
3 Precision Knee Drop R	2.00	4.00
4 Dynamic Punch C	.12	.25
5 Dynamic Hook C	.12	.25
6 Straight Clothesline C	.12	.25
7 Thrust Kick C	.12	.25
8 Shoot Punch U	.50	1.00
9 Dynamic Forearm U	.50	1.00
10 Technical Clothesline U	.50	1.00
11 Dynamic Knee Lift U	.50	1.00
12 Precision Kick U	.50	1.00
13 Blindside Tornado Strike R	2.00	4.00
14 Whirling Elbow R	2.00	4.00
15 Dynamic Lariat R	2.00	4.00
16 Punch After Punch R	2.00	4.00
17 Snap DDT C	.12	.25
18 Dynamic Throw C	.12	.25
19 Dynamic Drop C	.12	.25
20 Delayed Atomic Drop C	.12	.25
21 Blindside Beal Toss U	.50	1.00
22 Rolling Neck Breaker U	.50	1.00
23 Dynamic Takedown U	.50	1.00
24 Dynamic Slam U	.50	1.00

25 Precision Suplex U .50 1.00
26 Dynamic Driver R 2.00 4.00
27 Technical Power Bomb R 2.00 4.00
28 Vertical Power Bomb R 2.00 4.00
29 Atomic Power Slam R 2.00 4.00
30 Dynamic Arm Bar C .12 .25
31 Arm Twist C .12 .25
32 Dynamic Headlock C .12 .25
33 Blindside Abdominal Stretch C .12 .25
34 Arm Wrench U .50 1.00
35 Vise Lock U .50 1.00
36 Dynamic Stretch U .50 1.00
37 Dynamic Bear Hug U .50 1.00
38 Precision Sleeper U .50 1.00
39 Technical Crab R 2.00 4.00
40 Fujiwara Arm Bar R 2.00 4.00
41 Dynamic Figure Four R 2.00 4.00
42 Atomic Body Lock R 2.00 4.00
43 It's Great To Be Back Here In... C .12 .25
44 Just What the Game Needs C .12 .25
45 The Coach Says... U .50 1.00
46 Once Again, Kissing Up... R 2.00 4.00
47 You Can't Cheat an Honest Man... R 2.00 4.00
48 Contrary to Popular Opinion C .12 .25
49 Between the Ropes C .12 .25
50 Over the Ropes C .12 .25
51 Painfully Obvious Precision C .12 .25
52 ...And the Crowd Roars U .50 1.00
53 By Any Means Necessary U .50 1.00
54 Shoot Action R 2.00 4.00
55 Ashley: Pretty Punk R 2.00 4.00
56 Mickie: Fervent Fanatic R 2.00 4.00
57 Kick Out! R 2.00 4.00
58 Givin' 'Em High Fives C .12 .25
59 In The Interest Of Fairness C .12 .25
60 Technically Sound & Brutal C .12 .25
61 I Have A Major Announcement U .50 1.00
62 You Will Witness History U .50 1.00
63 There Is No Escape U .50 1.00
64 Denville, New Jersey R 2.00 4.00
65 WWE Homecoming R 2.00 4.00
66 That's Value! R 2.00 4.00
67 Go For the Cover! C .12 .25
68 Tormented Tomfoolery C .12 .25
69 A Punch That'll Take... C .12 .25
70 Precision Personified U .50 1.00
71 Shoot Counter U .50 1.00
72 Blindsided Rage U .50 1.00
73 A Great Deal Of Confusion R 2.00 4.00
74 Overwhelming Crowd Support R 2.00 4.00
75 Volley Finisher R 2.00 4.00
76 Carlito EX
77 Carlito's Apple UR 7.50 15.00
78 Carlito's Cabana UR 7.50 15.00
79 I Spit In the Face Of... EX
80 ...People Who Don't Want... EX
81 Carlito's Way DDT EX
82 Jake "the Snake" EX
83 Lucifer UR 7.50 15.00
84 Mind Games EX
85 The Snake Will Always.... EX
86 The Snake Bite DDT EX
87 The Million Dollar Man... EX
88 The Million Dollar Title Belt UR 7.50 15.00
89 Everybody's Got a Price EX
90 Everybody's Gonna Pay EX
91 The Million Dollar Dream EX
92 The Bookerman EX
93 Managed by Sharmell UR 7.50 15.00
94 Sharmell Interferes UR 7.50 15.00
95 You Didn't Just Try That... EX
96 Spinning Straight Elbow EX
97 Distracted by Sharmell EX
98 The Largest Athlete... EX
99 Mine Is Bigger Than Yours UR 7.50 15.00
100 The Biggest Precision... UR 7.50 15.00
101 Colossal Clubbing EX
102 Big Enough to Eat Somebody EX
103 The Big & The Small of It EX
104 X-treme Diva EX
105 It Just Feels Right UR 7.50 15.00
106 Just the Way I Planned... UR 7.50 15.00
107 Girly Choke EX
108 Don't Call Me A... EX
109 Love... Fury... Passion... EX
110 Chavo Guerrero PR
111 One for One UR 7.50 15.00
112 My Life For You PR
113 Guerreros por Siempre! PR
114 A Family Tradition PR
115 The Gory Bomb PR
116 Funaki PR
117 The Rising Sun UR 7.50 15.00
118 Japanese Flying Bulldog PR
119 I'll Do Anything For the... PR
120 ...I Do Ask the Tough Questions PR
121 Springboard Body Block PR
122 Mexicools PR
123 Lawn Maintenance... UR 7.50 15.00
124 Forget Your Stereotypes PR
125 Crazy Moonsault PR
126 Psychotic Guillotine Leg Drop PR
127 Mexi-Leg-Lace Powerbomb PR
128 Viscera PR
129 The Sex Drive UR 7.50 15.00
130 A Big Man Has A Big... Appetite PR
131 500 Pound Love Machine PR
132 Take It Like a Man PR
133 Flying Somersault Kick PR
134 STUNNER! PR
135 Death Waits for No Man PR
136 Bring the Hammer Down PR
137 This Is The Rock's Show PR
138 Journey Into Darkness PR
139 American By Birth... PR
140 I'm Driven by Anger PR
141 Liaison with Lita PR
142 It's Us vs. Them PR
143 Nobody Gets Higher PR
144 Walking a Golden Mile PR
145 24-inch Pythons PR
146 Walk That Aisle PR
147 Trish's Chick Kick PR
148 Old School Luche Libre... PR
149 Tuning Up the Band PR
150 One Issue On My Mind PR
151 The B!tch Is Back! PR
152 You Want Some? Come Get Some! PR
153 Too Hot For TV PR
154 Is Chloe Your Favorite Puppy? PR
155 Backed by Torrie & Candice PR
156 It's Good For Business PR
157 I Am a Wrestling God UR 7.50 15.00
158 The Ego Cutter UR 7.50 15.00
159 Hold On, Hotshot! UR 7.50 15.00
160 Shelton's Lunging Lariat UR 7.50 15.00
161 Dernier Slam UR 7.50 15.00
162 Unleashed Bomb UR 7.50 15.00
163 The Rowdy Sleeper UR 7.50 15.00
164 Listen Up, Playa! UR 7.50 15.00
165 No Fault Drop UR 7.50 15.00
166 Jillian Hall: The Fixer UR 7.50 15.00
167 The Brain UR 7.50 15.00
168 The Thump UR 7.50 15.00
169 At Ease, Soldier UR 7.50 15.00
170 The Intensity of Ten Cities UR 7.50 15.00
171 Should've Seen This Coming UR 7.50 15.00
172 Pails o' Fun UR 7.50 15.00

2006 Comic Images WWE Raw Deal Royal Rumble

COMPLETE SET (90)
1 Roundhouse Kick C .12 .25
2 Big Splash in the Corner U .50 1.00
3 Technical Tope R 2.00 4.00
4 Handcuffed C .12 .25
5 Fisticuffs C .12 .25
6 Armed & Dangerous U .50 1.00
7 Technical Drop Kick U .50 1.00
8 Ankle Breaker R 2.00 4.00
9 Running Clothesline R 2.00 4.00
10 Slingshot Into the Ring Post C .12 .25
11 Slam C .12 .25
12 Scoop Slam U .50 1.00
13 Thunder Bulldog U .50 1.00
14 Fall-away Suplex R 2.00 4.00
15 Technical Slam R 2.00 4.00
16 Hair Pull C .12 .25
17 Entangle in the Ropes C .12 .25
18 Key Lock U .50 1.00
19 Take Your Own Medicine U .50 1.00
20 Face Stretch R 2.00 4.00
21 Technical Body Lock R 2.00 4.00
22 How Many Do You Need? C .12 .25
23 Always Have a Plan B U .30 .75
24 Once is Enough R 2.00 4.00
25 Volley Call C .12 .25
26 Everyone Wants to Watch... C .12 .25
27 Everyone Wants to Watch... C .12 .25
28 Chained Aggression C .12 .25
29 No Pain, No Chain C .12 .25
30 Feel the Fire U .50 1.00
31 Sparks of Glory U .50 1.00
32 Underestimated Prowess U .50 1.00
33 Backed by Eric Bischoff U .25 .50
34 Backed by Theodore Long U .30 .60
35 Grab the Mic R 2.00 4.00
36 You Feeling Lucky? R 2.00 4.00
37 Face the Music R 2.00 4.00
38 Let the Heeling Begin R 2.00 4.00
39 I Waited Long Enough R 2.00 4.00
40 Chain Reaction C .12 .25
41 Argue With Tony Chimel C .15 .30
42 Product Endorsements C .12 .25
43 Unrelenting Assault U .50 1.00
44 Restart the Match U .50 1.00
45 Sit Right Here and Bide My Time U .50 1.00
46 It's Getting Hot in Here R 2.00 4.00
47 Let's Get It On! R 2.00 4.00
48 Managed by Lita R 2.00 4.00
49 A Technical Shoot C .50 1.00
50 Quick Poke C .12 .25
51 Small Concealed Foreign Object C .12 .25
52 USA! USA! USA! C .12 .25
53 Chain Barrier U .50 1.00
54 Heat Barrier U .50 1.00
55 Volley Barrier U .50 1.00
56 Too Hot to Handle U .50 1.00
57 Future Considerations R 2.00 4.00
58 The Sex, the Gods... R 2.00 4.00
59 Ready to Fight R 2.00 4.00
60 Break It Out, Break You... R 3.00 6.00
61 Hollywood Hulk Hogan PR 2.00 4.00
62 Whatcha Gonna Do, Brother? UR 7.50 15.00
63 When Hulkamania Runs... UR 7.50 15.00
64 I Live for My Hulkamaniacs... UR 7.50 15.00
65 Hulkin' Up UR 7.50 15.00
66 Original <WWE logo> Icon PR
67 Hollywood's Big Boot PR
68 Say Your Prayers... PR
69 Hollywood Leg Drop PR
70 Sgt. Slaughter PR
71 Real American Cobra Clutch UR 7.50 15.00
72 The Motor Pool PR
73 Boot Camp Match PR
74 At-Ten-HUT! PR
75 Gimme Ten, Maggot! PR
76 The Home Team PR
77 Because the Fans Demanded It UR 7.50 15.00
78 Flurry of Finishers UR 7.50 15.00
79 The Shhhhh Chop PR
80 Never Back Down - Never Quit PR
81 I Will Not Die PR
82 The Whole Dam Show PR
83 The Heat Seekers PR
84 On Your Home Turf UR 7.50 15.00
85 Good Old-Fashioned Mugging UR 7.50 15.00
86 I Know Cool ... And You're... PR
87 Kokubetsu PR
88 The Proper Punch PR
89 We're Not Mexicans... PR
90 Violent Vendetta UR 7.50 15.00

2002 Comic Images WWE Raw Deal Ruthless Aggression

1 The Dangerous Alliance
2 You Can't Stop 'em
3 Bad to the Bone
4 Twelve Years of Terror
5 Brock Lock
6 I'll Make You Tap
7 Managed by Paul Heyman
8 Do You Know Who I Am?
9 Settle Down, Son
10 The People's Team
11 Mutual Respect
12 Your Brush with Greatness is Over
13 Rock's Spit Punch
14 Original <WWE logo> Icon
15 Edge's Spear
16 Managed by Vince McMahon
17 Look Into My Eyes...
18 So Long Goodbye

2002 Comic Images WWE Raw Deal SummerSlam

1 Head Butt Drop C .12 .25
2 Inverted Body Block U .50 1.00
3 Back Splash R 2.00 4.00
4 Knife-Edge Chop C .12 .25
5 Spinning Back Fist C .12 .25
6 Atomic Back Body Drop C .12 .25
7 Back Rake C .12 .25
8 Brass Nuks Shot U .50 1.00
9 Short Arm Clothesline U .50 1.00
10 Kangaroo Kick U .50 1.00
11 360-Degree Clothesline R 2.00 4.00
12 Up and At 'em C .12 .25
13 Double Underhook Back Breaker C .12 .25
14 Snap Suplex C .12 .25
15 Bulldog Lariat C .12 .25
16 Face-buster Suplex U .50 1.00
17 Tilt-a-Whirl Powerslam U .50 1.00
18 Back Breaker Torture Rack R 2.00 4.00
19 Arm Wringer C .12 .25
20 Nerve Hold C .12 .25
21 Knee Lock U .50 1.00
22 Half Crab U .50 1.00
23 Dragon Sleeper R 2.00 4.00
24 Booby Trap C .12 .25
25 That's Enough Out of You C .12 .25
26 There Are Two Things... U .50 1.00
27 I Change the Questions R 2.00 4.00
28 Grab the Mic C .12 .25
29 Use 'em or Lose 'em C .12 .25
30 You Feeling Lucky? C .12 .25
31 I'm Gonna Try That Again C .12 .25
32 Battling the Voices C .12 .25
33 Springboard C .12 .25
34 Let's Pick Up the Pace C .12 .25
35 Filthy, Disgusting, Brutal... U .50 1.00
36 Energy Burst U .50 1.00
37 Mind Games U .50 1.00
38 Play the Game U .50 1.00
39 Give It All I Got U .50 1.00
40 Beating the Odds R 2.00 4.00
41 Smart Mark R 2.00 4.00
42 Hardcore 'Til the End R 2.00 4.00
43 Simply The Best R 2.00 4.00
44 Pencil-Necked Geek R 2.00 4.00
45 Go For the Cover R 2.00 4.00
46 Don't Hate da Playa, Hate da Game R 2.00 4.00
47 It's Showtime C .12 .25
48 J.R. Style Clubberin' C .12 .25
49 Pick Your Spots C .12 .25
50 Glass Ceiling C .12 .25
51 In the Interest of Fairness C .12 .25
52 Do You Know What... U .50 1.00
53 I'm The Biggest Dog on This Block U .50 1.00
54 Just Who in the Blue Hell... U .50 1.00
55 The Game Is Back... U .50 1.00
56 I'm Better Than You U .50 1.00
57 Bra and Panties Match R 2.00 4.00
58 Lethal nWo Poison R 2.00 4.00
59 Living Legend R 2.00 4.00
60 Managed by Stephanie... R 2.00 4.00
61 Managed by Torrie Wilson R 2.00 4.00
62 Managed by Stacy Keibler R 2.00 4.00
63 Managed by Terri Runnels R 2.00 4.00
64 I'm Not Outta It Yet C .12 .25
65 Shove C .12 .25
66 Business Is About to Pick Up C .12 .25
67 Get What You're Expectin' C .12 .25
68 Silent, But Violent C .12 .25
69 My God He's Broken in Half C .12 .25
70 Tag Out C .12 .25
71 It's All in the Teamwork C .12 .25

72 Save da Drama fo' yo' Mama U .50 1.00
73 Turn Up the Heat U .50 1.00
74 Greco-Roman Holiday U .50 1.00
75 That's a Near Fall U .50 1.00
76 You Suck You Suck U .50 1.00
77 Ham-and-Egger U .50 1.00
78 Not According to the Fine Print R 2.00 4.00
79 Squared Circle is No Place... R 2.00 4.00
80 Been There, Done That R 2.00 4.00
81 Human Highlight Reel R 2.00 4.00
82 To Be the Man... R 2.00 4.00
83 Ring General R 2.00 4.00
84 Hollywood Hogan EX
85 Whatcha Gonna Do, Brother? UR 7.50 15.00
86 Hulkin' Up UR
87 Hollywood's Big Boot EX
88 Say Your Prayers and... EX
89 Hollywood Leg Drop EX
90 Ric Flair EX
91 Stylin', Profilin', Limousine Ridin'... UR7.50 15.00
92 Woooooooooo UR 7.50 15.00
93 Diamonds are Forever... EX
94 Now You're Going to School EX
95 The Dirtiest Player in the Game EX
96 Hall and Nash EX
97 Too Sweet UR 7.50 15.00
98 Jack-knife UR
99 nWo Black and White EX
100 4 Life EX
101 Hall's Fall-Away Slam EX
102 Trish Stratus EX
103 The T and A Factor UR 7.50 15.00
104 100 Stratusfaction Guaranteed UR
105 Stratusfaction Bulldog EX
106 I've Been a Very Naughty Girl EX
107 Perhaps I Need a Spanking? EX
108 Billy and Chuck PU
109 Rico Enters UR 7.50 15.00
110 Oh, Baby, You Look So... PR
111 Chuck's Jungle Kick PR
112 Stretching is Good for the Groin PU
113 I've Had Many Partners... PU
114 Al Snow PU
115 Snow Plow UR 7.50 15.00
116 Head PR
117 What Does Everybody Need? PR
118 What Does Everybody Want? PU
119 Snow Slide PU
120 Tajiri PU
121 Kick of Death UR
122 Tarantula PR
123 Asian Mist PR
124 Tajiri's Handspring Elbow PU
125 Japanese Buzzsaw PU
126 Hurricane PU
127 Eye of the Hurricane UR
128 Stand Back There's a... PR
129 Caped Body Press PR
130 To the Hurricycle PU
131 Whassupwitdat??? PU
132 In the Presence of the Kanenites PR
133 I'm a Bad Man PR
134 Do YOU Live By the Three I's? PR
135 The Mood Is About to Change PR
136 The Best Technical Wrestler... PR
137 Whatchoo Talkin' 'bout, Ese? PR
138 Outsider Distraction PR
139 Brothers from Another Mother UR
140 Edge-acution UR
141 Temper Tantrum UR 7.50 15.00
142 Team X-Treme UR 7.50 15.00
143 Big All Over UR
144 Lita's Twist of Fate UR
145 Dude, Nice Hang Time UR
146 Tell Me You Didn't Just Say That UR7.50 15.00
147 Damn UR
148 Giant Killer UR
149 Listen Up, Sunshine UR
150 Raven's Shopping Cart UR 7.50 15.00
8/TR cUndisputed Heavyweight Title R 2.00 4.00
9/TR Women's Title Belt R 2.00 4.00

2003 Comic Images WWE Raw Deal Survivor Series 2

1 Spinning Crescent Kick (M) C .12 .25
2 Knee Smash (S) C .12 .25
3 Big Splash in the Corner (B) C .12 .25
4 Inverted Body Block (SS) U .50 1.00
5 Flying Body Press (PR) U .50 1.00
6 Flying Tope (M) U .50 1.00
7 Drive Opponent Thru... (B) U .50 1.00
8 Back Splash (SS) R 2.00 4.00
9 Superplex (F) R 2.00 4.00
10 Atomic Back Body Drop (SS) C .12 .25
11 Struck by a Kendo Stick (B) C .12 .25
12 Gut Punch (M) C .12 .25
13 Back Rake (SS) C .12 .25
14 Eye Rake (S) C .12 .25
15 Shoulder Block (S) U .50 1.00
16 Kick (S) U .50 1.00
17 Running Lariat (B) U .50 1.00
18 Discus Punch (P) U .50 1.00
19 Garbage Can Lid (B) U .50 1.00
20 Brass Nuks Shot (SS) U .50 1.00
21 Pump Kick (M) R 2.00 4.00
22 Superkick (S) R 2.00 4.00
23 European Uppercut (S) R 2.00 4.00
24 360-Degree Clothesline (SS) R 2.00 4.00
25 Running Clothesline (B) R 2.00 4.00
26 Chair Shot (S) R 2.00 4.00
27 Within Your Grasp (M) C .12 .25
28 Double Underhook... (SS) C .12 .25
29 Neck Breaker (B) C .12 .25
30 Headlock Takedown (S) U .50 1.00
31 Backslide (M) U .50 1.00
32 German Suplex (F) U .50 1.00
33 Spine Buster (B) U .50 1.00
34 Face-buster Suplex (SS) U .50 1.00
35 Tilt-a-Whirl Powerslam (SS) U .50 1.00
36 Samoan Drop (S) R 2.00 4.00
37 Fisherman's Suplex (S) R 2.00 4.00
38 DDT (S) R 2.00 4.00
39 Running Bulldog (M) R 2.00 4.00
40 Back Breaker Torture Rack (SS) R 2.00 4.00
41 Clutch onto Opponent (B) C .12 .25
42 Short Arm Hammerlock (M) C .12 .25
43 Nerve Hold (SS) C .12 .25
44 Ankle Lock (S) U .50 1.00
45 Standing Side Headlock (S) U .50 1.00
46 Strangle Hold (M) U .50 1.00
47 Apply Illegal Leverage (B) U .50 1.00
48 Half Crab (SS) U .50 1.00
49 Sleeper (S) R 2.00 4.00
50 Boston Crab (S) R 2.00 4.00
51 Claw (S) R 2.00 4.00
52 Sharpshooter (B) R 2.00 4.00
53 Step Aside (S) C .12 .25
54 Escape Move (S) C .12 .25
55 Break the Hold (S) C .12 .25
56 Roll Out of the Way (S) C .12 .25
57 Clumsy Opponent (B) C .12 .25
58 No Sell Maneuver (B) C .12 .25
59 Over Sell Maneuver (B) C .12 .25
60 All Talk, No Action (M) C .12 .25
61 Elbow to the Face (S) U .50 1.00
62 Knee to the Gut (S) U .50 1.00
63 Rolling Takedown (S) U .50 1.00
64 There Are Two Things... (SS) U .50 1.00
65 Clean Break (P) U .50 1.00
66 Just Bring It (S) U .50 1.00
67 Hebner Calls It (S) U .50 1.00
68 Kissing Up to the Stinkin'... (B) U .50 1.00
69 Partner Interference (S) U .50 1.00
70 Iron Will (M) R 2.00 4.00
71 Not Today, Pal (M) R 2.00 4.00
72 No Chance in Hell (S) R 2.00 4.00
73 I Change the Questions (SS) R 2.00 4.00
74 Manager Interferes (S) R 2.00 4.00
75 Tag in Partner (S) C .12 .25
76 You Feeling Lucky? (SS) C .12 .25
77 Great Technical Knowledge (B) C .12 .25
78 Jockeying for Position (S) C .12 .25
79 Turn the Match into a Pier... (B) C .12 .25
80 Irish Whip (S) C .12 .25
81 Throw Into the Corner... (S) C .12 .25
82 From the Top Rope (S) C .12 .25
83 Little She Devil (M) C .12 .25
84 Gut Wrench (M) C .12 .25
85 Amazing Display of Power (B) C .12 .25
86 Charismatic Style (B) C .12 .25
87 Cole Calls It Right (M) C .12 .25
88 Trailer Park Trash (M) C .12 .25
89 Where the Hell Are We? (PR) U .50 1.00
90 J.R. Style Slobber-knocker U .50 1.00
91 Roll Out of the Ring (S) U .50 1.00
92 Shake It Off (P) U .50 1.00
93 Defensive Posture (S) U .50 1.00
94 Energy Burst (SS) U .50 1.00
95 Table Table Table (FL) U .50 1.00
96 Backed by Stephanie... (S) U .50 1.00
97 Offer Handshake (S) U .50 1.00
98 Who Booked This Match? (F) U .50 1.00
99 Well Deserved Push (B) U .50 1.00
100 Get Crowd Support (S) U .50 1.00
101 Spit at Opponent (S) U .50 1.00
102 Beating the Odds (SS) R 2.00 4.00
103 Ego Boost (S) R 2.00 4.00
104 Lita to the Xtreme (B) R 2.00 4.00
105 Simply the Best (SS) R 2.00 4.00
106 Maintain Hold (S) R 2.00 4.00
107 Enter the Stratusphere (S) R 2.00 4.00
108 Puppies Puppies (S) R 2.00 4.00
109 Ring Steps (M) R 2.00 4.00
110 Diversion (P) R 2.00 4.00
111 Turn the Tide (S) R 2.00 4.00
112 Don't Hate da Playa... (SS) R 2.00 4.00
113 You're Not in My League (B) R 2.00 4.00
114 Awesome Pyro (B) C .12 .25
115 It's Showtime (SS) C .12 .25
116 J.R. Style Clubberin' (SS) C .12 .25
117 Pick Your Spots (SS) C .12 .25
118 Glass Ceiling (SS) C .12 .25
119 Givin' 'em High Fives (B) C .12 .25
120 Taunt the Fans (B) C .12 .25
121 Fans Love an Underdog (B) U .50 1.00
122 Chicago Street Fight (M) U .50 1.00
123 Trash Talkin' Interview (B) U .50 1.00
124 Snubbed by the Fans (M) U .50 1.00
125 Old School Wrestling Match (B) R 2.00 4.00
126 Underrated Superstar (B) R 2.00 4.00
127 Hell in a Cell Match (M) R 2.00 4.00
128 Indian Strap Match (M) R 2.00 4.00
129 Duchess of Queensbury Rules (M) R2.00 4.00
130 Handicap Match (M) R 2.00 4.00
131 Bra and Panties Match (SS) R 2.00 4.00
132 Managed by Stephanie... (SS) R 2.00 4.00
133 Managed by Torrie Wilson (SS) R 2.00 4.00
134 Managed by Terri Runnels (SS) R 2.00 4.00
135 Backlash (B) C .12 .25
136 Fortitude Surge (M) C .12 .25
137 Business Is About to Pick Up (SS) C .12 .25
138 Silent, But Violent (SS) C .12 .25
139 Fan Appreciation Day (M) C .12 .25
140 Dirty Low Blow (B) C .12 .25
141 Tag Out (SS) C .12 .25
142 When You Thought You Had... (B) U .50 1.00
143 Turn Up the Heat (SS) U .50 1.00
144 Over the Top Rope (M) U .50 1.00
145 Don't Mess with the Champ (B) R 2.00 4.00
146 Sustained Damage (M) R 2.00 4.00
147 Been There, Done That (SS) R 2.00 4.00
148 Fully Loaded (B) R 2.00 4.00
149 Ring General (SS) R 2.00 4.00
150 No Mercy (B) R 2.00 4.00
151 Dude Love Superstar Card R 2.00 4.00
152 Feel the Love (SS2) R 2.00 4.00
153 Psychedelic Dance Fever (SS2) R 2.00 4.00
154 Tree of Woe (SS2) R 2.00 4.00
156 Split Personalities... (SS2) UR 7.50 15.00
157 Get Softcore (S) UR 7.50 15.00
158 Three Faces of Foley (B) UR 7.50 15.00
159 Foley is Good (M) PR
160 Chris Jericho Superstar Card (S) R 2.00 4.00
161 Lionsault (S) R 2.00 4.00
162 Y2J (S) R 2.00 4.00
163 Don't You Never Eeeever (S) R 2.00 4.00
164 Walls of Jericho (S) UR 7.50 15.00
165 Ayatollah of Rock 'n' Roll-a (S) UR 7.50 15.00
166 Springboard Drop Kick (S) UR 7.50 15.00
167 Superior Acrobatics (B) UR 7.50 15.00
168 Would You Please Shut... (M) PR
169 Eddie Guerrero... (F) R 2.00 4.00
170 Snap Senton Splash (F) R 2.00 4.00
171 Study for Your GED (F) R 2.00 4.00
172 Latino Heeeeeeeat (F) R 2.00 4.00
173 Guerrero Frog Splash (F) UR 7.50 15.00
174 Get Your GED (F) UR 7.50 15.00
175 Eddie's Roll Up (B) UR 7.50 15.00
176 Ultimo Rechazo (M) UR 7.50 15.00
177 Whatchoo Talkin' 'bout, Ese (SS) PR
178 Edge Superstar Card (B) R 2.00 4.00
179 Listen, You Reekazoid (B) R 2.00 4.00
180 Sodas Rule (B) R 2.00 4.00
181 Million Dollar Smile (B) R 2.00 4.00
182 Edge-O-Matic (B) UR 7.50 15.00
183 You Think You Know Me? (M) UR 7.50 15.00
184 Edge-acution (SS) UR 7.50 15.00
185 Big Slide in the Ring (B) PR
186 Christian Superstar Card (B) R 2.00 4.00
187 This is So Totally Unfair (B) R 2.00 4.00
188 Greetings to Our Fans... (B) R 2.00 4.00
189 Kazoo Theme Songs (B) R 2.00 4.00
190 Unprettier (B) UR 7.50 15.00
191 Temper Tantrum (SS) UR 7.50 15.00
192 Christian's Shades (B) PR
193 Matt Hardy Superstar Card (B) R 2.00 4.00
194 M.Hardy's Patented Leg Drop (B) R 2.00 4.00
195 Put It All On the Line (B) R 2.00 4.00
196 Matt's Moonsault (B) R 2.00 4.00
197 Twist of Fate (B) UR 7.50 15.00
198 Live for the Moment (M) UR 7.50 15.00
199 Team X-Treme (SS) UR 7.50 15.00
200 Roar For the Fans (B) PR
201 Jeff Hardy Superstar Card (B) R 2.00 4.00
202 Whisper in the Wind (B) R 2.00 4.00
203 Incite the Fans (B) R 2.00 4.00
204 Ride the Barricade (B) R 2.00 4.00
205 Swanton Bomb (B) UR 7.50 15.00
206 No, Jeff, Don't Do It (B) PR
207 Big Show Superstar Card (M) R 2.00 4.00
208 Showstopper Chokeslam (M) R 2.00 4.00
209 Big Show Splash (M) R 2.00 4.00
210 500 lbs. of Raw Power (M) R 2.00 4.00
211 Final Cut (M) UR 7.50 15.00
212 Welllllll (M) UR 7.50 15.00
213 Big All Over (SS) UR 7.50 15.00
214 Lita Superstar Card (M) R 2.00 4.00
215 Lita-canrana (M) R 2.00 4.00
216 Lita Drop Kick (M) R 2.00 4.00
217 Crimson Goddess (M) R 2.00 4.00
218 Lita-sault (M) UR 7.50 15.00
219 X-Treme Thong (M) UR 7.50 15.00
220 Lita's Twist of Fate (SS) UR 7.50 15.00
221 Rob Van Dam Superstar Card (M) R 2.00 4.00
222 Five Star Frog Splash (M) R 2.00 4.00
223 Extreme Monkey Flip (M) R 2.00 4.00
224 Rolling Thunder (M) R 2.00 4.00
225 Van Daminator (M) UR 7.50 15.00
226 R-V-D (M) UR 7.50 15.00
227 Dude, Nice Hang Time (SS) UR 7.50 15.00
228 Booker T Superstar Card (M) R 2.00 4.00
229 Can You Dig It, Sucka? (M) R 2.00 4.00
230 Booker's Scissor Kick (M) R 2.00 4.00
231 Spinning T Kick (M) R 2.00 4.00
232 Bookend (M) UR 7.50 15.00
233 Spinnerooni (M) UR 7.50 15.00
234 Tell Me You Didn't Just... (SS) UR 7.50 15.00
235 Trish Stratus... (SS) R 2.00 4.00
236 Stratusfaction Bulldog (SS) R 2.00 4.00
237 I've Been a Very Naughty Girl (SS) R2.00 4.00
238 Perhaps I Need a Spanking? (SS) R 2.00 4.00
239 The TandA Factor (SS) UR 7.50 15.00
240 100 Stratusfaction... (SS) UR 7.50 15.00
241 Stone Cold Steve Austin... (S) PR
242 Austin Elbow Smash (S) PR
243 Double Digits (S) PR
244 Lou Thesz Press (S) PR
245 Stone Cold Stunner (S) UR 7.50 15.00
246 Open Up a Can of Whoop-A$ (S) UR7.50 15.00
247 Patented Austin Kick to the Gut (F) UR7.50 15.00
248 DTA (B) UR 7.50 15.00
249 What??? (M) PR
250 Deadman Inc... (S) PR
251 Bad Ass Chokeslam (S) PR
252 Old School Clothesline (S) PR
253 Dead Man Walking (S) PR

Card	Low	High
254 The Last Ride (S) UR	7.50	15.00
255 This is My Yard (S) UR	7.50	15.00
256 I'll Make You Famous (S) UR	7.50	15.00
257 Brothers 'til the End (B) UR	7.50	15.00
258 You Will Respect Me (M) PR		
259 Triple H Superstar Card (S) PR		
260 Leaping Knee to the Face (S) PR		
261 Facebuster (S) PR		
262 I Am the Game (S) PR		
263 Pedigree (S) UR	7.50	15.00
264 I've Got Two Words for Ya (F) UR	7.50	15.00
265 Triple H's Reverse Neck... (S) UR	7.50	15.00
266 Sledgehammer Shot (B) UR	7.50	15.00
267 Cerebral Assassin (M) PR		
268 The Rock Superstar Card (S) PR		
269 Take That Move... PR		
270 Rock Bottom (S) PR		
271 Smackdown Hotel (S) PR		
272 The People's Eyebrow (S) UR	7.50	15.00
273 The People's Elbow (S) UR	7.50	15.00
274 Patented Rock Footstomp (F) UR	7.50	15.00
275 The Brahma Bull (B) UR	7.50	15.00
276 Shades of the Great One (M) PR		
277 Kane Superstar Card (S) PR		
278 Kane's Chokeslam (S) PR		
279 Kane's Flying Clothesline (S) PR		
280 Kane's Return (S) PR		
281 Kane's Tombstone...(S) UR	7.50	15.00
282 Hellfire and Brimstone (S) UR	7.50	15.00
283 Masked Vengeance (S) UR	7.50	15.00
284 Born of Hellfire (M) PR		
285 In the Presence of... (SS) PR		
286 Rikishi Superstar Card (F) PR		
287 Drive, Rikishi, Drive (F) PR		
288 Back That A$ Up (F) PR		
289 Stink Face (F) PR		
290 Rikishi Driver (F) UR	7.50	15.00
291 A$ Drop (F) UR	7.50	15.00
292 I Did It for You (B) UR	7.50	15.00
294 I'm a Bad Man (SS) PR		
295 Kurt Angle Superstar Card (S) PR		
296 Intensity (S) PR		
297 Integrity (S) PR		
298 Intelligence (S) PR		
299 Olympic Slam (S) UR	7.50	15.00
300 It's True, It's True (S) UR	7.50	15.00
301 Where Are Your Medals? (B) UR	7.50	15.00
302 Angle Lock (M) UR	7.50	15.00
303 Do YOU Live by... (SS) PR		
304 Tazz (S) PR		
305 T-Bone Tazzplex (S) PR		
306 Head-and-Arms Tazzplex (S) PR		
307 Northern Lights Tazzplex (S) PR		
308 Tazzmission (S) UR	7.50	15.00
309 Thug It - Dead (S) UR	7.50	15.00
310 Just Another Victim (B) UR		
311 Tough Enough (M) UR	7.50	15.00
312 The Mood Is About... (SS) PR		
313 Chris Benoit Superstar Card (S) PR		
314 Kamikaze Headbutt (S) PR		
315 Series of Suplexes (S) PR		
316 Rabid Wolverine (S) PR		
317 Crippler Crossface (S) UR	7.50	15.00
318 Big Stupid Grin (S) UR	7.50	15.00
319 Prove Me Wrong (B) UR	7.50	15.00
320 First to Tap Out Match (M) UR	7.50	15.00
321 The Best Technical... (SS) PR		
322 Dudley Boyz Superstar Card (B) PR		
323 3D (B) UR	7.50	15.00
324 Wazzzuuup??? (B) PR		
325 Buh-Buh Ray Dudley... (B) PR		
326 Buh-Buh Bomb (B) UR	7.50	15.00
327 Catatonic Stare (B) PR		
328 My Name Is (B) PR		
329 Buh-Buh Drop (B) PR		
330 Buh-Buh Punch (B) PR		
331 D-Von Dudley Superstar Card (B) PR		
332 Testify (B) UR	7.50	15.00
333 Spinning Elbow (B) PR		
334 Doin' the D-Von (B) PR		
335 Thou Shall Not... (B) PR		
336 D-Von Get the Table (B) PR		
337 Greetings from Dudleyville... (M) UR	7.50	15.00
338 Brothers from Another... (SS) UR	7.50	15.00
339 Spike Dudley Superstar Card (M) PR		
340 Dudley Dog (M) UR	7.50	15.00
341 150 lbs. Soaking Wet (M) PR		
342 Good Golly, Miss Molly... (M) PR		
343 Psychotic Bump (M) PR		
344 Brotherly Love (M) PR		
345 Giant Killer (SS) UR	7.50	15.00
346 William Regal... (M) PR		
347 Union Jack (M) PR		
348 I've Been Besmirched (M) PR		
349 Goodwill Ambassador (M) PR		
350 Regal Stretch (M) UR	7.50	15.00
351 Commissioner Regal's... (M) PR		
352 Listen Up, Sunshine (SS) UR	7.50	15.00
353 Hollywood Hulk Hogan... (SS) PR		
354 Hollywood's Big Boot (SS) PR		
355 Say Your Prayers... (SS) PR		
356 Hollywood Leg Drop (SS) PR		
357 Whatcha Gonna Do... (SS) UR	7.50	15.00
358 Hulkin' Up (SS) UR	7.50	15.00
359 Ric Flair Superstar Card (SS) PR		
360 Diamonds are Forever... (SS) PR		
361 Now You're Going... (SS) PR		
362 The Dirtiest Player... (SS) PR		
363 Stylin', Profilin'... (SS) UR	7.50	15.00
364 Wooooooooo (SS) UR	7.50	15.00
365 Rico Enters (SS) UR	7.50	15.00
366 Al Snow Superstar Card (SS) PR		
367 What Does Everybody... (SS) PR		
368 What Does Everybody... (SS) PR		
369 Snow Slide (SS) PR		
370 Snow Plow (SS) UR	7.50	15.00
371 Head (SS) PR		
372 Tajiri Superstar Card (SS) PR		
373 Asian Mist (SS) PR		
374 Tajiri's Handspring Elbow (SS) PR		
375 Japanese Buzzsaw (SS) PR		
376 Kick of Death (SS) UR	7.50	15.00
377 Tarantula (SS) PR		
378 Hurricane Superstar Card (SS) PR		
379 Caped Body Press (SS) PR		
380 To the Hurricycle (SS) PR		
381 Whassupwitdat??? (SS) PR		
382 Eye of the Hurricane (SS) UR	7.50	15.00
383 Stand Back... (SS) PR		
155A The Love Handle (SS2) UR	7.50	15.00
155B Sweet Shin Music (SS2) UR	7.50	15.00
293A Gettin' Cheeky with It - A (M) UR	7.50	15.00
293B Gettin' Cheeky with It - B (M) UR	7.50	15.00
293C Gettin' Cheeky with It - C (M) UR	7.50	15.00

2005 Comic Images WWE Raw Deal Survivor Series 3

Card	Low	High
1 Diving Takedown C	.12	.25
2 Revolving Takedown TB U	.50	1.00
3 Flying Leg Scissors R	2.00	4.00
4 Suicide Dive R	2.00	4.00
5 Superplex TB R	2.00	4.00
6 Girly Punch C	.12	.25
7 Spinning Kick C	.12	.25
8 Right Cross Punch C	.12	.25
9 Left Cross Punch C	.12	.25
10 Atomic Back Body Drop C	.12	.25
11 Kick TB U	.50	1.00
12 Running Lariat U	.50	1.00
13 Lariat U	.50	1.00
14 Garbage Can Lid TB U	.50	1.00
15 Brass Nuks Shot U	.50	1.00
16 Steel Chain Shot TB U	.50	1.00
17 Superkick R	2.00	4.00
18 Lariat Takedown R	2.00	4.00
19 Short Arm Rib Breaker R	2.00	4.00
20 Atomic Lariat R	2.00	4.00
21 Blindside Kick R	2.00	4.00
22 360-Degree Clothesline R	2.00	4.00
23 Chair Shot R	2.00	4.00
24 Double Underhook Back Breaker C	.12	.25
25 Wheelbarrow Slam C	.12	.25
26 Snap Neckbreaker C	.12	.25
27 Face Driver C	.12	.25
28 Neck Breaker C	.12	.25
29 Vertical DDT Drop TB C	.12	.25
30 Shoot Slam U	.50	1.00
31 Judo Takedown U	.50	1.00
32 Quick Snap Body Slam U	.50	1.00
33 Double Underhook Power Bomb U	.50	1.00
34 Tilt-a-Whirl Powerslam U	.50	1.00
35 Blindside Slam U	.50	1.00
36 Suplex R	2.00	4.00
37 Rolling Headlock Vise R	2.00	4.00
38 Reverse Fall-away Slam R	2.00	4.00
39 Military Slam R	2.00	4.00
40 Takedown R	2.00	4.00
41 Death Valley Driver R	2.00	4.00
42 Back Breaker Torture Rack R	2.00	4.00
43 Faceplant TB R	2.00	4.00
44 Clutch onto Opponent C	.12	.25
45 Modified Clutch onto Opponent C	.12	.25
46 Triangle Choke C	.12	.25
47 Arm Breaker TB C	.12	.25
48 Body Lock C	.12	.25
49 Waist Lock TB U	.50	1.00
50 Shoot Headlock U	.50	1.00
51 Judo Choke TB U	.50	1.00
52 Wraparound Wrist Lock U	.50	1.00
53 Headlock U	.50	1.00
54 Strangle Hold TB U	.50	1.00
55 Apply Illegal Leverage U	.50	1.00
56 Front Chancery R	2.00	4.00
57 Apply Legal Leverage TB R	2.00	4.00
58 Blindside Choke R	2.00	4.00
59 Super Hold R	2.00	4.00
60 Inverted Leg Lock R	2.00	4.00
61 Sharpshooter TB R	2.00	4.00
62 Step Aside C	.12	.25
63 Escape Move C	.12	.25
64 No Sell Maneuver C	.12	.25
65 Over Sell Maneuver C	.12	.25
66 Clumsy Opponent C	.12	.25
67 I Already Warned You C	.12	.25
68 Quick Reflexes C	.12	.25
69 Unexpected Turn of Events C	.12	.25
70 Elbow to the Face U	.50	1.00
71 Hold the Phone U	.50	1.00
72 There Are Two Things... U	.50	1.00
73 Blindsided Ego TB U	.50	1.00
74 Overshot Your Mark U	.50	1.00
75 Leave Me Alone U	.50	1.00
76 Blindsided Control U	.50	1.00
77 Just Bring It U	.50	1.00
78 Reach for the Ropes U	.50	1.00
79 Iron Will TB R	2.00	4.00
80 Don't Try This at Home R	2.00	4.00
81 Too Many Rules... R	2.00	4.00
82 Headstrong R	2.00	4.00
83 Sloppy - Very Sloppy R	2.00	4.00
84 Manager Interferes R	2.00	4.00
85 Let's Wrestle Already C	.12	.25
86 Suplex into the Ring TB C	.12	.25
87 Chain Wrestling C	.12	.25
88 When Hell Freezes Over TB C	.12	.25
89 Commission-er Rules C	.12	.25
90 Battling the Voices TB C	.12	.25
91 Irish Whip C	.12	.25
92 Gut Wrench C	.12	.25
93 I've Got a Nice Bottom U	.50	1.00
94 Chained Heat U	.50	1.00
95 Roll Out of the Ring U	.50	1.00
96 Backed by Stephanie McMahon U	.50	1.00
97 Offer Handshake TB U	.50	1.00
98 Spit at Opponent U	.50	1.00
99 Ego Boost R	2.00	4.00
100 I Can't Be Reading This Right R	2.00	4.00
101 Why the Hell are We Back? R	2.00	4.00
102 Escape the Rules R	2.00	4.00
103 That's Broken R	2.00	4.00
104 Twisted Smile R	2.00	4.00
105 The End is Near R	2.00	4.00
106 Don't Hate da Playa... R	2.00	4.00
107 Enough with the Trash Talk TB R	2.00	4.00
108 No Disqualification Match TB C	.12	.25
109 Spontaneous Combustion C	.12	.25
110 This is Gonna Be a Rocket Buster C	.12	.25
111 Old School Psychology C	.12	.25
112 Taunt the Fans C	.12	.25
113 Old School Beating C	.12	.25
114 Chicago Street Fight U	.50	1.00
115 Pay-Per-View Main Event U	.50	1.00
116 Raw or Smackdown... U	.50	1.00
117 Smackdown #1 Announcer... TB U	.50	1.00
118 Calgary, Alberta, Canada U	.50	1.00
119 The Title is on the Line U	.50	1.00
120 You Rang? U	.50	1.00
121 Old School Wrestling Match R	2.00	4.00
122 Underrated Superstar TB R	2.00	4.00
123 Managed by Theodore Long R	2.00	4.00
124 Houston, Texas R	2.00	4.00
125 Philadelphia, Pennsylvania R	2.00	4.00
126 Bitter Rivals R	2.00	4.00
127 Managed by Dawn Marie R	2.00	4.00
128 Backlash C	.12	.25
129 Fortitude Surge C	.12	.25
130 Took That on the Chin C	.12	.25
131 Hardcore Style TB C	.12	.25
132 Skirt the Issue C	.12	.25
133 Check This Out C	.12	.25
134 Really, That's Enough C	.12	.25
135 Fan Appreciation Day C	.12	.25
136 Victory Roll C	.12	.25
137 Dirty Low Blow C	.12	.25
138 Grab the Ref C	.12	.25
139 Turn Up the Heat U	.50	1.00
140 Panic Assault U	.50	1.00
141 Panic Grab U	.50	1.00
142 Panic Throw U	.50	1.00
143 Immune to Pain TB U	.50	1.00
144 You're as Graceful... U	.50	1.00
145 This is Going Nowhere Fast U	.50	1.00
146 Chain Finisher U	.50	1.00
147 Sustained Damage R	2.00	4.00
148 The King Interferes R	2.00	4.00
149 Unscrupulous S.O.B. R	2.00	4.00
150 Reverse 180-Degree Chair Shot R	2.00	4.00
151 Stone Cold Steve Austin RUM		
152 Rattlesnake RUM		
153 Austin Elbow Smash RUM		
154 Double Digits RUM		
155 Lou Thesz Press TB RUM		
156 Stone Cold Stunner UR	7.50	15.00
157 Open Up a Can... UR	7.50	15.00
158 Patented Austin... UR	7.50	15.00
159 Do You Know What... TB RUM		
160 DTA TB UR	7.50	15.00
161 Rattlesnake Rulz RUM		
162 Cause Stone Cold Said So RUM		
163 And That's the Bottom Line RUM		
164 What??? RUM		
165 The Bionic Redneck UR	7.50	15.00
166 Gimme a Hell Yeah UR	7.50	15.00
167 Stomp a Mudhole RUM		
168 Don't Trust Nobody RUM		
169 Walk it Dry RUM		
170 Do You Want a Hug? RUM		
171 Undertaker RUM		
172 Undertaker's Chokeslam RUM		
173 Undertaker's Flying... TB RUM		
174 Undertaker Sits Up RUM		
175 Undertaker's Tombstone... UR	7.50	15.00
176 Power of Darkness UR	7.50	15.00
177 Rest in Peace UR	7.50	15.00
178 Throttled Within an Inch... RUM		
179 Rollin' - Rollin' - Rollin' RUM		
180 I'm the Biggest Dog... TB RUM		
181 Bad to the Bone RUM		
182 Twelve Years of Terror RUM		
183 Brothers 'til the End UR	7.50	15.00
184 You Will Respect Me RUM		
185 Throwin' Big Ol' Soup... RUM		
186 Big Evil - Red Devil RUM		
187 Your'e Gonna Pay TB RUM		
188 Managed by Paul Bearer RUM		
189 HHH RUM		
190 The Game RUM		
191 Leaping Knee to the Face RUM		
192 Facebuster TB RUM		
193 I Am the Game TB RUM		
194 Ric Flair Interferes UR	7.50	15.00
195 Pedigree UR	7.50	15.00
196 I've Got Two Words for Ya UR	7.50	15.00
197 Triple H's Reverse... UR	7.50	15.00
198 Cause I am That Damn Good RUM		
199 Flip Over the Corner Ringpost RUM		
200 It's Time to Play the Game RUM		
201 Sledgehammer Shot UR	7.50	15.00
202 Cerebral Assassin RUM		

203	The Game is Back... TB RUM		
204	Game Over? UR	7.50	15.00
205	The Game's Sleeper RUM		
206	Lunging Choke Hold RUM		
207	You Don't Want to Play Me RUM		
208	It's All About Control RUM		
209	Screw the Rules RUM		
210	A Beating You'll Never Forget RUM		
211	The Rock RUM		
212	The People's Champion RUM		
213	Take That Move... RUM		
214	Rock Bottom TB RUM		
215	Smackdown Hotel RUM		
216	The People's Eyebrow UR	7.50	15.00
217	The People's Elbow UR	7.50	15.00
218	Patented Rock Footstomp TB UR	7.50	15.00
219	Do You Smell... RUM		
220	Your Brush with... TB RUM		
221	Rock's Spit Punch RUM		
222	The Brahma Bull UR	7.50	15.00
223	Who in the Blue Hell... TB RUM		
224	Shades of the Great One RUM		
225	The People's Kip-Up UR	7.50	15.00
226	Remove the People's... TB RUM		
227	It Doesn't Matter... RUM		
228	You Bring the A$... RUM		
229	The People's DDT RUM		
230	Get Ready... TB RUM		
231	The Peep's Champ RUM		
232	Know Your Role... RUM		
233	Kane RUM		
234	The Big Freak'n Machine RUM		
235	Kane's Chokeslam RUM		
236	Kane's Flying Clothesline TB RUM		
237	Kane's Return RUM		
238	Kane's Tombstone Piledriver UR	7.50	15.00
239	Hellfire and Brimstone UR	7.50	15.00
240	Help's on the Way UR	7.50	15.00
241	Masked Vengeance UR	7.50	15.00
242	Boot to the Face RUM		
243	Chains of Destruction RUM		
244	Born of Hellfire RUM		
245	In the Presence... RUM		
246	Freaks are Cool TB UR	7.50	15.00
247	The Fire Still Burns RUM		
248	Big Freak'n Uppercut RUM		
249	My Path is Chosen RUM		
250	Hellfire Chokeslam TB RUM		
251	Big Freak'n Powerslam RUM		
252	Unmasked Vengeance RUM		
253	Kane's Rage RUM		
254	Chris Jericho RUM		
255	Highlight of the Night TB RUM		
256	Lionsault RUM		
257	Y2J RUM		
258	Don't You Never - Eeeever RUM		
259	Walls of Jericho UR	7.50	15.00
260	Ayatollah of Rock 'n' Roll-a TB UR	7.50	15.00
261	Springboard Drop Kick TB UR	7.50	15.00
262	Jerichoholics TB RUM		
263	Superior Acrobatics UR	7.50	15.00
264	Would You Please... RUM		
265	Happy You're Here... TB RUM		
266	I'm Better Than You TB RUM		
267	The Breakdown RUM		
268	I'm the King of the World RUM		
269	Highlight Reel RUM		
270	You Sanctimonious... UR	7.50	15.00
271	Listen Up, Junior... UR	7.50	15.00
272	My Obscenely Expensive... RUM		
273	Roll the Footage, Monkeys RUM		
274	Jericho's Ensugiri RUM		
275	Kurt Angle TB RUM		
276	Your Freaking Hero RUM		
277	Intensity RUM		
278	Integrity RUM		
279	Intelligence RUM		
280	Olympic Slam UR	7.50	15.00
281	It's True, It's True UR	7.50	15.00
282	I'll Make You Tap RUM		
283	Where Are Your Medals? UR	7.50	15.00
284	Angle Lock UR	7.50	15.00
285	Do YOU Live by... RUM		
286	Just Hold On a Second... RUM		
287	Collegiate Champions UR	7.50	15.00
288	Submit RUM		
289	Wrestling with a... TB RUM		
290	The Straps are Down UR	7.50	15.00
291	Oh, It's True UR	7.50	15.00
292	Angle's German Suplex RUM		
293	Whoo RUM		
294	Angle's Moonsault RUM		
295	Chris Benoit TB RUM		
296	The Crippler RUM		
297	Kamikaze Headbutt RUM		
298	Series of Suplexes RUM		
299	Rabid Wolverine TB RUM		
300	Crippler Crossface UR	7.50	15.00
301	Big Stupid Grin UR	7.50	15.00
302	Prove Me Wrong UR	7.50	15.00
303	First to Tap Out Match TB UR	7.50	15.00
304	Best Technical Wrestler... RUM		
305	A Victim of the Crippler TB RUM		
306	There's No Holding Me Back UR	7.50	15.00
307	Toothless Aggression UR	7.50	15.00
308	Cripple Opponent RUM		
309	Rabid Attack in the Corner TB RUM		
310	Surprise Drop Kick RUM		
311	Benoit's German Suplex RUM		
312	Pain is Inevitable RUM		
313	Eddie Guerrero RUM		
314	Snap Senton Splash RUM		
315	Study for Your GED RUM		
316	Latino Heeeeeeeat RUM		
317	Guerrero Frog Splash UR	7.50	15.00
318	Get Your GED TB UR	7.50	15.00
319	Eddie's Roll Up TB UR	7.50	15.00
320	Ultimo Rechazo UR	7.50	15.00
321	Whatchoo Talkin' 'bout... RUM		
322	Yo, Ese, I Know Your... TB RUM		
323	Lasso from El Paso RUM		
324	Gory Special RUM		
325	Viva La Raza Low Rider TB RUM		
326	Dudley Boyz RUM		
327	3D TB UR	7.50	15.00
328	Wazzzzuuup??? RUM		
329	TLC Match TB UR	7.50	15.00
330	Dudler Tough RUM		
331	Dudleyz3 RUM		
332	Beatings from Dudleyville RUM		
333	Blood is Thicker than Wood RUM		
334	Buh-Buh Ray Dudley TB RUM		
335	Buh-Buh Bomb TB UR	7.50	15.00
336	Catatonic Stare RUM		
337	My Name Is TB RUM		
338	Buh-Buh Drop RUM		
339	Buh-Buh Punch RUM		
340	D-Von Dudley RUM		
341	Testify TB UR	7.50	15.00
342	Spinning Elbow TB RUM		
343	Doin' the D-Von TB RUM		
344	Thou Shall Not... TB RUM		
345	D-Von -- Get the Table RUM		
346	Greetings from Dudleyville... TB UR	7.50	15.00
347	Brothers from Another Mother UR	7.50	15.00
348	Edge RUM		
349	Leader of the Edge... TB RUM		
350	Listen, You Reekazoid RUM		
351	Soda's Rule RUM		
352	Million Dollar Smile RUM		
353	Edge-O-Matic UR	7.50	15.00
354	You Think You Know Me? UR	7.50	15.00
355	Edge's Spear TB RUM		
356	Edge-acution UR	7.50	15.00
357	Big Slide in the Ring RUM		
358	Never Gonna Stop Me RUM		
359	You're a Human Vacuum... RUM		
360	Edgeucation of Adam... UR	7.50	15.00
361	Downward Spiral UR	7.50	15.00
362	Edge Kick RUM		
363	Scream if You Want It RUM		
364	'Cause I Want More RUM		
365	Christian RUM		
366	This is so Totally Unfair RUM		
367	Greetings to Our Fans... RUM		
368	Kazoo Theme Song RUM		
369	Unprettier UR	7.50	15.00
370	Temper Tantrum UR	7.50	15.00
371	Christian's Shades TB RUM		
372	Impaler RUM		
373	I Ain't No Sucka Neitha RUM		
374	To All My Peeps... RUM		
375	Matt Hardy RUM		
376	M.Hardy's Patented Leg Drop RUM		
377	Put It All on the Line TB RUM		
378	Matt's Moonsault TB RUM		
379	Twist of Fate UR	7.50	15.00
380	Live for the Moment UR	7.50	15.00
381	Team X-Treme UR	7.50	15.00
382	Roar for the Fans RUM		
383	Mattitude Adjustment RUM		
384	Version 1.0 TB RUM		
385	Side Effect RUM		
386	Era Mattitude Has Arrived RUM		
387	Big Show RUM		
388	Showstopper Chokeslam RUM		
389	Bog Show Splash RUM		
390	500 lbs. of Raw Power RUM		
391	Final Cut UR		
392	Welllllll UR	7.50	15.00
393	Big All Over UR	7.50	15.00
394	Mountain of a Man UR	7.50	15.00
395	You Can't Manhandle... RUM		
396	Showdown RUM		
397	Lita RUM		
398	Lita-canrana RUM		
399	Lita Drop Kick RUM		
400	Crimson Goddess RUM		
401	Lita-sault UR	7.50	15.00
402	X-Treme Thong UR	7.50	15.00
403	Lita's Twist of Fate UR	7.50	15.00
404	If You've Got It, Flaunt It UR	7.50	15.00
405	X-Treme Hedonism UR	7.50	15.00
406	The Goddess Returns RUM		
407	Lita's DDT TB RUM		
408	Rob Van Dam RUM		
409	Five Star Frog Splash TB RUM		
410	Extreme Monkey Flip TB RUM		
411	Rolling Thunder RUM		
412	Van Daminator UR	7.50	15.00
413	R-V-D UR	7.50	15.00
414	Dude, Nice Hang Time TB UR	7.50	15.00
415	Everything's Cool When... UR	7.50	15.00
416	Dude Whatever RUM		
417	Mr. Monday Night RUM		
418	Van Terminator RUM		
419	Booker T RUM		
420	Can You Dig It, Sucka? RUM		
421	Booker's Scissor Kick TB RUM		
422	Spinning T Kick RUM		
423	Bookend UR	7.50	15.00
424	Spinnerooni UR	7.50	15.00
425	Tell Me You Didn't Just... UR	7.50	15.00
426	Five Time Five Time... UR	7.50	15.00
427	Yo Dawg... RUM		
428	Houston Hangover RUM		
429	How Many Times? RUM		
430	Spike Dudley RUM		
431	Dudley Dog UR	7.50	15.00
432	150 lbs. Soaking Wet RUM		
433	Get Him, Boyz RUM		
434	Psychotic Bump RUM		
435	Brotherly Love RUM		
436	Giant Killer UR	7.50	15.00
437	Pound 4 Pound UR	7.50	15.00
438	William Regal RUM		
439	Union Jack RUM		
440	I've Been Besmirched RUM		
441	Goodwill Ambassador TB RUM		
442	Regal Stretch UR	7.50	15.00
443	Commissioner Regal's... RUM		
444	Listen Up, Sunshine UR	7.50	15.00
445	Regal Upper Class Punch UR	7.50	15.00
446	Proper Planning Prevents... RUM		
447	Keep It Simple, Sir RUM		
448	Ric Flair RUM		
449	Summer of Slam TB RUM		
450	Diamonds are Forever... RUM		
451	Now You're Going to School RUM		
452	The Dirtiest Player... TB RUM		
453	Stylin', Profilin', Limousine Ridin' UR	7.50	15.00
454	Woooooooooo UR	7.50	15.00
455	The Game Interferes TB UR	7.50	15.00
456	You're Going to Space... TB UR	7.50	15.00
457	The Flair Flop RUM		
458	Trish Stratus RUM		
459	Stratusfaction Bulldog TB RUM		
460	I've Been a Very Naughty Girl RUM		
461	Perhaps I Need a Spanking? RUM		
462	The TandA Factor UR	7.50	15.00
463	100 Stratusfaction... UR	7.50	15.00
464	Puppy Power RUM		
465	The StratusFear RUM		
466	Tajiri RUM		
467	Asian Mist TB RUM		
468	Tajiri's Handspring Elbow TB RUM		
469	Japanese Buzzsaw TB RUM		
470	Kick of Death UR	7.50	15.00
471	Tarantula TB RUM		
472	Octopus UR	7.50	15.00
473	Double Face Kick UR	7.50	15.00
474	Series of Kicks RUM		
475	Managed by Kyo Dai TB RUM		
476	Hurricane RUM		
477	Caped Body Press TB RUM		
478	To the Hurricycle TB RUM		
479	Whassupwitdat??? TB RUM		
480	Eye of the Hurricane UR	7.50	15.00
481	Stand Back There's... RUM		
482	Hurrislam UR	7.50	15.00
483	Shining Wizard Kick UR	7.50	15.00
484	Gregory Helms... RUM		
485	I've Got Hurri-Powers RUM		
486	Rey Mysterio RUM		
487	Luche Libre Extravaganza UR	7.50	15.00
488	The West Coast Pop TB UR	7.50	15.00
489	Too Fast For You RUM		
490	The 619 RUM		
491	Rey-Rey's Tope RUM		
492	West Coast Bronco Buster UR	7.50	15.00
493	Flying Body Press UR	7.50	15.00
494	Who's That Jumpin'... TB RUM		
495	Shawn Michaels RUM		
496	The Icon, The Showstoppa... UR	7.50	15.00
497	Sweet Chin Music UR	7.50	15.00
498	Don't Hunt What You... RUM		
499	Top Rope Elbow Drop RUM		
500	The Heart Break Kid RUM		
501	I'm Just a Sexy Boy UR	7.50	15.00
502	All Things are Possible UR	7.50	15.00
503	Rhyno RUM		
504	Gore Gore Gore UR	7.50	15.00
505	Extreme Warfare RUM		
506	Rhyno's Garbage Can RUM		
507	The Manbeast TB RUM		
508	Rhyno Stampede RUM		
509	Unstoppable RUM		
510	Unleash the Beast UR	7.50	15.00
511	Stacy Keibler RUM		
512	Straddle the Ropes UR	7.50	15.00
513	Superior Leg Work TB UR	7.50	15.00
514	Test or Freakzilla? RUM		
515	Pump Me Up RUM		
516	I Know How to Use Them RUM		
517	I Should've Been in that Magazine UR	7.50	15.00
518	Gail Kim and Molly Holly RUM		
519	Change Reality UR	7.50	15.00
520	Gail's Hurricanrana UR	7.50	15.00
521	Wake Up RUM		
522	Look Around RUM		
523	Molly-Go-Round RUM		
524	Control Your World UR	7.50	15.00
525	Bald is Beautiful UR	7.50	15.00
526	John Cena RUM		
527	Yo Kill da Beat UR	7.50	15.00
528	F-U UR		
529	You Can't See Me TB RUM		
530	Word Life TB RUM		
531	I'm Gonna Teach You... RUM		
532	So You Think You're... UR	7.50	15.00
533	Torrie Wilson RUM		
534	WWE Centerfold of the Year UR	7.50	15.00
535	Torrie's DDT UR	7.50	15.00
536	Does This Look Good on Me? RUM		
537	Strike a Pose RUM		
538	The Boise Beauty RUM		
539	Golden Thong Award UR	7.50	15.00
540	Victoria RUM		
541	Widow's Peak UR	7.50	15.00
542	Managed by Stevie Richards RUM		

543 All the Things She Said RUM		
544 Yes, I've Lost My Mind TB RUM		
545 Stevie Interferes RUM		
546 This is Not Enough UR	7.50	15.00
547 Evolution RUM		
548 Evolution is a Mystery UR	7.50	15.00
549 Paid, Laid, and Made UR	7.50	15.00
550 Yesterday is So Long Ago RUM		
551 I See the Line in the Sand RUM		
552 Nothing Ever Stays the Same RUM		
553 Paul Heyman RUM		
554 Let the Bodies Hit the Floor UR	7.50	15.00
555 You're Dangerously Close RUM		
556 Coach, Cole, or Finkel? RUM		
557 Big Boys Club RUM		
558 Do You Know Who... RUM		
559 Raw GM Eric Bischoff RUM		
560 Smackdown GM RUM		
561 Chavo's Inverted Powerbomb UR	7.50	15.00
562 It's All About the Benjamins RUM		
563 Greco Roman Specialists UR	7.50	15.00
564 Stone Cold Steve Austin... RUM		
565 Chris Jericho, Kane... RUM		
566 Rock, Deadman... RUM		
567 Rikishi, Chris Benoit... RUM		
568 APA or A-Train? RUM		
569 RVD or Booker T? UR	7.50	15.00
570 Edge or Big Show? UR	7.50	15.00
571 The People's Champ... RUM		
572 Mankind / Cactus Jack... RUM		
573 Backed by Mr. McMahon TB RUM		
574 Calling You Out RUM		
575 Chain Lashing TB RUM		
576 Managed by Vince... TB RUM		
577 Managed by Paul Heyman RUM		
578 Overhand Chairshot RUM		
579 Suicide Lariat RUM		
580 Atomic Knee Drop RUM		
581 Banned from Ringside RUM		
582 Divas Divas Divas RUM		
583 Vince McMahon Interferes RUM		
584 That Won't Make the Cut RUM		
585 Testicular Fortitude RUM		
586 I'm Hardcore I'm Hardcore RUM		
587 Back to Basics RUM		
588 Arm Bar RUM		
589 Arm Bar Takedown RUM		
590 Arm Drag RUM		
591 Atomic Drop RUM		
592 Belly to Back Suplex RUM		
593 Belly to Belly Suplex RUM		
594 Body Slam RUM		
595 Chop RUM		
596 Clothesline RUM		
597 Collar and Elbow Lockup RUM		
598 Drop Kick RUM		
599 Haymaker RUM		
600 Head Butt RUM		
601 Hip Toss RUM		
602 Press Slam RUM		
603 Punch RUM		
604 Roundhouse Punch RUM		
605 Russian Leg Sweep RUM		
606 Snap Mare RUM		
607 Vertical Suplex RUM		
608 Wrist Lock RUM		
609 Backhand Slap RUM		
610 Drop Toe Hold RUM		
611 Elbow Drop RUM		
612 Foot Stomp RUM		
613 Hammerlock RUM		
614 Comeback TB RUM		
615 Dem Damn Dudleyz TB RUM		
616 Hurricanrana TB RUM		
617 Chop to the Chest TB RUM		
618 Single Arm DDT TB RUM		
619 Ladder in the Ring TB RUM		
620 Drawing Extra Heat TB RUM		
621 Knife-Edge Chop TB RUM		
622 Springboard TB RUM		
623 Gut Punch TB RUM		
624 Spine Buster TB RUM		
625 DDT TB RUM		
626 Ankle Lock TB RUM		
627 No Chance in Hell TB RUM		
628 Great Technical... TB RUM		
629 Throw Into the Corner... RUM		
630 Charismatic Style TB RUM		
631 Table Table Table TB RUM		
632 Who Booked This Match? TB RUM		
633 Maintain Hold TB RUM		
634 Enter the Stratusphere RUM		
635 Puppies Puppies TB RUM		
636 Diversion TB RUM		
637 Hell in a Cell Match RUM		
638 Indian Strap Match RUM		
639 Duchess of Queensbury... RUM		
640 Bulldog Takedown TB RUM		
641 Corkscrew DDT TB RUM		
642 Did I Just Say... TB RUM		
643 Don't Cross the Boss TB RUM		

2005 Comic Images WWE Raw Deal Unforgiven

1 Counter Slash C	.12	.25
2 Corkscrew Elbow C	.12	.25
3 Body Block C	.12	.25
4 Spinning Leg Drop C	.12	.25
5 Missile Dropkick TB U	.50	1.00
6 Shooting Star Press TB U	.50	1.00
7 Girly Slap C	.12	.25
8 Shoulder Block TB C	.12	.25
9 Running Elbow Smash TB C	.12	.25
10 Kidney Punch C	.12	.25
11 Standing Drop Kick TB C	.12	.25
12 Knee Breaker TB U	.50	1.00
13 Back Fist TB U	.50	1.00
14 Back Body Drop TB U	.50	1.00
15 Reverse Clothesline U	.50	1.00
16 Everything and the Kitchen Sink U	.50	1.00
17 Ap Chaki Kick R	2.00	4.00
18 Precision Clothesline R	2.00	4.00
19 Baseball Slide TB R	2.00	4.00
20 Lock, Stock, and Barrel R	2.00	4.00
21 Rolling Hip Toss C	.12	.25
22 Japanese Arm Drag TB C	.12	.25
23 Sidewalk Slam TB C	.12	.25
24 Flip C	.12	.25
25 Running Spinebuster TB C	.12	.25
26 Shoot Suplex C	.12	.25
27 Snap Suplex TB U	.50	1.00
28 Headlock Takedown TB U	.50	1.00
29 Small Package TB U	.50	1.00
30 Swinging Neck Breaker U	.50	1.00
31 Pendulum Back Breaker U	.50	1.00
32 Powerbomb TB U	.50	1.00
33 Full Nelson Slam TB R	2.00	4.00
34 Shoot Russian Leg Sweep R	2.00	4.00
35 German Suplex TB R	2.00	4.00
36 Sit Out Powerbomb TB R	2.00	4.00
37 Tornado DDT TB R	2.00	4.00
38 Workin' on the Knee TB R	2.00	4.00
39 Precision Power Slam R	2.00	4.00
40 Side Headlock C	.12	.25
41 Bear Hug TB C	.12	.25
42 Full Nelson TB C	.12	.25
43 Bow and Arrow TB C	.12	.25
44 Guillotine Stretch TB C	.12	.25
45 Wrist Breaker U	.50	1.00
46 Arm Stretch U	.50	1.00
47 Sleeper TB U	.50	1.00
48 Side Chinlock U	.50	1.00
49 Camel Clutch TB U	.50	1.00
50 Spinning Toe Hold R	2.00	4.00
51 Boston Crab TB R	2.00	4.00
52 Precision Leg Lock R	2.00	4.00
53 Torture Rack TB R	2.00	4.00
54 Choke Hold TB R	2.00	4.00
55 Lift a Boot TB C	.12	.25
56 Spot Adjustment U	.50	1.00
57 A Revolution of the Mind R	2.00	4.00
58 Build Momentum C	.12	.25
59 Viva Las Divas C	.12	.25
60 Shake It Off TB C	.12	.25
61 Listen Loud and Clear C	.12	.25
62 Hardcore Timekeeper's Bell C	.12	.25
63 Not Yet TB C	.12	.25
64 Afterburn U	.50	1.00
65 Stagger TB U	.50	1.00
66 Kickin' It Old School U	.50	1.00
67 That's It U	.50	1.00
68 Marking Out TB U	.50	1.00
69 Grab WWE Timekeeper... U	.50	1.00
70 Sharmell: Sizzling Spouse R	2.00	4.00
71 Maria: Ideal Interviewer R	2.00	4.00
72 Christy: Curvy Cutie R	2.00	4.00
73 Melina: Naughty Manager R	2.00	4.00
74 Lilian: Amazing Announcer R	2.00	4.00
75 Candice: Internet Icon R	2.00	4.00
76 Hello, Ladies C	.12	.25
77 Rochester, New York C	.12	.25
78 Trash Talkin' Interview TB C	.12	.25
79 Who's Cooler... C	.12	.25
80 Blindsided Precision U	.50	1.00
81 Backstage Shenanigans U	.50	1.00
82 Pyrotechnic Volley U	.50	1.00
83 You Can't Spell... U	.50	1.00
84 Fans Love an Underdog R	2.00	4.00
85 Frankie Takes Hollywood R	2.00	4.00
86 Inferno Match TB R	2.00	4.00
87 The Old Switcheroo R	2.00	4.00
88 Not in Front of the Kids C	.12	.25
89 The GM of Stevie Night Heat C	.12	.25
90 This is Just the Beginning C	.12	.25
91 You Knew it Would End This Way C	.12	.25
92 Here I Stand: the Champion U	.50	1.00
93 WWE Divas: the Next Generation U	.50	1.00
94 Eviscerated by Viscera U	.50	1.00
95 WWE Divas Rule U	.50	1.00
96 I'm Just Hitting My Stride R	2.00	4.00
97 In This Ring, I Just Might Be R	2.00	4.00
98 Introduce Your Brain... R	2.00	4.00
99 One More Time... R	2.00	4.00
100 Batista EX		
101 The Destroyer UR	7.50	15.00
102 Batista Bomb UR	7.50	15.00
103 The Animal EX		
104 Physically Dominant Force EX		
105 Batista's Spinebuster EX		
106 Leader of the Peepulation EX		
107 Managed by Tyson Tomko UR	7.50	15.00
108 Just Close Your Eyes UR	7.50	15.00
109 That's How I Roll EX		
110 The Christian Coalition EX		
111 Tomakazi DDT EX		
112 Christy EX		
113 Temecula, California UR	7.50	15.00
114 2004 Diva Search Winner UR	7.50	15.00
115 Ain't It Fair? EX		
116 Christy's Twist EX		
117 Redheaded Sparkplug EX		
118 Immortal One EX		
119 Feathered Boa UR	7.50	15.00
120 I am a Real American UR	7.50	15.00
121 Hogan's Patented... EX		
122 Fight For the Rights... EX		
123 In My Day, a Maneuver... EX		
124 Rowdy Roddy Piper EX		
125 Bagpipe Introduction UR	7.50	15.00
126 Piper's Pit UR	7.50	15.00
127 Over Sell: Hot Rod Style EX		
128 Hot Rod EX		
129 Cowboy Bob Orton Interferes EX		
130 Smackdown GM... EX		
131 Haterade UR	7.50	15.00
132 Holla Holla Holla UR	7.50	15.00
133 Your Freaking Hero... EX		
134 Thuggin' and Buggin' EX		
135 The Mack Militant EX		
136 Heidenreich PR		
137 Disasterpiece UR	7.50	15.00
138 Heidenreich's Elbow Drop PR		
139 Who Wants to be My... PR		
140 A Friendly Boot PR		
141 Running Shoulder Block PR		
142 Gene Snitsky PR		
143 Baby Carriage UR	7.50	15.00
144 You Have Tasty Toes PR		
145 It's Not My Fault PR		
146 No Fault Clothesline PR		
147 No Fault Pump Handle... PR		
148 MNM PR		
149 The Snapshot UR	7.50	15.00
150 Managed by Melina PR		
151 There's Nothing Sweeter PR		
152 A-List Attack PR		
153 Melina Interferes PR		
154 Hurri-Friends PR		
155 The Hurri-Friends Armory UR	7.50	15.00
156 Super Masks... PR		
157 Super Storm Front PR		
158 Greetings, Citizen PR		
159 Stacy's Roundhouse Kick PR		
160 Unleash Hell PR		
161 Nobody's Safe PR		
162 Making the Game PR		
163 Finally The Rock... PR		
164 Another Big Freak'n... PR		
165 Chris Jericho PR		
166 Wolverine's Sharpshooter PR		
167 Addicted to the Heat PR		
168 Kurt Angle Invitational PR		
169 Edge's Running Spear PR		
170 Big Show's F5 PR		
171 When I Get You Alone PR		
172 The Hidden Dragon... PR		
173 Booker's Thrust Kick PR		
174 The Power of the Punch PR		
175 Flair's Chop Block PR		
176 The MaTrish Move PR		
177 Educated Hands PR		
178 Restricted Use in This Area PR		
179 Forever PR		
180 Flying Forearm PR		
181 Uncle Eric's Karate Kick PR		
182 Daddy's Little Girl TB PR		
183 Five Knuckle Shuffle PR		
184 Managed by Stacy Keibler PR		
185 Want to Take My Test? PR		
186 Spider Web Moonsault PR		
187 Girly Grab PR		
188 When You Run... PR		
189 Never Forgive... PR		
190 McMahon-us Interrupt-us UR	7.50	15.00
191 Gentlemen's Establishment UR	7.50	15.00
192 Hardcore Originator of ECW UR	7.50	15.00
193 Orlando Jordan... UR	7.50	15.00
194 Destiny UR	7.50	15.00
195 Here Comes the Money TB UR	7.50	15.00
196 Incredible Athleticism UR	7.50	15.00
197 Hello, My Name is Eugene UR	7.50	15.00
198 Le Bonsoir UR	7.50	15.00

2003 Comic Images WWE Raw Deal Velocity

1 Flying Mare C	.12	.25
2 Diving Takedown C	.12	.25
3 Quick Follow Through U	.50	1.00
4 Shoot Aerial 360-Degree Kick U	.50	1.00
5 Missile Shoulder Block R	2.00	4.00
6 Roll Up R	2.00	4.00
7 Standing Drop Kick C	.12	.25
8 Abdominal Rake C	.12	.25
9 Shoot Punch U	.50	1.00
10 Rapid-Fire Punches U	.50	1.00
11 Lariat Takedown R	2.00	4.00
12 Bionic Elbow R	2.00	4.00
13 Lock-up C	.12	.25
14 Oklahoma Roll C	.12	.25
15 Fall-Away Suplex C	.12	.25
16 Single Leg Takedown U	.50	1.00
17 Shoot Slam U	.50	1.00
18 Corkscrew DDT U	.50	1.00
19 Bulldog Takedown R	2.00	4.00
20 Rolling Headlock Vise R	2.00	4.00
21 Slam Bomb R	2.00	4.00
22 Body Scissors C	.12	.25
23 Breather Hold C	.12	.25
24 Waist Lock U	.50	1.00
25 Shoot Headlock U	.50	1.00
26 Sleeper Bomb R	2.00	4.00
27 Flying Body Lock R	2.00	4.00
28 Cartwheel C	.12	.25
29 Hold the Phone U	.50	1.00
30 Get the F Out R	2.00	4.00
31 He's as Crazy as a Pet Raccoon C	.12	.25
32 I'm Sorry, But You're Boring Me C	.12	.25
33 Measure Him C	.12	.25

34 Not on My Broadcast C .12 .25
35 Wanna Know What I'm Gonna Do? C .12 .25
36 Hot Tag [Tag Team Only Symbol] C .12 .25
37 Back-and-Forth Action U .50 1.00
38 Fire Extinguisher U .50 1.00
39 Caught Red-handed U .50 1.00
40 Gettin' Beat Like a... U .50 1.00
41 Good Things Sometimes Happen U .50 1.00
42 It Pays to be Evil U .50 1.00
43 Here's a Ratings Booster R 2.00 4.00
44 Did I Just Say Three Minutes? R 2.00 4.00
45 One of a Kind R 2.00 4.00
46 Defensive Stance R 2.00 4.00
47 He's Runnin' Like a Scalded Dawg R 2.00 4.00
48 Singapore Cane R 2.00 4.00
49 Don't You Usually Wrestle... C .12 .25
50 Educated Feet C .12 .25
51 Ring Psychology: Back C .12 .25
52 Ring Psychology: Neck C .12 .25
53 Unorthodox Style of Wrestling C .12 .25
54 Lumberjack Match U .50 1.00
55 Pay-Per-View Main Event U .50 1.00
56 Raw or Smackdown... U .50 1.00
57 Velocity U .50 1.00
58 Proper Conditioning U .50 1.00
59 I Aims ta be Startin' Sump'tin' R 2.00 4.00
60 Managed by Eric Bischoff R 2.00 4.00
61 Managed by Shane O'Mac R 2.00 4.00
62 I'm the Champ... R 2.00 4.00
63 My Sacrifice R 2.00 4.00
64 You Can't Spell Furniture... C .12 .25
65 Check This Out C .12 .25
66 Desire C .12 .25
67 Dragged to the Center of the Ring C .12 .25
68 See How It Feels C .12 .25
69 Reap the Rewards U .50 1.00
70 The Ref Got in the Way U .50 1.00
71 Hold On It's Not Time... U .50 1.00
72 Human Suplex Machine U .50 1.00
73 Beg For Mercy U .50 1.00
74 Justice for All R 2.00 4.00
75 The King Interferes R 2.00 4.00
76 That's J.R.'s Animal Hat Trick... R 2.00 4.00
77 Title Belt Clubberin' R 2.00 4.00
78 The Big Freak'n Machine EX
79 Freaks Are Cool UR 7.50 15.00
80 The Fire Still Burns PR
81 Big Freak'n Uppercut EX
82 My Path is Chosen EX
83 Hellfire Chokeslam EX
84 The Game EX
85 Game Over? UR 7.50 15.00
86 The Game's Sleeper PR
87 Lunging Choke Hold EX
88 You Don't Want to Play Me EX
89 It's All About Control EX
90 Goldust EX
91 Shattered Dreams Production UR 7.50 15.00
92 Shattered Dreams UR 7.50 15.00
93 <inhale> Goooooooooldust EX
94 Butt Bump EX
95 Director's Cut EX
96 Brock Lesnar EX
97 Backstage Warm-up Routine UR 7.50 15.00
98 F-5 UR 7.50 15.00
99 An Irresistible Force... EX
100 The Next Big Thing EX
101 Series of Back Breakers EX
102 The People's Champion EX
103 The People's Kip-up UR 7.50 15.00
104 Remove the People's... PR
105 It Doesn't Matter... EX
106 You Bring the A$... EX
107 The People's DDT EX
108 Rey Mysterio EX
109 Luche Libre Extravaganza UR 7.50 15.00
110 The West Coast Pop UR 7.50 15.00
111 Too Fast For You EX
112 The 619 EX
113 Rey-Rey's Tope EX
114 3 Minute Warning PR
115 Jamal's Top Rope Splash UR 7.50 15.00
116 Your Three Minutes Are Up PR
117 Jamal's Atomic Samoan Drop PR
118 Victim of the Revolving... PR
119 Double Elbow Drop PR
120 Jamie Noble PR
121 The Trailer Hitch UR 7.50 15.00
122 Managed by Nidia PR
123 Now I'm Gonna Get... PR
124 I'm Jamie Noble, Boy PR
125 Go On - Give 'im Some Sugar PR
126 Throwin' Big Ol' Soup Bones... PR
127 The Breakdown PR
128 Raisin' the Roof PR
129 Just Hold On a Second, Mister PR
130 Red Hook's Premiere... PR
131 A Victim of the Crippler PR
132 Yo, Ese, I Know You, Homes PR
133 Dudley Tough PR
134 Never Gonna Stop Me PR
135 Impaler PR
136 Mattitude Adjustment PR
137 That's Suicide PR
138 Mountain of a Man UR 7.50 15.00
139 If You've Got It, Flaunt It UR 7.50 15.00
140 Everything's Cool When You're UR 7.50 15.00
141 Five Time Five Time... UR 7.50 15.00
142 Pound 4 Pound UR 7.50 15.00
143 Regal Upper Class Punch UR 7.50 15.00
144 Raven's Playground UR 7.50 15.00
145 When Hulkamania Runs... UR 7.50 15.00
146 The Game Interferes UR 7.50 15.00
147 We're Sorry But This Has... UR 7.50 15.00
148 eM pleH UR 7.50 15.00
149 Octopus UR 7.50 15.00
150 Hurrislam UR 7.50 15.00
10/TR World Heavyweight Title Belt R 2.00 4.00
11/TR Cruiserweight Title Belt R 2.00 4.00

2004 Comic Images WWE Raw Deal Vengeance

1 Leaping Neck Snap C .12 .25
2 Revolving Takedown U .50 1.00
3 Flying Leg Scissors R 2.00 4.00
4 Spinning Kick C .12 .25
5 Right Cross Punch C .12 .25
6 Left Cross Punch C .12 .25
7 Judo Thrust U .50 1.00
8 Lariat U .50 1.00
9 Steel Chain Shot U .50 1.00
10 Short Arm Rib Breaker R 2.00 4.00
11 Blindside Kick R 2.00 4.00
12 Struck by an Unknown... R 2.00 4.00
13 Snap Neckbreaker C .12 .25
14 Pretzel Jerk C .12 .25
15 Face Driver C .12 .25
16 Vertical DDT Drop C .12 .25
17 Judo Takedown U .50 1.00
18 Quick Snap Body Slam U .50 1.00
19 Double Underhook Power Bomb U .50 1.00
20 Blindside Slam U .50 1.00
21 Suplex R 2.00 4.00
22 Military Slam R 2.00 4.00
23 Takedown R 2.00 4.00
24 Death Valley Driver R 2.00 4.00
25 Ankle Torque C .12 .25
26 Triangle Choke C .12 .25
27 Body Lock C .12 .25
28 Judo Choke U .50 1.00
29 Wraparound Wrist Lock U .50 1.00
30 Headlock U .50 1.00
31 Apply Legal Leverage R 2.00 4.00
32 Blindside Choke R 2.00 4.00
33 Super Hold R 2.00 4.00
34 I Already Warned You C .12 .25
35 Quick Reflexes C .12 .25
36 Unexpected Turn of Events C .12 .25
37 Blindsided Ego U .50 1.00
38 Leave Me Alone U .50 1.00
39 Blindsided Control U .50 1.00
40 Two R 2.00 4.00
41 Headstrong R 2.00 4.00
42 SloppyVery Sloppy R 2.00 4.00
43 Suplex into the Ring C .12 .25
44 Chain Wrestling C .12 .25
45 When Hell Freezes Over C .12 .25
46 Minute Hold C .12 .25
47 Throw Into the Ring C .12 .25
48 J.R. Style Donnybrook C .12 .25
49 Chained Heat U .50 1.00
50 Down and Out U .50 1.00
51 According to the Contract Table U .50 1.00
52 Last Chance U .50 1.00
53 J.R. Style Authentic BBQ Sauce U .50 1.00
54 For the Love of God - Why, King, Why? U .50 1.00
55 Escape the Rules R 2.00 4.00
56 That's Broken R 2.00 4.00
57 He's Playing Possum? R 2.00 4.00
58 J.R. Style Push R 2.00 4.00
59 Now or Never R 2.00 4.00
60 Enough With the Trash Talk R 2.00 4.00
61 Anaheim, California C .12 .25
62 Atlanta, Georgia C .12 .25
63 Newcastle, England C .12 .25
64 Omaha, Nebraska C .12 .25
65 Calgary, Alberta, Canada U .50 1.00
66 Las Vegas, Nevada U .50 1.00
67 New York, New York U .50 1.00
68 Saskatoon, Saskatchewan... U .50 1.00
69 Houston, Texas R 2.00 4.00
70 Philadelphia, Pennsylvania R 2.00 4.00
71 Raleigh, North Carolina R 2.00 4.00
72 Springfield, Illinois R 2.00 4.00
73 A Chorus of Boos C .12 .25
74 Spontaneous Combustion C .12 .25
75 This is Gonna Be a Rocket Buster C .12 .25
76 Old School Beating C .12 .25
77 First Blood Match U .50 1.00
78 The Title is on the Line U .50 1.00
79 You Rang? U .50 1.00
80 You, Me, and Whoever? U .50 1.00
81 Bad Blood R 2.00 4.00
82 Bitter Rivals R 2.00 4.00
83 It's All About the Game R 2.00 4.00
84 Managed by Dawn Marie R 2.00 4.00
85 Hardcore Style C .12 .25
86 Immune to Pain C .12 .25
87 Number One Contender C .12 .25
88 The Beautiful People C .12 .25
89 Grab the Ref C .12 .25
90 Desperate Tag U .50 1.00
91 Ringside Assistance U .50 1.00
92 You're as Graceful... U .50 1.00
93 Revolutionizing the Business U .50 1.00
94 Chain Finisher U .50 1.00
95 All Thatand Nothing? R 2.00 4.00
96 Divas Revealed R 2.00 4.00
97 To the Rescue R 2.00 4.00
98 Unscrupulous S.O.B. R 2.00 4.00
99 Cheap Accolades R 2.00 4.00
100 Evolution EX
101 Evolution is a Mystery UR 7.50 15.00
102 Paid, Laid, and Made UR 7.50 15.00
103 Yesterday is So Long Ago EX
104 I See the Line in the Sand EX
105 Nothing Ever Stays the Same EX
106 The Highlight of the Night EX
107 You Sanctimounious... UR 7.50 15.00
108 Listen Up, Junior... UR 7.50 15.00
109 My Obscenely Expensive... EX
110 Roll the Footage, Monkeys EX
111 Jericho's Ensugiri EX
112 The Mystery Wrestler EX
113 You Don't Want to Go... UR 7.50 15.00
114 Mankind / Cactus Jack... EX
115 Testicular Fortitude EX
116 I'm Hardcore I'm Hardcore EX
117 Leader of the Edge Army EX
118 Edgeucation of Adam... UR 7.50 15.00
119 Downward Spiral UR 7.50 15.00
120 Edge Kick EX
121 Scream If You Want It EX
122 Cause I Want More EX
123 Paul Heyman EX
124 Let the Bodies Hit the Floor UR 7.50 15.00
125 You're Dangerously Close PR
126 Coach, Cole, or Finkel? EX
127 Big Boys Club EX
128 Do You Know Who... EX
129 Your Freaking Hero EX
130 The Straps are Down UR 7.50 15.00
131 Oh, It's True UR 7.50 15.00
132 Angle's German Suplex EX
133 Woooooo EX
134 Angle's Moonsault EX
135 FBI PR
136 It's a Numbers Game UR 7.50 15.00
137 FBI Hit List PR
138 The Arrivederci PR
139 The Whack PR
140 The Fuhgeddaboutit PR
141 The A-Train PR
142 Snot Rocket UR 7.50 15.00
143 Who Do You Think You Are? PR
144 Chugga-chugga... PR
145 Derailer PR
146 Train Wreck PR
147 Managed by Paul Bearer PR
148 Know Your Role... PR
149 Kane's Rage PR
150 Rikishi's Hip Toss PR
151 Pain is Inevitable PR
152 Viva La Raza Low Rider PR
153 WWE Commentators PR
154 The Best Surprises... PR
155 Blood is Thicker Than Wood PR
156 To All My Peeps... PR
157 Era of Mattitude Has Arrived PR
158 Lita's DDT PR
159 Van Terminator PR
160 How Many Times? PR
161 Keep It Simple, Sir PR
162 The StratusFear PR
163 Managed by Kyo Dai PR
164 I've Got Hurri-Powers PR
165 Who's That Jumpin'... PR
166 Noble Bomb PR
167 Didn't I Already Fire You? PR
168 The People's Champ... PR
169 Belly-to-Belly Steinerplex UR 7.50 15.00
170 All Things Are Possible UR 7.50 15.00
171 Greco Roman Specialists UR 7.50 15.00
172 Test's Top Rope... UR 7.50 15.00
173 Unleash the Beast UR 7.50 15.00
174 I Should've Been in That Magazine UR7.50 15.00
175 Control Your World UR 7.50 15.00
176 Bald is Beautiful UR 7.50 15.00
177 So You Think You're... UR 7.50 15.00
178 The Boss's Main Squeeze UR 7.50 15.00
179 Golden Thong Award UR 7.50 15.00
180 This is Not Enough UR 7.50 15.00
181 Nidia's Mink Coat UR 7.50 15.00

2004 Comic Images WWE Raw Deal WrestleMania and SummerSlam Deck Tins

1 WrestleMania
2 Jerry the King Lawler
3 Absolutely Raw
4 Ultimate Smackdown
5 Summerslam
6 Fabulous Moolah
7 The Older the Berry
8 That Won't Make the Cut

2000 Comic Images WWF Raw Deal

COMPLETE SET ()
1 Chop C .12 .25
2 Punch C .12 .25
3 Head Butt C .12 .25
4 Roundhouse Punch C .12 .25
5 Haymaker C .12 .25
6 Back Body Drop C .12 .25
7 Big Boot C .12 .25
8 Shoulder Block U .50 1.00
9 Kick U .50 1.00
10 Cross Body Block U .50 1.00
11 Cheap Shot From the Corner U .50 1.00
12 Ensugiri U .50 1.00
13 Running Elbow Smash U .50 1.00
14 Drop Kick U .50 1.00
15 Discus Punch U .50 1.00
16 Superkick R 2.00 4.00
17 Spinning Heel Kick R 2.00 4.00
18 Spear R 2.00 4.00
19 Clothesline R 2.00 4.00
20 Chair Shot R 2.00 4.00

21 Hurricanrana R	2.00	4.00
22 Arm Bar Takedown C	.12	.25
23 Hip Toss C	.12	.25
24 Arm Drag C	.12	.25
25 Russian Leg Sweep C	.12	.25
26 Snap Mare C	.12	.25
27 Gut Buster C	.12	.25
28 Body Slam C	.12	.25
29 Back Breaker C	.12	.25
30 Double Leg Takedown U	.50	1.00
31 Fireman's Carry U	.50	1.00
32 Headlock Takedown U	.50	1.00
33 Belly to Belly Suplex U	.50	1.00
34 Atomic Facebuster U	.50	1.00
35 Atomic Drop U	.50	1.00
36 Inverse Atomic Drop U	.50	1.00
37 Vertical Suplex U	.50	1.00
38 Belly to Back Suplex U	.50	1.00
39 Pump Handle Slam U	.50	1.00
40 Reverse DDT U	.50	1.00
41 Samoan Drop R	2.00	4.00
42 Sit Out Powerbomb R	2.00	4.00
43 Bulldog R	2.00	4.00
44 Fisherman's Suplex R	2.00	4.00
45 DDT R	2.00	4.00
46 Power Slam R	2.00	4.00
47 Powerbomb R	2.00	4.00
48 Press Slam R	2.00	4.00
49 Collar and Elbow Lockup C	.12	.25
50 Wrist Lock C	.12	.25
51 Arm Bar C	.12	.25
52 Chin Lock C	.12	.25
53 Bear Hug C	.12	.25
54 Full Nelson C	.12	.25
55 Choke Hold C	.12	.25
56 Step Over Toe Hold C	.12	.25
57 Ankle Lock U	.50	1.00
58 Standing Side Headlock U	.50	1.00
59 Cobra Clutch U	.50	1.00
60 Bow and Arrow U	.50	1.00
61 Chicken Wing U	.50	1.00
62 Sleeper R	2.00	4.00
63 Camel Clutch R	2.00	4.00
64 Boston Crab R	2.00	4.00
65 Guillotine Stretch R	2.00	4.00
66 Abdominal Stretch R	.75	1.50
67 Torture Rack R	2.00	4.00
68 Figure Four Leg Lock R	2.00	4.00
69 Combination Attack R	2.00	4.00
70 Step Aside C	.12	.25
71 Escape Move C	.12	.25
72 Break the Hold C	.12	.25
73 Trip C	.12	.25
74 Rolling Takedown U	.50	1.00
75 Knee to the Gut U	.50	1.00
76 Elbow to the Face U	.50	1.00
77 Clean Break U	.50	1.00
78 Partner Interference R	2.00	4.00
79 Manager Interferes R	2.00	4.00
80 Disqualification R	2.00	4.00
81 No Chance in Hell R	2.00	4.00
82 Hmmm C	.12	.25
83 Don't Think Too Hard C	.12	.25
84 Tag in Partner C	.12	.25
85 Whaddya Got? C	.12	.25
86 Not Yet C	.12	.25
87 Jockeying for Position C	.12	.25
88 Irish Whip C	.12	.25
89 Flash in the Pan C	.12	.25
90 View of Villainy C	.12	.25
91 Shake It Off U	.50	1.00
92 Offer Handshake U	.50	1.00
93 Roll Out of the Ring U	.50	1.00
94 Distract the Ref U	.50	1.00
95 Recovery U	.50	1.00
96 Spit At Opponent U	.50	1.00
97 Double Team U	.50	1.00
98 Get Crowd Support U	.50	1.00
99 Comeback R	2.00	4.00
100 Ego Boost R	2.00	4.00
101 Deluding Yourself R	2.00	4.00
102 Stagger R	2.00	4.00
103 Diversion R	2.00	4.00
104 Marking Out R	2.00	4.00
105 Puppies Puppies R	2.00	4.00
106 Shane O'Mac R	2.00	4.00
107 Maintain Hold R	2.00	4.00
108 Pat and Gerry R	2.00	4.00
109 Stone Cold Stunner UR	7.50	15.00
110 Open Up a Can of Whoop-A$ UR	7.50	15.00
111 Undertaker's Tombstone... UR	7.50	15.00
112 Power of Darkness UR	7.50	15.00
113 Mandible Claw UR	7.50	15.00
114 Mr. Socko UR	7.50	15.00
115 Pedigree UR	7.50	15.00
116 Chyna Interferes UR	7.50	15.00
117 The People's Eyebrow UR	7.50	15.00
118 The People's Elbow UR	7.50	15.00
119 Kane's Tombstone Piledriver UR	7.50	15.00
120 Hellfire and Brimstone UR	7.50	15.00
121 Walls of Jericho UR	7.50	15.00
122 Ayatollah of Rock 'n' Roll-a UR	7.50	15.00
123 STONE COLD STEVE AUSTIN EX		
124 Austin Elbow Smash EX		
125 Lou Thesz Press EX		
126 Double Digits EX		
127 THE UNDERTAKER EX		
128 Undertaker's Chokeslam EX		
129 Undertaker's Flying Clothesline EX		
130 Undertaker Sits Up EX		
131 MANKIND EX		
132 Have a Nice Day EX		
133 Double Arm DDT EX		
134 Tree of Woe EX		
135 HHH EX		
136 Leaping Knee to the Face EX		
137 Facebuster EX		
138 I Am the Game. EX		
139 THE ROCK EX		
140 Smackdown Hotel EX		
141 Take That Move EX		
142 Rock Bottom EX		
143 KANE EX		
144 Kane's Chokeslam EX		
145 Kane's Flying Clothesline EX		
146 Kane's Return EX		
147 CHRIS JERICHO EX		
148 Lionsault EX		
149 Y2J EX		
150 Don't You Never EVER EX		
1TR WWF Heavyweight Title Belt		
2TR WWF Intercontinental Title Belt		
3TR WWF European Title Belt		

2001 Comic Images WWF Raw Deal Backlash

1 Flying Head Scissors C	.12	.25
2 Big Splash in the Corner C	.12	.25
3 Flying Clothesline U	.50	1.00
4 Drive Opponent Thru Announcer's Table U	.50	1.00
5 Crucifix Rollup R	2.00	4.00
6 Chop to the Chest C	.12	.25
7 Slap the Taste Out of Your Mouth C	.12	.25
8 Leg Sweep C	.12	.25
9 Struck by a Kendo Stick C	.12	.25
10 Pop the Guy On the Apron U	.50	1.00
11 Running Lariat U	.50	1.00
12 Garbage Can Lid U	.50	1.00
13 Stun Gun R	2.00	4.00
14 Hung Out to Dry R	2.00	4.00
15 Running Clothesline R	2.00	4.00
16 Scoop Slam C	.12	.25
17 Leg Drag C	.12	.25
18 Neck Breaker C	.12	.25
19 Rib Breaker C	.12	.25
20 Tiger Bomb C	.12	.25
21 Single Arm DDT U	.50	1.00
22 Tandem Atomic Drop U	.50	1.00
23 Brainbuster U	.50	1.00
24 Spine Buster U	.50	1.00
25 Workin' on the Knee R	2.00	4.00
26 Half Hour Suplex R	2.00	4.00
27 Clutch onto Opponent C	.12	.25
28 Captive Tag Out C	.12	.25
29 Arm Wrench C	.12	.25
30 Entangle In the Ropes C	.12	.25
31 Apply Illegal Leverage U	.50	1.00
32 Texas Cloverleaf U	.50	1.00
33 Microphone Cord R	2.00	4.00
34 Sharpshooter R	2.00	4.00
35 Clumsy Opponent C	.12	.25
36 No Sell Maneuver C	.12	.25
37 Over Sell Maneuver C	.12	.25
38 Kissing Up to the Stinkin' Fans U	.50	1.00
39 Hey That's Cheap Heat U	.50	1.00
40 Blown Spot R	2.00	4.00
41 Charismatic Style C	.12	.25
42 Set Him Up C	.12	.25
43 Great Technical Knowledge C	.12	.25
44 Turn the Match... C	.12	.25
45 Amazing Display of Power C	.12	.25
46 Adrenaline Rush C	.12	.25
47 Let's Take it Home C	.12	.25
48 Drawing Extra Heat U	.50	1.00
49 Well-Deserved Push U	.50	1.00
50 Propel Partner U	.50	1.00
51 Ladder In the Ring U	.50	1.00
52 Giving Away the Business U	.50	1.00
53 Heel Turn R	2.00	4.00
54 Lita to the Xtreme R	2.00	4.00
55 You're Not in My League R	2.00	4.00
56 Busted Wide Open R	2.00	4.00
57 Seeing Stars R	2.00	4.00
58 Announcer's Table R	2.00	4.00
59 I'm Gonna Put You... R	2.00	4.00
60 Watching My Back R	2.00	4.00
61 Study the Tapes C	.12	.25
62 Student of the Sport C	.12	.25
63 Awesome Pyro C	.12	.25
64 Givin' 'em High Fives C	.12	.25
65 Taunt the Fans C	.12	.25
66 Fans Love an Underdog U	.50	1.00
67 Trash Talkin' Interview U	.50	1.00
68 Jump the Bell U	.50	1.00
69 Old School Wrestling Match R	2.00	4.00
70 Here a Mark, There a Mark... R	2.00	4.00
71 Premiere WWF (logo) Superstar R	2.00	4.00
72 Underrated Superstar R	2.00	4.00
73 Backlash C	.12	.25
74 Dirty Low Blow C	.12	.25
75 Small Concealed Foreign Object C	.12	.25
76 Armageddon (WWF Logo) Style C	.12	.25
77 Per Order of the Chairman U	.50	1.00
78 Spectacular Ring Entrance U	.50	1.00
79 When You Thought You... U	.50	1.00
80 Referee Finally Catches... U	.50	1.00
81 Don't Mess with the Champ R	2.00	4.00
82 Fully Loaded R	2.00	4.00
83 Again With This Crap?? R	2.00	4.00
84 No Mercy R	2.00	4.00
85 Dudley Boyz EX		
86 3D UR	7.50	15.00
87 Wazzzzuuup??? EX		
88 Buh-Buh Ray Dudley U	.50	1.00
89 Buh-Buh Bomb UR	7.50	15.00
90 Catatonic Stare R	2.00	4.00
91 My Name Is U	.50	1.00
92 Buh-Buh Drop EX		
93 Buh-Buh Punch R	2.00	4.00
94 D-Von Dudley U	.50	1.00
95 Testify UR	7.50	15.00
96 Spinning Elbow R	2.00	4.00
97 Doin' the D-Von U	.50	1.00
98 Thou Shall Not ####... EX		
99 D-Von Get the Table R	2.00	4.00
100 Edge and Christian EX		
101 Con-Chair-To UR	7.50	15.00
102 For the Benefit of Those... EX		
103 Edge U	.50	1.00
104 Edge-O-Matic UR	7.50	15.00
105 Million Dollar Smile R	2.00	4.00
106 Big Slide Into the Ring U	.50	1.00
107 Listen, You Reekazoid EX		
108 Sodas Rule R	2.00	4.00
109 Christian U	.50	1.00
110 Unprettier UR	7.50	15.00
111 Kazoo Theme Songs R	2.00	4.00
112 Christian's Shades U	.50	1.00
113 This Is So Totally Unfair EX		
114 Greetings to Our Fans... R	2.00	4.00
115 Hardy Boyz EX		
116 Poetry in Motion UR	7.50	15.00
117 Spin Cycle EX		
118 Matt Hardy U	.50	1.00
119 Twist of Fate UR	7.50	15.00
120 Matt's Moonsault R	2.00	4.00
121 Roar for the Fans U	.50	1.00
122 Matt Hardy's Patented Leg Drop EX		
123 Put It All On the Line R	2.00	4.00
124 Jeff Hardy U	.50	1.00
125 Swanton Bomb UR	7.50	15.00
126 Ride the Barricade R	2.00	4.00
127 No, Jeff, Don't Do It U	.50	1.00
128 Whisper in the Wind EX		
129 Incite the Fans R	2.00	4.00
130 Right to Censor EX		
131 Right to (Censor) Interfere UR	7.50	15.00
132 We're Doing This For... R	2.00	4.00
133 What's Wrong with You People? R	2.00	4.00
134 We're Here to Clean Up... EX		
135 This is Unacceptable Behavior EX		
136 Censored EX		
137 DTA UR	7.50	15.00
138 Brothers 'til the End UR	7.50	15.00
139 Three Faces of Foley UR	7.50	15.00
140 The Brahma Bull UR	7.50	15.00
141 Sledge Hammer Shot UR	7.50	15.00
142 Superior Acrobatics UR	7.50	15.00
143 I Did It For You UR	7.50	15.00
144 Where Are Your Medals? UR	7.50	15.00
145 Ovicular Fortitude UR	7.50	15.00
146 Just Another Victim UR	7.50	15.00
147 Prove Me Wrong UR	7.50	15.00
148 Eddie's Roll Up UR	7.50	15.00
149 Pac's Back UR	7.50	15.00
150 The One Billy Gunn UR	7.50	15.00

2001 Comic Images WWF Raw Deal Fully Loaded

1 Falling Fist C	.12	.25
2 Knee Smash C	.12	.25
3 Elbow Drop C	.12	.25
4 Foot Stomp C	.12	.25
5 Splash U	.50	1.00
6 Leg Drop U	.50	1.00
7 Double Axe Handle U	.50	1.00
8 Shooting Star Press U	.50	1.00
9 Missile Dropkick R	2.00	4.00
10 Suicide Plancha R	2.00	4.00
11 Superplex R	2.00	4.00
12 Moonsault R	2.00	4.00
13 Backhand Slap C	.12	.25
14 Turnbuckle Smash C	.12	.25
15 Eye Rake C	.12	.25
16 Knee Lift U	.50	1.00
17 Baseball Slide U	.50	1.00
18 Surprise Hit U	.50	1.00
19 European Uppercut R	2.00	4.00
20 Trash Can R	2.00	4.00
21 Double Clothesline R	2.00	4.00
22 Jaw Jammer C	.12	.25
23 Japanese Arm Drag C	.12	.25
24 Jackhammer C	.12	.25
25 Drop Toe Hold C	.12	.25
26 Shoulder Breaker C	.12	.25
27 Small Package C	.12	.25
28 Monkey Flip U	.50	1.00
29 Knee Breaker U	.50	1.00
30 Full Nelson Slam U	.50	1.00
31 German Suplex U	.50	1.00
32 Airplane Spin U	.50	1.00
33 Swinging Neck Breaker U	.50	1.00
34 Fall-Away Slam R	2.00	4.00
35 Double Underhook Suplex R	2.00	4.00
36 Sidewalk Slam R	2.00	4.00
37 Giant Swing R	2.00	4.00
38 Northern Lights Suplex R	2.00	4.00
39 Hair Pull C	.12	.25
40 Front Face Lock C	.12	.25
41 Hammerlock C	.12	.25
42 Head Vise U	.50	1.00
43 Surfboard U	.50	1.00
44 Stump Puller U	.50	1.00
45 Claw R	2.00	4.00
46 STF R	2.00	4.00
47 Roll Out of the Way C	.12	.25
48 Borrring Borrring C	.12	.25
49 Shove Off the Top Rope C	.12	.25

50 Tornado DDT C .12 .25
51 Just Bring It U .50 1.00
52 Hebner Calls It U .50 1.00
53 Lift a Boot U .50 1.00
54 That's Gonna Cost You Reversa
55 Ref KO'd R 2.00 4.00
56 Attitude Adjustment R 2.00 4.00
57 In This Very Ring C .12 .25
58 Defensive Cover C .12 .25
59 Ho Train C .12 .25
60 Playing With Fire C .12 .25
61 Stare Down Opponent C .12 .25
62 Moongoose In the House C .12 .25
63 Commission-er Rules C .12 .25
64 McMahon-Helmsley Era C .12 .25
65 Throw Into the Corner Turnbuckle C .12 .25
66 From the Top Rope C .12 .25
67 Hardyz' Ambush C .12 .25
68 American Bad A$ C .12 .25
69 Do You Like Pie? C .12 .25
70 Doing the Job C .12 .25
71 Go for the Cheap Pop U .50 1.00
72 Predictable Opponent U .50 1.00
73 Who Booked This Match? U .50 1.00
74 JR Style Slobberknocker U .50 1.00
75 Bait Opponent U .50 1.00
76 Defensive Posture U .50 1.00
77 Table Table Table U .50 1.00
78 Backed by Stephanie McMahon U .50 1.00
79 Here Kitty, Kitty U .50 1.00
80 Throw Opponent Out of the Ring U .50 1.00
81 Quick Count Ref U .50 1.00
82 Turn the Tide R 2.00 4.00
83 Time Keeper's Bell R 2.00 4.00
84 Inferno Match R 2.00 4.00
85 Call to the Crowd R 2.00 4.00
86 Dem Damn Dudleyz R 2.00 4.00
87 Reeking of Awesomeness Action
88 Enter the Stratus-phere R 2.00 4.00
89 Kick Out R 2.00 4.00
90 Acolyte Protection Agency R 2.00 4.00
91 Rikishi Driver UR 7.50 15.00
92 A$ Drop UR 7.50 15.00
93 Rikishi EX
94 Drive, Rikishi, Drive EX
95 Back That A$ Up EX
96 Stink Face EX
97 Olympic Slam UR 7.50 15.00
98 It's True, It's True UR 7.50 15.00
99 Kurt Angle EX
100 Intensity EX
101 Integrity EX
102 Intelligence EX
103 Chyna's Pedigree UR 7.50 15.00
104 The 9th Wonder of the World UR 7.50 15.00
105 Chyna EX
106 Handspring Elbow EX
107 I'd Rather Be In Chyna EX
108 Chyna's Patented Low Blow EX
109 Tazzmission UR 7.50 15.00
110 Thug It - Dead UR 7.50 15.00
111 Tazz EX
112 T-Bone Tazzplex EX
113 Head-and-Arms Tazzplex EX
114 Northern Lights Tazzplex EX
115 Crippler Crossface UR 7.50 15.00
116 Big Stupid Grin UR 7.50 15.00
117 Chris Benoit EX
118 Kamikaze Headbutt EX
119 Series of Suplexes EX
120 Rabid Wolverine EX
121 Guerrero Frog Splash... UR 7.50 15.00
122 Get Your GED UR 7.50 15.00
123 Eddie Guerrero EX
124 Snap Senton Splash EX
125 Study for Your GED EX
126 Latino Heeeeeeeat EX
127 Doggy Pump Handle Slam UR 7.50 15.00
128 Road Dogg EX
129 Kickin' The Shizt-nit... EX
130 Juke N Jive EX
131 Let's Make Some Noise EX
132 X-Factor UR 7.50 15.00
133 X-Pac EX
134 Leaping Spin Kick EX
135 Bronco Buster EX
136 Huge Bump Out of the Ring EX
137 Fame-A$-er UR 7.50 15.00
138 B. A. Billy Gunn EX
139 I'm an A$ Man EX
140 B.A.'s Military Press Slam EX
141 The Federation's Purest Athlete EX
142 I've Got Two Words For Ya... UR 7.50 15.00
143 Tori Enters the Fray UR 7.50 15.00
144 Patented Rock Footstomp UR 7.50 15.00
145 Patented Austin Kick... UR 7.50 15.00
146 Rest In Peace UR 7.50 15.00
147 Get Hardcore UR 7.50 15.00
148 Triple H's Reverse... UR 7.50 15.00
149 Masked Vengence UR 7.50 15.00
150 Springboard Drop Kick UR 7.50 15.00

2002 Comic Images WWF Raw Deal Mania

1 Spinning Crescent Kick C .12 .25
2 Flying Reverse Elbow C .12 .25
3 Flying TopE U .50 1.00
4 Stackplex U .50 1.00
5 Asai Moonsault R 2.00 4.00
6 Forearm Shot C .12 .25
7 Feign Strike C .12 .25
8 Gut Punch C .12 .25
9 Step on Opponent's Noggin U .50 1.00
10 Into the Barricade U .50 1.00
11 Pump Kick R 2.00 4.00
12 Catapult C .12 .25
13 Within Your Grasp C .12 .25
14 Butterfly Suplex C .12 .25
15 Beal Toss C .12 .25
16 Backslide U .50 1.00
17 Tandem Flapjack U .50 1.00
18 Running Bulldog R 2.00 4.00
19 Short Arm Hammerlock C .12 .25
20 Knee Bar C .12 .25
21 Strangle Hold U .50 1.00
22 Arm Grapevine U .50 1.00
23 Indian Deathlock R 2.00 4.00
24 All Talk, No Action C .12 .25
25 Iron Will R 2.00 4.00
26 Not Today, Pal R 2.00 4.00
27 Out Think the Fink C .12 .25
28 Stratusfied C .12 .25
29 Got Wood? C .12 .25
30 Playing by the Rules C .12 .25
31 Kay-Fabe C .12 .25
32 Totally Bogus C .12 .25
33 Little She Devil C .12 .25
34 Gut Wrench C .12 .25
35 X-treme Measures C .12 .25
36 Cole Calls It Right C .12 .25
37 Trailer Park Trash C .12 .25
38 Veteran Referee: Tim White U .50 1.00
39 Daddy's Little Girl U .50 1.00
40 Messing With the Champ U .50 1.00
41 Everybody Wants... U .50 1.00
42 Wooden Palette U .50 1.00
43 Judgment Day U .50 1.00
44 Mania U .50 1.00
45 Torrie Wilson, On It R 2.00 4.00
46 Keibler's Cookies R 2.00 4.00
47 V.K.M.'s Patented Big Gulp R 2.00 4.00
48 Money Talks, BS Walks R 2.00 4.00
49 Ring Rats R 2.00 4.00
50 Billion Dollar Princess R 2.00 4.00
51 Unforgiven R 2.00 4.00
52 Ring Steps R 2.00 4.00
53 No Way Out R 2.00 4.00
54 Superior Training C .12 .25
55 Slandered Online C .12 .25
56 Product Endorsements C .12 .25
57 Backstage Ambush Attempt C .12 .25
58 No Disqualification Match C .12 .25
59 Personal Appearance U .50 1.00
60 Snubbed by the Fans U .50 1.00
61 Not Done with Any Flair U .50 1.00
62 Chicago Street Fight U .50 1.00
63 Four Corners Match U .50 1.00
64 Hell in a Cell Match R 2.00 4.00
65 Indian Strap Match R 2.00 4.00
66 Duchess of Queensbury Rules R 2.00 4.00
67 Handicap Match R 2.00 4.00
68 Signed Contract with Linda McMahon R2.00 4.00
69 Fortitude Surge C .12 .25
70 Fan Appreciation Day C .12 .25
71 Here Comes the Money C .12 .25
72 Remove Corner Turnbuckle C .12 .25
73 Over the Barricade C .12 .25
74 Touch Turnbuckle #1 U .50 1.00
75 Touch Turnbuckle #2 U .50 1.00
76 Touch Turnbuckle #3 U .50 1.00
77 Touch Turnbuckle #4 U .50 1.00
78 Over the Top Rope U .50 1.00
79 Second Wind R 2.00 4.00
80 Sustained Damage R 2.00 4.00
81 Happy You're Here... R 2.00 4.00
82 Test of Strength R 2.00 4.00
83 Debilitating Injury: Concussion R 2.00 4.00
84 Big Show EX
85 Final Cut UR 7.50 15.00
86 Wellllllllll UR 7.50 15.00
87 Showstopper Chokeslam EX
88 Big Show Splash EX
89 500lbs. of Raw Power EX
90 Lita EX
91 Lita-sault UR 7.50 15.00
92 X-treme Thong UR 7.50 15.00
93 Lita-canrana EX
94 Lita's Drop Kick EX
95 Crimson Goddess EX
96 Rob Van Dam EX
97 Van Daminator UR 7.50 15.00
98 R - V - D UR 7.50 15.00
99 Five Star Frog Splash EX
100 Extreme Monkey Flip EX
101 Rolling Thunder EX
102 Booker T EX
103 Bookend UR 7.50 15.00
104 Spinnerooni UR 7.50 15.00
105 Can You Dig It, Sucka? EX
106 Booker's Scissor Kick EX
107 Spinning T Kick EX
108 APA PU
109 Beer, Cards, and More Beer UR 7.50 15.00
110 Dominator PR
111 Clothesline from Hell PR
112 Faarooq's Spike Spine Buster PU
113 Bradshaw's Fall Away Slam PU
114 Spike Dudley PU
115 Dudley Dog UR 7.50 15.00
116 150 lbs. Soaking Wet PR
117 Good Golly, Miss Molly Holly PR
118 Psychotic Bump PU
119 Brotherly Love PU
120 William Regal PU
121 Regal Stretch UR 7.50 15.00
122 Commissioner Regal's Decree PR
123 Union Jack PR
124 I've Been Besmirched PU
125 Goodwill Ambassador PU
126 Raven PU
127 Raven Effect DDT UR 7.50 15.00
128 From the Bowery PR
129 What About Me? PR
130 Quoth the Raven Nevermore PU
131 I Feel Your Pain PU
132 What??? PR
133 You Will Respect Me PR
134 Foley is Good PR
135 Shades of the Great One PR
136 Cerebral Assassin PR
137 Born of Hellfire PR
138 Would You Please... PR
139 Gettin' Cheeky with It UR 7.50 15.00
140 Angle Lock UR 7.50 15.00
141 Tough Enough UR 7.50 15.00
142 First to Tap Out Match UR 7.50 15.00
143 /timo Rechazo UR 7.50 15.00
144 Pac's Pack UR 7.50 15.00
145 The One and Only UR 7.50 15.00
146 Greetings from Dudleyville... UR 7.50 15.00
147 You Think You Know Me? UR 7.50 15.00
148 Live for the Moment UR 7.50 15.00
149 TLC Match UR 7.50 15.00
150 Censorship Match UR 7.50 15.00
6/TR WCW Title Belt R 2.00 4.00
7/TR WWF Light Heavyweight Title R 2.00 4.00

2001 Comic Images WWF Raw Deal Survivor Series 1

COMPLETE SET ()
2a Punch V1.1
2b Knee Smash V2.1
3a Head Butt V1.1
3b Elbow Drop V2.1
5b Splash V2.1
8a Shoulder Block V1.1
9a Kick V1.1
12b Moonsault V2.1
13b Backhand Slap V2.1
15b Eye Rake V2.1
16a Superkick V1.1
16b Superkick V1.2
17a Spinning Heel Kick V1.1
19b European Uppercut V2.1
19c European Uppercut V2.2
20a Chair Shot V1.1
20b Trash Can V2.1
21a Hurricanrana V1.1
22b Jaw Jammer V2.1
23a Hip Toss V1.1
24a Arm Drag V1.1
25b Drop Toe Hold V2.1
30a Double Leg Takedown V1.1
32a Headlock Takedown V1.1
33a Belly to Belly Suplex V1.1
35b Double Underhook Suplex V2.1
36b Sidewalk Slam V2.1
37b Giant Swing V2.1
39b Hair Pull V2.1
41a Samoan Drop V1.1
41b Samoan Drop V1.2
42a Sit Out Powerbomb V1.1
43a Bulldog V1.1
44a Fisherman's Suplex V1.1
45a DDT V1.1
45b Claw V2.1
45c Claw V2.2
47b Roll Out of the Way V2.1
48b Boring Boring V2.1
50a Wrist Lock V1.1
51a Arm Bar V1.1
51b Just Bring It V2.1
51c Just Bring It V2.2
52b Hebner Calls It V2.1
53b Lift a Boot V2.1
55a Choke Hold V1.1
56b Attitude Adjustment V2.1
57a Ankle Lock V1.1
58a Standing Side Headlock V1.1
61a Chicken Wing V1.1
62a Sleeper V1.1
63b Commissioner Rules V2.1
64a Boston Crab V1.1
65a Guillotine Stretch V1.1
65b Throw into the Corner... V2.1
66b From the Top Rope V2.1
69a Combination Attack V1.1
70a Step Aside V1.1
71a Escape Move V1.1
71b Go for the Cheap Pop V2.1
72a Break the Hold V1.1
74a Rolling Takedown V1.1
74b JR Style Slobberknocker V2.1
75a Knee to the Gut V1.1
75b Bait Opponent V2.1
76a Elbow to the Face V1.1
76b Elbow to the Face V1.2
76c Defensive Posture V2.1
78a Partner Interference V1.1
78b Backed by Stephanie... V2.1
78c Backed by Stephanie... V2.2
79a Manager Interferes V1.1
79b Manager Interferes V1.2
80a Disqualification V1.1
81a No Chance in Hell V1.1
81b No Chance in Hell V1.2
82b Turn the Tide V2.1
82c Turn the Tide V2.2

84a Tag in Partner V1.1
84b Inferno Match V2.1
87a Jockeying for Position V1.1
88a Irish Whip V1.1
88b Enter the Stratusphere V2.1
92a Offer Handshake V1.1
93a Roll Out of the Ring V1.1
93b Roll Out of the Ring V1.2
95a Recovery V1.1
96a Spit At Opponent V1.1
97b Olympic Slam V2.1
98a Get Crowd Support V1.1
98b It's True, It's True V2.1
99b Kurt Angle V2.1
100a Ego Boost V1.1
100b Intensity V2.1
101b Integrity V2.1
102a Stagger V1.1
102b Intelligence V2.1
104a Marking Out V1.1
105a Puppies Puppies V1.1
105b Puppies Puppies V1.2
107a Maintain Hold V1.1
109a Stone Cold Stunner V1.1
109b Tazzmission V2.1
110a Open a Can of... V1.1
110b Thug It - Dead V2.1
111a The Last Ride V1.1
111b Tazz V2.1
112a This Is My Yard V1.1
112b T-Bone Tazzplex V2.1
113a Cactus's Double Arm DDT V1.1
113b Head-and-Arms Tazzplex V2.1
114a Barbed Wire Baseball Bat V1.1
114b Northern Lights Tazzplex V2.1
115a Pedigree V1.1
115b Crippler Crossface V2.1
116a Stephanie Interferes V1.1
116b Big Stupid Grin V2.1
117a The People's Eyebrow V1.1
117b Chris Benoit V2.1
118a The People's Elbow V1.1
118b Kamikazee Headbutt V2.1
119a Kane's Tombstone... V1.1
119b Series of Suplexes V2.1
120a Hellfire and Brimstone V1.1
120b Rabid Wolverine V2.1
121a Walls of Jericho V1.1
122a Ayatollah of Rock'n'Roll-a V1.1
123a Stone Cold Steve Austin V1.1
124a Austin Elbow Smash V1.1
125a Lou Thesz Press V1.1
126a Double Digits V1.1
127a Dead Man Inc. V1.1
128a Bad Ass Chokeslam V1.1
129a Old School Clothesline V1.1
130a Dead Man Walking V1.1
131a Cactus Jack V1.1
132a Bang Bang V1.1
133a Cactus Clothesline V1.1
134a Tree of Woe V1.1
135a Triple H V1.1
136a Leaping Knee to the Face V1.1
137a Facebuster V1.1
138a I Am the Game V1.1
139a The Rock V1.1
140a Smackdown Hotel V1.1
141a Take That Move V1.1
142a Rock Bottom V1.1
143a Kane V1.1
144a Kane's Chokeslam V1.1
145a Kane's Flying Clothesline V1.1
146a Kane's Return V1.1
146b I'll Make You Famous V2.1
147a Chris Jericho V1.1
147b Get Hardcore V2.1
148a Lionsault V1.1
148b Triple H's Reverse... V2.1
149a Y2J V1.1
149b Masked Vengence V2.1
150a Don't You Never Eeeever V1.1
150b Springboard Drop Kick V2.1

2000 Comic Images WWF Axxess Fan Fest

COMPLETE SET (3)		
1 Big Show	4.00	10.00
2 Triple H	6.00	15.00
3 The Rock	10.00	25.00

2000 Comic Images WWF The Divas Promos

COMPLETE SET (8)	12.00	30.00
P1 Chyna	3.00	8.00
P2 Debra	2.50	6.00
P3 Ivory	2.00	5.00
P4 Jacqueline	2.00	5.00
P5 The Kat	2.00	5.00
P6 Terri	3.00	8.00
P7 Tori	2.00	5.00
P8 Trish	4.00	10.00

2000 Comic Images WWF No Mercy

COMPLETE SET (81)	8.00	20.00
1 Mankind	.50	1.25
2 Cactus Jack	.50	1.25
3 Stone Cold Steve Austin	.75	2.00
4 Hardcore Holly	.20	.50
5 Al Snow	.20	.50
6 Road Dogg	.12	.30
7 Big Boss Man	.20	.50
8 The Undertaker	.60	1.50
9 Kane	.50	1.25
10 The Rock	.75	2.00
11 Vince McMahon	.50	1.25
12 Shane McMahon	.30	.75
13 Edge/Christian	.50	1.25
14 The Hardy Boyz	.30	.75
15 The Dudley Boyz	.20	.50
16 The Acolytes	.30	.75
17 Faarooq	.12	.30
18 Bradshaw	.30	.75
19 X-Pac	.20	.50
20 The Big Show	.30	.75
21 Viscera	.12	.30
22 Prince Albert	.12	.30
23 Test	.20	.50
24 Mr. Ass	.12	.30
25 Triple H	.75	2.00
26 Chyna	.50	1.25
27 Ken Shamrock	.20	.50
28 Godfather	.12	.30
29 Chris Jericho	.30	.75
30 Tazz RC	.20	.50
31 Hardcore Belt	.12	.30
32 D-Generation X	.30	.75
33 Gangrel	.12	.30
34 The Headbangers	.12	.30
35 British Bulldog	.20	.50
36 D'Lo Brown	.12	.30
37 Mark Henry	.12	.30
38 Kurt Angle RC	12.00	30.00
39 Mean Street Posse	.12	.30
40 Rikishi Phatu	.20	.50
41 Too Cool	.12	.30
42 Mick Foley	.50	1.25
43 Shawn Michaels	.50	1.25
44 The Undertaker	.60	1.50
45 Stone Cold Steve Austin	.75	2.00
46 Legion Of Doom	.40	1.00
47 Wild Samoans	.20	.50
48 Sgt. Slaughter	.30	.75
49 Mankind/The Rock	.75	2.00
50 Mankind/The Rock	.75	2.00
51 Mankind/The Undertaker	.60	1.50
52 Mankind/Triple H	.75	2.00
53 Mankind/Ken Shamrock	.50	1.25
54 The Rock/Triple H	.75	2.00
55 The Undertaker/Shawn Michaels	.60	1.50
56 The Hardy Boyz/Edge/Christian	.50	1.25
57 The Undertaker/Kane	.60	1.50
58 Undertaker/Kane/Austin	.75	2.00
59 Kane/Vince McMahon/Undertaker	.60	1.50
60 Steve Austin/Kane	.75	2.00
61 Steve Austin/Dude Love	.75	2.00
62 Steve Austin/Undertaker	.75	2.00
63 Steve Austin/Undertaker	.75	2.00
64 Steve Austin/Vince McMahon	.75	2.00
65 Steve Austin/The McMahons	.75	2.00
66 Shane McMahon/Test	.30	.75
67 Al Snow/Big Boss Man	.20	.50
68 Al Snow/Hardcore Holly	.20	.50
69 Al Snow/Minis	.20	.50
70 Ivory/Luna	.50	1.25
71 Ken Shamrock/Steve Blackman	.20	.50
72 Mr. Ass/Hardcore Holly	.20	.50
73 The Acolytes	.30	.75
74 New Age Outlaws/Mankind/Kane	.50	1.25
75 Vince McMahon/Mankind	.50	1.25
76 Sgt. Slaughter/Triple H	.75	2.00
77 Shawn Michaels/The Undertaker	.60	1.50
78 The Rock/Mankind	.75	2.00
79 Triple H/Cactus Jack	.75	2.00
80 The Hardy Boyz/The Dudley Boyz	.30	.75
81 Checklist	.12	.30

2000 Comic Images WWF No Mercy Hardcore Champions Holofoil

COMPLETE SET (8)	3.00	8.00
RANDOMLY INSERTED INTO PACKS		
C1 Mankind	1.25	3.00
C2 Big Bossman	.50	1.25
C3 Road Dogg	.50	1.25
C4 Hardcore Holly	.50	1.25
C5 Al Snow	.50	1.25
C6 Mr. Ass	.50	1.25
C7 British Bulldog	.50	1.25
C8 Test	.50	1.25

2000 Comic Images WWF No Mercy Piece of the Ring Relics

COMPLETE SET (4)	12.00	30.00
RANDOMLY INSERTED INTO PACKS		
P1 Ring Mat	6.00	15.00
P2 Road Dogg Hat	4.00	10.00
P3 Chris Jericho Shirt	8.00	20.00
P4 D-Generation X Shirt	5.00	12.00

2000 Comic Images WWF No Mercy Promos

COMPLETE SET (3)	1.50	4.00
RANDOMLY INSERTED INTO PACKS		
P1 Mankind/The Rock	.75	2.00
P2 The Undertaker/Kane	.75	2.00
P3 Vince McMahon	.75	2.00

2000 Comic Images WWF Rock Solid

COMPLETE SET (72)	10.00	25.00
UNOPENED BOX (36 PACKS)	100.00	150.00
UNOPENED PACK (7 CARDS)	3.00	4.00
1 Title Card	.30	.75
2 Reeling 'Em In	.30	.75
3 Catching Up	.30	.75
4 The People's Threads	.30	.75
5 Sweet Ride	.30	.75
6 The Rock's Roots	.30	.75
7 Shirt Off His Back	.30	.75
8 Electrifying Threads	.30	.75
9 In For A Trim	.30	.75
10 Laying It Down In Miami	.30	.75
11 Electrifying Author	.30	.75
12 The Little People's Champ	.30	.75
13 A Class Act	.30	.75
14 The Fans Bring It	.30	.75
15 They Smell It	.30	.75
16 Another Happy Customer	.30	.75
17 Author, Author	.30	.75
18 Who's The Champ	.15	.75
19 Rocky Rocky Rocky	.30	.75
20 Action, Rock	.30	.75
21 The People's Host	.30	.75
22 Hot, Hot, Hot	.30	.75
23 Getting Cheffy With It	.30	.75
24 The Best-Selling Author	.30	.75
25 The People's Show	.30	.75
26 Check Right In	.30	.75
27 Stretch 'Em Out, Rock	.30	.75
28 Electrifying	.30	.75
29 Rough Landing	.30	.75
30 Goin' Down	.30	.75
31 Off With The Pad	.30	.75
32 Table For One	.30	.75
33 Rock Bottom	.30	.75
34 Over The Top	.30	.75
35 His Own Medicine	.30	.75
36 Not A Friendly Hug	.30	.75
37 Who's The Game	.30	.75
38 The End In Near	.30	.75
39 Say Cheese	.30	.75
40 Respect	.30	.75
41 Taker Takes One	.30	.75
42 Some Pain For Kane	.30	.75
43 Big Blow To The Big Show	.30	.75
44 One Giant Hit For Mankind	.30	.75
45 Crippling The Crippler	.30	.75
46 Take That, Boss	.30	.75
47 Shane Can Smell It	.30	.75
48 Double Trouble	.30	.75
49 Olympic Zero	.30	.75
50 Turn That Camera Sideways And	.30	.75
51 Raw Is Who	.30	.75
52 Rock vs. Brooklyn Brawler	.30	.75
53 Rock vs. Faarooq	.30	.75
54 Rock vs. Triple H	.30	.75
55 Rock vs. Ken Shamrock & Mankind	.30	.75
56 Rock vs. Mr. Ass	.30	.75
57 Rock vs. Steve Austin	.30	.75
58 Rock vs. Mankind	.30	.75
59 Rock vs. Mankind	.30	.75
60 Rock vs. Chris Benoit	.30	.75
61 Rock vs. Triple H	.30	.75
62 Rock vs. Vince McMahon	.30	.75
63 Rock vs. Triple H	.30	.75
64 Rock vs. Mankind	.30	.75
65 Rock 'N' Sock Wins First Title	.30	.75
66 Rock 'N' Sock Wins Third Title	.30	.75
67 CL Rock on runway	.30	.75
68 CL Rock in crowd	.30	.75
69 CL Rock w/Mick Foley	.30	.75
70 CL Rock w/Kane	.30	.75
71 CL Rock w/Steve Austin	.30	.75
72 CL Rock w/Stevie Richards	.30	.75

2000 Comic Images WWF Rock Solid Holofoil

COMPLETE SET (6)	8.00	20.00
STATED ODDS 1:18		
C1 Rock Bottom	2.50	6.00
C2 Lethal Style	2.50	6.00
C3 The People's Champ	2.50	6.00
C4 The People's Elbow	2.50	6.00
C5 Kickin' Back	2.50	6.00
C6 Lights, Camera, Rock	2.50	6.00

2000 Comic Images WWF Rock Solid Promos

P1 Rock w/Sunglasses	1.50	4.00
P2 Rock on Ropes	1.50	4.00
P3 Rock Lounging	1.50	4.00

1999 Comic Images WWF SmackDown

COMPLETE SET (72)	6.00	15.00
*CHROMIUM: .5X TO 1.2X BASIC CARDS		
1 Title Card	.10	.25
2 Stone Cold Steve Austin	.60	1.50
3 The Rock	.60	1.50
4 The Big Show	.15	.40
5 Mankind	.30	.75
6 The Undertaker	.40	.75
7 X-Pac	.15	.40
8 Triple H	.50	1.25
9 The Road Dogg	.15	.40
10 Mr. Ass	.15	.40
11 Al Snow	.15	.40
12 Big Boss Man	.15	.40
13 Kane	.20	.50
14 D'Lo Brown	.10	.25
15 Droz	.10	.25
16 Edge	.50	1.25
17 Gangrel RC	.10	.25
18 Christian RC	.15	.40

19 Godfather	.15	.40
20 Prince Albert RC	.10	.25
21 Mark Henry	.10	.40
22 Jeff Jarrett	.15	.40
23 Chyna	.50	1.25
24 Mideon RC	.10	.25
25 Hardcore Holly	.15	.40
26 Test RC	.10	.25
27 Val Venis	.10	.25
28 Viscera	.10	.25
29 Too Cool	.10	.25
30 The Hardy Boyz	.20	.50
31 Debra RC	.20	.50
32 Tori RC	.20	.50
33 P.M.S.	.20	.50
34 Ken Shamrock	.20	.50
35 Jerry The King Lawler	.15	.40
36 Meat RC	.10	.25
37 Steve Blackman	.10	.25
38 Paul Bearer	.15	.40
39 Ivory RC	.20	.50
40 Shane McMahon RC	.15	.40
41 Vince McMahon	.30	.75
42 Stone Cold Steve Austin	.60	1.50
43 The Undertaker	.40	1.00
44 The Big Show	.15	.40
45 The Rock	.60	1.50
46 Mankind	.30	.75
47 Triple H/Chyna	.50	1.25
48 X-Pac	.15	.40
49 Kane	.20	.50
50 Ken Shamrock	.20	.50
51 Mean Street Posse	.10	.25
52 Test RC	.10	.25
53 Steve Austin/Undertaker	.40	1.00
54 The Rock/Triple H	.40	1.00
55 S.McMahon/The Rock/V.McMahon	.40	1.00
56 The Undertaker/Kane	.30	.75
57 Vince McMahon	.20	.60
58 The Rock/Mick Foley	.40	1.00
59 The Big Show	.15	.40
60 Stone Cold Steve Austin/The Rock	.40	1.00
61 Vince McMahon	.20	.50
62 Mankind/Vince McMahon	.30	.75
63 The Big Show	.20	.50
64 X-Pac/Shane McMahon	.10	.25
65 Mr. Ass	.10	.25
66 Vince McMahon/Shane McMahon	.20	.50
67 Stone Cold Steve Austin	.30	.75
68 The Rock	.40	1.00
69 The Brood	.30	.75
70 X-Pac/Road Dogg	.15	.40
71 Jeff Jarrett/Debra	.15	.40
72 Checklist	.10	.25

1999 Comic Images WWF SmackDown Chromium

COMPLETE SET (90)	6.00	15.00
1 Title Card	.12	.30
2 Stone Cold Steve Austin	.75	2.00
3 The Rock	.75	2.00
4 The Big Show	.20	.50
5 Mankind	.30	.75
6 The Undertaker	.40	1.00
7 X-Pac	.20	.50
8 Triple H	.60	1.50
9 The Road Dogg	.20	.50
10 Mr. Ass	.12	.30
11 Al Snow	.20	.50
12 Big Boss Man	.20	.50
13 Kane	.25	.60
14 D'Lo Brown	.12	.30
15 Droz	.12	.30
16 Edge	.60	1.50
17 Gangrel RC	.12	.30
18 Christian RC	.20	.50
19 Godfather	.20	.50
20 Prince Albert RC	.12	.30
21 Mark Henry	.12	.30
22 Jeff Jarrett	.20	.50
23 Chyna	.25	.60
24 Mideon RC	.12	.30
25 Hardcore Holly	.20	.50
26 Test RC	.12	.30
27 Val Venis	.12	.30
28 Viscera	.12	.30
29 Shawn Michaels	.40	1.00
30 The Hardy Boyz	.30	.75
31 Debra RC	.30	.75
32 Tori RC	.30	.75
33 P.M.S.	.30	.75
34 Ken Shamrock	.12	.30
35 Jerry The King Lawler	.20	.50
36 Meat RC	.12	.30
37 Steve Blackman	.12	.30
38 Paul Bearer	.20	.50
39 Ivory RC	.30	.75
40 Shane McMahon RC	.20	.50
41 Vince McMahon	.40	1.00
42 Stone Cold Steve Austin	.75	2.00
43 The Undertaker	.40	1.00
44 The Big Show	.20	.50
45 The Rock	.75	2.00
46 Mankind	.30	.75
47 Triple H/Chyna	.60	1.50
48 X-Pac	.20	.50
49 Kane	.25	.60
50 Ken Shamrock	.12	.30
51 Mean Street Posse	.12	.30
52 Test RC	.12	.30
53 Steve Austin/Undertaker	.50	1.25
54 The Rock/Triple H	.50	1.25
55 S.McMahon/The Rock/V.McMahon	.50	1.25
56 The Undertaker/Kane	.40	1.00
57 Vince McMahon	.30	.75
58 The Rock/Mick Foley	.30	.75
59 The Big Show	.25	.60
60 Stone Cold Steve Austin/The Rock	.50	1.25
61 Vince McMahon	.30	.75
62 Mankind/Vince McMahon	.30	.75
63 The Big Show	.25	.60
64 X-Pac/Shane McMahon	.20	.50
65 Mr. Ass	.12	.30
66 Vince McMahon/Shane McMahon	.25	.60
67 Stone Cold Steve Austin	.50	1.25
68 The Rock	.50	1.25
69 The Brood	.30	.75
70 X-Pac/Road Dogg	.20	.50
71 Jeff Jarrett/Debra	.20	.50
72 The Undertaker/Big Boss Man	.25	.60
73 Four-Way Match	.20	.50
74 Triple Threat Match	.20	.50
75 Shane McMahon/X-Pac	.20	.50
76 Triple H/Kane	.50	1.25
77 Stone Cold Steve Austin	.75	2.00
78 Mr. Ass	.20	.50
79 Road Dogg/Chyna	.20	.50
80 Road Dogg/X-Pac	.20	.50
81 Shane/Vince McMahon	.30	.75
82 Kane/The Big Show	.30	.75
83 X-Pac/Hardcore Holly	.20	.50
84 Triple H/The Rock	.60	1.50
85 Undertaker/Steve Austin	.60	1.50
86 Jeff Jarrett/Edge	.50	1.25
87 D'Lo Brown/Mideon	.12	.30
88 Big Boss Man/Al Snow	.20	.50
89 Acolytes/Hardy Boyz	.30	.75
90 Checklist	.12	.30

1999 Comic Images WWF SmackDown 22KT Gold Signatures

COMPLETE SET (6)	50.00	100.00
STATED ODDS 1:80		
1 Stone Cold Steve Austin	12.00	30.00
2 The Undertaker	10.00	25.00
3 The Rock	20.00	50.00
4 Triple H	12.00	30.00
5 The Big Show	12.00	30.00
6 Mankind	8.00	20.00
SE Stone Cold Steve Austin Special Edition		

1999 Comic Images WWF SmackDown Autographs

STATED ODDS 1:80		
NNO Al Snow	6.00	15.00
NNO Big Boss Man	15.00	40.00
NNO D'Lo Brown	6.00	15.00
NNO Godfather	6.00	15.00
NNO The Hardy Boyz	15.00	40.00
NNO Hardcore Holly	6.00	15.00
NNO Ivory	12.00	30.00
NNO Tori	6.00	15.00

1999 Comic Images WWF SmackDown Chrome Inserts

COMPLETE SET (6)	5.00	12.00
STATED ODDS 1:18		
C1 Stone Cold Steve Austin	1.50	4.00
C2 The Corporate Ministry	1.00	2.50
C3 X-Pac/Kane	.60	1.50
C4 The Brood	1.00	2.50
C5 Mankind	1.00	2.50
C6 The Rock	1.50	4.00

1999 Comic Images WWF SmackDown Promos

P1 Stone Cold Steve Austin NSU	1.50	4.00
P2 The Rock	2.00	5.00
P3 Mankind	1.00	2.50

1999-05 Danbury Mint WWF/WWE 22kt Gold

COMPLETE SET (124)	250.00	500.00
1 Andre The Giant	3.00	8.00
2 Ken Shamrock	2.00	5.00
3 Stone Cold Steve Austin	4.00	10.00
3 Bob Backlund	2.00	5.00
4 The Rock	4.00	10.00
5 B.A. Billy Gunn	1.50	4.00
6 Road Dogg	1.50	4.00
7 Gorilla Monsoon	1.50	4.00
8 Val Venis	1.00	2.50
9 Al Snow	1.25	3.00
10 Kane	2.00	5.00
11 Jesse The Body Ventura	2.50	6.00
12 Undertaker	5.00	12.00
13 Shawn Michaels	6.00	15.00
14 Jerry The King Lawler	4.00	10.00
15 Lita	3.00	8.00
16 Fabulous Moolah	2.50	6.00
17 Rikishi Fatu	1.25	3.00
18 Big Boss Man	1.00	2.50
19 Jim Ross	4.00	10.00
20 The Iron Sheik	1.25	3.00
21 Hardy Boyz	3.00	8.00
22 Trish Stratus	6.00	15.00
23 Chris Jericho	4.00	10.00
24 Sgt. Slaughter	1.50	4.00
25 Triple H	2.50	6.00
26 Stephanie McMahon-Helmsley	2.00	5.00
27 Chris Benoit	8.00	20.00
28 Captain Lou Albano	2.50	6.00
29 George The Animal Steele	2.00	5.00
30 X-Pac	1.25	3.00
31 Vince McMahon	2.00	5.00
32 Shane O Mac	2.50	6.00
33 Stone Cold Steve Austin	3.00	8.00
33 Bob Backlund	2.00	5.00
34 Chyna	3.00	8.00
35 Dudley Boyz	2.50	6.00
36 British Bulldog	2.50	6.00
37 Jimmy Superfly Snuka	1.50	4.00
38 Mankind	4.00	10.00
39 Tazz	2.00	5.00
40 Big Show	1.50	4.00
41 Kurt Angle	2.50	6.00
42 Eddie Guerrero	4.00	10.00
43 Debra	2.00	5.00
44 Mr. Fuji	1.25	3.00
45 The Godfather	2.50	6.00
46 Edge/Christian	2.50	6.00
47 Too Cool	1.25	3.00
48 Test	1.25	3.00
49 The Acolytes	1.50	4.00
50 Steve Blackman	2.50	6.00
51 William Regal	2.00	5.00
52 Ric Flair	5.00	12.00
53 Tajiri	2.00	5.00
54 Rhyno	1.25	3.00
55 Stacy Keibler	6.00	15.00
56 K-Kwik	1.25	3.00
57 Crash Holly	1.25	3.00
58 Molly Holly	1.50	4.00
59 Albert	1.50	4.00
60 Perry Saturn	2.00	5.00
61 Booker T	2.50	6.00
62 Kaientai	1.25	3.00
63 Jacqueline	1.25	3.00
64 Steven Richards	1.25	3.00
65 Raven	1.50	4.00
66 Rob Van Dam	2.00	5.00
67 Earl Hebner	2.50	6.00
68 Spike Dudley	1.25	3.00
69 Hardcore Holly	3.00	8.00
70 Linda McMahon	1.50	4.00
71 Hollywood Hulk Hogan	12.00	30.00
72 Nidia	2.50	6.00
73 Garrison Cade	4.00	10.00
74 Luther Reigns	4.00	10.00
75 Eric Bischoff	3.00	8.00
76 Gail Kim	8.00	20.00
77 Matt Hardy	2.50	6.00
78 Scott Steiner	8.00	20.00
79 Tyson Tomko	6.00	15.00
80 Miss Jackie	3.00	8.00
81 Ivory	4.00	10.00
82 Billy/Chuck	2.00	5.00
83 Chavo Guerrero	3.00	8.00
84 Jamie Noble	2.00	5.00
85 Mark Henry	3.00	8.00
86 Tommy Dreamer	2.50	6.00
87 Diamond Dallas Page	2.00	5.00
88 Mark Jindrak	2.50	6.00
89 Victoria	2.50	6.00
90 Kevin Nash	3.00	8.00
91 Eugene	3.00	8.00
92 John Cena	6.00	15.00
93 Rey Mysterio	4.00	10.00
94 Muhammad Hassan	5.00	12.00
95 The Hurricane	2.00	5.00
96 Matt Morgan	2.50	6.00
97 Sable	5.00	12.00
98 Rene/Kenzo	2.50	6.00
99 Billy Kidman	2.00	5.00
100 Goldust	2.00	5.00
101 Theodore Long	2.50	6.00
102 JBL	6.00	15.00
103 Lance Storm	2.00	5.00
104 Zach Gowen	3.00	8.00
105 FBI	1.25	3.00
106 Edge	6.00	15.00
107 Randy Orton	2.50	6.00
108 Maven	1.50	4.00
109 La Resistance	2.00	5.00
110 Chavo Guerrero	3.00	8.00
111 Basham Brothers	2.50	6.00
112 Bubba Ray Dudley	2.50	6.00
113 The Coach	4.00	10.00
114 Heidenreich	5.00	12.00
115 Benjamin/Haas	2.50	6.00
116 Jazz	2.50	6.00
117 Batista	2.50	6.00
118 Goldberg	6.00	15.00
119 Torrie Wilson	4.00	10.00
120 Brock Lesnar	3.00	8.00
B1 Mankind Bonus	15.00	40.00
B2 Cactus Jack Bonus	15.00	40.00

1991 Diamond WWF SuperStars Stickers

COMPLETE SET (150)	12.00	30.00
1 Hulk Hogan	.60	1.50
2 Hulk Hogan (Puzzle)	.60	1.50
3 Hulk Hogan (Puzzle)	.60	1.50
4 Hulk Hogan (Puzzle)	.60	1.50
5 Hulk Hogan (Puzzle)	.60	1.50
6 Nasty Boys	.12	.30
7 Nasty Boys	.12	.30
8 Earthquake	.12	.30
9 Earthquake	.12	.30
10 Earthquake	.12	.30
11 Jimmy Hart	.20	.50
12 Dino Bravo	.12	.30
13 Dino Bravo (Puzzle)	.12	.30
14 Dino Bravo (Puzzle)	.12	.30

15 British Bulldog (Puzzle) .15 .40
16 British Bulldog (Puzzle) .15 .40
17 British Bulldog (Puzzle) .15 .40
18 British Bulldog (Puzzle) .15 .40
19 British Bulldog .15 .40
20 British Bulldog .15 .40
21 Bobby The Brain Heenan .15 .40
22 Mr. Perfect .20 .50
23 Mr. Perfect (Puzzle) .20 .50
24 Mr. Perfect (Puzzle) .20 .50
25 Texas Tornado .15 .40
26 Texas Tornado (Puzzle) .15 .40
27 Texas Tornado (Puzzle) .15 .40
28 Tugboat .12 .30
29 Tugboat (Puzzle) .12 .30
30 Tugboat (Puzzle) .12 .30
31 Hacksaw Jim Duggan (Puzzle) .15 .40
32 Hacksaw Jim Duggan (Puzzle) .15 .40
33 Hacksaw Jim Duggan (Puzzle) .15 .40
34 Hacksaw Jim Duggan (Puzzle) .15 .40
35 Hacksaw Jim Duggan .15 .40
36 Big Boss Man (Puzzle) .12 .30
37 Big Boss Man (Puzzle) .12 .30
38 Big Boss Man .12 .30
39 Big Boss Man .12 .30
40 Power & Glory (Puzzle) .12 .30
41 Power & Glory (Puzzle) .12 .30
42 Power & Glory (Puzzle) .12 .30
43 Power & Glory (Puzzle) .12 .30
44 Hercules .12 .30
45 Paul Roma .12 .30
46 Slick .12 .30
47 Ultimate Warrior (Puzzle) .40 1.00
48 Ultimate Warrior (Puzzle) .40 1.00
49 Ultimate Warrior (Puzzle) .40 1.00
50 Ultimate Warrior (Puzzle) .40 1.00
51 Ultimate Warrior (Puzzle) .40 1.00
52 Ultimate Warrior (Puzzle) .40 1.00
53 Ultimate Warrior .40 1.00
54 Ultimate Warrior (Puzzle) .40 1.00
55 Ultimate Warrior (Puzzle) .40 1.00
56 Ultimate Warrior (Puzzle) .40 1.00
57 Ultimate Warrior (Puzzle) .40 1.00
58 Rockers (Puzzle) .20 .50
59 Rockers (Puzzle) .20 .50
60 Rockers (Puzzle) .20 .50
61 Rockers (Puzzle) .20 .50
62 Marty Jannetty .12 .30
63 Shawn Michaels .20 .50
64 Rockers .20 .50
65 Rockers .20 .50
66 The Model Rick Martel (Puzzle) .12 .30
67 The Model Rick Martel (Puzzle) .12 .30
68 The Model Rick Martel (Puzzle) .12 .30
69 The Model Rick Martel (Puzzle) .12 .30
70 The Model Rick Martel .12 .30
71 The Model Rick Martel .12 .30
72 The Model Rick Martel .12 .30
73 Hulk Hogan .60 1.50
74 Hulk Hogan (Puzzle) .60 1.50
75 Hulk Hogan (Puzzle) .60 1.50
76 Hulk Hogan (Puzzle) .60 1.50
77 Hulk Hogan (Puzzle) .60 1.50
78 Hulk Hogan .60 1.50
79 Hulk Hogan .60 1.50
80 Hulk Hogan (Puzzle) .60 1.50
81 Hulk Hogan (Puzzle) .60 1.50
82 Hulk Hogan (Puzzle) .60 1.50
83 Hulk Hogan (Puzzle) .60 1.50
84 Warlord .12 .30
85 Warlord .12 .30
86 Barbarian .12 .30
87 Barbarian .12 .30
88 Orient Express .12 .30
89 Orient Express .12 .30
90 Mr. Fuji .12 .30
91 Superfly Jimmy Snuka (Puzzle) .20 .50
92 Superfly Jimmy Snuka (Puzzle) .20 .50
93 Superfly Jimmy Snuka .20 .50
94 Superfly Jimmy Snuka .20 .50
95 Bushwackers (Puzzle) .12 .30
96 Bushwackers (Puzzle) .12 .30
97 Bushwackers (Puzzle) .12 .30
98 Bushwackers (Puzzle) .12 .30
99 Bushwackers .12 .30
100 Macho Man .40 1.00
101 Macho Man (Puzzle) .40 1.00
102 Macho Man (Puzzle) .40 1.00
103 Macho Man & Queen Sherri .40 1.00
104 Sensational Queen Sherri .15 .40
105 Sensational Queen Sherri .15 .40
106 Million Dollar Man (Puzzle) .15 .40
107 Million Dollar Man (Puzzle) .15 .40
108 Million Dollar Man (Puzzle) .15 .40
109 Million Dollar Man (Puzzle) .15 .40
110 Ted DiBiase .15 .40
111 Ted DiBiase .15 .40
112 Rowdy Roddy Piper (Puzzle) .50 1.25
113 Rowdy Roddy Piper (Puzzle) .50 1.25
114 Rowdy Roddy Piper .50 1.25
115 Legion of Doom .20 .50
116 Animal .20 .50
117 Legion of Doom .20 .50
118 Legion of Doom .20 .50
119 Legion of Doom (Puzzle) .20 .50
120 Legion of Doom (Puzzle) .20 .50
121 Legion of Doom (Puzzle) .20 .50
122 Legion of Doom (Puzzle) .20 .50
123 Haku (Puzzle) .12 .30
124 Haku (Puzzle) .12 .30
125 Haku .12 .30
126 Virgil (Puzzle) .12 .30
127 Virgil (Puzzle) .12 .30
128 Sgt. Slaughter (Puzzle) .20 .50
129 Sgt. Slaughter (Puzzle) .20 .50
130 Sgt. Slaughter (Puzzle) .20 .50
131 Sgt. Slaughter (Puzzle) .20 .50
132 Sgt. Slaughter .20 .50
133 Sgt. Slaughter (Puzzle) .20 .50
134 Sgt. Slaughter (Puzzle) .20 .50
135 Jake The Snake Roberts (Puzzle) .25 .60
136 Jake The Snake Roberts (Puzzle) .25 .60
137 Jake The Snake Roberts .25 .60
138 Jake The Snake Roberts (Puzzle) .25 .60
139 Jake The Snake Roberts (Puzzle) .25 .60
140 Jake The Snake Roberts (Puzzle) .25 .60
141 Jake The Snake Roberts (Puzzle) .25 .60
142 Koko B. Ware .12 .30
143 Koko B. Ware .12 .30
144 The Undertaker (Puzzle) .50 1.25
145 The Undertaker (Puzzle) .50 1.25
146 Undertaker/Paul Bearer (Puzzle) .50 1.25
147 Undertaker/Paul Bearer (Puzzle) .50 1.25
148 Undertaker/Paul Bearer (Puzzle) .50 1.25
149 Undertaker/Paul Bearer (Puzzle) .50 1.25
150 Paul Bearer .15 .40

1992 Disney's Limit Comic Stars of the WWF Magazine German

COMPLETE SET (8)
NNO The Big Boss Man
NNO Bret The Hit Man Hart
NNO The British Bulldog
NNO The Mountie
NNO Papa Shango
NNO Randy Macho Man Savage
NNO The Ultimate Warrior
NNO The Undertaker

2023 Donruss Elite WWE

*GREEN: X TO X BASIC CARDS
*PINK: X TO X BASIC CARDS
*RAZZLE DAZZLE: X TO X BASIC CARDS
*RED: X TO X BASIC CARDS
*STATUS EXPLOSION/275: X TO X BASIC CARDS
*BLUE/149: X TO X BASIC CARDS
*PURPLE/99: X TO X BASIC CARDS
*STATUS/80: X TO X BASIC CARDS
*ASPIRATIONS SWIRL/75: X TO X BASIC CARDS
*ASPIRATIONS/53: X TO X BASIC CARDS
*ORANGE/49: X TO X BASIC CARDS
*TEAL/25: UNPRICED DUE TO SCARCITY
*ASPIRATIONS DIE-CUTS/24: UNPRICED DUE TO SCARCITY
*STATUS DIE-CUTS/24: UNPRICED DUE TO SCARCITY
*GOLD/10: UNPRICED DUE TO SCARCITY
*BLACK/1: UNPRICED DUE TO SCARCITY
PRODUCT NEWLY RELEASED AT PRESS TIME

1 Tony D'Angelo
2 Liv Morgan
3 Quincy Elliott
4 Andre Chase
5 Dolph Ziggler
6 Alexa Bliss
7 Joe Gacy
8 Sami Zayn
9 Piper Niven
10 Damian Priest
11 Tyler Bate
12 Matt Riddle
13 Tatum Paxley
14 Ava
15 Dragon Lee
16 Becky Lynch
17 Karrion Kross
18 AJ Styles
19 Ricochet
20 Dominik Mysterio
21 Wes Lee
22 Nathan Frazer
23 Top Dolla
24 Braun Strowman
25 Elektra Lopez
26 Bianca Belair
27 Kofi Kingston
28 Asuka
29 Riddick Moss
30 Drew McIntyre
31 Xavier Woods
32 Paul Heyman
33 B-Fab
34 Bronson Reed
35 Elias
36 Brock Lesnar
37 LA Knight
38 Bobby Lashley
39 Sheamus
40 Edge
41 Zelina Vega
42 Raquel Rodriguez
43 Alba Fyre
44 Candice LeRae
45 Gigi Dolin
46 Charlotte Flair
47 Montez Ford
48 Bayley
49 Shinsuke Nakamura
50 Finn Balor
51 Arianna Grace
52 Rey Mysterio
53 Butch
54 Carmella
55 Grayson Waller
56 Cody Rhodes
57 Natalya
58 Austin Theory
59 Shotzi
60 Gunther
61 Stacks Lorenzo
62 Roxanne Perez
63 Johnny Gargano
64 Chad Gable
65 Ilja Dragunov
66 Randy Orton
67 Nikki Cross
68 Bray Wyatt
69 Sol Ruca
70 IYO SKY
71 Hank Walker
72 Scarlett
73 Santos Escobar
74 Chelsea Green
75 Jacy Jayne
76 Rhea Ripley
77 Nikkita Lyons
78 Bron Breakker
79 Sonya Deville
80 Jey Uso
81 Kiana James
82 Seth Freakin Rollins
83 Rick Boogs
84 Dakota Kai
85 Ivy Nile
86 Roman Reigns
87 Omos
88 Carmelo Hayes
89 The Miz
90 Jimmy Uso
91 Maxxine Dupri
92 Solo Sikoa
93 Xia Li
94 Dijak
95 JD McDonagh
96 Lola Vice
97 Otis
98 Cora Jade
99 Tiffany Stratton
100 Kevin Owens
101 Mankind
102 Rowdy Roddy Piper
103 Stacy Keibler
104 Undertaker
105 Stone Cold Steve Austin
106 Iron Sheik
107 Diesel
108 Tito Santana
109 Kane
110 Dusty Rhodes
111 Ricky Steamboat
112 Sherri Martel
113 The Godfather
114 1-2-3 Kid
115 Batista
116 Miss Elizabeth
117 Eric Bischoff
118 William Regal
119 Ken Shamrock
120 Eddie Guerrero
121 Rob Van Dam
122 Ultimate Warrior
123 Torrie Wilson
124 Million Dollar Man
125 Booker T
126 Rikishi
127 Hulk Hogan
128 Andre the Giant
129 Kurt Angle
130 Mr. Perfect
131 Scott Steiner
132 Red Rooster
133 Triple H
134 Bob Backlund
135 Bret Hart
136 Road Dogg
137 Jerry Lawler
138 British Bulldog
139 Lex Luger
140 Razor Ramon
141 Shawn Michaels
142 The Rock
143 Trish Stratus
144 Bubba Ray Dudley
145 Diamond Dallas Page
146 The Honky Tonk Man
147 John Cena
148 Bruno Sammartino
149 Lita
150 Rick Rude

2023 Donruss Elite WWE Elite Deck

*GREEN: X TO X BASIC CARDS
*RED/99: X TO X BASIC CARDS
*ORANGE/49: X TO X BASIC CARDS
*TEAL/25: UNPRICED DUE TO SCARCITY
*GOLD/10: UNPRICED DUE TO SCARCITY
*BLACK/1: UNPRICED DUE TO SCARCITY
RANDOMLY INSERTED INTO PACKS

1 Roman Reigns
2 Edge
3 John Cena
4 Bianca Belair
5 Steve Austin
6 Trish Stratus
7 Hulk Hogan
8 Bron Breakker
9 Randy Orton
10 Triple H

11 Brock Lesnar
12 Becky Lynch
13 The Rock
14 Charlotte Flair
15 Undertaker

2023 Donruss Elite WWE Elite Impressions

*GOLD/10: UNPRICED DUE TO SCARCITY
*BLACK/1: UNPRICED DUE TO SCARCITY
RANDOMLY INSERTED INTO PACKS

1 Oro Mensah
2 Edris Enofe
3 Booker T
4 Wendy Choo
5 Jim Duggan
6 Rick Boogs
7 Axiom
9 Rip Fowler
10 Mace
11 Wolfgang
12 Elektra Lopez
14 Yulisa Leon
15 Rob Van Dam
16 Ridge Holland
17 Boa
19 Steve Austin
20 Shelton Benjamin
21 Dijak
22 Fallon Henley
23 Kane
24 Angelo Dawkins
25 Sika
27 Brutus Creed
28 Angel
29 Von Wagner
31 Batista
32 Ilja Dragunov
33 Bret Hart
34 Chad Gable
35 Afa
36 R-Truth
38 Cedric Alexander
39 Wes Lee
41 Hulk Hogan
42 Josh Briggs
43 Don Muraco
44 Dana Brooke
45 Simon Dean
48 Cruz Del Toro
49 Blair Davenport
50 Amari Miller
51 Ivan Putski
52 Malik Blade
53 Bob Orton
54 Erik
55 Jerry Lawler
56 Emma
57 Ivy Nile
58 Dexter Lumis
59 Charlie Dempsey
60 Andre Chase
61 Torrie Wilson
62 Mr. Stone
63 Alundra Blayze
64 Ivar
65 The Boogeyman
66 Joaquin Wilde
67 Jagger Reid
68 Giovanni Vinci
70 Brooks Jensen
71 Paul Heyman
72 Nathan Frazer
73 Gerald Brisco
74 Mustafa Ali
75 Alba Fyre
76 Valhalla
77 Julius Creed
78 Humberto
79 Joe Coffey
80 Damon Kemp
81 Kevin Nash
82 Trick Williams
83 Michael Hayes
84 MVP
85 Bron Breakker
86 The Honky Tonk Man
87 Kayden Carter
88 LA Knight
89 Lyra Valkyria
90 Dante Chen
91 Diamond Dallas Page
92 Valentina Feroz
94 Nikki Cross
95 Cora Jade
96 Scrypts
98 Ludwig Kaiser
99 Mark Coffey
100 Duke Hudson

2023 Donruss Elite WWE Elite Signatures

*GREEN: X TO X BASIC CARDS
*RED/49: X TO X BASIC CARDS
*BLUE/25: UNPRICED DUE TO SCARCITY
*GOLD/10: UNPRICED DUE TO SCARCITY
*BLACK/1: UNPRICED DUE TO SCARCITY
RANDOMLY INSERTED INTO PACKS

1 Grayson Waller
2 John Cena
3 Steve Austin
5 Baron Corbin
6 Rey Mysterio
8 Shinsuke Nakamura
9 Damian Priest
11 Gunther
12 Karl Anderson
13 Cody Rhodes
14 Liv Morgan
15 Batista
16 Rhea Ripley
17 Bret Hart
18 Shotzi
19 Dolph Ziggler
20 Trish Stratus
21 Hulk Hogan
22 Karrion Kross
23 Alba Fyre
24 Luke Gallows
25 Bayley
26 Sami Zayn
28 Solo Sikoa
29 Dominik Mysterio
30 Undertaker
31 Jimmy Uso
32 Katana Chance
33 Alexa Bliss
35 Bianca Belair
36 Shawn Michaels
37 Carmella
38 The Miz
39 Drew McIntyre
40 Xavier Woods
41 Joe Gacy
42 Kofi Kingston
43 Austin Theory
44 Natalya
45 Big E
46 Shayna Baszler
47 Carmelo Hayes
48 Tiffany Stratton
50 Zelina Vega

2023 Donruss Elite WWE Family Lineage

*GREEN: X TO X BASIC CARDS
*RED/99: X TO X BASIC CARDS
*ORANGE/49: X TO X BASIC CARDS
*TEAL/25: UNPRICED DUE TO SCARCITY
*GOLD/10: UNPRICED DUE TO SCARCITY
*BLACK/1: UNPRICED DUE TO SCARCITY
RANDOMLY INSERTED INTO PACKS

1 Rikishi/Jimmy Uso
2 Natalya/Jim Neidhart
3 Sika/Roman Reigns
4 Randy Orton/Bob Orton
5 Rikishi/Solo Sikoa
6 Bron Breakker/Rick Steiner
7 Dominik Mysterio/Rey Mysterio
8 Charlie Dempsey/William Regal
9 The Rock/Rocky Johnson
10 Dusty Rhodes/Cody Rhodes

2023 Donruss Elite WWE Full Throttle

COMPLETE SET (15)
*GREEN: X TO X BASIC CARDS
*RED/99: X TO X BASIC CARDS
*ORANGE/49: X TO X BASIC CARDS
*TEAL/25: UNPRICED DUE TO SCARCITY
*GOLD/10: UNPRICED DUE TO SCARCITY
*BLACK/1: UNPRICED DUE TO SCARCITY
RANDOMLY INSERTED INTO PACKS

1 Kofi Kingston
2 Carmelo Hayes
3 Shawn Michaels
4 X-Pac
5 Seth Freakin Rollins
6 Matt Riddle
7 Jey Uso
8 Dolph Ziggler
9 Jimmy Uso
10 Montez Ford
11 AJ Styles
12 Austin Theory
13 Xavier Woods
14 Finn Balor
15 Rob Van Dam

2023 Donruss Elite WWE New Breed Autographs

*GREEN: X TO X BASIC CARDS
*RED/49: X TO X BASIC CARDS
*BLUE/25: UNPRICED DUE TO SCARCITY
*GOLD/10: UNPRICED DUE TO SCARCITY
*BLACK/1: UNPRICED DUE TO SCARCITY
RANDOMLY INSERTED INTO PACKS

1 JD McDonagh
3 Sol Ruca
5 Arianna Grace
6 Blair Davenport
7 Tatum Paxley
8 Dijak
9 Bron Breakker
10 Noam Dar
11 Joe Gacy
12 Ivy Nile
13 Tyler Bate
14 Rip Fowler
15 Stacks Lorenzo
16 Charlie Dempsey
17 Thea Hail
18 Gigi Dolin
19 Alba Fyre
20 Scrypts
21 Katana Chance
22 Jagger Reid
23 Zoey Stark
24 Von Wagner
25 Kiana James
26 Fallon Henley
27 Tiffany Stratton
28 Jacy Jayne
29 Carmelo Hayes
30 Axiom
31 Quincy Elliott
32 Julius Creed
33 Cameron Grimes
34 Wes Lee
35 Nikkita Lyons
36 Nathan Frazer
37 Tony D'Angelo
38 Ava
39 Grayson Waller
40 Brutus Creed

2023 Donruss Elite WWE Passing the Torch Signatures

*GOLD/10: UNPRICED DUE TO SCARCITY
*BLACK/1: UNPRICED DUE TO SCARCITY
RANDOMLY INSERTED INTO PACKS

1 S.Michaels/S.Austin
2 HHH/S.Rollins
3 JBL/B.Corbin
4 R.Reigns/J.Cena
5 B.Corbin/K.Angle
6 J.Cena/K.Angle
7 R.Reigns/Undertaker
8 D.Muraco/Cactus Jack
9 R.Mysterio/D.Mysterio
10 R.Steiner/B.Breakker

2023 Donruss Elite WWE Pen Pals

*GREEN: X TO X BASIC CARDS
*RED/49: X TO X BASIC CARDS
*BLUE/25: UNPRICED DUE TO SCARCITY
*GOLD/10: UNPRICED DUE TO SCARCITY
*BLACK/1: UNPRICED DUE TO SCARCITY
RANDOMLY INSERTED INTO PACKS

1 Charlotte Flair
3 Jey Uso
4 Cora Jade
5 Asuka
6 Quincy Elliott
7 Montez Ford
8 Dakota Kai
9 Roman Reigns
10 Scarlett
11 Finn Balor
12 Michin
13 Sheamus
14 Gigi Dolin
15 Kevin Owens
16 Roxanne Perez
17 B-Fab
18 IYO SKY
20 Raquel Rodriguez
21 Seth Freakin Rollins
22 Santos Escobar
23 Braun Strowman
24 Ava
25 Apollo Crews
26 Thea Hail
27 Butch
28 Johnny Gargano
30 Sonya Deville
31 Bobby Lashley
32 Bron Breakker
33 AJ Styles
34 Nikkita Lyons
35 Gable Steveson
36 Jacy Jayne
37 Candice LeRae
38 Maxxine Dupri
39 Becky Lynch
40 Top Dolla

2023 Donruss Elite WWE Powerhouses

*GREEN: X TO X BASIC CARDS
*RED/99: X TO X BASIC CARDS
*ORANGE/49: X TO X BASIC CARDS
*TEAL/25: UNPRICED DUE TO SCARCITY
*GOLD/10: UNPRICED DUE TO SCARCITY
*BLACK/1: UNPRICED DUE TO SCARCITY
RANDOMLY INSERTED INTO PACKS

1 Andre the Giant
2 Bianca Belair
3 Chyna
4 Braun Strowman
5 John Cena

2023 Donruss Elite WWE Spellbound

*GREEN: X TO X BASIC CARDS
*RED/99: X TO X BASIC CARDS
*ORANGE/49: X TO X BASIC CARDS
*TEAL/25: UNPRICED DUE TO SCARCITY
*GOLD/10: UNPRICED DUE TO SCARCITY
*BLACK/1: UNPRICED DUE TO SCARCITY
RANDOMLY INSERTED INTO PACKS

1 Roman Reigns
2 Roman Reigns
3 Roman Reigns
4 Roman Reigns
5 Roman Reigns

6 Brock Lesnar
7 Brock Lesnar
8 Brock Lesnar
9 Brock Lesnar
10 Brock Lesnar
11 John Cena
12 John Cena
13 John Cena
14 John Cena
15 Steve Austin
16 Steve Austin
17 Steve Austin
18 Steve Austin
19 Steve Austin
20 Steve Austin
21 Steve Austin
22 Steve Austin
23 Steve Austin
24 Lita
25 Lita
26 Lita
27 Lita
28 Rey Mysterio
29 Rey Mysterio
30 Rey Mysterio

2023 Donruss Elite WWE Star Status

*GREEN: X TO X BASIC CARDS
*RED/99: X TO X BASIC CARDS
*ORANGE/49: X TO X BASIC CARDS
*TEAL/25: UNPRICED DUE TO SCARCITY
*GOLD/10: UNPRICED DUE TO SCARCITY
*BLACK/1: UNPRICED DUE TO SCARCITY
RANDOMLY INSERTED INTO PACKS

1 Undertaker
2 Steve Austin
3 Lita
4 Hulk Hogan
5 Bray Wyatt
6 Randy Orton
7 Brock Lesnar
8 Roman Reigns
9 The Rock
10 John Cena
11 Bayley
12 Trish Stratus
13 Bobby Lashley
14 Sami Zayn
15 Cody Rhodes
16 Triple H
17 Becky Lynch
18 Edge
19 Charlotte Flair
20 Bianca Belair

2023 Donruss Elite WWE Title Waves

*GREEN: X TO X BASIC CARDS
*RED/99: X TO X BASIC CARDS
*ORANGE/49: X TO X BASIC CARDS
*TEAL/25: UNPRICED DUE TO SCARCITY
*GOLD/10: UNPRICED DUE TO SCARCITY
*BLACK/1: UNPRICED DUE TO SCARCITY
RANDOMLY INSERTED INTO PACKSc

1 John Cena
2 Charlotte Flair
3 Triple H
4 Becky Lynch
5 Randy Orton

2023 Donruss Elite WWE Turn of the Century Signatures

*RED/49: X TO X BASIC CARDS
*BLUE/25: UNPRICED DUE TO SCARCITY
*GOLD/10: UNPRICED DUE TO SCARCITY
*BLACK/1: UNPRICED DUE TO SCARCITY
RANDOMLY INSERTED INTO PACKS

1 Road Dogg
2 Diamond Dallas Page
4 JBL
5 Kurt Angle
7 Jim Duggan
8 Michael Hayes
9 Beth Phoenix
10 Rob Van Dam
11 Don Muraco
12 Tatanka
13 Madusa
14 Bradshaw
15 Million Dollar Man
16 Dok Hendrix
17 Terry Taylor
18 Papa Shango
19 Faarooq
20 Jerry Lawler
21 Kane
22 The Shockmaster
23 Bad News Barrett
24 Booker T
25 Greg Valentine
26 The Godfather
27 D-Lo Brown
28 Wade Barrett
29 Ivan Putski
30 1-2-3 Kid
31 Torrie Wilson
32 Jimmy Hart
33 Johnny Rodz
34 Wendi Richter
35 Scotty 2 Hotty
36 Brutus Beefcake
37 Stevie Ray
38 Hulk Hogan
39 Tyson Kidd
40 Eric Bischoff
41 The Honky Tonk Man
43 X-Pac
44 Jason Jordan
45 Rikishi
46 Eve Torres
47 Fit Finlay
48 Scott Steiner
49 Red Rooster
50 Rick Steiner
51 Mighty Molly
52 Bob Orton
53 Jimmy Garvin
54 Lex Luger
55 Albert
56 Undertaker
57 Tyler Breeze
58 The Boogeyman
59 Norman Smiley
60 Mike Rotunda

2002 Doritos WWF Super Stars

COMPLETE SET (12)	5.00	12.00
1 The Rock	.75	2.00
2 Stone Cold Steve Austin	.75	2.00
3 Kurt Angle	.50	1.25
4 Booker T	.25	.60
5 Triple H	.75	2.00
6 Edge	.50	1.25
7 Rob Van Dam	.25	.60
8 Chris Jericho	.40	1.00
9 Undertaker	.50	1.25
10 Jeff Hardy	.40	1.00
11 Lita	.75	2.00
12 Trish Stratus	1.25	3.00

1998 DuoCards WWF

COMPLETE SET (72)	40.00	100.00
1 WWF Attitude	.10	.25
2 Mr. Vince McMahon RC	1.25	3.00
3 Commissioner Slaughter	.20	.50
4 Mr. Pat Patterson RC	.10	.25
5 Mr. Gerald Brisco RC	.15	.40
6 WWF Champion	.60	1.50
7 WWF Tag Team Champions	.20	.50
8 WWF IC Champ/The Rock	8.00	20.00
9 WWF European Champion	.10	.25
10 WWF Light Heavyweight Champion	.10	.25
11 Stone Cold Steve Austin	3.00	8.00
12 Undertaker	3.00	8.00
13 Shawn Michaels	2.50	6.00
14 Ken Shamrock	2.00	5.00
15 The Rock RC	6.00	15.00
16 Triple H RC	2.50	6.00
17 Kane RC	5.00	12.00
18 Owen Hart	.30	1.00
19 Mankind RC	.30	.75
20 Dude Love RC	.30	.75
21 Cactus Jack RC	1.50	4.00
22 Sable RC	.30	.75
23 X-Pac	.20	.50
24 D'Lo Brown RC	.10	.25
25 Mark Henry RC	.10	.25
26 Bradshaw RC	.50	1.25
27 The Godfather	.10	.25
28 Double J	.10	.25
29 Dustin Runnels	.10	.25
30 Marvelous Marc Mero	.10	.25
31 Steve Blackman RC	.40	1.00
32 Al Snow and Head RC	.15	.40
33 Taka Michinoku RC	.10	.25
34 Badd Ass Billy Gunn RC	.20	.50
35 Savio Vega	.10	.25
36 Dr. Death Steve Williams	.10	.25
37 Steven Regal	.15	.40
38 Faarooq	.15	.40
39 Scorpio RC	.10	.25
40 Kurrgan RC	.10	.25
41 Luna	.10	.25
42 Dan The Beast Severn	.15	.40
43 Golga	.10	.25
44 Giant Silva RC	.10	.25
45 Road Dog Jesse James RC	.20	.50
46 Edge RWT RC	2.00	5.00
47 Darren Droz Drozdov RWT RC	.10	.25
48 Val Venis RWT RC	.15	.40
49 Papi Chulo RWT RC	.10	.25
50 Tiger Ali Singh RWT RC	.15	.40
51 D-Generation X FW	.20	.50
52 The Nation FW	.20	.60
53 Kaientai FW	.10	.25
54 Kane w/Mankind DD	1.50	4.00
55 New Age Outlaws DD	.20	.50
56 Headbangers DD	.10	.25
57 D.O.A. DD	.10	.25
58 L.O.D. 2000 DD	.15	.40
59 Southern Justice DD	.10	.25
60 Too Much DD	.10	.25
61 Los Boricuas DD	.10	.25
62 Paul Bearer BBB	.10	.25
63 Chyna BBB RC	2.00	5.00
64 Jackyl BBB RC	.10	.25
65 Jim Cornette BBB	.15	.40
66 Yamaguchi-San BBB RC	.10	.25
67 Jacqueline BBB RC	.15	.40
68 Paul Ellering BBB	.10	.25
69 Jim Ross MTR	.15	.40
70 Jerry The King Lawler MTR	1.50	4.00
71 Raw is War	.10	.25
72 Checklist	.10	.25

1998 DuoCards WWF Autographs

STATED ODDS 1:100		
NNO Billy Gunn	25.00	60.00
NNO Chyna	150.00	400.00
NNO Hawk	125.00	300.00
NNO Jacqueline	40.00	100.00
NNO Mankind	25.00	60.00
NNO Owen Hart	250.00	600.00
NNO Paul Bearer	60.00	150.00
NNO Road Dog Jesse James	25.00	60.00
NNO Sable	75.00	200.00
NNO Steve Blackman	30.00	60.00
NNO The Rock	750.00	2000.00

1998 DuoCards WWF Stone Cold's Greatest Hitz

COMPLETE SET (8)	15.00	30.00
STATED ODDS 1:20		
OMNI1 1996 King of the Ring	2.00	5.00
OMNI2 WM 13 Submission Match	2.00	5.00
OMNI3 1998 Royal Rumble	2.00	5.00
OMNI4 Wrestlemania XIV	2.00	5.00
OMNI5 King of the Ring	2.00	5.00
OMNI6 Raw is War	2.00	5.00
BONUS1 D-X In Your House	2.00	5.00
BONUS2 Arrest That Hyperlink	2.00	5.00

1998 DuoCards WWF Promos

1 Stone Cold Steve Austin	3.00	8.00
2 Sable	1.25	3.00
3 D-Generation X	2.00	5.00
4 Dude Love/Steve Austin	2.00	5.00

1999 Eastman Kodak WWF Collectible Motion

COMPLETE SET (6)	15.00	40.00
NNO Mankind	3.00	8.00
NNO The Rock	6.00	15.00
NNO Stone Cold Hell Yeah	6.00	15.00
NNO Stone Cold Stuns McMahon	6.00	15.00
NNO The Undertaker	5.00	12.00

2004 Edibas WWE Lamincards

COMPLETE SET (120)	15.00	40.00
1 Chris Benoit	.75	2.00
2 Randy Orton	.75	2.00
3 Kane	1.25	3.00
4 Chris Jericho	.75	2.00
5 Ric Flair	1.50	4.00
6 Rob Conway RC	.30	.75
7 Val Venis	.50	1.25
8 Chuck Palumbo	.50	1.25
9 Rosey	.30	.75
10 Tyson Tomko RC	.50	1.25
11 Shawn Michaels	2.00	5.00
12 The Rock	2.00	5.00
13 Shelton Benjamin RC	.30	.75
14 Christian	1.00	2.50
15 Mark Henry	.50	1.25
16 Test	.50	1.25
17 A-Train	.30	.75
18 Eric Bischoff	.50	1.25
19 Jonathan Coachman RC	.30	.75
20 Jerry The King Lawler	.75	2.00
21 Jim Ross	.50	1.25
22 Gail Kim RC	1.25	3.00
23 Ivory	1.25	3.00
24 Jazz	.75	2.00
25 Lita	2.00	5.00
26 Molly	1.50	4.00
27 Nidia	.75	2.00
28 Stacy Keibler	3.00	8.00
29 Trish Stratus	3.00	8.00
30 Victoria	1.50	4.00
31 Undertaker	1.50	4.00
32 JBL	.75	2.00
33 Eddie Guerrero	1.50	4.00
34 Booker T	1.25	3.00
35 Kurt Angle	1.25	3.00
36 John Cena	2.00	5.00
37 Rob Van Dam	1.25	3.00
38 Rene Dupree RC	.50	1.25
39 Rey Mysterio	.75	2.00
40 Paul Heyman	.30	.75
41 Hardcore Holly	.50	1.25
42 Paul London RC	.30	.75
43 Charlie Haas	.30	.75
44 Bubba Ray	.50	1.25
45 Billy Kidman	.30	.75
46 D-Von Dudley	.50	1.25
47 Chavo Guerrero	.50	1.25
48 Nunzio	.30	.75
49 Scotty 2 Hotty	.50	1.25
50 Johnny Stamboli	.30	.75
51 Danny Basham RC	.30	.75
52 Luther Reigns RC	.30	.75
53 Orlando Jordan RC	.30	.75
54 Akio RC	.30	.75
55 Big Show	1.25	3.00
56 Rico	.30	.75
57 Tazz	.50	1.25
58 Kenzo Suzuki RC	.30	.75
59 Theodore Long	.30	.75
60 Jon Heidenreich RC	.30	.75
61 Funaki	.50	1.25
62 Spike Dudley	.50	1.25
63 Hiroko RC	.30	.75
64 Dawn Marie	.75	2.00
65 Miss Jackie	1.25	3.00
66 Torrie Wilson	3.00	8.00

67 Chris Benoit LOGO .75 2.00
68 Randy Orton LOGO .75 2.00
69 Triple H LOGO 2.00 5.00
70 Batista LOGO 1.25 3.00
71 Kane LOGO 1.25 3.00
72 Chris Jericho LOGO .75 2.00
73 Ric Flair LOGO 1.50 4.00
74 Shawn Michaels LOGO 2.00 5.00
75 Rob Conway LOGO .30 .75
76 Stacy Keibler LOGO 3.00 8.00
77 Ivory LOGO 1.25 3.00
78 Molly Holly LOGO 1.50 4.00
79 Eddie Guerrero LOGO 1.50 4.00
80 Undertaker LOGO 1.50 4.00
81 Booker T LOGO 1.25 3.00
82 Kurt Angle LOGO 1.25 3.00
83 Rob Van Dam LOGO 1.25 3.00
84 Rey Mysterio LOGO .75 2.00
85 Hardcore Holly LOGO .50 1.25
86 Paul London LOGO .30 .75
87 Billy Kidman LOGO .30 .75
88 Dawn Marie LOGO .75 2.00
89 Miss Jackie LOGO 1.25 3.00
90 Torrie Wilson LOGO 3.00 8.00
91 Chavo Guerrero LOGO .50 1.25
92 Chuck Palumbo LOGO .50 1.25
93 Mark Henry LOGO .50 1.25
94 Orlando Jordan LOGO .30 .75
95 Rico LOGO .30 .75
96 The Rock LOGO 2.00 5.00
97 Scotty 2 Hotty LOGO .50 1.25
98 Lita LOGO 2.00 5.00
99 Victoria LOGO 1.50 4.00
100 Gail Kim LOGO 1.25 3.00
101 Benoit vs. Flair IA 1.50 4.00
102 Jericho vs. Michaels IA 2.00 5.00
103 Hurricane vs. The Rock IA 2.00 5.00
104 Orton vs. Benoit IA .75 2.00
105 Kane vs. Jericho IA 1.25 3.00
106 Test vs. Richards IA .50 1.25
107 HHH vs. Benoit IA 2.00 5.00
108 Benjamin vs. Orton IA .75 2.00
109 Conway vs. Hurricane IA .40 1.00
110 Jericho vs. Edge IA 1.25 3.00
111 Guerrero vs. Angle IA 1.50 4.00
112 Orton vs. The Rock IA 2.00 5.00
113 Akio vs. Moore IA .30 .75
114 Big Show vs. RVD IA 1.25 3.00
115 Dudleys vs. La Resistance IA .40 1.00
116 Cena vs. Big Show IA 2.00 5.00
117 JBL vs. Mysterio IA .75 2.00
118 Nunzio vs. Chavo IA .50 1.25
119 Booker T vs. Guerrero IA 1.50 4.00
120 Undertaker vs. Cena IA 2.00 5.00

2005 Edibas WWE Lamincards

COMPLETE SET (150) 15.00 40.00
1 Al Snow .30 .75
2 Batista .60 1.50
3 Booker T .50 1.25
4 Candice RC .75 2.00
5 Chris Benoit .75 2.00
6 Christian 1.00 2.50
7 Doug Basham .30 .75
8 Eddie Guerrero .75 2.00
9 Funaki .30 .75
10 Hardcore Holly .50 1.25
11 Heidenreich .30 .75
12 John Bradshaw Layfield .50 1.25
13 Joey Mercury RC .30 .75
14 Johnny Nitro RC .75 2.00
15 Melina RC 1.50 4.00
16 Michelle McCool RC 1.50 4.00
17 Nunzio .30 .75
18 Orlando Jordan .30 .75
19 Paul London .30 .75
20 Randy Orton .30 .75
21 Rey Mysterio .75 2.00
22 Scotty 2 Hotty .50 1.25
23 Sylvain Grenier RC .30 .75
24 Torrie Wilson 1.00 2.50
25 Undertaker 1.50 4.00
26 William Regal .50 1.25
27 Antonio RC .30 .75
28 Big Show 1.25 3.00
29 Carlito RC .60 1.50
30 Chris Jericho 1.00 2.50
31 Christy Hemme RC 1.00 2.50
32 Danny Basham .30 .75
33 Edge .75 2.00
34 Eugene .75 2.00
35 Gene Snitzky RC .30 .75
36 Jerry The King Lawler .75 2.00
37 John Cena 1.50 4.00
38 Kane 1.00 2.50
39 Kerwin White RC .30 .75
40 Kurt Angle .75 2.00
41 Lita 2.00 5.00
42 Rene Dupree .30 .75
43 Ric Flair 1.25 3.00
44 Rob Van Dam .75 2.00
45 Romeo RC .30 .75
46 Rosey .30 .75
47 Shawn Michaels 1.00 2.50
48 Shelton Benjamin .30 .75
49 Stacy Keibler 3.00 8.00
50 Tajiri .30 .75
51 The Hurricane .30 .75
52 The Rock 1.50 4.00
53 Triple H .75 2.00
54 Trish Stratus 3.00 8.00
55 Tyson Tomko .30 .75
56 Val Venis .50 1.25
57 Victoria 2.00 5.00
58 Viscera .30 .75
59 Sicilian Slide .30 .75
60 The Worm .50 1.25
61 Clothesline from Hell .50 1.25
62 Tombstone Piledriver 1.50 4.00
63 Frog Splash .75 2.00
64 Crippler Crossface .75 2.00
65 ChokeSlam 1.50 4.00
66 Scissors Kick .50 1.25
67 619 .75 2.00
68 Flying Headbutt .75 2.00
69 Book-End .50 1.25
70 The Walls of Jericho 1.00 2.50
71 Moonsault 2.00 5.00
72 Gory Bomb .40 1.00
73 FU 1.50 4.00
74 Rock Bottom 1.50 4.00
75 Super Splash .30 .75
76 Sweet Chin Music 1.00 2.50
77 Show Stopper 1.25 3.00
78 Ankle Lock .75 2.00
79 Twist of Fate 1.00 2.50
80 Chick Kick 3.00 8.00
81 Five Star Frog Splash .75 2.00
82 Bear Hug .30 .75
83 Clothesline .20 .50
84 Head Lock .30 .75
85 Boston Crab .75 2.00
86 Chinlock .20 .50
87 Jumping Foot Stomp .20 .50
88 Shoulder Block .30 .75
89 Right Hand .20 .50
90 Hip Toss 1.50 4.00
91 Sleeper Hold .30 .75
92 Hard Kick .20 .50
93 Leap Frog .20 .50
94 Head Lock 1.00 2.50
95 Pescado .75 2.00
96 Chinlock .60 1.50
97 Spinebuster 1.50 4.00
98 Chinlock .20 .50
99 Vertical Suplex .20 .50
100 Moonsault .75 2.00
101 One Leg Boston Crab .75 2.00
102 One Leg Boston Crab .30 .75
103 Rope Walk 1.50 4.00
104 Bulldog .20 .50
105 Drop Kick .75 2.00
106 Clothesline .30 .75
107 Back Kick .75 2.00
108 Clothesline .30 .75
109 Forearm .75 2.00
110 Face Slam .20 .50
111 Head Lock .20 .50
112 Belly to Back Suplex 1.00 2.50
113 Shoulder Tackle 1.50 4.00
114 Armbar .75 2.00
115 Big Boot 1.50 4.00
116 Armbar 1.00 2.50
117 Sharpshooter 1.50 4.00
118 Gorilla Press Slam 1.25 3.00
119 Double Flying Clothesline .20 .50
120 Batista .60 1.50
121 Booker T .50 1.25
122 Chris Benoit .75 2.00
123 Christian 1.00 2.50
124 Eddie Guerrero .75 2.00
125 John Bradshaw Layfield .50 1.25
126 Randy Orton .30 .75
127 Rey Mysterio .75 2.00
128 Undertaker 1.50 4.00
129 Big Show 1.25 3.00
130 Carlito RC .60 1.50
131 John Cena 1.50 4.00
132 Kane 1.00 2.50
133 Kurt Angle .75 2.00
134 Shawn Michaels 1.00 2.50
135 The Hurricane .30 .75
136 Triple H .75 2.00
137 Val Venis .50 1.25
138 The Rock 1.50 4.00
139 Hulk Hogan 1.50 4.00
140 Sgt. Slaughter .75 2.00
141 The Iron Sheik .75 2.00
142 WWE Champion .20 .50
143 WWE Intercontinental Champion .20 .50
144 WWE Tag Team Champion .20 .50
145 WWE Champion .20 .50
146 WWE Tag Team Champion .20 .50
147 WWE U.S. Champion .20 .50
148 WWE Heavyweight Champion .20 .50
149 WWE Cruiserweight Champion .20 .50
150 WWE Women's Champion .20 .50

2008 Edibas WWE Lamincards

COMPLETE SET (162)
1 Batista 1.25 3.00
2 Big Daddy V .50 1.25
3 Big Show .75 2.00
4 Brian Kendrick .50 1.25
5 Carlito .75 2.00
6 Curt Hawkins .30 .75
7 DH Smith RC .30 .75
8 Domino .30 .75
9 Edge 1.25 3.00
10 Festus RC .30 .75
11 Funaki .30 .75
12 Gregory Helms .40 1.00
13 Jeff Hardy 1.25 3.00
14 Jesse RC .30 .75
15 Jimmy Wang Yang .30 .75
16 Jim Ross .60 1.50
17 Jonathan Coachman .30 .75
18 Justin Roberts RC .30 .75
19 Kenny Dykstra .50 1.25
20 Mick Foley 1.50 4.00
21 MVP .50 1.25
22 Shannon Moore .30 .75
23 Shelton Benjamin .30 .75
24 The Great Khali .30 .75
25 Trevor Murdock .30 .75
26 Triple H 2.00 5.00
27 Umaga .50 1.25
28 Undertaker 1.50 4.00
29 Vladimir Kozlov RC .30 .75
30 Zack Ryder .30 .75
31 Cherry 1.25 3.00
32 Eve Torres RC .60 1.50
33 Maria 1.25 3.00
34 Maryse 1.25 3.00
35 Michelle McCool 1.50 4.00
36 Natalya RC .60 1.50
37 Vickie Guerrero .40 1.00
38 Victoria 1.50 4.00
39 Charlie Haas .30 .75
40 Chris Jericho .75 2.00
41 Chuck Palumbo .50 1.25
42 Cody Rhodes .30 .75
43 CM Punk .30 .75
44 Deuce .30 .75
45 Hacksaw Jim Duggan .75 2.00
46 Hardcore Holly .50 1.25
47 Jamie Noble .30 .75
48 JBL .30 .75
49 Jerry Lawler .60 1.50
50 John Cena 2.00 5.00
51 JTG .30 .75
52 Kane 1.25 3.00
53 Kofi Kingston RC .75 2.00
54 Lance Cade .30 .75
55 Matt Striker .30 .75
56 Michael Cole .30 .75
57 Mr. Kennedy .75 2.00
58 Paul Burchill .30 .75
59 Paul London .30 .75
60 Randy Orton .75 2.00
61 Rey Mysterio .75 2.00
62 Robbie McAllister .30 .75
63 Ron Simmons .30 .75
64 Rory McAllister .30 .75
65 Santino Marella .30 .75
66 Shad .30 .75
67 Shawn Michaels 2.00 5.00
68 Snitsky .50 1.25
69 Stone Cold Steve Austin 2.00 5.00
70 Todd Grisham .30 .75
71 Val Venis .40 1.00
72 William Regal .75 2.00
73 Beth Phoenix 1.50 4.00
74 Candice 1.50 4.00
75 Jillian 1.25 3.00
76 Layla .75 2.00
77 Katie Lea Burchill RC .40 1.00
78 Lilian Garcia .75 2.00
79 Melina 1.25 3.00
80 Mickie James 2.00 5.00
81 Armando Estrada .30 .75
82 Bam Neely RC .30 .75
83 Boogeyman .50 1.25
84 Chavo Guerrero .50 1.25
85 Colin Delaney RC .30 .75
86 Elijah Burke .30 .75
87 Finlay .50 1.25
88 Hornswoggle .50 1.25
89 John Morrison .30 .75
90 Mark Henry .50 1.25
91 Matt Hardy 1.25 3.00
92 Mike Adamle .30 .75
93 Mike Knox .30 .75
94 Nunzio .30 .75
95 Stevie Richards .50 1.25
96 Super Crazy .50 1.25
97 Tazz .50 1.25
98 The Miz .50 1.25
99 Theordore Long .40 1.00
100 Tommy Dreamer .30 .75
101 Tony Chimel RC .30 .75
102 Kelly Kelly 1.25 3.00
103 Lena Yada .40 1.00
104 Akeem .30 .75
105 Bam Bam Bigelow .75 2.00
106 Bobby Heenan .75 2.00
107 British Bulldog .75 2.00
108 Bushwhackers .40 1.00
109 Chief Jay Strongbow .75 2.00
110 Bob Orton .75 2.00
111 Doink the Clown .30 .75
112 Don Muraco .50 1.25
113 Dusty Rhodes .75 2.00
114 Earthquake .50 1.25
115 Freddie Blassie .40 1.00
116 Gorilla Monsoon .75 2.00
117 Hillbilly Jim .30 .75
118 Iron Sheik 1.25 3.00
119 Jake Roberts .75 2.00
120 Jimmy Hart .50 1.25
121 Jimmy Snuka .75 2.00
122 Junkyard Dog .50 1.25
123 Kamala .50 1.25
124 Koko B. Ware .30 .75
125 Michael Hayes .40 1.00
126 Ted DiBiase .75 2.00
127 Mr. Perfect .75 2.00
128 Paul Orndorff .60 1.50

129 Nikolai Volkoff	.50	1.25
130 One Man Gang	.30	.75
131 Papa Shango	.40	1.00
132 Paul Bearer	.50	1.25
133 Rick Rude	.75	2.00
134 Sgt. Slaughter	.75	2.00
135 Billy Graham	.40	1.00
136 Vader	.50	1.25
137 Body Smash	.75	2.00
138 Elbow Smash	.75	2.00
139 Whisper in the Wind	2.00	5.00
140 Sleeper Hold	.30	.75
141 Irish Whip	.75	2.00
142 Walls of Jericho	.75	2.00
143 Springboard Drop	.30	.75
144 Whisper in the Wind	1.25	3.00
145 619	1.25	3.00
146 Boston Crab	.50	1.25
147 Chin Lock	1.25	3.00
148 Elbow Drop	2.00	5.00
149 Jumping Knee Drop	.75	2.00
150 Chin Lock	.75	2.00
151 Spear	.30	.75
152 Headlock	1.25	3.00
153 Chin Lock	.30	.75
154 Springboard Drop	.75	2.00
155 Choke Slam	1.50	4.00
156 Clothesline	1.25	3.00
157 Elbow Smash	1.25	3.00
158 Armbar	1.25	3.00
159 Forearm Smash	1.50	4.00
160 SmackDown!	.30	.75
161 Raw	.30	.75
162 ECW	.30	.75

2014 Edibas WWE Lamincards

COMPLETE SET (160)

1 AJ Lee	1.50	4.00
2 Alberto Del Rio	.75	2.00
3 Alberto Del Rio	.75	2.00
4 Alex Riley	.30	.75
5 Bad News Barrett	.30	.75
6 Batista	1.00	2.50
7 Batista	1.00	2.50
8 Big E	.30	.75
9 Big Show	.75	2.00
10 Big Show	.75	2.00
11 Brad Maddox RC	.30	.75
12 Brock Lesnar	1.25	3.00
13 Brodus Clay	.30	.75
14 Camacho	.30	.75
15 Cesaro	.30	.75
16 Chris Jericho	.75	2.00
17 Christian	.30	.75
18 Curtis Axel	.30	.75
19 Damien Sandow	.30	.75
20 Daniel Bryan	.50	1.25
21 Daniel Bryan	.50	1.25
22 Darren Young	.30	.75
23 David Otunga	.30	.75
24 Dolph Ziggler	.50	1.25
25 Drew McIntyre	.30	.75
26 Heath Slater	.30	.75
27 Hornswoggle	.50	1.25
28 Jack Swagger	.50	1.25
29 Jinder Mahal	.30	.75
30 John Cena	1.50	4.00
31 John Cena	1.50	4.00
32 John Cena	1.50	4.00
33 John Cena	1.50	4.00
34 Justin Gabriel	.30	.75
35 Kane	.75	2.00
36 Kofi Kingston	.30	.75
37 Mark Henry	.50	1.25
38 Natalya	1.00	2.50
39 Randy Orton	1.25	3.00
40 Randy Orton	1.25	3.00
41 Rey Mysterio	.75	2.00
42 Rey Mysterio	.75	2.00
43 Rob Van Dam	.75	2.00
44 R-Truth	.30	.75
45 Ryback	.30	.75
46 Santino Marella	.50	1.25
47 Sheamus	.75	2.00
48 Sheamus	.75	2.00
49 Sin Cara	.75	2.00
50 Tensai	.30	.75
51 The Great Khali	.30	.75
52 The Miz	.50	1.25
53 The Rock	1.50	4.00
54 The Rock	1.50	4.00
55 The Rock	1.50	4.00
56 Titus O'Neil	.30	.75
57 Triple H	1.25	3.00
58 Triple H	1.25	3.00
59 Tyson Kidd	.30	.75
60 Undertaker	1.25	3.00
61 Undertaker	1.25	3.00
62 Zack Ryder	.30	.75
63 Fandango	.50	1.25
64 Summer Rae RC	1.25	3.00
65 Bray Wyatt	.75	2.00
66 Erick Rowan RC	.50	1.25
67 Luke Harper RC	.50	1.25
68 The Wyatt Family		
69 Cody Rhodes	.30	.75
70 Goldust	.30	.75
71 The Brotherhood	.30	.75
72 Dean Ambrose	.75	2.00
73 Roman Reigns	.75	2.00
74 Seth Rollins	.30	.75
75 The Shield		
76 The Usos		
77 Los Matadores	.30	.75
78 New Age Outlaws	.50	1.25
79 The Bella Twins	1.00	2.50
80 Naomi	.50	1.25
81 Rock Bottom	1.50	4.00
82 People's Elbow	1.50	4.00
83 Sister Abigail	.75	2.00
84 Pedigree	1.25	3.00
85 Samoan Splash	.30	.75
86 Drop Kick	.75	2.00
87 Diving Senton	.75	2.00
88 Irish Curse	.75	2.00
89 Cloverleaf	.75	2.00
90 Brogue Kick	.75	2.00
91 Cobra	.50	1.25
92 Shell Shocked	.30	.75
93 West Coast Pop	.75	2.00
94 619	.75	2.00
95 RKO	1.25	3.00
96 World's Strongest Slam	.50	1.25
97 Rough Ryder	.30	.75
98 Disaster Kick	.30	.75
99 Chop	.30	.75
100 Skull-Crushing Finale	.50	1.25
101 Figure-Four Leglock	.50	1.25
102 F5	1.25	3.00
103 Running Clothesline	.30	.75
104 Yes! Lock	.50	1.25
105 Moonsault	.30	.75
106 Running Bulldog	.30	.75
107 Killswitch	.30	.75
108 KO Punch	.75	2.00
109 STF	1.50	4.00
110 Attitude Adjustment	1.50	4.00
111 Arm Bar	.30	.75
112 Giant Swing	.30	.75
113 Five Star Frog Splash	.75	2.00
114 DDT	1.25	3.00
115 Spinebuster	1.00	2.50
116 Tombstone	1.25	3.00
117 Cross Rhodes	.30	.75
118 Lie Detector	.30	.75
119 5 Knuckle Shuffle	1.50	4.00
120 Elbow of Disdain	.30	.75
121 Christian/A.Del Rio	.75	2.00
122 S.Rollins/Big Show	.75	2.00
123 D.Bryan/D.Sandow	.50	1.25
124 J.Cena/Ryback	1.50	4.00
125 R.Mysterio/D.Sandow	.75	2.00
126 Sheamus/Big Show	.75	2.00
127 Ryback/M.Henry	.50	1.25
128 R.Orton/A.Del Rio	1.25	3.00
129 J.Cena/R.Reigns	1.50	4.00
130 Great Khali/Big Show	.75	2.00
131 Sheamus/D.Sandow	.75	2.00
132 Kane/Sheamus	.75	2.00
133 D.McIntyre/D.Young	.30	.75
134 C.Jericho/Fandango	.75	2.00
135 Big Show/Sheamus	.75	2.00
136 B.Wyatt/D.Bryan	.75	2.00
137 Ryback/Cesaro	.30	.75
138 Usos/D.Young	.30	.75
139 D.Bryan/D.Ziggler	.50	1.25
140 New Age Outlaws/Brotherhood	.50	1.25
141 Triple H/B.Lesnar	1.25	3.00
142 Miz/D.Ziggler	.50	1.25
143 J.Cena/Big Show	1.50	4.00
144 J.Swagger/A.Del Rio	.75	2.00
145 J.Mahal/Los Matadores	.30	.75
146 D.Bryan/The Shield	.50	1.25
147 Z.Ryder/W.Barrett	.30	.75
148 Fandango/C.Jericho	.75	2.00
149 Big Show/D.Ambrose	.75	2.00
150 Miz/Christian	.50	1.25
151 Camacho/Usos	.30	.75
152 The Rock/J.Cena	1.50	4.00
153 Booker T/Batista	1.00	2.50
154 R.Orton/H.Slater	1.25	3.00
155 Sin Cara/Ryback	.75	2.00
156 NXT Championship		
157 WWE Tag Team Championship		
158 Divas Championship		
159 WWE World Heavyweight Championship		
160 United States Championship		

2007 Edibas WWE Lamincards

COMPLETE SET (162)

1 Batista	.75	2.00
2 Brett Major RC	.50	1.25
3 Brian Major RC	.30	.75
4 Chavo Guerrero	.50	1.25
5 Dave Taylor RC	.30	.75
6 Deuce RC	.30	.75
7 Domino RC	.30	.75
8 Edge	.75	2.00
9 Finlay	.75	2.00
10 Funaki	.50	1.25
11 Gregory Helms	.30	.75
12 Hardcore Holly	.75	2.00
13 Jamie Noble	.30	.75
14 JBL	.75	2.00
15 Jimmy Wang Yang	.30	.75
16 Kane	.75	2.00
17 Kenny Dykstra RC	.50	1.25
18 Mark Henry	.50	1.25
19 Matt Hardy	.75	2.00
20 Michael Cole	.30	.75
21 Montel Vontavious Porter RC	.50	1.25
22 Rey Mysterio	.75	2.00
23 Ric Flair	1.25	3.00
24 Shannon Moore	.30	.75
25 The Great Khali	.30	.75
26 Theodore Long	.40	1.00
27 Undertaker	1.50	4.00
28 Ashley	.60	1.50
29 Cherry RC	.30	.75
30 Maryse RC	.60	1.50
31 Michelle McCool	1.50	4.00
32 Torrie Wilson	2.50	6.00
33 Vickie Guerrero RC	.40	1.00
34 Victoria	.60	1.50
35 Bobby Lashley	.75	2.00
36 Brien Kendrick	.50	1.25
37 Carlito	1.25	3.00
38 Charlie Haas	.30	.75
39 Hacksaw Jim Duggan	.50	1.25
40 Jeff Hardy	.75	2.00
41 Jerry The King Lawler	.75	2.00
42 Jim Ross	.40	1.00
43 John Cena	2.00	5.00
44 Jonathan Coachman	.30	.75
45 Mr. Kennedy	.75	2.00
46 Lance Cade	.30	.75
47 Paul London	.75	2.00
48 Randy Orton	1.25	3.00
49 Robbie McAllister RC	.30	.75
50 Rowdy Roddy Piper	1.25	3.00
51 Rory McAllister RC	.30	.75
52 Santino Marella RC	.40	1.00
53 Shawn Michaels	1.25	3.00
54 Shelton Benjamin	.30	.75
55 Snitsky	.30	.75
56 Stone Cold Steve Austin	2.00	5.00
57 Super Crazy	.50	1.25
58 Todd Grisham RC	.30	.75
59 Trevor Murdoch	.30	.75
60 Triple H	1.25	3.00
61 Umaga	.50	1.25
62 Val Venis	.75	2.00
63 William Regal	.75	2.00
64 Candice	1.50	4.00
65 Jillian	1.50	4.00
66 Lilian Garcia	.75	2.00
67 Maria	1.25	3.00
68 Melina	1.25	3.00
69 Mickie James	1.00	2.50
70 Armando Estrada RC	.30	.75
71 Balls Mahoney RC	.30	.75
72 Boogeyman	.30	.75
73 CM Punk	1.25	3.00
74 Elijah Burke RC	.30	.75
75 Joey Styles	.30	.75
76 John Morrison	.50	1.25
77 Kevin Thorn RC	.30	.75
78 Matt Striker	.30	.75
79 Mike Knox RC	.30	.75
80 Nunzio	.30	.75
81 Stevie Richards	.50	1.25
82 Tazz	.50	1.25
83 The Miz RC	.60	1.50
84 Tommy Dreamer	.40	1.00
85 Big Daddy V	.75	2.00
86 Kelly Kelly RC	.75	2.00
87 Layla RC	1.25	3.00
88 Akeem	.50	1.25
89 Bam Bam Bigelow	.75	2.00
90 Bobby The Brain Heenan	.60	1.50
91 British Bulldog	.50	1.25
92 Bushwhackers	.30	.75
93 Chief Jay Strongbow	.75	2.00
94 Cowboy Bob Orton	.40	1.00
95 Doink The Clown	.30	.75
96 Don Muraco	.50	1.25
97 Dusty Rhodes	.75	2.00
98 Earthquake	.50	1.25
99 Classy Freddie Blassie	.40	1.00
100 Gorilla Monsoon	.60	1.50
101 Hillbilly Jim	.30	.75
102 Iron Sheik	1.25	3.00
103 Jake The Snake Roberts	.75	2.00
104 Jimmy Hart	.50	1.25
105 Jimmy Superfly Snuka	.50	1.25
106 Junkyard Dog	.60	1.50
107 Kamala	.40	1.00
108 Koko B. Ware	.30	.75
109 Mean Gene Okerlund	.75	2.00
110 Michael Hayes	.40	1.00
111 Ted DiBiase	.60	1.50
112 Mr. Perfect	.50	1.25
113 Mr. Wonderful Paul Orndorff	.60	1.50
114 Nikolai Volkoff	.60	1.50
115 One Man Gang	.50	1.25
116 Papa Shango	.40	1.00
117 Paul Bearer	.50	1.25
118 Ravishing Rick Rude	.75	2.00
119 Sgt. Slaughter	.75	2.00
120 Superstar Billy Graham	.50	1.25
121 Vader	.50	1.25
122 Abdominal Stretch	.75	2.00
123 Air Mysterio	.75	2.00
124 Back Body Drop	.75	2.00
125 Belly-to-Back Suplex	.30	.75
126 Batista Bomb	.75	2.00
127 Belly-to-Back Suplex	.30	.75
128 Bodyslam	.30	.75
129 Choke Slam	1.50	4.00
130 Dropkick	.30	.75
131 Dropkick	.30	.75
132 Elbow Drop	.75	2.00
133 Gutbuster	.30	.75
134 Legdrop	1.50	4.00
135 Legdrop	2.00	5.00
136 Legdrop	1.50	4.00
137 Sleeper	2.00	5.00
138 Stomp	1.25	3.00

139 Irish Whip .75 2.00
140 Bodyslam .30 .75
141 Lionsault .75 2.00
142 Back Body Drop .30 .75
143 Elbow Smash .75 2.00
144 German Suplex .30 .75
145 Sleeper 1.25 3.00
146 Beth Phoenix .75 2.00
147 Batista .75 2.00
148 Edge .75 2.00
149 Randy Orton 1.25 3.00
150 Undertaker 1.50 4.00
151 Batista .75 2.00
152 MVP RC .50 1.25
153 Matt Hardy .75 2.00
154 Randy Orton 1.25 3.00
155 Jeff Hardy .75 2.00
156 Cade & Murdock .30 .75
157 CM Punk 1.25 3.00
158 Beth Phoenix .75 2.00
159 WWE Legends .30 .75
160 SmackDown! .30 .75
161 Raw .30 .75
162 ECW .30 .75

2007 eTopps WWE

COMPLETE SET W/O AU (6) 50.00 100.00
STATED PRINT RUN 999 SERIAL #'d SETS
WILSON AU STATED PRINT RUN TO 867*

1 Batista 2.00 5.00
2 John Cena 3.00 8.00
3 Shawn Michaels 8.00 20.00
4 The Rock 125.00 250.00
5 Undertaker 10.00 25.00
6 Rowdy Roddy Piper 2.50 6.00
7 Torrie Wilson AU/867 50.00 100.00

1991 Euroflash WCW Stickers

1 Sting .75 2.00
2 Sting .75 2.00
3 Sting .75 2.00
4 Sting .75 2.00
5 Sting .75 2.00
6 Sting .75 2.00
7 Sting .75 2.00
8 Sting .75 2.00
9 Sting .75 2.00
10 Sting .75 2.00
11 Sting .75 2.00
12 Sting .75 2.00
13 Sting .75 2.00
14 Sting .75 2.00
15 Sting .75 2.00
16 Sting .75 2.00
17 Sting .75 2.00
18 Rick Rude .50 1.25
19 Rick Rude .50 1.25
20 Rick Rude .50 1.25
21 Rick Rude .50 1.25
22 Rick Rude .50 1.25
23 Rick Rude .50 1.25
24 Rick Rude .50 1.25
25 Rick Rude .50 1.25
26 Rick Rude .50 1.25
27 Rick Rude .50 1.25
28 Rick Rude .50 1.25
29 Rick Rude .50 1.25
30 Rick Rude .50 1.25
31 Rick Rude & Madusa .50 1.25
32 Rick Rude & Madusa .50 1.25
33 Rick Rude & Madusa .50 1.25
34 Rick Rude & Madusa .50 1.25
35 Nikita Koloff .30 .75
36 Nikita Koloff .30 .75
37 Nikita Koloff .30 .75
38 Nikita Koloff .30 .75
39 Nikita Koloff .30 .75
40 Nikita Koloff .30 .75
41 Scotty Flamingo .25 .60
42 Scotty Flamingo .25 .60
43 Scotty Flamingo .25 .60
44 Scotty Flamingo .25 .60
45 Scotty Flamingo .25 .60
46 Scotty Flamingo .25 .60
47 The Steiner Brothers .50 1.25
48 The Steiner Brothers .50 1.25
49 The Steiner Brothers .50 1.25
50 The Steiner Brothers .50 1.25
51 The Steiner Brothers .50 1.25
52 The Steiner Brothers .50 1.25
53 The Steiner Brothers .50 1.25
54 The Steiner Brothers .50 1.25
55 The Steiner Brothers .50 1.25
56 The Steiner Brothers .50 1.25
57 The Steiner Brothers .50 1.25
58 The Steiner Brothers .50 1.25
59 The Steiner Brothers .50 1.25
60 The Steiner Brothers .50 1.25
61 The Steiner Brothers .50 1.25
62 The Steiner Brothers .50 1.25
63 The Steiner Brothers .50 1.25
64 The Steiner Brothers .50 1.25
65 The Steiner Brothers .50 1.25
66 The Steiner Brothers .50 1.25
67 The Steiner Brothers .50 1.25
68 The Steiner Brothers .50 1.25
69 The Steiner Brothers .50 1.25
70 The Steiner Brothers .50 1.25
71 The Steiner Brothers .50 1.25
72 Paul E. Dangerously .40 1.00
73 Paul E. Dangerously .40 1.00
74 Paul E. Dangerously .40 1.00
75 Paul E. Dangerously .40 1.00
76 Paul E. Dangerously .40 1.00
77 Paul E. Dangerously .40 1.00
78 Rick Rude & Madusa .50 1.25
79 Rick Rude & Madusa .50 1.25
80 WCW Action .20 .50
81 WCW Action .20 .50
82 WCW Action .20 .50
83 WCW Action .20 .50
84 WCW Action .20 .50
85 WCW Action .20 .50
86 WCW Action .20 .50
87 WCW Action .20 .50
88 WCW Action .20 .50
89 WCW Action .20 .50
90 Ricky Morton .25 .60
91 Ricky Morton .25 .60
92 Ricky Morton .25 .60
93 Ricky Morton .25 .60
94 Ricky Morton .25 .60
95 Brian Pillman .30 .75
96 Brian Pillman .30 .75
97 Brian Pillman .30 .75
98 Brian Pillman .30 .75
99 Brian Pillman .30 .75
100 Brian Pillman .30 .75
101 Brian Pillman .30 .75
102 Brian Pillman .30 .75
103 Brian Pillman .30 .75
104 Brian Pillman .30 .75
105 Brian Pillman .30 .75
106 Brian Pillman .30 .75
107 Brian Pillman .30 .75
108 Brian Pillman .30 .75
109 Brian Pillman .30 .75
110 Terry Taylor .25 .60
111 Terry Taylor .25 .60
112 Terry Taylor .25 .60
113 Terry Taylor .25 .60
114 Terry Taylor .25 .60
115 Terry Taylor .25 .60
116 Van Hammer .25 .60
117 Van Hammer .25 .60
118 Van Hammer .25 .60
119 Van Hammer .25 .60
120 Van Hammer .25 .60
121 Big Van Vader .50 1.25
122 Big Van Vader .50 1.25
123 Big Van Vader .50 1.25
124 Big Van Vader .50 1.25
125 Big Van Vader .50 1.25
126 Big Van Vader .50 1.25
127 Big Van Vader .50 1.25
128 Big Van Vader .50 1.25
129 Big Van Vader .50 1.25
130 Big Van Vader .50 1.25
131 Big Van Vader .50 1.25
132 Big Van Vader .50 1.25
133 Madusa .40 1.00
134 Madusa .40 1.00
135 Madusa .40 1.00
136 Madusa .40 1.00
137 Madusa .40 1.00
138 Madusa .40 1.00
139 Madusa .40 1.00
140 Madusa .40 1.00
141 Madusa .40 1.00
142 Madusa .40 1.00
143 Madusa .40 1.00
144 Madusa .40 1.00
145 Tom Zenk .25 .60
146 Tom Zenk .25 .60
147 Tom Zenk .25 .60
148 Tom Zenk .25 .60
149 Tom Zenk .25 .60
150 Tom Zenk .25 .60
151 Tom Zenk .25 .60
152 Tom Zenk .25 .60
153 Tom Zenk .25 .60
154 Tom Zenk .25 .60
155 Tom Zenk .25 .60
156 Jim Ross .40 1.00
157 Jim Ross .40 1.00
158 Jesse Ventura .50 1.25
159 Jesse Ventura & Jim Ross .50 1.25
160 Tony Schiavone .30 .75
161 Jesse Ventura .50 1.25
162 Jesse Ventura .50 1.25
163 Jesse Ventura & Jim Ross .50 1.25
164 Big Josh .25 .60
165 Big Josh .25 .60
166 Big Josh .25 .60
167 Big Josh .25 .60
168 Johnny B. Badd .30 .75
169 Johnny B. Badd .30 .75
170 Johnny B. Badd .30 .75
171 Johnny B. Badd .30 .75
172 Johnny B. Badd .30 .75
173 The Freebirds .30 .75
174 The Freebirds .30 .75
175 The Freebirds .30 .75
176 The Freebirds .30 .75
177 The Freebirds .30 .75
178 The Freebirds .30 .75
179 The Freebirds .30 .75
180 The Freebirds .30 .75
181 The Freebirds .30 .75
182 The Freebirds .30 .75
183 Dustin Rhodes .30 .75
184 Dustin Rhodes .30 .75
185 Dustin Rhodes .30 .75
186 Dustin Rhodes .30 .75
187 Dustin Rhodes .30 .75
188 Dustin Rhodes .30 .75
189 Dustin Rhodes .30 .75
190 Dustin Rhodes .30 .75
191 Dustin Rhodes .30 .75
192 Missy Hyatt .40 1.00
193 Missy Hyatt .40 1.00
194 Missy Hyatt .40 1.00
195 Missy Hyatt .40 1.00
196 Missy Hyatt .40 1.00
197 Missy Hyatt .40 1.00
198 Steve Austin .75 2.00
199 Steve Austin .75 2.00
200 Steve Austin .75 2.00
201 Steve Austin .75 2.00
202 Steve Austin .75 2.00
203 Steve Austin .75 2.00
204 Tag Teams .20 .50
205 Tag Teams .20 .50
206 Tag Teams .20 .50
207 Tag Teams .20 .50
208 Tag Teams .20 .50
209 Tag Teams .20 .50
210 Tag Teams .20 .50
211 Barry Windham .40 1.00
212 Barry Windham .40 1.00
213 Barry Windham .40 1.00
214 Barry Windham .40 1.00
215 Barry Windham .40 1.00
216 Barry Windham .40 1.00
217 Ron Simmons .30 .75
218 Ron Simmons .30 .75
219 Ron Simmons .30 .75
220 Big Van Vader .50 1.25
221 Big Van Vader .50 1.25
222 Big Van Vader .50 1.25
223 WCW Airborne .20 .50
224 WCW Airborne .20 .50
225 WCW Airborne .20 .50
226 WCW Airborne .20 .50
227 Marcus Alexander Bagwell .25 .60
228 Marcus Alexander Bagwell .25 .60
229 Marcus Alexander Bagwell .25 .60
230 Marcus Alexander Bagwell .25 .60
231 Marcus Alexander Bagwell .25 .60
232 Marcus Alexander Bagwell .25 .60
233 Super Invader .25 .60
234 Super Invader .25 .60
235 Super Invader .25 .60
236 Super Invader .25 .60
237 Tracey Smothers .25 .60
238 Mr. Hughes .25 .60
239 Junkyard Dog .40 1.00
240 Larry Zbyszko .30 .75

1991 Euroflash WWF SuperStars Stickers

COMPLETE SET (150)

1 Hulk Hogan .75 2.00
2 Hulk Hogan (Puzzle) .75 2.00
3 Hulk Hogan (Puzzle) .75 2.00
4 Hulk Hogan (Puzzle) .75 2.00
5 Hulk Hogan (Puzzle) .75 2.00
6 Nasty Boys .15 .40
7 Nasty Boys .15 .40
8 Earthquake .15 .40
9 Earthquake .15 .40
10 Earthquake .15 .40
11 Jimmy Hart .25 .60
12 Dino Bravo .15 .40
13 Dino Bravo (Puzzle) .15 .40
14 Dino Bravo (Puzzle) .15 .40
15 British Bulldog (Puzzle) .20 .50
16 British Bulldog (Puzzle) .20 .50
17 British Bulldog (Puzzle) .20 .50
18 British Bulldog (Puzzle) .20 .50
19 British Bulldog .20 .50
20 British Bulldog .20 .50
21 Bobby The Brain Heenan .20 .50
22 Mr. Perfect .25 .60
23 Mr. Perfect (Puzzle) .25 .60
24 Mr. Perfect (Puzzle) .25 .60
25 Texas Tornado .20 .50
26 Texas Tornado (Puzzle) .20 .50
27 Texas Tornado (Puzzle) .20 .50
28 Tugboat .15 .40
29 Tugboat (Puzzle) .15 .40
30 Tugboat (Puzzle) .15 .40
31 Hacksaw Jim Duggan (Puzzle) .20 .50
32 Hacksaw Jim Duggan (Puzzle) .20 .50
33 Hacksaw Jim Duggan (Puzzle) .20 .50
34 Hacksaw Jim Duggan (Puzzle) .20 .50
35 Hacksaw Jim Duggan .20 .50
36 Big Boss Man (Puzzle) .15 .40
37 Big Boss Man (Puzzle) .15 .40
38 Big Boss Man .15 .40
39 Big Boss Man .15 .40
40 Power & Glory (Puzzle) .15 .40
41 Power & Glory (Puzzle) .15 .40
42 Power & Glory (Puzzle) .15 .40
43 Power & Glory (Puzzle) .15 .40
44 Hercules .15 .40
45 Paul Roma .15 .40
46 Slick .15 .40
47 Ultimate Warrior (Puzzle) .50 1.25
48 Ultimate Warrior (Puzzle) .50 1.25
49 Ultimate Warrior (Puzzle) .50 1.25
50 Ultimate Warrior (Puzzle) .50 1.25
51 Ultimate Warrior (Puzzle) .50 1.25
52 Ultimate Warrior (Puzzle) .50 1.25
53 Ultimate Warrior .50 1.25
54 Ultimate Warrior (Puzzle) .50 1.25
55 Ultimate Warrior (Puzzle) .50 1.25
56 Ultimate Warrior (Puzzle) .50 1.25

57 Ultimate Warrior (Puzzle)	.50	1.25
58 Rockers (Puzzle)	.25	.60
59 Rockers (Puzzle)	.25	.60
60 Rockers (Puzzle)	.25	.60
61 Rockers (Puzzle)	.25	.60
62 Marty Jannetty	.15	.40
63 Shawn Michaels	.25	.60
64 Rockers	.25	.60
65 Rockers	.25	.60
66 The Model Rick Martel (Puzzle)	.15	.40
67 The Model Rick Martel (Puzzle)	.15	.40
68 The Model Rick Martel (Puzzle)	.15	.40
69 The Model Rick Martel (Puzzle)	.15	.40
70 The Model Rick Martel	.15	.40
71 The Model Rick Martel	.15	.40
72 The Model Rick Martel	.15	.40
73 Hulk Hogan	.75	2.00
74 Hulk Hogan (Puzzle)	.75	2.00
75 Hulk Hogan (Puzzle)	.75	2.00
76 Hulk Hogan (Puzzle)	.75	2.00
77 Hulk Hogan (Puzzle)	.75	2.00
78 Hulk Hogan	.75	2.00
79 Hulk Hogan	.75	2.00
80 Hulk Hogan (Puzzle)	.75	2.00
81 Hulk Hogan (Puzzle)	.75	2.00
82 Hulk Hogan (Puzzle)	.75	2.00
83 Hulk Hogan (Puzzle)	.75	2.00
84 Warlord	.15	.40
85 Warlord	.15	.40
86 Barbarian	.15	.40
87 Barbarian	.15	.40
88 Orient Express	.15	.40
89 Orient Express	.15	.40
90 Mr. Fuji	.15	.40
91 Superfly Jimmy Snuka (Puzzle)	.25	.60
92 Superfly Jimmy Snuka (Puzzle)	.25	.60
93 Superfly Jimmy Snuka	.25	.60
94 Superfly Jimmy Snuka	.25	.60
95 Bushwackers (Puzzle)	.15	.40
96 Bushwackers (Puzzle)	.15	.40
97 Bushwackers (Puzzle)	.15	.40
98 Bushwackers (Puzzle)	.15	.40
99 Bushwackers	.15	.40
100 Macho Man	.50	1.25
101 Macho Man (Puzzle)	.50	1.25
102 Macho Man (Puzzle)	.50	1.25
103 Macho Man & Queen Sherri	.50	1.25
104 Sensational Queen Sherri	.20	.50
105 Sensational Queen Sherri	.20	.50
106 Million Dollar Man (Puzzle)	.20	.50
107 Million Dollar Man (Puzzle)	.20	.50
108 Million Dollar Man (Puzzle)	.20	.50
109 Million Dollar Man (Puzzle)	.20	.50
110 Ted DiBiase	.20	.50
111 Ted DiBiase	.20	.50
112 Rowdy Roddy Piper (Puzzle)	.60	1.50
113 Rowdy Roddy Piper (Puzzle)	.60	1.50
114 Rowdy Roddy Piper	.60	1.50
115 Legion of Doom	.25	.60
116 Animal	.25	.60
117 Legion of Doom	.25	.60
118 Legion of Doom	.25	.60
119 Legion of Doom (Puzzle)	.25	.60
120 Legion of Doom (Puzzle)	.25	.60
121 Legion of Doom (Puzzle)	.25	.60
122 Legion of Doom (Puzzle)	.25	.60
123 Haku (Puzzle)	.15	.40
124 Haku (Puzzle)	.15	.40
125 Haku	.15	.40
126 Virgil (Puzzle)	.15	.40
127 Virgil (Puzzle)	.15	.40
128 Sgt. Slaughter (Puzzle)	.25	.60
129 Sgt. Slaughter (Puzzle)	.25	.60
130 Sgt. Slaughter (Puzzle)	.25	.60
131 Sgt. Slaughter (Puzzle)	.25	.60
132 Sgt. Slaughter	.25	.60
133 Sgt. Slaughter (Puzzle)	.25	.60
134 Sgt. Slaughter (Puzzle)	.25	.60
135 Jake The Snake Roberts (Puzzle)	.30	.75
136 Jake The Snake Roberts (Puzzle)	.30	.75
137 Jake The Snake Roberts	.30	.75
138 Jake The Snake Roberts (Puzzle)	.30	.75
139 Jake The Snake Roberts (Puzzle)	.30	.75
140 Jake The Snake Roberts (Puzzle)	.30	.75
141 Jake The Snake Roberts (Puzzle)	.30	.75
142 Koko B. Ware	.15	.40
143 Koko B. Ware	.15	.40
144 The Undertaker (Puzzle)	.60	1.50
145 The Undertaker (Puzzle)	.60	1.50
146 Undertaker/Paul Bearer (Puzzle)	.60	1.50
147 Undertaker/Paul Bearer (Puzzle)	.60	1.50
148 Undertaker/Paul Bearer (Puzzle)	.60	1.50
149 Undertaker/Paul Bearer (Puzzle)	.60	1.50
150 Paul Bearer	.20	.50

1960 Exhibit

COMPLETE SET (10)		
1 Bob Ortin	12.00	30.00
2 Hans Herman	4.00	10.00
3 Hans Schmidt	5.00	12.00
4 George Macricosta	8.00	20.00
5 Pat O'Connor	6.00	15.00
6 Rasputin	4.00	10.00
7 Roy McClarity	4.00	10.00
8 Tarzan White	4.00	10.00
9 Verne Gagne	10.00	25.00
10 Yukon Eric	6.00	15.00

1964 Exhibit

COMPLETE SET (16)	50.00	100.00
NNO Andre Drapp	5.00	12.00
NNO Antonio Rocca	3.00	8.00
NNO Bruno Sammartino	15.00	40.00
NNO Buddy Rogers	8.00	20.00
NNO Count Billy Vargo	3.00	8.00
NNO Cowboy Bob Ellis	3.00	8.00
NNO Don Leo Jonathan	3.00	8.00
NNO Enrique Torres	3.00	8.00
NNO Hard Boiled Haggerty	3.00	8.00
NNO Haystacks Calhoun	6.00	15.00
NNO Jerry Graham	3.00	8.00
NNO Lou Thesz	8.00	20.00
NNO Pat O'Connor	3.00	8.00
NNO Pepper Gomez	3.00	8.00
NNO Roy Heffernan	3.00	8.00
NNO Sailor Art Thomas	3.00	8.00

2010 FCW Summer Slamarama

NNO Bo Rotunda	12.00	30.00
NNO Darren Young	10.00	25.00
NNO Duke Rotunda	75.00	200.00
NNO Heath Slater	8.00	20.00
NNO Joe Hennig	12.00	30.00
NNO Justin Angel	8.00	20.00
NNO Kaval	10.00	25.00
NNO Naomi Knight	30.00	75.00
NNO Savannah	10.00	25.00
NNO Skip Sheffield (Ryback)	8.00	20.00
NNO Tyler Reks	8.00	20.00
NNO Wade Barrett	10.00	25.00

2011 FCW Summer Slamarama

NNO AJ	60.00	150.00
NNO Aksana	8.00	20.00
NNO Bo Rotundo	10.00	25.00
NNO Brad Maddox	3.00	8.00
NNO Briley Pierce	3.00	8.00
NNO Brodus Clay	5.00	12.00
NNO Calvin Raines	2.50	6.00
NNO Conor O'Brian	2.50	6.00
NNO Damien Sandow	8.00	20.00
NNO Dean Ambrose	20.00	50.00
NNO Hunico	3.00	8.00
NNO Husky Harris	60.00	150.00
NNO Jinder Mahal	8.00	20.00
NNO Kenneth Cameron	2.50	6.00
NNO Leo Kruger	4.00	10.00
NNO Mason Ryan	3.00	8.00
NNO Peter Orlov	2.50	6.00
NNO Raquel Diaz	3.00	8.00
NNO Richie Steamboat	6.00	15.00
NNO Roman Leakee	100.00	250.00
NNO Seth Rollins	75.00	200.00
NNO Titus O'Neill	5.00	12.00
NNO Xavier Woods	6.00	15.00

2012 FCW Summer Slamarama

NNO Bo Dallas	3.00	8.00
NNO Brad Maddox	2.00	5.00
NNO Briley Pierce	2.00	5.00
NNO Caylee Turner	1.50	4.00
NNO CJ Parker	1.50	4.00
NNO Jake Carter	1.50	4.00
NNO Mike Dalton	6.00	15.00
NNO Paige	125.00	250.00
NNO Raquel Diaz	3.00	8.00
NNO Richie Steamboat	2.00	5.00
NNO Rick Victor	1.50	4.00
NNO Sofia Cortez	2.50	6.00
NNO Summer Rae	30.00	75.00

2020 Finest WWE

COMPLETE SET W/SP (125)
COMPLETE SET W/O SP (100) 25.00 60.00
COMMON SP (101-125)
*REFRACTOR: .5X TO 1.2X BASIC CARDS
*X-FRACTOR: .6X TO 1.5X BASIC CARDS
*BLUE/150: .75X TO 2X BASIC CARDS
*GREEN/99: 1X TO 2.5X BASIC CARDS
*ORANGE/50: 1.2X TO 3X BASIC CARDS
*BLACK/25: 4X TO 10X BASIC CARDS
*GOLD/10: UNPRICED DUE TO SCARCITY
*RED/5: UNPRICED DUE TO SCARCITY
*SUPERFR/1: UNPRICED DUE TO SCARCITY
SP STATED ODDS (101-125) 1:80

1 Angel Garza RC	.60	1.50
2 Akam	.60	1.50
3 Aleister Black	1.00	2.50
4 Andrade	.75	2.00
5 Angelo Dawkins	.50	1.25
6 Asuka	2.00	5.00
7 Austin Theory RC	.75	2.00
8 Becky Lynch	2.00	5.00
9 Bianca Belair	1.25	3.00
10 Bobby Lashley	1.00	2.50
11 Murphy	.60	1.50
12 Charlotte Flair	2.00	5.00
13 Drew McIntyre	1.00	2.50
14 Edge	1.00	2.50
15 Erik	.50	1.25
16 Humberto Carrillo	.75	2.00
17 Ivar	.50	1.25
18 Kairi Sane	1.00	2.50
19 Kevin Owens	.60	1.50
20 Lana	1.25	3.00
21 Liv Morgan	1.25	3.00
22 Montez Ford	.50	1.25
23 Nia Jax	.75	2.00
24 R-Truth	.50	1.25
25 Randy Orton	1.25	3.00
26 Rezar	.50	1.25
27 Ricochet	.75	2.00
28 Riddick Moss	.50	1.25
29 Ruby Riott	.75	2.00
30 Samoa Joe	.75	2.00
31 Seth Rollins	1.00	2.50
32 Shayna Baszler	1.50	4.00
33 Zelina Vega	1.00	2.50
34 AJ Styles	1.50	4.00
35 Alexa Bliss	3.00	8.00
36 Bayley	1.00	2.50
37 Big E	.50	1.25
38 Braun Strowman	1.25	3.00
39 The Fiend Bray Wyatt	1.50	4.00
40 Carmella	1.25	3.00
41 Cesaro	.50	1.25
42 Daniel Bryan	1.50	4.00
43 Dolph Ziggler	.50	1.25
44 Elias	1.00	2.50
45 Jeff Hardy	1.25	3.00
46 Jey Uso	.50	1.25
47 Jimmy Uso	.50	1.25
48 John Morrison	.50	1.25
49 King Corbin	.60	1.50
50 Kofi Kingston	.75	2.00
51 Lacey Evans	1.25	3.00
52 Mandy Rose	2.50	6.00
53 Matt Riddle	1.00	2.50
54 Mojo Rawley	.50	1.25
55 Mustafa Ali	.75	2.00
56 Naomi	1.00	2.50
57 Nikki Cross	1.00	2.50
58 Otis	.75	2.00
59 Robert Roode	.50	1.25
60 Roman Reigns	1.25	3.00
61 Sami Zayn	.60	1.50
62 Sasha Banks	2.50	6.00
63 Sheamus	.60	1.50
64 Shinsuke Nakamura	1.00	2.50
65 Shorty G	.50	1.25
66 Sonya Deville	1.25	3.00
67 Tamina	.60	1.50
68 The Miz	.75	2.00
69 Tucker	.50	1.25
70 Xavier Woods	.50	1.25
71 Adam Cole	1.25	3.00
72 Bobby Fish	.50	1.25
73 Cameron Grimes RC	.50	1.25
74 Candice LeRae	1.50	4.00
75 Chelsea Green	2.50	6.00
76 Dakota Kai	1.00	2.50
77 Damian Priest RC	.50	1.25
78 Dominik Dijakovic	.50	1.25
79 Finn Balor	1.25	3.00
80 Io Shirai	.75	2.00
81 Isaiah Swerve Scott RC	.60	1.50
82 Johnny Gargano	1.00	2.50
83 Kacy Catanzaro	1.00	2.50
84 Karrion Kross RC	1.00	2.50
85 Keith Lee	.50	1.25
86 Kushida RC	.60	1.50
87 Kyle OiReilly	.60	1.50
88 Mia Yim	1.00	2.50
89 Pete Dunne	.50	1.25
90 Rhea Ripley	2.00	5.00
91 Roderick Strong	1.00	2.50
92 Scarlett RC	2.00	5.00
93 Shotzi Blackheart RC	1.50	4.00
94 Tegan Nox RC	1.25	3.00
95 Tommaso Ciampa	1.00	2.50
96 Tyler Breeze	.60	1.50
97 Velveteen Dream	.60	1.50
98 Kay Lee Ray RC	.75	2.00
99 Toni Storm	1.25	3.00
100 Walter RC	1.00	2.50
101 Big Show SP	1.50	4.00
102 Jinder Mahal SP	1.25	3.00
103 Natalya SP	2.50	6.00
104 Ember Moon SP	2.50	6.00
105 Dana Brooke SP	2.00	5.00
106 Jaxson Ryker SP RC	1.50	4.00
107 Kalisto SP	1.25	3.00
108 Kane SP	1.50	4.00
109 Aliyah SP	2.50	6.00
110 Bronson Reed SP RC	1.25	3.00
111 Robert Stone SP	1.25	3.00
112 Santos Escobar SP RC	1.25	3.00
113 Jordan Devlin SP RC	1.25	3.00
114 Mercedes Martinez SP RC	2.00	5.00
115 John Cena SP	5.00	12.00
116 Rob Gronkowski SP	2.00	5.00
117 Ronda Rousey SP	6.00	15.00
118 The Rock SP	6.00	15.00
119 Triple H SP	3.00	8.00
120 Undertaker SP	5.00	12.00
121 Batista SP	2.00	5.00
122 Bret Hit Man Hart SP	3.00	8.00
123 Goldberg SP	5.00	12.00
124 Shawn Michaels SP	3.00	8.00
125 Stone Cold Steve Austin SP	6.00	15.00

2020 Finest WWE Autographs

*GREEN/99: .6X TO 1.2X BASIC AUTOS
*ORANGE/50 .6X TO 1.5X BASIC AUTOS
*BLACK/25: UNPRICED DUE TO SCARCITY
*GOLD/10: UNPRICED DUE TO SCARCITY
*RED/5: UNPRICED DUE TO SCARCITY
*SUPERFR/1: UNPRICED DUE TO SCARCITY
STATED ODDS 1:17

AAB Aleister Black	8.00	20.00
AAC Adam Cole	10.00	25.00
AAD Angelo Dawkins	5.00	12.00
AAG Angel Garza	12.00	30.00
AAJ AJ Styles	15.00	40.00
AAN Andrade	5.00	12.00
AAS Asuka	30.00	75.00
ABA Bayley	25.00	60.00

ABB Bianca Belair 15.00 40.00
ABD Roman Reigns 15.00 40.00
ABE Big E 6.00 15.00
ABM Murphy 5.00 12.00
ABO Bobby Lashley 8.00 20.00
ABW The Fiend Bray Wyatt 30.00 75.00
ACG Cameron Grimes 10.00 25.00
ACS Cesaro 6.00 15.00
ADD Dominik Dijakovic 5.00 12.00
ADK Dakota Kai 20.00 50.00
ADM Drew McIntyre 15.00 40.00
ADZ Dolph Ziggler 6.00 15.00
AEK Erik 5.00 12.00
AFB Finn Balor 10.00 25.00
AIO Io Shirai 30.00 75.00
AIS Isaiah Swerve Scott 8.00 20.00
AJE Jey Uso 6.00 15.00
AJG Johnny Gargano 5.00 12.00
AJH Jeff Hardy 12.00 30.00
AKC King Corbin 6.00 15.00
AKL Keith Lee 10.00 25.00
AKU Kushida 5.00 12.00
ALM Liv Morgan 20.00 50.00
AMA Mandy Rose 25.00 60.00
AMF Montez Ford 6.00 15.00
AMY Mia Yim 10.00 25.00
ANC Nikki Cross 10.00 25.00
AOT Otis 8.00 20.00
AQS Shayna Baszler 10.00 25.00
ARC Ricochet 10.00 25.00
ARH Rhea Ripley 50.00 100.00
ARR Ruby Riott 15.00 40.00
ART R-Truth 8.00 20.00
ASB Sasha Banks 50.00 100.00
ASG Shorty G 5.00 12.00
ASH Sheamus 6.00 15.00
ASJ Samoa Joe 5.00 12.00
ASN Shinsuke Nakamura 8.00 20.00
ASR Seth Rollins 10.00 25.00
ATB Tyler Breeze 5.00 12.00
ATC Tucker 6.00 15.00
ATN Tegan Nox 30.00 75.00
ATO Tommaso Ciampa 10.00 25.00
AVD Velveteen Dream 5.00 12.00
AZV Zelina Vega 15.00 40.00

2020 Finest WWE Decade's Finest Debuts

COMPLETE SET (9) 6.00 15.00
*GOLD/50: .6X TO 1.5X BASIC CARDS
*RED/5: UNPRICED DUE TO SCARCITY
*SUPERFR/1: UNPRICED DUE TO SCARCITY
STATED ODDS 1:11

D1 Daniel Bryan 2.00 5.00
D2 Roman Reigns 1.50 4.00
D3 Seth Rollins 1.25 3.00
D4 Kevin Owens .75 2.00
D5 Samoa Joe 1.00 2.50
D6 Braun Strowman 1.50 4.00
D7 AJ Styles 2.00 5.00
D8 Shinsuke Nakamura 1.25 3.00
D9 Adam Cole 1.50 4.00
D10 Ronda Rousey 3.00 8.00

2020 Finest WWE Decade's Finest Debuts Autographs

*GOLD/50: .5X TO 1.2X BASIC AUTOS
*RED/5: UNPRICED DUE TO SCARCITY
*SUPERFR/1: UNPRICED DUE TO SCARCITY
STATED ODDS 1:124

DAC Adam Cole 12.00 30.00
DAJ AJ Styles 12.00 30.00
DKO Kevin Owens 6.00 15.00
DSJ Samoa Joe 6.00 15.00
DSN Shinsuke Nakamura 8.00 20.00

2020 Finest WWE Decade's Finest Returns

COMPLETE SET (17) 12.00 30.00
*GOLD/50: .6X TO 1.5X BASIC CARDS
*RED/5: UNPRICED DUE TO SCARCITY
*SUPERFR/1: UNPRICED DUE TO SCARCITY
STATED ODDS 1:7

R1 Bret Hit Man Hart 1.50 4.00
R2 Booker T 1.25 3.00
R3 Diesel 1.00 2.50
R4 The Rock 3.00 8.00
R5 Kane .75 2.00
R6 Undertaker 2.50 6.00
R7 Ultimate Warrior 1.50 4.00
R9 Shane McMahon 1.00 2.50
R10 Seth Rollins 1.25 3.00
R11 Goldberg 2.50 6.00
R12 Paige 1.50 4.00
R13 Daniel Bryan 2.00 5.00
R14 Bobby Lashley 1.25 3.00
R15 Roman Reigns 1.50 4.00
R16 Trish Stratus 3.00 8.00
R17 Batista 1.00 2.50
R18 Sasha Banks 3.00 8.00

2020 Finest WWE Decade's Finest Returns Autographs

*GOLD/50: .5X TO 1.2X BASIC AUTOS
*RED/5: UNPRICED DUE TO SCARCITY
*SUPERFR/1: UNPRICED DUE TO SCARCITY
STATED ODDS 1:106

RBL Bobby Lashley 8.00 20.00
RRR Roman Reigns 20.00 50.00
RSB Sasha Banks 50.00 100.00
RSR Seth Rollins 8.00 20.00

2020 Finest WWE Decade's Finest Superstars

COMPLETE SET (10) 10.00 25.00
*GOLD/50: .6X TO 1.5X BASIC CARDS
*RED/5: UNPRICED DUE TO SCARCITY
*SUPERFR/1: UNPRICED DUE TO SCARCITY
STATED ODDS 1:11

S1 Becky Lynch 2.50 6.00
S2 Charlotte Flair 2.50 6.00
S3 Daniel Bryan 2.00 5.00
S4 John Cena 2.50 6.00
S5 Kofi Kingston 1.00 2.50
S6 Randy Orton 1.50 4.00
S7 Roman Reigns 1.50 4.00
S8 Seth Rollins 1.25 3.00
S9 Sheamus .75 2.00
S10 The Miz 1.00 2.50

2020 Finest WWE Decade's Finest Superstars Autographs

*GOLD/50: .5X TO 1.2X BASIC AUTOS
*RED/5: UNPRICED DUE TO SCARCITY
*SUPERFR/1: UNPRICED DUE TO SCARCITY
STATED ODDS 1:123

SKK Kofi Kingston 6.00 15.00
SRR Roman Reigns 15.00 40.00
SSR Seth Rollins 12.00 30.00

2020 Finest WWE Finest Careers Die-Cuts

COMPLETE SET (10) 30.00 75.00
*GOLD/50: .6X TO 1.5X BASIC CARDS
*RED/5: UNPRICED DUE TO SCARCITY
*SUPERFR/1: UNPRICED DUE TO SCARCITY
STATED ODDS 1:48

C1 Austin 3:16 Is Born 6.00 15.00
C2 Stunner Heard Around World 6.00 15.00
C3 First WWE Championship 6.00 15.00
C4 Zamboni Mayhem 6.00 15.00
C5 Cementing the Boss' Car 6.00 15.00
C6 Raining on Corporation's Parade 6.00 15.00
C7 Stone Cold's Final Match 6.00 15.00
C8 Chasing Down Mr. McMahon 6.00 15.00
C9 Mr. McMahon Inducts Austin 6.00 15.00
C10 Celebrating Raw's 25th Anniversary 6.00 15.00

2020 Finest WWE Finest Tag Teams

COMPLETE SET (17) 12.00 30.00
*GOLD/50: .6X TO 1.5X BASIC CARDS
*RED/5: UNPRICED DUE TO SCARCITY
*SUPERFR/1: UNPRICED DUE TO SCARCITY
STATED ODDS 1:7

TT1 Akam/Rezar 1.00 2.50
TT2 Montez Ford/Angelo Dawkins .75 2.00
TT3 Kairi Sane/Asuka 3.00 8.00
TT4 Billie Kay/Peyton Royce 1.50 4.00
TT5 Ivar/Erik .75 2.00
TT6 Alexa Bliss/Nikki Cross 5.00 12.00
TT7 Sasha Banks/Bayley 4.00 10.00
TT8 Big E/Kofi Kingston 1.25 3.00
TT9 John Morrison/The Miz 1.25 3.00
TT10 Jimmy Uso/Jey Uso .75 2.00
TT11 Tucker/Otis 1.25 3.00
TT12 Bobby Fish/Kyle OiReilly 1.00 2.50
TT13 Pete Dunne/Matt Riddle 1.50 4.00
TT14 Wesley Blake/Steve Cutler 1.00 2.50
TT15 Wolfgang/Mark Coffey 1.00 2.50
TT16 James Drake/Zack Gibson 1.00 2.50
TT17 Marcel Barthel/Fabian Aichner .75 2.00

2020 Finest WWE Finest Tag Teams Autographs

*GOLD REF/25: UNPRICED DUE TO SCARCITY
*RED REF/5: UNPRICED DUE TO SCARCITY
*SUPERFR/1: UNPRICED DUE TO SCARCITY
STATED ODDS 1:74

TTBC Alexa Bliss/Nikki Cross 75.00 150.00
TTBH Sasha Banks/Bayley 100.00 200.00
TTHM Tucker/Otis 20.00 50.00
TTII Billie Kay/Peyton Royce 60.00 120.00
TTIM Marcel Barthel/Fabian Aichner 10.00 25.00
TTMM John Morrison/The Miz 30.00 75.00
TTSP Angelo Dawkins/Montez Ford 15.00 40.00
TTUE Bobby Fish/Kyle O'Reilly 15.00 40.00
TTVR Ivar/Erik 10.00 25.00

2021 Finest WWE

*REF: .5X TO 1.2X BASIC CARDS
*XFRAC: .6X TO 1.5X BASIC CARDS
*BLUE/150: .75X TO 2X BASIC CARDS
*GREEN/99: 1X TO 2.5X BASIC CARDS
*ROSE G/75: 1.2X TO 3X BASIC CARDS
*GOLD/50: 1.5X TO 4X BASIC CARDS
*ORANGE/25: 2X TO 5X BASIC CARDS
*ORANGE SP/25: UNPRICED DUE TO SCARCITY
*BLACK/10: UNPRICED DUE TO SCARCITY
*RED/5: UNPRICED DUE TO SCARCITY
*SUPER/1: UNPRICED DUE TO SCARCITY

1 AJ Styles 1.50 4.00
2 Akira Tozawa .60 1.50
3 Alexa Bliss 3.00 8.00
4 Asuka 2.00 5.00
5 Becky Lynch 2.00 5.00
6 Bobby Lashley 1.25 3.00
7 Charlotte Flair 2.50 6.00
8 Cedric Alexander .50 1.25
9 Damian Priest .75 2.00
10 Dana Brooke .50 1.25
11 Drew McIntyre 1.25 3.00
12 Elias .50 1.25
13 Humberto Carrillo .50 1.25
14 Jaxson Ryker .50 1.25
15 Jeff Hardy 1.25 3.00
16 Jinder Mahal .60 1.50
17 John Morrison 1.00 2.50
18 Keith Lee 1.00 2.50
19 Kofi Kingston 1.25 3.00
20 Lacey Evans 1.25 3.00
21 MACE .50 1.25
22 Mandy Rose 2.50 6.00
23 Mustafa Ali .60 1.50
24 MVP .50 1.25
25 Naomi .60 1.50
26 Nia Jax 1.00 2.50
27 Nikki A.S.H. 1.00 2.50
28 Omos RC 1.00 2.50
29 R-Truth .60 1.50
30 Randy Orton 1.50 4.00
31 Reggie RC .60 1.50
32 Rhea Ripley 1.50 4.00
33 Ricochet 1.00 2.50
34 Riddle 1.25 3.00
35 Shayna Baszler 1.00 2.50
36 Sheamus .75 2.00
37 Shelton Benjamin .75 2.00
38 T-BAR .60 1.50
39 Titus O'Neil .50 1.25
40 The Miz .75 2.00
41 Xavier Woods .50 1.25
42 Angelo Dawkins .60 1.50
43 Apollo Crews .60 1.50
44 Bayley 1.25 3.00
45 Bianca Belair 1.25 3.00
46 Big E 1.00 2.50
47 Carmella 1.25 3.00
48 Cesaro .50 1.25
49 Chad Gable .50 1.25
50 Commander Azeez RC .60 1.50
51 Dolph Ziggler 1.00 2.50
52 Dominik Mysterio RC .60 1.50
53 Edge 2.00 5.00
54 Finn Balor 1.25 3.00
55 Jey Uso .50 1.25
56 Kevin Owens 1.00 2.50
57 Baron Corbin .50 1.25
58 Liv Morgan 2.00 5.00
59 Montez Ford .50 1.25
60 Tegan Nox 1.25 3.00
61 Otis .60 1.50
62 Paul Heyman .60 1.50
63 Rey Mysterio 1.25 3.00
64 Rick Boogs RC .50 1.25
65 Robert Roode .60 1.50
66 Roman Reigns 2.50 6.00
67 Sasha Banks 2.50 6.00
68 Sami Zayn .75 2.00
69 Seth Rollins 1.25 3.00
70 Shinsuke Nakamura 1.25 3.00
71 Shotzi 2.00 5.00
72 Sonya Deville 1.25 3.00
73 Toni Storm 1.50 4.00
74 Zelina Vega 1.00 2.50
75 Aliyah 1.00 2.50
76 Adam Cole 1.50 4.00
77 Austin Theory 1.00 2.50
78 Candice LeRae 2.00 5.00
79 Cameron Grimes 1.00 2.50
80 Dakota Kai 1.00 2.50
81 Danny Burch .60 1.50
82 Drake Maverick .50 1.25
83 Ember Moon .60 1.50
84 Indi Hartwell RC 1.50 4.00
85 Io Shirai 1.00 2.50
86 Isaiah Swerve Scott .75 2.00
87 James Drake .50 1.25
88 Johnny Gargano 1.00 2.50
89 Karrion Kross 2.00 5.00
90 Kyle O'Reilly .75 2.00
91 Oney Lorcan .50 1.25
92 Pete Dunne 1.00 2.50
93 Raquel Gonzalez 1.25 3.00
94 Roderick Strong .75 2.00
95 Santos Escobar .75 2.00
96 Scarlett 2.50 6.00
97 Timothy Thatcher RC .50 1.25
98 Tommaso Ciampa 1.25 3.00
99 Zack Gibson .50 1.25
100 John Cena 2.50 6.00
101 Angel Garza SP 2.50 6.00
102 Eva Marie SP 5.00 12.00
103 Mansoor SP RC 2.00 5.00
104 Jimmy Uso SP 2.00 5.00
105 Tamina SP 2.50 6.00
106 Cameron Grimes SP 4.00 10.00
107 Dexter Lumis SP 2.00 5.00
108 Isaiah Swerve Scott SP 3.00 8.00
109 Kushida SP 3.00 8.00
110 Zoey Stark SP RC 2.50 6.00
111 Fabian Aichner SP 2.50 6.00
112 Kay Lee Ray SP 5.00 12.00
113 Marcel Barthel SP 2.50 6.00
114 Trent Seven SP 2.50 6.00
115 Tyler Bate SP 2.50 6.00
116 Walter SP 5.00 12.00
117 John Cena SP 10.00 25.00
118 Kane SP 3.00 8.00
119 Goldberg SP 8.00 20.00
120 Booker T SP 4.00 10.00
121 Rob Van Dam SP 4.00 10.00
122 Stacy Keibler SP 6.00 15.00

2021 Finest WWE Autographs

*GREEN/99: .6X TO 1.5X BASIC AUTOS
*GOLD/50: .75X TO 2X BASIC AUTOS
*ORANGE/25: UNPRICED DUE TO SCARCITY
*BLACK/10: UNPRICED DUE TO SCARCITY
*RED/5: UNPRICED DUE TO SCARCITY
*SUPER/1: UNPRICED DUE TO SCARCITY
RANDOMLY INSERTED INTO PACKS

RAAC Apollo Crews	5.00	12.00
RAAD Angelo Dawkins	5.00	12.00
RAAT Austin Theory	12.00	30.00
RABI Big E	8.00	20.00
RACE Cesaro	6.00	15.00
RACG Chad Gable	5.00	12.00
RACL Candice LeRae	8.00	20.00
RACR Carmella	10.00	25.00
RADK Dakota Kai	12.00	30.00
RADO Dominik Mysterio	10.00	25.00
RADP Damian Priest	6.00	15.00
RAEM Ember Moon	8.00	20.00
RAHC Humberto Carrillo	5.00	12.00
RAIH Indi Hartwell	12.00	30.00
RAIS Io Shirai	10.00	25.00
RAJG Johnny Gargano	5.00	12.00
RAJM John Morrison	6.00	15.00
RAJR Jaxson Ryker	6.00	15.00
RAKC King Corbin	5.00	12.00
RAKK Karrion Kross	10.00	25.00
RAKO Kyle O'Reilly	5.00	12.00
RAKT Commander Azeez	8.00	20.00
RALM Liv Morgan	25.00	60.00
RAMR Mandy Rose	25.00	60.00
RAMV MVP	5.00	12.00
RANJ Nia Jax	5.00	12.00
RAOM Omos	25.00	60.00
RAOT Otis	6.00	15.00
RARB Robert Roode	5.00	12.00
RARC Ricochet	10.00	25.00
RARE Mia Yim	10.00	25.00
RARG Raquel Gonzalez	12.00	30.00
RARH R-Truth	5.00	12.00
RARI Riddle	12.00	30.00
RARR Rhea Ripley	10.00	25.00
RASB Shayna Baszler	6.00	15.00
RASC Scarlett	20.00	50.00
RASE Santos Escobar	6.00	15.00
RASO Shotzi Blackheart	25.00	60.00
RASZ Sami Zayn	6.00	15.00
RATO Titus O'Neil	5.00	12.00
RAXW Xavier Woods	6.00	15.00

2021 Finest WWE Autographs Gold Refractors

*GOLD: .75X TO 2X BASIC AUTOS

RAA Asuka	25.00	60.00
RAE Edge	30.00	75.00
RAAB Alexa Bliss	125.00	250.00
RAAS AJ Styles	25.00	60.00
RABE Becky Lynch	100.00	200.00
RABL Bobby Lashley	15.00	40.00
RADM Drew McIntyre	15.00	40.00
RADZ Dolph Ziggler	12.00	30.00
RAJH Jeff Hardy	30.00	75.00
RAKF Kofi Kingston	12.00	30.00
RARM Rey Mysterio	30.00	75.00
RASA Sasha Banks	100.00	200.00
RASM Sheamus	8.00	20.00
RASR Seth Rollins	50.00	100.00
RATM The Miz	15.00	40.00

2021 Finest WWE Autographs Green Refractors

*GREEN: X TO X BASIC AUTOS

RASN Shinsuke Nakamura	8.00	20.00

2021 Finest WWE Deadman's Tombstone Career Tribute Die-Cuts

COMPLETE SET (13)	25.00	60.00

*ORANGE/25: 4X TO 10X BASIC CARDS
*RED/5: UNPRICED DUE TO SCARCITY
*SUPER/1: UNPRICED DUE TO SCARCITY
RANDOMLY INSERTED INTO PACKS

UT1 Debut of the Deadman	3.00	8.00
UT2 Defeating the Doppelganger	3.00	8.00
UT3 Deadman's Hand	3.00	8.00
UT4 Burning Brothers	3.00	8.00
UT5 Fall of Mankind	3.00	8.00
UT6 Stephanie's Teddy Bear	3.00	8.00
UT7 The Deadman Returns	3.00	8.00
UT8 Lightning Fright	3.00	8.00
UT9 Royal Rumble Match Winner	3.00	8.00
UT10 Rated-R Chokeslam	3.00	8.00
UT11 Career vs. Streak	3.00	8.00
UT12 End of an Era	3.00	8.00
UT13 A Phenomenal Ending	3.00	8.00

2021 Finest WWE Legacies

*ORANGE/25: UNPRICED DUE TO SCARCITY
*RED/5: UNPRICED DUE TO SCARCITY
*SUPER/1: UNPRICED DUE TO SCARCITY
RANDOMLY INSERTED INTO PACKS

L1 AJ Styles/HBK	2.50	6.00
L2 Bayley/Macho Man	3.00	8.00
L3 Bianca Belair/Mr. Perfect	2.00	5.00
L4 Carmella/Elizabeth	2.00	5.00
L5 Cesaro/Bruno Sammartino	.75	2.00
L6 Jeff Hardy/Undertaker	2.00	5.00
L7 Mandy Rose/Trish Stratus	4.00	10.00
L8 Montez Ford/Booker T	.75	2.00
L9 Rhea Ripley/Beth Phoenix	2.50	6.00
L10 Roman Reigns/The Rock	8.00	20.00
L11 R-Truth/John Cena	1.00	2.50
L12 Sasha Banks/Eddie Guerrero	4.00	10.00
L13 Miz/Ult.Warrior	3.00	8.00
L14 Bobby Lashley/Ron Simmons	2.00	5.00
L15 Randy Orton/Jake Roberts	2.50	6.00
L16 Dave Mastiff/Vader	.75	2.00
L17 Paul Heyman/Bobby Heenan	1.00	2.50

2021 Finest WWE Legacies Autographs

*ORANGE/25: UNPRICED DUE TO SCARCITY
*RED/5: UNPRICED DUE TO SCARCITY
*SUPER/1: UNPRICED DUE TO SCARCITY
RANDOMLY INSERTED INTO PACKS

LC Carmella	15.00	40.00
LAC Cesaro	10.00	25.00
LAS AJ Styles	12.00	30.00
LBB Bianca Belair	20.00	50.00
LJH Jeff Hardy	25.00	60.00
LMR Mandy Rose	30.00	75.00
LRR Rhea Ripley	25.00	60.00
LRT R-Truth	10.00	25.00
LTM The Miz	10.00	25.00

2021 Finest WWE Rumble Pops

*ORANGE/25: UNPRICED DUE TO SCARCITY
*RED/5: UNPRICED DUE TO SCARCITY
*SUPER/1: UNPRICED DUE TO SCARCITY
RANDOMLY INSERTED INTO PACKS

RP1 Mick Foley	2.00	5.00
RP2 John Cena	5.00	12.00
RP3 Diesel	1.50	4.00
RP4 Triple H	4.00	10.00
RP5 AJ Styles	3.00	8.00
RP6 Goldberg	4.00	10.00
RP7 Trish Stratus	5.00	12.00
RP8 Rey Mysterio	2.50	6.00
RP9 Becky Lynch	4.00	10.00
RP10 Edge	4.00	10.00

2021 Finest WWE Rumble Pops Autographs

*ORANGE/25: UNPRICED DUE TO SCARCITY
*RED/5: UNPRICED DUE TO SCARCITY
*SUPER/1: UNPRICED DUE TO SCARCITY
RANDOMLY INSERTED INTO PACKS

RG Goldberg	50.00	100.00
RAJ AJ Styles	10.00	25.00
RBL Becky Lynch	60.00	120.00
RMF Mick Foley	25.00	60.00
RRM Rey Mysterio	20.00	50.00

2021 Finest WWE Sole Survivors

*ORANGE/25: UNPRICED DUE TO SCARCITY
*RED/5: UNPRICED DUE TO SCARCITY
*SUPER/1: UNPRICED DUE TO SCARCITY
RANDOMLY INSERTED INTO PACKS

SS1 Hulk Hogan	4.00	10.00
SS2 Lex Luger	1.00	2.50
SS3 Razor Ramon	1.25	3.00
SS4 Randy Orton	2.50	6.00
SS5 Kofi Kingston	2.00	5.00
SS6 Dolph Ziggler	1.50	4.00
SS7 Roman Reigns	4.00	10.00
SS8 Asuka	3.00	8.00
SS9 Nia Jax	1.50	4.00
SS10 The British Bulldog	1.25	3.00

2021 Finest WWE Sole Survivors Autographs

*ORANGE/25: UNPRICED DUE TO SCARCITY
*RED/5: UNPRICED DUE TO SCARCITY
*SUPER/1: UNPRICED DUE TO SCARCITY
RANDOMLY INSERTED INTO PACKS

SA Asuka	20.00	50.00
SDZ Dolph Ziggler	6.00	15.00
SKK Kofi Kingston	8.00	20.00
SLL Lex Luger	15.00	40.00
SRR Roman Reigns	75.00	150.00

2021 Finest WWE Triple Autographs

COMMON AUTO	30.00	75.00

*ORANGE/25: UNPRICED DUE TO SCARCITY
*RED/5: UNPRICED DUE TO SCARCITY
RANDOMLY INSERTED INTO PACKS

TAAN The Usos/Reigns	250.00	500.00
TALA Barrett/McIntyre/Sheamus	30.00	75.00
TALF Mendoza/Wilde/Escobar	30.00	75.00
TAND Big E/Woods/Kingston	75.00	150.00

2021 Finest WWE Uncrowned Greatness

COMPLETE SET (20)	10.00	25.00

*ORANGE/25: UNPRICED DUE TO SCARCITY
*RED/5: UNPRICED DUE TO SCARCITY
*SUPER/1: UNPRICED DUE TO SCARCITY
RANDOMLY INSERTED INTO PACKS

UG1 Bam Bam Bigelow	1.25	3.00
UG2 Brutus The Barber Beefcake	.75	2.00
UG3 DDP	1.00	2.50
UG4 Dusty Rhodes	2.00	5.00
UG5 Harley Race	.60	1.50
UG6 Jake The Snake Roberts	1.00	2.50
UG7 Jerry The King Lawler	1.00	2.50
UG8 Junkyard Dog	.60	1.50
UG9 Lex Luger	.75	2.00
UG10 Ted DiBiase	1.25	3.00
UG11 Mr. Perfect	2.00	5.00
UG12 Ravishing Rick Rude	.75	2.00
UG13 Ricky The Dragon Steamboat	1.00	2.50
UG14 Rikishi	.75	2.00
UG15 Ron Simmons	1.00	2.50
UG16 Rowdy Roddy Piper	1.50	4.00
UG17 Scott Hall	1.00	2.50
UG18 The British Bulldog	1.00	2.50
UG19 Wade Barrett	.60	1.50
UG20 William Regal	1.00	2.50

2021 Finest WWE Uncrowned Greatness Autographs

*ORANGE/25: UNPRICED DUE TO SCARCITY
*RED/5: UNPRICED DUE TO SCARCITY
*SUPER/1: UNPRICED DUE TO SCARCITY
RANDOMLY INSERTED INTO PACKS

UR Rikishi	10.00	25.00
UBB Brutus The Barber Beefcake	12.00	30.00
UFR Ron Simmons	12.00	30.00
UJL Jerry The King Lawler	20.00	50.00
UJR Jake The Snake Roberts	25.00	60.00
ULL Lex Luger	15.00	40.00
URS Ricky The Dragon Steamboat	15.00	40.00
UTD Ted DiBiase	15.00	40.00
UWB Wade Barrett	10.00	25.00
UWR William Regal	10.00	25.00
UDDP DDP	20.00	50.00

2002 Fleer WWE Absolute Divas

COMPLETE SET (100)	15.00	40.00

*DIVA GEM: .75X TO 2X BASIC CARDS

1 Trish Stratus	1.25	3.00
2 Terri	.60	1.50
3 Ivory	.50	1.25
4 Lita	.75	2.00
5 Jackie RC	.50	1.25
6 Stacy Keibler RC	1.25	3.00
7 Torrie Wilson RC	1.25	3.00
8 Jacqueline	.30	.75
9 Molly	.30	.75
10 Jazz RC	.30	.75
11 Stephanie McMahon	.60	1.50
12 Nidia RC	.30	.75
13 Dawn Marie RC	.30	.75
14 Victoria RC	.60	1.50
15 Linda RC	.30	.75
16 Trish Stratus	1.25	3.00
17 Terri	1.25	3.00
18 Ivory	.50	1.25
19 Lita	.75	2.00
20 Jazz RC	.30	.75
21 Stacy Keibler RC	1.25	3.00
22 Torrie Wilson RC	1.25	3.00
23 Jacqueline	.30	.75
24 Molly	.30	.75
25 Stephanie McMahon	.60	1.50
26 Trish Stratus	1.25	3.00
27 Terri	.60	1.50
28 Ivory	.50	1.25
29 Lita	.75	2.00
30 Jackie RC	.50	1.25
31 Stacy Keibler RC	1.25	3.00
32 Torrie Wilson RC	1.25	3.00
33 Jacqueline	.30	.75
34 Molly	.30	.75
35 Jazz RC	.30	.75
36 Trish Stratus	1.25	3.00
37 Terri	.60	1.50
38 Ivory	.50	1.25
39 Lita	.75	2.00
40 Stacy Keibler RC	1.25	3.00
41 Torrie Wilson RC	1.25	3.00
42 Jacqueline	.30	.75
43 Molly	.30	.75
44 Jazz RC	.30	.75
45 Lita PS	.75	2.00
46 Bubba Ray PS	.20	.50
47 Jamie Noble PS RC	.20	.50
48 Matt Hardy PS	.30	.75
49 Brock Lesnar with Paul Heyman PS	1.25	3.00
50 William Regal PS	.20	.50
51 Triple H PS	.75	2.00
52 Vince McMahon PS	.50	1.25
53 Booker T PS	.50	1.25
54 Tajiri PS	.20	.50
55 Steven Richards PS	.20	.50
56 Chris Jericho PS	.30	.75
57 D-Von Dudley PS	.20	.50
58 Rob Van Dam PS RC	.50	1.25
59 The Rock PS	.75	2.00
60 Ric Flair PS	.60	1.50
61 Bradshaw PS	.30	.75
62 Hollywood Hulk Hogan PS	1.25	3.00
63 Hurricane PS RC	.20	.50
64 Jeff Hardy PS	.30	.75
65 Kurt Angle PS	.50	1.25
66 Jazz DM	.30	.75
67 Trish Stratus DM	1.25	3.00
68 Molly DM	.30	.75
69 Lita DM	.75	2.00
70 Stacy Keibler DM	1.25	3.00
71 Torrie Wilson DM	1.25	3.00
72 Trish Stratus DM	1.25	3.00
73 Jacqueline DM	.30	.75
74 Ivory DM	.50	1.25
75 Trish Stratus DM	1.25	3.00
76 Lita DM	.75	2.00
77 Terri DM	.60	1.50

78 Jacqueline DM	.30	.75
79 Molly DM	.30	.75
80 Dawn Marie DM	.30	.75
81 Lita GOF	.75	2.00
82 Jacqueline GOF	.30	.75
83 Molly GOF	.30	.75
84 Stacy Keibler GOF	1.25	3.00
85 Ivory GOF	.50	1.25
86 Trish Stratus GOF	1.25	3.00
87 Torrie Wilson GOF	1.25	3.00
88 Terri GOF	.60	1.50
89 Victoria GOF	.60	1.50
90 Jazz GOF	.30	.75
91 Trish Stratus GOF	1.25	3.00
92 Torrie Wilson GOF	1.25	3.00
93 Ivory GOF	.50	1.25
94 Lita GOF	.75	2.00
95 Dawn Marie GOF	.30	.75
96 Terri GOF	.60	1.50
97 Linda GOF	.30	.75
98 Stacy Keibler GOF	1.25	3.00
99 Molly GOF	.30	.75
100 Jackie GOF	.50	1.25

2002 Fleer WWE Absolute Divas Cover Shots

COMPLETE SET (10)	12.00	30.00
STATED ODDS 1:12 HOBBY		
1 Ivory	1.25	3.00
2 Jacqueline	.75	2.00
3 Lita	2.50	6.00
4 Dawn Marie	.75	2.00
5 Stacy Keibler (w/Dudley Boyz)	5.00	12.00
6 Terri	1.50	4.00
7 Torrie Wilson	3.00	8.00
8 Trish Stratus	5.00	12.00
9 Stephanie McMahon	6.00	15.00
10 Stacy & Torrie	4.00	10.00

2002 Fleer WWE Absolute Divas Diva Ink

STATED ODDS 1:198 HOBBY		
CARDS AVAILABLE BY EXCH ONLY		
NNO Dawn Marie	20.00	50.00
NNO Jackie	15.00	40.00
NNO Linda	10.00	25.00
NNO Stacy Keibler	125.00	250.00
NNO Torrie Wilson	100.00	200.00

2002 Fleer WWE Absolute Divas Inter-Actions

COMPLETE SET (20)	10.00	25.00
STATED ODDS 1:6 HOBBY		
1 Swimsuit Competition	1.50	4.00
2 Terri Wins Hardcore Title	.75	2.00
3 Six-Person Intergender Match	1.50	4.00
4 Bra & Panties Paddle on Pole Match	.75	2.00
5 Mixed Tag Team Match	1.50	4.00
6 Tag Team	1.50	4.00
7 Bikini Match	1.50	4.00
8 Table Match	.40	1.00
9 Mixed Tag Team Match	1.50	4.00
10 Tag Hardcore Women's Title Match	1.50	4.00
11 Tag Team	1.50	4.00
12 Judgment Day Match	1.50	4.00
13 Gravy Bowl Match	1.50	4.00
14 Tag Team Match	1.50	4.00
15 Wrestlemania X-8 Triple Threat	1.00	2.50
16 Tag Team	.40	1.00
17 Swimsuit Competition	.40	1.00
18 Women's Title Match-KOTR	1.50	4.00
19 Bra & Panties Match (Women's Title)	1.50	4.00
20 Lingerie Match	1.50	4.00

2002 Fleer WWE Absolute Divas Lip Service

STATED PRINT RUN 50 SER. #'d SETS		
CARDS AVAILABLE BY EXCH ONLY		
NNO Dawn Marie	50.00	100.00
NNO Jackie	20.00	50.00
NNO Linda	6.00	15.00
NNO Stacy Keibler	200.00	400.00
NNO Torrie Wilson	150.00	300.00

2002 Fleer WWE Absolute Divas Material Girls

STATED ODDS 1:36 HOBBY		
NNO Dawn Marie Skirt	4.00	10.00
NNO Ivory/Mat	2.00	5.00
NNO Jazz/Mat	2.00	5.00
NNO Lita/Mat	3.00	8.00
NNO Lita/Top	6.00	15.00
NNO Molly/Top	4.00	10.00
NNO Nidia/Shorts	4.00	10.00
NNO Stacy Keibler/Top	30.00	75.00
NNO Stacy Keibler/T-Shirt	15.00	40.00
NNO Terri/Outfit	6.00	15.00
NNO Torrie Wilson/Bikini	8.00	20.00
NNO Trish Stratus/Mat	10.00	25.00
NNO Trish Stratus/Top	20.00	50.00
NNO Victoria/Shorts	6.00	15.00

2002 Fleer WWE Absolute Divas Mini-Posters

COMPLETE SET (30)	8.00	20.00
STATED ODDS 1:1 HOBBY		
NNO Booker T	.40	1.00
NNO Brock Lesnar/Paul Heyman	1.00	2.50
NNO Chris Jericho	.25	.60
NNO Dawn Marie	.25	.60
NNO Hollywood Hulk Hogan	1.00	2.50
NNO Ivory	.40	1.00
NNO Jackie (orange border)	.40	1.00
NNO Jackie (yellow border)	.40	1.00
NNO Jacqueline	.25	.60
NNO Jazz	.25	.60
NNO Jeff Hardy	.25	.60
NNO Kurt Angle	.40	1.00
NNO Lita (blue border)	.60	1.50
NNO Lita (purple border)	.60	1.50
NNO Matt Hardy	.25	.60
NNO Molly	.25	.60
NNO Nidia	.25	.60
NNO Rob Van Dam	.40	1.00
NNO The Rock	.60	1.50
NNO Stacy Keibler (purple border)	1.00	2.50
NNO Stacy Keibler (red border)	1.00	2.50
NNO Stephanie McMahon	.50	1.25
NNO Terri (orange border)	.50	1.25
NNO Terri (purple border)	.50	1.25
NNO Torrie Wilson (black outfit)	1.00	2.50
NNO Torrie Wilson (blue outfit)	1.00	2.50
NNO Triple H	.60	1.50
NNO Trish Stratus (red border)	1.00	2.50
NNO Trish Stratus (yellow border)	1.00	2.50
NNO Victoria	.50	1.25

2002 Fleer WWE Absolute Divas Signed with a Kiss

STATED PRINT RUN 50 SER. #'d SETS		
AVAILABLE BY EXCH ONLY		
NNO Dawn Marie	60.00	120.00
NNO Ivory	20.00	50.00
NNO Jackie	25.00	60.00
NNO Linda	15.00	40.00
NNO Lita	50.00	100.00
NNO Stacy Keibler	500.00	1000.00
NNO Torrie Wilson	200.00	400.00

2002 Fleer WWE Absolute Divas Tropical Pleasures

COMPLETE SET (10)	12.00	30.00
STATED ODDS 1:12 HOBBY		
1 Ivory	1.25	3.00
2 Trish Stratus	3.00	8.00
3 Lita	2.00	5.00
4 Lita and Trish Stratus	3.00	8.00
5 Stacy Keibler	3.00	8.00
6 Terri	1.50	4.00
7 Torrie Wilson	3.00	8.00
8 Jacqueline	.75	2.00
9 Molly Holly	.75	2.00
10 Victoria	1.50	4.00

2002 Fleer WWE Absolute Divas Wardrobe Closet

STATED ODDS 1:23 HOBBY		
NNO Lita Jacket	6.00	15.00
NNO Molly/Top	4.00	10.00
NNO Nidia/Shorts	3.00	8.00
NNO Stacy Keibler/T-Shirt	15.00	40.00
NNO Torrie Wilson/Pants	12.00	30.00
NNO Torrie Wilson/Top	12.00	30.00
NNO Trish Stratus/Top	20.00	50.00
NNO Victoria/Top	5.00	12.00

2003 Fleer WWE Aggression

COMPLETE SET (89)	10.00	25.00
1 Goldberg	.75	2.00
2 Batista	.50	1.25
3 Booker T	.50	1.25
4 Bradshaw	.30	.75
5 Bubba Ray Dudley	.20	.50
6 Chief Morley	.20	.50
7 Chris Jericho	.30	.75
8 Chris Nowinski	.12	.30
9 Christian	.30	.75
10 D-Von Dudley	.20	.50
11 Eric Bischoff	.20	.50
12 Goldust	.12	.30
13 Ivory	.50	1.25
14 Jacqueline	.30	.75
15 Jazz	.20	.50
16 Jamal RC	.20	.50
17 Charlie Haas RC	.12	.30
18 Kane	.50	1.25
19 Kevin Nash	.60	1.50
20 Lance Storm	.12	.30
21 Al Snow	.12	.30
22 Lita	.75	2.00
23 Maven	.12	.30
24 Molly	.60	1.50
25 Randy Orton	.30	.75
26 Ric Flair	.60	1.50
27 Rico	.12	.30
28 Rob Van Dam	.50	1.25
29 Rosey RC	.12	.30
30 Scott Steiner	.60	1.50
31 Shawn Michaels	.75	2.00
32 Spike Dudley	.20	.50
33 Stacy Keibler	1.25	3.00
34 Steven Richards	.20	.50
35 Stone Cold Steve Austin	.75	2.00
36 Terri	.60	1.50
37 Test	.20	.50
38 The Hurricane	.12	.30
39 Tommy Dreamer	.12	.30
40 Trish Stratus	1.25	3.00
41 Triple H	.75	2.00
42 Victoria	.60	1.50
43 William Regal	.30	.75
44 Big Show	.50	1.25
45 Bill DeMott	.12	.30
46 Billy Kidman	.12	.30
47 Brock Lesnar	1.25	3.00
48 Chavo Guerrero	.20	.50
49 Chuck Palumbo	.20	.50
50 Chris Benoit	.30	.75
51 Crash	.12	.30
52 Dawn Marie	.60	1.50
53 Edge	.50	1.25
54 Eddie Guerrero	.60	1.50
55 Funaki	.20	.50
56 Sable	.75	2.00
57 Hulk Hogan	.75	2.00
58 Jamie Noble	.12	.30
59 John Cena	.75	2.00
60 Johnny Stamboli RC	.12	.30
61 Kurt Angle	.50	1.25
62 Mark Henry	.20	.50
63 Matt Hardy	.30	.75
64 Nathan Jones RC	.12	.30
65 Nidia	.30	.75
66 Nunzio RC	.12	.30
67 Rey Mysterio	.30	.75
68 Rhyno	.50	1.25
69 Rikishi	.30	.75
70 Shannon Moore RC	.12	.30
71 The Rock	.75	2.00
72 Tajiri	.12	.30
73 Torrie Wilson	1.25	3.00
74 Tazz	.20	.50
75 Undertaker	.60	1.50
76 A-Train	.12	.30
77 Paul Heyman	.12	.30
78 Brian Kendrick RC	.20	.50
79 Torrie Wilson DL	1.25	3.00
80 Sable DL	.75	2.00
81 Lita DL	.75	2.00
82 Ivory DL	.50	1.25
83 Jacqueline DL	.30	.75
84 Jazz DL	.20	.50
85 Molly DL	.60	1.50
86 Stacy Keibler DL	1.25	3.00
87 Terri DL	.60	1.50
88 Trish Stratus DL	1.25	3.00
89 Nidia DL	.30	.75

2003 Fleer WWE Aggression Matitude

COMPLETE SET (10)	10.00	25.00
STATED ODDS 1:12 HOBBY		
1 Triple H	2.00	5.00
2 The Rock	2.00	5.00
3 Brock Lesnar	3.00	8.00
4 Stone Cold Steve Austin	2.00	5.00
5 Kurt Angle	1.25	3.00
6 Chris Jericho	.75	2.00
7 Hulk Hogan	2.00	5.00
8 Scott Steiner	1.50	4.00
9 Rob Van Dam	1.25	3.00
10 Undertaker	1.50	4.00

2003 Fleer WWE Aggression Matitude Event Used

MR The Rock	4.00	10.00
MU Undertaker	3.00	8.00
MBL Brock Lesnar	3.00	8.00
MCJ Chris Jericho	2.50	6.00
MHH Hollywood Hulk Hogan	6.00	15.00
MKA Kurt Angle	4.00	10.00
MSA Stone Cold Steve Austin	3.00	8.00
MSS Scott Steiner	2.00	5.00
MTR Triple H	3.00	8.00
MRVD Rob Van Dam	2.00	5.00

2003 Fleer WWE Aggression Matitude Event Used Jumbo Images

STATED PRINT RUN 50 SER.#'d SETS		
MR The Rock	15.00	40.00
MU Undertaker	15.00	40.00
MBL Brock Lesnar	20.00	50.00
MCJ Chris Jericho	10.00	25.00
MHH Hollywood Hulk Hogan	25.00	60.00
MKA Kurt Angle	12.00	30.00
MSA Stone Cold Steve Austin	15.00	40.00
MSS Scott Steiner	12.00	30.00
MTH Triple H	15.00	40.00
MRVD Rob Van Dam	10.00	25.00

2003 Fleer WWE Aggression Queens of the Ring

COMPLETE SET (10)	25.00	60.00
STATED ODDS 1:8 HOBBY		
1 Lita	3.00	8.00
2 Ivory	2.00	5.00
3 Jacqueline	1.25	3.00
4 Jazz	.75	2.00
5 Molly	2.50	6.00
6 Stacy Keibler	5.00	12.00
7 Terri	2.50	6.00
8 Trish Stratus	5.00	12.00
9 Nidia	1.25	3.00
10 Torrie Wilson	5.00	12.00

2003 Fleer WWE Aggression Queens of the Ring Autographs

STATED PRINT RUN 50 SER.#'d SETS
SK AVAILABLE AT NATIONAL ONLY

SK STATED PRINT RUN 1500 CARDS

NNO Ivory/50	30.00	75.00
NNO Molly Holly/50	50.00	75.00
NNO Stacy Keibler/50	125.00	250.00
NNO Stacy Keibler NSCC	30.00	75.00
NNO Terri/50	60.00	125.00
NNO Trish Stratus/50	125.00	250.00

2003 Fleer WWE Aggression Queens of the Ring Event Used

STATED ODDS 1:115 HOBBY

QRI Ivory	10.00	25.00
QRJ Jacqueline	8.00	20.00
QRL Lita	12.00	30.00
QRN Nidia	8.00	20.00
QRT Terri	12.00	30.00
QRJA Jazz	8.00	20.00
QRMH Molly Holly	8.00	20.00
QRSK Stacy Keibler	20.00	50.00
QRTS Trish Stratus	15.00	40.00
QRTW Torrie Wilson	20.00	50.00

2003 Fleer WWE Aggression Ring Leaders

COMPLETE SET (15)	8.00	20.00
STATED ODDS 1:4 HOBBY		
1 Triple H	1.25	3.00
2 The Rock	1.25	3.00
3 Brock Lesnar	2.00	5.00
4 Stone Cold Steve Austin	1.25	3.00
5 The Hurricane	.20	.50
6 Undertaker	1.00	2.50
7 Kane	.75	2.00
8 Chris Jericho	.50	1.25
9 Hulk Hogan	1.25	3.00
10 Scott Steiner	1.00	2.50
11 Rob Van Dam	.75	2.00
12 Shawn Michaels	1.25	3.00
13 Chris Benoit	.50	1.25
14 Edge	.75	2.00
15 Booker T	.75	2.00

2003 Fleer WWE Aggression Ring Leaders Event Used

STATED ODDS 1:29 HOBBY

RLE Edge	6.00	15.00
RLH The Hurricane	3.00	8.00
RLK Kane	4.00	10.00
RLR The Rock	8.00	20.00
RLU Undertaker	6.00	15.00
RLBL Brock Lesnar	8.00	20.00
RLBT Booker T	3.00	8.00
RLCB Chris Benoit	4.00	10.00
RLCJ Chris Jericho	4.00	10.00
RLHH Hollywood Hulk Hogan	8.00	20.00
RLSA Stone Cold Steve Austin	8.00	20.00
RLSM Shawn Michaels	4.00	10.00
RLSS Scott Steiner	4.00	10.00
RLTH Triple H	6.00	15.00
RLRVD Rob Van Dam	4.00	10.00

2004 Fleer WWE Chaos

COMPLETE SET (95)	10.00	25.00
UNOPENED BOX (24 PACKS)		
UNOPENED PACK (5 CARDS)		
*GOLD: 1X TO 2.5X BASIC CARDS		
1 Stone Cold Steve Austin	1.25	3.00
2 Test	.30	.75
3 Jazz	.50	1.25
4 Kurt Angle	.75	2.00
5 Batista	.75	2.00
6 The Hurricane	.25	.60
7 Rey Mysterio	.50	1.25
8 Steven Richards	.30	.75
9 Goldberg	1.50	4.00
10 Chris Benoit	.50	1.25
11 Doug Basham	.20	.50
12 Torrie Wilson	2.00	5.00
13 Booker T	.75	2.00
14 Lance Storm	.20	.50
15 Rhyno	.75	2.00
16 Matt Hardy	.50	1.25
17 Maven	.20	.50
18 Rico	.20	.50
19 Rodney Mack RC	.20	.50
20 Jacqueline	.60	1.50
21 Rosey	.20	.50
22 Rikishi	.50	1.25
23 Scotty 2 Hotty	.30	.75
24 Mark Jindrak RC	.20	.50
25 Spike Dudley	.30	.75
26 Shawn Michaels	1.25	3.00
27 Paul Heyman	.20	.50
28 Val Venis	.30	.75
29 Shannon Moore	.20	.50
30 Triple H	1.25	3.00
31 Rob Conway RC	.20	.50
32 Edge	.75	2.00
33 A-Train	.20	.50
34 Big Show	.75	2.00
35 Theodore Long	.20	.50
36 Shelton Benjamin RC	.20	.50
37 Billy Gunn	.25	.60
38 Billy Kidman	.20	.50
39 Bradshaw	.50	1.25
40 Kane	.75	2.00
41 Charlie Haas	.20	.50
42 Chavo Guerrero	.30	.75
43 The Rock	1.25	3.00
44 Danny Basham RC	.20	.50
45 Chuck Palumbo	.30	.75
46 D-Von Dudley	.30	.75
47 Eddie Guerrero	1.00	2.50
48 Rene Dupree RC	.30	.75
49 Tajiri	.20	.50
50 Undertaker	1.00	2.50
51 Rob Van Dam	.75	2.00
52 Ric Flair	1.00	2.50
53 Matt Morgan RC	.25	.60
54 Eric Bischoff	.30	.75
55 Garrison Cade RC	.20	.50
56 Funaki	.30	.75
57 Brock Lesnar	2.00	5.00
58 Chris Jericho	.50	1.25
59 Hardcore Holly	.30	.75
60 Ultimo Dragon	.20	.50
61 Jamie Noble	.20	.50
62 Scott Steiner	1.00	2.50
63 John Cena	1.25	3.00
64 Randy Orton	.50	1.25
65 Johnny Stamboli	.20	.50
66 Nunzio	.20	.50
67 Bubba Ray Dudley	.30	.75
68 Mark Henry	.30	.75
69 Christian	.60	1.50
70 Jazz SI	.50	1.25
71 Torrie Wilson SI	2.00	5.00
72 Trish Stratus SI	2.00	5.00
73 Dawn Marie SI	.50	1.25
74 Stacy Keibler SI	2.00	5.00
75 Nidia SI	.50	1.25
76 Shaniqua SI RC	.50	1.25
77 Lita SI	1.25	3.00
78 Jacqueline SI	.60	1.50
79 Victoria SI	1.00	2.50
80 Terri SI	1.00	2.50
81 Ivory SI	.75	2.00
82 Gail Kim SI RC	.75	2.00
83 Miss Jackie SI	.75	2.00
84 Molly SI	1.00	2.50
85 Sable SI	1.25	3.00
86 Brock Lesnar PI	2.00	5.00
87 Triple H PI	1.25	3.00
88 Kurt Angle PI	.75	2.00
89 Batista PI	.75	2.00
90 Test PI	.30	.75
91 Randy Orton PI	.50	1.25
92 Scott Steiner PI	1.00	2.50
93 Booker T PI	.75	2.00
94 The Rock PI	1.25	3.00
95 Goldberg PI	1.50	4.00

2004 Fleer WWE Chaos Controlled Chaos

COMPLETE SET (15)	8.00	20.00
STATED ODDS 1:6 HOBBY AND RETAIL		
1 Brock Lesnar	2.00	5.00
2 Chris Benoit	.50	1.25
3 Triple H	1.25	3.00
4 Kurt Angle	.75	2.00
5 Kane	.75	2.00
6 Shawn Michaels	1.25	3.00
7 Edge	.75	2.00
8 Chris Jericho	.50	1.25
9 Stone Cold	1.25	3.00
10 Big Poppa Pump	1.00	2.50
11 Undertaker	1.00	2.50
12 Rob Van Dam	.75	2.00
13 Ric Flair	1.00	2.50
14 The Rock	1.25	3.00
15 Goldberg	1.50	4.00

2004 Fleer WWE Chaos Showing Off

COMPLETE SET (16)	12.50	30.00
STATED ODDS 1:4 HOBBY AND RETAIL		
1 Lita	1.50	4.00
2 Jacqueline	.75	2.00
3 Ivory	1.00	2.50
4 Dawn Marie	.60	1.50
5 Stacy Keibler	2.50	6.00
6 Nidia	.60	1.50
7 Molly Holly	1.25	3.00
8 Jazz	.60	1.50
9 Torrie Wilson	2.50	6.00
10 Victoria	1.25	3.00
11 Terri	1.25	3.00
12 Trish Stratus	2.50	6.00
13 Sable	1.50	4.00
14 Miss Jackie	1.00	2.50
15 Shaniqua	.60	1.50
16 Gail Kim	1.00	2.50

2004 Fleer WWE Chaos Showing Off Autographs

STATED PRINT RUN 25 SER.#'d SETS

NNO Dawn Marie	50.00	100.00
NNO Gail Kim	60.00	125.00
NNO Ivory	60.00	125.00
NNO Jacqueline	30.00	75.00
NNO Jazz	50.00	100.00
NNO Lita	75.00	150.00
NNO Molly	50.00	100.00
NNO Miss Jackie	60.00	125.00
NNO Nidia	30.00	75.00
NNO Sable	75.00	150.00
NNO Shaniqua	30.00	75.00
NNO Stacy Keibler	100.00	200.00
NNO Terri	100.00	200.00
NNO Torrie Wilson	60.00	120.00
NNO Trish Stratus	125.00	250.00
NNO Victoria	30.00	75.00

2004 Fleer WWE Chaos Showing Off Memorabilia

STATED ODDS 1:36 HOBBY; 1:72 RETAIL

SOI Ivory	5.00	12.00
SOJ Jacqueline	4.00	10.00
SOJ Jazz	4.00	10.00
SOL Lita	6.00	15.00
SOM Molly	5.00	12.00
SON Nidia	4.00	10.00
SOS Sable	6.00	15.00
SOS Shaniqua	4.00	10.00
SOT Terri	6.00	15.00
SOV Victoria	5.00	12.00
SODM Dawn Marie	5.00	12.00
SOGK Gail Kim	6.00	15.00
SOMJ Miss Jackie	6.00	15.00
SOSK Stacy Keibler	10.00	25.00
SOTS Trish Stratus	10.00	25.00
SOTW Torrie Wilson	10.00	25.00

2004 Fleer WWE Chaos Tuff Guys

COMPLETE SET (12)	12.00	30.00
STATED ODDS 1:12 HOBBY AND RETAIL		
1 The Rock	2.50	6.00
2 Eddie Guerrero	2.00	5.00
3 Triple H	2.50	6.00
4 Kurt Angle	1.50	4.00
5 Undertaker	2.00	5.00
6 Shawn Michaels	2.50	6.00
7 Rob Van Dam	1.50	4.00
8 Stone Cold Steve Austin	2.50	6.00
9 Chris Benoit	1.00	2.50
10 Brock Lesnar	4.00	10.00
11 Chris Jericho	1.00	2.50
12 Kane	1.50	4.00

2004 Fleer WWE Chaos Tuff Guys Event Used Mat

STATED ODDS 1:8 RETAIL

TGK Kane	2.00	5.00
TGU Undertaker	2.50	6.00
TGBL Brock Lesnar	6.00	15.00
TGCB Chris Benoit	1.50	4.00
TGCJ Chris Jericho	1.50	4.00
TGEG Eddie Guerrero	1.50	4.00
TGKA Kurt Angle	2.00	5.00
TGRV Rob Van Dam	1.50	4.00
TGSA Stone Cold Steve Austin	3.00	8.00
TGSM Shawn Michaels	2.50	6.00
TGTH Triple H	2.50	6.00
TGTR The Rock	3.00	8.00

2004 Fleer WWE Chaos Tuff Guys Event Worn Memorabilia

STATED ODDS 1:12 HOBBY EXCLUSIVE

TGK Kane	3.00	8.00
TGU Undertaker	4.00	10.00
TGBL Brock Lesnar	5.00	12.00
TGCB Chris Benoit	5.00	15.00
TGCJ Chris Jericho	2.50	6.00
TGEG Eddie Guerrero	3.00	10.00
TGKA Kurt Angle	4.00	10.00
TGRV Rob Van Dam	2.50	6.00
TGSA Stone Cold Steve Austin	5.00	12.00
TGSM Shawn Michaels	3.00	8.00
TGTH Triple H	4.00	10.00
TGTR The Rock	5.00	12.00

2003 Fleer WWE Divine Divas

COMPLETE SET (90)	10.00	25.00
1 Lita	.60	1.50
2 Jacqueline	.25	.60
3 Ivory	.40	1.00
4 Dawn Marie	.50	1.25
5 Stacy Keibler	1.00	2.50
6 Nidia	.25	.60
7 Molly	.50	1.25
8 Jazz	.15	.40
9 Torrie Wilson	1.00	2.50
10 Victoria	.50	1.25
11 Terri	.50	1.25
12 Trish Stratus	1.00	2.50
13 Sable	.60	1.50
14 Lita	.60	1.50
15 Jacqueline	.25	.60
16 Ivory	.40	1.00
17 Dawn Marie	.50	1.25
18 Stacy Keibler	1.00	2.50
19 Nidia	.25	.60
20 Molly	.50	1.25
21 Jazz	.15	.40
22 Torrie Wilson	1.00	2.50
23 Victoria	.50	1.25
24 Terri	.50	1.25
25 Trish Stratus	1.00	2.50
26 Sable	.60	1.50
27 Lita	.60	1.50
28 Jacqueline	.25	.60
29 Ivory	.40	1.00
30 Dawn Marie	.50	1.25
31 Stacy Keibler	1.00	2.50
32 Nidia	.25	.60
33 Molly	.50	1.25
34 Jazz	.15	.40
35 Torrie Wilson	1.00	2.50
36 Victoria	.50	1.25
37 Terri	.50	1.25
38 Trish Stratus	1.00	2.50
39 Sable	.60	1.50
40 Lita	.60	1.50
41 Jacqueline	.25	.60

Card	Low	High
42 Ivory	.40	1.00
43 Dawn Marie	.50	1.25
44 Stacy Keibler	1.00	2.50
45 Nidia	.25	.60
46 Molly	.50	1.25
47 Jazz	.15	.40
48 Torrie Wilson	1.00	2.50
49 Victoria	.50	1.25
50 Terri	.50	1.25
51 Trish Stratus	1.00	2.50
52 Sable	.60	1.50
53 Lita	.60	1.50
54 Jacqueline	.25	.60
55 Ivory	.40	1.00
56 Dawn Marie	.50	1.25
57 Stacy Keibler	1.00	2.50
58 Nidia	.25	.60
59 Molly	.50	1.25
60 Jazz	.15	.40
61 Torrie Wilson	1.00	2.50
62 Victoria	.50	1.25
63 Terri	.50	1.25
64 Trish Stratus	1.00	2.50
65 Sable	.60	1.50
66 Lita	.60	1.50
67 Jacqueline	.25	.60
68 Ivory	.40	1.00
69 Dawn Marie	.50	1.25
70 Stacy Keibler	1.00	2.50
71 Nidia	.25	.60
72 Molly	.50	1.25
73 Jazz	.15	.40
74 Torrie Wilson	1.00	2.50
75 Victoria	.50	1.25
76 Terri	.50	1.25
77 Trish Stratus	1.00	2.50
78 Sable	.60	1.50
79 Triple H/Victoria DT	.60	1.50
80 Trish Stratus/The Rock DT	1.00	2.50
81 Sable/Brock Lesnar DT	1.00	2.50
82 Lita/Edge DT	.60	1.50
83 Stacy Keibler/Scott Steiner DT	1.00	2.50
84 Terri/Stone Cold Steve Austin DT	.60	1.50
85 Chris Jericho/Ivory DT	.25	.60
86 Kurt Angle/Torrie Wilson DT	1.00	2.50
87 Booker T/Jazz DT	.40	1.00
88 Gail Kim/Kane DT	.40	1.00
89 Nidia/Jamie Noble DT	.25	.60
90 Zach Gowen/Stephanie DT	.50	1.25

2003 Fleer WWE Divine Divas Dress Code Memorabilia

STATED ODDS 1:288 HOBBY

Card	Low	High
NNO Dawn Marie	10.00	25.00
NNO Ivory	30.00	75.00
NNO Molly	12.00	30.00
NNO Nidia	12.00	30.00
NNO Sable	20.00	50.00
NNO Stacy Keibler	50.00	100.00
NNO Trish Stratus	25.00	60.00
NNO Victoria	10.00	25.00

2003 Fleer WWE Divine Divas Hugs and Kisses

Card	Low	High
COMPLETE SET (14)	15.00	40.00
STATED ODDS 1:8		
NNO Dawn Marie	1.50	4.00
NNO Gail Kim	1.25	3.00
NNO Ivory	1.25	3.00
NNO Lita	2.00	5.00
NNO Miss Jackie	1.25	3.00
NNO Molly	1.50	4.00
NNO Nidia	.75	2.00
NNO Sable	2.00	5.00
NNO Shaniqua	.75	2.00
NNO Stacy Keibler	3.00	8.00
NNO Terri	1.50	4.00
NNO Torrie Wilson	3.00	8.00
NNO Trish Stratus	3.00	8.00
NNO Victoria	1.50	4.00

2003 Fleer WWE Divine Divas Hugs and Kisses Autographs

STATED PRINT RUN 25 SER #'d SETS

Card	Low	High
NNO Dawn Marie	50.00	100.00
NNO Gail Kim	60.00	125.00
NNO Ivory	30.00	75.00
NNO Jazz	30.00	75.00
NNO Miss Jackie	60.00	125.00
NNO Lita	75.00	150.00
NNO Molly	50.00	100.00
NNO Nidia	30.00	75.00
NNO Sable	125.00	250.00
NNO Shaniqua	30.00	75.00
NNO Stacy Keibler	200.00	350.00
NNO Terri	100.00	200.00
NNO Trish Stratus	125.00	250.00
NNO Victoria	60.00	125.00
NNO Torrie Wilson	125.00	250.00

2003 Fleer WWE Divine Divas On Location

Card	Low	High
COMPLETE SET (16)	20.00	50.00
STATED ODDS 1:12 HOBBY AND RETAIL		
1 Jacqueline	1.00	2.50
2 Jazz	.60	1.50
3 Nidia	1.00	2.50
4 Dawn Marie	2.00	5.00
5 Torrie Wilson	4.00	10.00
6 Lita	2.50	6.00
7 Sable	2.50	6.00
8 Ivory	1.50	4.00
9 Stacy Keibler	4.00	10.00
10 Trish Stratus	4.00	10.00
11 Terri	2.00	5.00
12 Victoria	2.00	5.00
13 Molly	2.00	5.00
14 Miss Jackie	1.50	4.00
15 Shaniqua	1.00	2.50
16 Gail Kim	1.50	4.00

2003 Fleer WWE Divine Divas On Location Memorabilia

STATED ODDS 1:24 HOBBY: 1:96 RETAIL

Card	Low	High
NNO Dawn Marie	5.00	12.00
NNO Ivory	6.00	15.00
NNO Miss Jackie	6.00	15.00
NNO Molly	5.00	12.00
NNO Nidia	4.00	10.00
NNO Sable	8.00	20.00
NNO Shaniqua	4.00	10.00
NNO Victoria	6.00	15.00

2003 Fleer WWE Divine Divas With Love

Card	Low	High
1 Lita	1.25	3.00
2 Jacqueline	.50	1.25
3 Ivory	.75	2.00
4 Dawn Marie	1.00	2.50
5 Stacy Keibler	2.00	5.00
6 Nidia	.50	1.25
7 Molly	1.00	2.50
8 Jazz	.30	.75
9 Torrie Wilson	2.00	5.00
10 Victoria	1.00	2.50
11 Terri	1.00	2.50
12 Trish Stratus	2.00	5.00
13 Sable	1.25	3.00
14 Shaniqua	.50	1.25
15 Gail Kim	.75	2.00
16 Miss Jackie	.75	2.00

2003 Fleer WWE Divine Divas With Love Autographs

STATED PRINT RUN 100 SER.#'d SETS

Card	Low	High
NNO Dawn Marie	12.00	30.00
NNO Gail Kim	15.00	40.00
NNO Ivory	20.00	50.00
NNO Jacqueline	12.00	30.00
NNO Jazz	12.00	30.00
NNO Miss Jackie	15.00	40.00
NNO Molly	15.00	40.00
NNO Nidia	12.00	30.00
NNO Sable	100.00	200.00
NNO Shaniqua	12.00	30.00
NNO Stacy Keibler	75.00	150.00
NNO Trish Stratus	50.00	100.00
NNO Victoria	15.00	40.00

2003 Fleer WWE Divine Divas With Love Memorabilia

Card	Low	High
NNO Dawn Marie	4.00	10.00
NNO Gail Kim	6.00	15.00
NNO Ivory	6.00	15.00
NNO Jacqueline	3.00	8.00
NNO Miss Jackie	5.00	12.00
NNO Molly	4.00	10.00
NNO Nidia	3.00	8.00
NNO Sable	15.00	40.00
NNO Shaniqua	3.00	8.00
NNO Stacy Keibler	20.00	50.00
NNO Trish Stratus	8.00	20.00
NNO Victoria	4.00	10.00

2003 Fleer WWE Divine Divas Promo

Card	Low	High
5 Stacy Keibler	1.50	4.00

2004 Fleer WWE Divine Divas 2005

Card	Low	High
COMPLETE SET (80)	10.00	25.00
1 Lita	.50	1.25
2 Ivory	.30	.75
3 Dawn Marie	.20	.50
4 Stacy Keibler	.75	2.00
5 Nidia	.20	.50
6 Molly Holly	.40	1.00
7 Jazz	.20	.50
8 Torrie Wilson	.75	2.00
9 Victoria	.40	1.00
10 Trish Stratus	.75	2.00
11 Sable	.50	1.25
12 Miss Jackie	.30	.75
13 Gail Kim RC	.30	.75
14 Lita	.50	1.25
15 Ivory	.30	.75
16 Dawn Marie	.20	.50
17 Stacy Keibler	.75	2.00
18 Nidia	.20	.50
19 Molly Holly	.40	1.00
20 Jazz	.20	.50
21 Torrie Wilson	.75	2.00
22 Victoria	.40	1.00
23 Trish Stratus	.75	2.00
24 Sable	.50	1.25
25 Miss Jackie	.30	.75
26 Gail Kim RC	.30	.75
27 Lita	.50	1.25
28 Ivory	.30	.75
29 Dawn Marie	.20	.50
30 Stacy Keibler	.75	2.00
31 Torrie Wilson	.20	.50
32 Molly Holly	.40	1.00
33 Jazz	.20	.50
34 Torrie Wilson	.75	2.00
35 Victoria	.40	1.00
36 Trish Stratus	.75	2.00
37 Sable	.50	1.25
38 Miss Jackie	.30	.75
39 Gail Kim RC	.30	.75
40 Lita	.50	1.25
41 Ivory	.30	.75
42 Dawn Marie	.20	.50
43 Stacy Keibler	.75	2.00
44 Stacy Keibler	.75	2.00
45 Molly Holly	.40	1.00
46 Jazz	.20	.50
47 Torrie Wilson	.75	2.00
48 Victoria	.40	1.00
49 Trish Stratus	.75	2.00
50 Sable	.50	1.25
51 Miss Jackie	.30	.75
52 Gail Kim RC	.30	.75
53 Trish/Victoria CF	.75	2.00
54 Jazz & Gail Kim CF	.30	.75
55 Victoria & Molly Holly CF	.40	1.00
56 Sable/Torri/Stacy/Jackie CF	.75	2.00
57 Gail Kim & Lita CF	.50	1.25
58 Molly Holly & Gail Kim CF	.40	1.00
59 Jazz & Trish Stratus CF	.75	2.00
60 Lita & Trish Stratus CF	.75	2.00
61 Stacy Keibler & Miss Jackie CF	.75	2.00
62 Victoria & Gail Kim CF	.40	1.00
63 Molly Holly & Trish Stratus CF	.75	2.00
64 Sable & Torrie Wilson CF	.75	2.00
65 Victoria & Jazz CF	.40	1.00
66 Triple H OS	.50	1.25
67 Chris Jericho OS	.20	.50
68 Kurt Angle OS	.30	.75
69 Christian OS	.25	.60
70 Eric Bischoff OS	.12	.30
71 Shawn Michaels OS	.50	1.25
72 Eddie Guerrero OS	.40	1.00
73 Undertaker OS	.40	1.00
74 Booker T OS	.30	.75
75 Tyson Tomko OS RC	.12	.30
76 Chris Benoit OS	.20	.50
77 Eugene OS RC	.12	.30
78 Randy Orton OS	.20	.50
79 Edge OS	.30	.75
80 Babe of the Year Trish Stratus	.75	2.00

2004 Fleer WWE Divine Divas 2005 Body and Soul

Card	Low	High
COMPLETE SET (10)	8.00	20.00
STATED ODDS 1:8 HOBBY		
1 Dawn Marie	.60	1.50
2 Stacy Keibler	2.50	6.00
3 Torrie Wilson	2.50	6.00
4 Trish Stratus	2.50	6.00
5 Victoria	1.25	3.00
6 Miss Jackie	1.00	2.50
7 Lita	1.50	4.00
8 Ivory	1.00	2.50
9 Nidia	.60	1.50
10 Sable	1.50	4.00

2004 Fleer WWE Divine Divas 2005 Body and Soul Memorabilia

STATED ODDS 1:288 HOBBY

Card	Low	High
BSDM Dawn Marie	4.00	10.00
BSIV Ivory	6.00	15.00
BSLI Lita	8.00	20.00
BSMJ Miss Jackie	5.00	12.00
BSNI Nidia	4.00	10.00
BSSA Sable	8.00	20.00
BSSK Stacy Keibler	10.00	25.00
BSTS Trish Stratus	10.00	25.00
BSTW Torrie Wilson	8.00	20.00
BSVI Victoria	6.00	15.00

2004 Fleer WWE Divine Divas 2005 Divas Uncensored

Card	Low	High
COMPLETE SET (13)	15.00	40.00
STATED ODDS 1:12 HOBBY		
1 Dawn Marie	1.25	3.00
2 Jazz	1.25	3.00
3 Sable	3.00	8.00
4 Nidia	1.25	3.00
5 Victoria	2.50	6.00
6 Gail Kim	2.00	5.00
7 Ivory	2.00	5.00
8 Molly Holly	2.50	6.00
9 Trish Stratus	5.00	12.00
10 Lita	3.00	8.00
11 Stacy Keibler	5.00	12.00
12 Torrie Wilson	5.00	12.00
13 Miss Jackie	2.00	5.00

2004 Fleer WWE Divine Divas 2005 Divas Uncensored Memorabilia

STATED ODDS 1:24 HOBBY

Card	Low	High
DUL Lita	6.00	15.00
DUDM Dawn Marie	4.00	10.00
DUGK Gail Kim	4.00	10.00
DUIV Ivory	5.00	12.00
DUJA Jazz	3.00	8.00
DUMH Molly Holly	4.00	10.00
DUMJ Miss Jackie	5.00	12.00
DUNI Nidia	3.00	8.00
DUSA Sable	6.00	15.00
DUSK Stacy Keibler	12.00	30.00

DUTS Trish Stratus 8.00 20.00
DUTW Torrie Wilson 12.00 30.00
DUVI Victoria 4.00 10.00

2004 Fleer WWE Divine Divas 2005 Femme Physique

COMPLETE SET (13) 8.00 20.00
STATED ODDS 1:4 HOBBY

1 Lita 1.25 3.00
2 Ivory .75 2.00
3 Dawn Marie .50 1.25
4 Stacy Keibler 2.00 5.00
5 Nidia .50 1.25
6 Molly Holly 1.00 2.50
7 Jazz .50 1.25
8 Torrie Wilson 2.00 5.00
9 Victoria 1.00 2.50
10 Trish Stratus 2.00 5.00
11 Sable 1.25 3.00
12 Miss Jackie .75 2.00
13 Gail Kim .75 2.00

2004 Fleer WWE Divine Divas 2005 Femme Physique Memorabilia

STATED ODDS 1:28 HOBBY

FPL Lita 6.00 15.00
FPDM Dawn Marie 3.00 8.00
FPGK Gail Kim 3.00 8.00
FPIV Ivory 4.00 10.00
FPJA Jazz 3.00 8.00
FPMH Molly Holly 4.00 10.00
FPMJ Miss Jackie 5.00 12.00
FPNI Nidia 3.00 8.00
FPSA Sable 6.00 15.00
FPSK Stacy Keibler 8.00 20.00
FPTS Trish Stratus 8.00 20.00
FPTW Torrie Wilson 8.00 20.00
FPVI Victoria 4.00 10.00

2004 Fleer WWE Divine Divas 2005 Hugs and Kisses Autographs

STATED PRINT RUN 15 SER.#'d SETS

HKDM Dawn Marie 50.00 100.00
HKIV Ivory 60.00 125.00
HKLI Lita 150.00 300.00
HKMJ Miss Jackie 60.00 125.00
HKNI Nidia 50.00 100.00
HKSA Sable 250.00 500.00
HKSK Stacy Keibler 250.00 500.00
HKTM Torrie Wilson 125.00 250.00
HKTS Trish Stratus 200.00 400.00
HKVI Victoria 60.00 125.00

2004 Fleer WWE Divine Divas 2005 With Love Wardrobe Autographs

STATED PRINT RUN 5 SER #'d SETS
UNPRICED DUE TO SCARCITY

WLDM Dawn Marie
WLIV Ivory
WLLI Lita
WLMJ Miss Jackie
WLNI Nidia
WLSA Sable
WLSK Stacy Keibler
WLTS Trish Stratus
WLTW Torrie Wilson
WLVI Victoria

2002 Fleer WWE KB Toys SmackDown! Shut Your Mouth

1 Kurt Angle 2.00 5.00
2 The Rock 5.00 12.00
3 Undertaker 2.50 6.00
4 Trish Stratus 4.00 10.00
5 Stacy Keibler 4.00 10.00
6 Triple H 2.50 6.00
7 Chris Jericho 2.00 5.00
8 Booker T 1.25 3.00
9 Rob Van Dam 1.25 3.00
10 Hollywood Hulk Hogan 4.00 10.00

2002 Fleer WWE Raw vs. SmackDown

COMPLETE SET (90) 12.00 30.00

1 The Rock .75 2.00
2 Undertaker .60 1.50
3 Kurt Angle .50 1.25
4 Kevin Nash .60 1.50
5 Jim Ross .20 .50
6 X-Pac .20 .50
7 Chris Benoit .30 .75
8 Kane .50 1.25
9 Hollywood Hulk Hogan 1.25 3.00
10 Rob Van Dam RC .50 1.25
11 Billy Gunn .20 .50
12 Chuck Palumbo RC .20 .50
13 Booker T .50 1.25
14 Edge .50 1.25
15 Big Show .50 1.25
16 Rikishi .30 .75
17 Bubba Ray Dudley .20 .50
18 D-Von Dudley .20 .50
19 Brock Lesnar 6.00 15.00
20 Mark Henry .20 .50
21 William Regal .20 .50
22 Maven RC .12 .30
23 Lita .75 2.00
24 Billy Kidman .12 .30
25 Bradshaw .30 .75
26 Tajiri .20 .50
27 Steven Richards .20 .50
28 Chris Jericho .30 .75
29 Matt Hardy .30 .75
30 Ivory .50 1.25
31 Raven .20 .50
32 Albert .12 .30
33 Jeff Hardy .30 .75
34 The Hurricane RC .20 .50
35 Jerry Lawler .30 .75
36 Al Snow .20 .50
37 D'Lo Brown .12 .30
38 Diamond Dallas Page .20 .50
39 Shawn Stasiak .12 .30
40 Torrie Wilson RC 1.25 3.00
41 Terri .60 1.50
42 Scotty 2 Hotty .20 .50
43 Jacqueline .30 .75
44 Stacy Keibler RC 1.25 3.00
45 Goldust .12 .30
46 Christian .30 .75
47 Trish Stratus 1.25 3.00
48 Test .20 .50
49 Justin Credible .12 .30
50 Faarooq .12 .30
51 Boss Man .12 .30
52 Tazz .20 .50
53 Tommy Dreamer RC .12 .30
54 Hardcore Holly .20 .50
55 Crash .12 .30
56 The Big Valbowski .20 .50
57 Molly Holly .30 .75
58 Perry Saturn .12 .30
59 Spike Dudley .20 .50
60 Lance Storm RC .12 .30
61 Triple H .75 2.00
62 Vince McMahon .50 1.25
63 Ric Flair .60 1.50
64 nWo .20 .50
65 Rico RC .12 .30
66 Debra QR .30 .75
67 Jazz QR RC .30 .75
68 Lita QR .75 2.00
69 Ivory QR .50 1.25
70 Terri QR .60 1.50
71 Torrie Wilson QR 1.25 3.00
72 Jacqueline QR .30 .75
73 Stacy Keibler QR 1.25 3.00
74 Trish Stratus QR 1.25 3.00
75 Molly Holly QR .30 .75
76 Rob Van Dam/Kurt Angle RVS .50 1.25
77 Big Show/Rikishi RVS .50 1.25
78 Undertaker/DDP RVS .60 1.50
79 Stone Cold/The Rock RVS 2.00 5.00
80 William Regal/Chris Jericho RVS .20 .50
81 Bubba Ray & D-Von Dudley RVS .20 .50
82 Trish Stratus/Torrie Wilson RVS 1.25 3.00
83 Lita/Stacy Keibler RVS 1.25 3.00
84 Jacqueline/Ivory RVS .50 1.25
85 Raven/Tajiri RVS .20 .50
86 Brock Lesnar/The Rock RVS 5.00 12.00
87 Booker T/Edge RVS .50 1.25
88 Goldust/The Hurricane RVS .20 .50
89 Bradshaw/Faarooq RVS .30 .75
90 Kane/Hulk Hogan RVS 1.25 3.00

2002 Fleer WWE Raw vs. SmackDown Catch Phrases

COMPLETE SET (15) 6.00 15.00
STATED ODDS 1:4 HOBBY

CP1 The Rock 1.25 3.00
CP2 Ric Flair 1.00 2.50
CP3 Kurt Angle .75 2.00
CP4 Stone Cold Steve Austin 1.25 3.00
CP5 Tazz .30 .75
CP6 Raven .30 .75
CP7 Trish Stratus 2.00 5.00
CP8 Triple H 1.25 3.00
CP9 The Big Valbowski .30 .75
CP10 Booker T .75 2.00
CP11 Chris Jericho .50 1.25
CP12 Hollywood Hulk Hogan 2.00 5.00
CP13 nWo .30 .75
CP14 Jim Ross .30 .75
CP15 Chris Benoit .50 1.25

2002 Fleer WWE Raw vs. SmackDown Exposure

COMPLETE SET (10) 8.00 20.00
STATED ODDS 1:8 HOBBY

XP1 Debra .60 1.50
XP2 Ivory 1.00 2.50
XP3 Jacqueline .60 1.50
XP4 Jazz .60 1.50
XP5 Lita 1.50 4.00
XP6 Molly Holly .60 1.50
XP7 Stacy Keibler 2.50 6.00
XP8 Terri 1.25 3.00
XP9 Torrie Wilson 2.50 6.00
XP10 Trish Stratus 2.50 6.00

2002 Fleer WWE Raw vs. SmackDown Pay-Per-View Relics

COMPLETE SET (5) 30.00 75.00
STATED ODDS 1:33 HOBBY

NNO K.Angle/Kane 6.00 15.00
NNO R.Flair/Undertaker 10.00 25.00
NNO Rock/H.Hogan 20.00 50.00
NNO S.Hall/S.Austin 10.00 25.00
NNO W.Regal/RVD 6.00 15.00

2002 Fleer WWE Raw vs. SmackDown Pop-Ups

COMPLETE SET (10) 20.00 50.00
STATED ODDS 1:HOBBY BOX

NNO Chris Jericho 1.25 3.00
NNO Hollywood Hulk Hogan 5.00 12.00
NNO Kurt Angle 2.00 5.00
NNO Lita 3.00 8.00
NNO The Rock 3.00 8.00
NNO Stacy Keibler 5.00 12.00
NNO Stone Cold Steve Austin 3.00 8.00
NNO Triple H 3.00 8.00
NNO Trish Stratus 5.00 12.00
NNO Undertaker 2.50 6.00

2002 Fleer WWE Raw vs. SmackDown Raw Certified

STATED ODDS 1:72

NNO Kevin Nash 10.00 25.00
NNO Rob Van Dam 8.00 20.00
NNO Spike Dudley 8.00 20.00
NNO William Regal 8.00 20.00
NNO X-Pac 8.00 20.00

2002 Fleer WWE Raw vs. SmackDown SmackDown Authentics

STATED ODDS 1:36 HOBBY

NNO Billy Gunn/Headband 4.00 10.00
NNO Chuck Palumbo/Headband 4.00 10.00
NNO DDP/Pants 5.00 12.00
NNO Edge/Shirt 6.00 15.00
NNO Hollywood Hogan/Shirt 8.00 20.00
NNO Triple H/Shirt 6.00 15.00
NNO Undertaker/Shirt 6.00 15.00

2002 Fleer WWE Raw vs. SmackDown Triple Exposure

NNO Lita/Debra/Molly 25.00 60.00
NNO Molly/Stacy Keibler/Debra 30.00 75.00
NNO Terri/Torrie/Stacy 75.00 150.00

2002 Fleer WWE Raw vs. SmackDown Ultimate Exposure

STATED ODDS 1:96 HOBBY

NNO Debra 8.00 20.00
Jacket
NNO Lita/Top 10.00 25.00
NNO Molly Holly/Swimsuit 6.00 15.00
NNO Molly Holly/Top 6.00 15.00
NNO Stacy Keibler/Shirt 12.00 30.00
NNO Terri/Dress 10.00 25.00
NNO Torrie Wilson/Stocking 12.00 30.00

2002 Fleer WWE Royal Rumble

1 Big Show .50 1.25
2 Booker T .50 1.25
3 Bradshaw .30 .75
4 Brock Lesnar RC 12.00 30.00
5 Bubba Ray Dudley .20 .50
6 Chris Nowinski RC .12 .30
7 John Cena RC 20.00 50.00
8 D'Lo Brown .12 .30
9 Eddie Guerrero .60 1.50
10 Goldust .12 .30
11 Jacqueline .30 .75
12 Jazz RC .30 .75
13 Jeff Hardy .30 .75
14 Randy Orton RC 8.00 20.00
15 Kane .50 1.25
16 Kevin Nash .60 1.50
17 Lita .75 2.00
18 Mark Henry .20 .50
19 Matt Hardy .30 .75
20 Molly .30 .75
21 Rob Van Dam RC .50 1.25
22 Raven .20 .50
23 Shawn Michaels .75 2.00
24 Shawn Stasiak .12 .30
25 Spike Dudley .20 .50
26 Steven Richards .20 .50
27 Terri .60 1.50
28 Ric Flair .60 1.50
29 William Regal .20 .50
30 X-Pac .20 .50
31 Al Snow .20 .50
32 Billy .20 .50
33 Billy Kidman .12 .30
34 Chris Benoit .30 .75
35 Christian .30 .75
36 Chuck RC .20 .50
37 D-Von .20 .50
38 Paul Heyman .12 .30
39 Edge .50 1.25
40 Faarooq .12 .30
41 Funaki .20 .50
42 Chris Jericho .30 .75
43 Hollywood Hulk Hogan 1.25 3.00
44 The Hurricane RC .20 .50
45 Ivory .50 1.25
46 Kurt Angle .50 1.25
47 Maven RC .12 .30
48 Nidia RC .30 .75
49 Rico RC .12 .30
50 The Rock .75 2.00
51 Tajiri .20 .50
52 Torrie Wilson RC 1.25 3.00
53 Triple H .75 2.00

54 Scotty 2 Hotty	.20	.50
55 Stacy Keibler RC	1.25	3.00
56 Lance Storm RC	.12	.30
57 Tazz	.20	.50
58 Test	.20	.50
59 Eric Bischoff	.12	.30
60 Jackie RC	.50	1.25
61 Victoria RC	.60	1.50
62 Stephanie	.60	1.50
63 Vince McMahon	.50	1.25
64 Rikishi	.30	.75
65 Jerry Lawler	.30	.75
66 Jim Ross	.20	.50
67 Deacon Batista RC	6.00	15.00
68 Shane McMahon	.30	.75
69 Albert	.12	.30
70 Trish Stratus	1.25	3.00
71 Undertaker	.60	1.50
72 Dawn Marie RC	.30	.75
73 Chavo Guerrero	.20	.50
74 Rey Mysterio	.30	.75
75 Tommy Dreamer RC	.12	.30
76 Eddie Guerrero AKA	.60	1.50
77 Brock Lesnar AKA	6.00	15.00
78 Chris Benoit AKA	.30	.75
79 Triple H AKA	.75	2.00
80 Undertaker AKA	.60	1.50
81 The Rock AKA	.75	2.00
82 Jim Ross AKA	.20	.50
83 Jerry Lawler AKA	.30	.75
84 Ric Flair AKA	.60	1.50
85 Shawn Stasiak AKA	.12	.30
86 Kurt Angle AKA	.50	1.25
87 Shawn Michaels AKA	.75	2.00
88 Hulk Hogan AKA	1.25	3.00
89 Rob Van Dam AKA	.50	1.25
90 J.Hardy/M.Hardy/Lita AKA	.75	2.00

2002 Fleer WWE Royal Rumble AKA Memorabilia

STATED ODDS 1:24 HOBBY		
NNO HHH/Ring Mat	4.00	10.00
NNO Undertaker/Ring Mat	4.00	10.00

2002 Fleer WWE Royal Rumble Divastating

COMPLETE SET (15)	10.00	25.00
STATED ODDS 1:8 HOBBY		
D1 Ivory	1.00	2.50
D2 Torrie Wilson	2.50	6.00
D3 Terri	1.25	3.00
D4 Stacy Keibler	2.50	6.00
D5 Trish Stratus	2.50	6.00
D6 Molly	.60	1.50
D7 Stephanie McMahon	4.00	10.00
D8 Jazz	.60	1.50
D9 Jacqueline	.60	1.50
D10 Lita	1.50	4.00
D11 Dawn Marie	.60	1.50
D12 Nidia	.60	1.50
D13 Linda	.60	1.50
D14 Jackie	1.00	2.50
D15 Victoria	1.25	3.00

2002 Fleer WWE Royal Rumble Divastating Autographs

PRINT RUN 100 SER. #'d SETS		
NNO Lita	50.00	100.00
NNO Stacy Keibler	75.00	150.00
NNO Terri	25.00	60.00
NNO Torrie Wilson	60.00	120.00

2002 Fleer WWE Royal Rumble Divastating Memorabilia

STATED ODDS 1:48 HOBBY		
NNO Dawn Marie Dress	8.00	20.00
NNO Ivory/Undergarment	6.00	15.00
NNO Jazz/Ring Mat	4.00	10.00
NNO Stacy Keibler/Shirt	10.00	25.00
NNO Torrie Wilson/Skirt	10.00	25.00
NNO Trish Stratus/Pants	15.00	40.00

2002 Fleer WWE Royal Rumble Factions

COMPLETE SET (5)	20.00	50.00
STATED ODDS 1:120		
F1 The Nation of Domination	6.00	15.00
F2 The Corporation	6.00	15.00
F3 The Radicalz	6.00	15.00
F4 D-Generation X	6.00	15.00
F5 New World Order	6.00	15.00

2002 Fleer WWE Royal Rumble Factions Memorabilia

STATED ODDS 1:48 HOBBY		
NNO The Rock Shirt	8.00	20.00
NNO Shawn Michaels/D-X Shirt	6.00	15.00
NNO Shawn Michaels/nWo Shirt	6.00	15.00
NNO X-Pac/Shirt	4.00	10.00

2002 Fleer WWE Royal Rumble Gimmick Matches

COMPLETE SET (10)	6.00	15.00
STATED ODDS 1:4 HOBBY		
GM1 Triple H/C.Jericho	1.25	3.00
GM2 Undertaker/J.Hardy	1.00	2.50
GM3 RVD/E.Guerrero	1.00	2.50
GM4 K.Angle/Edge	.75	2.00
GM5 RVD/J.Hardy	.75	2.00
GM6 S.Keibler/T.Stratus	2.00	5.00
GM7 The Rock/T.Stratus	2.00	5.00
GM8 K.Angle/S.McMahon	.75	2.00
GM9 C.Jericho/Kane	.75	2.00
GM10 K.Angle/Edge	.75	2.00

2002 Fleer WWE Royal Rumble Gimmick Matches Dual Memorabilia

STATED PRINT RUN 25 SER. #'d SETS		
NNO The Rock/T.Stratus	15.00	40.00
NNO S.Keibler/T.Stratus	20.00	50.00
NNO Triple H/C.Jericho	20.00	50.00
NNO Undertaker/J.Hardy	50.00	100.00

2002 Fleer WWE Royal Rumble Gimmick Matches Memorabilia

STATED ODDS 1:24 HOBBY		
NNO Chris Jericho/Shirt HIAC	6.00	15.00
NNO Chris Jericho/Shirt Last Man	6.00	15.00
NNO Edge/Shirt Cage Match	8.00	20.00
NNO Edge/Shirt Hair vs. Hair	8.00	20.00
NNO Jeff Hardy/Shirt	8.00	20.00
NNO Jeff Hardy/Tank Top	8.00	20.00
NNO Stacy Keibler/Shirt	10.00	25.00
NNO Triple H/Shirt	8.00	20.00
NNO Trish Stratus/Pants	10.00	25.00
NNO Trish Stratus/Shirt	10.00	25.00
NNO Trish Stratus/Shirt Gravy Bowl	10.00	25.00
NNO Undertaker/Shirt	8.00	20.00

2002 Fleer WWE Royal Rumble Memorabilia

STATED ODDS 1:24 HOBBY		
NNO Brock Lesnar/Shirt	30.00	75.00
NNO Chris Benoit/Ring Skirt	6.00	15.00
NNO Edge/Ring Mat	6.00	15.00
NNO Funaki/Shirt	3.00	8.00
NNO Hollywood Hulk Hogan/T-Shirt	15.00	40.00
NNO The Hurricane/Ring Mat	3.00	8.00
NNO Kane/Ring Mat	5.00	12.00
NNO Kurt Angle/Ring Mat	5.00	12.00
NNO Maven/T-Shirt	3.00	8.00
NNO Rey Mysterio/Shirt	10.00	25.00
NNO Rob Van Dam/Ring Mat	4.00	10.00
NNO The Rock/Ring Mat	10.00	25.00
NNO Scotty 2 Hotty/Jeans	4.00	10.00
NNO Shawn Michaels/Shirt	5.00	12.00
NNO Tazz/Sweat Pants	3.00	8.00

2002 Fleer WWE Royal Rumble Recap

COMPLETE SET (10)	15.00	40.00
STATED ODDS 1:24 HOBBY		
RR1 Kane	1.50	4.00
RR2 Kane vs The Undertaker	2.00	5.00
RR3 Triple H vs Cactus Jack	2.50	6.00
RR4 Vince McMahon	1.50	4.00
RR5 Stone Cold	2.50	6.00
RR6 Hollywood Hulk Hogan	4.00	10.00
RR7 Ric Flair	2.00	5.00
RR8 The Rock vs Mankind	2.50	6.00
RR9 Shawn Michaels	2.50	6.00
RR10 Mae Young	1.00	2.50

2003 Fleer WWE WrestleMania XIX

COMPLETE SET (90)	12.50	30.00
1 Scott Steiner	.60	1.50
2 Scotty 2 Hotty	.20	.50
3 Albert	.12	.30
4 Kurt Angle	.50	1.25
5 Batista	.50	1.25
6 Chris Benoit	.30	.75
7 Big Show	.50	1.25
8 Billy	.20	.50
9 Eric Bischoff	.20	.50
10 Bradshaw	.30	.75
11 D'Lo Brown	.20	.50
12 John Cena	.75	2.00
13 Christian	.30	.75
14 Chuck	.20	.50
15 Tommy Dreamer	.12	.30
16 Bubba Ray Dudley	.20	.50
17 Spike Dudley	.20	.50
18 D-Von	.20	.50
19 Edge	.50	1.25
20 Ron Simmons	.20	.50
21 Ric Flair	.60	1.50
22 Funaki	.20	.50
23 Goldust	.12	.30
24 Crash	.12	.30
25 Eddie Guerrero	.60	1.50
26 Triple H	.75	2.00
27 Jeff Hardy	.30	.75
28 Matt Hardy	.30	.75
29 Hollywood Hulk Hogan	.75	2.00
30 The Hurricane	.12	.30
31 Chris Jericho	.30	.75
32 Kane	.50	1.25
33 Billy Kidman	.12	.30
34 Jerry Lawler	.30	.75
35 Brock Lesnar	1.25	3.00
36 Mark Henry	.20	.50
37 Maven	.12	.30
38 Godfather	.12	.30
39 Johnny Stamboli RC	.12	.30
40 Shawn Michaels	.75	2.00
41 Rey Mysterio	.30	.75
42 Kevin Nash	.60	1.50
43 Chris Nowinski	.12	.30
44 Randy Orton	.30	.75
45 Raven	.30	.75
46 William Regal	.30	.75
47 Steven Richards	.20	.50
48 Rico	.12	.30
49 Rikishi	.30	.75
50 The Rock	.75	2.00
51 Jim Ross	.20	.50
52 Al Snow	.12	.30
53 Jamie Noble	.12	.30
54 Lance Storm	.12	.30
55 Booker T	.50	1.25
56 Tajiri	.12	.30
57 Tazz	.20	.50
58 Test	.20	.50
59 Undertaker	.60	1.50
60 Rob Van Dam	.50	1.25
61 Lilian Garcia RC	1.50	4.00
62 Dawn Marie	.60	1.50
63 Trish Stratus	1.25	3.00
64 Jackie	.50	1.25
65 Victoria	.60	1.50
66 Stephanie	.60	1.50
67 Torrie Wilson	1.25	3.00
68 Stacy Keibler	1.25	3.00
69 Nidia	.30	.75
70 Ivory	.50	1.25
71 Terri	.60	1.50
72 Jacqueline	.30	.75
73 Jazz	.20	.50
74 Lita	.75	2.00
75 Molly	.60	1.50
76 Undertaker MM	.60	1.50
77 Kane MM	.50	1.25
78 Hollywood Hulk Hogan MM	.75	2.00
79 The Rock MM	.75	2.00
80 Triple H MM	.75	2.00
81 Kurt Angle MM	.50	1.25
82 Chris Jericho MM	.30	.75
83 Trish Stratus MM	1.25	3.00
84 Shawn Michaels MM	.75	2.00
85 Ivory MM	.50	1.25
86 Lita MM	.75	2.00
87 Jeff Hardy MM	.30	.75
88 Ric Flair MM	.60	1.50
89 Rikishi MM	.30	.75
90 Stone Cold Steve Austin MM	.75	2.00

2003 Fleer WWE WrestleMania XIX Diva Las Vegas

COMPLETE SET (2)		
NNO Dawn Marie/1350	8.00	20.00
NNO Torrie Wilson/150	20.00	50.00

2003 Fleer WWE WrestleMania XIX Flashbacks

COMPLETE SET (6)	30.00	60.00
STATED ODDS 1:48 HOBBY		
NNO Chris Jericho	4.00	10.00
NNO Hollywood Hulk Hogan	12.00	30.00
NNO Kurt Angle	6.00	15.00
NNO Stone Cold Steve Austin	6.00	15.00
NNO Triple H	10.00	25.00
NNO Undertaker	10.00	25.00

2003 Fleer WWE WrestleMania XIX Mat Finish

COMPLETE SET (10)	40.00	80.00
STATED ODDS 1:24 HOBBY		
NNO Brock Lesnar	6.00	15.00
NNO Edge	5.00	12.00
NNO The Hurricane	4.00	10.00
NNO Kurt Angle	5.00	12.00
NNO Rob Van Dam	4.00	10.00
NNO The Rock	6.00	15.00
NNO Stone Cold Steve Austin	6.00	15.00
NNO Triple H	5.00	12.00
NNO Trish Stratus	6.00	15.00
NNO Undertaker	5.00	12.00

2003 Fleer WWE WrestleMania XIX Title Shots

COMPLETE SET (7)	50.00	100.00
STATED ODDS 1:48 HOBBY		
NNO Brock Lesnar	10.00	25.00
NNO Kane	6.00	15.00
NNO Kurt Angle	8.00	20.00
NNO Rob Van Dam	6.00	15.00
NNO The Rock	12.00	30.00
NNO Triple H	8.00	20.00
NNO Undertaker	8.00	20.00

2004 Fleer WWE WrestleMania XX

COMPLETE SET (84)	10.00	25.00
*GOLD: .75X TO 2X BASIC CARDS		
1 Batista	.50	1.25
2 A-Train	.12	.30
3 Chris Jericho	.30	.75
4 Bill DeMott	.12	.30
5 Goldberg	1.00	2.50
6 Undertaker	.60	1.50
7 Kevin Nash	.60	1.50
8 Eddie Guerrero	.60	1.50
9 Mark Henry	.20	.50
10 John Cena	.75	2.00
11 Ric Flair	.60	1.50
12 Shannon Moore	.12	.30
13 Scott Steiner	.60	1.50
14 Brock Lesnar	1.25	3.00
15 Shawn Michaels	.75	2.00
16 Basham Brothers	.12	.30

17 Mark Jindrak & Garrison Cade	.12	.30
18 Chavo Guerrero	.20	.50
19 Eric Bischoff	.20	.50
20 Ultimo Dragon	.12	.30
21 Triple H	.75	2.00
22 The World's Greatest Tag Team	.12	.30
23 La Resistance	.12	.30
24 Rhyno	.50	1.25
25 Rico	.12	.30
26 Edge	.50	1.25
27 Steven Richards	.20	.50
28 Jerry The King Lawler	.30	.75
29 Vince McMahon	.50	1.25
30 Linda McMahon	.20	.50
31 Stephanie McMahon	.60	1.50
32 Shane McMahon	.30	.75
33 Jim Ross	.20	.50
34 Chris Nowinski	.12	.30
35 Tazz	.20	.50
36 Maven	.12	.30
37 Sean O'Haire RC	.12	.30
38 Dudley Boyz	.20	.50
39 The Hurricane	.15	.40
40 Rey Mysterio	.30	.75
41 Test	.20	.50
42 Tajiri	.12	.30
43 Stone Cold Steve Austin	.75	2.00
44 Chris Benoit	.30	.75
45 The Rock	.75	2.00
46 APA	.30	.75
47 Rosey	.12	.30
48 Rodney Mack RC	.12	.30
49 Matt Hardy	.30	.75
50 Randy Orton	.30	.75
51 Kurt Angle	.50	1.25
52 Lance Storm	.12	.30
53 FBI	.12	.30
54 Kane	.50	1.25
55 Billy Kidman	.12	.30
56 Christian	.40	1.00
57 Big Show	.50	1.25
58 Booker T	.50	1.25
59 Sable RD	.75	2.00
60 Lita RD	.75	2.00
61 Ivory RD	.50	1.25
62 Stacy Keibler RD	1.25	3.00
63 Molly RD	.60	1.50
64 Torrie Wilson RD	1.25	3.00
65 Terri RD	.60	1.50
66 Shaniqua RD RC	.30	.75
67 Gail Kim RC	.50	1.25
68 Miss Jackie RD	.50	1.25
69 Victoria RD	.60	1.50
70 Jazz RD	.30	.75
71 Nidia RD	.30	.75
72 Dawn Marie RD	.30	.75
73 Jacqueline RD	.40	1.00
74 Trish Stratus RD	1.25	3.00
75 Ric Flair MM	.60	1.50
76 Shawn Michaels MM	.75	2.00
77 Shawn Michaels MM	.75	2.00
78 Undertaker MM	.60	1.50
79 Stone Cold Steve Austin MM	.75	2.00
80 The Rock MM	.75	2.00
81 Triple H MM	.75	2.00
82 Steve Austin & The Rock MM	.75	2.00
83 Triple H MM	.75	2.00
84 Brock Lesnar MM	1.25	3.00

2004 Fleer WWE WrestleMania XX Champions and Contenders

COMPLETE SET (17)	8.00	20.00
STATED ODDS 1:4 HOBBY AND RETAIL		
1 Kurt Angle/Brock Lesnar	1.50	4.00
2 Steve Austin/The Rock	2.00	5.00
3 Trish Stratus/Jazz	1.50	4.00
4 Triple H/Booker T	1.00	2.50
5 Kane/Big Show	.60	1.50
6 Eddie Guerrero/Test	.75	2.00
7 Undertaker/Ric Flair	.75	2.00
8 Edge & Christian/Dudley Boyz	.60	1.50
9 Jazz/Lita	1.00	2.50
10 Triple H/The Rock	1.00	2.50
11 Shane & Vince McMahon	.60	1.50
12 Chris Benoit/Chris Jericho	.40	1.00
13 Rob Van Dam/William Regal	.60	1.50
14 Trish Stratus/Victoria	1.50	4.00
15 Matt Hardy/Rey Mysterio	.40	1.00
16 Steve Austin/Shawn Michaels	1.00	2.50
17 Triple H/Chris Jericho	1.00	2.50

2004 Fleer WWE WrestleMania XX Champions and Contenders Dual Memorabilia

STATED ODDS 1:144 HOBBY		
CCDJ/L Jazz/Lita	6.00	12.00
CCDK/BS Kane/Big Show	6.00	12.00
CCDSA/R S.Austin/The Rock	10.00	20.00
CCDTS/J T.Stratus/Jazz	10.00	20.00
CCDCB/CJ C.Benoit/C.Jericho	5.00	10.00
CCDKA/BL K.Angle/B.Lesnar	7.50	15.00
CCDMH/RM M.Hardy/R.Mysterio	6.00	12.00
CCDSA/SM S.Austin/S.Michaels	7.50	15.00
CCDTH/BT HHH/Booker T	6.00	12.00
CCDTH/CJ HHH/C.Jericho	6.00	12.00

2004 Fleer WWE WrestleMania XX Champions and Contenders Memorabilia

STATED ODDS 1:18 HOBBY		
CCSJ Jazz	3.00	8.00
CCSK Kane	4.00	10.00
CCSL Lita	5.00	12.00
CCSR The Rock	6.00	15.00
CCST Test	3.00	8.00
CCSU Undertaker	5.00	12.00
CCSBL Brock Lesnar	6.00	15.00
CCSBT Booker T	3.00	8.00
CCSCB Chris Benoit	3.00	8.00
CCSCJ Chris Jericho	3.00	8.00
CCSKA Kurt Angle	4.00	10.00
CCSMH Matt Hardy	5.00	12.00
CCSSA Stone Cold Steve Austin	6.00	15.00
CCSSM Shawn Michaels	5.00	12.00
CCSTH Triple H	5.00	12.00
CCSTS Trish Stratus	6.00	15.00
CCSRVD Rob Van Dam	3.00	8.00

2004 Fleer WWE WrestleMania XX Road to WrestleMania

COMPLETE SET (10)	20.00	50.00
STATED ODDS 1:24 HOBBY AND RETAIL		
1 Shawn Michaels	3.00	8.00
2 Trish Stratus	5.00	12.00
3 Brock Lesnar	5.00	12.00
4 Stone Cold Steve Austin	3.00	8.00
5 Undertaker	2.50	6.00
6 Scott Steiner	2.50	6.00
7 Lita	3.00	8.00
8 Triple H	3.00	8.00
9 The Rock	3.00	8.00
10 Kurt Angle	2.00	5.00

2004 Fleer WWE WrestleMania XX To the Mat Memorabilia

STATED ODDS 1:48 HOBBY		
1 Lita	6.00	15.00
2 Stacy Keibler	8.00	20.00
3 Molly	4.00	10.00
4 Torrie Wilson	8.00	20.00
5 Gail Kim	4.00	10.00
6 Victoria	5.00	12.00
7 Miss Jackie	5.00	12.00
8 Trish Stratus	8.00	20.00
9 Sable	6.00	15.00
10 Ivory	5.00	12.00

2004 Fleer WWE WrestleMania XX To the Mat Memorabilia Autographs

STATED PRINT RUN 50 SER.#'d SETS		
TTML Lita	50.00	100.00
TTMS Sable	30.00	75.00
TTMSK Stacy Keibler	60.00	120.00
TTMTS Trish Stratus	75.00	150.00
TTMTW Torrie Wilson	30.00	75.00

2002 Fleer WWF All Access

COMPLETE SET (100)	8.00	20.00
16 The Rock	2.00	5.00
1 Justin Credible	.12	.30
2 Shane McMahon	.30	.75
3 Tajiri	.20	.50
4 Jerry Lynn	.12	.30
5 Christian	.30	.75
6 Haku	.12	.30
7 Kurt Angle	.50	1.25
8 Albert	.12	.30
9 Chris Jericho	.30	.75
10 Jeff Hardy	.30	.75
11 Triple H	.75	2.00
12 The One Billy Gunn	.20	.50
13 Booker T	.50	1.25
14 Funaki	.20	.50
15 Chris Benoit	.30	.75
17 Bradshaw	.30	.75
18 Stephanie McMahon-Helmsley	2.00	5.00
19 Crash Holly	.12	.30
20 Rhyno	.30	.75
21 Faarooq	.12	.30
22 Al Snow	.20	.50
23 Hardcore Holly	.20	.50
24 Rikishi	.30	.75
25 Rob Van Dam RC	.50	1.25
26 X-Pac	.20	.50
27 D-Von Dudley	.20	.50
28 Kane	.50	1.25
29 Spike Dudley	.20	.50
30 William Regal	.20	.50
31 Taka Michinoku	.12	.30
32 Mick Foley	.50	1.25
33 Undertaker	.60	1.50
34 Edge	.50	1.25
35 Stone Cold Steve Austin	.75	2.00
36 Jim Ross	.20	.50
37 Bubba Ray Dudley	.20	.50
38 Steve Blackman	.12	.30
39 Test	.20	.50
40 Molly Holly	.30	.75
41 Vince Mcmahon	.50	1.25
42 Stacy Keibler RC	1.25	3.00
43 Torrie Wilson RC	1.25	3.00
44 Perry Saturn	.12	.30
45 Raven	.20	.50
46 Scotty 2 Hotty	.20	.50
47 Big Show	.50	1.25
48 Matt Hardy	.30	.75
49 Tazz	.20	.50
50 The Hurricane RC	.20	.50
51 Kane OTM	.50	1.25
52 Mick Foley OTM	.50	1.25
53 Lita OTM	.75	2.00
54 Justin Credible OTM	.12	.30
55 Big Show OTM	.50	1.25
56 Chris Benoit OTM	.30	.75
57 Stone Cold OTM	.75	2.00
58 Edge OTM	.50	1.25
59 Trish Stratus OTM	2.50	6.00
60 Faarooq OTM	.12	.30
61 Linda McMahon OTM	.20	.50
62 Matt Hardy OTM	.30	.75
63 Diamond Dallas Page OTM	.20	.50
64 The Hurricane OTM	.20	.50
65 Kurt Angle OTM	.50	1.25
66 Ric Flair OTM	.60	1.50
67 Undertaker OTM	.60	1.50
68 Tajiri OTM	.20	.50
69 Vince McMahon OTM	.50	1.25
70 Chris Jericho OTM	.30	.75
71 Triple H OTM	.75	2.00
72 Tazz OTM	.20	.50
73 Rob Van Dam OTM	.50	1.25
74 Sgt. Slaughter OTM	.30	.75
75 The Rock OTM	.75	2.00
76 Jim Ross OTM	.20	.50
77 Bradshaw OTM	.30	.75
78 Matt Hardy OTM	.30	.75
79 Perry Saturn OTM	.12	.30
80 X-Pac OTM	.20	.50
81 Maven RR RC	.12	.30
82 Molly Holly RR	.30	.75
83 Big Show RR	.50	1.25
84 Edge RR	.50	1.25
85 Stone Cold Steve Austin RR	.75	2.00
86 Vince McMahon RR	.50	1.25
87 Jeff Hardy RR	.30	.75
88 Kane RR	.50	1.25
89 Lita RR	.75	2.00
90 Ivory RR	.50	1.25
91 Kurt Angle RR	.50	1.25
92 Triple H RR	.75	2.00
93 Rob Van Dam RR	.50	1.25
94 Trish Stratus RR	1.25	3.00
95 Nidia RR RC	.30	.75
96 Matt Hardy RR	.30	.75
97 Christian RR	.30	.75
98 Mick Foley RR	.50	1.25
99 The Rock RR	.75	2.00
100 Undertaker RR	.60	1.50

2002 Fleer WWF All Access All Access Memorabilia

STATED ODDS 1:15		
AAMF Funaki	3.00	8.00
AAMH The Hurricane SP		
AAMK Kane	12.00	30.00
AAMU Undertaker	20.00	50.00
AAMA Stone Cold Steve Austin	12.00	30.00
AAMJH Jeff Hardy	5.00	12.00
AAMKA Kurt Angle		
AAMMH Molly Holly	5.00	12.00
AAMSH Scotty 2 Hotty	4.00	10.00
AAMSK Stacy Keibler	15.00	40.00
AAMT1 Tajiri	3.00	8.00
AAMT2 Tazz	3.00	8.00
AAMTH Triple H	6.00	15.00
AAMTW Torrie Wilson	8.00	20.00
AAMDVD D-Von Dudley	5.00	12.00
AAMRVD Rob Van Dam	4.00	10.00

2002 Fleer WWF All Access Famous Rides

COMPLETE SET (12)	5.00	12.00
STATED ODDS 1:6		
FR1 DDP's Pink Cadillac	.30	.75
FR2 Stone Cold's Truck	1.25	3.00
FR3 The Rock's Limo	1.25	3.00
FR4 D-X's Tank Jeep	.30	.75
FR5 Stone Cold Destroys Vince's Vette	1.25	3.00
FR6 Vince McMahon's Jet	.75	2.00
FR7 Big Show's Purple Car	.75	2.00
FR8 Kurt Angle's Scooter	.75	2.00
FR9 Jeff Hardy's Motorcycle	.50	1.25
FR10 Stone Cold's 18-Wheeler	1.25	3.00
FR11 D-Generation X's Bus	.30	.75
FR12 Al Snow's Lil' Racecar	.30	.75

2002 Fleer WWF All Access Match Makers

COMPLETE SET (15)	6.00	15.00
STATED ODDS 1:6		
MM1 Triple H & Stephanie	1.00	2.50
MM2 Kane & Undertaker	.75	2.00
MM3 Debra & Stone Cold	1.00	2.50
MM4 Dudley Boyz	.25	.60
MM5 The Rock & Mick Foley	1.00	2.50
MM6 Edge & Christian	.60	1.50
MM7 Stephanie & Chris Jericho	.75	2.00
MM8 Kurt Angle & Triple H	1.00	2.50
MM9 The Rock & Stone Cold	1.00	2.50
MM10 Kaientai	.25	.60
MM11 Benoit & Jericho	.40	1.00
MM12 Stone Cold & Undertaker	1.00	2.50
MM13 Kurt Angle & The Rock	1.00	2.50
MM14 Matt Hardy, Lita & Jeff Hardy	1.00	2.50
MM15 Mr. McMahon & Stone Cold	1.00	2.50

2002 Fleer WWF All Access Match Makers Memorabilia

STATED ODDS 1:95		
MMDB Dudley Boyz	15.00	40.00
MMEC Edge & Christian	12.00	30.00
MMKU Kane & Undertaker	10.00	25.00
MMRKA Kurt Angle & The Rock	12.00	30.00

Card	Low	High
MMRMF The Rock & Mick Foley	12.00	30.00
MMRSA The Rock & Stone Cold	15.00	40.00
MMSAU Stone Cold & Undertaker	12.00	30.00

2002 Fleer WWF All Access Off the Mat Autographs

RANDOMLY INSERTED INTO PACKS

Card	Low	High
NNO The Hurricane	12.00	30.00
NNO Jim Ross	30.00	75.00
NNO Lita	50.00	100.00
NNO Rob Van Dam	25.00	60.00
NNO Stacy Keibler	100.00	200.00
NNO Torrie Wilson	30.00	80.00
NNO Triple H	250.00	500.00
NNO Trish Stratus	60.00	120.00

2002 Fleer WWF All Access Pay-Per-View Posters

Card	Low	High
COMPLETE SET (8)	15.00	40.00
STATED ODDS 1:33		
PPV1 Backlash	3.00	8.00
PPV2 Invasion	2.00	5.00
PPV3 Judgment Day	3.00	8.00
PPV4 No Mercy	2.00	5.00
PPV5 No Way Out	2.00	5.00
PPV6 SummerSlam	3.00	8.00
PPV7 Unforgiven	3.00	8.00
PPV8 Vengeance	3.00	8.00
PPV9 WrestleMania X-7	3.00	8.00
PPV10 Survivor Series	5.00	12.00

2001 Fleer WWF Championship Clash

Card	Low	High
COMPLETE SET (80)	8.00	20.00
1 The Rock	4.00	10.00
2 K-Kwik RC	.12	.30
3 Steve Blackman	.12	.30
4 Eddie Guerrero	.30	.75
5 Jerry Lynn RC	.12	.30
6 Christian	.30	.75
7 Kane	.30	.75
8 Tazz	.20	.50
9 Stone Cold Steve Austin	.75	2.00
10 Crash Holly RC	.12	.30
11 Matt Hardy RC	.30	.75
12 Undertaker	.60	1.50
13 Al Snow	.15	.40
14 Tajiri RC	.12	.30
15 Scotty 2 Hotty RC	.20	.50
16 Dean Malenko	.12	.30
17 Raven	.12	.30
18 Big Show	.50	1.25
19 Jeff Hardy RC	.30	.75
20 Spike Dudley RC	.20	.50
21 Chris Jericho	.30	.75
22 Kurt Angle	.30	.75
23 Test	.20	.50
24 Chris Benoit	.30	.75
25 William Regal	.20	.50
26 Rikishi	.20	.50
27 D-Von Dudley RC	.20	.50
28 Mick Foley	.50	1.25
29 Triple H	.50	1.25
30 Albert	.12	.30
31 Haku	.12	.30
32 Perry Saturn	.12	.30
33 The One Billy Gunn	.12	.30
34 Hardcore Holly	.20	.50
35 Shane McMahon	.30	.75
36 Edge	.25	.60
37 Rhyno RC	.20	.50
38 Bubba Ray Dudley RC	.20	.50
39 Justin Credible RC	.12	.30
40 X-Pac	.20	.50
41 The Rock PC	2.50	6.00
42 K-Kwik PC	.12	.30
43 Steve Blackman PC	.12	.30
44 Eddie Guerrero PC	.30	.75
45 Jerry Lynn PC	.12	.30
46 Christian PC	.30	.75
47 Kane PC	.30	.75
48 Tazz PC	.20	.50
49 Stone Cold Steve Austin PC	.75	2.00
50 Crash Holly PC	.12	.30
51 Matt Hardy PC	.30	.75
52 Undertaker PC	.60	1.50
53 Al Snow PC	.15	.40
54 Tajiri PC	.12	.30
55 Scotty 2 Hotty PC	.20	.50
56 Dean Malenko PC	.12	.30
57 Raven PC	.12	.30
58 Big Show PC	.50	1.25
59 Jeff Hardy PC	.30	.75
60 Spike Dudley PC	.20	.50
61 Chris Jericho PC	.30	.75
62 Kurt Angle PC	.30	.75
63 Test PC	.20	.50
64 Chris Benoit PC	.30	.75
65 William Regal PC	.20	.50
66 Rikishi PC	.20	.50
67 D-Von Dudley PC	.20	.50
68 Mick Foley PC	.50	1.25
69 Triple H PC	.50	1.25
70 Albert PC	.12	.30
71 Haku PC	.12	.30
72 Perry Saturn PC	.12	.30
73 The One Billy Gunn PC	.12	.30
74 Hardcore Holly PC	.20	.50
75 Shane McMahon PC	.30	.75
76 Edge PC	.25	.60
77 Rhyno PC	.20	.50
78 Bubba Ray Dudley PC	.20	.50
79 Justin Credible PC	.12	.30
80 X-Pac PC	.20	.50

2001 Fleer WWF Championship Clash Divas Private Collection

STATED ODDS 1:30 HOBBY; 1:576 RETAIL

Card	Low	High
DPDE Debra/Skirt	10.00	25.00
DPTO Tori/Skirt & Tights	6.00	15.00
DPCIV Ivory/Scarf	8.00	20.00
DPCMH Molly Holly/Halter Top	4.00	10.00
DPCTE Terri/Dress	7.50	15.00
DPCLBT Lita/Bikini Top	25.00	50.00
DPCLTS Lita/T-Shirt	10.00	25.00

2001 Fleer WWF Championship Clash Divas Private Signing

Card	Low	High
COMPLETE SET (8)	175.00	350.00
STATED ODDS 1:120		
CARDS 1-4 AVAIL.IN CHAMP.CLASH		
CARDS 5-8 AVAIL.IN ULT DIVA COL.		
HOBBY EXCLUSIVE		
DPSD Debra	100.00	200.00
DPSI Ivory	30.00	75.00
DPSJ Jacqueline	20.00	40.00
DPSL Lita	25.00	50.00
DPSMH Molly Holly	75.00	150.00
DPSSM S.McMahon-Helmsley	200.00	400.00
DPSTE Terri	25.00	50.00
DPSTS Trish Stratus	150.00	300.00

2001 Fleer WWF Championship Clash Females

Card	Low	High
COMPLETE SET (9)	12.00	30.00
STATED ODDS 1:4 HOBBY; 1:7 RETAIL		
WF1 Ivory	.75	2.00
WF2 Trish Stratus	6.00	15.00
WF3 Lita	1.00	2.50
WF4 Molly Holly	4.00	10.00
WF5 Debra	3.00	8.00
WF6 Stephanie McMahon	5.00	12.00
WF7 Terri	1.00	2.50
WF8 Jacqueline	.75	2.00
WF9 Tori	1.00	2.50

2001 Fleer WWF Championship Clash Main Event Memorabilia

Card	Low	High
COMPLETE SET (9)	25.00	60.00
STATED ODDS 1:24 HOBBY; 1:144 RETAIL		
SA Steve Austin/Ring Skirt	5.00	12.00
BKR Big Show & Kane & Raven/Mat	3.00	8.00
EGT Test vs. E.Guerrero/Mat	2.50	6.00
CBCJ C.Benoit vs. C.Jericho/Ring Skirt	12.00	30.00
CJWR W.Regal vs. C.Jericho/Mat	3.00	8.00
KATH HHH vs. K.Angle/Ring Skirt	6.00	15.00
SATR S.Austin vs. Rock/Mat	5.00	12.00
SMKA S.McMahon vs. K.Angle Garbage Can SP	3.00	8.00
SAKACJ K.Angle & Y2J & S.Austin Steel Chair SP	4.00	10.00

2001 Fleer WWF Championship Clash Piece of the Champion

STATED ODDS 1:24 HOBBY; 1:576 RETAIL

Card	Low	High
PCB Bradshaw/T-Shirt	10.00	20.00
PCCJ C.Jericho/T-Shirt	12.00	30.00
PCER E.Rios/Pants	6.00	12.00
PCFA Faarooq/Knee Brace UER SP		
PCFN Funaki/T-Shirt	6.00	12.00
PCJH J.Hardy/T-Shirt	15.00	40.00
PCKA K.Angle/Gold Medal Strap SP	125.00	250.00
PCKA2 K.Angle/T-Shirt	15.00	30.00
PCMH M.Hardy/T-Shirt	15.00	30.00
PCSA S.Austin/T-Shirt	15.00	30.00
PCSH Scotty 2 Hotty/Pants	10.00	25.00
PCTM T.Michinoku/T-Shirt	6.00	12.00
PCXP X- Pac/Bandana	10.00	20.00

2002 Fleer WWF Divas Magazine Series 1

Card	Low	High
1 Lita	.40	1.00
2 Lita	.40	1.00
3 Lita	.40	1.00
4 Jacqueline	.20	.50
5 Jacqueline	.20	.50
6 Jacqueline	.20	.50
7 Torrie	.60	1.50
8 Torrie	.60	1.50
9 Torrie	.60	1.50

2002 Fleer WWF Divas Magazine Series 2

Card	Low	High
1 Trish	.60	1.50
2 Trish	.60	1.50
3 Trish	.60	1.50
4 Ivory	.20	.50
5 Ivory	.20	.50
6 Ivory	.20	.50
7 Terri	.30	.75
8 Terri	.30	.75
9 Terri	.30	.75

2002 Fleer WWF Divas Magazine Series 3

Card	Low	High
1 Stacy	.60	1.50
2 Stacy	.60	1.50
3 Stacy	.60	1.50
4 Sharmell	.20	.50
5 Sharmell	.20	.50
6 Sharmell	.20	.50
7 Molly	.20	.50
8 Molly	.20	.50
9 Molly	.20	.50

2001 Fleer WWF KB Toys Get Real

Card	Low	High
COMPLETE SET (18)	12.00	30.00
UNOPENED PACK (3 CARDS)	1.50	2.00
1 The Rock	2.50	6.00
2 Undertaker	2.50	6.00
3 Kane	1.25	3.00
4 Stone Cold Steve Austin	2.00	5.00
5 Kurt Angle	.75	2.00
6 Triple H	.75	2.00
7 Albert	.50	1.25
8 The Dudley Boyz	1.25	3.00
9 The Hardy Boyz	1.50	4.00
10 Lita	3.00	8.00
11 Edge	1.50	4.00
12 Christian	.60	1.50
13 Tazz	.50	1.25
14 Raven	.75	2.00
15 Chris Jericho	2.00	5.00
16 Jacqueline	.75	2.00
17 Ivory	.75	2.00
18 Trish Stratus	2.50	6.00

2001 Fleer WWF Raw Is War

Card	Low	High
COMPLETE SET (100)	25.00	60.00
1 Stone Cold Steve Austin	.75	2.00
2 Triple H	.50	1.25
3 Mick Foley	.50	1.25
4 Dean Malenko	.12	.30
5 Chris Jericho	.30	.75
6 Lita RC	3.00	8.00
7 Bubba Ray Dudley RC	.20	.50
8 JR	.20	.50
9 Bull Buchanan RC	.12	.30
10 Kane	.30	.75
11 Gerald Brisco	.20	.50
12 The Goodfather	.20	.50
13 Matt Hardy RC	.30	.75
14 Rikishi	.20	.50
15 Vince McMahon	.50	1.25
16 Ivory	.50	1.25
17 Trish Stratus RC	3.00	8.00
18 Test	.20	.50
19 Raven	.12	.30
20 Albert	.12	.30
21 Val Venis	.20	.50
22 Tazz	.20	.50
23 Chyna	.30	.75
24 Molly Holly RC	.50	1.25
25 Christian	.30	.75
26 Edge	.25	.60
27 William Regal	.20	.50
28 Crash Holly RC	.12	.30
29 Jeff Hardy RC	.30	.75
30 Kurt Angle	.30	.75
31 K-Kwik RC	.12	.30
32 Bradshaw	.30	.75
33 Terri RC	.60	1.50
34 Bob Hardcore Holly	.20	.50
35 Grandmaster Sexay RC	.12	.30
36 Perry Saturn	.12	.30
37 D-Von Dudley RC	.20	.50
38 The One Billy Gunn	.12	.30
39 The Rock	2.50	6.00
40 Eddie Guerrero	.30	.75
41 Steven Richards RC	.20	.50
42 Pat Patterson	.20	.50
43 Chris Benoit	.30	.75
44 Big Show	.50	1.25
45 Faarooq	.12	.30
46 Steve Blackman	.12	.30
47 Undertaker	.60	1.50
48 Jacqueline	.50	1.25
49 Scotty Too Hotty RC	.20	.50
50 Chris Jericho WZ	.30	.75
51 APA WZ	.30	.75
52 Billy Gunn vs. Val Venis WZ	.20	.50
53 Taka Michinoku WZ	.12	.30
54 Triple H vs.The Rock WZ	.75	2.00
55 Edge & Christian WZ	.30	.75
56 Big Show WZ	.50	1.25
57 Hardy Boyz vs. Edge & Christian WZ	.30	.75
58 Debra WZ	.60	1.50
59 Kurt Angle WZ	.30	.75
60 Kaientai WZ	.12	.30
61 Rock & Undertaker vs. Edge & Christian WZ	.75	2.00
62 Right to Censor WZ	.50	1.25
63 Undertaker WZ	.60	1.50
64 Billy Gunn with Chyna WZ	.30	.75
65 Dudleyz vs. Edge & Christian WZ	.30	.75
66 Lita vs. Trish Stratus WZ	.75	2.00
67 The Rock WZ	2.50	6.00
68 S.McMahon-Helmsley WZ RC	3.00	8.00
69 Dudley Boyz WZ	.20	.50
70 Triple H WZ	.50	1.25
71 Steve Austin vs. Vince WZ	2.50	6.00
72 Shane McMahon WZ	.30	.75
73 Perry Saturn with Terri WZ	.60	1.50
74 Too Cool WZ	.20	.50
75 Triple H WZ	.50	1.25
76 Hardy Boyz WZ	2.00	5.00
77 Stone Cold Steve Austin WZ	2.50	6.00
78 Undertaker vs. Kane WZ	.60	1.50
79 Hardcore/Molly/Crash Holly WZ	.50	1.25
80 William Regal WZ	.20	.50
81 Steve Austin vs. Kurt Angle WZ	.75	2.00

82 Vince McMahon WZ	.50	1.25
83 Right to Censor vs. Hardy Boyz WZ	.30	.75
84 Kane WZ	.30	.75
85 The Rock vs. Undertaker SE	.60	1.50
86 Steve Austin vs. William Regal SE	.60	1.50
87 Steve Austin vs. Chris Benoit SE	.60	1.50
88 Steve Austin vs. Rikishi vs. Angle SE	.60	1.50
89 Chris Jericho vs. The Rock SE	.60	1.50
90 Steve Austin vs. Kurt Angle SE	.60	1.50
91 S.Austin vs. Edge & Christian & Angle SE	.60	1.50
92 Triple H vs. Kurt Angle SE	.40	1.00
93 Undertaker vs. The Rock SE	.60	1.50
94 Chris Jericho vs. Benoit SE	.30	.75
95 Rock vs. HHH vs. Kurt Angle SE	.60	1.50
96 Shane McMahon vs. The Rock SE	.60	1.50
97 Triple H vs. The Rock SE	.60	1.50
98 The Rock vs. Kane SE	.60	1.50
99 Lita vs. Stephanie SE	.50	1.25
100 The Rock vs. Benoit SE	.60	1.50

2001 Fleer WWF Raw Is War Booty

STATED ODDS 1:26 HOBBY; 1:134 RETAIL

NNO Chris Benoit/Ring Skirt	12.00	30.00
NNO Chris Jericho/Ring Skirt	10.00	25.00
NNO Dudley Boyz/Ring Skirt	8.00	20.00
NNO Edge & Christian/Ring Skirt	10.00	25.00
NNO Hardy Boyz/Ring Mat	10.00	25.00
NNO Kane/Ring Skirt	6.00	15.00
NNO Kurt Angle/T-Shirt	12.00	30.00
NNO Mick Foley/Ring Mat	10.00	25.00
NNO Billy Gunn/Ring Trunks	12.00	30.00
NNO The Rock/Ring Mat	20.00	50.00
NNO Steve Austin/Ring Mat	10.00	30.00
NNO Triple H/Ring Mat	10.00	25.00
NNO Undertaker/Ring Mat	10.00	25.00
NNO Vince McMahon/Ring Mat	8.00	20.00
NNO William Regal/Ring Skirt	6.00	15.00

2001 Fleer WWF Raw Is War Booty Autographs

STATED ODDS 1:354
EXCH.EXPIRATION: 07/01/2002

NNO Christian	30.00	75.00
NNO Edge	40.00	100.00
NNO Undertaker	300.00	750.00

2001 Fleer WWF Raw Is War Famous Nicknames

COMPLETE SET (14)	25.00	60.00

STATED ODDS 1:15 HOBBY; 1:20 RETAIL

FN1 Chyna	3.00	8.00
FN2 Steve Austin	4.00	10.00
FN3 Kurt Angle	3.00	8.00
FN4 Billy Gunn	1.50	4.00
FN5 Triple H	3.00	8.00
FN6 Lita	5.00	12.00
FN7 Steve Blackman	1.50	4.00
FN8 The Rock	4.00	10.00
FN9 Shawn Michaels	3.00	8.00
FN10 Chris Jericho	3.00	8.00
FN11 Chris Benoit	2.50	6.00
FN12 Undertaker	3.00	8.00
FN13 Jim Ross	1.25	3.00
FN14 Eddie Guerrero	1.50	4.00

2001 Fleer WWF Raw Is War Femme Fatale

COMPLETE SET (20)	10.00	25.00

STATED ODDS 1:2 HOBBY AND RETAIL

FF1 Trish Stratus	2.50	6.00
FF2 Molly Holly	.25	.60
FF3 Terri	.40	1.00
FF4 Lita	2.00	5.00
FF5 Tori	.30	.75
FF6 Trish Stratus	2.50	6.00
FF7 Molly Holly	.25	.60
FF8 Terri	.40	1.00
FF9 Lita	2.00	5.00
FF10 Tori	.30	.75
FF11 Trish Stratus	2.50	6.00
FF12 Molly Holly	.25	.60
FF13 Terri	.40	1.00
FF14 Lita	2.00	5.00
FF15 Tori	.30	.75
FF16 Trish Stratus	2.50	6.00
FF17 Molly Holly	.25	.60
FF18 Terri	.40	1.00
FF19 Lita	2.00	5.00
FF20 Tori	.30	.75

2001 Fleer WWF Raw Is War Raw Is Jericho

COMPLETE SET (15)	6.00	15.00

STATED ODDS 1:2 HOBBY AND RETAIL

RJ1 The Rock	2.00	5.00
RJ2 Stone Cold Steve Austin	1.50	4.00
RJ3 Chris Benoit	.50	1.25
RJ4 Kurt Angle	.60	1.50
RJ5 Edge and Christian	.60	1.50
RJ6 Kane	.50	1.25
RJ7 Undertaker	1.25	3.00
RJ8 Chyna	.60	1.50
RJ9 Triple H	.60	1.50
RJ10 McMahon Family	.50	1.25
RJ11 Dudley Boyz	.50	1.25
RJ12 Hardy Boyz	.50	1.25
RJ13 Divas	.75	2.00
RJ14 Mick Foley	.60	1.50
RJ15 Chris Jericho	.60	1.50

2001 Fleer WWF Raw Is War TLC

COMPLETE SET (15)	10.00	25.00

STATED ODDS 1:5 HOBBY; 1:10 RETAIL

TLC1 Hardyz vs. Dudleyz vs. Edge & Christian	.60	1.50
TLC2 Hardy Boyz	1.25	3.00
TLC3 Dudley Boyz	1.25	3.00
TLC4 Edge & Christian	1.25	3.00
TLC5 Rock/Dudleyz vs. Angle/Edge/Christian	.60	1.50
TLC6 Jericho/Dudleyz vs. Angle/Edge/Christian	.60	1.50
TLC7 Bob Holly vs. Steve Blackman	.60	1.50
TLC8 Triple H	1.25	3.00
TLC9 Stone Cold Steve Austin	1.50	4.00
TLC10 Kane	1.00	2.50
TLC11 Chris Jericho	1.25	3.00
TLC12 Kurt Angle	1.25	3.00
TLC13 Big Show	1.00	2.50
TLC14 Undertaker	1.25	3.00
TLC15 The Rock	1.50	4.00

2001 Fleer WWF The Ultimate Diva Collection

COMPLETE SET (100)	20.00	50.00
COMPLETE SET W/O SP (85)	10.00	25.00

*GOLD (1-85): 1X TO 2.5X BASIC CARDS
*GOLD SP (86-100): 2X TO 5X BASIC CARDS
HEDONISM STATED ODDS 1:4

1 Trish Stratus RC	.40	1.00
2 Debra	.30	.75
3 Ivory	.25	.60
4 Jacqueline	.25	.60
5 Lita RC	.30	.75
6 Molly Holly RC	.25	.60
7 Terri RC	.30	.75
8 Trish Stratus RC	.40	1.00
9 Debra	.30	.75
10 Ivory	.25	.60
11 Jacqueline	.25	.60
12 Lita RC	.30	.75
13 Molly Holly RC	.25	.60
14 Debra	.30	.75
15 Trish Stratus RC	.40	1.00
16 Debra	.30	.75
17 Ivory	.25	.60
18 Jacqueline	.25	.60
19 Lita RC	.30	.75
20 Molly Holly RC	.25	.60
21 Terri RC	.30	.75
22 Trish Stratus RC	.40	1.00
23 Debra	.30	.75
24 Ivory	.25	.60
25 Jacqueline	.25	.60
26 Lita RC	.30	.75
27 Molly Holly RC	.25	.60
28 Terri RC	.30	.75
29 Trish Stratus RC	.40	1.00
30 Debra	.30	.75
31 Ivory	.25	.60
32 Jacqueline	.25	.60
33 Lita RC	.30	.75
34 Molly Holly RC	.25	.60
35 Terri RC	.30	.75
36 Trish Stratus RC	.40	1.00
37 Debra	.30	.75
38 Ivory	.25	.60
39 Jacqueline	.25	.60
40 Lita RC	.30	.75
41 Molly Holly RC	.25	.60
42 Terri RC	.30	.75
43 Trish Stratus RC	.40	1.00
44 Debra	.30	.75
45 Ivory	.25	.60
46 Jacqueline	.25	.60
47 Lita RC	.30	.75
48 Molly Holly RC	.25	.60
49 Terri RC	.30	.75
50 Trish Stratus RC	.40	1.00
51 Debra	.30	.75
52 Ivory	.25	.60
53 Jacqueline	.25	.60
54 Lita RC	.30	.75
55 Molly Holly RC	.25	.60
56 The Rock RP	.60	1.50
57 Stone Cold Steve Austin RP	.60	1.50
58 Triple H RP	.40	1.00
59 Undertaker RP	.50	1.25
60 APA RP	.25	.60
61 The Hardy Boyz RP	.25	.60
62 Dudley Boyz RP	.15	.40
63 Chris Jericho RP	.25	.60
64 Kurt Angle RP	.25	.60
65 Kane RP	.25	.60
66 Debra ITR	.30	.75
67 Jacqueline ITR	.25	.60
68 Lita ITR	.30	.75
69 Trish Stratus ITR	.40	1.00
70 Lita ITR	.30	.75
71 Molly Holly ITR	.25	.60
72 Jacqueline ITR	.25	.60
73 Terri ITR	.30	.75
74 Ivory ITR	.25	.60
75 Debra ITR	.30	.75
76 Molly Holly ITR	.25	.60
77 Lita ITR	.30	.75
78 Ivory ITR	.25	.60
79 Terri ITR	.30	.75
80 Trish Stratus ITR	.40	1.00
81 M.Holly/T.Stratus ITR	.40	1.00
82 M.Holly/Jacqueline ITR	.25	.60
83 Lita/T.Stratus ITR	.40	1.00
84 M.Holly/Lita ITR	.30	.75
85 Terri/T.Stratus ITR	.40	1.00
86 Debra HED SP	.75	2.00
87 Terri HED SP	.75	2.00
88 Lita HED SP	.75	2.00
89 Trish Stratus HED SP	1.00	2.50
90 Jacqueline HED SP	.60	1.50
91 Debra HED SP	.75	2.00
92 Terri HED SP	.75	2.00
93 Lita HED SP	.75	2.00
94 Trish Stratus HED SP	1.00	2.50
95 Jacqueline HED SP	.60	1.50
96 Debra HED SP	.75	2.00
97 Terri HED SP	.75	2.00
98 Lita HED SP	.75	2.00
99 Trish Stratus HED SP	1.00	2.50
100 Jacqueline HED SP	.60	1.50

2001 Fleer WWF The Ultimate Diva Collection The Bad and The Beautiful

COMPLETE SET (15)	10.00	20.00

STATED ODDS 1:4 HOBBY; 1:8 RETAIL

1 Trish Stratus	.75	2.00
2 Jacqueline	.50	1.25
3 Ivory	.50	1.25
4 Molly Holly	.50	1.25
5 Lita	.60	1.50
6 Terri	.60	1.50
7 Trish Stratus	.75	2.00
8 Jacqueline	.50	1.25
9 Debra	.60	1.50
10 Ivory	.50	1.25
11 Molly Holly	.50	1.25
12 Debra	.60	1.50
13 Terri	.60	1.50
14 Lita	.60	1.50
15 Trish Stratus	.75	2.00

2001 Fleer WWF The Ultimate Diva Collection Diva Ink

COMPLETE SET (2)	150.00	300.00

STATED ODDS 1:104 HOBBY; 1:1,787 RETAIL
EXCH.EXPIRATION: 1/1/2003

NNO Debra	20.00	40.00
NNO Ivory	30.00	60.00
NNO Jacqueline	20.00	40.00
NNO Lita	30.00	60.00
NNO Molly Holly	20.00	40.00
NNO Terri	30.00	60.00
NNO Trish Stratus	40.00	80.00

2001 Fleer WWF The Ultimate Diva Collection Kiss and Tell

COMPLETE SET (12)	15.00	30.00

STATED ODDS 1:12 HOBBY; 1:20 RETAIL

1 Vince McMahon/Trish Stratus	2.00	5.00
2 Kurt Angle/S.McMahon-Helmsley	1.50	4.00
3 Chris Jericho/Terri	1.50	4.00
4 Steve Austin/Debra	2.00	5.00
5 Triple H/S.McMahon-Helmsley	1.50	4.00
6 APA/Jacqueline	1.25	3.00
7 Perry Saturn/Terri	1.50	4.00
8 Undertaker/Ivory	1.50	4.00
9 The Hardy Boyz/Lita	1.50	4.00
10 The Rock/Trish Stratus	2.00	5.00
11 Dudley Boyz/Molly Holly	1.25	3.00
12 Kane/Ivory	1.25	3.00

2001 Fleer WWF The Ultimate Diva Collection Matching Set

COMPLETE SET (8)	25.00	60.00
COMMON CARD (1-8)	4.00	10.00
SEMISTARS	5.00	12.00
UNLISTED STARS	6.00	15.00
NNO Debra/Stone Cold	8.00	20.00
NNO Jacqueline/APA	4.00	10.00
NNO Jacqueline/Bradshaw	5.00	12.00
NNO Lita/Jeff Hardy	6.00	15.00
NNO Lita/Matt Hardy	8.00	20.00
NNO Molly Holly/Spike Dudley	5.00	12.00
NNO Terri/Perry Saturn	6.00	15.00
NNO Trish Stratus/Big Show	6.00	15.00

2001 Fleer WWF The Ultimate Diva Collection National Assets

COMPLETE SET (15)	15.00	30.00

STATED ODDS 1:12 HOBBY; 1:20 RETAIL

1 Lita	1.25	3.00
2 Debra	1.25	3.00
3 Ivory	1.00	2.50
4 Terri	1.25	3.00
5 Trish Stratus	1.50	4.00
6 Terri	1.25	3.00
7 Molly Holly	1.00	2.50
8 Jacqueline	1.00	2.50
9 Debra	1.25	3.00
10 Molly Holly	1.00	2.50
11 Trish Stratus	1.50	4.00
12 Terri	1.25	3.00
13 Ivory	1.00	2.50
14 Jacqueline	1.00	2.50
15 Lita	1.25	3.00

2001 Fleer WWF The Ultimate Diva Collection Ring Accessories

COMPLETE SET (7)	20.00	50.00
COMMON CARD (1-7)	4.00	8.00
SEMISTARS	4.00	10.00
UNLISTED STARS	5.00	12.00
NNO Debra	4.00	8.00
NNO Ivory	5.00	12.00

Card	Low	High
NNO Jacqueline	4.00	10.00
NNO Lita	7.50	15.00
NNO Molly Holly	5.00	10.00
NNO Terri	5.00	12.00
NNO Trish Stratus	15.00	40.00

2001 Fleer WWF The Ultimate Diva Collection Signed with a Kiss

RANDOMLY INSERTED INTO PACKS
STATED PRINT RUN 50 SERIAL #'d SETS
EXCH.EXPIRATION: 1/1/2003

Card	Low	High
NNO Debra	30.00	75.00
NNO Ivory	20.00	50.00
NNO Jacqueline	15.00	40.00
NNO Lita	75.00	150.00
NNO Molly Holly	75.00	150.00
NNO Terri Runnels	15.00	40.00
NNO Trish Stratus	600.00	1200.00

2001 Fleer WWF WrestleMania

COMPLETE SET (100) 8.00 20.00
*CH GOLD: 1.2X TO 3X BASIC CARDS

Card	Low	High
1 The Rock	2.00	5.00
2 D-Von Dudley RC	.20	.50
3 Matt Hardy RC	.30	.75
4 Test	.20	.50
5 Raven	.12	.30
6 Chris Benoit	.30	.75
7 Jeff Hardy RC	.30	.75
8 Shane McMahon	.30	.75
9 Brooklyn Brawler	.12	.30
10 Gerald Brisco	.20	.50
11 Linda McMahon RC	.20	.50
12 Albert	.12	.30
13 Eddie Guerrero	.30	.75
14 Mick Foley	.50	1.25
15 The Goodfather	.20	.50
16 Buh-Buh Ray Dudley RC	.20	.50
17 Grandmaster Sexay RC	.20	.50
18 Scotty 2 Hotty RC	.20	.50
19 William Regal	.20	.50
20 Big Boss Man	.20	.50
21 Edge	.25	.60
22 Mideon	.12	.30
23 Al Snow	.15	.40
24 Stephanie McMahon-Helmsley RC	8.00	20.00
25 Dean Malenko	.12	.30
26 Tazz	.20	.50
27 Bull Buchanan RC	.12	.30
28 Hardcore Holly	.20	.50
29 Sgt. Slaughter	.30	.75
30 X-Pac	.20	.50
31 Christian	.30	.75
32 Jim JR Ross	.20	.50
33 Steve Blackman	.12	.30
34 Fabulous Moolah	.20	.50
35 Gangrel	.12	.30
36 Rikishi	.20	.50
37 Vince McMahon	.50	1.25
38 Essa Rios	.12	.30
39 Pat Patterson	.20	.50
40 Triple H	.50	1.25
41 K-Kwik RC	.12	.30
42 Crash Holly RC	.12	.30
43 Kane	.30	.75
44 Steven Richards RC	.20	.50
45 Joey Abs RC	.12	.30
46 The One Billy Gunn	.12	.30
47 Faarooq	.12	.30
48 Undertaker	.60	1.50
49 Tiger Ali Singh	.12	.30
50 D'Lo Brown	.12	.30
51 Kurt Angle	.30	.75
52 Stone Cold Steve Austin	.75	2.00
53 Chaz RC	.12	.30
54 Chris Jericho	.30	.75
55 Jerry The King Lawler	.20	.50
56 Mae Young RC	.20	.50
57 Bradshaw	.30	.75
58 Funaki RC	.12	.30
59 Perry Saturn	.12	.30
60 Val Venis	.20	.50
61 Tori DIVAS	.60	1.50
62 Debra DIVAS	.60	1.50
63 Chyna DIVAS	.30	.75
64 Ivory DIVAS	.50	1.25
65 Jacqueline DIVAS	.50	1.25
66 The Kat DIVAS RC	.15	.40
67 Lita DIVAS RC	2.50	6.00
68 Trish Stratus DIVAS RC	3.00	8.00
69 Molly Holly DIVAS RC	.50	1.25
70 Terri DIVAS RC	.60	1.50
71 Edge & Christian TT	.30	.75
72 Hardy Boyz TT	.30	.75
73 Dudley Boyz TT	.20	.50
74 T & A TT	.20	.50
75 Right to Censor TT	.20	.50
76 The Radicalz TT	.30	.75
77 The Hollys TT	.20	.50
78 K-Kwik & Road Dogg TT	.12	.30
79 Lo Down TT	.12	.30
80 Too Cool TT	.20	.50
81 I Pity the Fool WR	.20	.50
82 Hulkamania Runs Wild WR	.60	1.50
83 Rage in the Cage WR	.60	1.50
84 A New Attendance Record WR	.12	.30
85 The Proud Chairman WR	.50	1.25
86 Brain Awakens Sleeping Giant WR	.40	1.00
87 Stars and Stripes Challenge WR	.12	.30
88 Don't Do It, Roddy WR	.30	.75
89 When in Rome WR	.20	.50
90 Megabucks vs. Megamaniacs WR	1.50	4.00
91 Good Friends, Better Enemies WR	.15	.40
92 Enter the Rattlesnake WR	.75	2.00
93 Dark Days Cometh WR	.60	1.50
94 Rock/Rikishi Early Years WR	.75	2.00
95 Hardcore Highlight WR	.12	.30
96 Rough Night for Charlie Hustle WR	.12	.30
97 The Stone Cold Age Begins WR	.75	2.00
98 Strike Two for the Hit King WR	.20	.50
99 The Rattlesnake Reigns Supreme WR	.75	2.00
100 Tag Team Daredevils WR	.12	.30

2001 Fleer WWF WrestleMania Foreign Objects

COMPLETE SET (9) 150.00 300.00
UNLISTED STARS 20.00 50.00
STATED ODDS 1:63 HOBBY EXCLUSIVE

Card	Low	High
NNO Chris Jericho/Jersey	10.00	25.00
NNO Dudley Boyz/Table SP	75.00	150.00
NNO The Rock/T-Shirt	15.00	40.00
NNO Steve Austin/T-Shirt	12.00	30.00
NNO Triple H/Jeans	10.00	25.00
NNO Triple H/T-Shirt	10.00	25.00
NNO Trish Stratus/Shirt	20.00	50.00
NNO Trish Stratus/Skirt	30.00	75.00
NNO Undertaker/T-Shirt	10.00	25.00

2001 Fleer WWF WrestleMania Lip Service

STATED PRINT RUN 50 SERIAL #'d SETS
EXCH.EXPIRATION: 04/01/2002
HOBBY EXCLUSIVE

Card	Low	High
NNO Chyna	200.00	400.00
NNO Ivory	50.00	100.00
NNO Jacqueline	25.00	60.00
NNO Lita	175.00	350.00
NNO Molly Holly	75.00	150.00
NNO Terri	50.00	100.00
NNO Tori	30.00	75.00
NNO Trish Stratus	250.00	500.00

2001 Fleer WWF WrestleMania The People's Champion

COMPLETE SET (15) 2.00 5.00
STATED ODDS 1:2

Card	Low	High
PC1 The People's Elbow	.20	.50
PC2 The Rock on the Mic	.20	.50
PC3 The People's Eyebrow	.20	.50
PC4 Blood From a Rock	.20	.50
PC5 Football Career	.20	.50
PC6 The Rock, The Author	.20	.50
PC7 The Great One	.20	.50
PC8 The Brahma Bull	.20	.50
PC9 Layeth the Smackdown	.20	.50
PC10 The Rock Bottom	.20	.50
PC11 Can You Smell?	.20	.50
PC12 Just Bring It Jabroni	.20	.50
PC13 Five-Time WWF Champion	.20	.50
PC14 The Millions And Millions	.20	.50
PC15 Not Just a WWF Superstar	.20	.50

2001 Fleer WWF WrestleMania Signature Moves

COMPLETE SET (15) 40.00 80.00
STATED ODDS 1:24 HOBBY EXCLUSIVE

Card	Low	High
SM1 The Rock	6.00	12.00
SM2 Stone Cold Steve Austin	6.00	12.00
SM3 Kurt Angle	5.00	10.00
SM4 Triple H	5.00	10.00
SM5 Chris Jericho	5.00	10.00
SM6 Chris Benoit	4.00	8.00
SM7 Undertaker	5.00	10.00
SM8 Kane	4.00	8.00
SM9 Too Cool	4.00	8.00
SM10 Hardy Boyz	5.00	10.00
SM11 Dudley Boyz	5.00	10.00
SM12 Tazz	5.00	10.00
SM13 Eddie Guerrero	2.00	5.00
SM14 The One Billy Gunn	2.00	5.00
SM15 Lita	7.50	15.00

2001 Fleer WWF WrestleMania Signature Moves Autographs

RANDOMLY INSERTED INTO PACKS
STATED PRINT RUN 500 SERIAL #'d SETS
STRATUS PROMO ONLY AVAILABLE AT '01 NSCC

Card	Low	High
NNO Bubba Ray Dudley	20.00	50.00
NNO D-Von Dudley	15.00	40.00
NNO Kurt Angle	50.00	100.00
NNO Stone Cold Steve Austin	400.00	750.00
NNO Trish Stratus NSCC		

2001 Fleer WWF WrestleMania Stone Cold Said So

COMPLETE SET (15) 5.00 12.00
STATED ODDS 1:2

Card	Low	High
SC1 The Rock	2.50	6.00
SC2 Kurt Angle	.50	1.25
SC3 Rikishi	.30	.75
SC4 Chris Benoit	.40	1.00
SC5 Chris Jericho	.50	1.25
SC6 Triple H	.50	1.25
SC7 Vince McMahon	.40	1.00
SC8 Undertaker	.50	4.00
SC9 Kane	.40	1.00
SC10 Stephanie McMahon-Helmsley	1.50	4.00
SC11 X-Pac	.30	.75
SC12 Mick Foley	.50	1.25
SC13 Tazz	.50	1.25
SC14 Shane McMahon	.40	1.00
SC15 The One Billy Gunn	.30	.75

2015 Frame By Frame WWE Flip Madness Collection

COMMON GOLD SP (21-30) 1.25 3.00
COMMON TITANIUM SP (31-36) 2.00 5.00

Card	Low	High
1 Batista	1.50	4.00
2 Big Show	1.50	4.00
3 Brock Lesnar	2.50	6.00
4 Cesaro	.60	1.50
5 Roman Reigns	1.50	4.00
6 Daniel Bryan	2.50	6.00
7 Dean Ambrose	1.50	4.00
8 Dolph Ziggler	1.00	2.50
9 Goldust	.60	1.50
10 John Cena	3.00	8.00
11 Kofi Kingston	.60	1.50
12 Mark Henry	1.00	2.50
13 Randy Orton	2.50	6.00
14 Ryback	.60	1.50
15 Seth Rollins	1.00	2.50
16 Sheamus	1.50	4.00
17 The Miz	1.00	2.50
18 King Barrett	.60	1.50
19 Triple H	2.50	6.00
20 Undertaker	2.50	6.00
21 Big Show SP	3.00	8.00
22 Brock Lesnar SP	5.00	12.00
23 Cesaro SP	1.25	3.00
24 Dolph Ziggler SP	2.00	5.00
25 Goldust SP	1.25	3.00
26 Roman Reigns SP	3.00	8.00
27 Ryback SP	1.25	3.00
28 Sheamus SP	3.00	8.00
29 Triple H SP	5.00	12.00
30 Undertaker SP	5.00	12.00
31 Daniel Bryan SP	8.00	20.00
32 Dean Ambrose SP	5.00	12.00
33 John Cena SP	10.00	25.00
34 Randy Orton SP	8.00	20.00
35 Seth Rollins SP	3.00	8.00
36 King Barrett SP	2.00	5.00

1988 Gold Bond WWF

COMPLETE SET (12) 15.00 40.00

Card	Low	High
NNO Andre the Giant	5.00	12.00
NNO Bobby The Brain Heenan	4.00	10.00
NNO Elizabeth	3.00	8.00
NNO George The Animal Steele	2.50	6.00
NNO Hillbilly Jim	2.00	5.00
NNO Honky Tonk Man	2.00	5.00
NNO Hulk Hogan	5.00	12.00
NNO Koko B. Ware	1.50	4.00
NNO Ted DiBiase	3.00	8.00
NNO Randy Macho Man Savage	3.00	8.00
NNO Ricky The Dragon Steamboat	1.50	4.00
NNO Strike Force	1.50	4.00

1989 Gold Bond WWF

COMPLETE SET (12)

Card	Low	High
NNO Andre the Giant	3.00	8.00
NNO Bobby The Brain Heenan		
NNO Brutus The Barber Beefcake	1.50	4.00
NNO Demolition (Ax & Smash)		
NNO Hacksaw Jim Duggan	2.50	6.00
NNO Hercules		
NNO Hulk Hogan	6.00	15.00
NNO Jake The Snake Roberts	3.00	8.00
NNO Macho Man Randy Savage	4.00	10.00
NNO Ted DiBiase	1.50	4.00
NNO Miss Elizabeth	3.00	8.00
NNO Ultimate Warrior		

1990 Gold Bond WWF

COMPLETE SET (12) 12.00 30.00

Card	Low	High
NNO Andre the Giant	2.50	6.00
NNO Bobby The Brain Heenan	2.00	5.00
NNO Brutus The Barber Beefcake	1.50	4.00
NNO Demolition	1.50	4.00
NNO Hulk Hogan	3.00	8.00
NNO Hulk Hogan No Holds Barred	4.00	10.00
NNO Macho Man Randy Savage	3.00	8.00
NNO Ted DiBiase	1.50	4.00
NNO Ravishing Rick Rude	1.50	4.00
NNO Rowdy Roddy Piper	3.00	8.00
NNO Ultimate Warrior	3.00	8.00
NNO Wrestlemania III	1.00	2.50

1991 Gold Bond WWF

COMPLETE SET (12)

Card	Low	High
NNO Big Boss Man		
NNO Honky Tonk Man		
NNO Hulk Hogan	3.00	8.00
NNO Jake The Snake Roberts	2.00	5.00
NNO Macho King Randy Savage	3.00	8.00
NNO Ted DiBiase	5.00	12.00
NNO Mr. Perfect	4.00	10.00
NNO Rowdy Roddy Piper	3.00	8.00
NNO Sensational Queen Sherri	10.00	25.00
NNO Sgt. Slaughter	2.50	6.00
NNO Superfly Jimmy Snuka		
NNO Ultimate Warrior		

1985 Golden Hulk Hogan's Rock 'n' Wrestling Card Game

Card	Low	High
NNO Andre the Giant	6.00	15.00
NNO Big John Studd	1.50	4.00
NNO Fabulous Moolah	1.50	4.00
NNO Hillbilly Jim	1.50	4.00
NNO Hulk Hogan	6.00	15.00
NNO Hulk Hogan/Iron Sheik Flip	6.00	15.00

NNO Iron Sheik	2.00	5.00
NNO Jimmy Superfly Snuka	1.50	4.00
NNO Junkyard Dog	2.00	5.00
NNO Mr. Fuji	1.25	3.00
NNO Nikolai Volkoff	1.25	3.00
NNO Rowdy Roddy Piper	3.00	8.00
NNO Tito Santana	1.25	3.00
NNO Wendi Richter	2.00	5.00

1992 Good Humor WWF

COMPLETE SET (12)		
NNO Big Boss Man		
NNO Bret Hit Man Hart	6.00	15.00
NNO Elizabeth	3.00	8.00
NNO Hulk Hogan	12.00	30.00
NNO Legion of Doom		
NNO Macho Man Randy Savage	5.00	12.00
NNO Ted DiBiase	3.00	8.00
NNO Mr. Perfect		
NNO Rowdy Roddy Piper	5.00	12.00
NNO Sid Justice		
NNO The Nasty Boys		
NNO The Undertaker	6.00	15.00

2002 Good Humor WWF

COMPLETE SET (10)	15.00	40.00
NNO Chris Jericho	1.50	4.00
NNO Dudley Boyz	1.50	4.00
NNO Edge & Christian	2.50	6.00
NNO Hardy Boyz	1.50	4.00
NNO Kane	2.50	6.00
NNO Kurt Angle	2.50	6.00
NNO The Rock	4.00	10.00
NNO Stone Cold Steve Austin	4.00	10.00
NNO Triple H	4.00	10.00
NNO The Undertaker	3.00	8.00

1990 Hasbro WWF Flips Trading Cards

COMPLETE SET (10)		
NNO Big Boss Man	1.25	3.00
NNO Brutus The Barber Beefcake	1.50	4.00
NNO The Bushwhackers		
NNO Hacksaw Jim Duggan	4.00	10.00
NNO Hulk Hogan	6.00	15.00
NNO Jake The Snake Roberts		
NNO Macho King Randy Savage	5.00	12.00
NNO Ted DiBiase		
NNO The Rockers		
NNO Ultimate Warrior		

1988 Hostess WWF WrestleMania IV Stickers

1 Jake The Snake Roberts	1.00	2.50
2 Billy Jack Haynes	.50	1.25
3 Brutus The Barber Beefcake	.75	2.00
4 Macho Man and Elizabeth	2.00	5.00
5 Koko B. Ware	.50	1.25
6 George The Animal Steele	.60	1.50
7 Hulk Hogan	2.50	6.00
8 Junkyard Dog	.60	1.50
9 Magnificent Muraco	.60	1.50
10 Bam Bam Bigelow	.75	2.00
11 Elizabeth	1.00	2.50
12 The Honky Tonk Man	.50	1.25
13 Ted DiBiase	.75	2.00
14 The Natural Butch Reed	.50	1.25
15 Ravishing Rick Rude	1.00	2.50
16 Killer Khan	.50	1.25
17 Bobby The Brain Heenan	1.00	2.50
18 Jimmy Hart	.60	1.50
19 Slick The Doctor of Style	.50	1.25
20 Hulk Hogan	2.50	6.00
21 Mr. Fuji	.50	1.25
22 Oliver Humperdink	.50	1.25
23 Strike Force	.60	1.50
24 The British Bulldogs	.75	2.00
25 The Killer Bees	.50	1.25
26 Demolition Ax and Smash	.75	2.00
27 The Islanders	.50	1.25
28 Ken Patera	.50	1.25
29 The Rougeau Brothers	.50	1.25
30 The Hart Foundation	.75	2.00
31 Strike Force	.60	1.50
32 Jesse The Body Ventura	1.00	2.50
33 Hillbilly Jim	.50	1.25
34 Randy Macho Man Savage	2.00	5.00

1987 Hostess Munchies WWF Stickers

COMPLETE SET (20)	10.00	20.00
NNO British Bulldogs	.20	.50
NNO Don Muraco	.15	.40
NNO George The Animal Steele	.40	1.00
NNO Hillbilly Jim	.20	.50
NNO Honky Tonk Man	.20	.50
NNO Hulk Hogan	3.00	8.00
NNO Hulk Hogan	3.00	8.00
NNO Iron Sheik and Nikoli Volkoff	.25	.60
NNO Jake The Snake Roberts	.50	1.25
NNO Junkyard Dog	.20	.50
NNO Kamala	.15	.40
NNO King Kong Bundy	.20	.50
NNO Koko B. Ware	.15	.40
NNO Outback Jack	.15	.40
NNO Paul Mr. Wonderful Orndorff	.20	.50
NNO Randy Savage and Elizabeth	1.50	4.00
NNO Ricky The Dragon Steamboat	.20	.50
NNO Rowdy Roddy Piper	1.25	3.00
NNO Sika	.40	1.00
NNO Tito Santana	.15	.40

1999 Hot Shots WWF Stickers

COMPLETE SET (212)	12.00	30.00
1 Stone Cold Steve Austin	.75	2.00
2 Stone Cold Steve Austin	.75	2.00
3 Stone Cold Steve Austin	.75	2.00
4 Stone Cold Steve Austin	.75	2.00
5 Stone Cold Steve Austin	.75	2.00
6 Stone Cold Steve Austin	.75	2.00
7 Stone Cold Steve Austin	.75	2.00
8 Stone Cold Steve Austin	.75	2.00
9 Stone Cold Steve Austin	.75	2.00
10 Stone Cold Steve Austin	.75	2.00
11 Stone Cold Steve Austin	.75	2.00
12 Stone Cold Steve Austin	.75	2.00
13 Stone Cold Steve Austin	.75	2.00
14 Stone Cold Steve Austin	.75	2.00
15 Stone Cold Steve Austin	.75	2.00
16 Stone Cold Steve Austin	.75	2.00
17 Stone Cold Steve Austin	.75	2.00
18 Stone Cold Steve Austin	.75	2.00
19 The Rock	.75	2.00
20 The Rock	.75	2.00
21 The Rock	.75	2.00
22 The Rock	.75	2.00
23 The Rock	.75	2.00
24 The Rock	.75	2.00
25 The Rock	.75	2.00
26 The Rock	.75	2.00
27 The Rock	.75	2.00
28 The Rock	.75	2.00
29 The Rock	.75	2.00
30 The Rock	.75	2.00
31 The Rock	.75	2.00
32 The Rock	.75	2.00
33 The Rock	.75	2.00
34 The Rock	.75	2.00
35 The Rock	.75	2.00
36 The Rock	.75	2.00
37 Big Show	.25	.60
38 Big Show	.25	.60
39 Big Show	.25	.60
40 Big Show	.25	.60
41 Big Show	.25	.60
42 Big Show	.25	.60
43 Undertaker	.60	1.50
44 Undertaker	.60	1.50
45 Undertaker	.60	1.50
46 Undertaker	.60	1.50
47 Undertaker	.60	1.50
48 Undertaker	.60	1.50
49 Undertaker	.60	1.50
50 Undertaker	.60	1.50
51 Undertaker	.60	1.50
52 Undertaker	.60	1.50
53 Undertaker	.60	1.50
54 Undertaker	.60	1.50
55 Undertaker	.60	1.50
56 Undertaker	.60	1.50
57 Undertaker	.60	1.50
58 Undertaker	.60	1.50
59 Undertaker	.60	1.50
60 Undertaker	.60	1.50
61 Acolytes	.12	.30
62 Corporate Ministry	.12	.30
63 Viscera	.12	.30
64 Chyna	.20	.50
65 Chyna	.20	.50
66 Big Boss Man	.12	.30
67 Big Boss Man	.12	.30
68 Viscera	.12	.30
69 Corporate Ministry	.12	.30
70 Big Boss Man	.12	.30
71 Acolytes	.12	.30
72 Paul Bearer	.15	.40
73 Ken Shamrock	.15	.40
74 Ken Shamrock	.15	.40
75 Ken Shamrock	.15	.40
76 Ken Shamrock	.15	.40
77 Ken Shamrock	.15	.40
78 Ken Shamrock	.15	.40
79 Mankind	.30	.75
80 Mankind	.30	.75
81 Mankind	.30	.75
82 Mankind	.30	.75
83 Mankind	.30	.75
84 Mankind	.30	.75
85 Mankind	.30	.75
86 Mankind	.30	.75
87 Mankind	.30	.75
88 Mankind	.30	.75
89 Mankind	.30	.75
90 Mankind	.30	.75
91 Vince McMahon	.20	.50
92 Vince McMahon	.20	.50
93 Vince McMahon	.20	.50
94 Vince McMahon	.20	.50
95 Vince McMahon	.20	.50
96 Vince McMahon	.20	.50
97 Shane McMahon	.20	.50
98 Shane McMahon	.20	.50
99 Shane McMahon	.20	.50
100 Shane McMahon	.20	.50
101 Shane McMahon	.20	.50
102 Shane McMahon	.20	.50
103 Triple H	.30	.75
104 Triple H	.30	.75
105 Triple H	.30	.75
106 Triple H	.30	.75
107 Triple H	.30	.75
108 Triple H	.30	.75
109 Jeff Jarrett	.25	.60
110 Jeff Jarrett	.25	.60
111 Jeff Jarrett	.25	.60
112 Jeff Jarrett	.25	.60
113 Jeff Jarrett	.25	.60
114 Jeff Jarrett	.25	.60
115 Debra	.30	.75
116 Debra	.30	.75
117 Debra	.30	.75
118 Debra	.30	.75
119 Debra	.30	.75
120 Debra	.30	.75
121 Kane	.25	.60
122 Kane	.25	.60
123 Kane	.25	.60
124 Kane	.25	.60
125 Kane	.25	.60
126 Kane	.25	.60
127 Kane	.25	.60
128 Kane	.25	.60
129 Kane	.25	.60
130 Kane	.25	.60
131 Kane	.25	.60
132 Kane	.25	.60
133 X-Pac	.25	.60
134 X-Pac	.25	.60
135 X-Pac	.25	.60
136 X-Pac	.25	.60
137 X-Pac	.25	.60
138 X-Pac	.25	.60
139 Road Dogg	.25	.60
140 Road Dogg	.25	.60
141 Road Dogg	.25	.60
142 Road Dogg	.25	.60
143 Road Dogg	.25	.60
144 Road Dogg	.25	.60
145 Billy Gunn	.25	.60
146 Billy Gunn	.25	.60
147 Billy Gunn	.25	.60
148 Billy Gunn	.25	.60
149 Billy Gunn	.25	.60
150 Billy Gunn	.25	.60
151 Al Snow	.15	.40
152 Al Snow	.15	.40
153 Al Snow	.15	.40
154 Al Snow	.15	.40
155 Al Snow	.15	.40
156 Al Snow	.15	.40
157 Val Venis	.15	.40
158 Val Venis	.15	.40
159 Val Venis	.15	.40
160 Val Venis	.15	.40
161 Val Venis	.15	.40
162 Val Venis	.15	.40
163 The Brood	.30	.75
164 Edge	.30	.75
165 The Brood	.30	.75
166 Christian	.25	.60
167 Edge	.30	.75
168 Christian	.25	.60
169 Gangrel	.12	.30
170 Gangrel	.12	.30
171 Gangrel	.12	.30
172 Gangrel	.12	.30
173 Gangrel	.12	.30
174 Gangrel	.12	.30
175 D-Lo Brown	.12	.30
176 D-Lo Brown	.12	.30
177 D-Lo Brown	.12	.30
178 D-Lo Brown	.12	.30
179 Mark Henry	.15	.40
180 Mark Henry	.15	.40
181 Goldust	.25	.60
182 Goldust	.25	.60
183 Goldust	.25	.60
184 Goldust	.25	.60
185 Goldust	.25	.60
186 Goldust	.25	.60
187 Godfather	.20	.50
188 Godfather	.20	.50
189 Godfather	.20	.50
190 Godfather	.20	.50
191 Godfather	.20	.50
192 Godfather	.20	.50
193 PMS	.15	.40
194 PMS	.15	.40
195 PMS	.15	.40
196 PMS	.15	.40
197 PMS	.15	.40
198 PMS	.15	.40
199 Nicole Bass	.12	.30
200 Droz	.12	.30
201 Shawn Michaels	.40	1.00
202 Ivory	.20	.50
203 Droz	.12	.30
204 Hardcore Holly	.12	.30
205 Test	.12	.30
206 Tiger Ali Singh	.12	.30
207 Tiger Ali Singh	.12	.30
208 Kurrgan	.12	.30
209 Test	.12	.30
210 Shawn Michaels	.40	1.00
211 Test	.12	.30
212 Raw Is War	.12	.30

1991 Imagine Wrestling Legends

COMPLETE SET (60)	25.00	60.00
1 Bruno Sammartino	1.25	3.00
2 Buddy Rogers	.75	2.00
3 Ivan Koloff	.75	2.00
4 Lou Albano	.40	1.00
5 Billy Graham	1.00	2.50
6 Killer Kowalski	1.00	2.50
7 Lou Thesz	1.25	3.00

8 Domenic DeNucci	.40	1.00
9 Bruno Sammartino	1.25	3.00
10 Buddy Rogers	.75	2.00
11 Ivan Koloff	.75	2.00
12 Lou Albano	.40	1.00
13 Billy Graham	1.00	2.50
14 Killer Kowalski	1.00	2.50
15 Lou Thesz	1.25	3.00
16 Bill Miller	.40	1.00
17 Domenic DeNucci	.40	1.00
18 Bruno Sammartino	1.25	3.00
19 Antonio Rocca	.40	1.00
20 Buddy Rogers	.75	2.00
21 Ivan Koloff	.75	2.00
22 Primo Carnerra	.75	2.00
23 Lou Albano	.40	1.00
24 Bruno Sammartino	1.25	3.00
25 Crusher Lisowski	.75	2.00
26 Billy Graham	1.00	2.50
27 Killer Kowalski	1.00	2.50
28 Domenic DeNucci	.40	1.00
29 Rocca & Perez	.75	2.00
30 Bill Watts	.40	1.00
31 BoBo Brazil	.75	2.00
32 Lou Thesz	1.25	3.00
33 Pedro Morales	1.00	2.50
34 Johnny Valentine	.75	2.00
35 Argentine Apollo	.40	1.00
36 Billy Graham	1.00	2.50
37 Haystacks Calhoun	.40	1.00
38 Bruno Sammartino	1.25	3.00
39 The Destroyer	.75	2.00
40 Buddy Rogers	.75	2.00
41 Ray Stevens	.75	2.00
42 Lou Albano	.40	1.00
43 Edouard Carpentier	.40	1.00
44 Killer Kowalski	1.00	2.50
45 Bob Backlund	1.00	2.50
46 Killer Kowalski	1.00	2.50
47 Mil Mascaras	1.00	2.50
48 Domenic DeNucci	.40	1.00
49 Smasher Sloan	.40	1.00
50 Ivan Koloff	.75	2.00
51 Lou Albano	.40	1.00
52 Lou Thesz	1.25	3.00
53 Harly Race UER	1.25	3.00
54 Billy Graham	1.00	2.50
55 Domenic DeNucci	.40	1.00
56 Hawk & Hansen	.75	2.00
57 Lou Thesz	1.25	3.00
58 Ivan Koloff	.75	2.00
59 Buddy Rogers	.75	2.00
60 Bruno Sammartino	1.25	3.00
61 Bruno Sammartino AU	50.00	100.00
62 Buddy Rogers AU	25.00	60.00
63 Lou Thesz AU	25.00	60.00
64 Billy Graham AU	15.00	40.00
65 Ivan Koloff AU	15.00	40.00
66 Killer Kowalski AU	30.00	75.00
67 Lou Albano AU	20.00	50.00
68 Domenic DeNucci AU	12.00	30.00

2022 Immaculate Collection WWE

*RED/40: .5X TO 1.2X BASIC CARDS
*GOLD/10: UNPRICED DUE TO SCARCITY
*GREEN/5: UNPRICED DUE TO SCARCITY
*PLATINUM/1: UNPRICED DUE TO SCARCITY
STATED PRINT RUN 65 SER.#'d SETS

1 Shawn Michaels	10.00	25.00
2 Dakota Kai	30.00	75.00
3 Triple H	8.00	20.00
4 Finn Balor	6.00	15.00
5 Junkyard Dog	3.00	8.00
6 Macho Man Randy Savage	12.00	30.00
7 Matt Riddle	6.00	15.00
8 Asuka	15.00	40.00
9 Razor Ramon	8.00	20.00
10 Booker T	5.00	12.00
11 Shayna Baszler	10.00	25.00
12 Damian Priest	5.00	12.00
13 Trish Stratus	12.00	30.00
14 Gigi Dolin	30.00	75.00
15 Kane	10.00	25.00
16 Ted DiBiase	6.00	15.00
17 Natalya	5.00	12.00
18 Bam Bam Bigelow	10.00	25.00
19 Rey Mysterio	8.00	20.00
20 Bret "Hit Man" Hart	10.00	25.00
21 Shinsuke Nakamura	5.00	12.00
22 Diesel	5.00	12.00
23 Tyler Bate	3.00	8.00
24 Goldberg	10.00	25.00
25 Karrion Kross	10.00	20.00
26 Mr. Perfect	8.00	20.00
27 Nikki Bella	15.00	40.00
28 Batista	8.00	20.00
29 Rhea Ripley	15.00	40.00
30 British Bulldog	4.00	10.00
31 Shotzi	12.00	30.00
32 Dolph Ziggler	3.00	8.00
33 Ultimate Warrior	15.00	40.00
34 Gunther	5.00	12.00
35 Katana Chance	10.00	25.00
36 Rowdy Roddy Piper	10.00	25.00
37 Nikkita Lyons	60.00	150.00
38 Bayley	12.00	30.00
39 Ricochet	4.00	10.00
40 Brock Lesnar	12.00	30.00
41 Solo Sikoa	20.00	50.00
42 Dominik Mysterio	6.00	15.00
43 Umaga	8.00	20.00
44 Hollywood Hogan	25.00	60.00
45 Kevin Owens	8.00	20.00
46 Stone Cold Steve Austin	20.00	50.00
47 Braun Strowman	6.00	15.00
48 Becky Lynch	25.00	60.00
49 The Rock	40.00	100.00
50 Bruno Sammartino	4.00	10.00
51 Sonya Deville	8.00	20.00
52 Drew McIntyre	6.00	15.00
53 Vader	4.00	10.00
54 Ilja Dragunov	5.00	12.00
55 Kofi Kingston	6.00	15.00
56 Bobby Lashley	5.00	12.00
57 Omos	3.00	8.00
58 Bianca Belair	15.00	40.00
59 Roman Reigns	10.00	25.00
60 Butch	3.00	8.00
61 Stacy Keibler	25.00	60.00
62 Dusty Rhodes	6.00	15.00
63 Xavier Woods	5.00	12.00
64 IYO SKY	6.00	15.00
65 Lacey Evans	5.00	12.00
66 Cody Rhodes	20.00	50.00
67 Paul Bearer	10.00	25.00
68 Big Boss Man	5.00	12.00
69 Ronda Rousey	12.00	30.00
70 Carmella	10.00	25.00
71 Terry Funk	5.00	12.00
72 Eddie Guerrero	12.00	30.00
73 X-Pac	3.00	8.00
74 Jey Uso	6.00	15.00
75 Liv Morgan	40.00	100.00
76 Alba Fyre	6.00	15.00
77 Paul Heyman	6.00	15.00
78 Big E	3.00	8.00
79 Roxanne Perez	50.00	125.00
80 Charlotte Flair	15.00	40.00
81 The Miz	6.00	15.00
82 Edge	12.00	30.00
83 Yokozuna	8.00	20.00
84 Jimmy Uso	3.00	8.00
85 Mandy Rose	25.00	60.00
86 Alexa Bliss	40.00	100.00
87 Randy Orton	10.00	25.00
88 Big John Studd	5.00	12.00
89 Scarlett	20.00	50.00
90 Chyna	10.00	25.00
91 Austin Theory	6.00	15.00
92 Elektra Lopez	10.00	25.00
93 Johnny Gargano	8.00	20.00
94 John Cena	12.00	30.00
95 Mankind	10.00	25.00
96 Andre the Giant	12.00	30.00
97 Raquel Rodriguez	15.00	40.00
98 Bobby Heenan	10.00	25.00
99 Seth Rollins	6.00	15.00
100 Tommaso Ciampa	4.00	10.00

2022 Immaculate Collection WWE All-Time Greats Signatures

*GOLD/10: UNPRICED DUE TO SCARCITY
*PLATINUM/1: UNPRICED DUE TO SCARCITY
RANDOMLY INSERTED INTO PACKS

AGBTS Batista/99 EXCH	60.00	150.00
AGCBO Cowboy Bob Orton/60	20.00	50.00
AGCJK Cactus Jack/75	75.00	200.00
AGGBG Goldberg/75	50.00	125.00
AGGBS Gerald Brisco/99	15.00	40.00
AGHHG Hulk Hogan/35 EXCH	400.00	1000.00
AGJCN John Cena/99 EXCH	125.00	300.00
AGJJT Jeff Jarrett/49 EXCH	15.00	40.00
AGJKL Jerry Lawler/75	30.00	75.00
AGLTA Lita/99	25.00	60.00
AGMDM Ted DiBiase/99	20.00	50.00
AGNBL Nikki Bella/75	50.00	125.00
AGRDG Road Dogg/75 EXCH	15.00	40.00
AGSBG Superstar Billy Graham/99	15.00	40.00
AGSCA Stone Cold Steve Austin/49	300.00	750.00
AGSML Shawn Michaels/75	75.00	200.00
AGTPH Triple H/99	125.00	300.00
AGTST Trish Stratus/99	40.00	100.00
AGUND Undertaker/49		
AGXPC X-Pac/75	25.00	60.00

2022 Immaculate Collection WWE The Bloodline Autograph

STATED PRINT RUN 25 SER.#'d SETS

NNO Sikoa/Reigns/Usos Afa/Sika/Rikishi	2000.00	5000.00

2022 Immaculate Collection WWE Dual Autographed Memorabilia

*PLATINUM/1: UNPRICED DUE TO SCARCITY
STATED PRINT RUN 10 SER.#'d SETS

DM R.Orton/M.Riddle EXCH
DM Shanky/J.Mahal EXCH
DM Edge/D.Priest EXCH
DM B.Lynch/B.Belair
DM AJ Styles/Edge EXCH
DMACC Azeez/A.Crews
DMBBD D.Ziggler/B.Breakker EXCH
DMBLO B.Lashley/Omos
DMBLR R.Reigns/B.Lesnar EXCH
DMCBB Ciampa/B.Breakker EXCH
DMCRD Brutus & Julius Creed
DMDMB B.Lesnar/D.McIntyre
DMDMH D.McIntyre/H.Corbin
DMGGJ J.Jayne/G.Dolin
DMGLA LA Knight/Gunther
DMJGM R.Ripley/D.Priest
DMJRR J.Reid/R.Fowler
DMKCK K.Carter/K.Chance
DMMRC M.Rose/C.Jade
DMMST Dominik & Rey Mysterio
DMNSH Natalya/S.Baszler EXCH
DMOMM MVP/Omos
DMPDL K.Wilson/E.Prince
DMSBL S.Rollins/B.Lesnar
DMSPF A.Dawkins/M.Ford
DMUSO Jimmy & Jey Uso
DMVRD Ivar/Erik

2022 Immaculate Collection WWE Dual Autographs

*PLATINUM/1: UNPRICED DUE TO SCARCITY
STATED PRINT RUN 25 SER.#'d SETS

DA K.Angle/G.Steveson EXCH		
DA R.Orton/C.Rhodes EXCH	250.00	600.00
DA Undertaker/Kane EXCH		
DA R.Orton/M.Riddle EXCH		
DA Edge/AJ Styles EXCH		
DA HHH/S.McMahon EXCH	250.00	600.00
DAACC Azeez/A.Crews	20.00	50.00
DAAPA Faarooq/Bradshaw		
DABLA The Bella Twins	100.00	250.00
DABLB B.Lynch/B.Belair	200.00	500.00
DABLG B.Lesnar/G.Steveson EXCH		
DABLO B.Lashley/Omos	75.00	200.00
DABLR B.Lesnar/R.Reigns EXCH		
DABWK The Bushwhackers	75.00	200.00
DACFR R.Rousey/C.Flair EXCH	300.00	750.00
DACRD Julius & Brutus Creed	60.00	150.00
DACRS C.Rhodes/S.Rollins EXCH		
DADMH H.Corbin/D.McIntyre		
DADPE D.Priest/Edge		
DAFHS S.Baszler/R.Rousey EXCH		
DAHHS I.Sheik/H.Hogan EXCH	300.00	750.00
DAJDI I.Dragunov/J.Devlin EXCH		
DAJGM D.Priest/R.Ripley	100.00	250.00
DAJMS J.Mahal/Shanky EXCH		
DAJRR J.Reid/R.Fowler		
DAKCK K.Chance/K.Carter	50.00	125.00
DALTT T.Stratus/Lita EXCH		
DAMST Rey & Dominik Mysterio		
DANOD Kama/Faarooq	50.00	125.00
DANSH S.Baszler/Natalya EXCH		
DAPDL K.Wilson/E.Prince	50.00	125.00
DARRV M.Riddle/RVD	75.00	200.00
DASCK K.Owens/S.Austin EXCH		
DASPF A.Dawkins/M.Ford	50.00	125.00
DATXA J.Jayne/G.Dolin	200.00	500.00
DAUSO Jey & Jimmy Uso	150.00	400.00
DAVKR Erik/Ivar	30.00	75.00
DAWSM Afa/Sika	100.00	250.00

2022 Immaculate Collection WWE Heralded Signatures

*GOLD/10: UNPRICED DUE TO SCARCITY
*PLATINUM/1: UNPRICED DUE TO SCARCITY
STATED PRINT RUN 95-99 SETS

HS123 1-2-3 Kid/99	20.00	50.00
HSABZ Alundra Blayze/99	10.00	25.00
HSASN Al Snow/99	15.00	40.00
HSBBK Brutus Beefcake/99	12.00	30.00
HSBGM The Boogeyman/99	25.00	60.00
HSBKB Brian Knobs/99	10.00	25.00
HSBKT Booker T/99	15.00	40.00
HSBPH Beth Phoenix/95	15.00	40.00
HSBWL Bushwhacker Luke/99	12.00	30.00
HSCBO Cowboy Bob Orton/99	12.00	25.00
HSDDP Diamond Dallas Page/99	20.00	50.00
HSDMR Don Muraco/99	12.00	25.00
HSGBS Gerald Brisco/99	10.00	30.00
HSGVL Greg Valentine/99	12.00	30.00
HSHJD Hacksaw Jim Duggan/99	20.00	50.00
HSISH Iron Sheik/99	20.00	50.00
HSIVY Ivory/99	10.00	25.00
HSJHT Jimmy Hart/99	15.00	40.00
HSJLW Jerry Lawler/99	20.00	50.00
HSJRZ Johnny Rodz/99	12.00	30.00
HSJSG Jerry Sags/99	12.00	30.00
HSKAG Kurt Angle/99	30.00	75.00
HSKLY Kelly Kelly/99	30.00	75.00
HSMDM Ted DiBiase/99	15.00	40.00
HSMHY Michael Hayes/99	12.00	30.00
HSMMC Michelle McCool/99	15.00	40.00
HSPED Paul Heyman/99 (unnumbered)	40.00	100.00
HSPSH Papa Shango/99	10.00	25.00
HSRDG Road Dogg/99	15.00	40.00
HSRKS Rikishi/99	15.00	40.00
HSRSM Ron Simmons/99	12.00	30.00
HSRVD Rob Van Dam/99	20.00	50.00
HSSBG Superstar Billy Graham/99	15.00	40.00
HSSHS Stan Hansen/99	30.00	75.00
HSSMN The Sandman/99	25.00	60.00
HSTKD Tyson Kidd/99	12.00	25.00
HSTLG Teddy Long/99	10.00	25.00
HSTRI Terri Runnels/99	15.00	40.00

2022 Immaculate Collection WWE Immaculate Celebrations Autographs

RANDOMLY INSERTED INTO PACKS

ICBGE Big E/49 EXCH	20.00	50.00
ICBKT Booker T/49	30.00	75.00
ICBLS Bobby Lashley/49	50.00	125.00
ICDDP Diamond Dallas Page/75	50.00	125.00
ICGBG Goldberg/75 EXCH	75.00	200.00
ICHHG Hulk Hogan/49	200.00	500.00
ICJCN John Cena/99	100.00	250.00
ICROR Randy Orton/49	75.00	200.00
ICSML Shawn Michaels/60	200.00	500.00
ICUND Undertaker/49 EXCH	300.00	750.00

2022 Immaculate Collection WWE Immaculate Inductions Autographs

RANDOMLY INSERTED INTO PACKS

IIBWB Bushwhacker Butch/75 12.00 30.00
IIBWL Bushwhacker Luke/75 20.00 50.00
IIDMR Don Muraco/75 15.00 40.00
IIGBG Goldberg/75 EXCH 50.00 125.00
IIHJD Hacksaw Jim Duggan/99 15.00 40.00
IIHTM The Honky Tonk Man/49 40.00 100.00
IIJJT Jeff Jarrett/49 15.00 40.00
IIJLW Jerry Lawler/75 30.00 75.00
IIJRZ Johnny Rodz/99 12.00 30.00
IIKNH Kevin Nash/75 30.00 75.00
IIMDM Ted DiBiase/99 20.00 50.00
IIMHY Michael Hayes/99 15.00 40.00
IIRDS Ricky The Dragon Steamboat/49 40.00 100.00
IISBG Superstar Billy Graham/99 25.00 60.00
IISCA Stone Cold Steve Austin 150.00 400.00
IISHS Stan Hansen/49 25.00 60.00
IITLG Teddy Long/49 20.00 50.00
IITWS Torrie Wilson/10 125.00 300.00
IIUND Undertaker/49 EXCH 200.00 500.00

2022 Immaculate Collection WWE Immaculate Ink

*GOLD/10: UNPRICED DUE TO SCARCITY
*PLATINUM/1: UNPRICED DUE TO SCARCITY
STATED PRINT RUN 99 SER.#'d SETS

IIACR Apollo Crews 10.00 25.00
IIADW Angelo Dawkins 8.00 20.00
IIBMN The Blue Meanie 15.00 40.00
IIBTH Butch 8.00 20.00
IIDFJ Dory Funk Jr. 30.00 75.00
IIDPR Damian Priest 15.00 40.00
IIERK Erik 8.00 20.00
IIHKU Haku 25.00 60.00
IIIVR Ivar 8.00 20.00
IIJJD Jason Jordan 10.00 25.00
IIJUS Jey Uso 15.00 40.00
IIKOW Kevin Owens 15.00 40.00
IILLK Leilani Kai 12.00 30.00
IIMIZ The Miz 15.00 40.00
IIMSH Mosh 8.00 20.00
IIMVP MVP 10.00 25.00
IIMZF Montez Ford 15.00 40.00
IIRCT Ricochet 12.00 30.00
IISDN Simon Dean 20.00 50.00
IISRH Stevie Richards 12.00 30.00
IITHR Thrasher 10.00 25.00
IITHR Austin Theory 20.00 50.00
IITPR Tom Prichard 15.00 40.00

2022 Immaculate Collection WWE Immaculate Milestones Autographs

RANDOMLY INSERTED INTO PACKS

IMBKT Booker T/49 40.00 100.00
IMDMI Drew McIntyre/49 40.00 100.00
IMHHG Hulk Hogan/49 EXCH 250.00 600.00
IMJCN John Cena/99 100.00 250.00
IMKNE Kane/75 50.00 125.00
IMNTL Natalya/49 EXCH 20.00 50.00
IMRMY Rey Mysterio/49 75.00 200.00
IMROR Randy Orton/49 EXCH 100.00 250.00
IMRRN Roman Reigns/49 EXCH 125.00 300.00
IMUND Undertaker/49 200.00 500.00

2022 Immaculate Collection WWE Immaculate Moments Autographs

RANDOMLY INSERTED INTO PACKS

MOCDR Cody Rhodes/99 75.00 200.00
MOGBG Goldberg/75 50.00 100.00
MOHHG Hulk Hogan/49 EXCH 300.00 800.00
MOKKG Kofi Kingston/49 40.00 100.00
MOKNE Kane/75 40.00 100.00
MOMKN Mankind/75 200.00 500.00
MORRN Roman Reigns/49 125.00 300.00
MOSCA Stone Cold Steve Austin/49 250.00 600.00
MOSML Shawn Michaels/60 125.00 300.00
MOTPH Triple H/99 100.00 250.00

2022 Immaculate Collection WWE Immaculate Nicknames Autographs

STATED PRINT RUN 25 SER.#'d SETS
UNPRICED DUE TO SCARCITY

INABS Alexa Bliss
INAJS AJ Styles
INBHH Bret "Hit Man" Hart
INBPH Beth Phoenix
INBTS Batista
INCBO Cowboy Bob Orton
INCFL Charlotte Flair
INDMR Don Muraco
INDSL Diesel
INDZG Dolph Ziggler
INGVL Greg Valentine
INHHG Hulk Hogan
INJHT Jimmy Hart
INJLW Jerry Lawler
INKNE Kane
INKOW Kevin Owens
INLLG Lex Luger
INMDM Ted DiBiase
INMFL Mick Foley
INMIZ The Miz
INNTL Natalya
INRCT Ricochet
INROR Randy Orton
INRRS Ronda Rousey
INRVD Rob Van Dam
INSBZ Shayna Baszler
INSFR Seth Rollins
INSML Shawn Michaels
INTPH Triple H
INUND Undertaker

2022 Immaculate Collection WWE The Immaculate Standard Memorabilia

STATED PRINT RUN 99 SER.#'d SETS

ISABS Alexa Bliss 60.00 150.00
ISAFY Alba Fyre 5.00 12.00
ISAJS AJ Styles 10.00 25.00
ISASH Nikki A.S.H. 5.00 12.00
ISASK Asuka 15.00 40.00
ISBBK Bron Breakker 6.00 15.00
ISBBL Bianca Belair 8.00 20.00
ISBCR Brutus Creed 5.00 12.00
ISBLN Becky Lynch 30.00 75.00
ISBLS Bobby Lashley 5.00 12.00
ISBLS Brock Lesnar 12.00 30.00
ISBRO Matt Riddle 6.00 15.00
ISBTL Bayley 10.00 25.00
ISCFL Charlotte Flair 12.00 30.00
ISCHY Carmelo Hayes 5.00 12.00
ISCJD Cora Jade 30.00 75.00
ISCML Carmella 8.00 20.00
ISDMI Drew McIntyre 5.00 12.00
ISDMY Dominik Mysterio 6.00 15.00
ISEGE Edge 8.00 20.00
ISFBL Finn Balor 15.00 40.00
ISGGD Gigi Dolin 20.00 50.00
ISGSV Gable Steveson 6.00 15.00
ISGWL Grayson Waller 10.00 25.00
ISIOS IYO SKY 10.00 25.00
ISIVN Ivy Nile 10.00 25.00
ISJCR Julius Creed 5.00 12.00
ISJJN Jacy Jayne 12.00 30.00
ISJMU Jimmy Uso 5.00 12.00
ISJUS Jey Uso 8.00 20.00
ISKCH Katana Chance 8.00 20.00
ISKKG Kofi Kingston 6.00 15.00
ISKOW Kevin Owens 10.00 25.00
ISLEV Lacey Evans 8.00 20.00
ISLVM Liv Morgan 40.00 100.00
ISMIZ The Miz 6.00 15.00
ISMRS Mandy Rose 15.00 40.00
ISNTL Natalya 6.00 15.00
ISOMS Omos 5.00 12.00
ISQZL Queen Zelina 10.00 25.00
ISRMY Rey Mysterio 10.00 25.00
ISROR Randy Orton 10.00 25.00
ISRRN Roman Reigns 15.00 40.00
ISRRP Rhea Ripley 20.00 50.00
ISSDV Sonya Deville 10.00 25.00
ISSFR Seth Rollins 10.00 25.00
ISSHM Sheamus 5.00 12.00
ISSHZ Shotzi 12.00 30.00
ISTHR Austin Theory 12.00 30.00
ISXWD Xavier Woods 10.00 25.00

2022 Immaculate Collection WWE Jumbo Memorabilia Hoodie

RANDOMLY INSERTED INTO PACKS
UNDER /24 UNPRICED DUE TO SCARCITY

JMABS Alexa Bliss/50 150.00 400.00
JMBCR Brutus Creed/4
JMBTH Butch/27 40.00 100.00
JMCHY Carmelo Hayes/50 30.00 75.00
JMDMI Drew McIntyre/26 30.00 75.00
JMEGE Edge/14
JMERK Erik/10
JMGWL Grayson Waller/18
JMIOS IYO SKY/4
JMIVR Ivar/12
JMJCR Julius Creed/4
JMJMU Jimmy Uso/24 20.00 50.00
JMJUS Jey Uso/24 15.00 40.00
JMRGH Ridge Holland/29 15.00 40.00
JMRST Roderick Strong/1
JMSFR Seth Rollins/26
JMSHM Sheamus/22

2022 Immaculate Collection WWE Jumbo Memorabilia Shirt

RANDOMLY INSERTED INTO PACKS

JMABS Alexa Bliss/50 125.00 300.00
JMACR Apollo Crews/50 10.00 25.00
JMADW Angelo Dawkins/50 15.00 40.00
JMAFY Alba Fyre/35 25.00 60.00
JMAJS AJ Styles/50 20.00 50.00
JMAOV Aoife Valkyrie/27 15.00 40.00
JMASH Nikki A.S.H./50 50.00 125.00
JMASK Asuka/50 75.00 200.00
JMAXM Axiom/13 10.00 25.00
JMBBK Bron Breakker/50 60.00 150.00
JMBBL Bianca Belair/50 60.00 150.00
JMBCR Brutus Creed/50 8.00 20.00
JMBDV Blair Davenport/22
JMBLN Becky Lynch/19 40.00 100.00
JMBLS Bobby Lashley/50 15.00 40.00
JMBOA Boa/30
JMBRO Matt Riddle/42 15.00 40.00
JMBTH Butch/50 25.00 60.00
JMCAZ Commander Azeez/38 8.00 20.00
JMCHY Carmelo Hayes/40 20.00 50.00
JMCJD Cora Jade/20
JMCMG Cameron Grimes/50 20.00 50.00
JMCML Carmella/50 25.00 60.00
JMDBK Dana Brooke/26 50.00 125.00
JMDDR Doudrop/50 25.00 60.00
JMDGL Drew Gulak/50 20.00 50.00
JMDMI Drew McIntyre/24
JMDMY Dominik Mysterio/50 20.00 50.00
JMDPR Damian Priest/50 20.00 50.00
JMDZG Dolph Ziggler/28 20.00 50.00
JMERK Erik/38 10.00 25.00
JMEZK Ezekiel/37 15.00 40.00
JMGGD Gigi Dolin/50 100.00 250.00
JMGWL Grayson Waller/7
JMHCB Happy Corbin/50 15.00 40.00
JMIHW Indi Hartwell/50 30.00 75.00
JMIJD Ilja Dragunov/50 20.00 50.00
JMIOS IYO SKY/36
JMIVR Ivar/50 12.00 30.00
JMJCF Joe Coffey/27 30.00 75.00
JMJCR Julius Creed/50 12.00 30.00
JMJDM JD McDonagh/27 10.00 25.00
JMJGC Joe Gacy/40 20.00 50.00
JMJJN Jacy Jayne/50 60.00 150.00
JMJMH Jinder Mahal/50 12.00 30.00
JMJMU Jimmy Uso/50 12.00 30.00
JMJNY Jinny/22
JMJUS Jey Uso/44 15.00 40.00
JMJWL Joaquin Wilde/50 12.00 30.00
JMKCT Kayden Carter/50 15.00 40.00
JMKKG Kofi Kingston/50 15.00 40.00
JMKOW Kevin Owens/50 50.00 125.00
JMLEV Lacey Evans/50 30.00 75.00
JMLLG Lash Legend/32 12.00 30.00
JMLVM Liv Morgan/50 60.00 150.00
JMMCF Mark Coffey/27 10.00 25.00
JMMIZ The Miz/50 15.00 40.00
JMMKS Meiko Satomura/50
JMMRS Mandy Rose/50 50.00 125.00
JMMSR man.soor/50 12.00 30.00
JMMVP MVP/47 25.00 60.00
JMMXD Max Dupri/41 15.00 40.00
JMMZF Montez Ford/50 25.00 60.00
JMNDR Noam Dar/27 10.00 25.00
JMNTL Natalya/20
JMOJN Odyssey Jones/31
JMOTS Otis/50 30.00 75.00
JMRBR Rampage Brown/27
JMRCT Ricochet/50 20.00 50.00
JMRGE Reggie/50 8.00 20.00
JMRGH Ridge Holland/50 12.00 30.00
JMRMY Rey Mysterio/50 25.00 60.00
JMRQG Raquel Rodriguez/50 20.00 50.00
JMRRN Roman Reigns/50 75.00 200.00
JMRRP Rhea Ripley/50 150.00 400.00
JMRST Roderick Strong/50 15.00 40.00
JMSBZ Shayna Baszler/40 15.00 40.00
JMSDV Sonya Deville/50 25.00 60.00
JMSES Santos Escobar/50 20.00 50.00
JMSFR Seth Rollins/29 60.00 150.00
JMSHK Shanky/50 12.00 30.00
JMSHM Sheamus/24
JMSHN Shinsuke Nakamura/50 25.00 60.00
JMSHZ Shotzi/50 100.00 250.00
JMSZN Sami Zayn/50 40.00 100.00
JMTBT Tyler Bate/50 8.00 20.00
JMTCM Tommaso Ciampa/29 25.00 60.00
JMVMH Veer Mahaan/34 15.00 40.00
JMVWG Von Wagner/24 15.00 40.00
JMWFG Wolfgang/18
JMWLE Wes Lee/50 12.00 30.00
JMXLI Xia Li/50 30.00 75.00
JMXQN Xyon Quinn/34 12.00 30.00
JMXWD Xavier Woods/50 30.00 75.00
JMZST Zoey Stark/30 15.00 40.00

2022 Immaculate Collection WWE Jumbo Memorabilia Specialty

RANDOMLY INSERTED INTO PACKS

JMADW Angelo Dawkins/50 25.00 60.00
JMBLN Becky Lynch/35 150.00 400.00
JMBRO Matt Riddle/8
JMFBL Finn Balor/9
JMMZF Montez Ford/50 25.00 60.00
JMRRP Rhea Ripley/41 200.00 500.00

2022 Immaculate Collection WWE Jumbo Ring Canvas

STATED PRINT RUN 99 SER.#'d SETS

RCAJS AJ Styles 12.00 30.00
RCBBK Bron Breakker 12.00 30.00
RCBRO Matt Riddle 5.00 12.00
RCCDR Cody Rhodes 30.00 75.00
RCCFL Charlotte Flair 30.00 75.00
RCCHY Carmelo Hayes 4.00 10.00
RCCJD Cora Jade 25.00 60.00
RCCMG Cameron Grimes 4.00 10.00
RCDMI Drew McIntyre 8.00 20.00
RCDPR Damian Priest 8.00 20.00
RCDZG Dolph Ziggler 6.00 15.00
RCEGE Edge 8.00 20.00
RCFBL Finn Balor 15.00 40.00
RCGSV Gable Steveson 8.00 20.00
RCGTH Gunther 4.00 10.00
RCKOW Kevin Owens 15.00 40.00
RCLVM Liv Morgan 25.00 60.00
RCMRS Mandy Rose 15.00 40.00
RCROR Randy Orton 12.00 30.00
RCRQG Raquel Gonzalez 6.00 15.00
RCSCA Stone Cold Steve Austin 30.00 75.00
RCSFR Seth Rollins 15.00 40.00
RCTCM Tommaso Ciampa 8.00 20.00
RCTDA Tony D'Angelo 4.00 10.00
RCBBL1 Bianca Belair 20.00 50.00
RCBBL2 Bianca Belair 20.00 50.00
RCBLN1 Becky Lynch 30.00 75.00

RCBLN2 Becky Lynch 30.00 75.00
RCBLS1 Bobby Lashley 10.00 25.00
RCBLS1 Brock Lesnar 30.00 75.00
RCBLS2 Bobby Lashley 10.00 25.00
RCBLS2 Brock Lesnar 30.00 75.00
RCDMY1 Dominik Mysterio 5.00 12.00
RCDMY2 Dominik Mysterio 5.00 12.00
RCJMU1 Jimmy Uso 6.00 15.00
RCJMU2 Jimmy Uso 6.00 15.00
RCJUS1 Jey Uso 6.00 15.00
RCJUS2 Jey Uso 6.00 15.00
RCMIZ1 The Miz 4.00 10.00
RCMIZ2 The Miz 4.00 10.00
RCPMC1 Pat McAfee 40.00 100.00
RCPMC2 Pat McAfee 40.00 100.00
RCRMY1 Rey Mysterio 10.00 25.00
RCRMY2 Rey Mysterio 10.00 25.00
RCRRN1 Roman Reigns 20.00 50.00
RCRRN2 Roman Reigns 20.00 50.00
RCRRS1 Ronda Rousey 15.00 40.00
RCRRS2 Ronda Rousey 15.00 40.00
RCTHR1 Theory 10.00 25.00
RCTHR2 Theory 10.00 25.00

2022 Immaculate Collection WWE Marks of Greatness Autographs

*GOLD/10: UNPRICED DUE TO SCARCITY
*PLATINUM/1: UNPRICED DUE TO SCARCITY
RANDOMLY INSERTED INTO PACKS

MGABS Alexa Bliss/49 100.00 250.00
MGAFY Alba Fyre/49 12.00 30.00
MGASK Asuka/49 60.00 150.00
MGBBK Bron Breakker/49 60.00 125.00
MGBBL Bianca Belair/49 60.00 150.00
MGBGE Big E/49 EXCH 12.00 30.00
MGBTL Bayley/49 40.00 100.00
MGCHY Carmelo Hayes/49 25.00 60.00
MGCJD Cora Jade/49 100.00 250.00
MGCMG Cameron Grimes/49 12.00 30.00
MGCML Carmella/49 40.00 100.00
MGEZK Ezekiel/99 8.00 20.00
MGFAI Giovanni Vinci/99 6.00 15.00
MGFBL Finn Balor/49 15.00 40.00
MGGBG Goldberg/75 EXCH
MGGTH Gunther/49 30.00 75.00
MGILU Brother Love/99 12.00 30.00
MGIOS Io Shirai/49
MGJMU Jimmy Uso/49 12.00 30.00
MGJUS Jey Uso/49 25.00 60.00
MGLVM Liv Morgan/49 75.00 200.00
MGLWK Ludwig Kaiser/99 15.00 40.00
MGMKS Meiko Satomura/60 10.00 25.00
MGMRS Mandy Rose/49 50.00 125.00
MGMSR man.soor/99 6.00 15.00
MGMZF Montez Ford/49 20.00 50.00
MGOTS Otis/99 12.00 30.00
MGRMY Rey Mysterio/49 25.00 60.00
MGRQG Raquel Rodriguez/49 20.00 50.00
MGRRS Ronda Rousey/99 100.00 250.00
MGSES Santos Escobar/49 15.00 40.00
MGSFR Seth Rollins/49 60.00 150.00
MGSHN Shinsuke Nakamura/49 12.00 30.00
MGSSK Solo Sikoa/99 50.00 125.00
MGTCM Ciampa/49 EXCH

2022 Immaculate Collection WWE Memorabilia Autographs

*RED/25: UNPRICED DUE TO SCARCITY
*GOLD/10: UNPRICED DUE TO SCARCITY
*ACETATE/8: UNPRICED DUE TO SCARCITY
*ACE.FOTL/3-6: UNPRICED DUE TO SCARCITY
*GREEN/5: UNPRICED DUE TO SCARCITY
*PLATINUM/1: UNPRICED DUE TO SCARCITY
STATED PRINT RUN 99 SER.#'d SETS

MAABS Alexa Bliss 100.00 250.00
MAACR Apollo Crews 10.00 25.00
MAAJS AJ Styles 20.00 50.00
MAASH Nikki A.S.H. 10.00 25.00
MAASK Asuka 25.00 60.00
MABBL Bianca Belair 30.00 75.00
MABLN Becky Lynch 60.00 150.00
MABLS Bobby Lashley 15.00 40.00
MACFL Charlotte Flair 40.00 100.00
MACML Carmella 40.00 100.00
MADMI Drew McIntyre 20.00 50.00
MADMY Dominik Mysterio 12.00 30.00
MADPR Damian Priest 12.00 30.00
MADZG Dolph Ziggler 10.00 25.00
MAEGE Edge 30.00 75.00
MAFBL Finn Balor 12.00 30.00
MAGGD Gigi Dolin 50.00 125.00
MAGTH Gunther 20.00 50.00
MAIOS Io Shirai
MAJMU Jimmy Uso 15.00 40.00
MAJUS Jey Uso 25.00 60.00
MAKKG Kofi Kingston 10.00 25.00
MAKOW Kevin Owens 15.00 40.00
MALVM Liv Morgan 60.00 150.00
MAMIZ The Miz 10.00 25.00
MAMRS Mandy Rose 50.00 125.00
MANTL Natalya EXCH 12.00 30.00
MAOMS Omos 10.00 25.00
MARCT Ricochet 10.00 25.00
MARMY Rey Mysterio 25.00 60.00
MAROR Randy Orton 40.00 100.00
MARQG Raquel Rodriguez 25.00 60.00
MARRP Rhea Ripley 40.00 100.00
MASFR Seth Rollins 50.00 125.00
MASHN Shinsuke Nakamura 12.00 30.00
MATCM Ciampa EXCH 10.00 25.00
MAXLI Xia Li 10.00 25.00
MAXWD Xavier Woods 15.00 40.00

2022 Immaculate Collection WWE Modern Marks Autographs

*GOLD/10: UNPRICED DUE TO SCARCITY
*PLATINUM/1: UNPRICED DUE TO SCARCITY
STATED PRINT RUN 99 SER.#'d SETS

MMASH Nikki A.S.H./99 10.00 25.00
MMBOA Boa/99 5.00 12.00
MMBRO Matt Riddle/99 15.00 40.00
MMCML Carmella/99 25.00 60.00
MMDBK Dana Brooke/99 12.00 30.00
MMDPR Damian Priest/49 10.00 25.00
MMEPC Elton Prince/99 6.00 15.00
MMJNY Jinny/99 10.00 25.00
MMJRD Jagger Reid/99 5.00 12.00
MMKKG Kofi Kingston/99 10.00 25.00
MMKWL Kit Wilson/99 5.00 12.00
MMLVM Liv Morgan/99 60.00 150.00
MMMSR man.soor/99 6.00 15.00
MMOMS Omos/99 10.00 25.00
MMOTS Otis/99 10.00 20.00
MMQZL Queen Zelina/99 12.00 30.00
MMRGE Reggie/99 5.00 12.00
MMRGH Ridge Holland/99 6.00 15.00
MMRPF Rip Fowler/99 6.00 15.00
MMRRD Robert Roode/99 6.00 15.00
MMSDV Sonya Deville/99 15.00 40.00
MMSHM Sheamus/99 8.00 20.00
MMSHZ Shotzi/99 25.00 60.00
MMSTN Stevie Turner/99 20.00 50.00
MMXQN Xyon Quinn/99 8.00 20.00

2022 Immaculate Collection WWE Premium Memorabilia Autographs

*RED/25: UNPRICED DUE TO SCARCITY
*GOLD/10: UNPRICED DUE TO SCARCITY
*ACETATE/8: UNPRICED DUE TO SCARCITY
*ACE.FOTL/3-6: UNPRICED DUE TO SCARCITY
*GREEN/5: UNPRICED DUE TO SCARCITY
*PLATINUM/1: UNPRICED DUE TO SCARCITY
STATED PRINT RUN 49-99 SETS

PMABS Alexa Bliss/99 125.00 300.00
PMAFY Alba Fyre/49
PMAJS AJ Styles/99 15.00 40.00
PMASK Asuka/99 25.00 60.00
PMBBL Bianca Belair/99 30.00 75.00
PMBLN Becky Lynch/99 100.00 250.00
PMBLS Brock Lesnar/49 75.00 200.00
PMBLS Bobby Lashley/99 15.00 40.00
PMBRO Matt Riddle/99 15.00 40.00
PMCFL Charlotte Flair/99 50.00 125.00
PMCMG Cameron Grimes/99 10.00 25.00
PMCML Carmella/99 25.00 60.00
PMDBK Dana Brooke/99 12.00 30.00
PMDDR Doudrop/99 EXCH
PMDGL Drew Gulak/99 6.00 15.00
PMDMI Drew McIntyre/49 15.00 40.00
PMDZG Dolph Ziggler/99 15.00 40.00
PMEGE Edge/99 40.00 100.00
PMFBL Finn Balor/75 20.00 50.00
PMGTH Gunther/99 30.00 75.00
PMIOS Io Shirai/49
PMJMU Jimmy Uso/99 15.00 40.00
PMJUS Jey Uso/99 12.00 30.00
PMKCH Katana Chance/99 15.00 40.00
PMKKG Kofi Kingston/99 15.00 40.00
PMKOW Kevin Owens/99 15.00 40.00
PMMIZ The Miz/99 20.00 50.00
PMMRS Mandy Rose/99 50.00 125.00
PMMZF Montez Ford/99 15.00 40.00
PMNTL Natalya/99 EXCH
PMOMS Omos/99 12.00 30.00
PMQZL Queen Zelina/99 25.00 60.00
PMRGE Reggie/99 10.00 25.00
PMRKB Rick Boogs/99 20.00 50.00
PMRMY Rey Mysterio/99 30.00 75.00
PMROR Randy Orton/49 EXCH
PMRRN Roman Reigns/49 150.00 400.00
PMSBZ Shayna Baszler/99 20.00 50.00
PMSDV Sonya Deville/99 20.00 50.00
PMSES Santos Escobar/49 8.00 20.00
PMSFR Seth Rollins/49 75.00 200.00
PMSHM Sheamus/99 15.00 40.00
PMSHN Shinsuke Nakamura/99 15.00 40.00
PMSHZ Shotzi/99 50.00 125.00
PMSZN Sami Zayn/99 20.00 50.00
PMTCM Ciampa/49 EXCH
PMTHR Theory/99 25.00 60.00

2022 Immaculate Collection WWE Quad Autographs

*PLATINUM/1: UNPRICED DUE TO SCARCITY
STATED PRINT RUN 5 SER.#'d SETS
UNPRICED DUE TO SCARCITY

QA HBK/HHH/X-Pac/Road Dogg
QA HBK/Edge/Orton/Cena
QA Miz/Ziggler/RVD/Edge
QA Rousey/Lesnar/Baszler/Riddle
QA Undertaker/Austin/Mankind./HHH
QA Goldberg/Lashley
QAAMJ Usos/Dawkins/Ford
QAASJ Usos/Sika/Afa
QAKXF Faarooq/Kane/X-Pac/Bradshaw
QAWMTB Bliss/Asuka/Carmella/Bayley

2022 Immaculate Collection WWE Rookie Memorabilia Autographs

*RED/25: UNPRICED DUE TO SCARCITY
*GOLD/10: UNPRICED DUE TO SCARCITY
*ACETATE/8: UNPRICED DUE TO SCARCITY
*ACE.FOTL/6: UNPRICED DUE TO SCARCITY
*GREEN/5: UNPRICED DUE TO SCARCITY
*PLATINUM/1: UNPRICED DUE TO SCARCITY
STATED PRINT RUN 99 SER.#'d SETS

101 Von Wagner 6.00 15.00
102 Grayson Waller 25.00 60.00
103 Jacy Jayne 40.00 100.00
104 Bron Breakker 60.00 150.00
105 Joe Gacy 10.00 25.00
106 Carmelo Hayes 20.00 50.00
107 Ivy Nile 15.00 40.00
108 Cora Jade 100.00 250.00
109 Veer Mahaan EXCH 8.00 20.00
110 Gable Steveson 30.00 75.00

2022 Immaculate Collection WWE Shadowbox Signatures

*GOLD/10: UNPRICED DUE TO SCARCITY
*PLATINUM/1: UNPRICED DUE TO SCARCITY
STATED PRINT RUN 49-99 SETS

SHADW Angelo Dawkins/49 12.00 30.00
SHAOV Aoife Valkyrie/99 12.00 30.00
SHAXM Axiom/99 10.00 25.00
SHBCR Brutus Creed/49 10.00 25.00
SHBDV Blair Davenport/99 12.00 30.00
SHBTH Butch/49 10.00 25.00
SHCDR Cody Rhodes/99 EXCH 100.00 250.00
SHDGL Drew Gulak/49 6.00 15.00
SHDPR Damian Priest/49 15.00 40.00
SHEPC Elton Prince/49 12.00 30.00
SHGGD Gigi Dolin/49 50.00 125.00
SHGWL Grayson Waller/49 20.00 50.00
SHIHW Indi Hartwell/99 20.00 50.00
SHIVN Ivy Nile/49 20.00 50.00
SHJCR Julius Creed/49 15.00 40.00
SHJGC Joe Gacy/49 15.00 40.00
SHJJN Jacy Jayne/49 50.00 125.00
SHJNY Jinny/99 8.00 20.00
SHKCH Katana Chance/49 15.00 40.00
SHKCT Kayden Carter/49 12.00 30.00
SHKWL Kit Wilson/49 6.00 15.00
SHLEV Lacey Evans/99 EXCH 12.00 30.00
SHLLG Lash Legend/99 10.00 25.00
SHMXD Max Dupri/49 6.00 15.00
SHNDR Noam Dar/99 6.00 15.00
SHOJN Odyssey Jones/99 6.00 15.00
SHSSK Solo Sikoa/99 40.00 100.00
SHSTN Stevie Turner/99 30.00 75.00
SHVWG Von Wagner/49 6.00 15.00
SHWLE Wes Lee/99 6.00 15.00
SHXQN Xyon Quinn/99 6.00 15.00

2022 Immaculate Collection WWE Standout Memorabilia

*RED/25: UNPRICED DUE TO SCARCITY
*GOLD/10: UNPRICED DUE TO SCARCITY
*PLATINUM/1: UNPRICED DUE TO SCARCITY
STATED PRINT RUN 99 SER.#'d SETS

SMABS Alexa Bliss 50.00 125.00
SMACR Apollo Crews 6.00 15.00
SMAJS AJ Styles 8.00 20.00
SMBBK Bron Breakker 10.00 25.00
SMBBL Bianca Belair 10.00 25.00
SMBLS Bobby Lashley 6.00 15.00
SMBTH Butch 4.00 10.00
SMCAZ Commander Azeez 3.00 8.00
SMCHY Carmelo Hayes 6.00 15.00
SMCML Carmella 12.00 30.00
SMDBK Dana Brooke 12.00 30.00
SMDDR Doudrop 5.00 12.00
SMERK Erik 6.00 15.00
SMGGD Gigi Dolin 20.00 50.00
SMIHW Indi Hartwell 10.00 25.00
SMIVR Ivar 3.00 8.00
SMJDM JD McDonagh 6.00 15.00
SMJMH Jinder Mahal 3.00 8.00
SMJUS Jey Uso 8.00 20.00
SMJWL Joaquin Wilde 3.00 8.00
SMKCT Kayden Carter 10.00 25.00
SMKKG Kofi Kingston 10.00 25.00
SMLEV Lacey Evans 8.00 20.00
SMLVM Liv Morgan 30.00 75.00
SMMSR man.soor 3.00 8.00
SMMZF Montez Ford 8.00 20.00
SMOJN Odyssey Jones 4.00 10.00
SMRBR Rampage Brown 3.00 8.00
SMRCT Ricochet 6.00 15.00
SMRGE Reggie 3.00 8.00
SMRGH Ridge Holland 6.00 15.00
SMRRN Roman Reigns 12.00 30.00
SMSBZ Shayna Baszler 12.00 30.00
SMSES Santos Escobar 5.00 12.00
SMSFR Seth Rollins 15.00 40.00
SMSHN Shinsuke Nakamura 5.00 12.00
SMVMH Veer Mahaan 6.00 15.00
SMWFG Wolfgang 5.00 12.00
SMXQN Xyon Quinn 5.00 12.00
SMXWD Xavier Woods 5.00 12.00

2022 Immaculate Collection WWE Superstar Swatches

*RED/25: UNPRICED DUE TO SCARCITY
*GOLD/10: UNPRICED DUE TO SCARCITY
*PLATINUM/1: UNPRICED DUE TO SCARCITY
STATED PRINT RUN 99 SER.#'d SETS

SSADW Angelo Dawkins 5.00 12.00
SSAFY Alba Fyre 5.00 12.00
SSASH Nikki A.S.H. 3.00 8.00
SSASK Asuka 15.00 40.00
SSBCR Brutus Creed 3.00 8.00
SSBDV Blair Davenport 10.00 25.00
SSBOA Boa
SSBRO Matt Riddle 6.00 15.00

Card	Low	High
SSCMG Cameron Grimes	3.00	8.00
SSCML Carmella	12.00	30.00
SSDGL Drew Gulak	4.00	10.00
SSDPR Damian Priest	8.00	20.00
SSEZK Ezekiel	5.00	12.00
SSHCB Happy Corbin		
SSIOS IYO SKY	8.00	20.00
SSJCR Julius Creed	8.00	20.00
SSJGC Joe Gacy	3.00	8.00
SSJJN Jacy Jayne	15.00	40.00
SSJMU Jimmy Uso		
SSJNY Jinny		
SSKOW Kevin Owens	8.00	20.00
SSLLG Lash Legend	3.00	8.00
SSMIZ The Miz	6.00	15.00
SSMKS Meiko Satomura	3.00	8.00
SSMRS Mandy Rose	30.00	75.00
SSMVP MVP		
SSMXD Max Dupri		
SSOTS Otis	4.00	10.00
SSRQG Raquel Rodriguez	8.00	20.00
SSRRP Rhea Ripley	30.00	75.00
SSRST Roderick Strong	5.00	12.00
SSSHK Shanky	6.00	15.00
SSSHM Sheamus	3.00	8.00
SSSHZ Shotzi	10.00	25.00
SSSZN Sami Zayn	10.00	25.00
SSTBT Tyler Bate	4.00	10.00
SSTCM Tommaso Ciampa	6.00	15.00
SSWLE Wes Lee	4.00	10.00
SSXLI Xia Li	12.00	30.00
SSZST Zoey Stark	8.00	20.00

2022 Immaculate Collection WWE Triple Autographs

*PLATINUM/1: UNPRICED DUE TO SCARCITY
STATED PRINT RUN 5-10 SETS

TA Undertaker/HBK/HHH/10
TA Orton/HHH/Batista/10
TA Wilson/McCool/Kelly/10
TA Mark & Joe Coffey/Wolfgang/10
TA Ziggler/Breakker/Ciampa/10
TA Woods/Big E/Kingston/10
TA Kelly/McCool/Phoenix/10
TA Rollins/McMahon/HHH/10
TA Faarooq/Undertaker/Bradshaw/10
TA The Usos/Reigns/10
TA D-Von/Spike/Bubba Ray/10
TAHSW Flair/Lynch/Bayley/10
TAMDB DiBiase/Knight/Grimes/10
TANOW Nash/Hart/Jarrett/5
TANXT Waller/Breakker/Hayes/10
TARAB Hart/Honky Tonk Man/Valentine/10
TASRB Butch/Holland/Sheamus/10
TATXA Rose/Dolin/Jayne/10

2021 Impact Wrestling Complete Series

Card	Low	High
1 Mike Tenay	1.25	3.00
2 Abyss	1.25	3.00
3 Bobby Roode	1.50	4.00
4 Christian Cage	2.50	6.00
5 Gail Kim	4.00	10.00
6 Madison Rayne	5.00	12.00
7 Scott D'Amore	1.25	3.00
8 Chris Sabin	1.25	3.00
9 Matt Cardona	6.00	15.00
10 Matthew Rehwoldt	1.25	3.00
11 Brian Myers	6.00	15.00
12 Deonna Purrazzo	10.00	25.00
13 Moose	8.00	20.00
14 Big LG	2.50	6.00
15 Karl Anderson	3.00	8.00
16 Eric Young	2.50	6.00
17 Rich Swann	2.00	5.00
18 Sami Callihan	1.25	3.00
19 Suicide	5.00	12.00
20 Rosemary	2.00	5.00
21 Tasha Steelz	1.50	4.00
22 Ace Austin	6.00	15.00
23 Chris Bey	1.50	4.00
24 Eddie Edwards	3.00	8.00
25 Heath	3.00	8.00
26 Havok	1.25	3.00
27 Jordynne Grace	6.00	15.00
28 Josh Alexander	1.25	3.00
29 Willie Mack	2.00	5.00
30 Crazzy Steve	1.25	3.00
31 VBD		
32 Hernandez	1.25	3.00
33 Jake Something	1.25	3.00
34 Johnny Swinger	3.00	8.00
35 Tenille Dashwood	4.00	10.00
36 Taylor Wilde	3.00	8.00
37 Trey Miguel	2.00	5.00
38 Rohit Raju	1.25	3.00
39 Petey Williams	1.25	3.00
40 Steve Maclin	1.25	3.00

2021 Impact Wrestling Complete Series Autographs

STATED ODDS 1:SET

Card	Low	High
M3 Moose	20.00	50.00
AA2 Ace Austin	15.00	40.00
BM1 Brian Myers	15.00	40.00
CS1 Chris Sabin	15.00	40.00
DP2 Deonna Purrazzo	50.00	100.00
JG3 Jordynne Grace	25.00	60.00
JS1 Johnny Swinger	10.00	25.00
LG1 Big LG	12.00	30.00
MC2 Matt Cardona	30.00	75.00
TD2 Tenille Dashwood	20.00	50.00
TM3 Trey Miguel	15.00	40.00
TS3 Tasha Steelz	30.00	75.00

2023 Impact Wrestling Series One

NNO Ace Austin
NNO Brian Myers
NNO Bully Ray
NNO Callihan
NNO Chris Bey
NNO Deonna Purrazzo
NNO Dirty Dango
NNO Eddie Edwards
NNO Frankie Kazarian
NNO Heath
NNO Joe Hendry
NNO Jordynne Grace
NNO Josh Alexander
NNO Killer Kelly
NNO Mickie James
NNO Moose
NNO Motor City Machine Guns
NNO Trey Miguel

2023 Impact Wrestling Series Two

NNO Alex Shelley
NNO Bhupinder Gujjar
NNO Courtney Rush
NNO Gisele Shaw
NNO Johnny Swinger
NNO Kylinn King
NNO Masha Slamovich
NNO Mike Bailey
NNO PCO
NNO Santino Marella DOA
NNO Steve Maclin
NNO The Coven
NNO Tommy Dreamer
NNO Trinity

2023 Impact Wrestling Series Two Foil

NNO Trinity
NNO Killer Kelly

2023 Impact Wrestling Series Two PPV

NNO Bound For Glory
NNO Hard To Kill
NNO Slammiversay
NNO Rebellion

1991 Impel WCW

Card	Low	High
COMPLETE SET (162)	6.00	15.00
1 Sting	.25	.60
2 Sting	.25	.60
3 Sting	.25	.60
4 Sting	.25	.60
5 Sting	.25	.60
6 Sting	.25	.60
7 Sting	.25	.60
8 Sting	.25	.60
9 Sting	.25	.60
10 Sting	.25	.60
11 Sting	.25	.60
12 Sting	.25	.60
13 Sting	2.50	6.00
14 Lex Luger	.10	.25
15 Lex Luger	.10	.25
16 Lex Luger	.10	.25
17 Lex Luger	.10	.25
18 Lex Luger	.10	.25
19 Lex Luger	.10	.25
20 Lex Luger	.10	.25
21 Lex Luger	.10	.25
22 Lex Luger	.10	.25
23 Lex Luger	.10	.25
24 Sid Vicious RC	.07	.20
25 Sid Vicious RC	.07	.20
26 Sid Vicious RC	.07	.20
27 Sid Vicious RC	.07	.20
28 Sid Vicious RC	.07	.20
29 Sid Vicious RC	.07	.20
30 Sid Vicious RC	.07	.20
31 Sid Vicious RC	.07	.20
32 Sid Vicious RC	.07	.20
33 Sid Vicious RC	.07	.20
34 Sid Vicious RC	.07	.20
35 Sid Vicious RC	.07	.20
36 Ric Flair	.30	.75
37 Ric Flair	.30	.75
38 Ric Flair	.30	.75
39 Ric Flair	.30	.75
40 Ric Flair	.30	.75
41 Ric Flair	.30	.75
42 Ric Flair	.30	.75
43 Ric Flair	.30	.75
44 Ric Flair	.30	.75
45 Ric Flair	.30	.75
46 Ric Flair	.30	.75
47 Ric Flair	2.00	5.00
48 Arn Anderson	.10	.25
49 Arn Anderson	.10	.25
50 Arn Anderson	.10	.25
51 Arn Anderson	.10	.25
52 Arn Anderson	.10	.25
53 Arn Anderson	.10	.25
54 Arn Anderson	.10	.25
55 Flyin Brian	.10	.25
56 Flyin Brian	.10	.25
57 Flyin Brian	.10	.25
58 Flyin Brian	.10	.25
59 Flyin Brian	.10	.25
60 Flyin Brian	.10	.25
61 Flyin Brian	.10	.25
62 Flyin Brian	.10	.25
63 Flyin Brian	.10	.25
64 Flyin Brian	.10	.25
65 Z-Man RC	.07	.20
66 Z-Man RC	.07	.20
67 Z-Man RC	.07	.20
68 Terry Taylor	.07	.20
69 Terry Taylor	.07	.20
70 Terry Taylor	.07	.20
71 Terry Taylor	.07	.20
72 Terry Taylor	.07	.20
73 Terry Taylor	.07	.20
74 Terry Taylor	.07	.20
75 Terry Taylor	.07	.20
76 Dutch Mantell RC	.10	.25
77 Dutch Mantell RC	.10	.25
78 Dutch Mantell RC	.10	.25
79 Dutch Mantell RC	.10	.25
80 Dutch Mantell RC	.10	.25
81 Dutch Mantell RC	.10	.25
82 Mr. Wall Street	.07	.20
83 Mr. Wall Street	.07	.20
84 Mr. Wall Street	.07	.20
85 El Gigante RC	.07	.20
86 El Gigante RC	.07	.20
87 El Gigante RC	.07	.20
88 El Gigante RC	.07	.20
89 El Gigante RC	.07	.20
90 El Gigante RC	.07	.20
91 El Gigante RC	.07	.20
92 El Gigante RC	.07	.20
93 Tommy Rich RC	.07	.20
94 Tommy Rich RC	.07	.20
95 Tommy Rich RC	.07	.20
96 Tommy Rich RC	.07	.20
97 Ricky Morton	.07	.20
98 Ricky Morton	.07	.20
99 Ricky Morton	.07	.20
100 Ricky Morton	.07	.20
101 Ricky Morton	.07	.20
102 Ricky Morton	.07	.20
103 Steiner Brothers	.15	.40
104 Steiner Brothers	.15	.40
105 Steiner Brothers	.15	.40
106 Steiner Brothers	.15	.40
107 Steiner Brothers	.15	.40
108 Steiner Brothers	.15	.40
109 Steiner Brothers	.15	.40
110 Steiner Brothers	.15	.40
111 Steiner Brothers	.15	.40
112 Steiner Brothers	.15	.40
113 Steiner Brothers	.15	.40
114 Steiner Brothers	.15	.40
115 Steiner Brothers	.15	.40
116 Steiner Brothers	.15	.40
117 Fabulous Freebirds	.10	.25
118 Fabulous Freebirds	.10	.25
119 Fabulous Freebirds	.10	.25
120 Fabulous Freebirds	.10	.25
121 Fabulous Freebirds	.10	.25
122 Fabulous Freebirds	.10	.25
123 Fabulous Freebirds	.10	.25
124 Fabulous Freebirds	.10	.25
125 Fabulous Freebirds	.10	.25
126 Fabulous Freebirds	.10	.25
127 Fabulous Freebirds	.10	.25
128 Fabulous Freebirds	.10	.25
129 Southern Boys	.07	.20
130 Southern Boys	.07	.20
131 Southern Boys	.07	.20
132 Southern Boys	.07	.20
133 Southern Boys	.07	.20
134 Southern Boys	.07	.20
135 Southern Boys	.07	.20
136 Southern Boys	.07	.20
137 Southern Boys	.07	.20
138 Southern Boys	.07	.20
139 Doom	.10	.25
140 Doom	.10	.25
141 Doom	.10	.25
142 Doom	.10	.25
143 Doom	.10	.25
144 Doom	.10	.25
145 Doom	.10	.25
146 Doom	.10	.25
147 Doom	.10	.25
148 Doom	.10	.25
149 Doom	.10	.25
150 Doom	.10	.25
151 Teddy Long	.07	.20
152 Teddy Long	.07	.20
153 Teddy Long	.07	.20
154 Jim Ross RC	.12	.30
155 Jim Ross RC	.12	.30
156 Jim Ross RC	.12	.30
157 Missy Hyatt	.12	.30
158 Missy Hyatt	.12	.30
159 Missy Hyatt	.12	.30
160 Missy Hyatt	.12	.30
161 Checklist	.07	.20
162 Checklist	.07	.20
NNO Sting HOLO	8.00	20.00

1990 International Games WCW Slam-A-Rama Wrestling Card Game

COMPLETE SET (49)

1 Arn Anderson (body slam)
2 Arn Anderson (drop kick)
3 Arn Anderson (pin)
4 Arn Anderson (press)

5 Barry Windham (body slam)		
6 Barry Windham (drop kick)		
7 Barry Windham (pin)		
8 Barry Windham (press)		
9 Brian Pillman (body slam)		
10 Brian Pillman (drop kick)		
11 Brian Pillman (pin)		
12 Brian Pillman (press)		
13 Butch Reed (body slam)		
14 Butch Reed (drop kick)		
15 Butch Reed (pin)		
16 Butch Reed (press)		
17 Lex Luger (body slam)		
18 Lex Luger (drop kick)		
19 Lex Luger (pin)		
20 Lex Luger (press)		
21 Ric Flair (body slam)		
22 Ric Flair (drop kick)		
23 Ric Flair (pin)		
24 Ric Flair (press)		
25 Rick Steiner (body slam)		
26 Rick Steiner (drop kick)		
27 Rick Steiner (pin)		
28 Rick Steiner (press)		
29 Ron Simmons (body slam)		
30 Ron Simmons (drop kick)		
31 Ron Simmons (pin)		
32 Ron Simmons (press)		
33 Scott Steiner (body slam)		
34 Scott Steiner (drop kick)		
35 Scott Steiner (pin)		
36 Scott Steiner (press)		
37 Sid Vicious (body slam)		
38 Sid Vicious (drop kick)		
39 Sid Vicious (pin)		
40 Sid Vicious (press)		
41 Sting (body slam)		
42 Sting (drop kick)		
43 Sting (pin)		
44 Sting (press)		
45 Tag Team (header)		
46 Tom Zenk (body slam)		
47 Tom Zenk (drop kick)		
48 Tom Zenk (pin)		
49 Tom Zenk (press)		

2008 KOCH Vision ROH Limited Edition

COMPLETE SET (6)

NNO Austin Aries	8.00	20.00
NNO Bryan Danielson	50.00	125.00
NNO Chris Hero	4.00	10.00
NNO Mark and Jay Briscoe	12.00	30.00
NNO Nigel McGuinness	6.00	15.00
NNO Roderick Strong	6.00	15.00

2023 Leaf Heroes of Wrestling

*BLUE: SAME VALUE
*GOLD: SAME VALUE
*GREEN: SAME VALUE
*PURPLE: SAME VALUE
*RED: SAME VALUE

B1 Bret Hart	1.00	2.50
B2 Chris Jericho	1.25	3.00
B3 Cody Rhodes	.75	2.00
B4 Hulk Hogan	1.50	4.00
B5 John Cena	1.50	4.00
B6 Kane	.75	2.00
B7 Ric Flair	1.25	3.00
B8 Sasha Banks	1.00	2.50
B9 Steve Austin	1.50	4.00
B10 Ted DiBiase	.75	2.00

2023 Leaf Heroes of Wrestling Autographs

*BLUE: SAME VALUE
*GOLD: SAME VALUE
*GREEN: SAME VALUE
*PURPLE: SAME VALUE
*RED: SAME VALUE

BAA1 Angelico	6.00	15.00
BAE1 Evil	6.00	15.00
BAG1 Godfather	8.00	20.00
BAH1 Homicide	5.00	12.00
BAK1 Kane	12.00	30.00
BAM1 Moose	5.00	12.00
BAP1 Pagano	5.00	12.00
BAS1 Sabu	10.00	25.00
BAS2 Sanada	8.00	20.00
BAW1 Warlord	5.00	12.00
BAAA1 Arn Anderson	15.00	40.00
BAAB1 Adam Bomb	6.00	15.00
BAAO1 Atsushi Onita	10.00	25.00
BAAP1 Adam Page	12.00	30.00
BAAS1 Al Snow	6.00	15.00
BABC1 Big Cass	4.00	10.00
BABC2 Brian Cage	6.00	15.00
BABF1 Bad Luck Fale	4.00	10.00
BABF2 Bobby Fulton	5.00	12.00
BABG1 Billy Gunn	8.00	20.00
BABH1 Barry Horowitz	5.00	12.00
BABH2 Bret Hart	30.00	75.00
BABR1 Brandi Rhodes	12.00	30.00
BABR2 Bronson Reed	5.00	12.00
BABR3 Butch Reed	6.00	15.00
BABT4 Black Tiger IV	4.00	10.00
BACJ1 Chris Jericho	25.00	60.00
BACR1 Cody Rhodes	25.00	60.00
BADB1 DiLo Brown	4.00	10.00
BADDP Diamond Dallas Page	12.00	30.00
BADF1 David Finlay	6.00	15.00
BAEA1 Enzo Amore	8.00	20.00
BAEB1 Eric Bischoff	10.00	25.00
BAEC3 EC3	5.00	12.00
BAEHV El Hijo del Vikingo	15.00	40.00
BAEM1 Ernest Miller	5.00	12.00
BAER1 Erick Rowan	5.00	12.00
BAFG1 Flip Gordon	5.00	12.00
BAGM1 The Great Muta	30.00	75.00
BAGS1 The Great Sasuke	6.00	15.00
BAGV1 Greg Valentine	6.00	15.00
BAHG1 Hirooki Goto	5.00	12.00
BAHH1 Hulk Hogan	60.00	150.00
BAHT1 Hiromu Takahashi	12.00	30.00
BAIV1 Ivelisse	10.00	25.00
BAJD1 Jim Duggan	8.00	20.00
BAJD2 J.J. Dillon	5.00	12.00
BAJF1 Jackie Fulton	6.00	15.00
BAJH1 Jimmy Hart	10.00	25.00
BAJL1 Jushin Liger	15.00	40.00
BAJW1 Jay White	30.00	75.00
BAJWY Jimmy Wang Yang	6.00	15.00
BAKH1 Kiera Hogan	12.00	30.00
BAKI1 Kota Ibushi	15.00	40.00
BAKK1 Kaleb Konley	5.00	12.00
BAKO1 Konnan	10.00	25.00
BAKS1 Kevin Sullivan	6.00	15.00
BALA1 Lance Archer	5.00	12.00
BALH1 La Hiedra	8.00	20.00
BALK1 Laredo Kid	6.00	15.00
BALK2 Leilani Kai	5.00	12.00
BAME1 Michael Elgin	5.00	12.00
BAMH1 Mark Henry	6.00	15.00
BAMR1 Matt Riddle	6.00	15.00
BAMS1 Minoru Suzuki	10.00	25.00
BAMT1 Masato Tanaka	6.00	15.00
BAPE1 Penta El Zero M	15.00	40.00
BAPS1 Perry Saturn	6.00	15.00
BAPW1 Paul Wight	12.00	30.00
BARF1 Rey Fenix	10.00	25.00
BARF2 Rikishi Fatu	8.00	20.00
BARF3 Ric Flair	40.00	100.00
BARR1 Rocky Romero	6.00	15.00
BARS1 Rich Swann	5.00	12.00
BARS2 Ron Simmons	8.00	20.00
BART1 Ryusuke Taguchi	4.00	10.00
BAS2H Scotty 2 Hotty	10.00	25.00
BASB1 Scarlett Bordeaux	10.00	25.00
BASB2 Sasha Banks	30.00	75.00
BASC1 Sami Callihan	6.00	15.00
BASD1 Shane Douglas	5.00	12.00
BASK1 Steve Keirn	5.00	12.00
BAST1 Shingo Takagi	6.00	15.00
BATA1 Tony Atlas	6.00	15.00
BATB1 The Barbarian	6.00	15.00
BATB2 Trent Baretta	5.00	12.00
BATD1 Ted DiBiase	6.00	15.00
BATDJ Ted DiBiase, Jr.	8.00	20.00
BATI1 Taiji Ishimori	8.00	20.00
BATI2 Tomohiro Ishii	12.00	30.00
BATL1 Tanga Loa	4.00	10.00
BATN1 Tetsuya Naito	12.00	30.00
BATR1 Tommy Rich	6.00	15.00
BATS1 Tasha Steelz	10.00	25.00
BATW1 Torrie Wilson	10.00	25.00
BATY1 Toru Yano	8.00	20.00
BATZ1 Taz	10.00	25.00
BAUG1 Ultimo Guerrero	5.00	12.00
BAVG1 Vickie Guerrero	6.00	15.00
BAVV1 Val Venis	5.00	12.00
BAYH1 Yoshi-Hashi	5.00	12.00
BAYT1 Yoshihiro Tajiri	8.00	20.00

2018 Leaf Legends of Wrestling Autographs

*GREEN/15: UNPRICED DUE TO SCARCITY
*GOLD/10: UNPRICED DUE TO SCARCITY
*PURPLE/5: UNPRICED DUE TO SCARCITY
*RED/1: UNPRICED DUE TO SCARCITY

LWC1 Christian	5.00	12.00
LWE1 Edge	8.00	20.00
LWK1 Konnan	4.00	10.00
LWR1 Ricochet	15.00	40.00
LWS1 Slick	5.00	12.00
LW2CS 2 Cold Scorpio	4.00	10.00
LWAS1 Alexis Smirnoff	12.00	30.00
LWBF1 Bad Luck Fale	6.00	15.00
LWBH1 Bret Hart	8.00	20.00
LWBL1 Bobby Lashley	6.00	15.00
LWBVR Baron Von Raschke	10.00	25.00
LWBW1 Barry Windham	5.00	12.00
LWCJ1 Chris Jericho	8.00	20.00
LWCK1 Corporal Kirchner	5.00	12.00
LWCR1 Cody Rhodes	15.00	40.00
LWDK1 Dynamite Kid	12.00	30.00
LWGS1 The Great Sasuke	6.00	15.00
LWGV1 Greg Valentine	5.00	12.00
LWHT1 Hiroshi Tanahashi	6.00	15.00
LWJB1 Jim Brunzell	4.00	10.00
LWJH1 Jimmy Hart	5.00	12.00
LWJR1 Jacques Rougeau	4.00	10.00
LWJR2 Jake Roberts	6.00	15.00
LWJR3 Jim Ross	6.00	15.00
LWJV1 Jesse Ventura	20.00	50.00
LWJV2 Jesse Ventura	20.00	50.00
LWKF1 Kazuyuki Fujita	8.00	20.00
LWKI1 Kota Ibushi	10.00	25.00
LWKK1 Kendo Kashin	4.00	10.00
LWKN1 Kevin Nash	6.00	15.00
LWKO1 Kazuchika Okada	12.00	30.00
LWKO2 Kenny Omega	25.00	60.00
LWKS1 Katsuyori Shibata	8.00	20.00
LWLH1 Larry Hennig	12.00	30.00
LWMS1 Minoru Suzuki	8.00	20.00
LWMW1 Mikey Whipwreck	4.00	10.00
LWPE1 Penta El Zero M	10.00	25.00
LWPO1 Pierre Ouellet	6.00	15.00
LWRF1 Ric Flair	15.00	40.00
LWRR1 Rocky Romero	4.00	10.00
LWSD1 Shane Douglas	4.00	10.00
LWSH1 Sam Houston	5.00	12.00
LWTI1 Tomohiro Ishii	12.00	30.00
LWTL1 Tanga Loa	12.00	30.00
LWTN1 Tetsuya Naito	12.00	30.00
LWTT1 Tama Tonga	10.00	25.00
LWWO1 Will Ospreay	12.00	30.00

2018 Leaf Legends of Wrestling Dual Autographs

LWD1 Edge /Christian	12.00	30.00
LWD2 C.Jericho/Christian	10.00	25.00
LWD3 K.Ibushi/B.L.Fale	8.00	20.00
LWD4 B.Hart/K.Nash		
LWD5 K.Nash/Konnan	10.00	25.00
LWD6 Konnan/S.Douglas		
LWD7 S.Douglas/2 Cold Scorpio	8.00	20.00
LWD8 J.Rougeau/P.Ouellet		
LWD9 2 Cold Scorpio/M.Whipwreck		
LWD10 B.L.Fale/T.Loa	12.00	30.00
LWD11 B.Windham/2 Cold Scorpio	8.00	20.00
LWD12 C.Rhodes/Christian		
LWD13 G.Valentine/J.Roberts	8.00	20.00
LWD14 L.Hennig/B.Von Raschke		
LWD15 Minoru Suzuki	15.00	40.00
Tomohiro Ishii		

2018 Leaf Legends of Wrestling Originals Update Autographs

E1 Edge (2014)	6.00	15.00
S3 Sunny (2014)	8.00	20.00
BW1 The Bushwackers (2014)	15.00	40.00
DB1 Dick Beyer (2017)	8.00	20.00
FE1 Fedor Emelianenko (2016)	12.00	30.00
JB1 Jim Brunzell (2017)	6.00	15.00
KS1 Kazuski Sakuraba (2016)	8.00	20.00
MTA Magnum T.A. (2017)	6.00	15.00
PP1 Pat Patterson (2014)	6.00	15.00
PVZ Paige VanZant (2016)	10.00	25.00
RG1 Royce Gracie (2016)	12.00	30.00
RMJ Rey Mysterio Jr. (2017)	10.00	25.00
RS1 Ricky Steamboat (2017)	8.00	20.00
RS2 Ryan Shamrock (2017)	5.00	12.00
SL1 Stan Lane (2014)	5.00	12.00
SR2 Stevie Richards (2014)	5.00	12.00

2012 Leaf Originals Wrestling

*YELLOW/99: .5X TO 1.2X BASIC AUTOS
*BLUE/25: .6X TO 1.5X BASIC AUTOS
*RED/10: UNPRICED DUE TO SCARCITY
*BLACK/1: UNPRICED DUE TO SCARCITY
*P.P.BLACK/1: UNPRICED DUE TO SCARCITY
*P.P.CYAN/1: UNPRICED DUE TO SCARCITY
*P.P.MAGENTA/1: UNPRICED DUE TO SCARCITY
*P.P.YELLOW/1: UNPRICED DUE TO SCARCITY
*A.A.: SAME VALUE AS BASIC AUTOS
*A.A.YELLOW/25: .6X TO 1.5X BASIC AUTOS
*A.A.BLUE/10: UNPRICED DUE TO SCARCITY
*A.A.RED/5: UNPRICED DUE TO SCARCITY
*A.A.BLACK/1: UNPRICED DUE TO SCARCITY
*A.A.P.P.BLACK/1: UNPRICED DUE TO SCARCITY
*A.A.P.P.CYAN/1: UNPRICED DUE TO SCARCITY
*A.A.P.P.MAGENTA/1: UNPRICED DUE TO SCARCITY
*A.A.P.P.YELLOW/1: UNPRICED DUE TO SCARCITY

ATB Abdullah the Butcher	10.00	25.00
BB1 Bob Backlund	10.00	25.00
BB2 Brutus Beefcake	8.00	20.00
BB3 Buff Bagwell	8.00	20.00
BH1 Bobby Heenan	12.00	30.00
BH2 Bret Hart	40.00	80.00
BO1 Cowboy Bob Orton Jr.	8.00	20.00
BS1 Bruno Sammartino	15.00	40.00
DDP Diamond Dallas Page	8.00	20.00
DS1 Dan Severn	6.00	15.00
GJG Jimmy Garvin	6.00	15.00
GS1 George Steele	10.00	25.00
GV1 Greg Valentine	8.00	20.00
HH1 Hulk Hogan	60.00	120.00
HJ1 Hillbilly Jim	10.00	25.00
HTM The Honky Tonk Man	10.00	25.00
IK1 Ivan Koloff	8.00	20.00
IP1 The Polish Hammer Ivan Putski	8.00	20.00
JD1 Hacksaw Jim Duggan	12.00	30.00
JH1 Jimmy Hart	10.00	25.00
JN1 Jim Neidhart	8.00	20.00
JR1 Jake Roberts	12.00	30.00
KA1 Kamala	8.00	20.00
KBW Koko B. Ware	8.00	20.00
KN1 Kevin Nash	15.00	40.00
KS1 Ken Shamrock	8.00	20.00
LL1 Lex Luger	10.00	25.00
LP1 Lanny Poffo	6.00	15.00
LZ1 Larry Zbyszko	6.00	15.00
MH1 Missy Hyatt	6.00	15.00
MJ1 Marty Jannetty	6.00	15.00
NK1 Nikita Koloff	8.00	20.00
NV1 Nikolai Volkoff	8.00	20.00
OMG One Man Gang	8.00	20.00
PO1 Paul Orndorff	25.00	60.00
PR1 Pete Rose	12.00	30.00
RM1 Rick Martel	6.00	15.00
RRP Rowdy Roddy Piper	75.00	150.00
RS1 Rick Steiner	6.00	15.00
SBG Billy Graham	25.00	50.00
SH1 Scott Hall	12.00	30.00
SID Sid	8.00	20.00
SS1 Scott Steiner	8.00	20.00

TA1 Tony Atlas	6.00	15.00
TAT Tatanka	8.00	20.00
TDB Ted DiBiase	10.00	25.00
TIS The Iron Sheik	15.00	40.00
TNB Ric Flair	30.00	75.00
TS1 Tito Santana	8.00	20.00
VAD Vader	25.00	60.00
WR1 Wendi Richter	8.00	20.00
PARWA Road Warrior Animal LOS	30.00	75.00

2014 Leaf Originals Wrestling

*YELLOW/99: SAME VALUE AS BASIC AUTOS
*BLUE/25: .5X TO 1.2X BASIC AUTOS
*RED/10: UNPRICED DUE TO SCARCITY
*BLACK/1: UNPRICED DUE TO SCARCITY
*P.P.BLACK/1: UNPRICED DUE TO SCARCITY
*P.P.CYAN/1: UNPRICED DUE TO SCARCITY
*P.P.MAGENTA/1: UNPRICED DUE TO SCARCITY
*P.P.YELLOW/1: UNPRICED DUE TO SCARCITY
*ALT.ART./ .5X TO 1.2X BASIC AUTOS
*A.A.YELLOW/25: .6X TO 1.5X BASIC AUTOS
*A.A.BLUE/10: UNPRICED DUE TO SCARCITY
*A.A.RED/5: UNPRICED DUE TO SCARCITY
*A.A.BLACK/1: UNPRICED DUE TO SCARCITY
*A.A.P.P.BLACK/1: UNPRICED DUE TO SCARCITY
*A.A.P.P.CYAN/1: UNPRICED DUE TO SCARCITY
*A.A.P.P.MAGENTA/1: UNPRICED DUE TO SCARCITY
*A.A.P.P.YELLOW/1: UNPRICED DUE TO SCARCITY

AF1 Francine	5.00	12.00
AG1 Gangrel SP	6.00	15.00
AG2 Godfather	5.00	12.00
AG3 Goldberg	50.00	100.00
AM1 Maryse	6.00	15.00
AR1 Raven	5.00	12.00
AS1 Sabu	12.00	30.00
AS2 Samu	6.00	15.00
AS2 Sting	25.00	60.00
AS3 Sandman	5.00	12.00
AW1 Warlord	5.00	12.00
AZ1 Zeus	5.00	12.00
A2CS 2 Cold Scorpio SP	5.00	12.00
AAB1 Adam Bomb	5.00	12.00
AAS1 Al Snow	5.00	12.00
ABH1 Bob Holly	5.00	12.00
ABH1 Bobby Heenan SP	12.00	30.00
ABM1 Balls Mahoney	5.00	12.00
ABM1 Blue Meanie	5.00	12.00
ACM1 Candice Michelle SP	10.00	25.00
ADA1 Demolition Ax	5.00	12.00
ADK1 Dynamite Kid SP	12.00	30.00
ADM1 Don Muraco	5.00	12.00
ADR1 Dennis Rodman SP	15.00	40.00
ADS1 Demolition Smash	5.00	12.00
AGB1 Gerald Brisco	5.00	12.00
AHH1 Hulk Hogan SP	75.00	150.00
AIS1 Iron Sheik	6.00	15.00
AJD1 J.J. Dillon	5.00	12.00
AJH1 Jeff Hardy SP	10.00	25.00
AJR2 Jake Roberts SP	10.00	25.00
AKK1 Kelly Kelly	6.00	15.00
AKKB King Kong Bundy	15.00	40.00
AKN1 Kevin Nash	8.00	20.00
AKP1 Ken Patera	5.00	12.00
AKVE Kevin Von Erich	6.00	15.00
ALS1 Lance Storm	5.00	12.00
AMK1 Maria Kanellis	6.00	15.00
AMT1 Mike Tyson SP	80.00	150.00
AOA1 Ole Anderson	25.00	60.00
ARF1 Ric Flair SP	75.00	150.00
ARF2 Rikishi Fatu	10.00	25.00
ARG1 Robert Gibson	5.00	12.00
ARM1 Ricky Morton	5.00	12.00
ARP1 Roddy Piper SP	50.00	100.00
ARS1 Ron Simmons	6.00	15.00
ASH1 Scott Hall	15.00	40.00
ASR1 Stevie Ray SP	6.00	15.00
ATB1 The Barbarian	5.00	12.00
ATD1 Tommy Dreamer	5.00	12.00
ATF1 Terry Funk	25.00	60.00
ATNB The Nasty Boys	8.00	20.00
ATS1 Trish Stratus	20.00	50.00
AVV1 Val Venis	5.00	12.00

2014 Leaf Originals Wrestling Flair's Epic Battles

*BLUE/10: UNPRICED DUE TO SCARCITY
*RED/5: UNPRICED DUE TO SCARCITY
*BLACK/1: UNPRICED DUE TO SCARCITY
*P.P.BLACK/1: UNPRICED DUE TO SCARCITY
*P.P.CYAN/1: UNPRICED DUE TO SCARCITY
*P.P.MAGENTA/1: UNPRICED DUE TO SCARCITY
*P.P.YELLOW/1: UNPRICED DUE TO SCARCITY

RFBH1 Ric Flair/Bret Hart	80.00	150.00
RFHH1 Ric Flair/Hulk Hogan	120.00	250.00
RFRM1 Ric Flair/Ricky Morton	20.00	50.00
RFRP1 Ric Flair/Roddy Piper	80.00	150.00

2017 Leaf Originals Wrestling Autographs

*YELLOW/99: .6X TO 1.5X BASIC AUTOS
*BLUE/25: .75X TO 2X BASIC AUTOS
*RED/10: 1X TO 2.5X BASIC CARDS
*BLACK/1: UNPRICED DUE TO SCARCITY
*ALT.ART: SAME VALUE AS BASIC AUTOS
*ALT.YELLOW/25: .75X TO 2X BASIC AUTOS
*ALT.BLUE/10: 1X TO 2.5X BASIC AUTOS
*ALT.RED/5: UNPRICED DUE TO SCARCITY
*ALT.BLACK/1: UNPRICED DUE TO SCARCITY

K1 Konnan	8.00	20.00
V2 Victoria	5.00	12.00
BB1 B. Brian Blair	5.00	12.00
BL1 Bobby Lashley	5.00	12.00
BW1 Barry Windham	6.00	15.00
DFJ Dory Funk Jr.	6.00	15.00
DLB D'Lo Brown	5.00	12.00
DM2 Dutch Mantel	5.00	12.00
JR1 Jacques Rougeau	5.00	12.00
JR2 Jim Ross	8.00	20.00
LK1 Leilani Kai	5.00	12.00
MF1 Manny Fernandez	5.00	12.00
MM1 Marc Mero	5.00	12.00
MVP MVP	6.00	15.00
SB1 Shelton Benjamin	6.00	15.00
SD1 Shane Douglas	5.00	12.00
TW1 Torrie Wilson	8.00	20.00

2017 Leaf Originals Wrestling '14 Design Autographs

*YELLOW/50-99: .6X TO 1.5X BASIC AUTOS
*BLUE/25: .75X TO 2X BASIC AUTOS
*RED/10: 1X TO 2.5X BASIC AUTOS
*BLACK/1: UNPRICED DUE TO SCARCITY
*P.P.BLACK/1: UNPRICED DUE TO SCARCITY
*P.P.CYAN/1: UNPRICED DUE TO SCARCITY
*P.P.MAGENTA/1: UNPRICED DUE TO SCARCITY
*P.P.YELLOW/1: UNPRICED DUE TO SCARCITY
*ALT.ART: SAME VALUE AS BASIC AUTOS
*ALT.YELLOW/25: .75X TO 2X BASIC AUTOS
*ALT.BLUE/10: 1X TO 2.5X BASIC AUTOS
*ALT.RED/5: UNPRICED DUE TO SCARCITY
*ALT.BLACK/1: UNPRICED DUE TO SCARCITY
*ALT.P.P.BLACK/1: UNPRICED DUE TO SCARCITY
*ALT.P.P.CYAN/1: UNPRICED DUE TO SCARCITY
*ALT.P.P.MAGENTA/1: UNPRICED DUE TO SCARCITY
*ALT.P.P.YELLOW/1: UNPRICED DUE TO SCARCITY

C1 Chyna	20.00	50.00
H1 Haku	6.00	15.00
S1 Slick	5.00	12.00
BE1 Bobby Eaton	5.00	12.00
BG1 Billy Gunn	5.00	12.00
BH2 Bret Hart	15.00	40.00
BR1 Butch Reed	5.00	12.00
BT1 Booker T	8.00	20.00
CH1 Christy Hemme	6.00	15.00
CJ1 Chris Jericho	8.00	20.00
DC1 Dennis Condrey	5.00	12.00
DH1 Danny Hodge	6.00	15.00
EB1 Eric Bischoff	5.00	12.00
JC1 Jim Cornette	6.00	15.00
JJ1 Jeff Jarrett	6.00	15.00
JL1 Jushin Liger	8.00	20.00
KS1 Kevin Sullivan	5.00	12.00
MF1 Mick Foley	8.00	20.00
MH1 Matt Hardy	5.00	12.00
RVD Rob Van Dam	5.00	12.00
TB1 Tully Blanchard	5.00	12.00
TR1 Terri Runnels	6.00	15.00
WS1 Wild Samoans	8.00	20.00
XP1 X-Pac	6.00	15.00

2017 Leaf Originals Wrestling '16 Design Autographs

*YELLOW/50: .6X TO 1.5X BASIC AUTOS
*BLUE/25: .75X TO 2X BASIC AUTOS
*RED/10: 1X TO 2.5X BASIC AUTOS
*BLACK/1: UNPRICED DUE TO SCARCITY
*ALT.ART: SAME VALUE AS BASIC AUTOS
*ALT.YELLOW/25: .75X TO 2X BASIC AUTOS
*ALT.BLUE/10: 1X TO 2.5X BASIC AUTOS
*ALT.RED/5: UNPRICED DUE TO SCARCITY
*ALT.BLACK/1: UNPRICED DUE TO SCARCITY

HH1 Hulk Hogan	20.00	50.00
KS1 Kazushi Sakuraba	12.00	30.00

2016 Leaf Signature Series Wrestling

*BLUE/7-50: UNPRICED DUE TO SCARCITY
*GREEN/5-25: UNPRICED DUE TO SCARCITY
*RED/3-10: UNPRICED DUE TO SCARCITY
*BLACK/2-5: UNPRICED DUE TO SCARCITY
*PURPLE/1: UNPRICED DUE TO SCARCITY
*P.P.BLACK/1: UNPRICED DUE TO SCARCITY
*P.P.CYAN/1: UNPRICED DUE TO SCARCITY
*P.P.MAGENTA/1: UNPRICED DUE TO SCARCITY
*P.P.BLACK/1: UNPRICED DUE TO SCARCITY

1 6-Pac	8.00	20.00
2 Adam Bomb	8.00	20.00
3 Adam Pearce	8.00	20.00
4 Al Snow	6.00	15.00
5 Balls Mahoney	10.00	25.00
6 The Barbarian	8.00	20.00
7 Barry Windham	10.00	25.00
8 Goldberg	25.00	60.00
9 Blue Meanie	8.00	20.00
10 Bob Holly	6.00	15.00
11 Bobby Heenan	30.00	75.00
12 Bolo Mongol/Ax	10.00	25.00
13 Brutus Beefcake	8.00	20.00
14 Bushwacker Luke	8.00	20.00
15 Carlito	6.00	15.00
16 Carlos Colon	10.00	25.00
17 Chris Masters	6.00	15.00
18 Christopher Daniels	6.00	15.00
19 Christy Hemme	12.00	30.00
20 Debra McMichael	10.00	25.00
21 Dennis Condrey	6.00	15.00
22 Dennis Rodman	15.00	40.00
23 Dynamite Kid	10.00	25.00
24 Ezekiel Jackson	6.00	15.00
25 Fifi/Wendy Barlow	10.00	25.00
26 Francine	10.00	25.00
27 Frankie Kazarian	6.00	15.00
28 Gangrel	6.00	15.00
29 Greg Valentine	10.00	25.00
30 Harley Race	12.00	30.00
31 Headshrinker Fatu	8.00	20.00
32 Hulk Hogan	30.00	80.00
33 Jeff Jarrett	10.00	25.00
34 Gerald Brisco	6.00	15.00
35 Jesus	6.00	15.00
36 Jimmy Garvin	6.00	15.00
37 Jimmy Hart	8.00	20.00
38 J.J. Dillon	8.00	20.00
39 Jushin Liger	15.00	40.00
40 Kama/Kama Mustafa	6.00	15.00
41 Kamala	8.00	20.00
42 Kelly Kelly	15.00	40.00
43 Ken Patera	8.00	20.00
44 Kevin Nash	10.00	25.00
45 Kevin Sullivan	10.00	25.00
46 King Kong Bundy	10.00	25.00
47 King Mo	6.00	15.00
48 Lanny Poffo	6.00	15.00
49 Larry Zbyszko	8.00	20.00
50 Lita	15.00	40.00
51 Maria Kanellis	10.00	25.00
52 Marlena	12.00	30.00
53 Masato Tanaka	8.00	20.00
54 Matt Hardy	8.00	20.00
55 Matt Striker	6.00	15.00
56 Mike Tyson	50.00	100.00
57 Mil Mascaras	30.00	80.00
58 Nick Bockwinkel	30.00	75.00
59 Nikita Koloff	8.00	20.00
60 Nikolai Volkoff	8.00	20.00
61 Ole Anderson	10.00	25.00
62 Papa Shango	8.00	20.00
63 Pat Tanaka	6.00	15.00
64 Pete Rose	15.00	40.00
65 Reby Sky	8.00	20.00
66 Repo Man	12.00	30.00
67 Ric Flair	20.00	50.00
68 Rick Steiner	10.00	25.00
69 Ricky Morton	8.00	20.00
70 Robert Gibson	8.00	20.00
71 Ron Simmons	8.00	20.00
72 Sabu	8.00	20.00
73 Samu	6.00	15.00
74 Scott Hall	15.00	40.00
75 Scott Norton	6.00	15.00
76 Sid Vicious	10.00	25.00
77 Steve Corino	6.00	15.00
78 Stevie Ray	8.00	20.00
79 Sunny	12.00	30.00
80 Terri Runnels	10.00	25.00
81 The Godfather	6.00	15.00
82 Iron Sheik	12.00	30.00
83 Tito Santana	10.00	25.00
84 Tommy Dreamer	8.00	20.00
85 Tully Blanchard	10.00	25.00
86 Val Venis	6.00	15.00
87 Warlord	6.00	15.00
88 Wendi Richter	15.00	40.00
89 Wrath	8.00	20.00
90 X-Pac	8.00	20.00
91 Zeus	12.00	30.00
92 Zodiac	8.00	20.00

2016 Leaf Signature Series Wrestling Adversaries

*BLUE/15-25: UNPRICED DUE TO SCARCITY
*GREEN/10: UNPRICED DUE TO SCARCITY
*RED/5: UNPRICED DUE TO SCARCITY
*BLACK/3: UNPRICED DUE TO SCARCITY
*PURPLE/1: UNPRICED DUE TO SCARCITY
*P.P.BLACK/1: UNPRICED DUE TO SCARCITY
*P.P.CYAN/1: UNPRICED DUE TO SCARCITY
*P.P.MAGENTA/1: UNPRICED DUE TO SCARCITY
*P.P.YELLOW/1: UNPRICED DUE TO SCARCITY
RANDOMLY INSERTED INTO PACKS

ADV01 S.Corino/T.Funk	15.00	40.00
ADV02 R.Flair/J.Garvin	20.00	50.00
ADV03 123 Kid/S.Hall	12.00	30.00
ADV05 B.Windham/B.Beefcake	12.00	30.00
ADV06 B.Eaton/R.Morton	12.00	30.00
ADV07 Carlito/Sabu	10.00	25.00
ADV09 S.Douglas/C.Daniels	10.00	25.00
ADV10 C.Hemme/V.Sky	20.00	50.00
ADV11 T.Dreamer/Francine	15.00	40.00
ADV12 Raven /F.Kazarian	10.00	25.00
ADV13 Animal/K.Sullivan	12.00	30.00
ADV14 Sandman/M.Striker	10.00	25.00
ADV15 Bushwacker Luke/P.Tanaka	12.00	30.00
ADV16 T.Dreamer/Sabu	15.00	40.00
ADV17 Zeus/H.Hogan	60.00	120.00

2016 Leaf Signature Series Wrestling Hall of Fame

*BLUE/15-50: UNPRICED DUE TO SCARCITY
*GREEN/10-25: UNPRICED DUE TO SCARCITY
*RED/5-10: UNPRICED DUE TO SCARCITY
*BLACK/3-5: UNPRICED DUE TO SCARCITY
*PURPLE/1: UNPRICED DUE TO SCARCITY
*P.P.BLACK/1: UNPRICED DUE TO SCARCITY
*P.P.CYAN/1: UNPRICED DUE TO SCARCITY
*P.P.MAGENTA/1: UNPRICED DUE TO SCARCITY
*P.P.YELLOW/1: UNPRICED DUE TO SCARCITY
RANDOMLY INSERTED INTO PACKS

HOF01 Bobby Heenan	20.00	50.00
HOF02 Carlos Colon	10.00	25.00
HOF03 Iron Sheik	10.00	25.00
HOF04 Wendi Richter	10.00	25.00
HOF05 Ron Simmons	10.00	25.00
HOF06 Nick Bockwinkel	50.00	100.00

HOF07 Ric Flair 25.00 60.00
HOF08 Mil Mascaras 30.00 80.00
HOF09 Harley Race 12.00 30.00
HOF10 Pete Rose 15.00 40.00
HOF11 Mike Tyson 50.00 100.00

2016 Leaf Signature Series Wrestling Ring Showdowns

*BLUE/7-50: UNPRICED DUE TO SCARCITY
*GREEN/5-10: UNPRICED DUE TO SCARCITY
*RED/3-5: UNPRICED DUE TO SCARCITY
*BLACK/2-3: UNPRICED DUE TO SCARCITY
*PURPLE/1: UNPRICED DUE TO SCARCITY
*P.P.BLACK/1: UNPRICED DUE TO SCARCITY
*P.P.CYAN/1: UNPRICED DUE TO SCARCITY
*P.P.MAGENTA/1: UNPRICED DUE TO SCARCITY
*P.P.YELLOW/1: UNPRICED DUE TO SCARCITY
RANDOMLY INSERTED INTO PACKS

RS201 Steve Corino/Greg Valentine 12.00 30.00
RS202 B.Bagwell/S.Norton 10.00 25.00
RS203 X-Pac /V.Venis 10.00 25.00
RS204 123 Kid/P.Tanaka 10.00 25.00
RS206 A.Bomb/Virgil 8.00 20.00
RS207 A.Snow/Raven 10.00 25.00
RS208 B.Mahoney/Sabu 15.00 40.00
RS209 Gangrel/Blue Meanie 10.00 25.00
RS210 H.Hogan/B.Beefcake 25.00 60.00
RS211 B.Beefcake/Masked Superstar 20.00 50.00
RS213 X-Pac /Gangrel 8.00 20.00
RS214 Gangrel /Godfather 8.00 20.00
RS215 K.Patera/T.Atlas 12.00 30.00
RS216 M.Bennett/S.Richards 8.00 20.00
RS217 M.Hardy/M.Bennett 12.00 30.00
RS218 R.Steiner/Vincent 8.00 20.00
RS219 K.Nash/R.Steiner 15.00 40.00
RS220 K.Nash/S.Vicious 15.00 40.00
RS222 T.Runnels/S.Richards 10.00 25.00
RS224 H.Hogan/D.Rodman 50.00 100.00

2016 Leaf Signature Series Wrestling Team Effort

*BLUE/7-50: UNPRICED DUE TO SCARCITY
*GREEN/5-25: UNPRICED DUE TO SCARCITY
*RED/3-10: UNPRICED DUE TO SCARCITY
*BLACK/2-5: UNPRICED DUE TO SCARCITY
*PURPLE/1: UNPRICED DUE TO SCARCITY
*P.P.BLACK/1: UNPRICED DUE TO SCARCITY
*P.P.CYAN/1: UNPRICED DUE TO SCARCITY
*P.P.MAGENTA/1: UNPRICED DUE TO SCARCITY
*P.P.YELLOW/1: UNPRICED DUE TO SCARCITY
RANDOMLY INSERTED INTO PACKS

TE01 S.Corino/A.Pearce 12.00 30.00
TE02 K.Patera/S.Norton 10.00 25.00
TE03 Konnan/S.Norton 20.00 50.00
TE05 J.Garvin/Precious 15.00 40.00
TE06 Ax/Smash 20.00 50.00
TE08 B.Eaton/D.Condrey 12.00 30.00
TE09 S.Lane/B.Eaton 12.00 30.00
TE10 S.Too Hotty/B.Christopher 15.00 40.00
TE11 B.Knobbs/J.Sags 12.00 30.00
TE13 J.Cornette/D.Condrey 10.00 25.00
TE14 Kama/Tatanka 10.00 25.00
TE15 C.Michelle/K.Kelly 12.00 30.00
TE16 N.Koloff/K.Kruschev 15.00 40.00
TE18 T.Runnels/V.Venis 15.00 40.00
TE19 N.Jackson/M.Jackson 8.00 20.00
TE20 M.Kanellis/M.Bennett 15.00 40.00
TE21 R.Steiner/S.Steiner 20.00 50.00
TE22 R.Morton/R.Gibson 12.00 30.00
TE23 R.Fatu/Samu 8.00 20.00
TE24 Tori/X-Pac 12.00 30.00

2020 Leaf Ultimate Wrestling Ultimate Stars Autographs

*PLATINUM/25>: UNPRICED DUE TO SCARCITY
*RED/10>: UNPRICED DUE TO SCARCITY
*EMERALD/5>: UNPRICED DUE TO SCARCITY
*SILVER/3>: UNPRICED DUE TO SCARCITY
*GOLD/1: UNPRICED DUE TO SCARCITY
*P.P.BLACK/1: UNPRICED DUE TO SCARCITY
*P.P.CYAN/1: UNPRICED DUE TO SCARCITY
*P.P.MAGENTA/1: UNPRICED DUE TO SCARCITY
*P.P.YELLOW/1: UNPRICED DUE TO SCARCITY

USE1 Edge 12.00 30.00
USG1 Goldberg 25.00 60.00
USK1 Kamala 10.00 25.00
UST1 Tugboat/Typhoon/Shockmaster 20.00 50.00
USW1 Warlord 8.00 20.00
USAA1 Arn Anderson 12.00 30.00
USAP1 Adam Page 15.00 40.00
USBB1 Britt Baker 12.00 30.00
USBB1 Brutus Beefcake 6.00 15.00
USBH1 Bret Hart 15.00 40.00
USBL1 Brother Love 8.00 20.00
USBOJ Bob Orton Jr. 6.00 15.00
USBP1 Brian Pillman Jr. 6.00 15.00
USBV1 Baron Von Raschke 10.00 25.00
USBW1 Barry Windham 10.00 25.00
USCC1 Colt Cabana 6.00 15.00
USCM1 Cima 5.00 12.00
USCR1 Cody Rhodes 15.00 40.00
USDA1 Demolition Ax 8.00 20.00
USDF1 Don Frye 6.00 15.00
USDS1 Demolition Smash 12.00 30.00
USEB1 Eric Bischoff 10.00 25.00
USED1 El Hijo del Fantasma 6.00 15.00
USFG1 Flip Gordon 5.00 12.00
USFL1 Flamita 5.00 12.00
USFU1 Funaki 6.00 15.00
USGM1 The Great Muta 15.00 40.00
USHH1 Hulk Hogan 60.00 120.00
USHT1 Hiroshi Tanahashi 8.00 20.00
USHTM The Honky Tonk Man 10.00 25.00
USJB1 Josh Barnett 10.00 25.00
USJH1 Jimmy Hart 8.00 20.00
USJL1 Jushin Liger 15.00 40.00
USKBW Koko B. Ware 10.00 25.00
USKI1 Kota Ibushi 15.00 40.00
USKO1 Kenny Omega 15.00 40.00
USKS1 Ken Shamrock 15.00 40.00
USLH1 Larry Hennig 10.00 25.00
USMF1 Manny Fernandez 6.00 15.00
USMF1 Mick Foley 15.00 40.00
USMS1 Minoru Suzuki 10.00 25.00
USPE1 Penta El Zero M 10.00 25.00
USPF1 Penelope Ford 10.00 25.00
USPS1 Perry Saturn 5.00 12.00
USRF1 Ric Flair 25.00 60.00
USRS1 Ricky Steamboat 10.00 25.00
USSS1 Sumie Sakai 5.00 12.00
USSV1 Sid Vicious 6.00 15.00
USTA1 Tony Atlas 6.00 15.00
USTB1 The Barbarian 6.00 15.00
USTB1 Tully Blanchard 10.00 25.00
USTD1 Ted DiBiase 10.00 25.00
USTF1 Terry Funk 15.00 40.00
USTS1 Tito Santana 8.00 20.00
USTZ1 Tazz 8.00 20.00
USVP1 Vampiro 8.00 20.00
USYH1 Yoshi-Hashi 6.00 15.00

2020 Leaf Ultimate Wrestling Clearly Dominant Autographs

*PINK/10-15: UNPRICED DUE TO SCARCITY
*PLATINUM/10: UNPRICED DUE TO SCARCITY
*GREEN/4-6: UNPRICED DUE TO SCARCITY
*RED/3-5: UNPRICED DUE TO SCARCITY
*SILVER/2-3: UNPRICED DUE TO SCARCITY
*GOLD/1: UNPRICED DUE TO SCARCITY
STATED PRINT RUN 25 SER.#'d SETS

CDG1 Goldberg 20.00 50.00
CDAA1 Arn Anderson 15.00 40.00
CDBH1 Bret Hart 20.00 50.00
CDCJ1 Chris Jericho 15.00 40.00
CDGM1 The Great Muta 30.00 75.00
CDHH1 Hulk Hogan 75.00 150.00
CDHT1 Hiroshi Tanahashi 12.00 30.00
CDJL1 Jushin Liger 20.00 50.00
CDJV1 Jesse Ventura
CDKK1 Kenta Kobashi 25.00 60.00
CDKN1 Kevin Nash 12.00 30.00
CDKO1 Kenny Omega 25.00 60.00
CDMF1 Mick Foley 15.00 40.00
CDRF1 Ric Flair 50.00 100.00

2020 Leaf Ultimate Wrestling Enshrined Autographs

*PURPLE/35>: UNPRICED DUE TO SCARCITY
*PLATINUM/10-15: UNPRICED DUE TO SCARCITY
*RED/7-10: UNPRICED DUE TO SCARCITY
*EMERALD/5: UNPRICED DUE TO SCARCITY
*SILVER/3: UNPRICED DUE TO SCARCITY
*GOLD/1: UNPRICED DUE TO SCARCITY
*P.P.BLACK/1: UNPRICED DUE TO SCARCITY
*P.P.CYAN/1: UNPRICED DUE TO SCARCITY
*P.P.MAGENTA/1: UNPRICED DUE TO SCARCITY
*P.P.YELLOW/1: UNPRICED DUE TO SCARCITY
RANDOMLY INSERTED INTO PACKS

EBB1 Brutus Beefcake 6.00 15.00
EBH1 Bret Hart 15.00 40.00
EBOJ Bob Orton Jr. 8.00 20.00
EHH1 Hulk Hogan 50.00 100.00
EJH1 Jimmy Hart 6.00 15.00
EKBW Koko B. Ware 6.00 15.00
EKN1 Kevin Nash 10.00 25.00
ERS1 Ricky Steamboat 12.00 30.00
ETA1 Tony Atlas 6.00 15.00

2020 Leaf Ultimate Wrestling Ultimate Ring Queens Autographs

*PURPLE/6-25: UNPRICED DUE TO SCARCITY
*PLATINUM/5-10: UNPRICED DUE TO SCARCITY
*RED/4-7: UNPRICED DUE TO SCARCITY
*EMERALD/3-5: UNPRICED DUE TO SCARCITY
*SILVER/2-3: UNPRICED DUE TO SCARCITY
*GOLD/1: UNPRICED DUE TO SCARCITY
*P.P.BLACK/1: UNPRICED DUE TO SCARCITY
*P.P.CYAN/1: UNPRICED DUE TO SCARCITY
*P.P.MAGENTA/1: UNPRICED DUE TO SCARCITY
*P.P.YELLOW/1: UNPRICED DUE TO SCARCITY
RANDOMLY INSERTED INTO PACKS

RQBB1 Britt Baker 25.00 60.00
RQBR1 Brandi Rhodes 15.00 40.00
RQIV1 Ivelisse 8.00 20.00
RQJH1 Jackie Haas 8.00 20.00
RQPF1 Penelope Ford 12.00 30.00
RQRS1 Ryan Shamrock 6.00 15.00
RQSB1 Scarlett Bordeaux 25.00 60.00
RQTB1 Tessa Blanchard 15.00 40.00
RQVI1 Victoria 6.00 15.00

2020 Leaf Ultimate Wrestling Ultimate Signatures 2

*PLATINUM/25>: UNPRICED DUE TO SCARCITY
*RED/15>: UNPRICED DUE TO SCARCITY
*EMERALD/5>: UNPRICED DUE TO SCARCITY
*SILVER/2-3: UNPRICED DUE TO SCARCITY
*GOLD/1: UNPRICED DUE TO SCARCITY
*P.P.BLACK/1: UNPRICED DUE TO SCARCITY
*P.P.CYAN/1: UNPRICED DUE TO SCARCITY
*P.P.MAGENTA/1: UNPRICED DUE TO SCARCITY
*P.P.YELLOW/1: UNPRICED DUE TO SCARCITY
RANDOMLY INSERTED INTO PACKS

US201 Ax/Smash 20.00 50.00
US202 Barbarian/Warlord 15.00 40.00
US203 B.Baker/P.Ford 25.00 60.00
US204 B.Beefcake/H.Hogan 60.00 120.00
US205 C.Cabana/T.Yano 15.00 40.00
US206 K.Omega/Cima 20.00 50.00
US207 E.Bischoff/T.Funk 20.00 50.00
US208 Honky Tonk Man/J.B. Badd 10.00 25.00
US209 T.DiBiase/J.Hart 12.00 30.00
US210 K.B. Ware/Bushwacker Luke 12.00 30.00
US211 S.Vicious/Vampiro 12.00 30.00
US212 Tazz/Funaki 12.00 30.00
US213 Tully & Tessa Blanchard 25.00 60.00
US214 T.Santana/T.DiBiase 15.00 40.00
US215 K.B. Ware/Warlord 10.00 25.00
US216 M.Foley/Edge 20.00 50.00
US217 Kat/Victoria 10.00 25.00
US218 Victoria/B.Reed 10.00 25.00
US219 T.Tonga/T.Loa 12.00 30.00
US220 A.Page/Y.Takahashi 15.00 40.00
US221 H.Hogan/D.Rodman 100.00 200.00

2020 Leaf Ultimate Wrestling Ultimate Signatures 4

*PURPLE/10-25: UNPRICED DUE TO SCARCITY
*PLATINUM/7-10: UNPRICED DUE TO SCARCITY
*RED/6-7: UNPRICED DUE TO SCARCITY
*EMERALD/4-5: UNPRICED DUE TO SCARCITY
*SILVER/3: UNPRICED DUE TO SCARCITY
*GOLD/1: UNPRICED DUE TO SCARCITY
*P.P.BLACK/1: UNPRICED DUE TO SCARCITY
*P.P.CYAN/1: UNPRICED DUE TO SCARCITY
*P.P.MAGENTA/1: UNPRICED DUE TO SCARCITY
*P.P.YELLOW/1: UNPRICED DUE TO SCARCITY
RANDOMLY INSERTED INTO PACKS

US401 Anderson/Blanchard/Flair/Windham
US402 Barbarian/Warlord/Ax/Smash 60.00 120.00

1999 Little Caesar's WCW/nWo Lenticular

COMPLETE SET (4) 3.00 8.00
NNO Diamond Dallas Page 1.25 3.00
NNO Goldberg 2.50 6.00
NNO Hollywood Hogan 2.00 5.00
NNO Sting 2.50 6.00

2001 Magic Box International WWF Metal Stickers

1 WWF LOGO .20 .50
2 Livewire LOGO .20 .50
3 RAW Is War LOGO .20 .50
4 SmackDown LOGO .20 .50
5 War Zone LOGO .20 .50
6 The Rock 1.50 4.00
7 The Rock 1.50 4.00
8 The Rock 1.50 4.00
9 The Rock 1.50 4.00
10 The Rock 1.50 4.00
11 The Rock 1.50 4.00
12 The Rock 1.50 4.00
13 The Rock 1.50 4.00
14 The Rock 1.50 4.00
15 The Rock 1.50 4.00
16 The Rock 1.50 4.00
17 The Rock 1.50 4.00
18 The Rock 1.50 4.00
19 The Rock 1.50 4.00
20 The Rock 1.50 4.00
21 The Rock 1.50 4.00
22 The Rock 1.50 4.00
23 The Rock 1.50 4.00
24 The Rock 1.50 4.00
25 The Rock 1.50 4.00
26 The Rock 1.50 4.00
27 The Rock 1.50 4.00
28 The Rock 1.50 4.00
29 Triple H 1.00 2.50
30 Triple H 1.00 2.50
31 Triple H 1.00 2.50
32 Triple H 1.00 2.50
33 Triple H 1.00 2.50
34 Triple H 1.00 2.50
35 Triple H 1.00 2.50
36 Triple H 1.00 2.50
37 Triple H 1.00 2.50
38 Triple H 1.00 2.50
39 Triple H 1.00 2.50
40 Triple H 1.00 2.50
41 Triple H 1.00 2.50
42 Triple H 1.00 2.50
43 Triple H 1.00 2.50
44 Triple H 1.00 2.50
45 Triple H 1.00 2.50
46 Triple H 1.00 2.50
47 Triple H 1.00 2.50
48 Triple H 1.00 2.50
49 Triple H 1.00 2.50
50 Triple H 1.00 2.50
51 Stone Cold Steve Austin 1.50 4.00
52 Stone Cold Steve Austin 1.50 4.00
53 Stone Cold Steve Austin 1.50 4.00
54 Stone Cold Steve Austin 1.50 4.00
55 Stone Cold Steve Austin 1.50 4.00
56 Stone Cold Steve Austin 1.50 4.00
57 Stone Cold Steve Austin 1.50 4.00

58 Stone Cold Steve Austin 1.50 4.00
59 Stone Cold Steve Austin 1.50 4.00
60 Stone Cold Steve Austin 1.50 4.00
61 Stone Cold Steve Austin 1.50 4.00
62 Stone Cold Steve Austin 1.50 4.00
63 Stone Cold Steve Austin 1.50 4.00
64 Stone Cold Steve Austin 1.50 4.00
65 Stone Cold Steve Austin 1.50 4.00
66 Stone Cold Steve Austin 1.50 4.00
67 Stone Cold Steve Austin 1.50 4.00
68 Stone Cold Steve Austin 1.50 4.00
69 Stone Cold Steve Austin 1.50 4.00
70 Kurt Angle .60 1.50
71 Kurt Angle .60 1.50
72 Kurt Angle .60 1.50
73 Kurt Angle .60 1.50
74 Kurt Angle .60 1.50
75 Kurt Angle .60 1.50
76 Kurt Angle .60 1.50
77 Kurt Angle .60 1.50
78 Kurt Angle .60 1.50
79 Kurt Angle .60 1.50
80 Kurt Angle .60 1.50
81 Kurt Angle .60 1.50
82 Kurt Angle .60 1.50
83 Kurt Angle .60 1.50
84 Kurt Angle .60 1.50
85 Kurt Angle .60 1.50
86 Kurt Angle .60 1.50
87 Kurt Angle .60 1.50
88 Undertaker 1.25 3.00
89 Undertaker 1.25 3.00
90 Undertaker 1.25 3.00
91 Undertaker 1.25 3.00
92 Undertaker 1.25 3.00
93 Undertaker 1.25 3.00
94 Undertaker 1.25 3.00
95 Undertaker 1.25 3.00
96 Undertaker 1.25 3.00
97 Undertaker 1.25 3.00
98 Undertaker 1.25 3.00
99 Undertaker 1.25 3.00
100 Kane .60 1.50
101 Kane .60 1.50
102 Kane .60 1.50
103 Kane .60 1.50
104 Kane .60 1.50
105 Kane .60 1.50
106 Kane .60 1.50
107 Kane .60 1.50
108 Kane .60 1.50
109 Kane .60 1.50
110 Kane .60 1.50
111 Kane .60 1.50
112 Chris Jericho .60 1.50
113 Chris Jericho .60 1.50
114 Chris Jericho .60 1.50
115 Chris Jericho .60 1.50
116 Chris Jericho .60 1.50
117 Chris Jericho .60 1.50
118 Chris Jericho .60 1.50
119 Chris Jericho .60 1.50
120 Chris Jericho .60 1.50
121 Chris Jericho .60 1.50
122 Chris Jericho .60 1.50
123 Chris Jericho .60 1.50
124 Chris Jericho .60 1.50
125 Chris Jericho .60 1.50
126 Chris Jericho .60 1.50
127 Edge & Christian .60 1.50
128 Edge & Christian .60 1.50
129 Edge & Christian .60 1.50
130 Edge & Christian .60 1.50
131 Edge & Christian .60 1.50
132 Edge & Christian .60 1.50
133 Edge & Christian .60 1.50
134 Eddie Guerrero .60 1.50
135 Eddie Guerrero .60 1.50
136 Eddie Guerrero .60 1.50
137 Eddie Guerrero .60 1.50
138 Eddie Guerrero .60 1.50
139 Rikishi .40 1.00
140 Rikishi .40 1.00
141 Rikishi .40 1.00
142 Rikishi .40 1.00
143 Rikishi .40 1.00
144 Chris Benoit .60 1.50
145 Chris Benoit .60 1.50
146 Chris Benoit .60 1.50
147 Chris Benoit .60 1.50
148 Chris Benoit .60 1.50
149 Big Bossman .40 1.00
150 Big Bossman .40 1.00
151 Big Bossman .40 1.00
152 Big Bossman .40 1.00
153 Big Bossman .40 1.00
154 Dean Malenko .25 .60
155 Dean Malenko .25 .60
156 Dean Malenko .25 .60
157 D'Lo Brown .25 .60
158 D'Lo Brown .25 .60
159 D'Lo Brown .25 .60
160 X-Pac .40 1.00
161 X-Pac .40 1.00
162 X-Pac .40 1.00
163 X-Pac .40 1.00
164 X-Pac .40 1.00
165 X-Pac .40 1.00
166 Al Snow .30 .75
167 Al Snow .30 .75
168 Al Snow .30 .75
169 Al Snow .30 .75
170 Al Snow .30 .75
171 Al Snow .30 .75
172 Tazz .40 1.00
173 Tazz .40 1.00
174 Tazz .40 1.00
175 Tazz .40 1.00
176 Tazz .40 1.00
177 Tazz & Jim Ross .40 1.00
178 Chyna .60 1.50
179 Chyna .60 1.50
180 Chyna .60 1.50
181 Chyna .60 1.50
182 Chyna .60 1.50
183 Chyna .60 1.50
184 Chyna .60 1.50
185 Chyna .60 1.50
186 Chyna .60 1.50
187 Chyna .60 1.50
188 Chyna .60 1.50
189 Chyna .60 1.50
190 Jacqueline 1.00 2.50
191 Jacqueline 1.00 2.50
192 Kat .25 .60
193 Kat .25 .60
194 Stephanie McMahon-Helmsley 1.25 3.00
195 Stephanie McMahon-Helmsley 1.25 3.00
196 Ivory 1.00 2.50
197 Trish Stratus 1.50 4.00
198 Lita 1.25 3.00
199 Lita 1.25 3.00
200 Lita 1.25 3.00
201 Terri Runnels 1.25 3.00
202 Too Cool .25 .60
203 Too Cool .25 .60
204 Too Cool .25 .60
205 Too Cool .25 .60
206 Too Cool .25 .60
207 Hardy Boyz w/Lita 1.25 3.00
208 Hardy Boyz .60 1.50
209 Hardy Boyz .60 1.50
210 Hardy Boyz .60 1.50
211 Hardy Boyz .60 1.50
212 Hardy Boyz .60 1.50
213 The Hollys 1.00 2.50
214 The Hollys 1.00 2.50
215 The Hollys 1.00 2.50
216 The Hollys 1.00 2.50
217 The Hollys 1.00 2.50
218 The Dudley Boyz .40 1.00
219 The Dudley Boyz .40 1.00
220 The Dudley Boyz .40 1.00
221 The Dudley Boyz .40 1.00
222 The Dudley Boyz .40 1.00
223 The Dudley Boyz .40 1.00
224 Right to Censor .25 .60
225 Right to Censor .25 .60
226 Right to Censor .25 .60
227 Right to Censor .25 .60
228 APA .60 1.50

2000 Magic Box WWF SmackDown Stickers

1 WWF LOGO .20 .50
2 Vince McMahon .75 2.00
3 The Rock 1.50 4.00
4 The Rock 1.50 4.00
5 The Rock 1.50 4.00
6 The Rock 1.50 4.00
7 The Rock 1.50 4.00
8 The Rock 1.50 4.00
9 The Rock 1.50 4.00
10 The Rock 1.50 4.00
11 The Rock 1.50 4.00
12 The Rock 1.50 4.00
13 The Rock 1.50 4.00
14 The Rock 1.50 4.00
15 The Rock 1.50 4.00
16 The Rock 1.50 4.00
17 The Rock 1.50 4.00
18 The Rock 1.50 4.00
19 The Rock 1.50 4.00
20 The Rock 1.50 4.00
21 The Rock 1.50 4.00
22 The Rock 1.50 4.00
23 The Rock 1.50 4.00
24 The Rock 1.50 4.00
25 The Rock 1.50 4.00
26 The Rock 1.50 4.00
27 Stone Cold Steve Austin 1.50 4.00
28 Stone Cold Steve Austin 1.50 4.00
29 Stone Cold Steve Austin 1.50 4.00
30 Stone Cold Steve Austin 1.50 4.00
31 Stone Cold Steve Austin 1.50 4.00
32 Stone Cold Steve Austin 1.50 4.00
33 Stone Cold Steve Austin 1.50 4.00
34 Stone Cold Steve Austin 1.50 4.00
35 Stone Cold Steve Austin 1.50 4.00
36 Stone Cold Steve Austin 1.50 4.00
37 Stone Cold Steve Austin 1.50 4.00
38 Stone Cold Steve Austin 1.50 4.00
39 Stone Cold Steve Austin 1.50 4.00
40 Stone Cold Steve Austin 1.50 4.00
41 Stone Cold Steve Austin 1.50 4.00
42 Stone Cold Steve Austin 1.50 4.00
43 Stone Cold Steve Austin 1.50 4.00
44 Stone Cold Steve Austin 1.50 4.00
45 Stone Cold Steve Austin 1.50 4.00
46 Stone Cold Steve Austin 1.50 4.00
47 Stone Cold Steve Austin 1.50 4.00
48 Stone Cold Steve Austin 1.50 4.00
49 Stone Cold Steve Austin 1.50 4.00
50 Stone Cold Steve Austin 1.50 4.00
51 Stone Cold Steve Austin 1.50 4.00
52 Undertaker 1.25 3.00
53 Undertaker 1.25 3.00
54 Undertaker 1.25 3.00
55 Undertaker 1.25 3.00
56 Undertaker 1.25 3.00
57 Undertaker 1.25 3.00
58 Undertaker 1.25 3.00
59 Undertaker 1.25 3.00
60 Undertaker 1.25 3.00
61 Undertaker 1.25 3.00
62 Undertaker 1.25 3.00
63 Undertaker 1.25 3.00
64 Undertaker 1.25 3.00
65 Undertaker 1.25 3.00
66 Undertaker 1.25 3.00
67 Undertaker 1.25 3.00
68 Undertaker 1.25 3.00
69 Undertaker 1.25 3.00
70 Kane .50 1.25
71 Kane .50 1.25
72 Kane .50 1.25
73 Kane .50 1.25
74 Kane .50 1.25
75 Kane .50 1.25
76 Kane .50 1.25
77 Kane .50 1.25
78 Kane .50 1.25
79 Kane .50 1.25
80 Kane .50 1.25
81 Kane .50 1.25
82 Kane .50 1.25
83 Kane .50 1.25
84 Kane .50 1.25
85 Kane .50 1.25
86 Kane .50 1.25
87 Triple H 1.00 2.50
88 Triple H 1.00 2.50
89 Triple H 1.00 2.50
90 Triple H 1.00 2.50
91 Triple H 1.00 2.50
92 Triple H 1.00 2.50
93 Triple H 1.00 2.50
94 Triple H 1.00 2.50
95 Triple H 1.00 2.50
96 Triple H 1.00 2.50
97 Triple H 1.00 2.50
98 X-Pac
99 X-Pac
100 X-Pac
101 X-Pac
102 X-Pac
103 X-Pac
104 X-Pac
105 X-Pac
106 X-Pac
107 X-Pac
108 X-Pac
109 X-Pac
110 Road Dogg .30 .75
111 Road Dogg .30 .75
112 Road Dogg .30 .75
113 Road Dogg .30 .75
114 Road Dogg .30 .75
115 Chris Jericho .50 1.25
116 Chris Jericho .50 1.25
117 Chris Jericho .50 1.25
118 Chris Jericho .50 1.25
119 Chris Jericho .50 1.25
120 Chris Jericho .50 1.25
121 WWF Get It LOGO .20 .50
122 War Zone LOGO .20 .50
123 Livewire LOGO .20 .50
124 WWF Jakked LOGO .20 .50
125 WWF SmackDown LOGO .20 .50
126 War Zone LOGO .20 .50
127 RAW Is War LOGO .20 .50
128 WWF Metal LOGO .20 .50
129 WWF Attitude LOGO .20 .50
130 WWF Superstars LOGO .20 .50
131 The Rock LOGO 1.50 4.00
132 Stone Cold Steve Austin LOGO 1.50 4.00
133 Kane LOGO .50 1.25
134 X-Pac LOGO
135 Triple H LOGO 1.00 2.50
136 Undertaker LOGO 1.25 3.00
137 Godfather LOGO .30 .75
138 Al Snow LOGO .25 .60
139 Val Venis LOGO .25 .60
140 Chris Jericho LOGO .50 1.25
141 Road Dogg LOGO .30 .75
142 Big Show LOGO .50 1.25
143 Gangrel LOGO .25 .60
144 Big Boss Man LOGO .40 1.00
145 Edge & Christian .50 1.25
146 Edge & Christian .50 1.25
147 Edge & Christian .50 1.25
148 Edge & Christian .50 1.25
149 Edge & Christian .50 1.25
150 Edge & Christian .50 1.25
151 Edge & Christian .50 1.25
152 Edge & Christian .50 1.25
153 Big Show .50 1.25
154 Big Show .50 1.25
155 Big Show .50 1.25
156 Big Show .50 1.25
157 Big Show .50 1.25
158 Big Show .50 1.25
159 Val Venis .25 .60
160 Val Venis .25 .60
161 Val Venis .25 .60
162 Val Venis .25 .60

163 Val Venis	.25	.60
164 D'Lo Brown	.25	.60
165 D'Lo Brown	.25	.60
166 D'Lo Brown	.25	.60
167 D'Lo Brown	.25	.60
168 D'Lo Brown	.25	.60
169 Al Snow	.25	.60
170 Al Snow	.25	.60
171 Al Snow	.25	.60
172 Al Snow	.25	.60
173 Al Snow	.25	.60
174 Godfather	.30	.75
175 Godfather	.30	.75
176 Godfather	.30	.75
177 Godfather	.30	.75
178 Godfather	.30	.75
179 Gangrel	.25	.60
180 Gangrel	.25	.60
181 Gangrel	.25	.60
182 Gangrel	.25	.60
183 Gangrel	.25	.60
184 Rikishi	.30	.75
185 Rikishi	.30	.75
186 Rikishi	.30	.75
187 Big Boss Man	.40	1.00
188 Big Boss Man	.40	1.00
189 Big Boss Man	.40	1.00
190 Big Boss Man	.40	1.00
191 British Bulldog	.40	1.00
192 Viscera	.25	.60
193 Viscera	.25	.60
194 Viscera	.25	.60
195 Prince Albert	.25	.60
196 Prince Albert	.25	.60
197 Prince Albert	.25	.60
198 Prince Albert	.25	.60
199 Tazz	.30	.75
200 Tazz	.30	.75
201 Paul Bearer	.40	1.00
202 Test	.25	.60
203 Mark Henry	.30	.75
204 Blue Meanie	.25	.60
205 Mantaur	.25	.60
206 Kurt Angle	.60	1.50
207 Chyna	.60	1.50
208 Chyna	.60	1.50
209 Chyna	.60	1.50
210 Chyna	.60	1.50
211 Chyna	.60	1.50
212 Debra	.40	1.00
213 Terri Runnels	.50	1.25
214 Torri	.25	.60
215 Jacqueline	.25	.60
216 Ivory	.30	.75
217 Ivory	.30	.75
218 Chyna	.60	1.50
219 Jacqueline	.25	.60
220 Ivory	.30	.75
221 Ivory	.30	.75
222 Ivory	.30	.75
223 DX	.75	2.00
224 DX	.75	2.00
225 DX	.75	2.00
226 Hardy Boyz	.50	1.25
227 Hardy Boyz	.50	1.25
228 Hardy Boyz	.50	1.25
229 Headbangers	.30	.75
230 Headbangers	.30	.75
231 Headbangers	.30	.75
232 Too Cool	.30	.75
233 Too Cool	.30	.75
234 Too Cool	.30	.75
235 APA	.30	.75
236 APA	.30	.75
237 APA	.30	.75
238 Dudley Boyz	.40	1.00
239 Dudley Boyz	.40	1.00
240 Dudley Boyz	.40	1.00
241 Mean Street Posse	.25	.60
242 Mean Street Posse	.25	.60
243 Mean Street Posse	.25	.60
244 The Hollys	.30	.75
245 The Hollys	.30	.75
246 The Hollys	.30	.75
247 The Rock	1.50	4.00
248 Stone Cold Steve Austin	1.50	4.00
249 Undertaker	1.25	3.00
250 Kane	.50	1.25
251 Triple H	1.00	2.50
252 X-Pac		
253 Road Dogg	.30	.75
254 Chris Jericho	.50	1.25
255 Christian	.30	.75
256 Edge	.50	1.25
257 Big Show	.50	1.25
258 Val Venis	.25	.60
259 Fans	.20	.50
260 Fans	.20	.50
261 Fans	.20	.50
262 Fans	.20	.50
263 Fans	.20	.50
264 Fans	.20	.50

1991 Mello Smello WWF Stickers

COMPLETE SET (6)	15.00	40.00
1 Hulk Hogan	10.00	25.00
2 The Bushwhackers	3.00	8.00
3 Big Boss Man	3.00	8.00
4 The Ultimate Warrior	6.00	15.00
5 The Legion of Doom	6.00	15.00
6 Jake The Snake Roberts	4.00	10.00

2006 Merlin WWE Champions Stickers

COMPLETE SET (250)		
1 WWE Logo LG	.20	.50
2 Raw Logo FOIL	.20	.50
3 SmackDown! Logo FOIL	.20	.50
4 Spirit Squad	.25	.60
5 Mickie James	1.50	4.00
6 Shelton Benjamin	.25	.60
7 Triple H	1.00	2.50
8 Big Show	1.00	2.50
9 John Cena LG	1.50	4.00
10 Kane FOIL	1.00	2.50
11 Ric Flair	1.25	3.00
12 Jim Ross	.30	.75
13 Stone Cold Steve Austin	1.50	4.00
14 Hulk Hogan	1.25	3.00
15 Edge	1.00	2.50
16 Batista	1.00	2.50
17 Lita	1.50	4.00
18 JBL	.60	1.50
19 Gregory Helms	.25	.60
20 Paul London	.25	.60
21 Brian Kendrick	.25	.60
22 Rey Mysterio LG	.60	1.50
23 Undertaker	1.25	3.00
24 Chris Benoit FOIL	1.00	2.50
25 Kurt Angle	1.00	2.50
26 Randy Orton	.60	1.50
27 Booker T	.60	1.50
28 Boogeyman	.60	1.50
29 Paul Burchill	.25	.60
30 Judgment Day Logo FOIL	.20	.50
31 John Cena	1.50	4.00
32 JBL	.60	1.50
33 John Cena	1.50	4.00
34 Eddie Guerrero	1.00	2.50
35 Rey Mysterio LG	.60	1.50
36 Eddie Guerrero	1.00	2.50
37 Rey Mysterio	.60	1.50
38 Booker T LG	.60	1.50
39 Kurt Angle	1.00	2.50
40 Chavo Guerrero	.40	1.00
41 Chavo Guerrero	.40	1.00
42 Paul London	.25	.60
43 ECW One Night Stand FOIL	.20	.50
44 Eddie Guerrero	1.00	2.50
45 Chris Benoit	1.00	2.50
46 Eddie Guerrero	1.00	2.50
47 Rey Mysterio	.60	1.50
48 Psicosis LG	.25	.60
49 Nunzio	.25	.60
50 Super Crazy	.40	1.00
51 Nunzio LG	.25	.60
52 Tajiri	.25	.60
53 RVD	.60	1.50
54 RVD	.60	1.50
55 Paul Heyman	.40	1.00
56 Vengeance Logo FOIL	.20	.50
57 Batista	1.00	2.50
58 Triple H	1.00	2.50
59 Batista LG	1.00	2.50
60 Triple H	1.00	2.50
61 Carlito	1.00	2.50
62 Shelton Benjamin	.25	.60
63 Carlito	1.00	2.50
64 Shawn Michaels LG	1.00	2.50
65 Kurt Angle	1.00	2.50
66 Kane	1.00	2.50
67 Edge FOIL	1.00	2.50
68 Kane	1.00	2.50
69 Great American Bash Logo FOIL	.20	.50
70 JBL	.60	1.50
71 Batista	1.00	2.50
72 Batista	1.00	2.50
73 JBL	.60	1.50
74 JBL LG	.60	1.50
75 JBL	.60	1.50
76 Melina	.50	1.25
77 Torrie Wilson LG	1.00	2.50
78 Melina	.50	1.25
79 Torrie Wilson	1.00	2.50
80 Melina	.50	1.25
81 Torrie Wilson	1.00	2.50
82 SummerSlam Logo FOIL	.20	.50
83 Shawn Michaels	1.00	2.50
84 Hulk Hogan	1.25	3.00
85 Hulk Hogan	1.25	3.00
86 Randy Orton FOIL	.60	1.50
87 Undertaker LG	1.25	3.00
88 Randy Orton	.60	1.50
89 Kurt Angle	1.00	2.50
90 Eugene LG	.25	.60
91 Edge	1.00	2.50
92 Matt Hardy	.60	1.50
93 Edge	1.00	2.50
94 Matt Hardy	.60	1.50
95 Unforgiven Logo FOIL	.20	.50
96 John Cena	1.50	4.00
97 Kurt Angle	1.00	2.50
98 John Cena	1.50	4.00
99 Carlito LG	1.00	2.50
100 Ric Flair FOIL	1.25	3.00
101 Ric Flair	1.25	3.00
102 Big Show LG	1.00	2.50
103 Snitsky	.40	1.00
104 Trish & Ashley	1.50	4.00
105 Victoria, Torrie, & Candice	1.50	4.00
106 Torrie Wilson	1.00	2.50
107 No Mercy Logo FOIL	.20	.50
108 Batista	1.00	2.50
109 Eddie Guerrero	1.00	2.50
110 Batista	1.00	2.50
111 Eddie Guerrero	1.00	2.50
112 Randy Orton LG	.60	1.50
113 Undertaker	1.25	3.00
114 Randy Orton	.60	1.50
115 Undertaker LG	1.25	3.00
116 Bobby Lashley	.60	1.50
117 Simon Dean	.25	.60
118 Simon Dean	.25	.60
119 Bobby Lashley	.60	1.50
120 John Cena LG	1.50	4.00
121 Rey Mysterio LG	.60	1.50
122 Batista FOIL	1.00	2.50
123 Triple H	1.00	2.50
124 Kurt Angle FOIL	1.00	2.50
125 Ric Flair	1.25	3.00
126 RVD	.60	1.50
127 Chris Benoit	1.00	2.50
128 Big Show & Kane	1.00	2.50
129 MNM	.40	1.00
130 Trish Stratus	1.50	4.00
131 Nunzio	.25	.60
132 Gregory Helms	.25	.60
133 Taboo Tuesday Logo FOIL	.20	.50
134 John Cena	1.50	4.00
135 Kurt Angle	1.00	2.50
136 Kurt Angle	1.00	2.50
137 Ric Flair	1.25	3.00
138 Triple H	1.00	2.50
139 Ric Flair	1.25	3.00
140 Triple H	1.00	2.50
141 Mick Foley	.75	2.00
142 Carlito	1.00	2.50
143 Divas Battle Royal	.20	.50
144 Divas Battle Royal LG	.20	.50
145 Survivor Series Logo FOIL	.20	.50
146 Shawn Michaels	1.00	2.50
147 Kane	1.00	2.50
148 Big Show FOIL	1.00	2.50
149 Carlito	1.00	2.50
150 Chris Masters	.40	1.00
151 Batista	1.00	2.50
152 Randy Orton	.60	1.50
153 JBL LG	.60	1.50
154 Rey Mysterio FOIL	.60	1.50
155 Bobby Lashley	.60	1.50
156 Shawn Michaels	1.00	2.50
157 Team Raw vs Team SmackDown!	.20	.50
158 Armageddon Logo FOIL	.20	.50
159 Undertaker	1.25	3.00
160 Randy Orton	.60	1.50
161 Undertaker	1.25	3.00
162 Randy Orton	.60	1.50
163 Rey Mysterio & Batista LG	1.00	2.50
164 Kane and Big Show	1.00	2.50
165 Kane	1.00	2.50
166 Chris Benoit	1.00	2.50
167 Booker T	.60	1.50
168 Chris Benoit	1.00	2.50
169 Matt Hardy	.60	1.50
170 JBL LG	.60	1.50
171 Revolution Logo FOIL	.20	.50
172 John Cena	1.50	4.00
173 Shawn Michaels	1.00	2.50
174 Kurt Angle	1.00	2.50
175 Chris Masters	.40	1.00
176 Carlito LG	1.00	2.50
177 Kane	1.00	2.50
178 John Cena	1.50	4.00
179 John Cena	1.50	4.00
180 Edge	1.00	2.50
181 Big Show	1.00	2.50
182 Triple H	1.00	2.50
183 Big Show LG	1.00	2.50
184 Royal Rumble Logo FOIL	.20	.50
185 Joey Mercury	.25	.60
186 Chris Benoit	1.00	2.50
187 Chris Masters	.40	1.00
188 Viscera	.40	1.00
189 Rey Mysterio LG	.60	1.50
190 Shawn Michaels	1.00	2.50
191 Viscera	.40	1.00
192 RVD	.60	1.50
193 Big Show	1.00	2.50
194 Jonathan Coachman	.25	.60
195 Rey Mysterio	.60	1.50
196 Rey Mysterio LG	.60	1.50
197 No Way Out Logo FOIL	.20	.50
198 Kurt Angle	1.00	2.50
199 Undertaker	1.25	3.00
200 Kurt Angle	1.00	2.50
201 Randy Orton	.60	1.50
202 Rey Mysterio	.60	1.50
203 Randy Orton	.60	1.50
204 Tatanka & Matt Hardy	.60	1.50
205 Nitro & Mercury LG	.40	1.00
206 Tatanka	.25	.60
207 JBL	.60	1.50
208 Bobby Lashley	.60	1.50
209 JBL LG	.60	1.50
210 WrestleMania 22 Logo FOIL	.20	.50
211 John Cena	1.50	4.00
212 Triple H FOIL	1.00	2.50
213 John Cena	1.50	4.00
214 Rey Mysterio	.60	1.50
215 Randy Orton LG	.60	1.50
216 Kurt Angle	1.00	2.50
217 Rey Mysterio	.60	1.50
218 Booker T FOIL	.60	1.50
219 Boogeyman	.60	1.50
220 Boogeyman	.60	1.50
221 Booker T	.60	1.50
222 Boogeyman LG	.60	1.50
223 Judgment Day Logo FOIL	.20	.50
224 Rey Mysterio	.60	1.50

225 JBL .60 1.50
226 Rey Mysterio .60 1.50
227 JBL .60 1.50
228 MNM LG .40 1.00
229 Johnny Nitro .40 1.00
230 London & Kendrick .25 .60
231 Bobby Lashley .60 1.50
232 Booker T .60 1.50
233 Booker T .60 1.50
234 Bobby Lashley LG .60 1.50
235 ECW Logo FOIL .20 .50
236 RVD .60 1.50
237 John Cena 1.50 4.00
238 RVD .60 1.50
239 RVD .60 1.50
240 Sabu LG .25 .60
241 Rey Mysterio .60 1.50
242 Rey Mysterio .60 1.50
243 Sabu .25 .60
244 Tazz .40 1.00
245 Jerry Lawler FOIL .75 2.00
246 Tazz LG .40 1.00
247 Rey Mysterio .60 1.50
248 Randy Orton .60 1.50
249 Kurt Angle 1.00 2.50
250 Rey Mysterio LG .60 1.50

2006 Merlin WWE Champions Stickers Rey Mysterio

RANDOMLY INSERTED INTO PACKS
R1 Mysterio vs Angle LG .40 1.00
R2 Mysterio vs Angle LG .40 1.00
R3 Mysterio vs Angle LG .40 1.00
R4 Mysterio vs Khali LG .40 1.00
R5 Mysterio vs Henry .40 1.00
R6 Rey Mysterio .40 1.00
R7 Mysterio vs Kane .40 1.00
R8 Mysterio Posing .40 1.00
R9 Mysterio vs Finlay .40 1.00
R10 Mysterio vs. JBL .40 1.00

2008 Merlin WWE Heroes Stickers

COMPLETE SET (230) 50.00 100.00
1 RAW Logo .15 .40
2 SmackDown Logo .15 .40
3 ECW Logo .15 .40
4 Randy Orton .40 1.00
5 Randy Orton .40 1.00
6 Randy Orton .40 1.00
7 Randy Orton .40 1.00
8 Randy Orton .40 1.00
9 Randy Orton .40 1.00
10 Randy Orton .40 1.00
11 Randy Orton .40 1.00
12 Randy Orton .40 1.00
13 Randy Orton .40 1.00
14 Randy Orton .40 1.00
15 Undertaker .75 2.00
16 Undertaker .75 2.00
17 Undertaker .75 2.00
18 Undertaker .75 2.00
19 Undertaker .75 2.00
20 Undertaker .75 2.00
21 Undertaker .75 2.00
22 Undertaker .75 2.00
23 Undertaker .75 2.00
24 Undertaker .75 2.00
25 Undertaker .75 2.00
26 Shawn Michaels 1.00 2.50
27 Shawn Michaels 1.00 2.50
28 Shawn Michaels 1.00 2.50
29 Shawn Michaels 1.00 2.50
30 Shawn Michaels 1.00 2.50
31 Shawn Michaels 1.00 2.50
32 Shawn Michaels 1.00 2.50
33 Shawn Michaels 1.00 2.50
34 Shawn Michaels 1.00 2.50
35 Shawn Michaels 1.00 2.50
36 Shawn Michaels 1.00 2.50
37 MVP .25 .60
38 MVP .25 .60
39 MVP .25 .60
40 MVP .25 .60
41 MVP .25 .60
42 MVP .25 .60
43 Michelle McCool .75 2.00
44 Michelle McCool .75 2.00
45 Michelle McCool .75 2.00
46 Michelle McCool .75 2.00
47 Michelle McCool .75 2.00
48 Triple H 1.00 2.50
49 Triple H 1.00 2.50
50 Triple H 1.00 2.50
51 Triple H 1.00 2.50
52 Triple H 1.00 2.50
53 Triple H 1.00 2.50
54 Triple H 1.00 2.50
55 Triple H 1.00 2.50
56 Triple H 1.00 2.50
57 Triple H 1.00 2.50
58 Triple H 1.00 2.50
59 Batista .60 1.50
60 Batista .60 1.50
61 Batista .60 1.50
62 Batista .60 1.50
63 Batista .60 1.50
64 Batista .60 1.50
65 Batista .60 1.50
66 Batista .60 1.50
67 Batista .60 1.50
68 Batista .60 1.50
69 Batista .60 1.50
70 Umaga .25 .60
71 Umaga .25 .60
72 Umaga .25 .60
73 Umaga .25 .60
74 Umaga .25 .60
75 Umaga .25 .60
76 Hornswoggle .25 .60
77 Hornswoggle .25 .60
78 Hornswoggle .25 .60
79 Hornswoggle .25 .60
80 Hornswoggle .25 .60
81 Matt Hardy .60 1.50
82 Matt Hardy .60 1.50
83 Matt Hardy .60 1.50
84 Matt Hardy .60 1.50
85 Matt Hardy .60 1.50
86 Matt Hardy .60 1.50
87 Matt Hardy .60 1.50
88 Matt Hardy .60 1.50
89 Matt Hardy .60 1.50
90 Matt Hardy .60 1.50
91 Matt Hardy .60 1.50
92 CM Punk .15 .40
93 CM Punk .15 .40
94 CM Punk .15 .40
95 CM Punk .15 .40
96 CM Punk .15 .40
97 CM Punk .15 .40
98 The Miz .25 .60
99 The Miz .25 .60
100 The Miz .25 .60
101 The Miz .25 .60
102 The Miz .25 .60
103 Ken Kennedy .40 1.00
104 Ken Kennedy .40 1.00
105 Ken Kennedy .40 1.00
106 Ken Kennedy .40 1.00
107 Ken Kennedy .40 1.00
108 Ken Kennedy .40 1.00
109 Melina .60 1.50
110 Melina .60 1.50
111 Melina .60 1.50
112 Melina .60 1.50
113 Melina .60 1.50
114 John Morrison .15 .40
115 John Morrison .15 .40
116 John Morrison .15 .40
117 John Morrison .15 .40
118 John Morrison .15 .40
119 Elijah Burke .15 .40
120 Elijah Burke .15 .40
121 Elijah Burke .15 .40
122 Elijah Burke .15 .40
123 Elijah Burke .15 .40
124 Elijah Burke .15 .40
125 Kane .60 1.50
126 Kane .60 1.50
127 Kane .60 1.50
128 Kane .60 1.50
129 Kane .60 1.50
130 Kane .60 1.50
131 Kane .60 1.50
132 Kane .60 1.50
133 Kane .60 1.50
134 Kane .60 1.50
135 Kane .60 1.50
136 John Cena 1.00 2.50
137 John Cena 1.00 2.50
138 John Cena 1.00 2.50
139 John Cena 1.00 2.50
140 John Cena 1.00 2.50
141 John Cena 1.00 2.50
142 John Cena 1.00 2.50
143 John Cena 1.00 2.50
144 John Cena 1.00 2.50
145 John Cena 1.00 2.50
146 John Cena 1.00 2.50
147 Rey Mysterio .40 1.00
148 Rey Mysterio .40 1.00
149 Rey Mysterio .40 1.00
150 Rey Mysterio .40 1.00
151 Rey Mysterio .40 1.00
152 Rey Mysterio .40 1.00
153 Rey Mysterio .40 1.00
154 Rey Mysterio .40 1.00
155 Rey Mysterio .40 1.00
156 Rey Mysterio .40 1.00
157 Rey Mysterio .40 1.00
158 Chris Jericho .40 1.00
159 Chris Jericho .40 1.00
160 Chris Jericho .40 1.00
161 Chris Jericho .40 1.00
162 Chris Jericho .40 1.00
163 Chris Jericho .40 1.00
164 Beth Phoenix .75 2.00
165 Beth Phoenix .75 2.00
166 Beth Phoenix .75 2.00
167 Beth Phoenix .75 2.00
168 Beth Phoenix .75 2.00
169 Chavo Guerrero .25 .60
170 Chavo Guerrero .25 .60
171 Chavo Guerrero .25 .60
172 Chavo Guerrero .25 .60
173 Chavo Guerrero .25 .60
174 The Great Khali .15 .40
175 The Great Khali .15 .40
176 The Great Khali .15 .40
177 The Great Khali .15 .40
178 The Great Khali .15 .40
179 The Great Khali .15 .40
180 Shelton Benjamin .15 .40
181 Shelton Benjamin .15 .40
182 Shelton Benjamin .15 .40
183 Shelton Benjamin .15 .40
184 Shelton Benjamin .15 .40
185 Boogeyman .25 .60
186 Boogeyman .25 .60
187 Boogeyman .25 .60
188 Boogeyman .25 .60
189 Boogeyman .25 .60
190 Boogeyman .25 .60
191 Edge .60 1.50
192 Edge .60 1.50
193 Edge .60 1.50
194 Edge .60 1.50
195 Edge .60 1.50
196 Edge .60 1.50
197 Edge .60 1.50
198 Edge .60 1.50
199 Edge .60 1.50
200 Edge .60 1.50
201 Edge .60 1.50
202 Jeff Hardy .60 1.50
203 Jeff Hardy .60 1.50
204 Jeff Hardy .60 1.50
205 Jeff Hardy .60 1.50
206 Jeff Hardy .60 1.50
207 Jeff Hardy .60 1.50
208 Jeff Hardy .60 1.50
209 Jeff Hardy .60 1.50
210 Jeff Hardy .60 1.50
211 Jeff Hardy .60 1.50
212 Jeff Hardy .60 1.50
213 Undertaker/Mark Henry .75 2.00
214 CM Punk/Miz .25 .60
215 Carlito/Mr. Anderson .40 1.00
F1 Undertaker .75 2.00
P2 World Title .15 .40
P3 Randy Orton .40 1.00
P4 Batista .60 1.50
P5 Rey Mysterio .40 1.00
P6 Triple H 1.00 2.50
P7 WWE Title .15 .40
P8 John Cena 1.00 2.50
P9 Randy Orton .40 1.00
P10 Edge .60 1.50
P11 JBL .15 .40
P12 Beth Phoenix .75 2.00
P13 WWE Women's Title .15 .40
P14 Melina .60 1.50
P15 Mickie James 1.00 2.50

2004 Merlin WWE RAW and SmackDown Explosion Stickers

R1 RAW LOGO .20 .50
R2 Eric Bischoff .40 1.00
R3 Triple H 1.50 4.00
R4 Triple H 1.50 4.00
R5 Triple H 1.50 4.00
R6 Triple H 1.50 4.00
R7 Triple H 1.50 4.00
R8 Triple H 1.50 4.00
R9 Triple H 1.50 4.00
S1 SmackDown LOGO .20 .50
S2 Stephanie McMahon 1.25 3.00
S3 Brock Lesnar 2.50 6.00
S4 Brock Lesnar FOIL 2.50 6.00
S5 Brock Lesnar 2.50 6.00
S6 Brock Lesnar 2.50 6.00
S7 Brock Lesnar 2.50 6.00
S8 Brock Lesnar 2.50 6.00
S9 Brock Lesnar 2.50 6.00
W1 Stone Cold Steve Austin 1.50 4.00
W2 Stone Cold Steve Austin 1.50 4.00
W3 Stone Cold Steve Austin 1.50 4.00
W4 Stone Cold Steve Austin 1.50 4.00
W5 Stone Cold Steve Austin 1.50 4.00
W6 Stone Cold Steve Austin 1.50 4.00
W7 Stone Cold Steve Austin 1.50 4.00
W8 Stone Cold Steve Austin 1.50 4.00
W9 Stone Cold Steve Austin 1.50 4.00
R10 Triple H FOIL 1.50 4.00
R11 Triple H 1.50 4.00
R12 Rob Van Dam 1.00 2.50
R13 Rob Van Dam 1.00 2.50
R14 Rob Van Dam FOIL 1.00 2.50
R15 Rob Van Dam 1.00 2.50
R16 Rob Van Dam 1.00 2.50
R17 Rob Van Dam 1.00 2.50
R18 Rob Van Dam 1.00 2.50
R19 Rob Van Dam 1.00 2.50
R20 Rob Van Dam 1.00 2.50
R21 Big Poppa Pump 1.25 3.00
R22 Big Poppa Pump 1.25 3.00
R23 Big Poppa Pump 1.25 3.00
R24 Big Poppa Pump FOIL 1.25 3.00
R25 Big Poppa Pump 1.25 3.00
R26 Booker T 1.00 2.50
R27 Booker T 1.00 2.50
R28 Booker T FOIL 1.00 2.50
R29 Booker T 1.00 2.50
R30 Booker T 1.00 2.50
R31 Chris Jericho .60 1.50
R32 Chris Jericho .60 1.50
R33 Chris Jericho FOIL .60 1.50
R34 Chris Jericho .60 1.50
R35 Chris Jericho .60 1.50
R36 Jeff Hardy .60 1.50
R37 Jeff Hardy .60 1.50
R38 Jeff Hardy .60 1.50
R39 Jeff Hardy FOIL .60 1.50
R40 Jeff Hardy .60 1.50
R41 Kane 1.00 2.50
R42 Kane FOIL 1.00 2.50
R43 Kane 1.00 2.50
R44 Kane 1.00 2.50

Card	Low	High
R45 Kane	1.00	2.50
R46 Bubba Ray Dudley	.40	1.00
R47 D-Von Dudley	.40	1.00
R48 Dudley Boyz	.40	1.00
R49 Rosey	.25	.60
R50 3 Minute Warning	.40	1.00
R51 Rosey	.25	.60
R52 Goldust	.40	1.00
R53 Goldust	.40	1.00
R54 Chris Nowinski	.25	.60
R55 Chris Nowinski	.25	.60
R56 Shawn Michaels FOIL	1.50	4.00
R57 Shawn Michaels	1.50	4.00
R58 Christian	.75	2.00
R59 Christian	.75	2.00
R60 William Regal	.30	.75
R61 William Regal	.30	.75
R62 Randy Orton	.60	1.50
R63 Randy Orton FOIL	.60	1.50
R64 Lance Storm	.25	.60
R65 Lance Storm	.25	.60
R66 Rico	.25	.60
R67 Rico	.25	.60
R68 Batista FOIL	1.00	2.50
R69 Batista	1.00	2.50
R70 The Hurricane	.30	.75
R71 The Hurricane	.30	.75
R72 Maven	.25	.60
R73 Maven	.25	.60
R74 Test	.40	1.00
R75 Test FOIL	.40	1.00
R76 Stacy Keibler	2.50	6.00
R77 Stacy Keibler	2.50	6.00
R78 Stacy Keibler	2.50	6.00
R79 Stacy Keibler FOIL	2.50	6.00
R80 Stacy Keibler	2.50	6.00
R81 Trish Stratus FOIL	2.50	6.00
R82 Trish Stratus	2.50	6.00
R83 Trish Stratus	2.50	6.00
R84 Trish Stratus	2.50	6.00
R85 Trish Stratus	2.50	6.00
R86 Molly Holly	1.25	3.00
R87 Molly Holly	1.25	3.00
R88 Molly Holly	1.25	3.00
R89 Molly Holly	1.25	3.00
R90 Jacqueline FOIL	.75	2.00
R91 Jackie Gayda	1.00	2.50
R92 Victoria FOIL	1.25	3.00
R93 Jazz	.60	1.50
R94 Ivory	1.00	2.50
R95 Triple H / Shawn Michaels	1.50	4.00
R96 D-Von Dudley	.40	1.00
R97 Big Poppa Pump	1.25	3.00
R98 Test	.40	1.00
S10 Brock Lesnar	2.50	6.00
S11 Brock Lesnar	2.50	6.00
S12 Kurt Angle	1.00	2.50
S13 Kurt Angle	1.00	2.50
S14 Kurt Angle	1.00	2.50
S15 Kurt Angle	1.00	2.50
S16 Shelton Benjamin	.25	.60
S17 Charlie Haas	.25	.60
S18 Kurt Angle	1.00	2.50
S19 Kurt Angle FOIL	1.00	2.50
S20 Kurt Angle	1.00	2.50
S21 Rey Mysterio	.60	1.50
S22 Rey Mysterio	.60	1.50
S23 Rey Mysterio	.60	1.50
S24 Rey Mysterio	.60	1.50
S25 Rey Mysterio	.60	1.50
S26 Rey Mysterio	.60	1.50
S27 Rey Mysterio	.60	1.50
S28 Rey Mysterio FOIL	.60	1.50
S29 Rey Mysterio	.60	1.50
S30 The Rock	1.50	4.00
S31 The Rock	1.50	4.00
S32 The Rock	1.50	4.00
S33 The Rock FOIL	1.50	4.00
S34 The Rock	1.50	4.00
S35 The Rock	1.50	4.00
S36 The Rock	1.50	4.00
S37 The Rock	1.50	4.00
S38 The Rock	1.50	4.00
S39 Edge	1.00	2.50
S40 Edge FOIL	1.00	2.50
S41 Edge	1.00	2.50
S42 Edge	1.00	2.50
S43 Edge	1.00	2.50
S44 Chris Benoit	.60	1.50
S45 Chris Benoit FOIL	.60	1.50
S46 Chris Benoit	.60	1.50
S47 Chris Benoit	.60	1.50
S48 Chris Benoit	.60	1.50
S49 Hulk Hogan	1.50	4.00
S50 Hulk Hogan	1.50	4.00
S51 Hulk Hogan FOIL	1.50	4.00
S52 Hulk Hogan	1.50	4.00
S53 Hulk Hogan	1.50	4.00
S54 The Undertaker	1.25	3.00
S55 The Undertaker	1.25	3.00
S56 The Undertaker FOIL	1.25	3.00
S57 The Undertaker	1.25	3.00
S58 The Undertaker	1.25	3.00
S59 Matt Hardy	.60	1.50
S60 Matt Hardy	.60	1.50
S61 Eddie Guerrero	1.25	3.00
S62 Eddie Guerrero	1.25	3.00
S63 Chavo Guerrero FOIL	.40	1.00
S64 Chavo Guerrero	.40	1.00
S65 Big Show	1.00	2.50
S66 Big Show	1.00	2.50
S67 A-Train	.25	.60
S68 A-Train	.25	.60
S69 Mark Henry	.40	1.00
S70 Mark Henry FOIL	.40	1.00
S71 Rikishi	.60	1.50
S72 Rikishi	.60	1.50
S73 John Cena	1.50	4.00
S74 John Cena	1.50	4.00
S75 Chuck Palumbo FOIL	.40	1.00
S76 Chuck Palumbo	.40	1.00
S77 Tajiri	.25	.60
S78 Tajiri	.25	.60
S79 Billy Kidman	.25	.60
S80 Billy Kidman	.25	.60
S81 Jamie Noble	.25	.60
S82 Jamie Noble FOIL	.25	.60
S83 Dawn Marie	.60	1.50
S84 Dawn Marie	.60	1.50
S85 Dawn Marie FOIL	.60	1.50
S86 Nidia FOIL	.60	1.50
S87 Nidia	.60	1.50
S88 Torrie Wilson FOIL	2.50	6.00
S89 Torrie Wilson	2.50	6.00
S90 Torrie Wilson	2.50	6.00
S91 Torrie Wilson	2.50	6.00
S92 Torrie Wilson	2.50	6.00
S93 Tajiri	.25	.60
S94 The Undertaker	1.25	3.00
S95 Brock Lesnar	2.50	6.00
S96 Chavo Guerrero	.40	1.00
S97 Jamie Noble	.25	.60
S98 Kurt Angle	1.00	2.50
W10 Stone Cold Steve Austin	1.50	4.00
W11 Stone Cold Steve Austin	1.50	4.00
W12 Stone Cold Steve Austin	1.50	4.00
W13 Stone Cold Steve Austin	1.50	4.00
W14 Stone Cold Steve Austin	1.50	4.00
W15 Stone Cold Steve Austin	1.50	4.00
W16 Stone Cold Steve Austin	1.50	4.00
W17 Stone Cold Steve Austin	1.50	4.00
W18 Stone Cold Steve Austin	1.50	4.00

2007 Merlin WWE Superstar Stickers

Card	Low	High
1 Raw LOGO	.20	.50
2 SmackDown! LOGO	.20	.50
3 ECW LOGO	.20	.50
4 Undertaker FOIL	1.25	3.00
5 Undertaker	1.25	3.00
6 Undertaker LG	1.25	3.00
7 Undertaker	1.25	3.00
8 Undertaker	1.25	3.00
9 Undertaker	1.25	3.00
10 Undertaker	1.25	3.00
11 Undertaker LG	1.25	3.00
12 Undertaker	1.25	3.00
13 Undertaker	1.25	3.00
14 Undertaker	1.25	3.00
15 John Cena FOIL	1.50	4.00
16 John Cena	1.50	4.00
17 John Cena LG	1.50	4.00
18 John Cena	1.50	4.00
19 John Cena	1.50	4.00
20 John Cena	1.50	4.00
21 John Cena LG	1.50	4.00
22 John Cena	1.50	4.00
23 John Cena	1.50	4.00
24 John Cena	1.50	4.00
25 John Cena	1.50	4.00
26 Edge FOIL	.60	1.50
27 Edge	.60	1.50
28 Edge LG	.60	1.50
29 Edge	.60	1.50
30 Edge	.60	1.50
31 Edge	.60	1.50
32 Edge LG	.60	1.50
33 Edge	.60	1.50
34 Edge	.60	1.50
35 Edge	.60	1.50
36 Edge	.60	1.50
37 Matt Hardy	.60	1.50
38 Matt Hardy	.60	1.50
39 Jeff Hardy LG	.60	1.50
40 Matt Hardy	.60	1.50
41 Matt Hardy	.60	1.50
42 Matt Hardy	.60	1.50
43 Matt Hardy LG	.60	1.50
44 Matt Hardy	.60	1.50
45 Jeff Hardy	.60	1.50
46 Matt Hardy	.60	1.50
47 Matt Hardy	.60	1.50
48 MVP FOIL	.40	1.00
49 MVP	.40	1.00
50 MVP	.40	1.00
51 MVP	.40	1.00
52 MVP	.40	1.00
53 The Great Khali	.25	.60
54 The Great Khali LG	.25	.60
55 The Great Khali	.25	.60
56 The Great Khali	.25	.60
57 The Great Khali	.25	.60
58 The Great Khali	.25	.60
59 D-Generation X FOIL	1.00	2.50
60 Triple H	1.00	2.50
61 Triple H LG	1.00	2.50
62 Shawn Michaels	1.00	2.50
63 Triple H	1.00	2.50
64 Shawn Michaels	1.00	2.50
65 Shawn Michaels LG	1.00	2.50
66 Triple H	1.00	2.50
67 Triple H	1.00	2.50
68 Shawn Michaels	1.00	2.50
69 Shawn Michaels	1.00	2.50
70 Batista FOIL	.60	1.50
71 Batista	.60	1.50
72 Batista LG	.60	1.50
73 Batista	.60	1.50
74 Batista	.60	1.50
75 Batista	.60	1.50
76 Batista LG	.60	1.50
77 Batista	.60	1.50
78 Batista	.60	1.50
79 Batista	.60	1.50
80 Batista	.60	1.50
81 Randy Orton FOIL	1.00	2.50
82 Randy Orton	1.00	2.50
83 Randy Orton	1.00	2.50
84 Randy Orton LG	1.00	2.50
85 Randy Orton	1.00	2.50
86 Umaga	.40	1.00
87 Umaga LG	.40	1.00
88 Umaga	.40	1.00
89 Umaga	.40	1.00
90 Umaga	.40	1.00
91 Umaga	.40	1.00
92 Melina FOIL	1.00	2.50
93 Melina	1.00	2.50
94 Candice	1.25	3.00
95 Torrie Wilson	2.00	5.00
96 Mickie James	.75	2.00
97 Ashley	.50	1.25
98 Ashley FOIL	.50	1.25
99 Victoria	.50	1.25
100 Cherry	.25	.60
101 Kelly Kelly	.60	1.50
102 Layla	1.00	2.50
103 Rowdy Roddy Piper	1.00	2.50
104 Don Muraco	.40	1.00
105 Dusty Rhodes	.60	1.50
106 Jimmy Snuka	.40	1.00
107 Sgt. Slaughter	.60	1.50
108 Bobby Heenan	.50	1.25
109 Mr. Perfect	.40	1.00
110 Nikolai Volkoff	.50	1.25
111 The Samoans	.30	.75
112 Superstar Billy Graham	.40	1.00
113 Junkyard Dog	.50	1.25
114 Rey Mysterio FOIL	.60	1.50
115 Rey Mysterio	.60	1.50
116 Rey Mysterio LG	.60	1.50
117 Rey Mysterio	.60	1.50
118 Rey Mysterio	.60	1.50
119 Rey Mysterio	.60	1.50
120 Rey Mysterio LG	.60	1.50
121 Rey Mysterio	.60	1.50
122 Rey Mysterio	.60	1.50
123 Rey Mysterio	.60	1.50
124 John Morrison	.40	1.00
125 John Morrison	.40	1.00
126 John Morrison	.40	1.00
127 John Morrison FOIL	.40	1.00
128 John Morrison	.40	1.00
129 John Morrison	.40	1.00
130 Boogeyman	.25	.60
131 Boogeyman	.25	.60
132 Boogeyman FOIL	.25	.60
133 Boogeyman	.25	.60
134 Boogeyman	.25	.60
135 Boogeyman	.25	.60
136 Cryme Tyme FOIL	.25	.60
137 Cryme Tyme	.25	.60
138 JTG LG	.25	.60
139 JTG	.25	.60
140 Shad	.25	.60
141 Shad	.25	.60
142 Shad LG	.25	.60
143 JTG	.25	.60
144 JTG	.25	.60
145 JTG	.25	.60
146 Shad	.25	.60
147 Elijah Burke	.25	.60
148 Elijah Burke	.25	.60
149 Elijah Burke	.25	.60
150 Elijah Burke LG	.25	.60
151 Elijah Burke	.25	.60
152 Tommy Dreamer FOIL	.30	.75
153 Tommy Dreamer LG	.30	.75
154 Tommy Dreamer	.30	.75
155 Tommy Dreamer	.30	.75
156 Tommy Dreamer	.30	.75
157 Tommy Dreamer	.30	.75
158 Deuce & Domino	.25	.60
159 Deuce	.25	.60
160 Deuce LG	.25	.60
161 Domino	.25	.60
162 Domino	.25	.60
163 Deuce	.25	.60
164 Domino LG	.25	.60
165 Deuce	.25	.60
166 Deuce & Domino	.25	.60
167 Deuce	.25	.60
168 Deuce	.25	.60
169 Marcus Cor Von FOIL	.25	.60
170 Marcus Cor Von	.25	.60
171 Marcus Cor Von	.25	.60
172 Marcus Cor Von LG	.25	.60
173 Marcus Cor Von	.25	.60
174 Marcus Cor Von	.25	.60
175 CM Punk	1.00	2.50
176 CM Punk LG	1.00	2.50
177 CM Punk	1.00	2.50
178 CM Punk	1.00	2.50
179 CM Punk	1.00	2.50
180 King Booker FOIL	.60	1.50
181 King Booker	.60	1.50
182 King Booker LG	.60	1.50
183 King Booker	.60	1.50
184 King Booker	.60	1.50
185 King Booker	.60	1.50
186 Queen Sharmell LG	.30	.75

187 Queen Sharmell .30 .75
188 King Booker .60 1.50
189 Queen Sharmell .30 .75
190 King Booker .60 1.50
191 Kane FOIL .60 1.50
192 Kane .60 1.50
193 Kane .60 1.50
194 Kane LG .60 1.50
195 Kane .60 1.50
196 Chavo Guerrero FOIL .40 1.00
197 Chavo Guerrero LG .40 1.00
198 Chavo Guerrero .40 1.00
199 Chavo Guerrero .40 1.00
200 Chavo Guerrero .40 1.00
201 Chavo Guerrero .40 1.00
202 Bobby Lashley FOIL .60 1.50
203 Bobby Lashley .60 1.50
204 Bobby Lashley .60 1.50
205 Bobby Lashley LG .60 1.50
206 Bobby Lashley .60 1.50
207 Bobby Lashley .60 1.50
208 Snitsky .25 .60
209 Snitsky LG .25 .60
210 Snitsky .25 .60
211 Snitsky .25 .60
212 Snitsky .25 .60
213 King Booker .60 1.50
214 Rey Mysterio .60 1.50
215 Undertaker 1.25 3.00
216 Edge .60 1.50
217 CM Punk 1.00 2.50
218 Shawn Michaels 1.00 2.50

2007 Merlin WWE Superstar Stickers Superstar Inserts

RANDOMLY INSERTED INTO PACKS

P1 John Cena 1.50 4.00
P2 King Booker .60 1.50
P3 John Cena 1.50 4.00
P4 Rey Mysterio vs Mark Henry .60 1.50
P5 CM Punk vs Ken Kennedy 1.00 2.50
P6 Edge .60 1.50
P7 Ric Flair 1.00 2.50
P8 Kane .60 1.50
P9 Chavo Guerrero .40 1.00
P10 Triple H 1.00 2.50
P11 Ken Kennedy .60 1.50
P12 Bobby Lashley .60 1.50
P13 Batista .60 1.50
P14 Gregory Helms .25 .60

2005 Merlin WWE Ultimate Stickers

1 Jim Ross .40 1.00
2 WWE LOGO .20 .50
3 RAW LOGO .20 .50
4 SmackDown LOGO .20 .50
5 John Cena 1.25 3.00
6 John Cena 1.25 3.00
7 John Cena 1.25 3.00
8 John Cena 1.25 3.00
9 John Cena 1.25 3.00
10 John Cena 1.25 3.00
11 John Cena 1.25 3.00
12 John Cena 1.25 3.00
13 John Cena 1.25 3.00
14 John Cena 1.25 3.00
15 John Cena 1.25 3.00
16 Batista .50 1.25
17 Batista .50 1.25
18 Batista .50 1.25
19 Batista .50 1.25
20 Batista .50 1.25
21 Batista .50 1.25
22 Batista .50 1.25
23 Batista .50 1.25
24 Batista .50 1.25
25 Batista .50 1.25
26 Batista .50 1.25
27 Undertaker 1.25 3.00
28 Undertaker 1.25 3.00
29 Undertaker 1.25 3.00
30 Undertaker 1.25 3.00
31 Undertaker 1.25 3.00
32 Undertaker 1.25 3.00
33 Undertaker 1.25 3.00
34 Undertaker 1.25 3.00
35 Undertaker 1.25 3.00
36 Undertaker 1.25 3.00
37 Undertaker 1.25 3.00
38 Triple H .60 1.50
39 Triple H .60 1.50
40 Triple H .60 1.50
41 Triple H .60 1.50
42 Triple H .60 1.50
43 Triple H .60 1.50
44 Triple H .60 1.50
45 Triple H .60 1.50
46 Triple H .60 1.50
47 Triple H .60 1.50
48 Triple H .60 1.50
49 Eddie Guerrero .60 1.50
50 Eddie Guerrero .60 1.50
51 Eddie Guerrero .60 1.50
52 Eddie Guerrero .60 1.50
53 Eddie Guerrero .60 1.50
54 Eddie Guerrero .60 1.50
55 Eddie Guerrero .60 1.50
56 Eddie Guerrero .60 1.50
57 Eddie Guerrero .60 1.50
58 Eddie Guerrero .60 1.50
59 Eddie Guerrero .60 1.50
60 Shawn Michaels .75 2.00
61 Shawn Michaels .75 2.00
62 Shawn Michaels .75 2.00
63 Shawn Michaels .75 2.00
64 Shawn Michaels .75 2.00
65 Shawn Michaels .75 2.00
66 Shawn Michaels .75 2.00
67 Shawn Michaels .75 2.00
68 Shawn Michaels .75 2.00
69 Shawn Michaels .75 2.00
70 Shawn Michaels .75 2.00
71 Rey Mysterio .60 1.50
72 Rey Mysterio .60 1.50
73 Rey Mysterio .60 1.50
74 Rey Mysterio .60 1.50
75 Rey Mysterio .60 1.50
76 Rey Mysterio .60 1.50
77 Rey Mysterio .60 1.50
78 Rey Mysterio .60 1.50
79 Rey Mysterio .60 1.50
80 Rey Mysterio .60 1.50
81 Rey Mysterio .60 1.50
82 Rey Mysterio .60 1.50
83 Kane .75 2.00
84 Kane .75 2.00
85 Kane .75 2.00
86 Kane .75 2.00
87 Kane .75 2.00
88 Kane .75 2.00
89 Kane .75 2.00
90 Kane .75 2.00
91 Kane .75 2.00
92 Kane .75 2.00
93 Kane .75 2.00
94 Kurt Angle .60 1.50
95 Kurt Angle .60 1.50
96 Kurt Angle .60 1.50
97 Kurt Angle .60 1.50
98 Kurt Angle .60 1.50
99 Kurt Angle .60 1.50
100 Kurt Angle .60 1.50
101 Kurt Angle .60 1.50
102 Kurt Angle .60 1.50
103 Kurt Angle .60 1.50
104 Kurt Angle .60 1.50
105 Randy Orton .25 .60
106 Randy Orton .25 .60
107 Randy Orton .25 .60
108 Randy Orton .25 .60
109 Randy Orton .25 .60
110 Randy Orton .25 .60
111 Randy Orton .25 .60
112 Randy Orton .25 .60
113 Randy Orton .25 .60
114 Randy Orton .25 .60
115 Randy Orton .25 .60
116 JBL .40 1.00
117 JBL .40 1.00
118 JBL .40 1.00
119 JBL .40 1.00
120 JBL .40 1.00
121 JBL .40 1.00
122 Edge .60 1.50
123 Edge .60 1.50
124 Edge .60 1.50
125 Edge .60 1.50
126 Edge .60 1.50
127 Big Show 1.00 2.50
128 Big Show 1.00 2.50
129 Big Show 1.00 2.50
130 Big Show 1.00 2.50
131 Big Show 1.00 2.50
132 Big Show 1.00 2.50
133 Chris Benoit .60 1.50
134 Chris Benoit .60 1.50
135 Chris Benoit .60 1.50
136 Chris Benoit .60 1.50
137 Chris Benoit .60 1.50
138 Carlito .50 1.25
139 Carlito .50 1.25
140 Carlito .50 1.25
141 Carlito .50 1.25
142 Carlito .50 1.25
143 Chris Jericho .75 2.00
144 Chris Jericho .75 2.00
145 Chris Jericho .75 2.00
146 Chris Jericho .75 2.00
147 Chris Jericho .75 2.00
148 Chris Jericho .75 2.00
149 WrestleMania 21 .20 .50
150 SummerSlam .20 .50
151 Royal Rumble .20 .50
152 Survivor Series .20 .50
153 Rey Mysterio .60 1.50
154 John Cena 1.25 3.00
155 Eddie Guerrero .60 1.50
156 Undertaker 1.25 3.00
157 Batista .50 1.25
158 Triple H .60 1.50
159 Booker T .40 1.00
160 Booker T .40 1.00
161 Booker T .40 1.00
162 Booker T .40 1.00
163 Booker T .40 1.00
164 Booker T .40 1.00
165 Booker T .40 1.00
166 Shelton Benjamin .25 .60
167 Shelton Benjamin .25 .60
168 Shelton Benjamin .25 .60
169 Shelton Benjamin .25 .60
170 Shelton Benjamin .25 .60
171 Rob Van Dam .60 1.50
172 Rob Van Dam .60 1.50
173 Rob Van Dam .60 1.50
174 Rob Van Dam .60 1.50
175 Rob Van Dam .60 1.50
176 Rob Van Dam .60 1.50
177 Christian .75 2.00
178 Christian .75 2.00
179 Christian .75 2.00
180 Christian .75 2.00
181 Christian .75 2.00
182 La Resistance .25 .60
183 William Regal .40 1.00
184 William Regal .40 1.00
185 Hurricane & Rosey .25 .60
186 Rosey .25 .60
187 Basham Brothers .25 .60
188 Basham Brothers .25 .60
189 MNM .30 .75
190 MNM .30 .75
191 The Dudley Boyz .40 1.00
192 The Dudley Boyz .40 1.00
193 Heidenreich .25 .60
194 Heidenreich .25 .60
195 Orlando Jordan .25 .60
196 Orlando Jordan .25 .60
197 Billy Kidman .30 .75
198 Muhammad Hassan .25 .60
199 Stone Cold Steve Austin 1.50 4.00
200 Stone Cold Steve Austin 1.50 4.00
201 Gene Snitsky .25 .60
202 Val Venis .40 1.00
203 Chris Masters .25 .60
204 Paul London .25 .60
205 Paul London .25 .60
206 Spike Dudley .25 .60
207 Spike Dudley .25 .60
208 Hardcore Holly .40 1.00
209 Charlie Haas .25 .60
210 Maven .25 .60
211 Eugene .60 1.50
212 Eugene .60 1.50
213 Tyson Tomko .25 .60
214 Kenzo Suzuki .25 .60
215 Steven Richards .25 .60
216 Steven Richards .25 .60
217 Nunzio .25 .60
218 Nunzio .25 .60
219 Nunzio .25 .60
220 Rene Dupree .25 .60
221 Chavo Guerrero .30 .75
222 Chavo Guerrero .30 .75
223 Mark Henry .30 .75
224 Garrison Cade .25 .60
225 Viscera .25 .60
226 Hulk Hogan 1.25 3.00
227 Hulk Hogan 1.25 3.00
228 Hulk Hogan 1.25 3.00
229 Hulk Hogan 1.25 3.00
230 Hulk Hogan 1.25 3.00
231 Hulk Hogan 1.25 3.00
232 Hulk Hogan 1.25 3.00
233 Rowdy Roddy Piper 1.00 2.50
234 Rowdy Roddy Piper 1.00 2.50
235 Rowdy Roddy Piper 1.00 2.50
236 Rowdy Roddy Piper 1.00 2.50
237 British Bulldog .40 1.00
238 British Bulldog .40 1.00
239 British Bulldog .40 1.00
240 British Bulldog .40 1.00
241 British Bulldog .40 1.00
242 Jake The Snake Roberts .60 1.50
243 Jake The Snake Roberts .60 1.50
244 Jake The Snake Roberts .60 1.50
245 Jake The Snake Roberts .60 1.50
246 Jake The Snake Roberts .60 1.50
247 Sgt. Slaughter .60 1.50
248 Sgt. Slaughter .60 1.50
249 Sgt. Slaughter .60 1.50
250 Sgt. Slaughter .60 1.50
251 Sgt. Slaughter .60 1.50
252 Sgt. Slaughter .60 1.50
253 The Bushwhackers .30 .75
254 The Bushwhackers .30 .75
255 The Bushwhackers .30 .75
256 The Bushwhackers .30 .75
257 The Bushwhackers .30 .75
258 Ric Flair 1.00 2.50
259 Ric Flair 1.00 2.50
260 Ric Flair 1.00 2.50
261 Ric Flair 1.00 2.50
262 Ric Flair 1.00 2.50
263 Ric Flair 1.00 2.50
264 Ric Flair 1.00 2.50
265 Ric Flair 1.00 2.50
266 Ric Flair 1.00 2.50
267 Ric Flair 1.00 2.50
268 Ric Flair 1.00 2.50
269 Trish Stratus 2.50 6.00
270 Trish Stratus 2.50 6.00
271 Trish Stratus 2.50 6.00
272 Lita 1.50 4.00
273 Stacy Keibler 2.50 6.00
274 Stacy Keibler 2.50 6.00
275 Christy Hemme .75 2.00
276 Christy Hemme .75 2.00
277 Candice Michelle .60 1.50
278 Victoria 1.50 4.00
279 Maria 1.50 4.00
280 Torrie Wilson .75 2.00
281 Torrie Wilson .75 2.00
282 Torrie Wilson .75 2.00
283 Miss Jackie .25 .60
284 Miss Jackie .25 .60
285 Dawn Marie
286 Dawn Marie
287 Joy Giovanni .25 .60

288 Joy Giovanni .25 .60
289 Michelle McCool 1.25 3.00
290 Michelle McCool 1.25 3.00
291 WWE Title .20 .50
292 World Title .20 .50
293 Money Title .75 2.00
294 RAW Title .20 .50
295 Tag Team Title .20 .50
296 US Title .20 .50
297 Tag Team Title .20 .50
298 Tag Team Title .20 .50
299 Cruiserweight Title .20 .50
300 Women's Title .20 .50
301 US Title .20 .50
302 Batista .50 1.25
303 John Cena 1.25 3.00
304 Batista & John Cena 1.25 3.00

1993 Merlin WWF SuperStars Stickers

1 WWF Logo FOIL .10 .25
2 Battle Royal (Puzzle) .10 .25
3 Battle Royal (Puzzle) .10 .25
4 Battle Royal (Puzzle) .10 .25
5 Lex Luger Logo FOIL .40 1.00
6 Lex Luger .40 1.00
7 Lex Luger .40 1.00
8 Lex Luger (Puzzle) .40 1.00
9 Lex Luger (Puzzle) .40 1.00
10 Lex Luger .40 1.00
11 Lex Luger (Puzzle) .40 1.00
12 Lex Luger (Puzzle) .40 1.00
13 Lex Luger FOIL .40 1.00
14 Lex Luger .40 1.00
15 Bob Backlund .30 .75
16 Bob Backlund Logo FOIL .30 .75
17 Bob Backlund .30 .75
18 Bob Backlund .30 .75
19 Bob Backlund FOIL .30 .75
20 Bob Backlund (Puzzle) .30 .75
21 Bob Backlund (Puzzle) .30 .75
22 Bob Backlund .30 .75
23 The Undertaker Logo FOIL 1.00 2.50
24 The Undertaker 1.00 2.50
25 The Undertaker 1.00 2.50
26 The Undertaker 1.00 2.50
27 The Undertaker FOIL 1.00 2.50
28 The Undertaker 1.00 2.50
29 The Undertaker (Puzzle) 1.00 2.50
30 The Undertaker (Puzzle) 1.00 2.50
31 The Undertaker (Puzzle) 1.00 2.50
32 The Undertaker (Puzzle) 1.00 2.50
33 Paul Bearer (Puzzle) .30 .75
34 Paul Bearer (Puzzle) .30 .75
35 Paul Bearer .30 .75
36 Paul Bearer (Puzzle) .30 .75
37 Paul Bearer (Puzzle) .30 .75
38 The Model Rick Martel Logo FOIL .30 .75
39 The Model Rick Martel (Puzzle) .30 .75
40 The Model Rick Martel (Puzzle) .30 .75
41 The Model Rick Martel (Puzzle) .30 .75
42 The Model Rick Martel (Puzzle) .30 .75
43 Bret Hit Man Hart Logo FOIL .50 1.25
44 Bret Hit Man Hart .50 1.25
45 Bret Hit Man Hart .50 1.25
46 Bret Hit Man Hart (Puzzle) .50 1.25
47 Bret Hit Man Hart (Puzzle) .50 1.25
48 Bret Hit Man Hart .50 1.25
49 Bret Hit Man Hart .50 1.25
50 Bret Hit Man Hart (Puzzle) .50 1.25
51 Bret Hit Man Hart (Puzzle) .50 1.25
52 Bret Hit Man Hart .50 1.25
53 Diesel (Puzzle) .40 1.00
54 Diesel (Puzzle) .40 1.00
55 Diesel .40 1.00
56 Diesel (Puzzle) .40 1.00
57 Diesel (Puzzle) .40 1.00
58 Diesel (Puzzle) .40 1.00
59 Diesel (Puzzle) .40 1.00
60 Diesel .40 1.00
61 Hulk Hogan Logo FOIL 1.00 2.50
62 Hulk Hogan (Puzzle) 1.00 2.50
63 Hulk Hogan (Puzzle) 1.00 2.50
64 Hulk Hogan 1.00 2.50
65 Hulk Hogan FOIL 1.00 2.50
66 Hulk Hogan 1.00 2.50
67 Hulk Hogan 1.00 2.50
68 Hulk Hogan 1.00 2.50
69 Hulk Hogan (Puzzle) 1.00 2.50
70 Hulk Hogan (Puzzle) 1.00 2.50
71 Irwin R. Schyster .30 .75
72 Irwin R. Schyster Logo FOIL .30 .75
73 Irwin R. Schyster .30 .75
74 Irwin R. Schyster (Puzzle) .30 .75
75 Irwin R. Schyster (Puzzle) .30 .75
76 Irwin R. Schyster .30 .75
77 Irwin R. Schyster .30 .75
78 Irwin R. Schyster FOIL .30 .75
79 Irwin R. Schyster .30 .75
80 Yokozuna Logo FOIL .50 1.25
81 Yokozuna (Puzzle) .50 1.25
82 Yokozuna (Puzzle) .50 1.25
83 Yokozuna .50 1.25
84 Yokozuna FOIL .50 1.25
85 Yokozuna .50 1.25
86 Yokozuna (Puzzle) .50 1.25
87 Yokozuna (Puzzle) .50 1.25
88 Yokozuna .50 1.25
89 Yokozuna .50 1.25
90 Mr. Fuji .25 .60
91 Mr. Fuji FOIL .25 .60
92 Mr. Fuji .25 .60
93 Mr. Fuji (Puzzle) .25 .60
94 Mr. Fuji (Puzzle) .25 .60
95 Shawn Michaels Logo FOIL .75 2.00
96 Shawn Michaels (Puzzle) .75 2.00
97 Shawn Michaels (Puzzle) .75 2.00
98 Shawn Michaels .75 2.00
99 Shawn Michaels .75 2.00
100 Adam Bomb FOIL .20 .50
101 Adam Bomb .20 .50
102 Adam Bomb .20 .50
103 Adam Bomb (Puzzle) .20 .50
104 Adam Bomb (Puzzle) .20 .50
105 Adam Bomb (Puzzle) .20 .50
106 Adam Bomb (Puzzle) .20 .50
107 Adam Bomb (Puzzle) .20 .50
108 Adam Bomb (Puzzle) .20 .50
109 Adam Bomb FOIL .20 .50
110 Randy Savage Logo FOIL .75 2.00
111 Randy Savage (Puzzle) .75 2.00
112 Randy Savage (Puzzle) .75 2.00
113 Randy Savage .75 2.00
114 Randy Savage .75 2.00
115 Randy Savage (Puzzle) .75 2.00
116 Randy Savage (Puzzle) .75 2.00
117 Randy Savage .75 2.00
118 Randy Savage .75 2.00
119 Randy Savage FOIL .75 2.00
120 Marty Jannetty .25 .60
121 Marty Jannetty .25 .60
122 Marty Jannetty (Puzzle) .25 .60
123 Marty Jannetty (Puzzle) .25 .60
124 Marty Jannetty Logo FOIL .25 .60
125 Marty Jannetty (Puzzle) .25 .60
126 Marty Jannetty (Puzzle) .25 .60
127 Marty Jannetty (Puzzle) .25 .60
128 Marty Jannetty (Puzzle) .25 .60
129 Tatanka Logo FOIL .25 .60
130 Tatanka (Puzzle) .25 .60
131 Tatanka (Puzzle) .25 .60
132 Tatanka FOIL .25 .60
133 Tatanka (Puzzle) .25 .60
134 Tatanka (Puzzle) .25 .60
135 Tatanka .25 .60
136 Tatanka (Puzzle) .25 .60
137 Tatanka (Puzzle) .25 .60
138 Tatanka .25 .60
139 Ludvig Borga Logo FOIL .20 .50
140 Ludvig Borga (Puzzle) .20 .50
141 Ludvig Borga (Puzzle) .20 .50
142 Ludvig Borga .20 .50
143 Ludvig Borga (Puzzle) .20 .50
144 Ludvig Borga (Puzzle) .20 .50
145 Ludvig Borga FOIL .20 .50
146 Ludvig Borga .20 .50
147 Ludvig Borga .20 .50
148 King of the Ring Logo FOIL .10 .25
149 Summer Slam Logo FOIL .10 .25
150 Survivor Series Logo FOIL .10 .25
151 Royal Rumble Logo FOIL .10 .25
152 WrestleMania Logo FOIL .10 .25
153 123 Kid Logo FOIL .25 .60
154 123 Kid (Puzzle) .25 .60
155 123 Kid (Puzzle) .25 .60
156 123 Kid .25 .60
157 123 Kid .25 .60
158 123 Kid .25 .60
159 123 Kid (Puzzle) .25 .60
160 123 Kid (Puzzle) .25 .60
161 123 Kid (Puzzle) .25 .60
162 123 Kid (Puzzle) .25 .60
163 Razor Ramon Logo FOIL .50 1.25
164 Razor Ramon .50 1.25
165 Razor Ramon .50 1.25
166 Razor Ramon (Puzzle) .50 1.25
167 Razor Ramon (Puzzle) .50 1.25
168 Razor Ramon (Puzzle) .50 1.25
169 Razor Ramon (Puzzle) .50 1.25
170 Razor Ramon FOIL .50 1.25
171 Razor Ramon (Puzzle) .50 1.25
172 Razor Ramon (Puzzle) .50 1.25
173 Bam Bam Bigelow Logo FOIL .40 1.00
174 Bam Bam Bigelow .40 1.00
175 Bam Bam Bigelow .40 1.00
176 Bam Bam Bigelow (Puzzle) .40 1.00
177 Bam Bam Bigelow (Puzzle) .40 1.00
178 Bam Bam Bigelow (Puzzle) .40 1.00
179 Bam Bam Bigelow (Puzzle) .40 1.00
180 Bam Bam Bigelow .40 1.00
181 Bam Bam Bigelow FOIL .40 1.00
182 Bam Bam Bigelow .40 1.00
183 Luna Vachon .25 .60
184 Luna Vachon Logo FOIL .25 .60
185 Luna Vachon .25 .60
186 Luna Vachon .25 .60
187 Luna Vachon .25 .60
188 Luna Vachon .25 .60
189 Luna Vachon FOIL .25 .60
190 Luna Vachon (Puzzle) .25 .60
191 Luna Vachon (Puzzle) .25 .60
192 Bastion Booger (Puzzle) .20 .50
193 Bastion Booger (Puzzle) .20 .50
194 Bastion Booger .20 .50
195 Bastion Booger .20 .50
196 Bastion Booger (Puzzle) .20 .50
197 Bastion Booger (Puzzle) .20 .50
198 Bastion Booger .20 .50
199 Bastion Booger (Puzzle) .20 .50
200 Bastion Booger (Puzzle) .20 .50
201 Crush FOIL .25 .60
202 Crush (Puzzle) .25 .60
203 Crush (Puzzle) .25 .60
204 Crush Logo FOIL .25 .60
205 Crush .25 .60
206 MVP .30 .75
207 MVP (Puzzle) .30 .75
208 MVP (Puzzle) .30 .75
209 MVP (Puzzle) .30 .75
210 MVP (Puzzle) .30 .75
211 Harvey Wippleman .20 .50
212 Harvey Wippleman .20 .50
213 Harvey Wippleman (Puzzle) .20 .50
214 Harvey Wippleman (Puzzle) .20 .50
215 Bobby Heenan (Puzzle) .40 1.00
216 Bobby Heenan (Puzzle) .40 1.00
217 Bobby Heenan Logo FOIL .40 1.00
218 Doink Logo FOIL .25 .60
219 Doink .25 .60
220 Doink (Puzzle) .25 .60
221 Doink (Puzzle) .25 .60
222 Doink .25 .60
223 Doink FOIL .25 .60
224 Doink .25 .60
225 Doink (Puzzle) .25 .60
226 Doink (Puzzle) .25 .60
227 Doink .25 .60
228 Rick of the Steiner Brother .30 .75
229 The Steiner Brothers FOIL .50 1.25
230 The Steiner Brothers (Puzzle) .50 1.25
231 The Steiner Brothers (Puzzle) .50 1.25
232 Scott of the Steiner Brother .50 1.25
233 The Steiner Brothers (Puzzle) .50 1.25
234 The Steiner Brothers (Puzzle) .50 1.25
235 The Steiner Brothers Logo FOIL .50 1.25
236 The Steiner Brothers (Puzzle) .50 1.25
237 The Steiner Brothers (Puzzle) .50 1.25
238 Men On A Mission (Puzzle) .25 .60
239 Men On A Mission (Puzzle) .25 .60
240 Men On A Mission FOIL .25 .60
241 Mabel of Men On A Mission
242 Men On A Mission (Puzzle) .25 .60
243 Men On A Mission (Puzzle) .25 .60
244 Mo of Men On A Mission .20 .50
245 Men On A Mission Logo FOIL .25 .60
246 Men On A Mission (Puzzle) .25 .60
247 Men On A Mission (Puzzle) .25 .60
248 Well Dunn Logo FOIL .25 .60
249 Well Dunn (Puzzle) .25 .60
250 Well Dunn (Puzzle) .25 .60
251 Well Dunn (Puzzle) .25 .60
252 Well Dunn (Puzzle)
253 Quebecers (Puzzle) .25 .60
254 Quebecers (Puzzle) .25 .60
255 Quebecers .25 .60
256 Quebecers Logo FOIL .25 .60
257 Jacques of the Quebecers .20 .50
258 Head Shrinkers Logo FOIL .25 .60
259 Head Shrinkers .25 .60
260 Head Shrinkers (Puzzle) .25 .60
261 Head Shrinkers (Puzzle) .25 .60
262 Fatu of the Head Shrinkers .25 .60
263 Head Shrinkers (Puzzle) .25 .60
264 Head Shrinkers (Puzzle) .25 .60
265 Head Shrinkers .25 .60
266 Head Shrinkers and Afa (Puzzle) .25 .60
267 Head Shrinkers and Afa (Puzzle) .25 .60
268 Tom Prichard of Heavenly Bodies .20 .50
269 Heavenly Bodies (Puzzle) .25 .60
270 Heavenly Bodies (Puzzle) .25 .60
271 Jimmy Del Ray of Heavenly Bodies .20 .50
272 Heavenly Bodies/J.Cornette (Puzzle) .25 .60
273 Heavenly Bodies/J.Cornette (Puzzle) .25 .60
274 Jim Cornette .25 .60
275 Heavenly Bodies/J.Cornette (Puzzle) .25 .60
276 Heavenly Bodies/J.Cornette (Puzzle) .25 .60
277 Jim Cornette .25 .60
278 Smoking Gunns Logo FOIL .30 .75
279 Smoking Gunns (Puzzle) .30 .75
280 Smoking Gunns (Puzzle) .30 .75
281 Bart of Smoking Gunns .25 .60
282 Billy of Smoking Gunns .30 .75
283 Smoking Gunns (Puzzle) .30 .75
284 Smoking Gunns (Puzzle) .30 .75
285 Smoking Gunns FOIL .30 .75
286 Smoking Gunns (Puzzle) .30 .75
287 Smoking Gunns (Puzzle) .30 .75
288 The Bushwhackers Logo FOIL .25 .60
289 The Bushwhackers (Puzzle) .25 .60
290 The Bushwhackers (Puzzle) .25 .60
291 Luke of The Bushwhackers .25 .60
292 The Bushwhackers (Puzzle) .25 .60
293 The Bushwhackers (Puzzle) .25 .60
294 Butch of The Bushwhackers .25 .60
295 The Bushwhackers FOIL .25 .60
296 The Bushwhackers (Puzzle) .25 .60
297 The Bushwhackers (Puzzle) .25 .60
298 WWF Title Belt FOIL .10 .25
299 WWF Intercontinental Belt FOIL .10 .25
300 WWF Tag Team Title Belt FOIL .10 .25

1986 Monty Gum Wrestling

COMPLETE SET (100) 75.00 150.00
1 Rip Rogers .40 1.00
2 Chris Adams .25 .75
3 Black Bart .20 .50
4 Steve Regal .60 1.50
5 Gino Hernandez .40 1.00
6 Ricky Steamboat .75 2.00
7 The Road Warriors 1.00 2.50
8 Joe LeDuc .60 1.50
9 Fritz Von Erich .60 1.50
10 Kevin Von Erich .60 1.50
11 Kerry Von Erich .60 1.50
12 Baron Von Raschke UER .20 .50
13 Sgt. Slaughter .75 2.00
14 Magnificent Don Muraco .40 1.00
15 Bobby Jaggers .20 .50

16 Wahoo McDaniel	2.00	5.00
17 The Great Kabuki & Sunshine	1.00	2.50
18 The Iron Sheik	.30	.75
19 Greg Valentine	.50	1.25
20 Rick Martel	.40	1.00
21 The Road Warriors	1.00	2.50
22 Hulk Hogan	4.00	10.00
23 Kerry Von Erich	1.00	2.50
24 David Schultz	1.25	3.00
25 The Road Warriors	1.25	3.00
26 Nikita Koloff	.25	.60
27 Baron Von Raschke	.20	.50
28 Hercules Hernandez	.50	1.25
29 The RPM's	.30	.75
30 Buzz Sawyer	1.00	2.50
31 Junkyard Dog UER	.40	1.00
32 Nikita Koloff	.40	1.00
33 Krusher Khruschev & Ivan Koloff	.20	.50
34 Kevin Von Erich (Ric Flair) UER	.75	2.00
35 Kerry Von Erich	.75	2.00
36 Bobby Fulton & Tommy Rogers	.75	2.00
37 Magnificent Don Muraco	.20	.50
38 Rick Martel	.40	1.00
39 Rick Martel	.20	.50
40 Rick Martel	.75	2.00
41 Gino Hernandez	.20	.50
42 Terry Taylor	.50	1.25
43 Rock 'N Roll Express	.75	2.00
44 Billy Jack Haynes & Rick Rude	.50	1.25
45 Billy Jack Haynes & Rick Rude	.50	1.25
46 Arn Anderson & Brett Sawyer	.40	1.00
47 Kerry Von Erich	.75	2.00
48 Rick Martel & Nick Bockwinkel	.20	.50
49 Hulk Hogan (w/Joan Rivers)	8.00	20.00
50 Hulk Hogan & Cyndi Lauper	4.00	10.00
51 Hulk Hogan & Muhammed Ali	8.00	20.00
52 Hulk Hogan & M.Ali (Stallone) UER	4.00	10.00
53 Tully Blanchard	1.25	3.00
54 Bruno Sammartino/Nikolai Volkoff	.75	2.00
55 Bruno Sammartino	1.25	3.00
56 B.Sammartino & Killer Kowalski	.50	1.25
57 B.Sammartino & Johnny Valentine	.75	2.00
58 Ric Flair & Kerry Von Erich	1.00	2.50
59 Ric Flair	5.00	12.00
60 Ric Flair & Dusty Rhodes	4.00	10.00
61 Hulk Hogan & Nick Bockwinkel	5.00	12.00
62 Hulk Hogan	8.00	20.00
63 Hulk Hogan & Ken Patera	3.00	8.00
64 Dusty Rhodes & Manny Fernandez	.30	.75
65 Dusty Rhodes	3.00	8.00
66 Dusty Rhodes & King Curtis	.75	2.00
67 The Missing Link	.75	2.00
68 The Road Warriors	1.00	2.50
69 Precious Paul Ellering	.20	.50
70 Fabulous Free-Birds: Terry Gordy	.75	2.00
71 Fabulous Freebirds: Michael Hayes	1.25	3.00
72 Jim Cornette UER	.75	2.00
73 Jesse Barr	.25	.60
74 Rip Rogers & Bugsy McGraw	.30	.75
75 Konga, the Barbarian	.40	1.00
76 Eric Embry	.20	.50
77 Magnum T.A. Terry Allen	1.50	4.00
78 Magnum T.A. Terry Allen	1.25	3.00
79 Greg Allen (Valentine) UER	.30	.75
80 Tully Blanchard	.40	1.00
81 The Sheepherders	.75	2.00
82 Tito Santana	.40	1.00
83 The One Man Gang	.75	2.00
84 Gary Hart	.20	.50
85 Brett Sawyer	.20	.50
86 Ron Bass	.20	.50
87 Hulk Hogan	6.00	15.00
88 Rick Flair UER	2.00	5.00
89 Rick Flair & Sgt. Slaughter UER	1.50	4.00
90 Rick Flair UER	6.00	15.00
91 Sgt. Slaughter	.75	2.00
92 Rick Steamboat	1.25	3.00
93 King Kong Brody	.50	1.25
94 Randy Savage	12.00	30.00
95 Dusty Rhodes	1.00	2.50
96 King Kong Bundy	.50	1.25
97 Nikita Koloff	.75	2.00
98 Nikita Koloff & Dusty Rhodes	.50	1.25
99 Butch Reed	.40	1.00
100 Konga, the Barbarian	.75	2.00

2005 NBC Universal WWE RAW Ringside Sweepstakes

COMPLETE SET (4)	4.00	10.00
NNO Carlito	1.25	3.00
NNO John Cena	2.00	5.00
NNO Torrie Wilson	1.50	4.00
NNO Triple H	1.25	3.00

1985 O'Quinn Wrestling All-Stars

COMPLETE SET (54) 150.00 300.00
ONLY AVAILABLE IN WRESTLING ALL STARS MAGAZINE

1 Hulk Hogan	30.00	75.00
2 Ric Flair	20.00	50.00
3 Rick Martel	2.50	6.00
4 Sergeant Slaughter	3.00	8.00
5 The Iron Sheik	6.00	15.00
6 Kamala	3.00	8.00
7 Dusty Rhodes	3.00	8.00
8 Paul Orndorff	2.50	6.00
9 The Fabulous Freebirds	3.00	8.00
10 Big John Studd	2.50	6.00
11 Kerry Von Erich	2.50	6.00
12 Jimmy Valiant	2.50	6.00
13 Baron Von Raschke	6.00	15.00
14 Missing Link	2.50	6.00
15 Roddy Piper	12.00	30.00
16 Terry Taylor	2.50	6.00
17 Superstar Billy Graham	3.00	8.00
18 Carlos Colon	2.50	6.00
19 Kevin Sullivan	3.00	8.00
20 Tommy Rich	2.50	6.00
21 (Jesse) The Body Ventura	8.00	20.00
22 Kevin Von Erich	2.50	6.00
23 King Kong Bundy	4.00	10.00
24 Wahoo McDaniel	3.00	8.00
25 Greg Valentine	3.00	8.00
26 Ken Patera	2.50	6.00
27 Terry Allen	2.50	6.00
28 Rock n Roll Express	4.00	10.00
29 Jerry Lawler	6.00	15.00
30 Junkyard Dog	3.00	8.00
31 Barry Windham	3.00	8.00
32 The Youngbloods	2.50	6.00
33 Ricky Steamboat	4.00	10.00
34 Superfly Snuka	3.00	8.00
35 The Road Warriors	12.00	30.00
36 Bob Orton	5.00	12.00
37 Mil Mascaras	3.00	8.00
38 Ivan Putski	2.50	6.00
39 Jimmy Garvin	2.50	6.00
40 Mike Von Erich	2.50	6.00
41 Chris Adams	2.50	6.00
42 Brad Armstrong	2.50	6.00
43 Gino Hernandez	4.00	10.00
44 Tully Blanchard	4.00	10.00
45 The Sheepherders	2.50	6.00
46 Andre The Giant	25.00	60.00
47 The Fabulous Ones	2.50	6.00
48 The Tonga Kid	2.50	6.00
49 Masked Superstar	3.00	8.00
50 Billy Haynes	3.00	8.00
51 Adrian Street	2.50	6.00
52 Pedro Morales	3.00	8.00
53 David Sammartino	3.00	8.00
54 Bruno Sammartino	5.00	12.00

1985 O-Pee-Chee WWF

COMPLETE SET W/HOGAN (66) 200.00 400.00
COMPLETE SET W/O HOGAN (60) 30.00 75.00
RINGSIDE ACTION (22-56)
SUPERSTARS SPEAK (57-66)

1 Hulk Hogan RC	75.00	150.00
2 The Iron Sheik RC	1.00	2.50
3 Captain Lou Albano RC	.75	2.00
4 Junk Yard Dog RC	1.00	2.50
5 Paul Mr. Wonderful Orndorff RC	.60	1.50
6 Jimmy Superfly Snuka RC	.60	1.50
7 Rowdy Roddy Piper RC	6.00	15.00
8 Wendi Richter RC	.75	2.00
9 Greg The Hammer Valentine RC	1.00	2.50
10 Brutus Beefcake RC	1.00	2.50
11 Jesse The Body Ventura RC	3.00	8.00
12 Big John Studd RC	.60	1.50
13 Fabulous Moolah RC	1.25	3.00
14 Tito Santana RC	1.25	3.00
15 Hillbilly Jim RC	1.00	2.50
16 Hulk Hogan RC	100.00	200.00
17 Mr. Fuji RC	.75	2.00
18 Rotundo RC & Windham RC	.75	2.00
19 Moondog Spot RC	.50	1.25
20 Chief Jay Strongbow RC	.50	1.25
21 George The Animal Steele RC	1.25	3.00
22 Let Go of My Toe! RA	.50	1.25
23 Lock 'Em Up! RA	.50	1.25
24 Scalp 'Em! RA	.50	1.25
25 Going for the Midsection! RA	.75	2.00
26 Up in the Air! RA	.60	1.50
27 All Tied Up! RA	1.50	4.00
28 Here She Comes! RA	.50	1.25
29 Stretched to the Limit! RA	3.00	8.00
30 Over He Goes! RA	1.00	2.50
31 An Appetite for Mayhem! RA	.60	1.50
32 Putting on Pressure! RA	.50	1.25
33 Smashed on a Knee! RA	.75	2.00
34 A Fist Comes Flying! RA	.50	1.25
35 Lemme' Out of This! RA	.50	1.25
36 No Fair Chokin'! RA	.50	1.25
37 Attacked by an Animal! RA	.50	1.25
38 One Angry Man! RA	1.25	3.00
39 Someone's Going Down! RA	1.25	3.00
40 Strangle Hold! RA	2.00	5.00
41 Bending an Arm! RA	.50	1.25
42 Ready for a Pile Driver! RA	.75	2.00
43 Face to the Canvas! RA	.50	1.25
44 Paul Wants It All! RA	.75	2.00
45 Kick to the Face! RA	3.00	8.00
46 Ready for Action! RA	.50	1.25
47 Putting on the Squeeze! RA	.60	1.50
48 Giants in Action! RA	1.50	4.00
49 Camel Clutch! RA	.60	1.50
50 Pile Up! RA	2.00	5.00
51 Can't Get Away! RA	.60	1.50
52 Going for the Pin! RA	.50	1.25
53 Ready to Fly! RA	2.00	5.00
54 Crusher in a Crusher! RA	.50	1.25
55 Fury of the Animal! RA	.75	2.00
56 Wrong Kind of Music! RA	6.00	15.00
57 Who's your next challenger? SS	2.50	6.00
58 This dog has got a mean bite! SS	.75	2.00
59 I don't think I'll ask that... SS	1.25	3.00
60 You Hulkster fans lift... SS	8.00	20.00
61 This ain't my idea... SS	1.00	2.50
62 You mean Freddie Blassie is... SS	1.25	3.00
63 Mpggh Ecch Oong. SS	1.00	2.50
64 It's the rock n' wrestling... SS	.75	2.00
65 Arrrgghhhh! SS	.60	1.50
66 They took my reindeer! SS	.60	1.50

1985 O-Pee-Chee WWF Stickers

COMPLETE SET W/HOGAN (22) 50.00 100.00
COMPLETE SET W/O HOGAN (17) 12.00 30.00
STATED ODDS 1:1

1 Hulk Hogan	15.00	40.00
2 Captain Lou Albano	.75	2.00
3 Brutus Beefcake	1.25	3.00
4 Jesse Ventura	2.00	5.00
5 The Iron Sheik	1.50	4.00
6 Wendi Richter	1.25	3.00
7 Jimmy Snuka	.75	2.00
8 Ivan Putski	1.00	2.50
9 Hulk Hogan	4.00	10.00
10 Junk Yard Dog	1.25	3.00
11 Hulk Hogan	6.00	15.00
12 Captain Lou Albano	.75	2.00
13 Captain Lou Albano	.75	2.00
14 Freddy Blassie & Iron Sheik	.75	2.00
15 Jimmy Snuka	.75	2.00
16 Hulk Hogan	10.00	25.00
17 Iron Sheik	1.50	4.00
18 Rene Goulet & S.D. Jones	1.25	3.00
19 Junk Yard Dog	.75	2.00
20 Wendi Richter	1.25	3.00
21 Le gÈant FerrÈ	3.00	8.00
22 Hulk Hogan	8.00	20.00

1985-86 O-Pee-Chee WWF Series 2

COMPLETE SET (75) 60.00 120.00
UNOPENED BOX (36 PACKS)
UNOPENED PACK (10 CARDS)

1 Nikolai Volkoff RC	4.00	10.00
2 The Magnificent Muraco RC	1.25	3.00
3 Tony Atlas RC	2.00	5.00
4 Jim The Anvil Neidhart RC	.40	1.00
5 Ricky Steamboat RC	.75	2.00
6 The British Bulldogs	1.50	4.00
7 King Kong Bundy RC	3.00	8.00
8 Bobby The Brain Heenan RC	1.25	3.00
9 Lei Lani Kai RC	.40	1.00
10 Snaky Squeeze!	.75	2.00
11 Savage Attack!	15.00	40.00
12 Cowboy Bob Orton RC	.50	1.25
13 Showing the Flag	1.25	3.00
14 Showboating!	1.50	4.00
15 Terry Funk RC	1.25	3.00
16 Martial Artist!	1.25	3.00
17 Don't Call Me Beach Bum	.75	2.00
18 Up and Over!	.30	1.00
19 Brewing Up Trouble!	.40	1.00
20 A Leg Up!	.75	2.00
21 About To Explode	.40	1.00
22 Twister!	.50	1.25
23 Headed For the Turnbuckle	5.00	12.00
24 Hercules Hernandez RC	2.50	6.00
25 Leggo' My Head!	.40	1.00
26 The Dragon Has Struck!	.40	1.00
27 Top Dog	1.00	2.50
28 Watch Out For Me	1.25	3.00
29 It's Time For A Little Road Work!	.60	1.50
30 Karate Chop!	.60	1.50
31 Crafty Fuji	.75	2.00
32 Bulldog Grip!	.60	1.50
33 Jake The Snake RC	4.00	10.00
34 Siva Afi RC	.60	1.50
35 This Is Gonna' Hurt!	1.25	3.00
36 Military Press!	.60	1.50
37 Tower Of Strength!	.40	1.00
38 Bulldog Grip!	.40	1.00
39 Piggyback!	2.00	5.00
40 Shove Off!	.40	1.00
41 Jimmy Mouth of the South Hart RC	1.25	3.00
42 Fliperoo!	.50	1.25
43 Ring Toss!	.50	1.25
44 Uncle Elmer RC	.50	1.25
45 Iran and Russia - Number One?	1.25	3.00
46 The Killer Bees	.50	1.25
47 Secret Plans	.50	1.25
48 Davey Boy Smith RC	1.50	4.00
49 Aerial Escape!	.40	1.00
50 Caught by Kong!	.60	1.50
51 Banging Away!	1.50	4.00
52 All American Boy!	.40	1.00
53 Fiji Fury!	.40	1.00
54 What d'ya mean...	1.00	2.50
55 Do you know any way...	.40	1.00
56 Those are the biggest feet...	.40	1.00
57 I make sukiyaki...	1.25	3.00
58 This guy really looks sick.	.40	1.00
59 Nikolai, he sings...	.40	1.00
60 The Animal In Love!	.40	1.00
61 Hoss Funk RC	.75	2.00
62 Can I autograph your cast?	.60	1.50
63 Randy Savage RC & Elizabeth RC	12.00	30.00
64 I don't know...	.40	1.00
65 If anybody calls you...	.40	1.00
66 It's rock and wrestling - forever!	2.00	5.00
67 Wrestlers vs. Football Greats	1.25	3.00
68 Big Men Battle	.50	1.25
69 Help Coming	.40	1.00
70 The Body Struts His Stuff	.40	1.00
71 In the Corner	1.25	3.00
72 Plenty of Beef	.75	2.00
73 Battle Royal Winner	.50	1.25
74 Working for a Position	.40	1.00
75 Ready for a War!	1.50	4.00

1987 O-Pee-Chee WWF

COMPLETE SET (75)	60.00	120.00
1 Bret "Hit Man" Hart RC	25.00	60.00
2 Andre the Giant RC	6.00	15.00
3 Hulk Hogan	5.00	12.00
4 Frankie	.75	2.00
5 Koko B. Ware RC	.75	2.00
6 Tito Santana	.60	1.50
7 Randy Savage & Elizabeth	10.00	25.00
8 Billy Jack Haynes RC	.40	1.00
9 Hercules & Bobby Heenan	.40	1.00
10 King Harley Race RC	.60	1.50
11 Kimchee & Kamala	.40	1.00
12 Bravo/Johnny V/Valentine	.50	1.25
13 Honky Tonk Man RC	1.00	2.50
14 Outback Jack RC	.40	1.00
15 King Kong Bundy	1.25	3.00
16 The Magnificent Muraco	.40	1.00
17 Mr. Fuji and Killer Khan	.75	2.00
18 The Natural Butch Reed RC	.60	1.50
19 Davey Boy Smith	.75	2.00
20 The Dynamite Kid RC	.40	1.00
21 Ricky The Dragon Steamboat	1.50	4.00
22 Two-Man Clothesline RA	.40	1.00
23 Ref Turned Wrestler RA	.75	2.00
24 Ready to Strike RA	.60	1.50
25 In the Outback RA	.40	1.00
26 The Hulkster Explodes RA	2.00	5.00
27 Double Whammy RA	.40	1.00
28 Spoiling for a Fight RA	.40	1.00
29 Flip Flop RA	.40	1.00
30 Islanders Attack RA	.40	1.00
31 King Harley Parades RA	.40	1.00
32 Backbreaker RA	.40	1.00
33 Double Dropkick RA	.40	1.00
34 The Loser Must Bow RA	.40	1.00
35 American-Made RA	2.50	6.00
36 A Challenge Answered RA	2.00	5.00
37 Champ in the Ring RA	4.00	10.00
38 Listening to Hulkamania RA	2.00	5.00
39 Heading for the Ring RA	.40	1.00
40 Out to Destroy RA	.40	1.00
41 Tama Takes a Beating RA	.40	1.00
42 Bundy in Mid-Air RA	.40	1.00
43 Karate Stance RA	.40	1.00
44 Her Eyes on Randy RA	2.50	6.00
45 The Olympian Returns RA	.40	1.00
46 Reed Is Riled RA	.40	1.00
47 Flying Bodypress RA	.40	1.00
48 Hooking the Leg RA	.40	1.00
49 A Belly Buster WMIII	.40	1.00
50 Revenge on Randy WMIII	.75	2.00
51 Fighting the Full Nelson WMIII	.40	1.00
52 Honky Tonk Goes Down WMIII	.40	1.00
53 Over the Top WMIII	.40	1.00
54 The Giant Is Slammed WMIII	1.25	3.00
55 Out of the Ring WMIII	.75	2.00
56 And Still Champion WMIII	1.50	4.00
57 Harts Hit Concrete WMIII	.40	1.00
58 The Challenge RA	1.25	3.00
59 Bearhug RA	.40	1.00
60 Fantastic Bodypress RA	.40	1.00
61 Aerial Maneuvers RA	.40	1.00
62 Ready to Sting! RA	.40	1.00
63 Showing Off RA	.40	1.00
64 Scare Tactics RA	.40	1.00
65 Taking a Bow RA	.60	1.50
66 Out to Eat a Turnbuckle RA	.40	1.00
67 Nice guys finish last! SS	.40	1.00
68 Here's how we keep... SS	.40	1.00
69 Urrggh. Nice! SS	.40	1.00
70 No Kamala...him not dinner! SS	.40	1.00
71 We are the original destroyers. SS	.40	1.00
72 I think the fans are mad at me. SS	.40	1.00
73 You ain't nothin'... SS	.40	1.00
74 I'm gonna take a big bit... SS	.40	1.00
75 Good! SS	.40	1.00

2004 Pacific TNA

COMPLETE SET (75)	10.00	25.00
UNOPENED BOX (24 PACKS)	85.00	100.00
UNOPENED PACK (5 CARDS)	4.00	5.00
*RED: .6X TO 1.5X BASIC CARDS		
1 April RC	.20	.50
2 Chelsea RC	.12	.30
3 Goldylocks RC	.75	2.00
4 Lollipop RC	.30	.75
5 Athena RC	.20	.50
6 Abyss RC	.30	.75
7 Jeremy Borash RC	.12	.30
8 Traci RC	.50	1.25
9 D'Lo Brown	.20	.50
10 Christopher Daniels RC	.12	.30
11 Delirious RC	.12	.30
12 Simon Diamond RC	.12	.30
13 Julio Dinero RC	.12	.30
14 Shane Douglas	.12	.30
15 Sonjay Dutt RC	.12	.30
16 Ekmo Fatu	.20	.50
17 Glenn Gilberti	.12	.30
18 Juventud Guerrera	.12	.30
19 Chris Harris RC	.12	.30
20 Don Harris RC	.12	.30
21 Ron Harris RC	.12	.30
22 Chris Hero RC	.12	.30
23 BG James	.20	.50
24 Jeff Jarrett	.60	1.50
25 Kid Kash RC	.12	.30
26 Frankie Kazarian RC	.12	.30
27 Ron Killings	.25	.60
28 Konnan	.12	.30
29 Lazz RC	.12	.30
30 Jerry Lynn	.12	.30
31 Father James Mitchell RC	.12	.30
32 Kevin Northcutt RC	.12	.30
33 Nosawa RC	.12	.30
34 CM Punk RC	40.00	100.00
35 Raven	.50	1.25
36 Dusty Rhodes	.30	.75
37 Vince Russo RC	.12	.30
38 Chris Sabin RC	.12	.30
39 Sandman	.20	.50
40 Rick Santel RC	.12	.30
41 Michael Shane RC	.12	.30
42 Shark Boy RC	.12	.30
43 Sonny Siaki	.12	.30
44 Sinn RC	.12	.30
45 Slash RC	.12	.30
46 James Storm RC	.20	.50
47 AJ Styles RC	8.00	20.00
48 Johnny Swinger RC	.12	.30
49 Terry Taylor	.12	.30
50 Trinity RC	.20	.50
51 Chris Vaughn RC	.12	.30
52 Ryan Wilson RC	.12	.30
53 David Young RC	.12	.30
54 Scott Hudson RC	.12	.30
55 Mike Tenay RC	.12	.30
56 Don West RC	.12	.30
57 Don Callis	.12	.30
58 Erik Watts RC	.12	.30
59 Rudy Charles RC	.12	.30
60 Mike Posey RC	.12	.30
61 Andrew Thomas RC	.12	.30
62 3Live Kru	.25	.60
63 America's Most Wanted	.20	.50
64 D'Lo Brown	.20	.50
65 Simon Diamond	.12	.30
66 Jeff Jarrett	.60	1.50
67 Raven	.50	1.25
68 Dusty Rhodes	.30	.75
69 Chris Sabin	.12	.30
70 Sonny Siaki RC	.12	.30
71 AJ Styles RC	6.00	15.00
72 Chris Vaughn RC	.12	.30
73 Trinity RC	.20	.50
74 Goldylocks RC	.75	2.00
75 Lollipop RC	.30	.75

2004 Pacific TNA Red

1 April	.30	.75
2 Chelsea	.20	.50
3 Goldylocks	1.25	3.00
4 Lollipop	.50	1.25
5 Athena	.30	.75
6 Abyss	.50	1.25
7 Jeremy Borash	.20	.50
8 Traci	.75	2.00
9 D'Lo Brown	.30	.75
10 Christopher Daniels	.20	.50
11 Delirious	.20	.50
12 Simon Diamond	.20	.50
13 Julio Dinero	.20	.50
14 Shane Douglas	.20	.50
15 Sonjay Dutt	.20	.50
16 Ekmo Fatu	.30	.75
17 Glenn Gilberti	.20	.50
18 Juventud Guerrera	.20	.50
19 Chris Harris	.20	.50
20 Don Harris	.20	.50
21 Ron Harris	.20	.50
22 Chris Hero	.20	.50
23 BG James	.30	.75
24 Jeff Jarrett	1.00	2.50
25 Kid Kash	.20	.50
26 Frankie Kazarian	.20	.50
27 Ron Killings	.40	1.00
28 Konnan	.20	.50
29 Lazz	.20	.50
30 Jerry Lynn	.20	.50
31 Father James Mitchell	.20	.50
32 Kevin Northcutt	.20	.50
33 Nosawa	.20	.50
34 CM Punk	60.00	150.00
35 Raven	.75	2.00
36 Dusty Rhodes	.50	1.25
37 Vince Russo	.20	.50
38 Chris Sabin	.20	.50
39 Sandman	.30	.75
40 Rick Santel	.20	.50
41 Michael Shane	.20	.50
42 Shark Boy	.20	.50
43 Sonny Siaki	.20	.50
44 Sinn	.20	.50
45 Slash	.20	.50
46 James Storm	.30	.75
47 AJ Styles	12.00	30.00
48 Johnny Swinger	.20	.50
49 Terry Taylor	.20	.50
50 Trinity	.30	.75
51 Chris Vaughn	.20	.50
52 Ryan Wilson	.20	.50
53 David Young	.20	.50
54 Scott Hudson	.20	.50
55 Mike Tenay	.20	.50
56 Don West	.20	.50
57 Don Callis	.20	.50
58 Erik Watts	.20	.50
59 Rudy Charles	.20	.50
60 Mike Posey	.20	.50
61 Andrew Thomas	.20	.50
62 3Live Kru	.40	1.00
63 America's Most Wanted	.30	.75
64 D'Lo Brown	.30	.75
65 Simon Diamond	.20	.50
66 Jeff Jarrett	1.00	2.50
67 Raven	.75	2.00
68 Dusty Rhodes	.50	1.25
69 Chris Sabin	.20	.50
70 Sonny Siaki	.20	.50
71 AJ Styles	8.00	20.00
72 Chris Vaughn	.20	.50
73 Trinity	.30	.75
74 Goldylocks	1.25	3.00
75 Lollipop	.50	1.25

2004 Pacific TNA Event-Used

STATED PRINT RUN 1,525 SER.#'d SETS		
1 America's Most Wanted	4.00	8.00
2 AJ Styles	15.00	40.00
3 D'Lo Brown	4.00	8.00
4 Raven	4.00	8.00
5 BG James	4.00	8.00

2004 Pacific TNA Event-Used Limited Edition

NOT AVAILABLE IN PACKS		
1 TNA Babes	15.00	40.00
2 America's Most Wanted	15.00	40.00

2004 Pacific TNA Legends and Superstars Autographs

STATED ODDS 1:24 HOBBY		
1 Rowdy Roddy Piper	75.00	200.00
3 Jeff Jarrett	8.00	20.00
4 Terry Taylor	8.00	20.00
5 Dusty Rhodes	150.00	400.00
6 Harley Race	50.00	125.00
7 Raven	8.00	20.00

2004 Pacific TNA Main Event Autographs

STATED ODDS 1:24 HOBBY		
NNO AJ Styles Red Border SP	30.00	75.00
NNO AJ Styles Gold Border SP	30.00	75.00
NNO AMW DUAL AU	6.00	15.00
NNO April	4.00	10.00
NNO Goldylocks	4.00	10.00
NNO Lollipop	5.00	12.00
NNO Chris Vaughn	4.00	10.00
NNO Trinity	4.00	10.00

2004 Pacific TNA Tag Teams

STATED ODDS 1:5 HOBBY		
1 Diamond/Swinger	.30	.75
2 The Naturals	.30	.75
3 3Live Kru	.60	1.50
4 The Gathering	15.00	40.00
5 Red Shirt Security	.30	.75
6 Black Shirt Security	.30	.75
7 Gilberti/Young	.30	.75
8 America's Most Wanted	.50	1.25

2004 Pacific TNA Tattoos

COMPLETE SET (28)	3.00	8.00
STATED ODDS 1:1 HOBBY		
1 TNA Logo 1	.12	.30
2 TNA Logo 2	.12	.30
3 TNA Logo 3	.12	.30
4 Total Non-Stop Action	.12	.30
5 PTC Logo 1	.12	.30
6 PTC Logo 2	.12	.30
7 PTC Logo 3	.12	.30
8 Raven	.50	1.25
9 AJ Styles	6.00	15.00
10 Jeff Jarrett	.60	1.50
11 D'Lo Brown	.20	.50
12 Chris Harris	.12	.30
13 James Storm	.20	.50
14 Shark Boy	.12	.30
15 Ron Killings	.25	.60
16 Konnan	.12	.30
17 BG James	.20	.50
18 Chris Sabin	.12	.30
19 Michael Shane	.12	.30
20 Sonny Siaki	.12	.30
21 Chris Vaughn	.12	.30
22 Trinity	.20	.50
23 America's Most Wanted	.20	.50
24 3Live Kru	.25	.60
25 Red Shirt Security	.12	.30
26 Black Shirt Security	.12	.30
27 Lollipop	.30	.75
28 Goldylocks	.75	2.00

2022 Panini Chronicles WWE

*BRONZE: .6X TO 1.5X BASIC CARDS
*SILVER: .75X TO 2X BASIC CARDS
*RED/199: 1.2X TO 3X BASIC CARDS
*BLUE/99: 2X TO 5X BASIC CARDS
*GREEN/99: 2X TO 5X BASIC CARDS
*PURPLE/49: 4X TO 10X BASIC CARDS
*GREEN SP/25: UNPRICED DUE TO SCARCITY
*GOLD/10: UNPRICED DUE TO SCARCITY
*BLACK/1: UNPRICED DUE TO SCARCITY
*GOLD VINYL/1: UNPRICED DUE TO SCARCITY
*NEBULA/1: UNPRICED DUE TO SCARCITY
*PLATINUM/1: UNPRICED DUE TO SCARCITY
GALA STATED PRINT RUN 8 SER.#'d SETS

1 Alexa Bliss	1.50	4.00
2 Happy Corbin	.30	.75
3 Liv Morgan	1.25	3.00
4 Josh Briggs RC	.25	.60

5 Bam Bam Bigelow	.40	1.00
6 Molly Holly	.30	.75
7 Robert Roode	.30	.75
8 Akira Tozawa	.30	.75
9 Bron Breakker RC	1.00	2.50
10 Commander Azeez	.30	.75
11 Asuka	1.00	2.50
12 The Honky Tonk Man	.30	.75
13 Mandy Rose	1.25	3.00
14 Junkyard Dog	.30	.75
15 D-Lo Brown	.25	.60
16 Montez Ford	.25	.60
17 R-Truth	.30	.75
18 Angel	.25	.60
19 Cora Jade RC	.75	2.00
20 Cowboy Bob Orton	.25	.60
21 Becky Lynch	1.00	2.50
22 Humberto	.25	.60
23 Rhea Ripley	.75	2.00
24 Ken Shamrock	.30	.75
25 Rick Steiner	.40	1.00
26 Mr. T	.50	1.25
27 Shelton Benjamin	.40	1.00
28 Angelo Dawkins	.30	.75
29 Gable Steveson RC	1.25	3.00
30 Dana Brooke	.25	.60
31 Brock Lesnar	1.25	3.00
32 Ilja Dragunov	.25	.60
33 Roman Reigns	1.50	4.00
34 Lex Luger	.30	.75
35 Karrion Kross	.50	1.25
36 Mustafa Ali	.30	.75
37 Sid Vicious	.30	.75
38 Big Boss Man	.40	1.00
39 Bayley	.60	1.50
40 Dominik Mysterio	.30	.75
41 Charlotte Flair	1.00	2.50
42 Ivar	.25	.60
43 Ronda Rousey	1.50	4.00
44 Ludwig Kaiser	.30	.75
45 Hulk Hogan	1.25	3.00
46 MVP	.25	.60
47 Tamina	.30	.75
48 Big John Studd	.25	.60
49 Nikkita Lyons RC	.60	1.50
50 Don Muraco	.25	.60
51 Cody Rhodes	.60	1.50
52 Jagger Reid	.25	.60
53 Elektra Lopez RC	.60	1.50
54 Mace	.25	.60
55 Macho Man Randy Savage	1.00	2.50
56 Otis	.30	.75
57 T-Bar	.25	.60
58 British Bulldog	.40	1.00
59 Roxanne Perez RC	.75	2.00
60 Erik	.25	.60
61 Edge	1.00	2.50
62 Jey Uso	.30	.75
63 Bret "Hit Man" Hart	.60	1.50
64 Madcap Moss	.25	.60
65 Stone Cold Steve Austin	1.25	3.00
66 Ravishing Rick Rude	.50	1.25
67 Umaga	.25	.60
68 Captain Lou Albano	.30	.75
69 Solo Sikoa RC	.60	1.50
70 Ezekiel	.25	.60
71 Finn Balor	.60	1.50
72 Jim "The Anvil" Neidhart	.30	.75
73 Goldberg	1.00	2.50
74 man.soor	.25	.60
75 Triple H	1.00	2.50
76 Reggie	.30	.75
77 Vader	.30	.75
78 Cedric Alexander	.25	.60
79 Tony D'Angelo RC	.75	2.00
80 Freddie Blassie	.30	.75
81 Gigi Dolin	1.00	2.50
82 Jimmy Uso	.30	.75
83 The Rock	2.50	6.00
84 Meiko Satomura RC	.75	2.00
85 Ultimate Warrior	1.00	2.50
86 Ridge Holland	.25	.60
87 Xavier Woods	.30	.75
88 Chad Gable	.25	.60
89 Veer Mahaan	.60	1.50
90 The Godfather	.25	.60
91 John Cena	.75	2.00
92 Jinder Mahal	.30	.75
93 Shawn Michaels	1.00	2.50
94 Michael Hayes	.25	.60
95 Undertaker	1.25	3.00
96 Road Dogg	.30	.75
97 X-Pac	.30	.75
98 Chief Jay Strongbow	.40	1.00
99 AJ Styles	.75	2.00
100 Greg Valentine	.25	.60
101 Asuka/Contenders	1.00	2.50
102 Finn Balor/Contenders	.60	1.50
103 Becky Lynch/Contenders	1.00	2.50
104 John Cena/Contenders	.75	2.00
105 Brock Lesnar/Contenders	1.25	3.00
106 Charlotte Flair/Contenders	1.00	2.50
107 AJ Styles/Contenders	.75	2.00
108 Cody Rhodes/Contenders	.60	1.50
109 Alexa Bliss/Contenders	1.50	4.00
110 Edge/Contenders	1.00	2.50
111 Carmelo Hayes/Rated Rookies	.30	.75
112 Nikkita Lyons/Rated Rookies	.60	1.50
113 Joe Gacy/Rated Rookies	.60	1.50
114 Roxanne Perez/Rated Rookies	.75	2.00
115 Solo Sikoa/Rated Rookies	.60	1.50
116 Bron Breakker/Rated Rookies	1.00	2.50
117 Tony D'Angelo/Rated Rookies	.75	2.00
118 Cora Jade/Rated Rookies	.75	2.00
119 Veer Mahaan/Rated Rookies	.60	1.50
120 Gable Steveson/Rated Rookies	1.25	3.00
121 Liv Morgan/Absolute	1.25	3.00
122 Bret "Hit Man" Hart/Absolute	.60	1.50
123 Mandy Rose/Absolute	1.25	3.00
124 The Rock/Absolute	2.50	6.00
125 Rhea Ripley/Absolute	.75	2.00
126 Goldberg/Absolute	1.00	2.50
127 Roman Reigns/Absolute	1.50	4.00
128 Ronda Rousey/Absolute	1.50	4.00
129 Gigi Dolin/Absolute	1.00	2.50
130 Solo Sikoa/Absolute	.60	1.50
131 Damian Priest/Origins	.50	1.25
132 Randy Orton/Origins	.60	1.50
133 Eddie Guerrero/Origins	.75	2.00
134 Gunther/Origins	.60	1.50
135 Axiom/Origins	.30	.75
136 Jake Roberts/Origins	.40	1.00
137 Batista/Origins	.50	1.25
138 Kit Wilson/Origins	.25	.60
139 Brie Bella/Origins	.50	1.25
140 Nathan Frazer/Origins	.25	.60
141 Shawn Michaels/Legacy	1.00	2.50
142 Andre The Giant/Legacy	1.00	2.50
143 Chyna/Legacy	.50	1.25
144 Hulk Hogan/Legacy	1.25	3.00
145 Macho Man Randy Savage/Legacy	1.00	2.50
146 Stone Cold Steve Austin/Legacy	1.25	3.00
147 Triple H/Legacy	1.00	2.50
148 Ultimate Warrior/Legacy	1.00	2.50
149 Undertaker/Legacy	1.25	3.00
150 Batista/Legacy	.50	1.25
151 Edris Enofe/Luminance	.25	.60
152 Rowdy Roddy Piper/Luminance	.60	1.50
153 Big E/Luminance	.50	1.25
154 Shinsuke Nakamura/Luminance	.60	1.50
155 Brooks Jensen/Luminance	.25	.60
156 Carmella/Luminance	.60	1.50
157 Bayley/Luminance	.60	1.50
158 Valentina Feroz/Luminance	.40	1.00
159 Alba Fyre/Luminance	.60	1.50
160 Guru Raaj/Luminance	.25	.60
161 Aleah James/Playoff		
162 Raquel Rodriguez/Playoff	.60	1.50
163 Beth Phoenix/Playoff	.50	1.25
164 Roderick Strong/Playoff	.40	1.00
165 Shotzi/Playoff	1.00	2.50
166 John Bradshaw Layfield/Playoff	.25	.60
167 Terry Funk/Playoff	.40	1.00
168 Kofi Kingston/Playoff	.60	1.50
169 Von Wagner/Playoff	.25	.60
170 Nikki A.S.H./Playoff	.40	1.00
171 Dante Chen/Prestige	.25	.60
172 Nikki Bella/Prestige	.60	1.50
173 Elektra Lopez/Prestige	.60	1.50
174 Ru Feng/Prestige	.25	.60
175 Ikemen Jiro/Prestige	.25	.60
176 Sonya Deville/Prestige	.60	1.50
177 Jerry Lawler/Prestige	.50	1.25
178 Kevin Owens/Prestige	.50	1.25
179 Bruno Sammartino/Prestige	.60	1.50
180 Razor Ramon/Prestige	.50	1.25
181 Tiffany Stratton/Rookies & Stars	.40	1.00
182 Grayson Waller/Rookies & Stars	.60	1.50
183 Blair Davenport/Rookies & Stars	.25	.60
184 Ivy Nile/Rookies & Stars	.25	.60
185 Shanky/Rookies & Stars	.25	.60
186 Jacy Jayne/Rookies & Stars	.60	1.50
187 Brutus Creed/Rookies & Stars	.30	.75
188 Julius Creed/Rookies & Stars	.60	1.50
189 Elton Prince/Rookies & Stars	.30	.75
190 Wendy Choo/Rookies & Stars	.50	1.25
191 Drew McIntyre/Score	.50	1.25
192 Trish Stratus/Score	1.25	3.00
193 IYO SKY/Score	.50	1.25
194 Kayden Carter/Score	.50	1.25
195 Alundra Blayze/Score	.30	.75
196 Odyssey Jones/Score	.25	.60
197 Bianca Belair/Score	.75	2.00
198 Queen Zelina/Score	.40	1.00
199 Cameron Grimes/Score	.50	1.25
200 Superstar Billy Graham/Score	.25	.60
201 Carmelo Hayes/Black	.30	.75
202 Kevin Owens/Black	.50	1.25
203 Nikki Bella/Black	.60	1.50
204 Brutus Creed/Black	.30	.75
205 Aliyah/Black	.50	1.25
206 Gorilla Monsoon/Black	.40	1.00
207 Kofi Kingston/Black	.60	1.50
208 AJ Styles/Black	.75	2.00
209 Ricky Steamboat/Black	.50	1.25
210 Asuka/Black	1.00	2.50
211 Xia Li/Black	.50	1.25
212 Bayley/Black	.60	1.50
213 Andre Chase/Black	.25	.60
214 Doudrop/Black	.40	1.00
215 Amari Miller/Black	.25	.60
216 Jacy Jayne/Black	.60	1.50
217 Odyssey Jones/Black	.25	.60
218 Alexa Bliss/Black	1.50	4.00
219 Shanky/Black	.25	.60
220 Bron Breakker/Black	1.00	2.50
221 Charlotte Flair/Certified	1.00	2.50
222 Terry Funk/Certified	.40	1.00
223 Tiffany Stratton/Certified	.40	1.00
224 Rowdy Roddy Piper/Certified	.60	1.50
225 Butch/Certified	.50	1.25
226 Aoife Valkyrie/Certified	.50	1.25
227 Grayson Waller/Certified	.60	1.50
228 The Miz/Certified	.40	1.00
229 Becky Lynch/Certified	1.00	2.50
230 Ricochet/Certified	.50	1.25
231 Cora Jade/Certified	.75	2.00
232 Yokozuna/Certified	.30	.75
233 Beth Phoenix/Certified	.50	1.25
234 Bodhi Hayward/Certified	.30	.75
235 Drew McIntyre/Certified	.50	1.25
236 Big E/Certified	.50	1.25
237 Jake Roberts/Certified	.40	1.00
238 Oliver Carter/Certified	.25	.60
239 Brock Lesnar/Certified	1.25	3.00
240 Shayna Baszler/Certified	.50	1.25
241 Finn Balor/Elite	.60	1.50
242 Alba Fyre/Elite	.60	1.50
243 Axiom/Elite	.30	.75
244 Shinsuke Nakamura/Elite	.60	1.50
245 Cactus Jack/Elite	.50	1.25
246 Bobby "The Brain" Heenan/Elite	.40	1.00
247 John "Bradshaw" Layfield/Elite	.25	.60
248 Omos/Elite	.50	1.25
249 Cody Rhodes/Elite	.60	1.50
250 Sheamus/Elite	.40	1.00
251 Gable Steveson/Elite	1.25	3.00
252 Yulisa Leon/Elite	.25	.60
253 Bianca Belair/Elite	.75	2.00
254 Stacy Keibler/Elite	.75	2.00
255 The Great Khali/Elite	.30	.75
256 Bobby Lashley/Elite	.50	1.25
257 Lacey Evans/Elite	.60	1.50
258 Matt Riddle/Elite	.60	1.50
259 Edge/Elite	1.00	2.50
260 The Miz/Elite	.40	1.00
261 Liv Morgan/Illusions	1.25	3.00
262 Shinsuke Nakamura/Illusions	.60	1.50
263 Bret "Hit Man" Hart/Illusions	.60	1.50
264 Trick Williams/Illusions	.25	.60
265 Big E/Illusions	.50	1.25
266 Butch/Illusions	.50	1.25
267 Duke Hudson/Illusions	.25	.60
268 Jerry Lawler/Illusions	.50	1.25
269 Gigi Dolin/Illusions	1.00	2.50
270 Paul Bearer/Illusions	.30	.75
271 Mandy Rose/Illusions	1.25	3.00
272 Theory/Illusions	.60	1.50
273 Dude Love/Illusions	.50	1.25
274 Booker T/Illusions	.50	1.25
275 Cameron Grimes/Illusions	.50	1.25
276 Carmella/Illusions	.60	1.50
277 Gunther/Illusions	.60	1.50
278 Lash Legend/Illusions	.25	.60
279 John Cena/Illusions	.75	2.00
280 Rikishi/Illusions	.30	.75
281 Blair Davenport/XR	.25	.60
282 Diamond Dallas Page/XR	.30	.75
283 Dusty Rhodes/XR	.60	1.50
284 Jinny/XR	.25	.60
285 Rhea Ripley/XR	.75	2.00
286 Paul Heyman/XR	.40	1.00
287 Ronda Rousey/XR	1.50	4.00
288 Shotzi/XR	1.00	2.50
289 Goldberg/XR	1.00	2.50
290 Cactus Jack/XR	.50	1.25
291 Carmella/XR	.60	1.50
292 Cruz Del Toro/XR	.40	1.00
293 Guru Raaj/XR	.25	.60
294 Malik Blade/XR	.25	.60
295 Roman Reigns/XR	1.50	4.00
296 Rob Van Dam/XR	.50	1.25
297 Solo Sikoa/XR	.60	1.50
298 Bobby Lashley/XR	.50	1.25
299 Aleah James/XR	.30	.75
300 Ciampa/XR	.60	1.50
301 Ciampa/Phoenix	.60	1.50
302 Mr. Perfect Curt Hennig/Phoenix	.50	1.25
303 Joaquin Wilde/Phoenix	.40	1.00
304 Rowdy Roddy Piper/Phoenix	.60	1.50
305 Roxanne Perez/Phoenix	.75	2.00
306 Alundra Blayze/Phoenix	.30	.75
307 Rhea Ripley/Phoenix	.75	2.00
308 Cruz Del Toro/Phoenix	.40	1.00
309 Aliyah/Phoenix	.50	1.25
310 Indi Hartwell/Phoenix	.75	2.00
311 Eddie Guerrero/Phoenix	.75	2.00
312 Queen Zelina/Phoenix	.40	1.00
313 Mankind/Phoenix	.50	1.25
314 Sonya Deville/Phoenix	.60	1.50
315 Ronda Rousey/Phoenix	1.50	4.00
316 Bobby Lashley/Phoenix	.50	1.25
317 The Rock/Phoenix	2.50	6.00
318 Edris Enofe/Phoenix	.25	.60
319 Bobby "The Brain" Heenan/Phoenix	.40	1.00
320 Julius Creed/Phoenix	.60	1.50
321 Ikemen Jiro/Phoenix	.25	.60
322 Roderick Strong/Phoenix	.40	1.00
323 Trish Stratus/Phoenix	1.25	3.00
324 Torrie Wilson/Phoenix	.60	1.50
325 Roman Reigns/Phoenix	1.50	4.00
326 Mandy Rose/Flux	1.25	3.00
327 Torrie Wilson/Flux	.60	1.50
328 Gigi Dolin/Flux	1.00	2.50
329 Doudrop/Flux	.40	1.00
330 Elektra Lopez/Flux	.60	1.50
331 Dusty Rhodes/Flux	.60	1.50
332 Solo Sikoa/Flux	.60	1.50
333 Faarooq/Flux	.30	.75
334 Ru Feng/Flux	.25	.60
335 Trish Stratus/Flux	1.25	3.00
336 Liv Morgan/Flux	1.25	3.00
337 Andre Chase/Flux	.25	.60
338 Shawn Michaels/Flux	1.00	2.50
339 Dude Love/Flux	.50	1.25
340 IYO SKY/Flux	.50	1.25
341 Scott Steiner/Flux	.40	1.00
342 Randy Orton/Flux	.60	1.50
343 Gene Okerlund/Flux	.40	1.00
344 Stevie Turner/Flux	.25	.60

345 Trick Williams/Flux .25 .60
346 John Cena/Flux .75 2.00
347 Kevin Nash/Flux .40 1.00
348 Damian Priest/Flux .50 1.25
349 Duke Hudson/Flux .25 .60
350 Katana Chance/Flux .50 1.25
351 Cody Rhodes/Donruss Optic .60 1.50
352 Lacey Evans/Donruss Optic .60 1.50
353 Andre The Giant/Donruss Optic 1.00 2.50
354 Paul Heyman/Donruss Optic .40 1.00
355 Nikki Bella/Donruss Optic .60 1.50
356 Sami Zayn/Donruss Optic .40 1.00
357 Ted DiBiase/Donruss Optic .40 1.00
358 Bruno Sammartino/Donruss Optic .60 1.50
359 Finn Balor/Donruss Optic .60 1.50
360 Superstar Billy Graham/Donruss Optic.25 .60
361 Charlotte Flair/Donruss Optic 1.00 2.50
362 Rikishi/Donruss Optic .30 .75
363 Diesel/Donruss Optic .40 1.00
364 Rey Mysterio/Donruss Optic .60 1.50
365 Rick Boogs/Donruss Optic .30 .75
366 Seth ìFreakinî Rollins/Donruss Optic .60 1.50
367 Brie Bella/Donruss Optic .50 1.25
368 Stacy Keibler/Donruss Optic .75 2.00
369 Edge/Donruss Optic 1.00 2.50
370 Kevin Owens/Donruss Optic .50 1.25
371 Brock Lesnar/Donruss Optic 1.25 3.00
372 Omos/Donruss Optic .50 1.25
373 Gene Okerlund/Donruss Optic .40 1.00
374 Undertaker/Donruss Optic 1.25 3.00
375 Terry Gordy/Donruss Optic .25 .60
376 The Miz/Spectra .40 1.00
377 Iron Sheik/Spectra .30 .75
378 Raquel Rodriguez/Spectra .60 1.50
379 AJ Styles/Spectra .75 2.00
380 Bodhi Hayward/Spectra .30 .75
381 Becky Lynch/Spectra 1.00 2.50
382 Ricochet/Spectra .50 1.25
383 Amari Miller/Spectra .25 .60
384 Shayna Baszler/Spectra .50 1.25
385 Kurt Angle/Spectra .60 1.50
386 Theory/Spectra .60 1.50
387 Kayden Carter/Spectra .50 1.25
388 Sami Zayn/Spectra .40 1.00
389 Alexa Bliss/Spectra 1.50 4.00
390 Billy Gunn/Spectra .30 .75
391 Chyna/Spectra .50 1.25
392 Matt Riddle/Spectra .60 1.50
393 Booker T/Spectra .50 1.25
394 Sheamus/Spectra .40 1.00
395 Randy Orton/Spectra .60 1.50
396 Xia Li/Spectra .50 1.25
397 Natalya/Spectra .40 1.00
398 Johnny Rodz/Spectra .25 .60
399 Asuka/Spectra 1.00 2.50
400 Trick Williams/Spectra .25 .60
401 Stone Cold Steve Austin/Noir 1.25 3.00
402 Rikishi/Noir .30 .75
403 Elton Prince/Noir .30 .75
404 Nathan Frazer/Noir .25 .60
405 AJ Styles/Noir .75 2.00
406 Valentina Feroz/Noir .40 1.00
407 Gigi Dolin/Noir 1.00 2.50
408 IRS/Noir .30 .75
409 Bron Breakker/Noir 1.00 2.50
410 Ken Shamrock/Noir .30 .75
411 Undertaker/Noir 1.25 3.00
412 Drew McIntyre/Noir .50 1.25
413 Isla Dawn/Noir .30 .75
414 Razor Ramon/Noir .50 1.25
415 Becky Lynch/Noir 1.00 2.50
416 1-2-3 Kid/Noir .30 .75
417 Mandy Rose/Noir 1.25 3.00
418 Joaquin Wilde/Noir .40 1.00
419 Bret "Hit Man" Hart/Noir .60 1.50
420 Nikolai Volkoff/Noir .25 .60
421 Dante Chen/Noir .25 .60
422 Stevie Turner/Noir .25 .60
423 Bianca Belair/Noir .75 2.00
424 Santos Escobar/Noir .40 1.00
425 Cody Rhodes/Noir .60 1.50
426 The Great Khali/Noir .30 .75
427 Ronda Rousey/Noir 1.50 4.00
428 Malik Blade/Noir .25 .60
429 Shawn Michaels/Noir 1.00 2.50
430 Paul Bearer/Noir .30 .75
431 John Cena/National Treasures .75 2.00
432 Mr. Perfect/National Treasures .50 1.25
433 Cora Jade/National Treasures .75 2.00
434 Papa Shango/National Treasures .25 .60
435 Triple H/National Treasures 1.00 2.50
436 The Hurricane/National Treasures .25 .60
437 Brooks Jensen/National Treasures .25 .60
438 Ivy Nile/National Treasures .25 .60
439 Alexa Bliss/National Treasures 1.50 4.00
440 Rey Mysterio/National Treasures .60 1.50
441 Roxanne Perez/National Treasures .75 2.00
442 Randy Orton/National Treasures .60 1.50
443 Goldberg/National Treasures 1.00 2.50
444 Santos Escobar/National Treasures .40 1.00
445 Andre The Giant/National Treasures 1.00 2.50
446 Von Wagner/National Treasures .25 .60
447 DDP/National Treasures .30 .75
448 Kevin Owens/National Treasures .50 1.25
449 Brock Lesnar/National Treasures 1.25 3.00
450 Karrion Kross/National Treasures .50 1.25
451 Rhea Ripley/National Treasures .75 2.00
452 Ricky Steamboat/National Treasures .50 1.25
453 Hulk Hogan/National Treasures 1.25 3.00
454 Stephanie McMahon/National Treasures.40 1.00
455 Aoife Valkyrie/National Treasures .50 1.25
456 Yulisa Leon/National Treasures .25 .60
457 Faarooq/National Treasures .30 .75
458 Nikki A.S.H./National Treasures .40 1.00
459 Edge/National Treasures 1.00 2.50
460 Lash Legend/National Treasures .25 .60
461 Liv Morgan/One 1.25 3.00
462 The Rock/One 2.50 6.00
463 Stacy Keibler/One .75 2.00
464 Chyna/One .50 1.25
465 Gorilla Monsoon/One .40 1.00
466 Rey Mysterio/One .60 1.50
467 Isla Dawn/One .30 .75
468 Yokozuna/One .30 .75
469 Asuka/One 1.00 2.50
470 Kit Wilson/One .25 .60
471 Roman Reigns/One 1.50 4.00
472 Batista/One .50 1.25
473 Macho Man Randy Savage/One 1.00 2.50
474 Ted DiBiase/One .40 1.00
475 Tiffany Stratton/One .40 1.00
476 Torrie Wilson/One .60 1.50
477 Indi Hartwell/One .75 2.00
478 Jinny/One .25 .60
479 Charlotte Flair/One 1.00 2.50
480 Mankind/One .50 1.25
481 Gable Steveson/One 1.25 3.00
482 Rob Van Dam/One .50 1.25
483 Ultimate Warrior/One 1.00 2.50
484 The Boogeyman/One .25 .60
485 Captain Lou Albano/One .30 .75
486 Wendy Choo/One .50 1.25
487 Iron Sheik/One .30 .75
488 Katana Chance/One .50 1.25
489 Finn Balor/One .60 1.50
490 Oliver Carter/One
491 Roxanne Perez/Gala
492 Gable Steveson/Gala
493 Solo Sikoa/Gala
494 Bron Breakker/Gala
495 Carmelo Hayes/Gala
496 Tony D'Angelo/Gala
497 Nikkita Lyons/Gala
498 Cora Jade/Gala
499 Joe Gacy/Gala
500 Veer Mahaan/Gala

2022 Panini Chronicles WWE Absolute Tools of the Trade Signatures

*PRIME/10: UNPRICED DUE TO SCARCITY
*SUPER PRIME/1: UNPRICED DUE TO SCARCITY
STATED PRINT RUN 75-99

TTADK Angelo Dawkins/99 5.00 12.00
TTASK Asuka/99 20.00 50.00
TTATH Theory/99 20.00 50.00
TTBTC Butch/99 10.00 25.00
TTCGR Cameron Grimes/99 12.00 30.00
TTCHY Carmelo Hayes/49 20.00 50.00
TTDBK Dana Brooke/99 8.00 20.00
TTDDP Doudrop/99 10.00 25.00
TTDPR Damian Priest/99 6.00 15.00
TTDZG Dolph Ziggler/99 8.00 20.00
TTGGD Gigi Dolin/75 60.00 150.00
TTGTH Gunther/99 12.00 30.00
TTIDG Ilja Dragunov/99 5.00 12.00
TTISH IYO SKY/99 25.00 60.00
TTJGC Joe Gacy/99 6.00 15.00
TTJJN Jacy Jayne/99 25.00 60.00
TTJUS Jey Uso/99 12.00 30.00
TTJUS Jimmy Uso/99 15.00 40.00
TTKCC Katana Chance/99 15.00 40.00
TTKCO Kayden Carter/99 10.00 25.00
TTKWD Xavier Woods/99 8.00 20.00
TTLEV Lacey Evans/99 25.00 60.00
TTLVM Liv Morgan/99 60.00 150.00
TTMIZ The Miz/99 10.00 25.00
TTMSM Meiko Satomura/75 6.00 15.00
TTMVP MVP/99 6.00 15.00
TTMZF Montez Ford/99 8.00 20.00
TTNTL Natalya/99 10.00 25.00
TTODY Odyssey Jones/99 5.00 12.00
TTOTS Otis/99 8.00 20.00
TTQZL Queen Zelina/99 15.00 40.00
TTRCH Ricochet/99 12.00 30.00
TTRGE Reggie/99 5.00 12.00
TTRHL Ridge Holland/99 6.00 15.00
TTRRP Rhea Ripley/99 30.00 75.00
TTRST Roderick Strong/99 5.00 12.00
TTSBZ Shayna Baszler/99 15.00 40.00
TTSES Santos Escobar/75 5.00 12.00
TTSZI Shotzi/99 30.00 75.00
TTVMH Veer Mahaan/99 8.00 20.00

2022 Panini Chronicles WWE Contenders Rookie Ticket Autographs

*RED: .6X TO 1.5X BASIC AUTOS
*CRACKED ICE/10: UNPRICED DUE TO SCARCITY
*CHAMPIONSHIP/1: UNPRICED DUE TO SCARCITY
RANDOMLY INSERTED INTO PACKS

RSAVK Aoife Valkyrie 12.00 30.00
RSAXM Axiom 6.00 15.00
RSBBK Bron Breakker 25.00 60.00
RSBCR Brutus Creed 6.00 15.00
RSGSV Gable Steveson EXCH 30.00 75.00
RSJNY Jinny 8.00 20.00
RSLLG Lash Legend 6.00 15.00
RSSSK Solo Sikoa 40.00 100.00
RSSTN Stevie Turner 12.00 30.00
RSVMH Veer Mahaan 6.00 15.00

2022 Panini Chronicles WWE Crown Royale Silhouettes Autographs

*PRIME/10: UNPRICED DUE TO SCARCITY
*SUPER PRIME/1: UNPRICED DUE TO SCARCITY
STATED PRINT RUN 99 SER.#'d SETS

SLACR Apollo Crews/99 5.00 12.00
SLADK Angelo Dawkins/99 5.00 12.00
SLASH Nikki A.S.H./99 15.00 40.00
SLBCD Brutus Creed/99 6.00 15.00
SLCJD Cora Jade/99 75.00 200.00
SLDMY Dominik Mysterio/99 10.00 25.00
SLDPR Damian Priest/99 10.00 25.00
SLERK Erik/99 6.00 15.00
SLGVC Giovanni Vinci/99 6.00 15.00
SLGWL Grayson Waller/99 12.00 30.00
SLHPC Happy Corbin/99 6.00 15.00
SLIHW Indi Hartwell/99 15.00 40.00
SLIVR Ivar/99 8.00 20.00
SLJCD Julius Creed/99 6.00 15.00
SLJMH Jinder Mahal/99 6.00 15.00
SLJQW Joaquin Wilde/99 6.00 15.00
SLJRD Jagger Reid/99 6.00 15.00
SLJUS Jey Uso/99 12.00 30.00
SLKKG Kofi Kingston/99 10.00 25.00
SLKLR Alba Fyre/49 20.00 50.00
SLKOW Kevin Owens/99 20.00 50.00
SLLLG Lash Legend/99 12.00 30.00
SLMBT Ludwig Kaiser/99 8.00 20.00
SLMFD Montez Ford/99 8.00 20.00
SLMXD Max Dupri/99 12.00 30.00
SLOMS Omos/99 6.00 15.00
SLRBG Rick Boogs/99 10.00 25.00
SLRDL Matt Riddle/99 15.00 40.00
SLRMY Rey Mysterio/99 30.00 75.00
SLRQG Raquel Rodriguez/99 25.00 60.00
SLRST Roderick Strong/99 5.00 12.00
SLSDV Sonya Deville/99 20.00 50.00
SLSHM Sheamus/99 10.00 25.00
SLSZN Sami Zayn/99 15.00 40.00
SLTBT Tyler Bate/99 5.00 12.00
SLTCP Ciampa/49 6.00 15.00
SLVWG Von Wagner/99 8.00 20.00
SLZST Zoey Stark/99 12.00 30.00

2022 Panini Chronicles WWE Donruss Optic Rated Rookie Signatures

*RED: .6X TO 1.5X BASIC AUTOS
*GOLD/10: UNPRICED DUE TO SCARCITY
*GOLD VINYL/1: UNPRICED DUE TO SCARCITY
RANDOMLY INSERTED INTO PACKS

RRGSV Gable Steveson EXCH 20.00 50.00
RRAOF Aoife Valkyrie 12.00 30.00
RRAXM Axiom 8.00 20.00
RRBBK Bron Breakker 30.00 75.00
RRCJD Cora Jade 75.00 150.00
RRINY Ivy Nile 15.00 40.00
RRJCD Julius Creed 6.00 15.00
RROJN Odyssey Jones 6.00 15.00
RRSHY Shanky 6.00 15.00
RRSSK Solo Sikoa 60.00 150.00

2022 Panini Chronicles WWE Flux Autographs

*RED: .6X TO 1.5X BASIC AUTOS
*GOLD/10: UNPRICED DUE TO SCARCITY
*BLACK/1: UNPRICED DUE TO SCARCITY
RANDOMLY INSERTED INTO PACKS

FXABS Alexa Bliss 100.00 250.00
FXACR Apollo Crews 5.00 12.00
FXADK Angelo Dawkins 4.00 10.00
FXAJS AJ Styles 15.00 40.00
FXBTH Butch 6.00 15.00
FXCAZ Commander Azeez 4.00 10.00
FXCOR Cody Rhodes EXCH 75.00 200.00
FXDGL Drew Gulak 5.00 12.00
FXDMY Dominik Mysterio 10.00 25.00
FXDPS Damian Priest 8.00 20.00
FXDZG Dolph Ziggler 6.00 15.00
FXEZK Ezekiel 6.00 15.00
FXHPC Happy Corbin 6.00 15.00
FXJMH Jinder Mahal 6.00 15.00
FXJMU Jimmy Uso 10.00 25.00
FXJUS Jey Uso 12.00 30.00
FXJWD Joaquin Wilde 4.00 10.00
FXKOW Kevin Owens 15.00 40.00
FXMFD Montez Ford 10.00 25.00
FXMIZ The Miz 12.00 30.00
FXMVP MVP 6.00 15.00
FXRDL Matt Riddle 12.00 30.00
FXRHL Ridge Holland 10.00 25.00
FXRRP Rhea Ripley 25.00 60.00
FXRRS Roman Reigns 50.00 125.00
FXSDV Sonya Deville 12.00 30.00
FXSZI Shotzi 30.00 75.00
FXTON Titus O'Neil 4.00 10.00
FXXLI Xia Li 15.00 40.00
FXZST Zoey Stark 10.00 25.00

2022 Panini Chronicles WWE Hall of Fame Autographs

*RED: .6X TO 1.5X BASIC AUTOS
*GOLD/10: UNPRICED DUE TO SCARCITY
*PLATINUM/1: UNPRICED DUE TO SCARCITY
RANDOMLY INSERTED INTO PACKS

HFDDP Diamond Dallas Page 12.00 30.00
HFDSL Diesel 25.00 60.00
HFHHG Hulk Hogan 125.00 300.00
HFISH Iron Sheik 20.00 50.00
HFKAG Kurt Angle 15.00 40.00
HFMDM Ted DiBiase 15.00 40.00

HFRVD Rob Van Dam	12.00	30.00
HFSCA Stone Cold Steve Austin	125.00	300.00
HFTSH Trish Stratus	40.00	100.00

2022 Panini Chronicles WWE It's All About the Game

COMPLETE SET (50)	500.00	1200.00

RANDOMLY INSERTED INTO PACKS

1 Hunter Hearst Helmsley	15.00	40.00
2 Hunter Hearst Helmsley	15.00	40.00
3 Hunter Hearst Helmsley	15.00	40.00
4 Hunter Hearst Helmsley	15.00	40.00
5 Hunter Hearst Helmsley	15.00	40.00
6 Hunter Hearst Helmsley	15.00	40.00
7 Triple H	15.00	40.00
8 Triple H	15.00	40.00
9 Triple H	15.00	40.00
10 Triple H	15.00	40.00
11 Triple H	15.00	40.00
12 Triple H	15.00	40.00
13 Triple H	15.00	40.00
14 Triple H	15.00	40.00
15 Triple H	15.00	40.00
16 Triple H	15.00	40.00
17 Triple H	15.00	40.00
18 Triple H	15.00	40.00
19 Triple H	15.00	40.00
20 Triple H	15.00	40.00
21 Triple H	15.00	40.00
22 Triple H	15.00	40.00
23 Triple H	15.00	40.00
24 Triple H	15.00	40.00
25 Triple H	15.00	40.00
26 Triple H	15.00	40.00
27 Triple H	15.00	40.00
28 Triple H	15.00	40.00
29 Triple H	15.00	40.00
30 Triple H	15.00	40.00
31 Triple H	15.00	40.00
32 Triple H	15.00	40.00
33 Triple H	15.00	40.00
34 Triple H	15.00	40.00
35 Triple H	15.00	40.00
36 Triple H	15.00	40.00
37 Triple H	15.00	40.00
38 Triple H	15.00	40.00
39 Triple H	15.00	40.00
40 Triple H	15.00	40.00
41 Triple H	15.00	40.00
42 Triple H	15.00	40.00
43 Triple H	15.00	40.00
44 Triple H	15.00	40.00
45 Triple H	15.00	40.00
46 Triple H	15.00	40.00
47 Triple H	15.00	40.00
48 Triple H	15.00	40.00
49 Triple H	15.00	40.00
50 Triple H	15.00	40.00

2022 Panini Chronicles WWE National Pride Signatures

*RED: .6X TO 1.5X BASIC AUTOS
*GOLD/10: UNPRICED DUE TO SCARCITY
*BLACK/1: UNPRICED DUE TO SCARCITY
RANDOMLY INSERTED INTO PACKS

NPASK Asuka	20.00	50.00
NPEGE Edge	15.00	40.00
NPFBL Finn Balor	12.00	30.00
NPGSV Gable Steveson EXCH	20.00	50.00
NPGTH Gunther	10.00	25.00
NPHHG Hulk Hogan	125.00	300.00
NPISH Iron Sheik	15.00	40.00
NPJDG Hacksaw Jim Duggan	12.00	30.00
NPKAG Kurt Angle	20.00	50.00
NPMCF Mark Coffey	6.00	15.00
NPMSR man.soor	6.00	15.00
NPNTL Natalya	8.00	20.00
NPSHK Shinsuke Nakamura	10.00	25.00
NPSHY Shanky	6.00	15.00
NPTSH Trish Stratus	30.00	75.00
NPWBT Wade Barrett	10.00	25.00
NPWGN Wolfgang	6.00	15.00
NPWRG William Regal	12.00	30.00

2022 Panini Chronicles WWE National Treasures Memorabilia Autographs

*GOLD/10: UNPRICED DUE TO SCARCITY
*PLATINUM/1: UNPRICED DUE TO SCARCITY
STATED PRINT RUN 49 SER.#'d SETS

NTMRS Mandy Rose	75.00	200.00
NTBBL Bianca Belair	50.00	125.00
NTRRN Roman Reigns	100.00	250.00
NTBLS Brock Lesnar	100.00	250.00
NTSFR Seth ìFreakinì Rollins	50.00	125.00
NTCML Carmella	50.00	125.00
NTDMC Drew McIntyre	25.00	60.00
NTAJS AJ Styles	25.00	60.00
NTFBL Finn Balor	25.00	60.00
NTKOW Kevin Owens	30.00	75.00
NTASK Asuka	60.00	125.00
NTRMY Rey Mysterio	40.00	100.00
NTBBK Bron Breakker	50.00	125.00
NTSKN Shinsuke Nakamura	25.00	60.00
NTCFL Charlotte Flair EXCH	60.00	150.00
NTEGE Edge	30.00	75.00
NTABS Alexa Bliss	150.00	400.00
NTGSV Gable Steveson	40.00	100.00
NTBLY Becky Lynch EXCH	150.00	400.00

2022 Panini Chronicles WWE Origins Autographs

*RED: .6X TO 1.5X BASIC AUTOS
*GOLD/10: UNPRICED DUE TO SCARCITY
*PLATINUM/1: UNPRICED DUE TO SCARCITY
RANDOMLY INSERTED INTO PACKS

OAAFA Afa	8.00	20.00
OABBF Brutus Beefcake	15.00	40.00
OABGM The Boogeyman	8.00	20.00
OABHH Bret "Hit Man" Hart	50.00	125.00
OABKT Booker T	12.00	30.00
OABLV Brother Love	12.00	30.00
OABPH Beth Phoenix	15.00	40.00
OABWB Bushwhacker Butch	12.00	30.00
OABWL Bushwhacker Luke	12.00	30.00
OADDP Diamond Dallas Page	10.00	25.00
OADMR Don Muraco	12.00	30.00
OAFRQ Faarooq	10.00	25.00
OAGFT The Godfather	10.00	25.00
OAGVL Greg Valentine	12.00	30.00
OAHHH Triple H EXCH	75.00	200.00
OAISH Iron Sheik	25.00	60.00
OAIVY Ivory	8.00	20.00
OAJBL John "Bradshaw" Layfield	10.00	25.00
OAJDG Hacksaw Jim Duggan	15.00	40.00
OAJHT Jimmy Hart	12.00	30.00
OAJLW Jerry Lawler	15.00	40.00
OAKAG Kurt Angle	15.00	40.00
OAKKL Kelly Kelly	12.00	30.00
OAKNE Kane	15.00	40.00
OAKNS Kevin Nash	20.00	50.00
OALLC Lex Luger	12.00	30.00
OAMDM Ted DiBiase	15.00	40.00
OAMHY Molly Holly	10.00	25.00
OAMMC Michelle McCool	12.00	30.00
OARDG Road Dogg	10.00	25.00
OARKI Rikishi	10.00	25.00
OARRS Ronda Rousey	75.00	200.00
OARVD Rob Van Dam	15.00	40.00
OASBG Superstar Billy Graham	12.00	30.00
OASHM Shane Helms	8.00	20.00
OASKA Sika	8.00	20.00
OATON Titus O'Neil	8.00	20.00
OAWBT Wade Barrett	8.00	20.00
OAWRG William Regal	12.00	30.00
OAXPC X-Pac	15.00	40.00

2022 Panini Chronicles WWE Phoenix Autographs

*RED: .6X TO 1.5X BASIC AUTOS
*GOLD/10: UNPRICED DUE TO SCARCITY
*GOLD VINYL/1: UNPRICED DUE TO SCARCITY
RANDOMLY INSERTED INTO PACKS

PAACR Apollo Crews	5.00	12.00
PAADK Angelo Dawkins	5.00	12.00
PAASH Nikki A.S.H.	8.00	20.00
PAATH Theory	15.00	40.00
PABBL Bianca Belair	20.00	50.00
PABCH Butch	6.00	15.00
PABDV Blair Davenport	10.00	25.00
PABGE Big E	6.00	15.00
PABLY Bayley	15.00	40.00
PACAZ Commander Azeez	5.00	12.00
PACFL Charlotte Flair EXCH	30.00	75.00
PACOR Cody Rhodes EXCH	75.00	200.00
PADDP Doudrop	10.00	25.00
PADGL Drew Gulak	5.00	12.00
PADPS Damian Priest	8.00	20.00
PADZG Dolph Ziggler	8.00	20.00
PAERK Erik	5.00	12.00
PAEZK Ezekiel	6.00	15.00
PAHCB Happy Corbin	6.00	15.00
PAIVR Ivar	5.00	12.00
PAJMH Jinder Mahal	5.00	12.00
PAJMU Jimmy Uso	15.00	40.00
PAJQW Joaquin Wilde	5.00	12.00
PAJRD Jagger Reid	5.00	12.00
PAJUS Jey Uso	12.00	30.00
PALEV Lacey Evans	12.00	30.00
PAMFD Montez Ford	6.00	15.00
PAMVP MVP	6.00	15.00
PAOMS Omos	5.00	12.00
PAOTS Otis	6.00	15.00
PAQZL Queen Zelina	12.00	30.00
PARGE Reggie	5.00	12.00
PARHL Ridge Holland	6.00	15.00
PARMY Rey Mysterio	20.00	50.00
PARPF Rip Fowler	5.00	12.00
PASDV Sonya Deville	12.00	30.00
PASHM Sheamus	8.00	20.00
PATON Titus O'Neil	5.00	12.00
PAXLI Xia Li	12.00	30.00
PAXWD Xavier Woods	6.00	15.00

2022 Panini Chronicles WWE Signatures

*RED: .6X TO 1.5X BASIC AUTOS
*GOLD/10: UNPRICED DUE TO SCARCITY
*PLATINUM/1: UNPRICED DUE TO SCARCITY
RANDOMLY INSERTED INTO PACKS

CSBBL Brie Bella	15.00	40.00
CSBHH Bret "Hit Man" Hart	40.00	100.00
CSBOA Boa	6.00	15.00
CSBTS Batista	50.00	125.00
CSDDP Diamond Dallas Page	12.00	30.00
CSEPC Elton Prince	6.00	15.00
CSGBG Goldberg	40.00	100.00
CSGVC Giovanni Vinci	6.00	15.00
CSJCF Joe Coffey	6.00	15.00
CSJCN John Cena	75.00	200.00
CSJDM JD McDonagh	6.00	15.00
CSJLW Jerry Lawler	20.00	50.00
CSJQW Joaquin Wilde	8.00	20.00
CSJRD Jagger Reid	6.00	15.00
CSJRZ Johnny Rodz	8.00	20.00
CSKAG Kurt Angle	15.00	40.00
CSKCT Kayden Carter	10.00	25.00
CSKNE Kane	30.00	75.00
CSKNH Kevin Nash	15.00	40.00
CSKWL Kit Wilson	6.00	15.00
CSLTA Lita	20.00	50.00
CSMBT Ludwig Kaiser	6.00	15.00
CSMCF Mark Coffey	6.00	15.00
CSMDM Ted DiBiase	12.00	30.00
CSMKN Mankind	30.00	75.00
CSNBL Nikki Bella	20.00	50.00
CSRDG Road Dogg	10.00	25.00
CSRKI Rikishi	10.00	25.00
CSRPF Rip Fowler	6.00	15.00
CSRSM Ron Simmons	12.00	30.00
CSSHM Shawn Michaels	75.00	200.00
CSTBT Tyler Bate	6.00	15.00
CSTSH Trish Stratus	30.00	75.00
CSUTK Undertaker	125.00	300.00
CSWGG Wolfgang	6.00	15.00
CSWLE Wes Lee	6.00	15.00
CSXNQ Xyon Quinn	6.00	15.00

2022 Panini Impeccable WWE

UNOPENED BOX (1 PACK)
UNOPENED PACK (9 CARDS)
*SILVER/49: .6X TO 1.5X BASIC CARDS
*GOLD/35: .75X TO 2X BASIC CARDS
*HOLO SILVER/25: UNPRICED DUE TO SCARCITY
*HOLO GOLD/10: UNPRICED DUE TO SCARCITY
*PLATINUM/1: UNPRICED DUE TO SCARCITY
STATED PRINT RUN 99 SER.#'d SETS

1 The Rock	12.00	30.00
2 Rhea Ripley	5.00	12.00
3 Ivar	2.00	5.00
4 AJ Styles	4.00	10.00
5 Ricochet	3.00	8.00
6 Damian Priest	4.00	10.00
7 Ronda Rousey	15.00	40.00
8 Otis	2.50	6.00
9 Cameron Grimes	2.50	6.00
10 Alexa Bliss	30.00	75.00
11 Stone Cold Steve Austin	20.00	50.00
12 Tamina	2.00	5.00
13 Jey Uso	2.50	6.00
14 Akira Tozawa	3.00	8.00
15 Ridge Holland	2.00	5.00
16 Dolph Ziggler	2.50	6.00
17 Chyna	10.00	25.00
18 Randy Orton	4.00	10.00
19 Eddie Guerrero	10.00	25.00
20 Becky Lynch	20.00	50.00
21 Undertaker	15.00	40.00
22 Angel	2.00	5.00
23 Jimmy Uso	2.50	6.00
24 Angelo Dawkins	2.00	5.00
25 Roman Reigns	8.00	20.00
26 Dominik Mysterio	2.50	6.00
27 Shayna Baszler	3.00	8.00
28 Reggie	2.00	5.00
29 Dusty Rhodes	4.00	10.00
30 Bianca Belair	6.00	15.00
31 Triple H	5.00	12.00
32 Big E	2.50	6.00
33 Jinder Mahal	2.00	5.00
34 Apollo Crews	2.00	5.00
35 Sami Zayn	3.00	8.00
36 Edge	5.00	12.00
37 Shotzi	12.00	30.00
38 Rey Mysterio	4.00	10.00
39 Solo Sikoa	10.00	25.00
40 Carmella	10.00	25.00
41 Cactus Jack	8.00	20.00
42 Cody Rhodes	25.00	60.00
43 Xavier Woods	2.50	6.00
44 Theory	4.00	10.00
45 Sheamus	3.00	8.00
46 Finn Balor	6.00	15.00
47 Xia Li	5.00	12.00
48 Riddle	5.00	12.00
49 Ciampa	3.00	8.00
50 Dana Brooke	2.00	5.00
51 Bruno Sammartino	2.50	6.00
52 Drew Gulak	2.50	6.00
53 Kofi Kingston	3.00	8.00
54 Bobby Lashley	3.00	8.00
55 Shinsuke Nakamura	4.00	10.00
56 Kevin Owens	5.00	12.00
57 Asuka	12.00	30.00
58 Robert Roode	2.00	5.00
59 Santos Escobar	2.00	5.00
60 Doudrop	2.00	5.00
61 Ultimate Warrior	8.00	20.00
62 Drew McIntyre	5.00	12.00
63 Mace	2.00	5.00
64 Brock Lesnar	8.00	20.00
65 Aliyah	2.00	5.00
66 The Miz	2.50	6.00
67 Bayley	6.00	15.00
68 R-Truth	2.00	5.00
69 Goldberg	4.00	10.00
70 Liv Morgan	30.00	75.00
71 Andre the Giant	10.00	25.00
72 Erik	2.00	5.00
73 Madcap Moss	2.00	5.00
74 Cedric Alexander	2.00	5.00
75 Charlotte Flair	8.00	20.00

Card	Low	High
76 Montez Ford	2.00	5.00
77 John Cena	6.00	15.00
78 Seth Freakin Rollins	6.00	15.00
79 Raquel Rodriguez	15.00	40.00
80 Maryse	12.00	30.00
81 Meiko Satomura	2.00	5.00
82 Happy Corbin	2.00	5.00
83 Mansoor	2.00	5.00
84 Chad Gable	2.00	5.00
85 Hulk Hogan	25.00	60.00
86 MVP	2.00	5.00
87 Lacey Evans	8.00	20.00
88 Shelton Benjamin	2.00	5.00
89 Alba Fyre	5.00	12.00
90 Nikki A.S.H.	3.00	8.00
91 Ilja Dragunov	2.00	5.00
92 Humberto	2.00	5.00
93 Rick Boogs	2.00	5.00
94 Commander Azeez	2.00	5.00
95 Natalya	3.00	8.00
96 Omos	2.00	5.00
97 Shanky	2.00	5.00
98 T-Bar	2.00	5.00
99 Mandy Rose	20.00	50.00
100 Queen Zelina	6.00	15.00

2022 Panini Impeccable WWE Elegance Memorabilia Autographs

*HOLO SILVER/25: .6X TO 1.5X BASIC AUTOS
*HOLO GOLD/10: UNPRICED DUE TO SCARCITY
*PLATINUM/1: UNPRICED DUE TO SCARCITY
RANDOMLY INSERTED INTO PACKS

Card	Low	High
EMABS Alexa Bliss	100.00	250.00
EMACR Apollo Crews	8.00	20.00
EMADK Angelo Dawkins	10.00	25.00
EMAJS AJ Styles	20.00	50.00
EMASK Asuka	30.00	75.00
EMBBL Bianca Belair	30.00	75.00
EMBLS Bobby Lashley	12.00	30.00
EMBLS Brock Lesnar	75.00	200.00
EMBLY Becky Lynch	40.00	100.00
EMCFL Charlotte Flair EXCH	60.00	150.00
EMCGR Cameron Grimes	8.00	20.00
EMCML Carmella	20.00	50.00
EMDDR Doudrop	8.00	20.00
EMDMC Drew McIntyre	25.00	60.00
EMDMY Dominik Mysterio	8.00	20.00
EMDPS Damian Priest	10.00	25.00
EMDZG Dolph Ziggler	10.00	25.00
EMEGD Edge	30.00	75.00
EMFBL Finn Balor	15.00	40.00
EMGGD Gigi Dolin	60.00	150.00
EMGTH Gunther	10.00	25.00
EMIDG Ilja Dragunov	12.00	30.00
EMISH Io Shirai	25.00	60.00
EMJMH Jinder Mahal	8.00	20.00
EMJMU Jimmy Uso	15.00	40.00
EMJUS Jey Uso	15.00	40.00
EMKKG Kofi Kingston	8.00	20.00
EMKOW Kevin Owens	15.00	40.00
EMLAK LA Knight	15.00	40.00
EMLVM Liv Morgan	100.00	250.00
EMMFD Montez Ford	12.00	30.00
EMMIZ The Miz	15.00	40.00
EMNTA Natalya	10.00	25.00
EMOMS Omos	12.00	30.00
EMOTS Otis	8.00	20.00
EMRDL Riddle	20.00	50.00
EMRMY Rey Mysterio	25.00	60.00
EMROR Randy Orton EXCH	40.00	100.00
EMRQG Raquel Rodriguez		
EMRRN Roman Reigns EXCH	60.00	150.00
EMRRP Rhea Ripley	40.00	100.00
EMSDV Sonya Deville	15.00	40.00
EMSHM Sheamus	10.00	25.00
EMSHN Shinsuke Nakamura	15.00	40.00
EMSHZ Shotzi	30.00	75.00
EMSRL Seth Freakin Rollins	30.00	75.00
EMSZN Sami Zayn	15.00	40.00
EMTCP Ciampa	10.00	25.00

2022 Panini Impeccable WWE Elegance Rookie Memorabilia Autographs

*HOLO SILVER/25: .6X TO 1.5X BASIC AUTOS
*HOLO GOLD/10: UNPRICED DUE TO SCARCITY
*PLATINUM/1: UNPRICED DUE TO SCARCITY
STATED PRINT RUN 99 SER.#'d SETS

Card	Low	High
101 Bron Breakker	60.00	150.00
102 Carmelo Hayes	20.00	50.00
103 Gable Steveson EXCH	25.00	60.00
104 Grayson Waller	12.00	30.00
105 Ivy Nile	20.00	50.00
106 Joe Gacy	12.00	30.00
107 Von Wagner	12.00	30.00
108 Cora Jade	75.00	200.00
109 Jacy Jayne	40.00	100.00
110 Veer Mahaan	12.00	30.00

2022 Panini Impeccable WWE Illustrious Ink

*HOLO SILVER/25: .6X TO 1.5X BASIC AUTOS
*HOLO GOLD/10: UNPRICED DUE TO SCARCITY
*PLATINUM/1: UNPRICED DUE TO SCARCITY
STATED PRINT RUN 99 SER.#'d SETS

Card	Low	High
ILAFA Afa	15.00	40.00
ILAML Amale	12.00	30.00
ILBOA Boa	6.00	15.00
ILCJD Cora Jade	75.00	200.00
ILCJK Cactus Jack	60.00	150.00
ILCML Carmella	30.00	75.00
ILDBK Dana Brooke	8.00	20.00
ILDDP Diamond Dallas Page	30.00	75.00
ILDGL Drew Gulak	12.00	30.00
ILDMR Don Muraco	15.00	40.00
ILDMS Dave Mastiff	6.00	15.00
ILDMY Dominik Mysterio	12.00	30.00
ILFRQ Faarooq	12.00	30.00
ILIVR Ivar EXCH	6.00	15.00
ILJCR Julius Creed	8.00	20.00
ILJDG Hacksaw Jim Duggan	25.00	60.00
ILJLW Jerry Lawler	25.00	60.00
ILJNY Jinny	10.00	25.00
ILJWL Joaquin Wilde	6.00	15.00
ILKWD Xavier Woods	12.00	30.00
ILKWL Kenny Williams	6.00	15.00
ILMCF Mark Coffey	6.00	15.00
ILMRS Mandy Rose	50.00	125.00
ILODY Odyssey Jones	6.00	15.00
ILOTS Otis	10.00	25.00
ILRHL Ridge Holland	6.00	15.00
ILSDV Sonya Deville	12.00	30.00
ILSKA Sika	10.00	25.00
ILTMN Teoman	6.00	15.00
ILZST Zoey Stark	15.00	40.00

2022 Panini Impeccable WWE Immortal Ink

*HOLO SILVER/25: .6X TO 1.5X BASIC AUTOS
*HOLO GOLD/10: UNPRICED DUE TO SCARCITY
*PLATINUM/1: UNPRICED DUE TO SCARCITY
STATED PRINT RUN 99 SER.#'d SETS

Card	Low	High
IMABZ Alundra Blayze	15.00	40.00
IMBBK Brutus Beefcake	20.00	50.00
IMBBL Brie Bella	25.00	60.00
IMBHT Bret "Hit Man" Hart	100.00	250.00
IMBKT Booker T	25.00	60.00
IMBLV Brother Love	12.00	30.00
IMBOR Cowboy Bob Orton	12.00	30.00
IMBPX Beth Phoenix	12.00	30.00
IMBWB Bushwhacker Butch	15.00	40.00
IMBWL Bushwhacker Luke	15.00	40.00
IMGFT The Godfather	12.00	30.00
IMGVL Greg Valentine	12.00	30.00
IMISH Iron Sheik	25.00	60.00
IMIVY Ivory	20.00	50.00
IMJBL John "Bradshaw" Layfield	12.00	30.00
IMJHT Jimmy Hart	12.00	30.00
IMJLW Jerry Lawler	25.00	60.00
IMKLY Kelly Kelly	25.00	60.00
IMLTA Lita	40.00	100.00
IMMDM Ted DiBiase	20.00	50.00
IMMHL Molly Holly	15.00	40.00
IMMHY Michael Hayes	12.00	30.00
IMNBL Nikki Bella	40.00	100.00
IMPGE Paige	50.00	125.00
IMRKI Rikishi	15.00	40.00
IMRVD Rob Van Dam	25.00	60.00
IMSBG Superstar Billy Graham	12.00	30.00
IMSML Shawn Michaels	100.00	250.00
IMUTK Undertaker	250.00	500.00
IMXPC X-Pac	20.00	50.00

2022 Panini Impeccable WWE Impeccable Championship Debuts Autographs

STATED PRINT RUN 1-99

Card	Low	High
CDABS Alexa Bliss/16		
CDAJS AJ Styles/16		
CDASK Asuka/18		
CDBBL Bianca Belair/21	250.00	600.00
CDBLS Brock Lesnar/2		
CDBLS Bobby Lashley/21	150.00	400.00
CDBLY Becky Lynch/16		
CDBPX Beth Phoenix/11		
CDBTS Batista/5		
CDCFL Charlotte Flair/15		
CDDMI Drew McIntyre/20	100.00	250.00
CDDZG Dolph Ziggler/11		
CDEGE Edge/6		
CDFBL Finn Balor/16		
CDGLB Goldberg/98	100.00	250.00
CDHHG Hulk Hogan/84	500.00	1200.00
CDISH Iron Sheik/83	75.00	200.00
CDJBL John "Bradshaw" Layfield/4		
CDJCN John Cena/5		
CDKKG Kofi Kingston/19		
CDKLY Kelly Kelly/9		
CDLTA Lita/1		
CDMFL Mankind/99	150.00	400.00
CDMMC Michelle McCool/8 EXCH		
CDPGE Paige/14		
CDROR Randy Orton/4		
CDRYM Rey Mysterio/6		
CDSCA Stone Cold Steve Austin/98	400.00	1000.00
CDSHM Sheamus/9		
CDSRL Seth Freakin Rollins/15		

2022 Panini Impeccable WWE Impeccable Championships Signatures

STATED PRINT RUN 2-16
UNPRICED DUE TO SCARCITY

ICABS Alexa Bliss/5 EXCH
ICABZ Alundra Blayze/3
ICAJS AJ Styles/2
ICBHT Bret "Hit Man" Hart/7
ICBLS Brock Lesnar/10
ICBLY Becky Lynch/6
ICBTS Batista/6
ICCFL Charlotte Flair/13
ICEGE Edge/11
ICGLB Goldberg/4
ICHHG Hulk Hogan/12
ICJCN John Cena/16
ICMKN Mankind/3
ICROR Randy Orton/14
ICRRN Roman Reigns/5
ICSCA Stone Cold Steve Austin/6
ICSRL Seth Freakin Rollins/4
ICTPH Triple H/14
ICTSH Trish Stratus/7
ICUKT Undertaker/7

2022 Panini Impeccable WWE Impeccable Hall of Fame Signatures

STATED PRINT RUN 4-96

Card	Low	High
HFABZ Alundra Blayze/15		
HFBBF Brutus Beefcake/19		
HFBHT Bret "Hit Man" Hart/6		
HFBKT Booker T/13		
HFBOR Cowboy Bob Orton/5		
HFBPX Beth Phoenix/17		
HFDDP Diamond Dallas Page/17		
HFEGE Edge/12		
HFFRQ Ron Simmons/12		
HFGFT The Godfather/17		
HFGLB Goldberg/18		
HFGVL Greg Valentine/4		
HFHHG Hulk Hogan/5		
HFIPT Ivan Putski/95 EXCH	40.00	100.00
HFISH Iron Sheik/5		
HFIVY Ivory/18		
HFJBL JBL/20	100.00	250.00
HFJHT Jimmy Hart/5		
HFJKL Jerry Lawler/7		
HFJRZ Johnny Rodz/96	40.00	100.00
HFKNE Kane/21	200.00	500.00
HFLTA Lita/14		
HFMDM Ted DiBiase/10		
HFMHL Molly Holly/21	75.00	200.00
HFRKI Rikishi/15		
HFRVD Rob Van Dam/21	100.00	250.00
HFSML Shawn Michaels/11		
HFTSH Trish Stratus/13		
HFTWL Torrie Wilson/19		
HFUKT Undertaker/22	1500.00	4000.00

2022 Panini Impeccable WWE Impeccable Jumbo Materials

STATED PRINT RUN 35 SER.#'d SETS

Card	Low	High
JMABS Alexa Bliss	30.00	75.00
JMAJS AJ Styles	8.00	20.00
JMASK Asuka	15.00	40.00
JMBBL Bianca Belair	10.00	25.00
JMBLS Brock Lesnar	25.00	60.00
JMBLS Bobby Lashley	6.00	15.00
JMBLY Becky Lynch	40.00	100.00
JMBRK Bron Breakker	12.00	30.00
JMCFL Charlotte Flair	25.00	60.00
JMCML Carmella	40.00	100.00
JMCRD Cody Rhodes	20.00	50.00
JMDMI Drew McIntyre	6.00	15.00
JMEGE Edge	12.00	30.00
JMFBL Finn Balor	12.00	30.00
JMLVM Liv Morgan	75.00	200.00
JMROR Randy Orton	12.00	30.00
JMRRN Roman Reigns	12.00	30.00
JMRYM Rey Mysterio	10.00	25.00
JMSCA Stone Cold Steve Austin	20.00	50.00
JMSRL Seth Freakin Rollins	15.00	40.00

2022 Panini Impeccable WWE Impeccable WrestleMania Signatures

STATED PRINT RUN 7-27

Card	Low	High
IWAJS AJ Styles/7		
IWBLS Brock Lesnar/11		
IWBTS Batista/7		
IWEGE Edge/13		
IWHHG Hulk Hogan/12		
IWJBL JBL/10		
IWJCA John Cena/15		
IWKAN Kurt Angle/9		
IWKKG Kofi Kingston/11		
IWKNE Kane/17		
IWMIZ The Miz/10		
IWROR Randy Orton/18		
IWRRN Roman Reigns/9 EXCH		
IWRYM Rey Mysterio/13		
IWSCA Stone Cold Steve Austin/8		
IWSHM Sheamus/10		
IWSML Shawn Michaels/17		
IWSRL Seth Freakin Rollins/11		
IWTPH Triple H/23 EXCH	500.00	1200.00
IWUTK Undertaker/27	800.00	1500.00

2022 Panini Impeccable WWE Indelible Ink

*HOLO SILVER/25: UNPRICED DUE TO SCARCITY
*HOLO GOLD/10: UNPRICED DUE TO SCARCITY
*PLATINUM/1: UNPRICED DUE TO SCARCITY
STATED PRINT RUN 99 SER.#'d SETS

Card	Low	High
INASH Nikki A.S.H.	10.00	25.00
INBGM The Boogeyman	15.00	40.00
INBTS Batista EXCH	30.00	75.00
INCAZ Commander Azeez	6.00	15.00
INDDR Doudrop	8.00	20.00
INDLN Dani Luna EXCH	8.00	20.00
INEPC Elton Prince	8.00	20.00

INERK Erik	5.00	12.00
INFAB Fabian Aichner	5.00	12.00
INFMW Flash Morgan Webster	5.00	12.00
INGBS Gerald Brisco	12.00	30.00
INGSV Gable Steveson EXCH	25.00	60.00
INHCN The Hurricane	12.00	30.00
ININY Ivy Nile	12.00	30.00
INJDV Jordan Devlin	6.00	15.00
INKAN Kurt Angle EXCH	30.00	75.00
INKCY Katana Chance	20.00	50.00
INKNS Diesel EXCH	25.00	60.00
INKWS Kit Wilson	6.00	15.00
INLEV Lacey Evans	15.00	40.00
INLLG Lex Luger	20.00	50.00
INMAD Mark Andrews EXCH	6.00	15.00
INMMC Michelle McCool EXCH	20.00	50.00
INMRS Mandy Rose	50.00	125.00
INMSR Mansoor	5.00	12.00
INMVP MVP	6.00	15.00
INOMS Omos	6.00	15.00
INRBG Rick Boogs	10.00	25.00
INRCO Ricochet	12.00	30.00
INRRD Robert Roode	6.00	15.00
INRRP Rhea Ripley	30.00	75.00
INSHY Shanky	6.00	15.00
INSHZ Shotzi	40.00	100.00
INSTN Stevie Turner	12.00	30.00
INTBT Tyler Bate	5.00	12.00
INWRG William Regal	12.00	30.00
INXLI Xia Li	30.00	75.00
INXQN Xyon Quinn	8.00	20.00
INZGB Zack Gibson	5.00	12.00

2022 Panini Impeccable WWE Silver WWE Legends Logos

*GOLD/1: UNPRICED DUE TO SCARCITY
STATED PRINT RUN 35 SER.#'d SETS

1 Junkyard Dog	75.00	200.00
2 Paul Bearer	60.00	150.00
3 Alundra Blayze	40.00	100.00
4 Rowdy Roddy Piper	100.00	250.00
5 Bret "Hit Man" Hart	125.00	300.00
6 Stone Cold Steve Austin	125.00	300.00
7 Diesel	75.00	200.00
8 Triple H	100.00	250.00
9 Hulk Hogan	200.00	500.00
10 Undertaker	200.00	500.00
11 Macho Man Randy Savage	150.00	400.00
12 Razor Ramon	100.00	250.00
13 Andre the Giant	125.00	300.00
14 Terry Gordy	30.00	100.00
15 Brie Bella	60.00	150.00
16 Ted DiBiase	75.00	200.00
17 Dusty Rhodes	75.00	200.00
18 Trish Stratus	125.00	300.00
19 Iron Sheik	40.00	100.00
20 Vader	50.00	125.00
21 Mankind	100.00	250.00
22 Rob Van Dam	60.00	150.00
23 Batista	60.00	150.00
24 Shawn Michaels	125.00	300.00
25 Bruno Sammartino	60.00	150.00
26 Superstar Billy Graham	75.00	200.00
27 Eddie Guerrero	100.00	250.00
28 Ultimate Warrior	200.00	500.00
29 JBL	40.00	100.00
30 X-Pac	60.00	150.00
31 Nikki Bella	75.00	200.00
32 The Rock	250.00	600.00
33 Booker T	50.00	125.00
34 Stacy Keibler	125.00	300.00
35 Chyna	100.00	250.00
36 Terry Funk	60.00	150.00
37 Goldberg	100.00	250.00
38 Umaga	40.00	100.00
39 Jerry Lawler	60.00	150.00
40 Yokozuna	60.00	150.00

2022 Panini Impeccable WWE Silver WWE Logos

*GOLD/1: UNPRICED DUE TO SCARCITY
STATED PRINT RUN 35 SER.#'d SETS

1 Jimmy Uso	60.00	150.00
2 Seth Freakin Rollins	60.00	150.00
3 Big E	50.00	125.00
4 Cora Jade	150.00	400.00
5 Solo Sikoa	75.00	200.00
6 Kofi Kingston	50.00	125.00
7 AJ Styles	100.00	250.00
8 Asuka	125.00	300.00
9 Jey Uso	60.00	150.00
10 Bayley	50.00	125.00
11 Roman Reigns	100.00	250.00
12 Raquel Rodriguez	40.00	100.00
13 Sami Zayn	60.00	150.00
14 Bron Breakker	75.00	200.00
15 Carmella	100.00	250.00
16 Bobby Lashley	60.00	150.00
17 Damian Priest	40.00	100.00
18 Drew McIntyre	60.00	150.00
19 Cody Rhodes	125.00	300.00
20 Liv Morgan	200.00	500.00
21 Dominik Mysterio	40.00	100.00
22 Ilja Dragunov	50.00	125.00
23 Edge	50.00	125.00
24 Grayson Waller	50.00	125.00
25 Riddle	50.00	125.00
26 Shinsuke Nakamura	75.00	200.00
27 Ronda Rousey	200.00	500.00
28 Brock Lesnar	125.00	300.00
29 Randy Orton	75.00	200.00
30 Charlotte Flair	125.00	300.00
31 Bianca Belair	60.00	150.00
32 Mandy Rose	200.00	500.00
33 Rey Mysterio	60.00	150.00
34 Finn Balor	100.00	250.00
35 Ciampa	40.00	100.00
36 Kevin Owens	75.00	200.00
37 Alexa Bliss	250.00	600.00
38 The Miz	50.00	125.00
39 Becky Lynch	100.00	250.00
40 John Cena	125.00	300.00

2022 Panini Impeccable WWE Stainless Stars

*ORANGE/25: UNPRICED DUE TO SCARCITY
*RED FOTL/15: UNPRICED DUE TO SCARCITY
*GOLD/10: UNPRICED DUE TO SCARCITY
*PLATINUM/1: UNPRICED DUE TO SCARCITY
STATED PRINT RUN 99 SER.#'d SETS

1 Undertaker	20.00	50.00
2 Mandy Rose	20.00	50.00
3 Triple H	12.00	30.00
4 Solo Sikoa	10.00	25.00
5 The Rock	30.00	75.00
6 Drew McIntyre	6.00	15.00
7 Stone Cold Steve Austin	20.00	50.00
8 Charlotte Flair	15.00	40.00
9 Randy Orton	8.00	20.00
10 Seth Freakin Rollins	10.00	25.00
11 Roman Reigns	15.00	40.00
12 Bron Breakker	15.00	40.00
13 Edge	10.00	25.00
14 Ciampa	6.00	15.00
15 Ronda Rousey	25.00	60.00
16 Brock Lesnar	12.00	30.00
17 Cody Rhodes	40.00	100.00
18 John Cena	15.00	40.00
19 Becky Lynch	15.00	40.00
20 Raquel Rodriguez	8.00	20.00
21 Bianca Belair	10.00	25.00
22 Cora Jade	30.00	75.00
23 Rey Mysterio	8.00	20.00
24 Bobby Lashley	6.00	15.00
25 Alexa Bliss	40.00	100.00

2022 Panini Impeccable WWE Stainless Stars Autographs

*BLUE/75: .5X TO 1.2X BASIC AUTOS
*PURPLE/49: .6X TO 1.5X BASIC AUTOS
*ORANGE/25: .75X TO 2X BASIC AUTOS
*GOLD/10: UNPRICED DUE TO SCARCITY
*PLATINUM/1: UNPRICED DUE TO SCARCITY
STATED PRINT RUN 99 SER.#'d SETS

SSAKD A-Kid	5.00	12.00
SSAOV Aoife Valkyrie	12.00	30.00
SSBBK Bron Breakker	40.00	100.00
SSBLS Brock Lesnar	60.00	150.00
SSBLY Becky Lynch	30.00	75.00
SSDBC Drew McIntyre	12.00	30.00
SSFBL Finn Balor	12.00	30.00
SSGBG Goldberg	40.00	100.00
SSIHW Indi Hartwell	20.00	50.00
SSIOS Io Shirai	15.00	40.00
SSKCZ Katana Chance	12.00	30.00
SSMSM Meiko Satomura	10.00	25.00
SSNDR Noam Dar	5.00	12.00
SSRMY Rey Mysterio	15.00	40.00
SSROR Randy Orton EXCH	30.00	75.00
SSRQG Raquel Rodriguez	20.00	50.00
SSRRN Roman Reigns EXCH	60.00	150.00
SSSES Santos Escobar	12.00	30.00
SSSRL Seth Freakin Rollins	20.00	50.00
SSSRY Sarray EXCH	8.00	20.00
SSTON Titus O'Neil	8.00	20.00
SSTSH Trish Stratus	40.00	100.00
SSTWL Torrie Wilson	30.00	75.00
SSWLE Wes Lee	8.00	20.00
SSZGB Zack Gibson	5.00	12.00

2022 Panini Impeccable WWE Superstar Autographs

*HOLO SILVER/25: .6X TO 1.5X BASIC AUTOS
*HOLO GOLD/10: UNPRICED DUE TO SCARCITY
*PLATINUM/1: UNPRICED DUE TO SCARCITY
STATED PRINT RUN 99 SER.#'d SETS

SAABS Alexa Bliss	125.00	300.00
SAADK Angelo Dawkins	6.00	15.00
SAAJS AJ Styles	20.00	50.00
SAASK Asuka	25.00	60.00
SAATH Theory	15.00	40.00
SABBL Bianca Belair	25.00	60.00
SABCR Brutus Creed	6.00	15.00
SABGE Big E	8.00	20.00
SABLS Bobby Lashley	15.00	40.00
SABLY Bayley	30.00	75.00
SABNB Bad News Barrett	8.00	20.00
SABTS Batista EXCH	50.00	125.00
SACFL Charlotte Flair EXCH	40.00	100.00
SAELS Ezekiel	10.00	25.00
SAEMK Emilia McKenzie	12.00	30.00
SAGBG Goldberg	60.00	150.00
SAHCB Happy Corbin	6.00	15.00
SAHHG Hulk Hogan	250.00	500.00
SAJCF Joe Coffey	5.00	12.00
SAJCN John Cena EXCH	60.00	150.00
SAJDK James Drake	5.00	12.00
SAJJN Jacy Jayne	50.00	125.00
SAKCT Kayden Carter	12.00	30.00
SAKLR Alba Fyre	15.00	40.00
SALLG Lash Legend	10.00	25.00
SALVM Liv Morgan	75.00	200.00
SAMBT Ludwig Kaiser	6.00	15.00
SAMFD Montez Ford	8.00	20.00
SANTL Natalya	10.00	25.00
SAQZL Queen Zelina	20.00	50.00
SARBR Rampage Brown	5.00	12.00
SARDG Road Dogg	15.00	40.00
SARDL Riddle	15.00	40.00
SARGE Reggie	5.00	12.00
SARST Roderick Strong	8.00	20.00
SASBG Superstar Billy Graham	20.00	50.00
SASBZ Shayna Baszler	8.00	20.00
SASCA Stone Cold Steve Austin	250.00	500.00
SATPH Triple H EXCH	75.00	200.00
SAWFG Wolfgang	5.00	12.00

2022 Panini Instant WWE

*VERSICOLOR/5: UNPRICED DUE TO SCARCITY
*BLACK/1: UNPRICED DUE TO SCARCITY

1 Undertaker/472*	6.00	15.00
2 Raquel Gonzalez/Dakota Kai/130*	6.00	15.00
3 Cameron Grimes/121*	2.50	6.00
4 Tommaso Ciampa/122*	2.50	6.00
5 MSK/126*	2.50	6.00
6 Mandy Rose/210*	8.00	20.00
7 Dolph Ziggler/120*		
8 The Usos/167*	3.00	8.00
9 Bianca Belair/167*	5.00	12.00
10 Cody Rhodes/316*	8.00	20.00
11 Charlotte Flair/283*	6.00	15.00
12 Stone Cold Steve Austin/384*	5.00	12.00
13 Triple H/268*		
14 RK-Bro/176*		
15 Gable Steveson/908*	6.00	15.00
16 Sasha Banks & Naomi/272*	4.00	10.00
17 Edge & Damian Priest/166*		
18 Roman Reigns/412*	3.00	8.00
19 Bron Breakker/588*		
20 Toxic Attraction/180*	6.00	15.00
21 Nikkita Lyons/629*	10.00	25.00
22 Cody Rhodes/130*	5.00	12.00
23 Omos/76*	3.00	8.00
24 Edge/105*		
25 Rhea Ripley/133*	4.00	10.00
26 Ronda Rousey/176*	6.00	15.00
27 Roman Reigns/Usos/117*	8.00	20.00
28 The Usos/97*	5.00	12.00
29 Bianca Belair/144*	4.00	10.00
30 Theory/123*	3.00	8.00
31 Cody Rhodes/242*	6.00	15.00
32 Finn Balor/114*	6.00	15.00
33 Gunther/120*	5.00	12.00
34 Brock Lesnar/95*		
35 John Cena/254*	5.00	12.00
36 John Cena/254*	5.00	12.00
37 John Cena/254*	5.00	12.00
38 John Cena/254*	5.00	12.00
39 John Cena/254*	5.00	12.00
40 John Cena/254*	5.00	12.00
41 John Cena/254*	5.00	12.00
42 John Cena/254*	5.00	12.00
43 John Cena/254*	5.00	12.00
44 John Cena/254*	5.00	12.00
45 John Cena/254*	5.00	12.00
46 John Cena/254*	5.00	12.00
47 John Cena/254*	5.00	12.00
48 John Cena/254*	5.00	12.00
49 John Cena/254*	5.00	12.00
50 John Cena/254*	5.00	12.00
51 John Cena/254*	5.00	12.00
52 Bobby Lashley	6.00	15.00
53 The Usos/69*	5.00	12.00
54 Liv Morgan/287*	8.00	20.00
55 Riddle/79*	6.00	15.00
56 Theory/78*	4.00	10.00
57 Cora Jade/Roxanne Perez/233*	10.00	25.00
58 Bianca Belair/95*	4.00	10.00
59 Edge/68*		
60 Pat McAfee/684*	5.00	12.00
61 Roman Reigns/145*	5.00	12.00
62 Raquel Rodriguez & Aliyah/91*		
63 Damage CTRL/67*	4.00	10.00
64 Gunther/		
65 Dominik Mysterio/		
66 Seth "Freakin" Rollins/		
67 Roman Reigns/83*	5.00	12.00
68 Pretty Deadly/84*	5.00	12.00
69 Mandy Rose/113*	6.00	15.00
70 Bron Breakker/		
71 Braun Strowman/		
72 Damage CTRL/		
73 Solo Sikoa/		
74 Ronda Rousey/69*		
75 Karrion Kross/84*		
76 Matt Riddle/83*		
77 Bray Wyatt/149*		
78 Wes Lee/84*		
79 Roxanne Perez/96*		
80 Mandy Rose/105*		
81 Bron Breakker/90*		
82 Ava Rayne/633*		
83 Becky Lynch/82*		
84 AJ Styles/87*		
85 Austin Theory/62*		
86 Sami Zayn/64*	8.00	20.00
87 Roxanne Perez/291*		
88 The American Nightmare Cody Rhodes/197*		
89 Rhea Ripley/160*		
90 Sami Zayn/150*	6.00	15.00

2022 Panini Instant WWE Autographs Versicolor

STATED PRINT RUN 5 SER.#'d SETS
UNPRICED DUE TO SCARCITY

35 John Cena

36 John Cena
37 John Cena
38 John Cena
39 John Cena
40 John Cena
41 John Cena
42 John Cena
43 John Cena
44 John Cena
45 John Cena
46 John Cena
47 John Cena
48 John Cena
49 John Cena
50 John Cena
51 John Cena

2023 Panini Instant WWE

1 Stacy Keibler/85*
2 Rey Mysterio/71*
3 Ava/163*
4 Indi Hartwell/80*
5 Dragon Lee/137*
6 Alba Fyre & Isla Dawn/79*
7 Carmelo Hayes/88*
8 The Street Profits/84*
9 Seth ìFreakinî Rollins/87*
10 Trish Status, Becky Lynch & Lita/91*
11 Rey Mysterio/87*
12 Rhea Ripley/156*
13 Kevin Owens & Sami Zayn/65*
14 Brock Lesnar/84*
15 Gunther/86*
16 Edge/90*
24 Damian Priest/54*
25 Liv Morgan & Raquel Rodrigeuz/
26 Gunther/
27 John Cena/
28 IYO SKY/
29 Seth Freakiní Rollins/
30 Jimmy & Jey Uso/
31 Tony DíAngelo/
32 Roxanne Perez/
33 Dominik Mysterio/
34 Tiffany Stratton/
35 Carmelo Hayes/
36 ìThe American Nightmareî Cody Rhodes/
37 ìThe American Nightmareî Cody Rhodes & Brock Lesnar/
38 LA Knight/
39 Shayna Baszler/
40 Gunther/
41 Seth ìFreakinî Rollins/
42 Bianca Belair/
43 IYO SKY/
44 Roman Reigns/
45 Jimmy Uso/
46 CM Punk
47 Roman Reigns/
48 The American Nightmare Cody Rhodes/
49 Bayley/
50 Jade Cargill/

2022 Panini Prizm WWE

*GREEN: .5X TO 1.2X BASIC CARDS
*HYPER: .6X TO 1.5X BASIC CARDS
*ICE: .6X TO 1.5X BASIC CARDS
*RW&B: .75X TO 2X BASIC CARDS
*RUBY WAVE: .75X TO 2X BASIC CARDS
*SILVER: 1X TO 2.5X BASIC CARDS
*RED/299: 1.2X TO 3X BASIC CARDS
*BLUE/199: 1.5X TO 4X BASIC CARDS
*PREMIUM BOX/199: 1.5X TO 4X BASIC CARDS
*PURPLE/149: 2X TO 5X BASIC CARDS
*ORANGE/99: 2.5X TO 6X BASIC CARDS
*TEAL/49: 3X TO 8X BASIC CARDS
*GREEN PULSAR/25: UNPRICED DUE TO SCARCITY
*MOJO/25: UNPRICED DUE TO SCARCITY
*WHITE SPARKLE/20: X TO X BASIC CARDS
*BLUE SHIM./10: UNPRICED DUE TO SCARCITY
*GOLD/10: UNPRICED DUE TO SCARCITY
*LUCKY ENV./8: UNPRICED DUE TO SCARCITY
*GOLD SHIM./3: UNPRICED DUE TO SCARCITY
*BLACK/1: UNPRICED DUE TO SCARCITY

1 Dana Brooke .40 1.00
2 Shelton Benjamin .60 1.50
3 Fabian Aichner .50 1.25
4 Von Wagner RC .40 1.00
5 Rikishi .50 1.25
6 Kenny Williams RC .40 1.00
7 AJ Styles 3.00 8.00
8 Mustafa Ali .50 1.25
9 Bianca Belair 1.25 3.00
10 Rick Boogs 1.00 2.50
11 Lita 1.50 4.00
12 Shotzi 1.50 4.00
13 Flash Morgan Webster .50 1.25
14 Wes Lee .40 1.00
15 Jimmy Uso .50 1.25
16 Kofi Kingston 1.00 2.50
17 A-Kid RC .50 1.25
18 Naomi .60 1.50
19 Blair Davenport RC .40 1.00
20 Riddle 1.00 2.50
21 Dave Mastiff .40 1.00
22 Stevie Turner RC .40 1.00
23 Gable Steveson RC 15.00 40.00
24 King Woods .50 1.25
25 Jinny RC .40 1.00
26 Harland RC .40 1.00
27 Akira Tozawa .50 1.25
28 Natalya .60 1.50
29 Bobby Lashley 1.00 2.50
30 Robert Roode .50 1.25
31 Dolph Ziggler .75 2.00
32 T-Bar .40 1.00
33 Goldberg 1.50 4.00
34 Xyon Quinn RC .40 1.00
35 Joe Coffey .40 1.00
36 Lewis Howley RC .40 1.00
37 Alexa Bliss 6.00 15.00
38 Nikki A.S.H. .60 1.50
39 Bron Breakker RC 12.00 30.00
40 Roman Reigns 2.00 5.00
41 Doudrop .60 1.50
42 Teoman RC .40 1.00
43 Grayson Waller RC .40 1.00
44 Queen Zelina .60 1.50
45 John Cena 3.00 8.00
46 Liv Morgan 2.00 5.00
47 Aliyah .75 2.00
48 Odyssey Jones RC 1.00 2.50
49 Cameron Grimes .75 2.00
50 Sam Stoker RC .40 1.00
51 Drew Gulak .50 1.25
52 Shane McMahon 1.25 3.00
53 Ilja Dragunov .40 1.00
54 Amale RC .40 1.00
55 Paul Heyman .75 2.00
56 Madcap Moss .40 1.00
57 Angel .40 1.00
58 Guru Raaj RC .40 1.00
59 Carmella 1.00 2.50
60 Beth Phoenix .75 2.00
61 Duke Hudson RC .40 1.00
62 Tommaso Ciampa 1.00 2.50
63 Io Shirai .75 2.00
64 Angelo Dawkins .50 1.25
65 Joseph Conners RC .40 1.00
66 Mansoor .40 1.00
67 Aoife Valkyrie RC .50 1.25
68 Pete Dunne .75 2.00
69 Cedric Alexander .40 1.00
70 Sarray .50 1.25
71 Elektra Lopez RC .50 1.25
72 Tony D'Angelo RC 1.25 3.00
73 Ivar .40 1.00
74 Apollo Crews .50 1.25
75 Julius Creed RC .40 1.00
76 Mark Andrews .40 1.00
77 Eddie Guerrero 2.00 5.00
78 Randy Orton 1.25 3.00
79 Chad Gable .40 1.00
80 The Great Khali .50 1.25
81 Ikemen Jiro RC .40 1.00
82 Trent Seven .50 1.25
83 Jacy Jayne RC .40 1.00
84 Asuka 1.50 4.00
85 Malcolm Bivens RC .40 1.00
86 Wendy Choo RC .75 2.00
87 Austin Theory 1.50 4.00
88 Raul Mendoza .60 1.50
89 Commander Azeez .50 1.25
90 Jerry Lawler .75 2.00
91 Erik .40 1.00
92 Valentina Feroz RC .60 1.50
93 Ultimate Warrior 2.50 6.00
94 Malik Blade RC .40 1.00
95 Kayden Carter .75 2.00
96 Robert Stone RC .40 1.00
97 Becky Lynch 2.00 5.00
98 Rey Mysterio 1.00 2.50
99 Dakota Kai .75 2.00
100 Shayna Baszler .75 2.00
101 Damian Priest 1.25 3.00
102 Sasha Banks 2.50 6.00
103 Saurav .40 1.00
104 Tiffany Stratton RC .60 1.50
105 James Drake .40 1.00
106 Kay Lee Ray 1.00 2.50
107 Mark Coffey .40 1.00
108 Bayley 1.00 2.50
109 Rampage Brown RC .40 1.00
110 Dani Luna RC .40 1.00
111 Seth Rollins 1.25 3.00
112 The Demon Finn Balor 2.50 6.00
113 Kevin Nash .75 2.00
114 Solo Sikoa RC 1.50 4.00
115 Jack Starz RC .40 1.00
116 Meiko Satomura RC .50 1.25
117 Big E .75 2.00
118 Raquel Gonzalez 1.00 2.50
119 Dante Chen RC .40 1.00
120 Shanky RC .40 1.00
121 Primate RC .40 1.00
122 Tyler Bate .50 1.25
123 Jey Uso .50 1.25
124 Kevin Owens 1.25 3.00
125 Montez Ford .40 1.00
126 Boa .40 1.00
127 Reggie .50 1.25
128 Dexter Lumis .40 1.00
129 Sheamus .60 1.50
130 Gigi Dolin 3.00 8.00
131 Veer Mahaan 1.00 2.50
132 Jinder Mahal .50 1.25
133 Kushida .60 1.50
134 MVP .40 1.00
135 Brock Lesnar 3.00 8.00
136 Rhea Ripley 1.50 4.00
137 Dominik Mysterio .50 1.25
138 Shinsuke Nakamura 1.00 2.50
139 Wild Boar RC .40 1.00
140 Walter 1.00 2.50
141 Joaquin Wilde .60 1.50
142 LA Knight .60 1.50
143 Nash Carter .40 1.00
144 Brutus Creed RC .50 1.25
145 Ricochet .75 2.00
146 Booker T .75 2.00
147 Sonya Deville 1.00 2.50
148 Happy Corbin .50 1.25
149 Wolfgang .40 1.00
150 Joe Gacy RC .40 1.00
151 Lash Legend RC .40 1.00
152 Stacy Keibler 2.00 5.00
153 Candice LeRae 1.25 3.00
154 Ridge Holland .40 1.00
155 Drew McIntyre 1.00 2.50
156 Tamina .50 1.25
157 Humberto .40 1.00
158 Xia Li .75 2.00
159 Bruno Sammartino 1.00 2.50
160 Santos Escobar .60 1.50
161 Noam Dar .50 1.25
162 Carmelo Hayes RC .50 1.25
163 Roderick Strong .60 1.50
164 Edge 2.50 6.00
165 Chyna 2.00 5.00
166 Indi Hartwell 1.25 3.00
167 Zack Gibson .40 1.00
168 Jordan Devlin .40 1.00
169 Mace .40 1.00
170 Omos .75 2.00
171 Cesaro .40 1.00
172 R-Truth .50 1.25
173 Elias .40 1.00
174 The Miz 1.50 4.00
175 Dusty Rhodes 1.00 2.50
176 Zoey Stark .50 1.25
177 Josh Briggs RC .40 1.00
178 Mandy Rose 2.00 5.00
179 Otis .50 1.25
180 Charlotte Flair 2.00 5.00
181 Sami Zayn .60 1.50
182 Emilia McKenzie RC .60 1.50
183 Titus O'Neil .40 1.00
184 Ivy Nile RC .40 1.00
185 Kacy Catanzaro .75 2.00
186 Marcel Barthel .50 1.25
187 Persia Pirotta RC 1.50 4.00
188 Cora Jade RC 6.00 15.00
189 Lacey Evans 1.00 2.50
190 Mick Foley 1.25 3.00
191 The Rock 6.00 15.00
192 Stone Cold Steve Austin 5.00 12.00
193 Undertaker 5.00 12.00
194 Triple H 3.00 8.00
195 Hulk Hogan 2.50 6.00
196 Batista 1.25 3.00
197 Trish Stratus 3.00 8.00
198 Bret "Hit Man" Hart 1.50 4.00
199 Shawn Michaels 1.50 4.00
200 Andre the Giant 2.50 6.00

2022 Panini Prizm WWE Champion Signatures

*GREEN: .5X TO 1.2X BASIC AUTOS
*SILVER: .6X TO 1.5X BASIC AUTOS
*RED/99: .75X TO 2X BASIC AUTOS
*BLUE/49: 1X TO 2.5X BASIC AUTOS
*MOJO/25: UNPRICED DUE TO SCARCITY
*GREEN PULS./25: UNPRICED DUE TO SCARCITY
*PREMIUM BOX/20: UNPRICED DUE TO SCARCITY
*GOLD/10: UNPRICED DUE TO SCARCITY
*BLACK/1: UNPRICED DUE TO SCARCITY
*WHITE SPARKLE/1: UNPRICED DUE TO SCARCITY
RANDOMLY INSERTED INTO PACKS

CSBGE Big E 20.00 50.00
CSBLY Becky Lynch 75.00 200.00
CSCFL Charlotte Flair 60.00 150.00
CSDPS Damian Priest 15.00 40.00
CSHHO Hulk Hogan 300.00 800.00
CSRRS Roman Reigns 200.00 500.00
CSSCA Stone Cold Steve Austin 400.00 800.00
CSSKN Shinsuke Nakamura 15.00 40.00
CSTPH Triple H 250.00 600.00
CSUND Undertaker 500.00 1200.00

2022 Panini Prizm WWE Color Blast

RANDOMLY INSERTED INTO PACKS

1 Brock Lesnar 1000.00 2500.00
2 Charlotte Flair 1000.00 2500.00
3 Roman Reigns 1500.00 4000.00
4 Alexa Bliss 1500.00 4000.00
5 Goldberg 600.00 1500.00
6 Becky Lynch 1000.00 2500.00
7 John Cena 1200.00 3000.00
8 Sasha Banks 750.00 2000.00
9 Big E 750.00 2000.00
10 Bianca Belair 750.00 2000.00

2022 Panini Prizm WWE Fearless

*GREEN: .5X TO 1.2X BASIC CARDS
*SILVER: .6X TO 1.5X BASIC CARDS
*GREEN PULS./25: UNPRICED DUE TO SCARCITY
*MOJO/25: UNPRICED DUE TO SCARCITY
*GOLD/10: UNPRICED DUE TO SCARCITY
*BLACK/1: UNPRICED DUE TO SCARCITY
RANDOMLY INSERTED INTO PACKS

1 Big E 1.25 3.00
2 Asuka 2.50 6.00
3 Shinsuke Nakamura 2.50 6.00
4 Riddle 2.00 5.00
5 Alexa Bliss 10.00 25.00
6 Rhea Ripley 3.00 8.00
7 Edge 2.00 5.00
8 Sasha Banks 5.00 12.00

9 Bayley	2.50	6.00
10 The Miz	1.50	4.00
11 Roman Reigns	5.00	12.00
12 Randy Orton	3.00	8.00
13 The Demon Finn Balor	2.00	5.00
14 Brock Lesnar	3.00	8.00
15 Kofi Kingston	1.25	3.00
16 Bobby Lashley	3.00	8.00
17 AJ Styles	3.00	8.00
18 Drew McIntyre	2.50	6.00
19 Rey Mysterio	1.50	4.00
20 Goldberg	2.50	6.00
21 Charlotte Flair	4.00	10.00
22 Bianca Belair	2.50	6.00
23 John Cena	3.00	8.00
24 Seth Rollins	3.00	8.00
25 Becky Lynch	4.00	10.00

2022 Panini Prizm WWE Iconic Rivals Dual Autographs

*GOLD/10: UNPRICED DUE TO SCARCITY
*BLACK/1: UNPRICED DUE TO SCARCITY
STATED PRINT RUN 25 SER.#'d SETS

IRAC Asuka/C.Flair	625.00	1250.00
IRBA S.Austin/B.Hart	2000.00	4000.00
IRBB B.Lynch/B.Belair	200.00	400.00
IRBC B.Lynch/C.Flair	250.00	500.00
IRBD B.Lashley/D.McIntyre EXCH	100.00	200.00
IRBG B.Lashley/Goldberg EXCH	200.00	400.00
IRCL C.Grimes/LA Knight	60.00	120.00
IRDR D.Kai/R.Gonzalez	75.00	150.00
IRER Edge/R.Orton	250.00	500.00
IRGH Goldberg/H.Hogan	750.00	1500.00
IRIW I.Dragunov/Walter	100.00	200.00
IRJR J.Cena/R.Reigns	1250.00	2500.00
IRKB B.Lesnar/K.Angle	300.00	600.00
IRKS K.Owens/S.Zayn	125.00	250.00
IRMT M.Foley/Triple H	400.00	700.00
IRRJ J.Cena/R.Orton	1500.00	3000.00
IRRU R.Reigns/Undertaker	750.00	1500.00
IRSA S.Austin/S.Michaels	750.00	1500.00
IRSB B.Lesnar/S.Rollins	400.00	700.00
IRST S.Michaels/Triple H	500.00	1000.00

2022 Panini Prizm WWE Legendary Signatures

*GREEN: .5X TO 1.2X BASIC AUTOS
*SILVER: .6X TO 1.5X BASIC AUTOS
*RED/99: .75X TO 2X BASIC AUTOS
*BLUE/49: 1X TO 2.5X BASIC AUTOS
*MOJO/25: UNPRICED DUE TO SCARCITY
*GREEN PULS./25: UNPRICED DUE TO SCARCITY
*GOLD/10: UNPRICED DUE TO SCARCITY
*BLACK/1: UNPRICED DUE TO SCARCITY
*WHITE SPARKLE/1: UNPRICED DUE TO SCARCITY
RANDOMLY INSERTED INTO PACKS

LSBAT Batista EXCH	300.00	600.00
LSBBL Brie Bella	15.00	40.00
LSBHT Bret "Hit Man" Hart	60.00	150.00
LSBKT Booker T	15.00	40.00
LSISH Iron Sheik	30.00	75.00
LSJLW Jerry Lawler	25.00	60.00
LSKAN Kurt Angle	25.00	60.00
LSKNE Kane	50.00	100.00
LSKNS Kevin Nash	50.00	100.00
LSLTA Lita	30.00	75.00
LSMFL Mick Foley	30.00	75.00
LSNBL Nikki Bella EXCH	60.00	120.00
LSRDG Road Dogg	15.00	40.00
LSRKS Rikishi	15.00	40.00
LSSLT Sgt. Slaughter	30.00	75.00
LSSMC Shawn Michaels	125.00	250.00
LSTST Trish Stratus	50.00	125.00

2022 Panini Prizm WWE Next Level

*GREEN: .5X TO 1.2X BASIC CARDS
*SILVER: .6X TO 1.5X BASIC CARDS
*GREEN PULS./25: UNPRICED DUE TO SCARCITY
*MOJO/25: UNPRICED DUE TO SCARCITY
*GOLD/10: UNPRICED DUE TO SCARCITY
*BLACK/1: UNPRICED DUE TO SCARCITY
RANDOMLY INSERTED INTO PACKS

1 The Demon Finn Balor	2.00	5.00
2 Big E	1.25	3.00
3 Bobby Lashley	2.50	6.00
4 Riddle	3.00	8.00
5 Rey Mysterio	2.50	6.00
6 Edge	4.00	10.00
7 Bianca Belair	3.00	8.00
8 Bayley	2.00	5.00
9 Seth Rollins	3.00	8.00
10 Roman Reigns	4.00	10.00
11 Brock Lesnar	4.00	10.00
12 Asuka	3.00	8.00
13 AJ Styles	2.50	6.00
14 Alexa Bliss	6.00	15.00
15 Goldberg	2.50	6.00
16 Sasha Banks	3.00	8.00
17 John Cena	4.00	10.00
18 The Miz	1.25	3.00
19 Becky Lynch	3.00	8.00
20 Randy Orton	2.00	5.00
21 Kofi Kingston	1.25	3.00
22 Shinsuke Nakamura	1.50	4.00
23 Drew McIntyre	2.50	6.00
24 Rhea Ripley	2.50	6.00
25 Charlotte Flair	3.00	8.00

2022 Panini Prizm WWE Prizmatic Entrances

*GREEN: .5X TO 1.2X BASIC CARDS
*SILVER: .6X TO 1.5X BASIC CARDS
*GREEN PULS./25: UNPRICED DUE TO SCARCITY
*MOJO/25: UNPRICED DUE TO SCARCITY
*GOLD/10: UNPRICED DUE TO SCARCITY
*BLACK/1: UNPRICED DUE TO SCARCITY
RANDOMLY INSERTED INTO PACKS

1 Carmella	1.50	4.00
2 Sheamus	1.25	3.00
3 Edge	3.00	8.00
4 Stone Cold Steve Austin	5.00	12.00
5 AJ Styles	1.50	4.00
6 Kane	1.50	4.00
7 Bayley	1.50	4.00
8 Rey Mysterio	2.00	5.00
9 Big E	1.25	3.00
10 Roman Reigns	4.00	10.00
11 Charlotte Flair	3.00	8.00
12 Shinsuke Nakamura	1.50	4.00
13 The Demon Finn Balor	2.50	6.00
14 John Cena	3.00	8.00
15 Alexa Bliss	6.00	15.00
16 Kofi Kingston	1.50	4.00
17 Becky Lynch	3.00	8.00
18 Rhea Ripley	2.00	5.00
19 Bobby Lashley	1.50	4.00
20 Sasha Banks	3.00	8.00
21 Drew McIntyre	2.00	5.00
22 The Miz	1.25	3.00
23 Goldberg	2.50	6.00
24 Undertaker	6.00	15.00
25 Asuka	2.50	6.00
26 Randy Orton	2.00	5.00
27 Bianca Belair	3.00	8.00
28 Riddle	2.50	6.00
29 Brock Lesnar	4.00	10.00
30 Seth Rollins	2.50	6.00

2022 Panini Prizm WWE Sensational Signatures

*GREEN: .6X TO 1.5X BASIC AUTOS
*GREEN PULS./25: UNPRICED DUE TO SCARCITY
*GOLD/10: UNPRICED DUE TO SCARCITY
*BLACK/1: UNPRICED DUE TO SCARCITY
*WHITE SPARKLE/1: UNPRICED DUE TO SCARCITY
RANDOMLY INSERTED INTO PACKS

SSACR Apollo Crews	5.00	12.00
SSADK Angelo Dawkins	5.00	12.00
SSAKD A-Kid	8.00	20.00
SSAML Amale	10.00	25.00
SSATH Austin Theory	30.00	75.00
SSBCR Brutus Creed	10.00	25.00
SSBDV Blair Davenport	10.00	25.00
SSCAZ Commander Azeez	5.00	12.00
SSCGR Cameron Grimes	8.00	20.00
SSCLR Candice LeRae	12.00	30.00
SSCMH Carmelo Hayes	25.00	60.00
SSCSR Cesaro	6.00	15.00
SSDBK Dana Brooke	10.00	25.00
SSDDP Diamond Dallas Page	15.00	40.00
SSDDR Doudrop	12.00	30.00
SSDGL Drew Gulak	5.00	12.00
SSDKI Dakota Kai	15.00	40.00
SSDLM Dexter Lumis	8.00	20.00
SSDMY Dominik Mysterio	10.00	25.00
SSDZG Dolph Ziggler	8.00	20.00
SSELS Elias	8.00	20.00
SSERK Erik	5.00	12.00
SSFAC Fabian Aichner	5.00	12.00
SSGWL Grayson Waller	20.00	50.00
SSHCB Happy Corbin	10.00	25.00
SSIHW Indi Hartwell	15.00	40.00
SSILD Ilja Dragunov	10.00	25.00
SSINL Ivy Nile	25.00	60.00
SSIVR Ivar	5.00	12.00
SSJCR Julius Creed	20.00	50.00
SSJDV Jordan Devlin	12.00	30.00
SSJJN Jacy Jayne	25.00	60.00
SSJMH Jinder Mahal	8.00	20.00
SSJMU Jimmy Uso	10.00	25.00
SSJUS Jey Uso	10.00	25.00
SSKLR Kay Lee Ray	12.00	30.00
SSKOW Kevin Owens	15.00	40.00
SSKSH Kushida	5.00	12.00
SSLAK LA Knight	15.00	40.00
SSLEV Lacey Evans	20.00	50.00
SSLVE Brother Love	15.00	40.00
SSMBT Marcel Barthel	6.00	15.00
SSMSR Mansoor	8.00	20.00
SSMST Meiko Satomura	15.00	40.00
SSMTF Montez Ford	12.00	30.00
SSMVP MVP	6.00	15.00
SSNDR Noam Dar	6.00	15.00
SSNKA Nikki A.S.H.	25.00	60.00
SSNOM Naomi	12.00	30.00
SSNSH Nash Carter	6.00	15.00
SSNTL Natalya	12.00	30.00
SSOJN Odyssey Jones	8.00	20.00
SSOTS Otis	8.00	20.00
SSPDN Pete Dunne	10.00	25.00
SSPGE Paige	100.00	200.00
SSPHE Paul Heyman EXCH	60.00	150.00
SSPPT Persia Pirotta	15.00	40.00
SSRCC Ricochet	12.00	30.00
SSRHL Ridge Holland	8.00	20.00
SSRRD Robert Roode	6.00	15.00
SSRST Roderick Strong	8.00	20.00
SSRVD Rob Van Dam EXCH	50.00	100.00
SSSBG Superstar Billy Graham	30.00	75.00
SSSBZ Shayna Baszler	10.00	25.00
SSSES Santos Escobar	10.00	25.00
SSSHK Shanky	6.00	15.00
SSSRY Sarray	12.00	30.00
SSSZY Sami Zayn	12.00	30.00
SSTBT Tyler Bate	6.00	15.00
SSTCP Tommaso Ciampa	10.00	25.00
SSTDB Ted DiBiase	50.00	100.00
SSTGK The Great Khali EXCH	15.00	40.00
SSTSV Trent Seven	6.00	15.00
SSVMH Veer Mahaan	25.00	60.00
SSVWG Von Wagner	6.00	15.00
SSWLE Wes Lee	6.00	15.00
SSXWD King Woods	12.00	30.00
SSZST Zoey Stark	10.00	25.00
SSZVG Queen Zelina	20.00	50.00

2022 Panini Prizm WWE Superstar Autographs

*GREEN: .5X TO 1.2X BASIC AUTOS
*SILVER: .6X TO 1.5X BASIC AUTOS
*RED/99: .75X TO 2X BASIC AUTOS
*BLUE/49: 1X TO 2.5X BASIC AUTOS
*GREEN PULS./25: UNPRICED DUE TO SCARCITY
*MOJO/25: UNPRICED DUE TO SCARCITY
*GOLD/10: UNPRICED DUE TO SCARCITY
*BLACK/1: UNPRICED DUE TO SCARCITY
*WHITE SPARKLE/1: UNPRICED DUE TO SCARCITY
RANDOMLY INSERTED INTO PACKS

SAABL Alexa Bliss EXCH	125.00	250.00
SAAJS AJ Styles	20.00	50.00
SAASK Asuka	30.00	75.00
SABBK Bron Breakker	250.00	500.00
SABBL Bianca Belair	25.00	60.00
SABLA Bobby Lashley EXCH	25.00	60.00
SABLS Brock Lesnar	125.00	300.00
SABLY Bayley	25.00	60.00
SACJD Cora Jade	75.00	150.00
SACML Carmella	15.00	40.00
SADMT Drew McIntyre	30.00	75.00
SAEDG Edge	30.00	75.00
SAFBL The Demon Finn Balor	30.00	75.00
SAGBG Goldberg	60.00	150.00
SAGGD Gigi Dolin	60.00	120.00
SAGST Gable Steveson	300.00	600.00
SAIDR Ilja Dragunov	10.00	25.00
SAISH Io Shirai	25.00	60.00
SAJCN John Cena	150.00	300.00
SAJGC Joe Gacy	25.00	60.00
SAKCZ Kacy Catanzaro	15.00	40.00
SAKKS Kofi Kingston	25.00	60.00
SALMG Liv Morgan	125.00	250.00
SAMRS Mandy Rose	60.00	120.00
SAOMS Omos	20.00	50.00
SARDL Riddle	30.00	75.00
SARGE Reggie	8.00	20.00
SARKB Rick Boogs	15.00	40.00
SARMS Rey Mysterio	50.00	125.00
SAROR Randy Orton	75.00	150.00
SARQG Raquel Gonzalez	25.00	60.00
SARRP Rhea Ripley	100.00	200.00
SASBK Sasha Banks	125.00	250.00
SASDV Sonya Deville	25.00	60.00
SASHM Sheamus	15.00	40.00
SASHZ Shotzi	25.00	60.00
SASRL Seth Rollins	50.00	100.00
SATMZ The Miz	25.00	60.00
SAWTR Walter	15.00	40.00
SAXLI Xia Li	15.00	40.00

2022 Panini Prizm WWE WWE Gold

*GREEN: .6X TO 1.5X BASIC CARDS
*SILVER: .75X TO 2X BASIC CARDS
*GREEN PULS./25: UNPRICED DUE TO SCARCITY
*MOJO/25: UNPRICED DUE TO SCARCITY
*GOLD/10: UNPRICED DUE TO SCARCITY
*BLACK/1: UNPRICED DUE TO SCARCITY
RANDOMLY INSERTED INTO PACKS

1 Randy Orton	2.50	6.00
2 Drew McIntyre	2.00	5.00
3 Seth Rollins	2.00	5.00
4 Tommaso Ciampa	1.50	4.00
5 The Miz	1.25	3.00
6 Alexa Bliss	15.00	40.00
7 Rey Mysterio	1.50	4.00
8 Sasha Banks	6.00	15.00
9 Triple H	3.00	8.00
10 Big E	1.25	3.00
11 Edge	3.00	8.00
12 Kofi Kingston	2.00	5.00
13 Roman Reigns	5.00	12.00
14 Bayley	2.00	5.00
15 Dolph Ziggler	2.00	5.00
16 Asuka	3.00	8.00
17 Ilja Dragunov	1.25	3.00
18 Charlotte Flair	5.00	12.00
19 Shawn Michaels	3.00	8.00
20 AJ Styles	2.50	6.00

2023 Panini Prizm WWE

*GREEN: .5X TO 1.2X BASIC CARDS
*HYPER: .5X TO 1.2X BASIC CARDS
*ICE: .6X TO 1.5X BASIC CARDS
*BLUE WAVE: .75X TO 2X BASIC CARDS
*RUBY WAVE: .75X TO 2X BASIC CARDS
*SILVER: 1X TO 2.5X BASIC CARDS
*RED/299: 1.2X TO 3X BASIC CARDS
*BLUE:/199: 1.5X TO 4X BASIC CARDS
*PREMIUM BOX/199: 1.5X TO 4X BASIC CARDS
*PURPLE/149: 2X TO 5X BASIC CARDS
*ORANGE/99: 2.5X TO 6X BASIC CARDS
*TEAL/49: 3X TO 8X BASIC CARDS
*GREEN PULS./25: UNPRICED DUE TO SCARCITY
*MOJO/25: UNPRICED DUE TO SCARCITY
*UC BLUE/25: UNPRICED DUE TO SCARCITY
*BLUE SHIM./11: UNPRICED DUE TO SCARCITY

*GOLD/10: UNPRICED DUE TO SCARCITY
*UC GOLD/10: UNPRICED DUE TO SCARCITY
*LUCKY ENV./8: UNPRICED DUE TO SCARCITY
*GOLD SHIM./5: UNPRICED DUE TO SCARCITY
*BLACK/1: UNPRICED DUE TO SCARCITY

1 Cody Rhodes 1.50 4.00
1 Stardust UC SP 6.00 15.00
2 Edris Enofe .40 1.00
3 Luke Gallows .50 1.25
4 Jagger Reid .50 1.25
5 Kofi Kingston .60 1.50
6 Bobby Lashley .75 2.00
7 Mustafa Ali .40 1.00
8 Batista .75 2.00
8 Deacon Batista UC SP 8.00 20.00
9 Rob Van Dam .75 2.00
10 Karl Anderson .50 1.25
11 Tamina .40 1.00
12 Elton Prince .40 1.00
13 Von Wagner .40 1.00
14 Jerry Lawler .75 2.00
15 Liv Morgan 1.50 4.00
16 Solo Sikoa 1.25 3.00
17 Natalya .60 1.50
18 Becky Lynch 1.50 4.00
19 Rowdy Roddy Piper 1.00 2.50
20 Tommaso Ciampa .60 1.50
20 Tommaso Ciampa UC SP 6.00 15.00
21 Candice LeRae 1.00 2.50
22 Fallon Henley .50 1.25
23 Wendy Choo .60 1.50
24 Jimmy Uso .75 2.00
25 Ludwig Kaiser .40 1.00
26 Alba Fyre 1.00 2.50
27 Nikki Cross .60 1.50
28 Bianca Belair 1.25 3.00
29 Roman Reigns 2.00 5.00
30 Cora Jade 1.50 4.00
31 The Miz .60 1.50
32 Gable Steveson .75 2.00
33 Wes Lee .50 1.25
34 Joaquin Wilde .60 1.50
35 Randy Savage 1.25 3.00
36 Aliyah .60 1.50
37 Noam Dar .40 1.00
38 Blair Davenport .60 1.50
39 Roxanne Perez 1.00 2.50
40 Dakota Kai .75 2.00
41 The Rock 2.00 5.00
41 Rocky Maivia UC SP 10.00 25.00
42 Giovanni Vinci .50 1.25
43 Xavier Woods .50 1.25
44 Joe Gacy .50 1.25
45 Malik Blade .40 1.00
46 Andre Chase .40 1.00
47 Omos .50 1.25
48 Scott Steiner .60 1.50
49 Sami Zayn 1.00 2.50
50 Damon Kemp .40 1.00
51 Tiffany Stratton .75 2.00
52 Grayson Waller .60 1.50
53 X-Pac .50 1.25
53 1-2-3 Kid UC SP 5.00 12.00
54 John Cena UC SP 10.00 25.00
54 John Cena 1.50 4.00
55 Mankind .75 2.00
55 Cactus Jack UC SP 6.00 15.00
56 Ava Raine RC 2.50 6.00
57 Zelina Vega .75 2.00
58 Bret Hit Man Hart 1.00 2.50
59 Santos Escobar .40 1.00
60 Dante Chen .40 1.00
61 Top Dolla RC 2.00 5.00
62 Baron Corbin .40 1.00
63 Yokozuna .75 2.00
64 Josh Briggs .40 1.00
65 man.soor .40 1.00
66 Aoife Valkyrie .50 1.25
67 Razor Ramon .75 2.00
67 Scott Hall UC SP 5.00 12.00
68 Brooks Jensen .50 1.25
69 Scarlett 1.50 4.00
70 Dolph Ziggler .50 1.25
71 Triple H 1.00 2.50
71 Hunter Hearst Helmsley UC SP 6.00 15.00
72 Ilja Dragunov .60 1.50
73 Yulisa Leon .40 1.00
74 Mia Yim .75 2.00
75 Matt Riddle 1.00 2.50
76 Arianna Grace RC 2.50 6.00
77 Emma .75 2.00
78 Butch .50 1.25
79 Shawn Michaels 1.50 4.00
80 Doudrop .50 1.25
81 Tyler Bate .50 1.25
82 Isla Dawn .60 1.50
83 Zoey Stark .60 1.50
84 Katana Chance .75 2.00
85 Maxxine Dupri RC 3.00 8.00
86 Ashante Thee Adonis .50 1.25
87 Rick Boogs .40 1.00
88 Carmella .75 2.00
89 Sheamus .60 1.50
90 Duke Hudson .40 1.00
91 Vader .60 1.50
92 Ivy Nile .60 1.50
93 Wolfgang .40 1.00
94 Kevin Owens .75 2.00
95 Montez Ford .60 1.50
96 Austin Theory .75 2.00
97 Ricochet .60 1.50
98 Cedric Alexander .50 1.25
99 Shotzi 1.00 2.50
100 Edge 1.50 4.00
100 Edge UC SP
101 B-Fab RC 2.00 5.00
102 Tatum Paxley RC 2.00 5.00
103 Chad Gable .50 1.25
104 Quincy Elliott .40 1.00
105 Sol Ruca RC 4.00 10.00
106 Humberto .50 1.25
107 R-Truth .40 1.00
108 Karrion Kross .75 2.00
109 Mr. Perfect .75 2.00
110 Joe Coffey .50 1.25
111 Bayley 1.00 2.50
112 Rey Mysterio 1.25 3.00
113 Channing Lorenzo RC 2.00 5.00
114 Terry Funk .50 1.25
115 Eliza Alexander RC 2.00 5.00
116 Indi Hartwell .75 2.00
117 Sanga .40 1.00
118 Kayden Carter .60 1.50
119 AJ Styles 1.00 2.50
120 LA Knight .60 1.50
121 Big E .60 1.50
122 Thea Hail .40 1.00
123 Charlotte Flair 1.25 3.00
124 Meiko Satomura .40 1.00
125 Erik .40 1.00
126 Ivar .40 1.00
127 Sarray .40 1.00
128 Kevin Nash .60 1.50
128 Diesel UC SP
129 Akira Tozawa .50 1.25
130 Mr. T .75 2.00
131 Boa .40 1.00
132 Tony D'Angelo .40 1.00
133 Cruz Del Toro .50 1.25
134 Rhea Ripley 2.00 5.00
135 Elias .50 1.25
135 Ezekiel UC SP
136 IYO SKY 1.00 2.50
137 Seth Rollins 1.00 2.50
138 Kiana James RC 2.50 6.00
139 Alexa Bliss 2.00 5.00
140 Mr. Stone .40 1.00
141 Braun Strowman .60 1.50
142 Trick Williams .40 1.00
143 Damian Priest 1.00 2.50
144 Ricky Steamboat .75 2.00
145 Finn Balor 1.00 2.50
146 Jacy Jayne .75 2.00
147 Shayna Baszler .75 2.00
148 Kit Wilson .40 1.00
149 Amari Miller .50 1.25
150 MVP .50 1.25
151 Brock Lesnar 1.25 3.00
151 Brock Lesnar UC SP
152 The Shockmaster UC SP
152 Typhoon .40 1.00
153 Dana Brooke .40 1.00
154 Ridge Holland .40 1.00
155 Gigi Dolin 1.00 2.50
156 JD McDonagh .50 1.25
157 Bray Wyatt .75 2.00
158 Lacey Evans .75 2.00
159 Andre The Giant 1.50 4.00
160 Nathan Frazer .40 1.00
161 Bron Breakker 1.00 2.50
162 Ultimate Warrior 1.25 3.00
163 Dexter Lumis .50 1.25
164 Rip Fowler .40 1.00
165 The Godfather .50 1.25
165 Papa Shango UC SP
166 Jey Uso .75 2.00
167 Shinsuke Nakamura .60 1.50
168 Mace .40 1.00
169 Angelo Dawkins .40 1.00
170 Nikkita Lyons 1.25 3.00
171 Brutus Creed .40 1.00
172 Undertaker 2.00 5.00
172 Mean Mark Callous UC SP
173 Dominik Mysterio .75 2.00
174 Robert Roode .50 1.25
175 Goldberg 1.00 2.50
176 Jinder Mahal .50 1.25
177 Bubba Ray Dudley .50 1.25
178 Madcap Moss .50 1.25
179 Apollo Crews .40 1.00
180 Oro Mensah .50 1.25
181 Cameron Grimes .50 1.25
182 Valentina Feroz .40 1.00
183 Roderick Strong .50 1.25
184 Drew McIntyre 1.00 2.50
185 Gunther 1.00 2.50
186 Johnny Gargano .75 2.00
186 Johnny Gargano UC SP
187 Sonya Deville .75 2.00
188 Valhalla .40 1.00
189 Asuka 1.50 4.00
190 Otis .40 1.00
191 Carmelo Hayes .60 1.50
192 Raquel Rodriguez 1.25 3.00
193 Eddie Guerrero 1.25 3.00
194 Ronda Rousey 2.00 5.00
195 Hulk Hogan 1.50 4.00
195 Hollywood Hogan UC SP
196 Julius Creed .40 1.00
197 Stone Cold Steve Austin 2.00 5.00
197 Stunning Steve Austin UC SP
198 Mark Coffey .40 1.00
199 Axiom .40 1.00
200 Randy Orton 1.00 2.50
200 Randy Orton UC SP

2023 Panini Prizm WWE Champion Signatures

*GREEN: SAME VALUE AS BASIC
*SILVER: SAME VALUE AS BASIC
*RED/99: .5X TO 1.2X BASIC AUTOS
*BLUE/49: .75X TO 2X BASIC AUTOS
*MOJO/25: UNPRICED DUE TO SCARCITY
*GOLD/10: UNPRICED DUE TO SCARCITY
*GREEN PULS/10: UNPRICED DUE TO SCARCITY
*BLACK/1: UNPRICED DUE TO SCARCITY
*WHITE SPARK/1: UNPRICED DUE TO SCARCITY
RANDOMLY INSERTED INTO PACKS

CSBBK Bron Breakker 20.00 50.00
CSBBL Bianca Belair 15.00 40.00
CSBSM Braun Strowman 12.00 30.00
CSDMI Drew McIntyre 10.00 25.00
CSGTH Gunther 12.00 30.00
CSJMU Jimmy Uso 10.00 25.00
CSJUS Jey Uso 10.00 25.00
CSLVM Liv Morgan 25.00 60.00
CSMIZ The Miz 10.00 25.00
CSRXP Roxanne Perez 30.00 75.00

2023 Panini Prizm WWE Color Blast

RANDOMLY INSERTED INTO PACKS

1 Bray Wyatt 150.00 400.00
2 Bron Breakker 75.00 200.00
3 Edge 100.00 250.00
4 Cody Rhodes 150.00 400.00
5 Undertaker 250.00 600.00
6 Ronda Rousey 125.00 300.00
7 Hulk Hogan 200.00 500.00
8 Roman Reigns 150.00 400.00
9 Triple H 100.00 250.00
10 Randy Orton 125.00 300.00

2023 Panini Prizm WWE Iconic Rivals Dual Autographs

*GOLD/10: UNPRICED DUE TO SCARCITY
*BLACK/1: UNPRICED DUE TO SCARCITY
STATED PRINT RUN 25 SER.#'d SETS

IRAJJ AJ Styles/J.Cena 125.00 300.00
IRBHS B.Hart/HBK 150.00 400.00
IRBTH Batista/HHH 125.00 300.00
IRKNX Kane/X-Pac 60.00 150.00
IRLVR L.Morgan/R.Rousey 125.00 300.00
IRRRD R.Reigns/D.McIntyre 150.00 400.00
IRTCJ T.Ciampa/J.Gargano 30.00 75.00
IRTSL T.Stratus/Lita 150.00 400.00
IRUTM Undertaker/Mankind

2023 Panini Prizm WWE Legendary Signatures

*GREEN: SAME VALUE AS BASIC
*SILVER: SAME VALUE AS BASIC
*RED/99: .5X TO 1.2X BASIC AUTOS
*BLUE/49: .75X TO 2X BASIC AUTOS
*MOJO/25: UNPRICED DUE TO SCARCITY
*GOLD/10: UNPRICED DUE TO SCARCITY
*GREEN PULS/10: UNPRICED DUE TO SCARCITY
*BLACK/1: UNPRICED DUE TO SCARCITY
*WHITE SPARK/1: UNPRICED DUE TO SCARCITY
RANDOMLY INSERTED INTO PACKS

LS Dude Love EXCH
LS Diesel EXCH
LSBHH Bret Hart 20.00 50.00
LSBKT Booker T 12.00 30.00
LSBPX Beth Phoenix 10.00 25.00
LSDDP Diamond Dallas Page 12.00 30.00
LSEBS Eric Bischoff 15.00 40.00
LSGBG Goldberg 30.00 75.00
LSISH Iron Sheik 15.00 40.00
LSJBL JBL EXCH 6.00 15.00
LSKNE Kane 15.00 40.00
LSLTA Lita 15.00 40.00
LSMDM Ted DiBiase 12.00 30.00
LSRKS Rikishi 8.00 20.00
LSSKB Stacy Keibler EXCH 15.00 40.00
LSSML Shawn Michaels 50.00 125.00
LSTST Trish Stratus 25.00 60.00
LSTWL Torrie Wilson 20.00 50.00

2023 Panini Prizm WWE Legends of the Hall

*GREEN: SAME VALUE AS BASIC
*SILVER: SAME VALUE AS BASIC
*GREEN PULS/25: UNPRICED DUE TO SCARCITY
*MOJO/25: UNPRICED DUE TO SCARCITY
*GOLD/10: UNPRICED DUE TO SCARCITY
*BLACK/1: UNPRICED DUE TO SCARCITY
RANDOMLY INSERTED INTO PACKS

1 Kevin Nash .75 2.00
2 Dusty Rhodes 1.25 3.00
3 Kane .60 1.50
4 Ted DiBiase .75 2.00
5 Bruno Sammartino .75 2.00
6 Andre The Giant 2.00 5.00
7 Booker T .60 1.50
8 Rowdy Roddy Piper 1.25 3.00
9 Razor Ramon 1.00 2.50
10 Bret Hart 1.25 3.00
11 Kurt Angle 1.00 2.50
12 Stone Cold Steve Austin 2.50 6.00
13 Rob Van Dam 1.00 2.50
14 Shawn Michaels 2.00 5.00
15 Mick Foley 1.00 2.50
16 Hulk Hogan 2.00 5.00
17 Ultimate Warrior 1.50 4.00
18 Iron Sheik .60 1.50
19 Randy Savage 1.50 4.00

20 Eddie Guerrero	1.50	4.00
21 Goldberg	1.25	3.00
22 Ricky Steamboat	1.00	2.50
23 Undertaker	2.50	6.00
24 Yokozuna	1.00	2.50
25 Trish Stratus	2.00	5.00

2023 Panini Prizm WWE Prizmatic Entrances

*GREEN: SAME VALUE AS BASIC
*SILVER: SAME VALUE AS BASIC
*GREEN PULS/25: UNPRICED DUE TO SCARCITY
*MOJO/25: UNPRICED DUE TO SCARCITY
*GOLD/10: UNPRICED DUE TO SCARCITY
*BLACK/1: UNPRICED DUE TO SCARCITY
RANDOMLY INSERTED INTO PACKS

1 Ultimate Warrior	1.50	4.00
2 Charlotte Flair	1.50	4.00
3 Bianca Belair	1.50	4.00
4 Eddie Guerrero	1.50	4.00
5 Undertaker	2.50	6.00
6 Karrion Kross	1.00	2.50
7 Edge	2.00	5.00
8 Randy Savage	1.50	4.00
9 Cody Rhodes	2.00	5.00
10 The Sandman	.50	1.25
11 Mr. Perfect	1.00	2.50
12 Becky Lynch	2.00	5.00
13 JBL	.50	1.25
14 Ronda Rousey	2.50	6.00
15 Triple H	1.25	3.00
16 Roman Reigns	2.50	6.00
17 Brock Lesnar	1.50	4.00
18 Shawn Michaels	2.00	5.00
19 Stone Cold Steve Austin	2.50	6.00
20 AJ Styles	1.25	3.00

2023 Panini Prizm WWE Ring Royalty

*GREEN: .5X TO 1.2X BASIC CARDS
*SILVER: .6X TO 1.5X BASIC CARDS
*GREEN PULS/25: UNPRICED DUE TO SCARCITY
*MOJO/25: UNPRICED DUE TO SCARCITY
*GOLD/10: UNPRICED DUE TO SCARCITY
*BLACK/1: UNPRICED DUE TO SCARCITY
RANDOMLY INSERTED INTO PACKS

1 Stone Cold Steve Austin	2.50	6.00
2 Wade Barrett	.50	1.25
3 Ted DiBiase	.75	2.00
4 Booker T	.60	1.50
5 Edge	2.00	5.00
6 Xavier Woods	.60	1.50
7 Ken Shamrock	.60	1.50
8 Queen Zelina	1.00	2.50
9 Triple H	1.25	3.00
10 Baron Corbin	.50	1.25
11 Bret Hart	1.25	3.00
12 Sheamus	.75	2.00
13 Randy Savage	1.50	4.00
14 Brock Lesnar	1.50	4.00
15 Kurt Angle	1.00	2.50

2023 Panini Prizm WWE Sensational Signatures

*GREEN: SAME VALUE AS BASIC
*SILVER: SAME VALUE AS BASIC
*RED/99: .5X TO 1.2X BASIC AUTOS
*BLUE/49: .75X TO 2X BASIC AUTOS
*MOJO/25: UNPRICED DUE TO SCARCITY
*GOLD/10: UNPRICED DUE TO SCARCITY
*GREEN PULS/10: UNPRICED DUE TO SCARCITY
*BLACK/1: UNPRICED DUE TO SCARCITY
*WHITE SPARK/1: UNPRICED DUE TO SCARCITY
RANDOMLY INSERTED INTO PACKS

SNACH Andre Chase	6.00	15.00
SNACR Apollo Crews	6.00	15.00
SNAFR Alba Fyre	8.00	20.00
SNAGD Angelo Dawkins	5.00	12.00
SNAGL Angel	5.00	12.00
SNAGR Arianna Grace	12.00	30.00
SNAKT Akira Tozawa	6.00	15.00
SNAML Amari Miller	6.00	15.00
SNASN Al Snow	5.00	12.00
SNAVR Ava Raine	30.00	75.00
SNBBR Bubba Ray Dudley	6.00	15.00
SNBFB B-Fab	6.00	15.00
SNBJN Brooks Jensen	6.00	15.00
SNBKB Brian Knobs	6.00	15.00
SNBWY Bray Wyatt EXCH	60.00	150.00
SNCAL Cedric Alexander	5.00	12.00
SNCDT Cruz Del Toro	5.00	12.00
SNCGR Cameron Grimes	6.00	15.00
SNCHG Chad Gable	5.00	12.00
SNCJD Cora Jade	30.00	75.00
SNCSL Channing "Stacks" Lorenzo	6.00	15.00
SNDBK Dana Brooke EXCH	6.00	15.00
SNDCH Dante Chen	5.00	12.00
SNDFJ Dory Funk Jr.	6.00	15.00
SNDHS Duke Hudson	5.00	12.00
SNDKP Damon Kemp	4.00	10.00
SNDXL Dexter Lumis	10.00	25.00
SNEEF Edris Enofe	6.00	15.00
SNELK Elektra Lopez	10.00	25.00
SNERK Erik	4.00	10.00
SNFHR Fallon Henley	30.00	75.00
SNGGD Gigi Dolin	20.00	50.00
SNGSV Gable Steveson EXCH	8.00	20.00
SNGVC Giovanni Vinci	10.00	25.00
SNHKU Haku	15.00	40.00
SNHMB Humberto	5.00	12.00
SNIJD Ilja Dragunov	8.00	20.00
SNIVR Ivar	4.00	10.00
SNJBR Josh Briggs	5.00	12.00
SNJCJ Jacy Jayne		
SNJGR Juventud Guerrera	6.00	15.00
SNJGR Johnny Gargano	8.00	20.00
SNJRZ Johnny Rodz	4.00	10.00
SNJSG Jerry Sags	6.00	15.00
SNKJN Kiana James	20.00	50.00
SNLAK LA Knight	30.00	75.00
SNLKI Leilani Kai	5.00	12.00
SNLWK Ludwig Kaiser	12.00	30.00
SNMAL Mustafa Ali	4.00	10.00
SNMCE Mace	4.00	10.00
SNMCM Madcap Moss	4.00	10.00
SNMKB Malik Blade	4.00	10.00
SNMSH Mosh	5.00	12.00
SNMVP MVP	6.00	15.00
SNMXI Maxxine Dupri	15.00	40.00
SNNCS Nikki Cross	10.00	25.00
SNNFZ Nathan Frazer	5.00	12.00
SNNKL Nikkita Lyons	40.00	100.00
SNNVA Nova	5.00	12.00
SNRBG Rick Boogs	8.00	20.00
SNRHL Ridge Holland	4.00	10.00
SNRRB Rockin' Robin	5.00	12.00
SNRRD Robert Roode	6.00	15.00
SNRSB Ricky "The Dragon" Steamboat	12.00	30.00
SNRTR R-Truth	10.00	25.00
SNRXP Roxanne Perez	40.00	100.00
SNSDL Spike Dudley	4.00	10.00
SNSDV Sonya Deville	10.00	25.00
SNSGS Sanga	6.00	15.00
SNSHB Shelton Benjamin	6.00	15.00
SNSHM Sheamus	8.00	20.00
SNSHN Shinsuke Nakamura	12.00	30.00
SNSHS Stan Hansen	20.00	50.00
SNSMN The Sandman	12.00	30.00
SNSRS Stevie Richards	5.00	12.00
SNSSK Solo Sikoa	25.00	60.00
SNSTN Mr. Stone	5.00	12.00
SNTBM The Blue Meanie	5.00	12.00
SNTDA Tony D'Angelo	4.00	10.00
SNTDL Top Dolla	6.00	15.00
SNTHL Thea Hail	15.00	40.00
SNTHR Thrasher	5.00	12.00
SNTLG Teddy Long	5.00	12.00
SNTMN Tamina	8.00	20.00
SNTPH Typhoon	8.00	20.00
SNTPR Tom Prichard	6.00	15.00
SNTPX Tatum Paxley	15.00	40.00
SNTRN Terri Runnels	12.00	30.00
SNTSN Tito Santana	10.00	25.00
SNTST Tiffany Stratton	30.00	75.00
SNTWL Trick Williams	20.00	50.00
SNVFR Valentina Feroz		
SNVMH Veer Mahaan	5.00	12.00
SNWCH Wendy Choo	10.00	25.00
SNXWD Xavier Woods	5.00	12.00
SNYLN Yulisa Leon	8.00	20.00

2023 Panini Prizm WWE Superstar Autographs

*GREEN: SAME VALUE AS BASIC
*SILVER: SAME VALUE AS BASIC
*RED/99: .5X TO 1.2X BASIC AUTOS
*BLUE/49: .75X TO 2X BASIC AUTOS
*MOJO/25: UNPRICED DUE TO SCARCITY
*GOLD/10: UNPRICED DUE TO SCARCITY
*GREEN PULS/10: UNPRICED DUE TO SCARCITY
*BLACK/1: UNPRICED DUE TO SCARCITY
*WHITE SPARK/1: UNPRICED DUE TO SCARCITY
RANDOMLY INSERTED INTO PACKS

SAAJS AJ Styles EXCH	15.00	40.00
SAASK Asuka	20.00	50.00
SAATH Austin Theory	8.00	20.00
SAAXB Alexa Bliss	40.00	100.00
SABGE Big E	6.00	15.00
SABLY Becky Lynch	20.00	50.00
SABTC Butch	6.00	15.00
SABYL Bayley	15.00	40.00
SACFL Charlotte Flair EXCH	25.00	60.00
SACML Carmella	10.00	25.00
SACRD Cody Rhodes	60.00	150.00
SADDP Doudrop	10.00	25.00
SADKI Dakota Kai	15.00	40.00
SADMY Dominik Mysterio	25.00	60.00
SADZG Dolph Ziggler	6.00	15.00
SAEDG Edge	20.00	50.00
SAELS Elias	5.00	12.00
SAFBL Finn Balor	10.00	25.00
SAIYO IYO SKY	12.00	30.00
SAJMH Jinder Mahal	5.00	12.00
SAKKG Kofi Kingston	6.00	15.00
SAKKR Karrion Kross	8.00	20.00
SAKOW Kevin Owens	10.00	25.00
SALEV Lacey Evans	12.00	30.00
SAMFD Montez Ford	5.00	12.00
SANTL Natalya	8.00	20.00
SAOMS Omos	5.00	12.00
SAOTS Otis	5.00	12.00
SARCH Ricochet	10.00	25.00
SARDL Matt Riddle EXCH	8.00	20.00
SARMY Rey Mysterio	20.00	50.00
SARRG Raquel Rodriguez	12.00	30.00
SARRP Rhea Ripley	50.00	125.00
SASCL Scarlett	12.00	30.00
SASFR Seth Rollins	15.00	40.00
SASHB Shayna Baszler	8.00	20.00
SASHZ Shotzi	12.00	30.00
SASZN Sami Zayn	8.00	20.00
SATCP Tommaso Ciampa EXCH	6.00	15.00
SAZLV Zelina Vega	12.00	30.00

2023 Panini Prizm WWE Throwback Signatures

*MOJO/25: UNPRICED DUE TO SCARCITY
*GOLD/10: UNPRICED DUE TO SCARCITY
*GREEN PULS/10: UNPRICED DUE TO SCARCITY
*BLACK/1: UNPRICED DUE TO SCARCITY
*WHITE SPARK/1: UNPRICED DUE TO SCARCITY
RANDOMLY INSERTED INTO PACKS

TBBLS Brock Lesnar	50.00	125.00
TBBTS Batista	60.00	150.00
TBHHG Hulk Hogan	125.00	300.00
TBHHH Triple H	60.00	150.00
TBJCN John Cena	50.00	125.00
TBRRN Roman Reigns	75.00	200.00
TBRRS Ronda Rousey	75.00	200.00
TBSCA Stone Cold Steve Austin	200.00	500.00
TBUTK Undertaker	150.00	400.00

2023 Panini Prizm WWE Top Tier

*GREEN: .5X TO 1.2X BASIC CARDS
*SILVER: .6X TO 1.5X BASIC CARDS
*GREEN PULS/25: UNPRICED DUE TO SCARCITY
*MOJO/25: UNPRICED DUE TO SCARCITY
*GOLD/10: UNPRICED DUE TO SCARCITY
*BLACK/1: UNPRICED DUE TO SCARCITY
RANDOMLY INSERTED INTO PACKS

1 Brock Lesnar	2.00	5.00
2 Seth Rollins	1.50	4.00
3 Dolph Ziggler	.75	2.00
4 Austin Theory	1.25	3.00
5 Gunther	1.50	4.00
6 Kevin Owens	1.25	3.00
7 Bobby Lashley	1.25	3.00
8 Roxanne Perez	1.50	4.00
9 Asuka	2.50	6.00
10 Rey Mysterio	2.00	5.00
11 Bron Breakker	1.50	4.00
12 Shinsuke Nakamura	1.00	2.50
13 Drew McIntyre	1.50	4.00
14 Shotzi	1.50	4.00
15 Jey Uso	1.25	3.00
16 Kofi Kingston	1.00	2.50
17 Cody Rhodes	2.50	6.00
18 Natalya	1.00	2.50
19 Bayley	1.50	4.00
20 Rhea Ripley	3.00	8.00
21 Carmella	1.25	3.00
22 The Miz	1.00	2.50
23 Edge	2.50	6.00
24 Johnny Gargano	1.25	3.00
25 Jimmy Uso	1.25	3.00
26 Lacey Evans	1.25	3.00
27 AJ Styles	1.50	4.00
28 Nikkita Lyons	2.00	5.00
29 Becky Lynch	2.50	6.00
30 Roman Reigns	3.00	8.00
31 Charlotte Flair	2.00	5.00
32 Matt Riddle	1.50	4.00
33 Finn Balor	1.50	4.00
34 Braun Strowman	1.00	2.50
35 Karrion Kross	1.25	3.00
36 Liv Morgan	2.50	6.00
37 Alexa Bliss	3.00	8.00
38 Randy Orton	1.50	4.00
39 Bianca Belair	2.00	5.00
40 Ronda Rousey	3.00	8.00

1998 Panini WCW/nWo Photocards

COMPLETE SET (108)	15.00	40.00
1 Goldberg	.50	1.25
2 Goldberg	.50	1.25
3 Goldberg	.50	1.25
4 Goldberg	.50	1.25
5 Goldberg	.50	1.25
6 Goldberg	.50	1.25
7 Goldberg	.50	1.25
8 Goldberg	.50	1.25
9 Goldberg	.50	1.25
10 Goldberg	.50	1.25
11 Goldberg Logo	.50	1.25
12 Goldberg	.50	1.25
13 Goldberg	.50	1.25
14 Goldberg	.50	1.25
15 Goldberg vs. Konnan	.50	1.25
16 Disco Inferno	.12	.30
17 Sting	.50	1.25
18 Sting	.50	1.25
19 Sting	.50	1.25
20 Sting	.50	1.25
21 Sting	.50	1.25
22 Sting Logo	.75	2.00
23 Sting	.50	1.25
24 Sting	.50	1.25
25 Hollywood Hogan	.60	1.50
26 Hollywood Hogan	.60	1.50
27 Hollywood Hogan	.60	1.50
28 Hollywood Hogan Logo	.60	1.50
29 Hollywood Hogan	.60	1.50
30 Hogan vs. Luger	.60	1.50
31 Hollywood Hogan	.60	1.50
32 Ric Flair	.40	1.00
33 Diamond Dallas Page	.30	.75
34 Diamond Dallas Page	.30	.75
35 Dallas Page Logo	.30	.75
36 Diamond Dallas Page	.30	.75
37 Scott Hall	.30	.75
38 Hall vs. Piper	.30	.75
39 Scott Hall	.30	.75

40 Scott Hall .30 .75
41 Kevin Nash .25 .60
42 Kevin Nash .25 .60
43 Kevin Nash Logo .25 .60
44 Kevin Nash .25 .60
45 Macho Man .40 1.00
46 Macho Man Logo .40 1.00
47 Macho Man .40 1.00
48 Macho Man vs. Hart .40 1.00
49 Public Enemy .12 .30
50 Public Enemy .12 .30
51 Lex Luger .20 .50
52 Lex Luger .20 .50
53 Luger vs. Hogan .30 .75
54 Lex Luger .20 .50
55 Lex Luger Logo .20 .50
56 Lex Luger .20 .50
57 Buff Bagwell .12 .30
58 Bagwell vs. Booker T .15 .40
59 Buff Bagwell .12 .30
60 Anvil .15 .40
61 Rick Steiner .15 .40
62 Rick Steiner .15 .40
63 Scott Steiner .15 .40
64 Scott Steiner .15 .40
65 Raven .15 .40
66 Raven Logo .15 .40
67 Raven .15 .40
68 Glacier .12 .30
69 Roddy Piper .40 1.00
70 Piper vs. Hogan .50 1.25
71 Roddy Piper .40 1.00
72 Scott Norton .12 .30
73 Rey Mysterio .30 .75
74 Rey Mysterio Logo .30 .75
75 Chris Benoit .25 .60
76 Benoit vs. Malenko .25 .60
77 Alex Wright .12 .30
78 Alex Wright .12 .30
79 Brian Adams .12 .30
80 Brian Adams .12 .30
81 Guerrero vs Konnan .12 .30
82 Eddie Guerrero .40 1.00
83 Guerrero vs Malenko .40 1.00
84 Wrath .15 .40
85 Chris Jericho .40 1.00
86 Chris Jericho .40 1.00
87 Jericho vs. Wright .40 1.00
88 Chris Jericho .40 1.00
89 Dean Malenko .15 .40
90 Malenko vs. Benoit .15 .40
91 Dean Malenko Logo .15 .40
92 Dean Malenko .15 .40
93 Dragon vs Wright .15 .40
94 Dragon vs Mysterio .25 .60
95 Konnan .20 .50
96 Konnan .20 .50
97 Bret Hart .40 1.00
98 Bret Hart .40 1.00
99 Bret Hart .40 1.00
100 British Bulldog .30 .75
101 Juventud vs Kidman .15 .40
102 Juventud vs Kidman .15 .40
103 Juventud vs Kidman .15 .40
104 Curt Hennig .25 .60
105 Saturn .12 .30
106 Saturn .12 .30
107 Saturn .12 .30
108 Nitro Girls .75 2.00

1999 Panini WCW/nWo Stickers

COMPLETE SET (120) 20.00 50.00
1 Bill Goldberg .60 1.50
2 Kevin Nash .30 .75
3 Diamond Dallas Page .30 .75
4 Hollywood Hogan .60 1.50
5 Ric Flair .50 1.25
6 Nash & Luger Rule! .30 .75
7 Kevin Nash .30 .75
8 Kevin Nash .30 .75
9 Goldberg-Nash Bash!!! .75 2.00
10 Kevin Nash .30 .75
11 Kevin Nash .25 .60
12 Kevin Nash .30 .75
13 Kevin Nash .30 .75
14 Kevin Nash .30 .75
15 Red & Black Attack .25 .60
16 Who's Next? .40 1.00
17 Bill Goldberg .60 1.50
18 Bill Goldberg .60 1.50
19 Bill Goldberg .60 1.50
20 Raven's Wings Are Clipped! .40 1.00
21 A Crushing Headlock On Konnan .40 1.00
22 Goldberg Tattoo .75 2.00
23 Bill Goldberg .60 1.50
24 Bill Goldberg .60 1.50
25 Bill Goldberg .60 1.50
26 Hogan Hands Out A Beating! .60 1.50
27 Hollywood Hogan .60 1.50
28 Hollywood Hogan .60 1.50
29 Hollywood Hogan .60 1.50
30 Hollywood Hogan .60 1.50
31 Hogan And His Buddy Bischoff! .60 1.50
32 No Mercy! .25 .60
33 Hollywood Hogan .60 1.50
34 Hollywood Hogan .60 1.50
35 Hollywood Hogan .60 1.50
36 Ric Flair Struts His Stuff! .50 1.25
37 Horsemen/Arn Anderson .40 1.00
38 Chris Benoit .25 .60
39 Dean Makenko .15 .40
40 Steve McMichael .12 .30
41 Malenko Mauls Benoit! .20 .50
42 Ric Flair Tells It Like It Is... .60 1.50
43 WOOOOOOOOO!!! .50 1.25
44 Ric Flair In Action... .40 1.00
45 Four Horsemen .25 .60
46 Eddie Guerrero .40 1.00
47 Juventud Guerrera .15 .40
48 Rey Mysterio .40 1.00
49 Juventud Jumps Kidman! .15 .40
50 Guerrero Airborne! .40 1.00
51 Eddie Guerrero .40 1.00
52 Hector Garza .12 .30
53 La Parka .12 .30
54 Damian .12 .30
55 Psychosis .12 .30
56 Che, Fyre, and Spice .40 1.00
57 Tigress .40 1.00
58 The Happy Loving Couple... .60 1.50
59 AC Jazz .40 1.00
60 Whisper .40 1.00
61 Alex Wright... .12 .30
62 Kidman Gets Drop... .15 .40
63 Kidman .15 .40
64 Wrath's Guillotine Drop! .12 .30
65 Kidman Hangs Tough! .15 .40
66 Konnan Krushes Eddie Guerrero! .30 .75
67 Konnan .20 .50
68 Whisper .40 1.00
69 British Bulldog .30 .75
70 Disco Inferno .12 .30
71 Van Hammer Slams Alex Wright! .12 .30
72 Booker T. .25 .60
73 Saturn .12 .30
74 Ernest Miller Wrestling... .15 .40
75 Chavo and Pepe .15 .40
76 Diamond Dallas Page .30 .75
77 Diamond Dallas Page .30 .75
78 DDP Has Hart! .40 1.00
79 DDP Gets The Drop On Sting! .40 1.00
80 Diamond Dallas Page .30 .75
81 Bret Hart .40 1.00
82 Hart Gets A Leg up! .40 1.00
83 Hart Puts The Hurt On DDP! .40 1.00
84 DDP Gets Hit By The Hitman! .40 1.00
85 Your Seat Is Ready! .40 1.00
86 Scott Hall .30 .75
87 The Pac In The House! .30 .75
88 Scott Hall .30 .75
89 Scott Hall .30 .75
90 Scott Hall .30 .75
91 Luger Lights It Up! .20 .50
92 Luger's Got A Flair For Winning! .20 .50
93 Lex Luger .20 .50
94 Lex Luger .20 .50
95 Lex Luger .20 .50
96 Big Poppa Pump Pumps It Up! .15 .40
97 Big Poppa Pump Pummels XXX! .15 .40
98 NWO Bad Boy Buff Bagwell! .12 .30
99 Big Poppa Pump Makes His Point! .15 .40
100 Steiner's Super Bod! .15 .40
101 Hollywood Hogan Gets Stung! .40 1.00
102 Sting .50 1.25
103 Scorpion .50 1.25
104 Sting .50 1.25
105 Sting .50 1.25
106 Alex Wright .12 .30
107 Chris Jericho .40 1.00
108 Eric Bischoff .25 .60
109 Scott Norton .12 .30
110 Glacier .12 .30
111 Rick Steiner .15 .40
112 Public Enemy .12 .30
113 Brian Adams .12 .30
114 Bagwell Bags Rick Steiner! .15 .40
115 The Announcers .12 .30
116 Kendall Windham Slam... .12 .30
117 Where The Big Boys Play! .25 .60
118 Raven At Rest! .15 .40
119 Wright Or Wrong? .12 .30
120 Anvil!!! (Bam Bam Bigelow) .20 .50

2015 Panini WWE Action Cards

1 RAW LOGO .20 .50
2 John Cena 1.25 3.00
3 SmackDown LOGO .20 .50
4 Brock Lesnar 1.00 2.50
5 WWE LOGO .20 .50
6 Randy Orton 1.00 2.50
7 Total Divas LOGO .20 .50
8 Paige RC 1.25 3.00
9 NXT LOGO .20 .50
10 John Cena 1.25 3.00
11 John Cena 1.25 3.00
12 John Cena 1.25 3.00
13 John Cena 1.25 3.00
14 John Cena 1.25 3.00
15 John Cena 1.25 3.00
16 John Cena 1.25 3.00
17 John Cena 1.25 3.00
18 John Cena 1.25 3.00
19 Daniel Bryan 1.00 2.50
20 Daniel Bryan 1.00 2.50
21 Daniel Bryan 1.00 2.50
22 Dean Ambrose .60 1.50
23 Dean Ambrose .60 1.50
24 Dean Ambrose .60 1.50
25 Sheamus .60 1.50
26 Sheamus .60 1.50
27 Sheamus .60 1.50
28 Chris Jericho .60 1.50
29 Chris Jericho .60 1.50
30 Chris Jericho .60 1.50
31 Randy Orton 1.00 2.50
32 Randy Orton 1.00 2.50
33 Randy Orton 1.00 2.50
34 Dolph Ziggler .40 1.00
35 Dolph Ziggler .40 1.00
36 Dolph Ziggler .40 1.00
37 The Miz .40 1.00
38 The Miz .40 1.00
39 The Miz .40 1.00
40 Kofi Kingston .25 .60
41 Kofi Kingston .25 .60
42 Kofi Kingston .25 .60
43 Roman Reigns .60 1.50
44 Roman Reigns .60 1.50
45 Roman Reigns .60 1.50
46 Big E .40 1.00
47 Xavier Woods .40 1.00
48 Erick Rowan .40 1.00
49 R-Truth .25 .60
50 Jack Swagger .40 1.00
51 Zack Ryder .25 .60
52 Ryback .25 .60
53 Darren Young .25 .60
54 Sin Cara .40 1.00
55 Bray Wyatt 1.00 2.50
56 Bray Wyatt 1.00 2.50
57 Bray Wyatt 1.00 2.50
58 King Barrett .25 .60
59 King Barrett .25 .60
60 King Barrett .25 .60
61 Rusev .60 1.50
62 Rusev .60 1.50
63 Rusev .60 1.50
64 Cesaro .25 .60
65 Cesaro .25 .60
66 Cesaro .25 .60
67 Big Show .60 1.50
68 Big Show .60 1.50
69 Big Show .60 1.50
70 Seth Rollins .40 1.00
71 Seth Rollins .40 1.00
72 Seth Rollins .40 1.00
73 Luke Harper .40 1.00
74 Mark Henry .40 1.00
75 Adam Rose .30 .75
76 Titus O'Neil .25 .60
77 Curtis Axel .25 .60
78 Bo Dallas .25 .60
79 Heath Slater .25 .60
80 David Otunga .25 .60
81 Tyson Kidd .25 .60
82 Kevin Owens .75 2.00
83 Macho Mandow .25 .60
84 Fandango .25 .60
85 Christian .25 .60
86 Paul Heyman .25 .60
87 Zeb Colter .40 1.00
88 Stephanie McMahon .40 1.00
89 Triple H 1.00 2.50
90 J&J Security .25 .60
91 Goldust .25 .60
92 Stardust .25 .60
93 Hornswoggle .40 1.00
94 Jey Uso .25 .60
95 Jimmy Uso .25 .60
96 The Usos .25 .60
97 Diego .25 .60
98 Fernando .25 .60
99 El Torito .25 .60
100 Brock Lesnar 1.00 2.50
101 Brock Lesnar 1.00 2.50
102 Brock Lesnar 1.00 2.50
103 The Rock 1.25 3.00
104 The Rock 1.25 3.00
105 The Rock 1.25 3.00
106 Batista .60 1.50
107 Batista .60 1.50
108 Batista .60 1.50
109 Undertaker 1.00 2.50
110 Undertaker 1.00 2.50
111 Undertaker 1.00 2.50
112 Kane .60 1.50
113 Kane .60 1.50
114 Kane .60 1.50
115 Sting .60 1.50
116 Sting .60 1.50
117 Sting .60 1.50
118 Nikki Bella .75 2.00
119 Brie Bella .75 2.00
120 The Bella Twins .75 2.00
121 Natalya .75 2.00
122 Natalya .75 2.00
123 Natalya .75 2.00
124 Paige 1.25 3.00
125 Emma .40 1.00
126 Naomi .40 1.00
127 Alicia Fox .50 1.25
128 Cameron .40 1.00
129 Eva Marie 1.00 2.50
130 Charlotte .75 2.00
131 Rosa Mendes .40 1.00
132 Summer Rae 1.00 2.50
133 Tamina .40 1.00
134 Lana 1.00 2.50
135 Sasha Banks .50 1.25
136 Michael Cole .25 .60
137 JBL .25 .60
138 Lilian Garcia .60 1.50
139 Jerry "The King" Lawler .40 1.00
140 Jerry "The King" Lawler .40 1.00
141 Renee Young 1.00 2.50
142 Howard Finkel .25 .60
143 Gene Okerlund .30 .75
144 Tony Chimel .25 .60
145 Ric Flair 1.25 3.00

#	Card	Low	High
146	Roman Reigns	.60	1.50
147	Santino Marella	.25	.60
148	WWE Tag Team Championship	.20	.50
149	WWE World Heavyweight Championship	.20	.50
150	United States Championship	.20	.50
151	Trish Stratus	1.25	3.00
152	Trish Stratus	1.25	3.00
153	Lita	1.00	2.50
154	Stone Cold Steve Austin	1.25	3.00
155	Stone Cold Steve Austin	1.25	3.00
156	Stone Cold Steve Austin	1.25	3.00
157	Triple H	1.00	2.50
158	Triple H	1.00	2.50
159	Triple H	1.00	2.50
160	Edge	.60	1.50
161	Edge	.60	1.50
162	Edge	.60	1.50
163	Ultimate Warrior	.75	2.00
164	Ultimate Warrior	.75	2.00
165	Ultimate Warrior	.75	2.00
166	Bret "Hit Man" Hart	.75	2.00
167	Bret "Hit Man" Hart	.75	2.00
168	Bret "Hit Man" Hart	.75	2.00
169	Shawn Michaels	1.00	2.50
170	Shawn Michaels	1.00	2.50
171	Shawn Michaels	1.00	2.50
172	Rowdy Roddy Piper	.75	2.00
173	Jake "The Snake" Roberts	.40	1.00
174	British Bulldog	.40	1.00
175	Ted DiBiase	.40	1.00
176	Mr. Perfect	.40	1.00
177	Yokozuna	.40	1.00
178	Big Boss Man	.25	.60
179	Ric Flair	1.25	3.00
180	Sgt. Slaughter	.40	1.00

2022 Panini WWE Debut Edition

*RED: .75X TO 2X BASIC CARDS
*GREEN: 1.2X TO 3X BASIC CARDS
*GOLD: 2X TO 5X BASIC CARDS

#	Card	Low	High
1	Ivar	.30	.75
2	AJ Styles	1.00	2.50
3	Rick Boogs	.40	1.00
4	Damian Priest	.60	1.50
5	Naomi	.50	1.25
6	Otis	.40	1.00
7	Lacey Evans	.75	2.00
8	Veer Mahaan	.75	2.00
9	Santos Escobar	.50	1.25
10	Rhea Ripley	1.00	2.50
11	Jey Uso	.40	1.00
12	Akira Tozawa	.40	1.00
13	Ricochet	.60	1.50
14	Dolph Ziggler	.60	1.50
15	Natalya	.50	1.25
16	Randy Orton	.75	2.00
17	Carmelo Hayes RC	.40	1.00
18	Alexa Bliss	2.00	5.00
19	Cora Jade RC	2.50	6.00
20	Tamina	.40	1.00
21	Jimmy Uso	.40	1.00
22	Angelo Dawkins	.40	1.00
23	Ridge Holland	.30	.75
24	Dominik Mysterio	.40	1.00
25	Sasha Banks	2.00	5.00
26	Reggie	.40	1.00
27	Fabian Aichner	.40	1.00
28	Becky Lynch	1.25	3.00
29	Gigi Dolin	1.25	3.00
30	Angel	.30	.75
31	Jinder Mahal	.40	1.00
32	Apollo Crews	.40	1.00
33	Roman Reigns	2.00	5.00
34	Edge	1.25	3.00
35	Shayna Baszler	.60	1.50
36	Rey Mysterio	.75	2.00
37	Marcel Barthel	.40	1.00
38	Bianca Belair	1.00	2.50
39	Mandy Rose	1.50	4.00
40	Brock Lesnar	1.50	4.00
41	King Woods	.40	1.00
42	Austin Theory	.75	2.00
43	Sami Zayn	.50	1.25
44	Finn Balor	.75	2.00
45	Shotzi	1.25	3.00
46	Robert Roode	.40	1.00
47	Roderick Strong	.50	1.25
48	Carmella	.75	2.00
49	Raquel Gonzalez	.75	2.00
50	Solo Sikoa RC	2.00	5.00
51	Kofi Kingston	.75	2.00
52	Big E	.60	1.50
53	Shanky RC	.30	.75
54	Kevin Owens	.60	1.50
55	Tiffany Stratton RC	.50	1.25
56	Riddle	.75	2.00
57	Tommaso Ciampa	.75	2.00
58	Dana Brooke	.30	.75
59	Ikja Dragunov	.30	.75
60	Drew Gulak	.40	1.00
61	Mace	.30	.75
62	Bobby Lashley	.60	1.50
63	Sheamus	.50	1.25
64	The Miz	.50	1.25
65	Xia Li	.60	1.50
66	R-Truth	.40	1.00
67	Maryse	.50	1.25
68	Doudrop	.50	1.25
69	Meiko Satomura RC	1.00	2.50
70	Drew McIntyre	.60	1.50
71	Madcap Moss	.30	.75
72	Cedric Alexander	.30	.75
73	Shinsuke Nakamura	.75	2.00
74	Montez Ford	.30	.75
75	Asuka	1.25	3.00
76	Seth Rollins	.75	2.00
77	Bron Breakker RC	2.50	6.00
78	Liv Morgan	1.50	4.00
79	Trent Seven	.40	1.00
80	Erik	.30	.75
81	Mansoor	.30	.75
82	Chad Gable	.30	.75
83	Aliyah	.60	1.50
84	MVP	.30	.75
85	Bayley	.75	2.00
86	Shelton Benjamin	.50	1.25
87	Dexter Lumis	.30	.75
88	Nikki A.S.H.	.50	1.25
89	Tyler Bate	.40	1.00
90	Happy Corbin	.40	1.00
91	Jacy Jayne RC	1.50	4.00
92	Commander Azeez	.40	1.00
93	Charlotte Flair	1.25	3.00
94	Omos	.60	1.50
95	John Cena	1.00	2.50
96	T-Bar	.30	.75
97	Joe Gacy RC	.75	2.00
98	Queen Zelina	.50	1.25
99	Noam Dar	.40	1.00
100	Humberto	.30	.75
101	Humberto L	.30	.75
102	Dusty Rhodes L	.75	2.00
103	Terry Funk L	.50	1.25
104	The Great Khali L	.40	1.00
105	Undertaker L	1.50	4.00
106	Jerry Lawler L	.60	1.50
107	Mick Foley L	.60	1.50
108	Batista L	.60	1.50
109	Rob Van Dam L	.60	1.50
110	Bret Hit Man Hart L	.75	2.00
111	Shawn Michaels L	1.25	3.00
112	Eddie Guerrero L	1.00	2.50
113	Triple H L	1.25	3.00
114	Hulk Hogan L	1.50	4.00
115	Vader L	.40	1.00
116	Diesel L	.50	1.25
117	Nikki Bella L	.75	2.00
118	Beth Phoenix L	.60	1.50
119	The Rock L	3.00	8.00
120	Brie Bella L	.60	1.50
121	Stacy Keibler L	1.00	2.50
122	The Godfather L	.30	.75
123	Ultimate Warrior L	1.25	3.00
124	Iron Sheik L	.40	1.00
125	X-Pac L	.40	1.00
126	Lex Luger L	.40	1.00
127	Rikishi L	.40	1.00
128	Big John Studd L	.30	.75
129	Ron Simmons L	.40	1.00
130	Bruno Sammartino L	.75	2.00
131	Stone Cold Steve Austin L	1.50	4.00
132	Goldberg L	1.25	3.00
133	Trish Stratus L	1.50	4.00
134	John Bradshaw Layfield L	.30	.75
135	Yokozuna L	.40	1.00
136	Macho Man Randy Savage L	1.25	3.00
137	Road Dogg L	.40	1.00
138	Booker T L	.60	1.50
139	Rowdy Roddy Piper L	.75	2.00
140	Chyna L	.60	1.50
141	Ted DiBiase CH	.50	1.25
142	Brock Lesnar CH	1.50	4.00
143	Big E CH	.60	1.50
144	John Cena CH	1.00	2.50
145	Damian Priest CH	.60	1.50
146	Edge CH	1.25	3.00
147	Charlotte Flair CH	1.25	3.00
148	Stone Cold Steve Austin L	1.50	4.00
149	Tommaso Ciampa CH	.75	2.00
150	Hulk Hogan CH	1.50	4.00
151	Ilja Dragunov CH	.30	.75
152	Triple H CH	1.25	3.00
153	Becky Lynch CH	1.25	3.00
154	Randy Orton CH	.75	2.00
155	Roman Reigns CH	2.00	5.00
156	The Rock CH	3.00	8.00
157	Shinsuke Nakamura CH	.75	2.00
158	Undertaker CH	1.50	4.00
159	Mandy Rose CH	1.50	4.00
160	Bret Hit Man Hart CH	.75	2.00

2022 Panini WWE NXT

*GREEN: .5X TO 1.2X BASIC CARDS
*SILVER: .5X TO 1.2X BASIC CARDS
*RED/199: .6X TO 1.5X BASIC CARDS
*BLUE/149: .75X TO 2X BASIC CARDS
*PURPLE/99: 1.2X TO 3X BASIC CARDS
*BLACK&GOLD/75: 1.2X TO 3X BASIC CARDS
*TEAL/49: 1.5X TO 4X BASIC CARDS
*2.0/25: UNPRICED DUE TO SCARCITY
*GOLD/10: UNPRICED DUE TO SCARCITY
*BLACK/1: UNPRICED DUE TO SCARCITY

#	Card	Low	High
1	Sanga	.30	.75
2	Tyler Bate	.40	1.00
3	Fallon Henley RC	.30	.75
4	Alba Fyre	.75	2.00
5	Andre Chase RC	.30	.75
6	Zoey Stark	.40	1.00
7	Giovanni Vinci	.40	1.00
8	Xia Brookside RC	2.00	5.00
9	Jack Starz RC	.30	.75
10	Mark Andrews	.30	.75
11	Solo Sikoa RC	1.50	4.00
12	Wolfgang	.30	.75
13	Cora Jade RC	3.00	8.00
14	Kayden Carter	.60	1.50
15	Boa	.30	.75
16	Tiger Turan RC	.30	.75
17	Grayson Waller RC	.75	2.00
18	A-Kid RC	1.25	3.00
19	Oliver Carter RC	.30	.75
20	Mark Coffey	.30	.75
21	Nathan Frazer RC	.30	.75
22	Dani Luna RC	1.25	3.00
23	Damon Kemp RC	.30	.75
24	Lash Legend RC	1.00	2.50
25	Bron Breakker RC	1.50	4.00
26	Santos Escobar	.50	1.25
27	Ashton Smith RC	.40	1.00
28	Dave Mastiff	.30	.75
29	Malik Blade RC	.30	.75
30	Noam Dar	.40	1.00
31	Tony D'Angelo RC	1.00	2.50
32	Emilia McKenzie RC	1.00	2.50
33	Elektra Lopez RC	1.25	3.00
34	Mandy Rose	2.00	5.00
35	Brooks Jensen RC	1.25	3.00
36	Amale RC	.30	.75
37	Charlie Dempsey RC	.30	.75
38	Eddie Dennis RC	.30	.75
39	Sam Gradwell RC	.30	.75
40	Rampage Brown RC	.30	.75
41	Trick Williams RC	.30	.75
42	Stevie Turner RC	.75	2.00
43	Gigi Dolin	2.00	5.00
44	Aleah James RC	.75	2.00
45	Brutus Creed RC	1.25	3.00
46	Aoife Valkyrie RC	.60	1.50
47	Ikemen Jiro RC	.30	.75
48	Flash Morgan Webster	.40	1.00
49	Roxanne Perez RC	2.50	6.00
50	Kit Wilson RC	.30	.75
51	Von Wagner RC	.30	.75
52	Wild Boar RC	.30	.75
53	Indi Hartwell	1.00	2.50
54	Bodhi Hayward RC	.40	1.00
55	Carmelo Hayes RC	.40	1.00
56	Blair Davenport RC	1.25	3.00
57	James Drake	.30	.75
58	Ilja Dragunov	.30	.75
59	Odyssey Jones RC	.30	.75
60	Saxon Huxley RC	.30	.75
61	Wes Lee	.30	.75
62	Primate RC	.30	.75
63	Io Shirai	.60	1.50
64	Sarray	.40	1.00
65	Cameron Grimes	.60	1.50
66	Isla Dawn RC	.40	1.00
67	Joaquin Wilde	.50	1.25
68	Joe Coffey	.30	.75
69	Nikkita Lyons RC	2.50	6.00
70	Sha Samuels RC	.30	.75
71	Xyon Quinn RC	1.50	4.00
72	Roderick Strong	.50	1.25
73	Ivy Nile RC	.30	.75
74	Tiffany Stratton RC	1.50	4.00
75	Dante Chen RC	.30	.75
76	Jinny RC	.30	.75
77	Joe Gacy RC	.75	2.00
78	Jordan Devlin	.30	.75
79	Cruz Del Toro	.50	1.25
80	Teoman RC	.30	.75
81	Zack Gibson	.30	.75
82	Edris Enofe RC	.30	.75
83	Jacy Jayne RC	1.50	4.00
84	Valentina Feroz RC	.50	1.25
85	T-Bone RC	.30	.75
86	Meiko Satomura RC	1.00	2.50
87	Josh Briggs RC	.30	.75
88	Kenny Williams RC	.30	.75
89	Robert Stone RC	.30	.75
90	Trent Seven	.40	1.00
91	Amari Miller RC	.30	.75
92	Yulisa Leon RC	.30	.75
93	Katana Chance	.60	1.50
94	Wendy Choo RC	.60	1.50
95	Duke Hudson RC	.30	.75
96	Nina Samuels	.40	1.00
97	Julius Creed RC	.75	2.00
98	Elton Prince RC	.40	1.00
99	Johnny Saint RC	.30	.75
100	Triple H	1.25	3.00
101	Kevin Owens	.60	1.50
102	Bianca Belair	1.00	2.50
103	Drew McIntyre	.60	1.50
104	Montez Ford	.30	.75
105	Bayley	.75	2.00
106	Apollo Crews	.40	1.00
107	Seth Freakin Rollins	.75	2.00
108	Charlotte Flair	1.25	3.00
109	Big E	.60	1.50
110	Shayna Baszler	.60	1.50
111	Finn Balor	.75	2.00
112	Damian Priest	.60	1.50
113	Alexa Bliss	2.00	5.00
114	Angelo Dawkins	.40	1.00
115	Becky Lynch	1.25	3.00
116	Asuka	1.25	3.00
117	Tyler Breeze	.30	.75
118	Otis	.40	1.00
119	Sami Zayn	.50	1.25
120	Ricochet	.60	1.50
121	Shinsuke Nakamura	.75	2.00
122	Chad Gable	.30	.75
123	Rhea Ripley	1.00	2.50
124	Roman Reigns	2.00	5.00
125	Corey Graves	.30	.75

2022 Panini WWE NXT All-Time Highlights

*GREEN: .5X TO 1.2X BASIC CARDS
*SILVER: .5X TO 1.2X BASIC CARDS
*BLACK&GOLD/75: .75X TO 2X BASIC CARDS
*2.0/25: UNPRICED DUE TO SCARCITY
*GOLD/10: UNPRICED DUE TO SCARCITY
*BLACK/1: UNPRICED DUE TO SCARCITY
RANDOMLY INSERTED INTO PACKS

1 Seth Freakin Rollins	1.25	3.00
2 Big E	1.00	2.50
3 Tyler Breeze	.50	1.25
4 Shayna Baszler	1.00	2.50
5 Charlotte Flair	2.00	5.00
6 Charlotte Flair	2.00	5.00
7 Sami Zayn	.75	2.00
8 The Demon Finn Balor	1.25	3.00
9 Tyler Bate	.60	1.50
10 Kevin Owens	1.00	2.50
11 Pete Dunne	1.00	2.50
12 WALTER	1.25	3.00
13 The Demon Finn Balor	1.25	3.00
14 Bayley	1.25	3.00
15 The Demon Finn Balor	1.25	3.00
16 Asuka	2.00	5.00
17 Bayley	1.25	3.00
18 Bayley	1.25	3.00
19 The Demon Finn Balor	1.25	3.00
20 Shinsuke Nakamura	1.25	3.00
21 Asuka	2.00	5.00
22 Asuka	2.00	5.00
23 Shinsuke Nakamura	1.25	3.00
24 Asuka	2.00	5.00
25 Shinsuke Nakamura	1.25	3.00

2022 Panini WWE NXT Alumni Signatures

*GREEN: .5X TO 1.2X BASIC AUTOS
*RED/49: .6X TO 1.5X BASIC AUTOS
*2.0/25: UNPRICED DUE TO SCARCITY
*BLACK&GOLD/25: UNPRICED DUE TO SCARCITY
*GOLD/10: UNPRICED DUE TO SCARCITY
*BLACK/1: UNPRICED DUE TO SCARCITY
RANDOMLY INSERTED INTO PACKS

ASABS Alexa Bliss	75.00	200.00
ASACR Apollo Crews	6.00	15.00
ASASK Asuka	15.00	40.00
ASBBL Bianca Belair	15.00	40.00
ASBGE Big E	8.00	20.00
ASBLN Becky Lynch	50.00	125.00
ASBLY Bayley	15.00	40.00
ASCFL Charlotte Flair EXCH	25.00	60.00
ASCML Carmella	15.00	40.00
ASDMI Drew McIntyre	12.00	30.00
ASFBL Finn Balor	12.00	30.00
ASKOW Kevin Owens	15.00	40.00
ASLVM Liv Morgan	50.00	125.00
ASPGE Paige EXCH	60.00	150.00
ASRRN Roman Reigns	50.00	125.00
ASSBZ Shayna Baszler	10.00	25.00
ASSNK Shinsuke Nakamura	10.00	25.00
ASSRL Seth Freakin Rollins	20.00	50.00
ASSZY Sami Zayn	8.00	20.00

2022 Panini WWE NXT Dual Autographs

*GOLD/10: UNPRICED DUE TO SCARCITY
*BLACK/1: UNPRICED DUE TO SCARCITY
STATED PRINT RUN 25 SER.#'d SETS

DAAJG AJ Styles/G.Waller		
DABSE B.Breakker/S.Escobar	60.00	150.00
DABTC B.Breakker/T.Ciampa	50.00	125.00
DACGL C.Grimes/LA Knight	20.00	50.00
DACRD B.Creed/J.Creed	60.00	150.00
DAGLS M.Coffey/Wolfgang		
DAGYV J.Drake/Z.Gibson	15.00	40.00
DAIMP F.Aichner/M.Barthel		
DAIZS Io Shirai/Z.Stark	40.00	100.00
DAKCK K.Catanzaro/K.Carter	30.00	75.00
DAKWE K.Wilson/E.Prince	30.00	75.00
DAMBD M.Satomura/B.Davenport	50.00	125.00
DAMRG M.Rose/R.Gonzalez		
DATSB T.Seven/T.Bate	25.00	60.00
DATXC G.Dolin/J.Jayne	125.00	300.00

2022 Panini WWE NXT Gold Inserts

*GREEN: .5X TO 1.2X BASIC CARDS
*SILVER: .5X TO 1.2X BASIC CARDS
*BLACK&GOLD/75: .75X TO 2X BASIC CARDS
*2.0/25: UNPRICED DUE TO SCARCITY
*GOLD/10: UNPRICED DUE TO SCARCITY
*BLACK/1: UNPRICED DUE TO SCARCITY
RANDOMLY INSERTED INTO PACKS

1 Drew McIntyre	1.25	3.00
2 Raquel Rodriguez	1.50	4.00
3 Trent Seven	.75	2.00
4 Gigi Dolin	2.50	6.00
5 Roderick Strong	1.00	2.50
6 Charlotte Flair	2.50	6.00
7 Seth Freakin Rollins	1.50	4.00
8 Bayley	1.50	4.00
9 Finn Balor	1.50	4.00
10 Shayna Baszler	1.25	3.00
11 Bron Breakker	2.50	6.00
12 Tyler Bate	.75	2.00
13 Fabian Aichner	.75	2.00
14 Jacy Jayne	1.50	4.00
15 Ilja Dragunov	.60	1.50
16 Io Shirai	1.25	3.00
17 Kevin Owens	1.25	3.00
18 Asuka	2.50	6.00
19 Shinsuke Nakamura	1.50	4.00
20 Mandy Rose	3.00	8.00
21 Carmelo Hayes	.75	2.00
22 Ciampa	1.50	4.00
23 Ludwig Kaiser	.75	2.00
24 Corey Graves	.60	1.50
25 Dolph Ziggler	1.25	3.00

2022 Panini WWE NXT Highlights

*GREEN: .5X TO 1.2X BASIC CARDS
*SILVER: .5X TO 1.2X BASIC CARDS
*BLACK&GOLD/75: .75X TO 2X BASIC CARDS
*2.0/25: UNPRICED DUE TO SCARCITY
*GOLD/10: UNPRICED DUE TO SCARCITY
*BLACK/1: UNPRICED DUE TO SCARCITY
RANDOMLY INSERTED INTO PACKS

1 Santos Escobar	.60	1.50
2 Raquel Rodriguez	1.00	2.50
3 Finn Balor	1.00	2.50
4 Santos Escobar	.60	1.50
5 Io Shirai	.75	2.00
6 Finn Balor	1.00	2.50
7 Io Shirai	.75	2.00
8 LA Knight	.60	1.50
9 Pete Dunne	.75	2.00
10 WALTER	1.00	2.50
11 Raquel Rodriguez	1.00	2.50
12 Santos Escobar	.60	1.50
13 Kushida	.60	1.50
14 Sarray	.50	1.25
15 Indi Hartwell/Candice LeRae	1.25	3.00
16 Raquel Rodriguez	1.00	2.50
17 Kushida	.60	1.50
18 Kushida	.60	1.50
19 LA Knight	.60	1.50
20 Raquel Rodriguez	1.00	2.50
21 Kushida	.60	1.50
22 Io Shirai/Zoey Stark	.75	2.00
23 Raquel Rodriguez	1.00	2.50
24 Cameron Grimes	.75	2.00
25 Raquel Rodriguez	1.00	2.50
26 Bron Breakker	1.50	4.00
27 Ciampa	1.00	2.50
28 Roderick Strong	.60	1.50
29 Raquel Rodriguez	1.00	2.50
30 Carmelo Hayes	.50	1.25
31 Jacy Jayne/Gigi Dolin	1.50	4.00
32 Mandy Rose	2.00	5.00
33 Fabian Aichner/Ludwig Kaiser	.50	1.25
34 Ciampa	1.00	2.50
35 Solo Sikoa	1.00	2.50
36 Carmelo Hayes	.50	1.25
37 Cora Jade	1.25	3.00
38 Fabian Aichner/Ludwig Kaiser	.50	1.25
39 Cameron Grimes	.75	2.00
40 Bron Breakker	1.50	4.00
41 Cameron Grimes	.75	2.00
42 Meiko Satomura	1.25	3.00
43 Raquel Rodriguez	1.00	2.50
44 WALTER	1.00	2.50
45 Tyler Bate	.50	1.25
46 Meiko Satomura	1.25	3.00
47 A-Kid	.50	1.25
48 Ilja Dragunov	.40	1.00
49 Noam Dar	.50	1.25
50 Tyler Bate/Trent Seven	.50	1.25

2022 Panini WWE NXT Memorabilia

*GREEN: .5X TO 1.2X BASIC MEM
*RED/99: .6X TO 1.5X BASIC MEM
*BLUE/49: .75X TO 2X BASIC MEM
*2.0/25: UNPRICED DUE TO SCARCITY
*BLACK&GOLD/25: UNPRICED DUE TO SCARCITY
*GOLD/10: UNPRICED DUE TO SCARCITY
*BLACK/1: UNPRICED DUE TO SCARCITY
RANDOMLY INSERTED INTO PACKS

NXMAKD A-Kid	2.00	5.00
NXMAML Amale	2.50	6.00
NXMAOV Aoife Valkyrie	2.00	5.00
NXMBBK Bron Breakker	8.00	20.00
NXMBCD Brutus Creed	2.50	6.00
NXMBDV Blair Davenport	6.00	15.00
NXMBOA Boa	2.50	6.00
NXMCGR Cameron Grimes	2.00	5.00
NXMCHY Carmelo Hayes	2.50	6.00
NXMCJD Cora Jade	12.00	30.00
NXMDLN Dani Luna	2.50	6.00
NXMDMS Dave Mastiff	2.00	5.00
NXMELP Elton Prince	2.50	6.00
NXMEMK Emilia McKenzie	2.50	6.00
NXMFAH Giovanni Vinci	5.00	12.00
NXMFMW Flash Morgan Webster	2.00	5.00
NXMGGD Gigi Dolin	10.00	25.00
NXMGTH Gunther	2.50	6.00
NXMGWL Grayson Waller	2.50	6.00
NXMIHW Indi Hartwell	8.00	20.00
NXMIOS Io Shirai	12.00	30.00
NXMIVN Ivy Nile	2.50	6.00
NXMJCD Julius Creed	2.50	6.00
NXMJCF Joe Coffey	4.00	10.00
NXMJDR James Drake	2.50	6.00
NXMJGC Joe Gacy	5.00	12.00
NXMJJN Jacy Jayne	12.00	30.00
NXMJNY Jinny	2.50	6.00
NXMJWD Joaquin Wilde	6.00	15.00
NXMKCC Katana Chance	5.00	12.00
NXMKDC Kayden Carter	6.00	15.00
NXMKLR Alba Fyre	4.00	10.00
NXMKWL Kenny Williams	2.50	6.00
NXMKWS Kit Wilson	6.00	15.00
NXMLLG Lash Legend	2.50	6.00
NXMMAW Mark Andrews	2.50	6.00
NXMMBT Ludwig Kaiser	10.00	25.00
NXMMCF Mark Coffey	3.00	8.00
NXMMDP Max Dupri	2.00	5.00
NXMMRS Mandy Rose	12.00	30.00
NXMMSM Meiko Satomura	2.00	5.00
NXMNMD Noam Dar	2.00	5.00
NXMODJ Odyssey Jones	2.50	6.00
NXMRQG Raquel Rodriguez	5.00	12.00
NXMRST Roderick Strong	3.00	8.00
NXMSES Santos Escobar	4.00	10.00
NXMSRY Sarray	5.00	12.00
NXMSTN Stevie Turner	8.00	20.00
NXMTBT Tyler Bate	2.50	6.00
NXMTCP Ciampa	2.50	6.00
NXMTEO Teoman	2.50	6.00
NXMVWG Von Wagner	3.00	8.00
NXMWFG Wolfgang	4.00	10.00
NXMWLE Wes Lee	2.50	6.00
NXMXYQ Xyon Quinn	8.00	20.00
NXMYSV Trent Seven	3.00	8.00
NXMZGB Zack Gibson	2.50	6.00
NXMZST Zoey Stark	3.00	8.00

2022 Panini WWE NXT Memorabilia Signatures

*2.0/25: UNPRICED DUE TO SCARCITY
*GOLD/10: UNPRICED DUE TO SCARCITY
*BLACK/1: UNPRICED DUE TO SCARCITY
STATED PRINT RUN 24-99

MSBCD Brutus Creed/99	8.00	20.00
MSBOA Boa/99	6.00	15.00
MSCGR Cameron Grimes/99	10.00	25.00
MSCHY Carmelo Hayes/49	15.00	40.00
MSCJD Cora Jade/99	60.00	150.00
MSFAH Giovanni Vinci/99	6.00	15.00
MSGGD Gigi Dolin/49	40.00	100.00
MSGTH Gunther/99	12.00	30.00
MSGWL Grayson Waller/99	10.00	25.00
MSIHW Indi Hartwell/99	12.00	30.00
MSIOS Io Shirai/49	30.00	75.00
MSIVN Ivy Nile/49	15.00	40.00
MSJCD Julius Creed/99	12.00	30.00
MSJDR James Drake/99	6.00	15.00
MSJGC Joe Gacy/99	15.00	40.00
MSJJN Jacy Jayne/99	40.00	100.00
MSJWD Joaquin Wilde/99	6.00	15.00
MSKCC Katana Chance/99	15.00	40.00
MSKDC Kayden Carter/99	10.00	25.00
MSKLR Alba Fyre/99	20.00	50.00
MSLLG Lash Legend/99	8.00	20.00
MSMBT Ludwig Kaiser/49	8.00	20.00
MSMDP Max Dupri/49	15.00	40.00
MSMRS Mandy Rose/99	40.00	100.00
MSMSM Meiko Satomura/24	12.00	30.00
MSODJ Odyssey Jones/99	10.00	25.00
MSRQG Raquel Rodriguez/49	15.00	40.00
MSRST Roderick Strong/99	8.00	20.00
MSSES Santos Escobar/99	6.00	15.00
MSSRY Sarray/99	8.00	20.00
MSTBT Tyler Bate/99	8.00	20.00
MSTCP Ciampa/49	8.00	20.00
MSVWG Von Wagner/99	6.00	15.00
MSWLE Wes Lee/99	6.00	15.00
MSXYQ Xyon Quinn/99	6.00	15.00
MSYSV Trent Seven/99	6.00	15.00
MSZGB Zack Gibson/99	8.00	20.00
MSZST Zoey Stark/99	6.00	15.00
NXMBBK Bron Breakker/99	40.00	100.00

2022 Panini WWE NXT Signatures

*GREEN: .5X TO 1.2X BASIC AUTOS
*RED/49: .6X TO 1.5X BASIC AUTOS
*2.0/25: UNPRICED DUE TO SCARCITY
*BLACK & GOLD/25: UNPRICED DUE TO SCARCITY
*GOLD/10: UNPRICED DUE TO SCARCITY
*BLACK/1: UNPRICED DUE TO SCARCITY
RANDOMLY INSERTED INTO PACKS

NSAKD A-Kid	8.00	20.00
NSAML Amale	10.00	25.00
NSAOV Aoife Valkyrie	10.00	25.00
NSBBK Bron Breakker	30.00	75.00
NSBCD Brutus Creed	10.00	25.00
NSBDV Blair Davenport	10.00	25.00
NSBOA Boa	5.00	12.00
NSCGR Cameron Grimes	8.00	20.00
NSCHY Carmelo Hayes	12.00	30.00
NSCJD Cora Jade	40.00	100.00
NSDLN Dani Luna	8.00	20.00
NSDMS Dave Mastiff	5.00	12.00
NSELP Elton Prince	8.00	20.00
NSEMK Emilia McKenzie	8.00	20.00
NSFAH Fabian Aichner	5.00	12.00
NSFMW Flash Morgan Webster	5.00	12.00
NSGGD Gigi Dolin	40.00	100.00
NSGTH Gunther	12.00	30.00
NSGWL Grayson Waller	10.00	25.00
NSIHW Indi Hartwell	15.00	40.00
NSILD Ilja Dragunov	10.00	25.00
NSIOS Io Shirai	10.00	25.00
NSIVN Ivy Nile	10.00	25.00
NSJCD Julius Creed	12.00	30.00
NSJCF Joe Coffey	5.00	12.00
NSJGC Joe Gacy	10.00	25.00
NSJJN Jacy Jayne	25.00	60.00
NSJNY Jinny	6.00	15.00
NSKCC Kacy Catanzaro	15.00	40.00

NSKDC Kayden Carter 10.00 25.00
NSKLR Kay Lee Ray 25.00 60.00
NSKWL Kenny Williams 5.00 12.00
NSKWS Kit Wilson 6.00 15.00
NSLAK LA Knight 8.00 20.00
NSLLG Lash Legend 6.00 15.00
NSMBT Marcel Barthel 6.00 15.00
NSMRS Mandy Rose 30.00 75.00
NSMSM Meiko Satomura 10.00 25.00
NSNMD Noam Dar 6.00 15.00
NSODJ Odyssey Jones 8.00 20.00
NSRPB Rampage Brown 6.00 15.00
NSRQG Raquel Gonzalez 12.00 30.00
NSRST Roderick Strong 5.00 12.00
NSSES Santos Escobar 12.00 30.00
NSSRY Sarray 12.00 30.00
NSSTN Stevie Turner 10.00 25.00
NSTBT Tyler Bate 6.00 15.00
NSTCP Tommaso Ciampa 6.00 15.00
NSTEO Teoman 5.00 12.00
NSVWG Von Wagner 6.00 15.00
NSWFG Wolfgang 6.00 15.00
NSWLE Wes Lee 6.00 15.00
NSXYQ Xyon Quinn 6.00 15.00
NSYSV Trent Seven 6.00 15.00

2022 Panini WWE Sticker Collection

1 WWE LOGO FOIL .20 .50
2 Panini LOGO FOIL .20 .50
3 RAW Puzzle 1 .20 .50
4 RAW Puzzle 2 .20 .50
5 World Title Belt .20 .50
6 RAW Women's Title Belt .20 .50
7 NXT 2.0 Puzzle 1 .20 .50
8 NXT 2.0 Puzzle 2 .20 .50
9 NXT Championship Belt .20 .50
10 SmackDown Puzzle 1 .20 .50
11 SmackDown Puzzle 2 .20 .50
12 Universal Title Belt .20 .50
13 SmackDown Women's Title Belt .20 .50
14 NXT Women's Title Belt .20 .50
15 WWE 24/7 Championship Belt .20 .50
16 RAW LOGO FOIL .20 .50
17 Akira Tozawa .30 .75
18 Angelo Dawkins .30 .75
19 Becky Lynch 1.00 2.50
20 Becky Lynch LOGO 1.00 2.50
21 Becky Lynch FOIL 1.00 2.50
22 Bobby Lashley .50 1.25
23 Bobby Lashley LOGO .50 1.25
24 Bobby Lashley FOIL .50 1.25
25 Apollo Crews .30 .75
26 Commander Azeez .30 .75
27 Carmella .60 1.50
28 Omos .50 1.25
29 Tommaso Ciampa .60 1.50
30 Damian Priest LOGO .50 1.25
31 Damian Priest FOIL .50 1.25
32 Damian Priest .50 1.25
33 AJ Styles .75 2.00
34 AJ Styles LOGO .75 2.00
35 AJ Styles FOIL .75 2.00
36 Cedric Alexander .25 .60
37 Chad Gable .25 .60
38 Bianca Belair LOGO .75 2.00
39 Bianca Belair FOIL .75 2.00
40 Bianca Belair .75 2.00
41 Rey Mysterio .60 1.50
42 Rey Mysterio LOGO .60 1.50
43 Rey Mysterio FOIL .60 1.50
44 Riddle .60 1.50
45 Riddle FOIL .60 1.50
46 Riddle LOGO .60 1.50
47 Corey Graves .25 .60
48 Dolph Ziggler .50 1.25
49 Alexa Bliss LOGO 1.50 4.00
50 Alexa Bliss FOIL 1.50 4.00
51 Alexa Bliss 1.50 4.00
52 Edge LOGO 1.00 2.50
53 Edge FOIL 1.00 2.50
54 Edge 1.00 2.50
55 Seth Freakin Rollins .60 1.50
56 Seth Freakin Rollins FOIL .60 1.50
57 Seth Freakin Rollins LOGO .60 1.50
58 Doudrop .40 1.00
59 Dominik Mysterio .30 .75
60 Randy Orton LOGO .60 1.50
61 Randy Orton FOIL .60 1.50
62 Randy Orton .60 1.50
63 Liv Morgan 1.25 3.00
64 Liv Morgan LOGO 1.25 3.00
65 Liv Morgan FOIL 1.25 3.00
66 Finn Balor LOGO .60 1.50
67 Finn Balor FOIL .60 1.50
68 Finn Balor .60 1.50
69 Kevin Owens .50 1.25
70 Montez Ford .25 .60
71 MVP .25 .60
72 Nikki A.S.H. .40 1.00
73 Rhea Ripley LOGO .75 2.00
74 Rhea Ripley FOIL .75 2.00
75 Rhea Ripley .75 2.00
76 Theory .60 1.50
77 Otis .30 .75
78 Queen Zelina .40 1.00
79 Dana Brooke .25 .60
80 Reggie .30 .75
81 Robert Roode .30 .75
82 R-Truth .30 .75
83 Shelton Benjamin .40 1.00
84 Sonya Deville .60 1.50
85 Cody Rhodes LOGO .60 1.50
86 Cody Rhodes FOIL .60 1.50
87 Cody Rhodes .60 1.50
88 Veer .60 1.50
89 Tamina .30 .75
90 Ezekiel .25 .60
91 T-Bar .25 .60
92 The Miz .40 1.00
93 Stephanie McMahon .40 1.00
94 SmackDown FOIL .20 .50
95 Aliyah .50 1.25
96 Cesaro .25 .60
97 Roman Reigns FOIL 1.50 4.00
98 Roman Reigns 1.50 4.00
99 Roman Reigns LOGO 1.50 4.00
100 The Bloodline 1.50 4.00
101 The Bloodline LOGO .20 .50
102 The Usos .60 1.50
103 Paul Heyman .40 1.00
104 Ivar .25 .60
105 Erik .25 .60
106 Brock Lesnar LOGO 1.25 3.00
107 Brock Lesnar FOIL 1.25 3.00
108 Brock Lesnar 1.25 3.00
109 Charlotte Flair LOGO 1.00 2.50
110 Charlotte Flair FOIL 1.00 2.50
111 Charlotte Flair 1.00 2.50
112 Sami Zayn .40 1.00
113 Sami Zayn LOGO .40 1.00
114 Sami Zayn FOIL .40 1.00
115 Mustafa Ali .30 .75
116 Drew Gulak .30 .75
117 Jinder Mahal .30 .75
118 Xavier Woods .30 .75
119 Kofi Kingston .60 1.50
120 Humberto .25 .60
121 Drew McIntyre LOGO .50 1.25
122 Drew McIntyre FOIL .50 1.25
123 Drew McIntyre .50 1.25
124 Naomi .40 1.00
125 Naomi LOGO .40 1.00
126 Naomi FOIL .40 1.00
127 Mace .25 .60
128 Madcap Moss .25 .60
129 Mansoor .25 .60
130 Jimmy Uso .30 .75
131 Jey Uso .30 .75
132 Sasha Banks LOGO 1.50 4.00
133 Sasha Banks 1.50 4.00
134 Sasha Banks FOIL 1.50 4.00
135 Ricochet .50 1.25
136 Ricochet LOGO .50 1.25
137 Ricochet FOIL .50 1.25
138 Natalya .40 1.00
139 Ludwig Kaiser .30 .75
140 Gunther .60 1.50
141 Rick Boogs .30 .75
142 Ridge Holland .25 .60
143 Shanky .25 .60
144 Happy Corbin LOGO .30 .75
145 Happy Corbin FOIL .30 .75
146 Happy Corbin .30 .75
147 Big E .50 1.25
148 Big E LOGO .50 1.25
149 Big E FOIL .50 1.25
150 Shayna Baszler .50 1.25
151 Sheamus .40 1.00
152 Butch .50 1.25
153 Sonya Deville .60 1.50
154 Angelo Dawkins .30 .75
155 The New Day LOGO .60 1.50
156 The New Day FOIL .60 1.50
157 The New Day .60 1.50
158 Shinsuke Nakamura .60 1.50
159 Shinsuke Nakamura LOGO .60 1.50
160 Shinsuke Nakamura FOIL .60 1.50
161 Xia Li .50 1.25
162 Shotzi 1.00 2.50
163 NXT 2.0 LOGO .20 .50
164 Amari Miller .25 .60
165 Bron Breakker LOGO 1.00 2.50
166 Bron Breakker FOIL 1.00 2.50
167 Bron Breakker 1.00 2.50
168 Andre Chase .25 .60
169 Boa .25 .60
170 Bodhi Hayward .30 .75
171 Brooks Jensen .25 .60
172 Brutus Creed .30 .75
173 Cameron Grimes .50 1.25
174 Cora Jade .75 2.00
175 Dakota Kai .50 1.25
176 Dante Chen .25 .60
177 Dexter Lumis .25 .60
178 Draco Anthony .25 .60
179 Mandy Rose LOGO 1.25 3.00
180 Mandy Rose FOIL 1.25 3.00
181 Mandy Rose 1.25 3.00
182 Duke Hudson .25 .60
183 Edris Enofe .25 .60
184 Elektra Lopez .60 1.50
185 Fabian Aichner .30 .75
186 Gigi Dolin 1.00 2.50
187 Grayson Waller .60 1.50
188 Guru Raaj .25 .60
189 Harland .25 .60
190 Ilja Dragunov LOGO .25 .60
191 Ilja Dragunov FOIL .25 .60
192 Ilja Dragunov .25 .60
193 Ikemen Jiro .25 .60
194 Indi Hartwell .75 2.00
195 Io Shirai .50 1.25
196 Ivy Nile .25 .60
197 Jacy Jayne .60 1.50
198 James Drake .25 .60
199 Joaquin Wilde .40 1.00
200 Joe Gacy .60 1.50
201 Meiko Satomura LOGO .75 2.00
202 Meiko Satomura FOIL .75 2.00
203 Meiko Satomura .75 2.00
204 Josh Briggs .25 .60
205 Julius Creed .60 1.50
206 Kacy Catanzaro .50 1.25
207 Alba Fyre .60 1.50
208 Kayden Carter .50 1.25
209 Kushida .40 1.00
210 LA Knight .40 1.00
211 Lash Legend .25 .60
212 Noam Dar LOGO .30 .75
213 Noam Dar FOIL .30 .75
214 Noam Dar .30 .75
215 Nathan Frazer .25 .60
216 Malik Blade .25 .60
217 Roxanne Perez .75 2.00
218 Nikkita Lyons .60 1.50
219 Carmelo Hayes LOGO .30 .75
220 Carmelo Hayes FOIL .30 .75
221 Carmelo Hayes .30 .75
222 Odyssey Jones .25 .60
223 Persia Pirotta .25 .60
224 Raul Mendoza .40 1.00
225 Raquel Rodriguez .60 1.50
226 Robert Stone .25 .60
227 Roderick Strong .40 1.00
228 Ru Feng .25 .60
229 Sanga .25 .60
230 Santos Escobar .40 1.00
231 Sarray .30 .75
232 Solo Sikoa .60 1.50
233 Tiffany Stratton .40 1.00
234 Tony D'Angelo .75 2.00
235 Trick Williams .25 .60
236 Valentina Feroz .40 1.00
237 Von Wagner .25 .60
238 Wendy Choo .50 1.25
239 Wes Lee .25 .60
240 Xyon Quinn .25 .60
241 Yulisa Leon .25 .60
242 Zack Gibson .25 .60
243 Zoey Stark .30 .75
244 Alpha Academy Puzzle 1 .25 .60
245 Alpha Academy Puzzle 2 .30 .75
246 Otis/Chad Gable FOIL .30 .75
247 Carmella/Queen Zelina FOIL .60 1.50
248 Carmella Puzzle 1 .60 1.50
249 Queen Zelina Puzzle 2 .40 1.00
250 RK-Bro Puzzle 1 .60 1.50
251 RK-Bro Puzzle 2 .60 1.50
252 Randy Orton/Riddle FOIL .60 1.50
253 M.Ford/A.Dawkins FOIL .30 .75
254 Street Profits Puzzle 1 .30 .75
255 Street Profits Puzzle 2 .25 .60
256 The Usos Puzzle 1 .60 1.50
257 The Usos Puzzle 2 .60 1.50
258 Jey Uso/Jimmy Uso FOIL .30 .75
259 Gigi Dolin/Jacy Jayne FOIL 1.00 2.50
260 Toxic Attraction Puzzle 1 1.00 2.50
261 Toxic Attraction Puzzle 2 .60 1.50
262 Moustache Mountain Puzzle 1 .30 .75
263 Moustache Mountain Puzzle 2 .30 .75
264 Tyler Bate/Trent Seven FOIL .30 .75
265 Kit Wilson/Elton Prince FOIL .30 .75
266 Pretty Deadly Puzzle 1 .25 .60
267 Pretty Deadly Puzzle 2 .30 .75
268 Sasha Banks 1.50 4.00
269 Becky Lynch 1.00 2.50
270 Randy Orton .60 1.50
271 Goldberg 1.00 2.50
272 The Rock Puzzle 1 2.50 6.00
273 The Rock Puzzle 2 2.50 6.00
274 Brock Lesnar 1.25 3.00
275 Bret Hart .60 1.50
276 Finn Balor .60 1.50
277 Steve Austin Puzzle 1 1.25 3.00
278 Steve Austin Puzzle 2 1.25 3.00
279 Roman Reigns Puzzle 1 1.50 4.00
280 Roman Reigns Puzzle 2 1.50 4.00
281 Triple H 1.00 2.50
282 Shawn Michaels Puzzle 1 1.00 2.50
283 Shawn Michaels Puzzle 2 1.00 2.50
284 Razor Ramon .50 1.25
285 Ted DiBiase .40 1.00
286 Randy Savage 1.00 2.50
287 Diesel .40 1.00
288 AJ Styles .75 2.00
289 Sheamus .40 1.00
290 Undertaker Puzzle 1 1.25 3.00
291 Undertaker Puzzle 2 1.25 3.00
292 Batista .50 1.25
293 Eddie Guerrero .75 2.00
294 John Cena Puzzle 1 .75 2.00
295 John Cena Puzzle 2 .75 2.00
296 WrestleMania III Poster 1.00 2.50
297 WrestleMania IV Poster 1.25 3.00
298 WrestleMania XII Poster 1.00 2.50
299 WrestleMania X-Seven Poster 2.50 6.00
300 WrestleMania 25th Ann. Poster 1.25 3.00
301 WrestleMania LOGO .20 .50
302 WrestleMania 35 Poster 1.50 4.00
303 WrestleMania 28 Poster 2.50 6.00
304 WrestleMania 38 Poster 1.50 4.00
305 Super Showdown LOGO .20 .50
306 Extreme Rules LOGO .20 .50
307 Money in the Bank LOGO .20 .50
308 Elimination Chamber LOGO .20 .50
309 WrestleMania BackLash LOGO .20 .50
310 SummerSlam '92 Poster .60 1.50
311 Royal Rumble LOGO .20 .50
312 Royal Rumble 2000 Poster 1.00 2.50
313 SummerSlam LOGO .20 .50

314 SummerSlam '16 Poster .75 2.00
315 Clash of Champions LOGO .20 .50
316 SummerSlam '95 Poster 1.00 2.50
317 Hell in a Cell LOGO .20 .50
318 Survivor Series LOGO .20 .50
319 NXT TakeOver Brooklyn Poster 1.50 4.00
320 No Way Out 2004 Poster 1.25 3.00
321 TLC LOGO .20 .50
322 KOTR/Queens Crown Tournament LOGO.20 .50
323 Rob Van Dam L .50 1.25
324 Batista L .50 1.25
325 Hulk Hogan L FOIL 1.25 3.00
326 Hulkamania L LOGO 1.25 3.00
327 Hulk Hogan L 1.25 3.00
328 Goldberg L 1.00 2.50
329 Eddie Guerrero L .75 2.00
330 Sgt. Slaughter L .40 1.00
331 John Cena L FOIL .75 2.00
332 John Cena L LOGO .75 2.00
333 John Cena L .75 2.00
334 Trish Stratus L 1.25 3.00
335 Triple H L 1.00 2.50
336 Alundra Blayze L .30 .75
337 Jerry Lawler L .50 1.25
338 The Rock L FOIL 2.50 6.00
339 The Rock L LOGO 2.50 6.00
340 The Rock L 2.50 6.00
341 Mean Gene Okerlund L .40 1.00
342 Jake The Snake Roberts L .40 1.00
343 Razor Ramon L .50 1.25
344 Undertaker L FOIL 1.25 3.00
345 Undertaker L LOGO 1.25 3.00
346 Undertaker L 1.25 3.00
347 Iron Sheik L .30 .75
348 Big John Studd L .25 .60
349 X-Pac (1-2-3 Kid) L .30 .75
350 Dusty Rhodes L .60 1.50
351 Stone Cold Steve Austin L FOIL 1.25 3.00
352 Stone Cold Steve Austin L LOGO 1.25 3.00
353 Stone Cold Steve Austin L 1.25 3.00
354 Ravishing Rick Rude L .50 1.25
355 Molly Holly L .30 .75
356 Bobby The Brain Heenan L .40 1.00
357 Ultimate Warrior L FOIL 1.00 2.50
358 Ultimate Warrior L LOGO 1.00 2.50
359 Ultimate Warrior L 1.00 2.50
360 British Bulldog L .40 1.00
361 Ricky The Dragon Steamboat L .50 1.25
362 Greg The Hammer Valentine L .25 .60
363 Yokozuna L .30 .75
364 Andre the Giant L FOIL 1.00 2.50
365 Andre the Giant L LOGO 1.00 2.50
366 Andre the Giant L 1.00 2.50
367 Big Boss Man L .40 1.00
368 Beth Phoenix L .50 1.25
369 Booker T L .50 1.25
370 Macho Man Randy Savage L FOIL 1.00 2.50
371 Macho Man Randy Savage L LOGO 1.00 2.50
372 Macho Man Randy Savage L 1.00 2.50
373 Diesel L .40 1.00
374 Chyna L .50 1.25
375 Don Muraco L .25 .60
376 Honky Tonk Man L .30 .75
377 Shawn Michaels L FOIL 1.00 2.50
378 Shawn Michaels L LOGO 1.00 2.50
379 Shawn Michaels L 1.00 2.50
380 The Great Khali L .30 .75
381 Rikishi L .30 .75
382 Nikki Bella L .60 1.50
383 Rowdy Roddy Piper L FOIL .60 1.50
384 Rowdy Roddy Piper L LOGO .60 1.50
385 Rowdy Roddy Piper L .60 1.50
386 Harley Race L .30 .75
387 George "The Animal" Steele L .40 1.00
388 Ted DiBiase L FOIL .40 1.00
389 Ted DiBiase L LOGO .40 1.00
390 Ted DiBiase L .40 1.00
391 Lex Luger L .30 .75
392 Stacy Keibler L .75 2.00
393 Mick Foley L FOIL .50 1.25
394 Mick Foley L LOGO .50 1.25
395 Mick Foley L .50 1.25
396 Vader L .30 .75
397 Bret Hitman Hart L FOIL .60 1.50
398 Bret Hitman Hart L LOGO .60 1.50
399 Bret Hitman Hart L .60 1.50
400 Nikolai Volkoff L .25 .60
401 Curt Hennig L .50 1.25
402 JBL HOF 2020 .25 .60
403 British Bulldog HOF 2020 .40 1.00
404 Titus O'Neil HOF 2020 .25 .60
405 The Bella Twins HOF 2020 .60 1.50
406 The nWo HOF 2020 1.25 3.00
407 Molly Holly HOF 2021 .30 .75
408 Kane HOF 2021 .40 1.00
409 The Great Khali HOF 2021 .30 .75
410 Rob Van Dam HOF 2021 .50 1.25
411 HOF 2022 LOGO Puzzle 1 .20 .50
412 HOF 2022 LOGO Puzzle 2 .20 .50
413 Undertaker HOF 2022 1.25 3.00
414 Vader HOF 2022 .30 .75

1954-55 Parkhurst Wrestling

COMPLETE SET (75) 350.00 600.00
*PREMIUM BACKS: SAME VALUE

1 Lou Thesz RC 10.00 25.00
2 Sky Hi Lee RC 4.00 10.00
3 Whipper Billy Watson RC 4.00 10.00
4 Johnny Barend RC 4.00 10.00
5 Antonio Argentina Rocca RC 6.00 15.00
6 Dirty Dick Raines RC 4.00 10.00
7 Frank Valois RC 4.00 10.00
8 Hombre Montana RC 4.00 10.00
9 Lou Plummer RC 4.00 10.00
10 Chief Big Heart RC 4.00 10.00
11 Man Mountain Dean Jr. RC 4.00 10.00
12 Primo Carnera 10.00 25.00
13 Paul Baillargeon RC 4.00 10.00
14 Nick Roberts RC 4.00 10.00
15 Tim Geohagen RC 4.00 10.00
16 The Togo Brothers 4.00 10.00
17 Verne Gagne RC 12.00 30.00
18 Maurice Tillet RC 4.00 10.00
19 Yukon Eric RC 4.00 10.00
20 Toar Morgan RC 4.00 10.00
21 Mighty Schultz RC 4.00 10.00
22 Bill Stack RC 4.00 10.00
23 Argentina Rocca RC 6.00 15.00
24 Big Ben Morgan RC 4.00 10.00
25 Lou Pitoscia RC 4.00 10.00
26 Earl McCready & Billy Watson 4.00 10.00
27 Hans Schmidt RC 4.00 10.00
28 Lu Kim RC 4.00 10.00
29 Roy McLarity RC 4.00 10.00
30 Lord Jan Blears 4.00 10.00
31 Lee Henning & Fred Atkins 4.00 10.00
32 Jim Goon Henry RC 4.00 10.00
33 Wee Willie Davis RC 4.00 10.00
34 Yvon Robert RC 4.00 10.00
35 Joe Killer Christie RC 4.00 10.00
36 Bo Bo Brazil RC 8.00 20.00
37 The Sharpe Brothers 4.00 10.00
38 Larry Moquin RC 4.00 10.00
39 Nanjo Singh RC 4.00 10.00
40 Wladek Kowalski RC 10.00 25.00
41 Frank Sexton RC 4.00 10.00
42 George Bollas RC 4.00 10.00
43 Ray Villmer RC 4.00 10.00
44 Steve Stanlee RC 4.00 10.00
45 Tuffy McCrae & Little Beaver 4.00 10.00
46 Johnny Rougeau RC 4.00 10.00
47 Harry Lewis RC 4.00 10.00
48 Pat Flanagan RC 4.00 10.00
49 Ovila Asselin RC 4.00 10.00
50 Sammy Berg RC 4.00 10.00
51 The Mighty Ursus 4.00 10.00
52 Lou Newman RC 4.00 10.00
53 George Scott RC 4.00 10.00
54 Hans Hermann RC 4.00 10.00
55 Bob Wagner RC 4.00 10.00
56 Little Beaver/Salassi 4.00 10.00
57 Sandor Kovacs RC 4.00 10.00
58 The Mills Brothers 4.00 10.00
59 Roberto Pico RC 4.00 10.00
60 Fred Atkins RC 4.00 10.00
61 Wild Bill Longson RC 4.00 10.00
62 Bobby Managoff RC 4.00 10.00
63 Athol Layton RC 4.00 10.00
64 Warren Bockwinkle RC 4.00 10.00
65 The Mighty Atlas RC 4.00 10.00
66 Mike Sharpe RC 4.00 10.00
67 Ernie Dusek 4.00 10.00
68 Danno O'Shocker RC 4.00 10.00
69 Gorgeous George RC 20.00 50.00
70 The Great Togo RC 4.00 10.00
71 Bob Langevin RC 4.00 10.00
72 Emil Dusek RC 4.00 10.00
73 Chief Sunni War Cloud RC 4.00 10.00
74 Pat O'Connor RC 4.00 10.00
75 Baron Leone RC 5.00 12.00

1955-56 Parkhurst Wrestling

COMPLETE SET (121) 450.00 800.00

1 Frank Valois 6.00 15.00
2 Johnny Barend 4.00 10.00
3 Sky Hi Lee 4.00 10.00
4 Hans Schmidt 4.00 10.00
5 Hans Hermann 4.00 10.00
6 Bo Bo Brazil 8.00 20.00
7 Chief Sunni War Cloud 4.00 10.00
8 The Mills Brothers 4.00 10.00
9 Roy McLarity 4.00 10.00
10 Danno O'Shocker 4.00 10.00
11 Chief Big Heart 4.00 10.00
12 Bob Wagner 4.00 10.00
13 Lou Pitoscia 4.00 10.00
14 Ernie Dusek 4.00 10.00
15 Whipper Watson 4.00 10.00
16 Johnny Rougeau 4.00 10.00
17 Ovila Asselin 4.00 10.00
18 Bill Stack 4.00 10.00
19 Ken Kenneth RC 4.00 10.00
20 Lou Newman 4.00 10.00
21 Warren Bockwinkle 4.00 10.00
22 The Sharpe Brothers 4.00 10.00
23 Bobby Managoff 4.00 10.00
24 Nick Roberts 4.00 10.00
25 Lee Henning RC 4.00 10.00
26 Joe Christie 4.00 10.00
27 Larry Moquin 4.00 10.00
28 Jim Goon Henry 4.00 10.00
29 Bob Langevin 4.00 10.00
30 Roberto Pico 4.00 10.00
31 Sammy Berg 4.00 10.00
32 Mighty Atlas 4.00 10.00
33 Baron Leone 4.00 10.00
34 Hassen Bay RC 4.00 10.00
35 Allen Garfield RC 4.00 10.00
36 Don Evans RC 4.00 10.00
37 Dory Funk RC 8.00 20.00
38 Art Neilson RC 4.00 10.00
39 Don Lee Jonathan RC 4.00 10.00
40 Argentina Rocca 6.00 15.00
41 Tex McKenzie RC 4.00 10.00
42 Pat Flanagan 4.00 10.00
43 Verne Gagne 8.00 20.00
44 Selassi & Little Beaver 4.00 10.00
45 Steve Stanlee 4.00 10.00
46 Frank Sexton 4.00 10.00
47 Pat O'Connor 4.00 10.00
48 Nanjo Singh 4.00 10.00
49 Toar Morgan 4.00 10.00
50 Harry Lewis 4.00 10.00
51 Doug Hepburn RC 4.00 10.00
52 Reggie Lisowski RC 4.00 10.00
53 Kenny Ackles RC 4.00 10.00
54 Argentina Rocca 6.00 15.00
55 Herb Parks RC 4.00 10.00
56 Bearcat Wright RC 4.00 10.00
57 Yvon Robert 4.00 10.00
58 Waldo Von Sieber RC 4.00 10.00
59 Harold Nelson RC 4.00 10.00
60 Sumo Wrestlers 4.00 10.00
61 Golden Hawk RC 4.00 10.00
62 Wee Willie Davis 4.00 10.00
63 Mike Sharpe 4.00 10.00
64 Sandor Kovacs 4.00 10.00
65 Lord Blears 4.00 10.00
66 Tim Goehagen 4.00 10.00
67 Jack Laskin RC 4.00 10.00
68 Emil Dusek 4.00 10.00
69 Ben Morgan 4.00 10.00
70 Lu Kim 4.00 10.00
71 Frank Marconi RC 4.00 10.00
72 Prince Maiava RC 4.00 10.00
73 Larry Kasaboski RC 4.00 10.00
74 Frank Thompson RC 4.00 10.00
75 Yukon Eric 4.00 10.00
76 Lou Thesz 6.00 15.00
77 Bill Longson 4.00 10.00
78 Fred Atkins 4.00 10.00
79 Lord Layton 4.00 10.00
80 Dusek Brothers 4.00 10.00
81 Zorra RC 4.00 10.00
82 Lou Thesz 10.00 25.00
83 Luther Lindsey RC 4.00 10.00
84 Jack Bence RC 4.00 10.00
85 Primo Carnera 8.00 20.00
86 Kalmikoff Brothers 4.00 10.00
87 The Great Togo 4.00 10.00
88 Lou Plummer 4.00 10.00
89 Bates Ford RC 4.00 10.00
90 Ursus and Montana 4.00 10.00
91 Paul Baillargeon 4.00 10.00
92 Bill McDaniels RC 4.00 10.00
93 Ray Villmer 4.00 10.00
94 Yvon Robert 4.00 10.00
95 Gorgeous George 15.00 40.00
96 Scott Brothers 4.00 10.00
97 Bronko Nagurski 50.00 100.00
98 Pete Managoff RC 4.00 10.00
99 The Togo Brothers 4.00 10.00
100 Don Lee RC 4.00 10.00
101 Steve Patrick RC 4.00 10.00
102 George Gordienko RC 4.00 10.00
103 Vic Holbrook RC 4.00 10.00
104 Gil Mains 4.00 10.00
105 Firpo Zbyszko RC 4.00 10.00
106 Mike Paidousis RC 4.00 10.00
107 Al Oeming RC 4.00 10.00
108 Matt Murphy RC 4.00 10.00
109 Martin Hutzler RC 4.00 10.00
110 Tommy O'Toole RC 4.00 10.00
111 Steve Gob RC 4.00 10.00
112 Riot Call Wright RC 4.00 10.00
113 Leo Newman RC 4.00 10.00
114 Frank Hurley RC 4.00 10.00
115 Jack Claybourne RC 4.00 10.00
116 Ken Colley RC 4.00 10.00
117 Whipper Watson 4.00 10.00
118 Steve McGill RC 4.00 10.00
119 Buddy Rogers RC 4.00 10.00
120 Gino Garibaldi RC 4.00 10.00
121 Ed Gardenia RC 5.00 12.00

2006 Popeye's WWE Mania Moments

COMPLETE SET (21) 15.00 40.00

1 Andre the Giant 1.50 4.00
2 Rowdy Roddy Piper 1.50 4.00
3 Hulk Hogan 1.50 4.00
4 Ted DiBiase 1.25 3.00
5 Jake The Snake Roberts 1.50 4.00
6 Skydome .60 1.50
7 Sgt. Slaughter 1.50 4.00
8 Ric Flair 1.50 4.00
9 Bobby Heenan .75 2.00
10 Mr. Perfect 1.00 2.50
11 Bam Bam Bigelow 1.00 2.50
12 Shawn Michaels 1.25 3.00
13 Undertaker 1.50 4.00
14 Stone Cold Steve Austin 2.00 5.00
15 The Rock 2.00 5.00
16 Mick Foley 1.00 2.50
17 Kurt Angle 1.25 3.00
18 Triple H 1.25 3.00
19 Rey Mysterio .75 2.00
20 Chris Benoit 1.25 3.00
21 Batista / John Cena 2.00 5.00

1989 Post Honeycomb WWE Posters

NNO Andre the Giant 20.00 50.00
NNO Brutus Beefcake 5.00 12.00
NNO Bushwhackers 4.00 10.00
NNO Demolition 6.00 15.00

NNO Hulk Hogan	20.00	50.00
NNO Macho Man	12.00	30.00
NNO Rockers	6.00	15.00
NNO Ultimate Warrior	15.00	40.00

1982 PWE Wrestling All-Stars Series A

COMPLETE SET (36) 750.00 2000.00
CARDS PRICED IN NR-MT CONDITION

1 Andre the Giant	400.00	1000.00
2 Hulk Hogan	250.00	600.00
3 Mil Mascaras	20.00	50.00
4 Ted DiBiase	30.00	75.00
5 The Junkyard Dog	25.00	60.00
6 Dusty Rhodes	30.00	75.00
7 Jack Brisco	6.00	15.00
8 Harley Race	25.00	60.00
9 Dory Funk Jr.	6.00	15.00
10 Terry Funk	30.00	75.00
11 Nick Bockwinkel	10.00	25.00
12 Bob Backlund	20.00	50.00
13 Bruno Sammartino	20.00	50.00
14 Pedro Morales	6.00	15.00
15 Don Muraco	20.00	50.00
16 Bill Dundee	15.00	40.00
17 Steve Olsonoski	6.00	15.00
18 Tommy Rich	10.00	25.00
19 Angelo Mosca	8.00	20.00
20 Bruiser Brody	30.00	75.00
21 The Fabulous Moolah	20.00	50.00
22 Wahoo McDaniel	12.00	30.00
23 Billy Robinson	6.00	15.00
24 Ivan Koloff	10.00	25.00
25 Tony Atlas	10.00	25.00
26 Pat Patterson	10.00	25.00
27 Ric Flair	250.00	600.00
28 Ivan Putski	8.00	20.00
29 Dick Murdoch	8.00	20.00
30 The Crusher	8.00	20.00
31 Ken Patera	12.00	30.00
32 Ernie Ladd	12.00	30.00
33 Dick the Bruiser	8.00	20.00
34 Jerry Lawler	40.00	100.00
35 Cowboy Bill Watts	10.00	25.00
36 The Destroyer	10.00	25.00

1983 PWE Wrestling All-Stars Series A

COMPLETE SET (36) 200.00 500.00
CARDS PRICED IN NR-MT CONDITION

1 Superstar (Billy) Graham	20.00	50.00
2 Tiger Mask	6.00	15.00
3 Sheik El Kaissey	6.00	15.00
4 Sgt. Jacque Goulet	5.00	12.00
5 Curt Hennig	30.00	75.00
6 Tully Blanchard	12.00	30.00
7 Jimmy Superfly Snuka	20.00	50.00
8 Gino Hernandez	10.00	25.00
9 Lou Thesz	8.00	20.00
10 Hacksaw (Jim) Duggan	20.00	50.00
11 Mr. Olympia	6.00	15.00
12 Iron Mike Sharpe	10.00	25.00
13 Jimmy Hart	20.00	50.00
14 Spike Huber	6.00	15.00
15 Steve Regal	6.00	15.00
16 Buddy Rogers	8.00	20.00
17 Jules Strongbow	10.00	25.00
18 Salvatore Bellomo	6.00	15.00
19 Bob Sweetan	6.00	15.00
20 Scott Casey	5.00	12.00
21 The Grappler	5.00	12.00
22 Big John Studd	10.00	25.00
23 Buddy Rose	8.00	20.00
24 Rocky Johnson	25.00	60.00
25 Jake Roberts	50.00	100.00
26 The Super Destroyer	4.00	10.00
27 Antonio Inoki	10.00	25.00
28 Dick Slater	6.00	15.00
29 Ken Lucas	4.00	10.00
30 Ricky Morton	15.00	40.00
31 Fred Blassie	12.00	30.00
32 Lou Albano	12.00	30.00
33 The Grand Wizard	4.00	10.00
34 Candi Divine	5.00	12.00
35 Austin Idol	12.00	30.00
36 Matt Borne	5.00	12.00

1982 PWE Wrestling All-Stars Series B

COMPLETE SET (36) 300.00 750.00
CARDS PRICED IN NR-MT CONDITION

1 Rick Martel	12.00	30.00
2 Tony Garea	10.00	25.00
3 Bob Roop	8.00	20.00
4 Greg Gagne	12.00	30.00
5 Jim Brunzell	6.00	15.00
6 Jay Strongbow	10.00	25.00
7 Kerry Von Erich	50.00	125.00
8 S.D. Jones	6.00	15.00
9 Brad Rheingans	6.00	15.00
10 Killer Khan	15.00	40.00
11 Ricky Steamboat	50.00	125.00
12 Paul Orndorff	15.00	40.00
13 Tito Santana	40.00	100.00
14 Sergeant Slaughter	40.00	100.00
15 Verne Gagne	10.00	25.00
16 Bobby Heenan	20.00	50.00
17 Jerry Blackwell	12.00	30.00
18 Les Thornton	4.00	10.00
19 Adrian Adonis	12.00	30.00
20 Jesse Ventura	30.00	75.00
21 Buck Zum Hofe	8.00	20.00
22 Jimmy Valiant	8.00	20.00
23 Steve Keirn	5.00	12.00
24 Ray Stevens	10.00	25.00
25 The Iron Sheik	30.00	75.00
26 Mr. Wrestling II	15.00	40.00
27 Col. Buck Robley	6.00	15.00
28 Bobby Duncum	5.00	12.00
29 Mike George	4.00	10.00
30 Dino Bravo	6.00	15.00
31 Baron Von Raschke	12.00	30.00
32 Bobo Brazil	6.00	15.00
33 Greg Valentine	15.00	40.00
34 Joyce Grable	6.00	15.00
35 Sweet Brown Sugar	10.00	25.00
36 Dutch Mantell	10.00	25.00

2022 Revolution WWE

COMPLETE SET (150) 75.00 200.00
*ASTRO: .5X TO 1.2X BASIC CARDS
*FRACTAL: .6X TO 1.5X BASIC CARDS
*GALACTIC: .75X TO 2X BASIC CARDS
*GROOVE: 1X TO 2.5X BASIC CARDS
*ANGULAR/199: 1.2X TO 3X BASIC CARDS
*COSMIC/149: 1.5X TO 4X BASIC CARDS
*SUNBURST/99: 2X TO 5X BASIC CARDS
*CUBIC/49: 2.5X TO 6X BASIC CARDS
*LAVA/10: UNPRICED DUE TO SCARCITY

1 Tony D'Angelo RC	1.25	3.00
2 Brock Lesnar	2.00	5.00
3 Meiko Satomura RC	1.25	3.00
4 Rick Boogs	.50	1.25
5 Natalya	.60	1.50
6 AJ Styles	1.25	3.00
7 Sonya Deville	1.00	2.50
8 Kevin Owens	.75	2.00
9 Nash Carter	.40	1.00
10 Alexa Bliss	2.50	6.00
11 Von Wagner RC	.40	1.00
12 Chad Gable	.40	1.00
13 Gigi Dolin	1.50	4.00
14 Ricochet	.75	2.00
15 Sasha Banks	2.50	6.00
16 Apollo Crews	.50	1.25
17 Bron Breakker RC	3.00	8.00
18 The Miz	.60	1.50
19 Wes Lee	.40	1.00
20 Becky Lynch	1.50	4.00
21 Xyon Quinn RC	.40	1.00
22 Drew McIntyre	.75	2.00
23 Jacy Jayne RC	1.50	4.00
24 Roman Reigns	2.50	6.00
25 Shayna Baszler	.75	2.00
26 Big E	.75	2.00
27 Cameron Grimes	.75	2.00
28 Montez Ford	.40	1.00
29 Odyssey Jones RC	.40	1.00
30 Bianca Belair	1.25	3.00
31 Zack Gibson	.40	1.00
32 Happy Corbin	.50	1.25
33 Mandy Rose	2.00	5.00
34 Sami Zayn	.60	1.50
35 Shotzi	1.50	4.00
36 Bobby Lashley	.75	2.00
37 Carmelo Hayes RC	.50	1.25
38 Angelo Dawkins	.50	1.25
39 Pete Dunne	.75	2.00
40 Carmella	1.00	2.50
41 James Drake	.40	1.00
42 Jey Uso	.50	1.25
43 Indi Hartwell	1.25	3.00
44 Sheamus	.60	1.50
45 Theory	1.00	2.50
46 Damian Priest	.75	2.00
47 Dexter Lumis	.40	1.00
48 Omos	.75	2.00
49 Rey Mysterio	1.00	2.50
50 Ronda Rousey	2.50	6.00
51 Candice LeRae	1.25	3.00
52 Jimmy Uso	.50	1.25
53 Io Shirai	.75	2.00
54 Shanky RC	.40	1.00
55 Xia Li	.75	2.00
56 Dolph Ziggler	.75	2.00
57 Fabian Aichner	.50	1.25
58 Randy Orton	1.00	2.50
59 Roderick Strong	.60	1.50
60 Doudrop	.60	1.50
61 Cora Jade RC	2.50	6.00
62 Jinder Mahal	.50	1.25
63 Katana Chance	.75	2.00
64 Shinsuke Nakamura	1.00	2.50
65 Asuka	1.50	4.00
66 Dominik Mysterio	.50	1.25
67 Grayson Waller RC	1.00	2.50
68 Riddle	1.00	2.50
69 Santos Escobar	.60	1.50
70 Liv Morgan	2.00	5.00
71 Dakota Kai	.75	2.00
72 King Woods	.50	1.25
73 Alba Fyre	1.00	2.50
74 Aliyah	.75	2.00
75 Bayley	1.00	2.50
76 Edge	1.50	4.00
77 Kushida	.60	1.50
78 Reggie	.50	1.25
79 Solo Sikoa RC	2.00	5.00
80 Nikki A.S.H.	.60	1.50
81 Gunther	1.00	2.50
82 Kofi Kingston	1.00	2.50
83 Raquel Rodriguez	1.00	2.50
84 Charlotte Flair	1.50	4.00
85 John Cena	1.25	3.00
86 Finn Balor	1.00	2.50
87 LA Knight	.60	1.50
88 Seth ìFreakinî Rollins	1.00	2.50
89 Elektra Lopez RC	1.00	2.50
90 Queen Zelina	.60	1.50
91 Ilja Dragunov	.40	1.00
92 Mansoor	.40	1.00
93 Sarray	.50	1.25
94 Naomi	.60	1.50
95 Lacey Evans	1.00	2.50
96 Gable Steveson RC	4.00	10.00
97 Ludwig Kaiser	.50	1.25
98 Veer Mahaan	1.00	2.50
99 Ciampa	1.00	2.50
100 Rhea Ripley	1.25	3.00
101 Andre The Giant	1.50	4.00
102 Bret "Hit Man" Hart	1.00	2.50
103 Faarooq	.50	1.25
104 Cactus Jack	.75	2.00
105 Ultimate Warrior	1.50	4.00
106 Dusty Rhodes	1.00	2.50
107 Hulk Hogan	2.00	5.00
108 Eddie Guerrero	1.25	3.00
109 Jerry Lawler	.75	2.00
110 Shawn Michaels	1.50	4.00
111 Rikishi	.50	1.25
112 Nikki Bella	1.00	2.50
113 Stone Cold Steve Austin	2.00	5.00
114 Chyna	.75	2.00
115 Undertaker	2.00	5.00
116 The Godfather	.40	1.00
117 Iron Sheik	.50	1.25
118 Triple H	1.50	4.00
119 Lex Luger	.50	1.25
120 Batista	.75	2.00
121 Rob Van Dam	.75	2.00
122 Bruno Sammartino	1.00	2.50
123 Ted DiBiase	.60	1.50
124 Diesel	.60	1.50
125 X-Pac	.50	1.25
126 The Great Khali	.50	1.25
127 JBL	.40	1.00
128 The Rock	4.00	10.00
129 Macho Man Randy Savage	1.50	4.00
130 Booker T	.75	2.00
131 Macho Man/Hulk Hogan	2.00	5.00
132 Fabian Aichner/Ludwig Kaiser	.50	1.25
133 Kane/Undertaker	2.00	5.00
134 Shawn Michaels/Triple H	1.50	4.00
135 Bret "Hit Man" Hart/Jim Neidhart	1.00	2.50
136 Erik/Ivar	.40	1.00
137 Mankind/The Rock	4.00	10.00
138 King Woods/Kofi Kingston	1.00	2.50
139 Bradshaw/Faarooq	.50	1.25
140 Randy Orton/Riddle	1.00	2.50
141 Booker T/Stevie Ray	.75	2.00
142 Gigi Dolin/Jacy Jayne	1.50	4.00
143 Edge/Randy Orton	1.50	4.00
144 Roman Reigns/Seth Rollins	2.50	6.00
145 Brie Bella/Nikki Bella	1.00	2.50
146 Angelo Dawkins/Montez Ford	.50	1.25
147 Diesel/Shawn Michaels	1.50	4.00
148 Chad Gable/Otis	.50	1.25
149 Gerald Brisco/Pat Patterson	.40	1.00
150 Jey Uso/Jimmy Uso	.50	1.25

2022 Revolution WWE Autographs

*SUNBURST/99: SAME VALUE AS BASIC
*CUBIC/49: .5X TO 1.2X BASIC AUTOS
*LAVA/10: UNPRICED DUE TO SCARCITY
*KALEIDO/1: UNPRICED DUE TO SCARCITY
RANDOMLY INSERTED INTO PACKS

AGABS Alexa Bliss	100.00	250.00
AGAJS AJ Styles	20.00	50.00
AGASK Asuka	30.00	75.00
AGBBL Bianca Belair	25.00	60.00
AGBGE Big E	8.00	20.00
AGBHT Bret "Hit Man" Hart	60.00	150.00
AGBLH Bobby Lashley	10.00	25.00
AGBLN Becky Lynch	50.00	125.00
AGBLS Brock Lesnar	100.00	250.00
AGBLY Bayley	25.00	60.00
AGBTS Batista	30.00	75.00
AGCLF Charlotte Flair	50.00	125.00
AGCML Carmella	15.00	40.00
AGDGZ Dolph Ziggler	8.00	20.00
AGDMC Drew McIntyre	12.00	30.00
AGDMY Dominik Mysterio	10.00	25.00
AGEGE Edge	30.00	75.00
AGFBL Finn Balor	12.00	30.00
AGGBG Goldberg	50.00	150.00
AGGSV Gable Steveson	60.00	150.00
AGGTH Gunther	12.00	30.00
AGHHG Hulk Hogan	200.00	500.00
AGHHH Triple H	100.00	250.00
AGIOS Io Shirai	20.00	50.00
AGJCN John Cena EXCH	75.00	200.00
AGKCZ Katana Chance	10.00	25.00
AGKKG Kofi Kingston	10.00	25.00
AGLIV Liv Morgan	40.00	100.00
AGMIZ The Miz	20.00	50.00
AGMRS Mandy Rose	75.00	200.00
AGOMS Omos	6.00	15.00
AGRDL Riddle	20.00	50.00
AGRMY Rey Mysterio	20.00	50.00
AGROR Randy Orton	50.00	125.00
AGRQG Raquel Rodriguez	12.00	30.00
AGRRN Roman Reigns EXCH	75.00	200.00
AGRRP Rhea Ripley	30.00	75.00
AGSBK Sasha Banks	60.00	150.00
AGSCA Stone Cold Steve Austin	300.00	750.00

AGSDV Sonya Deville 15.00 40.00
AGSHL Shawn Michaels 60.00 150.00
AGSHM Sheamus 10.00 25.00
AGSHZ Shotzi 40.00 100.00
AGSKN Shinsuke Nakamura 10.00 25.00
AGSMM Stephanie McMahon 100.00 250.00
AGSRL Seth Freakin Rollins 25.00 60.00
AGTSH Trish Stratus EXCH 40.00 100.00
AGUND Undertaker 200.00 500.00
AGXLI Xia Li 15.00 40.00

2022 Revolution WWE Liftoff

COMPLETE SET (10) 15.00 40.00
*GALACTIC: .6X TO 1.5X BASIC CARDS
*SUNBURST/99: .75X TO 2X BASIC CARDS
*CUBIC/49: 1.2X TO 3X BASIC CARDS
*LAVA/10: UNPRICED DUE TO SCARCITY
RANDOMLY INSERTED INTO PACKS

1 Bobby Lashley 1.25 3.00
2 Kofi Kingston 1.50 4.00
3 Charlotte Flair 2.50 6.00
4 Finn Balor 1.50 4.00
5 Alexa Bliss 10.00 25.00
6 Seth Rollins 1.50 4.00
7 Edge 2.50 6.00
8 Drew McIntyre 1.25 3.00
9 Rey Mysterio 1.50 4.00
10 AJ Styles 2.00 5.00

2022 Revolution WWE Liftoff Cubic

*CUBIC: 1.2X TO 3X BASIC CARDS

5 Alexa Bliss 30.00 75.00

2022 Revolution WWE Liftoff Galactic

*GALACTIC: .6X TO 1.5X BASIC CARDS

5 Alexa Bliss 15.00 40.00

2022 Revolution WWE Liftoff Sunburst

*SUNBURST: .75X TO 2X BASIC CARDS

5 Alexa Bliss 20.00 50.00

2022 Revolution WWE Shock Wave

COMPLETE SET (30) 30.00 75.00
*GALACTIC: .6X TO 1.5X BASIC CARDS
*SUNBURST/99: .75X TO 2X BASIC CARDS
*CUBIC/49: 1.2X TO 3X BASIC CARDS
*LAVA/10: UNPRICED DUE TO SCARCITY
RANDOMLY INSERTED INTO PACKS

1 Becky Lynch 2.50 6.00
2 Shinsuke Nakamura 1.50 4.00
3 Carmella 1.50 4.00
4 Xia Li 1.25 3.00
5 Doudrop 1.00 2.50
6 Roman Reigns 4.00 10.00
7 Jimmy Uso .75 2.00
8 Montez Ford .60 1.50
9 AJ Styles 2.00 5.00
10 Riddle 1.50 4.00
11 Big E 1.25 3.00
12 The Miz 1.00 2.50
13 Charlotte Flair 2.50 6.00
14 Bobby Lashley 1.25 3.00
15 Edge 2.50 6.00
16 Randy Orton 1.50 4.00
17 Kofi Kingston 1.50 4.00
18 Raquel Gonzalez 1.50 4.00
19 Apollo Crews .75 2.00
20 Sami Zayn 1.00 2.50
21 Brock Lesnar 3.00 8.00
22 Gunther 1.50 4.00
23 Dolph Ziggler 1.25 3.00
24 John Cena 2.00 5.00
25 Io Shirai 1.25 3.00
26 Sasha Banks 4.00 10.00
27 Mandy Rose 3.00 8.00
28 Rhea Ripley 2.00 5.00
29 Ronda Rousey 4.00 10.00
30 Seth "Freakin" Rollins 1.50 4.00

2022 Revolution WWE Supernova

COMPLETE SET (30) 60.00 150.00
*GALACTIC: .6X TO 1.5X BASIC CARDS
*SUNBURST/99: .75X TO 2X BASIC CARDS
*CUBIC/49: 1.2X TO 3X BASIC CARDS
*LAVA/10: UNPRICED DUE TO SCARCITY
RANDOMLY INSERTED INTO PACKS

1 Drew McIntyre 2.00 5.00
2 Shotzi 4.00 10.00
3 Jey Uso 1.25 3.00
4 Gunther 2.50 6.00
5 Kevin Owens 2.00 5.00
6 Mandy Rose 5.00 12.00
7 Alexa Bliss 12.00 30.00
8 Rey Mysterio 2.50 6.00
9 Bobby Lashley 2.00 5.00
10 Sasha Banks 6.00 15.00
11 Edge 4.00 10.00
12 The Miz 1.50 4.00
13 Jimmy Uso 1.25 3.00
14 Xia Li 2.00 5.00
15 Liv Morgan 5.00 12.00
16 Randy Orton 2.50 6.00
17 Becky Lynch 4.00 10.00
18 Rhea Ripley 3.00 8.00
19 Brock Lesnar 5.00 12.00
20 Seth "Freakin" Rollins 2.50 6.00
21 Finn Balor 2.50 6.00
22 Bayley 2.50 6.00
23 John Cena 3.00 8.00
24 Queen Zelina 1.50 4.00
25 AJ Styles 3.00 8.00
26 Raquel Gonzalez 2.50 6.00
27 Big E 2.00 5.00
28 Roman Reigns 6.00 15.00
29 Charlotte Flair 4.00 10.00
30 Shinsuke Nakamura 2.50 6.00

2022 Revolution WWE Supernova Cubic

*CUBIC: X TO X BASIC CARDS

7 Alexa Bliss 40.00 100.00

2022 Revolution WWE Supernova Sunburst

*SUNBURST: .75X TO 2X BASIC CARDS

7 Alexa Bliss 30.00 75.00

2022 Revolution WWE Vortex

COMPLETE SET (30) 60.00 150.00
*GALACTIC: .6X TO 1.5X BASIC CARDS
*SUNBURST/99: .75X TO 2X BASIC CARDS
*CUBIC/49: 1.2X TO 3X BASIC CARDS
*LAVA/10: UNPRICED DUE TO SCARCITY
RANDOMLY INSERTED INTO PACKS

1 Rey Mysterio 2.50 6.00
2 Bayley 2.50 6.00
3 Sasha Banks 6.00 15.00
4 Bobby Lashley 2.00 5.00
5 Brock Lesnar 5.00 12.00
6 Damian Priest 2.00 5.00
7 Finn Balor 2.50 6.00
8 John Cena 3.00 8.00
9 Liv Morgan 5.00 12.00
10 Apollo Crews 1.25 3.00
11 Ricochet 2.00 5.00
12 Becky Lynch 4.00 10.00
13 Sheamus 1.50 4.00
14 Bron Breakker 4.00 10.00
15 King Woods 1.25 3.00
16 Dominik Mysterio 1.25 3.00
17 Jey Uso 1.25 3.00
18 AJ Styles 3.00 8.00
19 Ronda Rousey 6.00 15.00
20 Asuka 4.00 10.00
21 Roman Reigns 6.00 15.00
22 Bianca Belair 3.00 8.00
23 Shotzi 4.00 10.00
24 Cora Jade 3.00 8.00
25 Queen Zelina 1.50 4.00
26 Drew McIntyre 2.00 5.00
27 Kevin Owens 2.00 5.00
28 Alexa Bliss 6.00 15.00
29 Randy Orton 2.50 6.00
30 Austin Theory 2.50 6.00

2022 Revolution WWE Vortex Cubic

*CUBIC: 1.2X TO 3X BASIC CARDS

28 Alexa Bliss 40.00 100.00

2022 Revolution WWE Vortex Sunburst

*SUNBURST: .75X TO 2X BASIC CARDS

28 Alexa Bliss 30.00 75.00

2023 Revolution WWE

LEGENDS (101-130)
TAG TEAMS (131-145)
FACTIONS (146-150)
*ASTRO: .5X TO 1.2X BASIC CARDS
*FRACTAL: .6X TO 1.5X BASIC CARDS
*GALACTIC: .75X TO 2X BASIC CARDS
*GROOVE: 1X TO 2.5X BASIC CARDS
*IMPACT/199: 1.2X TO 3X BASIC CARDS
*COSMIC/149: 1.5X TO 4X BASIC CARDS
*SUNBURST/99: 2X TO 5X BASIC CARDS
*CUBIC/49: 2.5X TO 6X BASIC CARDS
*LAVA/10: UNPRICED DUE TO SCARCITY
*KALEIDO/1: UNPRICED DUE TO SCARCITY

1 Brooks Jensen .50 1.25
2 Ronda Rousey 2.00 5.00
3 Dexter Lumis .50 1.25
4 Solo Sikoa 1.25 3.00
5 Ilja Dragunov .60 1.50
6 Karl Anderson .50 1.25
7 Bobby Lashley .75 2.00
8 Thea Hail .40 1.00
9 Bayley 1.00 2.50
10 Omos .50 1.25
11 Butch .50 1.25
12 Roxanne Perez 1.00 2.50
13 Dominik Mysterio .75 2.00
14 Sonya Deville .75 2.00
15 Indi Hartwell .75 2.00
16 Karrion Kross .75 2.00
17 Cody Rhodes 1.50 4.00
18 man.soor .40 1.00
19 Becky Lynch 1.50 4.00
20 Oro Mensah .50 1.25
21 Candice LeRae 1.00 2.50
22 Sami Zayn 1.00 2.50
23 Drew McIntyre 1.00 2.50
24 The Miz .60 1.50
25 IYO SKY 1.00 2.50
26 Katana Chance .75 2.00
27 AJ Styles 1.00 2.50
28 Matt Riddle 1.00 2.50
29 B-Fab RC 2.50 6.00
30 Otis .40 1.00
31 Carmella .75 2.00
32 Santos Escobar .40 1.00
33 Edge 1.50 4.00
34 Top Dolla RC 1.50 4.00
35 Jacy Jayne .75 2.00
36 Kayden Carter .60 1.50
37 Alba Fyre 1.00 2.50
38 Maxxine Dupri RC 3.00 8.00
39 Bianca Belair 1.25 3.00
40 Paul Heyman .50 1.25
41 Carmelo Hayes .60 1.50
42 Scarlett 1.50 4.00
43 Elias .50 1.25
44 Tyler Bate .50 1.25
45 JD McDonagh .50 1.25
46 Kevin Owens .75 2.00
47 Alexa Bliss 2.00 5.00
48 Meiko Satomura .40 1.00
49 Big E .60 1.50
50 Quincy Elliott .40 1.00
51 Chad Gable .50 1.25
52 Seth Rollins 1.00 2.50
53 Elton Prince .40 1.00
54 Von Wagner .40 1.00
55 Jey Uso .75 2.00
56 Kit Wilson .40 1.00
57 Apollo Crews .40 1.00
58 Mustafa Ali .40 1.00
59 Blair Davenport .60 1.50
60 Randy Orton 1.00 2.50
61 Charlotte Flair 1.25 3.00
62 Shayna Baszler .75 2.00
63 Emma .75 2.00
64 Wes Lee .50 1.25
65 Jimmy Uso .75 2.00
66 Kofi Kingston .60 1.50
67 Asuka 1.50 4.00
68 Natalya .60 1.50
69 Braun Strowman .60 1.50
70 Raquel Rodriguez 1.25 3.00
71 Cora Jade 1.50 4.00
72 Sheamus .60 1.50
73 Finn Balor 1.00 2.50
74 Xavier Woods .50 1.25
75 Joe Gacy .50 1.25
76 Liv Morgan 1.50 4.00
77 Austin Theory .75 2.00
78 Nathan Frazer .40 1.00
79 Bray Wyatt .75 2.00
80 Rey Mysterio 1.25 3.00
81 Dakota Kai .75 2.00
82 Shinsuke Nakamura .60 1.50
83 Gigi Dolin 1.00 2.50
84 Zelina Vega .75 2.00
85 Johnny Gargano .75 2.00
86 Luke Gallows .50 1.25
87 Ava RC 1.50 4.00
88 Nikki Cross .60 1.50
89 Brock Lesnar 1.25 3.00
90 Rhea Ripley 2.00 5.00
91 Damian Priest 1.00 2.50
92 Shotzi 1.00 2.50
93 Gunther 1.00 2.50
94 Zoey Stark .60 1.50
95 Josh Briggs .40 1.00
96 Mace .40 1.00
97 Baron Corbin .40 1.00
98 Nikkita Lyons 1.25 3.00
99 Bron Breakker 1.00 2.50
100 Roman Reigns 2.00 5.00
101 Big Boss Man L .50 1.25
102 Triple H L 1.00 2.50
103 Bret Hart 1.00 2.50
104 Undertaker L 2.00 5.00
105 Goldberg L 1.00 2.50
106 Mankind L .75 2.00
107 Miss Elizabeth L 1.00 2.50
108 Roddy Piper 1.00 2.50
109 Andre the Giant L 1.50 4.00
110 John Cena L 1.50 4.00
111 Bobby Heenan .60 1.50
112 Trish Stratus L 1.50 4.00
113 Diamond Dallas Page L .60 1.50
114 Vader L .60 1.50
115 Hulk Hogan L 1.50 4.00
116 Paul Bearer L .50 1.25
117 Steve Austin 2.00 5.00
118 Shawn Michaels L 1.50 4.00
119 Bam Bam Bigelow L .50 1.25
120 Terry Funk L .50 1.25
121 Scott Steiner L .60 1.50
122 Ultimate Warrior L 1.25 3.00
123 Eddie Guerrero L 1.25 3.00
124 Yokozuna L .75 2.00
125 Kevin Nash L .60 1.50
126 Razor Ramon L .75 2.00
127 Alundra Blayze L .60 1.50
128 Stacy Keibler L 1.00 2.50
129 Batista L .75 2.00
130 The Rock L 2.00 5.00
131 Typhoon/Earthquake TT .40 1.00
132 E.Prince/K.Wilson TT .40 1.00
133 The Steiners TT .60 1.50
134 A.Dawkins/M.Ford TT .60 1.50
135 K.Anderson/L.Gallows TT .50 1.25
136 The Usos TT .75 2.00
137 S.Zayn/K.Owens TT 1.00 2.50
138 Ivar/Erik TT .40 1.00
139 N.Volkoff/I.Sheik TT .40 1.00
140 The Creeds TT .40 1.00
141 B.Gunn/R.Dogg TT .60 1.50

142 J.Reid/R.Fowler TT	.50	1.25
143 Afa/Sika TT	.40	1.00
144 C.Gable/Otis TT	.50	1.25
145 Wolfgang/M.Coffey TT	.40	1.00
146 nWo FAC	1.50	4.00
147 Damage CTRL FAC	.75	2.00
148 D-Generation X FAC	2.00	5.00
149 The Bloodline FAC	2.50	6.00
150 The Judgment Day FAC	.75	2.00

2023 Revolution WWE Autographs

*SUNBURST/99: .6X TO 1.5X BASIC AUTOS
*CUBIC/49: .75X TO 2X BASIC AUTOS
*LAVA/10: UNPRICED DUE TO SCARCITY
*KALEIDO/1: UNPRICED DUE TO SCARCITY
RANDOMLY INSERTED INTO PACKS

AGFBL Finn Balor	10.00	25.00
AGRRP Rhea Ripley	30.00	75.00
AGSRL Seth Rollins	12.00	30.00
AGASK Asuka	15.00	40.00
AGSCA Steve Austin	75.00	200.00
AGLVM Liv Morgan	25.00	60.00
AGUTK Undertaker	150.00	400.00
AGBGE Big E	6.00	15.00
AGBLN Becky Lynch	20.00	50.00
AGSKY IYO SKY	12.00	30.00
AGDSL Diesel	12.00	30.00
AGSHZ Shotzi	10.00	25.00
AGSHL Shawn Michaels	60.00	150.00
AGBYL Bayley	10.00	25.00
AGBLS Brock Lesnar	25.00	60.00
AGDDP Diamond Dallas Page	15.00	40.00
AGBTS Batista	30.00	75.00
AGBKT Booker T	10.00	25.00
AGHMH Bret Hart	30.00	75.00
AGJBL JBL	8.00	20.00
AGLTA Lita	15.00	40.00
AGTCP Tommaso Ciampa	6.00	15.00
AGTSH Trish Stratus	25.00	60.00
AGBBL Bianca Belair	15.00	40.00
AGJCN John Cena	60.00	150.00
AGMDM Ted DiBiase	15.00	40.00
AGHHG Hulk Hogan	75.00	200.00
AGBCH Butch	6.00	15.00
AGKNE Kane	25.00	60.00
AGKON Kevin Owens	12.00	30.00
AGMKN Mankind	20.00	50.00
AGJGN Johnny Gargano	6.00	15.00
AGAJS AJ Styles	12.00	30.00
AGCFL Charlotte Flair	25.00	60.00
AGRRN Roman Reigns	60.00	150.00
AGATH Austin Theory	10.00	25.00
AGCRD Cody Rhodes	40.00	100.00
AGCML Carmella		
AGDMC Drew McIntyre	10.00	25.00
AGMRD Matt Riddle	10.00	25.00
AGRMY Rey Mysterio	12.00	30.00
AGSLS Solo Sikoa	15.00	40.00
AGABS Alexa Bliss	40.00	100.00
AGKKS Karrion Kross	8.00	20.00
AGGBG Goldberg	20.00	50.00
AGBPH Beth Phoenix	8.00	20.00
AGPHM Paul Heyman	30.00	75.00
AGDKI Dakota Kai	10.00	25.00
AGEGE Edge	20.00	50.00
AGZLV Zelina Vega	12.00	30.00

2023 Revolution WWE Kaboom!

RANDOMLY INSERTED INTO PACKS

1 Roman Reigns	400.00	1000.00
2 Edge	150.00	400.00
3 Triple H	200.00	500.00
4 Brock Lesnar	250.00	600.00
5 Cody Rhodes	300.00	750.00
6 The Rock	600.00	1500.00
7 Undertaker	300.00	750.00
8 Ronda Rousey	250.00	600.00
9 Andre the Giant	300.00	750.00
10 Bray Wyatt	150.00	400.00
11 John Cena	150.00	400.00
12 Randy Orton	150.00	400.00
13 Drew McIntyre	100.00	250.00
14 Hulk Hogan	500.00	1200.00
15 Alexa Bliss	500.00	1200.00
16 Charlotte Flair	150.00	400.00
17 Finn Balor	125.00	300.00
18 Shawn Michaels	250.00	600.00
19 Goldberg	125.00	300.00
20 Ultimate Warrior	300.00	750.00
21 Bianca Belair	125.00	300.00
22 Steve Austin	400.00	1000.00
23 Liv Morgan	150.00	400.00
24 Bayley	100.00	250.00
25 Becky Lynch	150.00	400.00

2023 Revolution WWE Liftoff!

*GALACTIC: .75X TO 2X BASIC CARDS
*SUNBURST/99: 1X TO 2.5X BASIC CARDS
*CUBIC/49: 1.2X TO 3X BASIC CARDS
*LAVA/10: UNPRICED DUE TO SCARCITY
*KALEIDO/1: UNPRICED DUE TO SCARCITY
RANDOMLY INSERTED INTO PACKS

1 Montez Ford	1.00	2.50
2 Kofi Kingston	1.00	2.50
3 Rey Mysterio	2.00	5.00
4 Eddie Guerrero	2.00	5.00
5 Rob Van Dam	1.25	3.00
6 Ricochet	1.00	2.50
7 Alexa Bliss	3.00	8.00
8 AJ Styles	1.50	4.00
9 Mustafa Ali	.60	1.50
10 Lita	1.50	4.00

2023 Revolution WWE Revolutionary Finishers

*GALACTIC: .75X TO 2X BASIC CARDS
*SUNBURST/99: 1X TO 2.5X BASIC CARDS
*CUBIC/49: 1.2X TO 3X BASIC CARDS
*KALEIDO/1: UNPRICED DUE TO SCARCITY
RANDOMLY INSERTED INTO PACKS

1 The Rock	4.00	10.00
2 Randy Orton	2.00	5.00
3 Steve Austin	4.00	10.00
4 Undertaker	4.00	10.00
5 Brock Lesnar	2.50	6.00
6 Curt Hennig	1.50	4.00
7 Shawn Michaels	3.00	8.00
8 Bret Hart	2.00	5.00
9 Roman Reigns	4.00	10.00
10 John Cena	3.00	8.00
11 Becky Lynch	3.00	8.00
12 Triple H	2.00	5.00
13 Sheamus	1.25	3.00
14 The Miz	1.25	3.00
15 Charlotte Flair	2.50	6.00
16 Bianca Belair	2.50	6.00
17 Austin Theory	1.50	4.00
18 Baron Corbin	.75	2.00
19 Braun Strowman	1.25	3.00
20 Bobby Lashley	1.50	4.00

2023 Revolution WWE Shock Wave

*GALACTIC: .75X TO 2X BASIC CARDS
*SUNBURST/99: 1X TO 2.5X BASIC CARDS
*CUBIC/49: 1.2X TO 3X BASIC CARDS
*LAVA/10: UNPRICED DUE TO SCARCITY
RANDOMLY INSERTED INTO PACKS

1 Bayley	1.50	4.00
2 Roman Reigns	3.00	8.00
3 Bobby Lashley	1.25	3.00
4 Seth Rollins	1.50	4.00
5 Carmelo Hayes	1.00	2.50
6 The Miz	1.00	2.50
7 Finn Balor	1.50	4.00
8 JD McDonagh	.75	2.00
9 AJ Styles	1.50	4.00
10 Roxanne Perez	1.50	4.00
11 Becky Lynch	2.50	6.00
12 Ronda Rousey	3.00	8.00
13 Braun Strowman	1.00	2.50
14 Sheamus	1.00	2.50
15 Cody Rhodes	2.50	6.00
16 Wes Lee	.75	2.00
17 Gunther	1.50	4.00
18 Johnny Gargano	1.25	3.00
19 Alba Fyre	1.50	4.00
20 Matt Riddle	1.50	4.00
21 Bianca Belair	2.00	5.00
22 Sami Zayn	1.50	4.00
23 Bron Breakker	1.50	4.00
24 Shinsuke Nakamura	1.00	2.50
25 Drew McIntyre	1.50	4.00
26 Zoey Stark	1.00	2.50
27 Ilja Dragunov	1.00	2.50
28 Kevin Owens	1.25	3.00
29 Austin Theory	1.25	3.00
30 Otis	.60	1.50

2023 Revolution WWE Star Gazing

*GALACTIC: .75X TO 2X BASIC CARDS
*SUNBURST/99: 1.2X TO 2.5X BASIC CARDS
*CUBIC/49: 1.5X TO 3X BASIC CARDS
*KALEIDO/1: UNPRICED DUE TO SCARCITY
RANDOMLY INSERTED INTO PACKS

1 Lita	2.00	5.00
2 Bron Breakker	2.00	5.00
3 Bret Hart	2.00	5.00
4 AJ Styles	2.00	5.00
5 Ricky Steamboat	1.50	4.00
6 Ultimate Warrior	2.50	6.00
7 Brock Lesnar	2.50	6.00
8 Hulk Hogan	3.00	8.00
9 JBL	.75	2.00
10 Triple H	2.00	5.00
11 Becky Lynch	3.00	8.00
12 Sami Zayn	2.00	5.00
13 Braun Strowman	1.25	3.00
14 Seth Rollins	2.00	5.00
15 Cody Rhodes	3.00	8.00
16 Andre the Giant	3.00	8.00
17 Trish Stratus	3.00	8.00
18 Undertaker	4.00	10.00
19 Booker T	1.00	2.50
20 Randy Orton	2.00	5.00
21 Bray Wyatt	1.50	4.00
22 Shawn Michaels	3.00	8.00
23 Roddy Piper	2.00	5.00
24 Eddie Guerrero	2.50	6.00
25 Gunther	2.00	5.00
26 Edge	3.00	8.00
27 Rey Mysterio	2.50	6.00
28 Steve Austin	4.00	10.00
29 Kofi Kingston	1.25	3.00
30 Roman Reigns	4.00	10.00
31 Rikishi	.75	2.00
32 Asuka	3.00	8.00
33 Batista	1.50	4.00
34 Alexa Bliss	4.00	10.00
35 Drew McIntyre	2.00	5.00
36 Mankind	1.50	4.00
37 The Miz	1.25	3.00
38 The Rock	4.00	10.00
39 John Cena	3.00	8.00
40 Charlotte Flair	2.50	6.00

1986 Scanlens WWF Australian

COMPLETE SET (66)	20.00	50.00
RINGSIDE ACTION (22-56)		
SUPERSTARS SPEAK (57-66)		
1 Hulk Hogan	100.00	200.00
2 The Iron Sheik	.20	.50
3 Captain Lou Albano	.20	.50
4 Junk Yard Dog	.20	.50
5 Paul Mr. Wonderful Orndorff	.15	.40
6 Jimmy Superfly Snuka	.15	.40
7 Rowdy Roddy Piper	2.00	5.00
8 Wendi Richter	.20	.50
9 Greg The Hammer Valentine	.15	.40
10 Brutus Beefcake	.12	.30
11 Jesse The Body Ventura	1.50	4.00
12 Big John Studd	.15	.40
13 Fabulous Moolah	.15	.40
14 Tito Santana	.12	.30
15 Hillbilly Jim	.15	.40
16 Hulk Hogan	125.00	250.00
17 Mr. Fuji	.12	.30
18 Rotundo & Windham	.12	.30
19 Moondog Spot	.12	.30
20 Chief Jay Strongbow	.12	.30
21 George "The Animal" Steele	.15	.40
22 Let Go of My Toe! RA	.15	.40
23 Lock 'Em Up! RA	.15	.40
24 Scalp 'Em! RA	.20	.50
25 Going for the Midsection! RA	.20	.50
26 Up in the Air! RA	.12	.30
27 All Tied Up! RA	.40	1.00
28 Here She Comes! RA	.12	.30
29 Stretched to the Limit! RA	2.00	5.00
30 Over He Goes! RA	.15	.40
31 An Appetite for Mayhem! RA	.15	.40
32 Putting on Pressure! RA	.20	.50
33 Smashed on a Knee! RA	.15	.40
34 A Fist Comes Flying! RA	.12	.30
35 Lemme' Out of This! RA	.12	.30
36 No Fair Chokin'! RA	.15	.40
37 Attacked by an Animal! RA	.15	.40
38 One Angry Man! RA	.40	1.00
39 Someone's Going Down! RA	.40	1.00
40 Strangle Hold! RA	.40	1.00
41 Bending an Arm! RA	.12	.30
42 Ready for a Pile Driver! RA	.15	.40
43 Face to the Canvas! RA	.12	.30
44 Paul Wants It All! RA	.15	.40
45 Kick to the Face! RA	.75	2.00
46 Ready for Action! RA	.12	.30
47 Putting on the Squeeze! RA	.20	.50
48 Giants in Action! RA	.40	1.00
49 Camel Clutch! RA	.20	.50
50 Pile Up! RA	.75	2.00
51 Can't Get Away! RA	.20	.50
52 Going for the Pin! RA	.12	.30
53 Ready to Fly! RA	.40	1.00
54 Crusher in a Crusher! RA	.20	.50
55 Fury of the Animal! RA	.15	.40
56 Wrong Kind of Music! RA	2.00	5.00
57 Who's your next challenger? SS	2.00	5.00
58 This dog has got a mean bite! SS	.20	.50
59 I don't think I'll ask... SS	.40	1.00
60 You Hulkster fans... SS	2.00	5.00
61 This ain't my idea... SS	.40	1.00
62 You mean Freddie Blassie... SS	.40	1.00
63 Mppgh Ecch Oong. SS	.20	.50
64 Rock n' wrestling... SS	.20	.50
65 Arrrggghhhh! SS	.15	.40
66 They took my reindeer! SS	.20	.50

2022 Select WWE

1 LA Knight	.50	1.25
2 Alba Fyre	.75	2.00
3 Alexa Bliss	2.00	5.00
4 Mansoor	.30	.75
5 Brock Lesnar	1.50	4.00
6 Raquel Rodriguez	.75	2.00
7 Eddie Guerrero	1.00	2.50
8 Seth Freakin Rollins	.75	2.00
9 The Godfather	.30	.75
10 The Miz	.50	1.25
11 Jey Uso	.40	1.00
12 Meiko Satomura RC	1.00	2.50
13 AJ Styles	1.00	2.50
14 Maryse	.50	1.25
15 Bron Breakker RC	3.00	8.00
16 Rhea Ripley	1.00	2.50
17 Dominik Mysterio	.40	1.00
18 Gunther	.75	2.00
19 Goldberg	1.25	3.00
20 The Rock	3.00	8.00
21 Jerry Lawler	.60	1.50
22 Montez Ford	.30	.75
23 Angel	.30	.75
24 Mick Foley	.60	1.50
25 Cedric Alexander	.30	.75
26 Ricochet	.60	1.50
27 Doudrop	.50	1.25
28 Shawn Michaels	1.25	3.00
29 The Great Khali	.40	1.00
30 Undertaker	1.50	4.00
31 Jimmy Uso	.40	1.00
32 Kevin Owens	.60	1.50
33 Angelo Dawkins	.40	1.00
34 Shotzi	1.25	3.00
35 Diamond Dallas Page	.40	1.00
36 Riddle	.75	2.00
37 Drew McIntyre	.60	1.50
38 Shelton Benjamin	.50	1.25
39 Harland RC	.30	.75
40 Triple H	1.25	3.00

41 Jinder Mahal .40 1.00
42 Xavier Woods .40 1.00
43 Apollo Crews .40 1.00
44 Liv Morgan 1.50 4.00
45 Charlotte Flair 1.25 3.00
46 Rikishi .40 1.00
47 Dusty Rhodes .75 2.00
48 Shinsuke Nakamura .75 2.00
49 Indi Hartwell 1.00 2.50
50 Sheamus .50 1.25
51 Happy Corbin .40 1.00
52 Kofi Kingston .75 2.00
53 Becky Lynch 1.25 3.00
54 Nikki A.S.H. .50 1.25
55 Stone Cold Steve Austin 1.50 4.00
56 Roman Reigns 2.00 5.00
57 Edge 1.25 3.00
58 Solo Sikoa RC 2.50 6.00
59 Julius Creed RC .75 2.00
60 Veer Mahaan .75 2.00
61 Joe Gacy RC .75 2.00
62 Kushida .50 1.25
63 Big E .60 1.50
64 Odyssey Jones RC .30 .75
65 Cora Jade RC 2.50 6.00
66 Ciampa .75 2.00
67 Dolph Ziggler .60 1.50
68 Sonya Deville .75 2.00
69 Hulk Hogan 1.50 4.00
70 Wes Lee .30 .75
71 John Cena 1.00 2.50
72 Macho Man Randy Savage 1.25 3.00
73 Blair Davenport RC 1.50 4.00
74 Omos .60 1.50
75 Damian Priest .60 1.50
76 Santos Escobar .50 1.25
77 Faarooq .40 1.00
78 Grayson Waller RC 1.25 3.00
79 Humberto .30 .75
80 Bayley .75 2.00
81 Jordan Devlin .30 .75
82 Rick Boogs .40 1.00
83 Bobby Lashley .60 1.50
84 Butch .60 1.50
85 Bret Hit Man Hart .75 2.00
86 Sasha Banks 2.00 5.00
87 Gigi Dolin 2.00 5.00
88 Ted DiBiase .50 1.25
89 Ilja Dragunov .30 .75
90 Ronda Rousey 2.00 5.00
91 Katana Chance .60 1.50
92 Rob Van Dam .60 1.50
93 Booker T .60 1.50
94 Randy Orton .75 2.00
95 Bruno Sammartino .75 2.00
96 Von Wagner RC .30 .75
97 Jacy Jayne RC 2.50 6.00
98 Tony D'Angelo RC 1.00 2.50
99 Io Shirai .60 1.50
100 Michael Cole .30 .75
101 Charlotte Flair 1.50 4.00
102 Shane McMahon .75 2.00
103 Edge 1.50 4.00
104 Typhoon .40 1.00
105 Jey Uso .50 1.25
106 Kevin Owens .75 2.00
107 AJ Styles 1.25 3.00
108 MVP .40 1.00
109 Big E .75 2.00
110 Ricochet .75 2.00
111 Chyna .75 2.00
112 Shayna Baszler .75 2.00
113 Elektra Lopez RC 1.00 2.50
114 Ultimate Warrior 1.50 4.00
115 Jimmy Hart .50 1.25
116 Xavier Woods .50 1.25
117 Finn Balor 1.00 2.50
118 Natalya .60 1.50
119 Boa .40 1.00
120 Riddle 1.00 2.50
121 Cora Jade 3.00 8.00
122 Sheamus .60 1.50
123 Gene Okerlund .60 1.50
124 Von Wagner .40 1.00
125 Jinny RC .40 1.00
126 LA Knight .60 1.50
127 Aliyah .75 2.00
128 Nina Samuels .50 1.25
129 Bret Hit Man Hart 1.00 2.50
130 Ridge Holland .40 1.00
131 Damian Priest .75 2.00
132 Shinsuke Nakamura 1.00 2.50
133 Gigi Dolin 2.00 5.00
134 Bad News Barrett .40 1.00
135 Joaquin Wilde .60 1.50
136 Elton Prince RC .50 1.25
137 Alundra Blayze .50 1.25
138 Oliver Carter RC .40 1.00
139 Brock Lesnar 2.00 5.00
140 Rob Van Dam .75 2.00
141 Dana Brooke .40 1.00
142 Shotzi 1.50 4.00
143 Grayson Waller 1.00 2.50
144 Wolfgang .40 1.00
145 John Cena 1.25 3.00
146 Madcap Moss .40 1.00
147 Aoife Valkyrie RC .75 2.00
148 Otis .50 1.25
149 Bruno Sammartino 1.00 2.50
150 Roderick Strong .60 1.50
151 Dave Mastiff .40 1.00
152 The Miz .60 1.50
153 Happy Corbin .50 1.25
154 Xia Li .75 2.00
155 Jordan Devlin .40 1.00
156 Mandy Rose 2.00 5.00
157 Apollo Crews .50 1.25
158 Queen Zelina .60 1.50
159 Bron Breakker 3.00 8.00
160 Roman Reigns 2.50 6.00
161 Dolph Ziggler .75 2.00
162 The Rock 4.00 10.00
163 Harland .40 1.00
164 Zack Gibson .40 1.00
165 Julius Creed 1.00 2.50
166 Mark Coffey .40 1.00
167 Asuka 1.50 4.00
168 Randy Orton 1.00 2.50
169 Cactus Jack .75 2.00
170 Kit Wilson RC .40 1.00
171 Drew Gulak .50 1.25
172 Ciampa 1.00 2.50
173 Indi Hartwell 2.50 6.00
174 Vader .50 1.25
175 Kama .40 1.00
176 Meiko Satomura 1.25 3.00
177 Becky Lynch 1.50 4.00
178 Cruz Del Toro .60 1.50
179 Cameron Grimes .75 2.00
180 Stone Cold Steve Austin 2.00 5.00
181 Drew McIntyre .75 2.00
182 Tony D'Angelo 1.25 3.00
183 Jacy Jayne 2.50 6.00
184 Umaga .40 1.00
185 Kayden Carter .75 2.00
186 Montez Ford .40 1.00
187 Beth Phoenix .75 2.00
188 Reggie .50 1.25
189 Carmella 1.00 2.50
190 Saxon Huxley RC .40 1.00
191 Eddie Guerrero 1.25 3.00
192 Trent Seven .50 1.25
193 Jerry Lawler .75 2.00
194 Nikkita Lyons RC 6.00 15.00
195 Kevin Nash .60 1.50
196 Mr. T .75 2.00
197 Big Boss Man .60 1.50
198 Rick Boogs .50 1.25
199 Chad Gable .40 1.00
200 Seth Freakin Rollins 1.00 2.50
201 Liv Morgan 3.00 8.00
202 AJ Styles 1.50 4.00
203 Nikki Bella 1.25 3.00
204 Big E 1.00 2.50
205 Ricky The Dragon Steamboat 1.00 2.50
206 Carmelo Hayes RC 1.50 4.00
207 Shawn Michaels 2.00 5.00
208 Gable Steveson RC 3.00 8.00
209 Trick Williams RC .50 1.25
210 Io Shirai 1.00 2.50
211 Macho Man Randy Savage 2.00 5.00
212 Alexa Bliss 3.00 8.00
213 Otis .60 1.50
214 Bobby Lashley 1.00 2.50
215 Riddle 1.25 3.00
216 Charlotte Flair 2.00 5.00
217 Sheamus .75 2.00
218 Finn Balor 1.25 3.00
219 Triple H 2.00 5.00
220 Joe Gacy 1.25 3.00
221 Madcap Moss .50 1.25
222 Amale RC .50 1.25
223 Paul Heyman .75 2.00
224 Bret Hit Man Hart 1.25 3.00
225 Rikishi .60 1.50
226 Dakota Kai 1.00 2.50
227 Shinsuke Nakamura 1.25 3.00
228 Gigi Dolin 4.00 10.00
229 Ultimate Warrior 2.00 5.00
230 John Cena 1.50 4.00
231 Mandy Rose 3.00 8.00
232 Aliyah 1.00 2.50
233 Nikkita Lyons 10.00 25.00
234 Brie Bella 1.00 2.50
235 Rob Van Dam 1.00 2.50
236 Damian Priest 1.00 2.50
237 Stone Cold Steve Austin 3.00 8.00
238 Goldberg 2.50 6.00
239 Undertaker 5.00 12.00
240 Jordan Devlin .50 1.25
241 Mankind 1.00 2.50
242 Apollo Crews .60 1.50
243 High Chief Peter Maivia .50 1.25
244 The British Bulldog .75 2.00
245 Roderick Strong .75 2.00
246 Dexter Lumis .50 1.25
247 Solo Sikoa 2.50 6.00
248 Grayson Waller 1.25 3.00
249 Xia Brookside RC 4.00 10.00
250 Kevin Owens 1.00 2.50
251 Ludwig Kaiser .60 1.50
252 Asuka 2.00 5.00
253 Randy Orton 1.25 3.00
254 Brock Lesnar 4.00 10.00
255 Roman Reigns 4.00 10.00
256 Diesel .75 2.00
257 Stacy Keibler 4.00 10.00
258 Gunther 1.25 3.00
259 X-Pac .60 1.50
260 Xavier Woods .60 1.50
261 Maryse .75 2.00
262 Theory 1.25 3.00
263 Raquel Rodriguez 1.25 3.00
264 Bron Breakker 5.00 12.00
265 Sami Zayn .75 2.00
266 Doudrop .75 2.00
267 Stephanie McMahon .75 2.00
268 Happy Corbin .60 1.50
269 Zoey Stark .60 1.50
270 Kofi Kingston 1.25 3.00
271 Ashton Smith RC .60 1.50
272 Bayley 1.25 3.00
273 Rey Mysterio 1.25 3.00
274 Cameron Grimes 1.00 2.50
275 Santos Escobar .75 2.00
276 Drew McIntyre 1.00 2.50
277 The Miz .75 2.00
278 Hulk Hogan 6.00 15.00
279 Ronda Rousey 5.00 12.00
280 Kushida .75 2.00
281 Meiko Satomura 1.50 4.00
282 Becky Lynch 2.00 5.00
283 Rhea Ripley 4.00 10.00
284 Candice LeRae 1.50 4.00
285 Sasha Banks 10.00 25.00
286 Edge 2.00 5.00
287 The Rock 10.00 25.00
288 Ilja Dragunov .50 1.25
289 Nathan Frazer RC .50 1.25
290 LA Knight .75 2.00
291 Montez Ford .50 1.25
292 Bianca Belair 1.50 4.00
293 Rick Boogs .60 1.50
294 Carmella 1.25 3.00
295 Seth Freakin Rollins 1.25 3.00
296 Fabian Aichner .60 1.50
297 Ciampa 1.25 3.00
298 Indi Hartwell 1.50 4.00
299 Cody Rhodes 12.00 30.00
300 Lex Luger .60 1.50
301 The Rock 6.00 15.00
302 Jimmy Uso .75 2.00
303 Mandy Rose 10.00 25.00
304 A-Kid RC .75 2.00
305 Nikki Bella 1.50 4.00
306 Bobby Lashley 1.25 3.00
307 Rey Mysterio 1.50 4.00
308 Damian Priest 1.25 3.00
309 Santos Escobar 1.00 2.50
310 Erik .60 1.50
311 Trent Seven .75 2.00
312 Jinny .60 1.50
313 Ludwig Kaiser .75 2.00
314 Akira Tozawa .75 2.00
315 Nikolai Volkoff .60 1.50
316 Brie Bella 1.25 3.00
317 Ravishing Rick Rude 1.25 3.00
318 Dana Brooke .60 1.50
319 Sarray .75 2.00
320 Ikemen Jiro RC .60 1.50
321 Tyler Bate .75 2.00
322 John Cena 2.00 5.00
323 Booker T 1.25 3.00
324 Amari Miller RC 5.00 12.00
325 Noam Dar .75 2.00
326 Brock Lesnar 3.00 8.00
327 Riddle 1.50 4.00
328 Dominik Mysterio .75 2.00
329 Sasha Banks 10.00 25.00
330 Iron Sheik .75 2.00
331 Undertaker 8.00 20.00
332 Don Muraco .60 1.50
333 Molly Holly .75 2.00
334 Andre Chase RC .60 1.50
335 Omos 1.25 3.00
336 Brutus Creed RC .75 2.00
337 Robert Roode .75 2.00
338 Drew McIntyre 1.25 3.00
339 Michelle McCool 1.00 2.50
340 Ivar .60 1.50
341 Xia Li 1.25 3.00
342 Stone Cold Steve Austin 3.00 8.00
343 Roxanne Perez RC 12.00 30.00
344 Theory 1.50 4.00
345 Paige 8.00 20.00
346 Carmelo Hayes .75 2.00
347 Robert Stone RC .60 1.50
348 Dude Love 1.25 3.00
349 Seth Freakin Rollins 1.50 4.00
350 Ivy Nile RC .60 1.50
351 Xyon Quinn RC .60 1.50
352 Josh Briggs RC .60 1.50
353 Mr. Perfect Curt Hennig 1.25 3.00
354 Batista 1.25 3.00
355 Papa Shango .60 1.50
356 Paul Heyman 1.00 2.50
357 Rocky Johnson .75 2.00
358 Duke Hudson RC .60 1.50
359 Shinsuke Nakamura 1.50 4.00
360 Jacy Jayne 8.00 20.00
361 Yulisa Leon RC 3.00 8.00
362 Kenny Williams RC .60 1.50
363 Trish Stratus 8.00 20.00
364 Bayley 1.50 4.00
365 Primate RC .60 1.50
366 Charlotte Flair 2.50 6.00
367 Rohan Raja RC .60 1.50
368 Eddie Dennis RC .60 1.50
369 Tamina .75 2.00
370 James Drake .60 1.50
371 Bron Breakker 8.00 20.00
372 Lacey Evans 1.50 4.00
373 Naomi 1.00 2.50
374 Becky Lynch 12.00 30.00
375 Queen Zelina 1.00 2.50
376 Superstar Billy Graham .60 1.50
377 Roman Reigns 4.00 10.00
378 Edge 2.50 6.00
379 T-Bar .60 1.50
380 JBL .60 1.50

381 Ronda Rousey 8.00 20.00
382 Lash Legend RC .60 1.50
383 Elton Prince .75 2.00
384 Bianca Belair 2.00 5.00
385 Rampage Brown RC .60 1.50
386 Commander Azeez .75 2.00
387 R-Truth .75 2.00
388 Ezekiel .60 1.50
389 Terry Funk 1.00 2.50
390 Jey Uso .75 2.00
391 Ken Shamrock .75 2.00
392 Mace .60 1.50
393 Natalya 1.00 2.50
394 Big E 1.25 3.00
395 Randy Orton 1.50 4.00
396 Corey Graves .60 1.50
397 Sami Zayn 1.00 2.50
398 Kit Wilson .60 1.50
399 The Miz 1.00 2.50
400 Jim The Anvil Neidhart .75 2.00

2022 Select WWE Autographed Memorabilia

*TIE-DYE/25: UNPRICED DUE TO SCARCITY
*GOLD/10: UNPRICED DUE TO SCARCITY
*BLACK/1: UNPRICED DUE TO SCARCITY
STATED PRINT RUN 199 SER.#'d SETS
B.LESNAR SER.#'d TO 49 CARDS

AMABL Alexa Bliss/199 50.00 125.00
AMACR Apollo Crews/199 8.00 20.00
AMADK Angelo Dawkins/199 6.00 15.00
AMAJS AJ Styles/199 12.00 30.00
AMASK Asuka/199 30.00 75.00
AMBBL Bianca Belair/199 15.00 40.00
AMBGE Big E EXCH/199
AMBLS Bobby Lashley/199 12.00 30.00
AMBLS Brock Lesnar/49 50.00 125.00
AMBLY Becky Lynch/199 30.00 75.00
AMBLY Bayley EXCH/199 25.00 60.00
AMCFL Charlotte Flair/199 25.00 60.00
AMCML Carmella/199 20.00 50.00
AMDBK Dana Brooke/199 10.00 25.00
AMDMI Drew McIntyre/199 10.00 25.00
AMDMY Dominik Mysterio/199 6.00 15.00
AMDPS Damian Priest/199 6.00 15.00
AMEDG Edge/199 30.00 75.00
AMFBL Finn Balor/199 15.00 40.00
AMJMU Jimmy Uso/199 10.00 25.00
AMJUS Jey Uso/199 10.00 25.00
AMKKG Kofi Kingston/199 6.00 15.00
AMKOW Kevin Owens/199 15.00 40.00
AMLVM Liv Morgan/199 60.00 150.00
AMMIZ The Miz/199 15.00 40.00
AMRDL Riddle/199 15.00 40.00
AMRHR Rhea Ripley/199 25.00 60.00
AMRMY Rey Mysterio/199 15.00 40.00
AMROR Randy Orton EXCH/199 30.00 75.00
AMRRN Roman Reigns/199 40.00 100.00
AMSBK Sasha Banks/199 60.00 150.00
AMSHM Sheamus/199 8.00 20.00
AMSHZ Shotzi/199 30.00 75.00
AMSKN Shinsuke Nakamura/199 10.00 25.00
AMSRL Seth Freakin Rollins/199 15.00 40.00

2022 Select WWE Championship

*FLASH: .5X TO 1.2X BASIC CARDS
*SILVER: .6X TO 1.5X BASIC CARDS
*GOLD/10: UNPRICED DUE TO SCARCITY
*BLACK/1: UNPRICED DUE TO SCARCITY
RANDOMLY INSERTED INTO PACKS

1 Bobby Lashley 1.25 3.00
2 Undertaker 3.00 8.00
3 Randy Orton 1.50 4.00
4 Becky Lynch 2.50 6.00
5 Stone Cold Steve Austin 3.00 8.00
6 John Cena 2.00 5.00
7 The Rock 6.00 15.00
8 Brock Lesnar 3.00 8.00
9 Roman Reigns 4.00 10.00
10 Charlotte Flair 2.50 6.00

2022 Select WWE Global Icons

*FLASH: .5X TO 1.2X BASIC CARDS
*SILVER: .6X TO 1.5X BASIC CARDS
*GOLD/10: UNPRICED DUE TO SCARCITY
*BLACK/1: UNPRICED DUE TO SCARCITY
RANDOMLY INSERTED INTO PACKS

1 Finn Balor 2.00 5.00
2 Hacksaw Jim Duggan 1.00 2.50
3 Bret "Hit Man" Hart 2.00 5.00
4 The Great Khali 1.00 2.50
5 Sheamus 1.25 3.00
6 Gunther 2.00 5.00
7 Trish Stratus 4.00 10.00
8 Drew McIntyre 1.50 4.00
9 Pat Patterson .75 2.00
10 Iron Sheik 1.00 2.50
11 Meiko Satomura 2.50 6.00
12 The British Bulldog 1.25 3.00
13 Becky Lynch 3.00 8.00
14 Asuka 3.00 8.00
15 Yokozuna 1.00 2.50
16 Rey Mysterio 2.00 5.00
17 Shinsuke Nakamura 2.00 5.00
18 Andre The Giant 3.00 8.00
19 Kevin Owens 1.50 4.00
20 Hulk Hogan 4.00 10.00

2022 Select WWE Hall of Fame Selections

*FLASH: .5X TO 1.2X BASIC CARDS
*SILVER: .6X TO 1.5X BASIC CARDS
*GOLD/10: UNPRICED DUE TO SCARCITY
*BLACK/1: UNPRICED DUE TO SCARCITY
RANDOMLY INSERTED INTO PACKS

1 Stone Cold Steve Austin 3.00 8.00
2 Booker T 1.25 3.00
3 Shawn Michaels 2.50 6.00
4 Ultimate Warrior 2.50 6.00
5 Trish Stratus 3.00 8.00
6 Macho Man Randy Savage 2.50 6.00
7 Kevin Nash 1.00 2.50
8 Edge 2.50 6.00
9 Ricky "The Dragon" Steamboat 1.25 3.00
10 Dusty Rhodes 1.50 4.00
11 Eddie Guerrero 2.00 5.00
12 Mick Foley 1.25 3.00
13 The British Bulldog 1.00 2.50
14 Rikishi .75 2.00
15 Superstar Billy Graham .60 1.50
16 Jerry Lawler 1.25 3.00
17 Hulk Hogan 3.00 8.00
18 Bret "Hit Man" Hart 1.50 4.00
19 Mr. Perfect Curt Hennig 1.25 3.00
20 Ted DiBiase 1.00 2.50

2022 Select WWE Legendary Signatures

*RED WAVE: SAME VALUE AS BASIC
*RED/99: .5X TO 1.2X BASIC AUTOS
*BLUE/49: .6X TO 1.5X BASIC AUTOS
*TIE-DYE/25: UNPRICED DUE TO SCARCITY
*GOLD/10: UNPRICED DUE TO SCARCITY
*GOLD WAVE/5: UNPRICED DUE TO SCARCITY
*BLACK/1: UNPRICED DUE TO SCARCITY
RANDOMLY INSERTED INTO PACKS

LSBKT Booker T 12.00 30.00
LSBPH Beth Phoenix 8.00 20.00
LSHHH Triple H 100.00 250.00
LSJCN John Cena EXCH 50.00 125.00
LSKNE Kane 10.00 25.00
LSLTA Lita 12.00 30.00
LSNBL Nikki Bella 12.00 30.00
LSRKI Rikishi 8.00 20.00
LSSCA Stone Cold Steve Austin 100.00 250.00
LSUND Undertaker 100.00 250.00

2022 Select WWE NXT 2.0

*FLASH: .5X TO 1.2X BASIC CARDS
*SILVER: .6X TO 1.5X BASIC CARDS
*GOLD/10: UNPRICED DUE TO SCARCITY
*BLACK/1: UNPRICED DUE TO SCARCITY
RANDOMLY INSERTED INTO PACKS

1 Gigi Dolin 2.50 6.00
2 LA Knight 1.00 2.50
3 Carmelo Hayes .75 2.00
4 Raquel Rodriguez 1.50 4.00
5 Ilja Dragunov .60 1.50
6 Ludwig Kaiser .75 2.00
7 Dakota Kai 1.25 3.00
8 Nikkita Lyons 1.50 4.00
9 Gunther 1.50 4.00
10 Jordan Devlin .60 1.50
11 Bron Breakker 2.50 6.00
12 Cameron Grimes 1.25 3.00
13 Ciampa 1.50 4.00
14 Jacy Jayne 1.50 4.00
15 Meiko Satomura 2.00 5.00
16 Fabian Aichner .75 2.00
17 Grayson Waller 1.50 4.00
18 Santos Escobar 1.00 2.50
19 Mandy Rose 3.00 8.00
20 Io Shirai 1.25 3.00

2022 Select WWE Phenomenon

*FLASH: .5X TO 1.2X BASIC CARDS
*SILVER: .6X TO 1.5X BASIC CARDS
*GOLD/10: UNPRICED DUE TO SCARCITY
*BLACK/1: UNPRICED DUE TO SCARCITY
RANDOMLY INSERTED INTO PACKS

1 Finn Balor 1.50 4.00
2 Bianca Belair 2.00 5.00
3 Omos 1.25 3.00
4 AJ Styles 2.00 5.00
5 Rey Mysterio 1.50 4.00
6 Seth Freakin Rollins 1.50 4.00
7 Shawn Michaels 2.50 6.00
8 Big E 1.25 3.00
9 Mankind 1.25 3.00
10 Stone Cold Steve Austin 3.00 8.00
11 Rob Van Dam 1.25 3.00
12 Becky Lynch 2.50 6.00
13 Kofi Kingston 1.50 4.00
14 Randy Orton 1.50 4.00
15 Roman Reigns 4.00 10.00
16 Kevin Owens 1.25 3.00
17 Shinsuke Nakamura 1.50 4.00
18 Undertaker 3.00 8.00
19 Drew McIntyre 1.25 3.00
20 The Miz 1.00 2.50
21 Edge 2.50 6.00
22 Rhea Ripley 2.00 5.00
23 Xavier Woods .75 2.00
24 Riddle 1.50 4.00
25 Sheamus 1.00 2.50
26 Brock Lesnar 3.00 8.00
27 Sasha Banks 4.00 10.00
28 The Rock 6.00 15.00
29 Bron Breakker 2.50 6.00
30 Charlotte Flair 2.50 6.00

2022 Select WWE Ringside Action Signatures

*RED WAVE: .5X TO 1.2X BASIC AUTOS
*RED/99: .6X TO 1.5X BASIC AUTOS
*BLUE/49: .75X TO 2X BASIC AUTOS
*TIE-DYE/25: UNPRICED DUE TO SCARCITY
*GOLD/10: UNPRICED DUE TO SCARCITY
*GOLD WAVE/5: UNPRICED DUE TO SCARCITY
*BLACK/1: UNPRICED DUE TO SCARCITY
RANDOMLY INSERTED INTO PACKS

RAABL Alexa Bliss 50.00 125.00
RAACR Apollo Crews 6.00 15.00
RABBK Bron Breakker 30.00 75.00
RABDV Blair Davenport 10.00 25.00
RABGE Big E 8.00 20.00
RABLY Bayley 15.00 40.00
RACAZ Commander Azeez 5.00 12.00
RACFL Charlotte Flair 25.00 60.00
RACGR Cameron Grimes 8.00 20.00
RACHY Carmelo Hayes 10.00 25.00
RACJD Cora Jade 40.00 100.00
RADDR Doudrop 8.00 20.00
RADGL Drew Gulak 5.00 12.00
RADKI Dakota Kai 15.00 40.00
RADMI Drew McIntyre 12.00 30.00
RADZG Dolph Ziggler 8.00 20.00
RAFBL Finn Balor 12.00 30.00
RAGTH Gunther 12.00 30.00
RAGWL Grayson Waller 10.00 25.00
RAIVR Ivar 5.00 12.00
RAJDV Jordan Devlin 6.00 15.00
RAJMH Jinder Mahal 8.00 20.00
RAJUS Jey Uso 10.00 25.00
RAKCT Katana Chance 10.00 25.00
RAKWD Xavier Woods 5.00 12.00
RALAK LA Knight 8.00 20.00
RALEV Lacey Evans 10.00 25.00
RAMIZ The Miz 8.00 20.00
RAMZF Montez Ford 8.00 20.00
RANKA Nikki A.S.H. 6.00 15.00
RANOM Naomi 6.00 15.00
RAOMS Omos 6.00 15.00
RARCC Ricochet 8.00 20.00
RARGE Reggie 5.00 12.00
RARHD Ridge Holland 5.00 12.00
RARMY Rey Mysterio 15.00 40.00
RARQG Raquel Rodriguez 12.00 30.00
RARRD Robert Roode 6.00 15.00
RARRN Roman Reigns 40.00 100.00
RASBZ Shayna Baszler 10.00 25.00
RASKN Shinsuke Nakamura 8.00 20.00
RASRL Seth Freakin Rollins 12.00 30.00
RAVWG Von Wagner 6.00 15.00
RAXLI Xia Li 12.00 30.00

2022 Select WWE Selective Swatches

*TIE-DYE/25: UNPRICED DUE TO SCARCITY
*GOLD/10: UNPRICED DUE TO SCARCITY
*BLACK/1: UNPRICED DUE TO SCARCITY
RANDOMLY INSERTED INTO PACKS

SWABL Alexa Bliss 12.00 30.00
SWACR Apollo Crews 3.00 8.00
SWADK Angelo Dawkins 2.50 6.00
SWAJS AJ Styles 5.00 12.00
SWASK Asuka 5.00 12.00
SWBBL Bianca Belair 4.00 10.00
SWBLS Bobby Lashley 3.00 8.00
SWBLS Brock Lesnar 5.00 12.00
SWBLY Becky Lynch 10.00 25.00
SWCFL Charlotte Flair 6.00 15.00
SWCML Carmella 5.00 12.00
SWDBK Dana Brooke 2.50 6.00
SWDMI Drew McIntyre 3.00 8.00
SWDMY Dominik Mysterio 2.50 6.00
SWDPS Damian Priest 2.50 6.00
SWEDG Edge 4.00 10.00
SWFBL Finn Balor 5.00 12.00
SWJMU Jimmy Uso 4.00 10.00
SWJUS Jey Uso 4.00 10.00
SWKKG Kofi Kingston 3.00 8.00
SWKOW Kevin Owens 4.00 10.00
SWLVM Liv Morgan 12.00 30.00
SWMIZ The Miz 2.50 6.00
SWRDL Riddle 3.00 8.00
SWRHR Rhea Ripley 5.00 12.00
SWRKO Randy Orton 3.00 8.00
SWRMY Rey Mysterio 3.00 8.00
SWRRN Roman Reigns 6.00 15.00
SWSBK Sasha Banks 8.00 20.00
SWSHM Sheamus 4.00 10.00
SWSHZ Shotzi 6.00 15.00
SWSKN Shinsuke Nakamura 3.00 8.00
SWSRL Seth Freakin Rollins 3.00 8.00

2022 Select WWE Signature Selections

*TIE-DYE/25: UNPRICED DUE TO SCARCITY
*GOLD/10: UNPRICED DUE TO SCARCITY
*GOLD FLASH/10: UNPRICED DUE TO SCARCITY
*BLACK/1: UNPRICED DUE TO SCARCITY
*BLACK FLASH/1: UNPRICED DUE TO SCARCITY
RANDOMLY INSERTED INTO PACKS
BLASTER EXCLUSIVE

SNAKD A-Kid 8.00 20.00
SNALB Alundra Blayze 15.00 40.00
SNAML Amale 10.00 25.00
SNAOF Aoife Valkyrie 10.00 25.00
SNBBF Brutus Beefcake 10.00 25.00
SNBBK Bron Breakker 30.00 75.00
SNBBL Brie Bella 15.00 40.00
SNBCD Brutus Creed 10.00 25.00
SNBDV Blair Davenport 10.00 25.00
SNBLS Brock Lesnar 100.00 250.00

Card	Low	High
SNBLY Becky Lynch	60.00	150.00
SNBOA Boa	5.00	12.00
SNBTA Batista	30.00	75.00
SNBWB Bushwhacker Butch	6.00	15.00
SNBWL Bushwhacker Luke	6.00	15.00
SNCBO Cowboy Bob Orton	6.00	15.00
SNCGR Cameron Grimes	8.00	20.00
SNCHY Carmelo Hayes	10.00	25.00
SNCJD Cora Jade	40.00	100.00
SNCLR Candice LeRae	12.00	30.00
SNDLM Dexter Lumis	8.00	20.00
SNDLN Dani Luna	8.00	20.00
SNDMI Drew McIntyre	12.00	30.00
SNDMS Dave Mastiff	5.00	12.00
SNEDG Edge	30.00	75.00
SNEMK Emilia McKenzie	8.00	20.00
SNEPC Elton Prince	8.00	20.00
SNFAI Fabian Aichner	5.00	12.00
SNFBL Finn Balor	12.00	30.00
SNFMW Flash Morgan Webster	5.00	12.00
SNGBS Gerald Brisco	8.00	20.00
SNGHV Greg Valentine	10.00	25.00
SNGSV Gable Steveson	40.00	100.00
SNGTH Gunther	12.00	30.00
SNGWL Grayson Waller	10.00	25.00
SNHCN The Hurricane	8.00	20.00
SNHHG Hulk Hogan	150.00	400.00
SNIHW Indi Hartwell	15.00	40.00
SNILU Brother Love	15.00	40.00
SNINY Ivy Nile	15.00	40.00
SNIOS Io Shirai	12.00	30.00
SNISH Iron Sheik	25.00	60.00
SNJBL JBL	8.00	20.00
SNJCD Julius Creed	12.00	30.00
SNJCF Joe Coffey	5.00	12.00
SNJDK James Drake	8.00	20.00
SNJDV Jordan Devlin	6.00	15.00
SNJHT Jimmy Hart	12.00	30.00
SNJJN Jacy Jayne	25.00	60.00
SNJKL Jerry Lawler	25.00	60.00
SNJNY Jinny EXCH	6.00	15.00
SNJWD Joaquin Wilde	6.00	15.00
SNKCY Katana Chance	10.00	25.00
SNKDC Kayden Carter	10.00	25.00
SNKLR Alba Fyre	6.00	15.00
SNKLY Kelly Kelly	10.00	25.00
SNKNY Kenny Williams	5.00	12.00
SNKSH Kushida	5.00	12.00
SNKWS Kit Wilson	6.00	15.00
SNLSH Lash Legend	6.00	15.00
SNLXL Lex Luger	12.00	30.00
SNMAD Mark Andrews	5.00	12.00
SNMBL Ludwig Kaiser	6.00	15.00
SNMCF Mark Coffey	5.00	12.00
SNMHL Molly Holly	10.00	25.00
SNMHY Michael Hayes	8.00	20.00
SNMKS Meiko Satomura	10.00	25.00
SNMRS Mandy Rose	40.00	100.00
SNNMD Noam Dar	6.00	15.00
SNNOM Naomi	6.00	15.00
SNODY Odyssey Jones	8.00	20.00
SNPDN Pete Dunne	10.00	25.00
SNPGE Paige	60.00	150.00
SNPSA Persia Pirotta	10.00	25.00
SNRKO Randy Orton EXCH	40.00	100.00
SNRMY Rey Mysterio	15.00	40.00
SNRPB Rampage Brown	6.00	15.00
SNRQG Raquel Rodriguez	12.00	30.00
SNRRD Robert Roode	6.00	15.00
SNRRN Roman Reigns	40.00	100.00
SNRST Roderick Strong	8.00	20.00
SNRVD Rob Van Dam	25.00	60.00
SNSGS Sgt. Slaughter	12.00	30.00
SNSHB Sasha Banks	40.00	100.00
SNSHM Shawn Michaels	60.00	150.00
SNSHY Shanky	6.00	15.00
SNSRL Seth Freakin Rollins	20.00	50.00
SNSRY Sarray	12.00	30.00
SNSTN Stevie Turner	10.00	25.00
SNTBT Tyler Bate EXCH	6.00	15.00
SNTEO Teoman	5.00	12.00
SNTSV Trent Seven	6.00	15.00
SNVWG Von Wagner	6.00	15.00
SNWFG Wolfgang	6.00	15.00
SNWSL Wes Lee	6.00	15.00
SNXLI Xia Li	12.00	30.00
SNXQN Xyon Quinn	6.00	15.00
SNZGB Zack Gibson	5.00	12.00
SNZST Zoey Stark	10.00	25.00

2022 Select WWE Signatures

*TIE-DYE/25: UNPRICED DUE TO SCARCITY
*GOLD/10: UNPRICED DUE TO SCARCITY
*GOLD WAVE/5: UNPRICED DUE TO SCARCITY
*BLACK/1: UNPRICED DUE TO SCARCITY
RANDOMLY INSERTED INTO PACKS

Card	Low	High
SGADW Angelo Dawkins	5.00	12.00
SGAJS AJ Styles	20.00	50.00
SGASK Asuka	30.00	75.00
SGATH Theory	8.00	20.00
SGBBL Bianca Belair	20.00	50.00
SGBLS Brock Lesnar	100.00	250.00
SGBLS Bobby Lashley	10.00	25.00
SGBLY Becky Lynch	60.00	150.00
SGCML Carmella	15.00	40.00
SGDBK Dana Brooke	10.00	25.00
SGDMY Dominik Mysterio	10.00	25.00
SGDPS Damian Priest	10.00	25.00
SGEDG Edge	30.00	75.00
SGELS Ezekiel	8.00	20.00
SGERK Erik	5.00	12.00
SGGGD Gigi Dolin	50.00	100.00
SGHCB Happy Corbin	10.00	25.00
SGIOS Io Shirai	12.00	30.00
SGJGC Joe Gacy	6.00	15.00
SGJMU Jimmy Uso	10.00	25.00
SGKKG Kofi Kingston	10.00	25.00
SGKLR Alba Fyre	6.00	15.00
SGKOW Kevin Owens	15.00	40.00
SGKSH Kushida	5.00	12.00
SGLVM Liv Morgan	40.00	100.00
SGMKS Meiko Satomura	10.00	25.00
SGMRS Mandy Rose	40.00	100.00
SGMSR Mansoor	6.00	15.00
SGMVP MVP	6.00	15.00
SGNTY Natalya	12.00	30.00
SGOTS Otis	8.00	20.00
SGPDN Pete Dunne	10.00	25.00
SGQZL Queen Zelina	15.00	40.00
SGRBG Rick Boogs	8.00	20.00
SGRDL Riddle	15.00	40.00
SGRHR Rhea Ripley	30.00	75.00
SGRKO Randy Orton	40.00	100.00
SGSBK Sasha Banks	40.00	100.00
SGSDV Sonya Deville	15.00	40.00
SGSES Santos Escobar	10.00	25.00
SGSHM Sheamus	10.00	25.00
SGSHZ Shotzi	25.00	60.00
SGSZN Sami Zayn	12.00	30.00
SGTMC Ciampa	8.00	20.00
SGVMH Veer Mahaan	12.00	30.00

2022 Select WWE Sparks

*TIE-DYE/25: UNPRICED DUE TO SCARCITY
*GOLD/10: UNPRICED DUE TO SCARCITY
*BLACK/1: UNPRICED DUE TO SCARCITY
RANDOMLY INSERTED INTO PACKS

Card	Low	High
1 Becky Lynch	10.00	25.00
2 Roman Reigns	8.00	20.00
3 Kofi Kingston	3.00	8.00
4 Rey Mysterio	5.00	12.00
5 Shinsuke Nakamura	5.00	12.00
6 Damian Priest	3.00	8.00
7 Shotzi	6.00	15.00
8 Bianca Belair	6.00	15.00
9 Brock Lesnar	4.00	10.00
10 Liv Morgan	12.00	30.00
12 Edge	5.00	12.00
13 Bobby Lashley	3.00	8.00
14 Sasha Banks	10.00	25.00
15 The Miz	3.00	8.00
16 Seth Freakin Rollins	3.00	8.00
17 AJ Styles	4.00	10.00
18 Asuka	4.00	10.00
19 Jimmy Uso	2.50	6.00
20 Rhea Ripley	8.00	20.00
21 Charlotte Flair	5.00	12.00
22 Drew McIntyre	3.00	8.00
23 Jey Uso	2.50	6.00
24 Apollo Crews	2.50	6.00
25 Randy Orton	3.00	8.00
26 Carmella	4.00	10.00
27 Alexa Bliss	12.00	30.00
28 Finn Balor	4.00	10.00
29 Kevin Owens	3.00	8.00

2023 Select WWE

Card	Low	High
1 Razor Ramon	.60	1.50
2 Big E	.50	1.25
3 Alba Fyre	.75	2.00
4 Ludwig Kaiser	.30	.75
5 Ivy Nile	.50	1.25
6 Xyon Quinn	.40	1.00
7 Thea Hail	.30	.75
8 Brock Lesnar	1.00	2.50
9 Diamond Dallas Page	.50	1.25
10 Mia Yim	.60	1.50
11 Shawn Michaels	1.25	3.00
12 Bray Wyatt	.60	1.50
13 Axiom	.30	.75
14 Raquel Rodriguez	1.00	2.50
15 Jacy Jayne	.60	1.50
16 AJ Styles	.75	2.00
17 Mr. Perfect	.60	1.50
18 Carmella	.60	1.50
19 Diesel	.50	1.25
20 Omos	.40	1.00
21 The Boogeyman	.30	.75
22 Charlotte Flair	1.00	2.50
23 Bron Breakker	.75	2.00
24 Rey Mysterio	1.00	2.50
25 Joe Coffey	.40	1.00
26 Akira Tozawa	.40	1.00
27 Rowdy Roddy Piper	.75	2.00
28 Cody Rhodes	1.25	3.00
29 Eddie Guerrero	1.00	2.50
30 Randy Orton	.75	2.00
31 The Rock	1.50	4.00
32 Drew McIntyre	.75	2.00
33 Cameron Grimes	.40	1.00
34 Ricochet	.50	1.25
35 Katana Chance	.60	1.50
36 Alexa Bliss	1.50	4.00
37 Steve Austin	1.50	4.00
38 Dexter Lumis	.40	1.00
39 George Steele	.50	1.25
40 R-Truth	.30	.75
41 Torrie Wilson	.60	1.50
42 Giovanni Vinci	.40	1.00
43 Charlie Dempsey	.30	.75
44 Roman Reigns	1.50	4.00
45 Kiana James RC	2.00	5.00
46 Asuka	1.25	3.00
47 Alundra Blayze	.50	1.25
48 Piper Niven	.40	1.00
49 Goldberg	.75	2.00
50 Seth Rollins	.75	2.00
51 Trish Stratus	1.25	3.00
52 Gunther	.75	2.00
53 Dabbo Kato RC	1.25	3.00
54 Sami Zayn	.75	2.00
55 Mark Coffey	.30	.75
56 Austin Theory	.60	1.50
57 Bam Bam Bigelow	.40	1.00
58 Edge	1.25	3.00
59 Hulk Hogan	1.25	3.00
60 Shelton Benjamin	.40	1.00
61 Ultimate Warrior	1.00	2.50
62 Ivar	.30	.75
63 Cora Jade	1.25	3.00
64 Sheamus	.50	1.25
65 Nathan Frazer	.30	.75
66 Bayley	.75	2.00
67 Batista	.60	1.50
68 Elias	.40	1.00
69 Jake Roberts	.50	1.25
70 The Miz	.50	1.25
71 Undertaker	1.50	4.00
72 Jimmy Uso	.60	1.50
73 Elektra Lopez	.40	1.00
74 Sonya Deville	.60	1.50
75 Nikkita Lyons	1.00	2.50
76 Becky Lynch	1.25	3.00
77 Booker T	.40	1.00
78 Johnny Gargano	.60	1.50
79 John Cena	1.25	3.00
80 Tommaso Ciampa	.50	1.25
81 X-Pac	.40	1.00
82 Karrion Kross	.60	1.50
83 Gigi Dolin	.75	2.00
84 Xavier Woods	.40	1.00
85 Roxanne Perez	.75	2.00
86 Bianca Belair	1.00	2.50
87 Bret Hart	.75	2.00
88 Luke Gallows	.40	1.00
89 Mankind	.60	1.50
90 Angel	.30	.75
91 Yokozuna	.60	1.50
92 Liv Morgan	1.25	3.00
93 Hank Walker RC	2.00	5.00
94 Top Dolla RC	1.00	2.50
95 Valentina Feroz	.30	.75
96 Bobby Lashley	.60	1.50
97 Brutus Beefcake	.40	1.00
98 Matt Riddle	.75	2.00
99 William Regal	.30	.75
100 Bronson Reed	.40	1.00
101 Randy Orton	1.00	2.50
102 Shawn Michaels	1.50	4.00
103 Cruz Del Toro	.50	1.25
104 Carmelo Hayes	.60	1.50
105 Mace	.40	1.00
106 Julius Creed	.40	1.00
107 Veer	.40	1.00
108 Rick Rude	.60	1.50
109 Brock Lesnar	1.25	3.00
110 Eddie Guerrero	1.25	3.00
111 Rhea Ripley	2.00	5.00
112 The Godfather	.50	1.25
113 Drew Gulak	.50	1.25
114 Cora Jade	1.50	4.00
115 Ridge Holland	.40	1.00
116 Chelsea Green	1.00	2.50
117 Yulisa Leon	.40	1.00
118 Rowdy Roddy Piper	1.00	2.50
119 Candice LeRae	1.00	2.50
120 Greg Valentine	.40	1.00
121 Tamina	.40	1.00
122 The Rock	2.00	5.00
123 Drew McIntyre	1.00	2.50
124 Dijak	.50	1.25
125 Roman Reigns	2.00	5.00
126 Lyra Valkyria	.50	1.25
127 AJ Styles	1.00	2.50
128 Steve Austin	2.00	5.00
129 Cody Rhodes	1.50	4.00
130 Hulk Hogan	1.50	4.00
131 The Miz	.60	1.50
132 Triple H	1.00	2.50
133 Emma	.75	2.00
134 Elton Prince	.40	1.00
135 Ronda Rousey	2.00	5.00
136 Meiko Satomura	.40	1.00
137 Alexa Bliss	2.00	5.00
138 Andre The Giant	1.50	4.00
139 Dakota Kai	.75	2.00
140 Jerry Lawler	.75	2.00
141 Aliyah	.60	1.50
142 Ultimate Warrior	1.25	3.00
143 Gunther	1.00	2.50
144 Gigi Dolin	1.00	2.50
145 Sami Zayn	1.00	2.50
146 Nikkita Lyons	1.25	3.00
147 Angelo Dawkins	.40	1.00
148 Batista	.75	2.00
149 Finn Balor	1.00	2.50
150 John Cena	1.50	4.00
151 Ashante Adonis	.50	1.25
152 Undertaker	2.00	5.00
153 Jey Uso	.75	2.00
154 Guru Raaj	.40	1.00
155 Santos Escobar	.40	1.00
156 Odyssey Jones	.40	1.00
157 Asuka	1.50	4.00
158 Beth Phoenix	1.00	2.50
159 IYO SKY	1.00	2.50
160 Lita	1.00	2.50
161 Big E	.60	1.50
162 Yokozuna	.75	2.00

163 Jimmy Uso .75 2.00
164 Hank Walker .40 1.00
165 Shinsuke Nakamura .60 1.50
166 Roxanne Perez 1.00 2.50
167 Baron Corbin .40 1.00
168 Booker T .50 1.25
169 Kevin Owens .75 2.00
170 Rick Steiner .50 1.25
171 Braun Strowman .60 1.50
172 Apollo Crews .40 1.00
173 Karrion Kross .75 2.00
174 Ilja Dragunov .60 1.50
175 Solo Sikoa 1.25 3.00
176 Sanga .40 1.00
177 Bayley 1.00 2.50
178 Cactus Jack .75 2.00
179 Matt Riddle 1.00 2.50
180 Rob Van Dam .75 2.00
181 Bray Wyatt .75 2.00
182 Bron Breakker 1.00 2.50
183 Kofi Kingston .60 1.50
184 Jagger Reid .50 1.25
185 Valhalla .40 1.00
186 Tatum Paxley RC 1.25 3.00
187 Becky Lynch 1.50 4.00
188 Chyna .75 2.00
189 Montez Ford .60 1.50
190 Scott Steiner .60 1.50
191 Charlotte Flair 1.25 3.00
192 Brooks Jensen .50 1.25
193 Liv Morgan 1.50 4.00
194 Josh Briggs .40 1.00
195 Xia Li .60 1.50
196 Tony D'Angelo .40 1.00
197 Bianca Belair 1.25 3.00
198 Diamond Dallas Page .60 1.50
199 Otis .40 1.00
200 Zeus .50 1.25
201 Mustafa Ali .50 1.25
202 Fit Finlay .50 1.25
203 Humberto .60 1.50
204 Rob Van Dam 1.00 2.50
205 Rey Mysterio 1.50 4.00
206 Trish Stratus 2.00 5.00
207 Joe Gacy .60 1.50
208 Hollywood Hogan 2.00 5.00
209 Cody Rhodes 2.00 5.00
210 Ava RC 2.50 6.00
211 Randy Orton 1.25 3.00
212 Goldberg 1.25 3.00
213 Jey Uso 1.00 2.50
214 Scott Hall 1.00 2.50
215 Roman Reigns 2.50 6.00
216 Ultimate Warrior 1.50 4.00
217 Nikkita Lyons 1.50 4.00
218 Dragon Lee RC 1.25 4.00
219 Damian Priest 1.25 3.00
220 Batista 1.00 2.50
221 Rhea Ripley 2.50 6.00
222 Howard Finkel .50 1.25
223 Jimmy Uso 1.00 2.50
224 Shane Helms .50 1.25
225 Ronda Rousey 2.50 6.00
226 Undertaker 2.50 6.00
227 Roxanne Perez 1.25 3.00
228 Steve Austin 2.50 6.00
229 Dolph Ziggler .60 1.50
230 Bayley 1.25 3.00
231 Seth îFreakinî Rollins 1.25 3.00
232 John Cena 2.00 5.00
233 Jinder Mahal .60 1.50
234 Shawn Michaels 2.00 5.00
235 Sami Zayn 1.25 3.00
236 Blair Davenport .75 2.00
237 Thea Hail .50 1.25
238 1-2-3 Kid .60 1.50
239 Dominik Mysterio 1.00 2.50
240 B-Fab RC 1.25 3.00
241 The Miz .75 2.00
242 Kevin Nash .75 2.00
243 LA Knight .75 2.00
244 Stephanie McMahon 1.00 2.50
245 Scarlett 2.00 5.00
246 Bron Breakker 1.25 3.00
247 Becky Lynch 2.00 5.00
248 AJ Styles 1.25 3.00
249 Edge 2.00 5.00
250 Billy Gunn .75 2.00
251 Braun Strowman .75 2.00
252 Lex Luger .60 1.50
253 Liv Morgan 2.00 5.00
254 The Blue Meanie .50 1.25
255 Shotzi 1.25 3.00
256 Carmelo Hayes .75 2.00
257 Bianca Belair 1.50 4.00
258 Alexa Bliss 2.50 6.00
259 Finn Balor 1.25 3.00
260 Bret Hart 1.25 3.00
261 Bray Wyatt 1.00 2.50
262 Lita 1.25 3.00
263 Riddick Moss .60 1.50
264 The Honky Tonk Man .60 1.50
265 Solo Sikoa 1.50 4.00
266 Cora Jade 2.00 5.00
267 Bobby Lashley 1.00 2.50
268 Andre The Giant 2.00 5.00
269 Gable Steveson 1.00 2.50
270 Captain Lou Albano .75 2.00
271 Charlotte Flair 1.50 4.00
272 Mr. T 1.00 2.50
273 Natalya .75 2.00
274 The Rock 2.50 6.00
275 Tegan Nox .75 2.00
276 Gigi Dolin 1.25 3.00
277 Brock Lesnar 1.50 4.00
278 Apollo Crews .50 1.25
279 Karl Anderson .60 1.50
280 Chyna 1.00 2.50
281 Drew McIntyre 1.25 3.00
282 Papa Shango .60 1.50
283 Pat McAfee 1.00 2.50
284 Torrie Wilson 1.00 2.50
285 Uncle Howdy .75 2.00
286 Indi Hartwell 1.00 2.50
287 Carmella 1.00 2.50
288 Asuka 2.00 5.00
289 Kevin Owens 1.00 2.50
290 Diamond Dallas Page .75 2.00
291 Erik .50 1.25
292 Ricky Steamboat 1.00 2.50
293 Paul Heyman .60 1.50
294 Triple H 1.25 3.00
295 Zelina Vega 1.00 2.50
296 Jacy Jayne 1.00 2.50
297 Chad Gable .60 1.50
298 Austin Theory 1.00 2.50
299 Matt Riddle 1.25 3.00
300 Madusa 1.00 2.50
301 Dory Funk Jr. .60 1.50
302 Dana Brooke .60 1.50
303 Steve Blackman .60 1.50
304 Big E 1.00 2.50
305 Undertaker 3.00 8.00
306 man.soor .60 1.50
307 Edris Enofe .60 1.50
308 Oro Mensah .75 2.00
309 Dijak .75 2.00
310 Zoey Stark 1.00 2.50
311 Eddie Guerrero 2.00 5.00
312 Edge 2.50 6.00
313 Paul Bearer .75 2.00
314 Braun Strowman 1.00 2.50
315 Tito Santana .75 2.00
316 Maxxine Dupri RC 4.00 10.00
317 Fallon Henley .75 2.00
318 Quincy Elliott .60 1.50
319 Million Dollar Man 1.00 2.50
320 Alexa Bliss 3.00 8.00
321 Al Snow .60 1.50
322 Finn Balor 1.50 4.00
323 Rob Van Dam 1.25 3.00
324 Butch .75 2.00
325 Andre Chase .60 1.50
326 Rey Mysterio 2.00 5.00
327 Grayson Waller 1.00 2.50
328 Rip Fowler .60 1.50
329 Rowdy Roddy Piper 1.50 4.00
330 Austin Theory 1.25 3.00
331 Freddie Blassie 1.00 2.50
332 Kevin Owens 1.25 3.00
333 Shawn Michaels 2.50 6.00
334 Charlotte Flair 2.00 5.00
335 Arianna Grace RC 2.50 6.00
336 Rick Boogs .60 1.50
337 Isla Dawn 1.00 2.50
338 Scrypts .60 1.50
339 Steve Austin 3.00 8.00
340 Becky Lynch 2.50 6.00
341 Goldberg 1.50 4.00
342 MVP .75 2.00
343 The Hurricane .60 1.50
344 Gunther 1.50 4.00
345 Ava RC 2.00 5.00
346 Roman Reigns 3.00 8.00
347 Jacy Jayne 1.25 3.00
348 Sol Ruca RC 3.00 8.00
349 Alundra Blayze 1.00 2.50
350 Bianca Belair 2.00 5.00
351 Hulk Hogan 2.50 6.00
352 Nikki Cross 1.00 2.50
353 The Sandman .60 1.50
354 Jey Uso 1.25 3.00
355 Brutus Creed .60 1.50
356 Ronda Rousey 3.00 8.00
357 JD McDonagh .75 2.00
358 Tiffany Stratton 1.25 3.00
359 Andre The Giant 2.50 6.00
360 Bobby Lashley 1.25 3.00
361 Iron Sheik .75 2.00
362 Randy Orton 1.50 4.00
363 Tom Prichard .60 1.50
364 Joaquin Wilde 1.00 2.50
365 Carmelo Hayes 1.00 2.50
366 Shanky .60 1.50
367 Katana Chance 1.25 3.00
368 Trick Williams .60 1.50
369 Bob Backlund 1.00 2.50
370 Brock Lesnar 2.00 5.00
371 Lola Vice RC 20.00 50.00
372 Rhea Ripley 3.00 8.00
373 Torrie Wilson 1.25 3.00
374 Karrion Kross 1.25 3.00
375 Channing Lorenzo 1.50 4.00
376 Solo Sikoa 2.00 5.00
377 Kayden Carter 1.00 2.50
378 Tyler Bate .75 2.00
379 Bobby Heenan 1.00 2.50
380 Carmella 1.25 3.00
381 Lita 1.50 4.00
382 Robert Roode .75 2.00
383 Triple H 1.50 4.00
384 Lacey Evans 1.25 3.00
385 Damon Kemp .60 1.50
386 Tony Atlas .60 1.50
387 Kit Wilson .60 1.50
388 Von Wagner .60 1.50
389 Booker T .75 2.00
390 Cedric Alexander .75 2.00
391 Virgil .60 1.50
392 Seth Rollins 1.50 4.00
393 Trish Stratus 2.50 6.00
394 Liv Morgan 2.50 6.00
395 Duke Hudson .60 1.50
396 Chelsea Green 1.50 4.00
397 Lash Legend .60 1.50
398 Wes Lee .75 2.00
399 Bret Hart 1.50 4.00
400 Cody Rhodes 2.50 6.00

2023 Select WWE And New

*PRZ GOLD/10: UNPRICED DUE TO SCARCITY
*PRZ GOLD FLASH/10: UNPRICED DUE TO SCARCITY
*PRZ GOLD WAVE/10: UNPRICED DUE TO SCARCITY
*PRZ BLACK/1: UNPRICED DUE TO SCARCITY
RANDOMLY INSERTED INTO PACKS

1 Hollywood Hogan 3.00 8.00
2 Gunther 2.00 5.00
3 The Rock 4.00 10.00
4 Roxanne Perez 2.00 5.00
5 Bron Breakker 2.00 5.00
6 Roman Reigns 4.00 10.00
7 Becky Lynch 3.00 8.00
8 Bianca Belair 2.50 6.00
9 Kevin Owens 1.50 4.00
10 Charlotte Flair 2.50 6.00

2023 Select WWE Artistic Selections

RANDOMLY INSERTED INTO PACKS

1 Roman Reigns 150.00 400.00
2 AJ Styles 50.00 125.00
3 Asuka 75.00 200.00
4 The Rock 150.00 400.00
5 Undertaker 100.00 250.00

2023 Select WWE Autographed Memorabilia

*PRZ RED/49: .5X TO 1.2X BASIC CARDS
*PRZ BLUE/35: .6X TO 1.5X BASIC CARDS
*PRZ TIEDYE/25: UNPRICED DUE TO SCARCITY
*PRZ GOLD/10: UNPRICED DUE TO SCARCITY
*PRZ BLACK/1: UNPRICED DUE TO SCARCITY
RANDOMLY INSERTED INTO PACKS

AMAJS AJ Styles 10.00 25.00
AMASK Asuka 25.00 60.00
AMATH Austin Theory 10.00 25.00
AMAXB Alexa Bliss 40.00 100.00
AMBBL Bianca Belair 15.00 40.00
AMBKL Becky Lynch 30.00 75.00
AMBLY Bayley 20.00 50.00
AMCFL Charlotte Flair 15.00 40.00
AMCML Carmella 12.00 30.00
AMDMI Drew McIntyre 15.00 40.00
AMDMY Dominik Mysterio 25.00 60.00
AMEGE Edge 15.00 40.00
AMFBL Finn Balor 12.00 30.00
AMGTH Gunther 15.00 40.00
AMJMU Jimmy Uso 12.00 30.00
AMJUS Jey Uso 12.00 30.00
AMKEV Kevin Owens 10.00 25.00
AMKKG Kofi Kingston 10.00 25.00
AMLEV Lacey Evans 15.00 40.00
AMLVM Liv Morgan 30.00 75.00
AMMIZ The Miz 10.00 25.00
AMMRD Matt Riddle 10.00 25.00
AMNTL Natalya 10.00 25.00
AMRMY Rey Mysterio 15.00 40.00
AMRRN Roman Reigns 60.00 150.00
AMRRP Rhea Ripley 30.00 75.00
AMSFR Seth Rollins 15.00 40.00
AMSHM Sheamus 10.00 25.00
AMSNK Shinsuke Nakamura 10.00 25.00
AMSZN Sami Zayn 8.00 20.00

2023 Select WWE Color Wheel

RANDOMLY INSERTED INTO PACKS

1 John Cena 200.00 500.00
2 Alexa Bliss 250.00 600.00
3 Bron Breakker 125.00 300.00
4 Charlotte Flair 125.00 300.00
5 Rey Mysterio 100.00 250.00
6 Ultimate Warrior 100.00 250.00
7 Cora Jade 250.00 600.00
8 Shawn Michaels 250.00 600.00
9 Hulk Hogan 300.00 750.00
10 Seth Rollins 150.00 400.00

2023 Select WWE Firestorm

RANDOMLY INSERTED INTO PACKS

1 Steve Austin 75.00 200.00
2 Ronda Rousey 75.00 200.00
3 Randy Orton 75.00 200.00
4 Kane 40.00 100.00
5 Becky Lynch 100.00 250.00
6 Bray Wyatt 60.00 150.00
7 Bret Hart 40.00 100.00
8 Brock Lesnar 60.00 150.00
9 Triple H 75.00 200.00
10 Cody Rhodes 100.00 250.00

2023 Select WWE Global Icons

*PRZ GOLD/10: UNPRICED DUE TO SCARCITY
*PRZ GOLD FLASH/10: UNPRICED DUE TO SCARCITY
*PRZ GOLD WAVE/10: UNPRICED DUE TO SCARCITY
RANDOMLY INSERTED INTO PACKS

1 Rowdy Roddy Piper 1.50 4.00
2 Sami Zayn 1.50 4.00
3 John Cena 2.50 6.00
4 Finn Balor 1.50 4.00
5 The Rock 3.00 8.00
6 Bruno Sammartino 1.00 2.50
7 Dakota Kai 1.25 3.00
8 Grayson Waller 1.00 2.50
9 Ivan Putski .60 1.50
10 Kevin Owens 1.25 3.00
11 Haku .60 1.50
12 Natalya 1.00 2.50
13 Gable Steveson 1.25 3.00
14 JD McDonagh .75 2.00
15 Tegan Nox 1.00 2.50
16 IYO SKY 1.50 4.00
17 Omos .75 2.00
18 Rhea Ripley 3.00 8.00
19 Ilja Dragunov 1.00 2.50
20 Maryse .75 2.00
21 Ronda Rousey 3.00 8.00
22 Butch .75 2.00
23 Kurt Angle 1.25 3.00
24 Becky Lynch 2.50 6.00
25 William Regal .60 1.50
26 Asuka 2.50 6.00
27 Ultimate Warrior 2.00 5.00
28 Emma 1.25 3.00
29 Alba Fyre 1.50 4.00
30 Bret Hart 1.50 4.00

2023 Select WWE Legendary Signatures

*PRZ FLASH: SAME VALUE AS BASIC
*PRZ RED WAVE: .5X TO 1.2X BASIC CARDS
*PRZ RED/60: .6X TO 1.5X BASIC CARDS
*PRZ BLUE/49: .6X TO 1.5X BASIC CARDS
*PRZ PURPLE/35: .75X TO 2X BASIC CARDS
*PRZ TIEDYE/25: UNPRICED DUE TO SCARCITY
*PRZ GOLD/10: UNPRICED DUE TO SCARCITY
*PRZ GOLD FLASH/10: UNPRICED DUE TO SCARCITY
*PRZ GOLD WAVE/10: UNPRICED DUE TO SCARCITY
*PRZ BLACK/1: UNPRICED DUE TO SCARCITY
RANDOMLY INSERTED INTO PACKS

LSBHM Bret Hart 30.00 75.00
LSBKT Booker T 8.00 20.00
LSBPH Beth Phoenix 8.00 20.00
LSBTS Batista 25.00 60.00
LSDSL Diesel EXCH 20.00 50.00
LSGBG Goldberg 40.00 100.00
LSHHG Hulk Hogan 100.00 250.00
LSHJD Jim Duggan 8.00 20.00
LSIVP Ivan Putski 8.00 20.00
LSJBL JBL 10.00 25.00
LSJCN John Cena 50.00 125.00
LSKNE Kane 15.00 40.00
LSLTA Lita 15.00 40.00
LSMDM Million Dollar Man 12.00 30.00
LSMKN Mankind 20.00 50.00
LSSCA Steve Austin 75.00 200.00
LSSHM Shawn Michaels 40.00 100.00
LSTST Trish Stratus 20.00 50.00
LSUDT Undertaker 50.00 125.00

2023 Select WWE Ringside Action Signatures

*PRZ FLASH: SAME VALUE AS BASIC
*PRZ RED WAVE: .5X TO 1.2X BASIC CARDS
*PRZ RED/60: .6X TO 1.5X BASIC CARDS
*PRZ BLUE/49: .6X TO 1.5X BASIC CARDS
*PRZ PURPLE/35: .75X TO 2X BASIC CARDS
*PRZ TIEDYE/25: UNPRICED DUE TO SCARCITY
*PRZ GOLD/10: UNPRICED DUE TO SCARCITY
*PRZ GOLD FLASH/10: UNPRICED DUE TO SCARCITY
*PRZ GOLD WAVE/10: UNPRICED DUE TO SCARCITY
*PRZ BLACK/1: UNPRICED DUE TO SCARCITY
RANDOMLY INSERTED INTO PACKS

RAAJS AJ Styles 12.00 30.00
RAAPC Adam Pearce 6.00 15.00
RAASK Asuka 15.00 40.00
RAATH Austin Theory 8.00 20.00
RAAXB Alexa Bliss 40.00 100.00
RABBL Bianca Belair 12.00 30.00
RABGE Big E 6.00 15.00
RABKL Becky Lynch 20.00 50.00
RABLY Bayley 12.00 30.00
RABTH Butch 6.00 15.00
RACBO Bob Orton 10.00 25.00
RACFL Charlotte Flair 20.00 50.00
RACML Carmella 12.00 30.00
RACRD Cody Rhodes 50.00 125.00
RADKI Dakota Kai 10.00 25.00
RADLB D-Lo Brown 6.00 15.00
RADMI Drew McIntyre 10.00 25.00
RAEGE Edge 15.00 40.00
RAETS Eve Torres 10.00 25.00
RAFBL Finn Balor 12.00 30.00
RAFLY Fit Finlay 8.00 20.00
RAHTM The Honky Tonk Man 15.00 40.00
RAIRS IRS 8.00 20.00
RAIYS IYO SKY 12.00 30.00
RAKEV Kevin Owens 10.00 25.00
RAKKR Karrion Kross 6.00 15.00
RALLG Lex Luger 8.00 20.00
RALVM Liv Morgan 30.00 75.00
RAMRD Matt Riddle 10.00 25.00
RAMRY Maryse 8.00 20.00
RAPHM Paul Heyman 15.00 40.00
RAPSH Papa Shango 10.00 25.00
RARMY Rey Mysterio 15.00 40.00
RARRP Rhea Ripley 40.00 100.00
RARST Rick Steiner 12.00 30.00
RASFR Seth Rollins 15.00 40.00
RASHZ Shotzi 12.00 30.00
RASST Scott Steiner 12.00 30.00
RATCP Tommaso Ciampa 6.00 15.00
RAZST Zoey Stark 10.00 25.00

2023 Select WWE Selective Swatches

*PRZ RED/49: .6X TO 1.5X BASIC CARDS
*PRZ BLUE/35: .75X TO 2X BASIC CARDS
*PRZ TIEDYE/25: UNPRICED DUE TO SCARCITY
*PRZ GOLD/10: UNPRICED DUE TO SCARCITY
*PRZ GOLD FLASH/10: UNPRICED DUE TO SCARCITY
*PRZ BLACK/1: UNPRICED DUE TO SCARCITY
RANDOMLY INSERTED INTO PACKS

SWACR Apollo Crews 4.00 10.00
SWAJS AJ Styles 6.00 15.00
SWATH Austin Theory 5.00 12.00
SWAXB Alexa Bliss 15.00 40.00
SWBBK Bron Breakker 6.00 15.00
SWBKL Becky Lynch 12.00 30.00
SWBLS Bobby Lashley 3.00 8.00
SWCGR Cameron Grimes 3.00 8.00
SWCML Carmella 6.00 15.00
SWDBK Dana Brooke 6.00 15.00
SWDKI Dakota Kai 8.00 20.00
SWDZG Dolph Ziggler 6.00 15.00
SWEGE Edge 5.00 12.00
SWGGD Gigi Dolin 8.00 20.00
SWGTH Gunther 4.00 10.00
SWIJD Ilja Dragunov 5.00 12.00
SWJGN Johnny Gargano 2.50 6.00
SWJJN Jacy Jayne 8.00 20.00
SWJMU Jimmy Uso 3.00 8.00
SWKEV Kevin Owens 2.00 5.00
SWLAK LA Knight 10.00 25.00
SWLVM Liv Morgan 10.00 25.00
SWMFD Montez Ford 2.50 6.00
SWNTL Natalya 6.00 15.00
SWOMS Omos 4.00 10.00
SWPPN Piper Niven 5.00 12.00
SWRCH Ricochet 3.00 8.00
SWRMY Rey Mysterio 2.50 6.00
SWSFR Seth Rollins 4.00 10.00
SWSHM Sheamus 2.00 5.00
SWSHZ Shotzi 3.00 8.00
SWSZN Sami Zayn 6.00 15.00
SWTCP Tommaso Ciampa 2.00 5.00
SWXLI Xia Li 5.00 12.00
SWZVG Zelina Vega 6.00 15.00

2023 Select WWE Sensations

*PRZ GOLD/10: UNPRICED DUE TO SCARCITY
*PRZ GOLD FLASH/10: UNPRICED DUE TO SCARCITY
*PRZ GOLD WAVE/10: UNPRICED DUE TO SCARCITY
*PRZ BLACK/1: UNPRICED DUE TO SCARCITY
RANDOMLY INSERTED INTO PACKS

1 Bayley 2.50 6.00
2 Roman Reigns 5.00 12.00
3 Bobby Lashley 2.00 5.00
4 Shawn Michaels 4.00 10.00
5 Charlotte Flair 3.00 8.00
6 The Rock 5.00 12.00
7 Drew McIntyre 2.50 6.00
8 Karrion Kross 2.00 5.00
9 Alexa Bliss 5.00 12.00
10 Matt Riddle 2.50 6.00
11 Becky Lynch 4.00 10.00
12 Sami Zayn 2.50 6.00
13 Bray Wyatt 2.00 5.00
14 Solo Sikoa 3.00 8.00
15 Cody Rhodes 4.00 10.00
16 Triple H 2.50 6.00
17 Gunther 2.50 6.00
18 Kevin Owens 2.00 5.00
19 Asuka 4.00 10.00
20 Randy Orton 2.50 6.00
21 Bianca Belair 3.00 8.00
22 Seth Rollins 2.50 6.00
23 Bron Breakker 2.50 6.00
24 Steve Austin 5.00 12.00
25 Cora Jade 4.00 10.00
26 Undertaker 5.00 12.00
27 John Cena 4.00 10.00
28 Liv Morgan 4.00 10.00
29 Austin Theory 2.00 5.00
30 Rey Mysterio 3.00 8.00

2023 Select WWE Signature Selections

RANDOMLY INSERTED INTO PACKS

SLAFR Alba Fyre 6.00 15.00
SLAGR Arianna Grace 10.00 25.00
SLASN Al Snow 5.00 12.00
SLATA Ashante Adonis 4.00 10.00
SLAXM Axiom 4.00 10.00
SLBBK Bron Breakker 12.00 30.00
SLBCR Brutus Creed 4.00 10.00
SLBDV Blair Davenport 8.00 20.00
SLBFB B-Fab 10.00 25.00
SLBGY The Boogeyman 10.00 25.00
SLBKN Brian Knobs 4.00 10.00
SLBOA Boa 3.00 8.00
SLBRD Bubba Ray Dudley 10.00 25.00
SLBST Braun Strowman 5.00 12.00
SLCDP Charlie Dempsey 6.00 15.00
SLCGR Cameron Grimes 4.00 10.00
SLCHY Carmelo Hayes 12.00 30.00
SLCLR Candice LeRae 6.00 15.00
SLCSL Channing Lorenzo 6.00 15.00
SLDFJ Dory Funk Jr. 6.00 15.00
SLDJK Dijak 4.00 10.00
SLDPR Damian Priest 10.00 25.00
SLELS Elias 4.00 10.00
SLEPC Elton Prince 6.00 15.00
SLGTH Gunther 10.00 25.00
SLGWL Grayson Waller 8.00 20.00
SLHCN The Hurricane 5.00 12.00
SLHKU Haku 10.00 25.00
SLIHW Indi Hartwell 12.00 30.00
SLISH Iron Sheik 20.00 50.00
SLISL Isla Dawn 20.00 50.00
SLIVN Ivy Nile 8.00 20.00
SLJCD Julius Creed 6.00 15.00
SLJCF Joe Coffey 5.00 12.00
SLJDM JD McDonagh 6.00 15.00
SLJGC Joe Gacy 3.00 8.00
SLJGR Juventud Guerrera 6.00 15.00
SLJMH Jinder Mahal 5.00 12.00
SLJMU Jimmy Uso 10.00 25.00
SLJRD Jagger Reid 5.00 12.00
SLJSG Jerry Sags 6.00 15.00
SLJUS Jey Uso 10.00 25.00
SLKAN Karl Anderson 4.00 10.00
SLKCH Katana Chance 6.00 15.00
SLKCT Kayden Carter 8.00 20.00
SLKJM Kiana James 12.00 30.00
SLKKG Kofi Kingston 10.00 25.00
SLKWL Kit Wilson 5.00 12.00
SLLEV Lacey Evans 12.00 30.00
SLLGL Luke Gallows 5.00 12.00
SLLLK Leilani Kai 6.00 15.00
SLLVK Lyra Valkyria 8.00 20.00
SLMCF Mark Coffey 3.00 8.00
SLMCM Riddick Moss 6.00 15.00
SLMFD Montez Ford 6.00 15.00
SLMIZ The Miz 6.00 15.00
SLMKS Meiko Satomura 4.00 10.00
SLMRD Scarlett 12.00 30.00
SLMRY Maryse 20.00 50.00
SLMSH Mosh 3.00 8.00
SLMXD Maxxine Dupri 20.00 50.00
SLMYM Mia Yim 6.00 15.00
SLNDR Noam Dar 4.00 10.00
SLNLY Nikkita Lyons 40.00 100.00
SLNTL Natalya 8.00 20.00
SLOMS Omos 5.00 12.00
SLORM Oro Mensah 3.00 8.00
SLOTS Otis 5.00 12.00
SLQEL Quincy Elliott 8.00 20.00
SLRCH Ricochet 10.00 25.00
SLRKI Rikishi 8.00 20.00
SLRPF Rip Fowler 3.00 8.00
SLRQR Raquel Rodriguez 15.00 40.00
SLRRB Rockin' Robin 8.00 20.00
SLSCH Scotty 2 Hotty 10.00 25.00
SLSDV Sonya Deville 8.00 20.00
SLSES Santos Escobar 3.00 8.00
SLSHS Stan Hansen 10.00 25.00
SLSHY Shayna Baszler 6.00 15.00
SLSRC Sol Ruca 50.00 125.00
SLSRS Stevie Richards 5.00 12.00
SLSZN Sami Zayn 10.00 25.00
SLTBM The Blue Meanie 6.00 15.00
SLTBT Tyler Bate 5.00 12.00
SLTDA Tony D'Angelo 3.00 8.00
SLTDL Top Dolla 4.00 10.00
SLTHL Thea Hail 30.00 75.00
SLTHR Thrasher 5.00 12.00
SLTLG Theodore Long 6.00 15.00
SLTPR Tom Prichard 5.00 12.00
SLTPX Tatum Paxley 8.00 20.00
SLTRN Terri Runnels 6.00 15.00
SLTSM The Sandman 5.00 12.00
SLTSN Tito Santana 6.00 15.00
SLTST Tiffany Stratton 30.00 75.00
SLTWL Torrie Wilson 15.00 40.00
SLVWG Von Wagner 3.00 8.00
SLWFG Wolfgang 3.00 8.00
SLWSL Wes Lee 4.00 10.00
SLXPC X-Pac 10.00 25.00

2023 Select WWE Signatures

*PRZ TIEDYE/25: UNPRICED DUE TO SCARCITY
*PRZ GOLD/10: UNPRICED DUE TO SCARCITY
*PRZ GOLD FLASH/10: UNPRICED DUE TO SCARCITY
*PRZ GOLD WAVE/10: UNPRICED DUE TO SCARCITY
*PRZ BLACK/1: UNPRICED DUE TO SCARCITY
RANDOMLY INSERTED INTO PACKS

SGABZ Alundra Blayze 6.00 15.00
SGACR Apollo Crews 3.00 8.00
SGAVR Ava 20.00 50.00
SGBBF Brutus Beefcake 8.00 20.00
SGBCB Baron Corbin 6.00 15.00
SGBLS Brock Lesnar EXCH 50.00 125.00
SGBWY Bray Wyatt 75.00 200.00
SGCJD Cora Jade 15.00 40.00
SGDMR Don Muraco 8.00 20.00
SGDMY Dominik Mysterio 12.00 30.00
SGDZG Dolph Ziggler 8.00 20.00
SGEMA Emma 10.00 25.00
SGFRQ Faarooq 6.00 15.00
SGGFT The Godfather 8.00 20.00
SGGGD Gigi Dolin 15.00 40.00
SGGSV Gable Steveson 10.00 25.00
SGGVL Greg Valentine 6.00 15.00
SGHJD Jim Duggan 12.00 30.00
SGJHT Jimmy Hart 6.00 15.00
SGJJN Jacy Jayne 12.00 30.00
SGJLW Jerry Lawler 10.00 25.00
SGJWD Joaquin Wilde 3.00 8.00
SGKAG Kurt Angle 12.00 30.00
SGKLY Kelly Kelly 8.00 20.00
SGMHL Molly Holly 6.00 15.00
SGMHY Michael Hayes 6.00 15.00

SGMMC Michelle McCool 10.00 25.00
SGMSR man.soor 3.00 8.00
SGPPN Piper Niven 5.00 12.00
SGRDG Road Dogg 6.00 15.00
SGRRN Roman Reigns 60.00 150.00
SGRVD Rob Van Dam 8.00 20.00
SGRXP Roxanne Perez 15.00 40.00
SGSBG Superstar Billy Graham 20.00 50.00
SGSCR Scrypts 4.00 10.00
SGSHM Sheamus EXCH 10.00 25.00
SGSNK Shinsuke Nakamura 10.00 25.00
SGVHL Valhalla 8.00 20.00
SGXWD Xavier Woods 6.00 15.00
SGZVG Zelina Vega 12.00 30.00

2023 Select WWE Snapshots

*PRZ GOLD/10: UNPRICED DUE TO SCARCITY
*PRZ GOLD FLASH/10: UNPRICED DUE TO SCARCITY
*PRZ GOLD WAVE/10: UNPRICED DUE TO SCARCITY
*PRZ BLACK/1: UNPRICED DUE TO SCARCITY
RANDOMLY INSERTED INTO PACKS

1 Lita 1.50 4.00
2 Carmelo Hayes 1.00 2.50
3 Otis .60 1.50
4 Damian Priest 1.50 4.00
5 Shawn Michaels 2.50 6.00
6 Dominik Mysterio 1.25 3.00
7 Ilja Dragunov 1.00 2.50
8 AJ Styles 1.50 4.00
9 Kane .75 2.00
10 Batista 1.25 3.00
11 Montez Ford 1.00 2.50
12 Chad Gable .75 2.00
13 Ricochet 1.00 2.50
14 Dexter Lumis .75 2.00
15 Shinsuke Nakamura 1.00 2.50
16 Elias .75 2.00
17 IYO SKY 1.50 4.00
18 Alba Fyre 1.50 4.00
19 Kofi Kingston 1.00 2.50
20 Big E 1.00 2.50
21 Nikkita Lyons 2.00 5.00
22 Dakota Kai 1.25 3.00
23 Rob Van Dam 1.25 3.00
24 Dolph Ziggler .75 2.00
25 Zoey Stark 1.00 2.50
26 Gigi Dolin 1.50 4.00
27 Jacy Jayne 1.25 3.00
28 Apollo Crews .60 1.50
29 LA Knight 1.00 2.50
30 Braun Strowman 1.00 2.50

2023 Select WWE Sparks Memorabilia

*PRZ TIEDYE/25: UNPRICED DUE TO SCARCITY
*PRZ GOLD/10: UNPRICED DUE TO SCARCITY
*PRZ BLACK/1: UNPRICED DUE TO SCARCITY
RANDOMLY INSERTED INTO PACKS

SPADW Angelo Dawkins 1.00 2.50
SPAFR Alba Fyre 2.50 6.00
SPASK Asuka 4.00 10.00
SPBBL Bianca Belair 3.00 8.00
SPBCB Baron Corbin 1.00 2.50
SPBTH Butch 1.25 3.00
SPCHY Carmelo Hayes 1.50 4.00
SPCJD Cora Jade 4.00 10.00
SPCLR Candice LeRae 2.50 6.00
SPDMI Drew McIntyre 2.50 6.00
SPDMY Dominik Mysterio 2.00 5.00
SPDPR Damian Priest 2.50 6.00
SPDXL Dexter Lumis 1.25 3.00
SPFBL Finn Balor 2.50 6.00
SPGWL Grayson Waller 1.50 4.00
SPIYS IYO SKY 2.50 6.00
SPJGC Joe Gacy 1.25 3.00
SPJUS Jey Uso 2.00 5.00
SPKCH Katana Chance 2.00 5.00
SPKKG Kofi Kingston 1.50 4.00
SPLEV Lacey Evans 2.00 5.00
SPMIZ The Miz 1.50 4.00
SPMRD Matt Riddle 2.50 6.00
SPMVP MVP 1.25 3.00
SPNCS Nikki Cross 1.50 4.00
SPOTS Otis 1.00 2.50
SPRQR Raquel Rodriguez 3.00 8.00
SPRRN Roman Reigns 5.00 12.00
SPRRP Rhea Ripley 5.00 12.00
SPSDV Sonya Deville 2.00 5.00
SPSES Santos Escobar 1.00 2.50
SPSHY Shayna Baszler 2.00 5.00
SPSNK Shinsuke Nakamura 1.50 4.00
SPXWD Xavier Woods 1.25 3.00
SPZST Zoey Stark 1.50 4.00

2006 7-11 WWE Slam Philippines

COMPLETE SET (36) 20.00 50.00

1 Finlay .75 2.00
2 William Regal .75 2.00
3 Batista 1.25 3.00
4 Matt Hardy .75 2.00
5 Lashley .75 2.00
6 Rey Mysterio .75 2.00
7 Brian Kendrick .30 .75
8 Paul London .30 .75
9 Vito .30 .75
10 Michelle McCool 1.50 4.00
11 Mr. Kennedy .75 2.00
12 Booker T .75 2.00
13 Undertaker 1.50 4.00
14 Ashley 1.25 3.00
15 Big Show 1.25 3.00
16 Rob Van Dam .75 2.00
17 Nitro .50 1.25
18 Hulk Hogan 1.50 4.00
19 Edge 1.25 3.00
20 Ric Flair 1.50 4.00
21 Carlito 1.25 3.00
22 Umaga .50 1.25
23 Torrie Wilson 1.25 3.00
24 John Cena 2.00 5.00
25 Randy Orton .75 2.00
26 Kane 1.25 3.00
27 Candice Michelle 2.00 5.00
28 Mickie James 2.00 5.00
29 Triple H 1.25 3.00
30 Shawn Michaels 1.25 3.00
31 Undertaker 1.50 4.00
32 Rey Mysterio .75 2.00
33 Batista 1.25 3.00
34 Triple H 1.25 3.00
35 John Cena 2.00 5.00
36 Shawn Michaels 1.25 3.00

2022 SkyBox Metal Universe AEW

COMPLETE SET W/SP (150) 50.00 125.00
COMPLETE SET W/OSP (100) 25.00 60.00
*BLUE SPECTRUM: 75X TO 2X BASIC CARDS
*PURPLE SPECTRUM/199: 2X TO 5X BASIC CARDS
*P.P.BLACK/1: UNPRICED DUE TO SCARCITY
*P.P.CYAN/1: UNPRICED DUE TO SCARCITY
*P.P.MAGENTA/1: UNPRICED DUE TO SCARCITY
*P.P.YELLOW/1: UNPRICED DUE TO SCARCITY
STATED SP ODDS 1:1 HOBBY/EPACK
STATED SP ODDS 1:5 BLASTER

1 Hangman Adam Page
2 Sammy Guevara 1.25 3.00
3 Adam Cole 1.25 3.00
4 Dante Martin RC 2.50 6.00
5 Powerhouse Hobbs .75 2.00
6 Lance Archer 1.00 2.50
7 Wardlow 1.00 2.50
8 Dr. Britt Baker 1.50 4.00
9 Jade Cargill 2.00 5.00
10 Thunder Rosa 1.00 2.50
11 Julia Hart RC 1.00 2.50
12 Serena Deeb .40 1.00
13 Anna Jay 1.50 4.00
14 Red Velvet .60 1.50
15 Jungle Boy Jack Perry 1.25 3.00
16 Kenny Omega 2.00 5.00
17 Jon Moxley 1.00 2.50
18 Chris Jericho 1.50 4.00
19 Hikaru Shida 1.00 2.50
20 Kris Statlander .75 2.00
21 RIHO .75 2.00
22 Athena .50 1.25
23 Tay Melo 1.50 4.00
24 Anthony Bowens .50 1.25
25 MJF 2.00 5.00
26 CM Punk 2.00 5.00
27 Scorpio Sky .75 2.00
28 Ricky Starks .75 2.00
29 Penta el Zero M 1.00 2.50
30 Keith Lee 1.00 2.50
31 The Bunny 1.00 2.50
32 Penelope Ford 2.00 5.00
33 Ruby Soho .75 2.00
34 Emi Sakura RC .40 1.00
35 Andrade El Idolo .50 1.25
36 Matt Menard RC .40 1.00
37 Austin Gunn .40 1.00
38 Colten Gunn RC .40 1.00
39 Darby Allin 2.00 5.00
40 Eddie Kingston 1.25 3.00
41 Jake Hager .50 1.25
42 John Silver .40 1.00
43 Matt Jackson 1.00 2.50
44 Max Caster .50 1.25
45 Miro .75 2.00
46 Malakai Black 1.00 2.50
47 Orange Cassidy 1.25 3.00
48 Christian Cage .60 1.50
49 Shawn Spears .60 1.50
50 Marq Quen .50 1.25
51 Angelo Parker RC .40 1.00
52 Kip Sabian .50 1.25
53 Matt Hardy .75 2.00
54 Matt Sydal .40 1.00
55 Ortiz .75 2.00
56 PAC .75 2.00
57 Preston Vance .40 1.00
58 QT Marshall .50 1.25
59 Rey Fenix 1.00 2.50
60 Claudio Castagnoli .40 1.00
61 Buddy Matthews .60 1.50
62 Sting 1.50 4.00
63 The Blade .40 1.00
64 The Butcher .40 1.00
65 Tony Nese .40 1.00
66 Trent Beretta .50 1.25
67 Luchasaurus .75 2.00
68 Toni Storm 1.50 4.00
69 Nyla Rose .75 2.00
70 Tony Schiavone .50 1.25
71 Jim Ross 1.00 2.50
72 William Regal .60 1.50
73 Excalibur .40 1.00
74 Taz .50 1.25
75 Mark Henry .50 1.25
76 Paul Turner .40 1.00
77 Aubrey Edwards .75 2.00
78 Stokely Hathaway .40 1.00
79 Lee Moriarty RC .40 1.00
80 Kyle O'Reilly .40 1.00
81 Bryan Danielson 1.50 4.00
82 Cash Wheeler .60 1.50
83 Danhausen RC 6.00 15.00
84 Chuck Taylor .40 1.00
85 Dax Harwood .60 1.50
86 Evil Uno .75 2.00
87 Isiah Kassidy .40 1.00
88 Brody King RC .50 1.25
89 Nick Jackson 1.00 2.50
90 Swerve Strickland .50 1.25
91 Dustin Rhodes .75 2.00
92 Brian Pillman Jr. RC 1.25 3.00
93 Alex Reynolds .40 1.00
94 Ethan Page 1.00 2.50
95 Wheeler Yuta RC 1.50 4.00
96 Jamie Hayter RC 2.00 5.00
97 Anthony Ogogo RC .40 1.00
98 HOOK RC 1.50 4.00
99 Daniel Garcia RC 1.25 3.00
100 Samoa Joe .75 2.00
101 Sammy Guevara SP 2.00 5.00
102 Jungle Boy Jack Perry SP 2.00 5.00
103 Hangman Adam Page SP 3.00 8.00
104 Orange Cassidy SP 2.00 5.00
105 Penta el Zero M SP 1.50 4.00
106 Hikaru Shida SP 1.50 4.00
107 Dr. Britt Baker SP 2.50 6.00
108 Nyla Rose SP 1.25 3.00
109 CM Punk SP 3.00 8.00
110 Toni Storm SP 2.50 6.00
111 Jade Cargill SP 3.00 8.00
112 Kenny Omega SP 3.00 8.00
113 Claudio Castagnoli SP .60 1.50
114 Powerhouse Hobbs SP 1.25 3.00
115 Red Velvet SP 1.00 2.50
116 Leyla Hirsch SP .75 2.00
117 Serena Deeb SP .60 1.50
118 Thunder Rosa SP 1.50 4.00
119 Anna Jay SP 2.50 6.00
120 Luchasaurus SP 1.25 3.00
121 Eddie Kingston SP 2.00 5.00
122 Bryan Danielson SP 2.50 6.00
123 Samoa Joe SP 1.25 3.00
124 Dante Martin SP .60 1.50
125 HOOK SP 2.50 6.00
126 Preston Vance SP .60 1.50
127 Ruby Soho SP 1.25 3.00
128 Penelope Ford SP 3.00 8.00
129 PAC SP 1.25 3.00
130 Dax Harwood SP 1.00 2.50
131 Darby Allin SP 3.00 8.00
132 Wardlow SP 1.50 4.00
133 Chris Jericho SP 2.50 6.00
134 MJF SP 3.00 8.00
135 Lance Archer SP 1.50 4.00
136 Jamie Hayter SP 3.00 8.00
137 Rey Fenix SP 1.50 4.00
138 Keith Lee SP 1.50 4.00
139 Tay Melo SP 2.50 6.00
140 Sting SP 2.50 6.00
141 RIHO SP 1.25 3.00
142 Adam Cole SP 2.00 5.00
143 Malakai Black SP 1.50 4.00
144 Kris Statlander SP 1.25 3.00
145 Jon Moxley SP 1.50 4.00
146 Cash Wheeler SP 1.00 2.50
147 Ricky Starks SP 1.25 3.00
148 John Silver SP .60 1.50
149 Scorpio Sky SP 1.25 3.00
150 Jay Lethal SP 1.00 2.50

2022 SkyBox Metal Universe AEW '97-98 Retro

*PURPLE SPECTRUM/199: .75X TO 2X BASIC CARDS
*P.P.BLACK/1: UNPRICED DUE TO SCARCITY
*P.P.CYAN/1: UNPRICED DUE TO SCARCITY
*P.P.MAGENTA/1: UNPRICED DUE TO SCARCITY
*P.P.YELLOW/1: UNPRICED DUE TO SCARCITY
STATED ODDS 1:5 HOBBY/EPACK
STATED ODDS 1:7.5 BLASTER

R1 Hangman Adam Page 3.00 8.00
R2 Sammy Guevara 2.00 5.00
R3 Kenny Omega 3.00 8.00
R4 Jon Moxley 1.50 4.00
R5 Orange Cassidy 2.00 5.00
R6 Penta el Zero M 1.50 4.00
R7 Hikaru Shida 1.50 4.00
R8 Dr. Britt Baker 2.50 6.00
R9 Nyla Rose 1.25 3.00
R10 Dante Martin .60 1.50
R11 Jade Cargill 3.00 8.00
R12 Jungle Boy Jack Perry 2.00 5.00
R13 CM Punk 3.00 8.00
R14 Powerhouse Hobbs 1.25 3.00
R15 Red Velvet 1.00 2.50
R16 Athena .75 2.00
R17 Serena Deeb .60 1.50
R18 Thunder Rosa 1.50 4.00
R19 Anna Jay 2.50 6.00
R20 Darby Allin 3.00 8.00
R21 Eddie Kingston 2.00 5.00
R22 Bryan Danielson 2.50 6.00
R23 Claudio Castagnoli .60 1.50
R24 Matt Jackson 1.50 4.00
R25 Nick Jackson 1.50 4.00
R26 Rey Fenix 1.50 4.00
R27 Keith Lee 1.50 4.00
R28 Tay Melo 2.50 6.00
R29 MJF 3.00 8.00
R30 RIHO 1.25 3.00
R31 HOOK 2.50 6.00
R32 Adam Cole 2.00 5.00
R33 Kris Statlander 1.25 3.00

R34 Cash Wheeler 1.00 2.50
R35 Toni Storm 2.50 6.00
R36 Ricky Starks 1.25 3.00
R37 John Silver .60 1.50
R38 Scorpio Sky 1.25 3.00
R39 W. Morrissey .75 2.00
R40 Malakai Black 1.50 4.00
R41 Ruby Soho 1.25 3.00
R42 Penelope Ford 3.00 8.00
R43 Matt Hardy 1.25 3.00
R44 Anthony Bowens .75 2.00
R45 Max Caster .75 2.00
R46 Wardlow 1.50 4.00
R47 Jamie Hayter 3.00 8.00
R48 Chris Jericho 2.50 6.00
R49 Lance Archer 1.50 4.00
R50 Sting 2.50 6.00

2022 SkyBox Metal Universe AEW '97-98 Retro Precious Metal Gems Red

*GREEN/10: UNPRICED DUE TO SCARCITY
*GOLD/1: UNPRICED DUE TO SCARCITY
STATED PRINT RUN 100 SER.#'d SETS

R1 Hangman Adam Page 30.00 75.00
R2 Sammy Guevara 30.00 75.00
R3 Kenny Omega 125.00 300.00
R4 Jon Moxley 100.00 250.00
R5 Orange Cassidy 100.00 250.00
R6 Penta el Zero M 30.00 75.00
R7 Hikaru Shida 60.00 150.00
R8 Dr. Britt Baker 150.00 400.00
R9 Nyla Rose 40.00 100.00
R10 Dante Martin 25.00 60.00
R11 Jade Cargill 100.00 250.00
R12 Jungle Boy Jack Perry 15.00 40.00
R13 CM Punk 125.00 300.00
R14 Powerhouse Hobbs
R15 Red Velvet 40.00 100.00
R16 Athena 15.00 40.00
R17 Serena Deeb 20.00 50.00
R18 Thunder Rosa
R19 Anna Jay 75.00 200.00
R20 Darby Allin 100.00 250.00
R21 Eddie Kingston 50.00 125.00
R22 Bryan Danielson 150.00 400.00
R23 Claudio Castagnoli 40.00 100.00
R24 Matt Jackson
R25 Nick Jackson 75.00 200.00
R26 Rey Fenix 40.00 100.00
R27 Keith Lee 25.00 60.00
R28 Tay Melo 50.00 125.00
R29 MJF 600.00 1500.00
R30 RIHO 20.00 50.00
R31 HOOK 60.00 150.00
R32 Adam Cole 40.00 100.00
R33 Kris Statlander 60.00 150.00
R34 Cash Wheeler 15.00 40.00
R35 Toni Storm 100.00 250.00
R36 Ricky Starks 25.00 60.00
R37 John Silver 15.00 40.00
R38 Scorpio Sky 12.00 30.00
R39 W. Morrissey
R40 Malakai Black 50.00 125.00
R41 Ruby Soho 30.00 75.00
R42 Penelope Ford 15.00 40.00
R43 Matt Hardy 20.00 50.00
R44 Anthony Bowens 15.00 40.00
R45 Max Caster
R46 Wardlow 25.00 60.00
R47 Jamie Hayter 100.00 250.00
R48 Chris Jericho 75.00 200.00
R49 Lance Archer 15.00 40.00
R50 Sting 300.00 800.00

2022 SkyBox Metal Universe AEW Autographs

*GREEN/10: UNPRICED DUE TO SCARCITY
*GOLD/1: UNPRICED DUE TO SCARCITY
GROUP A ODDS 1:31,006
GROUP B ODDS 1:351
GROUP C ODDS 1:321
GROUP D ODDS 1:136
STATED ODDS 1:75 HOBBY/EPACK
STOKELY HATHAWAY ONLY IN PARALLELS

1 Hangman Adam Page B 25.00 60.00
2 Sammy Guevara B 25.00 60.00
3 Adam Cole B 15.00 40.00
4 Dante Martin D 12.00 30.00
5 Powerhouse Hobbs D 10.00 25.00
6 Lance Archer B 12.00 30.00
7 Wardlow B 10.00 25.00
8 Dr. Britt Baker B
9 Jade Cargill B 60.00 150.00
10 Thunder Rosa B 20.00 50.00
11 Julia Hart B 60.00 150.00
12 Serena Deeb D 10.00 25.00
13 Anna Jay D 30.00 75.00
14 Red Velvet D 20.00 50.00
15 Jungle Boy Jack Perry B 20.00 50.00
16 Kenny Omega B 60.00 150.00
17 Jon Moxley B 40.00 100.00
18 Chris Jericho B 30.00 75.00
19 Hikaru Shida D 40.00 100.00
20 Kris Statlander B 20.00 50.00
21 RIHO D
22 Athena B 12.00 30.00
23 Tay Melo B 30.00 75.00
24 Anthony Bowens D 12.00 30.00
25 MJF C 150.00 400.00
26 CM Punk B 60.00 150.00
27 Scorpio Sky B 10.00 25.00
28 Ricky Starks D 25.00 60.00
29 Penta el Zero M D 12.00 30.00
30 Keith Lee B 10.00 25.00
31 The Bunny D 30.00 75.00
32 Penelope Ford D 50.00 125.00
33 Ruby Soho D 30.00 75.00
34 Emi Sakura D 15.00 40.00
35 Andrade El Idolo B 10.00 25.00
36 Matt Menard B
37 Austin Gunn C 10.00 25.00
38 Colten Gunn D 10.00 25.00
39 Darby Allin B 20.00 50.00
40 Eddie Kingston D 20.00 50.00
41 Jake Hager C 10.00 25.00
42 John Silver D 15.00 40.00
43 Matt Jackson D 25.00 60.00
44 Max Caster D 12.00 30.00
45 Miro D 10.00 25.00
46 Malakai Black D 15.00 40.00
47 Orange Cassidy C
48 Christian Cage D 20.00 50.00
49 Shawn Spears D 6.00 15.00
50 Marq Quen D 6.00 15.00
51 Angelo Parker B 8.00 20.00
52 Kip Sabian D 10.00 25.00
53 Matt Hardy C 8.00 20.00
54 Matt Sydal B 6.00 15.00
55 Ortiz D 10.00 25.00
56 PAC D 15.00 40.00
57 Preston Vance D 10.00 25.00
58 QT Marshall D 6.00 15.00
59 Rey Fenix D 20.00 50.00
60 Claudio Castagnoli B 8.00 20.00
61 Buddy Matthews B 15.00 30.00
62 Sting B 75.00 200.00
63 The Blade C 10.00 25.00
64 The Butcher D 10.00 25.00
65 Tony Nese B 8.00 20.00
66 Trent Beretta C 15.00 40.00
67 Luchasaurus B
68 Toni Storm B 100.00 250.00
69 Nyla Rose C 20.00 50.00
70 Tony Schiavone D
71 Jim Ross C 10.00 25.00
73 Excalibur D 12.00 30.00
74 Taz D
75 Mark Henry C 6.00 15.00
76 Paul Turner D 6.00 15.00
77 Aubrey Edwards D 15.00 40.00
79 Lee Moriarty A
80 Kyle O'Reilly C
81 Bryan Danielson C 30.00 75.00
82 Cash Wheeler C
83 Danhausen C 75.00 200.00
84 Chuck Taylor D 10.00 25.00
85 Dax Harwood C 15.00 40.00
86 Evil Uno D 10.00 25.00
87 Isiah Kassidy D 8.00 20.00
88 Brody King B
89 Nick Jackson C
90 Swerve Strickland B 20.00 50.00
91 Dustin Rhodes C 10.00 25.00
92 Brian Pillman Jr. B
93 Alex Reynolds C
94 Ethan Page C 20.00 50.00
95 Wheeler Yuta B 40.00 100.00
96 Jamie Hayter C 60.00 150.00
97 Anthony Ogogo C 10.00 25.00
98 HOOK B
99 Daniel Garcia D 15.00 40.00
100 Samoa Joe C 20.00 50.00

2022 SkyBox Metal Universe AEW Bonzo Gonzo

*GOLD/25: UNPRICED DUE TO SCARCITY
STATED ODDS 1:10 ALL BOXES

BG1 Orange Cassidy 6.00 15.00
BG2 Adam Cole 4.00 10.00
BG3 Jon Moxley 3.00 8.00
BG4 Bryan Danielson 2.50 6.00
BG5 Lee Moriarty 3.00 8.00
BG6 Jade Cargill 4.00 10.00
BG7 Dante Martin 2.50 6.00
BG8 Sammy Guevara 3.00 8.00
BG9 Marq Quen 1.50 4.00
BG10 Keith Lee 1.50 4.00
BG11 Penta el Zero M 3.00 8.00
BG12 Buddy Matthews 2.50 6.00
BG13 Brody King 1.50 4.00
BG14 Chris Jericho 3.00 8.00
BG15 Daniel Garcia 2.00 5.00
BG16 Jungle Boy Jack Perry 3.00 8.00
BG17 The Lucha Brothers 4.00 10.00
BG18 Brody King 2.50 6.00
BG19 Eddie Kingston 4.00 10.00
BG20 Hangman Adam Page 3.00 8.00
BG21 Claudio Castagnoli 1.50 4.00
BG22 Luchasaurus 3.00 8.00
BG23 Santana 1.50 4.00
BG24 Swerve Strickland 5.00 12.00
BG25 Dax Harwood 3.00 8.00
BG26 Max Caster 4.00 10.00
BG27 Nick Jackson 2.50 6.00
BG28 Cash Wheeler 2.00 5.00
BG29 Luchasaurus 3.00 8.00
BG30 Kris Statlander 3.00 8.00

2022 SkyBox Metal Universe AEW Competitive Advantage

COMPLETE SET (18)
STATED ODDS 1:600 HOBBY/EPACK

CA1 Adam Cole 40.00 100.00
CA2 Frankie Kazarian
CA3 Jon Moxley 40.00 100.00
CA4 Wardlow 25.00 60.00
CA5 Anna Jay
CA6 Hangman Adam Page 50.00 125.00
CA7 CM Punk 30.00 75.00
CA8 Sammy Guevara 50.00 125.00
CA9 Dr. Britt Baker 50.00 125.00
CA10 Jade Cargill
CA11 Red Velvet 15.00 40.00
CA12 Kenny Omega 150.00 400.00
CA13 Serena Deeb 25.00 60.00
CA14 Thunder Rosa 30.00 75.00
CA15 Jamie Hayter
CA16 Nyla Rose
CA17 Lance Archer
CA18 Jungle Boy Jack Perry 30.00 75.00

2022 SkyBox Metal Universe AEW Feeling the Love

*GOLD/25: UNPRICED DUE TO SCARCITY
*P.P.BLACK/1: UNPRICED DUE TO SCARCITY
*P.P.CYAN/1: UNPRICED DUE TO SCARCITY
*P.P.MAGENTA/1: UNPRICED DUE TO SCARCITY
*P.P.YELLOW/1: UNPRICED DUE TO SCARCITY
STATED ODDS 1:10 ALL BOXES

FL1 Adam Cole 4.00 10.00
FL2 Hangman Adam Page 8.00 20.00
FL3 Keith Lee 2.00 5.00
FL4 Danhausen 20.00 50.00
FL5 MJF 10.00 25.00
FL6 Dr. Britt Baker 8.00 20.00
FL7 Hikaru Shida 6.00 15.00
FL8 Thunder Rosa 6.00 15.00
FL9 Orange Cassidy 6.00 15.00
FL10 CM Punk 10.00 25.00
FL11 Malakai Black 5.00 12.00
FL12 Jungle Boy Jack Perry 6.00 15.00
FL13 Jade Cargill 15.00 40.00
FL14 Eddie Kingston 6.00 15.00
FL15 Athena 3.00 8.00
FL16 Samoa Joe 2.50 6.00
FL17 Bryan Danielson 2.50 6.00
FL18 Serena Deeb 2.00 5.00
FL19 Jay Lethal 4.00 10.00
FL20 Claudio Castagnoli 4.00 10.00

2022 SkyBox Metal Universe AEW Feeling the Love Autographs

GROUP A ODDS 1:5,091
GROUP B ODDS 1:3,294
STATED ODDS 1:2,000 HOBBY/EPACK

FL1 Adam Cole A
FL2 Hangman Adam Page A
FL3 Keith Lee A
FL4 Danhausen B 100.00 250.00
FL5 MJF B
FL6 Dr. Britt Baker A
FL7 Hikaru Shida B
FL8 Thunder Rosa B 40.00 100.00
FL9 Orange Cassidy B
FL10 CM Punk A
FL11 Malakai Black B
FL12 Jungle Boy Jack Perry A
FL13 Jade Cargill A 150.00 400.00
FL14 Eddie Kingston B
FL15 Athena A 60.00 150.00
FL16 Samoa Joe A
FL17 Bryan Danielson A
FL18 Serena Deeb B
FL19 Jay Lethal B 30.00 75.00
FL20 Claudio Castagnoli A

2022 SkyBox Metal Universe AEW Hardware

*GOLD SPECTRUM/25: UNPRICED DUE TO SCARCITY
STATED ODDS 1:38 ALL BOXES

HW1 Hangman Adam Page 8.00 20.00
HW2 Sammy Guevara 8.00 20.00
HW3 Scorpio Sky 6.00 15.00
HW4 Toni Storm 10.00 25.00
HW5 Jamie Hayter 12.00 30.00
HW6 Jade Cargill 8.00 20.00
HW7 Darby Allin 5.00 12.00
HW8 Matt Jackson 8.00 20.00
HW9 Nick Jackson 6.00 15.00
HW10 Max Caster 4.00 10.00
HW11 Rey Fenix 4.00 10.00
HW12 Miro 6.00 15.00
HW13 MJF 10.00 25.00
HW14 Kenny Omega 8.00 20.00
HW15 Jon Moxley 8.00 20.00
HW16 Chris Jericho 6.00 15.00
HW17 Dr. Britt Baker 10.00 25.00
HW18 Hikaru Shida 6.00 15.00
HW19 Luchasaurus 5.00 12.00
HW20 Jungle Boy Jack Perry 5.00 12.00

2022 SkyBox Metal Universe AEW Intimidation Nation

STATED ODDS 1:75 ALL BOXES

IN1 Adam Cole 8.00 20.00
IN2 Darby Allin 10.00 25.00
IN3 Jon Moxley 8.00 20.00
IN4 Jade Cargill 12.00 30.00
IN5 Anna Jay 10.00 25.00
IN6 Hangman Adam Page 5.00 12.00
IN7 CM Punk 15.00 40.00
IN8 Sammy Guevara 4.00 10.00
IN9 Dr. Britt Baker 10.00 25.00

- IN10 Hikaru Shida 15.00 40.00
- IN11 Keith Lee 4.00 10.00
- IN12 Kenny Omega 12.00 30.00
- IN13 Kris Statlander 15.00 40.00
- IN14 Thunder Rosa 8.00 20.00
- IN15 Jamie Hayter 12.00 30.00
- IN16 Nyla Rose 5.00 12.00
- IN17 Matt Hardy 6.00 15.00
- IN18 Jungle Boy Jack Perry 6.00 15.00
- IN19 Red Velvet 4.00 10.00
- IN20 Scorpio Sky 4.00 10.00

2022 SkyBox Metal Universe AEW Intimidation Nation Autographs

STATED PRINT RUN 25 SER.#'d SETS
HOBBY/EPACK EXCLUSIVE

- IN1 Adam Cole 50.00 125.00
- IN2 Darby Allin 60.00 150.00
- IN3 Jon Moxley 60.00 150.00
- IN4 Jade Cargill 150.00 400.00
- IN5 Anna Jay
- IN6 Hangman Adam Page
- IN7 CM Punk
- IN8 Sammy Guevara 75.00 200.00
- IN9 Dr. Britt Baker 150.00 400.00
- IN10 Hikaru Shida 50.00 125.00
- IN11 Keith Lee
- IN12 Kenny Omega
- IN13 Kris Statlander
- IN14 Thunder Rosa
- IN15 Jamie Hayter 150.00 400.00
- IN16 Nyla Rose
- IN17 Matt Hardy
- IN18 Jungle Boy Jack Perry
- IN19 Red Velvet
- IN20 Scorpio Sky

2022 SkyBox Metal Universe AEW Jambalaya

STATED ODDS 1:720 HOBBY/EPACK
STATED ODDS 1:2,160 BLASTER

- 1 Hangman Adam Page 125.00 300.00
- 2 Jon Moxley 150.00 400.00
- 3 MJF 500.00 1200.00
- 4 Sammy Guevara 100.00 250.00
- 5 Sting 400.00 1000.00
- 6 Jade Cargill 100.00 200.00
- 7 Red Velvet 60.00 150.00
- 8 Chris Jericho 125.00 300.00
- 9 Toni Storm 150.00 400.00
- 10 Orange Cassidy 60.00 150.00
- 11 Jungle Boy Jack Perry 50.00 125.00
- 12 Kenny Omega 600.00 1500.00
- 13 Tay Melo 50.00 125.00
- 14 Dr. Britt Baker 125.00 300.00
- 15 Scorpio Sky 50.00 125.00
- 16 Thunder Rosa 100.00 250.00
- 17 CM Punk 200.00 500.00
- 18 Serena Deeb 75.00 200.00
- 19 Anna Jay
- 20 Penta el Zero M 50.00 125.00

2022 SkyBox Metal Universe AEW The Merch

*GOLD/25: UNPRICED DUE TO SCARCITY
STATED ODDS 1:10 ALL BOXES

- TM1 Hangman Adam Page 4.00 10.00
- TM2 Adam Cole 5.00 12.00
- TM3 HOOK 3.00 8.00
- TM4 Chris Jericho 2.50 6.00
- TM5 CM Punk 5.00 12.00
- TM6 Toni Storm 3.00 8.00
- TM7 Bryan Danielson 3.00 8.00
- TM8 Dr. Britt Baker 6.00 15.00
- TM9 FTR 2.00 5.00
- TM10 Jon Moxley 4.00 10.00
- TM11 Kenny Omega 5.00 12.00
- TM12 Eddie Kingston 3.00 8.00
- TM13 Kris Statlander 2.50 6.00
- TM14 Lance Archer 6.00 15.00
- TM15 Malakai Black 3.00 8.00
- TM16 Darby Allin 4.00 10.00
- TM17 Miro 2.00 5.00
- TM18 Orange Cassidy 4.00 10.00
- TM19 Penta el Zero M 3.00 8.00
- TM20 Rey Fenix 2.50 6.00
- TM21 Ricky Starks 2.50 6.00
- TM22 Claudio Castagnoli 3.00 8.00
- TM23 Sting 4.00 10.00
- TM24 Tay Melo 3.00 8.00
- TM25 The Bunny 3.00 8.00
- TM26 The Butcher 2.00 5.00
- TM27 Thunder Rosa 3.00 8.00
- TM28 Matt Jackson/Nick Jackson 4.00 10.00
- TM29 Andrade El Idolo 2.50 6.00
- TM30 Danhausen 6.00 15.00

2022 SkyBox Metal Universe AEW Metal-X

STATED ODDS 1:240 HOBBY/EPACK
STATED ODDS 1:6,000 BLASTER

- MX1 Jade Cargill 30.00 75.00
- MX2 Sammy Guevara 10.00 25.00
- MX3 Claudio Castagnoli
- MX4 Orange Cassidy
- MX5 Cash Wheeler 25.00 60.00
- MX6 Dr. Britt Baker 60.00 150.00
- MX7 Penta el Zero M
- MX8 Wheeler Yuta 15.00 40.00
- MX9 Nyla Rose 50.00 125.00
- MX10 Dante Martin
- MX11 Hangman Adam Page 50.00 125.00
- MX12 Nick Comoroto
- MX13 Preston Vance 6.00 15.00
- MX14 Toni Storm
- MX15 Adam Cole 30.00 75.00
- MX16 Powerhouse Hobbs
- MX17 Red Velvet
- MX18 Leyla Hirsch 10.00 25.00
- MX19 Serena Deeb 15.00 40.00
- MX20 Thunder Rosa 15.00 40.00
- MX21 Anna Jay
- MX22 Luchasaurus
- MX23 Bryan Danielson 20.00 50.00
- MX24 CM Punk 30.00 75.00
- MX25 HOOK 20.00 50.00
- MX26 Danhausen 60.00 150.00
- MX27 Rey Fenix 60.00 150.00
- MX28 Lance Archer 6.00 15.00
- MX29 Dustin Rhodes 30.00 75.00
- MX30 MJF 125.00 300.00
- MX31 Tay Melo 15.00 40.00
- MX32 Chris Jericho 20.00 50.00
- MX33 Evil Uno
- MX34 Wardlow
- MX35 RIHO 25.00 60.00
- MX36 QT Marshall
- MX37 Jungle Boy Jack Perry 15.00 40.00
- MX38 Kris Statlander
- MX39 Jon Moxley
- MX40 Athena
- MX41 Ricky Starks
- MX42 John Silver 20.00 50.00
- MX43 Scorpio Sky 12.00 30.00
- MX44 Keith Lee
- MX45 Christian Cage
- MX46 Ruby Soho 15.00 40.00
- MX47 Penelope Ford 20.00 50.00
- MX48 Swerve Strickland
- MX49 The Bunny 30.00 75.00
- MX50 Darby Allin

2022 SkyBox Metal Universe AEW Palladium

*GOLD SPECTRUM/25: UNPRICED DUE TO SCARCITY
STATED ODDS 1:25 ALL BOXES

- P1 Kenny Omega 10.00 25.00
- P2 Jon Moxley 10.00 25.00
- P3 MJF 10.00 25.00
- P4 Sammy Guevara 4.00 10.00
- P5 Wardlow 6.00 15.00
- P6 Jade Cargill 10.00 25.00
- P7 Red Velvet 6.00 15.00
- P8 Kris Statlander 8.00 20.00
- P9 Toni Storm 8.00 20.00
- P10 Orange Cassidy 8.00 20.00
- P11 Matt Jackson 6.00 15.00
- P12 Hangman Adam Page 5.00 12.00
- P13 Nick Jackson 4.00 10.00
- P14 Rey Fenix 6.00 15.00
- P15 Ruby Soho 6.00 15.00
- P16 Thunder Rosa 5.00 12.00
- P17 CM Punk 8.00 20.00
- P18 Athena 4.00 10.00
- P19 Penelope Ford 5.00 12.00
- P20 Penta el Zero M 6.00 15.00
- P21 Dante Martin 3.00 8.00
- P22 Jungle Boy Jack Perry 5.00 12.00
- P23 Eddie Kingston 5.00 12.00
- P24 Lance Archer 3.00 8.00
- P25 Sting 10.00 25.00
- P26 Darby Allin 5.00 12.00
- P27 Hikaru Shida 6.00 15.00
- P28 Tay Melo 5.00 12.00
- P29 Dr. Britt Baker 8.00 20.00
- P30 Nyla Rose 5.00 12.00

2022 SkyBox Metal Universe AEW Planet Metal

STATED ODDS 1:20 ALL BOXES

- PM1 Ricky Starks 3.00 8.00
- PM2 Chris Jericho 4.00 10.00
- PM3 Nyla Rose 6.00 15.00
- PM4 Miro 3.00 8.00
- PM5 Jon Moxley 4.00 10.00
- PM6 Jade Cargill 10.00 25.00
- PM7 Kenny Omega 6.00 15.00
- PM8 Anna Jay 4.00 10.00
- PM9 Powerhouse Hobbs 5.00 12.00
- PM10 Red Velvet 3.00 8.00
- PM11 Toni Storm 5.00 12.00
- PM12 Hangman Adam Page 4.00 10.00
- PM13 Ruby Soho 4.00 10.00
- PM14 Jay Lethal 2.50 6.00
- PM15 Luchasaurus 2.50 6.00
- PM16 Jungle Boy Jack Perry 3.00 8.00
- PM17 Bryan Danielson 4.00 10.00
- PM18 Claudio Castagnoli 3.00 8.00
- PM19 Dante Martin 2.50 6.00
- PM20 Malakai Black 2.50 6.00
- PM21 Dr. Britt Baker 8.00 20.00
- PM22 Taz 2.50 6.00
- PM23 Tony Schiavone 2.00 5.00
- PM24 William Regal 2.00 5.00
- PM25 Eddie Kingston 3.00 8.00

2022 SkyBox Metal Universe AEW Precious Metal Gems Red

*GREEN/10: UNPRICED DUE TO SCARCITY
*GOLD/1: UNPRICED DUE TO SCARCITY
STATED PRINT RUN 100 SER.#'d SETS

- 1 Hangman Adam Page 30.00 75.00
- 2 Sammy Guevara 30.00 75.00
- 3 Adam Cole 40.00 100.00
- 4 Dante Martin 25.00 60.00
- 5 Powerhouse Hobbs
- 6 Lance Archer 15.00 40.00
- 7 Wardlow 25.00 60.00
- 8 Dr. Britt Baker 150.00 400.00
- 9 Jade Cargill 100.00 250.00
- 10 Thunder Rosa
- 11 Julia Hart 60.00 150.00
- 12 Serena Deeb 20.00 50.00
- 13 Anna Jay 75.00 200.00
- 14 Red Velvet 40.00 100.00
- 15 Jungle Boy Jack Perry 15.00 40.00
- 16 Kenny Omega 125.00 300.00
- 17 Jon Moxley 100.00 250.00
- 18 Chris Jericho 75.00 200.00
- 19 Hikaru Shida 60.00 150.00
- 20 Kris Statlander 60.00 150.00
- 21 RIHO 20.00 50.00
- 22 Athena 15.00 40.00
- 23 Tay Melo 50.00 125.00
- 24 Anthony Bowens 15.00 40.00
- 25 MJF 600.00 1500.00
- 26 CM Punk 125.00 300.00
- 27 Scorpio Sky 12.00 30.00
- 28 Ricky Starks 25.00 60.00
- 29 Penta el Zero M 30.00 75.00
- 30 Keith Lee 25.00 60.00
- 31 The Bunny 50.00 125.00
- 32 Penelope Ford 15.00 40.00
- 33 Ruby Soho 30.00 75.00
- 34 Emi Sakura 20.00 50.00
- 35 Andrade El Idolo 20.00 50.00
- 36 Matt Menard
- 37 Austin Gunn 15.00 40.00
- 38 Colten Gunn
- 39 Darby Allin 100.00 250.00
- 40 Eddie Kingston 50.00 125.00
- 41 Jake Hager 15.00 40.00
- 42 John Silver 15.00 40.00
- 43 Matt Jackson
- 44 Max Caster
- 45 Miro 30.00 75.00
- 46 Malakai Black 50.00 125.00
- 47 Orange Cassidy 100.00 250.00
- 48 Christian Cage
- 49 Shawn Spears 15.00 40.00
- 50 Marq Quen 12.00 30.00
- 51 Angelo Parker
- 52 Kip Sabian 25.00 60.00
- 53 Matt Hardy 20.00 50.00
- 54 Matt Sydal 20.00 50.00
- 55 Ortiz
- 56 PAC 25.00 60.00
- 57 Preston Vance 12.00 30.00
- 58 QT Marshall 15.00 40.00
- 59 Rey Fenix 40.00 100.00
- 60 Claudio Castagnoli 40.00 100.00
- 61 Buddy Matthews
- 62 Sting 300.00 800.00
- 63 The Blade 12.00 30.00
- 64 The Butcher 20.00 50.00
- 65 Tony Nese
- 66 Trent Beretta
- 67 Luchasaurus 20.00 50.00
- 68 Toni Storm 100.00 250.00
- 69 Nyla Rose 40.00 100.00
- 70 Tony Schiavone 12.00 30.00
- 71 Jim Ross
- 72 William Regal 30.00 75.00
- 73 Excalibur 12.00 30.00
- 74 Taz 12.00 30.00
- 75 Mark Henry
- 76 Paul Turner 12.00 30.00
- 77 Aubrey Edwards
- 78 Stokely Hathaway
- 79 Lee Moriarty 25.00 60.00
- 80 Kyle O'Reilly
- 81 Bryan Danielson 150.00 400.00
- 82 Cash Wheeler 15.00 40.00
- 83 Danhausen
- 84 Chuck Taylor 15.00 40.00
- 85 Dax Harwood 15.00 40.00
- 86 Evil Uno
- 87 Isiah Kassidy 20.00 50.00
- 88 Brody King 30.00 75.00
- 89 Nick Jackson 75.00 200.00
- 90 Swerve Strickland 60.00 150.00
- 91 Dustin Rhodes
- 92 Brian Pillman Jr.
- 93 Alex Reynolds 15.00 40.00
- 94 Ethan Page
- 95 Wheeler Yuta 40.00 100.00
- 96 Jamie Hayter 100.00 250.00
- 97 Anthony Ogogo 8.00 20.00
- 98 HOOK 60.00 150.00
- 99 Daniel Garcia 30.00 75.00
- 100 Samoa Joe 40.00 100.00
- 101 Sammy Guevara 30.00 75.00
- 102 Jungle Boy Jack Perry 15.00 40.00
- 103 Hangman Adam Page 30.00 75.00
- 104 Orange Cassidy 100.00 250.00
- 105 Penta el Zero M 30.00 75.00
- 106 Hikaru Shida 60.00 150.00
- 107 Dr. Britt Baker 150.00 400.00
- 108 Nyla Rose 40.00 100.00
- 109 CM Punk 125.00 300.00
- 110 Toni Storm 100.00 250.00
- 111 Jade Cargill 100.00 250.00
- 112 Kenny Omega 125.00 300.00
- 113 Claudio Castagnoli 40.00 100.00
- 114 Powerhouse Hobbs
- 115 Red Velvet 40.00 100.00

Card	Low	High
116 Leyla Hirsch	12.00	30.00
117 Serena Deeb	20.00	50.00
118 Thunder Rosa		
119 Anna Jay	75.00	200.00
120 Luchasaurus	20.00	50.00
121 Eddie Kingston	50.00	125.00
122 Bryan Danielson	150.00	400.00
123 Samoa Joe	40.00	100.00
124 Dante Martin	25.00	60.00
125 HOOK	60.00	150.00
126 Preston Vance	12.00	30.00
127 Ruby Soho	30.00	75.00
128 Penelope Ford	15.00	40.00
129 PAC	25.00	60.00
130 Dax Harwood	15.00	40.00
131 Darby Allin	100.00	250.00
132 Wardlow	25.00	60.00
133 Chris Jericho	75.00	200.00
134 MJF	600.00	1500.00
135 Lance Archer	15.00	40.00
136 Jamie Hayter	100.00	250.00
137 Rey Fenix	40.00	100.00
138 Keith Lee	25.00	60.00
139 Tay Melo	50.00	125.00
140 Sting	300.00	800.00
141 RIHO	20.00	50.00
142 Adam Cole	40.00	100.00
143 Malakai Black	50.00	125.00
144 Kris Statlander	60.00	150.00
145 Jon Moxley	100.00	250.00
146 Cash Wheeler	15.00	40.00
147 Ricky Starks	25.00	60.00
148 John Silver	15.00	40.00
149 Scorpio Sky	12.00	30.00
150 Jay Lethal	15.00	40.00

2022 SkyBox Metal Universe AEW SkyBox Premium

*STAR SAPPHIRES: 1X TO 2.5X BASIC CARDS
*STAR RUBIES/50: 1.5X TO 4X BASIC CARDS
*STAR EMERALDS/10: UNPRICED DUE TO SCARCITY
*STAR DIAMONDS/1: UNPRICED DUE TO SCARCITY
*P.P.BLACK/1: UNPRICED DUE TO SCARCITY
*P.P.CYAN/1: UNPRICED DUE TO SCARCITY
*P.P.MAGENTA/1: UNPRICED DUE TO SCARCITY
*P.P.YELLOW/1: UNPRICED DUE TO SCARCITY
STATED ODDS 1:5 HOBBY/EPACK
STATED ODDS 1:7.5 BLASTER

Card	Low	High
PP1 Adam Cole	2.50	6.00
PP2 Hikaru Shida	6.00	15.00
PP3 Hangman Adam Page	3.00	8.00
PP4 Thunder Rosa	6.00	15.00
PP5 Jade Cargill	5.00	12.00
PP6 Tay Melo	5.00	10.00
PP7 Kenny Omega	4.00	10.00
PP8 Darby Allin	5.00	12.00
PP9 Jon Moxley	2.00	5.00
PP10 Jungle Boy Jack Perry	2.50	6.00
PP11 Kris Statlander	4.00	10.00
PP12 Sammy Guevara	2.00	5.00
PP13 Dr. Britt Baker	4.00	10.00
PP14 Nyla Rose	2.00	5.00
PP15 CM Punk	6.00	15.00
PP16 Andrade El Idolo	3.00	8.00
PP17 Danhausen	8.00	20.00
PP18 HOOK	3.00	8.00
PP19 Claudio Castagnoli	3.00	8.00
PP20 Matt Jackson	4.00	10.00
PP21 Nick Jackson	4.00	10.00
PP22 Wheeler Yuta	2.50	6.00
PP23 The Blade	2.00	5.00
PP24 Scorpio Sky	2.00	5.00
PP25 Tony Nese	2.00	5.00
PP26 Cash Wheeler	2.00	5.00
PP27 Eddie Kingston	3.00	8.00
PP28 Julia Hart	10.00	25.00
PP29 Yuka Sakazaki	2.50	6.00
PP30 Bryan Danielson	3.00	8.00
PP31 Ethan Page	5.00	12.00
PP32 Jake Hager	2.00	5.00
PP33 Ortiz	2.00	5.00
PP34 PAC	2.00	5.00
PP35 Marq Quen	2.00	5.00
PP36 Jay Lethal	3.00	8.00
PP37 MJF	6.00	15.00
PP38 Swerve Strickland	3.00	8.00
PP39 Jamie Hayter	6.00	15.00
PP40 Penta el Zero M	5.00	12.00
PP41 Brody King	3.00	8.00
PP42 Athena	2.00	5.00
PP43 Justin Roberts	2.00	5.00
PP44 Rick Knox	2.00	5.00
PP45 Paul Turner	2.00	5.00
PP46 Kyle O'Reilly	3.00	8.00
PP47 Stokely Hathaway	3.00	8.00
PP48 William Regal	2.00	5.00
PP49 Mark Sterling	4.00	10.00
PP50 Alex Abrahantes	2.50	6.00

2022 SkyBox Metal Universe AEW SkyBox Premium Star Sapphires Autographs

*STAR EMERALDS/10: UNPRICED DUE TO SCARCITY
GROUP A ODDS 1:3,320
GROUP B ODDS 1:213
STATED ODDS 1:200 BLASTER

PP1 Adam Cole A
PP2 Hikaru Shida B
PP3 Hangman Adam Page B
PP4 Thunder Rosa A
PP5 Jade Cargill B
PP6 Tay Melo B
PP7 Kenny Omega A
PP8 Darby Allin B
PP9 Jon Moxley A
PP10 Jungle Boy Jack Perry A
PP11 Kris Statlander B
PP12 Sammy Guevara B
PP13 Dr. Britt Baker A
PP14 Nyla Rose B
PP15 CM Punk A
PP16 Andrade El Idolo B
PP17 Danhausen A
PP18 HOOK B
PP19 Claudio Castagnoli B
PP20 Matt Jackson B
PP21 Nick Jackson B
PP22 Wheeler Yuta B
PP23 The Blade B
PP24 Scorpio Sky B
PP25 Tony Nese B
PP26 Cash Wheeler B
PP27 Eddie Kingston B
PP28 Julia Hart B
PP29 Yuka Sakazaki B
PP30 Bryan Danielson B
PP31 Ethan Page B
PP32 Jake Hager B
PP33 Ortiz B
PP34 PAC B
PP35 Marq Quen B
PP36 Jay Lethal B
PP37 MJF A
PP38 Swerve Strickland B
PP39 Jamie Hayter B
PP40 Penta el Zero M B
PP41 Brody King B
PP42 Athena B
PP43 Justin Roberts B
PP44 Rick Knox B
PP45 Paul Turner B
PP46 Kyle O'Reilly B
PP47 Stokely Hathaway B
PP48 Alex Abrahantes B

2022 SkyBox Metal Universe AEW Technicians

*GOLD/25: UNPRICED DUE TO SCARCITY
STATED ODDS 1:7.5 ALL BOXES

Card	Low	High
TN1 Kenny Omega	2.50	6.00
TN2 Adam Cole	1.25	3.00
TN3 Bryan Danielson	6.00	15.00
TN4 Jay Lethal	1.25	3.00
TN5 CM Punk	6.00	15.00
TN6 Angelico	4.00	10.00
TN7 Chris Jericho	2.00	5.00
TN8 Wheeler Yuta	4.00	10.00
TN9 Evil Uno	1.00	2.50
TN10 Hikaru Shida	3.00	8.00
TN11 Wardlow	3.00	8.00
TN12 Dr. Britt Baker	4.00	10.00
TN13 Dax Harwood	1.50	4.00
TN14 Anna Jay	4.00	10.00
TN15 Eddie Kingston	1.50	4.00
TN16 PAC	1.25	3.00
TN17 Hangman Adam Page	2.50	6.00
TN18 Claudio Castagnoli	1.25	3.00
TN19 Darby Allin	6.00	15.00
TN20 Alex Reynolds	1.00	2.50
TN21 Sammy Guevara	1.00	2.50
TN22 Kris Statlander	1.50	4.00
TN23 Lance Archer	4.00	10.00
TN24 Malakai Black	6.00	15.00
TN25 Toni Storm	3.00	8.00
TN26 Powerhouse Hobbs	2.50	6.00
TN27 Jon Moxley	1.50	4.00
TN28 Daniel Garcia	2.50	6.00
TN29 Jungle Boy Jack Perry	5.00	12.00
TN30 MJF	6.00	15.00
TN31 Orange Cassidy	5.00	12.00
TN32 Rey Fenix	1.50	4.00
TN33 Thunder Rosa	5.00	12.00
TN34 Tay Melo	2.50	6.00
TN35 Ruby Soho	2.00	5.00
TN36 Penta el Zero M	2.50	6.00
TN37 Sting	2.50	6.00
TN38 Athena	1.00	2.50
TN39 Cash Wheeler	3.00	8.00
TN40 Scorpio Sky	2.00	5.00

2022 SkyBox Metal Universe AEW Turn Up the Heat

*GOLD/25: UNPRICED DUE TO SCARCITY
*P.P.BLACK/1: UNPRICED DUE TO SCARCITY
*P.P.CYAN/1: UNPRICED DUE TO SCARCITY
*P.P.MAGENTA/1: UNPRICED DUE TO SCARCITY
*P.P.YELLOW/1: UNPRICED DUE TO SCARCITY
STATED ODDS 1:38 ALL BOXES

Card	Low	High
TH1 Adam Cole	8.00	20.00
TH2 Anna Jay	10.00	25.00
TH3 Trent Beretta	2.50	6.00
TH4 Ruby Soho	6.00	15.00
TH5 Lee Moriarty	4.00	10.00
TH6 HOOK	6.00	15.00
TH7 Ethan Page	5.00	12.00
TH8 Tay Melo	4.00	10.00
TH9 Bryan Danielson	4.00	10.00
TH10 Brody King	6.00	15.00
TH11 Lance Archer	5.00	12.00
TH12 Sammy Guevara	4.00	10.00
TH13 Toni Storm	10.00	25.00
TH14 Luchasaurus	2.50	6.00
TH15 Serena Deeb	6.00	15.00
TH16 Rey Fenix	3.00	8.00
TH17 Red Velvet	5.00	12.00
TH18 Jamie Hayter	6.00	15.00
TH19 Ricky Starks	3.00	8.00
TH20 Scorpio Sky	3.00	8.00

2022 SkyBox Metal Universe AEW Turn Up the Heat Autographs

STATED ODDS 1:2,000 HOBBY/EPACK

Card	Low	High
TH1 Adam Cole		
TH2 Anna Jay	100.00	250.00
TH3 Trent Beretta		
TH4 Ruby Soho	60.00	150.00
TH5 Lee Moriarty	30.00	75.00
TH6 HOOK		
TH7 Ethan Page	40.00	100.00
TH8 Tay Melo	50.00	125.00
TH9 Bryan Danielson	75.00	200.00
TH10 Brody King		
TH11 Lance Archer		
TH12 Sammy Guevara	30.00	75.00
TH13 Toni Storm	60.00	150.00
TH14 Luchasaurus		
TH15 Serena Deeb		
TH16 Rey Fenix		
TH17 Red Velvet	40.00	100.00
TH18 Jamie Hayter		
TH19 Ricky Starks	25.00	60.00
TH20 Scorpio Sky		

1997 Stridex WWF

Card	Low	High
COMPLETE SET (7)	8.00	20.00
NNO Header Card	.75	2.00
NNO Ahmed Johnson	.75	2.00
NNO Bret Hit Man Hart	2.00	5.00
NNO Shawn Michaels	2.00	5.00
NNO Stone Cold Steve Austin	3.00	8.00
NNO Sycho Sid	1.25	3.00
NNO Undertaker	3.00	8.00

1987 Stuart WWF Canadian

COMPLETE SET (16) 15.00 40.00
*CUT: X TO X BASIC CARDS

Card	Low	High
1 Brutus The Barber Beefcake	1.25	3.00
2 Les Freres Rougeau Brothers	1.00	2.50
3 Strike Force	1.25	3.00
4 The Honky Tonk Man	1.25	3.00
5 Randy Savage with Elizabeth	4.00	10.00
6 Hulk Hogan	6.00	15.00
7 Demolition	1.25	3.00
8 Koko B. Ware	1.00	2.50
9 Ted DiBiase UER	1.50	4.00
10 Slick The Doctor of Style	1.25	3.00
11 British Bulldogs	1.25	3.00
12 Bobby The Brain Heenan	1.50	4.00
13 Jimmy Hart	1.25	3.00
14 George The Animal Steele	1.50	4.00
15 Jake The Snake Roberts	2.00	5.00
16 The Junk Yard Dog	1.25	3.00

1991 Swanson WWF Wrestling Canadian

Card	Low	High
COMPLETE SET (12)	30.00	75.00
NNO Big Boss Man	3.00	8.00
NNO Bret Hitman Hart	5.00	12.00
NNO The Bushwhackers	4.00	10.00
NNO Hulk Hogan	8.00	20.00
NNO Jake The Snake Roberts	2.50	6.00
NNO Legion of Doom	5.00	12.00
NNO Macho Man Randy Savage	6.00	15.00
NNO Ted DiBiase	3.00	8.00
NNO The Mountie	2.50	6.00
NNO Rockers Marty and Shawn	5.00	12.00
NNO Texas Tornado	2.50	6.00
NNO Ultimate Warrior	6.00	15.00

1994 Titan Sports WWF Vending Hologram Stickers

Card	Low	High
COMPLETE SET (10)	8.00	20.00
NNO Adam Bomb	1.00	2.50
NNO Bret Hitman Hart	2.00	5.00
NNO Doink	1.00	2.50
NNO Lex Luger	1.50	4.00
NNO Ludvig Borga	1.00	2.50
NNO Macho Man Randy Savage	2.00	5.00
NNO Razor Ramon	1.25	3.00
NNO Tatanka	1.00	2.50
NNO Undertaker	3.00	8.00
NNO Yokozuna	1.25	3.00

2013 Topps Best of WWE

COMPLETE SET (110) 8.00 20.00
*BLUE: .6X TO 1.5X BASIC CARDS
*BRONZE: .6X TO 1.5X BASIC CARDS
*SILVER: 2.5X TO 6X BASIC CARDS
*GOLD/10: 5X TO 12X BASIC CARDS
*P.P.BLACK/1: UNPRICED DUE TO SCARCITY
*P.P.CYAN/1: UNPRICED DUE TO SCARCITY
*P.P.MAGENTA/1: UNPRICED DUE TO SCARCITY
*P.P.YELLOW/1: UNPRICED DUE TO SCARCITY

Card	Low	High
1 The Rock	.75	2.00
2 Brock Lesnar/John Cena	.75	2.00
3 Daniel Bryan/AJ Lee	.75	2.00
4 Dusty Rhodes/Cody Rhodes	.25	.60
5 AJ Lee/Kaitlyn	.75	2.00
6 Layla/Nikki Bella	.30	.75
7 Cody Rhodes	.15	.40
8 CM Punk/Chris Jericho	.60	1.50
9 John Cena/Brock Lesnar	.75	2.00

Card	Low	High
10 Brock Lesnar/Triple H	.60	1.50
11 Kofi Kingston/R-Truth	.15	.40
12 Damien Sandow	.15	.40
13 John Laurinaitis/Big Show	.30	.75
14 Christian/Cody Rhodes	.15	.40
15 John Laurinaitis/John Cena	.75	2.00
16 AJ Lee/Kane	.75	2.00
17 Big Show/Mr. McMahon	.30	.75
18 CM Punk/Kane	.60	1.50
19 John Cena/John Laurinaitis	.75	2.00
20 Dolph Ziggler/Jack Swagger	.25	.60
21 AJ Lee	.75	2.00
22 Zack Ryder	.15	.40
23 AJ Lee/CM Punk	.75	2.00
24 Dolph Ziggler	.25	.60
25 John Cena	.75	2.00
26 AJ Lee/Daniel Bryan	.75	2.00
27 D-Generation X	.60	1.50
28 Dude Love/Brodus Clay	.60	1.50
29 Trish Stratus/Triple H	.75	2.00
30 AJ Lee/Daniel Bryan	.75	2.00
31 The Miz/Christian	.25	.60
32 APA/Heath Slater	.15	.40
33 Undertaker/Kane	.60	1.50
34 John Cena/Big Show	.75	2.00
35 CM Punk/The Rock	.75	2.00
36 Daniel Bryan	.40	1.00
37 Mr.McMahon/Booker T	.25	.60
38 Daniel Bryan	.40	1.00
39 Brock Lesnar/Shawn Michaels	.60	1.50
40 Antonio Cesaro/Santino Marella	.15	.40
41 Daniel Bryan/Kane	.40	1.00
42 Brock Lesnar/Triple H	.60	1.50
43 Dolph Ziggler/Chris Jericho	.60	1.50
44 Daniel Bryan/Kane	.40	1.00
45 CM Punk/Jerry Lawler	.60	1.50
46 Kane/Daniel Bryan	.40	1.00
47 CM Punk/Paul Heyman	.60	1.50
48 Kaitlyn	.30	.75
49 Kane/Bryan/Truth	.40	1.00
50 Eve	.60	1.50
51 CM Punk/John Cena	.75	2.00
52 CM Punk/Mr. McMahon	.60	1.50
53 Kofi Kingston/The Miz	.25	.60
54 AJ Lee/Vickie Guerrero	.75	2.00
55 Big Show/Sheamus	.30	.75
56 Brad Maddox/Ryback	.15	.40
57 Vickie Guerrero/John Cena	.75	2.00
58 Big Show/Sheamus	.30	.75
59 Randy Orton/Alberto Del Rio	.50	1.25
60 CM Punk/Jerry Lawler	.60	1.50
61 Ryback/Brad Maddox	.15	.40
62 Team Ziggler/Team Foley	.25	.60
63 Shield/Cena/Ryback	.75	2.00
64 John Cena/AJ Lee	.75	2.00
65 John Cena/Dolph Ziggler	.75	2.00
66 Vicki/AJ Lee/Maddox	.75	2.00
67 Cody Rhodes	.15	.40
68 Reigns/Bryan/Ambrose	.40	1.00
69 AJ Lee/Cena/Ziggler	.75	2.00
70 Big E Langston/John Cena	.75	2.00
71 8 Divas	.60	1.50
72 John Cena/Alberto Del Rio	.75	2.00
73 Great Khali	.15	.40
74 Wade Barrett/Kofi Kingston	.15	.40
75 Dolph Ziggler/AJ Lee	.75	2.00
76 Antonio Cesaro/Great Khali	.15	.40
77 CM Punk/Ryback	.60	1.50
78 The Rock/CM Punk	.75	2.00
79 Alberto Del Rio/Big Show	.30	.75
80 Kaitlyn/Eve	.60	1.50
81 Kane/Daniel Bryan	.40	1.00
82 Chris Jericho	.60	1.50
83 Bo Dallas	.15	.40
84 John Cena	.75	2.00
85 The Rock/CM Punk	.75	2.00
86 Brock Lesnar/Mr. McMahon	.60	1.50
87 Jack Swagger	.25	.60
88 Roman Reigns/Ryback	.25	.60
89 The Rock/CM Punk	.75	2.00
90 Vickie Guerrero/Brad Maddox	.25	.60
91 The Rock	.75	2.00
92 Heyman/McMahon/Brock/HHH	.60	1.50
93 John Cena/CM Punk	.75	2.00
94 The Deadman	.60	1.50
95 Ted DiBiase	.25	.60
96 Outlaws/Primo/Epico	.15	.40
97 CM Punk/Randy Orton	.60	1.50
98 Undertaker	.60	1.50
99 Brie Bella/Nikki Bella	.60	1.50
100 CM Punk/Undertaker	.60	1.50
101 Mick Foley/Chris Jericho	.60	1.50
102 Trish Stratus	.75	2.00
103 Booker T	.25	.60
104 Bob Backlund	.40	1.00
105 Bruno Sammartino	.40	1.00
106 The Miz/Wade Barrett	.25	.60
107 Fandango/Chris Jericho	.60	1.50
108 Undertaker/CM Punk	.60	1.50
109 Triple H/Brock Lesnar	.60	1.50
110 John Cena/The Rock	.75	2.00

2013 Topps Best of WWE Autographs

STATED ODDS 1:48 HOBBY AND RETAIL

Card	Low	High
NNO Dusty Rhodes	200.00	400.00
NNO Big E Langston	30.00	75.00
NNO Bob Backlund	15.00	40.00
NNO Brie Bella	15.00	40.00
NNO Bruno Sammartino	75.00	150.00
NNO Cactus Jack	15.00	40.00
NNO Damien Sandow	10.00	25.00
NNO Dean Ambrose	30.00	75.00
NNO Dude Love	150.00	300.00
NNO JBL	10.00	25.00
NNO Lilian Garcia	20.00	50.00
NNO Mankind	50.00	100.00
NNO Mick Foley	20.00	50.00
NNO Nikki Bella	15.00	40.00
NNO Paul Heyman	30.00	75.00
NNO Roman Reigns	150.00	300.00
NNO Seth Rollins	100.00	200.00
NNO Trish Stratus	30.00	75.00
NNO Vickie Guerrero	10.00	25.00

2013 Topps Best of WWE Dual Autographs

STATED PRINT RUN 10 SER. #'d SETS

Card	Low	High
NNO Brie Bella/Nikki Bella	75.00	150.00
NNO B.Sammartino/B.Backlund		
NNO D.Sandow/Big E	25.00	60.00
NNO D.Ambrose/P.Heyman	60.00	120.00
NNO J.Swagger/V.Guerrero	25.00	60.00
NNO JBL/L.Garcia	50.00	100.00
NNO M.Foley/T.Stratus	50.00	100.00
NNO R.Dogg/B.Gunn	75.00	150.00
NNO S.Rollins/R.Reigns	200.00	400.00
NNO S.Michaels/X-Pac	100.00	200.00

2013 Topps Best of WWE Jerry Lawler Portraits

COMPLETE SET (10) 30.00 80.00
*P.P.BLACK/1: UNPRICED DUE TO SCARCITY
*P.P.CYAN/1: UNPRICED DUE TO SCARCITY
*P.P.MAGENTA/1: UNPRICED DUE TO SCARCITY
*P.P.YELLOW/1: UNPRICED DUE TO SCARCITY
RANDOMLY INSERTED INTO RETAIL PACKS

Card	Low	High
1 CM Punk	6.00	15.00
2 R-Truth	1.50	4.00
3 Undertaker	6.00	15.00
4 Kane	3.00	8.00
5 Paul Bearer	2.50	6.00
6 Vickie Guerrero	2.50	6.00
7 Stone Cold Steve Austin	6.00	15.00
8 Sgt. Slaughter	2.50	6.00
9 Vader	1.50	4.00
10 Doink the Clown	1.50	4.00

2013 Topps Best of WWE Swatch Relics

STATED ODDS 1:24 HOBBY EXCLUSIVE

Card	Low	High
NNO AJ Lee/Shirt	20.00	50.00
NNO AJ Lee/Teddy Bear	60.00	120.00
NNO Brodus Clay/Shirt	4.00	10.00
NNO CM Punk/Shirt	6.00	15.00
NNO Damien Sandow/Shirt	4.00	10.00
NNO Daniel Bryan/Shirt	5.00	12.00
NNO Dean Ambrose/Shirt	5.00	12.00
NNO Dolph Ziggler/Shirt	5.00	12.00
NNO Great Khali/Referee Shirt	4.00	10.00
NNO John Cena/Hat	40.00	80.00
NNO John Cena/Headband		
NNO John Cena/Shirt	6.00	15.00
NNO John Cena/Wristband	40.00	80.00
NNO Miz/Shirt	4.00	10.00
NNO Randy Orton/Shirt	5.00	12.00
NNO Roman Reigns/Shirt	5.00	12.00
NNO Ryback/Shirt	4.00	10.00
NNO Seth Rollins/Shirt	6.00	15.00
NNO Sheamus/Shirt	4.00	10.00
NNO Wade Barrett/Shirt	4.00	10.00

2013 Topps Best of WWE Top 10 Catchphrases

COMPLETE SET (10) 4.00 10.00
*P.P.BLACK/1: UNPRICED DUE TO SCARCITY
*P.P.CYAN/1: UNPRICED DUE TO SCARCITY
*P.P.MAGENTA/1: UNPRICED DUE TO SCARCITY
*P.P.YELLOW/1: UNPRICED DUE TO SCARCITY
STATED ODDS OVERALL 3:1 HOBBY AND RETAIL

Card	Low	High
1 The Rock/If Ya Smell	3.00	8.00
2 Undertaker/Rest in Peace	1.50	4.00
3 John Cena/You Can't See Me!	1.25	3.00
4 Booker T/Can You Dig It, Sucka?	.30	.75
5 The Miz/Because I'm the Miz...	.30	.75
6 Daniel Bryan/Yes!	.50	1.25
7 CM Punk/Best in the World	.75	2.00
8 Zack Ryder/Woo Woo Woo	.20	.50
9 Damien Sandow/You're Welcome!	.20	.50
10 Vickie Guerrero/Excuse Me!	.30	.75

2013 Topps Best of WWE Top 10 Finishers

COMPLETE SET (10) 5.00 12.00
*P.P.BLACK/1: UNPRICED DUE TO SCARCITY
*P.P.CYAN/1: UNPRICED DUE TO SCARCITY
*P.P.MAGENTA/1: UNPRICED DUE TO SCARCITY
*P.P.YELLOW/1: UNPRICED DUE TO SCARCITY
STATED ODDS OVERALL 3:1 HOBBY AND RETAIL

Card	Low	High
1 Undertaker/Tombstone	2.50	6.00
2 Stone Cold Steve Austin/Stunner	1.50	4.00
3 Randy Orton/RKO	.75	2.00
4 Shawn Michaels/Sweet Chin Music	.75	2.00
5 Triple H/Pedigree	.75	2.00
6 The Rock/Rock Bottom	1.00	2.50
7 John Cena/Attitude Adjustment	1.00	2.50
8 CM Punk/GTS	.75	2.00
9 Rey Mysterio/619	.50	1.25
10 Eddie Guerrero/Frog Splash	.20	.50

2013 Topps Best of WWE Top 10 Greatest WWE Moments

COMPLETE SET (10) 5.00 12.00
*P.P.BLACK/1: UNPRICED DUE TO SCARCITY
*P.P.CYAN/1: UNPRICED DUE TO SCARCITY
*P.P.MAGENTA/1: UNPRICED DUE TO SCARCITY
*P.P.YELLOW/1: UNPRICED DUE TO SCARCITY
STATED ODDS OVERALL 3:1 HOBBY AND RETAIL

Card	Low	High
1 Undertaker/Shawn Michaels	2.50	6.00
2 Triple H	1.50	4.00
3 John Cena	1.25	3.00
4 The Rock/John Cena	1.00	2.50
5 Eddie Guerrero/Brock Lesnar	.75	2.00
6 The Rock/Hollywood Hogan	1.00	2.50
7 John Cena/JBL	1.00	2.50
8 CM Punk	.75	2.00
9 CM Punk/John Cena	1.00	2.50
10 Mr. McMahon	.20	.50

2013 Topps Best of WWE Top 10 Intercontinental Champions

COMPLETE SET (10) 3.00 8.00
*P.P.BLACK/1: UNPRICED DUE TO SCARCITY
*P.P.CYAN/1: UNPRICED DUE TO SCARCITY
*P.P.MAGENTA/1: UNPRICED DUE TO SCARCITY
*P.P.YELLOW/1: UNPRICED DUE TO SCARCITY
STATED ODDS OVERALL 3:1 HOBBY AND RETAIL

Card	Low	High
1 Randy Orton	2.00	5.00
2 Rey Mysterio	1.00	2.50
3 Christian	.25	.60
4 Kofi Kingston	.20	.50
5 Cody Rhodes	.20	.50
6 Wade Barrett	.20	.50
7 Dolph Ziggler	.30	.75
8 William Regal	.25	.60
9 Santino Marella	.20	.50
10 Ezekiel Jackson	.20	.50

2013 Topps Best of WWE Top 10 Rivalries

COMPLETE SET (10) 5.00 12.00
*P.P.BLACK/1: UNPRICED DUE TO SCARCITY
*P.P.CYAN/1: UNPRICED DUE TO SCARCITY
*P.P.MAGENTA/1: UNPRICED DUE TO SCARCITY
*P.P.YELLOW/1: UNPRICED DUE TO SCARCITY
STATED ODDS OVERALL 3:1 HOBBY AND RETAIL

Card	Low	High
1 Shawn Michaels/Undertaker	2.50	6.00
2 Undertaker/Triple H	1.50	4.00
3 John Cena/The Rock	1.25	3.00
4 Undertaker/Kane	.75	2.00
5 CM Punk/John Cena	1.00	2.50
6 Triple H/Shawn Michaels	.75	2.00
7 Triple H/Randy Orton	.75	2.00
8 John Cena/Brock Lesnar	1.00	2.50
9 Triple H/Batista	.75	2.00
10 Rey Mysterio/Eddie Guerrero	.50	1.25

2013 Topps Best of WWE Top 10 Trash Talkers

COMPLETE SET (10) 5.00 12.00
*P.P.BLACK/1: UNPRICED DUE TO SCARCITY
*P.P.CYAN/1: UNPRICED DUE TO SCARCITY
*P.P.MAGENTA/1: UNPRICED DUE TO SCARCITY
*P.P.YELLOW/1: UNPRICED DUE TO SCARCITY
STATED ODDS OVERALL 3:1 HOBBY AND RETAIL

Card	Low	High
1 Stone Cold Steve Austin	2.50	6.00
2 The Rock	2.00	5.00
3 CM Punk	1.00	2.50
4 Triple H	.75	2.00
5 Rowdy Roddy Piper	.50	1.25
6 John Cena	1.00	2.50
7 The Miz	.30	.75
8 Shawn Michaels	.75	2.00
9 Paul Heyman	.20	.50
10 AJ Lee	1.00	2.50

2013 Topps Best of WWE Top 10 2K14

COMPLETE SET (10) 60.00 120.00
RANDOMLY INSERTED INTO PACKS

Card	Low	High
1 John Cena	15.00	40.00
2 Triple H	8.00	20.00
3 The Rock	20.00	50.00
4 Undertaker	10.00	25.00
5 CM Punk	15.00	40.00
6 Sheamus	6.00	15.00
7 Brock Lesnar	8.00	20.00
8 Eddie Guerrero	8.00	20.00
9 The Miz	6.00	15.00
10 JBL	6.00	15.00

2013 Topps Best of WWE Top 10 Undertaker Matches

COMPLETE SET (10) 5.00 12.00
*P.P.BLACK/1: UNPRICED DUE TO SCARCITY
*P.P.CYAN/1: UNPRICED DUE TO SCARCITY
*P.P.MAGENTA/1: UNPRICED DUE TO SCARCITY
*P.P.YELLOW/1: UNPRICED DUE TO SCARCITY
STATED ODDS OVERALL 3:1 HOBBY AND RETAIL

Card	Low	High
1 Vs. Triple H	2.50	6.00
2 Vs. Shawn Michaels	1.50	4.00
3 Vs. Shawn Michaels	1.00	2.50
4 Vs. Triple H	.75	2.00
5 Vs. Stone Cold Steve Austin	.75	2.00
6 Wins Royal Rumble	.75	2.00
7 Vs. Batista	.75	2.00
8 Vs. Kane	.75	2.00
9 Vs. Randy Orton	.75	2.00
10 Vs. CM Punk	.75	2.00

2013 Topps Best of WWE Top 10 World Heavyweight Champions

COMPLETE SET (10) 4.00 10.00
*P.P.BLACK/1: UNPRICED DUE TO SCARCITY
*P.P.CYAN/1: UNPRICED DUE TO SCARCITY

*P.P.MAGENTA/1: UNPRICED DUE TO SCARCITY
*P.P.YELLOW/1: UNPRICED DUE TO SCARCITY
STATED ODDS OVERALL 3:1 HOBBY AND RETAIL

1	Undertaker	2.50	6.00
2	Triple H	1.50	4.00
3	Randy Orton	.75	2.00
4	Batista	.50	1.25
5	Sheamus	.40	1.00
6	Rey Mysterio	.50	1.25
7	Kane	.40	1.00
8	CM Punk	.75	2.00
9	Booker T	.30	.75
10	Daniel Bryan	.50	1.25

2013 Topps Best of WWE Top 10 WWE Champions

COMPLETE SET (10) 5.00 12.00
*P.P.BLACK/1: UNPRICED DUE TO SCARCITY
*P.P.CYAN/1: UNPRICED DUE TO SCARCITY
*P.P.MAGENTA/1: UNPRICED DUE TO SCARCITY
*P.P.YELLOW/1: UNPRICED DUE TO SCARCITY
STATED ODDS OVERALL 3:1 HOBBY AND RETAIL

1	John Cena	3.00	8.00
2	Triple H	1.50	4.00
3	The Rock	1.25	3.00
4	Undertaker	.75	2.00
5	CM Punk	.75	2.00
6	Sheamus	.40	1.00
7	Brock Lesnar	.75	2.00
8	Eddie Guerrero	.20	.50
9	The Miz	.30	.75
10	JBL	.30	.75

2013 Topps Best of WWE Top 10 WWE Tag Team Champions

COMPLETE SET (10) 3.00 8.00
*P.P.BLACK/1: UNPRICED DUE TO SCARCITY
*P.P.CYAN/1: UNPRICED DUE TO SCARCITY
*P.P.MAGENTA/1: UNPRICED DUE TO SCARCITY
*P.P.YELLOW/1: UNPRICED DUE TO SCARCITY
STATED ODDS OVERALL 3:1 HOBBY AND RETAIL

1	D-Generation X	2.50	6.00
2	Team Hell No	1.00	2.50
3	Rey Mysterio/Eddie Guerrero	.60	1.50
4	Big Show/Kane	.40	1.00
5	Kofi Kingston/R-Truth	.20	.50
6	Air Boom	.20	.50
7	ShoMiz	.40	1.00
8	Ted DiBiase/Cody Rhodes	.25	.60
9	Curt Hawkins/Zack Ryder	.20	.50
10	Primo & Epico	.20	.50

2013 Topps Best of WWE WrestleMania 29 Mat Relics

STATED ODDS 1:48 HOBBY AND RETAIL

NNO	Alberto Del Rio	4.00	10.00
NNO	Big E Langston	4.00	10.00
NNO	Big Show	4.00	10.00
NNO	Brock Lesnar	5.00	12.00
NNO	Chris Jericho	5.00	12.00
NNO	CM Punk	12.00	30.00
NNO	Daniel Bryan	5.00	12.00
NNO	Dolph Ziggler	4.00	10.00
NNO	Fandango	6.00	15.00
NNO	Jack Swagger	4.00	10.00
NNO	John Cena	6.00	20.00
NNO	Kane	5.00	12.00
NNO	Mark Henry	4.00	10.00
NNO	Randy Orton	6.00	15.00
NNO	Ryback	5.00	12.00
NNO	Sheamus	4.00	10.00
NNO	The Shield	6.00	15.00
NNO	Triple H	5.00	12.00
NNO	Undertaker	8.00	20.00
NNO	The Rock	15.00	40.00

2014 Topps Chrome WWE

COMPLETE SET (110) 8.00 20.00
*REF.: .4X TO 1.2X BASIC CARDS
*ATOMIC REF.: .6X TO 1.5X BASIC CARDS
*XFRACTOR: .6X TO 1.5X BASIC CARDS
*GOLD REF./50: 2X TO 5X BASIC CARDS
*SUPERFR./1: UNPRICED DUE TO SCARCITY
*P.P.BLACK/1: UNPRICE DUE TO SCARCITY
*P.P.CYAN/1: UNPRICE DUE TO SCARCITY
*P.P.MAGENTA/1: UNPRICE DUE TO SCARCITY
*P.P.YELLOW/1: UNPRICE DUE TO SCARCITY

1	AJ Lee	1.50	4.00
2	Alex Riley	.30	.75
3	Big E Langston	.30	.75
4	Bo Dallas RC	.30	.75
5	Brad Maddox RC	.30	.75
6	Bray Wyatt	.75	2.00
7	Brie Bella	1.00	2.50
8	Brock Lesnar	1.25	3.00
9	Brodus Clay	.30	.75
10	Cameron	.50	1.25
11	Chris Jericho	.75	2.00
12	CM Punk	1.25	3.00
13	Curtis Axel	.30	.75
14	Daniel Bryan	.50	1.25
15	David Otunga	.30	.75
16	Dean Ambrose	.75	2.00
17	Diego	.30	.75
18	Dolph Ziggler	.50	1.25
19	Erick Rowan RC	.50	1.25
20	Eva Marie RC	1.25	3.00
21	Fandango	.50	1.25
22	Fernando	.30	.75
23	Jack Swagger	.50	1.25
24	Jerry The King Lawler	.75	2.00
25	John Cena	1.50	4.00
26	JoJo RC	.50	1.25
27	Justin Roberts	.30	.75
28	Kane	.75	2.00
29	Kofi Kingston	.30	.75
30	Luke Harper RC	.50	1.25
31	El Torito RC	.30	.75
32	Michael Cole	.30	.75
33	The Miz	.50	1.25
34	Naomi	.50	1.25
35	Nikki Bella	1.00	2.50
36	Paul Heyman	.30	.75
37	R-Truth	.30	.75
38	Randy Orton	1.25	3.00
39	Rey Mysterio	.75	2.00
40	The Rock	1.50	4.00
41	Rob Van Dam	.75	2.00
42	Roman Reigns	.75	2.00
43	Ryback	.30	.75
44	Santino Marella	.50	1.25
45	Scott Stanford	.30	.75
46	Seth Rollins	.30	.75
47	Stephanie McMahon	.50	1.25
48	Summer Rae RC	1.25	3.00
49	Tamina Snuka	.50	1.25
50	Tensai	.30	.75
51	Triple H	1.25	3.00
52	Zack Ryder	.30	.75
53	Zeb Colter	.50	1.25
54	Aksana	.75	2.00
55	Alberto Del Rio	.75	2.00
56	Alicia Fox	.50	1.25
57	Antonio Cesaro	.30	.75
58	Big Show	.75	2.00
59	Booker T	.50	1.25
60	Camacho	.30	.75
61	Christian	.30	.75
62	Cody Rhodes	.30	.75
63	Curt Hawkins	.30	.75
64	Damien Sandow	.30	.75
65	Darren Young	.30	.75
66	Drew McIntyre	.30	.75
67	Ezekiel Jackson	.50	1.25
68	The Great Khali	.30	.75
69	Heath Slater	.30	.75
70	Hornswoggle	.50	1.25
71	Hunico	.30	.75
72	JBL	.50	1.25
73	Jey Uso	.30	.75
74	Jimmy Uso	.30	.75
75	Jinder Mahal	.30	.75
76	Josh Mathews	.30	.75
77	Justin Gabriel	.30	.75
78	Goldust	.30	.75
79	Layla	.75	2.00
80	Lilian Garcia	.75	2.00
81	Mark Henry	.50	1.25
82	Natalya	1.00	2.50
83	Renee Young RC	1.25	3.00
84	Ricardo Rodriguez	.30	.75
85	Rosa Mendes	.50	1.25
86	Sheamus	.75	2.00
87	Sin Cara	.75	2.00
88	Theodore Long	.30	.75
89	Titus O'Neil	.30	.75
90	Tony Chimel	.30	.75
91	Tyson Kidd	.30	.75
92	Undertaker	1.25	3.00
93	Vickie Guerrero	.50	1.25
94	Bad News Barrett	.30	.75
95	William Regal	.50	1.25
96	Andre the Giant L	1.25	3.00
97	Billy Gunn L	.50	1.25
98	Bob Backlund L	.50	1.25
99	Diamond Dallas Page L	.50	1.25
100	Eddie Guerrero L	.50	1.25
101	Honky Tonk Man L	.50	1.25
102	Jim Ross L	.50	1.25
103	Junkyard Dog L	.50	1.25
104	Kevin Nash L	.75	2.00
105	Larry Zbyszko L	.50	1.25
106	Mick Foley L	.75	2.00
107	Paul Bearer L	.50	1.25
108	Road Dogg L	.50	1.25
109	Shawn Michaels L	1.25	3.00
110	X-Pac L	.30	.75

2014 Topps Chrome WWE Autographs

*REFRACTOR/50: .5X TO 1.2X BASIC AUTOS
*RED REF./25: .75X TO 2X BASIC AUTOS
*GOLD REF./10: UNPRICED DUE TO SCARCITY
*SUPERFR./1: UNPRICE DUE TO SCARCITY

NNO	Aksana	15.00	40.00
NNO	Alicia Fox	5.00	12.00
NNO	Diamond Dallas Page	12.00	30.00
NNO	Dolph Ziggler	10.00	25.00
NNO	Fandango	6.00	15.00
NNO	Honky Tonk Man	8.00	20.00
NNO	Kane	20.00	50.00
NNO	Natalya	12.00	30.00
NNO	Roman Reigns	100.00	200.00
NNO	Sin Cara	5.00	12.00

2014 Topps Chrome WWE Championship Plates

*SUPERFR./1: UNPRICED DUE TO SCARCITY
SP CARDS ARE SER.#'d TO 25

NNO	AJ Lee SP	75.00	150.00
NNO	Alicia Fox	12.00	30.00
NNO	Batista	15.00	40.00
NNO	Brie Bella	15.00	40.00
NNO	Chris Jericho SP	20.00	50.00
NNO	Cody Rhodes	8.00	20.00
NNO	Cody Rhodes and Goldust	8.00	20.00
NNO	Daniel Bryan/World Title	12.00	30.00
NNO	Daniel Bryan/WWE Title	12.00	30.00
NNO	Dolph Ziggler	12.00	30.00
NNO	Edge and Christian	15.00	40.00
NNO	Greg The Hammer Valentine	8.00	20.00
NNO	Honky Tonk Man	12.00	30.00
NNO	John Cena SP	20.00	50.00
NNO	Natalya	15.00	40.00
NNO	Nikki Bella	15.00	40.00
NNO	Randy Orton	20.00	50.00
NNO	Ravishing Rick Rude	8.00	20.00
NNO	Rey Mysterio	12.00	30.00
NNO	Ricky The Dragon Steamboat	8.00	20.00
NNO	RVD and Rey Mysterio	12.00	30.00
NNO	Sgt. Slaughter	25.00	60.00
NNO	S.Michaels/World Title	20.00	50.00
NNO	S.Michaels/WWE Title	20.00	50.00
NNO	Sheamus	12.00	30.00
NNO	The Shield SP	120.00	200.00
NNO	ShoMiz	12.00	30.00
NNO	Stone Cold Steve Austin SP	25.00	60.00
NNO	Triple H	20.00	50.00
NNO	Undertaker SP	25.00	60.00

2014 Topps Chrome WWE Champions Tribute Batista

COMPLETE SET (5) 5.00 12.00
*P.P.BLACK/1: UNPRICED DUE TO SCARCITY
*P.P.CYAN/1: UNPRICED DUE TO SCARCITY
*P.P.MAGENTA/1: UNPRICED DUE TO SCARCITY
*P.P.YELLOW/1: UNPRICED DUE TO SCARCITY
STATED OVERALL ODDS 1:6

1	Batista	1.50	4.00
2	Batista	1.50	4.00
3	Batista	1.50	4.00
4	Batista	1.50	4.00
5	Batista	1.50	4.00

2014 Topps Chrome WWE Champions Tribute Eddie Guerrero

COMPLETE SET (5) 2.50 6.00
*P.P.BLACK/1: UNPRICED DUE TO SCARCITY
*P.P.CYAN/1: UNPRICED DUE TO SCARCITY
*P.P.MAGENTA/1: UNPRICED DUE TO SCARCITY
*P.P.YELLOW/1: UNPRICED DUE TO SCARCITY
STATED OVERALL ODDS 1:6

1	Eddie Guerrero	.75	2.00
2	Eddie Guerrero	.75	2.00
3	Eddie Guerrero	.75	2.00
4	Eddie Guerrero	.75	2.00
5	Eddie Guerrero	.75	2.00

2014 Topps Chrome WWE Champions Tribute Edge

COMPLETE SET (5) 4.00 10.00
*P.P.BLACK/1: UNPRICED DUE TO SCARCITY
*P.P.CYAN/1: UNPRICED DUE TO SCARCITY
*P.P.MAGENTA/1: UNPRICED DUE TO SCARCITY
*P.P.YELLOW/1: UNPRICED DUE TO SCARCITY
STATED OVERALL ODDS 1:6

1	Edge	1.25	3.00
2	Edge	1.25	3.00
3	Edge	1.25	3.00
4	Edge	1.25	3.00
5	Edge	1.25	3.00

2014 Topps Chrome WWE Champions Tribute Iron Sheik

COMPLETE SET (5)
*P.P.CYAN/1: UNPRICED DUE TO SCARCITY
*P.P.MAGENTA/1: UNPRICED DUE TO SCARCITY
*P.P.YELLOW/1: UNPRICED DUE TO SCARCITY
STATED OVERALL ODDS 1:6

1	Iron Sheik	.75	2.00
2	Iron Sheik	.75	2.00
3	Iron Sheik	.75	2.00
4	Iron Sheik	.75	2.00
5	Iron Sheik	.75	2.00

2014 Topps Chrome WWE Champions Tribute JBL

COMPLETE SET (5) 2.50 6.00
*P.P.BLACK/1: UNPRICED DUE TO SCARCITY
*P.P.CYAN/1: UNPRICED DUE TO SCARCITY
*P.P.MAGENTA/1: UNPRICED DUE TO SCARCITY
*P.P.YELLOW/1: UNPRICED DUE TO SCARCITY
STATED OVERALL ODDS 1:6

1	JBL	.75	2.00
2	JBL	.75	2.00
3	JBL	.75	2.00
4	JBL	.75	2.00
5	JBL	.75	2.00

2014 Topps Chrome WWE Champions Tribute Kevin Nash

COMPLETE SET (5) 4.00 10.00
*P.P.BLACK/1: UNPRICED DUE TO SCARCITY
*P.P.CYAN/1: UNPRICED DUE TO SCARCITY
*P.P.MAGENTA/1: UNPRICED DUE TO SCARCITY
*P.P.YELLOW/1: UNPRICED DUE TO SCARCITY
STATED OVERALL ODDS 1:6

1	Kevin Nash	1.25	3.00
2	Kevin Nash	1.25	3.00

3 Kevin Nash 1.25 3.00
4 Kevin Nash 1.25 3.00
5 Kevin Nash 1.25 3.00

2014 Topps Chrome WWE Champions Tribute Mick Foley

COMPLETE SET (5) 4.00 10.00
*P.P.BLACK/1: UNPRICED DUE TO SCARCITY
*P.P.CYAN/1: UNPRICED DUE TO SCARCITY
*P.P.MAGENTA/1: UNPRICED DUE TO SCARCITY
*P.P.YELLOW/1: UNPRICED DUE TO SCARCITY
STATED OVERALL ODDS 1:6

1 Mick Foley 1.25 3.00
2 Mick Foley 1.25 3.00
3 Mick Foley 1.25 3.00
4 Mick Foley 1.25 3.00
5 Mick Foley 1.25 3.00

2014 Topps Chrome WWE Champions Tribute Sgt. Slaughter

COMPLETE SET (5) 4.00 10.00
*P.P.BLACK/1: UNPRICED DUE TO SCARCITY
*P.P.CYAN/1: UNPRICED DUE TO SCARCITY
*P.P.MAGENTA/1: UNPRICED DUE TO SCARCITY
*P.P.YELLOW/1: UNPRICED DUE TO SCARCITY
STATED OVERALL ODDS 1:6

1 Sgt. Slaughter 1.25 3.00
2 Sgt. Slaughter 1.25 3.00
3 Sgt. Slaughter 1.25 3.00
4 Sgt. Slaughter 1.25 3.00
5 Sgt. Slaughter 1.25 3.00

2014 Topps Chrome WWE Champions Tribute Shawn Michaels

COMPLETE SET (5) 6.00 15.00
*P.P.BLACK/1: UNPRICED DUE TO SCARCITY
*P.P.CYAN/1: UNPRICED DUE TO SCARCITY
*P.P.MAGENTA/1: UNPRICED DUE TO SCARCITY
*P.P.YELLOW/1: UNPRICED DUE TO SCARCITY
STATED OVERALL ODDS 1:6

1 Shawn Michaels 2.00 5.00
2 Shawn Michaels 2.00 5.00
3 Shawn Michaels 2.00 5.00
4 Shawn Michaels 2.00 5.00
5 Shawn Michaels 2.00 5.00

2014 Topps Chrome WWE Champions Tribute Yokozuna

COMPLETE SET (5) 2.50 6.00
*P.P.BLACK/1: UNPRICED DUE TO SCARCITY
*P.P.CYAN/1: UNPRICED DUE TO SCARCITY
*P.P.MAGENTA/1: UNPRICED DUE TO SCARCITY
*P.P.YELLOW/1: UNPRICED DUE TO SCARCITY
STATED OVERALL ODDS 1:6

1 Yokozuna .75 2.00
2 Yokozuna .75 2.00
3 Yokozuna .75 2.00
4 Yokozuna .75 2.00
5 Yokozuna .75 2.00

2014 Topps Chrome WWE Dual Autographs

STATED PRINT RUN 5 SER.#'d SETS

NNO D.Bryan/B.Wyatt 150.00 300.00
NNO D.Rhodes/J.Swagger 100.00 200.00
NNO J.Cena/R.Orton 150.00 300.00
NNO L.Harper/E.Rowan 100.00 200.00

2014 Topps Chrome WWE Jerry Lawler's Tributes

COMPLETE SET (10) 10.00 25.00
*P.P.BLACK/1: UNPRICED DUE TO SCARCITY
*P.P.CYAN/1: UNPRICED DUE TO SCARCITY
*P.P.MAGENTA/1: UNPRICED DUE TO SCARCITY
*P.P.YELLOW/1: UNPRICED DUE TO SCARCITY
STATED ODDS 1:12 HOBBY AND RETAIL

1 The Iron Sheik 1.00 2.50
2 Sgt. Slaughter 1.50 4.00
3 Yokozuna 1.00 2.50
4 Kevin Nash 1.50 4.00
5 Shawn Michaels 2.50 6.00
6 Mick Foley 1.50 4.00
7 Eddie Guerrero 1.00 2.50
8 JBL 1.00 2.50
9 Batista 2.00 5.00
10 Edge 1.50 4.00

2014 Topps Chrome WWE Kiss

NNO AJ Lee 50.00 100.00
NNO Aksana 20.00 50.00
NNO Alicia Fox 20.00 50.00
NNO Cameron 30.00 60.00
NNO Eva Marie 30.00 80.00
NNO Naomi 30.00 60.00
NNO Tamina Snuka 12.00 30.00
NNO Vickie Guerrero 12.00 30.00

2014 Topps Chrome WWE Kiss Autographs

NNO AJ Lee 250.00 400.00
NNO Aksana 30.00 75.00
NNO Cameron 30.00 75.00
NNO Tamina Snuka 30.00 75.00
NNO Vickie Guerrero 75.00 150.00

2014 Topps Chrome WWE NXT Prospects

COMPLETE SET (20) 30.00 75.00
*P.P.BLACK/1: UNPRICED DUE TO SCARCITY
*P.P.CYAN/1: UNPRICED DUE TO SCARCITY
*P.P.MAGENTA/1: UNPRICED DUE TO SCARCITY
*P.P.YELLOW/1: UNPRICED DUE TO SCARCITY
STATED ODDS 1:3 HOBBY AND RETAIL

1 Adrian Neville 1.25 3.00
2 Alexander Rusev 1.50 4.00
3 Baron Corbin .60 1.50
4 Bayley 5.00 12.00
5 Charlotte 12.00 30.00
6 CJ Parker .60 1.50
7 Konnor O'Brian .60 1.50
8 Corey Graves .60 1.50
9 Emma 2.00 5.00
10 Enzo Amore 1.25 3.00
11 Jason Jordan .60 1.50
12 Leo Kruger .60 1.50
13 Mojo Rawley .60 1.50
14 Paige 8.00 20.00
15 Rick Viktor .60 1.50
16 Sami Zayn 1.25 3.00
17 Sasha Banks 10.00 25.00
18 Sylvester Lefort .60 1.50
19 Tyler Breeze .60 1.50
20 Xavier Woods .60 1.50

2014 Topps Chrome WWE Royal Rumble Mat Relics

*SUPERFR/1: UNPRICED DUE TO SCARCITY
STATED ODDS

NNO Alberto Del Rio 4.00 10.00
NNO Alexander Rusev 6.00 15.00
NNO Batista 10.00 25.00
NNO Big E 3.00 8.00
NNO Billy Gunn 5.00 12.00
NNO Bray Wyatt 8.00 20.00
NNO Brock Lesnar 8.00 20.00
NNO Cody Rhodes 3.00 8.00
NNO Daniel Bryan 8.00 20.00
NNO El Torito 3.00 8.00
NNO Goldust 3.00 8.00
NNO JBL 5.00 12.00
NNO John Cena 10.00 25.00
NNO Kane 6.00 15.00
NNO Kevin Nash 8.00 20.00
NNO Randy Orton 8.00 20.00
NNO Rey Mysterio 8.00 20.00
NNO Road Dogg 5.00 12.00
NNO Roman Reigns 10.00 25.00
NNO Sheamus 6.00 15.00

2014 Topps Chrome WWE Swatch Relics

NNO Alberto Del Rio 6.00 15.00
NNO Bray Wyatt 12.00 30.00
NNO Curtis Axel 3.00 8.00
NNO Damien Sandow 3.00 8.00
NNO Daniel Bryan 8.00 20.00
NNO Diego 3.00 8.00
NNO Dolph Ziggler 5.00 12.00
NNO Fernando 3.00 8.00
NNO Goldust 3.00 8.00
NNO Jack Swagger 6.00 15.00
NNO John Cena 12.00 30.00
NNO Kofi Kingston 3.00 8.00
NNO Mark Henry 5.00 12.00
NNO The Miz 5.00 12.00
NNO Rey Mysterio 8.00 20.00
NNO Undertaker 15.00 40.00

2014 Topps Chrome WWE WrestleMania DVD Promo

P1 John Cena

2015 Topps Chrome WWE

COMPLETE SET (100) 8.00 20.00
UNOPENED BOX (24 PACKS) 60.00 80.00
UNOPENED PACK (4 CARDS) 3.50 4.00
*REF.: .4X TO 1.2X BASIC CARDS
*ATOMIC: .6X TO 1.5X BASIC CARDS
*XFRACTOR: .6X TO 1.5X BASIC CARDS
*PULSAR/75: 1.5X TO 4X BASIC CARDS
*GOLD/50: 2X TO 5X BASIC CARDS
*SILVER WAVE/20: 3X TO 8X BASIC CARDS
*SHIMMER/10: 5X TO 12X BASIC CARDS
*RED/5: UNPRICED DUE TO SCARCITY
*SUPERFR./1: UNPRICED DUE TO SCARCITY
*P.P.BLACK/1: UNPRICED DUE TO SCARCITY
*P.P.CYAN/1: UNPRICED DUE TO SCARCITY
*P.P.MAGENTA/1: UNPRICED DUE TO SCARCITY
*P.P.YELLOW/1: UNPRICED DUE TO SCARCITY

1 Adam Rose RC .30 .75
2 AJ Lee 1.25 3.00
3 Alicia Fox .50 1.25
4 Bad News Barrett .25 .60
5 Batista .60 1.50
6 Big E .40 1.00
7 Big Show .60 1.50
8 Bo Dallas .25 .60
9 Booker T .40 1.00
10 Bray Wyatt 1.00 2.50
11 Brie Bella .75 2.00
12 Brock Lesnar 1.00 2.50
13 Cameron .40 1.00
14 Cesaro .25 .60
15 Chris Jericho .60 1.50
16 Christian .25 .60
17 Curtis Axel .25 .60
18 Damien Mizdow .40 1.00
19 Daniel Bryan 1.00 2.50
20 Darren Young .25 .60
21 David Otunga .25 .60
22 Dean Ambrose .60 1.50
23 Diego .25 .60
24 Dolph Ziggler .40 1.00
25 Eden .40 1.00
26 Emma RC .40 1.00
27 Erick Rowan .40 1.00
28 Eva Marie 1.00 2.50
29 Fandango .25 .60
30 Fernando .25 .60
31 Goldust .25 .60
32 Heath Slater .25 .60
33 Hornswoggle .40 1.00
34 Jack Swagger .40 1.00
35 Jerry The King Lawler .40 1.00
36 Jey Uso .25 .60
37 Jimmy Uso .25 .60
38 John Cena 1.25 3.00
39 Justin Gabriel .25 .60
40 Kane .60 1.50
41 Kofi Kingston .25 .60
42 Lana RC 1.00 2.50
43 Layla .60 1.50
44 Lilian Garcia .60 1.50
45 Luke Harper .40 1.00
46 Mark Henry .40 1.00
47 The Miz .40 1.00
48 Naomi .40 1.00
49 Natalya .75 2.00
50 Nikki Bella .75 2.00
51 Paige RC 1.25 3.00
52 Paul Heyman .25 .60
53 R-Truth .25 .60
54 Randy Orton 2.00 5.00
55 Renee Young 1.00 2.50
56 Rey Mysterio .60 1.50
57 The Rock 1.25 3.00
58 Rob Van Dam .60 1.50
59 Roman Reigns .60 1.50
60 Rosa Mendes .40 1.00
61 Rusev RC .60 1.50
62 Ryback .25 .60
63 Seth Rollins .40 1.00
64 Sheamus .60 1.50
65 Sin Cara .40 1.00
66 Stardust .25 .60
67 Stephanie McMahon .40 1.00
68 Summer Rae 1.00 2.50
69 Tamina Snuka .40 1.00
70 Titus O'Neil .25 .60
71 El Torito .25 .60
72 Triple H 1.00 2.50
73 Tyson Kidd .25 .60
74 Undertaker 1.00 2.50
75 William Regal .40 1.00
76 Xavier Woods .40 1.00
77 Zack Ryder .25 .60
78 Zeb Colter .40 1.00
79 Bret Hit Man Hart .75 2.00
80 Bruno Sammartino .60 1.50
81 George The Animal Steele .30 .75
82 Gerald Brisco .40 1.00
83 Hulk Hogan 1.25 3.00
84 Larry Zbyszko .40 1.00
85 Mouth of the South Jimmy Hart .30 .75
86 Pat Patterson .25 .60
87 Ric Flair 1.25 3.00
88 Rowdy Roddy Piper .75 2.00
89 Sting .60 1.50
90 Ultimate Warrior .75 2.00
91 Aiden English NXT RC .30 .75
92 Alexa Bliss NXT RC 12.00 30.00
93 Angelo Dawkins NXT RC .30 .75
94 Bull Dempsey NXT RC .40 1.00
95 Colin Cassady NXT RC .40 1.00
96 Hideo Itami NXT RC .25 .60
97 Kalisto NXT RC .40 1.00
98 Marcus Louis NXT RC .40 1.00
99 Sawyer Fulton NXT RC .40 1.00
100 Tye Dillinger NXT RC .40 1.00

2015 Topps Chrome WWE Autographs

*PULSAR/75: .5X TO 1.2X BASIC AUTOS
*GOLD/10: .75X TO 2X BASIC AUTOS
*RED/5: UNPRICED DUE TO SCARCITY

NNO Adam Rose 6.00 15.00
NNO Brie Bella 12.00 30.00
NNO Bruno Sammartino 15.00 40.00
NNO Eva Marie 20.00 50.00
NNO Hulk Hogan 200.00 400.00
NNO Lana 25.00 60.00
NNO Lita 20.00 50.00
NNO Nikki Bella 25.00 60.00
NNO Renee Young 12.00 30.00
NNO Roman Reigns 100.00 200.00

2015 Topps Chrome WWE Commemorative Championship Plates

*PULSAR/75: .6X TO 1.5X BASIC PLATES
*RED/5: UNPRICED DUE TO SCARCITY

NNO Adrian Neville 6.00 15.00
NXT Champion
NNO Adrian Neville 6.00 15.00
NXT Tag Champion
NNO Big E 5.00 12.00
NNO Bo Dallas 3.00 8.00
NNO Charlotte 10.00 25.00
NNO Corey Graves 6.00 15.00
NNO Erick Rowan 5.00 12.00
NNO Kalisto 5.00 12.00
NNO Konnor 8.00 20.00

Card	Low	High
NNO Luke Harper	5.00	12.00
NNO Paige	15.00	40.00
NNO Seth Rollins	6.00	15.00
NNO Sin Cara	5.00	12.00
NNO Viktor	8.00	20.00

2015 Topps Chrome WWE Diva Kiss

RANDOMLY INSERTED INTO PACKS

Card	Low	High
NNO Brie Bella	20.00	50.00
NNO Cameron	10.00	25.00
NNO Eden	10.00	25.00
NNO Emma	30.00	60.00
NNO Naomi	20.00	40.00
NNO Natalya	20.00	50.00
NNO Nikki Bella	40.00	80.00
NNO Renee Young	25.00	60.00
NNO Summer Rae	25.00	60.00
NNO Tamina Snuka	10.00	25.00

2015 Topps Chrome WWE Diva Kiss Autographs

*RED REF./5: UNPRICED DUE TO SCARCITY
*SUPERFR./1: UNPRICED DUE TO SCARCITY
STATED PRINT RUN 25 SER.#'d SETS

Card	Low	High
NNO Brie Bella	50.00	100.00
NNO Cameron	12.00	30.00
NNO Eden	15.00	40.00
NNO Emma	25.00	60.00
NNO Naomi	15.00	50.00
NNO Natalya	20.00	50.00
NNO Nikki Bella	50.00	100.00
NNO Renee Young	75.00	150.00
NNO Summer Rae	30.00	75.00
NNO Tamina Snuka	15.00	40.00

2015 Topps Chrome WWE Dual Autographs

STATED PRINT RUN 5 SER. #'d SETS
UNPRICED DUE TO SCARCITY

1 AJ Lee/Paige
2 D.Ambrose/S.Rollins
3 Emma/Eden
4 J.Cena/B.Wyatt

2015 Topps Chrome WWE King of the Ring Sign Relics

*RED/5: UNPRICED DUE TO SCARCITY
*SUPERFR./1: UNPRICED DUE TO SCARCITY
STATED ODDS 1:1,156 HOBBY

Card	Low	High
NNO Billy Gunn	5.00	12.00
NNO Bret Hit Man Hart	12.00	30.00
NNO Brock Lesnar	15.00	40.00
NNO Don Muraco	5.00	12.00
NNO Edge	8.00	20.00
NNO Harley Race	5.00	12.00
NNO King Booker	5.00	12.00
NNO Ted DiBiase	5.00	12.00
NNO Sheamus	8.00	20.00
NNO Stone Cold Steve Austin	10.00	25.00
NNO Tito Santana	5.00	12.00
NNO Triple H	8.00	20.00
NNO William Regal	5.00	12.00

2015 Topps Chrome WWE Night of Champions Mat Relics

RANDOMLY INSERTED INTO PACKS
*PULSAR/75: .6X TO 1.5X BASIC RELICS

Card	Low	High
1 AJ Lee	12.00	30.00
2 Brock Lesnar	10.00	25.00
3 Cesaro	2.50	6.00
4 Chris Jericho	6.00	15.00
5 Dean Ambrose	6.00	15.00
6 Dolph Ziggler	4.00	10.00
7 John Cena	12.00	30.00
8 Mark Henry	4.00	10.00
9 The Miz	4.00	10.00
10 Nikki Bella	8.00	20.00
11 Paige	12.00	30.00
12 Randy Orton	10.00	25.00
13 Rusev	6.00	15.00
14 Seth Rollins	4.00	10.00
15 Sheamus	6.00	15.00

2015 Topps Chrome WWE Night of Champions Turnbuckle Relics

*SUPERFR./1: UNPRICED DUE TO SCARCITY
STATED PRINT RUN 33 SER.#'d SETS

Card	Low	High
NNO AJ Lee	80.00	150.00
NNO Brock Lesnar	15.00	40.00
NNO Chris Jericho	12.00	30.00
NNO Dean Ambrose	25.00	50.00
NNO John Cena	25.00	60.00
NNO Nikki Bella	15.00	40.00
NNO Paige	25.00	60.00
NNO Randy Orton	15.00	40.00
NNO Seth Rollins	8.00	20.00

2015 Topps Chrome WWE NXT Autographs

*GOLD/10: .75X TO 2X BASIC AUTOS
*ATOMIC/5: UNPRICED DUE TO SCARCITY
*RED/5: UNPRICED DUE TO SCARCITY
*SUPERFR./1: UNPRICED DUE TO SCARCITY
RANDOMLY INSERTED INTO PACKS

Card	Low	High
NNO Aiden English	6.00	15.00
NNO Alexa Bliss	200.00	350.00
NNO Charlotte	30.00	80.00
NNO Colin Cassady	12.00	30.00
NNO Sawyer Fulton	5.00	12.00

2015 Topps Chrome WWE Swatch Relics

RANDOMLY INSERTED INTO PACKS
*PULSAR/75: .1X TO 2.5X BASIC RELICS

Card	Low	High
NNO Cesaro	1.50	4.00
NNO Curtis Axel	1.50	4.00
NNO Damien Mizdow	2.50	6.00
NNO Daniel Bryan	6.00	15.00
NNO Darren Young	1.50	4.00
NNO Diego	1.50	4.00
NNO Jack Swagger	2.50	6.00
NNO Jerry The King Lawler	2.50	6.00
NNO Jimmy Uso	1.50	4.00
NNO John Cena	8.00	20.00
NNO Kofi Kingston	1.50	4.00
NNO Mark Henry	2.50	6.00
NNO Paige	8.00	20.00
NNO Randy Orton	6.00	15.00
NNO Sheamus	4.00	10.00
NNO Titus O'Neil	1.50	4.00
NNO Tyson Kidd	1.50	4.00
NNO Zack Ryder	1.50	4.00

2015 Topps Chrome WWE Ultimate Warrior Commemorative Face Paint Plate

*PULSAR REF/75: 1.2X TO 3X BASIC MEM
RANDOMLY INSERTED INTO PACKS

Card	Low	High
NNO Ultimate Warrior	5.00	12.00

2020 Topps Chrome WWE

COMPLETE SET (100) 15.00 40.00
*REF: .5X TO 1.2X BASIC CARDS
*XFRAC: .6X TO 1.5X BASIC CARDS
*GREEN/99: 1.2X TO 3X BASIC CARDS
*GOLD/50: 2X TO 5X BASIC CARDS
*ORANGE/25: UNPRICED DUE TO SCARCITY
*BLACK/10: UNPRICED DUE TO SCARCITY
*RED/5: UNPRICED DUE TO SCARCITY
*SUPER/1: UNPRICED DUE TO SCARCITY

Card	Low	High
1 AJ Styles	1.25	3.00
2 Aleister Black	.75	2.00
3 Alexa Bliss	2.50	6.00
4 Mustafa Ali	.60	1.50
5 Andrade	.60	1.50
6 Asuka	1.50	4.00
7 King Corbin	.50	1.25
8 Bayley	.75	2.00
9 Becky Lynch	1.50	4.00
10 Big E	.40	1.00
11 Big Show	.50	1.25
12 Billie Kay	.75	2.00
13 Bobby Lashley	.75	2.00
14 Braun Strowman	1.00	2.50
15 The Fiend Bray Wyatt	1.25	3.00
16 Brock Lesnar	1.50	4.00
17 Murphy	.50	1.25
18 Carmella	1.00	2.50
19 Cesaro	.40	1.00
20 Charlotte Flair	1.50	4.00
21 Daniel Bryan	1.25	3.00
22 Drake Maverick	.40	1.00
23 Drew McIntyre	.75	2.00
24 Elias	.40	1.00
25 Erik	.40	1.00
26 Ember Moon	.75	2.00
27 Finn Balor	1.00	2.50
28 Humberto Carrillo	.60	1.50
29 Ivar	.40	1.00
30 Jeff Hardy	1.00	2.50
31 Jey Uso	.40	1.00
32 Jimmy Uso	.40	1.00
33 John Cena	1.50	4.00
34 Kairi Sane	.75	2.00
35 Kane	.50	1.25
36 Karl Anderson	.40	1.00
37 Kevin Owens	.50	1.25
38 Kofi Kingston	.60	1.50
39 Lana	1.00	2.50
40 Lacey Evans	1.00	2.50
41 Luke Gallows	.40	1.00
42 Mandy Rose	2.00	5.00
43 Naomi	.75	2.00
44 Natalya	.60	1.50
45 Nia Jax	.60	1.50
46 Nikki Cross	.75	2.00
47 Peyton Royce	.75	2.00
48 Randy Orton	1.00	2.50
49 Ricochet	.60	1.50
50 Roman Reigns	1.00	2.50
51 Ronda Rousey	2.00	5.00
52 R-Truth	.40	1.00
53 Ruby Riott	.60	1.50
54 Rusev	.50	1.25
55 Sami Zayn	.50	1.25
56 Samoa Joe	.60	1.50
57 Sasha Banks	2.00	5.00
58 Seth Rollins	.75	2.00
59 Sheamus	.50	1.25
60 Shinsuke Nakamura	.75	2.00
61 Shorty G	.40	1.00
62 Sonya Deville	1.00	2.50
63 The Miz	.60	1.50
64 The Rock	2.00	5.00
65 Triple H	1.00	2.50
66 Undertaker	1.50	4.00
67 Xavier Woods	.40	1.00
68 Zelina Vega	.75	2.00
69 Adam Cole	1.00	2.50
70 Angel Garza RC	.50	1.25
71 Angelo Dawkins	.40	1.00
72 Bianca Belair	1.00	2.50
73 Boa RC	.40	1.00
74 Bobby Fish	.40	1.00
75 Bronson Reed RC	.40	1.00
76 Cameron Grimes RC	.40	1.00
77 Candice LeRae	1.25	3.00
78 Damian Priest RC	.40	1.00
79 Dexter Lumis RC	.40	1.00
80 Io Shirai	.60	1.50
81 Isaiah Swerve Scott RC	.50	1.25
82 Joaquin Wilde RC	.40	1.00
83 Johnny Gargano	.75	2.00
84 Kushida RC	.50	1.25
85 Kyle O'Reilly	.50	1.25
86 Lio Rush	.40	1.00
87 Matt Riddle	.75	2.00
88 Mia Yim	.75	2.00
89 Montez Ford	.40	1.00
90 Roderick Strong	.75	2.00
91 Shayna Baszler	1.25	3.00
92 Velveteen Dream	.50	1.25
93 Alexander Wolfe	.40	1.00
94 Fabian Aichner	.40	1.00
95 Marcel Barthel RC	.40	1.00
96 Pete Dunne	.40	1.00
97 Rhea Ripley	1.50	4.00
98 Toni Storm	1.00	2.50
99 Travis Banks RC	.40	1.00
100 Walter RC	.75	2.00

2020 Topps Chrome WWE Autographs

*GREEN/99: .5X TO 1.2X BASIC AUTOS
*GOLD/50: .6X TO 1.5X BASIC AUTOS
*ORANGE/25: UNPRICED DUE TO SCARCITY
*BLACK/10: UNPRICED DUE TO SCARCITY
*RED/5: UNPRICED DUE TO SCARCITY
*SUPER/1: UNPRICED DUE TO SCARCITY
RANDOMLY INSERTED INTO PACKS

Card	Low	High
AAB Aleister Black	8.00	20.00
AAC Adam Cole	10.00	25.00
AAL Alexa Bliss	60.00	120.00
AAN Andrade	8.00	20.00
AAS AJ Styles	12.00	30.00
ABY Bayley	20.00	50.00
ACF Charlotte Flair	20.00	50.00
ADB Daniel Bryan	8.00	20.00
ADM Drew McIntyre	12.00	30.00
AFB Finn Balor	12.00	30.00
AHC Humberto Carrillo	6.00	15.00
AIS Io Shirai	30.00	75.00
AKC King Corbin	6.00	15.00
AKK Kofi Kingston	6.00	15.00
AKU Kushida	8.00	20.00
ALE Lacey Evans	15.00	40.00
AMA Mustafa Ali	8.00	20.00
ARH Rhea Ripley	30.00	75.00
ASB Shayna Baszler	10.00	25.00
ASD Johnny Gargano	6.00	15.00
ASJ Samoa Joe	6.00	15.00
ASN Shinsuke Nakamura	12.00	30.00
ASR Seth Rollins	8.00	20.00
ATM The Miz	8.00	20.00

2020 Topps Chrome WWE Big Legends

COMPLETE SET (25) 12.00 30.00
*GREEN/99: .75X TO 2X BASIC CARDS
*GOLD/50: 1.2X TO 3X BASIC CARDS
*ORANGE/25: UNPRICED DUE TO SCARCITY
*BLACK/10: UNPRICED DUE TO SCARCITY
*RED/5: UNPRICED DUE TO SCARCITY
*SUPER/1: UNPRICED DUE TO SCARCITY
RANDOMLY INSERTED INTO PACKS

Card	Low	High
BL1 Alundra Blayze	1.00	2.50
BL2 Boogeyman	.60	1.50
BL3 Booker T	1.25	3.00
BL4 Brutus The Barber Beefcake	.60	1.50
BL5 Christian	.75	2.00
BL6 Eve	1.25	3.00
BL7 Gerald Brisco	.60	1.50
BL8 The Godfather	.60	1.50
BL9 The Hurricane	.60	1.50
BL10 Jerry The King Lawler	1.50	4.00
BL11 Kerry Von Erich	1.00	2.50
BL12 Kevin Nash	1.00	2.50
BL13 Kurt Angle	1.50	4.00
BL14 Mick Foley	1.25	3.00
BL15 Molly Holly	.75	2.00
BL16 Pat Patterson	.60	1.50
BL17 Razor Ramon	1.00	2.50
BL18 Ric Flair	2.50	6.00
BL19 Rikishi	.60	1.50
BL20 Road Dogg Jesse James	.75	2.00
BL21 Ron Simmons	1.00	2.50
BL22 Sgt. Slaughter	1.25	3.00
BL23 Ted DiBiase	1.25	3.00
BL24 Wendi Richter	.75	2.00
BL25 X-Pac	.60	1.50

2020 Topps Chrome WWE Big Legends Autographs

*GREEN/99: .5X TO 1.2X BASIC CARDS
*GOLD/50: .6X TO 1.5X BASIC CARDS
*ORANGE/25: UNPRICED DUE TO SCARCITY
*BLACK/10: UNPRICED DUE TO SCARCITY
*RED/5: UNPRICED DUE TO SCARCITY
*SUPER/1: UNPRICED DUE TO SCARCITY
RANDOMLY INSERTED INTO PACKS

Card	Low	High
BLJJ Road Dogg Jesse James	10.00	25.00
BLJL Jerry The King Lawler	12.00	30.00
BLHBK Shawn Michaels		

2020 Topps Chrome WWE Fantasy Matches

COMPLETE SET (22) 15.00 40.00
*GREEN/99: .6X TO 1.5X BASIC CARDS
*GOLD/50: .75X TO 2X BASIC CARDS
*ORANGE/25: UNPRICED DUE TO SCARCITY
*BLACK/10: UNPRICED DUE TO SCARCITY
*RED/5: UNPRICED DUE TO SCARCITY
*SUPER/1: UNPRICED DUE TO SCARCITY
RANDOMLY INSERTED INTO PACKS

Card	Name	Low	High
FM1	Samoa Joe/John Cena	2.50	6.00
FM2	Beth Phoenix/Chyna	1.50	4.00
FM3	Batista/Ultimate Warrior	1.50	4.00
FM4	AJ Styles/Mr. Perfect	2.00	5.00
FM5	Drew McIntyre/Booker T	1.25	3.00
FM6	The Miz/Rowdy Roddy Piper	1.50	4.00
FM7	Roman Reigns/The Rock	3.00	8.00
FM8	Randy Orton/DDP	1.50	4.00
FM9	Bret Hit Man Hart/Daniel Bryan	2.00	5.00
FM10	Alexa Bliss/Trish Stratus	4.00	10.00
FM11	Charlotte Flair/Lita	2.50	6.00
FM12	The Fiend/Jake Roberts	2.00	5.00
FM13	Seth Rollins/Shawn Michaels	1.50	4.00
FM14	Kurt Angle/Ken Shamrock	1.50	4.00
FM15	Mankind/Jeff Hardy	1.50	4.00
FM16	Braun Strowman/Goldberg	2.50	6.00
FM17	Finn Balor/Undertaker	2.50	6.00
FM18	Rick Rude/Robert Roode	.75	2.00
FM19	KO/Stone Cold Steve Austin	3.00	8.00
FM20	Big Show/Vader	1.00	2.50
FM21	Randy Savage/Kofi Kingston	2.00	5.00
FM22	Andrade/Eddie Guerrero	1.50	4.00

2020 Topps Chrome WWE Fantasy Matches Autographs

*BLACK/10: UNPRICED DUE TO SCARCITY
*RED/5: UNPRICED DUE TO SCARCITY
*SUPER/1: UNPRICED DUE TO SCARCITY
STATED PRINT RUN 25 SER.#'d SETS

Card	Name	Low	High
FMKK	J.Hardy/Mankind	75.00	150.00
FMLC	C.Flair/Lita	125.00	250.00
FMSA	S.Rollins/S.Michaels	75.00	150.00
FMTA	A.Bliss/T.Stratus	250.00	500.00

2020 Topps Chrome WWE Image Variations

*GREEN/99: .5X TO 1.2X BASIC CARDS
*GOLD/50: .6X TO 1.5X BASIC CARDS
*ORANGE/25: UNPRICED DUE TO SCARCITY
*BLACK/10: UNPRICED DUE TO SCARCITY
*RED/5: UNPRICED DUE TO SCARCITY
*SUPER/1: UNPRICED DUE TO SCARCITY
RANDOMLY INSERTED INTO PACKS

Card	Name	Low	High
IV1	AJ Styles	2.00	5.00
IV2	Alexa Bliss	5.00	12.00
IV3	Mustafa Ali	1.50	4.00
IV4	Asuka	3.00	8.00
IV5	Bayley	1.50	4.00
IV6	Becky Lynch	6.00	15.00
IV7	Bianca Belair	2.50	6.00
IV8	The Fiend Bray Wyatt	4.00	10.00
IV9	Carmella	4.00	10.00
IV10	Charlotte Flair	5.00	12.00
IV11	Ember Moon	1.50	4.00
IV12	Finn Balor	2.00	5.00
IV13	Jeff Hardy	2.50	6.00
IV14	Kairi Sane	3.00	8.00
IV15	Kofi Kingston	1.50	4.00
IV16	Lacey Evans	3.00	8.00
IV17	Matt Riddle	2.50	6.00
IV18	Naomi	2.50	6.00
IV19	Nikki Cross	3.00	8.00
IV20	Ricochet	2.00	5.00
IV21	Samoa Joe	2.00	5.00
IV22	Seth Rollins	2.00	5.00
IV23	Sonya Deville	2.50	6.00
IV24	Velveteen Dream	2.00	5.00
IV25	King Corbin	1.50	4.00

2020 Topps Chrome WWE Shocking Wins

COMPLETE SET (25) 12.00 30.00
*GREEN/99: .5X TO 1.2X BASIC CARDS
*GOLD/50: .6X TO 1.5X BASIC CARDS
*ORANGE/25: UNPRICED DUE TO SCARCITY
*BLACK/10: UNPRICED DUE TO SCARCITY
*RED/5: UNPRICED DUE TO SCARCITY
*SUPER/1: UNPRICED DUE TO SCARCITY
RANDOMLY INSERTED INTO PACKS

Card	Name	Low	High
SW1	Ron Simmons	1.00	2.50
SW2	The 1-2-3 Kid	.60	1.50
SW3	Yokozuna	1.00	2.50
SW4	Shawn Michaels	1.50	4.00
SW5	Kevin Nash	1.00	2.50
SW6	Mankind	1.25	3.00
SW7	Jeff Hardy	1.50	4.00
SW8	Brock Lesnar	2.50	6.00
SW9	The Hurricane	.60	1.50
SW10	Eddie Guerrero	1.50	4.00
SW11	Shelton Benjamin	.75	2.00
SW12	Bobby Lashley	1.25	3.00
SW13	Sheamus	.75	2.00
SW14	The Miz	1.00	2.50
SW15	Sheamus	.75	2.00
SW16	Lord Tensai	.60	1.50
SW17	Bo Dallas	.60	1.50
SW18	Fandango	.60	1.50
SW19	Brock Lesnar	2.50	6.00
SW20	Paige	1.50	4.00
SW21	Charlotte Flair	2.50	6.00
SW22	Heath Slater	.60	1.50
SW23	Kevin Owens	.75	2.00
SW24	Finn Balor	1.50	4.00
SW25	Jinder Mahal	.60	1.50

2020 Topps Chrome WWE Shocking Wins Autographs

*GREEN/99: .5X TO 1.2X BASIC AUTOS
*GOLD/50: .6X TO 1.5X BASIC AUTOS
*ORANGE/25: UNPRICED DUE TO SCARCITY
*BLACK/10: UNPRICED DUE TO SCARCITY
*RED/5: UNPRICED DUE TO SCARCITY
*SUPER/1: UNPRICED DUE TO SCARCITY
RANDOMLY INSERTED INTO PACKS

Card	Name	Low	High
SWABD	Bo Dallas	5.00	12.00
SWACF	Charlotte Flair	15.00	40.00
SWAFB	Finn Balor	12.00	30.00
SWAJH	Jeff Hardy	10.00	25.00
SWAJL	Jerry The King Lawler		
SWAJM	Jinder Mahal		
SWAKO	Kevin Owens	6.00	15.00
SWALA	Bobby Lashley	5.00	12.00
SWALT	Lord Tensai	5.00	12.00
SWAMA	Mustafa Ali	5.00	12.00
SWAMK	Mankind		
SWASB	Shelton Benjamin	6.00	15.00
SWASH	Sheamus		
SWASM	Sheamus	8.00	20.00
SWATM	The Miz	8.00	20.00
SWAZR	Zack Ryder		

2021 Topps Chrome WWE

*REFRACTOR: .5X TO 1.2X BASIC CARDS
*AQUA/150: .75X TO 2X BASIC CARDS
*GREEN/99: 1X TO 2.5X BASIC CARDS
*GOLD/50: 1.5X TO 4X BASIC CARDS
*ORANGE/25: UNPRICED DUE TO SCARCITY
*BLACK/10: UNPRICED DUE TO SCARCITY
*RED/5: UNPRICED DUE TO SCARCITY
*SUPERFR/1: UNPRICED DUE TO SCARCITY

Card	Name	Low	High
1	AJ Styles	1.25	3.00
2	Akira Tozawa	.50	1.25
3	Alexa Bliss	2.50	6.00
4	Andrade	.60	1.50
5	Angel Garza	.50	1.25
6	Arturo Ruas RC	.40	1.00
7	Asuka	1.50	4.00
8	Becky Lynch	1.50	4.00
9	Bobby Lashley	1.00	2.50
10	Braun Strowman	1.00	2.50
11	The Fiend Bray Wyatt	1.50	4.00
12	Charlotte Flair	2.00	5.00
13	Charly Caruso	1.00	2.50
14	Dabba-Kato RC	.40	1.00
15	Drew Gulak	.50	1.25
16	Drew McIntyre	1.00	2.50
17	Gran Metalik	.40	1.00
18	John Morrison	.75	2.00
19	Edge	1.50	4.00
20	Erik	.40	1.00
21	Ivar	.40	1.00
22	Jeff Hardy	1.00	2.50
23	Keith Lee	.75	2.00
24	King Corbin	.40	1.00
25	Kofi Kingston	1.00	2.50
26	Lacey Evans	1.00	2.50
27	Lince Dorado	.40	1.00
28	Mandy Rose	2.00	5.00
29	Riddle	1.00	2.50
30	Naomi	.50	1.25
31	Nikki Cross	.75	2.00
32	Mustafa Ali	.50	1.25
33	MVP	.40	1.00
34	Nia Jax	.75	2.00
35	Peyton Royce	.75	2.00
36	R-Truth	.50	1.25
37	Randy Orton	1.25	3.00
38	Riddick Moss	.50	1.25
39	Samoa Joe	.75	2.00
40	Shayna Baszler	.75	2.00
41	Sheamus	.60	1.50
42	Shelton Benjamin	.60	1.50
43	Dominik Dijakovic	.50	1.25
44	The Miz	.60	1.50
45	Xavier Woods	.40	1.00
46	Aleister Black	1.00	2.50
47	Angelo Dawkins	.50	1.25
48	Apollo Crews	.50	1.25
49	Bayley	1.00	2.50
50	Bianca Belair	1.00	2.50
51	Big E	.75	2.00
52	Billie Kay	.75	2.00
53	Cesaro	.40	1.00
54	Daniel Bryan	1.50	4.00
55	Dolph Ziggler	.75	2.00
56	Kalisto	.50	1.25
57	Kayla Braxton	.75	2.00
58	Kevin Owens	.75	2.00
59	Liv Morgan	1.50	4.00
60	Montez Ford	.40	1.00
61	Murphy	.50	1.25
62	Natalya	.60	1.50
63	Otis	.50	1.25
64	Roman Reigns	2.00	5.00
65	Ruby Riott	.75	2.00
66	Sasha Banks	2.00	5.00
67	Sami Zayn	.60	1.50
68	Seth Rollins	1.00	2.50
69	Shinsuke Nakamura	1.00	2.50
70	Chad Gable	.40	1.00
71	Sonya Deville	1.00	2.50
72	Adam Cole	1.25	3.00
73	Aliyah	.75	2.00
74	Austin Theory	.75	2.00
75	Bobby Fish	.50	1.25
76	Bronson Reed	.50	1.25
77	Cameron Grimes	.75	2.00
78	Candice LeRae	1.50	4.00
79	Dakota Kai	.75	2.00
80	Damian Priest	.60	1.50
81	Dexter Lumis	.40	1.00
82	Finn Balor	1.00	2.50
83	Io Shirai	.75	2.00
84	Isaiah Swerve Scott	.60	1.50
85	Johnny Gargano	.75	2.00
86	Karrion Kross	1.50	4.00
87	Kyle O'Reilly	.60	1.50
88	Kushida	.60	1.50
89	Raquel Gonzalez	1.00	2.50
90	Rhea Ripley	1.25	3.00
91	Ridge Holland RC	.40	1.00
92	Robert Stone	.40	1.00
93	Roderick Strong	.60	1.50
94	Santos Escobar	.60	1.50
95	Scarlett	2.00	5.00
96	Shotzi Blackheart	1.50	4.00
97	Tegan Nox	1.00	2.50
98	Timothy Thatcher RC	.40	1.00
99	Tommaso Ciampa	1.00	2.50
100	Velveteen Dream	.50	1.25

2021 Topps Chrome WWE 5 Timers Club

COMPLETE SET (20) 20.00 50.00
*GREEN/99: .5X TO 1.2X BASIC CARDS
*GOLD/50: .6X TO 1.5X BASIC CARDS
*ORANGE/25: UNPRICED DUE TO SCARCITY
*BLACK/10: UNPRICED DUE TO SCARCITY
*RED/5: UNPRICED DUE TO SCARCITY
*SUPERFR/1: UNPRICED DUE TO SCARCITY
RANDOMLY INSERTED INTO PACKS

Card	Name	Low	High
5T1	Booker T	1.25	3.00
5T2	Bret Hit Man Hart	1.50	4.00
5T3	Charlotte Flair	3.00	8.00
5T4	Dolph Ziggler	1.25	3.00
5T5	Edge	2.50	6.00
5T6	John Cena	3.00	8.00
5T7	Kevin Nash	1.00	2.50
5T8	Kofi Kingston	1.50	4.00
5T9	Lex Luger	.75	2.00
5T10	Randy Orton	2.00	5.00
5T11	Rey Mysterio	1.50	4.00
5T12	Ric Flair	2.50	6.00
5T13	R-Truth	.75	2.00
5T14	Sasha Banks	3.00	8.00
5T15	Stone Cold Steve Austin	3.00	8.00
5T16	The Miz	1.00	2.50
5T17	The Rock	6.00	15.00
5T18	Triple H	2.50	6.00
5T19	Trish Stratus	3.00	8.00
5T20	William Regal	1.00	2.50

2021 Topps Chrome WWE 5 Timers Club Autographs

*GOLD/50: .5X TO 1.2X BASIC AUTOS
*ORANGE/25: .6X TO 1.5X BASIC AUTOS
*BLACK/10: UNPRICED DUE TO SCARCITY
*RED/5: UNPRICED DUE TO SCARCITY
*SUPERFR/1: UNPRICED DUE TO SCARCITY
*P.P.BLACK/1: UNPRICED DUE TO SCARCITY
*P.P.CYAN/1: UNPRICED DUE TO SCARCITY
*P.P.MAGENTA/1: UNPRICED DUE TO SCARCITY
*P.P.YELLOW/1: UNPRICED DUE TO SCARCITY
STATED PRINT RUN 99 SER.#'d SETS

Card	Name	Low	High
5TABT	Booker T	15.00	40.00
5TACF	Charlotte Flair	75.00	150.00
5TAKK	Kofi Kingston	12.00	30.00
5TARM	Rey Mysterio	50.00	100.00
5TASB	Sasha Banks	75.00	150.00
5TATM	The Miz	12.00	30.00
5TATS	Trish Stratus	75.00	150.00
5TAWR	William Regal	15.00	40.00

2021 Topps Chrome WWE Autographs

*GREEN/99: .5X TO 1.2X BASIC AUTOS
*GOLD/50: .6X TO 1.5X BASIC AUTOS
*ORANGE/25: UNPRICED DUE TO SCARCITY
*BLACK/10: UNPRICED DUE TO SCARCITY
*RED/5: UNPRICED DUE TO SCARCITY
*SUPERFR/1: UNPRICED DUE TO SCARCITY
*P.P.BLACK/1: UNPRICED DUE TO SCARCITY
*P.P.CYAN/1: UNPRICED DUE TO SCARCITY
*P.P.MAGENTA/1: UNPRICED DUE TO SCARCITY
*P.P.YELLOW/1: UNPRICED DUE TO SCARCITY
RANDOMLY INSERTED INTO PACKS

Card	Name	Low	High
AAA	Aliyah	12.00	30.00
AAB	Alexa Bliss	75.00	150.00
AAC	Apollo Crews	5.00	12.00
AAD	Angelo Dawkins	6.00	15.00
AAJ	AJ Styles	12.00	30.00
AAS	Asuka	15.00	40.00
ABA	Bayley	20.00	50.00
ABB	Bianca Belair	15.00	40.00
ABE	Big E	6.00	15.00
ABH	Shotzi Blackheart	25.00	60.00
ABK	Billie Kay	15.00	40.00
ABL	Bobby Lashley	10.00	25.00
ABR	Bronson Reed	5.00	12.00
ACL	Candice LeRae	12.00	30.00
ACS	Cesaro	6.00	15.00
ADL	Dexter Lumis	6.00	15.00
ADP	Damian Priest	8.00	20.00
AFB	Finn Balor	12.00	30.00

AGM Gran Metalik	6.00	15.00
AIS Io Shirai	15.00	40.00
AJG Johnny Gargano	5.00	12.00
AJM John Morrison	8.00	20.00
AKC King Corbin	6.00	15.00
AKO Kevin Owens	12.00	30.00
AKR Karrion Kross	15.00	40.00
AKY Kyle O'Reilly	6.00	15.00
ALM Liv Morgan	30.00	75.00
AMA Mustafa Ali	5.00	12.00
AMF Montez Ford	6.00	15.00
AMR Mandy Rose	20.00	50.00
ANC Nikki Cross	10.00	25.00
ANJ Nia Jax	8.00	20.00
AOT Otis	5.00	12.00
APR Peyton Royce	15.00	40.00
ARB Ruby Riott	15.00	40.00
ARG Raquel Gonzalez	20.00	50.00
ARP Rhea Ripley	20.00	50.00
ARS Robert Stone	5.00	12.00
ASB Shayna Baszler	10.00	25.00
ASC Scarlett	50.00	100.00
ASD Sonya Deville	15.00	40.00
ASG Chad Gable	5.00	12.00
ASM Sheamus	6.00	15.00
ASN Shinsuke Nakamura	10.00	25.00
ASR Seth Rollins	10.00	25.00
ASS Isaiah Swerve Scott	6.00	15.00
AST Roderick Strong	6.00	15.00
ATC Tommaso Ciampa	8.00	20.00
ATK Dakota Kai	12.00	30.00
ATT Timothy Thatcher	6.00	15.00
AXW Xavier Woods	6.00	15.00
ABAY Adam Cole	25.00	60.00
ABRO Riddle	15.00	40.00
ADMC Drew McIntyre		
ALEE Keith Lee	8.00	20.00
AMVP MVP	6.00	15.00

2021 Topps Chrome WWE Best of In Your House

COMPLETE SET (25) 25.00 60.00
*GREEN/99: .5X TO 1.2X BASIC CARDS
*GOLD/50: .6X TO 1.5X BASIC CARDS
*ORANGE/25: UNPRICED DUE TO SCARCITY
*BLACK/10: UNPRICED DUE TO SCARCITY
*RED/5: UNPRICED DUE TO SCARCITY
*SUPERFR/1: UNPRICED DUE TO SCARCITY
RANDOMLY INSERTED INTO PACKS

IYH1 Shawn Michaels	2.50	6.00
IYH2 Razor Ramon	1.00	2.50
IYH3 Hunter Hearst Helmsley	2.50	6.00
IYH4 Undertaker	3.00	8.00
IYH5 Razor Ramon	1.00	2.50
IYH6 Shawn Michaels	2.50	6.00
IYH7 Mark Henry	.60	1.50
IYH8 HBK	2.50	6.00
IYH9 Stone Cold Steve Austin	3.00	8.00
IYH10 Undertaker	3.00	8.00
IYH11 Ken Shamrock	.75	2.00
IYH12 Shawn Michaels/Undertaker	3.00	8.00
IYH13 Shawn Michaels	2.50	6.00
IYH14 Kane	1.00	2.50
IYH15 Triple H	2.50	6.00
IYH16 Shawn Michaels	2.50	6.00
IYH17 Undertaker	3.00	8.00
IYH18 Stone Cold Steve Austin	3.00	8.00
IYH19 Steve Austin/Undertaker	3.00	8.00
IYH20 Christian	1.00	2.50
IYH21 Ken Shamrock	.75	2.00
IYH22 Stone Cold Steve Austin	3.00	8.00
IYH23 Finn Balor	1.50	4.00
IYH24 Keith Lee	1.25	3.00
IYH25 Io Shirai	1.25	3.00

2021 Topps Chrome WWE Cruiserweight Greats

COMPLETE SET (10) 4.00 10.00
*GREEN/99: .5X TO 1.2X BASIC CARDS
*GOLD/50: .6X TO 1.5X BASIC CARDS
*ORANGE/25: UNPRICED DUE TO SCARCITY
*BLACK/10: UNPRICED DUE TO SCARCITY
*RED/5: UNPRICED DUE TO SCARCITY
*SUPERFR/1: UNPRICED DUE TO SCARCITY
FAT PACK EXCLUSIVES

CG1 Akira Tozawa	.60	1.50
CG2 Angel Garza	.60	1.50
CG3 Cedric Alexander	.50	1.25
CG4 Drew Gulak	.60	1.50
CG5 Jordan Devlin	.50	1.25
CG6 Kalisto	.60	1.50
CG7 Murphy	.60	1.50
CG8 Santos Escobar	.75	2.00
CG9 The Brian Kendrick	.50	1.25
CG10 Tony Nese	.50	1.25

2021 Topps Chrome WWE Cruiserweight Greats Autographs

*ORANGE/25: .5X TO 1.2X BASIC AUTOS
*BLACK/10: UNPRICED DUE TO SCARCITY
*RED/5: UNPRICED DUE TO SCARCITY
*SUPERFR/1: UNPRICED DUE TO SCARCITY
FAT PACK EXCLUSIVES
STATED PRINT RUN 50 SER.#'d SETS

CGAAG Angel Garza	5.00	15.00
CGAAT Akira Tozawa	6.00	15.00
CGACA Cedric Alexander	8.00	20.00
CGAKL Kalisto	6.00	15.00
CGAMP Murphy	6.00	15.00
CGASE Santos Escobar	10.00	25.00
CGATN Tony Nese	8.00	20.00

2021 Topps Chrome WWE Great Feats of Strength

COMPLETE SET (10) 6.00 15.00
*GREEN/99: .5X TO 1.2X BASIC CARDS
*GOLD/50: .6X TO 1.5X BASIC CARDS
*ORANGE/25: UNPRICED DUE TO SCARCITY
*BLACK/10: UNPRICED DUE TO SCARCITY
*RED/5: UNPRICED DUE TO SCARCITY
*SUPERFR/1: UNPRICED DUE TO SCARCITY
BLASTER BOX EXCLUSIVES

GF1 Beth Phoenix	1.00	2.50
GF2 Mark Henry	.50	1.25
GF3 Mark Henry	.50	1.25
GF4 Titus O'Neil	.50	1.25
GF5 Braun Strowman	1.25	3.00
GF6 Ronda Rousey	2.50	6.00
GF7 Bobby Lashley	1.25	3.00
GF8 Cesaro	.50	1.25
GF9 Tyler Bate	.60	1.50
GF10 Bianca Belair	1.25	3.00

2021 Topps Chrome WWE Great Feats of Strength Autographs

*BLACK/10: UNPRICED DUE TO SCARCITY
*RED/5: UNPRICED DUE TO SCARCITY
*SUPERFR/1: UNPRICED DUE TO SCARCITY
BLASTER BOX EXCLUSIVES

GFABB Bianca Belair
GFABE Big E
GFABP Beth Phoenix
GFACS Cesaro
GFARR Ronda Rousey
GFATO Titus O'Neil
GFATY Tyler Bate
GFAWS Mark Henry

2021 Topps Chrome WWE Image Variations

*GREEN/99: 1X TO 2.5X BASIC CARDS
*GOLD/50: 1.5X TO 4X BASIC CARDS
*ORANGE/25: UNPRICED DUE TO SCARCITY
*BLACK/10: UNPRICED DUE TO SCARCITY
*RED/5: UNPRICED DUE TO SCARCITY
*SUPERFR/1: UNPRICED DUE TO SCARCITY
RANDOMLY INSERTED INTO PACKS

IV1 AJ Styles	3.00	8.00
IV2 Angel Garza	1.25	3.00
IV3 Asuka	6.00	15.00
IV4 Bray Wyatt	3.00	8.00
IV5 Erik	1.25	3.00
IV6 Gran Metalik	1.25	3.00
IV7 Keith Lee	2.00	5.00
IV8 King Corbin	2.00	5.00
IV9 Lince Dorado	1.50	4.00
IV10 Mandy Rose	8.00	20.00
IV11 Riddle	2.00	5.00
IV12 MVP	1.25	3.00
IV13 Naomi	1.25	3.00
IV14 Samoa Joe	1.25	3.00
IV15 Shayna Baszler	1.50	4.00
IV16 Sheamus	1.25	3.00
IV17 The Miz	1.25	3.00
IV18 Bianca Belair	2.50	6.00
IV19 Seth Rollins	1.50	4.00
IV20 Bayley	2.00	5.00
IV21 Big E	1.50	4.00
IV22 Cesaro	1.25	3.00
IV23 Dolph Ziggler	1.25	3.00
IV24 Kalisto	1.25	3.00
IV25 Kayla Braxton	2.50	6.00
IV26 Sasha Banks	6.00	15.00
IV27 Shinsuke Nakamura	2.00	5.00
IV28 Santos Escobar	1.25	3.00
IV29 Shotzi Blackheart	5.00	12.00
IV30 Velveteen Dream	1.25	3.00

2021 Topps Chrome WWE Slam Attax

COMPLETE SET (200) 125.00 250.00
*REF.: .5X TO 1.2X BASIC CARDS
*SPECKLE: .6X TO 1.5X BASIC CARDS
*YELLOW/99: .75X TO 2X BASIC CARDS
*GREEN/50: 1.2X TO 3X BASIC CARDS
*ORANGE/25: UNPRICED DUE TO SCARCITY
*BLACK/10: UNPRICED DUE TO SCARCITY
*RED WAVE/5: UNPRICED DUE TO SCARCITY
*SUPERFR/1: UNPRICED DUE TO SCARCITY

1 Adam Cole	1.00	2.50
2 AJ Styles	1.00	2.50
3 Akira Tozawa	.40	1.00
4 Danny Burch	.40	1.00
5 Alexa Bliss	2.00	5.00
6 Angel Garza	.40	1.00
7 Angelo Dawkins	.40	1.00
8 Apollo Crews	.40	1.00
9 Asuka	1.25	3.00
10 Austin Theory	.60	1.50
11 Bayley	.75	2.00
12 Becky Lynch	1.25	3.00
13 Bianca Belair	.75	2.00
14 Big E	.60	1.50
15 Doudrop	.50	1.25
16 Bobby Lashley	.75	2.00
17 Fabian Aichner	.40	1.00
18 Jimmy Uso	.30	.75
19 Cameron Grimes	.60	1.50
20 Candice LeRae	1.25	3.00
21 Carmella	.75	2.00
22 Cedric Alexander	.30	.75
23 Cesaro	.30	.75
24 Chad Gable	.30	.75
25 Charlotte Flair	1.50	4.00
26 Dakota Kai	.60	1.50
27 Damian Priest	.50	1.25
28 Dana Brooke	.30	.75
29 Flash Morgan Webster	.40	1.00
30 Dexter Lumis	.30	.75
31 Dolph Ziggler	.60	1.50
32 Dominik Mysterio RC	.40	1.00
33 Drew McIntyre	.75	2.00
34 Edge	1.25	3.00
35 Elias	.30	.75
36 Ember Moon	.40	1.00
37 Dominik Mysterio RC	.40	1.00
38 Finn Balor	.75	2.00
39 Indi Hartwell RC	1.00	2.50
40 Io Shirai	.60	1.50
41 Isaiah "Swerve" Scott	.50	1.25
42 Ivar	.30	.75
43 James Drake	.30	.75
44 Jeff Hardy	.75	2.00
45 Jey Uso	.30	.75
46 John Morrison	.60	1.50
47 Johnny Gargano	.60	1.50
48 Jordan Devlin	.30	.75
49 Kacy Catanzaro	.60	1.50
50 Karrion Kross	1.25	3.00
51 Kay Lee Ray	.75	2.00
52 Keith Lee	.60	1.50
53 Kevin Owens	.60	1.50
54 Lince Dorado	.30	.75
55 Baron Corbin	.30	.75
56 Kofi Kingston	.75	2.00
57 Jinder Mahal	.40	1.00
58 Kushida	.50	1.25
59 Kyle OíReilly	.50	1.25
60 Lacey Evans	.75	2.00
61 Gran Metalik	.30	.75
62 Reggie RC	.40	1.00
63 Liv Morgan	1.25	3.00
64 Mace	.30	.75
65 Mandy Rose	1.50	4.00
66 Marcel Barthel	.40	1.00
67 Mark Andrews	.30	.75
68 Zelina Vega	.60	1.50
69 Montez Ford	.30	.75
70 Humberto Carrillo	.30	.75
71 Mustafa Ali	.40	1.00
72 Naomi	.40	1.00
73 Nash Carter RC	.30	.75
74 Natalya	.50	1.25
75 Nia Jax	.60	1.50
76 Nikki A.S.H.	.60	1.50
77 Oney Lorcan	.30	.75
78 Otis	.40	1.00
79 Pete Dunne	.60	1.50
80 R-Truth	.40	1.00
81 Randy Orton	1.00	2.50
82 Raquel Gonzalez	.75	2.00
83 Rey Mysterio	.75	2.00
84 Rhea Ripley	1.00	2.50
85 Ricochet	.60	1.50
86 Riddle	.75	2.00
87 Robert Roode	.40	1.00
88 Roderick Strong	.50	1.25
89 Roman Reigns	1.50	4.00
90 MVP	.30	.75
91 Sami Zayn	.50	1.25
92 Santos Escobar	.50	1.25
93 Sasha Banks	1.50	4.00
94 Scarlett	1.50	4.00
95 Seth Rollins	.75	2.00
96 Shayna Baszler	.60	1.50
97 Sheamus	.50	1.25
98 Shelton Benjamin	.50	1.25
99 Shinsuke Nakamura	.75	2.00
100 Shotzi	1.25	3.00
101 T-Bar	.40	1.00
102 Tamina	.40	1.00
103 Tegan Nox	.75	2.00
104 Omos RC	.60	1.50
105 The Miz	.50	1.25
106 Timothy Thatcher RC	.30	.75
107 Tommaso Ciampa	.75	2.00
108 Toni Storm	1.00	2.50
109 Trent Seven	.40	1.00
110 Tyler Bate	.40	1.00
111 Ilja Dragunov	.30	.75
112 Walter	.75	2.00
113 Wes Lee RC	.30	.75
114 Xavier Woods	.30	.75
115 Zack Gibson	.30	.75
116 Mankind 25th ANN	.60	1.50
117 Steve Austin 25th ANN	1.50	4.00
118 Hulk Hogan 25th ANN	1.50	4.00
119 The Rock 25th ANN	3.00	8.00
120 The Undertaker TYT	1.50	4.00
121 The Undertaker TYT	1.50	4.00
122 The Undertaker TYT	1.50	4.00
123 The Undertaker TYT	1.50	4.00
124 The Undertaker TYT	1.50	4.00
125 Apollo Crews BS	.40	1.00
126 Bianca Belair BS	.75	2.00
127 Big E BS	.60	1.50
128 Cesaro BS	.30	.75
129 Damian Priest BS	.50	1.25
130 Jey Uso BS	.30	.75
131 Liv Morgan BS	1.25	3.00
132 Rhea Ripley BS	1.00	2.50
133 Riddle BS	.75	2.00
134 Andre the Giant L	1.25	3.00
135 Batista L	.60	1.50
136 Bret Hart L	.75	2.00
137 Hulk Hogan L	1.50	4.00
138 Macho Man L	1.25	3.00

139 Mankind L .60 1.50
140 Shawn Michaels L 1.25 3.00
141 Steve Austin L 1.50 4.00
142 Trish Stratus L 1.50 4.00
143 Ultimate Warrior L 1.25 3.00
144 Apollo Crews BL .40 1.00
145 Bayley BL .75 2.00
146 Sasha Banks BL 1.50 4.00
147 Sheamus BL .50 1.25
148 Asuka ER 1.25 3.00
149 Cesaro ER .30 .75
150 Kevin Owens ER .60 1.50
151 Seth Rollins ER .75 2.00
152 Drew McIntyre SS .75 2.00
153 Mandy Rose SS 1.50 4.00
154 Montez Ford SS .30 .75
155 Roman Reigns SS 1.50 4.00
156 Dominik Mysterio PB .40 1.00
157 Keith Lee PB .60 1.50
158 Riddle PB .75 2.00
159 Shayna Baszler PB .60 1.50
160 Angelo Dawkins COC .40 1.00
161 Bobby Lashley COC .75 2.00
162 Sami Zayn COC .50 1.25
163 Shinsuke Nakamura COC .75 2.00
164 AJ Styles SRS 1.00 2.50
165 Lacey Evans SRS .75 2.00
166 Nia Jax SRS .60 1.50
167 The Miz SRS .50 1.25
168 Big E TLC .60 1.50
169 Cedric Alexander TLC .30 .75
170 Otis TLC .40 1.00
171 Randy Orton TLC 1.00 2.50
172 Bianca Belair RR .75 2.00
173 Edge RR 1.25 3.00
174 Rhea Ripley RR 1.00 2.50
175 Asuka ICONS 1.25 3.00
176 Bayley ICONS .75 2.00
177 Becky Lynch ICONS 1.25 3.00
178 Charlotte Flair ICONS 1.50 4.00
179 John Cena ICONS 1.50 4.00
180 Kofi Kingston ICONS .75 2.00
181 Randy Orton ICONS 1.00 2.50
182 Seth Rollins ICONS .75 2.00
183 Alexa Bliss 100 2.00 5.00
184 Bianca Belair 100 .75 2.00
185 Drew McIntyre 100 .75 2.00
186 Bobby Lashley 100 .75 2.00
187 Sasha Banks 100 1.50 4.00
188 Big E 100 .60 1.50
189 Edge 100 1.25 3.00
190 Hollywood Hulk Hogan nWo SR 1.50 4.00
191 Roman Reigns 100 1.50 4.00
192 AJ Styles F 1.00 2.50
193 Bobby Lashley F .75 2.00
194 Drew McIntyre F .75 2.00
195 Io Shirai F .60 1.50
196 Jey Uso F .30 .75
197 Randy Orton F 1.00 2.50
198 Rhea Ripley F 1.00 2.50
199 Roman Reigns F 1.50 4.00
200 John Cena nWo UR 6.00 15.00

2021 Topps Chrome WWE Slam Attax Autographs

*ORANGE/25: UNPRICED DUE TO SCARCITY
*RED WAVE/5: UNPRICED DUE TO SCARCITY
*SUPERFR/1: UNPRICED DUE TO SCARCITY
STATED ODDS 1:54
STATED PRINT RUN 50 SER.#'d SETS

AB Big E 5.00 12.00
AR Reckoning
AAB Alexa Bliss 40.00 100.00
AAC Adam Cole 8.00 20.00
AAJ AJ Styles 10.00 25.00
ABB Bianca Belair 15.00 40.00
ABH Bret Hart 25.00 60.00
ABL Becky Lynch 30.00 75.00
ACF Charlotte Flair 25.00 60.00
ACL Candice LeRae 10.00 25.00
ADM Drew McIntyre 8.00 20.00
AED Edge
AFA Fabian Aichner 5.00 12.00
AFB Finn Balor 10.00 25.00
AGM Gran Metalik 5.00 12.00
AHH Hulk Hogan
AIS Io Shirai 10.00 25.00
AJC John Cena
AJR Jaxson Ryker 6.00 15.00
AKR Kay Lee Ray 15.00 40.00
AKU Kushida 5.00 12.00
AKY Kyle O'Reilly 6.00 15.00
AMA Ali
AMF Mick Foley
AMY Mia Yim 8.00 20.00
ANC Nikki A.S.H. 10.00 25.00
ANM Naomi 12.00 30.00
ANT Natalya 10.00 25.00
ARC Ricochet
ARR Rhea Ripley
ARR Roman Reigns
ARS Roderick Strong
ASB Sasha Banks
ASH Shelton Benjamin 6.00 15.00
ASN Shinsuke Nakamura 8.00 20.00
AT7 Trent Seven 5.00 12.00
ATC Tommaso Ciampa 8.00 20.00
ATM The Miz 8.00 20.00
ATS Toni Storm 20.00 50.00
ATY Tyler Bate 5.00 12.00
AWT Walter 15.00 40.00
AXW Xavier Woods 6.00 15.00
AZV Zelina Vega 10.00 25.00
AHHH Triple H

2014 Topps The Complete A to Z of WWE Stickers

1 WWE Logo .20 .50
2 RAW Logo .20 .50
3 SmackDown Logo .20 .50
4 Jerry Lawler .60 1.50
5 Michael Cole .25 .60
6 AJ Lee FOIL 1.25 3.00
7 Alberto Del Rio .60 1.50
8 Alex Riley .25 .60
9 Cesaro .25 .60
10 Alicia Fox .40 1.00
11 Batista FOIL .75 2.00
12 Big E Langston .25 .60
13 Big Show .60 1.50
14 Billy Gunn .40 1.00
15 Bray Wyatt .60 1.50
16 Brock Lesnar 1.00 2.50
17 Cactus Jack FOIL .60 1.50
18 Christian .25 .60
19 Cody Rhodes .25 .60
20 Cameron .40 1.00
21 Curtis Axel .25 .60
22 Daniel Bryan FOIL .40 1.00
23 Damien Sandow .25 .60
24 Darren Young .25 .60
25 The Rock 1.25 3.00
26 Dolph Ziggler .40 1.00
27 Dean Ambrose .60 1.50
28 Eva Marie FOIL 1.00 2.50
29 Emma .40 1.00
30 Erick Rowan .40 1.00
31 Evan Bourne .25 .60
32 Ezekiel Jackson .40 1.00
33 El Torito .25 .60
34 Fandango FOIL .40 1.00
35 Ric Flair .75 2.00
36 Arn Anderson .30 .75
37 Tully Blanchard .30 .75
38 Barry Windham .30 .75
39 Goldust FOIL .25 .60
40 Great Khali .25 .60
41 Gene Okerlund .40 1.00
42 George "The Animal" Steele UER .40 1.00
43 Greg Valentine .25 .60
44 Hornswoggle FOIL .40 1.00
45 Heath Slater .25 .60
46 Harley Race .40 1.00
47 Jim Duggan .40 1.00
48 Hulk Hogan 1.25 3.00
49 Hulk Hogan 1.25 3.00
50 The Iron Sheik FOIL .40 1.00
51 Jack Swagger .40 1.00
52 JBL .40 1.00
53 Jimmy Uso .25 .60
54 Jey Uso .25 .60
55 John Cena FOIL 1.25 3.00
56 Jinder Mahal .25 .60
57 Jerry Lawler .60 1.50
58 JTG .25 .60
59 Justin Gabriel .25 .60
60 Jake "The Snake" Roberts .40 1.00
61 Kane FOIL .60 1.50
62 Kofi Kingston .25 .60
63 King of the Ring/Austin 1.25 3.00
64 KO Punch/Big Show .60 1.50
65 Killswitch/Christian .25 .60
66 Kicking Out!/Cesaro .25 .60
67 Layla FOIL .60 1.50
68 Lilian Garcia .60 1.50
69 Luke Harper .40 1.00
70 Lana .50 1.25
71 Daniel Bryan & Brie Bella .75 2.00
72 Lumberjack Match .20 .50
73 Mr. Perfect FOIL .30 .75
74 The Miz .40 1.00
75 Michael Cole .25 .60
76 Mark Henry .40 1.00
77 Million Dollar Man .30 .75
78 Money in the Bank .20 .50
79 Natalya FOIL .75 2.00
80 Naomi .40 1.00
81 Nikki Bella .75 2.00
82 NO DQ Match/Bray Wyatt .60 1.50
83 Neckbreaker/John Cena 1.25 3.00
84 Never Give Up/John Cena 1.25 3.00
85 KO Punch FOIL/Big Show .60 1.50
86 The Regal Stretch .40 1.00
87 Slap/Great Khali .25 .60
88 Figure-Four Leglock/Ric Flair .75 2.00
89 Yes! Lock/Daniel Bryan .40 1.00
90 The Sharpshooter/Natalya .75 2.00
91 Papa Shango FOIL .30 .75
92 Paul Heyman .25 .60
93 Stone Cold Steve Austin 1.25 3.00
94 Brock Lesnar 1.00 2.50
95 RVD .60 1.50
96 Curtis Axel .25 .60
97 JYD vs. Greg Valentine FOIL .40 1.00
98 Hulk Hogan vs. Ultimate Warrior 1.25 3.00
99 Rowdy Roddy Piper vs. Goldust .60 1.50
100 Steve Austin vs. Shawn Michaels 1.25 3.00
101 The Rock vs. Steve Austin 1.25 3.00
102 Chris Jericho vs. Triple H 1.00 2.50
103 Triple H vs. Batista FOIL 1.00 2.50
104 John Cena vs. Triple H 1.25 3.00
105 Edge vs. Undertaker 1.00 2.50
106 The Miz vs. John Cena 1.25 3.00
107 John Cena vs. The Rock 1.25 3.00
108 John Cena vs. The Rock 1.25 3.00
109 The Miz vs. Wade Barrett FOIL .40 1.00
110 Six-Man Tag Team Match .20 .50
111 Randy Orton vs. Big Show 1.00 2.50
112 Wade Barrett vs. The Miz vs. Curtis Axel.40 1.00
113 Dolph Ziggler vs. Alberto Del Rio .60 1.50
114 John Cena vs. Daniel Bryan 1.25 3.00
115 World Heavyweight Championship Match FOIL .25 .60
116 Daniel Bryan vs. Randy Orton 1.00 2.50
117 Alberto Del Rio vs. RVD .60 1.50
118 Shield vs. Cody & Goldust .25 .60
119 Alberto Del Rio vs. John Cena 1.25 3.00
120 Randy Orton vs. Daniel Bryan 1.00 2.50
121 Stephanie McMahon FOIL .40 1.00
122 AJ Lee 1.25 3.00
123 Vicky Guerrero .40 1.00
124 Brie Bella .75 2.00
125 Nikki Bella .75 2.00
126 Rosa Mendes .40 1.00
127 Rey Mysterio FOIL .60 1.50
128 Randy Orton 1.00 2.50
129 R-Truth .25 .60
130 Road Dogg .40 1.00
131 Roman Reigns .60 1.50
132 Ryback .25 .60
133 Sheamus FOIL .60 1.50
134 Santino Marella .40 1.00
135 Sin Cara .60 1.50
136 Seth Rollins .25 .60
137 Summer Rae 1.00 2.50
138 Stephanie McMahon .40 1.00
139 Triple H FOIL 1.00 2.50
140 Tyson Kidd .25 .60
141 Tensai .25 .60
142 Tamina .40 1.00
143 Titus O'Neil .25 .60
144 Theodore Long .25 .60
145 Undertaker vs. Shawn Michaels 1.00 2.50
146 Undertaker FOIL 1.00 2.50
147 Undertaker vs. Shawn Michaels 1.00 2.50
148 Undertaker vs. Triple H 1.00 2.50
149 Triple H vs. Big Show 1.00 2.50
150 Undertaker vs. CM Punk 1.00 2.50
151 Vicky Guerrero FOIL .40 1.00
152 Shawn Michaels 1.00 2.50
153 Mr. Wonderful .25 .60
154 Cody Rhodes .25 .60
155 Rick Rude .25 .60
156 William Regal FOIL .40 1.00
157 Trish Stratus 1.00 2.50
158 Diamond Dallas Page .40 1.00
159 Bill DeMott .25 .60
160 Chris Jericho .60 1.50
161 Xavier Woods .25 .60
162 John Cena vs. Ryback 1.25 3.00
163 Brock Lesnar vs. Triple H 1.00 2.50
164 Dean Ambrose vs. Kofi Kingston .60 1.50
165 Sheamus vs. Mark Henry .60 1.50
166 The Shield vs. Team Hell No .60 1.50
167 Yoshi Tatsu .25 .60
168 Cody Rhodes .25 .60
169 D-Generation X Invades WCW .50 1.25
170 Undertaker vs. Mankind 1.00 2.50
171 Hulk Hogan vs. The Iron Sheik 1.25 3.00
172 Big Show vs. Brock Lesnar 1.00 2.50
173 Zack Ryder FOIL .25 .60
174 Zeb Coulter .40 1.00
175 British Bulldog .50 1.25
176 Ricky "The Dragon" Steamboat .25 .60
177 Gorilla Monsoon .50 1.25
178 WWE World Heavyweight Championship.20 .50
179 Intercontinental Championship .20 .50
180 United States Championship .20 .50
181 Divas Championship .20 .50
182 Tag Team Championship .20 .50

2015 Topps The Complete A to Z of WWE Stickers Spanish

1 WWE LOGO .20 .50
2 RAW LOGO .20 .50
3 SmackDown LOGO .20 .50
4 Jerry "The King" Lawler .40 1.00
5 Michael Cole .25 .60
6 Adam Rose .30 .75
7 Alex Riley .25 .60
8 Alicia Fox .50 1.25
9 Batista FOIL .60 1.50
10 Big E .40 1.00
11 Big Show .60 1.50
12 Bo Dallas .25 .60
13 Bray Wyatt 1.00 2.50
14 Brock Lesnar 1.00 2.50
15 Cesaro FOIL .25 .60
16 Christian .25 .60
17 Chris Jericho .60 1.50
18 Cameron .40 1.00
19 Curtis Axel .25 .60
20 Daniel Bryan FOIL 1.00 2.50
21 Damien Sandow .25 .60
22 Darren Young .25 .60
23 The Rock 1.25 3.00
24 Dolph Ziggler .40 1.00
25 Dean Ambrose .60 1.50
26 Eva Marie FOIL 1.00 2.50
27 Emma .40 1.00
28 Erick Rowan .40 1.00
29 Edge .60 1.50
30 Eddie Guerrero .60 1.50
31 El Torito .25 .60
32 Ric Flair 1.25 3.00
33 Arn Anderson .30 .75
34 Tully Blanchard .30 .75

Card	Low	High
35 Barry Windham	.30	.75
36 Fandango FOIL	.25	.60
37 Goldust FOIL	.25	.60
38 The Godfather	.25	.60
39 Greg Valentine	.30	.75
40 Mean Gene Okerlund	.30	.75
41 George Steele	.30	.75
42 Hornswoggle FOIL	.40	1.00
43 Heath Slater	.25	.60
44 The King Harley Race	.40	1.00
45 Hacksaw Jim Duggan	.40	1.00
46 Iron Sheik FOIL	.40	1.00
47 Jack Swagger	.40	1.00
48 JBL	.25	.60
49 Jimmy Uso	.25	.60
50 Jey Uso	.25	.60
51 John Cena FOIL	1.25	3.00
52 John Cena	1.25	3.00
53 Junkyard Dog	.30	.75
54 Jerry "The King" Lawler	.40	1.00
55 John Cena	1.25	3.00
56 Jake "The Snake" Roberts	.40	1.00
57 Kane FOIL	.60	1.50
58 Kofi Kingston	.25	.60
59 King of the Ring/Austin	1.25	3.00
60 KO Punch/Big Show	.60	1.50
61 Killswitch/Christian	.25	.60
62 Kicking Out/Cesaro	.25	.60
63 Lilian Garcia	.60	1.50
64 Luke Harper	.40	1.00
65 Lana	1.00	2.50
66 Daniel Bryan & Brie Bella	1.00	2.50
67 Lumberjack Match	.20	.50
68 Mr. Perfect Curt Henning FOIL	.40	1.00
69 The Miz	.40	1.00
70 Michael Cole	.25	.60
71 Mark Henry	.40	1.00
72 Ted DiBiase	.40	1.00
73 Money in the Bank	.20	.50
74 Natalya FOIL	.75	2.00
75 Naomi	.40	1.00
76 Nikki Bella	.75	2.00
77 No Disqualification Match	.20	.50
78 Neckbreaker/John Cena	1.25	3.00
79 Never Give Up/John Cena	1.25	3.00
80 STF/John Cena	1.25	3.00
81 The Regal Stretch	.40	1.00
82 The Accolade/Rusev	.60	1.50
83 Figure-Four/Ric Flair	1.25	3.00
84 Yes! Lock	1.00	2.50
85 Sharpshooter/Natalya	.75	2.00
86 Paul Heyman	.25	.60
87 Brock Lesnar	1.00	2.50
88 Rob Van Dam	.60	1.50
89 Curtis Axel	.25	.60
90 Papa Shango FOIL	.25	.60
91 JYD vs. Greg Valentine FOIL	.30	.75
92 Rowdy Roddy Piper vs. Goldust	.75	2.00
93 Steve Austin vs. HBK	1.25	3.00
94 The Rock vs. Steve Austin	1.25	3.00
95 Chris Jericho vs. Triple H	1.00	2.50
96 Triple H vs. Batista FOIL	1.00	2.50
97 John Cena vs. Triple H	1.25	3.00
98 Edge vs. Undertaker	1.00	2.50
99 The Miz vs. John Cena	1.25	3.00
100 John Cena vs. The Rock	1.25	3.00
101 John Cena vs. The Rock	1.25	3.00
102 Andre the Giant Battle Royal FOIL	1.25	3.00
103 Six-Man Tag Team Match	.20	.50
104 Bad News Barrett vs. RVD	.60	1.50
105 Money in the Bank Ladder Match	.20	.50
106 Chris Jericho vs. Bray Wyatt	1.00	2.50
107 Roman Reigns vs. Randy Orton	1.00	2.50
108 Brock Lesnar vs. John Cena FOIL	1.25	3.00
109 Rusev vs. Mark Henry	.60	1.50
110 Seth Rollins vs. Dean Ambrose	.60	1.50
111 The Miz vs. Dolph Ziggler	.40	1.00
112 Bray Wyatt vs. Dean Ambrose	1.00	2.50
113 Elimination Match	.20	.50
114 Stephanie McMahon FOIL	.40	1.00
115 Paige	1.25	3.00
116 Brie Bella	.75	2.00
117 Nikki Bella	.75	2.00
118 Rosa Mendes	.40	1.00
119 Randy Orton FOIL	1.00	2.50
120 Randy Orton	1.00	2.50
121 R-Truth	.25	.60
122 Rusev	.60	1.50
123 Roman Reigns	.60	1.50
124 Ryback	.25	.60
125 Sheamus FOIL	.60	1.50
126 Santino Marella	.25	.60
127 Sin Cara	.40	1.00
128 Seth Rollins	.40	1.00
129 Summer Rae	1.00	2.50
130 Stephanie McMahon	.40	1.00
131 Triple H FOIL	1.00	2.50
132 Tyson Kidd	.25	.60
133 Trish Stratus	1.25	3.00
134 Tamina	.40	1.00
135 Titus O'Neil	.25	.60
136 Terry Funk	.30	.75
137 Undertaker FOIL	1.00	2.50
138 Undertaker vs. Shawn Michaels	1.00	2.50
139 Undertaker vs. Triple H	1.00	2.50
140 Undertaker vs. Triple H	1.00	2.50
141 Undertaker vs. Brock Lesnar	1.00	2.50
142 Undertaker vs. Brock Lesnar	1.00	2.50
143 Billy Gunn FOIL	.40	1.00
144 Shawn Michaels	1.00	2.50
145 Mr. Wonderful Paul Orndorff	.40	1.00
146 Dolph Ziggler	.40	1.00
147 Ravishing Rick Rude	.40	1.00
148 William Regal FOIL	.40	1.00
149 Trish Stratus	1.25	3.00
150 Diamond Dallas Page	.50	1.25
151 Lita	1.00	2.50
152 Xavier Woods FOIL	.40	1.00
153 John Cena vs. Ryback	1.25	3.00
154 John Cena vs. Seth Rollins	1.25	3.00
155 Sheamus vs. Mark Henry	.60	1.50
156 The Shield vs. Team Hell No	1.00	2.50
157 Yokozuna FOIL	.40	1.00
158 Dean Ambrose	.60	1.50
159 D-Generation X	.75	2.00
160 Big Show vs. Brock Lesnar	1.00	2.50
161 Zack Ryder FOIL	.25	.60
162 Zeb Colter	.40	1.00
163 British Bulldog	.40	1.00
164 Ricky "The Dragon" Steamboat	.40	1.00
165 Gorilla Monsoon	.30	.75
166 WWE Title Belt	.20	.50
167 WWE Intercontinental Belt	.20	.50
168 WWE US Title Belt	.20	.50
169 WWE Diva Title Belt	.20	.50
170 WWE Tag Team Belt	.20	.50

2006 Topps Heritage Chrome WWE

COMPLETE SET (90) 10.00 25.00
*REFRACTORS: .75X TO 2X BASIC CARDS
*X-FRACTORS: 1.5X TO 4X BASIC CARDS
*SUPERFR./25: 10X TO 25X BASIC CARDS

Card	Low	High
1 John Cena	4.00	10.00
2 Batista	.75	2.00
3 Carlito	.75	2.00
4 Orlando Jordan	.20	.50
5 Paul London	.20	.50
6 Johnny Nitro	.30	.75
7 Joey Mercury	.20	.50
8 The Hurricane	.20	.50
9 Rosey	.20	.50
10 The Rock	10.00	25.00
11 Stone Cold Steve Austin	1.25	3.00
12 Hulk Hogan	1.00	2.50
13 Big Show	.75	2.00
14 The Boogeyman RC	.30	.75
15 Danny Basham	.20	.50
16 Edge	.75	2.00
17 Finlay	.50	1.25
18 Eugene	.20	.50
19 Joey Styles RC	.20	.50
20 Jonathan Coachman	.20	.50
21 Kane	.75	2.00
22 Kid Kash	.20	.50
23 Kurt Angle	.75	2.00
24 Rene Dupree	.30	.75
25 Ric Flair	1.00	2.50
26 Rob Van Dam	.50	1.25
27 Shawn Michaels	.75	2.00
28 Triple H	.75	2.00
29 Chavo Guerrero	.30	.75
30 Val Venis	.30	.75
31 Viscera	.30	.75
32 Steven Richards	.30	.75
33 Booker T	.50	1.25
34 Chris Benoit	.75	2.00
35 Ken Kennedy RC	.50	1.25
36 Doug Basham	.30	.75
37 Lashley RC	.50	1.25
38 Funaki	.30	.75
39 Hardcore Holly	.30	.75
40 JBL	.50	1.25
41 Paul Burchill RC	.20	.50
42 Psicosis	.20	.50
43 Super Crazy	.30	.75
44 Shelton Benjamin	.20	.50
45 Chris Masters	.30	.75
46 Nunzio	.20	.50
47 Randy Orton	.50	1.25
48 Rey Mysterio	.50	1.25
49 Scotty 2 Hotty	.30	.75
50 Tazz	.30	.75
51 Theodore Long	.20	.50
52 Undertaker	1.00	2.50
53 William Regal	.50	1.25
54 Antonio	.20	.50
55 Romeo	.20	.50
56 Snitsky	.30	.75
57 Robert Conway	.30	.75
58 Mickie James DV RC	1.25	3.00
59 Sharmell DV	.75	2.00
60 Trish Stratus DV	1.25	3.00
61 Torrie Wilson DV	.75	2.00
62 Ashley DV RC	.75	2.00
63 Lita DV	1.25	3.00
64 Lilian Garcia DV	1.00	2.50
65 Maria DV	.75	2.00
66 Stacy Keibler DV	2.00	5.00
67 Victoria DV	1.25	3.00
68 Candice Michelle DV	1.25	3.00
69 Michelle McCool DV	1.00	2.50
70 Melina DV	.40	1.00
71 The British Bulldog L	.75	2.00
72 Chief Jay Strongbow L	.30	.75
73 Classy Freddie Blassie L	.30	.75
74 Cowboy Bob Orton L	.50	1.25
75 Bobby The Brain Heenan L	.50	1.25
76 Gorilla Monsoon L	.30	.75
77 Hillbilly Jim L	.30	.75
78 Iron Sheik L	.75	2.00
79 Jake The Snake Roberts L	.60	1.50
80 Jerry The King Lawler L	.60	1.50
81 Junkyard Dog L	.60	1.50
82 Mouth of the South Jimmy Hart L	.75	2.00
83 Mr. Wonderful Paul Orndorff L	.75	2.00
84 Nikolai Volkoff L	.50	1.25
85 Rowdy Roddy Piper L	1.00	2.50
86 Sgt. Slaughter L	.75	2.00
87 Superstar Billy Graham L RC	.30	.75
88 Ted DiBiase L	.75	2.00
89 Godfather L	.30	.75
90 Checklist	.20	.50

2006 Topps Heritage Chrome WWE Refractors

STATED ODDS 1:6 HOBBY AND RETAIL

Card	Low	High
1 John Cena	25.00	60.00
10 The Rock	60.00	120.00

2006 Topps Heritage Chrome WWE X-Fractors

STATED ODDS 1:12 HOBBY AND RETAIL

Card	Low	High
1 John Cena	60.00	120.00
10 The Rock	150.00	300.00

2006 Topps Heritage Chrome WWE Autographs

GROUP A ODDS: 1:404 HOBBY
GROUP B ODDS: 1:719 HOBBY
GROUP C ODDS: 1:167 HOBBY
GROUP D ODDS: 1:31 HOBBY

Card	Low	High
NNO Ashley D	12.00	30.00
NNO Big Show D	12.00	30.00
NNO Bobby The Brain Heenan D	125.00	250.00
NNO Boogeyman D	10.00	25.00
NNO Booker T A	8.00	20.00
NNO Carlito C	6.00	15.00
NNO Chavo Guerrero D	6.00	15.00
NNO Chief Jay Strongbow D	12.00	30.00
NNO Chris Benoit D	300.00	600.00
NNO Hillbilly Jim D	30.00	75.00
NNO JBL A	25.00	60.00
NNO Jerry The King Lawler D	15.00	40.00
NNO John Cena D	75.00	150.00
NNO Kane B	12.00	30.00
NNO Ken Kennedy D	6.00	15.00
NNO Kurt Angle C	10.00	25.00
NNO Lashley D	15.00	40.00
NNO Lilian Garcia D	12.00	30.00
NNO Lita D	15.00	40.00
NNO Mickie James D	15.00	40.00
NNO Rey Mysterio D	20.00	50.00
NNO Sgt. Slaughter D	20.00	50.00
NNO Shawn Michaels D	75.00	150.00
NNO Tazz C	15.00	40.00
NNO Torrie Wilson D	15.00	40.00
NNO Trish Stratus C	25.00	60.00
NNO Victoria D	12.00	30.00

2006 Topps Heritage Chrome WWE Ringside Relics

COMPLETE SET (2) 10.00 25.00
RETAIL EXCLUSIVE

Card	Low	High
NNO JBL/Batista	6.00	15.00
NNO Melina/T.Wilson	8.00	20.00

2007 Topps Heritage II Chrome WWE

COMPLETE SET (100) 10.00 25.00
*REFRACTORS: .8X TO 2X BASIC CARDS
*X-FRACTORS: 1.5X TO 4X BASIC CARDS
*SUPERFR/25: 10X TO 25X BASIC CARDS

Card	Low	High
1 John Cena	1.25	3.00
2 Batista	.50	1.25
3 Carlito	.75	2.00
4 Tatanka	.20	.50
5 Highlanders	.30	.75
6 Johnny Nitro	.30	.75
7 The Great Khali	.20	.50
8 Gregory Helms	.20	.50
9 Jeff Hardy	.50	1.25
10 The Rock	1.50	4.00
11 Stone Cold Steve Austin	1.25	3.00
12 Matt Striker	.20	.50
13 Montel Vontavious Porter RC	.30	.75
14 The Boogeyman	.20	.50
15 Mark Henry	.30	.75
16 Edge	.50	1.25
17 Finlay	.50	1.25
18 Eugene	.20	.50
19 Sandman	.30	.75
20 Sabu RC	.20	.50
21 Kane	.50	1.25
22 Brian Kendrick/Paul London	.50	1.25
23 Rene Dupree	.30	.75
24 Ric Flair	.75	2.00
25 Rob Van Dam	.75	2.00
26 Shawn Michaels	.75	2.00
27 Triple H	.75	2.00
28 Chavo Guerrero	.30	.75
29 Vito	.20	.50
30 Viscera	.50	1.25
31 King Booker	.50	1.25
32 Chris Benoit	.50	1.25
33 Ken Kennedy	.50	1.25
34 Bobby Lashley	.50	1.25
35 Funaki	.30	.75
36 Matt Hardy	.50	1.25
37 JBL	.50	1.25
38 Paul Burchill	.20	.50
39 CM Punk	.75	2.00
40 Super Crazy	.30	.75
41 Shelton Benjamin	.20	.50
42 Chris Masters	.75	2.00
43 Little Guido Maritato	.20	.50
44 Randy Orton	.75	2.00
45 Rey Mysterio	.50	1.25

46 Scotty 2 Hotty .30 .75
47 Kenny Dykstra RC .30 .75
48 Undertaker 1.00 2.50
49 William Regal .50 1.25
50 Charlie Haas .20 .50
51 Umaga .30 .75
52 Snitsky .20 .50
53 Rob Conway .20 .50
54 Mr. McMahon .75 2.00
55 Shane McMahon .50 1.25
56 Stephanie McMahon 1.00 2.50
57 Linda McMahon .30 .75
58 Mickie James DV .60 1.50
59 Sharmell DV .25 .60
60 Torrie Wilson DV 1.50 4.00
61 Ashley DV .40 1.00
62 Michelle McCool DV 1.00 2.50
63 Layla DV RC .75 2.00
64 Maria DV .75 2.00
65 Kristal DV .75 2.00
66 Victoria DV .40 1.00
67 Candice Michelle DV 1.00 2.50
68 Jillian Hall DV 1.00 2.50
69 Melina DV .75 2.00
70 Mean Gene Okerlund L .50 1.25
71 Don Muraco L .30 .75
72 Paul Bearer L .30 .75
73 One Man Gang L .30 .75
74 Dusty Rhodes L .50 1.25
75 Bushwhackers L .20 .50
76 The Wild Samoans L .30 .75
77 Bam Bam Bigelow L .50 1.25
78 Mr. Perfect Curt Hennig L .50 1.25
79 The British Bulldog L .75 2.00
80 Earthquake L .30 .75
81 Rocky Johnson L RC .30 .75
82 Papa Shango L .25 .60
83 Jerry The King Lawler .50 1.25
84 High Chief Peter Maivia L .20 .50
85 Arn Anderson L .20 .50
86 Mick Foley L .75 2.00
87 Ravishing Rick Rude L .50 1.25
88 Doink L .20 .50
89 Andre The Giant L .75 2.00
90 Batista TR .50 1.25
91 Triple H TR .75 2.00
92 Carlito TR .75 2.00
93 John Cena TR 1.25 3.00
94 Rey Mysterio TR .50 1.25
95 Andre The Giant TR .75 2.00
96 Iron Sheik TR .75 2.00
97 Jerry The King Lawler TR .50 1.25
98 Rowdy Roddy Piper TR .75 2.00
99 Superstar Billy Graham TR .30 .75
100 Cena/Booker/Ashley/Mysterio CL 1.25 3.00

2007 Topps Heritage II Chrome WWE Autographs

STATED ODDS 1:24 HOBBY EXCLUSIVE

NNO Ashley 12.00 30.00
NNO Jeff Hardy 15.00 40.00
NNO John Cena 25.00 60.00
NNO Ken Kennedy 8.00 20.00
NNO Layla 10.00 25.00
NNO Melina 10.00 25.00
NNO Michelle McCool 10.00 25.00
NNO Mickie James 15.00 40.00
NNO Sabu 10.00 25.00
NNO Sandman 15.00 40.00
NNO Sharmell 6.00 15.00
NNO Torrie Wilson 15.00 40.00
NNO William Regal 10.00 25.00

2007 Topps Heritage II Chrome WWE Mini

COMPLETE SET (5)

1 John Cena
2 Rey Mysterio
3 Andre The Giant
4 Hulk Hogan
5 Batista

2007 Topps Heritage II Chrome WWE Ringside Relics

STATED ODDS 1:24 RETAIL EXCLUSIVE

NNO Jeff Hardy/Carlito 4.00 10.00
NNO Kane/Umaga 4.00 10.00
NNO Lita/Mickie James 6.00 15.00

2008 Topps Heritage III Chrome WWE

COMPLETE SET (90) 8.00 20.00
*REFRACTORS: .8X TO 2X BASIC CARDS
*X-FRACTORS: 1.5X TO 4X BASIC CARDS
*SUPERFR./25: 10X TO 25X BASIC CARDS

1 John Cena 1.25 3.00
2 Batista .75 2.00
3 Rey Mysterio .50 1.25
4 Stone Cold 1.25 3.00
5 The Great Khali .20 .50
6 Chris Jericho .50 1.25
7 Edge .75 2.00
8 Hard Core Holly .30 .75
9 Umaga .30 .75
10 Montel Vontavious Porter .30 .75
11 Stevie Richards .30 .75
12 Deuce .20 .50
13 Lance Cade .20 .50
14 Super Crazy .30 .75
15 Chuck Palumbo .30 .75
16 Domino .20 .50
17 Trevor Murdoch .20 .50
18 Zack Ryder .20 .50
19 Festus RC .20 .50
20 Mark Henry .30 .75
21 Boogeyman .30 .75
22 Brian Kendrick .30 .75
23 Tommy Dreamer .20 .50
24 Charlie Haas .20 .50
25 JBL .20 .50
26 Armando Estrada .20 .50
27 CM Punk .20 .50
28 Triple H 1.25 3.00
29 Shannon Moore .20 .50
30 Hacksaw Jim Duggan .50 1.25
31 Jeff Hardy .75 2.00
32 Kane .75 2.00
33 Ron Simmons .20 .50
34 Finlay .30 .75
35 The Miz .30 .75
36 Kenny Dykstra .30 .75
37 Snitsky .30 .75
38 Jesse RC .20 .50
39 Santino Marella .20 .50
40 Cody Rhodes .20 .50
41 Shelton Benjamin .20 .50
42 Hornswoggle .30 .75
43 Big Daddy V .30 .75
44 Matt Striker .20 .50
45 Curt Hawkins .20 .50
46 William Regal .50 1.25
47 Jimmy Wang Yang .20 .50
48 Elijah Burke .20 .50
49 Chavo Guerrero .30 .75
50 Paul London .20 .50
51 Mr. Kennedy .50 1.25
52 John Morrison .20 .50
53 Matt Hardy .75 2.00
54 Shawn Michaels 1.25 3.00
55 Randy Orton .50 1.25
56 Ric Flair .75 2.00
57 Undertaker 1.00 2.50
58 Torrie Wilson DV 1.50 4.00
59 Candice DV 1.00 2.50
60 Michelle McCool DV 1.00 2.50
61 Melina DV .75 2.00
62 Cherry DV .75 2.00
63 Jillian DV .75 2.00
64 Ashley DV .75 2.00
65 Maria DV .75 2.00
66 Kelly Kelly DV .75 2.00
67 Mickie James DV 1.25 3.00
68 Maryse DV .75 2.00
69 Victoria DV 1.00 2.50
70 Anderson/Blanchard L .30 .75
71 Brian Pillman L .30 .75
72 Dean Malenko L .50 1.25
73 Funk Brothers L .30 .75
74 Dusty Rhodes L .50 1.25
75 The Freebirds L .30 .75
76 Jimmy Superfly Snuka L .50 1.25
77 Jimmy Garvin L .30 .75
78 Papa Shango L .25 .60
79 Pat Patterson L .20 .50
80 Bam Bam Bigelow L .50 1.25
81 Gorilla Monsoon L .50 1.25
82 Ted Dibiase L .50 1.25
83 Rocky Johnson L .30 .75
84 Bruiser Brody L RC .30 .75
85 Kamala L .30 .75
86 Earthquake L .30 .75
87 Vader L .30 .75
88 Jack and Gerry Brisco L .30 .75
89 Cowboy Bob Orton L .50 1.25
100 Checklist .20 .50

2008 Topps Heritage III Chrome WWE Allen and Ginter Superstars

COMPLETE SET (10) 6.00 15.00
*REFRACTORS: .8X TO 2X BASIC CARDS
*X-FRACTORS: 1.5X TO 4X BASIC CARDS
*SUPERFR/25: 10X TO 25X BASIC CARDS

1 John Cena 1.25 3.00
2 Batista .75 2.00
3 Rey Mysterio .50 1.25
4 Triple H 1.25 3.00
5 Shawn Michaels 1.25 3.00
6 Undertaker 1.00 2.50
7 Rowdy Roddy Piper .75 2.00
8 Chief Jay Strongbow .50 1.25
9 Sgt. Slaughter .50 1.25
10 Iron Sheik .75 2.00

2008 Topps Heritage III Chrome WWE Autographs

STATED ODDS 1:24 HOBBY EXCLUSIVE

NNO Ashley 25.00 60.00
NNO Carlito 6.00 15.00
NNO Cherry 8.00 20.00
NNO Chuck Palumbo 6.00 15.00
NNO Festus 6.00 15.00
NNO Jeff Hardy 15.00 40.00
NNO Jesse 8.00 20.00
NNO Kane 25.00 60.00
NNO Layla 8.00 20.00
NNO Montel Vontavious Porter 6.00 15.00
NNO Tommy Dreamer 6.00 15.00
NNO Trevor Murdoch 6.00 15.00

2008 Topps Heritage III Chrome WWE Mini-Cards

COMPLETE SET (5)

1 Stone Cold Steve Austin
2 John Cena
3 Edge
4 Umaga
5 The Great Khali

2008 Topps Heritage III Chrome WWE Ringside Relics

STATED ODDS 1:24 RETAIL EXCLUSIVE

NNO Hardcore Holly vs. Carlito 4.00 10.00
NNO Mickie James vs. Beth Phoenix 4.00 10.00
NNO Mr. Kennedy vs. Shawn Michaels 5.00 12.00

2006 Topps Heritage II WWE

COMPLETE SET (90) 8.00 20.00

1 John Cena .75 2.00
2 Batista .40 1.00
3 Carlito .30 .75
4 Tatanka .12 .30
5 Paul London/Brian Kendrick .30 .75
6 Johnny Nitro .12 .30
7 The Great Khali RC .40 1.00
8 Gregory Helms .12 .30
9 Gunnar Scott RC .30 .75
10 The Rock .75 2.00
11 Stone Cold Steve Austin .75 2.00
12 Hulk Hogan .75 2.00
13 Big Show .40 1.00
14 The Boogeyman RC .20 .50
15 Mark Henry .30 .75
16 Edge .40 1.00
17 Finlay .30 .75
18 Eugene .12 .30
19 Matt Striker RC .12 .30
20 Jake and Jesse Gymini .20 .50
21 Kane .50 1.25
22 Kid Kash .20 .50
23 Kurt Angle .75 2.00
24 Rene Dupree .12 .30
25 Ric Flair .60 1.50
26 Rob Van Dam .50 1.25
27 Shawn Michaels .60 1.50
28 Triple H .75 2.00
29 Chavo Guerrero .30 .75
30 Vito RC .12 .30
31 Viscera .20 .50
32 Steven Richards .20 .50
33 Booker T .30 .75
34 Chris Benoit .30 .75
35 Ken Kennedy RC .30 .75
36 Goldust .30 .75
37 Bobby Lashley RC .30 .75
38 Funaki .20 .50
39 Matt Hardy .20 .50
40 JBL .40 1.00
41 Paul Burchill RC .12 .30
42 Psicosis .12 .30
43 Super Crazy .20 .50
44 Shelton Benjamin .12 .30
45 Chris Masters .40 1.00
46 Little Guido Maritato RC .12 .30
47 Randy Orton .40 1.00
48 Rey Mysterio .30 .75
49 Scotty 2 Hotty .20 .50
50 Tazz .20 .50
51 Spirit Squad .20 .50
52 Undertaker .60 1.50
53 William Regal .30 .75
54 Charlie Haas .12 .30
55 Umaga .20 .50
56 Snitsky .20 .50
57 Rob Conway .12 .30
58 Mickie James DV RC .75 2.00
59 Sharmell DV .40 1.00
60 Torrie Wilson DV .75 2.00
61 Ashley DV RC .40 1.00
62 Lita DV .60 1.50
63 Beth Phoenix DV RC 1.50 4.00
64 Maria DV .50 1.25
65 Kristal DV RC .40 1.00
66 Victoria DV .60 1.50
67 Candice Michelle DV .60 1.50
68 Jillian Hall DV RC .50 1.25
69 Melina DV .50 1.25
70 Mean Gene Okerlund L .30 .75
71 Don Muraco L .20 .50
72 Paul Bearer L .20 .50
73 One Man Gang L .20 .50
74 Dusty Rhodes L .30 .75
75 Bushwhackers L .20 .50
76 The Wild Samoans L .30 .75
77 Bam Bam Bigelow L .20 .50
78 Mr. Perfect Curt Hennig L .30 .75
79 The British Bulldog L .50 1.25
80 Earthquake L .20 .50
81 Kamala L .30 .75
82 Koko B Ware L .20 .50
83 Jerry The King Lawler L .30 .75
84 High Chief Peter Maivia L RC .12 .30
85 Arn Anderson L .12 .30
86 Mick Foley L .50 1.25
87 Ravishing Rick Rude L .30 .75
88 Vader L .30 .75
89 Andre The Giant L .50 1.25
90 Checklist .12 .30

2006 Topps Heritage II WWE Autographs

STATED ODDS 1:24 HOBBY EXCLUSIVE

NNO Ashley 10.00 25.00
NNO Bobby Lashley 8.00 20.00

NNO Booker T 15.00 40.00
NNO Brian Kendrick 8.00 20.00
NNO Carlito 8.00 20.00
NNO Charlie Haas 6.00 15.00
NNO Chavo Guerrero 6.00 15.00
NNO Edge 20.00 50.00
NNO Gene Snitsky 6.00 15.00
NNO Jamie Noble 6.00 15.00
NNO Jillian Hall 10.00 25.00
NNO John Cena 60.00 120.00
NNO Johnny Nitro 8.00 20.00
NNO Kane 12.00 30.00
NNO Ken Kennedy 8.00 20.00
NNO Kurt Angle 12.00 30.00
NNO Melina 10.00 25.00
NNO Michelle McCool 15.00 40.00
NNO Mickie James 15.00 40.00
NNO The Miz 8.00 20.00
NNO Paul London 6.00 15.00
NNO Randy Orton 30.00 75.00
NNO Sharmell 8.00 20.00
NNO Shawn Michaels 75.00 150.00
NNO Umaga 15.00 40.00
NNO Vito 6.00 15.00

2006 Topps Heritage II WWE Magazine Promos

COMPLETE SET (9) 4.00 10.00
WWE MAGAZINE EXCLUSIVE

W1 John Cena 1.00 2.50
W2 Triple H 1.00 2.50
W3 Edge .75 2.00
W4 Batista .60 1.50
W5 Undertaker .60 1.50
W6 Rey Mysterio .60 1.50
W7 Hulk Hogan 1.00 2.50
W8 Rowdy Roddy Piper .75 2.00
W9 Sgt. Slaughter .75 2.00

2006 Topps Heritage II WWE Magnets

COMPLETE SET (9) 6.00 15.00
STATED ODDS 1:4 RETAIL EXCLUSIVE

1 John Cena 1.50 4.00
2 Batista 1.00 2.50
3 Carlito .60 1.50
4 Shawn Michaels 1.00 2.50
5 Triple H 1.00 2.50
6 Rey Mysterio .60 1.50
7 Edge 1.00 2.50
8 Hulk Hogan 1.25 3.00
9 Torrie Wilson 2.00 5.00

2006 Topps Heritage II WWE Raw vs. Smackdown

COMPLETE SET (2) .75 2.00
V1 John Cena .60 1.50
V2 Rey Mysterio .40 1.00

2006 Topps Heritage II WWE Ringside Relics

STATED ODDS 1:24 HOBBY

NNO Big Show 8.00 20.00
NNO Carlito 5.00 12.00
NNO Hulk Hogan 10.00 25.00
NNO John Cena/Hat 30.00 75.00
NNO John Cena/Shirt 10.00 25.00
NNO Psicosis 5.00 12.00
NNO Shawn Michaels 12.00 30.00
NNO Triple H 8.00 20.00

2006 Topps Heritage II WWE Ringside Relics Doubles

NNO G.Helms/Super Crazy 5.00 12.00
NNO K.Kennedy/G.Scott 5.00 12.00
NNO B.Lashley/K.Booker 5.00 12.00

2006 Topps Heritage II WWE Tin Inserts

COMPLETE SET (6) 6.00 15.00
STATED ODDS 1:RETAIL TIN

TLB1 John Cena 2.50 6.00
TLB2 Hulk Hogan 2.00 5.00
TLB3 Edge 1.50 4.00
TLB4 Triple H 2.00 5.00
TLB5 Rey Mysterio 1.00 2.50
TLB6 Andre The Giant 1.50 4.00

2006 Topps Heritage II WWE Toppers

COMPLETE SET (12) 4.00 10.00
B1-B3 STATED ODDS 1:HOBBY BOX
B4-B9 STATED ODDS 1:RETAIL TIN
B10-B12 STATED ODDS 1:2 RETAIL BLISTER

B1 D-Generation X 1.00 2.50
B2 Edge & Lita .75 2.00
B3 Armando Estrada/Umaga .30 .75
B4 Booker T & Sharmell .60 1.50
B5 Johnny Nitro & Melina .60 1.50
B6 Spirit Squad .30 .75
B7 D-Generation X 1.00 2.50
B8 Edge & Lita .75 2.00
B9 Armando Estrada/Umaga .30 .75
B10 The Great Khali/Daivari .30 .75
B11 Highlanders .30 .75
B12 Brian Kendrick/Paul London .60 1.50

2006 Topps Heritage II WWE Turkey Red Legends

COMPLETE SET (12) 6.00 15.00
STATED ODDS 1:6 HOBBY EXCLUSIVE

1 Rowdy Roddy Piper 1.00 2.50
2 Jake The Snake Roberts .60 1.50
3 Sgt. Slaughter .75 2.00
4 Chief Jay Strongbow .30 .75
5 Jerry The King Lawler .60 1.50
6 Gorilla Monsoon .30 .75
7 Iron Sheik .75 2.00
8 Junkyard Dog .75 2.00
9 Superstar Billy Graham .30 .75
10 Classy Freddie Blassie .30 .75
11 Bobby The Brain Heenan .50 1.25
12 Andre The Giant 1.00 2.50

2006 Topps Heritage II WWE Turkey Red Superstars

COMPLETE SET (12) 10.00 20.00
STATED ODDS 1:6 RETAIL EXCLUSIVE

1 John Cena 1.50 4.00
2 Batista 1.00 2.50
3 Carlito .60 1.50
4 Big Show 1.00 2.50
5 Shawn Michaels 1.00 2.50
6 Rey Mysterio .60 1.50
7 Kurt Angle 1.00 2.50
8 Edge 1.00 2.50
9 Rob Van Dam .60 1.50
10 Triple H 1.00 2.50
11 Hulk Hogan 1.25 3.00
12 Ric Flair 1.25 3.00

2007 Topps Heritage III WWE

COMPLETE SET (90) 8.00 20.00

1 John Cena 1.00 2.50
2 Batista .40 1.00
3 Rey Mysterio .40 1.00
4 Stone Cold Steve Austin 1.00 2.50
5 The Great Khali .15 .40
6 Carlito .60 1.50
7 Edge .40 1.00
8 Hardcore Holly .40 1.00
9 Umaga .25 .60
10 Montel Vontavious Porter RC .25 .60
11 Stevie Richards .25 .60
12 Deuce RC .15 .40
13 Lance Cade .15 .40
14 Super Crazy .25 .60
15 Chuck Palumbo .15 .40
16 Domino RC .15 .40
17 Trevor Murdoch .15 .40
18 Val Venis .40 1.00
19 Bobby Lashley .40 1.00
20 Mark Henry .25 .60
21 Boogeyman .15 .40
22 Brian Kendrick .25 .60
23 Tommy Dreamer .20 .50
24 Charlie Haas .15 .40
25 JBL .40 1.00
26 Armando Estrada RC .15 .40
27 CM Punk .60 1.50
28 Triple H .60 1.50
29 Shannon Moore .15 .40
30 Hacksaw Jim Duggan .25 .60
31 Jeff Hardy .40 1.00
32 Kane .40 1.00
33 Ron Simmons .25 .60
34 Finlay .40 1.00
35 The Miz RC .30 .75
36 Kenny Dykstra RC .25 .60
37 Snitsky .15 .40
38 Chris Masters .60 1.50
39 Santino Marella RC .20 .50
40 Cody Rhodes RC 8.00 20.00
41 Shelton Benjamin .15 .40
42 Hornswoggle RC .20 .50
43 Big Daddy V .40 1.00
44 Matt Striker .15 .40
45 Jamie Noble .15 .40
46 William Regal .40 1.00
47 Jimmy Wang Yang .15 .40
48 Elijah Burke RC .15 .40
49 Chavo Guerrero .25 .60
50 Paul London .40 1.00
51 Mr. Kennedy .40 1.00
52 John Morrison .25 .60
53 Matt Hardy .40 1.00
54 Shawn Michaels .60 1.50
55 Randy Orton .60 1.50
56 Ric Flair .60 1.50
57 Undertaker .75 2.00
58 Torrie Wilson DV 1.25 3.00
59 Candice DV .75 2.00
60 Michelle McCool DV .75 2.00
61 Melina DV .60 1.50
62 Cherry DV RC .15 .40
63 Jillian DV .75 2.00
64 Ashley DV .30 .75
65 Maria DV .60 1.50
66 Kelly Kelly DV RC .40 1.00
67 Mickie James DV .50 1.25
68 Maryse DV RC .30 .75
69 Victoria DV .30 .75
70 Anderson/Blanchard L .15 .40
71 Brian Pillman L .15 .40
72 Dean Malenko L .15 .40
73 Funk Brothers Dory & Terry L .15 .40
74 Dusty Rhodes L .40 1.00
75 The Freebirds L .15 .40
76 Jimmy Superfly Snuka L .25 .60
77 Jimmy Garvin L .15 .40
78 Papa Shango L .20 .50
79 Pat Patterson L .15 .40
80 Bam Bam Bigelow L .40 1.00
81 Gorilla Monsoon L .30 .75
82 Ted DiBiase L .30 .75
83 Rocky Johson L RC .25 .60
84 Bruiser Brody L RC .15 .40
85 Kamala L .20 .50
86 Earthquake L .25 .60
87 Vader L .25 .60
88 Jack and Gerry Brisco L .15 .40
89 Cowboy Bob Orton L .20 .50
90 John Cena CL 1.00 2.50

2007 Topps Heritage III WWE Allen and Ginter Legends

COMPLETE SET (12) 6.00 15.00
STATED ODDS 1:6 HOBBY EXCLUSIVE

1 Rowdy Roddy Piper 1.00 2.50
2 Chief Jay Strongbow .30 .75
3 Sgt. Slaughter .60 1.50
4 Iron Sheik .60 1.50
5 Don Muraco .20 .50
6 Ravishing Rick Rude .60 1.50
7 Classy Freddie Blassie .30 .75
8 Bobby The Brain Heenan .60 1.50
9 The British Bulldog .60 1.50
10 Jake The Snake Roberts .60 1.50
11 Nikolai Volkoff .60 1.50
12 Junkyard Dog 1.00 2.50

2007 Topps Heritage III WWE Allen and Ginter Superstars

COMPLETE SET (12) 10.00 25.00
STATED ODDS 1:6 RETAIL EXCLUSIVE

1 John Cena 1.50 4.00
2 Batista .75 2.00
3 Rey Mysterio .60 1.50
4 Carlito .60 1.50
5 Edge .75 2.00
6 Bobby Lashley .60 1.50
7 Mr. Kennedy .75 2.00
8 Triple H 1.50 4.00
9 Shawn Michaels 1.25 3.00
10 Undertaker 1.25 3.00
11 Ric Flair 1.25 3.00
12 Booker T .75 2.00

2007 Topps Heritage III WWE Allen and Ginter Tin Inserts

STATED ODDS 1:1 TIN EXCLUSIVES

1 John Cena
2 Batista
3 Ric Flair
4 Undertaker
5 Edge
6 Shawn Michaels

2007 Topps Heritage III WWE Autographs

STATED ODDS 1:24 HOBBY EXCLUSIVE

NNO Candice 8.00 20.00
NNO Carlito 6.00 15.00
NNO Cherry 6.00 15.00
NNO Chuck Palumbo 6.00 15.00
NNO CM Punk 75.00 150.00
NNO Deuce 6.00 15.00
NNO Domino 6.00 15.00
NNO Hacksaw Jim Duggan 15.00 40.00
NNO Jeff Hardy 20.00 50.00
NNO John Cena 75.00 150.00
NNO Kane 12.00 30.00
NNO Kelly Kelly 20.00 50.00
NNO Lance Cade 6.00 15.00
NNO Maria 12.00 30.00
NNO Miz 12.00 30.00
NNO Montel Vontavious Porter 8.00 20.00
NNO Randy Orton 25.00 60.00
NNO Stevie Richards 6.00 15.00
NNO Super Crazy 6.00 15.00
NNO Torrie Wilson 10.00 25.00
NNO Trevor Murdoch 6.00 15.00
NNO Victoria 12.00 30.00

2007 Topps Heritage III WWE Event-Used Mat Ringside Relics

STATED ODDS 1:24 RETAIL EXCLUSIVE

NNO John Cena/Randy Orton 4.00 10.00
NNO Rey Mysterio/Chavo Guerrero 3.00 8.00
NNO Triple H/King Booker 4.00 10.00

2007 Topps Heritage III WWE Ringside Relics

STATED ODDS 1:24 HOBBY EXCLUSIVE

NNO Bobby Lashley 5.00 10.00
NNO Carlito 5.00 10.00
NNO John Cena 6.00 12.00
NNO Matt Hardy 5.00 10.00
NNO Mr. Kennedy 5.00 10.00

2007 Topps Heritage III WWE Magnets

COMPLETE SET (9) 6.00 15.00
STATED ODDS 1:4 RETAIL

1 John Cena 1.50 4.00
2 Batista .60 1.50
3 Rey Mysterio .60 1.50
4 Carlito 1.00 2.50
5 Edge .60 1.50
6 Bobby Lashley .60 1.50

Card	Low	High
7 Mr. Kennedy	.60	1.50
8 Triple H	1.00	2.50
9 Ric Flair	1.00	2.50

2007 Topps Heritage III WWE Ringside Bonus

COMPLETE SET (16) 25.00 60.00
STATED ODDS 4:1 WAL-MART BLASTER

Card	Low	High
R1 John Cena	5.00	12.00
R2 Carlito	2.50	6.00
R3 CM Punk	2.50	6.00
R4 Randy Orton	4.00	10.00
R5 Hornswoggle	1.50	4.00
R6 Jamie Noble	1.50	4.00
R7 Super Crazy	1.50	4.00
R8 Great Khali	2.50	6.00
R9 Jeff Hardy	3.00	8.00
R10 Matt Hardy	3.00	8.00
R11 Chavo Guerrero	1.50	4.00
R12 Finlay	1.50	4.00
R13 Kane	3.00	8.00
R14 Hardcore Holly	2.50	6.00
R15 Rey Mysterio	3.00	8.00
R16 Jimmy Wang Yang	1.50	4.00

2007 Topps Heritage III WWE Ringside Rookie Bonus

COMPLETE SET (4) 10.00 25.00
STATED ODDS 1:1 WAL-MART BLASTER

Card	Low	High
RK1 Cody Rhodes	4.00	10.00
RK2 Santino Marella	4.00	10.00
RK3 Deuce	3.00	8.00
RK4 Domino	3.00	8.00

2007 Topps Heritage III WWE Superstar Team

Card	Low	High
1 Brian Kendrick/Paul London	.20	.50
2 C.Haas/S.Benjamin	.12	.30
3 Lance Cade/Trevor Murdoch	.12	.30

2007 Topps Heritage III WWE Superstar Team Oversized

COMPLETE SET (3)
STATED ODDS 1:1 HOBBY EXCLUSIVES

1 Brian Kendrick/Paul London
2 Charlie Haas/Shelton Benjamin
3 Lance Cade/Trevor Murdoch

2007 Topps Heritage III WWE Tin Inserts

COMPLETE SET (6)
STATED ODDS 1:1 TIN EXCLUSIVES

B1 John Cena
B2 Batista
B3 Ric Flair
B4 Undertaker
B5 Edge
B6 Shawn Michaels

2008 Topps Heritage IV WWE

COMPLETE SET (90) 8.00 20.00

Card	Low	High
1 Armando Estrada	.12	.30
2 Ricky Ortiz RC	.12	.30
3 Bam Neely RC	.12	.30
4 Batista	.50	1.25
5 Big Show	.30	.75
6 Brian Kendrick	.20	.50
7 Carlito	.30	.75
8 Chavo Guerrero	.20	.50
9 Chris Jericho	.30	.75
10 CM Punk	.12	.30
11 Cody Rhodes	.12	.30
12 Undertaker	.60	1.50
13 Curt Hawkins	.12	.30
14 D-Lo Brown	.20	.50
15 Edge	.50	1.25
16 Evan Bourne RC	.12	.30
17 Ezekiel RC	.20	.50
18 Festus RC	.12	.30
19 Finlay	.20	.50
20 The Great Khali	.12	.30
21 Hardcore Holly	.20	.50
22 Hornswoggle	.20	.50
23 Jamie Noble	.12	.30
24 John Bradshaw Layfield	.12	.30
25 Jeff Hardy	.50	1.25
26 Jesse RC	.12	.30
27 John Cena	.75	2.00
28 John Morrison	.12	.30
29 JTG	.12	.30
30 Kane	.50	1.25
31 Kofi Kingston RC	.20	.50
32 Lance Cade	.12	.30
33 Mark Henry	.20	.50
34 Matt Hardy	.50	1.25
35 Primo Colon RC	.12	.30
36 Mike Knox	.12	.30
37 The Miz	.20	.50
38 Mr. Kennedy	.30	.75
39 MVP	.20	.50
40 Paul Burchill	.12	.30
41 Randy Orton	.30	.75
42 Rey Mysterio	.30	.75
43 Santino Marella	.12	.30
44 Shad	.12	.30
45 Shawn Michaels	.75	2.00
46 Shelton Benjamin	.12	.30
47 Snitsky	.20	.50
48 Super Crazy	.20	.50
49 Ted DiBiase Jr. RC	.30	.75
50 Tommy Dreamer	.12	.30
51 Tony Atlas	.12	.30
52 Triple H	.75	2.00
53 Umaga	.20	.50
54 Vladimir Kozlov RC	.20	.50
55 Zack Ryder	.12	.30
56 Tiffany DV RC	.60	1.50
57 Beth Phoenix DV	.60	1.50
58 Candice DV	.60	1.50
59 Eve DV RC	.50	1.25
60 Jillian DV	.50	1.25
61 Katie Lea Burchill DV RC	.50	1.25
62 Kelly Kelly DV	.50	1.25
63 Layla DV	.50	1.25
64 Lilian Garcia DV	.50	1.25
65 Maria DV	.50	1.25
66 Maryse DV	.50	1.25
67 Melina DV	.50	1.25
68 Michelle McCool DV	.60	1.50
69 Mickie James DV	.75	2.00
70 Natalya DV RC	.50	1.25
71 Victoria DV	.60	1.50
72 Tazz/Jim Ross A	.12	.30
73 Jerry Lawler/Michael Cole A	.12	.30
74 Matt Striker/Todd Grisham A	.12	.30
75 Bobby The Brain Heenan	.50	1.25
76 Brian Pillman L	.20	.50
77 Gerald Brisco L	.20	.50
78 Jack Brisco L RC	.20	.50
79 Mr. Perfect Curt Hennig	.30	.75
80 Mr. Wonderful Paul Orndorff	.30	.75
81 Rowdy Roddy Piper	.50	1.25
82 Superfly Jimmy Snuka	.30	.75
83 British Bulldog L	.30	.75
84 Hillbilly Jim L	.30	.75
85 Junkyard Dog L	.30	.75
86 Mean Gene Okerlund	.30	.75
87 Ted DiBiase L	.30	.75
88 Tully Blanchard L	.20	.50
89 Dusty Rhodes L	.30	.75
90 Checklist	.12	.30

2008 Topps Heritage IV WWE Allen and Ginter Legends

COMPLETE SET (12) 6.00 15.00
STATED ODDS 1:6 HOBBY

Card	Low	High
1 Bobby The Brain Heenan	.60	1.50
2 Junkyard Dog	1.00	2.50
3 Hillbilly Jim	.60	1.50
4 British Bulldog	.60	1.50
5 Mean Gene Okerlund	.60	1.50
6 Mr. Perfect Curt Hennig	.40	1.00
7 Rowdy Roddy Piper	1.00	2.50
8 Jimmy Superfly Snuka	.60	1.50
9 Mr. Wonderful Paul Orndorff	.40	1.00
10 Ted DiBiase	.60	1.50
11 Tully Blanchard	.40	1.00
12 Brian Pillman	.40	1.00

2008 Topps Heritage IV WWE Allen and Ginter Superstars

COMPLETE SET (12) 10.00 25.00
STATED ODDS 1:6 RETAIL EXCLUSIVE

Card	Low	High
1 Batista	2.00	5.00
2 John Cena	3.00	8.00
3 Chavo Guerrero	1.25	3.00
4 Chris Jericho	1.25	3.00
5 Edge	2.00	5.00
6 Triple H	3.00	8.00
7 Jeff Hardy	2.00	5.00
8 Matt Hardy	2.00	5.00
9 Mr. Kennedy	1.25	3.00
10 CM Punk	1.25	3.00
11 Rey Mysterio	1.25	3.00
12 Undertaker	2.50	6.00

2008 Topps Heritage IV WWE Autographs

RANDOM INSERTS IN PACKS
STATED ODDS 1:24 HOBBY/TARGET/WALMART

Card	Low	High
NNO Beth Phoenix	12.00	30.00
NNO Carlito	25.00	60.00
NNO Chavo Guerrero	8.00	20.00
NNO Cody Rhodes	15.00	40.00
NNO Deuce	6.00	15.00
NNO John Cena	75.00	150.00
NNO Kofi Kingston	12.00	30.00
NNO Layla	15.00	40.00
NNO Matt Hardy	12.00	30.00
NNO Mickie James	75.00	150.00
NNO Natalya	12.00	30.00
NNO Tazz	6.00	15.00
NNO Ted DiBiase Jr.	12.00	30.00

2008 Topps Heritage IV WWE Blister Bonus

COMPLETE SET (3)
RANDOMLY INSERTED INTO PACKS
RETAIL EXCLUSIVE

1 Edge
2 John Cena
3 Matt Hardy

2008 Topps Heritage IV WWE Magnets

COMPLETE SET (9) 12.00 30.00
STATED ODDS 1:4 RETAIL EXCLUSIVE

Card	Low	High
1 John Cena	3.00	8.00
2 Mr. Kennedy	1.25	3.00
3 CM Punk	2.50	6.00
4 Chris Jericho	1.25	3.00
5 Batista	2.00	5.00
6 Triple H	3.00	8.00
7 Edge	2.00	5.00
8 Mickie James	3.00	8.00
9 Melina	2.00	5.00

2008 Topps Heritage IV WWE Mat Relics

STATED ODDS 1:24 RETAIL EXCLUSIVES

Card	Low	High
NNO Batista vs. Paul Burchill	3.00	8.00
NNO John Cena vs. Cody Rhodes	5.00	12.00
NNO John Cena vs. Ted DiBiase	5.00	12.00

2008 Topps Heritage IV WWE Ringside Rookies

COMPLETE SET (4) 15.00 40.00
STATED ODDS 1:WALMART BLASTER

Card	Low	High
RK1 Ted DiBiase Jr.	8.00	20.00
RK2 Vladimir Kozlov	4.00	10.00
RK3 Evan Bourne	5.00	12.00
RK4 Natalya	8.00	20.00

2008 Topps Heritage IV WWE Ringside Superstars

COMPLETE SET (16) 30.00 80.00
STATED ODDS 4:1 WALMART BLASTER

Card	Low	High
R1 John Cena	6.00	15.00
R2 Batista	4.00	10.00
R3 CM Punk	2.00	5.00
R4 Rey Mysterio	2.50	6.00
R5 Triple H	6.00	15.00
R6 Undertaker	5.00	12.00
R7 MVP	2.00	5.00
R8 Jeff Hardy	4.00	10.00
R9 Matt Hardy	4.00	10.00
R10 Tommy Dreamer	2.00	5.00
R11 Mark Henry	2.00	5.00
R12 John Morrison	2.00	5.00
R13 Mickie James	6.00	15.00
R14 Beth Phoenix	5.00	12.00
R15 Candice	5.00	12.00
R16 Michelle McCool	5.00	12.00

2008 Topps Heritage IV WWE Shirt Relics

STATED ODDS

Card	Low	High
NNO Jeff Hardy	7.50	15.00
NNO MVP	6.00	12.00
NNO Rey Mysterio	6.00	12.00

2008 Topps Heritage IV WWE Tin Inserts

COMPLETE SET (6) 12.00 30.00
STATED ODDS 1:TIN RETAIL EXCLUSIVE

Card	Low	High
1 John Cena	4.00	10.00
2 Rey Mysterio	2.50	6.00
3 Shawn Michaels	4.00	10.00
4 Edge	2.50	6.00
5 Randy Orton	2.50	6.00
6 Triple H	4.00	10.00

2005 Topps Heritage WWE

COMPLETE SET (90) 20.00 50.00

Card	Low	High
1 John Cena	1.25	3.00
2 Batista	.50	1.25
3 Carlito RC	.50	1.25
4 Orlando Jordan	.25	.60
5 Paul London	.25	.60
6 Johnny Nitro RC	.60	1.50
7 Joey Mercury RC	.25	.60
8 Hurricane	.25	.60
9 Rosey	.25	.60
10 The Rock	1.25	3.00
11 Stone Cold Steve Austin	1.50	4.00
12 Hulk Hogan	1.25	3.00
13 Big Show	1.00	2.50
14 Chris Jericho	.75	2.00
15 Danny Basham	.25	.60
16 Edge	.60	1.50
17 Eric Bischoff	.40	1.00
18 Eugene	.60	1.50
19 Jim Ross	.40	1.00
20 Jonathan Coachman	.25	.60
21 Kane	.75	2.00
22 Heidenreich	.25	.60
23 Kurt Angle	1.25	3.00
24 Rene Dupree	.25	.60
25 Ric Flair	1.00	2.50
26 Rob Van Dam	.60	1.50
27 Shawn Michaels	.75	2.00
28 Tajiri	.25	.60
29 Triple H	.60	1.50
30 Kerwin White RC	.25	.60
31 Val Venis	.40	1.00
32 Viscera	.25	.60
33 Steven Richards	.25	.60
34 Booker T	.40	1.00
35 Chris Benoit	.60	1.50
36 Christian	.75	2.00
37 Doug Basham	.25	.60
38 Eddie Guerrero	.60	1.50
39 Funaki	.25	.60
40 Hardcore Holly	.40	1.00
41 JBL	.40	1.00
42 Juventud	.25	.60
43 Psicosis	.25	.60
44 Super Crazy RC	.25	.60
45 Shelton Benjamin	.25	.60
46 Chris Masters RC	.25	.60

Card	Low	High
47 Nunzio	.25	.60
48 Randy Orton	.25	.60
49 Rey Mysterio	.60	1.50
50 Scotty 2 Hotty	.40	1.00
51 Tazz	.25	.60
52 Theodore Long	.25	.60
53 Undertaker	1.25	3.00
54 William Regal	.40	1.00
55 Antonio	.25	.60
56 Romeo RC	.25	.60
57 Snitsky RC	.25	.60
58 Robert Conway	.25	.60
59 Sharmell DV	1.25	3.00
60 Trish Stratus DV	2.50	6.00
61 Torrie Wilson DV	.75	2.00
62 Christy Hemme DV RC	.75	2.00
63 Lita DV	1.50	4.00
64 Lilian Garcia DV	1.25	3.00
65 Maria DV RC	1.50	4.00
66 Stacy Keibler DV	2.50	6.00
67 Victoria DV	1.50	4.00
68 Candice Michelle DV RC	.60	1.50
69 Michelle McCool DV RC	1.25	3.00
70 Melina DV RC	1.25	3.00
71 The British Bulldog L	.40	1.00
72 Chief Jay Strongbow L	.25	.60
73 Classy Freddie Blassie L	.25	.60
74 Cowboy Bob Orton L	.40	1.00
75 Bobby The Brain Heenan L	.40	1.00
76 Gorilla Monsoon L	.25	.60
77 Hillbilly Jim L	.40	1.00
78 Iron Sheik L	.60	1.50
79 Jake The Snake Roberts L	.60	1.50
80 Jerry The King Lawler L	.60	1.50
81 Junkyard Dog L	.60	1.50
82 Mouth of the South Jimmy Hart L	.75	2.00
83 Mr. Wonderful Paul Orndorff L	.75	2.00
84 Nikolai Volkoff L	.40	1.00
85 Rowdy Roddy Piper L	1.00	2.50
86 Sgt. Slaughter L	.60	1.50
87 Superstar Billy Graham L	.40	1.00
88 Ted DiBiase L	.75	2.00
89 Godfather L	.25	.60
90 Hogan/Cena/Batista CL	1.25	3.00

2005 Topps Heritage WWE Autographs

OVERALL STATED ODDS 1:36
HEMME ODDS 1:1574 H
ANGLE, HOGAN, SHIEK ODDS 1:530 H
MICHAELS, SLAUGHTER, WILSON ODDS 1:520 H
CENA, KANE, KIEBLER, LAWLER, PIPER, STRATUS, STRONBOW ODDS 1:510
HILLBILLY, HEENAN ODDS 1:473 RETAIL

Card	Low	High
NNO Bobby The Brain Heenan RET	60.00	150.00
NNO Chief Jay Strongbow	20.00	50.00
NNO Christy Hemme	40.00	100.00
NNO Hillbilly Jim RET	25.00	60.00
NNO Hulk Hogan	250.00	600.00
NNO Iron Sheik	15.00	100.00
NNO Jerry The King Lawler	25.00	60.00
NNO John Cena	150.00	400.00
NNO Kane	25.00	60.00
NNO Kurt Angle	25.00	60.00
NNO Lita	25.00	60.00
NNO Rowdy Roddy Piper	150.00	400.00
NNO Sgt. Slaughter	20.00	50.00
NNO Shawn Michaels	75.00	200.00
NNO Stacy Keibler	60.00	150.00
NNO Torrie Wilson	30.00	75.00
NNO Trish Stratus	40.00	100.00

2005 Topps Heritage WWE Event-Used Mat Ringside Relics

STATED ODDS 1:12 RETAIL EXCLUSIVES

Card	Low	High
NNO Booker T/Christian	2.50	6.00
NNO Rey Mysterio/Eddie Guerrero	6.00	15.00
NNO JBL/Batista	2.50	6.00

2005 Topps Heritage WWE Event-Worn Ringside Relics

OVERALL STATED ODDS 1:17
EUGENE ODDS 1:214
MICHAELS ODDS 1:196
ANGLE ODDS 1:185
JERICHO ODDS 1:158
TRIPLE H ODDS 1:104
CENA ODDS 1:89
HOGAN ODDS 1:70

Card	Low	High
NNO Chris Jericho	6.00	15.00
NNO Eugene	8.00	20.00
NNO Hulk Hogan	15.00	40.00
NNO John Cena	8.00	20.00
NNO Kurt Angle	8.00	20.00
NNO Shawn Michaels	10.00	25.00
NNO Triple H	10.00	25.00

2005 Topps Heritage WWE Stickers

Card	Low	High
COMPLETE SET (10)	8.00	20.00
STATED ODDS 1:4 HOBBY		
1 Hulk Hogan	2.00	5.00
2 The Rock	2.00	5.00
3 Batista	.75	2.00
4 Shawn Michaels	1.25	3.00
5 Carlito	.75	2.00
6 Kurt Angle	1.00	2.50
7 Triple H	1.00	2.50
8 John Cena	2.00	5.00
9 Torrie Wilson	1.25	3.00
10 Christy Hemme	1.25	3.00

2005 Topps Heritage WWE World's Greatest Wrestling Managers DVD Promos

STATED ODDS 1:SET PER DVD

Card	Low	High
V1 Bobby The Brain Heenan	1.25	3.00
V2 Classy Freddie Blassie	.60	1.50
V3 Mouth of the South Jimmy Hart	2.00	5.00
V4 Paul Bearer	1.25	3.00

2005 Topps Heritage WWE Promo

Card	Low	High
NNO John Cena	2.00	5.00

2012 Topps Heritage WWE

Card	Low	High
COMPLETE SET (110)	10.00	25.00
*SILVER: .75X TO 2X BASIC CARDS		
*BLACK: 5X TO 12X BASIC CARDS		
*GOLD/10: UNPRICED DUE TO SCARCITY		
1 AJ Lee	.75	2.00
2 Aksana RC	.40	1.00
3 Alberto Del Rio	.40	1.00
4 Alicia Fox	.25	.60
5 Beth Phoenix	.40	1.00
6 Big Show	.40	1.00
7 Brock Lesnar	.60	1.50
8 Brodus Clay	.15	.40
9 Cameron RC	.25	.60
10 Chris Jericho	.60	1.50
11 Christian	.15	.40
12 CM Punk	.60	1.50
13 Cody Rhodes	.15	.40
14 Damien Sandow RC	.15	.40
15 Daniel Bryan	.15	.40
16 Dolph Ziggler	.25	.60
17 Eve	.60	1.50
18 Jack Swagger	.25	.60
19 John Cena	.75	2.00
20 Kaitlyn	.40	1.00
21 Kane	.40	1.00
22 Ryback	.15	.40
23 Kofi Kingston	.15	.40
24 Layla	.40	1.00
25 Lilian Garcia	.40	1.00
26 Mark Henry	.25	.60
27 The Miz	.25	.60
28 Naomi RC	.25	.60
29 Natalya	.60	1.50
30 R-Truth	.15	.40
31 Randy Orton	.60	1.50
32 Rey Mysterio	.40	1.00
33 The Rock	.75	2.00
34 Rosa Mendes	.25	.60
35 Santino Marella	.25	.60
36 Sheamus	.40	1.00
37 Kama Mustafa	.15	.40
38 Tamina Snuka	.25	.60
39 Tensai	.15	.40
40 Triple H	.60	1.50
41 Tyson Kidd	.15	.40
42 Undertaker	.60	1.50
43 Zack Ryder	.15	.40
44 Batista	.25	.60
45 Booker T	.25	.60
46 Cactus Jack	.60	1.50
47 Dude Love	.60	1.50
48 Jerry The King Lawler	.40	1.00
49 Jim Ross	.15	.40
50 Kevin Nash	.25	.60
51 Mankind	.60	1.50
52 Mick Foley	.60	1.50
53 Shawn Michaels	.60	1.50
54 Stone Cold Steve Austin	.75	2.00
55 Trish Stratus	.75	2.00
56 Akeem	.15	.40
57 The American Dream Dusty Rhodes	.25	.60
58 Andre The Giant	.75	2.00
59 Arn Anderson	.25	.60
60 Barry Windham	.25	.60
61 Big Boss Man	.15	.40
62 Big John Studd	.25	.60
63 Bobby The Brain Heenan	.25	.60
64 Brian Pillman	.25	.60
65 The British Bulldog	.25	.60
66 Bushwhacker Butch	.15	.40
67 Bushwhacker Luke	.15	.40
68 Chief Jay Strongbow	.25	.60
69 Classy Freddie Blassie	.25	.60
70 Cowboy Bob Orton	.25	.60
71 Dean Malenko	.25	.60
72 Doink The Clown	.25	.60
73 Don Muraco	.25	.60
74 The Godfather	.15	.40
75 Gorilla Monsoon	.25	.60
76 Greg The Hammer Valentine	.25	.60
77 Hacksaw Jim Duggan	.25	.60
78 Harley Race	.25	.60
79 Hillbilly Jim	.25	.60
80 Howard Finkel RC	.25	.60
81 The Iron Sheik	.25	.60
82 Irwin R. Schyster	.15	.40
83 Jake The Snake Roberts	.25	.60
84 Jimmy Superfly Snuka	.25	.60
85 Junkyard Dog	.25	.60
86 Sin Cara	.40	1.00
87 Kamala	.25	.60
88 Koko B. Ware	.25	.60
89 Mean Gene Okerlund	.25	.60
90 Michael PS Hayes	.15	.40
91 Ted DiBiase	.25	.60
92 Mr. Perfect	.25	.60
93 Mr. Wonderful Paul Orndorff	.25	.60
94 Nikolai Volkoff	.25	.60
95 One Man Gang	.15	.40
96 Papa Shango	.15	.40
97 Paul Bearer	.15	.40
98 Ravishing Rick Rude	.25	.60
99 Ricky The Dragon Steamboat	.25	.60
100 Road Warrior Animal	.25	.60
101 Road Warrior Hawk	.25	.60
102 Rocky Johnson	.25	.60
103 Rowdy Roddy Piper	.40	1.00
104 Sgt. Slaughter	.25	.60
105 Terry Funk	.25	.60
106 Tito Santana	.25	.60
107 Tom Prichard RC	.15	.40
108 Tully Blanchard	.25	.60
109 Vader	.25	.60
110 Yokozuna	.25	.60

2012 Topps Heritage WWE Allen and Ginter

Card	Low	High
COMPLETE SET (30)	30.00	75.00
STATED ODDS 1:6 HOBBY AND RETAIL		
1 Brock Lesnar	3.00	8.00
2 Christian	.75	2.00
3 CM Punk	3.00	8.00
4 Daniel Bryan	.75	2.00
5 John Cena	4.00	10.00
6 Kelly Kelly	3.00	8.00
7 Kofi Kingston	.75	2.00
8 Layla	2.00	5.00
9 Randy Orton	3.00	8.00
10 Sheamus	2.00	5.00
11 Booker T	1.25	3.00
12 Diesel	1.25	3.00
13 Mankind	3.00	8.00
14 Stone Cold Steve Austin	4.00	10.00
15 Trish Stratus	4.00	10.00
16 The American Dream Dusty Rhodes	1.25	3.00
17 Andre The Giant	4.00	10.00
18 Big Boss Man	.75	2.00
19 Big John Studd	1.25	3.00
20 Cowboy Bob Orton	1.25	3.00
21 Doink The Clown	1.25	3.00
22 Hacksaw Jim Duggan	1.25	3.00
23 Kamala	1.25	3.00
24 Koko B. Ware	1.25	3.00
25 Papa Shango	.75	2.00
26 Paul Bearer	.75	2.00
27 Ricky The Dragon Steamboat	1.25	3.00
28 Terry Funk	1.25	3.00
29 Vader	1.25	3.00
30 Yokozuna	1.25	3.00

2012 Topps Heritage WWE Andre the Giant Tribute

Card	Low	High
COMPLETE SET (10)	8.00	20.00
*SILVER/85: 1X TO 2.5X BASIC CARDS		
*GOLD/10: UNPRICED DUE TO SCARCITY		
STATED ODDS 1:8 HOBBY AND RETAIL		
1 Andre the Giant	1.25	3.00
2 Andre the Giant	1.25	3.00
3 Andre the Giant	1.25	3.00
4 Andre the Giant	1.25	3.00
5 Andre the Giant	1.25	3.00
6 Andre the Giant	1.25	3.00
7 Andre the Giant	1.25	3.00
8 Andre the Giant	1.25	3.00
9 Andre the Giant	1.25	3.00
10 Andre the Giant	1.25	3.00

2012 Topps Heritage WWE Autographs

STATED ODDS HOBBY EXCLUSIVE 1:44
STATED ODDS RETAIL EXCLUSIVE 1:120

Card	Low	High
NNO Akeem	25.00	60.00
NNO Cameron	15.00	40.00
NNO CM Punk	50.00	100.00
NNO Doink The Clown	100.00	200.00
NNO The Godfather	25.00	60.00
NNO Howard Finkel	20.00	50.00
NNO Irwin R. Schyster	25.00	60.00
NNO Jake The Snake Roberts	20.00	50.00
NNO John Cena	75.00	150.00
NNO Kama Mustafa	10.00	25.00
NNO Kamala	15.00	40.00
NNO Layla	10.00	25.00
NNO Mean Gene Okerlund	15.00	40.00
NNO Michael PS Hayes	10.00	25.00
NNO Naomi	15.00	40.00
NNO Natalya	12.00	30.00
NNO One Man Gang	25.00	60.00
NNO Papa Shango	20.00	50.00
NNO Paul Bearer	75.00	150.00
NNO Vader	30.00	75.00

2012 Topps Heritage WWE Fabled Tag Teams

Card	Low	High
COMPLETE SET (10)	6.00	15.00
STATED ODDS 1:12 HOBBY AND RETAIL		
1 Nikolai Volkoff/Iron Sheik	.75	2.00
2 The Brain Busters	.75	2.00
3 Big Boss Man/Akeem	.50	1.25
4 The Road Warriors	.75	2.00
5 The Bushwhackers	.50	1.25
6 Money Inc	.75	2.00
7 The Rock N Sock Connection	2.50	6.00
8 The Brothers of Destruction	2.00	5.00
9 The Two-Man Power Trip	2.50	6.00
10 D-Generation X	2.00	5.00

2012 Topps Heritage WWE Family History

COMPLETE SET (10) 6.00 15.00
STATED ODDS 1:8 HOBBY AND RETAIL

1	B.Orton/R.Orton	2.00	5.00
2	T.DiBiase Sr./T.DiBiase Jr.	.75	2.00
3	J.Snuka/T.Snuka	.75	2.00
4	R.Johnson/The Rock	2.50	6.00
5	Yokozuna/The Usos	.75	2.00
6	B.Bulldog/Natalya	2.00	5.00
7	D.Rhodes/C.Rhodes	.75	2.00
8	Animal/J.Laurinaitis	.50	1.25
9	Mr. Perfect/M.McGillicutty	.75	2.00
10	P.Bearer/Kane	1.25	3.00

2012 Topps Heritage WWE Jerry the King Lawler Portraits

COMPLETE SET (10) 12.00 30.00
STATED ODDS 1:24 HOBBY AND RETAIL

1	Big Show	2.50	6.00
2	Brodus Clay	1.00	2.50
3	CM Punk	4.00	10.00
4	Hornswoggle	1.50	4.00
5	Kelly Kelly	4.00	10.00
6	Rey Mysterio	2.50	6.00
7	Santino Marella	1.50	4.00
8	Sheamus	2.50	6.00
9	The Miz	1.50	4.00
10	Undertaker	4.00	10.00

2012 Topps Heritage WWE Ringside Action

COMPLETE SET (55) 10.00 25.00
STATED ODDS 1:1 HOBBY AND RETAIL

1	Superfly Splash	.60	1.50
2	Double A Spinebuster	.60	1.50
3	Stone Cold Stunner	2.00	5.00
4	Perfect-Plex	.60	1.50
5	Cobra Clutch	.60	1.50
6	DDT	.60	1.50
7	Flying Fist Drop	1.00	2.50
8	Figure Four Leglock	.60	1.50
9	Mandible Claw	1.50	4.00
10	Jackknife Powerbomb	.60	1.50
11	Superplex	.60	1.50
12	Running Powerslam	.60	1.50
13	Doomsday Device	.60	1.50
14	Bionic Elbow	.60	1.50
15	Camel Clutch	.60	1.50
16	Flying Cross-body Press	.60	1.50
17	Three Point Stance Clothesline	.60	1.50
18	Scissor Kick	.60	1.50
19	Rude Awakening	.60	1.50
20	Chokeslam	1.00	2.50
21	Lariat	.60	1.50
22	Texas Cloverleaf	.60	1.50
23	Flying Splash	.60	1.50
24	Million Dollar Dream	.60	1.50
25	Rock Bottom	2.00	5.00
26	F-5	1.50	4.00
27	Battering Ram	.40	1.00
28	The Write-Off	.40	1.00
29	Killswitch	.40	1.00
30	Sidewalk Slam	.40	1.00
31	Flying Forearm	.60	1.50
32	Pimp Drop/The Godfather	.40	1.00
33	The Whoopie Cushion		
34	Diving Headbutt	.60	1.50
35	STF	.40	1.00
36	619	1.00	2.50
38	G.T.S. (Go to Sleep)	1.50	4.00
39	World's Strongest Slam	.60	1.50
40	RKO	1.50	4.00
41	Moonsault Side Slam	1.00	2.50
42	Vader Bomb	.60	1.50
43	Air Pillman	.60	1.50
44	The Claw	.40	1.00
45	Banzai Drop	.60	1.50
46	Wasteland	.40	1.00
47	Brogue Kick	1.00	2.50
48	Attitude Adjustment	2.00	5.00
49	Reverse Piledriver	.60	1.50
50	Knockout Punch	.60	1.50
51	The Walls of Jericho	1.50	4.00
52	Sweet Chin Music	1.50	4.00
53	Batista Bomb	.60	1.50
54	Pedigree	1.50	4.00
55	Yes! Lock	.40	1.00
86	Dream Street	.60	1.50

2012 Topps Heritage WWE Shirt Relics

TWO AUTO OR MEM PER HOBBY BOX
STATED ODDS 1:97 RETAIL

NNO	Alberto Del Rio/Scarf	6.00	15.00
NNO	Batista	6.00	15.00
NNO	CM Punk	6.00	15.00
NNO	Cody Rhodes	5.00	12.00
NNO	Daniel Bryan	5.00	12.00
NNO	Dolph Ziggler	6.00	15.00
NNO	John Cena	8.00	20.00
NNO	Kofi Kingston	5.00	12.00
NNO	Mark Henry	5.00	12.00
NNO	The Miz	5.00	12.00
NNO	Randy Orton	6.00	15.00
NNO	Rey Mysterio	6.00	15.00
NNO	R-Truth	5.00	12.00
NNO	Santino Marella	5.00	12.00
NNO	Sheamus	5.00	12.00
NNO	Stone Cold Steve Austin	8.00	20.00
NNO	Wade Barrett	5.00	12.00
NNO	Zack Ryder	5.00	12.00

2012 Topps Heritage WWE Stickers

COMPLETE SET (18) 10.00 25.00
STATED ODDS 1:4 HOBBY AND RETAIL

1	Ricky The Dragon Steamboat	.75	2.00
2	Rey Mysterio	1.25	3.00
3	Trish Stratus	2.50	6.00
4	Undertaker	2.00	5.00
5	Mankind	2.00	5.00
6	Ravishing Rick Rude	.75	2.00
7	Sin Cara	1.25	3.00
8	Vader	.75	2.00
9	Dude Love	2.00	5.00
10	Jake The Snake Roberts	.75	2.00
11	Gorilla Monsoon	.75	2.00
12	Greg The Hammer Valentine	.75	2.00
13	Rowdy Roddy Piper	1.25	3.00
14	Doink The Clown	.75	2.00
15	Booker T	.75	2.00
16	Koko B. Ware	.75	2.00
17	Kamala	.75	2.00
18	Kane	1.25	3.00

2012 Topps Heritage WWE The Superstars Speak

COMPLETE SET (20) 8.00 20.00
STATED ODDS 1:4 HOBBY AND RETAIL

1	Stone Cold Steve Austin	2.00	5.00
2	Cactus Jack	1.50	4.00
3	Booker T	.60	1.50
4	Road Warrior Hawk	.60	1.50
5	Gorilla Monsoon	.60	1.50
6	Rowdy Roddy Piper	1.00	2.50
7	The American Dream Dusty Rhodes	.60	1.50
8	Classy Freddie Blassie	.60	1.50
9	The Iron Sheik	.60	1.50
10	Trish Stratus	2.00	5.00
11	The Rock	2.00	5.00
12	Mr. Perfect	.60	1.50
13	Kevin Nash	.60	1.50
14	Mankind	1.50	4.00
15	Hacksaw Jim Duggan	.60	1.50
16	Jim Ross	.40	1.00
17	Vader	.60	1.50
18	Ted DiBiase	.60	1.50
19	Yokozuna	.40	1.00
20	Sgt. Slaughter	.60	1.50

2012 Topps Heritage WWE Wrestlemania XXVII Mat Relics

TWO AUTO OR MEM PER HOBBY BOX
STATED ODDS 1:97 RETAIL

NNO	Alberto Del Rio	6.00	15.00
NNO	Big Show	6.00	15.00
NNO	Booker T	4.00	10.00
NNO	Christian	4.00	10.00
NNO	CM Punk	6.00	15.00
NNO	Cody Rhodes	5.00	12.00
NNO	Dolph Ziggler	4.00	10.00
NNO	Ezekiel Jackson	4.00	10.00
NNO	Heath Slater	4.00	10.00
NNO	Jerry The King Lawler	5.00	12.00
NNO	John Cena	6.00	15.00
NNO	Justin Gabriel	5.00	12.00
NNO	Kane	5.00	12.00
NNO	Kofi Kingston	5.00	12.00
NNO	Layla	6.00	15.00
NNO	Michael Cole	4.00	10.00
NNO	The Miz	4.00	10.00
NNO	Randy Orton	6.00	15.00
NNO	The Rock	8.00	20.00
NNO	Santino Marella	5.00	12.00
NNO	Stone Cold Steve Austin	8.00	20.00
NNO	Triple H	6.00	15.00
NNO	Trish Stratus	8.00	20.00
NNO	Undertaker	6.00	15.00
NNO	Wade Barrett	5.00	12.00

2015 Topps Heritage WWE

COMPLETE SET (110) 12.00 30.00
*BLACK: .75X TO 2X BASIC CARDS
*SILVER: 5X TO 12X BASIC CARDS
*GOLD/10: 8X TO 20X BASIC CARDS
*RED/1: UNPRICED DUE TO SCARCITY
*P.P.BLACK/1: UNPRICED DUE TO SCARCITY
*P.P.CYAN/1: UNPRICED DUE TO SCARCITY
*P.P.MAGENTA/1: UNPRICED DUE TO SCARCITY
*P.P.YELLOW/1: UNPRICED DUE TO SCARCITY

1	The American Dream Dusty Rhodes	.25	.60
2	The Acolytes	.25	.60
3	Bob Backlund	.15	.40
4	Bam Bam Bigelow	.20	.50
5	Booker T	.25	.60
6	Bret Hit Man Hart	.50	1.25
7	The British Bulldog	.25	.60
8	Bruno Sammartino	.40	1.00
9	The Bushwhackers	.15	.40
10	Cowboy Bob Orton	.15	.40
11	D-Generation X	.60	1.50
12	Diamond Dallas Page	.30	.75
13	Doink the Clown	.15	.40
14	Earthquake	.15	.40
15	Edge	.40	1.00
16	The Foreign Legion	.25	.60
17	The Four Horsemen	.50	1.25
18	The Funks	.20	.50
19	Eddie Guerrero	.40	1.00
20	George The Animal Steele	.20	.50
21	Papa Shango	.15	.40
22	Hacksaw Jim Duggan	.25	.60
23	Hillbilly Jim	.25	.60
24	Rob Van Dam	.40	1.00
25	Jake The Snake Roberts	.25	.60
26	Jerry The King Lawler	.25	.60
27	Jim Ross	.25	.60
28	Junkyard Dog	.20	.50
29	Kamala	.20	.50
30	The King Harley Race	.25	.60
31	Koko B. Ware	.20	.50
32	Money Inc.	.25	.60
33	Mr. Perfect Curt Hennig	.25	.60
34	Mr. Wonderful Paul Orndorff	.25	.60
35	The Nasty Boys	.25	.60
36	The Outsiders	.40	1.00
37	Ravishing Rick Rude	.25	.60
38	Ricky The Dragon Steamboat	.25	.60
39	Rocky Johnson	.25	.60
40	Rowdy Roddy Piper	.50	1.25
41	Rhythm & Blues	.25	.60
42	Sgt. Slaughter	.25	.60
43	Lex Luger & Sting	.40	1.00
44	Stone Cold Steve Austin	.75	2.00
45	Tito Santana	.25	.60
46	The Twin Towers	.20	.50
47	Ultimate Warrior	.50	1.25
48	Vader	.20	.50
49	Virgil	.15	.40
50	Yokozuna	.25	.60
51	Eve	.30	.75
52	Lita	.60	1.50
53	Trish Stratus	.75	2.00
54	Alicia Fox	.30	.75
55	The Bella Twins	.50	1.25
56	Emma RC	.25	.60
57	Lana RC	.60	1.50
58	Naomi	.25	.60
59	Natalya	.50	1.25
60	Paige RC	.75	2.00
61	King Barrett	.15	.40
62	Batista	.40	1.00
63	Big Show	.40	1.00
64	Bo Dallas	.15	.40
65	Bray Wyatt	.60	1.50
66	Brock Lesnar	.60	1.50
67	Chris Jericho	.40	1.00
68	Christian	.15	.40
69	Damien Sandow	.15	.40
70	Daniel Bryan	.60	1.50
71	Dean Ambrose	.40	1.00
72	Dolph Ziggler	.25	.60
73	Goldust	.15	.40
74	J & J Security	.15	.40
75	John Cena	.75	2.00
76	Kalisto RC	.25	.60
77	Kane	.40	1.00
78	Luke Harper	.25	.60
79	Mark Henry	.25	.60
80	The Miz	.25	.60
81	Neville RC	.30	.75
82	The New Day	.25	.60
83	The Prime Time Players	.15	.40
84	R-Truth	.15	.40
85	Randy Orton	.60	1.50
86	The Rock	.75	2.00
87	Fandango	.15	.40
88	Roman Reigns	.40	1.00
89	Rusev RC	.40	1.00
90	Ryback	.15	.40
91	Santino Marella	.15	.40
92	Seth Rollins	.25	.60
93	Sheamus	.40	1.00
94	Sin Cara	.25	.60
95	Stardust	.15	.40
96	Cesaro	.15	.40
97	Undertaker	.60	1.50
98	The Usos	.15	.40
99	William Regal	.25	.60
100	Zack Ryder	.15	.40
101	Alexa Bliss RC	4.00	10.00
102	Baron Corbin RC	.25	.60
103	Bull Dempsey RC	.25	.60
104	Charlotte RC	.50	1.25
105	Finn Balor RC	.50	1.25
106	Hideo Itami RC	.15	.40
107	Kevin Owens RC	.50	1.25
108	Sami Zayn RC	.25	.60
109	Sasha Banks RC	6.00	15.00
110	Tyler Breeze RC	.15	.40
111	Steve Austin 2K16 SP		
111B	Steve Austin 2K16 SP Black		
111C	Steve Austin 2K16 SP Blue		
111D	Steve Austin 2K16 SP Yellow		

2015 Topps Heritage WWE 2K16

COMPLETE SET (8) 10.00 25.00
*BLACK/50: 1.2X TO 3X BASIC CARDS
*P.P.BLACK/1: UNPRICED DUE TO SCARCITY
*P.P.CYAN/1: UNPRICED DUE TO SCARCITY
*P.P.MAGENTA/1: UNPRICED DUE TO SCARCITY
*P.P.YELLOW/1: UNPRICED DUE TO SCARCITY

1	Stone Cold Steve Austin	4.00	10.00
2	Daniel Bryan	3.00	8.00
3	Finn Balor	2.50	6.00
4	King Barrett	.75	2.00
5	Paige	4.00	10.00
6	Paul Heyman	.75	2.00
7	Seth Rollins	1.25	3.00
8	Stone Cold Steve Austin	4.00	10.00

2015 Topps Heritage WWE Autographs

*BLACK/50: .5X TO 1.2X BASIC AUTOS
*SILVER/25: .75X TO 2X BASIC AUTOS
*GOLD/10: UNPRICED DUE TO SCARCITY
*RED/1: UNPRICED DUE TO SCARCITY

Card	Low	High
NNO Alundra Blayze	8.00	20.00
NNO Daniel Bryan	12.00	30.00
NNO Dean Ambrose	15.00	40.00
NNO Dolph Ziggler	10.00	25.00
NNO Eva Marie	15.00	40.00
NNO Finn Balor	20.00	50.00
NNO Hideo Itami	10.00	25.00
NNO John Cena	30.00	75.00
NNO Neville	10.00	25.00
NNO Pat Patterson	10.00	25.00
NNO Roman Reigns	60.00	120.00
NNO Sasha Banks	125.00	250.00
NNO Seth Rollins	15.00	40.00

2015 Topps Heritage WWE Money in the Bank Relics

*BLACK/50: .5X TO 1.2X BASIC MEM
*SILVER/25: .75X TO 2X BASIC MEM
*GOLD/10: UNPRICED DUE TO SCARCITY
*RED/1: UNPRICED DUE TO SCARCITY

Card	Low	High
NNO Big E	3.00	8.00
NNO Big Show	5.00	12.00
NNO Darren Young	2.00	5.00
NNO Dean Ambrose	5.00	12.00
NNO Dolph Ziggler	3.00	8.00
NNO John Cena	10.00	25.00
NNO Kane	5.00	12.00
NNO Kevin Owens	6.00	15.00
NNO King Barrett	2.00	5.00
NNO Kofi Kingston	2.00	5.00
NNO Neville	4.00	10.00
NNO Nikki Bella	6.00	15.00
NNO Paige	10.00	25.00
NNO Randy Orton	8.00	20.00
NNO Roman Reigns	5.00	12.00
NNO R-Truth	2.00	5.00
NNO Ryback	2.00	5.00
NNO Seth Rollins	3.00	8.00
NNO Sheamus	5.00	12.00
NNO Titus O'Neil	2.00	5.00
NNO Xavier Woods	3.00	8.00

2015 Topps Heritage WWE nWo Autographs

RANDOMLY INSERTED INTO PACKS

Card	Low	High
NNO Big Show	20.00	50.00
NNO Booker T	12.00	30.00
NNO Bret Hit Man Hart	25.00	60.00
NNO Kevin Nash	20.00	50.00
NNO Lex Luger	12.00	30.00
NNO Shawn Michaels	60.00	120.00
NNO X-Pac	15.00	40.00

2015 Topps Heritage WWE nWo Tribute

COMPLETE SET (10) 10.00 25.00
RANDOMLY INSERTED INTO PACKS

Card	Low	High
31 Scott Hall	2.50	6.00
32 Kevin Nash	2.50	6.00
33 The Giant	2.50	6.00
34 Syxx	2.00	5.00
35 Miss Elizabeth	2.00	5.00
36 Mr. Wallstreet	1.00	2.50
37 Big Bubba Rogers	1.00	2.50
38 Curt Hennig	1.50	4.00
39 Bret Hit Man Hart	3.00	8.00
40 Stevie Ray	1.00	2.50

2015 Topps Heritage WWE NXT Called Up

COMPLETE SET (30) 8.00 20.00
*P.P.BLACK/1: UNPRICED DUE TO SCARCITY
*P.P.CYAN/1: UNPRICED DUE TO SCARCITY
*P.P.MAGENTA/1: UNPRICED DUE TO SCARCITY
*P.P.YELLOW/1: UNPRICED DUE TO SCARCITY
STATED ODDS 1:1

Card	Low	High
1 Bad News Barrett	.30	.75
2 David Otunga	.30	.75
3 Heath Slater	.30	.75
4 Darren Young	.30	.75
5 Daniel Bryan	1.25	3.00
6 Ryback	.30	.75
7 Alex Riley	.30	.75
8 Curtis Axel	.30	.75
9 Naomi	.50	1.25
10 Titus OíNeil	.30	.75
11 Dean Ambrose	.75	2.00
12 Roman Reigns	.75	2.00
13 Seth Rollins	.50	1.25
14 Big E	.50	1.25
15 Bo Dallas	.30	.75
16 Bray Wyatt	1.25	3.00
17 Luke Harper	.50	1.25
18 Erick Rowan	.50	1.25
19 Adam Rose	.40	1.00
20 Summer Rae	1.25	3.00
21 Xavier Woods	.50	1.25
22 Emma	.50	1.25
23 Byron Saxton	.30	.75
24 Rusev	.75	2.00
25 Lana	1.25	3.00
26 Paige	1.50	4.00
27 Konnor	.40	1.00
28 Viktor	.30	.75
29 Kalisto	.50	1.25
30 Neville	.60	1.50

2015 Topps Heritage WWE Rookie of the Year

COMPLETE SET (30) 10.00 25.00
*P.P.BLACK/1: UNPRICED DUE TO SCARCITY
*P.P.CYAN/1: UNPRICED DUE TO SCARCITY
*P.P.MAGENTA/1: UNPRICED DUE TO SCARCITY
*P.P.YELLOW/1: UNPRICED DUE TO SCARCITY
STATED ODDS 1:1

Card	Low	High
1 Mr. Wonderful Paul Orndorff	.50	1.25
2 Rowdy Roddy Piper	1.00	2.50
3 Davey Boy Smith	.50	1.25
4 Jake The Snake Roberts	.50	1.25
5 Ultimate Warrior	1.00	2.50
6 Shawn Michaels	1.25	3.00
7 Earthquake	.30	.75
8 Undertaker	1.25	3.00
9 I.R.S.	.30	.75
10 Razor Ramon	.75	2.00
11 Diesel	.75	2.00
12 Kama	.30	.75
13 Hunter Hearst Helmsley	1.25	3.00
14 Mark Henry	.50	1.25
15 Kane	.75	2.00
16 Edge	.75	2.00
17 Chris Jericho	.75	2.00
18 Lita	1.25	3.00
19 Brock Lesnar	1.25	3.00
20 Joey Mercury	.30	.75
21 The Miz	.50	1.25
22 Santino Marella	.30	.75
23 Dolph Ziggler	.50	1.25
24 Sheamus	.75	2.00
25 Daniel Bryan	1.25	3.00
26 Sin Cara	.50	1.25
27 Dean Ambrose	.75	2.00
28 Bray Wyatt	1.25	3.00
29 Rusev	.75	2.00
30 Neville	.60	1.50

2015 Topps Heritage WWE Swatch Relics

*BLACK/50: .5X TO 1.2 BASIC MEM
*GOLD/10: UNPRICED DUE TO SCARCITY
*RED/1: UNPRICED DUE TO SCARCITY

Card	Low	High
NNO Aiden English	3.00	8.00
NNO Baron Corbin	4.00	10.00
NNO Bayley	5.00	12.00
NNO Becky Lynch	5.00	12.00
NNO Big E	4.00	10.00
NNO Big Show	6.00	15.00
NNO Bo Dallas	2.50	6.00
NNO Bray Wyatt	10.00	25.00
NNO Cesaro	2.50	6.00
NNO Charlotte	8.00	20.00
NNO Colin Cassady	4.00	10.00
NNO Curtis Axel	2.50	6.00
NNO Damien Sandow	2.50	6.00
NNO Daniel Bryan	10.00	25.00
NNO Darren Young	2.50	6.00
NNO Dean Ambrose	6.00	15.00
NNO Dolph Ziggler	4.00	10.00
NNO Enzo Amore	2.50	6.00
NNO Finn Balor	8.00	20.00
NNO Goldust	2.50	6.00
NNO Jack Swagger	4.00	10.00
NNO Jimmy Uso	2.50	6.00
NNO John Cena	12.00	30.00
NNO Kalisto	4.00	10.00
NNO Kevin Owens	8.00	20.00
NNO King Barrett	2.50	6.00
NNO Kofi Kingston	2.50	6.00
NNO Konnor	3.00	8.00
NNO Luke Harper	4.00	10.00
NNO Luke Harper	4.00	10.00
NNO Mojo Rawley	2.50	6.00
NNO Natalya	8.00	20.00
NNO Neville	5.00	12.00
NNO Randy Orton	10.00	25.00
NNO Roman Reigns	6.00	15.00
NNO Rusev	6.00	15.00
NNO Ryback	2.50	6.00
NNO Samoa Joe	6.00	15.00
NNO Sasha Banks	5.00	12.00
NNO Seth Rollins	4.00	10.00
NNO Sheamus	6.00	15.00
NNO Simon Gotch	2.50	6.00
NNO Sin Cara	4.00	10.00
NNO Tamina	4.00	10.00
NNO The Miz	4.00	10.00
NNO Titus O'Neil	2.50	6.00
NNO Tyler Breeze	2.50	6.00
NNO Viktor	2.50	6.00
NNO Xavier Woods	4.00	10.00
NNO Zack Ryder	2.50	6.00

2015 Topps Heritage WWE Then and Now

COMPLETE SET (30) 10.00 25.00
*P.P.BLACK/1: UNPRICED DUE TO SCARCITY
*P.P.CYAN/1: UNPRICED DUE TO SCARCITY
*P.P.MAGENTA/1: UNPRICED DUE TO SCARCITY
*P.P.YELLOW/1: UNPRICED DUE TO SCARCITY
STATED ODDS 1:1

Card	Low	High
1 Batista	.75	2.00
2 Big Show	.75	2.00
3 Booker T	.50	1.25
4 Brock Lesnar	1.25	3.00
5 Chris Jericho	.75	2.00
6 Christian	.30	.75
7 Daniel Bryan	1.25	3.00
8 Damien Sandow	.30	.75
9 Darren Young	.30	.75
10 Dean Ambrose	.75	2.00
11 Edge	.75	2.00
12 Goldust	.30	.75
13 Hornswoggle	.50	1.25
14 Jamie Noble	.30	.75
15 JBL	.30	.75
16 Joey Mercury	.30	.75
17 John Cena	1.50	4.00
18 Kane	.75	2.00
19 Mark Henry	.50	1.25
20 The Miz	.50	1.25
21 Randy Orton	1.25	3.00
22 Ryback	.30	.75
23 Seth Rollins	.50	1.25
24 Sting	.75	2.00
25 Stone Cold Steve Austin	1.50	4.00
26 Triple H	1.25	3.00
27 Trish Stratus	1.50	4.00
28 Undertaker	1.25	3.00
29 William Regal	.50	1.25
30 Zack Ryder	.30	.75

2016 Topps Heritage WWE

COMPLETE SET (110) 10.00 25.00
*BRONZE/99: .75X TO 2X BASIC CARDS
*SILVER/50: 1.2X TO 3X BASIC CARDS
*BLUE/25: 2X TO 5X BASIC CARDS
*GOLD/10: 4X TO 10X BASIC CARDS
*RED/1: UNPRICED DUE TO SCARCITY
*P.P.BLACK/1: UNPRICED DUE TO SCARCITY
*P.P.CYAN/1: UNPRICED DUE TO SCARCITY
*P.P.MAGENTA/1: UNPRICED DUE TO SCARCITY
*P.P.YELLOW/1: UNPRICED DUE TO SCARCITY

Card	Low	High
1 AJ Styles	1.00	2.50
2 Alberto Del Rio	.40	1.00
3 Big E	.25	.60
4 Big Show	.50	1.25
5 Braun Strowman RC	.30	.75
6 Bray Wyatt	1.00	2.50
7 Brock Lesnar	1.25	3.00
8 Bubba Ray Dudley	.50	1.25
9 Cesaro	.50	1.25
10 Chris Jericho	.60	1.50
11 D-Von Dudley	.40	1.00
12 Dean Ambrose	.75	2.00
13 Dolph Ziggler	.30	.75
14 Erick Rowan	.25	.60
15 Goldust	.40	1.00
16 Jack Swagger	.25	.60
17 Jey Uso	.25	.60
18 Jimmy Uso	.25	.60
19 John Cena	1.25	3.00
20 Kalisto	.60	1.50
21 Kane	.40	1.00
22 Kevin Owens	.60	1.50
23 Karl Anderson RC	.25	.60
24 Kofi Kingston	.25	.60
25 Luke Harper	.25	.60
26 Neville	.60	1.50
27 Randy Orton	.60	1.50
28 The Rock	1.25	3.00
29 Roman Reigns	.75	2.00
30 Rusev	.60	1.50
31 Luke Gallows	.30	.75
32 Seth Rollins	.40	1.00
33 Sheamus	.60	1.50
34 Sin Cara	.30	.75
35 Zack Ryder	.25	.60
36 Sting	.60	1.50
37 Triple H	1.00	2.50
38 Tyson Kidd	.25	.60
39 Undertaker	1.00	2.50
40 Xavier Woods	.25	.60
41 Alicia Fox	.40	1.00
42 Becky Lynch RC	.75	2.00
43 Brie Bella	.50	1.25
44 Charlotte	.75	2.00
45 Eva Marie	.50	1.25
46 Lana	1.00	2.50
47 Mandy Rose RC	6.00	15.00
48 Naomi	.40	1.00
49 Natalya	.40	1.00
50 Nikki Bella	.75	2.00
51 Paige	.75	2.00
52 Rosa Mendes	.25	.60
53 Sasha Banks	.75	2.00
54 Summer Rae	.60	1.50
55 Tamina	.30	.75
56 Aiden English	.25	.60
57 Angelo Dawkins	.25	.60
58 Apollo Crews RC	.25	.60
59 Asuka RC	1.00	2.50
60 Bayley RC	.60	1.50
61 Baron Corbin	.30	.75
62 Carmella RC	.60	1.50
63 Colin Cassady	.50	1.25
64 Enzo Amore RC	.50	1.25
65 Finn Balor	.75	2.00
66 Hideo Itami	.30	.75
67 Nia Jax RC	.40	1.00
68 Sami Zayn	.40	1.00
69 Samoa Joe	.60	1.50
70 Simon Gotch RC	.40	1.00
71 Alundra Blayze L	.40	1.00
72 American Dream Dusty Rhodes L	.25	.60
73 Andre The Giant L	.75	2.00
74 Bam Bam Bigelow L	.30	.75
75 Bret Hit Man Hart L	.60	1.50
76 The British Bulldog L	.30	.75

77 Bruno Sammartino L .30 .75
78 Daniel Bryan L 1.00 2.50
79 Diamond Dallas Page L .40 1.00
80 Eddie Guerrero L .60 1.50
81 Edge L .60 1.50
82 Eve L .50 1.25
83 The Honky Tonk Man L .25 .60
84 Irwin R. Schyster L .25 .60
85 Jake The Snake Roberts L .50 1.25
86 Jim The Anvil Neidhart L .25 .60
87 Kevin Nash L .60 1.50
88 Lex Luger L .40 1.00
89 Lita L .75 2.00
90 Macho Man Randy Savage L .60 1.50
91 Ted DiBiase L .30 .75
92 Miss Elizabeth L .25 .60
93 Mr. Perfect Curt Hennig L .60 1.50
94 Ravishing Rick Rude L .40 1.00
95 Ric Flair L 1.00 2.50
96 Ricky The Dragon Steamboat L .30 .75
97 Rikishi L .30 .75
98 Road Dogg L .40 1.00
99 Rob Van Dam L .50 1.25
100 Ron Simmons L .60 1.50
101 Rowdy Roddy Piper L .75 2.00
102 Scott Hall L .60 1.50
103 Sensational Sherri L .40 1.00
104 Shawn Michaels L 1.00 2.50
105 The Iron Sheik L .25 .60
106 Stone Cold Steve Austin L 1.25 3.00
107 Tatanka L .25 .60
108 Trish Stratus L 1.25 3.00
109 Ultimate Warrior L .60 1.50
110 X-Pac L .40 1.00
111 Seth Rollins SP 5.00 12.00
112 Roman Reigns SP 6.00 15.00
113 Macho Man Randy Savage SP 5.00 12.00

2016 Topps Heritage WWE All-Star Patches

*BRONZE/99: .5X TO 1.2X BASIC MEM
*SILVER/50: .6X TO 1.5X BASIC MEM
*BLUE/25: .75X TO 2X BASIC MEM
*GOLD/10: UNPRICED DUE TO SCARCITY
*P.P.BLACK/1: UNPRICED DUE TO SCARCITY
*P.P.CYAN/1: UNPRICED DUE TO SCARCITY
*P.P.MAGENTA/1: UNPRICED DUE TO SCARCITY
*P.P.YELLOW/1: UNPRICED DUE TO SCARCITY
RANDOMLY INSERTED INTO PACKS

NNO Andre the Giant 6.00 15.00
NNO Bam Bam Bigelow 2.50 6.00
NNO Bayley 5.00 12.00
NNO Big Van Vader 4.00 10.00
NNO Booker T 4.00 10.00
NNO Bret Hit Man Hart 5.00 12.00
NNO Brock Lesnar 10.00 25.00
NNO Bubba Ray Dudley 4.00 10.00
NNO Curt Hennig 5.00 12.00
NNO D-Von Dudley 3.00 8.00
NNO Finn Balor 6.00 15.00
NNO The Giant 4.00 10.00
NNO Hideo Itami 2.50 6.00
NNO John Cena 10.00 25.00
NNO Kevin Nash 5.00 12.00
NNO Lex Luger 3.00 8.00
NNO Macho Man Randy Savage 5.00 12.00
NNO Ric Flair 8.00 20.00
NNO Rob Van Dam 4.00 10.00
NNO The Rock 10.00 25.00
NNO Sami Zayn 3.00 8.00
NNO Samoa Joe 5.00 12.00
NNO Scott Hall 5.00 12.00
NNO Sting 5.00 12.00
NNO Stone Cold Steve Austin 10.00 25.00
NNO Syxx 3.00 8.00
NNO Terry Funk 2.00 5.00
NNO Triple H 8.00 20.00
NNO Ultimate Warrior 5.00 12.00
NNO Undertaker 8.00 20.00

2016 Topps Heritage WWE Autographs

*SILVER/50: .5X TO 1.2X BASIC AUTOS
*BLUE/25: .6X TO 1.5X BASIC AUTOS
*GOLD/10: 1X TO 2.5X BASIC AUTOS
*P.P.BLACK/1: UNPRICED DUE TO SCARCITY
*P.P.CYAN/1: UNPRICED DUE TO SCARCITY
*P.P.MAGENTA/1: UNPRICED DUE TO SCARCITY
*P.P.YELLOW/1: UNPRICED DUE TO SCARCITY
RANDOMLY INSERTED INTO PACKS

NNO Asuka 20.00 50.00
NNO Bayley 15.00 40.00
NNO Becky Lynch 30.00 75.00
NNO Big E 6.00 15.00
NNO Brian Knobbs 6.00 15.00
NNO Brie Bella 10.00 25.00
NNO Brock Lesnar 60.00 120.00
NNO Dean Ambrose 12.00 30.00
NNO Finn Balor 15.00 40.00
NNO Hideo Itami 10.00 25.00
NNO Jake The Snake Roberts 15.00 40.00
NNO Jerry Sags 6.00 15.00
NNO Jim The Anvil Neidhart 5.00 12.00
NNO John Cena 20.00 50.00
NNO Kevin Owens 10.00 25.00
NNO Kofi Kingston 6.00 15.00
NNO Nia Jax 8.00 20.00
NNO Nikki Bella 10.00 25.00
NNO Roman Reigns 30.00 75.00
NNO Sami Zayn 10.00 25.00
NNO Samoa Joe 12.00 30.00
NNO Sasha Banks 25.00 60.00
NNO Sting 25.00 60.00
NNO Tatanka 5.00 12.00
NNO Tyler Breeze 6.00 15.00
NNO Typhoon 5.00 12.00
NNO Xavier Woods 6.00 15.00

2016 Topps Heritage WWE Diva Kiss

GOLD/10: UNPRICED DUE TO SCARCITY
RANDOMLY INSERTED INTO PACKS

NNO Asuka 125.00 250.00
NNO Billie Kay 20.00 50.00
NNO Charlotte 25.00 60.00
NNO Dasha Fuentes 30.00 75.00
NNO Mandy Rose 60.00 120.00
NNO Naomi 12.00 30.00
NNO Nia Jax 20.00 50.00
NNO Peyton Royce 30.00 75.00

2016 Topps Heritage WWE Diva Kiss Autographs

*GOLD/10: UNPRICED DUE TO SCARCITY
*P.P.BLACK/1: UNPRICED DUE TO SCARCITY
*P.P.CYAN/1: UNPRICED DUE TO SCARCITY
*P.P.MAGENTA/1: UNPRICED DUE TO SCARCITY
*P.P.YELLOW/1: UNPRICED DUE TO SCARCITY
RANDOMLY INSERTED INTO PACKS

NNO Asuka 200.00 350.00
NNO Billie Kay 50.00 100.00
NNO Charlotte 100.00 200.00
NNO Dasha Fuentes 30.00 80.00
NNO Mandy Rose 50.00 100.00
NNO Naomi 20.00 50.00
NNO Nia Jax 60.00 120.00
NNO Peyton Royce 80.00 150.00

2016 Topps Heritage WWE Dual Autographs

STATED PRINT RUN 11 SER.#'d SETS

NNO Asuka/N.Jax 50.00 100.00
NNO B.Knobbs/J.Sags 25.00 60.00
NNO Charlotte/B.Lynch 125.00 250.00
NNO F.Balor/S.Joe 80.00 150.00
NNO J.Roberts/J.Neidhart 50.00 100.00
NNO J.Cena/Sting 100.00 200.00
NNO K.Owens/D.Ziggler 60.00 120.00
NNO N.Bella/B.Bella 60.00 120.00
NNO R.Reigns/D.Ambrose 50.00 100.00
NNO S.Zayn/H.Itami 25.00 60.00
NNO S.Banks/Bayley 125.00 250.00
NNO Tatanka/Typhoon 25.00 60.00

2016 Topps Heritage WWE NXT University of Central Florida Mat Relics

*BRONZE/99: .5X TO 1.2X BASIC MEM
GOLD/10: UNPRICED DUE TO SCARCITY
STATED PRINT RUN 99 SER.#'d SETS

NNO Alex Riley 2.50 6.00
NNO Asuka 10.00 25.00
NNO Bayley 6.00 15.00
NNO Carmella 6.00 15.00
NNO Colin Cassady 5.00 12.00
NNO Enzo Amore 5.00 12.00
NNO Nia Jax 4.00 10.00
NNO Sami Zayn 4.00 10.00
NNO Samoa Joe 6.00 15.00
NNO Tye Dillinger 3.00 8.00

2016 Topps Heritage WWE Record Breakers

COMPLETE SET (30) 12.00 30.00
*P.P.BLACK/1: UNPRICED DUE TO SCARCITY
*P.P.CYAN/1: UNPRICED DUE TO SCARCITY
*P.P.MAGENTA/1: UNPRICED DUE TO SCARCITY
*P.P.YELLOW/1: UNPRICED DUE TO SCARCITY

1 Bruno Sammartino .40 1.00
2 John Cena 1.50 4.00
3 Brock Lesnar 1.50 4.00
4 Andre the Giant 1.00 2.50
5 Ric Flair 1.25 3.00
6 Triple H 1.25 3.00
7 Randy Orton 1.00 2.50
8 Edge 1.00 2.50
9 Honky Tonk Man .40 1.00
10 Chris Jericho 1.00 2.50
11 Lex Luger .60 1.50
12 Ric Flair 1.50 4.00
13 Nikki Bella 1.25 3.00
14 Eve Torres .75 2.00
15 The Dudley Boyz .75 2.00
16 Edge 1.00 2.50
17 Finn Balor 1.25 3.00
18 Paige 1.25 3.00
19 The Ascension .40 1.00
20 Neville 1.00 2.50
21 The British Bulldog .50 1.25
22 Big Boss Man .60 1.50
23 Harlem Heat .75 2.00
24 Undertaker 1.50 4.00
25 Stone Cold Steve Austin 2.00 5.00
26 Roman Reigns 1.25 3.00
27 Kane .60 1.50
28 Triple H 1.50 4.00
29 Kane .60 1.50
30 Bret Hit Man Hart 1.00 2.50

2016 Topps Heritage WWE Survivor Series 2015 Mat Relics

*BRONZE/99: SAME VALUE AS BASIC MEM
*SILVER/50: .5X TO 1.2X BASIC MEM
*BLUE/25: .6X TO 1.5X BASIC MEM
*GOLD/10: UNPRICED DUE TO SCARCITY
*P.P.BLACK/1: UNPRICED DUE TO SCARCITY
*P.P.CYAN/1: UNPRICED DUE TO SCARCITY
*P.P.MAGENTA/1: UNPRICED DUE TO SCARCITY
*P.P.YELLOW/1: UNPRICED DUE TO SCARCITY
RANDOMLY INSERTED INTO PACKS

NNO Alberto Del Rio 4.00 10.00
NNO Bray Wyatt 10.00 25.00
NNO Bubba Ray Dudley 5.00 12.00
NNO Charlotte 8.00 20.00
NNO D-Von Dudley 4.00 10.00
NNO Dean Ambrose 8.00 20.00
NNO Dolph Ziggler 3.00 8.00
NNO Goldust 4.00 10.00
NNO Jey Uso 2.50 6.00
NNO Jimmy Uso 2.50 6.00
NNO Kalisto 6.00 15.00
NNO Kane 4.00 10.00
NNO Kevin Owens 6.00 15.00
NNO Luke Harper 2.50 6.00
NNO Paige 8.00 20.00
NNO Roman Reigns 8.00 20.00
NNO Sheamus 6.00 15.00
NNO Titus O'Neil 2.50 6.00
NNO Tyler Breeze 2.50 6.00
NNO Undertaker 10.00 25.00

2016 Topps Heritage WWE Swatch Relics

*BRONZE/150: SAME VALUE AS BASIC MEM
*SILVER/50: .5X TO 1.2X BASIC MEM
*BLUE/25: .6X TO 1.5X BASIC MEM
*GOLD/10: UNPRICED DUE TO SCARCITY
*P.P.BLACK/1: UNPRICED DUE TO SCARCITY
*P.P.CYAN/1: UNPRICED DUE TO SCARCITY
*P.P.MAGENTA/1: UNPRICED DUE TO SCARCITY
*P.P.YELLOW/1: UNPRICED DUE TO SCARCITY
RANDOMLY INSERTED INTO PACKS

1 Aiden English 2.50 6.00
2 Alberto Del Rio 4.00 10.00
3 Asuka 10.00 25.00
4 Bayley 6.00 15.00
5 Big E 2.50 6.00
6 Bray Wyatt 10.00 25.00
7 Brock Lesnar 12.00 30.00
8 Bubba Ray Dudley 5.00 12.00
9 Cesaro 5.00 12.00
10 Charlotte 8.00 20.00
11 D-Von Dudley 4.00 10.00
12 Dean Ambrose 8.00 20.00
13 Dolph Ziggler 3.00 8.00
14 Finn Balor 8.00 20.00
15 Jey Uso 2.50 6.00
16 Jimmy Uso 2.50 6.00
17 John Cena 12.00 30.00
18 Kevin Owens 6.00 15.00
19 Kofi Kingston 2.50 6.00
20 Paige 8.00 20.00
21 Roman Reigns 8.00 20.00
22 Samoa Joe 6.00 15.00
23 Sheamus 6.00 15.00
24 Simon Gotch 4.00 10.00
25 Xavier Woods 2.50 6.00
26 Zack Ryder 2.50 6.00

2016 Topps Heritage WWE Turn Back the Clock

COMPLETE SET (15) 10.00 25.00
*P.P.BLACK/1: UNPRICED DUE TO SCARCITY
*P.P.CYAN/1: UNPRICED DUE TO SCARCITY
*P.P.MAGENTA/1: UNPRICED DUE TO SCARCITY
*P.P.YELLOW/1: UNPRICED DUE TO SCARCITY
RANDOMLY INSERTED INTO PACKS

1 The Iron Sheik .50 1.25
2 Andre the Giant 1.50 4.00
3 Ricky The Dragon Steamboat .60 1.50
4 Jake The Snake Roberts 1.00 2.50
5 Texas Tornado .75 2.00
6 Big Boss Man .75 2.00
7 Hacksaw Jim Duggan .50 1.25
8 Rowdy Roddy Piper 1.50 4.00
9 Tatanka .50 1.25
10 Undertaker 2.00 5.00
11 Macho Man Randy Savage 1.25 3.00
12 Sgt. Slaughter .60 1.50
13 Shawn Michaels 2.00 5.00
14 Bret Hit Man Hart 1.25 3.00
15 The British Bulldog .60 1.50

2016 Topps Heritage WWE WCW/nWo All-Stars

COMPLETE SET (40) 20.00 50.00
*P.P.BLACK/1: UNPRICED DUE TO SCARCITY
*P.P.CYAN/1: UNPRICED DUE TO SCARCITY
*P.P.MAGENTA/1: UNPRICED DUE TO SCARCITY
*P.P.YELLOW/1: UNPRICED DUE TO SCARCITY

1 Scott Hall 1.50 4.00
2 Kevin Nash 1.50 4.00
3 Trillionaire Ted DiBiase .75 2.00
4 The Giant 1.25 3.00
5 Syxx 1.00 2.50
6 Vincent .60 1.50
7 Miss Elizabeth .60 1.50
8 Mr. Wallstreet .60 1.50
9 Big Bubba Rogers 1.00 2.50
10 Macho Man Randy Savage 1.50 4.00

11 Curt Hennig 1.50 4.00
12 Rick Rude 1.00 2.50
13 Dusty Rhodes .60 1.50
14 Bret Hit Man Hart 1.50 4.00
15 Stevie Ray .60 1.50
16 Lex Luger 1.00 2.50
17 Sting 1.50 4.00
18 Shawn Michaels 2.50 6.00
19 Booker T 1.25 3.00
20 Ric Flair 2.50 6.00
21 Arn Anderson .60 1.50
22 Diamond Dallas Page 1.00 2.50
23 Rowdy Roddy Piper 2.00 5.00
24 Ultimate Warrior 1.50 4.00
25 The British Bulldog .75 2.00
26 Jim The Anvil Neidhart .60 1.50
27 Hacksaw Jim Duggan .60 1.50
28 Chris Jericho 1.50 4.00
29 Eddie Guerrero 1.50 4.00
30 Dean Malenko .60 1.50
31 Mr. Wonderful Paul Orndorff .60 1.50
32 Terry Funk .60 1.50
33 Larry Zbyszko .60 1.50
34 John Tenta .60 1.50
35 Bam Bam Bigelow .75 2.00
36 Brian Pillman .75 2.00
37 Steven Regal .60 1.50
38 Brian Knobbs .60 1.50
39 Jerry Sags .75 2.00
40 Madusa .75 2.00

2017 Topps Heritage WWE

COMPLETE SET (100) 10.00 25.00
*BRONZE: .5X TO 1.2X BASIC CARDS
*BLUE/99: .75X TO 2X BASIC CARDS
*SILVER/25: 1.2X TO 3X BASIC CARDS
*GOLD/10: 2X TO 5X BASIC CARDS
*RED/1: UNPRICED DUE TO SCARCITY
*P.P.BLACK/1: UNPRICED DUE TO SCARCITY
*P.P.CYAN/1: UNPRICED DUE TO SCARCITY
*P.P.MAGENTA/1: UNPRICED DUE TO SCARCITY
*P.P.YELLOW/1: UNPRICED DUE TO SCARCITY

1 Asuka 1.25 3.00
2 Bobby Roode 1.00 2.50
3 Ember Moon RC 1.00 2.50
4 Eric Young .75 2.00
5 Hideo Itami .60 1.50
6 Johnny Gargano .40 1.00
7 Liv Morgan .60 1.50
8 Tommaso Ciampa .40 1.00
9 The Rock 2.00 5.00
10 Alicia Fox .60 1.50
11 Austin Aries .75 2.00
12 Bayley 1.25 3.00
13 Big Cass .50 1.25
14 Big E .50 1.25
15 Bob Backlund .40 1.00
16 The Brian Kendrick .40 1.00
17 Brock Lesnar 2.00 5.00
18 Cesaro .75 2.00
19 Charlotte Flair 1.50 4.00
20 Chris Jericho 1.00 2.50
21 Enzo Amore 1.25 3.00
22 Finn Balor 1.50 4.00
23 Goldberg 1.50 4.00
24 Karl Anderson .40 1.00
25 Kevin Owens 1.00 2.50
26 Kofi Kingston .50 1.25
27 Lana 1.25 3.00
28 Luke Gallows .60 1.50
29 Mick Foley 1.00 2.50
30 Roman Reigns 1.25 3.00
31 Rusev .75 2.00
32 Sami Zayn .50 1.25
33 Samoa Joe 1.25 3.00
34 Sasha Banks 1.25 3.00
35 Seth Rollins 1.25 3.00
36 Sheamus .75 2.00
37 Triple H 1.00 2.50
38 Xavier Woods .50 1.25
39 AJ Styles 2.00 5.00
40 Alexa Bliss 2.00 5.00
41 Baron Corbin .60 1.50
42 Becky Lynch 1.25 3.00
43 Bray Wyatt 1.00 2.50
44 Carmella 1.00 2.50
45 Chad Gable .50 1.25
46 Daniel Bryan 1.50 4.00
47 Dean Ambrose 1.25 3.00
48 Dolph Ziggler .60 1.50
49 Heath Slater .40 1.00
50 Jason Jordan .50 1.25
51 Jey Uso .50 1.25
52 Jimmy Uso .50 1.25
53 John Cena 2.00 5.00
54 Kalisto .60 1.50
55 Kane .50 1.25
56 Luke Harper .40 1.00
57 Maryse .75 2.00
58 The Miz .75 2.00
59 Mojo Rawley .50 1.25
60 Naomi .75 2.00
61 Natalya .75 2.00
62 Nikki Bella 1.00 2.50
63 Randy Orton 1.00 2.50
64 Rhyno .40 1.00
65 Shinsuke Nakamura 1.00 2.50
66 Undertaker 1.50 4.00
67 Zack Ryder .40 1.00
68 Alundra Blayze L .50 1.25
69 Andre the Giant L .75 2.00
70 Batista L .75 2.00
71 Bret Hit Man Hart L .75 2.00
72 British Bulldog L .40 1.00
73 Brutus The Barber Beefcake L .40 1.00
74 Diamond Dallas Page L .50 1.25
75 Dusty Rhodes L .50 1.25
76 Edge L 1.00 2.50
77 Fit Finlay L .40 1.00
78 Jake The Snake Roberts L .50 1.25
79 Jim The Anvil Neidhart L .40 1.00
80 Ken Shamrock L .40 1.00
81 Kevin Nash L .60 1.50
82 Lex Luger L .50 1.25
83 Terri Runnels L .40 1.00
84 Macho Man Randy Savage L .75 2.00
85 Ted DiBiase L .50 1.25
86 Mr. Perfect L .75 2.00
87 Ravishing Rick Rude L .60 1.50
88 Ric Flair L 1.00 2.50
89 Rob Van Dam L .75 2.00
90 Ron Simmons L .50 1.25
91 Rowdy Roddy Piper L .75 2.00
92 Scott Hall L .50 1.25
93 Sgt. Slaughter L .50 1.25
94 Shawn Michaels L 1.00 2.50
95 Sid Vicious L .50 1.25
96 Sting L 1.25 3.00
97 Stone Cold Steve Austin L 1.50 4.00
98 Trish Stratus L 1.50 4.00
99 Ultimate Warrior L .75 2.00
100 Wendi Richter L .50 1.25

2017 Topps Heritage WWE Thirty Years of SummerSlam

COMPLETE SET (50) 5.00 12.00
*P.P.BLACK/1: UNPRICED DUE TO SCARCITY
*P.P.CYAN/1: UNPRICED DUE TO SCARCITY
*P.P.MAGENTA/1: UNPRICED DUE TO SCARCITY
*P.P.YELLOW/1: UNPRICED DUE TO SCARCITY
STATED ODDS 2:1

1 Ultimate Warrior .50 1.25
2 The Mega Powers .50 1.25
3 Ultimate Warrior .50 1.25
4 Texas Tornado .25 .60
5 Hart Foundation .50 1.25
6 Ultimate Warrior .50 1.25
7 Bret Hit Man Hart .50 1.25
8 Virgil .25 .60
9 Ultimate Warrior .50 1.25
10 British Bulldog .25 .60
11 Lex Luger .30 .75
12 Alundra Blayze .30 .75
13 Razor Ramon .30 .75
14 Shawn Michaels .60 1.50
15 Diesel .40 1.00
16 Mankind .60 1.50
17 Shawn Michaels .60 1.50
18 Mankind .60 1.50
19 Bret Hit Man Hart .50 1.25
20 Triple H .60 1.50
21 Stond Cold Steve Austin 1.00 2.50
22 Unholy Alliance 1.00 2.50
23 Mankind .60 1.50
24 X-Pac .25 .60
25 X-Pac .25 .60
26 The Rock 1.25 3.00
27 Shawn Michaels .60 1.50
28 Brock Lesnar 1.25 3.00
29 Kane .30 .75
30 Kurt Angle .50 1.25
31 JBL .30 .75
32 John Cena 1.25 3.00
33 Edge .60 1.50
34 John Cena 1.25 3.00
35 Undertaker 1.00 2.50
36 Randy Orton .60 1.50
37 Randy Orton .60 1.50
38 Team WWE 1.00 2.50
39 Randy Orton .60 1.50
40 Brock Lesnar 1.25 3.00
41 Daniel Bryan 1.00 2.50
42 Randy Orton .60 1.50
43 Roman Reigns .75 2.00
44 Brock Lesnar 1.25 3.00
45 Seth Rollins .75 2.00
46 Undertaker 1.00 2.50
47 Charlotte 1.00 2.50
48 AJ Styles 1.25 3.00
49 Finn Balor 1.00 2.50
50 Brock Lesnar 1.25 3.00

2017 Topps Heritage WWE Autographed NXT TakeOver Toronto 2016 Mat Relics

STATED ODDS 1:9,056
STATED PRINT RUN 10 SER. #'d SETS
UNPRICED DUE TO SCARCITY

NNO Asuka
NNO Booby Roode
NNO Johnny Gargano
NNO Mickie James
NNO Samoa Joe
NNO Shinsuke Nakamura
NNO Tommaso Ciampa

2017 Topps Heritage WWE Autographed Survivor Series 2016 Mat Relics

STATED ODDS 1:3,544
STATED PRINT RUN 10 SER. #'d SETS
UNPRICED DUE TO SCARCITY

NNO AJ Styles
NNO Alexa Bliss
NNO Alicia Fox
NNO Bayley
NNO Becky Lynch
NNO Braun Strowman
NNO Bray Wyatt
NNO Brock Lesnar
NNO Carmella
NNO Charlotte Flair
NNO Chris Jericho
NNO Goldberg
NNO Kevin Owens
NNO Natalya
NNO Randy Orton
NNO Roman Reigns
NNO Sasha Banks
NNO Seth Rollins

2017 Topps Heritage WWE Autographs

*BLUE/50: .5X TO 1.2X BASIC AUTOS
*SILVER/25: .6X TO 1.5X BASIC AUTOS
*GOLD/10: UNPRICED DUE TO SCARCITY
*RED/1: UNPRICED DUE TO SCARCITY
*P.P.BLACK/1: UNPRICED DUE TO SCARCITY
*P.P.CYAN/1: UNPRICED DUE TO SCARCITY
*P.P.MAGENTA/1: UNPRICED DUE TO SCARCITY
*P.P.YELLOW/1: UNPRICED DUE TO SCARCITY
STATED ODDS 1:24

NNO AJ Styles 15.00 40.00
NNO Alexa Bliss 60.00 120.00
NNO Asuka 25.00 60.00
NNO Bayley 15.00 40.00
NNO Becky Lynch 50.00 100.00
NNO Bobby Roode 12.00 30.00
NNO Bray Wyatt 12.00 30.00
NNO Bret Hit Man Hart 20.00 50.00
NNO Brutus The Barber Beefcake 12.00 30.00
NNO Charlotte Flair 20.00 50.00
NNO Chris Jericho 10.00 25.00
NNO Dean Ambrose 8.00 20.00
NNO Ember Moon 6.00 15.00
NNO Eric Young 6.00 15.00
NNO Finn Balor 15.00 40.00
NNO Fit Finlay 10.00 25.00
NNO Goldberg 30.00 80.00
NNO Kevin Owens 8.00 20.00
NNO Sasha Banks 20.00 50.00
NNO Shinsuke Nakamura 15.00 40.00
NNO Sting 20.00 50.00

2017 Topps Heritage WWE Autographs Blue

STATED ODDS 1:93
STATED PRINT RUN 50 SER.#'d SETS

NNO Undertaker 120.00 250.00

2017 Topps Heritage WWE Autographs Silver

NNO Brock Lesnar 30.00 75.00

2017 Topps Heritage WWE Bizarre SummerSlam Matches

COMPLETE SET (10) 3.00 8.00
*P.P.BLACK/1: UNPRICED DUE TO SCARCITY
*P.P.CYAN/1: UNPRICED DUE TO SCARCITY
*P.P.MAGENTA/1: UNPRICED DUE TO SCARCITY
*P.P.YELLOW/1: UNPRICED DUE TO SCARCITY
STATED ODDS 1:3

1 Big Boss Man .40 1.00
2 Undertaker 1.25 3.00
3 Mankind .75 2.00
4 British Bulldog .30 .75
5 X-Pac .30 .75
6 Ken Shamrock .30 .75
7 Kane .40 1.00
8 Ric Flair .75 2.00
9 Bray Wyatt .75 2.00
10 Rusev .60 1.50

2017 Topps Heritage WWE Commemorative Patches

*BRONZE/99: .5X TO 1.2X BASIC MEM
*BLUE/50: .6X TO 1.5X BASIC MEM
*SILVER/25: .75X TO 2X BASIC MEM
*GOLD/10: UNPRICED DUE TO SCARCITY
*RED/1: UNPRICED DUE TO SCARCITY
*P.P.BLACK/1: UNPRICED DUE TO SCARCITY
*P.P.CYAN/1: UNPRICED DUE TO SCARCITY
*P.P.MAGENTA/1: UNPRICED DUE TO SCARCITY
*P.P.YELLOW/1: UNPRICED DUE TO SCARCITY
STATED ODDS 1:115

NNO AJ Styles 6.00 15.00
NNO Asuka 4.00 10.00
NNO Bobby Roode 3.00 8.00
NNO Charlotte Flair 5.00 12.00
NNO Chris Jericho 3.00 8.00
NNO Dean Ambrose 4.00 10.00
NNO Dolph Ziggler 2.00 5.00
NNO Ember Moon 3.00 8.00
NNO Eric Young 2.50 6.00
NNO Hideo Itami 2.00 5.00
NNO John Cena 6.00 15.00
NNO Kevin Owens 3.00 8.00
NNO The Miz 2.50 6.00
NNO Ric Flair 3.00 8.00
NNO Roman Reigns 4.00 10.00
NNO Rowdy Roddy Piper 2.50 6.00

NNO Seth Rollins	4.00	10.00
NNO Shawn Michaels	3.00	8.00
NNO Sting	4.00	10.00
NNO Trish Stratus	5.00	12.00

2017 Topps Heritage WWE Dual Autographs

STATED ODDS 1:2,264
STATED PRINT RUN 10 SER.#'d SETS
RANDOMLY INSERTED INTO PACKS

NNO Big E/K.Kingston/10	30.00	75.00
NNO B.Sammartino/L.Zbyszko/9	100.00	200.00
NNO J.Lawler/M.Cole/10	50.00	100.00
NNO Primo/Epico/10	25.00	60.00
NNO S.Rollins/R.Reigns/10	60.00	120.00

2017 Topps Heritage WWE Kiss

*GOLD/10: UNPRICED DUE TO SCARCITY
*RED/1: UNPRICED DUE TO SCARCITY
STATED ODDS 1:685

NNO Alexa Bliss	150.00	300.00
NNO Asuka	25.00	60.00
NNO Carmella	60.00	120.00
NNO Charlotte Flair	100.00	200.00
NNO Dana Brooke	30.00	75.00
NNO Ember Moon	20.00	50.00
NNO Liv Morgan	75.00	150.00

2017 Topps Heritage WWE Kiss Autographs

*GOLD/10: UNPRICED DUE TO SCARCITY
*RED/1: UNPRICED DUE TO SCARCITY
STATED ODDS 1:2,717

NNO Alexa Bliss	500.00	1000.00
NNO Asuka	75.00	150.00
NNO Carmella	60.00	120.00
NNO Charlotte Flair	60.00	120.00
NNO Dana Brooke	75.00	150.00
NNO Ember Moon	50.00	100.00
NNO Liv Morgan	50.00	100.00

2017 Topps Heritage WWE NXT TakeOver Toronto 2016 Mat Relics

*BRONZE/99: .5X TO 1.2X BASIC MEM
*BLUE/50: .6X TO 1.5X BASIC MEM
*SILVER/25: .75X TO 2X BASIC MEM
*GOLD/10: UNPRICED DUE TO SCARCITY
*RED/1: UNPRICED DUE TO SCARCITY
*P.P.BLACK/1: UNPRICED DUE TO SCARCITY
*P.P.CYAN/1: UNPRICED DUE TO SCARCITY
*P.P.MAGENTA/1: UNPRICED DUE TO SCARCITY
*P.P.YELLOW/1: UNPRICED DUE TO SCARCITY
RANDOMLY INSERTED INTO PACKS

NNO Akam	1.50	4.00
NNO Asuka	5.00	12.00
NNO Bobby Roode	4.00	10.00
NNO Johnny Gargano	1.50	4.00
NNO Mickie James	2.50	6.00
NNO Rezar	1.50	4.00
NNO Samoa Joe	5.00	12.00
NNO Shinsuke Nakamura	4.00	10.00
NNO Tommaso Ciampa	1.50	4.00
NNO Tye Dillinger	1.50	4.00

2017 Topps Heritage WWE Roster Updates

COMPLETE SET (10)	12.00	30.00

*P.P.BLACK/1: UNPRICED DUE TO SCARCITY
*P.P.CYAN/1: UNPRICED DUE TO SCARCITY
*P.P.MAGENTA/1: UNPRICED DUE TO SCARCITY
*P.P.YELLOW/1: UNPRICED DUE TO SCARCITY
RANDOMLY INSERTED INTO PACKS

R1 Alexander Wolfe	2.00	5.00
R2 Kassius Ohno	1.50	4.00
R3 Nikki Cross	3.00	8.00
R4 Roderick Strong	2.00	5.00
R5 Tye Dillinger	1.50	4.00
R6 Cedric Alexander	2.50	6.00
R7 Gentleman Jack Gallagher	3.00	8.00
R8 Neville	2.50	6.00
R9 Rich Swann	1.50	4.00
R10 TJ Perkins	1.50	4.00

2017 Topps Heritage WWE Shirt Relics

*BLUE/50: .5X TO 1.2X BASIC MEM
*SILVER/25: .6X TO 1.5X BASIC MEM
*GOLD/10: UNPRICED DUE TO SCARCITY
*RED/1: UNPRICED DUE TO SCARCITY

RC Carmella	5.00	12.00
RN Naomi	4.00	10.00
RS Sheamus	4.00	10.00
RAA Andrade Cien Almas	2.00	5.00
RAC Apollo Crews	2.50	6.00
RAE Aiden English	2.00	5.00
RAF Alicia Fox	3.00	8.00
RBK Becky Lynch	6.00	15.00
RBL Brock Lesnar	10.00	25.00
RBR Bobby Roode	5.00	12.00
RCA Curtis Axel	2.00	5.00
RCF Charlotte Flair	8.00	20.00
RDY Darren Young	2.00	5.00
RHI Hideo Itami	3.00	8.00
RJC John Cena	10.00	25.00
RJG Johnny Gargano	2.00	5.00
RJJ JoJo	3.00	8.00
RKA Karl Anderson	2.00	5.00
RLH Luke Harper	2.00	5.00
RNJ No Way Jose	2.00	5.00
RNN Natalya	4.00	10.00
RRO Randy Orton	5.00	12.00
RSB Sasha Banks	6.00	15.00
RSN Shinsuke Nakamura	5.00	12.00
RSR Seth Rollins	6.00	15.00
RSU Summer Rae	5.00	12.00
RTC Tommaso Ciampa	2.00	5.00
RZR Zack Ryder	2.00	5.00

2017 Topps Heritage WWE SummerSlam All-Stars

COMPLETE SET (30)	6.00	15.00

*P.P.BLACK/1: UNPRICED DUE TO SCARCITY
*P.P.CYAN/1: UNPRICED DUE TO SCARCITY
*P.P.MAGENTA/1: UNPRICED DUE TO SCARCITY
*P.P.YELLOW/1: UNPRICED DUE TO SCARCITY
STATED ODDS 1:1

1 Undertaker	1.50	4.00
2 Edge	1.00	2.50
3 Triple H	1.00	2.50
4 Bret Hit Man Hart	.75	2.00
5 Shawn Michaels	1.00	2.50
6 Randy Orton	1.00	2.50
7 Kane	.50	1.25
8 Ultimate Warrior	.75	2.00
9 Rob Van Dam	.75	2.00
10 Brock Lesnar	2.00	5.00
11 Big Show	.50	1.25
12 Chris Jericho	1.00	2.50
13 Kurt Angle	.75	2.00
14 John Cena	2.00	5.00
15 Tatanka	.40	1.00
16 Jerry The King Lawler	.50	1.25
17 Earthquake	.40	1.00
18 Irwin R. Schyster	.40	1.00
19 British Bulldog	.30	.75
20 Stone Cold Steve Austin	1.50	4.00
21 Daniel Bryan	1.50	4.00
22 Mick Foley	1.00	2.50
23 The Rock	1.50	4.00
24 Sheamus	.75	2.00
25 Kofi Kingston	.50	1.25
26 X-Pac	.40	1.00
27 Dolph Ziggler	.60	1.50
28 Ric Flair	1.00	2.50
29 Texas Tornado	.40	1.00
30 Typhoon	.40	1.00

2017 Topps Heritage WWE Survivor Series 2016 Mat Relics

*BRONZE/99: .5X TO 1.2X BASIC MEM
*BLUE/50: .6X TO 1.5X BASIC MEM
*SILVER/25: .75X TO 2X BASIC MEM
*GOLD/10: UNPRICED DUE TO SCARCITY
*RED/1: UNPRICED DUE TO SCARCITY
*P.P.BLACK/1: UNPRICED DUE TO SCARCITY
*P.P.CYAN/1: UNPRICED DUE TO SCARCITY
*P.P.MAGENTA/1: UNPRICED DUE TO SCARCITY
*P.P.YELLOW/1: UNPRICED DUE TO SCARCITY
STATED ODDS 1:175

NNO AJ Styles	6.00	15.00
NNO Alexa Bliss	15.00	40.00
NNO Alicia Fox	5.00	12.00
NNO Bayley	6.00	15.00
NNO Becky Lynch	6.00	15.00
NNO Braun Strowman	5.00	12.00
NNO Bray Wyatt	6.00	15.00
NNO Brock Lesnar	8.00	20.00
NNO Carmella	5.00	12.00
NNO Charlotte Flair	6.00	15.00
NNO Chris Jericho	6.00	15.00
NNO Dean Ambrose	4.00	10.00
NNO Goldberg	6.00	15.00
NNO Kevin Owens	5.00	12.00
NNO Natalya	4.00	10.00
NNO Randy Orton	5.00	12.00
NNO Roman Reigns	5.00	12.00
NNO Sasha Banks	8.00	20.00
NNO Seth Rollins	5.00	12.00
NNO Shane McMahon	6.00	15.00

2018 Topps Heritage WWE

COMPLETE SET W/SP (119)	25.00	60.00
COMPLETE SET W/O SP (110)	10.00	25.00

*BRONZE: .6X TO 1.5X BASIC CARDS
*BLUE/99: .75X TO 2X BASIC CARDS
*SILVER/25: 2X TO 5X BASIC CARDS
*GOLD/10: UNPRICED DUE TO SCARCITY
*RED/1: UNPRICED DUE TO SCARCITY
*P.P.BLACK/1: UNPRICED DUE TO SCARCITY
*P.P.CYAN/1: UNPRICED DUE TO SCARCITY
*P.P.MAGENTA/1: UNPRICED DUE TO SCARCITY
*P.P.YELLOW/1: UNPRICED DUE TO SCARCITY

1 AJ Styles	1.00	2.50
2 Akira Tozawa	.40	1.00
3 Alexa Bliss	1.25	3.00
4 Alicia Fox	.40	1.00
5 Apollo Crews	.25	.60
6 Ariya Daivari	.25	.60
7 Asuka	.75	2.00
8 Baron Corbin	.40	1.00
9 Bayley	.40	1.00
10 Becky Lynch	.60	1.50
11 Big Cass	.30	.75
12 Big E	.30	.75
13 Big Show	.25	.60
14 Bobby Roode	.40	1.00
15 Braun Strowman	.60	1.50
16 Bray Wyatt	.60	1.50
17 Brie Bella	.50	1.25
18 Carmella	.50	1.25
19 Cedric Alexander	.25	.60
20 Cesaro	.50	1.25
21 Chad Gable	.25	.60
22 Charlotte Flair	.75	2.00
23 Chris Jericho	.60	1.50
24 Dean Ambrose	.50	1.25
25 Drew Gulak	.25	.60
26 Elias	.60	1.50
27 Fandango	.25	.60
28 Finn Balor	.60	1.50
29 Gentleman Jack Gallagher	.30	.75
30 Goldust	.50	1.25
31 Jason Jordan	.25	.60
32 Jeff Hardy	.50	1.25
33 Jey Uso	.25	.60
34 Jimmy Uso	.25	.60
35 Jinder Mahal	.30	.75
36 John Cena	1.00	2.50
37 Kalisto	.25	.60
38 Kane	.40	1.00
39 Karl Anderson	.25	.60
40 Kevin Owens	.60	1.50
41 Kofi Kingston	.30	.75
42 Kurt Angle	.60	1.50
43 Lana	.60	1.50
44 Liv Morgan	.50	1.25
45 Luke Gallows	.30	.75
46 Mandy Rose	.60	1.50
47 Maria Kanellis	.60	1.50
48 Maryse	.50	1.25
49 Woken Matt Hardy	.60	1.50
50 Mickie James	.50	1.25
51 Mojo Rawley	.25	.60
52 Mustafa Ali	.25	.60
53 Naomi	.30	.75
54 Natalya	.30	.75
55 Nia Jax	.40	1.00
56 Nikki Bella	.50	1.25
57 Noam Dar	.25	.60
58 Paige	.60	1.50
59 Pete Dunne RC	.25	.60
60 R-Truth	.30	.75
61 Randy Orton	.60	1.50
62 Rhyno	.25	.60
63 Roman Reigns	.60	1.50
64 Ruby Riott	.40	1.00
65 Rusev	.40	1.00
66 Sami Zayn	.25	.60
67 Samoa Joe	.50	1.25
68 Sarah Logan RC	.25	.60
69 Sasha Banks	.75	2.00
70 Seth Rollins	.60	1.50
71 Shane McMahon	.50	1.25
72 Sheamus	.50	1.25
73 Shelton Benjamin	.30	.75
74 Shinsuke Nakamura	.60	1.50
75 Sin Cara	.30	.75
76 Sonya Deville	.50	1.25
77 Stephanie McMahon	.50	1.25
78 Tamina	.25	.60
79 The Brian Kendrick	.40	1.00
80 The Miz	.50	1.25
81 The Rock	1.25	3.00
82 Titus O'Neil	.25	.60
83 Tony Nese	.25	.60
84 Triple H	.60	1.50
85 Tye Dillinger	.25	.60
86 Tyler Bate	.25	.60
87 Tyler Breeze	.25	.60
88 Undertaker	1.00	2.50
89 Xavier Woods	.30	.75
90 Zack Ryder	.25	.60
91 Adam Cole RC	.30	.75
92 Aleister Black	.30	.75
93 Alexander Wolfe	.25	.60
94 Andrade Cien Almas	.40	1.00
95 Billie Kay	.50	1.25
96 Bobby Fish RC	.25	.60
97 Drew McIntyre	.40	1.00
98 Ember Moon	.50	1.25
99 Eric Young	.30	.75
100 Johnny Gargano	.25	.60
101 Kairi Sane RC	.60	1.50
102 Kassius Ohno	.25	.60
103 Killian Dain	.30	.75
104 Kyle O'Reilly RC	.30	.75
105 Nikki Cross	.40	1.00
106 Oney Lorcan	.30	.75
107 Peyton Royce	.60	1.50
108 Roderick Strong	.25	.60
109 Tommaso Ciampa	.25	.60
110 Velveteen Dream	.25	.60
111 Aiden English SP	1.25	3.00
112 Ariya Daivari SP	1.25	3.00
113 Dash Wilder SP	1.50	4.00
114 Harper SP	2.00	5.00
115 Konnor SP	1.25	3.00
116 R-Truth SP	1.50	4.00
117 Rowan SP	2.00	5.00
118 Scott Dawson SP	1.50	4.00
119 Viktor SP	1.25	3.00

2018 Topps Heritage WWE Autographed NXT TakeOver War Games 2017 Mat Relics

STATED PRINT RUN 10 SER.#'d SETS
UNPRICED DUE TO SCARCITY

NXTAAC Adam Cole
NXTABF Bobby Fish
NXTADM Drew McIntyre
NXTAEM Ember Moon
NXTAKD Killian Dain
NXTAKO Kyle O'Reilly
NXTARS Roderick Strong

2018 Topps Heritage WWE Autographed Survivor Series 2017 Mat Relics

STATED PRINT RUN 10 SER.#'d SETS
UNPRICED DUE TO SCARCITY

SSAAJ AJ Styles
SSAAS Asuka
SSABR Booby Roode
SSABS Braun Strowman
SSAKA Kurt Angle
SSANJ Nia Jax
SSARO Randy Orton
SSASB Sasha Banks
SSASJ Samoa Joe
SSASN Shinsuke Nakamura
SSATH Triple H

2018 Topps Heritage WWE Autographed TLC 2017 Mat Relics

STATED PRINT RUN 10 SER.#'d SETS
UNPRICED DUE TO SCARCITY

TLCAAJ AJ Styles
TLCABS Braun Strowman
TLCAKA Kurt Angle
TLCASH Sheamus
TLCATM The Miz

2018 Topps Heritage WWE Autographed TLC Commemorative Medallion Relics

STATED PRINT RUN 10 SER.#'d SETS
UNPRICED DUE TO SCARCITY

CTMAAJ AJ Styles
CTMABC Baron Corbin
CTMABS Braun Strowman
CTMADZ Dolph Ziggler
CTMAKA Kane
CTMAKA Kurt Angle
CTMAMZ The Miz
CTMASA Sheamus
CTMASH Sheamus
CTMATM The Miz

2018 Topps Heritage WWE Autographs

*BLUE/50: .5X TO 1.2X BASIC AUTOS
*SILVER/25: .6X TO 1.5X BASIC AUTOS
*GOLD/10: UNPRICED DUE TO SCARCITY
*RED/1: UNPRICED DUE TO SCARCITY
STATED PRINT RUN 99 SER.#'d SETS

AAB Alexa Bliss 50.00 100.00
AAC Adam Cole 15.00 40.00
AAS AJ Styles 15.00 40.00
AAS Asuka 12.00 30.00
ABA Bayley 12.00 30.00
ABE Big E 5.00 12.00
ABL Becky Lynch 15.00 40.00
ABS Braun Strowman 12.00 30.00
ACF Charlotte Flair 15.00 40.00
AFB Finn Balor 12.00 30.00
AJH Jeff Hardy 12.00 30.00
AKA Kurt Angle 10.00 25.00
AKK Kofi Kingston 6.00 15.00
AKO Kevin Owens 6.00 15.00
ALM Liv Morgan 10.00 25.00
AMH Matt Hardy 10.00 25.00
AMR Mandy Rose 15.00 40.00
ASB Sasha Banks 12.00 30.00
ASN Shinsuke Nakamura 10.00 25.00
AXW Xavier Woods 5.00 12.00
AALB Aleister Black 6.00 15.00

2018 Topps Heritage WWE Autographs Silver

ACA Carmella 12.00 30.00
ASM Stephanie McMahon 75.00 150.00
ATH Triple H 150.00 300.00
AUN Undertaker 125.00 250.00

2018 Topps Heritage WWE Big Legends

COMPLETE SET (50) 12.00 30.00
*BRONZE/99: .75X TO 2X BASIC CARDS
*BLUE/50: 1.2X TO 3X BASIC CARDS
*SILVER/25: 1.5X TO 4X BASIC CARDS
*GOLD/10: UNPRICED DUE TO SCARCITY
*RED/1: UNPRICED DUE TO SCARCITY
*P.P.BLACK/1: UNPRICED DUE TO SCARCITY
*P.P.CYAN/1: UNPRICED DUE TO SCARCITY
*P.P.MAGENTA/1: UNPRICED DUE TO SCARCITY
*P.P.YELLOW/1: UNPRICED DUE TO SCARCITY
STATED ODDS 2:1; 4:1 FAT PACK

BL1 Alundra Blayze .30 .75
BL2 Andre the Giant .60 1.50
BL3 Bam Bam Bigelow .50 1.25
BL4 Bob Backlund .30 .75
BL5 Booker T .50 1.25
BL6 Bret Hit Man Hart .75 2.00
BL7 British Bulldog .60 1.50
BL8 Bruno Sammartino .50 1.25
BL9 Brutus The Barber Beefcake .30 .75
BL10 Cowboy Bob Orton .30 .75
BL11 Dean Malenko .30 .75
BL12 Diamond Dallas Page .50 1.25
BL13 Dusty Rhodes .60 1.50
BL14 Eddie Guerrero .75 2.00
BL15 Edge .75 2.00
BL16 George The Animal Steele .40 1.00
BL17 Greg The Hammer Valentine .30 .75
BL18 Hacksaw Jim Duggan .30 .75
BL19 Harley Race .30 .75
BL20 The Honky Tonk Man .30 .75
BL21 Iron Sheik .30 .75
BL22 Irwin R. Schyster .30 .75
BL23 Jake The Snake Roberts .40 1.00
BL24 Jerry The King Lawler .60 1.50
BL25 Jim The Anvil Neidhart .50 1.25
BL26 Kerry Von Erich .30 .75
BL27 Kevin Nash .60 1.50
BL28 Kevin Von Erich .50 1.25
BL29 Larry Zbyszko .30 .75
BL30 Lex Luger .40 1.00
BL31 Lita .75 2.00
BL32 Macho Man Randy Savage 1.00 2.50
BL33 Michael P.S. Hayes .30 .75
BL34 Mick Foley .60 1.50
BL35 Ted DiBiase .40 1.00
BL36 Mr. Perfect .40 1.00
BL37 Mr. Wonderful Paul Orndorff .30 .75
BL38 Nikolai Volkoff .30 .75
BL39 Ravishing Rick Rude .40 1.00
BL40 Ric Flair 1.00 2.50
BL41 Ricky The Dragon Steamboat .50 1.25
BL42 Ron Simmons .40 1.00
BL43 Rowdy Roddy Piper .75 2.00
BL44 Scott Hall .60 1.50
BL45 Sgt. Slaughter .40 1.00
BL46 Sid Vicious .30 .75
BL47 Sting .75 2.00
BL48 Stone Cold Steve Austin 1.50 4.00
BL49 Trish Stratus 1.25 3.00
BL50 Ultimate Warrior 1.25 3.00

2018 Topps Heritage WWE Big Legends Autographs

*SILVER/25: UNPRICED DUE TO SCARCITY
*GOLD/10: UNPRICED DUE TO SCARCITY
*RED/1: UNPRICED DUE TO SCARCITY

BLAAB Alundra Blayze 6.00 15.00
BLABB Brutus The Barber Beefcake 6.00 15.00
BLABH Bret Hit Man Hart 25.00 60.00
BLAIS Irwin R. Schyster 10.00 25.00
BLAJD Hacksaw Jim Duggan 8.00 20.00
BLAJR Jake The Snake Roberts 15.00 40.00
BLAST Sting 25.00 60.00
BLATD Ted DiBiase 12.00 30.00
BLATS Trish Stratus 30.00 75.00
BLADDP Diamond Dallas Page 10.00 25.00

2018 Topps Heritage WWE Dual Autographs

STATED PRINT RUN 10 SER.#'d SETS
UNPRICED DUE TO SCARCITY

DACC Epico/Primo/9
DAKR B.Kay/P.Royce/10
DALC M.Cole/J.Lawler/10
DATM S.McMahon/Triple H/10
DAUT Triple H/Undertaker/10

2018 Topps Heritage WWE Kiss

*GOLD/10: UNPRICED DUE TO SCARCITY
*RED/1: UNPRICED DUE TO SCARCITY

KCAB Alexa Bliss 60.00 120.00
KCAF Alicia Fox 15.00 40.00
KCAS Asuka 30.00 75.00
KCCC Charly Caruso 50.00 100.00
KCDB Dana Brooke 20.00 50.00
KCDF Dasha Fuentes 15.00 40.00
KCMR Mandy Rose 50.00 100.00
KCNA Natalya 15.00 40.00
KCNA Naomi 15.00 40.00
KCRY Renee Young 20.00 50.00

2018 Topps Heritage WWE Kiss Autographs

*GOLD/10: UNPRICED DUE TO SCARCITY
*RED/1: UNPRICED DUE TO SCARCITY
STATED PRINT RUN 25 SER.#'d SETS

KAAB Alexa Bliss 150.00 300.00
KAAF Alicia Fox 50.00 100.00
KAAS Asuka 60.00 120.00
KACC Charly Caruso 30.00 75.00
KADB Dana Brooke 50.00 100.00
KADF Dasha Fuentes 30.00 75.00
KAMR Mandy Rose 75.00 150.00
KANA Natalya 25.00 60.00
KARY Renee Young 30.00 75.00

2018 Topps Heritage WWE Manufactured Coins

1 John Cena 8.00 20.00
2 Brock Lesnar 6.00 15.00
3 AJ Styles 5.00 12.00
4 Roman Reigns 5.00 12.00
5 Seth Rollins 5.00 12.00
6 Dean Ambrose 4.00 10.00
7 Braun Strowman 4.00 10.00
8 Samoa Joe 4.00 10.00
9 Shinsuke Nakamura 5.00 12.00
10 Kevin Owens 4.00 10.00

2018 Topps Heritage WWE NXT TakeOver War Games 2017 Mat Relics

*BRONZE/99: .5X TO 1.2X BASIC MEM
*BLUE/50: .6X TO 1.5X BASIC MEM
*SILVER/25: .75X TO 2X BASIC MEM
*GOLD/10: UNPRICED DUE TO SCARCITY
*RED/1: UNPRICED DUE TO SCARCITY
STATED PRINT RUN 299 SER.#'d SETS

NXTAA Andrade Cien Almas 2.50 6.00
NXTAC Adam Cole 8.00 20.00
NXTAW Alexander Wolfe 2.50 6.00
NXTBF Bobby Fish 4.00 10.00
NXTDM Drew McIntyre 2.50 6.00
NXTEM Ember Moon 3.00 8.00
NXTEY Eric Young 3.00 8.00
NXTKD Killian Dain 3.00 8.00
NXTKO Kyle O'Reilly 3.00 8.00
NXTRS Roderick Strong 2.50 6.00

2018 Topps Heritage WWE Shirt Relics

*BLUE/50: .5X TO 1.2X BASIC MEM
*SILVER/25: .6X TO 1.5X BASIC MEM
*GOLD/10: UNPRICED DUE TO SCARCITY
*RED/1: UNPRICED DUE TO SCARCITY
STATED PRINT RUN 99 SER.#'d SETS

SRAB Alexa Bliss 12.00 30.00
SRAE Aiden English 4.00 10.00
SRAF Alicia Fox 3.00 8.00
SRAK Akam 3.00 8.00
SRAW Alexander Wolfe 3.00 8.00
SRBE Becky Lynch 5.00 12.00
SRBL Brock Lesnar 6.00 15.00
SRCA Carmella 5.00 12.00
SRDW Dash Wilder 3.00 8.00
SREM Ember Moon 5.00 12.00
SREY Eric Young 3.00 8.00
SRGD Goldust 3.00 8.00
SRJC John Cena 6.00 15.00
SRJJ JoJo 5.00 12.00
SRNC Nikki Cross 5.00 12.00
SRRE Rezar 3.00 8.00
SRRR Roman Reigns 8.00 20.00
SRRY Renee Young 5.00 12.00
SRSD Scott Dawson 3.00 8.00
SRSR Seth Rollins 5.00 12.00

2018 Topps Heritage WWE Survivor Series 2017 Mat Relics

*BRONZE/99: .5X TO 1.2X BASIC MEM
*BLUE/50: .6X TO 1.5X BASIC MEM
*SILVER/25: .75X TO 2X BASIC MEM
*GOLD/10: UNPRICED DUE TO SCARCITY
*RED/1: UNPRICED DUE TO SCARCITY
STATED PRINT RUN 299 SER.#'d SETS

SSAB Alexa Bliss 10.00 25.00
SSAJ AJ Styles 3.00 8.00
SSAS Asuka 5.00 12.00
SSBA Bayley 3.00 8.00
SSBL Brock Lesnar 4.00 10.00
SSBR Bobby Roode 3.00 8.00
SSBS Braun Strowman 4.00 10.00
SSCF Charlotte Flair 5.00 12.00
SSDA Dean Ambrose 2.50 6.00
SSFB Finn Balor 3.00 8.00
SSJC John Cena 4.00 10.00
SSKA Kurt Angle 2.50 6.00
SSNJ Nia Jax 2.50 6.00
SSRO Randy Orton 2.50 6.00
SSRR Roman Reigns 3.00 8.00
SSSB Sasha Banks 6.00 15.00
SSSJ Samoa Joe 4.00 10.00
SSSN Shinsuke Nakamura 3.00 8.00
SSSR Seth Rollins 3.00 8.00
SSTH Triple H 4.00 10.00

2018 Topps Heritage WWE Tag Teams and Stables

COMPLETE SET (20) 6.00 15.00
*BRONZE/99: .5X TO 1.2X BASIC CARDS
*BLUE/50: .6X TO 1.5X BASIC CARDS
*SILVER/25: 1.2X TO 3X BASIC CARDS
*GOLD/10: UNPRICED DUE TO SCARCITY
*RED/1: UNPRICED DUE TO SCARCITY
STATED ODDS 1:2; 2:1 FAT PACK

TT1 Cesaro & Sheamus .75 2.00
TT2 The Shield 1.00 2.50
TT3 The Hardy Boyz 1.00 2.50
TT4 Heath Slater & Rhyno .40 1.00
TT5 Luke Gallows & Karl Anderson .50 1.25
TT6 The Miz & The Miztourage .75 2.00
TT7 The Revival .50 1.25
TT8 Bludgeon Brothers .60 1.50
TT9 Breezango .40 1.00
TT10 Shelton Benjamin & Chad Gable .50 1.25
TT11 Kevin Owens & Sami Zayn 1.00 2.50
TT12 The Hype Bros .40 1.00
TT13 Jinder Mahal & The Singhs .50 1.25
TT14 The New Day .60 1.50
TT15 The Authors of Pain .40 1.00
TT16 Heavy Machinery .40 1.00
TT17 The Ilconics 1.00 2.50
TT18 SAnitY .60 1.50
TT19 The Street Profits .40 1.00
TT20 Undisputed ERA .50 1.25

2018 Topps Heritage WWE TLC 2017 Mat Relics

*BRONZE/99: .5X TO 1.2X BASIC MEM
*BLUE/50: .6X TO 1.5X BASIC MEM
*SILVER/25: .75X TO 2X BASIC MEM
*GOLD/10: UNPRICED DUE TO SCARCITY

*RED/1: UNPRICED DUE TO SCARCITY
STATED PRINT RUN 299 SER.#'d SETS

TLCAJ AJ Styles 4.00 10.00
TLCBS Braun Strowman 2.00 5.00
TLCCE Cesaro 2.00 5.00
TLCDA Dean Ambrose 3.00 8.00
TLCFB Finn Balor 4.00 10.00
TLCKA Kurt Angle 4.00 10.00
TLCKN Kane 3.00 8.00
TLCSH Sheamus 2.00 5.00
TLCSR Seth Rollins 5.00 12.00
TLCTM The Miz 2.00 5.00

2018 Topps Heritage WWE TLC Commemorative Medallion Relics

*BRONZE/99: .5X TO 1.2X BASIC MEM
*BLUE/50: .6X TO 1.5X BASIC MEM
*SILVER/25: .75X TO 2X BASIC MEM
*GOLD/10: UNPRICED DUE TO SCARCITY
*RED/1: UNPRICED DUE TO SCARCITY
STATED PRINT RUN 199 SER.#'d SETS

CTMAB Alexa Bliss 10.00 25.00
CTMAJ AJ Styles 5.00 12.00
CTMBC Baron Corbin 4.00 10.00
CTMBL Becky Lynch 6.00 15.00
CTMBS Braun Strowman 5.00 12.00
CTMCE Cesaro 3.00 8.00
CTMDA Dean Ambrose 3.00 8.00
CTMDE Dean Ambrose 3.00 8.00
CTMDZ Dolph Ziggler 3.00 8.00
CTMJC John Cena 5.00 12.00
CTMKA Kurt Angle 3.00 8.00
CTMKA Kane 3.00 8.00
CTMKL Kalisto 3.00 8.00
CTMMZ The Miz 3.00 8.00
CTMRL Seth Rollins 4.00 10.00
CTMRR Roman Reigns 5.00 12.00
CTMSA Sheamus 3.00 8.00
CTMSH Sheamus 3.00 8.00
CTMSR Seth Rollins 3.00 8.00
CTMTM The Miz 3.00 8.00

2018 Topps Heritage WWE Top 10 Rookies

COMPLETE SET (10) 4.00 10.00
*BRONZE/99: .5X TO 1.2X BASIC CARDS
*BLUE/50: .6X TO 1.5X BASIC CARDS
*SILVER/25: .75X TO 2X BASIC CARDS
*GOLD/10: UNPRICED DUE TO SCARCITY
*RED/1: UNPRICED DUE TO SCARCITY
*P.P.BLACK/1: UNPRICED DUE TO SCARCITY
*P.P.CYAN/1: UNPRICED DUE TO SCARCITY
*P.P.MAGENTA/1: UNPRICED DUE TO SCARCITY
*P.P.YELLOW/1: UNPRICED DUE TO SCARCITY
STATED ODDS 1:3; 1:1 FAT PACK

TR1 Asuka 1.25 3.00
TR2 Shinsuke Nakamura 1.00 2.50
TR3 Bobby Roode .60 1.50
TR4 Samoa Joe .75 2.00
TR5 Tyler Bate .40 1.00
TR6 Pete Dunne .40 1.00
TR7 Dash Wilder .50 1.25
TR8 Scott Dawson .50 1.25
TR9 Elias 1.00 2.50
TR10 Tye Dillinger .40 1.00

2018 Topps Heritage WWE Top 10 Rookies Autographs

*SILVER/25: .5X TO 1.2X BASIC AUTOS
*GOLD/10: UNPRICED DUE TO SCARCITY
*RED/1: UNPRICED DUE TO SCARCITY
STATED PRINT RUN 50 SER.#'d SETS

TTRAAS Asuka 15.00 40.00
TTRABR Bobby Roode 10.00 25.00
TTRADW Dash Wilder 5.00 12.00
TTRAEL Elias 25.00 60.00
TTRASD Scott Dawson 5.00 12.00
TTRASJ Samoa Joe 10.00 25.00
TTRASN Shinsuke Nakamura 12.00 30.00
TTRATD Tye Dillinger 6.00 15.00

2018 Topps Heritage WWE Triple Mat Relics

*SILVER/25: .5X TO 1.2X BASIC MEM
*GOLD/10: UNPRICED DUE TO SCARCITY
*RED/1: UNPRICED DUE TO SCARCITY
STATED PRINT RUN 50 SER.#'d SETS

TMBL Brock Lesnar 8.00 20.00
TMCF Charlotte Flair 12.00 30.00
TMDA Dean Ambrose 10.00 25.00
TMJC John Cena 10.00 25.00
TMKO Kevin Owens 8.00 20.00
TMTH Triple H 8.00 20.00
TMTM The Miz 8.00 20.00
TMUD Undertaker 15.00 40.00

2021 Topps Heritage WWE

COMPLETE SET (100) 10.00 25.00
*FOIL: .6X TO 1.5X BASIC CARDS
*GREEN/99: .75X TO 2X BASIC CARDS
*BLUE/25: 1.5X TO 4X BASIC CARDS
*RED/10: UNPRICED DUE TO SCARCITY
*FOILFRACTOR/1: UNPRICED DUE TO SCARCITY

1 AJ Styles 1.00 2.50
2 Akira Tozawa .40 1.00
3 Alexa Bliss 2.00 5.00
4 Angel Garza .40 1.00
5 Asuka 1.25 3.00
6 Bobby Lashley .75 2.00
7 Cedric Alexander .30 .75
8 Charlotte Flair 1.50 4.00
8 Charlotte Flair SP/Peacock 30.00 75.00
9 Damian Priest .50 1.25
10 Dana Brooke .30 .75
11 Drew McIntyre .75 2.00
12 Doudrop .50 1.25
13 Elias .30 .75
14 Erik .30 .75
15 Eva Marie .75 2.00
16 Gran Metalik .30 .75
17 Humberto Carrillo .30 .75
18 Ivar .30 .75
19 Jeff Hardy .75 2.00
20 John Morrison .60 1.50
21 Keith Lee .60 1.50
22 Kofi Kingston .75 2.00
23 Lacey Evans .75 2.00
24 Lince Dorado .30 .75
25 MACE .30 .75
26 Mandy Rose 1.50 4.00
26 Mandy Rose SP/Roses 30.00 75.00
27 Mustafa Ali .40 1.00
28 MVP .30 .75
29 Naomi .40 1.00
30 Nia Jax .60 1.50
31 Nikki ASH .60 1.50
32 Omos RC .60 1.50
33 Randy Orton 1.00 2.50
33 Randy Orton SP/Viper 15.00 40.00
34 Rhea Ripley 1.00 2.50
35 Ricochet .60 1.50
36 Riddick Moss .40 1.00
37 Riddle .75 2.00
38 R-Truth .40 1.00
39 Shayna Baszler .60 1.50
40 Sheamus .50 1.25
40 Sheamus SP/Shark 12.00 30.00
41 Shelton Benjamin .50 1.25
42 T-BAR .40 1.00
43 The Fiend 1.25 3.00
44 The Miz .50 1.25
45 Titus O'Neil .30 .75
46 Xavier Woods .30 .75
47 Angelo Dawkins .40 1.00
48 Apollo Crews .40 1.00
49 Baron Corbin .30 .75
49 Baron Corbin SP/Wolf 8.00 20.00
50 Bayley .75 2.00
51 Bianca Belair .75 2.00
52 Big E .60 1.50
53 Carmella .75 2.00
54 Cesaro .30 .75
55 Chad Gable .30 .75
56 Commander Azeez RC .40 1.00
57 Dolph Ziggler .60 1.50
58 Dominik Mysterio RC .40 1.00
59 Edge 1.25 3.00
60 Jey Uso .30 .75
61 Jimmy Uso .30 .75
62 Kevin Owens .60 1.50
63 Liv Morgan 1.25 3.00
64 Mia Yim .40 1.00
65 Montez Ford .30 .75
66 Natalya .50 1.25
67 Otis .40 1.00
67 Otis SP/Worm 15.00 40.00
68 Rey Mysterio .75 2.00
69 Robert Roode .40 1.00
70 Roman Reigns 1.50 4.00
70 Roman Reigns SP/Dog 30.00 75.00
71 Sami Zayn .50 1.25
72 Sasha Banks 1.50 4.00
72 Sasha Banks SP/Cash 25.00 60.00
73 Seth Rollins .75 2.00
74 Shinsuke Nakamura .75 2.00
74 Nakamura SP/Crown 10.00 25.00
75 Tamina .40 1.00
76 Zelina Vega .60 1.50
77 Adam Cole 1.00 2.50
78 Boa .30 .75
79 Cameron Grimes .60 1.50
80 Candice LeRae 1.25 3.00
81 Dakota Kai .60 1.50
82 Ember Moon .40 1.00
83 Finn Balor .75 2.00
84 Io Shirai .60 1.50
85 Indi Hartwell RC 1.00 2.50
86 Johnny Gargano .60 1.50
87 Karrion Kross 1.25 3.00
88 Kushida .50 1.25
89 Kyle O'Reilly .50 1.25
90 Santos Escobar .50 1.25
91 Samoa Joe .60 1.50
92 Scarlett 1.50 4.00
93 Shotzi 1.25 3.00
94 Timothy Thatcher RC .30 .75
95 Tommaso Ciampa .75 2.00
96 Toni Storm 1.00 2.50
97 Xia Li .60 1.50
98 Becky Lynch 1.25 3.00
99 John Cena 1.50 4.00
100 Triple H 1.25 3.00

2021 Topps Heritage WWE Allen and Ginter

COMPLETE SET (30) 12.00 30.00
RANDOMLY INSERTED INTO PACKS

AG1 AJ Styles 1.00 2.50
AG2 Alexa Bliss 2.00 5.00
AG3 Asuka 1.25 3.00
AG4 Bayley .75 2.00
AG5 Becky Lynch 1.25 3.00
AG6 Big E .60 1.50
AG7 Charlotte Flair 1.50 4.00
AG8 Diesel .50 1.25
AG9 Drew McIntyre .75 2.00
AG10 Eddie Guerrero 1.50 4.00
AG11 Kane .50 1.25
AG12 Kevin Owens .60 1.50
AG13 Mr. Perfect 1.00 2.50
AG14 Macho Man Randy Savage 1.25 3.00
AG15 Ted DiBiase .60 1.50
AG16 Razor Ramon .50 1.25
AG17 Rikishi .40 1.00
AG18 Roman Reigns 1.50 4.00
AG19 Sasha Banks 1.50 4.00
AG20 Seth Rollins .75 2.00
AG21 Shinsuke Nakamura .75 2.00
AG22 Typhoon .30 .75
AG23 Sycho Sid .50 1.25
AG24 The 1-2-3 Kid .40 1.00
AG25 The Fiend Bray Wyatt 1.25 3.00
AG26 The Miz .50 1.25
AG27 The Rock 3.00 8.00
AG28 Ultimate Warrior 1.25 3.00
AG29 Vader .50 1.25
AG30 The Godfather .40 1.00

2021 Topps Heritage WWE Autographs

*GREEN/99: .5X TO 1.2X BASIC AUTOS
*PURPLE/50: .6X TO 1.5X BASIC AUTOS
*BLUE/25: 1.2X TO 3X BASIC AUTOS
*RED/10: UNPRICED DUE TO SCARCITY
*GOLD/1: UNPRICED DUE TO SCARCITY
STATED ODDS 1:264
STATED PRINT RUN 199 SER.#'d SETS

AS Sasha Banks 60.00 120.00
AAB Alexa Bliss 75.00 150.00
AAC Apollo Crews 6.00 15.00
AAJ AJ Styles 10.00 25.00
AAS Asuka 15.00 40.00
ABE Big E 6.00 15.00
ABL Bobby Lashley 8.00 20.00
ACI Tommaso Ciampa 6.00 15.00
ACM Carmella 8.00 20.00
ACS Cesaro 6.00 15.00
ADM Drew McIntyre 8.00 20.00
ADZ Dolph Ziggler 6.00 15.00
AEM Ember Moon 5.00 12.00
AFB Finn Balor 10.00 25.00
AIS Io Shirai 10.00 25.00
AJC John Cena
AJM John Morrison 8.00 20.00
AKK Karrion Kross 10.00 25.00
AKO Kevin Owens 6.00 15.00
AKU Kushida 5.00 12.00
ALD Lince Dorado 6.00 15.00
ALM Liv Morgan 25.00 60.00
AMA Mustafa Ali 5.00 12.00
ANJ Nia Jax 5.00 12.00
ARH Rhea Ripley 15.00 40.00
ART R-Truth 5.00 12.00
ASB Shayna Baszler 5.00 12.00
ASE Santos Escobar 6.00 15.00
ASH Shotzi Blackheart 25.00 60.00
ASL Scarlett 20.00 50.00
ASN Shinsuke Nakamura 8.00 20.00
ASR Seth Rollins 10.00 25.00
ASZ Sami Zayn 8.00 20.00
ATT Timothy Thatcher 6.00 15.00
ABRO Riddle 12.00 30.00
AJEY Jey Uso 5.00 12.00
AKOR Kyle O'Reilly 8.00 20.00
AMVP MVP 5.00 12.00
AREY Rey Mysterio 15.00 40.00

2021 Topps Heritage WWE Dual Autographs

*BLUE/25: .5X TO 1.2X BASIC AUTOS
*RED/10: UNPRICED DUE TO SCARCITY
*GOLD/1: UNPRICED DUE TO SCARCITY
STATED ODDS 1:3,796
STATED PRINT RUN 50 SER.#'d SETS

DAJB S.Baszler/N.Jax 25.00 60.00
DAND K.Kingston/X.Woods 20.00 50.00
DART Mace/T-Bar 15.00 40.00
DASP M.Ford/A.Dawkins 20.00 50.00
DAVR Ivar/Erik 12.00 30.00
DAGYV J.Drake/Z.Gibson 12.00 30.00
DALHP G.Metalik/L.Dorado 20.00 50.00

2021 Topps Heritage WWE The Miz Superstar Tribute

COMPLETE SET (20) 6.00 15.00
STATED ODDS 1:3

TM1 The Miz .60 1.50
TM2 The Miz .60 1.50
TM3 The Miz .60 1.50
TM4 The Miz .60 1.50
TM5 The Miz .60 1.50
TM6 The Miz .60 1.50
TM7 The Miz .60 1.50
TM8 The Miz .60 1.50
TM9 The Miz .60 1.50
TM10 The Miz .60 1.50
TM11 The Miz .60 1.50
TM12 The Miz .60 1.50
TM13 The Miz .60 1.50
TM14 The Miz .60 1.50
TM15 The Miz .60 1.50

TM16 The Miz	.60	1.50
TM17 The Miz	.60	1.50
TM18 The Miz	.60	1.50
TM19 The Miz	.60	1.50
TM20 The Miz	.60	1.50

2021 Topps Heritage WWE The Miz Superstar Tribute Autographs

*RED/10: UNPRICED DUE TO SCARCITY
STATED ODDS 1:4,181
STATED PRINT RUN 25 SER.#'d SETS

AMZ6 The Miz
AMZ9 The Miz
AMZ11 The Miz
AMZ15 The Miz
AMZ19 The Miz

2021 Topps Heritage WWE Sketch Card Reproduction

COMPLETE SET (10)
STATED ODDS 1:24

SCR1 Eddie Guerrero
SCR2 Edge
SCR3 John Cena
SCR4 Randy Orton
SCR5 Triple H
SCR6 Undertaker
SCR7 Jeff Hardy
SCR8 Kane
SCR9 MVP
SCR10 Rey Mysterio

2021 Topps Heritage WWE Superstar Stickers

COMPLETE SET (18)	12.00	30.00
STATED ODDS 1:4		
S1 AJ Styles	1.00	2.50
S2 Alexa Bliss	2.00	5.00
S3 Bayley	.75	2.00
S4 Becky Lynch	1.25	3.00
S5 Charlotte Flair	1.50	4.00
S6 D-Generation X	1.25	3.00
S7 Finn Balor	.75	2.00
S8 Jeff Hardy	.75	2.00
S9 John Cena	1.50	4.00
S10 Randy Orton	1.00	2.50
S11 Asuka	1.25	3.00
S12 Rey Mysterio	.75	2.00
S13 Roman Reigns	1.50	4.00
S14 Sasha Banks	1.50	4.00
S15 Seth Rollins	.75	2.00
S16 Shinsuke Nakamura	.75	2.00
S17 The Miz	.50	1.25
S18 The New Day	.75	2.00
S19 Naomi	.40	1.00
S20 Undertaker	1.50	4.00

2021 Topps Heritage WWE Superstars Speak

COMPLETE SET (10)	8.00	20.00
STATED ODDS 1:12		
SS1 Batista	.75	2.00
SS2 Booker T	.75	2.00
SS3 Goldberg	1.50	4.00
SS4 John Cena	2.00	5.00
SS5 Macho Man Randy Savage	1.50	4.00
SS6 Ric Flair	1.50	4.00
SS7 The Fiend Bray Wyatt	1.50	4.00
SS8 The Miz	.60	1.50
SS9 Undertaker	2.00	5.00
SS10 Ron Simmons	.60	1.50

2011 Topps Jim Ross JR's BarBQ Sauce Autograph Exclusive

NNO Jim Ross	30.00	75.00

2017 Topps Legends of WWE

COMPLETE SET (100)	8.00	20.00
*BRONZE: .6X TO 1.5X BASIC CARDS		
*SILVER/99: .75X TO 2X BASIC CARDS		
*BLUE/50: 1.2X TO 3X BASIC CARDS		
*GOLD/10: UNPRICED DUE TO SCARCITY		
*RED/1: UNPRICED DUE TO SCARCITY		
1 Brock Lesnar	1.25	3.00
2 Goldberg	1.00	2.50
3 The Rock	1.25	3.00
4 Hunter Hearst Helmsley	.60	1.50
5 Undertaker	1.00	2.50
6 Afa	.25	.60
7 Alundra Blayze	.30	.75
8 Andre the Giant	.50	1.25
9 Bam Bam Bigelow	.40	1.00
10 The Berzerker	.25	.60
11 Big Boss Man	.30	.75
12 Big John Studd	.30	.75
13 Bob Backlund	.25	.60
14 Bobby The Brain Heenan	.40	1.00
15 The Boogeyman	.25	.60
16 Booker T	.30	.75
17 Bret Hit Man Hart	.50	1.25
18 Brian Knobbs	.25	.60
19 British Bulldog	.25	.60
20 Bruno Sammartino	.40	1.00
21 Brutus The Barber Beefcake	.25	.60
22 Cowboy Bob Orton	.40	1.00
23 D'Lo Brown	.25	.60
24 Daniel Bryan	1.00	2.50
25 Dean Malenko	.30	.75
26 Diamond Dallas Page	.30	.75
27 Don Muraco	.25	.60
28 Dory Funk Jr.	.25	.60
29 Dusty Rhodes	.30	.75
30 Earthquake	.25	.60
31 Eddie Guerrero	.50	1.25
32 Edge	.60	1.50
33 Eve Torres	.40	1.00
34 Fit Finlay	.25	.60
35 General Adnan	.25	.60
36 George The Animal Steele	.40	1.00
37 Gerald Brisco	.25	.60
38 The Goon RC	.25	.60
39 Greg The Hammer Valentine	.30	.75
40 Hacksaw Jim Duggan	.40	1.00
41 Haku	.25	.60
42 Harley Race	.30	.75
43 The Honky Tonk Man	.30	.75
44 Iron Sheik	.30	.75
45 Irwin R. Schyster	.25	.60
46 Jake The Snake Roberts	.30	.75
47 The Godfather	.25	.60
48 Jerry The King Lawler	.30	.75
49 Jerry Sags	.25	.60
50 Jim The Anvil Neidhart	.25	.60
51 Junkyard Dog	.30	.75
52 Mike Rotunda	.25	.60
53 Ken Shamrock	.25	.60
54 Kerry Von Erich	.25	.60
55 Kevin Nash	.40	1.00
56 Kevin Von Erich	.40	1.00
57 Larry Zbyszko	.30	.75
58 Lex Luger	.30	.75
59 Macho Man Randy Savage	.50	1.25
60 Magnum T.A.	.25	.60
61 Michael P.S. Hayes	.30	.75
62 Mick Foley	.60	1.50
63 Ted DiBiase	.30	.75
64 Miss Elizabeth	.40	1.00
65 Mr. Perfect	.50	1.25
66 Mr. Wonderful Paul Orndorff	.30	.75
67 Nikolai Volkoff	.30	.75
68 Norman Smiley	.30	.75
69 Papa Shango	.25	.60
70 Pat Patterson	.25	.60
71 Ravishing Rick Rude	.40	1.00
72 Ric Flair	.60	1.50
73 Ricky The Dragon Steamboat	.50	1.25
74 Road Dogg	.40	1.00
75 Rob Van Dam	.50	1.25
76 Rocky Johnson	.25	.60
77 Ron Simmons	.30	.75
78 Rowdy Roddy Piper	.50	1.25
79 Scott Hall	.30	.75
80 Sgt. Slaughter	.30	.75
81 Sensational Sherri	.30	.75
82 Sid Vicious	.30	.75
83 Sika RC	.25	.60
84 Stevie Ray	.25	.60
85 Sting	.75	2.00
86 Stone Cold Steve Austin	1.00	2.50
87 Tatanka	.25	.60
88 Tatsumi Fujinami	.25	.60
89 Terri Runnels	.25	.60
90 Terry Taylor	.25	.60
91 Trish Stratus	1.00	2.50
92 Tully Blanchard	.30	.75
93 Typhoon	.25	.60
94 Ultimate Warrior	.50	1.25
95 Umaga	.25	.60
96 Virgil	.25	.60
97 The Warlord	.25	.60
98 Wendi Richter	.30	.75
99 X-Pac	.25	.60
100 Yokozuna	.40	1.00

2017 Topps Legends of WWE Autographed Retired Championship Belt Relics

*GOLD/10: UNPRICED DUE TO SCARCITY		
*BLACK/5: UNPRICED DUE TO SCARCITY		
*RED/1: UNPRICED DUE TO SCARCITY		
RANDOMLY INSERTED INTO PACKS		
ARCAB Alundra Blayze	8.00	20.00
ARCBH Bret Hit Man Hart	15.00	40.00
ARCBP Beth Phoenix	8.00	20.00
ARCBR Bret Hit Man Hart	15.00	40.00
ARCBS Big Show	10.00	25.00
ARCBT Booker T	15.00	40.00
ARCCF Charlotte Flair	15.00	40.00
ARCCH Chris Jericho	20.00	50.00
ARCCJ Chris Jericho	20.00	50.00
ARCDM Dean Malenko	6.00	15.00
ARCET Eve Torres	12.00	30.00
ARCGO Goldberg	30.00	75.00
ARCIV Ivory	8.00	20.00
ARCJA Jim The Anvil Neidhart	6.00	15.00
ARCJB JBL	8.00	20.00
ARCMA Maryse	12.00	30.00
ARCMD Alundra Blayze	6.00	15.00
ARCRD Road Dogg	6.00	15.00
ARCRF Ric Flair	60.00	120.00
ARCST Sting	30.00	75.00
ARCTD Ted DiBiase	10.00	25.00
ARCTS Trish Stratus	25.00	60.00
ARCWR Wendi Richter	10.00	25.00

2017 Topps Legends of WWE Autographed Shirt Relics

*GOLD/10: UNPRICED DUE TO SCARCITY
*BLACK/5: UNPRICED DUE TO SCARCITY
*RED/1: UNPRICED DUE TO SCARCITY
STATED ODDS

ARBH Bret Hit Man Hart
ARBS Big Show
ARDP Diamond Dallas Page
ARED Edge
ARIR The Iron Sheik
ARKN Kevin Nash
ARLL Lex Luger
ARMA Mankind
ARMF Mick Foley
ARRD Road Dogg
ARRS Ricky The Dragon Steamboat
ARSM Shawn Michaels
ARST Sting
ARTB Tully Blanchard
ARTD Ted DiBiase

2017 Topps Legends of WWE Autographs

*BRONZE/99: .5X TO 1.2X BASIC AUTOS		
*SILVER/50: .6X TO 1.5X BASIC AUTOS		
*BLUE/25: .75X TO 2X BASIC AUTOS		
*GOLD/10: UNPRICED DUE TO SCARCITY		
*BLACK/5: UNPRICED DUE TO SCARCITY		
*RED/1: UNPRICED DUE TO SCARCITY		
STATED PRINT RUN 199 SER.#'d SETS		
LAAB Alundra Blayze	8.00	20.00
LAAL Albert	6.00	15.00
LABF Brutus The Barber Beefcake	12.00	30.00
LABM Bret Hit Man Hart	30.00	75.00
LABT Booker T	6.00	15.00
LADP Diamond Dallas Page	12.00	30.00
LAED Edge	12.00	30.00
LAET Eve Torres	10.00	25.00
LAFF Fit Finlay	6.00	15.00
LAGD Goldust	8.00	20.00
LAGV Greg The Hammer Valentine	6.00	15.00
LAHA Hacksaw Jim Duggan	12.00	30.00
LAIR Irwin R. Schyster	5.00	12.00
LAJA Jim The Anvil Neidhart	20.00	50.00
LAKE Kane	10.00	25.00
LAKN Kevin Nash	12.00	30.00
LAKS Ken Shamrock	10.00	25.00
LALL Lex Luger	12.00	30.00
LAMF Mick Foley	20.00	50.00
LAMP Michael P.S. Hayes	6.00	15.00
LANS Norman Smiley	5.00	12.00
LAPE Paul Ellering	10.00	25.00
LARS Ricky The Dragon Steamboat	15.00	40.00
LASM Shawn Michaels	15.00	40.00
LASS Sgt. Slaughter	10.00	25.00
LAST Sting	25.00	60.00
LASV Sid Vicious	6.00	15.00
LATA Tatanka	10.00	25.00
LATD Ted DiBiase	15.00	40.00
LATH The Boogeyman	6.00	15.00
LAWE Wendi Richter	6.00	15.00
LAWR William Regal	6.00	15.00

2017 Topps Legends of WWE Autographs Bronze

*BRONZE: .5X TO 1.2X BASIC AUTOS		
LAGO Goldberg	20.00	50.00

2017 Topps Legends of WWE Autographs Silver

STATED PRINT RUN 50 SER.#'d SETS		
LAUN Undertaker	150.00	300.00

2017 Topps Legends of WWE Dual Autographs

STATED PRINT RUN 10 SER.#'d SETS		
RANDOMLY INSERTED INTO PACKS		
DADS T.DiBiase/IRS	50.00	100.00
DAFB R.Flair/T.Blanchard	50.00	100.00
DAHN J.Neidhart/B.Hart	75.00	150.00
DARB A.Blayze/W.Richter	30.00	60.00
DASV I.Sheik/N.Volkoff	30.00	75.00
DASZ L.Zbyszko/B.Sammartino	30.00	75.00
DATM HHH/S.McMahon	500.00	1000.00
DAUK Kane/Undertaker	300.00	500.00
DAUS Sting/Undertaker	300.00	600.00
DASTL L.Luger/Sting	100.00	200.00

2017 Topps Legends of WWE Legendary Bouts

COMPLETE SET (20)	6.00	15.00
RANDOMLY INSERTED INTO PACKS		
1 Undertaker/Shawn Michaels	1.25	3.00
2 Bret Hart/Steve Austin	1.25	3.00
3 Randy Savage/Ricky Steamboat	.60	1.50
4 Ultimate Warrior/Randy Savage	.60	1.50
5 Bret Hart/The British Bulldog	.30	.75
6 Bret Hart/Shawn Michaels	.75	2.00
7 The Rock/Steve Austin	1.50	4.00
8 Undertaker/Shawn Michaels	1.25	3.00
9 John Cena/Brock Lesnar	1.50	4.00
10 Mr. Perfect/Bret Hart	.60	1.50
11 Razor Ramon/Shawn Michaels	.75	2.00
12 Ric Flair/Mr. Perfect	.60	1.50
13 Randy Orton/Cactus Jack	.75	2.00
14 Ric Flair Wins 1992 Royal Rumble	.75	2.00
15 Undertaker/Triple H	1.25	3.00
16 Ric Flair/Randy Savage	.75	2.00
17 Chris Jericho/Shawn Michaels	.75	2.00
18 Triple H/Cactus Jack	.75	2.00
19 Sting's Squad./Dangerous Alliance	1.00	2.50
20 Edge/John Cena	1.50	4.00

2017 Topps Legends of WWE Retired Titles

COMPLETE SET (22)	5.00	12.00
RANDOMLY INSERTED INTO PACKS		
1 Bret Hit Man Hart	.75	2.00
2 Ric Flair	1.00	2.50
3 Terry Funk	.40	1.00
4 Triple H	1.00	2.50
5 Money Inc.	.50	1.25
6 The Outsiders	.60	1.50
7 Terry Taylor & Greg Valentine	.50	1.25
8 The Glamour Girls	.40	1.00
9 Trish Stratus	1.50	4.00
10 Nikki Bella	1.00	2.50
11 Ted DiBiase	.50	1.25
12 Tatsumi Fujinami	.40	1.00
13 British Bulldog	.40	1.00
14 Ricky Steamboat	.75	2.00
15 Rob Van Dam	.75	2.00
16 Chris Jericho	1.00	2.50
17 Dean Malenko	.50	1.25
18 Tatsumi Fujinami	.40	1.00
19 Brian Pillman	.40	1.00
20 Bradshaw	.50	1.25
21 Norman Smiley	.50	1.25
22 Virgil	.40	1.00

2017 Topps Legends of WWE Shirt Relics

STATED PRINT RUN 299 SER.#'d SETS

ARBH Bret Hit Man Hart	5.00	12.00
ARBL Brock Lesnar	4.00	10.00
ARBS Big Show	3.00	8.00
ARDP Diamond Dallas Page	3.00	8.00
ARED Edge	3.00	8.00
ARIR The Iron Sheik	2.50	6.00
ARKN Kevin Nash	2.50	6.00
ARLL Lex Luger	2.50	6.00
ARMA Mankind	2.50	6.00
ARMF Mick Foley	3.00	8.00
ARRD Road Dogg	2.50	6.00
ARRS Ricky The Dragon Steamboat	3.00	8.00
ARSM Shawn Michaels	6.00	15.00
ARST Sting	6.00	15.00
ARTB Tully Blanchard	2.50	6.00
ARTD Ted DiBiase	3.00	8.00

2017 Topps Legends of WWE Triple Autographs

TAFSG Flair/Sting/Goldberg	150.00	300.00
TAHNH Neidhart/J.Hart/B.Hart	125.00	250.00
TALJM D.Love/C.Jack/Mankind	100.00	250.00
TANSL Luger/Nash/Sting	100.00	200.00

2018 Topps Legends of WWE

COMPLETE SET (100)	15.00	40.00
*BRONZE: .6X TO 1.5X BASIC CARDS		
*SILVER/50: 1X TO 2.5X BASIC CARDS		
*BLUE/25: 1.5X TO 4X BASIC CARDS		
*GOLD/10: UNPRICED DUE TO SCARCITY		
*BLACK/5: UNPRICED DUE TO SCARCITY		
*RED/1: UNPRICED DUE TO SCARCITY		
*P.P.BLACK/1: UNPRICED DUE TO SCARCITY		
*P.P.CYAN/1: UNPRICED DUE TO SCARCITY		
*P.P.MAGENTA/1: UNPRICED DUE TO SCARCITY		
*P.P.YELLOW/1: UNPRICED DUE TO SCARCITY		
1 Andre the Giant	.60	1.50
2 Bam Bam Bigelow	.50	1.25
3 Batista	.50	1.25
4 Big John Studd	.30	.75
5 Bob Backlund	.30	.75
6 Bobby The Brain Heenan	.50	1.25
7 Booker T	.50	1.25
8 Bret Hit Man Hart	.75	2.00
9 Chief Jay Strongbow	.50	1.25
10 Classy Freddie Blassie	.30	.75
11 Cowboy Bob Orton	.30	.75
12 D'Lo Brown	.30	.75
13 Diamond Dallas Page	.50	1.25
14 Don Muraco	.30	.75
15 Dusty Rhodes	.60	1.50
16 Eddie Guerrero	.75	2.00
17 Edge	.75	2.00
18 Fit Finlay	.30	.75
19 George The Animal Steele	.40	1.00
20 Gorilla Monsoon	.60	1.50
21 Hacksaw Jim Duggan	.30	.75
22 Harley Race	.30	.75
23 Honky Tonk Man	.30	.75
24 Jake The Snake Roberts	.40	1.00
25 Jim Ross	.50	1.25
26 Jerry The King Lawler	.60	1.50
27 Jim The Anvil Neidhart	.50	1.25
28 Junkyard Dog	.30	.75
29 Ken Shamrock	.40	1.00
30 Kevin Nash	.60	1.50
31 Kevin Von Erich	.50	1.25
32 Kurt Angle	.75	2.00
33 Lex Luger	.40	1.00
34 Mark Henry	.40	1.00
35 Ted DiBiase	.40	1.00
36 Mr. Perfect	.40	1.00
37 Mr. Wonderful Paul Orndorff	.30	.75
38 Papa Shango	.30	.75
39 Pat Patterson	.30	.75
40 Ravishing Rick Rude	.40	1.00
41 Ric Flair	1.00	2.50
42 Ricky The Dragon Steamboat	.50	1.25
43 Rowdy Roddy Piper	.75	2.00
44 Sgt. Slaughter	.40	1.00
45 Shawn Michaels	1.00	2.50
46 Sid Vicious	.30	.75
47 Stevie Ray	.30	.75
48 Sting	.75	2.00
49 Stone Cold Steve Austin	1.50	4.00
50 Tatanka	.30	.75
51 Tatsumi Fujinami	.30	.75
52 Ultimate Warrior	1.25	3.00
53 Vader	.40	1.00
54 William Regal	.50	1.25
55 Yokozuna	.40	1.00
56 Big Show	.30	.75
57 Bobby Lashley	.60	1.50
58 The Brian Kendrick	.50	1.25
59 Daniel Bryan	.75	2.00
60 Dolph Ziggler	.40	1.00
61 Jeff Hardy	.60	1.50
62 Goldust	.60	1.50
63 John Cena	1.25	3.00
64 Kane	.50	1.25
65 Woken Matt Hardy	.75	2.00
66 Randy Orton	.75	2.00
67 The Rock	1.50	4.00
68 Shelton Benjamin	.40	1.00
69 Undertaker	1.25	3.00
70 Triple H	.75	2.00
IC1 X-Pac/1-2-3 Kid	.40	1.00
IC2 Albert/Tensai	.30	.75
IC3 Big Bubba Rogers/Big Boss Man	.30	.75
IC4 Brutus Beefcake/The Zodiac	.30	.75
IC5 The Booty Man/The Disciple	.30	.75
IC6 Earthquake/The Shark	.30	.75
IC7 Kama Mustafa/Kama	.30	.75
IC8 The Godfather/Goodfather	.30	.75
IC9 Trillionaire/Million Dollar Man	.40	1.00
WD1 Alundra Blayze	.30	.75
WD2 Beth Phoenix	.60	1.50
WD3 Eve Torres	.60	1.50
WD4 Lita	.75	2.00
WD5 Miss Elizabeth	.75	2.00
WD6 Sherri Martel	.60	1.50
WD7 Stephanie McMahon	.60	1.50
WD8 Terri Runnels	.40	1.00
WD9 Trish Stratus	1.25	3.00
IC10 Colonel Mustafa/Iron Sheik	.30	.75
IC11 Michael Wallstreet/IRS	.30	.75
IC12 Umaga/Jamal	.30	.75
IC13 Road Dogg/Jesse James	.30	.75
IC14 Macho Man/Macho King	1.00	2.50
IC15 Dok Hendrix/Michael P.S. Hayes	.30	.75
IC16 Scott Hall/Razor Ramon	.60	1.50
IC17 Faarooq/Ron Simmons	.40	1.00
IC18 Terry Taylor/Red Rooster	.30	.75
IC19 Tugboat/Typhoon	.30	.75
IC20 Virgil/Vincent	.30	.75
WD10 Wendi Richter	.30	.75

2018 Topps Legends of WWE Autographed Commemorative Hall of Fame Rings

*SILVER/50: .5X TO 1.2X BASIC AUTOS
*BLUE/25: .6X TO 1.5X BASIC AUTOS
*GOLD/10: UNPRICED DUE TO SCARCITY
*BLACK/5: UNPRICED DUE TO SCARCITY
*RED/1: UNPRICED DUE TO SCARCITY
STATED PRINT RUN 99 SER.#'d SETS

HOFAB Alundra Blayze	10.00	25.00
HOFBH Bret Hit Man Hart	15.00	40.00
HOFBP Beth Phoenix	12.00	30.00
HOFBT Booker T	15.00	40.00
HOFDP Diamond Dallas Page	10.00	25.00
HOFEG Edge	10.00	25.00
HOFHR Harley Race	15.00	40.00
HOFJD Hacksaw Jim Duggan	10.00	25.00
HOFJL Jerry The King Lawler	20.00	50.00
HOFJR Jake The Snake Roberts	12.00	30.00
HOFKA Kurt Angle	12.00	30.00
HOFKN Kevin Nash	12.00	30.00
HOFLT Lita	20.00	50.00
HOFMH Mark Henry	10.00	25.00
HOFPO Mr. Wonderful Paul Orndorff	12.00	30.00
HOFRD Ricky The Dragon Steamboat	10.00	25.00
HOFRF Ric Flair/84	30.00	75.00
HOFRR Razor Ramon	15.00	40.00
HOFSS Sgt. Slaughter	12.00	30.00
HOFST Sting	25.00	60.00
HOFWR Wendi Richter	10.00	25.00

2018 Topps Legends of WWE Autographed Dual Relics

*GOLD/10: UNPRICED DUE TO SCARCITY
*BLACK/5: UNPRICED DUE TO SCARCITY
*RED/1: UNPRICED DUE TO SCARCITY
STATED PRINT RUN 25 SER.#'d SETS

ADRGD Goldust	12.00	30.00
ADRJH Jeff Hardy	15.00	40.00
ADRMH Woken Matt Hardy	20.00	50.00

2018 Topps Legends of WWE Autographed Shirt Relics

*SILVER/50: .5X TO 1.2X BASIC AUTOS
*BLUE/25: .6X TO 1.5X BASIC AUTOS
*GOLD/10: UNPRICED DUE TO SCARCITY
*BLACK/5: UNPRICED DUE TO SCARCITY
*RED/1: UNPRICED DUE TO SCARCITY
STATED PRINT RUN 99 SER.#'d SETS

ASRDP Diamond Dallas Page	10.00	25.00
ASREG Edge	12.00	30.00
ASRIS The Iron Sheik	10.00	25.00
ASRKN Kevin Nash	15.00	40.00
ASRLL Lex Luger	10.00	25.00
ASRMH Woken Matt Hardy	8.00	20.00
ASRRD Road Dogg		
ASRRS Ricky The Dragon Steamboat	8.00	20.00
ASRST Sting	15.00	40.00

2018 Topps Legends of WWE Autographs

*BRONZE/99: SAME VALUE AS BASIC AUTOS
*SILVER/50: .5X TO 1.2X BASIC AUTOS
*BLUE/25: .6X TO 1.5X BASIC AUTOS
*GOLD/10: UNPRICED DUE TO SCARCITY
*BLACK/5: UNPRICED DUE TO SCARCITY
*RED/1: UNPRICED DUE TO SCARCITY
*P.P.BLACK/1: UNPRICED DUE TO SCARCITY
*P.P.CYAN/1: UNPRICED DUE TO SCARCITY
*P.P.MAGENTA/1: UNPRICED DUE TO SCARCITY
*P.P.YELLOW/1: UNPRICED DUE TO SCARCITY

AAB Alundra Blayze	6.00	15.00
AAF Afa	5.00	12.00
ABE Brutus The Barber Beefcake	8.00	20.00
ABH Bret Hit Man Hart	12.00	30.00
ABN Brian Knobbs	6.00	15.00
ABS Big Show	8.00	20.00
ABT Booker T	8.00	20.00
ACB Cowboy Bob Orton	5.00	12.00
ACJ Chris Jericho	12.00	30.00
ADB Daniel Bryan	10.00	25.00
ADP Diamond Dallas Page	6.00	15.00
AED Edge	12.00	30.00
AFA Faarooq	5.00	12.00
AFF Fit Finlay	6.00	15.00
AGD Goldust	6.00	15.00
AGO The Goon	10.00	25.00
AHA Haku	8.00	20.00
AHR Harley Race	8.00	20.00
AHT Honky Tonk Man	6.00	15.00
AIR Irwin R. Schyster	5.00	12.00
AJD Hacksaw Jim Duggan	10.00	25.00
AJH Jimmy Hart	6.00	15.00
AJJ JJ Dillon	6.00	15.00
AJL Jerry The King Lawler	8.00	20.00
AJS Jake The Snake Roberts	10.00	25.00
AKA Kurt Angle	12.00	30.00
AKE Kane	6.00	15.00
AKN Kevin Nash	6.00	15.00
ALL Lex Luger	8.00	20.00
ALT Lita	12.00	30.00
AMA Mankind	6.00	15.00
AMC Michael Cole	5.00	12.00
AMD Ted DiBiase	8.00	20.00
ANB Jerry Sags	5.00	12.00
ANS Norman Smiley	6.00	15.00
APE Paul Ellering	8.00	20.00
APS Michael P.S. Hayes	6.00	15.00
ARH Rhyno	5.00	12.00
ARO Randy Orton	10.00	25.00
ARS Ricky The Dragon Steamboat	10.00	25.00
ASI Sika	6.00	15.00
ASR Stevie Ray	6.00	15.00
ASS Sgt. Slaughter	6.00	15.00
AST Sting	15.00	40.00
ASV Sid Vicious	6.00	15.00
ATA Magnum T.A.	6.00	15.00
ATG The Godfather	6.00	15.00
ATK Tatanka	5.00	12.00
ATS Trish Stratus	20.00	50.00
ATT Terry Taylor	5.00	12.00
ATW The Warlord	5.00	12.00
AWD Wendi Richter	6.00	15.00
AWR William Regal	8.00	20.00

2018 Topps Legends of WWE Autographs Silver

STATED PRINT RUN 50 SER.#'d SETS

ASM Stephanie McMahon	75.00	150.00
ATH Triple H	125.00	250.00
AUD Undertaker	100.00	200.00

2018 Topps Legends of WWE Dual Autographs

*BLACK/5: UNPRICED DUE TO SCARCITY
*RED/1: UNPRICED DUE TO SCARCITY
STATED PRINT RUN 10 SER.#'d SETS
UNPRICED DUE TO SCARCITY

DABW Bushwhackers
DADX HHH/HBK
DAGG J.Martin/L.Kai
DAHF P.Orndorff/H.Race
DAHH Booker T/S.Ray

2018 Topps Legends of WWE Relics

RANDOMLY INSERTED INTO PACKS

SRBH Bret Hit Man Hart	5.00	12.00
SRDP Diamond Dallas Page	3.00	8.00
SREG Edge	3.00	8.00
SRGD Goldust	2.50	6.00
SRIS The Iron Sheik	2.50	6.00
SRJC John Cena	5.00	12.00
SRKN Kevin Nash	3.00	8.00
SRLL Lex Luger	2.50	6.00
SRMH Woken Matt Hardy	2.00	5.00
SRRD Road Dogg	2.00	5.00
SRRS Ricky The Dragon Steamboat	2.00	5.00
SRST Sting	3.00	8.00
SRTD Ted DiBiase	2.00	5.00

2018 Topps Legends of WWE Triple Autographs

STATED PRINT RUN 10 SER.#'d SETS
UNPRICED DUE TO SCARCITY

TAMHF K.Angle/HHH/S.McMahon
TAMOD Faarooq/Edge/Undertaker
TATCM HHH/Undertaker/Faarooq

2021 Topps Living WWE

1 Stone Cold Steve Austin/5,521* 8.00 20.00
2 Trish Stratus/3,546* 8.00 20.00
3 The Miz/1,582* 2.50 6.00
4 Maryse/1,592* 2.50 6.00
5 Erik/1,116* 1.50 4.00
6 Ivar/1,135* 1.50 4.00
7 Bobby Lashley/1,031* 4.00 10.00
8 MVP/1,024* 1.50 4.00
9 Jeff Hardy/1,699* 4.00 10.00
10 Undertaker/3,231* 8.00 20.00
11 Shinsuke Nakamura/962* 4.00 10.00
12 Akira Tozawa/968* 2.00 5.00
13 Jey Uso/800* 1.50 4.00
14 Jimmy Uso/785* 1.50 4.00
15 Mia Yim/792* 2.00 5.00
16 Keith Lee/786* 3.00 8.00
17 Sami Zayn/825* 2.50 6.00
18 Edge/1,022* 6.00 15.00
19 Sheamus/758* 2.50 6.00
20 Cesaro/744* 1.50 4.00
21 Titus O'Neil/696* 1.50 4.00
22 Roman Reigns/1,105* 8.00 20.00
23 Braun Strowman/839 4.00 10.00
24 Alexa Bliss/1,601* 10.00 25.00
25 Drew McIntyre/674* 4.00 10.00
26 Jinder Mahal/718* 2.00 5.00
27 Carmella/683* 4.00 10.00
28 R-Truth/619* 2.00 5.00
29 Aleister Black/606* 4.00 10.00
30 Ricochet/565* 3.00 8.00
31 Eddie Guerrero/925* 8.00 20.00
32 Sasha Banks/1,242* 8.00 20.00
33 Nikki Cross/541* 3.00 8.00
34 Finn Balor/570* 4.00 10.00
35 Angelo Dawkins/529* 2.00 5.00
36 Montez Ford/529* 1.50 4.00
37 Dolph Ziggler/551* 3.00 8.00
38 Robert Roode/512* 2.00 5.00
39 Karrion Kross/686* 6.00 15.00
40 Scarlett/936* 8.00 20.00
41 Bianca Belair/671* 4.00 10.00
42 Naomi/621* 2.00 5.00
43 Kayden Carter/483* 3.00 8.00
44 Kacy Catanzaro/554* 3.00 8.00
45 Mr. America (Hulk Hogan)/1,216* 8.00 20.00
46 Lex Luger/713* 2.00 5.00
47 Rey Mysterio/676* 4.00 10.00
48 Dominik Mysterio/563* 2.00 5.00
49 Miss Elizabeth/1,142* 3.00 8.00
50 Macho Man Randy Savage/1,866* 6.00 15.00
51 Beth Phoenix/1,142* 3.00 8.00
52 Lacey Evans/564* 4.00 10.00
53 Bobby "The Brain" Heenan/701* 2.50 6.00
54 Razor Ramon/769* 2.50 6.00
55 AJ Styles//574* 5.00 12.00
56 Omos/544* 3.00 8.00
57 Kane/658* 2.50 6.00
58 Rob Van Dam/527* 3.00 8.00
59 Seth Rollins/643* 4.00 10.00
60 Becky Lynch/932* 6.00 15.00
61 British Bulldog/646* 2.50 6.00
62 Bret Hart/1,013* 4.00 10.00
63 Cedric Alexander/430* 1.50 4.00
64 Shelton Benjamin/431* 2.50 6.00
65 Dakota Kai/490* 3.00 8.00
66 Raquel Gonzalez/572* 4.00 10.00
67 John Morrison/426* 3.00 8.00
68 Franky Monet/483* 3.00 8.00
69 Natalya/442* 2.50 6.00
70 Tamina/404* 2.00 5.00
71 Rikishi/485* 2.00 5.00
72 Yokozuna/506* 2.50 6.00
73 Asuka/767* 6.00 15.00
74 Io Shirai/663* 3.00 8.00
75 Apollo Crews/412* 2.00 5.00
76 Commander Azeez/412* 2.00 5.00
77 Papa Shango/648* 2.00 5.00
78 Ultimate Warrior/1,267* 6.00 15.00
79 Riddle/509* 4.00 10.00
80 Randy Orton/601* 5.00 12.00
81 Rocky Johnson/827* 3.00 8.00
82 The Rock/3,671* 15.00 40.00
83 Gobbledy Gooker/565* 1.50 4.00
84 Big E/485* 3.00 8.00
85 Kofi Kingston/424* 4.00 10.00
86 Xavier Woods/419* 1.50 4.00
87 Shotzi Blackheart/769* 6.00 15.00
88 Charlotte Flair/796* 8.00 20.00
89 Billy Gunn/491* 2.00 5.00
90 Road Dogg/496* 2.00 5.00
91 Chyna/596* 3.00 8.00
92 X-Pac/516* 2.00 5.00
93 John Cena/
94 Mick Foley/
95 Shawn Michaels/
96 Triple H/

2021 Topps Living WWE Rainbow Foil

STATED PRINT RUN 50 SER.#'d SETS
VIP PARTY EXCLUSIVE
1 Stone Cold Steve Austin 100.00 200.00

2006 Topps Lollipops WWE Superstars Stickers German

1 John Cena
2 Batista
3 Rey Mysterio
4 Triple H
5 Boogeyman
6 Chris Masters
7 The Big Show
8 Undertaker
9 Christy Hemme
10 Edge
11 Shelton Benjamin
12 JBL John "Bradshaw" Layfield
13 Kane
14 Melina
15 Randy Orton
16 Carlito
17 Stone Cold Steve Austin
18 Kurt Angle
19 Ric Flair
20 Rob Van Dam

2016-18 Topps Now WWE

1 Brock Lesnar/132* 6.00 15.00
2 Finn Balor/221* 5.00 12.00
3 Dean Ambrose/114* 6.00 15.00
4 Charlotte/124* 6.00 15.00
5 AJ Styles/127* 8.00 20.00
6 AJ Styles/191* 6.00 15.00
7 Becky Lynch/212* 8.00 20.00
8 Heath Slater and Rhyno/104* 4.00 10.00
9 Kane/81* 12.00 30.00
10 The Miz/85* 6.00 15.00
11 Kevin Owens/68* 5.00 12.00
12 The New Day/61* 15.00 40.00
13 Charlotte/88* 5.00 12.00
14 Roman Reigns/61* 8.00 20.00
15 Chris Jericho/62* 10.00 25.00
16 AJ Styles/73* 5.00 12.00
17 Naomi/70* 8.00 20.00
18 Heath Slater & Rhyno/65* 8.00 20.00
19 Dolph Ziggler/73* 5.00 12.00
20 Bray Wyatt/86* 5.00 12.00
21 Nikki Bella/87* 5.00 12.00
22 Goldberg/249* 6.00 15.00
23 Kevin Owens/98* 8.00 20.00
24 Charlotte Flair/151* 6.00 15.00
25 Roman Reigns/69* 5.00 12.00
26 New Day/70* 5.00 12.00
27 Brian Kendrick/72* 5.00 12.00
28 The Miz/59* 5.00 12.00
29 Edge/58* 5.00 12.00
30 Undertaker/126* 8.00 20.00
31 Goldberg/125* 6.00 15.00
32 Team Smackdown Live Men/62* 5.00 12.00
33 Team Raw Women/88* 4.00 10.00
34 Team Raw Tag Team/60* 5.00 12.00
35 The Brian Kendrick/59* 5.00 12.00
36 The Miz/60* 5.00 12.00
37 AJ Styles/122* 4.00 10.00
38 Alexa Bliss/180* 15.00 40.00
39 The Miz/82* 4.00 10.00
40 Nikki Bella/93* 6.00 15.00
41 Baron Corbin/91* 4.00 10.00
42 Randy Orton & Bray Wyatt/115* 5.00 12.00
43A Kevin Owens/65* 4.00 10.00
44 Cesaro & Sheamus/65* 4.00 10.00
45 Sami Zayn/68* 4.00 10.00
46 Seth Rollins/63* 4.00 10.00
47 Rich Swann/65* 4.00 10.00
48A Charlotte Flair/108* 6.00 15.00
49 Naomi/Nikki Bella/Becky Lynch/88* 4.00 10.00
50 Luke Gallows & Karl Anderson/64* 4.00 10.00
51 Charlotte Flair/100* 4.00 10.00
52 Kevin Owens/62* 6.00 15.00
53 Neville/61* 5.00 12.00
54A John Cena/82* 6.00 15.00
55 Goldberg/Undertaker/73* 6.00 15.00
56A Randy Orton/85* 5.00 12.00
57 Nia Jax/83* 6.00 15.00
58 Bray Wyatt/102* 5.00 12.00
59 Naomi/82* 6.00 15.00
60 Randy Orton/54* 6.00 15.00
61 Nikki Bella & Natalya/74* 6.00 15.00
62 American Alpha/39* 4.00 10.00
63 Becky Lynch/73* 6.00 15.00
64 Bayley/288* 6.00 15.00
65 Goldberg/223* 8.00 20.00
66 Bayley/153* 5.00 12.00
67 Roman Reigns/64* 5.00 12.00
68 Neville/73* 5.00 12.00
69 Sasha Banks/141* 5.00 12.00
70 Luke Gallows & Karl Anderson/74* 5.00 12.00
71 Samoa Joe/81* 5.00 12.00
72 Undertaker/172* 6.00 15.00
73 Naomi/72* 5.00 12.00
74 Goldberg/64* 8.00 20.00
75 Randy Orton/69* 5.00 12.00
76 John Cena/Nikki Bella/91* 5.00 12.00
77 Hardy Boyz/114* 8.00 20.00
78 Bayley/97* 5.00 12.00
79 Kevin Owens/71* 5.00 12.00
80 Shinsuke Nakamura/78* 8.00 20.00
82 Tye Dillinger/37* 10.00 25.00
81 Finn Balor/46* 10.00 25.00
83 The Revival/46* 5.00 12.00
84 Dean Ambrose/Miz/Maryse/40* 5.00 12.00
85 Alexa Bliss/123* 10.00 25.00
86 Kevin Owens/49* 5.00 12.00
87 Charlotte Flair/57* 8.00 20.00
88 Braun Strowman/55* 5.00 12.00
89 Bray Wyatt/49* 5.00 12.00
90 Seth Rollins/50* 5.00 12.00
91 Alexa Bliss/223* 10.00 25.00
92 The Hardy Boyz/65* 5.00 12.00
93 Chris Jericho/56* 5.00 12.00
94 Shinsuka Nakamura/96* 5.00 12.00
95 The Usos/
96 Sami Zayn/41* 5.00 12.00
97 Natalya Carmella Tamina/49* 5.00 12.00
98 Kevin Owens/44* 5.00 12.00
99 Jinder Mahal/69* 5.00 12.00
100 The Miz/60* 5.00 12.00
101 Sasha Banks/Rich Swann/78* 6.00 15.00
102 Alexa Bliss/264* 8.00 20.00
103 Cesaro & Sheamus/53* 4.00 10.00
104 Neville/53* 4.00 10.00
105 Samoa Joe/56* 4.00 10.00
106 Carmella/112* 6.00 15.00
107 The Usos/41* 5.00 12.00
108 Naomi/49* 5.00 12.00
109 Jinder Mahal/41* 4.00 10.00
110 Baron Corbin/60* 4.00 10.00
111 Brock Lesnar/61* 6.00 15.00
112 Braun Strowman/39* 4.00 10.00
113 The Miz/33* 4.00 10.00
114 Sasha Banks/103* 5.00 12.00
115 Cesaro & Sheamus/33* 4.00 10.00
116 Big Cass/32* 4.00 10.00
117 Bray Wyatt/37* 4.00 10.00
118 Neville/32* 4.00 10.00
119 Jinder Mahal/50* 4.00 10.00
120 The New Day/49* 4.00 10.00
121 John Cena/59* 4.00 10.00
122 Kevin Owens/44* 4.00 10.00
123 Natalya/44* 4.00 10.00
124 Baron Corbin/38* 4.00 10.00
125 HHH & Stephanie/Connor's Cure/216*4.00 10.00
126 Natalya/62* 4.00 10.00
127 Sasha Banks/114* 6.00 15.00
128 Dean Ambrose & Seth Rollins/80* 5.00 12.00
129 AJ Styles/63* 5.00 12.00
130 Jinder Mahal/38* 5.00 12.00
131 Brock Lesnar/50* 5.00 12.00
132 Brock Lesnar/51* 5.00 12.00
133 Enzo Amore/48* 5.00 12.00
134 Roman Reigns/46* 5.00 12.00
135 Alexa Bliss/138* 10.00 25.00
136 Ambrose/Rollins/38* 5.00 12.00
137 Finn Balor/40* 5.00 12.00
138 Kevin Owens/39* 5.00 12.00
139 Bobby Roode/32* 5.00 12.00
140 Jinder Mahal/29* 5.00 12.00
141 Natalya/53* 5.00 12.00
142 Baron Corbin/30* 5.00 12.00
143 The Usos/32* 5.00 12.00
144 Angle/Rollins/Ambrose/75* 5.00 12.00
145 Alexa Bliss/191* 8.00 20.00
146 The Demon Finn Balor/94* 5.00 12.00
147 Asuka/146* 6.00 15.00
148 Enzo Amore/55* 4.00 10.00
149 Sasha Banks/100* 5.00 12.00
150 The Shield/50* 4.00 10.00
151 Team Raw Women/35* 4.00 10.00
152 Charlotte Flair/102* 6.00 15.00
153 Team Raw Men/ 4.00 10.00
154 AJ Styles/65* 4.00 10.00
155 Kevin Owens & Sami Zayn/34* 4.00 10.00
156 Charlotte Flair/63* 6.00 15.00
157 The Usos/33* 4.00 10.00
158 Dolph Ziggler/33* 4.00 10.00
159 Scott Hall/89* 4.00 10.00
160 Undertaker/147* 6.00 15.00
161 The Miz/88* 4.00 10.00
162 John Cena/91* 6.00 15.00
163 Stone Cold Steve Austin/153* 8.00 20.00

2016-18 Topps Now WWE Relics

STATED PRINT RUN 25 SER.#'d SETS
43B Kevin Owens 20.00 50.00
48B Charlotte Flair 60.00 120.00
54B John Cena 50.00 100.00
56B Randy Orton 25.00 60.00
72A Undertaker 80.00 150.00
74A Goldberg 15.00 40.00
75A Randy Orton 20.00 50.00
76A John Cena/Nikki Bella 30.00 75.00
127A Sasha Banks 60.00 120.00
128A Dean Ambrose & Seth Rollins 30.00 75.00
131A Brock Lesnar 30.00 75.00
144A Kurt Angle 30.00 75.00
147A Asuka 50.00 100.00
163A Stone Cold Steve Austin 60.00 120.00

2018 Topps Now WWE

COMPLETE SET (72) 300.00 600.00
1 AJ Styles/99* 6.00 15.00
2 Shinsuke Nakamura/127* 5.00 12.00
3 Cesaro & Sheamus/82* 5.00 12.00
4 Lita/102* 6.00 15.00
5 Trish Stratus/186* 8.00 20.00
6 Asuka/145* 6.00 15.00
7 Alexa Bliss/171* 10.00 25.00
8 Asuka/140* 6.00 15.00
9 Woken Matt Hardy/56* 6.00 15.00
10 Roman Reigns/59* 6.00 15.00
11 AJ Styles/53* 5.00 12.00
12 Asuka/103* 6.00 15.00
13 Charlotte Flair/101* 6.00 15.00
14 Randy Orton/67* 5.00 12.00
15 Shinsuke Nakamura/50* 5.00 12.00
16 Daniel Bryan/125* 6.00 15.00
17 Woken Matt Hardy/76* 8.00 20.00
18 Cedric Alexander/74* 8.00 20.00
19 Naomi/87* 8.00 20.00
20 Seth Rollins/77* 8.00 20.00
21 Charlotte Flair/261* 8.00 20.00
22 Jinder Mahal/64* 5.00 12.00
23 The Bludgeon Brothers/67* 5.00 12.00

24 The Undertaker/145* 8.00 20.00
25 Daniel Bryan/93* 8.00 20.00
26 Nia Jax/115* 5.00 12.00
27 AJ Styles/85* 5.00 12.00
28 Braun Strowman/67* 5.00 12.00
29 Brock Lesnar/44* 5.00 12.00
30 Ronda Rousey/1342* 12.00 30.00
31 Braun Strowman/66* 5.00 12.00
32 Daniel Bryan/52* 6.00 15.00
33 Undertaker/62* 8.00 20.00
34 AJ Styles/52* 6.00 15.00
35 John Cena/66* 5.00 12.00
36 Seth Rollins/37* 6.00 15.00
37 Daniel Bryan/30* 12.00 30.00
38 Roman Reigns/33* 8.00 20.00
39 Alexa Bliss/301* 8.00 20.00
40 AJ Styles/101* 6.00 15.00
41 Alexa Bliss/304* 10.00 25.00
42 Braun Strowman/101* 5.00 12.00
43 Bobby Lashley/47* 8.00 20.00
44 Alexa Bliss/175* 10.00 25.00
45 AJ Styles/58* 8.00 20.00
46 Dolph Ziggler/48* 6.00 15.00
47 Seth Rollins/80* 6.00 15.00
48 Charlotte Flair/191* 8.00 20.00
49 Ronda Rousey/970* 8.00 20.00
50 Roman Reigns/79* 12.00 30.00
51 Becky Lynch/172* 5.00 12.00
52 Dolph Ziggler/Drew McIntyre/73* 5.00 12.00
53 AJ Styles/74* 5.00 12.00
54 Ronda Rousey/299* 6.00 15.00
55 John Cena/64* 5.00 12.00
56 Iconics/146* 5.00 12.00
57 AJ Styles/64* 4.00 10.00
58 Ronda Rousey/Bellas/166* 6.00 15.00
59 Triple H/72* 4.00 10.00
60 Buddy Murphy/64* 10.00 25.00
61 Trish Stratus & Lita/212* 6.00 15.00
62 Nia Jax/139* 12.00 30.00
63 Toni Storm/239* 8.00 20.00
64 Shayna Baszler/149* 6.00 15.00
65 Becky Lynch/325* 5.00 12.00
66 Ronda Rousey/324* 5.00 12.00
67 Seth Rollins/63* 10.00 25.00
68 Charlotte Flair/143* 8.00 20.00
69 Brock Lesnar/63* 10.00 25.00
70 Asuka/270* 4.00 10.00
71 Daniel Bryan/70* 6.00 15.00
72 Ronda Rousey/295* 5.00 12.00

2018 Topps Now WWE Relics

*GOLD/1: UNPRICED/SCARCITY

2A Shinsuke Nakamura 25.00 60.00
6A Asuka 75.00 150.00
24A The Undertaker 25.00 60.00
25A Daniel Bryan 30.00 75.00
29A Brock Lesnar 60.00 120.00
30A Ronda Rousey 150.00 300.00
48A Charlotte Flair 30.00 75.00
49A Ronda Rousey 100.00 200.00
50A Roman Reigns
68A Charlotte Flair 50.00 100.00
69A Brock Lesnar

2019 Topps Now WWE

1 Women's Royal Rumble/166* 8.00 20.00
2 Men's Royal Rumble/75* 5.00 12.00
3 Asuka/186* 6.00 15.00
4 Ronda Rousey/268* 6.00 15.00
5 Daniel Bryan/90* 5.00 12.00
6 Brock Lesnar/91* 6.00 15.00
7 Becky Lynch/279* 6.00 15.00
8 Seth Rollins/113* 5.00 12.00
9 WM35 Men's Preview/100* 4.00 10.00
10 WM35 Women's Preview/215* 5.00 12.00
11 Seth Rollins/157* 4.00 10.00
12 Roman Reigns/119* 4.00 10.00
13 Kurt Angle/127* 6.00 15.00
14 Kofi Kingston/217* 4.00 10.00
15 The Iconics/211* 3.00 8.00
16 Triple H/95* 3.00 8.00
17 John Cena/136* 4.00 10.00
18 Becky Lynch/710* 6.00 15.00
19 Seth Rollins/58* 6.00 15.00
20 Kofi Kingston/49* 5.00 12.00
21 Rey Mysterio/48* 8.00 20.00
22 Bayley/164* 5.00 12.00
23 Charlotte Flair/140* 6.00 15.00
24 Becky Lynch/163* 5.00 12.00
25 Bayley/138* 5.00 12.00
26 Brock Lesnar/49* 5.00 12.00
27 Mansoor/29* 12.00 30.00
28 Randy Orton/26* 6.00 15.00
29 Undertaker/31* 6.00 15.00
30 Drew Gulak/45* 5.00 12.00
31 Becky Lynch/109* 6.00 15.00
32 Ricochet/48* 5.00 12.00
33 Bayley/81* 8.00 20.00
34 Seth Rollins w/Becky Lynch/111* 6.00 15.00
35 Undertaker & Roman Reigns/58* 6.00 15.00
36 AJ Styles/57* 5.00 12.00
37 Bayley/81* 5.00 12.00
38 Seth Rollins & Becky Lynch/91* 5.00 12.00
39 Brock Lesnar/55* 5.00 12.00
40 Becky Lynch vs. Natalya/58* 6.00 15.00
41 Kofi Kingston vs. Randy Orton/29* 4.00 10.00
42 Brock Lesnar vs. Seth Rollins/29* 8.00 20.00
43 Becky Lynch/159* 8.00 20.00
44 AJ Styles/67* 4.00 10.00
45 Charlotte Flair/171* 6.00 15.00
46 The Fiend Bray Wyatt/ 8.00 20.00
47 Seth Rollins//96* 4.00 10.00
48 Bayley//96* 5.00 12.00
49 Samoa Joe/26* 6.00 15.00
50 Cedric Alexander/26* 3.00 8.00
51 Elias/29* 3.00 8.00
52 Andrade/28* 5.00 12.00
53 Ricochet/31* 4.00 10.00
54 Baron Corbin/31* 4.00 10.00
55 Ali/20*
56 Chad Gable/56* 6.00 15.00
57 Baron Corbin/21*
58 Samoa Joe and Ricochet/21*
59 Elias/21*
60 Chad Gable/20*
61 Baron Corbin/30*
62 Chad Gable/31* 6.00 15.00
63 Bayley/101*
64 Sasha Banks/172* 5.00 12.00
65 Kofi Kingston/55*
66 Erick Rowan/55*
67 Seth Rollins/66*
68 Baron Corbin/
69 Rock & Becky Lynch/118* 6.00 15.00
70 Becky & Charlotte/81* 6.00 15.00
71 Kevin Owens/41* 5.00 12.00
72 Roman Reigns/38*
73 Roman Reigns & Daniel Bryan/44*
74 Kabuki Warriors/74* 5.00 12.00
75 Charlotte Flair/75* 6.00 15.00
76 Becky Lynch/110* 4.00 10.00
77 The Fiend Bray Wyatt/182* 8.00 20.00
78 Team Hogan/36* 5.00 12.00
79 Natalya/Lacey Evans/104*
80 AJ Styles/34*
81 Mansoor/34*
82 The OC/34* 5.00 12.00
83 Brock Lesnar/34* 6.00 15.00
84 Team NXT Women/79* 6.00 15.00
85 Roderick Strong/43* 6.00 15.00
86 Adam Cole/43* 6.00 15.00
87 The Fiend Bray Wyatt/80* 8.00 20.00
88 Team SmackDown Men/38* 8.00 20.00
89 Brock Lesnar/43* 5.00 12.00
90 Shayna Baszler/61* 8.00 20.00
91 The New Day/29*
92 Aleister Black/29*
93 King Corbin/24*
94 Bray Wyatt/50* 6.00 15.00
95 The Kabuki Warriors/70* 5.00 12.00

2020 Topps Now WWE

1 Roman Reigns/51* 6.00 15.00
2 Charlotte Flair/170* 6.00 15.00
3 Bayley/77* 3.00 8.00
4 The Fiend/85* 5.00 12.00
5 Becky Lynch/152* 6.00 15.00
6 Drew McIntyre/*76 3.00 8.00
7 Undertaker/77* 6.00 15.00
8 The Miz & John Morrison/40*
9 Roman Reigns/41* 6.00 15.00
10 Bayley/83* 3.00 8.00
11 Goldberg/67* 6.00 15.00
12 Alexa Bliss & Nikki Cross/160* 10.00 25.00
13 Becky Lynch/162* 6.00 15.00
14 Sami Zayn/66* 3.00 8.00
15 John Morrison/56* 4.00 10.00
16 Kevin Owens/61* 3.00 8.00
17 Braun Strowman/75* 6.00 15.00
18 Undertaker/141* 6.00 15.00
19 Rob Gronkowski/393* 2.50 6.00
20 Charlotte Flair/153* 6.00 15.00
21 Aleister Black/55*
22 Edge/96* 4.00 10.00
23 Street Profits/71* 4.00 10.00
24 Bayley/105* 8.00 20.00
25 The Fiend Bray Wyatt/107* 6.00 15.00
26 Drew McIntyre/105* 3.00 8.00
27 The New Day/45*
28 Bayley/75* 3.00 8.00
29 Braun Strowman/55*
30 Drew McIntyre/59*
31 Asuka/155* 6.00 15.00
32 Otis/78* 2.50 6.00
33 Bayley & Sasha Banks/148* 8.00 20.00
34 Sheamus/38*
35 Braun Strowman/40*
36 Drew McIntyre/41*
37 Randy Orton/84* 4.00 10.00
38 Cesaro & Nakamura/38*
39 Seth Rollins/31*
40 Drew McIntyre/36*
41 Bayley/73* 3.00 8.00
42 The Fiend Bray Wyatt/116* 5.00 12.00
43 Drew McIntyre/79* 3.00 8.00
44 Asuka/209* 6.00 15.00
45 Seth Rollins/57*
46 Mandy Rose/93* 8.00 20.00
47 Bayley/128* 3.00 8.00
48 Roman Reigns/86* 4.00 10.00
49 Roman Reigns/73* 4.00 10.00
50 Rey & Dominik Mysterio/97* 3.00 8.00
51 Shayna Baszler & Nia Jax/72* 5.00 12.00
52 Bobby Lashley/45*
53 Roman Reigns/62* 4.00 10.00
54 Drew McIntyre/52*
55 Asuka/102* 6.00 15.00
56 Sami Zayn/52*
57 Roman Reigns/61* 4.00 10.00
58 The Miz/39*
59 Sasha Banks/163* 8.00 20.00
60 Randy Orton/73* 4.00 10.00
61 Team RAW (men)/68* 5.00 12.00
62 Street Profits/55*
63 Bobby Lashley/65* 3.00 8.00
64 Sasha Banks/261* 8.00 20.00
65 Team RAW (women)/129* 4.00 10.00
66 Roman Reigns/65* 4.00 10.00
67 Undertaker/736* 6.00 15.00
68 Drew McIntyre
69 Sasha Banks 8.00 20.00
70 The Hurt Business
71 Asuka & Charlotte Flair 6.00 15.00
72 Roman Reigns
73 Randy Orton

2020 Topps Now WWE Autographs

*RED/10: UNPRICED DUE TO SCARCITY
*GOLD/1: UNPRICED DUE TO SCARCITY
STATED PRINT RUN 25 SER.#'d SETS

31A Asuka 75.00 150.00
32A Otis 30.00 75.00
DMA Dominik Mysterio 60.00 120.00

2020 Topps Now WWE Relics

1A Drew McIntyre 30.00 75.00
2A Charlotte Flair 50.00 100.00

2021 Topps Now WWE

1 Drew McIntyre/181* 3.00 8.00
2 Sasha Banks/426* 6.00 15.00
3 Bianca Belair/342* 3.00 8.00
4 Roman Reigns/160* 6.00 15.00
5 Edge/224* 5.00 12.00
6 Bobby Lashley/132* 3.00 8.00
7 Alexa Bliss/679* 8.00 20.00
8 The Fiend Bray Wyatt/487* 8.00 20.00
9 Bobby Lashley/118* 3.00 8.00
10 Cesaro/130* 1.25 3.00
11 AJ Styles & Omos/141* 4.00 10.00
12 Braun Strowman/153* 3.00 8.00
13 Bianca Belair/286* 3.00 8.00
14 Randy Orton/
15 Kevin Owens/116* 2.50 6.00
16 Sheamus/144* 3.00 8.00
17 Apollo Crews/118* 1.50 4.00
18 Shayna Baszler & Nia Jax/135* 2.50 6.00
19 Rhea Ripley/475* 4.00 10.00
20 Roman Reigns/193* 6.00 15.00
21 John Cena/293* 6.00 15.00
22 RK-Bro/197* 4.00 10.00
23 Becky Lynch/437* 5.00 12.00
24 Roman Reigns/189* 6.00 15.00
25 Damian Priest/201* 2.00 5.00
26 Edge/207* 5.00 12.00
27 Charlotte Flair/285* 6.00 15.00
28 Bobby Lashley/120* 3.00 8.00
29 Big E/

2021 Topps Now WWE Autographs

STATED PRINT RUN 25 SER.#'d SETS

6A Bobby Lashley
29A Big E

2021 Topps Now WWE Mat Relics

STATED PRINT RUN 25 SER.#'d SETS

13A Bianca Belair
20A Roman Reigns
23A Becky Lynch 50.00 100.00
24A Roman Reigns
27A Charlotte Flair 30.00 75.00
SS1A Goldberg
SS2A John Cena

2017 Topps Now WWE Countdown to NXT TakeOver Orlando

1 Asuka vs. Ember Moon 5.00 12.00
2 Bobby Roode vs. Nakamura 5.00 12.00
3 AOP vs. Revival vs. #DIY 5.00 12.00
4 Aleister Black vs. Andrade 5.00 12.00
5 Dillinger/Strong/Jose/Ruby vs. Sanity 5.00 12.00

2017 Topps Now WWE Countdown to WrestleMania

1 Goldberg vs. Brock Lesnar 5.00 12.00
2 Bray Wyatt vs. Randy Orton 5.00 12.00
3 Chris Jericho vs. Kevin Owens 6.00 15.00
4 Undertaker vs. Roman Reigns 8.00 20.00
5 Bayley/Charlotte/Sasha/Nia 8.00 20.00
6 SD Women's Title Match 12.00 30.00
7 Cena & Nikki vs. Miz & Maryse 5.00 12.00
8 Seth Rollins vs. HHH 5.00 12.00
9 AJ Styles vs. Shane McMahon 5.00 12.00
10 Dean Ambrose vs. Baron Corbin 5.00 12.00
11 Neville vs. Austin Aries 5.00 12.00

2017 Topps Now WWE SummerSlam

STATED PRINT RUN 36 SER.#'d SETS
UNPRICED DUE TO SCARCITY

1 Lesnar/Reigns/Samoa Joe/Strowman
2 Jinder Mahal vs. Nakamura
3 Alexa Bliss vs. Sasha Banks
4 Naomi vs. Natalya
5 AJ Styles vs. Kevin Owens
6 Akira Tozawa vs. Neville
7 Cesaro/Sheamus vs. Ambrose/Rollins
8 New Day vs. Usos
9 John Cena vs. Baron Corbin
10 Randy Orton vs. Rusev
11 The Demon Finn Balor vs. Bray Wyatt
12 Big Show vs. Big Cass

2021 Topps Now WWE Turn Back the Clock

COMPLETE SET (9)
1 Ron Simmons/149*

2 King Booker/113*
3 Alicia Fox/109*
4 Mark Henry/107*
5 Big E/104*
6 Sasha Banks/257*
7 Naomi/110*
8 Ember Moon/108*
9 Kofi Kingston/146*

2016-18 Topps Now WWE NXT

1 Samoa Joe/43*
2 Asuka/77* 20.00 50.00
3 DIY/58*
4 Authors of Pain/44*
5 Bobby Roode/40*
7 Eric Young/50* 6.00 15.00
8 Roderick Strong/71* 6.00 15.00
9 The Authors of Pain/49* 5.00 12.00
10 Asuka/87* 5.00 12.00
11 Bobby Roode/56* 6.00 15.00
12 Seth Rollins/62* 6.00 15.00
13 Bobby Roode/74* 5.00 12.00
14 Asuka/117* 5.00 12.00
15 Roderick Strong/27* 4.00 10.00
16 Asuka/74* 4.00 10.00
17 Bobby Roode/25* 4.00 10.00
18 The Authors of Pain/27* 4.00 10.00
19 Tommaso Ciampa/43* 4.00 10.00
20 Sanity/47* 5.00 12.00
21 Asuka/86* 5.00 12.00
22 Drew McIntyre/46* 5.00 12.00
23 Adam Cole/104* 5.00 12.00
24 Undisputed Era/57* 5.00 12.00
25 Andrade Cien Almas/46* 5.00 12.00
26 Ember Moon/63* 5.00 12.00

2016-18 Topps Now WWE NXT Relics

4B Asuka 30.00 75.00
5B Bobby Roode 8.00 20.00

2018 Topps Now WWE NXT

1 The Undisputed Era/38* 5.00 12.00
2 Ember Moon/56* 5.00 12.00
3 Aleister Black/54* 5.00 12.00
4 Andrade Cien Almas/31* 5.00 12.00
5 Adam Cole/80* 8.00 20.00
6 Shayna Baszler/80* 8.00 20.00
7 The Undisputed Era/50* 8.00 20.00
8 Aleister Black/56* 8.00 20.00
9 Johnny Gargano/51* 8.00 20.00
10 Kairi Sane/196*
11 Tommaso Ciampa/66*

2019 Topps Now WWE NXT

1 War Raiders/67* 6.00 15.00
2 Johnny Gargano/77* 3.00 8.00
3 Shayna Baszler/71* 6.00 15.00
4 Tommaso Ciampa/65* 4.00 10.00
5 War Raiders/91* 4.00 10.00
6 Johnny Gargano/131* 4.00 10.00
7 Shayna Baszler/104* 5.00 12.00
8 Velveteen Dream/93* 6.00 15.00
9 Matt Riddle/36* 4.00 10.00
10 Street Profits/34* 5.00 12.00
11 Velveteen Dream/36* 5.00 12.00
12 Shayna Baszler/36* 5.00 12.00
13 Adam Cole/56* 5.00 12.00
14 The Street Profits/64* 4.00 10.00
15 Io Shirai/93* 5.00 12.00
16 The Velveteen Dream/65* 4.00 10.00
17 Shayna Baszler/80* 5.00 12.00
18 Adam Cole/86* 4.00 10.00
19 Candice LeRae/110* 8.00 20.00
20 Roderick Strong/31* 6.00 15.00
21 Team Ripley/79*
22 Pete Dunne/46*
23 Finn Balor/38*
25 The Undisputed Era/22*
26 Tyler Bate/24*
27 Kay Lee Ray/45*
28 Gallus/36*

2020 Topps Now WWE NXT

1 Jordan Devlin/48* 6.00 15.00
2 #DIY/
3 Rhea Ripley/131* 5.00 12.00
4 Imperium/37* 8.00 20.00
5 Adam Cole/35* 5.00 12.00
6 The Broserweights/38* 6.00 15.00
7 Rhea Ripley/81* 5.00 12.00
8 Finn Balor/29* 8.00 20.00
9 Dakota Kai/88* 4.00 10.00
10 Keith Lee/34* 5.00 12.00
11 Finn Balor/42*
12 Keith Lee/48*
13 Adam Cole/64*
14 Karrion Kross/88*
15 Io Shirai/314*
16 Io Shirai/94*
17 Dexter Lumis/67*
18 Tegan Nox/227*
19 Candice LeRae/85*
20 Keith Lee/125*
21A Karrion Kross/
21B Damian Priest/35*
22A Io Shirai/
22B Kushida/57*
23A Damian Priest/
23B Santos Escobar/47*
24 Io Shirai/110*
25 Finn Balor/*40
26 Johnny Gargano/28*
27 Dexter Lumis/36*
28 Rhea Ripley/83*
29 Io Shirai/96*
30 Team Candice/95* 15.00 40.00
31 Johnny Gargano/42*
32 The Undisputed Era/61*
LR Leon Ruff/148* 5.00 12.00

2020 Topps Now WWE NXT Autograph

LRA Leon Ruff 30.00 75.00

2017 Topps Now WWE NXT TakeOver Brooklyn III

1 Bobby Roode vs. Drew McIntyre 6.00 15.00
2 Asuka vs. Ember Moon 8.00 20.00
3 AOP vs. SAnitY 6.00 15.00
4 Aleister Black vs. Hideo Itami 6.00 15.00
5 Andrade vs. Johnny Gargano 6.00 15.00

2021 Topps On-Demand WWE Best of British

*GREEN/99: .5X TO 1.2X BASIC CARDS
*BLUE/49: .6X TO 1.5X BASIC CARDS
*PURPLE/25: UNPRICED DUE TO SCARCITY
*RED/10: UNPRICED DUE TO SCARCITY
*ORANGE/5: UNPRICED DUE TO SCARCITY
*GOLD/1: UNPRICED DUE TO SCARCITY

1 British Bulldog 1.50 4.00
2 Drew McIntyre 2.50 6.00
3 Paige 2.50 6.00
4 Bret Hart vs. B.Bulldog 2.50 6.00
5 Macho Man vs. Ultimate Warrior 4.00 10.00
6 Papa Shango vs. Tito Santana 1.25 3.00
7 Grizzled Young Veterans 1.00 2.50
8 William Regal 1.50 4.00
9 Wade Barrett 1.00 2.50
10 Tyler Bate 1.25 3.00
11 Pete Dunne 2.00 5.00
12 Flash Morgan Webster 1.25 3.00
13 Piper Niven 1.50 4.00
14 Zack Gibson 1.00 2.50
15 Joe Coffey 1.00 2.50
16 Mark Coffey 1.00 2.50
17 Wolfgang 1.00 2.50
18 Danny Burch 1.25 3.00
19 Trent Seven 1.25 3.00
20 Mark Andrews 1.00 2.50
21 Gallus 1.25 3.00
22 Nikki Cross 2.00 5.00
23 Kay Lee Ray 2.50 6.00
24 James Drake 1.00 2.50
25 AJ Styles vs. Jinder Mahal 3.00 8.00
26 Becky Lynch 4.00 10.00
27 Finn Balor 2.50 6.00
28 Sheamus 1.50 4.00
29 Jordan Devlin 1.00 2.50
30 Killian Dain 1.00 2.50

2021 Topps On-Demand WWE Best of British Autographs

*PURPLE/25: UNPRICED DUE TO SCARCITY
*RED/10: UNPRICED DUE TO SCARCITY
*ORANGE/5: UNPRICED DUE TO SCARCITY
*GOLD/1: UNPRICED DUE TO SCARCITY
RANDOMLY INSERTED INTO PACKS

NNO AJ Styles
NNO Becky Lynch
NNO Bret Hart
NNO Drew McIntyre
NNO Finn Balor
NNO James Drake
NNO Kay Lee Ray
NNO Killian Dain
NNO Mark Andrews
NNO Mark Coffey
NNO Nikki Cross
NNO Pete Dunne
NNO Sheamus
NNO Trent Seven
NNO Tyler Bate
NNO Wade Barrett
NNO William Regal
NNO Wolfgang

2019 Topps On-Demand WWE Mother's Day

COMPLETE SET (9) 12.00 30.00
STATED PRINT RUN 107 ANNCD SETS

1 Beth Phoenix 2.00 5.00
2 Eve Torres 1.50 4.00
3 Lacey Evans 2.50 6.00
4 Maryse 1.50 4.00
5 Mickie James 3.00 8.00
6 Naomi 2.00 5.00
7 Tamina 1.25 3.00
8 Trish Stratus 6.00 15.00
9 Stephanie McMahon 3.00 8.00

2021 Topps On-Demand WWE Summer of Cena

COMPLETE SET (15) 20.00 50.00
*PURPLE/25: 2X TO 5X BASIC CARDS
*RED/10: UNPRICED DUE TO SCARCITY
*ORANGE/5: UNPRICED DUE TO SCARCITY
*GOLD/1: UNPRICED DUE TO SCARCITY
STATED PRINT RUN ANNCD SETS

NNO John Cena 2.50 6.00
NNO Shocking Return 2.50 6.00
NNO The Ultimate Face-Off 2.50 6.00
NNO Opening RAW 2.50 6.00
NNO Meeting the Bro 2.50 6.00
NNO Crushing Corbin 2.50 6.00
NNO Contract Is Signed 2.50 6.00
NNO Masters of the Mic 2.50 6.00
NNO Vegas Can See Him! 2.50 6.00
NNO Vegas Classic 2.50 6.00
NNO John Cena vs. Booker T 2.50 6.00
NNO John Cena vs. Randy Orton 2.50 6.00
NNO John Cena vs. Batista 2.50 6.00
NNO John Cena By the Numbers 2.50 6.00
NNO SummerSlam 2021 Poster Image 2.50 6.00

2020 Topps On-Demand WWE 30 Years of the Deadman

COMPLETE SET (40) 12.00 30.00
STATED PRINT RUN 278 SER.#'d SETS

1 Legend of the Undertaker .75 2.00
2 Legend of the Undertaker .75 2.00
3 Legend of the Undertaker .75 2.00
4 Legend of the Undertaker .75 2.00
5 Legend of the Undertaker .75 2.00
6 Legend of the Undertaker .75 2.00
7 Legend of the Undertaker .75 2.00
8 Legend of the Undertaker .75 2.00
9 Legend of the Undertaker .75 2.00
10 Legend of the Undertaker .75 2.00
11 Legend of the Undertaker .75 2.00
12 Legend of the Undertaker .75 2.00
13 Legend of the Undertaker .75 2.00
14 Legend of the Undertaker .75 2.00
15 Legend of the Undertaker .75 2.00
16 Legend of the Undertaker .75 2.00
17 Legend of the Undertaker .75 2.00
18 Legend of the Undertaker .75 2.00
19 Legend of the Undertaker .75 2.00
20 Legend of the Undertaker .75 2.00
21 The Streak .75 2.00
22 The Streak .75 2.00
23 The Streak .75 2.00
24 The Streak .75 2.00
25 The Streak .75 2.00
26 The Streak .75 2.00
27 The Streak .75 2.00
28 The Streak .75 2.00
29 The Streak .75 2.00
30 The Streak .75 2.00
31 The Streak .75 2.00
32 The Streak .75 2.00
33 The Streak .75 2.00
34 The Streak .75 2.00
35 The Streak .75 2.00
36 The Streak .75 2.00
37 The Streak .75 2.00
38 The Streak .75 2.00
39 The Streak .75 2.00
40 The Streak .75 2.00

2020 Topps On-Demand WWE 30 Years of the Deadman Rest in Peace Relic

*NAVY BLUE/50: .75X TO 2X BASIC MEM
*PURPLE/30: 1X TO 2.5X BASIC MEM
*GRAY/15: UNPRICED DUE TO SCARCITY
*BLACK/5: UNPRICED DUE TO SCARCITY
*GOLD/1: UNPRICED DUE TO SCARCITY
STATED PRINT RUN 99 SER.#'d SETS

C1 Undertaker 12.00 30.00

2019 Topps On-Demand WWE WrestleMania 35 Roster

COMPLETE SET (10) 25.00 60.00
STATED PRINT RUN 75 SER.#'d SETS

1 Kurt Angle 3.00 8.00
2 Kofi Kingston 2.50 6.00
3 The New Daniel Bryan 4.00 10.00
4 Becky Lynch 6.00 15.00
5 Charlotte Flair 6.00 15.00
6 Ronda Rousey 8.00 20.00
7 Seth Rollins 4.00 10.00
8 Brock Lesnar 6.00 15.00
9 Triple H 4.00 10.00
10 Dave Batista 4.00 10.00

2010 Topps Platinum WWE

COMPLETE SET (125) 12.00 30.00
*RAINBOW: .8X TO 2X BASIC CARDS
*X-FRACTOR: 1X TO 2.5X BASIC CARDS
*GREEN/499: 1.25X TO 3X BASIC CARDS
*BLUE/199: 2X TO 5X BASIC CARDS
*GOLD/50: 3X TO 8X BASIC CARDS
*RED/1: UNPRICED DUE TO SCARCITY
*P.P.BLACK/1: UNPRICED DUE TO SCARCITY
*P.P.CYAN/1: UNPRICED DUE TO SCARCITY
*P.P.MAGENTA/1: UNPRICED DUE TO SCARCITY
*P.P.YELLOW/1: UNPRICED DUE TO SCARCITY

1 John Cena 1.00 2.50
2 Finlay .30 .75
3 Shad .20 .50
4 Dean Malenko .30 .75
5 Christian .30 .75
6 Kane .50 1.25
7 Luke Gallows .20 .50
8 The Miz .30 .75
9 Gail Kim .50 1.25
10 Iron Sheik .50 1.25
11 Eli Cottonwood RC .20 .50
12 High Chief Peter Maivia .20 .50
13 Earthquake .30 .75

14 Melina	.75	2.00
15 Paul Bearer	.30	.75
16 Rosa Mendes RC	.30	.75
17 Ricky The Dragon Steamboat	.30	.75
18 Darren Young RC	.30	.75
19 Animal UER/Hawk on Front	.20	.50
20 JTG	.20	.50
21 Evan Bourne	.20	.50
22 Jake The Snake Roberts	.50	1.25
23 Edge	.75	2.00
24 Beth Phoenix	.75	2.00
25 Jey Uso RC	.20	.50
26 The Great Khali	.20	.50
27 Jimmy Superfly Snuka	.50	1.25
28 Layla	.50	1.25
29 Mark Henry	.30	.75
30 Arn Anderson	.30	.75
31 Jimmy Uso RC	.20	.50
32 Bushwhacker Luke	.20	.50
33 Jerry The King Lawler	.30	.75
34 Chris Masters	.20	.50
35 Bushwhacker Butch	.20	.50
36 Hawk UER/Animal on Front	.20	.50
37 Big Show	.50	1.25
38 Tamina RC	.20	.50
39 Hacksaw Jim Duggan	.30	.75
40 Cowboy Bob Orton	.30	.75
41 Percy Watson RC	.20	.50
42 Ted DiBiase	.30	.75
43 Curt Hawkins	.20	.50
44 Husky Harris RC	.40	1.00
45 Tyler Reks RC	.20	.50
46 Mr. Perfect Curt Hennig	.30	.75
47 Jillian	.75	2.00
48 CM Punk	.75	2.00
49 Vance Archer	.20	.50
50 Tiffany	.30	.75
51 Hillbilly Jim	.30	.75
52 David Otunga RC	.30	.75
53 Jack Swagger	.20	.50
54 Maryse	.75	2.00
55 Triple H	1.00	2.50
56 Michelle McCool	.75	2.00
57 Alex Riley RC	.20	.50
58 One Man Gang	.30	.75
59 Kofi Kingston	.30	.75
60 Zack Ryder	.20	.50
61 Doink	.20	.50
62 Sergeant Slaughter	.50	1.25
63 Dusty Rhodes	.50	1.25
64 Kelly Kelly	.75	2.00
65 Theodore Long	.20	.50
66 Chris Jericho	.50	1.25
67 Heath Slater RC	.30	.75
68 Natalya	.75	2.00
69 Rocky Johnson	.20	.50
70 Kaval RC	.20	.50
71 Eve	.75	2.00
72 Bobby The Brain Heenan	.30	.75
73 Undertaker	.75	2.00
74 Bam Bam Bigelow	.30	.75
75 Classy Freddie Blassie	.50	1.25
76 MVP	.30	.75
77 Goldust	.30	.75
78 Chavo Guerrero	.30	.75
79 Brian Pillman	.50	1.25
80 Lucky Cannon RC	.20	.50
81 Drew McIntyre RC	.30	.75
82 Ranjin Singh	.20	.50
83 Papa Shango	.20	.50
84 William Regal	.50	1.25
85 Titus O'Neil RC	.20	.50
86 Trent Barreta RC	.20	.50
87 Nikki Bella	.75	2.00
88 R-Truth	.20	.50
89 Vader	.30	.75
90 Skip Sheffield RC	.30	.75
91 Tyson Kidd	.20	.50
92 Michael Tarver RC	.30	.75
93 John Morrison	.30	.75
94 Michael McGillicutty RC	.20	.50
95 Koko B. Ware	.30	.75
96 Don Muraco	.30	.75
97 Randy Orton	.75	2.00
98 Harley Race	.30	.75
99 British Bulldog	.30	.75
100 Sheamus RC	.30	.75
101 Justin Gabriel RC	.30	.75
102 Yoshi Tatsu RC	.20	.50
103 Ezekiel Jackson	.20	.50
104 Terry Funk	.50	1.25
105 Mr. Wonderful Paul Orndorff	.50	1.25
106 David Hart Smith	.20	.50
107 Ravishing Rick Rude	.30	.75
108 Nikolai Volkoff	.30	.75
109 Cody Rhodes	.20	.50
110 Hornswoggle	.30	.75
111 Primo	.20	.50
112 Santino Marella	.20	.50
113 Rey Mysterio	.50	1.25
114 Wade Barrett RC	.30	.75
115 Dolph Ziggler	.30	.75
116 Ted DiBiase	.30	.75
117 Chief Jay Strongbow	.20	.50
118 Vladimir Kozlov	.30	.75
119 Junkyard Dog	.50	1.25
120 Vickie Guerrero	.20	.50
121 Rowdy Roddy Piper	.75	2.00
122 Kamala	.30	.75
123 Brie Bella	.75	2.00
124 Caylen Croft RC	.20	.50
125 Alicia Fox	.30	.75
CL Checklist	.20	.50

2010 Topps Platinum WWE Autographed Relics

*BLUE/99: .75X TO 1.5X BASIC AUTOS
*GOLD/25: 1X TO 2X BASIC AUTOS
STATED PRINT RUN 275 SER. #'d SETS

1 John Cena	20.00	50.00
5 Christian	10.00	25.00
8 The Miz	10.00	25.00
21 Evan Bourne	12.00	30.00
23 Edge	15.00	40.00
37 Big Show	15.00	40.00
48 CM Punk	35.00	70.00
59 Kofi Kingston	12.00	30.00
76 MVP	10.00	25.00
97 Randy Orton	15.00	40.00

2010 Topps Platinum WWE Autographs

*BLUE/99: .75X TO 1.5X BASIC AUTOS
*GOLD/25: 1X TO 2X BASIC AUTOS
*RED/1: UNPRICED DUE TO SCARCITY
*P.P.BLACK/1: UNPRICED DUE TO SCARCITY
*P.P.CYAN/1: UNPRICED DUE TO SCARCITY
*P.P.MAGENTA/1: UNPRICED DUE TO SCARCITY
*P.P.YELLOW/1: UNPRICED DUE TO SCARCITY
STATED PRINT RUN 271 SER.#'d SETS

6 Kane	15.00	40.00
42 Ted DiBiase	12.00	30.00
43 Curt Hawkins	6.00	15.00
45 Tyler Reks	6.00	15.00
52 David Otunga	8.00	20.00
54 Maryse	20.00	50.00
56 Michelle McCool	20.00	50.00
60 Zack Ryder	8.00	20.00
64 Kelly Kelly	20.00	50.00
65 Theodore Long	8.00	20.00
66 Chris Jericho	25.00	60.00
81 Drew McIntyre	12.00	30.00
86 Trent Barreta	8.00	20.00
114 Wade Barrett	12.00	30.00
115 Dolph Ziggler	12.00	30.00
124 Caylen Croft UER/Misspelled Caylan	8.00	20.00
125 Alicia Fox	12.00	30.00

2010 Topps Platinum WWE Legendary Superstars

COMPLETE SET (25) 5.00 12.00
*GREEN/499: .5X TO 1.25X BASIC CARDS
*BLUE/199: .6X TO 1.5X BASIC CARDS
*GOLD/50: 1.2X TO 3X BASIC CARDS
*RED/1: UNPRICED DUE TO SCARCITY
STATED ODDS 1:4

LS1 Evan Bourne/Jimmy Snuka	.60	1.50
LS2 Dolph Ziggler/Paul Orndorff	.60	1.50
LS3 Randy Orton/Jake Roberts	1.00	2.50
LS4 Goldust/Papa Shango	.40	1.00
LS5 R-Truth/Koko B. Ware	.40	1.00
LS6 The Miz/Michael Hayes	.40	1.00
LS7 Mark Henry/One Man Gang	.40	1.00
LS8 Big Show/Vader	.60	1.50
LS9 William Regal/Arn Anderson	.60	1.50
LS10 John Cena/Dusty Rhodes	1.25	3.00
LS11 Drew McIntyre/Rick Rude	.40	1.00
LS12 Edge/Brian Pillman	1.00	2.50
LS13 Chris Jericho/Roddy Piper	1.00	2.50
LS14 The Usos/Wild Samoans	.40	1.00
LS15 Kane/Bam Bam Bigelow	.60	1.50
LS16 Daniel Bryan/Dean Malenko	.40	1.00
LS17 Sheamus/Iron Sheik	.60	1.50
LS18 Triple H/Harley Race	1.25	3.00
LS19 Curt Hawkins/Curt Hennig	.40	1.00
LS20 Ted DiBiase/Tully Blanchard	.40	1.00
LS21 MVP/Ted DiBiase	.40	1.00
LS22 Rey Mysterio/Ricky Steamboat	.60	1.50
LS23 CM Punk/Terry Funk	1.00	2.50
LS24 Bros. of Destruction/LOD	1.00	2.50
LS25 Wade Barrett/British Bulldog	.40	1.00

2010 Topps Platinum WWE Platinum Performance

COMPLETE SET (25) 6.00 15.00
*GREEN/499: .5X TO 1.25X BASIC CARDS
*BLUE/199: .6X TO 1.5X BASIC CARDS
*GOLD/50: 1.2X TO 3X BASIC CARDS
*RED/1: UNPRICED DUE TO SCARCITY
STATED ODDS 1:4

PP1 Pat Patterson	.40	1.00
PP2 Bobby The Brain Heenan	.40	1.00
PP3 Chris Jericho	.60	1.50
PP4 Randy Orton	1.00	2.50
PP5 Hacksaw Jim Duggan	.40	1.00
PP6 Triple H	1.25	3.00
PP7 CM Punk	1.00	2.50
PP8 The British Bulldog	.40	1.00
PP9 Beth Phoenix	1.00	2.50
PP10 John Cena	1.25	3.00
PP11 Jimmy Superfly Snuka	.60	1.50
PP12 Sheamus	.40	1.00
PP13 Chris Jericho	.60	1.50
PP14 Big Show	.60	1.50
PP15 Rey Mysterio	.60	1.50
PP16 The Hart Dynasty	.40	1.00
PP17 Undertaker	1.00	2.50
PP18 Ted DiBiase	.40	1.00
PP19 Vladimir Kozlov	.40	1.00
PP20 Edge	1.00	2.50
PP21 John Morrison	.40	1.00
PP22 Harley Race	.40	1.00
PP23 MVP	.40	1.00
PP24 Eve	1.00	2.50
PP25 Ricky The Dragon Steamboat	.40	1.00

2010 Topps Platinum WWE Relics

*GREEN/399: .5X TO 1.25X BASIC MEM
*BLUE/99: .6X TO 1.5X BASIC MEM
*GOLD/50: 1.2X TO 3X BASIC MEM
*RED/10: UNPRICED DUE TO SCARCITY
STATED ODDS ONE PER HOBBY BOX

1 John Cena	8.00	20.00
5 Christian	5.00	12.00
8 The Miz	5.00	12.00
23 Edge	6.00	15.00
37 Big Show	6.00	15.00
48 CM Punk	8.00	20.00
55 Triple H	8.00	20.00
59 Kofi Kingston	5.00	12.00
76 MVP	5.00	12.00
88 R-Truth	5.00	12.00
91 Tyson Kidd	6.00	15.00
93 John Morrison	8.00	20.00
97 Randy Orton	10.00	25.00
100 Sheamus	6.00	15.00
106 David Hart Smith	5.00	12.00

2010 Topps Platinum WWE Triple Relics

STATED PRINT RUN 99 SER.#'d SETS

FTR1 TripleH/Cena/Edge	25.00	50.00
FTR2 Morrison/Kingston/Miz	20.00	40.00
FTR3 Bourne/Truth/Christian	20.00	40.00
FTR4 Rhodes/Bourne/MVP	20.00	40.00
FTR5 Christian/Edge/Kidd	20.00	40.00
FTR6 Sheamus/Mysterio/Orton/75	25.00	50.00
FTR7 Cena/Sheamus/Morrison	25.00	50.00
FTR8 Orton/Smith/Marella	25.00	50.00
FTR9 Show/Edge/Punk	20.00	40.00
FTR10 Punk/Miz/Mysterio/75	20.00	40.00

2006 Topps UK WWE Insider English

COMPLETE SET (82)

1 Antonio
2 Big Show FOIL
3 Carlito
4 Chris Masters
5 Christy Hemme FOIL
6 Danny Basham
7 Edge
8 Eric Bischoff
9 Eugene
10 Gene Snitsky
11 Hulk Hogan FOIL
12 Jerry The King Lawler
13 Jim Ross
14 John Cena FOIL
15 Jonathan Coachman
16 Kane FOIL
17 Chavo Guerrero
18 Kurt Angle FOIL
19 Lance Cade FOIL
20 Lilian Garcia
21 Lita
22 Maria
23 Matt Hardy
24 Rene Dupree
25 Ric Flair FOIL
26 Rob Conway
27 Rob Van Dam
28 Romeo
29 Rosey
30 Shawn Michaels
31 Shelton Benjamin
32 Stacy Keibler
33 Stone Cold Steve Austin
34 Tajiri
35 The Hurricane
36 Trevor Murdoch FOIL RC
37 Triple H
38 Trish Stratus
39 Tyson Tomko
40 Val Venis
41 Victoria
42 Viscera
43 Batista FOIL
44 Booker T
45 Candice
46 Chris Benoit FOIL
47 Christian
48 Doug Basham
49 The Boogeyman FOIL RC
50 Funaki
51 Hardcore Holly
52 Heidenreich FOIL
53 JBL
54 Joey Mercury
55 Johnny Nitro
56 Josh Mathews RC
57 Juventud
58 Ken Kennedy RC
59 Melina
60 Michael Cole RC
61 Michelle McCool
62 Nunzio FOIL
63 Orlando Jordan
64 Paul London
65 Psicosis
66 Randy Orton
67 Rey Mysterio FOIL

68 Road Warrior Animal FOIL
69 Scotty 2 Hotty
70 Sharmell
71 Simon Dean RC
72 Steven Richards
73 Super Crazy
74 Sylvan
75 Tazz
76 Theodore Long
77 Torrie Wilson
78 Undertaker FOIL
79 Vito RC
80 William Regal
81 WWE Logo FOIL
82 WrestleMania 22 Logo

2006 Topps UK WWE Insider English Checklists

CK1 Checklist 1
CK2 Checklist 2

1999 Topps WCW Embossed

COMPLETE SET (72)	10.00	25.00
1 Title Card	.12	.30
2 Buff Bagwell	.12	.30
3 Lash LeRoux RC	.12	.30
4 Chris Benoit	.20	.50
5 Rick Steiner	.20	.50
6 Diamond Dallas Page	.25	.60
7 Disco Inferno	.12	.30
8 Bobby Duncum, Jr. RC	.12	.30
9 Vampiro RC	.12	.30
10 Rowdy Roddy Piper	.40	1.00
11 Arn Anderson	.25	.60
12 Sid Vicious	.12	.30
13 Macho Man Randy Savage	.40	1.00
14 Ric Flair	1.00	2.50
15 Saturn	.12	.30
16 Goldberg	.30	1.00
17 Steven Regal	.12	.30
18 Juventud Guerrera	.20	.50
19 Chavo Guerrero, Jr.	.12	.30
20 Eddy Guerrero	.20	.50
21 Shane Douglas RC	.12	.30
22 Sting	.60	1.50
23 Rey Mysterio, Jr.	.30	.75
24 Booker T.	.20	.50
25 Stevie Ray	.12	.30
26 Bret Hart	.20	.50
27 Barry Windham	.12	.30
28 Scott Norton	.12	.30
29 Curt Hennig	.25	.60
30 Kaos RC	.12	.30
31 Scotty Riggs	.12	.30
32 Hugh Morrus	.12	.30
33 Ernest The Cat Miller	.12	.30
34 Kanyon	.12	.30
35 Kaz Hayashi	.12	.30
36 Billy Kidman	.12	.30
37 Konnan	.12	.30
38 Psychosis	.12	.30
39 Lenny Lane RC	.12	.30
40 Lodi	.12	.30
41 Meng	.12	.30
42 Dean Malenko	.12	.30
43 Prince Iaukea RC	.12	.30
44 Berlyn	.12	.30
45 David Flair RC	.12	.30
46 Evan Karagias RC	.12	.30
47 Jimmy Hart P	.20	.50
48 JJ Dillon P	.12	.30
49 Charles Robinson P RC	.12	.30
50 Hardcore Hak DHD RC	.12	.30
51 Brian Knobs DHD	.12	.30
52 Bam Bam Bigelow DHD	.20	.50
53 Jerry Flynn DHD RC	.12	.30
54 Fit Finlay DHD	.12	.30
55 Hulk Hogan	2.00	5.00
56 Kevin Nash	.30	.75
57 Scott Steiner	.30	.75
58 Lex Luger	.25	.60
59 Scott Hall	.12	.30
60 Horace Hogan RC	.12	.30
61 Vincent	.12	.30
62 Kimberly WOW	.20	.50
63 Chae WOW	.20	.50
64 Spice WOW	.20	.50
65 Tygress WOW	.20	.50
66 Fyre WOW	.20	.50
67 A.C. Jazz WOW	.20	.50
68 Storm WOW RC	.20	.50
69 Asya WOW RC	.20	.50
70 Madusa WOW	.20	.50
71 Gorgeous George WOW RC	.20	.50
72 Miss Elizabeth WOW	.30	.75
NNO Hulk Hogan RR	25.00	50.00

1999 Topps WCW Embossed Authentic Signatures

STATED ODDS 1:49

NNO Asya	20.00	50.00
NNO Barbarian	50.00	100.00
NNO Blitzkrieg	15.00	40.00
NNO Brad Armstrong	25.00	60.00
NNO Buff Bagwell	150.00	400.00
NNO Chastity	30.00	75.00
NNO Chris Adams	50.00	100.00
NNO Dave Taylor	20.00	50.00
NNO Doug Dillinger	15.00	40.00
NNO Eric Watts	30.00	75.00
NNO Gorgeous George	200.00	500.00
NNO Hacksaw Jim Duggan	30.00	75.00
NNO Horace Hogan	60.00	150.00
NNO Jerry Flynn	25.00	60.00
NNO Kendall Windham	75.00	150.00
NNO Lash Laroux	20.00	50.00
NNO Lex Luger	60.00	120.00
NNO Lizmark, Jr.	20.00	50.00
NNO Madusa	50.00	100.00
NNO Outrageous Evan Karagios	20.00	50.00
NNO Sarge Buddy Lee Parker	20.00	50.00
NNO Scott Hudson	30.00	75.00
NNO Scotty Putsky	25.00	60.00
NNO Steve Regal	100.00	250.00
NNO Tank Abbott	50.00	100.00
NNO Tough Tom	20.00	50.00
NNO Van Hammer	30.00	75.00

1999 Topps WCW Embossed Chrome

STATED ODDS 1:6

1 Buff Bagwell/Lex Luger	1.50	4.00
2 Goldberg/Kevin Nash	2.50	6.00
3 Randy Savage/Gorgeous George	2.50	6.00
4 Ric Flair/David Flair	2.00	5.00
5 Scott Steiner/Rick Steiner	1.25	3.00

1999 Topps WCW Embossed Promos

P1 Buff Bagwell	1.00	2.50
P2 Gorgeous George	1.50	4.00

1992 Topps UK WCW

COMPLETE SET (66)

1 Lex Luger
2 Sting
3 Brian Pillman
4 Arn Anderson
5 Tom Zenk
6 Scott Steiner
7 Rick Steiner
8 Barry Windham
9 Butch Reed
10 Ron Simmons
11 Doom
12 El Gigante
13 Michael PS Hayes
14 Jimmy Garvin
15 The Fabulous Freebirds
16 The Steiner Brothers
17 Brian Pillman
18 Diamond Studd RC
19 P.N. News RC
20 Johnny B. Badd RC
21 Paul E. Dangerously
22 Bobby Eaton
23 Richard Morton
24 One Man Gang
25 Diamond Dallas Page RC
26 Checklist
27 Tommy Rich
28 P.N. News RC
29 Van Hammer RC
30 Lex Luger
31 Missy Hyatt
32 Van Hammer RC
33 Arn Anderson
34 Bobby Eaton
35 Jimmy Garvin UER/Scott Hall Image
36 Big Josh RC
37 Dustin Rhodes RC
38 Tom Zenk
39 Johnny B. Badd RC
40 Lex Luger
41 Sting
42 Terrence Taylor
43 Big Van Vader RC
44 Arn Anderson
45 Barry Windham
46 One Man Gang
47 Sting
48 Checklist
49 Jimmy Garvin UER/Scott Hall Image
50 Lex Luger
51 Dustin Rhodes RC
52 Diamond Studd RC
53 Tommy Rich
54 Lex Luger
55 Bobby Eaton
56 Johnny B. Badd RC
57 Sting
58 Big Josh RC
59 Tracy Smothers RC
60 Brian Pillman
61 Big Van Vader RC
62 Terrence Taylor
63 Ron Simmons
64 Tom Zenk
65 P.N. News RC
66 El Gigante

1999 Topps WCW VHS Promos

COMPLETE SET (5)

1 Hollywood Hogan
2 Ric Flair
3 Sting
4 Lex Luger
5 Randy Savage

1998 Topps WCW/nWo

COMPLETE SET (72)	30.00	75.00
1 Hollywood Hogan	4.00	10.00
2 Sting	1.25	3.00
3 Kevin Nash	.40	1.00
4 Macho Man Randy Savage	1.25	3.00
5 Bret Hart	1.25	3.00
6 Lex Luger	.30	.75
7 Giant RC	3.00	8.00
8 Diamond Dallas Page	.40	1.00
9 Goldberg RC	4.00	10.00
10 Scott Hall	.75	2.00
11 Rick Steiner	.20	.50
12 Scott Steiner	.30	.75
13 Buff Bagwell	.60	1.50
14 Scott Norton RC	.12	.30
15 Booker T	.20	.50
16 Rowdy Roddy Piper	1.50	4.00
17 Chris Benoit RC	2.00	5.00
18 Raven RC	.12	.30
19 Chris Jericho RC	2.00	5.00
20 Ravishing Rick Rude	.30	.75
21 Konnan RC	.12	.30
22 Saturn RC	.12	.30
23 Sick Boy RC	.12	.30
24 British Bulldog	.20	.50
25 Juventud Guerrera RC	.12	.30
26 Dean Malenko RC	.40	1.00
27 Eddy Guerrero RC	2.50	6.00
28 Chavo Guerrero Jr. RC	.40	1.00
29 Ultimo Dragon RC	.40	1.00
30 Disco Inferno RC	.12	.30
31 Wrath	.12	.30
32 Rey Mysterio Jr. RC	6.00	15.00
33 Psychosis RC	.12	.30
34 Stevie Ray	.12	.30
35 Jimmy Hart	.20	.50
36 Steve McMichael	.20	.50
37 Curt Hennig	.30	.75
38 Meng	.12	.30
39 Vincent	.12	.30
40 Fit Finley RC	.40	1.00
41 Jay Leno	3.00	8.00
42 Alex Wright	.12	.30
43 Tenay/Schiavone/Heenan	.12	.30
44 Hugh Morrus RC	.20	.50
45 Kaz Hayashi RC	.12	.30
46 Kanyon RC	.20	.50
47 The Disciple	.20	.50
48 Jim Neidhart	.12	.30
49 Arn Anderson	.20	.50
50 Eric Bischoff	1.25	3.00
51 Ernest Miller RC	.20	.50
52 Miss Elizabeth	2.00	5.00
53 Gene Okerlund	.20	.50
54 Ric Flair	.75	2.00
55 Brian Adams	.20	.50
56 Lodi RC	.12	.30
57 Riggs RC	.12	.30
58 Fyre NG RC	1.25	3.00
59 Chae NG RC	1.25	3.00
60 Kimberly NG	1.25	3.00
61 Spice NG RC	1.25	3.00
62 A.C. Jazz NG RC	1.25	3.00
63 Tygress NG RC	1.25	3.00
64 Whisper NG RC	1.25	3.00
65 Hollywood Hogan ICON	2.00	5.00
66 Macho Man Randy Savage ICON	1.25	3.00
67 Rowdy Roddy Piper ICON	1.50	4.00
68 Goldberg CH	1.50	4.00
69 Chris Jericho CH	1.25	3.00
70 Bret Hart CH	.30	.75
71 Kidman CH RC	.12	.30
72 Hogan/Goldberg CL	.12	2.00

1998 Topps WCW/nWo Authentic Signatures

STATED ODDS 1:40 HOBBY

NNO Alex Wright	50.00	125.00
NNO Arn Anderson	60.00	150.00
NNO Bobby Heenan	100.00	250.00
NNO Chris Benoit	600.00	1500.00
NNO Chris Jericho	400.00	1000.00
NNO Dean Malenko	75.00	200.00
NNO Diamond Dallas Page	100.00	250.00
NNO The Disciple	25.00	60.00
NNO Disco Inferno	25.00	60.00
NNO Eddy Guerrero	600.00	1500.00
NNO Ernest Miller	75.00	200.00
NNO Fit Finley	30.00	75.00
NNO Fyre	30.00	75.00
NNO Gene Okerlund	75.00	200.00
NNO Giant	100.00	250.00
NNO Hollywood Hogan	200.00	500.00
NNO Jimmy Hart	30.00	75.00
NNO Juventud Guerrera	30.00	75.00
NNO Kanyon	25.00	60.00
NNO Kaz Hayashi	30.00	75.00
NNO Kevin Nash	40.00	100.00
NNO Kidman	50.00	125.00
NNO Konnan	30.00	75.00
NNO Lodi	20.00	50.00
NNO Meng	30.00	75.00
NNO Mike Tenay	15.00	40.00
NNO Psychosis	60.00	150.00
NNO Raven	40.00	100.00
NNO Riggs	40.00	100.00
NNO Saturn	30.00	75.00
NNO Sick Boy	40.00	100.00
NNO Spice	30.00	75.00
NNO Tony Schiavone	50.00	125.00
NNO Tygress	25.00	60.00
NNO Vincent	15.00	40.00
NNO Whisper	25.00	60.00
NNO Wrath	30.00	75.00

1998 Topps WCW/nWo Chrome

Card	Low	High
COMPLETE SET (10)	50.00	125.00
STATED ODDS 1:12 HOBBY EXCLUSIVE		
C1 Goldberg	12.00	30.00
C2 Diamond Dallas Page	3.00	8.00
C3 Macho Man Randy Savage	6.00	15.00
C4 Sting	6.00	15.00
C5 Hollywood Hogan	20.00	50.00
C6 Kevin Nash	6.00	15.00
C7 Konnan	3.00	8.00
C8 Bret Hart	15.00	40.00
C9 Giant	8.00	20.00
C10 Lex Luger	3.00	8.00

1998 Topps WCW/nWo Retail Stickers

Card	Low	High
COMPLETE SET (10)	5.00	12.00
STATED ODDS 1:1 RETAIL EXCLUSIVE		
S1 Goldberg	1.00	2.50
S2 Diamond Dallas Page	.60	1.50
S3 Macho Man Randy Savage	1.25	3.00
S4 Sting	3.00	8.00
S5 Hollywood Hogan	2.00	5.00
S6 Kevin Nash	.50	1.25
S7 Konnan	.40	1.00
S8 Bret Hart	1.25	3.00
S9 Giant	.60	1.50
S10 Lex Luger	.40	1.00

1998 Topps WCW/nWo Promos

Card	Low	High
COMPLETE SET (5)	4.00	10.00
P1 Hollywood Hogan	2.50	6.00
P2 Sting	2.00	5.00
P3 Macho Man	1.25	3.00
P4 DDP	1.00	2.50
P5 Goldberg	1.00	2.50

1999 Topps WCW/nWo Nitro

Card	Low	High
COMPLETE SET (72)	6.00	15.00
1 Checklist	.12	.30
2 Bret Hart	.25	.60
3 Diamond Dallas Page	.25	.60
4 Goldberg	.30	.75
5 Rick Steiner	.20	.50
6 Booker T	.20	.50
7 Chris Jericho	.20	.50
8 Saturn	.12	.30
9 Bam Bam Bigelow	.20	.50
10 Chavo Guerrero, Jr.	.12	.30
11 Disco Inferno	.12	.30
12 Wrath	.12	.30
13 Rey Misterio, Jr.	.25	.60
14 Meng	.12	.30
15 Super Calo RC	.12	.30
16 Glacier RC	.12	.30
17 Silver King RC	.12	.30
18 Kaos RC	.12	.30
19 Lenny Lane RC	.12	.30
20 Norman Smiley RC	.40	1.00
21 Kidman	.12	.30
22 Alex Wright	.12	.30
23 Kanyon	.12	.30
24 Raven	.12	.30
25 Lodi	.12	.30
26 Ernest Miller	.20	.50
27 The Disciple	.20	.50
28 Bobby Duncum, Jr. RC	.12	.30
29 Barry Windham	.12	.30
30 Konnan	.12	.30
31 Buff Bagwell	.12	.30
32 Eric Bischoff	.12	.30
33 Hollywood Hogan	1.50	4.00
34 Scott Hall	.12	.30
35 Horace Hogan RC	.12	.30
36 Scott Steiner	.25	.60
37 Stevie Ray	.12	.30
38 Brian Adams	.12	.30
39 Vincent	.12	.30
40 Curt Hennig	.25	.60
41 Macho Man Randy Savage	.40	1.00
42 Sting	.60	1.50
43 Kevin Nash	.30	.75
44 Lex Luger	.25	.60
45 Ric Flair	1.00	2.50
46 Arn Anderson	.20	.50
47 Dean Malenko	.12	.30
48 Chris Benoit	.25	.60
49 Steve McMichael	.20	.50
50 Juventud Guerrera	.12	.30
51 Eddie Guerrero	.20	.50
52 Psychosis	.12	.30
53 La Parka RC	.12	.30
54 Damian RC	.12	.30
55 Hector Garza RC	.12	.30
56 Miss Elizabeth	.30	.75
57 Kimberly	.20	.50
58 Spice	.20	.50
59 A.C. Jazz	.20	.50
60 Tygress	.20	.50
61 Whisper	.20	.50
62 Chae	.20	.50
63 Fyre	.20	.50
64 Storm RC	.20	.50
65 Goldberg Triumphant	.30	.75
66 The Venomous Bite of Sting	.40	1.00
67 Hogan for President	.60	1.50
68 Kevin Nash Is God	.30	.75
69 DDP Is Back Again	.25	.60
70 Larry Zbyszko/Bobby Heenan	.20	.50
71 Doug Dellinger	.12	.30
72 Sonny Onoo RC	.12	.30

1999 Topps WCW/nWo Nitro Authentic Signatures

Card	Low	High
STATED ODDS 1:40 HOBBY		
NNO A.C. Jazz	25.00	60.00
NNO Bam Bam Bigelow	200.00	500.00
NNO Billy Silverman	30.00	75.00
NNO Bret Hart	300.00	800.00
NNO Brian Adams	125.00	300.00
NNO Chae	20.00	50.00
NNO Charles Robinson	25.00	60.00
NNO Chavo Guerrero, Jr.	15.00	40.00
NNO Curt Hennig	250.00	400.00
NNO Cyclope	12.00	30.00
NNO Damian	50.00	100.00
NNO David Penzer	15.00	40.00
NNO El Dandy	10.00	25.00
NNO Glacier	75.00	150.00
NNO Goldberg	200.00	400.00
NNO Hector Garza	12.00	30.00
NNO Hugh Morrus	25.00	60.00
NNO Jim Neidhart	50.00	100.00
NNO Kenny Kaos	15.00	40.00
NNO Kimberly	125.00	250.00
NNO La Parka	50.00	100.00
NNO Larry Zbyszko	25.00	60.00
NNO Lenny Lane	25.00	60.00
NNO Macho Man Randy Savage	1000.00	2500.00
NNO Ms. Elizabeth	500.00	1200.00
NNO Nick Patrick	10.00	25.00
NNO Norman Smiley	12.00	30.00
NNO Prince Iaukea	10.00	25.00
NNO Rick Steiner	100.00	200.00
NNO Scott Hall	400.00	1000.00
NNO Scott Norton	20.00	50.00
NNO Silver King	10.00	25.00
NNO Sonny Onoo	30.00	75.00
NNO Sting	150.00	300.00
NNO Storm	50.00	100.00
NNO Super Calo	10.00	25.00
NNO Ultimo Dragon	30.00	75.00

1999 Topps WCW/nWo Nitro Chrome

Card	Low	High
COMPLETE SET (12)	30.00	60.00
STATED ODDS 1:12 HOBBY		
C1 Sting/Luger v. Hogan/Nash	3.00	8.00
C2 Hogan v. Sting	4.00	10.00
C3 Hogan v. Savage	3.00	8.00
C4 Savage v. Sting	2.50	6.00
C5 Nash v. Giant	3.00	8.00
C6 Hogan/Hart v. Savage/Piper	4.00	10.00
C7 DDP v. Hogan	3.00	8.00
C8 DDP v. Hogan	3.00	8.00
C9 WCW v. The Pac v. Hollywood	3.00	8.00
C10 Goldberg v. DDP	2.50	6.00
C11 60 Man 3 Ring Battle Royal	1.50	4.00
C12 Nash v. Goldberg	3.00	8.00

1999 Topps WCW/nWo Nitro Stickers

Card	Low	High
COMPLETE SET (12)	3.00	6.00
STATED ODDS 1:1 RETAIL		
S1 Sting/Luger v. Hogan/Nash	.40	1.00
S2 Hogan v. Sting	.40	1.00
S3 Hogan v. Savage	.30	.75
S4 Savage v. Sting	.20	.50
S5 Nash v. Giant	.20	.50
S6 Hogan/Hart v. Savage/Piper	.40	1.00
S7 DDP v. Hogan	.40	1.00
S8 DDP v. Hogan	.40	1.00
S9 WCW v. The Pac v. Hollywood	.40	1.00
S10 Goldberg v. DDP	.30	.75
S11 60 Man 3 Ring Battle Royal	.20	.50
S12 Nash v. Goldberg	.30	.75

1999 Topps WCW/nWo Nitro Promos

Card	Low	High
D1 IS DEALER EXCLUSIVE		
B1 Nash and Nitro Girls DE	3.00	8.00
H1 Goldberg	2.00	5.00
H2 Kevin Nash	.75	2.00
H3 Goldberg	1.25	3.00
R1 Goldberg		

2009 Topps WWE

Card	Low	High
COMPLETE SET (90)	15.00	30.00
*GOLD/500: 1.2X TO 3X BASIC CARDS		
*BLACK/40: 5X TO 12X BASIC CARDS		
*PLATINUM/1: UNPRICED DUE TO SCARCITY		
1 Hurricane Helms	.15	.40
2 Carlito	.40	1.00
3 CM Punk	.25	.60
4 Maria	.60	1.50
5 Kofi Kingston	.15	.40
6 Primo	.15	.40
7 Rey Mysterio	.40	1.00
8 Natalya	.60	1.50
9 Tommy Dreamer	.15	.40
10 Michelle McCool	.60	1.50
11 Undertaker	.75	2.00
12 Big Show	.40	1.00
13 Charlie Haas	.15	.40
14 Chris Jericho	.40	1.00
15 Evan Bourne	.15	.40
16 Layla	.40	1.00
17 Christian	.40	1.00
18 Cody Rhodes	.15	.40
19 Dolph Ziggler RC	.25	.60
20 Randy Orton	.40	1.00
21 Edge	.60	1.50
22 Mickie James	.75	2.00
23 Festus	.15	.40
24 Finlay	.25	.60
25 Ted DiBiase	.25	.60
26 Goldust	.25	.60
27 Melina	.60	1.50
28 Hornswoggle	.25	.60
29 Jack Swagger RC	.15	.40
30 Jim Ross	.15	.40
31 Mark Henry	.25	.60
32 Katie Lea Burchill	.40	1.00
33 Mike Knox	.15	.40
34 Kelly Kelly	.60	1.50
35 Matt Hardy	.60	1.50
36 Montel Vontavious Porter	.25	.60
37 R-Truth	.15	.40
38 John Cena	1.00	2.50
39 William Regal	.40	1.00
40 Santino Marella	.15	.40
41 Tyson Kidd RC	.15	.40
42 Maryse	.40	1.00
43 Shelton Benjamin	.15	.40
44 The Brian Kendrick	.25	.60
45 The Great Khali	.15	.40
46 Eve	.60	1.50
47 The Miz	.25	.60
48 Triple H	1.00	2.50
49 Vladimir Kozlov	.25	.60
50 Alicia Fox RC	.25	.60
51 Beth Phoenix	.75	2.00
52 Gail Kim	.40	1.00
53 Jerry The King Lawler	.25	.60
54 Theodore Long	.15	.40
55 Batista	.60	1.50
56 Tiffany	.25	.60
57 Ranjin Singh RC	.15	.40
58 Tony Atlas	.15	.40
59 Kane	.60	1.50
60 Shawn Michaels	1.00	2.50
61 Chavo Guerrero	.25	.60
62 John Morrison	.25	.60
63 Jamie Noble	.15	.40
64 Jimmy Wang Yang	.15	.40
65 Kung Fu Naki	.15	.40
66 Paul Burchill	.15	.40
67 Jillian Hall	.60	1.50
68 David Hart Smith	.15	.40
69 Curt Hawkins	.15	.40
70 DJ Gabriel RC	.15	.40
71 Ezekiel Jackson	.15	.40
72 Jesse	.15	.40
73 Zack Ryder	.15	.40
74 JTG	.15	.40
75 Shad Gaspard	.15	.40
76 Ricky Ortiz	.15	.40
77 Brie Bella RC	5.00	12.00
78 Nikki Bella RC	6.00	15.00
79 CM Punk	.25	.60
80 Santina Marella	.15	.40
81 Chris Jericho	.40	1.00
82 Matt Hardy	.60	1.50
83 Rey Mysterio	.40	1.00
84 Undertaker/Shawn Michaels	1.00	2.50
85 Edge	.60	1.50
86 John Cena	1.00	2.50
87 Randy Orton	.40	1.00
88 Triple H	1.00	2.50
89 Stone Cold Steve Austin	1.00	2.50
90 John Cena CL	1.00	2.50

2009 Topps WWE Autographs

Card	Low	High
STATED ODDS 1:54 HOBBY; 1:172 RETAIL		
NNO Arn Anderson	20.00	50.00
NNO Beth Phoenix	12.00	30.00
NNO Evan Bourne	6.00	15.00
NNO Gail Kim	12.00	30.00
NNO Jim Ross	10.00	25.00
NNO John Cena	30.00	75.00
NNO John Morrison	15.00	40.00
NNO Maryse	30.00	75.00
NNO Michelle McCool	12.00	30.00
NNO Mickie James	15.00	40.00
NNO Ricky Steamboat	12.00	30.00
NNO Santino Marella	6.00	15.00
NNO Tiffany	12.00	30.00

2009 Topps WWE Dual Autographs

Card	Low	High
STATED ODDS 1:55 HOBBY EXCLUSIVE		
NNO Bob & Randy Orton	60.00	120.00
NNO Carlito/Primo	12.00	30.00
NNO Dusty & Cody Rhodes	150.00	300.00
NNO Ted DiBiase Sr. & Jr.	12.00	30.00

2009 Topps WWE Event-Worn Ringside Relics

Card	Low	High
STATED ODDS 1:24 HOBBY; 1:84 RETAIL		
NNO Christian	6.00	15.00
NNO Cody Rhodes	6.00	15.00
NNO Miz (looking left)	5.00	12.00
NNO Miz (looking right)	5.00	12.00
NNO Santino Marella (hands apart)	6.00	15.00
NNO Santino Marella (hands clasped)	6.00	15.00
NNO Shawn Michaels (no hat)	8.00	20.00
NNO Shawn Michaels (w/hat)	8.00	20.00
NNO Ted DiBiase	6.00	15.00
NNO Triple H	8.00	20.00

2009 Topps WWE Historical Commemorative Patches

Card	Low	High
COMPLETE SET (4)	12.00	30.00
STATED ODDS 1:RETAIL BLASTER BOX		
P1 John Cena/WrestleMania	6.00	15.00
P2 John Cena/The Bash	6.00	15.00

P3 John Cena/SummerSlam 6.00 15.00
P4 John Cena/Royal Rumble 6.00 15.00

2009 Topps WWE Judgment Day Mat Relic Autographs

STATED ODDS 1:215 HOBBY EXCLUSIVE

NNO Christian 25.00 60.00
NNO Edge 30.00 75.00
NNO Randy Orton 30.00 75.00
NNO Rey Mysterio 20.00 50.00

2009 Topps WWE Legends of the Ring

COMPLETE SET (20) 8.00 20.00
*GOLD/2250: .75X TO 2X BASIC CARDS
*PLATINUM/1: UNPRICED DUE TO SCARCITY
STATED ODDS 1:1 HOBBY AND RETAIL

1 Bam Bam Bigelow 1.00 2.50
2 British Bulldog 1.00 2.50
3 Chief Jay Strongbow .60 1.50
4 Dean Malenko 1.00 2.50
5 Don Muraco .40 1.00
6 Dusty Rhodes 1.00 2.50
7 Iron Sheik 1.00 2.50
8 Jake The Snake Roberts 1.00 2.50
9 Jimmy Superfly Snuka 1.00 2.50
10 Junkyard Dog 1.00 2.50
11 Mr. Perfect 1.00 2.50
12 Nikolai Volkoff .60 1.50
13 Ravishing Rick Rude 1.00 2.50
14 Sgt. Slaughter 1.00 2.50
15 Superstar Billy Graham 1.00 2.50
16 Terry Funk .60 1.50
17 Vader .60 1.50
18 The Wild Samoans .60 1.50
19 Gorilla Monsoon 1.00 2.50
20 Mr. Wonderful Paul Orndorff .60 1.50

2009 Topps WWE Reign of Honor

COMPLETE SET (10) 6.00 15.00
STATED ODDS 1:6 HOBBY AND RETAIL

1 John Cena 1.50 4.00
2 Triple H 1.50 4.00
3 Jack Swagger .25 .60
4 Rey Mysterio .60 1.50
5 MVP .40 1.00
6 Melina 1.00 2.50
7 Maryse .60 1.50
8 Primo & Carlito .60 1.50
9 Shawn Michaels 1.50 4.00
10 Undertaker 1.25 3.00

2009 Topps WWE Sketches

STATED ODDS 1:2,857 HOBBY EXCLUSIVE
UNPRICED DUE TO SCARCITY

NNO Eve/Beauty...Eye of Beholder
NNO Eve/Musical Notes
NNO Eve/Passion
NNO Eve/Speak What You Feel
NNO J.Lawler/Batista
NNO J.Lawler/Big Show
NNO J.Lawler/Edge
NNO J.Lawler/Jack Swagger
NNO J.Lawler/Rey Mysterio
NNO J.Lawler/Triple H
NNO J.Lawler/Undertaker
NNO Natalya/Balance
NNO Natalya/Calm
NNO Natalya/Energy
NNO Natalya/Glory
NNO Natalya/Happy
NNO Natalya/Honour
NNO Natalya/Peace
NNO Natalya/Pride
NNO Natalya/Sparkle
NNO Natalya/Spirit
NNO Santino/Island
NNO Santino/Landscape
NNO Santino/Map of Italy
NNO Santino/Muscle
NNO Santino/Santina
NNO Santino/Santino
NNO Santino/Self Portrait 1
NNO Santino/Self Portrait 2
NNO Santino/Self Portrait 3
NNO Santino/Self Portrait w/belt

2009 Topps WWE Tin Inserts

COMPLETE SET (4)

1 Jack Swagger
2 Triple H
3 Chris Jericho
4 Rey Mysterio

2009 Topps WWE Topps Town

COMPLETE SET (30) 6.00 15.00
STATED ODDS 1:1 HOBBY AND RETAIL

1 Batista .50 1.25
2 Beth Phoenix .60 1.50
3 Chris Jericho .30 .75
4 Christian .30 .75
5 CM Punk .20 .50
6 Cody Rhodes .12 .30
7 Dolph Ziggler .20 .50
8 Edge .50 1.25
9 Evan Bourne .12 .30
10 Gail Kim .30 .75
11 Jack Swagger .12 .30
12 John Cena .75 2.00
13 John Morrison .20 .50
14 Kofi Kingston .12 .30
15 Maria .50 1.25
16 Maryse .30 .75
17 Matt Hardy .50 1.25
18 Melina .50 1.25
19 Michelle McCool .50 1.25
20 Mickie James .60 1.50
21 Montel Vontavious Porter .20 .50
22 Randy Orton .30 .75
23 Rey Mysterio .30 .75
24 R-Truth .12 .30
25 Santino Marella .12 .30
26 Shawn Michaels .75 2.00
27 Ted DiBiase .20 .50
28 The Miz .20 .50
29 Triple H .75 2.00
30 Undertaker .60 1.50

2010 Topps WWE

COMPLETE SET (110) 10.00 25.00
*BLUE/2010: 1X TO 2.5X BASIC CARDS
*SILVER/999: 1.2X TO 3X BASIC CARDS
*GOLD/50: 4X TO 10X BASIC CARDS
*RED/1: UNPRICED DUE TO SCARCITY
*P.P.BLACK/1: UNPRICED DUE TO SCARCITY
*P.P.CYAN/1: UNPRICED DUE TO SCARCITY
*P.P.MAGENTA/1: UNPRICED DUE TO SCARCITY
*P.P.YELLOW/1: UNPRICED DUE TO SCARCITY

1 John Cena .75 2.00
2 Layla .40 1.00
3 William Regal .40 1.00
4 John Morrison .25 .60
5 Matt Hardy .40 1.00
6 Alicia Fox .25 .60
7 Yoshi Tatsu RC .15 .40
8 Nikki Bella .60 1.50
9 Randy Orton .60 1.50
10 Luke Gallows .15 .40
11 MVP .25 .60
12 Michelle McCool .60 1.50
13 JTG .15 .40
14 Rosa Mendes RC .25 .60
15 Beth Phoenix .60 1.50
16 Chris Jericho .40 1.00
17 Kane .40 1.00
18 Mark Henry .25 .60
19 Tyson Kidd .15 .40
20 Santino Marella .15 .40
21 Theodore Long .15 .40
22 Big Show .40 1.00
23 Kofi Kingston .25 .60
24 Vladimir Kozlov .25 .60
25 Vance Archer .15 .40
26 Brie Bella .60 1.50
27 Ezekiel Jackson .15 .40
28 David Hart Smith .15 .40
29 Trent Baretta RC .15 .40
30 Kelly Kelly .60 1.50
31 Goldust .25 .60
32 Maryse .60 1.50
33 Tyler Reks RC .15 .40
34 Serena RC .25 .60
35 Melina .60 1.50
36 CM Punk .60 1.50
37 Drew McIntyre RC .25 .60
38 Jillian .60 1.50
39 Cody Rhodes .15 .40
40 Ted DiBiase .25 .60
41 Finlay .25 .60
42 Dolph Ziggler .25 .60
43 Triple H .75 2.00
44 Hornswoggle .25 .60
45 R-Truth .15 .40
46 The Miz .25 .60
47 Primo .15 .40
48 Jack Swagger .15 .40
49 Caylen Croft RC .15 .40
50 Rey Mysterio .40 1.00
51 Chris Masters .15 .40
52 Chavo Guerrero .25 .60
53 Shad .15 .40
54 Ranjin Singh .15 .40
55 Sheamus RC .25 .60
56 Vickie Guerrero .15 .40
57 Evan Bourne .15 .40
58 Edge .60 1.50
59 The Undertaker .60 1.50
60 Zack Ryder .15 .40
61 Natalya .60 1.50
62 The Great Khali .15 .40
63 Eve .60 1.50
64 Christian .25 .60
65 Michael Tarver RC .25 .60
66 Skip Sheffield RC .25 .60
67 Wade Barrett RC .25 .60
68 Daniel Bryan RC 8.00 20.00
69 Darren Young RC .25 .60
70 David Otunga RC .25 .60
71 Heath Slater RC .25 .60
72 Justin Gabriel RC .25 .60
73 Undertaker 18-0 .60 1.50
74 ShowMiz .40 1.00
75 The Dude Busters .15 .40
76 The Straight Edge Society .60 1.50
77 Hart Dynasty .60 1.50
78 Mr. Perfect Curt Hennig .25 .60
79 Dean Malenko .25 .60
80 Don Muraco .25 .60
81 Akeem .25 .60
82 Doink the Clown .15 .40
83 Earthquake .25 .60
84 Hillbilly Jim .25 .60
85 Mr. Wonderful Paul Orndorff .40 1.00
86 Nikolai Volkoff .25 .60
87 Papa Shango .15 .40
88 Vader .25 .60
89 Sgt. Slaughter .40 1.00
90 Junkyard Dog .40 1.00
91 Bobby The Brain Heenan .25 .60
92 Harley Race .25 .60
93 The American Dream Dusty Rhodes .40 1.00
94 Jake The Snake Roberts .40 1.00
95 The Iron Sheik .40 1.00
96 Koko B. Ware .25 .60
97 Brian Pillman .40 1.00
98 Jimmy Superfly Snuka .40 1.00
99 Mean Gene Okerland UER .25 .60
100 Ted DiBiase .25 .60
101 The Bushwackers .15 .40
102 Paul Bearer .25 .60
103 Rowdy Roddy Piper .60 1.50
104 Terry Funk .40 1.00
105 Kamala .25 .60
106 Cowboy Bob Orton .25 .60
107 The Road Warriors .40 1.00
108 Ravishing Rick Rude .25 .60
109 Bam Bam Bigelow .25 .60
110 Classy Freddie Blassie .40 1.00
CH1 Checklist 1/2 .15 .40
CH3 Checklist 3/4 .15 .40

2010 Topps WWE Autographs

*GOLD/25: .6X TO 1.5X BASIC AUTOS
*RED/1: UNPRICED DUE TO SCARCITY
*P.P.BLACK/1: UNPRICED DUE TO SCARCITY
*P.P.CYAN/1: UNPRICED DUE TO SCARCITY
*P.P.MAGENTA/1: UNPRICED DUE TO SCARCITY
*P.P.YELLOW/1: UNPRICED DUE TO SCARCITY
OVERALL AUTO ODDS 1:BOX

ABP Beth Phoenix
ABS Big Show 12.00 30.00
ACC Caylen Croft 6.00 15.00
ACH Christian
ACM CM Punk 20.00 50.00
ACR Cody Rhodes 8.00 20.00
ADM Drew McIntyre 10.00 25.00
ADS David Hart Smith 8.00 20.00
AEB Evan Bourne 6.00 15.00
AED Edge 12.00 30.00
AEJ Ezekiel Jackson 6.00 15.00
AGK Gail Kim 12.00 30.00
AJC John Cena 30.00 75.00
AJM John Morrison 10.00 25.00
AJT JTG 6.00 15.00
AKK Kofi Kingston 8.00 20.00
ALG Luke Gallows 6.00 15.00
AMM Michelle McCool 12.00 30.00
ARM Rosa Mendes 10.00 25.00
ARO Randy Orton 20.00 50.00
ART R-Truth 8.00 20.00
ASE Serena 10.00 25.00
ASH Shad 6.00 15.00
ATB Trent Baretta 6.00 15.00
ATD Ted DiBiase 10.00 25.00
ATH Triple H
ATK Tyson Kidd 8.00 20.00
ATM Miz 12.00 30.00
AVA Vance Archer 6.00 15.00
AZR Zack Ryder 8.00 20.00
ASAN Santino Marella 10.00 25.00
ASHE Sheamus 12.00 30.00
JCA1 John Cena 50.00 100.00

2010 Topps WWE Championship Material

COMPLETE SET (50) 20.00 50.00
*PUZZLE BACK: .5X TO 1.2X BASIC CARDS
*IC PUZZLE: .5X TO 1.2X BASIC CARDS
STATED ODDS 1:6 HOBBY AND RETAIL

C1 Christian .50 1.25
C2 John Morrison .50 1.25
C3 John Morrison .50 1.25
C4 The Miz & John Morrison .50 1.25
C5 CM Punk 1.25 3.00
C6 CM Punk 1.25 3.00
C7 Kofi Kingston & CM Punk 1.25 3.00
C8 The Miz .50 1.25
C9 The Hart Dynasty 1.25 3.00
C10 Goldust .50 1.25
C11 Triple H 1.50 4.00
C12 Edge & Chris Jericho 1.25 3.00
C13 Christian .50 1.25
C14 Chris Jericho & Big Show .75 2.00
C15 Chris Jericho .75 2.00
C16 Randy Orton 1.25 3.00
C17 Big Show & The Miz .75 2.00
C18 Edge & Christian 1.25 3.00
C19 Edge 1.25 3.00
C20 Mark Henry .50 1.25
C21 Chavo Guerrero .50 1.25
C22 Matt Hardy .75 2.00
C23 Undertaker & Kane 1.25 3.00
C24 Kane .75 2.00
C25 Kane .75 2.00
C26 R-Truth .30 .75
C27 John Cena 1.50 4.00
C28 Big Show .75 2.00
C29 Ted DiBiase & Cody Rhodes .50 1.25
C30 Drew McIntyre .50 1.25
C31 Rey Mysterio .75 2.00
C32 Jack Swagger .30 .75
C33 William Regal .75 2.00
C34 Kofi Kingston .50 1.25
C35 Santino Marella .30 .75

C36 Ted DiBiase .75 2.00
C37 Michelle McCool 1.25 3.00
C38 Maryse 1.25 3.00
C39 Edge & Randy Orton 1.25 3.00
C40 Jillian 1.25 3.00
C41 Melina 1.25 3.00
C42 MVP .50 1.25
C43 Kofi Kingston .50 1.25
C44 Matt Hardy .75 2.00
C45 Finlay .50 1.25
C46 Mr. Perfect .50 1.25
C47 Don Muraco .50 1.25
C48 Ravishing Rick Rude .50 1.25
C49 Rowdy Roddy Piper 1.25 3.00
C50 British Bulldog .50 1.25

2010 Topps WWE Dual Autographs

*GOLD/25: .5X TO 1.2X BASIC AUTOS
*RED/1: UNPRICED DUE TO SCARCITY
*P.P.BLACK/1: UNPRICED DUE TO SCARCITY
*P.P.CYAN/1: UNPRICED DUE TO SCARCITY
*P.P.MAGENTA/1: UNPRICED DUE TO SCARCITY
*P.P.YELLOW/1: UNPRICED DUE TO SCARCITY
STATED PRINT RUN 99 SER.#'d SETS

DABM E.Bourne/D.McIntyre 10.00 25.00
DACB C.Croft/T.Baretta 8.00 20.00
DACO J.Cena/R.Orton 50.00 100.00
DADR T.DiBiase/C.Rhodes 12.00 30.00
DAES Edge/Big Show 15.00 40.00
DAJC E.Jackson/Christian
DAJS JTG/Shad 8.00 20.00
DAJT E.Jackson/R-Truth 8.00 20.00
DAKM K.Kingston/Miz 12.00 30.00
DAMP J.Morrison/CM Punk 20.00 50.00
DAPG CM Punk/L.Gallows 20.00 50.00
DAPS CM Punk/Serena 15.00 40.00
DARM Z.Ryder/R.Mendes 12.00 30.00
DASK D.Smith/T.Kidd 8.00 20.00
DASP S.Marella/B.Phoenix
DASS S.Marella/Sheamus 12.00 30.00
DAKMC G.Kim/M.McCool 15.00 40.00

2010 Topps WWE Elimination Chamber Canvas

COMPLETE SET (19) 60.00 120.00
*GOLD/50: .75X TO 2X BASIC CARDS
*RED/1: UNPRICED DUE TO SCARCITY
OVERALL RELIC ODDS 1:2 RETAIL EXCLUSIVE

EC1 John Cena 8.00 20.00
EC2 Sheamus 2.50 6.00
EC3 Triple H 8.00 20.00
EC4 Randy Orton 6.00 15.00
EC5 Ted DiBiase Jr. 2.50 6.00
EC6 Kofi Kingston 2.50 6.00
EC7 Drew McIntyre 2.50 6.00
EC8 Kane 4.00 10.00
EC9 Michelle McCool 6.00 15.00
EC10 Layla 4.00 10.00
EC11 Maryse 6.00 15.00
EC12 The Miz 2.50 6.00
EC13 MVP 2.50 6.00
EC14 Chris Jericho 4.00 10.00
EC15 The Undertaker 6.00 15.00
EC16 John Morrison 2.50 6.00
EC17 CM Punk 6.00 15.00
EC18 Rey Mysterio 4.00 10.00
EC19 R-Truth 2.50 6.00

2010 Topps WWE Favorite Finishers

COMPLETE SET (25) 8.00 20.00
STATED ODDS 1:4 HOBBY AND RETAIL

FF1 Dolph Ziggler .40 1.00
FF2 Jack Swagger .25 .60
FF3 Edge 1.00 2.50
FF4 CM Punk 1.00 2.50
FF5 Sheamus .40 1.00
FF6 Evan Bourne .25 .60
FF7 Undertaker 1.00 2.50
FF8 John Cena 1.25 3.00
FF9 The Hart Dynasty 1.00 2.50
FF10 Yoshi Tatsu .25 .60
FF11 Drew McIntyre .40 1.00
FF12 MVP .40 1.00
FF13 John Morrison .40 1.00
FF14 Randy Orton 1.00 2.50
FF15 Big Show .60 1.50
FF16 Kofi Kingston .40 1.00
FF17 Matt Hardy .60 1.50
FF18 Kane .60 1.50
FF19 Christian .40 1.00
FF20 Mark Henry .40 1.00
FF21 Triple H 1.25 3.00
FF22 Beth Phoenix 1.00 2.50
FF23 Rey Mysterio .60 1.50
FF24 Chris Jericho .60 1.50
FF25 The Miz .40 1.00

2010 Topps WWE History Of

COMPLETE SET (25) 10.00 25.00
STATED ODDS 1:8 HOBBY AND RETAIL

HO1 Chris Jericho .75 2.00
HO2 Triple H 1.50 4.00
HO3 Edge 1.25 3.00
HO4 Jack Swagger .30 .75
HO5 John Morrison .50 1.25
HO6 The Undertaker 1.25 3.00
HO7 Kane .75 2.00
HO8 The Miz .50 1.25
HO9 Finlay .50 1.25
HO10 Michelle McCool 1.25 3.00
HO11 Rey Mysterio .75 2.00
HO12 Natalya 1.25 3.00
HO13 John Cena 1.50 4.00
HO14 Kelly Kelly 1.25 3.00
HO15 Ted DiBiase .50 1.25
HO16 Randy Orton 1.25 3.00
HO17 Kofi Kingston .50 1.25
HO18 Big Show .75 2.00
HO19 Santino Marella .30 .75
HO20 Goldust .50 1.25
HO21 Christian .50 1.25
HO22 William Regal .75 2.00
HO23 British Bulldog .50 1.25
HO24 Junkyard Dog .75 2.00
HO25 Mr. Perfect .50 1.25

2010 Topps WWE National Heroes

COMPLETE SET (25) 10.00 25.00
STATED ODDS 1:8 HOBBY AND RETAIL

NH1 John Cena 1.50 4.00
NH2 Maryse 1.25 3.00
NH3 Jack Swagger .30 .75
NH4 Edge 1.25 3.00
NH5 Chris Jericho .75 2.00
NH6 William Regal .75 2.00
NH7 Finlay .50 1.25
NH8 Yoshi Tatsu .30 .75
NH9 Sheamus .50 1.25
NH10 Sgt. Slaughter .75 2.00
NH11 Vladimir Kozlov .50 1.25
NH12 The Great Khali .30 .75
NH13 Kamala .50 1.25
NH14 Nikolai Volkoff .50 1.25
NH15 Iron Shiek .75 2.00
NH16 Wild Samoans .30 .75
NH17 Kofi Kingston .50 1.25
NH18 Drew McIntyre .50 1.25
NH19 Santino Marella .30 .75
NH20 Rey Mysterio .75 2.00
NH21 Mark Henry .50 1.25
NH22 Christian .50 1.25
NH23 Tyson Kidd .30 .75
NH24 Chavo Guerrero .50 1.25
NH25 The British Bulldog .50 1.25

2010 Topps WWE Signature Swatches

STATED PRINT RUN 25 SER. #'d SETS

SSSBS Big Show 60.00 120.00
SSSCG Chavo Guerrero 25.00 60.00
SSSCH Christian 30.00 80.00
SSSCJ Chris Jericho 50.00 100.00
SSSCM CM Punk 60.00 120.00
SSSCR Cody Rhodes 25.00 60.00
SSSDS David Hart Smith 25.00 60.00
SSSEB Evan Bourne 25.00 60.00
SSSED Edge 50.00 100.00
SSSJC John Cena 100.00 200.00
SSSJM John Morrison 50.00 100.00
SSSKK Kofi Kingston 30.00 80.00
SSSMH Matt Hardy 30.00 80.00
SSSRM Rey Mysterio 50.00 100.00
SSSRO Randy Orton 100.00 200.00
SSSSA Santino Marella EXCH 50.00 100.00
SSSSH Shad 25.00 60.00
SSSTD Ted DiBiase Jr. 25.00 60.00
SSSTK Tyson Kidd 30.00 80.00
SSSTM The Miz 30.00 80.00
SSSJTG JTG 25.00 60.00
SSSMVP MVP 30.00 80.00

2010 Topps WWE Superstar Jumbo Swatches

STATED PRINT RUN 30 SER.#'d SETS

SSSBS Big Show 50.00 100.00
SSSCG Chavo Guerrero
SSSCH Christian 40.00 80.00
SSSCJ Chris Jericho
SSSCM CM Punk 50.00 100.00
SSSCR Cody Rhodes 20.00 50.00
SSSDS David Hart Smith 25.00 60.00
SSSEB Evan Bourne 25.00 60.00
SSSED Edge 50.00 100.00
SSSJC John Cena 60.00 120.00
SSSJM John Morrison 40.00 80.00
SSSKK Kofi Kingston 40.00 80.00
SSSMH Matt Hardy EXCH 50.00 100.00
SSSRM Rey Mysterio 40.00 80.00
SSSRO Randy Orton 40.00 80.00
SSSSA Santino Marella EXCH 25.00 60.00
SSSSH Shad
SSSTD Ted DiBiase Jr.
SSSTH Triple H
SSSTK Tyson Kidd 25.00 60.00
SSSTM The Miz 40.00 80.00
SSSTU The Undertaker
SSSJTG JTG
SSSMVP MVP 25.00 60.00

2010 Topps WWE Superstar Swatches

*GOLD/99: .5X TO 1.2X BASIC CARDS
*RED/1: UNPRICED DUE TO SCARCITY
OVERALL RELIC ODDS 1:BOX

JCR1 John Cena 15.00 30.00
SBS Big Show 5.00 12.00
SCG Chavo Guerrero
SCH Christian 5.00 12.00
SCJ Chris Jericho
SCM CM Punk 5.00 12.00
SCR Cody Rhodes 4.00 10.00
SDS David Hart Smith 4.00 10.00
SEB Evan Bourne 5.00 12.00
SED Edge 6.00 15.00
SJC John Cena 10.00 25.00
SJM John Morrison 6.00 15.00
SKK Kofi Kingston 5.00 12.00
SMH Matt Hardy EXCH 8.00 20.00
SRM Rey Mysterio 8.00 20.00
SRO Randy Orton 10.00 25.00
SSA Santino Marella EXCH 5.00 12.00
SSH Shad
STD Ted DiBiase EXCH 6.00 15.00
STH Triple H EXCH 20.00 50.00
STK Tyson Kidd 4.00 10.00
STM The Miz 4.00 10.00
STU The Undertaker
SJTG JTG
SMVP MVP 4.00 10.00

2010 Topps WWE Topps Town

COMPLETE SET (25) 10.00 25.00
STATED ODDS 1:6 HOBBY AND RETAIL

TT1 John Cena 1.25 3.00
TT2 Jack Swagger .25 .60
TT3 Rey Mysterio .60 1.50
TT4 The Miz .40 1.00
TT5 Kane .60 1.50
TT6 Triple H 1.25 3.00
TT7 MVP .40 1.00
TT8 The Undertaker 1.00 2.50
TT9 John Morisson .40 1.00
TT10 Randy Orton 1.00 2.50
TT11 Kofi Kingston .40 1.00
TT12 Michelle McCool 1.00 2.50
TT13 Cody Rhodes .25 .60
TT14 Edge 1.00 2.50
TT15 Kelly Kelly 1.00 2.50
TT16 Ted DiBiase .40 1.00
TT17 Chris Jericho .60 1.50
TT18 CM Punk 1.00 2.50
TT19 Big Show .60 1.50
TT20 Beth Phoenix 1.00 2.50
TT21 Sheamus .40 1.00
TT22 Christian .40 1.00
TT23 R-Truth .25 .60
TT24 Ezekiel Jackson .25 .60
TT25 Maryse 1.00 2.50

2010 Topps WWE When They Were Young

RANDOMLY INSERTED INTO PACKS

WTWY1 John Cena
WTWY2 William Regal
WTWY3 Jack Swagger
WTWY4 Chris Jericho
WTWY5 Big Show
WTWY6 Natalya
WTWY7 The Miz
WTWY8 Sheamus
WTWY9 Chavo Guerrero
WTWY10 Shad
WTWY11 Hornswoggle
WTWY12 Jerry Lawler
WTWY13 Santino Marella
WTWY14 Melina
WTWY15 Ted DiBiase Jr.
WTWY16 Cody Rhodes
WTWY17 Christian
WTWY18 Kelly Kelly
WTWY19 Rosa Mendes
WTWY20 CM Punk
WTWY21 Shelton Benjamin
WTWY22 Evan Bourne
WTWY23 R-Truth
WTWY24 Zack Ryder
WTWY25 Triple H

2010 Topps WWE World Championship Material

COMPLETE SET (25) 12.00 30.00
*PUZZLE: .5X TO 1.2X BASIC CARDS
STATED ODDS 1:6 HOBBY AND RETAIL

W1 John Cena 1.50 4.00
W2 John Cena 1.50 4.00
W3 Triple H 1.50 4.00
W4 Triple H 1.50 4.00
W5 Chris Jericho .75 2.00
W6 Superstar Billy Graham .75 2.00
W7 Chris Jericho .75 2.00
W8 Sheamus .50 1.25
W9 Randy Orton 1.25 3.00
W10 Randy Orton 1.25 3.00
W11 Kane .75 2.00
W12 Undertaker 1.25 3.00
W13 Undertaker 1.25 3.00
W14 Rey Mysterio .75 2.00
W15 Jack Swagger .30 .75
W16 Melina 1.25 3.00
W17 Edge 1.25 3.00
W18 Beth Phoenix 1.25 3.00
W19 Edge 1.25 3.00
W20 Michelle McCool 1.25 3.00
W21 Big Show .75 2.00
W22 CM Punk 1.25 3.00
W23 Sgt. Slaughter .75 2.00
W24 The Iron Sheik .75 2.00
W25 John Cena 1.50 4.00

2011 Topps WWE

COMPLETE SET (113) 10.00 25.00
*BLUE/2011: .8X TO 2X BASIC CARDS
*BLACK/999: 1.5X TO 4X BASIC CARDS
*GOLD/50: 4X TO 10X BASIC CARDS
*RED/1: UNPRICED DUE TO SCARCITY

*P.P.BLACK/1: UNPRICED DUE TO SCARCITY
*P.P.CYAN/1: UNPRICED DUE TO SCARCITY
*P.P.MAGENTA/1: UNPRICED DUE TO SCARCITY
*P.P.YELLOW/1: UNPRICED DUE TO SCARCITY

1 John Cena .75 2.00
2 Randy Orton .60 1.50
3 Rey Mysterio .40 1.00
4 Wade Barrett .15 .40
5 John Morrison .25 .60
6 Natalya .60 1.50
7 Primo .15 .40
8 Justin Gabriel .15 .40
9 Johnny Curtis RC .15 .40
10 Josh Mathews .15 .40
11 Michael McGillicutty .15 .40
12 Jey Uso .15 .40
13 Dolph Ziggler .25 .60
14 Alex Riley .15 .40
15 Kharma .25 .60
16 Ranjin Singh .15 .40
17 Chris Masters .15 .40
18 Ted DiBiase .25 .60
19 Percy Watson .15 .40
20 Hornswoggle .25 .60
21 David Otunga .15 .40
22 Booker T .25 .60
23 Mason Ryan RC .15 .40
24 Tamina .15 .40
25 CM Punk .40 1.00
26 Jack Korpela RC .15 .40
27 Kelly Kelly .60 1.50
28 William Regal .25 .60
29 Beth Phoenix .40 1.00
30 The Great Khali .15 .40
31 Michael Cole .15 .40
32 Brodus Clay RC .15 .40
33 Goldust .15 .40
34 Jimmy Uso .15 .40
35 Kofi Kingston .15 .40
36 Matt Striker .15 .40
37 Nikki Bella .60 1.50
38 Yoshi Tatsu .15 .40
39 Ricardo Rodriguez RC .15 .40
40 Cody Rhodes .15 .40
41 Brie Bella .60 1.50
42 Ezekiel Jackson .25 .60
43 Vladimir Kozlov .25 .60
44 Sheamus .25 .60
45 Vickie Guerrero .25 .60
46 Alicia Fox .25 .60
47 Drew McIntyre .15 .40
48 Todd Grisham .15 .40
49 Jack Swagger .25 .60
50 Tyson Kidd .15 .40
51 Alberto Del Rio RC .40 1.00
52 Heath Slater .15 .40
53 Evan Bourne .15 .40
54 JTG .15 .40
55 Kaitlyn RC .40 1.00
56 Big Show .40 1.00
57 Tyler Reks .15 .40
58 Layla .40 1.00
59 Justin Roberts .15 .40
60 R-Truth .15 .40
61 Daniel Bryan .15 .40
62 Gail Kim .40 1.00
63 The Miz .25 .60
64 Chavo Guerrero .15 .40
65 Curt Hawkins .15 .40
66 Maryse .60 1.50
67 Kane .40 1.00
68 Santino Marella .25 .60
69 Mark Henry .25 .60
70 David Hart Smith .15 .40
71 Rosa Mendes .25 .60
72 Jerry The King Lawler .40 1.00
73 Undertaker .75 2.00
74 Melina .60 1.50
75 Sin Cara RC .40 1.00
76 Eve .60 1.50
77 Theodore Long .15 .40
78 Zack Ryder .15 .40
79 Christian .15 .40
80 Triple H .60 1.50
81 Edge .60 1.50
82 The Rock .75 2.00
83 Darren Young .15 .40
84 Lucky Cannon .15 .40
85 Titus O'Neil .15 .40
86 Byron Saxton RC .15 .40
87 Conor O'Brian RC .15 .40
88 Jacob Novak RC .15 .40
89 The American Dream Dusty Rhodes .25 .60
90 The British Bulldog .25 .60
91 Ted DiBiase .25 .60
92 Rowdy Roddy Piper .60 1.50
93 Mr. Perfect .40 1.00
94 The Iron Sheik .40 1.00
95 Cowboy Bob Orton .25 .60
96 Jake The Snake Roberts .40 1.00
97 Ravishing Rick Rude .25 .60
98 Doink the Clown .25 .60
99 Big Boss Man .25 .60
100 Bushwhacker Luke .25 .60
101 Bushwhacker Butch .25 .60
102 Yokozuna .25 .60
103 Sgt. Slaughter .40 1.00
104 Papa Shango .15 .40
105 Hawk .40 1.00
106 Animal .40 1.00
107 Kamala .25 .60
108 Terry Funk .25 .60
109 Junkyard Dog .40 1.00
110 Hacksaw Jim Duggan .40 1.00
CL1 Checklist 1 .15 .40
CL2 Checklist 2 .15 .40
CL3 Checklist 3 .15 .40

2011 Topps WWE Autographs

NNO Alberto Del Rio 15.00 40.00
NNO Alex Riley 10.00 25.00
NNO Big Show 12.00 30.00
NNO Brie Bella 20.00 50.00
NNO Christian 10.00 25.00
NNO David Otunga 6.00 15.00
NNO Drew McIntyre 8.00 20.00
NNO Evan Bourne 6.00 15.00
NNO Eve 12.00 30.00
NNO Ezekiel Jackson 10.00 25.00
NNO John Cena 25.00 60.00
NNO Kane 12.00 30.00
NNO Kofi Kingston 10.00 25.00
NNO Mark Henry 10.00 25.00
NNO Michael McGillicutty 6.00 15.00
NNO Nikki Bella 20.00 50.00
NNO Randy Orton 20.00 50.00
NNO R-Truth 8.00 20.00
NNO Sin Cara 10.00 25.00
NNO The Miz 10.00 25.00

2011 Topps WWE Catchy Phrases

COMPLETE SET (10) 5.00 10.00
*P.P.BLACK/1: UNPRICED DUE TO SCARCITY
*P.P.CYAN/1: UNPRICED DUE TO SCARCITY
*P.P.MAGENTA/1: UNPRICED DUE TO SCARCITY
*P.P.YELLOW/1: UNPRICED DUE TO SCARCITY
STATED ODDS 1:8 HOBBY AND RETAIL

CP1 John Cena 1.50 4.00
CP2 The Miz .50 1.25
CP3 The Rock 1.50 4.00
CP4 Undertaker 1.50 4.00
CP5 Triple H 1.25 3.00
CP6 Rey Mysterio .75 2.00
CP7 Christian .30 .75
CP8 Zack Ryder .30 .75
CP9 Goldust .30 .75
CP10 Vickie Guerrero .50 1.25

2011 Topps WWE Dual Autographs

STATED PRINT RUN 70 SER.#'d SETS

NNO A.Del Rio/Christian 25.00 60.00
NNO Big Show/M.Henry 20.00 50.00
NNO Brie Bella & Nikki Bella 60.00 120.00
NNO D.Otunga/M.McGillicutty 12.00 30.00
NNO Eve/K.Kingston 25.00 60.00
NNO J.Cena/R-Truth 30.00 75.00
NNO Kane/E.Jackson 15.00 40.00
NNO R.Orton/E.Bourne 25.00 60.00
NNO S.Cara/D.McIntyre 15.00 40.00
NNO Miz/A.Riley 20.00 50.00

2011 Topps WWE Electrifying Entrances

COMPLETE SET (25) 10.00 25.00
*P.P.BLACK/1: UNPRICED DUE TO SCARCITY
*P.P.CYAN/1: UNPRICED DUE TO SCARCITY
*P.P.MAGENTA/1: UNPRICED DUE TO SCARCITY
*P.P.YELLOW/1: UNPRICED DUE TO SCARCITY
STATED ODDS 1:8 HOBBY AND RETAIL

EE1 Undertaker 1.50 4.00
EE2 John Cena 1.50 4.00
EE3 Triple H 1.25 3.00
EE4 Rey Mysterio .75 2.00
EE5 R-Truth .30 .75
EE6 Randy Orton 1.25 3.00
EE7 The Miz .50 1.25
EE8 Big Show .75 2.00
EE9 Kofi Kingston .30 .75
EE10 Sheamus .50 1.25
EE11 Alberto Del Rio .75 2.00
EE12 Kane .75 2.00
EE13 Christian .30 .75
EE14 Jack Swagger .50 1.25
EE15 Sin Cara .75 2.00
EE16 Wade Barrett .30 .75
EE17 John Morrison .50 1.25
EE18 Drew McIntyre .30 .75
EE19 Daniel Bryan .30 .75
EE20 Cody Rhodes .30 .75
EE21 Ted DiBiase .50 1.25
EE22 Dolph Ziggler .50 1.25
EE23 Santino Marella .50 1.25
EE24 The Great Khali .30 .75
EE25 Kharma .50 1.25

2011 Topps WWE Heritage

COMPLETE SET (50) 12.00 30.00
P.P.BLACK/1: UNPRICED DUE TO SCARCITY
P.P.CYAN/1: UNPRICED DUE TO SCARCITY
P.P.MAGENTA/1: UNPRICED DUE TO SCARCITY
P.P.YELLOW/1: UNPRICED DUE TO SCARCITY
STATED ODDS 1:4 HOBBY AND RETAIL

H1 Stone Cold Steve Austin 1.00 2.50
H2 Shawn Michaels 1.00 2.50
H3 Trish Stratus 1.25 3.00
H4 Booker T .40 1.00
H5 Jerry The King Lawler .60 1.50
H6 Michael PS Hayes .25 .60
H7 The American Dream Dusty Rhodes .40 1.00
H8 The British Bulldog .40 1.00
H9 Ted DiBiase .40 1.00
H10 Rowdy Roddy Piper 1.00 2.50
H11 Mr. Perfect .60 1.50
H12 Mean Gene Okerlund .40 1.00
H13 Jimmy Superfly Snuka .60 1.50
H14 Paul Bearer .40 1.00
H15 Irwin R. Schyster .25 .60
H16 Vader .40 1.00
H17 Akeem .25 .60
H18 Bobby The Brain Heenan .40 1.00
H19 Kama Mustafa .25 .60
H20 Howard Finkel .25 .60
H21 Don Muraco .40 1.00
H22 Harley Race .40 1.00
H23 Brian Pillman .40 1.00
H24 The Iron Sheik .60 1.50
H25 Koko B. Ware .40 1.00
H26 Gorilla Monsoon .40 1.00
H27 Jake The Snake Roberts .60 1.50
H28 Ravishing Rick Rude .40 1.00
H29 Doink the Clown .25 .60
H30 Big Boss Man .40 1.00
H31 Jim Ross .25 .60
H32 Rocky Johnson .40 1.00
H33 Terry Funk .40 1.00
H34 Big John Studd .25 .60
H35 The Godfather .25 .60
H36 Hillbilly Jim .40 1.00
H37 Barry Windham .25 .60
H38 Tito Santana .25 .60
H39 Nikolai Volkoff .40 1.00
H40 Arn Anderson .40 1.00
H41 Tully Blanchard .40 1.00
H42 One Man Gang .25 .60
H43 Dean Malenko .25 .60
H44 Classy Freddie Blassie .40 1.00
H45 Tom Prichard .25 .60
H46 Yokozuna .40 1.00
H47 Mr. Wonderful Paul Orndorff .40 1.00
H48 Sgt. Slaughter .60 1.50
H49 Diesel .40 1.00
H50 Batista .40 1.00

2011 Topps WWE Masters of the Mat Relics

*GOLD/50: 1X TO 2.5X BASIC MEM
*RED/1: UNPRICED DUE TO SCARCITY
STATED ODDS 1:69

NNO Alberto Del Rio 2.50 6.00
NNO Big Show 2.50 6.00
NNO Christian 2.50 6.00
NNO Cody Rhodes 2.50 6.00
NNO Daniel Bryan 2.50 6.00
NNO Dolph Ziggler 2.50 6.00
NNO Drew McIntyre 2.50 6.00
NNO Jack Swagger 2.50 6.00
NNO John Cena 5.00 12.00
NNO John Morrison 2.50 6.00
NNO Kane 2.50 6.00
NNO Kofi Kingston 2.50 6.00
NNO Mark Henry 2.50 6.00
NNO Randy Orton 4.00 10.00
NNO Rey Mysterio 3.00 8.00
NNO R-Truth 2.50 6.00
NNO Santino Marella 2.50 6.00
NNO Sheamus 2.50 6.00
NNO Sin Cara 2.50 6.00
NNO Ted DiBiase 2.50 6.00
NNO The Great Khali 2.50 6.00
NNO The Miz 2.50 6.00
NNO Triple H 4.00 10.00
NNO Undertaker 4.00 10.00
NNO Wade Barrett 2.50 6.00

2011 Topps WWE Prestigious Pairings

COMPLETE SET (15) 6.00 15.00
*P.P.BLACK/1: UNPRICED DUE TO SCARCITY
*P.P.CYAN/1: UNPRICED DUE TO SCARCITY
*P.P.MAGENTA/1: UNPRICED DUE TO SCARCITY
*P.P.YELLOW/1: UNPRICED DUE TO SCARCITY
STATED ODDS 1:8 HOBBY AND RETAIL

PP1 Big Show/Kane .75 2.00
PP2 Marella/Kozlov .50 1.25
PP3 Phoenix/Kelly 1.25 3.00
PP4 Lawler/Ross .75 2.00
PP5 Swagger/Cole .50 1.25
PP6 Orton/Mysterio 1.25 3.00
PP7 Cena/Cara 1.50 4.00
PP8 Jimmy Uso/Jay Uso .30 .75
PP9 Ziggler/Guerrero .50 1.25
PP10 Edge/Christian 1.25 3.00
PP11 Del Rio/Clay .75 2.00
PP12 Ziggler/Sheamus .50 1.25
PP13 Morrison/Bryan .50 1.25
PP14 Torres/Kim 1.25 3.00
PP15 R-Truth/Morrison .50 1.25

2011 Topps WWE Ringside Relics Ring Skirts

*GOLD/50: .6X TO 1.5X BASIC MEM
*RED/1: UNPRICED DUE TO SCARCITY
STATED ODDS 1:180

NNO Alberto Del Rio 3.00 8.00
NNO Big Show 3.00 8.00
NNO Christian 3.00 8.00
NNO Daniel Bryan 3.00 8.00
NNO Dolph Ziggler 3.00 8.00
NNO Jack Swagger 3.00 8.00
NNO John Cena 6.00 15.00
NNO John Morrison 3.00 8.00
NNO Kane 3.00 8.00
NNO Kofi Kingston 3.00 8.00
NNO Randy Orton 5.00 12.00

NNO Rey Mysterio	4.00	10.00
NNO R-Truth	3.00	8.00
NNO Santino Marella	3.00	8.00
NNO Sheamus	3.00	8.00
NNO Sin Cara	3.00	8.00
NNO The Miz	3.00	8.00
NNO Triple H	5.00	12.00
NNO Undertaker	6.00	15.00
NNO Wade Barrett	3.00	8.00

2011 Topps WWE Superstar Swatches

*GOLD/50: .6X TO 1.5X BASIC CARDS
*RED/1: UNPRICED DUE TO SCARCITY
STATED ODDS 1:126

NNO Christian	4.00	10.00
NNO Cody Rhodes	4.00	10.00
NNO Daniel Bryan	5.00	12.00
NNO Drew McIntyre	4.00	10.00
NNO Heath Slater	4.00	10.00
NNO Jack Swagger	4.00	10.00
NNO Kofi Kingston	4.00	10.00
NNO Randy Orton	5.00	12.00
NNO R-Truth	4.00	10.00
NNO Santino Marella	4.00	10.00
NNO Sheamus	4.00	10.00
NNO Stone Cold Steve Austin	6.00	15.00
NNO Ted DiBiase	4.00	10.00
NNO The Miz	4.00	10.00
NNO Wade Barrett	4.00	10.00

2012 Topps WWE

COMPLETE SET (93)	15.00	40.00
COMPLETE SET W/O SP (90)	10.00	25.00

*BLUE: 1X TO 2.5X BASIC CARDS
*GOLD: 2.5X TO 6X BASIC CARDS
*PURPLE: 2.5X TO 6X BASIC CARDS
*RED: 2.5X TO 6X BASIC CARDS
*SILVER: 2.5X TO 6X BASIC CARDS
*BLACK: 8X TO 20X BASIC CARDS
*PLATINUM/1: UNPRICED DUE TO SCARCITY
*P.P.BLACK/1: UNPRICED DUE TO SCARCITY
*P.P.CYAN/1: UNPRICED DUE TO SCARCITY
*P.P.MAGENTA/1: UNPRICED DUE TO SCARCITY
*P.P.YELLOW/1: UNPRICED DUE TO SCARCITY

1 John Cena	.75	2.00
2 Randy Orton	.60	1.50
3 Beth Phoenix	.40	1.00
4 Sheamus	.40	1.00
5 Brock Lesnar	.60	1.50
6 Daniel Bryan	.15	.40
7A Mick Foley	.60	1.50
7B Cactus Jack SP	4.00	10.00
7C Dude Love SP	4.00	10.00
7D Mankind SP	4.00	10.00
8 Cody Rhodes	.15	.40
9 Cameron RC	.25	.60
10 Christian	.15	.40
11 Kelly Kelly	.60	1.50
12 Hornswoggle	.25	.60
13 Brodus Clay	.15	.40
14 Aksana RC	.40	1.00
15 Epico RC	.15	.40
16 Mark Henry	.25	.60
17 Maxine RC	.40	1.00
18 Jey Uso	.15	.40
19 Zack Ryder	.15	.40
20 Ricardo Rodriguez	.15	.40
21 JTG	.15	.40
22 Hunico RC	.15	.40
23 Kofi Kingston	.15	.40
24 Matt Striker	.15	.40
25 Kane	.40	1.00
26 Jimmy Uso	.15	.40
27 Naomi RC	.25	.60
28 The Great Khali	.15	.40
29 Tyler Reks	.15	.40
30 Josh Matthews	.15	.40
31 Derrick Bateman RC	.15	.40
32 Camacho RC	.15	.40
33 Kharma	.25	.60
34 Heath Slater	.15	.40
35 Evan Bourne	.15	.40
36 Yoshi Tatsu	.15	.40
37 Big Show	.40	1.00
38 Ryback	.15	.40
39 Percy Watson	.15	.40
40 Kaitlyn	.40	1.00
41 The Miz	.25	.60
42 William Regal	.25	.60
43 Michael Cole	.15	.40
44 Wade Barrett	.15	.40
45 Rey Mysterio	.40	1.00
46 Alicia Fox	.25	.60
47 Triple H	.60	1.50
48 Layla	.40	1.00
49 Chris Jericho	.60	1.50
50 Jinder Mahal	.15	.40
51 Eve	.60	1.50
52 Johnny Curtis	.15	.40
53 Tensai	.15	.40
54 Titus O'Neil	.15	.40
55 Vickie Guerrero	.25	.60
56 Justin Gabriel	.15	.40
57 Primo	.15	.40
58 Booker T	.25	.60
59 Goldust	.15	.40
60 Natalya	.60	1.50
61 Jack Swagger	.25	.60
62 Ezekiel Jackson	.25	.60
63 John Laurinaitis	.15	.40
64 Ted DiBiase	.25	.60
65 R-Truth	.15	.40
66 Trent Barreta	.15	.40
67 Jerry The King Lawler	.40	1.00
68 Tyson Kidd	.15	.40
69 David Otunga	.15	.40
70 Rosa Mendes	.25	.60
71 Michael McGillicutty	.15	.40
72 Drew McIntyre	.15	.40
73 Alex Riley	.15	.40
74 Theodore Long	.15	.40
75 Dolph Ziggler	.25	.60
76 Sin Cara	.40	1.00
77 Justin Roberts	.15	.40
78 Alberto Del Rio	.40	1.00
79 Curt Hawkins	.15	.40
80 Tamina Snuka	.25	.60
81 Mason Ryan	.15	.40
82 Darren Young	.15	.40
83 Scott Stanford RC	.15	.40
84 Lilian Garcia	.40	1.00
85 Santino Marella	.25	.60
86 Antonio Cesaro RC	.15	.40
87 The Rock	.75	2.00
88 AJ	.75	2.00
89 CM Punk	.60	1.50
90 Undertaker	.60	1.50

2012 Topps WWE Autographs

STATED ODDS 1:470 HOBBY AND RETAIL

NNO Booker T	15.00	40.00
NNO Cactus Jack	50.00	100.00
NNO Chris Jericho	30.00	75.00
NNO Dude Love	50.00	100.00
NNO Epico	8.00	20.00
NNO Hunico	8.00	20.00
NNO John Laurinaitis	12.00	30.00
NNO Mankind	50.00	100.00
NNO Mick Foley	30.00	75.00
NNO Primo	8.00	20.00
NNO Triple H		

2012 Topps WWE Classic Hall of Famers

COMPLETE SET (35)	10.00	25.00

*P.P.BLACK/1: UNPRICED DUE TO SCARCITY
*P.P.CYAN/1: UNPRICED DUE TO SCARCITY
*P.P.MAGENTA/1: UNPRICED DUE TO SCARCITY
*P.P.YELLOW/1: UNPRICED DUE TO SCARCITY
STATED ODDS 1:4 HOBBY AND RETAIL

1 Chief Jay Strongbow	.40	1.00
2 Classy Freddie Blassie	.40	1.00
3 Gorilla Monsoon	.40	1.00
4 Jimmy Superfly Snuka	.40	1.00
5 Big John Studd	.40	1.00
6 Bobby The Brain Heenan	.40	1.00
7 Don Muraco	.40	1.00
8 Greg The Hammer Valentine	.40	1.00
9 Harley Race	.40	1.00
10 Junkyard Dog	.40	1.00
11 Sgt. Slaughter	.40	1.00
12 Tito Santana	.40	1.00
13 Cowboy Bob Orton	.40	1.00
14 The Iron Sheik	.40	1.00
15 Mr. Wonderful Paul Orndorff	.40	1.00
16 Nikolai Volkoff	.40	1.00
17 Rowdy Roddy Piper	.60	1.50
18 Mean Gene Okerlund	.40	1.00
19 The American Dream Dusty Rhodes	.40	1.00
20 Mr. Perfect Curt Hennig	.40	1.00
21 Rocky Johnson	.40	1.00
22 Terry Funk	.40	1.00
23 Howard Finkel	.40	1.00
24 Koko B. Ware	.40	1.00
25 Ricky The Dragon Steamboat	.40	1.00
26 Stone Cold Steve Austin	1.25	3.00
27 Ted DiBiase	.40	1.00
28 Hacksaw Jim Duggan	.40	1.00
29 Road Warrior Hawk	.40	1.00
30 Road Warrior Animal	.40	1.00
31 Shawn Michaels	1.00	2.50
32 Edge	.60	1.50
33 Arn Anderson	.40	1.00
34 Barry Windham	.40	1.00
35 Tully Blanchard	.40	1.00

2012 Topps WWE Classic Hall of Famers Autographs

STATED ODDS 1:269 HOBBY AND RETAIL

NNO Animal	25.00	60.00
NNO Barry Windham	12.00	30.00
NNO Don Muraco	20.00	50.00
NNO Greg The Hammer Valentine	25.00	60.00
NNO Harley Race	50.00	100.00
NNO Jimmy Superfly Snuka	100.00	200.00
NNO Koko B. Ware	15.00	40.00
NNO Mr. Wonderful Paul Orndorff	100.00	200.00
NNO Nikolai Volkoff	15.00	30.00
NNO Terry Funk	75.00	150.00
NNO Tito Santana	20.00	50.00
NNO Tully Blanchard	15.00	40.00

2012 Topps WWE Diva Kiss

STATED ODDS 1:1,125

NNO AJ	100.00	175.00
NNO Aksana	30.00	80.00
NNO Alicia Fox	30.00	80.00
NNO Beth Phoenix	30.00	80.00
NNO Kaitlyn	20.00	50.00
NNO Kelly Kelly	25.00	60.00
NNO Layla	50.00	100.00
NNO Maxine	20.00	50.00
NNO Natalya	30.00	80.00
NNO Rosa Mendes	30.00	80.00
NNO Cameron	20.00	50.00
NNO Naomi	30.00	80.00
NNO Tamina Snuka	30.00	80.00

2012 Topps WWE Divas Class of 2012

COMPLETE SET (15)	8.00	20.00

*P.P.BLACK/1: UNPRICED DUE TO SCARCITY
*P.P.CYAN/1: UNPRICED DUE TO SCARCITY
*P.P.MAGENTA/1: UNPRICED DUE TO SCARCITY
*P.P.YELLOW/1: UNPRICED DUE TO SCARCITY
STATED ODDS 1:4 HOBBY AND RETAIL

1 AJ	2.50	6.00
2 Aksana	1.25	3.00
3 Alicia Fox	.75	2.00
4 Beth Phoenix	1.25	3.00
5 Cameron	.75	2.00
6 Eve	2.00	5.00
7 Kaitlyn	1.25	3.00
8 Kelly Kelly	2.00	5.00
9 Layla	1.25	3.00
10 Lilian Garcia	1.25	3.00
11 Maxine	1.25	3.00
12 Naomi	.75	2.00
13 Natalya	2.00	5.00
14 Rosa Mendes	.75	2.00
15 Tamina Snuka	.75	2.00

2012 Topps WWE Divas Class of 2012 Autographs

STATED ODDS 1:364

NNO Aksana	20.00	50.00
NNO Alicia Fox	15.00	40.00
NNO Beth Phoenix	15.00	40.00
NNO Kaitlyn	30.00	75.00
NNO Kelly Kelly	30.00	75.00
NNO Lilian Garcia	20.00	50.00
NNO Maxine	15.00	40.00
NNO Rosa Mendes	15.00	40.00
NNO Tamina Snuka	20.00	50.00

2012 Topps WWE Dual Autographs

STATED ODDS 1:2,245 HOBBY EXCLUSIVE

NNO Jimmy & Tamina Snuka	100.00	200.00
NNO Maxine/Kaitlyn	30.00	75.00
NNO Primo/Epico	20.00	50.00
NNO T.Blanchard/B.Windham	25.00	60.00

2012 Topps WWE First Class Champions

COMPLETE SET (20)	10.00	25.00

*P.P.BLACK/1: UNPRICED DUE TO SCARCITY
*P.P.CYAN/1: UNPRICED DUE TO SCARCITY
*P.P.MAGENTA/1: UNPRICED DUE TO SCARCITY
*P.P.YELLOW/1: UNPRICED DUE TO SCARCITY
STATED ODDS 1:6 HOBBY AND RETAIL

1 The Iron Shiek	.50	1.25
2 Sgt. Slaughter	.50	1.25
3 Undertaker	1.25	3.00
4 Yokozuna	.50	1.25
5 Diesel	.50	1.25
6 Shawn Michaels	1.25	3.00
7 Stone Cold Steve Austin	1.50	4.00
8 The Rock	1.50	4.00
9 Mankind	1.25	3.00
10 Triple H	1.25	3.00
11 Big Show	.75	2.00
12 Chris Jericho	1.25	3.00
13 Brock Lesnar	1.25	3.00
14 John Cena	1.50	4.00
15 Edge	.75	2.00
16 Randy Orton	1.25	3.00
17 Batista	.50	1.25
18 Sheamus	.75	2.00
19 The Miz	.50	1.25
20 CM Punk	1.25	3.00

2012 Topps WWE Shirt Relics

*BLACK/50: .8X TO 2X BASIC MEM
*PLATINUM/1: UNPRICED DUE TO SCARCITY
STATED ODDS 1:112

NNO Alberto Del Rio	5.00	12.00
NNO Big Show	6.00	15.00
NNO Brodus Clay	5.00	12.00
NNO Camacho	5.00	12.00
NNO CM Punk	6.00	15.00
NNO Cody Rhodes	5.00	12.00
NNO Daniel Bryan	5.00	12.00
NNO Dolph Ziggler	6.00	15.00
NNO Hornswoggle	5.00	12.00
NNO Hunico	4.00	10.00
NNO Jerry Lawler	6.00	15.00
NNO John Cena	10.00	25.00
NNO Kofi Kingston	5.00	12.00
NNO Mark Henry	4.00	10.00
NNO Randy Orton	6.00	15.00
NNO R-Truth	4.00	10.00
NNO Santino Marella	4.00	10.00
NNO Sheamus	5.00	12.00
NNO The Miz	5.00	12.00
NNO Zack Ryder	5.00	12.00
NNO Natalya	5.00	12.00
NNO Christian	5.00	12.00
NNO Chris Jericho	6.00	15.00
NNO Evan Bourne	3.00	8.00
NNO Heath Slater	4.00	10.00
NNO Jack Swagger	4.00	10.00

NNO Justin Gabriel 3.00 8.00
NNO Michael McGillicutty 3.00 8.00
NNO Ted DiBiase 3.00 8.00
NNO Wade Barrett 4.00 10.00

2012 Topps WWE Top Class Matches Punk's Picks

COMPLETE SET (10) 5.00 12.00
*P.P.BLACK/1: UNPRICED DUE TO SCARCITY
*P.P.CYAN/1: UNPRICED DUE TO SCARCITY
*P.P.MAGENTA/1: UNPRICED DUE TO SCARCITY
*P.P.YELLOW/1: UNPRICED DUE TO SCARCITY
STATED ODDS 1:6

1 Wins ECW Championship 1.00 2.50
2 Wins Money in the Bank 1.00 2.50
3 Wins Intercontinental Title 1.00 2.50
4 Wins World Heavyweight Championship 1.00 2.50
5 Loses His Hair 1.00 2.50
6 Wins the WWE Championship 1.00 2.50
7 Unifies the WWE Championship 1.00 2.50
8 Reclaims the WWE Championship 1.00 2.50
9 Victorious at WrestleMania XXVIII 1.00 2.50
10 Turns Back Jericho Again 1.00 2.50

2012 Topps WWE World Class Events

COMPLETE SET (10) 5.00 12.00
*P.P.BLACK/1: UNPRICED DUE TO SCARCITY
*P.P.CYAN/1: UNPRICED DUE TO SCARCITY
*P.P.MAGENTA/1: UNPRICED DUE TO SCARCITY
*P.P.YELLOW/1: UNPRICED DUE TO SCARCITY
STATED ODDS 1:6

1 WrestleMania XXVII 1.00 2.50
2 Money in the Bank 2011 1.00 2.50
3 SummerSlam 2011 1.00 2.50
4 Hell in a Cell 2011 1.00 2.50
5 Vengeance 2011 1.00 2.50
6 Survivor Series 2011 1.00 2.50
7 Tables, Ladders and Chairs 2011 1.00 2.50
8 Royal Rumble 2012 1.00 2.50
9 Elimination Chamber 2012 1.00 2.50
10 WrestleMania XXVIII 1.00 2.50

2012 Topps WWE WrestleMania XXVIII Mat Relics

*BLACK/50: .8X TO 2X BASIC MEM
*PLATINUM/1: UNPRICED DUE TO SCARCITY
STATED ODDS 1:109

NNO Beth Phoenix 6.00 15.00
NNO Big Show 6.00 15.00
NNO Booker T 5.00 12.00
NNO Chris Jericho 6.00 15.00
NNO CM Punk 10.00 25.00
NNO Cody Rhodes 5.00 12.00
NNO Daniel Bryan 5.00 12.00
NNO David Otunga 5.00 12.00
NNO Dolph Ziggler 5.00 12.00
NNO Eve 6.00 15.00
NNO Jack Swagger 6.00 15.00
NNO John Cena 10.00 25.00
NNO Kane 6.00 15.00
NNO Kelly Kelly 8.00 20.00
NNO Kofi Kingston 5.00 12.00
NNO Mark Henry 5.00 12.00
NNO Randy Orton 6.00 15.00
NNO R-Truth 5.00 12.00
NNO Santino Marella 5.00 12.00
NNO Sheamus 6.00 15.00
NNO The Miz 5.00 12.00
NNO The Rock 10.00 25.00
NNO Triple H 8.00 20.00
NNO Undertaker 10.00 25.00
NNO Zack Ryder 6.00 15.00

2013 Topps WWE

COMPLETE SET (110) 8.00 20.00
*BLACK: 2.5X TO 6X BASIC CARDS
*SILVER: 4X TO 10X BASIC CARDS
*GOLD/10: 15X TO 40X BASIC CARDS
*P.P.BLACK/1: UNPRICED DUE TO SCARCITY
*P.P.CYAN/1: UNPRICED DUE TO SCARCITY
*P.P.MAGENTA/1: UNPRICED DUE TO SCARCITY
*P.P.YELLOW/1: UNPRICED DUE TO SCARCITY

1 AJ Lee .75 2.00
2 Alex Riley .15 .40
3 Big E Langston RC .15 .40
4 Big Show .30 .75
5 Brock Lesnar .60 1.50
6 Brodus Clay .15 .40
7 Cameron .25 .60
8 CM Punk .60 1.50
9 Daniel Bryan .40 1.00
10 David Otunga .15 .40
11 Dean Ambrose RC .25 .60
12 Dolph Ziggler .25 .60
13 Epico .15 .40
14 Evan Bourne .15 .40
15 Eve .60 1.50
16 Jack Swagger .25 .60
17 Jerry The King Lawler .30 .75
18 John Cena .75 2.00
19 JTG .15 .40
20 Justin Roberts .15 .40
21 Kane .30 .75
22 Kofi Kingston .15 .40
23 Mason Ryan .15 .40
24 Michael Cole .15 .40
25 Michael McGillicutty .15 .40
26 The Miz .25 .60
27 Naomi .40 1.00
28 Paul Heyman .15 .40
29 Primo .15 .40
30 R-Truth .15 .40
31 Rey Mysterio .40 1.00
32 The Rock .75 2.00
33 Roman Reigns RC 30.00 75.00
34 Rosa Mendes .25 .60
35 Ryback .15 .40
36 Santino Marella .15 .40
37 Scott Stanford .15 .40
38 Seth Rollins RC 10.00 25.00
39 Tamina Snuka .20 .50
40 Tensai .15 .40
41 Triple H .60 1.50
42 Vickie Guerrero .25 .60
43 Zack Ryder .15 .40
44 Aksana .25 .60
45 Alberto Del Rio .30 .75
46 Alicia Fox .25 .60
47 Antonio Cesaro .15 .40
48 Booker T .25 .60
49 Camacho .15 .40
50 Christian .15 .40
51 Cody Rhodes .15 .40
52 Damien Sandow .15 .40
53 Darren Young .15 .40
54 Drew McIntyre .15 .40
55 Ezekiel Jackson .15 .40
56 The Great Khali .15 .40
57 Heath Slater .15 .40
58 Hornswoggle .15 .40
59 Hunico .15 .40
60 Jey Uso .15 .40
61 Jimmy Uso .15 .40
62 Jinder Mahal .15 .40
63 Fandango .15 .40
64 Josh Mathews .15 .40
65 Justin Gabriel .15 .40
66 Kaitlyn .30 .75
67 Layla .30 .75
68 Lilian Garcia .40 1.00
69 Mark Henry .20 .50
70 Matt Striker .15 .40
71 Natalya .30 .75
72 Percy Watson .15 .40
73 Randy Orton .50 1.25
74 Ricardo Rodriguez .15 .40
75 Sheamus .30 .75
76 Sin Cara .25 .60
77 Ted DiBiase .20 .50
78 Theodore Long .15 .40
79 Titus O'Neil .15 .40
80 Tyson Kidd .15 .40
81 Undertaker .60 1.50
82 Wade Barrett .15 .40
83 William Regal .20 .50
84 Yoshi Tatsu .15 .40
85 The American Dream Dusty Rhodes .25 .60
86 Big John Studd .25 .60
87 The British Bulldog .25 .60
88 The Bushwhackers .15 .40
89 Cowboy Bob Orton .25 .60
90 Dean Malenko .15 .40
91 Hacksaw Jim Duggan .25 .60
92 Greg The Hammer Valentine .15 .40
93 Harley Race .25 .60
94 The Iron Sheik .25 .60
95 Jake The Snake Roberts .25 .60
96 Jimmy Superfly Snuka .25 .60
97 Junkyard Dog .25 .60
98 Ted DiBiase .25 .60
99 Mr. Perfect .25 .60
100 Mr. Wonderful Paul Orndorff .25 .60
101 Nikolai Volkoff .25 .60
102 Ravishing Rick Rude .25 .60
103 Ricky The Dragon Steamboat .25 .60
104 Rowdy Roddy Piper .40 1.00
105 Sgt. Slaughter .25 .60
106 Terry Funk .25 .60
107 Tito Santana .25 .60
108 Tom Prichard .15 .40
109 Vader .15 .40
110 Yokozuna .15 .40

2013 Topps WWE Autographed Relics

STATED ODDS 1:9,550
UNPRICED DUE TO SCARCITY

NNO Alicia Fox
NNO Daniel Bryan
NNO Dolph Ziggler
NNO Kofi Kingston
NNO Ryback
NNO Sin Cara

2013 Topps WWE Autographs

STATED ODDS 1:79 HOBBY AND RETAIL

NNO AJ Lee 75.00 150.00
NNO Alicia Fox 8.00 20.00
NNO Antonio Cesaro 10.00 25.00
NNO Bushwhacker Butch 12.00 30.00
NNO Bushwhacker Luke 8.00 20.00
NNO Cowboy Bob Orton 10.00 25.00
NNO Daniel Bryan 15.00 40.00
NNO Dean Malenko 12.00 30.00
NNO Dolph Ziggler 12.00 30.00
NNO Eve 12.00 30.00
NNO Jack Swagger 10.00 25.00
NNO Kaitlyn 15.00 40.00
NNO Kofi Kingston 8.00 20.00
NNO Michael Cole 8.00 20.00
NNO Ted DiBiase 15.00 40.00
NNO Randy Orton 20.00 50.00
NNO Rosa Mendes 10.00 25.00
NNO Ryback 10.00 25.00
NNO Sin Cara 10.00 25.00
NNO Tom Prichard 8.00 20.00

2013 Topps WWE Diva Kiss

STATED ODDS 1:568 HOBBY AND RETAIL

NNO AJ Lee 100.00 175.00
NNO Aksana 25.00 50.00
NNO Alicia Fox 15.00 40.00
NNO Cameron 25.00 50.00
NNO Eve 40.00 80.00
NNO Kaitlyn 40.00 80.00
NNO Layla 30.00 60.00
NNO Naomi 15.00 40.00
NNO Natalya 30.00 60.00
NNO Rosa Mendes 25.00 50.00

2013 Topps WWE Diva Snapshots

COMPLETE SET (10) 20.00 40.00
STATED ODDS 1:24 HOBBY AND RETAIL

NNO AJ Lee 6.00 15.00
NNO Aksana 2.00 5.00
NNO Alicia Fox 2.00 5.00
NNO Cameron 2.00 5.00
NNO Eve 5.00 12.00
NNO Kaitlyn 2.50 6.00
NNO Layla 2.50 6.00
NNO Naomi 3.00 8.00
NNO Natalya 2.50 6.00
NNO Rosa Mendes 2.00 5.00

2013 Topps WWE Shirt Relics

STATED ODDS 1:24 HOBBY; 1:96 RETAIL

NNO Alicia Fox/Skirt 6.00 15.00
NNO Big Show/Hat 6.00 15.00
NNO Brodus Clay/Pants 4.00 10.00
NNO CM Punk/Shirt 9.00 20.00
NNO Damien Sandow/Shirt 5.00 12.00
NNO Daniel Bryan/Shirt 5.00 12.00
NNO Dolph Ziggler/Shirt 5.00 12.00
NNO Kofi Kingston/Shirt 5.00 12.00
NNO Paul Heyman/Suit 6.00 15.00
NNO R-Truth/Shirt 5.00 12.00
NNO Rey Mysterio/Shirt 6.00 15.00
NNO Ryback/Shirt 8.00 20.00
NNO Santino Marella/Puppet 6.00 15.00
NNO Sheamus/Shirt 6.00 15.00
NNO Sin Cara/Shirt 5.00 12.00
NNO The Miz/Shirt 4.00 10.00
NNO Titus O'Neil/Shirt 4.00 10.00
NNO Wade Barrett/Shirt 5.00 12.00
NNO CM Punk/Sock SP 30.00 60.00

2013 Topps WWE SummerSlam Mat Relics

STATED ODDS 1:102

NNO AJ Lee 8.00 20.00
NNO Aksana 4.00 10.00
NNO Alberto Del Rio 5.00 12.00
NNO Antonio Cesaro 4.00 10.00
NNO Big Show 4.00 10.00
NNO Brock Lesnar 6.00 15.00
NNO CM Punk 6.00 15.00
NNO Daniel Bryan 4.00 10.00
NNO Darren Young 4.00 10.00
NNO Dolph Ziggler 5.00 12.00
NNO Jerry The King Lawler 5.00 12.00
NNO John Cena 8.00 20.00
NNO Kane 5.00 12.00
NNO Kofi Kingston 4.00 10.00
NNO Paul Heyman 5.00 12.00
NNO R-Truth 4.00 10.00
NNO Santino Marella 4.00 10.00
NNO Sheamus 4.00 10.00
NNO The Miz 4.00 10.00
NNO Titus O'Neil 4.00 10.00
NNO Triple H 6.00 15.00
NNO Vickie Guerrero 4.00 10.00

2013 Topps WWE Triple Autographs

STATED ODDS 1:12,637 HOBBY AND RETAIL
UNPRICED DUE TO SCARCITY

NNO Luke/Butch/DiBiase
NNO Bryan/Cesaro/Kaitlyn
NNO Eve/Fox/Mendes
NNO Swagger/SinCara/Ryback
NNO R.Orton/B.Orton/Cole

2013 Topps WWE Triple Threat Tier Three

COMPLETE SET (30) 5.00 12.00
*TIER TWO: .5X TO 1.2X TIER THREE
*TIER ONE: .8X TO 2X TIER THREE
*T3 P.P.BLACK/1: UNPRICED DUE TO SCARCITY
*T3 P.P.CYAN/1: UNPRICED DUE TO SCARCITY
*T3 P.P.MAGENTA/1: UNPRICED DUE TO SCARCITY
*T3 P.P.YELLOW/1: UNPRICED DUE TO SCARCITY
*T2 P.P.BLACK/1: UNPRICED DUE TO SCARCITY
*T2 P.P.CYAN/1: UNPRICED DUE TO SCARCITY
*T2 P.P.MAGENTA/1: UNPRICED DUE TO SCARCITY
*T2 P.P.YELLOW/1: UNPRICED DUE TO SCARCITY
*T1 P.P.BLACK/1: UNPRICED DUE TO SCARCITY
*T1 P.P.CYAN/1: UNPRICED DUE TO SCARCITY
*T1 P.P.MAGENTA/1: UNPRICED DUE TO SCARCITY
*T1 P.P.YELLOW/1: UNPRICED DUE TO SCARCITY
STATED ODDS 1:2 HOBBY AND RETAIL

TT1 Dolph Ziggler .30 .75
TT2 John Cena 1.00 2.50
TT3 Jack Swagger .30 .75
TT4 The Miz .30 .75
TT5 Prime Time Players .20 .50
TT6 Wade Barrett .20 .50
TT7 Santino Marella .20 .50
TT8 Brock Lesnar .75 2.00

TT9 Sin Cara	.30	.75
TT10 Rey Mysterio	.50	1.25
TT11 Damien Sandow	.20	.50
TT12 Randy Orton	.60	1.50
TT13 Cody Rhodes	.20	.50
TT14 Eve	.75	2.00
TT15 Kane	.40	1.00
TT16 Big Show	.40	1.00
TT17 AJ Lee	1.00	2.50
TT18 Mark Henry	.25	.60
TT19 Triple H	.75	2.00
TT20 Ryback	.20	.50
TT21 Zack Ryder	.20	.50
TT22 Daniel Bryan	.50	1.25
TT23 Alberto Del Rio	.40	1.00
TT24 Christian	.20	.50
TT25 Tyson Kidd	.20	.50
TT26 CM Punk	.75	2.00
TT27 The Rock	1.00	2.50
TT28 Undertaker	.75	2.00
TT29 Kofi Kingston	.20	.50
TT30 Sheamus	.40	1.00

2013 Topps WWE 2K14 Phenom Edition Promo

NNO Undertaker

2014 Topps WWE

COMPLETE SET (110) 10.00 25.00
*BLACK: .75X TO 2X BASIC CARDS
*SILVER: 1.5X TO 4X BASIC CARDS
*GOLD/10: 6X TO 15X BASIC CARDS
*RED/1: UNPRICED DUE TO SCARCITY
*P.P.BLACK/1: UNPRICED DUE TO SCARCITY
*P.P.CYAN/1: UNPRICED DUE TO SCARCITY
*P.P.MAGENTA/1: UNPRICED DUE TO SCARCITY
*P.P.YELLOW/1: UNPRICED DUE TO SCARCITY

1 AJ Lee	.75	2.00
2 Alex Riley	.15	.40
3 Big E Langston	.15	.40
4 Bo Dallas RC	.15	.40
5 Brad Maddox RC	.15	.40
6 Bray Wyatt	.40	1.00
7 Brie Bella	.50	1.25
8 Brock Lesnar	.60	1.50
9 Brodus Clay	.15	.40
10 Cameron	.25	.60
11 Chris Jericho	.40	1.00
12 CM Punk	.60	1.50
13 Curtis Axel	.15	.40
14 Daniel Bryan	.25	.60
15 David Otunga	.15	.40
16 Dean Ambrose	.40	1.00
17 Diego	.15	.40
18 Dolph Ziggler	.25	.60
19 Erick Rowan RC	.25	.60
20 Eva Marie RC	.60	1.50
21 Fandango	.25	.60
22 Fernando	.15	.40
23 Jack Swagger	.25	.60
24 Jerry The King Lawler	.40	1.00
25 John Cena	.75	2.00
26 Jojo RC	.25	.60
27 Justin Roberts	.15	.40
28 Kane	.40	1.00
29 Kofi Kingston	.15	.40
30 Luke Harper RC	.25	.60
31 El Torito RC	.15	.40
32 Michael Cole	.15	.40
33 The Miz	.25	.60
34 Naomi	.25	.60
35 Nikki Bella	.50	1.25
36 Paul Heyman	.15	.40
37 R-Truth	.15	.40
38 Randy Orton	.60	1.50
39 Rey Mysterio	.40	1.00
40 The Rock	.75	2.00
41 Rob Van Dam	.40	1.00
42 Roman Reigns	.40	1.00
43 Ryback	.15	.40
44 Santino Marella	.25	.60
45 Scott Stanford	.15	.40
46 Seth Rollins	.15	.40
47 Stephanie McMahon	.25	.60
48 Summer Rae RC	.60	1.50
49 Tamina Snuka	.25	.60
50 Tensai	.15	.40
51 Triple H	.60	1.50
52 Zack Ryder	.15	.40
53 Zeb Colter	.25	.60
54 Aksana	.40	1.00
55 Alberto Del Rio	.40	1.00
56 Alicia Fox	.25	.60
57 Antonio Cesaro	.15	.40
58 Big Show	.40	1.00
59 Booker T	.25	.60
60 Camacho	.15	.40
61 Christian	.15	.40
62 Cody Rhodes	.15	.40
63 Curt Hawkins	.15	.40
64 Damien Sandow	.15	.40
65 Darren Young	.15	.40
66 Drew McIntyre	.15	.40
67 Ezekiel Jackson	.25	.60
68 The Great Khali	.15	.40
69 Heath Slater	.15	.40
70 Hornswoggle	.25	.60
71 Hunico	.15	.40
72 JBL	.25	.60
73 Jey Uso	.15	.40
74 Jimmy Uso	.15	.40
75 Jinder Mahal	.15	.40
76 Josh Mathews	.15	.40
77 Justin Gabriel	.15	.40
78 Kaitlyn	.40	1.00
79 Layla	.40	1.00
80 Lilian Garcia	.40	1.00
81 Mark Henry	.25	.60
82 Natalya	.50	1.25
83 Renee Young RC	.60	1.50
84 Ricardo Rodriguez	.15	.40
85 Rosa Mendes	.25	.60
86 Sheamus	.40	1.00
87 Sin Cara	.40	1.00
88 Theodore Long	.15	.40
89 Titus O'Neil	.15	.40
90 Tony Chimel	.15	.40
91 Tyson Kidd	.15	.40
92 Undertaker	.60	1.50
93 Vickie Guerrero	.25	.60
94 Wade Barrett	.15	.40
95 William Regal	.25	.60
96 Andre The Giant L	.60	1.50
97 Billy Gunn L	.25	.60
98 Bob Backlund L	.25	.60
99 Diamond Dallas Page L	.25	.60
100 Eddie Guerrero L	.25	.60
101 Honky Tonk Man L	.25	.60
102 Jim Ross L	.25	.60
103 Junkyard Dog L	.25	.60
104 Kevin Nash L	.40	1.00
105 Larry Zbyszko L	.25	.60
106 Mick Foley L	.40	1.00
107 Paul Bearer L	.25	.60
108 Road Dogg L	.25	.60
109 Shawn Michaels L	.60	1.50
110 X-Pac L	.15	.40

2014 Topps WWE Autographs

*BLACK/50: .5X TO 1.2X BASIC AUTOS
*SILVER/25: .6X TO 1.5X BASIC AUTOS
*GOLD/10: UNPRICED DUE TO SCARCITY
*RED/1: UNPRICED DUE TO SCARCITY
*P.P.BLACK/1: UNPRICED DUE TO SCARCITY
*P.P.CYAN/1: UNPRICED DUE TO SCARCITY
*P.P.MAGENTA/1: UNPRICED DUE TO SCARCITY
*P.P.YELLOW/1: UNPRICED DUE TO SCARCITY

NNO AJ Lee	60.00	120.00
NNO Billy Gunn	8.00	20.00
NNO Bray Wyatt	30.00	75.00
NNO Daniel Bryan	15.00	40.00
NNO Erick Rowan	6.00	15.00
NNO Eva Marie	12.00	30.00
NNO Jack Swagger	8.00	20.00
NNO John Cena	75.00	150.00
NNO JoJo	6.00	15.00
NNO Luke Harper	8.00	20.00
NNO Randy Orton	30.00	75.00
NNO Renee Young	15.00	40.00
NNO Road Dogg	12.00	30.00
NNO Shawn Michaels	30.00	75.00
NNO Summer Rae	15.00	40.00
NNO X-Pac	8.00	20.00

2014 Topps WWE Champions

COMPLETE SET (30) 10.00 25.00
*P.P.BLACK/1: UNPRICED DUE TO SCARCITY
*P.P.CYAN/1: UNPRICED DUE TO SCARCITY
*P.P.MAGENTA/1: UNPRICED DUE TO SCARCITY
*P.P.YELLOW/1: UNPRICED DUE TO SCARCITY
STATED ODDS 1:4 HOBBY AND RETAIL

1 Bruno Sammartino	.40	1.00
2 Bob Backlund	.40	1.00
3 The Iron Sheik	.40	1.00
4 Andre The Giant	1.00	2.50
5 Sgt. Slaughter	.60	1.50
6 Undertaker	1.00	2.50
7 Yokozuna	.40	1.00
8 Diesel	.60	1.50
9 Shawn Michaels	1.00	2.50
10 Stone Cold Steve Austin	1.25	3.00
11 Kane	.60	1.50
12 The Rock	1.25	3.00
13 Mankind	.60	1.50
14 Triple H	1.00	2.50
15 Big Show	.60	1.50
16 Chris Jericho	.60	1.50
17 Brock Lesnar	1.00	2.50
18 Eddie Guerrero	.40	1.00
19 JBL	.40	1.00
20 John Cena	1.25	3.00
21 Edge	.60	1.50
22 Rob Van Dam	.60	1.50
23 Randy Orton	1.00	2.50
24 Batista	.75	2.00
25 Sheamus	.60	1.50
26 The Miz	.40	1.00
27 CM Punk	1.00	2.50
28 Rey Mysterio	.60	1.50
29 Alberto Del Rio	.60	1.50
30 Daniel Bryan	.40	1.00

2014 Topps WWE Championship Belts

STATED PRINT RUN 400 SETS

NNO AJ Lee	10.00	25.00
NNO Andre The Giant	8.00	20.00
NNO Brie Bella	6.00	15.00
NNO British Bulldog	4.00	10.00
NNO Chris Jericho	5.00	12.00
NNO Christian	2.00	5.00
NNO CM Punk	12.00	30.00
NNO Daniel Bryan	3.00	8.00
NNO D-Generation X	8.00	20.00
NNO Edge	5.00	12.00
NNO Jeri-Show	5.00	12.00
NNO Jimmy Superfly Snuka	3.00	8.00
NNO John Cena	10.00	25.00
NNO Kaitlyn	5.00	12.00
NNO Kofi Kingston	2.00	5.00
NNO Kofi Kingston/R-Truth	2.00	5.00
NNO Layla	5.00	12.00
NNO The Miz	3.00	8.00
NNO Mr. Perfect Curt Hennig	2.50	6.00
NNO Nikki Bella	6.00	15.00
NNO Randy Orton	8.00	20.00
NNO Ravishing Rick Rude	2.00	5.00
NNO Rey Mysterio/Eddie Guerrero	5.00	12.00
NNO Ricky The Dragon Steamboat	2.00	5.00
NNO The Rock	10.00	25.00
NNO Rowdy Roddy Piper	5.00	12.00
NNO Stone Cold Steve Austin	10.00	25.00
NNO Team Hell No	5.00	12.00
NNO Triple H	8.00	20.00
NNO Undertaker	8.00	20.00

2014 Topps WWE Diva Kiss

STATED PRINT RUN 100 SETS

NNO AJ Lee	150.00	225.00
NNO Brie Bella	50.00	100.00
NNO Eva Marie	30.00	75.00
NNO JoJo	25.00	60.00
NNO Kaitlyn	25.00	60.00
NNO Lilian Garcia	25.00	60.00
NNO Natalya	25.00	60.00
NNO Nikki Bella	50.00	100.00
NNO Renee Young	35.00	75.00
NNO Summer Rae	60.00	120.00

2014 Topps WWE Diva Kiss Autographs

COMMON AUTO 60.00 120.00
STATED PRINT RUN 20 SETS

NNO AJ Lee	200.00	400.00
NNO Eva Marie	125.00	250.00
NNO JoJo	60.00	120.00
NNO Renee Young	75.00	150.00
NNO Summer Rae	125.00	250.00

2014 Topps WWE Greatest Championship Contenders

COMPLETE SET (10) 5.00 12.00
*P.P.BLACK/1: UNPRICED DUE TO SCARCITY
*P.P.CYAN/1: UNPRICED DUE TO SCARCITY
*P.P.MAGENTA/1: UNPRICED DUE TO SCARCITY
*P.P.YELLOW/1: UNPRICED DUE TO SCARCITY
STATED ODDS 1:12

1 Ricky The Dragon Steamboat	.50	1.25
2 Mr. Perfect	.60	1.50
3 Ravishing Rick Rude	.50	1.25
4 Ted DiBiase	.60	1.50
5 Rowdy Roddy Piper	1.25	3.00
6 Mr. Wonderful Paul Orndorff	.50	1.25
7 Jake The Snake Roberts	.75	2.00
8 Jimmy Superfly Snuka	.75	2.00
9 The British Bulldog	1.00	2.50
10 The American Dream Dusty Rhodes	1.00	2.50

2014 Topps WWE Greatest Championship Matches

COMPLETE SET (20) 8.00 20.00
*P.P.BLACK/1: UNPRICED DUE TO SCARCITY
*P.P.CYAN/1: UNPRICED DUE TO SCARCITY
*P.P.MAGENTA/1: UNPRICED DUE TO SCARCITY
*P.P.YELLOW/1: UNPRICED DUE TO SCARCITY
STATED ODDS 1:8 HOBBY AND RETAIL

1 The Rock/Steve Austin	.75	2.00
2 John Cena/CM Punk	.75	2.00
3 John Cena/HBK	.75	2.00
4 The Rock/Mankind	.75	2.00
5 Triple H/Cactus Jack	.60	1.50
6 HBK/Mankind	.60	1.50
7 John Cena/RVD	.75	2.00
8 Brock Lesnar/Undertaker	.60	1.50
9 Rey Mysterio/John Cena	.75	2.00
10 HHH/Chris Jericho	.60	1.50
11 Steve Austin/The Rock	.75	2.00
12 Randy Orton/John Cena	.75	2.00
13 CM Punk/John Cena	.75	2.00
14 The Rock/HHH	.75	2.00
15 Brock Lesnar/Eddie Guerrero	.60	1.50
16 John Cena/JBL	.75	2.00
17 The Rock/Brock Lesnar	.75	2.00
18 Steve Austin/Chris Jericho	.75	2.00
19 CM Punk/Chris Jericho	.60	1.50
20 Mankind/The Rock	.75	2.00

2014 Topps WWE NXT Prospects

COMPLETE SET (20) 15.00 40.00
*P.P.BLACK/1: UNPRICED DUE TO SCARCITY
*P.P.CYAN/1: UNPRICED DUE TO SCARCITY
*P.P.MAGENTA/1: UNPRICED DUE TO SCARCITY
*P.P.YELLOW/1: UNPRICED DUE TO SCARCITY
STATED ODDS 1:2 HOBBY AND RETAIL

1 Adrian Neville	.60	1.50
2 Alexander Rusev	.75	2.00
3 Baron Corbin	.30	.75
4 Bayley	3.00	8.00
5 Charlotte	6.00	15.00
6 CJ Parker	.30	.75
7 Konnor O'Brian	.30	.75
8 Corey Graves	.30	.75
9 Emma	1.50	4.00
10 Enzo Amore	.60	1.50
11 Jason Jordan	.30	.75

12 Leo Kruger .30 .75
13 Mojo Rawley .30 .75
14 Paige 5.00 12.00
15 Rick Viktor .30 .75
16 Sami Zayn .60 1.50
17 Sasha Banks 6.00 15.00
18 Sylvester Lefort .30 .75
19 Tyler Breeze .30 .75
20 Xavier Woods .30 .75

2014 Topps WWE Quad Autograph

STATED PRINT RUN 5 SER.#'d SETS
UNPRICED DUE TO SCARCITY

NNO HBK/X-Pac/Dogg/Gunn

2014 Topps WWE Stone Cold Steve Austin Tribute

COMPLETE SET (10) 5.00 12.00
*P.P.BLACK/1: UNPRICED DUE TO SCARCITY
*P.P.CYAN/1: UNPRICED DUE TO SCARCITY
*P.P.MAGENTA/1: UNPRICED DUE TO SCARCITY
*P.P.YELLOW/1: UNPRICED DUE TO SCARCITY
STATED ODDS 1:12 HOBBY AND RETAIL

1 Stone Cold Steve Austin 1.00 2.50
2 Stone Cold Steve Austin 1.00 2.50
3 Stone Cold Steve Austin 1.00 2.50
4 Stone Cold Steve Austin 1.00 2.50
5 Stone Cold Steve Austin 1.00 2.50
6 Stone Cold Steve Austin 1.00 2.50
7 Stone Cold Steve Austin 1.00 2.50
8 Stone Cold Steve Austin 1.00 2.50
9 Stone Cold Steve Austin 1.00 2.50
10 Stone Cold Steve Austin 1.00 2.50

2014 Topps WWE SummerSlam Mat Relics

NNO AJ Lee 12.00 30.00
NNO Alberto Del Rio 6.00 15.00
NNO Big E Langston 2.50 6.00
NNO Bray Wyatt 6.00 15.00
NNO Brie Bella 8.00 20.00
NNO Brock Lesnar 10.00 25.00
NNO Christian 2.50 6.00
NNO CM Punk 10.00 25.00
NNO Cody Rhodes 2.50 6.00
NNO Damien Sandow 2.50 6.00
NNO Daniel Bryan 4.00 10.00
NNO Dean Ambrose 10.00 25.00
NNO Dolph Ziggler 4.00 10.00
NNO John Cena 12.00 30.00
NNO Kaitlyn 6.00 15.00
NNO Kane 6.00 15.00
NNO Natalya 8.00 20.00
NNO Randy Orton 10.00 25.00
NNO Rob Van Dam 6.00 15.00
NNO Triple H 10.00 25.00

2014 Topps WWE Swatch Relics

NNO Brodus Clay/Shirt 3.00 8.00
NNO Christian/Shirt 3.00 8.00
NNO CM Punk/Shirt 6.00 15.00
NNO Damien Sandow/Shirt 3.00 8.00
NNO Daniel Bryan/Shirt 4.00 10.00
NNO Darren Young/Shirt 3.00 8.00
NNO Dean Ambrose/Shirt 8.00 20.00
NNO Dolph Ziggler/Shirt 5.00 12.00
NNO Hornswoggle/Shirt 3.00 8.00
NNO John Cena/Shirt 8.00 20.00
NNO Mark Henry/Shirt 4.00 10.00
NNO The Miz/Shirt 3.00 8.00
NNO Randy Orton/Shirt 6.00 15.00
NNO Roman Reigns/Shirt 12.00 30.00
NNO Ryback/Shirt 3.00 8.00
NNO Seth Rollins/Shirt 6.00 15.00
NNO Undertaker/Pants 12.00 30.00
NNO Wade Barrett/Shirt 3.00 8.00

2014 Topps WWE Triple Autographs

STATED PRINT RUN 25 SER.#'d SETS
UNPRICED DUE TO SCARCITY

NNO Lee/Rae/Young
NNO Wyatt/Harper/Rowan
NNO Marie/JoJo/Swagger
NNO Cena/Bryan/Orton

2014 Topps WWE Promo

P1 HBK/WWE 50 Book 4.00 10.00

2015 Topps WWE

COMPLETE SET (100) 8.00 20.00
*BLACK: 2X TO 5X BASIC CARDS
*SILVER: 3X TO 8X BASIC CARDS
*GOLD/10: 6X TO 15X BASIC CARDS
*RED/1: UNPRICED DUE TO SCARCITY
*P.P.BLACK/1: UNPRICED DUE TO SCARCITY
*P.P.CYAN/1: UNPRICED DUE TO SCARCITY
*P.P.MAGENTA/1: UNPRICED DUE TO SCARCITY
*P.P.YELLOW/1: UNPRICED DUE TO SCARCITY

1 Adam Rose RC .20 .50
2 AJ Lee .75 2.00
3 Alex Riley .15 .40
4 Alicia Fox .30 .75
5 Bad News Barrett .15 .40
6 Batista .40 1.00
7 Big E .25 .60
8 Big Show .40 1.00
9 Bo Dallas .15 .40
10 Booker T .25 .60
11 Bray Wyatt .60 1.50
12 Brie Bella .50 1.25
13 Brock Lesnar .60 1.50
14 Byron Saxton .15 .40
15 Cameron .25 .60
16 Cesaro .15 .40
17 Chris Jericho .40 1.00
18 Christian .15 .40
19 Curtis Axel .15 .40
20 Damien Mizdow .15 .40
21 Daniel Bryan .60 1.50
22 Darren Young .15 .40
23 David Otunga .15 .40
24 Dean Ambrose .40 1.00
25 Diego .15 .40
26 Dolph Ziggler .25 .60
27 Eden .25 .60
28 Emma RC .25 .60
29 Erick Rowan .25 .60
30 Eva Marie .60 1.50
31 Fandango .15 .40
32 Fernando .15 .40
33 Goldust .15 .40
34 Heath Slater .15 .40
35 Hornswoggle .25 .60
36 Jack Swagger .25 .60
37 Jason Albert .15 .40
38 JBL .15 .40
39 Jerry The King Lawler .25 .60
40 Jey Uso .15 .40
41 Jimmy Uso .15 .40
42 John Cena .75 2.00
43 Justin Gabriel .15 .40
44 Kane .40 1.00
45 Kofi Kingston .15 .40
46 Lana RC .60 1.50
47 Layla .40 1.00
48 Lilian Garcia .40 1.00
49 Luke Harper .25 .60
50 Mark Henry .25 .60
51 Michael Cole .15 .40
52 The Miz .25 .60
53 Naomi .25 .60
54 Natalya .50 1.25
55 Nikki Bella .50 1.25
56 Paige RC .75 2.00
57 Paul Heyman .15 .40
58 R-Truth .15 .40
59 Randy Orton .60 1.50
60 Renee Young .60 1.50
61 Rey Mysterio .40 1.00
62 The Rock .75 2.00
63 Rob Van Dam .40 1.00
64 Roman Reigns .40 1.00
65 Rosa Mendes .25 .60
66 Rusev RC .40 1.00
67 Ryback .15 .40
68 Santino Marella .15 .40
69 Scott Stanford .15 .40
70 Seth Rollins .25 .60
71 Sheamus .40 1.00
72 Sin Cara .25 .60
73 Stardust .15 .40
74 Stephanie McMahon .25 .60
75 Summer Rae .60 1.50
76 Tamina Snuka .25 .60
77 Titus O'Neil .15 .40
78 Tom Phillips RC .15 .40
79 Tony Chimel .15 .40
80 El Torito .15 .40
81 Triple H .60 1.50
82 Tyson Kidd .15 .40
83 Undertaker .60 1.50
84 William Regal .25 .60
85 Xavier Woods .25 .60
86 Zack Ryder .15 .40
87 Zeb Colter .25 .60
88 Bret The Hit Man Hart .50 1.25
89 Bruno Sammartino .40 1.00
90 George The Animal Steele .20 .50
91 Gerald Brisco .25 .60
92 Hulk Hogan .75 2.00
93 Larry Zbyszko .25 .60
94 Mouth of the South Jimmy Hart .20 .50
95 Pat Patterson .15 .40
96 Ric Flair .75 2.00
97 Rowdy Roddy Piper .50 1.25
98 Sting .40 1.00
99 Ultimate Warrior .50 1.25
100 Virgil .15 .40

2015 Topps WWE Athletic Tape Relics

*RED/1: UNPRICED DUE TO SCARCITY
STATED PRINT RUN 20 SER.#'d SETS

NNO Cesaro 30.00 80.00
NNO Curtis Axel 25.00 60.00
NNO Daniel Bryan 120.00 200.00
NNO Darren Young 15.00 40.00
NNO Jack Swagger 15.00 40.00
NNO Rey Mysterio 30.00 80.00
NNO Ryback 25.00 60.00
NNO Zack Ryder 50.00 100.00

2015 Topps WWE Autographs

*BLACK/50: .6X TO 1.5X BASIC AUTOS
*SILVER/25: .75X to 2X BASIC AUTOS
*GOLD/10: 1X TO 2.5X BASIC AUTOS
*RED/1: UNPRICED DUE TO SCARCITY
*P.P.BLACK/1: UNPRICED DUE TO SCARCITY
*P.P.CYAN/1: UNPRICED DUE TO SCARCITY
*P.P.MAGENTA/1: UNPRICED DUE TO SCARCITY
*P.P.YELLOW/1: UNPRICED DUE TO SCARCITY
RANDOMLY INSERTED INTO PACKS

NNO AJ Lee 75.00 150.00
NNO Bray Wyatt 15.00 40.00
NNO Bret Hit Man Hart 25.00 60.00
NNO Eden 20.00 50.00
NNO Emma 15.00 40.00
NNO George The Animal Steele 15.00 40.00
NNO Hulk Hogan 125.00 250.00
NNO Jack Swagger 6.00 15.00
NNO John Cena 25.00 60.00
NNO Larry Zbyszko 6.00 15.00
NNO Mouth of the South Jimmy Hart 6.00 15.00
NNO Paige 75.00 150.00
NNO Ric Flair 15.00 40.00
NNO Rowdy Roddy Piper 25.00 60.00
NNO Rusev 20.00 50.00
NNO Seth Rollins 15.00 40.00

2015 Topps WWE Championship Plates

*GOLD/10: UNPRICED DUE TO SCARCITY
*RED/1: UNPRICED DUE TO SCARCITY
RANDOMLY INSERTED INTO PACKS

NNO AJ Lee 15.00 40.00
NNO Batista and Rey Mysterio 6.00 15.00
NNO Big Show 6.00 15.00
NNO Booker T 6.00 15.00
NNO Brie Bella 8.00 20.00
NNO Brock Lesnar 8.00 20.00
NNO Bruno Sammartino 6.00 15.00
NNO Cesaro 6.00 15.00
NNO Dean Ambrose 8.00 20.00
NNO Dolph Ziggler 8.00 20.00
NNO Edge and Chris Jericho 6.00 15.00
NNO Eve 10.00 25.00
NNO Hulk Hogan 12.00 30.00
NNO John Cena 10.00 25.00
NNO Kane 6.00 15.00
NNO Kane and Big Show 6.00 15.00
NNO Lex Luger 6.00 15.00
NNO New Age Outlaws 8.00 20.00
NNO Nikki Bella 12.00 30.00
NNO Paige 15.00 40.00
NNO Randy Orton 6.00 15.00
NNO Razor Ramon 8.00 20.00
NNO Rey Mysterio 6.00 15.00
NNO Ric Flair/US Title 10.00 25.00
NNO Ric Flair/WWE Title 12.00 30.00
NNO Rock 8.00 20.00
NNO Triple H 6.00 15.00
NNO Ultimate Warrior/IC Title 6.00 15.00
NNO Ultimate Warrior/WWE Title 10.00 25.00
NNO Usos 8.00 20.00

2015 Topps WWE Crowd Chants Oh No

COMPLETE SET (10) 4.00 10.00
*P.P.BLACK/1: UNPRICED DUE TO SCARCITY
*P.P.CYAN/1: UNPRICED DUE TO SCARCITY
*P.P.MAGENTA/1: UNPRICED DUE TO SCARCITY
*P.P.YELLOW/1: UNPRICED DUE TO SCARCITY
RANDOMLY INSERTED INTO PACKS

1 The Montreal Incident .40 1.00
2 Mr. McMahon/The Rock .40 1.00
3 Eve/Zack Ryder 1.00 2.50
4 Brad Maddox/Ryback .40 1.00
5 Damien Sandow/Cody Rhodes .40 1.00
6 Big Show/John Cena .40 1.00
7 Randy Orton/Daniel Bryan 1.25 3.00
8 Triple H/Daniel Bryan .75 2.00
9 Wyatt Family/John Cena .50 1.25
10 Streak Ends 1.00 2.50

2015 Topps WWE Crowd Chants One More Match

COMPLETE SET (10) 4.00 10.00
*P.P.BLACK/1: UNPRICED DUE TO SCARCITY
*P.P.CYAN/1: UNPRICED DUE TO SCARCITY
*P.P.MAGENTA/1: UNPRICED DUE TO SCARCITY
*P.P.YELLOW/1: UNPRICED DUE TO SCARCITY
RANDOMLY INSERTED INTO PACKS

1 Cowboy Bob Orton .40 1.00
2 Edge .50 1.25
3 Shawn Michaels .50 1.25
4 Ted DiBiase .40 1.00
5 Bruno Sammartino .40 1.00
6 Ric Flair .75 2.00
7 Rowdy Roddy Piper .50 1.25
8 Hulk Hogan 1.25 3.00
9 Jake The Snake Roberts .40 1.00
10 Stone Cold Steve Austin 1.25 3.00

2015 Topps WWE Crowd Chants This Is Awesome

COMPLETE SET (10) 4.00 10.00
*P.P.BLACK/1: UNPRICED DUE TO SCARCITY
*P.P.CYAN/1: UNPRICED DUE TO SCARCITY
*P.P.MAGENTA/1: UNPRICED DUE TO SCARCITY
*P.P.YELLOW/1: UNPRICED DUE TO SCARCITY
RANDOMLY INSERTED INTO PACKS

1 Rock beats Cena .75 2.00
2 DX Reunites .75 2.00
3 Bob Backlund HOF .40 1.00
4 Dolph Ziggler/Alberto Del Rio .40 1.00
5 Big Show/Triple H .40 1.00
6 Kofi Kingston .40 1.00
7 Wyatt Family/The Shield .40 1.00
8 Hogan/Austin/Rock 1.25 3.00
9 Daniel Bryan .40 1.00
10 Paige/AJ Lee 2.50 6.00

2015 Topps WWE Crowd Chants USA

COMPLETE SET (10) 5.00 12.00
*P.P.BLACK/1: UNPRICED DUE TO SCARCITY
*P.P.CYAN/1: UNPRICED DUE TO SCARCITY
*P.P.MAGENTA/1: UNPRICED DUE TO SCARCITY
*P.P.YELLOW/1: UNPRICED DUE TO SCARCITY
RANDOMLY INSERTED INTO PACKS

1 Hulk Hogan 1.50 4.00
2 Sgt. Slaughter .75 2.00
3 Hacksaw Jim Duggan .40 1.00
4 Lex Luger .40 1.00
5 The US Express .40 1.00
6 Jack Swagger .40 1.00
7 The American Dream Dusty Rhodes .40 1.00
8 John Cena 1.25 3.00
9 The Rock 1.50 4.00
10 Undertaker 1.25 3.00

2015 Topps WWE Crowd Chants WOOOOOO

COMPLETE SET (10) 4.00 10.00
*P.P.BLACK/1: UNPRICED DUE TO SCARCITY
*P.P.CYAN/1: UNPRICED DUE TO SCARCITY
*P.P.MAGENTA/1: UNPRICED DUE TO SCARCITY
*P.P.YELLOW/1: UNPRICED DUE TO SCARCITY
RANDOMLY INSERTED INTO PACKS

1 Ric Flair/Royal Rumble .75 2.00
2 Ric Flair/Randy Savage .60 1.50
3 Ric Flair/Eric Bischoff .60 1.50
4 Ric Flair/Jeff Jarrett .60 1.50
5 Evolution .60 1.50
6 Ric Flair/Carlito .60 1.50
7 Ric Flair/Roddy Piper .60 1.50
8 Ric Flair HOF 1.25 3.00
9 Shawn Michaels/Ric Flair .60 1.50
10 Four Horsemen HOF 1.25 3.00

2015 Topps WWE Crowd Chants YES! YES! YES!

COMPLETE SET (10) 5.00 12.00
*P.P.BLACK/1: UNPRICED DUE TO SCARCITY
*P.P.CYAN/1: UNPRICED DUE TO SCARCITY
*P.P.MAGENTA/1: UNPRICED DUE TO SCARCITY
*P.P.YELLOW/1: UNPRICED DUE TO SCARCITY
RANDOMLY INSERTED INTO PACKS

1 Daniel Bryan/Kane .75 2.00
2 Team Hell No/Tag Champs 1.25 3.00
3 Team Hell No/Ziggler & Big E .75 2.00
4 Daniel Bryan/WWE Title .75 2.00
5 Locker Room/Daniel Bryan .75 2.00
6 Daniel Bryan/Second Title .75 2.00
7 Daniel Bryan/Wyatt Family .75 2.00
8 Yes Movement .75 2.00
9 Daniel Bryan/Triple H .75 2.00
10 Daniel Bryan 1.25 3.00
WWE World TItle

2015 Topps WWE Crowd Chants You Still Got It

COMPLETE SET (10) 2.50 6.00
*P.P.BLACK/1: UNPRICED DUE TO SCARCITY
*P.P.CYAN/1: UNPRICED DUE TO SCARCITY
*P.P.MAGENTA/1: UNPRICED DUE TO SCARCITY
*P.P.YELLOW/1: UNPRICED DUE TO SCARCITY
RANDOMLY INSERTED INTO PACKS

1 Ricky The Dragon Steamboat .40 1.00
2 Booker T .40 1.00
3 Chris Jericho .40 1.00
4 Vader .40 1.00
5 Road Warrior Animal .40 1.00
6 Jerry The King Lawler .40 1.00
7 Rob Van Dam .40 1.00
8 Goldust .40 1.00
9 Billy Gunn .40 1.00
10 Road Dogg .40 1.00

2015 Topps WWE Diva Kiss

*GOLD/10: .5X TO 1.2X BASIC KISS
*RED/1: UNPRICED DUE TO SCARCITY
RANDOMLY INSERTED INTO PACKS

NNO Alicia Fox 20.00 50.00
NNO Eva Marie 25.00 60.00
NNO Eve Torres 25.00 60.00
NNO Lana 30.00 80.00
NNO Layla 15.00 40.00
NNO Lilian Garcia 15.00 40.00
NNO Paige 150.00 300.00
NNO Rosa Mendes 15.00 40.00
NNO Trish Stratus 30.00 80.00
NNO Lita 25.00 60.00

2015 Topps WWE Diva Kiss Autographs

*GOLD/10: UNPRICED DUE TO SCARCITY
*RED/1: UNPRICED DUE TO SCARCITY
STATED PRINT RUN 15 SER.#'d SETS

NNO Alicia Fox 40.00 100.00
NNO Eva Marie 80.00 200.00
NNO Eve Torres 40.00 100.00
NNO Lana 80.00 200.00
NNO Layla 50.00 125.00
NNO Lilian Garcia 50.00 125.00
NNO Paige 100.00 250.00
NNO Rosa Mendes 30.00 80.00
NNO Trish Stratus 100.00 250.00
NNO Lita 80.00 200.00

2015 Topps WWE King of the Ring Relics

*RED/1: UNPRICED DUE TO SCARCITY
RANDOMLY INSERTED INTO PACKS

NNO Billy Gunn 12.00 30.00
NNO Bret Hit Man Hart 25.00 60.00
NNO Brock Lesnar 15.00 40.00
NNO Don Muraco 12.00 30.00
NNO Edge 20.00 50.00
NNO Harley Race 20.00 50.00
NNO King Booker 15.00 40.00
NNO Ted DiBiase 20.00 50.00
NNO Sheamus 15.00 40.00
NNO Stone Cold Steve Austin 25.00 60.00
NNO Tito Santana 15.00 40.00
NNO Triple H 25.00 60.00
NNO William Regal 12.00 30.00

2015 Topps WWE NXT Prospects

COMPLETE SET (10) 6.00 15.00
STATED ODDS 1:3

1 Aiden English 1.00 2.50
2 Alexa Bliss 12.00 30.00
3 Angelo Dawkins 1.00 2.50
4 Bull Dempsey 1.50 4.00
5 Colin Cassady 1.25 3.00
6 Hideo Itami 2.00 5.00
7 Kalisto 1.25 3.00
8 Marcus Louis 1.00 2.50
9 Sawyer Fulton 1.00 2.50
10 Tye Dillinger 1.00 2.50

2015 Topps WWE SummerSlam Mat Relics

*GOLD/10: UNPRICED DUE TO SCARCITY
*RED/1: UNPRICED DUE TO SCARCITY
RANDOMLY INSERTED INTO PACKS

NNO AJ Lee 12.00 30.00
NNO Bray Wyatt 6.00 15.00
NNO Brie Bella 6.00 15.00
NNO Brock Lesnar 8.00 20.00
NNO Cesaro 5.00 12.00
NNO Chris Jericho 8.00 20.00
NNO Dean Ambrose 6.00 15.00
NNO Dolph Ziggler 8.00 20.00
NNO Jack Swagger 5.00 12.00
NNO John Cena 6.00 15.00
NNO Miz 5.00 12.00
NNO Nikki Bella 6.00 15.00
NNO Paige 15.00 40.00
NNO Randy Orton 5.00 12.00
NNO Rob Van Dam 5.00 12.00
NNO Roman Reigns 8.00 20.00
NNO Rusev 6.00 15.00
NNO Seth Rollins 5.00 12.00
NNO Stephanie McMahon 8.00 20.00
NNO Triple H 8.00 20.00

2015 Topps WWE Swatch Relics

*GOLD/10: UNPRICED DUE TO SCARCITY
*RED/1: UNPRICED DUE TO SCARCITY
RANDOMLY INSERTED INTO PACKS

NNO AJ Lee 15.00 40.00
NNO Big E 5.00 12.00
NNO Big Show 5.00 12.00
NNO Bo Dallas 6.00 15.00
NNO Bray Wyatt 10.00 25.00
NNO Brie Bella 6.00 15.00
NNO Dolph Ziggler 6.00 15.00
NNO Fandango 5.00 12.00
NNO Goldust 5.00 12.00
NNO Jey Uso 5.00 12.00
NNO John Cena 6.00 15.00
NNO The Miz 5.00 12.00
NNO Natalya 6.00 15.00
NNO Nikki Bella 6.00 15.00
NNO Paige 15.00 40.00
NNO Randy Orton 6.00 15.00
NNO Seth Rollins 6.00 15.00
NNO Stardust 5.00 12.00

2015 Topps WWE Triple Autographs

STATED PRINT RUN 5 SER.#'d SETS
UNPRICED DUE TO SCARCITY

NNO AJ/Paige/Emma
NNO Wyatt/Rusev/Hart
NNO Hogan/Flair/Piper
NNO Cena/Ambrose/Rollins
NNO Paige/Emma/Eden

2016 Topps WWE

COMPLETE SET (100) 10.00 25.00
*BRONZE: 1.2X TO 3X BASIC CARDS
*SILVER: 2X TO 5X BASIC CARDS
*GOLD/10: UNPRICED DUE TO SCARCITY
*RED/1: UNPRICED DUE TO SCARCITY
*P.P.BLACK/1: UNPRICED DUE TO SCARCITY
*P.P.CYAN/1: UNPRICED DUE TO SCARCITY
*P.P.MAGENTA/1: UNPRICED DUE TO SCARCITY
*P.P.YELLOW/1: UNPRICED DUE TO SCARCITY

1 Adam Rose .20 .50
2 Alberto Del Rio .30 .75
3 Alicia Fox .30 .75
4 The Ascension .20 .50
5 Becky Lynch RC .60 1.50
6 Big Show .40 1.00
7 Bo Dallas .20 .50
8 Booker T .40 1.00
9 Brie Bella .40 1.00
10 Bubba Ray Dudley .40 1.00
11 The Bunny .20 .50
12 Byron Saxton .20 .50
13 Cesaro .40 1.00
14 Charlotte .60 1.50
15 Corey Graves RC .12 .30
16 Curtis Axel .20 .50
17 D-Von Dudley .30 .75
18 Damien Sandow .20 .50
19 Dolph Ziggler .25 .60
20 Fandango .20 .50
21 Goldust .30 .75
22 Jason Albert .20 .50
23 JBL .25 .60
24 Jerry The King Lawler .40 1.00
25 Kalisto .50 1.25
26 Kevin Owens .50 1.25
27 Lana .75 2.00
28 Mandy Rose RC 2.00 5.00
29 Mark Henry .25 .60
30 The Miz .30 .75
31 Naomi .30 .75
32 Natalya .30 .75
33 Neville .50 1.25
34 Nikki Bella .60 1.50
35 Paige .60 1.50
36 Titus O'Neil .20 .50
37 R-Truth .20 .50
38 Rusev .50 1.25
39 Ryback .25 .60
40 Sasha Banks .60 1.50
41 Sin Cara .25 .60
42 Stardust .20 .50
43 Summer Rae .50 1.25
44 Tamina .25 .60
45 Tyler Breeze .20 .50
46 Tyson Kidd .20 .50
47 The Usos .20 .50
48 William Regal .20 .50
49 Zeb Colter .20 .50
50 Alundra Blayze L .25 .60
51 American Dream Dusty Rhodes L .20 .50
52 Andre the Giant L .60 1.50
53 Bam Bam Bigelow L .25 .60
54 Barry Windham L .20 .50
55 Batista L .40 1.00
56 The Brain Busters L .20 .50
57 The British Bulldog L .25 .60
58 The Bushwhackers L .20 .50
59 Christian L .30 .75
60 Dangerous Danny Davis L .20 .50
61 Doink the Clown L .20 .50
62 Edge L .50 1.25
63 Eve Torres L .40 1.00
64 George The Animal Steele L .25 .60
65 The Godfather L .25 .60
66 Irwin R. Schyster L .20 .50
67 Jake The Snake Roberts L .40 1.00
68 Jim Ross L .30 .75
69 J.J. Dillon L .20 .50
70 Kamala L .20 .50
71 Kerry Von Erich L .30 .75
72 Kevin Nash L .50 1.25
73 Kevin Von Erich L RC .30 .75
74 Lita L .60 1.50
75 Macho King Randy Savage L .50 1.25
76 Mike Rotunda L .20 .50
77 Ted DiBiase L .25 .60
78 Miss Elizabeth L .20 .50
79 Mr. X L .20 .50
80 The Nasty Boys L .20 .50
81 The Natural Disasters L .20 .50
82 Bret Hit Man Hart L .50 1.25
83 Papa Shango L .25 .60
84 Ric Flair L .75 2.00
85 Rikishi L .25 .60
86 Road Dogg L .30 .75
87 Rob Van Dam L .40 1.00
88 Faarooq L .50 1.25
89 Rowdy Roddy Piper L .60 1.50
90 Santino Marella L .25 .60
91 Scott Hall L .50 1.25
92 Sensational Sherri L .30 .75
93 Shawn Michaels L .75 2.00
94 Stevie Ray L .20 .50
95 Superstar Billy Graham L .20 .50
96 Tatsumi Fujinami L RC .20 .50
97 Trish Stratus L 1.00 2.50
98 Ultimate Warrior L .50 1.25
99 Virgil L .20 .50
100 X-Pac L .30 .75

2016 Topps WWE 2K17 NXT TakeOver London Mat Relics

*PURPLE/299: SAME VALUE AS BASIC
*GREEN/199: .5X TO 1.2X BASIC MEM
*BRONZE/99: .6X TO 1.5X BASIC MEM
*SILVER/50: .75X TO 2X BASIC MEM
*BLUE/25: UNPRICED DUE TO SCARCITY
*GOLD/10: UNPRICED DUE TO SCARCITY
RANDOMLY INSERTED INTO PACKS

NNO Asuka 5.00 12.00
NNO Emma 6.00 15.00
NNO Dana Brooke 3.00 8.00
NNO Dash Wilder 2.50 6.00
NNO Scott Dawson 2.50 6.00
NNO Enzo Amore 3.00 8.00
NNO Colin Cassady 3.00 8.00
NNO Carmella 6.00 15.00
NNO Baron Corbin 4.00 10.00
NNO Apollo Crews 3.00 8.00
NNO Bayley 5.00 12.00
NNO Nia Jax 3.00 8.00
NNO Finn Balor 5.00 12.00
NNO Samoa Joe 3.00 8.00

2016 Topps WWE Authority Perspectives

COMPLETE SET (18) 12.00 30.00
*P.P.BLACK/1: UNPRICED DUE TO SCARCITY
*P.P.CYAN/1: UNPRICED DUE TO SCARCITY
*P.P.MAGENTA/1: UNPRICED DUE TO SCARCITY
*P.P.YELLOW/1: UNPRICED DUE TO SCARCITY
RANDOMLY INSERTED INTO PACKS
*ANTI-AUTHORITY: SAME VALUE

1A Triple H 2.50 6.00
2A Stephanie McMahon 1.00 2.50
3A Seth Rollins 1.00 2.50
4A Kane 1.00 2.50
5A J&J Security .60 1.50
6A The New Day 1.50 4.00
7A The Wyatt Family 1.25 3.00
8A King Barrett .60 1.50
9A Sheamus 1.50 4.00
10A John Cena 3.00 8.00
11A Sting 1.50 4.00
12A The Rock 3.00 8.00
13A Reigns/Ambrose 2.00 5.00
14A Randy Orton 1.50 4.00
15A Brock Lesnar 3.00 8.00
16A Undertaker 2.50 6.00
17A Chris Jericho 1.50 4.00
18A Daniel Bryan 2.50 6.00

2016 Topps WWE Autographs

*BRONZE/50: .5X TO 1.2X BASIC AUTOS
*SILVER/25: .75X TO 2X BASIC AUTOS
*GOLD/10: UNPRICED DUE TO SCARCITY
*RED/1: UNPRICED DUE TO SCARCITY
*P.P.BLACK/1: UNPRICED DUE TO SCARCITY
*P.P.CYAN/1: UNPRICED DUE TO SCARCITY
*P.P.MAGENTA/1: UNPRICED DUE TO SCARCITY
*P.P.YELLOW/1: UNPRICED DUE TO SCARCITY
RANDOMLY INSERTED INTO PACKS

NNO Apollo Crews 10.00 25.00
NNO Alberto Del Rio 10.00 25.00
NNO Asuka 30.00 80.00
NNO Bayley 25.00 60.00
NNO Becky Lynch 15.00 40.00
NNO Braun Strowman 10.00 25.00
NNO Bray Wyatt 10.00 25.00
NNO Bubba Ray Dudley 8.00 20.00
NNO Charlotte 12.00 30.00
NNO D-Von Dudley 6.00 15.00
NNO Dean Ambrose 10.00 25.00
NNO Finn Balor 15.00 40.00
NNO JJ Dillion 6.00 15.00
NNO John Cena 15.00 40.00
NNO Luke Harper 25.00 60.00
NNO Natalya 8.00 20.00
NNO Nia Jax 12.00 30.00
NNO Ric Flair 30.00 75.00
NNO Rikishi 6.00 15.00
NNO Roman Reigns 10.00 25.00
NNO Samoa Joe 8.00 20.00
NNO Seth Rollins 8.00 20.00
NNO Sting 25.00 60.00
NNO Superstar Billy Graham 15.00 40.00

2016 Topps WWE Diva Kiss

*GOLD/10: UNPRICED DUE TO SCARCITY
*RED/1: UNPRICED DUE TO SCARCITY
STATED PRINT RUN 99 SER.#'d SETS

NNO Alicia Fox 30.00 75.00
NNO Alundra Blayze 60.00 120.00
NNO Bayley 75.00 150.00
NNO Becky Lynch 150.00 300.00
NNO Brie Bella 30.00 75.00
NNO Charlotte 125.00 250.00
NNO Lana 50.00 100.00
NNO Lita 25.00 60.00
NNO Nikki Bella 60.00 120.00
NNO Sasha Banks 150.00 300.00
NNO Trish Stratus 200.00 400.00

2016 Topps WWE Diva Kiss Autographs

*GOLD/10: UNPRICED DUE TO SCARCITY
*RED/1: UNPRICED DUE TO SCARCITY
*P.P.BLACK/1: UNPRICED DUE TO SCARCITY
*P.P.CYAN/1: UNPRICED DUE TO SCARCITY
*P.P.MAGENTA/1: UNPRICED DUE TO SCARCITY
*P.P.YELLOW/1: UNPRICED DUE TO SCARCITY
STATED PRINT RUN 25 SER.#'d SETS

NNO Alicia Fox 30.00 80.00
NNO Alundra Blayze 30.00 80.00
NNO Bayley 100.00 200.00
NNO Becky Lynch 400.00 800.00
NNO Brie Bella 150.00 300.00
NNO Charlotte 150.00 300.00
NNO Lana 60.00 120.00
NNO Lita 50.00 100.00
NNO Nikki Bella 50.00 100.00
NNO Sasha Banks 250.00 500.00
NNO Trish Stratus 250.00 500.00

2016 Topps WWE Medallions

*BRONZE/50: .5X TO 1.2X BASIC MEM
*SILVER/25: .6X TO 1.5X BASIC MEM
*GOLD/10: UNPRICED DUE TO SCARCITY
*RED/1: UNPRICED DUE TO SCARCITY
STATED PRINT RUN 299 SER.#'d SETS

NNO Big E 2.00 5.00
NNO Braun Strowman 2.50 6.00
NNO Bray Wyatt 8.00 20.00
NNO Brock Lesnar 10.00 25.00
NNO Chris Jericho 5.00 12.00
NNO Daniel Bryan 8.00 20.00
NNO Dean Ambrose 6.00 15.00
NNO Jamie Noble 2.00 5.00
NNO Joey Mercury 2.00 5.00
NNO John Cena 10.00 25.00
NNO Kane 3.00 8.00
NNO King Barrett 2.00 5.00
NNO Kofi Kingston 2.00 5.00
NNO Luke Harper 2.00 5.00
NNO Randy Orton 5.00 12.00
NNO The Rock 10.00 25.00
NNO Roman Reigns 6.00 15.00
NNO Seth Rollins 3.00 8.00
NNO Sheamus 5.00 12.00
NNO Stephanie McMahon 3.00 8.00
NNO Sting 5.00 12.00
NNO Triple H 8.00 20.00
NNO Undertaker 8.00 20.00
NNO Xavier Woods 2.00 5.00

2016 Topps WWE NXT Inserts

COMPLETE SET (28) 8.00 20.00
*P.P.BLACK/1: UNPRICED DUE TO SCARCITY
*P.P.CYAN/1: UNPRICED DUE TO SCARCITY
*P.P.MAGENTA/1: UNPRICED DUE TO SCARCITY
*P.P.YELLOW/1: UNPRICED DUE TO SCARCITY
STATED ODDS 1:1

1 Aiden English .30 .75
2 Alexa Bliss 4.00 10.00
3 Angelo Dawkins .30 .75
4 Apollo Crews .30 .75
5 Asuka 4.00 10.00
6 Baron Corbin .40 1.00
7 Bayley .75 2.00
8 Billie Kay .75 2.00
9 Blake .30 .75
10 Carmella .75 2.00
11 Chad Gable .40 1.00
12 Colin Cassady .60 1.50
13 Dana Brooke .75 2.00
14 Dash Wilder .40 1.00
15 Scott Dawson .30 .75
16 Enzo Amore .60 1.50
17 Finn Balor 2.00 5.00
18 Hideo Itami .40 1.00
19 Jason Jordan .40 1.00
20 Mojo Rawley .30 .75
21 Murphy .30 .75
22 Nia Jax .50 1.25
23 Peyton Royce .75 2.00
24 Sami Zayn .50 1.25
25 Samoa Joe .75 2.00
26 Sawyer Fulton .40 1.00
27 Simon Gotch .50 1.25
28 Tye Dillinger .40 1.00

2016 Topps WWE NXT TakeOver Brooklyn Mat Relics

*BRONZE/50: .5X TO 1.2X BASIC MEM
*SILVER/25: .6X TO 1.5X BASIC MEM
*GOLD/10: UNPRICED DUE TO SCARCITY
*RED/1: UNPRICED DUE TO SCARCITY
*P.P.BLACK/1: UNPRICED DUE TO SCARCITY
*P.P.CYAN/1: UNPRICED DUE TO SCARCITY
*P.P.MAGENTA/1: UNPRICED DUE TO SCARCITY
*P.P.YELLOW/1: UNPRICED DUE TO SCARCITY
STATED PRINT RUN 199 SER.#'d SETS

NNO Aiden English 2.50 6.00
NNO Alexa Bliss 12.00 30.00
NNO Apollo Crews 2.50 6.00
NNO Baron Corbin 3.00 8.00
NNO Bayley 6.00 15.00
NNO Blake 2.50 6.00
NNO Finn Balor 8.00 20.00
NNO Kevin Owens 6.00 15.00
NNO Murphy 2.50 6.00
NNO Samoa Joe 6.00 15.00
NNO Sasha Banks 8.00 20.00
NNO Simon Gotch 4.00 10.00
NNO Tye Dillinger 3.00 8.00
NNO Tyler Breeze 2.50 6.00

2016 Topps WWE Shirt Relics

*BRONZE/50: .5X TO 1.2X BASIC MEM
*SILVER/25: .6X TO 1.5X BASIC MEM
*GOLD/10: UNPRICED DUE TO SCARCITY
*RED/1: UNPRICED DUE TO SCARCITY
*P.P.BLACK/1: UNPRICED DUE TO SCARCITY
*P.P.CYAN/1: UNPRICED DUE TO SCARCITY
*P.P.MAGENTA/1: UNPRICED DUE TO SCARCITY
*P.P.YELLOW/1: UNPRICED DUE TO SCARCITY
RANDOMLY INSERTED INTO PACKS

NNO Aiden English 3.00 8.00
NNO Alberto Del Rio 5.00 12.00
NNO Alicia Fox 5.00 12.00
NNO Apollo Crews 3.00 8.00
NNO Bayley 8.00 20.00
NNO Becky Lynch 10.00 25.00
NNO Braun Strowman 4.00 10.00
NNO Bray Wyatt 12.00 30.00
NNO Brie Bella 6.00 15.00
NNO Bubba Ray Dudley 6.00 15.00
NNO Cesaro 6.00 15.00
NNO Charlotte 10.00 25.00
NNO Dean Ambrose 10.00 25.00
NNO D-Von Dudley 5.00 12.00
NNO Finn Balor 10.00 25.00
NNO John Cena 15.00 40.00
NNO Kevin Owens 8.00 20.00
NNO Luke Harper 3.00 8.00
NNO Naomi 5.00 12.00
NNO Natalya 5.00 12.00
NNO Neville 8.00 20.00
NNO Paige 10.00 25.00
NNO Roman Reigns 10.00 25.00
NNO Samoa Joe 8.00 20.00
NNO Sasha Banks 10.00 25.00
NNO Seth Rollins 5.00 12.00
NNO Simon Gotch 5.00 12.00
NNO Tamina 4.00 10.00
NNO Tyler Breeze 3.00 8.00
NNO Zack Ryder 3.00 8.00

2016 Topps WWE SummerSlam Mat Relics

*BRONZE/50: .5X TO 1.2X BASIC MEM
*SILVER/25: .6X TO 1.5X BASIC MEM
*GOLD/10: UNPRICED DUE TO SCARCITY
*RED/1: UNPRICED DUE TO SCARCITY
*P.P.BLACK/1: UNPRICED DUE TO SCARCITY
*P.P.CYAN/1: UNPRICED DUE TO SCARCITY
*P.P.MAGENTA/1: UNPRICED DUE TO SCARCITY
*P.P.YELLOW/1: UNPRICED DUE TO SCARCITY
STATED PRINT RUN 199 SER.#'d SETS

NNO Big Show 4.00 10.00
NNO Bray Wyatt 8.00 20.00
NNO Brock Lesnar 10.00 25.00
NNO Cesaro 4.00 10.00
NNO Dean Ambrose 6.00 15.00
NNO Dolph Ziggler 2.50 6.00
NNO John Cena 10.00 25.00
NNO Kevin Owens 5.00 12.00
NNO King Barrett 2.00 5.00
NNO Luke Harper 2.00 5.00
NNO The Miz 3.00 8.00
NNO Neville 5.00 12.00
NNO Randy Orton 5.00 12.00
NNO Roman Reigns 6.00 15.00
NNO Rusev 5.00 12.00
NNO Ryback 2.50 6.00
NNO Seth Rollins 3.00 8.00
NNO Sheamus 5.00 12.00
NNO Stardust 2.00 5.00
NNO Undertaker 8.00 20.00

2016 Topps WWE Superstars of Canada Autographs

STATED PRINT RUN 25 SER.#'d SETS

NNO Chris Jericho 15.00 40.00
NNO Christian 12.00 30.00
NNO Edge 25.00 60.00
NNO Kevin Owens 12.00 30.00
NNO Natalya 12.00 30.00
NNO Renee Young 15.00 40.00
NNO Sami Zayn 10.00 25.00
NNO Trish Stratus 50.00 100.00
NNO Tyson Kidd 6.00 15.00
NNO Viktor 6.00 15.00

2016 Topps WWE Triple Autographs

STATED PRINT RUN 11 SER.#'d SETS

NNO Del Rio/Graham/Rikishi 50.00 100.00
NNO Bayley/Asuka/Jax 75.00 150.00
NNO Wyatt/Harper/Strowman 100.00 200.00
NNO Charlotte/Lynch/Natalya 100.00 200.00
NNO Balor/Samoa Joe/Crews 100.00 200.00
NNO Cena/Dudley Boyz 75.00 150.00
NNO Rollins/Ambrose/Reigns 125.00 250.00
NNO Sting/Flair/Dillon 150.00 300.00

2017 Topps WWE

COMPLETE SET W/O SP (100) 8.00 20.00
*BRONZE: .5X TO 1.2X BASIC CARDS
*BLUE/99: 1X TO 2.5X BASIC CARDS
*SILVER/25: 2X TO 5X BASIC CARDS
*GOLD/10: 4X TO 10X BASIC CARDS
*RED/1: UNPRICED DUE TO SCARCITY
*P.P.BLACK/1: UNPRICED DUE TO SCARCITY
*P.P.CYAN/1: UNPRICED DUE TO SCARCITY
*P.P.MAGENTA/1: UNPRICED DUE TO SCARCITY
*P.P.YELLOW/1: UNPRICED DUE TO SCARCITY

1A The Rock 1.25 3.00
1B The Rock SP/Just Bring It 10.00 25.00
2 Tyson Kidd .25 .60
3 Booker T .30 .75
4 Byron Saxton .25 .60
5A Bayley .75 2.00
5B Bayley SP/Leaping 5.00 12.00
6 Big Cass .30 .75
7A Big E .30 .75
7B Big E SP/Big Splash 3.00 8.00
8 Bob Backlund .25 .60
9A Brian Kendrick .25 .60
9B Brian Kendrick SP/Jacket 3.00 8.00
10A Brock Lesnar 1.25 3.00
10B Brock Lesnar SP/Outside Ring 8.00 20.00
11 Chad Patton RC .25 .60
12 Charly Caruso RC .25 .60
13A Chris Jericho .60 1.50
13B Chris Jericho SP/Walls of Jericho 6.00 15.00
14 Corey Graves .25 .60
15 Darrick Moore RC .25 .60
16 Enzo Amore .75 2.00
17A Finn Balor 1.00 2.50
17B Finn Balor SP/Entrance 10.00 25.00
18A Goldberg 1.00 2.50
18B Goldberg SP/Jacket 12.00 30.00
19 JoJo .40 1.00
20 John Cone RC .25 .60
21 Karl Anderson .25 .60
22A Kofi Kingston .30 .75
22B Kofi Kingston SP/Leaping 6.00 15.00
23 Luke Gallows .40 1.00

24 Michael Cole	.25	.60
25 Mick Foley	.60	1.50
26A Nia Jax	.40	1.00
26B Nia Jax SP/Pink Gear	5.00	12.00
27 Paige	.60	1.50
28 Paul Heyman	.25	.60
29 Rod Zapata RC	.25	.60
30 Shawn Bennett RC	.25	.60
31 TJ Perkins RC	.25	.60
32 Titus O'Neil	.25	.60
33A Triple H	.60	1.50
33B Triple H SP/No Mic	10.00	25.00
34A Xavier Woods	.30	.75
34B Xavier Woods	2.50	6.00
35A AJ Styles	1.25	3.00
35B AJ Styles	12.00	30.00
36A Alexa Bliss	1.25	3.00
36B Alexa Bliss SP/Flip	15.00	40.00
37 Andrea D'Marco RC	.25	.60
38A Carmella	.60	1.50
38B Carmella SP/Microphone	6.00	15.00
39 Chad Gable	.30	.75
40 Charles Robinson	.25	.60
41 Dan Engler RC	.25	.60
42 David Otunga	.25	.60
43 Greg Hamilton	.25	.60
44 Jason Ayers RC	.25	.60
45 Jason Jordan	.30	.75
46 JBL	.30	.75
47A John Cena	1.25	3.00
47B John Cena SP		
48A Kane	.30	.75
48B Kane SP/Facing Forward	8.00	20.00
49 Luke Harper	.25	.60
50 Maryse	.50	1.25
51 Mauro Ranallo	.25	.60
52 Mike Chioda RC	.25	.60
53A The Miz	.50	1.25
53B Miz SP/In Ring	8.00	20.00
54 Mojo Rawley	.30	.75
55A Randy Orton	.60	1.50
55B Randy Orton SP/RKO	6.00	15.00
56 Renee Young	.40	1.00
57 Ryan Tran RC	.25	.60
58A Undertaker	1.00	2.50
58B Undertaker SP/Silhouette	20.00	50.00
59 Zack Ryder	.25	.60
60 Alexander Wolfe RC	.30	.75
61 Aliyah	.30	.75
62A Asuka	.75	2.00
62B Asuka SP/Mask	8.00	20.00
63A Austin Aries	.50	1.25
63B Austin Aries SP/Cape	6.00	15.00
64 Billie Kay	.30	.75
65A Bobby Roode	.60	1.50
65B Bobby Roode SP	8.00	20.00
66 Cathy Kelley	.25	.60
67 Dash Wilder	.25	.60
68 Dasha Fuentes	.30	.75
69 Danilo Anfibio RC	.25	.60
70 Drake Wuertz RC	.25	.60
71 Eddie Orengo RC	.25	.60
72 Ember Moon RC	.60	1.50
73 Eric Young	.50	1.25
74 Hideo Itami	.40	1.00
75 Johnny Gargano	.25	.60
76 Liv Morgan	.40	1.00
77 Nick Miller RC	.25	.60
78 Nikki Cross RC	.50	1.25
79 Oney Lorcan	.25	.60
80 Paul Ellering	.25	.60
81 Peyton Royce	.40	1.00
82 Roderick Strong RC	.30	.75
83A Samoa Joe	.75	2.00
83B Samoa Joe SP		
84 Scott Dawson	.25	.60
85 Shane Thorne RC	.25	.60
86A Shinsuke Nakamura	.60	1.50
86B Nakamura SP/Jacket	6.00	15.00
87 Tommaso Ciampa	.25	.60
88 Tye Dillinger	.25	.60
89 William Regal	.30	.75
90 Norman Smiley	.30	.75
91 Ric Flair	.60	1.50
92 Terri Runnels	.25	.60
93 Beth Phoenix	.25	.60
94 Eric Bischoff	.25	.60
95 Ivory	.25	.60
96 Judy Martin RC	.25	.60
97 Kelly Kelly	.50	1.25
98 Leilani Kai	.25	.60
99 Princess Victoria RC	.25	.60
100 Torrie Wilson	.60	1.50

2017 Topps WWE Autographed Shirt Relics

STATED ODDS 1:3,524

NNO Bayley	30.00	75.00
NNO Big E	15.00	40.00
NNO Bray Wyatt	30.00	75.00
NNO Carmella	25.00	60.00
NNO Cesaro	15.00	40.00
NNO Dolph Ziggler	15.00	40.00
NNO John Cena	50.00	100.00
NNO Karl Anderson	15.00	40.00
NNO Kevin Owens	15.00	40.00
NNO Kofi Kingston	15.00	40.00
NNO The Miz	30.00	75.00
NNO Randy Orton	30.00	80.00
NNO Roman Reigns		
NNO Seth Rollins	25.00	60.00
NNO Shinsuke Nakamura		
NNO Xavier Woods		

2017 Topps WWE Autographs

*BLUE/50: .6X TO 1.5X BASIC AUTOS
*SILVER/25: .75X TO 2X BASIC AUTOS
*GOLD/10: UNPRICED DUE TO SCARCITY
*RED/1: UNPRICED DUE TO SCARCITY
STATED ODDS 1:50

5 Bayley	15.00	40.00
6 Big Cass	8.00	20.00
7 Big E	6.00	15.00
10 Brock Lesnar	50.00	100.00
13 Chris Jericho	12.00	30.00
16 Enzo Amore	10.00	25.00
18 Goldberg	50.00	100.00
21 Karl Anderson	6.00	15.00
22 Kofi Kingston	6.00	15.00
23 Luke Gallows	5.00	12.00
34 Xavier Woods	6.00	15.00
38 Carmella	10.00	25.00
53 The Miz	5.00	12.00
62 Asuka	15.00	40.00
64 Billie Kay	8.00	20.00
81 Peyton Royce	10.00	25.00
83 Samoa Joe	6.00	15.00
91 Ric Flair	15.00	40.00
92 Terri Runnels	10.00	25.00
93 Beth Phoenix	6.00	15.00
94 Eric Bischoff	8.00	20.00
96 Judy Martin	6.00	15.00
97 Kelly Kelly	15.00	40.00
98 Leilani Kai	6.00	15.00
100 Torrie Wilson	10.00	25.00

2017 Topps WWE Autographs Blue

STATED ODDS 1:99
STATED PRINT RUN 50 SER.#'d SETS

58 Undertaker	150.00	300.00

2017 Topps WWE Autographs Silver

STATED ODDS 1:116
STATED PRINT RUN 25 SER.#'d SETS

25 Mick Foley	15.00	40.00

2017 Topps WWE Breaking Ground

COMPLETE SET (10)	5.00	12.00
STATED ODDS 1:2		
1 Baron Corbin	1.00	2.50
2 Dana Brooke	1.25	3.00
3 Tyler Breeze	.60	1.50
4 Jason Jordan	.75	2.00
5 Tyler Breeze	.60	1.50
6 The Superstars	1.00	2.50
7 Bayley	2.00	5.00
8 Scott Hall	.75	2.00
9 Sami Zayn	.75	2.00
10 Tyler Breeze	.60	1.50

2017 Topps WWE Championship Relics

*BLUE/50: .5X TO 1.2X BASIC MEM
*SILVER/25: .6X TO 1.5X BASIC MEM
*GOLD/10: 1X TO 2.5X BASIC MEM
*RED/1: UNPRICED DUE TO SCARCITY
STATED ODDS 1:277

NNO AJ Styles	10.00	25.00
NNO Becky Lynch	6.00	15.00
NNO Charlotte Flair	8.00	20.00
NNO Dean Ambrose	6.00	15.00
NNO Dean Ambrose	6.00	15.00
NNO Dolph Ziggler	3.00	8.00
NNO Finn Balor	8.00	20.00
NNO Kalisto	3.00	8.00
NNO Kevin Owens/NXT Title	5.00	12.00
NNO Kevin Owens/Universal Title	5.00	12.00
NNO The Miz	4.00	10.00
NNO The New Day	4.00	10.00
NNO Rhyno & Heath Slater	2.00	5.00
NNO Roman Reigns/US Title	6.00	15.00
NNO Roman Reigns/WWE Title	6.00	15.00
NNO Rusev	4.00	10.00
NNO Sasha Banks	6.00	15.00
NNO Seth Rollins	6.00	15.00
NNO Triple H	5.00	12.00
NNO Zack Ryder	2.00	5.00

2017 Topps WWE Kiss

*GOLD/10: .6X TO 1.5X BASIC KISS
*RED/1: UNPRICED DUE TO SCARCITY
STATED ODDS 1:125

NNO Asuka	25.00	60.00
NNO Becky Lynch	15.00	40.00
NNO Charlotte Flair	25.00	60.00
NNO Maryse	20.00	50.00
NNO Naomi	15.00	40.00
NNO Summer Rae	12.00	30.00

2017 Topps WWE NXT Autographed TakeOver Brooklyn II Mat Relics

STATED PRINT RUN 10 SER.#'d SETS

NNO Asuka
NNO Austin Aries
NNO Bayley
NNO Samoa Joe
NNO Shinsuke Nakamura

2017 Topps WWE NXT TakeOver Brooklyn II Mat Relics

*BRONZE/199: SAME VALUE AS BASIC MEM
*BLUE/50: .5X TO 1.2X BASIC MEM
*SILVER/25: .6X TO 1.5X BASIC MEM
*GOLD/10: 1X TO 2.5X BASIC MEM
*RED/1: UNPRICED DUE TO SCARCITY
STATED ODDS 1:369

NNO Andrade Cien Almas	2.00	5.00
NNO Asuka	6.00	15.00
NNO Austin Aries	4.00	10.00
NNO Bayley	6.00	15.00
NNO Bobby Roode	5.00	12.00
NNO Johnny Gargano	2.00	5.00
NNO No Way Jose	2.00	5.00
NNO Samoa Joe	6.00	15.00
NNO Shinsuke Nakamura	5.00	12.00
NNO Tommaso Ciampa	2.00	5.00

2017 Topps WWE Roster Updates

COMPLETE SET (20)	8.00	20.00
RANDOMLY INSERTED INTO PACKS		
R1 Tamina	1.25	3.00
R2 Cedric Alexander	1.50	4.00
R3 Gran Metalik	2.00	5.00
R4 Jack Gallagher	2.00	5.00
R5 Lince Dorado	1.25	3.00
R6 Noam Dar	1.00	2.50
R7 Rich Swann	1.00	2.50
R8 Stephanie McMahon	1.25	3.00
R9 Shane McMahon	1.50	4.00
R10 Tom Phillips	1.00	2.50
R11 Andrade Cien Almas	1.00	2.50
R12 Mandy Rose	1.25	3.00
R13 Mike Rome	1.00	2.50
R14 No Way Jose	1.00	2.50
R15 Otis Dozovic	1.25	3.00
R16 Riddick Moss	1.25	3.00
R17 Tian Bing	1.00	2.50
R18 Tino Sabbatelli	1.25	3.00
R19 Tye Dillinger	1.00	2.50
R20 Tucker Knight	2.50	6.00

2017 Topps WWE Shirt Relics

*BLUE/50: .5X TO 1.2X BASIC MEM
*SILVER/25: .6X TO 1.5X BASIC MEM
*GOLD/10: 1X TO 2.5X BASIC MEM
*RED/1: UNPRICED DUE TO SCARCITY
STATED ODDS 1:185
STATED PRINT RUN 199 SER.#'d SETS

NNO Andrade Cien Almas	2.00	5.00
NNO Baron Corbin	3.00	8.00
NNO Bayley	6.00	15.00
NNO Big E	2.50	6.00
NNO Bobby Roode	5.00	12.00
NNO Bray Wyatt	5.00	12.00
NNO Carmella	5.00	12.00
NNO Cesaro	4.00	10.00
NNO Chad Gable	2.50	6.00
NNO Dolph Ziggler	3.00	8.00
NNO Heath Slater	2.00	5.00
NNO Jason Jordan	2.50	6.00
NNO John Cena	10.00	25.00
NNO Johnny Gargano	2.00	5.00
NNO Karl Anderson	2.00	5.00
NNO Kevin Owens	5.00	12.00
NNO Kofi Kingston	2.50	6.00
NNO The Miz	4.00	10.00
NNO No Way Jose	2.00	5.00
NNO Randy Orton	5.00	12.00
NNO Roman Reigns	6.00	15.00
NNO Seth Rollins	6.00	15.00
NNO Shinsuke Nakamura	5.00	12.00
NNO Tommaso Ciampa	2.00	5.00
NNO Xavier Woods	2.50	6.00

2017 Topps WWE Stone Cold Podcast

COMPLETE SET (8)	8.00	20.00
STATED ODDS 1:4		
1 Triple H	2.00	5.00
2 Paul Heyman	.75	2.00
3 Edge & Christian	2.00	5.00
4 Brock Lesnar	4.00	10.00
5 Big Show	1.00	2.50
6 Mick Foley	2.00	5.00
7 AJ Styles	4.00	10.00
8 Dean Ambrose	2.50	6.00

2017 Topps WWE Autographed SummerSlam 2016 Mat Relics

STATED PRINT RUN 10 SER.#'d SETS
UNPRICED DUE TO SCARCITY

NNO AJ Styles
NNO Big Cass
NNO Brock Lesnar
NNO Charlotte Flair
NNO Chris Jericho
NNO Dean Ambrose
NNO Dolph Ziggler
NNO Enzo Amore
NNO Finn Balor
NNO John Cena
NNO Karl Anderson
NNO Kevin Owens
NNO Kofi Kingston
NNO Luke Gallows
NNO Randy Orton
NNO Roman Reigns
NNO Rusev
NNO Sasha Banks
NNO Seth Rollins
NNO Xavier Woods

2017 Topps WWE SummerSlam 2016 Mat Relics

*BRONZE/199: SAME VALUE AS BASIC MEM
*BLUE/50: .5X TO 1.2X BASIC MEM
*SILVER/25: .6X TO 1.5X BASIC MEM
*GOLD/10: 1X TO 2.5X BASIC MEM
*RED/1: UNPRICED DUE TO SCARCITY
STATED ODDS 1:184
STATED PRINT RUN 299 SER.#'d SETS

NNO AJ Styles 10.00 25.00
NNO Big Cass 2.50 6.00
NNO Brock Lesnar 10.00 25.00
NNO Charlotte Flair 8.00 20.00
NNO Chris Jericho 5.00 12.00
NNO Dean Ambrose 6.00 15.00
NNO Dolph Ziggler 3.00 8.00
NNO Enzo Amore 6.00 15.00
NNO Finn Balor 8.00 20.00
NNO John Cena 10.00 25.00
NNO Karl Anderson 2.00 5.00
NNO Kevin Owens 5.00 12.00
NNO Kofi Kingston 2.50 6.00
NNO Luke Gallows 3.00 8.00
NNO Randy Orton 5.00 12.00
NNO Roman Reigns 6.00 15.00
NNO Rusev 4.00 10.00
NNO Sasha Banks 6.00 15.00
NNO Seth Rollins 6.00 15.00
NNO Xavier Woods 2.50 6.00

2017 Topps WWE Total Divas

COMPLETE SET (20) 12.00 30.00
STATED ODDS 1:2

1 Nikki Bella 1.25 3.00
2 Brie Bella 1.25 3.00
3 Natalya 1.00 2.50
4 The Bellas 1.25 3.00
5 Mandy Rose .60 1.50
6 Natalya 1.00 2.50
7 Nikki Bella 1.25 3.00
8 Nikki Bella 1.25 3.00
9 Alicia Fox .75 2.00
10 Natalya 1.00 2.50
11 Brie Bella 1.25 3.00
12 Brie Bella 1.25 3.00
13 John Cena 2.50 6.00
14 Daniel Bryan 2.00 5.00
15 Natalya 1.00 2.50
16 The Bella Twins 1.25 3.00
17 Nikki Bella 1.25 3.00
18 Mandy Rose .60 1.50
19 Alicia Fox .75 2.00
20 Nikki Bella 1.25 3.00

2017 Topps WWE Triple Autographs

STATED ODDS 1:1,762

NNO Bayley/Jax/Morgan
NNO Big E/Kingston/Woods 60.00 120.00
NNO Kay/Royce/Aliyah
NNO Lesnar/Goldberg/Bischoff 250.00 400.00
NNO C.Kelly/Fuentes/Young 75.00 150.00
NNO Martin/Kai/Victoria
NNO K.Kelly/Wilson/Phoenix 75.00 150.00

2017 Topps WWE Undertaker Tribute

COMPLETE SET (40) 15.00 40.00

1 Undertaker 2.00 5.00
2 Undertaker 2.00 5.00
3 Undertaker 2.00 3.00
4 Undertaker 2.00 5.00
5 Undertaker 2.00 5.00
6 Undertaker 2.00 5.00
7 Undertaker 2.00 5.00
8 Undertaker 2.00 5.00
9 Undertaker 2.00 5.00
10 Undertaker 2.00 5.00
11 Undertaker 2.00 5.00
12 Undertaker 2.00 5.00
13 Undertaker 2.00 5.00
14 Undertaker 2.00 5.00
15 Undertaker 2.00 5.00
16 Undertaker 2.00 5.00
17 Undertaker 2.00 5.00
18 Undertaker 2.00 5.00
19 Undertaker 2.00 5.00
20 Undertaker 2.00 5.00
21 Undertaker 2.00 5.00
22 Undertaker 2.00 5.00
23 Undertaker 2.00 5.00
24 Undertaker 2.00 5.00
25 Undertaker 2.00 5.00
26 Undertaker 2.00 5.00
27 Undertaker 2.00 5.00
28 Undertaker 2.00 5.00
29 Undertaker 2.00 5.00
30 Undertaker 2.00 5.00
31 Undertaker 2.00 5.00
32 Undertaker 2.00 5.00
33 Undertaker 2.00 5.00
34 Undertaker 2.00 5.00
35 Undertaker 2.00 5.00
36 Undertaker 2.00 5.00
37 Undertaker 2.00 5.00
38 Undertaker 2.00 5.00
39 Undertaker 2.00 5.00
40 Undertaker 2.00 5.00

2018 Topps WWE

COMPLETE SET W/O SP (100) 8.00 20.00
*BRONZE: .5X TO 1.2X BASIC CARDS
*BLUE/99: .75X TO 2X BASIC CARDS
*SILVER/25: 2X TO 5X BASIC CARDS
*GOLD/10: UNPRICED DUE TO SCARCITY
*RED/1: UNPRICED DUE TO SCARCITY
*P.P.BLACK/1: UNPRICED DUE TO SCARCITY
*P.P.CYAN/1: UNPRICED DUE TO SCARCITY
*P.P.MAGENTA/1: UNPRICED DUE TO SCARCITY
*P.P.YELLOW/1: UNPRICED DUE TO SCARCITY

1A Adam Cole RC .30 .75
1B Adam Cole SP/Shirtless 12.00 30.00
2A AJ Styles 1.00 2.50
2B AJ Styles SP/Shirtless 20.00 50.00
3 Akam .25 .60
4 Akira Tozawa .40 1.00
5A Aleister Black .30 .75
5B Aleister Black SP/Mid-Air 6.00 15.00
6 Alicia Fox .40 1.00
7 Andrade Cien Almas .40 1.00
8 Apollo Crews .25 .60
9 Ariya Daivari .25 .60
10 Asuka .75 2.00
11A Big E .30 .75
11B Big E SP/Microphone 2.50 6.00
12 Billie Kay .50 1.25
13 Bo Dallas .25 .60
14A Bobby Roode .40 1.00
14B Bobby Roode SP/In Action 10.00 25.00
15 Bobby Fish RC .25 .60
16 Booker T .40 1.00
17 The Brian Kendrick .40 1.00
18 Brie Bella .50 1.25
19 Byron Saxton .25 .60
20A Carmella .50 1.25
20B Carmella SP/In Ring 12.00 30.00
21 Cathy Kelley .50 1.25
22 Cedric Alexander .25 .60
23 Chad Gable .25 .60
24A Charlotte Flair .75 2.00
24B Charlotte Flair SP/Close-Up 12.00 30.00
25 Christy St. Cloud RC .30 .75
26 Curt Hawkins .25 .60
27 Curtis Axel .25 .60
28 Daniel Bryan .60 1.50
29 Drew Gulak .25 .60
30A Drew McIntyre .40 1.00
30B Drew McIntyre SP/Close-Up 2.50 6.00
31 Elias .60 1.50
32A Ember Moon .50 1.25
32B Ember Moon SP/Between Ropes 6.00 15.00
33 Gentleman Jack Gallagher .30 .75
34 Gran Metalik .25 .60
35 Greg Hamilton .40 1.00
36 Heath Slater .25 .60
37 Hideo Itami .25 .60
38 Jerry The King Lawler .50 1.25
39 Jey Uso .25 .60
40 Jim Ross .40 1.00
41 Jimmy Uso .25 .60
42A Jinder Mahal .30 .75
42B Jinder Mahal SP/Shirtless
43 John Cena 1.00 2.50
44 Johnny Gargano .25 .60
45A Kairi Sane RC .60 1.50
45B Kairi Sane SP/Mid-Air
46 Kayla Braxton RC .25 .60
47A Kevin Owens .60 1.50
47B Kevin Owens SP/Red Background 8.00 20.00
48A Kofi Kingston .30 .75
48B Kofi Kingston SP/Cross Body 2.50 6.00
49 Kurt Angle .60 1.50
50A Kyle O'Reilly RC .30 .75
50B Kyle O'Reilly SP/Straightfaced 2.50 6.00
51 Lana .60 1.50
52 Lita .60 1.50
53 Maria Kanellis .60 1.50
54 Maryse .50 1.25
55 Mauro Ranallo .25 .60
56 Mean Gene Okerlund .30 .75
57 Michael Cole .25 .60
58 Mickie James .50 1.25
59 Mike Kanellis .60 1.50
60 Mike Rome .25 .60
61 The Miz .50 1.25
62 Montez Ford .25 .60
63 Mr. McMahon .50 1.25
64 Mustafa Ali .25 .60
65 Naomi .30 .75
66A Natalya .30 .75
66B Natalya SP/Pointing Up 12.00 30.00
67 Neville .40 1.00
68 Nia Jax .40 1.00
69 Nigel McGuinness RC .25 .60
70 Noam Dar .25 .60
71 Paige .60 1.50
72 Paul Ellering .30 .75
73 Percy Watson .25 .60
74 Pete Dunne RC .25 .60
75 Peyton Royce .60 1.50
76 Rezar .25 .60
77 Rhyno .25 .60
78 Big Cass .30 .75
79 The Rock 1.25 3.00
80 Roderick Strong .25 .60
81 Samir Singh RC .25 .60
82 Shane McMahon .50 1.25
83 Shelton Benjamin .30 .75
84 Sin Cara .30 .75
85 Sonya Deville .50 1.25
86 Stephanie McMahon .50 1.25
87 Sunil Singh RC .25 .60
88 Tamina .25 .60
89 Titus O'Neil .25 .60
90 TJP .30 .75
91 Tommaso Ciampa .25 .60
92 Tony Nese .25 .60
93 Tony Chimel .25 .60
94 Triple H .60 1.50
95 Tyler Bate .25 .60
96A Undertaker 1.00 2.50
96B Undertaker SP/Kneeling 10.00 25.00
97 William Regal .40 1.00
98A Xavier Woods .30 .75
98B Xavier Woods SP/Cross Body 5.00 12.00
99 Zack Ryder .25 .60
100 Zelina Vega RC .25 .60

2018 Topps WWE Autographed Commemorative Championship Medallions

STATED PRINT RUN 10 SER.#'d SETS
UNPRICED DUE TO SCARCITY

CCAJ AJ Styles
CCAT Akira Tozawa
CCBW Bray Wyatt
CCCJ Chris Jericho
CCJM Jinder Mahal
CCKO Kevin Owens
CCNA Natalya
CCNO Naomi
CCRO Randy Orton
CCTM The Miz

2018 Topps WWE Autographed Dual Mat Relics

STATED PRINT RUN 10 SER.#'d SETS
UNPRICED DUE TO SCARCITY

DMRDB Daniel Bryan
DMRSM Stephanie McMahon
DMRTH Triple H
DMRUT Undertaker
DNRDA Dean Ambrose

2018 Topps WWE Autographed NXT TakeOver Brooklyn III Mat Relics

STATED PRINT RUN 10 SER.#'d SETS
UNPRICED DUE TO SCARCITY

TBRAB Aleister Black
TBRAC Adam Cole
TBRAS Asuka
TBRBR Bobby Roode
TBRDM Drew McIntyre
TBREM Ember Moon
TBREY Eric Young
TBRHI Hideo Itami
TBRJG Johnny Gargano

2018 Topps WWE Autographed Shirt Relics

STATED PRINT RUN 10 SER.#'d SETS
UNPRICED DUE TO SCARCITY

SRAE Aiden English
SRAF Alicia Fox
SREY Eric Young
SRGD Goldust
SRJJ JoJo
SRNA Natalya
SRRY Renee Young
SRSJ Samoa Joe

2018 Topps WWE Autographed SummerSlam 2017 Mat Relics

STATED PRINT RUN 10 SER.#'d SETS
UNPRICED DUE TO SCARCITY

SMRAJ AJ Styles
SMRBC Baron Corbin
SMRBS Braun Strowman
SMRBW Bray Wyatt
SMRCO Cesaro
SMRDA Dean Ambrose
SMRJM Jinder Mahal
SMRKO Kevin Owens
SMRNA Natalya
SMRNO Naomi
SMRSB Sasha Banks
SMRSH Sheamus
SMRSJ Samoa Joe
SMRSN Shinsuke Nakamura

2018 Topps WWE Autographs

*BLUE/50: .5X TO 1.2X BASIC AUTOS
*SILVER/25: .6X TO 1.5X BASIC AUTOS
*GOLD/10: UNPRICED DUE TO SCARCITY
*RED/1: UNPRICED DUE TO SCARCITY

1 Adam Cole 20.00 50.00
2 AJ Styles 15.00 40.00
4 Akira Tozawa 5.00 12.00
5 Aleister Black 10.00 25.00
8 Apollo Crews 4.00 10.00
10 Asuka 15.00 40.00
11 Big E 8.00 20.00
14 Bobby Roode 6.00 15.00
15 Bobby Fish 12.00 30.00
18 Brie Bella 10.00 25.00
20 Carmella 12.00 30.00
24 Charlotte Flair 15.00 40.00
30 Drew McIntyre 8.00 20.00
32 Ember Moon 10.00 25.00
42 Jinder Mahal 5.00 12.00
45 Kairi Sane 30.00 75.00
47 Kevin Owens 6.00 15.00
48 Kofi Kingston 6.00 15.00
49 Kurt Angle 12.00 30.00
50 Kyle O'Reilly 12.00 30.00
61 The Miz 5.00 12.00

65 Naomi 4.00 10.00
66 Natalya 6.00 15.00
68 Nia Jax 10.00 25.00
80 Roderick Strong 5.00 12.00
83 Shelton Benjamin 5.00 12.00
88 Tamina 4.00 10.00
89 Titus O'Neil 5.00 12.00
98 Xavier Woods 6.00 15.00

2018 Topps WWE Commemorative Championship Medallions

*BRONZE/99: .5X TO 1.2X BASIC MEM
*BLUE/50: .6X TO 1.5X BASIC MEM
*SILVER/25: .75X TO 2X BASIC MEM
*GOLD/10: UNPRICED DUE TO SCARCITY
*RED/1: UNPRICED DUE TO SCARCITY

CCAA American Alpha 3.00 8.00
CCAB Alexa Bliss 10.00 25.00
CCAJ AJ Styles 6.00 15.00
CCAS Dean Ambrose & Seth Rollins 8.00 20.00
CCAT Akira Tozawa 3.00 8.00
CCAX Alexa Bliss 8.00 20.00
CCBA Bayley 8.00 20.00
CCBL Brock Lesnar 10.00 25.00
CCBW Bray Wyatt 3.00 8.00
CCCJ Chris Jericho 4.00 10.00
CCCS Cesaro & Sheamus 2.50 6.00
CCGA Luke Gallows & Karl Anderson 2.50 6.00
CCHB The Hardy Boyz 6.00 15.00
CCJC John Cena 5.00 12.00
CCJM Jinder Mahal 2.50 6.00
CCKA Kalisto 2.50 6.00
CCKO Kevin Owens 4.00 10.00
CCNA Natalya 2.50 6.00
CCND The New Day 2.50 6.00
CCNO Naomi 2.50 6.00
CCRO Randy Orton 4.00 10.00
CCTM The Miz 2.50 6.00
CCTU The Usos 3.00 8.00
CCWF The Wyatt Family 5.00 12.00

2018 Topps WWE Dual Mat Relics

*SILVER/25: .6X TO 1.5X BASIC MEM
*GOLD/10: UNPRICED DUE TO SCARCITY
*RED/1: UNPRICED DUE TO SCARCITY

DMRBL Brock Lesnar 10.00 25.00
DMRBY Bayley 10.00 25.00
DMRDA Dean Ambrose 6.00 15.00
DMRDB Daniel Bryan 8.00 20.00
DMRRR Roman Reigns 6.00 15.00
DMRSM Stephanie McMahon 15.00 40.00
DMRSR Seth Rollins 5.00 12.00
DMRTH Triple H 6.00 15.00
DMRTR The Rock 8.00 20.00
DMRUT Undertaker 12.00 30.00

2018 Topps WWE Evolution

COMPLETE SET (50) 15.00 40.00
E1 The Giant .40 1.00
E2 Big Show .40 1.00
E3 Big Show .40 1.00
E4 Booker T .60 1.50
E5 G.I. Bro .60 1.50
E6 King Booker .60 1.50
E7 Booker T .60 1.50
E8 Brock Lesnar 1.50 4.00
E9 Brock Lesnar 1.50 4.00
E10 Chris Jericho 1.00 2.50
E11 Chris Jericho 1.00 2.50
E12 Daniel Bryan 1.00 2.50
E13 Daniel Bryan 1.00 2.50
E14 Daniel Bryan 1.00 2.50
E15 The Rock 2.00 5.00
E16 The Rock 2.00 5.00
E17 Goldust .75 2.00
E18 Seven .75 2.00
E19 American Nightmare Dustin Rhodes .75 2.00
E20 Goldust .75 2.00
E21 Jerry The King Lawler .75 2.00
E22 Jerry The King Lawler .75 2.00
E23 John Cena 1.50 4.00
E24 Doctor of Thuganomics John Cena 1.50 4.00
E25 John Cena 1.50 4.00
E26 Kane .60 1.50
E27 Kane .60 1.50
E28 Corporate Kane .60 1.50
E29 Kane .60 1.50
E30 Kurt Angle 1.00 2.50
E31 Kurt Angle 1.00 2.50
E32 Mark Henry .50 1.25
E33 Mark Henry .50 1.25
E34 Mark Henry .50 1.25
E35 Cactus Jack .75 2.00
E36 Mankind .75 2.00
E37 Dude Love .75 2.00
E38 Mick Foley .75 2.00
E39 Randy Orton 1.00 2.50
E40 Randy Orton 1.00 2.50
E41 Hunter Hearst Helmsley 1.00 2.50
E42 Triple H 1.00 2.50
E43 The Game Triple H 1.00 2.50
E44 COO Triple H 1.00 2.50
E45 Undertaker 1.50 4.00
E46 Undertaker 1.50 4.00
E47 Undertaker 1.50 4.00
E48 The American Bad-Ass Undertaker 1.50 4.00
E49 Big Evil Undertaker 1.50 4.00
E50 Undertaker 1.50 4.00

2018 Topps WWE Kiss

*GOLD/10: UNPRICED DUE TO SCARCITY
*RED/1: UNPRICED DUE TO SCARCITY

KBX Billie Kay 20.00 50.00
KDB Dana Brooke 15.00 40.00
KEM Ember Moon 20.00 50.00
KKS Kairi Saine 30.00 75.00
KLM Liv Morgan 25.00 60.00
KMA Maryse 15.00 40.00
KNA Natalya 15.00 40.00
KPR Peyton Royce 25.00 60.00
KSD Sonya Deville 50.00 100.00

2018 Topps WWE Kiss Autographs

*GOLD/10: UNPRICED DUE TO SCARCITY
*RED/1: UNPRICED DUE TO SCARCITY
STATED PRINT RUN 25 SER.#'d SETS

NNO Billie Kay 30.00 75.00
NNO Dana Brooke 30.00 75.00
NNO Ember Moon 60.00 120.00
NNO Kairi Saine 50.00 100.00
NNO Liv Morgan 50.00 100.00
NNO Maryse 50.00 100.00
NNO Mickie James 75.00 150.00
NNO Natalya 30.00 75.00
NNO Peyton Royce 30.00 75.00
NNO Sonya Deville 60.00 120.00

2018 Topps WWE NXT TakeOver Brooklyn III Mat Relics

*BRONZE/199: .5X TO 1.2X BASIC MEM
*BLUE/50: .6X TO 1.5X BASIC MEM
*SILVER/25: .75X TO 2X BASIC MEM
*GOLD/10: UNPRICED DUE TO SCARCITY
*RED/1: UNPRICED DUE TO SCARCITY

TBRAA Andrade Cien Almas 3.00 8.00
TBRAB Aleister Black 3.00 8.00
TBRAC Adam Cole 6.00 15.00
TBRAS Asuka 6.00 15.00
TBRBR Bobby Roode 3.00 8.00
TBRDM Drew McIntyre 3.00 8.00
TBREM Ember Moon 4.00 10.00
TBREY Eric Young 3.00 8.00
TBRHI Hideo Itami 3.00 8.00
TBRJG Johnny Gargano 3.00 8.00

2018 Topps WWE Roster Updates

COMPLETE SET (20) 15.00 40.00
R1 Aiden English 1.00 2.50
R2 Aliyah 1.50 4.00
R3 Angelo Dawkins 1.00 2.50
R4 Buddy Murphy 1.25 3.00
R5 Charly Caruso 1.50 4.00
R6 Corey Graves 1.25 3.00
R7 Dana Brooke 2.00 5.00
R8 Dasha Fuentes 1.50 4.00
R9 Epico Colon 1.00 2.50
R10 JoJo 1.00 2.50
R11 Konnor 1.00 2.50
R12 Lars Sullivan 1.00 2.50
R13 Lio Rush 1.00 2.50
R14 Primo Colon 1.00 2.50
R15 R-Truth 1.25 3.00
R16 Renee Young 1.50 4.00
R17 Sarah Logan 1.00 2.50
R18 Tom Phillips 1.00 2.50
R19 Viktor 1.00 2.50
R20 Wesley Blake 1.25 3.00

2018 Topps WWE Shirt Relics

*BLUE/50: .6X TO 1.5X BASIC MEM
*SILVER/25: .75X TO 2X BASIC MEM
*GOLD/10: UNPRICED DUE TO SCARCITY
*RED/1: UNPRICED DUE TO SCARCITY

SRAE Aiden English 3.00 8.00
SRAF Alicia Fox 3.00 8.00
SRAW Alexander Wolfe 2.50 6.00
SRBL Brock Lesnar 6.00 15.00
SRDW Dash Wilder 2.50 6.00
SREY Eric Young 3.00 8.00
SRGD Goldust 3.00 8.00
SRJC John Cena 8.00 20.00
SRJJ JoJo 5.00 12.00
SRNA Natalya 3.00 8.00
SRNC Nikki Cross 6.00 15.00
SRRR Roman Reigns 4.00 10.00
SRRY Renee Young 6.00 15.00
SRSD Scott Dawson 3.00 8.00
SRSJ Samoa Joe 4.00 10.00

2018 Topps WWE SummerSlam 2017 Mat Relics

*BRONZE/199: .5X TO 1.2X BASIC MEM
*BLUE/50: .6X TO 1.5X BASIC MEM
*SILVER/25: .75X TO 2X BASIC MEM
*GOLD/10: UNPRICED DUE TO SCARCITY
*RED/1: UNPRICED DUE TO SCARCITY

SMRAB Alexa Bliss 8.00 20.00
SMRAJ AJ Styles 5.00 12.00
SMRBC Baron Corbin 2.50 6.00
SMRBL Brock Lesnar 4.00 10.00
SMRBS Braun Strowman 5.00 12.00
SMRBW Bray Wyatt 2.50 6.00
SMRCO Cesaro 2.50 6.00
SMRDA Dean Ambrose 2.50 6.00
SMRFB Finn Balor 4.00 10.00
SMRJC John Cena 5.00 12.00
SMRJM Jinder Mahal 2.50 6.00
SMRKO Kevin Owens 2.50 6.00
SMRNA Natalya 3.00 8.00
SMRNO Naomi 2.50 6.00
SMRRR Roman Reigns 3.00 8.00
SMRSB Sasha Banks 8.00 20.00
SMRSH Sheamus 2.50 6.00
SMRSJ Samoa Joe 2.50 6.00
SMRSN Shinsuke Nakamura 4.00 10.00
SMRSR Seth Rollins 2.50 6.00

2018 Topps WWE Triple Autographs

STATED PRINT RUN 10 SER.#'d SETS
UNPRICED DUE TO SCARCITY

TADAY Big E/Kingston/Woods
TAERA Cole/Fish/O'Reilly
TAHOJ Ambrose/Rollins/Reigns
TAMIZ Miz/Axel/Dallas
TARAW HHH/S.McMahon/Angle
TATWF Wyatt/Harper/Rowan

2021 Topps WWE

COMPLETE SET (200) 15.00 40.00
*FOILBOARD: .6X TO 1.5X BASIC CARDS
*AQUA/299: .75X TO 2X BASIC CARDS
*LT GREEN/199: 1.2X TO 3X BASIC CARDS
*DK GREEN/99: 1.5X TO 4X BASIC CARDS
*CITRINE/75: 2X TO 5X BASIC CARDS
*ORANGE/50: 2.5X TO 6X BASIC CARDS
*PURPLE/25: UNPRICED DUE TO SCARCITY
*BLUE/10: UNPRICED DUE TO SCARCITY
*BLACK/5: UNPRICED DUE TO SCARCITY
*RED/1: UNPRICED DUE TO SCARCITY
*P.P.BLACK/1: UNPRICED DUE TO SCARCITY
*P.P.CYAN/1: UNPRICED DUE TO SCARCITY
*P.P.MAGENTA/1: UNPRICED DUE TO SCARCITY
*P.P.YELLOW/1: UNPRICED DUE TO SCARCITY

1 Kofi Kingston .60 1.50
2 Otis .30 .75
3 Usos .50 1.25
4 Miz .40 1.00
5 King Corbin's Court .50 1.25
6 Drew McIntyre .60 1.50
7 John Morrison .50 1.25
8 John Morrison .50 1.25
9 Roman Reigns 1.25 3.00
10 Edge 1.00 2.50
11 Drew McIntyre .60 1.50
12 Miz & John Morrison .50 1.25
13 King Corbin .25 .60
14 Randy Orton .75 2.00
15 Angel Garza .30 .75
16 Drew McIntyre .60 1.50
17 Angel Garza .30 .75
18 King Corbin .25 .60
19 Drew McIntyre .60 1.50
20 Street Profits .50 1.25
21 Usos .60 1.50
22 Seth Rollins .60 1.50
23 Randy Orton .75 2.00
24 Roman Reigns 1.25 3.00
25 Undertaker 1.25 3.00
26 Miz & John Morrison .50 1.25
27 Angel Garza .30 .75
28 Goldberg 1.00 2.50
29 Usos .40 1.00
30 Angel Garza .30 .75
31 Randy Orton .75 2.00
32 Dolph Ziggler .50 1.25
33 Miz & John Morrison .50 1.25
34 Sami Zayn .60 1.50
35 AJ Styles .75 2.00
36 Edge 1.00 2.50
37 Elias .25 .60
38 Edge 1.00 2.50
39 Elias .25 .60
40 Dolph Ziggler .50 1.25
41 Street Profits .30 .75
42 Miz & John Morrison .50 1.25
43 King Corbin .25 .60
44 Kevin Owens & Street Profits .25 .60
45 Cesaro .25 .60
46 John Morrison .50 1.25
47 Kevin Owens .50 1.25
48 Undertaker 1.25 3.00
49 Elias .25 .60
50 Otis .30 .75
51 Edge 1.00 2.50
52 Street Profits .50 1.25
53 Drew McIntyre .60 1.50
54 Drew McIntyre .60 1.50
55 Sheamus .40 1.00
56 Seth Rollins .60 1.50
57 Big E .50 1.25
58 Apollo Crews .30 .75
59 Rey Mysterio .60 1.50
60 Drew McIntyre .60 1.50
61 King Corbin .25 .60
62 Lucha House Party .40 1.00
63 Drew McIntyre .60 1.50
64 Otis .30 .75
65 AJ Styles .75 2.00
66 Viking Raiders .25 .60
67 New Day .50 1.25
68 Drew McIntyre .60 1.50
69 Otis .30 .75
70 Bobby Lashley .60 1.50
71 Rey Mysterio .60 1.50
72 Randy Orton 1.00 2.50
73 Elias .25 .60
74 Bobby Lashley .25 .60
75 Drew McIntyre .60 1.50
76 AJ Styles .75 2.00
77 Jeff Hardy .60 1.50
78 Apollo Crews .30 .75
79 Drew McIntyre .60 1.50
80 Drew McIntyre .60 1.50
81 Sheamus .40 1.00
82 Jeff Hardy .60 1.50

83 Bobby Lashley .60 1.50
84 Bobby Lashley & MVP .60 1.50
85 AJ Styles .75 2.00
86 Cesaro & Nakamura .60 1.50
87 Sheamus .40 1.00
88 Drew McIntyre .60 1.50
89 Randy Orton .75 2.00
90 Cesaro & Nakamura .60 1.50
91 Seth Rollins .60 1.50
92 Drew McIntyre .60 1.50
93 Street Profits .30 .75
94 Seth Rollins .60 1.50
95 Drew McIntyre .60 1.50
96 AJ Styles .75 2.00
97 Alexa Bliss 1.50 4.00
98 Aliyah .50 1.25
99 Asuka 1.00 2.50
100 Becky Lynch 1.00 2.50
101 Bobby Lashley .60 1.50
102 Cedric Alexander .25 .60
103 Charlotte Flair 1.25 3.00
104 Damian Priest .40 1.00
105 Dana Brooke .25 .60
106 Drew Gulak .30 .75
107 Drew McIntyre .60 1.50
108 Doudrop .40 1.00
109 Elias .25 .60
110 Eva Marie .60 1.50
111 Jeff Hardy .60 1.50
112 Jaxson Ryker .25 .60
113 John Morrison .50 1.25
114 Keith Lee .50 1.25
115 Kofi Kingston .60 1.50
116 Lacey Evans .60 1.50
117 Mace .25 .60
118 Mansoor RC .25 .60
119 MVP .25 .60
120 Mustafa Ali .30 .75
121 Naomi .30 .75
122 Nia Jax .50 1.25
123 Nikki A.S.H. .50 1.25
124 Omos RC .50 1.25
125 Randy Orton .75 2.00
126 Reggie RC .30 .75
127 Rhea Ripley .75 2.00
128 Ricochet .50 1.25
129 Riddle .60 1.50
130 Shayna Baszler .50 1.25
131 Sheamus .40 1.00
132 Shelton Benjamin .40 1.00
133 T-Bar .30 .75
134 The Miz .40 1.00
135 Xavier Woods .25 .60
136 Angelo Dawkins .30 .75
137 Apollo Crews .30 .75
138 Baron Corbin .25 .60
139 Bayley .60 1.50
140 Bianca Belair .60 1.50
141 Big E .50 1.25
142 Carmella .60 1.50
143 Cesaro .25 .60
144 Chad Gable .25 .60
145 Commander Azeez RC .30 .75
146 Dolph Ziggler .50 1.25
147 Dominik Mysterio RC .30 .75
148 Finn Balor .60 1.50
149 Jey Uso .25 .60
150 Jimmy Uso .25 .60
151 Kevin Owens .50 1.25
152 King Nakamura .60 1.50
153 Liv Morgan 1.00 2.50
154 Montez Ford .25 .60
155 Natalya .40 1.00
156 Nox .60 1.50
157 Otis .30 .75
158 Rey Mysterio .60 1.50
159 Rick Boogs RC .25 .60
160 Robert Roode .30 .75
161 Roman Reigns 1.25 3.00
162 Sami Zayn .40 1.00
163 Sasha Banks 1.25 3.00
164 Seth Rollins .60 1.50
165 Shotzi 1.00 2.50
166 Sonya Deville .60 1.50
167 Tamina .30 .75
168 Toni Storm .75 2.00
169 Zelina Vega .50 1.25
170 Austin Theory .50 1.25
171 Candice LeRae 1.00 2.50
172 Dakota Kai .50 1.25
173 Dexter Lumis .25 .60
174 Ember Moon .30 .75
175 Io Shirai .50 1.25
176 Indi Hartwell RC .75 2.00
177 Isaiah "Swerve" Scott .40 1.00
178 Johnny Gargano .50 1.25
179 Karrion Kross 1.00 2.50
180 Kyle O'Reilly .40 1.00
181 Mandy Rose 1.25 3.00
182 Pete Dunne .50 1.25
183 Raquel Gonzalez .60 1.50
184 Roderick Strong .40 1.00
185 Samoa Joe .50 1.25
186 Santos Escobar .40 1.00
187 Sarray RC .30 .75
188 Scarlett 1.25 3.00
189 Timothy Thatcher RC .25 .60
190 Tommaso Ciampa .60 1.50
191 Walter .60 1.50
192 Batista .50 1.25
193 British Bulldog .40 1.00
194 Edge 1.00 2.50
195 Goldberg 1.00 2.50
196 JBL .25 .60
197 Kane .40 1.00
198 Molly Holly .30 .75
199 Rob Van Dam .50 1.25
200 John Cena 1.25 3.00

2021 Topps WWE Autographed Mat Relics

*RED/1: UNPRICED DUE TO SCARCITY
STATED ODDS 1:4,986
STATED PRINT RUN 10 SER.#'d SETS

MRAB Big E
MRAR Riddle
MRMY Mia Yim
MRAAG Angel Garza
MRAFA Fabian Aichner
MRAFB Finn Balor
MRAJD Jordan Devlin
MRAJG Johnny Gargano
MRAKL Keith Lee
MRAMB Marcel Barthel
MRARM Rey Mysterio
MRARR Rhea Ripley
MRARS Roderick Strong
MRATC Tommaso Ciampa
MRAWT WALTER
MRABOB Bobby Lashley
MRADOM Dominik Mysterio
MRANIA Nia Jax
MRAROM Roman Reigns
MRASHA Shayna Baszler

2021 Topps WWE Autographs

*GREEN/99: .6X TO 1.5X BASIC AUTOS
*ORANGE/50: .75X TO 2X BASIC AUTOS
*PURPLE/25: UNPRICED DUE TO SCARCITY
*BLUE/10: UNPRICED DUE TO SCARCITY
*BLACK/5: UNPRICED DUE TO SCARCITY
*RED/1: UNPRICED DUE TO SCARCITY
*P.P.BLACK/1: UNPRICED DUE TO SCARCITY
*P.P.CYAN/1: UNPRICED DUE TO SCARCITY
*P.P.MAGENTA/1: UNPRICED DUE TO SCARCITY
*P.P.YELLOW/1: UNPRICED DUE TO SCARCITY
STATED PRINT RUN 150 SER.#'d SETS

AC Carmella 12.00 30.00
AE Big E 6.00 15.00
AAS AJ Styles 10.00 25.00
AAT Austin Theory 5.00 12.00
ABB Bianca Belair 12.00 30.00
ABE Becky Lynch 50.00 100.00
ABL Bobby Lashley 10.00 25.00
ACF Charlotte Flair 30.00 75.00
ADM Drew McIntyre 15.00 40.00
ADP Damian Priest 6.00 15.00
AED Edge 25.00 60.00
AFB Finn Balor 10.00 25.00
AJH Jeff Hardy 15.00 40.00
AJU Jey Uso 6.00 15.00
AKC King Corbin 5.00 12.00
AKF Kofi Kingston 6.00 15.00
AKK Karrion Kross
AKL Keith Lee
AKN Asuka 25.00 60.00
AKO Kevin Owens 8.00 20.00
ALM Liv Morgan 30.00 75.00
AMR Riddle 10.00 25.00
AOT Otis 6.00 15.00
AQS Shayna Baszler 6.00 15.00
ARH Rhea Ripley 12.00 30.00
ARM Rey Mysterio 15.00 40.00
ARR Roman Reigns 30.00 75.00
ARU Robert Roode 5.00 12.00
ASB Sasha Banks 50.00 100.00
ASD Sonya Deville 8.00 20.00
ASN Shinsuke Nakamura 10.00 25.00
ASR Seth Rollins 10.00 25.00
ASZ Sami Zayn 6.00 15.00
AUN Apollo Crews 5.00 12.00
AXW Xavier Woods 5.00 12.00
AMVP MVP 5.00 12.00

2021 Topps WWE Coolest Mixed Tag Teams

COMPLETE SET (11) 6.00 15.00
STATED ODDS 1:10

MT1 Charlotte Flair/AJ Styles 1.50 4.00
MT2 Finn Balor/Bayley .75 2.00
MT3 John Cena/Trish Stratus 1.50 4.00
MT4 Sasha Banks/Roman Reigns 1.50 4.00
MT5 R-Truth/Carmella .75 2.00
MT6 The Miz/Asuka 1.25 3.00
MT7 Stephanie McMahon/Triple H 1.25 3.00
MT8 Jimmy Uso/Naomi .40 1.00
MT9 Seth Rollins/Becky Lynch 1.25 3.00
MT10 Johnny Gargano/Candice LeRae 1.25 3.00
MT11 Natalya/Shinsuke Nakamura .75 2.00

2021 Topps WWE Hall of Fame Tribute

COMPLETE SET (18) 8.00 20.00
STATED ODDS 1:12

HOF1 Razor .50 1.25
HOF2 Diesel .50 1.25
HOF3 ...The New World Order .50 1.25
HOF4 Hollywood Hulk Hogan 1.50 4.00
HOF5 The Outsiders .50 1.25
HOF6 The nWo PPV 1.50 4.00
HOF7 Syxx .40 1.00
HOF8 Kevin Nash .50 1.25
HOF9 Fingerpoke of Doom .50 1.25
HOF10 Scott Hall .75 2.00
HOF11 Hollywood Hulk Hogan 1.50 4.00
HOF12 Kevin Nash .50 1.25
HOF13 Scott Hall .50 1.25
HOF14 Scott Hall .50 1.25
HOF15 The nWo 1.50 4.00
HOF16 The nWo .50 1.25
HOF17 Scott Hall .50 1.25
HOF18 Icon vs. Icon 3.00 8.00

2021 Topps WWE Hall of Fame Tribute Autographs

STATED PRINT RUN 25 SER.#'d SETS

NWOKN Kevin Nash 15.00 40.00
NWOSW Syxx 12.00 30.00

2021 Topps WWE Locker Room Veterans Booklet Autograph

ABC Miz/R-Truth/Rey/Orton/J.Hardy/Benjamin
Sheamus/Natalya/Edge/Lashley/MVP/Kingston

2021 Topps WWE Manufactured Match Film Strip Relics

*AQUA/299: .5X TO 1.2X BASIC MEM
*LT GREEN/199: .6X TO 1.5X BASIC MEM
*DK GREEN/99: .75X TO 2X BASIC MEM
*CITRINE/75: 1X TO 2.5X BASIC MEM
*ORANGE/50: 1.2X TO 3X BASIC MEM
*PURPLE/25: UNPRICED DUE TO SCARCITY
*BLUE/10: UNPRICED DUE TO SCARCITY
*BLACK/5: UNPRICED DUE TO SCARCITY
*RED/1: UNPRICED DUE TO SCARCITY
STATED ODDS 1:74

FSAJ AJ Styles/John Cena 6.00 15.00
FSBB Bret Hart/British Bulldog 5.00 12.00
FSBC Becky Lynch/Charlotte Flair 8.00 20.00
FSBP Bret Hart/Mr. Perfect 5.00 12.00
FSHA Bret Hart/Steve Austin 6.00 15.00
FSHG Hulk Hogan/Andre the Giant 10.00 25.00
FSHM Bret Hart/Shawn Michaels 5.00 12.00
FSHU Hulk Hogan/Ultimate Warrior 15.00 40.00
FSJE John Cena/Edge
FSKU Undertaker/Kane 5.00 12.00
FSLU Bobby Lashley/Umaga 5.00 12.00
FSMF Shawn Michaels/Ric Flair 5.00 12.00
FSMR Macho Man Randy Savage/Ric Flair6.00 15.00
FSNC Natalya/Charlotte Flair
FSPR Mr. Perfect/Ric Flair 4.00 12.00
FSRC The Rock/John Cena 6.00 15.00
FSRH The Rock/Hulk Hogan 10.00 25.00
FSRS Razor Ramon/Shawn Michaels 10.00 25.00
FSSB Sasha Banks/Bayley 6.00 15.00
FSSC Sami Zayn/Cesaro 4.00 12.00
FSSM Shawn Michaels/Mankind 5.00 12.00
FSSS Macho Man Randy
Savage/Ricky Steamboat 12.00 30.00
FSST Shawn Michaels/Triple H 5.00 12.00
FSSW Macho King Randy Savage
Ultimate Warrior 8.00 20.00
FSTJ The Miz/John Cena
FSBCA Becky Lynch/Charlotte Flair/Asuka6.00 15.00
FSFBL Charlotte Flair/Sasha
Banks/Becky Lynch 5.00 12.00
FSRA2 The Rock/Steve Austin 8.00 20.00
FSRA3 The Rock/Steve Austin 8.00 20.00
FSRC2 The Rock/John Cena 6.00 15.00
FSUH2 Undertaker/Triple H 6.00 15.00
FSUH3 Undertaker/Triple H 6.00 15.00
FSUM1 Undertaker/Shawn Michaels 6.00 15.00
FSUM2 Undertaker/Shawn Michaels 6.00 15.00
FSUM3 Undertaker/Shawn Michaels 6.00 15.00
FSUMK Undertaker/Mankind 5.00 12.00
FSACJG Adam Cole/Johnny Gargano 5.00 12.00
FSKOSZ Kevin Owens/Sami Zayn 5.00 12.00
FSTCJG Tommaso Ciampa/Johnny Gargano5.00 12.00

2021 Topps WWE Mat Relics

*AQUA/299: .5X TO 1.2X BASIC MEM
*LT GREEN/199: .6X TO 1.5X BASIC MEM
*DK GREEN/99: .75X TO 2X BASIC MEM
*CITRINE/75: 1X TO 2.5X BASIC MEM
*ORANGE/50: 1.2X TO 3X BASIC MEM
*PURPLE/25: UNPRICED DUE TO SCARCITY
*BLUE/10: UNPRICED DUE TO SCARCITY
*BLACK/5: UNPRICED DUE TO SCARCITY
*RED/1: UNPRICED DUE TO SCARCITY
STATED ODDS 1:49

MRB Big E 1.25 3.00
MRR Riddle 1.50 4.00
MRAC Adam Cole 2.00 5.00
MRAG Angel Garza .75 2.00
MRAS Asuka 2.50 6.00
MRBA Bayley 1.50 4.00
MRBB Bianca Belair 1.50 4.00
MRBF Bobby Fish .75 2.00
MRBL Becky Lynch 8.00 20.00
MRBR Robert Roode 2.50 6.00
MRCS Cesaro 2.00 5.00
MRDA Dana Brooke 2.00 5.00
MRDK Dakota Kai 4.00 10.00
MRDM Finn Balor 5.00 12.00
MRFA Fabian Aichner 2.50 6.00
MRFB Finn Balor 5.00 12.00
MRGM Gran Metalik 2.00 5.00
MRID Ilja Dragunov 2.00 5.00
MRIS Isaiah "Swerve" Scott 3.00 8.00
MRJD Jordan Devlin 2.00 5.00
MRJG Johnny Gargano 4.00 10.00
MRJH Jeff Hardy 5.00 12.00
MRJM Jinder Mahal 2.50 6.00
MRKL Keith Lee 4.00 10.00
MRKO Kevin Owens 4.00 10.00
MRKR Kyle O'Reilly 3.00 8.00

MRLA Bobby Lashley 5.00 12.00
MRLM Liv Morgan 8.00 20.00
MRMA Mustafa Ali 2.50 6.00
MRMB Marcel Barthel 2.50 6.00
MRMY Mia Yim 2.50 6.00
MRNJ Nia Jax 4.00 10.00
MROT Otis 2.50 6.00
MRRM Rey Mysterio 5.00 12.00
MRRR Rhea Ripley 6.00 15.00
MRRS Roderick Strong 3.00 8.00
MRSB Sasha Banks 10.00 25.00
MRSD Sonya Deville 5.00 12.00
MRSG Chad Gable 2.00 5.00
MRSN Shinsuke Nakamura 5.00 12.00
MRSR Seth Rollins 5.00 12.00
MRT7 Trent Seven 2.50 6.00
MRTC Tommaso Ciampa 5.00 12.00
MRTO Titus O'Neil 2.00 5.00
MRTS Toni Storm 6.00 15.00
MRTY Tyler Bate 2.50 6.00
MRWT WALTER 5.00 12.00
MRBOB Bobby Lashley 5.00 12.00
MRDOM Dominik Mysterio 2.50 6.00
MRKLR Kay Lee Ray 5.00 12.00
MRMIZ The Miz 3.00 8.00
MRNIA Nia Jax 4.00 10.00
MRROM Roman Reigns 10.00 25.00
MRSHA Shayna Baszler 4.00 10.00

2021 Topps WWE Memorable Entrances

COMPLETE SET (9) 6.00 15.00
STATED ODDS 1:10
ME1 Rhythm & Blues .40 1.00
ME2 Bobby The Brain Heenan .50 1.25
ME3 Macho King Randy Savage 1.25 3.00
ME4 Shawn Michaels 1.25 3.00
ME5 John Cena 1.50 4.00
ME6 Undertaker 1.50 4.00
ME7 Triple H 1.25 3.00
ME8 Sasha Banks 1.50 4.00
ME9 Roman Reigns 1.50 4.00

2021 Topps WWE RKO Outta Nowhere

COMPLETE SET (10) 6.00 15.00
STATED ODDS 1:10
RKO1 Undertaker 1.50 4.00
RKO2 Hulk Hogan 1.50 4.00
RKO3 Jeff Hardy .75 2.00
RKO4 Triple H 1.25 3.00
RKO5 Dolph Ziggler .60 1.50
RKO6 Seth Rollins .75 2.00
RKO7 Rey Mysterio .75 2.00
RKO8 Ricochet .60 1.50
RKO9 AJ Styles 1.00 2.50
RKO10 Alexa Bliss 2.00 5.00

2021 Topps WWE Tag Team Autographs

*BLUE/10: UNPRICED DUE TO SCARCITY
*RED/1: UNPRICED DUE TO SCARCITY
RANDOMLY INSERTED INTO PACKS
STATED PRINT RUN 25 SER.#'d SETS
DADD R.Roode/D.Ziggler 15.00 40.00
DASN S.Baszler/N.Jax 15.00 40.00
DALHP L.Dorado/G.Metalik 12.00 30.00

2007 Topps WWE Action

COMPLETE SET (90) 8.00 20.00
1 John Cena .60 1.50
2 Carlito .40 1.00
3 Charlie Haas .10 .25
4 Chris Masters .40 1.00
5 Edge .25 .60
6 Eugene .10 .25
7 Jim Duggan .40 1.00
8 John Morrison .10 .25
9 JTG RC .10 .25
10 Kenny Dykstra RC .15 .40
11 Lance Cade .15 .40
12 Randy Orton .40 1.00
13 Robbie McAllister RC .10 .25
14 Rory McAllister RC .10 .25
15 Shad RC .10 .25
16 Shawn Michaels .40 1.00
17 Shelton Benjamin .10 .25
18 Super Crazy .15 .40
19 Trevor Murdoch .10 .25
20 Triple H .40 1.00
21 Umaga .15 .40
22 Val Venis .25 .60
23 Viscera .25 .60
24 Ric Flair .40 1.00
25 The Great Khali .10 .25
26 Jeff Hardy .25 .60
27 Matt Hardy .25 .60
28 Batista .25 .60
29 Boogeyman .10 .25
30 Brian Kendrick .15 .40
31 Chavo Guerrero .15 .40
32 Santino Marella RC .25 .60
33 Dave Taylor RC .10 .25
34 Deuce RC .10 .25
35 Domino RC .10 .25
36 Finlay .25 .60
37 Funaki .15 .40
38 Gregory Helms .10 .25
39 Hornswoggle RC .15 .40
40 Jamie Noble .10 .25
41 Jimmy Wang Yang .10 .25
42 Kane .25 .60
43 King Booker .25 .60
44 Mark Henry .15 .40
45 Montel Vontavious Porter RC .15 .40
46 Mr. Kennedy .25 .60
47 Paul London .25 .60
48 Rey Mysterio .25 .60
49 Scotty 2 Hotty .15 .40
50 The Miz RC .40 1.00
51 Balls Mahoney RC .10 .25
52 Bobby Lashley .25 .60
53 CM Punk .40 1.00
54 Elijah Burke RC .10 .25
55 Hardcore Holly .25 .60
56 Kevin Thorn RC .10 .25
57 Nunzio .10 .25
58 Marcus CorVan RC .10 .25
59 Matt Striker .10 .25
60 Tazz .15 .40
61 Joey Styles .10 .25
62 Sabu RC .10 .25
63 Sandman .15 .40
64 Snitsky .10 .25
65 Steve Richards .15 .40
66 Tommy Dreamer .15 .40
67 Undertaker/Batista .50 1.25
68 Undertaker/Batista .50 1.25
69 Undertaker/Batista .50 1.25
70 J. Cena/S. Michaels .60 1.50
71 J. Cena/S. Michaels .60 1.50
72 J. Cena/S. Michaels .60 1.50
73 Bobby Lashley/Umaga .25 .60
74 Bobby Lashley/Umaga .25 .60
75 Bobby Lashley/Umaga .25 .60
76 Mr. Kennedy .25 .60
77 Mr. Kennedy .25 .60
78 Mr. Kennedy .25 .60
79 ECW Originals/New Breed .10 .25
80 ECW Originals/New Breed .10 .25
81 ECW Originals/New Breed .10 .25
82 The Great Khali/Kane .25 .60
83 The Great Khali/Kane .25 .60
84 The Great Khali/Kane .25 .60
85 The Great Khali/Kane .25 .60
86 Mr. McMahon .40 1.00
87 Mr. McMahon .40 1.00
88 Mr. McMahon .40 1.00
89 Mr. McMahon .40 1.00
90 Checklist Card .10 .25

2007 Topps WWE Action Autographs

STATED ODDS 1:48 HOBBY EXCLUSIVE
WILLIAM PERRY ODDS 1:1,392
NNO Bobby Lashley 10.00 25.00
NNO Carlito 5.00 12.00
NNO CM Punk 30.00 60.00
NNO Edge 10.00 25.00
NNO Jeff Hardy 20.00 40.00
NNO John Cena 25.00 50.00
NNO Matt Hardy 10.00 25.00
NNO Mr. Kennedy 10.00 25.00
NNO William Refrigerator Perry 40.00 80.00

2007 Topps WWE Action Lenticular Motion

COMPLETE SET (10) 5.00 12.00
STATED ODDS 1:8 RETAIL EXCLUSIVE
1 John Cena 1.25 3.00
2 Carlito .60 1.50
3 Shawn Michaels 1.00 2.50
4 Batista 1.00 2.50
5 Mr. Kennedy .40 1.00
6 Bobby Lashley .40 1.00
7 Ric Flair 1.50 4.00
8 Edge .75 2.00
9 Rey Mysterio .75 2.00
10 Rob Van Dam .40 1.00

2007 Topps WWE Action Ringside Relics

COMPLETE SET (4) 10.00 25.00
STATED ODDS 1:48 HOBBY EXCLUSIVE
NNO Carlito 3.00 8.00
NNO Edge 4.00 10.00
NNO Mr. Kennedy 3.00 8.00
NNO Shawn Michaels 5.00 12.00

2007 Topps WWE Action Tattoos

COMPLETE SET (10) 4.00 10.00
STATED ODDS 1:4 RETAIL EXCLUSIVE
1 Batista .30 .75
2 Booker T .30 .75
3 John Cena .75 2.00
4 Edge .30 .75
5 Triple H .50 1.25
6 Undertaker .60 1.50
7 Carlito .50 1.25
8 Ric Flair .50 1.25
9 Rob Van Dam .50 1.25
10 Rey Mysterio .30 .75

2015-16 Topps WWE Bret Hart Tribute

COMPLETE SET (20) 15.00 40.00
CANADIAN EXCLUSIVES
1 Bret Hit Man Hart 2.50 6.00
2 Bret Hit Man Hart 2.50 6.00
3 Bret Hit Man Hart 2.50 6.00
4 Bret Hit Man Hart 2.50 6.00
5 Bret Hit Man Hart 2.50 6.00
6 Bret Hit Man Hart 2.50 6.00
7 Bret Hit Man Hart 2.50 6.00
8 Bret Hit Man Hart 2.50 6.00
9 Bret Hit Man Hart 2.50 6.00
10 Bret Hit Man Hart 2.50 6.00
11 Bret Hit Man Hart 2.50 6.00
12 Bret Hit Man Hart 2.50 6.00
13 Bret Hit Man Hart 2.50 6.00
14 Bret Hit Man Hart 2.50 6.00
15 Bret Hit Man Hart 2.50 6.00
16 Bret Hit Man Hart 2.50 6.00
17 Bret Hit Man Hart 2.50 6.00
18 Bret Hit Man Hart 2.50 6.00
19 Bret Hit Man Hart 2.50 6.00
20 Bret Hit Man Hart 2.50 6.00

2015-16 Topps WWE Bret Hart Tribute Autographs and Relics

NNO Bret Hart AU/100 50.00 100.00
NNO Bret Hart MEM/100 30.00 80.00
NNO Bret Hart AU MEM/10 150.00 300.00

2016 Topps WWE Brock Lesnar Tribute

COMPLETE SET (10) 15.00 40.00
WALMART EXCLUSIVE
1 Brock Lesnar 1.00 2.50
2 Brock Lesnar 1.00 2.50
3 Brock Lesnar 1.00 2.50
4 Brock Lesnar 1.00 2.50
5 Brock Lesnar 1.00 2.50
6 Brock Lesnar 1.00 2.50
7 Brock Lesnar 1.00 2.50
8 Brock Lesnar 1.00 2.50
9 Brock Lesnar 1.00 2.50
10 Brock Lesnar 1.00 2.50
11 Brock Lesnar 1.00 2.50
12 Brock Lesnar 1.00 2.50
13 Brock Lesnar 1.00 2.50
14 Brock Lesnar 1.00 2.50
15 Brock Lesnar 1.00 2.50
16 Brock Lesnar 1.00 2.50
17 Brock Lesnar 1.00 2.50
18 Brock Lesnar 1.00 2.50
19 Brock Lesnar 1.00 2.50
20 Brock Lesnar 1.00 2.50
21 Brock Lesnar 1.00 2.50
22 Brock Lesnar 1.00 2.50
23 Brock Lesnar 1.00 2.50
24 Brock Lesnar 1.00 2.50
25 Brock Lesnar 1.00 2.50
26 Brock Lesnar 1.00 2.50
27 Brock Lesnar 1.00 2.50
28 Brock Lesnar 1.00 2.50
29 Brock Lesnar 1.00 2.50
30 Brock Lesnar 1.00 2.50
31 Brock Lesnar 1.00 2.50
32 Brock Lesnar 1.00 2.50
33 Brock Lesnar 1.00 2.50
34 Brock Lesnar 1.00 2.50
35 Brock Lesnar 1.00 2.50
36 Brock Lesnar 1.00 2.50
37 Brock Lesnar 1.00 2.50
38 Brock Lesnar 1.00 2.50
39 Brock Lesnar 1.00 2.50
40 Brock Lesnar 1.00 2.50

2016 Topps WWE Brock Lesnar Tribute Autographs and Relics

NNO Brock Lesnar AUTO
NNO Brock Lesnar RELIC
NNO Brock Lesnar RELIC AUTO

2011 Topps WWE Champions

COMPLETE SET (90) 10.00 25.00
UNOPENED BOX (24 PACKS)
UNOPENED PACK (7 CARDS)
1 Undertaker/Shawn Michaels .75 2.00
2 ShowMiz/Morrison & R-Truth .40 1.00
3 Randy Orton/Rhodes & DiBiase .60 1.50
4 Jack Swagger MITB .25 .60
5 Triple H/Sheamus .60 1.50
6 Rey Mysterio/CM Punk .40 1.00
7 10-Diva Tag Match .60 1.50
8 John Cena/Batista .75 2.00
9 Sheamus .25 .60
10 Randy Orton .60 1.50
11 The Miz .60 1.50
12 Rey Mysterio .40 1.00
13 Kane .40 1.00
14 Edge .60 1.50
15 Dolph Ziggler .25 .60
16 Edge .60 1.50
17 Kofi Kingston .15 .40
18 Dolph Ziggler .25 .60
19 Kofi Kingston .15 .40
20 Wade Barrett .15 .40
21 R-Truth .15 .40
22 The Miz .25 .60
23 Daniel Bryan .15 .40
24 Sheamus .25 .60
25 David Hart Smith/Tyson Kidd .15 .40
26 Cody Rhodes/Drew McIntyre .15 .40
27 David Otunga/John Cena .75 2.00
28 Heath Slater/Justin Gabriel .15 .40
29 Santino Marella/Vladimir Kozlov .25 .60
30 Heath Slater/Justin Gabriel .15 .40
31 John Cena/The Miz .75 2.00
32 Heath Slater/Justin Gabriel .15 .40
33 Eve .60 1.50
34 Alicia Fox .25 .60
35 Melina .60 1.50
36 Michelle McCool .60 1.50

Card	Low	High
37 Natalya	.60	1.50
38 Eve	.60	1.50
39 Beth Phoenix	.40	1.00
40 Layla	.40	1.00
41 Nexus	.15	.40
42 Alberto Del Rio	.40	1.00
43 Alex Riley	.15	.40
44 Mason Ryan	.15	.40
45 Sin Cara	.40	1.00
46 Ted DiBiase	.25	.60
47 Big Show/Miz	.40	1.00
48 Randy Orton/Evan Bourne	.60	1.50
49 Big Show/CM Punk	.40	1.00
50 Kane MITB	.40	1.00
51 The Miz MITB	.25	.60
52 Kane/Undertaker	.75	2.00
53 Team SmackDown	.60	1.50
54 Sheamus KOTR	.25	.60
55 Team Mysterio	.40	1.00
56 CM Punk	.40	1.00
57 Wade Barrett	.15	.40
58 John Morrison	.25	.60
59 Booker T	.25	.60
60 Diesel	.25	.60
61 Alberto Del Rio	.40	1.00
62 Edge	.60	1.50
63 John Cena	.75	2.00
64 The Rock Returns	.75	2.00
65 Stone Cold Steve Austin	.60	1.50
66 Trish Stratus/Vickie Guerrero.	.75	2.00
67 Mean Gene Okerlund	.25	.60
68 Cowboy Bob Orton	.25	.60
69 Nikolai Volkoff	.25	.60
70 Jimmy Superfly Snuka	.40	1.00
71 Tito Santana	.15	.40
72 Sgt. Slaughter	.40	1.00
73 Jim Ross	.15	.40
74 Rowdy Roddy Piper	.60	1.50
75 Daniel Bryan	.15	.40
76 The Miz	.25	.60
77 CM Punk/John Cena	.75	2.00
78 Wade Barrett	.15	.40
79 John Morrison	.25	.60
80 Drew McIntyre	.15	.40
81 Daniel Bryan	.15	.40
82 Cody Rhodes	.15	.40
83 Edge/Alberto Del Rio	.60	1.50
84 Big Show/Kane/Santino/Kofi	.40	1.00
85 Randy Orton/CM Punk	.60	1.50
86 Michael Cole/Jerry Lawler	.40	1.00
87 Undertaker/Triple H	.75	2.00
88 Trish & Morrison/LayCool & Ziggler	.75	2.00
89 The Miz/John Cena	.75	2.00
90 Checklist	.15	.40

2011 Topps WWE Champions Autographs

STATED ODDS 1:150

Card	Low	High
NNO Dolph Ziggler	8.00	20.00
NNO Edge	15.00	40.00
NNO John Cena	25.00	60.00
NNO Kofi Kingston	12.00	30.00
NNO Layla	10.00	25.00
NNO Michelle McCool	12.00	30.00
NNO The Miz	12.00	30.00
NNO Natalya	12.00	30.00
NNO Randy Orton	20.00	50.00
NNO Santino Marella	8.00	20.00
NNO Sheamus	12.00	30.00
NNO Vladimir Kozlov	8.00	20.00

2011 Topps WWE Champions Foil

Card	Low	High
COMPLETE SET (10)	4.00	10.00
STATED ODDS 1:3		
F1 Stone Cold Steve Austin	1.00	2.50
F2 Triple H	1.00	2.50
F3 Ravishing Rick Rude	.40	1.00
F4 John Morrison	.40	1.00
F5 Edge & Christian	1.00	2.50
F6 Michelle McCool	1.00	2.50
F7 Melina	1.00	2.50
F8 The British Bulldog	.40	1.00
F9 Terry Funk	.40	1.00
F10 Booker T	.40	1.00

2009 Topps WWE Chipz

Card	Low	High
COMPLETE SET (63)	15.00	30.00
1 John Cena	1.00	2.50
2 Randy Orton	.40	1.00
3 Charlie Haas	.15	.40
4 JTG	.15	.40
5 Snitsky	.25	.60
6 Shad	.15	.40
7 Shawn Michaels	1.00	2.50
8 Santino Marella	.15	.40
9 D-Lo Brown	.25	.60
10 William Regal	.40	1.00
11 Jerry Lawler	.25	.60
12 Chris Jericho	.40	1.00
13 Ted DiBiase	.40	1.00
14 Cody Rhodes	.15	.40
15 Hardcore Holly	.25	.60
16 JBL	.25	.60
17 Michael Cole	.15	.40
18 Rey Mysterio	.40	1.00
19 Batista	.60	1.50
20 Chuck Palumbo	.25	.60
21 Jamie Noble	.15	.40
22 CM Punk	.25	.60
23 Kofi Kingston	.15	.40
24 Kane	.60	1.50
25 Triple H	1.00	2.50
26 Brian Kendrick	.25	.60
27 Undertaker	.75	2.00
28 Jeff Hardy	.60	1.50
29 Umaga	.25	.60
30 Jim Ross	.15	.40
31 Edge	.60	1.50
32 Big Show	.40	1.00
33 Kenny Dykstra	.25	.60
34 Jimmy Wang Yang	.15	.40
35 Zack Ryder	.15	.40
36 Curt Hawkins	.15	.40
37 Deuce	.15	.40
38 Kung Fu Naki	.15	.40
39 R-Truth	.15	.40
40 MVP	.25	.60
41 Vladimir Kozlov	.25	.60
42 Primo	.15	.40
43 Jesse	.15	.40
44 Festus	.15	.40
45 Tazz	.15	.40
46 Shelton Benjamin	.15	.40
47 Elijah Burke	.15	.40
48 Hornswoggle	.25	.60
49 Tommy Dreamer	.15	.40
50 Mike Knox	.15	.40
51 Evan Bourne	.15	.40
52 Matt Striker	.15	.40
53 Matt Hardy	.60	1.50
54 John Morrison	.25	.60
55 Chavo Guerrero	.25	.60
56 Candice	.75	2.00
57 Jillian	.60	1.50
58 Maria	.60	1.50
59 Melina	.60	1.50
60 Michelle McCool	.60	1.50
61 Eve	.60	1.50
62 Kelly Kelly	.60	1.50
63 Victoria	.60	1.50

2009 Topps WWE Chipz Foil

Card	Low	High
COMPLETE SET (17)	10.00	20.00
STATED ODDS 1:2		
1 Randy Orton	.50	1.25
2 Shawn Michaels	1.25	3.00
3 Mr. Kennedy	.50	1.25
4 Carlito	.50	1.25
5 Shad	.20	.50
6 Chris Jericho	.50	1.25
7 The Great Khali	.20	.50
8 Matt Hardy	.75	2.00
9 MVP	.30	.75
10 Hurricane Helms	.20	.50
11 Mark Henry	.30	.75
12 Finlay	.30	.75
13 John Morrison	.30	.75
14 Boogeyman	.30	.75
15 The Miz	.30	.75
16 Beth Phoenix	1.00	2.50
17 Mickie James	1.00	2.50

2009 Topps WWE Chipz Silver

SILVER STATED ODDS 1:24
GOLD STATED ODDS 1:72

Card	Low	High
1 Shawn Michaels	12.00	30.00
2 Rey Mysterio	10.00	25.00
3 CM Punk	8.00	20.00
4 Kane	10.00	25.00
5 Triple H	10.00	25.00
6 Batista	10.00	25.00
7 Jeff Hardy	10.00	25.00
8 Edge	8.00	20.00
9 Randy Orton	10.00	25.00
10 John Cena GOLD	10.00	25.00

2011 Topps WWE Classic

Card	Low	High
COMPLETE SET (90)	8.00	20.00
*GOLD: 4X TO 10X BASIC CARDS		
1 AJ RC	8.00	20.00
2 Alberto Del Rio	.40	1.00
3 Alex Riley	.15	.40
4 Alicia Fox	.25	.60
5 Batista	.25	.60
6 Beth Phoenix	.40	1.00
7 Big Show	.40	1.00
8 Booker T	.25	.60
9 Brie Bella	.60	1.50
10 Brodus Clay	.15	.40
11 Christian	.15	.40
12 CM Punk	.40	1.00
13 Cody Rhodes	.15	.40
14 Curt Hawkins	.15	.40
15 Daniel Bryan	.15	.40
16 David Otunga	.15	.40
17 Dolph Ziggler	.25	.60
18 Drew McIntyre	.15	.40
19 Eden Stiles RC	.60	1.50
20 Edge	.60	1.50
21 Evan Bourne	.15	.40
22 Eve	.60	1.50
23 Ezekiel Jackson	.25	.60
24 Goldust	.15	.40
25 Heath Slater	.15	.40
26 Hornswoggle	.25	.60
27 Jack Swagger	.25	.60
28 Jerry The King Lawler	.40	1.00
29 Jey Uso	.15	.40
30 Jim Ross	.15	.40
31 Jimmy Uso	.15	.40
32 Jinder Mahal RC	.25	.60
33 John Cena	.75	2.00
34 John Morrison	.25	.60
35 Johnny Curtis	.15	.40
36 JTG	.15	.40
37 Justin Gabriel	.15	.40
38 Kaitlyn	.40	1.00
39 Kane	.40	1.00
40 Kelly Kelly	.60	1.50
41 Kofi Kingston	.15	.40
42 Layla	.40	1.00
43 Mark Henry	.25	.60
44 Mason Ryan	.15	.40
45 Matt Striker	.15	.40
46 Michael Cole	.15	.40
47 Michael McGillicutty	.15	.40
48 The Miz	.25	.60
49 Natalya	.60	1.50
50 Nikki Bella	.60	1.50
51 Percy Watson	.15	.40
52 Primo	.15	.40
53 R-Truth	.15	.40
54 Randy Orton	.60	1.50
55 Rey Mysterio	.40	1.00
56 Ricardo Rodriguez	.15	.40
57 The Rock	.75	2.00
58 Rosa Mendes	.25	.60
59 Santino Marella	.25	.60
60 Shawn Michaels	.60	1.50
61 Sheamus	.25	.60
62 Sin Cara RC	.40	1.00
63 Stone Cold Steve Austin	.60	1.50
64 Tamina	.15	.40
65 Ted DiBiase	.25	.60
66 Theodore Long	.15	.40
67 Trent Barreta	.15	.40
68 Triple H	.60	1.50
69 Trish Stratus	.75	2.00
70 Tyler Reks	.15	.40
71 Tyson Kidd	.15	.40
72 Undertaker	.75	2.00
73 Vickie Guerrero	.25	.60
74 Wade Barrett	.15	.40
75 William Regal	.25	.60
76 Yoshi Tatsu	.15	.40
77 Zack Ryder	.15	.40
78 The American Dream Dusty Rhodes	.25	.60
79 Arn Anderson	.25	.60
80 Big Boss Man	.25	.60
81 Bobby The Brain Heenan	.25	.60
82 Diesel	.25	.60
83 Jimmy Superfly Snuka	.40	1.00
84 Junkyard Dog	.40	1.00
85 Michael PS Hayes	.15	.40
86 Ricky The Dragon Steamboat	.40	1.00
87 The Road Warriors	.40	1.00
88 Rowdy Roddy Piper	.60	1.50
89 Sgt. Slaughter	.40	1.00
90 Yokozuna	.25	.60

2011 Topps WWE Classic Autographs

STATED ODDS 1:24 HOBBY; 1:153 RETAIL

Card	Low	High
NNO AJ	75.00	150.00
NNO CM Punk	15.00	40.00
NNO Daniel Bryan	15.00	40.00
NNO Dolph Ziggler	8.00	20.00
NNO Hornswoggle	8.00	20.00
NNO Jack Swagger	8.00	20.00
NNO Jinder Mahal	15.00	40.00
NNO Johnny Curtis	8.00	20.00
NNO Justin Gabriel	8.00	20.00
NNO Mason Ryan	8.00	20.00
NNO Rey Mysterio	20.00	50.00
NNO R-Truth	10.00	25.00
NNO Santino Marella	8.00	20.00
NNO Sheamus	12.00	30.00
NNO Wade Barrett	8.00	20.00
NNO Zack Ryder	8.00	20.00

2011 Topps WWE Classic Relics

STATED ODDS 1:24 HOBBY; 1:48 RETAIL

Card	Low	High
NNO Alberto Del Rio	5.00	12.00
NNO Christian	5.00	12.00
NNO CM Punk	8.00	20.00
NNO Daniel Bryan	5.00	12.00
NNO Dolph Ziggler	6.00	15.00
NNO Drew McIntyre	5.00	12.00
NNO Hornswoggle	5.00	12.00
NNO Jack Swagger	5.00	12.00
NNO Kofi Kingston	5.00	12.00
NNO The Miz	5.00	12.00
NNO Santino Marella	8.00	20.00
NNO Sheamus	5.00	12.00
NNO Zack Ryder	6.00	15.00

2011 Topps WWE Classic Promo

Card	Low	High
P1 Rock vs. Cena/WWE '12	4.00	10.00

2020 Topps WWE Countdown to WrestleMania

Card	Low	High
COMPLETE SET (20)	75.00	200.00
1 Hulk Hogan/Andre the Giant/207*	6.00	15.00
2 Hulk Hogan/Randy Savage/207*	5.00	12.00
3 Ultimate Warrior/Hulk Hogan/208*	6.00	15.00
4 Razor Ramon/170*	4.00	10.00
5 Shawn Michaels/Bret Hart/147*	5.00	12.00
6 Bret Hart/Steve Austin/149*	5.00	12.00
7 Stone Cold Steve Austin/164*	5.00	12.00
8 The Rock/172*	4.00	10.00
9 Brock Lesnar/132*	4.00	10.00
10 Eddie Guerrero/134*	4.00	10.00
11 Undertaker/123*	5.00	12.00
12 Undertaker/129*	4.00	10.00
13 John Cena/113*	4.00	10.00
14 Daniel Bryan/116*	10.00	25.00
15 Brock Lesnar/106*	8.00	20.00
16 Seth Rollins/116*	4.00	10.00

17 Charlotte Flair/183* 5.00 12.00
18 Kurt Angle & Ronda Rousey/194* 10.00 25.00
19 Becky Lynch/206* 8.00 20.00
20 Kofi Kingston/113* 4.00 10.00

2017 Topps WWE Daniel Bryan Tribute

COMPLETE SET (20) 8.00 20.00
1 Daniel Bryan 1.25 3.00
2 Daniel Bryan 1.25 3.00
3 Daniel Bryan 1.25 3.00
4 Daniel Bryan 1.25 3.00
5 Daniel Bryan 1.25 3.00
6 Daniel Bryan 1.25 3.00
7 Daniel Bryan 1.25 3.00
8 Daniel Bryan 1.25 3.00
9 Daniel Bryan 1.25 3.00
10 Daniel Bryan 1.25 3.00
11 Daniel Bryan 1.25 3.00
12 Daniel Bryan 1.25 3.00
13 Daniel Bryan 1.25 3.00
14 Daniel Bryan 1.25 3.00
15 Daniel Bryan 1.25 3.00
16 Daniel Bryan 1.25 3.00
17 Daniel Bryan 1.25 3.00
18 Daniel Bryan 1.25 3.00
19 Daniel Bryan 1.25 3.00
20 Daniel Bryan 1.25 3.00
21 Daniel Bryan 1.25 3.00
22 Daniel Bryan 1.25 3.00
23 Daniel Bryan 1.25 3.00
24 Daniel Bryan 1.25 3.00
25 Daniel Bryan 1.25 3.00
26 Daniel Bryan 1.25 3.00
27 Daniel Bryan 1.25 3.00
28 Daniel Bryan 1.25 3.00
29 Daniel Bryan 1.25 3.00
30 Daniel Bryan 1.25 3.00
31 Daniel Bryan 1.25 3.00
32 Daniel Bryan 1.25 3.00
33 Daniel Bryan 1.25 3.00
34 Daniel Bryan 1.25 3.00
35 Daniel Bryan 1.25 3.00
36 Daniel Bryan 1.25 3.00
37 Daniel Bryan 1.25 3.00
38 Daniel Bryan 1.25 3.00
39 Daniel Bryan 1.25 3.00
40 Daniel Bryan 1.25 3.00

2017 Topps WWE Daniel Bryan Tribute Autographs and Relics

NNO Daniel Bryan AU
NNO Daniel Bryan MEM
NNO Daniel Bryan AU MEM

2017 Topps WWE Daniel Bryan Tribute Topps Heritage WWE Autographs and Relics

RANDOMLY INSERTED INTO PACKS
1 Daniel Bryan AUTO
2 Daniel Bryan RELIC
3 Daniel Bryan AUTO RELIC

2017 Topps WWE Daniel Bryan Tribute Topps WWE Road to WrestleMania Autographs and Relics

NNO Daniel Bryan AU
NNO Daniel Bryan MEM
NNO Daniel Bryan AU MEM

2017 Topps WWE Daniel Bryan Tribute Topps WWE Then Now Forever Autographs and Relics

STATED ODDS
NNO Daniel Bryan AUTO 12.00 30.00
NNO Daniel Bryan RELIC 8.00 20.00
NNO Daniel Bryan AUTO RELIC

2008 Topps WWE Decade of Decadence Ultimate Fan Edition DVD Memorabilia Promo

NNO Edge/Shirt 10.00 25.00

2016 Topps WWE Divas Revolution

COMPLETE SET (43) 15.00 40.00
*SILVER/50: 1X TO 2.5X BASIC CARDS
*PINK/25: 2.5X TO 6X BASIC CARDS
*GOLD/10: 4X TO 10X BASIC CARDS
*RED/1: UNPRICED DUE TO SCARCITY
1 Wendi Richter .25 .60
2 Miss Elizabeth .25 .60
3 Sensational Sherri .40 1.00
4 Alundra Blayze .30 .75
5 Ivory .25 .60
6 Lita .75 2.00
7 Trish Stratus 1.25 3.00
8 Torrie Wilson .60 1.50
9 Leilani Kai .25 .60
10 Kelly Kelly .40 1.00
11 Beth Phoenix .40 1.00
12 Eve Torres .50 1.25
13 Alexa Bliss 6.00 15.00
14 Alicia Fox .40 1.00
15 Cathy Kelley RC .25 .60
16 Becky Lynch RC 4.00 10.00
17 Brie Bella .50 1.25
18 Carmella RC .60 1.50
19 Charlotte 3.00 8.00
20 Dana Brooke RC .60 1.50
21 Dasha Fuentes RC .25 .60
22 Emma .50 1.25
23 Eva Marie .50 1.25
24 JoJo .25 .60
25 Lana 1.00 2.50
26 Maryse .50 1.25
27 Naomi .40 1.00
28 Natalya .40 1.00
29 Nia Jax RC .40 1.00
30 Nikki Bella .75 2.00
31 Renee Young .60 1.50
32 Rosa Mendes .25 .60
33 Sasha Banks 3.00 8.00
34 Stephanie McMahon .40 1.00
35 Summer Rae .60 1.50
36 Tamina .30 .75
37 Aliyah RC .30 .75
38 Asuka RC 2.50 6.00
39 Bayley RC .60 1.50
40 Billie Kay RC .60 1.50
41 Liv Morgan RC 6.00 15.00
42 Peyton Royce RC .60 1.50
43 Mandy Rose RC 3.00 8.00

2016 Topps WWE Divas Revolution Autographs

*SILVER/50: .6X TO 1.5X BASIC AUTOS
*PINK/25: .75X TO 2X BASIC AUTOS
*GOLD/10: 1.2X TO 3X BASIC AUTOS
*RED/1: UNPRICED DUE TO SCARCITY
STATED ODDS 1:9
1 Wendi Richter 12.00 30.00
4 Alundra Blayze 10.00 25.00
6 Lita 15.00 40.00
7 Trish Stratus 20.00 50.00
8 Torrie Wilson 20.00 50.00
9 Leilani Kai 6.00 15.00
10 Kelly Kelly 15.00 40.00
11 Beth Phoenix 10.00 25.00
12 Eve Torres 20.00 50.00
13 Alexa Bliss 60.00 120.00
14 Alicia Fox 12.00 30.00
16 Becky Lynch 25.00 60.00
17 Brie Bella 12.00 30.00
18 Carmella 15.00 40.00
19 Charlotte 20.00 50.00
22 Emma 15.00 40.00
26 Maryse 12.00 30.00
27 Naomi 10.00 25.00
28 Natalya 12.00 30.00
30 Nikki Bella 15.00 40.00
32 Rosa Mendes 6.00 15.00
33 Sasha Banks 20.00 50.00
35 Summer Rae 10.00 25.00
36 Tamina 10.00 25.00
38 Asuka 15.00 40.00
43 Mandy Rose 50.00 100.00

2016 Topps WWE Divas Revolution Best Matches

COMPLETE SET (9) 6.00 15.00
*SILVER/50: .5X TO 1.5X BASIC CARDS
*PINK/25: X TO 2X BASIC CARDS
*GOLD/10: 1.2X TO 3X BASIC CARDS
*RED/1: UNPRICED DUE TO SCARCITY
1 Alundra Blayze/Bull Nakano .60 1.50
2 Trish Stratus/Lita 2.50 6.00
3 Charlotte/Natalya 1.50 4.00
4 Stephanie McMahon/Brie Bella .75 2.00
5 Charlotte/Sasha Banks 1.50 4.00
6 Sasha Banks/Becky Lynch 1.50 4.00
7 Bayley 1.25 3.00
8 Bayley/Sasha Banks 1.25 3.00
9 Asuka/Bayley 2.00 5.00

2016 Topps WWE Divas Revolution Diva Kiss

*GOLD/10: .75X TO 2X BASIC KISS
*RED/1: UNPRICED DUE TO SCARCITY
STATED ODDS 1:15
NNO Alexa Bliss 60.00 120.00
NNO Alicia Fox 12.00 30.00
NNO Asuka 25.00 60.00
NNO Becky Lynch 20.00 50.00
NNO Billie Kay 25.00 60.00
NNO Carmella 25.00 60.00
NNO Charlotte 20.00 50.00
NNO Dana Brooke 25.00 60.00
NNO Emma 25.00 60.00
NNO Mandy Rose 20.00 40.00
NNO Maryse 20.00 50.00
NNO Natalya 20.00 50.00
NNO Nia Jax 12.00 30.00
NNO Peyton Royce 12.00 30.00
NNO Renee Young 20.00 50.00

2016 Topps WWE Divas Revolution Diva Kiss Autographs

*GOLD/10: .75X TO 2X BASIC AUTOS
*RED/1: UNPRICED DUE TO SCARCITY
STATED ODDS 1:56
NNO Alexa Bliss 120.00 200.00
NNO Alicia Fox 15.00 40.00
NNO Asuka 40.00 100.00
NNO Becky Lynch 60.00 120.00
NNO Billie Kay 25.00 60.00
NNO Carmella 60.00 120.00
NNO Charlotte 60.00 120.00
NNO Dana Brooke 25.00 60.00
NNO Emma 25.00 60.00
NNO Mandy Rose 25.00 60.00
NNO Maryse 25.00 60.00
NNO Natalya 15.00 40.00
NNO Nia Jax 15.00 40.00
NNO Peyton Royce 15.00 40.00
NNO Renee Young 20.00 50.00

2016 Topps WWE Divas Revolution Historic Women's Champions

COMPLETE SET (10) 6.00 15.00
*SILVER/50: .75X TO 2X BASIC CARDS
*PINK/25: 2X TO 5X BASIC CARDS
*GOLD/10: 3X TO 8X BASIC CARDS
*RED/1: UNPRICED DUE TO SCARCITY
1 Alundra Blayze .50 1.25
2 Lita 1.25 3.00
3 Trish Stratus 2.00 5.00
4 Maryse .75 2.00
5 Eve Torres .75 2.00
6 Nikki Bella 1.25 3.00
7 Charlotte 1.25 3.00
8 Charlotte 1.25 3.00
9 Bayley 1.00 2.50
10 Charlotte 1.25 3.00

2016 Topps WWE Divas Revolution Mat Relics

*SILVER/50: .5X TO 1.2X BASIC MEM
*PINK/25: .6X TO 1.5X BASIC MEM
*GOLD/10: .75X TO 2X BASIC MEM
*RED/1: UNPRICED DUE TO SCARCITY
STATED ODDS 1:8
NNO Alexa Bliss Belfast 10.00 25.00
NNO Alexa Bliss DMF 10.00 25.00
NNO Alicia Fox Summerslam 3.00 8.00
NNO Alicia Fox WrestleMania 3.00 8.00
NNO Asuka Belfast 8.00 20.00
NNO Asuka DMF 8.00 20.00
NNO Bayley Takeover 5.00 12.00
NNO Bayley DMF 5.00 12.00
NNO Bayley Belfast 5.00 12.00
NNO Becky Lynch SummerSlam 6.00 15.00
NNO Becky Lynch NXT 6.00 15.00
NNO Brie Bella SummerSlam 4.00 10.00
NNO Brie Bella WrestleMania 4.00 10.00
NNO Carmella Belfast 5.00 12.00
NNO Carmella DMF 5.00 12.00
NNO Charlotte SummerSlam 6.00 15.00
NNO Charlotte NXT 6.00 15.00
NNO Dana Brooke NXT 5.00 12.00
NNO Emma WrestleMania 4.00 10.00
NNO Emma NXT 4.00 10.00
NNO Eve Torres WrestleMania 4.00 10.00
NNO Naomi SummerSlam 3.00 8.00
NNO Naomi WrestleMania 3.00 8.00
NNO Naomi WrestleMania 3.00 8.00
NNO Nia Jax Belfast 3.00 8.00
NNO Nia Jax DMF 3.00 8.00
NNO Nikki Bella MITB 6.00 15.00
NNO Nikki Bella SummerSlam 6.00 15.00
NNO Nikki Bella WrestleMania 6.00 15.00
NNO Peyton Royce Belfast 5.00 12.00
NNO Peyton Royce DMF 5.00 12.00
NNO Rosa Mendes WrestleMania 2.00 5.00
NNO Sasha Banks Takeover 6.00 15.00
NNO Sasha Banks SummerSlam 6.00 15.00
NNO Tamina SummerSlam 2.50 6.00

2016 Topps WWE Divas Revolution Power Couples

COMPLETE SET (10) 6.00 15.00
*RED/50: .75X TO 2X BASIC CARDS
*PINK/25: 1.2X TO 3X BASIC CARDS
*GOLD/10: 2X TO 5X BASIC CARDS
RANDOMLY INSERTED INTO PACKS
1 Miss Elizabeth/Randy Savage 1.00 2.50
2 Stephanie McMahon/HHH 1.50 4.00
3 Lita/Edge 1.25 3.00
4 Sensational Sherri/HBK 1.50 4.00
5 Trish Stratus/Christian 2.00 5.00
6 Brie Bella/Daniel Bryan 1.50 4.00
7 Queen Sherri/Randy Savage 1.00 2.50
8 Naomi/Jimmy Uso .60 1.50
9 Rusev/Lana 1.50 4.00
10 Lita/Kane 1.25 3.00

2016 Topps WWE Divas Revolution The Revolution

COMPLETE SET (4) 4.00 10.00
*SILVER/50: .75X TO 2X BASIC CARDS
*PINK/25: 1.2X TO 3X BASIC CARDS
*GOLD/10: 1.5X TO 4X BASIC CARDS
*RED/1: UNPRICED DUE TO SCARCITY
1 Charlotte 1.50 4.00
2 Team PCB 1.25 3.00
3 Charlotte 1.50 4.00
4 Charlotte 1.50 4.00

2016 Topps WWE Divas Revolution Rivalries

COMPLETE SET (8) 5.00 12.00
*SILVER/50: 1X TO 2.5X BASIC CARDS
*PINK/25: 1.2X TO 3X BASIC CARDS
*GOLD/10: 1.5X TO 4X BASIC CARDS
*RED//1: UNPRICED DUE TO SCARCITY
RANDOMLY INSERTED INTO PACKS
1 Trish Stratus/Lita 2.00 5.00
2 Trish Stratus/Stephanie McMahon 2.00 5.00
3 Bayley/Sasha Banks 1.25 3.00
4 Charlotte/Sasha Banks 1.25 3.00
5 Charlotte/Nikki Bella 1.25 3.00

6 Becky Lynch/Charlotte	1.25	3.00
7 Brie Bella/Nikki Bella	1.25	3.00
8 Miss Elizabeth	.60	1.50
Sensational Sherri		

2016 Topps WWE Divas Revolution Shirt Relics

*SILVER/50: .5X TO 1.2X BASIC MEM
*PINK/25: .6X TO 1.5X BASIC MEM
*GOLD/10: UNPRICED DUE TO SCARCITY
*RED/1: UNPRICED DUE TO SCARCITY

NNO Alexa Bliss	12.00	30.00
NNO Alicia Fox	4.00	10.00
NNO Asuka	10.00	25.00
NNO Becky Lynch	8.00	20.00
NNO Brie Bella	5.00	12.00
NNO Carmella	6.00	15.00
NNO Charlotte	8.00	20.00
NNO JoJo	2.50	6.00
NNO Lana	10.00	25.00
NNO Naomi	4.00	10.00
NNO Natalya	4.00	10.00
NNO Renee Young	6.00	15.00
NNO Sasha Banks	8.00	20.00
NNO Summer Rae	6.00	15.00
NNO Tamina	3.00	8.00

2007 Topps WWE Dog Tags

COMPLETE SET (24)	40.00	80.00
*GOLD: 1X TO 2.5X BASIC TAGS		
1 John Cena	4.00	10.00
2 Batista	1.50	4.00
3 Johnny Nitro	1.00	2.50
4 Carlito	2.50	6.00
5 Ric Flair	2.50	6.00
6 Undertaker	3.00	8.00
7 Chris Benoit	1.50	4.00
8 CM Punk	2.50	6.00
9 Booker T	1.50	4.00
10 Rob Van Dam	2.50	6.00
11 Ken Kennedy	1.50	4.00
12 Shawn Michaels	2.50	6.00
13 The Rock	5.00	12.00
14 Jeff Hardy	1.50	4.00
15 Stone Cold Steve Austin	4.00	10.00
16 Edge	1.50	4.00
17 Rey Mysterio	1.50	4.00
18 Kane	1.50	4.00
19 Randy Orton	2.50	6.00
20 Triple H	2.50	6.00
21 Sabu	.60	1.50
22 Umaga	1.00	2.50
23 Sandman	1.00	2.50
24 Bobby Lashley	1.50	4.00

2007 Topps WWE Dog Tags Trading Cards

COMPLETE SET (25)	15.00	40.00
1 John Cena	2.00	5.00
2 Batista	.75	2.00
3 Johnny Nitro	.50	1.25
4 Carlito	1.25	3.00
5 Ric Flair	1.25	3.00
6 Undertaker	1.50	4.00
7 Chris Benoit	.75	2.00
8 CM Punk	1.25	3.00
9 Booker T	.75	2.00
10 Rob Van Dam	1.25	3.00
11 Ken Kennedy	.75	2.00
12 Shawn Michaels	1.25	3.00
13 The Rock	2.50	6.00
14 Jeff Hardy	.75	2.00
15 Stone Cold Steve Austin	2.00	5.00
16 Edge	.75	2.00
17 Rey Mysterio	.75	2.00
18 Kane	.75	2.00
19 Randy Orton	1.25	3.00
20 Triple H	1.25	3.00
21 Sabu	.30	.75
22 Umaga	.50	1.25
23 Sandman	.50	1.25
24 Bobby Lashley	.75	2.00
NNO Checklist	.30	.75

2015 Topps WWE Dog Tags

COMPLETE SET (30)	15.00	40.00
*GOLD: .6X TO 1.5X BASIC TAGS		
1 AJ Lee	1.50	4.00
2 Bad News Barrett	.30	.75
3 Batista	.75	2.00
4 Big Show	.75	2.00
5 Bray Wyatt	1.25	3.00
6 Brock Lesnar	1.25	3.00
7 Cesaro	.30	.75
8 Chris Jericho	.75	2.00
9 Daniel Bryan	1.25	3.00
10 Dean Ambrose	.75	2.00
11 Dolph Ziggler	.50	1.25
12 Edge	.75	2.00
13 Hulk Hogan	1.50	4.00
14 Jake The Snake Roberts	.50	1.25
15 John Cena	1.50	4.00
16 Kane	.75	2.00
17 Kofi Kingston	.30	.75
18 Randy Orton	1.25	3.00
19 Rey Mysterio	.75	2.00
20 Ric Flair	1.50	4.00
21 Rob Van Dam	.75	2.00
22 The Rock	1.50	4.00
23 Roman Reigns	.75	2.00
24 Seth Rollins	.50	1.25
25 Shawn Michaels	1.25	3.00
26 Sheamus	.75	2.00
27 Stone Cold Steve Austin	1.50	4.00
28 Triple H	1.25	3.00
29 Ultimate Warrior	1.00	2.50
30 Undertaker	1.25	3.00

2015 Topps WWE Dog Tags Trading Cards

COMPLETE SET (30)	8.00	20.00
STATED ODDS 1:1		
1 AJ Lee	.75	2.00
2 Bad News Barrett	.15	.40
3 Batista	.40	1.00
4 Big Show	.40	1.00
5 Bray Wyatt	.60	1.50
6 Brock Lesnar	.60	1.50
7 Cesaro	.15	.40
8 Chris Jericho	.40	1.00
9 Daniel Bryan	.60	1.50
10 Dean Ambrose	.40	1.00
11 Dolph Ziggler	.25	.60
12 Edge	.40	1.00
13 Hulk Hogan	.75	2.00
14 Jake The Snake Roberts	.25	.60
15 John Cena	.75	2.00
16 Kane	.40	1.00
17 Kofi Kingston	.15	.40
18 Randy Orton	.60	1.50
19 Rey Mysterio	.40	1.00
20 Ric Flair	.75	2.00
21 Rob Van Dam	.40	1.00
22 The Rock	.75	2.00
23 Roman Reigns	.40	1.00
24 Seth Rollins	.25	.60
25 Shawn Michaels	.60	1.50
26 Sheamus	.40	1.00
27 Stone Cold Steve Austin	.75	2.00
28 Triple H	.60	1.50
29 Ultimate Warrior	.50	1.25
30 Undertaker	.60	1.50

2015 Topps WWE Dog Tags Relic Tags

*GOLD: X TO X BASIC MEM		
STATED ODDS		
1 Bad News Barrett	4.00	10.00
2 Big Show	4.00	10.00
3 Bray Wyatt	12.00	30.00
4 Cesaro	4.00	10.00
5 Chris Jericho	5.00	12.00
6 Daniel Bryan	8.00	20.00
7 Dolph Ziggler	6.00	15.00
8 Edge	6.00	15.00
9 Hulk Hogan	15.00	40.00
10 Kofi Kingston	5.00	12.00
11 John Cena	25.00	60.00
12 Randy Orton	8.00	20.00
13 Rey Mysterio	6.00	15.00
14 Rob Van Dam	6.00	15.00
15 Roman Reigns	8.00	20.00
16 Seth Rollins	8.00	20.00

2010 Topps WWE Dog Tags Pyrotechno Edition

COMPLETE SET (24)	12.00	30.00
*GOLD: .75X TO 2X BASIC TAGS		
1 John Cena	2.50	6.00
2 Kofi Kingston	.75	2.00
3 Big Show	1.25	3.00
4 Cody Rhodes	.50	1.25
5 Ted DiBiase	.75	2.00
6 Santino Marella	.50	1.25
7 The Miz	.75	2.00
8 Triple H	2.50	6.00
9 Shawn Michaels	3.00	8.00
10 CM Punk	2.00	5.00
11 John Morrison	.75	2.00
12 Chris Jericho	1.25	3.00
13 Matt Hardy	1.25	3.00
14 Christian	.75	2.00
15 Tommy Dreamer	.50	1.25
16 Undertaker	2.00	5.00
17 Yoshi Tatsu	.50	1.25
18 Sheamus	.75	2.00
19 Finlay	.75	2.00
20 Hornswoggle	.75	2.00
21 Edge	2.00	5.00
22 Batista	2.00	5.00
23 Evan Bourne	.50	1.25
24 Randy Orton	2.00	5.00

2010 Topps WWE Dog Tags Pyrotechno Edition Trading Cards

COMPLETE SET (24)	10.00	25.00
1 John Cena	2.00	5.00
2 Kofi Kingston	.60	1.50
3 Big Show	1.00	2.50
4 Cody Rhodes	.40	1.00
5 Ted DiBiase	.60	1.50
6 Santino Marella	.40	1.00
7 The Miz	.60	1.50
8 Triple H	2.00	5.00
9 Shawn Michaels	2.50	6.00
10 CM Punk	1.50	4.00
11 John Morrison	.60	1.50
12 Chris Jericho	1.00	2.50
13 Matt Hardy	1.00	2.50
14 Christian	.60	1.50
15 Tommy Dreamer	.40	1.00
16 Undertaker	1.50	4.00
17 Yoshi Tatsu	.40	1.00
18 Sheamus	.60	1.50
19 Finlay	.60	1.50
20 Hornswoggle	.60	1.50
21 Edge	1.50	4.00
22 Batista	1.50	4.00
23 Evan Bourne	.40	1.00
24 Randy Orton	1.50	4.00

2011 Topps WWE Dog Tags Ringside Relic Edition

COMPLETE SET (24)	10.00	20.00
1 CM Punk	1.00	2.50
2 Daniel Bryan	.40	1.00
3 David Otunga	.40	1.00
4 John Cena	2.00	5.00
5 John Morrison	.60	1.50
6 Justin Gabriel	.40	1.00
7 Ezekiel Jackson	.60	1.50
8 Randy Orton	1.50	4.00
9 Sheamus	.60	1.50
10 The Miz	.60	1.50
11 Wade Barrett	.40	1.00
12 Heath Slater	.40	1.00
13 Dolph Ziggler	.60	1.50
14 Edge	1.50	4.00
15 Kane	1.00	2.50
16 Undertaker	2.00	5.00
17 Alberto Del Rio	1.00	2.50
18 Jack Swagger	.60	1.50
19 Tyler Reks	.40	1.00
20 Drew McIntyre	.40	1.00
21 Rey Mysterio	1.00	2.50
22 Kaval	1.00	2.50
23 Kofi Kingston	.40	1.00
24 Big Show	1.00	2.50

2011 Topps WWE Dog Tags Ringside Relic Edition Memorabilia Tags

STATED ODDS 1:24		
1 Hornswoggle	2.50	6.00
2 Sheamus	2.50	6.00
3 Kofi Kingston	2.50	6.00
4 Edge	6.00	15.00
5 Jack Swagger	2.50	6.00
6 Justin Gabriel	2.50	6.00
7 David Hart Smith	2.50	6.00
8 The Miz	2.50	6.00
9 John Cena	8.00	20.00
10 Randy Orton	6.00	15.00
11 Alex Riley	2.50	6.00
12 Heath Slater	2.50	6.00
13 Wade Barrett	2.50	6.00
14 John Morrison	2.50	6.00
15 David Otunga	2.50	6.00
16 Tyson Kidd	2.50	6.00
17 Rey Mysterio	4.00	10.00
18 Big Show	4.00	10.00

2011 Topps WWE Dog Tags Ringside Relic Edition Trading Cards

COMPLETE SET (24)	4.00	10.00
1 CM Punk	.40	1.00
2 Daniel Bryan	.15	.40
3 David Otunga	.15	.40
4 John Cena	.75	2.00
5 John Morrison	.25	.60
6 Justin Gabriel	.15	.40
7 Ezekiel Jackson	.25	.60
8 Randy Orton	.60	1.50
9 Sheamus	.25	.60
10 The Miz	.25	.60
11 Wade Barrett	.15	.40
12 Heath Slater	.15	.40
13 Dolph Ziggler	.25	.60
14 Edge	.60	1.50
15 Kane	.40	1.00
16 Undertaker	.75	2.00
17 Alberto Del Rio	.40	1.00
18 Jack Swagger	.25	.60
19 Tyler Reks	.15	.40
20 Drew McIntyre	.15	.40
21 Rey Mysterio	.40	1.00
22 Kaval	.40	1.00
23 Kofi Kingston	.15	.40
24 Big Show	.40	1.00

2011 Topps WWE Dog Tags Ringside Relic Edition Silver Insert Cards

COMPLETE SET (18)	4.00	10.00
STATED ODDS 1:24		
1 Hornswoggle	.40	1.00
2 Sheamus	.40	1.00
3 Kofi Kingston	.25	.60
4 Edge	1.00	2.50
5 Jack Swagger	.40	1.00
6 Justin Gabriel	.25	.60
7 David Hart Smith	.25	.60
8 The Miz	.40	1.00
9 John Cena	1.25	3.00
10 Randy Orton	1.00	2.50
11 Alex Riley	.25	.60
12 Heath Slater	.25	.60
13 Wade Barrett	.25	.60
14 John Morrison	.40	1.00
15 David Otunga	.25	.60
16 Tyson Kidd	.25	.60
17 Rey Mysterio	.60	1.50
18 Big Show	.60	1.50

2012 Topps WWE Dog Tags Ringside Relic Edition

COMPLETE SET (24) 15.00 40.00
STATED ODDS 1:1

1 CM Punk 2.50 6.00
2 Ted Dibiase 1.00 2.50
3 Sheamus 1.50 4.00
4 David Otunga .60 1.50
5 The Miz 1.00 2.50
6 Jack Swagger 1.00 2.50
7 R-Truth .60 1.50
8 Heath Slater .60 1.50
9 Christian .60 1.50
10 John Cena 3.00 8.00
11 Zack Ryder .60 1.50
12 Daniel Bryan .60 1.50
13 Hornswoggle 1.00 2.50
14 Rey Mysterio 1.50 4.00
15 Dolph Ziggler 1.00 2.50
16 Kofi Kingston .60 1.50
17 Evan Bourne .60 1.50
18 Santino Marella 1.00 2.50
19 Triple H 2.50 6.00
20 Sin Cara 1.50 4.00
21 The Miz 1.00 2.50
22 Stone Cold Steve Austin 3.00 8.00
23 Undertaker 2.50 6.00
24 Randy Orton 2.50 6.00

2012 Topps WWE Dog Tags Ringside Relic Edition Memorabilia Tags

STATED ODDS 1:24

1 CM Punk 6.00 15.00
2 Ted Dibiase 2.50 6.00
3 Sheamus 4.00 10.00
4 David Otunga 1.50 4.00
5 The Miz 2.50 6.00
6 Jack Swagger 2.50 6.00
7 R-Truth 1.50 4.00
8 Heath Slater 1.50 4.00
9 Christian 1.50 4.00
10 John Cena 8.00 20.00
11 Zack Ryder 1.50 4.00
12 Daniel Bryan 1.50 4.00
13 Hornswoggle 2.50 6.00
14 Rey Mysterio 4.00 10.00
15 Dolph Ziggler 2.50 6.00
16 Kofi Kingston 1.50 4.00
17 Evan Bourne 1.50 4.00

2012 Topps WWE Dog Tags Ringside Relic Edition Trading Cards

COMPLETE SET (24) 5.00 12.00

1 CM Punk 1.00 2.50
2 Ted Dibiase .40 1.00
3 Sheamus .60 1.50
4 David Otunga .25 .60
5 The Miz .40 1.00
6 Jack Swagger .40 1.00
7 R-Truth .25 .60
8 Heath Slater .25 .60
9 Christian .25 .60
10 John Cena 1.25 3.00
11 Zack Ryder .25 .60
12 Daniel Bryan .25 .60
13 Hornswoggle .40 1.00
14 Rey Mysterio .60 1.50
15 Dolph Ziggler .40 1.00
16 Kofi Kingston .25 .60
17 Evan Bourne .25 .60
18 Santino Marella .40 1.00
19 Triple H 1.00 2.50
20 Sin Cara .60 1.50
21 The Miz .40 1.00
22 Stone Cold Steve Austin 1.25 3.00
23 Undertaker 1.00 2.50
24 Randy Orton 1.00 2.50

2013 Topps WWE Dog Tags Signature Series

STATED ODDS 1:1

1 John Cena 3.00 8.00
2 CM Punk 2.50 6.00
3 Ryback .60 1.50
4 Sheamus 1.25 3.00
5 Big Show 1.25 3.00
6 Randy Orton 2.00 5.00
7 Alberto Del Rio 1.25 3.00
8 Christian .60 1.50
9 Cody Rhodes .60 1.50
10 Rey Mysterio 1.50 4.00
11 Sin Cara 1.00 2.50
12 Dolph Ziggler 1.00 2.50
13 Zack Ryder .60 1.50
14 Santino .60 1.50
15 Triple H 2.50 6.00
16 Undertaker 2.50 6.00
17 Kane 1.25 3.00
18 Daniel Bryan 1.50 4.00
19 The Miz 1.00 2.50
20 Kofi Kingston .60 1.50
21 R-Truth .60 1.50
22 Brodus Clay .60 1.50
23 Wade Barrett .60 1.50
24 The Rock 3.00 8.00
25 Cactus Jack 2.50 6.00
26 Jerry King Lawler 1.25 3.00
27 Shawn Michaels 2.50 6.00
28 Kevin Nash .75 2.00
29 Booker T 1.00 2.50
30 Stone Cold Steve Austin 2.50 6.00

2013 Topps WWE Dog Tags Signature Series Autographed Tags

STATED ODDS 1:107

NNO AJ Lee 75.00 150.00
NNO Aksana 6.00 15.00
NNO Booker T 12.00 30.00
NNO Brodus Clay 6.00 15.00
NNO Daniel Bryan 15.00 40.00
NNO Kane 12.00 30.00
NNO Layla 6.00 15.00
NNO Natalya 10.00 25.00
NNO Tamina 6.00 15.00
NNO Zack Ryder 6.00 15.00

2013 Topps WWE Dog Tags Signature Series Divas Trading Cards

COMPLETE SET (5)
STATED ODDS 1:107

1 AJ Lee 15.00 40.00
2 Aksana 5.00 12.00
3 Layla 6.00 15.00
4 Natalya 6.00 15.00
5 Tamina 4.00 10.00

2013 Topps WWE Dog Tags Signature Series Memorabilia Tags

STATED ODDS 1:24

NNO Alberto Del Rio 3.00 8.00
NNO Brodus Clay 1.50 4.00
NNO CM Punk 6.00 15.00
NNO Cody Rhodes 1.50 4.00
NNO Daniel Bryan 4.00 10.00
NNO Dolph Ziggler 2.50 6.00
NNO John Cena 8.00 20.00
NNO Kofi Kingston 1.50 4.00
NNO The Miz 2.50 6.00
NNO Rey Mysterio 4.00 10.00
NNO R-Truth 1.50 4.00
NNO Ryback 1.50 4.00
NNO Santino 1.50 4.00
NNO Shawn Michaels 6.00 15.00
NNO Sheamus 3.00 8.00
NNO Sin Cara 2.50 6.00
NNO Wade Barrett 1.50 4.00
NNO Zack Ryder 1.50 4.00

2013 Topps WWE Dog Tags Signature Series Trading Cards

COMPLETE SET (30) 6.00 15.00

1 John Cena 1.25 3.00
2 CM Punk 1.00 2.50
3 Ryback .25 .60
4 Sheamus .50 1.25
5 Big Show .50 1.25
6 Randy Orton .75 2.00
7 Alberto Del Rio .50 1.25
8 Christian .25 .60
9 Cody Rhodes .25 .60
10 Rey Mysterio .60 1.50
11 Sin Cara .40 1.00
12 Dolph Ziggler .40 1.00
13 Zack Ryder .25 .60
14 Santino .25 .60
15 Triple H 1.00 2.50
16 Undertaker 1.00 2.50
17 Kane .50 1.25
18 Daniel Bryan .60 1.50
19 The Miz .40 1.00
20 Kofi Kingston .25 .60
21 R-Truth .25 .60
22 Brodus Clay .25 .60
23 Wade Barrett .25 .60
24 The Rock 1.25 3.00
25 Cactus Jack 1.00 2.50
26 Jerry King Lawler .50 1.25
27 Shawn Michaels 1.00 2.50
28 Kevin Nash .30 .75
29 Booker T .40 1.00
30 Stone Cold Steve Austin 1.00 2.50

2007 Topps WWE Dog Tags UK

COMPLETE SET (21) 25.00 60.00
*GOLD: 1X TO 2.5X BASIC TAGS

1 John Cena 4.00 10.00
2 Batista 1.50 4.00
3 Johnny Nitro 1.00 2.50
4 Carlito 2.50 6.00
5 Ric Flair 2.50 6.00
6 Undertaker 3.00 8.00
7 CM Punk 2.50 6.00
8 Booker T 1.50 4.00
9 Ken Kennedy 1.50 4.00
10 Shawn Michaels 2.50 6.00
11 The Rock 5.00 12.00
12 Jeff Hardy 1.50 4.00
13 Stone Cold Steve Austin 4.00 10.00
14 Edge 1.50 4.00
15 Rey Mysterio 1.50 4.00
16 Kane 1.50 4.00
17 Randy Orton 2.50 6.00
18 Triple H 2.50 6.00
19 Umaga 1.00 2.50
20 Sandman 1.00 2.50
21 Bobby Lashley 1.50 4.00

2007 Topps WWE Dog Tags UK Trading Cards

COMPLETE SET (21) 12.00 30.00

1 John Cena 2.00 5.00
2 Batista .75 2.00
3 Johnny Nitro .50 1.25
4 Carlito 1.25 3.00
5 Ric Flair 1.25 3.00
6 Undertaker 1.50 4.00
7 CM Punk 1.25 3.00
8 Booker T .75 2.00
9 Ken Kennedy .75 2.00
10 Shawn Michaels 1.25 3.00
11 The Rock 2.50 6.00
12 Jeff Hardy .75 2.00
13 Stone Cold Steve Austin 2.00 5.00
14 Edge .75 2.00
15 Rey Mysterio .75 2.00
16 Kane .75 2.00
17 Randy Orton 1.25 3.00
18 Triple H 1.25 3.00
19 Umaga .50 1.25
20 Sandman .50 1.25
21 Bobby Lashley .75 2.00
CL Checklist .30 .75

2007-08 Topps WWE DVD Collection

COMPLETE SET (17)

D1 Iron Sheik & Nikolai Volkoff
D2 Ravishing Rick Rude
D3 Mr. Perfect/Roddy Piper
D4 The Rock
D5 Ted DiBiase
D6 The British Bulldog Davey Boy Smith
D7 Mankind
D8 Shawn Michaels
D9 Jake The Snake Roberts
D10 Sgt. Slaughter
D11 Undertaker
D12 Edge
D13 Hacksaw Jim Duggan
D14 Ric Flair
D15 Stone Cold Steve Austin
D16 Triple H
CL Checklist

2007 Topps WWE Face-Off

COMPLETE SET (132) 20.00 50.00

1 Bobby Lashley .75 2.00
2 Armando Estrada RC .30 .75
3 Brian Kendrick .50 1.25
4 Carlito 1.25 3.00
5 Charlie Haas .30 .75
6 Daivari RC .30 .75
7 Jim Duggan .50 1.25
8 Jeff Hardy .75 2.00
9 Jerry Lawler .75 2.00
10 Jim Ross .40 1.00
11 John Cena 2.00 5.00
12 Jonathan Coachman .30 .75
13 JTG RC .30 .75
14 King Booker .75 2.00
15 Lance Cade .30 .75
16 Mr. Kennedy .75 2.00
17 Paul London .75 2.00
18 Randy Orton 1.25 3.00
19 Robbie McAllister RC .30 .75
20 Rory McAllister RC .30 .75
21 Roddy Piper 1.25 3.00
22 Sandman .50 1.25
23 Santino Marella RC .40 1.00
24 Shad RC .30 .75
25 Shane McMahon .75 2.00
26 Shawn Michaels 1.25 3.00
27 Shelton Benjamin .30 .75
28 Snitsky .30 .75
29 Stone Cold 2.00 5.00
30 Super Crazy .50 1.25
31 Todd Grisham RC .30 .75
32 Trevor Murdoch .30 .75
33 Triple H 1.25 3.00
34 Umaga .50 1.25
35 Val Venis .75 2.00
36 William Regal .75 2.00
37 Batista .75 2.00
38 Brett Major RC .50 1.25
39 Brian Major RC .30 .75
40 Chavo Guerrero .50 1.25
41 Chris Masters 1.25 3.00
42 Dave Taylor RC .30 .75
43 Deuce RC .30 .75
44 Domino RC .30 .75
45 Edge .75 2.00
46 Eugene .30 .75
47 Finlay .75 2.00
48 Funaki .50 1.25
49 Gregory Helms .30 .75
50 Hardcore Holly .75 2.00
51 Hornswoggle RC .40 1.00
52 Jamie Noble .30 .75
53 JBL .75 2.00
54 Jimmy Wang Yang .30 .75
55 Kane .75 2.00
56 Kenny Dykstra RC .50 1.25
57 Mark Henry .50 1.25
58 Matt Hardy .75 2.00
59 Michael Cole .30 .75
60 MVP RC .50 1.25
61 Rey Mysterio .75 2.00
62 Ric Flair 1.25 3.00
63 Shannon Moore .30 .75
64 The Great Khali .30 .75
65 Theodore Long .40 1.00
66 Undertaker 1.50 4.00
67 Ashley .60 1.50
68 Candice 1.50 4.00

69 Cherry RC	.30	.75
70 Jillian	1.50	4.00
71 Kelly Kelly RC	.75	2.00
72 Maria	1.25	3.00
73 Melina	1.25	3.00
74 Michelle McCool	1.50	4.00
75 Mickie James	1.00	2.50
76 Queen Sharmell	.40	1.00
77 Torrie Wilson	2.50	6.00
78 Victoria	.60	1.50
79 Balls Mahoney RC	.30	.75
80 Boogeyman	.30	.75
81 CM Punk	1.25	3.00
82 Elijah Burke RC	.30	.75
83 Joey Styles	.30	.75
84 John Morrison	.50	1.25
85 Kevin Thorn RC	.30	.75
86 Nunzio	.30	.75
87 Marcus Cor Von RC	.30	.75
88 Matt Striker	.30	.75
89 Mike Knox RC	.30	.75
90 Stevie Richards	.50	1.25
91 Tazz	.50	1.25
92 The Miz RC	.60	1.50
93 Tommy Dreamer	.40	1.00
94 Big Daddy V	.30	.75
95 Kendrick / London	.75	2.00
96 Hass / Benjamin	.30	.75
97 Carlito / Masters	1.25	3.00
98 Cryme Tyme	.30	.75
99 Taylor / Regal	.75	2.00
100 Deuce / Domino	.30	.75
101 D-Generation X	1.00	2.50
102 Burke / Cor Von	.30	.75
103 Undertaker / Kane	1.50	4.00
104 Finlay / Hornswoggle	.75	2.00
105 Michaels / Cena	2.00	5.00
106 Cade / Murdoch	.30	.75
107 Kane / Boogeyman	.75	2.00
108 Flair / Piper	1.25	3.00
109 Hardy Boys	.75	2.00
110 Highlanders	.50	1.25
111 Major Brothers	.50	1.25
112 Dusty / Cody Rhodes	.75	2.00
113 Candice / Victoria	1.50	4.00
114 Vince / Shane McMahon	1.25	3.00
115 Junkyard Dog	.60	1.50
116 British Bulldog	1.25	3.00
117 Bushwhacker Butch	.50	1.25
118 Bushwhacker Luke	.50	1.25
119 Curt Hennig	.50	1.25
120 Doink the Clown	.30	.75
121 Dusty Rhodes	.75	2.00
122 Jake Roberts	.75	2.00
123 Jimmy Snuka	.50	1.25
124 Ted DiBiase	.60	1.50
125 Nikolai Volkoff	.60	1.50
126 Paul Bearer	.50	1.25
127 Sgt. Slaughter	.75	2.00
128 Billy Graham	.50	1.25
129 Terry Funk	.30	.75
130 Bobby Heenan	.60	1.50
131 Checklist 1 CL		
132 Checklist 2 CL		.75

2007 Topps WWE Face-Off Royal Rumble Champions

COMPLETE SET (10)	12.00	30.00
RANDOMLY INSERTED INTO PACKS		
R1 Batista	1.25	3.00
R2 Triple H	2.00	5.00
R3 The Rock	4.00	10.00
R4 Jim Duggan	.75	2.00
R5 Rey Mysterio	1.25	3.00
R6 Ric Flair	2.00	5.00
R7 Shawn Michaels	2.00	5.00
R8 Stone Cold Steve Austin	3.00	8.00
R9 Undertaker	2.50	6.00
R10 Mr. McMahon	2.00	5.00

2007 Topps WWE Face-Off Superstar Foil

COMPLETE SET (22)	12.00	30.00
RANDOMLY INSERTED INTO PACKS		
S1 Bobby Lashley	1.00	2.50
S2 Boogeyman	.40	1.00
S3 Carlito	1.50	4.00
S4 Chavo Guerrero	.60	1.50
S5 Chris Masters	1.50	4.00
S6 CM Punk	1.50	4.00
S7 Edge	1.00	2.50
S8 Fit Finlay	1.00	2.50
S9 Jeff Hardy	1.00	2.50
S10 John Cena	2.50	6.00
S11 John Morrison	.60	1.50
S12 Kane	1.00	2.50
S13 King Booker	1.00	2.50
S14 Mark Henry	.60	1.50
S15 Matt Hardy	1.00	2.50
S16 Mr. Kennedy	1.00	2.50
S17 MVP	.60	1.50
S18 Randy Orton	1.50	4.00
S19 Shelton Benjamin	.40	1.00
S20 The Great Khali	.40	1.00
S21 Tommy Dreamer	.50	1.25
S22 Umaga	.60	1.50

2020 Topps WWE Fully Loaded Autographed Gear Relics

*GREEN/50: .5X TO 1.2X BASIC AUTOS
*PURPLE/25: UNPRICED DUE TO SCARCITY
*BLUE/10: UNPRICED DUE TO SCARCITY
*RED/5: UNPRICED DUE TO SCARCITY
*GOLD/1: UNPRICED DUE TO SCARCITY
STATED ODDS 1:23
STATED PRINT RUN 199 SER.#'d SETS

SGAJ AJ Styles	20.00	50.00
SGBL Becky Lynch	75.00	150.00
SGFB Finn Balor	20.00	50.00
SGSN Shinsuke Nakamura	20.00	50.00

2020 Topps WWE Fully Loaded Autographed Chair Relics

*GREEN/50: .5X TO 1.2X BASIC AUTOS
*PURPLE/25: UNPRICED DUE TO SCARCITY
*BLUE/10: UNPRICED DUE TO SCARCITY
*RED/5: UNPRICED DUE TO SCARCITY
*GOLD/1: UNPRICED DUE TO SCARCITY
STATED ODDS 1:20
STATED PRINT RUN 99 SER.#'d SETS

CAS Asuka	50.00	100.00
CCL Candice LeRae	30.00	75.00
CDK Dakota Kai	30.00	75.00
CKC King Corbin	12.00	30.00
CRR Rhea Ripley	60.00	120.00
CSB Shayna Baszler	15.00	40.00
CTN Tegan Nox	30.00	75.00

2020 Topps WWE Fully Loaded Autographed Kiss

*PURPLE/25: .5X TO 1.2X BASIC AUTOS
*BLUE/10: UNPRICED DUE TO SCARCITY
*RED/5: UNPRICED DUE TO SCARCITY
*GOLD/1: UNPRICED DUE TO SCARCITY
STATED ODDS 1:118
STATED PRINT RUN 50 SER.#'d SETS

KBK Billie Kay	30.00	75.00
KBL Becky Lynch	125.00	300.00
KCC Charly Caruso	30.00	75.00
KCF Charlotte Flair	100.00	250.00
KCM Carmella	40.00	100.00
KEM Ember Moon	25.00	60.00
KLM Liv Morgan	125.00	300.00
KMJ Mickie James	75.00	150.00
KMM Maryse	30.00	75.00
KMR Mandy Rose	100.00	250.00
KNC Nikki Cross	60.00	150.00
KNJ Nia Jax	25.00	60.00
KNT Natalya	50.00	100.00
KPR Peyton Royce	30.00	75.00
KRR Ruby Riott	40.00	100.00
KRY Renee Young	25.00	60.00
KSD Sonya Deville	40.00	100.00
KVB Vanessa Borne	30.00	75.00

2020 Topps WWE Fully Loaded Autographed Ladder Relics

*GREEN/50: .5X TO 1.2X BASIC AUTOS
*PURPLE/25: UNPRICED DUE TO SCARCITY
*BLUE/10: UNPRICED DUE TO SCARCITY
*RED/5: UNPRICED DUE TO SCARCITY
*GOLD/1: UNPRICED DUE TO SCARCITY
STATED ODDS 1:15
STATED PRINT RUN 99 SER.#'d SETS

LAJ AJ Styles	25.00	60.00
LAS Asuka	30.00	75.00
LBE Big E	15.00	40.00
LCS Cesaro	15.00	40.00
LKC King Corbin	12.00	30.00
LKK Kofi Kingston	15.00	40.00
LKO Kevin Owens	25.00	60.00
LLE Lacey Evans	30.00	75.00
LNJ Nia Jax	20.00	50.00
LOT Otis	12.00	30.00
LSZ Sami Zayn	12.00	30.00

2020 Topps WWE Fully Loaded Autographed Microphone Box Relics

*GOLD/1: UNPRICED DUE TO SCARCITY
STATED PRINT RUN 5 SER.#'d SETS
UNPRICED DUE TO SCARCITY

MCBE Big E
MCRT R-Truth
MCTM The Miz

2020 Topps WWE Fully Loaded Autographed Oversized Mat Relics

*GREEN/50: .5X TO 1.2X BASIC AUTOS
*PURPLE/25: UNPRICED DUE TO SCARCITY
*BLUE/10: UNPRICED DUE TO SCARCITY
*RED/5: UNPRICED DUE TO SCARCITY
*GOLD/1: UNPRICED DUE TO SCARCITY
STATED ODDS 1:6
STATED PRINT RUN 199 SER.#'d SETS

MAB Alexa Bliss	75.00	150.00
MAJ AJ Styles	20.00	50.00
MBA Bayley	30.00	75.00
MBL The Fiend Bray Wyatt	60.00	120.00
MBS Braun Strowman	15.00	40.00
MCF Becky Lynch	60.00	120.00
MCM Carmella	30.00	75.00
MJG Johnny Gargano	12.00	30.00
MKK Kofi Kingston	12.00	30.00
MSB Sasha Banks	75.00	150.00
MSH Sheamus	15.00	40.00
MSN Shinsuke Nakamura	15.00	40.00
MSR Seth Rollins	20.00	50.00
MTM The Miz	15.00	40.00

2020 Topps WWE Fully Loaded Autographed Table Relics

*GREEN/50: .5X TO 1.2X BASIC AUTOS
*PURPLE/25: UNPRICED DUE TO SCARCITY
*BLUE/10: UNPRICED DUE TO SCARCITY
*RED/5: UNPRICED DUE TO SCARCITY
*GOLD/1: UNPRICED DUE TO SCARCITY
STATED ODDS 1:11
STATED PRINT RUN 99 SER.#'d SETS

TAB Aleister Black	20.00	50.00
TAC Adam Cole	20.00	50.00
TAJ AJ Styles	20.00	50.00
TAS Asuka	50.00	100.00
TBF Bobby Fish	15.00	40.00
TBS Braun Strowman	15.00	40.00
TCM Carmella	30.00	75.00
TCS Cesaro	15.00	40.00
TDD Dominik Dijakovic	12.00	30.00
TKL Keith Lee	15.00	40.00
TKO Kevin Owens	15.00	40.00
TKR Kyle O'Reilly	12.00	30.00
TLA Bobby Lashley	12.00	30.00
TRS Roderick Strong	15.00	40.00
TSN Shinsuke Nakamura	15.00	40.00
TTC Tommaso Ciampa	15.00	40.00

2020 Topps WWE Fully Loaded Autographed Turnbuckle Relics

*GREEN/50: .5X TO 1.2X BASIC AUTOS
*PURPLE/25: UNPRICED DUE TO SCARCITY
*BLUE/10: UNPRICED DUE TO SCARCITY
*RED/5: UNPRICED DUE TO SCARCITY
*GOLD/1: UNPRICED DUE TO SCARCITY
STATED ODDS 1:11
STATED PRINT RUN 99 SER.#'d SETS

AAC Apollo Crews	12.00	30.00
AAG Angel Garza	12.00	30.00
AAN Andrade	15.00	40.00
AAT Austin Theory	100.00	250.00
ADM Drew McIntyre	20.00	50.00
ADZ Dolph Ziggler	12.00	30.00
AJH Jeff Hardy	25.00	60.00
ALE Lacey Evans	25.00	60.00
AMA Mustafa Ali	12.00	30.00
AMR Mandy Rose	75.00	150.00
AOT Otis	15.00	40.00
ARC Ricochet	12.00	30.00
ART R-Truth	15.00	40.00
ASB Shayna Baszler	15.00	40.00
ASJ Samoa Joe	15.00	40.00
ATM The Miz	12.00	30.00

2020 Topps WWE Fully Loaded Autographs

STATED ODDS 1:430

AVM Mr. McMahon	300.00	600.00

2021 Topps WWE Fully Loaded Future Stars Autographs

*GOLD/99: .5X TO 1.2X BASIC AUTOS
*CITRINE/75: .6X TO 1.5X BASIC AUTOS
*ONYX/50: .75X TO 2X BASIC AUTOS
*SAPPHIRE/25: UNPRICED DUE TO SCARCITY
*RUBY/1: UNPRICED DUE TO SCARCITY
*P.P.BLACK/1: UNPRICED DUE TO SCARCITY
*P.P.CYAN/1: UNPRICED DUE TO SCARCITY
*P.P.MAGENTA/1: UNPRICED DUE TO SCARCITY
*P.P.YELLOW/1: UNPRICED DUE TO SCARCITY
STATED ODDS 1:12

SS Sarray	25.00	60.00
SW WALTER	15.00	40.00
SAT Austin Theory	12.00	30.00
SDM Dominik Mysterio	20.00	50.00
SIH Indi Hartwell	20.00	50.00
SKK Karrion Kross		
SLK LA Knight	30.00	75.00
SNC Nash Carter	8.00	20.00
SSB Shotzi Blackheart	30.00	75.00
SSC Scarlett	50.00	100.00
STB Tyler Bate	8.00	20.00
STS Toni Storm	25.00	60.00
STV Franky Monet	20.00	50.00
SWL Wes Lee	8.00	20.00
SZS Zoey Stark	15.00	40.00

2021 Topps WWE Fully Loaded Autographed Ladder Relics

*CITRINE/75: .6X TO 1.5X BASIC AUTOS
*ONYX/50: .75X TO 2X BASIC AUTOS
*SAPPHIRE/25: UNPRICED DUE TO SCARCITY
*RUBY/1: UNPRICED DUE TO SCARCITY
*DIE-CUT/1: UNPRICED DUE TO SCARCITY
STATED ODDS 1:26
STATED PRINT RUN 99 SER.#'d SETS

LCG Cameron Grimes	15.00	40.00
LCL Candice LeRae	25.00	60.00
LDP Damian Priest	12.00	30.00
LIS Io Shirai	50.00	100.00
LJG Johnny Gargano	15.00	40.00
LJU Jimmy Uso	12.00	30.00
LSZ Sami Zayn	15.00	40.00

2021 Topps WWE Fully Loaded Autographed Metal Chair Relics

*CITRINE/75: .6X TO 1.5X BASIC AUTOS
*ONYX/50: .75X TO 2X BASIC AUTOS
*SAPPHIRE/25: UNPRICED DUE TO SCARCITY
*RUBY/1: UNPRICED DUE TO SCARCITY

*DIE-CUT/1: UNPRICED DUE TO SCARCITY
STATED ODDS 1:23
STATED PRINT RUN 99 SER.#'d SETS

CO Omos 25.00 60.00
CBB Bianca Belair 30.00 75.00
CDR Drew McIntyre 20.00 50.00
CIS Io Shirai 30.00 75.00
CJM John Morrison 12.00 30.00
CKO Kevin Owens 15.00 40.00
CRG Raquel Gonzalez 30.00 75.00
CSB Sasha Banks 60.00 120.00
CROM Roman Reigns 75.00 150.00

2021 Topps WWE Fully Loaded Autographed Oversized Mat Relics

*GOLD/99: SAME VALUE AS BASIC
*CITRINE/75: .6X TO 1.5X BASIC AUTOS
*ONYX/50: .75X TO 2X BASIC AUTOS
*SAPPHIRE/25: UNPRICED DUE TO SCARCITY
*RUBY/1: UNPRICED DUE TO SCARCITY
STATED ODDS 1:26

MA Asuka 30.00 75.00
ME Edge 25.00 60.00
MBC Baron Corbin 12.00 30.00
MCF Charlotte Flair 50.00 100.00
MFB The Demon King Finn Balor 25.00 60.00

2021 Topps WWE Fully Loaded Autographed Trash Can Relics

*GOLD/99: SAME VALUE AS BASIC
*CITRINE/75: .6X TO 1.5X BASIC AUTOS
*ONYX/50: .75X TO 2X BASIC AUTOS
*SAPPHIRE/25: UNPRICED DUE TO SCARCITY
*RUBY/1: UNPRICED DUE TO SCARCITY
STATED ODDS 1:34

TIS Io Shirai 50.00 100.00
TRM Raul Mendoza 10.00 25.00
TSE Santos Escobar 10.00 25.00

2021 Topps WWE Fully Loaded Autographed Superstar Gear Relics

*CITRINE/75: .6X TO 1.5X BASIC AUTOS
*ONYX/50: .75X TO 2X BASIC AUTOS
*SAPPHIRE/25: UNPRICED DUE TO SCARCITY
*RUBY/1: UNPRICED DUE TO SCARCITY
*DIE-CUT/1: UNPRICED DUE TO SCARCITY
STATED ODDS 1:34
STATED PRINT RUN 99 SER.#'d SETS

GC Carmella 30.00 75.00
GR Ricochet 12.00 30.00
GBE Big E 15.00 40.00
GSB Shayna Baszler 12.00 30.00
GXW Xavier Woods 12.00 30.00
GKOR Kyle O'Reilly 12.00 30.00

2021 Topps WWE Fully Loaded Autographed Table Relics

*CITRINE/75: .6X TO 1.5X BASIC AUTOS
*ONYX/50: .75X TO 2X BASIC AUTOS
*SAPPHIRE/25: UNPRICED DUE TO SCARCITY
*RUBY/1: UNPRICED DUE TO SCARCITY
*DIE-CUT/1: UNPRICED DUE TO SCARCITY
STATED ODDS 1:19
STATED PRINT RUN 99 SER.#'d SETS

TE Elias 10.00 25.00
TAS AJ Styles 15.00 40.00
TJH Jeff Hardy 20.00 50.00
TJU Jey Uso 10.00 25.00
TKK Kofi Kingston 15.00 40.00
TPD Pete Dunne 10.00 25.00
TRM Rey Mysterio 20.00 50.00
TRR Rhea Ripley 30.00 75.00
TSR Seth Rollins 15.00 40.00
TTM The Miz 15.00 40.00

2021 Topps WWE Fully Loaded Autographed Turnbuckle Pad Relics

*GOLD/99: SAME VALUE AS BASIC
*CITRINE/75: .6X TO 1.5X BASIC AUTOS
*ONYX/50: .75X TO 2X BASIC AUTOS
*SAPPHIRE/25: UNPRICED DUE TO SCARCITY
*RUBY/1: UNPRICED DUE TO SCARCITY
STATED ODDS 1:23

PN Natalya 15.00 40.00
PAD Angelo Dawkins 10.00 25.00
PKL Keith Lee 12.00 30.00
PMF Montez Ford 10.00 25.00
PSR Seth Rollins

2021 Topps WWE Fully Loaded Legends Autographs

*GOLD/99: SAME VALUE AS BASIC
*CITRINE/75: .6X TO 1.5X BASIC AUTOS
*ONYX/50: .75X TO 2X BASIC AUTOS
*SAPPHIRE/25: UNPRICED DUE TO SCARCITY
*RUBY/1: UNPRICED DUE TO SCARCITY
*P.P.BLACK/1: UNPRICED DUE TO SCARCITY
*P.P.CYAN/1: UNPRICED DUE TO SCARCITY
*P.P.MAGENTA/1: UNPRICED DUE TO SCARCITY
*P.P.YELLOW/1: UNPRICED DUE TO SCARCITY
STATED ODDS 1:23

LG Goldberg
LK Kane 20.00 50.00
LU Undertaker 125.00 300.00
LBH Bret "Hit Man" Hart 50.00 125.00
LDL Dude Love 60.00 150.00
LPS Papa Shango 20.00 50.00
LSA Stone Cold Steve Austin
LSK Stacy Keibler 40.00 100.00
LSM Shawn Michaels
LTS Trish Stratus 30.00 75.00
L123 1-2-3 Kid
LDDP Diamond Dallas Page 25.00 60.00
LHHH Triple H
LJBL John "Bradshaw" Layfield 10.00 25.00

2018 Topps WWE Hall of Fame Tribute

1 Andre the Giant .60 1.50
2 Andre the Giant .60 1.50
3 Andre the Giant .60 1.50
4 Andre the Giant .60 1.50
5 Andre the Giant .60 1.50
6 Andre the Giant .60 1.50
7 Andre the Giant .60 1.50
8 Andre the Giant .60 1.50
9 Andre the Giant .60 1.50
10 Andre the Giant .60 1.50
11 Ultimate Warrior .60 1.50
12 Ultimate Warrior .60 1.50
13 Ultimate Warrior .60 1.50
14 Ultimate Warrior .60 1.50
15 Ultimate Warrior .60 1.50
16 Ultimate Warrior .60 1.50
17 Ultimate Warrior .60 1.50
18 Ultimate Warrior .60 1.50
19 Ultimate Warrior .60 1.50
20 Ultimate Warrior .60 1.50
21 Ric Flair .60 1.50
22 Ric Flair .60 1.50
23 Ric Flair .60 1.50
24 Ric Flair .60 1.50
25 Ric Flair .60 1.50
26 Ric Flair .60 1.50
27 Ric Flair .60 1.50
28 Ric Flair .60 1.50
29 Ric Flair .60 1.50
30 Ric Flair .60 1.50
31 Rowdy Roddy Piper .60 1.50
32 Rowdy Roddy Piper .60 1.50
33 Rowdy Roddy Piper .60 1.50
34 Rowdy Roddy Piper .60 1.50
35 Rowdy Roddy Piper .60 1.50
36 Rowdy Roddy Piper .60 1.50
37 Rowdy Roddy Piper .60 1.50
38 Rowdy Roddy Piper .60 1.50
39 Rowdy Roddy Piper .60 1.50
40 Rowdy Roddy Piper .60 1.50

2015 Topps WWE Hulk Hogan Tribute

COMPLETE SET (30) 12.00 30.00
*GOLD/10: 4X TO 10X BASIC CARDS
*RED/1: UNPRICED DUE TO SCARCITY

1 Hulk Hogan .75 2.00
2 Hulk Hogan .75 2.00
3 Hulk Hogan .75 2.00
4 Hulk Hogan .75 2.00
5 Hulk Hogan .75 2.00
6 Hulk Hogan .75 2.00
7 Hulk Hogan .75 2.00
8 Hulk Hogan .75 2.00
9 Hulk Hogan .75 2.00
10 Hulk Hogan .75 2.00
11 Hulk Hogan .75 2.00
12 Hulk Hogan .75 2.00
13 Hulk Hogan .75 2.00
14 Hulk Hogan .75 2.00
15 Hulk Hogan .75 2.00
16 Hulk Hogan .75 2.00
17 Hulk Hogan .75 2.00
18 Hulk Hogan .75 2.00
19 Hulk Hogan .75 2.00
20 Hulk Hogan .75 2.00
21 Hulk Hogan .75 2.00
22 Hulk Hogan .75 2.00
23 Hulk Hogan .75 2.00
24 Hulk Hogan .75 2.00
25 Hulk Hogan .75 2.00
26 Hulk Hogan .75 2.00
27 Hulk Hogan .75 2.00
28 Hulk Hogan .75 2.00
29 Hulk Hogan .75 2.00
30 Hulk Hogan .75 2.00

2007 Topps WWE Payback

1 Shawn Michaels 1.25 3.00
2 Triple H 1.25 3.00
3 Edge .75 2.00
4 John Cena 2.00 5.00
5 Randy Orton 1.25 3.00
6 Val Venis .75 2.00
7 Kane .75 2.00
8 Eugene .30 .75
9 Jerry Lawler .75 2.00
10 Lita 1.25 3.00
11 Viscera .75 2.00
12 Rob Conway .30 .75
13 Chris Masters 1.25 3.00
14 Shelton Benjamin .30 .75
15 Mickie James 1.00 2.50
16 Ric flair 1.25 3.00
17 Victoria .60 1.50
18 Umaga .50 1.25
19 Carlito 1.25 3.00
20 Johnny Nitro .50 1.25
21 Candice 1.50 4.00
22 Torrie Wilson 2.50 6.00
23 Mick Foley 1.25 3.00
24 Hulk Hogan 1.50 4.00
25 Kenny .50 1.25
26 Jeff Hardy .75 2.00
27 Stone Cold Steve Austin 2.00 5.00
28 Charlie Haas .30 .75
29 Mikey .30 .75
30 Melina 1.25 3.00
31 Rory McAllister RC .30 .75
32 Robbie McAllister RC .30 .75
33 Rey Mysterio .75 2.00
34 Undertaker 1.50 4.00
35 JBL .75 2.00
36 Jillian Hall 1.50 4.00
37 Brian Kendrick .50 1.25
38 Chris Benoit .75 2.00
39 King Booker .75 2.00
40 Batista .75 2.00
41 Paul London .75 2.00
42 Chavo Guerrero Jr. .50 1.25
43 Gregory Helms .30 .75
44 Matt Hardy .75 2.00
45 Tatanka .30 .75
46 Paul Burchill .30 .75
47 Bobby Lashley .75 2.00
48 Snitsky .30 .75
49 Finlay .75 2.00
50 The Miz .60 1.50
51 Ashley .60 1.50
52 Joey Mercury .30 .75
53 Psicosis .50 1.25
54 Super Crazy .50 1.25
55 The Great Khali .30 .75
56 Kid Kash .40 1.00
57 Ken Kennedy .75 2.00
58 Funaki .50 1.25
59 Scotty 2 Hotty .50 1.25
60 William Regal .75 2.00
61 Vito .30 .75
62 Michelle McCool 1.50 4.00
63 Mark Henry .50 1.25
64 Jamie Noble .30 .75
65 Al Snow .30 .75
66 Test .30 .75
67 Little Guido Maritato .30 .75
68 Jazz .40 1.00
69 Justin Credible .40 1.00
70 Roadkill RC .30 .75
71 Sandman .50 1.25
72 Big Show .50 1.25
73 Tommy Dreamer .40 1.00
74 Tony Mamaluke .30 .75
75 CM Punk 1.25 3.00
76 Hardcore Holly .75 2.00
77 Francine .60 1.50
78 Tazz .50 1.25
79 Rob Van Dam 1.25 3.00
80 Sabu .30 .75
81 Balls Mahoney RC .30 .75
82 C.W. Anderson .30 .75
83 Danny Doring RC .30 .75
84 Matt Striker .30 .75
85 Mike Knox RC .30 .75
86 Stevie Richards .50 1.25
87 Kevin Thorn RC .30 .75
88 Terry Funk .30 .75
89 British Bulldog 1.25 3.00
90 Sgt. Slaughter .75 2.00
91 Rowdy Roddy Piper 1.25 3.00
92 Million Dollar Man Ted DiBiase .60 1.50
93 Dusty Rhodes .75 2.00
94 Junkyard Dog .60 1.50
95 Doink The Clown .30 .75
96 Jake "The Snake" Roberts .75 2.00

2010 Topps WWE Icons Stickers

1 WWE Logo
2 HHH 1.25 3.00
3 John Cena 1.25 3.00
4 Raw Logo
5 Mark Henry .40 1.00
6 Vladimir Kozlov .40 1.00
7 Sheamus .40 1.00
8 R-Truth .25 .60
9 The Miz .40 1.00
10 David Hart Smith .25 .60
11 John Cena 1.25 3.00
12 Ezekiel Jackson .25 .60
13 William Regal .60 1.50
14 Smakdown Logo
15 Kane .60 1.50
16 Cody Rhodes .25 .60
17 Kofi Kingston .40 1.00
18 Drew McIntyre .40 1.00
19 Matt Hardy .60 1.50
20 Chris Masters .25 .60
21 Jack Swagger .25 .60
22 Rey Mysterio .60 1.50
23 Vance Archer .25 .60
24 NXT Logo
25 Matt Striker .25 .60
26 NXT Team
27 Wade Barrett .40 1.00
28 Skip Sheffield .40 1.00
29 Heath Slater .40 1.00
30 David Otunga .40 1.00
31 Justin Gabriel .40 1.00
32 Darren Young .40 1.00
33 Michael Tarver .40 1.00
34 Royal Rumble Logo
35 The Miz .40 1.00
36 The Miz vs MVP .40 1.00
37 The Miz vs MVP .40 1.00
38 The Miz vs MVP .40 1.00
39 Sheamus vs Randy Orton 1.00 2.50
40 Sheamus vs Randy Orton 1.00 2.50
41 Sheamus vs Randy Orton 1.00 2.50
42 Sheamus vs Randy Orton 1.00 2.50

43 Sheamus .40 1.00
44 Undertaker vs Rey Mysterio 1.00 2.50
45 Undertaker vs Rey Mysterio 1.00 2.50
46 Undertaker vs Rey Mysterio 1.00 2.50
47 Undertaker vs Rey Mysterio 1.00 2.50
48 Royal Rumble Moments
49 Royal Rumble Moments
50 Royal Rumble Moments
51 Edge 1.00 2.50
52 Edge 1.00 2.50
53 Edge 1.00 2.50
54 Elimination Chamber Logo
55 Undertaker 1.00 2.50
56 CM Punk vs R-Truth 1.00 2.50
57 Chris Jericho vs John Morrison .60 1.50
58 Chris Jericho vs John Morrison .60 1.50
59 Sheamus .40 1.00
60 HHH vs Sheamus 1.25 3.00
61 HHH vs Sheamus 1.25 3.00
62 John Cena vs HHH 1.25 3.00
63 John Cena vs Randy Orton 1.25 3.00
64 Wrestlemania Logo .20 .50
65 John Morrison .40 1.00
66 Randy Orton vs Cody Rhodes 1.00 2.50
67 Randy Orton vs Cody Rhodes 1.00 2.50
68 Randy Orton vs Cody Rhodes 1.00 2.50
69 Randy Orton 1.00 2.50
70 Edge 1.00 2.50
71 Chris Jericho vs Edge 1.00 2.50
72 John Cena vs. Batista 1.25 3.00
73 John Cena vs. Batista 1.25 3.00
74 Undertaker Logo 1.00 2.50
75 Shawn Michaels Logo 1.50 4.00
76 Undertaker vs Shawn Michaels 1.50 4.00
77 Undertaker vs Shawn Michaels 1.50 4.00
78 Undertaker vs Shawn Michaels 1.50 4.00
79 Undertaker vs Shawn Michaels 1.50 4.00
80 Undertaker vs Shawn Michaels 1.50 4.00
81 Undertaker vs Shawn Michaels 1.50 4.00
82 Undertaker vs Shawn Michaels 1.50 4.00
83 Undertaker vs Shawn Michaels 1.50 4.00
84 Extreme Rules Logo .20 .50
85 Jack Swagger vs Randy Orton 1.00 2.50
86 Jack Swagger vs Randy Orton 1.00 2.50
87 HHH vs Sheamus 1.25 3.00
88 HHH vs Sheamus 1.25 3.00
89 Chris Jericho vs Edge 1.00 2.50
90 Chris Jericho vs Edge 1.00 2.50
91 John Cena vs Batista 1.25 3.00
92 John Cena vs Batista 1.25 3.00
93 John Cena vs Batista 1.25 3.00
94 Sheamus .40 1.00
95 Sheamus .40 1.00
96 Sheamus vs Santino Marella .40 1.00
97 R-Truth .25 .60
98 R-Truth .25 .60
99 Ted DiBiase .40 1.00
100 Ted DiBiase .40 1.00
101 Ted DiBiase .40 1.00
102 Mark Henry .40 1.00
103 Mark Henry .40 1.00
104 Jack Swagger .25 .60
105 Jack Swagger .25 .60
106 Jack Swagger .25 .60
107 Kofi Kingston .40 1.00
108 Kofi Kingston .40 1.00
109 CM Punk Team 1.00 2.50
110 CM Punk 1.00 2.50
111 CM Punk Team 1.00 2.50
112 Dolph Ziggler .40 1.00
113 Dolph Ziggler .40 1.00
114 Heath Slater .40 1.00
115 Skip Sheffield .40 1.00
116 Michael Tarver .40 1.00
117 John Cena vs Michael Tarver 1.25 3.00
118 Michael Tarver .40 1.00
119 Wade Barrett .40 1.00
120 Wade Barrett .40 1.00
121 Justin Gabriel .40 1.00
122 Darren Young .40 1.00
123 Darren Young .40 1.00
124 WWE Champion Belt .20 .50
125 John Cena 1.25 3.00
126 John Cena 1.25 3.00
127 Sheamus .40 1.00
128 Sheamus .40 1.00
129 Randy Orton 1.00 2.50
130 Randy Orton 1.00 2.50
131 Randy Orton 1.00 2.50
132 HHH 1.25 3.00
133 HHH 1.25 3.00
134 WWE World Heavywight Belt .20 .50
135 Jack Swagger .25 .60
136 Jack Swagger .25 .60
137 Jack Swagger .25 .60
138 Undertaker 1.00 2.50
139 Undertaker 1.00 2.50
140 CM Punk 1.00 2.50
141 CM Punk 1.00 2.50
142 Chris Jericho .60 1.50
143 Chris Jericho .60 1.50
144 WWE Intercontinental Belt .20 .50
145 Kofi Kingston .40 1.00
146 Kofi Kingston .40 1.00
147 Chris Jericho .60 1.50
148 Chris Jericho .60 1.50
149 Drew McIntyre .40 1.00
150 Drew McIntyre .40 1.00
151 Drew McIntyre .40 1.00
152 Rey Mysterio .60 1.50
153 Rey Mysterio .60 1.50
154 WWE Divas Belt .20 .50
155 Eve 1.00 2.50
156 Eve 1.00 2.50
157 Maryse 1.00 2.50
158 Maryse 1.00 2.50
159 WWE Woman's Championship Belt .20 .50
160 Michelle McCool 1.00 2.50
161 Mickie James 1.25 3.00
162 Layla .60 1.50
163 Melina 1.00 2.50
164 WWE US Championship Belt .20 .50
165 R-Truth .25 .60
166 R-Truth .25 .60
167 The Miz .40 1.00
168 The Miz .40 1.00
169 The Miz .40 1.00
170 MVP .40 1.00
171 MVP .40 1.00
172 Matt Hardy .60 1.50
173 Matt Hardy .60 1.50
174 WWE Tag Team Title Belt .20 .50
175 David Hart Smith & Tyson Kidd .25 .60
176 David Hart Smith & Tyson Kidd .25 .60
177 Big Show & The Miz .60 1.50
178 Big Show & The Miz .60 1.50
179 WWE Tag Team Title Belt .20 .50
180 D-Generation X
181 D-Generation X
182 Caylen Croft & Trent Barreta .25 .60
183 Caylen Croft & Trent Barreta .25 .60
184 Tyson Kidd .25 .60
185 Chris Jericho .60 1.50
186 Evan Bourne .25 .60
187 HHH 1.25 3.00
188 Santino Marella .25 .60
189 Edge 1.00 2.50
190 Ted DiBiase .40 1.00
191 Randy Orton 1.00 2.50
192 Yoshi Tatsu .25 .60
193 John Morrison .40 1.00
194 MVP .40 1.00
195 Caylen Croft .25 .60
196 CM Punk 1.00 2.50
197 Undertaker 1.00 2.50
198 Luke Gallows .25 .60
199 Christian .40 1.00
200 Shad .25 .60
201 Big Show .60 1.50
202 Trent Barreta .25 .60
203 Dolph Ziggler .40 1.00
204 R-Truth and Morrison .40 1.00
205 R-Truth and Morrison .40 1.00
206 Hart-Dynasty .20 .50
207 Hart-Dynasty .20 .50
208 Edge 1.00 2.50
209 Edge 1.00 2.50
210 Edge 1.00 2.50
211 Evan Bourne .25 .60
212 Evan Bourne .25 .60
213 Evan Bourne .25 .60
214 Big Show .60 1.50
215 Big Show .60 1.50
216 Big Show .60 1.50
217 Shad .25 .60
218 Shad .25 .60
219 Christian .40 1.00
220 Christian .40 1.00
221 Kane .60 1.50
222 Kane .60 1.50
223 Kane .60 1.50
224 John Cena 1.25 3.00
225 Ted DiBiase .40 1.00
226 Theodore Long .25 .60
227 Heath Slater .40 1.00
228 Christian .40 1.00
229 Michelle McCool 1.00 2.50
230 HHH 1.25 3.00
231 Wrestlemania VII Logo .20 .50
232 Dusty Rhodes .60 1.50
233 Primo .25 .60
234 Randy Orton 1.00 2.50
235 Rey Mysterio .60 1.50
236 Undertaker 1.00 2.50
P1 Undertaker 1.00 2.50
P2 Sheamus .40 1.00
P3 Rey Mysterio .60 1.50
P4 Randy Orton 1.00 2.50
P5 Cody Rhodes .25 .60
P6 The Miz .40 1.00
P7 Chris Masters .25 .60
P8 Edge 1.00 2.50
P9 CM Punk 1.00 2.50
P10 Matt Hardy .60 1.50
P11 Kane .60 1.50
P12 Mark Henry .40 1.00
P13 Drew McIntyre .40 1.00
P14 Dolph Ziggler .40 1.00

2013 Topps WWE Icons Stickers

1 WWE LOGO .20 .50
2 Brock Lesnar 1.00 2.50
3 The Rock 1.25 3.00
4 SmackDown .20 .50
5 Great Khali .25 .60
6 Kofi Kingston .25 .60
7 Brock Lesnar 1.00 2.50
8 Brock Lesnar 1.00 2.50
9 Brock Lesnar 1.00 2.50
10 Brock Lesnar 1.00 2.50
11 Brock Lesnar 1.00 2.50
12 Brock Lesnar 1.00 2.50
13 Brock Lesnar 1.00 2.50
14 Brock Lesnar 1.00 2.50
15 Brock Lesnar 1.00 2.50
16 Brock Lesnar 1.00 2.50
17 Brock Lesnar 1.00 2.50
18 Brock Lesnar 1.00 2.50
19 The Rock 1.25 3.00
20 The Rock 1.25 3.00
21 The Rock 1.25 3.00
22 The Rock 1.25 3.00
23 The Rock 1.25 3.00
24 The Rock 1.25 3.00
25 The Rock 1.25 3.00
26 The Rock 1.25 3.00
27 The Rock 1.25 3.00
28 The Rock 1.25 3.00
29 The Rock 1.25 3.00
30 The Rock 1.25 3.00
31 Alberto Del Rio .50 1.25
32 Alberto Del Rio .50 1.25
33 Alberto Del Rio .50 1.25
34 Alberto Del Rio .50 1.25
35 Alberto Del Rio .50 1.25
36 Alberto Del Rio .50 1.25
37 Alberto Del Rio .50 1.25
38 Alberto Del Rio .50 1.25
39 Alberto Del Rio .50 1.25
40 Alberto Del Rio .50 1.25
41 Alberto Del Rio .50 1.25
42 Alberto Del Rio .50 1.25
43 Antonio Cesaro .25 .60
44 Antonio Cesaro .25 .60
45 Antonio Cesaro .25 .60
46 Antonio Cesaro .25 .60
47 Antonio Cesaro .25 .60
48 Daniel Bryan .60 1.50
49 Daniel Bryan .60 1.50
50 Daniel Bryan .60 1.50
51 Daniel Bryan .60 1.50
52 Daniel Bryan .60 1.50
53 Dolph Ziggler .40 1.00
54 Dolph Ziggler .40 1.00
55 Dolph Ziggler .40 1.00
56 Dolph Ziggler .40 1.00
57 Dolph Ziggler .40 1.00
58 Ryback .25 .60
59 Ryback .25 .60
60 Ryback .25 .60
61 Ryback .25 .60
62 Ryback .25 .60
63 Kofi Kingston .25 .60
64 Kofi Kingston .25 .60
65 Kofi Kingston .25 .60
66 Kofi Kingston .25 .60
67 Kofi Kingston .25 .60
68 Sin Cara .40 1.00
69 Sin Cara .40 1.00
70 Sin Cara .40 1.00
71 Sin Cara .40 1.00
72 Sin Cara .40 1.00
73 Jack Swagger .40 1.00
74 Jack Swagger .40 1.00
75 Jack Swagger .40 1.00
76 Jack Swagger .40 1.00
77 Jack Swagger .40 1.00
78 Jack Swagger .40 1.00
79 Jack Swagger .40 1.00
80 Jack Swagger .40 1.00
81 Jack Swagger .40 1.00
82 Jack Swagger .40 1.00
83 Jack Swagger .40 1.00
84 CM Punk 1.00 2.50
85 CM Punk 1.00 2.50
86 CM Punk 1.00 2.50
87 CM Punk 1.00 2.50
88 CM Punk 1.00 2.50
89 CM Punk 1.00 2.50
90 CM Punk 1.00 2.50
91 CM Punk 1.00 2.50
92 CM Punk 1.00 2.50
93 CM Punk 1.00 2.50
94 CM Punk 1.00 2.50
95 Sheamus .50 1.25
96 Sheamus .50 1.25
97 Sheamus .50 1.25
98 Sheamus .50 1.25
99 Sheamus .50 1.25
100 Sheamus .50 1.25
101 Sheamus .50 1.25
102 Sheamus .50 1.25
103 Sheamus .50 1.25
104 Sheamus .50 1.25
105 Sheamus .50 1.25
106 Sheamus .50 1.25
107 Mark Henry .30 .75
108 Mark Henry .30 .75
109 Mark Henry .30 .75
110 Mark Henry .30 .75
111 Mark Henry .30 .75
112 Big Show .50 1.25
113 Big Show .50 1.25
114 Big Show .50 1.25
115 Big Show .50 1.25
116 Big Show .50 1.25
117 Great Khali .25 .60
118 Great Khali .25 .60
119 Great Khali .25 .60
120 Great Khali .25 .60
121 Great Khali .25 .60
122 Brodus Clay .25 .60
123 Brodus Clay .25 .60
124 Brodus Clay .25 .60
125 Brodus Clay .25 .60
126 Brodus Clay .25 .60
127 Kane .50 1.25
128 Kane .50 1.25
129 Kane .50 1.25
130 Kane .50 1.25

131 Kane .50 1.25
132 The Miz .40 1.00
133 The Miz .40 1.00
134 The Miz .40 1.00
135 The Miz .40 1.00
136 The Miz .40 1.00
137 John Cena 1.25 3.00
138 John Cena 1.25 3.00
139 John Cena 1.25 3.00
140 John Cena 1.25 3.00
141 John Cena 1.25 3.00
142 John Cena 1.25 3.00
143 John Cena 1.25 3.00
144 John Cena 1.25 3.00
145 John Cena 1.25 3.00
146 John Cena 1.25 3.00
147 John Cena 1.25 3.00
148 John Cena 1.25 3.00
149 The Shield .40 1.00
150 The Shield .40 1.00
151 The Shield .40 1.00
152 The Shield .40 1.00
153 The Shield .40 1.00
154 The Shield .40 1.00
155 The Shield .40 1.00
156 The Shield .40 1.00
157 The Shield .40 1.00
158 The Shield .40 1.00
159 The Shield .40 1.00
160 Randy Orton .75 2.00
161 Randy Orton .75 2.00
162 Randy Orton .75 2.00
163 Randy Orton .75 2.00
164 Randy Orton .75 2.00
165 Randy Orton .75 2.00
166 Randy Orton .75 2.00
167 Randy Orton .75 2.00
168 Randy Orton .75 2.00
169 Randy Orton .75 2.00
170 Randy Orton .75 2.00
171 Rey Mysterio .60 1.50
172 Rey Mysterio .60 1.50
173 Rey Mysterio .60 1.50
174 Rey Mysterio .60 1.50

2006 Topps WWE Insider

COMPLETE SET (72) 8.00 20.00
1 Lashley RC .30 .75
2 Big Show .50 1.25
3 Carlito .50 1.25
4 Chris Masters .20 .50
5 Edge .50 1.25
6 Gene Snitsky .20 .50
7 Hulk Hogan .60 1.50
8 Jerry The King Lawler .40 1.00
9 John Cena .75 2.00
10 Jonathan Coachman .12 .30
11 Kane .50 1.25
12 Chavo Guerrero .20 .50
13 Kurt Angle .50 1.25
14 Lance Cade .12 .30
15 Lilian Garcia .60 1.50
16 Lita .75 2.00
17 Maria .50 1.25
18 Matt Hardy .30 .75
19 Rene Dupree .20 .50
20 Ric Flair .60 1.50
21 Rob Conway .20 .50
22 Rob Van Dam .30 .75
23 Paul Burchill RC .12 .30
24 Kid Kash .12 .30
25 Shawn Michaels .50 1.25
26 Shelton Benjamin .12 .30
27 Mickie James RC .75 2.00
28 Stone Cold .75 2.00
29 Gregory Helms .12 .30
30 Trevor Murdoch RC .12 .30
31 Triple H .50 1.25
32 Trish Stratus .75 2.00
33 Mark Henry .20 .50
34 Val Venis .20 .50
35 Victoria .75 2.00
36 Viscera .20 .50
37 Batista .50 1.25
38 Booker T .30 .75
39 Candice Michelle .75 2.00
40 Chris Benoit .50 1.25
41 Boogeyman RC .20 .50
42 Funaki .20 .50
43 Hardcore Holly .20 .50
44 Joey Styles RC .12 .30
45 JBL .30 .75
46 Joey Mercury .12 .30
47 Johnny Nitro .20 .50
48 Ashley RC .50 1.25
49 Finlay .30 .75
50 Ken Kennedy RC .30 .75
51 Melina .25 .60
52 Michael Cole RC .12 .30
53 Nunzio .12 .30
54 Orlando Jordan .12 .30
55 Paul London .12 .30
56 Psicosis .12 .30
57 Randy Orton .30 .75
58 Rey Mysterio .30 .75
59 Road Warrior Animal .25 .60
60 Kristal RC .30 .75
61 Sharmell .50 1.25
62 Simon Dean RC .12 .30
63 Steven Richards .20 .50
64 Super Crazy .20 .50
65 Goldust .20 .50
66 Tazz .20 .50
67 Theodore Long .12 .30
68 Torrie Wilson .50 1.25
69 Undertaker .60 1.50
70 Vito RC .12 .30
71 William Regal .30 .75
72 Checklist .10 .25

2006 Topps WWE Insider Autographs

STATED ODDS 1:24 HOBBY EXCLUSIVE
NNO Ashley 6.00 15.00
NNO Candice Michelle 12.00 30.00
NNO Carlito 30.00 80.00
NNO Chris Masters 6.00 15.00
NNO Edge 15.00 40.00
NNO Eugene 12.00 30.00
NNO Goldust 8.00 20.00
NNO Gregory Helms 8.00 20.00
NNO John Cena 75.00 150.00
NNO Kristal 8.00 20.00
NNO Lita 12.00 30.00
NNO Maria 20.00 50.00
NNO Matt Hardy 12.00 30.00
NNO Melina 8.00 20.00
NNO Mickie James 20.00 50.00
NNO Randy Orton 25.00 60.00
NNO Road Warrior (Animal) 15.00 50.00
NNO Shelton Benjamin 12.00 30.00
NNO Torrie Wilson 30.00 75.00
NNO Trish Stratus 50.00 100.00
NNO Victoria 12.00 30.00
NNO Viscera 15.00 40.00

2006 Topps WWE Insider Champions

COMPLETE SET (12) 5.00 12.00
STATED ODDS 1:6 RETAIL EXCLUSIVE
C1 John Cena .75 2.00
C2 Ric Flair .60 1.50
C3 Trish Stratus .75 2.00
C4 Rey Mysterio .30 .75
C5 Eddie Guerrero .50 1.25
C6 Booker T .30 .75
C7 Chris Benoit .50 1.25
C8 Kurt Angle .50 1.25
C9 Undertaker .60 1.50
C10 Triple H .50 1.25
C11 Stone Cold .75 2.00
C12 Hulk Hogan .60 1.50

2006 Topps WWE Insider Coins

COMPLETE SET (24) 12.00 30.00
STATED ODDS 1:1 RETAIL EXCLUSIVE
1 John Cena 1.50 4.00
2 Edge 1.00 2.50
3 Carlito 1.00 2.50
4 Kurt Angle 1.00 2.50
5 Randy Orton .60 1.50
6 Shawn Michaels 1.00 2.50
7 Undertaker 1.25 3.00
8 Batista 1.00 2.50
9 Ric Flair 1.25 3.00
10 Chris Masters .40 1.00
11 Triple H 1.00 2.50
12 Kane 1.00 2.50
13 Boogeyman .40 1.00
14 Steve Austin 1.50 4.00
15 Trish Stratus 1.50 4.00
16 Rob Van Dam .60 1.50
17 Chris Benoit 1.00 2.50
18 Hulk Hogan 1.25 3.00
19 JBL .60 1.50
20 Rey Mysterio .60 1.50
21 Big Show 1.00 2.50
22 Booker T .60 1.50
23 Torrie Wilson 1.00 2.50
24 Candice Michelle 1.50 4.00

2006 Topps WWE Insider Divas

COMPLETE SET (12) 10.00 25.00
STATED ODDS 1:3 RETAIL EXCLUSIVE
D1 Candice Michelle .60 1.50
D2 Ashley 4.00 10.00
D3 Mickie James .60 1.50
D4 Sharmell .40 1.00
D5 Torrie Wilson 6.00 15.00
D6 Trish Stratus 5.00 12.00
D7 Jillian Hall .40 1.00
D8 Lilian Garcia .50 1.25
D9 Lita .60 1.50
D10 Maria .40 1.00
D11 Kristal .25 .60
D12 Victoria .60 1.50

2006 Topps WWE Insider Memorabilia

STATED ODDS 1:24 HOBBY EXCLUSIVE
NNO John Cena 6.00 15.00
NNO Kurt Angle 3.00 8.00
NNO Matt Hardy 2.00 5.00
NNO Rey Mysterio 2.00 5.00
NNO Shawn Michaels 8.00 20.00

2006 Topps WWE Insider Promos

COMPLETE SET (2)
P1 Undertaker 4.00 10.00
P2 Batista 1.50 4.00

2019 Topps WWE Intercontinental Championship 40th Anniversary

COMPLETE SET (40) 15.00 40.00
RANDOMLY INSERTED INTO PACKS
IC1 Don Muraco .50 1.25
IC2 Macho Man Randy Savage 1.25 3.00
IC3 Ricky The Dragon Steamboat .60 1.50
IC4 The Honky Tonk Man .50 1.25
IC5 Ultimate Warrior 1.25 3.00
IC6 Ravishing Rick Rude .60 1.50
IC7 Mr. Perfect .75 2.00
IC8 Texas Tornado .75 2.00
IC9 Bret Hit Man Hart 1.25 3.00
IC10 Rowdy Roddy Piper 1.25 3.00
IC11 Shawn Michaels 1.25 3.00
IC12 Razor Ramon .75 2.00
IC13 Diesel .75 2.00
IC14 Triple H 1.25 3.00
IC15 The Rock 2.50 6.00
IC16 Stone Cold Steve Austin 2.50 6.00
IC17 Ken Shamrock .75 2.00
IC18 Road Dogg .50 1.25
IC19 The Godfather .50 1.25
IC20 Edge 1.25 3.00
IC21 D'Lo Brown .50 1.25
IC22 Kurt Angle 1.00 2.50
IC23 Eddie Guerrero 1.25 3.00
IC24 Billy Gunn .60 1.50
IC25 Jeff Hardy 1.25 3.00
IC26 Kane .75 2.00
IC27 Albert .50 1.25
IC28 William Regal .75 2.00
IC29 Booker T 1.25 3.00
IC30 Randy Orton 1.25 3.00
IC31 Shelton Benjamin .60 1.50
IC32 Ric Flair 1.50 4.00
IC33 Umaga .50 1.25
IC34 Kofi Kingston .75 2.00
IC35 Rey Mysterio 1.25 3.00
IC36 Drew McIntyre .60 1.50
IC37 Dolph Ziggler 1.00 2.50
IC38 Big Show .75 2.00
IC39 The Miz 1.00 2.50
IC40 Curtis Axel .60 1.50

2017 Topps WWE John Cena Tribute

COMPLETE SET (40) 6.00 15.00
STATED ODDS 1:6
1 John Cena 1.00 2.50
2 John Cena 1.00 2.50
3 John Cena 1.00 2.50
4 John Cena 1.00 2.50
5 John Cena 1.00 2.50
6 John Cena 1.00 2.50
7 John Cena 1.00 2.50
8 John Cena 1.00 2.50
9 John Cena 1.00 2.50
10 John Cena 1.00 2.50
11 John Cena 1.00 2.50
12 John Cena 1.00 2.50
13 John Cena 1.00 2.50
14 John Cena 1.00 2.50
15 John Cena 1.00 2.50
16 John Cena 1.00 2.50
17 John Cena 1.00 2.50
18 John Cena 1.00 2.50
19 John Cena 1.00 2.50
20 John Cena 1.00 2.50
21 John Cena 1.00 2.50
22 John Cena 1.00 2.50
23 John Cena 1.00 2.50
24 John Cena 1.00 2.50
25 John Cena 1.00 2.50
26 John Cena 1.00 2.50
27 John Cena 1.00 2.50
28 John Cena 1.00 2.50
29 John Cena 1.00 2.50
30 John Cena 1.00 2.50
31 John Cena 1.00 2.50
32 John Cena 1.00 2.50
33 John Cena 1.00 2.50
34 John Cena 1.00 2.50
35 John Cena 1.00 2.50
36 John Cena 1.00 2.50
37 John Cena 1.00 2.50
38 John Cena 1.00 2.50
39 John Cena 1.00 2.50
40 John Cena 1.00 2.50

2018 Topps WWE Macho Man Randy Savage Tribute

1 Macho Man Randy Savage 1.25 3.00
2 Macho Man Randy Savage 1.25 3.00
3 Macho Man Randy Savage 1.25 3.00
4 Macho Man Randy Savage 1.25 3.00
5 Macho Man Randy Savage 1.25 3.00
6 Macho Man Randy Savage 1.25 3.00
7 Macho Man Randy Savage 1.25 3.00
8 Macho Man Randy Savage 1.25 3.00
9 Macho Man Randy Savage 1.25 3.00
10 Macho Man Randy Savage 1.25 3.00
11 Macho Man Randy Savage 1.25 3.00
12 Macho Man Randy Savage 1.25 3.00
13 Macho Man Randy Savage 1.25 3.00
14 Macho Man Randy Savage 1.25 3.00
15 Macho Man Randy Savage 1.25 3.00
16 Macho Man Randy Savage 1.25 3.00
17 Macho Man Randy Savage 1.25 3.00
18 Macho Man Randy Savage 1.25 3.00
19 Macho Man Randy Savage 1.25 3.00
20 Macho Man Randy Savage 1.25 3.00
21 Macho Man Randy Savage 1.25 3.00
22 Macho Man Randy Savage 1.25 3.00
23 Macho Man Randy Savage 1.25 3.00
24 Macho Man Randy Savage 1.25 3.00
25 Macho Man Randy Savage 1.25 3.00

26	Macho Man Randy Savage	1.25	3.00
27	Macho Man Randy Savage	1.25	3.00
28	Macho Man Randy Savage	1.25	3.00
29	Macho Man Randy Savage	1.25	3.00
30	Macho Man Randy Savage	1.25	3.00
31	Macho Man Randy Savage	1.25	3.00
32	Macho Man Randy Savage	1.25	3.00
33	Macho Man Randy Savage	1.25	3.00
34	Macho Man Randy Savage	1.25	3.00
35	Macho Man Randy Savage	1.25	3.00
36	Macho Man Randy Savage	1.25	3.00
37	Macho Man Randy Savage	1.25	3.00
38	Macho Man Randy Savage	1.25	3.00
39	Macho Man Randy Savage	1.25	3.00
40	Macho Man Randy Savage	1.25	3.00

2019 Topps WWE Money in the Bank

COMPLETE SET (90) 10.00 25.00
*BRONZE: .5X TO 1.2X BASIC CARDS
*GREEN/99: .75X TO 2X BASIC CARDS
*BLUE/50: 1.2X TO 3X BASIC CARDS
*PURPLE/25: 2X TO 5X BASIC CARDS
*GOLD/10: UNPRICED DUE TO SCARCITY
*BLACK/5: UNPRICED DUE TO SCARCITY
*RED/1: UNPRICED DUE TO SCARCITY

1	Aiden English	.25	.60
2	AJ Styles	1.25	3.00
3	Alexa Bliss	1.25	3.00
4	Alicia Fox	.50	1.25
5	Andrade	.30	.75
6	Ariya Daivari	.25	.60
7	Apollo Crews	.30	.75
8	Asuka	.75	2.00
9	Baron Corbin	.40	1.00
10	Bayley	.50	1.25
11	Becky Lynch	1.00	2.50
12	Beth Phoenix	.40	1.00
13	Big Show	.40	1.00
14	Big E	.25	.60
15	Bobby Lashley	.50	1.25
16	Robert Roode	.50	1.25
17	Booker T	.60	1.50
18	Braun Strowman	.60	1.50
19	Bray Wyatt	.60	1.50
20	Brock Lesnar	1.00	2.50
21	Carmella	.60	1.50
22	Cesaro	.30	.75
23	Charlotte Flair	1.00	2.50
24	Christian	.40	1.00
25	Curt Hawkins	.25	.60
26	Curtis Axel	.30	.75
27	Dana Brooke	.50	1.25
28	Daniel Bryan	.60	1.50
29	Drew McIntyre	.30	.75
30	Elias	.50	1.25
31	Ember Moon	.60	1.50
32	Eve Torres	.30	.75
33	Fandango	.25	.60
34	Finlay	.25	.60
35	Finn Balor	.50	1.25
36	Gran Metalik	.25	.60
37	Heath Slater	.25	.60
38	Jeff Hardy	.60	1.50
39	Jey Uso	.30	.75
40	Jimmy Uso	.30	.75
41	Jinder Mahal	.50	1.25
42	John Cena	1.25	3.00
43	Kalisto	.25	.60
44	Kane	.40	1.00
45	Karl Anderson	.40	1.00
46	Kevin Owens	.60	1.50
47	Kofi Kingston	.40	1.00
48	Lacey Evans	.50	1.25
49	Lince Dorado	.25	.60
50	Luke Gallows	.40	1.00
51	Mark Henry	.30	.75
52	Maria Kanellis	.60	1.50
53	Mandy Rose	.60	1.50
54	Matt Hardy	.50	1.25
55	Mike Kanellis	.25	.60
56	Mojo Rawley	.30	.75
57	Ali	.25	.60
58	Naomi	.40	1.00
59	Natalya	.50	1.25
60	Nikki Cross	.40	1.00
61	Nia Jax	.50	1.25
62	Paige	1.00	2.50
63	Paul Heyman	.30	.75
64	Randy Orton	.60	1.50
65	Rey Mysterio	.60	1.50
66	Ric Flair	.75	2.00
67	Ricochet	.60	1.50
68	Roman Reigns	.60	1.50
69	Ronda Rousey	1.25	3.00
70	Rowan	.25	.60
71	R-Truth	.30	.75
72	Sami Zayn	.50	1.25
73	Samir Singh	.25	.60
74	Samoa Joe	.50	1.25
75	Sonya Deville	.50	1.25
76	Seth Rollins	.60	1.50
77	Sheamus	.40	1.00
78	Shelton Benjamin	.30	.75
79	Shinsuke Nakamura	.60	1.50
80	Sunil Singh	.25	.60
81	Tamina	.25	.60
82	Lord Tensai	.25	.60
83	The Miz	.50	1.25
84	Titus O'Neil	.30	.75
85	Tony Nese	.25	.60
86	Tyler Breeze	.30	.75
87	Xavier Woods	.30	.75
88	William Regal	.40	1.00
89	Zack Ryder	.30	.75
90	Zelina Vega	.40	1.00

2019 Topps WWE Money in the Bank Autographed Mat Relics

COMMON AUTO 5.00 12.00
*BLUE/50: .5X TO 1.2X BASIC AUTOS
*PURPLE/25: UNPRICED DUE TO SCARCITY
*GOLD/10: UNPRICED DUE TO SCARCITY
*BLACK/5: UNPRICED DUE TO SCARCITY
*RED/1: UNPRICED DUE TO SCARCITY
STATED ODDS 1:227
STATED PRINT RUN 99 SER.#'d SETS

MRACM	Carmella	12.00	30.00
MRAFB	Finn Balor	10.00	25.00
MRAKA	Karl Anderson	8.00	20.00
MRAKK	Kofi Kingston	6.00	15.00
MRAKO	Kevin Owens	8.00	20.00
MRALG	Luke Gallows	6.00	15.00
MRANT	Natalya	6.00	15.00
MRART	R-Truth	6.00	15.00
MRASA	Samir Singh	5.00	12.00
MRASJ	Samoa Joe	6.00	15.00
MRASM	Sheamus	8.00	20.00
MRASN	Shinsuke Nakamura	6.00	15.00
MRASR	Seth Rollins	8.00	20.00
MRASU	Sunil Singh	5.00	12.00
MRATO	Titus O'Neil	5.00	12.00
MRATS	Tamina	5.00	12.00
MRAXW	Xavier Woods	5.00	12.00
MRAZR	Zack Ryder	6.00	15.00

2019 Topps WWE Money in the Bank Autographed Shirt Relics

*BLUE/50: .5X TO 1.2X BASIC AUTOS
*PURPLE/25: .6X TO 1.5X BASIC AUTOS
*GOLD/10: UNPRICED DUE TO SCARCITY
*BLACK/5: UNPRICED DUE TO SCARCITY
*RED/1: UNPRICED DUE TO SCARCITY
STATED ODDS 1:453
STATED PRINT RUN 99 SER.#'d SETS

SRAAC	Apollo Crews	5.00	12.00
SRAAJ	AJ Styles	10.00	25.00
SRABS	Braun Strowman	12.00	30.00
SRACS	Cesaro	5.00	12.00
SRAHS	Heath Slater	5.00	12.00
SRAKK	Kofi Kingston	6.00	15.00
SRARI	Ricochet	10.00	25.00
SRARR	Roman Reigns		
SRASR	Seth Rollins	12.00	30.00
SRASZ	Sami Zayn	10.00	25.00

2019 Topps WWE Money in the Bank Autographs

*GREEN/99: .5X TO 1.2X BASIC AUTOS
*BLUE/50: .6X TO 1.5X BASIC AUTOS
*PURPLE/25: UNPRICED DUE TO SCARCITY
*GOLD/10: UNPRICED DUE TO SCARCITY
*BLACK/5: UNPRICED DUE TO SCARCITY
*RED/1: UNPRICED DUE TO SCARCITY
STATED ODDS 1:41
STATED PRINT RUN 99 SER.#'d SETS

AAB	Alexa Bliss	20.00	50.00
AAD	Andrade	4.00	10.00
AAE	Aiden English	4.00	10.00
AAJ	AJ Styles	8.00	20.00
AAK	Asuka	10.00	25.00
AAL	Ali	4.00	10.00
ABC	Baron Corbin	4.00	10.00
ABE	Big E	4.00	10.00
ABJ	Shelton Benjamin	4.00	10.00
ABK	Dana Brooke	10.00	25.00
ABL	Becky Lynch	12.00	30.00
ABM	Matt Hardy	5.00	12.00
ABR	Robert Roode	4.00	10.00
ABS	Braun Strowman	5.00	12.00
ABW	Bray Wyatt	6.00	15.00
ACF	Charlotte Flair EXCH	12.00	30.00
ACM	Carmella	6.00	15.00
ACS	Cesaro	4.00	10.00
ADB	Daniel Bryan	6.00	15.00
ADM	Drew McIntyre	4.00	10.00
ADZ	Dolph Ziggler	4.00	10.00
AEL	Elias	5.00	12.00
AEM	Ember Moon	6.00	15.00
AFB	Finn Balor	5.00	12.00
AKK	Kofi Kingston	4.00	10.00
AKL	Kalisto	4.00	10.00
AKO	Kevin Owens	5.00	12.00
AMA	Maria Kanellis	8.00	20.00
AMG	Karl Anderson	4.00	10.00
AMI	Mike Kanellis	4.00	10.00
ANT	Natalya	5.00	12.00
ARM	Rey Mysterio	10.00	25.00
ARS	Rusev	4.00	10.00
ARW	Rowan	4.00	10.00
ASA	Samir Singh	4.00	10.00
ASB	Sasha Banks	10.00	25.00
ASJ	Samoa Joe	4.00	10.00
ASM	Sheamus	4.00	10.00
ASN	Shinsuke Nakamura	5.00	12.00
ASR	Seth Rollins	.60	15.00
ASU	Sunil Singh	4.00	10.00
ASZ	Sami Zayn	4.00	10.00
ATM	The Miz	5.00	12.00
ATO	Titus O'Neil	4.00	10.00
AXW	Xavier Woods	4.00	10.00
AZR	Zack Ryder	5.00	12.00
AZV	Zelina Vega	8.00	20.00

2019 Topps WWE Money in the Bank Cash-In Moments

COMPLETE SET (13) 8.00 20.00
STATED ODDS 1:6

CM1	Kane	.60	1.50
CM2	The Miz	.75	2.00
CM3	Daniel Bryan	1.00	2.50
CM4	John Cena	2.00	5.00
CM5	Randy Orton	1.00	2.50
CM6	Seth Rollins	1.00	2.50
CM7	Sheamus	.60	1.50
CM8	Baron Corbin	.60	1.50
CM9	Braun Strowman	1.00	2.50
CM10	Carmella	1.00	2.50
CM11	Alexa Bliss	2.00	5.00
CM12	Bayley	.75	2.00
CM13	Brock Lesnar	1.50	4.00

2019 Topps WWE Money in the Bank Dual Autographs

*GOLD/10: UNPRICED DUE TO SCARCITY
*BLACK/5: UNPRICED DUE TO SCARCITY
*RED/1: UNPRICED DUE TO SCARCITY
STATED ODDS 1:3,663
STATED PRINT RUN 25 SER.#'d SETS

DANEW	X.Woods/Big E	25.00	60.00
DABROS	The Singhs	25.00	60.00
DAGOOD	K.Anderson/L.Gallows	20.00	50.00
DAHRDY	The Hardys	30.00	75.00

2019 Topps WWE Money in the Bank Greatest Matches and Moments

COMPLETE SET (22) 6.00 15.00
STATED ODDS 1:3

GMM1	Shelton Benjamin	.40	1.00
GMM2	Matt Hardy	.60	1.50
GMM3	Kofi Kingston	.50	1.25
GMM4	Kofi Kingston	.50	1.25
GMM5	Kofi Kingston	.50	1.25
GMM6	The Miz	.60	1.50
GMM7	Daniel Bryan	.75	2.00
GMM8	Christian	.50	1.25
GMM9	Big Show	.50	1.25
GMM10	The Shield	.75	2.00
GMM11	John Cena	1.50	4.00
GMM12	Seth Rollins	.75	2.00
GMM13	John Cena	1.50	4.00
GMM14	Bray Wyatt	.75	2.00
GMM15	AJ Styles	1.50	4.00
GMM16	Seth Rollins	.75	2.00
GMM17	Mike & Maria Kanellis	.75	2.00
GMM18	Carmella	.75	2.00
GMM19	AJ Styles and Nakamura	1.50	4.00
GMM20	Carmella	.75	2.00
GMM21	Ember Moon	.75	2.00
GMM22	Brock Lesnar	1.25	3.00

2019 Topps WWE Money in the Bank Mat Relics

*GREEN/99: .5X TO 1.2X BASIC MEM
*BLUE/50: .6X TO 1.5X BASIC MEM
*PURPLE/25: UNPRICED DUE TO SCARCITY
*GOLD/10: UNPRICED DUE TO SCARCITY
*BLACK/5: UNPRICED DUE TO SCARCITY
*RED/1: UNPRICED DUE TO SCARCITY
STATED ODDS 1:20

MRBC	Baron Corbin	2.50	6.00
MRBE	Big E	2.50	6.00
MRBL	Bobby Lashley	2.50	6.00
MRBR	Robert Roode	2.50	6.00
MRCM	Carmella	4.00	10.00
MRFB	Finn Balor	5.00	12.00
MRJE	Jey Uso	2.50	6.00
MRJI	Jimmy Uso	2.50	6.00
MRKK	Kofi Kingston	3.00	8.00
MRKO	Kevin Owens	4.00	10.00
MRLK	Becky Lynch	5.00	12.00
MRNM	Naomi	2.50	6.00
MRNT	Natalya	2.50	6.00
MRRO	Randy Orton	3.00	8.00
MRRT	R-Truth	3.00	8.00
MRSJ	Samoa Joe	2.50	6.00
MRSM	Sheamus	2.50	6.00
MRSR	Seth Rollins	4.00	10.00
MRTO	Titus O'Neil	2.50	6.00
MRTS	Tamina	2.50	6.00
MRXW	Xavier Woods	2.50	6.00
MRZR	Zack Ryder	2.50	6.00

2019 Topps WWE Money in the Bank Money Cards

COMPLETE SET (13) 8.00 20.00
STATED ODDS 1:6

MC1	Kane	.60	1.50
MC2	The Miz	.75	2.00
MC3	Daniel Bryan	1.00	2.50
MC4	John Cena	2.00	5.00
MC5	Randy Orton	1.00	2.50
MC6	Seth Rollins	1.00	2.50
MC7	Sheamus	.60	1.50
MC8	Baron Corbin	.60	1.50
MC9	Braun Strowman	1.00	2.50
MC10	Carmella	1.00	2.50
MC11	Alexa Bliss	2.00	5.00
MC12	Bayley	.75	2.00
MC13	Brock Lesnar	1.50	4.00

2019 Topps WWE Money in the Bank Quad Autograph

STATED ODDS 1:47,616
STATED PRINT RUN 5 SER.#'d SETS
UNPRICED DUE TO SCARCITY

QABC Owens/Styles/Nakamura/Corbin

2019 Topps WWE Money in the Bank Shirt Relics

*GREEN/99: .5X TO 1.2X BASIC MEM
*BLUE/50: .6X TO 1.5X BASIC MEM
*PURPLE/25: UNPRICED DUE TO SCARCITY
*GOLD/10: UNPRICED DUE TO SCARCITY
*BLACK/5: UNPRICED DUE TO SCARCITY
*RED/1: UNPRICED DUE TO SCARCITY
STATED ODDS 1:23
STATED PRINT RUN 199 SER.#'d SETS

SRAC Apollo Crews 1.50 4.00
SRAJ AJ Styles 3.00 8.00
SRBL Brock Lesnar 5.00 12.00
SRBS Braun Strowman 2.50 6.00
SRCS Cesaro 4.00 10.00
SRFB Finn Balor 4.00 10.00
SRHS Heath Slater 1.50 4.00
SRJE Jey Uso 2.50 6.00
SRJI Jimmy Uso 2.50 6.00
SRKB Booker T 3.00 8.00
SRKK Kofi Kingston 3.00 8.00
SRKO Kevin Owens 3.00 8.00
SRLA Bobby Lashley 2.50 6.00
SRMZ The Miz 3.00 8.00
SRRI Ricochet 5.00 12.00
SRRM Rey Mysterio 5.00 12.00
SRRR Roman Reigns 6.00 15.00
SRSR Seth Rollins 5.00 12.00
SRSZ Sami Zayn 2.50 6.00

2019 Topps WWE Money in the Bank Triple Autographs

*GOLD/10: UNPRICED DUE TO SCARCITY
*BLACK/5: UNPRICED DUE TO SCARCITY
*RED/1: UNPRICED DUE TO SCARCITY
STATED ODDS 1:6,802
STATED PRINT RUN SER.#'d SETS

TABC Anderson/Gallows/Styles 60.00 120.00
TANEW Woods/Big E/Kingston 50.00 100.00

2019 Topps WWE Money in the Bank Promo

NYCC19 John Cena NYCC 5.00 12.00

2016 Topps WWE NXT

*BRONZE/50: .6X TO 1.5X BASIC CARDS
*SILVER/25: .75X TO 2X BASIC CARDS
*GOLD/10: 1.5X TO 4X BASIC CARDS
*RED/1: UNPRICED DUE TO SCARCITY

1 Aliyah RC .75 2.00
2 Akam RC .60 1.50
3 Andrade "Cien" Almas RC .60 1.50
4 Angelo Dawkins .60 1.50
5 Asuka RC 2.50 6.00
6 Austin Aries .75 2.00
7 Billie Kay RC 1.50 4.00
8 Blake RC .60 1.50
9 Dash Wilder RC .75 2.00
10 Elias Samson RC .60 1.50
11 Hideo Itami .75 2.00
12 Johnny Gargano RC .60 1.50
13 Liv Morgan RC .75 2.00
14 Buddy Murphy RC .60 1.50
15 No Way Jose RC .60 1.50
16 Peyton Royce RC 1.50 4.00
17 Rezar RC .60 1.50
18 Samoa Joe 1.50 4.00
19 Sawyer Fulton .75 2.00
20 Scott Dawson RC .60 1.50
21 Shinsuke Nakamura RC 2.50 6.00
22 Tommaso Ciampa RC .75 2.00
23 Tye Dillinger .75 2.00
24 Roman Reigns 2.00 5.00
25 Seth Rollins 1.00 2.50
26 Big E .60 1.50
27 Bray Wyatt 2.50 6.00
28 Xavier Woods .60 1.50
29 Rusev 1.50 4.00
30 Kalisto 1.50 4.00
31 Neville 1.50 4.00
32 Kevin Owens 1.50 4.00
33 Charlotte 2.00 5.00
34 Sasha Banks 2.00 5.00
35 Becky Lynch 2.00 5.00
36 Sami Zayn 1.00 2.50
37 Baron Corbin .75 2.00
38 Big Cass 1.25 3.00
39 Enzo Amore RC 1.25 3.00
40 Aiden English .60 1.50
41 Simon Gotch RC 1.00 2.50
42 Dana Brooke RC 1.50 4.00
43 Alexa Bliss 3.00 8.00
44 Carmella RC 1.50 4.00
45 Chad Gable RC .75 2.00
46 Finn Balor 2.00 5.00
47 Jason Jordan RC .75 2.00
48 Mojo Rawley RC .60 1.50
49 Nia Jax RC 1.00 2.50
50 Bayley RC 1.50 4.00

2016 Topps WWE NXT Autographs

*BRONZE/50: .5X TO 1.2X BASIC AUTOS
*SILVER/25: .6X TO 1.5X BASIC AUTOS
*GOLD/10: UNPRICED DUE TO SCARCITY
*RED/1: UNPRICED DUE TO SCARCITY
STATED OVERALL ODDS 1:MINIBOX

NNO Alexa Bliss 50.00 100.00
NNO Aliyah 8.00 15.00
NNO Andrade Cien Almas 6.00 15.00
NNO Angelo Dawkins 6.00 15.00
NNO Asuka 20.00 50.00
NNO Austin Aries 10.00 25.00
NNO Bayley 15.00 40.00
NNO Billie Kay 20.00 50.00
NNO Blake 6.00 15.00
NNO Buddy Murphy 6.00 15.00
NNO Dash Wilder 12.00 30.00
NNO Elias Samson 15.00 40.00
NNO Finn Balor 15.00 40.00
NNO Hideo Itami 6.00 15.00
NNO Johnny Gargano 6.00 15.00
NNO Liv Morgan 40.00 100.00
NNO Nia Jax 8.00 20.00
NNO No Way Jose 10.00 25.00
NNO Peyton Royce 15.00 40.00
NNO Samoa Joe 10.00 25.00
NNO Sawyer Fulton 10.00 25.00
NNO Scott Dawson 6.00 15.00
NNO Shinsuke Nakamura 10.00 25.00
NNO Tommaso Ciampa 6.00 15.00
NNO Tye Dillinger 10.00 25.00

2017 Topps WWE NXT

*BRONZE: .6X TO 1.5X BASIC CARDS
*BLUE/50: .75X TO 2X BASIC CARDS
*SILVER/25: 1.2X TO 3X BASIC CARDS
*GOLD/10: UNPRICED DUE TO SCARCITY
*RED/1: UNPRICED DUE TO SCARCITY
*P.P.BLACK/1: UNPRICED DUE TO SCARCITY
*P.P.CYAN/1: UNPRICED DUE TO SCARCITY
*P.P.MAGENTA/1: UNPRICED DUE TO SCARCITY
*P.P.YELLOW/1: UNPRICED DUE TO SCARCITY

1 Asuka 1.25 3.00
2 Akam .40 1.00
3 Alexander Wolfe RC .50 1.25
4 Aliyah .50 1.25
5 Andrade Cien Almas .40 1.00
6 Angelo Dawkins .40 1.00
7 Killian Dain RC .40 1.00
8 Billie Kay .50 1.25
9 Bobby Roode 1.00 2.50
10 Buddy Murphy .40 1.00
11 Elias Samson .60 1.50
12 Ember Moon 1.00 2.50
13 Eric Young .75 2.00
14 Hideo Itami .60 1.50
15 Johnny Gargano .40 1.00
16 Liv Morgan .60 1.50
17 Mandy Rose .50 1.25
18 Nick Miller RC .40 1.00
19 Nikki Cross RC .75 2.00
20 No Way Jose .40 1.00
21 Oney Lorcan .40 1.00
22 Otis Dozovic RC .50 1.25
23 Peyton Royce .60 1.50
24 Rezar .40 1.00
25 Riddick Moss RC .50 1.25
26 Roderick Strong .50 1.25
27 Ruby Riot RC .50 1.25
28 Sawyer Fulton .40 1.00
29 Shane Thorne RC .40 1.00
30 Tian Bing RC .40 1.00
31 Tino Sabbatelli .50 1.25
32 Tommaso Ciampa .40 1.00
33 Tucker Knight RC 1.00 2.50
34 Wesley Blake .40 1.00
35 Cathy Kelley .40 1.00
36 Charly Caruso RC .40 1.00
37 Mike Rome RC .40 1.00
38 Paul Ellering .40 1.00
39 Tom Phillips .40 1.00
40 William Regal .50 1.25
41 Corey Graves .40 1.00
42 Dasha Fuentes .50 1.25
43 Baron Corbin .60 1.50
44 Bayley 1.25 3.00
45 Dash Wilder .40 1.00
46 Finn Balor 1.50 4.00
47 Samoa Joe 1.25 3.00
48 Scott Dawson .40 1.00
49 Shinsuke Nakamura 1.00 2.50
50 Tye Dillinger .40 1.00

2017 Topps WWE NXT Autographs

*BRONZE/99: .5X TO 1.2X BASIC AUTOS
*BLUE/50: .6X TO 1.5X BASIC AUTOS
*SILVER/25: .75X TO 2X BASIC AUTOS
*GOLD/10: UNPRICED DUE TO SCARCITY
*RED/1: UNPRICED DUE TO SCARCITY
*P.P.BLACK/1: UNPRICED DUE TO SCARCITY
*P.P.CYAN/1: UNPRICED DUE TO SCARCITY
*P.P.MAGENTA/1: UNPRICED DUE TO SCARCITY
*P.P.YELLOW/1: UNPRICED DUE TO SCARCITY
RANDOMLY INSERTED INTO PACKS

RAAC Andrade Cien Almas 5.00 12.00
RAAD Angelo Dawkins 5.00 12.00
RAAK Akam 8.00 20.00
RAAL Aliyah 6.00 15.00
RAAS Asuka 20.00 50.00
RAAW Alexander Wolfe 8.00 20.00
RABD Killian Dain 5.00 12.00
RABK Billie Kay 10.00 25.00
RABM Buddy Murphy 5.00 12.00
RABR Bobby Roode 10.00 25.00
RACC Charly Caruso 8.00 20.00
RACK Cathy Kelley 8.00 20.00
RADF Dasha Fuentes 8.00 20.00
RADW Dash Wilder 5.00 12.00
RAEM Ember Moon 10.00 25.00
RAEY Eric Young 6.00 15.00
RAHI Hideo Itami 5.00 12.00
RAJG Johnny Gargano 5.00 12.00
RALM Liv Morgan 15.00 40.00
RAMR Mandy Rose 20.00 50.00
RANC Nikki Cross 10.00 25.00
RANM Nick Miller 5.00 12.00
RANW No Way Jose 5.00 12.00
RAOD Otis Dozovic 5.00 12.00
RAOL Oney Lorcan 6.00 15.00
RAPR Peyton Royce 8.00 20.00
RARE Rezar 5.00 12.00
RARM Riddick Moss 5.00 12.00
RARS Roderick Strong 5.00 12.00
RASD Scott Dawson 5.00 12.00
RASF Sawyer Fulton 5.00 12.00
RASN Shinsuke Nakamura 12.00 30.00
RAST Shane Thorne 5.00 12.00
RATB Tian Bing 5.00 12.00
RATC Tommaso Ciampa 5.00 12.00
RATK Tucker Knight 5.00 12.00
RATP Tom Phillips 5.00 12.00
RATS Tino Sabbatelli 5.00 12.00
RAWB Wesley Blake 5.00 12.00

2017 Topps WWE NXT Dual Relics

RANDOMLY INSERTED INTO PACKS
STATED PRINT RUN 25 SER.#'d SETS
UNPRICED DUE TO SCARCITY

DRAA Andrade Cien Almas
DRAS Asuka
DRBR Bobby Roode
DRBY Bayley
DREM Ember Moon
DRFB Finn Balor
DRJG Johnny Gargano
DRNJ No Way Jose
DRSD Scott Dawson
DRSJ Samoa Joe
DRSN Shinsuke Nakamura
DRTC Tommaso Ciampa

2017 Topps WWE NXT Mat Relics

*BRONZE/99: .5X TO 1.2X BASIC MEM
*BLUE/50: .6X TO 1.5X BASIC MEM
*SILVER/25: .75X TO 2X BASIC MEM
*GOLD/10: UNPRICED DUE TO SCARCITY
*RED/1: UNPRICED DUE TO SCARCITY
RANDOMLY INSERTED INTO PACKS

MRAA Andrade Cien Almas 2.00 5.00
MRAC Apollo Crews 2.50 6.00
MRAE Aiden English 2.00 5.00
MRAK Asuka 6.00 15.00
MRAS Asuka 6.00 15.00
MRAU Austin Aries 4.00 10.00
MRBC Big Cass 2.50 6.00
MRBR Bobby Roode 5.00 12.00
MRBY Bayley 6.00 15.00
MRCG Chad Gable 2.50 6.00
MRDW Dash Wilder 2.00 5.00
MREA Enzo Amore 6.00 15.00
MREM Ember Moon 5.00 12.00
MRFB Finn Balor 8.00 20.00
MRJG Johnny Gargano 2.00 5.00
MRJJ Jason Jordan 2.50 6.00
MRKO Kevin Owens 5.00 12.00
MRMR Mojo Rawley 2.50 6.00
MRSB Sasha Banks 6.00 15.00
MRSD Scott Dawson 2.00 5.00
MRSH Shinsuke Nakamura 5.00 12.00
MRSJ Samoa Joe 6.00 15.00
MRSK Asuka 6.00 15.00
MRSN Shinsuke Nakamura 5.00 12.00
MRSZ Sami Zayn 2.50 6.00
MRTB Tyler Breeze 2.00 5.00
MRTC Tommaso Ciampa 2.00 5.00
MRTD Tye Dillinger 2.00 5.00
MRZR Zack Ryder 2.00 5.00
MRBCB Baron Corbin 3.00 8.00
MRBEY Bayley 6.00 15.00
MRBLY Bayley 6.00 15.00
MRBRD Bobby Roode 5.00 12.00
MRBRH Bobby Roode 5.00 12.00
MRBYY Bayley 6.00 15.00
MRFBL Finn Balor 8.00 20.00
MRFBR Finn Balor 8.00 20.00
MRNWJ No Way Jose 2.00 5.00
MRNYJ No Way Jose 2.00 5.00
MRSJE Samoa Joe 6.00 15.00
MRSJO Samoa Joe 6.00 15.00
MRSNK Shinsuke Nakamura 5.00 12.00
MRSZN Sami Zayn 2.50 6.00
MRTDL Tye Dillinger 2.00 5.00

2017 Topps WWE NXT Matches and Moments

*BRONZE: .5X TO 1.5X BASIC CARDS
*BLUE/50: .75X TO 2X BASIC CARDS
*SILVER/25: 1.2X TO 3X BASIC CARDS
*GOLD/10: UNPRICED DUE TO SCARCITY
*RED/1: UNPRICED DUE TO SCARCITY
*P.P.BLACK/1: UNPRICED DUE TO SCARCITY
*P.P.CYAN/1: UNPRICED DUE TO SCARCITY
*P.P.MAGENTA/1: UNPRICED DUE TO SCARCITY
*P.P.YELLOW/1: UNPRICED DUE TO SCARCITY

1 Jason Jordan & Chad Gable .50 1.25
2 Finn Balor/Samoa Joe 1.50 4.00
3 Apollo Crews .50 1.25

4 Finn Balor/Samoa Joe 1.50 4.00
5 Finn Balor/Samoa Joe 1.50 4.00
6 Bayley 1.25 3.00
7 Apollo Crews .50 1.25
8 Baron Corbin .60 1.50
9 Samoa Joe 1.25 3.00
10 Samoa Joe 1.25 3.00
11 Dash/Dawson .75 2.00
12 Dash/Dawson .75 2.00
13 Jason Jordan/Chad Gable .50 1.25
14 Samoa Joe/Baron Corbin 1.25 3.00
15 Dash/Dawson .75 2.00
16 Finn Balor 1.50 4.00
17 Elias Samson .60 1.50
18 Sami Zayn .50 1.25
19 Finn Balor 1.50 4.00
20 Sami Zayn vs. Samoa Joe 1.25 3.00
21 Baron Corbin .60 1.50
22 Finn Balor 1.50 4.00
23 Samoa Joe 1.25 3.00
24 The Revival .75 2.00
25 American Alpha .50 1.25
26 Finn Balor 1.50 4.00
27 American Alpha .50 1.25
28 Shinsuke Nakamura 1.00 2.50
29 Asuka 1.25 3.00
30 Finn Balor 1.50 4.00
31 Apollo Crews .50 1.25
32 Shinsuke Nakamura 1.00 2.50
33 No Way Jose .40 1.00
34 Samoa Joe 1.25 3.00
35 Samoa Joe 1.50 4.00
36 Shinsuke Nakamura 1.00 2.50
37 Finn Balor 1.50 4.00
38 Blake/Murphy .40 1.00
39 Johnny Gargano/Tommaso Ciampa .40 1.00
40 Andrade Cien Almas .40 1.00
41 The Revival .50 1.25
42 The Authors of Pain .40 1.00
43 Samoa Joe 1.50 4.00
44 TM-61 .40 1.00
45 Oney Lorcan .40 1.00
46 Johnny Gargano/Tommaso Ciampa .40 1.00
47 The Revival .50 1.25
48 Shinsuke Nakamura 1.50 4.00
49 Shinsuke Nakamura 1.00 2.50
50 Bobby Roode 1.00 2.50

2017 Topps WWE NXT Shirt Relics

*BRONZE/99: .5X TO 1.2X BASIC MEM
*BLUE/50: .6X TO 1.5X BASIC MEM
*SILVER/25: .75X TO 2X BASIC MEM
*GOLD/10: UNPRICED DUE TO SCARCITY
*RED/1: UNPRICED DUE TO SCARCITY
RANDOMLY INSERTED INTO PACKS

SRAK Akam 2.00 5.00
SRAW Alexander Wolfe 2.50 6.00
SRBR Bobby Roode 5.00 12.00
SREM Ember Moon 5.00 12.00
SREY Eric Young 4.00 10.00
SRHI Hideo Itami 3.00 8.00
SRNC Nikki Cross 4.00 10.00
SRRZ Rezar 2.00 5.00
SRSD Scott Dawson 2.00 5.00
SRSN Shinsuke Nakamura 5.00 12.00
SRACA Andrade Cien Almas 2.00 5.00
SRAKA Asuka 6.00 15.00
SRBLY Bayley 6.00 15.00
SRNWJ No Way Jose 2.00 5.00

2018 Topps WWE NXT

*BRONZE: .6X TO 1.5X BASIC CARDS
*BLUE/50: .75X TO 2X BASIC CARDS
*SILVER/25: 1.2X TO 3X BASIC CARDS
*GOLD/10: UNPRICED DUE TO SCARCITY
*RED/1: UNPRICED DUE TO SCARCITY
*P.P.BLACK/1: UNPRICED DUE TO SCARCITY
*P.P.CYAN/1: UNPRICED DUE TO SCARCITY
*P.P.MAGENTA/1: UNPRICED DUE TO SCARCITY
*P.P.YELLOW/1: UNPRICED DUE TO SCARCITY

R1 Adam Cole RC .50 1.25
R2 Akam .40 1.00
R3 Aleister Black .50 1.25
R4 Alexander Wolfe .40 1.00
R5 Andrade Cien Almas .60 1.50
R6 Angelo Dawkins .40 1.00
R7 Bobby Fish RC .40 1.00
R8 Buddy Murphy .50 1.25
R9 Cezar Bononi RC .40 1.00
R10 Drew McIntyre .60 1.50
R11 Eric Young .50 1.25
R12 Fabian Aichner RC .40 1.00
R13 Gabriel Ealy RC .40 1.00
R14 Kassius Ohno .40 1.00
R15 Killian Dain .50 1.25
R16 Kyle O'Reilly RC .50 1.25
R17 Lars Sullivan RC .40 1.00
R18 Lio Rush RC .40 1.00
R19 Montez Ford .40 1.00
R20 Nick Miller .40 1.00
R21 No Way Jose .50 1.25
R22 Oney Lorcan .50 1.25
R23 Otis Dozovic .40 1.00
R24 Paul Ellering .50 1.25
R25 Pete Dunne RC .40 1.00
R26 Rezar .40 1.00
R27 Riddick Moss .40 1.00
R28 Roderick Strong .40 1.00
R29 Shane Thorne .40 1.00
R30 Tino Sabbatelli .50 1.25
R31 Tommaso Ciampa .40 1.00
R32 Tucker Knight .40 1.00
R33 Tyler Bate .40 1.00
R34 Trent Seven RC .40 1.00
R35 Velveteen Dream .40 1.00
R36 Wesley Blake .50 1.25
R37 Aliyah .60 1.50
R38 Bianca Belair RC 2.00 5.00
R39 Billie Kay .75 2.00
R40 Ember Moon .75 2.00
R41 Kairi Sane RC 1.00 2.50
R42 Lacey Evans .50 1.25
R43 Nikki Cross .60 1.50
R44 Peyton Royce 1.00 2.50
R45 Shayna Baszler 1.00 2.50
R46 Taynara Conti RC .40 1.00
R47 Vanessa Borne .40 1.00
R48 Zelina Vega .40 1.00
R49 William Regal .50 1.25
R50 Triple H 1.00 2.50

2018 Topps WWE NXT Autographed Shirt Relics

*BLUE/50: .5X TO 1.2X BASIC AUTOS
*SILVER/25: .6X TO 1.5X BASIC AUTOS
*GOLD/10: UNPRICED DUE TO SCARCITY
*RED/1: UNPRICED DUE TO SCARCITY
STATED PRINT RUN 99 SER.#'d SETS

ARAA Andrade Cien Almas 8.00 20.00
ARAK Akam 6.00 15.00
ARAW Alexander Wolfe 5.00 12.00
AREM Ember Moon 12.00 30.00
AREY Eric Young 8.00 20.00
ARNC Nikki Cross 10.00 25.00
ARNW No Way Jose 8.00 20.00
ARRZ Rezar 6.00 15.00

2018 Topps WWE NXT Autographs

*BRONZE/99: SAME VALUE AS BASIC
*BLUE/50: .5X TO 1.2X BASIC AUTOS
*SILVER/25: .6X TO 1.5X BASIC AUTOS
*GOLD/10: UNPRICED DUE TO SCARCITY
*RED/1: UNPRICED DUE TO SCARCITY
*P.P.BLACK/1: UNPRICED DUE TO SCARCITY
*P.P.CYAN/1: UNPRICED DUE TO SCARCITY
*P.P.MAGENTA/1: UNPRICED DUE TO SCARCITY
*P.P.YELLOW/1: UNPRICED DUE TO SCARCITY
RANDOMLY INSERTED INTO PACKS

AAA Andrade Cien Almas 4.00 10.00
AAB Aleister Black 6.00 15.00
AAC Adam Cole 8.00 20.00
AAD Angelo Dawkins 4.00 10.00
AAK Akam 4.00 10.00
AAW Alexander Wolfe 4.00 10.00
AAY Aliyah 6.00 15.00
ABB Bianca Belair 50.00 100.00
ABF Bobby Fish 10.00 25.00
ABK Billie Kay 10.00 25.00
ABM Buddy Murphy 5.00 12.00
ABY Bayley 8.00 20.00
ACB Cezar Bononi 5.00 12.00
ADA Dean Ambrose 20.00 50.00
ADM Drew McIntyre 8.00 20.00
AEM Ember Moon 8.00 20.00
AEY Eric Young 5.00 12.00
AFA Fabian Aichner 6.00 15.00
AJG Johnny Gargano 6.00 15.00
AKD Killian Dain 5.00 12.00
AKS Kairi Sane 20.00 50.00
ALE Lacey Evans 10.00 25.00
ALR Lio Rush 10.00 25.00
ALS Lars Sullivan 10.00 25.00
AMF Montez Ford 10.00 25.00
ANC Nikki Cross 6.00 15.00
ANM Nick Miller 5.00 12.00
ANW No Way Jose 4.00 10.00
AOD Otis Dozovic 5.00 12.00
AOL Oney Lorcan 5.00 12.00
AON Kassius Ohno 4.00 10.00
APD Pete Dunne 15.00 40.00
APR Peyton Royce 6.00 15.00
ARE Rezar 4.00 10.00
ARM Riddick Moss 4.00 10.00
ARS Roderick Strong 4.00 10.00
ASH Shayna Baszler 12.00 30.00
AST Shane Thorne 5.00 12.00
ATB Tyler Bate 10.00 25.00
ATC Tommaso Ciampa 5.00 12.00
ATK Tucker Knight 4.00 10.00
ATS Tino Sabbatelli 4.00 10.00
ATY Taynara Conti 20.00 50.00
AUA Kyle O'Reilly 6.00 15.00
AVB Vanessa Borne 12.00 30.00
AVD Velveteen Dream 6.00 15.00
AWB Wesley Blake 4.00 10.00
AZV Zelina Vega 20.00 50.00

2018 Topps WWE NXT Dual Autographs

*GOLD/10: UNPRICED DUE TO SCARCITY
*RED/1: UNPRICED DUE TO SCARCITY
STATED PRINT RUN 25 SER.#'d SETS

DADY Triple H/William Regal 75.00 150.00
DAID Peyton Royce/Billie Kay 75.00 150.00

2018 Topps WWE NXT Matches and Moments

*BRONZE: .6X TO 1.5X BASIC CARDS
*BLUE/50: .75X TO 2X BASIC CARDS
*SILVER/25: 1.2X TO 3X BASIC CARDS
*GOLD/10: UNPRICED DUE TO SCARCITY
*RED/1: UNPRICED DUE TO SCARCITY
*P.P.BLACK/1: UNPRICED DUE TO SCARCITY
*P.P.CYAN/1: UNPRICED DUE TO SCARCITY
*P.P.MAGENTA/1: UNPRICED DUE TO SCARCITY
*P.P.YELLOW/1: UNPRICED DUE TO SCARCITY

1 Samoa Joe .75 2.00
2 Bobby Roode .60 1.50
3 The Revival .50 1.25
4 Shinsuke Nakamura 1.00 2.50
5 The Authors of Pain .50 1.25
6 Tye Dillinger .40 1.00
7 Bobby Roode .60 1.50
8 Andrade "Cien" Almas .60 1.50
9 SAnitY Debut .60 1.50
10 #DIY Advance .40 1.00
11 Shane Thorne .40 1.00
12 The Authors of Pain .50 1.25
13 Andrade "Cien" Almas .60 1.50
14 Bobby Roode .60 1.50
15 The Authors of Pain .50 1.25
16 #DIY .40 1.00
17 Samoa Joe .75 2.00
18 SAnitY .60 1.50
19 Samoa Joe .75 2.00
20 Shinsuke Nakamura 1.00 2.50
21 Shinsuke Nakamura 1.00 2.50
22 Bobby Roode .60 1.50
23 #DIY .40 1.00
24 #DIY .50 1.25
25 TM61 .50 1.25
26 Eric Young .50 1.25
27 The Authors of Pain .50 1.25
28 Seth Rollins 1.00 2.50
29 Bobby Roode 1.00 2.50
30 SAnitY .50 1.25
31 Kassius Ohno .40 1.00
32 The Authors of Pain .50 1.25
33 Shinsuke Nakamura 1.00 2.50
34 Bobby Roode .60 1.50
35 Kassius Ohno 1.00 2.50
36 SAnitY .50 1.25
37 Aleister Black .50 1.25
38 The Authors of Pain .50 1.25
39 Bobby Roode 1.00 2.50
40 Oney Lorcan .50 1.25
41 Drew McIntyre .60 1.50
42 Tye Dillinger .40 1.00
43 Tyler Bate .50 1.25
44 Hideo Itami .40 1.00
45 Hideo Itami .40 1.00
46 Roderick Strong .50 1.25
47 Pete Dunne .40 1.00
48 Bobby Roode .60 1.50
49 The Authors of Pain .40 1.00
50 Tommaso Ciampa .40 1.00

2018 Topps WWE NXT Triple Autographs

*GOLD/10: UNPRICED DUE TO SCARCITY
*RED/1: UNPRICED DUE TO SCARCITY
STATED ODDS

TAERA Cole/Fish/O'Reilly 50.00 100.00
TAMAG McIntyre/Almas/Gargano 30.00 75.00
TAMCA Moon/Cross/Aliyah 50.00 100.00
TASAY Young/Wolfe/Dain 25.00 60.00

2019 Topps WWE NXT

COMPLETE SET (100) 12.00 30.00
*BRONZE: .6X TO 1.5X BASIC CARDS
*BLUE/50: .75X TO 2X BASIC CARDS
*SILVER/25: 2X TO 5X BASIC CARDS
*GOLD/10: UNPRICED DUE TO SCARCITY
*RED/1: UNPRICED DUE TO SCARCITY

1 Velveteen Dream .50 1.25
2 The Undisputed Era .40 1.00
3 Aleister Black .30 .75
4 Andrade .30 .75
5 Roderick Strong .50 1.25
6 Pete Dunne .50 1.25
7 Johnny Gargano .25 .60
8 Pete Dunne & Roderick Strong .50 1.25
9 Adam Cole .30 .75
10 Johnny Gargano .25 .60
11 Pete Dunne & Roderick Strong .50 1.25
12 EC3 .25 .60
13 Ricochet .60 1.50
14 Adam Cole .30 .75
15 Roderick Strong .50 1.25
16 Aleister Black .30 .75
17 Johnny Gargano .50 1.25
18 The Viking Raiders .30 .75
19 Ricochet .60 1.50
20 Lars Sullivan .25 .60
21 Kona Reeves .30 .75
22 Pete Dunne .50 1.25
23 The Viking Raiders .30 .75
24 Tommaso Ciampa .40 1.00
25 Kona Reeves .30 .75
26 Dunne/Danny Burch/Oney Lorcan .50 1.25
27 Lars Sullivan .25 .60
28 EC3 .40 1.00
29 Pete Dunne .50 1.25
30 The Undisputed Era .50 1.25
31 Ricochet .60 1.50
32 Aleister Black .30 .75
33 Tommaso Ciampa .25 .60
34 British Strong Style .50 1.25
35 Aleister Black & Ricochet .60 1.50
36 Moustache Mountain .40 1.00
37 The Undisputed Era .50 1.25
38 Johnny Gargano .25 .60
39 The Undisputed Era .50 1.25
40 Tommaso Ciampa .30 .75
41 EC3 .25 .60
42 Aleister Black .30 .75

43 Keith Lee	.25	.60
44 The Undisputed Era	.50	1.25
45 Velveteen Dream	.50	1.25
46 Ricochet	.60	1.50
47 Tommaso Ciampa	.25	.60
48 Lars Sullivan	.25	.60
49 The Undisputed Era	.50	1.25
50 The Forgotten Sons	.40	1.00
51 Jaxson Ryker	.25	.60
52 Pete Dunne	.60	1.50
53 Lars Sullivan	.25	.60
54 Keith Lee	.25	.60
55 Ricochet	.60	1.50
56 Bobby Fish	.40	1.00
57 Pete Dunne	.50	1.25
58 EC3	.25	.60
59 Johnny Gargano	.30	.75
60 Matt Riddle	.40	1.00
61 Heavy Machinery	.25	.60
62 Pete Dunne	.50	1.25
63 Aleister Black	.30	.75
64 Tommaso Ciampa	.25	.60
65 Dunne/Ricochet/Viking Raiders	.60	1.50
66 The Forgotten Sons	.40	1.00
67 EC3	.25	.60
68 Ricochet	.60	1.50
69 Dominik Dijakovic	.25	.60
70 Walter	.50	1.25
71 Tommaso Ciampa	.25	.60
72 The Viking Raiders	.30	.75
73 Johnny Gargano	.25	.60
74 Matt Riddle	.40	1.00
75 Black/Ricochet/Velveteen Dream	.25	.60
76 Rik Bugez	.40	1.00
77 Ricochet	.60	1.50
78 Velveteen Dream	.50	1.25
79 Keith Lee	.25	.60
80 DIY	.25	.60
81 Aleister Black/Ricochet	.60	1.50
82 Aleister Black/Ricochet	.60	1.50
83 Johnny Gargano	.25	.60
84 Adam Cole	.30	.75
85 Aleister Black & Ricochet	.60	1.50
86 The Viking Raiders	.30	.75
87 Velveteen Dream	.50	1.25
88 Walter	.50	1.25
89 Johnny Gargano	.50	1.25
90 Velveteen Dream	.50	1.25
91 Kushida	.25	.60
92 Matt Riddle	.40	1.00
93 The Viking Raiders	.30	.75
94 Tyler Breeze	.30	.75
95 Walter	.50	1.25
96 Imperium	.50	1.25
97 Matt Riddle	.50	1.25
98 The Street Profits	.30	.75
99 Velveteen Dream	.50	1.25
100 Adam Cole	.30	.75

2019 Topps WWE NXT Autographed Shirt Relics

*BLUE/50: .5X TO 1.2X BASIC AUTOS
*SILVER/25: UNPRICED DUE TO SCARCITY
*GOLD/10: UNPRICED DUE TO SCARCITY
*RED/1: UNPRICED DUE TO SCARCITY
STATED ODDS 1:364
STATED PRINT RUN 99 SER.#'d SETS

ASAC Adam Cole	8.00	20.00
ASRS Roderick Strong	6.00	15.00
ASSB Shayna Baszler	10.00	25.00
ASVD Velveteen Dream	6.00	15.00

2019 Topps WWE NXT Autographs

*BRONZE/99: SAME VALUE AS BASIC
*BLUE/50: .5X TO 1.2X BASIC AUTOS
*SILVER/25: UNPRICE DUE TO SCARCITY
*GOLD/10: UNPRICED DUE TO SCARCITY
*RED/1: UNPRICED DUE TO SCARCITY
*P.P.BLACK/1: UNPRICED DUE TO SCARCITY
*P.P.CYAN/1: UNPRICED DUE TO SCARCITY
*P.P.MAGENTA/1: UNPRICED DUE TO SCARCITY
*P.P.YELLOW/1: UNPRICED DUE TO SCARCITY
STATED ODDS 1:20

AE Erik	5.00	12.00
AI Ivar	5.00	12.00
AAC Adam Cole	8.00	20.00
ABB Bianca Belair	12.00	30.00
ABF Bobby Fish	5.00	12.00
ABM Buddy Murphy	5.00	12.00
ACG Chelsea Green	15.00	40.00
ACL Candice LeRae	6.00	15.00
ADD Dominik Dijakovic	6.00	15.00
ADP Deonna Purrazzo	6.00	15.00
AIS Io Shirai	25.00	60.00
AJD Jessamyn Duke	8.00	20.00
AJG Johnny Gargano	5.00	12.00
AKL Keith Lee	12.00	30.00
AKY Kyle O'Reilly	5.00	12.00
ALE Lacey Evans	15.00	40.00
AMS Marina Shafir	5.00	12.00
AMY Mia Yim	10.00	25.00
ANC Nikki Cross	8.00	20.00
AOD Otis	6.00	15.00
AOH Kassius Ohno	5.00	12.00
APD Pete Dunne	8.00	20.00
APM Damian Priest	5.00	12.00
ARC Ricochet	12.00	30.00
ARS Roderick Strong	5.00	12.00
ASB Shayna Baszler	6.00	15.00
ATK Tucker	5.00	12.00
ATM Tommaso Ciampa	8.00	20.00
ATS Toni Storm	75.00	150.00
AVD Velveteen Dream	5.00	12.00
AWT Walter	15.00	40.00
ABRO Matt Riddle	15.00	40.00

2019 Topps WWE NXT Dual Autographs

*GOLD/10: UNPRICED DUE TO SCARCITY
*RED/1: UNPRICED DUE TO SCARCITY
STATED ODDS 1:1,149
STATED PRINT RUN 25 SER.#'d SETS

DAAB M.Barthel/F.Aichner	25.00	60.00
DAGL C.LeRae/J.Gargano	60.00	120.00
DAMG V.Borne/Aliyah	50.00	100.00
DASO K.O'Reilly/R.Strong	20.00	50.00

2019 Topps WWE NXT Kiss Autographs

*GOLD/10: UNPRICED DUE TO SCARCITY
*RED/1: UNPRICED DUE TO SCARCITY
STATED ODDS 1:1,910
STATED PRINT RUN 25 SER.#'d SETS

AKAL Aliyah	50.00	100.00
AKBB Bianca Belair	125.00	250.00
AKCG Chelsea Green	100.00	200.00
AKIS Io Shirai	200.00	350.00

2019 Topps WWE NXT Roster

COMPLETE SET (50)	15.00	40.00
STATED ODDS 2:1		
1 Adam Cole	.60	1.50
2 Jordan Myles	.30	.75
3 Aliyah	.50	1.25
4 Angelo Dawkins	.50	1.25
5 Bianca Belair	.30	.75
6 Bobby Fish	.75	2.00
7 Candice LeRae	1.00	2.50
8 Cathy Kelly	1.25	3.00
9 Chelsea Green	.50	1.25
10 Dakota Kai	1.00	2.50
11 Damian Priest	.50	1.25
12 Danny Burch	.50	1.25
13 Deonna Purrazzo	.50	1.25
14 Dominik Dijakovic	.50	1.25
15 Fabian Aichner	1.00	2.50
16 Humberto Carrillo	1.00	2.50
17 Io Shirai	.50	1.25
18 Jaxson Ryker	.50	1.25
19 Jessamyn Duke	.60	1.50
20 Jessi Kamea	.50	1.25
21 Johnny Gargano	.50	1.25
22 Kacy Catanzaro	1.25	3.00
23 Kassius Ohno	.75	2.00
24 Keith Lee	.50	1.25
25 Kona Reeves	.60	1.50
26 Kushida	.50	1.25
27 Kyle O'Reilly	.75	2.00
28 Marcel Barthel	1.00	2.50
29 Marina Shafir	.50	1.25
30 Matt Riddle	.75	2.00
31 Mauro Ranallo	.50	1.25
32 Mia Yim	.50	1.25
33 Montez Ford	.50	1.25
34 Oney Lorcan	.60	1.50
35 Pete Dunne	1.00	2.50
36 Raul Mendoza	.50	1.25
37 Rik Bugez	.50	1.25
38 Riddick Moss	.50	1.25
39 Roderick Strong	1.00	2.50
40 Shayna Baszler	1.00	2.50
41 Steve Cutler	.75	2.00
42 Toni Storm	2.00	5.00
43 Trent Seven	.75	2.00
44 Tyler Bate	.60	1.50
45 Vanessa Borne	.60	1.50
46 Velveteen Dream	1.00	2.50
47 Walter	1.00	2.50
48 Wesley Blake	.75	2.00
49 William Regal	.75	2.00
50 Xia Li	.50	1.25

2019 Topps WWE NXT Triple Autographs

*GOLD/10: UNPRICED DUE TO SCARCITY
*RED/1: UNPRICED DUE TO SCARCITY
STATED ODDS 1:1,442
STATED PRINT RUN 25 SER.#'d SETS

TA4H Shafir/Baszler/Duke	60.00	120.00
TAFS Ryker/Blake/Cutler	30.00	75.00
TAMYC Purrazzo/Shirai/Yim	100.00	200.00

2020 Topps WWE NXT

COMPLETE SET (100)	8.00	20.00

*BRONZE: .5X TO 1.2X BASIC CARDS
*BLUE/50: .75X TO 2X BASIC CARDS
*SILVER/25: UNPRICED DUE TO SCARCITY
*GOLD/10: UNPRICED DUE TO SCARCITY
*RED/1: UNPRICED DUE TO SCARCITY

1 Imperium	.60	1.50
2 Alexander Wolfe	.60	1.50
3 Angel Garza	.40	1.00
4 Adam Cole	.75	2.00
5 Imperium	.50	1.25
6 Isaiah Swerve Scott	.40	1.00
7 Trent Seven	.30	.75
8 Killian Dain	.40	1.00
9 Johnny Gargano	.75	2.00
10 WALTER	.60	1.50
11 Pete Dunne	.30	.75
12 Tyler Bate	.50	1.25
13 Pete Dunne	.60	1.50
14 Dave Mastiff	.40	1.00
15 Street Profits	.30	.75
16 Velveteen Dream	.40	1.00
17 Adam Cole	.75	2.00
18 Flash Morgan Webster	.40	1.00
19 Mark Andrews	.30	.75
20 Moustache Mountain	.60	1.50
21 Killian Dain	.40	1.00
22 Dominik Dijakovic	.30	.75
23 Undisputed ERA	.75	2.00
24 Joe Coffey	.40	1.00
25 Mark Andrews	.40	1.00
26 WALTER	.60	1.50
27 Roderick Strong	.60	1.50
28 Mark Andrews & Flash Webster	.40	1.00
29 Roderick Strong	.60	1.50
30 Matt Riddle	.60	1.50
31 Keith Lee	.30	.75
32 Matt Riddle	.60	1.50
33 Adam Cole	.75	2.00
34 Undisputed ERA	.60	1.50
35 Finn Balor	.75	2.00
36 Tommaso Ciampa	.75	2.00
37 Gallus	.40	1.00
38 Roderick Strong	.60	1.50
39 Tommaso Ciampa	.60	1.50
40 Pete Dunne	.30	.75
41 Damian Priest	.30	.75
42 Gallus	.40	1.00
43 Angel Garza	.40	1.00
44 Roderick Strong	.60	1.50
45 Finn Balor	.75	2.00
46 Undisputed ERA	.75	2.00
47 NXT Invades SmackDown	1.00	2.50
48 Adam Cole	.75	2.00
49 Pete Dunne	.30	.75
50 Angel Garza	.40	1.00
51 Ilja Dragunov	.60	1.50
52 Imperium	.50	1.25
53 WALTER	.60	1.50
54 Finn Balor	.75	2.00
55 Keith Lee	.60	1.50
56 Damian Priest	.30	.75
57 Adam Cole	.75	2.00
58 Alexander Wolfe	.30	.75
59 NXT Invades SD DX-Style	.75	2.00
60 Pete Dunne	.30	.75
61 Finn Balor	.75	2.00
62 Team Ciampa	.60	1.50
63 Roderick Strong	.60	1.50
64 Adam Cole	.75	2.00
65 Keith Lee	.75	2.00
66 Undisputed ERA	.75	2.00
67 Finn Balor	.75	2.00
68 Gallus & Ilja Dragunov	.60	1.50
69 Tommaso Ciampa	.30	.75
70 Imperium	.60	1.50
71 Angel Garza	.40	1.00
72 Finn Balor	.75	2.00
73 Brawl Leads to Ladder Match	.30	.75
74 Johnny Gargano	.60	1.50
75 Isaiah Swerve Scott	.40	1.00
76 Austin Theory	.50	1.25
77 Ilja Dragunov	.50	1.25
78 Austin Theory	.50	1.25
79 Imperium	.30	.75
80 Undisputed ERA	.75	2.00
81 Keith Lee	.30	.75
82 Tyler Bate	.50	1.25
83 Gallus	.40	1.00
84 WALTER	.60	1.50
85 Undisputed ERA	.75	2.00
86 BroserWeights	.60	1.50
87 Johnny Gargano	.60	1.50
88 Grizzled Young Veterans	.40	1.00
89 Isaiah Swerve Scott	.40	1.00
90 Imperium	.75	2.00
91 Grizzled Young Veterans	.40	1.00
92 BroserWeights	.60	1.50
93 Keith Lee	.60	1.50
94 Jordan Devlin	.30	.75
95 Travis Banks	.30	.75
96 Finn Balor	.75	2.00
97 Jordan Devlin	.40	1.00
98 Imperium	.60	1.50
99 #DIY	.60	1.50
100 BroserWeights	.60	1.50

2020 Topps WWE NXT Autographed Mat Relics

*BLUE/50: .5X TO 1.2X BASIC AUTOS
*SILVER/25: UNPRICED DUE TO SCARCITY
*GOLD/10: UNPRICED DUE TO SCARCITY
*RED/1: UNPRICED DUE TO SCARCITY
STATED ODDS 1:12
STATED PRINT RUN 99 SER.#'d SETS

MRAAC Adam Cole	20.00	50.00
MRABB Bianca Belair	15.00	40.00
MRABF Bobby Fish	12.00	30.00
MRACL Candice LeRae	25.00	60.00
MRADK Dakota Kai	30.00	75.00
MRAIS Io Shirai	30.00	75.00
MRAJG Johnny Gargano	10.00	25.00
MRAKL Keith Lee	12.00	30.00
MRAKO Kyle O'Reilly	10.00	25.00
MRAMR Matt Riddle	15.00	40.00
MRARR Rhea Ripley	50.00	100.00
MRATC Tommaso Ciampa	12.00	30.00
MRATN Tegan Nox	25.00	60.00
MRAVT Velveteen Dream	12.00	30.00

2020 Topps WWE NXT Autographed Shirt Relics

*SILVER/25: UNPRICED DUE TO SCARCITY
*GOLD/10: UNPRICED DUE TO SCARCITY
*RED/1: UNPRICED DUE TO SCARCITY
STATED ODDS 1:33
STATED PRINT RUN 50 SER.#'d SETS

SRAAC Adam Cole	20.00	50.00
SRABF Bobby Fish	12.00	30.00
SRAFB Finn Balor	15.00	40.00
SRAJG Johnny Gargano	12.00	30.00
SRAKO Kyle O'Reilly	10.00	25.00
SRAKU Kushida	10.00	25.00
SRAMY Mia Yim	12.00	30.00
SRAT7 Trent Seven	20.00	50.00
SRATC Tommaso Ciampa	10.00	25.00
SRAVD Velveteen Dream		

2020 Topps WWE NXT Called Up

COMPLETE SET (9) 6.00 15.00
RANDOMLY INSERTED INTO PACKS

CU1 Aleister Black	1.50	4.00
CU2 Angelo Dawkins	.75	2.00
CU3 Lacey Evans	2.00	5.00
CU4 Lars Sullivan	.75	2.00
CU5 Montez Ford	.75	2.00
CU6 Nikki Cross	1.50	4.00
CU7 Otis	1.25	3.00
CU8 Ricochet	1.25	3.00
CU9 Tucker	.75	2.00

2020 Topps WWE NXT Called Up Autographs

STATED PRINT RUN 25 SER.#'d SETS

CUAAB Aleister Black	15.00	40.00
CUAAD Angelo Dawkins	6.00	15.00
CUALE Lacey Evans	12.00	30.00
CUAMF Montez Ford	15.00	40.00
CUANC Nikki Cross	12.00	30.00
CUAOT Otis	6.00	15.00
CUARC Ricochet	10.00	25.00

2020 Topps WWE NXT Dual Autographs

STATED PRINT RUN 25 SER.#'d SETS

DABB V.Borne/Aliyah	100.00	200.00
DATK T.Nox/D.Kai	125.00	250.00
DAUE B.Fish/K.O'Reilly	25.00	60.00

2020 Topps WWE NXT Johnny Gargano Tribute

COMPLETE SET (20) 12.00 30.00
RANDOMLY INSERTED INTO PACKS

JG1 Johnny Gargano	1.50	4.00
JG2 Johnny Gargano	1.50	4.00
JG3 Johnny Gargano	1.50	4.00
JG4 Johnny Gargano	1.50	4.00
JG5 Johnny Gargano	1.50	4.00
JG6 Johnny Gargano	1.50	4.00
JG7 Johnny Gargano	1.50	4.00
JG8 Johnny Gargano	1.50	4.00
JG9 Johnny Gargano	1.50	4.00
JG10 Johnny Gargano	1.50	4.00
JG11 Johnny Gargano	1.50	4.00
JG12 Johnny Gargano	1.50	4.00
JG13 Johnny Gargano	1.50	4.00
JG14 Johnny Gargano	1.50	4.00
JG15 Johnny Gargano	1.50	4.00
JG16 Johnny Gargano	1.50	4.00
JG17 Johnny Gargano	1.50	4.00
JG18 Johnny Gargano	1.50	4.00
JG19 Johnny Gargano	1.50	4.00
JG20 Johnny Gargano	1.50	4.00

2020 Topps WWE NXT Johnny Gargano Tribute Autographs

*GOLD/10: UNPRICED DUE TO SCARCITY
*RED/1: UNPRICED DUE TO SCARCITY
STATED PRINT RUN 25 SER.#'d SETS

JG15 Johnny Gargano	10.00	25.00
JG16 Johnny Gargano	10.00	25.00
JG17 Johnny Gargano	10.00	25.00
JG18 Johnny Gargano	10.00	25.00
JG19 Johnny Gargano	10.00	25.00

2020 Topps WWE NXT Roster

COMPLETE SET (66) 15.00 40.00
RANDOMLY INSERTED INTO PACKS

NXT1 Adam Cole	.75	2.00
NXT2 Aliyah	.60	1.50
NXT3 Angel Garza	.40	1.00
NXT4 Austin Theory	.50	1.25
NXT5 Bianca Belair	.75	2.00
NXT6 Boa	.30	.75
NXT7 Bobby Fish	.30	.75
NXT8 Bronson Reed	.30	.75
NXT9 Cameron Grimes	.30	.75
NXT10 Candice LeRae	1.00	2.50
NXT11 Chelsea Green	1.50	4.00
NXT12 Dakota Kai	.60	1.50
NXT13 Damian Priest	.30	.75
NXT14 Danny Burch	.40	1.00
NXT15 Dexter Lumis	.30	.75
NXT16 Dominik Dijakovic	.30	.75
NXT17 Fandango	.30	.75
NXT18 Finn Balor	.75	2.00
NXT19 Io Shirai	.50	1.25
NXT20 Isaiah "Swerve" Scott	.40	1.00
NXT21 Jaxson Ryker	.40	1.00
NXT22 Jessamyn Duke	.50	1.25
NXT23 Joaquin Wilde	.30	.75
NXT24 Johnny Gargano	.60	1.50
NXT25 Keith Lee	.30	.75
NXT26 Killian Dain	.40	1.00
NXT27 Kona Reeves	.30	.75
NXT28 Kyle O'Reilly	.40	1.00
NXT29 Kushida	.40	1.00
NXT30 Mansoor	.30	.75
NXT31 Marina Shafir	.50	1.25
NXT32 Matt Riddle	.60	1.50
NXT33 Mia Yim	.60	1.50
NXT34 Oney Lorcan	.40	1.00
NXT35 Pete Dunne	.30	.75
NXT36 Raul Mendoza	.30	.75
NXT37 Rhea Ripley	1.25	3.00
NXT38 Roderick Strong	.60	1.50
NXT39 Santana Garrett	.30	.75
NXT40 Shane Thorne	.30	.75
NXT41 Shayna Baszler	1.00	2.50
NXT42 Shotzi Blackheart	1.00	2.50
NXT43 Steve Cutler	.30	.75
NXT44 Tegan Nox	.75	2.00
NXT45 Tommaso Ciampa	.60	1.50
NXT46 Tyler Breeze	.40	1.00
NXT47 Vanessa Borne	.60	1.50
NXT48 Velveteen Dream	.40	1.00
NXT49 Wesley Blake	.40	1.00
NXT50 Xia Li	.60	1.50
NXT51 Alexander Wolfe	.30	.75
NXT52 Fabian Aichner	.30	.75
NXT53 Flash Morgan Webster	.40	1.00
NXT54 Joe Coffey	.30	.75
NXT55 Jordan Devlin	.30	.75
NXT56 Kay Lee Ray	.50	1.25
NXT57 Marcel Barthel	.30	.75
NXT58 Mark Andrews	.30	.75
NXT59 Mark Coffey	.40	1.00
NXT60 Toni Storm	.75	2.00
NXT61 Trent Seven	.30	.75
NXT62 Tyler Bate	.50	1.25
NXT63 WALTER	.60	1.50
NXT64 Wolfgang	.30	.75
NXT65 James Drake	.40	1.00
NXT66 Zack Gibson	.30	.75

2020 Topps WWE NXT Roster Autographs

*BRONZE/99: .5X TO 1.2X BASIC AUTOS
*BLUE/50: .6X TO 1.5X BASIC AUTOS
*SILVER/25: UNPRICED DUE TO SCARCITY
*GOLD/10: UNPRICED DUE TO SCARCITY
*RED/1: UNPRICED DUE TO SCARCITY

AAC Adam Cole	10.00	25.00
AAG Angel Garza	6.00	15.00
AAL Aliyah	10.00	25.00
AAR Arturo Ruas	6.00	15.00
AAT Austin Theory	12.00	30.00
ABB Bianca Belair	20.00	50.00
ABF Bobby Fish	5.00	12.00
ABL Shotzi Blackheart	60.00	120.00
ABR Bronson Reed	10.00	25.00
ACG Cameron Grimes	6.00	15.00
ACL Candice LeRae	20.00	50.00
ADD Dominik Dijakovic	5.00	12.00
ADK Dakota Kai	15.00	40.00
ADL Dexter Lumis	20.00	50.00
ADP Damian Priest	6.00	15.00
AFA Fabian Aichner	5.00	12.00
AFB Finn Balor	10.00	25.00
AIO Io Shirai	20.00	50.00
AIS Isaiah Swerve Scott	5.00	12.00
AJG Johnny Gargano	8.00	20.00
AJW Joaquin Wilde	8.00	20.00
AKC Kayden Carter	10.00	25.00
AKL Keith Lee	6.00	15.00
AKU Kushida	10.00	25.00
AMB Marcel Barthel	5.00	12.00
AMR Matt Riddle	15.00	40.00
AMY Mia Yim	8.00	20.00
AOL Oney Lorcan	5.00	12.00
ARM Raul Mendoza	6.00	15.00
ARR Rhea Ripley	50.00	100.00
ARS Roderick Strong	5.00	12.00
ATN Tegan Nox	30.00	75.00
ATO Tommaso Ciampa	6.00	15.00
AVD Velveteen Dream	5.00	12.00

2021 Topps WWE NXT

COMPLETE SET (100) 10.00 25.00
*PURPLE: .75X TO 2X BASIC CARDS
*BLUE/50: 1.5X TO 4X BASIC CARDS
*RED/25: 2X TO 5X BASIC CARDS
*GOLD/10: UNPRICED DUE TO SCARCITY
*PLATINUM/1: UNPRICED DUE TO SCARCITY

1 Roderick Strong	.50	1.25
2 Keith Lee	.60	1.50
3 The BroserWeights	.75	2.00
4 Adam Cole	1.00	2.50
5 Johnny Gargano	.60	1.50
6 The BroserWeights	.75	2.00
7 Tommaso Ciampa	.75	2.00
8 Keith Lee	.60	1.50
9 Johnny Gargano	.60	1.50
10 Timothy Thatcher	.30	.75
11 Karrion Kross	1.50	4.00
12 Akira Tozawa	.50	1.25
13 El Hijo	.50	1.25
14 Jake Atlas	.30	.75
15 Kushida	.50	1.25
16 Isaiah "Swerve" Scott	.50	1.25
17 Imperium	.40	1.00
18 Drake Maverick	.40	1.00
19 Keith Lee	.60	1.50
20 Johnny Gargano	.60	1.50
21 Karrion Kross	1.50	4.00
22 Adam Cole	1.00	2.50
23 Akira Tozawa	.40	1.00
24 Kushida	.50	1.25
25 Jake Atlas	.30	.75
26 Imperium	.40	1.00
27 Damian Priest	.75	2.00
28 Riddle	.75	2.00
29 El Hijo	.50	1.25
30 Roderick Strong	.50	1.25
31 Drake Maverick	.50	1.25
32 Tommaso Ciampa	.75	2.00
33 Timothy Thatcher	.30	.75
34 El Hijo	.50	1.25
35 Finn B·lor	.75	2.00
36 Keith Lee	.60	1.50
37 Karrion Kross	1.25	3.00
38 El Hijo	.50	1.25
39 Adam Cole	1.00	2.50
40 Imperium	.40	1.00
41 Karrion Kross	1.25	3.00
42 Dexter Lumis	.30	.75
43 Keith Lee	.60	1.50
44 Dexter Lumis	.30	.75
45 Legado del Fantasma	.50	1.25
46 Keith Lee	.60	1.50
47 Keith Lee	.60	1.50
48 Breezango	.50	1.25
49 Bronson Reed	.40	1.00
50 Karrion Kross	1.25	3.00
51 Imperium	.40	1.00
52 Dexter Lumis	.30	.75
53 Damian Priest	.50	1.25
54 Keith Lee	.60	1.50
55 Imperium	.50	1.25
56 Karrion Kross	1.25	3.00
57 Bronson Reed	.40	1.00
58 Cameron Grimes	.60	1.50
59 Breezango	.50	1.25
60 Finn B·lor	.75	2.00
61 Damian Priest	.50	1.25
62 Karrion Kross	1.25	3.00
63 Karrion Kross	1.50	4.00
64 Breezango	.50	1.25
65 Adam Cole	1.00	2.50
66 Finn B·lor	.75	2.00
67 Breezango	.50	1.25
68 Damian Priest	.50	1.25
69 Damian Priest	.50	1.25
70 Roderick Strong & Danny Burch	.50	1.25
71 Kyle O'Reilly	.50	1.25
72 Damian Priest	.50	1.25
73 Santos Escobar	.50	1.25
74 Finn B·lor	.75	2.00
75 Cameron Grimes	.60	1.50
76 Johnny Gargano	.60	1.50
77 Undisputed ERA	.50	1.25
78 Damian Priest	.50	1.25
79 Legado del Fantasma	.50	1.25
80 Oney Lorcan & Danny Burch	.40	1.00
81 Pete Dunne	.60	1.50
82 Johnny Gargano	.60	1.50
83 Dexter Lumis	.60	1.50
84 Kushida	.50	1.25
85 Leon Ruff	.30	.75
86 Santos Escobar	.50	1.25
87 Oney Lorcan & Danny Burch	.30	.75
88 Damian Priest	.60	1.50
89 Dexter Lumis and Cameron Grimes	.60	1.50
90 Kushida	.50	1.25
91 Tommaso Ciampa	.75	2.00
92 Dexter Lumis	.60	1.50
93 Johnny Gargano	.60	1.50
94 Finn B·lor	1.50	4.00
95 Karrion Kross	1.25	3.00
96 The Way	.60	1.50
97 Kyle O'Reilly	.50	1.25
98 Leon Ruff	.30	.75
99 Damian Priest	1.25	3.00
100 Johnny Gargano	1.25	3.00

2021 Topps WWE NXT Finn Balor Tribute

COMPLETE SET (10) 5.00 12.00
RANDOMLY INSERTED INTO PACKS

FB1 Finn Balor	1.00	2.50
FB2 Finn Balor	1.00	2.50
FB3 Finn Balor	1.00	2.50
FB4 Finn Balor	1.00	2.50
FB5 Finn Balor	1.00	2.50
FB6 Finn Balor	1.00	2.50
FB7 Finn Balor	1.00	2.50
FB8 Finn Balor	1.00	2.50
FB9 Finn Balor	1.00	2.50
FB10 Finn Balor	1.00	2.50

2021 Topps WWE NXT Finn Balor Tribute Autographs

*GOLD/10: UNPRICED DUE TO SCARCITY
*PLATINUM/1: UNPRICED DUE TO SCARCITY
STATED PRINT RUN 25 SER.#'d SETS

FB14 Finn Balor	25.00	60.00
FB15 Finn Balor	25.00	60.00
FB16 Finn Balor	25.00	60.00
FB19 Finn Balor	25.00	60.00
FB20 Finn Balor	25.00	60.00

2021 Topps WWE NXT Migs Media Illustrations

COMPLETE SET (10) 6.00 15.00
RANDOMLY INSERTED INTO PACKS

Card	Low	High
MM1 Cameron Grimes	1.25	3.00
MM2 Dakota Kai	1.25	3.00
MM3 Damian Priest	1.00	2.50
MM4 Io Shirai	1.25	3.00
MM5 Kushida	1.00	2.50
MM6 Rhea Ripley	2.00	5.00
MM7 Santos Escobar	1.00	2.50
MM8 Bronson Reed	.75	2.00
MM9 Tegan Nox	1.50	4.00
MM10 Timothy Thatcher	.60	1.50

2021 Topps WWE NXT NXT Alumni

COMPLETE SET (9) 5.00 12.00
RANDOMLY INSERTED INTO PACKS

Card	Low	High
NA1 Angel Garza	.75	2.00
NA2 Bianca Belair	1.50	4.00
NA3 Jaxson Ryker	.60	1.50
NA4 Keith Lee	1.25	3.00
NA5 Riddle	1.50	4.00
NA6 Riddick Moss	.75	2.00
NA7 Shayna Baszler	1.25	3.00
NA8 Damian Priest	1.00	2.50
NA9 Rhea Ripley	2.00	5.00

2021 Topps WWE NXT NXT Alumni Autographs

*GOLD/10: UNPRICED DUE TO SCARCITY
*PLATINUM/1: UNPRICED DUE TO SCARCITY
RANDOMLY INSERTED INTO PACKS

Card	Low	High
NAAG Angel Garza	8.00	20.00
NAJR Jaxson Ryker	8.00	20.00
NAKL Keith Lee	10.00	25.00
NAMR Riddle	15.00	40.00
NARM Riddick Moss	20.00	50.00
NASB Shayna Baszler	15.00	40.00

2021 Topps WWE NXT Tag Team Autographs

*GOLD/10: UNPRICED DUE TO SCARCITY
*PLATINUM/1: UNPRICED DUE TO SCARCITY
STATED PRINT RUN 25 SER.#'d SETS

Card	Low	High
DABZ T.Breeze/Fandango	15.00	40.00
DAER C.Parker/M.Martel	50.00	100.00
DAIP M.Barthel/F.Aichner	30.00	75.00
DAJC C.LeRae/J.Gargano	100.00	200.00
DAKS Scarlett/K.Kross	250.00	500.00
DALF J.Wilde/R.Mendoza		
DAOD D.Burch/O.Lorcan	30.00	75.00
DATN K.Catanzaro/K.Carter	100.00	200.00
DAUE B.Fish/K.O'Reilly	20.00	50.00
DAGYV J.Drake/Z.Gibson	15.00	40.00

2021 Topps WWE NXT We Are NXT

RANDOMLY INSERTED INTO PACKS

Card	Low	High
NXT1 Adam Cole	1.25	3.00
NXT2 Aliyah	.75	2.00
NXT3 Austin Theory	.75	2.00
NXT4 Arturo Ruas	.40	1.00
NXT5 Bobby Fish	.50	1.25
NXT6 Bronson Reed	.50	1.25
NXT7 Cameron Grimes	.75	2.00
NXT8 Candice LeRae	1.50	4.00
NXT9 Chase Parker	.40	1.00
NXT10 Dakota Kai	.75	2.00
NXT11 Danny Burch	.50	1.25
NXT12 Dave Mastiff	.40	1.00
NXT13 Dexter Lumis	.40	1.00
NXT14 Drake Maverick	.40	1.00
NXT15 Fabian Aichner	.50	1.25
NXT16 Fandango	.60	1.50
NXT17 Finn Balor	1.00	2.50
NXT18 Flash Morgan Webster	.50	1.25
NXT19 Ilja Dragunov	.40	1.00
NXT20 Indi Hartwell	1.25	3.00
NXT21 Io Shirai	.75	2.00
NXT22 Isaiah Swerve Scott	.60	1.50
NXT23 Jake Atlas	.40	1.00
NXT24 James Drake	.40	1.00
NXT25 Jessi Kamea	.75	2.00
NXT26 Joaquin Wilde	.60	1.50
NXT27 Johnny Gargano	.75	2.00
NXT28 Kacy Catanzaro	.75	2.00
NXT29 Karrion Kross	1.50	4.00
NXT30 Kay Lee Ray	1.00	2.50
NXT31 Kayden Carter	.75	2.00
NXT32 Killian Dain	.40	1.00
NXT33 Kushida	.60	1.50
NXT34 Kyle O'Reilly	.60	1.50
NXT35 Malcolm Bivens	.40	1.00
NXT36 Marcel Barthel	.50	1.25
NXT37 Marina Shafir	.75	2.00
NXT38 Matt Martel	.50	1.25
NXT39 Noam Dar	.50	1.25
NXT40 Oney Lorcan	.40	1.00
NXT41 Pete Dunne	.75	2.00
NXT42 Piper Niven	.60	1.50
NXT43 Raquel Gonzalez	1.00	2.50
NXT44 Raul Mendoza	.60	1.50
NXT45 Ridge Holland	.40	1.00
NXT46 Robert Stone	.40	1.00
NXT47 Roderick Strong	.60	1.50
NXT48 Santos Escobar	.60	1.50
NXT49 Saurav	.40	1.00
NXT50 Scarlett	2.00	5.00
NXT51 Shotzi Blackheart	1.50	4.00
NXT52 Tegan Nox	1.00	2.50
NXT53 Ashante Thee Adonis	.50	1.25
NXT54 Timothy Thatcher	.40	1.00
NXT55 Tommaso Ciampa	1.00	2.50
NXT56 Toni Storm	1.25	3.00
NXT57 Trent Seven	.50	1.25
NXT58 Tyler Bate	.50	1.25
NXT59 Tyler Breeze	.50	1.25
NXT60 WALTER	1.00	2.50
NXT61 Xia Li	.75	2.00
NXT62 Zack Gibson	.40	1.00

2021 Topps WWE NXT We Are NXT Autographs

*GREEN/99: .5X TO 1.2X BASIC AUTOS
*PURPLE/75: .6X TO 1.5X BASIC AUTOS
*BLUE/50: .75X TO 2X BASIC AUTOS
*RED/25: 1.2X TO 3X BASIC AUTOS
*GOLD/10: UNPRICED DUE TO SCARCITY
*PLATINUM/1: UNPRICED DUE TO SCARCITY
*P.P.BLACK/1: UNPRICED DUE TO SCARCITY
*P.P.CYAN/1: UNPRICED DUE TO SCARCITY
*P.P.MAGENTA/1: UNPRICED DUE TO SCARCITY
*P.P.YELLOW/1: UNPRICED DUE TO SCARCITY
RANDOMLY INSERTED INTO PACKS

Card	Low	High
AAC Adam Cole		
AAL Aliyah		
AAT Austin Theory	10.00	25.00
ABA Marcel Barthel	6.00	15.00
ABF Bobby Fish	5.00	12.00
ABR Bronson Reed	10.00	25.00
ACG Cameron Grimes	6.00	15.00
ACL Candice LeRae		
ACP Chase Parker	8.00	20.00
ADB Danny Burch		
ADK Dakota Kai	15.00	40.00
ADL Dexter Lumis	10.00	25.00
ADM Dave Mastiff	6.00	15.00
ADR Drake Maverick	5.00	12.00
AFA Fabian Aichner	6.00	15.00
AFD Fandango	5.00	12.00
AFS Kayden Carter	8.00	20.00
AID Ilja Dragunov	15.00	40.00
AIH Indi Hartwell	20.00	50.00
AIS Io Shirai	15.00	40.00
AJA Jake Atlas	5.00	12.00
AJD James Drake	5.00	12.00
AJG Johnny Gargano		
AJK Jessi Kamea	10.00	25.00
AJW Joaquin Wilde	5.00	12.00
AKC Kacy Catanzaro	15.00	40.00
AKD Killian Dain		
AKK Karrion Kross	25.00	60.00
AKS Kushida	8.00	20.00
AMM Matt Martel	6.00	15.00
AOL Oney Lorcan		
APD Pete Dunne	6.00	15.00
APN Piper Niven		
ARE Robert Stone	4.00	12.00
ARG Raquel Gonzalez	30.00	75.00
ARH Ridge Holland	6.00	15.00
ARM Raul Mendoza	5.00	12.00
ARS Roderick Strong	8.00	20.00
ASB Shotzi Blackheart	20.00	50.00
ASC Scarlett		
ASE Santos Escobar	5.00	12.00
ASW Isaiah Swerve Scott	5.00	12.00
AT7 Trent Seven	6.00	15.00
ATB Tyler Breeze	5.00	10.00
ATC Tommaso Ciampa		
ATM Ashante Thee Adonis	5.00	12.00
ATN Tegan Nox	10.00	25.00
ATO Toni Storm	25.00	60.00
ATT Timothy Thatcher	6.00	15.00
ATY Tyler Bate		
AWT WALTER	10.00	25.00
AXL Xia Li	10.00	25.00
AZG Zack Gibson	6.00	15.00
AKLR Kay Lee Ray		
AKOR Kyle O'Reilly	6.00	15.00

2011 Topps WWE Power Chipz

Card	Low	High
1 Undertaker	2.00	5.00
2 Edge	1.50	4.00
3 John Cena	2.00	5.00
4 Triple H	1.50	4.00
5 Rey Mysterio	1.00	2.50
6 CM Punk	1.00	2.50
7 Randy Orton	1.50	4.00
8 The Miz	.60	1.50
9 Big Show	1.00	2.50
10 Kofi Kingston	.40	1.00
11 Sheamus	.60	1.50
12 Alberto Del Rio	1.00	2.50
13 Stone Cold Steve Austin	1.50	4.00
14 Shawn Michaels	1.50	4.00
15 Christian	.40	1.00
16 Kane	1.00	2.50
17 Jack Swagger	.60	1.50
18 Daniel Bryan	.40	1.00
19 Eve	1.50	4.00
20 John Morrison	.60	1.50
21 The Great Khali	.40	1.00
22 Dolph Ziggler	.60	1.50
23 Mark Henry	.60	1.50
24 Chavo Guerrero	.40	1.00
25 Wade Barrett	.40	1.00
26 Natalya	1.50	4.00
27 Batista	.60	1.50
28 Santino Marella	.60	1.50
29 Cody Rhodes	.40	1.00
30 Ted DiBiase, Jr.	.60	1.50
31 Hornswoggle	.60	1.50
32 Drew McIntyre	.40	1.00
33 Alex Riley	.40	1.00
34 William Regal	.60	1.50
35 Vladimir Kozlov	.60	1.50
36 Primo	.40	1.00
37 Ezekiel Jackson	.60	1.50
38 R-Truth	.40	1.00
39 Beth Phoenix	1.00	2.50
40 Trish Stratus	2.00	5.00
41 Goldust	.40	1.00
42 David Hart Smith	.40	1.00
43 Jerry Lawler	1.00	2.50
44 Curt Hawkins	.40	1.00
45 Tyson Kidd	.40	1.00
46 Zack Ryder	.40	1.00
47 Melina	1.50	4.00
48 JTG	.40	1.00
49 Evan Bourne	.40	1.00
50 Michael McGillicutty	.40	1.00
51 Yoshi Tatsu	.40	1.00
52 Chris Masters	.40	1.00
53 Tyler Reks	.40	1.00
54 Skip Sheffield	.50	1.25
55 Darren Young	.40	1.00
56 Husky Harris	1.00	2.50
57 Jey Uso	.40	1.00
58 Jimmy Uso	.40	1.00
59 David Otunga	.40	1.00
60 Heath Slater	.40	1.00
61 Justin Gabriel	.40	1.00
62 Trent Barreta	.40	1.00
63 Kaitlyn	1.00	2.50
64 Gail Kim	1.00	2.50
65 Alicia Fox	.60	1.50
66 Kelly Kelly	1.50	4.00
67 Layla	1.00	2.50
68 Brie Bella	1.50	4.00
69 Nikki Bella	1.50	4.00
70 Maryse	1.50	4.00
71 Tamina	.40	1.00
72 Rosa Mendes	.60	1.50
73 Vickie Guerrero	.60	1.50
74 Teddy Long	.40	1.00

2011 Topps WWE Power Chipz Finishing Moves

RANDOMLY INSERTED INTO PACKS

Card	Low	High
F1 John Cena/Attitude Adjustment	3.00	8.00
F2 Randy Orton/RKO	2.50	6.00
F3 Undertaker/Last Ride	3.00	8.00
F4 Edge/Spear	2.50	6.00
F5 Triple H/Pedigree	2.50	6.00
F6 Rey Mysterio/619	1.50	4.00
F7 CM Punk/Go To Sleep	1.50	4.00
F8 The Miz/Skull-Crushing Finale	1.00	2.50
F9 Big Show/Choke Slam	1.50	4.00
F10 Kofi Kingston/Trouble In Paradise	.60	1.50
F11 Sheamus/High Cross	1.00	2.50
F12 Kane/Tombstone Piledriver	1.50	4.00

2011 Topps WWE Power Chipz Gold

RANDOMLY INSERTED INTO PACKS

Card	Low	High
G1 Undertaker	4.00	10.00
G2 Edge	3.00	8.00
G3 John Cena	4.00	10.00
G4 Triple H	3.00	8.00
G5 Rey Mysterio	2.00	5.00
G6 CM Punk	2.00	5.00
G7 Randy Orton	3.00	8.00
G8 The Miz	1.25	3.00
G9 Big Show	2.00	5.00
G10 Kofi Kingston	.75	2.00
G11 Sheamus	1.25	3.00
G12 Alberto Del Rio	2.00	5.00

2011 Topps WWE Power Chipz Legends

RANDOMLY INSERTED INTO PACKS

Card	Low	High
L1 Booker T	1.50	4.00
L2 Rowdy Roddy Piper	4.00	10.00
L3 Jake The Snake Roberts	2.50	6.00
L4 Mr. Perfect	2.50	6.00
L5 The British Bulldog	1.50	4.00
L6 Ted DiBiase	1.50	4.00
L7 Dusty Rhodes The American Dream	1.50	4.00
L8 Cowboy Bob Orton	1.50	4.00
L9 Junkyard Dog	2.50	6.00
L10 One Man Gang	1.00	2.50
L11 Papa Shango	1.00	2.50
L12 Sgt. Slaughter	2.50	6.00
L13 Hacksaw Jim Duggan	2.50	6.00
L14 Yokozuna	1.50	4.00
L15 Vader	1.50	4.00
L16 Doink The Clown	1.00	2.50
L17 Ravishing Rick Rude	1.50	4.00
L18 Jimmy Superfly Snuka	2.50	6.00
L19 Big Boss Man	1.50	4.00
L20 Terry Funk	1.50	4.00
L21 Kamala	1.50	4.00
L22 Hillbilly Jim	1.50	4.00
L23 Classy Freddie Blassie	1.50	4.00
L24 Mean Gene Okerlund	1.50	4.00

2011 Topps WWE Power Chipz Ruby

COMPLETE SET (12)
RANDOMLY INSERTED INTO PACKS

Card	Low	High
R1 Santino Marella	1.25	3.00
R2 Cody Rhodes	.75	2.00
R3 Ted DiBiase, Jr.	1.25	3.00
R4 Hornswoggle	1.25	3.00
R5 Drew McIntyre	.75	2.00
R6 Alex Riley	.75	2.00

R7 William Regal 1.25 3.00
R8 Vladimir Kozlov 1.25 3.00
R9 Primo .75 2.00
R10 Ezekiel Jackson 1.25 3.00
R11 R-Truth .75 2.00
R12 Beth Phoenix 2.00 5.00

2011 Topps WWE Power Chipz Silver

COMPLETE SET (12)
RANDOMLY INSERTED INTO PACKS

S1 Christian .75 2.00
S2 Kane 2.00 5.00
S3 Jack Swagger 1.25 3.00
S4 Daniel Bryan .75 2.00
S5 Eve 3.00 8.00
S6 John Morrison 1.25 3.00
S7 The Great Khali .75 2.00
S8 Dolph Ziggler 1.25 3.00
S9 Mark Henry 1.25 3.00
S10 Chavo Guerrero .75 2.00
S11 Wade Barrett .75 2.00
S12 Natalya 3.00 8.00

2019 Topps WWE RAW

COMPLETE SET (90) 10.00 25.00
*BRONZE: .6X TO 1.5X BASIC CARDS
*BLUE/99: .75X TO 2X BASIC CARDS
*SILVER/25: 2X TO 5X BASIC CARDS
*GOLD/10: UNPRICED DUE TO SCARCITY
*BLACK/1: UNPRICED DUE TO SCARCITY
*P.P.BLACK/1: UNPRICED DUE TO SCARCITY
*P.P.CYAN/1: UNPRICED DUE TO SCARCITY
*P.P.MAGENTA/1: UNPRICED DUE TO SCARCITY
*P.P.YELLOW/1: UNPRICED DUE TO SCARCITY

1 Akam .25 .60
2 Alexa Bliss 1.25 3.00
3 Alicia Fox .50 1.25
4 Apollo Crews .30 .75
5 Baron Corbin .40 1.00
6 Batista .60 1.50
7 Bayley .50 1.25
8 Bo Dallas .30 .75
9 Bobby Lashley .50 1.25
10 Bobby Roode .50 1.25
11 Booker T .60 1.50
12 Braun Strowman .60 1.50
13 Bray Wyatt .60 1.50
14 Brie Bella .60 1.50
15 Brock Lesnar 1.00 2.50
16 Chad Gable .25 .60
17 Charly Caruso .40 1.00
18 Corey Graves .30 .75
19 Curt Hawkins .25 .60
20 Curtis Axel .30 .75
21 Dana Brooke .50 1.25
22 Dash Wilder .25 .60
23 David Otunga .25 .60
24 Dean Ambrose .60 1.50
25 Dolph Ziggler .50 1.25
26 Drake Maverick .25 .60
27 Drew McIntyre .30 .75
28 Elias .50 1.25
29 Ember Moon .60 1.50
30 Fandango .25 .60
31 Finn Balor .50 1.25
32 Gran Metalik .25 .60
33 Heath Slater .25 .60
34 Jason Jordan .30 .75
35 Jinder Mahal .50 1.25
36 Jonathan Coachman .25 .60
37 John Cena 1.25 3.00
38 JoJo .40 1.00
39 Kalisto .25 .60
40 Kane .40 1.00
41 Kayla Braxton .40 1.00
42 Kevin Owens .60 1.50
43 Konnor .25 .60
44 Kurt Angle .50 1.25
45 Lince Dorado .25 .60
46 Lio Rush .30 .75
47 Liv Morgan .75 2.00
48 Michael Cole .25 .60
49 Mickie James .60 1.50
50 Mike Rome .30 .75
51 Mojo Rawley .30 .75
52 Natalya .50 1.25
53 Nia Jax .50 1.25
54 Nikki Bella .60 1.50
55 No Way Jose .30 .75
56 Paul Heyman .30 .75
57 Renee Young .40 1.00
58 Rezar .25 .60
59 Rhyno .25 .60
60 Roman Reigns .60 1.50
61 Ronda Rousey 1.25 3.00
62 Ruby Riott .50 1.25
63 Sami Zayn .50 1.25
64 Samir Singh .25 .60
65 Sarah Logan .30 .75
66 Sasha Banks 1.00 2.50
67 Scott Dawson .25 .60
68 Seth Rollins .60 1.50
69 Stephanie McMahon .60 1.50
70 Sunil Singh .25 .60
71 Titus O'Neil .30 .75
72 Tyler Breeze .30 .75
73 Viktor .25 .60
74 Zack Ryder .30 .75
75 Akira Tozawa .25 .60
76 Ariya Daivari .25 .60
77 Buddy Murphy .30 .75
78 Cedric Alexander .25 .60
79 Drew Gulak .25 .60
80 Gentleman Jack Gallagher .30 .75
81 Hideo Itami .25 .60
82 Maria Kanellis .60 1.50
83 Mark Andrews .25 .60
84 Mike Kanellis .25 .60
85 Nigel McGuinness .25 .60
86 Noam Dar .25 .60
87 The Brian Kendrick .40 1.00
88 TJP .40 1.00
89 Tony Nese .25 .60
90 Vic Joseph RC .25 .60

2019 Topps WWE RAW Autographed Commemorative Intercontinental Championship Relics

STATED PRINT RUN 10 SER.#'d SETS

ICRAHH Triple H
ICRASM Shawn Michaels

2019 Topps WWE RAW Autographed Commemorative RAW Championship Relics

STATED PRINT RUN 10 SER.#'d SETS
UNPRICED DUE TO SCARCITY

RACAB Alexa Bliss
RACBL Bayley
RACBS Braun Strowman
RACCF Charlotte Flair
RACDA Dean Ambrose
RACFB Finn Balor
RACKO Kevin Owens
RACRRR Ronda Rousey
RACSB Sasha Banks
RACSR Seth Rollins
RACTM The Miz

2019 Topps WWE RAW Autographed Mat Relics

STATED PRINT RUN 10 SER.#'d SETS
UNPRICED DUE TO SCARCITY

DMARAB Aleister Black
DMARAJ AJ Styles
DMARAK Asuka
DMARAS Shayna Baszler
DMARBL Bobby Lashley
DMARBR Bobby Roode
DMARBS Braun Strowman
DMARCF Charlotte Flair
DMAREM Ember Moon
DMARFB Finn Balor
DMARJG Johnny Gargano
DMARJN Natalya
DMARKK Kofi Kingston
DMARKO Kevin Owens
DMARKR Kyle O'Reilly
DMARLK Becky Lynch
DMARMB Alexa Bliss
DMARNC Nikki Cross
DMARNM Naomi
DMARRC Ricochet
DMARRD Rusev
DMARRS Roderick Strong
DMARSB Sasha Banks
DMARSJ Samoa Joe
DMARSN Shinsuke Nakamura
DMARSR Seth Rollins
DMARSZ Sami Zayn
DMARTC Tomasso Ciampa
DMARTM The Miz
DMARVD Velveteen Dream
DMARRRR Ronda Rousey

2019 Topps WWE RAW Autographed Shirt Relics

STATED PRINT RUN 10 SER.#'d SETS
UNPRICED DUE TO SCARCITY

SARAB Alexa Bliss
SARDA Dean Ambrose
SARFB Finn Balor
SARKO Kevin Owens
SARRY Renee Young
SARSR Seth Rollins
SARWJ No Way Jose

2019 Topps WWE RAW Autographed Women's Revolution Relics

STATED PRINT RUN 10 SER.#'d SETS
UNPRICED DUE TO SCARCITY

DRACAB Alexa Bliss
DRACSB Sasha Banks
DRACRRR Ronda Rousey

2019 Topps WWE RAW Autographs

*BLUE/50: .5X TO 1.2X BASIC AUTOS
*SILVER/25: .6X TO 1.5X BASIC AUTOS
*GOLD/10: UNPRICED DUE TO SCARCITY
*BLACK/1: UNPRICED DUE TO SCARCITY
STATED PRINT RUN 99 SER.#'d SETS

AAB Alexa Bliss 25.00 60.00
AAC Apollo Crews 6.00 15.00
ABC Baron Corbin 5.00 12.00
ABL Bobby Lashley 8.00 20.00
ABR Bobby Roode 4.00 10.00
ABS Braun Strowman/94 5.00 12.00
ABT Booker T 5.00 12.00
ACA Cedric Alexander 4.00 10.00
ACC Charly Caruso 6.00 15.00
ACG Chad Gable 3.00 8.00
ADA Dean Ambrose 6.00 15.00
ADB Dana Brooke 6.00 15.00
ADM Drew McIntyre 5.00 12.00
AEM Ember Moon/63 8.00 20.00
AFB Finn Balor/88 12.00 30.00
AGR Corey Graves 6.00 15.00
AHO Hideo Itami 3.00 8.00
AJG Gentleman Jack Gallagher 12.00 30.00
AJJ Jason Jordan/77 5.00 12.00
AJN Natalya 10.00 25.00
AKA Kurt Angle 8.00 20.00
AKT Kalisto 4.00 10.00
ALD Lince Dorado/98 10.00 25.00
ALR Lio Rush 6.00 15.00
ARY Renee Young 6.00 12.00
ASL Sarah Logan 6.00 15.00
ASR Seth Rollins 8.00 20.00
ATB Tyler Breeze 4.00 10.00
ATN Titus O'Neil 4.00 10.00

2019 Topps WWE RAW Commemorative Intercontinental Championship Relics

RANDOMLY INSERTED INTO PACKS

ICRED Edge
ICRHH Triple H
ICRRM The Rock
ICRRR Razor Ramon
ICRSM Shawn Michaels

2019 Topps WWE RAW Commemorative RAW Championship Relics

*BRONZE/99: SAME VALUE AS BASIC
*BLUE/50: .5X TO 1.2X BASIC MEM
*SILVER/25: .6X TO 1.5X BASIC MEM
*GOLD/10: UNPRICED DUE TO SCARCITY
*BLACK/1: UNPRICED DUE TO SCARCITY
RANDOMLY INSERTED INTO PACKS

RCAB Alexa Bliss 10.00 25.00
RCBC Karl Anderson/Luke Gallows 2.00 5.00
RCBD Roman Reigns 5.00 12.00
RCBL Bayley 5.00 12.00
RCBS Braun Strowman 2.50 6.00
RCBT Curtis Axel/Bo Dallas 2.50 6.00
RCCF Charlotte Flair 4.00 10.00
RCDA Dean Ambrose 5.00 12.00
RCDZ Dolph Ziggler 2.50 6.00
RCFB Finn Balor 3.00 8.00
RCGB Goldberg 6.00 15.00
RCKO Kevin Owens 2.00 5.00
RCNJ Nia Jax 2.00 5.00
RCRR Roman Reigns 5.00 12.00
RCSB Sasha Banks 6.00 15.00
RCSD Seth Rollins/Dean Ambrose 3.00 8.00
RCSR Seth Rollins 4.00 10.00
RCTB Cesaro/Sheamus 2.00 5.00
RCTM The Miz 2.00 5.00
RCZM Drew McIntyre/Dolph Ziggler 2.50 6.00
RCRRR Ronda Rousey 12.00 30.00

2019 Topps WWE RAW Hometown Heroes

COMPLETE SET (48) 12.00 30.00
RANDOMLY INSERTED INTO PACKS

HH1 Alexa Bliss 2.00 5.00
HH2 Apollo Crews .50 1.25
HH3 Baron Corbin .60 1.50
HH4 Bayley .75 2.00
HH5 Big Show .60 1.50
HH6 Bo Dallas .50 1.25
HH7 Bobby Lashley .75 2.00
HH8 Bobby Roode .75 2.00
HH9 Booker T 1.00 2.50
HH10 Curtis Axel .50 1.25
HH11 Dana Brooke .75 2.00
HH12 Dean Ambrose 1.00 2.50
HH13 Dolph Ziggler .75 2.00
HH14 Drew McIntyre .50 1.25
HH15 Elias .75 2.00
HH16 Ember Moon 1.00 2.50
HH17 Finn Balor .75 2.00
HH18 Heath Slater .40 1.00
HH19 Jason Jordan .50 1.25
HH20 Jinder Mahal .75 2.00
HH21 John Cena 2.00 5.00
HH22 Kevin Owens 1.00 2.50
HH23 Liv Morgan 1.25 3.00
HH24 Mickie James 1.00 2.50
HH25 Mojo Rawley .50 1.25
HH26 Natalya .75 2.00
HH27 Nia Jax .75 2.00
HH28 No Way Jose .50 1.25
HH29 Lince Dorado .40 1.00
HH30 Lio Rush .50 1.25
HH31 Rhyno .40 1.00
HH32 Roman Reigns 1.00 2.50
HH33 Ronda Rousey 2.00 5.00
HH34 Ruby Riott .75 2.00
HH35 Sarah Logan .50 1.25
HH36 Sasha Banks 1.50 4.00
HH37 Seth Rollins 1.00 2.50
HH38 Titus O'Neil .50 1.25
HH39 Zack Ryder .50 1.25
HH40 Buddy Murphy .50 1.25
HH41 Cedric Alexander .40 1.00
HH42 Drew Gulak .40 1.00
HH43 Gentleman Jack Gallagher .50 1.25
HH44 Gran Metalik .40 1.00
HH45 Hideo Itami .40 1.00
HH46 Kalisto .40 1.00
HH47 Mark Andrews .40 1.00
HH48 TJP .60 1.50

2019 Topps WWE RAW Image Variations

RANDOMLY INSERTED INTO PACKS

IVAB Alexa Bliss	30.00	75.00
IVAC Apollo Crews	2.50	6.00
IVBL Bobby Lashley	12.00	30.00
IVBR Bobby Roode	3.00	8.00
IVBY Bayley	8.00	20.00
IVDG Drew Gulak	3.00	8.00
IVDM Drew McIntyre	3.00	8.00
IVDZ Dolph Ziggler	3.00	8.00
IVEM Ember Moon	4.00	10.00
IVFB The Demon Finn Balor	15.00	40.00
IVJN Natalya	5.00	12.00
IVKO Kevin Owens	4.00	10.00
IVLL Kalisto	2.50	6.00
IVLR Lio Rush	3.00	8.00
IVMK Mike Kanellis	4.00	10.00
IVMR Mojo Rawley	4.00	10.00
IVNJ Nia Jax	4.00	10.00
IVRR Roman Reigns	6.00	15.00
IVRS Drake Maverick	6.00	15.00
IVSB Sasha Banks	12.00	30.00
IVSR Seth Rollins	5.00	12.00
IVSZ Sami Zayn	3.00	8.00
IVTJ TJP	5.00	12.00
IVZR Zack Ryder	8.00	20.00

2019 Topps WWE RAW Intercontinental Champions Autographs

*GOLD/10: UNPRICED DUE TO SCARCITY
STATED PRINT RUN 25 SER.#'d SETS

ICAHH Triple H	100.00	200.00
ICASM Shawn Michaels	50.00	100.00

2019 Topps WWE RAW Kiss

*SILVER/25: .6X TO 1.5X BASIC KISS
*GOLD/10: UNPRICED DUE TO SCARCITY
*BLACK/1: UNPRICED DUE TO SCARCITY
STATED PRINT RUN 50 SER.#'d SETS

KCAF Alicia Fox	15.00	40.00
KCEM Ember Moon	15.00	40.00
KCNJ Nia Jax	12.00	30.00

2019 Topps WWE RAW Kiss Autographs

*GOLD/10: UNPRICED DUE TO SCARCITY
*BLACK/1: UNPRICED DUE TO SCARCITY
STATED PRINT RUN 25 SER.#'d SETS

KARAF Alicia Fox	30.00	75.00
KARMJ Mickie James	60.00	120.00
KARNJ Nia Jax	20.00	50.00

2019 Topps WWE RAW Legends of RAW

COMPLETE SET (20)	6.00	15.00

RANDOMLY INSERTED INTO PACKS

LR1 Batista	.60	1.50
LR2 Bret Hitman Hart	.60	1.50
LR3 Edge	.60	1.50
LR4 Faarooq	.40	1.00
LR5 Goldberg	.75	2.00
LR6 Jerry The King Lawler	.50	1.25
LR7 Ken Shamrock	.40	1.00
LR8 Lita	.60	1.50
LR9 Mr. Perfect	.40	1.00
LR10 Mark Henry	.30	.75
LR11 Mankind	.50	1.25
LR12 Sycho Sid	.25	.60
LR13 Rikishi	.25	.60
LR14 Ric Flair	.75	2.00
LR15 Road Dogg	.25	.60
LR16 Shawn Michaels	.60	1.50
LR17 Stone Cold Steve Austin	1.25	3.00
LR18 Trish Stratus	1.25	3.00
LR19 Vader	.30	.75
LR20 X-Pac	.25	.60

2019 Topps WWE RAW Mat Relics

SEMISTARS	2.00	5.00
UNLISTED STARS	2.50	6.00

*BRONZE/99: .5X TO 1.2X BASIC MEM
*BLUE/50: .6X TO 1.5X BASIC MEM
*SILVER/25: .75X TO 2X BASIC MEM
*GOLD/10: UNPRICED DUE TO SCARCITY
*BLACK/1: UNPRICED DUE TO SCARCITY
RANDOMLY INSERTED INTO PACKS

DMRAB Aleister Black	1.50	4.00
DMRAJ AJ Styles	3.00	8.00
DMRAK Asuka	6.00	15.00
DMRAS Shayna Baszler	4.00	10.00
DMRBL Bobby Lashley	1.50	4.00
DMRBR Bobby Roode	2.50	6.00
DMRBS Braun Strowman	2.00	5.00
DMRCF Charlotte Flair	4.00	10.00
DMRCM Carmella	5.00	12.00
DMRDB Daniel Bryan	2.50	6.00
DMRDN Danny Burch	2.50	6.00
DMREM Ember Moon	3.00	8.00
DMRFB Finn Balor	4.00	10.00
DMRJG Johnny Gargano	2.00	5.00
DMRJN Natalya	3.00	8.00
DMRKK Kofi Kingston	3.00	8.00
DMRKO Kevin Owens	2.50	6.00
DMRKR Kyle O'Reilly	3.00	8.00
DMRLD Lana	2.50	6.00
DMRLK Becky Lynch	6.00	15.00
DMRLS Lars Sullivan	1.50	4.00
DMRMB Alexa Bliss	12.00	30.00
DMRNC Nikki Cross	1.50	4.00
DMRNJ Nia Jax	2.00	5.00
DMRNM Naomi	2.50	6.00
DMROL Oney Lorcan	2.00	5.00
DMRRC Ricochet	3.00	8.00
DMRRD Rusev	2.50	6.00
DMRRR Roman Reigns	4.00	10.00
DMRRS Roderick Strong	2.00	5.00
DMRSB Sasha Banks	8.00	20.00
DMRSJ Samoa Joe	2.00	5.00
DMRSN Shinsuke Nakamura	3.00	8.00
DMRSR Seth Rollins	4.00	10.00
DMRSZ Sami Zayn	2.00	5.00
DMRTC Tommaso Ciampa	2.00	5.00
DMRTM The Miz	2.50	6.00
DMRVD Velveteen Dream	2.00	5.00
DMRWE Elias	2.00	5.00
DMRRRR Ronda Rousey	10.00	25.00

2019 Topps WWE RAW Shirt Relics

*BRONZE/99: .5X TO 1.2X BASIC MEM
*BLUE/50: .6X TO 1.5X BASIC MEM
*SILVER/25: .75X TO 2X BASIC MEM
*GOLD/10: UNPRICED DUE TO SCARCITY
*BLACK/1: UNPRICED DUE TO SCARCITY
STATED PRINT RUN 199 SER.#'d SETS

SRAB Alexa Bliss	15.00	40.00
SRDA Dean Ambrose	6.00	15.00
SREL Elias	4.00	10.00
SRFB Finn Balor	8.00	20.00
SRKO Kevin Owens	3.00	8.00
SRRR Roman Reigns	5.00	15.00
SRSR Seth Rollins	6.00	15.00
SRWJ No Way Jose	3.00	6.00

2019 Topps WWE RAW Triple Autographs

*BLACK/1: UNPRICED DUE TO SCARCITY
STATED PRINT RUN 10 SER.#'d SETS
UNPRICED DUE TO SCARCITY

TAAB Bliss/Fox/James
TARS Morgan/Riott/Logan

2019 Topps WWE RAW Women's Revolution Autographs

*GOLD/10: UNPRICED DUE TO SCARCITY
*BLACK/1: UNPRICED DUE TO SCARCITY
RANDOMLY INSERTED INTO PACKS

WABL Bayley	20.00	50.00
WARR Ronda Rousey		
WASB Sasha Banks	30.00	75.00

2019 Topps WWE RAW Women's Revolution Relics

RANDOMLY INSERTED INTO PACKS

DRCAB Alexa Bliss
DRCNJ Nia Jax
DRCSB Sasha Banks

2004 Topps WWE RAW and SmackDown Apocalypse

C1 Checklist 1	.25	.60
C2 Checklist 2	.25	.60
D1 Torrie Wilson	3.00	8.00
D2 Dawn Marie	.75	2.00
D3 Miss Jackie	1.25	3.00
D4 Lita	2.00	5.00
D5 Nidia	.75	2.00
D6 Stacy Keibler	3.00	8.00
D7 Trish Stratus	3.00	8.00
F1 In-Ring Action FOIL	.25	.60
F2 Triple H	2.00	5.00
F3 Chris Benoit	.75	2.00
F4 Shawn Michaels	2.00	5.00
F5 Edge	1.25	3.00
F6 Chris Jericho	.75	2.00
F7 Kane	1.25	3.00
F8 The Rock	2.00	5.00
F9 Ric Flair	1.50	4.00
P1 Eddie Guerrero	1.50	4.00
P2 JBL John "Bradshaw" Layfield	.75	2.00
P3 Kurt Angle	1.25	3.00
P4 Rey Mysterio	.75	2.00
P5 John Cena	2.00	5.00
P6 Undertaker	1.50	4.00
P7 Booker T	1.25	3.00
P8 Dawn Marie	.75	2.00
P9 Miss Jackie	1.25	3.00
R1 RAW Superstars	.25	.60
R2 Jerry "The King" Lawler	.75	2.00
R3 Jim Ross	.50	1.25
R4 Tajiri	.30	.75
R5 The Rock FOIL	2.00	5.00
R6 Maven	.30	.75
R7 Molly Holly	1.50	4.00
R8 Nidia FOIL	.75	2.00
R9 Trish Stratus FOIL	3.00	8.00
S1 Smackdown! Superstars	.25	.60
S2 Michael Cole		
S3 Tazz	.50	1.25
S4 Akio		
S5 Big Show FOIL	1.25	3.00
S6 Chavo Guerrero	.50	1.25
S7 D-Von Dudley	.50	1.25
S8 JBL John "Bradshaw" Layfield FOIL	.75	2.00
S9 Johnny Stamboli	.30	.75
F10 Randy Orton	.75	2.00
F11 Batista	1.25	3.00
F12 Shelton Benjamin	.30	.75
F13 Eugene	.50	1.25
F14 Maven	.30	.75
F15 The Hurricane	.40	1.00
F16 Matt Hardy	.75	2.00
F17 Trish Stratus	3.00	8.00
F18 Lita	2.00	5.00
F19 Eddie Guerrero	1.50	4.00
F20 Kurt Angle	1.25	3.00
F21 JBL John "Bradshaw" Layfield	.75	2.00
F22 John Cena	2.00	5.00
F23 Rey Mysterio	.75	2.00
F24 Undertaker	1.50	4.00
F25 Rob Van Dam	1.25	3.00
F26 Booker T	1.25	3.00
F27 Chavo Guerrero	.50	1.25
F28 Charlie Haas	.30	.75
F29 Rico	.30	.75
F30 Big Show	1.25	3.00
F31 Heidenreich	.30	.75
F32 Billy Kidman	.30	.75
F33 Bubba Ray Dudley	.50	1.25
F34 Rene Dupree	.50	1.25
F35 Spike Dudley	.50	1.25
P10 Kane	1.25	3.00
P11 Chris Benoit	.75	2.00
P12 Triple H	2.00	5.00
P13 Edge	1.25	3.00
P14 The Rock	2.00	5.00
P15 Chris Jericho	.75	2.00
P16 Jim Ross	.50	1.25
P17 Jerry "The King" Lawler	.75	2.00
P18 Trish Stratus	3.00	8.00
R10 Triple H FOIL	2.00	5.00
R11 Ric Flair FOIL	1.50	4.00
R12 Rob Conway	.30	.75
R13 Rosey	.30	.75
R14 Shawn Michaels FOIL	2.00	5.00
R15 Shelton Benjamin	.30	.75
R16 Eric Bischoff	.50	1.25
R17 Eugene FOIL	.50	1.25
R18 Gail Kim FOIL	1.25	3.00
R19 Garrison Cade	.30	.75
R20 A-Train	.30	.75
R21 Batista FOIL	1.25	3.00
R22 Chris Benoit FOIL	.75	2.00
R23 Chris Jericho FOIL	.75	2.00
R24 Christian	1.00	2.50
R25 Joanathan Coachman	.30	.75
R26 Kane FOIL	1.25	3.00
R27 Lita FOIL	.25	.60
R28 Ivory	1.25	3.00
R29 Matt Hardy FOIL	.75	2.00
R30 Edge FOIL	1.25	3.00
R31 Stacy Kiebler FOIL	3.00	8.00
R32 Sylvain Grenier		
R33 Rhyno	1.25	3.00
R34 The Hurricane	.40	1.00
R35 Randy Orton FOIL	.75	2.00
R36 Tyson Tomko	.50	1.25
R37 Victoria FOIL	1.50	4.00
R38 William Regal	.40	1.00
S10 Kurt Angle FOIL	1.25	3.00
S11 Eddie Guerrero FOIL	1.50	4.00
S12 Rico	.30	.75
S13 John Cena FOIL	2.00	5.00
S14 Theodore Long	.30	.75
S15 Heidenreich FOIL	.30	.75
S16 Undertaker FOIL	1.50	4.00
S17 Miss Jackie FOIL	1.25	3.00
S18 Nunzio	.30	.75
S19 Rene Dupree	.50	1.25
S20 Danny Basham	.30	.75
S21 Dawn Marie FOIL	.75	2.00
S22 Doug Basham	.30	.75
S23 Scotty 2 Hotty	.50	1.25
S24 Spike	.50	1.25
S25 Booker T FOIL	1.25	3.00
S26 Bubba Ray Dudley	.50	1.25
S27 Charlie Haas	.30	.75
S28 Billy Gunn	.40	1.00
S29 Rob Van Dam FOIL	1.25	3.00
S30 Torrie Wilson FOIL	3.00	8.00
S31 Billy Kidman	.30	.75
S32 Rey Mysterio FOIL	.75	2.00

2009 Topps WWE Rivals Stickers

1 Emblem WWE	.12	.30
2 WWE 1	.12	.30
3 WWE 2	.12	.30
4 John Cena	.75	2.00
5 John Cena	.75	2.00
6 John Cena	.75	2.00
7 John Cena	.75	2.00
8 John Cena	.75	2.00
9 John Cena	.75	2.00
10 John Cena	.75	2.00
11 John Cena	.75	2.00
12 John Cena	.75	2.00
13 John Cena	.75	2.00
14 Edge	.50	1.25
15 Edge	.50	1.25
16 Edge	.50	1.25
17 Edge	.50	1.25
18 Edge	.50	1.25
19 Edge	.50	1.25
20 Edge	.50	1.25
21 Edge	.50	1.25
22 Edge	.50	1.25
23 Edge	.50	1.25
24 Kane	.50	1.25
25 Kane	.50	1.25

26 Kane .50 1.25
27 Kane .50 1.25
28 Kane .50 1.25
29 The Miz .20 .50
30 The Miz .20 .50
31 The Miz .20 .50
32 The Miz .20 .50
33 The Miz .20 .50
34 Mr. Kennedy .30 .75
35 Mr. Kennedy .30 .75
36 Mr. Kennedy .30 .75
37 Mr. Kennedy .30 .75
38 Mr. Kennedy .30 .75
39 William Regal .30 .75
40 William Regal .30 .75
41 William Regal .30 .75
42 William Regal .30 .75
43 William Regal .30 .75
44 Chavo Guerrero .20 .50
45 Chavo Guerrero .20 .50
46 Chavo Guerrero .20 .50
47 Chavo Guerrero .20 .50
48 Chavo Guerrero .20 .50
49 Chavo Guerrero .20 .50
50 Chavo Guerrero .20 .50
51 Chavo Guerrero .20 .50
52 Chavo Guerrero .20 .50
53 Chavo Guerrero .20 .50
54 CM Punk .20 .50
55 CM Punk .20 .50
56 CM Punk .20 .50
57 CM Punk .20 .50
58 CM Punk .20 .50
59 CM Punk .20 .50
60 CM Punk .20 .50
61 CM Punk .20 .50
62 CM Punk .20 .50
63 CM Punk .20 .50
64 The Great Khali .12 .30
65 The Great Khali .12 .30
66 The Great Khali .12 .30
67 The Great Khali .12 .30
68 The Great Khali .12 .30
69 Finlay & Hornswoggle .20 .50
70 Finlay & Hornswoggle .20 .50
71 Finlay & Hornswoggle .20 .50
72 Finlay & Hornswoggle .20 .50
73 Finlay & Hornswoggle .20 .50
74 Kofi Kingston .12 .30
75 Kofi Kingston .12 .30
76 Kofi Kingston .12 .30
77 Kofi Kingston .12 .30
78 Kofi Kingston .12 .30
79 Carlito .30 .75
80 Carlito .30 .75
81 Carlito .30 .75
82 Carlito .30 .75
83 Carlito .30 .75
84 Jeff Hardy .50 1.25
85 Jeff Hardy .50 1.25
86 Jeff Hardy .50 1.25
87 Jeff Hardy .50 1.25
88 Jeff Hardy .50 1.25
89 Jeff Hardy .50 1.25
90 Jeff Hardy .50 1.25
91 Jeff Hardy .50 1.25
92 Jeff Hardy .50 1.25
93 Jeff Hardy .50 1.25
94 John Morrison .20 .50
95 John Morrison .20 .50
96 John Morrison .20 .50
97 John Morrison .20 .50
98 John Morrison .20 .50
99 John Morrison .20 .50
100 John Morrison .20 .50
101 John Morrison .20 .50
102 John Morrison .20 .50
103 John Morrison .20 .50
104 Shawn Michaels .75 2.00
105 Shawn Michaels .75 2.00
106 Shawn Michaels .75 2.00
107 Shawn Michaels .75 2.00
108 Shawn Michaels .75 2.00
109 Vladimir Kozlov .20 .50
110 Vladimir Kozlov .20 .50
111 Vladimir Kozlov .20 .50
112 Vladimir Kozlov .20 .50
113 Vladimir Kozlov .20 .50
114 Big Show .30 .75
115 Big Show .30 .75
116 Big Show .30 .75
117 Big Show .30 .75
118 Big Show .30 .75
119 JBL .20 .50
120 JBL .20 .50
121 JBL .20 .50
122 JBL .20 .50
123 JBL .20 .50
124 Beth Phoenix .60 1.50
125 Beth Phoenix .60 1.50
126 Maria .50 1.25
127 Maria .50 1.25
128 Candice .60 1.50
129 Melina .50 1.25
130 Mickie James .60 1.50
131 Candice .60 1.50
132 Melina .50 1.25
133 Mickie James .60 1.50
134 Matt Hardy .50 1.25
135 Matt Hardy .50 1.25
136 Matt Hardy .50 1.25
137 Matt Hardy .50 1.25
138 Matt Hardy .50 1.25
139 Matt Hardy .50 1.25
140 Matt Hardy .50 1.25
141 Matt Hardy .50 1.25
142 Matt Hardy .50 1.25
143 Matt Hardy .50 1.25
144 MVP .20 .50
145 MVP .20 .50
146 MVP .20 .50
147 MVP .20 .50
148 MVP .20 .50
149 Chris Jericho .30 .75
150 Chris Jericho .30 .75
151 Chris Jericho .30 .75
152 Chris Jericho .30 .75
153 Chris Jericho .30 .75
154 Cody Rhodes & Ted Dibiase .20 .50
155 Cody Rhodes & Ted Dibiase .20 .50
156 Cody Rhodes & Ted Dibiase .20 .50
157 Cody Rhodes & Ted Dibiase .20 .50
158 Cody Rhodes & Ted Dibiase .20 .50
159 Cryme Tyme .12 .30
160 Cryme Tyme .12 .30
161 Cryme Tyme .12 .30
162 Cryme Tyme .12 .30
163 Cryme Tyme .12 .30
164 Triple H .75 2.00
165 Triple H .75 2.00
166 Triple H .75 2.00
167 Triple H .75 2.00
168 Triple H .75 2.00
169 Triple H .75 2.00
170 Triple H .75 2.00
171 Triple H .75 2.00
172 Triple H .75 2.00
173 Triple H .75 2.00
174 Rey Mysterio .30 .75
175 Rey Mysterio .30 .75
176 Rey Mysterio .30 .75
177 Rey Mysterio .30 .75
178 Rey Mysterio .30 .75
179 Rey Mysterio .30 .75
180 Rey Mysterio .30 .75
181 Rey Mysterio .30 .75
182 Rey Mysterio .30 .75
183 Rey Mysterio .30 .75
184 Shelton Benjamin .12 .30
185 Shelton Benjamin .12 .30
186 Shelton Benjamin .12 .30
187 Shelton Benjamin .12 .30
188 Shelton Benjamin .12 .30
189 Tommy Dreamer .12 .30
190 Tommy Dreamer .12 .30
191 Tommy Dreamer .12 .30
192 Tommy Dreamer .12 .30
193 Tommy Dreamer .12 .30
194 Santino Marella .12 .30
195 Santino Marella .12 .30
196 Santino Marella .12 .30
197 Santino Marella .12 .30
198 Santino Marella .12 .30
199 Umaga .20 .50
200 Umaga .20 .50
201 Umaga .20 .50
202 Umaga .20 .50
203 Umaga .20 .50
204 Randy Orton .30 .75
205 Randy Orton .30 .75
206 Randy Orton .30 .75
207 Randy Orton .30 .75
208 Randy Orton .30 .75
209 Randy Orton .30 .75
210 Randy Orton .30 .75
211 Randy Orton .30 .75
212 Randy Orton .30 .75
213 Randy Orton .30 .75
214 Undertaker .60 1.50
215 Undertaker .60 1.50
216 Undertaker .60 1.50
217 Undertaker .60 1.50
218 Undertaker .60 1.50
219 Undertaker .60 1.50
220 Undertaker .60 1.50
221 Undertaker .60 1.50
222 Undertaker .60 1.50
223 Undertaker .60 1.50
224 Mark Henry .20 .50
225 Mark Henry .20 .50
226 Mark Henry .20 .50
227 Mark Henry .20 .50
228 Mark Henry .20 .50
229 Batista .50 1.25
230 Batista .50 1.25
231 Batista .50 1.25
232 Batista .50 1.25
233 Batista .50 1.25
234 Jack Swagger .12 .30
235 Jack Swagger .12 .30
236 Jack Swagger .12 .30
P1 RAW .12 .30
P2 John Cena .75 2.00
P3 Randy Orton .30 .75
P4 JBL .20 .50
P5 Rey Mysterio .30 .75
P6 ECW .12 .30
P7 John Morrison .20 .50
P8 Mark Henry .20 .50
P9 Chavo Guerrero .20 .50
P10 SMACK DOWN .12 .30
P11 Edge .50 1.25
P12 Triple H .75 2.00
P13 Jeff Hardy .50 1.25
P14 Vladimir Kozlov .20 .50

2014 Topps WWE Road to WrestleMania

COMPLETE SET (110) 12.00 30.00
*BRONZE: .6X TO 1.5X BASIC CARDS
*BLUE: .75X TO 2X BASIC CARDS
*PURPLE: .75X TO 2X BASIC CARDS
*BLACK: 2.5X TO 6X BASIC CARDS
*GOLD/10: UNPRICED DUE TO SCARCITY
*P.P.BLACK/1: UNPRICED DUE TO SCARCITY
*P.P.CYAN/1: UNPRICED DUE TO SCARCITY
*P.P.MAGENTA/1: UNPRICED DUE TO SCARCITY
*P.P.YELLOW/1: UNPRICED DUE TO SCARCITY

1 Wade Barrett .15 .40
2 Dolph Ziggler .25 .60
3 Ryback .15 .40
4 Kofi Kingston .15 .40
5 Undertaker .60 1.50
6 AJ Lee .75 2.00
7 Brock Lesnar .60 1.50
8 Mark Henry .15 .40
9 Dean Ambrose .60 1.50
10 The Shield .75 2.00
11 Brock Lesnar .60 1.50
12 Curtis Axel .15 .40
13 Team Hell No .50 1.25
14 Curtis Axel .15 .40
15 AJ Lee .75 2.00
16 Alberto Del Rio .40 1.00
17 John Cena .75 2.00
18 Mark Henry .15 .40
19 Brad Maddox .15 .40
20 Wyatt Family .60 1.50
21 Damien Sandow .25 .60
22 John Cena .75 2.00
23 Randy Orton .60 1.50
24 AJ Lee .75 2.00
25 Rob Van Dam .40 1.00
26 Vickie Guerrero .15 .40
27 Eva Marie and JoJo .15 .40
28 Cody Rhodes .15 .40
29 Daniel Bryan .75 2.00
30 Alberto Del Rio .40 1.00
31 Bray Wyatt .75 2.00
32 Cody Rhodes .15 .40
33 Daniel Bryan .75 2.00
34 Randy Orton .60 1.50
35 Daniel Bryan .75 2.00
36 Randy Orton .60 1.50
37 Randy Orton .60 1.50
38 Edge .60 1.50
39 Randy Orton .60 1.50
40 The Miz .25 .60
41 Natalya & Tyson Kidd .75 2.00
42 Daniel Bryan .75 2.00
43 Triple H .60 1.50
44 Daniel Bryan .75 2.00
45 The Rhodes Brothers .25 .60
46 Los Matadores .15 .40
47 The Rhodes Brothers .25 .60
48 Big Show .40 1.00
49 The Rhodes Brothers .25 .60
50 The Rhodes Brothers .25 .60
51 John Cena .75 2.00
52 Randy Orton .60 1.50
53 John Cena .75 2.00
54 The Authority .25 .60
55 Big E .15 .40
56 Xavier Woods .15 .40
57 Rey Mysterio .40 1.00
58 The Shield .75 2.00
59 Team Total Divas 1.25 3.00
60 Titus O'Neil .15 .40
61 Sin Cara .15 .40
62 Triple H .60 1.50
63 Daniel Bryan .75 2.00
64 Randy Orton .60 1.50
65 Brodus Clay .15 .40
66 The Total Divas 1.25 3.00
67 Brock Lesnar .60 1.50
68 Jake The Snake Roberts .40 1.00
69 Daniel Bryan .75 2.00
70 Batista .60 1.50
71 New Age Outlaws .25 .60
72 Rusev .40 1.00
73 Kevin Nash .40 1.00
74 Sheamus .40 1.00
75 Batista .40 1.00
76 Titus O'Neil .15 .40
77 Christian .25 .60
78 Emma .40 1.00
79 The Wyatt Family .60 1.50
80 Randy Orton .60 1.50
81 Hulk Hogan .75 2.00
82 Undertaker .60 1.50
83 Lana .60 1.50
84 The Usos .25 .60
85 Big Show .40 1.00
86 Hulk Hogan .75 2.00
87 Daniel Bryan .75 2.00
88 The Shield .75 2.00
89 Kane .40 1.00
90 The Wyatt Family .60 1.50
91 Undertaker .60 1.50
92 Brock Lesnar .60 1.50
93 The Wyatt Family .60 1.50
94 Rowdy Roddy Piper .40 1.00
95 Jake The Snake Roberts .40 1.00
96 Kane .40 1.00
97 Razor Ramon .40 1.00
98 Ultimate Warrior .40 1.00
99 The Usos .25 .60
100 The Real Americans .25 .60
101 Triple H .60 1.50

102 Daniel Bryan	.75	2.00
103 The Shield	.75	2.00
104 Kofi Kingston	.15	.40
105 Cesaro	.25	.60
106 John Cena	.75	2.00
107 Brock Lesnar	.60	1.50
108 AJ Lee	.75	2.00
109 Daniel Bryan	.75	2.00
110 Daniel Bryan	.75	2.00

2014 Topps WWE Road to WrestleMania 30 Years of WrestleMania

COMPLETE SET (60) 12.00 30.00
*P.P.BLACK/1: UNPRICED DUE TO SCARCITY
*P.P.CYAN/1: UNPRICED DUE TO SCARCITY
*P.P.MAGENTA/1: UNPRICED DUE TO SCARCITY
*P.P.YELLOW/1: UNPRICED DUE TO SCARCITY
STATED ODDS 2:1

1 The Foreign Legion	.20	.50
2 Hulk Hogan & Mr. T	1.25	3.00
3 The British Bulldogs	.20	.50
4 Hulk Hogan/King Kong Bundy	1.25	3.00
5 Ricky "The Dragon" Steamboat	.20	.50
6 Hulk Hogan vs. Andre	1.25	3.00
7 Hulk Hogan vs. Andre	1.25	3.00
8 Randy Savage	.20	.50
9 Rick Rude	.20	.50
10 Hulk Hogan	1.25	3.00
11 Ted DiBiase	.20	.50
12 Ultimate Warrior	1.50	4.00
13 Ultimate Warrior	.60	1.50
14 Hulk Hogan	1.25	3.00
15 Macho Man Randy Savage	.75	2.00
16 Hulk Hogan	1.25	3.00
17 Yokozuna	.20	.50
18 Hulk Hogan	1.25	3.00
19 Yokozuna	.20	.50
20 Bret "Hit Man" Hart	.20	.50
21 Yokozuna & Owen Hart	.20	.50
22 Diesel	.20	.50
23 Ultimate Warrior	.60	1.50
24 Shawn Michaels	.60	1.50
25 British Bulldog & Owen Hart	.40	1.00
26 Bret "Hit Man" Hart	1.00	2.50
27 Triple H	.75	2.00
28 Stone Cold Steve Austin	1.25	3.00
29 Road Dogg	.20	.50
30 Stone Cold Steve Austin	2.00	5.00
31 Edge & Christian	.60	1.50
32 Triple H	.75	2.00
33 Edge & Christian	.60	1.50
34 Stone Cold Steve Austin	1.00	2.50
35 The Rock	2.00	5.00
36 Triple H	.75	2.00
37 Triple H	.75	2.00
38 Brock Lesnar	.75	2.00
39 Eddie Guerrero	.20	.50
40 Triple Threat Match	1.25	3.00
41 John Cena	1.00	2.50
42 Batista	.20	.50
43 Rey Mysterio	.20	.50
44 John Cena	1.25	3.00
45 Vince McMahon	.20	.50
46 John Cena	1.25	3.00
47 Shawn Michaels Retires Ric Flair	.60	1.50
48 Randy Orton	1.25	3.00
49 John Cena	1.25	3.00
50 Triple H	.75	2.00
51 Chris Jericho	.60	1.50
52 John Cena	1.25	3.00
53 Edge	.60	1.50
54 The Miz	1.25	3.00
55 CM Punk	.50	1.25
56 The Rock	1.50	4.00
57 Triple H	1.00	2.50
58 John Cena	1.50	4.00
59 Daniel Bryan	1.25	3.00
60 Daniel Bryan	1.25	3.00

2014 Topps WWE Road to WrestleMania Autographed WrestleMania 30 Mat Relics

RANDOMLY INSERTED INTO PACKS

NNO Bray Wyatt	40.00	100.00
NNO Cameron	12.00	30.00
NNO Cesaro	15.00	40.00
NNO Eve	20.00	50.00
NNO Hulk Hogan	150.00	300.00
NNO Jimmy Hart	20.00	30.00
NNO Kane	25.00	60.00
NNO Kevin Nash	30.00	80.00
NNO Layla	12.00	30.00
NNO Lex Luger	30.00	80.00
NNO Naomi	20.00	50.00
NNO Nikki Bella	30.00	80.00
NNO Roman Reigns	40.00	100.00
NNO Ron Simmons	30.00	80.00
NNO Summer Rae	40.00	100.00
NNO Trish Stratus	60.00	120.00

2014 Topps WWE Road to WrestleMania Dual Autographs

RANDOMLY INSERTED INTO PACKS

NNO B.Wyatt/R.Reigns	150.00	400.00
NNO H.Hogan/J.Hart	125.00	300.00
NNO Kane/Layla	20.00	50.00
NNO K.Nash/R.Simmons	30.00	80.00
NNO Lex Luger/Cesaro	40.00	100.00
NNO Naomi/N.Bella	25.00	60.00
NNO T.Stratus/Eve	50.00	100.00

2014 Topps WWE Road to WrestleMania Queen of WrestleMania

COMPLETE SET (8) 10.00 25.00
*P.P.BLACK/1: UNPRICED DUE TO SCARCITY
*P.P.CYAN/1: UNPRICED DUE TO SCARCITY
*P.P.MAGENTA/1: UNPRICED DUE TO SCARCITY
*P.P.YELLOW/1: UNPRICED DUE TO SCARCITY
STATED ODDS 1:12

1 Leads T&A to Victory	2.00	5.00
2 Triple Threat Match/Women's Title	2.00	5.00
3 Defeats Victoria and Jazz	2.00	5.00
4 Turns on Chris Jericho	2.00	5.00
5 Defeats Christy Hemme	2.00	5.00
6 Battles Mickie James	2.00	5.00
7 With John Morrison and Snooki	2.00	5.00
8 Hall of Fame Induction	2.00	5.00

2014 Topps WWE Road to WrestleMania The Streak

COMPLETE SET (22) 8.00 20.00
*P.P.BLACK/1: UNPRICED DUE TO SCARCITY
*P.P.CYAN/1: UNPRICED DUE TO SCARCITY
*P.P.MAGENTA/1: UNPRICED DUE TO SCARCITY
*P.P.YELLOW/1: UNPRICED DUE TO SCARCITY
STATED ODDS 1:1

1 Jimmy Superfly Snuka	.60	1.50
2 Jake The Snake Roberts	.60	1.50
3 Giant Gonzales	.60	1.50
4 King Kong Bundy	.60	1.50
5 Diesel	.60	1.50
6 Sycho Sid	.60	1.50
7 Kane	.60	1.50
8 Big Boss Man	.60	1.50
9 Triple H	.60	1.50
10 Ric Flair	.60	1.50
11 Big Show/A-Train	.60	1.50
12 Kane	.60	1.50
13 Randy Orton	.60	1.50
14 Mark Henry	.60	1.50
15 Batista	.60	1.50
16 Edge	.60	1.50
17 Shawn Michaels	.60	1.50
18 Shawn Michaels	.60	1.50
19 Triple H	.60	1.50
20 Triple H	.60	1.50
21 CM Punk	.60	1.50
22 Brock Lesnar	2.00	5.00

2014 Topps WWE Road to WrestleMania Swatch Relics

*P.P.BLACK/1: UNPRICED DUE TO SCARCITY
*P.P.CYAN/1: UNPRICED DUE TO SCARCITY
*P.P.MAGENTA/1: UNPRICED DUE TO SCARCITY
*P.P.YELLOW/1: UNPRICED DUE TO SCARCITY
RANDOMLY INSERTED INTO PACKS

NNO Alberto Del Rio/Shirt	3.00	8.00
NNO Big Show/Shirt	3.00	8.00
NNO Billy Gunn/Shirt	3.00	8.00
NNO Bray Wyatt/Shirt	4.00	10.00
NNO Curtis Axel/Shirt	3.00	8.00
NNO Damien Sandow/Shirt	3.00	8.00
NNO Daniel Bryan/Shirt	10.00	25.00
NNO Darren Young/Shirt	4.00	10.00
NNO Dolph Ziggler/Shirt	5.00	12.00
NNO Goldust/Shirt	3.00	8.00
NNO Jack Swagger/Shirt	3.00	8.00
NNO Jey Uso/Shirt	8.00	20.00
NNO John Cena/Shirt	120.00	200.00
NNO John Cena/Shoe	8.00	20.00
NNO Mark Henry/Shirt	4.00	10.00
NNO The Miz/Shirt	3.00	8.00
NNO Natalya/Shirt	4.00	10.00
NNO Ryback/Shirt	3.00	8.00
NNO Tamina Snuka/Shirt	3.00	8.00
NNO T.Stratus/Green Pants	30.00	60.00
NNO T.Stratus/Purple Pants	30.00	60.00
NNO Undertaker/Pants & Hat	150.00	300.00

2014 Topps WWE Road to WrestleMania Ultimate Warrior Tribute

COMPLETE SET (10) 5.00 12.00
*P.P.BLACK/1: UNPRICED DUE TO SCARCITY
*P.P.CYAN/1: UNPRICED DUE TO SCARCITY
*P.P.MAGENTA/1: UNPRICED DUE TO SCARCITY
*P.P.YELLOW/1: UNPRICED DUE TO SCARCITY
STATED ODDS 1:4

1 Defeats Honky Tonk Man	.75	2.00
2 Defeats Ravishing Rick Rude	.75	2.00
3 Defeats The Heenan Family	.75	2.00
4 Defeats Hulk Hogan for WWE Title	.75	2.00
5 Defeats Ravishing Rick Rude	.75	2.00
6 Wins Match at Survivor Series	.75	2.00
7 Defeats Macho King Randy Savage	.75	2.00
8 Returns to WWE, Defeats Triple H	.75	2.00
9 Joins WCW	.75	2.00
10 Addresses WWE Universe	.75	2.00

2014 Topps WWE Road to WrestleMania WrestleMania 30 Mat Relics

RANDOMLY INSERTED INTO PACKS

NNO AJ Lee	12.00	30.00
NNO Batista	4.00	10.00
NNO Big Show	5.00	12.00
NNO Bray Wyatt	6.00	15.00
NNO Brock Lesnar	4.00	10.00
NNO Cesaro	3.00	8.00
NNO Daniel Bryan	8.00	20.00
NNO Dean Ambrose	5.00	12.00
NNO Hulk Hogan	10.00	25.00
NNO Jey Uso	3.00	8.00
NNO Jimmy Uso	3.00	8.00
NNO John Cena	8.00	20.00
NNO Randy Orton	6.00	15.00
NNO The Rock	6.00	15.00
NNO Roman Reigns	8.00	20.00
NNO Seth Rollins	6.00	15.00
NNO Sheamus	3.00	8.00
NNO Stone Cold Steve Austin	6.00	15.00
NNO Triple H	5.00	12.00
NNO Undertaker	6.00	15.00

2014 Topps WWE Road to WrestleMania WrestleMania Autographs

*BRONZE/25: .5X TO 1.2X BASIC AUTOS
RANDOMLY INSERTED INTO PACKS

NNO Bray Wyatt	15.00	40.00
NNO Cameron	8.00	20.00
NNO Cesaro	12.00	30.00
NNO Eve	12.00	20.00
NNO Hulk Hogan	100.00	200.00
NNO Jimmy Hart	12.00	25.00
NNO Kane	15.00	40.00
NNO Kevin Nash	15.00	40.00
NNO Layla	12.00	25.00
NNO Lex Luger	12.00	30.00
NNO Naomi	12.00	30.00
NNO Nikki Bella	15.00	40.00
NNO Roman Reigns	20.00	50.00
NNO Ron Simmons	12.00	30.00
NNO Summer Rae	15.00	40.00
NNO Trish Stratus	30.00	75.00

2014 Topps WWE Road to WrestleMania WWE 2K15

STATED ODDS 1:613

1 AJ Lee	50.00	100.00
2 Bray Wyatt	15.00	40.00
3 Brock Lesnar	10.00	25.00
4 Cesaro	8.00	20.00
5 Daniel Bryan	15.00	40.00
6 Dolph Ziggler	8.00	20.00
7 Hulk Hogan	30.00	80.00
8 John Cena	30.00	80.00
9 Roman Reigns	20.00	50.00
10 Seth Rollins	20.00	50.00

2015 Topps WWE Road to WrestleMania

COMPLETE SET (110) 10.00 25.00
*BRONZE: .6X TO 1.5X BASIC CARDS
*BLUE: .75X TO 2X BASIC CARDS
*PURPLE: .75X TO 2X BASIC CARDS
*SILVER: 2.5X TO 6X BASIC CARDS
*GOLD/10: UNPRICED DUE TO SCARCITY
*RED/1: UNPRICED DUE TO SCARCITY
*P.P. BLACK/1: UNPRICED DUE TO SCARCITY
*P.P. CYAN/1: UNPRICED DUE TO SCARCITY
*P.P. MAGENTA/1: UNPRICED DUE TO SCARCITY
*P.P. YELLOW/1: UNPRICED DUE TO SCARCITY

1 Paige	.60	1.50
2 The Shield/Daniel Bryan	.30	.75
3 Daniel Bryan/Hulk Hogan	.50	1.25
4 Fandango/Summer Rae/Layla	.12	.30
5 Ultimate Warrior Tribute	.12	.30
6 Cesaro/Mark Henry	.12	.30
7 Evolution/The Shield	.50	1.25
8 Jimmy Uso/Naomi	.12	.30
9 Kane/Daniel Bryan	.30	.75
10 Bray Wyatt/John Cena	.50	1.25
11 Kane/Brie Bella	.30	.75
12 Bad News Barrett/Big E	.12	.30
13 The Shield/Evolution	.30	.75
14 Bray Wyatt/John Cena	.50	1.25
15 Daniel Bryan/Kane	.50	1.25
16 Sheamus/Dean Ambrose	.30	.75
17 Adam Rose	.15	.40
18 Bo Dallas	.12	.30
19 The Authority/Brad Maddox	.50	1.25
20 Daniel Bryan/Brie Bella	.50	1.25
21 Brie Bella	.40	1.00
22 John Cena/Bray Wyatt	.60	1.50
23 The Shield/Evolution	.30	.75
24 Batista	.30	.75
25 Seth Rollins/The Shield	.20	.50
26 The Authority/Daniel Bryan	.50	1.25
27 John Cena/Shield/Wyatts	.60	1.50
28 Stardust	.12	.30
29 John Cena/Kane	.60	1.50
30 Seth Rollins MITB	.20	.50
31 John Cena	.60	1.50
32 Bret Hit Man Hart/Damien Sandow	.40	1.00
33 Funkadactyls	.20	.50
34 Summer Rae/Layla/Fandango	.50	1.25
35 The Miz	.20	.50
36 John Cena	.60	1.50
37 Brock Lesnar/John Cena	.50	1.25
38 Stephanie McMahon/Brie Bella	.20	.50
39 Brock Lesnar/Hulk Hogan	.50	1.25
40 Dolph Ziggler/The Miz	.20	.50
41 Paige/AJ Lee	.60	1.50
42 Seth Rollins/Dean Ambrose	.20	.50

43 Roman Reigns/Randy Orton	.30	.75
44 Brock Lesnar/John Cena	.50	1.25
45 Gold & Stardust/Usos	.12	.30
46 The Miz/Dolph Ziggler	.20	.50
47 Dean Ambrose/Seth Rollins	.30	.75
48 John Cena/Brock Lesnar	.60	1.50
49 Dolph Ziggler/The Miz	.20	.50
50 The Bunny	.12	.30
51 Seth Rollins/Dean Ambrose	.20	.50
52 The Rock/Rusev	.60	1.50
53 Dean Ambrose/The Authority	.30	.75
54 Dean Ambrose/John Cena	.30	.75
55 Nikki Bella/Brie Bella	.40	1.00
56 John Cena/Randy Orton	.60	1.50
57 Bray Wyatt/Dean Ambrose	.50	1.25
58 The Authority/Randy Orton	.50	1.25
59 Rusev/Sheamus	.30	.75
60 Luke Harper/Dolph Ziggler	.20	.50
61 Miz & Mizdow/Goldust & Stardust	.20	.50
62 Divas Survivor Series Match	.12	.30
63 Nikki Bella/AJ Lee	.40	1.00
64 Sting WWE Debut	.30	.75
65 Team Cena/Team Authority	.60	1.50
66 Dolph Ziggler/Luke Harper	.20	.50
67 John Cena/Seth Rollins	.60	1.50
68 Roman Reigns	.30	.75
69 Bray Wyatt/Dean Ambrose	.50	1.25
70 Brock Lesnar/Chris Jericho	.50	1.25
71 Seth Rollins/John Cena	.20	.50
72 Dean Ambrose/Bray Wyatt	.30	.75
73 Edge & Christian	.30	.75
74 Usos/The Miz & Mizdow	.12	.30
75 The Ascension/Miz & Mizdow	.12	.30
76 Seth Rollins/John Cena	.20	.50
77 Bad New Barrett/Dolph Ziggler	.12	.30
78 Authority/Ziggler/Ryback/Rowan	.50	1.25
79 Rollins/Cena/Lesnar	.20	.50
80 Daniel Bryan	.50	1.25
81 The Ascension/nWo	.12	.30
82 Sting/Team Cena	.30	.75
83 Lesnar/Rollins/Cena	.50	1.25
84 Kane	.30	.75
85 Roman Reigns	.30	.75
86 Daniel Bryan/Kane	.50	1.25
87 Daniel Bryan/Seth Rollins	.50	1.25
88 Stardust/Goldust	.12	.30
89 Ric Flair/Triple H	.60	1.50
90 Prime Time Players	.12	.30
91 Randy Orton/The Authority	.50	1.25
92 Tyson Kidd & Cesaro/Usos	.12	.30
93 Sting/Triple H	.30	.75
94 Rusev/John Cena	.30	.75
95 Roman Reigns/Daniel Bryan	.30	.75
96 Sting/Randy Orton	.30	.75
97 Larry Zbyszko HOF	.20	.50
98 Bushwhackers HOF	.12	.30
99 Hulk Hogan/Macho Man HOF	.60	1.50
100 Kevin Nash HOF	.30	.75
101 Tyson Kidd & Cesaro	.12	.30
102 Big Show	.30	.75
103 Daniel Bryan	.50	1.25
104 Randy Orton/Seth Rollins	.50	1.25
105 Triple H/Sting	.50	1.25
106 AJ Lee & Paige/Bella Twins	.60	1.50
107 John Cena/Rusev	.60	1.50
108 The Rock/The Authority	.60	1.50
109 Undertaker/Bray Wyatt	.50	1.25
110 Rollins/Lesnar/Reigns	.20	.50

2015 Topps WWE Road to WrestleMania Autographs

*BRONZE/50: .5X TO 1.2X BASIC AUTOS
*SILVER/25: .6X TO 1.5X BASIC AUTOS
*GOLD/10: .75X TO 2X BASIC AUTOS
*RED/1: UNPRICED DUE TO SCARCITY
*P.P.BLACK/1: UNPRICED DUE TO SCARCITY
*P.P.CYAN/1: UNPRICED DUE TO SCARCITY
*P.P.MAGENTA/1: UNPRICED DUE TO SCARCITY
*P.P.YELLOW/1: UNPRICED DUE TO SCARCITY
RANDOMLY INSERTED INTO PACKS

NNO Afa	8.00	20.00
NNO Alicia Fox	6.00	15.00
NNO Bray Wyatt	12.00	30.00
NNO Brie Bella	12.00	30.00
NNO Brock Lesnar	60.00	120.00
NNO Damien Mizdow	6.00	15.00
NNO Daniel Bryan	12.00	30.00
NNO Dean Ambrose	12.00	30.00
NNO Dolph Ziggler	8.00	20.00
NNO Emma	10.00	25.00
NNO Hulk Hogan	125.00	250.00
NNO Jack Swagger	6.00	15.00
NNO Jimmy Hart	10.00	25.00
NNO Nikki Bella	15.00	40.00
NNO Razor Ramon	20.00	50.00
NNO Roman Reigns	15.00	40.00
NNO R-Truth	8.00	20.00
NNO Ryback	8.00	20.00
NNO Sika	8.00	20.00

2015 Topps WWE Road to WrestleMania Bizarre WrestleMania Matches

COMPLETE SET (10) 5.00 12.00
*P.P.BLACK/1: UNPRICED DUE TO SCARCITY
*P.P.CYAN/1: UNPRICED DUE TO SCARCITY
*P.P.MAGENTA/1: UNPRICED DUE TO SCARCITY
*P.P.YELLOW/1: UNPRICED DUE TO SCARCITY
STATED ODDS 1:4

1 Andre the Giant/Big John Studd	1.00	2.50
2 Mr.T/Rowdy Roddy Piper	1.00	2.50
3 Corporal Kirchner/Nikolai Volkoff	1.00	2.50
4 Battle Royal	1.00	2.50
5 Rowdy Roddy Piper/Adrian Adonis	1.00	2.50
6 Jake Roberts/Rick Martel	1.00	2.50
7 Rowdy Roddy Piper/Goldust	1.00	2.50
8 C.Jack & C.Charlie/New Age Outlaws	1.00	2.50
9 Gimmick Battle Royal	1.00	2.50
10 Akebono/Big Show	1.00	2.50

2015 Topps WWE Road to WrestleMania Classic WrestleMania Matches

COMPLETE SET (30) 6.00 15.00
*P.P.BLACK/1: UNPRICED DUE TO SCARCITY
*P.P.CYAN/1: UNPRICED DUE TO SCARCITY
*P.P.MAGENTA/1: UNPRICED DUE TO SCARCITY
*P.P.YELLOW/1: UNPRICED DUE TO SCARCITY
RANDOMLY INSERTED INTO PACKS

1 Harley Race/JYD	.50	1.25
2 Honky Tonk Man/Jake Roberts	.50	1.25
3 Twin Towers/Rockers	.50	1.25
4 Nasty Boys/Hart Foundation	.50	1.25
5 Bret Hart/Rowdy Roddy Piper	.50	1.25
6 Money Inc/Mega-Maniacs	.50	1.25
7 Lex Luger/Mr. Perfect	.50	1.25
8 Bret Hit Man Hart	.50	1.25
9 Razor Ramon/Shawn Michaels	.50	1.25
10 Steve Austin/Savio Vega	.50	1.25
11 Chris Jericho/Kurt Angle	.50	1.25
12 Chris Jericho/William Regal	.50	1.25
13 Eddie Guerrero/Test	.50	1.25
14 Steve Austin/Chris Jericho	.50	1.25
15 Shawn Michaels/Chris Jericho	.50	1.25
16 John Cena/Big Show	.50	1.25
17 Christian/Chris Jericho	.50	1.25
18 Goldberg/Brock Lesnar	.50	1.25
19 Rey Mysterio/Eddie Guerrero	.50	1.25
20 Edge MITB	.50	1.25
21 Kurt Angle/Shawn Michaels	.50	1.25
22 Rob Van Dam MITB	.50	1.25
23 Edge/Mick Foley	.50	1.25
24 Shawn Michaels/Mr. McMahon	.50	1.25
25 Jack Swagger MITB	.50	1.25
26 Bret Hart/Mr. McMahon	.50	1.25
27 Randy Orton/CM Punk	.50	1.25
28 Sheamus/Daniel Bryan	.50	1.25
29 Shield/Orton Sheamus Big Show	.50	1.25
30 Team Hell No/Ziggler & Big E	.50	1.25

2015 Topps WWE Road to WrestleMania Dual Autographs

STATED PRINT RUN 10 SER.#'d SETS
UNPRICED DUE TO SCARCITY

NNO Afa/Sika
NNO Brie & Nikki Bella
NNO D.Mizdow/J.Hart
NNO D.Bryan/B.Wyatt
NNO D.Ambrose/R.Reigns
NNO D.Ziggler/Ryback
NNO Emma/A.Fox
NNO H.Hogan/R.Ramon

2015 Topps WWE Road to WrestleMania Hall of Fame

COMPLETE SET (30) 4.00 10.00
*P.P.BLACK/1: UNPRICED DUE TO SCARCITY
*P.P.CYAN/1: UNPRICED DUE TO SCARCITY
*P.P.MAGENTA/1: UNPRICED DUE TO SCARCITY
*P.P.YELLOW/1: UNPRICED DUE TO SCARCITY
STATED ODDS 1:1

1 Chief Jay Strongbow	.40	1.00
2 Classy Freddie Blassie	.25	.60
3 Gorilla Monsoon	.30	.75
4 George The Animal Steele	.30	.75
5 Jimmy Superfly Snuka	.40	1.00
6 Pat Patterson	.25	.60
7 The Magnificent Don Muraco	.40	1.00
8 Greg The Hammer Valentine	.30	.75
9 The King Harley Race	.40	1.00
10 Sgt. Slaughter	.40	1.00
11 Tito Santana	.40	1.00
12 Hulk Hogan	1.25	3.00
13 Rowdy Roddy Piper	.75	2.00
14 Cowboy Bob Orton	.25	.60
15 Mr. Wonderful Paul Orndorff	.40	1.00
16 Nikolai Volkoff	.25	.60
17 The Iron Sheik	.40	1.00
18 Bret Hit Man Hart	.75	2.00
19 The American Dream Dusty Rhodes	.40	1.00
20 Jerry The King Lawler	.40	1.00
21 Nature Boy Ric Flair	1.25	3.00
22 Rocky Johnson	.40	1.00
23 Stone Cold Steve Austin	1.25	3.00
24 Ricky The Dragon Steamboat	.40	1.00
25 Koko B. Ware	.30	.75
26 Ted DiBiase	.40	1.00
27 Heartbreak Kid Shawn Michaels	1.00	2.50
28 Hacksaw Jim Duggan	.40	1.00
29 Edge	.60	1.50
30 Ron Simmons	.40	1.00

2015 Topps WWE Road to WrestleMania HHH at WrestleMania

COMPLETE SET (10) 4.00 10.00
*P.P.BLACK/1: UNPRICED DUE TO SCARCITY
*P.P.CYAN/1: UNPRICED DUE TO SCARCITY
*P.P.MAGENTA/1: UNPRICED DUE TO SCARCITY
*P.P.YELLOW/1: UNPRICED DUE TO SCARCITY
STATED ODDS 1:2

1 Defeats Goldust	.75	2.00
2 Battles Kane	.75	2.00
3 Wins 4-Way Elimination Match	.75	2.00
4 Defeats Y2J for WWE Title	.75	2.00
5 Defeats Booker T	.75	2.00
6 Defeats Randy Orton	.75	2.00
7 Defeats Sheamus	.75	2.00
8 Faces Undertaker No Holds Barred	.75	2.00
9 Faces Undertaker Hell in a Cell	.75	2.00
10 Defeats Brock Lesnar	.75	2.00

2015 Topps WWE Road to WrestleMania Mat Relics

*SILVER/25: .6X TO 1.5X BASIC MEM
*GOLD/10: UNPRICED DUE TO SCARCITY
*RED/1: UNPRICED DUE TO SCARCITY
*P.P.BLACK/1: UNPRICED DUE TO SCARCITY
*P.P.CYAN/1: UNPRICED DUE TO SCARCITY
*P.P.MAGENTA/1: UNPRICED DUE TO SCARCITY
*P.P.YELLOW/1: UNPRICED DUE TO SCARCITY
RANDOMLY INSERTED INTO PACKS

NNO Bad News Barrett	2.00	5.00
NNO Big Show	2.50	6.00
NNO Bray Wyatt	3.00	8.00
NNO Brie Bella	4.00	10.00
NNO Brock Lesnar	3.00	8.00
NNO Damien Mizdow	2.50	6.00
NNO Daniel Bryan	5.00	12.00
NNO Dean Ambrose	3.00	8.00
NNO Dolph Ziggler	2.00	5.00
NNO John Cena	4.00	10.00
NNO Nikki Bella	4.00	10.00
NNO Paige	6.00	15.00
NNO Randy Orton	3.00	8.00
NNO Roman Reigns	4.00	10.00
NNO Rusev	2.50	6.00
NNO Ryback	2.00	5.00
NNO Seth Rollins	3.00	8.00
NNO Sting	6.00	15.00
NNO Triple H	3.00	8.00
NNO Undertaker	5.00	12.00

2015 Topps WWE Road to WrestleMania Rocking WrestleMania

COMPLETE SET (8) 5.00 12.00
*P.P.BLACK/1: UNPRICED DUE TO SCARCITY
*P.P.CYAN/1: UNPRICED DUE TO SCARCITY
*P.P.MAGENTA/1: UNPRICED DUE TO SCARCITY
*P.P.YELLOW/1: UNPRICED DUE TO SCARCITY
RANDOMLY INSERTED INTO PACKS

1 Faces Stone Cold Steve Austin	1.25	3.00
2 Takes on Stone Cold Steve Austin	1.25	3.00
3 Defeats Hollywood Hulk Hogan	1.25	3.00
4 Defeats Stone Cold Steve Austin	1.25	3.00
5 Rock 'n' Sock Reunite	1.25	3.00
6 Rock Bottoms John Cena	1.25	3.00
7 Defeats John Cena	1.25	3.00
8 Battles John Cena	1.25	3.00

2015 Topps WWE Road to WrestleMania Superstars of Canada

COMPLETE SET (10) 25.00 60.00
RANDOMLY INSERTED INTO PACKS

1 Chris Jericho	5.00	12.00
2 Christian	2.00	5.00
3 Edge	5.00	12.00
4 Kevin Owens	6.00	15.00
5 Natalya	6.00	15.00
6 Renee Young	8.00	20.00
7 Sami Zayn	3.00	8.00
8 Trish Stratus	10.00	25.00
9 Tyson Kidd	2.00	5.00
10 Viktor	2.00	5.00

2015 Topps WWE Road to WrestleMania Superstars of Canada Autographs

RANDOMLY INSERTED INTO PACKS
STATED PRINT RUN 25 SER.#'d SETS
CANADIAN EXCLUSIVES

NNO Chris Jericho	50.00	100.00
NNO Christian	25.00	60.00
NNO Edge	50.00	100.00
NNO Kevin Owens	15.00	40.00
NNO Natalya	20.00	50.00
NNO Renee Young	20.00	50.00
NNO Sami Zayn	10.00	25.00
NNO Trish Stratus	100.00	200.00
NNO Tyson Kidd	6.00	15.00
NNO Viktor	6.00	15.00

2015 Topps WWE Road to WrestleMania Swatch Relics

*P.P.BLACK/1: UNPRICED DUE TO SCARCITY
*P.P.CYAN/1: UNPRICED DUE TO SCARCITY
*P.P.MAGENTA/1: UNPRICED DUE TO SCARCITY
*P.P.YELLOW/1: UNPRICED DUE TO SCARCITY
RANDOMLY INSERTED INTO PACKS

NNO Adam Rose	4.00	10.00
NNO Brie Bella	6.00	15.00
NNO Cesaro	4.00	10.00
NNO Charlotte	10.00	25.00
NNO Dean Ambrose	8.00	20.00
NNO Damien Mizdow	4.00	10.00
NNO Dolph Ziggler	4.00	10.00
NNO Goldust	6.00	15.00
NNO Hulk Hogan	10.00	25.00
NNO John Cena	6.00	15.00
NNO Jack Swagger	5.00	12.00
NNO Nikki Bella	10.00	25.00
NNO Paige	12.00	30.00
NNO Roman Reigns	8.00	20.00
NNO Rusev	5.00	12.00

NNO Ryback 5.00 12.00
NNO Stardust 5.00 12.00
NNO Sami Zayn 6.00 15.00

2015 Topps WWE Road to WrestleMania Turnbuckle Pad Relics

RANDOMLY INSERTED INTO PACKS
STATED PRINT RUN 25 SER.#'d SETS

NNO Bad News Barrett 6.00 15.00
NNO Big Show 15.00 40.00
NNO Bray Wyatt 25.00 60.00
NNO Brie Bella 20.00 50.00
NNO Brock Lesnar 25.00 60.00
NNO Damien Mizdow 6.00 15.00
NNO Daniel Bryan 25.00 60.00
NNO Dean Ambrose 15.00 40.00
NNO Dolph Ziggler 10.00 25.00
NNO John Cena 30.00 80.00
NNO Nikki Bella 20.00 50.00
NNO Paige 30.00 80.00
NNO Randy Orton 25.00 60.00
NNO Roman Reigns 15.00 40.00
NNO Rusev 15.00 40.00
NNO Ryback 6.00 15.00
NNO Seth Rollins 10.00 25.00
NNO Sting 15.00 40.00
NNO Triple H 25.00 60.00
NNO Undertaker 25.00 60.00

2016 Topps WWE Road to WrestleMania

COMPLETE SET (110) 12.00 30.00
*BRONZE: .5X TO 1.2X BASIC CARDS
*SILVER: 2X TO 5X BASIC CARDS
*GOLD/10: UNPRICED DUE TO SCARCITY
*RED/1: UNPRICED DUE TO SCARCITY
*PP BLACK/1: UNPRICED DUE TO SCARCITY
*PP CYAN/1: UNPRICED DUE TO SCARCITY
*PP MAGENTA/1: UNPRICED DUE TO SCARCITY
*PP YELLOW/1: UNPRICED DUE TO SCARCITY
NUMBERS 111-113 ARE WWE DVD EXCLUSIVES

1 Daniel Bryan .75 2.00
2 The Usos .20 .50
3 Alundra Blayze .25 .60
4 Ric Flair .75 2.00
5 Triple H .75 2.00
6 Hideo Itami .25 .60
7 Damien Mizdow .30 .75
8 Sting .50 1.25
9 Triple H .75 2.00
10 D-Generation X .60 1.50
11 Rusev .50 1.25
12 Bray Wyatt .75 2.00
13 Roman Reigns 1.00 2.50
14 Sheamus .50 1.25
15 Kalisto .50 1.25
16 Brock Lesnar 1.00 2.50
17 Neville .50 1.25
18 Big Show .60 1.50
19 Fandango .20 .50
20 Daniel Bryan/John Cena 1.00 2.50
21 The Miz .30 .75
22 The New Day .50 1.25
23 Roman Reigns .60 1.50
24 Seth Rollins .30 .75
25 Bad New Barrett .20 .50
26 Sami Zayn 1.00 2.50
27 Erick Rowan .20 .50
28 Neville 1.00 2.50
29 Daniel Bryan .75 2.00
30 John Cena 1.00 2.50
31 Seth Rollins .30 .75
32 Rusev .75 2.00
33 Kevin Owens 1.00 2.50
34 Lana .75 2.00
35 The New Day .50 1.25
36 Kalisto .50 1.25
37 The New Day .50 1.25
38 Nikki Bella .60 1.50
39 Kevin Owens .50 1.25
40 Ryback .25 .60
41 Dean Ambrose .60 1.50
42 Dusty Rhodes Tribute .20 .50
43 Bray Wyatt .75 2.00
44 Sheamus .50 1.25
45 Nikki Bella .60 1.50
46 John Cena 1.00 2.50
47 The Prime Time Players .20 .50
48 Seth Rollins .60 1.50
49 Brock Lesnar 1.00 2.50
50 Brock Lesnar 1.00 2.50
51 Cesaro 1.00 2.50
52 Chris Jericho .50 1.25
53 Nikki Bella .60 1.50
54 Brock Lesnar 1.00 2.50
55 Rusev/Summer Rae .75 2.00
56 Brock Lesnar 1.00 2.50
57 John Cena 1.00 2.50
58 Rusev .50 1.25
59 Stardust .20 .50
60 Brock Lesnar 1.00 2.50
61 Cesaro .50 1.25
62 Bray Wyatt .75 2.00
63 Charlotte .60 1.50
64 John Cena 1.00 2.50
65 Undertaker 1.00 2.50
66 Brock Lesnar 1.00 2.50
67 John Cena/Cesaro/Randy Orton 1.00 2.50
68 Seth Rollins .30 .75
69 John Cena 1.00 2.50
70 Dean Ambrose/Cesaro .60 1.50
71 Rowdy Roddy Piper Tribute .60 1.50
72 Ambrose/Reigns/Orton .50 1.25
73 The New Day .50 1.25
74 Undertaker 1.00 2.50
75 Ryback .30 .75
76 Roman Reigns/Dean Ambrose .75 2.00
77 Seth Rollins .30 .75
78 Team PCB .60 1.50
79 Undertaker 1.00 2.50
80 Brock Lesnar 1.00 2.50
81 The Dudley Boyz .40 1.00
82 Braun Strowman .25 .60
83 Sting .50 1.25
84 Charlotte .60 1.50
85 Sting/John Cena 1.00 2.50
86 Hideo Itami .25 .60
87 Sami Zayn .30 .75
88 Becky Lynch .60 1.50
89 Kevin Owens .50 1.25
90 Tyler Breeze/Adam Rose .20 .50
91 Finn Balor .60 1.50
92 Charlotte/Bayley .60 1.50
93 Sasha Banks .60 1.50
94 Kevin Owens .50 1.25
95 Samoa Joe .50 1.25
96 Kevin Owens .50 1.25
97 Samoa Joe .50 1.25
98 Samoa Joe .50 1.25
99 Finn Balor/Samoa Joe .60 1.50
100 Finn Balor .60 1.50
101 The Vaudevillains .20 .50
102 Sasha Banks .60 1.50
103 Blake/Murphy .20 .50
104 Bayley .60 1.50
105 Bayley .50 1.25
106 The Vaudevillains .20 .50
107 Apollo Crews .20 .50
108 Samoa Joe .50 1.25
109 Bayley .50 1.25
110 Finn Balor .60 1.50
111 The Dudley Boyz SP
112 Stone Cold Steve Austin SP
113 Daniel Bryan SP

2016 Topps WWE Road to WrestleMania Autographs

*BRONZE/50: .5X TO 1.2X BASIC AUTOS
*SILVER/25: .60X TO 1.5X BASIC AUTOS
*GOLD/10: UNPRICED DUE TO SCARCITY
*RED/1: UNPRICED DUE TO SCARCITY
*PP BLACK/1: UNPRICED DUE TO SCARCITY
*PP CYAN/1: UNPRICED DUE TO SCARCITY
*PP MAGENTA/1: UNPRICED DUE TO SCARCITY
*PP YELLOW/1: UNPRICED DUE TO SCARCITY
STATED PRINT RUN 99 SER.#'d SETS

NNO Baron Corbin 10.00 25.00
NNO Bayley 15.00 40.00
NNO Becky Lynch 25.00 60.00
NNO Brie Bella 10.00 25.00
NNO Brock Lesnar 100.00 200.00
NNO Charlotte 25.00 60.00
NNO Daniel Bryan 10.00 25.00
NNO Dean Ambrose 10.00 25.00
NNO Dory Funk Jr. 12.00 30.00
NNO Dusty Rhodes 50.00 100.00
NNO Eva Marie 15.00 40.00
NNO Gerald Brisco 6.00 15.00
NNO John Cena 20.00 50.00
NNO Kalisto 12.00 30.00
NNO Kevin Von Erich 25.00 60.00
NNO Lana 20.00 50.00
NNO Michael P.S. Hayes 10.00 25.00
NNO Neville 6.00 15.00
NNO Nikki Bella 15.00 40.00
NNO Pat Patterson 6.00 15.00
NNO Ric Flair 15.00 40.00
NNO Roman Reigns 12.00 30.00
NNO Samoa Joe 8.00 20.00
NNO Sasha Banks 25.00 60.00
NNO Seth Rollins 10.00 25.00
NNO Sting 30.00 80.00
NNO Terry Funk 50.00 100.00

2016 Topps WWE Road to WrestleMania Battleground Mat Relics

*BRONZE/50: .5X TO 1.2X BASIC MEM
*SILVER/25: .6X TO 1.5X BASIC MEM
*GOLD/10: UNPRICED DUE TO SCARCITY
*RED/1: UNPRICED DUE TO SCARCITY
*PP BLACK/1: UNPRICED DUE TO SCARCITY
*PP CYAN/1: UNPRICED DUE TO SCARCITY
*PP MAGENTA/1: UNPRICED DUE TO SCARCITY
*PP YELLOW/1: UNPRICED DUE TO SCARCITY
STATED PRINT RUN 199 SER.#'d SETS

NNO Big E 2.00 5.00
NNO Bray Wyatt 8.00 20.00
NNO Brie Bella 4.00 10.00
NNO Brock Lesnar 10.00 25.00
NNO Charlotte 6.00 15.00
NNO Darren Young 2.00 5.00
NNO John Cena 10.00 25.00
NNO Kevin Owens 5.00 12.00
NNO Kofi Kingston 2.00 5.00
NNO Luke Harper 2.00 5.00
NNO Randy Orton 5.00 12.00
NNO Roman Reigns 6.00 15.00
NNO R-Truth 2.00 5.00
NNO Sasha Banks 6.00 15.00
NNO Seth Rollins 3.00 8.00
NNO Sheamus 5.00 12.00
NNO Titus O'Neil 2.00 5.00
NNO Undertaker 8.00 20.00
NNO Wade Barrett 2.00 5.00
NNO Xavier Woods 2.00 5.00

2016 Topps WWE Road to WrestleMania Battleground Turnbuckle Pad Relics

STATED PRINT RUN 25 SER.#'d SETS

NNO Big E 5.00 12.00
NNO Bray Wyatt 20.00 50.00
NNO Brie Bella 10.00 25.00
NNO Brock Lesnar 25.00 60.00
NNO Charlotte 15.00 40.00
NNO Darren Young 5.00 12.00
NNO John Cena 25.00 60.00
NNO Kevin Owens 12.00 30.00
NNO Kofi Kingston 5.00 12.00
NNO Luke Harper 5.00 12.00
NNO Randy Orton 12.00 30.00
NNO Roman Reigns 15.00 40.00
NNO R-Truth 5.00 12.00
NNO Sasha Banks 15.00 40.00
NNO Seth Rollins 8.00 20.00
NNO Sheamus 12.00 30.00
NNO Titus O'Neil 5.00 12.00
NNO Undertaker 20.00 50.00
NNO Wade Barrett 5.00 12.00
NNO Xavier Woods 5.00 12.00

2016 Topps WWE Road to WrestleMania Dual Autographs

STATED PRINT RUN 11 SER.#'d SETS

NNO Charlotte/Bayley 75.00 200.00
NNO Lana/E.Marie 75.00 200.00
NNO Neville/Kalisto 30.00 75.00
NNO P.Patterson/G.Brisco 25.00 60.00
NNO Samoa Joe/B.Corbin 40.00 100.00
NNO S.Banks/B.Lynch 125.00 300.00
NNO Sting/R.Flair 150.00 400.00
NNO T.Funk/D.Funk Jr. 40.00 100.00

2016 Topps WWE Road to WrestleMania Dusty Rhodes Tribute

COMPLETE SET (10) 3.00 8.00
STATED ODDS 1:6

1 Dusty Rhodes .60 1.50
2 Dusty Rhodes .60 1.50
3 Dusty Rhodes .60 1.50
4 Dusty Rhodes 1.00 2.50
5 Dusty Rhodes .60 1.50
6 Dusty Rhodes 1.00 2.50
7 Dusty Rhodes .60 1.50
8 Dusty Rhodes .60 1.50
9 Dusty Rhodes .60 1.50
10 Dusty Rhodes 1.50 4.00

2016 Topps WWE Road to WrestleMania Immortals

COMPLETE SET (10) 6.00 15.00
STATED ODDS 1:6

1 Roman Reigns 1.00 2.50
2 Daniel Bryan 1.25 3.00
3 Randy Orton .75 2.00
4 The Bellas 1.00 2.50
5 Paige 1.00 2.50
6 Triple H 1.25 3.00
7 Undertaker 1.25 3.00
8 The Rock 1.50 4.00
9 Brock Lesnar 1.50 4.00
10 John Cena 1.50 4.00

2016 Topps WWE Road to WrestleMania NXT Diva Kiss

STATED PRINT RUN 99 SER.#'d SETS

NNO Alexa Bliss 50.00 100.00
NNO Bayley 80.00 150.00
NNO Becky Lynch 50.00 100.00
NNO Carmella 25.00 60.00
NNO Charlotte 50.00 100.00
NNO Dana Brooke 20.00 50.00
NNO Eva Marie 30.00 80.00
NNO JoJo 20.00 50.00
NNO Sasha Banks 100.00 200.00

2016 Topps WWE Road to WrestleMania NXT Diva Kiss Autographs

*GOLD/10: UNPRICED DUE TO SCARCITY
*RED/1: UNPRICED DUE TO SCARCITY
*PP BLACK/1: UNPRICED DUE TO SCARCITY
*PP CYAN/1: UNPRICED DUE TO SCARCITY
*PP MAGENTA/1: UNPRICED DUE TO SCARCITY
*PP YELLOW/1: UNPRICED DUE TO SCARCITY
STATED PRINT RUN 25 SER.#'d SETS

NNO Alexa Bliss 250.00 500.00
NNO Bayley 75.00 150.00
NNO Becky Lynch 120.00 200.00
NNO Carmella 60.00 120.00
NNO Charlotte 150.00 250.00
NNO Dana Brooke 50.00 100.00
NNO Eva Marie 50.00 100.00
NNO JoJo 50.00 100.00
NNO Sasha Banks 150.00 250.00

2016 Topps WWE Road to WrestleMania Roster

COMPLETE SET (30) 10.00 25.00
*P.P.BLACK/1: UNPRICED DUE TO SCARCITY
*P.P.CYAN/1: UNPRICED DUE TO SCARCITY
*P.P.MAGENTA/1: UNPRICED DUE TO SCARCITY

*P.P.YELLOW/1: UNPRICED DUE TO SCARCITY
STATED ODDS 1:1

1 The Rock 1.50 4.00
2 Triple H 1.25 3.00
3 Undertaker 1.25 3.00
4 Sting .75 2.00
5 Brock Lesnar 1.50 4.00
6 Seth Rollins .50 1.25
7 Roman Reigns 1.00 2.50
8 Randy Orton .75 2.00
9 Dean Ambrose 1.00 2.50
10 John Cena 1.50 4.00
11 Rusev .75 2.00
12 Daniel Bryan 1.25 3.00
13 Dolph Ziggler .40 1.00
14 King Barrett .30 .75
15 Luke Harper .30 .75
16 Bray Wyatt 1.25 3.00
17 The Miz .50 1.25
18 Ryback .40 1.00
19 Big Show .60 1.50
20 Cesaro .60 1.50
21 Tyson Kidd .30 .75
22 Kofi Kingston .30 .75
23 Big E .30 .75
24 Xavier Woods .30 .75
25 Brie Bella .60 1.50
26 Nikki Bella 1.00 2.50
27 Paige 1.00 2.50
28 Naomi .50 1.25
29 Natalya .50 1.25
30 Lana 1.25 3.00

2016 Topps WWE Road to WrestleMania Rowdy Roddy Piper Tribute

COMPLETE SET (10) 4.00 10.00
STATED ODDS 1:6

1 Rowdy Roddy Piper .75 2.00
2 Rowdy Roddy Piper 1.25 3.00
3 Rowdy Roddy Piper .75 2.00
4 Rowdy Roddy Piper .75 2.00
5 Rowdy Roddy Piper .75 2.00
6 Rowdy Roddy Piper .75 2.00
7 Rowdy Roddy Piper .75 2.00
8 Rowdy Roddy Piper .75 2.00
9 Rowdy Roddy Piper .75 2.00
10 Rowdy Roddy Piper .75 2.00

2016 Topps WWE Road to WrestleMania Shirt Relics

*BRONZE/50: .5X TO 1.2X BASIC MEM
*SILVER/25: .6X TO 1.5X BASIC MEM
*GOLD/10: UNPRICED DUE TO SCARCITY
*RED/1: UNPRICED DUE TO SCARCITY
*PP BLACK/1: UNPRICED DUE TO SCARCITY
*PP CYAN/1: UNPRICED DUE TO SCARCITY
*PP MAGENTA/1: UNPRICED DUE TO SCARCITY
*PP YELLOW/1: UNPRICED DUE TO SCARCITY
STATED PRINT RUN 350 SER.#'d SETS

NNO Alicia Fox 3.00 8.00
NNO Baron Corbin 2.50 6.00
NNO Bayley 10.00 25.00
NNO Becky Lynch 10.00 25.00
NNO Big Show 4.00 10.00
NNO Bray Wyatt 8.00 20.00
NNO Colin Cassady 4.00 10.00
NNO Darren Young 2.00 5.00
NNO Dean Ambrose 6.00 15.00
NNO John Cena 10.00 25.00
NNO Kalisto 5.00 12.00
NNO Kevin Owens 5.00 12.00
NNO Kofi Kingston 2.00 5.00
NNO Miz 3.00 8.00
NNO Mojo Rawley 2.00 5.00
NNO Neville 5.00 12.00
NNO Paige 8.00 20.00
NNO Randy Orton 5.00 12.00
NNO Rob Van Dam 4.00 10.00
NNO Roman Reigns 6.00 15.00
NNO Ryback 2.50 6.00
NNO Sami Zayn 3.00 8.00
NNO Samoa Joe 5.00 12.00
NNO Sasha Banks 8.00 20.00
NNO Seth Rollins 3.00 8.00
NNO Sheamus 5.00 12.00
NNO Sin Cara 2.50 6.00
NNO Summer Rae 5.00 12.00
NNO Tyler Breeze 2.00 5.00
NNO Xavier Woods 2.00 5.00

2016 Topps WWE Road to WrestleMania SP Inserts

STATED ODDS 1:24 HOBBY EXCLUSIVE

1 Kevin Owens 4.00 10.00
2 Charlotte 5.00 12.00
3 John Cena 8.00 20.00
4 Seth Rollins 4.00 10.00
5 Brock Lesnar 8.00 20.00
6 Tyler Breeze 1.50 4.00
7 Alberto Del Rio 8.00 20.00
8 Roman Reigns 6.00 15.00
9 Seth Rollins 2.50 6.00
10 Brock Lesnar 8.00 20.00
11 Paige 5.00 12.00
12 Goldust 2.50 6.00
13 Ryback 2.00 5.00
14 Undertaker/Kane 6.00 15.00
15 Roman Reigns 5.00 12.00
16 Sheamus 5.00 12.00
17 The New Day 1.50 4.00
18 Alberto Del Rio 2.50 6.00
19 Dean Ambrose 5.00 12.00
20 Sheamus 5.00 12.00

2016 Topps WWE Road to WrestleMania Triple Threat Autographed Dual Relics

STATED PRINT RUN 11 SER.#'d SETS

NNO Bray Wyatt 50.00 100.00
NNO Daniel Bryan 100.00 150.00
NNO Dean Ambrose 25.00 60.00
NNO John Cena 50.00 100.00
NNO Nikki Bella 60.00 120.00
NNO Roman Reigns 60.00 120.00
NNO Seth Rollins 30.00 80.00

2016 Topps WWE Road to WrestleMania WWE Hall of Fame Commemorative Ring Relics

*BRONZE/50: .5X TO 1.2X BASIC MEM
*SILVER/25: .6X TO 1.5X BASIC MEM
*GOLD/10: UNPRICED DUE TO SCARCITY
RED/1: UNPRICED DUE TO SCARCITY
*P.P. BLACK/1: UNPRICED DUE TO SCARCITY
*P.P. CYAN/1: UNPRICED DUE TO SCARCITY
*P.P. MAGENTA/1: UNPRICED DUE TO SCARCITY
*P.P. YELLOW/1: UNPRICED DUE TO SCARCITY
STATED PRINT RUN 299 SER.#'d SETS

NNO Alundra Blayze 2.00 5.00
NNO American Dream Dusty Rhodes 1.50 4.00
NNO Bob Backlund 1.50 4.00
NNO Booker T 3.00 8.00
NNO Bret Hit Man Hart 4.00 10.00
NNO Bruno Sammartino 2.00 5.00
NNO Don Muraco 1.50 4.00
NNO Edge 4.00 10.00
NNO George The Animal Steele 2.00 5.00
NNO Hacksaw Jim Duggan 1.50 4.00
NNO Harley Race 1.50 4.00
NNO Iron Sheik 1.50 4.00
NNO Jake The Snake Roberts 3.00 8.00
NNO Jerry The King Lawler 3.00 8.00
NNO Kevin Nash 4.00 10.00
NNO Koko B. Ware 1.50 4.00
NNO Larry Zbyszko 1.50 4.00
NNO Lita 5.00 12.00
NNO Ted DiBiase 2.00 5.00
NNO Mr. Wonderful Paul Orndorff 1.50 4.00
NNO Razor Ramon 4.00 10.00
NNO Ric Flair 6.00 15.00
NNO Ricky The Dragon Steamboat 2.00 5.00
NNO Ron Simmons 4.00 10.00
NNO Rowdy Roddy Piper 5.00 12.00
NNO Sgt. Slaughter 2.00 5.00
NNO Shawn Michaels 6.00 15.00
NNO Stone Cold Steve Austin 8.00 20.00
NNO Trish Stratus 8.00 20.00
NNO Ultimate Warrior 4.00 10.00

2017 Topps WWE Road to WrestleMania

COMPLETE SET (100) 10.00 25.00
*BRONZE: .5X TO 1.2X BASIC CARDS
*BLUE/99: 1X TO 2.5X BASIC CARDS
*SILVER/25: 1.5X TO 4X BASIC CARDS
*GOLD/10: 3X TO 8X BASIC CARDS
*RED/1: UNPRICED DUE TO SCARCITY
*P.P.BLACK/1: UNPRICED DUE TO SCARCITY
*P.P.CYAN/1: UNPRICED DUE TO SCARCITY
*P.P.MAGENTA/1: UNPRICED DUE TO SCARCITY
*P.P.YELLOW/1: UNPRICED DUE TO SCARCITY

1 Roman Reigns .60 1.50
2 Dean Ambrose .60 1.50
3 Dean Ambrose .60 1.50
4 John Cena 1.00 2.50
5 Charlotte .75 2.00
6 Kalisto .30 .75
7 Brock Lesnar 1.00 2.50
8 The Wyatt Family .50 1.25
9 Dean Ambrose .60 1.50
10 Kalisto .30 .75
11 Sasha Banks .60 1.50
12 AJ Styles 1.00 2.50
13 The Wyatt Family .50 1.25
14 Triple H .50 1.25
15 Triple H .50 1.25
16 AJ Styles 1.00 2.50
17 The Rock 1.00 2.50
18 Roman Reigns/Dean Ambrose .60 1.50
19 Brock Lesnar 1.00 2.50
20 Brock Lesnar 1.00 2.50
21 Daniel Bryan Retires .75 2.00
22 Chris Jericho .50 1.25
23 Kevin Owens .50 1.25
24 Brock Lesnar 1.00 2.50
25 Kalisto .30 .75
26 Charlotte .75 2.00
27 AJ Styles 1.00 2.50
28 Roman Reigns/Dean Ambrose .60 1.50
29 Brock Lesnar 1.00 2.50
30 Roman Reigns .60 1.50
31 Shane McMahon .30 .75
32 Dean Ambrose .60 1.50
33 Triple H .50 1.25
34 Undertaker .75 2.00
35 Triple H .50 1.25
36 Shane McMahon .30 .75
37 Sami Zayn .25 .60
38 The New Day .40 1.00
39 Dean Ambrose .60 1.50
40 Brock Lesnar 1.00 2.50
41 Triple H .50 1.25
42 Triple H .50 1.25
43 Roman Reigns .60 1.50
44 Undertaker .75 2.00
45 Brock Lesnar 1.00 2.50
46 Shane McMahon .30 .75
47 The Godfather .20 .50
48 Vader .20 .50
49 The Fabulous Freebirds .20 .50
50 John Cena 1.00 2.50
51 Sting Retires .60 1.50
52 Kalisto .30 .75
53 Team Total Divas .20 .50
54 Lita .40 1.00
55 The Usos .25 .60
56 Zack Ryder .20 .50
57 Chris Jericho .50 1.25
58 Brock Lesnar 1.00 2.50
59 Charlotte .75 2.00
60 Shane McMahon .30 .75
61 Undertaker .75 2.00
62 Diamond Dallas Page .25 .60
63 Tatanka .20 .50
64 Baron Corbin .30 .75
65 The Rock 1.00 2.50
66 HHH/Stephanie .50 1.25
67 Roman Reigns .60 1.50
68 Apollo Crews .25 .60
69 The Miz .40 1.00
70 Maryse .40 1.00
71 Enzo Amore/Big Cass .60 1.50
72 Cesaro .40 1.00
73 AJ Styles 1.00 2.50
74 Vaudevillains .20 .50
75 Cesaro .40 1.00
76 Gallows & Anderson .30 .75
77 Roman Reigns .60 1.50
Bray Wyatt
78 Sami Zayn .25 .60
79 League of Nations .20 .50
80 Dean Ambrose .60 1.50
81 Charlotte .75 2.00
82 Shane & Stephanie McMahon .30 .75
83 Roman Reigns .60 1.50
84 Dana Brooke .40 1.00
85 Rusev .40 1.00
86 Dean Ambrose .60 1.50
87 Charlotte .75 2.00
88 Roman Reigns .60 1.50
89 Seth Rollins .60 1.50
90 The Club .20 .50
91 AJ Styles 1.00 2.50
92 Dean Ambrose .60 1.50
93 Seth Rollins .60 1.50
94 Dean Ambrose .60 1.50
95 Team USA .20 .50
96 Daniel Bryan .75 2.00
Mick Foley
97 WWE Draft .20 .50
98 Sasha Banks/Bayley .60 1.50
99 John Cena/Enzo & Cass 1.00 2.50
100 Dean Ambrose .60 1.50

2017 Topps WWE Road to WrestleMania Autographed Andre the Giant Battle Royal Trophy Relics

STATED ODDS 1:33,024
UNPRICED DUE TO SCARCITY

NNO Big Show
NNO Cesaro
NNO Curtis Axel
NNO Darren Young
NNO Goldust
NNO Heath Slater
NNO Hideo Itami
NNO Jack Swagger
NNO Kane
NNO Konnor
NNO Mark Henry
NNO The Miz
NNO Viktor

2017 Topps WWE Road to WrestleMania Andre the Giant Battle Royal Trophy Relics

*BLUE/50: .5X TO 1.2X BASIC MEM
*SILVER/25: .6X TO 1.5X BASIC MEM
*GOLD/10: .75X TO 2X BASIC MEM
*RED/1: UNPRICED DUE TO SCARCITY
*P.P.BLACK/1: UNPRICED DUE TO SCARCITY
*P.P.CYAN/1: UNPRICED DUE TO SCARCITY
*P.P.MAGENTA/1: UNPRICED DUE TO SCARCITY
*P.P.YELLOW/1: UNPRICED DUE TO SCARCITY
STATED ODDS 1:1,296

NNO Baron Corbin 3.00 8.00
NNO Big Show 2.50 6.00
NNO Bo Dallas 2.00 5.00
NNO Cesaro 4.00 10.00
NNO Curtis Axel 2.00 5.00
NNO Darren Young 2.00 5.00
NNO Diamond Dallas Page 2.50 6.00
NNO Fandango 2.00 5.00
NNO Goldust 2.50 6.00
NNO Heath Slater 2.00 5.00
NNO Hideo Itami 3.00 8.00
NNO Jack Swagger 2.00 5.00
NNO Kane 2.50 6.00
NNO Konnor 2.00 5.00
NNO Mark Henry 2.00 5.00
NNO R-Truth 2.00 5.00
NNO Tatanka 2.00 5.00

NNO The Miz 4.00 10.00
NNO Tyler Breeze 2.00 5.00
NNO Viktor 2.00 5.00

2017 Topps WWE Road to WrestleMania Autographed Shirt Relics

STATED ODDS 1:22,016
UNPRICED DUE TO SCARCITY

NNO Asuka
NNO Austin Aries
NNO Bayley
NNO Becky Lynch
NNO Big Cass
NNO Big E
NNO Bray Wyatt
NNO Cesaro
NNO Darren Young
NNO Dolph Ziggler
NNO Enzo Amore
NNO Hideo Itami
NNO John Cena
NNO Kevin Owens
NNO Kofi Kingston
NNO Natalya
NNO Randy Orton
NNO Roman Reigns
NNO Sami Zayn
NNO Sasah Banks
NNO Seth Rollins
NNO Shinsuke Nakamura
NNO Simon Gotch
NNO Xavier Woods
NNO Zack Ryder

2017 Topps WWE Road to WrestleMania Autographs

*BLUE/50: .6X TO 1.5X BASIC AUTOS
*SILVER/25: .75X TO 2X BASIC AUTOS
*GOLD/10: 1X TO 2.5X BASIC AUTOS
*RED/1: UNPRICED DUE TO SCARCITY
*P.P.BLACK/1: UNPRICED DUE TO SCARCITY
*P.P.CYAN/1: UNPRICED DUE TO SCARCITY
*P.P.MAGENTA/1: UNPRICED DUE TO SCARCITY
*P.P.YELLOW/1: UNPRICED DUE TO SCARCITY
STATED ODDS 1:36

NNO Asuka 15.00 40.00
NNO Austin Aries 8.00 20.00
NNO Bayley 20.00 50.00
NNO Becky Lynch 15.00 40.00
NNO Big E 8.00 20.00
NNO Bray Wyatt 12.00 30.00
NNO Cesaro 10.00 25.00
NNO Charlotte 12.00 30.00
NNO Dean Ambrose 12.00 30.00
NNO Finn Balor 12.00 30.00
NNO Hideo Itami 6.00 15.00
NNO John Cena
NNO Kevin Owens 15.00 40.00
NNO Kofi Kingston 6.00 15.00
NNO Lana 8.00 20.00
NNO Lex Luger 10.00 25.00
NNO Maryse 12.00 30.00
NNO The Miz 6.00 15.00
NNO Nikki Bella 15.00 40.00
NNO Roman Reigns 30.00 75.00
NNO Rusev 6.00 15.00
NNO Sasha Banks 30.00 75.00
NNO Seth Rollins 12.00 30.00
NNO Shinsuke Nakamura 20.00 50.00
NNO Sting 25.00 60.00

2017 Topps WWE Road to WrestleMania Kiss

*GOLD/10: .6X TO 1.5X BASIC KISS
*RED/1: UNPRICED DUE TO SCARCITY
STATED ODDS 1:91

NNO Alexa Bliss 60.00 120.00
NNO Becky Lynch 20.00 50.00
NNO Carmella 20.00 50.00
NNO Charlotte 15.00 40.00
NNO Liv Morgan 20.00 50.00
NNO Natalya 12.00 30.00
NNO Nia Jax 12.00 30.00
NNO Renee Young 12.00 30.00

2017 Topps WWE Road to WrestleMania Kiss Autographs

*GOLD/10: UNPRICED DUE TO SCARCITY
*RED/1: UNPRICED DUE TO SCARCITY
STATED ODDS 1:354

NNO Alexa Bliss 250.00 500.00
NNO Becky Lynch 150.00 300.00
NNO Carmella 30.00 80.00
NNO Charlotte 125.00 250.00
NNO Liv Morgan 60.00 120.00
NNO Natalya 25.00 60.00
NNO Nia Jax 20.00 50.00
NNO Nikki Bella 60.00 120.00
NNO Renee Young 25.00 60.00

2017 Topps WWE Road to WrestleMania Dual Autographs

STATED ODDS 1:726
STATED PRINT RUN 10 SER.#'d SETS

NNO Asuka/Bayley 100.00 200.00
NNO Charlotte/R.Flair 100.00 200.00
NNO F.Balor/H.Itami 60.00 120.00
NNO J.Cena/N.Bella 125.00 250.00
NNO K.Kingston/Big E 30.00 75.00
NNO Miz/Maryse 60.00 120.00
NNO R.Reigns/D.Ambrose
NNO Rusev/Lana 75.00 150.00
NNO S.Banks/B.Lynch 100.00 200.00
NNO S.Rollins/Cesaro 60.00 120.00
NNO S.Nakamura/A.Aries
NNO Sting/L.Luger 75.00 150.00

2017 Topps WWE Road to WrestleMania Autographed NXT TakeOver Dallas Mat Relics

STATED PRINT RUN 10 SER.#'d SETS
UNPRICED DUE TO SCARCITY

NNO Asuka
NNO Austin Aries
NNO Bayley
NNO Sami Zayn
NNO Samoa Joe
NNO Shinsuke Nakamura

2017 Topps WWE Road to WrestleMania NXT TakeOver Dallas Mat Relics

*BLUE/50: .5X TO 1.2X BASIC MEM
*SILVER/25: .6X TO 1.5X BASIC MEM
*GOLD/10: .75X TO 2X BASIC MEM
*RED/1: UNPRICED DUE TO SCARCITY
*P.P.BLACK/1: UNPRICED DUE TO SCARCITY
*P.P.CYAN/1: UNPRICED DUE TO SCARCITY
*P.P.MAGENTA/1: UNPRICED DUE TO SCARCITY
*P.P.YELLOW/1: UNPRICED DUE TO SCARCITY
STATED ODDS 1:2,642

NNO Asuka 5.00 12.00
NNO Austin Aries 3.00 8.00
NNO Baron Corbin 2.50 6.00
NNO Bayley 5.00 12.00
NNO Chad Gable 2.00 5.00
NNO Finn Balor 6.00 15.00
NNO Jason Jordan 2.00 5.00
NNO Sami Zayn 2.00 5.00
NNO Samoa Joe 5.00 12.00
NNO Shinsuke Nakamura 4.00 10.00

2017 Topps WWE Road to WrestleMania Shirt Relics

*BLUE/50: .5X TO 1.2X BASIC MEM
*SILVER/25: .6X TO 1.5X BASIC MEM
*GOLD/10: UNPRICED DUE TO SCARCITY
*RED/1: UNPRICED DUE TO SCARCITY
*P.P.BLACK/1: UNPRICED DUE TO SCARCITY
*P.P.CYAN/1: UNPRICED DUE TO SCARCITY
*P.P.MAGENTA/1: UNPRICED DUE TO SCARCITY
*P.P.YELLOW/1: UNPRICED DUE TO SCARCITY
STATED ODDS 1:870

NNO Asuka 4.00 10.00
NNO Austin Aries 2.50 6.00
NNO Becky Lynch 4.00 10.00
NNO Big Cass 1.50 4.00
NNO Bray Wyatt 3.00 8.00
NNO Cesaro 2.50 6.00
NNO Charlotte 5.00 12.00
NNO Darren Young 1.25 3.00
NNO Dolph Ziggler 2.00 5.00
NNO Finn Balor 5.00 12.00
NNO Hideo Itami 2.00 5.00
NNO John Cena 6.00 15.00
NNO Kofi Kingston 1.50 4.00
NNO Natalya 2.50 6.00
NNO No Way Jose 1.25 3.00
NNO Randy Orton 3.00 8.00
NNO Roman Reigns 4.00 10.00
NNO Sasha Banks 4.00 10.00
NNO Seth Rollins 4.00 10.00
NNO Shinsuke Nakamura 3.00 8.00
NNO Simon Gotch 1.25 3.00
NNO Zack Ryder 1.25 3.00

2017 Topps WWE Road to WrestleMania Autographed Triple Threat Dual Relics

STATED ODDS 1:66,048
STATED PRINT RUN 10 SER.#'d SETS

NNO Brock Lesnar 125.00 250.00
NNO John Cena 125.00 200.00
NNO Roman Reigns 60.00 120.00
NNO Sasha Banks 120.00 200.00

2017 Topps WWE Road to WrestleMania Autographed WrestleMania 32 Mat Relics

STATED ODDS 1:33,024
UNPRICED DUE TO SCARCITY

NNO AJ Styles
NNO Becky Lynch
NNO Bray Wyatt
NNO Brie Bella
NNO Brock Lesnar
NNO Chris Jericho
NNO Dean Ambrose
NNO John Cena
NNO Kevin Owens
NNO Natalya
NNO Roman Reigns
NNO Sasha Banks
NNO Zack Ryder

2017 Topps WWE Road to WrestleMania WrestleMania 32 Mat Relics

*BLUE/50: .5X TO 1.2X BASIC MEM
*SILVER/25: .6X TO 1.5X BASIC MEM
*GOLD/10: .75X TO 2X BASIC MEM
*RED/1: UNPRICED DUE TO SCARCITY
*P.P.BLACK/1: UNPRICED DUE TO SCARCITY
*P.P.CYAN/1: UNPRICED DUE TO SCARCITY
*P.P.MAGENTA/1: UNPRICED DUE TO SCARCITY
*P.P.YELLOW/1: UNPRICED DUE TO SCARCITY
STATED ODDS 1:1,296

NNO AJ Styles 10.00 25.00
NNO Baron Corbin 3.00 8.00
NNO Becky Lynch 6.00 15.00
NNO Bray Wyatt 5.00 12.00
NNO Brie Bella 5.00 12.00
NNO Brock Lesnar 10.00 25.00
NNO Charlotte 8.00 20.00
NNO Chris Jericho 5.00 12.00
NNO Dean Ambrose 6.00 15.00
NNO John Cena 10.00 25.00
NNO Kevin Owens 5.00 12.00
NNO Lana 6.00 15.00
NNO Natalya 4.00 10.00
NNO The Rock 10.00 25.00
NNO Roman Reigns 6.00 15.00
NNO Sasha Banks 6.00 15.00
NNO Shane McMahon 3.00 8.00
NNO Triple H 5.00 12.00
NNO Undertaker 8.00 20.00
NNO Zack Ryder 2.00 5.00

2017 Topps WWE Road to WrestleMania WrestleMania 33 Roster

COMPLETE SET (50) 10.00 25.00
STATED ODDS 2:1

WMR1 Triple H .75 2.00
WMR2 Stephanie McMahon .40 1.00
WMR3 Roman Reigns 1.00 2.50
WMR4 The Rock 1.50 4.00
WMR5 John Cena 1.50 4.00
WMR6 Bray Wyatt .75 2.00
WMR7 Erick Rowan .30 .75
WMR8 Braun Strowman .40 1.00
WMR9 Luke Harper .30 .75
WMR10 Undertaker 1.25 3.00
WMR11 Shane McMahon .50 1.25
WMR12 Brock Lesnar 1.50 4.00
WMR13 Dean Ambrose 1.00 2.50
WMR14 Charlotte 1.25 3.00
WMR15 Ric Flair .75 2.00
WMR16 Sasha Banks 1.00 2.50
WMR17 Becky Lynch 1.00 2.50
WMR18 Chris Jericho .75 2.00
WMR19 AJ Styles 1.50 4.00
WMR20 Baron Corbin .50 1.25
WMR21 Kane .40 1.00
WMR22 Big Show .40 1.00
WMR23 Mark Henry .30 .75
WMR24 Zack Ryder .30 .75
WMR25 Kevin Owens .75 2.00
WMR26 Sami Zayn .40 1.00
WMR27 The Miz .60 1.50
WMR28 Dolph Ziggler .50 1.25
WMR29 Sin Cara .40 1.00
WMR30 Kalisto .50 1.25
WMR31 Kofi Kingston .40 1.00
WMR32 Big E .40 1.00
WMR33 Xavier Woods .40 1.00
WMR34 Sheamus .60 1.50
WMR35 Rusev .60 1.50
WMR36 Jey Uso .40 1.00
WMR37 Jimmy Uso .40 1.00
WMR38 Darren Young .30 .75
WMR39 R-Truth .30 .75
WMR40 Goldust .40 1.00
WMR41 Heath Slater .30 .75
WMR42 Brie Bella .75 2.00
WMR43 Natalya .60 1.50
WMR44 Alicia Fox .50 1.25
WMR45 Eva Marie .75 2.00
WMR46 Lana 1.00 2.50
WMR47 Naomi .60 1.50
WMR48 Tamina .40 1.00
WMR49 Emma .75 2.00
WMR50 Summer Rae .75 2.00

2018 Topps WWE Road to WrestleMania

COMPLETE SET (100) 8.00 20.00
*BRONZE: .5X TO 1.2X BASIC CARDS
*BLUE/99: .75X TO 2X BASIC CARDS
*SILVER/25: 2X TO 5X BASIC CARDS
*GOLD/10: UNPRICED DUE TO SCARCITY
*RED/1: UNPRICED DUE TO SCARCITY
*P.P.BLACK/1: UNPRICED DUE TO SCARCITY
*P.P.CYAN/1: UNPRICED DUE TO SCARCITY
*P.P.MAGENTA/1: UNPRICED DUE TO SCARCITY
*P.P.YELLOW/1: UNPRICED DUE TO SCARCITY

1 Roman Reigns .60 1.50
2 Cesaro & Sheamus .50 1.25
3 Roman Reigns .60 1.50
4 Universal Champion Kevin Owens .60 1.50
5 Roman Reigns .60 1.50
6 Kevin Owens .60 1.50
7 Team Raw defeats Team SmackDown .50 1.25
8 Cesaro & Sheamus .50 1.25
9 Undertaker Returns 1.00 2.50
10 Chris Jericho .60 1.50
11 Luke Gallows & Karl Anderson .30 .75
12 Kevin Owens .60 1.50
13 Samoa Joe Debuts .50 1.25
14 Kevin Owens .60 1.50
15 Roman Reigns .60 1.50

16 Kevin Owens	1.00	2.50
17 Roman Reigns	1.00	2.50
18 Mick Foley	.60	1.50
19 Undertaker	1.00	2.50
20 Undertaker	1.00	2.50
21 Ricky The Dragon Steamboat	.40	1.00
22 Diamond Dallas Page	.40	1.00
23 Kurt Angle Returns	.60	1.50
24 Kevin Owens	.60	1.50
25 The Hardy Boyz Return	.60	1.50
26 Seth Rollins	.60	1.50
27 Brock Lesnar	1.00	2.50
28 Roman Reigns	.60	1.50
29 Kurt Angle	.60	1.50
30 The Revival	.30	.75
31 Finn Balor	.60	1.50
32 Alexa Bliss	1.25	3.00
33 Elias	.60	1.50
34 Chris Jericho	.60	1.50
35 Bray Wyatt	.60	1.50
36 Braun Strowman	.60	1.50
37 Goldust	.50	1.25
38 The Miz	.50	1.25
39 Cesaro & Sheamus	.50	1.25
40 Samoa Joe	.50	1.25
41 Big Cass Turns	.30	.75
42 Cesaro & Sheamus	.50	1.25
43 Universal Champion Brock Lesnar	1.00	2.50
44 Kurt Angle	.60	1.50
45 Braun Strowman	.60	1.50
46 Dean Ambrose	.60	1.50
47 TJP	.30	.75
48 The Brian Kendrick	.40	1.00
49 The Brian Kendrick	.40	1.00
50 Rich Swann	.30	.75
51 Neville Returns	.40	1.00
52 Neville	.40	1.00
53 Neville	.40	1.00
54 Noam Dar	.40	1.00
55 Akira Tozawa	.40	1.00
56 WWE Champion AJ Styles	1.00	2.50
57 Dolph Ziggler	.50	1.25
58 Bray Wyatt	.60	1.50
59 Randy Orton	.60	1.50
60 The Miz	.50	1.25
61 Edge and Undertaker Return	1.00	2.50
62 Team SmackDown defeats Team Raw	1.00	2.50
63 James Ellsworth	.25	.60
64 The New Wyatt Family	.60	1.50
65 The Miz	.50	1.25
66 Baron Corbin	.40	1.00
67 AJ Styles	1.00	2.50
68 American Alpha	.25	.60
69 Dean Ambrose	.50	1.25
70 John Cena	1.00	2.50
71 Randy Orton	.60	1.50
72 Randy Orton	.60	1.50
73 Bray Wyatt	.60	1.50
74 Randy Orton	.60	1.50
75 The Usos	.40	1.00
76 Shane McMahon	1.00	2.50
77 Mojo Rawley	.25	.60
78 Dean Ambrose	.50	1.25
79 AJ Styles	1.00	2.50
80 John Cena Proposes to Nikki Bella	1.00	2.50
81 Randy Orton	.60	1.50
82 Tye Dillinger	.25	.60
83 Shinsuke Nakamura	.60	1.50
84 The Superstar Shake-Up	.75	2.00
85 Jinder Mahal	.30	.75
86 Kevin Owens	.60	1.50
87 Shinsuke Nakamura	.60	1.50
88 The Usos	.40	1.00
89 Jinder Mahal	.30	.75
90 Maria Kanellis	.60	1.50
91 WWE Champion Jinder Mahal	.30	.75
92 Baron Corbin	.40	1.00
93 AJ Styles	1.00	2.50
94 The New Day	.40	1.00
95 Kevin Owens	.60	1.50
96 John Cena	1.00	2.50
97 WWE Champion Jinder Mahal	.30	.75
98 AJ Styles	1.00	2.50
99 Shinsuke Nakamura	1.00	2.50
100 Jinder Mahal	.30	.75

2018 Topps WWE Road to WrestleMania Commemorative Andre the Giant Battle Royal Trophy Relics

*BRONZE/99: .5X TO 1.2X BASIC MEM
*BLUE/50: .6X TO 1.5X BASIC MEM
*SILVER/25: .75X TO 2X BASIC MEM
*GOLD/10: UNPRICED DUE TO SCARCITY
*RED/1: UNPRICED DUE TO SCARCITY
STATED ODDS 1:936

ACBR Braun Strowman	6.00	15.00
ACBS Big Show	2.50	6.00
ACCG Chad Gable	2.50	6.00
ACDZ Dolph Ziggler	2.50	6.00
ACFA Fandango	5.00	12.00
ACGO Goldust	2.50	6.00
ACHS Heath Slater	2.50	6.00
ACJI Jimmy Uso	5.00	12.00
ACJJ Jason Jordan	2.50	6.00
ACJM Jinder Mahal	2.50	6.00
ACJU Jey Uso	2.50	6.00
ACKD Killian Dain	3.00	8.00
ACLH Luke Harper	3.00	8.00
ACMH Mark Henry	2.50	6.00
ACMR Mojo Rawley	3.00	8.00
ACRH Rhyno	3.00	8.00
ACRT R-Truth	2.50	6.00
ACSZ Sami Zayn	4.00	10.00
ACTB Tian Bing	2.50	6.00
ACTBR Tyler Breeze	2.50	6.00

2018 Topps WWE Road to WrestleMania Autographed Commemorative Andre the Giant Battle Royal Trophy Relics

STATED ODDS 1:24,096
STATED PRINT RUN 10 SER.#'d SETS
UNPRICED DUE TO SCARCITY

NNO Big Show
NNO Braun Strowman
NNO Dolph Ziggler
NNO Fandango
NNO Goldust
NNO Heath Slater
NNO Jey Uso
NNO Jimmy Uso
NNO Jinder Mahal
NNO Killian Dain
NNO Luke Harper
NNO Mark Henry
NNO Mojo Rawley
NNO Sami Zayn
NNO Tyler Breeze

2018 Topps WWE Road to WrestleMania Autographed Dual Relics

STATED ODDS 1:96,384
STATED PRINT RUN 10 SER.#'d SETS
UNPRICED DUE TO SCARCITY

NNO Alexa Bliss
NNO John Cena
NNO Kevin Owens
NNO Naomi
NNO Roman Reigns
NNO Shinsuke Nakamura

2018 Topps WWE Road to WrestleMania Autographed NXT TakeOver Orlando Mat Relics

STATED ODDS 1:32,128
STATED PRINT RUN 10 SER.#'d SETS
UNPRICED DUE TO SCARCITY

NNO Aleister Black
NNO Asuka
NNO Bobby Roode
NNO Eric Young
NNO Johnny Gargano
NNO Kassius Ohno
NNO Nikki Cross
NNO Roderick Strong
NNO Ruby Riot
NNO Shinsuke Nakamura
NNO Tommaso Ciampa

2018 Topps WWE Road to WrestleMania Autographed Shirt Relics

STATED ODDS 1:32,128
STATED PRINT RUN 10 SER.#'d SETS
UNPRICED DUE TO SCARCITY

NNO Becky Lynch
NNO Carmella
NNO Cesaro
NNO Goldust
NNO Karl Anderson
NNO Kevin Owens
NNO Luke Gallows
NNO Luke Harper
NNO Naomi
NNO Roman Reigns
NNO Sting
NNO Xavier Woods

2018 Topps WWE Road to WrestleMania Autographed Wrestlemania 33 Mat Relics

STATED ODDS 1:24,096
STATED PRINT RUN 10 SER.#'d SETS
UNPRICED DUE TO SCARCITY

NNO AJ Styles
NNO Charlotte Flair
NNO Chris Jericho
NNO Jeff Hardy
NNO Kevin Owens
NNO Maryse
NNO Naomi
NNO Randy Orton
NNO Roman Reigns
NNO Sasha Banks
NNO Stephanie McMahon
NNO The Miz
NNO Triple H
NNO Undertaker

2018 Topps WWE Road to WrestleMania Autographs

*BLUE/50: .5X TO 1.2X BASIC AUTOS
*SILVER/25: .6X TO 1.5X BASIC AUTOS
*GOLD/10: UNPRICED DUE TO SCARCITY
*RED/1: UNPRICED DUE TO SCARCITY
*P.P.BLACK/1: UNPRICED DUE TO SCARCITY
*P.P.CYAN/1: UNPRICED DUE TO SCARCITY
*P.P.MAGENTA/1: UNPRICED DUE TO SCARCITY
*P.P.YELLOW/1: UNPRICED DUE TO SCARCITY
STATED ODDS 1:32

AAB Aleister Black	12.00	30.00
AAL Alexa Bliss	30.00	75.00
AAS AJ Styles	15.00	40.00
ABA Bayley	12.00	30.00
ABL Becky Lynch	15.00	40.00
ABW Bray Wyatt	8.00	20.00
ACA Carmella	10.00	25.00
ACF Charlotte Flair	15.00	40.00
ADA Dean Ambrose	12.00	30.00
ADW Dash Wilder	6.00	15.00
AEM Ember Moon	12.00	30.00
AEY Eric Young	5.00	12.00
AFB Finn Balor	15.00	40.00
AJG Johnny Gargano	10.00	25.00
AJH Jeff Hardy	15.00	40.00
AJM Jinder Mahal	10.00	25.00
AKA Kassius Ohno	6.00	15.00
AKO Kevin Owens	8.00	20.00
AMH Matt Hardy	15.00	40.00
ANA Naomi	6.00	15.00
ANC Nikki Cross	10.00	25.00
ARS Roderick Strong	5.00	12.00
ASB Sasha Banks	20.00	50.00
ASD Scott Dawson	5.00	12.00
ASJ Samoa Joe	8.00	20.00
ASN Shinsuke Nakamura	12.00	30.00
ASR Seth Rollins	12.00	30.00
ATC Tommaso Ciampa	5.00	12.00
ATD Tye Dillinger	6.00	15.00
ATM The Miz	8.00	20.00
AASU Asuka	15.00	40.00
ABOR Bobby Roode	10.00	25.00
AKUA Kurt Angle	15.00	40.00
ARRI Ruby Riot	12.00	30.00

2018 Topps WWE Road to WrestleMania Autographs Silver

STATED ODDS 1:105
STATED PRINT RUN 25 SER.#'d SETS

ASM Stephanie McMahon	125.00	250.00
ATH Triple H	150.00	300.00
AUN Undertaker	150.00	300.00
ANAT Natalya	10.00	25.00

2018 Topps WWE Road to WrestleMania Dual Autographs

STATED ODDS 1:1,928
STATED PRINT RUN 10 SER.#'d SETS

DABR A.Black/B.Roode/10	60.00	120.00
DAFS F.Balor/Samoa Joe/4		
DAJT T.Ciampa/J.Gargano/10	30.00	75.00
DAMJ Matt & Jeff Hardy/10	30.00	75.00
DARK K.Ohno/R.Strong/10		
DARN N.Cross/R.Riot/10	20.00	50.00
DAUK K.Angle/Undertaker/10	250.00	400.00

2018 Topps WWE Road to WrestleMania Dual Relics

*SILVER/25: .5X TO 1.2X BASIC MEM
*GOLD/10: UNPRICED DUE TO SCARCITY
*RED/1: UNPRICED DUE TO SCARCITY
STATED PRINT RUN 50 SER.#'d SETS

DRAB Alexa Bliss	30.00	75.00
DRBL Brock Lesnar	10.00	25.00
DRJC John Cena	15.00	40.00
DRKO Kevin Owens	10.00	25.00
DRNA Naomi	12.00	30.00
DRRR Roman Reigns	10.00	25.00
DRSN Shinsuke Nakamura		
DRSR Seth Rollins	12.00	30.00

2018 Topps WWE Road to WrestleMania Kiss

*GOLD/10: UNPRICED DUE TO SCARCITY
*RED/1: UNPRICED DUE TO SCARCITY
STATED ODDS 1:112

KAB Alexa Bliss	60.00	120.00
KAS Asuka	30.00	75.00
KCA Carmella	25.00	60.00
KCF Charlotte Flair/99	25.00	60.00
KMA Maryse	20.00	50.00
KNA Naomi	12.00	30.00
KRR Ruby Riot	20.00	50.00

2018 Topps WWE Road to WrestleMania Kiss Autographs

*GOLD/10: UNPRICED DUE TO SCARCITY
*RED/1: UNPRICED DUE TO SCARCITY
STATED ODDS 1:445

NNO Alexa Bliss	120.00	250.00
NNO Asuka	50.00	100.00
NNO Becky Lynch	60.00	120.00
NNO Carmella	50.00	100.00
NNO Charlotte Flair	75.00	150.00
NNO Goldust	75.00	150.00
NNO Maryse	50.00	100.00
NNO Nikki Cross	50.00	100.00
NNO Ruby Riot	50.00	100.00

2018 Topps WWE Road to WrestleMania NXT TakeOver Orlando Mat Relics

*BRONZE/99: SAME VALUE AS BASIC MEM
*BLUE/50: .5X TO 1.2X BASIC MEM
*SILVER/25: .6X TO 1.5X BASIC MEM
*GOLD/10: UNPRICED DUE TO SCARCITY
*RED/1: UNPRICED DUE TO SCARCITY
STATED ODDS 1:1,236

MRAB Aleister Black	6.00	15.00
MRAS Asuka	6.00	15.00
MRBR Bobby Roode	6.00	15.00

MRDW Dash Wilder	2.50	6.00
MREM Ember Moon	3.00	8.00
MREY Eric Young	2.50	6.00
MRJG Johnny Gargano	3.00	8.00
MRKO Kassius Ohno	6.00	15.00
MRNC Nikki Cross	4.00	10.00
MRRR Ruby Riot	5.00	12.00
MRRS Roderick Strong	2.50	6.00
MRSD Scott Dawson	3.00	8.00
MRSN Shinsuke Nakamura	4.00	10.00
MRTC Tommaso Ciampa	3.00	8.00
MRTD Tye Dillinger	3.00	8.00

2018 Topps WWE Road to WrestleMania Road to WrestleMania 34

RTW1 The Miz & Miztourage	1.25	3.00
RTW2 Big Cass	.75	2.00
RTW3 Finn Balor	1.50	4.00
RTW4 Dean Ambrose & Seth Rollins	1.50	4.00
RTW5 Brock Lesnar	2.50	6.00
RTW6 Braun Strowman	1.50	4.00
RTW7 John Cena	2.50	6.00
RTW8 Jeff Hardy	1.25	3.00
RTW9 John Cena and Roman Reigns	2.50	6.00
RTW10 Neville	1.00	2.50
RTW11 Enzo Amore	.60	1.50
RTW12 The Brian Kendrick	1.00	2.50
RTW13 The Usos	.60	1.50
RTW14 John Cena	2.50	6.00
RTW15 Randy Orton	1.50	4.00
RTW16 AJ Styles	2.50	6.00
RTW17 Jinder Mahal	.75	2.00
RTW18 Bobby Roode	1.00	2.50
RTW19 Shelton Benjamin	.75	2.00
RTW20 Shinsuke Nakamura	1.50	4.00

2018 Topps WWE Road to WrestleMania Shirt Relics

*BLUE/50: .5X TO 1.2X BASIC MEM
*SILVER/25: .6X TO 1.5X BASIC MEM
*GOLD/10: UNPRICED DUE TO SCARCITY
*RED/1: UNPRICED DUE TO SCARCITY
STATED ODDS 1:1,890
STATED PRINT RUN 99 SER.#'d SETS

SRAB Alexa Bliss	12.00	30.00
SRBL Becky Lynch	10.00	25.00
SRBR Brock Lesnar	5.00	12.00
SRCA Carmella	6.00	15.00
SRCE Cesaro	3.00	8.00
SRCG Chad Gable	2.50	6.00
SRGO Goldust	3.00	8.00
SRJC John Cena	6.00	15.00
SRJI Jimmy Uso	2.50	6.00
SRJJ Jason Jordan	3.00	8.00
SRKA Karl Anderson	2.50	6.00
SRKO Kevin Owens	2.50	6.00
SRLG Luke Gallows	2.50	6.00
SRLH Luke Harper	3.00	8.00
SRNA Naomi	4.00	10.00
SRNW No Way Jose	2.50	6.00
SRRR Roman Reigns	4.00	10.00
SRSR Seth Rollins	4.00	10.00
SRST Sting	10.00	25.00
SRXW Xavier Woods	2.50	6.00

2018 Topps WWE Road to WrestleMania WrestleMania 33 Mat Relics

*BRONZE/99: SAME VALUE AS BASIC MEM
*BLUE/50: .5X TO 1.2X BASIC MEM
*SILVER/25: .6X TO 1.5X BASIC MEM
*GOLD/10: UNPRICED DUE TO SCARCITY
*RED/1: UNPRICED DUE TO SCARCITY
STATED ODDS 1:748
STATED PRINT RUN 199 SER.#'d SETS

WMAB Alexa Bliss	10.00	25.00
WMAS AJ Styles	8.00	20.00
WMBA Bayley	6.00	15.00
WMBR Brock Lesnar	6.00	15.00
WMBY Bray Wyatt	10.00	25.00
WMCA Carmella	5.00	12.00
WMCF Charlotte Flair	6.00	15.00
WMCJ Chris Jericho	4.00	10.00
WMDA Dean Ambrose	5.00	12.00
WMJC John Cena	6.00	15.00
WMJH Jeff Hardy	6.00	15.00
WMKO Kevin Owens	4.00	10.00
WMMA Maryse	6.00	15.00
WMMH Matt Hardy	4.00	10.00
WMNA Naomi	4.00	10.00
WMNB Nikki Bella	5.00	12.00
WMRO Randy Orton	3.00	8.00
WMRR Roman Reigns	10.00	25.00
WMSB Sasha Banks	6.00	15.00
WMSM Stephanie McMahon	6.00	15.00
WMSR Seth Rollins	5.00	12.00
WMTH Triple H	8.00	20.00
WMTM The Miz	3.00	8.00
WMUN Undertaker	15.00	40.00
WMNAT Natalya	3.00	8.00

2018 Topps WWE Road to WrestleMania WrestleMania 34 Roster

COMPLETE SET (50)	12.00	30.00
R1 Roman Reigns	.75	2.00
R2 Brock Lesnar	1.25	3.00
R3 Randy Orton	.75	2.00
R4 Bray Wyatt	.75	2.00
R5 Seth Rollins	.75	2.00
R6 Triple H	.75	2.00
R7 John Cena	1.25	3.00
R8 The Miz	.60	1.50
R9 Kevin Owens	.75	2.00
R10 Chris Jericho	.75	2.00
R11 AJ Styles	1.25	3.00
R12 Dean Ambrose	.60	1.50
R13 Baron Corbin	.50	1.25
R14 Mojo Rawley	.30	.75
R15 Jinder Mahal	.40	1.00
R16 Asuka	1.00	2.50
R17 Matt Hardy	.75	2.00
R18 Jeff Hardy	.60	1.50
R19 Luke Gallows	.40	1.00
R20 Karl Anderson	.30	.75
R21 Cesaro	.60	1.50
R22 Sheamus	.60	1.50
R23 Enzo Amore	.30	.75
R24 Big Cass	.40	1.00
R25 Bayley	.50	1.25
R26 Charlotte Flair	1.00	2.50
R27 Sasha Banks	1.00	2.50
R28 Nia Jax	.50	1.25
R29 Naomi	.40	1.00
R30 Alexa Bliss	1.50	4.00
R31 Becky Lynch	.75	2.00
R32 Mickie James	.60	1.50
R33 Natalya	.40	1.00
R34 Carmella	.60	1.50
R35 Braun Strowman	.75	2.00
R36 Big Show	.30	.75
R37 Sami Zayn	.30	.75
R38 Luke Harper	.50	1.25
R39 Dolph Ziggler	.40	1.00
R40 Fandango	.30	.75
R41 Tyler Breeze	.30	.75
R42 Jason Jordan	.30	.75
R43 Chad Gable	.30	.75
R44 Jey Uso	.30	.75
R45 Jimmy Uso	.30	.75
R46 Heath Slater	.30	.75
R47 Rhyno	.30	.75
R48 Goldust	.60	1.50
R49 R-Truth	.40	1.00
R50 Titus O'Neil	.30	.75

2019 Topps WWE Road to WrestleMania

COMPLETE SET (100) 10.00 25.00
*BRONZE: .5X TO 1.2X BASIC CARDS
*BLUE/99: .75X TO 2X BASIC CARDS
*SILVER/25: 2X TO 5X BASIC CARDS
*GOLD/10: UNPRICED DUE TO SCARCITY
*RED/1: UNPRICED DUE TO SCARCITY
*P.P.BLACK/1: UNPRICED DUE TO SCARCITY
*P.P.CYAN/1: UNPRICED DUE TO SCARCITY
*P.P.MAGENTA/1: UNPRICED DUE TO SCARCITY
*P.P.YELLOW/1: UNPRICED DUE TO SCARCITY

1 Braun Strowman	.60	1.50
2 Braun Strowman	1.25	3.00
3 Roman Reigns	1.25	3.00
4 The Shield	.60	1.50
5 Kane	.40	1.00
6 Demon Finn Balor	.50	1.25
7 Kurt Angle	.50	1.25
8 SmackDown Live Siege	.50	1.25
9 Cesaro & Sheamus	.40	1.00
10 The Shield	.60	1.50
11 Triple H	.60	1.50
12 Braun Strowman	.60	1.50
13 The Shield	.60	1.50
14 Team Raw Defeat Team SmackDown	.60	1.50
15 Roman Reigns	.60	1.50
16 Matt Hardy Snaps	.50	1.25
17 Braun Strowman	.60	1.50
18 Seth Rollins & Jason Jordan	.60	1.50
19 Roman Reigns	.60	1.50
20 The Balor Club	.50	1.25
21 Stone Cold Steve Austin Returns	1.25	3.00
22 The Miz	.50	1.25
23 Cesaro & Sheamus	.40	1.00
24 John Cena	1.25	3.00
25 Elias	.50	1.25
26 Finn Balor and Seth Rollins	.60	1.50
27 Braun Strowman	.60	1.50
28 Roman Reigns	.60	1.50
29 Kurt Angle	.50	1.25
30 Braun Strowman	.60	1.50
31 John Cena	1.25	3.00
32 Braun Strowman	.60	1.50
33 John Cena	1.25	3.00
34 Woken Matt Hardy	.60	1.50
35 Seth Rollins	.60	1.50
36 Kurt Angle & Ronda Rousey	1.25	3.00
37 Undertaker	1.25	3.00
38 Braun Strowman	.60	1.50
39 Breezango	.30	.75
40 Gentleman Jack Gallagher	.40	1.00
41 Kalisto	.25	.60
42 Kalisto	.25	.60
43 Drew Gulak	.25	.60
44 Akira Tozawa	.25	.60
45 Hideo Itami	.25	.60
46 Cedric Alexander & Goldust	.25	.60
47 Drake Maverick	.25	.60
48 Mark Andrews	.25	.60
49 Buddy Murphy	.30	.75
50 Cedric Alexander	.25	.60
51 Mustafa Ali	.25	.60
52 Cedric Alexander	.25	.60
53 Buddy Murphy	.30	.75
54 Cedric Alexander	.25	.60
55 Shinsuke Nakamura	.60	1.50
56 The New Day	.40	1.00
57 Rusev	.50	1.25
58 Kevin Owens	.60	1.50
59 The Usos	.30	.75
60 Baron Corbin	.40	1.00
61 Jinder Mahal	.60	1.50
62 Kevin Owens	.60	1.50
63 Kevin Owens and Sami Zayn	.60	1.50
64 Baron Corbin	.40	1.00
65 Kevin Owens & Sami Zayn	.60	1.50
66 Shinsuka Nakamura	.60	1.50
67 AJ Styles	1.25	3.00
68 Raw Launches Counter-Siege	.60	1.50
69 Baron Corbin	.40	1.00
70 The Usos	.30	.75
71 Kevin Owens & Sami Zayn	.60	1.50
72 Mojo Rawley	.30	.75
73 Kevin Owens	.60	1.50
74 Rusev & Aiden English	.50	1.25
75 Kevin Owens & Sami Zayn	.60	1.50
76 Kevin Owens	.60	1.50
77 Dolph Ziggler	.50	1.25
78 Kevin Owens & Sami Zayn	.60	1.50
79 AJ Styles	1.25	3.00
80 Dolph Ziggler	.50	1.25
81 Kevin Owens	.60	1.50
82 Sami Zayn	1.25	3.00
83 Bobby Roode	.50	1.25
84 AJ Styles	1.25	3.00
85 Shinsuke Nakamura	.60	1.50
86 AJ Styles & Nakamura	1.25	3.00
87 John Cena	1.25	3.00
88 Sami Zayn	.50	1.25
89 Randy Orton	.60	1.50
90 AJ Styles	1.25	3.00
91 Daniel Bryan	.60	1.50
92 Daniel Bryan	.60	1.50
93 Jinder Mahal	.60	1.50
94 Bludgeon Brothers	.30	.75
95 Daniel Bryan & Shane McMahon	.60	1.50
96 AJ Styles	1.25	3.00
97 Braun Strowman	.60	1.50
98 Shinsuka Nakamura	.60	1.50
99 The Usos	.30	.75
100 Woken Matt Hardy	.50	1.25

2019 Topps WWE Road to WrestleMania Autographed Commemorative Andre the Giant Battle Royal Trophy Relics

STATED PRINT RUN 10 SER.#'d SETS
UNPRICED DUE TO SCARCITY

BRABC Baron Corbin
BRACG Chad Gable
BRADZ Dolph Ziggler
BRAFN Fandango
BRAGD Goldust
BRAKA Karl Anderson
BRALG Luke Gallows
BRAMH Woken Matt Hardy
BRAMR Mojo Rawley
BRASB Shelton Benjamin
BRASC Sin Cara
BRATB Tyler Breeze
BRATO Titus O'Neil

2019 Topps WWE Road to WrestleMania Autographed Commemorative Intercontinental Championship Relics

STATED PRINT RUN 10 SER.#'d SETS
UNPRICED DUE TO SCARCITY

ICRBH Bret Hit Man Hart
ICRRS Ricky The Dragon Steamboat

2019 Topps WWE Road to WrestleMania Autographed Divas Revolution Relic

UNPRICED DUE TO SCARCITY

DRRABB Brie Bella

2019 Topps WWE Road to WrestleMania Autographed Mat Relics

STATED PRINT RUN 10 SER.#'d SETS
UNPRICED DUE TO SCARCITY

MRAAB Alexa Bliss
MRAAC Adam Cole
MRAAS Asuka
MRACF Charlotte Flair
MRAEM Ember Moon
MRAJG Johnny Gargano
MRAKA Kurt Angle
MRAKD Killian Dain
MRAKO Kevin Owens
MRAMH Woken Matt Hardy
MRANA Naomi
MRARC Ricochet
MRASB Shayna Baszler
MRASN Shinsuke Nakamura
MRASR Seth Rollins
MRASZ Sami Zayn
MRATC Tommaso Ciampa
MRAUN Undertaker
MRAALB Aleister Black

MRAERA Kyle O'Reilly
MRAHHH Triple H
MRARRR Ronda Rousey
MRASMC Stephanie McMahon

2019 Topps WWE Road to WrestleMania Autographed Shirt Relics

STATED PRINT RUN 10 SER.#'d SETS
UNPRICED DUE TO SCARCITY

SRAAB Alexa Bliss
SRAAF Alicia Fox
SRACM Carmella
SRAFB Finn Balor
SRAMH Woken Matt Hardy
SRARD Rusev
SRARY Renee Young
SRASR Seth Rollins

2019 Topps WWE Road to WrestleMania Autographs

*BLUE/50: .5X TO 1.2X BASIC AUTOS
*SILVER/25: .6X TO 1.5X BASIC AUTOS
*GOLD/10: UNPRICED DUE TO SCARCITY
*RED/1: UNPRICED DUE TO SCARCITY
*P.P.BLACK/1: UNPRICED DUE TO SCARCITY
*P.P.CYAN/1: UNPRICED DUE TO SCARCITY
*P.P.MAGENTA/1: UNPRICED DUE TO SCARCITY
*P.P.YELLOW/1: UNPRICED DUE TO SCARCITY
RANDOMLY INSERTED INTO PACKS

AAB Alexa Bliss 30.00 75.00
AAE Aiden English 5.00 12.00
AAJ AJ Styles 15.00 40.00
AAS Asuka 15.00 40.00
ABE Big E 6.00 15.00
ABR Bobby Roode 6.00 15.00
ABS Braun Strowman 15.00 40.00
ACE Cesaro 5.00 12.00
ACF Charlotte Flair 20.00 50.00
ACM Carmella 12.00 30.00
ADB Daniel Bryan 10.00 25.00
AEM Ember Moon 10.00 25.00
AFB Finn Balor 15.00 40.00
AJH Jeff Hardy 15.00 40.00
AKA Kurt Angle 10.00 25.00
AKK Kofi Kingston 6.00 15.00
AKO Kevin Owens 10.00 25.00
ALM Liv Morgan EXCH 15.00 40.00
AMH Woken Matt Hardy 8.00 20.00
ANA Naomi 8.00 20.00
ANJ Nia Jax 6.00 15.00
ARD Rusev 8.00 20.00
ARW Rowan 5.00 12.00
ASB Sasha Banks 20.00 50.00
ASH Sheamus 6.00 15.00
ASJ Samoa Joe 8.00 20.00
ASN Shinsuke Nakamura 10.00 25.00
ASR Seth Rollins 10.00 25.00
ASZ Sami Zayn 5.00 12.00
ATM The Miz 6.00 15.00
AXW Xavier Woods 6.00 15.00
ARRR Ronda Rousey 125.00 250.00
ARTT Ruby Riott 12.00 30.00
AWWE Elias 12.00 30.00

2019 Topps WWE Road to WrestleMania Autographs Blue

AJM Jinder Mahal 8.00 20.00
AJEY Jey Uso 6.00 15.00
AJIM Jimmy Uso 6.00 15.00

2019 Topps WWE Road to WrestleMania Autographs Silver

AUN Undertaker 125.00 250.00
AHHH Triple H 100.00 200.00
ASMC Stephanie McMahon 75.00 150.00

2019 Topps WWE Road to WrestleMania Commemorative Andre the Giant Battle Royal Trophy Relics

*BRONZE/99: .5X TO 1.2X BASIC MEM
*BLUE/50: .6X TO 1.5X BASIC MEM
*SILVER/25: .75X TO 2X BASIC MEM
*GOLD/10: UNPRICED DUE TO SCARCITY
*RED/1: UNPRICED DUE TO SCARCITY
RANDOMLY INSERTED INTO PACKS

BRAE Aiden English 2.00 5.00
BRBC Baron Corbin 2.50 6.00
BRCG Chad Gable 3.00 8.00
BRDZ Dolph Ziggler 2.50 6.00
BRFN Fandango 2.00 5.00
BRGD Goldust 2.50 6.00
BRHS Heath Slater 2.00 5.00
BRKA Karl Anderson 2.50 6.00
BRKN Kane 3.00 8.00
BRLG Luke Gallows 2.50 6.00
BRMH Woken Matt Hardy 3.00 8.00
BRMR Mojo Rawley 2.00 5.00
BRRT R-Truth 2.00 5.00
BRRY Rhyno 2.50 6.00
BRSB Shelton Benjamin 3.00 8.00
BRSC Sin Cara 4.00 10.00
BRTB Tyler Breeze 2.50 6.00
BRTD Tye Dillinger 2.50 6.00
BRTO Titus O'Neil 2.50 6.00
BRZR Zack Ryder 3.00 8.00

2019 Topps WWE Road to WrestleMania Divas Revolution Autographs

RANDOMLY INSERTED INTO PACKS

DRABB Brie Bella
DRABL Becky Lynch
DRACF Charlotte Flair

2019 Topps WWE Road to WrestleMania Divas Revolution Relics

RANDOMLY INSERTED INTO PACKS

DRRBB Brie Bella
DRRNB Nikki Bella

2019 Topps WWE Road to WrestleMania Dual Autographs

STATED PRINT RUN 10 SER.#'d SETS
UNPRICED DUE TO SCARCITY

DAAP Akam/Rezar
DABB Rowan/Harper
DABR T.Breeze/Fandango
DABT B.Dallas/C.Axel
DADW B.Wyatt/M.Hardy
DAUSO The Usos
DAYEP S.Zayn/K.Owens

2019 Topps WWE Road to WrestleMania Intercontinental Champions Autographs

*GOLD/10: UNPRICED DUE TO SCARCITY
*RED/1: UNPRICED DUE TO SCARCITY
*P.P.BLACK/1: UNPRICED DUE TO SCARCITY
*P.P.CYAN/1: UNPRICED DUE TO SCARCITY
*P.P.MAGENTA/1: UNPRICED DUE TO SCARCITY
*P.P.YELLOW/1: UNPRICED DUE TO SCARCITY
RANDOMLY INSERTED INTO PACKS

ICABH Bret Hit Man Hart
ICARS Ricky The Dragon Steamboat

2019 Topps WWE Road to WrestleMania Kiss

*SILVER/25: .6X TO 1.2X BASIC KISS
*GOLD/10: UNPRICED DUE TO SCARCITY
*RED/1: UNPRICED DUE TO SCARCITY
STATED PRINT RUN 50 SER.#'d SETS

KCEM Ember Moon 20.00 50.00
KCKS Kairi Sane 25.00 60.00
KCLE Lacey Evans 30.00 75.00
KCNA Naomi 15.00 40.00
KCTC Taynara Conti 30.00 75.00
KCVB Vanessa Borne 15.00 40.00

2019 Topps WWE Road to WrestleMania Mat Relics

*BRONZE/99: .5X TO 1.2X BASIC MEM
*BLUE/50: .6X TO 1.5X BASIC MEM
*SILVER/25: .75X TO 2X BASIC MEM
*GOLD/10: UNPRICED DUE TO SCARCITY
*RED/1: UNPRICED DUE TO SCARCITY
RANDOMLY INSERTED INTO PACKS

MRAA Andrade Cien Almas 2.50 6.00
MRAB Alexa Bliss 10.00 25.00
MRAC Adam Cole 3.00 8.00
MRAJ AJ Styles 3.00 8.00
MRAS Asuka 5.00 12.00
MRBA Batista 4.00 10.00
MRBS Braun Strowman 2.50 6.00
MRCA Cedric Alexander 2.00 5.00
MRCF Charlotte Flair 5.00 12.00
MRDB Daniel Bryan 3.00 8.00
MREM Ember Moon 3.00 8.00
MRFB Finn Balor 3.00 8.00
MRJC John Cena 4.00 10.00
MRJG Johnny Gargano 2.50 6.00
MRKA Kurt Angle 3.00 8.00
MRKD Killian Dain 2.00 5.00
MRKO Kevin Owens 2.00 5.00
MRLS Lars Sullivan 1.50 4.00
MRMH Woken Matt Hardy 2.50 6.00
MRNA Naomi 4.00 10.00
MRNJ Nia Jax 2.00 5.00
MRPD Pete Dunne 3.00 8.00
MRRC Ricochet 3.00 8.00
MRRR Roman Reigns 4.00 10.00
MRRS Roderick Strong 2.50 6.00
MRSB Shayna Baszler 3.00 8.00
MRSN Shinsuke Nakamura 2.50 6.00
MRSR Seth Rollins 3.00 8.00
MRSZ Sami Zayn 1.50 4.00
MRTC Tommaso Ciampa 2.50 6.00
MRTM The Miz 2.00 5.00
MRUN Undertaker 5.00 12.00
MRVD Velveteen Dream 3.00 8.00
MRALB Aleister Black 3.00 8.00
MREC3 EC3 1.50 4.00
MRERA Kyle O'Reilly 2.50 6.00
MRHHH Triple H 3.00 8.00
MRRRR Ronda Rousey 6.00 15.00
MRSMC Stephanie McMahon 3.00 8.00
MRWWE Elias 2.00 5.00

2019 Topps WWE Road to WrestleMania Shirt Relics

*BRONZE/99: .5X TO 1.2X BASIC MEM
*BLUE/50: .6X TO 1.5X BASIC MEM
*SILVER/25: .75X TO 2X BASIC MEM
*GOLD/10: UNPRICED DUE TO SCARCITY
*RED/1: UNPRICED DUE TO SCARCITY
RANDOMLY INSERTED INTO PACKS

SRAB Alexa Bliss 15.00 30.00
SRAE Aiden English 2.50 6.00
SRAF Alicia Fox 5.00 12.00
SRBS Braun Strowman 2.50 6.00
SRCM Carmella 4.00 10.00
SRDB Daniel Bryan 3.00 8.00
SRFB Finn Balor 3.00 8.00
SRJC John Cena 4.00 10.00
SRJH Jeff Hardy 2.50 6.00
SRMH Woken Matt Hardy 4.00 10.00
SRRD Rusev 3.00 8.00
SRRR Roman Reigns 5.00 12.00
SRRY Renee Young 2.50 6.00
SRSR Seth Rollins 4.00 10.00
SRTM The Miz 2.50 6.00
SRWWE Elias 5.00 12.00

2019 Topps WWE Road to WrestleMania Update

COMPLETE SET (20) 8.00 20.00
RANDOMLY INSERTED INTO PACKS

U1 No Way Jose .50 1.25
U2 Jeff Hardy 1.00 2.50
U3 Bobby Lashley .75 2.00
U4 Samoa Joe .75 2.00
U5 Jeff Hardy 1.00 2.50
U6 AOP .60 1.50
U7 Kevin Owens and Sami Zayn 1.00 2.50
U8 Dolph Ziggler and Drew McIntyre .75 2.00
U9 Kalisto .40 1.00
U10 Drew Gulak .40 1.00
U11 Buddy Murphy .50 1.25
U12 Lince Dorado .40 1.00
U13 Paige 1.50 4.00
U14 Usos .50 1.25
U15 Randy Orton 1.00 2.50
U16 Shinsuke Nakamura 1.00 2.50
U17 Jeff Hardy 1.00 2.50
U18 Harper .50 1.25
U19 Samoa Joe .75 2.00
U20 AJ Styles & Daniel Bryan 2.00 5.00

2019 Topps WWE Road to WrestleMania WrestleMania 35 Roster

COMPLETE SET (50) 6.00 15.00
RANDOMLY INSERTED INTO PACKS

WM1 Paul Heyman .40 1.00
WM2 AJ Styles 1.50 4.00
WM3 Shinsuke Nakamura .75 2.00
WM4 Undertaker 1.50 4.00
WM5 John Cena 1.50 4.00
WM6 Elias .60 1.50
WM7 Kurt Angle .60 1.50
WM8 Ronda Rousey 1.50 4.00
WM9 Triple H .75 2.00
WM10 Stephanie McMahon .75 2.00
WM11 Charlotte Flair 1.25 3.00
WM12 Asuka 1.00 2.50
WM13 Nia Jax .60 1.50
WM14 Alexa Bliss 1.50 4.00
WM15 Daniel Bryan .75 2.00
WM16 Shane McMahon .75 2.00
WM17 Kevin Owens .75 2.00
WM18 Sami Zayn .60 1.50
WM19 Seth Rollins .75 2.00
WM20 The Miz .60 1.50
WM21 Finn Balor .60 1.50
WM22 Jinder Mahal .60 1.50
WM23 Randy Orton .75 2.00
WM24 Bobby Roode .60 1.50
WM25 Rusev .60 1.50
WM26 Aiden English .30 .75
WM27 Braun Strowman .75 2.00
WM28 Cesaro .40 1.00
WM29 Sheamus .50 1.25
WM30 Harper .40 1.00
WM31 Rowan .30 .75
WM32 Jey Uso .40 1.00
WM33 Jimmy Uso .40 1.00
WM34 Big E .30 .75
WM35 Kofi Kingston .50 1.25
WM36 Xavier Woods .40 1.00
WM37 Cedric Alexander .30 .75
WM38 Mustafa Ali .30 .75
WM39 Woken Matt Hardy .60 1.50
WM40 Bray Wyatt .75 2.00
WM41 Naomi .50 1.25
WM42 Bayley .60 1.50
WM43 Sasha Banks 1.25 3.00
WM44 Samoa Joe .60 1.50
WM45 Jeff Hardy .75 2.00
WM46 Bobby Lashley .60 1.50
WM47 Ember Moon .75 2.00
WM48 Carmella .75 2.00
WM49 Ruby Riott .60 1.50
WM50 Liv Morgan 1.00 2.50

2020 Topps WWE Road to WrestleMania

COMPLETE SET (100) 12.00 30.00
*FOILBOARD: .5X TO 1.2X BASIC CARDS
*BLUE/99: 1.2X TO 3X BASIC CARDS
*SILVER/25: UNPRICED DUE TO SCARCITY
*GOLD/10: UNPRICED DUE TO SCARCITY
*RED/1: UNPRICED DUE TO SCARCITY
*P.P.BLACK/1: UNPRICED DUE TO SCARCITY
*P.P.CYAN/1: UNPRICED DUE TO SCARCITY
*P.P.MAGENTA/1: UNPRICED DUE TO SCARCITY
*P.P.YELLOW/1: UNPRICED DUE TO SCARCITY

1 Lince Dorado & Gran Metalik .25 .60
2 Buddy Murphy .30 .75
3 Buddy Murphy .30 .75

#	Card	Low	High
4	Buddy Murphy	.30	.75
5	Buddy Murphy	.30	.75
6	Noam Dar	.25	.60
7	Buddy Murphy	.40	1.00
8	Buddy Murphy	.30	.75
9	Tony Nese	.25	.60
10	Buddy Murphy	.30	.75
11	Tony Nese	.25	.60
12	Tony Nese	.25	.60
13	Tony Nese	.25	.60
14	Tony Nese	.25	.60
15	Roman Reigns	.60	1.50
16	Seth Rollins	.50	1.25
17	Dolph Ziggler & Drew McIntyre	.50	1.25
18	Brock Lesnar	1.00	2.50
19	Dolph Ziggler & Drew McIntyre	.50	1.25
20	Seattle Hates The Elias & KO Show	.30	.75
21	Triple H	1.00	2.50
22	Roman Reigns	.60	1.50
23	Dolph Ziggler	.25	.60
24	Brock Lesnar	1.00	2.50
25	D-Generation X	1.00	2.50
26	Drew McIntyre	.50	1.25
27	AOP	.30	.75
28	Seth Rollins	.50	1.25
29	Brock Lesnar	1.00	2.50
30	Team RAW Def. Team SmackDown	.60	1.50
31	AOP	.30	.75
32	Robert Roode & Chad Gable	.25	.60
33	Finn Balor	.60	1.50
34	Cena/Balor/Rollins	.60	1.50
35	Bobby Lashley	.50	1.25
36	Seth Rollins	.50	1.25
37	Brock Lesnar	1.00	2.50
38	The Revival	.25	.60
39	Baron Corbin	.30	.75
40	Seth Rollins	1.00	2.50
41	The Revival	.25	.60
42	Finn Balor	.60	1.50
43	Baron Corbin	.30	.75
44	Batista Returns	.40	1.00
45	Roman Reigns Returns	.60	1.50
46	Seth Rollins	.50	1.25
47	Bobby Lashley	.50	1.25
48	Kurt Angle	.60	1.50
49	Kurt Angle	.60	1.50
50	Drew McIntyre	.50	1.25
51	Baron Corbin	.30	.75
52	Curt Hawkins & Zack Ryder	.25	.60
53	Braun Strowman	.60	1.50
54	Seth Rollins	.50	1.25
55	Roman Reigns	.60	1.50
56	Triple H	.60	1.50
57	Baron Corbin	.30	.75
58	The Demon Finn Balor	.60	1.50
59	The New Day	.40	1.00
60	Daniel Bryan	.75	2.00
61	Randy Orton	.60	1.50
62	AJ Styles	.75	2.00
63	Shinsuke Nakamura	.50	1.25
64	The New Day	.40	1.00
65	AJ Styles	.75	2.00
66	Randy Orton	.60	1.50
67	Big Show Helps The Bar	.30	.75
68	The Miz	.40	1.00
69	The Miz	.50	1.25
70	Rey Mysterio	.50	1.25
71	Daniel Bryan	.75	2.00
72	The New Daniel Bryan	.75	2.00
73	The New Daniel Bryan	.75	2.00
74	The Bar	.30	.75
75	AJ Styles & Mustafa Ali	.75	2.00
76	Mustafa Ali	.40	1.00
77	Rusev	.30	.75
78	AJ Styles	.75	2.00
79	Samoa Joe & Andrade	.40	1.00
80	Andrade	.50	1.25
81	Rey Mysterio and Andrade	.50	1.25
82	Shinsuke Nakamura	.50	1.25
83	The Miz & Shane McMahon	.40	1.00
84	Erick Rowan	.25	.60
85	R-Truth	.25	.60
86	R-Truth	.25	.60
87	The Usos	.25	.60
88	The New Daniel Bryan	.75	2.00
89	Samoa Joe	.40	1.00
90	The Usos	.25	.60
91	The Bar	.30	.75
92	Samoa Joe	.40	1.00
93	The New Daniel Bryan	.75	2.00
94	Kofi Kingston	.40	1.00
95	The New Day	.25	.60
96	AJ Styles	.75	2.00
97	The Usos	.25	.60
98	Shane McMahon	.40	1.00
99	Samoa Joe	.40	1.00
100	Kofi Kingston	.75	2.00

2020 Topps WWE Road to WrestleMania Andre the Giant Battle Royal Commemorative Trophy Relics

*BRONZE/99: .5X TO 1.2X BASIC MEM
*BLUE/50: .6X TO 1.5X BASIC MEM
*SILVER/25: UNPRICED DUE TO SCARCITY
*GOLD/10: UNPRICED DUE TO SCARCITY
*RED/1: UNPRICED DUE TO SCARCITY
STATED PRINT RUN 199 SER.#'d SETS

Code	Card	Low	High
AGAC	Apollo Crews	2.00	5.00
AGAD	Andrade	2.50	6.00
AGAL	Ali	2.50	6.00
AGBS	Braun Strowman	4.00	10.00
AGCA	Curtis Axel	2.00	5.00
AGGM	Gran Metalik	4.00	10.00
AGJH	Jeff Hardy	5.00	12.00
AGJM	Jinder Mahal	2.00	5.00
AGKA	Karl Anderson	2.50	6.00
AGKL	Kalisto	2.50	6.00
AGLD	Lince Dorado	2.00	5.00
AGMH	Matt Hardy	4.00	10.00
AGOT	Otis	6.00	15.00
AGRR	Robert Roode	3.00	8.00
AGSB	Shelton Benjamin	2.50	6.00
AGTB	Tyler Breeze	2.50	6.00
AGTK	Tucker	2.00	5.00

2020 Topps WWE Road to WrestleMania Autographed Andre the Giant Battle Royal Commemorative Trophy Relics

*RED/1: UNPRICED DUE TO SCARCITY
STATED PRINT RUN 10 SER.#'d SETS
UNPRICED DUE TO SCARCITY

AGAAC Apollo Crews
AGAAD Andrade
AGAAL Ali
AGABS Braun Strowman
AGAGM Gran Metalik
AGAJH Jeff Hardy
AGAJM Jinder Mahal
AGAMH Matt Hardy
AGAOT Otis
AGATK Tucker

2020 Topps WWE Road to WrestleMania Autographed Hall of Fame Headliner Tribute Relic

HOFHTM Honky Tonk Man

2020 Topps WWE Road to WrestleMania Autographed Mat Relics

*RED/1: UNPRICED DUE TO SCARCITY
STATED PRINT RUN 10 SER.#'d SETS
UNPRICED DUE TO SCARCITY

MRAAC Adam Cole
MRAAJ AJ Styles
MRABC Becky Lynch
MRABK Billie Kay
MRABP Beth Phoenix
MRACM Carmella
MRAKA Kurt Angle
MRAKK Kofi Kingston
MRAPR Peyton Royce
MRARR Roman Reigns
MRASB Shayna Baszler
MRASJ Samoa Joe
MRAVD Velveteen Dream
MRAZR Zack Ryder

2020 Topps WWE Road to WrestleMania Autographed Shirt Relics

*RED/1: UNPRICED DUE TO SCARCITY
STATED PRINT RUN 10 SER.#'d SETS
UNPRICED DUE TO SCARCITY

SRAAB Aleister Black
SRAAD Andrade
SRAAJ AJ Styles
SRABB Bobby Lashley
SRABD Bo Dallas
SRABS Braun Strowman
SRACA Curtis Axel
SRAEL Elias
SRAFB Finn Balor
SRANJ No Way Jose
SRARC Ricochet
SRARR Ronda Rousey
SRAZR Zack Ryder

2020 Topps WWE Road to WrestleMania Autographed Women's WrestleMania Battle Royal Commemorative Trophy Relics

*RED/1: UNPRICED DUE TO SCARCITY
STATED PRINT RUN 10 SER.#'d SETS
UNPRICED DUE TO SCARCITY

WRAAS Asuka
WRACM Carmella
WRADB Dana Brooke
WRAEM Ember Moon
WRAKS Kairi Sane
WRAMJ Mickie James
WRAMK Maria Kanellis
WRAMR Mandy Rose
WRANC Nikki Cross
WRANM Naomi
WRASD Sonya Deville
WRASL Sarah Logan
WRAZV Zelina Vega

2020 Topps WWE Road to WrestleMania Autographs

*BLUE/50: .5X TO 1.2X BASIC AUTOS
*SILVER/25: UNPRICED DUE TO SCARCITY
*GOLD/10: UNPRICED DUE TO SCARCITY
*RED/1: UNPRICED DUE TO SCARCITY
*P.P.BLACK/1: UNPRICED DUE TO SCARCITY
*P.P.CYAN/1: UNPRICED DUE TO SCARCITY
*P.P.MAGENTA/1: UNPRICED DUE TO SCARCITY
*P.P.YELLOW/1: UNPRICED DUE TO SCARCITY
STATED PRINT RUN 99 SER.#'d SETS

Code	Card	Low	High
AAB	Alexa Bliss	60.00	120.00
AAJ	AJ Styles	10.00	25.00
AAL	Aleister Black	12.00	30.00
AAS	Asuka	25.00	60.00
ABK	Becky Lynch	30.00	75.00
ABS	Braun Strowman	15.00	40.00
ABW	Bray Wyatt	12.00	30.00
ACM	Carmella	15.00	40.00
ADB	Daniel Bryan	10.00	25.00
AKK	Kofi Kingston	6.00	15.00
AKO	Kevin Owens	8.00	20.00
AKS	Kairi Sane	15.00	40.00
ALE	Lacey Evans	12.00	30.00
AMA	Ali	6.00	15.00
ARC	Ricochet	10.00	25.00
ARR	Roman Reigns	10.00	25.00
ASB	Sasha Banks	25.00	60.00
ASJ	Samoa Joe	6.00	15.00
ASN	Shinsuke Nakamura	8.00	20.00
ASR	Seth Rollins	12.00	30.00
ATM	The Miz	6.00	15.00

2020 Topps WWE Road to WrestleMania Dual Autographs

*GOLD/10: UNPRICED DUE TO SCARCITY
*RED/1: UNPRICED DUE TO SCARCITY
STATED PRINT RUN 25 SER.#'d SETS

Code	Card	Low	High
DAGB	K.Anderson/L.Gallows	25.00	60.00
DAHB	The Hardy Boyz	100.00	200.00
DAHM	Tucker/Otis	60.00	120.00
DAIG	Andrade/Z.Vega	30.00	75.00
DAII	B.Kay/P.Royce	100.00	200.00
DARV	S.Dawson/D.Wilder		

2020 Topps WWE Road to WrestleMania Hall of Fame Headliner Tribute

Code	Card	Low	High
	COMPLETE SET (16)	10.00	25.00
	FANDOMLY INSERTED INTO PACKS		
HF1	Honky Tonk Man	1.00	2.50
HF2	Honky Tonk Man	1.00	2.50
HF3	Honky Tonk Man	1.00	2.50
HF4	Honky Tonk Man	1.50	4.00
HF5	Honky Tonk Man	1.00	2.50
HF6	Honky Tonk Man	1.00	2.50
HF7	Honky Tonk Man	1.00	2.50
HF8	Honky Tonk Man	1.00	2.50
HF9	Honky Tonk Man	1.00	2.50
HF10	Honky Tonk Man	1.00	2.50
HF11	Honky Tonk Man	1.00	2.50
HF12	Honky Tonk Man	1.00	2.50
HF13	Honky Tonk Man	1.00	2.50
HF14	Honky Tonk Man	1.00	2.50
HF15	Honky Tonk Man	1.00	2.50
HF16	Honky Tonk Man	1.00	2.50

2020 Topps WWE Road to WrestleMania Hall of Fame Headliner Tribute Autographs

STATED PRINT RUN 10 SER.#'d SETS
UNPRICED DUE TO SCARCITY

HFA1 Honky Tonk Man
HFA2 Honky Tonk Man
HFA3 Honky Tonk Man
HFA4 Honky Tonk Man
HFA5 Honky Tonk Man
HFA6 Honky Tonk Man
HFA7 Honky Tonk Man
HFA8 Honky Tonk Man
HFA9 Honky Tonk Man
HFA10 Honky Tonk Man
HFA11 Honky Tonk Man
HFA12 Honky Tonk Man
HFA13 Honky Tonk Man
HFA14 Honky Tonk Man
HFA15 Honky Tonk Man
HFA16 Honky Tonk Man

2020 Topps WWE Road to WrestleMania Mat Relics

*BRONZE/99: .5X TO 1.2X BASIC MEM
*BLUE/50: .6X TO 1.5X BASIC MEM
*SILVER/25: UNPRICED DUE TO SCARCITY
*GOLD/10: UNPRICED DUE TO SCARCITY
*RED/1: UNPRICED DUE TO SCARCITY
STATED PRINT RUN 199 SER.#'d SETS

Code	Card	Low	High
MRAB	Aleister Black	2.00	5.00
MRAC	Adam Cole	5.00	12.00
MRAJ	AJ Styles	5.00	12.00
MRBB	Bianca Belair	4.00	10.00
MRBC	Becky Lynch	10.00	25.00
MRBK	Billie Kay	8.00	20.00
MRBM	Buddy Murphy	2.00	5.00
MRBP	Beth Phoenix	2.50	6.00
MRBS	Braun Strowman	4.00	10.00
MRBT	Batista	6.00	15.00
MRCF	Charlotte Flair	6.00	15.00
MRCH	Curt Hawkins	2.00	5.00
MRCM	Carmella	5.00	12.00
MRDB	Daniel Bryan	3.00	8.00
MRDM	Drew McIntyre	4.00	10.00
MRER	Erik	2.00	5.00
MRIS	Io Shirai	2.00	5.00
MRIV	Ivar	2.00	5.00

MRJG Johnny Gargano 2.50 6.00
MRKA Kurt Angle 3.00 8.00
MRKK Kofi Kingston 4.00 10.00
MRKS Kairi Sane 2.50 6.00
MRMR Matt Riddle 2.00 5.00
MRNT Natalya 3.00 8.00
MRPD Pete Dunne 2.00 5.00
MRPR Peyton Royce 6.00 15.00
MRRC Ricochet 2.50 6.00
MRRM Rey Mysterio 2.50 6.00
MRRR Roman Reigns 4.00 10.00
MRRS Ronda Rousey 8.00 20.00
MRSB Shayna Baszler 5.00 12.00
MRSJ Samoa Joe 3.00 8.00
MRTH Triple H 3.00 8.00
MRTM The Miz 2.50 6.00
MRTN Tony Nese 2.00 5.00
MRVD Velveteen Dream 2.00 5.00
MRWT Walter 2.50 6.00
MRZR Zack Ryder 10.00 25.00
MRJEY Jey Uso 2.50 6.00
MRJIM Jimmy Uso 2.50 6.00

2020 Topps WWE Road to WrestleMania Shirt Relics

*BRONZE/99: .5X TO 1.2X BASIC MEM
*BLUE/50: .6X TO 1.5X BASIC MEM
*SILVER/25: UNPRICED DUE TO SCARCITY
*GOLD/10: UNPRICED DUE TO SCARCITY
*RED/1: UNPRICED DUE TO SCARCITY
STATED PRINT RUN 199 SER.#'d SETS

SRAB Aleister Black 4.00 10.00
SRAD Andrade 2.50 6.00
SRAJ AJ Styles 5.00 12.00
SRBB Bobby Lashley 3.00 8.00
SRBD Bo Dallas 2.00 5.00
SRBH Bret Hit Man Hart 8.00 20.00
SRBL Brock Lesnar 4.00 10.00
SRBS Braun Strowman 3.00 8.00
SRBT Booker T 3.00 8.00
SRCA Curtis Axel 2.50 6.00
SREL Elias 2.50 6.00
SRFB Finn Balor 5.00 12.00
SRNJ No Way Jose 2.00 5.00
SRRR Ronda Rousey 20.00 50.00
SRSM Shawn Michaels 5.00 12.00
SRSR Stevie Ray 2.00 5.00
SRZR Zack Ryder 2.50 6.00

2020 Topps WWE Road to WrestleMania Six-Person Autograph Booklet

STATED PRINT RUN 10 SER.#'d SETS
UNPRICED DUE TO SCARCITY

ABCMITB Rousey/Flair/Rollins/Reigns/Kingston/Lynch

2020 Topps WWE Road to WrestleMania Triple Autographs

*GOLD/10: UNPRICED DUE TO SCARCITY
*RED/1: UNPRICED DUE TO SCARCITY
STATED PRINT RUN 25 SER.#'d SETS

TALP Dorado/Metalik/Kalisto 60.00 120.00
TAND Woods/Big E/Kingston 75.00 150.00

2020 Topps WWE Road to WrestleMania Winningest Superstars in WrestleMania History

COMPLETE SET (10) 6.00 15.00
RANDOMLY INSERTED INTO PACKS

WS1 Randy Orton 1.00 2.50
WS2 Shawn Michaels 1.00 2.50
WS3 Seth Rollins .75 2.00
WS4 Macho Man Randy Savage 1.25 3.00
WS5 Rey Mysterio .75 2.00
WS6 Kane .50 1.25
WS7 Bret Hit Man Hart 1.00 2.50
WS8 Triple H 1.00 2.50
WS9 John Cena 1.50 4.00
WS10 Undertaker 1.50 4.00

2020 Topps WWE Road to WrestleMania Winningest Superstars in WrestleMania History Autographs

*RED/1: UNPRICED DUE TO SCARCITY
STATED PRINT RUN 10 SER.#'d SETS
UNPRICED DUE TO SCARCITY

WSA1 Randy Orton
WSA2 Shawn Michaels
WSA3 Seth Rollins
WSA4 Rey Mysterio
WSA5 Bret Hit Man Hart

2020 Topps WWE Road to WrestleMania Women's WrestleMania Battle Royal Commemorative Trophy Relics

*BRONZE/99: .5X TO 1.2X BASIC MEM
*BLUE/50: .6X TO 1.5X BASIC MEM
*SILVER/25: UNPRICED DUE TO SCARCITY
*GOLD/10: UNPRICED DUE SCARCITY
*RED/1: UNPRICED DUE TO SCARCITY
STATED PRINT RUN 199 SER.#'d SETS

WRAS Asuka 6.00 15.00
WRCM Carmella 5.00 12.00
WRDB Dana Brooke 2.50 6.00
WREM Ember Moon 3.00 8.00
WRKS Kairi Sane 2.50 6.00
WRMJ Mickie James 4.00 10.00
WRMK Maria Kanellis 5.00 12.00
WRMR Mandy Rose 8.00 20.00
WRNC Nikki Cross 4.00 10.00
WRNM Naomi 2.50 6.00
WRSD Sonya Deville 3.00 8.00
WRSL Sarah Logan 2.50 6.00
WRZV Zelina Vega 3.00 8.00

2020 Topps WWE Road to WrestleMania WrestleMania Roster

COMPLETE SET (50) 12.00 30.00
RANDOMLY INSERTED INTO PACKS

WM1 AJ Styles 1.00 2.50
WM2 Aleister Black .60 1.50
WM3 Alexa Bliss 2.00 5.00
WM4 Mustafa Ali .50 1.25
WM5 Andrade .50 1.25
WM6 Asuka 1.25 3.00
WM7 King Corbin .40 1.00
WM8 Bayley .60 1.50
WM9 Becky Lynch 1.25 3.00
WM10 Big E .30 .75
WM11 Billie Kay .60 1.50
WM12 Bobby Lashley .60 1.50
WM13 Braun Strowman .75 2.00
WM14 The Fiend Bray Wyatt 1.00 2.50
WM15 Brock Lesnar 1.25 3.00
WM16 Buddy Murphy .40 1.00
WM17 Carmella .75 2.00
WM18 Cesaro .30 .75
WM19 Charlotte Flair 1.25 3.00
WM20 Daniel Bryan 1.00 2.50
WM21 Drew McIntyre .60 1.50
WM22 Elias .30 .75
WM23 Ember Moon .60 1.50
WM24 Erik .30 .75
WM25 Finn Balor .75 2.00
WM26 Ivar .30 .75
WM27 Jeff Hardy .75 2.00
WM28 John Cena 1.25 3.00
WM29 Kairi Sane .60 1.50
WM30 Kevin Owens .40 1.00
WM31 Kofi Kingston .50 1.25
WM32 Lacey Evans .75 2.00
WM33 Lars Sullivan .30 .75
WM34 Mandy Rose 1.50 4.00
WM35 Matt Hardy .60 1.50
WM36 Nikki Cross .60 1.50
WM37 Peyton Royce .60 1.50
WM38 Randy Orton .75 2.00
WM39 Rey Mysterio .60 1.50
WM40 Ricochet .50 1.25
WM41 Roman Reigns .75 2.00
WM42 R-Truth .30 .75
WM43 Sami Zayn .40 1.00
WM44 Samoa Joe .50 1.25
WM45 Seth Rollins .60 1.50
WM46 Shinsuke Nakamura .60 1.50
WM47 Sonya Deville .75 2.00
WM48 The Miz .50 1.25
WM49 Xavier Woods .30 .75
WM50 Zelina Vega .60 1.50

2020 Topps WWE Road to WrestleMania Yearly Records

COMPLETE SET (10) 8.00 20.00
BLASTER EXCLUSIVE

YR1 Asuka 2.50 6.00
YR2 Braun Strowman 1.50 4.00
YR3 Brock Lesnar 2.50 6.00
YR4 Carmella 1.50 4.00
YR5 Charlotte Flair 2.50 6.00
YR6 Daniel Bryan 2.00 5.00
YR7 Kofi Kingston 1.00 2.50
YR8 Mickie James 1.00 2.50
YR9 Pete Dunne .60 1.50
YR10 Seth Rollins 1.25 3.00

2020 Topps WWE Road to WrestleMania Yearly Records Autographs

*RED/1: UNPRICED DUE TO SCARCITY
STATED PRINT RUN 10 SER.#'d SETS
UNPRICED DUE TO SCARCITY

YRA1 Asuka
YRA2 Braun Strowman
YRA3 Carmella
YRA4 Kofi Kingston
YRA5 Seth Rollins

2021 Topps WWE Road to WrestleMania Stickers

1 Intro .15 .40
2 Intro .15 .40
3 Intro .15 .40
4 Intro .15 .40
5 Drew McIntyre .60 1.50
6 Drew McIntyre .60 1.50
7 Drew McIntyre .60 1.50
8 Drew McIntyre .60 1.50
9 Drew McIntyre .60 1.50
10 Drew McIntyre .60 1.50
11 Drew McIntyre .60 1.50
12 Drew McIntyre .60 1.50
13 Drew McIntyre .60 1.50
14 Drew McIntyre .60 1.50
15 Becky Lynch 1.00 2.50
16 Becky Lynch 1.00 2.50
17 Becky Lynch 1.00 2.50
18 Becky Lynch 1.00 2.50
19 Becky Lynch 1.00 2.50
20 Becky Lynch 1.00 2.50
21 Becky Lynch 1.00 2.50
22 Becky Lynch 1.00 2.50
23 Becky Lynch 1.00 2.50
24 Becky Lynch 1.00 2.50
25 The Fiend Bray Wyatt 1.00 2.50
26 The Fiend Bray Wyatt 1.00 2.50
27 The Fiend Bray Wyatt 1.00 2.50
28 The Fiend Bray Wyatt 1.00 2.50
29 The Fiend Bray Wyatt 1.00 2.50
30 The Fiend Bray Wyatt 1.00 2.50
31 The Fiend Bray Wyatt 1.00 2.50
32 The Fiend Bray Wyatt 1.00 2.50
33 The Fiend Bray Wyatt 1.00 2.50
34 The Fiend Bray Wyatt 1.00 2.50
35 Charlotte Flair 1.25 3.00
36 Charlotte Flair 1.25 3.00
37 Charlotte Flair 1.25 3.00
38 Charlotte Flair 1.25 3.00
39 Angel Garza .30 .75
40 Drew Gulak .30 .75
41 Big Show .50 1.25
42 Shayna Baszler .50 1.25
43 Lacey Evans .60 1.50
44 AJ Styles .75 2.00
45 AJ Styles .75 2.00
46 AJ Styles .75 2.00
47 AJ Styles .75 2.00
48 Mandy Rose 1.25 3.00
49 Dana Brooke .25 .60
50 Elias .25 .60
51 Nia Jax .50 1.25
52 Braun Strowman .60 1.50
53 Braun Strowman .60 1.50
54 Bobby Lashley .60 1.50
55 Bobby Lashley .60 1.50
56 Cedric Alexander .25 .60
57 MVP .25 .60
58 Shelton Benjamin .40 1.00
59 Akira Tozawa .30 .75
60 Randy Orton .75 2.00
61 Viking Raiders .25 .60
62 R-Truth .30 .75
63 Naomi .30 .75
64 Andrade .40 1.00
65 Nikki Cross .50 1.25
66 The New Day .50 1.25
67 The New Day .50 1.25
68 The Miz .40 1.00
69 Ricochet .50 1.25
70 Keith Lee .50 1.25
71 Keith Lee .50 1.25
72 Keith Lee .50 1.25
73 Keith Lee .50 1.25
74 Ali .30 .75
75 Retribution .25 .60
76 Retribution .25 .60
77 Lana .30 .75
78 Sheamus .40 1.00
79 Alexa Bliss 1.50 4.00
80 Alexa Bliss 1.50 4.00
81 Alexa Bliss 1.50 4.00
82 Gran Metalik .25 .60
83 John Morrison .50 1.25
84 Humberto Carrillo .25 .60
85 Humberto Carrillo .25 .60
86 Humberto Carrillo .25 .60
87 Jeff Hardy .60 1.50
88 Tucker .25 .60
89 Asuka 1.00 2.50
90 Asuka 1.00 2.50
91 Asuka 1.00 2.50
92 Edge 1.00 2.50
93 Edge 1.00 2.50
94 Charlotte Flair 1.25 3.00
95 Number One .15 .40
96 Surprise .15 .40
97 Most Eliminations .15 .40
98 Most Wins .15 .40
99 Champion .15 .40
100 History Maker .15 .40
101 1988 .15 .40
102 The People's Rumble .15 .40
103 Undertaker The Streak 1.25 3.00
104 Undertaker The Streak #1 1.25 3.00
105 Undertaker The Streak #6 1.25 3.00
106 Undertaker The Streak #7 1.25 3.00
107 Undertaker The Streak #9 1.25 3.00
108 Undertaker The Streak #12 1.25 3.00
109 Undertaker The Streak #14 1.25 3.00
110 Undertaker The Streak #17 1.25 3.00
111 Undertaker The Streak #21 1.25 3.00
112 WrestleMania .15 .40
113 WrestleMania X .15 .40
114 WrestleMania 13 .15 .40
115 WrestleMania XV .15 .40
116 WrestleMania X-Seven .15 .40
117 WrestleMania XX .15 .40
118 WrestleMania 25 .15 .40
119 WrestleMania XXX .15 .40
120 WrestleMania 36 .15 .40
121 Adam Cole .75 2.00
122 Adam Cole .75 2.00
123 Adam Cole .75 2.00
124 The Undisputed Era .40 1.00
125 Shotzi Blackheart 1.00 2.50
126 Dexter Lumis .25 .60
127 Johnny Gargano .50 1.25
128 Candice LeRae 1.00 2.50
129 Rhea Ripley .75 2.00
130 Damian Priest .40 1.00

131 Finn Balor .60 1.50
132 Karrion Kross 1.00 2.50
133 Dakota Kai .50 1.25
134 Pete Dunne .50 1.25
135 Kushida .40 1.00
136 Kushida .40 1.00
137 Kushida .40 1.00
138 Ember Moon .30 .75
139 Tommaso Ciampa .60 1.50
140 NXT UK .15 .40
141 Moustache Mountain .25 .60
142 Moustache Mountain .25 .60
143 Trent Seven .30 .75
144 Tyler Bate .30 .75
145 Ilja Dragunov .25 .60
146 Jordan Devlin .25 .60
147 Piper Niven .40 1.00
148 Gallus .30 .75
149 Kay Lee Ray .60 1.50
150 Andre the Giant 1.00 2.50
151 Macho Man Randy Savage 1.00 2.50
152 Ultimate Warrior 1.00 2.50
153 Rowdy Roddy Piper .60 1.50
154 Bret "Hit Man" Hart .60 1.50
155 Shawn Michaels 1.00 2.50
156 Undertaker 1.25 3.00
157 Stone Cold Steve Austin 1.25 3.00
158 The Rock 2.50 6.00
159 Triple H 1.00 2.50
160 Trish Stratus 1.25 3.00
161 Eddie Guerrero 1.25 3.00
162 Edge 1.00 2.50
163 John Cena 1.25 3.00
164 Randy Orton .75 2.00
165 Batista .50 1.25
166 Charlotte Flair 1.25 3.00
167 Becky Lynch 1.00 2.50
168 Roman Reigns 1.25 3.00
169 Roman Reigns 1.25 3.00
170 Roman Reigns 1.25 3.00
171 Roman Reigns 1.25 3.00
172 Roman Reigns 1.25 3.00
173 Roman Reigns 1.25 3.00
174 Roman Reigns 1.25 3.00
175 Roman Reigns 1.25 3.00
176 Roman Reigns 1.25 3.00
177 Roman Reigns 1.25 3.00
178 Roman Reigns 1.25 3.00
179 Sasha Banks 1.25 3.00
180 Sasha Banks 1.25 3.00
181 Sasha Banks 1.25 3.00
182 Sasha Banks 1.25 3.00
183 Sasha Banks 1.25 3.00
184 Sasha Banks 1.25 3.00
185 Sasha Banks 1.25 3.00
186 Sasha Banks 1.25 3.00
187 Sasha Banks 1.25 3.00
188 Sasha Banks 1.25 3.00
189 Seth Rollins .60 1.50
190 Seth Rollins .60 1.50
191 Seth Rollins .60 1.50
192 Seth Rollins .60 1.50
193 Seth Rollins .60 1.50
194 Seth Rollins .60 1.50
195 Seth Rollins .60 1.50
196 Seth Rollins .60 1.50
197 Seth Rollins .60 1.50
198 Seth Rollins .60 1.50
199 Bayley .60 1.50
200 Bayley .60 1.50
201 Bayley .60 1.50
202 Bayley .60 1.50
203 Rey Mysterio .60 1.50
204 Rey Mysterio .60 1.50
205 Rey Mysterio .60 1.50
206 Baron Corbin .25 .60
207 Baron Corbin .25 .60
208 SmackDown Fact .15 .40
209 Usos .25 .60
210 Usos .25 .60
211 Kevin Owens .50 1.25
212 Bo Dallas .25 .60
213 Big E .50 1.25
214 Big E .50 1.25
215 Big E .50 1.25
216 Mojo Rawley .25 .60
217 Tamina .30 .75
218 Cesaro .25 .60
219 Cesaro .25 .60
220 Cesaro .25 .60
221 Billie Kay .50 1.25
222 Dolph Ziggler .50 1.25
223 Dolph Ziggler .50 1.25
224 Dolph Ziggler .50 1.25
225 Street Profits .25 .60
226 Street Profits .25 .60
227 Street Profits .25 .60
228 Chad Gable .25 .60
229 Apollo Crews .30 .75
230 Murphy .30 .75
231 The Riott Squad .40 1.00
232 The Riott Squad .40 1.00
233 Aleister Black .60 1.50
234 Bianca Belair .60 1.50
235 Bianca Belair .60 1.50
236 Bianca Belair .60 1.50
237 Sami Zayn .40 1.00
238 Kalisto .30 .75
239 SmackDown Fact .15 .40
240 Daniel Bryan 1.00 2.50
241 Daniel Bryan 1.00 2.50
242 Daniel Bryan 1.00 2.50
243 Natalya .40 1.00
244 Lars Sullivan .25 .60
245 Otis .30 .75
246 Otis .30 .75
247 Kane .40 1.00
248 Shinsuke Nakamura .60 1.50
249 Shinsuke Nakamura .60 1.50
250 Wesley Blake .25 .60
251 Jaxson Ryker .25 .60
252 Steve Cutler .25 .60
253 Carmella .60 1.50
254 Carmella .60 1.50
255 Carmella .60 1.50
256 Robert Roode .30 .75
257 Mickie James .50 1.25
258 Main Event Shocker .15 .40
259 Fantastic Flair .15 .40
260 Super Cena 1.25 3.00
261 Hardcore Hell .15 .40
262 Air Shane .50 1.25
263 Macho Marathon 1.00 2.50
264 Asuka's Run Ended 1.00 2.50
265 Magic Mysterio .60 1.50
266 Money, Money, Money .15 .40
267 Mega Match .15 .40
268 Bret Wins Big .60 1.50
269 His Time Is Now 1.25 3.00
270 KO to Big Show .15 .40
271 The Last Ride .15 .40
272 I'm Sorry, I Love You .15 .40
273 You Never Saw It Coming .15 .40
274 Warrior to the Rescue 1.00 2.50
275 Greatest Rivals .15 .40
276 Wyatt's World 1.00 2.50
277 Legends of the Ladder .15 .40
278 Super Spear .15 .40
279 The Boyz Are Back .60 1.50
280 Dream Match .15 .40
281 Austin Era Begins 1.25 3.00
282 Match Made in Heaven .15 .40
283 Kofi-Mania .60 1.50
284 The Ultimate Challenge .15 .40
285 Best of British .15 .40
286 The Boyhood Dream 1.00 2.50
287 Becky Two Belts 1.00 2.50
288 Stone Cold Classic 1.25 3.00
289 Icon vs. Icon 2.50 6.00
290 Drama in the Cell .15 .40
291 Yes .15 .40
292 End of the Streak 1.25 3.00
293 Heist of the Century .15 .40
294 The Greatest of Them All .15 .40
295 Sami Zayn .40 1.00
296 Bianca Belair .60 1.50
297 Seth Rollins .60 1.50
298 Alexa Bliss 1.50 4.00
299 Kofi Kingston .60 1.50
300 Big Show .50 1.25
301 Becky Lynch 1.00 2.50
302 Charlotte Flair 1.25 3.00
303 Cesaro .25 .60
304 Mandy Rose 1.25 3.00

2021 Topps WWE Road to WrestleMania Stickers Autographs

STATED PRINT RUN 100 ANNCD SETS
AA1 Big E 20.00 50.00
AA2 Becky Lynch 60.00 120.00
AA3 Walter 30.00 75.00
AA4 Trent Seven 30.00 75.00
AA5 Naomi 50.00 100.00

2021 Topps WWE Road to WrestleMania Stickers Firefly Funhouse Pop-Up Card

NNO Bray Wyatt 2.00 5.00

2021 Topps WWE Road to WrestleMania Stickers Gold XL

T1 Icons
T2 Superstars
T3 Future Legends

2021 Topps WWE Road to WrestleMania Stickers Limited Edition

LE1 The Rock 2.00 5.00
LE2 The Fiend Bray Wyatt 2.50 6.00
LE3 Roman Reigns 1.50 4.00
LE4 Sasha Banks 1.50 4.00

2021 Topps WWE Road to WrestleMania Stickers Tins

NNO McIntyre/Bliss/Orton/Lashley/Strowman
NNO Rose/Banks/Bayley/Rollins/Styles
NNO Ripley/Fiend/Shirai/Reigns/Big E

2016 Topps WWE The Rock Tribute

COMPLETE SET (40) 6.00 15.00
STATED ODDS 1:6
1 The Rock 1.00 2.50
2 The Rock 1.00 2.50
3 The Rock 1.00 2.50
4 The Rock 1.00 2.50
5 The Rock 1.00 2.50
6 The Rock 1.00 2.50
7 The Rock 1.00 2.50
8 The Rock 1.00 2.50
9 The Rock 1.00 2.50
10 The Rock 1.00 2.50
11 The Rock 1.00 2.50
12 The Rock 1.00 2.50
13 The Rock 1.00 2.50
14 The Rock 1.00 2.50
15 The Rock 1.00 2.50
16 The Rock 1.00 2.50
17 The Rock 1.00 2.50
18 The Rock 1.00 2.50
19 The Rock 1.00 2.50
20 The Rock 1.00 2.50
21 The Rock 1.00 2.50
22 The Rock 1.00 2.50
23 The Rock 1.00 2.50
24 The Rock 1.00 2.50
25 The Rock 1.00 2.50
26 The Rock 1.00 2.50
27 The Rock 1.00 2.50
28 The Rock 1.00 2.50
29 The Rock 1.00 2.50
30 The Rock 1.00 2.50
31 The Rock 1.00 2.50
32 The Rock 1.00 2.50
33 The Rock 1.00 2.50
34 The Rock 1.00 2.50
35 The Rock 1.00 2.50
36 The Rock 1.00 2.50
37 The Rock 1.00 2.50
38 The Rock 1.00 2.50
39 The Rock 1.00 2.50
40 The Rock 1.00 2.50

2019 Topps WWE Roman Reigns Leukemia and Lymphoma Society Set

COMPLETE SET (11) 8.00 20.00
STATED PRINT RUN 101 ANNCD SETS
1 Survivor Series 2013 1.25 3.00
2 Royal Rumble 2014 1.25 3.00
3 Fastlane 2015 1.25 3.00
4 Extreme Rules 2015 1.25 3.00
5 WrestleMania 32 1.25 3.00
6 Extreme Rules 2016 1.25 3.00
7 WrestleMania 33 1.25 3.00
8 No Mercy 2017 1.25 3.00
9 SummerSlam 2018 1.25 3.00
10 RAW Return 2019 1.25 3.00
11 LLS 1.25 3.00

2019 Topps WWE Ronda Rousey Spotlight Complete Series

COMPLETE SET (40) 25.00 60.00
CARDS (1-10) EXCLUSIVE TO ROAD TO WRESTLE-MANIA
CARDS (11-20) EXCLUSIVE TO WWE RAW
CARDS (21-30) EXCLUSIVE TO WWE SUMMERSLAM
CARDS (31-40) EXCLUSIVE TO SMACKDOWN LIVE
1 Helps Rock Fend Off HHH/Stephanie 1.25 3.00
2 Crashes Women's Royal Rumble 1.25 3.00
3 WWE Contract 1.25 3.00
4 Confronts HHH & Stephanie 1.25 3.00
5 Takes Down Stephanie 1.25 3.00
6 Rebuffs Absolution 1.25 3.00
7 Teams w/Kurt Angle 1.25 3.00
8 Armbars Stephanie Twice 1.25 3.00
9 Helps Natalya 1.25 3.00
10 Armbars Mickie James 1.25 3.00
11 Chases off Alexa Bliss 1.25 3.00
12 Confronts Nia Jax 1.25 3.00
13 Signs Contract for Title Match 1.25 3.00
14 Armbars Nia Jax 1.25 3.00
15 Defeats Nia Jax by DQ 1.25 3.00
16 Is Suspended 1.25 3.00
17 Violates Her Suspension 1.25 3.00
18 Wins Her RAW Debut 1.25 3.00
19 Defeats Alexa Bliss for Title 1.25 3.00
20 Attacks Stephanie McMahon 1.25 3.00
21 Works with Trish Stratus 1.25 3.00
22 Stops Alexa Bliss & Alicia Fox 1.25 3.00
23 Teams with Natalya 1.25 3.00
24 Defends Title Against Bliss 1.25 3.00
25 Defeats Rudy Riott 1.25 3.00
26 Crashes Negotiations 1.25 3.00
27 Toe-to-Toe w/Charlotte Flair 1.25 3.00
28 Defeats Mickie James 1.25 3.00
29 Teams with Ember Moon 1.25 3.00
30 Watches Ember Moon's Back 1.25 3.00
31 Defends Women's Title Against Nia 1.25 3.00
32 Tries to Issue Open Challenge 1.25 3.00
33 Defeats Natalya to Retain Title 1.25 3.00
34 Teams with Natalya 1.25 3.00
35 Appears A Moment of Bliss 1.25 3.00
36 Tags with Sasha Banks 1.25 3.00
37 Defeats Bayley in Open Challenge 1.25 3.00
38 Defeats Liv Morgan & Sarah Logan 1.25 3.00
39 Attacks Becky Lynch 1.25 3.00
40 Defeats Dana Brooke 1.25 3.00

2010 Topps WWE Rumble Pack

COMPLETE SET (50) 5.00 12.00
1 Big Show .30 .75
2 Big Show .30 .75
3 Carlito .30 .75
4 Chris Jericho .30 .75
5 Christian .20 .50
6 Christian .20 .50
7 CM Punk .50 1.25
8 Cody Rhodes .12 .30
9 Cody Rhodes .12 .30
10 Evan Bourne .12 .30
11 Evan Bourne .12 .30
12 Hornswoggle .20 .50
13 Hornswoggle .20 .50
14 Yoshi Tatsu .12 .30
15 Yoshi Tatsu .12 .30

16 Jack Swagger .12 .30
17 Jack Swagger .12 .30
18 John Cena .60 1.50
19 John Cena .60 1.50
20 John Morrison .15 .40
21 John Morrison .15 .40
22 Kane .30 .75
23 Kane .30 .75
24 Kofi Kingston .20 .50
25 Kofi Kingston .20 .50
26 Kung Fu Naki .12 .30
27 Matt Hardy .30 .75
28 MVP .20 .50
29 MVP .20 .50
30 Primo .12 .30
31 R-Truth .12 .30
32 R-Truth .12 .30
33 Randy Orton .50 1.25
34 Randy Orton .50 1.25
35 Rey Mysterio .30 .75
36 Rey Mysterio .30 .75
37 Santino Marella .12 .30
38 Shawn Michaels .75 2.00
39 Shawn Michaels .75 2.00
40 Sheamus .20 .50
41 Ted DiBiase .20 .50
42 The Miz .20 .50
43 Undertaker .50 1.25
44 Triple H .60 1.50
45 Triple H .60 1.50
46 Edge .50 1.25
47 Edge .50 1.25
48 Batista .50 1.25
49 Batista .50 1.25
50 Checklist .12 .30

2010 Topps WWE Rumble Pack Finger Puppets

COMPLETE SET (10) 3.00 8.00
STATED ODDS 1:4

1 Shawn Michaels 1.25 3.00
2 Rey Mysterio .50 1.25
3 CM Punk .75 2.00
4 Hornswoggle .30 .75
5 Mark Henry .30 .75
6 Hurricane Helms .20 .50
7 Triple H 1.00 2.50
8 R-Truth .20 .50
9 Dolph Ziggler .30 .75
10 MVP .30 .75

2010 Topps WWE Rumble Pack Glow-in-the-Dark

COMPLETE SET (10) 4.00 10.00
STATED ODDS 1:6

1 John Cena 1.25 3.00
2 Undertaker 1.00 2.50
3 Rey Mysterio .60 1.50
4 Yoshi Tatsu .25 .60
5 The Miz .40 1.00
6 Big Show .60 1.50
7 Shawn Michaels 1.50 4.00
8 Triple H 1.25 3.00
9 Carlito .60 1.50
10 Jack Swagger .25 .60

2010 Topps WWE Rumble Pack Hidden Images

COMPLETE SET (10) 4.00 10.00
STATED ODDS 1:6

1 John Cena 1.25 3.00
2 MVP .40 1.00
3 Undertaker 1.00 2.50
4 Evan Bourne .25 .60
5 CM Punk 1.00 2.50
6 Triple H 1.25 3.00
7 Christian .40 1.00
8 Kane .60 1.50
9 Chris Jericho .60 1.50
10 Rey Mysterio .60 1.50

2010 Topps WWE Rumble Pack Pop-Ups

COMPLETE SET (9) 3.00 8.00
STATED ODDS 1:4

1 John Cena 1.00 2.50
2 Sheamus .30 .75
3 Undertaker .75 2.00
4 Triple H 1.00 2.50
5 Evan Bourne .20 .50
6 Randy Orton .75 2.00
7 John Morrison .25 .60
8 The Miz .30 .75
9 Edge .75 2.00

2010 Topps WWE Rumble Pack Stickers

COMPLETE SET (30) 6.00 15.00
STATED ODDS 2:1

1 John Cena .75 2.00
2 John Cena .75 2.00
3 John Cena .75 2.00
4 Triple H .75 2.00
5 Triple H .75 2.00
6 Triple H .75 2.00
7 Undertaker .60 1.50
8 Undertaker .60 1.50
9 Undertaker .60 1.50
10 Rey Mysterio .40 1.00
11 Rey Mysterio .40 1.00
12 Rey Mysterio .40 1.00
13 Edge .60 1.50
14 Edge .60 1.50
15 Edge .60 1.50
16 Batista .60 1.50
17 Batista .60 1.50
18 Batista .60 1.50
19 Shawn Michaels 1.00 2.50
20 Shawn Michaels 1.00 2.50
21 Shawn Michaels 1.00 2.50
22 CM Punk .60 1.50
23 CM Punk .60 1.50
24 CM Punk .60 1.50
25 Randy Orton .60 1.50
26 Randy Orton .60 1.50
27 Randy Orton .60 1.50
28 Kane .40 1.00
29 Kofi Kingston .25 .60
30 DX CL 1.00 2.50

2010 Topps WWE Rumble Pack Tattoos

COMPLETE SET (10) 5.00 12.00
STATED ODDS 1:6

1 Kofi Kingston/Randy Orton 1.00 2.50
2 Christian/William Regal .60 1.50
3 Triple H/Edge 1.25 3.00
4 Kane/Big Show .60 1.50
5 Batista/The Undertaker 1.00 2.50
6 MVP/Jack Swagger .40 1.00
7 Shawn Michaels/Chris Jericho 1.50 4.00
8 Rey Mysterio/CM Punk 1.00 2.50
9 John Morrison/The Miz .40 1.00
10 John Cena/Sheamus 1.25 3.00

2018 Topps WWE Shawn Michaels Tribute

1 Shawn Michaels 1.25 3.00
2 Shawn Michaels 1.25 3.00
3 Shawn Michaels 1.25 3.00
4 Shawn Michaels 1.25 3.00
5 Shawn Michaels 1.25 3.00
6 Shawn Michaels 1.25 3.00
7 Shawn Michaels 1.25 3.00
8 Shawn Michaels 1.25 3.00
9 Shawn Michaels 1.25 3.00
10 Shawn Michaels 1.25 3.00
11 Shawn Michaels 1.25 3.00
12 Shawn Michaels 1.25 3.00
13 Shawn Michaels 1.25 3.00
14 Shawn Michaels 1.25 3.00
15 Shawn Michaels 1.25 3.00
16 Shawn Michaels 1.25 3.00
17 Shawn Michaels 1.25 3.00
18 Shawn Michaels 1.25 3.00
19 Shawn Michaels 1.25 3.00
20 Shawn Michaels 1.25 3.00
21 Shawn Michaels 1.25 3.00
22 Shawn Michaels 1.25 3.00
23 Shawn Michaels 1.25 3.00
24 Shawn Michaels 1.25 3.00
25 Shawn Michaels 1.25 3.00
26 Shawn Michaels 1.25 3.00
27 Shawn Michaels 1.25 3.00
28 Shawn Michaels 1.25 3.00
29 Shawn Michaels 1.25 3.00
30 Shawn Michaels 1.25 3.00
31 Shawn Michaels 1.25 3.00
32 Shawn Michaels 1.25 3.00
33 Shawn Michaels 1.25 3.00
34 Shawn Michaels 1.25 3.00
35 Shawn Michaels 1.25 3.00
36 Shawn Michaels 1.25 3.00
37 Shawn Michaels 1.25 3.00
38 Shawn Michaels 1.25 3.00
39 Shawn Michaels 1.25 3.00
40 Shawn Michaels 1.25 3.00

2018 Topps WWE Shawn Michaels Tribute Topps Heritage WWE Autographs and Relics

SMA1 Shawn Michaels AU 30.00 75.00
SMR1 Shawn Michaels RELIC 8.00 20.00
SMAR1 Shawn Michaels AU RELIC 60.00 120.00

2018 Topps WWE Shawn Michaels Tribute Topps WWE Road to WrestleMania Autographs and Relics

SM Shawn Michaels AU 30.00 75.00
SMR Shawn Michaels RELIC 10.00 25.00
SMAR Shawn Michaels AU RELIC 50.00 100.00

2020 Topps WWE Signature Performance Autographs

*BLUE/25: UNPRICED DUE TO SCARCITY
*RED/10: UNPRICED DUE TO SCARCITY
*ORANGE/5: UNPRICED DUE TO SCARCITY
*GOLD/1: UNPRICED DUE TO SCARCITY
STATED PRINT RUN 50 SER.#'d SETS

NNO Drew McIntyre 50.00 100.00

2008 Topps WWE Slam Attax

COMPLETE SET (172) 15.00 40.00

1 John Cena CH 1.25 3.00
2 Edge CH .75 2.00
3 Chavo Guerrero CH .30 .75
4 Matt Hardy CH .75 2.00
5 Chris Jericho CH .50 1.25
6 Triple H CH 1.25 3.00
7 Jeff Hardy CH .75 2.00
8 Rey Mysterio CH .50 1.25
9 Randy Orton CH .50 1.25
10 CM Punk CH .20 .50
11 William Regal CH .50 1.25
12 Batista CH .75 2.00
13 Shawn Michaels CH 1.25 3.00
14 Beth Phoenix CH 1.00 2.50
15 Kofi Kingston CH .50 1.25
16 Undertaker CH 1.00 2.50
17 Montel Vontavious Porter FM .30 .75
18 Kane FM .75 2.00
19 Mr. Kennedy FM .50 1.25
20 Big Show FM .50 1.25
21 Carlito FM .50 1.25
22 D-Generation X FM .60 1.50
23 The Hardys FM .75 2.00
24 Cryme Tyme FM .25 .60
25 Umaga FM .30 .75
26 JBL FM .20 .50
27 Mark Henry FM .30 .75
28 John Morrison FM .20 .50
29 The Great Khali FM .20 .50
30 Snitsky FM .30 .75
31 Shelton Benjamin FM .20 .50
32 Stone Cold Steve Austin FM 1.25 3.00
33 Mickie James FM 1.25 3.00
34 Finlay FM .30 .75
35 Vladimir Kozlov FM .20 .50
36 WWE Title TC .20 .50
37 Intercontinental Title TC .20 .50
38 Womenís Title TC .20 .50
39 World Tag Team Title TC .20 .50
40 World Heavyweight Title TC .20 .50
41 United States Title TC .20 .50
42 WWE Tag Team Title TC .20 .50
43 WWE Diva Title TC .20 .50
44 ECW Title TC .20 .50
45 WWE MITB Briefcase TC .20 .50
46 Deuce .20 .50
47 Kofi Kingston RC .50 1.25
48 JBL .20 .50
49 Charlie Haas .20 .50
50 Ron Simmons .20 .50
51 CM Punk .20 .50
52 Chuck Palumbo .30 .75
53 William Regal .50 1.25
54 Paul Burchill .20 .50
55 Rey Mysterio .50 1.25
56 Snitsky .30 .75
57 Paul London .20 .50
58 Chris Jericho .50 1.25
59 Val Venis .25 .60
60 Jerry Lawler .40 1.00
61 Ted DiBiase Jr. RC .50 1.25
62 Stone Cold Steve Austin 1.25 3.00
63 Hacksaw Jim Duggan .50 1.25
64 Todd Grisham .20 .50
65 Jamie Noble .20 .50
66 Batista .75 2.00
67 D'Lo Brown .30 .75
68 Santino Marella .20 .50
69 Shawn Michaels 1.25 3.00
70 Michael Cole .20 .50
71 John Cena 1.25 3.00
72 JTG .20 .50
73 Shad .20 .50
74 Randy Orton .50 1.25
75 Lance Cade .20 .50
76 Hardcore Holly .30 .75
77 Cody Rhodes .20 .50
78 Kane .75 2.00
79 Mike Adamle .20 .50
80 Ezekiel Jackson RC .20 .50
81 Montel Vontavious Porter .30 .75
82 Funaki .20 .50
83 Undertaker 1.00 2.50
84 DH Smith RC .20 .50
85 Gregory Helms .25 .60
86 Jeff Hardy .75 2.00
87 Vladimir Kozlov RC .20 .50
88 The Great Khali .20 .50
89 Jesse RC .20 .50
90 Festus RC .20 .50
91 Edge .75 2.00
92 Carlito .50 1.25
93 Vickie Guerrero .25 .60
94 Kenny Dykstra .30 .75
95 Mr. Kennedy .50 1.25
96 Shelton Benjamin .20 .50
97 Triple H 1.25 3.00
98 Justin Roberts RC .20 .50
99 Jimmy Wang Yang .20 .50
100 Curt Hawkins .20 .50
101 Zack Ryder .20 .50
102 Brian Kendrick .30 .75
103 Big Show .50 1.25
104 Jim Ross .40 1.00
105 Umaga .30 .75
106 Tazz .30 .75
107 John Morrison .20 .50
108 Tommy Dreamer .20 .50
109 Mike Knox .20 .50
110 Super Crazy .30 .75
111 Boogeyman .30 .75
112 Mark Henry .30 .75
113 Chavo Guerrero .30 .75
114 Tony Chimel RC .20 .50
115 Finlay .30 .75
116 Bam Neely RC .20 .50
117 Matt Hardy .75 2.00
118 Armando Estrada .20 .50
119 Elijah Burke .20 .50

120 Hornswoggle .30 .75
121 The Miz .30 .75
122 Ricky Ortiz RC .20 .50
123 Evan Bourne RC .20 .50
124 Theodore Long .25 .60
125 Matt Striker .20 .50
126 Natalya DV RC .40 1.00
127 Eve DV RC .40 1.00
128 Maria DV .75 2.00
129 Tiffany DV RC .30 .75
130 Katie Lea Burchill DV RC .25 .60
131 Kelly Kelly DV .75 2.00
132 Layla DV .50 1.25
133 Beth Phoenix DV 1.00 2.50
134 Candice DV 1.00 2.50
135 Lilian Garcia DV .50 1.25
136 Lena Yada DV .25 .60
137 Victoria DV 1.00 2.50
138 Melina DV .75 2.00
139 Maryse DV .75 2.00
140 Michelle McCool DV 1.00 2.50
141 Jillian DV .75 2.00
142 Mickie James DV 1.25 3.00
143 Kane & Undertaker 1.00 2.50
144 The Bushwhackers .25 .60
145 Curt Hawkins & Zack Ryder .20 .50
146 Finlay & Hornswoggle .30 .75
147 Chris Jericho & Lance Cade .50 1.25
148 Cody Rhodes & Ted Dibiase .50 1.25
149 John Morrison & The Miz .30 .75
150 The Hardys TT .75 2.00
151 Jesse & Festus TT .20 .50
152 Cryme Tyme TT .25 .60
153 D-Generation X TT .60 1.50
154 Chavo Guerrero / Bam Neely TT .30 .75
155 Sgt. Slaughter HOF .50 1.25
156 Jimmy Hart HOF .30 .75
157 Cowboy Bob Orton HOF .50 1.25
158 The Iron Sheik HOF .75 2.00
159 Rowdy Roddy Piper HOF .75 2.00
160 Pat Patterson HOF .20 .50
161 Gerald Brisco HOF .20 .50
162 Junkyard Dog HOF .30 .75
163 Dusty Rhodes HOF .50 1.25
164 Jimmy Superfly Snuka .50 1.25
165 Tony Atlas HOF .20 .50
166 Bobby The Brain Heenan .50 1.25
167 Superstar Billy Graham .25 .60
168 Gorilla Monsoon L .50 1.25
169 Nikolai Volkoff L .30 .75
170 Curt Hennig L .50 1.25
171 Vader L .30 .75
172 Stone Cold Steve Austin L 1.25 3.00

2010 Topps WWE Slam Attax

COMPLETE SET (130) 12.00 30.00

1 Kofi Kingston .20 .50
2 Carlito .30 .75
3 Primo .12 .30
4 Jerry Lawler .20 .50
5 Ted DiBiase .20 .50
6 Jim Duggan .20 .50
7 Festus .12 .30
8 Chris Masters .12 .30
9 Hornswoggle .20 .50
10 Jamie Noble .12 .30
11 Mark Henry .20 .50
12 Justin Roberts .12 .30
13 Santino Marella .12 .30
14 Shawn Michaels .75 2.00
15 Jack Swagger .12 .30
16 Michael Cole .12 .30
17 The Miz .20 .50
18 Triple H .60 1.50
19 Chavo Guerrero .20 .50
20 Evan Bourne .12 .30
21 Big Show .30 .75
22 Montel Vontavious Porter .20 .50
23 John Cena .60 1.50
24 Randy Orton .50 1.25
25 Cody Rhodes .12 .30
26 Eve .50 1.25
27 Melina .50 1.25
28 Alicia Fox .20 .50
29 Kelly Kelly .50 1.25
30 Gail Kim .30 .75
31 Jillian .50 1.25
32 Maryse .50 1.25
33 Sheamus RC .20 .50
34 Brie Bella .50 1.25
35 Nikki Bella .50 1.25
36 Kung Fu Naki .12 .30
37 Undertaker .50 1.25
38 Charlie Haas .12 .30
39 Kane .30 .75
40 CM Punk .50 1.25
41 Dolph Ziggler .20 .50
42 Rey Mysterio .30 .75
43 Chris Jericho .30 .75
44 The Great Khali .12 .30
45 Slam Master J .12 .30
46 Matt Hardy .30 .75
47 Edge .50 1.25
48 JTG .12 .30
49 Shad .12 .30
50 David Hart Smith .12 .30
51 Tyson Kidd .12 .30
52 Mike Knox .12 .30
53 R-Truth .12 .30
54 John Morrison .20 .50
55 Finlay .20 .50
56 Beth Phoenix .50 1.25
57 Batista .50 1.25
58 Theodore Long .12 .30
59 Todd Grisham .12 .30
60 Ranjin Singh .12 .30
61 Jimmy Wang Yang .12 .30
62 Curt Hawkins .12 .30
63 Jim Ross .12 .30
64 Natalya .50 1.25
65 Michelle McCool .50 1.25
66 Mickie James .60 1.50
67 Layla .30 .75
68 Maria .50 1.25
69 Tommy Dreamer .12 .30
70 The Hurricane .12 .30
71 Vladimir Kozlov .20 .50
72 Tony Chimel .12 .30
73 Ezekiel Jackson .12 .30
74 Shelton Benjamin .12 .30
75 Josh Mathews .12 .30
76 William Regal .30 .75
77 Paul Burchill .12 .30
78 Gabriel .12 .30
79 Goldust .20 .50
80 Zack Ryder .12 .30
81 Yoshi Tatsu .12 .30
82 Abraham Washington RC .12 .30
83 Tyler Reks RC .12 .30
84 Savannah RC .20 .50
85 Matt Striker .12 .30
86 Christian .20 .50
87 Rosa Mendes .20 .50
88 Katie Lea Burchill .30 .75
89 Tiffany .20 .50
90 C.Rhodes/T.DiBiase .20 .50
91 Cryme Tyme .12 .30
92 D.Smith/T.Kidd .12 .30
93 S.Benjamin/C.Haas .12 .30
94 C.Jericho/Big Show .30 .75
95 M.Henry/Hornswoggle .20 .50
96 Iron Sheik .30 .75
97 Ted DiBiase .20 .50
98 Jake Roberts .30 .75
99 Koko B. Ware .20 .50
100 British Bulldog .20 .50
101 Sgt. Slaughter .30 .75
102 Rick Rude .20 .50
103 Bam Bam Bigelow .20 .50
104 Junkyard Dog .30 .75
105 Roddy Piper .50 1.25
106 Paul Orndorff .30 .75
107 Jimmy Snuka .30 .75
108 Nikolai Volkoff .20 .50
109 Dusty Rhodes .30 .75
110 Bobby Heenan .20 .50
111 Hillbilly Jim .20 .50
112 Curt Hennig .20 .50
113 Bob Orton .20 .50
114 Jerry Lawler .20 .50
115 Earthquake .20 .50
116 TLC Match .12 .30
117 Steel Cage Match .12 .30
118 Hell in a Cell Match .12 .30
119 Stretcher Match .12 .30
120 Casket Match .12 .30
121 Royal Rumble .12 .30
122 No Way Out .12 .30
123 WrestleMania .12 .30
124 Backlash .12 .30
125 Judgement Day .12 .30
126 Extreme Rules .12 .30
127 The Bash .12 .30
128 Night Of Champions .12 .30
129 Summerslam .12 .30
130 Survivor Series .12 .30

2010 Topps WWE Slam Attax Champions

COMPLETE SET (16) 8.00 20.00
STATED ODDS 1:5

1 John Cena 2.00 5.00
2 Edge 1.50 4.00
3 Matt Hardy 1.00 2.50
4 Chris Jericho 1.00 2.50
5 Triple H 2.00 5.00
6 Rey Mysterio 1.00 2.50
7 Randy Orton 1.50 4.00
8 CM Punk 1.50 4.00
9 Batista 1.50 4.00
10 C.Jericho/Big Show 1.00 2.50
11 Michelle McCool 1.50 4.00
12 Kofi Kingston .60 1.50
13 Christian .60 1.50
14 Montel Vontavious Porter .60 1.50
15 Maryse 1.50 4.00
16 Undertaker 1.50 4.00

2010 Topps WWE Slam Attax Finishing Moves

COMPLETE SET (19) 6.00 15.00
STATED ODDS 1:6

1 Kane .75 2.00
2 Cody Rhodes .30 .75
3 Ted DiBiase .50 1.25
4 Shawn Michaels 2.00 5.00
5 John Morrison .50 1.25
6 Carlito .75 2.00
7 Beth Phoenix 1.25 3.00
8 Jack Swagger .30 .75
9 Mark Henry .50 1.25
10 Tommy Dreamer .30 .75
11 Evan Bourne .30 .75
12 The Great Khali .30 .75
13 Chavo Guerrero .50 1.25
14 Melina 1.25 3.00
15 Finlay .50 1.25
16 Big Show .75 2.00
17 Shelton Benjamin .30 .75
18 R-Truth .30 .75
19 Maria 1.25 3.00

2010 Topps WWE Slam Attax Props

COMPLETE SET (10) 5.00 12.00
STATED ODDS 1:5

1 Steel Chair .75 2.00
2 Sledgehammer .75 2.00
3 Table .75 2.00
4 Trash Can .75 2.00
5 Ladder .75 2.00
6 Steel Steps .75 2.00
7 Ring Bell .75 2.00
8 Brass Knuckles .75 2.00
9 Shillelagh .75 2.00
10 Kendo Stick .75 2.00

2010 Topps WWE Slam Attax Starter Box Exclusives

COMPLETE SET (5) 6.00 15.00
STATED ODDS ONE PER STARTER BOX

1 Chris Jericho 1.25 3.00
2 Undertaker 2.00 5.00
3 Randy Orton 2.00 5.00
4 Triple H 2.50 6.00
5 John Cena 2.50 6.00

2010 Topps WWE Slam Attax Titles

COMPLETE SET (11) 5.00 12.00
STATED ODDS 1:6

1 WWE Championship .75 2.00
2 Intercontinental Championship .75 2.00
3 Women's Championship .75 2.00
4 Word Tag Team Championship .75 2.00
5 World Heavyweight Championship .75 2.00
6 United States Championship .75 2.00
7 WWE Tag Team Championship .75 2.00
8 WWE Divas Championship .75 2.00
9 ECW Championship .75 2.00
10 WWE Money in the Bank Briefcase .75 2.00
11 WWE Slammy Award .75 2.00

2010 Topps WWE Slam Attax WrestleMania XXVI

COMPLETE SET (5) 6.00 15.00
ONE SET PER WRESTLEMANIA XXVI TIN

1 Chris Jericho 1.00 2.50
2 John Cena 2.00 5.00
3 Randy Orton 1.50 4.00
4 Triple H 2.00 5.00
5 Undertaker 1.50 4.00

2018 Topps WWE Slam Attax Live!

COMPLETE SET (392) 25.00 60.00

1 Alexa Bliss FOIL 1.00 2.50
2 Baron Corbin FOIL .30 .75
3 Bobby Roode FOIL .30 .75
4 Braun Strowman FOIL .50 1.25
5 Elias FOIL .50 1.25
6 Finn Balor FOIL .50 1.25
7 John Cena FOIL .75 2.00
8 Kevin Owens FOIL .50 1.25
9 Nia Jax FOIL .30 .75
10 Roman Reigns FOIL .50 1.25
11 Sami Zayn FOIL .20 .50
12 Seth Rollins FOIL .50 1.25
13 AJ Styles FOIL .75 2.00
14 Rusev FOIL .30 .75
15 Asuka FOIL .60 1.50
16 Bludgeon Brothers FOIL .30 .75
17 Carmella FOIL .40 1.00
18 Charlotte Flair FOIL .60 1.50
19 Jeff Hardy FOIL .40 1.00
20 The Miz FOIL .40 1.00
21 Rusev FOIL .30 .75
22 Samoa Joe FOIL .40 1.00
23 Shinsuke Nakamura FOIL .50 1.25
24 The Usos FOIL .30 .75
25 Adam Cole FOIL RC .25 .60
26 Aleister Black FOIL .25 .60
27 Kairi Sane FOIL RC .50 1.25
28 Pete Dunne FOIL RC .20 .50
29 Roderick Strong FOIL .20 .50
30 Shayna Baszler FOIL .50 1.25
31 Undisputed Era FOIL .25 .60
32 Cedric Alexander FOIL .20 .50
33 Alexa Bliss/Nia Jax FOIL 1.00 2.50
34 Bray Wyatt/Woken Matt Hardy FOIL .50 1.25
35 Roman Reigns/Jinder Mahal FOIL .50 1.25
36 Seth Rollins/Finn Balor FOIL .50 1.25
37 AJ Styles/Nakamura FOIL .75 2.00
38 Asuka/Charlotte Flair FOIL .60 1.50
39 Bobby Roode/Randy Orton FOIL .50 1.25
40 Daniel Bryan/The Miz FOIL .50 1.25
41 Adam Cole/Velveteen Dream FOIL .25 .60
42 Andrade/Aleister Black FOIL .30 .75
43 Ember Moon/Shayna Baszler FOIL .50 1.25
44 Bret Hart/Shawn Michaels FOIL .60 1.50
45 Ric Flair/Chris Jericho FOIL .60 1.50
46 Trish Stratus/Lita FOIL .75 2.00
47 Undertaker/Kane FOIL .75 2.00
48 X-Pac/Shane McMahon FOIL .40 1.00
49 1-2-3 Kid .25 .60
50 Braun Strowman .50 1.25
51 Bret Hit Man Hart .50 1.25
52 Chris Jericho .50 1.25
53 Chris Jericho .50 1.25

Card	Low	High
54 D-Generation X	.60	1.50
55 Daniel Bryan	.50	1.25
56 Daniel Bryan	.50	1.25
57 Finn Balor	.50	1.25
58 Jeff Hardy	.40	1.00
59 John Cena	.75	2.00
60 John Cena & Shawn Michaels	.75	2.00
61 Kane	.30	.75
62 Mark Henry	.25	.60
63 The Miz	.40	1.00
64 Paige	.50	1.25
65 Randy Orton	.50	1.25
66 Ric Flair	.60	1.50
67 Roman Reigns	.50	1.25
68 Sasha Banks	.60	1.50
69 Seth Rollins	.50	1.25
70 Shane McMahon	.40	1.00
71 Stephanie McMahon	.40	1.00
72 Sting	.50	1.25
73 Stone Cold Steve Austin	1.00	2.50
74 Stone Cold Steve Austin	1.00	2.50
75 Stone Cold Steve Austin	1.00	2.50
76 The Rock	1.00	2.50
77 Trish Stratus & Lita	.75	2.00
78 Ultimate Warrior	.75	2.00
79 Undertaker & Triple H	.75	2.00
80 Yokozuna	.25	.60
81 Akam	.20	.50
82 Alexa Bliss	1.00	2.50
83 Alicia Fox	.30	.75
84 Apollo Crews	.20	.50
85 Baron Corbin	.30	.75
86 Bayley	.30	.75
87 Big Show	.20	.50
88 Bo Dallas	.20	.50
89 Bobby Roode	.30	.75
90 Braun Strowman	.50	1.25
91 Bray Wyatt	.50	1.25
92 Chad Gable	.20	.50
93 Charly Caruso	.30	.75
94 Corey Graves	.25	.60
95 Curt Hawkins	.20	.50
96 Curtis Axel	.20	.50
97 Dana Brooke	.40	1.00
98 Dash Wilder	.25	.60
99 David Otunga	.25	.60
100 Dean Ambrose	.40	1.00
101 Drew McIntyre	.30	.75
102 Elias	.50	1.25
103 Ember Moon	.40	1.00
104 Fandango	.20	.50
105 Finn Balor	.50	1.25
106 Goldust	.40	1.00
107 Heath Slater	.20	.50
108 Jason Jordan	.20	.50
109 Jinder Mahal	.25	.60
110 John Cena	.75	2.00
111 JoJo	.20	.50
112 Jonathan Coachman	.20	.50
113 Kane	.30	.75
114 Kevin Owens	.50	1.25
115 Konnor	.20	.50
116 Kurt Angle	.50	1.25
117 Bobby Lashley	.40	1.00
118 Liv Morgan	.40	1.00
119 Maryse	.40	1.00
120 Woken Matt Hardy	.50	1.25
121 Michael Cole	.20	.50
122 Mickie James	.40	1.00
123 Mike Kanellis RC	.20	.50
124 Mike Rome	.20	.50
125 Mojo Rawley	.20	.50
126 Natalya	.25	.60
127 Nia Jax	.30	.75
128 No Way Jose	.25	.60
129 Renee Young	.30	.75
130 Rezar	.20	.50
131 Rhyno	.20	.50
132 Roman Reigns	.50	1.25
133 Ronda Rousey	1.00	2.50
134 Ruby Riott	.30	.75
135 Sami Zayn	.20	.50
136 Sarah Logan RC	.20	.50
137 Sasha Banks	.60	1.50
138 Scott Dawson	.25	.60
139 Seth Rollins	.50	1.25
140 Stephanie McMahon	.40	1.00
141 Titus O'Neil	.20	.50
142 Triple H	.50	1.25
143 Tyler Breeze	.20	.50
144 Viktor	.20	.50
145 Zack Ryder	.20	.50
146 Aiden English	.20	.50
147 AJ Styles	.75	2.00
148 Alexander Wolfe	.20	.50
149 Andrade Cien Almas	.30	.75
150 Asuka	.60	1.50
151 Becky Lynch	.50	1.25
152 Big Cass	.25	.60
153 Big E	.25	.60
154 Billie Kay	.40	1.00
155 Byron Saxton	.20	.50
156 Carmella	.40	1.00
157 Cesaro	.40	1.00
158 Charlotte Flair	.60	1.50
159 Chris Jericho	.50	1.25
160 Daniel Bryan	.50	1.25
161 Dasha Fuentes	.30	.75
162 Eric Young	.25	.60
163 Greg Hamilton	.30	.75
164 Harper	.30	.75
165 Jeff Hardy	.40	1.00
166 Jey Uso	.20	.50
167 Jimmy Uso	.20	.50
168 Karl Anderson	.20	.50
169 Killian Dain	.25	.60
170 Kofi Kingston	.25	.60
171 Lana	.50	1.25
172 Luke Gallows	.25	.60
173 Mandy Rose	.50	1.25
174 Maria Kanellis	.50	1.25
175 The Miz	.40	1.00
176 Naomi	.25	.60
177 Nikki Bella	.40	1.00
178 Paige	.50	1.25
179 Peyton Royce	.50	1.25
180 R-Truth	.25	.60
181 Randy Orton	.50	1.25
182 Rowan	.30	.75
183 Rusev	.30	.75
184 Samir Singh RC	.20	.50
185 Samoa Joe	.40	1.00
186 Shane McMahon	.40	1.00
187 Sheamus	.40	1.00
188 Shelton Benjamin	.25	.60
189 Shinsuke Nakamura	.50	1.25
190 Sin Cara	.25	.60
191 Sonya Deville	.40	1.00
192 Sunil Singh RC	.20	.50
193 Tamina	.20	.50
194 Tom Phillips	.20	.50
195 Tye Dillinger	.20	.50
196 Xavier Woods	.25	.60
197 Zelina Vega RC	.20	.50
198 Adam Cole RC	.25	.60
199 Aleister Black	.25	.60
200 Aliyah	.30	.75
201 Angelo Dawkins	.20	.50
202 Bianca Belair RC	1.00	2.50
203 Bobby Fish RC	.20	.50
204 Buddy Murphy	.25	.60
205 Cezar Bononi RC	.20	.50
206 Danny Burch RC	.20	.50
207 EC3	.20	.50
208 Fabian Aichner RC	.20	.50
209 Johnny Gargano	.20	.50
210 Kairi Sane RC	.50	1.25
211 Kassius Ohno	.20	.50
212 Kyle O'Reilly RC	.25	.60
213 Lacey Evans	.25	.60
214 Lars Sullivan RC	.20	.50
215 Lio Rush RC	.20	.50
216 Mauro Ranallo	.20	.50
217 Montez Ford	.20	.50
218 Nick Miller	.20	.50
219 Nigel McGuinness	.20	.50
220 Nikki Cross	.30	.75
221 Oney Lorcan	.25	.60
222 Otis Dozovic	.20	.50
223 Percy Watson	.20	.50
224 Pete Dunne RC	.20	.50
225 Ricochet RC	.40	1.00
226 Riddick Moss	.20	.50
227 Roderick Strong	.20	.50
228 Shane Thorne	.20	.50
229 Shayna Baszler	.50	1.25
230 Taynara Conti RC	.20	.50
231 Tino Sabatelli	.25	.60
232 Tommaso Ciampa	.20	.50
233 Trent Seven RC	.20	.50
234 Tucker Knight	.20	.50
235 Tyler Bate	.20	.50
236 Vanessa Borne	.20	.50
237 Velveteen Dream	.20	.50
238 Wesley Blake	.25	.60
239 William Regal	.30	.75
240 Akira Tozawa	.30	.75
241 Ariya Daivari RC	.20	.50
242 The Brian Kendrick	.30	.75
243 Cedric Alexander	.20	.50
244 Drake Maverick RC	.25	.60
245 Drew Gulak	.20	.50
246 Gentleman Jack Gallagher	.25	.60
247 Gran Metalik	.20	.50
248 Hideo Itami	.20	.50
249 Kalisto	.20	.50
250 Lince Dorado	.20	.50
251 Mustafa Ali	.20	.50
252 Neville	.30	.75
253 Noam Dar	.20	.50
254 TJP	.25	.60
255 Tony Nese	.20	.50
256 Alundra Blayze	.20	.50
257 Andre the Giant	.40	1.00
258 Bam Bam Bigelow	.30	.75
259 Batista	.30	.75
260 Beth Phoenix	.40	1.00
261 Big Boss Man	.20	.50
262 Billy Gunn	.25	.60
263 Bob Backlund	.20	.50
264 Bobby The Brain Heenan	.30	.75
265 Booker T	.30	.75
266 Bret Hit Man Hart	.50	1.25
267 British Bulldog	.30	.75
268 Bruno Sammartino	.30	.75
269 Chief Jay Strongbow	.30	.75
270 Classy Freddie Blassie	.20	.50
271 Cowboy Bob Orton	.20	.50
272 D'Lo Brown	.20	.50
273 Dean Malenko	.20	.50
274 Diamond Dallas Page	.30	.75
275 Dusty Rhodes	.40	1.00
276 Eddie Guerrero	.50	1.25
277 Edge	.50	1.25
278 Eve	.40	1.00
279 The Godfather	.20	.50
280 Hacksaw Jim Duggan	.20	.50
281 Harley Race	.20	.50
282 Honky Tonk Man	.20	.50
283 Howard Finkel	.20	.50
284 Iron Sheik	.20	.50
285 Irwin R. Schyster	.20	.50
286 Jake The Snake Roberts	.25	.60
287 Jerry The King Lawler	.40	1.00
288 Jim The Anvil Neidhart	.30	.75
289 Jimmy Hart	.30	.75
290 Junkyard Dog	.20	.50
291 Ken Shamrock	.25	.60
292 Kevin Nash	.40	1.00
293 Lex Luger	.25	.60
294 Lita	.50	1.25
295 Macho Man Randy Savage	.60	1.50
296 Magnificent Don Muraco	.20	.50
297 Mark Henry	.25	.60
298 Mean Gene Okerlund	.25	.60
299 Ted DiBiase	.25	.60
300 Mr. Perfect Curt Hennig	.25	.60
301 Mr. Wonderful Paul Orndorff	.20	.50
302 Norman Smiley	.20	.50
303 Papa Shango	.20	.50
304 Paul Bearer	.30	.75
305 Prince Albert	.20	.50
306 Psycho Sid	.20	.50
307 Ravishing Rick Rude	.25	.60
308 Razor Ramon	.40	1.00
309 Ric Flair	.60	1.50
310 Ricky The Dragon Steamboat	.30	.75
311 Rikishi	.20	.50
312 Road Dogg	.20	.50
313 The Rock	1.00	2.50
314 Rowdy Roddy Piper	.50	1.25
315 Sgt. Slaughter	.25	.60
316 Shawn Michaels	.60	1.50
317 Sting	.50	1.25
318 Stone Cold Steve Austin	1.00	2.50
319 Tatanka	.20	.50
320 Trish Stratus	.75	2.00
321 Ultimate Warrior	.75	2.00
322 Umaga	.20	.50
323 Undertaker	.75	2.00
324 Viscera	.20	.50
325 X-Pac	.25	.60
326 Yokozuna	.25	.60
327 The Ascension	.20	.50
328 Authors of Pain	.20	.50
329 Bray Wyatt & Woken Matt Hardy	.50	1.25
330 Breezango	.20	.50
331 Heath Slater & Rhyno	.20	.50
332 The Miztourage	.40	1.00
333 The Revival	.25	.60
334 The Riott Squad	.40	1.00
335 The Shield	.50	1.25
336 Titus Worldwide	.40	1.00
337 Absolution	.50	1.25
338 The Bar	.40	1.00
339 Bludgeon Brothers	.30	.75
340 Gallows & Anderson	.25	.60
341 The New Day	.30	.75
342 Rusev Day	.30	.75
343 The IIconics	.50	1.25
344 SanitY	.30	.75
345 The Singh Brothers	.25	.60
346 The Usos	.30	.75
347 Danny Burch & Oney Lorcan	.25	.60
348 Heavy Machinery	.20	.50
349 Moustache Mountain	.20	.50
350 Riddick Moss & Tino Sabbatelli	.25	.60
351 The Street Profits	.20	.50
352 TM-61	.20	.50
353 Undisputed Era	.25	.60
354 Bushwhackers	.20	.50
355 D-Generation X	.60	1.50
356 Nasty Boys	.20	.50
357 nWo	.40	1.00
358 WWE Title	.20	.50
359 Intercontinental Title	.20	.50
360 RAW Women's Title	.20	.50
361 WWE UK Title	.20	.50
362 SmackDown Women's Title	.20	.50
363 NXT Title	.20	.50
364 WWE Universal Title	.20	.50
365 NXT Women's Title	.20	.50
366 RAW Tag Team Title	.20	.50
367 SmackDown Tag Team Title	.20	.50
368 United States Title	.20	.50
369 WWE Cruiserweight Title	.20	.50
370 NXT Tag Team Title	.20	.50
371 Puzzle	.50	1.25
372 Puzzle	.75	2.00
373 Puzzle	.30	.75
374 Puzzle	.50	1.25
375 Puzzle	1.00	2.50
376 Puzzle	.50	1.25
377 Puzzle	.40	1.00
378 Puzzle	.75	2.00
379 Puzzle	.50	1.25
380 Puzzle	.50	1.25
381 Puzzle	.75	2.00
382 Puzzle	.60	1.50
383 Puzzle	1.00	2.50
384 Puzzle	1.00	2.50
385 Puzzle	.75	2.00
386 Puzzle	.20	.50
387 Puzzle	.20	.50
388 Puzzle	.20	.50
389 Steel Chair	.20	.50
390 Table	.20	.50
391 Ladder	.20	.50
392 Trash Can	.20	.50

2018 Topps WWE Slam Attax Live! Authentic Ring Mat Memorabilia

RMAA John Cena & Nikki Bella
RMAB Triple H & Stephanie McMahon
RMAC Seth Rollins
RMBA The Usos
RMBB Carmella
RMBC Baron Corbin
RMCA Sasha Banks
RMCB Braun Strowman
RMCC AJ Styles
RMDA Kurt Angle
RMDB The Miz
RMDC Dean Ambrose/Seth Rollins
RMEA Charlotte Flair
RMEB Alexa Bliss
RMEC Finn Balor
RMFA Shinsuke Nakamura
RMFB Kevin Owens
RMFC Asuka
RMGA Drew McIntyre
RMGB Braun Strowman
RMGC Andrade Cien Almas
RMHA Undisputed Era
RMHB Velveteen Dream
RMHC Kairi Sane
RMIA Aleister Black
RMIB Adam Cole
RMIC Ember Moon
RMJA Finn Balor
RMJB Elias
RMJC Jason Jordan

2018 Topps WWE Slam Attax Live! Authentic T-Shirt Memorabilia

TS1 AJ Styles
TS3 Bayley
TS5 John Cena
TS7 Karl Anderson
TS9 Roman Reigns
TS10 Sami Zayn
TS11 Tye Dillinger

2018 Topps WWE Slam Attax Live! Collector Cards

CC1 Bret Hit Man Hart
CC2 Eddie Guerrero
CC3 Shawn Michaels
CC4 Sting
CC5 Stone Cold Steve Austin
CC6 Ultimate Warrior

2018 Topps WWE Slam Attax Live! Gold Limited Edition

LEPA Roman Reigns
LEPB Daniel Bryan
LEPC Andrade Cien Almas
LEPD Sasha Banks
LEPE Asuka
LEPF Seth Rollins
LEPG John Cena
LEPH Kevin Owens

2018 Topps WWE Slam Attax Live! Silver Limited Edition

LEMB Braun Strowman
LEMC Adam Cole
LEMD Charlotte Flair
LEMF Randy Orton
LESA Ronda Rousey

2010 Topps WWE Slam Attax Mayhem

COMPLETE SET (161)	12.00	30.00
1 Chris Jericho	.30	.75
2 David Hart Smith	.12	.30
3 Edge	.50	1.25
4 Evan Bourne	.12	.30
5 Ezekiel Jackson	.12	.30
6 Goldust	.20	.50
7 Jerry Lawler	.20	.50
8 Jay Uso RC	.12	.30
9 Jimmy Uso RC	.12	.30
10 John Cena	.60	1.50
11 John Morrison	.20	.50
12 Justin Roberts	.12	.30
13 Mark Henry	.20	.50
14 Michael Cole	.12	.30
15 Primo	.12	.30
16 R-Truth	.12	.30
17 Randy Orton	.50	1.25
18 Ranjin Singh	.12	.30
19 Santino Marella	.12	.30
20 Sheamus RC	.20	.50
21 Ted DiBiase	.20	.50
22 The Great Khali	.12	.30
23 The Miz	.20	.50
24 Triple H	.60	1.50
25 Tyson Kidd	.12	.30
26 Vladimir Kozlov	.20	.50
27 William Regal	.30	.75
28 Yoshi Tatsu	.12	.30
29 Zack Ryder	.12	.30
30 Alicia Fox	.20	.50
31 Brie Bella	.50	1.25
32 Eve	.50	1.25
33 Gail Kim	.30	.75
34 Jillian	.50	1.25
35 Maryse	.50	1.25
36 Melina	.50	1.25
37 Natalya	.50	1.25
38 Nikki Bella	.50	1.25
39 Tamina RC	.12	.30
40 Big Show	.30	.75
41 Caylen Croft RC	.12	.30
42 Chavo Guerrero	.20	.50
43 Chris Masters	.12	.30
44 Christian	.20	.50
45 CM Punk	.50	1.25
46 Cody Rhodes	.12	.30
47 Curt Hawkins	.12	.30
48 Dolph Ziggler	.20	.50
49 Drew McIntyre RC	.20	.50
50 Finlay	.20	.50
51 Hornswoggle	.20	.50
52 Jack Swagger	.12	.30
53 JTG	.12	.30
54 Kane	.30	.75
55 Kofi Kingston	.20	.50
56 Luke Gallows	.12	.30
57 Matt Hardy	.30	.75
58 Matt Striker	.12	.30
59 Montel Vontavious Porter	.20	.50
60 Rey Mysterio	.30	.75
61 Shad	.12	.30
62 Theodore Long	.12	.30
63 Todd Grisham	.12	.30
64 Tony Chimel	.12	.30
65 Trent Barreta RC	.12	.30
66 Tyler Reks RC	.12	.30
67 Undertaker	.50	1.25
68 Vance Archer	.12	.30
69 Beth Phoenix	.50	1.25
70 Kelly Kelly	.50	1.25
71 Layla	.30	.75
72 Michelle McCool	.50	1.25
73 Rosa Mendes	.20	.50
74 Serena RC	.20	.50
75 Darren Young	.20	.50
76 David Otunga RC	.20	.50
77 Heath Slater RC	.20	.50
78 Justin Gabriel	.20	.50
79 Michael Tarver RC	.20	.50
80 Skip Sheffield RC	.20	.50
81 Wade Barrett RC	.20	.50
82 Alex Riley RC	.12	.30
83 Husky Harris	.25	.60
84 Kaval RC	.12	.30
85 Lucky Cannon	.12	.30
86 Eli Cottonwood RC	.12	.30
87 Michael McGillicutty RC	.12	.30
88 Percy Watson RC	.12	.30
89 Titus O'Neil RC	.12	.30
90 Jamie Keyes RC	.12	.30
91 David Hart Smith/Tyson Kidd	.12	.30
92 Trent Barreta/Caylen Croft	.12	.30
93 Chris Jericho/The Miz	.30	.75
94 Montel Vontavious Porter/JTG	.20	.50
95 Curt Hawkins/Vance Archer	.12	.30
96 William Regal/Vladimir Kozlov	.30	.75
97 THE USO Brothers	.12	.30
98 Iron Sheik	.30	.75
99 Jake The Snake Roberts	.30	.75
100 Koko B. Ware	.20	.50
101 British Bulldog	.20	.50
102 Sgt. Slaughter	.30	.75
103 Ravishing Rick Rude	.20	.50
104 Bam Bam Bigelow	.20	.50
105 Junkyard Dog	.30	.75
106 Ted DiBiase	.20	.50
107 Rowdy Roddy Piper	.50	1.25
108 Mr. Wonderful Paul Orndorff	.30	.75
109 Jimmy Superfly Snuka	.30	.75
110 Nikolai Volkoff	.20	.50
111 Dusty Rhodes	.30	.75
112 Bobby The Brain Heenan	.20	.50
113 Hillbilly Jim	.20	.50
114 Mr. Perfect Curt Hennig	.20	.50
115 Barry Windham	.20	.50
116 Cowboy Bob Orton	.20	.50
117 Jerry The King Lawler	.20	.50
118 Earthquake	.20	.50
119 Ricky Dragon Steamboat	.20	.50
120 Vader	.20	.50
121 Gorilla Monsoon	.12	.30
122 Terry Funk	.30	.75
123 IRS	.12	.30
124 Yokozuna	.12	.30
125 Steel Chair	.12	.30
126 Sledgehammer	.12	.30
127 Table	.12	.30
128 Trash Can	.12	.30
129 Ladder	.12	.30
130 Steel Steps	.12	.30
131 Ring Bell	.12	.30
132 Brass Knuckles	.12	.30
133 Baseball Bat	.12	.30
134 Handcuffs	.12	.30
135 Fire Extinguisher	.12	.30
136 Announcers Table	.12	.30
137 Steel Pipe	.12	.30
138 Microphone	.12	.30
139 Steel Cage Match	.12	.30
140 Hell in a Cell Match	.12	.30
141 Stretcher Match	.12	.30
142 Casket Match	.12	.30
143 Elimination Chamber Match	.12	.30
144 Ambulance Match	.12	.30
145 Backstage Brawl	.12	.30
146 Royal Rumble	.12	.30
147 Elimination Chamber	.12	.30
148 WrestleMania XXVI	.12	.30
149 Extreme Rules	.12	.30
150 WWE Over The Limit	.12	.30
151 Fatal 4 Way	.12	.30
152 Money In The Bank	.12	.30
153 SummerSlam	.12	.30
154 Night Of Champions	.12	.30
155 Hell In A Cell	.12	.30
156 WWE Bragging Rights	.12	.30
157 TLC:Tables, Ladders and Chairs	.12	.30
158 John Cena	.60	1.50
159 The Miz	.20	.50
160 Undertaker	.50	1.25
161 Rey Mysterio	.30	.75

2010 Topps WWE Slam Attax Mayhem Champions

COMPLETE SET (16)	8.00	20.00
STATED ODDS 1:6		
1 Jack Swagger	.40	1.00
2 Drew McIntyre	.60	1.50
3 John Cena	2.00	5.00
4 The Miz	.60	1.50
5 David Hart Smith/Tyson Kidd	.40	1.00
6 Eve	1.50	4.00
7 Layla	1.00	2.50
8 Triple H	2.00	5.00
9 Randy Orton	1.50	4.00
10 Chris Jericho	1.00	2.50
11 Undertaker	1.50	4.00
12 Big Show	1.00	2.50
13 Edge	1.50	4.00
14 Sheamus	.60	1.50
15 Melina	1.50	4.00
16 Kofi Kingston	.60	1.50

2010 Topps WWE Slam Attax Mayhem Finishing Moves

COMPLETE SET (26)	10.00	25.00
STATED ODDS		
1 Chavo Guerrero	.50	1.25
2 Chris Masters	.30	.75
3 Christian	.50	1.25
4 Dolph Ziggler	.50	1.25
5 Kane	.75	2.00
6 Luke Gallows	.30	.75
7 Matt Hardy	.75	2.00
8 Montel Vontavious Porter	.50	1.25
9 Undertaker	1.25	3.00
10 Evan Bourne	.30	.75
11 Mark Henry	.50	1.25
12 Rey Mysterio	.75	2.00
13 R-Truth	.30	.75
14 Ted DiBiase	.50	1.25
15 The Great Khali	.30	.75
16 The Miz	.50	1.25
17 Zack Ryder	.30	.75
18 Edge	1.25	3.00
19 Randy Orton	1.25	3.00
20 John Cena	1.50	4.00
21 John Morrison	.50	1.25
22 Jack Swagger	.30	.75
23 Beth Phoenix	1.25	3.00
24 Michelle McCool	1.25	3.00
25 Maryse	1.25	3.00
26 Gail Kim	.75	2.00

2010 Topps WWE Slam Attax Mayhem General Managers

COMPLETE SET (6)	2.50	6.00
STATED ODDS 1:6		
1 T.Long/You're Kicked Out	.75	2.00
2 T.Long/You're Kicked Out	.75	2.00
3 T.Long/You're Kicked Out	.75	2.00
4 T.Long/Return to the Ring	.75	2.00
5 T.Long/Return to the Ring	.75	2.00
6 T.Long/Return to the Ring	.75	2.00

2010 Topps WWE Slam Attax Mayhem Starter Box Exclusives

COMPLETE SET (3)	2.50	6.00
STATED ODDS ONE PER STARTER BOX		
1 Montel Vontavious Porter	.75	2.00
2 Triple H	2.50	6.00
3 Drew McIntyre	.75	2.00

2010 Topps WWE Slam Attax Mayhem Titles

COMPLETE SET (10)	5.00	12.00
STATED ODDS		
1 WWE Championship	.75	2.00
2 Intercontinental Championship	.75	2.00
3 Women's Championship	.75	2.00
4 World Tag Team Championship	.75	2.00
5 World Heavyweight Championship	.75	2.00
6 United States Championship	.75	2.00
7 WWE Tag Team Championship	.75	2.00
8 WWE Divas Championship	.75	2.00
9 WWE Money in the Bank Briefcase	.75	2.00
10 WWE Slammy Award	.75	2.00

2020 Topps WWE Slam Attax Reloaded

COMPLETE SET (352)	20.00	50.00
1 Akam	.40	1.00
2 Akira Tozawa	.30	.75
3 Aleister Black	.60	1.50
4 Andrade	.50	1.25
5 Angel Garza RC	.40	1.00
6 Angelo Dawkins	.30	.75
7 Apollo Crews	.40	1.00
8 Asuka	1.25	3.00
9 Becky Lynch	1.25	3.00

No.	Name	Low	High
10	Bianca Belair	.75	2.00
11	Big Show	.40	1.00
12	Billie Kay	.60	1.50
13	Bobby Lashley	.60	1.50
14	Cedric Alexander	.30	.75
15	Charlotte Flair	1.25	3.00
16	Drew McIntyre	.60	1.50
17	Edge	.60	1.50
18	Erik	.30	.75
19	Humberto Carrillo	.50	1.25
20	Ivar	.30	.75
21	Jason Jordan	.30	.75
22	Jinder Mahal	.30	.75
23	Kairi Sane	.60	1.50
24	Kevin Owens	.40	1.00
25	Liv Morgan	.75	2.00
26	Montez Ford	.30	.75
27	Murphy	.40	1.00
28	Natalya	.50	1.25
29	Nia Jax	.50	1.25
30	Peyton Royce	.60	1.50
31	R-Truth	.30	.75
32	Randy Orton	.75	2.00
33	Rey Mysterio	.60	1.50
34	Rezar	.30	.75
35	Ricochet	.50	1.25
36	Shayna Baszler	1.00	2.50
37	Ruby Riott	.50	1.25
38	Samoa Joe	.50	1.25
39	Seth Rollins	.60	1.50
40	Shelton Benjamin	.40	1.00
41	Titus O'Neil	.30	.75
42	Undertaker	1.25	3.00
43	Zelina Vega	.60	1.50
44	AJ Styles	1.00	2.50
45	Alexa Bliss	2.00	5.00
46	Bayley	.60	1.50
47	Big E	.30	.75
48	Bo Dallas	.30	.75
49	Braun Strowman	.75	2.00
50	Carmella	.75	2.00
51	Cesaro	.30	.75
52	Dana Brooke	.50	1.25
53	Daniel Bryan	1.00	2.50
54	Dolph Ziggler	.30	.75
55	Elias	.30	.75
56	Ember Moon	.60	1.50
57	Goldberg	1.25	3.00
58	Gran Metalik	.30	.75
59	Jaxson Ryker RC	.40	1.00
60	Jeff Hardy	.75	2.00
61	Jey Uso	.30	.75
62	Jimmy Uso	.30	.75
63	John Morrison	.30	.75
64	Kalisto	.30	.75
65	Kane	.40	1.00
66	King Corbin	.40	1.00
67	Kofi Kingston	.50	1.25
68	Lacey Evans	.75	2.00
69	Lars Sullivan	.30	.75
70	Lince Dorado	.30	.75
71	Mandy Rose	1.50	4.00
72	Maryse	.60	1.50
73	Mickie James	.50	1.25
74	Mojo Rawley	.30	.75
75	Mustafa Ali	.50	1.25
76	Naomi	.60	1.50
77	Nikki Cross	.60	1.50
78	Otis	.50	1.25
79	Robert Roode	.30	.75
80	Roman Reigns	.75	2.00
81	Sami Zayn	.40	1.00
82	Sasha Banks	1.50	4.00
83	Sheamus	.40	1.00
84	Shinsuke Nakamura	.60	1.50
85	Shorty G	.30	.75
86	Sonya Deville	.75	2.00
87	Steve Cutler	.30	.75
88	Tamina	.40	1.00
89	The Fiend Bray Wyatt	1.00	2.50
90	The Miz	.50	1.25
91	Tucker	.30	.75
92	Wesley Blake	.40	1.00
93	Xavier Woods	.30	.75
94	Adam Cole	.75	2.00
95	Aliyah	.60	1.50
96	Arturo Ruas	.30	.75
97	Mercedes Martinez	.50	1.25
98	Boa RC	.30	.75
99	Bobby Fish	.30	.75
100	Bronson Reed RC	.30	.75
101	Cameron Grimes RC	.30	.75
102	Candice LeRae	1.00	2.50
103	Chelsea Green	1.50	4.00
104	Dakota Kai	.60	1.50
105	Damian Priest	.30	.75
106	Danny Burch	.40	1.00
107	Dexter Lumis RC	.30	.75
108	Dominik Dijakovic	.30	.75
109	Fandango	.30	.75
110	Finn Balor	.75	2.00
111	Io Shirai	.50	1.25
112	Isaiah Swerve Scott RC	.40	1.00
113	Jessamyn Duke	.50	1.25
114	Joaquin Wilde RC	.30	.75
115	Johnny Gargano	.60	1.50
116	Kacy Catanzaro	.60	1.50
117	Karrion Kross RC	.60	1.50
118	Keith Lee	.30	.75
119	Killian Dain	.40	1.00
120	Kona Reeves	.30	.75
121	Kushida	.40	1.00
122	Kyle O'Reilly	.40	1.00
123	Mansoor	.30	.75
124	Marina Shafir	.50	1.25
125	Matt Riddle	.60	1.50
126	Mia Yim	.60	1.50
127	Pete Dunne	.30	.75
128	Racquel Gonzalez RC	.50	1.25
129	Rhea Ripley	1.25	3.00
130	Roderick Strong	.60	1.50
131	Scarlett RC	1.25	3.00
132	Shane Thorne	.30	.75
133	Santana Garrett RC	.30	.75
134	Shotzi Blackheart RC	1.00	2.50
135	Tegan Nox RC	.75	2.00
136	Tommaso Ciampa	.60	1.50
137	Tyler Breeze	.40	1.00
138	Vanessa Borne	.60	1.50
139	Velveteen Dream	.40	1.00
140	Xia Li	.60	1.50
141	Alexander Wolfe	.30	.75
142	Dave Mastiff RC	.40	1.00
143	Fabian Aichner	.12	.30
144	Flash Morgan Webster RC	.40	1.00
145	Ilja Dragunov RC	.50	1.25
146	James Drake RC	.40	1.00
147	Joe Coffey RC	.30	.75
148	Jordan Devlin RC	.30	.75
149	Kay Lee Ray RC	.50	1.25
150	Ligero RC	.30	.75
151	Marcel Barthel RC	.30	.75
152	Mark Andrews	.30	.75
153	Mark Coffey RC	.40	1.00
154	Noam Dar	.30	.75
155	Piper Niven RC	.40	1.00
156	Toni Storm	.75	2.00
157	Travis Banks RC	.30	.75
158	Trent Seven	.30	.75
159	Tyler Bate	.50	1.25
160	Walter RC	.60	1.50
161	Wolfgang RC	.30	.75
162	Zack Gibson RC	.30	.75
163	Ariya Daivari	.30	.75
164	Gentleman Jack Gallagher	.40	1.00
165	Oney Lorcan	.40	1.00
166	Raul Mendoza	.30	.75
167	Samir Singh	.30	.75
168	Sunil Singh	.30	.75
169	The Brian Kendrick	.30	.75
170	Tony Nese	.30	.75
171	AOP TT	.40	1.00
172	Murphy/Austin Theory TT	.50	1.25
173	Miz/John Morrison TT	.50	1.25
174	Seth Rollins/Murphy TT	.60	1.50
175	Usos TT	.30	.75
176	Heavy Machinery TT	.50	1.25
177	Robert Roode/Dolph Ziggler TT	.30	.75
178	Street Profits TT	.30	.75
179	Viking Raiders TT	.30	.75
180	Broserweights TT	.60	1.50
181	Ever Rise TT		
182	Danny Burch/Oney Lorcan TT	.40	1.00
183	Ricochet/Cedric Alexander TT	.50	1.25
184	Grizzled Young Veterans TT	.40	1.00
185	Alexa Bliss/Nikki Cross TT	2.00	5.00
186	Kabuki Warriors TT	1.25	3.00
187	Nakamura/Cesaro TT	.60	1.50
188	Lucha House Party TT	.30	.75
189	New Day TT	.50	1.25
190	Forgotten Sons TT	.40	1.00
191	British Strong Style TT	.50	1.25
192	Gallus TT	.40	1.00
193	The Undisputed Era TT	.75	2.00
194	Imperium TT	.60	1.50
195	Adam Cole FL	.75	2.00
196	Aleister Black FL	.60	1.50
197	Bianca Belair FL	.75	2.00
198	Dominik Dijakovic FL	.30	.75
199	Io Shirai FL	.50	1.25
200	Keith Lee FL	.30	.75
201	King Corbin FL	.40	1.00
202	Liv Morgan FL	.75	2.00
203	Matt Riddle FL	.60	1.50
204	Pete Dunne FL	.30	.75
205	Rhea Ripley FL	1.25	3.00
206	Ricochet FL	.50	1.25
207	Shayna Baszler FL	1.00	2.50
208	Tommaso Ciampa FL	.60	1.50
209	Velveteen Dream FL	.40	1.00
210	Walter FL	.60	1.50
211	Angel Garza FL	.40	1.00
212	Austin Theory FL RC	.50	1.25
213	Cameron Grimes FL	.30	.75
214	Candice LeRae FL	1.00	2.50
215	Dakota Kai FL	.60	1.50
216	Johnny Gargano FL	.60	1.50
217	Montez Ford FL	.30	.75
218	Toni Storm FL	.75	2.00
219	Lacey Evans FL	.75	2.00
220	Otis FL	.50	1.25
221	AJ Styles R	1.00	2.50
222	Asuka R	1.25	3.00
223	Rey Mysterio R	.60	1.50
224	Ruby Riott R	.50	1.25
225	Table	.20	.50
226	Ladder	.20	.50
227	Steel Chair	.20	.50
228	Trash Can	.20	.50
229	The Fiend Bray Wyatt FFH	1.00	2.50
230	Bray Wyatt FFH	1.00	2.50
231	Mercy the Buzzard FFH	.40	1.00
232	Huskus the Pig Boy FFH	.40	1.00
233	Ramblin' Rabbit FFH	.40	1.00
234	Abby the Witch FFH	1.00	2.50
235	Beth Phoenix HOF	.50	1.25
236	Brutus Beefcake HOF	.30	.75
237	Dusty Rhodes HOF	.60	1.50
238	Jerry Lawler HOF	.75	2.00
239	Mark Henry HOF	.50	1.25
240	Road Dogg HOF	.40	1.00
241	Faarooq HOF	.50	1.25
242	X-Pac HOF	.30	.75
243	Big Boss Man HOF	.50	1.25
244	British Bulldog HOF	.50	1.25
245	Diamond Dallas Page HOF	.60	1.50
246	Hacksaw Jim Duggan HOF	.60	1.50
247	Kevin Nash HOF	.50	1.25
248	Mr. Perfect HOF	.50	1.25
249	Rick Rude HOF	.40	1.00
250	Razor Ramon HOF	.50	1.25
251	Ricky Steamboat HOF	.50	1.25
252	Rikishi HOF	.30	.75
253	Rowdy Roddy Piper HOF	.75	2.00
254	Sgt. Slaughter HOF	.60	1.50
255	The Honky Tonk Man HOF	.50	1.25
256	Million Dollar Man HOF	.60	1.50
257	Andre the Giant HOF	.75	2.00
258	Batista HOF	.50	1.25
259	Booker T HOF	.60	1.50
260	Bret Hit Man Hart HOF	.75	2.00
261	Chyna HOF	.75	2.00
262	Eddie Guerrero HOF	.75	2.00
263	Lita HOF	.75	2.00
264	Randy Savage HOF	1.00	2.50
265	Mick Foley HOF	.60	1.50
266	Ric Flair HOF	1.25	3.00
267	Shawn Michaels HOF	.75	2.00
268	Diesel HOF	.50	1.25
269	Sting HOF	1.00	2.50
270	Trish Stratus HOF	1.50	4.00
271	Ultimate Warrior HOF	.75	2.00
272	Yokozuna HOF	.50	1.25
273	Andrade B	.50	1.25
274	Charlotte Flair B	1.25	3.00
275	Drew McIntyre B	.60	1.50
276	Edge B	.60	1.50
277	Sheamus B	.40	1.00
278	AJ Styles B	1.00	2.50
279	Alexa Bliss B	2.00	5.00
280	Murphy B	.40	1.00
281	The Fiend Bray Wyatt B	1.00	2.50
282	Nikki Cross B	.60	1.50
283	Adam Cole B	.75	2.00
284	Dolph Ziggler B	.30	.75
285	Rhea Ripley B	1.25	3.00
286	Io Shirai B	.50	1.25
287	Shayna Baszler B	1.00	2.50
288	Seth Rollins B	.60	1.50
289	Angel Garza B	.40	1.00
290	Goldberg B	1.25	3.00
291	Roman Reigns B	.75	2.00
292	The Miz B	.50	1.25
293	Bayley B	.60	1.50
294	Natalya B	.50	1.25
295	Randy Orton B	.75	2.00
296	Daniel Bryan B	1.00	2.50
297	Kairi Sane B	.60	1.50
298	Shorty G B	.30	.75
299	Aleister Black B	.60	1.50
300	Kevin Owens B	.40	1.00
301	Kofi Kingston B	.50	1.25
302	Shinsuke Nakamura B	.60	1.50
303	Asuka MITB	1.25	3.00
304	Otis MITB	.50	1.25
305	Universal Title	.20	.50
306	WWE Title	.20	.50
307	RAW Women's Title	.20	.50
308	SmackDown Women's Title	.20	.50
309	Intercontinental Title	.20	.50
310	United States Title	.20	.50
311	24/7 Title	.20	.50
312	RAW Tag Team Title	.20	.50
313	SmackDown Tag Team Title	.20	.50
314	WWE Women's Tag Team Title	.20	.50
315	NXT Title	.20	.50
316	NXT Women's Title	.20	.50
317	NXT North American Title	.20	.50
318	NXT Cruiserweight Title	.20	.50
319	NXT Tag Team Title	.20	.50
320	NXT UK Title	.20	.50
321	NXT UK Women's Title	.20	.50
322	NXT UK Tag Team Title	.20	.50
323	Orton/RKO	.75	2.00
324	Balor/Coup de Grace	.75	2.00
325	Goldberg/Jackhammer	1.25	3.00
326	Black/Black Mass	.60	1.50
327	Edge/Spear	.60	1.50
328	Styles/Phenomenal Forearm	1.00	2.50
329	Hardy/Swanton Bomb	.75	2.00
330	McIntyre/Claymore Kick	.60	1.50
331	Hart/Sharpshooter	.75	2.00
332	Austin/Stone Cold Stunner	1.50	4.00
333	Undertaker/Tombstone	1.25	3.00
334	Triple H/Pedigree	.75	2.00
335	Kane/Chokeslam	.40	1.00
336	Cena/Attitude Adjustment	1.25	3.00
337	Braun Strowman B	.75	2.00
338	Otis B	.50	1.25
339	Sasha Banks ICONS	1.50	4.00
340	Charlotte Flair ICONS	1.25	3.00
341	Daniel Bryan ICONS	1.00	2.50
342	Seth Rollins ICONS	.60	1.50
343	Triple H ICONS	.75	2.00
344	The Rock ICONS	1.50	4.00
345	Bret Hart ICONS	.75	2.00
346	Steve Austin ICONS	1.50	4.00
347	Roman Reigns 100 CLUB	.75	2.00
348	Asuka 100 CLUB	1.25	3.00
349	Drew McIntyre 100 CLUB	.60	1.50

350 Bray Wyatt 100 CLUB 1.00 2.50
351 Undertaker SR 1.25 3.00
352 John Cena SR 1.25 3.00

2020 Topps WWE Slam Attax Reloaded Autographs

AAB Alexa Bliss
AAC Adam Cole
AAD Angelo Dawkins
AAJ AJ Styles
AAN Andrade
AAS Asuka
ABA Bayley
ABB Bianca Belair
ABE Big E
ABL Becky Lynch
ABM Murphy
ACS Cesaro
ADB Daniel Bryan
ADM Drew McIntyre
AED Edge
AEL Elias
AEM Ember Moon
AFB Finn Balor
AJG Johnny Gargano
AKO Kevin Owens
AKS Kairi Sane
ALA Bobby Lashley
ALE Lacey Evans
AMA Mustafa Ali
AMR Mandy Rose
ANJ Nia Jax
ANM Naomi
ANT Natalya
AOO Otis
APD Pete Dunne
ARB Ruby Riott
ARC Ricochet
ARR Robert Roode
ARS Roderick Strong
ART R-Truth
ASB Shayna Baszler
ASD Sonya Deville
ASG Shorty G
ASH Shinsuke Nakamura
ATB Tyler Bate
ATC Tommaso Ciampa
ATE Aleister Black
ATM The Miz
ATS Trent Seven
AVD Velveteen Dream/50
(Topps.com Exclusive)
AXW Xavier Woods

2020 Topps WWE Slam Attax Reloaded Collector Tins

NNO Edge
NNO John Cena
NNO Sasha Banks

2020 Topps WWE Slam Attax Reloaded Exclusives

T1 Bret Hit Man Hart
T2 British Bulldog
T3 Eddie Guerrero
T4 Yokozuna
T5 Batista
T6 Diesel
T7 Lita
T8 Bayley
T9 The Fiend Bray Wyatt
T10 Kofi Kingston
T11 Velveteen Dream
T12 Kevin Owens
T13 Rhea Ripley
T14 Sasha Banks
T15 Macho Man Randy Savage
T16 Ric Flair
T17 Shawn Michaels
T18 Stone Cold Steve Austin
T19 Papa Shango
T20 Vader
T21 Booker T
T22 Daniel Bryan
T23 Drew McIntyre
T24 Randy Orton
T25 Roman Reigns
T26 King Corbin
T27 Alexa Bliss
T28 Becky Lynch
T29 Andre the Giant
T30 Bam Bam Bigelow
T31 Ultimate Warrior
T32 Rowdy Roddy Piper
T33 Razor Ramon
T34 Chyna
T35 Trish Stratus
T36 AJ Styles
T37 Braun Strowman
T38 The Miz
T39 Seth Rollins
T40 Adam Cole
T41 Charlotte Flair
T42 Asuka

2020 Topps WWE Slam Attax Reloaded Limited Edition Bronze

LEBB Becky Lynch
LECB Drew McIntyre
LERB Roman Reigns

2020 Topps WWE Slam Attax Reloaded Limited Edition Gold

LEDA The Rock
(Mega Tins Exclusive)
LEDB Undertaker
(Mega Tins Exclusive)
LEDC Stone Cold Steve Austin
(Mega Tins Exclusive)
LESA The Fiend Bray Wyatt
LETA John Cena
(Collector Tins Exclusive)
LETB Sasha Banks
(Collector Tins Exclusive)
LETC Edge
(Collector Tins Exclusive)
LEXA Daniel Bryan
(Web Wednesday Exclusive)
LEXB Charlotte Flair
(WWE Kids Magazine Exclusive)
LEXC Seth Rollins
(Web Wednesday Exclusive)
LEXD Nikki Cross
(Web Wednesday Exclusive)

2020 Topps WWE Slam Attax Reloaded Relics

M1 Drew McIntyre/T-Shirt
M2 Humberto Carrllo/T-Shirt
M3 Samoa Joe/T-Shirt
M4 Shayna Baszler/T-Shirt
M5 Sonya Deville/T-Shirt
M6 Roman Reigns vs. King Corbin/Table
M7 Triple H vs. Batista/Mat

2020 Topps WWE Slam Attax Reloaded XL

XL1 John Cena
XL2 Charlotte Flair
XL3 Braun Strowman
XL4 Bayley
XL5 Becky Lynch
XL6 Roman Reigns
XL7 Undertaker
XL8 The Fiend Bray Wyatt
XL9 Drew McIntyre
XL10 Rhea Ripley
XL11 Kofi Kingston

2016 Topps WWE Slam Attax TakeOver

COMPLETE SET (299) 25.00 60.00
1 AJ Styles .50 1.25
2 Asuka RC .50 1.25
3 Alberto Del Rio .20 .50
4 Brock Lesnar .60 1.50
5 Charlotte .40 1.00
6 Dean Ambrose .40 1.00
7 Finn Balor .40 1.00
8 John Cena .60 1.50
9 Kalisto .30 .75
10 Kevin Owens .30 .75
11 Roman Reigns .40 1.00
12 Samoa Joe .30 .75
13 Sasha Banks .40 1.00
14 Seth Rollins .20 .50
15 The New Day .30 .75
16 Triple H .50 1.25
17 AJ Styles .50 1.25
18 Asuka RC .50 1.25
19 Alberto Del Rio .20 .50
20 Brock Lesnar .60 1.50
21 Charlotte .40 1.00
22 Dean Ambrose .40 1.00
23 Finn Balor .40 1.00
24 John Cena .60 1.50
25 Kalisto .30 .75
26 Kevin Owens .30 .75
27 Roman Reigns .40 1.00
28 Samoa Joe .30 .75
29 Sasha Banks .40 1.00
30 Seth Rollins .20 .50
31 The New Day .30 .75
32 Triple H .50 1.25
33 Becky Lynch RC .40 1.00
34 Big E .12 .30
35 Bo Dallas .12 .30
36 Bray Wyatt .50 1.25
37 Charlotte .40 1.00
38 Kalisto .30 .75
39 Kevin Owens .30 .75
40 Luke Harper .12 .30
41 Neville .25 .60
42 Paige .40 1.00
43 Roman Reigns .40 1.00
44 Rusev .30 .75
45 Sasha Banks .40 1.00
46 Seth Rollins .20 .50
47 Tyler Breeze .12 .30
48 Xavier Woods .12 .30
49 MITB Briefcase .12 .30
50 NXT Women's Title .12 .30
51 NXT Title .12 .30
52 NXT Tag Team Title .12 .30
53 WWE Tag Team Title .12 .30
54 WWE Women's Title .12 .30
55 WWE United States Title .12 .30
56 WWE Title .12 .30
57 AJ Styles .50 1.25
58 Alberto Del Rio .20 .50
59 Apollo Crews .12 .30
60 Asuka RC .50 1.25
61 Baron Corbin .15 .40
62 Bayley RC .30 .75
63 Becky Lynch RC .40 1.00
64 Big Cass .25 .60
65 Braun Strowman RC .15 .40
66 Bray Wyatt .50 1.25
67 Brock Lesnar .60 1.50
68 Charlotte .40 1.00
69 Chris Jericho .30 .75
70 Dean Ambrose .40 1.00
71 Dolph Ziggler .15 .40
72 Elias Samson RC .12 .30
73 Erick Rowan .12 .30
74 Heath Slater .12 .30
75 Hideo Itami .15 .40
76 Jason Jordan RC .15 .40
77 John Cena .60 1.50
78 Kalisto .30 .75
79 Kevin Owens .30 .75
80 Mojo Rawley RC .12 .30
81 Neville .25 .60
82 Paige .40 1.00
83 Roman Reigns .40 1.00
84 Rusev .30 .75
85 Samoa Joe .30 .75
86 Sasha Banks .40 1.00
87 Sheamus .30 .75
88 Triple H .50 1.25
89 Aiden English .12 .30
90 AJ Styles .50 1.25
91 Alberto Del Rio .20 .50
92 Alicia Fox .20 .50
93 Apollo Crews .12 .30
94 Baron Corbin .15 .40
95 Becky Lynch RC .40 1.00
96 Big Cass .25 .60
97 Big E .12 .30
98 Big Show .25 .60
99 Bo Dallas .12 .30
100 Booker T .25 .60
101 Braun Strowman RC .15 .40
102 Bray Wyatt .50 1.25
103 Brie Bella .25 .60
104 Brock Lesnar .60 1.50
105 Bubba Ray Dudley .25 .60
106 Byron Saxton .12 .30
107 Cesaro .25 .60
108 Charlotte .40 1.00
109 Chris Jericho .30 .75
110 Curtis Axel .12 .30
111 Dana Brooke RC .30 .75
112 Daniel Bryan .50 1.25
113 Darren Young .12 .30
114 David Otunga .12 .30
115 Dean Ambrose .40 1.00
116 Dolph Ziggler .15 .40
117 D-Von Dudley .20 .50
118 Emma .25 .60
119 Enzo Amore RC .25 .60
120 Epico .12 .30
121 Erick Rowan .12 .30
122 Eva Marie .25 .60
123 Fandango .12 .30
124 Goldust .20 .50
125 Heath Slater .12 .30
126 Jack Swagger .12 .30
127 JBL .15 .40
128 Jerry Lawler .25 .60
129 Jey Uso .12 .30
130 Jimmy Uso .12 .30
131 John Cena .60 1.50
132 JoJo .12 .30
133 Kalisto .30 .75
134 Kane .20 .50
135 Karl Anderson RC .12 .30
136 Kevin Owens .30 .75
137 Kofi Kingston .12 .30
138 Konnor .12 .30
139 Lana .50 1.25
140 Luke Gallows .15 .40
141 Luke Harper .12 .30
142 Mark Henry .15 .40
143 Maryse .25 .60
144 Mauro Ranallo RC .12 .30
145 Michael Cole .12 .30
146 Naomi .20 .50
147 Natalya .20 .50
148 Neville .25 .60
149 Nikki Bella .40 1.00
150 Paige .40 1.00
151 Primo .12 .30
152 Randy Orton .30 .75
153 Renee Young .30 .75
154 Roman Reigns .40 1.00
155 Rosa Mendes .12 .30
156 R-Truth .12 .30
157 Rusev .30 .75
158 Ryback .15 .40
159 Sami Zayn .20 .50
160 Sasha Banks .40 1.00
161 Seth Rollins .20 .50
162 Sheamus .30 .75
163 Simon Gotch RC .20 .50
164 Sin Cara .15 .40
165 Summer Rae .30 .75
166 Tamina .15 .40
167 The Miz .20 .50
168 The Rock .60 1.50
169 Titus O'Neil .12 .30
170 Tony Chimel .12 .30
171 Triple H .50 1.25
172 Tyler Breeze .12 .30
173 Tyson Kidd .12 .30
174 Undertaker .50 1.25
175 Viktor .12 .30

176 Xavier Woods .12 .30
177 Zack Ryder .12 .30
178 Alexa Bliss .60 1.50
179 Angelo Dawkins .12 .30
180 Asuka RC .50 1.25
181 Austin Aries .15 .40
182 Bayley RC .30 .75
183 Billie Kay RC .30 .75
184 Blake RC .12 .30
185 Carmella RC .30 .75
186 Cathy Kelley RC .12 .30
187 Chad Gable RC .15 .40
188 Corey Graves RC .12 .30
189 Dash Wilder RC .15 .40
190 Dasha Fuentes .12 .30
191 Elias Samson RC .12 .30
192 Finn Balor .40 1.00
193 Greg Hamilton RC .12 .30
194 Hideo Itami .15 .40
195 Jason Jordan RC .15 .40
196 Mandy Rose RC 2.00 5.00
197 Mojo Rawley RC .12 .30
198 Murphy RC .12 .30
199 Nia Jax RC .20 .50
200 No Way Jose RC .12 .30
201 Peyton Royce RC .30 .75
202 Samoa Joe .30 .75
203 Sawyer Fulton .15 .40
204 Scott Dawson RC .12 .30
205 Shinsuke Nakamura RC .50 1.25
206 Tom Phillips .12 .30
207 Tye Dillinger .15 .40
208 William Regal .12 .30
209 Adrienne Reese .30 .75
210 Bronson Matthews RC .12 .30
211 Oney Lorcan RC .12 .30
212 Hugo Knox RC .12 .30
213 King Constantine RC .12 .30
214 Manny Andrade .20 .50
215 Noah Kekoa RC .12 .30
216 Tino Sabbatelli RC .12 .30
217 Bam Bam Bigelow .15 .40
218 Big Boss Man .20 .50
219 Bob Backlund .12 .30
220 Bobby Heenan .20 .50
221 Booker T .25 .60
222 Bret Hart .30 .75
223 Brian Pillman .15 .40
224 British Bulldog .15 .40
225 Bruno Sammartino .15 .40
226 Chief Jay Strongbow .20 .50
227 Freddie Blassie .15 .40
228 Bob Orton .20 .50
229 Dean Malenko .12 .30
230 Diamond Dallas Page .20 .50
231 Diesel .30 .75
232 Doink The Clown .12 .30
233 Dusty Rhodes .12 .30
234 Eddie Guerrero .30 .75
235 Edge .30 .75
236 Greg Valentine .15 .40
237 Jim Duggan .12 .30
238 Harley Race .12 .30
239 Honky Tonk Man .12 .30
240 Iron Shiek .12 .30
241 Irwin R. Schyster .12 .30
242 Jake Roberts .25 .60
243 Jim Neidhart .12 .30
244 Jimmy Hart .15 .40
245 Junkyard Dog .20 .50
246 Kevin Nash .30 .75
247 Lex Luger .20 .50
248 Lita .40 1.00
249 Randy Savage .30 .75
250 Don Muraco .12 .30
251 Gene Okerlund .15 .40
252 Ted DiBiase .15 .40
253 Curt Hennig .30 .75
254 Paul Orndorf .12 .30
255 Paul Bearer .20 .50
256 Rick Rude .20 .50
257 Razor Ramon .30 .75
258 Ric Flair .50 1.25
259 Ricky Steamboat .15 .40
260 Rikishi .15 .40
261 Rhyno .12 .30
262 Road Dogg .20 .50
263 Ron Simmons .30 .75
264 Rowdy Roddy Piper .40 1.00
265 Sgt. Slaughter .15 .40
266 Shawn Michaels .50 1.25
267 Sting .30 .75
268 Stone Cold Steve Austin .60 1.50
269 Terry Funk .12 .30
270 The Godfather .15 .40
271 Trish Stratus .60 1.50
272 Ultimate Warrior .30 .75
273 Vader .25 .60
274 X-Pac .20 .50
275 Yokozuna .25 .60
276 American Alpha .15 .40
277 Blake/Murphy .12 .30
278 Enzo/Cass .25 .60
279 Gargano/Ciampa .15 .40
280 Gallows/Anderson .15 .40
281 The Shining Stars .12 .30
282 Team B.A.D. .40 1.00
283 The Ascension .12 .30
284 The Bella Twins .40 1.00
285 The Bushwhackers .12 .30
286 The Dudley Boyz .25 .60
287 The Hype Bros .12 .30
288 The Lucha Dragons .30 .75
289 The New Day .30 .75
290 The Prime Time Players .12 .30
291 The Revival .15 .40
292 The Social Outcasts .12 .30
293 The Usos .12 .30
294 The Vaudevillains .20 .50
295 The Wyatt Family .50 1.25
296 Ladder .12 .30
297 Steel Chair .12 .30
298 Table .12 .30
299 Trash Can .12 .30

2021 Topps WWE Slam Attax

COMPLETE SET (368) 100.00 200.00
1 Adam Cole .60 1.50
2 AJ Styles .60 1.50
3 Akira Tozawa .25 .60
4 Aleister Black .50 1.25
5 Alexa Bliss 1.25 3.00
6 Alexander Wolfe .20 .50
7 Aliyah .40 1.00
8 August Grey RC .20 .50
9 Angel Garza .25 .60
10 Angelo Dawkins .25 .60
11 Apollo Crews .25 .60
12 Ariya Daivari .25 .60
13 Arturo Ruas RC .20 .50
14 Asuka .75 2.00
15 Austin Theory .40 1.00
16 Bayley .50 1.25
17 Becky Lynch .75 2.00
18 Bianca Belair .50 1.25
19 Big E .40 1.00
20 Billie Kay .40 1.00
21 Bo Dallas .20 .50
22 Boa .20 .50
23 Bobby Fish .25 .60
24 Bobby Lashley .50 1.25
25 Braun Strowman .50 1.25
26 Bronson Reed .25 .60
27 Cameron Grimes .40 1.00
28 Candice LeRae .75 2.00
29 Carmella .50 1.25
30 Cedric Alexander .20 .50
31 Cesaro .20 .50
32 Chad Gable .20 .50
33 Charlotte Flair 1.00 2.50
34 Chelsea Green .50 1.25
35 Dabba Kato RC .25 .60
36 Dakota Kai .40 1.00
37 Damian Priest .30 .75
38 Dana Brooke .20 .50
39 Daniel Bryan .75 2.00
40 Danny Burch .25 .60
41 Dave Mastiff .20 .50
42 Dexter Lumis .20 .50
43 Dolph Ziggler .40 1.00
44 Dominik Mysterio RC .25 .60
45 Drew Gulak .25 .60
46 Drew McIntyre .50 1.25
47 Edge .75 2.00
48 Elias .20 .50
49 Ember Moon .25 .60
50 Erik .20 .50
51 Fabian Aichner .25 .60
52 Fandango .30 .75
53 Finn Balor .50 1.25
54 Flash Morgan .25 .60
55 Gran Metalik .20 .50
56 Humberto Carrillo .20 .50
57 Ilja Dragunov .20 .50
58 Indi Hartwell RC .60 1.50
59 Io Shirai .40 1.00
60 Isaiah "Swerve" Scott .30 .75
61 Ivar .20 .50
62 Jake Atlas RC .20 .50
63 James Drake .20 .50
64 Jaxson Ryker .20 .50
65 Jeff Hardy .50 1.25
66 Jessamyn Duke .20 .50
67 Jey Uso .20 .50
68 Jimmy Uso .20 .50
69 Jinder Mahal .25 .60
70 Joaquin Wilde .30 .75
71 Joe Coffey .20 .50
72 John Morrison .40 1.00
73 Johnny Gargano .40 1.00
74 Jordan Devlin .20 .50
75 Kacy Catanzaro .40 1.00
76 Kalisto .25 .60
77 Kane .30 .75
78 Karrion Kross .75 2.00
79 Kay Lee Ray .50 1.25
80 Kayden Carter .40 1.00
81 Keith Lee .40 1.00
82 Kevin Owens .40 1.00
83 Killian Dain .20 .50
84 King Corbin .20 .50
85 Kofi Kingston .50 1.25
86 Kona Reeves .20 .50
87 Kushida .30 .75
88 Kyle O'Reilly .30 .75
89 Lacey Evans .50 1.25
90 Lana .25 .60
91 Leon Ruff RC .20 .50
92 Lince Dorado .20 .50
93 Liv Morgan .75 2.00
94 Mace .20 .50
95 Mandy Rose 1.00 2.50
96 Mansoor RC .20 .50
97 Marcel Barthel .25 .60
98 Marina Shafir .40 1.00
99 Mark Andrews .20 .50
100 Mark Coffey .20 .50
101 Mercedes Martinez .30 .75
102 Montez Ford .20 .50
103 Murphy .25 .60
104 Mustafa Ali .25 .60
105 MVP .20 .50
106 Naomi .25 .60
107 Nash Carter RC .20 .50
108 Natalya .30 .75
109 Nia Jax .40 1.00
110 Nikki Cross .40 1.00
111 Noam Dar .25 .60
112 Oney Lorcan .20 .50
113 Otis .25 .60
114 Pete Dunne .40 1.00
115 Peyton Royce .40 1.00
116 Piper Niven .30 .75
117 R-Truth .25 .60
118 Randy Orton .60 1.50
119 Raquel Gonzalez .50 1.25
120 Raul Mendoza .30 .75
121 Reckoning .25 .60
122 Rey Mysterio .50 1.25
123 Rhea Ripley .60 1.50
124 Ricochet .40 1.00
125 Riddick Moss .25 .60
126 Riddle .50 1.25
127 Rinku (Veer Mahaan) RC .20 .50
128 Robert Roode .25 .60
129 Roderick Strong .30 .75
130 Roman Reigns 1.00 2.50
131 Ruby Riott .40 1.00
132 Sami Zayn .30 .75
133 Samir Singh .20 .50
134 Santos Escobar .30 .75
135 Sasha Banks 1.00 2.50
136 Saurav RC .20 .50
137 Scarlett 1.00 2.50
138 Seth Rollins .50 1.25
139 Shayna Baszler .40 1.00
140 Sheamus .30 .75
141 Shelton Benjamin .30 .75
142 Shinsuke Nakamura .50 1.25
143 Shotzi Blackheart .75 2.00
144 Slapjack .20 .50
145 Sunil Singh .20 .50
146 T-Bar .25 .60
147 Tamina .25 .60
148 Tegan Nox .50 1.25
149 The Brian Kendrick .20 .50
150 The Fiend Bray Wyatt .75 2.00
151 The Miz .30 .75
152 Timothy Thatcher RC .20 .50
153 Tomasso Ciampa .50 1.25
154 Toni Storm .60 1.50
155 Tony Nese .20 .50
156 Trent Seven .25 .60
157 Tucker .20 .50
158 Tyler Bate .25 .60
159 Tyler Breeze .25 .60
160 Tyler Rust RC .20 .50
161 Vanessa Borne .25 .60
162 Velveteen Dream .25 .60
163 Walter .50 1.25
164 Wes Lee RC .20 .50
165 Wesley Blake .20 .50
166 Wolfgang .20 .50
167 Xavier Woods .20 .50
168 Xia Lee .40 1.00
169 Zack Gibson .20 .50
170 Ariya Daivari & Tony Nese TT .25 .60
171 Asuka & Charlotte TT 1.00 2.50
172 Breezango TT .30 .75
173 Cesaro & Daniel Bryan TT .75 2.00
174 Dakota Kai & Raquel TT .40 1.00
175 Danny Burch & Oney Lorcan TT .25 .60
176 Elias & Jaxson TT .20 .50
177 Ever Rise TT .25 .60
178 Flash Webster & Mark Andrews TT .25 .60
179 Alpha Academy TT .25 .60
180 Gallus TT .25 .60
181 Grizzled Young Veterans TT .20 .50
182 The Hurt Business TT .30 .75
183 Imperium TT .25 .60
184 Indus Sher TT .20 .50
185 K. Catanzaro & K. Carter TT .40 1.00
186 Kushida & Leon Ruff TT .30 .75
187 Legado Del Fantasma TT .25 .60
188 Mandy Rose & Dana Brooke TT 1.00 2.50
189 Moustache Mountain TT .25 .60
190 MSK TT .20 .50
191 Retribution TT .20 .50
192 Shayna Baszler & Nia Jax TT .40 1.00
193 Shotzi & Ember Moon TT .75 2.00
194 The Bollywood Boys TT .20 .50
195 The Dirty Dawgs TT .40 1.00
196 The Lucha House Party TT .20 .50
197 The Miz & John Morrison TT .40 1.00
198 The New Day TT .40 1.00
199 The Riott Squad TT .30 .75
200 The Robert Stone Brand TT .20 .50
201 The Street Profits TT .25 .60
202 The Viking Raiders TT .20 .50
203 The Way TT .20 .50
204 Ciampa & Timothy Thatcher TT .50 1.25
205 The Way FAC .20 .50
206 The Hurt Business FAC .30 .75
207 Imperium FAC .25 .60
208 Retribution FAC .20 .50
209 Styles Clash .60 1.50
210 Twisted Bliss 1.25 3.00
211 Bayley-to-Belly .50 1.25
212 Big Ending .40 1.00

213 The Hurt Lock .50 1.25
214 Powerslam .50 1.25
215 Figure-Eight Leg-Lock 1.00 2.50
216 Claymore .50 1.25
217 Moonsault .40 1.00
218 Uso Splash .20 .50
219 RKO .60 1.50
220 Riptide .60 1.50
221 Spear 1.00 2.50
222 Brogue Kick .30 .75
223 Sister Abigail .75 2.00
224 Skull-Crushing Finale .30 .75
225 Sasha Banks 1.00 2.50
226 Sasha Banks 1.00 2.50
227 Sasha Banks 1.00 2.50
228 Riddle .50 1.25
229 Riddle .50 1.25
230 Riddle .50 1.25
231 Mankind .40 1.00
232 Stone Cold Steve Austin 1.00 2.50
233 Hulk Hogan 1.00 2.50
234 The Rock 2.00 5.00
235 Universal Title .15 .40
236 WWE Title .15 .40
237 RAW Women's Title .15 .40
238 SmackDown Women's Title .15 .40
239 Intercontinental Title .15 .40
240 United States Title .15 .40
241 24/7 Title .15 .40
242 RAW Tag Team Title .15 .40
243 SmackDown Title .15 .40
244 WWE Women's Tag Team Title .15 .40
245 NXT Title .15 .40
246 NXT Women's Title .15 .40
247 NXT North American Title .15 .40
248 NXT Cruiserweight Title .15 .40
249 NXT Tag Team Title .15 .40
250 NXT UK Title .15 .40
251 NXT UK Women's Title .15 .40
252 NXT UK Tag Team Title .15 .40
253 AJ Styles .60 1.50
254 Alexa Bliss 1.25 3.00
255 Charlotte Flair 1.00 2.50
256 Drew McIntyre .50 1.25
257 Randy Orton .60 1.50
258 The Fiend Bray Wyatt .75 2.00
259 Bayley .50 1.25
260 Bianca Belair .50 1.25
261 Daniel Bryan .75 2.00
262 Kevin Owens .40 1.00
263 Roman Reigns 1.00 2.50
264 Sasha Banks 1.00 2.50
265 Adam Cole .60 1.50
266 Finn Balor .50 1.25
267 Io Shirai .40 1.00
268 Karrion Kross .75 2.00
269 Pete Dunne .40 1.00
270 Toni Storm .60 1.50
271 Flash Morgan Webster .25 .60
272 Ilja Dragunov .20 .50
273 Kay Lee Ray .50 1.25
274 Trent Seven .25 .60
275 Walter .50 1.25
276 Wolfgang .20 .50
277 Thank You Taker 1.00 2.50
278 Thank You Taker 1.00 2.50
279 Thank You Taker 1.00 2.50
280 Thank You Taker 1.00 2.50
281 Thank You Taker 1.00 2.50
282 Daniel Bryan .75 2.00
283 Ricochet .40 1.00
284 Shotzi Blackheart .75 2.00
285 WWE Logo .15 .40
286 RAW Logo .15 .40
287 SmackDown Logo .15 .40
288 NXT Logo .15 .40
289 NXT UK Logo .15 .40
290 Andre the Giant L .75 2.00
291 Batista L .40 1.00
292 Bret "Hit Man" Hart L .50 1.25
293 Hulk Hogan L 1.00 2.50
294 Macho Man Randy Savage L .75 2.00
295 Mankind L .40 1.00
296 Ric Flair L .75 2.00
297 Stone Cold Steve Austin L 1.00 2.50
298 Trish Stratus L 1.00 2.50
299 Ultimate Warrior L .75 2.00
300 Apollo Crews .25 .60
301 Bianca Belair .50 1.25
302 Big E .40 1.00
303 Billie Kay .40 1.00
304 Cesaro .20 .50
305 Damien Priest .30 .75
306 Jey Uso .20 .50
307 Liv Morgan .75 2.00
308 Rhea Ripley .60 1.50
309 Riddle .50 1.25
310 Firefly Funhouse Logo .15 .40
311 Mercy the Buzzard .15 .40
312 Huskus the Pig Boy .15 .40
313 Abby the Witch .15 .40
314 Ramblin' Rabbit .15 .40
315 The Boss 1.00 2.50
316 Friendship Frog .15 .40
317 Apollo Crews .25 .60
318 Bayley .50 1.25
319 Braun Strowman .50 1.25
320 Sheamus .30 .75
321 Asuka .75 2.00
322 Cesaro .20 .50
323 Kevin Owens .40 1.00
324 Seth Rollins .50 1.25
325 Drew McIntyre .50 1.25
326 Mandy Rose 1.00 2.50
327 Montez Ford .20 .50
328 Roman Reigns 1.00 2.50
329 Dominik Mysterio RC .25 .60
330 Keith Lee .40 1.00
331 Riddle .50 1.25
332 Shayna Baszler .40 1.00
333 Angelo Dawkins .25 .60
334 Bobby Lashley .50 1.25
335 Sami Zayn .30 .75
336 Shinsuke Nakamura .50 1.25
337 AJ Styles .60 1.50
338 Lacey Evans .50 1.25
339 Lana .25 .60
340 The Miz .30 .75
341 Big E .40 1.00
342 Cedric Alexander .20 .50
343 Daniel Bryan .75 2.00
344 Randy Orton .60 1.50
345 Bianca Belair .50 1.25
346 Billie Kay .40 1.00
347 Edge .75 2.00
348 Rhea Ripley .60 1.50
349 Asuka ICON .75 2.00
350 Bayley ICON .50 1.25
351 Becky Lynch ICON .75 2.00
352 Charlotte Flair ICON 1.00 2.50
353 Daniel Bryan ICON .75 2.00
354 Kofi Kingston ICON .50 1.25
355 Randy Orton ICON .60 1.50
356 Seth Rollins ICON .50 1.25
357 Hollywood Hulk Hogan SR 1.00 2.50
358 Alexa Bliss 100C 1.25 3.00
359 Bianca Belair 100C .50 1.25
360 Drew McIntyre 100C .50 1.25
361 Bobby Lashley 100C .50 1.25
362 Sasha Banks 100C 1.00 2.50
363 The Fiend Bray Wyatt 100C .75 2.00
364 Edge 100C .75 2.00
365 Roman Reigns 100C 1.00 2.50
366 Alexa Bliss/Firefly Funhouse 1.25 3.00
367 Bray Wyatt/Firefly Funhouse .75 2.00
368 John Cena nWo UR 1.00 2.50

2021 Topps WWE Slam Attax Autographs

RANDOMLY INSERTED INTO PACKS

AT1 Adam Cole
AT2 Alexa Bliss
AT3 Becky Lynch
AT4 Bianca Belair
AT5 Billie Kay
AT6 The Fiend Bray Wyatt
AT7 Candice LeRae
AT8 Carmella 30.00 75.00
AT9 Cesaro
AT10 Elias
AT11 Ember Moon
AT12 Finn Balor
AT13 Flash Morgan Webster
AT14 Io Shirai
AT15 Kevin Owens
AT17 Mark Coffey
AT18 Mustafa Ali
AT19 Finn Balor
AT20 Riddle 60.00 120.00
AT21 Ruby Riott
AT22 Pete Dunne
AT23 Rhea Ripley
AT24 Sasha Banks
AT25 Shinsuke Nakamura
AT26 Shotzi Blackheart
AT27 The Miz 15.00 40.00
AT28 Tommaso Ciampa 25.00 60.00
AT29 Wolfgang
AT30 Xavier Woods 15.00 40.00
AT34 Keith Lee 15.00 40.00
AT35 Lacey Evans 25.00 60.00
AT37 Asuka 50.00 100.00
AT38 Bayley
AT39 Charlotte Flair
AT40 Naomi 12.00 30.00
AT41 Natalya 20.00 50.00
AT42 Nikki Cross 20.00 50.00
AT43 Peyton Royce 30.00 75.00
AT44 Trish Stratus 50.00 100.00
FINDDREW Drew McIntyre/99

2021 Topps WWE Slam Attax Boneyard Match Relics

STATED PRINT RUN 200 SER.#'d SETS

BY1 Undertaker vs. AJ Styles 50.00 100.00

2021 Topps WWE Slam Attax Champion Edition

STATED PRINT RUN 100 SER.#'d SETS

NNO Nikki A.S.H. 15.00 40.00
NNO Reggie 4.00 10.00
NNO Roman Reigns 12.00 30.00

2021 Topps WWE Slam Attax The Impossible Autographs

STATED PRINT RUN 1 SER.#'d SET
UNPRICED DUE TO SCARCITY

AT31 The Fiend/Alexa Bliss
AT32 John Cena
AT33 Roman Reigns

2021 Topps WWE Slam Attax Limited Edition Bronze

RANDOMLY INSERTED INTO PACKS

LE3B The Fiend Bray Wyatt 2.00 5.00
LE4B Alexa Bliss 2.50 6.00
LE5B Roman Reigns 2.00 5.00

2021 Topps WWE Slam Attax Limited Edition Gold

COMPLETE SET (24) 75.00 150.00
RANDOMLY INSERTED INTO PACKS

LE1G Drew McIntyre 1.50 4.00
LE2G Sasha Banks 3.00 8.00
LE3G The Fiend Bray Wyatt 4.00 10.00
LE4G Alexa Bliss 6.00 15.00
LE5G Roman Reigns 4.00 10.00
LE6G Bianca Belair 2.00 5.00
LE7G AJ Styles 2.50 6.00
LE8G Billie Kay 2.00 5.00
LE9G Big E 1.50 4.00
LE10G Daniel Bryan 2.50 6.00
LE11G Keith Lee 1.50 4.00
LE12G Liv Morgan 2.00 5.00
LE13G Riddle 3.00 8.00
LE14G Charlotte Flair 3.00 8.00
LE15G Bobby Lashley 2.00 5.00
LE16G Seth Rollins 1.50 4.00
LE17G Rhea Ripley 2.50 6.00
LE18G Becky Lynch 4.00 10.00
LE19G The Rock 6.00 15.00
LE20G John Cena 4.00 10.00
LE21G Randy Orton 3.00 8.00
LE22G Mandy Rose 4.00 10.00
LE23G Sami Zayn 1.50 4.00
LE24G Bayley 15.00 40.00

2021 Topps WWE Slam Attax Limited Edition Platinum Blue

RANDOMLY INSERTED INTO PACKS

LE3R The Fiend Bray Wyatt 10.00 25.00
LE4R Alexa Bliss 20.00 50.00
LE5R Roman Reigns 10.00 25.00

2021 Topps WWE Slam Attax Limited Edition Silver

RANDOMLY INSERTED INTO PACKS

LE3S The Fiend Bray Wyatt 3.00 8.00
LE4S Alexa Bliss 5.00 12.00
LE5S Roman Reigns 3.00 8.00

2021 Topps WWE Slam Attax Oversized

COMPLETE SET (20) 30.00 75.00

OV1 Roman Reigns 4.00 10.00
OV2 Hulk Hogan 4.00 10.00
OV3 Batista 1.50 4.00
OV4 Bret "Hit Man" Hart 2.00 5.00
OV5 Stone Cold Steve Austin 4.00 10.00
OV6 Becky Lynch 3.00 8.00
OV7 Drew McIntyre 2.00 5.00
OV8 Trish Stratus 4.00 10.00
OV9 Ultimate Warrior 3.00 8.00
OV10 Ric Flair 3.00 8.00
OV11 Karrion Kross 3.00 8.00
OV12 The Fiend Bray Wyatt 3.00 8.00
OV13 Alexa Bliss 5.00 12.00
OV14 Apollo Crews 1.00 2.50
OV15 Kevin Owens 1.50 4.00
OV16 Bianca Belair 2.00 5.00
OV17 Asuka 3.00 8.00
OV18 Cesaro .75 2.00
OV19 Sasha Banks 4.00 10.00
OV20 Big E 1.50 4.00

2021 Topps WWE Slam Attax SP

STATED PRINT RUN 100 SER.#'d SETS

NNO The Fiend Bray Wyatt 12.00 30.00
NNO Lilly 8.00 20.00
NNO Omos 6.00 15.00

2021 Topps WWE Slam Attax Tactic Cards

COMPLETE SET (4) 3.00 8.00
RANDOMLY INSERTED INTO PACKS

T1 Ladder 1.00 2.50
T2 Table 1.00 2.50
T3 Steel Chair 1.00 2.50
T4 Special Counsel Paul Heyman 1.00 2.50

2021 Topps WWE Slam Attax Women of WWE

COMPLETE SET (32) 10.00 25.00
RANDOMLY INSERTED INTO PACKS

W1 Alexa Bliss 1.50 4.00
W2 Asuka 1.00 2.50
W3 Bayley .60 1.50
W4 Becky Lynch 1.00 2.50
W5 Bianca Belair .60 1.50
W6 Billie Kay .50 1.25
W7 Candice LeRae 1.00 2.50
W8 Carmella .60 1.50
W9 Charlotte Flair 1.25 3.00
W10 Dakota Kai .50 1.25
W11 Dana Brooke .25 .60
W12 Ember Moon .30 .75
W13 Io Shirai .50 1.25
W14 Kacy Catanzaro .50 1.25
W15 Kay Lee Ray .60 1.50
W16 Lacey Evans .60 1.50
W17 Lana .30 .75
W18 Liv Morgan 1.00 2.50
W19 Mandy Rose 1.25 3.00

W20 Naomi	.30	.75
W21 Natalya	.40	1.00
W22 Nia Jax	.50	1.25
W23 Nikki Cross	.50	1.25
W24 Peyton Royce	.50	1.25
W25 Piper Niven	.40	1.00
W26 Rhea Ripley	.75	2.00
W27 Ruby Riott	.50	1.25
W28 Sasha Banks	1.25	3.00
W29 Scarlett	1.25	3.00
W30 Shayna Baszler	.50	1.25
W31 Tamina	.30	.75
W32 Toni Storm	.75	2.00

2019 Topps WWE SmackDown Live

COMPLETE SET (90) 10.00 25.00
*GREEN: .5X TO 1.5X BASIC CARDS
*PURPLE/99: .75X TO 3X BASIC CARDS
*20TH ANN./20: UNPRICED DUE TO SCARCITY
*GOLD/10: UNPRICED DUE TO SCARCITY
*RED/1: UNPRICED DUE TO SCARCITY
*P.P.BLACK/1: UNPRICED DUE TO SCARCITY
*P.P.CYAN/1: UNPRICED DUE TO SCARCITY
*P.P.MAGENTA/1: UNPRICED DUE TO SCARCITY
*P.P.YELLOW/1: UNPRICED DUE TO SCARCITY

1 Aiden English	.25	.60
2 Aleister Black	.30	.75
3 Ali	.25	.60
4 Andrade	.30	.75
5 Apollo Crews	.30	.75
6 Asuka	.75	2.00
7 Bayley	.50	1.25
8 Becky Lynch	1.00	2.50
9 Big E	.25	.60
10 Billie Kay	.50	1.25
11 Bo Dallas	.30	.75
12 Buddy Murphy	.30	.75
13 Byron Saxton	.25	.60
14 Carmella	.60	1.50
15 Cesaro	.30	.75
16 Chad Gable	.25	.60
17 Charlotte Flair	1.00	2.50
18 Corey Graves	.30	.75
19 Curtis Axel	.30	.75
20 Daniel Bryan	.60	1.50
21 Elias	.50	1.25
22 Ember Moon	.60	1.50
23 Finn Balor	.50	1.25
24 Greg Hamilton	.25	.60
25 Jeff Hardy	.60	1.50
26 Jinder Mahal	.50	1.25
27 Kairi Sane	.50	1.25
28 Kevin Owens	.60	1.50
29 Kofi Kingston	.40	1.00
30 Lana	.50	1.25
31 Lars Sullivan	.25	.60
32 Liv Morgan	.75	2.00
33 Mandy Rose	.60	1.50
34 Maryse	.30	.75
35 Matt Hardy	.50	1.25
36 Mickie James	.60	1.50
37 Otis	.25	.60
38 Paige	1.00	2.50
39 Peyton Royce	.60	1.50
40 R-Truth	.30	.75
41 Randy Orton	.60	1.50
42 Roman Reigns	.60	1.50
43 Rowan	.25	.60
44 Rusev	.50	1.25
45 Samir Singh	.25	.60
46 Sarah Schreiber RC	.25	.60
47 Sheamus	.40	1.00
48 Shelton Benjamin	.30	.75
49 Shinsuke Nakamura	.60	1.50
50 Sin Cara	.25	.60
51 Sonya Deville	.50	1.25
52 Sunil Singh	.25	.60
53 Tom Phillips	.25	.60
54 Tucker	.25	.60
55 Xavier Woods	.30	.75
56 Zelina Vega	.40	1.00
57 Big Show	.40	1.00
58 The Rock	1.25	3.00
59 Triple H	.60	1.50
60 Undertaker	1.25	3.00
61 Albert	.25	.60
62 Beth Phoenix	.40	1.00
63 Big Boss Man	.30	.75
64 The British Bulldog	.60	1.50
65 Boogeyman	.25	.60
66 King Booker	.60	1.50
67 Cactus Jack	.50	1.25
68 Christian	.40	1.00
69 Chyna	.50	1.25
70 Cowboy Bob Orton	.25	.60
71 D-Lo Brown	.25	.60
72 Diamond Dallas Page	.50	1.25
73 Eddie Guerrero	.60	1.50
74 Faarooq	.40	1.00
75 Finlay	.25	.60
76 The Godfather	.25	.60
77 Goldberg	.75	2.00
78 Jerry The King Lawler	.50	1.25
79 Kevin Nash	.40	1.00
80 Lita	.60	1.50
81 Mankind	.50	1.25
82 Paul Bearer	.30	.75
83 Rikishi	.25	.60
84 Road Dogg Jesse James	.25	.60
85 Rowdy Roddy Piper	.60	1.50
86 Scott Hall	.40	1.00
87 Stone Cold Steve Austin	1.25	3.00
88 Tatanka	.25	.60
89 Trish Stratus	1.25	3.00
90 X-Pac	.25	.60

2019 Topps WWE SmackDown Live 20 Years of SmackDown

COMPLETE SET (46) 12.00 30.00
RANDOMLY INSERTED INTO PACKS

SD1 Undertaker & Big Show	1.50	4.00
SD2 The Rock & Mankind	1.50	4.00
SD3 Stone Cold Steve Austin	1.50	4.00
SD4 Jeff Hardy	.75	2.00
SD5 Kurt Angle	.60	1.50
SD6 Batista	.75	2.00
SD7 Rey Mysterio	.75	2.00
SD8 John Cena	1.50	4.00
SD9 Kurt Angle	.60	1.50
SD10 Kurt Angle	.60	1.50
SD11 Rey Mysterio	.75	2.00
SD12 Brock Lesnar	1.25	3.00
SD13 Brock Lesnar	1.25	3.00
SD14 Eddie Guerrero	.75	2.00
SD15 Stone Cold Steve Austin	1.50	4.00
SD16 Eddie Guerrero	.75	2.00
SD17 Undertaker	1.50	4.00
SD18 Kurt Angle	.60	1.50
SD19 Eddie Guerrero	.75	2.00
SD20 Undertaker	1.50	4.00
SD21 Kurt Angle	.60	1.50
SD22 Booker T	.75	2.00
SD23 Shawn Michaels	.75	2.00
SD24 Jeff Hardy	.75	2.00
SD25 Jeff Hardy	.75	2.00
SD26 Shawn Michaels	.75	2.00
SD27 Randy Orton	.75	2.00
SD28 Daniel Bryan	.75	2.00
SD29 Beth Phoenix	.50	1.25
SD30 Daniel Bryan	.75	2.00
SD31 John Cena	1.50	4.00
SD32 Cesaro	.40	1.00
SD33 Batista	.75	2.00
SD34 Wyatt Family	.40	1.00
SD35 Kevin Owens	.75	2.00
SD36 The Miz	.60	1.50
SD37 Alexa Bliss	1.50	4.00
SD38 Bray Wyatt	.75	2.00
SD39 The Usos	.40	1.00
SD40 Carmella	.75	2.00
SD41 Shinsuke Nakamura	.75	2.00
SD42 The New Day	.60	1.50
SD43 AJ Styles	1.50	4.00
SD44 John Cena	1.50	4.00
SD45 Rusev	.60	1.50
SD46 The New Day	.60	1.50

2019 Topps WWE SmackDown Live Autographed Intercontinental Championship 40th Anniversary Relics

RANDOMLY INSERTED INTO PACKS

ICRKK Kofi Kingston
ICRSB Shelton Benjamin
ICRTM The Miz

2019 Topps WWE SmackDown Live Autographed Mat Relics

STATED PRINT RUN 10 SER.#'d SETS
UNPRICED DUE TO SCARCITY

MRAAJ AJ Styles
MRABD Daniel Bryan
MRABE Big E
MRABM Buddy Murphy
MRACM Carmella
MRAJE Jey Uso
MRAJH Jeff Hardy
MRAJI Jimmy Uso
MRAKA Karl Anderson
MRAKK Kofi Kingston
MRAKS Shinsuke Nakamura
MRALG Luke Gallows
MRAMA Ali
MRAMR Mandy Rose
MRARJ Rey Mysterio
MRARM Rey Mysterio
MRART R-Truth
MRASD Sonya Deville
MRASN Shinsuke Nakamura
MRAXW Xavier Woods

2019 Topps WWE SmackDown Live Autographed Shirt Relics

STATED PRINT RUN 10 SER.#'d SETS
UNPRICED DUE TO SCARCITY

SRAC Apollo Crews
SREM Ember Moon
SRMH Matt Hardy
SRXW Xavier Woods
SRAAA Andrade
SRAAB Aleister Black
SRAEL Elias
SRAKK Kofi Kingston

2019 Topps WWE SmackDown Live Autographed SmackDown Championship Commemorative Relics

STATED PRINT RUN 10 SER.#'d SETS
UNPRICED DUE TO SCARCITY

ASCAB Alexa Bliss
ASCAJ AJ Styles
ASCBC Baron Corbin
ASCBL Becky Lynch
ASCBR Robert Roode
ASCCM Carmella
ASCKK Kofi Kingston
ASCKO Kevin Owens
ASCNM Naomi
ASCNT Natalya
ASCRO Randy Orton
ASCRT R-Truth
ASCSJ Samoa Joe
ASCSN Shinsuke Nakamura

2019 Topps WWE SmackDown Live Autographed Women's Evolution Relics

DRACCM Carmella

2019 Topps WWE SmackDown Live Autographs

*ORANGE/50: .5X TO 1.2X BASIC AUTOS
*20TH ANN./20: UNPRICED DUE TO SCARCITY
*GOLD/10: UNPRICED DUE TO SCARCITY
*RED/1: UNPRICED DUE TO SCARCITY
STATED PRINT RUN 99 SER.#'d SETS

AAA Andrade	4.00	10.00
AAL Aleister Black	12.00	30.00
ABA Bayley	10.00	25.00
ABE Becky Lynch		
ABK Billie Kay	8.00	20.00
ABL Big E	4.00	10.00
ABU Buddy Murphy	8.00	20.00
ACH Chad Gable	4.00	10.00
ACM Carmella	10.00	25.00
AEL Elias	4.00	10.00
AEM Ember Moon	8.00	20.00
AFI Finn Balor	12.00	30.00
AGH Greg Hamilton	4.00	10.00
AKE Kevin Owens	6.00	15.00
AKK Kofi Kingston	6.00	15.00
ALI Liv Morgan	15.00	40.00
AMA Ali	4.00	10.00
AMH Matt Hardy	6.00	15.00
AMR Mandy Rose	15.00	40.00
AOT Otis	10.00	25.00
APR Peyton Royce	10.00	25.00
ARR Roman Reigns	10.00	25.00
ART R-Truth	5.00	12.00
ARW Rowan	4.00	10.00
ASD Sonya Deville	6.00	15.00
ASN Shinsuke Nakamura	5.00	12.00
ATU Tucker	4.00	10.00
AXW Xavier Woods	5.00	12.00
AZV Zelina Vega	12.00	30.00

2019 Topps WWE SmackDown Live Corey Says

COMPLETE SET (19) 6.00 15.00
RANDOMLY INSERTED INTO PACKS

CG1 AJ Styles	1.50	4.00
CG2 Asuka	1.00	2.50
CG3 Becky Lynch	1.25	3.00
CG4 Carmella	.75	2.00
CG5 Cesaro	.40	1.00
CG6 Charlotte Flair	1.25	3.00
CG7 Daniel Bryan	.75	2.00
CG8 Jeff Hardy	.75	2.00
CG9 Randy Orton	.75	2.00
CG10 Rey Mysterio	.75	2.00
CG11 Rusev	.60	1.50
CG12 Samoa Joe	.60	1.50
CG13 Shane McMahon	.75	2.00
CG14 Sheamus	.50	1.25
CG15 Shinsuke Nakamura	.75	2.00
CG16 The Miz	.60	1.50
CG17 The New Day	.60	1.50
CG18 The Usos	.40	1.00
CG19 Undertaker	1.50	4.00

2019 Topps WWE SmackDown Live Dual Autographs

*GOLD/10: UNPRICED DUE TO SCARCITY
*RED/1: UNPRICED DUE TO SCARCITY
STATED PRINT RUN 25 SER.#'d SETS

DADB R-Truth/Carmella	20.00	50.00
DAGB K.Anderson/L.Gallows	30.00	75.00
DAII B.Kay/P.Royce	75.00	150.00
DATQ Z.Vega/Andrade	20.00	50.00
DAABS S.Deville/M.Rose	75.00	150.00

2019 Topps WWE SmackDown Live Image Variations

IV1 Aleister Black		
IV2 Andrade	6.00	15.00
IV3 Big E		
IV4 Billie Kay	6.00	15.00
IV5 Charlotte Flair	15.00	40.00
IV6 Daniel Bryan	12.00	30.00
IV7 Jeff Hardy	4.00	10.00
IV8 Killian Dain		
IV9 Kofi Kingston	6.00	15.00
IV10 Mandy Rose	12.00	30.00
IV11 Peyton Royce		
IV12 R-Truth		
IV13 Shinsuke Nakamura		
IV14 Sheamus		
IV15 Shelton Benjamin	8.00	20.00
IV16 Sonya Deville	10.00	25.00
IV17 Xavier Woods	4.00	10.00

IV18 Zelina Vega
IV19 Ali
IV20 Matt Hardy 8.00 20.00

2019 Topps WWE SmackDown Live Intercontinental Championship 40th Anniversary Autographs

ICAKK Kofi Kingston 8.00 20.00
ICASB Shelton Benjamin 12.00 30.00
ICATM The Miz 10.00 25.00

2019 Topps WWE SmackDown Live Intercontinental Championship 40th Anniversary Relics

RANDOMLY INSERTED INTO PACKS

ICRDM Drew McIntyre
ICRKK Kofi Kingston
ICRRM Rey Mysterio
ICRSB Shelton Benjamin
ICRTM The Miz

2019 Topps WWE SmackDown Live Mat Relics

*PURPLE/99: .6X TO 1.5X BASIC MEM
*ORANGE/50: .75X TO 2X BASIC MEM
*20TH ANN./20: UNPRICED DUE TO SCARCITY
*GOLD/10: UNPRICED DUE TO SCARCITY
*RED/1: UNPRICED DUE TO SCARCITY
STATED PRINT RUN 199 SER.#'d SETS

MR4H Charlotte Flair 8.00 20.00
MRAJ AJ Styles 4.00 10.00
MRAS Asuka 6.00 15.00
MRAW Alexander Wolfe 3.00 8.00
MRBD Daniel Bryan 4.00 10.00
MRBE Big E 2.50 6.00
MRBL Becky Lynch 6.00 15.00
MRBM Buddy Murphy 2.50 6.00
MRBS Big Show 2.50 6.00
MRBT Batista 3.00 8.00
MRCF Charlotte Flair 6.00 15.00
MRCM Carmella 4.00 10.00
MRCS Cesaro 2.50 6.00
MRDB Daniel Bryan 4.00 10.00
MREY Eric Young 2.50 6.00
MRJE Jey Uso 2.50 6.00
MRJH Jeff Hardy 4.00 10.00
MRJI Jimmy Uso 2.50 6.00
MRKA Karl Anderson 2.50 6.00
MRKD Killian Dain 2.50 6.00
MRKK Kofi Kingston 3.00 8.00
MRKS Shinsuke Nakamura 3.00 8.00
MRLG Luke Gallows 2.50 6.00
MRLN Lana 3.00 8.00
MRMA Ali 2.50 6.00
MRMH Stephanie McMahon 4.00 10.00
MRMR Mandy Rose 6.00 15.00
MRRF Ric Flair 5.00 12.00
MRRJ Rey Mysterio 4.00 10.00
MRRM Rey Mysterio 4.00 10.00
MRRO Randy Orton 4.00 10.00
MRRS Rusev 2.50 6.00
MRRT R-Truth 2.50 6.00
MRSD Sonya Deville 3.00 8.00
MRSH Sheamus 2.50 6.00
MRSJ Samoa Joe 2.50 6.00
MRSN Shinsuke Nakamura 3.00 8.00
MRTH Triple H 3.00 8.00
MRTM The Miz 2.50 6.00
MRUT Undertaker 6.00 15.00
MRXW Xavier Woods 2.50 6.00

2019 Topps WWE SmackDown Live Shirt Relics

*PURPLE/99: .6X TO 1.5X BASIC MEM
*ORANGE/50: .75X TO 2X BASIC MEM
20TH ANN./20: UNPRICED DUE TO SCARCITY
*GOLD/10: UNPRICED DUE TO SCARCITY
*RED/1: UNPRICED DUE TO SCARCITY
STATED PRINT RUN 199 SER.#'d SETS

SRAA Andrade/199 5.00 12.00
SRAB Aleister Black/199 5.00 12.00
SRAC Apollo Crews/199 4.00 10.00
SREL Elias/199 5.00 12.00
SREM Ember Moon/199 6.00 15.00
SRJH Jeff Hardy/199 5.00 12.00
SRKA Karl Anderson/199 4.00 10.00
SRKK Kofi Kingston/199 4.00 10.00
SRKS Kairi Sane/199 5.00 12.00
SRLG Luke Gallows/199 4.00 10.00
SRLM Liv Morgan/160 12.00 30.00
SRMH Matt Hardy/199 4.00 10.00
SRSM Sheamus/199 4.00 10.00
SRXW Xavier Woods/199 6.00 15.00

2019 Topps WWE SmackDown Live SmackDown Championship Commemorative Relics

*PURPLE/99: .6X TO 1.5X BASIC MEM
*ORANGE/50: .75X TO 2X BASIC MEM
20TH ANN./20: UNPRICED DUE TO SCARCITY
*GOLD/10: UNPRICED DUE TO SCARCITY
*RED/1: UNPRICED DUE TO SCARCITY
STATED PRINT RUN 199 SER.#'d SETS

SCAB Alexa Bliss 8.00 20.00
SCAJ AJ Styles 5.00 12.00
SCAS Asuka 6.00 15.00
SCBC Baron Corbin 2.50 6.00
SCBL Becky Lynch 10.00 25.00
SCBR Robert Roode 2.50 6.00
SCBW Bray Wyatt 6.00 15.00
SCCF Charlotte Flair 4.00 10.00
SCCM Carmella 8.00 20.00
SCDB Daniel Bryan 5.00 12.00
SCJC John Cena 6.00 15.00
SCJH Jeff Hardy 5.00 12.00
SCKK Kofi Kingston 5.00 12.00
SCKO Kevin Owens 2.50 6.00
SCMH Jinder Mahal 2.50 6.00
SCNM Naomi 2.50 6.00
SCNT Natalya 2.50 6.00
SCRO Randy Orton 5.00 12.00
SCRT R-Truth 3.00 8.00
SCRV Rusev 2.50 6.00
SCSJ Samoa Joe 2.50 6.00
SCSN Shinsuke Nakamura 4.00 10.00
SCVP Randy Orton 5.00 12.00

2019 Topps WWE SmackDown Live SmackDown Tag Team Championship Commemorative Relics

*PURPLE/99: .6X TO 1.5X BASIC MEM
*ORANGE/50: .75X TO 2X BASIC MEM
20TH ANN./20: UNPRICED DUE TO SCARCITY
*GOLD/10: UNPRICED DUE TO SCARCITY
*RED/1: UNPRICED DUE TO SCARCITY
STATED PRINT RUN 199 SER.#'d SETS

SCAA J.Jordan/C.Gable 4.00 10.00
SCBB Matt & Jeff Hardy 6.00 15.00
SCND X.Woods/K.Kingston 5.00 12.00
SCPE Rowan/D.Bryan 4.00 10.00
SCTB Cesaro/Sheamus 4.00 10.00
SCUS Jey & Jimmy Uso 6.00 15.00
SCWF R.Orton/B.Wyatt 5.00 12.00

2019 Topps WWE SmackDown Live Triple Autographs

*GOLD/10: UNPRICED DUE TO SCARCITY
*RED/1: UNPRICED DUE TO SCARCITY
STATED PRINT RUN 25 SER.#'d SETS

TAND Woods/Big E/Kingston 100.00 200.00

2019 Topps WWE SmackDown Live Women's Evolution Autographs

RANDOMLY INSERTED INTO PACKS

WACM Carmella
WAMR Mandy Rose
WASD Sonya Deville

2019 Topps WWE SmackDown Live Women's Evolution Relics

RANDOMLY INSERTED INTO PACKS

DRCAK Asuka
DRCCM Carmella
DRCKS Kairi Sane

2015 Topps WWE Sting Tribute

COMPLETE SET (40) 15.00 40.00
*GOLD/10: 2X TO 5X BASIC CARDS
*RED/1: UNPRICED DUE TO SCARCITY

1 Sting 1.25 3.00
2 Sting 1.25 3.00
3 Sting 1.25 3.00
4 Sting 1.25 3.00
5 Sting 1.25 3.00
6 Sting 1.25 3.00
7 Sting 1.25 3.00
8 Sting 1.25 3.00
9 Sting 1.25 3.00
10 Sting 1.25 3.00
11 Sting 1.25 3.00
12 Sting 1.25 3.00
13 Sting 1.25 3.00
14 Sting 1.25 3.00
15 Sting 1.25 3.00
16 Sting 1.25 3.00
17 Sting 1.25 3.00
18 Sting 1.25 3.00
19 Sting 1.25 3.00
20 Sting 1.25 3.00
21 Sting 1.25 3.00
22 Sting 1.25 3.00
23 Sting 1.25 3.00
24 Sting 1.25 3.00
25 Sting 1.25 3.00
26 Sting 1.25 3.00
27 Sting 1.25 3.00
28 Sting 1.25 3.00
29 Sting 1.25 3.00
30 Sting 1.25 3.00
31 Sting 1.25 3.00
32 Sting 1.25 3.00
33 Sting 1.25 3.00
34 Sting 1.25 3.00
35 Sting 1.25 3.00
36 Sting 1.25 3.00
37 Sting 1.25 3.00
38 Sting 1.25 3.00
39 Sting 1.25 3.00
40 Sting 1.25 3.00

2015 Topps WWE Sting Tribute Autographs and Relics

*GOLD/10: UNPRICED DUE TO SCARCITY
*RED/1: UNPRICED DUE TO SCARCITY

NNO Sting AU/Red White Blue 25.00 60.00
NNO Sting MEM/Shirt 10.00 25.00
NNO Sting AU MEM/Shirt 50.00 100.00

2015 Topps WWE Sting Tribute Topps Chrome WWE Autographs and Relics

*GOLD/10: UNPRICED DUE TO SCARCITY

NNO Sting AU/WCW Belt 50.00 100.00
NNO Sting MEM/Tights 15.00 40.00
NNO Sting AU MEM/Tights 75.00 150.00

2015 Topps WWE Sting Tribute Topps Heritage WWE Autographs and Relics

*GOLD/10: UNPRICED DUE TO SCARCITY
*RED/1: UNPRICED DUE TO SCARCITY

NNO Sting AU 50.00 100.00
NNO Sting AU MEM/Glove

2015 Topps WWE Sting Tribute Topps WWE Road to WrestleMania Autographs and Relics

*GOLD/10: UNPRICED DUE TO SCARCITY
*RED/1: UNPRICED DUE TO SCARCITY

NNO Sting AU 50.00 100.00
NNO Sting MEM/Boots 30.00 75.00
NNO Sting AU MEM/Boots 75.00 150.00

2019 Topps WWE SummerSlam

COMPLETE SET (100) 10.00 25.00
*BRONZE: .6X TO 1.5X BASIC CARDS
*BLUE/99: .75X TO 2X BASIC CARDS
*SILVER/25: 2X TO 5X BASIC CARDS
*GOLD/10: UNPRICED DUE TO SCARCITY
*RED/1: UNPRICED DUE TO SCARCITY
*P.P.BLACK/1: UNPRICED DUE TO SCARCITY
*P.P.CYAN/1: UNPRICED DUE TO SCARCITY
*P.P.MAGENTA/1: UNPRICED DUE TO SCARCITY
*P.P.YELLOW/1: UNPRICED DUE TO SCARCITY

1 Akam .25 .60
2 Baron Corbin .40 1.00
3 Bobby Lashley .50 1.25
4 Braun Strowman .60 1.50
5 Bray Wyatt .60 1.50
6 Brock Lesnar 1.00 2.50
7 Dolph Ziggler .50 1.25
8 Drew McIntyre .30 .75
9 Elias .50 1.25
10 Finn Balor .50 1.25
11 Kevin Owens .60 1.50
12 Kurt Angle .50 1.25
13 Rezar .25 .60
14 Roman Reigns .60 1.50
15 Sami Zayn .50 1.25
16 Seth Rollins .60 1.50
17 Titus O'Neil .30 .75
18 Alexa Bliss 1.25 3.00
19 Bayley .50 1.25
20 Ember Moon .60 1.50
21 Liv Morgan .75 2.00
22 Natalya .50 1.25
23 Nia Jax .50 1.25
24 Ronda Rousey 1.25 3.00
25 Ruby Riott .50 1.25
26 Sarah Logan .30 .75
27 Sasha Banks 1.00 2.50
28 Ali .25 .60
29 AJ Styles 1.25 3.00
30 Andrade .30 .75
31 Big E .25 .60
32 Cesaro .30 .75
33 Daniel Bryan .60 1.50
34 Jeff Hardy .60 1.50
35 Kofi Kingston .40 1.00
36 The Miz .50 1.25
37 Randy Orton .60 1.50
38 Rey Mysterio .60 1.50
39 Samoa Joe .50 1.25
40 Sheamus .40 1.00
41 Shinsuke Nakamura .60 1.50
42 Xavier Woods .30 .75
43 Asuka .75 2.00
44 Becky Lynch 1.00 2.50
45 Carmella .60 1.50
46 Charlotte Flair 1.00 2.50
47 Mandy Rose .60 1.50
48 Naomi .40 1.00
49 Peyton Royce .60 1.50
50 Zelina Vega .40 1.00
51 Matt Hardy & Bray Wyatt .60 1.50
52 Shelton Benjamin .60 1.50
53 Nakamura, Rusev & English 1.25 3.00
54 The Deleters of Worlds .60 1.50
55 Cedric Alexander .25 .60
56 Jeff Hardy .60 1.50
57 The Bludgeon Brothers .30 .75
58 Seth Rollins .60 1.50
59 AJ Styles 1.25 3.00
60 Brock Lesnar 1.00 2.50
61 Seth Rollins .60 1.50
62 Jeff Hardy .60 1.50
63 AJ Styles and Nakamura .60 1.50
64 Braun Strowman .60 1.50
65 The Deleters of Worlds .60 1.50
66 Finn Balor .50 1.25
67 Rusev .60 1.50
68 Andrade .40 1.00
69 Cedric Alexander .30 .75
70 The B-Team .30 .75
71 Braun Strowman .60 1.50
72 Shinsuke Nakamura .60 1.50
73 Seth Rollins .60 1.50
74 AJ Styles 1.25 3.00
75 Braun Strowman .60 1.50
76 Dolph Ziggler .50 1.25
77 Rusev 1.25 3.00
78 Drew McIntyre .30 .75

79 AJ Styles & Jeff Hardy 1.25 3.00
80 The B-Team .30 .75
81 Bobby Lashley .50 1.25
82 AJ Styles 1.25 3.00
83 Dolph Ziggler .60 1.50
84 Roman Reigns .60 1.50
85 Bobby Lashley .50 1.25
86 Randy Orton .60 1.50
87 Drew Gulak .25 .60
88 Baron Corbin .50 1.25
89 Nakamura & Randy Orton .60 1.50
90 The New Day .40 1.00
91 Brock Lesnar 1.00 2.50
92 Cedric Alexander .25 .60
93 Seth Rollins .60 1.50
94 The New Day .25 .60
95 Braun Strowman .60 1.50
96 Samoa Joe .50 1.25
97 The Miz .60 1.50
98 Finn Balor .50 1.25
99 Shinsuke Nakamura .60 1.50
100 Roman Reigns .60 1.50

2019 Topps WWE SummerSlam Autographed Intercontinental Championship Manufactured Relics

UNPRICED DUE TO SCARCITY
ICRAJH Jeff Hardy
ICRAKA Kurt Angle
ICRAWR William Regal

2019 Topps WWE SummerSlam Autographed Manufactured Logo Relics

STATED PRINT RUN 10 SER.#'d SETS
UNPRICED DUE TO SCARCITY
LRABS Braun Strowman
LRAKA Kurt Angle
LRALL Lex Luger
LRAMK Mankind
LRARO Randy Orton
LRATD Ted DiBiase

2019 Topps WWE SummerSlam Autographed Mat Relics

STATED PRINT RUN 10 SER.#'d SETS
UNPRICED DUE TO SCARCITY
MRAAB Alexa Bliss
MRAAC Adam Cole
MRAAJ AJ Styles
MRABC Baron Corbin
MRABE Big E
MRABL Becky Lynch
MRABM Drew McIntyre
MRABS Braun Strowman
MRACM Carmella
MRADB Daniel Bryan
MRAEC Velveteen Dream
MRAFB Finn Balor
MRAJG Johnny Gargano
MRAJH Jeff Hardy
MRAKK Kofi Kingston
MRAKO Kevin Owens
MRAKR Kyle O'Reilly
MRAKS Kairi Sane
MRANT Natalya
MRARC Ricochet
MRARS Roderick Strong
MRARW Rowan
MRASB Shayna Baszler
MRASJ Samoa Joe
MRASN Shinsuke Nakamura
MRASR Seth Rollins
MRATB Tyler Bate
MRATM The Miz
MRATS Trent Seven
MRAVD EC3
MRAXW Xavier Woods

2019 Topps WWE SummerSlam Autographed Superstar Relics

STATED PRINT RUN 10 SER.#'d SETS
UNPRICED DUE TO SCARCITY
SRAAE Aiden English
SRAAW Alexander Wolfe
SRABS Braun Strowman
SRACS Cesaro
SRADW Dash Wilder
SRAEY Eric Young
SRAKD Killian Dain
SRASD Scott Dawson
SRASM Shawn Michaels
SRASZ Sami Zayn

2019 Topps WWE SummerSlam Autographed Women's Evolution Relics

UNPRICED DUE TO SCARCITY
ERARR Ruby Riott
ERATS Tamina

2019 Topps WWE SummerSlam Autographs

*BLUE/50: .5X TO 1.2X BASIC AUTOS
*SILVER/25: .6X TO 1.5X BASIC AUTOS
*GOLD/10: UNPRICED DUE TO SCARCITY
*RED/1: UNPRICED DUE TO SCARCITY
*P.P.BLACK/1: UNPRICED DUE TO SCARCITY
*P.P.CYAN/1: UNPRICED DUE TO SCARCITY
*P.P.MAGENTA/1: UNPRICED DUE TO SCARCITY
*P.P.YELLOW/1: UNPRICED DUE TO SCARCITY
STATED ODDS 1:24
OCAA Andrade 4.00 10.00
OCAB Alexa Bliss 30.00 75.00
OCAJ AJ Styles 12.00 30.00
OCBE Big E 4.00 10.00
OCBL Bayley 10.00 25.00
OCBR Bobby Roode 5.00 12.00
OCBS Braun Strowman 6.00 15.00
OCCF Charlotte Flair 15.00 40.00
OCCM Carmella 8.00 20.00
OCDM Drew McIntyre 6.00 15.00
OCEL Elias 8.00 20.00
OCFB Finn Balor 12.00 30.00
OCJH Jeff Hardy 12.00 30.00
OCKK Kofi Kingston 8.00 20.00
OCKO Kevin Owens 5.00 12.00
OCMM Bobby Lashley 5.00 12.00
OCMR Mandy Rose 20.00 50.00
OCRM Rey Mysterio 12.00 30.00
OCRR Ruby Riott 15.00 40.00
OCRT R-Truth 4.00 10.00
OCSD Sonya Deville 10.00 25.00
OCSJ Samoa Joe 6.00 15.00
OCSN Shinsuke Nakamura 8.00 20.00
OCTM The Miz 6.00 15.00
OCXW Xavier Woods 4.00 10.00
OCZV Zelina Vega 12.00 30.00

2019 Topps WWE SummerSlam Dual Autographs

STATED PRINT RUN 10 SER.#'d SETS
UNPRICED DUE TO SCARCITY
DAAB S.Deville/M.Rose
DABT B.Dallas/C.Axel
DAII B.Kay/P.Royce
DAMK Maria & Mike Kanellis
DAND X.Woods/K.Kingston

2019 Topps WWE SummerSlam Greatest Matches and Moments

COMPLETE SET (40) 6.00 15.00
RANDOMLY INSERTED INTO PACKS
GM1 Ult.Warrior Def. Honky Tonk Man .50 1.25
GM2 Warrior/Rick Rude .60 1.50
GM3 Dusty Rhodes/Honky Tonk Man .50 1.25
GM4 Texas Tornado Def. Mr. Perfect .30 .75
GM5 Macho Man Marries Elizabeth .60 1.50
GM6 Virgil/Ted DiBiase .25 .60
GM7 British Bulldog/Bret Hart .50 1.25
GM8 Warrior/Randy Savage .60 1.50
GM9 Lex Luger/Yokozuna .30 .75
GM10 Alundra Blayze/Bull Nakano .25 .60
GM11 Shawn Michaels/Razor Ramon .50 1.25
GM12 Mankind/Undertaker .40 1.00
GM13 Shawn Michaels/Vader .60 1.50
GM14 Mankind/Triple H .50 1.25
GM15 Steve Austin wins IC Title 1.00 2.50
GM16 Ken Shamrock/Owen Hart .40 1.00
GM17 Steve Austin/Undertaker 1.25 3.00
GM18 Mankind/Steve Austin/HHH .50 1.25
GM19 Rock/HHH/Kurt Angle 1.00 2.50
GM20 Kurt Angle/Steve Austin 1.25 3.00
GM21 Shawn Michaels/HHH .60 1.50
GM22 Kurt Angle/Rey Mysterio .40 1.00
GM23 Kurt Angle/Brock Lesnar .50 1.25
GM24 Kurt Angle/Eddie Guerrero .40 1.00
GM25 Rey Mysterio/Eddie Guerrero .60 1.50
GM26 Ric Flair/Mick Foley .75 2.00
GM27 John Cena/Randy Orton 1.25 3.00
GM28 Batista/John Cena .50 1.25
GM29 Rey Mysterio/Dolph Ziggler .60 1.50
GM30 Randy Orton/Sheamus .50 1.25
GM31 Randy Orton/Christian .60 1.50
GM32 Kane/Rey Mysterio/Undertaker .30 .75
GM33 Miz/Rey Mysterio .50 1.25
GM34 Daniel Bryan/John Cena .50 1.25
GM35 Roman Reigns/Randy Orton .60 1.50
GM36 Seth Rollins/John Cena .50 1.25
GM37 Charlotte Flair/Sasha Banks 1.00 2.50
GM38 Finn Balor/Seth Rollins .50 1.25
GM39 AJ Styles/John Cena 1.25 3.00
GM40 Usos/New Day .30 .75

2019 Topps WWE SummerSlam Intercontinental Champion Autographs

STATED PRINT RUN 25 SER.#'d SETS
ICRJH Jeff Hardy 15.00 40.00
ICRWR William Regal 10.00 25.00

2019 Topps WWE SummerSlam Intercontinental Championship Manufactured Relics

RANDOMLY INSERTED INTO PACKS
ICRBT Booker T
ICRDL D'Lo Brown
ICRJH Jeff Hardy
ICRKA Kurt Angle
ICRWR William Regal

2019 Topps WWE SummerSlam Manufactured Logo Relics

*BRONZE/99: .5X TO 1.2X BASIC MEM
*BLUE/50: .6X TO 1.5X BASIC MEM
*SILVER/25: .75X TO 2X BASIC MEM
*GOLD/10: UNPRICED DUE TO SCARCITY
*RED/1: UNPRICED DUE TO SCARCITY
STATED ODDS 1:152
LRBH Bret Hit Man Hart 3.00 8.00
LRBL Brock Lesnar 6.00 15.00
LRBS Braun Strowman 3.00 8.00
LRBT Booker T 3.00 8.00
LRED Edge 3.00 8.00
LRJC John Cena 4.00 10.00
LRKA Kurt Angle 3.00 8.00
LRLL Lex Luger 2.50 6.00
LRMK Mankind 2.50 6.00
LRRO Randy Orton 4.00 10.00
LRSA Stone Cold Steve Austin 6.00 15.00
LRSM Shawn Michaels 4.00 10.00
LRTD Ted DiBiase 2.50 6.00
LRUT Undertaker 4.00 10.00
LRBDC Diesel 3.00 8.00

2019 Topps WWE SummerSlam Mat Relics

*BRONZE/99: .5X TO 1.2X BASIC MEM
*BLUE/50: .6X TO 1.5X BASIC MEM
*SILVER/25: .75X TO 2X BASIC MEM
*GOLD/10: UNPRICED DUE TO SCARCITY
*RED/1: UNPRICED DUE TO SCARCITY
RANDOMLY INSERTED INTO PACKS
MRAB Alexa Bliss 12.00 30.00
MRAC Adam Cole 3.00 8.00
MRAJ AJ Styles 3.00 8.00
MRBC Baron Corbin 1.50 4.00
MRBD Roman Reigns 3.00 8.00
MRBE Big E 1.50 4.00
MRBI Brock Lesnar 3.00 8.00
MRBL Becky Lynch 6.00 15.00
MRBM Drew McIntyre 2.50 6.00
MRBS Braun Strowman 2.50 6.00
MRCF Charlotte Flair 5.00 12.00
MRCM Carmella 4.00 10.00
MRDB Daniel Bryan
MRDZ Dolph Ziggler 2.50 6.00
MREC Velveteen Dream 2.50 6.00
MRFB Finn Balor 4.00 10.00
MRHP Harper 2.50 6.00
MRJG Johnny Gargano 2.50 6.00
MRJH Jeff Hardy 4.00 10.00
MRKK Kofi Kingston 3.00 8.00
MRKO Kevin Owens 2.00 5.00
MRKR Kyle O'Reilly 2.00 5.00
MRKS Kairi Sane 3.00 8.00
MRNT Natalya 3.00 8.00
MRPH Paul Heyman 2.50 6.00
MRRC Ricochet 3.00 8.00
MRRR Ronda Rousey 10.00 25.00
MRRS Roderick Strong 2.50 6.00
MRRW Rowan 1.50 4.00
MRSB Shayna Baszler
MRSJ Samoa Joe 2.00 5.00
MRSN Shinsuke Nakamura 2.00 5.00
MRSR Seth Rollins 3.00 8.00
MRTB Tyler Bate 2.50 6.00
MRTC Tommaso Ciampa 2.50 6.00
MRTM The Miz 2.00 5.00
MRTS Trent Seven 1.50 4.00
MRVD EC3 1.50 4.00
MRXW Xavier Woods 1.50 4.00

2019 Topps WWE SummerSlam Mr. SummerSlam

RANDOMLY INSERTED INTO PACKS
MSS1 Lesnar/Rock 1.25 3.00
MSS2 Lesnar/HHH 1.00 2.50
MSS3 Lesnar/Cena 1.25 3.00
MSS4 Lesnar/Orton 1.00 2.50
MSS5 Lesnar/Joe/Strowman/Reigns 1.00 2.50
MSS6 Undertaker Returns 1.25 3.00
MSS7 Undertaker/Kama 1.25 3.00
MSS8 Unholy Alliance/Kane/X-Pac .40 1.00
MSS9 Undertaker/Edge 1.25 3.00
MSS10 Undertaker/Brock Lesnar 1.25 3.00
MSS11 Edge & Christian .60 1.50
MSS12 Edge/Eddie Guerrero .60 1.50
MSS13 Edge IC Title .60 1.50
MSS14 Edge/Matt Hardy .60 1.50
MSS15 Edge/John Cena .60 1.50
MSS16 HHH PPV Debut .60 1.50
MSS17 Triple H/Rock 1.25 3.00
MSS18 DX/Mr. McMahon & Shane .60 1.50
MSS19 HHH/King Booker .60 1.50
MSS20 HHH/A Giant .60 1.50
MSS21 Hart Foundation .60 1.50
MSS22 Bret Hart/Mr. Perfect .60 1.50
MSS23 Bret Hart/Lawler .60 1.50
MSS24 Bret Hart/Undertaker .60 1.50
MSS25 Bret Hart Returns .60 1.50

2019 Topps WWE SummerSlam Posters Spotlight

COMPLETE SET (4) 3.00 8.00
STATED ODDS 1:6
SS14 '14 Cena/Lesnar 1.25 3.00
SS15 '15 Lesnar/Undertaker 1.00 2.50
SS16 '17 Collage 1.00 2.50
SS17 '18 Lesnar/Bliss/Rousey/Reigns 1.50 4.00

2019 Topps WWE SummerSlam Superstar Relics

*BRONZE/99: SAME VALUE AS BASIC
*BLUE/50: .5X TO 1.2X BASIC MEM
*SILVER/25: .6X TO 1.5X BASIC MEM
*GOLD/10: UNPRICED DUE TO SCARCITY
*RED/1: UNPRICED DUE TO SCARCITY
RANDOMLY INSERTED INTO PACKS
SRAC Apollo Crews 2.50 6.00
SRAW Alexander Wolfe 2.50 6.00

SRBS Braun Strowman	5.00	12.00
SRCS Cesaro	3.00	8.00
SRDW Dash Wilder	2.50	6.00
SRED Edge	4.00	10.00
SREY Eric Young	2.50	6.00
SRHS Heath Slater	2.50	6.00
SRJC John Cena	5.00	12.00
SRKD Killian Dain	2.50	6.00
SRRR Roman Reigns	4.00	10.00
SRSD Scott Dawson	2.50	6.00
SRSM Shawn Michaels	4.00	10.00
SRSR Seth Rollins	3.00	8.00
SRSZ Sami Zayn	2.50	6.00

2019 Topps WWE SummerSlam Women's Evolution Autographs

*GOLD/10: UNPRICED DUE TO SCARCITY
*P.P.BLACK/1: UNPRICED DUE TO SCARCITY
*P.P.CYAN/1: UNPRICED DUE TO SCARCITY
*P.P.MAGENTA/1: UNPRICED DUE TO SCARCITY
*P.P.YELLOW/1: UNPRICED DUE TO SCARCITY
STATED PRINT RUN 25 SER.#'d SETS
UNPRICED DUE TO SCARCITY

WAAF Alicia Fox
WAEM Ember Moon
WAMJ Mickie James
WANL Natalya
WARR Ruby Riott
WATS Tamina

2019 Topps WWE SummerSlam Women's Evolution Relics

STATED PRINT RUN 25 SER.#'d SETS
UNPRICED DUE TO SCARCITY

ERAF Alicia Fox
EREM Ember Moon
ERRR Ruby Riott
ERTS Tamina

2021 Topps WWE Superstars

COMPLETE SET (225)	30.00	80.00
1 Adam Cole	.60	1.50
2 AJ Styles	.60	1.50
3 Akira Tozawa	.25	.60
4 Alexa Bliss	1.25	3.00
5 Aliyah	.40	1.00
6 Angel Garza	.25	.60
7 Angelo Dawkins	.25	.60
8 Apollo Crews	.25	.60
9 Asuka	.75	2.00
10 Austin Theory	.40	1.00
11 Bayley	.40	1.00
12 Becky Lynch	.75	2.00
13 Bianca Belair	.50	1.25
14 Big E	.40	1.00
15 Bobby Lashley	.50	1.25
16 Cameron Grimes	.40	1.00
17 Candice LeRae	.75	2.00
18 Carmella	.50	1.25
19 Cedric Alexander	.20	.50
20 Cesaro	.20	.50
21 Chad Gable	.20	.50
22 Charlotte Flair	1.00	2.50
23 Commander Azeez RC	.25	.60
24 Dakota Kai	.40	1.00
25 Damian Priest	.30	.75
26 Dana Brooke	.20	.50
27 Danny Burch	.25	.60
28 Dave Mastiff	.20	.50
29 Dexter Lumis	.20	.50
30 Dolph Ziggler	.40	1.00
31 Dominik Mysterio RC	.25	.60
32 Drake Maverick	.20	.50
33 Drew Gulak	.25	.60
34 Drew McIntyre	.50	1.25
35 Edge	.75	2.00
36 Elias	.20	.50
37 Ember Moon	.25	.60
38 Erik	.20	.50
39 Eva Marie	.50	1.25
40 Fabian Aichner	.25	.60
41 Finn Balor	.50	1.25
42 Flash Morgan Webster	.25	.60
43 Franky Monet RC	.40	1.00
44 Gigi Dolin RC	.20	.50
45 Gran Metalik	.20	.50
46 Humberto Carrillo	.20	.50
47 Ilja Dragunov	.20	.50
48 Indi Hartwell RC	.60	1.50
49 Io Shirai	.40	1.00
50 Isaiah "Swerve" Scott	.30	.75
51 Ivar	.20	.50
52 James Drake	.20	.50
53 Jaxson Ryker	.20	.50
54 Jeff Hardy	.50	1.25
55 Jey Uso	.20	.50
56 Jimmy Uso	.20	.50
57 Jinder Mahal	.25	.60
58 Joaquin Wilde	.30	.75
59 Joe Coffey	.20	.50
60 John Morrison	.40	1.00
61 Johnny Gargano	.40	1.00
62 Jordan Devlin	.20	.50
63 Kacy Catanzaro	.40	1.00
64 Karrion Kross	.75	2.00
65 Kay Lee Ray	.50	1.25
66 Kayden Carter	.40	1.00
67 Keith Lee	.40	1.00
68 Kevin Owens	.40	1.00
69 Baron Corbin	.20	.50
70 Kofi Kingston	.50	1.25
71 Kushida	.30	.75
72 Kyle O'Reilly	.30	.75
73 LA Knight RC	.25	.60
74 Lacey Evans	.50	1.25
75 Liv Morgan	.75	2.00
76 Mace	.20	.50
77 Mandy Rose	1.00	2.50
78 Mansoor RC	.20	.50
79 Marcel Barthel	.25	.60
80 Mark Andrews	.20	.50
81 Mark Coffey	.20	.50
82 Montez Ford	.20	.50
83 Mustafa Ali	.25	.60
84 MVP	.25	.60
85 Naomi	.25	.60
86 Nash Carter RC	.20	.50
87 Natalya	.30	.75
88 Nia Jax	.40	1.00
89 Nikki A.S.H.	.40	1.00
90 Noam Dar	.25	.60
91 Oney Lorcan	.20	.50
92 Omos RC	.40	1.00
93 Otis	.25	.60
94 Pete Dunne	.40	1.00
95 Doudrop	.30	.75
96 R-Truth	.25	.60
97 Randy Orton	.60	1.50
98 Raquel Gonzalez	.50	1.25
99 Mia Yim	.25	.60
100 Reggie RC	.25	.60
101 Rey Mysterio	.50	1.25
102 Rhea Ripley	.60	1.50
103 Ricochet	.40	1.00
104 Riddick Moss	.25	.60
105 Riddle	.50	1.25
106 Robert Roode	.25	.60
107 Roderick Strong	.30	.75
108 Roman Reigns	1.00	2.50
109 Sami Zayn	.30	.75
110 Santos Escobar	.30	.75
111 Sarray RC	.25	.60
112 Sasha Banks	1.00	2.50
113 Scarlett	1.00	2.50
114 Seth Rollins	.50	1.25
115 Shayna Baszler	.40	1.00
116 Sheamus	.30	.75
117 Shelton Benjamin	.30	.75
118 Shinsuke Nakamura	.50	1.25
119 Shotzi	.75	2.00
120 Shane Thorne	.20	.50
121 T-Bar	.25	.60
122 Tamina	.25	.60
123 Tegan Nox	.50	1.25
124 Samoa Joe	.40	1.00
125 The Miz	.30	.75
126 Timothy Thatcher RC	.20	.50
127 Tommaso Ciampa	.50	1.25
128 Toni Storm	.60	1.50
129 Trent Seven	.25	.60
130 Tyler Bate	.25	.60
131 Walter	.50	1.25
132 Wes Lee RC	.20	.50
133 Wolfgang	.20	.50
134 Xavier Woods	.20	.50
135 Xia Li	.40	1.00
136 Zack Gibson	.20	.50
137 Zoey Stark RC	.25	.60
138 Andre the Giant L	.75	2.00
139 Bam Bam Bigelow L	.40	1.00
140 Batista L	.40	1.00
141 Big Boss Man L	.30	.75
142 Booker T L	.40	1.00
143 Bret "Hit Man" Hart L	.50	1.25
144 British Bulldog L	.30	.75
145 Chyna L	.40	1.00
146 Doink the Clown L	.20	.50
147 Eddie Guerrero L	1.00	2.50
148 Goldberg L	.75	2.00
149 Honky Tonk Man L	.20	.50
150 Hulk Hogan L	1.00	2.50
151 Jake "The Snake" Roberts L	.30	.75
152 Kevin Nash L	.30	.75
153 Lex Luger L	.25	.60
154 Macho Man Randy Savage L	.75	2.00
155 Mick Foley L	.40	1.00
156 Mr. Perfect L	.60	1.50
157 Papa Shango L	.25	.60
158 Razor Ramon L	.30	.75
159 Ricky "The Dragon" Steamboat L	.30	.75
160 Rikishi L	.25	.60
161 Rowdy Roddy Piper L	.50	1.25
162 RVD L	.40	1.00
163 Sgt. Slaughter L	.30	.75
164 Shawn Michaels L	.75	2.00
165 Stacy Keibler L	.60	1.50
166 Stone Cold Steve Austin L	1.00	2.50
167 Trish Stratus L	1.00	2.50
168 Ultimate Warrior L	.75	2.00
169 Undertaker L	1.00	2.50
170 Vader L	.30	.75
171 Yokozuna L	.30	.75
172 Bianca Belair UF	.50	1.25
173 Bobby Lashley UF	.50	1.25
174 Drew McIntyre UF	.50	1.25
175 Io Shirai UF	.40	1.00
176 Kevin Owens UF	.40	1.00
177 Randy Orton UF	.60	1.50
178 Rhea Ripley UF	.60	1.50
179 Roman Reigns UF	1.00	2.50
180 John Cena UF	1.00	2.50
181 The Austin Era Begins	1.00	2.50
182 Five-Star Classic	1.00	2.50
183 Ticket to the Title	1.00	2.50
184 First WWE Championship	1.00	2.50
185 Dominating the Dude	1.00	2.50
186 The People's Stunner	1.00	2.50
187 Third Royal Rumble Win	1.00	2.50
188 Main Event Shocker	1.00	2.50
189 Last-Ever Match	1.00	2.50
190 The Winning Business WMFB	.50	1.25
191 A Swiss Masterclass WMFB	.20	.50
192 Omos Makes His Mark WMFB	.40	1.00
193 Triumphant Turmoil WMFB	.30	.75
194 Bianca Becomes Great-est WMFB	.40	1.00
195 RKO Stuns the Fiend WMFB	.60	1.50
196 Owens KO's His Rival WMFB	.40	1.00
197 Sheamus Solves Riddle WMFB	.30	.75
198 Crews Control WMFB	.25	.60
199 Rhea Wins the Big One WMFB	.60	1.50
200 Smash 'Em/Stack 'Em/Pin 'Em WMFB	1.00	2.50
201 Alexa Bliss RTWM	1.25	3.00
202 Becky Lynch RTWM	.75	2.00
203 Bianca Belair RTWM	.50	1.25
204 Charlotte Flair RTWM	1.00	2.50
205 Drew McIntyre RTWM	.50	1.25
206 Kofi Kingston RTWM	.50	1.25
207 Randy Orton RTWM	.60	1.50
208 Roman Reigns RTWM	1.00	2.50
209 Seth Rollins RTWM	.50	1.25
210 The Rock	2.00	5.00
211 The Rock	2.00	5.00
212 The Rock	2.00	5.00
213 The Rock	2.00	5.00
214 The Rock	2.00	5.00
215 The Rock	2.00	5.00
216 The Rock	2.00	5.00
217 The Rock	2.00	5.00
218 SummerSlam 2020 SUW	1.00	2.50
219 Payback 2020 SUW	1.00	2.50
220 Clash of Champions 2020 SUW	1.00	2.50
221 Hell in a Cell 2020 SUW	1.00	2.50
222 Survivor Series 2020 SUW	1.00	2.50
223 Royal Rumble 2021 SUW	1.00	2.50
224 WrestleMania 37 SUW	1.00	2.50
225 WrestleMania Backlash SUW	1.00	2.50

2021 Topps WWE Superstars 25 Years of The Rock

COMPLETE SET (3)	8.00	20.00

*GREEN/50: .5X TO 1.2X BASIC CARDS
*PURPLE/25: .6X TO 1.5X BASIC CARDS
*TURQUOISE/10: UNPRICED DUE TO SCARCITY
*RED/5: UNPRICED DUE TO SCARCITY
*GOLD/1: UNPRICED DUE TO SCARCITY

TF1 Survivor Series Shocker	4.00	10.00
TF2 Icon vs. Icon	4.00	10.00
TF3 Magic in Miami	4.00	10.00

2021 Topps WWE Superstars Autographs Orange

*TURQUOISE/10: UNPRICED DUE TO SCARCITY
*RED/5: UNPRICED DUE TO SCARCITY
*GOLD/1: UNPRICED DUE TO SCARCITY
STATED PRINT RUN 99 SER.#'d SETS

NNO Big E
NNO Erik
NNO King Nakamura
NNO Naomi
NNO Roderick Strong
NNO Samoa Joe
NNO Tyler Bate
NNO Zelina Vega
NNO Kofi Kingston
(2021 Black Friday Exclusive)
NNO Kofi Kingston (Kofi-Mania)
(2021 Black Friday Exclusive)

2021 Topps WWE Superstars Crystal

COMPLETE SET (6)	15.00	40.00

RANDOMLY INSERTED INTO PACKS

CR1 Alexa Bliss	6.00	15.00
CR2 Bianca Belair	3.00	8.00
CR3 Drew McIntyre	6.00	15.00
CR4 Roman Reigns	5.00	12.00
CR5 Sasha Banks	6.00	15.00
CR6 John Cena	4.00	10.00

2021 Topps WWE Superstars Iconic Matches

*TURQUOISE/10: UNPRICED DUE TO SCARCITY
*RED/5: UNPRICED DUE TO SCARCITY
*GOLD/1: UNPRICED DUE TO SCARCITY
RANDOMLY INSERTED INTO PACKS

MA1 WrestleMania III
MA2 WrestleMania VI
MA3 SummerSlam 1992
MA4 SummerSlam 1995
MA5 WrestleMania XII
MA6 Royal Rumble 2000
MA7 WrestleMania X-Seven
MA8 WrestleMania 25
MA9 WrestleMania 28
MA10 NXT TakeOver: Brooklyn
MA11 SummerSlam 2016

2021 Topps WWE Superstars John Cena's Greatest Moments

COMPLETE SET (6)	12.00	30.00

*GREEN/50: .5X TO 1.2X BASIC CARDS
*PURPLE/25: .6X TO 1.5X BASIC CARDS
*TURQUOISE/10: UNPRICED DUE TO SCARCITY
*RED/5: UNPRICED DUE TO SCARCITY
*GOLD/1: UNPRICED DUE TO SCARCITY
RANDOMLY INSERTED INTO PACKS

JC1 First WWE Title	3.00	8.00

JC2 Legend of the Ladder 3.00 8.00
JC3 Rumble Shocker 3.00 8.00
JC4 Iconic Entrance 3.00 8.00
JC5 Revenge on the Rock 3.00 8.00
JC6 Thuganomics 4 Life 3.00 8.00

2021 Topps WWE Superstars Legends Autographs Orange

*TURQUOISE/10: UNPRICED DUE TO SCARCITY
*RED/5: UNPRICED DUE TO SCARCITY
*GOLD/1: UNPRICED DUE TO SCARCITY
STATED PRINT RUN 99 SER.#'d SETS

NNO Booker T
NNO Ted DiBiase

2021 Topps WWE Superstars Return of the Fans

COMPLETE SET (5) 6.00 15.00
*GREEN/50: .5X TO 1.2X BASIC CARDS
*PURPLE/25: .6X TO 1.5X BASIC CARDS
*TURQUOISE/10: UNPRICED DUE TO SCARCITY
*RED/5: UNPRICED DUE TO SCARCITY
*GOLD/1: UNPRICED DUE TO SCARCITY
RANDOMLY INSERTED INTO PACKS

RF1 Big E Wins the Big One 2.00 5.00
RF2 Roman Reigns Supreme 2.50 6.00
RF3 Return Heard Around the World 2.50 6.00
RF4 The Bro-Off 4.00 10.00
RF5 Superhero Cash-In 1.50 4.00

2021 Topps WWE Superstars Super Elite

COMPLETE SET (16) 15.00 40.00
*YELLOW: .5X TO 1.2X BASIC CARDS
*BLUE/299: .6X TO 1.5X BASIC CARDS
*ORANGE/99: .75X TO 2X BASIC CARDS
*GREEN/50: 1X TO 2.5X BASIC CARDS
*PURPLE/25: UNPRICED DUE TO SCARCITY
*TURQUOISE/10: UNPRICED DUE TO SCARCITY
*RED/5: UNPRICED DUE TO SCARCITY
*GOLD/1: UNPRICED DUE TO SCARCITY
RANDOMLY INSERTED INTO PACKS

SE1 AJ Styles 1.50 4.00
SE2 Alexa Bliss 3.00 8.00
SE3 Asuka 2.00 5.00
SE4 Bayley 1.00 2.50
SE5 Becky Lynch 2.00 5.00
SE6 Bianca Belair 1.25 3.00
SE7 Bobby Lashley 1.25 3.00
SE8 Charlotte Flair 2.50 6.00
SE9 Drew McIntyre 1.25 3.00
SE10 Riddle 1.25 3.00
SE11 Randy Orton 1.50 4.00
SE12 Roman Reigns 2.50 6.00
SE13 Sasha Banks 2.50 6.00
SE14 Seth Rollins 1.25 3.00
SE15 Shinsuke Nakamura 1.25 3.00
SE16 Big E 1.00 2.50

2021 Topps WWE Superstars Super Elite Icons

COMPLETE SET (9) 12.00 30.00
*YELLOW: .5X TO 1.2X BASIC CARDS
*BLUE/299: .6X TO 1.5X BASIC CARDS
*ORANGE/99: .75X TO 2X BASIC CARDS
*GREEN/50: 1X TO 2.5X BASIC CARDS
*PURPLE/25: UNPRICED DUE TO SCARCITY
*TURQUOISE/10: UNPRICED DUE TO SCARCITY
*RED/5: UNPRICED DUE TO SCARCITY
*GOLD/1: UNPRICED DUE TO SCARCITY
RANDOMLY INSERTED INTO PACKS

IC1 Andre the Giant 2.00 5.00
IC2 Bret Hit Man Hart 1.25 3.00
IC3 Hulk Hogan 2.50 6.00
IC4 John Cena 2.50 6.00
IC5 Shawn Michaels 2.00 5.00
IC6 Stone Cold Steve Austin 2.50 6.00
IC7 The Rock 5.00 12.00
IC8 Triple H 2.00 5.00
IC9 Undertaker 2.50 6.00

2016 Topps WWE Then Now Forever

COMPLETE SET (100) 10.00 25.00
*BRONZE: 1.2X TO 3X BASIC CARDS
*SILVER: 2X TO 5X BASIC CARDS
*GOLD/10: 4X TO 10X BASIC CARDS
*RED/1: UNPRICED DUE TO SCARCITY
*P.P.BLACK/1: UNPRICED DUE TO SCARCITY
*P.P.CYAN/1: UNPRICED DUE TO SCARCITY
*P.P.MAGENTA/1: UNPRICED DUE TO SCARCITY
*P.P.YELLOW/1: UNPRICED DUE TO SCARCITY

101 Aiden English .20 .50
102 AJ Styles .75 2.00
103 Apollo Crews RC .20 .50
104 Baron Corbin .25 .60
105 Big Cass .40 1.00
106 Big E .20 .50
107 Braun Strowman RC .25 .60
108 Bray Wyatt .75 2.00
109 Brock Lesnar 1.00 2.50
110 Cathy Kelley RC .20 .50
111 Chris Jericho .50 1.25
112 Dana Brooke RC .50 1.25
113 Darren Young .20 .50
114 Dasha Fuentes RC .20 .50
115 David Otunga .20 .50
116 Dean Ambrose .60 1.50
117 Emma .40 1.00
118 Enzo Amore RC .40 1.00
119 Epico .20 .50
120 Erick Rowan .20 .50
121 Eva Marie .40 1.00
122 Greg Hamilton RC .20 .50
123 Heath Slater .20 .50
124 Jack Swagger .20 .50
125 John Cena 1.00 2.50
126 JoJo .20 .50
127 Kane .30 .75
128 Karl Anderson RC .20 .50
129 Kofi Kingston .20 .50
130 Luke Gallows .25 .60
131 Luke Harper .20 .50
132 Maryse .40 1.00
133 Mauro Ranallo RC .20 .50
134 Primo .20 .50
135 Randy Orton .50 1.25
136 Renee Young .50 1.25
137 The Rock 1.00 2.50
138 Roman Reigns .60 1.50
139 Rosa Mendes .20 .50
140 Sami Zayn .30 .75
141 Scott Stanford .20 .50
142 Seth Rollins .30 .75
143 Shane McMahon .30 .75
144 Sheamus .50 1.25
145 Simon Gotch RC .30 .75
146 Stephanie McMahon .30 .75
147 Tom Phillips .20 .50
148 Tony Chimel .20 .50
149 Triple H .75 2.00
150 Undertaker .75 2.00
151 Xavier Woods .20 .50
152 Zack Ryder .20 .50
153 Big Boss Man L .30 .75
154 Big John Studd L .30 .75
155 Bob Backlund L .20 .50
156 Bobby The Brain Heenan L .30 .75
157 Brian Pillman L .25 .60
158 Bruno Sammartino L .25 .60
159 Chief Jay Strongbow L .30 .75
160 Cowboy Bob Orton L .30 .75
161 Daniel Bryan L .75 2.00
162 Dean Malenko L .20 .50
163 Diamond Dallas Page L .30 .75
164 Eddie Guerrero L .50 1.25
165 The Funks L .20 .50
166 Gerald Brisco L .20 .50
167 Gorilla Monsoon L .30 .75
168 General Adnan L .20 .50
169 Greg The Hammer Valentine L .25 .60
170 Hacksaw Jim Duggan L .20 .50
171 High Chief Peter Maivia L .20 .50
172 The Honky Tonk Man L .20 .50
173 Howard Finkel L .20 .50
174 Jamie Noble L .20 .50
175 Jim The Anvil Neidhart L .20 .50
176 Joey Mercury L .20 .50
177 Junkyard Dog L .30 .75
178 The King Harley Race L .20 .50
179 Larry Zbyszko L .20 .50
180 Lex Luger L .30 .75
181 Mean Gene Okerlund L .25 .60
182 Michael P.S. Hayes L .20 .50
183 Mouth of the South Jimmy Hart L .25 .60
184 Mr. Perfect Curt Henning L .50 1.25
185 Mr. Wonderful Paul Orndorff L .20 .50
186 Nikolai Volkoff L .25 .60
187 Norman Smiley L .20 .50
188 Pat Patterson L .20 .50
189 Paul Bearer L .30 .75
190 Ravishing Rick Rude L .30 .75
191 Ricky The Dragon Steamboat L .25 .60
192 Rocky Johnson L .25 .60
193 Sgt. Slaughter L .25 .60
194 Sting L .50 1.25
195 Stone Cold Steve Austin L 1.00 2.50
196 Tatanka L .20 .50
197 Tom Prichard L .20 .50
198 Vader L .40 1.00
199 Viscera L .20 .50
200 Yokozuna L .40 1.00

2016 Topps WWE Then Now Forever Autographs

*BRONZE/50: .5X TO 1.2X BASIC AUTOS
*SILVER/25: .75X TO 2X BASIC AUTOS
*GOLD/10: 1.2X TO 3X BASIC AUTOS
*RED/1: UNPRICED DUE TO SCARCITY
*P.P.BLACK/1: UNPRICED DUE TO SCARCITY
*P.P.CYAN/1: UNPRICED DUE TO SCARCITY
*P.P.MAGENTA/1: UNPRICED DUE TO SCARCITY
*P.P.YELLOW/1: UNPRICED DUE TO SCARCITY
STATED ODDS 1:51

NNO Aiden English 6.00 15.00
NNO AJ Styles 20.00 50.00
NNO Becky Lynch 15.00 60.00
NNO Charlotte 20.00 50.00
NNO Chris Jericho 15.00 40.00
NNO Dean Ambrose 10.00 25.00
NNO Enzo Amore 12.00 30.00
NNO Hideo Itami 6.00 15.00
NNO Karl Anderson 8.00 20.00
NNO Luke Gallows 8.00 20.00
NNO Maryse 12.00 30.00
NNO Naomi 6.00 15.00
NNO Natalya 8.00 20.00
NNO Norman Smiley 6.00 15.00
NNO Ric Flair 60.00 120.00
NNO Roman Reigns 20.00 50.00
NNO R-Truth 6.00 15.00
NNO Sami Zayn 10.00 25.00
NNO Samoa Joe 6.00 15.00
NNO Sasha Banks 50.00 100.00
NNO Seth Rollins 8.00 20.00
NNO Shinsuke Nakamura 30.00 80.00
NNO Simon Gotch 6.00 15.00
NNO Sting 20.00 50.00

2016 Topps WWE Then Now Forever Diva Kiss

*GOLD/10: UNPRICED DUE TO SCARCITY
*RED/1: UNPRICED DUE TO SCARCITY
STATED ODDS 1:125
STATED PRINT RUN 99 SER.#'d SETS

NNO Alicia Fox 15.00 40.00
NNO Asuka 30.00 80.00
NNO Bayley 30.00 80.00
NNO Becky Lynch 25.00 60.00
NNO Brie Bella 20.00 50.00
NNO Carmella 25.00 60.00
NNO Charlotte 20.00 50.00
NNO Lana 20.00 50.00
NNO Nikki Bella 20.00 50.00
NNO Sasha Banks 30.00 80.00

2016 Topps WWE Then Now Forever Diva Kiss Autographs

*GOLD/10: UNPRICED DUE TO SCARCITY
*RED/1: UNPRICED DUE TO SCARCITY
STATED ODDS 1:482
STATED PRINT RUN 25 SER.#'d SETS

NNO Alicia Fox 25.00 60.00
NNO Asuka 80.00 150.00
NNO Bayley 150.00 300.00
NNO Becky Lynch 60.00 120.00
NNO Brie Bella 80.00 150.00
NNO Carmella 50.00 100.00
NNO Charlotte 60.00 120.00
NNO Lana 50.00 100.00
NNO Nikki Bella 60.00 120.00
NNO Sasha Banks 150.00 300.00

2016 Topps WWE Then Now Forever Mask and Face Paint Medallions

*BRONZE: .5X TO 1.2X BASIC MEM
*SILVER: .6X TO 1.5X BASIC MEM
*GOLD/10: UNPRICED DUE TO SCARCITY
*RED/1: UNPRICED DUE TO SCARCITY
*P.P.BLACK/1: UNPRICED DUE TO SCARCITY
*P.P.CYAN/1: UNPRICED DUE TO SCARCITY
*P.P.MAGENTA/1: UNPRICED DUE TO SCARCITY
*P.P.YELLOW/1: UNPRICED DUE TO SCARCITY
STATED ODDS 1:338

NNO Asuka 8.00 20.00
NNO Braun Strowman 5.00 12.00
NNO Goldust 10.00 25.00
NNO Kalisto 6.00 15.00
NNO Kane 5.00 12.00
NNO Papa Shango 5.00 12.00
NNO Sin Cara 5.00 12.00
NNO Sting 8.00 20.00
NNO Undertaker 10.00 25.00

2016 Topps WWE Then Now Forever NXT Prospects

COMPLETE SET (15) 12.00 30.00
STATED ODDS 1:1

1 Angelo Dawkins 1.00 2.50
2 Austin Aries 1.25 3.00
3 Asuka 4.00 10.00
4 Billie Kay 2.50 6.00
5 Blake 1.00 2.50
6 Dash Wilder 1.25 3.00
7 Elias Samson 1.00 2.50
8 Hideo Itami 1.25 3.00
9 No Way Jose 1.00 2.50
10 Peyton Royce 2.50 6.00
11 Samca Joe 2.50 6.00
12 Sawyer Fulton 1.25 3.00
13 Scott Dawson 1.00 2.50
14 Shinsuke Nakamura 2.50 6.00
15 Tye Dillinger 1.25 3.00

2016 Topps WWE Then Now Forever NXT Rivalries

COMPLETE SET (20) 10.00 25.00
STATED ODDS 1:2

1 Shinsuke Nakamura vs. Samoa Joe 2.00 5.00
2 Finn Balor vs. Samoa Joe 1.25 3.00
3 Kevin Owens vs. Finn Balor 1.25 3.00
4 Asuka vs. Bayley .75 2.00
5 Nia Jax vs. Asuka 1.25 3.00
6 Nia Jax vs. Bayley 1.50 4.00
7 Emma vs. Asuka .75 2.50
8 No Way Jose vs. Austin Aries .75 2.00
9 Baron Corbin vs. Austin Aries .75 2.00
10 Elias Samson vs. Apollo Crews .75 2.00
11 Baron Corbin vs. Samoa Joe 1.25 3.00
12 Emma vs. Bayley 1.25 3.00
13 Sami Zayn vs. Cesaro .75 2.00
14 Tyler Breeze vs. Hideo Itami .75 2.00
15 Tyler Breeze vs. Neville .75 2.00
16 Summer Rae vs. Paige 2.00 5.00
17 Bo Dallas vs. Neville .75 2.00
18 Bray Wyatt vs. Neville .75 2.00
19 Big E vs. Bo Dallas .75 2.00
20 Big E vs. Seth Rollins .75 2.00

2016 Topps WWE Then Now Forever Royal Rumble 2016 Mat Relics

*BRONZE/50: .5X TO 1.2X BASIC MEM
*SILVER/25: .6X TO 1.5X BASIC MEM
*GOLD/10: UNPRICED DUE TO SCARCITY

*RED/1: UNPRICED DUE TO SCARCITY
*P.P.BLACK/1: UNPRICED DUE TO SCARCITY
*P.P.CYAN/1: UNPRICED DUE TO SCARCITY
*P.P.MAGENTA/1: UNPRICED DUE TO SCARCITY
*P.P.YELLOW/1: UNPRICED DUE TO SCARCITY
STATED ODDS 1:92

NNO AJ Styles 8.00 20.00
NNO Alberto Del Rio 3.00 8.00
NNO Becky Lynch 6.00 15.00
NNO Big E 2.00 5.00
NNO Big Show 4.00 10.00
NNO Braun Strowman 2.50 6.00
NNO Bray Wyatt 8.00 20.00
NNO Brock Lesnar 10.00 25.00
NNO Charlotte 6.00 15.00
NNO Chris Jericho 5.00 12.00
NNO Dean Ambrose 6.00 15.00
NNO Dolph Ziggler 2.50 6.00
NNO Erick Rowan 2.00 5.00
NNO Kalisto 5.00 12.00
NNO Kane 3.00 8.00
NNO Kevin Owens 5.00 12.00
NNO Kofi Kingston 2.00 5.00
NNO Luke Harper 2.00 5.00
NNO The Miz 3.00 8.00
NNO Ric Flair 8.00 20.00
NNO Roman Reigns 6.00 15.00
NNO Sami Zayn 3.00 8.00
NNO Sheamus 5.00 12.00
NNO Triple H 8.00 20.00
NNO Xavier Woods 2.00 5.00

2016 Topps WWE Then Now Forever Shirt Relics

*BRONZE/50: .5X TO 1.2X BASIC MEM
*SILVER/25: .6X TO 1.5X BASIC MEM
*GOLD/10: UNPRICED DUE TO SCARCITY
*RED/1: UNPRICED DUE TO SCARCITY
*P.P.BLACK/1: UNPRICED DUE TO SCARCITY
*P.P.CYAN/1: UNPRICED DUE TO SCARCITY
*P.P.MAGENTA/1: UNPRICED DUE TO SCARCITY
*P.P.YELLOW/1: UNPRICED DUE TO SCARCITY
STATED ODDS 1:102

1 Aiden English 2.00 5.00
2 Alberto Del Rio 3.00 8.00
3 Apollo Crews 2.00 5.00
4 Asuka 8.00 20.00
5 Austin Aries 2.50 6.00
6 Baron Corbin 2.50 6.00
7 Bayley 5.00 12.00
8 Big Cass 4.00 10.00
9 Big Show 4.00 10.00
10 Bo Dallas 2.00 5.00
11 Braun Strowman 2.50 6.00
12 Bray Wyatt 8.00 20.00
13 Bubba Ray Dudley 4.00 10.00
14 Cesaro 4.00 10.00
15 Curtis Axel 2.00 5.00
16 Darren Young 2.00 5.00
17 Finn Balor 6.00 15.00
18 Heath Slater 2.00 5.00
19 Jey Uso 2.00 5.00
20 Jimmy Uso 2.00 5.00
21 John Cena 10.00 25.00
22 Kalisto 5.00 12.00
23 Kevin Owens 5.00 12.00
24 Luke Harper 2.00 5.00
25 Randy Orton 5.00 12.00
26 Roman Reigns 6.00 15.00
27 Sheamus 5.00 12.00
28 Simon Gotch 3.00 8.00
29 Xavier Woods 2.00 5.00
30 Zack Ryder 2.00 5.00

2016 Topps WWE Then Now Forever Triple Autographs

STATED ODDS 1:1,362
STATED PRINT RUN 11 SER.#'d SETS

NNO English/Gotch/Amore 50.00 100.00
NNO Styles/Anderson/Gallows 125.00 250.00
NNO Cena/Jericho/R-Truth 75.00 150.00
NNO Naomi/Banks/Bayley 125.00 250.00
NNO Natalya/Charlotte/Lynch 125.00 250.00
NNO Samoa Joe/Balor/Itami 100.00 200.00
NNO Rollins/Ambrose/Reigns 120.00 250.00
NNO Nakamura/Zayn/Asuka 100.00 200.00

2016 Topps WWE Then Now Forever WWE Rivalries

COMPLETE SET (20) 10.00 25.00
STATED ODDS 1:2

1 AJ Styles vs. John Cena 1.00 2.50
2 Seth Rollins vs. Roman Reigns 1.00 2.50
3 Seth Rollins vs. Dean Ambrose 1.25 3.00
4 Dean Ambrose vs. Chris Jericho 1.25 3.00
5 Roman Reigns vs. AJ Styles 1.50 4.00
6 Chris Jericho vs. AJ Styles .75 2.00
7 Sami Zayn vs. Kevin Owens 1.25 3.00
8 Kevin Owens vs. Cesaro 1.50 4.00
9 Kevin Owens vs. Dolph Ziggler 1.25 3.00
10 Undertaker vs. Brock Lesnar 2.00 5.00
11 Roman Reigns vs. Triple H 1.25 3.00
12 Dean Ambrose vs. Triple H 1.25 3.00
13 Natalya vs. Charlotte 1.00 2.50
14 Natalya vs. Becky Lynch 1.25 3.00
15 Dolph Ziggler vs. Baron Corbin .75 2.00
16 Enzo Amore vs. Chris Jericho 1.00 2.50
17 Kalisto vs. Rusev .75 2.00
18 Rusev vs. Jack Swagger .75 2.00
19 Lana vs. Brie Bella 1.50 4.00
20 Dolph Ziggler vs. The Miz .75 2.00

2017 Topps WWE Then Now Forever

COMPLETE SET (100) 10.00 25.00
*BRONZE: .5X TO 1.2X BASIC CARDS
*BLUE/99: 1X TO 2.5X BASIC CARDS
*SILVER/25: 2X TO 5X BASIC CARDS
*GOLD/10: 4X TO 10X BASIC CARDS
*RED/1: UNPRICED DUE TO SCARCITY
*P.P.BLACK/1: UNPRICED DUE TO SCARCITY
*P.P.CYAN/1: UNPRICED DUE TO SCARCITY
*P.P.MAGENTA/1: UNPRICED DUE TO SCARCITY
*P.P.YELLOW/1: UNPRICED DUE TO SCARCITY

101 Tyler Bate RC
102 Brie Bella .60 1.50
103 Jerry The King Lawler .30 .75
104A Akira Tozawa RC .25 .60
104B Akira Tozawa SP/Arms Up 8.00 20.00
105 Alicia Fox .40 1.00
106 Apollo Crews .30 .75
107 Ariya Daivari .25 .60
108 Harley Race .30 .75
109A Big Show .30 .75
109B Big Show SP/Red/White/Blue 4.00 10.00
110 Bo Dallas .25 .60
111A Braun Strowman .30 .75
111B Braun Strowman SP/Stomping 5.00 12.00
112A Bray Wyatt .60 1.50
112B Bray Wyatt SP/White Ropes 5.00 12.00
113A Cesaro .50 1.25
113B Cesaro SP/Mid-Air 5.00 12.00
114 Charly Caruso RC .25 .60
115 Curt Hawkins .25 .60
116 Curtis Axel .25 .60
117 Dana Brooke .50 1.25
118 Darren Young .25 .60
119 Dean Ambrose .75 2.00
120 Emma .60 1.50
121 Jeff Hardy .50 1.25
122 Goldust .30 .75
123 Heath Slater .25 .60
124 JoJo .40 1.00
125 Kalisto .40 1.00
126 Kurt Angle .50 1.25
127 Mark Henry .25 .60
128 Matt Hardy .60 1.50
129 Mickie James .40 1.00
130 Neville .40 1.00
131 R-Truth .25 .60
132 Rhyno .25 .60
133 Roman Reigns .75 2.00
134 Sasha Banks .75 2.00
135 Seth Rollins .75 2.00
136A Sheamus .50 1.25
136B Sheamus SP/Mid-Air 4.00 10.00
137 Summer Rae .60 1.50
138 Aiden English .25 .60
139 Baron Corbin .40 1.00
140 Becky Lynch .75 2.00
141 Charlotte Flair 1.00 2.50
142A Daniel Bryan 1.00 2.50
142B Daniel Bryan SP/YES! 5.00 12.00
143A Dolph Ziggler .40 1.00
143B Dolph Ziggler SP/Drops Elbow 5.00 12.00
144 Epico .25 .60
145 Erick Rowan .25 .60
146 Fandango .25 .60
147 James Ellsworth RC .25 .60
148 Jey Uso .30 .75
149 Jimmy Uso .30 .75
150 Jinder Mahal .40 1.00
151A Kevin Owens .60 1.50
151B Kevin Owens SP/Red/White/Blue 5.00 12.00
152 Konnor .25 .60
153 Lana .75 2.00
154 Naomi .50 1.25
155A Natalya .50 1.25
155B Natalya SP/Arms Raised 6.00 15.00
156 Nikki Bella .60 1.50
157 Primo .25 .60
158A Rusev .50 1.25
158B Rusev SP/Man Bun 5.00 12.00
159 Sami Zayn .30 .75
160 Shinsuke Nakamura .60 1.50
161 Sin Cara .30 .75
162 Tyler Breeze .25 .60
163 Viktor .25 .60
164 Akam .25 .60
165 Aleister Black RC .25 .60
166 Andrade Cien Almas .25 .60
167 Angelo Dawkins .25 .60
168 Buddy Murphy .25 .60
169 Drew McIntyre .25 .60
170 Elias .40 1.00
171 Kassius Ohno RC .25 .60
172 Killian Dain RC .25 .60
173 Abbey Laith RC .25 .60
174 Lacey Evans RC .40 1.00
175 Mandy Rose .30 .75
176 No Way Jose .25 .60
177 Rezar .25 .60
178 Ruby Riot RC .30 .75
179 Sawyer Fulton .25 .60
180 Wesley Blake .25 .60
181 Alundra Blayze .30 .75
182 Andre the Giant .50 1.25
183 Bret Hit Man Hart .50 1.25
184 British Bulldog .25 .60
185 Bruno Sammartino .40 1.00
186 Dusty Rhodes .30 .75
187 Edge .60 1.50
188 Jake The Snake Roberts .30 .75
189 Lex Luger .30 .75
190 Macho Man Randy Savage .50 1.25
191 Ted DiBiase .30 .75
192 Mr. Perfect .50 1.25
193 Ravishing Rick Rude .40 1.00
194 Rowdy Roddy Piper .50 1.25
195 Shawn Michaels .60 1.50
196 Sting .75 2.00
197 Stone Cold Steve Austin 1.00 2.50
198 Trish Stratus 1.00 2.50
199 Ultimate Warrior .50 1.25
200 Wendi Richter .30 .75

2017 Topps WWE Then Now Forever Autographed Dual Relics

STATED PRINT RUN 10 SER. #'d SETS
UNPRICED DUE TO SCARCITY

NNO Asuka
NNO Bayley
NNO Bobby Roode
NNO Bray Wyatt
NNO Charlotte Flair
NNO John Cena
NNO Nikki Bella
NNO Randy Orton
NNO Shinsuke Nakamura

2017 Topps WWE Then Now Forever Autographed NXT TakeOver San Antonio 2017 Mat Relics

STATED PRINT RUN 10 SER.#'d SETS
UNPRICED DUE TO SCARCITY

NNO Asuka
NNO Billie Kay
NNO Bobby Roode
NNO Eric Young
NNO Peyton Royce
NNO Roderick Strong
NNO Shinsuke Nakamura

2017 Topps WWE Then Now Forever Autographed Royal Rumble 2017 Mat Relics

STATED PRINT RUN 10 SER. #'d SETS
UNPRICED DUE TO SCARCITY

NNO AJ Styles
NNO Braun Strowman
NNO Bray Wyatt
NNO Charlotte Flair
NNO Chris Jericho
NNO Goldberg
NNO Karl Anderson
NNO Kevin Owens
NNO Luke Gallows
NNO Naomi
NNO Neville
NNO Nia Jax
NNO Nikki Bella
NNO Randy Orton
NNO Roman Reigns
NNO Undertaker

2017 Topps WWE Then Now Forever Autographed Shirt Relics

STATED PRINT RUN 10 SER.#'d SETS
UNPRICED DUE TO SCARCITY

NNO Aiden English
NNO Becky Lynch
NNO Big Show
NNO Charlotte Flair
NNO Curtis Axel
NNO JoJo
NNO Kevin Owens
NNO Naomi
NNO Natalya
NNO Sasha Banks
NNO Seth Rollins
NNO Sheamus
NNO Sting
NNO Summer Rae

2017 Topps WWE Then Now Forever Autographs

*BLUE/50: .6X TO 1.5X BASIC AUTOS
*SILVER/25: .75X TO 2X BASIC AUTOS
*GOLD/10: UNPRICED DUE TO SCARCITY
*RED/1: UNPRICED DUE TO SCARCITY
STATED ODDS

102 Brie Bella 10.00 25.00
104 Akira Tozawa 8.00 20.00
105 Alicia Fox 8.00 20.00
106 Apollo Crews 6.00 15.00
111 Braun Strowman 12.00 30.00
112 Bray Wyatt 8.00 20.00
113 Cesaro 6.00 15.00
119 Dean Ambrose 10.00 25.00
121 Jeff Hardy 15.00 40.00
123 Heath Slater 5.00 12.00
126 Kurt Angle 15.00 40.00
128 Matt Hardy 15.00 40.00
134 Sasha Banks 25.00 60.00
136 Sheamus 5.00 12.00
139 Baron Corbin 5.00 12.00
140 Becky Lynch 15.00 40.00
154 Naomi 10.00 25.00
159 Sami Zayn 5.00 12.00
160 Shinsuke Nakamura 15.00 40.00
165 Aleister Black 8.00 20.00
169 Drew McIntyre 8.00 20.00
171 Kassius Ohno 6.00 15.00
172 Killian Dain 6.00 15.00
174 Lacey Evans 12.00 30.00
178 Ruby Riot 15.00 40.00
189 Lex Luger 8.00 20.00

2017 Topps WWE Then Now Forever Championship Medallion Relics

*BRONZE/99: .5X TO 1.2X BASIC MEM
*BLUE/50: .6X TO 1.5X BASIC MEM
*SILVER/25: .75X TO 2X BASIC MEM
*GOLD/10: UNPRICED DUE TO SCARCITY
*RED/1: UNPRICED DUE TO SCARCITY
RANDOMLY INSERTED INTO PACKS

NNO Aiden English	1.50	4.00
NNO American Alpha	2.00	5.00
NNO Asuka	5.00	12.00
NNO The Authors of Pain	1.50	4.00
NNO Bayley	5.00	12.00
NNO Blake & Murphy	1.50	4.00
NNO Bobby Roode	4.00	10.00
NNO The Brian Kendrick	1.50	4.00
NNO DIY	3.00	8.00
NNO Finn Balor	6.00	15.00
NNO Kevin Owens	4.00	10.00
NNO Neville	2.50	6.00
NNO The Revival	3.00	8.00
NNO Rich Swann	1.50	4.00
NNO Sami Zayn	2.00	5.00
NNO Samoa Joe	5.00	12.00
NNO Sasha Banks	5.00	12.00
NNO Shinsuke Nakamura	4.00	10.00
NNO TJ Perkins	1.50	4.00

2017 Topps WWE Then Now Forever Dual Relics

*SILVER/25: .6X TO 1.5X BASIC MEM
*GOLD/10: UNPRICED DUE TO SCARCITY
*RED/1: UNPRICED DUE TO SCARCITY
STATED PRINT RUN 50 SER.#'d SETS

NNO Asuka		
NNO Bayley		
NNO Bobby Roode	10.00	25.00
NNO Bray Wyatt		
NNO Brock Lesnar		
NNO Charlotte Flair		
NNO John Cena	12.00	30.00
NNO Nikki Bella	10.00	25.00
NNO Randy Orton		
NNO Shinsuke Nakamura	20.00	50.00

2017 Topps WWE Then Now Forever Finishers and Signature Moves

COMPLETE SET (50)	10.00	25.00
STATED ODDS 2:1		
F1 John Cena	1.50	4.00
F2 John Cena	1.50	4.00
F3 Brock Lesnar	1.50	4.00
F4 Brock Lesnar	1.50	4.00
F5 Goldberg	1.25	3.00
F6 Goldberg	1.25	3.00
F7 The Rock	1.50	4.00
F8 The Rock	1.50	4.00
F9 Triple H	.75	2.00
F10 Randy Orton	.75	2.00
F11 Undertaker	1.25	3.00
F12 Undertaker	1.25	3.00
F13 Undertaker	1.25	3.00
F14 Kane	.40	1.00
F15 Big Show	.40	1.00
F16 Big Show	.40	1.00
F17 Chris Jericho	.75	2.00
F18 Chris Jericho	.75	2.00
F19 Chris Jericho	.75	2.00
F20 Daniel Bryan	1.25	3.00
F21 Mick Foley	.75	2.00
F22 Mick Foley	.75	2.00
F23 Booker T	.40	1.00
F24 AJ Styles	1.50	4.00
F25 AJ Styles	1.50	4.00
F26 AJ Styles	1.50	4.00
F27 Finn Balor	1.25	3.00
F28 Finn Balor	1.25	3.00
F29 The Miz	.60	1.50
F30 The Miz	.60	1.50
F31 Bobby Roode	.75	2.00
F32 Shinsuke Nakamura	.75	2.00
F33 Drew McIntyre	.30	.75
F34 Aliyah	.40	1.00
F35 Andrade Cien Almas	.30	.75
F36 Dean Ambrose	1.00	2.50
F37 No Way Jose	.30	.75
F38 Ember Moon	.75	2.00
F39 Eric Young	.60	1.50
F40 Hideo Itami	.50	1.25
F41 Nikki Cross	.60	1.50
F42 Billie Kay	.40	1.00
F43 Tye Dillinger	.30	.75
F44 Buddy Murphy	.30	.75
F45 Peyton Royce	.50	1.25
F46 The Authors of Pain	.30	.75
F47 The Revival	.60	1.50
F48 TM-61	.30	.75
F49 The Hype Bros.	.40	1.00
F50 #DIY	.60	1.50

2017 Topps WWE Then Now Forever Kiss

*GOLD/10: UNPRICED DUE TO SCARCITY
*RED/1: UNPRICED DUE TO SCARCITY
STATED PRINT RUN 99 SER.#'d SETS

NNO Alexa Bliss	200.00	400.00
NNO Asuka	50.00	100.00
NNO Becky Lynch	125.00	250.00
NNO Billie Kay	15.00	40.00
NNO Charlotte Flair	125.00	250.00
NNO Ember Moon	30.00	75.00
NNO Liv Morgan	100.00	200.00
NNO Peyton Royce	15.00	40.00

2017 Topps WWE Then Now Forever Kiss Autographs

*GOLD/10: UNPRICED DUE TO SCARCITY
*RED/1: UNPRICED DUE TO SCARCITY
STATED PRINT RUN 25 SER.#'d SETS

NNO Alexa Bliss		
NNO Asuka	50.00	100.00
NNO Becky Lynch	50.00	100.00
NNO Billie Kay	30.00	75.00
NNO Charlotte Flair	60.00	120.00
NNO Ember Moon	25.00	60.00
NNO Liv Morgan	50.00	100.00
NNO Mickie James	60.00	120.00
NNO Nikki Bella	50.00	100.00
NNO Peyton Royce	30.00	75.00

2017 Topps WWE Then Now Forever NXT TakeOver San Antonio 2017 Mat Relics

*BRONZE/99: .5X TO 1.2X BASIC MEM
*BLUE/50: .6X TO 1.5X BASIC MEM
*SILVER/25: .75X TO 2X BASIC MEM
*GOLD/10: UNPRICED DUE TO SCARCITY
*RED/1: UNPRICED DUE TO SCARCITY
STATED PRINT RUN 350 SER.#'d SETS

NNO Akam	1.50	4.00
NNO Asuka	5.00	12.00
NNO Billie Kay	2.00	5.00
NNO Bobby Roode	4.00	10.00
NNO Eric Young	3.00	8.00
NNO Peyton Royce	2.50	6.00
NNO Rezar	1.50	4.00
NNO Roderick Strong	2.00	5.00
NNO Shinsuke Nakamura	4.00	10.00
NNO Tye Dillinger	1.50	4.00

2017 Topps WWE Then Now Forever Roster Updates

COMPLETE SET (20)	12.00	30.00
R21 Alexa Bliss	5.00	12.00
R22 Dash Wilder	1.00	2.50
R23 Jason Jordan	1.25	3.00
R24 Maryse	2.00	5.00
R25 The Miz	2.00	5.00
R26 Mustafa Ali	1.00	2.50
R27 Scott Dawson	1.00	2.50
R28 Tony Nese	1.00	2.50
R29 The New Day	2.00	5.00
R30 Samir Singh	1.00	2.50
R31 Sunil Singh	1.00	2.50
R32 Tamina	1.25	3.00
R33 Tye Dillinger	1.00	2.50
R34 Dan Matha	1.00	2.50
R35 Vanessa Borne	1.25	3.00
R36 Gabriel Ealy	1.00	2.50
R37 Kona Reeves	1.00	2.50
R38 The Velveteen Dream	1.25	3.00
R39 Steve Cutler	1.00	2.50
R40 Uriel Ealy	1.00	2.50

2017 Topps WWE Then Now Forever Royal Rumble 2017 Mat Relics

*BRONZE/99: .5X TO 1.2X BASIC MEM
*BLUE/50: .6X TO 1.5X BASIC MEM
*SILVER/25: .75X TO 2X BASIC MEM
*GOLD/10: UNPRICED DUE TO SCARCITY
*RED/1: UNPRICED DUE TO SCARCITY
RANDOMLY INSERTED INTO PACKS

NNO AJ Styles	6.00	15.00
NNO Bayley	4.00	10.00
NNO Braun Strowman	1.50	4.00
NNO Bray Wyatt	3.00	8.00
NNO Brock Lesnar	6.00	15.00
NNO Charlotte Flair	5.00	12.00
NNO Chris Jericho	3.00	8.00
NNO Goldberg	5.00	12.00
NNO John Cena	6.00	15.00
NNO Karl Anderson	1.25	3.00
NNO Kevin Owens	3.00	8.00
NNO Luke Gallows	2.00	5.00
NNO Naomi	2.50	6.00
NNO Neville	2.00	5.00
NNO Nia Jax	2.00	5.00
NNO Nikki Bella	3.00	8.00
NNO Randy Orton	3.00	8.00
NNO Rich Swann	1.25	3.00
NNO Roman Reigns	4.00	10.00
NNO Undertaker	5.00	12.00

2017 Topps WWE Then Now Forever Shirt Relics

*BLUE/50: .5X TO 1.2X BASIC MEM
*SILVER/25: .6X TO 1.5X BASIC MEM
*GOLD/10: UNPRICED DUE TO SCARCITY
*RED/1: UNPRICED DUE TO SCARCITY
RANDOMLY INSERTED INTO PACKS

NNO Aiden English	1.25	3.00
NNO Andrade Cien Almas	1.25	3.00
NNO Becky Lynch	4.00	10.00
NNO Big Show	1.50	4.00
NNO Brock Lesnar	6.00	15.00
NNO Charlotte Flair	5.00	12.00
NNO Curtis Axel	1.25	3.00
NNO Darren Young	1.25	3.00
NNO John Cena	6.00	15.00
NNO JoJo	2.00	5.00
NNO Kevin Owens	3.00	8.00
NNO Naomi	2.50	6.00
NNO Natalya	2.50	6.00
NNO No Way Jose	1.25	3.00
NNO Sasha Banks	4.00	10.00
NNO Seth Rollins	4.00	10.00
NNO Sheamus	2.50	6.00
NNO Sting	4.00	10.00
NNO Summer Rae	3.00	8.00

2017 Topps WWE Then Now Forever Triple Autographs

STATED PRINT RUN 10 SER.#'d SETS
RANDOMLY INSERTED INTO PACKS

NNO Bayley/Banks/Flair	125.00	250.00
NNO Wyatt/Orton/Harper	75.00	150.00
NNO Rollins/Reigns/Ambrose	150.00	300.00
NNO Undertaker/Lesnar/Goldberg	400.00	600.00
NNO Undertaker/Kane/Bryan	250.00	400.00

2018 Topps WWE Then Now Forever

COMPLETE SET W/O SP (100) 8.00 20.00
*BRONZE: .5X TO 1.2X BASIC CARDS
*BLUE/99: .75X TO 2X BASIC CARDS
*SILVER/25: 2X TO 5X BASIC CARDS
*GOLD/10: UNPRICED DUE TO SCARCITY
*RED/1: UNPRICED DUE TO SCARCITY
*P.P.BLACK/1: UNPRICED DUE TO SCARCITY
*P.P.CYAN/1: UNPRICED DUE TO SCARCITY
*P.P.MAGENTA/1: UNPRICED DUE TO SCARCITY
*P.P.YELLOW/1: UNPRICED DUE TO SCARCITY

101 Ronda Rousey	2.50	6.00
102 Alexa Bliss	1.25	3.00
102A Alexa Bliss SP		
103 Akam	.25	.60
104 Alexander Wolfe	.25	.60
105 Andrade	.40	1.00
105A Andrade SP		
106 Constable Baron Corbin	.40	1.00
107 Bayley	.40	1.00
107A Bayley SP		
108 Becky Lynch	.60	1.50
108A Becky Lynch SP		
109 Bianca Belair RC	1.25	3.00
110 Big Show	.25	.60
111 Billie Kay	.50	1.25
112 Bobby Lashley	.50	1.25
112A Bobby Lashley SP		
113 Braun Strowman	.60	1.50
113A Braun Strowman SP		
114 Bray Wyatt	.60	1.50
114A Bray Wyatt SP		
115 Candice LeRae RC	.30	.75
116 Cesaro	.50	1.25
116A Cesaro SP		
117 Cezar Bononi RC	.25	.60
118 Dakota Kai RC	.30	.75
119 Danny Burch RC	.25	.60
120 Dash Wilder	.30	.75
121 David Otunga	.30	.75
122 Dean Ambrose	.50	1.25
122A Dean Ambrose SP		
123 Dolph Ziggler	.30	.75
124 Drake Maverick RC	.30	.75
125 Drew McIntyre	.40	1.00
125A Drew McIntyre SP		
126 EC3	.25	.60
127 Ember Moon	.50	1.25
127A Ember Moon SP		
128 Eric Young	.30	.75
128A Eric Young SP		
129 Fabian Aichner RC	.25	.60
130 Fandango	.25	.60
131 Finn Balor	.60	1.50
131A Finn Balor SP		
132 Goldust	.50	1.25
133 Hanson RC	.30	.75
134 Harper	.40	1.00
135 Hideo Itami	.25	.60
136 Jason Jordan	.25	.60
137 Jeff Hardy	.50	1.25
137A Jeff Hardy SP		
138 Jonathan Coachman	.25	.60
139 Kalisto	.25	.60
140 Kane	.40	1.00
141 Karl Anderson	.25	.60
142 Kassius Ohno	.25	.60
143 Killian Dain	.30	.75
144 Kona Reeves	.25	.60
145 Lacey Evans	.30	.75
146 Lince Dorado	.25	.60
147 Liv Morgan	.50	1.25
148 Luke Gallows	.30	.75
149 Mandy Rose	.60	1.50
150 Mark Andrews RC	.25	.60
151 Woken Matt Hardy	.60	1.50
152 Mojo Rawley	.25	.60
153 Nick Miller	.25	.60
154 Nikki Bella	.50	1.25
155 Nikki Cross	.40	1.00
156 No Way Jose	.30	.75
157 Otis Dozovic	.25	.60
158 Peyton Royce	.60	1.50
159 Randy Orton	.60	1.50
159A Randy Orton SP		
160 Raul Mendoza RC	.25	.60
161 Rezar	.25	.60
162 Ricochet RC	.50	1.25
163 Riddick Moss	.25	.60
164 Roman Reigns	.60	1.50
164A Roman Reigns SP		
165 Rowan	.40	1.00
166 Rowe RC	.25	.60

167 Ruby Riott .40 1.00
167A Ruby Riott SP
168 Rusev .40 1.00
168A Rusev SP
169 Sami Zayn .25 .60
169A Sami Zayn SP
170 Samoa Joe .50 1.25
170A Samoa Joe SP
171 Sasha Banks .75 2.00
171A Sasha Banks SP
172 Scott Dawson .30 .75
173 Scott Stanford .25 .60
174 Seth Rollins .60 1.50
174A Seth Rollins SP
175 Shane Thorne .25 .60
176 Shayna Baszler .60 1.50
177 Sheamus .50 1.25
177A Sheamus SP
178 Shinsuke Nakamura .60 1.50
178A Shinsuke Nakamura SP
179 Taynara Conti RC .25 .60
180 Tino Sabbatelli .30 .75
181 Trent Seven RC .25 .60
182 Tucker Knight .25 .60
183 Tye Dillinger .25 .60
184 Tyler Breeze .25 .60
185 Vanessa Borne .25 .60
186 Velveteen Dream .25 .60
187 Zelina Vega RC .25 .60
188 Andre the Giant .50 1.25
189 Beth Phoenix .50 1.25
190 Bret Hit Man Hart .60 1.50
191 Eddie Guerrero .60 1.50
192 Edge .60 1.50
193 Jake The Snake Roberts .30 .75
194 Lita .60 1.50
195 Macho Man Randy Savage .75 2.00
196 Ted DiBiase .30 .75
197 Mr. Perfect .30 .75
198 Shawn Michaels .75 2.00
199 Sting .60 1.50
200 Stone Cold Steve Austin 1.25 3.00

2018 Topps WWE Then Now Forever 25 Years of RAW

COMPLETE SET (50) 12.00 30.00
RANDOMLY INSERTED INTO PACKS

RAW1 Monday Night RAW Premieres .40 1.00
RAW2 Mr. Perfect Def. Ric Flair .40 1.00
RAW3 123 Kid vs. Bret Hart .40 1.00
RAW4 Ringmaster Debuts 1.50 4.00
RAW5 Bret Hart Snaps .75 2.00
RAW6 Austin injures Bret Hart 1.50 4.00
RAW7 NA Outlaws/Chainsaw Charlie .40 1.00
RAW8 HHH Leads DX .75 2.00
RAW9 DX Invades WCW .75 2.00
RAW10 Stone Cold/Zamboni 1.50 4.00
RAW11 Undertaker Captures Austin 1.25 3.00
RAW12 Stone Cold/Beer Truck 1.50 4.00
RAW13 The Higher Power .40 1.00
RAW14 Rock/This Is Your Life .40 1.00
RAW15 HHH and Stephanie Elope .75 2.00
RAW16 Angle/Milk Truck .75 2.00
RAW17 HHH Returns .75 2.00
RAW18 WWE Draft .40 1.00
RAW19 Hardy/Undertaker .60 1.50
RAW20 HHH Turns on HBK .75 2.00
RAW21 HHH/Evolution .75 2.00
RAW22 Goldberg Debuts 1.25 3.00
RAW23 HHH Def. Ric Flair .75 2.00
RAW24 Lita Def. Trish .75 2.00
RAW25 Batista Thumbs Down .50 1.25
RAW26 Cena Joins RAW 1.25 3.00
RAW27 HBK/Montreal 1.00 2.50
RAW28 Mr. McMahon's Limo .60 1.50
RAW29 Hardy Swantons Orton .60 1.50
RAW30 Ric Flair Retires 1.00 2.50
RAW31 Bret Hart Returns .75 2.00
RAW32 HBK Farewell 1.00 2.50
RAW33 Nexus Invades .40 1.00
RAW34 Miz Cashes In .60 1.50
RAW35 HHH/Taker WrestleMania .75 2.00
RAW36 Edge Retires .75 2.00
RAW37 Daniel Bryan Kane Hug .75 2.00
RAW38 Dolph Ziggler Cashes In .40 1.00
RAW39 Mark Henry Fake Retires .40 1.00
RAW40 Yes! Movement .75 2.00
RAW41 Seth Rollins Turns .75 2.00
RAW42 Kevin Owens Debuts .75 2.00
RAW43 Shane McMahon Returns .60 1.50
RAW44 Styles Confronts Cena 1.25 3.00
RAW45 Goldberg Returns 1.25 3.00
RAW46 Angle New GM .75 2.00
RAW47 Roman Reigns/My Yard .75 2.00
RAW48 The Shield Reunite .40 1.00
RAW49 Miz Wins 8th IC Title .60 1.50
RAW50 Scott Hall Returns .60 1.50

2018 Topps WWE Then Now Forever Autographed Royal Rumble 2018 Mat Relics

STATED PRINT RUN 10 SER.#'d SETS
UNPRICED DUE TO SCARCITY

MRARRAC Adam Cole
MRARRAJ AJ Styles
MRARRAS Asuka
MRARRBS Braun Strowman
MRARRFB Finn Balor
MRARRKK Kofi Kingston
MRARRKO Kevin Owens
MRARRMH Woken Matt Hardy
MRARRRS Rusev
MRARRSN Shinsuke Nakamura
MRARRSR Seth Rollins
MRARRSZ Sami Zayn

2018 Topps WWE Then Now Forever Autographed Shirt Relics

STATED PRINT RUN 10 SER.#'d SETS
UNPRICED DUE TO SCARCITY

SRAB Alexa Bliss
SRAK Akam
SRCG Chad Gable
SRCR Carmella
SRDZ Dolph Ziggler
SRJC John Cena
SRJJ Jason Jordan
SRKA Karl Anderson
SRLG Luke Gallows
SRNA Naomi
SRRZ Rezar
SRSR Seth Rollins

2018 Topps WWE Then Now Forever Autographs

*BLUE/99: .5X TO 1.2X BASIC AUTOS
*SILVER/25: .6X TO 1.5X BASIC AUTOS
*GOLD/10: UNPRICED DUE TO SCARCITY
*RED/1: UNPRICED DUE TO SCARCITY
RANDOMLY INSERTED INTO PACKS

102 Alexa Bliss 30.00 75.00
106 Baron Corbin 4.00 10.00
108 Becky Lynch 15.00 40.00
111 Billie Kay 10.00 25.00
113 Braun Strowman 10.00 25.00
114 Bray Wyatt 8.00 20.00
115 Candice LeRae 12.00 30.00
125 Drew McIntyre 6.00 15.00
126 EC3 10.00 25.00
127 Ember Moon 8.00 20.00
128 Eric Young 5.00 12.00
131 Finn Balor 8.00 20.00
133 Hanson 12.00 30.00
137 Jeff Hardy 8.00 20.00
142 Kassius Ohno 4.00 10.00
147 Liv Morgan 15.00 40.00
151 Woken Matt Hardy 8.00 20.00
152 Mojo Rawley 5.00 12.00
158 Peyton Royce 12.00 30.00
162 Ricochet 25.00 60.00
166 Rowe 8.00 20.00
167 Ruby Riott 12.00 30.00
168 Rusev 6.00 15.00
169 Sami Zayn 6.00 15.00
170 Samoa Joe 5.00 12.00
178 Shinsuke Nakamura 10.00 25.00
189 Beth Phoenix 10.00 25.00

2018 Topps WWE Then Now Forever Four Corner Mat Relics

*SILVER/25: .5X TO 1.2X BASIC MEM
*GOLD/10: UNPRICED DUE TO SCARCITY
STATED PRINT RUN 50 SER.#'d SETS

FCAJ AJ Styles 12.00 30.00
FCAS Asuka 10.00 25.00
FCDA Dean Ambrose 4.00 10.00
FCJC John Cena 12.00 30.00
FCRO Randy Orton 6.00 15.00
FCRR Roman Reigns 6.00 15.00
FCSN Shinsuke Nakamura 10.00 25.00
FCSR Seth Rollins 12.00 30.00
FCTH Triple H 10.00 25.00
FCUN Undertaker 15.00 40.00

2018 Topps WWE Then Now Forever Kiss

*GOLD/10: UNPRICED DUE TO SCARCITY
*RED/1: UNPRICED DUE TO SCARCITY

KCAB Alexa Bliss 75.00 200.00
KCAS Asuka 50.00 125.00
KCMR Mandy Rose 40.00 100.00

2018 Topps WWE Then Now Forever Kiss Autographs

*GOLD/10: UNPRICED DUE TO SCARCITY
*RED/1: UNPRICED DUE TO SCARCITY
STATED PRINT RUN 25 SER.#'d SETS

KCMJ Mickie James 50.00 125.00
KCMR Mandy Rose 125.00 300.00
KCRR Ruby Riott 50.00 125.00

2018 Topps WWE Then Now Forever Money in the Bank 2017 Mat Relics

*BRONZE/99: .5X TO 1.2X BASIC MEM
*BLUE/50: .6X TO 1.5X BASIC MEM
*SILVER/25: .75X TO 2X BASIC MEM
*GOLD/10: UNPRICED DUE TO SCARCITY
*RED/1: UNPRICED DUE TO SCARCITY

MRMBAJ AJ Styles 8.00 20.00
MRMBBC Baron Corbin 2.50 6.00
MRMBBL Becky Lynch 6.00 15.00
MRMBCF Charlotte Flair 10.00 25.00
MRMBCR Carmella 5.00 12.00
MRMBDZ Dolph Ziggler 3.00 8.00
MRMBKO Kevin Owens 2.50 6.00
MRMBNT Natalya 3.00 8.00
MRMBSN Shinsuke Nakamura 4.00 10.00
MRMBSZ Sami Zayn 2.50 6.00
MRMBTA Tamina 2.50 6.00

2018 Topps WWE Then Now Forever NXT TakeOver Philadelphia 2018 Mat Relics

*BRONZE/99: .5X TO 1.2X BASIC MEM
*BLUE/50: .6X TO 1.5X BASIC MEM
*SILVER/25: .75X TO 2X BASIC MEM
*GOLD/10: UNPRICED DUE TO SCARCITY
*RED/1: UNPRICED DUE TO SCARCITY

MRPHAA Andrade Cien Almas 4.00 10.00
MRPHAB Aleister Black 2.50 6.00
MRPHAC Adam Cole 3.00 8.00
MRPHBF Bobby Fish 2.00 5.00
MRPHEM Ember Moon 3.00 8.00
MRPHJG Johnny Gargano 2.00 5.00
MRPHKO Kassius Ohno 3.00 8.00
MRPHOR Kyle O'Reilly 4.00 10.00
MRPHSB Shayna Baszler 3.00 8.00
MRPHVD Velveteen Dream 5.00 12.00

2018 Topps WWE Then Now Forever RAW 25 Mat Relics

*BRONZE/99: .5X TO 1.2X BASIC MEM
*BLUE/50: .6X TO 1.5X BASIC MEM
*SILVER/25: .75X TO 2X BASIC MEM
*GOLD/10: UNPRICED DUE TO SCARCITY
*RED/1: UNPRICED DUE TO SCARCITY

MR25AS Asuka 5.00 12.00
MR25EL Elias 2.50 6.00
MR25JC John Cena 6.00 15.00
MR25RR Roman Reigns 4.00 10.00
MR25SA Stone Cold Steve Austin 12.00 30.00
MR25TM The Miz 3.00 8.00

2018 Topps WWE Then Now Forever Roster Updates

COMPLETE SET (20) 15.00 40.00
RANDOMLY INSERTED INTO PACKS

R21 Asuka 2.50 6.00
R22 Bobby Roode 1.25 3.00
R23 Chad Gable .75 2.00
R24 Jinder Mahal 1.00 2.50
R25 Kevin Owens 2.00 5.00
R26 Konnor .75 2.00
R27 Maria Kanellis 2.00 5.00
R28 Mike Kanellis 2.00 5.00
R29 Natalya 1.00 2.50
R30 Paige 2.00 5.00
R31 R-Truth 1.00 2.50
R32 Samir Singh .75 2.00
R33 Sarah Logan .75 2.00
R34 Sonya Deville 1.50 4.00
R35 Sunil Singh .75 2.00
R36 The Miz 1.50 4.00
R37 Vic Joseph .75 2.00
R38 Viktor .75 2.00
R39 Zack Ryder .75 2.00
R40 Maryse 1.50 4.00

2018 Topps WWE Then Now Forever Royal Rumble 2018 Mat Relics

*BRONZE/199: .5X TO 1.2X BASIC MEM
*BLUE/99: .6X TO 1.5X BASIC MEM
*SILVER/25: .75X TO 2X BASIC MEM
*GOLD/10: UNPRICED DUE TO SCARCITY
*RED/1: UNPRICED DUE TO SCARCITY

MRRRAA Andrade Cien Almas 2.00 5.00
MRRRAC Adam Cole 4.00 10.00
MRRRAJ AJ Styles 6.00 15.00
MRRRAS Asuka 4.00 10.00
MRRRBE Big E 2.00 5.00
MRRRBS Braun Strowman 3.00 8.00
MRRRCE Cesaro 2.50 6.00
MRRRDZ Dolph Ziggler 2.50 6.00
MRRREL Elias 3.00 8.00
MRRRFB Finn Balor 5.00 12.00
MRRRJC John Cena 6.00 15.00
MRRRJJ Jason Jordan 2.50 6.00
MRRRJM Jinder Mahal 2.00 5.00
MRRRKK Kofi Kingston 2.50 6.00
MRRRKN Kane 2.50 6.00
MRRRKO Kevin Owens 2.00 5.00
MRRRMH Woken Matt Hardy 2.50 6.00
MRRRNB Nikki Bella 5.00 12.00
MRRRRO Randy Orton 4.00 10.00
MRRRRR Roman Reigns 4.00 10.00
MRRRRS Rusev 2.50 6.00
MRRRSH Sheamus 3.00 8.00
MRRRSN Shinsuke Nakamura 3.00 8.00
MRRRSR Seth Rollins 4.00 10.00
MRRRSZ Sami Zayn 2.50 6.00
MRRRTM The Miz 2.50 6.00
MRRRXW Xavier Woods 2.50 6.00

2018 Topps WWE Then Now Forever Shirt Relics

*BLUE/99: .5X TO 1.2X BASIC MEM
*SILVER/25: .75X TO 2X BASIC MEM
*GOLD/10: UNPRICED DUE TO SCARCITY
*RED/1: UNPRICED DUE TO SCARCITY

SRAB Alexa Bliss 8.00 20.00
SRAK Akam 1.50 4.00
SRCG Chad Gable 1.50 4.00
SRCR Carmella 3.00 8.00
SRDZ Dolph Ziggler 1.50 4.00
SRJC John Cena 4.00 10.00
SRJJ Jason Jordan 2.00 5.00
SRKA Karl Anderson 2.00 5.00
SRLG Luke Gallows 2.00 5.00
SRNA Naomi 3.00 8.00
SRRZ Rezar 1.50 4.00
SRSR Seth Rollins 4.00 10.00

2018 Topps WWE Then Now Forever Triple Autographs

STATED PRINT RUN 10 SER.#'d SETS
UNPRICED DUE TO SCARCITY

TAABS	Paige/Rose/Deville
TACLB	Styles/Gallows/Anderson
TATRS	Riott/Morgan/Logan
TATWW	O'Neil/Crews/Brooke

2018 Topps WWE Then Now Forever Promo

NYCC2	Alexa Bliss NYCC	4.00	10.00

2016 Topps WWE Then Now Forever Stickers

1	WWE Logo FOIL	.20	.50
2	Raw Logo	.20	.50
3	Smackdown Logo	.20	.50
4	NXT Logo	.20	.50
5	WWE Legends Logo	.20	.50
6	Brock Lesnar FOIL	.60	1.50
7	Brock Lesnar	.60	1.50
8	Brock Lesnar	.60	1.50
9	Brock Lesnar	.60	1.50
10	Brock Lesnar	.60	1.50
11	Neville	.30	.75
12	Neville	.30	.75
13	Neville	.30	.75
14	Neville	.30	.75
15	Neville	.30	.75
16	The New Day FOIL	.30	.75
17	The New Day	.30	.75
18	The New Day	.30	.75
19	The New Day	.30	.75
20	The New Day	.30	.75
21	Dudley Boyz	.12	.30
22	Dudley Boyz	.12	.30
23	D-Von Dudley	.20	.50
24	Bubba Ray Dudley	.25	.60
25	Dudley Boyz	.12	.30
26	Finn Balor FOIL	.40	1.00
27	Finn Balor	.40	1.00
28	Finn Balor	.40	1.00
29	Finn Balor	.40	1.00
30	Finn Balor	.40	1.00
31	Samoa Joe	.30	.75
32	Samoa Joe	.30	.75
33	Samoa Joe	.30	.75
34	Samoa Joe	.30	.75
35	Samoa Joe	.30	.75
36	Apollo Crews	.12	.30
37	Apollo Crews	.12	.30
38	Apollo Crews	.12	.30
39	Apollo Crews	.12	.30
40	Apollo Crews	.12	.30
41	Baron Corbin	.15	.40
42	Baron Corbin	.15	.40
43	Baron Corbin	.15	.40
44	Baron Corbin	.15	.40
45	Baron Corbin	.15	.40
46	John Cena FOIL	.60	1.50
47	John Cena	.60	1.50
48	John Cena	.60	1.50
49	John Cena	.60	1.50
50	John Cena	.60	1.50
51	Seth Rollins	.20	.50
52	Seth Rollins	.20	.50
53	Seth Rollins	.20	.50
54	Seth Rollins	.20	.50
55	Seth Rollins	.20	.50
56	Roman Reigns FOIL	.40	1.00
57	Roman Reigns	.40	1.00
58	Roman Reigns	.40	1.00
59	Roman Reigns	.40	1.00
60	Roman Reigns	.40	1.00
61	Dean Ambrose FOIL	.40	1.00
62	Dean Ambrose	.40	1.00
63	Dean Ambrose	.40	1.00
64	Dean Ambrose	.40	1.00
65	Dean Ambrose	.40	1.00
66	The Wyatt Family FOIL	.50	1.25
67	Bray Wyatt	.50	1.25
68	Braun Strowman	.15	.40
69	Luke Harper	.12	.30
70	Erick Rowan	.12	.30
71	Kalisto FOIL	.30	.75
72	Kalisto	.30	.75
73	Kalisto	.30	.75
74	Kalisto	.30	.75
75	Kalisto	.30	.75
76	Bret Hart FOIL	.30	.75
77	Bret Hart	.30	.75
78	Bret Hart	.30	.75
79	Bret Hart	.30	.75
80	Bret Hart	.30	.75
81	Edge FOIL	.30	.75
82	Edge	.30	.75
83	Edge	.30	.75
84	Edge	.30	.75
85	Edge	.30	.75
86	Sting	.30	.75
87	Sting	.30	.75
88	Sting	.30	.75
89	Sting	.30	.75
90	Sting	.30	.75
91	Shawn Michaels FOIL	.50	1.25
92	Shawn Michaels	.50	1.25
93	Shawn Michaels	.50	1.25
94	Shawn Michaels	.50	1.25
95	Shawn Michaels	.50	1.25
96	Charlotte FOIL	.40	1.00
97	Alicia Fox	.20	.50
98	Becky Lynch	.40	1.00
99	Brie Bella	.25	.60
100	Lana	.50	1.25
101	Nikki Bella FOIL	.40	1.00
102	Natalya	.20	.50
103	Paige	.40	1.00
104	Sasha Banks	.40	1.00
105	Summer Rae	.30	.75
106	Naomi	.20	.50
107	Bayley FOIL	.30	.75
108	Alexa Bliss	.60	1.50
109	Asuka	.50	1.25
110	Billie Kay	.30	.75
111	Carmella	.30	.75
112	Eva Marie FOIL	.25	.60
113	Dana Brooke	.30	.75
114	Emma	.25	.60
115	Nia Jax	.20	.50
116	Peyton Royce	.30	.75
117	Dasha Fuentes	.12	.30
118	Randy Orton FOIL	.30	.75
119	Randy Orton	.30	.75
120	Randy Orton	.30	.75
121	Randy Orton	.30	.75
122	Randy Orton	.30	.75
123	Daniel Bryan FOIL	.50	1.25
124	Daniel Bryan	.50	1.25
125	Daniel Bryan	.50	1.25
126	Daniel Bryan	.50	1.25
127	Daniel Bryan	.50	1.25
128	Ryback FOIL	.15	.40
129	Ryback	.15	.40
130	Ryback	.15	.40
131	Ryback	.15	.40
132	Ryback	.15	.40
133	Dolph Ziggler FOIL	.15	.40
134	Dolph Ziggler	.15	.40
135	Dolph Ziggler	.15	.40
136	Dolph Ziggler	.15	.40
137	Dolph Ziggler	.15	.40
138	Chris Jericho	.30	.75
139	Shawn Michaels	.50	1.25
140	Steve Austin/Beer Truck	.60	1.50
141	Samoa Joe	.30	.75
142	The Shield		
143	Randy Orton	.30	.75
144	Bayley/Sasha Banks	.40	1.00
145	Bray Wyatt	.50	1.25
146	no info		
147	The Rock	.60	1.50
148	Ric Flair	.50	1.25
149	Daniel Bryan	.50	1.25
150	Brock Lesnar	.60	1.50
151	Kevin Owens	.30	.75
152	Finn Balor	.40	1.00
153	Bret Hart	.30	.75
154	The Rock/John Cena	.60	1.50
155	The Bellas	.40	1.00
156	Seth Rollins		
157	Divas Revolution		
158	Ultimate Warrior	.30	.75
159	Roman Reigns	.40	1.00
160	League of Nations FOIL	.30	.75
161	Alberto Del Rio	.20	.50
162	Sheamus	.30	.75
163	Wade Barrett		
164	Rusev	.30	.75
165	Kane FOIL	.20	.50
166	Kane	.20	.50
167	Kane	.20	.50
168	Kane	.20	.50
169	Kane	.20	.50
170	Kevin Owens FOIL	.30	.75
171	Kevin Owens	.30	.75
172	Kevin Owens	.30	.75
173	Kevin Owens	.30	.75
174	Kevin Owens	.30	.75
175	Chris Jericho FOIL	.30	.75
176	Chris Jericho	.30	.75
177	Chris Jericho	.30	.75
178	Chris Jericho	.30	.75
179	Chris Jericho	.30	.75
180	Dash/Dawson	.15	.40
181	Dash/Dawson	.15	.40
182	Dash/Dawson	.15	.40
183	Dash/Dawson	.15	.40
184	Dash/Dawson	.15	.40
185	Blake/Murphy FOIL	.12	.30
186	Murphy	.12	.30
187	Blake	.12	.30
188	Alexa Bliss/Murphy/Blake	.60	1.50
189	Blake	.12	.30
190	Enzo Amore	.25	.60
191	Enzo Amore	.25	.60
192	Enzo Amore	.25	.60
193	Enzo Amore	.25	.60
194	Enzo Amore	.25	.60
195	Colin Cassady FOIL	.25	.60
196	Colin Cassady	.25	.60
197	Colin Cassady	.25	.60
198	Colin Cassady	.25	.60
199	Colin Cassady	.25	.60
200	Eddie Guerrero FOIL	.30	.75
201	Eddie Guerrero	.30	.75
202	Eddie Guerrero	.30	.75
203	Eddie Guerrero	.30	.75
204	Eddie Guerrero	.30	.75
205	Stone Cold Steve Austin FOIL	.60	1.50
206	Stone Cold Steve Austin	.60	1.50
207	Stone Cold Steve Austin	.60	1.50
208	Stone Cold Steve Austin	.60	1.50
209	Stone Cold Steve Austin	.60	1.50
210	Razor Ramon	.30	.75
211	Razor Ramon	.30	.75
212	Razor Ramon	.30	.75
213	Razor Ramon	.30	.75
214	Razor Ramon	.30	.75
215	Ultimate Warrior FOIL	.30	.75
216	Ultimate Warrior	.30	.75
217	Ultimate Warrior	.30	.75
218	Ultimate Warrior	.30	.75
219	Ultimate Warrior	.30	.75
220	The Usos FOIL	.12	.30
221	The Usos	.12	.30
222	The Usos	.12	.30
223	The Usos	.12	.30
224	The Usos	.12	.30
225	Cesaro	.25	.60
226	Cesaro	.25	.60
227	Cesaro	.25	.60
228	Cesaro	.25	.60
229	Cesaro	.25	.60
230	The Rock FOIL	.60	1.50
231	The Rock	.60	1.50
232	The Rock	.60	1.50
233	The Rock/John Cena	.60	1.50
234	The Rock	.60	1.50
235	Undertaker FOIL	.50	1.25
236	Undertaker	.50	1.25
237	Undertaker	.50	1.25
238	Undertaker	.50	1.25
239	Undertaker	.50	1.25
240	Brock Lesnar	.60	1.50
241	Kalisto	.30	.75
242	Brock Lesnar/Undertaker	.60	1.50
243	Sting	.30	.75
244	Seth Rollins	.20	.50

2020-21 Topps WWE This Month in History

1	Jeff Hardy/95*
2	Evolution/85*
3	Boogeyman/85*
4	Trish Stratus/188*
5	Wade Barrett/78*
6	Sgt. Slaughter/89*
7	Eddie Guerrero/122*
8	Daniel Bryan/102*
9	Andre the Giant/282*
10	Mr. T/269*
11	Bret Hit Man Hart/187*
12	Road Dogg/130*
13	Mankind/147*
14	Shelton Benjamin/70*
15	Asuka/110*
16	Rob Van Dam/103*
17	Hulk Hogan/175*
18	Scott Hall/96*
19	Honky Tonk Man/
20	Yokozuna/
21	Diamond Dallas Page/
22	Sherri Martel/
23	Goldberg/
24	Undertaker/
25	Ultimate Warrior/
26	Macho Man & Elizabeth/
27	British Bulldog/
28	Stone Cold Steve Austin/
29	Shawn Michaels/
30	Trish Stratus/
31	Bayley/
32	Batista/
33	Alundra Blayze/

2020 Topps WWE 3:16 Day

COMPLETE SET (6) 15.00 40.00
STATED PRINT RUN 137 SETS

1	Stone Cold Steve Austin	4.00	10.00
2	Stone Cold Steve Austin	4.00	10.00
3	Stone Cold Steve Austin	4.00	10.00
4	Stone Cold Steve Austin	4.00	10.00
5	Stone Cold Steve Austin	4.00	10.00
6	Stone Cold Steve Austin	6.00	15.00

2019 Topps WWE Transcendent

*BLUE/15: UNPRICED DUE TO SCARCITY
*PURPLE/10: UNPRICED DUE TO SCARCITY
*BLACK/5: UNPRICED DUE TO SCARCITY
*GOLD/1: UNPRICED DUE TO SCARCITY
*RED/1: UNPRICED DUE TO SCARCITY
STATED PRINT RUN 25 SER.#'d SETS

AAB	Alexa Bliss	150.00	300.00
AAC	Adam Cole	50.00	100.00
AAJ	AJ Styles	75.00	150.00
AAL	Aleister Black	50.00	100.00
AAS	Asuka	100.00	200.00
ABB	Brie Bella	30.00	75.00
ABE	Becky Lynch	75.00	150.00
ABH	Bret Hit Man Hart	60.00	120.00
ABK	Billie Kay	30.00	75.00
ABL	Brock Lesnar	50.00	100.00
ABO	Bobby Lashley	25.00	60.00
ABR	Bobby Roode	20.00	50.00
ABS	Braun Strowman	30.00	75.00
ABY	Bayley	50.00	100.00
ACA	Carmella	30.00	75.00
ACF	Charlotte Flair	100.00	200.00
ACJ	Chris Jericho	60.00	120.00
ADA	Dean Ambrose	30.00	75.00
ADB	Daniel Bryan	50.00	100.00
AEL	Elias	15.00	40.00
AFB	Finn Balor	20.00	50.00
AJC	John Cena	100.00	200.00
AJG	Johnny Gargano	30.00	75.00
AKO	Kevin Owens	15.00	40.00

ALL Lex Luger 25.00 60.00
ALV Liv Morgan 75.00 150.00
AMA Maryse 20.00 50.00
AMJ Mickie James 30.00 75.00
AMM Mr. McMahon 500.00 1000.00
AMR Mandy Rose 60.00 120.00
ANA Naomi 15.00 40.00
ANB Nikki Bella 50.00 100.00
ANT Natalya 25.00 60.00
APG Paige 100.00 200.00
APR Peyton Royce 75.00 150.00
ARD Ricky The Dragon Steamboat 20.00 50.00
ARO Randy Orton 30.00 75.00
ASA Stone Cold Steve Austin 225.00 450.00
ASB Sasha Banks 75.00 150.00
ASH Shane McMahon 200.00 400.00
ASJ Samoa Joe 15.00 40.00
ASM Stephanie McMahon 100.00 200.00
ASN Shinsuke Nakamura 25.00 60.00
ASR Seth Rollins 20.00 50.00
AST Sting 60.00 120.00
ASW Shawn Michaels 100.00 200.00
ATH Triple H 150.00 300.00
ATS Trish Stratus 75.00 150.00
AUN Undertaker 175.00 350.00
ARRR Ronda Rousey 200.00 400.00

2019 Topps WWE Transcendent Autographed Championship Titles

NNO Dean Ambrose
NNO Jeff Hardy
NNO Randy Orton
NNO Rey Mysterio
NNO Seth Rollins

2019 Topps WWE Transcendent Autographed Kiss

*BLACK/5: UNPRICED DUE TO SCARCITY
*GOLD/1: UNPRICED DUE TO SCARCITY
*RED/1: UNPRICED DUE TO SCARCITY
STATED PRINT RUN 10 SER.#'d SETS
UNPRICED DUE TO SCARCITY

KAS Asuka
KBB Brie Bella
KNB Nikki Bella
KPR Peyton Royce

2019 Topps WWE Transcendent Autographed Sketches

STATED PRINT RUN 1 SER.#'d SET
UNPRICED DUE TO SCARCITY

1 Adam Cole
2 AJ Styles
3 Aleister Black
4 Alexa Bliss
5 Asuka
6 Bayley
7 Becky Lynch
8 Billie Kay
9 Bobby Lashley
10 Bobby Roode
11 Braun Strowman
12 Bray Wyatt
13 Bret Hart
14 Brie Bella
15 Charlotte Flair
16 Daniel Bryan
17 Dean Ambrose
18 Dolph Ziggler
19 Drew McIntyre
20 Elias
21 Ember Moon
22 Finn Balor
23 Jeff Hardy
24 John Cena
25 Johnny Gargano
26 Kairi Sane
27 Kane
28 Kevin Owens
29 Kofi Kingston
30 Matt Hardy
31 Naomi
32 Nikki Bella
33 Randy Orton
34 Ric Flair
35 Ricochet
36 Roman Reigns
37 Ronda Rousey
38 Samoa Joe
39 Sasha Banks
40 Seth Rollins
41 Shawn Michaels
42 Shinsuke Nakamura
43 Sting
44 Stone Cold Steve Austin
45 The Miz
46 The Rock
47 Tommaso Ciampa
48 Triple H
49 Trish Stratus
50 Undertaker

2019 Topps WWE Transcendent Oversized Tribute Cut Signatures

STATED PRINT RUN 1 SER.#'d SET
UNPRICED DUE TO SCARCITY

CAG Andre The Giant
CBH Bobby Heenan
CBS Bruno Sammartino
CCH Mr. Perfect
CDR Dusty Rhodes
CEG Eddie Guerrero
CFB Freddie Blassie
CGM Gorilla Monsoon
CGS George Steele
CJN Jim The Anvil Neidhart
CJS Chief Jay Strongbow
CKV Kerry Von Erich
CME Miss Elizabeth
CMY Mae Young
CPB Paul Bearer
CRR Ravishing Rick Rude
CRS Macho Man Randy Savage
CSM Sherri Martel
CUG Umaga
CUM Ultimate Warrior
CYK Yokozuna
CBBB Bam Bam Bigelow
CBJS Big John Studd
CBVV Vader
CJYD Junkyard Dog
CRRR Rowdy Roddy Piper

2019 Topps WWE Transcendent Oversized Tribute Dual Cut Signatures

STATED PRINT RUN 1 SER.#'d SET
UNPRICED DUE TO SCARCITY

DCAB Andre the Giant/B.Heenan
DCBC P. Bearer/Vader
DCDS G.Steele/Junkyard Dog
DCEM Elizabeth/S.Martel
DCES G.Steele/Elizabeth
DCHH Mr. Perfect/B.Heenan
DCPE K.Von Erich/R.Piper
DCPG E.Guerrero/R.Piper
DCPW Warrior/R.Piper
DCRE D.Rhodes/Elizabeth
DCRS R.Savage/S.Martel
DCSB G.Steele/F.Blassie
DCSE R.Savage/Elizabeth
DCSH B.Heenan/J.Studd
DCSN J.Neidhart/R.Savage
DCSR B.Sammartino/R.Piper
DCSS B.Sammartino/J.Strongbow
DCSW Warrior/R.Savage
DCVB B.Bigelow/Vader
DCVM Vader/R.Savage
DCYU Umaga/Yokozuna
DCYV Vader/Yokozuna
DCNW01 C.Hennig/D.Rhodes
DCNW02 R.Savage/C.Hennig

2019 Topps WWE Transcendent VIP Party Autographs

B1 Big Show 15.00 40.00
B2 Big Show 15.00 40.00
F1 Ric Flair 75.00 150.00
F2 Ric Flair 75.00 150.00
S1 Sting 50.00 100.00
S2 Sting 50.00 100.00

2019 Topps WWE Transcendent VIP Party Dual Autograph

NNO Stephanie McMahon/Triple H 225.00 450.00

2020 Topps WWE Transcendent

COMPLETE SET (50) 500.00 750.00
STATED PRINT RUN 50 SER.#'d SETS

1 Adam Cole 15.00 40.00
2 Andre the Giant 30.00 75.00
3 Angelo Dawkins 6.00 15.00
4 Bianca Belair 15.00 40.00
5 Big Show 8.00 20.00
6 Bruno Sammartino 15.00 40.00
7 Cain Velasquez 6.00 15.00
8 Cameron Grimes RC 6.00 15.00
9 Candice LeRae 20.00 50.00
10 Chyna 15.00 40.00
11 Damian Priest 6.00 15.00
12 Dusty Rhodes 12.00 30.00
13 Eddie Guerrero 15.00 40.00
14 Harley Race 10.00 25.00
15 Hulk Hogan 20.00 50.00
16 Io Shirai 10.00 25.00
17 Jim The Anvil Neidhart 8.00 20.00
18 John Cena 25.00 60.00
19 John Morrison 6.00 15.00
20 Johnny Gargano 12.00 30.00
21 Keith Lee 6.00 15.00
22 Kevin Nash 10.00 25.00
23 Lana 15.00 40.00
24 Lio Rush 6.00 15.00
25 Macho Man Randy Savage 20.00 50.00
26 Mandy Rose 30.00 80.00
27 Mr. Perfect Curt Hennig 10.00 25.00
28 Montez Ford 6.00 15.00
29 Mustafa Ali 10.00 25.00
30 Naomi 12.00 30.00
31 Natalya 10.00 25.00
32 Nikki Cross 12.00 30.00
33 Paul Heyman 6.00 15.00
34 Ravishing Rick Rude 8.00 20.00
35 Renee Young 8.00 20.00
36 Rhea Ripley 25.00 60.00
37 Robert Roode 6.00 15.00
38 Roderick Strong 12.00 30.00
39 Rowdy Roddy Piper 15.00 40.00
40 Rusev 8.00 20.00
41 Scott Hall 10.00 25.00
42 Shorty G 6.00 15.00
43 Sting 20.00 50.00
44 Sonya Deville 15.00 40.00
45 The British Bulldog 10.00 25.00
46 The Rock 30.00 80.00
47 Ultimate Warrior 30.00 75.00
48 Undertaker 25.00 60.00
49 Vader 10.00 25.00
50 Yokozuna 10.00 25.00

2020 Topps WWE Transcendent Autographed Replica Championship Side Plates

UNPRICED DUE TO SCARCITY

NNO AJ Styles
NNO Becky Lynch
NNO Charlotte Flair
NNO Daniel Bryan
NNO Kofi Kingston
NNO Randy Orton
NNO Roman Reigns
NNO Seth Rollins
NNO Triple H

2020 Topps WWE Transcendent Autographs

*GREEN/15: UNPRICED DUE TO SCARCITY
*PURPLE/10: UNPRICED DUE TO SCARCITY
*BLUE/5: UNPRICED DUE TO SCARCITY
*RED/1: UNPRICED DUE TO SCARCITY

AAA Andrade 25.00 60.00
AAB Aleister Black 30.00 75.00
AAJ AJ Styles 60.00 120.00
AAK Asuka 100.00 200.00
AAX Alexa Bliss 150.00 300.00
ABC King Corbin 25.00 60.00
ABD Diesel 30.00 75.00
ABH Bret Hit Man Hart 75.00 150.00
ABI Brock Lesnar 125.00 250.00
ABL Becky Lynch 75.00 150.00
ABR Braun Strowman 50.00 100.00
ABT Booker T 30.00 75.00
ABW The Fiend Bray Wyatt 100.00 200.00
ABY Bayley 50.00 100.00
ACF Charlotte Flair 100.00 200.00
ACW Sheamus 25.00 60.00
ADB Daniel Bryan 50.00 100.00
ADR Drew McIntyre 60.00 120.00
AFB Finn Balor 50.00 100.00
AGB Goldberg 75.00 150.00
AHH Hulk Hogan 250.00 500.00
AJH Jeff Hardy 60.00 120.00
AKA Kurt Angle 50.00 100.00
AKK Kofi Kingston 60.00 120.00
AKN Kane 50.00 100.00
AKO Kevin Owens 50.00 100.00
AKS Kairi Sane 75.00 150.00
ALE Lacey Evans 60.00 120.00
ALT Lita 75.00 150.00
AMF Mick Foley 30.00 75.00
AMR Matt Riddle 60.00 120.00
AQS Shayna Baszler 50.00 100.00
ARC Ricochet 25.00 60.00
ARO Randy Orton 60.00 120.00
ARR Roman Reigns 75.00 150.00
ASB Sasha Banks 125.00 250.00
ASC Stone Cold Steve Austin 350.00 700.00
ASM Shane McMahon 125.00 250.00
ASN Shinsuke Nakamura 30.00 75.00
ASR Seth Rollins 50.00 100.00
AST Stephanie McMahon 250.00 400.00
ATC Tommaso Ciampa 50.00 100.00
ATM The Miz 30.00 75.00
AUT Undertaker 300.00 500.00
AZV Zelina Vega 60.00 120.00
AHBK Shawn Michaels 125.00 250.00
AHHH Triple H 250.00 400.00
AVKM Mr. McMahon 600.00 1000.00

2020 Topps WWE Transcendent Bat Relic Autographs

RCST Sting 250.00 400.00

2020 Topps WWE Transcendent Dual Autographs

*GREEN/15: UNPRICED DUE TO SCARCITY
*PURPLE/10: UNPRICED DUE TO SCARCITY
*BLUE/5: UNPRICED DUE TO SCARCITY
*RED/1: UNPRICED DUE TO SCARCITY
STATED PRINT RUN 25 SER.#'d SETS

DAVR Erik/Ivar 75.00 150.00
DAUSO Jimmy Uso/Jey Uso 75.00 150.00

2020 Topps WWE Transcendent Image Variation Autographs

STATED PRINT RUN 1 SER.#'d SET
UNPRICED DUE TO SCARCITY

AIVAA Andrade
AIVAB Aleister Black
AIVAJ AJ Styles
AIVAK Asuka
AIVAX Alexa Bliss
AIVBC King Corbin
AIVBD Diesel
AIVBH Bret Hit Man Hart
AIVBI Brock Lesnar
AIVBL Becky Lynch
AIVBR Braun Strowman
AIVBT Booker T
AIVBW Bray Wyatt
AIVBY Bayley
AIVCF Charlotte Flair
AIVCW Sheamus

AIVDB Daniel Bryan
AIVDR Drew McIntyre
AIVFB Finn Balor
AIVGB Goldberg
AIVHH Hulk Hogan
AIVJH Jeff Hardy
AIVKA Kurt Angle
AIVKK Kofi Kingston
AIVKN Kane
AIVKO Kevin Owens
AIVKS Kairi Sane
AIVLE Lacey Evans
AIVLT Lita
AIVMF Mick Foley
AIVMR Matt Riddle
AIVQS Shayna Baszler
AIVRC Ricochet
AIVRO Randy Orton
AIVRR Roman Reigns
AIVSB Sasha Banks
AIVSC Stone Cold Steve Austin
AIVSJ Samoa Joe
AIVSM Shane McMahon
AIVSN Shinsuke Nakamura
AIVSR Seth Rollins
AIVST Stephanie McMahon
AIVTC Tommaso Ciampa
AIVTM The Miz
AIVUT Undertaker
AIVZV Zelina Vega
AIVHBK Shawn Michaels
AIVHHH Triple H
AIVVKM Mr. McMahon

2020 Topps WWE Transcendent Image Variation Dual Autographs

STATED PRINT RUN 1 SER.#'d SET
UNPRICED DUE TO SCARCITY

DAIVVR Erik/Ivar
DAIVUSO Jimmy Uso/Jey Uso

2020 Topps WWE Transcendent John Cena Superstar Tribute

COMPLETE SET (50)	250.00	500.00
JCRP1 John Cena	10.00	25.00
JCRP2 John Cena	10.00	25.00
JCRP3 John Cena	10.00	25.00
JCRP4 John Cena	10.00	25.00
JCRP5 John Cena	10.00	25.00
JCRP6 John Cena	10.00	25.00
JCRP7 John Cena	10.00	25.00
JCRP8 John Cena	10.00	25.00
JCRP9 John Cena	10.00	25.00
JCRP10 John Cena	10.00	25.00
JCRP11 John Cena	10.00	25.00
JCRP12 John Cena	10.00	25.00
JCRP13 John Cena	10.00	25.00
JCRP14 John Cena	10.00	25.00
JCRP15 John Cena	10.00	25.00
JCRP16 John Cena	10.00	25.00
JCRP17 John Cena	10.00	25.00
JCRP18 John Cena	10.00	25.00
JCRP19 John Cena	10.00	25.00
JCRP20 John Cena	10.00	25.00
JCRP21 John Cena	10.00	25.00
JCRP22 John Cena	10.00	25.00
JCRP23 John Cena	10.00	25.00
JCRP24 John Cena	10.00	25.00
JCRP25 John Cena	10.00	25.00
JCRP26 John Cena	10.00	25.00
JCRP27 John Cena	10.00	25.00
JCRP28 John Cena	10.00	25.00
JCRP29 John Cena	10.00	25.00
JCRP30 John Cena	10.00	25.00
JCRP31 John Cena	10.00	25.00
JCRP32 John Cena	10.00	25.00
JCRP33 John Cena	10.00	25.00
JCRP34 John Cena	10.00	25.00
JCRP35 John Cena	10.00	25.00
JCRP36 John Cena	10.00	25.00
JCRP37 John Cena	10.00	25.00
JCRP38 John Cena	10.00	25.00
JCRP39 John Cena	10.00	25.00
JCRP40 John Cena	10.00	25.00
JCRP41 John Cena	10.00	25.00
JCRP42 John Cena	10.00	25.00
JCRP43 John Cena	10.00	25.00
JCRP44 John Cena	10.00	25.00
JCRP45 John Cena	10.00	25.00
JCRP46 John Cena	10.00	25.00
JCRP47 John Cena	10.00	25.00
JCRP48 John Cena	10.00	25.00
JCRP49 John Cena	10.00	25.00
JCRP50 John Cena	10.00	25.00

2020 Topps WWE Transcendent John Cena Superstar Tribute Autographs

STATED PRINT RUN 1 SER.#'d SET
UNPRICED DUE TO SCARCITY

2020 Topps WWE Transcendent Sketches

STATED PRINT RUN 1 SER.#'d SET
UNPRICED DUE TO SCARCITY
ART BY DAN BERGREN

NNO AJ Styles
NNO Alexa Bliss
NNO Andrade
NNO Angel Garza
NNO Asuka
NNO Batista
NNO Bayley
NNO Becky Lynch
NNO Braun Strowman
NNO The Fiend Bray Wyatt
NNO Bret Hit Man Hart
NNO Brock Lesnar
NNO Charlotte Flair
NNO Eddie Guerrero
NNO Ember Moon
NNO Finn Balor
NNO Goldberg
NNO Hulk Hogan
NNO Jeff Hardy
NNO John Cena
NNO Kairi Sane
NNO Kane
NNO Keith Lee
NNO Kevin Owens
NNO Kofi Kingston
NNO Lacey Evans
NNO Lita
NNO Matt Riddle
NNO Mustafa Ali
NNO Pete Dunne
NNO Randy Orton
NNO Macho Man Randy Savage
NNO Ricochet
NNO Rowdy Roddy Piper
NNO Roman Reigns
NNO Ronda Rousey
NNO Sami Zayn
NNO Samoa Joe
NNO Sasha Banks
NNO Seth Rollins
NNO Shawn Michaels
NNO Shayna Baszler
NNO Shinsuke Nakamura
NNO Sting
NNO Stone Cold Steve Austin
NNO The Miz
NNO The Rock
NNO Triple H
NNO Ultimate Warrior
NNO Undertaker

2020 Topps WWE Transcendent VIP Party Black and White Pattern 1

*BLACK/WHITE 2: UNPRICED DUE TO SCARCITY
*BLACK/WHITE 3: UNPRICED DUE TO SCARCITY
*BLACK/WHITE 4: UNPRICED DUE TO SCARCITY
*BLACK/WHITE 5: UNPRICED DUE TO SCARCITY
*AQUA/PURPLE 1: UNPRICED DUE TO SCARCITY
*AQUA/PURPLE 2: UNPRICED DUE TO SCARCITY
*AQUA/PURPLE 3: UNPRICED DUE TO SCARCITY
*AQUA/PURPLE 4: UNPRICED DUE TO SCARCITY
*AQUA/PURPLE 5: UNPRICED DUE TO SCARCITY
*GREEN/YELLOW 1: UNPRICED DUE TO SCARCITY
*GREEN/YELLOW 2: UNPRICED DUE TO SCARCITY
*GREEN/YELLOW 3: UNPRICED DUE TO SCARCITY
*GREEN/YELLOW 4: UNPRICED DUE TO SCARCITY
*GREEN/YELLOW 5: UNPRICED DUE TO SCARCITY
*PURPLE/RED 1: UNPRICED DUE TO SCARCITY
*PURPLE/RED 2: UNPRICED DUE TO SCARCITY
*PURPLE/RED 3: UNPRICED DUE TO SCARCITY
*PURPLE/RED 4: UNPRICED DUE TO SCARCITY
*PURPLE/RED 5: UNPRICED DUE TO SCARCITY
*RED/YELLOW 1: UNPRICED DUE TO SCARCITY
*RED/YELLOW 2: UNPRICED DUE TO SCARCITY
*RED/YELLOW 3: UNPRICED DUE TO SCARCITY
*RED/YELLOW 4: UNPRICED DUE TO SCARCITY
*RED/YELLOW 5: UNPRICED DUE TO SCARCITY
STATED PRINT RUN 1 SER.#'d SET
UNPRICED DUE TO SCARCITY
SUMMERSLAM VIP EXCLUSIVE
ALL CARDS ARE 1/1

1 AJ Styles
2 Akira Tozawa
3 Alexa Bliss
4 Apollo Crews
5 Asuka
6 Batista
7 Bayley
8 Bianca Belair
9 Bobby Lashley
10 Bray Wyatt
11 Carmella
12 Cesaro
13 Dakota Kai
14 Dolph Ziggler
15 Dominik Mysterio
16 Drew McIntyre
17 Edge
18 Finn Balor
19 Hulk Hogan
20 Jey Uso
21 Jinder Mahal
22 TBD
23 Kevin Owens
24 Kofi Kingston
25 Kushida
26 MVP
27 Nia Jax
28 Omos
29 Pete Dunne
30 Randy Orton
31 Raquel Gonzalez
32 Razor Ramon
33 Rey Mysterio
34 Rhea Ripley
35 Ric Flair
36 Riddle
37 Roman Reigns
38 Sami Zayn
39 Santos Escobar
40 Sasha Banks
41 Scarlett
42 Seth Rollins
43 Sgt. Slaughter
44 Shayna Baszler
45 Sheamus
46 Shotzi Blackheart
47 The Miz
48 Walter
49 Xavier Woods
50 X-Pac

2020 Topps WWE Transcendent VIP Party Autographs

*AQUA/PURPLE 1: UNPRICED DUE TO SCARCITY
*AQUA/PURPLE 2: UNPRICED DUE TO SCARCITY
*BLACK/WHITE 1: UNPRICED DUE TO SCARCITY
*BLACK/WHITE 2: UNPRICED DUE TO SCARCITY
*GREEN/YELLOW 1: UNPRICED DUE TO SCARCITY
*GREEN/YELLOW 2: UNPRICED DUE TO SCARCITY
*PURPLE/RED 1: UNPRICED DUE TO SCARCITY
*PURPLE/RED 2: UNPRICED DUE TO SCARCITY
*RED/YELLOW 1: UNPRICED DUE TO SCARCITY
*RED/YELLOW 2: UNPRICED DUE TO SCARCITY
STATED PRINT RUN 1 SER.#'d SET
UNPRICED DUE TO SCARCITY
SUMMERSLAM VIP EXCLUSIVE
ALL CARDS 1/1

ABE Big E
ABP Beth Phoenix
AEM Ember Moon
AJC John Cena
AJL Jerry Lawler
AJN Jim Neidhart
AJR Jaxson Ryker
AMK Mankind
ANN Natalya
ATA Tamina
ATR Trish Stratus
ATS Toni Storm
AJBL JBL
AKOR Kyle OíReilly

2020 Topps WWE Transcendent VIP Party On-Card Autographs

STATED PRINT RUN 25 SER.#'d SETS
SUMMERSLAM VIP EXCLUSIVE

VIPDM1 Drew McIntyre	30.00	75.00
VIPDM2 Drew McIntyre	30.00	75.00
VIPJH1 Jeff Hardy		
VIPJH2 Jeff Hardy		
VIPNC1 Nikki Ash	50.00	100.00
VIPNC2 Nikki Ash	50.00	100.00
VIPRR1 Rhea Ripley		
VIPRR2 Rhea Ripley		

2021 Topps WWE Transcendent

COMPLETE SET (50)	200.00	500.00
1 Aleister Black	8.00	20.00
2 Andre the Giant	12.00	30.00
3 Apollo Crews	4.00	10.00
4 Bam Bam Bigelow	6.00	15.00
5 Beth Phoenix	6.00	15.00
6 Big Boss Man	5.00	12.00
7 Braun Strowman	8.00	20.00
8 Candice LeRae	12.00	30.00
9 Cedric Alexander	3.00	8.00
10 Diamond Dallas Page	5.00	12.00
11 Dusty Rhodes	10.00	25.00
12 Earthquake	8.00	20.00
13 Eddie Guerrero	15.00	40.00
14 Faarooq	5.00	12.00
15 Finlay	3.00	8.00
16 Finn Balor	8.00	20.00
17 George The Animal Steele	6.00	15.00
18 Gorilla Monsoon	6.00	15.00
19 Indi Hartwell RC	10.00	25.00
20 Jerry The King Lawler	5.00	12.00
21 Jimmy Hart	4.00	10.00
22 Junkyard Dog	3.00	8.00
23 Kay Lee Ray	8.00	20.00
24 Kevin Owens	6.00	15.00
25 King Corbin	3.00	8.00
26 Lacey Evans	8.00	20.00
27 Mae Young	5.00	12.00
28 Macho King Randy Savage	12.00	30.00
29 Marlena	5.00	12.00
30 Michael Cole	3.00	8.00
31 Mr. Perfect	10.00	25.00
32 Naomi	4.00	10.00
33 Natalya	5.00	12.00
34 Nikolai Volkoff	3.00	8.00
35 Nikki Cross	6.00	15.00
36 Paul Bearer	6.00	15.00
37 Ricky The Dragon Steamboat	5.00	12.00
38 Raquel Gonzalez	8.00	20.00
39 Rob Van Dam	6.00	15.00
40 Roderick Strong	5.00	12.00
41 Rowdy Roddy Piper	8.00	20.00
42 Shayna Baszler	6.00	15.00
43 Sheamus	5.00	12.00
44 Sensational Sherri Martel	8.00	20.00
45 Shinsuke Nakamura	8.00	20.00
46 The Brian Kendrick	3.00	8.00
47 The Honky Tonk Man	3.00	8.00
48 Trent Seven	4.00	10.00
49 Tyler Bate	4.00	10.00
50 Ultimate Warrior	12.00	30.00

2021 Topps WWE Transcendent Autographed Championships

NNO AJ Styles/WWE Title
NNO B.Lashley/WWE Title

NNO B.Strowman/SD Universal Title
NNO D.McIntyre/WWE Title
NNO F.Balor/RAW Universal Title
NNO Goldberg/RAW Universal Title
NNO K.Owens/RAW Universal Title
NNO K.Kingston/WWE Title
NNO R.Reigns/SD Universal Title
NNO S.Rollins/RAW Universal Title

2021 Topps WWE Transcendent Autographs

*GREEN/15: UNPRICED DUE TO SCARCITY
*PURPLE/10: UNPRICED DUE TO SCARCITY
*BLUE/5: UNPRICED DUE TO SCARCITY
*RED/1: UNPRICED DUE TO SCARCITY
*SUPERFR/1: UNPRICED DUE TO SCARCITY
STATED PRINT RUN 25 SER.#'d SETS

AAB Alexa Bliss	200.00	400.00
AAC Adam Cole	50.00	100.00
AAJ AJ Styles	25.00	60.00
AAS Asuka	100.00	200.00
ABA Bayley	30.00	75.00
ABB Bianca Belair	50.00	100.00
ABE Big E	20.00	50.00
ABH Bret "Hit Man" Hart	150.00	300.00
ABL Becky Lynch EXCH	100.00	200.00
ACF Charlotte Flair	75.00	150.00
ACS Cesaro	15.00	40.00
ADK Dakota Kai	50.00	100.00
ADP Damian Priest	15.00	40.00
ADR Drew McIntyre	25.00	60.00
AED Edge	60.00	120.00
AGB Goldberg	75.00	150.00
AIR Iron Sheik	50.00	100.00
AIS Io Shirai	75.00	150.00
AJC John Cena	150.00	300.00
AJR Jake "The Snake" Roberts	75.00	150.00
AJU Jey Uso	15.00	40.00
AKK Karrion Kross	20.00	50.00
AKL Keith Lee	15.00	40.00
AKN Kane	50.00	100.00
ALA Bobby Lashley	20.00	50.00
AMK Mankind	100.00	200.00
ANJ Nia Jax	25.00	60.00
ARM Rey Mysterio	100.00	200.00
ARO Randy Orton	50.00	100.00
ARP Rhea Ripley	60.00	120.00
ARR Roman Reigns	125.00	250.00
ASA Stone Cold Steve Austin	500.00	800.00
ASC Scarlett	60.00	120.00
ASD Sonya Deville	20.00	50.00
ASR Seth Rollins	30.00	75.00
ASS Sgt. Slaughter	50.00	100.00
AST Stephanie McMahon	150.00	300.00
ATD Ted DiBiase	30.00	75.00
ATS Toni Storm	75.00	150.00
AUT Undertaker	300.00	500.00
AVM Mr. McMahon	750.00	1500.00
AWT WALTER	15.00	40.00
AXP X-Pac	30.00	75.00
ABRO Riddle	15.00	40.00
AHBK Shawn Michaels	150.00	300.00
AHHH Triple H	200.00	400.00
AMVP MVP	15.00	40.00

2021 Topps WWE Transcendent Dual Autographs

*GREEN/15: UNPRICED DUE TO SCARCITY
*PURPLE/10: UNPRICED DUE TO SCARCITY
*BLUE/5: UNPRICED DUE TO SCARCITY
*RED/1: UNPRICED DUE TO SCARCITY
*SUPERFR/1: UNPRICED DUE TO SCARCITY
STATED PRINT RUN 25 SER.#'d SETS

TAKW The New Day	30.00	75.00
TAMM The Miz & John Morrison	25.00	60.00
TASP The Street Profits	25.00	60.00

2021 Topps WWE Transcendent Quad Autograph

*GREEN/15: UNPRICED DUE TO SCARCITY
*PURPLE/10: UNPRICED DUE TO SCARCITY
*BLUE/5: UNPRICED DUE TO SCARCITY
*RED/1: UNPRICED DUE TO SCARCITY
STATED PRINT RUN 25 SER.#'d SETS

QA4HW Becky/Sasha/Charlotte/Bayley	600.00	1000.00

2021 Topps WWE Transcendent Ric Flair Legends Tribute

COMPLETE SET (25) 125.00 300.00
STATED ODDS 1:SET PER BOX
STATED PRINT RUN 50 SER.#'d SETS

RF1 Ric Flair	8.00	20.00
RF2 Ric Flair	8.00	20.00
RF3 Ric Flair	8.00	20.00
RF4 Ric Flair	8.00	20.00
RF5 Ric Flair	8.00	20.00
RF6 Ric Flair	8.00	20.00
RF7 Ric Flair	8.00	20.00
RF8 Ric Flair	8.00	20.00
RF9 Ric Flair	8.00	20.00
RF10 Ric Flair	8.00	20.00
RF11 Ric Flair	8.00	20.00
RF12 Ric Flair	8.00	20.00
RF13 Ric Flair	8.00	20.00
RF14 Ric Flair	8.00	20.00
RF15 Ric Flair	8.00	20.00
RF16 Ric Flair	8.00	20.00
RF17 Ric Flair	8.00	20.00
RF18 Ric Flair	8.00	20.00
RF19 Ric Flair	8.00	20.00
RF20 Ric Flair	8.00	20.00
RF21 Ric Flair	8.00	20.00
RF22 Ric Flair	8.00	20.00
RF23 Ric Flair	8.00	20.00
RF24 Ric Flair	8.00	20.00
RF25 Ric Flair	8.00	20.00

2021 Topps WWE Transcendent The Rock Legends Tribute

COMPLETE SET (25) 200.00 500.00
STATED ODDS 1:SET PER BOX
STATED PRINT RUN 50 SER.#'d SETS

DJ1 The Rock	15.00	40.00
DJ2 The Rock	15.00	40.00
DJ3 The Rock	15.00	40.00
DJ4 The Rock	15.00	40.00
DJ5 The Rock	15.00	40.00
DJ6 The Rock	15.00	40.00
DJ7 The Rock	15.00	40.00
DJ8 The Rock	15.00	40.00
DJ9 The Rock	15.00	40.00
DJ10 The Rock	15.00	40.00
DJ11 The Rock	15.00	40.00
DJ12 The Rock	15.00	40.00
DJ13 The Rock	15.00	40.00
DJ14 The Rock	15.00	40.00
DJ15 The Rock	15.00	40.00
DJ16 The Rock	15.00	40.00
DJ17 The Rock	15.00	40.00
DJ18 The Rock	15.00	40.00
DJ19 The Rock	15.00	40.00
DJ20 The Rock	15.00	40.00
DJ21 The Rock	15.00	40.00
DJ22 The Rock	15.00	40.00
DJ23 The Rock	15.00	40.00
DJ24 The Rock	15.00	40.00
DJ25 The Rock	15.00	40.00

2021 Topps WWE Transcendent Sketches

UNPRICED DUE TO SCARCITY

NNO Alexa Bliss
NNO Asuka
NNO Batista
NNO Bayley
NNO Becky Lynch
NNO Booker T
NNO Braun Strowman
NNO Bray Wyatt
NNO Bret "Hit Man" Hart
NNO Charlotte Flair
NNO Daniel Bryan
NNO Drew McIntyre
NNO Eddie Guerrero
NNO Edge
NNO Finn Balor
NNO Goldberg
NNO Hulk Hogan
NNO Jeff Hardy
NNO John Cena
NNO Kane
NNO Keith Lee
NNO Kevin Owens
NNO King Corbin
NNO Macho Man Randy Savage
NNO Mick Foley
NNO Ted DiBiase
NNO Mr. Perfect
NNO Nia Jax
NNO Otis
NNO Randy Orton
NNO Razor Ramon
NNO Rey Mysterio
NNO Ric Flair
NNO Riddle
NNO Rikishi
NNO Roman Reigns
NNO Rowdy Roddy Piper
NNO Sasha Banks
NNO Sami Zayn
NNO Seth Rollins
NNO Shawn Michaels
NNO Sheamus
NNO Sgt. Slaughter
NNO Shinsuke Nakamura
NNO Stone Cold Steve Austin
NNO The New Day
NNO The Rock
NNO Ultimate Warrior
NNO Undertaker

2016 Topps WWE Triple H Tribute

COMPLETE SET (10) 12.00 30.00
TARGET EXCLUSIVES

1 Triple H	.50	1.25
2 Triple H	.50	1.25
3 Triple H	.50	1.25
4 Triple H	.50	1.25
5 Triple H	.50	1.25
6 Triple H	1.25	3.00
7 Triple H	1.50	4.00
8 Triple H	1.25	3.00
9 Triple H	1.25	3.00
10 Triple H	1.25	3.00
11 Triple H	.50	1.25
12 Triple H	.50	1.25
13 Triple H	.50	1.25
14 Triple H	.50	1.25
15 Triple H	.50	1.25
16 Triple H	1.25	3.00
17 Triple H	1.25	3.00
18 Triple H	1.25	3.00
19 Triple H	1.25	3.00
20 Triple H	1.25	3.00
21 Triple H	.50	1.25
22 Triple H	.50	1.25
23 Triple H	.50	1.25
24 Triple H	.50	1.25
25 Triple H	.50	1.25
26 Triple H	1.25	3.00
27 Triple H	1.25	3.00
28 Triple H	1.25	3.00
29 Triple H	1.25	3.00
30 Triple H	1.25	3.00
31 Triple H	.50	1.25
32 Triple H	.50	1.25
33 Triple H	.50	1.25
34 Triple H	.50	1.25
35 Triple H	.50	1.25
36 Triple H	1.25	3.00
37 Triple H	1.25	3.00
38 Triple H	1.25	3.00
39 Triple H	1.25	3.00
40 Triple H	1.25	3.00

2020 Topps WWE Triple H 25th Anniversary

COMPLETE SET (25) 8.00 20.00

1 Triple H	.75	2.00
2 Triple H	.75	2.00
3 Triple H	.75	2.00
4 Triple H	.75	2.00
5 Triple H	.75	2.00
6 Triple H	.75	2.00
7 Triple H	.75	2.00
8 Triple H	.75	2.00
9 Triple H	.75	2.00
10 Triple H	.75	2.00
11 Triple H	.75	2.00
12 Triple H	.75	2.00
13 Triple H	.75	2.00
14 Triple H	.75	2.00
15 Triple H	.75	2.00
16 Triple H	.75	2.00
17 Triple H	.75	2.00
18 Triple H	.75	2.00
19 Triple H	.75	2.00
20 Triple H	.75	2.00
21 Triple H	.75	2.00
22 Triple H	.75	2.00
23 Triple H	.75	2.00
24 Triple H	.75	2.00
25 Triple H	.75	2.00

2020 Topps WWE Triple H 25th Anniversary Autographs

COMMON AUTO (1A-5A) 100.00 200.00
*GREEN/15: UNPRICED DUE TO SCARCITY
*GOLD/1: UNPRICED DUE TO SCARCITY
STATED OVERALL ODDS 1:2 W/RELICS
STATED PRINT RUN 99 SER.#'d SETS

1A Triple H	100.00	200.00
2A Triple H	100.00	200.00
3A Triple H	100.00	200.00
4A Triple H	100.00	200.00
5A Triple H	100.00	200.00

2020 Topps WWE Triple H 25th Anniversary Cerebral Moments

COMPLETE SET (11) 5.00 12.00
STATED PRINT RUN 260 SETS

C1 Triple H	.75	2.00
C2 Triple H	.75	2.00
C3 Triple H	.75	2.00
C4 Triple H	.75	2.00
C5 Triple H	.75	2.00
C6 Triple H	.75	2.00
C7 Triple H	.75	2.00
C8 Triple H	.75	2.00
C9 Triple H	.75	2.00
C10 Triple H	.75	2.00
C11 Triple H	.75	2.00
C12 Triple H	.75	2.00

2020 Topps WWE Triple H 25th Anniversary Relics

COMMON MEM 30.00 75.00
*GREEN/9: UNPRICED DUE TO SCARCITY
*GOLD/1: UNPRICED DUE TO SCARCITY
STATED OVERALL ODDS 1:2 W/AUTOGRAPHS
STATED PRINT RUN 15 SER.#'d SETS

1R Triple H	30.00	75.00
2R Triple H	30.00	75.00
3R Triple H	30.00	75.00
4R Triple H	30.00	75.00
5R Triple H	30.00	75.00

2020 Topps WWE Triple H 25th Anniversary World Title Victories

COMPLETE SET (14) 6.00 15.00
STATED PRINT RUN 260 SETS

T1 Triple H	.75	2.00
T2 Triple H	.75	2.00
T3 Triple H	.75	2.00
T4 Triple H	.75	2.00
T5 Triple H	.75	2.00
T6 Triple H	.75	2.00
T7 Triple H	.75	2.00
T8 Triple H	.75	2.00
T9 Triple H	.75	2.00
T10 Triple H	.75	2.00
T11 Triple H	.75	2.00
T12 Triple H	.75	2.00
T13 Triple H	.75	2.00

2017 Topps WWE Ultimate Collection Stickers

1 General Managers .15 .40
2 General Managers .15 .40
3 General Managers .15 .40
4 General Managers .15 .40
5 General Managers .15 .40
6 Enzo Amore & Big Cass .60 1.50
7 Enzo Amore & Big Cass .60 1.50
8 Enzo Amore & Big Cass .60 1.50
9 Enzo Amore & Big Cass .60 1.50
10 Enzo Amore & Big Cass .60 1.50
11 American Alpha .25 .60
12 American Alpha .25 .60
13 American Alpha .25 .60
14 American Alpha .25 .60
15 American Alpha .25 .60
16 AJ Styles 1.00 2.50
17 AJ Styles 1.00 2.50
18 AJ Styles 1.00 2.50
19 AJ Styles 1.00 2.50
20 AJ Styles 1.00 2.50
21 Finn Balor .75 2.00
22 Finn Balor .75 2.00
23 Finn Balor .75 2.00
24 Finn Balor .75 2.00
25 Finn Balor .75 2.00
26 Austin Aries .40 1.00
27 Austin Aries .40 1.00
28 Austin Aries .40 1.00
29 Austin Aries .40 1.00
30 Austin Aries .40 1.00
31 Bobby Roode .50 1.25
32 Bobby Roode .50 1.25
33 Bobby Roode .50 1.25
34 Bobby Roode .50 1.25
35 Bobby Roode .50 1.25
36 Braun Strowman .25 .60
37 Braun Strowman .25 .60
38 Braun Strowman .25 .60
39 Braun Strowman .25 .60
40 Braun Strowman .25 .60
41 Baron Corbin .30 .75
42 Baron Corbin .30 .75
43 Baron Corbin .30 .75
44 Baron Corbin .30 .75
45 Baron Corbin .30 .75
46 Chris Jericho .50 1.25
47 Chris Jericho .50 1.25
48 Chris Jericho .50 1.25
49 Chris Jericho .50 1.25
50 Chris Jericho .50 1.25
51 Randy Orton .50 1.25
52 Randy Orton .50 1.25
53 Randy Orton .50 1.25
54 Randy Orton .50 1.25
55 Randy Orton .50 1.25
56 Tye Dillinger .20 .50
57 Tye Dillinger .20 .50
58 Tye Dillinger .20 .50
59 Tye Dillinger .20 .50
60 Tye Dillinger .20 .50
61 No Way Jose .20 .50
62 No Way Jose .20 .50
63 No Way Jose .20 .50
64 No Way Jose .20 .50
65 No Way Jose .20 .50
66 Brock Lesnar 1.00 2.50
67 Brock Lesnar 1.00 2.50
68 Brock Lesnar 1.00 2.50
69 Brock Lesnar 1.00 2.50
70 Brock Lesnar 1.00 2.50
71 Dean Ambrose .60 1.50
72 Dean Ambrose .60 1.50
73 Dean Ambrose .60 1.50
74 Dean Ambrose .60 1.50
75 Dean Ambrose .60 1.50
76 Kevin Owens .50 1.25
77 Kevin Owens .50 1.25
78 Kevin Owens .50 1.25
79 Kevin Owens .50 1.25
80 Kevin Owens .50 1.25
81 Bray Wyatt .50 1.25
82 Bray Wyatt .50 1.25
83 Bray Wyatt .50 1.25
84 Bray Wyatt .50 1.25
85 Bray Wyatt .50 1.25
86 Samoa Joe .60 1.50
87 Samoa Joe .60 1.50
88 Samoa Joe .60 1.50
89 Samoa Joe .60 1.50
90 Samoa Joe .60 1.50
91 Shinsuke Nakamura .50 1.25
92 Shinsuke Nakamura .50 1.25
93 Shinsuke Nakamura .50 1.25
94 Shinsuke Nakamura .50 1.25
95 Shinsuke Nakamura .50 1.25
96 Women's Division .15 .40
97 Women's Division .15 .40
98 Women's Division .15 .40
99 Women's Division .15 .40
100 Women's Division .15 .40
101 Women's Division .15 .40
102 Women's Division .15 .40
103 Women's Division .15 .40
104 Women's Division .15 .40
105 Women's Division .15 .40
106 Women's Division .15 .40
107 Women's Division .15 .40
108 Women's Division .15 .40
109 Women's Division .15 .40
110 Women's Division .15 .40
111 Women's Division .15 .40
112 Women's Division .15 .40
113 Women's Division .15 .40
114 Women's Division .15 .40
115 Women's Division .15 .40
116 Women's Division .15 .40
117 Women's Division .15 .40
118 Roman Reigns .60 1.50
119 Roman Reigns .60 1.50
120 Roman Reigns .60 1.50
121 Roman Reigns .60 1.50
122 Roman Reigns .60 1.50
123 John Cena 1.00 2.50
124 John Cena 1.00 2.50
125 John Cena 1.00 2.50
126 John Cena 1.00 2.50
127 John Cena 1.00 2.50
128 Sami Zayn .25 .60
129 Sami Zayn .25 .60
130 Sami Zayn .25 .60
131 Sami Zayn .25 .60
132 Sami Zayn .25 .60
133 The Miz .40 1.00
134 The Miz .40 1.00
135 The Miz .40 1.00
136 The Miz .40 1.00
137 The Miz .40 1.00
138 Hall of Fame .15 .40
139 Hall of Fame .15 .40
140 Hall of Fame .15 .40
141 Hall of Fame .15 .40
142 Hall of Fame .15 .40
143 Hall of Fame .15 .40
144 Hall of Fame .15 .40
145 Hall of Fame .15 .40
146 Hall of Fame .15 .40
147 Hall of Fame .15 .40
148 Hall of Fame .15 .40
149 Hall of Fame .15 .40
150 Hall of Fame .15 .40
151 Hall of Fame .15 .40
152 Hall of Fame .15 .40
153 Hall of Fame .15 .40
154 Hall of Fame .15 .40
155 Hall of Fame .15 .40
156 Hall of Fame .15 .40
157 Hall of Fame .15 .40
158 Hall of Fame .15 .40
159 Hall of Fame .15 .40
160 Cesaro & Sheamus .40 1.00
161 Cesaro & Sheamus .40 1.00
162 Cesaro & Sheamus .40 1.00
163 Cesaro & Sheamus .40 1.00
164 Cesaro & Sheamus .40 1.00
165 Apollo Crews .25 .60
166 Apollo Crews .25 .60
167 Apollo Crews .25 .60
168 Apollo Crews .25 .60
169 Apollo Crews .25 .60
170 Rusev .40 1.00
171 Rusev .40 1.00
172 Rusev .40 1.00
173 Rusev .40 1.00
174 Rusev .40 1.00
175 Dolph Ziggler .30 .75
176 Dolph Ziggler .30 .75
177 Dolph Ziggler .30 .75
178 Dolph Ziggler .30 .75
179 Dolph Ziggler .30 .75
180 #DIY .40 1.00
181 #DIY .40 1.00
182 #DIY .40 1.00
183 #DIY .40 1.00
184 #DIY .40 1.00
185 The Revival .40 1.00
186 The Revival .40 1.00
187 The Revival .40 1.00
188 The Revival .40 1.00
189 The Revival .40 1.00
190 Pay-Per-View .15 .40
191 Pay-Per-View .15 .40
192 Pay-Per-View .15 .40
193 Pay-Per-View .15 .40
194 Pay-Per-View .15 .40
195 Pay-Per-View .15 .40
196 Pay-Per-View .15 .40
197 Pay-Per-View .15 .40
198 Pay-Per-View .15 .40
199 Pay-Per-View .15 .40
200 Championship .15 .40
201 Championship .15 .40
202 Championship .15 .40
203 Championship .15 .40
204 Championship .15 .40
205 Championship .15 .40
206 Championship .15 .40
207 Championship .15 .40
208 Championship .15 .40
209 Championship .15 .40
210 Eric Young .40 1.00
211 Eric Young .40 1.00
212 Eric Young .40 1.00
213 Eric Young .40 1.00
214 Eric Young .40 1.00
215 Elias Samson .30 .75
216 Elias Samson .30 .75
217 Elias Samson .30 .75
218 Elias Samson .30 .75
219 Elias Samson .30 .75
220 Seth Rollins .60 1.50
221 Seth Rollins .60 1.50
222 Seth Rollins .60 1.50
223 Seth Rollins .60 1.50
224 Seth Rollins .60 1.50
225 The Usos .50 1.25
226 The Usos .50 1.25
227 The Usos .50 1.25
228 The Usos .50 1.25
229 The Usos .50 1.25
230 The New Day .40 1.00
231 The New Day .40 1.00
232 The New Day .40 1.00
233 The New Day .40 1.00
234 The New Day .40 1.00
235 Heath Slater & Rhyno .20 .50
236 Heath Slater & Rhyno .20 .50
237 Heath Slater & Rhyno .20 .50
238 Heath Slater & Rhyno .20 .50
239 Heath Slater & Rhyno .20 .50
240 Cruiserweight .15 .40
241 Cruiserweight .15 .40
242 Cruiserweight .15 .40
243 Cruiserweight .15 .40
244 Cruiserweight .15 .40

2008 Topps WWE Ultimate Rivals

COMPLETE SET (90) 8.00 20.00
1 Kane vs. Chavo Guerrero .40 1.00
2 Batista vs. Mark Henry .40 1.00
3 Batisita vs. The Great Khali .40 1.00
4 Batista vs. Undertaker .50 1.25
5 Big Daddy V vs. Boogeyman .15 .40
6 Kendrick/London vs. Regal/Taylor .25 .60
7 Chris Jericho vs. JBL .25 .60
8 CM Punk vs. John Morrison .10 .25
9 CM Punk vs. Mike Knox .10 .25
10 CM Punk vs. Shannon Moore .10 .25
11 C.Rhodes vs. Hardcore Holly .15 .40
12 D-Generation X vs. Rated RKO .25 .60
13 Elijah Burke vs. CM Punk .10 .25
14 Finlay vs. Rey Mysterio .25 .60
15 Finlay vs. JBL .15 .40
16 Jamie Noble vs. The Hurricane .12 .30
17 Jamie Noble vs. Hornswoggle .15 .40
18 Jeff Hardy vs. John Morrison .40 1.00
19 Jeff Hardy vs. Umaga .40 1.00
20 John Cena vs. Carlito .60 1.50
21 John Cena vs. Edge .60 1.50
22 John Cena vs. Randy Orton .60 1.50
23 Kane vs. MVP .40 1.00
24 Kane vs. Snitsky .40 1.00
25 Umaga vs. Kane .40 1.00
26 Kane vs. Undertaker .50 1.25
27 K.Dykstra vs. Chuck Palumbo .15 .40
28 K.Dykstra vs. Shawn Michaels .60 1.50
29 Cade/Murdoch vs. Rhodes/Holly .15 .40
30 Deuce/Domino vs. London/Kendrick .15 .40
31 Matt Hardy vs. Edge .40 1.00
32 Matt Hardy vs. MVP .40 1.00
33 T.Dreamer vs. Matt Striker .10 .25
34 Mr. Kennedy vs. Undertaker .50 1.25
35 Big Show vs. John Cena .60 1.50
36 R.Mysterio vs. Chavo Guerrero .25 .60
37 Rey Mysterio vs. MVP .25 .60
38 Ric Flair vs. Carlito .40 1.00
39 S.Marella vs. Steve Austin .60 1.50
40 Shawn Michaels vs. Undertaker .60 1.50
41 Funaki vs. Val Venis .10 .25
42 Steve Austin vs. Mr. McMahon .60 1.50
43 Kevin Thorn vs. Stevie Richards .15 .40
44 Tommy Dreamer vs. Mick Foley .50 1.25
45 Triple H vs. Batista .60 1.50
46 Triple H vs. Mick Foley .60 1.50
47 Randy Orton vs. Triple H .60 1.50
48 Triple H vs. Umaga .60 1.50
49 Shane McMahon vs. Mr. McMahon .25 .60
50 Randy Orton vs. Jeff Hardy .40 1.00
51 Steve Austin vs. Brian Pillman .60 1.50
52 S.Michaels vs. British Bulldog .60 1.50
53 Chris Jericho vs. Dean Malenko .25 .60
54 Big Show vs. Undertaker .50 1.25
55 Randy Orton vs. Dusty Rhodes .25 .60
56 Shane McMahon vs. Chris Jericho .25 .60
57 Jerry Lawler vs. Tazz .25 .60
58 Ric Flair vs. Terry Funk .40 1.00
59 Paul Bearer vs. Undertaker .50 1.25
60 Rey Mysterio vs. JBL .25 .60
61 Arn Anderson vs. Ric Flair .40 1.00
62 Ric Flair vs. Mr.Perfect .40 1.00
63 Ric Flair vs. Dusty Rhodes .40 1.00
64 Kama Mustafa vs. Undertaker .50 1.25
65 Santino Marella vs. Maria .40 1.00
66 Mickie James vs. Melina .60 1.50
67 Candice Michelle vs. Beth Phoenix .50 1.25
68 Melina vs. Candice Michelle .50 1.25
69 Kelly Kelly vs. Layla .40 1.00
70 Victoria vs. Michelle McCool .50 1.25
71 Mickie James vs. Beth Phoenix .60 1.50
72 Maria vs. Melina .40 1.00
73 Doink vs. Bam Bam Bigelow .25 .60
74 Iron Shiek vs. Sgt. Slaughter .40 1.00
75 Paul Orndorff vs. Bobby Heenan .25 .60
76 J.Strongbow vs. Peter Maivia .25 .60
77 Mick Foley vs. Terry Funk .25 .60
78 Dusty Rhodes vs. Billy Graham .25 .60
79 Ron Simmons vs. Vader .15 .40
80 Jake Roberts vs. Kamala .25 .60
81 Jake Roberts vs. Rick Rude .25 .60
82 Jake Roberts vs. Ted DiBiase .25 .60
83 Jake Roberts vs. Jerry Lawler .25 .60
84 Bam Bam vs. One Man Gang .25 .60
85 Ric Flair vs. Roddy Piper .40 1.00
86 Rocky Johnson vs. Wild Samoans .15 .40
87 Ted DiBiase vs. Dusty Rhodes .25 .60
88 Sgt. Slaughter vs. Pat Patterson .25 .60
89 Gorilla Monsoon vs. Vader .25 .60
90 Checklist .10 .25

2008 Topps WWE Ultimate Rivals Autographs

STATED ODDS 1:48 HOBBY EXCLUSIVE

NNO CM Punk 100.00 200.00
NNO Edge 20.00 50.00
NNO Elijah Burke 6.00 15.00
NNO John Morrison 8.00 20.00
NNO Matt Hardy 8.00 20.00
NNO Michelle McCool 12.00 30.00
NNO The Miz 8.00 20.00
NNO Stevie Richards 6.00 15.00
NNO Super Crazy 6.00 15.00
NNO Victoria 8.00 20.00

2008 Topps WWE Ultimate Rivals Motion Cards

COMPLETE SET (10) 4.00 10.00
STATED ODDS 1:8 HOBBY AND RETAIL

1 Batista vs. Edge .60 1.50
2 Lance Cade vs. Hardcore Holly .20 .50
3 Carlito vs. Brian Kendrick .30 .75
4 Chavo Guerrero vs. CM Punk .30 .75
5 Hornswoggle/Finley vs. Edge .60 1.50
6 Lance Cade .20 .50
7 Jeff Hardy vs. Randy Orton .60 1.50
8 Rey Mysterio vs. Edge .60 1.50
9 Triple H vs. Umaga 1.00 2.50
10 Undertaker vs. MVP 1.00 2.50

2008 Topps WWE Ultimate Rivals Ringside Relics

STATED ODDS 1:48 HOBBY EXCLUSIVE

NNO Carlito 3.00 8.00
NNO Charlie Haas 3.00 8.00
NNO CM Punk 3.00 8.00
NNO Edge 4.00 10.00
NNO John Cena 6.00 15.00
NNO Matt Hardy 5.00 12.00
NNO Mr. Kennedy 3.00 8.00

2008 Topps WWE Ultimate Rivals Tattoos

COMPLETE SET (10) 4.00 10.00
STATED ODDS 1:4 RETAIL EXCLUSIVE

1 John Cena 1.00 3.00
2 Batista .60 1.50
3 Shawn Michaels 1.00 2.50
4 Edge .60 1.50
5 Mr. Kennedy .30 .75
6 The Undertaker .60 1.50
7 Ric Flair .60 1.50
8 Triple H 1.00 2.50
9 Rey Mysterio .30 .75
10 John Morrison .30 .75

2008 Topps WWE Ultimate Rivals Promos

P1 John Cena vs. Edge 1.00 2.50

2015 Topps WWE Undisputed

COMPLETE SET (100) 30.00 80.00
*RED: .5X TO 1.2X BASIC CARDS
*BLACK/99: .6X TO 1.5X BASIC CARDS
*PURPLE/50: .75X TO 2X BASIC CARDS
*SILVER/25: 1.2X TO 3X BASIC CARDS
*GOLD/1: UNPRICED DUE TO SCARCITY
*PP BLACK/1: UNPRICED DUE TO SCARCITY
*PP CYAN/1: UNPRICED DUE TO SCARCITY
*PP MAGENTA/1: UNPRICED DUE TO SCARCITY
*PP YELLOW/1: UNPRICED DUE TO SCARCITY

1 Undertaker 2.50 6.00
2 Rosa Mendes 1.00 2.50
3 Lita 2.50 6.00
4 Kofi Kingston .60 1.50
5 George The Animal Steele .75 2.00
6 Titus O'Neil .60 1.50
7 Stardust .60 1.50
8 The American Dream Dusty Rhodes 1.00 2.50
9 Alicia Fox 1.25 3.00
10 Brock Lesnar 2.50 6.00
11 Zack Ryder .60 1.50
12 Summer Rae 2.50 6.00
13 The Miz 1.00 2.50
14 Roman Reigns 1.50 4.00
15 Natalya 2.00 5.00
16 Rob Van Dam 1.50 4.00
17 Lana RC 2.50 6.00
18 Shawn Michaels 2.50 6.00
19 R-Truth .60 1.50
20 Nature Boy Ric Flair 3.00 8.00
21 Jey Uso .60 1.50
22 Hacksaw Jim Duggan 1.00 2.50
23 Booker T 1.00 2.50
24 Randy Orton 2.50 6.00
25 John Cena 3.00 8.00
26 Big Show 1.50 4.00
27 Cesaro .60 1.50
28 Kevin Nash 1.50 4.00
29 Honky Tonk Man 1.00 2.50
30 Bret Hit Man Hart 2.00 5.00
31 Paige RC 3.00 8.00
32 Dolph Ziggler 1.00 2.50
33 Christian .60 1.50
34 Ricky The Dragon Steamboat 1.00 2.50
35 Chris Jericho 1.50 4.00
36 Jerry The King Lawler 1.00 2.50
37 Kane 1.50 4.00
38 Bo Dallas .60 1.50
39 Darren Young .60 1.50
40 Daniel Bryan 2.50 6.00
41 Paul Heyman .60 1.50
42 Big E 1.00 2.50
43 Sin Cara 1.00 2.50
44 Doink The Clown .60 1.50
45 Naomi 1.00 2.50
46 Paul Bearer 1.00 2.50
47 Rusev RC 1.50 4.00
48 Mark Henry 1.00 2.50
49 Erick Rowan 1.00 2.50
50 Triple H 2.50 6.00
51 Diamond Dallas Page 1.25 3.00
52 Tyson Kidd .60 1.50
53 The British Bulldog 1.00 2.50
54 Razor Ramon 1.50 4.00
55 Ted DiBiase 1.00 2.50
56 King Barrett .60 1.50
57 Seth Rollins 1.00 2.50
58 Rowdy Roddy Piper 2.00 5.00
59 Ultimate Warrior 2.00 5.00
60 Trish Stratus 3.00 8.00
61 Eve Torres 1.25 3.00
62 Adam Rose RC .75 2.00
63 Bruno Sammartino 1.50 4.00
64 JBL .60 1.50
65 The Iron Sheik 1.00 2.50
66 Emma RC 1.00 2.50
67 Jack Swagger 1.00 2.50
68 Luke Harper 1.00 2.50
69 Konnor .75 2.00
70 Sting 1.50 4.00
71 Bray Wyatt 2.50 6.00
72 Bob Backlund .60 1.50
73 Eva Marie 2.50 6.00
74 Jake The Snake Roberts 1.00 2.50
75 Yokozuna 1.00 2.50
76 Nikki Bella 2.00 5.00
77 Sheamus 1.50 4.00
78 Jimmy Uso .60 1.50
79 Fandango .60 1.50
80 Neville RC 1.25 3.00
81 Viktor RC .60 1.50
82 Cowboy Bob Orton .60 1.50
83 Arn Anderson .75 2.00
84 Damien Sandow .60 1.50
85 Edge 1.50 4.00
86 Classy Freddie Blassie .60 1.50
87 Dean Ambrose 1.50 4.00
88 Stephanie McMahon 1.00 2.50
89 Sgt. Slaughter 1.00 2.50
90 Mr. Perfect Curt Hennig 1.00 2.50
91 Ryback .60 1.50
92 Big Boss Man .60 1.50
93 Bam Bam Bigelow .75 2.00
94 Pat Patterson .60 1.50
95 Brie Bella 2.00 5.00
96 Cameron 1.00 2.50
97 Kalisto RC 1.00 2.50
98 The Rock 3.00 8.00
99 Goldust .60 1.50
100 Ravishing Rick Rude 1.00 2.50

2015 Topps WWE Undisputed Autographed Relics

*BLACK/50: .6X TO 1.5X BASIC AUTOS
*PURPLE/25: 1X TO 2.5X BASIC AUTOS
*GOLD/1: UNPRICED DUE TO SCARCITY

UARAF Alicia Fox 6.00 15.00
UARAR Adam Rose 5.00 12.00
UARBB Brie Bella 12.00 30.00
UARBD Bo Dallas 5.00 12.00
UARBS Big Show 8.00 20.00
UARBW Bray Wyatt 12.00 30.00
UARCA Curtis Axel 5.00 12.00
UARCE Cesaro 10.00 25.00
UARDA Dean Ambrose 12.00 30.00
UARDB Daniel Bryan 15.00 40.00
UARDM Damien Sandow 5.00 12.00
UARDY Darren Young 5.00 12.00
UARDZ Dolph Ziggler 6.00 15.00
UARFA Fandango 5.00 12.00
UARGO Goldust 8.00 20.00
UARHS Heath Slater 5.00 12.00
UARJC John Cena 25.00 60.00
UARJS Jack Swagger 5.00 12.00
UARJU Jimmy Uso 8.00 20.00
UARKO Konnor 5.00 12.00
UARMH Mark Henry 6.00 15.00
UARNA Natalya 8.00 20.00
UARNB Nikki Bella 50.00 100.00
UARRO Randy Orton 12.00 30.00
UARRR Roman Reigns 25.00 60.00
UARSH Sheamus 10.00 25.00
UARSR Seth Rollins 15.00 40.00
UARTK Tyson Kidd 5.00 12.00
UARTM The Miz 8.00 20.00
UARTO Titus O'Neil 5.00 12.00
UARVI Viktor 5.00 12.00
UARZR Zack Ryder 5.00 12.00
UARBNB King Barrett 6.00 15.00
UARJKL Jerry The King Lawler 15.00 40.00
UARSRA Summer Rae 10.00 25.00

2015 Topps WWE Undisputed Autographs

*BLACK/50: .6X TO 1.5X BASIC AUTOS
*PURPLE/25: .75X TO 2X BASIC AUTOS
*GOLD/1: UNPRICED DUE TO SCARCITY

UAAB Alundra Blayze 8.00 20.00
UABB Brie Bella 12.00 30.00
UABL Brock Lesnar 120.00 200.00
UABS Bruno Sammartino 10.00 25.00
UABW Bray Wyatt 8.00 20.00
UACJ Chris Jericho 15.00 40.00
UADA Dean Ambrose 8.00 20.00
UADB Daniel Bryan 10.00 25.00
UADZ Dolph Ziggler 6.00 15.00
UAED Edge 10.00 25.00
UAEV Eve Torres 6.00 15.00
UAIS The Iron Sheik 20.00 50.00
UAJC John Cena 75.00 150.00
UAJL Jerry The King Lawler 8.00 20.00
UALI Lita 10.00 25.00
UALT Lawrence Taylor 75.00 150.00
UAMM Ted DiBiase 12.00 30.00
UANA Natalya 6.00 15.00
UANB Nikki Bella 12.00 30.00
UANE Neville 6.00 15.00
UAPH Paul Heyman 8.00 20.00
UAPR Pete Rose 20.00 50.00
UARF Nature Boy Ric Flair 15.00 40.00
UARO Randy Orton 25.00 60.00
UARR Razor Ramon 60.00 120.00
UARU Rusev 6.00 15.00
UARY Ryback 6.00 15.00
UASM Shawn Michaels 50.00 100.00
UASR Seth Rollins 15.00 40.00
UATM The Miz 8.00 20.00
UATS Trish Stratus 50.00 100.00
UABHH Bret Hit Man Hart 50.00 100.00
UABSH Big Show 6.00 15.00
UARRE Roman Reigns 50.00 100.00
UASRA Summer Rae 12.00 30.00

2015 Topps WWE Undisputed Cage Evolution Moments

COMPLETE SET (20) 10.00 25.00
*RED: .5X TO 1.2X BASIC CARDS
*BLACK/99: .6X TO 1.5X BASIC CARDS
*PURPLE/50: .75X TO 2X BASIC CARDS
*SILVER/25: 1.2X TO 3X BASIC CARDS
*GOLD/1: UNPRICED DUE TO SCARCITY
*PP BLACK/1: UNPRICED DUE TO SCARCITY
*PP CYAN/1: UNPRICED DUE TO SCARCITY
*PP MAGENTA/1: UNPRICED DUE TO SCARCITY
*PP YELLOW/1: UNPRICED DUE TO SCARCITY

CEM1 Ultimate Warrior/Rick Rude 1.25 3.00
CEM2 Undertaker/Shawn Michaels 1.50 4.00
CEM3 Edge/Christian 1.00 2.50
CEM4 John Cena/Big Show 2.00 5.00
CEM5 Sheamus/Ryback/R-Truth 1.00 2.50
Barrett/Ziggler/Henry
CEM6 Triple H/Randy Orton 1.50 4.00
CEM7 JBL/Big Show 1.00 2.50
CEM8 John Cena/Edge 2.00 5.00
CEM9 Undertaker/Edge 1.50 4.00
CEM10 Mark Henry/Big Show 1.00 2.50
CEM11 Big Show/Bryan/Henry 1.50 4.00
CEM12 Undertaker/Triple H 1.50 4.00
CEM13 Triple H/Brock Lesnar 1.50 4.00
CEM14 Cesaro/Orton/Bryan 2.00 5.00
Cena/Christian/Sheamus
CEM15 John Cena/Bray Wyatt 2.00 5.00
CEM16 RVD/Jericho/HHH 1.50 4.00
Booker T/Kane/HBK
CEM17 Shawn Michaels/Triple H 1.50 4.00
CEM18 Dean Ambrose/Seth Rollins 1.00 2.50
CEM19 Randy Orton/Seth Rollins 1.50 4.00
CEM20 John Cena/Seth Rollins 2.00 5.00

2015 Topps WWE Undisputed Cut Signatures

STATED PRINT RUN 1 SER.#'d SET
UNPRICED DUE TO SCARCITY

CUTBB British Bulldog
CUTJD Junkyard Dog
CUTMP Mr. Perfect Curt Hennig
CUTBBM Big Boss Man
CUTCJS Chief Jay Strongbow

2015 Topps WWE Undisputed Famous Finishers

COMPLETE SET (30) 12.00 30.00
*RED: .5X TO 1.2X BASIC CARDS
*BLACK/99: .6X TO 1.5X BASIC CARDS
*PURPLE/50: .75X TO 2X BASIC CARDS
*SILVER/25: 1.2X TO 3X BASIC CARDS
*GOLD/1: UNPRICED DUE TO SCARCITY
*PP BLACK/1: UNPRICED DUE TO SCARCITY
*PP CYAN/1: UNPRICED DUE TO SCARCITY
*PP MAGENTA/1: UNPRICED DUE TO SCARCITY
*PP YELLOW/1: UNPRICED DUE TO SCARCITY

FF1 Sweet Chin Music 2.00 5.00
FF2 Pedigree 2.00 5.00
FF3 Stratusfaction 2.50 6.00
FF4 Zig Zag .75 2.00
FF5 Tombstone 2.00 5.00
FF6 Figure-4 Leglock 2.50 6.00
FF7 RKO 2.00 5.00
FF8 Rude Awakening .75 2.00
FF9 Codebreaker 1.25 3.00
FF10 Brogue Kick 1.25 3.00
FF11 Sharpshooter 1.50 4.00
FF12 Attitude Adjustment 2.50 6.00
FF13 Million Dollar Dream .75 2.00
FF14 KO Punch 1.25 3.00
FF15 Sister Abigail 2.00 5.00
FF16 F-5 2.00 5.00
FF17 Running Knee Smash 2.00 5.00
FF18 Camel Clutch .75 2.00
FF19 Texas Cloverleaf .75 2.00
FF20 World's Strongest Slam .75 2.00
FF21 Razor's Edge 1.25 3.00
FF22 Banzai Drop .75 2.00
FF23 Patriot Lock .75 2.00
FF24 Spear 1.25 3.00
FF25 Perfectplex .75 2.00

FF26 DDT .75 2.00
FF27 Coup de Grace 1.50 4.00
FF28 Figure Eight 1.50 4.00
FF29 Skull-Crushing Finale .75 2.00
FF30 Red Arrow 1.00 2.50

2015 Topps WWE Undisputed Famous Rivalries Dual Autographed Jumbo Relics

STATED PRINT RUN 5 SER.#'d SETS
UNPRICED DUE TO SCARCITY

FRARAR D.Ambrose/S.Rollins
FRARBB Nikki & Brie Bella
FRARCO J.Cena/R.Orton
FRARSH Big Show/M.Henry
FRARZM D.Ziggler/Miz

2015 Topps WWE Undisputed Famous Rivalries Dual Autographs

STATED PRINT RUN 25 SER.#'d SETS

FRACO J.Cena/R.Orton 150.00 300.00
FRAHL B.Hart/J.Lawler 75.00 150.00
FRAMR S.Michaels/R.Ramon 100.00 200.00

2015 Topps WWE Undisputed Fistographs

STATED PRINT RUN 10 SER.#'d SETS

NNO Big Show 75.00 200.00
NNO Bray Wyatt 75.00 200.00
NNO Bret Hit Man Hart 100.00 250.00
NNO Bruno Sammartino 100.00 250.00
NNO Daniel Bryan 125.00 300.00
NNO Dean Ambrose 125.00 300.00
NNO Edge 100.00 250.00
NNO Jack Swagger 60.00 150.00
NNO John Cena 150.00 400.00
NNO Kane 75.00 200.00
NNO King Barrett 60.00 150.00
NNO Lita 125.00 300.00
NNO Mark Henry 60.00 150.00
NNO Randy Orton 100.00 250.00
NNO Ric Flair 125.00 300.00
NNO Roman Reigns 200.00 500.00
NNO Rowdy Roddy Piper 125.00 300.00
NNO Rusev 60.00 150.00
NNO Shawn Michaels 150.00 400.00
NNO Sheamus 60.00 150.00
NNO Trish Stratus 150.00 400.00

2015 Topps WWE Undisputed Four Corners Quadragraphs

STATED PRINT RUN 10 SER.#'d SETS

FCQBBSL Lita/Trish/Bellas 300.00 600.00
FCQBBYS Bryan/Young/Barrett/Slater 125.00 250.00
FCQDNZO Dallas/Neville/Zayn/Owens 125.00 250.00
FCQHHLD J.Hart/B.Hart/Lawler/DiBiase 150.00 300.00

2015 Topps WWE Undisputed NXT In Line Autographs

*BLACK/50: .6X TO 1.5X BASIC AUTOS
*PURPLE/25: .75X TO 2X BASIC AUTOS
*GOLD/1: UNPRICED DUE TO SCARCITY

NABD Bull Dempsey 5.00 12.00
NABL Becky Lynch 150.00 300.00
NABM Murphy 5.00 12.00
NACC Colin Cassady 6.00 15.00
NACH Charlotte 125.00 250.00
NAEA Enzo Amore 10.00 25.00
NAFB Finn Balor 50.00 100.00
NAHI Hideo Itami 8.00 20.00
NAKO Kevin Owens 25.00 60.00
NASB Sasha Banks 150.00 300.00
NASJ Samoa Joe 10.00 25.00
NASZ Sami Zayn 10.00 25.00
NATB Tyler Breeze 8.00 20.00
NAWB Blake 5.00 12.00
NABCO Baron Corbin 6.00 15.00

2015 Topps WWE Undisputed NXT Prospects

COMPLETE SET (25) 100.00 200.00
*RED: .5X TO 1.2X BASIC CARDS
*BLACK/99: .6X TO 1.5X BASIC CARDS
*PURPLE/50: .75X TO 2X BASIC CARDS
*SILVER/25: 1.2X TO 3X BASIC CARDS
*GOLD/1: UNPRICED DUE TO SCARCITY
*PP BLACK/1: UNPRICED DUE TO SCARCITY
*PP CYAN/1: UNPRICED DUE TO SCARCITY
*PP MAGENTA/1: UNPRICED DUE TO SCARCITY
*PP YELLOW/1: UNPRICED DUE TO SCARCITY

NXT1 Angelo Dawkins 1.50 4.00
NXT2 Sasha Banks 12.00 30.00
NXT3 Finn Balor 4.00 10.00
NXT4 Sami Zayn 2.00 5.00
NXT5 Charlotte 10.00 25.00
NXT6 Blake 1.25 3.00
NXT7 Murphy 1.25 3.00
NXT8 Carmella 5.00 12.00
NXT9 Enzo Amore 1.25 3.00
NXT10 Baron Corbin 2.00 5.00
NXT11 Hideo Itami 1.25 3.00
NXT12 Tyler Breeze 1.25 3.00
NXT13 Solomon Crowe 1.25 3.00
NXT14 Becky Lynch 15.00 40.00
NXT15 Bayley 5.00 12.00
NXT16 Bull Dempsey 2.00 5.00
NXT17 Alexa Bliss 50.00 100.00
NXT18 Tye Dillinger 2.00 5.00
NXT19 Jason Jordan 1.25 3.00
NXT20 Colin Cassady 2.00 5.00
NXT21 Aiden English 1.50 4.00
NXT22 Simon Gotch 1.25 3.00
NXT23 Mojo Rawley 1.25 3.00
NXT24 Marcus Louis 2.00 5.00
NXT25 Samoa Joe 3.00 8.00

2016 Topps WWE Undisputed

COMPLETE SET (100) 25.00 60.00
*BRONZE/99: .5X TO 1.2X BASIC CARDS
*SILVER/50: .75X TO 2X BASIC CARDS
*BLUE/25: 1.2X TO 3X BASIC CARDS
*GOLD/10: 2X TO 5X BASIC CARDS
*RED/1: UNPRICED DUE TO SCARCITY
*P.P.BLACK/1: UNPRICED DUE TO SCARCITY
*P.P.CYAN/1: UNPRICED DUE TO SCARCITY
*P.P.MAGENTA/1: UNPRICED DUE TO SCARCITY
*P.P.YELLOW/1: UNPRICED DUE TO SCARCITY

1 Alberto Del Rio 1.00 2.50
2 Big E .60 1.50
3 Big Show 1.25 3.00
4 Braun Strowman RC .75 2.00
5 Bray Wyatt 2.50 6.00
6 Brock Lesnar 3.00 8.00
7 Bubba Ray Dudley 1.25 3.00
8 Cesaro 1.25 3.00
9 Chris Jericho 1.50 4.00
10 D-Von Dudley 1.00 2.50
11 Dean Ambrose 2.00 5.00
12 Dolph Ziggler .75 2.00
13 Erick Rowan .60 1.50
14 Goldust 1.00 2.50
15 Jerry The King Lawler 1.25 3.00
16 John Cena 3.00 8.00
17 Kane 1.00 2.50
18 Kevin Owens 1.50 4.00
19 King Barrett .60 1.50
20 Kofi Kingston .60 1.50
21 Luke Harper .60 1.50
22 Mark Henry .75 2.00
23 The Miz 1.00 2.50
24 Neville 1.50 4.00
25 Paul Heyman .75 2.00
26 R-Truth .60 1.50
27 Randy Orton 1.50 4.00
28 The Rock 3.00 8.00
29 Roman Reigns 2.00 5.00
30 Rusev 1.50 4.00
31 Ryback .75 2.00
32 Seth Rollins 1.00 2.50
33 Sheamus 1.50 4.00
34 Sting 1.50 4.00
35 Triple H 2.50 6.00
36 Tyler Breeze .60 1.50
37 Tyson Kidd .60 1.50
38 Undertaker 2.50 6.00
39 Xavier Woods .60 1.50
40 Zack Ryder .60 1.50
41 The American Dream Dusty Rhodes .60 1.50
42 Andre the Giant 2.00 5.00
43 Bam Bam Bigelow .75 2.00
44 Batista 1.25 3.00
45 Big Boss Man 1.00 2.50
46 Big John Studd 1.00 2.50
47 Bob Backlund .60 1.50
48 Bobby The Brain Heenan 1.00 2.50
49 Bret Hit Man Hart 1.50 4.00
50 Brian Pillman .75 2.00
51 The British Bulldog .75 2.00
52 Cowboy Bob Orton 1.00 2.50
53 Diamond Dallas Page 1.00 2.50
54 Doink the Clown .60 1.50
55 Eddie Guerrero 1.50 4.00
56 Edge 1.50 4.00
57 General Adnan .60 1.50
58 George The Animal Steele .75 2.00
59 Hacksaw Jim Duggan .60 1.50
60 High Chief Peter Maivia .60 1.50
61 Honky Tonk Man .60 1.50
62 Jake The Snake Roberts 1.25 3.00
63 Jim The Anvil Neidhart .60 1.50
64 Jim Ross 1.00 2.50
65 J.J. Dillon .60 1.50
66 Junkyard Dog 1.00 2.50
67 Kamala .60 1.50
68 The King Harley Race .60 1.50
69 Kevin Nash 1.50 4.00
70 Lex Luger 1.00 2.50
71 Macho Man Randy Savage 1.50 4.00
72 Mean Gene Okerlund .75 2.00
73 Michael P.S. Hayes .60 1.50
74 Ted DiBiase .75 2.00
75 The Mouth of the South Jimmy Hart .75 2.00
76 Mr. Perfect Curt Hennig 1.50 4.00
77 Mr. Wonderful Paul Orndorff .60 1.50
78 Papa Shango .75 2.00
79 Paul Bearer 1.00 2.50
80 Ravishing Rick Rude 1.00 2.50
81 Ric Flair 2.50 6.00
82 Ricky The Dragon Steamboat .75 2.00
83 Rikishi .75 2.00
84 Road Dogg 1.00 2.50
85 Rob Van Dam 1.25 3.00
86 Rocky Johnson .75 2.00
87 Rowdy Roddy Piper 2.00 5.00
88 Scott Hall 1.50 4.00
89 Sgt. Slaughter .75 2.00
90 Shawn Michaels 2.50 6.00
91 Superstar Billy Graham .60 1.50
92 Stone Cold Steve Austin 3.00 8.00
93 Tatanka .60 1.50
94 Tatsumi Fujinami RC .60 1.50
95 Tito Santana .75 2.00
96 Ultimate Warrior 1.50 4.00
97 Vader 1.25 3.00
98 Virgil .60 1.50
99 X-Pac 1.00 2.50
100 Yokozuna 1.25 3.00

2016 Topps WWE Undisputed Autographed Diva Kiss and Relic Booklets

STATED PRINT RUN 5 SER. #'d SETS
UNPRICED DUE TO SCARCITY

ADRAF Alicia Fox
ADRBA Bayley
ADRBB Brie Bella
ADRLA Lana
ADRNB Nikki Bella

2016 Topps WWE Undisputed Autographed Relics

*SILVER/50: .6X TO 1.5X BASIC AUTOS
*BLUE/25: 1X TO 2.5X BASIC MEM
*GOLD/10: 1.2X TO 3X BASIC AUTOS
*RED/1: UNPRICED DUE TO SCARCITY
*P.P.BLACK/1: UNPRICED DUE TO SCARCITY
*P.P.CYAN/1: UNPRICED DUE TO SCARCITY
*P.P.MAGENTA/1: UNPRICED DUE TO SCARCITY
*P.P.YELLOW/1: UNPRICED DUE TO SCARCITY
STATED PRINT RUN 99 SER.#'d SETS

UARAC Alicia Fox 6.00 15.00
UARAE Aiden English 6.00 15.00
UARBB Brie Bella 12.00 30.00
UARBC Baron Corbin 6.00 15.00
UARBE Big E 6.00 15.00
UARBL Becky Lynch 20.00 50.00
UARBW Bray Wyatt 10.00 25.00
UARCC Colin Cassady 8.00 20.00
UARCH Charlotte 15.00 40.00
UARDA Dean Ambrose 12.00 30.00
UARDD D-Von Dudley 6.00 15.00
UARDZ Dolph Ziggler 6.00 15.00
UAREA Enzo Amore 12.00 30.00
UARFB Finn Balor 15.00 40.00
UARJU Jey Uso 6.00 15.00
UARKA Kalisto 6.00 15.00
UARKK Kofi Kingston 6.00 15.00
UARKO Kevin Owens 12.00 30.00
UARMR Mojo Rawley 6.00 15.00
UARNE Neville 8.00 20.00
UARRR Roman Reigns 10.00 25.00
UARRY Ryback 6.00 15.00
UARSB Sasha Banks 25.00 60.00
UARSC Sin Cara 8.00 20.00
UARSG Simon Gotch 6.00 15.00
UARSH Sheamus 6.00 15.00
UARSJ Samoa Joe 6.00 15.00
UARSR Seth Rollins 10.00 25.00
UARTB Tyler Breeze 6.00 15.00
UARTM The Miz 6.00 15.00
UARXW Xavier Woods 6.00 15.00
UARZR Zack Ryder 6.00 15.00
UARADR Alberto Del Rio 6.00 15.00
UARAPC Apollo Crews 6.00 15.00
UARBAY Bayley 20.00 50.00
UARBRD Bubba Ray Dudley 6.00 15.00
UARJIU Jimmy Uso 8.00 20.00

2016 Topps WWE Undisputed Autographs

*BRONZE/99: .5X TO 1.2X BASIC AUTOS
*SILVER/50: .75X TO 2X BASIC AUTOS
*BLUE/25: 1.2X TO 3X BASIC AUTOS
*GOLD/10: 1.5X TO 4X BASIC AUTOS
*RED/1: UNPRICED DUE TO SCARCITY
*P.P.BLACK/1: UNPRICED DUE TO SCARCITY
*P.P.CYAN/1: UNPRICED DUE TO SCARCITY
*P.P.MAGENTA/1: UNPRICED DUE TO SCARCITY
*P.P.YELLOW/1: UNPRICED DUE TO SCARCITY
RANDOMLY INSERTED INTO PACKS

UAAF Alicia Fox 5.00 12.00
UAAS Asuka 25.00 60.00
UABA Bayley 15.00 40.00
UABB Brie Bella 8.00 20.00
UABE Big E 6.00 15.00
UABH Bret Hit Man Hart 12.00 30.00
UABL Becky Lynch 30.00 75.00
UABS Braun Strowman 6.00 15.00
UABT Booker T 6.00 15.00
UACA Carmella 10.00 25.00
UACC Colin Cassady 6.00 15.00
UACE Cesaro 6.00 15.00
UACH Charlotte 25.00 60.00
UADA Dean Ambrose 10.00 25.00
UADB Daniel Bryan 10.00 25.00
UADD D-Von Dudley 6.00 15.00
UAEA Enzo Amore 10.00 25.00
UAER Erick Rowan 5.00 12.00
UAFB Finn Balor 10.00 25.00
UAGO Goldust 10.00 25.00
UAHI Hideo Itami 5.00 12.00
UAJC John Cena 75.00 150.00
UAJN Jim The Anvil Neidhart 6.00 15.00
UAKA Kalisto 5.00 12.00
UAKK Kofi Kingston 10.00 25.00
UALA Lana 10.00 25.00
UALH Luke Harper 6.00 15.00
UALI Lita 25.00 60.00
UANA Natalya 10.00 25.00
UANB Nikki Bella 10.00 25.00
UANJ Nia Jax 5.00 12.00
UARR Roman Reigns 20.00 50.00
UASB Sasha Banks 30.00 75.00
UASC Sin Cara 6.00 15.00

UASJ Samoa Joe	5.00	12.00
UASR Seth Rollins	8.00	20.00
UAST Sting	25.00	60.00
UATS Trish Stratus	30.00	75.00
UAXW Xavier Woods	5.00	12.00
UAAJS AJ Styles	10.00	25.00
UABAC Baron Corbin	6.00	15.00
UABRD Bubba Ray Dudley	6.00	15.00
UABRW Bray Wyatt	6.00	15.00
UANAO Naomi	5.00	12.00
UASTR Stevie Ray	5.00	12.00

2016 Topps WWE Undisputed Cut Signatures

STATED PRINT RUN 1 SER.#'d SET
UNPRICED DUE TO SCARCITY

UCSRS Macho Man Randy Savage
UCSCFB Classy Freddie Blassie
UCSMIE Miss Elizabeth

2016 Topps WWE Undisputed Divas Revolution

COMPLETE SET (30) 60.00 120.00
*BRONZE/99: .5X TO 1.2X BASIC CARDS
*SILVER/50: .75X TO 2X BASIC CARDS
*BLUE/25: 1.2X TO 3X BASIC CARDS
*GOLD/10: UNPRICED DUE TO SCARCITY
*RED/1: UNPRICED DUE TO SCARCITY
*P.P.BLACK/1 UNPRICED DUE TO SCARCITY
*P.P.CYAN/1 UNPRICED DUE TO SCARCITY
*P.P.MAGENTA/1 UNPRICED DUE TO SCARCITY
*P.P.YELLOW/1 UNPRICED DUE TO SCARCITY
RANDOMLY INSERTED INTO PACKS

DR1 Alundra Blayze	1.50	4.00
DR2 Eve	2.50	6.00
DR3 Lita	4.00	10.00
DR4 Miss Elizabeth	1.25	3.00
DR5 Sensational Sherri	2.00	5.00
DR6 Trish Stratus	6.00	15.00
DR7 Alicia Fox	2.00	5.00
DR8 Asuka	5.00	12.00
DR9 Bayley	3.00	8.00
DR10 Becky Lynch	4.00	10.00
DR11 Brie Bella	2.50	6.00
DR12 Cameron	1.25	3.00
DR13 Charlotte	4.00	10.00
DR14 Dasha Fuentes	1.25	3.00
DR15 Eden	1.50	4.00
DR16 Emma	2.50	6.00
DR17 Eva Marie	2.50	6.00
DR18 JoJo	1.25	3.00
DR19 Lana	5.00	12.00
DR20 Mandy Rose	3.00	8.00
DR21 Naomi	2.00	5.00
DR22 Natalya	2.00	5.00
DR23 Nikki Bella	4.00	10.00
DR24 Paige	4.00	10.00
DR25 Renee Young	3.00	8.00
DR26 Rosa Mendes	1.25	3.00
DR27 Sasha Banks	4.00	10.00
DR28 Maryse	2.50	6.00
DR29 Summer Rae	3.00	8.00
DR30 Tamina	1.50	4.00

2016 Topps WWE Undisputed Faction Triple Autograph Booklets

STATED PRINT RUN 10 SER. #'d SETS

FTAARR Ambrose/Rollins/Reigns	125.00	250.00
FTABBF The Bellas/Fox	100.00	200.00
FTAKBW Kingston/Big E/Woods	75.00	150.00
FTANBT Naomi/Banks/Tamina	125.00	250.00
FTASKV Stardust/Konnor/Viktor	60.00	120.00

2016 Topps WWE Undisputed Family Ties Dual Autographs

STATED PRINT RUN 25 SER.#'d SETS

FTABB Nikki & Brie Bella	120.00	200.00
FTAFC Ric & Charlotte Flair	120.00	200.00
FTAGS Goldust/Stardust	60.00	120.00
FTANN J.Neidhart/Natalya	60.00	120.00
FTATR Booker T/S. Ray	30.00	75.00

2016 Topps WWE Undisputed NXT Prospects

COMPLETE SET (30) 30.00 80.00
*BRONZE/99: .5X TO 1.2X BASIC CARDS
*SILVER/50: .75X TO 2X BASIC CARDS
*BLUE/25: 1.2X TO 3X BASIC CARDS
*GOLD/10: UNPRICED DUE TO SCARCITY
*RED/1: UNPRICED DUE TO SCARCITY
*P.P.BLACK/1: UNPRICED DUE TO SCARCITY
*P.P.CYAN/1: UNPRICED DUE TO SCARCITY
*P.P.MAGENTA/1: UNPRICED DUE TO SCARCITY
*P.P.YELLOW/1: UNPRICED DUE TO SCARCITY
RANDOMLY INSERTED INTO PACKS

NXT1 Aiden English	1.25	3.00
NXT2 Alexa Bliss	6.00	15.00
NXT3 Angelo Dawkins	1.25	3.00
NXT4 Apollo Crews	1.25	3.00
NXT5 Asuka	5.00	12.00
NXT6 Austin Aries	1.50	4.00
NXT7 Baron Corbin	1.50	4.00
NXT8 Bayley	3.00	8.00
NXT9 Billie Kay	3.00	8.00
NXT10 Blake	1.25	3.00
NXT11 Carmella	3.00	8.00
NXT12 Chad Gable	1.50	4.00
NXT13 Colin Cassady	2.50	6.00
NXT14 Dana Brooke	3.00	8.00
NXT15 Dash Wilder	1.50	4.00
NXT16 Elias Samson	1.25	3.00
NXT17 Enzo Amore	2.50	6.00
NXT18 Finn Balor	4.00	10.00
NXT19 Hideo Itami	1.50	4.00
NXT20 Jason Jordan	1.50	4.00
NXT21 Mojo Rawley	1.25	3.00
NXT22 Murphy	1.25	3.00
NXT23 Nia Jax	2.00	5.00
NXT24 Peyton Royce	3.00	8.00
NXT25 Sami Zayn	2.00	5.00
NXT26 Samoa Joe	3.00	8.00
NXT27 Sawyer Fulton	1.50	4.00
NXT28 Scott Dawson	1.25	3.00
NXT29 Simon Gotch	2.00	5.00
NXT30 Tye Dillinger	1.50	4.00

2016 Topps WWE Undisputed Relics

STATED PRINT RUN 175 SER.#'d SETS

UARAC Alicia Fox	3.00	8.00
UARAE Aiden English	2.00	5.00
UARBB Brie Bella	4.00	10.00
UARBC Baron Corbin	2.50	6.00
UARBE Big E	2.00	5.00
UARBL Becky Lynch	6.00	15.00
UARBW Bray Wyatt	8.00	20.00
UARCC Colin Cassady	4.00	10.00
UARCH Charlotte	6.00	15.00
UARDA Dean Ambrose	6.00	15.00
UARDD D-Von Dudley	3.00	8.00
UARDZ Dolph Ziggler	2.50	6.00
UAREA Enzo Amore	4.00	10.00
UARFB Finn Balor	6.00	15.00
UARJU Jey Uso	2.00	5.00
UARKA Kalisto	5.00	12.00
UARKB King Barrett	2.00	5.00
UARKK Kofi Kingston	2.00	5.00
UARKO Kevin Owens	5.00	12.00
UARMR Mojo Rawley	2.00	5.00
UARNE Neville	5.00	12.00
UARRR Roman Reigns	6.00	15.00
UARRY Ryback	2.50	6.00
UARSB Sasha Banks	6.00	15.00
UARSC Sin Cara	2.50	6.00
UARSG Simon Gotch	3.00	8.00
UARSH Sheamus	5.00	12.00
UARSJ Samoa Joe	5.00	12.00
UARSR Seth Rollins	3.00	8.00
UARTB Tyler Breeze	2.00	5.00
UARTM The Miz	3.00	8.00
UARXW Xavier Woods	2.00	5.00
UARZR Zack Ryder	2.00	5.00
UARADR Alberto Del Rio	3.00	8.00
UARAPC Apollo Crews	2.00	5.00
UARBAY Bayley	5.00	12.00
UARBRD Bubba Ray Dudley	4.00	10.00
UARJIU Jimmy Uso	2.00	5.00

2016 Topps WWE Undisputed Tag Teams

COMPLETE SET (40) 50.00 100.00
*BRONZE/99: .5X TO 1.2X BASIC CARDS
*SILVER/50: .75X TO 2X BASIC CARDS
*BLUE/25: 1.2X TO 3X BASIC CARDS
*GOLD/10: UNPRICED DUE TO SCARCITY
*RED/1: UNPRICED DUE TO SCARCITY
*P.P.BLACK/1: UNPRICED DUE TO SCARCITY
*P.P.CYAN/1: UNPRICED DUE TO SCARCITY
*P.P.MAGENTA/1: UNPRICED DUE TO SCARCITY
*P.P.YELLOW/1: UNPRICED DUE TO SCARCITY
RANDOMLY INSERTED INTO PACKS

UTT1 The Allied Powers	1.50	4.00
UTT2 The APA	2.50	6.00
UTT3 The Ascension	1.00	2.50
UTT4 Blake and Murphy	1.00	2.50
UTT5 The Brain Busters	1.00	2.50
UTT6 Brothers of Destruction	4.00	10.00
UTT7 The Bushwhackers	1.00	2.50
UTT8 D-Generation X	3.00	8.00
UTT9 The Dudley Boyz	2.00	5.00
UTT10 Edge and Christian	2.50	6.00
UTT11 The Enforcers	1.00	2.50
UTT12 The Foreign Legion	1.25	3.00
UTT13 The Funks	1.00	2.50
UTT14 Gold and Stardust	1.50	4.00
UTT15 Harlem Heat	2.00	5.00
UTT16 The Hart Foundation	2.50	6.00
UTT17 The Hollywood Blonds	5.00	12.00
UTT18 The Hype Bros.	1.00	2.50
UTT19 J and J Security	1.00	2.50
UTT20 Jeri-Show	2.50	6.00
UTT21 The Insiders	2.50	6.00
UTT22 The Lucha Dragons	2.50	6.00
UTT23 The Mega Bucks	3.00	8.00
UTT24 Money Inc.	1.25	3.00
UTT25 The Nasty Boys	1.25	3.00
UTT26 The Natural Disasters	1.00	2.50
UTT27 The Outsiders	2.50	6.00
UTT28 The Prime Time Players	1.00	2.50
UTT29 Rated-RKO	2.50	6.00
UTT30 Rhythm and Blues	1.25	3.00
UTT31 ShoMiz	2.00	5.00
UTT32 Team Hell No	4.00	10.00
UTT33 Team Rhodes Scholars	1.00	2.50
UTT34 Dudes with Attitude	4.00	10.00
UTT35 Two Man Power Trip	5.00	12.00
UTT36 Unholy Alliance	4.00	10.00
UTT37 Miz/Mizdow	1.50	4.00
UTT38 The Usos	1.00	2.50
UTT39 The Vaudevillains	1.50	4.00
UTT40 The Revival	1.25	3.00

2017 Topps WWE Undisputed

COMPLETE SET (70) 20.00 50.00
*BRONZE/99: .5X TO 1.2X BASIC CARDS
*SILVER/50: .75X TO 2X BASIC CARDS
*GREEN/25: 1.2X TO 3X BASIC CARDS
*GOLD/10: 2X TO 5X BASIC CARDS
*RED/1: UNPRICED DUE TO SCARCITY
*P.P.BLACK/1: UNPRICED DUE TO SCARCITY
*P.P.CYAN/1: UNPRICED DUE TO SCARCITY
*P.P.MAGENTA/1: UNPRICED DUE TO SCARCITY
*P.P.YELLOW/1: UNPRICED DUE TO SCARCITY

1 John Cena	3.00	8.00
2 AJ Styles	3.00	8.00
3 Big Cass	.75	2.00
4 Big E	.75	2.00
5 The Brian Kendrick	.60	1.50
6 Bray Wyatt	1.50	4.00
7 Brock Lesnar	3.00	8.00
8 Cesaro	1.25	3.00
9 Chad Gable	.75	2.00
10 Chris Jericho	1.50	4.00
11 Daniel Bryan	2.50	6.00
12 Dean Ambrose	2.00	5.00
13 Dolph Ziggler	1.00	2.50
14 Finn Balor	2.50	6.00
15 Goldberg	2.50	6.00
16 James Ellsworth RC	.60	1.50
17 Jason Jordan	.75	2.00
18 Kane	.75	2.00
19 Karl Anderson	.60	1.50
20 Kevin Owens	1.50	4.00
21 Kofi Kingston	.75	2.00
22 Luke Gallows	1.00	2.50
23 Luke Harper	.60	1.50
24 Mick Foley	1.50	4.00
25 The Miz	1.25	3.00
26 Neville	1.00	2.50
27 Randy Orton	1.50	4.00
28 Rich Swann RC	.60	1.50
29 The Rock	3.00	8.00
30 Roman Reigns	2.00	5.00
31 Rusev	1.25	3.00
32 Sami Zayn	.75	2.00
33 Seth Rollins	2.00	5.00
34 Shane McMahon	1.00	2.50
35 Sheamus	1.25	3.00
36 TJ Perkins RC	.60	1.50
37 Triple H	1.50	4.00
38 Undertaker	2.50	6.00
39 Xavier Woods	.75	2.00
40 Zack Ryder	.60	1.50
41 Alexander Wolfe RC	.75	2.00
42 Andrade Cien Almas	.60	1.50
43 Austin Aries	1.25	3.00
44 Bobby Roode	1.50	4.00
45 Dash Wilder	.60	1.50
46 Eric Young	1.25	3.00
47 Hideo Itami	1.00	2.50
48 Johnny Gargano	.60	1.50
49 Nick Miller RC	.60	1.50
50 No Way Jose	.60	1.50
51 Oney Lorcan	.60	1.50
52 Roderick Strong RC	.75	2.00
53 Samoa Joe	2.00	5.00
54 Sawyer Fulton	.60	1.50
55 Scott Dawson	.60	1.50
56 Shane Thorne RC	.60	1.50
57 Shinsuke Nakamura	1.50	4.00
58 Tommaso Ciampa	.60	1.50
59 Tye Dillinger	.60	1.50
60 William Regal	.75	2.00
61 Andre the Giant	1.25	3.00
62 Bret Hit Man Hart	1.25	3.00
63 Macho Man Randy Savage	1.25	3.00
64 Ted DiBiase	.75	2.00
65 Ric Flair	1.50	4.00
66 Rowdy Roddy Piper	1.25	3.00
67 Shawn Michaels	1.50	4.00
68 Sting	2.00	5.00
69 Stone Cold Steve Austin	2.50	6.00
70 Ultimate Warrior	1.25	3.00

2017 Topps WWE Undisputed Autographed Relics

*SILVER/50: .5X TO 1.2X BASIC AUTOS
*GREEN/25: .6X TO 1.5X BASIC AUTOS
*GOLD/10: UNPRICED DUE TO SCARCITY
*RED/1: UNPRICED DUE TO SCARCITY
RANDOMLY INSERTED INTO PACKS

UARAE Aiden English	5.00	12.00
UARAB Alexa Bliss	60.00	120.00
UARAF Alicia Fox	6.00	15.00
UARAS Asuka	25.00	60.00
UARAA Austin Aries	5.00	12.00
UARBC Baron Corbin	6.00	15.00
UARBE Becky Lynch	25.00	60.00
UARBCA Big Cass	5.00	12.00
UARBIG Big E	6.00	15.00
UARBS Big Show	6.00	15.00
UARBD Bo Dallas	6.00	15.00
UARBR Bobby Roode	6.00	15.00
UARBRS Braun Strowman	15.00	40.00
UARBW Bray Wyatt	10.00	25.00
UARBB Brie Bella	12.00	30.00
UARCA Carmella	12.00	30.00
UARCU Curtis Axel	5.00	12.00
UARDY Darren Young	6.00	15.00
UARDZ Dolph Ziggler	6.00	15.00
UARFA Fandango	5.00	12.00
UARFB Finn Balor	12.00	30.00
UARGO Goldust	6.00	15.00
UARHS Heath Slater	5.00	12.00
UARJG Johnny Gargano	5.00	12.00

UARJO JoJo	6.00	15.00
UARKA Kalisto	8.00	20.00
UARLH Luke Harper	50.00	100.00
UARMR Mojo Rawley	5.00	12.00
UARNA Natalya	6.00	15.00
UARNE Neville	8.00	20.00
UARRO Randy Orton	15.00	40.00
UARRY Renee Young	8.00	20.00
UARRR Roman Reigns	15.00	40.00
UARSJ Samoa Joe	6.00	15.00
UARSB Sasha Banks	60.00	120.00
UARSR Seth Rollins	12.00	30.00
UARSH Sheamus	6.00	15.00
UARSG Simon Gotch	5.00	12.00
UARSU Summer Rae	8.00	20.00
UARTA Tamina	6.00	15.00
UARTC Tommaso Ciampa	8.00	20.00
UARVI Viktor	5.00	12.00
UARZR Zack Ryder	6.00	15.00

2017 Topps WWE Undisputed Autographs

*BRONZE/99: SAME VALUE AS BASIC AUTOS

*SILVER/50: .5X TO 1.2X BASIC AUTOS

*GREEN/25: .6X TO 1.5X BASIC AUTOS

*GOLD/10: UNPRICED DUE TO SCARCITY

*BLACK/5: UNPRICED DUE TO SCARCITY

*RED/1: UNPRICED DUE TO SCARCITY

*P.P.BLACK/1: UNPRICED DUE TO SCARCITY

*P.P.CYAN/1: UNPRICED DUE TO SCARCITY

*P.P.MAGENTA/1: UNPRICED DUE TO SCARCITY

*P.P.YELLOW/1: UNPRICED DUE TO SCARCITY

RANDOMLY INSERTED INTO PACKS

UAA Asuka	15.00	40.00
UAC Cesaro	6.00	15.00
UAE Edge	10.00	25.00
UAM Maryse	12.00	30.00
UAN Natalya	8.00	20.00
UAR Rhyno	6.00	15.00
UAS Sting	25.00	60.00
UAAA Austin Aries	6.00	15.00
UAAB Alexa Bliss	60.00	120.00
UAAF Alicia Fox	8.00	20.00
UAAS AJ Styles	20.00	50.00
UABA Bayley	15.00	40.00
UABC Big Cass	6.00	15.00
UABE Big E	5.00	12.00
UABH Bret Hit Man Hart	15.00	40.00
UABL Becky Lynch	25.00	60.00
UABR Bobby Roode	10.00	25.00
UABW Bray Wyatt	8.00	20.00
UACA Carmella	12.00	30.00
UACF Charlotte Flair	15.00	40.00
UACJ Chris Jericho	10.00	25.00
UADA Dean Ambrose	10.00	25.00
UADB Dana Brooke	10.00	25.00
UADD Diamond Dallas Page	12.00	30.00
UAEA Enzo Amore	8.00	20.00
UAEM Ember Moon	8.00	20.00
UAEY Eric Young	6.00	15.00
UAFB Finn Balor	15.00	40.00
UAHS Heath Slater	5.00	12.00
UAJG Johnny Gargano	6.00	15.00
UAKA Karl Anderson	6.00	15.00
UAKO Kevin Owens	8.00	20.00
UALG Luke Gallows	5.00	12.00
UALM Liv Morgan	12.00	30.00
UANA Naomi	8.00	20.00
UANB Nikki Bella	10.00	25.00
UARR Roman Reigns	25.00	60.00
UARS Roderick Strong	6.00	15.00
UARY Renee Young	8.00	20.00
UASB Sasha Banks	15.00	40.00
UASH Sheamus	5.00	12.00
UASN Shinsuke Nakamura	20.00	50.00
UASR Seth Rollins	10.00	25.00
UASZ Sami Zayn	6.00	15.00
UATC Tommaso Ciampa	6.00	15.00
UATM The Miz	5.00	12.00
UATP TJ Perkins	5.00	12.00
UATS Trish Stratus	25.00	60.00
UAXW Xavier Woods	5.00	12.00
UABAC Baron Corbin	8.00	20.00
UAEMM Emma	10.00	25.00
UAKOK Kofi Kingston	5.00	12.00

2017 Topps WWE Undisputed Autographs Bronze

UAG Goldberg	50.00	100.00
UAU Undertaker	150.00	300.00
UARO Randy Orton	15.00	40.00
UABRL Brock Lesnar	50.00	100.00

2017 Topps WWE Undisputed Dream Matches

COMPLETE SET (10)	10.00	25.00

*BRONZE/99: .5X TO 1.2X BASIC CARDS

*SILVER/50: .6X TO 1.5X BASIC CARDS

*GREEN/25: .75X TO 2X BASIC CARDS

*GOLD/10: UNPRICED DUE TO SCARCITY

*RED/1: UNPRICED DUE TO SCARCITY

*P.P.BLACK/1: UNPRICED DUE TO SCARCITY

*P.P.CYAN/1: UNPRICED DUE TO SCARCITY

*P.P.MAGENTA/1: UNPRICED DUE TO SCARCITY

*P.P.YELLOW/1: UNPRICED DUE TO SCARCITY

STATED ODDS 1:

D1 Sting/Undertaker	2.00	5.00
D2 Goldberg/Steve Austin	1.50	4.00
D3 Steve Austin/Brock Lesnar	1.50	4.00
D4 Shawn Michaels/The Rock	2.00	5.00
D5 Shawn Michaels/Eddie Guerrero	1.25	3.00
D6 John Cena/Steve Austin	1.50	4.00
D7 Edge/Bret Hit Man Hart	1.00	2.50
D8 Undertaker/Goldberg	1.50	4.00
D9 Batista/Brock Lesnar	1.25	3.00
D10 Nakamura/Daniel Bryan	1.00	2.50

2017 Topps WWE Undisputed Dual Autographs

STATED PRINT RUN 25 SER.#'d SETS

UDAAE Asuka/E.Moon	60.00	120.00
UDABA B.Roode/A.Aries	30.00	75.00
UDABG B.Lesnar/Goldberg	120.00	250.00
UDACR Charlotte & Ric Flair	75.00	150.00
UDAJT J.Gargano/T.Ciampa	50.00	100.00
UDAKC K.Owens/C.Jericho	60.00	120.00
UDASB S.Banks/Bayley	75.00	150.00
UDASR S.Rollins/R.Reigns	100.00	200.00

2017 Topps WWE Undisputed Quad Autographed Booklets

STATED PRINT RUN 5 SER.#'d SETS

UNPRICED DUE TO SCARCITY

UQACSBB Charlotte/Banks/Lynch/Bayley

UQAFAKL Balor/Styles/Anderson/Gallows

UQAGBJR Goldberg/Lesnar/Cena/Orton

UQASBER Nakamura/Roode/Young/Strong

2017 Topps WWE Undisputed Relics

*SILVER/50: .5X TO 1.2X BASIC MEM

*GREEN/25: .6X TO 1.5X BASIC MEM

*GOLD/10: UNPRICED DUE TO SCARCITY

*RED/1: UNPRICED DUE TO SCARCITY

RANDOMLY INSERTED INTO PACKS

URAA Austin Aries	3.00	8.00
URAB Alexa Bliss	8.00	20.00
URAE Aiden English	1.50	4.00
URAF Alicia Fox	2.50	6.00
URAS Asuka	5.00	12.00
URBB Brie Bella	4.00	10.00
URBD Bo Dallas	1.50	4.00
URBE Becky Lynch	5.00	12.00
URBL Brock Lesnar	8.00	20.00
URBR Bobby Roode	4.00	10.00
URBS Big Show	2.00	5.00
URBW Bray Wyatt	4.00	10.00
URCA Carmella	4.00	10.00
URCU Curtis Axel	1.50	4.00
URDY Darren Young	1.50	4.00
URFB Finn Balor	6.00	15.00
URGO Goldust	2.00	5.00
URJC John Cena	8.00	20.00
URJO JoJo	2.50	6.00
URLH Luke Harper	1.50	4.00
URMR Mojo Rawley	2.00	5.00
URNA Natalya	3.00	8.00
URNE Neville	2.50	6.00
URRO Randy Orton	4.00	10.00
URRY Renee Young	2.50	6.00
URSB Sasha Banks	5.00	12.00
URSG Simon Gotch	1.50	4.00
URSH Sheamus	3.00	8.00
URSJ Samoa Joe	5.00	12.00
URSR Seth Rollins	5.00	12.00
URSR Summer Rae	4.00	10.00
URTA Tamina	2.00	5.00
URVI Viktor	1.50	4.00
URXW Xavier Woods	2.00	5.00
URZR Zack Ryder	1.50	4.00
URBCA Big Cass	2.00	5.00
URBIG Big E	2.00	5.00

2017 Topps WWE Undisputed Cut Signature

STATED PRINT RUN 1 SER.#'d SET

UNPRICED DUE TO SCARCITY

UTCYO Yokozuna

2017 Topps WWE Undisputed Triple Autographs

STATED PRINT RUN 10 SER.#'d SETS

UTAAKL Styles/Anderson/Gallows	100.00	200.00
UTABAE Bayley/Asuka/Moon	150.00	300.00
UTACSB Flair/Banks/Lynch	250.00	400.00
UTADSR Ambrose/Rollins/Reigns	125.00	250.00
UTANCA N.Bella/Carmella/Bliss	200.00	350.00

2017 Topps WWE Undisputed Women's Division

*BRONZE/99: .75X TO 2X BASIC CARDS

*SILVER/50: 1X TO 2.5X BASIC CARDS

*GREEN/25: 1.5X TO 4X BASIC CARDS

*GOLD/10: UNPRICED DUE TO SCARCITY

*RED/1: UNPRICED DUE TO SCARCITY

*P.P.BLACK/1: UNPRICED DUE TO SCARCITY

*P.P.CYAN/1: UNPRICED DUE TO SCARCITY

*P.P.MAGENTA/1: UNPRICED DUE TO SCARCITY

*P.P.YELLOW/1: UNPRICED DUE TO SCARCITY

RANDOMLY INSERTED INTO PACKS

W1 Alexa Bliss	4.00	10.00
W2 Alicia Fox	1.25	3.00
W3 Bayley	2.50	6.00
W4 Becky Lynch	2.50	6.00
W5 Carmella	2.00	5.00
W6 Charlotte Flair	3.00	8.00
W7 Dana Brooke	1.50	4.00
W8 Eva Marie	2.00	5.00
W9 Lana	2.50	6.00
W10 Maryse	1.50	4.00
W11 Mickie James	1.25	3.00
W12 Naomi	1.50	4.00
W13 Natalya	1.50	4.00
W14 Nia Jax	1.25	3.00
W15 Nikki Bella	2.00	5.00
W16 Sasha Banks	2.50	6.00
W17 Asuka	2.50	6.00
W18 Ember Moon	2.00	5.00
W19 Liv Morgan	1.25	3.00

2018 Topps WWE Undisputed

COMPLETE SET (50)	20.00	50.00
UNOPENED BOX (10 PACKS)	200.00	250.00
UNOPENED PACK (5 CARDS)	20.00	25.00

*ORANGE/99: .6X TO 1.5X BASIC CARDS

*GREEN/50: .75X TO 2X BASIC CARDS

*BLUE/25: 1X TO 2.5X BASIC CARDS

*GOLD/10: 2X TO 5X BASIC CARDS

*PURPLE/5: UNPRICED DUE TO SCARCITY

*RED/1: UNPRICED DUE TO SCARCITY

*P.P.BLACK/1: UNPRICED DUE TO SCARCITY

*P.P.CYAN/1: UNPRICED DUE TO SCARCITY

*P.P.MAGENTA/1: UNPRICED DUE TO SCARCITY

*P.P.YELLOW/1: UNPRICED DUE TO SCARCITY

1 AJ Styles	2.50	6.00
2 Alexa Bliss	3.00	8.00
3 Asuka	2.00	5.00
4 Bayley	1.00	2.50
5 Becky Lynch	1.50	4.00
6 Big E	.75	2.00
7 Bobby Roode	1.00	2.50
8 Brie Bella	1.25	3.00
9 Braun Strowman	1.50	4.00
10 Bray Wyatt	1.50	4.00
11 Brock Lesnar	2.50	6.00
12 Carmella	1.25	3.00
13 Cesaro	1.25	3.00
14 Charlotte Flair	2.00	5.00
15 Chris Jericho	1.50	4.00
16 Daniel Bryan	1.50	4.00
17 Dean Ambrose	1.25	3.00
18 Finn Balor	1.50	4.00
19 Jason Jordan	.60	1.50
20 Jeff Hardy	1.25	3.00
21 John Cena	2.50	6.00
22 Kane	1.00	2.50
23 Kevin Owens	1.50	4.00
24 Kofi Kingston	.75	2.00
25 Kurt Angle	1.50	4.00
26 Woken Matt Hardy	1.50	4.00
27 Mickie James	1.25	3.00
28 Naomi	.75	2.00
29 Natalya	.75	2.00
30 Nia Jax	1.00	2.50
31 Nikki Bella	1.25	3.00
32 Paige	1.50	4.00
33 Randy Orton	1.50	4.00
34 Roman Reigns	1.50	4.00
35 Ruby Riott	1.00	2.50
36 Sami Zayn	.60	1.50
37 Samoa Joe	1.25	3.00
38 Sasha Banks	2.00	5.00
39 Seth Rollins	1.50	4.00
40 Sheamus	1.25	3.00
41 Shinsuke Nakamura	1.50	4.00
42 The Miz	1.25	3.00
43 Triple H	1.50	4.00
44 Undertaker	2.50	6.00
45 Xavier Woods	.75	2.00
46 Adam Cole RC	.75	2.00
47 Aleister Black	.75	2.00
48 Drew McIntyre	1.00	2.50
49 Ember Moon	1.25	3.00
50 Kairi Sane RC	1.50	4.00

2018 Topps WWE Undisputed 30 Years of Royal Rumble

COMPLETE SET (25)	12.00	30.00

*ORANGE/99: .5X TO 1.2X BASIC CARDS

*GREEN/50: .6X TO 1.5X BASIC CARDS

*BLUE/25: .75X TO 2X BASIC CARDS

*GOLD/10: 1.2X TO 3X BASIC CARDS

*PURPLE/5: UNPRICED DUE TO SCARCITY

*RED/1: UNPRICED DUE TO SCARCITY

*P.P.BLACK/1: UNPRICED DUE TO SCARCITY

*P.P.CYAN/1: UNPRICED DUE TO SCARCITY

*P.P.MAGENTA/1: UNPRICED DUE TO SCARCITY

*P.P.YELLOW/1: UNPRICED DUE TO SCARCITY

RANDOMLY INSERTED INTO PACKS

RR1 Hacksaw Jim Duggan	.60	1.50
RR2 Big John Studd	.60	1.50
RR3 Ric Flair	2.00	5.00
RR4 Yokozuna	.75	2.00
RR5 Bret Hit Man Hart	1.50	4.00
RR6 Lex Luger	.75	2.00
RR7 Shawn Michaels	2.00	5.00
RR8 Shawn Michaels	2.00	5.00
RR9 Stone Cold Steve Austin	3.00	8.00
RR10 Stone Cold Steve Austin	3.00	8.00
RR11 The Rock	3.00	8.00
RR12 Stone Cold Steve Austin	3.00	8.00
RR13 Triple H	1.50	4.00
RR14 Brock Lesnar	2.50	6.00
RR15 Batista	1.00	2.50
RR16 Undertaker	2.50	6.00
RR17 John Cena	2.50	6.00
RR18 Randy Orton	1.50	4.00
RR19 Edge	1.50	4.00
RR20 Sheamus	1.25	3.00
RR21 John Cena	2.50	6.00
RR22 Batista	1.00	2.50
RR23 Roman Reigns	1.50	4.00
RR24 Triple H	1.50	4.00
RR25 Randy Orton	1.50	4.00

2018 Topps WWE Undisputed 30 Years of Survivor Series

COMPLETE SET (25) 12.00 30.00
*ORANGE/99: .5X TO 1.2X BASIC CARDS
*GREEN/50: .6X TO 1.5X BASIC CARDS
*BLUE/25: .75X TO 2X BASIC CARDS
*GOLD/10: 1.2X TO 3X BASIC CARDS
*PURPLE/5: UNPRICED DUE TO SCARCITY
*RED/1: UNPRICED DUE TO SCARCITY
*P.P.BLACK/1: UNPRICED DUE TO SCARCITY
*P.P.CYAN/1: UNPRICED DUE TO SCARCITY
*P.P.MAGENTA/1: UNPRICED DUE TO SCARCITY
*P.P.YELLOW/1: UNPRICED DUE TO SCARCITY
RANDOMLY INSERTED INTO PACKS

SS1 Andre The Giant 1.25 3.00
SS2 Macho Man Randy Savage 2.00 5.00
SS3 Ultimate Warrior 2.50 6.00
SS4 Ultimate Warrior 2.50 6.00
SS5 Big Boss Man .60 1.50
SS6 The Nasty Boys .60 1.50
SS7 Lex Luger .75 2.00
SS8 Ted DiBiase .75 2.00
SS9 Shawn Michaels 2.00 5.00
SS10 Ken Shamrock .75 2.00
SS11 The Rock 3.00 8.00
SS12 Chris Jericho 1.50 4.00
SS13 Randy Orton 1.50 4.00
SS14 Batista 1.00 2.50
SS15 John Cena 2.50 6.00
SS16 Randy Orton 1.50 4.00
SS17 Mickie James 1.25 3.00
SS18 Kofi Kingston .75 2.00
SS19 Dolph Ziggler .75 2.00
SS20 Dolph Ziggler .75 2.00
SS21 Natalya .75 2.00
SS22 John Cena 2.50 6.00
SS23 The Usos 1.00 2.50
SS24 AJ Styles 2.50 6.00
SS25 Kurt Angle 1.50 4.00

2018 Topps WWE Undisputed Autographed Kiss and Shirt Relic Booklets

STATED ODDS 1:1,500
STATED PRINT RUN 5 SER.#'d SETS
UNPRICED DUE TO SCARCITY

KSAF Alicia Fox
KSEM Ember Moon
KSNA Natalya
KSNB Nikki Bella
KSRY Renee Young

2018 Topps WWE Undisputed Autographed Relics

*SILVER/50: .5X TO 1.2X BASIC AUTOS
*BLUE/25: UNPRICED DUE TO SCARCITY
*GOLD/10: UNPRICED DUE TO SCARCITY
*PURPLE/5: UNPRICED DUE TO SCARCITY
*RED/1: UNPRICED DUE TO SCARCITY
*P.P.BLACK/1: UNPRICED DUE TO SCARCITY
*P.P.CYAN/1: UNPRICED DUE TO SCARCITY
*P.P.MAGENTA/1: UNPRICED DUE TO SCARCITY
*P.P.YELLOW/1: UNPRICED DUE TO SCARCITY
STATED ODDS 1:10
STATED PRINT RUN 99 SER.#'d SETS

URAA Andrade Cien Almas 8.00 20.00
URAB Alexa Bliss 60.00 120.00
URAE Aiden English 5.00 12.00
URAF Alicia Fox 15.00 40.00
URAK Akam 6.00 15.00
URAP Apollo Crews 5.00 12.00
URAW Alexander Wolfe 6.00 15.00
URAX Curtis Axel 5.00 12.00
URBK Becky Lynch 30.00 75.00
URCA Carmella 20.00 50.00
URCF Charlotte Flair 20.00 50.00
URCG Chad Gable 6.00 15.00
URDW Dash Wilder 6.00 15.00
UREY Eric Young 8.00 20.00
URFN Fandango 5.00 12.00
URGD Goldust 10.00 25.00
URHA Harper 6.00 15.00
URJJ JoJo 15.00 40.00
URJO Jason Jordan 5.00 12.00
URJU Jimmy Uso 6.00 15.00
URKA Karl Anderson 5.00 12.00
URLG Luke Gallows 6.00 15.00
URNA Naomi 10.00 25.00
URNC Nikki Cross 10.00 25.00
URNT Natalya 12.00 30.00
URNW No Way Jose 8.00 20.00
URRE Rezar 6.00 15.00
URRY Renee Young 15.00 40.00
URSB Sasha Banks 25.00 60.00
URSD Scott Dawson 6.00 15.00
URSR Seth Rollins 15.00 40.00
URTC Tommaso Ciampa 8.00 20.00
URZR Zack Ryder 6.00 15.00

2018 Topps WWE Undisputed Autographs

*ORANGE/99: .5X TO 1.2X BASIC AUTOS
*GREEN/50: .6X TO 1.5X BASIC AUTOS
*BLUE/25: UNPRICED DUE TO SCARCITY
*GOLD/10: UNPRICED DUE TO SCARCITY
*PURPLE/5: UNPRICED DUE TO SCARCITY
*RED/1: UNPRICED DUE TO SCARCITY
*P.P.BLACK/1: UNPRICED DUE TO SCARCITY
*P.P.CYAN/1: UNPRICED DUE TO SCARCITY
*P.P.MAGENTA/1: UNPRICED DUE TO SCARCITY
*P.P.YELLOW/1: UNPRICED DUE TO SCARCITY
RANDOMLY INSERTED INTO PACKS

UAAB Alexa Bliss 30.00 75.00
UAAC Adam Cole 12.00 30.00
UAAJ AJ Styles 20.00 50.00
UAAS Asuka 15.00 40.00
UABA Bayley 15.00 40.00
UABC Baron Corbin 6.00 15.00
UABE Big E 6.00 15.00
UABF Bobby Fish 8.00 20.00
UABL Becky Lynch 25.00 60.00
UABR Bobby Roode 10.00 25.00
UABW Bray Wyatt 10.00 25.00
UACA Carmella 12.00 30.00
UACE Cesaro 6.00 15.00
UACF Charlotte Flair 15.00 40.00
UACG Chad Gable 4.00 10.00
UADA Dean Ambrose 8.00 20.00
UADB Daniel Bryan 15.00 40.00
UADM Drew McIntyre 10.00 25.00
UADW Dash Wilder 5.00 12.00
UAEL Elias 15.00 40.00
UAEY Eric Young 5.00 12.00
UAFA Fandango 8.00 20.00
UAFB Finn Balor 15.00 40.00
UAHI Hideo Itami 6.00 15.00
UAJH Jeff Hardy 12.00 30.00
UAJJ Jason Jordan 6.00 15.00
UAJM Jinder Mahal 6.00 15.00
UAKA Karl Anderson 4.00 10.00
UAKK Kofi Kingston 4.00 10.00
UAKO Kevin Owens 12.00 30.00
UAKS Kairi Sane 25.00 60.00
UALA Lana 8.00 20.00
UAMH Matt Hardy 10.00 25.00
UAMK Maria Kanellis 8.00 20.00
UAMR Mojo Rawley 4.00 10.00
UANA Naomi 5.00 12.00
UANJ Nia Jax 10.00 25.00
UARS Roderick Strong 6.00 15.00
UARU Rusev 5.00 12.00
UASB Sasha Banks 20.00 50.00
UASD Scott Dawson 4.00 10.00
UASH Sheamus 6.00 15.00
UASJ Samoa Joe 10.00 25.00
UASN Shinsuke Nakamura 10.00 25.00
UASR Seth Rollins 12.00 30.00
UAST Sting 15.00 40.00
UASZ Sami Zayn 5.00 12.00
UATB Tyler Breeze 6.00 15.00
UATD Tye Dillinger 5.00 12.00
UATM The Miz 8.00 20.00
UAVD Velveteen Dream 15.00 40.00
UAXW Xavier Woods 5.00 12.00
UAZR Zack Ryder 4.00 10.00
UAABL Aleister Black 10.00 20.00
UABCA Big Cass 5.00 12.00
UABRS Braun Strowman 12.00 30.00
UAEMB Ember Moon 12.00 30.00
UAKOH Kassius Ohno 6.00 15.00
UAKUA Kurt Angle 12.00 30.00
UAKYO Kyle O'Reilly 6.00 15.00
UAMAR Maryse 10.00 25.00
UANAT Natalya 8.00 20.00
UARRI Ruby Riott 8.00 20.00
UASBE Shelton Benjamin 6.00 15.00

2018 Topps WWE Undisputed Classic Matches Dual Autographed Relics

*PURPLE/5: UNPRICED DUE TO SCARCITY
*RED/1: UNPRICED DUE TO SCARCITY
STATED ODDS 1:766
STATED PRINT RUN 10 SER.#'d SETS
UNPRICED DUE TO SCARCITY

ARBH HHH/D.Bryan
ARDS Sheamus/D.Bryan
ARRH HHH/S.Rollins
ARRU Undertaker/R.Reigns

2018 Topps WWE Undisputed Cut Signatures

STATED ODDS 1:19,120
STATED PRINT RUN 1 SER.#'d SET
UNPRICED DUE TO SCARCITY

CSCH Mr. Perfect Curt Hennig
CSEG Eddie Guerrero

2018 Topps WWE Undisputed Dual Autographs

*GOLD/10: UNPRICED DUE TO SCARCITY
*PURPLE/5: UNPRICED DUE TO SCARCITY
*RED/1: UNPRICED DUE TO SCARCITY
STATED ODDS 1:154
STATED PRINT RUN 25 SER.#'d SETS

DAAJ K.Angle/J.Jordan 25.00 60.00
DAAR D.Ambrose/S.Rollins 30.00 75.00
DABG S.Benjamin/C.Gable 15.00 40.00
DACS Sheamus/Cesaro 15.00 40.00
DAFB T.Breeze/Fandango 30.00 75.00
DAGA K.Anderson/L.Gallows 25.00 60.00
DAHH J.Hardy/M.Hardy 60.00 120.00
DARR M.Rawley/Z.Ryder 30.00 75.00
DATM HHH/S.McMahon 150.00 300.00
DAWD S.Dawson/D.Wilder 15.00 40.00

2018 Topps WWE Undisputed Quad Autographed Booklets

STATED ODDS 1:1,500
STATED PRINT RUN 5 SER.#'d SETS
UNPRICED DUE TO SCARCITY

QAAUTH HHH/McMahon/Rollins/Orton
QATEAMA Benjamin/Jordan/Gable/Angle
QAWYATT Wyatt/Strowman/Harper/Rowan
QASANITY Cross/Wolfe/Dain/Young
QATHEMIZ Axel/Maryse/Miz/Dallas

2018 Topps WWE Undisputed Relics

*GREEN/50: .6X TO 1.2X BASIC MEM
*BLUE/25: .75X TO 2X BASIC MEM
*GOLD/10: 1.5X TO 4X BASIC MEM
*PURPLE/5: UNPRICED DUE TO SCARCITY
*RED/1: UNPRICED DUE TO SCARCITY
*P.P.BLACK/1: UNPRICED DUE TO SCARCITY
*P.P.CYAN/1: UNPRICED DUE TO SCARCITY
*P.P.MAGENTA/1: UNPRICED DUE TO SCARCITY
*P.P.YELLOW/1: UNPRICED DUE TO SCARCITY
STATED ODDS 1:10
STATED PRINT RUN 99 SER.#'d SETS

URAA Andrade Cien Almas 5.00 12.00
URAB Alexa Bliss 12.00 30.00
URAE Aiden English 2.00 5.00
URAF Alicia Fox 5.00 12.00
URAK Akam 2.00 5.00
URAW Alexander Wolfe 2.50 6.00
URAX Curtis Axel 3.00 8.00
URBC Baron Corbin 2.50 6.00
URBE Big E 2.50 6.00
URBK Becky Lynch 10.00 25.00
URBL Brock Lesnar 6.00 15.00
URBR Bobby Roode 2.50 6.00
URCA Carmella 8.00 20.00
URCF Charlotte Flair 6.00 15.00
URCG Chad Gable 2.50 6.00
URDB Daniel Bryan 5.00 12.00
URDW Dash Wilder 3.00 8.00
UREM Ember Moon 5.00 12.00
UREY Eric Young 2.50 6.00
URGD Goldust 3.00 8.00
URHA Harper 2.00 5.00
LRHI Hideo Itami 2.00 5.00
LRJC John Cena 10.00 25.00
LRJJ JoJo 6.00 15.00
LRJO Jason Jordan 2.00 5.00
LRJU Jimmy Uso 3.00 8.00
LRKA Karl Anderson 3.00 8.00
URKK Kofi Kingston 2.50 6.00
URKO Kevin Owens 2.50 6.00
URLG Luke Gallows 2.00 5.00
URNA Naomi 2.50 6.00
URNC Nikki Cross 6.00 15.00
URNT Natalya 3.00 8.00
URNW No Way Jose 2.00 5.00
URRE Rezar 2.00 5.00
URRR Roman Reigns 6.00 15.00
URRY Renee Young 5.00 12.00
JRSB Sasha Banks 12.00 30.00
JRSD Scott Dawson 2.00 5.00
JRSR Seth Rollins 2.50 6.00
JRTC Tommaso Ciampa 6.00 15.00
JRXW Xavier Woods 2.50 6.00

2018 Topps WWE Undisputed Rivals Dual Autograph and Championship Booklets

STATED ODDS 1:1,500
STATED PRINT RUN 5 SER.#'d SETS
UNPRICED DUE TO SCARCITY

ACAC B.Corbin/D.Ambrose
ACBF Bayley/C.Flair
ACNB A.Bliss/Naomi
ACOJ C.Jericho/K.Owens
ACOW B.Wyatt/R.Orton

2018 Topps WWE Undisputed Triple Autographs

*PURPLE/5: UNPRICED DUE TO SCARCITY
*RED/1: UNPRICED DUE TO SCARCITY
STATED ODDS 1:475
STATED PRINT RUN 10 SER.#'d SETS

TACFO O'Reilly/Cole/Fish
TAKBW Kingston/Woods/Big E
TAMAD Miz/Axel/Dallas
TAOTC O'Neil/Crews/Tozawa
TASGA Anderson/Gallows/Styles
TAUUN J.Uso/J.Uso/Naomi
TAYWD Dain/Young/Wolfe

2018 Topps WWE Undisputed Triple Shirt Relics

*GOLD/10: UNPRICED DUE TO SCARCITY
*PURPLE/5: UNPRICED DUE TO SCARCITY
*RED/1: UNPRICED DUE TO SCARCITY
STATED ODDS 1:310
STATED PRINT RUN 25 SER.#'d SETS

TSBGA Gallows/Balor/Anderson 20.00 50.00
TSDAY Woods/Kingston/Big E 12.00 30.00
TSNUU The Usos/Naomi 15.00 40.00
TSOZB Zayn/Bryan/Owens 12.00 30.00
TSRRJ Rollins/Reigns/Jordan 15.00 40.00

2019 Topps WWE Undisputed

COMPLETE SET (100) 25.00 60.00
*ORANGE/99: .6X TO 1.5X BASIC CARDS
*GREEN/50: .75X TO 2X BASIC CARDS
*BLUE/25: 1X TO 2.5X BASIC CARDS
*GOLD/10: UNPRICED DUE TO SCARCITY
*PURPLE/5: UNPRICED DUE TO SCARCITY
*RED/1: UNPRICED DUE TO SCARCITY
*P.P.BLACK/1: UNPRICED DUE TO SCARCITY
*P.P.CYAN/1: UNPRICED DUE TO SCARCITY
*P.P.MAGENTA/1: UNPRICED DUE TO SCARCITY
*P.P.YELLOW/1: UNPRICED DUE TO SCARCITY

1 Aiden English .50 1.25
2 AJ Styles 2.50 6.00

3 Alexa Bliss 2.50 6.00
4 Alexander Wolfe .50 1.25
5 Andrade .60 1.50
6 Asuka 1.50 4.00
7 Baron Corbin .75 2.00
8 Bayley 1.00 2.50
9 Becky Lynch 2.00 5.00
10 Big E .50 1.25
11 Billie Kay 1.00 2.50
12 Bo Dallas .60 1.50
13 Bobby Lashley 1.00 2.50
14 Bobby Roode 1.00 2.50
15 Braun Strowman 1.25 3.00
16 Bray Wyatt 1.25 3.00
17 Carmella 1.25 3.00
18 Cedric Alexander .50 1.25
19 Cesaro .60 1.50
20 Charlotte Flair 2.00 5.00
21 Curtis Axel .60 1.50
22 Daniel Bryan 1.25 3.00
23 Dash Wilder .50 1.25
24 Dolph Ziggler 1.00 2.50
25 Drake Maverick .50 1.25
26 Drew Gulak .50 1.25
27 Drew McIntyre .60 1.50
28 Elias 1.00 2.50
29 Ember Moon 1.25 3.00
30 Eric Young .60 1.50
31 Finn Balor 1.00 2.50
32 Harper .60 1.50
33 Jeff Hardy 1.25 3.00
34 Jey Uso .60 1.50
35 Jimmy Uso .60 1.50
36 Jinder Mahal 1.00 2.50
37 John Cena 2.50 6.00
38 Karl Anderson .75 2.00
39 Kevin Owens 1.25 3.00
40 Killian Dain .50 1.25
41 Kofi Kingston .75 2.00
42 Kurt Angle 1.00 2.50
43 Lacey Evans 1.00 2.50
44 Lio Rush .60 1.50
45 Liv Morgan 1.50 4.00
46 Luke Gallows .75 2.00
47 Mustafa Ali .50 1.25
48 Naomi .75 2.00
49 Natalya 1.00 2.50
50 Nia Jax 1.00 2.50
51 Paige 2.00 5.00
52 Peyton Royce 1.25 3.00
53 Randy Orton 1.25 3.00
54 Rey Mysterio 1.25 3.00
55 Roman Reigns 1.25 3.00
56 Ronda Rousey 2.50 6.00
57 Rowan .50 1.25
58 Ruby Riott 1.00 2.50
59 Rusev 1.00 2.50
60 Sami Zayn 1.00 2.50
61 Samoa Joe 1.00 2.50
62 Sarah Logan .60 1.50
63 Sasha Banks 2.00 5.00
64 Scott Dawson .50 1.25
65 Seth Rollins 1.25 3.00
66 Sheamus .75 2.00
67 Shelton Benjamin .60 1.50
68 Shinsuke Nakamura 1.25 3.00
69 The Miz 1.00 2.50
70 The Rock 2.50 6.00
71 Titus O'Neil .60 1.50
72 Triple H 1.25 3.00
73 Undertaker 2.50 6.00
74 Xavier Woods .60 1.50
75 Zelina Vega .75 2.00
76 Adam Cole .60 1.50
77 Aleister Black .60 1.50
78 Deonna Purrazzo RC .50 1.25
79 EC3 .50 1.25
80 Johnny Gargano .50 1.25
81 Kairi Sane 1.00 2.50
82 Keith Lee RC .50 1.25
83 Nikki Cross .75 2.00
84 Ricochet 1.25 3.00
85 Shayna Baszler 1.00 2.50
86 Tommaso Ciampa .50 1.25
87 Goldberg 1.50 4.00
88 Shawn Michaels 1.25 3.00
89 Sting 1.25 3.00
90 Trish Stratus 2.50 6.00
RS1 Finn Balor 1.00 2.50
RS2 Jeff Hardy 1.25 3.00
RS3 Sasha Banks 2.00 5.00
RS4 Bayley 1.00 2.50
RS5 Seth Rollins 1.25 3.00
RS6 Shinsuke Nakamura 1.25 3.00
RS7 Aleister Black .60 1.50
RS8 Ricochet 1.25 3.00
RS9 Sting 1.25 3.00
RS10 Ric Flair 1.50 4.00

2019 Topps WWE Undisputed Autographed Kiss and Shirt Relic Booklet

STATED PRINT RUN 5 SER.#'d SETS
UNPRICED DUE TO SCARCITY
AKSAF Alicia Fox

2019 Topps WWE Undisputed Autographed Relics

*GREEN/50: .5X TO 1.2X BASIC AUTOS
*BLUE/25: .6X TO 1.5X BASIC AUTOS
*GOLD/10: UNPRICED DUE TO SCARCITY
*PURPLE/5: UNPRICED DUE TO SCARCITY
*RED/1: UNPRICED DUE TO SCARCITY
STATED PRINT RUN 120 SER.#'d SETS
UAR4H Shayna Baszler 10.00 25.00
UARAA Andrade 12.00 30.00
UARAB Alexa Bliss 60.00 120.00
UARAC Adam Cole 10.00 25.00
UARAE Aiden English 6.00 15.00
UARAK Asuka 20.00 50.00
UARBD Bo Dallas 6.00 15.00
UARBS Braun Strowman 12.00 30.00
UARCA Curtis Axel 6.00 15.00
UARCM Carmella 15.00 40.00
UARCS Cesaro 6.00 15.00
UARDW Dash Wilder 6.00 15.00
UAREL Elias 10.00 25.00
UARFB Finn Balor 12.00 30.00
UARJH Jeff Hardy 12.00 30.00
UARKD Killian Dain 6.00 15.00
UARKK Kofi Kingston 12.00 30.00
UARLG Luke Gallows 6.00 15.00
UARLM Liv Morgan 25.00 60.00
UARMG Karl Anderson 6.00 15.00
UARNJ Nia Jax 8.00 20.00
UARNM Naomi 8.00 20.00
UARNN Natalya 10.00 25.00
UARNW No Way Jose 6.00 15.00
UARRB Ruby Riott 12.00 30.00
UARRC Ricochet 20.00 50.00
UARSB Sasha Banks 20.00 50.00
UARSD Scott Dawson 6.00 15.00
UARSM Sheamus 6.00 15.00
UARSR Seth Rollins 8.00 20.00
UARSZ Sami Zayn 6.00 15.00
UARTC Tommaso Ciampa 10.00 25.00
UARTM The Miz 10.00 25.00
UARVD Velveteen Dream 10.00 25.00
UARXW Xavier Woods 6.00 15.00
UARZR Zack Ryder 6.00 15.00

2019 Topps WWE Undisputed Autographed Relics Blue

UARCH Curt Hawkins 10.00 25.00

2019 Topps WWE Undisputed Autographed Relics Green

UARAF Alicia Fox 8.00 20.00

2019 Topps WWE Undisputed Autographed Tag Team Championship Medallion Booklets

STATED PRINT RUN 5 SER.#'d SETS
UNPRICED DUE TO SCARCITY
DACBT C.Axel/B.Dallas
DACND X.Woods/K.Kingston
DACTB Cesaro/Sheamus
DACUSO Jey and Jimmy Uso

2019 Topps WWE Undisputed Autographs

*GOLD/10: UNPRICED DUE TO SCARCITY
*PURPLE/5: UNPRICED DUE TO SCARCITY
*RED/1: UNPRICED DUE TO SCARCITY
*P.P.BLACK/1: UNPRICED DUE TO SCARCITY
*P.P.CYAN/1: UNPRICED DUE TO SCARCITY
*P.P.MAGENTA/1: UNPRICED DUE TO SCARCITY
*P.P.YELLOW/1: UNPRICED DUE TO SCARCITY
STATED PRINT RUN 199 SER.#'d SETS
AAA Andrade Almas 5.00 12.00
AAB Alexa Bliss 50.00 100.00
AAC Adam Cole 10.00 25.00
AAL Aleister Black 8.00 20.00
AAS AJ Styles 15.00 40.00
AAW Alexander Wolfe 5.00 12.00
ABC Baron Corbin 5.00 12.00
ABD Bo Dallas 5.00 12.00
ABE Big E 6.00 15.00
ABL Becky Lynch 25.00 60.00
ABR Bobby Roode 8.00 20.00
ABS Braun Strowman 10.00 25.00
ACA Cedric Alexander 5.00 12.00
ACE Cesaro 5.00 12.00
ACF Charlotte Flair 20.00 50.00
ACJ Cactus Jack 15.00 40.00
ACU Curtis Axel 5.00 12.00
ADK Dakota Kai 12.00 30.00
ADM Drew McIntyre 6.00 15.00
ADP Deonna Purrazzo 20.00 50.00
AEC EC3 5.00 12.00
AEY Eric Young 5.00 12.00
AFB Finn Balor 12.00 30.00
AJF Jeff Hardy 12.00 30.00
AJG Johnny Gargano 6.00 15.00
AJM Jinder Mahal 5.00 12.00
AKA Kurt Angle 10.00 25.00
AKD Killian Dain 5.00 12.00
AKK Kofi Kingston 10.00 25.00
AKL Keith Lee 6.00 15.00
AKR Kyle O'Reilly 5.00 12.00
AKS Kairi Sane 15.00 40.00
ALR Lio Rush 5.00 12.00
AMA Maryse 10.00 25.00
AME Carmella 10.00 25.00
AMR Mandy Rose 15.00 40.00
ANA Naomi 6.00 15.00
ANJ Nia Jax 8.00 20.00
ANN Natalya 5.00 12.00
APD Pete Dunne 6.00 15.00
ARI Ricochet 20.00 50.00
ARM Rey Mysterio 12.00 30.00
ARS Roderick Strong 5.00 12.00
ARU Rusev 5.00 12.00
ARY Renee Young 6.00 15.00
ASD Sonya Deville 12.00 30.00
ASH Sheamus 5.00 12.00
ASN Shinsuke Nakamura 10.00 25.00
AST Sting 15.00 40.00
ASU Asuka 15.00 40.00
ASZ Sami Zayn 5.00 12.00
ATC Tommaso Ciampa 8.00 20.00
ATM The Miz 10.00 25.00
ATN Titus O'Neil 5.00 12.00
AVD Velveteen Dream 10.00 25.00
AXW Xavier Woods 5.00 12.00
AZV Zelina Vega 12.00 30.00
ABAS Shayna Baszler 10.00 25.00
AE Elias 8.00 20.00

2019 Topps WWE Undisputed Cut Signatures

STATED PRINT RUN 1 SER.#'d SET
UNPRICED DUE TO SCARCITY
CSDR Dusty Rhodes
CSEG Eddie Guerrero
CSJN Jim "The Anvil" Neidhart

2019 Topps WWE Undisputed Dual Autographs

*GOLD/10: UNPRICED DUE TO SCARCITY
*PURPLE/5: UNPRICED DUE TO SCARCITY
*RED/1: UNPRICED DUE TO SCARCITY
STATED PRINT RUN 25 SER.#'d SETS
DTI B.Kay/P.Royce 125.00 250.00
DTR D.Wilder/S.Dawson 50.00 100.00
DUE R.Strong/K.O'Reilly 25.00 60.00
DWR Hanson/Rowe 100.00 200.00

2019 Topps WWE Undisputed Quad Autographs Booklets

STATED PRINT RUN 5 SER.#'d SETS
UNPRICED DUE TO SCARCITY
QHW Flair/Lynch/Banks/Bayley
QUE Strong/O'Reilly/Fish/Cole

2019 Topps WWE Undisputed Relics

*GREEN/50: .5X TO 1.2X BASIC MEM
*BLUE/25: .6X TO 1.5X BASIC MEM
*GOLD/10: UNPRICED DUE TO SCARCITY
*PURPLE/5: UNPRICED DUE TO SCARCITY
*RED/1: UNPRICED DUE TO SCARCITY
STATED PRINT RUN 99 SER.#'d SETS
UR4H Shayna Baszler 4.00 10.00
URAA Andrade 4.00 10.00
URAB Alexa Bliss 12.00 30.00
URAC Adam Cole 6.00 15.00
URAF Alicia Fox 4.00 10.00
URAK Asuka 5.00 12.00
URBD Bo Dallas 4.00 10.00
URBS Braun Strowman 5.00 12.00
URCA Curtis Axel 5.00 12.00
URCF Charlotte Flair 10.00 25.00
URCM Carmella 6.00 15.00
URCS Cesaro 3.00 8.00
URDW Dash Wilder 3.00 8.00
URDZ Dolph Ziggler 4.00 10.00
UREL Elias 3.00 8.00
UREM Ember Moon 5.00 12.00
URFB Finn Balor 5.00 12.00
URJC John Cena 6.00 15.00
URJH Jeff Hardy 5.00 12.00
URKD Killian Dain 5.00 12.00
URKK Kofi Kingston 4.00 10.00
URKO Kevin Owens 5.00 12.00
URLG Luke Gallows 4.00 10.00
URLM Liv Morgan 10.00 25.00
URMG Karl Anderson 4.00 10.00
URNJ Nia Jax 5.00 12.00
URNM Naomi 3.00 8.00
URNN Natalya 4.00 10.00
URNW No Way Jose 4.00 10.00
URRB Ruby Riott 4.00 10.00
URRC Ricochet 5.00 12.00
URRR Roman Reigns 6.00 15.00
URSB Sasha Banks 8.00 20.00
URSD Scott Dawson 3.00 8.00
URSM Sheamus 3.00 8.00
URSR Seth Rollins 5.00 12.00
URSZ Sami Zayn 3.00 8.00
URTC Tommaso Ciampa 5.00 12.00
URTM The Miz 3.00 8.00
URVD Velveteen Dream 4.00 10.00
URXW Xavier Woods 4.00 10.00
URZR Zack Ryder 5.00 12.00
URUCE Jey Uso 3.00 8.00
URUSO Jimmy Uso 3.00 8.00

2019 Topps WWE Undisputed Triple Autographs

*PURPLE/5: UNPRICED DUE TO SCARCITY
*RED/1: UNPRICED DUE TO SCARCITY
STATED PRINT RUN 10 SER.#'d SETS
UNPRICED DUE TO SCARCITY
TLP Kalisto/Metalik/Dorado
TND Big E/Woods/Kingston
TRD Rusev/Lana/English
TRS Logan/Riott/Morgan

2020 Topps WWE Undisputed

COMPLETE SET (90) 25.00 60.00
*ORANGE/99: .75X TO 2X BASIC CARDS
*GREEN/50: 1.2X TO 3X BASIC CARDS
*BLUE/25: UNPRICED DUE TO SCARCITY
*GOLD/10: UNPRICED DUE TO SCARCITY
*PURPLE/5: UNPRICED DUE TO SCARCITY

*RED/1: UNPRICED DUE TO SCARCITY
*P.P.BLACK/1: UNPRICED DUE TO SCARCITY
*P.P.CYAN/1: UNPRICED DUE TO SCARCITY
*P.P.MAGENTA/1: UNPRICED DUE TO SCARCITY
*P.P.YELLOW/1: UNPRICED DUE TO SCARCITY

1 Aleister Black 1.00 2.50
2 Andrade .75 2.00
3 Asuka 2.00 5.00
4 Becky Lynch 2.00 5.00
5 Bianca Belair 1.25 3.00
6 Bobby Lashley 1.00 2.50
7 Buddy Murphy .60 1.50
8 Charlotte Flair 2.00 5.00
9 Drew McIntyre 1.00 2.50
10 Edge 1.00 2.50
11 Erik .50 1.25
12 Humberto Carrillo .75 2.00
13 Ivar .50 1.25
14 Kairi Sane 1.00 2.50
15 Kevin Owens .60 1.50
16 Lana 1.25 3.00
17 Nia Jax .75 2.00
18 Randy Orton 1.25 3.00
19 Ricochet .75 2.00
20 Ruby Riott .75 2.00
21 R-Truth .50 1.25
22 Samoa Joe .75 2.00
23 Seth Rollins 1.00 2.50
24 Zelina Vega 1.00 2.50
25 AJ Styles 1.50 4.00
26 Alexa Bliss 3.00 8.00
27 Bayley 1.00 2.50
28 Big E .50 1.25
29 Braun Strowman 1.25 3.00
30 The Fiend Bray Wyatt 1.50 4.00
31 Carmella 1.25 3.00
32 Cesaro .50 1.25
33 Dana Brooke .75 2.00
34 Daniel Bryan 1.50 4.00
35 Dolph Ziggler .50 1.25
36 Elias .50 1.25
37 King Corbin .60 1.50
38 Kofi Kingston .75 2.00
39 Lacey Evans 1.25 3.00
40 Matt Riddle 1.00 2.50
41 Mustafa Ali .75 2.00
42 Naomi 1.00 2.50
43 Nikki Cross 1.00 2.50
44 Robert Roode .50 1.25
45 Roman Reigns 1.25 3.00
46 Sami Zayn .60 1.50
47 Sasha Banks 2.50 6.00
48 Sheamus .60 1.50
49 Shinsuke Nakamura 1.00 2.50
50 The Miz .75 2.00
51 Xavier Woods .50 1.25
52 Adam Cole 1.25 3.00
53 Bobby Fish .50 1.25
54 Candice LeRae 1.50 4.00
55 Dakota Kai 1.00 2.50
56 Damian Priest RC .50 1.25
57 Dominik Dijakovic .50 1.25
58 Finn Balor 1.25 3.00
59 Io Shirai .75 2.00
60 Johnny Gargano 1.00 2.50
61 Kay Lee Ray RC .75 2.00
62 Karrion Kross RC 1.00 2.50
63 Keith Lee .50 1.25
64 Kushida RC .60 1.50
65 Kyle OíReilly .60 1.50
66 Mia Yim 1.00 2.50
67 Pete Dunne .50 1.25
68 Rhea Ripley 2.00 5.00
69 Roderick Strong 1.00 2.50
70 Scarlett RC 2.00 5.00
71 Shayna Baszler 1.50 4.00
72 Tommaso Ciampa 1.00 2.50
73 Toni Storm 1.25 3.00
74 Velveteen Dream .60 1.50
75 Walter RC 1.00 2.50
76 John Cena 2.00 5.00
77 Ronda Rousey 2.50 6.00
78 Undertaker 2.00 5.00
79 Batista .75 2.00
80 Booker T 1.00 2.50
81 Bret Hit Man Hart 1.25 3.00
82 Diesel .75 2.00
83 Howard Finkel .50 1.25
84 Hulk Hogan 1.50 4.00
85 Lita 1.25 3.00
86 Mr. T 1.00 2.50
87 Razor Ramon .75 2.00
88 Rowdy Roddy Piper 1.25 3.00
89 Trish Stratus 2.50 6.00
90 Stone Cold Steve Austin 2.50 6.00

2020 Topps WWE Undisputed Autographed Dual Relics

*GREEN/50: .75X TO 2X BASIC AUTOS
*BLUE/25: UNPRICED DUE TO SCARCITY
*GOLD/10: UNPRICED DUE TO SCARCITY
*PURPLE/5: UNPRICED DUE TO SCARCITY
*RED/1: UNPRICED DUE TO SCARCITY
*P.P.BLACK/1: UNPRICED DUE TO SCARCITY
*P.P.CYAN/1: UNPRICED DUE TO SCARCITY
*P.P.MAGENTA/1: UNPRICED DUE TO SCARCITY
*P.P.YELLOW/1: UNPRICED DUE TO SCARCITY
STATED PRINT RUN 99 SER.#'d SETS

DRAAB Aleister Black 12.00 30.00
DRAAC Adam Cole 8.00 20.00
DRAAD Angelo Dawkins 8.00 20.00
DRAAJ AJ Styles 15.00 40.00
DRAAN Andrade/62 8.00 20.00
DRABB Bianca Belair 15.00 40.00
DRABF Bobby Fish 8.00 20.00
DRABO Bobby Lashley 8.00 20.00
DRABS Braun Strowman 10.00 25.00
DRACC Cesaro 6.00 15.00
DRACF Charlotte Flair 25.00 60.00
DRACS Cesaro 6.00 15.00
DRADZ Dolph Ziggler 6.00 15.00
DRAEK Erik 6.00 15.00
DRAFB Finn Balor 10.00 25.00
DRAJD Mia Yim 12.00 30.00
DRAJG Johnny Gargano 10.00 25.00
DRAKD Killian Dain 6.00 15.00
DRAKE Kevin Owens 8.00 20.00
DRAKK Kofi Kingston 8.00 20.00
DRAKO Kevin Owens 8.00 20.00
DRAKR Kyle OíReilly 6.00 15.00
DRALE Lacey Evans 15.00 40.00
DRALS Bobby Lashley 8.00 20.00
DRAMR Matt Riddle 12.00 30.00
DRAMZ The Miz 8.00 20.00
DRANJ Nia Jax 6.00 15.00
DRANT Natalya 10.00 25.00
DRAOT Otis 12.00 30.00
DRAPD The Demon Finn Balor 15.00 40.00
DRAPP Ricochet 10.00 25.00
DRARB Ruby Riott 15.00 40.00
DRARC Ricochet 10.00 25.00
DRARH Rhea Ripley 50.00 100.00
DRARS Roderick Strong 6.00 15.00
DRASH Shayna Baszler 15.00 40.00
DRASR Seth Rollins 8.00 20.00
DRATC Tommaso Ciampa 6.00 15.00
DRAVD Velveteen Dream/46
DRAXW Xavier Woods 6.00 15.00

2020 Topps WWE Undisputed Autographed Match Books

STATED PRINT RUN 5 SER.#'d SETS
UNPRICED DUE TO SCARCITY

MBCAS AJ Styles/Samoa Joe
MBCDT D.Bryan/Miz
MBCJT J.Gargano/T.Ciampa

2020 Topps WWE Undisputed Autographed Oversized Boxloaders

STATED PRINT RUN 5 SER.#'d SETS
UNPRICED DUE TO SCARCITY

BLAC Adam Cole
BLAJ AJ Styles
BLBA Bayley
BLBW The Fiend Bray Wyatt
BLKK Kofi Kingston
BLMR Matt Riddle
BLSB Sasha Banks
BLSN Shinsuke Nakamura
BLTM The Miz
BL4HW Shayna Baszler

2020 Topps WWE Undisputed Autographs

*ORANGE/99: .5X TO 1.2X BASIC AUTOS
*GREEN/50: .6X TO 1.5X BASIC AUTOS
*BLUE/25: UNPRICED DUE TO SCARCITY
*GOLD/10: UNPRICED DUE TO SCARCITY
*PURPLE/5: UNPRICED DUE TO SCARCITY
*RED/1: UNPRICED DUE TO SCARCITY
*P.P.BLACK/1: UNPRICED DUE TO SCARCITY
*P.P.CYAN/1: UNPRICED DUE TO SCARCITY
*P.P.MAGENTA/1: UNPRICED DUE TO SCARCITY
*P.P.YELLOW/1: UNPRICED DUE TO SCARCITY
STATED PRINT RUN 199 SER.#'d SETS

AAB Alexa Bliss 50.00 100.00
AAC Adam Cole 10.00 25.00
AAJ AJ Styles 12.00 30.00
AAN Andrade 6.00 15.00
AAS Asuka 30.00 75.00
AAT Aleister Black 8.00 20.00
AAZ Zelina Vega 15.00 40.00
ABA Bayley EXCH 15.00 40.00
ABB Bianca Belair 12.00 30.00
ABD Daniel Bryan 10.00 25.00
ABE Big E 6.00 15.00
ABF Bobby Fish 8.00 20.00
ABM Buddy Murphy 6.00 15.00
ABS Braun Strowman EXCH 10.00 25.00
ABT Booker T 10.00 25.00
ABW The Fiend Bray Wyatt 50.00 100.00
ACF Charlotte Flair 20.00 50.00
ACL Candice LeRae 15.00 40.00
ACM Carmella EXCH 15.00 40.00
ACS Cesaro 5.00 15.00
ADB Dana Brooke 10.00 25.00
ADD Dominik Dijakovic 8.00 20.00
ADK Dakota Kai 20.00 50.00
ADM Drew McIntyre 12.00 30.00
ADP Damian Priest 8.00 20.00
ADZ Dolph Ziggler 8.00 20.00
AHC Humberto Carrillo 6.00 15.00
AIO Io Shirai 30.00 75.00
AIV Ivar 6.00 15.00
AJG Johnny Gargano 6.00 15.00
AKC King Corbin 8.00 20.00
AKK Kofi Kingston 6.00 15.00
AKO Kevin Owens 6.00 15.00
AKS Kairi Sane 20.00 50.00
AKU Kushida 8.00 20.00
ALE Lacey Evans 15.00 40.00
ALN Lana EXCH 10.00 25.00
ALT Lita 20.00 50.00
AMA Mustafa Ali 8.00 20.00
AMR Matt Riddle 12.00 30.00
AMY Mia Yim 10.00 25.00
ANC Nikki Cross 10.00 25.00
ARB Ruby Riott 12.00 30.00
ARC Ricochet 8.00 20.00
ARD Kyle OíReilly 6.00 15.00
ARR Roman Reigns EXCH 15.00 40.00
ART R-Truth 12.00 30.00
ASB Sasha Banks 30.00 75.00
ASG Shorty G EXCH 8.00 20.00
ASJ Samoa Joe 6.00 15.00
ASM Sheamus 8.00 20.00
ASN Shinsuke Nakamura 6.00 15.00
ASR Seth Rollins 10.00 25.00
ASZ Sami Zayn 6.00 15.00
ATC Tommaso Ciampa 8.00 20.00
ATM The Miz 8.00 20.00
AVD Velveteen Dream EXCH 6.00 15.00
AVR Erik 8.00 20.00
A4HW Shayna Baszler 12.00 30.00
ABOB Bobby Lashley 8.00 20.00
ALEE Keith Lee 10.00 25.00
ARIP Rhea Ripley 60.00 120.00
AROD Roderick Strong EXCH 8.00 20.00

2020 Topps WWE Undisputed Cut Signatures

STATED PRINT RUN 1 SER.#'d SET
UNPRICED DUE TO SCARCITY

CSBB Bam Bam Bigelow
CSBH Bobby The Brain Heenan
CSBM Big Boss Man
CSBS Bruno Sammartino
CSDR Dusty Rhodes
CSEG Eddie Guerrero
CSGO Mean Gene Okerlund
CSJN Jim The Anvil Neidhart
CSJS Big John Studd
CSJT Earthquake
CSMP Mr. Perfect
CSNV Nikolai Volkoff
CSPB Paul Bearer
CSRP Rowdy Roddy Piper
CSRR Ravishing Rick Rude
CSRS Macho Man Randy Savage
CSUM Umaga
CSUW Ultimate Warrior
CSVD Big Van Vader
CSYO Yokozuna
CSDBS Davey Boy Smith

2020 Topps WWE Undisputed Dual Relics

*GREEN/50: .75X TO 2X BASIC MEM
*BLUE/25: UNPRICED DUE TO SCARCITY
*GOLD/10: UNPRICED DUE TO SCARCITY
*PURPLE/5: UNPRICED DUE TO SCARCITY
*RED/1: UNPRICED DUE TO SCARCITY
*P.P.BLACK/1: UNPRICED DUE TO SCARCITY
*P.P.CYAN/1: UNPRICED DUE TO SCARCITY
*P.P.MAGENTA/1: UNPRICED DUE TO SCARCITY
*P.P.YELLOW/1: UNPRICED DUE TO SCARCITY
STATED PRINT RUN 99 SER.#'d SETS

DRAB Aleister Black 3.00 8.00
DRAC Adam Cole 2.50 6.00
DRAD Angelo Dawkins 2.50 6.00
DRAJ AJ Styles 4.00 10.00
DRAN Andrade 2.00 5.00
DRBB Bianca Belair 3.00 8.00
DRBF Bobby Fish 2.00 5.00
DRBO Bobby Lashley 2.50 6.00
DRBS Braun Strowman 3.00 8.00
DRCF Charlotte Flair 5.00 12.00
DRCM Carmella 8.00 20.00
DRCS Cesaro 2.50 6.00
DRDZ Dolph Ziggler 2.50 6.00
DREK Erik 2.00 5.00
DREL Elias 2.50 6.00
DRFB Finn Balor 6.00 15.00
DRJD Mia Yim 5.00 12.00
DRJG Johnny Gargano 4.00 10.00
DRKD Killian Dain 2.00 5.00
DRKE Kevin Owens 3.00 8.00
DRKK Kofi Kingston 3.00 8.00
DRKO Kevin Owens 3.00 8.00
DRKR Kyle OíReilly 2.50 6.00
DRKS Kairi Sane 12.00 30.00
DRLE Lacey Evans 6.00 15.00
DRMR Matt Riddle 4.00 10.00
DRMZ The Miz 2.50 6.00
DRNJ Nia Jax 2.50 6.00
DRNT Natalya 3.00 8.00
DROT Otis 2.00 5.00
DRPD The Demon Finn Balor 6.00 15.00
DRRB Ruby Riott 5.00 12.00
DRRC Ricochet 3.00 8.00
DRRO Randy Orton 3.00 8.00
DRRR Roman Reigns 4.00 10.00
DRRS Roderick Strong 2.00 5.00
DRSM Shawn Michaels 4.00 10.00
DRSR Seth Rollins 3.00 8.00
DRTC Tommaso Ciampa 2.50 6.00
DRVD Velveteen Dream 2.00 5.00
DRXW Xavier Woods 2.50 6.00
DRHHH Triple H 4.00 10.00

2020 Topps WWE Undisputed Framed Autograph

STATED PRINT RUN 150 SER.#'d SETS

AFF Bray Wyatt 50.00 100.00

2020 Topps WWE Undisputed Quad Autographs

STATED PRINT RUN 5 SER.#'d SETS
UNPRICED DUE TO SCARCITY

QHW Banks/Flair/Lynch/Bayley
QIP Walter/Barthel/Aichner/Wolfe
QUE Cole/Fish/O'Reilly/Strong

2020 Topps WWE Undisputed Schamberger Art

COMPLETE SET (10) 20.00 50.00
RANDOMLY INSERTED INTO PACKS

RS1 Mustafa Ali 3.00 8.00
RS2 Asuka 5.00 12.00
RS3 Becky Lynch 5.00 12.00
RS4 Bianca Belair 3.00 8.00
RS5 Eddie Guerrero 4.00 10.00
RS6 Macho Man Randy Savage 6.00 15.00
RS7 The Miz 2.50 6.00
RS8 Toni Storm 6.00 15.00
RS9 Undertaker 4.00 10.00
RS10 Walter 2.00 5.00

2020 Topps WWE Undisputed Schamberger Art Autographs

STATED PRINT RUN 10 SER.#'d SETS
UNPRICED DUE TO SCARCITY

RSRSAS Schamberger/Ali
RSRSBB Schamberger/Asuka
RSRSBL Schamberger/Lynch
RSRSMA Schamberger/Belair
RSRSRG Schamberger/Guerrero
RSRSRS Schamberger/Savage
RSRSTM Schamberger/Miz
RSRSTS Schamberger/Storm
RSRSUT Schamberger/Undertaker
RSRSWT Schamberger/WALTER

2020 Topps WWE Undisputed Schamberger Art Superstar Autographs

STATED PRINT RUN 10 SER.#'d SETS
UNPRICED DUE TO SCARCITY

ARSAS Asuka
ARSBB Bianca Belair
ARSMA Mustafa Ali
ARSTM The Miz

2020 Topps WWE Undisputed Tag Team Autographs

*GOLD/10: UNPRICED DUE TO SCARCITY
*PURPLE/5: UNPRICED DUE TO SCARCITY
*RED/1: UNPRICED DUE TO SCARCITY
STATED PRINT RUN 25 SER.#'d SETS

DAKW K.Sane/Asuka 125.00 250.00
DASP A.Dawkins/M.Ford 30.00 75.00
DAVR Erik/Ivar 20.00 50.00

2020 Topps WWE Undisputed Triple Autographs

*PURPLE/5: UNPRICED DUE TO SCARCITY
*RED/1: UNPRICED DUE TO SCARCITY
STATED PRINT RUN 10 SER.#'d SETS
UNPRICED DUE TO SCARCITY

TALP Dorado/Metalik/Kalisto
TAND Woods/Big E/Kingston

2021 Topps WWE Undisputed

COMPLETE SET (74) 20.00 50.00
*PURPLE/99: .75X TO 2X BASIC CARDS
*GREEN/50: 1.2X TO 3X BASIC CARDS
*BLACK/25: UNPRICED DUE TO SCARCITY
*BLUE/10: UNPRICED DUE TO SCARCITY
*RED/5: UNPRICED DUE TO SCARCITY
*GOLD/1: UNPRICED DUE TO SCARCITY
*P.P.BLACK/1: UNPRICED DUE TO SCARCITY
*P.P.CYAN/1: UNPRICED DUE TO SCARCITY
*P.P.MAGENTA/1: UNPRICED DUE TO SCARCITY
*P.P.YELLOW/1: UNPRICED DUE TO SCARCITY

1 AJ Styles 1.50 4.00
2 Alexa Bliss 3.00 8.00
3 Angel Garza .60 1.50
4 Becky Lynch 2.00 5.00
5 Bobby Lashley 1.25 3.00
6 The Fiend Bray Wyatt 2.00 5.00
7 Charlotte Flair 2.50 6.00
8 Damian Priest .75 2.00
9 Dana Brooke .50 1.25
10 Drew McIntyre 1.25 3.00
11 Elias .50 1.25
12 Eva Marie 1.25 3.00
13 John Morrison 1.00 2.50
14 Keith Lee 1.00 2.50
15 MACE .50 1.25
16 Mandy Rose 2.50 6.00
17 Mustafa Ali .60 1.50
18 MVP .50 1.25
19 Nia Jax 1.00 2.50
20 Omos RC 1.00 2.50
21 Rhea Ripley 1.50 4.00
22 Riddle 1.25 3.00
23 R-Truth .60 1.50
24 Shayna Baszler 1.00 2.50
25 Sheamus .75 2.00
26 T-BAR .60 1.50
27 Xavier Woods .50 1.25
28 Angelo Dawkins .60 1.50
29 Apollo Crews .60 1.50
30 Bianca Belair 1.25 3.00
31 Big E 1.00 2.50
32 Carmella 1.25 3.00
33 Cesaro .50 1.25
34 Chad Gable .50 1.25
35 Commander Azeez RC .60 1.50
36 Dominik Mysterio RC .60 1.50
37 Jey Uso .50 1.25
38 Jimmy Uso .50 1.25
39 Kevin Owens 1.00 2.50
40 Baron Corbin .50 1.25
41 Liv Morgan 2.00 5.00
42 Mia Yim .60 1.50
43 Montez Ford .50 1.25
44 Natalya .75 2.00
45 Otis .60 1.50
46 Sami Zayn .75 2.00
47 Shinsuke Nakamura 1.25 3.00
48 Tamina .60 1.50
49 Adam Cole 1.50 4.00
50 Candice LeRae 2.00 5.00
51 Dakota Kai 1.00 2.50
52 Danny Burch .60 1.50
53 Ember Moon .60 1.50
54 Finn Balor 1.25 3.00
55 Indi Hartwell RC 1.50 4.00
56 Io Shirai 1.00 2.50
57 Johnny Gargano 1.00 2.50
58 Karrion Kross 2.00 5.00
59 Kushida .75 2.00
60 LA Knight RC .60 1.50
61 Nash Carter RC .50 1.25
62 Oney Lorcan .50 1.25
63 Pete Dunne 1.00 2.50
64 Santos Escobar .75 2.00
65 Tommaso Ciampa 1.25 3.00
66 Toni Storm 1.50 4.00
67 Wes Lee RC .50 1.25
68 Lex Luger .60 1.50
69 Ric Flair 2.00 5.00
70 The Godfather .60 1.50
71 Undertaker 2.50 6.00
72 William Regal .75 2.00
73 Yokozuna .75 2.00
74 John Cena 2.50 6.00

2021 Topps WWE Undisputed Autographed Framed Boxloaders

*BLUE/25: UNPRICED DUE TO SCARCITY
*GOLD/10: UNPRICED DUE TO SCARCITY
*BLACK/5: UNPRICED DUE TO SCARCITY
*ORANGE/3: UNPRICED DUE TO SCARCITY
STATED PRINT RUN 150 SER.#'d SETS

FRA Asuka 30.00 75.00
FRK Kane 25.00 60.00
FRM MVP 8.00 20.00
FRR Riddle 15.00 40.00
FRAB Alexa Bliss 100.00 200.00
FRCA Cedric Alexander 10.00 25.00
FRIS Io Shirai 20.00 50.00
FRJH Jeff Hardy 30.00 75.00
FRJM John Morrison 12.00 30.00
FRKU Kushida
FRLL Lex Luger 15.00 40.00
FRMA Mustafa Ali 8.00 20.00
FRRM Rey Mysterio 25.00 60.00
FRRR Robert Roode 8.00 20.00
FRSB Shelton Benjamin 10.00 25.00
FRTC Tommaso Ciampa 12.00 30.00
FRWR William Regal 15.00 40.00

2021 Topps WWE Undisputed Autographed Mat Relics

*GREEN/50: .5X TO 1.2X BASIC AUTOS
*BLUE/25: UNPRICED DUE TO SCARCITY
*GOLD/10: UNPRICED DUE TO SCARCITY
*BLACK/5: UNPRICED DUE TO SCARCITY
STATED PRINT RUN 99 SER.#'d SETS

MB Bayley 15.00 40.00
MC Cesaro 8.00 20.00
ME Edge 20.00 50.00
MG Goldberg
MM MVP 6.00 15.00
MO Otis 6.00 15.00
M$$ Sasha Banks 30.00 75.00
MAC Adam Cole 15.00 40.00
MAD Angelo Dawkins 5.00 12.00
MAG Angel Garza 5.00 12.00
MAN Angelo Dawkins 5.00 12.00
MAP Apollo Crews 5.00 12.00
MAS Asuka 15.00 40.00
MAT Austin Theory 6.00 15.00
MBF Bobby Fish 5.00 12.00
MBL Becky Lynch 30.00 75.00
MBO Bobby Lashley 10.00 25.00
MBW The Fiend Bray Wyatt
MCF Charlotte Flair
MDD Dominik Dijakovic
MDG Drew Gulak 5.00 12.00
MDM Drew McIntyre 10.00 25.00
MDO Dominik Mysterio 12.00 30.00
MDR Drew McIntyre 10.00 25.00
MES Elias 6.00 15.00
MFB Finn Balor 10.00 25.00
MGA Angel Garza 5.00 12.00
MJC John Cena 100.00 200.00
MJG Johnny Gargano 5.00 12.00
MJM John Morrison
MJU Jimmy Uso 5.00 12.00
MKC King Corbin 5.00 12.00
MKK Kofi Kingston 6.00 15.00
MKL Keith Lee 10.00 25.00
MKO Kevin Owens 8.00 20.00
MKR Kyle O'Reilly 8.00 20.00
MMF Montez Ford 5.00 12.00
MMO Montez Ford 5.00 12.00
MMR Matt Riddle 12.00 30.00
MPD Pete Dunne 6.00 15.00
MRR Rhea Ripley 25.00 60.00
MSB Shayna Baszler 6.00 15.00
MSE Seth Rollins 12.00 30.00
MSR Seth Rollins 12.00 30.00
MTC Tommaso Ciampa 8.00 20.00

2021 Topps WWE Undisputed Autographed Match-Up Dual Relics

*GOLD/10: UNPRICED DUE TO SCARCITY
*BLACK/5: UNPRICED DUE TO SCARCITY
STATED PRINT RUN 25 SER.#'d SETS

AMABN Natalya/B.Lynch
AMABS S.Baszler/B.Lynch
AMACD D.Gulak/Cesaro
AMACT C.Flair/T.Stratus
AMADG Goldberg/D.McIntyre
AMADO D.Gulak/O.Lorcan
AMADT T.Nox/D.Kai
AMAEK Elias/K.Corbin
AMAFJ J.Gargano/F.Balor
AMAFR C.Flair/R.Ripley
AMAIC Io Shirai/C.LeRae
AMAKD K.Lee/D.Dijakovic
AMAKS S.Rollins/K.Owens
AMALK Asuka/Bayley
AMALN Natalya/L.Morgan
AMAMS M.Rose/S.Deville
AMARJ Ricochet/J.Gargano
AMARO K.Owens/R.Reigns
AMART R.Ripley/T.Storm
AMASA S.Banks/Asuka
AMASC S.Banks/Carmella
AMASM M.Yim/S.Baszler

2021 Topps WWE Undisputed Autographed Oversized Boxloaders

STATED ODDS 1:93 BOXES
STATED PRINT RUN 5 SER.#'d SETS
UNPRICED DUE TO SCARCITY

OAC Carmella
OAR Ricochet
OAAG Angel Garza
OACF Charlotte Flair
OADZ Dolph Ziggler
OAJG Johnny Gargano
OAJU Jey Uso
OAKO Kevin Owens
OANJ Nia Jax
OAPD Pete Dunne
OASZ Sami Zayn

2021 Topps WWE Undisputed Autographs

*PURPLE/99: .5X TO 1.2X BASIC AUTOS
*GREEN/50: .6X TO 1.5X BASIC AUTOS
*BLUE/25: UNPRICED DUE TO SCARCITY
*GOLD/10: UNPRICED DUE TO SCARCITY
*BLACK/5: UNPRICED DUE TO SCARCITY
*RED/1: UNPRICED DUE TO SCARCITY
*P.P.BLACK/1: UNPRICED DUE TO SCARCITY
*P.P.CYAN/1: UNPRICED DUE TO SCARCITY
*P.P.MAGENTA/1: UNPRICED DUE TO SCARCITY
*P.P.YELLOW/1: UNPRICED DUE TO SCARCITY
STATED PRINT RUN 199 SER.#'d SETS

AC Carmella 12.00 30.00
AE Elias 6.00 15.00
AK Kushida 4.00 10.00
AM MACE 4.00 10.00
AO Omos 12.00 30.00
AR Riddle 10.00 25.00
AU Undertaker
AAB Alexa Bliss 30.00 75.00
AAC Adam Cole 10.00 25.00
AAD Angelo Dawkins 6.00 15.00
AAG Angel Garza 3.00 8.00
AAS AJ Styles 10.00 25.00
ABB Bianca Belair EXCH 15.00 40.00
ABE Big E 4.00 10.00
ABL Becky Lynch 25.00 60.00
ABO Bobby Lashley EXCH 8.00 20.00
ACF Charlotte Flair EXCH 20.00 50.00
ACG Chad Gable 6.00 15.00
ACL Candice LeRae 10.00 25.00
ACS Cesaro 5.00 12.00
ADB Danny Burch 3.00 8.00
ADK Dakota Kai 10.00 25.00
ADM Drew McIntyre
ADO Dominik Mysterio 6.00 15.00
ADZ Dolph Ziggler 5.00 12.00
AEM Ember Moon 6.00 15.00
AFB Finn Balor 8.00 20.00
AIH Indi Hartwell 10.00 25.00
AIS Io Shirai 12.00 30.00
AJC John Cena
AJG Johnny Gargano 5.00 12.00
AJU Jey Uso 4.00 10.00
AKC King Corbin 5.00 12.00
AKK Karrion Kross 8.00 20.00
AKL Keith Lee 6.00 15.00
AKO Kevin Owens 8.00 20.00
ALL Lex Luger 12.00 30.00
AMA Mustafa Ali 4.00 10.00
AMF Montez Ford 4.00 10.00
AMR Mandy Rose 20.00 50.00
AMVP MVP 5.00 12.00
ANJ Nia Jax 4.00 10.00
AOD Otis 6.00 15.00

ARP Rhea Ripley	15.00	40.00
ARR Robert Roode	5.00	12.00
ART R-Truth	4.00	10.00
ASB Shayna Baszler	5.00	12.00
ASE Santos Escobar	5.00	12.00
ASH Sheamus	6.00	15.00
ASN Shinsuke Nakamura	8.00	20.00
ASZ Sami Zayn	6.00	15.00
ATB T-BAR	5.00	12.00
ATC Tommaso Ciampa	6.00	15.00
ATG The Godfather	8.00	20.00
ATS Toni Storm	12.00	30.00
AWR William Regal	10.00	25.00
AXW Xavier Woods	4.00	10.00

2021 Topps WWE Undisputed Cut Signatures

STATED PRINT RUN 1 SER.#'d SET
UNPRICED DUE TO SCARCITY

CSBB Bam Bam Bigelow
CSBH Bobby "The Brain" Heenan
CSCJS Chief Jay Strongbow

2021 Topps WWE Undisputed Dual Autographs

*BLUE/25: UNPRICED DUE TO SCARCITY
*GOLD/10: UNPRICED DUE TO SCARCITY
*BLACK/5: UNPRICED DUE TO SCARCITY
*RED/1: UNPRICED DUE TO SCARCITY
STATED PRINT RUN 50 SER.#'d SETS

DACS Cesaro/S.Nakamura	25.00	60.00
DADM D.Brooke/M.Rose		
DADR R.Gonzalez/D.Kai	20.00	50.00
DAHB S.Benjamin/C.Alexander		
DAIM M.Barthel/F.Aichner	10.00	25.00
DAKS Scarlett/K.Kross	50.00	100.00
DALF J.Wilde/R.Mendoza	12.00	30.00
DALH G.Metalik/L.Dorado	12.00	30.00
DAMF Dominik & Rey Mysterio	30.00	75.00
DAND K.Kingston/X.Woods	10.00	25.00
DANS N.Jax/S.Baszler	10.00	25.00
DAOD O.Lorcan/D.Burch	10.00	25.00
DAPC C.LeRae/J.Gargano	50.00	100.00
DARB Mace/T-Bar	10.00	25.00
DAVR Ivar/Erik	10.00	25.00
DAZR D.Ziggler/R.Roode	10.00	25.00
DAGYZ Z.Gibson/J.Drake	10.00	25.00

2021 Topps WWE Undisputed Fistographs

STATED ODDS 1:19 BOXES
STATED PRINT RUN 25 SER.#'d SETS

FIO Omos	125.00	250.00
FIAS AJ Styles	200.00	400.00
FIBB Bianca Belair	200.00	400.00
FIBE Big E	100.00	200.00
FIDM Drew McIntyre	200.00	400.00
FIOD Otis	100.00	200.00
FIRR Rhea Ripley	250.00	500.00
FISB Sasha Banks	400.00	800.00
FISN Shinsuke Nakamura	200.00	400.00
FISR Seth Rollins	250.00	500.00

2021 Topps WWE Undisputed Grand Slam Champions

COMPLETE SET (16)	20.00	50.00
RANDOMLY INSERTED INTO PACKS		
GS1 Asuka	3.00	8.00
GS2 Bayley	2.00	5.00
GS3 Booker T	1.50	4.00
GS4 Eddie Guerrero	4.00	10.00
GS5 Edge	3.00	8.00
GS6 Jeff Hardy	2.00	5.00
GS7 Kane	1.25	3.00
GS8 Kofi Kingston	2.00	5.00
GS9 Randy Orton	2.50	6.00
GS10 Rey Mysterio	2.00	5.00
GS11 Roman Reigns	4.00	10.00
GS12 Sasha Banks	4.00	10.00
GS13 Seth Rollins	2.00	5.00
GS14 Shawn Michaels	3.00	8.00
GS15 The Miz	1.25	3.00
GS16 Triple H	3.00	8.00

2021 Topps WWE Undisputed Grand Slam Champions Autographs

*PURPLE/99: .5X TO 1.2X BASIC AUTOS
*GREEN/50: .6X TO 1.5X BASIC AUTOS
*BLUE/25: UNPRICED DUE TO SCARCITY
*GOLD/10: UNPRICED DUE TO SCARCITY
*BLACK/5: UNPRICED DUE TO SCARCITY
*RED/1: UNPRICED DUE TO SCARCITY
*P.P.BLACK/1: UNPRICED DUE TO SCARCITY
*P.P.CYAN/1: UNPRICED DUE TO SCARCITY
*P.P.MAGENTA/1: UNPRICED DUE TO SCARCITY
*P.P.YELLOW/1: UNPRICED DUE TO SCARCITY
STATED PRINT RUN 199 SER.#'d SETS

GAA Asuka	15.00	40.00
GAE Edge	15.00	40.00
GAK Kane	20.00	50.00
GABT Booker T	12.00	30.00
GAJH Jeff Hardy	12.00	30.00
GAKK Kofi Kingston	6.00	15.00
GARM Rey Mysterio	15.00	40.00
GATM The Miz	10.00	25.00

2021 Topps WWE Undisputed Grand Slam Champions Autographs Purple

STATED PRINT RUN 99 SER.#'d SETS

GASB Sasha Banks	50.00	100.00
GASR Seth Rollins	12.00	30.00

2021 Topps WWE Undisputed Mat Relics

*GREEN/50: .5X TO 1.2X BASIC MEM
*BLUE/25: UNPRICED DUE TO SCARCITY
*GOLD/10: UNPRICED DUE TO SCARCITY
*BLACK/5: UNPRICED DUE TO SCARCITY
*RED/1: UNPRICED DUE TO SCARCITY
*P.P.BLACK/1: UNPRICED DUE TO SCARCITY
*P.P.CYAN/1: UNPRICED DUE TO SCARCITY
*P.P.MAGENTA/1: UNPRICED DUE TO SCARCITY
*P.P.YELLOW/1: UNPRICED DUE TO SCARCITY
STATED PRINT RUN 99 SER.#'d SETS

MB Bayley	4.00	10.00
MC Cesaro	1.50	4.00
MG Goldberg	6.00	15.00
MM MVP	1.50	4.00
M$$ Sasha Banks	8.00	20.00
MAC Adam Cole	5.00	12.00
MAD Angelo Dawkins	2.00	5.00
MAG Angel Garza	2.00	5.00
MAP Apollo Crews	2.00	5.00
MBF Bobby Fish	2.00	5.00
MBL Becky Lynch	6.00	15.00
MCF Charlotte Flair	8.00	20.00
MDD Dominik Dijakovic	2.00	5.00
MDG Drew Gulak	2.00	5.00
MES Elias	1.50	4.00
MFB Finn Balor	4.00	10.00
MJG Johnny Gargano	3.00	8.00
MKC King Corbin	1.50	4.00
MKL Keith Lee	3.00	8.00
MKR Kyle O'Reilly	2.50	6.00
MMF Montez Ford	1.50	4.00
MMR Matt Riddle	4.00	10.00
MPD Pete Dunne	3.00	8.00
MRA Randy Orton	5.00	12.00
MRR Rhea Ripley	5.00	12.00
MSB Shayna Baszler	3.00	8.00
MSE Seth Rollins	4.00	10.00
MTC Tommaso Ciampa	4.00	10.00

2021 Topps WWE Undisputed Match-Up Dual Autographed Books

*GOLD/5: UNPRICED DUE TO SCARCITY
*RED/1: UNPRICED DUE TO SCARCITY
STATED PRINT RUN 10 SER.#'d SETS
UNPRICED DUE TO SCARCITY

MAC C.Flair/Asuka
MAS AJ Styles/S.Nakamura
MBS S.Banks/Bayley
MCS Cesaro/Sheamus
MEJ Edge/J.Hardy
MJR R.Reigns/J.Cena
MSR S.Rollins/F.Balor
MTM HHH/Mankind
MUK Kane/Undertaker

2021 Topps WWE Undisputed Match-Up Dual Relics

*GREEN/50: .5X TO 1.2X BASIC MEM
*BLUE/25: UNPRICED DUE TO SCARCITY
*RED/1: UNPRICED DUE TO SCARCITY
*GOLD/10: UNPRICED DUE TO SCARCITY
*P.P.BLACK/1: UNPRICED DUE TO SCARCITY
*P.P.CYAN/1: UNPRICED DUE TO SCARCITY
*P.P.MAGENTA/1: UNPRICED DUE TO SCARCITY
*P.P.YELLOW/1: UNPRICED DUE TO SCARCITY
STATED PRINT RUN 99 SER.#'d SETS

MABA Asuka/B.Lynch	6.00	15.00
MABJ B.Wyatt/J.Cena	8.00	20.00
MABL L.Evans/Bayley	4.00	10.00
MABS B.Lynch/S.Baszler	6.00	15.00
MACP A.Crews/MVP	2.00	5.00
MACS S.Baszler/C.Flair	8.00	20.00
MADG D.McIntyre/Goldberg	6.00	15.00
MADR R.Reigns/D.McIntyre	8.00	20.00
MAEK King Corbin/Elias	1.50	4.00
MAER R.Orton/Edge	6.00	15.00
MAFR C.Flair/R.Ripley	8.00	20.00
MAKS K.Owens/S.Rollins	4.00	10.00
MALK Bayley/Asuka	6.00	15.00
MAMO R.Orton/D.McIntyre	5.00	12.00
MAMS S.Deville/M.Rose	8.00	20.00
MARB B.Belair/R.Ripley	5.00	12.00
MARM D.Mysterio/S.Rollins	4.00	10.00
MARO K.Owens/R.Reigns	8.00	20.00
MASA S.Banks/Asuka	8.00	20.00
MASC S.Bannks/Carmella	8.00	20.00

2021 Topps WWE Undisputed Rob Schamberger Illustrations

COMPLETE SET (10)	12.00	30.00
RANDOMLY INSERTED INTO PACKS		
RS1 AJ Styles	2.00	5.00
RS2 Big E	1.25	3.00
RS3 Charlotte Flair	3.00	8.00
RS4 Johnny Gargano	1.25	3.00
RS5 Natalya	1.00	2.50
RS6 Rey Mysterio	1.50	4.00
RS7 Roman Reigns	3.00	8.00
RS8 Shotzi Blackheart	2.50	6.00
RS9 Stone Cold Steve Austin	3.00	8.00
RS10 The Fiend Bray Wyatt	2.50	6.00

2021 Topps WWE Undisputed Rob Schamberger Illustrations Artist Autographs

STATED PRINT RUN 10 SER.#'d SETS
UNPRICED DUE TO SCARCITY

AAAS Rob Schamberger
AABE Rob Schamberger
AABW Rob Schamberger
AACF Rob Schamberger
AAJG Rob Schamberger
AANT Rob Schamberger
AARM Rob Schamberger
AARR Rob Schamberger
AASA Rob Schamberger
AASB Rob Schamberger

2021 Topps WWE Undisputed Rob Schamberger Illustrations Superstar Autographs

STATED PRINT RUN 10 SER.#'d SETS
UNPRICED DUE TO SCARCITY

SAAS AJ Styles
SABE Big E
SABW The Fiend Bray Wyatt
SAJG Johnny Gargano
SANT Natalya
SARM Rey Mysterio
SASB Shotzi Blackheart

2017 Topps WWE Women's Division

UNOPENED BLASTER BOX (81 CARDS)
UNOPENED HANGER BOX (40 CARDS)
UNOPENED FAT PACK (18 CARDS)
*SILVER/50: 1.2X TO 3X BASIC CARDS
*BLUE/25: 2X TO 5X BASIC CARDS
*GOLD/10: UNPRICED DUE TO SCARCITY
*RED/1: UNPRICED DUE TO SCARCITY

R1 Aliyah	.40	1.00
R2 Asuka	1.00	2.50
R3 Billie Kay	.40	1.00
R4 Cathy Kelley	.30	.75
R5 Ember Moon	.75	2.00
R6 Kimberly Frankele RC	.30	.75
R7 Liv Morgan	.50	1.25
R8 Mandy Rose	.40	1.00
R9 Nikki Cross RC	.60	1.50
R10 Peyton Royce	.50	1.25
R11 Ruby Riot RC	.40	1.00
R12 Brie Bella	.75	2.00
R13 Alexa Bliss	1.50	4.00
R14 Alicia Fox	.50	1.25
R15 Bayley	1.00	2.50
R16 Charly Caruso RC	.30	.75
R17 Dana Brooke	.60	1.50
R18 Emma	.75	2.00
R19 JoJo	.50	1.25
R20 Maryse	.60	1.50
R21 Mickie James	.50	1.25
R22 Nia Jax	.50	1.25
R23 Sasha Banks	1.00	2.50
R24 Stephanie McMahon	.40	1.00
R25 Summer Rae	.75	2.00
R26 Lita	.60	1.50
R27 Becky Lynch	1.00	2.50
R28 Carmella	.75	2.00
R29 Charlotte Flair	1.25	3.00
R30 Dasha Fuentes	.40	1.00
R31 Lana	1.00	2.50
R32 Naomi	.60	1.50
R33 Natalya	.60	1.50
R34 Nikki Bella	.75	2.00
R35 Renee Young	.50	1.25
R36 Tamina	.40	1.00
R37 Alundra Blayze	.40	1.00
R38 Eve Torres	.50	1.25
R39 Miss Elizabeth	.50	1.25
R40 Sherri Martel	.40	1.00
R41 Terri Runnels	.30	.75
R42 Trish Stratus	1.25	3.00
R43 Wendi Richter	.40	1.00
R44 Beth Phoenix	.30	.75
R45 Ivory	.30	.75
R46 Judy Martin RC	.30	.75
R47 Kelly Kelly	.60	1.50
R48 Leilani Kai	.30	.75
R49 Princess Victoria RC	.30	.75
R50 Torrie Wilson	.75	2.00

2017 Topps WWE Women's Division Autographed Kiss and Mat Relics

STATED ODDS 1:1,054 BLASTER BOX EXCLUSIVE
STATED PRINT RUN 5 SER.#'d SETS
UNPRICED DUE TO SCARCITY

WARCA Carmella
WARNA Natalya

2017 Topps WWE Women's Division Autographed Mat Relics

STATED ODDS 1:68 BLASTER BOX
STATED ODDS 1:6,012 HANGER BOX
STATED ODDS 1:11,988 HANGER PACK
STATED PRINT RUN 10 SER.#'d SETS
UNPRICED DUE TO SCARCITY

MRAB Alexa Bliss
MRAF Alicia Fox
MRAS Asuka
MRBA Bayley
MRBL Becky Lynch
MRCA Carmella
MRCF Charlotte Flair
MRNJ Nia Jax
MRSR Summer Rae
MRSU Summer Rae
MRTA Tamina
MRASA Asuka

MRASU Asuka
MRBAY Bayley
MRBEC Becky Lynch
MRBLY Bayley
MRCAR Carmella
MRCHA Charlotte Flair
MRCHF Charlotte Flair
MRCRM Carmella
MREMM Emma
MRNAO Naomi
MRNAT Natalya
MRNIA Nia Jax
MRSUM Summer Rae
MRTAM Tamina
MRCHAR Charlotte Flair
MREMMA Emma

2017 Topps WWE Women's Division Autographs

*SILVER/50: .5X TO 1.2X BASIC AUTOS
*BLUE/25: .6X TO 1.5X BASIC AUTOS
*GOLD/10: UNPRICED DUE TO SCARCITY
*RED/1: UNPRICED DUE TO SCARCITY
STATED ODDS 1:13 BLASTER BOX
STATED ODDS 1:802 HANGER BOX
STATED ODDS 1:1,599 HANGER PACK
STATED PRINT RUN 99 OR FEWER SER.#'d SETS

R1 Aliyah/99 6.00 15.00
R2 Asuka/99 20.00 50.00
R3 Billie Kay/99 10.00 25.00
R4 Cathy Kelley/99 8.00 20.00
R5 Ember Moon/94 8.00 20.00
R7 Liv Morgan/99 25.00 60.00
R8 Mandy Rose/99 20.00 50.00
R10 Peyton Royce/99 10.00 25.00
R11 Ruby Riot/99 20.00 50.00
R12 Brie Bella/56 10.00 25.00
R13 Alexa Bliss/99 50.00 100.00
R14 Alicia Fox/61 10.00 25.00
R18 Emma/99 12.00 30.00
R19 JoJo/99 6.00 15.00
R22 Nia Jax/99 10.00 25.00
R23 Sasha Banks/68 25.00 60.00
R27 Becky Lynch/99 15.00 40.00
R28 Carmella/99 20.00 50.00
R29 Charlotte Flair/57 20.00 50.00
R30 Dasha Fuentes/99 6.00 15.00
R32 Naomi/99 8.00 20.00
R33 Natalya/78 8.00 20.00
R34 Nikki Bella/99 10.00 25.00
R36 Tamina/99 6.00 15.00
R37 Alundra Blayze/99 8.00 20.00
R41 Terri Runnels/99 10.00 25.00
R43 Wendi Richter/99 6.00 15.00
R44 Beth Phoenix/99 8.00 20.00
R45 Ivory/99 6.00 15.00
R46 Judy Martin/99 6.00 15.00
R47 Kelly Kelly/99 10.00 25.00
R48 Leilani Kai/99 6.00 15.00
R49 Princess Victoria/99 10.00 25.00
R50 Torrie Wilson/99 12.00 30.00

2017 Topps WWE Women's Division Autographs Blue

STATED ODDS 1:39 BLASTER BOX
STATED ODDS 1:3,280 HANGER BOX
STATED ODDS 1:6,539 HANGER PACK
STATED PRINT RUN 25 SER.#'d SETS

R25 Summer Rae 15.00 40.00

2017 Topps WWE Women's Division Autographs Silver

STATED ODDS 1:20 BLASTER BOX
STATED ODDS 1:1,569 HANGER BOX
STATED ODDS 1:3,128 HANGER PACK
STATED PRINT RUN 50 SER.#'d SETS

R15 Bayley 15.00 40.00
R20 Maryse 8.00 20.00
R38 Eve Torres 20.00 50.00
R42 Trish Stratus 25.00 60.00

2017 Topps WWE Women's Division Diva's Championship Medallions

*SILVER/50: .5X TO 1.2X BASIC MEM
*BLUE/25: .6X TO 1.5X BASIC MEM
*GOLD/10: UNPRICED DUE TO SCARCITY
*RED/1: UNPRICED DUE TO SCARCITY
STATED ODDS 1:15 BLASTER BOX
STATED ODDS 1:1,203 HANGER BOX
STATED ODDS 1:2,398 HANGER PACK
STATED PRINT RUN 99 SER.#'d SETS

DCM Maryse 5.00 12.00
DCN Natalya 5.00 12.00
DCAF Alicia Fox 4.00 10.00
DCBB Brie Bella 6.00 15.00
DCBP Beth Phoenix 2.50 6.00
DCCF Charlotte Flair 10.00 25.00
DCET Eve Torres 4.00 10.00
DCKK Kelly Kelly 5.00 12.00
DCMJ Mickie James 4.00 10.00
DCNB Nikki Bella 6.00 15.00

2017 Topps WWE Women's Division Finishers and Signature Moves

*SILVER/50: 1X TO 2.5X BASIC CARDS
*BLUE/25: 1.2X TO 3X BASIC CARDS
*GOLD/10: 2X TO 5X BASIC CARDS
*RED/1: UNPRICED DUE TO SCARCITY
STATED ODDS 5:1 HANGER BOX EXCLUSIVE

F1 Alexa Bliss 3.00 8.00
F2 Nikki Bella 1.50 4.00
F3 Bayley 2.00 5.00
F4 Natalya 1.25 3.00
F5 Brie Bella 1.50 4.00
F6 Sasha Banks 2.00 5.00
F7 Becky Lynch 2.00 5.00
F8 Beth Phoenix .60 1.50
F9 Sasha Banks 2.00 5.00
F10 Charlotte Flair 2.50 6.00
F11 Eve Torres 1.00 2.50
F12 Mickie James 1.00 2.50
F13 Trish Stratus 2.50 6.00
F14 Naomi 1.25 3.00
F15 Alicia Fox 1.00 2.50
F16 Tamina .75 2.00
F17 Dana Brooke 1.25 3.00
F18 Emma 1.50 4.00
F19 Carmella 1.50 4.00
F20 Summer Rae 1.50 4.00
F21 Nia Jax 1.00 2.50
F22 Stephanie McMahon .75 2.00
F23 Kelly Kelly 1.25 3.00
F24 Charlotte Flair 2.50 6.00

2017 Topps WWE Women's Division Kiss

*GOLD/10: UNPRICED DUE TO SCARCITY
*RED/1: UNPRICED DUE TO SCARCITY
STATED ODDS 1:67 BLASTER BOX
STATED ODDS 1:1,503 HANGER BOX
STATED ODDS 1:2,997 HANGER PACK
STATED PRINT RUN 99 SER.#'d SETS

KAF Alicia Fox/99 15.00 40.00
KBK Billie Kay/99 25.00 60.00
KCA Carmella/99 25.00 60.00
KDB Dana Brooke/69 15.00 40.00
KNA Naomi/54 15.00 40.00
KPR Peyton Royce/99 20.00 50.00
KRY Renee Young/68 25.00 60.00

2017 Topps WWE Women's Division Kiss Autographs

*GOLD/10: UNPRICED DUE TO SCARCITY
*RED/1: UNPRICED DUE TO SCARCITY
STATED ODDS 1:211 BLASTER BOX
STATED ODDS 1:6,012 HANGER BOX
STATED ODDS 1:11,988 HANGER PACK
STATED PRINT RUN 25 SER.#'d SETS

KAF Alicia Fox
KAS Asuka
KBK Billie Kay 50.00 100.00
KCA Carmella 50.00 100.00
KDB Dana Brooke 30.00 75.00
KMR Mandy Rose 125.00 250.00
KPR Peyton Royce 125.00 250.00
KRY Renee Young 30.00 75.00

2017 Topps WWE Women's Division Mat Relics

*SILVER/50: .5X TO 1.2X BASIC MEM
*BLUE/25: .6X TO 1.5X BASIC MEM
*GOLD/10: UNPRICED DUE TO SCARCITY
*RED/1: UNPRICED DUE TO SCARCITY
STATED ODDS 1:10 BLASTER BOX
STATED ODDS 1:262 HANGER BOX
STATED ODDS 1:522 HANGER PACK
STATED PRINT RUN 199 SER.#'d SETS

MRAB Alexa Bliss 8.00 20.00
MRAF Alicia Fox 2.50 6.00
MRAL Alexa Bliss 8.00 20.00
MRAS Asuka 5.00 12.00
MRBA Bayley 5.00 12.00
MRBB Brie Bella 4.00 10.00
MRBL Becky Lynch 5.00 12.00
MRBR Brie Bella 4.00 10.00
MRCA Carmella 4.00 10.00
MRCF Charlotte Flair 6.00 15.00
MRDB Dana Brooke 3.00 8.00
MRLA Lana 5.00 12.00
MRNB Nikki Bella 4.00 10.00
MRNC Nikki Cross 3.00 8.00
MRNI Nikki Bella 4.00 10.00
MRNJ Nia Jax 2.50 6.00
MRSB Sasha Banks 5.00 12.00
MRSM Stephanie McMahon 2.00 5.00
MRSR Summer Rae 4.00 10.00
MRSU Summer Rae 4.00 10.00
MRTA Tamina 2.00 5.00
MRASA Asuka 5.00 12.00
MRASU Asuka 5.00 12.00
MRBAY Bayley 5.00 12.00
MRBEC Becky Lynch 5.00 12.00
MRBLY Bayley 5.00 12.00
MRBRI Brie Bella 4.00 10.00
MRCAR Carmella 4.00 10.00
MRCHA Charlotte Flair 6.00 15.00
MRCHF Charlotte Flair 6.00 15.00
MRCRM Carmella 4.00 10.00
MREMM Emma 4.00 10.00
MRLAA Lana 5.00 12.00
MRLAN Lana 5.00 12.00
MRNAO Naomi 3.00 8.00
MRNAT Natalya 3.00 8.00
MRNIA Nia Jax 2.50 6.00
MRNIK Nikki Cross 3.00 8.00
MRSAS Sasha Banks 5.00 12.00
MRSTE Stephanie McMahon 2.00 5.00
MRSUM Summer Rae 4.00 10.00
MRTAM Tamina 2.00 5.00
MRCHAR Charlotte Flair 6.00 15.00
MREMMA Emma 4.00 10.00

2017 Topps WWE Women's Division NXT Matches and Moments

*SILVER/50: 1.2X TO 3X BASIC CARDS
*BLUE/25: 2X TO 5X BASIC CARDS
*GOLD/10: UNPRICED DUE TO SCARCITY
*RED/1: UNPRICED DUE TO SCARCITY

NXT1 Emma .75 2.00
NXT2 Billie Kay .40 1.00
NXT3 Peyton Royce .50 1.25
NXT4 Asuka 1.00 2.50
NXT5 Asuka 1.00 2.50
NXT6 Bayley 1.00 2.50
NXT7 Nia Jax .50 1.25
NXT8 Bayley 1.50 4.00
NXT9 Bayley 1.00 2.50
NXT10 Carmella 1.00 2.50
NXT11 Bayley 1.00 2.50
NXT12 Bayley 1.00 2.50
NXT13 Asuka 1.00 2.50
NXT14 Asuka 1.00 2.50
NXT15 Nia Jax .50 1.25
NXT16 Nia Jax .50 1.25
NXT17 Asuka 1.00 2.50
NXT18 Bayley 1.00 2.50
NXT19 Mandy Rose .40 1.00
NXT20 Ember Moon .75 2.00
NXT21 Asuka 1.00 2.50
NXT22 Asuka 1.00 2.50
NXT23 Nikki Cross .60 1.50
NXT24 Asuka 1.00 2.50
NXT25 Asuka 1.00 2.50
NXT26 Ember Moon .75 2.00

2017 Topps WWE Women's Division Rivalries

*SILVER/50: 1.2X TO 3X BASIC CARDS
*BLUE/25: 2X TO 5X BASIC CARDS
*GOLD/10: UNPRICED DUE TO SCARCITY
*RED/1: UNPRICED DUE TO SCARCITY
STATED ODDS 3:1 HANGER PACK EXCLUSIVE

RV1 Charlotte Flair/Bayley 1.25 3.00
RV2 Charlotte Flair/Dana Brooke 1.25 3.00
RV3 Sasha Banks/Dana Brooke 1.00 2.50
RV4 Sasha Banks/Nia Jax 1.00 2.50
RV5 Bayley/Dana Brooke 1.00 2.50
RV6 Nikki Bella/Maryse .75 2.00
RV7 Nikki Bella/Natalya .75 2.00
RV8 Nikki Bella/Carmella .75 2.00
RV9 Becky Lynch/Alexa Bliss 1.50 4.00
RV10 Becky Lynch/Mickie James 1.00 2.50
RV11 Alexa Bliss/Mickie James 1.50 4.00
RV12 Alexa Bliss/Naomi 1.50 4.00
RV13 Alexa Bliss/Bayley 1.50 4.00
RV14 Naomi/Charlotte Flair 1.25 3.00
RV15 Asuka/Ember Moon 1.00 2.50
RV16 Asuka/Peyton Royce 1.00 2.50
RV17 Asuka/Billie Kay 1.00 2.50
RV18 Asuka/Nikki Cross 1.00 2.50
RV19 Ruby Riot/Nikki Cross .60 1.50
RV20 Wendi Richter/Leilani Kai .40 1.00
RV21 Trish Stratus/Mickie James 1.25 3.00
RV22 Mickie James/Beth Phoenix .50 1.25
RV23 Mickie James/Maryse .60 1.50
RV24 Eve Torres/Maryse .60 1.50
RV25 Eve Torres/Natalya .60 1.50

2017 Topps WWE Women's Division Shirt Relics

*SILVER/50: .5X TO 1.2X BASIC MEM
*BLUE/25: .6X TO 1.5X BASIC MEM
*GOLD/10: UNPRICED DUE TO SCARCITY
*RED/1: UNPRICED DUE TO SCARCITY
STATED ODDS 1:12 BLASTER BOX
STATED ODDS 1:950 HANGER BOX
STATED ODDS 1:1,893 HANGER PACK
STATED PRINT RUN 199 SER.#'d SETS

SRAB Alexa Bliss 15.00 40.00
SRAF Alicia Fox 5.00 12.00
SRBA Bayley 10.00 25.00
SRBL Becky Lynch 10.00 25.00
SRCA Carmella 8.00 20.00
SRCF Charlotte Flair 12.00 30.00
SRJO JoJo 5.00 12.00
SRNA Naomi 6.00 15.00
SRNT Natalya 6.00 15.00
SRRY Renee Young 5.00 12.00
SRSB Sasha Banks 10.00 25.00
SRSR Summer Rae 8.00 20.00

2017 Topps WWE Women's Division Women's Championship Medallions

*SILVER/50: .5X TO 1.2X BASIC MEM
*BLUE/25: .6X TO 1.5X BASIC MEM
*GOLD/10: UNPRICED DUE TO SCARCITY
*RED/1: UNPRICED DUE TO SCARCITY
STATED ODDS 1:15 BLASTER BOX
STATED ODDS 1:1,203 HANGER BOX
STATED ODDS 1:2,398 HANGER PACK
STATED PRINT RUN 99 SER.#'d SETS

WCI Ivory 2.50 6.00
WCAB Alundra Blayze 3.00 8.00
WCBP Beth Phoenix 2.50 6.00
WCLK Leilani Kai 2.50 6.00
WCMJ Mickie James 4.00 10.00
WCSM Stephanie McMahon 3.00 8.00
WCSS Sensational Sherri 3.00 8.00
WCTS Trish Stratus 10.00 25.00
WCWR Wendi Richter 3.00 8.00

2017 Topps WWE Women's Division WWE Matches and Moments

*SILVER/50: 1.2X TO 3X BASIC CARDS
*BLUE/25: 2X TO 5X BASIC CARDS
*GOLD/10: UNPRICED DUE TO SCARCITY
*RED/1: UNPRICED DUE TO SCARCITY

Card	Low	High
WWE1 Sasha Banks	1.00	2.50
WWE2 Charlotte	1.25	3.00
WWE3 Nikki Bella	.75	2.00
WWE4 Bayley	1.00	2.50
WWE5 Becky Lynch	1.00	2.50
WWE6 Alexa Bliss	1.50	4.00
WWE7 Charlott Flair	1.25	3.00
WWE8 Alexa Bliss	1.50	4.00
WWE9 Charlotte Flair	1.25	3.00
WWE10 Sasha Banks	1.00	2.50
WWE11 Nikki Bella	.75	2.00
WWE12 Charlotte Flair	1.25	3.00
WWE13 Team Raw	1.25	3.00
WWE14 Sasha Banks	1.00	2.50
WWE15 Nikki Bella	.75	2.00
WWE16 Alexa Bliss	1.50	4.00
WWE17 Charlotte Flair	1.25	3.00
WWE18 Charlotte Flair	1.25	3.00
WWE19 Bayley	1.00	2.50
WWE20 Natalya	.75	2.00
WWE21 La Luchadora	.50	1.25
WWE22 Bayley	1.00	2.50
WWE23 Alexa Bliss	1.50	4.00
WWE24 Mickie James	1.50	4.00

2018 Topps WWE Women's Division

*SILVER/50: .6X TO 1.5X BASIC CARDS
*BLUE/25: 1.2X TO 3X BASIC CARDS
*GOLD/10: UNPRICED DUE TO SCARCITY
*RED/1: UNPRICED DUE TO SCARCITY

Card	Low	High
1 Alexa Bliss	2.00	5.00
2 Alicia Fox	.60	1.50
3 Asuka	1.25	3.00
4 Bayley	.60	1.50
5 Becky Lynch	1.00	2.50
6 Brie Bella	.75	2.00
7 Carmella	.75	2.00
8 Cathy Kelley	.75	2.00
9 Charlotte Flair	1.25	3.00
10 Charly Caruso	.60	1.50
11 Dana Brooke	.75	2.00
12 Dasha Fuentes	.60	1.50
13 JoJo	.40	1.00
14 Lana	1.00	2.50
15 Liv Morgan	.75	2.00
16 Mandy Rose	1.00	2.50
17 Maria Kanellis	1.00	2.50
18 Maryse	.75	2.00
19 Mickie James	.75	2.00
20 Naomi	.50	1.25
21 Natalya	.50	1.25
22 Nia Jax	.60	1.50
23 Nikki Bella	.75	2.00
24 Renee Young	.60	1.50
25 Ronda Rousey	2.00	5.00
26 Ruby Riott	.60	1.50
27 Sarah Logan RC	.40	1.00
28 Sasha Banks	1.25	3.00
29 Sonya Deville	.75	2.00
30 Stephanie McMahon	.75	2.00
31 Tamina	.40	1.00
32 Aliyah	.60	1.50
33 Bianca Belair RC	2.00	5.00
34 Billie Kay	.75	2.00
35 Candice LeRae RC	.50	1.25
36 Dakota Kai RC	.50	1.25
37 Ember Moon	.75	2.00
38 Kairi Sane RC	1.00	2.50
39 Kayla Braxton RC	.40	1.00
40 Lacey Evans	.50	1.25
41 Nikki Cross	.60	1.50
42 Peyton Royce	1.00	2.50
43 Shayna Baszler	1.00	2.50
44 Taynara Conti RC	.40	1.00
45 Vanessa Borne	.40	1.00
46 Zelina Vega RC	.40	1.00
47 Alundra Blayze	.40	1.00
48 Lita	1.00	2.50
49 Trish Stratus	1.50	4.00
50 Wendi Richter	.40	1.00

2018 Topps WWE Women's Division Autographed Kiss and Shirt Relic Booklets

STATED PRINT RUN 5 SER.#'d SETS
UNPRICED DUE TO SCARCITY

ASKAB Alexa Bliss
ASKCF Charlotte Flair
ASKCR Carmella
ASKEM Ember Moon

2018 Topps WWE Women's Division Autographed Mat Relics

STATED ODDS 1:1,866
STATED PRINT RUN 10 SER.#'d SETS
UNPRICED DUE TO SCARCITY

AMRAK Asuka
AMRAS Asuka
AMRBB Brie Bella
AMRBL Becky Lynch
AMRBP Beth Phoenix
AMRBY Bayley
AMRCR Carmella
AMRDB Dana Brooke
AMREB Ember Moon
AMREM Ember Moon
AMRKR Kairi Sane
AMRKS Kairi Sane
AMRLA Lana
AMRLM Liv Morgan
AMRLT Lita
AMRMJ Mickie James
AMRMR Mandy Rose
AMRNA Naomi
AMRNB Nikki Bella
AMRNC Nikki Cross
AMRNJ Nia Jax
AMRNT Natalya
AMRNY Natalya
AMRPR Peyton Royce
AMRRR Ruby Riott
AMRSB Sasha Banks
AMRSD Sonya Deville
AMRSL Sarah Logan
AMRTM Tamina
AMRTS Trish Stratus

2018 Topps WWE Women's Division Autographed Shirt Relics

STATED ODDS 1:4,547
STATED PRINT RUN 10 SER.#'d SETS
UNPRICED DUE TO SCARCITY

ASRAB Alexa Bliss
ASRAF Alicia Fox
ASRBL Becky Lynch
ASRCF Charlotte Flair
ASRCM Carmella
ASREM Ember Moon
ASRJO JoJo
ASRNA Naomi
ASRNC Nikki Cross
ASRNT Natalya
ASRRY Renee Young
ASRSB Sasha Banks

2018 Topps WWE Women's Division Autographs

*GREEN/150: SAME VALUE AS BASIC AUTOS
*PURPLE/99: .5X TO 1.2X BASIC AUTOS
*BRONZE/75: .6X TO 1.5X BASIC AUTOS
*SILVER/50: .75X TO 2X BASIC AUTOS
*BLUE/25: 1X TO 2.5X BASIC AUTOS
*GOLD/10: UNPRICED DUE TO SCARCITY
*BLACK/5: UNPRICED DUE TO SCARCITY
*RED/1: UNPRICED DUE TO SCARCITY
*P.P.BLACK/1: UNPRICED DUE TO SCARCITY
*P.P.CYAN/1: UNPRICED DUE TO SCARCITY
*P.P.MAGENTA/1: UNPRICED DUE TO SCARCITY
*P.P.YELLOW/1: UNPRICED DUE TO SCARCITY
STATED ODDS 1:86
STATED PRINT RUN 199 SER.#'d SETS

Card	Low	High
1 Alexa Bliss	30.00	75.00
2 Alicia Fox	5.00	12.00
3 Asuka	12.00	30.00
4 Bayley	10.00	25.00
5 Becky Lynch	12.00	30.00
6 Brie Bella	10.00	25.00
7 Carmella	8.00	20.00
9 Charlotte Flair	15.00	40.00
11 Dana Brooke	6.00	15.00
12 Dasha Fuentes	5.00	12.00
14 Lana	6.00	15.00
15 Liv Morgan	15.00	40.00
16 Mandy Rose	12.00	30.00
19 Mickie James	10.00	25.00
20 Naomi	6.00	15.00
21 Natalya	8.00	20.00
22 Nia Jax	12.00	30.00
23 Nikki Bella	10.00	25.00
26 Ruby Riott	15.00	40.00
27 Sarah Logan	10.00	25.00
28 Sasha Banks	15.00	40.00
29 Sonya Deville	8.00	20.00
31 Tamina	5.00	12.00
32 Aliyah	6.00	15.00
33 Bianca Belair	15.00	40.00
34 Billie Kay	10.00	25.00
35 Candice LeRae	15.00	40.00
36 Dakota Kai	25.00	60.00
37 Ember Moon	10.00	25.00
38 Kairi Sane	15.00	40.00
40 Lacey Evans	12.00	30.00
42 Peyton Royce	15.00	40.00
43 Shayna Baszler	8.00	20.00
44 Taynara Conti	12.00	30.00
45 Vanessa Borne	8.00	20.00

2018 Topps WWE Women's Division Autographs Green

Card	Low	High
24 Renee Young	6.00	15.00

2018 Topps WWE Women's Division Commemorative Championship Relics

*PURPLE/99: SAME VALUE AS BASIC
*SILVER/50: .5X TO 1.2X BASIC MEM
*BLUE/25: .6X TO 1.5X BASIC MEM
*GOLD/10: UNPRICED DUE TO SCARCITY
*BLACK/5: UNPRICED DUE TO SCARCITY
*RED/1: UNPRICED DUE TO SCARCITY
STATED ODDS 1:183
STATED PRINT RUN 199 SER.#'d SETS

Card	Low	High
CCAB Alundra Blayze	2.00	5.00
CCAL Alexa Bliss	10.00	25.00
CCAS Asuka	5.00	12.00
CCBL Becky Lynch	8.00	20.00
CCBP Beth Phoenix	2.50	6.00
CCBY Bayley	2.50	6.00
CCCF Charlotte Flair	6.00	15.00
CCCH Charlotte Flair	6.00	15.00
CCET Eve Torres	2.00	5.00
CCLT Lita	4.00	10.00
CCMJ Mickie James	5.00	12.00
CCMR Maryse	2.00	5.00
CCNA Naomi	2.50	6.00
CCNB Nikki Bella	3.00	8.00
CCNT Natalya	3.00	8.00
CCPG Paige	10.00	25.00
CCSB Sasha Banks	6.00	15.00
CCSS Sensational Sherri	2.00	5.00
CCTS Trish Stratus	4.00	10.00
CCWR Wendi Richter	2.00	5.00

2018 Topps WWE Women's Division Kiss

*GOLD/10: UNPRICED DUE TO SCARCITY
*RED/1: UNPRICED DUE TO SCARCITY
STATED ODDS 1:1,797
STATED PRINT RUN 99 SER.#'d SETS

Card	Low	High
KCCF Charlotte Flair	30.00	75.00
KCCR Carmella	25.00	60.00
KCEM Ember Moon	25.00	60.00
KCLM Liv Morgan	20.00	50.00

2018 Topps WWE Women's Division Kiss Autographs

*GOLD/10: UNPRICED DUE TO SCARCITY
*RED/1: UNPRICED DUE TO SCARCITY
STATED ODDS 1:7,658
STATED PRINT RUN 25 SER.#'d SETS

Card	Low	High
AKCAB Alexa Bliss	150.00	300.00
AKCCF Charlotte Flair	200.00	400.00
AKCLM Liv Morgan	60.00	120.00

2018 Topps WWE Women's Division Mat Relics

*GREEN/150: SAME AS BASIC MEM
*PURPLE/99: .5X TO 1.2X BASIC MEM
*BRONZE/75: .6X TO 1.5X BASIC MEM
*SILVER/50: .75X TO 2X BASIC MEM
*BLUE/25: 1X TO 2.5X BASIC MEM
*GOLD/10: UNPRICED DUE TO SCARCITY
*BLACK/5: UNPRICED DUE TO SCARCITY
*RED/1: UNPRICED DUE TO SCARCITY
STATED ODDS 1:123

Card	Low	High
AMRAK Asuka	4.00	10.00
AMRAS Asuka	4.00	10.00
AMRBB Brie Bella	3.00	8.00
AMRBL Becky Lynch	5.00	12.00
AMRBP Beth Phoenix	3.00	8.00
AMRBY Bayley	2.50	6.00
AMRCR Carmella	4.00	10.00
AMRDB Dana Brooke	2.50	6.00
AMREB Ember Moon	5.00	12.00
AMREM Ember Moon	5.00	12.00
AMRKR Kairi Sane	5.00	12.00
AMRKS Kairi Sane	5.00	12.00
AMRLA Lana	5.00	12.00
AMRLM Liv Morgan	4.00	10.00
AMRLT Lita	3.00	8.00
AMRMJ Mickie James	4.00	10.00
AMRMR Mandy Rose	3.00	8.00
AMRNA Naomi	2.00	5.00
AMRNB Nikki Bella	5.00	12.00
AMRNC Nikki Cross	2.00	5.00
AMRNJ Nia Jax	2.00	5.00
AMRNT Natalya	5.00	12.00
AMRNY Natalya	5.00	12.00
AMRPR Peyton Royce	3.00	8.00
AMRRR Ruby Riott	4.00	10.00
AMRSB Sasha Banks	6.00	15.00
AMRSD Sonya Deville	3.00	8.00
AMRSL Sarah Logan	3.00	8.00
AMRTM Tamina	2.00	5.00
AMRTS Trish Stratus	8.00	20.00

2018 Topps WWE Women's Division Matches and Moments

*SILVER/50: .6X TO 1.5X BASIC CARDS
*BLUE/25: 1.2X TO 3X BASIC CARDS
*GOLD/10: UNPRICED DUE TO SCARCITY
*RED/1: UNPRICED DUE TO SCARCITY

Card	Low	High
NXT1 Ember Moon	.75	2.00
NXT2 Asuka	1.25	3.00
NXT3 Asuka	1.25	3.00
NXT4 Ruby Riott	.60	1.50
NXT5 Asuka	1.25	3.00
NXT6 Asuka	1.25	3.00
NXT7 Asuka	1.25	3.00
NXT8 Sarah Logan	.40	1.00
NXT9 NXT Women's Triple Threat	1.25	3.00
NXT10 Asuka	1.25	3.00
NXT11 Bianca Belair	2.00	5.00
NXT12 Vanessa Borne	.40	1.00
NXT13 Ember Moon	.75	2.00
NXT14 Asuka	1.25	3.00
NXT15 Shayna Baszler	1.00	2.50
NXT16 Dakota Kai	.50	1.25
NXT17 Bianca Belair	2.00	5.00
NXT18 Candice LeRae	.50	1.25
NXT19 Lacey Evans	.50	1.25
NXT20 Kairi Sane	1.00	2.50
NXT21 Kairi Sane	2.00	5.00
NXT22 Shayna Baszler	1.00	2.50
NXT23 Dakota Kai	.50	1.25
NXT24 Candice LeRae	.50	1.25
NXT25 Shayna Baszler	1.00	2.50

NXT26 Kairi Sane 1.00 2.50
NXT27 Shayna Baszler 1.00 2.50
NXT28 Kairi Sane 1.00 2.50
NXT29 Asuka 1.25 3.00
NXT30 Kairi Sane 1.00 2.50
RAW1 Charlotte Flair 1.25 3.00
RAW2 Bayley .60 1.50
RAW3 Sasha Banks 1.25 3.00
RAW4 Sasha Banks 1.25 3.00
RAW5 Bayley .60 1.50
RAW6 Sasha Banks 1.25 3.00
RAW7 Nia Jax .60 1.50
RAW8 Bayley & Sasha Banks 1.25 3.00
RAW9 Bayley .60 1.50
RAW10 Alexa Bliss/Mickie James 2.00 5.00
SDL1 Becky Lynch 1.00 2.50
SDL2 Naomi .50 1.25
SDL3 Naomi .50 1.25
SDL4 Alexa Bliss 2.00 5.00
SDL5 Natalya .50 1.25
SDL6 Mickie James .75 2.00
SDL7 John Cena & Nikki Bella 1.50 4.00
SDL8 Naomi .50 1.25
SDL9 Charlotte Flair 1.25 3.00
SDL10 Charlotte Flair 1.25 3.00

2018 Topps WWE Women's Division Mixed Match Challenge

COMPLETE SET (24) 8.00 20.00
*SILVER/50: .6X TO 1.5X BASIC CARDS
*BLUE/25: .75X TO 2X BASIC CARDS
*GOLD/10: UNPRICED DUE TO SCARCITY
*RED/1: UNPRICED DUE TO SCARCITY
RANDOMLY INSERTED INTO PACKS

MM1 Bliss/Strowman 1.50 4.00
MM2 Banks/Balor 1.00 2.50
MM3 Jax/Crews .50 1.25
MM4 Miz/Asuka 1.00 2.50
MM5 Rose/Goldust .75 2.00
MM6 Bayley/Elias .75 2.00
MM7 Roode/Flair 1.00 2.50
MM8 Lana/Rusev .75 2.00
MM9 Natalya/Nakamura .75 2.00
MM10 Jimmy Uso/Naomi .40 1.00
MM11 Zayn/Lynch .75 2.00
MM12 Big E/Carmella .60 1.50
MM13 The Boss Club 1.00 2.50
MM14 Team Awe-ska 1.00 2.50
MM15 Team Little Big 1.50 4.00
MM16 Glowish .30 .75
MM17 Ravishing Rusev Day! .50 1.25
MM18 The Robe Warriors .50 1.25
MM19 Team Awe-ska 1.00 2.50
MM20 Team Little Big .75 2.00
MM21 The Robe Warriors 1.00 2.50
MM22 Team Awe-ska 1.00 2.50
MM23 Roode & Lynch .75 2.00
MM24 Team Awe-ska 1.00 2.50

2018 Topps WWE Women's Division Power Couples

*SILVER/50: .5X TO 1.2X BASIC CARDS
*BLUE/25: .6X TO 1.5X BASIC CARDS
*GOLD/10: UNPRICED DUE TO SCARCITY
*RED/1: UNPRICED DUE TO SCARCITY
RANDOMLY INSERTED INTO PACKS

PC1 Brie Bella/Daniel Bryan 1.50 4.00
PC2 Stephanie McMahon/Triple H 1.50 4.00
PC3 Maryse/The Miz 1.25 3.00
PC4 Renee Young/Dean Ambrose 1.25 3.00
PC5 Naomi/Jimmy Uso .75 2.00
PC6 Lana/Rusev 1.50 4.00
PC7 Maria Kanellis/Mike Kanellis 1.50 4.00
PC8 Candice LeRae/Johnny Gargano .75 2.00
PC9 Beth Phoenix/Edge 1.50 4.00
PC10 Alicia Fox/Noam Dar 1.00 2.50
PC11 Alicia Fox/Cedric Alexander 1.00 2.50
PC12 Lana/Dolph Ziggler 1.50 4.00
PC13 Eve Torres/Zack Ryder 1.25 3.00
PC14 Maria Kanellis/Dolph Ziggler 1.50 4.00
PC15 Stephanie McMahon/Kurt Angle 1.50 4.00
PC16 Trish Stratus/Chris Jericho 2.50 6.00
PC17 Trish Stratus/Jeff Hardy 2.50 6.00
PC18 Marlena/Goldust 1.25 3.00
PC19 Miss Elizabeth/Randy Savage 2.00 5.00
PC20 Queen Sherri/Randy Savage 2.00 5.00
PC21 Sherri/Shawn Michaels 2.00 5.00
PC22 Lita/Kane 1.50 4.00

2018 Topps WWE Women's Division Shirt Relics

*PURPLE/99: .5X TO 1.2X BASIC MEM
*SILVER/50: .6X TO 1.5X BASIC MEM
*BLUE/25: .75X TO 2X BASIC MEM
*GOLD/10: UNPRICED DUE TO SCARCITY
*BLACK/5: UNPRICED DUE TO SCARCITY
*RED/1: UNPRICED DUE TO SCARCITY
STATED ODDS 1:516

ASRAB Alexa Bliss 15.00 40.00
ASRAF Alicia Fox 5.00 12.00
ASRBL Becky Lynch 8.00 20.00
ASRCF Charlotte Flair 10.00 25.00
ASRCM Carmella 6.00 15.00
ASREM Ember Moon 6.00 15.00
ASRJO JoJo 5.00 10.00
ASRNA Naomi 5.00 12.00
ASRNC Nikki Cross 4.00 10.00
ASRNT Natalya 6.00 15.00
ASRRY Renee Young 5.00 12.00
ASRSB Sasha Banks 8.00 20.00

2018 Topps WWE Women's Division Women's Champion

COMPLETE SET (25) 10.00 25.00
RANDOMLY INSERTED INTO PACKS

WC1 Maryse .75 2.00
WC2 Mickie James .75 2.00
WC3 Eve Torres .75 2.00
WC4 Alicia Fox .60 1.50
WC5 Natalya .50 1.25
WC6 Brie Bella .75 2.00
WC7 Beth Phoenix .75 2.00
WC8 Nikki Bella .75 2.00
WC9 Paige 1.00 2.50
WC10 Charlotte Flair 1.25 3.00
WC11 Paige 1.00 2.50
WC12 Charlotte Flair 1.25 3.00
WC13 Sasha Banks 1.25 3.00
WC14 Bayley .60 1.50
WC15 Asuka 1.25 3.00
WC16 Ember Moon .75 2.00
WC17 Charlotte Flair 1.25 3.00
WC18 Sasha Banks 1.25 3.00
WC19 Bayley .60 1.50
WC20 Alexa Bliss 2.00 5.00
WC21 Becky Lynch 1.00 2.50
WC22 Alexa Bliss 2.00 5.00
WC23 Naomi .50 1.25
WC24 Natalya .50 1.25
WC25 Charlotte Flair 1.25 3.00

2018 Topps WWE Women's Division Women's Royal Rumble

COMPLETE SET (24) 12.00 30.00
*SILVER/50: .5X TO 1.5X BASIC CARDS
*BLUE/25: 1.2X TO 3X BASIC CARDS
*GOLD/10: UNPRICED DUE TO SCARCITY
*RED/1: UNPRICED DUE TO SCARCITY
STATED ODDS 1:2

RR1 Sasha Banks 2.00 5.00
RR2 Becky Lynch 1.50 4.00
RR3 Sarah Logan .60 1.50
RR4 Mandy Rose 1.50 4.00
RR5 Lita 1.50 4.00
RR6 Kairi Sane 1.50 4.00
RR7 Tamina .60 1.50
RR8 Dana Brooke 1.25 3.00
RR9 Sonya Deville 1.25 3.00
RR10 Liv Morgan 1.25 3.00
RR11 Lana 1.50 4.00
RR12 Ruby Riott 1.00 2.50
RR13 Carmella 1.25 3.00
RR14 Natalya .75 2.00
RR15 Naomi .75 2.00
RR16 Nia Jax 1.00 2.50
RR17 Ember Moon 1.25 3.00
RR18 Beth Phoenix 1.25 3.00
RR19 Asuka 2.00 5.00
RR20 Mickie James 1.25 3.00
RR21 Nikki Bella 1.25 3.00
RR22 Brie Bella 1.25 3.00
RR23 Bayley 1.00 2.50
RR24 Trish Stratus 2.50 6.00

2019 Topps WWE Women's Division

COMPLETE SET (100) 8.00 20.00
*PURPLE/99: .6X TO 1.5X BASIC CARDS
*BRONZE/75: .75X TO 2X BASIC CARDS
*ORANGE/50: 1X TO 2.5X BASIC CARDS
*BLUE/25: 1.5X TO 4X BASIC CARDS
*GOLD/10: UNPRICED DUE TO SCARCITY
*RED/1: UNPRICED DUE TO SCARCITY
*P.P.BLACK/1: UNPRICED DUE TO SCARCITY
*P.P.CYAN/1: UNPRICED DUE TO SCARCITY
*P.P.MAGENTA/1: UNPRICED DUE TO SCARCITY
*P.P.YELLOW/1: UNPRICED DUE TO SCARCITY

1 Alexa Bliss 1.25 3.00
2 Alicia Fox .50 1.25
3 Bayley .50 1.25
4 Dana Brooke .50 1.25
5 Ember Moon .60 1.50
6 Lacey Evans .50 1.25
7 Liv Morgan .75 2.00
8 Mickie James .60 1.50
9 Natalya .50 1.25
10 Nia Jax .50 1.25
11 Ronda Rousey 1.25 3.00
12 Ruby Riott .50 1.25
13 Sarah Logan .30 .75
14 Sasha Banks 1.00 2.50
15 Tamina .25 .60
16 Renee Young .40 1.00
17 Stephanie McMahon .60 1.50
18 Maria Kanellis .60 1.50
19 Asuka .75 2.00
20 Becky Lynch 1.00 2.50
21 Billie Kay .50 1.25
22 Carmella .60 1.50
23 Mandy Rose .60 1.50
24 Maryse .30 .75
25 Naomi .40 1.00
26 Nikki Cross .40 1.00
27 Peyton Royce .60 1.50
28 Sonya Deville .50 1.25
29 Zelina Vega .40 1.00
30 Paige 1.00 2.50
31 Aliyah .25 .60
32 Bianca Belair .25 .60
33 Candice LeRae .50 1.25
34 Chelsea Green RC .25 .60
35 Dakota Kai .50 1.25
36 Deonna Purrazzo RC .25 .60
37 Io Shirai RC .25 .60
38 Jessamyn Duke .30 .75
39 Jessi Kamea RC .25 .60
40 Kacy Catanzaro RC .60 1.50
41 Kairi Sane .50 1.25
42 Lacey Lane RC .25 .60
43 Marina Shafir RC .25 .60
44 Mia Yim RC .25 .60
45 MJ Jenkins RC .25 .60
46 Shayna Baszler .50 1.25
47 Taynara Conti .30 .75
48 Vanessa Borne .30 .75
49 Xia Li RC .25 .60
50 Toni Storm RC 1.00 2.50
51 Nina Samuels RC .30 .75
52 Alundra Blayze .30 .75
53 Beth Phoenix .40 1.00
54 Eve Torres .30 .75
55 Marlena .25 .60
56 Lita .60 1.50
57 Sherri Martel .40 1.00
58 Miss Elizabeth .50 1.25
59 Trish Stratus 1.25 3.00
60 Wendi Richter .25 .60
61 Asuka .75 2.00
62 Ember Moon .60 1.50
63 Asuka .75 2.00
64 Asuka .75 2.00
65 Alexa Bliss 1.25 3.00
66 Shayna Baszler .50 1.25
67 Naomi .40 1.00
68 Nia Jax 1.25 3.00
69 Ronda Rousey 1.25 3.00
70 Candice LeRae .50 1.25
71 Carmella .60 1.50
72 Asuka .75 2.00
73 Shayna Baszler .50 1.25
74 Kairi Sane .50 1.25
75 Shayna Baszler .50 1.25
76 Bayley .50 1.25
77 Alexa Bliss 1.25 3.00
78 Carmella .75 2.00
79 Alexa Bliss 1.25 3.00
80 Sasha Banks & Bayley 1.00 2.50
81 Kairi Sane .50 1.25
82 Ronda Rousey 1.25 3.00
83 Asuka .75 2.00
84 Ronda Rousey 1.25 3.00
85 Iiconics .60 1.50
86 Io Shirai .25 .60
87 Becky Lynch 1.00 2.50
88 Bianca Belair .25 .60
89 Shayna Baszler .50 1.25
90 Team RAW/Team SmackDown .75 2.00
91 Nikki Cross .40 1.00
92 Mia Yim .25 .60
93 Io Shirai .50 1.25
94 Natalya .50 1.25
95 Ronda Rousey 1.25 3.00
96 Asuka .75 2.00
97 Natalya .50 1.25
98 Asuka .75 2.00
99 Bayley/Sasha Banks/Ember Moon .60 1.50
100 Bianca Belair .25 .60

2019 Topps WWE Women's Division Autographed Mat Relics

*RED/1: UNPRICED DUE TO SCARCITY
STATED PRINT RUN 10 SER.#'d SETS
UNPRICED DUE TO SCARCITY

MRAAS Asuka
MRABL Becky Lynch
MRABY Bayley
MRACA Carmella
MRAIS Io Shirai
MRAKS Kairi Sane
MRANA Natalya
MRANM Naomi
MRAQA Shayna Baszler
MRASD Sonya Deville
MRATA Tamina

2019 Topps WWE Women's Division Autographed Shirt Relics

*RED/1: UNPRICED DUE TO SCARCITY
STATED PRINT RUN 10 SER.#'d SETS
UNPRICED DUE TO SCARCITY

SRAAB Alexa Bliss
SRACM Carmella
SRALE Lacey Evans
SRANM Naomi
SRANT Natalya
SRAQA Shayna Baszler
SRARY Renee Young
SRATM Tamina

2019 Topps WWE Women's Division Autographs

*GREEN/150: SAME VALUE AS BASIC
*PURPLE/99: .5X TO 1.2X BASIC AUTOS
*BRONZE/75: .5X TO 1.2X BASIC AUTOS
*ORANGE/50: .6X TO 1.5X BASIC AUTOS
*BLUE/25: UNPRICED DUE TO SCARCITY
*GOLD/10: UNPRICED DUE TO SCARCITY
*BLACK/5: UNPRICED DUE TO SCARCITY
*RED/1: UNPRICED DUE TO SCARCITY
*P.P.BLACK/1: UNPRICED DUE TO SCARCITY
*P.P.CYAN/1: UNPRICED DUE TO SCARCITY
*P.P.MAGENTA/1: UNPRICED DUE TO SCARCITY
*P.P.YELLOW/1: UNPRICED DUE TO SCARCITY
RANDOMLY INSERTED INTO PACKS

AAB Alexa Bliss 30.00 75.00

ABE Bayley	12.00	30.00
ABK Billie Kay	10.00	25.00
ABZ Shayna Baszler	8.00	20.00
ACG Chelsea Green	20.00	50.00
ACL Candice LeRae	10.00	25.00
ACM Carmella	12.00	30.00
ADB Dana Brooke	6.00	15.00
ADK Dakota Kai	10.00	25.00
ADP Deonna Purrazzo	6.00	15.00
AEM Ember Moon	8.00	20.00
AIS Io Shirai	30.00	75.00
AJD Jessamyn Duke	10.00	25.00
AJE Jessi Kamea	8.00	20.00
AKC Kacy Catanzaro	15.00	40.00
ALE Lacey Evans	10.00	25.00
AMR Mandy Rose	15.00	40.00
AMS Marina Shafir	8.00	20.00
AMY Mia Yim	12.00	30.00
ANC Nikki Cross	8.00	20.00
ANT Natalya	6.00	15.00
APR Peyton Royce	10.00	25.00
ARY Renee Young	6.00	15.00
ASD Sonya Deville	10.00	25.00
ATC Taynara Conti	6.00	15.00
ATM Tamina	6.00	15.00
AVB Vanessa Borne	6.00	15.00
AEST Bianca Belair	10.00	25.00

2019 Topps WWE Women's Division Championship Side Plate Commemorative Patches

*PURPLE/99: .5X TO 1.2X BASIC MEM
*ORANGE/50: .6X TO 1.5X BASIC MEM
*BLUE/25: .75X TO 2X BASIC MEM
*GOLD/10: UNPRICED DUE TO SCARCITY
*RED/1: UNPRICED DUE TO SCARCITY
STATED PRINT RUN 199 SER.#'d SETS

PCAB Alexa Bliss	15.00	40.00
PCAK Asuka	8.00	20.00
PCBL Becky Lynch	10.00	25.00
PCBY Bayley	8.00	20.00
PCCM Carmella	6.00	15.00
PCEM Ember Moon	5.00	12.00
PCKS Kairi Sane	12.00	30.00
PCNJ Nia Jax	5.00	12.00
PCNM Naomi	4.00	10.00
PCNT Natalya	4.00	10.00
PCQA Shayna Baszler	5.00	12.00
PCRR Ronda Rousey	12.00	30.00
PCSB Sasha Banks	8.00	20.00

2019 Topps WWE Women's Division Dual Autographs

*GOLD/10: UNPRICED DUE TO SCARCITY
*BLACK/5: UNPRICED DUE TO SCARCITY
*RED/1: UNPRICED DUE TO SCARCITY
RANDOMLY INSERTED INTO PACKS
STATED PRINT RUN 25 SER.#'d SETS

DABC A.Bliss/N.Cross	200.00	300.00
DADD B.Phoenix/Natalya	60.00	120.00
DAII B.Kay/P/Royce	125.00	250.00

2019 Topps WWE Women's Division Mat Relics

*GREEN/150: SAME VALUE AS BASIC
*PURPLE/99: .5X TO 1.2X BASIC MEM
*BRONZE/75: .6X TO 1.5X BASIC MEM
*ORANGE/50: .75X TO 2X BASIC MEM
*BLUE/25: 1.2X TO 3X BASIC MEM
*GOLD/10: UNPRICED DUE TO SCARCITY
*BLACK/5: UNPRICED DUE TO SCARCITY
*RED/1: UNPRICED DUE TO SCARCITY
RANDOMLY INSERTED INTO PACKS
STATED PRINT RUN 199 SER.#'d SETS

MRAB Alexa Bliss	10.00	25.00
MRAF Alicia Fox	3.00	8.00
MRAK Asuka	5.00	12.00
MRAS Asuka	4.00	10.00
MRBE Becky Lynch	10.00	25.00
MRBK Billie Kay	4.00	10.00
MRBL Becky Lynch	10.00	25.00
MRBP Beth Phoenix	3.00	8.00
MRBY Bayley	2.50	6.00
MRCA Carmella	3.00	8.00
MRCH Charlotte Flair	4.00	10.00
MRCM Carmella	3.00	8.00
MREM Ember Moon	4.00	10.00
MRIS Io Shirai	6.00	15.00
MRJJ JoJo	2.50	6.00
MRKS Kairi Sane	5.00	12.00
MRLI Liv Morgan	6.00	15.00
MRLM Liv Morgan	5.00	12.00
MRLT Lita	3.00	8.00
MRMD Alundra Blayze	2.50	6.00
MRMJ Mickie James	2.50	6.00
MRNA Natalya	2.50	6.00
MRNI Nia Jax	3.00	8.00
MRNJ Nia Jax	3.00	8.00
MRNM Naomi	2.50	6.00
MRNT Natalya	2.50	6.00
MRQA Shayna Baszler	2.50	6.00
MRRB Ruby Riott	3.00	8.00
MRRO Ronda Rousey	10.00	25.00
MRRR Ronda Rousey	10.00	25.00
MRRU Ruby Riott	3.00	8.00
MRRY Renee Young	3.00	8.00
MRSA Sarah Logan	2.50	6.00
MRSB Sasha Banks	6.00	15.00
MRSD Sonya Deville	5.00	12.00
MRSF Trish Stratus	4.00	10.00
MRSL Sarah Logan	2.50	6.00
MRTA Tamina	2.50	6.00
MRTM Tamina	2.50	6.00
MRTS Toni Storm	8.00	20.00

2019 Topps WWE Women's Division Mixed Match Challenge Season 2

COMPLETE SET (25) 8.00 20.00
*ORANGE/50: 1.2X TO 3X BASIC CARDS
*BLUE/25: 2X TO 5X BASIC CARDS
*GOLD/10: UNPRICED DUE TO SCARCITY
*RED/1: UNPRICED DUE TO SCARCITY
RANDOMLY INSERTED INTO PACKS

MMC1 Monster Eclipse	.60	1.50
MMC2 Country Dominance	.60	1.50
MMC3 B'N'B	.50	1.25
MMC4 Mahalicia	.50	1.25
MMC5 Team Pawz	.50	1.25
MMC6 Awe-ska	.75	2.00
MMC7 Day One Glow	.40	1.00
MMC8 Ravishing Rusev Day	.50	1.25
MMC9 Fabulous Truth	.60	1.50
MMC10 Monster Eclipse	.60	1.50
MMC11 Country Dominance	.60	1.50
MMC12 Awe-ska	.75	2.00
MMC13 B'N'B	.50	1.25
MMC14 Robert Roode/Team Pawz	.50	1.25
MMC15 Awe-ska	.75	2.00
MMC16 Monster Eclipse	.60	1.50
MMC17 Fabulous Truth	.60	1.50
MMC18 Curt Hawkins/Monster Eclipse	.60	1.50
MMC19 Mahalicia	.50	1.25
MMC20 B'N'B	.50	1.25
MMC21 Awe-ska	.75	2.00
MMC22 Apollo Crews/B'N'B	.50	1.25
MMC23 Mahalicia	.50	1.25
MMC24 Fabulous Truth	.60	1.50
MMC25 Fabulous Truth Win	.60	1.50

2019 Topps WWE Women's Division Shirt Relics

*PURPLE/99: .5X TO 1.2X BASIC CARDS
*ORANGE/50: .6X TO 1.5X BASIC CARDS
*BLUE/25: .75X TO 2X BASIC CARDS
*GOLD/10: UNPRICED DUE TO SCARCITY
*RED/1: UNPRICED DUE TO SCARCITY
STATED PRINT RUN 199 SER.#'d SETS

SRAB Alexa Bliss	12.00	30.00
SRAF Alicia Fox	5.00	12.00
SRAS Asuka	6.00	15.00
SRCM Carmella	5.00	12.00
SRJJ JoJo	4.00	10.00
SRLE Lacey Evans	5.00	12.00
SRNM Naomi	4.00	10.00
SRNT Natalya	4.00	10.00
SRQA Shayna Baszler	4.00	10.00
SRSB Sasha Banks		

2019 Topps WWE Women's Division Team Bestie

COMPLETE SET (20) 8.00 20.00
*ORANGE/50: 1.5X TO 4X BASIC CARDS
*BLUE/25: 2.5X TO 6X BASIC CARDS
*GOLD/10: UNPRICED DUE TO SCARCITY
*RED/1: UNPRICED DUE TO SCARCITY
RANDOMLY INSERTED INTO PACKS

TB1 Trish Stratus	.75	2.00
TB2 Trish Stratus	.75	2.00
TB3 Trish Stratus	.75	2.00
TB4 Trish Stratus	.75	2.00
TB5 Team Bestie	1.00	2.50
TB6 Trish Stratus	.75	2.00
TB7 Trish Stratus	.75	2.00
TB8 Trish Stratus	.75	2.00
TB9 Trish Stratus	1.25	3.00
TB10 Trish Stratus	.75	2.00
TB11 Lita	.60	1.50
TB12 Lita/The Rock	1.00	2.50
TB13 Lita	.60	1.50
TB14 Team Bestie	.75	2.00
TB15 Lita	.60	1.50
TB16 Lita	.60	1.50
TB17 Lita	.60	1.50
TB18 Lita	.60	1.50
TB19 Lita	.60	1.50
TB20 Lita	.60	1.50

2019 Topps WWE Women's Division Triple Autographs

STATED PRINT RUN 10 SER.#'d SETS
UNPRICED DUE TO SCARCITY

TA4H Shafir/Duke/Baszler

2019 Topps WWE Women's Division Women's Evolution

COMPLETE SET (10) 8.00 20.00
*ORANGE/50: 1.2X TO 1.5X BASIC CARDS
*BLUE/25: 2X TO 3X BASIC CARDS
*GOLD/10: UNPRICED DUE TO SCARCITY
*RED/1: UNPRICED DUE TO SCARCITY

WE1 Lita	1.50	4.00
WE2 Alundra Blayze	.75	2.00
WE3 Nia Jax/Tamina	.60	1.50
WE4 Carmella	1.50	4.00
WE5 Mandy Rose	1.50	4.00
WE6 Toni Storm	2.50	6.00
WE7 Sasha/Bayley/Natalya	2.50	6.00
WE8 Jessamyn Duke/Marina Shafir	.75	2.00
WE9 Becky Lynch	2.50	6.00
WE10 Women's Division	3.00	8.00

2019 Topps WWE Women's Division Women's Royal Rumble

COMPLETE SET (25) 12.00 30.00
*ORANGE/50: 2X TO 5X BASIC CARDS
*BLUE/25: 3X TO 8X BASIC CARDS
*GOLD/10: UNPRICED DUE TO SCARCITY
*RED/1: UNPRICED DUE TO SCARCITY
RANDOMLY INSERTED INTO PACKS

RR1 Lacey Evans	1.00	2.50
RR2 Natalya	1.00	2.50
RR3 Mandy Rose	1.25	3.00
RR4 Mickie James	1.25	3.00
RR5 Ember Moon	1.25	3.00
RR6 Billie Kay	1.00	2.50
RR7 Nikki Cross	.75	2.00
RR8 Peyton Royce	1.25	3.00
RR9 Tamina	.50	1.25
RR10 Kairi Sane	1.00	2.50
RR11 Naomi	.75	2.00
RR12 Candice LeRae	1.00	2.50
RR13 Alicia Fox	1.00	2.50
RR14 Kacy Catanzaro	1.25	3.00
RR15 Zelina Vega	.75	2.00
RR16 Ruby Riott	1.00	2.50
RR17 Io Shirai	.50	1.25
RR18 Sonya Deville	1.00	2.50
RR19 Alexa Bliss	2.50	6.00
RR20 Bayley	1.00	2.50
RR21 Becky Lynch	2.00	5.00
RR22 Nia Jax	1.00	2.50
RR23 Carmella	1.25	3.00
RR24 Maria Kanellis	1.25	3.00
RR25 Xia Li	.50	1.25

2020 Topps WWE Women's Division

COMPLETE SET (100) 15.00 40.00
*PURPLE/99: .6X TO 1.5X BASIC CARDS
*GREEN/75: .75X TO 2X BASIC CARDS
*ORANGE/50: 1X TO 2.5X BASIC CARDS
*BLUE/25: 1.5X TO 4X BASIC CARDS
*GOLD/10: UNPRICED DUE TO SCARCITY
*BLACK/5: UNPRICED DUE TO SCARCITY
*RED/1: UNPRICED DUE TO SCARCITY
*P.P.BLACK/1: UNPRICED DUE TO SCARCITY
*P.P.CYAN/1: UNPRICED DUE TO SCARCITY
*P.P.MAGENTA/1: UNPRICED DUE TO SCARCITY
*P.P.YELLOW/1: UNPRICED DUE TO SCARCITY

1 Becky Lynch	1.00	2.50
2 Toni Storm	.60	1.50
3 Nikki Cross	.50	1.25
4 Becky Lynch	1.00	2.50
5 Asuka	1.00	2.50
6 Shayna Baszler	.75	2.00
7 Ronda Rousey	1.25	3.00
8 Asuka	1.00	2.50
9 Lacey Evans	.60	1.50
10 Becky Lynch	1.00	2.50
11 Boss 'n' Hug Connection	1.25	3.00
12 Ronda Rousey	1.25	3.00
13 Mandy Rose	1.25	3.00
14 Shayna Baszler	.75	2.00
15 Asuka	1.00	2.50
16 Becky Lynch	1.00	2.50
17 Boss 'n' Hug Connection	1.25	3.00
18 IIconics	.50	1.25
19 Charlotte Flair	1.00	2.50
20 Shayna Baszler	.75	2.00
21 IIconics	.50	1.25
22 Becky Lynch	1.25	3.00
23 Lacey Evans	.60	1.50
24 Kairi Sane	.50	1.25
25 Shayna Baszler	.75	2.00
26 Charlotte Flair	1.00	2.50
27 Toni Storm	.60	1.50
28 Kabuki Warriors	.50	1.25
29 Bayley	.50	1.25
30 Becky Lynch	1.00	2.50
31 Charlotte Flair	1.00	2.50
32 Bayley	.50	1.25
33 Shayna Baszler	.75	2.00
34 Alexa Bliss	1.50	4.00
35 Kay Lee Ray	.40	1.00
36 Bayley	.50	1.25
37 Becky Lynch	1.00	2.50
38 Baron Corbin & Lacey Evans	.60	1.50
39 Nikki Cross	.50	1.25
40 Shayna Baszler	.75	2.00
41 Io Shirai	.75	2.00
42 Nikki Cross	1.50	4.00
43 Mia Yim	.50	1.25
44 Nikki Cross	.50	1.25
45 Seth Rollins & Becky Lynch	1.00	2.50
46 Io Shirai	.40	1.00
47 Bayley	.50	1.25
48 Seth Rollins & Becky Lynch	1.00	2.50
49 Natalya	.40	1.00
50 Bayley & Ember Moon	.50	1.25
51 Iiconics	.50	1.25
52 Ember Moon	.50	1.25
53 Candice LeRae	.75	2.00
54 Natalya	1.00	2.50
55 Alexa Bliss & Nikki Cross	1.50	4.00
56 Charlotte Flair	1.25	3.00
57 Shayna Baszler	.75	2.00
58 Becky Lynch & Charlotte Flair	1.00	2.50
59 Alexa Bliss & Nikki Cross	1.50	4.00
60 Io Shirai	.40	1.00
61 Shayna Baszler	.75	2.00
62 Alexa Bliss & Nikki Cross	1.50	4.00
63 Becky Lynch	1.00	2.50
64 Bayley	.50	1.25
65 Charlotte Flair	1.25	3.00
66 Alexa Bliss & Nikki Cross	1.50	4.00

67 Sasha Banks 1.25 3.00
68 Charlotte Flair 1.00 2.50
69 Alexa Bliss & Nikki Cross 1.50 4.00
70 Charlotte Flair 1.50 4.00
71 Mia Yim .50 1.25
72 Sasha Banks 1.25 3.00
73 Rhea Ripley 1.00 2.50
74 Kay Lee Ray .40 1.00
75 Sasha Banks 1.25 3.00
76 Bayley .50 1.25
77 Bayley & Sasha Banks 1.25 3.00
78 Fire & Desire 1.25 3.00
79 Becky Lynch & Charlotte Flair 1.00 2.50
80 Nikki Cross 1.50 4.00
81 Shayna Baszler 1.00 2.50
82 Alexa Bliss & Nikki Cross 1.50 4.00
83 Bayley .50 1.25
84 Sasha Banks 1.25 3.00
85 Becky Lynch & Charlotte Flair 1.00 2.50
86 Candice LeRae .75 2.00
87 Kabuki Warriors 1.00 2.50
88 Dakota Kai .50 1.25
89 Shayna Baszler .75 2.00
90 Charlotte Flair 1.00 2.50
91 Kabuki Warriors 1.00 2.50
92 Becky Lynch 1.00 2.50
93 Kabuki Warriors 1.00 2.50
94 Bayley 1.00 2.50
95 Tegan Nox .60 1.50
96 Nikki Cross .50 1.25
97 Rhea Ripley 1.00 2.50
98 Dakota Kai & Tegan Nox .60 1.50
99 Kabuki Warriors .60 1.50
100 Kabuki Warriors 1.00 2.50

2020 Topps WWE Women's Division Autographed Championship Plate Patches

*RED/1: UNPRICED DUE TO SCARCITY
STATED PRINT RUN 10 SER.#'d SETS
UNPRICED DUE TO SCARCITY

CPAB Alexa Bliss
CPAS Asuka
CPCM Carmella
CPKS Kairi Sane
CPNJ Nia Jax
CPNM Naomi
CPNT Natalya
CPQU Charlotte Flair
CPSB Sasha Banks
CPSP Shayna Baszler
CPALX Alexa Bliss
CPBAY Bayley
CPRIP Rhea Ripley

2020 Topps WWE Women's Division Autographed Mat Relics

*RED/1: UNPRICED DUE TO SCARCITY
STATED PRINT RUN 10 SER.#'d SETS
UNPRICED DUE TO SCARCITY

MRABA Bayley
MRABB Bianca Belair
MRABP Beth Phoenix
MRACG Chelsea Green
MRACL Candice LeRae
MRADB Dana Brooke
MRADK Dakota Kai
MRAKS Kairi Sane
MRALE Lacey Evans
MRALM Liv Morgan
MRAMM Mercedes Martinez
MRAMR Mandy Rose
MRAMY Mia Yim
MRANM Naomi
MRAZI Shotzi Blackheart
MRAZV Zelina Vega

2020 Topps WWE Women's Division Autographs

*PINK/150: SAME VALUE AS BASIC
*PURPLE/99: .5X TO 1.2X BASIC AUTO
*GREEN/75: .6X TO 1.5X BASIC AUTO
*ORANGE/50: .75X TO 2X BASIC AUTO
*BLUE/25: UNPRICED DUE TO SCARCITY
*GOLD/10: UNPRICED DUE TO SCARCITY
*BLACK/5: UNPRICED DUE TO SCARCITY
*RED/1: UNPRICED DUE TO SCARCITY
*P.P.BLACK/1: UNPRICED DUE TO SCARCITY
*P.P.CYAN/1: UNPRICED DUE TO SCARCITY
*P.P.MAGENTA/1: UNPRICED DUE TO SCARCITY
*P.P.YELLOW/1: UNPRICED DUE TO SCARCITY
STATED ODDS

AAB Alexa Bliss 60.00 120.00
AAL Aliyah 12.00 30.00
AAS Asuka 20.00 50.00
ABB Bianca Belair 25.00 60.00
ABI Billie Kay 10.00 25.00
ABL Bayley 15.00 40.00
ACC Charly Caruso 10.00 25.00
ACG Chelsea Green 15.00 40.00
ACL Candice LeRae 12.00 30.00
ACM Carmella 15.00 40.00
ADK Dakota Kai 20.00 50.00
AEM Ember Moon 8.00 20.00
AIS Io Shirai 30.00 75.00
AJD Jessamyn Duke 8.00 20.00
AKB Kayla Braxton 20.00 50.00
AKC Kayden Carter 10.00 25.00
ALE Lacey Evans 15.00 40.00
ALM Liv Morgan 20.00 50.00
ALN Lana 12.00 30.00
AMJ Mickie James 12.00 30.00
AMR Mandy Rose 15.00 40.00
AMS Marina Shafir 6.00 15.00
AMY Mia Yim 6.00 15.00
ANC Nikki Cross 10.00 25.00
ANJ Nia Jax 6.00 15.00
ANM Naomi 8.00 20.00
ANT Natalya 6.00 15.00
APR Peyton Royce 15.00 40.00
ARB Ruby Riott 12.00 30.00
ARR Rhea Ripley 50.00 100.00
ASB Sasha Banks 30.00 75.00
ASG Santana Garrett 15.00 40.00
ASH Shotzi Blackheart 75.00 150.00
ASP Shayna Baszler 10.00 25.00
ATN Tegan Nox 25.00 60.00
ATS Toni Storm 50.00 100.00
AXL Xia Li 20.00 50.00
AKLR Kay Lee Ray 20.00 50.00

2020 Topps WWE Women's Division Breaking Barriers

COMPLETE SET (10) 8.00 20.00
*BLUE/25: UNPRICED DUE TO SCARCITY
*GOLD/10: UNPRICED DUE TO SCARCITY
*BLACK/5: UNPRICED DUE TO SCARCITY
*RED/1: UNPRICED DUE TO SCARCITY
RANDOMLY INSERTED INTO PACKS

BB1 Chyna 1.25 3.00
BB2 Chyna 1.25 3.00
BB3 Chyna 1.25 3.00
BB4 Chyna 1.25 3.00
BB5 Alundra Blayze .75 2.00
BB6 Chyna 1.25 3.00
BB7 Ronda Rousey 2.50 6.00
BB8 WWE Evolution 2.00 5.00
BB9 Nia Jax .75 2.00
BB10 Main Event WrestleMania 2.00 5.00

2020 Topps WWE Women's Division Championship Plate Patches

*PURPLE/99: .5X TO 1.2X BASIC MEM
*GREEN/75: .6X TO 1.5X BASIC MEM
*ORANGE/50: .6X TO 1.5X BASIC MEM
*BLUE/25: UNPRICED DUE TO SCARCITY
*GOLD/10: UNPRICED DUE TO SCARCITY
*RED/1: UNPRICED DUE TO SCARCITY
STATED PRINT RUN 150 SER.#'d SETS

CPA Asuka 12.00 30.00
CPC Charlotte Flair 6.00 15.00
CPAB Alexa Bliss 15.00 40.00
CPAS Asuka 12.00 30.00
CPBL Becky Lynch 10.00 25.00
CPBS Sasha Banks 10.00 25.00
CPCF Charlotte Flair 6.00 15.00
CPCM Carmella 5.00 12.00
CPEM Ember Moon 4.00 10.00
CPHG Bayley 6.00 15.00
CPKS Kairi Sane 5.00 12.00
CPNJ Nia Jax 4.00 10.00
CPNM Naomi 3.00 8.00
CPNT Natalya 3.00 8.00
CPPG Paige
CPQU Charlotte Flair 6.00 15.00
CPRH Rhea Ripley 15.00 40.00
CPRM Bayley 6.00 15.00
CPRR Ronda Rousey 12.00 30.00
CPSB Sasha Banks 10.00 25.00
CPSP Shayna Baszler 10.00 25.00
CPTS Toni Storm 15.00 40.00
CPALX Alexa Bliss 15.00 40.00
CPBAY Bayley 6.00 15.00
CPKLR Kay Lee Ray 8.00 20.00
CPMAN Becky Lynch 10.00 25.00
CPRIP Rhea Ripley 15.00 40.00

2020 Topps WWE Women's Division Cut Signatures

STATED PRINT RUN 1 SER.#'d SET
UNPRICED DUE TO SCARCITY

CSCY Chyna
CSMA Mae Young
CSME Miss Elizabeth

2020 Topps WWE Women's Division Dual Autographs

*GOLD/10: UNPRICED DUE TO SCARCITY
*BLACK/5: UNPRICED DUE TO SCARCITY
*RED/1: UNPRICED DUE TO SCARCITY
RANDOMLY INSERTED INTO PACKS

DAAN A.Bliss/N.Cross 100.00 200.00
DAHI V.Borne/Aliyah 50.00 100.00
DAKW K.Sane/Asuka 125.00 250.00

2020 Topps WWE Women's Division Four Horsewomen of MMA Autographed Book

QMMA Shafir/Rousey/Baszler/Duke 500.00 1000.00

2020 Topps WWE Women's Division Four Horsewomen of WWE Autographed Book

QWWE Bayley/Lynch/Flair/Banks 1000.00 1500.00

2020 Topps WWE Women's Division Mat Relics

*PURPLE/99: .5X TO 1.2X BASIC MEM
*ORANGE/50: .6X TO 1.5X BASIC MEM
*BLUE/25: UNPRICED DUE TO SCARCITY
*GOLD/10: UNPRICED DUE TO SCARCITY
*RED/1: UNPRICED DUE TO SCARCITY
STATED PRINT RUN 150 SER.#'d SETS

MRAB Alexa Bliss 12.00 30.00
MRAS Asuka 10.00 25.00
MRBA Bayley 5.00 12.00
MRBB Bianca Belair 3.00 8.00
MRBL Becky Lynch 8.00 20.00
MRBP Beth Phoenix 2.00 5.00
MRCF Charlotte Flair 6.00 15.00
MRCG Chelsea Green 4.00 10.00
MRCL Candice LeRae 6.00 15.00
MRDB Dana Brooke 2.50 6.00
MRDK Dakota Kai 8.00 20.00
MRET Asuka 10.00 25.00
MRIS Io Shirai 5.00 12.00
MRKS Kairi Sane 6.00 15.00
MRLE Lacey Evans 4.00 10.00
MRLM Liv Morgan 8.00 20.00
MRMH Mighty Molly 3.00 8.00
MRMM Mercedes Martinez 3.00 8.00
MRMR Mandy Rose 6.00 15.00
MRMY Mia Yim 3.00 8.00
MRNC Nikki Cross 4.00 10.00
MRNM Naomi 3.00 8.00
MRNT Natalya 2.50 6.00
MRQU Charlotte Flair 6.00 15.00
MRRR Rhea Ripley 6.00 15.00
MRSB Shayna Baszler 6.00 15.00
MRSD Sonya Deville 2.00 5.00
MRTM Becky Lynch 8.00 20.00
MRTN Tegan Nox 5.00 12.00
MRTO Toni Storm 10.00 25.00
MRTS Tamina 2.00 5.00
MRXL Xia Li 4.00 10.00
MRZI Shotzi Blackheart 12.00 30.00
MRZV Zelina Vega 3.00 8.00
MREST Bianca Belair 3.00 8.00

2020 Topps WWE Women's Division Roster

COMPLETE SET (60) 20.00 50.00
*BLUE/25: UNPRICED DUE TO SCARCITY
*GOLD/10: UNPRICED DUE TO SCARCITY
*BLACK/5: UNPRICED DUE TO SCARCITY
*RED/1: UNPRICED DUE TO SCARCITY

RC1 Alexa Bliss 2.50 6.00
RC2 Alicia Taylor .40 1.00
RC3 Aliyah .75 2.00
RC4 Asuka 1.50 4.00
RC5 Bayley .75 2.00
RC6 Becky Lynch 1.50 4.00
RC7 Beth Phoenix .60 1.50
RC8 Bianca Belair 1.00 2.50
RC9 Billie Kay .75 2.00
RC10 Candice LeRae 1.25 3.00
RC11 Carmella 1.00 2.50
RC12 Charlotte Flair 1.50 4.00
RC13 Charly Caruso .40 1.00
RC14 Chelsea Green 2.00 5.00
RC15 Chyna 1.00 2.50
RC16 Dakota Kai .75 2.00
RC17 Dana Brooke .60 1.50
RC18 Ember Moon .75 2.00
RC19 Io Shirai .60 1.50
RC20 Jessamyn Duke .60 1.50
RC21 Jessi Kamea .40 1.00
RC22 Kairi Sane .75 2.00
RC23 Kay Lee Ray .60 1.50
RC24 Kayden Carter .40 1.00
RC25 Kayla Braxton .50 1.25
RC26 Lacey Evans 1.00 2.50
RC27 Lana 1.00 2.50
RC28 Liv Morgan 1.00 2.50
RC29 Lita 1.00 2.50
RC30 Mandy Rose 2.00 5.00
RC31 Marina Shafir .60 1.50
RC32 Maryse .75 2.00
RC33 Mia Yim .75 2.00
RC34 Mickie James .60 1.50
RC35 Naomi .75 2.00
RC36 Natalya .60 1.50
RC37 Nia Jax .60 1.50
RC38 Nikki Cross .75 2.00
RC39 Paige 1.00 2.50
RC40 Peyton Royce .75 2.00
RC41 Piper Niven .50 1.25
RC42 Renee Young .50 1.25
RC43 Rhea Ripley 1.50 4.00
RC44 Ronda Rousey 2.00 5.00
RC45 Ruby Riott .60 1.50
RC46 Santana Garrett .40 1.00
RC47 Sarah Schreiber .40 1.00
RC48 Sasha Banks 2.00 5.00
RC49 Shayna Baszler 1.25 3.00
RC50 Shotzi Blackheart 1.25 3.00
RC51 Sonya Deville 1.00 2.50
RC52 Stephanie McMahon 1.00 2.50
RC53 Tamina .50 1.25
RC54 Tegan Nox 1.00 2.50
RC55 Toni Storm 1.00 2.50
RC56 Trish Stratus 2.00 5.00
RC57 Vanessa Borne .75 2.00
RC58 Xia Li .75 2.00
RC59 Zelina Vega .75 2.00
RC60 Raquel Gonzalez .60 1.50

2020 Topps WWE Women's Division Superstar Transformations

COMPLETE SET (15) 20.00 50.00
*BLUE/25: UNPRICED DUE TO SCARCITY
*GOLD/10: UNPRICED DUE TO SCARCITY

*BLACK/5: UNPRICED DUE TO SCARCITY
*RED/1: UNPRICED DUE TO SCARCITY
ST1 Alexa Bliss 6.00 15.00
ST2 Asuka 3.00 8.00
ST3 Bayley 2.50 6.00
ST4 Becky Lynch 4.00 10.00
ST5 Carmella 2.00 5.00
ST6 Charlotte Flair 4.00 10.00
ST7 Io Shirai 2.50 6.00
ST8 Kairi Sane 3.00 8.00
ST9 Liv Morgan 2.50 6.00
ST10 Naomi 1.50 4.00
ST11 Paige 1.50 4.00
ST12 Peyton Royce 2.50 6.00
ST13 Ruby Riott 2.50 6.00
ST14 Sasha Banks 5.00 12.00
ST15 Sonya Deville 1.50 4.00

2020 Topps WWE Women's Division Triple Autographs

*GOLD/10: UNPRICED DUE TO SCARCITY
*BLACK/5: UNPRICED DUE TO SCARCITY
*RED/1: UNPRICED DUE TO SCARCITY
STATED PRINT RUN 25 SER.#'d SETS
TAUK Ray/Storm/Ripley 150.00 300.00
TABAD Naomi/Tamina/Banks 100.00 200.00

2021 Topps WWE Women's Division

COMPLETE SET (100) 10.00 25.00
*FOIL: .5X TO 1.2X BASIC CARDS
*PURPLE/99: .6X TO 1.5X BASIC CARDS
*ORANGE/75: .75X TO 2X BASIC CARDS
*GREEN/50: 1X TO 2.5X BASIC CARDS
*BLUE/25: 1.5X TO 4X BASIC CARDS
*GOLD/10: UNPRICED DUE TO SCARCITY
*BLACK/5: UNPRICED DUE TO SCARCITY
*RED/1: UNPRICED DUE TO SCARCITY
*P.P.BLACK/1: UNPRICED DUE TO SCARCITY
*P.P.CYAN/1: UNPRICED DUE TO SCARCITY
*P.P.MAGENTA/1: UNPRICED DUE TO SCARCITY
*P.P.YELLOW/1: UNPRICED DUE TO SCARCITY
1 Bianca Belair .60 1.50
2 Io Shirai .50 1.25
3 Alexa Bliss & Nikki Cross 1.50 4.00
4 Bayley 1.25 3.00
5 Sonya Deville 1.25 3.00
6 Tamina .30 .75
7 Charlotte Flair 1.25 3.00
8 Mia Yim .30 .75
9 Alexa Bliss & Nikki Cross 1.50 4.00
10 Charlotte Flair 1.25 3.00
11 Rhea Ripley .75 2.00
12 Sonya Deville 1.25 3.00
13 Tamina & Lacey Evans .60 1.50
14 Bayley .60 1.50
15 Asuka 1.00 2.50
16 Becky Lynch 1.00 2.50
17 Nia Jax 1.00 2.50
18 Charlotte Flair 1.25 3.00
19 Bayley .60 1.50
20 Nia Jax .50 1.25
21 Sasha Banks 1.50 4.00
22 Nia Jax .50 1.25
23 Golden Role Models 1.25 3.00
24 Io Shirai .50 1.25
25 Charlotte Flair 1.25 3.00
26 Golden Role Models 1.25 3.00
27 Asuka .50 1.25
28 Asuka 1.00 2.50
29 Golden Role Models 1.25 3.00
30 Sonya Deville 1.25 3.00
31 Asuka 1.00 2.50
32 Rhea Ripley .75 2.00
33 Nikki Cross .50 1.25
34 Sasha Banks 1.25 3.00
35 Rhea Ripley .75 2.00
36 Tegan Nox .60 1.50
37 Io Shirai 1.25 3.00
38 Nikki Cross .60 1.50
39 Asuka 1.00 2.50
40 Golden Role Models 1.25 3.00
41 Golden Role Models 1.25 3.00
42 Aliyah .50 1.25
43 Io Shirai .50 1.25
44 Dakota Kai .50 1.25
45 Golden Role Models 1.25 3.00
46 RAW Title Match Controversy .60 1.50
47 Bayley .60 1.50
48 Shotzi Blackheart 1.00 2.50
49 Nikki Cross .50 1.25
50 Nia Jax & Shayna Baszler .50 1.25
51 Mercedes Martinez .40 1.00
52 Bayley .60 1.50
53 The Fiend 1.50 4.00
54 Asuka 1.00 2.50
55 Dakota Kai .50 1.25
56 Asuka 1.00 2.50
57 Rhea Ripley & Shotzi Blackheart 1.00 2.50
58 Asuka 1.00 2.50
59 Rhea Ripley & Shotzi Blackheart 1.00 2.50
60 Dakota Kai .60 1.50
61 Sonya Deville .60 1.50
62 Sasha Banks 1.25 3.00
63 Io Shirai .50 1.25
64 Mandy Rose 1.25 3.00
65 Bayley .60 1.50
66 Asuka 1.00 2.50
67 Shayna Baszler & Nia Jax .50 1.25
68 Asuka 1.25 3.00
69 Dakota Kai & Raquel Gonzalez .60 1.50
70 Shayna Baszler & Nia Jax .50 1.25
71 Bayley 1.25 3.00
72 Rhea Ripley .75 2.00
73 Alexa Bliss 1.50 4.00
74 Candice LeRae 1.00 2.50
75 Alexa Bliss 1.50 4.00
76 Sasha Banks 1.25 3.00
77 Candice LeRae & Johnny Gargano 1.00 2.50
78 Io Shirai 1.00 2.50
79 Ember Moon .30 .75
80 Nia Jax & Shayna Baszler .50 1.25
81 Ember Moon & Rhea Ripley .75 2.00
82 Candice LeRae 1.00 2.50
83 Toni Storm .75 2.00
84 Dakota Kai .50 1.25
85 Sasha Banks 1.25 3.00
86 Sasha Banks 1.25 3.00
87 Rhea Ripley .75 2.00
88 Io Shirai .50 1.25
89 Nia Jax & Shayna Baszler .50 1.25
90 Dakota Kai .60 1.50
91 Toni Storm .75 2.00
92 Sasha Banks 1.25 3.00
93 Carmella .60 1.50
94 Candice LeRae 1.00 2.50
95 Carmella .60 1.50
96 Toni Storm & Ember Moon .75 2.00
97 Io Shirai .75 2.00
98 Sasha Banks 1.25 3.00
99 Alexa Bliss 1.50 4.00
100 Toni Storm .75 2.00

2021 Topps WWE Women's Division 5th Anniversary Women's Championship Autographs

*ORANGE/75: .5X TO 1.2X BASIC AUTOS
*GREEN/50: .6X TO 1.5X BASIC AUTOS
*BLUE/25: .75X TO 2X BASIC AUTOS
*GOLD/10: UNPRICED DUE TO SCARCITY
*RED/1: UNPRICED DUE TO SCARCITY
STATED PRINT RUN 99 SER.#'d SETS
UNPRICED DUE TO SCARCITY
5AAB Alexa Bliss 75.00 150.00
5AAS Asuka 30.00 75.00
5ABL Becky Lynch 50.00 100.00
5ACF Charlotte Flair 50.00 100.00
5ACM Carmella 15.00 40.00
5ANJ Nia Jax 10.00 25.00
5ANM Naomi 10.00 25.00
5ANT Natalya 10.00 25.00
5ASB Sasha Banks 60.00 120.00

2021 Topps WWE Women's Division 5th Anniversary Women's Championship Tribute

*BLUE/25: 1.2X TO 3X BASIC CARDS
*GOLD/10: UNPRICED DUE TO SCARCITY
*BLACK/5: UNPRICED DUE TO SCARCITY
*RED/1: UNPRICED DUE TO SCARCITY
RANDOMLY INSERTED INTO PACKS
RC1 Sasha Banks def. Charlotte Flair 2.50 6.00
RC2 Charlotte Flair def. Sasha Banks 2.50 6.00
RC3 Sasha Banks def. Charlotte Flair 2.50 6.00
RC4 Bayley def. Charlotte Flair 1.25 3.00
RC5 Alexa Bliss def. Bayley 3.00 8.00
RC6 Alexa Bliss 3.00 8.00
RC7 Becky Lynch def. Sasha Banks 2.00 5.00
RC8 Becky Lynch def. Sasha Banks 2.00 5.00
RC9 Becky Lynch def. Asuka 2.00 5.00
RC10 Sasha Banks def. Asuka 2.50 6.00
SC1 Alexa Bliss def. Becky Lynch 3.00 8.00
SC2 Charlotte Flair def. Asuka 2.50 6.00
SC3 Charlotte Flair def. Becky Lynch and Carmella 2.50 6.00
SC4 Becky Lynch def. Charlotte Flair 2.00 5.00
SC5 Charlotte Flair def. Becky Lynch 2.50 6.00
SC6 Becky Lynch def. Charlotte Flair 2.00 5.00
SC7 Asuka def. Becky Lynch and Charlotte Flair 2.00 5.00
SC8 Asuka def. Becky Lynch 2.00 5.00
SC9 Bayley def. Charlotte Flair 1.25 3.00
SC10 Sasha Banks def. Bayley 2.50 6.00

2021 Topps WWE Women's Division Autographed Mat Relics

STATED PRINT RUN 10 SER.#'d SETS
UNPRICED DUE TO SCARCITY
MC Carmella
MN Naomi
MT Tamina
MAB Alexa Bliss
MBB Bianca Belair
MBZ Shayna Baszler
MCF Charlotte Flair
MDB Dana Brooke
MDK Dakota Kai
MEM Ember Moon
MLM Liv Morgan
MMR Mandy Rose
MNC Nikki Cross
MNJ Nia Jax
MNT Natalya
MRP Rhea Ripley
MSB Shotzi Blackheart
MSD Sonya Deville
MTN Tegan Nox
MTS Toni Storm

2021 Topps WWE Women's Division Autographed Superstar Logo Patches

STATED PRINT RUN 10 SER.#'d SETS
UNPRICED DUE TO SCARCITY
ARAS Asuka
ARBB Bianca Belair
ARBZ Shayna Baszler
ARCF Charlotte Flair
ARCL Candice LeRae
ARCM Carmella
ARDB Dana Brooke
ARDK Dakota Kai
ARMR Mandy Rose
ARNJ Nia Jax
ARNT Natalya
ARRP Rhea Ripley
ARSD Sonya Deville
ARSZ Shotzi Blackheart

2021 Topps WWE Women's Division Autographs

*PURPLE/99: .5X TO 1.2X BASIC AUTOS
*ORANGE/75: .6X TO 1.5X BASIC AUTOS
*GREEN/50: .75X TO 2X BASIC AUTOS
*BLUE/25: 1X TO 2.5X BASIC AUTOS
*GOLD/10: UNPRICED DUE TO SCARCITY
*BLACK/5: UNPRICED DUE TO SCARCITY
*RED/1: UNPRICED DUE TO SCARCITY
*P.P.BLACK/1: UNPRICED DUE TO SCARCITY
*P.P.CYAN/1: UNPRICED DUE TO SCARCITY
*P.P.MAGENTA/1: UNPRICED DUE TO SCARCITY
*P.P.YELLOW/1: UNPRICED DUE TO SCARCITY
STATED PRINT RUN 199 SER.#'d SETS
AAA Alyse Ashton 12.00 30.00
AAB Alexa Bliss 75.00 150.00
AAL Aliyah 8.00 20.00
AAS Asuka 15.00 40.00
AAT Alicia Taylor 5.00 12.00
ABL Becky Lynch 30.00 75.00
ABP Beth Phoenix 8.00 20.00
ABZ Shayna Baszler 6.00 15.00
ACJ Cora Jade 75.00 150.00
ACL Candice LeRae 8.00 20.00
ACM Carmella 10.00 25.00
ADK Dakota Kai 10.00 25.00
AEM Ember Moon 6.00 15.00
AFM Franky Monet 12.00 30.00
AGD Gigi Dolin 75.00 150.00
AIH Indi Hartwell 15.00 40.00
AIS Io Shirai 12.00 30.00
AJK Jessi Kamea 6.00 15.00
AKB Kayla Braxton 6.00 15.00
AKC Kacy Catanzaro 12.00 30.00
AKD Kayden Carter 5.00 12.00
AKT Katrina Cortez 6.00 15.00
ALE Lacey Evans 10.00 25.00
ALM Liv Morgan 30.00 75.00
AMH Molly Holly 20.00 50.00
AMM McKenzie Mitchell 8.00 20.00
AMZ Maryse 10.00 25.00
ANC Nikki Cross 8.00 20.00
ANJ Nia Jax 5.00 12.00
ANT Natalya 6.00 15.00
APN Piper Niven 10.00 25.00
ARG Raquel Gonzalez 10.00 25.00
ARP Rhea Ripley 15.00 40.00
ASC Scarlett 30.00 75.00
ASD Sonya Deville 8.00 20.00
ASR Sarray 30.00 75.00
ASS Sarah Schreiber 10.00 25.00
AST Stephanie McMahon 125.00 250.00
ASZ Shotzi Blackheart 15.00 40.00
ATI Mei Ying 12.00 30.00
ATM Tamina 5.00 12.00
ATN Tegan Nox 12.00 30.00
ATS Toni Storm 15.00 40.00
AXL Xia Li 15.00 40.00
AZS Zoey Stark 6.00 15.00
AKLR Kay Lee Ray 6.00 15.00
ANEM Eva Marie 12.00 30.00

2021 Topps WWE Women's Division Autographs Purple

ACF Charlotte Flair 50.00 100.00
ANM Naomi 8.00 20.00

2021 Topps WWE Women's Division Best Roommates Ever Autograph Book

QBRE Kai/Duke/Baszler/Yim

2021 Topps WWE Women's Division Diamond Cuts

COMPLETE SET (14)
*BLUE/25: 2X TO 5X BASIC CARDS
*GOLD/10: UNPRICED DUE TO SCARCITY
*BLACK/5: UNPRICED DUE TO SCARCITY
*RED/1: UNPRICED DUE TO SCARCITY
RANDOMLY INSERTED INTO PACKS
DC1 Charlotte Flair 4.00 10.00
DC2 Lacey Evans 2.00 5.00
DC3 Mandy Rose 4.00 10.00
DC4 Jessi Kamea 1.50 4.00
DC5 Bianca Belair 2.00 5.00
DC6 Dana Brooke .75 2.00
DC7 Carmella 2.00 5.00
DC8 Franky Monet 1.50 4.00
DC9 Liv Morgan 3.00 8.00
DC10 Natalya 1.25 3.00
DC11 Sasha Banks 4.00 10.00
DC12 Aliyah 1.50 4.00
DC13 Dakota Kai 1.50 4.00
DC14 Indi Hartwell 2.50 6.00

2021 Topps WWE Women's Division Dual Autographs

*GOLD/10: UNPRICED DUE TO SCARCITY
*RED/1: UNPRICED DUE TO SCARCITY
STATED PRINT RUN 25 SER.#'d SETS
UNPRICED DUE TO SCARCITY

Card	Low	High
DADR D.Kai/R.Gonzalez		
DAKK K.Carter/K/Catanzaro	50.00	100.00
DAMD M.Rose/D.Brooke	60.00	120.00
DANS S.Baszler/N.Jax	15.00	40.00
DANT Tamina/Natalya	25.00	60.00
DASE E.Moon/S.Blackheart	50.00	100.00

2021 Topps WWE Women's Division Legends of the Women's Division Autograph Book

QWDL Eve/Holly/Stratus/Phoenix

2021 Topps WWE Women's Division Mat Relics

*PINK/150: SAME VALUE AS BASIC
*PURPLE/99: .5X TO 1.2X BASIC MEM
*ORANGE/75: .6X TO 1.5X BASIC MEM
*GREEN/50: .75X TO 2X BASIC MEM
*BLUE/25: 1X TO 2.5X BASIC MEM
*GOLD/10: UNPRICED DUE TO SCARCITY
*BLACK/5: UNPRICED DUE TO SCARCITY
*RED/1: UNPRICED DUE TO SCARCITY
STATED PRINT RUN 250 SER.#'d SETS

Card	Low	High
M$ Sasha Banks	10.00	25.00
MA Asuka	6.00	15.00
MB Bayley	6.00	15.00
MC Carmella	3.00	8.00
MN Naomi	3.00	8.00
MT Tamina	2.50	6.00
MAB Alexa Bliss	15.00	40.00
MAK Asuka	6.00	15.00
MAL Alexa Bliss	15.00	40.00
MBB Bianca Belair	5.00	12.00
MBE Becky Lynch	12.00	30.00
MBL Bayley	6.00	15.00
MBY Bayley	6.00	15.00
MBZ Shayna Baszler	5.00	12.00
MCF Charlotte Flair	6.00	15.00
MCH Charlotte Flair	6.00	15.00
MDA Dakota Kai	5.00	12.00
MDB Dana Brooke	2.50	6.00
MDK Dakota Kai	5.00	12.00
MEM Ember Moon	2.50	6.00
MLA Lacey Evans	4.00	10.00
MLE Lacey Evans	4.00	10.00
MLM Liv Morgan	10.00	25.00
MLV Liv Morgan	10.00	25.00
MMR Mandy Rose	6.00	15.00
MNC Nikki Cross	2.50	6.00
MNJ Nia Jax	2.50	6.00
MNT Natalya	3.00	8.00
MRP Rhea Ripley	8.00	20.00
MSA Sasha Banks	10.00	25.00
MSB Shotzi Blackheart	8.00	20.00
MSD Sonya Deville	4.00	10.00
MTN Tegan Nox	3.00	8.00
MTS Toni Storm	5.00	12.00
MALE Alexa Bliss	15.00	40.00
MASU Asuka	6.00	15.00
MBIA Bianca Belair	5.00	12.00
MMRS Mandy Rose	6.00	15.00
MNIA Nia Jax	2.50	6.00
MRHE Rhea Ripley	8.00	20.00
MSAS Sasha Banks	10.00	25.00
MSHA Shayna Baszler	5.00	12.00

2021 Topps WWE Women's Division Roster

Card	Low	High
COMPLETE SET (55)	12.00	30.00

*BLUE/25: 1.2X TO 3X BASIC CARDS
*GOLD/10: UNPRICED DUE TO SCARCITY
*BLACK/5: UNPRICED DUE TO SCARCITY
*RED/1: UNPRICED DUE TO SCARCITY
RANDOMLY INSERTED INTO PACKS

Card	Low	High
R1 Alexa Bliss	2.50	6.00
R2 Asuka	1.50	4.00
R3 Becky Lynch	1.50	4.00
R4 Charlotte Flair	2.00	5.00
R5 Dana Brooke	.40	1.00
R6 Doudrop	.60	1.50
R7 Lacey Evans	1.00	2.50
R8 Mandy Rose	2.00	5.00
R9 Maryse	.60	1.50
R10 Naomi	.50	1.25
R11 Nia Jax	.75	2.00
R12 Nikki A.S.H.	.75	2.00
R13 Rhea Ripley	1.25	3.00
R14 Sarah Schreiber	.40	1.00
R15 Shayna Baszler	.75	2.00
R16 Alyse Ashton	.40	1.00
R17 Bayley	1.00	2.50
R18 Bianca Belair	1.00	2.50
R19 Carmella	1.00	2.50
R20 Kayla Braxton	.75	2.00
R21 Liv Morgan	1.50	4.00
R22 Natalya	.60	1.50
R23 Sasha Banks	2.00	5.00
R24 Sonya Deville	1.00	2.50
R25 Tamina	.50	1.25
R26 Alicia Taylor	.40	1.00
R27 Aliyah	.75	2.00
R28 Beth Phoenix	.75	2.00
R29 Candice LeRae	1.50	4.00
R30 Dakota Kai	.75	2.00
R31 Ember Moon	.50	1.25
R32 Franky Monet	.75	2.00
R33 Gigi Dolin	.40	1.00
R34 Indi Hartwell	1.25	3.00
R35 Io Shirai	.75	2.00
R36 Jessi Kamea	.75	2.00
R37 Kacy Catanzaro	.75	2.00
R38 Kavita Devi	.40	1.00
R39 Kayden Carter	.75	2.00
R40 Mei Ying	.60	1.50
R41 McKenzie Mitchell	.50	1.25
R42 Mercedes Martinez	.60	1.50
R43 Raquel Gonzalez	1.00	2.50
R44 Sarray	.50	1.25
R45 Scarlett	2.00	5.00
R46 Shotzi	1.50	4.00
R47 Nox	1.00	2.50
R48 Toni Storm	1.25	3.00
R49 Xia Li	.75	2.00
R50 Zoey Stark	.50	1.25
R51 Kay Lee Ray	1.00	2.50
R52 Stephanie McMahon	1.00	2.50
R53 Eva Marie	1.00	2.50
R54 Marlena	.60	1.50
R55 Molly Holly	.50	1.25

2021 Topps WWE Women's Division Sketches

NNO Carlos Cabaleiro

2021 Topps WWE Women's Division Superstar Logo Patches

*PINK/150: SAME VALUE AS BASIC
*PURPLE/99: .5X TO 1.2X BASIC MEM
*ORANGE/75: .6X TO 1.5X BASIC MEM
*GREEN/50: .75X TO 2X BASIC MEM
*BLUE/25: 1X TO 2.5X BASIC MEM
*GOLD/10: UNPRICED DUE TO SCARCITY
*BLACK/5: UNPRICED DUE TO SCARCITY
*RED/1: UNPRICED DUE TO SCARCITY
STATED PRINT RUN 199 SER.#'d SETS

Card	Low	High
SLPAB Alexa Bliss	15.00	40.00
SLPAS Asuka	10.00	25.00
SLPBA Bayley	8.00	20.00
SLPBB Bianca Belair	6.00	15.00
SLPBL Becky Lynch	15.00	40.00
SLPBP Beth Phoenix	4.00	10.00
SLPBZ Shayna Baszler	3.00	8.00
SLPCF Charlotte Flair	6.00	15.00
SLPCL Candice LeRae	4.00	10.00
SLPCM Carmella	4.00	10.00
SLPDB Dana Brooke	3.00	8.00
SLPDK Dakota Kai	5.00	12.00
SLPEM Ember Moon	5.00	12.00
SLPEV Eve	3.00	8.00
SLPLE Lacey Evans	3.00	8.00
SLPLM Liv Morgan	10.00	25.00
SLPMM Mercedes Martinez	4.00	10.00
SLPMR Mandy Rose	6.00	15.00
SLPNJ Nia Jax	3.00	8.00
SLPNM Naomi	5.00	12.00
SLPNT Natalya	4.00	10.00
SLPRP Rhea Ripley	6.00	15.00
SLPSB Sasha Banks	8.00	20.00
SLPSC Scarlett	10.00	25.00
SLPSD Sonya Deville	3.00	8.00
SLPSZ Shotzi	5.00	12.00
SLPTN Nox	8.00	20.00
SLPTR Trish Stratus	8.00	20.00

2019 Topps WWE Women's Revolution

Card	Low	High
COMPLETE SET (40)	25.00	60.00
SEMISTARS	1.00	2.50
UNLISTED STARS	1.25	3.00

RANDOMLY INSERTED INTO PACKS

Card	Low	High
DR1 Paige	2.00	5.00
DR2 Charlotte/Becky/Sasha	2.00	5.00
DR3 Charlotte Flair	2.00	5.00
DR4 Team PCB	2.00	5.00
DR5 Charlotte Flair	2.00	5.00
DR6 Nikki Bella	2.00	5.00
DR7 Charlotte Flair	2.00	5.00
DR8 Paige	2.00	5.00
DR9 Natalya	2.00	5.00
DR10 Charlotte Flair	2.00	5.00
DR11 Paige	2.00	5.00
DR12 Charlotte Flair	2.00	5.00
DR13 Paige	2.00	5.00
DR14 Charlotte Flair	2.00	5.00
DR15 Charlotte Flair	2.00	5.00
DR16 Nikki Bella	1.25	3.00
DR17 Charlotte Flair	2.00	5.00
DR18 Sasha Banks	2.00	5.00
DR19 Brie Bella	1.25	3.00
DR20 Team B.A.D./Sasha Banks	2.00	5.00
DR21 Lita	1.25	3.00
DR22 Charlotte Flair	2.00	5.00
DR23 Charlotte Flair	2.00	5.00
DR24 SD Women's Championship	2.50	6.00
DR25 Becky Lynch	2.00	5.00
DR26 Charlotte Flair	2.00	5.00
DR27 Sasha Banks & Charlotte Flair	2.00	5.00
DR28 Mickie James & Asuka	1.25	3.00
DR29 Alexa Bliss	2.50	6.00
DR30 Mickie James & Alexa Bliss	2.50	6.00
DR31 Bayley	1.00	2.50
DR32 Naomi	.75	2.00
DR33 Naomi & Charlotte	.75	2.00
DR34 Alexa Bliss	2.50	6.00
DR35 Carmella	1.25	3.00
DR36 Asuka	1.50	4.00
DR37 Charlotte Flair	2.00	5.00
DR38 Absolution	2.00	5.00
DR39 Riott Squad	1.50	4.00
DR40 Asuka	1.50	4.00

1985 Topps WWF

Card	Low	High
COMPLETE SET W/HOGAN (66)	125.00	300.00
COMPLETE SET W/O HOGAN (60)	100.00	200.00
UNOPENED BOX (36 PACKS)	1000.00	1500.00
UNOPENED PACK (9 CARDS+1 STICKER)	30.00	40.00
RACK PACK (26 CARDS+3 STICKERS)	150.00	200.00

RINGSIDE ACTION (22-56)
SUPERSTARS SPEAK (57-66)
*OPC: SAME VALUE AS TOPPS

Card	Low	High
1 Hulk Hogan RC	50.00	125.00
2 The Iron Sheik RC	1.25	3.00
3 Captain Lou Albano RC	1.25	3.00
4 Junk Yard Dog RC	1.00	2.50
5 Paul Mr. Wonderful Orndorff RC	1.25	3.00
6 Jimmy Superfly Snuka RC	2.00	5.00
7 Rowdy Roddy Piper RC	8.00	20.00
8 Wendi Richter RC	1.25	3.00
9 Greg The Hammer Valentine RC	1.00	2.50
10 Brutus Beefcake RC	1.25	3.00
11 Jesse The Body Ventura RC	4.00	10.00
12 Big John Studd RC	1.00	2.50
13 Fabulous Moolah RC	2.00	5.00
14 Tito Santana RC	1.00	2.50
15 Hillbilly Jim RC	1.50	4.00
16 Hulk Hogan RC	40.00	100.00
17 Mr. Fuji RC	1.00	2.50
18 Rotundo RC & Windham RC	.75	2.00
19 Moondog Spot RC	.75	2.00
20 Chief Jay Strongbow RC	1.50	4.00
21 George The Animal Steele RC	1.25	3.00
22 Let Go of My Toe! RA	.50	1.25
23 Lock 'Em Up! RA	.50	1.25
24 Scalp 'Em! RA	.50	1.25
25 Going for the Midsection! RA	.75	2.00
26 Up in the Air! RA	.60	1.50
27 All Tied Up! RA	1.50	4.00
28 Here She Comes! RA	.50	1.25
29 Stretched to the Limit! RA	1.50	4.00
30 Over He Goes! RA	1.00	2.50
31 An Appetite for Mayhem! RA	.60	1.50
32 Putting on Pressure! RA	.50	1.25
33 Smashed on a Knee! RA	.75	2.00
34 A Fist Comes Flying! RA	.50	1.25
35 Lemme' Out of This! RA	.50	1.25
36 No Fair Chokin'! RA	.50	1.25
37 Attacked by an Animal! RA	.50	1.25
38 One Angry Man! RA	1.25	3.00
39 Someone's Going Down! RA	1.25	3.00
40 Strangle Hold! RA	2.00	5.00
41 Bending an Arm! RA	.50	1.25
42 Ready for a Pile Driver! RA	.75	2.00
43 Face to the Canvas! RA	.50	1.25
44 Paul Wants It All! RA	.75	2.00
45 Kick to the Face! RA	1.25	3.00
46 Ready for Action! RA	.50	1.25
47 Putting on the Squeeze! RA	.60	1.50
48 Giants in Action! RA	1.50	4.00
49 Camel Clutch! RA	.60	1.50
50 Pile Up! RA	2.00	5.00
51 Can't Get Away! RA	.60	1.50
52 Going for the Pin! RA	.50	1.25
53 Ready to Fly! RA	2.00	5.00
54 Crusher in a Crusher! RA	.50	1.25
55 Fury of the Animal! RA	.75	2.00
56 Wrong Kind of Music! RA	6.00	15.00
57 Who's your next challenger? SS	2.50	6.00
58 This dog has got a mean bite! SS	.75	2.00
59 I don't think I'll ask that... SS	1.25	3.00
60 You Hulkster fans lift... SS	8.00	20.00
61 This ain't my idea... SS	1.00	2.50
62 You mean Freddie Blassie is... SS	1.25	3.00
63 Mppgh Ecch Oong. SS	1.00	2.50
64 It's the rock n' wrestling... SS	.75	2.00
65 Arrrggghhhh! SS	.60	1.50
66 They took my reindeer! SS	.60	1.50

1985 Topps WWF Stickers

Card	Low	High
COMPLETE SET W/HOGAN (22)	30.00	75.00
COMPLETE SET W/O HOGAN (17)	20.00	50.00
1 Hulk Hogan	10.00	25.00
2 Captain Lou Albano	.75	2.00
3 Brutus Beefcake	1.25	3.00
4 Jesse Ventura	2.00	5.00
5 The Iron Sheik	1.50	4.00
6 Wendi Richter	1.25	3.00
7 Jimmy Snuka	.75	2.00
8 Ivan Putski	1.00	2.50
9 Hulk Hogan	4.00	10.00
10 Junk Yard Dog	1.25	3.00
11 Hulk Hogan	6.00	15.00
12 Captain Lou Albano	.75	2.00
13 Captain Lou Albano	.75	2.00
14 Freddie Blassie & The Iron Sheik	.75	2.00
15 Jimmy Snuka	.75	2.00
16 Hulk Hogan	10.00	25.00
17 Iron Sheik	1.50	4.00
18 Rene Goulet & S.D. Jones	1.25	3.00
19 Junk Yard Dog	.75	2.00
20 Wendi Richter	1.25	3.00
21 Andre the Giant	4.00	10.00
22 Hulk Hogan	8.00	20.00

1987 Topps WWF

Card	Low	High
COMPLETE SET (75)	60.00	120.00
1 Bret "Hit Man" Hart RC	25.00	60.00
2 Andre the Giant RC	6.00	15.00
3 Hulk Hogan	5.00	12.00

4 Frankie	.75	2.00
5 Koko B. Ware RC	.75	2.00
6 Tito Santana	.60	1.50
7 Randy Savage & Elizabeth	10.00	25.00
8 Billy Jack Haynes RC	.40	1.00
9 Hercules & Bobby Heenan	.40	1.00
10 King Harley Race RC	.60	1.50
11 Kimchee & Kamala RC	.75	2.00
12 Bravo/Johnny V/Valentine	.50	1.25
13 Honky Tonk Man RC	1.00	2.50
14 Outback Jack RC	.40	1.00
15 King Kong Bundy	1.25	3.00
16 The Magnificent Muraco	.40	1.00
17 Mr. Fuji and Killer Khan	.75	2.00
18 The Natural Butch Reed RC	.60	1.50
19 Davey Boy Smith	.75	2.00
20 The Dynamite Kid RC	.40	1.00
21 Ricky The Dragon Steamboat	1.50	4.00
22 Two-Man Clothesline RA	.40	1.00
23 Ref Turned Wrestler RA	.75	2.00
24 Ready to Strike RA	.60	1.50
25 In the Outback RA	.40	1.00
26 The Hulkster Explodes RA	2.00	5.00
27 Double Whammy RA	.40	1.00
28 Spoiling for a Fight RA	.40	1.00
29 Flip Flop RA	.40	1.00
30 Islanders Attack RA	.40	1.00
31 King Harley Parades RA	.40	1.00
32 Backbreaker RA	.40	1.00
33 Double Dropkick RA	.40	1.00
34 The Loser Must Bow RA	.40	1.00
35 American-Made RA	2.50	6.00
36 A Challenge Answered RA	2.00	5.00
37 Champ in the Ring RA	4.00	10.00
38 Listening to Hulkamania RA	2.00	5.00
39 Heading for the Ring RA	.40	1.00
40 Out to Destroy RA	.40	1.00
41 Tama Takes a Beating RA	.40	1.00
42 Bundy in Mid-Air RA	.40	1.00
43 Karate Stance RA	.40	1.00
44 Her Eyes on Randy RA	2.50	6.00
45 The Olympian Returns RA	.40	1.00
46 Reed Is Riled RA	.40	1.00
47 Flying Bodypress RA	.40	1.00
48 Hooking the Leg RA	.40	1.00
49 A Belly Buster WMIII	.40	1.00
50 Revenge on Randy WMIII	.75	2.00
51 Fighting the Full Nelson WMIII	.40	1.00
52 Honky Tonk Goes Down WMIII	.40	1.00
53 Over the Top WMIII	.40	1.00
54 The Giant Is Slammed WMIII	1.25	3.00
55 Out of the Ring WMIII	.75	2.00
56 And Still Champion WMIII	1.50	4.00
57 Harts Hit Concrete WMIII	.40	1.00
58 The Challenge RA	1.25	3.00
59 Bearhug RA	.40	1.00
60 Fantastic Bodypress RA	.40	1.00
61 Aerial Maneuvers RA	.40	1.00
62 Ready to Sting! RA	.40	1.00
63 Showing Off RA	.40	1.00
64 Scare Tactics RA	.40	1.00
65 Taking a Bow RA	.60	1.50
66 Out to Eat a Turnbuckle RA	.40	1.00
67 Nice guys finish last! SS	.40	1.00
68 Here's how we keep... SS	.40	1.00
69 Urrggh. Nice! SS	.40	1.00
70 No Kamala...him not dinner! SS	.40	1.00
71 We are the original destroyers. SS	.40	1.00
72 I think the fans are mad at me. SS	.40	1.00
73 You ain't nothin'... SS	.40	1.00
74 I'm gonna take a big bit... SS	.40	1.00
75 Good! SS	.40	1.00

1987 Topps WWF Stickers

COMPLETE SET (22)	20.00	50.00
1 Bret Hit Man Hart	5.00	12.00
2 Hulk Hogan	8.00	20.00
3 Koko B. Ware	.40	1.00
4 Randy Savage & Elizabeth	10.00	25.00
5 Billy Jack Haynes	.40	1.00
6 Hercules & Bobby Heenan	.60	1.50
7 King Harley Race	.60	1.50
8 Kimchee & Kamala	.40	1.00
9 Bravo/Johnny V/Valentine	.60	1.50
10 Honky Tonk Man	.60	1.50
11 Outback Jack	.40	1.00
12 King Kong Bundy	.60	1.50
13 Magnificent Muraco	.40	1.00
14 Mr. Fuji & Killer Khan	.40	1.00
15 Ricky The Dragon Steamboat	.60	1.50
16 Danny Davis	.40	1.00
17 Andre the Giant	6.00	15.00
18 Ken Patera	.40	1.00
19 Smash Demolition	.40	1.00
20 Jim The Anvil Neidhart	.40	1.00
21 George The Animal Steele	.60	1.50
22 WWF Logo	.40	1.00

1985 Topps WWF 3-D Pro Wrestling Stars

COMPLETE SET (12)	500.00	1000.00
1 Hulk Hogan	200.00	500.00
2 Wendi Richter	40.00	100.00
3 Jimmy Superfly Snuka	40.00	100.00
4 The Iron Sheik	50.00	125.00
5 Hillbilly Jim	30.00	75.00
6 Captain Lou Albano	40.00	100.00
7 Paul Orndorff	60.00	150.00
8 Jesse The Body Ventura	50.00	125.00
9 Brutus Beefcake	30.00	75.00
10 Andre the Giant	100.00	250.00
11 Rocky Johnson	30.00	75.00
12 Junk Yard Dog	50.00	125.00

1993 Topps Ireland Wacky Wrestling

COMPLETE SET (66)	15.00	40.00
1 Randy Savage	1.25	3.00
2 Undertaker	1.50	4.00
3 Papa Shango & Ultimate Warrior	.75	2.00
4 Hulk Hogan	1.50	4.00
5 Hacksaw Jim Duggan	.50	1.25
6 Sid Vicious	.40	1.00
7 Ric Flair & Rowdy Roddy Piper	1.25	3.00
8 El Matador	.60	1.50
9 Bushwhackers	.40	1.00
10 Scott Steiner	.75	2.00
11 Ultimate Warrior & Undertaker	1.50	4.00
12 Papa Shango	.40	1.00
13 Hulk Hogan	1.50	4.00
14 Shawn Michaels	1.25	3.00
15 Shawn Michaels & Virgil	1.25	3.00
16 Razor Ramon	.75	2.00
17 Bret Hart	.75	2.00
18 Bret Hart	.75	2.00
19 El Matador	.60	1.50
20 Papa Shango	.40	1.00
21 Big Bossman & The Mountie	.50	1.25
22 Hulk Hogan	1.50	4.00
23 Hulk Hogan & Ultimate Warrior	1.50	4.00
24 Ultimate Warrior	.75	2.00
25 Ric Flair & Michael Hayes	1.25	3.00
26 Ric Flair	1.25	3.00
27 Ric Flair	1.25	3.00
28 Ric Flair & El Gigante	1.25	3.00
29 Undertaker	1.50	4.00
30 Kamala & Bushwhacker Luke	.40	1.00
31 Kamala	.30	.75
32 Honky Tonk Man	.40	1.00
33 Honky Tonk Man	.40	1.00
34 Honky Tonk Man & Greg Valentine	.40	1.00
35 Sid Vicious	.40	1.00
36 Sid Vicious & Scott Steiner	.75	2.00
37 Lanny Poffo	.30	.75
38 Ted DiBiase	.60	1.50
39 Brian Knobbs & Scott Steiner	.75	2.00
40 Sgt. Slaughter	.40	1.00
41 Steiner Brothers	.75	2.00
42 Iron Sheik & Sgt. Slaughter	.40	1.00
43 Randy Savage	1.25	3.00
44 Koko B. Ware	.30	.75
45 Road Warrior Animal	.50	1.25
46 Road Warrior Animal	.50	1.25
47 Road Warrior Animal	.50	1.25
48 Hercules	.30	.75
49 Bam Bam Bigelow	.60	1.50
50 Bushwhackers	.40	1.00
51 Bushwhackers	.40	1.00
52 Brooklyn Brawler	.50	1.25
53 Ravishing Rick Rude	.50	1.25
54 Tony Atlas & Greg Valentine	.40	1.00
55 Jim Neidhart & Ivan Koloff	.40	1.00
56 Terry Taylor	.30	.75
57 Big Bossman & Nailz	.50	1.25
58 Davey Boy Smith	.50	1.25
59 Ravishing Rick Rude & Paul Orndorff	.50	1.25
60 Ric Flair & Sting	1.25	3.00
61 DDP & Diamond Studd	.75	2.00
62 Road Warrior Hawk & Ric Flair	1.25	3.00
63 Papa Shango	.40	1.00
64 Ric Flair & Lex Luger	1.25	3.00
65 Tony Atlas & Nikolai Volkoff	.40	1.00
66 Randy Savage	1.25	3.00

2009 TRISTAR Hulk Hogan Joins TNA Commemoratives

COMPLETE SET (2)
H1 Hulk Hogan
H2 Hulk Hogan

2008 TRISTAR TNA Cross the Line

COMPLETE SET (100) 8.00 20.00
*GOLD/50: 2X TO 5X BASIC CARDS
*RED/10: UNPRICED DUE TO SCARCITY
*PURPLE/1: UNPRICED DUE TO SCARCITY

1 A.J. Styles	.40	1.00
2 Motor City Machineguns	.15	.40
3 Brother Ray	.20	.50
4 LAX	.15	.40
5 Consequences Creed RC	.15	.40
6 Taylor Wilde RC	.60	1.50
7 Sheik Abdul Bashir RC	.20	.50
8 Main Event Mafia	.20	.50
9 Hector Guerrero & Willie Urbina	.12	.30
10 Lauren RC	.40	1.00
11 Kyra Angle RC	.40	1.00
12 Suicide	.12	.30
13 Rhaka Khan RC	.20	.50
14 Mick Foley	.60	1.50
15 Shane Sewell RC	.12	.30
16 Dutch Mantel	.12	.30
17 Beer Money Inc.	.15	.40
18 Prince Justice Brotherhood	.12	.30
19 Jeff Jarrett	.75	2.00
20 A.J. Styles	.40	1.00
21 Cowboy James Storm	.15	.40
22 Mike Tenay	.15	.40
23 Don West	.12	.30
24 Rudy Charles	.12	.30
25 Andrew Thomas	.12	.30
26 Jeremy Borash	.12	.30
27 Hermie Sadler	.12	.30
28 Kevin Nash	.60	1.50
29 Brother Devon	.20	.50
30 Beautiful People	.60	1.50
31 Roxxi RC	.40	1.00
32 Abyss	.40	1.00
33 Dixie Carter RC	.30	.75
34 Christian Cage	.30	.75
35 Booker T	.75	2.00
36 Shark Boy	.12	.30
37 Johnny Devine RC	.15	.40
38 Petey Williams RC	.12	.30
39 Homicide RC	.15	.40
40 Angelina Love RC	.60	1.50
41 Scott Steiner	.60	1.50
42 Alex Shelley RC	.15	.40
43 Jacqueline	.40	1.00
44 Curry Man	.12	.30
45 Kip James	.15	.40
46 Earl Hebner RC	.15	.40
47 Velvet Sky RC	.50	1.25
48 Kurt Angle	.75	2.00
49 Jim Cornette	.15	.40
50 Sting	.60	1.50
51 Traci Brooks	.50	1.25
52 Jay Lethal RC	.12	.30
53 Robert Roode RC	.12	.30
54 Petey Williams RC	.12	.30
55 Sonjay Dutt	.12	.30
56 Sharmell	.40	1.00
57 Chris Sabin	.12	.30
58 Matt Morgan	.15	.40
59 ODB RC	.40	1.00
60 Tomko	.12	.30
61 Kurt Angle	.75	2.00
62 Christian Cage	.30	.75
63 ODB RC	.40	1.00
64 Team 3D	.20	.50
65 A.J. Styles	.40	1.00
66 James Storm	.15	.40
67 Raisha Saeed RC	.30	.75
68 Sonjay Dutt	.12	.30
69 Kevin Nash	.60	1.50
70 Matt Morgan	.15	.40
71 BG James	.12	.30
72 Hernandez RC	.15	.40
73 A.J. Styles	.40	1.00
74 Kurt Angle	.75	2.00
75 Christian Cage	.30	.75
76 Jeff Jarrett	.75	2.00
77 Sting	.60	1.50
78 Christian Cage	.30	.75
79 Jeff Jarrett	.75	2.00
80 Kurt Angle Meets Samoa Joe	.75	2.00
81 Sharmell	.40	1.00
82 Sting	.60	1.50
83 Most Important Moment in TNA History	.12	.30
84 Christian Cage vs. Abyss	.40	1.00
85 Samoa Joe vs. Daniels vs. Styles	.40	1.00
86 Kurt Angle	.75	2.00
87 Styles vs. Angle	.75	2.00
88 Eric Young RC	.12	.30
89 Rhino	.30	.75
90 Samoa Joe RC	.20	.50
91 SoCal Val RC	.60	1.50
92 Curry Man	.12	.30
93 Lance Rock RC	.15	.40
94 Jimmy Rave RC	.15	.40
95 Sting vs. Samoa Joe	.60	1.50
96 Kurt Angle vs. Jeff Jarrett	.75	2.00
97 Awesome Kong/TNA Knockouts	.30	.75
98 Beer Money vs. LAX	.15	.40
99 Steve McMichael	.30	.75
100 Checklist	.12	.30

2008 TRISTAR TNA Cross the Line Autographed Memorabilia Silver

*GOLD/50: .6X TO 1.2X BASIC AU MEM
*RED/25: .75X TO 1.5 BASIC AU MEM
*GREEN/5: UNPRICED DUE TO SCARCITY
*PURPLE/1: UNPRICED DUE TO SCARCITY
STATED PRINT RUN 99 SER.#'d SETS

MAA Abyss	15.00	30.00
MOA ODB	15.00	30.00
MSA Sting	25.00	50.00
MABA Sheik Abdul Bashir	10.00	20.00
MALA Angelina Love	20.00	40.00
MASA A.J. Styles	20.00	40.00
MCCA Christian Cage	15.00	30.00
MCHA Christy Hemme	20.00	40.00
MCMA Curry Man	10.00	20.00
MDCA Dixie Carter	15.00	30.00
MJBA Jeremy Borash	10.00	20.00
MKAA Kurt Angle	15.00	30.00
MKNA Kevin Nash	20.00	40.00
MRCA Rudy Charles	10.00	20.00
MRSA Raisha Saeed	10.00	20.00
MSEA Super Eric	10.00	20.00
MSJA Samoa Joe	20.00	40.00
MSVA SoCal Val	15.00	30.00
MTWA Taylor Wilde	15.00	30.00
MVSA Velvet Sky	20.00	40.00

2008 TRISTAR TNA Cross the Line Autographs Silver

*GOLD/50: .5X TO 1.2X BASIC AUTOS
*RED/25: .6X TO 1.5X BASIC AUTOS
*PURPLE/1: UNPRICED DUE TO SCARCITY
*P.P.BLACK/1: UNPRICED DUE TO SCARCITY
*P.P.CYAN/1: UNPRICED DUE TO SCARCITY
*P.P.MAGENTA/1: UNPRICED DUE TO SCARCITY
*P.P.YELLOW/1: UNPRICED DUE TO SCARCITY

CA Abyss	8.00	20.00
CJ Jacqueline	6.00	15.00
CL Lauren	6.00	15.00

CO ODB 6.00 15.00
CS Sting 20.00 50.00
CAB Sheik Abdul Bashir 6.00 15.00
CAJ A.J. Styles 10.00 25.00
CAK Awesome Kong 6.00 15.00
CAL Angelina Love 10.00 25.00
CAS Alex Shelley 6.00 15.00
CAT Andrew Thomas 6.00 15.00
CBD Brother Devon 8.00 20.00
CBR Brother Ray 8.00 20.00
CBT Booker T 8.00 20.00
CCC Christian Cage 8.00 20.00
CCH Christy Hemme 10.00 25.00
CCM Curry Man 8.00 20.00
CCS Chris Sabin 6.00 15.00
CDC Dixie Carter 8.00 20.00
CDW Don West 8.00 20.00
CEH Earl Hebner 6.00 15.00
CEY Eric Young 6.00 15.00
CH1 Hernandez 6.00 15.00
CH2 Homicide 6.00 15.00
CHG Hector Guerrero 6.00 15.00
CHS Hermie Sadler 6.00 15.00
CJB Jeremy Borash 6.00 15.00
CJC Jim Cornette 6.00 15.00
CJD Johnny Devine 6.00 15.00
CJJ Jeff Jarrett 8.00 20.00
CJL Jay Lethal 6.00 15.00
CJR Jimmy Rave 6.00 15.00
CJS James Storm 6.00 15.00
CKA Kurt Angle 12.00 30.00
CKJ Kip James 6.00 15.00
CKN Kevin Nash 12.00 30.00
CLR Lance Rock 6.00 15.00
CMF Mick Foley 12.00 30.00
CMM Matt Morgan 8.00 20.00
CMT Mike Tenay 6.00 15.00
CPW Petey Williams 6.00 15.00
CR2 Roxxi 8.00 20.00
CRC Rudy Charles
CRR Robert Roode 6.00 15.00
CRS Raisha Saeed 8.00 20.00
CRS Rhino 6.00 15.00
CS2 Sharmell 6.00 15.00
CS3 Suicide 8.00 20.00
CSB Shark Boy 6.00 15.00
CSD Sonjay Dutt 6.00 15.00
CSE Super Eric 6.00 15.00
CSJ Slick Johnson 6.00 15.00
CSJ Samoa Joe 12.00 30.00
CSM Steve McMichael 8.00 20.00
CSS Scott Steiner 12.00 30.00
CSV SoCal Val 8.00 20.00
CTB Traci Brooks 8.00 20.00
CTW Taylor Wilde 8.00 20.00
CVS Velvet Sky 10.00 25.00
CWU Willie Urbina 8.00 20.00
CCC2 Consequences Creed 6.00 15.00
CKA2 Karen Angle 8.00 20.00
CSS2 Shane Sewell 6.00 15.00

2008 TRISTAR TNA Cross the Line Dual Autographs Silver

*GOLD/50: .5X TO 1.2X BASIC AUTOS
*RED/25: .6X TO 1.5X BASIC AUTOS
*BLUE/5: UNPRICED DUE TO SCARCITY
*PURPLE/1: UNPRICED DUE TO SCARCITY
*P.P.BLACK/1: UNPRICED DUE TO SCARCITY
*P.P.CYAN/1: UNPRICED DUE TO SCARCITY
*P.P.MAGENTA/1: UNPRICED DUE TO SCARCITY
*P.P.YELLOW/1: UNPRICED DUE TO SCARCITY
RANDOMLY INSERTED INTO PACKS

C2BS Booker T/Sharmell 15.00 30.00
C2CB J.Cornette/T.Brooks 12.50 25.00
C2CR C.Cage/Rhino 12.50 25.00
C2HH Hernandez/Homicide 7.50 15.00
C2JK S.Joe/K.Nash 15.00 30.00
C2KS A.Kong/R.Saeed 12.50 25.00
C2KW A.Kong/T.Wilde 20.00 40.00
C2LS A.Love/V.Sky 20.00 40.00
C2RD BroRay/BroDevon 15.00 30.00
C2SA A.J. Styles/K.Angle 15.00 30.00
C2SA Sting/K.Angle 20.00 40.00
C2SR J.Storm/R.Roode 15.00 30.00
C2SS A.Shelley/C.Sabin 15.00 30.00
C2SW S.Steiner/P.Williams 12.50 25.00
C2WC P.Williams/C.Creed 7.50 15.00

2008 TRISTAR TNA Cross the Line Dual Memorabilia Silver

*GOLD/50: .5X TO 1.2X BASIC MEM
*RED/25: .6X TO 1.5X BASIC MEM
*GREEN/5: UNPRICED DUE TO SCARCITY
*PURPLE/1: UNPRICED DUE TO SCARCITY
STATED PRINT RUN 99 SER.#'d SETS

MS2 Sting 20.00 50.00
MAS2 Kurt Angle/A.J. Styles 8.00 20.00
MDL2 Sonjay Dutt/Jay Lethal 6.00 15.00
MLV2 Jay Lethal 5.00 12.00
SoCal Val

2008 TRISTAR TNA Cross the Line High Impact Championship Inserts

STATED ODDS 1:CASE
NO PRICING DUE TO SCARCITY

NNO A.J. Styles Auto Baseball EXCH
NNO TNA Wrestler Auto Photo EXCH
NNO Velvet Sky Auto Baseball EXCH
NNO Booker T Auto Baseball EXCH

2008 TRISTAR TNA Cross the Line Memorabilia Silver

*GOLD/50: .5X TO 1.2X BASIC MEM
*RED/25: .6X TO 1.5X BASIC MEM
*GREEN/5: UNPRICED DUE TO SCARCITY
*PURPLE/1: UNPRICED DUE TO SCARCITY
STATED PRINT RUN 99 SER.#'d SETS

MA Abyss 8.00 20.00
MS Sting 10.00 25.00
MAB Sheik Abdul Bashir 6.00 15.00
MAS A.J. Styles 8.00 20.00
MBP The Beautiful People 10.00 25.00
MCC Christian Cage 8.00 20.00
MCM Curry Man 6.00 15.00
MDC Dixie Carter 8.00 20.00
MKA Kurt Angle 10.00 25.00
MKN Kevin Nash 8.00 20.00
MSE Super Eric 6.00 15.00
MTW Taylor Wilde 8.00 20.00

2008 TRISTAR TNA Cross the Line Quad Autographs Silver

*GOLD/50: .6X TO 1.2X BASIC AUTOS
*RED/25: .75X TO 1.5X BASIC AUTOS
*BLUE/5: UNPRICED DUE TO SCARCITY
*PURPLE/1: UNPRICED DUE TO SCARCITY
*P.P.BLACK/1: UNPRICED DUE TO SCARCITY
*P.P.CYAN/1: UNPRICED DUE TO SCARCITY
*P.P.MAGENTA/1: UNPRICED DUE TO SCARCITY
*P.P.YELLOW/1: UNPRICED DUE TO SCARCITY
RANDOMLY INSERTED INTO PACKS

1 Love/Sky/Brooks/Hemme 60.00 120.00
2 Sting/Nash/Jarrett/Steiner 125.00 200.00
3 Hebner/Johnson/Thomas/Charles 25.00 50.00
4 Tenay/West/Guerrero/Urbina 25.00 50.00
5 Storm/Roode/Homic/Hrndz 25.00 50.00
6 Love/Sky/Kong/Jacqueline 30.00 60.00
7 Bashir/Dutt/Curry/Guer 25.00 50.00

2008 TRISTAR TNA Cross the Line Triple Autographs Silver

*GOLD/50: .6X TO 1.2X BASIC AUTOS
*RED/25: .75X TO 1.5X BASIC AUTOS
*BLUE/5: UNPRICED DUE TO SCARCITY
*PURPLE/1: UNPRICED DUE TO SCARCITY
*P.P.BLACK/1: UNPRICED DUE TO SCARCITY
*P.P.CYAN/1: UNPRICED DUE TO SCARCITY
*P.P.MAGENTA/1: UNPRICED DUE TO SCARCITY
*P.P.YELLOW/1: UNPRICED DUE TO SCARCITY
RANDOMLY INSERTED INTO PACKS

C3B Tenay/West/Borash 20.00 40.00
C3BP Love/Sky/James 40.00 80.00
C3RR Hemme/Rock/Rave 25.00 50.00
C3BSS Booker/Sting/Samoa 40.00 80.00
C3LVD Lethal/SoCal/Dutt 25.00 50.00
C3PJB Shark/Curry/SuperEric 20.00 40.00

2010 TRISTAR TNA Icons

COMPLETE SET (100) 10.00 25.00
*GOLD/25: 2.5X TO 6X BASIC CARDS
*RED/5: UNPRICED DUE TO SCARCITY
*PURPLE/1: UNPRICED DUE TO SCARCITY

1 Hulk Hogan 1.00 2.50
2 Ric Flair .75 2.00
3 Sting .60 1.50
4 Jeff Hardy .60 1.50
5 Mick Foley .75 2.00
6 Kevin Nash .60 1.50
7 Rob Van Dam .40 1.00
8 Jeff Jarrett .40 1.00
9 Kurt Angle .60 1.50
10 Eric Bischoff .15 .40
11 Earl Hebner .15 .40
12 Mr. Anderson .25 .60
13 Team 3D .25 .60
14 AJ Styles .40 1.00
15 Tara .60 1.50
16 Tommy Dreamer .15 .40
17 Ric Flair .75 2.00
18 Sting .60 1.50
19 Jeff Hardy .60 1.50
20 Jeff Jarrett .40 1.00
21 Kevin Nash .60 1.50
22 Kurt Angle .60 1.50
23 Mick Foley .75 2.00
24 Rob Van Dam .40 1.00
25 Ric Flair .75 2.00
26 Sting .60 1.50
27 Jeff Hardy .60 1.50
28 Mick Foley .75 2.00
29 Kevin Nash .60 1.50
30 Rob Van Dam .40 1.00
31 Team 3D .25 .60
32 Kurt Angle .60 1.50
33 Eric Bischoff .15 .40
34 Dixie Carter .40 1.00
35 Desmond Wolfe RC .15 .40
36 Jay Lethal .15 .40
37 Matt Morgan .15 .40
38 Abyss .25 .60
39 AJ Styles .40 1.00
40 Hulk Hogan 1.00 2.50
41 Velvet Sky .75 2.00
42 Angelina Love .60 1.50
43 Taylor Wilde .40 1.00
44 Sarita .40 1.00
45 Daffney .60 1.50
46 Madison Rayne .60 1.50
47 Lacey Von Erich RC .75 2.00
48 Christy Hemme .60 1.50
49 SoCal Val .60 1.50
50 Chelsea .60 1.50
51 Miss Tessmacher RC .75 2.00
52 Rosie Lottalove RC .40 1.00
53 Motor City Machineguns .20 .50
54 Rob Terry .15 .40
55 Kazarian .15 .40
56 D'Angelo Dinero .15 .40
57 Douglas Williams .15 .40
58 Desmond Wolfe .15 .40
59 Eric Young .15 .40
60 Generation Me .15 .40
61 Beer Money Inc. .25 .60
62 Abyss .25 .60
63 Matt Morgan .15 .40
64 Samoa Joe .25 .60
65 Hernandez .15 .40
66 Ink Inc. .15 .40
67 Jay Lethal .15 .40
68 Magnus .15 .40
69 Lacey Von Erich RC .75 2.00
70 Hulk Hogan .75 2.00
71 Ric Flair .60 1.50
72 Sting .50 1.25
73 Jeff Hardy .50 1.25
74 Mick Foley .60 1.50
75 Kevin Nash .50 1.25
76 Rob Van Dam .30 .75
77 Jeff Jarrett .30 .75
78 Kurt Angle .50 1.25
79 Mr. Anderson .20 .50
80 Tommy Dreamer .15 .40
81 Hulk Hogan .75 2.00
82 Ric Flair .60 1.50
83 Sting .50 1.25
84 Jeff Hardy .50 1.25
85 Mick Foley .60 1.50
86 Kevin Nash .50 1.25
87 Rob Van Dam .30 .75
88 Jeff Jarrett .30 .75
89 Kurt Angle .50 1.25
90 Mick Foley .60 1.50
91 Mick Foley .60 1.50
92 Mick Foley .60 1.50
93 Mick Foley .60 1.50
94 Mick Foley .60 1.50
95 Sting .50 1.25
96 Kevin Nash .50 1.25
97 Rob Van Dam .30 .75
98 Mr. Anderson .20 .50
99 Jeff Jarrett .30 .75
100 Kurt Angle .50 1.25

2010 TRISTAR TNA Icons Dual Memorabilia Silver

STATED PRINT RUN 199 SER.#'d SETS

M8 Rob Van Dam
Jeff Hardy
M9 Ric Flair
AJ Styles

2010 TRISTAR TNA Icons Hogangraphs Green

OVERALL AUTO ODDS TWO PER BOX

H1 Hulk Hogan 75.00 150.00
H2 Hulk Hogan 75.00 150.00
H3 Hulk Hogan 75.00 150.00
H4 Hulk Hogan 75.00 150.00
H5 Hulk Hogan 75.00 150.00

2010 TRISTAR TNA Icons Hulk Hogan Die-Cut Letter Memorabilia Silver

*GOLD/50: .5X TO 1.2X BASIC MEM
*RED/25: .6X TO 1.5 BASIC MEM
*PURPLE/1: UNPRICED DUE TO SCARCITY
STATED ODDS OVERALL MEM 1:BOX
STATED PRINT RUN 199 SER.#'d SETS

HH1 Hulk Hogan Bandana H 12.00 30.00
HH2 Hulk Hogan Bandana O 12.00 30.00
HH3 Hulk Hogan Bandana G 12.00 30.00
HH4 Hulk Hogan Bandana A 12.00 30.00
HH5 Hulk Hogan Bandana N 12.00 30.00

2010 TRISTAR TNA Icons Hulk Hogan Dual Autographs Gold

*GREEN/50: UNPRICED DUE TO SCARCITY
*RED/5: UNPRICED DUE TO SCARCITY
*PURPLE/1: UNPRICED DUE TO SCARCITY
STATED PRINT RUN 99 SER.#'d SETS

H21 Hulk Hogan/Abyss
H22 Hulk Hogan/AJ Styles
H23 Hulk Hogan/Jeff Hardy
H24 Hulk Hogan/Jeff Jarrett
H25 Hulk Hogan/Kevin Nash
H26 Hulk Hogan/Kurt Angle
H27 Hulk Hogan/Lacey Von Erich
H28 Hulk Hogan/Mick Foley
H29 Hulk Hogan/Ric Flair
H210 Hulk Hogan/Rob Van Dam
H211 Hulk Hogan/Sting
H212 Hulk Hogan/Tara
H213 Hulk Hogan/Velvet Sky

2010 TRISTAR TNA Icons Hulk Hogan Quad Autographs Gold

*GREEN/50: UNPRICED DUE TO SCARCITY
*RED/5: UNPRICED DUE TO SCARCITY
*PURPLE/1: UNPRICED DUE TO SCARCITY
STATED PRINT RUN 99 SER. #'d SETS

H41 Hogan/Sky/Rayne/Von Erich
H42 Hogan/Magnus/Williams/Terry
H43 Hogan/Flair/Abyss/Styles
H44 Hogan/Flair/Sting/Foley

2010 TRISTAR TNA Icons Iconigraphs Gold

*GREEN/25: .5X TO 1.2X BASIC AUTOS
*RED/5: UNPRICED DUE TO SCARCITY
*PURPLE/1: UNPRICED DUE TO SCARCITY
STATED ODDS OVERALL 2:BOX
STATED PRINT RUN 50 SER.#'d SETS

Card	Low	High
I1 Ric Flair		
I2 Sting		
I3 Jeff Hardy	25.00	50.00
I4 Mick Foley	12.00	30.00
I5 Kevin Nash	10.00	20.00
I6 Rob Van Dam	20.00	40.00
I7 Jeff Jarrett	10.00	20.00
I8 Kurt Angle	12.00	25.00
I9 Earl Hebner	12.00	25.00
I10 Mr. Anderson	12.00	25.00
I11 AJ Styles	10.00	20.00
I12 Syxx-Pac	12.00	25.00
I13 Tara	12.00	25.00
I14 Tommy Dreamer	10.00	20.00
I15 Sting/Icon		
I16 Jeff Hardy/Twist of Fate		
I17 Mick Foley/Bang Bang		
I18 Kevin Nash (inscribed)		
I19 Rob Van Dam/Mr. Monday Night		
I20 Rob Van Dam/Whole F'n Show		
I21 Rob Van Dam/420		
I22 Jeff Jarrett/TNA Founder		
I23 Jeff Jarrett/Guitar Show		
I24 Jeff Jarrett/Slapnutz		
I25 Jeff Jarrett/The Chosen One		
I26 Jeff Jarrett/Music City USA		
I27 Kurt Angle/Olympic Champ		
I28 Kurt Angle/It's Real		
I29 Earl Hebner/Montreal Screw Job		
I30 Mr. Anderson/Mic Check		
I31 Mr. Anderson/Go Pack Go		
I32 AJ Styles/Grand Slam Winner		
I33 AJ Styles/Phenomenal		
I34 AJ Styles/TNA Original		
I35 Tommy Dreamer/Extreme Original		

2010 TRISTAR TNA Icons Memorabilia Silver

*GOLD: .5X TO 1.2X BASIC MEM
*RED: .6X TO 1.5X BASIC MEM
*PURPLE/1: UNPRICED DUE TO SCARCITY
STATED ODDS OVERALL 1:BOX
STATED PRINT RUN 199 SER.#'d SETS

Card	Low	High
M1 Ric Flair		
M2 Rob Van Dam	4.00	10.00
M3 Jeff Hardy	6.00	15.00
M4 Sting		
M5 Mick Foley	8.00	20.00
M6 Kevin Nash	6.00	15.00
M7 Tommy Dreamer	4.00	10.00

2010 TRISTAR TNA Icons Memorabilia Gold

*GOLD: .5X TO 1.2X BASIC MEM
STATED PRINT RUN 50 SER.#'d SETS

Card	Low	High
M1 Ric Flair		
M2 Rob Van Dam	5.00	12.00
M3 Jeff Hardy	8.00	20.00
M4 Sting	10.00	25.00
M5 Mick Foley	10.00	25.00
M6 Kevin Nash	8.00	20.00
M7 Tommy Dreamer	5.00	12.00

2010 TRISTAR TNA Icons The Next Generation Autographs Gold

*GREEN/25: .5X TO 1.2X BASIC AUTOS
*RED/5: UNPRICED DUE TO SCARCITY
*PURPLE/1: UNPRICED DUE TO SCARCITY
STATED ODDS OVERALL 2:BOX
STATED PRINT RUN 50 SER.#'d SETS

Card	Low	High
NEXT1 Alex Shelley	6.00	15.00
NEXT2 Chris Sabin	4.00	10.00
NEXT3 Rob Terry	4.00	10.00
NEXT4 Kazarian	4.00	10.00
NEXT5 D'Angelo Dinero	4.00	10.00
NEXT6 Douglas Williams	4.00	10.00
NEXT7 Desmond Wolfe	4.00	10.00
NEXT8 Eric Young	4.00	10.00
NEXT9 Abyss	6.00	15.00
NEXT10 Matt Morgan	4.00	10.00
NEXT11 Samoa Joe	6.00	15.00
NEXT12 Hernandez	4.00	10.00
NEXT13 Jay Lethal	4.00	10.00
NEXT14 Magnus	4.00	10.00

2010 TRISTAR TNA Icons Quad Memorabilia Silver

COMPLETE SET (1)

HH8 Hogan/Flair/Sting/Foley

2010 TRISTAR TNA Icons Six Autographs Gold

*GREEN/50: UNPRICED DUE TO SCARCITY
*RED/5: UNPRICED DUE TO SCARCITY
*PURPLE/1: UNPRICED DUE TO SCARCITY
STATED PRINT RUN 99 SER.#'d SETS

A61 Hogan/Foley/Sting/Nash/Flair/Jarr
A62 RVD/Moore/Hardy/Foley/Anderson/Angle
A63 Devon/Young/Ray/Storm/Nash/Roode
A64 Sky/Love/Rayne/Wilde/Von Erich/Sarita

2010 TRISTAR TNA Icons Sugar and Spice Autographs Gold

*GREEN/25: .5X TO 1.2X BASIC AUTOS
*RED/5: UNPRICED DUE TO SCARCITY
*PURPLE/1: UNPRICED DUE TO SCARCITY
STATED ODDS OVERALL 2:BOX
STATED PRINT RUN 50 SER.#'d SETS

Card	Low	High
SS1 Velvet Sky	10.00	25.00
SS2 Angelina Love	8.00	20.00
SS3 Taylor Wilde	8.00	20.00
SS4 Sarita	8.00	20.00
SS5 Daffney	10.00	25.00
SS6 Madison Rayne	8.00	20.00
SS7 Lacey Von Erich	12.00	30.00
SS8 Christy Hemme	8.00	20.00
SS9 SoCal Val	8.00	20.00
SS10 Chelsea	10.00	25.00
SS11 Miss Tessmacher	12.00	30.00
SS12 Rosie Lottalove	10.00	25.00

2010 TRISTAR TNA Icons Triple Memorabilia Silver

STATED PRINT RUN 199 SER.#'d SETS

HH6 Hulk Hogan/Bandana
HH7 Hulk Hogan/Bandana/Shirt/Mat
M10 Sky/Rayne/Von Erich

2008 TRISTAR TNA Impact

Card	Low	High
COMPLETE SET (69)	8.00	20.00
UNOPENED BOX (18 PACKS)	30.00	50.00
UNOPENED PACK (8 CARDS)		

*GOLD/50: 2X TO 5X BASIC CARDS
*RUBY/10: UNPRICED DUE TO SCARCITY
*P.P.BLACK/1: UNPRICED DUE TO SCARCITY
*P.P.CYAN/1: UNPRICED DUE TO SCARCITY
*P.P.MAGENTA/1: UNPRICED DUE TO SCARCITY
*P.P.YELLOW/1: UNPRICED DUE TO SCARCITY

Card	Low	High
1 Kurt Angle	.75	2.00
2 Christian Cage	.30	.75
3 Samoa Joe RC	.20	.50
4 A.J. Styles	.40	1.00
5 Tomko	.12	.30
6 Booker T	.75	2.00
7 Jay Lethal RC	.12	.30
8 Jeff Jarrett	.75	2.00
9 Rhino	.30	.75
10 Curry Man	.12	.30
11 Sting	.60	1.50
12 Scott Steiner	.60	1.50
13 Robert Roode RC	.12	.30
14 Eric Young RC	.12	.30
15 Homicide RC	.15	.40
16 Hernandez RC	.15	.40
17 Petey Williams RC	.12	.30
18 Shark Boy	.12	.30
19 Consequences Creed RC	.15	.40
20 Alex Shelley RC	.15	.40
21 Jimmy Rave RC	.15	.40
22 Rellik RC	.15	.40
23 Brother Devon	.20	.50
24 Brother Ray	.20	.50
25 Kip James	.15	.40
26 Abyss	.40	1.00
27 Lance Hoyt RC	.15	.40
28 BG James	.12	.30
29 Chris Sabin	.12	.30
30 Kaz	.12	.30
31 Johnny Devine RC	.15	.40
32 Super Eric RC	.12	.30
33 Black Reign RC	.15	.40
34 James Storm	.15	.40
35 Sonjay Dutt	.12	.30
36 A.Styles/Tomko	.40	1.00
37 Team 3D	.20	.50
38 LAX	.40	1.00
39 Rock n' Rave Infection	.75	2.00
40 Motor Sity Machineguns	.15	.40
41 Karen Angle RC	.50	1.25
42 ODB RC	.40	1.00
43 Awesome Kong RC	.30	.75
44 Traci Brooks	.50	1.25
45 Christy Hemme	.75	2.00
46 Sharmell	.40	1.00
47 Gail Kim	.40	1.00
48 Angelina Love RC	.60	1.50
49 Raisha Saeed RC	.30	.75
50 SoCal Val RC	.60	1.50
51 Velvet Sky RC	.50	1.25
52 Hermie Sadler	.40	1.00
53 Jacqueline	.40	1.00
54 Roxxi Laveaux RC	.40	1.00
55 Salinas RC	.40	1.00
56 Vince Russo	.12	.30
57 James Mitchell	.15	.40
58 Matt Morgan	.15	.40
59 Jim Cornette	.15	.40
60 Earl Hebner RC	.15	.40
61 Andrew Thomas	.12	.30
62 Rudy Charles	.12	.30
63 Mark Johnson RC	.12	.30
64 Mike Tenay	.15	.40
65 Don West	.12	.30
66 Jeremy Borash	.12	.30
67 Terry Taylor	.12	.30
68 Dixie Carter RC	.30	.75
69 Kevin Nash	.60	1.50

2008 TRISTAR TNA Impact Autographs Silver

*GOLD/50: .5X TO 1.2X BASIC AUTOS
*RED/25: .6X TO 1.5X BASIC AUTOS
*BLUE/5: UNPRICED DUE TO SCARCITY
*PURPLE/1: UNPRICED DUE TO SCARCITY

Card	Low	High
AA Abyss	6.00	15.00
AJ Jacqueline	4.00	10.00
AK Kaz	4.00	10.00
AO ODB	4.00	10.00
AR Rellik	4.00	10.00
AS Sting SP	40.00	80.00
AT Tomko	6.00	15.00
AAJ A.J. Styles	15.00	40.00
AAK Awesome Kong	5.00	12.00
AAL Angelina Love	6.00	15.00
AAS Alex Shelley	5.00	12.00
ABD Brother Devon	6.00	15.00
ABG BG James	5.00	12.00
ABR Black Reign	4.00	10.00
ABR Brother Ray	6.00	15.00
ABT Booker T SP	15.00	40.00
ACC Christian Cage SP	6.00	15.00
ACH Christy Hemme	10.00	25.00
ACM Curry Man	4.00	10.00
ACS Chris Sabin	5.00	12.00
ADC Dixie Carter SP	15.00	40.00
ADW Don West	4.00	10.00
AEY Eric Young	4.00	10.00
AGK Gail Kim	20.00	40.00
AH1 Hernandez	4.00	10.00
AH2 Homicide	4.00	10.00
AJB Jeremy Borash	4.00	10.00
AJC Jim Cornette	5.00	12.00
AJD Johnny Devine	4.00	10.00
AJJ Jeff Jarrett	6.00	15.00
AJL Jay Lethal	4.00	10.00
AJM James Mitchell	4.00	10.00
AJR Jimmy Rave	5.00	12.00
AJS James Storm	4.00	10.00
AKA Kurt Angle SP	30.00	60.00
AKJ Kip James	5.00	12.00
AKN Kevin Nash	12.00	30.00
ALH Lance Hoyt	4.00	10.00
AMM Matt Morgan	5.00	12.00
AMT Mike Tenay	4.00	10.00
APB Payton Banks	5.00	12.00
APW Petey Williams	4.00	10.00
AR2 Rhino	5.00	12.00
ARL Roxxi Laveaux	5.00	12.00
ARR Robert Roode	5.00	12.00
ARS Raisha Saeed	4.00	10.00
AS2 Sharmell	4.00	10.00
AS3 Salinas	5.00	12.00
ASB Shark Boy	4.00	10.00
ASD Sonjay Dutt	4.00	10.00
ASE Super Eric	4.00	10.00
ASJ Samoa Joe SP	15.00	40.00
ASS Scott Steiner	12.00	30.00
ASV SoCal Val	5.00	12.00
ATB Traci Brooks	5.00	12.00
AVS Velvet Sky	10.00	25.00
ACC2 Consequences Creed	4.00	10.00
AKA2 Karen Angle SP	20.00	40.00

2008 TRISTAR TNA Impact Dual Autographs Gold

COMPLETE SET (10)
*RED/25: .5X TO 1.2X BASIC AUTOS
*BLUE/5: UNPRICED DUE TO SCARCITY
*PURPLE/1: UNPRICED DUE TO SCARCITY
STATED PRINT RUN 50 SER.#'d SETS

Card	Low	High
A2AA Kurt & Karen Angle	50.00	100.00
A2BS Booker T/Sharmell	25.00	50.00
A2DR Brothers Devon & Ray	25.00	50.00
A2HH Homicide/Hernandez	20.00	40.00
A2LS A.Love/V.Sky	40.00	80.00
A2LV J.Lethal/S.Val	20.00	40.00
A2RB R.Roode/P.Banks	25.00	50.00
A2SJ J.Storm/Jacqueline	20.00	40.00
A2SS A.Shelley/C.Sabin	30.00	60.00
A2TW M.Tenay/D.West	15.00	30.00

2008 TRISTAR TNA Impact Memorabilia Black

*RAINBOW FOIL/10-50
*GOLD/25: .5X TO 1.2X BASIC MEM
*RED/1: UNPRICED DUE TO SCARCITY
STATED PRINT RUN 250 SER.#'d SETS

Card	Low	High
AAO ODB	6.00	15.00
AAS Sting	10.00	25.00
AAT Tomko	5.00	12.00
AAAL Angelina Love	10.00	25.00
AAAS A.J. Styles	6.00	15.00
AACC Christian Cage	5.00	12.00
AACH Christy Hemme	8.00	20.00
AAGK Gail Kim	8.00	20.00
AAJL Jay Lethal	6.00	15.00
AAKA Kurt Angle	8.00	20.00
AAKN Kevin Nash	8.00	20.00
AASD Sonjay Dutt	5.00	12.00
AASJ Samoa Joe	5.00	12.00
AASS Scott Steiner	8.00	20.00
AASV SoCal Val	8.00	20.00
AATB Traci Brooks	8.00	20.00
AAVS Velvet Sky	10.00	25.00
AAKA2 Karen Angle	10.00	25.00

2008 TRISTAR TNA Impact Mike's Magical Moments

Card	Low	High
COMPELETE SET (5)	1.00	2.50

*GOLD/50: 2X TO 5X BASIC CARDS
*RED/10: UNPRICED DUE TO SCARCITY
*PURPLE/1: UNPRICED DUE TO SCARCITY
*P.P.BLACK/1: UNPRICED DUE TO SCARCITY
*P.P.CYAN/1: UNPRICED DUE TO SCARCITY
*P.P.MAGENTA/1: UNPRICED DUE TO SCARCITY

*P.P.YELLOW/1: UNPRICED DUE TO SCARCITY
M1 First Night .12 .30
M2 Kurt Angle/Samoa Joe .75 2.00
M3 Big Name Newcomers/Arrivals .12 .30
M4 X Division .12 .30
M5 Sporting Superstars .12 .30

2008 TRISTAR TNA Impact Muscles Ink

COMPLETE SET (10) 3.00 8.00
*GOLD/50: 2X TO 5X BASIC CARDS
*RED/10: UNPRICED DUE TO SCARCITY
*PURPLE/1: UNPRICED DUE TO SCARCITY
*P.P.BLACK/1: UNPRICED DUE TO SCARCITY
*P.P.CYAN/1: UNPRICED DUE TO SCARCITY
*P.P.MAGENTA/1: UNPRICED DUE TO SCARCITY
*P.P.YELLOW/1: UNPRICED DUE TO SCARCITY
MI1 Scott Steiner .60 1.50
MI2 Robert Roode .12 .30
MI3 Petey Williams .12 .30
MI4 Traci Brooks .50 1.25
MI5 Brother Devon .20 .50
MI6 Booker T .75 2.00
MI7 Christy Hemme .75 2.00
MI8 Kevin Nash .60 1.50
MI9 Tomko .12 .30
MI10 Kurt Angle .75 2.00

2008 TRISTAR TNA Impact Then and Now

COMPLETE SET (4) 1.50 4.00
*GOLD/50: 2X TO 5X BASIC CARDS
*RED/10: UNPRICED DUE TO SCARCITY
*PURPLE/1: UNPRICED DUE TO SCARCITY
*P.P.BLACK/1: UNPRICED DUE TO SCARCITY
*P.P.CYAN/1: UNPRICED DUE TO SCARCITY
*P.P.MAGENTA/1: UNPRICED DUE TO SCARCITY
*P.P.YELLOW/1: UNPRICED DUE TO SCARCITY
TN1 Jeff Jarrett .75 2.00
TN2 Robert Roode .12 .30
TN3 Kevin Nash .60 1.50
TN4 Scott Steiner .60 1.50

2008 TRISTAR TNA Impact Thoughts by Big Sexy Kevin Nash

COMPLETE SET (5) 2.00 5.00
*GOLD/50: 2X TO 5X BASIC CARDS
*RED/10: UNPRICED DUE TO SCARCITY
*PURPLE/1: UNPRICED DUE TO SCARCITY
*P.P.BLACK/1: UNPRICED DUE TO SCARCITY
*P.P.CYAN/1: UNPRICED DUE TO SCARCITY
*P.P.MAGENTA/1: UNPRICED DUE TO SCARCITY
*P.P.YELLOW/1: UNPRICED DUE TO SCARCITY
BS1 TNA's X-Division .60 1.50
BS2 Samoa Joe .60 1.50
BS3 Sting .60 1.50
BS4 Scott Steiner .60 1.50
BS5 Trading Cards .60 1.50

2008 TRISTAR TNA Impact Triple Autographs Red

STATED PRINT RUN 25 SER.#'d SETS
A3AAS Angle/Angle/Styles 75.00 150.00
A3RHH Rave/Hoyt/Hemme 25.00 50.00

2008 TRISTAR TNA Impact We Are TNA

COMPLETE SET (7) 2.50 6.00
*GOLD/50: 2X TO 5X BASIC CARDS
*RED/10: UNPRICED DUE TO SCARCITY
*PURPLE/1: UNPRICED DUE TO SCARCITY
*P.P.BLACK/1: UNPRICED DUE TO SCARCITY
*P.P.CYAN/1: UNPRICED DUE TO SCARCITY
*P.P.MAGENTA/1: UNPRICED DUE TO SCARCITY
*P.P.YELLOW/1: UNPRICED DUE TO SCARCITY
T1 6-Sided Ring .40 1.00
T2 X-Division .20 .50
T3 History .75 2.00
T4 TNA World Championship .75 2.00
T5 TNA X-Division Championship .40 1.00
T6 TNA World Tag Team Champ. .40 1.00
T7 TNA Womens Championship .40 1.00

2009 TRISTAR TNA Impact

COMPLETE SET (100) 12.50 25.00
UNOPENED BOX (20 PACKS)
UNOPENED PACK (6 CARDS)
*WHITE: SAME VALUE
*SILVER/20: 4X TO 10X BASIC CARDS
*GOLD/5: UNPRICED DUE TO SCARCITY
*PURPLE/1: UNPRICED DUE TO SCARCITY
1 Sting .60 1.50
2 Mick Foley .60 1.50
3 Daniels .12 .30
4 Angelina Love .60 1.50
5 Bobby Lashley .30 .75
6 James Storm .15 .40
7 Jeff Jarrett .60 1.50
8 Taz .12 .30
9 Brother Ray .20 .50
10 Tara .50 1.25
11 Samoa Joe .20 .50
12 Kevin Nash .75 2.00
13 Suicide .12 .30
14 Velvet Sky .60 1.50
15 Scott Steiner .60 1.50
16 Daffney RC .30 .75
17 Amazing Red RC .12 .30
18 Matt Morgan .15 .40
19 Hernandez .15 .40
20 ODB .20 .50
21 AJ Styles .30 .75
22 Jay Lethal .12 .30
23 Awesome Kong .20 .50
24 Robert Roode .15 .40
25 Kurt Angle .75 2.00
26 Brutus Magnus RC .12 .30
27 SoCal Val .50 1.25
28 Mike Tenay .12 .30
29 Jenna Morasca RC .50 1.25
30 Booker T .12 .30
31 Alex Shelley .15 .40
32 Kiyoshi RC .12 .30
33 Sojournor Bolt RC .20 .50
34 Abyss .30 .75
35 Christy Hemme .75 2.00
36 Doug Williams RC .12 .30
37 Consequences Creed .12 .30
38 Taylor Wilde .50 1.25
39 Jesse Neal RC .12 .30
40 Brother Devon .20 .50
41 Lauren Brooke .30 .75
42 Shark Boy .12 .30
43 Homicide .15 .40
44 Sharmell .20 .50
45 Jim Cornette .12 .30
46 Cody Deaner RC .12 .30
47 Eric Young .12 .30
48 Raisha Saeed .20 .50
49 Rhino .20 .50
50 Sarita RC .30 .75
51 Don West .12 .30
52 Traci Brooks .50 1.25
53 Sheik Abdul Bashir .12 .30
54 Dr. Stevie .15 .40
55 Madison Rayne RC .50 1.25
56 Chris Sabin .12 .30
57 Kip James .15 .40
58 Dixie Carter .30 .75
59 Jeremy Borash .12 .30
60 Rob Terry RC .12 .30
61 Hermie Sadler .12 .30
62 Rocco & Sally Boy .12 .30
63 Ayako Hamada RC .30 .75
64 The Beautiful People .60 1.50
65 Beer Money, Inc. .15 .40
66 Danny Bonaduce .30 .75
67 Curtis Granderson .20 .50
68 THE ICON: STING .60 1.50
69 THE ICON: STING .60 1.50
70 THE ICON: STING .60 1.50
71 THE ICON: STING .60 1.50
72 THE ICON: STING .60 1.50
73 Mick Foley .60 1.50
74 Kurt Angle .75 2.00
75 Booker T .12 .30
76 AJ Styles .30 .75
77 Suicide .12 .30
78 Daniels .12 .30
79 Team 3D .20 .50
80 Sting/Kurt Angle .75 2.00
81 Angelina Love .60 1.50
82 Awesome Kong .20 .50
83 Kurt Angle .75 2.00
84 Jenna Morasca RC .50 1.25
85 Daniels .12 .30
86 Madison Rayne RC .50 1.25
87 Mike Tenay .12 .30
88 Alex Shelley .15 .40
89 Sheik Abdul Bashir .12 .30
90 Jeff Jarrett .60 1.50
91 Consequences Creed .12 .30
92 Lauren Brooke .30 .75
93 Mick Foley .60 1.50
94 James Storm .15 .40
95 Jenna Morasca RC .50 1.25
96 Kip James .15 .40
97 Mike Tenay .12 .30
98 Daniels .12 .30
99 Tweet n' Tweak Connection .20 .50
NNO Checklist .12 .30

2009 TRISTAR TNA Impact Autographs Silver

SEMISTARS (IA1-IA84)
UNLISTED STARS (IA1-IA84)
*GOLD/60: .5X TO 1.2X BASIC AUTOS
*BLUE/25: .6X TO 1.5X BASIC AUTOS
*GREEN/10: UNPRICED DUE TO SCARCITY
*PURPLE/1: UNPRICED DUE TO SCARCITY
IA1 Abyss 5.00 12.00
IA2 AJ Styles 6.00 15.00
IA3 Alex Shelley 4.00 10.00
IA4 Amazing Red 4.00 10.00
IA5 Angelina Love 8.00 20.00
IA6 Awesome Kong 5.00 12.00
IA7 Bobby Lashley
IA8 Booker T
IA9 Brother Devon 4.00 10.00
IA10 Brother Ray 4.00 10.00
IA11 Brutus Magnus 4.00 10.00
IA12 Chris Sabin 5.00 12.00
IA13 Christy Hemme
IA14 Cody Deaner 4.00 10.00
IA15 Consequences Creed 4.00 10.00
IA16 Curtis Granderson
IA17 Daffney 8.00 20.00
IA18 Daniels 5.00 12.00
IA19 Danny Bonaduce 6.00 15.00
IA20 Dixie Carter 5.00 12.00
IA21 Doug Williams 4.00 10.00
IA22 Dr. Stevie 5.00 12.00
IA23 Eric Young 4.00 10.00
IA24 Hernandez
IA25 Homicide 4.00 10.00
IA26 Hermie Sadler 4.00 10.00
IA27 James Storm 5.00 12.00
IA28 Jay Lethal 4.00 10.00
IA29 Jeff Jarrett 6.00 15.00
IA30 Jenna Morasca 6.00 15.00
IA31 Jesse Neal 4.00 10.00
IA32 Jeremy Borash 4.00 10.00
IA33 Jim Cornette
IA34 Kevin Nash
IA35 Kip James 4.00 10.00
IA36 Kiyoshi 4.00 10.00
IA37 Kurt Angle
IA38 Lauren Brooke 5.00 12.00
IA39 Madison Rayne 6.00 15.00
IA40 Matt Morgan
IA41 Mick Foley
IA42 ODB 4.00 10.00
IA43 Raisha Saeed 5.00 12.00
IA44 Rhino
IA45 Rob Terry 5.00 12.00
IA46 Robert Roode 5.00 12.00
IA47 Samoa Joe 5.00 12.00
IA48 Sarita 6.00 15.00
IA49 Scott Steiner
IA50 Shark Boy 5.00 12.00
IA51 Sharmell
IA52 Sheik Abdul Bashir 10.00
IA53 SoCal Val 6.00 15.00
IA54 Sojournor Bolt
IA55 Sting
IA56 Suicide 4.00 10.00
IA57 Tara 8.00 20.00
IA58 Taylor Wilde 8.00 20.00
IA59 Traci Brooks 6.00 15.00
IA60 Velvet Sky 8.00 20.00
IA61 Jeff Jarrett
Mick Foley
IA62 Angelina Love 12.00 30.00
Velvet Sky
IA63 Chris Sabin
Alex Shelley
IA64 Daffney 12.00 30.00
The Governor
IA65 Bobby Lashley
Kurt Angle
IA66 Kevin Nash
Jenna Morasca
IA67 Abyss
Lauren
IA68 Mick Foley
Sting
IA69 Consequences Creed
Jay Lethal
IA70 Jesse Neal
Rhino
IA71 Mike Tenay
Don West
IA72 ODB
Cody Deaner
IA73 Brother Devon
Brother Ray
IA74 Sting
Kurt Angle
IA75 Kevin Nash
Samoa Joe
IA76 Scott Steiner
Booker T
IA77 Angelina Love
Velvet Sky
Madison Rayne
IA78 Sting
Kurt Angle
Mick Foley
IA79 Tara
Christy Hemme
Traci Brooks
IA80 Brutus Magnus
Rob Terry
Doug Williams
IA81 Brother Devon
Brother Ray
James Storm
Robert Roode
IA82 Kurt Angle
Kevin Nash
Booker T
Scott Steiner
IA83 Angelina Love
Velvet Sky
Tara
Christy Hemme
IA84 Chris Sabin
Alex Shelley
Jay Lethal
Consequences Creed

2009 TRISTAR TNA Impact High Impact Championship Inserts

NNO Phone Call EXCH
NNO 2 Tickets and Backstage Pass EXCH
NNO 2 Tickets EXCH
NNO Autographed Baseball EXCH
NNO Autographed Photo EXCH

2009 TRISTAR TNA Impact Knockout Autographed Dual Kiss Gold

*BLUE/10: UNPRICED DUE TO SCARCITY
*PURPLE/1: UNPRICED DUE TO SCARCITY
STATED PRINT RUN 25 SER.#'d SETS
2K1 A.Love/V.Sky
2K2 C.Hemme/T.Brooks
2K3 J.Morasca/Sharmell 15.00 30.00
2K4 SoCal Val/L.Brooke 25.00 50.00

2009 TRISTAR TNA Impact Knockout Kiss Gold

*BLUE/25: .6X TO 1.5X BASIC KISS
*GREEN/10: UNPRICED DUE TO SCARCITY
*PURPLE/1: UNPRICED DUE TO SCARCITY
STATED PRINT RUN 99 SER.#'d SETS

K1 Angelina Love 15.00 40.00
K2 Awesome Kong 8.00 20.00
K3 Christy Hemme 15.00 40.00
K4 Jenna Morasca 10.00 25.00
K5 ODB 8.00 20.00
K6 Sharmell 8.00 20.00
K7 Tara 15.00 40.00
K8 Taylor Wilde 12.00 30.00
K9 Traci Brooks 12.00 30.00
K10 Velvet Sky 15.00 40.00

2009 TRISTAR TNA Impact Sting Autographed Face Paint Silver

STATED PRINT RUN 10 SER. #'d SETS
NOT PRICED DUE TO SCARCITY

S1 Sting Black
S2 Sting White

2009 TRISTAR TNA Impact Sting Event-Worn Face Paint Silver

*PURPLE/1: UNPRICED DUE TO SCARCITY
STATED PRINT RUN 5 SER. #'d SETS
UNPRICED DUE TO SCARCITY

S1 Sting Black
S2 Sting White

2009 TRISTAR TNA Impact Sting Face Paint Gold

*GREEN/10: UNPRICED DUE TO SCARCITY
*PURPLE/1: UNPRICED DUE TO SCARCITY
STATED PRINT RUN 60 SER.#'d SETS

S1 Sting Black 25.00 60.00
S2 Sting White 25.00 60.00

2013 TRISTAR TNA Impact Glory

COMPLETE SET (109) 20.00 50.00
COMPLETE SET W/O SP (100) 8.00 20.00
UNOPENED BOX (20 PACKS)
UNOPENED PACK (6 CARDS)
*RED/40: 2X TO 5X BASIC CARDS
*RED SP/40: .5X TO 1.2X BASIC CARDS
*BLUE/10: UNPRICED DUE TO SCARCITY
*BLUE SP/10: UNPRICED DUE TO SCARCITY
*RAINBOW/1: UNPRICED DUE TO SCARCITY
*RAINBOW SP/1: UNPRICED DUE TO SCARCITY
STATED ODDS SP 1:1 HOBBY BOX

1 Jeff Hardy .60 1.50
2 Hulk Hogan .75 2.00
3 Kurt Angle .25 .60
4 Sting .60 1.50
5 Rampage Jackson .25 .60
6 Tito Ortiz .25 .60
7 Mickie James .75 2.00
8 Chris Sabin .15 .40
9 Bully Ray .15 .40
10 Bobby Roode .15 .40
11 AJ Styles .25 .60
12 Gail Kim .40 1.00
13 Velvet Sky .60 1.50
14 Chavo Guerrero Jr. .15 .40
15 James Storm .15 .40
16 ODB .15 .40
17 Christopher Daniels .15 .40
18 Sting .60 1.50
19 Joseph Park .25 .60
20 Jessie Godderz .15 .40
21 Mr. Anderson .25 .60
22 Garett Bischoff .25 .60
23 Samoa Joe .15 .40
24 Austin Aries .25 .60
25 Hernandez .15 .40
26 Jeremy Borash .15 .40
27 Manik RC .15 .40
28 Velvet Sky .60 1.50
29 Jeff Hardy .60 1.50
30 Christy Hemme .50 1.25
31 Robbie E .15 .40
32 Dixie Carter .25 .60
33 Christopher Daniels .15 .40
34 Taryn Terrell .40 1.00
35 Eric Young .15 .40
36 Miss Tessmacher .40 1.00
37 Magnus .15 .40
38 AJ Styles .25 .60
39 Hulk Hogan .75 2.00
40 Sting .60 1.50
41 Gail Kim .40 1.00
42 Wes Brisco RC .15 .40
43 Rob Terry .15 .40
44 Chavo Guerrero Jr. .15 .40
45 Gunner .15 .40
46 Velvet Sky .60 1.50
47 Knux .15 .40
48 Jeff Hardy .60 1.50
49 Chris Sabin .15 .40
50 Kazarian .15 .40
51 King Mo .15 .40
52 Austin Aries .25 .60
53 Jay Bradley RC .15 .40
54 Kenny King RC .15 .40
55 Taz .15 .40
56 Hernandez .15 .40
57 Eric Young .15 .40
58 Hulk Hogan .75 2.00
59 Velvet Sky .60 1.50
60 Sting .60 1.50
61 AJ Styles .25 .60
62 Rockstar Spud RC .15 .40
63 Bully Ray .15 .40
64 Dixie Carter .25 .60
65 Velvet Sky .60 1.50
66 Rampage Jackson .25 .60
67 Jeff Hardy .60 1.50
68 Christopher Daniels .15 .40
69 Abyss .25 .60
70 Chris Sabin .15 .40
71 Mike Tenay .15 .40
72 Mickie James .75 2.00
73 AJ Styles .25 .60
74 ODB .15 .40
75 Magnus .15 .40
76 Hector Guerrero .15 .40
77 Hulk Hogan .75 2.00
78 Brooke Hogan .40 1.00
79 Austin Aries .25 .60
80 Jessie Godderz .15 .40
81 Jessie Godderz .15 .40
82 Jessie Godderz .15 .40
83 Garett Bischoff .25 .60
84 Chavo Guerrero Jr. .15 .40
85 Sam Shaw RC .15 .40
86 Bobby Roode .15 .40
87 Dixie Carter .25 .60
88 Jeff Hardy .60 1.50
89 Hulk Hogan .75 2.00
90 Jeff Hardy Original Art .50 1.25
91 Jeff Hardy Original Art .50 1.25
92 Jeff Hardy Original Art .50 1.25
93 Jeff Hardy Original Art .50 1.25
94 Jeff Hardy Original Art .50 1.25
95 Jeff Hardy Original Art .50 1.25
96 Jeff Hardy Original Art .50 1.25
97 Jeff Hardy Original Art .50 1.25
98 Jeff Hardy Original Art .50 1.25
99 Jeff Hardy Original Art .50 1.25
100 Aces and Eights SP 3.00 8.00
101 Jeff Hardy SP 3.00 8.00
102 Rampage Jackson SP 1.25 3.00
103 Velvet Sky SP 3.00 8.00
104 AJ Styles SP 1.25 3.00
105 Gail Kim SP 2.00 5.00
106 Sting SP 3.00 8.00
107 Jeff Hardy SP 3.00 8.00
108 Dixie Carter SP 1.25 3.00
109 Hulk Hogan SP 4.00 10.00

2013 TRISTAR TNA Impact Glory Autographed Mat Relics Gold

*BLUE/10: UNPRICED DUE TO SCARCITY
*RED/5: UNPRICED DUE TO SCARCITY
*RAINBOW/1: UNPRICED DUE TO SCARCITY
STATED PRINT RUN 50 SER.#'d SETS

MAS AJ Styles 12.00 30.00
MBH Brooke Hogan 20.00 50.00
MBR Bully Ray 8.00 20.00
MBR Bobby Roode 8.00 20.00
MCG Chavo Guerrero Jr. 8.00 20.00
MCH Christy Hemme 12.00 30.00
MCS Chris Sabin 8.00 20.00
MD Devon 8.00 20.00
MHH Hulk Hogan 50.00 100.00
MJG Jessie Godderz 8.00 20.00
MJH Jeff Hardy 20.00 50.00
MKA Kurt Angle 15.00 40.00
MMA Mr. Anderson 8.00 20.00
MMJ Mickie James 20.00 50.00
MRJ Rampage Jackson 12.00 30.00
MS Sting 30.00 60.00
MT Tara 8.00 20.00
MTT Taryn Terrell 12.00 30.00

2013 TRISTAR TNA Impact Glory Autographed Memorabilia Red

M1 Hulk Hogan
M2 Jeff Hardy
M3 Sting 40.00 80.00
M4 Austin Aries
M5 Rampage Jackson 15.00 40.00
M6 Tito Ortiz

2013 TRISTAR TNA Impact Glory Dual Autographs Gold

*RED/50: .5X TO 1.2X BASIC AUTOS
*BLUE/10: UNPRICED DUE TO SCARCITY
*GREEN/5: UNPRICED DUE TO SCARCITY
*RAINBOW/1: UNPRICED DUE TO SCARCITY
*P.P.BLACK/1: UNPRICED DUE TO SCARCITY
*P.P.CYAN/1: UNPRICED DUE TO SCARCITY
*P.P.MAGENTA/1: UNPRICED DUE TO SCARCITY
*P.P.YELLOW/1: UNPRICED DUE TO SCARCITY
STATED PRINT RUN 99 SER.#'d SETS

4 J.Park/Abyss 8.00 20.00
7 M.James/G.Kim 10.00 25.00
8 C.Daniels/Kazarian 4.00 10.00
10 E.Young/ODB 4.00 10.00
12 G.Kim/V.Sky 8.00 20.00
14 B.Roode/J.Storm 5.00 12.00
16 J.Storm/Gunner 5.00 12.00
20 A.Styles/S.Joe 8.00 20.00
21 C.Hemme/S.Val 8.00 20.00

2013 TRISTAR TNA Impact Glory Dual Memorabilia Gold

*RED/50: .5X TO 1.2X BASIC MEM
*BLUE/10: UNPRICED DUE TO SCARCITY
*GREEN/5: UNPRICED DUE TO SCARCITY
*RAINBOW/1: UNPRICED DUE TO SCARCITY
STATED PRINT RUN 99 SER.#'d SETS

M8 B.Ray/M.Tessmacher 5.00 12.00
M9 T.Ortiz/R.Jackson 5.00 12.00

2013 TRISTAR TNA Impact Glory Dual Memorabilia Red

*RED/50: .5X TO 1.2X BASIC MEM

M8 B.Ray/M.Tessmacher 6.00 15.00
M9 T.Ortiz/R.Jackson 6.00 15.00

2013 TRISTAR TNA Impact Glory Jeff Hardy Autographed Face Paint Green

H1 Jeff Hardy
H2 Jeff Hardy

2013 TRISTAR TNA Impact Glory Memorabilia Red

STATED PRINT RUN 50 SER.#'d SETS

M10 Tito Ortiz 5.00 12.00
M11 Rampage Jackson 5.00 12.00
M12 Bully Ray 5.00 12.00
M13 Mickie James 15.00 40.00
M14 Sting 12.00 30.00

2013 TRISTAR TNA Impact Glory On-Card Autographs Gold

*RED/50: .5X TO 1.2X BASIC AUTOS
*BLUE/10: UNPRICED DUE TO SCARCITY
*GREEN/5: UNPRICED DUE TO SCARCITY
*RAINBOW/1: UNPRICED DUE TO SCARCITY
STATED PRINT RUN 199 SER.#'d SETS

GAS AJ Styles 8.00 20.00
GBR Bobby Roode 6.00 15.00
GCH Christy Hemme 6.00 15.00
GGK Gail Kim 8.00 20.00
GJG Jessie Godderz 5.00 12.00
GJS James Storm 5.00 12.00
GKA Kurt Angle 12.00 30.00
GMJ Mickie James 8.00 20.00
GT Tara 6.00 15.00
GVS Velvet Sky 10.00 25.00

2013 TRISTAR TNA Impact Glory Quad Memorabilia Gold

*RED/50: X TO X BASIC MEM
*BLUE/10: UNPRICED DUE TO SCARCITY
*GREEN/5: UNPRICED DUE TO SCARCITY
*RAINBOW/1: UNPRICED DUE TO SCARCITY
STATED PRINT RUN 99 SER.#'d SETS

M7 Kim/James/Tessmacher/Sky

2013 TRISTAR TNA Impact Glory Autographs Gold

*RED/50: .5X TO 1.2X BASIC AUTOS
*BLUE/10: UNPRICED DUE TO SCARCITY
*GREEN/5: UNPRICED DUE TO SCARCITY
*RAINBOW/1: UNPRICED DUE TO SCARCITY
*P.P.BLACK/1: UNPRICED DUE TO SCARCITY
*P.P.CYAN/1: UNPRICED DUE TO SCARCITY
*P.P.MAGENTA/1: UNPRICED DUE TO SCARCITY
*P.P.YELLOW/1: UNPRICED DUE TO SCARCITY
STATED PRINT RUN 99 SER.#'d SETS

G5 Chris Sabin 4.00 10.00
G11 Manik 4.00 10.00
G15 Knux 4.00 10.00
G26 Wes Brisco 4.00 10.00
G27 Jay Bradley 4.00 10.00
G31 Brooke Hogan 15.00 40.00
G32 Garett Bischoff 4.00 10.00
G33 Magnus 4.00 10.00
G37 Devon 4.00 10.00

2013 TRISTAR TNA Impact Glory Triple Autographs Red

*BLUE/10: UNPRICED DUE TO SCARCITY
*GREEN/5: UNPRICED DUE TO SCARCITY
*RAINBOW/1: UNPRICED DUE TO SCARCITY
STATED PRINT RUN 50 SER.#'d SETS

1 Bobby Roode 8.00 20.00
Christopher Daniels
Kazarian
3 Brisco/G.Bischoff/Knux 8.00 20.00
5 James/ODB/Tessmacher 12.00 30.00

2013 TRISTAR TNA Impact Live

COMPLETE SET (109) 25.00 50.00
COMPLETE SET W/O SP (99) 8.00 20.00
UNOPENED BOX (20 PACKS)
UNOPENED PACK (6 CARDS)
*GOLD/50: 2X TO 5X BASIC CARDS
*GOLD SP/50: .6X TO 1.5X BASIC CARDS
*RED/10: UNPRICED DUE TO SCARCITY
*RED SP/10: UNPRICED DUE TO SCARCITY
*RAINBOW/1: UNPRICED DUE TO SCARCITY
*RAINBOW/1: UNPRICED DUE TO SCARCITY
STATED SP ODDS 1:BOX

1 Hulk Hogan .75 2.00
2 Brooke Hogan .40 1.00
3 Hulk Hogan/Brooke Hogan .75 2.00
4 Sting .60 1.50
5 Jeff Hardy .60 1.50
6 Austin Aries .25 .60
7 Gail Kim .40 1.00
8 AJ Styles .25 .60
9 Bobby Roode .15 .40
10 Bully Ray .15 .40

11	Kurt Angle	.25	.60
12	Garett Bischoff	.25	.60
13	Hernandez	.15	.40
14	King Mo	.15	.40
15	Jessie Godderz	.15	.40
16	Tara	.50	1.25
17	James Storm	.15	.40
18	Kazarian	.15	.40
19	Christopher Daniels	.15	.40
20	Matt Morgan	.15	.40
21	Rob Van Dam	.25	.60
22	Douglas Williams	.15	.40
23	SoCal Val	.40	1.00
24	Sting	.60	1.50
25	Christy Hemme	.50	1.25
26	Jesse Sorensen	.15	.40
27	Taz	.15	.40
28	Earl Hebner	.15	.40
29	Magnus	.15	.40
30	AJ Styles	.25	.60
31	Kenny King RC	.15	.40
32	Taryn Terrell	.40	1.00
33	Devon	.15	.40
34	Velvet Sky	.60	1.50
35	Jeff Hardy	.60	1.50
36	Joseph Park	.25	.60
37	Eric Young	.15	.40
38	Tara	.50	1.25
39	Chris Sabin	.15	.40
40	Sting	.60	1.50
41	Bully Ray	.15	.40
42	Robbie E	.15	.40
43	Rob Terry	.15	.40
44	James Storm	.15	.40
45	Crimson	.15	.40
46	DOC	.15	.40
47	Jessie Godderz	.15	.40
48	Samoa Joe	.15	.40
49	Rob Van Dam	.25	.60
50	Hulk Hogan	.75	2.00
51	Jeff Hardy	.60	1.50
52	Christy Hemme	.50	1.25
53	Jessie Godderz	.15	.40
54	Madison Rayne	.40	1.00
55	TNA Referees	.15	.40
56	Zema Ion RC	.15	.40
57	Christopher Daniels	.15	.40
58	Mr. Anderson	.25	.60
59	Garett Bischoff	.25	.60
60	AJ Styles	.25	.60
61	Mike Tenay	.15	.40
62	Aces and Eights	.15	.40
63	Matt Morgan	.15	.40
64	James Storm	.15	.40
65	Hernandez	.15	.40
66	Kurt Angle	.25	.60
67	Douglas Williams	.15	.40
68	Jeff Hardy	.60	1.50
69	ODB	.15	.40
70	Abyss	.25	.60
71	Bully Ray	.15	.40
72	Jeremy Borash	.15	.40
73	Gunner	.15	.40
74	Christopher Daniels	.15	.40
75	AJ Styles	.25	.60
76	Gut Check	.15	.40
77	Alex Silva	.15	.40
78	Christian York RC	.15	.40
79	Sam Shaw RC	.15	.40
80	Joey Ryan RC	.15	.40
81	Taeler Hendrix RC	.25	.60
82	Wes Brisco RC	.15	.40
83	Al Snow	.25	.60
84	D'Lo Brown	.15	.40
85	Chavo Guerrero Jr.	.15	.40
86	Hector Guerrero	.15	.40
87	World Tag Team Champions: Hernandez and Chavo Guerrero Jr.	.15	.40
88	The Guerrero Legacy	.15	.40
89	Gail Kim	.40	1.00
90	Mr. Anderson	.25	.60
91	Miss Tessmacher	.40	1.00
92	Robbie E	.15	.40
93	Tara	.50	1.25
94	Mickie James	.75	2.00
95	Chavo Guerrero Jr.	.15	.40
96	Destination X	.15	.40
97	Slammiversary	.15	.40
98	Bound For Glory	.15	.40
99	Sting's Hall of Fame Induction	.60	1.50
100	Hulk Hogan SP	4.00	10.00
101	Sting SP	3.00	8.00
102	Bully Ray SP	.75	2.00
103	Samoa Joe SP	.75	2.00
104	Kurt Angle SP	1.25	3.00
105	Hulk Hogan SP	4.00	10.00
106	Sting SP	3.00	8.00
107	Kurt Angle SP	1.25	3.00
108	Miss Tessmacher SP	2.00	5.00
109	Jeff Hardy SP	3.00	8.00
CL	Checklist	.15	.40

2013 TRISTAR TNA Impact Live Autographed Memorabilia Gold

M17 Gail Kim

2013 TRISTAR TNA Impact Live Autographed Memorabilia Rainbow

STATED PRINT RUN 1 SER.#'d SET
UNPRICED DUE TO SCARCITY

M15 Hulk Hogan
M16 Jeff Hardy
M17 Gail Kim
M18 Sting

2013 TRISTAR TNA Impact Live Autographs Gold

*GREEN/50: .5X TO 1.2X BASIC AUTOS
*BLUE/25: .6X TO 1.5X BASIC AUTOS
*RED/5: UNPRICED DUE TO SCARCITY
*RAINBOW/1: UNPRICED DUE TO SCARCITY
STATED PRINT RUN 99 SER. #'d SETS

L16	Gail Kim	8.00	20.00
L17	James Storm	5.00	12.00
L20	Mr. Anderson	6.00	15.00
L23	Taryn Terrell	12.00	30.00
L24	Doug Williams	3.00	8.00
L25	Matt Morgan	5.00	12.00
L26	Christy Hemme	10.00	25.00
L27	Abyss	3.00	8.00
L29	Samoa Joe	3.00	8.00
L32	Bully Ray	5.00	12.00
L33	Robbie E	3.00	8.00
L34	Winter	4.00	10.00
L35	Jesse Sorensen	3.00	8.00
L36	Kazarian	4.00	10.00
L37	Garett Bischoff	3.00	8.00
L38	Kenny King	6.00	15.00
L39	Christian York	8.00	20.00
L40	Hector Guerrero	3.00	8.00
L41	ODB	5.00	12.00
L42	Bobby Roode	3.00	8.00
L43	Chris Sabin	4.00	10.00
L44	SoCal Val	5.00	12.00
L45	Rosita	5.00	12.00
L46	Hernandez	3.00	8.00
L47	Kid Kash	3.00	8.00
L48	Austin Aries	8.00	20.00

2013 TRISTAR TNA Impact Live Dual Autographs Gold

*GREEN/50: .5X TO 1.2X BASIC AUTOS
*BLUE/25: .6X TO 1.5X BASIC AUTOS
*RED/5: UNPRICED DUE TO SCARCITY
*RAINBOW/1: UNPRICED DUE TO SCARCITY
STATED PRINT RUN 99 SER.#'d SETS

2	Chavo & Hector Guerrero		
3	K.Angle/W.Brisco		
4	E.Young/ODB		
5	C.Daniels/Kazarian	4.00	10.00
6	Tara/J.Godderz	6.00	15.00
7	C.Hemme/J.Borash	6.00	15.00
8	M.Morgan/J.Ryan	6.00	15.00
9	Sarita/Rosita	5.00	12.00
10	C.Guerrero/Hernandez		
11	G.Kim/M.James	12.00	30.00
12	J.Storm/B.Roode		
13	B.Roode/J.Hardy		
14	B.Hogan/B.Ray		
15	A.Aries/M.Morgan		
16	M.Tessmacher/Tara	8.00	20.00
17	W.Brisco/G.Bischoff	5.00	12.00
18	S.Shaw/C.York		
19	M.James/Tara		
20	C.Daniels/C.Sabin	4.00	10.00
21	C.Sabin/J.Sorensen	4.00	10.00
22	K.Angle/M.Anderson		
23	B.Roode/A.Aries		
24	M.Anderson/Devon		
25	Sting/J.Hardy		

2013 TRISTAR TNA Impact Live Dual Memorabilia Silver

*GOLD/50: .5X TO 1.2X BASIC MEM
*BLUE/25: .6X TO 1.5X BASIC MEM
*RED/5: UNPRICED DUE TO SCARCITY
*RAINBOW/1: UNPRICED DUE TO SCARCITY
STATED ODDS OVERALL 1:BOX

M11	Tara / Jessie Godderz	4.00	10.00
M12	C.Guerrero Jr./Hernandez	4.00	10.00

2013 TRISTAR TNA Impact Live Eight Autographs Gold

*GREEN/50: X TO X BASIC AUTOS
*BLUE/25: UNPRICED DUE TO SCARCITY
*RED/5: UNPRICED DUE TO SCARCITY
*RAINBOW/1: UNPRICED DUE TO SCARCTIY
STATED PRINT RUN 99 SER.#'d SETS

3 Brooke Hogan
Tara
Velvet Sky
Madison Rayne
Gail Kim
Mickie James
Christy Hemme
Ms. Tessmacher

2013 TRISTAR TNA Impact Live Jeff Hardy Die-Cut Letter Memorabilia Gold

*BLUE/25: .5X TO 1.2X BASIC MEM
*RED/5: .75X TO 2X BASIC MEM
*RAINBOW/1: UNPRICED DUE TO SCARCITY
STATED PRINT RUN 50 SER.#'d SETS

M1	Jeff Hardy H	15.00	40.00
M2	Jeff Hardy A	15.00	40.00
M3	Jeff Hardy R	15.00	40.00
M4	Jeff Hardy D	15.00	40.00
M5	Jeff Hardy Y	15.00	40.00

2013 TRISTAR TNA Impact Live Memorabilia Silver

*GOLD/50: .5X TO 1.2X BASIC MEM
*BLUE/25: .6X TO 1.5X BASIC MEM
*RED/5: UNPRICED DUE TO SCARCITY
*RAINBOW/1: UNPRICED DUE TO SCARCITY
STATED ODDS OVERALL 1:BOX

M6	Hulk Hogan	10.00	25.00
M7	Sting	8.00	20.00
M8	Kurt Angle	6.00	15.00
M9	Austin Aries	4.00	10.00
M10	Chavo Guerrero Jr.	4.00	10.00

2013 TRISTAR TNA Impact Live Quad Autographs Gold

*GREEN/50: X TO X BASIC AUTOS
*BLUE/25: UNPRICED DUE TO SCARCITY
*RED/5: UNPRICED DUE TO SCARCITY
*RAINBOW/1: UNPRICED DUE TO SCARCITY
STATED PRINT RUN 99 SER.#'d SETS

1 Gail Kim
Mickie James
Tara
Velvet Sky
2 Angle/Brisco/G.Bischoff/Samoa Joe

2013 TRISTAR TNA Impact Live Quad Memorabilia Silver

*GOLD/50: .5X TO 1.2X BASIC MEM
*BLUE/25: .6X TO 1.5X BASIC MEM
*RED/5: UNPRICED DUE TO SCARCITY
*RAINBOW/1: UNPRICED DUE TO SCARCITY
STATED ODDS OVERALL 1:BOX

M13	Hulk Hogan / Sting / Jeff Hardy / Kurt Angle		
M14	Kim/James/Tessmacher/Sky	12.00	30.00

2013 TRISTAR TNA Impact Live Six Autographs Gold

2 Kim/Tara/James
Sky/Tessmacher/Rayne

2013 TRISTAR TNA Impact Live Ten Autographs Gold

2 Styles/Morgan/Sabin/Daniels/Roode
Young/Hernandez/Kazarian/Storm/Robbie

2013 TRISTAR TNA Impact Live Triple Autographs Gold

2 Jeff Hardy
Austin Aries
Bobby Roode
4 Angle/Anderson/Hardy

2013 TRISTAR TNA Impact Live Twelve Autographs Gold

2 Brooke/Tara/Hemme/Sarita
Kim/Sky/Tessmacher/Terrell
James/Rayne/ODB/Val

2012 TRISTAR TNA Impact Reflexxions

COMPLETE SET (100) 10.00 25.00
UNOPENED BOX (20 PACKS)
UNOPENED PACK (6 CARDS)
*SILVER/40: 2.5X TO 6X BASIC CARDS
*GOLD/10: UNPRICED DUE TO SCARCITY
*PURPLE/1: UNPRICED DUE TO SCARCITY
SUBSET CARDS SAME PRICE AS BASE CARDS
EXCHANGE DEADLINE 6/1/2013

1	Hulk Hogan	1.00	2.50
2	Ric Flair	.75	2.00
3	Sting	.60	1.50
4	Bobby Roode	.15	.40
5	James Storm	.15	.40
6	Jeff Hardy	.60	1.50
7	AJ Styles	.25	.60
8	Dixie Carter	.40	1.00
9	Jeff Jarrett	.25	.60
10	Rob Van Dam	.25	.60
11	Velvet Sky	.75	2.00
12	Bully Ray	.15	.40
13	Angelina Love	.60	1.50
14	Kurt Angle	.25	.60
15	Crimson	.15	.40
16	Christy Hemme	.60	1.50
17	Gail Kim	.40	1.00
18	Austin Aries RC	.25	.60
19	Mickie James	1.00	2.50
20	Samoa Joe	.15	.40
21	Eric Bischoff	.15	.40
22	Garrett Bischoff	.25	.60
23	Mr. Anderson	.25	.60
24	Alex Shelley	.15	.40
25	Mark Haskins RC	.15	.40
26	Rob Terry	.15	.40
27	Karen Jarrett	.25	.60
28	Douglas Williams	.15	.40
29	Rosita	.25	.60
30	Kazarian	.15	.40
31	Scott Steiner	.25	.60
32	Zema Ion RC	.15	.40
33	Anarquia	.15	.40
34	Gunner	.15	.40
35	Kid Kash	.25	.60
36	D'Angelo Dinero	.15	.40
37	Magnus	.15	.40
38	Tara	.60	1.50
39	Abyss	.25	.60
40	Matt Morgan	.15	.40
41	ODB	.15	.40
42	Chris Sabin	.15	.40
43	Jesse Sorensen RC	.15	.40
44	Mike Tenay	.15	.40

45 Madison Rayne .40 1.00
46 Devon .15 .40
47 Sarita .25 .60
48 Eric Young .15 .40
49 Traci Brooks .40 1.00
50 Anthony Nese .15 .40
51 Taz .15 .40
52 Hernandez .15 .40
53 Brooke Tessmacher .40 1.00
54 Christopher Daniels .15 .40
55 Jesse Neal .15 .40
56 Robbie E .15 .40
57 SoCal Val .40 1.00
58 Brian Kendrick .15 .40
59 Jeremy Borash .15 .40
60 Shannon Moore .15 .40
61 Winter .60 1.50
62 Ric Flair US .75 2.00
63 Sting US .60 1.50
64 Christy Hemme US .60 1.50
65 Jeff Jarrett US .25 .60
66 Velvet Sky US .75 2.00
67 Mr. Anderson US .25 .60
68 Gail Kim US .40 1.00
69 Scott Steiner US .25 .60
70 Traci Brooks US .40 1.00
71 Jeff Hardy US .60 1.50
72 Dixie Carter US .40 1.00
73 Sting FT .60 1.50
74 Ric Flair FT .75 2.00
75 Velvet Sky FT .75 2.00
76 Jeff Jarrett FT .25 .60
77 Scott Steiner FT .25 .60
78 Jeff Hardy FT .60 1.50
79 Mr. Anderson FT .25 .60
80 Velvet Sky BMV .75 2.00
81 Christy Hemme BMV .60 1.50
82 Gail Kim BMV .40 1.00
83 Karen Jarrett BMV .25 .60
84 Traci Brooks BMV .40 1.00
85 Madison Rayne BMV .40 1.00
86 Brooke Tessmacher BMV .40 1.00
87 Hulk Hogan SW 1.00 2.50
88 Sting SW .60 1.50
89 Kurt Angle SW .25 .60
90 Crimson SW .15 .40
91 Jeff Hardy LH .60 1.50
92 Sting LH .60 1.50
93 Christy Hemme LH .60 1.50
94 Ric Flair LH .75 2.00
95 Mr. Anderson LH .25 .60
96 Velvet Sky LH .75 2.00
97 Scott Steiner LH .25 .60
98 Gail Kim LH .40 1.00
99 Jeff Jarrett LH .25 .60
CL Checklist .15 .40
NNO Jeff Hardy Art Redemption EXCH

2012 TRISTAR TNA Impact Reflexxions Autographed Mat Relics Gold

*BLUE/25: X TO X BASIC AU RELICS
*RED/5: UNPRICED DUE TO SCARCITY
*PURPLE/1: UNPRICED DUE TO SCARCITY
STATED PRINT RUN 50 SER.#'d SETS

M3 Kurt Angle
M4 Velvet Sky 25.00 50.00
M5 AJ Styles
M6 Bobby Roode
M7 Tara
M8 Mr. Anderson
M9 James Storm 15.00 30.00
M10 Angelina Love 20.00 40.00
M11 Jeff Jarrett
M12 Gail Kim 20.00 40.00
M13 Rob Van Dam

2012 TRISTAR TNA Impact Reflexxions Autographed Memorabilia Blue

*RED/5: UNPRICED DUE TO SCARCITY
*PURPLE/1: UNPRICED DUE TO SCARCITY
STATED PRINT RUN 25 SER.#'d SETS

M14 Hulk Hogan
M15 Ric Flair 75.00 125.00
M16 Sting 50.00 100.00
M17 Rob Van Dam 20.00 40.00
M18 Kurt Angle 25.00 50.00
M19 Mickie James 75.00 125.00
M20 Jeff Hardy 40.00 80.00
M21 Mr. Anderson 15.00 30.00
M22 Garett Bischoff 15.00 30.00
M23 Velvet Sky 40.00 80.00

2012 TRISTAR TNA Impact Reflexxions Autographs Silver

*GOLD/50: .5X TO 1.2X BASIC AUTOS
*RED/25: X TO X BASIC AUTOS
*GREEN/5: UNPRICED DUE TO SCARCITY
*PURPLE/1: UNPRICED DUE TO SCARCITY
STATED PRINT RUN 99 SER.#'d SETS

16 Christy Hemme 10.00 25.00
20 Samoa Joe 4.00 10.00
22 Garrett Bischoff 4.00 10.00
26 Rob Terry 4.00 10.00
29 Rosita 6.00 15.00
30 Kazarian 4.00 10.00
33 Anarquia 4.00 10.00
34 Gunner 4.00 10.00
35 Kid Kash 6.00 15.00
36 D'Angelo Dinero 4.00 10.00
37 Magnus 4.00 10.00
39 Abyss 5.00 12.00
41 ODB 4.00 10.00
43 Jesse Sorensen 5.00 12.00
45 Madison Rayne 6.00 15.00
47 Sarita 5.00 12.00
48 Eric Young 4.00 10.00
49 Traci Brooks 5.00 12.00
52 Hernandez 4.00 10.00
53 Brooke Tessmacher 8.00 20.00
55 Jesse Neal 4.00 10.00
56 Robbie E 4.00 10.00
57 SoCal Val 5.00 12.00
61 Winter 8.00 20.00

2012 TRISTAR TNA Impact Reflexxions Blue Foil Inserts

COMPLETE SET (50) 60.00 120.00
*RED/10: UNPRICED DUE TO SCARCITY
*PURPLE/1: UNPRICED DUE TO SCARCITY
STATED PRINT RUN 40 SER.#'d SETS

R1 Hulk Hogan 4.00 10.00
R2 Hulk Hogan 4.00 10.00
R3 Hulk Hogan 4.00 10.00
R4 Hulk Hogan 4.00 10.00
R5 Hulk Hogan 4.00 10.00
R6 Ric Flair 3.00 8.00
R7 Ric Flair 3.00 8.00
R8 Sting 2.50 6.00
R9 Sting 2.50 6.00
R10 Kurt Angle 1.00 2.50
R11 Kurt Angle 1.00 2.50
R12 Jeff Jarrett 1.00 2.50
R13 Rob Van Dam 1.00 2.50
R14 Velvet Sky 3.00 8.00
R15 AJ Styles 1.00 2.50
R16 Eric Bischoff .60 1.50
R17 Scott Steiner 1.00 2.50
R18 Angelina Love 2.50 6.00
R19 Mr. Anderson 1.00 2.50
R20 Bobby Roode .60 1.50
R21 James Storm .60 1.50
R22 Abyss 1.00 2.50
R23 Gail Kim 1.50 4.00
R24 Samoa Joe .60 1.50
R25 Crimson .60 1.50
R26 Dixie Carter 1.50 4.00
R27 Tara 2.50 6.00
R28 Hernandez .60 1.50
R29 Christopher Daniels .60 1.50
R30 Devon .60 1.50
R31 Mickie James 4.00 10.00
R32 Matt Morgan .60 1.50
R33 Bully Ray .60 1.50
R34 Garett Bischoff 1.00 2.50
R35 Brooke Tessmacher 1.50 4.00
R36 Karen Jarrett 1.00 2.50
R37 The Immortal Battles 4.00 10.00
R38 The Immortal Battles 4.00 10.00
R39 The Immortal Battles 4.00 10.00
R40 Jeff Hardy 2.50 6.00
R41 Jeff Hardy Original Art 5.00 12.00
R42 Jeff Hardy Original Art 5.00 12.00
R43 Jeff Hardy Original Art 5.00 12.00
R44 Jeff Hardy Original Art 5.00 12.00
R45 Jeff Hardy Original Art 5.00 12.00
R46 Jeff Hardy Original Art 5.00 12.00
R47 Jeff Hardy Original Art 5.00 12.00
R48 Jeff Hardy Original Art 5.00 12.00
R49 Jeff Hardy Original Art 5.00 12.00
R50 Jeff Hardy Original Art 5.00 12.00

2012 TRISTAR TNA Impact Reflexxions Dual Autographs Silver

*GOLD/50: .5X TO 1.25X BASIC AUTOS
*RED/25: .6X TO 1.5X BASIC AUTOS
*GREEN/5: UNPRICED DUE TO SCARCITY
*PURPLE/1: UNPRICED DUE TO SCARCITY
STATED PRINT RUN 99 SER.#'d SETS

7 Tara/Tessmacher 8.00 20.00
8 Crimson/Morgan 6.00 15.00
9 Kim/Sky 15.00 30.00
10 K.Jarrett/Brooks 10.00 25.00
12 Hernandez/Anarquia 5.00 12.00
14 Robbie E/Robbie T 5.00 12.00
15 Sarita/Rosita 8.00 20.00
17 Aries/Kash 8.00 20.00
19 Hemme/SoCal Val 8.00 20.00
20 Tenay/Borash 5.00 12.00
29 Aries/Kendrick 6.00 15.00
30 Sky/Love 8.00 20.00

2012 TRISTAR TNA Impact Reflexxions Dual Memorabilia Silver

*GOLD/50: .5X TO 1.2X BASIC MEM
*BLUE/25: .6X TO 1.5X BASIC MEM
*RED/5: UNPRICED DUE TO SCARCITY
*PURPLE/1: UNPRICED DUE TO SCARCITY
STATED PRINT RUN 199 SER.#'d SETS

M26 J.Jarrett/K.Jarrett 4.00 10.00
M27 Roode/Storm 4.00 10.00
M29 Jarrett/Brooks 5.00 12.00

2012 TRISTAR TNA Impact Reflexxions Quad Memorabilia Silver

*GOLD/50: X TO X BASIC MEM
*BLUE/25: X TO X BASIC MEM
*RED/5: UNPRICED DUE TO SCARCITY
*PURPLE/1: UNPRICED DUE TO SCARCITY
STATED PRINT RUN 199 SER.#'d SETS

M36 Styles/Abyss/Mrgn/Dnls 8.00 20.00

2012 TRISTAR TNA Impact Reflexxions Quad Memorabilia Gold

*GOLD: .5X TO 1.2X BASIC MEM
STATED PRINT RUN 50 SER.#'d SETS

M34 James/Tara/Sky/Love 15.00 40.00
M36 Styles/Abyss/Mrgn/Dnls 10.00 25.00

2012 TRISTAR TNA Impact Reflexxions Quad Memorabilia Red

STATED PRINT RUN 5 SER.#'d SETS
UNPRICED DUE TO SCARCITY

M34 James/Tara/Sky/Love
M35 Hulk/Flair/Sting/Angle
M36 Styles/Abyss/Mrgn/Dnls

2012 TRISTAR TNA Impact Reflexxions Six Autographs Red

*GREEN/5: UNPRICED DUE TO SCARCITY
*PURPLE/1: UNPRICED DUE TO SCARCITY
STATED PRINT RUN 25 SER.#'d SETS

1 Sky/Tara/Tess/Love/Wint/Rayn
3 Rood/Strm/Styl/VDam/Hard/Angle

2012 TRISTAR TNA Impact Reflexxions Triple Autographs Red

*GREEN/5: UNPRICED DUE TO SCARCITY
*PURPLE/1: UNPRICED DUE TO SCARCITY
STATED PRINT RUN 25 SER.#'d SETS

2 Angle/Jarrett/Jarrett 20.00 40.00
3 Roode/Styles/Hardy 40.00 80.00
4 Kim/James/Sky 40.00 80.00
5 Hemme/Kim/Brooks 30.00 60.00

2012 TRISTAR TNA Impact Reflexxions Triple Memorabilia Silver

*GOLD/50: .5X TO 1.2X BASIC MEM
*BLUE/25: X TO X BASIC MEM
*RED/5: UNPRICED DUE TO SCARCITY
*PURPLE/1: UNPRICED DUE TO SCARCITY
STATED PRINT RUN 199 SER.#'d SETS

M32 Sting/Steiner/Jarrett 8.00 20.00
M33 RVD/Anderson/Styles 6.00 15.00

2012 TRISTAR TNA Impact Reflexxions Triple Memorabilia Blue

*BLUE: .6X TO 1.5X BASIC MEM
STATED PRINT RUN 25 SER.#'d SETS

M31 Hogan/Flair/Sting
M32 Sting/Steiner/Jarrett 12.00 30.00
M33 RVD/Anderson/Styles 10.00 25.00

2012 TRISTAR TNA Impact Reflexxions Triple Memorabilia Purple

STATED PRINT RUN 1 SER.#'d SET
UNPRICED DUE TO SCARCITY

M31 Hogan/Flair/Sting
M32 Sting/Steiner/Jarrett
M33 RVD/Anderson/Styles

2012 TRISTAR TNA Impact TENacious

COMPLETE SET (120)
COMPLETE SET W/O SP (100) 8.00 20.00
UNOPENED BOX (20 PACKS)
UNOPENED PACK (6 CARDS)
*SILVER/30: 2.5X TO 6X BASIC CARDS
*GOLD/RED/10: UNPRICED DUE TO SCARCITY
*PURPLE/1: UNPRICED DUE TO SCARCITY

1 Jeff Jarrett .25 .60
2 AJ Styles .25 .60
3 James Storm .15 .40
4 Jeremy Borash .15 .40
5 Mike Tenay .15 .40
6 Hulk Hogan 1.00 2.50
7 Brooke Hogan .60 1.50
8 Sting .60 1.50
9 Gail Kim .40 1.00
10 Jeff Jarrett .25 .60
11 Jeff Hardy .60 1.50
12 Kurt Angle .25 .60
13 Chris Sabin .15 .40
14 Austin Aries RC .25 .60
15 Bully Ray .15 .40
16 Hector Guerrero RC .15 .40
17 Kazarian .15 .40
18 Eric Bischoff .15 .40
19 Hernandez .15 .40
20 Jeff Jarrett .25 .60
21 Mickie James 1.00 2.50
22 Christopher Daniels .15 .40
23 Mr. Anderson .25 .60
24 ODB .15 .40
25 Devon .15 .40
26 Matt Morgan .15 .40
27 Ric Flair .75 2.00
28 AJ Styles .25 .60
29 Rob Terry .15 .40
30 Jeff Jarrett .25 .60
31 Rob Van Dam .25 .60
32 Jeff Hardy .60 1.50
33 Kid Kash .25 .60
34 Robbie E .15 .40
35 Madison Rayne .40 1.00
36 Bobby Roode .15 .40
37 Bobby Roode .15 .40
38 Bobby Roode .15 .40
39 Bobby Roode .15 .40
40 Jeff Jarrett .25 .60
41 Jeremy Borash .15 .40

42 Jeremy Borash .15 .40
43 Jeremy Borash .15 .40
44 Joseph Park .25 .60
45 Alex Silva RC .15 .40
46 Gunner .15 .40
47 Mr. Anderson .25 .60
48 Rosita .25 .60
49 Samoa Joe .15 .40
50 Jeff Jarrett .25 .60
51 Sarita .25 .60
52 Eric Young .15 .40
53 Kurt Angle .25 .60
54 Miss Tessmacher .40 1.00
55 Sting .60 1.50
56 Tara .60 1.50
57 Garett Bischoff RC .25 .60
58 Taz .15 .40
59 SoCal Val .40 1.00
60 Jeff Jarrett .25 .60
61 Velvet Sky .75 2.00
62 Angelina Love .60 1.50
63 Jeff Hardy .60 1.50
64 Zema Ion RC .15 .40
65 Winter .60 1.50
66 James Storm .15 .40
67 Jessie Godderz RC .15 .40
68 Matt Morgan .15 .40
69 ODB .15 .40
70 Jeff Jarrett .25 .60
71 Christopher Daniels .15 .40
72 Gail Kim .40 1.00
73 Velvet Sky .75 2.00
74 Doug Williams .15 .40
75 Abyss .25 .60
76 Crimson .15 .40
77 Karen Jarrett .25 .60
78 Eric Young .15 .40
79 Magnus .15 .40
80 Jeff Jarrett .25 .60
81 D'Angelo Dinero .15 .40
82 Jesse Sorensen RC .15 .40
83 Jeff Hardy .60 1.50
84 Christy Hemme .60 1.50
85 Christopher Daniels .15 .40
86 Hulk Hogan 1.00 2.50
87 Tara .60 1.50
88 ODB .15 .40
89 Magnus .15 .40
90 AJ Styles .25 .60
91 Miss Tessmacher .40 1.00
92 Joe vs. Daniels vs. Styles .15 .40
93 MSG Hulk Hogan Press Conference 1.00 2.50
94 IMPACT Wrestling Live on 1/4/2010 1.00 2.50
95 Beer Money vs. MCMG Best of 5 .15 .40
96 RVD Defeats Hardy and Styles .25 .60
97 Sting Defeats Jarrett .60 1.50
98 Samoa Joe vs. Kurt Angle .25 .60
99 Gail Kim Wins 1st Knockouts Title .40 1.00
100 Jeff Hardy/100 8.00 20.00
101 Team 3D/100 2.50 6.00
102 Kurt Angle/100 3.00 8.00
103 Hulk Hogan/100 4.00 10.00
104 Ric Flair/100 4.00 10.00
105 Jeff Hardy ART/100 8.00 20.00
106 Jeff Hardy ART/100 8.00 20.00
107 Jeff Hardy ART/100 8.00 20.00
108 Jeff Hardy ART/100 8.00 20.00
109 Jeff Hardy ART/100 8.00 20.00
110 Hulk Hogan/100 4.00 10.00
111 Hulk Hogan/100 4.00 10.00
112 Hulk Hogan/100 4.00 10.00
113 Hulk Hogan/100 4.00 10.00
114 Hulk Hogan/100 4.00 10.00
115 Sting/100 3.00 8.00
116 Sting/100 3.00 8.00
117 Sting/100 3.00 8.00
118 Sting/100 3.00 8.00
119 Sting/100 3.00 8.00
CL Checklist .15 .40

2012 TRISTAR TNA Impact TENacious Autographed Memorabilia Silver

COMPLETE SET (5)
*GOLD/80: .5X TO 1.2X BASIC AU MEM
*BLUE/50: .6X TO 1.5X BASIC AU MEM
*RED/10: UNPRICED DUE TO SCARCITY
*PURPLE/1: UNPRICED DUE TO SCARCITY
STATED PRINT RUN 100 SER.#'d SETS

T2 Jeff Hardy 12.00 30.00
T3 Bobby Roode 5.00 12.00
T4 Sting 25.00 60.00
T5 Mickie James 15.00 40.00
T6 Rob Van Dam 10.00 25.00

2012 TRISTAR TNA Impact TENacious Autographed Memorabilia Blue

T2 Jeff Hardy 20.00 50.00
T3 Bobby Roode 8.00 20.00
T4 Sting 50.00 100.00
T5 Mickie James 30.00 60.00
T6 Rob Van Dam 15.00 40.00

2012 TRISTAR TNA Impact TENacious Autographs Gold

*RED/10: UNPRICED DUE TO SCARCITY
*PURPLE/1: UNPRICED DUE TO SCARCITY
STATED PRINT RUN 100 SER.#'d SETS

TEN1 Jeff Jarrett 6.00 15.00
TEN2 AJ Styles 5.00 12.00
TEN3 James Storm 4.00 10.00
TEN4 Gail Kim
TEN8 Sting
TEN9 Bobby Roode 4.00 10.00
TEN10 Jeff Hardy 25.00 50.00
TEN11 Kurt Angle 10.00 25.00
TEN12 Eric Bischoff
TEN13 Mickie James 12.00 30.00
TEN14 Mr. Anderson 5.00 12.00
TEN15 Ric Flair
TEN16 Rob Van Dam 10.00 25.00
TEN17 Austin Aries 10.00 25.00
TEN18 Brooke Tessmacher 10.00 25.00
TEN19 Samoa Joe 4.00 10.00
TEN20 Tara 8.00 20.00
TEN21 Bully Ray 5.00 12.00
TEN22 Devon 4.00 10.00
TEN23 Velvet Sky 8.00 20.00
TEN24 Garett Bischoff 4.00 10.00
TEN25 Abyss 4.00 10.00
TEN26 Christy Hemme 10.00 25.00
TEN27 Jeremy Borash 4.00 10.00
TEN28 ODB 4.00 10.00
TEN29 Magnus 4.00 10.00
TEN30 Crimson 4.00 10.00
TEN31 Doug Williams 4.00 10.00
TEN32 Robbie E 4.00 10.00
TEN33 Alex Shelley 4.00 10.00
TEN34 Rosita 5.00 12.00
TEN35 Gunner 5.00 12.00
TEN36 Kazarian 4.00 10.00
TEN37 Angelina Love 8.00 20.00
TEN38 Matt Morgan 4.00 10.00
TEN39 Chris Sabin 4.00 10.00
TEN40 Gail Kim 10.00 25.00
TEN41 Hernandez 5.00 12.00
TEN42 Madison Rayne 8.00 20.00
TEN43 Anarquia 4.00 10.00
TEN44 Winter 6.00 15.00
TEN45 Eric Young 4.00 10.00
TEN46 Sarita 5.00 12.00
TEN47 Shannon Moore 4.00 10.00
TEN48 Christopher Daniels 4.00 10.00
TEN49 Mike Tenay 4.00 10.00
TEN50 SoCal Val 5.00 12.00

2012 TRISTAR TNA Impact TENacious Celebrity Cut Signatures Gold

STATED PRINT RUN 5 SER.#'d SETS
UNPRICED DUE TO SCARCITY

1 Ace Young
2 Adam Pac-Man Jones
3 AJ Pierzynski
4 Brandon Jacobs
5 Brian Urlacher
6 Brooke Hogan
7 Chris Rock
8 Curtis Granderson
9 David Eckstein
10 Dennis Rodman
11 Johnny Damon
12 Juan Pablo Montoya
13 Ken Shamrock
14 Rowdy Roddy Piper
15 Steve McMichael
16 Tito Ortiz
17 Toby Keith
18 Tom Arnold

2012 TRISTAR TNA Impact TENacious Dual Autographs Gold

*RED/10: UNPRICED DUE TO SCARCITY
*PURPLE/1: UNPRICED DUE TO SCARCITY
STATED PRINT RUN 100 SER. #'d SETS

TEN21 B.Roode/J.Storm 8.00 20.00
TEN22 Eric & Garett Bischoff
TEN23 J.Hardy/K.Angle
TEN24 V.Sky/G.Kim 12.00 30.00
TEN25 K.Angle/AJ Styles
TEN26 Sting/J.Hardy
TEN28 ODB/E.Young 5.00 12.00
TEN210 B.Roode/E.Young 5.00 12.00
TEN211 A.Shelley/C.Sabin 5.00 12.00
TEN212 K.Angle/Samoa Joe 10.00 25.00
TEN213 Sting/B.Roode
TEN214 Sting/J.Jarrett
TEN215 B.Ray/Devon
TEN216 Jeff & Karen Jarrett
TEN217 Kazarian/T.Brooks 8.00 20.00
TEN218 K.Angle/Sting
TEN219 Hernandez/Anarquia 5.00 12.00
TEN220 Kazarian/C.Daniels 5.00 12.00

2012 TRISTAR TNA Impact TENacious Dual Memorabilia Silver

*GOLD/80: .5X TO 1.2X BASIC MEM
*BLUE/50: .6X TO 1.5X BASIC MEM
*RED/10: UNPRICED DUE TO SCARCITY
*PURPLE/1: UNPRICED DUE TO SCARCITY
STATED PRINT RUN 100 SER.#'d SETS

T10 Eric & Garett Bischoff 3.00 8.00
T11 Devon/B.Ray 3.00 8.00
T12 B.Roode/J.Storm 3.00 8.00
T13 J.Hardy/Mr.Anderson 6.00 15.00
T14 K.Angle/AJ Styles 3.00 8.00

2012 TRISTAR TNA Impact TENacious Quad Autographs Gold

*RED/10: UNPRICED DUE TO SCARCITY
*PURPLE/1: UNPRICED DUE TO SCARCITY

TEN41 Jarrett/Styles/Storm/Borash
TEN43 Storm/Roode/Sabin/Shelley 10.00 25.00

2012 TRISTAR TNA Impact TENacious Six Autographs Gold

*RED/10: UNPRICED DUE TO SCARCITY
*PURPLE/1: UNPRICED DUE TO SCARCITY
STATED ODDS

TEN61 Styles/Samoa Joe/Daniels
Aries/Sabin/Kash
TEN62 Young/Styles/Terry
Abyss/Williams/Devon
TEN63 Angle/Sting/Styles
Roode/RVD/Hardy
TEN64 Kim/Love/Tara
Rayne/James/Sky

2012 TRISTAR TNA Impact TENacious Triple Autographs Gold

*RED/10: UNPRICED DUE TO SCARCITY
*PURPLE/1: UNPRICED DUE TO SCARCITY
STATED ODDS

TEN31 Styles/Samoa Joe/Daniels
TEN32 Kurt & Karen Angle/Jarrett

2012 TRISTAR TNA Impact TENacious Triple Memorabilia Blue

T15 Jarrett/Storm/Styles 6.00 15.00
T17 Kim/Sky/James 10.00 25.00

2009 TRISTAR TNA Knockouts

COMPLETE SET W/SP (108) 20.00 50.00
COMPLETE SET W/O SP (90) 12.00 30.00
UNOPENED BOX (18 PACKS)
UNOPENED PACK (4 CARDS)
*SILVER: 4X TO 10X BASIC CARDS
*GOLD/10: UNPRICED DUE TO SCARCITY
*PURPLE/1: UNPRICED DUE TO SCARCITY
*P.P.BLACK/1: UNPRICED DUE TO SCARCITY
*P.P.CYAN/1: UNPRICED DUE TO SCARCITY
*P.P.MAGENTA/1: UNPRICED DUE TO SCARCITY
*P.P.YELLOW/1: UNPRICED DUE TO SCARCITY
INSTANT WIN CARD RANDOMLY INSERTED
90-107 ARE REVEALED PACKS EXCLUSIVE

1 Angelina Love .50 1.25
2 Awesome Kong .15 .40
3 Christy Hemme .60 1.50
4 The Governor .25 .60
5 Jacqueline .20 .50
6 Jenna Morasca .40 1.00
7 Lauren .25 .60
8 Madison Rayne KO RC .40 1.00
9 ODB .15 .40
10 Raisha Saeed .15 .40
11 Rhaka Khan .20 .50
12 Roxxi .20 .50
13 Sharmell .15 .40
14 SoCal Val .40 1.00
15 Sojournor Bolt KO RC .15 .40
16 Taylor Wilde .40 1.00
17 Traci Brooks .40 1.00
18 Velvet Sky .50 1.25
19 Cute Kip .12 .30
20 The Beautiful People .50 1.25
21 Angelina Love .50 1.25
22 Christy Hemme .60 1.50
23 Lauren .25 .60
24 ODB .15 .40
25 Roxxi .20 .50
26 Sharmell .15 .40
27 SoCal Val .40 1.00
28 Taylor Wilde .40 1.00
29 Traci Brooks .40 1.00
30 Velvet Sky .50 1.25
31 Angelina Love .50 1.25
32 Awesome Kong .15 .40
33 Dixie Carter .25 .60
34 Jacqueline .20 .50
35 Lauren .25 .60
36 ODB .15 .40
37 Raisha Saeed .15 .40
38 Traci Brooks .40 1.00
39 Christy Hemme .60 1.50
40 Rhaka Khan .20 .50
41 Roxxi .20 .50
42 Sharmell .15 .40
43 SoCal Val .40 1.00
44 Sojournor Bolt TT .15 .40
45 Taylor Wilde .40 1.00
46 Velvet Sky .50 1.25
47 Jacqueline .20 .50
48 Sojournor Bolt FF .15 .40
49 ODB .15 .40
50 Traci Brooks .40 1.00
51 Angelina Love .50 1.25
52 Awesome Kong .15 .40
53 Christy Hemme .60 1.50
54 Jacqueline .20 .50
55 Lauren .25 .60
56 ODB .15 .40
57 Sharmell .15 .40
58 SoCal Val .40 1.00
59 Sojournor Bolt OUT .15 .40
60 Taylor Wilde .40 1.00
61 Traci Brooks .40 1.00
62 Velvet Sky .50 1.25
63 Angelina Love .50 1.25
64 Awesome Kong .15 .40
65 Christy Hemme .60 1.50
66 Dixie Carter .25 .60
67 Roxxi .20 .50
68 Sharmell .15 .40
69 ODB .15 .40
70 Taylor Wilde .40 1.00
71 Traci Brooks .40 1.00
72 Velvet Sky .50 1.25
73 Angelina Love / AJ Styles .50 1.25
74 Awesome Kong / Samoa Joe .15 .40

75 Christy Hemme / Robert Roode .60 1.50
76 Dixie Carter / Mick Foley .50 1.25
77 Jacqueline / James Storm .20 .50
78 Jenna Morasca / Brother Ray .40 1.00
79 Lauren / Chris Sabin .25 .60
80 ODB / Rhino .15 .40
81 Raisha Saeed / Alex Shelley .15 .40
82 Rhaka Khan / Kurt Angle .60 1.50
83 Roxxi / Jim Cornette .20 .50
84 Sharmell / Mike Tenay .15 .40
85 SoCal Val / Consequences Creed .40 1.00
86 Sojournor Bolt/Don West MC .15 .40
87 Taylor Wilde / Jay Lethal .40 1.00
88 Traci Brooks / Sting .50 1.25
89 Velvet Sky / Brother Devon .50 1.25
90 Traci Brooks 1.25 3.00
91 Angelina Love 1.50 4.00
92 SoCal Val 1.25 3.00
93 Christy Hemme 2.00 5.00
94 Velvet Sky 1.50 4.00
95 Lauren .75 2.00
96 ODB .50 1.25
97 Traci Brooks 1.25 3.00
98 SoCal Val 1.25 3.00
99 Christy Hemme 2.00 5.00
100 Angelina Love 1.50 4.00
101 Roxxi .60 1.50
102 Jenna Morasca 1.25 3.00
103 Velvet Sky 1.50 4.00
104 SoCal Val 1.25 3.00
105 Christy Hemme 2.00 5.00
106 Angelina Love/Velvet Sky 1.50 4.00
107 Traci Brooks/SoCal Val 1.25 3.00
CL Checklist .20 .50
NNO Instant Winner

2009 TRISTAR TNA Knockouts Autographed Dual Kiss Gold

*TURQUOISE/10: UNPRICED DUE TO SCARCITY
*PURPLE/1: UNPRICED DUE TO SCARCITY
STATED PRINT RUN 25 SER.#'d SETS

2K1 A.Love/V.Sky
2K2 C.Hemme/T.Brooks
2K3 Jenna/Sharmell
2K4 S.Val/Lauren

2009 TRISTAR TNA Knockouts Autographed Kiss

STATED PRINT RUN 10 SER.#'d SETS

K1 Angelina Love
K2 Awesome Kong
K3 Jacqueline
K4 Jenna
K5 Lauren
K6 Madison Rayne
K7 ODB
K8 Roxxi
K9 Sharmell
K10 Sojournor Bolt
K11 Taylor Wilde
K12 Velvet Sky
K13 Christy Hemme
K14 SoCal Val
K15 Traci Brooks

2009 TRISTAR TNA Knockouts Knockout Kiss

*TURQUOISE/25: .5X TO 1.25X BASIC KISS
*GREEN/5: UNPRICED DUE TO SCARCITY
*PURPLE/1: UNPRICED DUE TO SCARCITY
*P.P.BLACK/1: UNPRICED DUE TO SCARCITY
*P.P.CYAN/1: UNPRICED DUE TO SCARCITY
*P.P.MAGENTA/1: UNPRICED DUE TO SCARCITY
*P.P.YELLOW/1: UNPRICED DUE TO SCARCITY
STATED PRINT RUN 75 SER.#'d SETS
K12-K15 ARE REVEALED PACKS EXCLUSIVE

K1 Angelina Love 30.00 60.00
K2 Awesome Kong 12.00 30.00
K3 Jacqueline 8.00 20.00
K4 Jenna 25.00 50.00
K5 Lauren 15.00 40.00
K6 Madison Rayne 25.00 50.00
K7 ODB 12.00 30.00
K8 Roxxi 10.00 25.00
K9 Sharmell 10.00 25.00
K10 Sojournor Bolt 8.00 20.00
K11 Taylor Wilde 25.00 50.00
K12 Velvet Sky 30.00 60.00
K13 Christy Hemme 25.00 50.00
K14 SoCal Val 15.00 40.00
K15 Traci Brooks 12.00 30.00

2009 TRISTAR TNA Knockouts Signature Curves

*GOLD/75: .5X TO 1.2X BASIC AUTOS
*TURQUOISE/25: UNPRICED DUE TO SCARCITY
*PINK/10: UNPRICED DUE TO SCARCITY
*GREEN/5: UNPRICED DUE TO SCARCITY
*PURPLE/1: UNPRICED DUE TO SCARCITY
*P.P.BLACK/1: UNPRICED DUE TO SCARCITY
*P.P.CYAN/1: UNPRICED DUE TO SCARCITY
*P.P.MAGENTA/1: UNPRICED DUE TO SCARCITY
*P.P.YELLOW/1: UNPRICED DUE TO SCARCITY
STATED ODDS 1:9

KA1 Angelina Love 10.00 25.00
KA2 Awesome Kong 6.00 15.00
KA3 Christy Hemme 10.00 25.00
KA4 Dixie Carter 6.00 15.00
KA5 Jacqueline 6.00 15.00
KA6 Jenna 8.00 20.00
KA7 Madison Rayne 10.00 25.00
KA8 Raisha Saeed 6.00 15.00
KA9 Roxxi 6.00 15.00
KA10 Sharmell 6.00 15.00
KA11 SoCal Val 8.00 20.00
KA12 Sojournor Bolt 8.00 20.00
KA13 Taylor Wilde 8.00 20.00
KA14 Traci Brooks 8.00 20.00
KA15 Velvet Sky 10.00 25.00
KA24 Lauren 10.00 25.00
KA25 ODB 8.00 20.00

2009 TRISTAR TNA Knockouts Six-Person Signature Curves Gold

*TURQUOISE/25: X TO X BASIC AUTOS
*GREEN/5: UNPRICED DUE TO SCARCITY
*PURPLE/1: UNPRICED DUE TO SCARCITY
*P.P.BLACK/1: UNPRICED DUE TO SCARCITY
*P.P.CYAN/1: UNPRICED DUE TO SCARCITY
*P.P.MAGENTA/1: UNPRICED DUE TO SCARCITY
*P.P.YELLOW/1: UNPRICED DUE TO SCARCITY
STATED ODDS

KA27 Sharmell/Booker T/Nash
Angle/Sting/Steiner

2009 TRISTAR TNA Knockouts Top Drawer Memorabilia Gold

*TURQUOISE/75: .5X TO 1.2X BASIC MEM
*PINK/10: UNPRICED DUE TO SCARCITY
*PURPLE/1: UNPRICED DUE TO SCARCITY
STATED PRINT RUN 175 SER.#'d SETS

TD1 Angelina Love 10.00 25.00
TD2 Christy Hemme 10.00 25.00
TD3 Jenna Morasca 6.00 15.00
TD4 Lauren 10.00 25.00
TD5 Madison Rayne 10.00 25.00
TD6 Roxxi 6.00 15.00
TD7 SoCal Val 8.00 20.00
TD8 Sojournor Bolt 6.00 15.00
TD9 Taylor Wilde 10.00 25.00
TD10 Traci Brooks 6.00 15.00
TD11 Velvet Sky 10.00 25.00

2010 TRISTAR TNA New Era

COMPLETE SET (101) 30.00 75.00
UNOPENED BOX (20 PACKS)
UNOPENED PACK (6 CARDS)
COMPLETE SET W/O SP (90) 10.00 25.00
*SILVER: 2.5X TO 6X BASIC CARDS
*GOLD/10: UNPRICED DUE TO SCARCITY
*PURPLE/1: UNPRICED DUE TO SCARCITY
OBAK STATED ODDS 2:HOBBY BOX
OBAK ANNOUNCED PRINT RUN 600

1 Hulk Hogan 1.00 2.50
2 Hulk Hogan 1.00 2.50
3 Hulk Hogan 1.00 2.50
4 Hulk Hogan 1.00 2.50
5 Hulk Hogan 1.00 2.50
6 Hulk Hogan 1.00 2.50
7 Hulk Hogan 1.00 2.50
8 Ric Flair .75 2.00
9 Jeff Hardy .60 1.50
10 Scott Hall .15 .40
11 Syxx-Pac .25 .60
12 Eric Bischoff .15 .40
13 Shannon Moore .15 .40
14 Orlando Jordan .15 .40
15 Bubba the Love Sponge RC .25 .60
16 Mr. Anderson .25 .60
17 The Nasty Boys .15 .40
18 Generation Me .15 .40
19 The Pope D'Angelo Dinero .15 .40
20 Desmond Wolfe RC .15 .40
21 Brian Kendrick .25 .60
22 Jimmy Hart .25 .60
23 Sting .60 1.50
24 Kurt Angle .60 1.50
25 Mick Foley .75 2.00
26 Kevin Nash .60 1.50
27 Jeff Jarrett .40 1.00
28 James Storm .25 .60
29 Alex Shelley .25 .60
30 AJ Styles .40 1.00
31 Team 3D .25 .60
32 British Invasion .15 .40
33 Taz & Mike Tenay .15 .40
34 Motor City Machineguns .25 .60
35 Matt Morgan .15 .40
36 Amazing Red .15 .40
37 Robert Roode .15 .40
38 Suicide .15 .40
39 Abyss .25 .60
40 Lethal Consequences .15 .40
41 Eric Young .15 .40
42 Beer Money, Inc. .25 .60
43 Samoa Joe .25 .60
44 Daniels .15 .40
45 Taylor Wilde .40 1.00
46 Homicide .20 .50
47 Daffney .60 1.50
48 Hernandez .15 .40
49 The Beautiful People .75 2.00
50 Rob Terry .15 .40
51 Lacey Von Erich RC .75 2.00
52 Tara .60 1.50
53 Hamada .40 1.00
54 Sarita .40 1.00
55 ODB .25 .60
56 Jesse Neal .15 .40
57 Velvet Sky .75 2.00
58 Magnus .15 .40
59 Angelina Love .60 1.50
60 Doug Williams .15 .40
61 Madison Rayne .60 1.50
62 Rhino .25 .60
63 Kazarian .15 .40
64 Chris Sabin .15 .40
65 Dr. Stevie .15 .40
66 Christy Hemme .60 1.50
67 Jeremy Borash .15 .40
68 Dixie Carter .40 1.00
69 Bob Carter RC .15 .40
70 Rob Van Dam .40 1.00
71 Destination X .15 .40
72 Lockdown .15 .40
73 Hulk Hogan/Eric Bischoff .75 2.00
74 Ric Flair/AJ Styles .60 1.50
75 Scott Hall/Syxx-Pac .20 .50
76 Hulk Hogan/Abyss .75 2.00
77 Matt Morgan/Hernandez .15 .40
78 Ric Flair .60 1.50
79 Ric Flair .60 1.50
80 Ric Flair .60 1.50
81 TNA iMPACT! Moves .75 2.00
82 Hogan's Wrestling Return .75 2.00
83 H.Hogan/R.Flair .75 2.00
84 The Main Event .75 2.00
85 Why, Sting, Why? .50 1.25
86 Van Dam Arrives in TNA .30 .75
87 The Band: Off Key .20 .50
88 Kurt Angle .50 1.25
89 Jeff Hardy Returns .50 1.25
90 What A Night! .75 2.00
91 Hulk Hogan OBAK SP 4.00 10.00
92 Ric Flair OBAK SP 3.00 8.00
93 Sting OBAK SP 2.50 6.00
94 Kevin Nash OBAK SP 2.50 6.00
95 Jeff Jarrett OBAK SP 1.50 4.00
96 Kurt Angle OBAK SP 2.50 6.00
97 Mick Foley OBAK SP 3.00 8.00
98 AJ Styles OBAK SP 1.50 4.00
99 Beautiful People OBAK SP 3.00 8.00
100 Hogan/Flair OBAK SP 4.00 10.00
CL Checklist .15 .40

2010 TRISTAR TNA New Era Autographed Hulk Hogan Bonus Red

*PURPLE/1: UNPRICED DUE TO SCARCITY
STATED PRINT RUN 9 SER.#'d SETS
UNPRICED DUE TO SCARCITY

H1 Hulk Hogan holding rope
H2 Hulk Hogan black shirt in ring
H3 Hulk Hogan ripping shirt
H4 Hulk Hogan no shirt white bkgrnd
H5 Hulk Hogan w/boa
H6 Hulk Hogan black shirt white bkgrnd

2010 TRISTAR TNA New Era Autographed Memorabilia Silver

STATED PRINT RUN 199 SER.#'d SETS

M13 Hulk Hogan
M14 Ric Flair
M15 Mick Foley
M16 Sting
M17 AJ Styles
M18 Velvet Sky 15.00 40.00

2010 TRISTAR TNA New Era Autographs Silver

*GOLD/50: .5X TO 1.2X BASIC AUTOS
*GREEN/15-25: X TO X BASIC AUTOS
*RED/5: UNPRICED DUE TO SCARCITY
*PURPLE/1: UNPRICED DUE TO SCARCITY

A1 Hulk Hogan
A2 Sting
A3 Mick Foley 10.00 25.00
A4 Kurt Angle 8.00 20.00
A5 Sean Morley 6.00 15.00
A6 Mr. Anderson 8.00 20.00
A7 Orlando Jordan 8.00 20.00
A8 D'Angelo Dinero 8.00 20.00
A9 Tara 6.00 15.00
A10 Desmond Wolfe 4.00 10.00
A11 Taz 4.00 10.00
A12 Kevin Nash 8.00 20.00
A13 Brian Kendrick 6.00 15.00
A14 AJ Styles 8.00 20.00
A15 Jeff Jarrett 5.00 12.00
A16 Sarita 6.00 15.00
A17 Amazing Red 4.00 10.00
A18 Lacey Von Erich 12.00 30.00
A19 Abyss 4.00 10.00
A20 Rob Van Dam 12.00 30.00
A21 Hernandez 4.00 10.00
A22 Taylor Wilde 6.00 15.00
A23 Samoa Joe 8.00 20.00
A24 Awesome Kong 5.00 12.00
A25 Dr. Stevie 5.00 12.00
A26 Brutus Magnus 4.00 10.00
A27 Velvet Sky 10.00 25.00
A28 Jeremy Borash 4.00 10.00
A29 Madison Rayne 8.00 20.00
A30 Doug Williams 4.00 10.00
A31 Christy Hemme 10.00 25.00
A32 Suicide 4.00 10.00
A33 Hamada 8.00 20.00
A34 Robert Roode 4.00 10.00
A35 Brian Knobs 4.00 10.00
A36 Dixie Carter 5.00 12.00
A37 Daniels 4.00 10.00
A38 Bubba the Love Sponge 10.00 25.00
A39 ODB 5.00 12.00
A40 Homicide 4.00 10.00
A41 Matt Morgan 4.00 10.00
A42 Daffney 10.00 25.00
A43 Jesse Neal 4.00 10.00

A44 James Storm 4.00 10.00
A45 SoCal Val 6.00 15.00
A46 Jeff Hardy 20.00 40.00
A47 Traci Brooks 6.00 15.00
A48 Jerry Sags 4.00 10.00
A49 Angelina Love 8.00 20.00
A50 Alex Shelley 4.00 10.00
A51 Syxx-Pac 6.00 15.00
A52 Shannon Moore 6.00 15.00
A53 Jay Lethal 4.00 10.00
A54 Rob Terry 4.00 10.00
A55 Ric Flair

2010 TRISTAR TNA New Era Dual Autographs Silver

*GOLD/50: X TO X BASIC AUTOS
*GREEN/25: X TO X BASIC AUTOS
*RED/5: UNPRICED DUE TO SCARCITY
*PURPLE/1: UNPRICED DUE TO SCARCITY
RANDOMLY INSERTED INTO RETAIL PACKS

1 H.Hogan/Sting
2 M.Foley/Abyss
3 H.Hogan/D.Carter
4 K.Angle/J.Jarrett
5 K.Nash/E.Young
6 H.Hogan/M.Foley
7 K.Angle/Mr.Anderson
8 Taz/M.Tenay
9 H.Hogan/K.Nash
10 A.Love/Lacey Von Erich
11 D.Dinero/O.Jordan
12 B.Knobs/J.Sags
13 A.Kong/Hamada
14 K.Angle/D.Wolfe
15 M.Morgan/Hernandez
16 V.Sky/M.Rayne
17 H.Hogan/K.Angle
18 A.Shelley/C.Sabin
19 J.Storm/R.Roode
20 R.Flair/AJ Styles
21 Sting/R.Flair
22 H.Hogan/R.Flair

2010 TRISTAR TNA New Era Dual Autographs Gold

STATED PRINT RUN 50 SER.#'d SETS

1 H.Hogan/Sting
2 M.Foley/Abyss
3 H.Hogan/D.Carter
4 K.Angle/J.Jarrett
5 K.Nash/E.Young
6 H.Hogan/M.Foley
7 K.Angle/Mr.Anderson
8 Taz/M.Tenay
9 H.Hogan/K.Nash
10 Angelina Love/L.Von Erich
11 D.Dinero/O.Jordan
12 B.Knobs/J.Sags
13 A.Kong/Hamada
14 K.Angle/D.Wolfe
15 M.Morgan/Hernandez
16 V.Sky/M.Rayne
17 H.Hogan/K.Angle
18 A.Shelley/C.Sabin
19 J.Storm/R.Roode
20 R.Flair/AJ Styles
21 Sting/R.Flair
22 H.Hogan/R.Flair

2010 TRISTAR TNA New Era Dual Autographs Green

*GREEN: X TO X BASIC AUTOS
STATED PRINT RUN 25 SER.#'d SETS

1 H.Hogan/Sting
2 M.Foley/Abyss 20.00 40.00
3 H.Hogan/D.Carter
4 K.Angle/J.Jarrett 25.00 50.00
5 K.Nash/E.Young 15.00 30.00
6 H.Hogan/M.Foley
7 K.Angle/Mr.Anderson 20.00 40.00
8 Taz/M.Tenay 10.00 20.00
9 H.Hogan/K.Nash
10 Angelina Love/L.Von Erich 20.00 40.00
11 D.Dinero/O.Jordan 20.00 40.00
12 B.Knobs/J.Sags 15.00 30.00
13 A.Kong/Hamada 15.00 30.00
14 K.Angle/D.Wolfe 20.00 40.00
15 M.Morgan/Hernandez 15.00 30.00
16 V.Sky/M.Rayne 20.00 40.00
17 H.Hogan/K.Angle
18 A.Shelley/C.Sabin 10.00 20.00
19 J.Storm/R.Roode 15.00 30.00
20 R.Flair/AJ Styles
21 Sting/R.Flair
22 H.Hogan/R.Flair

2010 TRISTAR TNA New Era Dual Memorabilia Silver

STATED ODDS

M10 J.Storm/R.Roode 4.00 10.00

2010 TRISTAR TNA New Era Memorabilia Silver

*GOLD/50: .5X TO 1.2X BASIC MEM
*RED/25: .6X TO 1.5X BASIC MEM
*PURPLE/1: UNPRICED DUE TO SCARCITY
OVERALL MEM ODDS ONE PER HOBBY BOX
STATED PRINT RUN 99-199

M1 Hulk Hogan
M2 Ric Flair
M3 Mick Foley 5.00 12.00
M4 Sting 6.00 15.00
M5 Kurt Angle 5.00 12.00
M6 Rob Van Dam 4.00 10.00
M7 Mr. Anderson 4.00 10.00
M8 Syxx-Pac 4.00 10.00

2010 TRISTAR TNA New Era Quad Autographs Silver

*GOLD/50: X TO X BASIC AUTOS
*GREEN/25: X TO X BASIC AUTOS
*RED/5: UNPRICED DUE TO SCARCITY
*PURPLE/1: UNPRICED DUE TO SCARCITY
RANDOMLY INSERTED INTO RETAIL PACKS

1 Hogan/Jarrett/Angle/Foley
2 Sky/Rayne/Von Erich/Love
3 Hogan/Flair/Sting/Nash
4 Wilde/Sarita/Hamada/A.Kong
5 Hogan/Abyss/Flair/Styles

2010 TRISTAR TNA New Era Triple Autographs Silver

*GOLD/50: X TO X BASIC AUTOS
*GREEN/25: X TO X BASIC AUTOS
*RED/5: UNPRICED DUE TO SCARCITY
*PURPLE/1: UNPRICED DUE TO SCARCITY
RANDOMLY INSERTED INTO RETAIL PACKS

1 Hogan/Nash/6-Pac
2 Sky/Rayne/Von Erich
3 Terry/Magnus/Williams
4 Tara/Hemme/Brooks

2010 TRISTAR TNA New Era Triple Autographs Green

*GREEN: X TO X BASIC AUTOS
STATED PRINT RUN 25 SER.#'d SETS

1 Hogan/Nash/6-Pac
2 Sky/Rayne/Von Erich 30.00 60.00
3 Terry/Magnus/Williams 15.00 30.00
4 Tara/Hemme/Brooks 20.00 40.00

2010 TRISTAR TNA New Era Triple Autographs Red

STATED PRINT RUN 5 SER.#'d SETS
UNPRICED DUE TO SCARCITY

1 Hogan/Nash/6-Pac
2 Sky/Rayne/Von Erich
3 Terry/Magnus/Williams
4 Tara/Hemme/Brooks

2010 TRISTAR TNA Obak National Convention

COMPLETE SET (3) 4.00 10.00
TNA1 Rob Van Dam 2.00 5.00
TNA2 Mick Foley 2.50 6.00
TNA3 Kurt Angle 2.00 5.00

2011 TRISTAR TNA Signature Impact

COMPLETE SET (100) 20.00 40.00
COMPLETE SET W/O SP (90) 10.00 25.00
UNOPENED BOX (20 PACKS)
UNOPENED PACK (6 CARDS)
*SILVER/50: 2.5X TO 6X BASIC CARDS
*SILVER SP/50: .75X TO 2X BASIC CARDS
*GOLD/5: UNPRICED DUE TO SCARCITY
*PURPLE/1: UNPRICED DUE TO SCARCITY

1 Hulk Hogan 1.00 2.50
2 Ric Flair .75 2.00
3 Sting .60 1.50
4 Jeff Jarrett .25 .60
5 Scott Steiner .25 .60
6 Jeff Hardy .60 1.50
7 Matt Hardy .40 1.00
8 Velvet Sky .75 2.00
9 Abyss .25 .60
10 Kurt Angle .25 .60
11 Sting .60 1.50
12 Ric Flair .75 2.00
13 Matt Hardy/Jeff Hardy .60 1.50
14 AJ Styles .25 .60
15 Velvet Sky .75 2.00
16 Scott Steiner .25 .60
17 Mr. Anderson .25 .60
18 Anarquia RC .15 .40
19 Devon .15 .40
20 Dixie Carter .40 1.00
21 Crimson .15 .40
22 Angelina Love .60 1.50
23 Eric Bischoff .15 .40
24 AJ Styles .25 .60
25 Daniels .15 .40
26 Gunner RC .15 .40
27 Murphy RC .15 .40
28 Tara .60 1.50
29 Ric Flair .75 2.00
30 Hulk Hogan 1.00 2.50
31 Mickie James 1.00 2.50
32 Sting .60 1.50
33 Abyss .25 .60
34 Mr. Anderson .25 .60
35 James Storm .15 .40
36 Karen Jarrett .25 .60
37 Bully Ray .15 .40
38 Douglas Williams .15 .40
39 Mickie James 1.00 2.50
40 Mr. Anderson .25 .60
41 Alex Shelley .15 .40
42 Chris Sabin .15 .40
43 Matt Morgan .15 .40
44 Rob Van Dam .25 .60
45 Hulk Hogan 1.00 2.50
46 Samoa Joe .15 .40
47 Taz .15 .40
48 RVD .25 .60
49 Madison Rayne .40 1.00
50 Orlando Jordan .15 .40
51 Mike Tenay .15 .40
52 Taz .15 .40
53 Jeremy Borash .15 .40
54 Christy Hemme .60 1.50
55 Eric Young .15 .40
56 Ms. Tessmacher .40 1.00
57 Rob Terry .15 .40
58 Amazing Red .15 .40
59 Hernandez .15 .40
60 Magnus .15 .40
61 K.Angle/J.Jarrett .25 .60
62 Lockdown 2011 .15 .40
63 Karen Jarrett's TNA Return .25 .60
64 Karen on Angle & Jarrett .25 .60
65 The Jarrett/Angle Bunch .15 .40
66 Robbie E .15 .40
67 Robert Roode .15 .40
68 Shannon Moore .15 .40
69 Jesse Neal .15 .40
70 Cookie .15 .40
71 D'Angelo Dinero .15 .40
72 Rosita RC .25 .60
73 Generation Me .15 .40
74 Samoa Joe .15 .40
75 Mexican America .15 .40
76 Sarita .25 .60
77 Suicide .15 .40
78 Brian Kendrick .15 .40
79 Winter .60 1.50
80 Kazarian .15 .40
81 Immortal .15 .40
82 Fortune .15 .40
83 Bully Ray .15 .40
84 Christy Hemme .60 1.50
85 Kurt Angle .25 .60
86 Beer Money .15 .40
87 Eric Bischoff .15 .40
88 Scott Steiner .25 .60
89 Samoa Joe .15 .40
90 Hogan/Flair/Sting 3.00 8.00
91 Hulk Hogan SP 3.00 8.00
92 Hulk Hogan SP 3.00 8.00
93 Hulk Hogan SP 3.00 8.00
94 Ric Flair SP 3.00 8.00
95 Ric Flair SP 3.00 8.00
96 Ric Flair SP 3.00 8.00
97 Sting SP 3.00 8.00
98 Sting SP 3.00 8.00
99 Sting SP 3.00 8.00
CL Checklist .15 .40

2011 TRISTAR TNA Signature Impact Autographs Silver

*GOLD/25: .6X TO 1.25X BASIC AUTOS
*RED/5: UNPRICED DUE TO SCARCITY
*PURPLE/1: UNPRICED DUE TO SCARCITY
STATED PRINT RUN 99 SER.#'d SETS

S8 Jeff Hardy 25.00 50.00
S9 Matt Hardy 15.00 30.00
S10 Rob Van Dam 15.00 30.00
S11 Mickie James 30.00 60.00
S12 Scott Steiner
S13 Anarquia 15.00 30.00
S14 Jeff Jarrett 12.00 25.00
S15 Kazarian 6.00 15.00
S16 Winter 12.00 25.00
S17 Kurt Angle 20.00 40.00
S18 Karen Jarrett 6.00 15.00
S19 Abyss 6.00 15.00
S20 Matt Morgan 6.00 15.00
S21 Kendrick 6.00 15.00
S22 Mr. Anderson 10.00 20.00
S23 Velvet Sky 20.00 40.00
S24 Robert Roode 10.00 20.00
S25 Ms. Tessmacher 12.00 25.00
S26 Sarita 6.00 15.00
S27 Jesse Neal 6.00 15.00
S28 Amazing Red 6.00 15.00
S29 D'Angelo Dinero 6.00 15.00
S30 Magnus 6.00 15.00
S31 Angelina Love 10.00 20.00
S32 Orlando Jordan 6.00 15.00
S33 Mick Foley 10.00 20.00
S34 Crimson 6.00 15.00
S35 Daniels 6.00 15.00
S36 Madison Rayne 10.00 20.00
S37 Murphy
S38 Tara 10.00 20.00
S39 James Storm 6.00 15.00
S40 Jeremy Buck 6.00 15.00
S41 Rosita 12.00 25.00
S42 Rob Terry 6.00 15.00
S43 SoCal Val 10.00 20.00
S44 Jay Lethal 6.00 15.00
S45 Mike Tenay 6.00 15.00
S46 Jeremy Borash 6.00 15.00
S47 Samoa Joe 6.00 15.00
S48 Eric Young 6.00 15.00
S49 AJ Styles 10.00 20.00
S50 Christy Hemme 10.00 20.00
S51 Shannon Moore 6.00 15.00
S52 Max Buck 6.00 15.00
S53 Chyna 10.00 25.00
S54 Eric Bischoff

2011 TRISTAR TNA Signature Impact Dual Autographs Silver

*GOLD/25: .6X TO 1.25X BASIC AUTOS
*RED/5: UNPRICED DUE TO SCARCITY
*PURPLE/1: UNPRICED DUE TO SCARCITY
STATED PRINT RUN 99 SER.#'d SETS

1 H.Hogan/R.Flair
2 Jeff & Matt Hardy
3 Jeff & Karen Jarrett
4 Sting/RVD
5 H.Hogan/Sting
6 M.Hardy/RVD
7 H.Hogan/M.Hardy
8 Sarita/Rosita 10.00 20.00
9 Hernandez/Anarquia
10 AJ Styles/Daniels 10.00 20.00
11 RVD/H.Hogan
12 M.James/Tara 20.00 40.00
13 Tara/M.Rayne 10.00 20.00
14 Gunner/Murphy 6.00 15.00
15 Magnus/D.Williams 6.00 15.00
16 Max & Jeremy Buck 6.00 15.00
17 S.Steiner/H.Hogan
18 Crimson/Abyss 6.00 15.00
19 K.Angle/J.Jarrett
20 S.Moore/J.Neal
21 M.Foley/RVD
22 C.Hemme/S.Val 10.00 20.00
23 Hernandez/M.Morgan 6.00 15.00
24 Robbie E/Cookie 6.00 15.00
25 Winter/A.Love 10.00 20.00
26 A.Love/V.Sky 15.00 30.00
27 Chyna/K.Angle

2011 TRISTAR TNA Signature Impact Dual Memorabilia Silver

STATED PRINT RUN 199 SER.#'d SETS

M11 Jeff & Matt Hardy

2011 TRISTAR TNA Signature Impact Eight Autographs Silver

*GOLD/25: UNPRICED DUE TO SCARCITY
*RED/5: UNPRICED DUE TO SCARCITY
*PURPLE/1: UNPRICED DUE TO SCARCITY
STATED PRINT RUN 99 SER.#'d SETS

1 Hogan/Flair/Sting/Steiner
Angle/J.Hardy/RVD/M.Hardy
2 Hogan/Tara/Flair/James
Sting/Sky/J.Hardy/Love
3 James/Tara/Love/Sky
Rayne/Winter/Rosita/Sarita

2011 TRISTAR TNA Signature Impact Five Autographs Silver

*GOLD/25: X TO X BASIC AUTOS
*RED/5: UNPRICED DUE TO SCARCITY
*PURPLE/1: UNPRICED DUE TO SCARCITY
STATED PRINT RUN 99 SER.#'d SETS

1 Hogan/Steiner/Sting/Jarrett/Flair
2 Love/Sky/Tara/James/Rayne 30.00 60.00
3 Jeff & Matt Hardy/RVD/Foley/Angle

2011 TRISTAR TNA Signature Impact Memorabilia Silver

*GOLD/50: .6X TO 1.25X BASIC MEM
*BLUE/25: .75X TO 1.5X BASIC MEM
*RED/5: UNPRICED DUE TO SCARCITY
*PURPLE/1: UNPRICED DUE TO SCARCITY
STATED PRINT RUN 199 SER.#'d SETS

M6 Hulk Hogan
M7 Sting 12.00 25.00
M8 Chyna 12.00 25.00
M9 Jeff Hardy
M10 Rob Van Dam 10.00 20.00

2011 TRISTAR TNA Signature Impact Quad Autographs Silver

*GOLD/25: .6X TO 1.25X BASIC AUTOS
*RED/5: UNPRICED DUE TO SCARCITY
*PURPLE/1: UNPRICED DUE TO SCARCITY
STATED PRINT RUN 99 SER.#'d SETS

1 Flair/Hardy/Abyss/Styles
2 Hogan/Flair/The Hardys
3 Hernandez/Anarquia/Sarita/Rosita 15.00 30.00
4 Angle/Chyna/Karen & Jeff Jarrett

2011 TRISTAR TNA Signature Impact Quad Memorabilia Silver

M14 Sky/Love/Winter/James 15.00 40.00
M15 Hernandez/Anarquia 8.00 20.00
Sarita/Rosita

2011 TRISTAR TNA Signature Impact Ric Flair Die-Cut Letter Memorabilia Silver

COMPLETE SET (5)

M1 Ric Flair F
M2 Ric Flair L
M3 Ric Flair A
M4 Ric Flair I
M5 Ric Flair R

2011 TRISTAR TNA Signature Impact Seven Autographs Silver

*GOLD/25: UNPRICED DUE TO SCARCITY
*RED/5: UNPRICED DUE TO SCARCITY
*PURPLE/1: UNPRICED DUE TO SCARCITY
STATED PRINT RUN 99 SER.#'d SETS
UNPRICED DUE TO SCARCITY

1 Sting/RVD/Anderson/Hogan
Flair/Jeff & Matt Hardy
2 Hogan/James/Flair
Love/RVD/Sky/J.Hardy

2011 TRISTAR TNA Signature Impact Six Autographs Silver

*GOLD/25: UNPRICED DUE TO SCARCITY
*RED/5: UNPRICED DUE TO SCARCITY
*PURPLE/1: UNPRICED DUE TO SCARCITY
STATED PRINT RUN 99 SER.#'d SETS
UNPRICED DUE TO SCARCITY

1 Hogan/Flair/Sting
Angle/Jarrett/Steiner
2 Tara/James/Sky
Love/Rayne/Hemme

2011 TRISTAR TNA Signature Impact Triple Autographs Silver

*GOLD/25: UNPRICED DUE TO SCARCITY
*RED/5: UNPRICED DUE TO SCARCITY
*PURPLE/1: UNPRICED DUE TO SCARCITY
STATED PRINT RUN 99 SER.#'d SETS
UNPRICED DUE TO SCARCITY

1 Jeff & Karen Jarrett/Angle
2 Sky/Winter/Love
3 Sting/RVD/Anderson
4 Hogan/Flair/Sting
5 Jeff & Matt Hardy/RVD

2011 TRISTAR TNA Signature Impact Triple Memorabilia Silver

M12 Hogan/Flair/Sting
M13 Jeff & Karen Jarrett/Angle 8.00 20.00

2010 TRISTAR TNA Xtreme

COMPLETE SET W/SP (111) 60.00 120.00
COMPLETE SET W/O SP (101) 10.00 25.00
UNOPENED BOX (20 PACKS)
UNOPENED PACK (6 CARDS)
*SILVER/40: 3X TO 8X BASIC CARDS
*GOLD/10: UNPRICED DUE TO SCARCITY
*PURPLE/1: UNPRICED DUE TO SCARCITY
SP STATED ODDS 1:BOX

1 Hulk Hogan 1.00 2.50
2 Eric Bischoff .15 .40
3 Jeff Jarrett .40 1.00
4 Samoa Joe .25 .60
5 Robbie E RC .15 .40
6 Sting .60 1.50
7 Ric Flair .75 2.00
8 AJ Styles .40 1.00
9 Matt Morgan .15 .40
10 Cowboy James Storm .25 .60
11 Robert Roode .15 .40
12 Kazarian .15 .40
13 Tommy Dreamer .15 .40
14 Mick Foley .75 2.00
15 Brother Devon .25 .60
16 Stevie Richards .15 .40
17 Rhino .25 .60
18 Brian Kendrick .25 .60
19 Raven .25 .60
20 Taz .15 .40
21 Sabu .15 .40
22 Al Snow .40 1.00
23 Hardcore Justice .15 .40
24 RVD/Sabu .40 1.00
25 Raven/Tommy Dreamer .25 .60
26 So.Philly Street Fight .15 .40
27 Rhino/Al Snow/Brother Runt .40 1.00
28 Stevie Richards/PJ Polaco .15 .40
29 Too Cold Scorpio/CW Anderson .15 .40
30 The FBI/Kash/Diamond/Swinger .15 .40
31 Jason Hervey .15 .40
32 Rob Van Dam .40 1.00
33 Jeff Hardy .60 1.50
34 Kurt Angle .60 1.50
35 D'Angelo Dinero .15 .40
36 Brother Ray .25 .60
37 Mr. Anderson .25 .60
38 TNA Tag Team Champ .15 .40
39 Falls Count Anywhere .25 .60
40 Jarrett/Joe/Sting/Nash .60 1.50
41 Tommy Dreamer/AJ Styles .40 1.00
42 Jeff Hardy/Kurt Angle .60 1.50
43 London Brawling .15 .40
44 Generation Me .15 .40
45 Rob Terry .15 .40
46 Douglas Williams .15 .40
47 Motorcity Machine Guns .25 .60
48 Amazing Red .15 .40
49 Magnus .15 .40
50 Hernandez .15 .40
51 Jeremy Borash .15 .40
52 Orlando Jordan .15 .40
53 TNA Tag Team Champ .15 .40
54 Classic Knockouts .25 .60
55 RVD Overcomes the Odds .40 1.00
56 Lethal Lockdown .15 .40
57 Cookie RC .25 .60
58 Mickie James .75 2.00
59 Angelina Love .60 1.50
60 Velvet Sky .75 2.00
61 Lacey Von Erich RC .75 2.00
62 Madison Rayne .60 1.50
63 Taylor Wilde .40 1.00
64 Hamada .40 1.00
65 Daffney .60 1.50
66 Sarita .40 1.00
67 SoCal Val .60 1.50
68 Tara .60 1.50
69 Miss Tessmacher RC .75 2.00
70 Ink Inc. .15 .40
71 Abyss SS .25 .60
72 AJ Styles SS .40 1.00
73 Hulk Hogan SS 1.00 2.50
74 Kurt Angle SS .60 1.50
75 Jeff Jarrett SS .40 1.00
76 Jeff Hardy SS .60 1.50
77 Dixie Carter SS .40 1.00
78 Rob Van Dam SS .40 1.00
79 Lacey Von Erich SS .75 2.00
80 Jay Lethal SS .15 .40
81 Tommy Dreamer SS .15 .40
82 Mick Foley SS .75 2.00
83 Sting PC .60 1.50
84 Madison Rayne PC .60 1.50
85 D'Angelo Dinero PC .15 .40
86 Christy Hemme PC .60 1.50
87 Jeff Hardy PC .60 1.50
88 Angelina Love PC .60 1.50
89 Mickie James PC .75 2.00
90 Dixie Carter PC .40 1.00
91 Kurt Angle PC .60 1.50
92 Mike Tenay PC .15 .40
93 Mickie James .75 2.00
94 Rob Van Dam UX .40 1.00
95 Sting UX .60 1.50
96 Jeff Hardy UX .60 1.50
97 Abyss UX .25 .60
98 Tommy Dreamer UX .15 .40
99 AJ Styles UX .40 1.00
100 Hulk Hogan UX 1.00 2.50
101 Jeff Hardy Original Art SP 6.00 15.00
102 Jeff Hardy Original Art SP 6.00 15.00
103 Jeff Hardy Original Art SP 6.00 15.00
104 Jeff Hardy Original Art SP 6.00 15.00
105 Jeff Hardy Original Art SP 6.00 15.00
106 Jeff Hardy Original Art SP 6.00 15.00
107 Jeff Hardy Original Art SP 6.00 15.00
108 Jeff Hardy Original Art SP 6.00 15.00
109 Jeff Hardy Original Art SP 6.00 15.00
110 Jeff Hardy Original Art SP 6.00 15.00
CL Checklist .15 .40

2010 TRISTAR TNA Xtreme Autographed Memorabilia Gold

*GREEN/25: UNPRICED DUE TO SCARCITY
*RED/5: UNPRICED DUE TO SCARCITY
*PURPLE/1: UNPRICED DUE TO SCARCITY
STATED PRINT RUN 99 SER.#'d SETS
UNPRICED DUE TO SCARCITY

XA1 Hulk Hogan
XA2 Mickie James
XA3 Rob Van Dam
XA4 Jeff Hardy
XA5 Sting
XA6 AJ Styles

2010 TRISTAR TNA Xtreme Autographs Gold

COMMON AUTO 5.00 12.00
*GREEN/25: .6X TO 1.5X BASIC AUTOS
*RED/5: UNPRICED DUE TO SCARCITY
*PURPLE/1: UNPRICED DUE TO SCARCITY
STATED PRINT RUN 99 SER.#'d SETS

X1 Rob Van Dam
X2 Rhino 6.00 15.00
X3 Mick Foley
X4 Tommy Dreamer 6.00 15.00
X5 Sabu 6.00 15.00
X6 Raven
X7 Stevie Richards 6.00 15.00
X8 Al Snow 8.00 20.00
X9 Kid Kash 5.00 12.00
X10 New Jack 5.00 12.00
X11 P.J. Polaco 5.00 12.00
X12 Tracy Smothers 5.00 12.00
X13 Axl Rotten 5.00 12.00
X14 Too Cold Scorpio 5.00 12.00
X15 Bill Alfonso 5.00 12.00
X16 Tony Luke 5.00 12.00
X17 Blue Tillie 5.00 12.00
X18 Swinger 5.00 12.00
X19 Brother Runt 5.00 12.00
X20 Stephen DeAngelis 5.00 12.00
X21 Simon Diamond 5.00 12.00
X22 Nova 5.00 12.00
X23 Guido Maritato 5.00 12.00
X24 Big Sal 5.00 12.00
X25 Mustafa 5.00 12.00
X26 C.W. Anderson 5.00 12.00
X27 Joel Gertner
X28 John Rechner
X29 Taz 5.00 12.00
X30 Brian Kendrick 6.00 15.00
X31 Tara 8.00 20.00
X32 Jason Hervey 6.00 15.00
X33 Mickie James 15.00 30.00
X34 Jeremy Borash 5.00 12.00
X35 Samoa Joe 8.00 20.00
X36 Alex Shelley 5.00 12.00
X37 Shannon Moore 8.00 20.00
X38 Jay Lethal 5.00 12.00
X39 Jeff Hardy
X40 Chris Sabin 5.00 12.00
X41 Kazarian 5.00 12.00
X42 Mr. Anderson 6.00 15.00
X43 Sting
X44 Abyss 6.00 15.00
X45 AJ Styles 8.00 20.00
X46 Angelina Love 10.00 25.00

X47 Madison Rayne 10.00 25.00
X48 Velvet Sky 10.00 25.00
X49 Lacey Von Erich 10.00 25.00
X50 Christy Hemme 10.00 25.00
X51 Kevin Nash 10.00 25.00
X52 Kurt Angle 10.00 25.00
X53 Ric Flair
X54 Hulk Hogan
X55 Hulk Hogan
X56 Hulk Hogan

2010 TRISTAR TNA Xtreme Autographs Green

*GREEN: .6X TO 1.5X BASIC AUTOS
STATED PRINT RUN 25 SER.#'d SETS

X1 Rob Van Dam
X2 Rhino 10.00 25.00
X3 Mick Foley
X4 Tommy Dreamer 10.00 25.00
X5 Sabu 10.00 25.00
X6 Raven
X7 Stevie Richards 10.00 25.00
X8 Al Snow 12.00 30.00
X9 Kid Kash 8.00 20.00
X10 New Jack 8.00 20.00
X11 P.J. Polaco 8.00 20.00
X12 Tracy Smothers 8.00 20.00
X13 Axl Rotten 8.00 20.00
X14 Too Cold Scorpio 8.00 20.00
X15 Bill Alfonso 8.00 20.00
X16 Tony Luke 8.00 20.00
X17 Blue Tillie 8.00 20.00
X18 Swinger 8.00 20.00
X19 Brother Runt 8.00 20.00
X20 Stephen DeAngelis 8.00 20.00
X21 Simon Diamond 8.00 20.00
X22 Nova 8.00 20.00
X23 Guido Maritato 8.00 20.00
X24 Big Sal 8.00 20.00
X25 Mustafa 8.00 20.00
X26 C.W. Anderson 8.00 20.00
X27 Joel Gertner
X28 John Rechner
X29 Taz 8.00 20.00
X30 Brian Kendrick 10.00 25.00
X31 Tara 15.00 30.00
X32 Jason Hervey 10.00 25.00
X33 Mickie James 25.00 50.00
X34 Jeremy Borash 8.00 20.00
X35 Samoa Joe 12.00 30.00
X36 Alex Shelley 8.00 20.00
X37 Shannon Moore 12.00 30.00
X38 Jay Lethal 8.00 20.00
X39 Jeff Hardy
X40 Chris Sabin 8.00 20.00
X41 Kazarian 8.00 20.00
X42 Mr. Anderson 10.00 25.00
X43 Sting
X44 Abyss 10.00 25.00
X45 AJ Styles 12.00 30.00
X46 Angelina Love 20.00 40.00
X47 Madison Rayne 20.00 40.00
X48 Velvet Sky 20.00 40.00
X49 Lacey Von Erich 20.00 40.00
X50 Christy Hemme 20.00 40.00
X51 Kevin Nash 20.00 40.00
X52 Kurt Angle 20.00 40.00
X53 Ric Flair
X54 Hulk Hogan
X55 Hulk Hogan
X56 Hulk Hogan

2010 TRISTAR TNA Xtreme Dual Autographed Memorabilia Gold

STATED PRINT RUN 50 SER.#'d SETS

XA7 RVD/Sabu
XA8 A.Love/V.Sky 35.00 70.00
XA9 J.Hardy/RVD

2010 TRISTAR TNA Xtreme Dual Autographs Gold

1 R.Flair/M.Foley
2 Sting/K.Nash
3 RVD/Sabu
4 A.Love/V.Sky 12.00 30.00
5 A.Shelley/C.Sabin 8.00 20.00
6 Max & Jeremy Buck 8.00 20.00
7 J.Neal/S.Moore 12.00 25.00
8 Robbie E/Cookie 12.00 30.00
9 Tommy & Trisa Dreamer 12.00 30.00
10 N.Jack/Mustafa
11 J.Finegan/M.Kehner
12 Scorpio/C.Anderson
13 M.Tenay/Taz
14 Raven/T.Dreamer
15 H.Hogan/R.Flair

2010 TRISTAR TNA Xtreme Dual Memorabilia

*GOLD/50: .5X TO 1.2X BASIC MEM
*GREEN/25: .6X TO 1.5X BASIC MEM
*RED/5: UNPRICED DUE TO SCARCITY
*PURPLE/1: UNPRICED DUE TO SCARCITY
STATED PRINT RUN 199 SER.#'d SETS

X12 Robbie E/Cookie 8.00 20.00
X13 Jeremy & Max Buck 6.00 15.00

2010 TRISTAR TNA Xtreme Dual Memorabilia Gold

*GOLD: .5X TO 1.2X BASIC MEM
STATED PRINT RUN 50 SER.#'d SETS

X12 Robbie E/Cookie 10.00 25.00
X13 Jeremy & Max Buck 8.00 20.00

2010 TRISTAR TNA Xtreme Lovely Locks Hair Autographs Turquoise

*PINK/1: UNPRICED DUE TO SCARCITY
STATED PRINT RUN 3 SER.#'d SETS
UNPRICED DUE TO SCARCITY

LL1 Velvet Sky
LL2 Angelina Love
LL3 SoCal Val
LL4 Christy Hemme

2010 TRISTAR TNA Xtreme Memorabilia

*GOLD/50: .5X TO 1.2X BASIC MEM
*GREEN/10: UNPRICED DUE TO SCARCITY
*RED/5: UNPRICED DUE TO SCARCITY
*PURPLE/1: UNPRICED DUE TO SCARCITY
OVERALL MEMORABILIA ODDS ONE PER HOBBY BOX
STATED PRINT RUN 199 SER.#'d SETS

X1 Hulk Hogan
X2 Rob Van Dam
X3 Jeff Hardy
X4 Mr. Anderson 6.00 15.00
X5 Kurt Angle 6.00 15.00
X6 Mickie James
X7 AJ Styles
X8 D'Angelo Dinero
X9 Sabu 6.00 15.00
X10 Al Snow 6.00 15.00
X11 Brother Runt 6.00 15.00

2010 TRISTAR TNA Xtreme Obak

COMPLETE SET (8) 15.00 40.00
STATED PRINT RUN 310 SER.#'d SETS

X1 Hulk Hogan 8.00 20.00
X2 Jeff Hardy 5.00 12.00
X3 Rob Van Dam 3.00 8.00
X4 Mickie James 6.00 15.00
X5 AJ Styles 3.00 8.00
X6 Tommy Dreamer 1.25 3.00
X7 Jeff Jarrett 3.00 8.00
X8 Sting 5.00 12.00

2010 TRISTAR TNA Xtreme Quad Autographs

*GOLD/99: UNPRICED DUE TO SCARCITY
*GREEN/25: UNPRICED DUE TO SCARCITY
*RED/5: UNPRICED DUE TO SCARCITY
*PURPLE/1: UNPRICED DUE TO SCARCITY
UNPRICED DUE TO SCARCITY

1 Hogan/Flair/Jarrett/Hardy
2 Angle/Sting/Nash/Foley
3 Sky/Love/Rayne/Tara
4 Tommy & Trisa Dreamer/Kimberly/Brianna

2010 TRISTAR TNA Xtreme Quad Memorabilia Gold

*GREEN/10: UNPRICED DUE TO SCARCITY
*RED/5: UNPRICED DUE TO SCARCITY
*PURPLE/1: UNPRICED DUE TO SCARCITY
STATED PRINT RUN 50 SER.#'d SETS

X14 Hogan/Sting/RVD/Hardy
X15 Sky/Love/Von Erich/Rayne
X16 Hogan/Flair/Foley/Sting
X17 Tara/James/Sky/Love
X18 Snow/B.Runt/Scorpio/Tillie 15.00 30.00
X19 Dreamer/RVD/Sabu/Snow 15.00 30.00

2010 TRISTAR TNA Xtreme Six Autographs

*GOLD/99: UNPRICED DUE TO SCARCITY
*GREEN/25: UNPRICED DUE TO SCARCITY
*RED/5: UNPRICED DUE TO SCARCITY
*PURPLE/1: UNPRICED DUE TO SCARCITY
UNPRICED DUE TO SCARCITY

1 Flair/Styles/Storm
Roode/Kazarian/Morgan
2 Hogan/Flair/Hardy
Jarrett/Angle/Sting
3 Dreamer/Foley/Richards
Rhino/Raven/Sabu
4 Smothers/Luke/Maritato
Kash/Diamond/Swinger

2010 TRISTAR TNA Xtreme Six Autographs Gold

STATED PRINT RUN 99 SER.#'d SETS

1 Flair/Styles/Storm
Roode/Kazarian/Morgan
2 Hogan/Flair/Hardy
Jarrett/Angle/Sting
3 Dreamer/Foley/Richards
Rhino/Raven/Sabu
4 Smothers/Luke/Maritato
Kash/Diamond/Swinger

2010 TRISTAR TNA Xtreme Sting Die-Cut Letter Memorabilia Green

STATED PRINT RUN 10 SER.#'d SETS

S1 Sting S 20.00 40.00
S2 Sting T 20.00 40.00
S3 Sting I 20.00 40.00
S4 Sting N 20.00 40.00
S5 Sting G 20.00 40.00

2010 TRISTAR TNA Xtreme Sting Face Paint Red

STATED PRINT RUN 5 SER.#'d SETS
UNPRICED DUE TO SCARCITY

S3 Sting
S4 Sting

2010 TRISTAR TNA Xtreme Triple Autographs Gold

STATED PRINT RUN 99 SER.#'d SETS

1 Hogan/Jarrett/Flair
2 Foley/Angle/Anderson
3 Raven/Dreamer/Foley
4 Richards/Nova/Polaco
5 Rhino/Runt/Snow
6 Ray/Devon/Gertner
7 Sabu/VanDam/Alfonso

2010 TRISTAR TNA Xtreme Velvet Sky Die-Cut Letter Memorabilia Gold

STATED PRINT RUN 50 SER.#'d SETS

VS1 Velvet Sky S 25.00 50.00
VS2 Velvet Sky K 25.00 50.00
VS3 Velvet Sky Y 25.00 50.00

2006 Unilever WWE

NNO Batista 5.00 12.00
NNO Booker T 3.00 8.00
NNO Carlito 5.00 12.00
NNO Hulk Hogan 6.00 15.00
NNO The Hurricane 1.25 3.00
NNO John Cena 8.00 20.00
NNO Kurt Angle 5.00 12.00
NNO Rey Mysterio 3.00 8.00
NNO Stone Cold Steve Austin 8.00 20.00
NNO The Undertaker 6.00 15.00

2021 Upper Deck AEW

COMPLETE SET W/SP (100) 100.00 200.00
COMPLETE SET W/O SP (60) 30.00 75.00
COMMON TT (61-70) .60 1.50
COMMON CREW (71-80) .60 1.50
COMMON MAG (81-100) 1.25 3.00
*GOLD: .5X TO 1.2X BASIC CARDS
*GOLD TT: .5X TO 1.2X BASIC CARDS
*GOLD CREW: .5X TO 1.2X BASIC CARDS
*GOLD MAG: .5X TO 1.2X BASIC CARDS
*PYRO: .75X TO 2X BASIC CARDS
*PYRO TT: .75X TO 2X BASIC CARDS
*PYRO CREW: .75X TO 2X BASIC CARDS
*PYRO MAG: .75X TO 2X BASIC CARDS
*DYNAMITE: 1.2X TO 3X BASIC CARDS
*DYNA.TT: 1.2X TO 3X BASIC CARDS
*DYNA.CREW: 1.2X TO 3X BASIC CARDS
*DYNA.MAG: 1.2X TO 3X BASIC CARDS
*FINISHER: 1.5X TO 4X BASIC CARDS
*FINISH.TT: 1.5X TO 4X BASIC CARDS
*FINISH.CREW: 1.5X TO 4X BASIC CARDS
*FINISH.MAG: 1.5X TO 4X BASIC CARDS
*YELLOW: X TO X BASIC CARDS
*EXCLUSIVES/100: 8X TO 20X BASIC CARDS
*HIGH GLOSS/10: UNPRICED DUE TO SCARCITY
*BLACK/1: UNPRICED DUE TO SCARCITY

1 Cody Rhodes 1.00 2.50
2 Kris Statlander RC .50 1.25
3 Shawn Spears .50 1.25
4 Dustin Rhodes .60 1.50
5 Lance Archer .75 2.00
6 Penelope Ford RC .50 1.25
7 Hangman Adam Page RC 2.00 5.00
8 Scorpio Sky RC .30 .75
9 Miro .60 1.50
10 QT Marshall RC .40 1.00
11 Dr. Britt Baker RC 1.50 4.00
12 Joey Janela RC .30 .75
13 Jon Moxley .75 2.00
14 Isiah Kassidy RC .40 1.00
15 Sammy Guevara RC .75 2.00
16 Kenny Omega RC 2.00 5.00
17 The Blade RC .50 1.25
18 John Silver RC .30 .75
19 Jake Hager .50 1.25
20 Nick Jackson RC 1.25 3.00
21 PAC .60 1.50
22 Abadon RC .30 .75
23 Jungle Boy RC 1.25 3.00
24 Marq Quen RC .40 1.00
25 RIHO RC 1.25 3.00
26 Ricky Starks RC .75 2.00
27 Frankie Kazarian .40 1.00
28 Anna Jay RC 1.50 4.00
29 Matt Jackson RC 1.25 3.00
30 Ortiz RC .50 1.25
31 Cash Wheeler .50 1.25
32 Stu Grayson RC .30 .75
33 Darby Allin RC 2.00 5.00
34 Chuck Taylor RC .40 1.00
35 Trent? .75 2.00
36 Alex Reynolds RC .30 .75
37 Matt Hardy .60 1.50
38 The Butcher RC .50 1.25
39 Tay Conti 1.25 3.00
40 Orange Cassidy RC .75 2.00
41 Big Swole RC .50 1.25
42 Penta el Zero M RC .75 2.00
43 Kip Sabian RC .60 1.50
44 Christopher Daniels .50 1.25
45 Brian Cage RC .40 1.00
46 Luchasaurus RC 1.00 2.50
47 Colt Cabana RC .40 1.00
48 The Bunny RC .75 2.00
49 Wardlow RC .60 1.50

50 Nyla Rose RC .60 1.50
51 MJF RC 2.00 5.00
52 Santana RC .50 1.25
53 Brandi Rhodes 1.50 4.00
54 Chris Jericho 1.25 3.00
55 Hikaru Shida RC 1.00 2.50
56 Powerhouse Hobbs RC .60 1.50
57 Dax Harwood .50 1.25
58 Rey Fenix RC .75 2.00
59 Evil Uno RC .60 1.50
60 Mr. Brodie Lee .75 2.00
61 Trent?/Chuck Taylor SP 1.25 3.00
62 The Butcher/The Blade SP .75 2.00
63 Dax Harwood/Cash Wheeler SP .75 2.00
64 Santana/Ortiz SP .75 2.00
65 Jungle Boy/Luchasaurus SP 2.00 5.00
66 Rey Fenix/Penta el Zero M SP 1.25 3.00
67 Evil Uno/Stu Grayson SP 1.00 2.50
68 Marq Quen/Isiah Kassidy SP .60 1.50
69 Frankie Kazarian/Scorpio Sky SP .60 1.50
70 Matt Jackson/Nick Jackson SP 2.00 5.00
71 Arn Anderson SP 1.00 2.50
72 Billy Gunn SP .75 2.00
73 Jake Roberts SP 1.00 2.50
74 Jim Ross SP 1.50 4.00
75 Justin Roberts SP .60 1.50
76 Paul Turner SP RC .60 1.50
77 Sting SP 2.50 6.00
78 Taz SP .75 2.00
79 Tony Schiavone SP .75 2.00
80 Tully Blanchard SP 1.00 2.50
81 Sting SP 4.00 10.00
82 Brian Cage SP 1.25 3.00
83 Dr. Britt Baker SP 5.00 12.00
84 Chris Jericho SP 4.00 10.00
85 Cody Rhodes SP 3.00 8.00
86 Colt Cabana SP 1.25 3.00
87 Darby Allin SP 6.00 15.00
88 Hikaru Shida SP 3.00 8.00
89 Jon Moxley SP 2.50 6.00
90 Kenny Omega SP 6.00 15.00
91 Lance Archer SP 2.50 6.00
92 Matt Hardy SP 2.00 5.00
93 Matt Jackson SP 4.00 10.00
94 MJF SP 6.00 15.00
95 Mr. Brodie Lee SP 2.50 6.00
96 Nick Jackson SP 4.00 10.00
97 Nyla Rose SP 2.00 5.00
98 Orange Cassidy SP 2.50 6.00
99 Rey Fenix SP 2.50 6.00
100 Sammy Guevara SP 2.50 6.00

2021 Upper Deck AEW Autographed Belt The Champion Achievement

BELT Jon Moxley

2021 Upper Deck AEW Autographed Champion Achievements

CA4A Chris Jericho 60.00 150.00
CA4B Cody Rhodes 75.00 200.00

2021 Upper Deck AEW Autographs

*PYRO/25: UNPRICED DUE TO SCARCITY
*DYNAMITE/5: UNPRICED DUE TO SCARCITY
*GOLD/1: UNPRICED DUE TO SCARCITY
*P.P.BLACK/1: UNPRICED DUE TO SCARCITY
*P.P.CYAN/1: UNPRICED DUE TO SCARCITY
*P.P.MAGENTA/1: UNPRICED DUE TO SCARCITY
*P.P.YELLOW/1: UNPRICED DUE TO SCARCITY
GROUP A ODDS 1:7,581
GROUP B ODDS 1:1,832
GROUP C ODDS 1:913
GROUP D ODDS 1:464
GROUP E ODDS 1:341
STATED ODDS 1:146 HOBBY/EPACK
STATED ODDS 1:113 BLASTER/FAT PACKS
STATED TT ODDS 1:2,048 HOBBY
STATED TT ODDS 1:1,700 EPACK/BLAST/FAT
STATED CREW ODDS 1:1,024 HOBBY/EPACK
STATED CREW ODDS 1:800 BLASTER/FAT
STATED MAG ODDS 1:768 HOBBY/EPACK
STATED MAG ODDS 1:600 BLASTER/FAT

1 Cody Rhodes B 60.00 150.00
2 Kris Statlander E 20.00 50.00
3 Shawn Spears D 20.00 50.00
4 Dustin Rhodes D 25.00 60.00
5 Lance Archer C 6.00 15.00
6 Penelope Ford E 20.00 50.00
7 Hangman Adam Page D 40.00 100.00
8 Scorpio Sky D 6.00 15.00
9 Miro D 10.00 25.00
10 QT Marshall E 6.00 15.00
11 Dr. Britt Baker C 60.00 150.00
12 Joey Janela D 6.00 15.00
13 Jon Moxley B 50.00 125.00
14 Isiah Kassidy C 6.00 15.00
15 Sammy Guevara C 20.00 50.00
16 Kenny Omega B 75.00 200.00
17 The Blade C 8.00 20.00
18 John Silver D 12.00 30.00
19 Jake Hager E 6.00 15.00
20 Nick Jackson A 20.00 50.00
21 PAC E 8.00 20.00
22 Abadon E 15.00 40.00
23 Jungle Boy D 25.00 60.00
24 Marq Quen D 10.00 25.00
25 RIHO E 40.00 100.00
26 Ricky Starks D 20.00 50.00
27 Frankie Kazarian C 6.00 15.00
28 Anna Jay E 60.00 150.00
29 Matt Jackson A 20.00 50.00
30 Ortiz D 6.00 15.00
31 Cash Wheeler D 15.00 40.00
32 Stu Grayson D 6.00 15.00
33 Darby Allin B 50.00 125.00
34 Chuck Taylor D 10.00 25.00
35 Trent? D 6.00 15.00
36 Alex Reynolds E 25.00 60.00
37 Matt Hardy B 12.00 30.00
38 The Butcher C 8.00 20.00
39 Tay Conti E 40.00 100.00
40 Orange Cassidy B 50.00 125.00
41 Big Swole E 10.00 25.00
42 Penta el Zero M C 15.00 40.00
43 Kip Sabian E 6.00 15.00
44 Christopher Daniels E 8.00 20.00
45 Brian Cage C 10.00 25.00
46 Luchasaurus C 25.00 60.00
47 Colt Cabana C 8.00 20.00
48 The Bunny E 30.00 75.00
49 Wardlow E 20.00 50.00
50 Nyla Rose C 10.00 25.00
51 MJF B 125.00 300.00
52 Santana D 8.00 20.00
53 Brandi Rhodes E 15.00 40.00
54 Chris Jericho B 50.00 125.00
55 Hikaru Shida B 75.00 200.00
56 Powerhouse Hobbs D 10.00 25.00
57 Dax Harwood D 10.00 25.00
58 Rey Fenix A 8.00 20.00
59 Evil Uno D 6.00 15.00
61 Chuck Taylor/Trent? B 30.00 75.00
62 The Butcher/The Blade B 20.00 50.00
63 Dax Harwood/Cash Wheeler B 75.00 150.00
64 Santana/Ortiz B 30.00 75.00
65 Jungle Boy/Luchasaurus B 50.00 125.00
66 Rey Fenix/Penta el Zero M B 20.00 50.00
67 Evil Uno/Stu Grayson B 40.00 100.00
68 Marq Quen/Isiah Kassidy B 20.00 50.00
69 Frankie Kazarian/Scorpio Sky B 12.00 30.00
70 Matt Jackson/Nick Jackson A 40.00 100.00
71 Arn Anderson B 30.00 75.00
72 Billy Gunn A 10.00 25.00
73 Jake Roberts B 15.00 40.00
74 Jim Ross B 15.00 40.00
75 Justin Roberts B 6.00 15.00
76 Paul Turner B 6.00 15.00
77 Sting A 75.00 200.00
78 Taz B 12.00 30.00
79 Tony Schiavone B 10.00 25.00
80 Tully Blanchard B 8.00 20.00
81 Sting B 50.00 125.00
82 Brian Cage C 10.00 25.00
83 Dr. Britt Baker C 60.00 150.00
84 Chris Jericho A 60.00 150.00
85 Cody Rhodes A 75.00 200.00
86 Colt Cabana C 8.00 20.00
87 Darby Allin C 40.00 100.00
88 Hikaru Shida C 60.00 150.00
89 Jon Moxley B 50.00 125.00
90 Kenny Omega C 60.00 150.00
91 Lance Archer C 6.00 15.00
92 Matt Hardy C 12.00 30.00
93 Matt Jackson B 20.00 50.00
94 MJF C 100.00 250.00
96 Nick Jackson B 20.00 50.00
97 Nyla Rose C 10.00 25.00
98 Orange Cassidy C 40.00 100.00
99 Rey Fenix B 10.00 25.00
100 Sammy Guevara C 20.00 50.00

2021 Upper Deck AEW Canvas

COMPLETE SET W/O SP (30) 30.00 75.00
STATED ODDS 1:5
STATED SP ODDS 1:40

C1 Matt Hardy 1.50 4.00
C2 Brian Cage 1.00 2.50
C3 Dustin Rhodes 1.50 4.00
C4 Jungle Boy 3.00 8.00
C5 Brandi Rhodes 4.00 10.00
C6 Darby Allin 5.00 12.00
C7 Dr. Britt Baker 4.00 10.00
C8 Austin Gunn 1.00 2.50
C9 Tay Conti 3.00 8.00
C10 PAC 1.50 4.00
C11 Best Friends 2.00 5.00
C12 Colt Cabana 1.00 2.50
C13 Taz 1.00 2.50
C14 Nyla Rose 1.50 4.00
C15 The Butcher/The Blade 1.25 3.00
C16 Santana/Ortiz 1.25 3.00
C17 Lance Archer 2.00 5.00
C18 Sting 3.00 8.00
C19 Ricky Starks 2.00 5.00
C20 Luchasaurus 2.50 6.00
C21 Scorpio Sky .75 2.00
C22 Anna Jay 4.00 10.00
C23 Dax Harwood/Cash Wheeler 1.25 3.00
C24 Jim Ross 2.00 5.00
C25 Big Swole 1.25 3.00
C26 Joey Janela .75 2.00
C27 Rey Fenix/Penta el Zero M 2.00 5.00
C28 Tony Schiavone 1.00 2.50
C29 Sammy Guevara 2.00 5.00
C30 Hikaru Shida 2.50 6.00
C31 Cody Rhodes SP 8.00 20.00
C32 Nick Jackson SP 8.00 20.00
C33 Matt Jackson SP 8.00 20.00
C34 Mr. Brodie Lee SP 10.00 25.00
C35 Chris Jericho SP 8.00 20.00
C36 Hangman Adam Page SP 12.00 30.00
C37 Orange Cassidy SP 8.00 20.00
C38 MJF SP 10.00 25.00
C39 Kenny Omega SP 15.00 40.00
C40 Jon Moxley SP 8.00 20.00

2021 Upper Deck AEW Champion Achievements

CA1 Kenny Omega/Hangman Adam Page6.00 15.00
CA2 Hikaru Shida 2.50 6.00
CA3 Jon Moxley 4.00 10.00
CA4C AEW Championship Belt 2.00 5.00

2021 Upper Deck AEW The Dotted Line Autographs

STATED ODDS 1:1,536 HOBBY/EPACK
STATED ODDS 1:3,072 BLASTER
STATED ODDS 1:6,144 FAT PACKS

DLCJ Chris Jericho 60.00 150.00
DLCR Cody Rhodes 125.00 300.00
DLDA Darby Allin 150.00 400.00
DLHS Hikaru Shida
DLJM Jon Moxley
DLKO Kenny Omega 200.00 500.00
DLMF MJF 250.00 600.00
DLMH Matt Hardy
DLMJ Matt Jackson
DLNJ Nick Jackson
DLOC Orange Cassidy 60.00 150.00

2021 Upper Deck AEW Main Features

COMPLETE SET (40) 30.00 75.00
*SILVER: .5X TO 1.2X BASIC CARDS
*GREEN/199: 1.5X TO 4X BASIC CARDS
*GOLD: .6X TO 1.5X BASIC CARDS
*RED/50: 2X TO 5X BASIC CARDS
*PURPLE/25: 2.5X TO 6X BASIC CARDS
*BLACK/1: UNPRICED DUE TO SCARCITY
STATED ODDS 1:1

MF1 Cody Rhodes 1.25 3.00
MF2 Darby Allin 2.50 6.00
MF3 Lance Archer 1.00 2.50
MF4 Chris Jericho 1.50 4.00
MF5 RIHO 1.50 4.00
MF6 Santana .60 1.50
MF7 Orange Cassidy 1.00 2.50
MF8 Hikaru Shida 1.25 3.00
MF9 Dax Harwood .60 1.50
MF10 Kenny Omega 2.50 6.00
MF11 Big Swole .60 1.50
MF12 Dustin Rhodes .75 2.00
MF13 Shawn Spears .60 1.50
MF14 PAC .75 2.00
MF15 Brandi Rhodes 2.00 5.00
MF16 Cash Wheeler .60 1.50
MF17 Frankie Kazarian .50 1.25
MF18 Tay Conti 1.50 4.00
MF19 Nick Jackson 1.50 4.00
MF20 Penta el Zero M 1.00 2.50
MF21 Nyla Rose .75 2.00
MF22 Brian Cage .50 1.25
MF23 Sting 1.50 4.00
MF24 Ortiz .60 1.50
MF25 Hangman Adam Page 2.50 6.00
MF26 Luchasaurus 1.25 3.00
MF27 Scorpio Sky .40 1.00
MF28 MJF 2.50 6.00
MF29 Jungle Boy 1.50 4.00
MF30 The Blade .60 1.50
MF31 Matt Jackson 1.50 4.00
MF32 Matt Hardy .75 2.00
MF33 Colt Cabana .50 1.25
MF34 Rey Fenix 1.00 2.50
MF35 Dr. Britt Baker 2.00 5.00
MF36 Anna Jay 2.00 5.00
MF37 Ricky Starks 1.00 2.50
MF38 Sammy Guevara 1.00 2.50
MF39 Jake Hager .60 1.50
MF40 Jon Moxley 1.00 2.50

2021 Upper Deck AEW Memorabilia

*GOLD/199: .75X TO 2X BASIC MEM
*RED/50: 1.5X TO 4X BASIC MEM

1 Cody Rhodes 3.00 8.00
2 Kris Statlander 1.50 4.00
3 Shawn Spears 1.50 4.00
4 Dustin Rhodes 2.00 5.00
5 Lance Archer 2.50 6.00
6 Penelope Ford 1.50 4.00
7 Hangman Adam Page 6.00 15.00
8 Scorpio Sky 1.00 2.50
9 Miro 2.00 5.00
10 QT Marshall 1.25 3.00
11 Dr. Britt Baker 5.00 12.00
12 Joey Janela 1.00 2.50
13 Jon Moxley 2.50 6.00
14 Isiah Kassidy 1.25 3.00
15 Sammy Guevara 2.50 6.00
16 Kenny Omega 6.00 15.00
17 The Blade 1.50 4.00
18 John Silver 1.00 2.50
19 Jake Hager 1.50 4.00
20 Nick Jackson 4.00 10.00
21 PAC 2.00 5.00
22 Abadon 1.00 2.50
23 Jungle Boy 4.00 10.00
24 Marq Quen 1.25 3.00
26 Ricky Starks 2.50 6.00
27 Frankie Kazarian 1.25 3.00
28 Anna Jay 5.00 12.00
29 Matt Jackson 4.00 10.00
30 Ortiz 1.50 4.00
31 Cash Wheeler 1.50 4.00
32 Stu Grayson 1.00 2.50
33 Darby Allin 6.00 15.00
34 Chuck Taylor 1.25 3.00
35 Trent? 2.50 6.00

36 Alex Reynolds	1.00	2.50
37 Matt Hardy	2.00	5.00
38 The Butcher	1.50	4.00
39 Tay Conti	4.00	10.00
40 Orange Cassidy	2.50	6.00
41 Big Swole	1.50	4.00
42 Penta el Zero M	2.50	6.00
43 Kip Sabian	2.00	5.00
44 Christopher Daniels	1.50	4.00
45 Brian Cage	1.25	3.00
46 Luchasaurus	3.00	8.00
47 Colt Cabana	1.25	3.00
48 The Bunny	2.50	6.00
49 Wardlow	2.00	5.00
50 Nyla Rose	2.00	5.00
51 MJF	6.00	15.00
52 Santana	1.50	4.00
53 Brandi Rhodes	5.00	12.00
54 Chris Jericho	4.00	10.00
55 Hikaru Shida	3.00	8.00
56 Powerhouse Hobbs	2.00	5.00
57 Dax Harwood	1.50	4.00
58 Rey Fenix	2.50	6.00
59 Evil Uno	2.00	5.00
61 Chuck Taylor/Trent?	2.50	6.00
62 The Butcher/The Blade	1.50	4.00
63 Dax Harwood/Cash Wheeler	1.50	4.00
64 Santana/Ortiz	1.50	4.00
65 Jungle Boy/Luchasaurus	4.00	10.00
66 Rey Fenix/Penta el Zero M	2.50	6.00
67 Evil Uno/Stu Grayson	2.00	5.00
68 Marq Quen/Isiah Kassidy	1.25	3.00
69 Frankie Kazarian/Scorpio Sky	1.25	3.00
70 Matt Jackson/Nick Jackson	4.00	10.00
71 Arn Anderson	1.50	4.00
72 Billy Gunn	1.25	3.00
73 Jake Roberts	1.50	4.00
74 Jim Ross	2.50	6.00
78 Taz	1.25	3.00
80 Tully Blanchard	1.50	4.00

2021 Upper Deck AEW NYCC Promo Sheet

PV1 Rhodes/Miro/Baker/Omega/Cover Jericho/Shida/Sting/Moxley	20.00	50.00

2021 Upper Deck AEW NYCC Promos

NNO Cover Card	1.50	4.00
PV1 Cody Rhodes	2.00	5.00
PV2 Miro	2.00	5.00
PV3 Dr. Britt Baker	12.00	30.00
PV4 Kenny Omega	8.00	20.00
PV5 Chris Jericho	3.00	8.00
PV6 Hikaru Shida	5.00	12.00
PV7 Sting	6.00	15.00
PV8 Jon Moxley	4.00	10.00

2021 Upper Deck AEW Preview

0 CM Punk	12.00	30.00
PP1 Adam Cole	2.50	6.00
PP2 Bryan Danielson	4.00	10.00
PP3 Keith Lee	2.50	6.00

2021 Upper Deck AEW Preview Autograph

0 CM Punk	60.00	150.00

2021 Upper Deck AEW Rhodes to Success

COMPLETE SET (10) 15.00 40.00
*SILVER: .5X TO 1.2X BASIC CARDS
*GOLD: .6X TO 1.5X BASIC CARDS
*RED/50: 1.5X TO 4X BASIC CARDS
*BLACK/1: UNPRICED DUE TO SCARCITY
STATED ODDS 1:10 HOBBY/EPACK/BLASTER
STATED ODDS 1:5 FAT PACKS

RS1 Cody Rhodes	2.00	5.00
RS2 Cody Rhodes	2.00	5.00
RS3 Cody Rhodes	2.00	5.00
RS4 Cody Rhodes	2.00	5.00
RS5 Cody Rhodes	2.00	5.00
RS6 Cody Rhodes	2.00	5.00
RS7 Cody Rhodes	2.00	5.00
RS8 Cody Rhodes	2.00	5.00
RS9 Cody Rhodes	2.00	5.00
RS10 Cody Rhodes	2.00	5.00

2021 Upper Deck AEW Top Rope

COMPLETE SET (10) 12.00 30.00
*SILVER: .5X TO 1.2X BASIC CARDS
*GOLD: .6X TO 1.5X BASIC CARDS
*RED/50: 2X TO 5X BASIC CARDS
*BLACK/1: UNPRICED DUE TO SCARCITY
STATED ODDS 1:10 HOBBY/EPACK/BLASTER
STATED ODDS 1:5 FAT PACKS

TR1 PAC	1.00	2.50
TR2 Darby Allin	3.00	8.00
TR3 Nick Jackson	2.00	5.00
TR4 RIHO	2.00	5.00
TR5 Kenny Omega	3.00	8.00
TR6 Joey Janela	.50	1.25
TR7 Rey Fenix	1.25	3.00
TR8 Hangman Adam Page	3.00	8.00
TR9 Marq Quen	.60	1.50
TR10 Sammy Guevara	1.25	3.00

2021 Upper Deck AEW Wednesday in Action

COMPLETE SET (33) 50.00 125.00
STATED ODDS 1:64

WIA1 Orange Cassidy	2.50	6.00
WIA2 Luchasaurus	3.00	8.00
WIA3 Chris Jericho	4.00	10.00
WIA4 Anna Jay	5.00	12.00
WIA5 Dax Harwood	1.50	4.00
WIA6 Matt Hardy	2.00	5.00
WIA7 Brian Cage	1.25	3.00
WIA8 Santana	1.50	4.00
WIA9 Jon Moxley	2.50	6.00
WIA10 Hikaru Shida	3.00	8.00
WIA11 Matt Jackson	4.00	10.00
WIA12 Nick Jackson	4.00	10.00
WIA13 Dustin Rhodes	2.00	5.00
WIA14 Ricky Starks	2.50	6.00
WIA15 Dr. Britt Baker	5.00	12.00
WIA16 MJF	6.00	15.00
WIA17 Lance Archer	2.50	6.00
WIA18 Kenny Omega	6.00	15.00
WIA19 Penta el Zero M	2.50	6.00
WIA20 Sammy Guevara	2.50	6.00
WIA21 Ortiz	1.50	4.00
WIA22 Tay Conti	4.00	10.00
WIA23 Cody Rhodes	3.00	8.00
WIA24 Joey Janela	1.00	2.50
WIA25 Scorpio Sky	1.00	2.50
WIA26 Rey Fenix	2.50	6.00
WIA27 Sting	4.00	10.00
WIA28 Brandi Rhodes	5.00	12.00
WIA29 Cash Wheeler	1.50	4.00
WIA30 Christopher Daniels	1.50	4.00
WIA31 Jungle Boy	4.00	10.00
WIA32 Nyla Rose	2.00	5.00
WIA33 Hangman Adam Page	6.00	15.00

2022 Upper Deck AEW

*GOLD: .75X TO 2X BASIC CARDS
*PYRO: 1.2X TO 3X BASIC CARDS
*GREEN PYRO/399: 1.5X TO 4X BASIC CARDS
*DYNAMITE/299: 2X TO 5X BASIC CARDS
*PURPLE PYRO/199: 2.5X TO 6X BASIC CARDS
*EXCLUSIVE/100: 4X TO 10X BASIC CARDS
*HIGH GLOSS/10: UNPRICED DUE TO SCARCITY
*BLACK/1: UNPRICED DUE TO SCARCITY

1 Chris Jericho	1.25	3.00
2 Colt Cabana	.40	1.00
3 MJF	1.50	4.00
4 Brian Pillman Jr. RC	1.25	3.00
5 The Bunny	.75	2.00
6 Powerhouse Hobbs	.60	1.50
7 Max Caster	.40	1.00
8 Ethan Page	.75	2.00
9 Christian Cage	.50	1.25
10 Luchasaurus	.60	1.50
11 Trent?	.40	1.00
12 Nyla Rose	.60	1.50
13 Sammy Guevara	1.00	2.50
14 Daniel Garcia RC	1.00	2.50
15 CM Punk	1.50	4.00
16 QT Marshall	.40	1.00
17 Ricky Starks	.60	1.50
18 Jake Hager	.50	1.25
19 The Blade	.30	.75
20 Jungle Boy	1.00	2.50
21 Penelope Ford	1.50	4.00
22 Santana	.60	1.50
23 Paul Wight	.60	1.50
24 Evil Uno	.60	1.50
25 John Silver	.30	.75
26 Scorpio Sky	.60	1.50
27 Adam Cole	1.00	2.50
28 Billy Gunn	.40	1.00
29 Ruby Soho	.60	1.50
30 Stu Grayson	.60	1.50
31 Red Velvet	.50	1.25
32 Jay Lethal	.50	1.25
33 Tay Conti	1.25	3.00
34 Lance Archer	.75	2.00
35 Kris Statlander	.60	1.50
36 Angelico RC	.40	1.00
37 The Butcher	.30	.75
38 Serena Deeb	.30	.75
39 PAC	.60	1.50
40 Jon Moxley	.75	2.00
41 Matt Hardy	.60	1.50
42 Dax Harwood	.50	1.25
43 Matt Sydal	.30	.75
44 Cash Wheeler	.50	1.25
45 Miro	.60	1.50
46 Dustin Rhodes	.60	1.50
47 Eddie Kingston	1.00	2.50
48 Rey Fenix	.75	2.00
49 Anthony Bowens	.40	1.00
50 Frankie Kazarian	.40	1.00
51 Malakai Black	.75	2.00
52 Orange Cassidy	1.00	2.50
53 Dante Martin RC	.60	1.50
54 RIHO	.60	1.50
55 Matt Jackson	.75	2.00
56 Nick Jackson	.75	2.00
57 Bryan Danielson	1.25	3.00
58 Hangman Adam Page	1.50	4.00
59 Darby Allin	1.50	4.00
60 Jamie Hayter RC	2.00	5.00
61 Kenny Omega	1.50	4.00
62 Andrade El Idolo	.40	1.00
63 Thunder Rosa	.75	2.00
64 Dr. Britt Baker	1.25	3.00
65 Chuck Taylor	.30	.75
66 Wardlow	.75	2.00
67 Keith Lee	.75	2.00
68 Diamante	.30	.75
69 Kyle O'Reilly	.30	.75
70 Ortiz	.60	1.50
71 Shawn Spears	.50	1.25
72 Alex Reynolds	.30	.75
73 Jade Cargill	1.50	4.00
74 Penta el Zero M	.75	2.00
75 Lee Johnson	.30	.75
76 Sting	1.25	3.00
77 Anna Jay	1.25	3.00
78 Hikaru Shida	.75	2.00
79 Griff Garrison	.30	.75
80 Hook RC	2.50	6.00
81 Dax Harwood/Cash Wheeler	.50	1.25
82 Rey Fenix/Penta El Zero M	.75	2.00
83 Griff Garrison/Brian Pillman Jr.	.50	1.25
84 Anthony Bowens/Max Caster	.40	1.00
85 Jeff Parker/Matt Lee	.40	1.00
86 Santana/Ortiz	.60	1.50
87 Jungle Boy/Luchasaurus	1.00	2.50
88 Marq Quen/Isiah Kassidy	.40	1.00
89 The Butcher/The Blade	.30	.75
90 Matt Jackson/Nick Jackson	.75	2.00
91 Jim Ross	.75	2.00
92 Tony Schiavone	.40	1.00
93 Vickie Guerrero	.30	.75
94 Bryce Remsburg RC	.40	1.00
95 Arn Anderson	.50	1.25
96 Justin Roberts	.30	.75
97 Tully Blanchard	.40	1.00
98 Rick Knox RC	.40	1.00
99 Mark Henry	.40	1.00
100 Taz	.40	1.00

2022 Upper Deck AEW Autographs

*PYRO/25: UNPRICED DUE TO SCARCITY
*DYNAMITE/5: UNPRICED DUE TO SCARCITY
*GOLD/1: UNPRICED DUE TO SCARCITY
*P.P.BLACK/1: UNPRICED DUE TO SCARCITY
*P.P.CYAN/1: UNPRICED DUE TO SCARCITY
*P.P.MAGENTA/1: UNPRICED DUE TO SCARCITY
*P.P.YELLOW/1: UNPRICED DUE TO SCARCITY
STATED OVERALL ODDS 1:144 HOBBY/EPACK
STATED OVERALL ODDS 1:187 BLASTER
TAG TEAM OVERALL ODDS 1:3,072 HOBBY/EPACK
TAG TEAM OVERALL ODDS 1:6,000 BLASTER
CREW OVERALL ODDS 1:768 HOBBY/EPACK
CREW OVERALL ODDS 1:1,000 BLASTER
GROUP A ODDS 1:14,037
GROUP B ODDS 1:2,562
GROUP C ODDS 1:154

1 Chris Jericho A		
2 Colt Cabana C	6.00	15.00
3 MJF C	200.00	500.00
4 Brian Pillman Jr. B	10.00	25.00
5 The Bunny C	25.00	60.00
6 Powerhouse Hobbs B		
7 Max Caster C	40.00	100.00
8 Ethan Page C	40.00	100.00
9 Christian Cage C	15.00	40.00
10 Luchasaurus C	20.00	50.00
11 Trent? C	10.00	25.00
12 Nyla Rose C	12.00	30.00
13 Sammy Guevara C	25.00	60.00
14 Daniel Garcia C	15.00	40.00
15 CM Punk A		
16 QT Marshall C	10.00	25.00
17 Ricky Starks B		
18 Jake Hager C	10.00	25.00
19 The Blade C	6.00	15.00
20 Jungle Boy C	30.00	75.00
21 Penelope Ford C	40.00	100.00
22 Santana C	10.00	25.00
23 Paul Wight B	10.00	25.00
24 Evil Uno C	15.00	40.00
25 John Silver C	8.00	20.00
26 Scorpio Sky C	10.00	25.00
27 Adam Cole C		
28 Billy Gunn C	20.00	50.00
29 Ruby Soho B		
30 Stu Grayson C	10.00	25.00
31 Red Velvet B		
32 Jay Lethal C	15.00	40.00
33 Tay Conti C	40.00	100.00
34 Lance Archer C	10.00	25.00
35 Kris Statlander C	60.00	150.00
36 Angelico C	12.00	30.00
37 The Butcher C	6.00	15.00
38 Serena Deeb C	15.00	40.00
39 PAC C	15.00	40.00
40 Jon Moxley A		
41 Matt Hardy B		
42 Dax Harwood C		
43 Matt Sydal C		
44 Cash Wheeler B		
45 Miro C	15.00	40.00
46 Dustin Rhodes B	15.00	40.00
47 Eddie Kingston C	50.00	125.00
48 Rey Fenix C	25.00	60.00
49 Anthony Bowens C	25.00	60.00
50 Frankie Kazarian B		
51 Malakai Black C	25.00	60.00
52 Orange Cassidy C		
53 Dante Martin C	50.00	125.00
54 RIHO C	30.00	75.00
55 Matt Jackson B	15.00	40.00
56 Nick Jackson B		
57 Bryan Danielson C	20.00	50.00
58 Hangman Adam Page C	60.00	150.00
59 Darby Allin C	60.00	150.00
60 Jamie Hayter C	125.00	300.00
61 Kenny Omega A		
62 Andrade El Idolo C	20.00	50.00
63 Thunder Rosa B	40.00	100.00
64 Dr. Britt Baker C	125.00	300.00
65 Chuck Taylor C	10.00	25.00
66 Wardlow C	25.00	60.00
67 Keith Lee A	25.00	60.00

68 Diamante C 10.00 25.00
69 Kyle O'Reilly C 12.00 30.00
70 Ortiz C 10.00 25.00
71 Shawn Spears C 10.00 25.00
72 Alex Reynolds C 6.00 15.00
73 Jade Cargill C 100.00 250.00
74 Penta el Zero M C 30.00 75.00
75 Lee Johnson C 15.00 40.00
76 Sting C 60.00 150.00
77 Anna Jay C 50.00 125.00
78 Hikaru Shida B 75.00 200.00
79 Griff Garrison C 10.00 25.00
80 HOOK C 150.00 400.00
81 Dax Harwood/Cash Wheeler 75.00 200.00
82 Rey Fenix/Penta El Zero M
83 Griff Garrison/Brian Pillman Jr. 25.00 60.00
84 Anthony Bowens/Max Caster 60.00 150.00
85 Jeff Parker/Matt Lee 40.00 100.00
86 Santana/Ortiz
87 Jungle Boy/Luchasaurus
88 Marq Quen/Isiah Kassidy
89 The Butcher/The Blade 30.00 75.00
90 Matt Jackson/Nick Jackson
91 Jim Ross 12.00 30.00
92 Tony Schiavone 12.00 30.00
93 Vickie Guerrero 12.00 30.00
94 Bryce Remsburg 10.00 25.00
95 Arn Anderson 15.00 40.00
96 Justin Roberts 12.00 30.00
97 Tully Blanchard 20.00 50.00
98 Rick Knox 15.00 40.00
99 Mark Henry
100 Taz 10.00 25.00

2022 Upper Deck AEW Breakouts

STATED ODDS 1:73 HOBBY/EPACK/BLASTER
SP ODDS 1:512 HOBBY/EPACK/BLASTER

BO1 Christian Cage 6.00 15.00
BO2 Thunder Rosa 15.00 40.00
BO3 Matt Hardy 6.00 15.00
BO4 Jade Cargill 40.00 100.00
BO5 Cash Wheeler 25.00 60.00
BO6 Adam Cole 20.00 50.00
BO7 Dustin Rhodes 10.00 25.00
BO8 Kris Statlander 15.00 40.00
BO9 Malakai Black 12.00 30.00
BO10 Paul Wight 4.00 15.00
BO11 Jungle Boy 12.00 30.00
BO12 Sting 20.00 50.00
BO13 Rey Fenix 12.00 30.00
BO14 Darby Allin 30.00 75.00
BO15 Max Caster 8.00 20.00
BO16 Luchasaurus 8.00 20.00
BO17 Tay Conti 12.00 30.00
BO18 Penta el Zero M 15.00 40.00
BO19 Bryan Danielson 15.00 40.00
BO20 Lance Archer 8.00 20.00
BO21 Dr. Britt Baker 25.00 60.00
BO22 Dax Harwood 6.00 15.00
BO23 Wardlow 12.00 30.00
BO24 Powerhouse Hobbs 10.00 25.00
BO25 Ricky Starks 8.00 20.00
BO26 Orange Cassidy SP 20.00 50.00
BO27 Chris Jericho SP 30.00 75.00
BO28 Keith Lee SP 30.00 75.00
BO29 Kenny Omega SP 60.00 150.00
BO30 Jon Moxley SP 30.00 75.00
BO31 Hangman Adam Page SP 100.00
BO32 Miro SP 20.00 50.00
BO33 CM Punk SP 40.00 100.00
BO34 Matt Jackson SP 20.00 50.00
BO35 Nick Jackson SP 20.00 50.00

2022 Upper Deck AEW Canvas

STATED ODDS 1:4 HOBBY/EPACK/BLASTER/FAT
SP ODDS 1:40 HOBBY/EPACK/BLASTER/FAT

C1 Brian Pillman Jr. 1.00 2.50
C2 Penta el Zero M 1.50 4.00
C3 Tay Conti 2.50 6.00
C4 Ruby Soho 1.25 3.00
C5 Dax Harwood 1.00 2.50
C6 Dustin Rhodes 1.25 3.00
C7 Rey Fenix 1.50 4.00
C8 Jungle Boy 2.00 5.00
C9 Luchasaurus 1.25 3.00
C10 Ricky Starks 1.25 3.00
C11 Dr. Britt Baker 2.50 6.00
C12 Thunder Rosa 1.50 4.00
C13 Sammy Guevara 2.00 5.00
C14 Mark Henry .75 2.00
C15 Isiah Kassidy/Marq Quen .75 2.00
C16 Jamie Hayter 3.00 8.00
C17 Anthony Bowens/Max Caster .75 2.00
C18 Dante Martin .60 1.50
C19 Lance Archer 1.50 4.00
C20 Bryan Danielson 2.50 6.00
C21 Matt Hardy 1.25 3.00
C22 Powerhouse Hobbs 1.25 3.00
C23 MJF 3.00 8.00
C24 Santana/Ortiz 1.25 3.00
C25 Paul Wight 1.25 3.00
C26 Jade Cargill 3.00 8.00
C27 Christian Cage 1.00 2.50
C28 CM Punk 3.00 8.00
C29 Hikaru Shida 1.50 4.00
C30 Cash Wheeler 1.00 2.50
C31 Hangman Adam Page SP 8.00 20.00
C32 Matt Jackson SP 4.00 10.00
C33 Orange Cassidy SP 5.00 12.00
C34 Kenny Omega SP 8.00 20.00
C35 Chris Jericho SP 6.00 15.00
C36 Miro SP 3.00 8.00
C37 Sting SP 6.00 15.00
C38 Nick Jackson SP 4.00 10.00
C39 Keith Lee SP 4.00 10.00
C40 Darby Allin SP 8.00 20.00

2022 Upper Deck AEW Debut Dates

COMPLETE SET (10) 10.00 25.00
*SILVER: .5X TO 1.2X BASIC CARDS
*GOLD: .6X TO 1.5X BASIC CARDS
*RED/50: .75X TO 2X BASIC CARDS
*GOLD SPECTRUM/1: UNPRICED DUE TO SCARCITY
STATED ODDS 1:10 HOBBY/EPACK/BLASTER
STATED ODDS 1:5 FAT PACKS

DD1 Thunder Rosa 1.50 4.00
DD2 Paul Wight 1.25 3.00
DD3 Ruby Soho 1.25 3.00
DD4 Christian Cage 1.00 2.50
DD5 Andrade El Idolo .75 2.00
DD6 Malakai Black 1.50 4.00
DD7 Adam Cole 2.00 5.00
DD8 CM Punk 3.00 8.00
DD9 Bryan Danielson 2.50 6.00
DD10 Mark Henry .75 2.00

2022 Upper Deck AEW Jumbo Mat Relic Signatures

STATED PRINT RUN 10 SER.#'d SETS
UNPRICED DUE TO SCARCITY

JMS2 Rey Fenix
JMS3 Chris Jericho
JMS5 Nick Jackson
JMS6 Kenny Omega
JMS7 Christian Cage
JMS8 Lance Archer
JMS9 Tay Conti
JMS10 Powerhouse Hobbs
JMS11 Darby Allin
JMS12 Miro
JMS14 Matt Jackson
JMS15 Orange Cassidy
JMS16 Matt Hardy
JMS17 Jungle Boy
JMS18 Brian Cage
JMS19 MJF

2022 Upper Deck AEW Main Features

*SILVER: .5X TO 1.2X BASIC CARDS
*GOLD: .6X TO 1.5X BASIC CARDS
*GREEN/199: .75X TO 2X BASIC CARDS
*RED/50: 1.2X TO 3X BASIC CARDS
*PURPLE/25: UNPRICED DUE TO SCARCITY
*GOLD SPECTRUM/1: UNPRICED DUE TO SCARCITY
STATED ODDS 1:1 HOBBY/EPACK/BLASTER
STATED ODDS 2:1 FAT PACKS

MF1 Kenny Omega 4.00 10.00
MF2 Thunder Rosa 2.00 5.00
MF3 Cash Wheeler 1.25 3.00
MF4 Darby Allin 4.00 10.00
MF5 Adam Cole 2.50 6.00
MF6 Dr. Britt Baker 3.00 8.00
MF7 Max Caster 1.00 2.50
MF8 Luchasaurus 1.50 4.00
MF9 MJF 4.00 10.00
MF10 Orange Cassidy 2.50 6.00
MF11 Sting 3.00 8.00
MF12 Christian Cage 1.25 3.00
MF13 Hangman Adam Page 4.00 10.00
MF14 Penta el Zero M 2.00 5.00
MF15 Ruby Soho 1.50 4.00
MF16 Tay Conti 3.00 8.00
MF17 PAC 1.50 4.00
MF18 Matt Jackson 2.00 5.00
MF19 Bryan Danielson 3.00 8.00
MF20 Chris Jericho 3.00 8.00
MF21 Powerhouse Hobbs 1.50 4.00
MF22 Jungle Boy 2.50 6.00
MF23 Lance Archer 2.00 5.00
MF24 Nyla Rose 1.50 4.00
MF25 Anthony Bowens 1.00 2.50
MF26 Keith Lee 2.00 5.00
MF27 Paul Wight 1.50 4.00
MF28 Rey Fenix 2.00 5.00
MF29 Dax Harwood 1.25 3.00
MF30 Dustin Rhodes 1.50 4.00
MF31 Nick Jackson 2.00 5.00
MF32 Mark Henry 1.00 2.50
MF33 Ricky Starks 1.50 4.00
MF34 Miro 1.50 4.00
MF35 Hikaru Shida 2.00 5.00
MF36 Brian Cage 1.00 2.50
MF37 Red Velvet 1.25 3.00
MF38 Sammy Guevara 2.50 6.00
MF39 CM Punk 4.00 10.00
MF40 Jon Moxley 2.00 5.00

2022 Upper Deck AEW Mat Relics

*GOLD: .5X TO 1.2X BASIC MEM
*RED/50: .6X TO 1.5X BASIC MEM
STATED ODDS 1:23 BLASTER

1 Chris Jericho 6.00 15.00
2 Colt Cabana 2.00 5.00
3 MJF 8.00 20.00
4 Brian Pillman Jr. 2.50 6.00
5 The Bunny 4.00 10.00
6 Powerhouse Hobbs 3.00 8.00
7 Max Caster 2.00 5.00
8 Ethan Page 4.00 10.00
9 Christian Cage 2.50 6.00
10 Luchasaurus 3.00 8.00
11 Trent? 2.00 5.00
12 Nyla Rose 3.00 8.00
13 Sammy Guevara 5.00 12.00
14 Daniel Garcia 2.00 5.00
15 CM Punk 8.00 20.00
16 QT Marshall 2.00 5.00
17 Ricky Starks 3.00 8.00
18 Jake Hager 2.50 6.00
19 The Blade 1.50 4.00
20 Jungle Boy 5.00 12.00
21 Penelope Ford 8.00 20.00
22 Santana 3.00 8.00
23 Paul Wight 3.00 8.00
24 Evil Uno 3.00 8.00
25 John Silver 1.50 4.00
26 Scorpio Sky 3.00 8.00
27 Adam Cole 5.00 12.00
28 Billy Gunn 2.00 5.00
29 Ruby Soho 3.00 8.00
30 Stu Grayson 3.00 8.00
31 Red Velvet 2.50 6.00
32 Jay Lethal 2.50 6.00
33 Tay Conti 6.00 15.00
34 Lance Archer 4.00 10.00
35 Kris Statlander 3.00 8.00
36 Angelico 1.50 4.00
37 The Butcher 1.50 4.00
38 Serena Deeb 1.50 4.00
39 PAC 3.00 8.00
40 Jon Moxley 4.00 10.00
41 Matt Hardy 3.00 8.00
42 Dax Harwood 2.50 6.00
43 Matt Sydal 1.50 4.00
44 Cash Wheeler 2.50 6.00
45 Miro 3.00 8.00
46 Dustin Rhodes 3.00 8.00
47 Eddie Kingston 5.00 12.00
48 Rey Fenix 4.00 10.00
49 Anthony Bowens 2.00 5.00
50 Frankie Kazarian 2.00 5.00
51 Malakai Black 4.00 10.00
52 Orange Cassidy 5.00 12.00
53 Dante Martin 1.50 4.00
54 RIHO 3.00 8.00
55 Matt Jackson 4.00 10.00
56 Nick Jackson 4.00 10.00
57 Bryan Danielson 6.00 15.00
58 Hangman Adam Page 8.00 20.00
59 Darby Allin 8.00 20.00
60 Jamie Hayter 8.00 20.00
61 Kenny Omega 8.00 20.00
62 Andrade El Idolo 2.00 5.00
63 Thunder Rosa 4.00 10.00
64 Dr. Britt Baker 6.00 15.00
65 Chuck Taylor 1.50 4.00
66 Wardlow 4.00 10.00
67 Keith Lee 4.00 10.00
68 Diamante 1.50 4.00
69 Kyle O'Reilly 1.50 4.00
70 Ortiz 3.00 8.00
71 Shawn Spears 2.50 6.00
72 Alex Reynolds 1.50 4.00
73 Jade Cargill 8.00 20.00
74 Penta el Zero M 4.00 10.00
75 Lee Johnson 1.50 4.00
76 Sting 6.00 15.00
77 Anna Jay 6.00 15.00
78 Hikaru Shida 4.00 10.00
79 Griff Garrison 1.50 4.00
80 HOOK 6.00 15.00
81 Dax Harwood/Cash Wheeler 2.50 6.00
82 Rey Fenix/Penta El Zero M 4.00 10.00
83 Griff Garrison/Brian Pillman Jr. 2.50 6.00
84 Anthony Bowens/Max Caster 2.00 5.00
85 Jeff Parker/Matt Lee 2.00 5.00
86 Santana/Ortiz 3.00 8.00
87 Jungle Boy/Luchasaurus 5.00 12.00
88 Marq Quen/Isiah Kassidy 2.00 5.00
89 The Butcher/The Blade 1.50 4.00
90 Matt Jackson/Nick Jackson 4.00 10.00
91 Jim Ross 4.00 10.00
92 Tony Schiavone 2.00 5.00
93 Vickie Guerrero 1.50 4.00
94 Bryce Remsburg 1.50 4.00
95 Arn Anderson 2.50 6.00
96 Justin Roberts 1.50 4.00
97 Tully Blanchard 2.00 5.00
98 Rick Knox 1.50 4.00
99 Mark Henry 2.00 5.00
100 Taz 2.00 5.00

2022 Upper Deck AEW Match Dated Moments Grand Slam

GS1 Toni Storm 2.00 5.00
GS2 The Wizard Chris Jericho 2.50 6.00
GS3 Jon Moxley 2.00 5.00
GS4 The Great Muta 1.25 3.00
GS5 HOOK and Action Bronson S 12.00 30.00
GS6 The Acclaimed G 30.00 75.00

2022 Upper Deck AEW Match Dated Moments Top Ranked Achievements

*SILVER: UNPRICED DUE TO SCARCITY
*GOLD: UNPRICED DUE TO SCARCITY

TR1 MJF
TR2 Jon Moxley
TR3 Bryan Danielson
TR4 Dr. Britt Baker DMD
TR5 Jade Cargill
TR6 Kenny Omega

2022 Upper Deck AEW Outside the Ring

COMPLETE SET (10) 6.00 15.00
*SILVER: .5X TO 1.2X BASIC CARDS
*GOLD: .6X TO 1.5X BASIC CARDS
*RED/50: .75X TO 2X BASIC CARDS

*GOLD SPECTRUM/1: UNPRICED DUE TO SCARCITY
STATED ODDS 1:10 HOBBY/EPACK/BLASTER
STATED ODDS 1:5 FAT PACKS

OTR1 Santana 1.25 3.00
OTR2 Ortiz 1.25 3.00
OTR3 Varsity Blonds 1.00 2.50
OTR4 Best Friends .75 2.00
OTR5 Tony Schiavone .75 2.00
OTR6 Hikaru Shida 1.50 4.00
OTR7 Shawn Spears 1.00 2.50
OTR8 Sammy Guevara 2.00 5.00
OTR9 Powerhouse Hobbs 1.25 3.00
OTR10 Mark Henry .75 2.00

2022 Upper Deck AEW Shirt Relics

*RED/50: .75X TO 2X BASIC MEM
RANDOMLY INSERTED INTO PACKS

1 Chris Jericho 6.00 15.00
2 Colt Cabana 2.00 5.00
3 MJF 8.00 20.00
4 Brian Pillman Jr. 2.50 6.00
5 The Bunny 4.00 10.00
6 Powerhouse Hobbs 3.00 8.00
7 Max Caster 2.00 5.00
8 Ethan Page 4.00 10.00
9 Christian Cage 2.50 6.00
10 Luchasaurus 3.00 8.00
11 Trent? 2.00 5.00
12 Nyla Rose 3.00 8.00
13 Sammy Guevara 5.00 12.00
14 Daniel Garcia 2.00 5.00
15 CM Punk 8.00 20.00
16 QT Marshall 2.00 5.00
17 Ricky Starks 3.00 8.00
18 Jake Hager 2.50 6.00
19 The Blade 1.50 4.00
20 Jungle Boy 5.00 12.00
21 Penelope Ford 8.00 20.00
22 Santana 3.00 8.00
23 Paul Wight 3.00 8.00
24 Evil Uno 3.00 8.00
25 John Silver 1.50 4.00
26 Scorpio Sky 3.00 8.00
27 Adam Cole 5.00 12.00
28 Billy Gunn 2.00 5.00
29 Ruby Soho 3.00 8.00
30 Stu Grayson 3.00 8.00
31 Red Velvet 2.50 6.00
32 Jay Lethal 2.50 6.00
33 Tay Conti 6.00 15.00
34 Lance Archer 4.00 10.00
35 Kris Statlander 3.00 8.00
36 Angelico 1.50 4.00
37 The Butcher 1.50 4.00
38 Serena Deeb 1.50 4.00
39 PAC 3.00 8.00
40 Jon Moxley 4.00 10.00
41 Matt Hardy 3.00 8.00
42 Dax Harwood 2.50 6.00
43 Matt Sydal 1.50 4.00
44 Cash Wheeler 2.50 6.00
45 Miro 3.00 8.00
46 Dustin Rhodes 3.00 8.00
47 Eddie Kingston 5.00 12.00
48 Rey Fenix 4.00 10.00
49 Anthony Bowens 2.00 5.00
50 Frankie Kazarian 2.00 5.00
51 Malakai Black 4.00 10.00
52 Orange Cassidy 5.00 12.00
53 Dante Martin 1.50 4.00
54 RIHO 3.00 8.00
55 Matt Jackson 4.00 10.00
56 Nick Jackson 4.00 10.00
57 Bryan Danielson 6.00 15.00
58 Hangman Adam Page 8.00 20.00
59 Darby Allin 8.00 20.00
60 Jamie Hayter 8.00 20.00
61 Kenny Omega 8.00 20.00
62 Andrade El Idolo 2.00 5.00
63 Thunder Rosa 4.00 10.00
64 Dr. Britt Baker 6.00 15.00
65 Chuck Taylor 1.50 4.00
66 Wardlow 4.00 10.00
67 Keith Lee 4.00 10.00
68 Diamante 1.50 4.00
69 Kyle O'Reilly 1.50 4.00
70 Ortiz 3.00 8.00
71 Shawn Spears 2.50 6.00
72 Alex Reynolds 1.50 4.00
73 Jade Cargill 8.00 20.00
74 Penta el Zero M 4.00 10.00
75 Lee Johnson 1.50 4.00
76 Sting 6.00 15.00
77 Anna Jay 6.00 15.00
78 Hikaru Shida 4.00 10.00
79 Griff Garrison 1.50 4.00
80 HOOK 6.00 15.00
81 Dax Harwood/Cash Wheeler 2.50 6.00
82 Rey Fenix/Penta El Zero M 4.00 10.00
83 Griff Garrison/Brian Pillman Jr. 2.50 6.00
84 Anthony Bowens/Max Caster 2.00 5.00
85 Jeff Parker/Matt Lee 2.00 5.00
86 Santana/Ortiz 3.00 8.00
87 Jungle Boy/Luchasaurus 5.00 12.00
88 Marq Quen/Isiah Kassidy 2.00 5.00
89 The Butcher/The Blade 1.50 4.00
90 Matt Jackson/Nick Jackson 4.00 10.00
91 Jim Ross 4.00 10.00
92 Tony Schiavone 2.00 5.00
93 Vickie Guerrero 1.50 4.00
94 Bryce Remsburg 1.50 4.00
95 Arn Anderson 2.50 6.00
96 Justin Roberts 1.50 4.00
97 Tully Blanchard 2.00 5.00
98 Rick Knox 1.50 4.00
99 Mark Henry 2.00 5.00
100 Taz 2.00 5.00

2023 Upper Deck AEW

*HIGH GLOSS/10: UNPRICED DUE TO SCARCITY
*BLACK/1: UNPRICED DUE TO SCARCITY

1 Bryan Danielson .75 2.00
1A Bryan Danielson VAR SP
2 Colten Gunn .40 1.00
3 Samoa Joe .60 1.50
4 Jake Hager .30 .75
5 Kris Statlander .75 2.00
5A Kris Statlander VAR SP
6 Taya Valkyrie .60 1.50
7 Orange Cassidy 1.00 2.50
8 MJF 1.50 4.00
9 Wheeler Yuta .60 1.50
10 Rey Fenix .50 1.25
11 Claudio Castagnoli .40 1.00
11A Claudio Castagnoli VAR SP
12 Riho .60 1.50
13 Daniel Garcia .40 1.00
14 Malakai Black .60 1.50
15 Preston Vance .40 1.00
16 Hook 1.00 2.50
16A HOOK VAR SP
17 Jade Cargill 1.50 4.00
17A Jade Cargill VAR SP
18 Adam Cole .75 2.00
18A Adam Cole VAR SP
19 Powerhouse Hobbs .60 1.50
20 Anna Jay 1.00 2.50
20A Anna Jay VAR SP
21 Hangman Adam Page 1.25 3.00
21A Hangman Adam Page VAR SP
22 Toni Storm .75 2.00
22A Toni Storm VAR SP
23 Austin Gunn .40 1.00
24 Ethan Page .50 1.25
25 Jack Perry .75 2.00
26 Lee Moriarty .50 1.25
26A Lee Moriarty VAR SP
27 Matt Jackson .75 2.00
28 Matt Hardy .60 1.50
29 Darius Martin RC 1.25 3.00
30 Hikaru Shida 1.00 2.50
31 Alex Reynolds .30 .75
32 Julia Hart .75 2.00
33 Dr. Britt Baker 1.25 3.00
33A Dr. Britt Baker VAR SP
34 Buddy Matthews .30 .75
35 Saraya 1.00 2.50
36 Rush RC 1.00 2.50
36A Lance Archer VAR SP
37 Swerve Strickland .50 1.25
38 Danhausen .75 2.00
39 Willow Nightingale RC 2.00 5.00
40 PAC .50 1.25
41 Nick Jackson .75 2.00
42 Jay Lethal .50 1.25
43 Anthony Bowens .30 .75
44 Sting 1.25 3.00
44A Sting VAR SP
45 Ricky Starks .30 .75
46 Sammy Guevara .75 2.00
46A Sammy Guevara VAR SP
47 Dante Martin .40 1.00
48 Darby Allin 1.25 3.00
48A Darby Allin VAR SP
49 Penta el Zero M .50 1.25
50 Dax Harwood .50 1.25
51 Jamie Hayter .75 2.00
52 Christian Cage .50 1.25
53 Ruby Soho .60 1.50
53A Ruby Soho VAR SP
54 Nyla Rose .50 1.25
55 Konosuke Takeshita 1.25 3.00
56 Athena .50 1.25
56A Athena VAR SP
57 Tay Melo .75 2.00
57A Tay Melo VAR SP
58 Matt Menard .30 .75
59 Chris Jericho .75 2.00
59A Chris Jericho VAR SP
60 Max Caster .40 1.00
60A Max Caster VAR SP
61 Kenny Omega 1.25 3.00
61A Kenny Omega VAR SP
62 Brody King .30 .75
63 Jon Moxley .75 2.00
63A Jon Moxley VAR SP
64 Jay White RC 1.00 2.50
65 Wardlow .60 1.50
65A Wardlow VAR SP
66 Angelo Parker RC 1.00 2.50
67 Trent Beretta .30 .75
68 Keith Lee .50 1.25
68A Keith Lee VAR SP
69 Cash Wheeler .40 1.00
6A Taya Valkyrie VAR SP
70 Eddie Kingston 1.00 2.50
71 Darius Martin/Dante Martin .40 1.00
72 Chuck Taylor/Trent Beretta .40 1.00
73 Dax Harwood/Cash Wheeler .50 1.25
74 Jericho Appreciation Society .75 2.00
75 Austin Gunn/Colten Gunn .40 1.00
76 Rey Fenix/Penta el Zero M .50 1.25
77 Max Caster/Anthony Bowens .40 1.00
78 Marq Quen/Isiah Kassidy .40 1.00
79 Matt Jackson/Nick Jackson .75 2.00
80 Andrade El Idolo/Rush .60 1.50
81 Stokely Hathaway .30 .75
82 Aubrey Edwards .50 1.25
83 Renee Paquette .50 1.25
84 Paul Turner .30 .75
85 Taz .50 1.25
86 Rick Knox .30 .75
87 Justin Roberts .30 .75
88 Bryce Remsburg .30 .75
89 Tony Schiavone .50 1.25
90 Jim Ross .60 1.50
91 Mark Sterling RC 1.00 2.50
92 Excalibur .30 .75
93 Matt Jackson/Nick Jackson .75 2.00
94 Renee Paquette/Jon Moxley .50 1.25
95 HOOK/Taz 1.00 2.50
96 Dante Martin/Darius Martin .40 1.00
97 Arn Anderson/Brock Anderson .60 1.50
98 Sammy Guevara/Tay Melo .75 2.00
99 Rey Fenix/Penta el Zero M .50 1.25
100 Colten Gunn/Austin Gunn .40 1.00

2023 Upper Deck AEW All Elite Women

*SILVER/199: .5X TO 1.2X BASIC CARDS
STATED ODDS 1:480 HOBBY/EPACK
STATED ODDS 1:180 BLASTER
STATED ODDS 1:40 PACK WARS

AEW1 Ruby Soho 2.00 5.00
AEW2 Jamie Hayter 2.50 6.00
AEW3 Hikaru Shida 3.00 8.00
AEW4 Athena 1.50 4.00
AEW5 Jade Cargill 5.00 12.00
AEW6 Marina Shafir 1.25 3.00
AEW7 Saraya 3.00 8.00
AEW8 Nyla Rose 1.50 4.00
AEW9 Thunder Rosa 2.50 6.00
AEW10 Tay Melo 2.50 6.00
AEW11 Kris Statlander 2.50 6.00
AEW12 Emi Sakura 1.50 4.00
AEW13 Julia Hart 2.50 6.00
AEW14 Dr. Britt Baker 4.00 10.00
AEW15 Red Velvet 1.50 4.00
AEW16 Willow Nightingale 1.25 3.00
AEW17 Anna Jay 3.00 8.00
AEW18 Toni Storm 2.50 6.00
AEW19 The Bunny 2.50 6.00
AEW20 Penelope Ford 2.50 6.00

2023 Upper Deck AEW Alliances Acetate

STATED ODDS 1:72 HOBBY/EPACK
STATED ODDS 1:490 BLASTER

AL1 Bryan Danielson/Jon Moxley 3.00 8.00
AL2 Max Caster/Anthony Bowens 1.50 4.00
AL3 Anna Jay/Tay Melo 4.00 10.00
AL4 Marq Quen/Isiah Kassidy 1.50 4.00
AL5 Cash Wheeler/Dax Harwood 2.00 5.00
AL6 Jamie Hayter/Dr. Britt Baker 5.00 12.00
AL7 Alex Reynolds/John Silver 1.50 4.00
AL8 The Butcher/The Blade 2.00 5.00
AL9 Kenny Omega/Don Callis 5.00 12.00
AL10 Matt Menard/Angelo Parker 2.00 5.00
AL11 Dante Martin/Darius Martin 1.50 4.00
AL12 Danhausen/Orange Cassidy 4.00 10.00
AL13 Chuck Taylor/Trent Beretta 1.50 4.00
AL14 Daniel Garcia/Sammy Guevara 3.00 8.00
AL15 Darby Allin/Sting 12.00 30.00
AL16 Colten Gunn/Austin Gunn 1.50 4.00
AL17 Toni Storm/Saraya 4.00 10.00
AL18 Lee Moriarty/Big Bill 2.00 5.00
AL19 QT Marshall/Aaron Solo 1.25 3.00
AL20 Chris Jericho/Jake Hager 3.00 8.00
AL21 Penta el Zero M/Rey Fenix 2.00 5.00
AL22 Jeff Hardy/Matt Hardy 2.50 6.00
AL23 Rush/Preston Vance 1.50 4.00
AL24 Malakai Black/Brody King 2.50 6.00
AL25 Claudio Castagnoli/Wheeler Yuta 2.50 6.00

2023 Upper Deck AEW Autographs

*PYRO/25: UNPRICED DUE TO SCARCITY
*DYNAMITE/5: UNPRICED DUE TO SCARCITY
*GOLD/1: UNPRICED DUE TO SCARCITY
OVERALL ODDS 1:166 HOBBY/EPACK
OVERALL ODDS 1:300 BLASTER
GROUP A ODDS 1:170,842
GROUP B ODDS 1:11,389
GROUP C ODDS 1:295
GROUP D ODDS 1:392
CARD #'s 71 & 72 NOT INCLUDED IN BASE

1 Bryan Danielson C 60.00 150.00
2 Colten Gunn C 10.00 25.00
3 Samoa Joe C 15.00 40.00
4 Jake Hager C 8.00 20.00
5 Kris Statlander C
6 Taya Valkyrie C 15.00 40.00
7 Orange Cassidy C
8 MJF B
9 Wheeler Yuta C
10 Rey Fenix C
11 Claudio Castagnoli C 15.00 40.00
12 RIHO C 60.00 150.00
13 Daniel Garcia C
14 Malakai Black C
15 Preston Vance C
16 HOOK C 25.00 60.00
17 Jade Cargill C
18 Adam Cole C 15.00 40.00
19 Powerhouse Hobbs C
20 Anna Jay C 60.00 150.00
21 Hangman Adam Page C 30.00 75.00
22 Toni Storm C
23 Austin Gunn C 6.00 15.00
24 Ethan Page C 12.00 30.00

25 Jack Perry C
26 Lee Moriarty C 10.00 25.00
27 Matt Jackson C
28 Matt Hardy C
29 Darius Martin C 20.00 50.00
30 Hikaru Shida C 60.00 150.00
31 Alex Reynolds C
32 Julia Hart C 60.00 150.00
33 Dr. Britt Baker B
34 Buddy Matthews C
36 Rush C
37 Swerve Strickland C
38 Danhausen C
40 PAC C 12.00 30.00
41 Nick Jackson C
42 Jay Lethal C
43 Anthony Bowens C 12.00 30.00
44 Sting B
45 Ricky Starks D 10.00 25.00
46 Sammy Guevara C 15.00 40.00
47 Dante Martin C
48 Darby Allin C
49 Penta el Zero M C
50 Dax Harwood C
51 Jamie Hayter C
52 Christian Cage C 10.00 25.00
53 Ruby Soho C
54 Nyla Rose D 15.00 40.00
55 Konosuke Takeshita C
56 Athena C
57 Tay Melo C
58 Matt Menard D 10.00 25.00
59 Chris Jericho B
60 Max Caster D
61 Kenny Omega B
62 Brody King C
63 Jon Moxley C
65 Wardlow C
66 Angelo Parker C
67 Trent Beretta C
68 Keith Lee C
69 Cash Wheeler C
70 Eddie Kingston C
73 Dax Harwood/Cash Wheeler A
75 Austin Gunn/Colten Gunn D
76 Rey Fenix/Penta el Zero M D
77 Max Caster/Anthony Bowens D
78 Marq Quen/Isiah Kassidy D
79 Matt Jackson/Nick Jackson D
80 Andrade El Idolo/Rush D
81 Stokely Hathaway D 10.00 25.00
82 Aubrey Edwards D
83 Renee Paquette D 20.00 50.00
84 Paul Turner D 10.00 25.00
85 Taz D 10.00 25.00
86 Rick Knox D 10.00 25.00
87 Justin Roberts D 12.00 30.00
88 Bryce Remsburg D 6.00 15.00
89 Tony Schiavone D 12.00 30.00
90 Jim Ross D
91 Mark Sterling D 20.00 50.00
92 Excalibur D 6.00 15.00

2023 Upper Deck AEW Breakouts Acetate Foilboard

STATED ODDS 1:480 HOBBY/EPACK
STATED ODDS 1:177 BLASTER

BO1 Malakai Black 10.00 25.00
BO2 Anna Jay 75.00 200.00
BO3 Athena 15.00 40.00
BO4 Action Andretti 10.00 25.00
BO5 Kyle O'Reilly 8.00 20.00
BO6 Willow Nightingale 15.00 40.00
BO7 Kris Statlander 30.00 75.00
BO8 Lee Moriarty 8.00 20.00
BO9 Rush 12.00 30.00
BO10 Mark Briscoe 8.00 20.00
BO11 Satnam Singh 8.00 20.00
BO12 Wheeler Yuta 15.00 40.00
BO13 Buddy Matthews 8.00 20.00
BO14 Big Bill 8.00 20.00
BO15 Danhausen 100.00 250.00
BO16 Ricky Starks 12.00 30.00
BO17 PAC 10.00 25.00
BO18 Ruby Soho 10.00 25.00
BO19 Daniel Garcia 8.00 20.00
BO20 Brody King 8.00 20.00
BO21 Lance Archer 10.00 25.00
BO22 Swerve Strickland 15.00 40.00
BO23 Skye Blue 100.00 250.00
BO24 Bandido 8.00 20.00
BO25 Powerhouse Hobbs 20.00 50.00

2023 Upper Deck AEW Breakouts Acetate Foilboard SP

STATED ODDS 1:960 HOBBY/EPACK
STATED ODDS 1:665 BLASTER

BR1 Saraya 40.00 100.00
BR2 Claudio Castagnoli 12.00 30.00
BR3 Keith Lee 20.00 50.00
BR4 Toni Storm 125.00 300.00
BR5 Willow Nightingale 15.00 40.00
BR6 HOOK 30.00 75.00
BR7 Wardlow 25.00 60.00
BR8 Jamie Hayter 40.00 100.00
BR9 Samoa Joe
BR10 Konosuke Takeshita

2023 Upper Deck AEW Championship Autographs

HOBBY EXCLUSIVE

CA4A Jon Moxley
CA5A MJF

2023 Upper Deck AEW Day With the Belt

STATED ODDS 1:2,400 HOBBY/EPACK

DB1 Wardlow
DB2 Chris Jericho
DB3 Jade Cargill
DB4 Max Caster
DB5 Jon Moxley
DB6 Toni Storm
DB7 Sammy Guevara
DB8 Anthony Bowens
DB9 Hikaru Shida
DB10 Kenny Omega
DB11 Dr. Britt Baker
DB12 Darby Allin
DB13 Thunder Rosa
DB14 PAC
DB15 Hangman Adam Page

2023 Upper Deck AEW Dazzlers Blue

*GREEN: SAME VALUE AS BASIC
*ORANGE: .5X TO 1.2X BASIC CARDS
STATED ODDS 1:6.4 HOBBY/EPACK

DZ1 Kenny Omega 5.00 12.00
DZ2 Powerhouse Hobbs 1.25 3.00
DZ3 Isiah Kassidy .75 2.00
DZ4 Nick Jackson 1.50 4.00
DZ5 Malakai Black 1.25 3.00
DZ6 Ethan Page 1.00 2.50
DZ7 Claudio Castagnoli .75 2.00
DZ8 Hangman Adam Page 2.50 6.00
DZ9 Jack Perry 1.50 4.00
DZ10 Jamie Hayter 1.50 4.00
DZ11 Danhausen 4.00 10.00
DZ12 Julia Hart 1.50 4.00
DZ13 Darby Allin 5.00 12.00
DZ14 Orange Cassidy 3.00 8.00
DZ15 Penta el Zero M 1.00 2.50
DZ16 Preston Vance .75 2.00
DZ17 Dr. Britt Baker 4.00 10.00
DZ18 Colten Gunn .75 2.00
DZ19 Lance Archer .60 1.50
DZ20 Samoa Joe 1.25 3.00
DZ21 Rey Fenix 1.00 2.50
DZ22 Yuka Sakazaki .60 1.50
DZ23 Matt Jackson 1.50 4.00
DZ24 Jade Cargill 10.00 25.00
DZ25 Kris Statlander 1.50 4.00
DZ26 Sting 2.50 6.00
DZ27 Bryan Danielson 1.50 4.00
DZ28 Austin Gunn .75 2.00
DZ29 Dante Martin .75 2.00
DZ30 Ricky Starks .60 1.50
DZ31 Ruby Soho 1.25 3.00
DZ32 HOOK 2.00 5.00
DZ33 Anna Jay 2.00 5.00
DZ34 Keith Lee 1.00 2.50
DZ35 Athena 1.00 2.50
DZ36 Jon Moxley 1.50 4.00
DZ37 Evil Uno .75 2.00
DZ38 Darius Martin .75 2.00
DZ39 Wardlow 1.25 3.00
DZ40 Tay Melo 1.50 4.00
DZ41 MJF 3.00 8.00
DZ42 Jay Lethal 1.00 2.50
DZ43 Sammy Guevara 1.50 4.00
DZ44 Toni Storm 1.50 4.00
DZ45 Juice Robinson .60 1.50
DZ46 Eddie Kingston 2.00 5.00
DZ47 Lee Moriarty 1.00 2.50
DZ48 Daniel Garcia .75 2.00
DZ49 Chris Jericho 1.50 4.00
DZ50 Adam Cole 1.50 4.00

2023 Upper Deck AEW Double or Nothing Playing Cards

STATED 2s to 10s ODDS 1:7.5 HOBBY/EPACK
STATED 2s to 10s ODDS 1:10 BLASTER
STATED 2s to 10s ODDS 1:15 PACK WARS
STATED JACKS AND KINGS ODDS 1:45 HOBBY/EPACK
STATED JACKS AND KINGS ODDS 1:60 BLASTER
STATED JACKS AND KINGS ODDS 1:90 PACK WARS
STATED ACES ODDS 1:135 HOBBY/EPACK
STATED ACES ODDS 1:180 BLASTER
STATED ACES ODDS 1:270 PACK WARS
STATED JOKERS ODDS 1:270 HOBBY/EPACK
STATED JOKERS ODDS 1:360 BLASTER
STATED JOKERS ODDS 1:540 PACK WARS

PC1 Chris Jericho
PC2 Hangman Adam Page
PC3 Jade Cargill
PC4 Jon Moxley
PC5 Kenny Omega
PC6 Wardlow
PC7 Bryan Danielson
PC8 Adam Cole
PC9 Jamie Hayter
PC10 Toni Storm
PC11 Dr. Britt Baker
PC12 Hikaru Shida
PC13 Powerhouse Hobbs
PC14 Anna Jay
PC15 Sammy Guevara
PC16 Claudio Castagnoli
PC17 Athena
PC18 HOOK
PC19 Rey Fenix
PC20 Keith Lee
PC21 Samoa Joe
PC22 Ruby Soho
PC23 PAC
PC24 Tay Melo
PC25 Ricky Starks
PC26 Jack Perry
PC27 Lee Moriarty
PC28 Penta el Zero M
PC29 Julia Hart
PC30 Lance Archer
PC31 Luchasaurus
PC32 RIHO
PC33 Eddie Kingston
PC34 Darby Allin
PC35 Sting
PC36 Kris Statlander
PC37 Konosuke Takeshita
PC38 Saraya
PC39 Matt Jackson
PC40 Nick Jackson
PC41 Penelope Ford
PC42 Cash Wheeler
PC43 Dax Harwood
PC44 Nyla Rose
PC45 Christian Cage
PC46 The Bunny
PC47 Jay Lethal
PC48 Malakai Black
PC49 Angelo Parker
PC50 Matt Menard
PC51 Brody King
PC52 Matt Hardy
PC53 Orange Cassidy
PC54 Danhausen

2023 Upper Deck AEW Excalibur's Picks

*SILVER/199: .5X TO 1.2X BASIC CARDS
*P.P.BLACK/1: UNPRICED DUE TO SCARCITY
*P.P.CYAN/1: UNPRICED DUE TO SCARCITY
*P.P.MAGENTA/1: UNPRICED DUE TO SCARCITY
*P.P.YELLOW/1: UNPRICED DUE TO SCARCITY
STATED ODDS 1:40 HOBBY/EPACK
STATED ODDS 1:35 BLASTER
STATED ODDS 1:80 PACK WARS

EP1 Jon Moxley 1.50 4.00
EP2 Jamie Hayter 1.50 4.00
EP3 HOOK 2.00 5.00
EP4 Eddie Kingston 2.00 5.00
EP5 Powerhouse Hobbs 1.25 3.00
EP6 Willow Nightingale .75 2.00
EP7 Konosuke Takeshita 2.50 6.00
EP8 Toni Storm 1.50 4.00
EP9 PAC 1.00 2.50
EP10 Top Flight .75 2.00

2023 Upper Deck AEW Fearsome Finishers Lenticular

STATED ODDS 1:480 HOBBY/EPACK
STATED ODDS 1:360 BLASTER

FF1 Jon Moxley 40.00 100.00
FF2 Wardlow
FF3 Jade Cargill 30.00 75.00
FF4 PAC 15.00 40.00
FF5 Kenny Omega
FF6 Hangman Adam Page 30.00 75.00
FF7 Ruby Soho 20.00 50.00
FF8 Kris Statlander 40.00 100.00
FF9 Daniel Garcia 10.00 25.00
FF10 Jay Lethal 12.00 30.00
FF11 Toni Storm 50.00 125.00
FF12 Eddie Kingston 15.00 40.00
FF13 Jamie Hayter 40.00 100.00
FF14 Bryan Danielson 20.00 50.00
FF15 Chris Jericho 15.00 40.00
FF16 HOOK 50.00 125.00
FF17 Willow Nightingale
FF18 Penta el Zero M 20.00 50.00
FF19 Sammy Guevara 20.00 50.00
FF20 Athena 15.00 40.00
FF21 Ricky Starks 10.00 25.00
FF22 Dante Martin 15.00 40.00
FF23 Dr. Britt Baker 75.00 200.00
FF24 Jack Perry 10.00 25.00
FF25 Powerhouse Hobbs

2023 Upper Deck AEW Intimidating Introductions Lenticular

STATED ODDS 1:480 HOBBY/EPACK
STATED ODDS 1:810 BLASTER

II1 Kenny Omega 60.00 150.00
II2 Kris Statlander 50.00 125.00
II3 Bryan Danielson
II4 Sting 50.00 125.00
II5 Thunder Rosa 30.00 75.00
II6 Tay Melo
II7 Malakai Black
II8 Nyla Rose
II9 Powerhouse Hobbs
II10 Ruby Soho 10.00 25.00
II11 HOOK
II12 Jade Cargill 30.00 75.00
II13 Toni Storm 75.00 200.00
II14 Lance Archer 12.00 30.00
II15 Chris Jericho
II16 Darby Allin 20.00 50.00
II17 Claudio Castagnoli
II18 John Silver
II19 Hangman Adam Page 30.00 75.00
II20 Wardlow
II21 Keith Lee
II22 Samoa Joe 15.00 40.00
II23 Swerve Strickland 60.00 150.00
II24 Adam Cole 12.00 30.00
II25 Jon Moxley

2023 Upper Deck AEW Mat Relics

1 Bryan Danielson
2 Colten Gunn
3 Samoa Joe
4 Jake Hager
5 Kris Statlander
6 Taya Valkyrie
7 Orange Cassidy
8 MJF
9 Wheeler Yuta
10 Rey Fenix
11 Claudio Castagnoli
12 RIHO
13 Daniel Garcia
14 Malakai Black
15 Preston Vance
16 HOOK
17 Jade Cargill
18 Adam Cole
19 Powerhouse Hobbs
20 Anna Jay
21 Hangman Adam Page
22 Toni Storm
23 Austin Gunn
24 Ethan Page
25 Jack Perry
26 Lee Moriarty
27 Matt Jackson
28 Matt Hardy
29 Darius Martin
30 Hikaru Shida
31 Alex Reynolds
32 Julia Hart
33 Dr. Britt Baker
34 Buddy Matthews
35 Saraya
36 Rush
37 Swerve Strickland
38 Danhausen
39 Willow Nightingale
40 PAC
41 Nick Jackson
42 Jay Lethal
43 Anthony Bowens
44 Sting
45 Ricky Starks
46 Sammy Guevara
47 Dante Martin
48 Darby Allin
49 Penta el Zero M
50 Dax Harwood
51 Jamie Hayter
52 Christian Cage
53 Ruby Soho
54 Nyla Rose
55 Konosuke Takeshita
56 Athena
57 Tay Melo
58 Matt Menard
59 Chris Jericho
60 Max Caster
61 Kenny Omega
62 Brody King
63 Jon Moxley
64 Switchblade Jay White
65 Wardlow
66 Angelo Parker
67 Trent Beretta
68 Keith Lee
69 Cash Wheeler
70 Eddie Kingston
71 Darius Martin/Dante Martin
72 Chuck Taylor/Trent Beretta
73 Dax Harwood/Cash Wheeler
74 Jericho Appreciation Society
75 Austin Gunn/Colten Gunn
76 Rey Fenix/Penta el Zero M
77 Max Caster/Anthony Bowens
78 Marq Quen/Isiah Kassidy
79 Young Bucks
80 Andrade El Idolo/Rush
81 Stokely Hathaway
82 Aubrey Edwards
83 Renee Paquette
84 Paul Turner
85 Taz
86 Rick Knox
87 Justin Roberts
88 Bryce Remsburg
89 Tony Schiavone
90 Jim Ross
91 Mark Sterling
92 Excalibur

2023 Upper Deck AEW Match Dated Moments

1 Ricky Starks
2 Jungle Boy Jack Perry
3 Ruby Soho
4 Hangman Adam Page
5 Wardlow
6 Cash Wheeler and Dax Harwood
7 The House of Black S
8 MJF G
9 Orange Cassidy
10 FTR
11 Wardlow
12 Toni Storm
13 House of Black
14 Kris Statlander
15 MJF S
16 Konosuke Takeshita G
17 Samoa Joe
18 Luchasaurus
19 Kris Statlander
20 Bullet Club Gold
21 Bryan Danielson
22 MJF and Adam Cole
23 Konosuke Takeshita S
24 Jon Moxley G
25 Adam Copeland, Sting and Darby Allin
26 Freshly Squeezed Orange Cassidy
27 Timeless Toni Storm
28 Absolute Ricky Starks
29 Julia Hart
30 Chris Jericho and Kenny Omega
31 Swerve Strickland
32 MJF

2023 Upper Deck AEW Match Dated Moments Special Edition

1 MJF
2 CM Punk
3 Jungle Boy Jack Perry
4 Sting, Darby Allin, Tetsuya Naito
5 American Dragon Bryan Danielson S
6 Kenny Omega and Will Ospreay G
7 FTR
8 Eddie Kingston, Penta El Zero M, Orange Cassidy and Best Friends
9 Darby Allin and Sting
10 Billy Gunn and The Acclaimed
11 Saraya S
12 MJF G
13 Saraya S
14 MJF
15 Darby Allin and Sting
16 The Righteous
17 Rey Fenix S
18 Eddie Kingston G
19 The Acclaimed
20 MJF
21 Kris Statlander
22 Swerve Strickland
23 Bryan Danielson S
24 Christian Cage G
25 Daniel Garcia
26 Timeless Toni Storm
27 Swerve Strickland
28 Christian Cage
29 Samoa Joe
30 Eddie Kingston

2023 Upper Deck AEW Match Dated Moments Battle Match Achievements

BM1 Saraya
BM2 Kris Statlander
BM3 Willow Nightingale
BM4 Toni Storm
BM5 Hikaru Shida
BM6 Skye Blue

2023 Upper Deck AEW Match Dated Moments PPV Aftermath Achievements

PPA1 Better Than You BayBay
PPA2 Toni Storm

2023 Upper Deck AEW Mic Check

*SILVER/199: .6X TO 1.5X BASIC CARDS
STATED ODDS 1:20 HOBBY/EPACK
STATED ODDS 1:17.5 BLASTER
STATED ODDS 1:40 PACK WARS

MC1 Switchblade Jay White	2.00	5.00
MC2 Ruby Soho	1.50	4.00
MC3 Anthony Bowens	.75	2.00
MC4 Orange Cassidy	2.50	6.00
MC5 Samoa Joe	1.50	4.00
MC6 MJF	4.00	10.00
MC7 Eddie Kingston	2.50	6.00
MC8 Sammy Guevara	2.00	5.00
MC9 Danhausen	2.00	5.00
MC10 Dr. Britt Baker	3.00	8.00
MC11 Kenny Omega	3.00	8.00
MC12 Thunder Rosa	2.00	5.00
MC13 Jon Moxley	2.00	5.00
MC14 Sting	3.00	8.00
MC15 Chris Jericho	2.00	5.00
MC16 PAC	1.25	3.00
MC17 Max Caster	1.00	2.50
MC18 Nyla Rose	1.25	3.00
MC19 Jake Hager	.75	2.00
MC20 Hangman Adam Page	3.00	8.00

2023 Upper Deck AEW New Arrivals

1 Juice Robinson	5.00	12.00
2 Mark Briscoe	2.00	5.00
3 Taya Valkyrie	4.00	10.00
4 Nigel McGuinness	2.50	6.00
5 Switchblade Jay White	3.00	8.00
6 Komander	4.00	10.00
7 Roderick Strong	2.00	5.00
8 Nick Wayne	5.00	12.00
9 Aussie Open	2.00	5.00
10 Adam Copeland	6.00	15.00
11 Ric Flair		
12 Dralistico		
13 CJ Perry		
14 Kota Ibushi		
15 Mariah May		
16 Will Ospreay		

2023 Upper Deck AEW Ring Masters Autographs

STATED ODDS 1:4,250 HOBBY/EPACK

RM1 Adam Cole
RM2 Jamie Hayter
RM3 Chris Jericho
RM4 Sammy Guevara
RM5 Kris Statlander
RM6 Jon Moxley
RM7 Claudio Castagnoli
RM8 Keith Lee
RM9 Wardlow
RM10 Ruby Soho
RM11 Hangman Adam Page
RM12 Jade Cargill
RM13 Samoa Joe
RM14 Dr. Britt Baker
RM15 Kenny Omega
RM16 Toni Storm
RM17 HOOK
RM18 Powerhouse Hobbs

2023 Upper Deck AEW Shirt Relics

*RED (71-80)/25: UNPRICED DUE TO SCARCITY
*RED (82-92)/10: UNPRICED DUE TO SCARCITY
STATED ODDS 1:120
STATED PRINT RUN (71-80) 25 SER.#'d SETS
STATED PRINT RUN (82-92) 10 SER.#'d SETS

1 Bryan Danielson
2 Colten Gunn
3 Samoa Joe
4 Jake Hager
5 Kris Statlander
6 Taya Valkyrie
7 Orange Cassidy
8 MJF
9 Wheeler Yuta
10 Rey Fenix
12 RIHO
13 Daniel Garcia
14 Malakai Black
15 Preston Vance
16 HOOK
17 Jade Cargill
18 Adam Cole
19 Powerhouse Hobbs
20 Anna Jay
21 Hangman Adam Page
22 Toni Storm
23 Austin Gunn
24 Ethan Page
25 Jack Perry
26 Lee Moriarty
27 Matt Jackson
28 Matt Hardy
29 Darius Martin
30 Hikaru Shida
31 Alex Reynolds
32 Julia Hart
33 Dr. Britt Baker
34 Buddy Matthews
36 Rush
37 Swerve Strickland
38 Danhausen
39 Willow Nightingale
40 PAC
41 Nick Jackson
42 Jay Lethal
43 Anthony Bowens
44 Sting
45 Ricky Starks
46 Sammy Guevara
47 Dante Martin
48 Darby Allin
49 Penta el Zero M
50 Dax Harwood
51 Jamie Hayter
52 Christian Cage
53 Ruby Soho
54 Nyla Rose
55 Konosuke Takeshita
56 Athena
57 Tay Melo
58 Matt Menard
59 Chris Jericho
60 Max Caster
61 Kenny Omega
62 Brody King
63 Jon Moxley
64 Switchblade Jay White
65 Wardlow
66 Angelo Parker
67 Trent Beretta
68 Keith Lee
69 Cash Wheeler
70 Eddie Kingston
71 Darius Martin/Dante Martin
72 Chuck Taylor/Trent Beretta
73 Dax Harwood/Cash Wheeler
74 Jericho Appreciation Society
75 Austin Gunn/Colten Gunn
76 Rey Fenix/Penta el Zero M
77 Max Caster/Anthony Bowens
78 Marq Quen/Isiah Kassidy
79 Young Bucks
80 Andrade El Idolo/Rush
82 Aubrey Edwards
83 Renee Paquette
84 Paul Turner
85 Taz
86 Rick Knox
87 Justin Roberts
88 Bryce Remsburg
89 Tony Schiavone

90 Jim Ross
91 Mark Sterling
92 Excalibur

2023 Upper Deck AEW Stare Down

STATED ODDS 1:35 HOBBY/EPACK
STATED ODDS 1:210 BLASTER

SD1 Sting
SD2 Dr. Britt Baker
SD3 Danhausen
SD4 Kris Statlander
SD5 Malakai Black
SD6 Stokely Hathaway
SD7 Thunder Rosa
SD8 Darby Allin
SD9 Preston Vance
SD10 Yuka Sakazaki
SD11 Evil Uno
SD12 Serpentico
SD13 Dustin Rhodes
SD14 Penta el Zero M
SD15 Rey Fenix
SD16 MJF
SD17 Mark Briscoe
SD18 Brody King
SD19 Buddy Matthews
SD20 Dax Harwood
SD21 Lance Archer
SD22 Cash Wheeler
SD23 Nick Comoroto
SD24 Jamie Hayter
SD25 Ruby Soho

2023 Upper Deck AEW Stepping Inside the Ring

*GOLD: .5X TO 1.2X BASIC CARDS
*SILVER: .6X TO 1.5X BASIC CARDS
*RED/50: 1.2X TO 3X BASIC CARDS
*GOLD SPECTRUM/1: UNPRICED DUE TO SCARCITY
*P.P.BLACK/1: UNPRICED DUE TO SCARCITY
*P.P.CYAN/1: UNPRICED DUE TO SCARCITY
*P.P.MAGENTA/1: UNPRICED DUE TO SCARCITY
*P.P.YELLOW/1: UNPRICED DUE TO SCARCITY
STATED ODDS 1:11 HOBBY/EPACK
STATED ODDS 1:35 BLASTER
STATED ODDS 1:23 PACK WARS

SR1 Danhausen 2.50 6.00
SR2 Claudio Castagnoli 1.25 3.00
SR3 Toni Storm 2.50 6.00
SR4 Samoa Joe 2.00 5.00
SR5 Athena 1.50 4.00
SR6 Julia Hart 2.50 6.00
SR7 HOOK 3.00 8.00
SR8 Swerve Strickland 1.50 4.00
SR9 Satnam Singh 1.00 2.50
SR10 Brody King 1.00 2.50

2023 Upper Deck AEW Total Access

*GOLD: .5X TO 1.2X BASIC CARDS
*SILVER: .6X TO 1.5X BASIC CARDS
*RED/50: 1.2X TO 3X BASIC CARDS
*GOLD SPECTRUM/1: UNPRICED DUE TO SCARCITY
*P.P.BLACK/1: UNPRICED DUE TO SCARCITY
*P.P.CYAN/1: UNPRICED DUE TO SCARCITY
*P.P.MAGENTA/1: UNPRICED DUE TO SCARCITY
*P.P.YELLOW/1: UNPRICED DUE TO SCARCITY
STATED ODDS 1:11 HOBBY/EPACK
STATED ODDS 1:35 BLASTER
STATED ODDS 1:23 PACK WARS

TA1 Jade Cargill 3.00 8.00
TA2 PAC 1.00 2.50
TA3 RIHO 1.25 3.00
TA4 Bryan Danielson 1.50 4.00
TA5 Hangman Adam Page 2.50 6.00
TA6 Swerve Strickland 1.00 2.50
TA7 Powerhouse Hobbs 1.25 3.00
TA8 Max Caster .75 2.00
TA9 Ricky Starks .60 1.50
TA10 Hikaru Shida 2.00 5.00

2023 Upper Deck AEW UD Canvas

STATED ODDS 1:6 HOBBY/EPACK
STATED ODDS 1:7 BLASTER
STATED ODDS 1:12 PACK WARS

C1 Penta el Zero M
C2 Chuck Taylor
C3 Ethan Page 2.00 5.00
C4 Satnam Singh 1.25 3.00
C5 Kris Statlander 3.00 8.00
C6 Jeff Jarrett 2.00 5.00
C7 Malakai Black 2.50 6.00
C8 Ortiz 1.50 4.00
C9 Konosuke Takeshita 5.00 12.00
C10 Jericho Appreciation Society 4.00 10.00
C11 Kenny Omega 5.00 12.00
C12 Rush 1.25 3.00
C13 Matt Hardy 2.50 6.00
C14 Taya Valkyrie 2.50 6.00
C15 Claudio Castagnoli 1.50 4.00
C16 Keith Lee 2.00 5.00
C17 Darius Martin 1.50 4.00
C18 Marina Shafir 1.50 4.00
C19 Skye Blue 5.00 12.00
C20 Jake Hager 1.25 3.00
C21 Eddie Kingston 4.00 10.00
C22 HOOK 4.00 10.00
C23 Daniel Garcia 1.50 4.00
C24 Colten Gunn 1.50 4.00
C25 Swerve Strickland 2.00 5.00
C26 Yuka Sakazaki 1.25 3.00
C27 Red Velvet 2.00 5.00
C28 Lee Moriarty 2.00 5.00
C29 Matt Jackson 3.00 8.00
C30 Sammy Guevara 3.00 8.00
C31 Action Andretti 1.25 3.00
C32 Jamie Hayter 3.00 8.00
C33 Matt Menard 1.25 3.00
C34 Bandido 1.50 4.00
C35 Adam Cole 3.00 8.00
C36 Dax Harwood 2.00 5.00
C37 Preston Vance 1.50 4.00
C38 Buddy Matthews 1.25 3.00
C39 FTR 2.00 5.00
C40 Rey Fenix 2.00 5.00
C41 Billy Gunn 2.00 5.00
C42 PAC 2.00 5.00
C43 The Acclaimed 1.50 4.00
C44 Nyla Rose 2.00 5.00
C45 MJF 6.00 15.00
C46 Brody King 1.25 3.00
C47 Blackpool Combat Club 3.00 8.00
C48 Powerhouse Hobbs 2.50 6.00
C49 Christian Cage 2.00 5.00
C50 Nick Jackson 3.00 8.00
C51 Dr. Britt Baker 5.00 12.00
C52 Penelope Ford 3.00 8.00
C53 Hangman Adam Page 5.00 12.00
C54 Angelo Parker 2.00 5.00
C55 Juice Robinson 1.25 3.00
C56 Julia Hart 3.00 8.00
C57 Anthony Bowens 1.25 3.00
C58 Trent Beretta 1.25 3.00
C59 Samoa Joe 2.50 6.00
C60 Toni Storm 3.00 8.00
C61 Switchblade Jay White 3.00 8.00
C62 RIHO 2.50 6.00
C63 QT Marshall 1.25 3.00
C64 Isiah Kassidy 1.50 4.00
C65 Tony Nese 1.50 4.00
C66 Dante Martin 1.50 4.00
C67 Ruby Soho 2.50 6.00
C68 Madison Rayne 2.50 6.00
C69 Cash Wheeler 1.50 4.00
C70 Danhausen 3.00 8.00
C71 Jon Moxley 3.00 8.00
C72 Orange Cassidy 4.00 10.00
C73 John Silver 1.50 4.00
C74 Max Caster 1.50 4.00
C75 Anna Jay 4.00 10.00
C76 Alex Reynolds 1.25 3.00
C77 Sting 5.00 12.00
C78 Jade Cargill 6.00 15.00
C79 Bryan Danielson 3.00 8.00
C80 Saraya 4.00 10.00
C81 Wheeler Yuta 2.50 6.00
C82 Hikaru Shida 4.00 10.00
C83 Tay Melo 3.00 8.00
C84 Chris Jericho 3.00 8.00
C85 The Blade 2.00 5.00
C86 Willow Nightingale 1.50 4.00
C87 Jack Perry 3.00 8.00
C88 Lance Archer 1.25 3.00
C89 Ricky Starks 1.25 3.00
C90 Athena 2.00 5.00
C91 Austin Gunn 1.50 4.00
C92 Evil Uno 1.50 4.00
C93 The Bunny 3.00 8.00
C94 Darby Allin 5.00 12.00
C95 The Butcher 2.00 5.00
C96 Wardlow 2.50 6.00
C97 Emi Sakura 2.00 5.00
C98 Jay Lethal 2.00 5.00
C99 Big Bill 1.50 4.00
C100 Mark Briscoe 1.50 4.00

2023 Upper Deck AEW We Are All Elite

*SILVER: .5X TO 1.2X BASIC CARDS
*GREEN/199: .75X TO 2X BASIC CARDS
*RED/50: 1.2X TO 3X BASIC CARDS
*PURPLE/25: UNPRICED DUE TO SCARCITY
*GOLD SPECTRUM/1: UNPRICED DUE TO SCARCITY
*P.P.BLACK/1: UNPRICED DUE TO SCARCITY
*P.P.CYAN/1: UNPRICED DUE TO SCARCITY
*P.P.MAGENTA/1: UNPRICED DUE TO SCARCITY
*P.P.YELLOW/1: UNPRICED DUE TO SCARCITY
STATED ODDS 1:1.5 HOBBY/EPACK
STATED ODDS 1:4.5 BLASTER
STATED ODDS 1:7 PACK WARS

AE1 Julia Hart 1.50 4.00
AE2 Keith Lee 1.00 2.50
AE3 Chris Jericho 1.50 4.00
AE4 HOOK 2.00 5.00
AE5 Dr. Britt Baker 2.50 6.00
AE6 Matt Hardy 1.25 3.00
AE7 Nyla Rose 1.00 2.50
AE8 Athena 1.00 2.50
AE9 Luchasaurus 1.00 2.50
AE10 Ruby Soho 1.25 3.00
AE11 Claudio Castagnoli .75 2.00
AE12 Powerhouse Hobbs 1.25 3.00
AE13 Adam Cole 1.50 4.00
AE14 PAC 1.00 2.50
AE15 Wheeler Yuta 1.25 3.00
AE16 Kenny Omega 2.50 6.00
AE17 Toni Storm 1.50 4.00
AE18 Jon Moxley 1.50 4.00
AE19 Kris Statlander 1.50 4.00
AE20 Anna Jay 2.00 5.00
AE21 Max Caster .75 2.00
AE22 Hangman Adam Page 2.50 6.00
AE23 Wardlow 1.25 3.00
AE24 Lee Moriarty 1.00 2.50
AE25 MJF 3.00 8.00
AE26 Bryan Danielson 1.50 4.00
AE27 Thunder Rosa 1.50 4.00
AE28 Ricky Starks .60 1.50
AE29 Jack Perry 1.50 4.00
AE30 Konosuke Takeshita 2.50 6.00
AE31 Sammy Guevara 1.50 4.00
AE32 Eddie Kingston 2.00 5.00
AE33 Samoa Joe 1.25 3.00
AE34 Scorpio Sky .75 2.00
AE35 Tay Melo 1.50 4.00
AE36 Lance Archer .60 1.50
AE37 Daniel Garcia .75 2.00
AE38 Jamie Hayter 1.50 4.00
AE39 Jade Cargill 3.00 8.00
AE40 Swerve Strickland 1.00 2.50

2023 Upper Deck AEW World Tour Lenticular

STATED ODDS 1:480 HOBBY/EPACK
STATED ODDS 1:180 BLASTER

WT1 Tay Melo 40.00 100.00
WT2 Claudio Castagnoli 15.00 40.00
WT3 Chris Jericho
WT4 PAC
WT5 Satnam Singh 12.00 30.00
WT6 Konosuke Takeshita
WT7 Malakai Black 20.00 50.00
WT8 RIHO 30.00 75.00
WT9 Jon Moxley 25.00 60.00
WT10 Kenny Omega 50.00 125.00
WT11 Dr. Britt Baker 75.00 200.00
WT12 Rush 12.00 30.00
WT13 Penta el Zero M 15.00 40.00
WT14 Angelico 12.00 30.00
WT15 Buddy Matthews 10.00 25.00
WT16 Jay White 20.00 50.00
WT17 Taya Valkyrie 25.00 60.00
WT18 Anthony Ogogo 25.00 60.00
WT19 Ethan Page 15.00 40.00
WT20 The Bunny 30.00 75.00
WT21 Thunder Rosa 25.00 60.00
WT22 Emi Sakura 15.00 40.00
WT23 Toni Storm 30.00 75.00
WT24 Jade Cargill 60.00 150.00
WT25 Jamie Hayter 60.00 150.00

2023 Upper Deck AEW Young Bucks

STATED ODDS 1:960 HOBBY/EPACK

YB1 Young Bucks 40.00 100.00
YB2 Young Bucks 40.00 100.00
YB3 Young Bucks 40.00 100.00
YB4 Young Bucks 40.00 100.00
YB5 Young Bucks 40.00 100.00

2023 Upper Deck AEW All In Promos

ALLAP Hangman Adam Page
ALLBB Dr. Britt Baker DMD
ALLDA Darby Allin
ALLOC Orange Cassidy
ALLTS Toni Storm

2022 Upper Deck AEW All Out Promos

AO1 Jon Moxley
AO2 Toni Storm
AO3 Darby Allin

2023 Upper Deck AEW Collision E-Pack

C1 CM Punk 12.00 30.00

2022 Upper Deck AEW Double or Nothing Promos

DNW Wardlow
DNAC Adam Cole
DNAJ Anna Jay
DNKS Kris Statlander
DNLH Leyla Hirsch
DNMB Malakai Black

2023 Upper Deck AEW Double or Nothing Promos

DNPH Powerhouse Hobbs
DNTG The Gunns
DNWN Willow Nightingale

2022 Upper Deck AEW Fan Fest Promos

FFAP Adam Page
FFBB Dr. Britt Baker DMD
FFCJ Chris Jericho
FFJB Jungle Boy
FFJC Jade Cargill
FFTR Thunder Rosa

2022 Upper Deck AEW Full Gear Promos

FG1 The Acclaimed
FG2 Saraya
FG3 Hook

2022 Upper Deck AEW Match Dated Moments

1 Hangman Adam Page 3.00 8.00
2 Jade Cargill 4.00 10.00
3 Sting/Darby Allin/Sammy Guevara 3.00 8.00
4 Dr. Britt Baker DMD 5.00 12.00
5 CM Punk S 10.00 25.00
6 Willam Regal G 25.00 60.00
7 Wardlow 2.00 5.00
8 Thunder Rosa 8.00 20.00
9 The Hardys 2.00 5.00

10 CM Punk	3.00	8.00
11 Adam Cole & Britt Baker S	6.00	15.00
12 Jericho Appreciation Society G	30.00	75.00
13 FTR	4.00	10.00
14 Jericho/Guevara/Suzuki	3.00	8.00
15 PAC	2.00	5.00
16 Jon Moxley	2.50	6.00
17 Orange Cassidy/Will Ospreay S	6.00	15.00
18 Allin/Sting/Takagi G	15.00	40.00
19 CM Punk	3.00	8.00
20 Toni Storm	2.50	6.00
21 Lionheart Chris Jericho	2.50	6.00
22 The Joker (MJF)	4.00	10.00
23 The Elite S	10.00	25.00
24 MJF G	40.00	100.00
25 Death Triangle		
26 Saraya	8.00	20.00
27 Danhausen	10.00	25.00
28 Jamie Hayter	6.00	15.00
29 MJF S	3.00	8.00
30 Jungle Boy G		

2023 Upper Deck AEW Match Dated Moments Special Edition Squared Circle Moments Achievements

SCM1 Kenny Omega
SCM2 MJF
SCM3 Eddie Kingston
SCM4 Christian Cage
SCM5 Toni Storm

2021 Upper Deck AEW Happy Holidays Promo

UDHC2021 Omega/Baker/Cargill/Punk

2022 Upper Deck AEW New Arrivals

*SILVER: .6X TO 1.5X BASIC CARDS

1 Athena	3.00	8.00
2 Stokely Hathaway	2.00	5.00
3 Claudio Castagnoli	4.00	10.00
4 Madison Rayne	3.00	8.00
5 Trustbusters	2.50	6.00
6 W. Morrissey	2.00	5.00
7 Saraya	5.00	12.00
8 Rush	2.00	5.00
9 Renee Paquette	2.00	5.00
10 Willow Nightingale	3.00	8.00
11 Jeff Jarrett	2.00	5.00
12 Bandido	3.00	8.00
13 Konosuke Takeshita	3.00	8.00
14 AR Fox	2.00	5.00
15 Action Andretti	6.00	15.00

2022 Upper Deck AEW New Arrivals First Encounter Achievements

FEA1 Danhausen	10.00	25.00
FEA2 Keith Lee and Swerve Strickland	8.00	20.00
FEA3 Claudio Castagnoli	4.00	10.00
FEA4 Athena	10.00	25.00
FEA5 Saraya	12.00	30.00
FEA6 Samoa Joe	8.00	20.00

2023 Upper Deck AEW New Arrivals First Encounter Achievements

FE1 Komander
FE2 Adam Copeland

2024 Upper Deck AEW New Arrivals

1 Deonna Purrazzo
2 Bounty Hunter Brian Keith

2023 Upper Deck AEW Oversized Convention Exclusives

GC23 Brandon Cutler GEN CON
NSCC Skye Blue/200* NSCC

2023 Upper Deck AEW Revolution Promos

REV1 Samoa Joe
REV2 Death Triangle
REV3 Jamie Hayter
REV4 Julia Hart

2021 Upper Deck AEW Spectrum

*DARK/99: .6X TO 1.5X BASIC CARDS
*RED/50: .75X TO 2X BASIC CARDS
*GREEN/25: UNPRICED DUE TO SCARCITY
*BEACH/10: UNPRICED DUE TO SCARCITY
*GOLD/1: UNPRICED DUE TO SCARCITY

1 Kenny Omega RC	6.00	15.00
2 Hikaru Shida RC	2.50	6.00
3 Joey Janela RC	1.50	4.00
4 Tay Conti	1.50	4.00
5 Isiah Kassidy RC	1.25	3.00
6 Jake Hager	.60	1.50
7 Rey Fenix RC	1.25	3.00
8 Anthony Bowens RC	1.50	4.00
9 Sonny Kiss RC	.75	2.00
10 Hangman Adam Page RC	4.00	10.00
11 MJF RC	10.00	25.00
12 Tony Schiavone	.50	1.25
13 Ricky Starks RC	1.25	3.00
14 Serpentico RC	.75	2.00
15 Christopher Daniels	.60	1.50
16 Wardlow RC	2.00	5.00
17 CM Punk	2.00	5.00
18 Trent?	.50	1.25
19 Penta el Zero M RC	1.50	4.00
20 Frankie Kazarian	.50	1.25
21 Chuck Taylor RC	.75	2.00
22 Darby Allin RC	3.00	8.00
23 Evil Uno RC	1.25	3.00
24 Paul Wight	.75	2.00
25 Leva Bates RC	.75	2.00
26 Powerhouse Hobbs RC	1.25	3.00
27 Aubrey Edwards RC	2.00	5.00
28 The Butcher RC	.75	2.00
29 Nyla Rose RC	1.50	4.00
30 Yuka Sakazaki RC	.75	2.00
31 Excalibur RC	.75	2.00
32 Cody Rhodes	1.25	3.00
33 Billy Gunn	.50	1.25
34 Marq Quen RC	.75	2.00
35 Ortiz RC	.75	2.00
36 Marko Stunt RC	.75	2.00
37 Malakai Black	1.00	2.50
38 Sting	1.50	4.00
39 Sammy Guevara RC	2.00	5.00
40 Miro	.75	2.00
41 The Bunny	1.00	2.50
42 Penelope Ford RC	3.00	8.00
43 Kip Sabian RC	1.00	2.50
44 The Blade RC	.75	2.00
45 Cash Wheeler	.60	1.50
46 Santana RC	.75	2.00
47 John Silver RC	.75	2.00
48 Matt Jackson RC	1.50	4.00
49 Colt Cabana RC	.75	2.00
50 RIHO RC	1.25	3.00
51 Eddie Kingston RC	2.00	5.00
52 Ryo Mizunami RC	.75	2.00
53 Stu Grayson RC	.75	2.00
54 Matt Sydal	.40	1.00
55 Jon Moxley	1.00	2.50
56 Luchasaurus RC	2.50	6.00
57 Nick Jackson RC	1.50	4.00
58 Jade Cargill RC	5.00	12.00
59 Adam Cole	1.25	3.00
60 Griff Garrison RC	.75	2.00
61 Pres10 Vance RC	.75	2.00
62 Red Velvet RC	.75	2.00
63 Bryan Danielson	1.50	4.00
64 Orange Cassidy RC	2.00	5.00
65 Serena Deeb	.40	1.00
66 Dax Harwood	.60	1.50
67 Jim Ross	1.00	2.50
68 Leyla Hirsch RC	1.25	3.00
69 Brandi Rhodes	2.00	5.00
70 Diamante RC	.75	2.00
71 Austin Gunn RC	.75	2.00
72 Shawn Spears	.60	1.50
73 Luther RC	.75	2.00
74 Scorpio Sky RC	1.25	3.00
75 Chris Jericho	1.50	4.00
76 Jungle Boy RC	3.00	8.00
77 Brian Cage RC	.75	2.00
78 Max Caster RC	1.25	3.00
79 Thunder Rosa RC	5.00	12.00
80 Ethan Page RC	1.50	4.00
81 Dustin Rhodes	.75	2.00
82 Lee Johnson RC	.75	2.00
83 Dr. Britt Baker RC	2.50	6.00
84 Lance Archer	1.00	2.50
85 Kris Statlander RC	1.25	3.00
86 Matt Hardy	.75	2.00
87 Christian Cage	.60	1.50
88 Taz	.50	1.25
89 Alex Reynolds RC	.75	2.00
90 PAC	.75	2.00

2021 Upper Deck AEW Spectrum Autographed Banner Year Relics

STATED PRINT RUN 5 SER.#'d SETS
UNPRICED DUE TO SCARCITY

BY1 Chris Jericho
BY2 Chris Jericho
BY3 Chris Jericho
BY4 Chris Jericho
BY5 Chris Jericho
BY6 Chris Jericho
BY7 Chris Jericho
BY8 Chris Jericho

2021 Upper Deck AEW Spectrum Autographed Diamond Battle Royale Relics

STATED PRINT RUN 12 SER.#'d SETS
UNPRICED DUE TO SCARCITY

DBR1 MJF
DBR2 Hangman Adam Page
DBR3 Sammy Guevara
DBR4 John Silver
DBR5 Alex Reynolds
DBR6 Isiah Kassidy
DBR7 Marq Quen
DBR8 Matt Hardy
DBR9 Scorpio Sky
DBR10 Shawn Spears
DBR11 Orange Cassidy
DBR12 Kip Sabian
DBR13 Miro
DBR14 Wardlow
DBR15 Jungle Boy

2021 Upper Deck AEW Spectrum Autographed Memorabilia

*DARK/10: UNPRICED DUE TO SCARCITY
*GOLD/1: UNPRICED DUE TO SCARCITY
STATED PRINT RUN 20 SER.#'d SETS

1 Kenny Omega
2 Hikaru Shida
3 Joey Janela
4 Tay Conti
5 Isiah Kassidy
6 Jake Hager
7 Rey Fenix
8 Anthony Bowens
9 Sonny Kiss
10 Hangman Adam Page
11 MJF
12 Tony Schiavone
13 Ricky Starks
14 Serpentico
15 Christopher Daniels
16 Wardlow
17 CM Punk
18 Trent?
19 Penta el Zero M
20 Frankie Kazarian
21 Chuck Taylor
22 Darby Allin
23 Evil Uno
24 Paul Wight
25 Leva Bates
26 Powerhouse Hobbs
27 Aubrey Edwards
28 The Butcher
29 Nyla Rose
31 Excalibur
32 Cody Rhodes
33 Billy Gunn
34 Marq Quen
35 Ortiz
36 Marko Stunt
37 Malakai Black
38 Sting
39 Sammy Guevara
40 Miro
41 The Bunny
42 Penelope Ford
43 Kip Sabian
44 The Blade
45 Cash Wheeler
46 Santana
47 John Silver
48 Matt Jackson
49 Colt Cabana
50 RIHO
51 Eddie Kingston
53 Stu Grayson
55 Jon Moxley
56 Luchasaurus
57 Nick Jackson
58 Jade Cargill
60 Griff Garrison
61 Pres10 Vance
62 Red Velvet
64 Orange Cassidy
65 Serena Deeb
66 Dax Harwood
67 Jim Ross
68 Leyla Hirsch
69 Brandi Rhodes
70 Diamante
71 Austin Gunn
72 Shawn Spears
73 Luther
74 Scorpio Sky
75 Chris Jericho
76 Jungle Boy
77 Brian Cage
78 Max Caster
79 Thunder Rosa
80 Ethan Page
81 Dustin Rhodes
82 Lee Johnson
83 Dr. Britt Baker
84 Lance Archer
85 Kris Statlander
86 Matt Hardy
87 Christian Cage
88 Taz
89 Alex Reynolds
90 PAC

2021 Upper Deck AEW Spectrum Autographed On the Mat Relics

STATED PRINT RUN 25 SER.#'d SETS

OTM1 Tay Conti		
OTM2 Ethan Page	60.00	150.00
OTM3 Penelope Ford	75.00	200.00
OTM4 Chuck Taylor		
OTM5 The Bunny	40.00	100.00
OTM6 Kris Statlander	60.00	150.00
OTM7 Austin Gunn		
OTM8 Diamante		
OTM9 Red Velvet	15.00	40.00
OTM10 Jake Hager		
OTM11 Dr. Britt Baker	125.00	300.00
OTM12 Jungle Boy	30.00	75.00
OTM13 Marko Stunt		
OTM14 Anthony Bowens	30.00	75.00
OTM15 Pres10 Vance	20.00	50.00
OTM16 Trent?		
OTM17 Lee Johnson		
OTM18 Jade Cargill	60.00	150.00
OTM19 Angelico		
OTM20 Ricky Starks	30.00	75.00
OTM21 Christopher Daniels	12.00	30.00
OTM22 Powerhouse Hobbs	15.00	40.00
OTM23 Max Caster	50.00	125.00
OTM24 RIHO	25.00	60.00

2021 Upper Deck AEW Spectrum Autographed Ring Generals Relics

STATED PRINT RUN 16 SER.#'d SETS
UNPRICED DUE TO SCARCITY

RL1 Rey Fenix
RL2 Cody Rhodes
RL3 Darby Allin
RL4 PAC
RL5 Thunder Rosa
RL6 Nick Jackson
RL7 Billy Gunn
RL8 Frankie Kazarian
RL9 Serena Deeb
RL10 Brian Cage
RL11 Powerhouse Hobbs
RL12 Jon Moxley
RL13 Sting
RL14 Hikaru Shida
RL15 Ortiz
RL16 Orange Cassidy
RL17 Matt Jackson
RL18 Paul Wight
RL19 MJF
RL20 Kenny Omega
RL21 Dr. Britt Baker
RL22 Miro
RL23 Santana
RL24 Chris Jericho

2021 Upper Deck AEW Spectrum Autographed Table for 2 Relics

STATED PRINT RUN 12 SER.#'d SETS
UNPRICED DUE TO SCARCITY

T21 PAC/A.Page
T22 J.Moxley/E.Kingston
T23 C.Rhodes/D.Rhodes
T24 B.Baker/T.Schiavone
T25 H.Shida/Abadon
T26 D.Allin/R.Starks
T27 M.Hardy/S.Guevara
T28 R.Velvet/J.Cargill
T29 N.Rose/Riho
T210 Sting/L.Archer
T211 C.Cage/K.Omega
T212 O.Cassidy/Miro
T213 MJF/C.Jericho

2021 Upper Deck AEW Spectrum Autographed Table for 4 Relics

STATED PRINT RUN 12 SER.#'d SETS
UNPRICED DUE TO SCARCITY

T41 Sting/Allin/Cage/Starks
T42 Wheeler/Harwood/Santana/Ortiz
T43 Miro/Sabian/Cassidy/Taylor
T44 Fenix/el Zero/Jacksons
T45 Butcher/Blade/Luchasaurus/Perry
T46 Pillman Jr./Garrison/Bowens/Caster
T47 Kassidy/Quen/Reynolds/Silver
T48 Page/Sky/Uno/Grayson

2021 Upper Deck AEW Spectrum Autographs

*DARK/25: UNPRICED DUE TO SCARCITY
*BEACH/5: UNPRICED DUE TO SCARCITY
*GOLD/1: UNPRICED DUE TO SCARCITY
*P.P.BLACK/1: UNPRICED DUE TO SCARCITY
*P.P.CYAN/1: UNPRICED DUE TO SCARCITY
*P.P.MAGENTA/1: UNPRICED DUE TO SCARCITY
*P.P.YELLOW/1: UNPRICED DUE TO SCARCITY
GROUP A ODDS 1:44
GROUP B ODDS 1:16
GROUP C ODDS 1:6
GROUP D ODDS 1:3
STATED ODDS 1:7 HOBBY/EPACK

1 Kenny Omega B 75.00 200.00
2 Hikaru Shida A 40.00 100.00
3 Joey Janela D 8.00 20.00
4 Tay Conti C 30.00 75.00
5 Isiah Kassidy D 8.00 20.00
6 Jake Hager B 10.00 25.00
7 Rey Fenix B 20.00 50.00
8 Anthony Bowens D 20.00 50.00
9 Sonny Kiss D 10.00 25.00
10 Hangman Adam Page A 50.00 125.00
11 MJF A 200.00 500.00
12 Tony Schiavone D 15.00 40.00
13 Ricky Starks D 30.00 75.00
14 Serpentico D 10.00 25.00
15 Christopher Daniels D 12.00 30.00
16 Wardlow D 30.00 75.00
17 CM Punk A 125.00 300.00
18 Trent? C 10.00 25.00
19 Penta el Zero M C 30.00 75.00
20 Frankie Kazarian C 12.00 30.00
21 Chuck Taylor D 12.00 30.00
22 Darby Allin B 60.00 150.00
23 Evil Uno D 12.00 30.00
24 Paul Wight B 12.00 30.00
25 Leva Bates D 10.00 25.00
26 Powerhouse Hobbs C 20.00 50.00
27 Aubrey Edwards D 30.00 75.00
28 The Butcher C 8.00 20.00
29 Nyla Rose C 12.00 30.00
30 Yuka Sakazaki B 12.00 30.00
31 Excalibur D 12.00 30.00
32 Cody Rhodes A 100.00 250.00
33 Billy Gunn C 12.00 30.00
34 Marq Quen D 8.00 20.00
35 Ortiz C 10.00 25.00
36 Marko Stunt D 8.00 20.00
37 Malakai Black C 30.00 75.00
38 Sting B 60.00 150.00
39 Sammy Guevara B 25.00 60.00
40 Miro B 10.00 25.00
41 The Bunny D 30.00 75.00
42 Penelope Ford D 40.00 100.00
43 Kip Sabian D 12.00 30.00
44 The Blade D 8.00 20.00
45 Cash Wheeler D 15.00 40.00
46 Santana C 12.00 30.00
47 John Silver D 10.00 25.00
48 Matt Jackson B 20.00 50.00
49 Colt Cabana D 12.00 30.00
50 RIHO D 30.00 75.00
51 Eddie Kingston C 30.00 75.00
53 Stu Grayson C 12.00 30.00
54 Matt Sydal C 8.00 20.00
55 Jon Moxley A 50.00 125.00
56 Luchasaurus D 30.00 75.00
57 Nick Jackson B 20.00 50.00
58 Jade Cargill D 75.00 200.00
59 Adam Cole A 40.00 100.00
60 Griff Garrison D 12.00 30.00
61 Pres10 Vance D 12.00 30.00
62 Red Velvet D 15.00 40.00
63 Bryan Danielson A 40.00 100.00
64 Orange Cassidy B 40.00 100.00
65 Serena Deeb D 12.00 30.00
66 Dax Harwood D 15.00 40.00
67 Jim Ross C 15.00 40.00
68 Leyla Hirsch D 10.00 25.00
69 Brandi Rhodes C 20.00 50.00
70 Diamante D 12.00 30.00
71 Austin Gunn D 12.00 30.00
72 Shawn Spears D 8.00 20.00
73 Luther D 15.00 40.00
74 Scorpio Sky C 8.00 20.00
75 Chris Jericho B 60.00 150.00
76 Jungle Boy D 25.00 60.00
77 Brian Cage C 12.00 30.00
78 Max Caster D 25.00 60.00
79 Thunder Rosa C 60.00 150.00
80 Ethan Page D 30.00 75.00
81 Dustin Rhodes C 12.00 30.00
82 Lee Johnson D 10.00 25.00
83 Dr. Britt Baker C 75.00 200.00
84 Lance Archer C 10.00 25.00
85 Kris Statlander D 50.00 125.00
86 Matt Hardy B 15.00 40.00
87 Christian Cage C 15.00 40.00
88 Taz C 10.00 25.00
89 Alex Reynolds C 12.00 30.00
90 PAC C 15.00 40.00

2021 Upper Deck AEW Spectrum Banner Year Relics

RANDOMLY INSERTED INTO PACKS

BY1 Chris Jericho 5/25/20 15.00 40.00
BY2 Chris Jericho 9/5/20 15.00 40.00
BY3 Chris Jericho 10/7/20 15.00 40.00
BY4 Chris Jericho 11/7/20 15.00 40.00
BY5 Chris Jericho 3/7/21 15.00 40.00
BY6 Chris Jericho 4/14/21 15.00 40.00
BY7 Chris Jericho 5/5/21 15.00 40.00
BY8 Chris Jericho 5/30/21 15.00 40.00

2021 Upper Deck AEW Spectrum Chair Shots

STATED ODDS 1:8 HOBBY/EPACK

CS1 Shawn Spears 3.00 8.00
CS2 Lance Archer 5.00 12.00
CS3 Dustin Rhodes 4.00 10.00
CS4 Dr. Britt Baker 10.00 25.00
CS5 Matt Hardy 4.00 10.00
CS6 Santana 3.00 8.00
CS7 Miro 4.00 10.00
CS8 Jon Moxley 5.00 12.00
CS9 The Blade 3.00 8.00
CS10 Penta el Zero M 5.00 12.00
CS11 Thunder Rosa 8.00 20.00
CS12 Sammy Guevara 5.00 12.00
CS13 Darby Allin 12.00 30.00
CS14 The Butcher 3.00 8.00
CS15 Joey Janela 2.00 5.00
CS16 Eddie Kingston 6.00 15.00
CS17 Ethan Page 5.00 12.00
CS18 Chris Jericho 8.00 20.00
CS19 Ortiz 3.00 8.00
CS20 Kenny Omega 12.00 30.00

2021 Upper Deck AEW Spectrum Diamond Battle Royale Relics

STATED PRINT RUN 25 SER.#'d SETS

DBR1 MJF 75.00 200.00
DBR2 Hangman Adam Page 75.00 200.00
DBR3 Sammy Guevara 30.00 75.00
DBR4 John Silver 25.00 60.00
DBR5 Alex Reynolds 20.00 50.00
DBR6 Isiah Kassidy 20.00 50.00
DBR7 Marq Quen 20.00 50.00
DBR8 Matt Hardy 25.00 60.00
DBR9 Scorpio Sky 25.00 60.00
DBR10 Shawn Spears 20.00 50.00
DBR11 Orange Cassidy 40.00 100.00
DBR12 Kip Sabian 30.00 75.00
DBR13 Miro 25.00 60.00
DBR14 Wardlow 60.00 150.00
DBR15 Jungle Boy 60.00 150.00

2021 Upper Deck AEW Spectrum Full Gear

STATED ODDS 1:4 HOBBY/EPACK

FG1 Jon Moxley 8.00 20.00
FG2 Dr. Britt Baker 20.00 50.00
FG3 Orange Cassidy 6.00 15.00
FG4 Darby Allin 12.00 30.00
FG5 MJF 15.00 40.00
FG6 Hangman Adam Page 12.00 30.00
FG7 RIHO 10.00 25.00
FG8 Nyla Rose 6.00 15.00
FG9 Cash Wheeler 6.00 15.00
FG10 Dax Harwood 6.00 15.00
FG11 Serena Deeb 5.00 12.00
FG12 Matt Jackson 12.00 30.00
FG13 Nick Jackson 12.00 30.00
FG14 Eddie Kingston 15.00 40.00
FG15 John Silver 5.00 12.00
FG16 Hikaru Shida 12.00 30.00
FG17 Chris Jericho 10.00 25.00
FG18 Cody Rhodes 12.00 30.00
FG19 Matt Hardy 5.00 12.00
FG20 Kenny Omega 30.00 75.00

2021 Upper Deck AEW Spectrum Memorabilia

*DARK/25: UNPRICED DUE TO SCARCITY
*GOLD/1: UNPRICED DUE TO SCARCITY
STATED ODDS 1:1 HOBBY/EPACK

1 Kenny Omega 8.00 20.00
2 Hikaru Shida 4.00 10.00
3 Joey Janela 1.25 3.00
4 Tay Conti 5.00 12.00
5 Isiah Kassidy 1.50 4.00
6 Jake Hager 2.00 5.00
7 Rey Fenix 3.00 8.00
8 Anthony Bowens 1.25 3.00
9 Sonny Kiss 1.25 3.00
10 Hangman Adam Page 8.00 20.00
11 MJF 8.00 20.00
12 Tony Schiavone 1.50 4.00
13 Ricky Starks 3.00 8.00
14 Serpentico 1.25 3.00
15 Christopher Daniels 2.00 5.00
16 Wardlow 2.50 6.00
17 CM Punk 6.00 15.00
18 Trent? 1.50 4.00
19 Penta el Zero M 3.00 8.00
20 Frankie Kazarian 1.50 4.00
21 Chuck Taylor 1.50 4.00
22 Darby Allin 8.00 20.00
23 Evil Uno 2.50 6.00
24 Paul Wight 2.50 6.00
25 Leva Bates 1.25 3.00
26 Powerhouse Hobbs 2.50 6.00
27 Aubrey Edwards 3.00 8.00
28 The Butcher 2.00 5.00
29 Nyla Rose 2.50 6.00
31 Excalibur 1.25 3.00
32 Cody Rhodes 4.00 10.00
33 Billy Gunn 1.50 4.00
34 Marq Quen 1.50 4.00
35 Ortiz 2.00 5.00
36 Marko Stunt 1.25 3.00
37 Malakai Black 3.00 8.00
38 Sting 5.00 12.00
39 Sammy Guevara 3.00 8.00
40 Miro 2.50 6.00
41 The Bunny 3.00 8.00
42 Penelope Ford 2.00 5.00
43 Kip Sabian 2.50 6.00
44 The Blade 2.00 5.00
45 Cash Wheeler 2.00 5.00
46 Santana 2.00 5.00
47 John Silver 1.25 3.00
48 Matt Jackson 5.00 12.00
49 Colt Cabana 1.50 4.00
50 RIHO 5.00 12.00
51 Eddie Kingston 4.00 10.00
53 Stu Grayson 1.25 3.00
55 Jon Moxley 3.00 8.00
56 Luchasaurus 4.00 10.00
57 Nick Jackson 5.00 12.00
58 Jade Cargill 6.00 15.00
60 Griff Garrison 1.25 3.00
61 Pres10 Vance 1.25 3.00
62 Red Velvet 1.25 3.00
64 Orange Cassidy 3.00 8.00
65 Serena Deeb 1.25 3.00
66 Dax Harwood 2.00 5.00
67 Jim Ross 3.00 8.00
68 Leyla Hirsch 1.50 4.00
69 Brandi Rhodes 6.00 15.00
70 Diamante 1.25 3.00
71 Austin Gunn 1.50 4.00
72 Shawn Spears 2.00 5.00
73 Luther 1.25 3.00
74 Scorpio Sky 1.25 3.00
75 Chris Jericho 5.00 12.00
76 Jungle Boy 5.00 12.00
77 Brian Cage 1.50 4.00
78 Max Caster 1.50 4.00
79 Thunder Rosa 5.00 12.00
80 Ethan Page 3.00 8.00
81 Dustin Rhodes 2.50 6.00
82 Lee Johnson 1.25 3.00
83 Dr. Britt Baker 6.00 15.00
84 Lance Archer 3.00 8.00
85 Kris Statlander 2.00 5.00
86 Matt Hardy 2.50 6.00
87 Christian Cage 2.00 5.00
88 Taz 1.50 4.00
89 Alex Reynolds 1.25 3.00
90 PAC 2.50 6.00

2021 Upper Deck AEW Spectrum On the Mat Relics

RANDOMLY INSERTED INTO PACKS

OTM1 Tay Conti 10.00 25.00
OTM2 Ethan Page 6.00 15.00

OTM3 Penelope Ford	4.00	10.00
OTM4 Chuck Taylor	3.00	8.00
OTM5 The Bunny	6.00	15.00
OTM6 Kris Statlander	4.00	10.00
OTM7 Austin Gunn	3.00	8.00
OTM8 Diamante	2.50	6.00
OTM9 Red Velvet	2.50	6.00
OTM10 Jake Hager	4.00	10.00
OTM11 Dr. Britt Baker	12.00	30.00
OTM12 Jungle Boy	10.00	25.00
OTM13 Marko Stunt	2.50	6.00
OTM14 Anthony Bowens	2.50	6.00
OTM15 Pres10 Vance	2.50	6.00
OTM16 Trent?	3.00	8.00
OTM17 Lee Johnson	2.50	6.00
OTM18 Jade Cargill	12.00	30.00
OTM19 Angelico	2.50	6.00
OTM20 Ricky Starks	6.00	15.00
OTM21 Christopher Daniels	4.00	10.00
OTM22 Powerhouse Hobbs	5.00	12.00
OTM23 Max Caster	3.00	8.00
OTM24 RIHO	10.00	25.00

2021 Upper Deck AEW Spectrum Ring Generals Relics

STATED PRINT RUN 50 SER.#'d SETS

RL1 Rey Fenix	15.00	40.00
RL2 Cody Rhodes	40.00	100.00
RL3 Darby Allin	30.00	75.00
RL4 PAC	20.00	50.00
RL5 Thunder Rosa	30.00	75.00
RL6 Nick Jackson	25.00	60.00
RL7 Billy Gunn	10.00	25.00
RL8 Frankie Kazarian	12.00	30.00
RL9 Serena Deeb	10.00	25.00
RL10 Brian Cage	15.00	40.00
RL11 Powerhouse Hobbs	15.00	40.00
RL12 Jon Moxley	15.00	40.00
RL13 Sting	40.00	100.00
RL14 Hikaru Shida	25.00	60.00
RL15 Ortiz	10.00	25.00
RL16 Orange Cassidy	20.00	50.00
RL17 Matt Jackson	20.00	50.00
RL18 Paul Wight	10.00	25.00
RL19 MJF	75.00	200.00
RL20 Kenny Omega	40.00	100.00
RL21 Dr. Britt Baker	40.00	100.00
RL22 Miro	12.00	30.00
RL23 Santana	12.00	30.00
RL24 Chris Jericho	30.00	75.00

2021 Upper Deck AEW Spectrum Table for 2 Relics

STATED ODDS 1:9 HOBBY/EPACK

T21 PAC/A.Page	15.00	40.00
T22 J.Moxley/E.Kingston	15.00	40.00
T23 C.Rhodes/D.Rhodes	30.00	75.00
T24 B.Baker/T.Schiavone	20.00	50.00
T25 H.Shida/Abadon	15.00	40.00
T26 D.Allin/R.Starks	20.00	50.00
T27 M.Hardy/S.Guevara	15.00	40.00
T28 R.Velvet/J.Cargill	30.00	75.00
T29 N.Rose/Riho	15.00	40.00
T210 Sting/L.Archer	25.00	60.00
T211 C.Cage/K.Omega	30.00	75.00
T212 O.Cassidy/Miro	15.00	40.00
T213 MJF/C.Jericho	20.00	50.00

2021 Upper Deck AEW Spectrum Table for 4 Relics

*GOLD/12: UNPRICED DUE TO SCARCITY
STATED ODDS 1:36 HOBBY/EPACK

T41 Sting/Allin/Cage/Starks	50.00	125.00
T42 Wheeler/Harwood/Santana/Ortiz	20.00	50.00
T43 Miro/Sabian/Cassidy/Taylor	12.00	30.00
T44 Fenix/el Zero/Jacksons	15.00	40.00
T45 Butcher/Blade/Luchasaurus/Perry	12.00	30.00
T46 Pillman Jr./Garrison/Bowens/Caster	12.00	30.00
T47 Kassidy/Quen/Reynolds/Silver	12.00	30.00
T48 Page/Sky/Uno/Grayson	20.00	50.00

2022 Upper Deck AEW Spectrum Revolution Fan Fest Promo Sheet

FF1 Conti/Page/MJF/Punk/Cover
Danielson/Cargill/Perry/Baker

2022 Upper Deck AEW Spectrum Revolution Fan Fest Promos

FF1 Tay Conti
FF2 Hangman Adam Page
FF3 MJF
FF4 CM Punk
FF5 Bryan Danielson
FF6 Jade Cargill
FF7 Jungle Boy
FF8 Dr. Britt Baker DMD
NNO Cover Card

2022 Upper Deck Allure AEW

*PURPLE DIAMOND/10: UNPRICED DUE TO SCARCITY
*GOLDEN TREASURES/1: UNPRICED DUE TO SCARCITY
*P.P.BLACK/1: UNPRICED DUE TO SCARCITY
*P.P.CYAN/1: UNPRICED DUE TO SCARCITY
*P.P.MAGENTA/1: UNPRICED DUE TO SCARCITY
*P.P.YELLOW/1: UNPRICED DUE TO SCARCITY
HORIZONTAL ODDS 1:2 HOBBY/EPACK/BLASTER
STAR FUTURES ODDS 1:2 HOBBY/EPACK/BLASTER

1 Adam Cole	1.00	2.50
2 Hangman Adam Page	1.50	4.00
3 Jade Cargill	1.50	4.00
4 Sammy Guevara	1.00	2.50
5 Dr. Britt Baker	1.25	3.00
6 Darby Allin	1.50	4.00
7 Keith Lee	.75	2.00
8 Kenny Omega	1.50	4.00
9 Powerhouse Hobbs	.60	1.50
10 Jack Perry	1.00	2.50
11 Red Velvet	.50	1.25
12 Tay Melo	1.25	3.00
13 Serena Deeb	.30	.75
14 Thunder Rosa	.75	2.00
15 Julia Hart RC	.75	2.00
16 Wheeler Yuta RC	1.25	3.00
17 Bryan Danielson	1.25	3.00
18 CM Punk	1.50	4.00
19 MJF	1.50	4.00
20 Anthony Ogogo RC	.30	.75
21 Eddie Kingston	1.00	2.50
22 Orange Cassidy	1.00	2.50
23 HOOK RC	1.25	3.00
24 Alex Reynolds	.30	.75
25 Danhausen RC	1.25	3.00
26 Anthony Bowens	.40	1.00
27 Samoa Joe	.60	1.50
28 Preston Vance	.30	.75
29 Ethan Page	.75	2.00
30 Konosuke Takeshita RC	.30	.75
31 Sting	1.25	3.00
32 Chris Jericho	1.25	3.00
33 Hikaru Shida	.75	2.00
34 Chuck Taylor	.30	.75
35 Lee Moriarty RC	.30	.75
36 Dante Martin RC	.30	.75
37 Jeff Jarrett	.60	1.50
38 Dax Harwood	.50	1.25
39 Jay Lethal	.50	1.25
40 Kyle O'Reilly	.30	.75
41 Evil Uno	.60	1.50
42 Emi Sakura RC	.30	.75
43 Satnam Singh RC	.30	.75
44 Yuka Sakazaki	.30	.75
45 Colten Gunn RC	.30	.75
46 Isiah Kassidy	.30	.75
47 Claudio Castagnoli	.30	.75
48 Lance Archer	.75	2.00
49 John Silver	.30	.75
50 Anna Jay	1.25	3.00
51 Swerve Strickland	.40	1.00
52 Andrade El Idolo	.40	1.00
53 Kris Statlander	.60	1.50
54 Daniel Garcia RC	.40	1.00
55 Luchasaurus	.60	1.50
56 Malakai Black	.75	2.00
57 Austin Gunn	.30	.75
58 Marq Quen	.40	1.00
59 Ricky Starks	.60	1.50
60 Matt Jackson	.75	2.00
61 PAC	.60	1.50
62 The Butcher	.30	.75
63 Dustin Rhodes	.60	1.50
64 Nick Jackson	.75	2.00
65 Ortiz	.60	1.50
66 Skye Blue RC	3.00	8.00
67 Jamie Hayter RC	1.50	4.00
68 Penelope Ford	1.50	4.00
69 Penta el Zero M	.75	2.00
70 QT Marshall	.40	1.00
71 Rey Fenix	.75	2.00
72 Matt Hardy	.60	1.50
73 RIHO	.60	1.50
74 Ruby Soho	.60	1.50
75 Jake Hager	.40	1.00
76 Scorpio Sky	.60	1.50
77 Trent Beretta	.40	1.00
78 Cash Wheeler	.50	1.25
79 Christian Cage	.50	1.25
80 Nyla Rose	.60	1.50
81 Jon Moxley	.75	2.00
82 Wardlow	.75	2.00
83 The Bunny	.60	1.50
84 Max Caster	.40	1.00
85 Abadon	.40	1.00
86 Matt Menard RC	.30	.75
87 Toni Storm	1.25	3.00
88 The Blade	.30	.75
89 Brody King RC	.40	1.00
90 Jim Ross	.75	2.00
91 Excalibur	.30	.75
92 Tony Nese	.30	.75
93 Taz	.40	1.00
94 Bryce Remsburg RC	.30	.75
95 Aubrey Edwards	.60	1.50
96 Rick Knox RC	.30	.75
97 Buddy Matthews	.50	1.25
98 Angelo Parker RC	.30	.75
99 Stokely Hathaway	.30	.75
100 Athena	.40	1.00
101 Adam Cole	1.00	2.50
102 Claudio Castagnoli	.50	1.25
103 Ricky Starks	1.00	2.50
104 Chris Jericho	2.00	5.00
105 Powerhouse Hobbs	1.00	2.50
106 Hangman Adam Page	2.50	6.00
107 Jon Moxley	1.25	3.00
108 Sammy Guevara	1.50	4.00
109 Dr. Britt Baker	2.00	5.00
110 Jade Cargill	2.50	6.00
111 Red Velvet	.75	2.00
112 Penta el Zero M	1.25	3.00
113 Kris Statlander	1.00	2.50
114 Thunder Rosa	1.25	3.00
115 Anna Jay	2.00	5.00
116 Bryan Danielson	2.00	5.00
117 CM Punk	2.50	6.00
118 MJF	2.50	6.00
119 Darby Allin	2.50	6.00
120 Sting	2.00	5.00
121 Orange Cassidy	1.50	4.00
122 Kenny Omega	2.50	6.00
123 Hikaru Shida	1.25	3.00
124 Jack Perry	1.50	4.00
125 Keith Lee	1.25	3.00
126 Anthony Ogogo	.50	1.25
127 Jade Cargill	2.50	6.00
128 Jamie Hayter	2.50	6.00
129 Darby Allin	2.50	6.00
130 Austin Gunn	.50	1.25
131 Abadon	.60	1.50
132 Dante Martin	.50	1.25
133 Kris Statlander	1.00	2.50
134 Wheeler Yuta	2.00	5.00
135 Wardlow	1.25	3.00
136 Anna Jay	2.00	5.00
137 Tay Melo	2.00	5.00
138 Daniel Garcia	.60	1.50
139 Isiah Kassidy	.50	1.25
140 Lee Moriarty	.50	1.25
141 Skye Blue	2.00	5.00
142 HOOK	2.00	5.00
143 Colten Gunn	.50	1.25
144 Marq Quen	.60	1.50
145 Konosuke Takeshita	.50	1.25
146 Yuka Sakazaki	.50	1.25
147 MJF	2.50	6.00
148 Julia Hart	1.25	3.00
149 Satnam Singh	.50	1.25
150 Jack Perry	1.50	4.00

2022 Upper Deck Allure AEW Autographs

*BLUE/35: .6X TO 1.5X BASIC CARDS
*PURPLE DIAMOND/10: UNPRICED DUE TO SCARCITY
*GOLDEN TREASURES/1: UNPRICED DUE TO SCARCITY
STATED ODDS 1:60 HOBBY/EPACK
STATED ODDS 1:240 BLASTER

1 Adam Cole	25.00	60.00
2 Hangman Adam Page	20.00	50.00
3 Jade Cargill	40.00	100.00
4 Sammy Guevara	15.00	40.00
5 Dr. Britt Baker	40.00	100.00
6 Darby Allin	30.00	75.00
7 Keith Lee	15.00	40.00
8 Kenny Omega	100.00	250.00
9 Powerhouse Hobbs	10.00	25.00
10 Jack Perry		
11 Red Velvet	12.00	30.00
12 Tay Melo	30.00	75.00
13 Serena Deeb	12.00	30.00
14 Thunder Rosa		
15 Julia Hart	100.00	250.00
16 Wheeler Yuta		
17 Bryan Danielson	50.00	125.00
18 CM Punk	75.00	200.00
19 MJF	60.00	150.00
20 Anthony Ogogo		
21 Eddie Kingston		
22 Orange Cassidy	50.00	125.00
23 HOOK	25.00	60.00
24 Alex Reynolds	10.00	25.00
25 Danhausen	30.00	75.00
26 Anthony Bowens	10.00	25.00
27 Samoa Joe	15.00	40.00
28 Preston Vance	6.00	15.00
29 Ethan Page	20.00	50.00
30 Konosuke Takeshita	75.00	200.00
31 Sting		
32 Chris Jericho	40.00	100.00
33 Hikaru Shida	40.00	100.00
34 Chuck Taylor	15.00	40.00
35 Lee Moriarty	8.00	20.00
36 Dante Martin	6.00	15.00
37 Jeff Jarrett	12.00	30.00
38 Dax Harwood		
39 Jay Lethal	10.00	25.00
40 Kyle O'Reilly	12.00	30.00
41 Evil Uno		
42 Emi Sakura	10.00	25.00
43 Satnam Singh		
44 Yuka Sakazaki	25.00	60.00
45 Colten Gunn	6.00	15.00
46 Isiah Kassidy	6.00	15.00
47 Claudio Castagnoli	12.00	30.00
48 Lance Archer	6.00	15.00
49 John Silver	8.00	20.00
50 Anna Jay	75.00	200.00
51 Swerve Strickland		
52 Andrade El Idolo		
53 Kris Statlander	60.00	150.00
54 Daniel Garcia	30.00	75.00
55 Luchasaurus		
56 Malakai Black		
57 Austin Gunn	10.00	25.00
58 Marq Quen	10.00	25.00
59 Ricky Starks		
60 Matt Jackson	30.00	75.00
61 PAC	10.00	25.00
62 The Butcher	12.00	30.00
63 Dustin Rhodes	8.00	20.00
64 Nick Jackson	20.00	50.00
65 Ortiz	8.00	20.00
66 Skye Blue	150.00	400.00
67 Jamie Hayter	150.00	400.00
68 Penelope Ford		
69 Penta el Zero M	20.00	50.00
70 QT Marshall	10.00	25.00
71 Rey Fenix	25.00	60.00
72 Matt Hardy	12.00	30.00
73 RIHO	40.00	100.00
74 Ruby Soho		
75 Jake Hager	6.00	15.00
76 Scorpio Sky	6.00	15.00
77 Trent Beretta		

78 Cash Wheeler 12.00 30.00
79 Christian Cage 15.00 40.00
80 Nyla Rose 20.00 50.00
81 Jon Moxley 30.00 75.00
82 Wardlow
83 The Bunny 20.00 50.00
84 Max Caster 15.00 40.00
85 Abadon 25.00 60.00
86 Matt Menard 6.00 15.00
87 Toni Storm
88 The Blade 10.00 25.00
89 Brody King 20.00 50.00
90 Jim Ross 8.00 20.00
91 Excalibur 8.00 20.00
92 Tony Nese 6.00 15.00
93 Taz 6.00 15.00
94 Bryce Remsburg 6.00 15.00
95 Aubrey Edwards
96 Rick Knox
97 Buddy Matthews 8.00 20.00
98 Angelo Parker
99 Stokely Hathaway 10.00 25.00
100 Athena 12.00 30.00
101 Adam Cole
102 Claudio Castagnoli
103 Ricky Starks
104 Chris Jericho
105 Powerhouse Hobbs
106 Hangman Adam Page
107 Jon Moxley
108 Sammy Guevara
109 Dr. Britt Baker
110 Jade Cargill
111 Red Velvet
112 Penta el Zero M
113 Kris Statlander
114 Thunder Rosa
115 Anna Jay
116 Bryan Danielson
117 CM Punk
118 MJF
119 Darby Allin
120 Sting
121 Orange Cassidy
122 Kenny Omega
123 Hikaru Shida
124 Jack Perry
125 Keith Lee
126 Anthony Ogogo
127 Jade Cargill
128 Jamie Hayter
129 Darby Allin
130 Austin Gunn
131 Abadon
132 Dante Martin
133 Kris Statlander
134 Wheeler Yuta
135 Wardlow
136 Anna Jay
137 Tay Melo
138 Daniel Garcia
139 Isiah Kassidy
140 Lee Moriarty
141 Skye Blue
142 HOOK
143 Colten Gunn
144 Marq Quen
145 Konosuke Takeshita
146 Yuka Sakazaki
147 MJF
148 Julia Hart
149 Satnam Singh
150 Jack Perry

2022 Upper Deck Allure AEW Buses

*GOLDEN TREASURES/1: UNPRICED DUE TO SCARCITY
STATED ODDS 1:160 HOBBY/EPACK
STATED ODDS 1:480 BLASTER

BU1 Lance Archer
BU2 Sting 50.00 125.00
BU3 MJF 60.00 150.00
BU4 Sammy Guevara 15.00 40.00
BU5 Thunder Rosa 12.00 30.00
BU6 Jade Cargill
BU7 Nyla Rose
BU8 Ruby Soho 12.00 30.00
BU9 Kris Statlander 30.00 75.00
BU10 Toni Storm 25.00 60.00
BU11 Orange Cassidy 12.00 30.00
BU12 Scorpio Sky 8.00 20.00
BU13 Keith Lee 15.00 40.00
BU14 Hangman Adam Page 15.00 40.00
BU15 Samoa Joe 15.00 30.00
BU16 Danhausen 30.00 75.00
BU17 Wardlow 10.00 25.00
BU18 CM Punk 60.00 150.00
BU19 Claudio Castagnoli 10.00 25.00
BU20 Anna Jay 50.00 125.00
BU21 Penta el Zero M 12.00 30.00
BU22 Swerve Strickland 40.00 100.00
BU23 Jack Perry 30.00 75.00
BU24 Jon Moxley
BU25 Kenny Omega 40.00 100.00
BU26 Chris Jericho 10.00 25.00
BU27 Darby Allin 40.00 100.00
BU28 HOOK 20.00 50.00
BU29 Tay Melo
BU30 Dr. Britt Baker 20.00 50.00

2022 Upper Deck Allure AEW Buses Autographs

STATED PRINT RUN 10 SER.#'d SETS
UNPRICED DUE TO SCARCITY
HOBBY/EPACK EXCLUSIVE

BU1 Lance Archer
BU2 Sting
BU3 MJF
BU4 Sammy Guevara
BU5 Thunder Rosa
BU6 Jade Cargill
BU7 Nyla Rose
BU8 Ruby Soho
BU9 Kris Statlander
BU10 Toni Storm
BU11 Orange Cassidy
BU12 Scorpio Sky
BU13 Keith Lee
BU14 Hangman Adam Page
BU15 Samoa Joe
BU16 Danhausen
BU17 Wardlow
BU18 CM Punk
BU19 Claudio Castagnoli
BU20 Anna Jay

2022 Upper Deck Allure AEW Color Flow

*ORANGE-YELLOW: SAME VALUE AS BASIC
*YELLOW-GREEN: .5X TO 1.2X BASIC CARDS
*GREEN-BLUE/299: .75X TO 2X BASIC CARDS
*BLUE-PURPLE/199: 1.2X TO 3X BASIC CARDS
*GOLDEN TREASURES/1: UNPRICED DUE TO SCARCITY
STATED ODDS 1:4 HOBBY/EPACK
STATED ODDS 1:8 BLASTER

R1 CM Punk 4.00 10.00
R2 Sammy Guevara 2.50 6.00
R3 Jack Perry 2.50 6.00
R4 Cash Wheeler 1.25 3.00
R5 Orange Cassidy 2.50 6.00
R6 Penta el Zero M 2.00 5.00
R7 Malakai Black 2.00 5.00
R8 Dr. Britt Baker 3.00 8.00
R9 Nyla Rose 1.50 4.00
R10 Dante Martin .75 2.00
R11 Jade Cargill 4.00 10.00
R12 Kenny Omega 4.00 10.00
R13 Danhausen 3.00 8.00
R14 PAC 1.50 4.00
R15 Athena 1.00 2.50
R16 Jay Lethal 1.25 3.00
R17 Serena Deeb .75 2.00
R18 Thunder Rosa 2.00 5.00
R19 Anna Jay 3.00 8.00
R20 Luchasaurus 1.50 4.00
R21 Eddie Kingston 2.50 6.00
R22 Andrade El Idolo 1.00 2.50
R23 Hangman Adam Page 4.00 10.00
R24 Powerhouse Hobbs 1.50 4.00
R25 HOOK 3.00 8.00
R26 Rey Fenix 2.00 5.00
R27 Keith Lee 2.00 5.00
R28 Tay Melo 3.00 8.00
R29 John Silver .75 2.00
R30 Toni Storm 3.00 8.00
R31 Brody King 1.00 2.50
R32 Bryan Danielson 3.00 8.00
R33 Kris Statlander 1.50 4.00
R34 Jon Moxley 2.00 5.00
R35 Adam Cole 2.50 6.00
R36 Ricky Starks 1.50 4.00
R37 Kyle O'Reilly .75 2.00
R38 Scorpio Sky 1.50 4.00
R39 Daniel Garcia 1.00 2.50
R40 Samoa Joe 1.50 4.00
R41 Ruby Soho 1.50 4.00
R42 Penelope Ford 4.00 10.00
R43 Claudio Castagnoli .75 2.00
R44 The Bunny 1.50 4.00
R45 Darby Allin 4.00 10.00
R46 Wardlow 2.00 5.00
R47 Chris Jericho 3.00 8.00
R48 MJF 4.00 10.00
R49 Lance Archer 2.00 5.00
R50 Wheeler Yuta 3.00 8.00

2022 Upper Deck Allure AEW Color Flow Autographs

*GOLDEN TREASURES/1: UNPRICED DUE TO SCARCITY
STATED ODDS 1:320 HOBBY/EPACK
STATED ODDS 1:640 BLASTER

R1 CM Punk
R2 Sammy Guevara
R3 Jack Perry
R4 Cash Wheeler
R5 Orange Cassidy
R6 Penta el Zero M
R7 Malakai Black
R8 Dr. Britt Baker
R9 Nyla Rose
R10 Dante Martin
R11 Jade Cargill
R12 Kenny Omega
R13 Danhausen
R14 PAC
R15 Athena
R16 Jay Lethal
R17 Serena Deeb
R18 Thunder Rosa
R19 Anna Jay
R20 Luchasaurus
R21 Eddie Kingston
R22 Andrade El Idolo
R23 Hangman Adam Page
R24 Powerhouse Hobbs
R25 HOOK
R26 Rey Fenix
R27 Keith Lee
R28 Tay Melo
R29 John Silver
R30 Toni Storm
R31 Brody King
R32 Bryan Danielson
R33 Kris Statlander
R34 Jon Moxley
R35 Adam Cole
R36 Ricky Starks
R37 Kyle O'Reilly
R38 Scorpio Sky
R39 Daniel Garcia
R40 Samoa Joe
R41 Ruby Soho
R42 Penelope Ford
R43 Claudio Castagnoli
R44 The Bunny
R45 Darby Allin
R46 Wardlow
R47 Chris Jericho
R48 MJF
R49 Lance Archer
R50 Wheeler Yuta

2022 Upper Deck Allure AEW I Scream For

*PINK/100: .75X TO 2X BASIC CARDS
*BLUE/35: 1.5X TO 4X BASIC CARDS
*PURPLE DIAMOND/10: UNPRICED DUE TO SCARCITY
*GOLDEN TREASURES/1: UNPRICED DUE TO SCARCITY
STATED ODDS 1:8 HOBBY/EPACK
STATED ODDS 1:16 BLASTER

ISF1 Tay Melo 2.50 6.00
ISF2 Jade Cargill 3.00 8.00
ISF3 Orange Cassidy 2.00 5.00
ISF4 Chris Jericho 2.50 6.00
ISF5 Toni Storm 2.50 6.00
ISF6 Thunder Rosa 1.50 4.00
ISF7 Anna Jay 2.50 6.00
ISF8 Adam Cole 2.00 5.00
ISF9 Sting 2.50 6.00
ISF10 Kenny Omega 3.00 8.00
ISF11 Darby Allin 3.00 8.00
ISF12 Jon Moxley 1.50 4.00
ISF13 Jack Perry 2.00 5.00
ISF14 Kris Statlander 1.25 3.00
ISF15 Malakai Black 1.50 4.00
ISF16 Hangman Adam Page 3.00 8.00
ISF17 CM Punk 3.00 8.00
ISF18 Wardlow 1.50 4.00
ISF19 Sammy Guevara 2.00 5.00
ISF20 Dr. Britt Baker 2.50 6.00

2022 Upper Deck Allure AEW I Scream For Autographs

STATED ODDS 1:800 HOBBY/EPACK

ISF1 Tay Melo
ISF2 Jade Cargill
ISF3 Orange Cassidy
ISF4 Chris Jericho
ISF5 Toni Storm
ISF6 Thunder Rosa
ISF7 Anna Jay
ISF8 Adam Cole
ISF9 Sting
ISF10 Kenny Omega
ISF11 Darby Allin
ISF12 Jon Moxley
ISF13 Jack Perry
ISF14 Kris Statlander
ISF15 Malakai Black
ISF16 Hangman Adam Page
ISF17 CM Punk
ISF18 Wardlow
ISF19 Sammy Guevara
ISF20 Dr. Britt Baker

2022 Upper Deck Allure AEW My Squad

*PURPLE DIAMOND/10: UNPRICED DUE TO SCARCITY
*GOLDEN TREASURES/1: UNPRICED DUE TO SCARCITY
STATED ODDS 1:6.4 HOBBY/EPACK
STATED ODDS 1:12.8 BLASTER

MC1 J.Perry/Luchasaurus 2.00 5.00
MC2 I.Kassidy/M.Quen .75 2.00
MC3 Austin, Colten & Billy Gunn .75 2.00
MC4 Andrade/Rush .75 2.00
MC5 D.Harwood/C.Wheeler 1.00 2.50
MC6 K.Lee/S.Strickland 1.50 4.00
MC7 Dante & Darius Martin .60 1.50
MC8 B.Pillman Jr./G.Garrison 1.00 2.50
MC9 The Young Bucks 1.50 4.00
MC10 Beretta/Taylor/Cassidy/Statlander 2.00 5.00
MC11 PAC/Penta/Fenix 1.50 4.00
MC12 Comoroto/Marshall/Solo/Ogogo .75 2.00
MC13 Omega/Young Bucks 3.00 8.00
MC14 A.Bowens/M.Caster .75 2.00
MC15 Penta/R.Fenix 1.50 4.00
MC16 Jericho/Garcia/Hager/Parker 2.50 6.00
Menard/Jay/Guevara/Melo
MC17 Hathaway/Moriarty/Austin & Colten Gunn/Morrissey/Page 1.50 4.00
MC18 Butcher/Blade/Bunny 1.25 3.00
MC19 Luther/Serpentico .60 1.50
MC20 Matthews/King/Black/Hart 1.50 4.00
MC21 Reynolds/Uno/Silver/Vance 1.25 3.00

MC22 S.Strickland/K.Lee	1.50	4.00
MC23 Danielson/Moxley/Yuta/Castagnoli	2.50	6.00
MC24 J.Perry/Luchasaurus	2.00	5.00
MC25 D.Harwood/C.Wheeler	1.00	2.50

2022 Upper Deck Allure AEW Photo Variations

STATED PRINT RUN 10 SER.#'d SETS
UNPRICED DUE TO SCARCITY
HOBBY/EPACK EXCLUSIVE

1 Sammy Guevara
2 Hangman Adam Page
3 Jade Cargill
4 Thunder Rosa
5 Adam Cole
6 Kris Statlander
7 Powerhouse Hobbs
8 Nyla Rose
9 Matt Jackson
10 Nick Jackson

2022 Upper Deck Allure AEW Title Ambitions

*PINK/100: .75X TO 2X BASIC CARDS
*BLUE/35: 1.5X TO 4X BASIC CARDS
*PURPLE DIAMOND/10: UNPRICED DUE TO SCARCITY
*GOLDEN TREASURES/1: UNPRICED DUE TO SCARCITY
STATED ODDS 1:4.5 HOBBY/EPACK
STATED ODDS 1:9 BLASTER

TA1 Daniel Garcia	.75	2.00
TA2 Tay Melo	2.50	6.00
TA3 Wheeler Yuta	2.50	6.00
TA4 Jamie Hayter	3.00	8.00
TA5 Lee Moriarty	.60	1.50
TA6 Orange Cassidy	2.00	5.00
TA7 Julia Hart	1.50	4.00
TA8 Ruby Soho	1.25	3.00
TA9 Skye Blue	2.50	6.00
TA10 Dante Martin	.60	1.50
TA11 Athena	.75	2.00
TA12 MJF	3.00	8.00
TA13 Andrade El Idolo	.75	2.00
TA14 Powerhouse Hobbs	1.25	3.00
TA15 Red Velvet	1.00	2.50
TA16 Leyla Hirsch	.75	2.00
TA17 Serena Deeb	.60	1.50
TA18 Penelope Ford	3.00	8.00
TA19 Anna Jay	2.50	6.00
TA20 Anthony Bowens	.75	2.00
TA21 Eddie Kingston	2.00	5.00
TA22 Bryan Danielson	2.50	6.00
TA23 Max Caster	.75	2.00
TA24 Colten Gunn	.60	1.50
TA25 Ethan Page	1.50	4.00
TA26 Adam Cole	2.00	5.00
TA27 Claudio Castagnoli	.60	1.50
TA28 Austin Gunn	.60	1.50
TA29 Evil Uno	1.25	3.00
TA30 Konosuke Takeshita	.60	1.50
TA31 Matt Hardy	1.25	3.00
TA32 Malakai Black	1.50	4.00
TA33 Jay Lethal	1.00	2.50
TA34 Lance Archer	1.50	4.00
TA35 Christian Cage	1.00	2.50

2022 Upper Deck Allure AEW Title Ambitions Autographs

STATED ODDS 1:800 HOBBY/EPACK

TA1 Daniel Garcia
TA2 Tay Melo
TA3 Wheeler Yuta
TA4 Jamie Hayter
TA5 Lee Moriarty
TA6 Orange Cassidy
TA7 Julia Hart
TA8 Ruby Soho
TA9 Skye Blue
TA10 Dante Martin
TA11 Athena
TA12 MJF
TA13 Andrade El Idolo
TA14 Powerhouse Hobbs
TA15 Red Velvet
TA16 Leyla Hirsch
TA17 Serena Deeb
TA18 Penelope Ford
TA19 Anna Jay
TA20 Anthony Bowens
TA21 Eddie Kingston
TA22 Bryan Danielson
TA23 Max Caster
TA24 Colten Gunn
TA25 Ethan Page
TA26 Adam Cole
TA27 Claudio Castagnoli
TA28 Austin Gunn
TA29 Evil Uno
TA30 Konosuke Takeshita
TA31 Matt Hardy
TA32 Malakai Black
TA33 Jay Lethal
TA34 Lance Archer
TA35 Christian Cage

2022 Upper Deck Allure AEW Title Fights

*PINK/100: .75X TO 2X BASIC CARDS
*BLUE/35: 1.5X TO 4X BASIC CARDS
*PURPLE DIAMOND/10: UNPRICED DUE TO SCARCITY
*GOLDEN TREASURES/1: UNPRICED DUE TO SCARCITY
STATED ODDS 1:4.5 HOBBY/EPACK
STATED ODDS 1:9 BLASTER

TF1 Hangman Adam Page	3.00	8.00
TF2 Bryan Danielson	2.50	6.00
TF3 Kenny Omega	3.00	8.00
TF4 Jon Moxley	1.50	4.00
TF5 Chris Jericho	2.50	6.00
TF6 Rey Fenix	1.50	4.00
TF7 Orange Cassidy	2.00	5.00
TF8 PAC	1.25	3.00
TF9 Jack Perry	2.00	5.00
TF10 Jake Hager	.75	2.00
TF11 Christian Cage	1.00	2.50
TF12 Lance Archer	1.50	4.00
TF13 Adam Cole	2.00	5.00
TF14 Dante Martin	.60	1.50
TF15 Penta el Zero M	1.50	4.00
TF16 Darby Allin	3.00	8.00
TF17 Ricky Starks	1.25	3.00
TF18 Scorpio Sky	1.25	3.00
TF19 CM Punk	3.00	8.00
TF20 MJF	3.00	8.00

2022 Upper Deck Allure AEW Title Fights Autographs

STATED ODDS 1:800 HOBBY/EPACK

TF1 Hangman Adam Page
TF2 Bryan Danielson
TF3 Kenny Omega
TF4 Jon Moxley
TF5 Chris Jericho
TF6 Rey Fenix
TF7 Orange Cassidy
TF8 PAC
TF9 Jack Perry
TF10 Jake Hager
TF11 Christian Cage
TF12 Lance Archer
TF13 Adam Cole
TF14 Dante Martin
TF15 Penta el Zero M
TF16 Darby Allin
TF17 Ricky Starks
TF18 Scorpio Sky
TF19 CM Punk
TF20 MJF

2023 Upper Deck National Convention AEW Iconic Entrances

IE1 Chris Jericho	3.00	8.00
IE2 MJF	5.00	12.00
IE3 Jade Cargill	8.00	20.00
IE4 Kenny Omega	15.00	40.00
IE5 Toni Storm	2.00	5.00

2023 Upper Deck National Convention AEW Iconic Entrance Autographs

IE1 Chris Jericho
IE2 MJF
IE3 Jade Cargill
IE4 Kenny Omega
IE5 Toni Storm

2023 Upper Deck AEW Vs. System 2PCG

AEW001 Adam Page L1
AEW002 Adam Page L2
AEW003 Chris Jericho L1
AEW004 Chris Jericho L2
AEW005 Jon Moxley L1
AEW006 Jon Moxley L2
AEW007 Darby Allin L1
AEW008 Darby Allin L2
AEW009 Kris Statlander L1
AEW010 Kris Statlander L2
AEW011 Thunder Rosa L1
AEW012 Thunder Rosa L2
AEW013 Sting 1
AEW014 Hikaru Shida 1
AEW015 Luchasaurus 2
AEW016 Danhausen 2
AEW017 Penta El Zero Miedo 3
AEW018 Claudio Castagnoli 3
AEW019 Eddie Kingston 4
AEW020 Jungle Boy 4
AEW021 Sammy Guevara 5
AEW022 Rey Fenix 5
AEW023 Samoa Joe 6
AEW024 Orange Cassidy 6
AEW025 Keith Lee 7
AEW026 Dynamite
AEW027 Elevation
AEW028 Pop
AEW029 Right Tunnel
AEW030 Adam Cole L1
AEW031 Adam Cole L2
AEW032 Bryan Danielson L1
AEW033 Bryan Danielson L2
AEW034 Dr. Britt Baker, D.M.D. L1
AEW035 Dr. Britt Baker, D.M.D. L2
AEW036 Jade Cargill L1
AEW037 Jade Cargill L2
AEW038 Malakai Black L1
AEW039 Malakai Black L2
AEW040 MJF L1
AEW041 MJF L2
AEW042 HOOK 1
AEW043 Nyla Rose 1
AEW044 Matt Hardy 2
AEW045 Andrade El Idolo 2
AEW046 Ethan Page 3
AEW047 Ricky Starks 3
AEW048 Matt Jackson 4
AEW049 Nick Jackson 4
AEW050 Scorpio Sky 5
AEW051 Lance Archer 5
AEW052 Miro 6
AEW053 Wardlow 6
AEW054 Kenny Omega 7
AEW055 Dark
AEW056 Heat
AEW057 Rampage
AEW058 Left Tunnel
AEW059 Ladder Match
AEW060 Lights Out
AEW061 Steel Cage Match
AEW062 Texas Death Match
AEW063 AEW World Championship Belt
AEW064 Table
AEW065 Chair
AEW066 Baseball Bat
AEW067 Revolution
AEW068 Full Gear
AEW069 All Out
AEW070 Double or Nothing

2000 Waldenbooks WWF Limited Edition

COMPLETE SET (2)	8.00	20.00
1 Have a Nice Day!	3.00	8.00
2 The Rock Says	6.00	15.00

1987 Wonderama NWA Wrestling Supercards

COMPLETE SET (51)

1 Ric Flair
2 Tommy Angel
3 Dusty Rhodes vs. Tully Blanchard
4 Baby Doll
5 Eddie Hotstuff Gilbert
6 Rocky King
7 Lex Luger vs. Arn Anderson
8 Mike Rotunda vs. Ivan Koloff
9 Barry Windham & Sting
10 Ron Simmons
11 Mighty Wilbur
12 Skandor Akbar
13 Precious
14 Shaska Whatley vs. Jimmy Valiant
15 Curtis Thompson
16 Kendall Windham
17 Sting
18 Paul Ellering
19 Johnny Ace
20 Kat Leroux & Linda Dallas
21 Michael P.S. Hayes
22 Terry Taylor
23 Barry Windham
24 Johnny Weaver vs. J.J. Dillion
25 Tully Blanchard
26 Dick Murdock
27 Sweet Stan Lane
28 Barbarian & Paul Jones
29 Linda Dallas & Misty Blue
30 Road Warriors
31 Stan Lane vs Sean Royal
32 Ricky Santana
33 Jimmy Valiant
34 Larry Zbyszko vs Kendall Windham
35 Lex Luger
36 Shaska Whatley
37 Warlord
38 Beautiful Bobby Eaton
39 Dusty Rhodes
40 Paul Jones
41 Eddie Gilbert vs. Sting
42 Rowdy Roddy Piper
43 Barry Windham vs. Arn Anderson
44 Michael Hayes
45 Larry Stephens
46 Black Bart
47 Gladiator #2
48 Ric Flair vs. Sting
49 Ivan Koloff
CL Checklist
NNO Ric Flair Header

1988 Wonderama NWA

COMPLETE SET (343)	300.00	600.00
1 Ric Flair RC	75.00	150.00
2 Tommy Angel RC	.40	1.00
3 Dusty Rhodes/Tully Blanchard	2.50	6.00
4 Baby Doll RC	1.25	3.00
5 Eddie Gilbert RC	2.00	5.00
6 Rocky King RC	.75	2.00
7 Lex Luger/Arn Anderson	1.50	4.00
8 Mike Rotunda vs. Ivan Koloff	.60	1.50
9 Barry Windham/Sting	5.00	12.00
10 Ron Simmons RC	.20	3.00
11 Mighty Wilbur RC	.40	1.00
12 Skandor Akbar RC	.60	1.50
13 Precious RC	1.50	4.00
14 Shaska Whatley vs. Jimmy Valiant	.40	1.00
15 Curtis Thompson RC	.75	2.00
16 Kendall Windham RC	2.00	5.00
17 Sting RC	20.00	50.00
18 Paul Ellering RC	1.25	3.00
19 Johnny Ace RC	.75	2.00
20 Kat Leroux w/Linda Dallas	.75	2.00

21 Michael Hayes RC 1.00 2.50
22 Terry Taylor RC .40 1.00
23 Barry Windham RC 2.50 6.00
24 Johnny Weaver vs. J.J. Dillon .40 1.00
25 Tully Blanchard RC 1.00 2.50
26 Dick Murdoch RC .75 2.00
27 Stan Lane RC .75 2.00
28 Barbarian w/Paul Jones .40 1.00
29 Linda Dallas w/Misty Blue .75 2.00
30 Road Warriors 15.00 40.00
31 Stan Lane vs. Sean Royal .50 1.25
32 Ricky Santana RC .40 1.00
33 Jimmy Valiant RC 1.25 3.00
34 Larry Zbyszko vs. Kendall Windham .75 2.00
35 Lex Luger RC 2.00 5.00
36 Shaska Whatley RC .40 1.00
37 Warlord RC .40 1.00
38 Bobby Eaton RC 2.00 5.00
39 Dusty Rhodes RC 2.50 6.00
40 Paul Jones RC .40 1.00
41 Eddie Gilbert/Sting 2.00 5.00
42 Butch Miller RC .40 1.00
43 Barry Windham/Arn Anderson 3.00 8.00
44 Michael Hayes RC 1.00 2.50
45 Larry Stephens RC .40 1.00
46 Black Bart RC .40 1.00
47 Gladiator #2 RC .40 .30
48 Ric Flair/Sting 3.00 8.00
49 Ivan Koloff RC 1.25 3.00
50 Jamie West RC .40 1.00
51 Larry Zbyszko RC .75 2.00
52 Sean Royal vs. Bobby Eaton .40 1.00
53 Arn Anderson vs. Lex Luger 2.00 5.00
54 Baby Doll RC .60 1.50
55 Tim Horner vs. Shaska Whatley .40 1.00
56 Jimmy Garvin vs. Tully Blanchard 1.00 2.50
57 Kendall Windham vs. Gladiator .40 1.00
58 Terry Taylor vs. Eddie Gilbert .75 2.00
59 Dick Murdoch RC .50 1.25
60 Stan Lane vs. Sean Royal .40 .30
61 Magnum T.A. RC .75 .75
62 Ricky Santana RC .40 .30
63 Luke Williams RC .40 .30
64 Robert Gibson RC 1.50 4.00
65 Ron Garvin RC .40 1.00
66 Ivan Koloff RC .50 .50
67 Larry Zbyszko vs. Kendall Windham .50 .50
68a Butch Miller RC 1.25 3.00
68b Ric Flair logo 6.00 15.00
69 Ricky Morton RC 1.50 4.00
70 Tommy Angel RC .40 1.00
71 Stan Lane vs. Sean Royal .40 .30
72 Kendall Windham RC .40 .30
73 Baby Doll RC .50 .50
74a Black Bart RC
74b Barry Windham logo 1.00 2.50
75 Road Warrior Hawk RC 1.50 4.00
76 Mike Rotunda .60 1.50
77 Ron Simmons/Arn Anderson 1.00 2.50
78 J.J. Dillon RC .40 1.00
79 Shaska Whatley vs. Jimmy Valiant .60 1.50
80 Kat Leroux RC .50 1.25
81 Kendall Windham vs. Larry Zbyszko .50 1.25
82 Road Warrior Animal RC 2.00 5.00
83 D.Murdoch/Steve Williams .50 1.25
84 Tully Blanchard RC 2.50 6.00
85 Barbarian RC .75 2.00
86 Robert Gibson RC 1.25 3.00
87 Ricky Santana RC .40 1.00
88 Jimmy Valiant RC .60 1.50
89 Nikita Koloff/Ric Flair 4.00 10.00
90 Kat Leroux vs. Misty Blue .50 1.25
91 Kevin Sullivan RC 6.00 15.00
92 Luke Williams RC .40 1.00
93 Lex Luger/Arn Anderson 1.00 2.50
94 Big Bubba Rogers RC 1.25 3.00
95 Bobby Eaton RC .60 1.50
96 Paul Jones RC .40 1.00
97 Butch Miller RC .40 .30
98 Jimmy Garvin w/Precious 1.25 3.00
99a Warlord vs. Sting 2.00 5.00
99b Dusty Rhodes logo 3.00 8.00
100 Ivan Koloff RC .50 1.25
101 Larry Zbyszko RC .50 .50
102 Sting RC 20.00 50.00
103 Larry Zbyszko/Baby Doll .60 1.50
104 Eddie Gilbert/Sting 1.00 2.50
105 Dusty Rhodes RC 2.00 5.00
106 Mighty Wilbur RC .40 1.00
107 Michael Hayes/Ric Flair .60 1.50
108 Brad Armstorng w/Tom Horner .40 .30
109 Terry Taylor RC .40 .30
110 Dick Murdoch RC .50 .50
111 Tully Blanchard RC .75 2.00
112 Ricky Santana vs. Warlord .40 1.00
113 Jimmy Valiant RC 1.25 3.00
114 Kevin Sullivan RC .60 1.50
115 Paul Jones RC .40 1.00
116 Lex Luger/Sting 8.00 20.00
117 Ivan Koloff RC .50 1.25
118 Larry Zbyszko/Barry Windham .50 .50
119 Italian Stallion RC .40 .30
120 Dusty Rhodes RC 2.00 5.00
121 Tim Horner vs. Chris Champion .40 1.00
122 Eddie Gilbert/Sting 1.50 4.00
123 Mighty Wilbur vs. Ivan Koloff .50 1.25
124 Barry Windham RC .50 .50
125 Dick Murdoch RC .50 1.25
126 Lex Luger RC 3.00 8.00
127 Dusty Rhodes/Nikita Koloff 1.00 2.50
128 Barbarian/Warlord/Ivan Koloff .50 1.25
129 Paul Jones RC .40 .30
130 Arn Anderson/Barry Windham .75 2.00
131 Ivan Koloff RC .75 2.00
132 Baby Doll/Dusty Rhodes 1.50 4.00
133 Eddie Gilbert w/Terry Taylor .60 1.50
134 Rocky King w/Kendall Windham .40 1.00
135 Jimmy Garvin vs. Tully Blanchard .75 2.00
136a Ricky Morton vs. Ric Flair 1.50 4.00
136b Lex Luger logo 1.50 4.00
137 Tim Horner vs. Gladiator .40 1.00
138 Kendall Windham RC .40 .30
139 Magnum T.A. RC .75 .75
140 Terry Taylor RC .40 .30
141 Dick Murdoch/Steve Williams .60 .60
142 Barbarian RC .40 .30
143 Mad Dog Debbie RC .40 .30
144 Dr. Death Steve Williams RC .50 .50
145 Italian Stallion RC .40 .30
146 Jimmy Valiant RC 3.00 8.00
147 Kevin Sullivan vs. Jimmy Garvin .40 1.00
148 Ron Garvin RC .40 .30
149 Ricky Morton RC 1.00 2.50
150 Luke Williams RC .40 1.00
151 Paul Jones RC .40 .30
152 Butch Miller RC .40 .30
153 Warlord/Sting 1.50 4.00
154 Ricky Morton/Ric Flair 1.25 3.00
155 Black Bart RC .40 1.00
156 Gladiators 1 & 2 .40 1.00
157 Ivan Koloff RC .50 1.25
158 Larry Zbyszko w/Baby Doll .60 1.50
159 Road Warrior Hawk RC 1.50 4.00
160 Bobby Eaton vs. Chris Champion .40 1.00
161 Paul Jones RC .40 1.00
162 Ric Flair RC 10.00 25.00
163 Luke Williams RC .40 .30
164 Dick Murdoch/Steve Williams .50 .50
165 J.J. Dillon RC .40 .30
166 Linda Dallas vs. Misty Blue .50 .50
167 Mike Rotunda .40 1.00
168 Tommy Angel RC .40 .30
169 Baby Doll RC .50 .50
170 Animal/I.Koloff .60 .60
171 Mike Rotunda w/Kevin Sullivan .40 .30
172 Ron Garvin RC .40 .30
173 Ron Simmons RC .50 .50
174 Robert Gibson RC .40 .30
175 Four Horsemen logo 4.00 10.00
176 Pee Wee Anderson RC .40 1.00
177 Tony Schiavone RC 1.50 4.00
178 Tiger Conway RC .40 1.00
179 Nikita Koloff RC .75 2.00
180 Chris Champion RC .40 1.00
181 Kendall Windham RC .40 .30
182 Paul Ellering vs. Paul Jones .40 .30
183 Lex Luger RC 1.50 4.00
184 Johnny Ace RC .40 1.00
185 Cougar Jay RC .40 1.00
186 Missy Hyatt w/Magnum T.A. .75 .75
187 Precious RC 1.00 2.50
188 Kat Leroux vs. Misty Blue .50 1.25
189 Denny Brown w/Nelson Royal .40 .30
190 Johnny Weaver RC .40 .30
191 Sting/Eddie Gilbert 6.00 15.00
192 Dick Murdoch RC .50 1.25
193 Ole Anderson RC .40 .30
194 Sting RC 20.00 50.00
195 Barbarian RC .40 1.00
196 Road Warrior Animal RC 2.00 5.00
197 Michael Hayes/Ric Flair .60 1.50
198 Paul Jones RC .40 .30
199 Ricky Santana RC .40 .30
200 Ron Garvin RC .40 .30
201 Jimmy Valiant RC .40 .30
202 Tully Blanchard RC .50 .50
203 Shaska Whatley RC .40 .30
204 Rock 'N Roll Express 5.00 12.00
205 Brad Armstrong RC .40 1.00
206 Misty Blue RC .50 .50
207 Road Warriors 5.00 12.00
208 Larry Zbyszko RC .50 1.25
209 Bobby Eaton RC .40 .30
210 Paul Jones w/Warlord .40 .30
211 Butch Miller RC .40 .30
212 Lex Luger RC .75 2.00
213 Larry Stephens RC .40 1.00
214 Warlord/Sting 1.25 3.00
215 Dr. Death Steve Williams RC .50 1.25
216 Tommy Young RC .40 .30
217 Nikita Koloff RC .40 .30
218 George South RC .40 .30
219 Dusty Rhodes/Ric Flair 3.00 8.00
220 Black Bart RC .40 1.00
221 Ivan Koloff RC .50 .50
222 Barry Windham RC .50 .50
223 Larry Zbyszko RC .50 .50
224 Sean Royal RC .40 .30
225 Kevin Sullivan vs. Jimmy Garvin .40 .30
226 Eddie Gilbert RC 1.00 2.50
227 Ric Flair/Robert Gibson 2.50 6.00
228 Eddie Gilbert RC 1.00 2.50
229 Rocky King vs. Nelson Royal .40 .30
230 Mike Rotunda .40 1.00
231 Arn Anderson RC .50 .50
232 Ron Simmons RC 1.25 3.00
233 Mighty Wilbur RC .40 .30
234 Tony Schiavone RC 1.50 4.00
235 Skandor Akbar RC .40 .30
236 Jimmy Garvin vs. Tully Blanchard .50 .50
237 Jive Tones .40 .30
238 Tim Horner RC .40 .30
239 Arn Anderson RC 1.25 3.00
240 Ivan Koloff w/Paul Jones .50 1.25
241 Paul Jones RC .40 .30
242 Magnum T.A./Arn Anderson .75 .75
243 Kevin Sullivan w/Mike Rotunda .40 .30
244 Ricky Santana RC .40 .30
245 Baby Doll RC .50 .50
246 Eddie Gilbert/Ron Garvin .50 .50
247 Dr. Death Steve Williams RC .50 .50
248 Mike Rotunda vs. Jimmy Garvin .40 .30
249 Mighty Wilbur RC .40 .30
250 Kevin Sullivan vs. Jimmy Garvin .40 .30
251 Dick Murdoch RC .50 .50
252 Ron Garvin/Ric Flair .60 1.50
253 Trent Knight RC .40 .30
254 Curtis Thompson RC .40 .30
255 Mighty Wilbur RC .40 .30
256 Luke Williams RC .40 .30
257 Ricky Morton/Ric Flair .60 1.50
258 Missy Hyatt RC 2.00 5.00
259 Road Warrior Animal RC 1.50 4.00
260 Nelson Royal RC .40 1.00
261 Magnum T.A. RC .75 .75
262 Road Warriors 2.00 5.00
263 Johnny Weaver RC .40 1.00
264 Precious RC .50 1.25
265 Robert Gibson RC .40 .30
266 Dick Murdoch RC .50 .50
267 Arn Anderson RC .50 .50
268 Ole Anderson RC .50 .50
269 Barbarian RC .40 .30
270 Ric Flair/Ron Garvin 2.00 5.00
271 Linda Dallas vs. Venus .50 .50
272 Gene Ligon RC .40 1.00
273 Ricky Santana RC .40 .30
274 Lex Luger/Nikita Koloff .40 1.00
275 Misty Blue vs. Linda Dallas .50 .50
276 J.J. Dillon RC .40 .30
277 David Isley RC .40 .30
278 Teddy Long RC .40 1.00
279 Road Warriors 2.00 5.00
280 Kevin Sullivan RC .40 1.00
281 Road Warrior Animal RC 1.25 3.00
282 Luke Williams RC .40 .30
283 Big Bubba Rogers RC 1.25 3.00
284 Jimmy Garvin RC .40 .30
285 Denny Brown RC .40 .30
286 Bobby Eaton RC .40 .30
287 Robert Gibson RC .40 .30
288 Paul Jones RC .40 .30
289 Butch Miller RC .40 .30
290 Warlord vs. Road Warrior Animal .60 1.50
291 Tommy Young RC .40 .30
292 Nikita Koloff RC .40 .30
293 Black Bart RC .40 .30
294 Gladiator #1 RC .40 .30
295 Ivan Koloff RC .50 .50
296 Ricky Nelson RC .40 .30
297 Dr. Death Steve Williams RC .50 .50
298 Rick Steiner RC .40 1.00
299 Larry Zbyszko RC .60 .60
300 Sean Royal RC .40 .30
301 Road Warriors .60 .60
302 Baby Doll RC .50 .50
303 J.J. Dillon/Lex Luger .50 1.25
304 Tim Horner RC .40 .30
305 Paul Ellering RC .40 .30
306 Lex Luger/Gladiator .40 1.00
307 J.J. Dillon RC .40 .30
308 Midnight Express .40 .30
309 Sheepherders w/Johnny Ace .40 .30
310 Jimmy Garvin w/Precious .40 .30
311 Kat Leroux RC .50 .50
312 Jimmy Garvin RC .40 .30
313 Road Warriors .60 .60
314 Ricky Morton RC .40 .30
315 Barbarian RC .40 .30
316 Linda Dallas RC .50 .50
317 Sting/Eddie Gilbert 2.50 6.00
318 Italian Stallion RC .40 .30
319 Ricky Santana RC .40 .30
320 Jimmy Valiant RC .40 .30
321 Shaska Whatley RC .40 .30
322 Michael Hayes RC .40 .30
323 Misty Blue RC .50 .50
324 Magnum T.A. RC .75 .75
325 Venus RC .40 1.00
326 Luke Williams RC .40 .30
327 Road Warrior Animal RC 1.25 3.00
328 Dr. Death Steve Williams RC .50 .50
329 Bobby Eaton RC .40 .30
330 Paul Jones RC .40 .30
331 Butch Miller RC .40 .30
332 Tully Blanchard RC 1.25 3.00
333 Warlord vs. Road Warrior Hawk .75 .75
334 Ivan Koloff w/Paul Jones .50 .50
335 Jamie West RC .40 .30
336 Larry Zbyszko/Dusty Rhodes .75 .75
337 Lex Luger RC .40 1.00
338 Sean Royal RC .40 .30
339 Four Horsemen 30.00 75.00
340 Jimmy Garvin RC .40 .30
341 Road Warriors/Paul Ellering .60 .60
342 Comrade Orga RC .40 .30
343 Magnum T.A. RC .75 .75
NNO Checklist 1 .75 2.00
NNO Checklist 2 .75 2.00
NNO Checklist 3 .75 2.00
NNO Checklist 4 .75 2.00

2019-20 WWE Bray Wyatt Collector's Boxes

Box 1 Firefly Funhouse/500* 125.00 250.00
Box 2 Wyatt Gym/1000* 30.00 75.00
Box 3 The Holidays w/Ramblin' Rabbit 30.00 75.00
Box 4 Mercy the Buzzard

Action Figures & Figurines

2024 Funko Bitty Pops WWE

11 Hulk Hogan CH
46 The Rock CH
47 Razor Ramon
50 Shawn Michaels
52 Triple H CH
61 Batista
68 Bret Hart
69 Undertaker
73 Mean Gene Okerlund
74 Diesel
84 Stone Cold Steve Austin CH
93 Rey Mysterio
97 Jerry Lawler
114 Dusty Rhodes
121 Ricky Steamboat
126 British Bulldog

2024 Funko Bitty Pops WWE 4-Packs

NNO Bret/HEK/Mean Gene/Chase
NNO Dusty/Lawler/Steamboat/Chase
NNO Razor/Diesel/Mysterio/Chase
NNO Undertaker/Bulldog/Batista/Chase

2015 Funko Mystery Minis WWE Series 1

COMPLETE SET (15)	55.00	110.00
UNOPENED CASE (12 BOXES)		
UNOPENED BOX (1 MINI)		
NNO Andre the Giant	3.00	6.00
NNO Brie Bella	3.00	6.00
NNO Daniel Bryan	3.00	6.00
NNO George The Animal Steele	6.00	12.00
NNO Hacksaw Jim Duggan WM	10.00	20.00
NNO Hulk Hogan	12.50	25.00
NNO Iron Sheik	6.00	12.00
NNO John Cena	3.00	6.00
NNO Nikki Bella	4.00	8.00
NNO Randy Savage WM	12.50	25.00
NNO Ric Flair	12.50	25.00
NNO Rock	7.50	15.00
NNO Rowdy Roddy Piper WM	15.00	30.00
NNO Ultimate Warrior	6.00	12.00
NNO Undertaker	4.00	8.00

2016 Funko Mystery Minis WWE Series 2

COMPLETE SET (15)	50.00	100.00
UNOPENED CASE (12 BOXES)		
UNOPENED BOX (1 MINI)		
NNO Bret Hitman Hart	3.00	6.00
NNO Brock Lesnar	4.00	8.00
NNO Dusty Rhodes	3.00	6.00
NNO Goldust	3.00	6.00
NNO Jake The Snake Roberts TAR	20.00	40.00
NNO John Cena	4.00	8.00
NNO Kevin Nash	3.00	6.00
NNO Ted DiBiase	3.00	6.00
NNO Randy Orton	3.00	6.00
NNO Razor Ramon TAR	15.00	30.00
NNO Roman Reigns	3.00	6.00
NNO Seth Rollins	3.00	6.00
NNO Sgt. Slaughter TAR	10.00	20.00
NNO Sting	3.00	6.00
NNO Stone Cold Steve Austin	6.00	12.00

2017 Funko Pint Size Heroes WWE

COMPLETE SET (19)	75.00	150.00
NNO Andre the Giant	10.00	20.00
NNO Big E	4.00	8.00
NNO Bray Wyatt	4.00	8.00
NNO Brock Lesnar	3.00	6.00
NNO Enzo Amore	5.00	10.00
NNO Finn Balor TRU	10.00	20.00
NNO John Cena	3.00	6.00
NNO Kevin Owens	4.00	8.00
NNO Kofi Kingston	5.00	10.00
NNO Macho Man Randy Savage	15.00	30.00
NNO Nikki Bella	4.00	8.00
NNO Ric Flair TRU	7.50	15.00
NNO Roman Reigns	4.00	8.00
NNO Sasha Banks	4.00	8.00
NNO Seth Rollins	3.00	6.00
NNO Stone Cold Steve Austin TRU	10.00	20.00
NNO Ultimate Warrior	7.50	15.00
NNO Undertaker	4.00	8.00
NNO Xavier Woods	3.00	6.00

2020-24 Funko Pop Vinyl Art Series

44 The Rock WM

2011-24 Funko Pop Vinyl Freddy Funko

COMMON FUNKO POP	12.50	25.00
34A Hulk Hogan/500* FD	600.00	1200.00
34B Hulk Hogan Injured /500* FD	600.00	1200.00
52 Sting/500* FD	600.00	1200.00

2022-24 Funko Pop Vinyl Magazine Covers

17 Hulk Hogan
(2023 Target Exclusive)
18 Mr. T
(2023 Target Exclusive)

2015-19 Funko Pop Vinyl Pocket Pop Keychains WWE

NNO Hulk Hogan	7.50	15.00
NNO John Cena V	7.50	15.00
NNO John Cena WM DVD	6.00	12.00
NNO Macho Man WM DVD	6.00	12.00
NNO The Rock WM DVD	6.00	12.00
NNO Sting WM DVD	5.00	10.00
NNO Ultimate Warrior WM DVD	7.50	15.00
NNO Undertaker WM DVD	10.00	20.00

2018-19 Funko Pop Vinyl Pro Wrestling

1 Kenny Omega	7.50	15.00
2 American Nightmare Cody	7.50	15.00

2018-19 Funko Pop Vinyl Pro Wrestling Multi-Packs

NNO Young Bucks	7.50	15.00
NNO Young Bucks Purple/Gold HT	10.00	20.00

2011-24 Funko Pop Vinyl WWE

1A John Cena	30.00	75.00
1B J.Cena Black Pants WWE.com	200.00	400.00
1C J.Cena Green-Orange	30.00	60.00
1D J.Cena Green Hat WWE.com	400.00	800.00
2A CM Punk V	125.00	250.00
2B CM Punk Pink Trunks HT	300.00	600.00
3 The Rock V	30.00	75.00
4 Sheamus V	40.00	80.00
5A Stone Cold Steve Austin V	30.00	75.00
5B SC Steve Austin 2K16 PRE	60.00	125.00
5C SC Steve Austin 2K16 GS	25.00	50.00
5D SC Steve Austin 2K16 EB	25.00	50.00
6A Rey Mysterio V	175.00	350.00
6B R.Mysterio Bright Blue 7-11	250.00	500.00
6C Rey Mysterio Dark SDCC	375.00	750.00
7A Daniel Bryan V	50.00	100.00
7B Daniel Bryan Red Trunks HT/UT	40.00	80.00
7C Daniel Bryan Patterned WWE.com	300.00	600.00
8 Undertaker	60.00	120.00
9 Triple H V	40.00	80.00
10A Macho Man Randy Savage V	30.00	60.00
10B Savage Pink WWE.com	250.00	500.00
10C Macho Man Randy Savage Purple FYE	30.00	75.00
11A Hulk Hogan	30.00	75.00
11B Hogan Hulk Rules WWE.com	250.00	500.00
11C Hollywood Hogan WWE 2K15	200.00	400.00
12 AJ Lee WWE.com	200.00	400.00
13 Brock Lesnar WM	50.00	100.00
14 Brie Bella	25.00	50.00
15 Nikki Bella	25.00	50.00
16 Paige V	75.00	150.00
17 Ric Flair TAR	25.00	50.00
18 Roddy Piper TAR	25.00	50.00
19A Sting	75.00	150.00
19B Wolfpac Sting GS	100.00	200.00
20 Ultimate Warrior	30.00	75.00
21 Andre the Giant	25.00	50.00
23 Roman Reigns	40.00	80.00
24A Seth Rollins V	30.00	60.00
24B Seth Rollins White Attire FYE	30.00	60.00
25 Bret Hart	30.00	75.00
26 Eva Marie	7.50	15.00
27 Kevin Owens V	25.00	50.00
28 Bray Wyatt V	75.00	150.00
29 Big E	10.00	20.00
30 Xavier Woods	7.50	15.00
31 Kofi Kingston	7.50	15.00
32 Shawn Michaels WG	25.00	50.00
33 Kane WG	40.00	80.00
34A Finn Balor	15.00	30.00
34B Finn Balor Demon Mask CH	40.00	80.00
35 Mick Foley	50.00	100.00
36 Goldberg	30.00	75.00
37 AJ Styles	12.50	25.00
38 The Demon Finn Balor FYE	15.00	30.00
39 Bayley TRU	17.50	35.00
40A Chris Jericho Red	25.00	50.00
40B Chris Jericho Blue FYE	17.50	35.00
41A Million Dollar Man Black	17.50	35.00
41B Million Dollar Man White CH	40.00	80.00
42 Sasha Banks	30.00	75.00
43A Iron Sheik White	17.50	35.00
43B Iron Sheik Red CH	30.00	60.00
44A Zack Ryder NYCC	30.00	75.00
44B Zack Ryder FCE	20.00	40.00
44C Zack Ryder Green Tights/500* FHQ	400.00	800.00
45 Shinsuke Nakamura TRU	20.00	40.00
46A The Rock	15.00	30.00
46B The Rock Black Jacket CH	20.00	40.00
46C The Rock Gold NYCC	25.00	50.00
46D The Rock Gold TAR	15.00	30.00
47A Razor Ramon	12.50	25.00
47B Razor Ramon nWo Trunks CH	40.00	80.00
47C Razor Ramon Purple GS	12.50	25.00
48 Braun Strowman	20.00	40.00
49 Alexa Bliss	25.00	50.00
50 Shawn Michaels	25.00	50.00
51A Jake The Snake Robers Green	20.00	40.00
51B Jake The Snake Roberts Blue CH	40.00	80.00
52A Triple H	12.50	25.00
52B Triple H Masked CH	50.00	100.00
53A Mr. McMahon	12.50	25.00
53B Mr. McMahon Pink Jacket CH	40.00	80.00
54 Sgt. Slaughter	20.00	40.00
55 Kurt Angle	30.00	75.00
56A Asuka SDCC	40.00	80.00
56B Asuka SCE	10.00	20.00
56C Asuka w/Mask WM	20.00	40.00
56D Asuka w/Mask TAR	20.00	40.00
57 Ric Flair Classic 2K19	60.00	120.00
58 Ronda Rousey	17.50	35.00
59 John Cena Clear AMZ	25.00	50.00
60 Randy Orton	15.00	30.00
61 Batista	12.50	25.00
62A Charlotte Flair	10.00	20.00
62B Charlotte Flair Blue Robe FL	15.00	30.00
63 Ric Flair Red Robe	30.00	60.00
64 Andre the Giant 6" WM	15.00	30.00
65 Becky Lynch	7.50	15.00
66A Trish Stratus	7.50	15.00
66B Trish Stratus DC Web Exclusive	15.00	30.00
67 Elias	10.00	20.00
68 Bret Hit Man Hart Pink	30.00	75.00
69A Undertaker Hooded	12.50	25.00
69B Undertaker Hooded Purple Translucent AMZ	10.00	20.00
70 Becky Lynch The Man AMZ	12.50	25.00
71 Hulk Hogan Python Power WM	12.50	25.00
72 The Miz	10.00	20.00

- 73 Mean Gene Okerlund 7.50 15.00
- 74A Diesel 12.50 25.00
- 74B Kevin Nash CH 40.00 80.00
- 75A Naomi 7.50 15.00
- 75B Naomi GITD CH 20.00 40.00
- 76 John Cena Thuganomics 12.50 25.00
- 77 The Fiend Bray Wyatt AMZ 25.00 50.00
- 78 The Rock w/Microphone 12.50 25.00
- 79 Macho Man Randy Savage DC GS 12.50 25.00
- 80 Mr. T 10.00 20.00
- 81 Undertaker ABA AMZ 10.00 20.00
- 82 Ric Flair '92 Royal Rumble GS 20.00 40.00
- 83 Macho Man Randy Savage Checkered Glasses GS 7.50 15.00
- 84 Stone Cold Steve Austin w/Belt 10.00 20.00
- 85 Chyna 7.50 15.00
- 86 Edge 7.50 15.00
- 87 Drew McIntyre 7.50 15.00
- 88 Otis MITB 7.50 15.00
- 89 Stone Cold Steve Austin 2 Belts 71115.00 30.00
- 90 Eddie Guerrero w/Pop Pin GS 12.50 25.00
- 91 The Rock Bring It Shirt EE 10.00 20.00
- 92 Xavier Woods Up Up Down Down MET TAR 10.00 20.00
- 93A Rey Mysterio 10.00 20.00
- 93B Rey Mysterio GITD AMZ 12.50 25.00
- 94 Angelo Dawkins 7.50 15.00
- 95 Montez Ford 7.50 15.00
- 96 Asuka 7.50 15.00
- 97 Jerry Lawler 7.50 15.00
- 98 Roman Reigns MET AMZ 12.50 25.00
- 99 Triple H DX GS 7.50 15.00
- 100 The Fiend Bray Wyatt Santa WM 15.00 30.00
- 101 Shawn Michaels DX GS 10.00 20.00
- 102 Becky Lynch w/Two Belts TAR 10.00 20.00
- 103 Mankind GS 17.50 35.00
- 104 Alexa Bliss w/Lilly WM 10.00 20.00
- 105 Cactus Jack GS 12.50 25.00
- 106 Undertaker Coffin GS 15.00 30.00
- 107A Alexa Bliss White Dress 10.00 20.00
- 107B Alexa Bliss Black Dress CH 20.00 40.00
- 108A Bianca Belair Purple 7.50 15.00
- 108B Bianca Belair Red 7.50 15.00
- 109 Dude Love 7.50 15.00
- 110 Brock Lesnar Cowboy 7.50 15.00
- 111 Roman Reigns HOTT WM 12.50 25.00
- 112 Macho Man Randy Savage EE 12.50 25.00
- 113 Paul Heyman GS 7.50 15.00
- 114 Dusty Rhodes 10.00 20.00
- 115 Riddle 7.50 15.00
- 116 Randy Orton 10.00 20.00
- 117 Rob Van Dam GS 7.50 15.00
- 118 Finn Balor AMZ 10.00 20.00
- 119 Bam Bam Bigelow GITD WM 10.00 20.00
- 120A Rocky Maivia 10.00 20.00
- 120B Rocky Maivia MET FS 15.00 30.00
- 121 Ricky The Dragon Steamboat 10.00 20.00
- 122 Rhea Ripley 20.00 40.00
- 123 Cody Rhodes WM 25.00 50.00
- 124A Ted DiBiase GS 10.00 20.00
- 124B Ted DiBiase DC GS CH 40.00 80.00
- 126 British Bulldog 10.00 20.00
- 127A Beth Phoenix 7.50 15.00
- 127B Beth Phoenix Street Gear CH 30.00 60.00
- 128 King Booker 12.50 25.00
- 130 Liv Morgan 10.00 20.00
- 131 Roman Reigns 12.50 25.00
- 134A Johnny Knoxville SDCC 30.00 60.00
- 134B Johnny Knoxville SCE 25.00 50.00
- 135 Big Boss Man GS 10.00 20.00
- 136 John Cena 7.50 15.00
- 137 The Rock 7.50 15.00
- 138 Vader 7.50 15.00
- 139 Triple H Skull King 15.00 30.00
- 140 Rick Rude 7.50 15.00
- 142 Ultimate Warrior HOF GS 17.50 35.00
- 143 Kane HOF SE
- 145 Braun Strowman
- 146 Kurt Angle
- 147 Rowdy Roddy Piper
- 148 Shotzi
- 149 Hulk Hogan
- 150 Rikishi TAR
- 151 Hurricane TAR
- 152 Cody Rhodes

1991 Galoob WCW Superstars 14-Inch

- NNO Lex Luger 50.00 100.00
- NNO Ric Flair 60.00 120.00
- NNO Sid Vicious 50.00 100.00
- NNO Sting 100.00 200.00

1991 Galoob WCW Superstars 14-Inch (loose)

- NNO Lex Luger 20.00 40.00
- NNO Ric Flair 30.00 75.00
- NNO Sid Vicious 30.00 75.00
- NNO Sting 30.00 60.00

1991 Galoob WCW Superstars Accessories

- NNO 12-Figure Collector's Case 30.00 75.00
- NNO Championship Belt 75.00 150.00
- NNO Slam Action Wrestling Arena 125.00 250.00

1991 Galoob WCW Superstars Series 1

- NNO Arn Anderson 30.00 60.00
- NNO Barry Windham 25.00 50.00
- NNO Brian Pillman 30.00 60.00
- NNO Butch Reed 20.00 40.00
- NNO Lex Luger 15.00 30.00
- NNO Ric Flair 50.00 90.00
- NNO Rick Steiner 20.00 40.00
- NNO Ron Simmons 20.00 40.00
- NNO Scott Steiner 20.00 40.00
- NNO Sid Vicious 30.00 60.00
- NNO Sting/Blue Tights 30.00 60.00
- NNO Sting/Orange Tights 150.00 300.00
- NNO Tom Zenk 20.00 40.00

1991 Galoob WCW Superstars Series 1 (loose)

- NNO Arn Anderson 7.50 15.00
- NNO Barry Windham 7.50 15.00
- NNO Brian Pillman 7.50 15.00
- NNO Butch Reed 10.00 20.00
- NNO Lex Luger 7.50 15.00
- NNO Ric Flair 10.00 20.00
- NNO Rick Steiner 7.50 15.00
- NNO Ron Simmons 7.50 15.00
- NNO Scott Steiner 7.50 15.00
- NNO Sid Vicious 10.00 20.00
- NNO Sting/Blue Tights 12.50 25.00
- NNO Sting/Orange Tights 25.00 50.00
- NNO Tom Zenk 6.00 12.00

1991 Galoob WCW Superstars Series 2

- NNO Arn Anderson/Red Trunks 125.00 250.00
- NNO Barry Windham/Blue Trunks 125.00 250.00
- NNO Brian Pillman/Lt Blue Trunks 100.00 200.00
- NNO Lex Luger/Green Trunks 125.00 250.00
- NNO Ric Flair/Red Trunks 150.00 300.00
- NNO Rick Steiner/Green Tights 100.00 200.00
- NNO Ron Simmons/Blue Tights 25.00 50.00
- NNO Scott Steiner/Red & Blue Tights 125.00 250.00
- NNO Sid Vicious/Pink Tights 100.00 200.00
- NNO Sting/Black Tights 150.00 300.00

1991 Galoob WCW Superstars Series 2 (loose)

- NNO Arn Anderson/Red Trunks 15.00 30.00
- NNO Barry Windham/Blue Trunks 12.50 25.00
- NNO Brian Pillman/Lt Blue Trunks 25.00 50.00
- NNO Lex Luger/Green Trunks 20.00 40.00
- NNO Ric Flair/Red Trunks 15.00 30.00
- NNO Rick Steiner/Green Tights 15.00 30.00
- NNO Ron Simmons/Blue Tights 20.00 40.00
- NNO Scott Steiner/Red & Blue Tights 25.00 50.00
- NNO Sid Vicious/Pink Tights 20.00 40.00
- NNO Sting/Black Tights 20.00 40.00

1991 Galoob WCW Superstars UK

- NNO Big Josh 500.00 1000.00
- NNO Dustin Rhodes 100.00 200.00
- NNO El Gigante 150.00 300.00
- NNO Jimmy Garvin 150.00 300.00
- NNO Lex Luger/Robe
- NNO Michael Hayes 200.00 350.00
- NNO Sting/Robe 250.00 400.00

1991 Galoob WCW Superstars UK (loose)

- NNO Big Josh 150.00 300.00
- NNO Dustin Rhodes 75.00 150.00
- NNO El Gigante 30.00 75.00
- NNO Jimmy Garvin 20.00 40.00
- NNO Lex Luger/Robe 75.00 150.00
- NNO Michael Hayes 20.00 40.00
- NNO Sting/Robe 60.00 120.00

1991 Galoob WCW Tag Team Superstars UK

- NNO Lex Luger/Sting
- NNO Michael Haynes/Jimmy Garvin
- NNO Ric Flair/Arn Anderson
- NNO Rick & Scott Steiner

1990 Galoob WCW Tag Team Superstars US

- NNO Lex Luger/Sting 75.00 150.00
- NNO Ric Flair/Arn Anderson 75.00 150.00
- NNO Rick & Scott Steiner 60.00 120.00
- NNO Ron Simmons/Butch Reed 100.00 200.00

1990 Hasbro WWF Series 1

- NNO Akeem 200.00 350.00
- NNO Andre the Giant 150.00 300.00
- NNO Ax 125.00 250.00
- NNO Big Boss Man 75.00 150.00
- NNO Brutus The Barber Beefcake 60.00 120.00
- NNO Hulk Hogan 150.00 300.00
- NNO Jake The Snake Roberts 100.00 200.00
- NNO Macho Man Randy Savage 300.00 600.00
- NNO Ted DiBiase 125.00 250.00
- NNO Ravishing Rick Rude 125.00 250.00
- NNO Smash 60.00 120.00
- NNO Ultimate Warrior 200.00 350.00

1990 Hasbro WWF Series 1 (loose)

- NNO Akeem 10.00 20.00
- NNO Andre the Giant 25.00 50.00
- NNO Ax 12.50 25.00
- NNO Big Boss Man 10.00 20.00
- NNO Brutus The Barber Beefcake 12.50 25.00
- NNO Hulk Hogan 15.00 30.00
- NNO Jake The Snake Roberts 12.50 25.00
- NNO Macho Man Randy Savage 20.00 40.00
- NNO Ted DiBiase 10.00 20.00
- NNO Ravishing Rick Rude 7.50 15.00
- NNO Smash 7.50 15.00
- NNO Ultimate Warrior 10.00 20.00

1991 Hasbro WWF Series 2

- NNO Dusty Rhodes 600.00 1000.00
- NNO Hacksaw Jim Duggan 75.00 150.00
- NNO Honky Tonk Man 60.00 120.00
- NNO Hulk Hogan 75.00 150.00
- NNO Macho King 150.00 300.00
- NNO Million Dollar Man 75.00 150.00
- NNO Rowdy Roddy Piper 75.00 150.00
- NNO Superfly Jim Snuka 60.00 120.00
- NNO Ultimate Warrior 125.00 250.00

1991 Hasbro WWF Series 2 (loose)

- NNO Dusty Rhodes 50.00 100.00
- NNO Hacksaw Jim Duggan 10.00 20.00
- NNO Honky Tonk Man 15.00 30.00
- NNO Hulk Hogan 12.50 25.00
- NNO Macho King 25.00 50.00
- NNO Million Dollar Man 7.50 15.00
- NNO Rowdy Roddy Piper 7.50 15.00
- NNO Superfly Jim Snuka 7.50 15.00
- NNO Ultimate Warrior 15.00 30.00

1991 Hasbro WWF Series 2 Tag Teams

- NNO The Bushwhackers 60.00 120.00
- NNO Demolition 150.00 300.00
- NNO The Rockers 60.00 120.00

1991 Hasbro WWF Series 2 Tag Teams (loose)

- NNO Butch 12.50 25.00
- NNO Crush 10.00 20.00
- NNO Luke 12.50 25.00
- NNO Marty Jannetty 10.00 20.00
- NNO Shawn Michaels 10.00 20.00
- NNO Smash 10.00 20.00

1992 Hasbro WWF Series 3

- NNO Big Boss Man 60.00 120.00
- NNO Brutus Beefcake/Zebra Tights 200.00 400.00
- NNO Earthquake 75.00 150.00
- NNO Greg The Hammer Valentine 50.00 100.00
- NNO Hulk Hogan 100.00 200.00
- NNO Koko B. Ware 75.00 150.00
- NNO Macho Man Randy Savage 90.00 175.00
- NNO Mr. Perfect 60.00 120.00
- NNO Sgt. Slaughter 60.00 120.00
- NNO Texas Tornado 60.00 120.00
- NNO Typhoon 50.00 100.00
- NNO Ultimate Warrior 125.00 250.00

1992 Hasbro WWF Series 3 (loose)

NNO	Big Boss Man	10.00	20.00
NNO	Brutus The Barber Beefcake	30.00	60.00
NNO	Earthquake	12.50	25.00
NNO	Greg The Hammer Valentine	10.00	20.00
NNO	Hulk Hogan	15.00	30.00
NNO	Koko B. Ware	15.00	30.00
NNO	Macho Man Randy Savage	10.00	20.00
NNO	Mr. Perfect	15.00	30.00
NNO	Sgt. Slaughter	15.00	30.00
NNO	Texas Tornado	12.50	25.00
NNO	Typhoon	10.00	20.00
NNO	Ultimate Warrior	25.00	50.00

1992 Hasbro WWF Series 3 Tag Teams

NNO	Legion of Doom	125.00	250.00
NNO	Nasty Boys	125.00	250.00

1992 Hasbro WWF Series 3 Tag Teams (loose)

NNO	Animal	20.00	40.00
NNO	Hawk	20.00	40.00
NNO	Knobbs	10.00	20.00
NNO	Sags	10.00	20.00

1992 Hasbro WWF Series 4

NNO	Bret Hart	200.00	350.00
NNO	British Bulldog	75.00	150.00
NNO	Ricky The Dragon Steamboat	50.00	100.00
NNO	Undertaker	75.00	150.00

1992 Hasbro WWF Series 4 (loose)

NNO	Bret Hart	20.00	40.00
NNO	British Bulldog	12.50	25.00
NNO	Ricky The Dragon Steamboat	12.50	25.00
NNO	Undertaker	20.00	40.00

1993 Hasbro WWF Series 5

NNO	Hulk Hogan	75.00	150.00
NNO	IRS	50.00	100.00
NNO	Jim Neidhart	60.00	120.00
NNO	Macho Man	100.00	200.00
NNO	Mountie	50.00	100.00
NNO	Rick Martel	50.00	100.00
NNO	Sid Justice	60.00	120.00
NNO	Skinner	50.00	100.00
NNO	Virgil	30.00	75.00
NNO	Warlord	60.00	120.00

1993 Hasbro WWF Series 5 (loose)

NNO	Hulk Hogan	12.50	25.00
NNO	IRS	10.00	20.00
NNO	Jim Neidhart	10.00	20.00
NNO	Macho Man	20.00	40.00
NNO	Mountie	20.00	40.00
NNO	Rick Martel	12.50	25.00
NNO	Sid Justice	12.50	25.00
NNO	Skinner	12.50	25.00
NNO	Virgil	10.00	20.00
NNO	Warlord	15.00	30.00

1993 Hasbro WWF Series 6

NNO	Berzerker	75.00	150.00
NNO	El Matador	30.00	75.00
NNO	Papa Shango	75.00	150.00
NNO	Repo Man	60.00	120.00
NNO	Ric Flair	125.00	250.00
NNO	Tatanka	50.00	100.00

1993 Hasbro WWF Series 6 (loose)

NNO	Berzerker	20.00	40.00
NNO	El Matador	12.50	25.00
NNO	Papa Shango	15.00	30.00
NNO	Repo Man	12.50	25.00
NNO	Ric Flair	15.00	30.00
NNO	Tatanka	10.00	20.00

1993 Hasbro WWF Series 7

NNO	Crush	75.00	150.00
NNO	Kamala/Star on Belly	100.00	200.00
NNO	Kamala/Crescent Moon Belly	4000.00	8000.00
NNO	Nailz	125.00	250.00
NNO	Owen Hart	150.00	300.00
NNO	Razor Ramon	75.00	150.00
NNO	Shawn Michaels	75.00	150.00

1993 Hasbro WWF Series 7 (loose)

NNO	Crush	15.00	30.00
NNO	Kamala/Star on Belly	20.00	40.00
NNO	Kamala/Crescent Moon Belly	750.00	1500.00
NNO	Nailz	25.00	50.00
NNO	Owen Hart	25.00	50.00
NNO	Razor Ramon	25.00	50.00
NNO	Shawn Michaels	25.00	50.00

1993 Hasbro WWF Series 8

NNO	Bam Bam Bigelow	125.00	250.00
NNO	Bret Hart	200.00	400.00
NNO	Lex Luger	75.00	150.00
NNO	Mr. Perfect	100.00	200.00
NNO	Undertaker	250.00	500.00
NNO	Yokozuna	100.00	200.00

1993 Hasbro WWF Series 8 (loose)

NNO	Bam Bam Bigelow	25.00	50.00
NNO	Bret Hart	30.00	75.00
NNO	Lex Luger	15.00	30.00
NNO	Mr. Perfect	15.00	30.00
NNO	Undertaker	60.00	120.00
NNO	Yokozuna	30.00	75.00

1993 Hasbro WWF Series 9

NNO	Doink the Clown	100.00	200.00
NNO	Hacksaw Jim Duggan	100.00	200.00
NNO	Million Dollar Man	75.00	150.00
NNO	Rick Steiner	60.00	120.00
NNO	Scott Steiner	50.00	100.00
NNO	Tatanka	60.00	120.00

1993 Hasbro WWF Series 9 (loose)

NNO	Doink the Clown	25.00	50.00
NNO	Hacksaw Jim Duggan	30.00	75.00
NNO	Million Dollar Man	20.00	40.00
NNO	Rick Steiner	20.00	40.00
NNO	Scott Steiner	15.00	30.00

1993 Hasbro WWF Series 10

NNO	Butch	50.00	100.00
NNO	Fatu	50.00	100.00
NNO	Giant Gonzalez	60.00	120.00
NNO	Luke	50.00	100.00
NNO	Marty Jannetty	30.00	75.00
NNO	Razor Ramon/Purple Shorts	125.00	250.00
NNO	Razor Ramon/Red Shorts	150.00	300.00
NNO	Samu	30.00	75.00
NNO	Shawn Michaels/Black Tights	200.00	400.00
NNO	Shawn Michaels/White Tights	150.00	300.00

1993 Hasbro WWF Series 10 (loose)

NNO	Butch	15.00	30.00
NNO	Fatu	10.00	20.00
NNO	Giant Gonzalez	12.50	25.00
NNO	Luke	15.00	30.00
NNO	Marty Jannetty	15.00	30.00
NNO	Razor Ramon/Purple Shorts	50.00	100.00
NNO	Razor Ramon/Red Shorts	15.00	30.00
NNO	Samu	10.00	20.00
NNO	Shawn Michaels/Black Tights	50.00	100.00
NNO	Shawn Michaels/White Tights	10.00	20.00

1994 Hasbro WWF Series 11

NNO	1-2-3 Kid	500.00	1000.00
NNO	Adam Bomb	125.00	250.00
NNO	Bart Gunn	150.00	300.00
NNO	Billy Gunn	150.00	300.00
NNO	Crush	300.00	600.00
NNO	Ludvig Borga	150.00	300.00
NNO	Yokozuna	300.00	600.00

1994 Hasbro WWF Series 11 (loose)

NNO	1-2-3 Kid	200.00	400.00
NNO	Adam Bomb	100.00	200.00
NNO	Bart Gunn	100.00	200.00
NNO	Billy Gunn	125.00	250.00
NNO	Crush	125.00	250.00
NNO	Ludvig Borga	75.00	150.00
NNO	Yokozuna	75.00	150.00

1992 Hasbro WWF Accessories and Playsets

NNO King of the Ring (yellow)
NNO Official Wrestling Ring (blue)
NNO Official Wrestling Ring (sound effects)

1993 Hasbro WWF Magazine Series

NNO	Bret Hart	600.00	1200.00
NNO	Hulk Hogan	600.00	1200.00
NNO	Undertaker	1500.00	2500.00

1993 Hasbro WWF Magazine Series (loose)

NNO	Bret Hart	50.00	100.00
NNO	Hulk Hogan	400.00	800.00
NNO	Undertaker	1000.00	1500.00

1992 Hasbro WWF Mini Wrestlers

NNO	Brutus Beefcake/Butch/Luke Greg Valentine	30.00	75.00
NNO	Mr. Perfect/Jim Duggan Roddy Piper/Texas Tornado	30.00	75.00
NNO	Typhoon/Earthquake/Animal/Hawk	25.00	60.00

1992 Hasbro WWF Mini Wrestlers Playset

NNO Royal Rumble Wrestling Ring (w/Hogan/Slaughter/Roberts/DiBiase/Boss Man/Savage

1992 Hasbro WWF Mini Wrestlers Playset Figures (loose)

NNO	Big Boss Man	10.00	20.00
NNO	Hulk Hogan	20.00	40.00
NNO	Jake The Snake Roberts	15.00	30.00
NNO	Macho Man Randy Savage	20.00	40.00
NNO	Ted DiBiase	10.00	20.00
NNO	Sgt. Slaughter	20.00	40.00

2019 HeroClix WWE Series 1 Mixed Match Challenge

107 Charlotte Flair
108 Sasha Banks
109 Finn Balor
110 AJ Styles
111 WWE Ring

2019 HeroClix WWE Series 1 Mixed Match Challenge Maps

M001 WWE Backstage Area
M001 WWE Arena

2019 HeroClix WWE Series 1 Rock 'N Sock Starter Set

101 The Rock
102 Mankind
103 Stone Cold Steve Austin
104 Triple H
105 Ric Flair
106 Shawn Michaels

2019 HeroClix WWE Series 1 Rock 'N Sock Starter Set Maps

M001 WWE Training Center
M002 WWE War Games

1998 The Idea Factory WCW Beanbag Brawlers Series 1

NNO Bret "Hit Man" Hart/21,000*
NNO Diamond Dallas Page/28,000*
NNO Goldberg/35,000*
NNO Hollywood Hogan/21,000*
NNO Kevin Nash/28,000*
NNO Sting/35,000*

1999 The Idea Factory WCW Beanbag Brawlers Series 2

NNO Booker T/
NNO Buff Bagwell/
NNO Goldberg/
NNO Jeff Jarrett/
NNO Scott Steiner/
NNO Sting/
NNO Vampiro/

2017 Jada Toys WWE Metalfigs 2.5-Inch

M228 John Cena
M229 Brock Lesnar
M230 Triple H
M231 Finn Balor
M232 Paige
M243 Sasha Banks

2017 Jada Toys WWE Metalfigs 4-Inch

M200 Finn Balor
M202 Paige
M203 Brock Lesnar
M205 John Cena
M206 Sami Zayn
M207 Sasha Banks
M210 Seth Rollins
M211 The Rock
M212 Charlotte Flair
M213 Kevin Owens
M218 AJ Styles
M220 The Rock

M242 John Cena
M275 Finn Balor

2017 Jada Toys WWE Metalfigs 6-Inch

M209 Triple H

2017 Jada Toys WWE Nano Metalfigs

W1 John Cena
W2 Triple H
W3 The Rock
W4 Roman Reigns
W5 Charlotte Flair
W6 Bayley
W7 Sami Zayn
W8 Chris Jericho
W9 Dean Ambrose
W10 Macho Man Randy Savage
W11 Sting
W12 Undertaker
W13 AJ Styles
W14 Kevin Owens
W15 Seth Rollins
W16 Finn Balor
W17 Sasha Banks
W18 Brock Lesnar
W19 Becky Lynch
W20 Kalisto
W21 Bray Wyatt
W22 Nikki Bella
W23 Ultimate Warrior
W24 Rowdy Roddy Piper

2017 Jada Toys WWE Nano Metalfigs 20-Pack

NNO Cena/Triple H/Rock/Reigns/Charlotte Bayley/Zayn/Jericho/Ambrose/Savage#{Sting/Undertaker/Styles/Owens/Rollins#{Balor/Banks/Lesnar/Kalisto/Wyatt#{(2017 Toys R Us Exclusive)

2007-08 Jakks Pacific ECW Wrestling Series 1

NNO CM Punk 20.00 40.00
NNO Kevin Thorn 25.00 50.00
NNO Rob Van Dam 15.00 30.00
NNO Sandman 25.00 50.00
NNO Tommy Dreamer 25.00 50.00

2007-08 Jakks Pacific ECW Wrestling Series 2

NNO Ariel 15.00 30.00
NNO Balls Mahoney 12.50 25.00
NNO Elijah Burke 25.00 50.00
NNO Joey Styles 20.00 40.00
NNO Kelly Kelly 25.00 50.00
NNO Mike Knox 15.00 30.00

2007-08 Jakks Pacific ECW Wrestling Series 3

NNO Layla 12.50 25.00
NNO Marcus Cor Von
NNO Matt Striker 7.50 15.00
NNO Nunzio 6.00 12.00
NNO Snitsky
NNO Stevie Richards
NNO Tazz

2007-08 Jakks Pacific ECW Wrestling Series 4

NNO Boogeyman
NNO CM Punk 7.50 15.00
NNO Elijah Burke 15.00 30.00
NNO John Morrison 10.00 20.00
NNO Matt Striker
NNO Tommy Dreamer

2007-08 Jakks Pacific ECW Wrestling Series 5

NNO Christian 12.50 25.00
NNO Evan Bourne
NNO Fit Finlay 12.50 25.00
NNO Jack Swagger
NNO Mark Henry
NNO Tyson Kidd 6.00 12.00

2010 Jakks Pacific TNA Wrestling Cross the Line Series 1

NNO James Storm/Bobby Roode 30.00 75.00
NNO Samoa Joe/Mick Foley 30.00 60.00
NNO Scott Steiner/Kevin Nash 25.00 50.00

2010 Jakks Pacific TNA Wrestling Cross the Line Series 2

NNO AJ Styles/Jeff Jarrett
NNO Alex Shelley/Chris Sabin 30.00 75.00
NNO Brother Ray/Brother Devon

2010 Jakks Pacific TNA Wrestling Cross the Line Series 3

NNO AJ Styles/Jeff Hardy
NNO Kurt Angle/Mr. Anderson 20.00 40.00
NNO Stevie Richards/Daffney 12.50 25.00

2010 Jakks Pacific TNA Wrestling Cross the Line Series 4

NNO Eric Young/Kevin Nash 15.00 30.00
NNO Hulk Hogan/Abyss 30.00 75.00
NNO Sting/Rob Van Dam 20.00 40.00

2010 Jakks Pacific TNA Wrestling Deluxe Impact Series 1

NNO AJ Styles/No Stubble
NNO AJ Styles/Stubble
NNO Jeff Jarrett/Dk Blonde Hair 10.00 20.00
NNO Jeff Jarrett/Lt Blonde Hair
NNO Kurt Angle 10.00 20.00
NNO Samoa Joe 15.00 30.00
NNO Sting
NNO Suicide

2010 Jakks Pacific TNA Wrestling Deluxe Impact Series 1 Slammin' Celebration Exclusives

NNO AJ Styles
NNO Jeff Jarrett
NNO Kurt Angle
NNO Samoa Joe
NNO Sting
NNO Suicide

2010 Jakks Pacific TNA Wrestling Deluxe Impact Series 2

NNO AJ Styles
NNO Amazing Red
NNO Eric Young
NNO Hernandez 25.00 50.00
NNO Hulk Hogan 40.00 80.00
NNO Mick Foley

2010 Jakks Pacific TNA Wrestling Deluxe Impact Series 3

NNO Jay Lethal 15.00 30.00
NNO Kevin Nash 12.50 25.00
NNO Matt Morgan 20.00 40.00
NNO Shark Boy 15.00 30.00
NNO Sting
NNO Velvet Sky 20.00 40.00

2010 Jakks Pacific TNA Wrestling Deluxe Impact Series 4

NNO Abyss 50.00 100.00
NNO D'Angelo Dinero
NNO Desmond Wolfe 25.00 50.00
NNO Hulk Hogan 30.00 60.00
NNO Jeff Hardy
NNO Rob Van Dam

2010 Jakks Pacific TNA Wrestling Deluxe Impact Series 5

NNO Angelina Love 20.00 40.00
NNO Jeff Hardy
NNO Mr. Anderson
NNO Raven LOTR
NNO Rob Terry 10.00 20.00
NNO Samoa Joe 20.00 40.00

2011 Jakks Pacific TNA Wrestling Deluxe Impact Series 6

NNO Doug Williams
NNO Kazarian 12.50 25.00
NNO Kurt Angle 15.00 30.00
NNO Madison Rayne 20.00 40.00
NNO Sting 15.00 30.00
NNO Terry Taylor LOTR 17.50 35.00

2012 Jakks Pacific TNA Wrestling Deluxe Impact Series 7

NNO Bobby Roode 10.00 20.00
NNO James Storm
NNO James Storm/Belt 30.00 75.00
NNO Jeff Hardy 30.00 60.00
NNO Mr. Anderson 10.00 20.00
NNO Velvet Sky 12.50 25.00

2012 Jakks Pacific TNA Wrestling Deluxe Impact Series 8

NNO AJ Styles
NNO Hulk Hogan 30.00 60.00
NNO Matt Morgan 7.50 15.00
NNO Rob Van Dam
NNO Rob Van Dam/Belt
NNO Sting

2013 Jakks Pacific TNA Wrestling Deluxe Impact Series 9

NNO Austin Aries
NNO Christopher Daniels
NNO Gail Kim
NNO Jeff Hardy
NNO Jeff Hardy/Belt
NNO Magnus

2013 Jakks Pacific TNA Wrestling Deluxe Impact Series 10

NNO Crimson
NNO Kurt Angle
NNO Miss Tessmacher
NNO Rob Terry
NNO Rob Van Dam

2013 Jakks Pacific TNA Wrestling Deluxe Impact Series 11

NNO AJ Styles
NNO Austin Aries
NNO Jeff Hardy
NNO Velvet Sky

2014 Jakks Pacific TNA Wrestling Deluxe Impact Series 12

NNO Bully Ray 12.50 25.00
NNO Chris Sabin 20.00 40.00
NNO Hernandez 12.50 25.00
NNO Magnus

2014 Jakks Pacific TNA Wrestling Deluxe Impact Series 13

NNO Angelina Love 12.50 25.00
NNO Mr. Anderson 7.50 15.00

2010 Jakks Pacific TNA Wrestling Genesis

NNO AJ Styles
NNO AJ Styles/Belt
NNO Jeff Jarrett
NNO Jeff Jarrett/Belt
NNO Kurt Angle
NNO Kurt Angle/Belt
NNO Samoa Joe
NNO Samoa Joe/Belt
NNO Sting
NNO Sting/Belt
NNO Suicide
NNO Suicide/Belt

2010 Jakks Pacific TNA Wrestling Genesis 3-Packs

NNO AJ Styles/Kurt Angle/Suicide
NNO Jeff Jarrett/Samoa Joe/Sting

2010 Jakks Pacific TNA Wrestling Genesis 4-Packs

NNO AJ Styles/Kurt Angle/Sting/Suicide
NNO Jeff Jarrett/Kurt Angle/Samoa Joe/Sting

2010 Jakks Pacific TNA Wrestling Impact Series 1

NNO Abyss 15.00 30.00
NNO Jay Lethal 10.00 20.00
NNO Kevin Nash 7.50 15.00
NNO Kurt Angle 7.50 15.00
NNO Sting 12.50 25.00
NNO Suicide 20.00 40.00

2010 Jakks Pacific TNA Wrestling Legends of the Ring

NNO Hulk Hogan
NNO Jeff Jarrett
NNO Kevin Nash
NNO Kurt Angle
NNO Sting
NNO Sting USA Gear RSC

2010 Jakks Pacific TNA Wrestling Micro Impact Series 1

NNO Abyss/Shark Boy/Suicide
NNO AJ Styles/Jeff Jarrett/Mick Foley
NNO C. Daniels/Creed/Jay Lethal
NNO Kevin Nash/Kurt Angle/Sting

2010 Jakks Pacific TNA Wrestling Micro Impact Series 1 10-Pack

NNO Sting/Shark Boy/Jeff Jarrett/Suicide/Abyss
Jay Lethal/AJ Styles/Mick Foley/Kurt Angle/Kevin Nash

2010 Jakks Pacific TNA Wrestling Micro Impact Series 2

NNO Abyss/Hulk Hogan/Jeff Hardy
NNO Eric Young/Lethal/Nash
NNO James Storm/Morgan/Roode 15.00 30.00
NNO Jeff Jarrett/RVD/Sting

1998 Jakks Pacific WWF 2 Tuff Series 1

NNO Chyna/HHH 12.50 25.00
NNO D.O.A. 7.50 15.00
NNO Goldust/Marlena 10.00 20.00
NNO Truth Commission 7.50 15.00

1998 Jakks Pacific WWF 2 Tuff Series 2

NNO B. Christopher/J. Lawler 7.50 15.00
NNO Kama Mustafa/D'Lo Brown 10.00 20.00
NNO Kurrgan/Jackal 7.50 15.00
NNO Road Dogg/B.A. Billy Gunn 12.50 25.00

1999 Jakks Pacific WWF 2 Tuff Series 3

NNO Kane/Corporate Mankind 10.00 20.00
NNO LOD 2000 15.00 30.00
NNO Steve Austin/Undertaker 12.50 25.00
NNO The Rock/Owen Hart 15.00 30.00

1999 Jakks Pacific WWF 2 Tuff Series 4

NNO Big Boss Man vs. Steve Austin 12.50 25.00
NNO The Rock vs. Mankind 10.00 20.00
NNO Undertaker vs. Kane 12.50 25.00
NNO Val Venis vs. B.A. Billy Gunn 7.50 15.00

1999 Jakks Pacific WWF 2 Tuff Series 5

NNO Billy Gunn vs. Road Dogg 10.00 20.00
NNO Debra McMichaels vs. Double J 7.50 15.00
NNO Stone Cold Steve Austin vs. The Rock12.5025.00
NNO Viscera vs. Undertaker 10.00 20.00

2003 Jakks Pacific WWE Adrenaline Series 1

NNO Big Show/Brock Lesnar 25.00 50.00
NNO Shawn Michaels/RVD 15.00 30.00
NNO Tommy Dreamer
Jeff Hardy

2003 Jakks Pacific WWE Adrenaline Series 2

NNO Johnny Stamboli 15.00 30.00
Chavo Guerrero
NNO Rey Mysterio/Matt Hardy 20.00 40.00
NNO Test/Stacy Keibler 20.00 40.00

2003 Jakks Pacific WWE Adrenaline Series 3

NNO Kurt Angle/Brock Lesnar 20.00 40.00
NNO Shawn Michaels/Y2J
NNO Steve Austin/Eric Bischoff 20.00 40.00

2003 Jakks Pacific WWE Adrenaline Series 4

NNO Billy Gunn/Torrie Wilson 12.50 25.00
NNO Chris Benoit/Rhyno 17.50 35.00
NNO Undertaker/John Cena 25.00 50.00

2003 Jakks Pacific WWE Adrenaline Series 5

NNO Eddie Guerrero 25.00 50.00
John Cena
NNO Rey Mysterio 15.00 30.00
Billy Kidman
NNO Shelton Benjamin 10.00 20.00
Charlie Haas

2003 Jakks Pacific WWE Adrenaline Series 6

NNO Eddie and Chavo Guerrero 15.00 30.00
NNO Faarooq/Bradshaw 10.00 20.00
NNO The Hurricane/Rosey 10.00 20.00

2004 Jakks Pacific WWE Adrenaline Series 7

NNO Batista/Randy Orton 17.50 35.00
NNO Chris Jericho/Christian
NNO Scott Steiner/Test 12.50 25.00

2004 Jakks Pacific WWE Adrenaline Series 8

NNO Bubba Ray/D-Von Dudley 10.00 20.00
NNO Rene Dupree 12.50 25.00
Rob Conway
NNO Steven Richards/Victoria 15.00 30.00

2004 Jakks Pacific WWE Adrenaline Series 9

NNO Charlie Haas/Rico 12.50 25.00
NNO Eddie Guerrero 20.00 40.00
John Bradshaw Layfield
NNO Matt Hardy/Lita 20.00 40.00

2004 Jakks Pacific WWE Adrenaline Series 10

NNO Christian/Trish Stratus 20.00 40.00
NNO Doug and Danny Basham 12.50 25.00
NNO Triple H/Randy Orton 20.00 40.00

2005 Jakks Pacific WWE Adrenaline Series 11

NNO Billy Kidman/Paul London 12.50 25.00
NNO Heidenreich/Paul Heyman 12.50 25.00
NNO John Cena/Funaki 20.00 40.00

2005 Jakks Pacific WWE Adrenaline Series 12

NNO Batista/Triple H 15.00 30.00
NNO JBL/Orlando Jordan 12.50 25.00
NNO RVD/Rey Mysterio 15.00 30.00

2005 Jakks Pacific WWE Adrenaline Series 13

NNO Luther Reigns/Kurt Angle 12.50 25.00
NNO Rey Mysterio/Teddy Long 15.00 30.00
NNO Rob Conway 12.50 25.00
Sylvain Grenier

2005 Jakks Pacific WWE Adrenaline Series 14

NNO Eddie Guerrero/Booker T 15.00 30.00
NNO M. Hassan/Daivari 20.00 40.00
NNO William Regal/Tajiri 12.50 25.00

2005 Jakks Pacific WWE Adrenaline Series 15

NNO John Cena/JBL 15.00 30.00
NNO Kane/Edge 20.00 40.00
NNO Rey Mysterio 25.00 50.00
Eddie Guerrero

2005 Jakks Pacific WWE Adrenaline Series 16

NNO Batista/JBL 15.00 30.00
NNO Chris Jericho/John Cena 20.00 40.00
NNO Johnny Nitro 12.50 25.00
Joey Mercury

2006 Jakks Pacific WWE Adrenaline Series 17

NNO John Cena/Kurt Angle 12.50 25.00
NNO Matt Hardy/Edge 12.50 25.00
NNO Super Crazy/Psicosis 15.00 30.00

2006 Jakks Pacific WWE Adrenaline Series 18

NNO Bobby Lashley 17.50 35.00
Orlando Jordan
NNO Lance Cade 15.00 30.00
Trevor Murdoch
NNO Johnny Nitro
Road Warrior Animal

2006 Jakks Pacific WWE Adrenaline Series 19

NNO John Cena/Edge 15.00 30.00
NNO Johnny Nitro 10.00 20.00
Joey Mercury
NNO Rey Mysterio/Mark Henry 20.00 40.00

2006 Jakks Pacific WWE Adrenaline Series 20

NNO Triple H/John Cena
NNO Trish Stratus/HBK 15.00 30.00
NNO William Regal 12.50 25.00
Paul Burchill

2006 Jakks Pacific WWE Adrenaline Series 21

NNO Booker T/Boogeyman 12.50 25.00
NNO Gymini 12.50 25.00
NNO Mikey vs. Big Show 15.00 30.00

2006 Jakks Pacific WWE Adrenaline Series 22

NNO Johnny/Mitch 10.00 20.00
NNO Psicosis/Super Crazy 15.00 30.00
NNO Umaga/Armando Estrada 15.00 30.00

2007 Jakks Pacific WWE Adrenaline Series 23

NNO Booker T vs. Batista 12.50 25.00
NNO Elijah Burke 15.00 30.00
Sylvester Terkay
NNO Jeff Hardy vs. Johnny Nitro 20.00 40.00

2007 Jakks Pacific WWE Adrenaline Series 24

NNO Brian Kendrick/Paul London 12.50 25.00
NNO HHH/Shawn Michaels 17.50 35.00
NNO Undertaker/Kane 15.00 30.00

2007 Jakks Pacific WWE Adrenaline Series 25

NNO Charlie Haas/Shelton Benjamin 12.50 25.00
NNO John Cena vs. The Great Khali 20.00 40.00
NNO MVP vs. Kane 15.00 30.00

2007 Jakks Pacific WWE Adrenaline Series 26

NNO Cryme Tyme 12.50 25.00
NNO The Highlanders 12.50 25.00
NNO King Booker/Queen Sharmell 15.00 30.00

2007 Jakks Pacific WWE Adrenaline Series 27

NNO Deuce/Domino 15.00 30.00
NNO Jeff and Matt Hardy 17.50 35.00
NNO Lance Cade/Trevor Murdoch 12.50 25.00

2007 Jakks Pacific WWE Adrenaline Series 28

NNO CM Punk/Elijah Burke 15.00 30.00
NNO Mr. Kennedy/Edge 12.50 25.00
NNO Umage/Vince McMahon 12.50 25.00

2008 Jakks Pacific WWE Adrenaline Series 29

NNO Cody & Dusty Rhodes 12.50 25.00
NNO Miz/Layla 12.50 25.00
NNO MVP/Matt Hardy 15.00 30.00

2008 Jakks Pacific WWE Adrenaline Series 30

NNO Balls Mahoney/Kelly Kelly 20.00 40.00
NNO HHH/Umaga 15.00 30.00
NNO Rey Mysterio/Finlay

2008 Jakks Pacific WWE Adrenaline Series 31

NNO Big Daddy V/Matt Striker 12.50 25.00
NNO Chuck Palumbo 15.00 30.00
Michelle McCool
NNO The Highlanders 12.50 25.00

2008 Jakks Pacific WWE Adrenaline Series 32

NNO Jesse/Festus 10.00 20.00
NNO John Morrison/The Miz 15.00 30.00
NNO Santino Marella/Maria 15.00 30.00

2008 Jakks Pacific WWE Adrenaline Series 33

NNO Chavo Guerrero/Kane 15.00 30.00
NNO Katie Lea/Paul Burchill 15.00 30.00
NNO Vickie Guerrero/Edge 20.00 40.00

2008 Jakks Pacific WWE Adrenaline Series 34

NNO Hornswoggle/Finlay 30.00 60.00
NNO Randy Orton/JBL
NNO Tommy Dreamer 20.00 40.00
Joey Styles

2009 Jakks Pacific WWE Adrenaline Series 35

NNO	Cody Rhodes/Ted DiBiase Jr.		
NNO	Curt Hawkins/Zach Ryder	15.00	30.00
NNO	Evan Bourne/Rey Mysterio		

2009 Jakks Pacific WWE Adrenaline Series 36

NNO	Brian Kendrick/Ezekiel Jackson	15.00	30.00
NNO	Mark Henry/Tony Atlas	15.00	30.00
NNO	Shad Gaspard/JTG	20.00	40.00

2009 Jakks Pacific WWE Adrenaline Series 37

NNO	Jeff Hardy/The Undertaker	20.00	40.00
NNO	Million Dollar Man/DiBiase Jr.		
NNO	Triple H/Randy Orton	12.50	25.00

2009 Jakks Pacific WWE Adrenaline Series 38

NNO	Edge vs. Big Show		
NNO	Finlay/Hornswoggle	25.00	50.00
NNO	Jack Swagger vs. Christian		

2009 Jakks Pacific WWE Adrenaline Series 39

NNO	Undertaker/HBK	12.50	25.00
NNO	Triple H/Stephanie		
NNO	Natalya/Tyson Kidd		

2000 Jakks Pacific WWF Back Talkin' Crushers Exclusive

NNO	Stone Cold Steve Austin TF	10.00	20.00

1999 Jakks Pacific WWF Back Talkin' Crushers Series 1

NNO	Big Show	6.00	12.00
NNO	The Rock	7.50	15.00
NNO	Steve Austin	10.00	20.00
NNO	Undertaker	7.50	15.00

2000 Jakks Pacific WWF Back Talkin' Crushers Series 2

NNO	Mankind	7.50	15.00
NNO	Road Dogg	6.00	12.00
NNO	The Rock	10.00	20.00

2000 Jakks Pacific WWF Back Talkin' Crushers Series 3

NNO	Chris Jericho	10.00	20.00
NNO	Steve Austin	10.00	20.00
NNO	Triple H	7.50	15.00

2001 Jakks Pacific WWF Back Talkin' Slammers Series 1

NNO	The Rock	12.50	25.00
NNO	Stone Cold Steve Austin	12.50	25.00
NNO	Triple H	10.00	20.00

2001 Jakks Pacific WWF Back Talkin' Slammers Series 2

NNO	Chris Jericho	10.00	20.00
NNO	Kurt Angle	12.50	25.00
NNO	Undertaker		

2001 Jakks Pacific WWF Back Talkin' Slammers Series 3

NNO	Chris Jericho	10.00	20.00
NNO	Kurt Angle	12.50	25.00
NNO	Stone Cold Steve Austin	10.00	20.00
NNO	The Rock	10.00	20.00
NNO	Triple H	7.50	15.00
NNO	Undertaker		

2002 Jakks Pacific WWF Back Talkin' Slammers Series 4

NNO	Chris Jericho		
NNO	Kurt Angle		
NNO	Triple H		

2000 Jakks Pacific WWF Backlash Series 1

NNO	Al Snow	12.50	25.00
NNO	Kane	6.00	12.00
NNO	Shawn Michaels	15.00	30.00
NNO	Stone Cold Steve Austin	10.00	20.00
NNO	The Rock	12.50	25.00
NNO	Triple H	10.00	20.00
NNO	Undertaker	10.00	20.00
NNO	X-Pac	7.50	15.00

2000 Jakks Pacific WWF Backlash Series 2

NNO	Big Boss Man		
NNO	Edge		
NNO	Hardcore Holly		
NNO	Road Dogg		
NNO	The Rock		
NNO	Stone Cold Steve Austin		
NNO	Triple H	7.50	15.00
NNO	X-Pac	6.00	12.00

2000 Jakks Pacific WWF Backlash Series 3

NNO	Billy Gunn	7.50	15.00
NNO	Edge	10.00	20.00
NNO	Kane	7.50	15.00
NNO	The Rock		
NNO	Stone Cold Steve Austin		
NNO	Test		
NNO	Triple H		
NNO	Undertaker		

2000 Jakks Pacific WWF Backlash Series 4

NNO	Big Boss Man	6.00	12.00
NNO	Billy Gunn	7.50	15.00
NNO	Edge	10.00	20.00
NNO	Kane	10.00	20.00
NNO	The Rock		
NNO	Stone Cold Steve Austin	12.50	25.00
NNO	Triple H		
NNO	Undertaker	15.00	30.00

2000 Jakks Pacific WWF Backlash Series 5

NNO	Al Snow		
NNO	Hardcore Holly	6.00	12.00
NNO	Rock		
NNO	Stone Cold Steve Austin	12.50	25.00
NNO	Test		
NNO	Undertaker	15.00	30.00
NNO	Val Venis		
NNO	X-Pac		

2005 Jakks Pacific WWE Backlash Series 7

NNO	Batista	12.50	25.00
NNO	Chris Benoit	12.50	25.00
NNO	Kurt Angle	10.00	20.00
NNO	Undertaker	15.00	30.00

2005 Jakks Pacific WWE Backlash Series 8

NNO	Batista	12.50	25.00
NNO	Edge	10.00	20.00
NNO	Kurt Angle	12.50	25.00
NNO	Triple H	10.00	20.00

2005 Jakks Pacific WWE Backlash Series 9

NNO	Carlito	12.50	25.00
NNO	Kurt Angle	20.00	40.00
NNO	Randy Orton	7.50	15.00
NNO	Rob Van Dam	12.50	25.00
NNO	Shawn Michaels		
NNO	Undertaker		

2005 Jakks Pacific WWE Backlash Series 10

NNO	Batista	12.50	25.00
NNO	Chris Benoit	7.50	15.00
NNO	John Cena	12.50	25.00
NNO	Rob Van Dam	7.50	15.00
NNO	Shawn Michaels	15.00	30.00
NNO	Triple H	10.00	20.00

2007 Jakks Pacific WWE Backlash Series 11

NNO	Bobby Lashley	12.50	25.00
NNO	Edge	15.00	30.00
NNO	Finlay	15.00	30.00
NNO	Jeff Hardy	15.00	30.00
NNO	Rey Mysterio	20.00	40.00
NNO	Undertaker	20.00	40.00

2008 Jakks Pacific WWE Backlash Series 12

NNO	Kane		
NNO	Matt Hardy		
NNO	Miz		
NNO	Mr. Kennedy		
NNO	Randy Orton		
NNO	Triple H		

2009 Jakks Pacific WWE Backlash Series 13

NNO	Batista		
NNO	Chavo Guerrero		
NNO	Chris Jericho		
NNO	Elijah Burke		
NNO	John Cena		
NNO	Nunzio		

2009 Jakks Pacific WWE Backlash Series 14

NNO	Chavo Guerrero		
NNO	Cody Rhodes		
NNO	Matt Hardy	10.00	20.00
NNO	Stone Cold Steve Austin		
NNO	Triple H		

2009 Jakks Pacific WWE Backlash Series 15

NNO	Chris Jericho	15.00	30.00
NNO	CM Punk		
NNO	John Cena	10.00	20.00
NNO	Rey Mysterio	20.00	40.00
NNO	Shawn Michaels	12.50	25.00
NNO	Triple H	15.00	30.00

2008 Jakks Pacific WWE Best of Classic Superstars

NNO	Andre the Giant	20.00	40.00
NNO	Bret Hit Man Hart	20.00	40.00
NNO	Eddie Guerrero	12.50	25.00
NNO	Rowdy Roddy Piper		
NNO	Shawn Michaels	12.50	25.00

2009 Jakks Pacific WWE Best of Deluxe Aggression

NNO	Chris Jericho		
NNO	John Cena		
NNO	Randy Orton		
NNO	Rey Mysterio		
NNO	Triple H		
NNO	Undertaker		

2006 Jakks Pacific WWE Best of Deluxe Aggression

NNO	Batista	7.50	15.00
NNO	John Cena	15.00	30.00
NNO	Kane	10.00	20.00
NNO	Rey Mysterio	10.00	20.00
NNO	Triple H	7.50	15.00
NNO	Undertaker	20.00	40.00

2008 Jakks Pacific WWE Best of Deluxe Aggression

NNO	Chris Jericho	15.00	30.00
NNO	CM Punk		
NNO	John Cena	10.00	20.00
NNO	Rey Mysterio	17.50	35.00
NNO	Shawn Michaels	12.50	25.00
NNO	Undertaker	20.00	40.00

2005 Jakks Pacific WWE Best of ECW

NNO	Bubba Ray Dudley	15.00	30.00
NNO	D-Von Dudley	12.50	25.00
NNO	Rey Mysterio	12.50	25.00
NNO	Rhyno	7.50	15.00
NNO	Rob Van Dam	15.00	30.00
NNO	Stevie Richards	7.50	15.00

2005 Jakks Pacific WWE Best of WCW

NNO	Billy Kidman	10.00	20.00
NNO	Chris Benoit	15.00	30.00
NNO	Chris Jericho	12.50	25.00
NNO	Eddie Guerrero	10.00	20.00
NNO	Rey Mysterio	15.00	30.00
NNO	Ric Flair	20.00	40.00

1998 Jakks Pacific WWF Bone Crunchin' Buddies

NNO	Animal		
NNO	Dude Love		
NNO	Hawk		
NNO	Shawn Michaels		

1999 Jakks Pacific WWF Bone Crunchin' Buddies

NNO	Kane		
NNO	The Rock		
NNO	Steve Austin/Ring Gear	20.00	40.00

NNO Steve Austin/Street Clothes
NNO Triple H 20.00 40.00
NNO Undertaker

2001 Jakks Pacific WWF Bone Crunchin' Buddies

NNO Animal
NNO Hawk
NNO The Rock
NNO Stone Cold Steve Austin
NNO Undertaker

1999 Jakks Pacific WWF Break Down In Your House

NNO D'Lo Brown 7.50 15.00
NNO Droz 6.00 12.00
NNO Goldust 6.00 12.00
NNO Mankind 12.50 25.00
NNO Steve Austin 10.00 20.00
NNO X-Pac 6.00 12.00

1999 Jakks Pacific WWF Break Down In Your House Multi-Packs

NNO Steve Austin/D'Lo Brown/Droz BJ
NNO Steve Austin/Droz/Goldust/X-Pac SC
NNO X-Pac/Mankind/Goldust BJ

2003 Jakks Pacific WWE Bring the Noise

NNO Matt Hardy 10.00 20.00
NNO Shawn Michaels 7.50 15.00
NNO The Rock 20.00 40.00
NNO Tommy Dreamer 12.50 25.00
NNO Triple H 12.50 25.00
NNO Undertaker

2008 Jakks Pacific WWE Build N' Brawl Playset

NNO Wrestling Ring
{w/HHH & Orton TRU

2008 Jakks Pacific WWE Build N' Brawl Series 1

NNO Batista
NNO Bobby Lashley
NNO Edge
NNO John Cena
NNO Triple H
NNO Undertaker

2008 Jakks Pacific WWE Build N' Brawl Series 2

NNO Batista
NNO Kane
NNO Mr. Kennedy
NNO Randy Orton
NNO Rey Mysterio
NNO Shawn Michaels

2008 Jakks Pacific WWE Build N' Brawl Series 3

NNO Boogeyman
NNO CM Punk
NNO Jeff Hardy
NNO Matt Hardy
NNO MVP
NNO Umaga

2008 Jakks Pacific WWE Build N' Brawl Series 4

NNO Chris Jericho
NNO Deuce
NNO Domino
NNO The Miz
NNO John Morrison
NNO Stone Cold Steve Austin

2008 Jakks Pacific WWE Build N' Brawl Series 5

NNO Chavo Guerrero
NNO Elijah Burke
NNO Finlay
NNO JBL
NNO Razor Ramon
NNO William Regal

2008 Jakks Pacific WWE Build N' Brawl Series 6

NNO Curt Hawkins
NNO Kofi Kingston
NNO Rey Mysterio
NNO Santino Marella
NNO Sgt. Slaughter
NNO Zack Ryder

2008 Jakks Pacific WWE Build N' Brawl Series 7

NNO Bret Hart
NNO John Cena
NNO Mark Henry
NNO Matt Hardy
NNO Rey Mysterio
NNO Undertaker

2008 Jakks Pacific WWE Build N' Brawl Series 8

NNO Batista
NNO Big Show
NNO Rey Mysterio
NNO The Rock
NNO Roddy Piper
NNO Shawn Michaels

2008 Jakks Pacific WWE Build N' Brawl Series 9

NNO John Cena
NNO Rey Mysterio
NNO Undertaker

2008 Jakks Pacific WWE Build N' Brawl WrestleMania

NNO John Cena
NNO Rey Mysterio 12.50 25.00
NNO Triple H 10.00 20.00

1999 Jakks Pacific WWF Camo Carnage

NNO B.A. Billy Gunn 6.00 12.00
NNO Billy Gunn SI 7.50 15.00
NNO Billy Gunn w/Gun 7.50 15.00
NNO Chyna 6.00 12.00
NNO Chyna SI 7.50 15.00
NNO Chyna w/Gun 7.50 15.00
NNO HHH 6.00 12.00
NNO HHH SI 7.50 15.00
NNO HHH w/Gun 7.50 15.00
NNO Road Dogg 5.00 10.00
NNO Road Dogg SI 6.00 12.00
NNO Road Dogg w/Gun 6.00 12.00
NNO Stone Cold Steve Austin 7.50 15.00
NNO Steve Austin SI 10.00 20.00
NNO Steve Austin w/Gun 10.00 20.00
NNO X-Pac 5.00 10.00
NNO X-Pac SI 6.00 12.00
NNO X-Pac w/Gun 6.00 12.00

2004 Jakks Pacific WWE Classic Superstars Series 1

NNO Andre the Giant 20.00 40.00
NNO Bret Hart 30.00 75.00
NNO Hunter Hearst Helmsley 10.00 20.00
NNO Shawn Michaels 25.00 50.00
NNO Ultimate Warrior 15.00 30.00
NNO Undertaker 15.00 30.00

2004 Jakks Pacific WWE Classic Superstars Series 2

NNO Big John Studd 12.50 25.00
Chair & Microphone
NNO Big John Studd 20.00 40.00
Ring Bell & Stretcher
NNO Dude Love 15.00 30.00
Tye-Dye Wrist Bands
NNO Dude Love 12.50 25.00
Yellow Wrist Bands
NNO George The Animal Steele 15.00 30.00
Painted Body Hair
NNO George The Animal Steele 25.00 50.00
Synthetic Body Hair
NNO Mankind 20.00 40.00
NNO Ric Flair 20.00 40.00
NNO Sgt. Slaughter/Jacket Off
NNO Sgt. Slaughter/Jacket On 15.00 30.00

2004 Jakks Pacific WWE Classic Superstars Series 3

NNO Ultimate Warrior
NNO Bret Hit Man Hart 15.00 30.00
NNO Jake The Snake Roberts 15.00 30.00
NNO Ted DiBiase 25.00 50.00
NNO Superfly Jimmy Snuka 15.00 30.00
NNO Undertaker 12.50 25.00

2004 Jakks Pacific WWE Classic Superstars Series 4

NNO Hacksaw Jim Duggan 20.00 40.00
NNO Hillbilly Jim 15.00 30.00
NNO Junkyard Dog 12.50 25.00
NNO Rowdy Roddy Piper 15.00 30.00
NNO Tito Santana 12.50 25.00
NNO Yokozuna
Smooth Belt Strap
NNO Yokozuna 20.00 40.00
Textured Belt Strap

2004 Jakks Pacific WWE Classic Superstars Series 5

NNO Brutus The Barber Beefcake 15.00 30.00
NNO Iron Sheik 15.00 30.00
NNO King Kong Bundy 20.00 40.00
NNO Mr. Wonderful Paul Orndorff 15.00 30.00
NNO Nikolai Volkoff 20.00 40.00
NNO Terry Funk 25.00 50.00

2005 Jakks Pacific WWE Classic Superstars Series 6

NNO Andre the Giant 15.00 30.00
NNO Bobby The Brain Heenan 12.50 25.00
NNO Doink 15.00 30.00
NNO Earthquake 10.00 20.00
Painted Chest Hair
NNO Earthquake 12.50 25.00
Synthetic Chest Hair
NNO Koko B. Ware 25.00 50.00
NNO One Man Gang 20.00 40.00
NNO Road Warrior Animal 20.00 40.00
NNO Road Warrior Hawk 15.00 30.00
NNO Shawn Michaels 12.50 25.00

2005 Jakks Pacific WWE Classic Superstars Series 7

NNO Andre the Giant 15.00 30.00
NNO British Bulldog 12.50 25.00
NNO Don Muraco 15.00 30.00
NNO Eddie Guerrero 10.00 20.00
NNO Gorilla Monsoon 12.50 25.00
NNO Jimmy Hart 15.00 30.00
NNO King Harley Race 20.00 40.00
NNO Superstar Billy Graham 12.50 25.00
NNO The Ultimate Warrior 15.00 30.00

2005 Jakks Pacific WWE Classic Superstars Series 8

NNO Vader 25.00 50.00
NNO Bruiser Brody 25.00 50.00
NNO Chief Jay Strongbow 15.00 30.00
NNO Classy Freddie Blassie 10.00 20.00
NNO Cowboy Bob Orton 20.00 40.00
Ace on Boots
NNO Cowboy Bob Orton 15.00 30.00
Plain Boots
NNO Hollywood Hogan 20.00 40.00
Large World Title
NNO Hollywood Hogan 15.00 30.00
Small World Title
NNO Hulk Hogan/'80s WWF Title 30.00 75.00
NNO Hulk Hogan/'90s WWF Title 20.00 40.00
NNO Jerry The King Lawler 15.00 30.00

2006 Jakks Pacific WWE Classic Superstars Series 9

NNO Akeem 12.50 25.00
NNO Bam Bam Bigelow 25.00 50.00
NNO The Godfather 15.00 30.00
NNO Kamala 15.00 30.00
NNO Papa Shango 20.00 40.00
NNO Paul Bearer/Bow Tie 15.00 30.00
NNO Paul Bearer/Windsor Tie 15.00 30.00
NNO Ric Flair/Smooth Wrists 15.00 30.00
NNO Ric Flair/Taped Wrists 10.00 20.00
NNO Road Warrior Animal 10.00 20.00
NNO Road Warrior Hawk 10.00 20.00

2006 Jakks Pacific WWE Classic Superstars Series 10

NNO Bruno Sammartino 12.50 25.00
NNO Dusty Rhodes 20.00 40.00
NNO Gorilla Monsoon 25.00 50.00
NNO Greg The Hammer Valentine 20.00 40.00
NNO Harley Race 15.00 30.00
NNO Mr. Perfect 15.00 30.00
NNO Rocky Maivia 20.00 40.00
NNO Sabu 20.00 40.00

2006 Jakks Pacific WWE Classic Superstars Series 11

NNO 123 Kid 20.00 40.00

NNO	Barry Windham	10.00	20.00
NNO	Diesel	15.00	30.00
NNO	Fabulous Moolah	10.00	20.00
NNO	Hulk Hogan Black Weightlifting Belt	12.50	25.00
NNO	Hulk Hogan Yellow Weightlifting Belt	20.00	40.00
NNO	Irwin R. Schyster	15.00	30.00
NNO	Ken Shamrock	12.50	25.00
NNO	Rick Steiner	15.00	30.00

2006 Jakks Pacific WWE Classic Superstars Series 12

NNO	Arn Anderson	12.50	25.00
NNO	Brooklyn Brawler	15.00	30.00
NNO	Captain Lou Albano	15.00	30.00
NNO	Dean Malenko	12.50	25.00
NNO	Handsome Jimmy Valiant	20.00	40.00
NNO	Hollywood Hulk Hogan	30.00	60.00
NNO	Killer Kowalski	12.50	25.00
NNO	Nasty Boy Brian Knobbs	12.50	25.00
NNO	Nasty Boy Jerry Sags	12.50	25.00
NNO	Ultimate Warrior Facing Back	15.00	30.00
NNO	Ultimate Warrior Facing Forward	15.00	30.00

2006 Jakks Pacific WWE Classic Superstars Series 13

NNO	Al Snow	15.00	30.00
NNO	Bad News Brown	10.00	20.00
NNO	Bret Hit Man Hart	15.00	30.00
NNO	Brother Love	25.00	50.00
NNO	Droz	10.00	20.00
NNO	Dusty Rhodes	15.00	30.00
NNO	Ernie Ladd	15.00	30.00
NNO	Luna Vachon	20.00	40.00
NNO	The Mountie	25.00	50.00
NNO	Mr. Perfect	15.00	30.00
NNO	Ravishing Rick Rude	20.00	40.00
NNO	Undertaker/LJN Style	25.00	50.00

2007 Jakks Pacific WWE Classic Superstars Series 14

NNO	Abdullah the Butcher	30.00	60.00
NNO	Bob Backlund	20.00	40.00
NNO	Demolition Ax	20.00	40.00
NNO	Demolition Smash	20.00	40.00
NNO	Diamond Dallas Page	20.00	40.00
NNO	Honky Tonk Man	17.50	35.00
NNO	Mean Gene Okerlund	30.00	60.00
NNO	Rick The Model Martel	25.00	50.00
NNO	Sensational Sherri	15.00	30.00
NNO	Steve Austin/LJN Black Card	15.00	30.00
NNO	Steve Austin/LJN Blue Card		
NNO	The Ultimate Warrior	15.00	30.00

2007 Jakks Pacific WWE Classic Superstars Series 15

NNO	The Genius	20.00	40.00
NNO	Johnny Rodz	12.50	25.00
NNO	Lex Luger	15.00	30.00
NNO	Outlaw Ron Bass	12.50	25.00
NNO	Razor Ramon	20.00	40.00
NNO	The Rock/LJN Style	12.50	25.00
NNO	Shawn Michaels w/Entrance Gear	15.00	30.00
NNO	Shawn Michaels w/o Entrance Gear	15.00	30.00
NNO	Tank Abbott w/Chair+Barbell	15.00	30.00
NNO	Tank Abbott w/Chair	20.00	40.00
NNO	Tully Blanchard	15.00	30.00
NNO	Zeus w/Chain+Pipe	40.00	80.00
NNO	Zeus w/Chain	20.00	40.00

2007 Jakks Pacific WWE Classic Superstars Series 16

NNO	Barbarian	20.00	40.00
NNO	Giant Gonzalez/Painted Fur	25.00	50.00
NNO	Giant Gonzalez Synthetic Fur/500*	60.00	120.00
NNO	Shawn Michaels/LJN Style	12.50	25.00
NNO	Sycho Sid w/Knee Pads & {WWF Belt by Feet	15.00	30.00
NNO	Sycho Sid w/Knee Pads & {WWF Belt by Waist	20.00	40.00
NNO	Sycho Sid w/o Knee Pads & {WWF Belt by Feet	20.00	40.00
NNO	Sycho Sid w/o Knee Pads & {WWF Belt by Waist	12.50	25.00
NNO	Vince McMahon	20.00	40.00
NNO	Warlord	20.00	40.00
NNO	The Ultimate Warrior	25.00	50.00
NNO	X-Pac/Belt by Feet	12.50	25.00
NNO	X-Pac/Belt by Waist		

2007 Jakks Pacific WWE Classic Superstars Series 17

NNO	Eddie Guerrero	17.50	35.00
NNO	Ivan Putski	15.00	30.00
NNO	Ken Patera	25.00	50.00
NNO	Repo Man	17.50	35.00
NNO	The Rock	20.00	40.00
NNO	Rocky Johnson	15.00	30.00
NNO	Shane McMahon Centered Jersey Logo	15.00	30.00
NNO	Shane McMahon Off-Centered Jersey Logo		
NNO	Triple H/LJN Style	15.00	30.00
NNO	Typhoon	17.50	35.00

2007 Jakks Pacific WWE Classic Superstars Series 18

NNO	Honky Tonk Man	15.00	30.00
NNO	Jim Ross	30.00	75.00
NNO	Kane	25.00	50.00
NNO	King Mabel	30.00	75.00
NNO	Mae Young	30.00	60.00
NNO	Ric Flair/LJN Style	15.00	30.00
NNO	Rikishi	15.00	30.00
NNO	Stone Cold Steve Austin	15.00	30.00
NNO	Sunny	20.00	40.00
NNO	Val Venis Cruiserweight Torso		
NNO	Val Venis Heavyweight Torso	20.00	40.00

2008 Jakks Pacific WWE Classic Superstars Series 19

NNO	Adam Bomb	30.00	75.00
NNO	Cactus Jack	12.50	25.00
NNO	Eddie Guerrero	15.00	30.00
NNO	Evil Doink	20.00	40.00
NNO	Howard Finkel	20.00	40.00
NNO	Kevin Sullivan	15.00	30.00
NNO	Mankind/LJN Style	17.50	35.00
NNO	Nikita Koloff	30.00	60.00
NNO	The Rock	15.00	30.00
NNO	Tatanka	15.00	30.00

2008 Jakks Pacific WWE Classic Superstars Series 20

NNO	Dynamite Kid	20.00	40.00
NNO	John Cena/LJN Style	12.50	25.00
NNO	Rey Mysterio	17.50	35.00
NNO	Ric Flair	25.00	50.00
NNO	The Rock	15.00	30.00
NNO	Ron Simmons	15.00	30.00
NNO	Tony Atlas	20.00	40.00

2008 Jakks Pacific WWE Classic Superstars Series 21

NNO	Brian Pillman	12.50	25.00
NNO	Buff Bagwell	30.00	60.00
NNO	Chris Jericho	15.00	30.00
NNO	Jeff Hardy	20.00	40.00
NNO	Jesse The Body Ventura	15.00	30.00
NNO	Rey Mysterio/LJN Style	20.00	40.00
NNO	Tazz	12.50	25.00

2008 Jakks Pacific WWE Classic Superstars Series 22

NNO	Andy Kaufman	50.00	100.00
NNO	Bob Spark Plugg Holly	15.00	30.00
NNO	Chainsaw Charlie	15.00	30.00
NNO	Earthquake	17.50	35.00
NNO	Eddie Guerrero/LJN Style	15.00	30.00
NNO	Matt Hardy	20.00	40.00
NNO	Mr. McMahon	15.00	30.00
NNO	Stone Cold Steve Austin	25.00	50.00

2009 Jakks Pacific WWE Classic Superstars Series 23

NNO	The Berzerker	25.00	50.00
NNO	Big Boss Man	30.00	60.00
NNO	Billy Kidman	15.00	30.00
NNO	Lance Storm	25.00	50.00
NNO	Road Warrior Animal	15.00	30.00
NNO	Road Warrior Hawk	15.00	30.00
NNO	Rob Van Dam	17.50	35.00
NNO	Spike Dudley	25.00	50.00
NNO	Trish Stratus/LJN Style	25.00	50.00

2009 Jakks Pacific WWE Classic Superstars Series 24

NNO	B. Brian Blair	20.00	40.00
NNO	Davey Boy Smith	15.00	30.00
NNO	Dynamite Kid	15.00	30.00
NNO	Hunter-Hearst-Helmsley	15.00	30.00
NNO	Jim Brunzell	15.00	30.00
NNO	Rey Mysterio	20.00	40.00
NNO	Rob Van Dam/LJN Style	15.00	30.00
NNO	Stephanie McMahon	15.00	30.00
NNO	Trish Stratus	30.00	60.00

2009 Jakks Pacific WWE Classic Superstars Series 25

NNO	Bastion Booger	30.00	75.00
NNO	Big Boss Man	15.00	30.00
NNO	Big Show	15.00	30.00
NNO	Goldberg	50.00	100.00
NNO	Haku	50.00	100.00
NNO	Jack Brisco	30.00	60.00
NNO	Jeff Hardy/LJN Style	20.00	40.00
NNO	Jerry Brisco	30.00	75.00
NNO	Jesse The Body Ventura	40.00	80.00

2009 Jakks Pacific WWE Classic Superstars Series 26

NNO	Bret Hit Man Hart	15.00	30.00
NNO	Dangerous Danny Davis	20.00	40.00
NNO	Dr. Death Steve Williams	30.00	60.00
NNO	Giant Machine/Andre	20.00	40.00
NNO	The Iron Sheik	20.00	40.00
NNO	Junkyard Dog	12.50	25.00
NNO	Matt Hardy/LJN Style	12.50	25.00
NNO	Meng	15.00	30.00
NNO	Mr. Fuji	20.00	40.00
NNO	The Sheik	25.00	50.00
NNO	The Shockmaster	25.00	50.00

2009 Jakks Pacific WWE Classic Superstars Series 27

NNO	The Barbarian	15.00	30.00
NNO	Bill Goldberg	50.00	100.00
NNO	Evil Doink	15.00	30.00
NNO	The Giant		
NNO	Kona Crush	50.00	100.00
NNO	Sgt. Slaughter	15.00	30.00
NNO	Steve Blackman	25.00	50.00
NNO	The Warlord	15.00	30.00

2009 Jakks Pacific WWE Classic Superstars Series 28

NNO	Bret Hit Man Hart	20.00	40.00
NNO	Rey Mysterio/LJN Style	30.00	60.00
NNO	Rowdy Roddy Piper	20.00	40.00
NNO	Shawn Michaels	12.50	25.00
NNO	Triple H	12.50	25.00
NNO	The Undertaker	25.00	50.00

2004 Jakks Pacific WWE Classic Superstars 2-Packs Series 1

NNO	Hart Foundation Back Knee Pads on Bret UK	75.00	150.00
NNO	Hart Foundation Pink Knee Pads	30.00	75.00
NNO	Road Warriors		
NNO	Rockers	30.00	75.00

2005 Jakks Pacific WWE Classic Superstars 2-Packs Series 2

NNO	Jake Roberts/Steve Austin	30.00	75.00
NNO	Mankind/Undertaker	30.00	60.00
NNO	Roddy Piper/Jimmy Snuka	30.00	60.00

2005 Jakks Pacific WWE Classic Superstars 2-Packs Series 3

NNO	Bushwhackers	25.00	50.00
NNO	Steve Austin/Roddy Piper	25.00	50.00
NNO	Wild Samoans	20.00	40.00

2006 Jakks Pacific WWE Classic Superstars 2-Packs Series 4

NNO	Hulk Hogan/Freddie Blassie	25.00	50.00
NNO	Sgt. Slaughter/Col. Mustafa	20.00	40.00
NNO	Undertaker/Paul Bearer	25.00	50.00

2006 Jakks Pacific WWE Classic Superstars 2-Packs Series 5

NNO	Demolition	40.00	80.00
NNO	Hulk Hogan/Ultimate Warrior	60.00	120.00
NNO	Hulk Hogan/Ultimate Warrior Head Variant		
NNO	Ted DiBiase/Virgil	20.00	40.00

2007 Jakks Pacific WWE Classic Superstars 2-Packs Series 6

NNO Hollywood Blondes 30.00 60.00
NNO Midnight Express 50.00 75.00
NNO Strike Force 30.00 60.00

2007 Jakks Pacific WWE Classic Superstars 2-Packs Series 7

NNO Arn Anderson/Tully Blanchard 25.00 50.00
NNO Lex Luger/Dean Malenko 25.00 50.00
NNO Ric Flair/Barry Windham 25.00 50.00

2008 Jakks Pacific WWE Classic Superstars 2-Packs Series 8

NNO Giant Gonzales 30.00 75.00
Harvey Wippleman
NNO Jerry Lawler vs. 50.00 100.00
{Andy Kaufman
NNO Killer Bees 40.00 80.00

2008 Jakks Pacific WWE Classic Superstars 2-Packs Series 9

NNO British Bulldogs 75.00 150.00
NNO Ivan & Nikita Koloff 30.00 75.00
NNO Rock 'n Roll Express 60.00 120.00

2009 Jakks Pacific WWE Classic Superstars 2-Packs Series 10

NNO Tony Atlas/Rocky Johnson
NNO Too Cool
NNO Yokozuna vs. Bret Hart 30.00 60.00

2009 Jakks Pacific WWE Classic Superstars 2-Packs Series 11

NNO Jake Roberts vs. Rick Martel
NNO Jake Roberts vs. Rick Martel/Blindfolds
NNO Rob Van Dam vs. Tazz 25.00 50.00
NNO Rowdy Roddy Piper vs. Mr. Fuji 40.00 80.00

2009 Jakks Pacific WWE Classic Superstars 2-Packs Series 12

NNO Cowboy Bob Orton/Randy Orton 30.00 60.00
NNO Jim Neidhart/Natalya 30.00 75.00
NNO Million Dollar Man/DiBiase Jr. 20.00 40.00

2009 Jakks Pacific WWE Classic Superstars 2-Packs Series 13

NNO Steve Austin vs. Rock 30.00 60.00
NNO Triple H/X-Pac 20.00 40.00
NNO Bobby Heenan/Abe Schwartz 30.00 60.00

2004 Jakks Pacific WWE Classic Superstars 3-Packs Series 1

NNO Jake Roberts/Andre Single Strap150.00 300.00
John Studd
NNO Jake Roberts/Andre Double Strap30.00 75.00
John Studd

2005 Jakks Pacific WWE Classic Superstars 3-Packs Series 2

NNO Bret Hart/Rock/HBK 30.00 75.00

2005 Jakks Pacific WWE Classic Superstars 3-Packs Series 3

NNO 3 Faces of Undertaker 60.00 120.00
NNO Jim Neidhart/Tito Santana 20.00 40.00
Marty Janetty

2005 Jakks Pacific WWE Classic Superstars 3-Packs Series 4

NNO King Kong Bundy 45.00 90.00
Volkoff & Sheik
NNO Hart Foundation w/J. Hart 30.00 75.00

2006 Jakks Pacific WWE Classic Superstars 3-Packs Series 5

NNO Fabulous Freebirds 30.00 60.00
NNO Fabulous Freebirds
Taped Wrists
NNO Mega-Maniacs 25.00 50.00
w/Jimmy Hart

2006 Jakks Pacific WWE Classic Superstars 3-Packs Series 6

NNO Captain Lou Albano 20.00 40.00
Wild Samoans
NNO Rowdy Roddy Piper/Cowboy
Bob Orton/Mr. Wonderful 25.00 50.00

2006 Jakks Pacific WWE Classic Superstars 3-Packs Series 7

NNO Terry Funk/Cactus Jack/Sabu 25.00 50.00
NNO Undertaker/Kane/Paul Bearer 25.00 50.00

2007 Jakks Pacific WWE Classic Superstars 3-Packs Series 8

NNO Jake Roberts/British 40.00 80.00
{Bulldog/Koko B. Ware
NNO Ric Flair/Perfect/Heenan 25.00 50.00

2008 Jakks Pacific WWE Classic Superstars 3-Packs Series 9

NNO Rhythm & Blues 30.00 75.00
{w/Jimmy Hart
NNO Rocky Johnson
Peter Maivia/The Rock 40.00 80.00

2009 WWE Classic Superstars 3-Packs Series 10

NNO Brainbusters w/Bobby Heenan 25.00 50.00
NNO Demolition/Ax/ 75.00 150.00
Smash/Crush

2009 Jakks Pacific WWE Classic Superstars 3-Packs Series 11

NNO LOD 2000 w/Sunny 75.00 150.00
NNO Nasty Boys w/Jimmy Hart 30.00 60.00

2009 Jakks Pacific WWE Classic Superstars 3-Packs Series 12

NNO Powers of Pain w/Mr. Fuji
NNO Tito Santana/HBK w/Sherri

1999 Jakks Pacific WWF Deadly Games

NNO Droz 6.00 12.00
NNO HHH 6.00 12.00
NNO Stone Cold Steve Austin 7.50 15.00

2005 Jakks Pacific WWE Deluxe Aggression Series 1

NNO Batista 20.00 40.00
NNO Kurt Angle 12.50 25.00
NNO John Cena 30.00 60.00
NNO Randy Orton 15.00 30.00
NNO Rey Mysterio 20.00 40.00
NNO Triple H 15.00 30.00

2006 Jakks Pacific WWE Deluxe Aggression Series 2

NNO Booker T 10.00 20.00
NNO Carlito Cool 10.00 20.00
NNO Edge 10.00 20.00
NNO Kane 15.00 30.00
NNO Rey Mysterio 15.00 30.00
NNO Undertaker 25.00 50.00

2006 Jakks Pacific WWE Deluxe Aggression Series 3

NNO Batista 12.50 25.00
NNO Chris Benoit 15.00 30.00
NNO John Cena
NNO Kurt Angle 12.50 25.00
NNO Lashley 7.50 15.00
NNO Shawn Michaels

2006 Jakks Pacific WWE Deluxe Aggression Series 4

NNO Boogeyman 12.50 25.00
NNO Chris Masters 10.00 20.00
NNO JBL 7.50 15.00
NNO Mr. Kennedy
NNO Randy Orton 10.00 20.00
NNO Rob Conway 7.50 15.00
NNO Shelton Benjamin

2006 Jakks Pacific WWE Deluxe Aggression Series 5

NNO Batista 10.00 20.00
NNO Big Show 15.00 30.00
NNO John Cena 20.00 40.00
NNO Matt Hardy 10.00 20.00
NNO Rob Van Dam 10.00 20.00
NNO Triple H

2007 Jakks Pacific WWE Deluxe Aggression Series 6

NNO Booker T
NNO Edge
NNO Finlay
NNO John Cena
NNO Kenny
NNO Rob Van Dam

2007 Jakks Pacific WWE Deluxe Aggression Series 7

NNO Carlito
NNO Chris Benoit
NNO Mr. Kennedy
NNO Jeff Hardy
NNO Sabu
NNO Rey Mysterio

2007 Jakks Pacific WWE Deluxe Aggression Series 8

NNO Bobby Lashley
NNO CM Punk
NNO Sandman
NNO Gregory Helms
NNO Undertaker
NNO Johnny Nitro

2007 Jakks Pacific WWE Deluxe Aggression Series 8 (loose)

NNO Bobby Lashley
NNO CM Punk
NNO Sandman
NNO Gregory Helms
NNO Undertaker
NNO Johnny Nitro

2007 Jakks Pacific WWE Deluxe Aggression Series 9

NNO Mr. McMahon
NNO Kenny Dykstra
NNO Kevin Thorn
NNO John Cena
NNO Jimmy Wang Yang
NNO Tommy Dreamer

2007 Jakks Pacific WWE Deluxe Aggression Series 10

NNO Batista
NNO Daivari
NNO JBL
NNO Matt Hardy
NNO Randy Orton
NNO Shawn Michaels

2007 Jakks Pacific WWE Deluxe Aggression Series 11

NNO Chavo Guerrero
NNO Elijah Burke
NNO John Cena
NNO MVP
NNO Snitsky
NNO William Regal

2007 Jakks Pacific WWE Deluxe Aggression Series 12

NNO Batista
NNO Boogeyman
NNO CM Punk
NNO Paul London
NNO Shawn Michaels
NNO Umaga

2008 Jakks Pacific WWE Deluxe Aggression Series 13

NNO Cody Rhodes 12.50 25.00
NNO John Cena 12.50 25.00
NNO Miz 10.00 20.00
NNO Rey Mysterio 12.50 25.00
NNO Stone Cold Steve Austin 15.00 30.00
NNO Triple H 17.50 35.00

2008 Jakks Pacific WWE Deluxe Aggression Series 14

NNO John Morrison 20.00 40.00
NNO Armando Estrada 10.00 20.00
NNO Brian Kendrick 10.00 20.00
NNO MVP 10.00 20.00
NNO Randy Orton 12.50 25.00
NNO Undertaker 20.00 40.00

2008 Jakks Pacific WWE Deluxe Aggression Series 15

NNO Chris Jericho
NNO Finlay
NNO Matt Striker 15.00 30.00
NNO Mr. Kennedy
NNO Tazz
NNO Undertaker

2008 Jakks Pacific WWE Deluxe Aggression Series 16

NNO Batista

NNO Edge 15.00 30.00
NNO JBL 10.00 20.00
NNO Nunzio
NNO Randy Orton
NNO Shelton Benjamin

2008 Jakks Pacific WWE Deluxe Aggression Series 17

NNO Curt Hawkins
NNO DH Smith 12.50 25.00
NNO Kofi Kingston 15.00 30.00
NNO Paul Burchill 10.00 20.00
NNO Santino Marella 10.00 20.00
NNO Zack Ryder

2008 Jakks Pacific WWE Deluxe Aggression Series 18

NNO Chris Jericho 15.00 30.00
NNO Festus 10.00 20.00
NNO Hardcore Holly 10.00 20.00
NNO Jesse 10.00 20.00
NNO John Morrison 10.00 20.00
NNO The Miz

2009 Jakks Pacific WWE Deluxe Aggression Series 19

NNO Chris Jericho
NNO John Cena 15.00 30.00
NNO JTG 10.00 20.00
NNO Matt Hardy 15.00 30.00
NNO Shad 10.00 20.00
NNO Ted DiBiase 12.50 25.00

2009 Jakks Pacific WWE Deluxe Aggression Series 20

NNO Big Show 10.00 20.00
NNO Evan Bourne
NNO Shawn Michaels
NNO Stone Cold Steve Austin
NNO R-Truth 10.00 20.00
NNO Rey Mysterio 17.50 35.00

2009 Jakks Pacific WWE Deluxe Aggression Series 21

NNO Edge 12.50 25.00
NNO Goldust
NNO Jeff Hardy 25.00 50.00
NNO John Cena 12.50 25.00
NNO Rey Mysterio 20.00 40.00
NNO Vladimir Kozlov 10.00 20.00

2009 Jakks Pacific WWE Deluxe Aggression Series 22

NNO Batista
NNO Christian 25.00 50.00
NNO CM Punk 30.00 60.00
NNO Jack Swagger 12.50 25.00
NNO Randy Orton
NNO Triple H

2009 Jakks Pacific WWE Deluxe Aggression Series 23

NNO Batista
NNO Big Show 10.00 20.00
NNO John Cena 10.00 20.00
NNO Randy Orton
NNO Rey Mysterio
NNO Triple H 15.00 30.00

2009 Jakks Pacific WWE Deluxe Aggression Series 24

NNO Kofi Kingston
NNO Matt Hardy
NNO MVP
NNO Rey Mysterio 15.00 30.00

2007 Jakks Pacific WWE Deluxe Aggression 2-Packs

NNO Edge/Batista
NNO Undertaker/Kane
NNO Shawn Michaels/Triple H

2006 Jakks Pacific WWE Deluxe Aggression 3-Packs Series 1

NNO Triple H/John Cena/Edge 15.00 30.00
NNO Rey Mysterio/Randy Orton/Kurt Angle25.0050.00

2007 Jakks Pacific WWE Deluxe Aggression 3-Packs Series 2

NNO DX & The Big Show
NNO Rey Mysterio
Lashley/Batista

2007 Jakks Pacific WWE Deluxe Aggression 3-Packs Series 3

NNO Lashley/Sabu/RVD
NNO Randy Orton/Edge/Jeff Hardy

2008 Jakks Pacific WWE Deluxe Aggression 3-Packs Series 4

NNO Shawn Michaels/John Cena/Edge
NNO Mr. Kennedy/Undertaker/Fit Finlay20.00 40.00

2008 Jakks Pacific WWE Deluxe Aggression 3-Packs Series 5

NNO Umaga/Triple H/Randy Orton 25.00 50.00
NNO Rey Mysterio/Undertaker/Fit Finlay25.00 50.00

2009 Jakks Pacific WWE Deluxe Aggression 3-Packs Series 6

NNO Chris Jericho/Kane/Shawn Michaels
NNO CM Punk/Edge/Chavo Guerrero

2006 Jakks Pacific WWE Deluxe Classic Superstars Series 1

NNO Hulk Hogan 25.00 50.00
NNO Ric Flair 25.00 50.00
NNO Rowdy Roddy Piper (black tape) 15.00 30.00
NNO Rowdy Roddy Piper (gold tape)
NNO Stone Cold Steve Austin 15.00 30.00
NNO The Rock 20.00 40.00

2007 Jakks Pacific WWE Deluxe Classic Superstars Series 2

NNO Bret Hart
NNO British Bulldog
NNO Kevin Nash
NNO Mr. Perfect
NNO Shawn Michaels

2007 Jakks Pacific WWE Deluxe Classic Superstars Series 3

NNO Jake The Snake Roberts
NNO Lex Luger
NNO Ravishing Rick Rude
NNO Scott Hall
NNO Undertaker

2007 Jakks Pacific WWE Deluxe Classic Superstars Series 4

NNO Brutus Beefcake
NNO Honky Tonk Man
NNO Iron Sheik
NNO Ted DiBiase
NNO Shawn Michaels

2008 Jakks Pacific WWE Deluxe Classic Superstars Series 5

NNO Buff Bagwell 12.50 25.00
NNO Diamond Dallas Page
NNO Jim The Anvil Neidhart 20.00 40.00
NNO Jimmy Superfly Snuka 12.50 25.00

2008 Jakks Pacific WWE Deluxe Classic Superstars Series 6

NNO Eddie Guerrero 25.00 50.00
NNO Hillbilly Jim 20.00 40.00
NNO Kane 30.00 60.00
NNO Sgt. Slaughter 17.50 35.00
NNO Triple H 12.50 25.00

2009 Jakks Pacific WWE Deluxe Classic Superstars Series 7

NNO Bret Hart 20.00 40.00
NNO Shawn Michaels 15.00 30.00
NNO The Rock 15.00 30.00
NNO Tito Santana 12.50 25.00
NNO Undertaker 20.00 40.00

2009 Jakks Pacific WWE Deluxe Classic Superstars Series 8

NNO Big John Studd 30.00 40.00
NNO British Bulldog 12.50 25.00
NNO Chainsaw Charlie 10.00 20.00
NNO Dynamite Kid 20.00 40.00
NNO Stone Cold Steve Austin 25.00 50.00

2000 Jakks Pacific WWF Double Slam Series 1

NNO Edge/Christian 17.50 35.00
NNO Kane/X-Pac 10.00 20.00
NNO Stone Cold Steve Austin 15.00 30.00
Shane McMahon
NNO Vince McMahon/Undertaker 10.00 20.00

2000 Jakks Pacific WWF Double Slam Series 2

NNO Big Show 12.50 25.00
Stone Cold Steve Austin
NNO HHH/X-Pac
NNO The Rock/Billy Gunn 10.00 20.00
NNO Undertaker/Kane

2000 Jakks Pacific WWF Double Slam Series 3

NNO Big Show/Test 7.50 15.00
NNO Billy Gunn/Hardcore Holly 7.50 15.00
NNO Debra/Stone Cold Steve Austin 15.00 30.00
NNO Mankind/Undertaker 15.00 30.00

2000 Jakks Pacific WWF Double Slam Series 4

NNO Chyna/Chris Jericho 17.50 35.00
NNO Matt Hardy/Jeff Hardy 17.50 35.00
NNO Triple H/Billy Gunn 10.00 20.00

2000 Jakks Pacific WWF Double Slam Series 5

NNO Bradshaw/Faarooq 10.00 20.00
NNO Edge/Christian 12.50 25.00
NNO Triple H/The Rock

1998 Jakks Pacific WWF DTA Tour Series 1

NNO 8-Ball 6.00 12.00
NNO Chainz 7.50 15.00
NNO Dude Love 7.50 15.00
NNO Faarooq 6.00 12.00
NNO HHH 6.00 12.00
NNO Kane 12.50 25.00
NNO Shawn Michaels 10.00 20.00
NNO Vader 6.00 12.00

1999 Jakks Pacific WWF DTA Tour Series 2

NNO Double J Jeff Jarrett 6.00 12.00
NNO Al Snow 6.00 12.00
NNO Blue Blazer 15.00 30.00
NNO Edge 7.50 15.00
NNO Steve Blackman 6.00 12.00
NNO Undertaker 10.00 20.00

1999 Jakks Pacific WWF DTA Tour Series 3

NNO Christian 5.00 10.00
NNO Godfather 5.00 10.00
NNO HHH 7.50 15.00
NNO Ken Shamrock 7.50 15.00
NNO Stone Cold Steve Austin 12.50 25.00
NNO X-Pac 6.00 12.00

2004 Jakks Pacific WWE Exclusives

NNO Legion of Doom 150.00 300.00
(Ringside Collectibles Exclusive)
NNO Roddy Piper/100* TFM 1000.00 2000.00
NNO Roddy Piper/1800* RSF 150.00 300.00
NNO Roddy Piper/3000* TFM 75.00 150.00
NNO Ultimate Warrior/100* NYC TF1500.00 3000.00

2005 Jakks Pacific WWE Exclusives

NNO Hillbilly Jim/5000* 30.00 75.00
RTWM21 TOUR
NNO Hulk Hogan vs. Shawn Michaels/3000* RSC
75.00 150.00
NNO Mankind vs. Terry Funk KM 25.00 50.00
NNO Sgt. Slaughter/100* TFM 500.00 1000.00
NNO Sgt. Slaughter/3000* TFM 30.00 60.00
NNO Superstar B. Graham/3000* TRU CAN
NNO Superstar B.Graham
Blue Jeans/14000* TRU
NNO Superstar B. Graham
Green Gear/7000* TRU
NNO Superstar B. Graham
Pink Suit/7000 TRU
NNO Superstar B. Graham
Red Suit/400* TRU Orland
NNO Terry Funk/100* NYC TF

2006 Jakks Pacific WWE Exclusives

NNO Bobby Heenan Weasel/100* NYC TF300.00
500.00
NNO Bret Hart vs. Shawn Michaels RSF125.00 250.00
NNO British Bulldog & William Regal 50.00 100.00
Best of British ARGO UK
NNO Diesel & Shawn Michaels 60.00 120.00
2 Dudes with Attitudes RSC

NNO Dusty Rhodes/3000* OL 50.00 100.00
NNO Hulk Hogan/Blue Trunks & 30.00 75.00
{White Boots WM CAN
NNO Hulk Hogan/Blue Trunks & 25.00 60.00
{White Boots WM US
NNO Hulk Hogan/Tye Dye &
{Knee Brace WM US
NNO Hulk Hogan/Tye Dye & 30.00 75.00
{No Knee Brace WM US
NNO Hulk Hogan/Tye Dye WM CAN
NNO Hulk Hogan 2-in-1 MANIA TIX 75.00 150.00
NNO Hulk Hogan vs. 60.00 120.00
{Andre the Giant ARGO/BL
NNO Hulk Hogan/100* TFM 1500.00 3000.00
NNO Hulk Hogan/3000* TFM 60.00 120.00
NNO Jimmy Hart/100* NYC TF 600.00 1200.00
NNO Steve Austin WWE SZ 30.00 75.00
NNO Tazz/Towel Around Waist RSC
NNO Tazz/Towel in Package RSC 60.00 120.00

2007 Jakks Pacific WWE Exclusives

NNO Bret Hart vs. Jeff Hardy OL 100.00 200.00
NNO Razor Ramon vs. HBK RSC 60.00 120.00
NNO Roddy Piper Deluxe/100* NYC TF1000.00 2000.00
NNO Scott Hall & Kevin Nash 75.00 150.00
The Outsiders RSC
NNO Steve Austin vs. Bret Hart RSF 150.00 300.00
NNO Ultimate Warrior Classic
Superstars Marble Finish/20*
NNO Ultimate Warrior
Classic Superstars 2000.00 3500.00
One Warrior Nation/20*
NNO Ultimate Warrior Classic
Superstars Warrior America/5*
NNO Ultimate Warrior Classic
Superstars WCW 1998/20*
NNO Ultimate Warrior Ring Giant 1800.00 3000.00
Warrior America/25*
NNO Ultimate Warrior
Unmatched Fury 4000.00 6000.00
Warrior America Gear/15*

2008 Jakks Pacific WWE Exclusives

NNO Cactus Jack/3000* TFM 50.00 100.00
NNO D-Generation X RSC 75.00 150.00
NNO Eddie Guerrero vs. Rey Mysterio 400.00 750.00
{Halloween Havoc RSC
NNO Eddie Guerrero/100* NYC TF 1000.00 2000.00
NNO Hardy Boys RSC
NNO Hardy Boys WWE SZ
NNO Hart Foundation PROFIG
NNO Ric Flair/3000* WWE 24/7 30.00 75.00
NNO Stephanie & Triple H RSC 60.00 120.00
NNO Undertaker vs. Kane RSC 300.00 600.00
NNO Undertaker GITD/100* TFM 1000.00 2000.00
NNO Undertaker/3000* TFM 75.00 150.00

2009 Jakks Pacific WWE Exclusives

NNO Edge/3000* TFM 125.00 250.00
NNO Goldust Shattered RSC 125.00 250.00
NNO Kane vs. Vader OL 30.00 60.00
NNO Rey Mysterio/100* TFM 300.00 600.00
NNO Shawn Michaels/ 125.00 250.00
Multi-Belts PROFIG
NNO Shawn Michaels vs. 75.00 150.00
{Steve Austin WWE SZ
NNO Shawn Michaels vs. 100.00 200.00
{Undertaker RSC
NNO Sunny/100* TFM 300.00 500.00
NNO Sunny/3000* TFM 30.00 75.00
NNO Undertaker vs. 100.00 200.00
{Triple H WWE SZ

2005 Jakks Pacific WWE Face Flippin' Fighters

NNO Batista 12.50 25.00
NNO Chris Benoit 10.00 20.00
NNO Eddie Guerrero 12.50 25.00
NNO John Cena 20.00 40.00
NNO Randy Orton 12.50 25.00
NNO Undertaker 20.00 40.00

2001 Jakks Pacific WWF Famous Scenes Series 1

NNO Jeff Hardy/Matt Hardy 15.00 30.00
NNO Mick Foley/Undertaker 20.00 50.00
NNO The Rock/Triple H 12.50 25.00

2001 Jakks Pacific WWF Famous Scenes Series 2

NNO Chris Benoit/Chris Jericho 12.50 25.00
NNO HHH/Cactus Jack 20.00 40.00
NNO Kurt Angle/Rikishi 15.00 30.00

2001 Jakks Pacific WWF Famous Scenes Series 3

NNO Bubba Ray Dudley/D-Von Dudley15.00 30.00
NNO Stone Cold Steve Austin
Vince McMahon

2001 Jakks Pacific WWF Famous Scenes Series 4

NNO Lita/Test 15.00 30.00
NNO The Rock/Billy Gunn
NNO Stone Cold Steve Austin 12.50 25.00
Undertaker

1998 Jakks Pacific WWF Fantasy Warfare

NNO Stone Cold Steve
Austin vs. Andre the Giant 12.50 25.00
NNO Undertaker vs. Mankind 15.00 30.00

2002 Jakks Pacific WWF Fatal 4-Way Series 1

NNO Bubba Ray Dudley 6.00 12.00
NNO Edge 10.00 20.00
NNO Jeff Hardy 15.00 30.00
NNO Lita 12.50 25.00

2002 Jakks Pacific WWF Fatal 4-Way Series 2

NNO Chris Jericho 20.00 40.00
NNO Christian 7.50 15.00
NNO Stone Cold Steve Austin 12.50 25.00
NNO Undertaker 20.00 40.00

2002 Jakks Pacific WWF Fatal 4-Way Series 3

NNO Bubba Ray Dudley 6.00 12.00
NNO Chris Jericho 10.00 20.00
NNO Christian 10.00 20.00
NNO Jeff Hardy 12.50 25.00

1999 Jakks Pacific WWF Federation Fighters

NNO Kane
(two sleeves)
NNO Stone Cold Steve Austin 15.00 30.00
NNO Steve Austin/Jumpsuit 20.00 40.00

1999 Jakks Pacific WWF Federation Fighters Series 2

NNO Big Show 15.00 30.00
NNO Rock 25.00 50.00
NNO Stone Cold Steve Austin 15.00 30.00
NNO Undertaker 20.00 40.00

2001 Jakks Pacific WWF-WWE Final Count Series 1

NNO Billy Gunn vs. Edge
Downward Spiral
NNO Billy Gunn vs. Edge
Famous-er
NNO Lita vs. Matt Hardy
Litacanrana
NNO Lita vs. Matt Hardy
Twist of Fate
NNO Undertaker vs. Steve Austin
The Last Ride
NNO Undertaker vs. Steve Austin
Stone Cold Stunner

2002 Jakks Pacific WWF-WWE Final Count Series 2

NNO Kane vs. Steve Austin
NNO Kurt Angle vs. Triple H 12.50 25.00
NNO The Rock vs. Chris Jericho 20.00 40.00

2002 Jakks Pacific WWF-WWE Final Count Series 3

NNO Billy Gunn/Jeff Hardy 12.50 25.00
NNO Chris Jericho/Steve Austin
NNO Rikishi/Bubba Ray Dudley

2002 Jakks Pacific WWF-WWE Final Count Series 4

NNO Albert/Scotty Too Hotty
NNO The Rock/Kurt Angle 15.00 30.00
NNO Test/Christian

2002 Jakks Pacific WWF-WWE Final Count Series 5

NNO Bradshaw/Undertaker
NNO Jeff Hardy/Trish Stratus 12.50 25.00
NNO Rob Van Dam 25.00 50.00
Eddie Guerrero

2002 Jakks Pacific WWF-WWE Final Count Series 6

NNO Billy vs. Chuck 10.00 20.00
Famous-er
NNO Billy vs. Chuck 10.00 20.00
Jungle Kick
NNO C.Jericho vs. C.Benoit 15.00 30.00
Crippler Crossface
NNO C.Jericho vs. C.Benoit 15.00 30.00
Walls of Jericho
NNO Hulk Hogan vs. HHH 12.50 25.00
Pedigree
NNO Hulk Hogan vs. HHH 12.50 25.00
Running Leg Drop

2002 Jakks Pacific WWF-WWE Final Count Series 7

NNO Batista
NNO Billy Kidman
NNO Hurricane

2001 Jakks Pacific WWF Finishing Moves Series 1

NNO Chris Jericho/Kurt Angle
NNO The Hardy Boyz
NNO Triple H/The Rock

2001 Jakks Pacific WWF Finishing Moves Series 2

NNO Chris Jericho/The Rock
NNO Kane/Undertaker
NNO Rikishi/Triple H

2001 Jakks Pacific WWF Finishing Moves Series 3

NNO Chris Benoit/Chris Jericho
NNO Eddie Guerrero/Billy Gunn
NNO The Hardy Boyz

2001 Jakks Pacific WWF Finishing Moves Series 4

NNO Kane/Edge
NNO Lita/Buh Buh Dudley
NNO The Rock/Stone Cold Steve Austin

2002 Jakks Pacific WWE Flex 'Ems Series 1

NNO Chris Jericho 7.50 15.00
NNO Edge 7.50 15.00
NNO Hulk Hogan 10.00 20.00
NNO Kurt Angle 7.50 15.00
NNO The Rock 10.00 20.00
NNO Triple H 7.50 15.00

2002 Jakks Pacific WWE Flex 'Ems Series 2

NNO Batista 10.00 20.00
NNO Booker T 7.50 15.00
NNO Brock Lesnar 6.00 12.00
NNO Chris Benoit 6.00 12.00
NNO Hurricane 7.50 15.00
NNO Rob Van Dam 7.50 15.00

2002 Jakks Pacific WWE Flex 'Ems Series 3

NNO Batista 7.50 15.00
NNO Chris Benoit 7.50 15.00
NNO Chris Jericho 7.50 15.00
NNO Hurricane 7.50 15.00
NNO Rob Van Dam 7.50 15.00
NNO The Rock 10.00 20.00

2003 Jakks Pacific WWE Flex 'Ems Series 4

NNO Booker T
NNO Kane
NNO Kurt Angle
NNO Rey Mysterio
NNO Triple H
NNO Undertaker

2003 Jakks Pacific WWE Flex 'Ems Series 5

NNO Booker T

NNO Brock Lesnar
NNO Chris Benoit
NNO Chris Jericho
NNO Rey Mysterio
NNO Rob Van Dam

2003 Jakks Pacific WWE Flex 'Ems Series 8

NNO Chris Jericho
NNO Eddie Guerrero
NNO Kurt Angle
NNO Matt Hardy
NNO Randy Orton
NNO Rey Mysterio

2003 Jakks Pacific WWE Flex 'Ems Series 9

NNO Batista
NNO Chris Benoit
NNO Eddie Guerrero
NNO Randy Orton
NNO Rey Mysterio
NNO Rob Van Dam

2003 Jakks Pacific WWE Flex 'Ems Series 10

NNO Batista
NNO Booker T
NNO Chris Benoit
NNO Chris Jericho
NNO Eddie Guerrero
NNO Rey Mysterio

2003 Jakks Pacific WWE Flex 'Ems Series 11

NNO Batista
NNO Kurt Angle
NNO Randy Orton
NNO Rey Mysterio
NNO Triple H
NNO Undertaker

2003 Jakks Pacific WWE Flex 'Ems Series 12

NNO Kane
NNO Rey Mysterio
NNO Shawn Michaels
NNO Triple H

2003 Jakks Pacific WWE Flex 'Ems Series 13

NNO Batista
NNO Chris Benoit
NNO Randy Orton
NNO Rob Van Dam

2003 Jakks Pacific WWE Flex 'Ems Series 14

NNO Rey Mysterio
NNO Shawn Michaels
NNO Triple H
NNO Undertaker

1998 Jakks Pacific WWF Fully Loaded Series 1

NNO Al Snow 6.00 12.00
NNO B.A. Billy Gunn 7.50 15.00
NNO HHH 6.00 12.00
NNO Kane 7.50 15.00
NNO Road Dogg 5.00 10.00
NNO The Rock 10.00 20.00

1999 Jakks Pacific WWF Fully Loaded Series 2

NNO Road Dogg Jesse James 6.00 12.00
NNO The Rock 10.00 20.00
NNO Shane McMahon 12.50 25.00
NNO Stone Cold Steve Austin 10.00 20.00
NNO Test
NNO X-Pac 7.50 15.00

2003 Jakks Pacific WWE Grudge Brawlers

NNO Christian
NNO Chris Jericho
NNO Kurt Angle
NNO Jeff Hardy 30.00 60.00
NNO Triple H
NNO Undertaker

1997 Jakks Pacific WWF Grudge Match

NNO Bret Hitman Hart vs. Stone Cold Steve Austin 10.00 20.00
NNO Goldust vs. Savio Vega 6.00 12.00
NNO Shawn Michaels vs. Owen Hart 7.50 15.00
NNO Sycho Sid vs. Vader 10.00 20.00
NNO The Undertaker vs. Mankind 15.00 30.00
NNO Yokozuna vs. Ahmed Johnson 6.00 12.00

1998 Jakks Pacific WWF Grudge Match Series 1

NNO HHH vs. Owen Hart 7.50 15.00
NNO Ken Shamrock vs. Dan Severn 7.50 15.00
NNO Luna vs. Sable 20.00 40.00
NNO Marvelous Marc Mero vs. Lethal Weapon Steve Blackman
NNO Stone Cold Steve Austin vs. Shawn Michaels 10.00 20.00
NNO Undertaker vs. Kane 10.00 20.00

1998 Jakks Pacific WWF Grudge Match Series 2

NNO HHH vs. Shawn Michaels 7.50 15.00
NNO Road Dogg Jesse James vs. Al Snow
NNO Stone Cold Steve Austin vs. Vince McMahon 12.50 25.00

1998 Jakks Pacific WWF Grudge Match Series 3

NNO Stone Cold Steve Austin vs. The Rock7.50 15.00
NNO X-Pac vs. Double J Jeff Jarrett 10.00 20.00

2005 Jakks Pacific WWE Havoc Unleashed Series 1

NNO Booker T 10.00 20.00
NNO Chris Benoit 7.50 15.00
NNO Edge 7.50 15.00
NNO Kurt Angle 12.50 25.00
NNO Scotty 2 Hotty 10.00 20.00
NNO Triple H 10.00 20.00

2006 Jakks Pacific WWE Havoc Unleashed Series 2

NNO Batista 10.00 20.00
NNO JBL 7.50 15.00
NNO RVD 12.50 25.00
NNO Shawn Michaels 12.50 25.00

2007 Jakks Pacific WWE Havoc Unleashed Series 3

NNO Bobby Lashley
NNO Edge
NNO HHH
NNO John Cena
NNO Kane
NNO Matt Hardy

2009 Jakks Pacific WWE Havoc Unleashed Series 4

NNO Batista 10.00 20.00
NNO HHH 6.00 12.00
NNO JBL 7.50 15.00
NNO Matt Hardy 7.50 15.00
NNO Undertaker 10.00 20.00

1997 Jakks Pacific WWF Heroes of Wrestling

NNO Sycho Sid 10.00 20.00
NNO Undertaker 12.50 25.00

2000 Jakks Pacific WWF House of Pain

NNO HHH 7.50 15.00
NNO Rock 12.50 25.00
NNO Stone Cold Steve Austin 12.50 25.00
NNO Tori 7.50 15.00
NNO Undertaker 12.50 25.00
NNO X-Pac 6.00 12.00

2000 Jakks Pacific WWF House of Pain (loose)

NNO HHH
NNO The Rock
NNO Stone Cold Steve Austin
NNO Tori
NNO Undertaker
NNO X-Pac

1998 Jakks Pacific WWF Jakk'd Up

NNO Sable
NNO Stone Cold Steve Austin
NNO Kane
NNO Undertaker

1998 Jakks Pacific WWF Jakk'd Up (loose)

NNO Sable
NNO Stone Cold Steve Austin
NNO Kane
NNO Undertaker

1997 Jakks Pacific WWF Boxed Sets

NNO Championship Title Series
Undertaker/Rocky/Bulldog/Owen
NNO King of the Iron Rungs
Hart/Austin/Ref/Johnson
NNO Nation of Domination
Mason/Faarooq/Vega/Crush
NNO RAW Is War 1
Sunny/Bret Hart/Sid/Vince
NNO Survivor Series 1996
Bearer/Mankind/Undertaker/Executioner
NNO Triple Threat
Johnson/Mero/Yokozuna

1998 Jakks Pacific WWF Boxed Sets

NNO Bad to the Bonz Steve Austin TRU
NNO Badd Blood
Bearer/Undertaker/Kane/Austin WM CAN
NNO DX
HHH/Chyna/Billy/Road Dogg MEI
NNO Go Mental
HHH/Dude Love/Austin/Undertaker SAM
NNO Legends of the Past and Present
Andre/Undertaker/Austin WM
NNO Mankind Grapple KM
NNO No Holds Barred
Kane/Austin/Cactus Jack KB
NNO Off the Mat
Austin/Rock/Billy Gunn/Road Dogg TRU
NNO RAW Is War 2
Austin/Undertaker/Rock/Mankind)
NNO Rock Bottom KM
NNO Shotgun Saturday Night
Austin/Kane/HBK/The Rock
NNO Slammers
Mankind/HBK/Undertaker/Austin
NNO Stone Cold Steve Austin Breakaway Table KM
NNO Stone Cold Steve Austin Grapple KM
NNO Stone Cold Steve Austin Special Collection HILLS
NNO Survivor Series
Undertaker/Kane/Austin/Rock
NNO Undertaker Special Collection HILLS
NNO WrestleMania XV Fully Loaded
Undertaker/Austin/Road Dogg/Billy Gunn
NNO WrestleMania XV Judgment Day
Undertaker/Austin/Vince

1999 Jakks Pacific WWF Boxed Sets

NNO Buried Alive 30.00 75.00
HHH/Vince/Undertaker/Austin
NNO Championship Title Series 20.00 40.00
Austin/X-Pac/Kane/The Rock TRU
NNO Hardcore Champions 20.00 40.00
Big Boss Man/Mankind/Al Snow/Hardcore Holly
NNO Mick Foley's Triple Threat 25.00 50.00
Mankind/Dude Love/Cactus Jack KB
NNO No Chance 20.00 40.00
Vince/Austin/Paul Wight
NNO Over the Edge 15.00 30.00
Austin/Rock/HHH/Kane
NNO Perfect 10
Austin/Rock/Kane/Undertaker/Mankind/Big Show#(X-Pac/HHH/Road Dogg/Billy Gunn TRU
NNO SummerSlam '99 Camo Carnage17.50 35.00
HHH/Billy Gunn/Ausin
NNO SummerSlam Expect No Mercy
Austin/Rock/Vince/Undertaker
NNO SummerSlam '99 Last Man Standing20.00 40.00
Austin/Rock/Vince/Shane
NNO Survivor Series Mayhem 17.50 35.00
HHH/Rock/Austin
NNO WWF Attitude 20.00 40.00
HBK/Animal/Austin/Hawk KM

2001 Jakks Pacific WWF Boxed Sets

NNO 2 Extreme 30.00 75.00
Lita & The Hardys
NNO Back in the Ring/Undertaker 25.00 50.00
Stone Cold Steve Austin/Mick Foley KM
NNO Brothers of Destruction
Austin/Undertaker/Kane TRU
NNO Cold Day in Dudleyville 30.00 60.00
Rock/D-Von/Buh Buh Ray TRU
NNO Get in the Groove 50.00 100.00
(Scottie/Rikishi/Sexay MEI
NNO Insurrextion

HHH/Austin/Bubba/Edge/Kane#(Rock/Test/Jeff Hardy/Y2J/Regal UK
NNO KOTR Lead Me to My Throne
D-Von/Edge/Austin/Angle/Hardys
NNO Picture Perfect 20.00 40.00
Edge/Christian KM
NNO Renegades
Raven/Austin/Shane McMahon KM
NNO Team Extreme 20.00 40.00
Matt & Jeff Hardy/Lita
NNO Triple Threat 12.50 25.00
Y2J/Rock/HHH

2002 Jakks Pacific WWE Boxed Sets

NNO nWo Federation Poison 25.00 50.00
Nash/X-Pac/Hall
NNO RAW Draft
Bubba Ray/Undertaker/Flair/Austin
NNO Rock Solid 20.00 40.00
Rock/Scorpion King
NNO SmackDown Draft
Y2J/Hogan/Vince/Rock

2004 Jakks Pacific WWE Employee Gift Exclusives

NNO Ric Flair/25*
NNO Rowdy Roddy Piper/20*
NNO Sgt. Slaughter/20*

2002 Jakks Pacific WWF-WWE King of the Ring Series 1

NNO D-Von Dudley 7.50 15.00
NNO Edge 20.00 40.00
NNO Jeff Hardy 12.50 25.00
NNO Kurt Angle 10.00 20.00
NNO Matt Hardy 7.50 15.00
NNO Stone Cold Steve Austin

2002 Jakks Pacific WWF-WWE King of the Ring Series 2

NNO Brock Lesnar 15.00 30.00
NNO Chris Jericho 12.50 25.00
NNO Hardcore Holly 12.50 25.00
NNO Rob Van Dam 15.00 30.00
NNO Test 10.00 20.00
NNO X-Pac 10.00 20.00

1998 Jakks Pacific WWF Legends

NNO Andre the Giant 20.00 40.00
NNO Captain Lou Albano 7.50 15.00
NNO Classy Freddie Blassie 7.50 15.00
NNO Jimmy Superfly Snuka 10.00 20.00

1999 Jakks Pacific WWF Live Wire Series 1

NNO Chyna 10.00 20.00
NNO Ken Shamrock 7.50 15.00
NNO Mankind 10.00 20.00
NNO Stone Cold Steve Austin 12.50 25.00
NNO Undertaker 15.00 30.00
NNO Vader 7.50 15.00

1999 Jakks Pacific WWF Live Wire Series 2

NNO Mark Henry 7.50 15.00
NNO Marvelous Marc Mero 6.00 12.00
NNO Rock 10.00 20.00
NNO Shawn Michaels 7.50 15.00
NNO Val Venis 6.00 12.00
NNO X-Pac 7.50 15.00

2003 Jakks Pacific WWE Main Event

NNO Hulk Hogan 12.50 25.00
NNO Shawn Michaels
NNO Spike Dudley 15.00 30.00
NNO Stacy Keibler 10.00 20.00
NNO Tazz
NNO Torrie Wilson 10.00 20.00
NNO Triple H

1997 Jakks Pacific WWF Managers Series 1

NNO Bob Backlund/Sultan 12.50 25.00
NNO Clarence Mason/Crush 10.00 20.00
NNO Paul Bearer/Mankind 12.50 25.00
NNO Sable/Marc Mero 10.00 20.00

2002 Jakks Pacific WWE Match Champs

NNO Booker T 10.00 20.00
NNO Jeff Hardy 10.00 20.00
NNO Ric Flair 7.50 15.00
NNO Rob Van Dam 7.50 15.00
NNO The Rock 10.00 20.00
NNO Triple H 7.50 15.00

2002 Jakks Pacific WWF Match Enders

NNO Billy Gunn/Famous-er
NNO Edge/Downward Spiral
NNO Lita/Litacanrana
NNO Matt Hardy/Twist of Fate
NNO Triple H/Pedigree
NNO Undertaker/Last Ride 12.50 25.00

2007 Jakks Pacific WWE Maximum Aggression Series 1

NNO Bobby Lashley
NNO Carlito
NNO CM Punk
NNO Rey Mysterio
NNO Triple H

2008 Jakks Pacific WWE Maximum Aggression Series 2

NNO Carlito 20.00 40.00
NNO Chris Jericho
NNO Elijah Burke 25.00 50.00
NNO Undertaker 20.00 40.00

2008 Jakks Pacific WWE Maximum Aggression Series 3

NNO Edge 20.00 40.00
NNO John Cena 15.00 30.00
NNO John Morrison
NNO Randy Orton 15.00 30.00

2008 Jakks Pacific WWE Maximum Aggression Series 4

NNO Matt Hardy
NNO Kane
NNO Mr. Kennedy
NNO Shelton Benjamin

2009 Jakks Pacific WWE Maximum Aggression Series 5

NNO CM Punk 15.00 30.00
NNO John Cena 20.00 40.00
NNO Matt Hardy
NNO Triple H 15.00 30.00

2009 Jakks Pacific WWE Maximum Aggression Series 6

NNO Rey Mysterio 25.00 50.00
NNO Shawn Michaels
NNO Triple H 15.00 30.00
NNO Undertaker 20.00 40.00

1999 Jakks Pacific WWF Maximum Sweat Series 1

NNO Hunter Hearst-Helmsley 6.00 12.00
NNO Kane/Mask Off 10.00 20.00
NNO Kane/Mask On 12.50 25.00
NNO Rock The People's Champion 15.00 30.00
NNO Shawn Michaels 12.50 25.00
NNO Stone Cold Steve Austin 10.00 20.00
NNO Undertaker 15.00 30.00

1999 Jakks Pacific WWF Maximum Sweat Series 2

NNO B.A. Billy Gunn 10.00 20.00
NNO Edge 7.50 15.00
NNO Ken Shamrock 7.50 15.00
NNO Road Dogg 10.00 20.00
NNO Stone Cold Steve Austin 12.50 25.00
NNO Undertaker 10.00 20.00

1999 Jakks Pacific WWF Maximum Sweat Series 3

NNO Big Show 10.00 20.00
NNO Gangrel/Blue Shirt
NNO Gangrel/Lt. Blue Shirt 12.50 25.00
NNO Mankind 7.50 15.00
NNO The Rock 10.00 20.00
NNO Stone Cold Steve Austin 10.00 20.00

1999 Jakks Pacific WWF Maximum Sweat Series 4

NNO Billy Gunn 7.50 15.00
NNO Droz 7.50 15.00
NNO Kane 7.50 15.00
NNO Road Dogg 7.50 15.00
NNO Stone Cold Steve Austin 10.00 20.00
NNO Undertaker

1999 Jakks Pacific WWF Maximum Sweat Special Series

NNO B.A. Billy Gunn
NNO Edge
NNO Ken Shamrock
NNO Road Dogg

2008 Jakks Pacific WWE Micro Aggression 10-Packs

NNO Batista/Jeff Hardy/HBK/Kennedy/Cena
Mysterio/Undertaker/Carlito/HHH/Kane
NNO John Cena/Kennedy/HBK/CM Punk/Batista
Kane/HHH/Carlito/Undertaker/Mysterio
NNO John Cena/Matt Hardy/Orton/MVP/Primo
Kane/HHH/Carlito/Undertaker/Mysterio

2006 Jakks Pacific WWE Micro Aggression Playset

NNO Crash and Bash Playset 30.00 75.00
Chris Benoit/Triple H/Kane/Rey Mysterio

2007 Jakks Pacific WWE Micro Aggression Playset

NNO Crash and Bash Arena
w/John Cena/HBK/Lashley/Edge

2008 Jakks Pacific WWE Micro Aggression Playsets

NNO Crash and Bash Cell 60.00 120.00
w/Cena/Undertaker/HBK/CM Punk
NNO Crash and Bash El. Chamber 30.00 75.00
w/Cena/Rey Mysterio/Umaga/Kane

2006 Jakks Pacific WWE Micro Aggression Series 1

NNO Kane/Undertaker/Chris Benoit 15.00 30.00
NNO Rey Mysterio/John Cena/Rob Van Dam 12.50 25.00
NNO Triple H/Shawn Michaels/John Cena12.50 25.00

2007 Jakks Pacific WWE Micro Aggression Series 2

NNO Edge/Cena/RVD
NNO Rey Mysterio/Batista/Hogan
NNO Triple H/HBK/Orton

2007 Jakks Pacific WWE Micro Aggression Series 3

NNO Jeff Hardy/Cena/Carlito
NNO Jimmy Wang Yang/Undertaker/Kennedy
NNO Shawn Michaels/CM Punk/Tommy Dreamer

2007 Jakks Pacific WWE Micro Aggression Series 4

NNO Batista/Finlay/Rey Mysterio
NNO CM Punk/Lashley/Hardcore Holly
NNO Edge/Cena/Orton

2008 Jakks Pacific WWE Micro Aggression Series 5

NNO CM Punk/Lashley/T.Dreamer
NNO Jeff Hardy/Cena/HBK
NNO Undertaker/Kennedy/Batista

2008 Jakks Pacific WWE Micro Aggression Series 6

NNO Carlito/King Booker/HHH
NNO Chris Masters/MVP/Edge
NNO Hardcore Holly/Burke/Boogeyman

2008 Jakks Pacific WWE Micro Aggression Series 7

NNO John Cena/Umaga/Kennedy
NNO John Morrison/CM Punk/Tommy Dreamer
NNO Matt Hardy/Batista/Rey Mysterio

2008 Jakks Pacific WWE Micro Aggression Series 8

NNO Edge/Kane/Finlay
NNO Miz/Boogeyman/Burke
NNO Triple H/Jeff Hardy/Lashley

2008 Jakks Pacific WWE Micro Aggression Series 9

NNO CM Punk/Finlay/Morrison
NNO Rey Mysterio/MVP/Undertaker
NNO Shawn Michaels/Cena/Kennedy

2008 Jakks Pacific WWE Micro Aggression Series 10

NNO Chris Jericho/John Cena/JBL
NNO CM Punk/Elijah Burke/Domino
NNO Great Khali/Undertaker/Deuce

2008 Jakks Pacific WWE Micro Aggression Series 11

NNO Chavo/Big Daddy V/Benjamin
NNO Edge/Ric Flair/Kane
NNO Triple H/Cody Rhodes/Umaga

2008 Jakks Pacific WWE Micro Aggression Series 12

NNO Carlito/Santino/Orton
NNO Matt Hardy/Ryder/Hawkins
NNO Tommy Dreamer/Kofi/Miz

2009 Jakks Pacific WWE Micro Aggression Series 13

NNO Kane/Mysterio/Cena 10.00 20.00
NNO MVP/Undertaker/Jeff Hardy
NNO Shawn Michaels/CM Punk/Y2J 12.50 25.00

2009 Jakks Pacific WWE Micro Aggression Series 14

NNO Carlito/Ryder/Hawkins 7.50 15.00
NNO Cody Rhodes/DiBiase/JBL 7.50 15.00
NNO Finlay/Dreamer/Matt Hardy

2009 Jakks Pacific WWE Micro Aggression Series 15

NNO Cody Rhodes/Mysterio/Cena 10.00 20.00
NNO Edge/Jeff Hardy/HHH 7.50 15.00
NNO MVP/Matt Hardy/Morrison

Jakks Pacific WWE Micro Aggression Series 16

NNO John Cena/Mysterio/Undertaker 12.50 25.00
NNO Randy Orton/Rhodes/DiBiase
NNO Triple H/MVP/Edge 10.00 20.00

2009 Jakks Pacific WWE Micro Aggression Series 17

NNO Finlay/Dreamer/Morrison
NNO John Cena/Mysterio/Kane 12.50 25.00
NNO Undertaker/Hawkins/Ryder

2001 Jakks Pacific WWF No Way Out Series 1

NNO Chris Jericho 10.00 20.00
NNO Grandmaster Sexay 7.50 15.00
NNO Kurt Angle
NNO The Rock 15.00 30.00
NNO Scotty 2 Hotty 7.50 15.00
NNO Stone Cold Steve Austin 12.50 25.00

2001 Jakks Pacific WWF No Way Out Series 2

NNO Chris Benoit 15.00 30.00
NNO Chris Jericho 15.00 30.00
NNO Christian 10.00 20.00
NNO Kurt Angle 12.50 25.00
NNO Lita 10.00 20.00
NNO Matt Hardy 12.50 25.00
NNO Raven 10.00 20.00
NNO Undertaker 15.00 30.00

2002 Jakks Pacific WWE nWo

NNO Hulk Hogan/Tights 15.00 30.00
NNO Hulk Hogan/T-Shirt 12.50 25.00
NNO Kevin Nash/Tights 12.50 25.00
NNO Kevin Nash/T-Shirt 10.00 20.00
NNO Scott Hall/Tights 12.50 25.00
NNO Scott Hall/T-Shirt 10.00 20.00

2002 Jakks Pacific WWE nWo 2-Packs

NNO Hulk Hogan vs. The Rock 12.50 25.00
NNO Kane vs. Kevin Nash 20.00 40.00
NNO Steve Austin vs. Scott Hall 20.00 40.00

2002 Jakks Pacific WWE nWo Playset

NNO Metal Match 30.00 60.00

2002 Jakks Pacific WWE Off the Ropes Series 1

NNO Booker T 7.50 15.00
NNO Brock Lesnar 10.00 20.00
NNO Edge 7.50 15.00
NNO Hollywood Hulk Hogan 15.00 30.00
NNO Triple H 10.00 20.00
NNO Trish Stratus 20.00 40.00

2003 Jakks Pacific WWE Off the Ropes Series 2

NNO Chris Benoit 12.50 25.00
NNO Hurricane 15.00 30.00
NNO Kurt Angle 10.00 20.00
NNO Matt Hardy
NNO Rikishi

2003 Jakks Pacific WWE Off the Ropes Series 2 (loose)

NNO Brock Lesnar 12.50 25.00
NNO Chris Jericho 10.00 20.00
NNO Christian 10.00 20.00
NNO Rey Mysterio 15.00 30.00

2003 Jakks Pacific WWE Off the Ropes Series 4

NNO Jamie Noble 7.50 15.00
NNO Rob Van Dam 10.00 20.00
NNO Scott Steiner 4.00 15.00
NNO Undertaker

2003 Jakks Pacific WWE Off the Ropes Series 5

NNO Billy Gunn 10.00 20.00
NNO Brock Lesnar 12.50 25.00
NNO Eddie Guerrero 10.00 20.00
NNO Ric Flair 7.50 15.00
NNO Stone Cold Steve Austin 12.50 25.00
NNO Triple H 10.00 20.00

2003 Jakks Pacific WWE Off the Ropes Series 6

NNO Al Snow 12.50 25.00
NNO A-Train 10.00 20.00
NNO Big Show 7.50 15.00
NNO Spike Dudley 10.00 20.00
NNO Tajiri 12.50 25.00

2004 Jakks Pacific WWE Off the Ropes Series 7

NNO Brock Lesnar 10.00 20.00
NNO Chris Benoit 10.00 20.00
NNO Lance Storm 7.50 15.00
NNO Matt Hardy 12.50 25.00
NNO Rob Van Dam 12.50 25.00
NNO Triple H 10.00 20.00

2004 Jakks Pacific WWE Off the Ropes Series 8

NNO JBL 10.00 20.00
NNO Maven 10.00 20.00
NNO Rob Van Dam 10.00 20.00
NNO The Rock 15.00 30.00
NNO Stacy Keibler 20.00 40.00
NNO Steven Richards 7.50 15.00

2005 Jakks Pacific WWE Off the Ropes Series 9

NNO Chris Benoit 12.50 25.00
NNO Rey Mysterio 10.00 20.00
NNO Triple H 10.00 20.00

2006 Jakks Pacific WWE Off the Ropes Series 10

NNO Batista 7.50 15.00
NNO Chris Masters 7.50 15.00
NNO John Cena 10.00 20.00
NNO Kurt Angle 10.00 20.00
NNO Shawn Michaels 12.50 25.00

2007 Jakks Pacific WWE Off the Ropes Series 11

NNO Boogeyman
NNO JBL
NNO John Cena
NNO Randy Orton
NNO Ric Flair
NNO Shawn Michaels

2007 Jakks Pacific WWE Off the Ropes Series 12

NNO Batista
NNO Elijah Burke
NNO The Great Khali
NNO Jeff Hardy
NNO Mr. Kennedy
NNO Tommy Dreamer

2009 Jakks Pacific WWE Off the Ropes Series 13

NNO Big Show 10.00 20.00
NNO Chris Jericho 15.00 30.00
NNO Festus 7.50 15.00
NNO Hornswoggle
NNO JBL 7.50 15.00
NNO Kofi Kingston 7.50 15.00

2003 Jakks Pacific WWE Pay Per View Series 1

NNO Booker T 12.50 25.00
NNO Goldberg 20.00 40.00
NNO Ric Flair 10.00 20.00
NNO Scott Steiner 30.00 75.00
NNO Stone Cold Steve Austin
NNO Triple H

2003 Jakks Pacific WWE Pay Per View Series 2

NNO Eddie Guerrero
NNO Goldberg
NNO Kurt Angle
NNO Stone Cold Steve Austin
NNO Triple H
NNO Undertaker

2003 Jakks Pacific WWE Pay Per View Series 3

NNO Eric Bischoff
NNO Goldberg
NNO John Cena
NNO Kane
NNO Kurt Angle
NNO Randy Orton

2004 Jakks Pacific WWE Pay Per View Series 4

NNO Chris Benoit 10.00 20.00
NNO Chris Jericho 15.00 30.00
NNO Edge 10.00 20.00
NNO Hurricane 12.50 25.00
NNO Randy Orton 15.00 30.00
NNO Shelton Benjamin 12.50 25.00

2004 Jakks Pacific WWE Pay Per View Series 6

NNO Chris Jericho 10.00 20.00
NNO Edge 15.00 30.00
NNO JBL 10.00 20.00
NNO John Cena 12.50 25.00
NNO Kane 7.50 15.00
NNO Torrie Wilson 20.00 40.00

2004 Jakks Pacific WWE Pay Per View Series 7

NNO Eddie Guerrero 10.00 20.00
NNO Edge 7.50 15.00
NNO JBL 6.00 12.00
NNO Randy Orton 12.50 25.00
NNO Trish Stratus 15.00 30.00
NNO Undertaker 12.50 25.00

2005 Jakks Pacific WWE Pay Per View Series 8

NNO Batista 12.50 25.00
NNO Eugene 10.00 20.00
NNO Kane 15.00 30.00
NNO Maven 7.50 15.00
NNO Shawn Michaels/Ref Gear 15.00 30.00
NNO Triple H 7.50 15.00

2005 Jakks Pacific WWE Pay Per View Series 9

NNO Bubba Ray Dudley 12.50 25.00
NNO D-Von Dudley 10.00 20.00
NNO Eric Bischoff
NNO JBL 7.50 15.00
NNO Kurt Angle/Referee Gear
NNO Paul Heyman 10.00 20.00
NNO Rey Mysterio 15.00 30.00
NNO Rob Van Dam 10.00 20.00
NNO Stone Cold Steve Austin
NNO Tajiri 12.50 25.00
NNO Tazz 7.50 15.00
NNO Tommy Dreamer 15.00 30.00

2006 Jakks Pacific WWE Pay Per View Series 10

NNO Animal 7.50 15.00
NNO Batista 7.50 15.00
NNO JBL/Vest
NNO Orlando Jordan 12.50 25.00

NNO	Rey Mysterio	12.50	25.00
NNO	Undertaker	15.00	30.00

2006 Jakks Pacific WWE Pay Per View Series 11

NNO	Batista	15.00	30.00
NNO	Daivari/Ref Gear		
NNO	John Cena		
NNO	Kurt Angle	7.50	15.00
NNO	Randy Orton	10.00	20.00
NNO	Undertaker		

2006 Jakks Pacific WWE Pay Per View Series 12

NNO	Gregory Helms	10.00	20.00
NNO	Kurt Angle	12.50	25.00
NNO	Matt Hardy	12.50	25.00
NNO	Randy Orton	15.00	30.00
NNO	Rey Mysterio	15.00	30.00
NNO	Undertaker	12.50	25.00

2006 Jakks Pacific WWE Pay Per View Series 13

NNO	Carlito		
NNO	Edge	15.00	30.00
NNO	John Cena	20.00	40.00
NNO	Ric Flair	12.50	25.00
NNO	Rob Van Dam	10.00	20.00
NNO	Shawn Michaels		

2007 Jakks Pacific WWE Pay Per View Series 14

NNO	Carlito
NNO	Eric Bischoff/Ref Gear
NNO	Jeff Hardy
NNO	John Cena
NNO	King Booker
NNO	Umaga

2007 Jakks Pacific WWE Pay Per View Series 15

NNO	Batista
NNO	Brian Kendrick
NNO	Finlay
NNO	John Cena
NNO	Johnny Nitro
NNO	Kane

2007 Jakks Pacific WWE Pay Per View Series 16

NNO	Bobby Lashley
NNO	Deuce
NNO	Edge
NNO	John Cena
NNO	Mark Henry
NNO	Matt Hardy

2008 Jakks Pacific WWE Pay Per View Series 17

NNO	Batista
NNO	CM Punk
NNO	Randy Orton
NNO	Rey Mysterio
NNO	Triple H
NNO	Umaga

2008 Jakks Pacific WWE Pay Per View Series 18

NNO	Chavo Guerrero
NNO	Edge
NNO	JBL
NNO	John Cena
NNO	Triple H
NNO	Undertaker

2008 Jakks Pacific WWE Pay Per View Series 19

NNO	Batista
NNO	Big Show
NNO	JBL
NNO	Triple H
NNO	Umaga
NNO	Undertaker

2008 Jakks Pacific WWE Pay Per View Series 20

NNO	Batista
NNO	Jeff Hardy
NNO	Matt Hardy
NNO	Rey Mysterio
NNO	Triple H
NNO	Undertaker

2008 Jakks Pacific WWE Pay Per View Series 21

NNO	Edge
NNO	Jack Swagger
NNO	Randy Orton
NNO	Shane McMahon
NNO	Shawn Michaels
NNO	Triple H

2001 Jakks Pacific WWF Playsets

NNO	Attitude Ring	25.00	50.00
NNO	Hardcore Action Ring w/Ref/Jim Ross	20.00	40.00
NNO	Hardcore Action Ring w/Ref/Jim Ross/Mick Foley	20.00	40.00

2016-17 Jakks Pacific WWE Plush Hangers

NNO	AJ Styles
NNO	Brock Lesnar
NNO	Dean Ambrose
NNO	Finn Balor
NNO	John Cena
NNO	Roman Reigns
NNO	Seth Rollins
NNO	Undertaker

2000 Jakks Pacific WWF Prop Boxes

NNO	Back Alley Street Fight	12.50	25.00
NNO	Break Room Brawl		
NNO	House of Pain	20.00	40.00

2004 Jakks Pacific WWE Pump 'N Flex Series 1

NNO	Chris Benoit	7.50	15.00
NNO	Eddie Guerrero	15.00	30.00
NNO	John Cena	20.00	40.00
NNO	Kane	12.50	25.00
NNO	Kurt Angle	10.00	20.00
NNO	Triple H	10.00	20.00

2004 Jakks Pacific WWE Pump 'N Flex Series 2

NNO	Batista		
NNO	Booker T	12.50	25.00
NNO	John Cena	12.50	25.00
NNO	Randy Orton	7.50	15.00
NNO	Rene Dupree		

2003 Jakks Pacific WWE RAW 10th Anniversary

NNO	Goldust	10.00	20.00
NNO	Jeff Hardy	15.00	30.00
NNO	Jerry Lawler	12.50	25.00
NNO	Kurt Angle	10.00	20.00
NNO	The Rock	15.00	30.00
NNO	RVD	12.50	25.00
NNO	Shane McMahon	15.00	30.00
NNO	Shawn Michaels	12.50	25.00
NNO	Steve Austin	20.00	40.00
NNO	Triple H	10.00	20.00
NNO	Trish Stratus	15.00	30.00
NNO	Undertaker	17.50	35.00

2002 Jakks Pacific WWE RAW Draft

1	Undertaker/27,500*	12.50	25.00
2A	Kevin Nash/8,750*	12.50	25.00
2B	Scott Hall/8,750*	12.50	25.00
2C	X-Pac/10,000*	7.50	15.00
3	Kane/25,000*	12.50	25.00
4	Rob Van Dam/21,250*	10.00	20.00
5	Booker T/20,000*	12.50	25.00
6	Big Show/18,750*	10.00	20.00
7	Bubba Ray/18,750*	12.50	25.00
8	Brock Lesnar		
9	William Regal/16,250*	10.00	20.00
10	Lita/16,250*	15.00	30.00
11	Bradshaw/13,750*	7.50	15.00
12	Steven Richards/12,500*		
13	Matt Hardy/11,250*	10.00	20.00
14	Raven/8,750*	12.50	25.00
15	Jeff Hardy/7,500*	20.00	40.00
16	Mr. Perfect		
17	Spike Dudley/5,000*		
18	D'Lo Brown		
19	Shawn Stasiak		
20	Terri		

1999 Jakks Pacific WWF RAW Is War

NNO	Mankind	7.50	15.00
NNO	The Rock	15.00	30.00
NNO	Stone Cold Steve Austin	7.50	15.00
NNO	Undertaker	10.00	20.00

2003 Jakks Pacific WWE RAW Uncovered

NNO	Jeff Hardy	20.00	40.00
NNO	Kane	50.00	100.00
NNO	Kurt Angle	15.00	30.00
NNO	Matt Hardy	15.00	30.00
NNO	Rey Mysterio	20.00	40.00
NNO	Rob Van Dam	12.50	25.00

2002 Jakks Pacific WWF Real Reaction R-3 Tech Series 1

NNO	Chris Benoit	12.50	25.00
NNO	Chris Jericho	10.00	20.00
NNO	Kane	15.00	30.00
NNO	Matt Hardy	10.00	20.00
NNO	The Rock	10.00	20.00
NNO	Stone Cold Steve Austin	12.50	25.00

2002 Jakks Pacific WWF Real Reaction R-3 Tech Series 2

NNO	Big Show	12.50	25.00
NNO	Edge	10.00	20.00
NNO	Jeff Hardy	15.00	30.00
NNO	Rock	10.00	20.00
NNO	Stone Cold Steve Austin	10.00	20.00
NNO	Undertaker	15.00	30.00

2002 Jakks Pacific WWF Real Reaction R-3 Tech Series 3

NNO	Big Show	12.50	25.00
NNO	Jeff Hardy	15.00	30.00
NNO	Kane		
NNO	Matt Hardy	7.50	15.00
NNO	Stone Cold Steve Austin		
NNO	Undertaker	10.00	20.00

2002 Jakks Pacific WWF Real Reaction R-3 Tech Series 4

NNO	Billy Gunn	7.50	15.00
NNO	Chuck Palumbo	7.50	15.00
NNO	Kurt Angle	7.50	15.00
NNO	Rikishi	7.50	15.00
NNO	Test	6.00	12.00
NNO	Triple H	12.50	25.00

2002 Jakks Pacific WWF Real Reaction R-3 Tech Series 5

NNO	Booker T	7.50	15.00
NNO	Chris Benoit	7.50	15.00
NNO	Jeff Hardy	10.00	20.00
NNO	Kevin Nash	7.50	15.00
NNO	Rob Van Dam	6.00	12.00
NNO	Undertaker	12.50	25.00

2000 Jakks Pacific WWF Rebellion Series 1

NNO	Chris Benoit	10.00	20.00
NNO	Chris Jericho	12.50	25.00
NNO	Jeff Hardy	7.50	15.00
NNO	The Rock	12.50	25.00
NNO	Undertaker	15.00	30.00
NNO	X-Pac	7.50	15.00

2001 Jakks Pacific WWF Rebellion Series 2

NNO	Chris Benoit	10.00	20.00
NNO	Chris Jericho	7.50	15.00
NNO	Crash Holly	10.00	20.00
NNO	Kurt Angle	10.00	20.00
NNO	The Rock	15.00	30.00

2001 Jakks Pacific WWF Rebellion Series 3

NNO	D-Von Dudley	7.50	15.00
NNO	Jeff Hardy	12.50	25.00
NNO	Kurt Angle	10.00	20.00
NNO	Stone Cold Steve Austin	20.00	40.00
NNO	The Rock	12.50	25.00
NNO	Triple H	7.50	15.00
NNO	Undertaker	12.50	25.00

2001 Jakks Pacific WWF Rebellion Series 4

NNO	Billy Gunn	7.50	15.00
NNO	Chris Benoit	10.00	20.00
NNO	Edge	10.00	20.00
NNO	HHH	10.00	20.00
NNO	Lita	10.00	20.00
NNO	X-Pac	7.50	15.00

2002 Jakks Pacific WWE Relentless

NNO Booker T
NNO Edge 10.00 20.00
NNO Rob Van Dam 15.00 30.00
NNO Triple H

2005 Jakks Pacific WWE Ring Giants Classic Series 1

NNO Rowdy Roddy Piper 30.00 60.00
NNO Ted DiBiase 25.00 50.00
NNO Ultimate Warrior 30.00 75.00

2005 Jakks Pacific WWE Ring Giants Series 1

NNO Chris Benoit 20.00 40.00
NNO Eddie Guerrero 15.00 30.00
NNO John Cena 15.00 30.00
NNO Triple H 15.00 30.00

2005 Jakks Pacific WWE Ring Giants Series 2

NNO Batista 12.50 25.00
NNO Booker T 15.00 30.00
NNO Kurt Angle 20.00 40.00
NNO Randy Orton 15.00 30.00

2005 Jakks Pacific WWE Ring Giants Series 3

NNO Carlito/Hair 20.00 40.00
NNO Carlito/No Hair
NNO Kane 12.50 25.00
NNO Rey Mysterio 30.00 75.00
Red White Blue Pants
NNO Shawn Michaels 20.00 40.00

2005 Jakks Pacific WWE Ring Giants Series 4

NNO Batista 15.00 30.00
NNO John Cena 20.00 40.00
NNO Rey Mysterio 15.00 30.00
NNO Undertaker 20.00 40.00

2006 Jakks Pacific WWE Ring Giants Series 5

NNO Batista
NNO John Cena
NNO Kurt Angle
NNO Rey Mysterio

2006 Jakks Pacific WWE Ring Giants Series 6

NNO Bobby Lashley
NNO Boogeyman
NNO Kurt Angle
NNO Rey Mysterio

2006 Jakks Pacific WWE Ring Giants Series 7

NNO Batista
NNO Hulk Hogan
NNO John Cena
NNO Rob Van Dam

2007 Jakks Pacific WWE Ring Giants Series 8

NNO Edge
NNO John Cena
NNO Rey Mysterio
NNO Shawn Michaels

2007 Jakks Pacific WWE Ring Giants Series 9

NNO Carlito
NNO Shawn Michaels
NNO Triple H
NNO Undertaker

2007 Jakks Pacific WWE Ring Giants Series 10

NNO Batista
NNO Jeff Hardy
NNO Mr. Kennedy
NNO Randy Orton

2007 Jakks Pacific WWE Ring Giants Series 11

NNO Boogeyman
NNO Edge
NNO Fit Finlay
NNO Matt Hardy

2007 Jakks Pacific WWE Ring Giants Series 12

NNO Jeff Hardy
NNO John Cena
NNO Rey Mysterio
NNO Triple H

2007 Jakks Pacific WWE Ring Giants Series 13

NNO Boogeyman
NNO Finlay
NNO Matt Hardy
NNO Randy Orton

1997 Jakks Pacific WWF Ring Masters

NNO Bret Hit Man Hart 10.00 20.00
NNO Goldust 6.00 12.00
NNO Shawn Michaels 10.00 20.00
NNO Sycho Sid 6.00 12.00
NNO Undertaker 7.50 15.00
NNO Yokozuna

2002 Jakks Pacific WWE Ringleader Collection

NNO Chris Jericho 10.00 20.00
NNO Hollywood Hulk Hogan 17.50 35.00
NNO The Rock 10.00 20.00
NNO Triple H 15.00 30.00
NNO Undertaker 15.00 30.00

2002 Jakks Pacific WWE Ringside Rebels Series 1

NNO The Rock 20.00 40.00
NNO Stone Cold Steve Austin
NNO Undertaker 25.00 50.00

2002 Jakks Pacific WWE Ringside Rebels Series 2

NNO Chris Jericho 15.00 30.00
NNO The Rock 15.00 30.00
NNO Triple H 12.50 25.00

2002 Jakks Pacific WWE Ringside Rebels Series 3

NNO Booker T 10.00 20.00
NNO Rob Van Dam 15.00 30.00
NNO Triple H 12.50 25.00

2002 Jakks Pacific WWE Ringside Rebels Series 4

NNO Hulk Hogan 20.00 40.00
NNO Jeff Hardy 15.00 30.00

2002 Jakks Pacific WWE Ringside Rivals Fatal Showdown

NNO Chris Jericho vs. Triple H
NNO Jeff Hardy vs. Eddie Guerrero
NNO Undertaker vs. Hollywood Hogan

2002 Jakks Pacific WWE Ringside Rivals Head to Head

NNO Edge vs. Kurt Angle
NNO Rob Van Dam vs. Booker T
NNO Test vs. Tajiri

2002 Jakks Pacific WWE Ringside Rivals New Series

NNO Billy Gunn vs. Chuck Palumbo
NNO Matt Hardy vs. Jeff Hardy
NNO The Rock vs. Brock Lesnar

2002 Jakks Pacific WWE Ringside Rivals Raging Tempers

NNO Rob Van Dam vs. Test
NNO The Rock vs. Booker T
NNO Vince McMahon vs. Ric Flair

2001 Jakks Pacific WWF Ringside Rivals Series 1

NNO Bradshaw vs. Test 10.00 20.00
NNO Father (Vince) vs. Son (Shane) 12.50 25.00
NNO The Rock vs. Stone Cold Steve Austin15.0030.00

2001 Jakks Pacific WWF Ringside Rivals Series 2

NNO Edge vs. Christian 25.00 50.00
NNO Kurt Angle vs. Undertaker 15.00 30.00
NNO Matt Hardy vs. Bubba Ray Dudley12.50 25.00
NNO The Rock vs. Chris Jericho 25.00 50.00
NNO Triple H vs. Stone Cold Steve Austin20.00 40.00
NNO William Regal vs. Mick Foley 20.00 40.00

2002 Jakks Pacific WWF Ringside Rivals Series 3

NNO D-Von vs. Spike
NNO Edge vs. William Regal
NNO Triple H vs. Kurt Angle

1998 Jakks Pacific WWF Ringside Collection Series 1

NNO Referee 5.00 10.00
NNO Sable 7.50 15.00
NNO Sunny 10.00 20.00
NNO Vince McMahon 6.00 12.00

1998 Jakks Pacific WWF Ringside Collection Series 2

NNO Honky Tonk Man 6.00 12.00
NNO Jim Cornette 15.00 30.00
NNO Jim Ross 12.50 25.00
NNO Referee 5.00 10.00
NNO Sgt. Slaughter 7.50 15.00
NNO Vince McMahon 7.50 15.00

1997 Jakks Pacific WWF Ripped and Ruthless Series 1

NNO Goldust 5.00 10.00
NNO Mankind 7.50 15.00
NNO Stone Cold Steve Austin 10.00 20.00
NNO Undertaker 12.50 25.00

1998 Jakks Pacific WWF Ripped and Ruthless Series 2

NNO Kane 15.00 30.00
NNO Sable 12.50 25.00
NNO Shawn Michaels 10.00 20.00
NNO Triple H 10.00 20.00

1998 Jakks Pacific WWF Ripped and Ruthless 2-Pack

NNO Undertaker/Stone Cold Steve Austin

1999 Jakks Pacific WWF Road Rage

NNO Al Snow 7.50 15.00
NNO Gangrel 7.50 15.00
NNO Godfather 10.00 20.00
NNO Hardcore Holly 6.00 12.00
NNO The Rock 12.50 25.00
NNO Test 6.00 12.00

2002 Jakks Pacific WWF Road to WrestleMania

NNO Bubba Ray Dudley
NNO Chris Benoit
NNO Chris Jericho
NNO D-Von Dudley
NNO Jeff Hardy
NNO Undertaker

2006 Jakks Pacific WWE Road to WrestleMania 22 Gear and Figure Sets

NNO Kane/Glove & Elbow Pad
NNO Rey Mysterio/Mask
NNO Triple H/Crown

2006 Jakks Pacific WWE Road to WrestleMania 22 Series 1

NNO Chris Benoit
NNO Eddie Guerrero
NNO John Cena
NNO Kurt Angle
NNO Rey Mysterio
NNO Shawn Michaels
NNO Shawn Michaels
Hulk Hogan Costume

2006 Jakks Pacific WWE Road to WrestleMania 22 2-Packs Series 1

NNO Batista/JBL
NNO Edge/Matt Hardy
NNO Undertaker/Randy Orton

2006 Jakks Pacific WWE Road to WrestleMania 22 Series 2

NNO Batista
NNO Carlito
NNO Chris Masters
NNO John Cena
NNO Kurt Angle
NNO Shawn Michaels

2006 Jakks Pacific WWE Road to WrestleMania 22 2-Packs Series 2

NNO Kane/Big Show
NNO Rey Mysterio/Matt Hardy
NNO Rob Conway/Tyson Tomko

2006 Jakks Pacific WWE Road to WrestleMania 22 Series 3

NNO Bobby Lashley
NNO Finlay
NNO Matt Hardy
NNO Ric Flair
NNO RVD
NNO Shelton Benjamin

2006 Jakks Pacific WWE Road to WrestleMania 22 2-Packs Series 3

NNO John Cena/Edge
NNO Kurt Angle/Rey Mysterio
NNO Undertaker/Mark Henry

2007 Jakks Pacific WWE Road to WrestleMania 23 Series 1

NNO Batista
NNO King Booker
NNO Rey Mysterio
NNO Ric Flair
NNO Shawn Michaels
NNO Triple H

2007 Jakks Pacific WWE Road to WrestleMania 23 2-Packs Series 1

NNO John Cena/Edge
NNO Randy Orton/Hulk Hogan
NNO Sabu/Big Show

2007 Jakks Pacific WWE Road to WrestleMania 23 Series 2

NNO Batista
NNO Chris Benoit
NNO CM Punk
NNO Ron Simmons
NNO Triple H

2007 Jakks Pacific WWE Road to WrestleMania 23 2-Packs Series 2

NNO Bobby Lashley/John Cena
NNO Matt Hardy/Jeff Hardy
NNO Undertaker/Mr. Kennedy

2007 Jakks Pacific WWE Road to WrestleMania 23 Series 3

NNO CM Punk
NNO Elijah Burke
NNO Jeff Hardy
NNO Matt Hardy
NNO Mr. Kennedy
NNO MVP

2007 Jakks Pacific WWE Road to WrestleMania 23 2-Packs Series 3

NNO Batista/Undertaker
NNO Bobby Lashley/Umaga
NNO John Cena/Shawn Michaels

2008 Jakks Pacific WWE Road to WrestleMania 24 Series 1

NNO Batista
NNO Carlito
NNO CM Punk/Blue Trunks
NNO Kane
NNO Mr. Kennedy
NNO Umaga

2008 Jakks Pacific WWE Road to WrestleMania 24 Series 1 2-Packs

NNO Randy Orton/John Cena
NNO Rey Mysterio/Chavo Guerrero 15.00 30.00
NNO Triple H/Mr. McMahon

2008 Jakks Pacific WWE Road to WrestleMania 24 Series 2

NNO Batista
NNO CM Punk/Red Trunks
NNO Kane
NNO Triple H
NNO Umaga
NNO Undertaker

2008 Jakks Pacific WWE Road to WrestleMania 24 Series 2 2-Packs

NNO Finlay & Mysterio
NNO Mr. Kennedy & Jeff Hardy
NNO Shawn Michaels & Randy Orton

2008 Jakks Pacific WWE Road to WrestleMania 24 Series 3

NNO Chris Jericho
NNO CM Punk/Black Trunks
NNO Finlay
NNO John Cena
NNO Kane
NNO Randy Orton

2008 Jakks Pacific WWE Road to WrestleMania 24 Series 3 2-Packs

NNO Batista & Umaga
NNO Edge & Undertaker
NNO Ric Flair & Shawn Michaels

2008 Jakks Pacific WWE Road to WrestleMania 24 Best of WrestleMania

NNO Batista
NNO John Cena
NNO Kane
NNO Rey Mysterio
NNO Shawn Michaels
NNO Triple H

2008 Jakks Pacific WWE Road to WrestleMania 24 Mask and Figure Sets

NNO Rey Mysterio
Black and Green Pants
NNO Rey Mysterio/Blue Pants
NNO Rey Mysterio/Silver Pants

2002 Jakks Pacific WWE Rollin' Rebels

NNO Hulk Hogan 30.00 75.00
NNO Undertaker 30.00 60.00

2002 Jakks Pacific WWE Royal Rumble

NNO Chris Jericho 7.50 15.00
NNO Referee Earl Hebner 6.00 12.00
NNO Ric Flair 10.00 20.00
NNO Tazz 6.00 12.00
NNO Triple H 7.50 15.00
NNO William Regal 6.00 12.00

2006 Jakks Pacific WWE Royal Rumble

NNO Carlito
NNO Randy Orton
NNO Rey Mysterio
NNO Rob Van Dam 12.50 25.00
NNO Shawn Michaels
NNO Triple H

2007 Jakks Pacific WWE Royal Rumble

NNO Batista
NNO Bobby Lashley
NNO John Cena
NNO Mr. Kennedy
NNO Shawn Michaels
NNO Undertaker

2008 Jakks Pacific WWE Royal Rumble

NNO Chris Jericho
NNO Edge
NNO JBL
NNO John Cena
NNO Randy Orton
NNO Ric Flair

2009 Jakks Pacific WWE Royal Rumble

NNO Cody Rhodes
NNO Great Khali
NNO Kane
NNO Mark Henry
NNO Ted DiBiase
NNO Vladimir Kozlov

2008 Jakks Pacific WWE Royal Rumble Playset

NNO Deluxe Ring
(w/Cena/Y2J/Mysterio/Edge

2000 Jakks Pacific WWF Rulers of the Ring Series 1

NNO Al Snow 6.00 12.00
NNO Buh Buh Ray 7.50 15.00
NNO D-Von 7.50 15.00
NNO Edge 6.00 12.00
NNO Ivory 10.00 20.00
NNO Tazz 10.00 20.00

2000 Jakks Pacific WWF Rulers of the Ring Series 2

NNO Big Boss Man 7.50 15.00
NNO Brian Christopher 7.50 15.00
NNO Crash Holly 6.00 12.00
NNO Rikishi 7.50 15.00
NNO Scotty 2 Hotty 6.00 12.00
NNO Steve Blackman 10.00 20.00

2001 Jakks Pacific WWF Rulers of the Ring Series 3

NNO Eddie Guerrero 12.50 25.00
NNO Perry Saturn 10.00 20.00
NNO Prince Albert 10.00 20.00
NNO Raven 12.50 25.00
NNO Stephanie McMahon-Helmsley 10.00 20.00
NNO Steven Richards 7.50 15.00

2001 Jakks Pacific WWF Rulers of the Ring Series 4

NNO Bob Holly 10.00 20.00
NNO Christian 7.50 15.00
NNO Justin Credible 10.00 20.00
NNO Molly Holly 10.00 20.00
NNO Shane McMahon 15.00 30.00

2003 Jakks Pacific WWE Ruthless Aggression Best of 2003

NNO A-Train
NNO Chavo Guerrero
NNO Eric Bischoff
NNO Goldust
NNO Rey Mysterio
NNO Rico
NNO Scott Steiner

2006 Jakks Pacific WWE Ruthless Aggression Best of 2006

NNO Boogeyman
NNO Carlito
NNO Chris Masters
NNO Edge
NNO John Cena
NNO Kurt Angle
NNO Rey Mysterio
NNO Rob Van Dam
NNO Shawn Michaels

2007 Jakks Pacific WWE Ruthless Aggression Best of 2007

NNO Great Khali 15.00 30.00
NNO John Cena 10.00 20.00
NNO Rey Mysterio 12.50 25.00
NNO Shawn Michaels 10.00 20.00
NNO Umaga
NNO Undertaker

2008 Jakks Pacific WWE Ruthless Aggression Best of 2008

NNO Batista
NNO John Cena 10.00 20.00
NNO Ric Flair 12.50 25.00
NNO Triple H 10.00 20.00
NNO Umaga 10.00 20.00
NNO Undertaker

2009 Jakks Pacific WWE Ruthless Aggression Best of 2009

NNO Batista
NNO Hornswoggle
NNO John Cena
NNO Randy Orton
NNO Rey Mysterio 15.00 30.00
NNO Triple H

2002 Jakks Pacific WWE Ruthless Aggression Series 1

NNO Brock Lesnar 15.00 30.00
NNO Chavo Guerrero 7.50 15.00
NNO Eric Bischoff 20.00 40.00
NNO John Cena 15.00 30.00
NNO Randy Orton 10.00 20.00
NNO Rey Mysterio

2003 Jakks Pacific WWE Ruthless Aggression Series 2

NNO Batista 6.00 12.00

NNO	Billy Kidman	7.50	15.00
NNO	Jamie Noble	6.00	12.00
NNO	Rico	6.00	12.00
NNO	Scott Steiner	7.50	15.00
NNO	Tommy Dreamer	15.00	30.00

2003 Jakks Pacific WWE Ruthless Aggression Series 3

NNO	A-Train		
NNO	Goldust	10.00	20.00
NNO	John Cena	15.00	30.00
NNO	Rey Mysterio	12.50	25.00
NNO	Rob Van Dam	12.50	25.00
NNO	Scott Steiner	25.00	50.00

2003 Jakks Pacific WWE Ruthless Aggression Series 3.5

NNO	Chavo Guerrero		
NNO	Eric Bischoff	12.50	25.00
NNO	Goldust		
NNO	Rey Mysterio		
NNO	Rico		
NNO	Scott Steiner		

2003 Jakks Pacific WWE Ruthless Aggression Series 4

NNO	Bill Goldberg	25.00	50.00
NNO	Chris Benoit	15.00	30.00
NNO	Eddie Guerrero	10.00	20.00
NNO	The Hurricane	15.00	30.00
NNO	The Rock	25.00	50.00
NNO	Undertaker	12.50	25.00

2003 Jakks Pacific WWE Ruthless Aggression Series 5

NNO	Billy Kidman	7.50	15.00
NNO	John Cena	15.00	30.00
NNO	Kane	15.00	30.00
NNO	Kevin Nash	7.50	15.00
NNO	Shawn Michaels	12.50	25.00
NNO	Tajiri	7.50	15.00

2003 Jakks Pacific WWE Ruthless Aggression Series 6

NNO	Bill Goldberg	30.00	60.00
NNO	Kurt Angle	7.50	15.00
NNO	Maven	6.00	12.00
NNO	Rey Mysterio	12.50	25.00
NNO	Rob Van Dam	6.00	12.00
NNO	Triple H	20.00	40.00

2003 Jakks Pacific WWE Ruthless Aggression Series 7

NNO	Brock Lesnar	15.00	30.00
NNO	Chris Benoit	25.00	50.00
NNO	Chris Jericho	12.50	25.00
NNO	Kane/Unmasked	10.00	20.00
NNO	Matt Hardy	10.00	20.00
NNO	Randy Orton	10.00	20.00

2003 Jakks Pacific WWE Ruthless Aggression Series 7.5

NNO	Bill Goldberg		
NNO	Chris Jericho		
NNO	Goldust		
NNO	Rey Mysterio	6.00	12.00
NNO	Rob Van Dam		
NNO	Stone Cold Steve Austin		

2004 Jakks Pacific WWE Ruthless Aggression Series 8

NNO	Bill Goldberg	30.00	75.00
NNO	Christian (long sleeves)	12.50	25.00
NNO	Christian (short sleeves)		
NNO	Kurt Angle	6.00	12.00
NNO	Test		
NNO	The Rock	15.00	30.00
NNO	Ultimo Dragon	20.00	40.00

2004 Jakks Pacific WWE Ruthless Aggression Series 8.5

NNO	A-Train		
NNO	Big Show	6.00	12.00
NNO	Eddie Guerrero	7.50	15.00
NNO	John Cena	6.00	12.00
NNO	Rey Mysterio		
NNO	Undertaker		

2004 Jakks Pacific WWE Ruthless Aggression Series 9

NNO	Booker T SE	15.00	30.00
NNO	Jamie Noble	7.50	15.00
NNO	Kane	10.00	20.00
NNO	Matt Hardy	12.50	25.00
NNO	Matt Morgan	10.00	20.00
NNO	Rob Van Dam	10.00	20.00
NNO	Stone Cold Steve Austin	12.50	25.00

2004 Jakks Pacific WWE Ruthless Aggression Series 10

NNO	Chris Benoit	10.00	20.00
NNO	Chris Jericho	7.50	15.00
NNO	Edge	15.00	30.00
NNO	Kurt Angle	10.00	20.00
NNO	Rey Mysterio	12.50	25.00
NNO	Ultimo Dragon	12.50	25.00

2004 Jakks Pacific WWE Ruthless Aggression Series 10.5

NNO	Charlie Haas		
NNO	Jamie Noble	7.50	15.00
NNO	John Bradshaw Layfield		
NNO	Matt Hardy	10.00	20.00
NNO	Shelton Benjamin		
NNO	Tajiri		

2004 Jakks Pacific WWE Ruthless Aggression Series 11

NNO	Batista	7.50	15.00
NNO	Booker T	12.50	25.00
NNO	Eugene	7.50	15.00
NNO	John Cena	7.50	15.00
NNO	Rene Dupree	6.00	12.00
NNO	Undertaker	10.00	20.00

2004 Jakks Pacific WWE Ruthless Aggression Series 11.5

NNO	Charlie Haas		
NNO	John Cena		
NNO	Randy Orton	10.00	20.00
NNO	Rene Dupree		
NNO	Rob Conway		
NNO	Shelton Benjamin		

2004 Jakks Pacific WWE Ruthless Aggression Series 12

NNO	Booker T	7.50	15.00
NNO	Chris Jericho	7.50	15.00
NNO	Eric Bischoff	10.00	20.00
NNO	Kurt Angle	12.50	25.00
NNO	Randy Orton	7.50	15.00
NNO	Rey Mysterio	12.50	25.00

2004 Jakks Pacific WWE Ruthless Aggression Series 12.5

NNO	Chris Benoit		
NNO	Edge		
NNO	Eric Bischoff		
NNO	Randy Orton		
NNO	Shelton Benjamin		
NNO	Triple H		

2005 Jakks Pacific WWE Ruthless Aggression Series 13

NNO	Chavo Guerrero	7.50	15.00
NNO	Kurt Angle	10.00	20.00
NNO	Rosey	12.50	25.00
NNO	Shelton Benjamin	10.00	20.00
NNO	Tyson Tomko	7.50	15.00
NNO	William Regal	10.00	20.00

2005 Jakks Pacific WWE Ruthless Aggression Series 14

NNO	John Cena	15.00	30.00
NNO	Ric Flair	10.00	20.00
NNO	Shelton Benjamin	7.50	15.00
NNO	Triple H	10.00	20.00
NNO	Trish Stratus	12.50	25.00
NNO	Undertaker	7.50	15.00

2005 Jakks Pacific WWE Ruthless Aggression Series 15

NNO	Big Show	17.50	35.00
NNO	Carlito	7.50	15.00
NNO	Christian	12.50	25.00
NNO	Gene Snitsky	15.00	30.00
NNO	Johnathan Coachman	7.50	15.00
NNO	Mark Jindrak	7.50	15.00

2005 Jakks Pacific WWE Ruthless Aggression Series 15.5

NNO	Chris Masters		
NNO	Eric Bischoff		
NNO	Heidenreich		
NNO	Scotty 2 Hotty		
NNO	Shannon Moore		
NNO	Simon Dean		

2005 Jakks Pacific WWE Ruthless Aggression Series 16

NNO	Batista	10.00	20.00
NNO	Kurt Angle	12.50	25.00
NNO	Rey Mysterio	12.50	25.00
NNO	Stone Cold Steve Austin	10.00	20.00
NNO	Triple H	10.00	20.00
NNO	Undertaker	12.50	25.00

2005 Jakks Pacific WWE Ruthless Aggression Series 16.5

NNO	Chris Jericho		
NNO	John Cena		
NNO	Rob Van Dam		
NNO	Shawn Michaels		
NNO	Undertaker		
NNO	Viscera	15.00	30.00

2005 Jakks Pacific WWE Ruthless Aggression Series 17

NNO	Hardcore Holly	10.00	20.00
NNO	Nunzio	7.50	15.00
NNO	Orlando Jordan	7.50	15.00
NNO	Paul London	7.50	15.00
NNO	Steven Richards	10.00	20.00
NNO	Tajiri	6.00	12.00

2005 Jakks Pacific WWE Ruthless Aggression Series 17.5

NNO	Batista	10.00	20.00
NNO	The Hurricane	20.00	40.00
NNO	John Cena	7.50	15.00
NNO	Rey Mysterio	10.00	20.00
NNO	Shawn Michaels		
NNO	Undertaker		

2006 Jakks Pacific WWE Ruthless Aggression Series 18

NNO	Batista		
NNO	Carlito	20.00	40.00
NNO	Eddie Guerrero	10.00	20.00
NNO	Heidenreich	12.50	25.00
NNO	John Cena	20.00	40.00
NNO	Shawn Michaels		

2006 Jakks Pacific WWE Ruthless Aggression Series 18.5

NNO	Batista		
NNO	Chris Benoit		
NNO	Edge		
NNO	John Cena		
NNO	Matt Hardy		
NNO	Randy Orton		

2006 Jakks Pacific WWE Ruthless Aggression Series 19

NNO	Chris Benoit		
NNO	Ken Kennedy		
NNO	Kurt Angle	15.00	30.00
NNO	Randy Orton	7.50	15.00
NNO	Rey Mysterio		
NNO	Rob Conway		

2006 Jakks Pacific WWE Ruthless Aggression Series 20

NNO	Boogeyman	10.00	20.00
NNO	Booker T		
NNO	Chris Masters	7.50	15.00
NNO	Kid Kash		
NNO	Ric Flair	15.00	30.00

2006 Jakks Pacific WWE Ruthless Aggression Series 20.5

NNO	Batista		
NNO	Ken Kennedy		
NNO	Randy Orton		
NNO	Rey Mysterio		
NNO	Undertaker		

2006 Jakks Pacific WWE Ruthless Aggression Series 21

NNO	Carlito		
NNO	Chavo Guerrero		
NNO	Edge		
NNO	John Cena		
NNO	Rob Van Dam		
NNO	Triple H		

2006 Jakks Pacific WWE Ruthless Aggression Series 22

NNO Kurt Angle 15.00 30.00
NNO Matt Striker 12.50 25.00
NNO Nicky 6.00 12.00
NNO Rey Mysterio
NNO Torrie Wilson 12.50 25.00
NNO Victoria 20.00

2006 Jakks Pacific WWE Ruthless Aggression Series 22.5

NNO Big Show
NNO Edge
NNO Lita
NNO Psicosis
NNO Rey Mysterio
NNO Shawn Michaels
NNO Undertaker

2006 Jakks Pacific WWE Ruthless Aggression Series 23

NNO John Cena
NNO Paul London
NNO Rey Mysterio 15.00 30.00
NNO Shelton Benjamin
NNO Tatanka
NNO Triple H

2006 Jakks Pacific WWE Ruthless Aggression Series 23.5

NNO Carlito
NNO Chris Masters
NNO Edge
NNO John Cena
NNO Rob Van Dam
NNO Shawn Michaels

2006 Jakks Pacific WWE Ruthless Aggression Series 24

NNO Big Show
NNO Booker T
NNO Kane
NNO Kenny 10.00 20.00
NNO Sabu 15.00 30.00
NNO The Great Khali 20.00 40.00

2006 Jakks Pacific WWE Ruthless Aggression Series 24.5

NNO Batista
NNO John Cena
NNO Paul Heyman 15.00 30.00
NNO Tommy Dreamer
NNO Triple H
NNO Undertaker

2006 Jakks Pacific WWE Ruthless Aggression Series 25

NNO Batista
NNO Brian Kendrick
NNO Carlito
NNO Rey Mysterio 6.00 12.00
NNO Shawn Michaels
NNO Test

2007 Jakks Pacific WWE Ruthless Aggression Series 26

NNO Candice Michelle 12.50 25.00
NNO Chris Benoit 15.00 30.00
NNO Finlay 10.00 20.00
NNO Hardcore Holly 7.50 15.00
NNO John Cena 7.50 15.00
NNO William Regal 15.00 30.00

2007 Jakks Pacific WWE Ruthless Aggression Series 27

NNO Batista 6.00 12.00
NNO Bobby Lashley 15.00 30.00
NNO Chris Masters 7.50 15.00
NNO John Cena 6.00 12.00
NNO Mr. Kennedy 7.50 15.00
NNO Rey Mysterio 6.00 12.00

2007 Jakks Pacific WWE Ruthless Aggression Series 28

NNO Kenny Dykstra
NNO Miz 10.00 20.00
NNO Mr. McMahon
NNO Rey Mysterio 12.50 25.00
NNO Super Crazy 10.00 20.00
NNO Torrie Wilson 20.00 40.00
NNO Victoria 15.00 30.00

2007 Jakks Pacific WWE Ruthless Aggression Series 29

NNO Batista 7.50 15.00
NNO Candice Michelle 12.50 25.00
NNO Edge 12.50 25.00
NNO Ken Kennedy 10.00 20.00
NNO Matt Hardy 12.50 25.00
NNO Melina 15.00 30.00
NNO Shawn Michaels 12.50 25.00

2007 Jakks Pacific WWE Ruthless Aggression Series 30

NNO Boogeyman 12.50 25.00
NNO John Cena 7.50 15.00
NNO Mark Henry 10.00 20.00
NNO MVP 10.00 20.00
NNO Sandman 12.50 25.00
NNO Triple H 10.00 20.00

2007 Jakks Pacific WWE Ruthless Aggression Series 31

NNO Batista 6.00 12.00
NNO Jillian Hall 12.50 25.00
NNO John Cena 7.50 15.00
NNO John Morrison 10.00 20.00
NNO Kelly Kelly 12.50 25.00
NNO Kevin Thorn 10.00 20.00
NNO Ric Flair 12.50 25.00

2007 Jakks Pacific WWE Ruthless Aggression Series 31.5

NNO Batista 10.00 20.00
NNO Boogeyman 10.00 20.00
NNO CM Punk 12.50 25.00
NNO John Morrison 10.00 20.00
NNO Matt Hardy 10.00 20.00
NNO Randy Orton 12.50 25.00

2007 Jakks Pacific WWE Ruthless Aggression Series 32

NNO Carlito 12.50 25.00
NNO John Morrison 12.50 25.00
NNO Randy Orton 10.00 20.00
NNO Triple H 10.00 20.00
NNO Umaga 10.00 20.00
NNO Undertaker 12.50 25.00

2008 Jakks Pacific WWE Ruthless Aggression Series 33

NNO Candice Michelle 15.00 30.00
NNO CM Punk 15.00 30.00
NNO John Cena 7.50 15.00
NNO Melina 20.00 40.00
NNO Randy Orton 7.50 15.00
NNO Rey Mysterio 15.00 30.00
NNO Triple H 12.50 25.00

2008 Jakks Pacific WWE Ruthless Aggression Series 34

NNO Chris Jericho 10.00 20.00
NNO Funaki 7.50 15.00
NNO Great Khali
NNO Lilian Garcia 12.50 25.00
NNO Mickie James 15.00 30.00
NNO Nunzio
NNO Shelton Benjamin

2008 Jakks Pacific WWE Ruthless Aggression Series 34.5

NNO Batista
NNO Cody Rhodes
NNO Jamie Noble
NNO The Miz
NNO Ric Flair 10.00 20.00
NNO Great Khali

2008 Jakks Pacific WWE Ruthless Aggression Series 35

NNO Beth Phoenix 6.00 12.00
NNO Edge 7.50 15.00
NNO Hornswoggle 15.00 30.00
NNO Joey Styles 6.00 12.00
NNO Rey Mysterio
NNO Santino
NNO Victoria 15.00 30.00

2008 Jakks Pacific WWE Ruthless Aggression Series 35.5

NNO Carlito 10.00 20.00
NNO Edge 7.50 15.00
NNO Elijah Burke 10.00 20.00
NNO Matt Hardy 10.00 20.00
NNO Ken Kennedy
NNO Triple H 15.00 30.00

2008 Jakks Pacific WWE Ruthless Aggression Series 36

NNO Big Show 12.50 25.00
NNO Charlie Haas 10.00 20.00
NNO David Hart Smith 15.00 30.00
NNO Kofi Kingston 15.00 30.00
NNO Maryse 12.50 25.00
NNO Mickie James 15.00 30.00
NNO Umaga 12.50 25.00

2008 Jakks Pacific WWE Ruthless Aggression Series 37

NNO Cherry 17.50 35.00
NNO Colin Delaney 15.00 30.00
NNO Festus 7.50 15.00
NNO Katie Lee Burchill 20.00 40.00
NNO MVP
NNO Paul Burchill
NNO Santino Marella 12.50 25.00

2008 Jakks Pacific WWE Ruthless Aggression Series 38

NNO Batista 10.00 20.00
NNO The Brian Kendrick 15.00 30.00
NNO Hornswoggle 12.50 25.00
NNO Jesse
NNO John Cena 10.00 20.00
NNO Rey Mysterio 15.00 30.00

2008 Jakks Pacific WWE Ruthless Aggression Series 38.5

NNO Big Show
NNO Chris Jericho
NNO Festus 10.00 20.00
NNO Jesse
NNO Kane
NNO Kofi Kingston 12.50 25.00

2009 Jakks Pacific WWE Ruthless Aggression Series 39

NNO Evan Bourne 10.00 20.00
NNO Jeff Hardy 15.00 30.00
NNO Mark Henry
NNO Rey Mysterio 15.00 30.00
NNO Ted DiBiase 15.00 30.00
NNO Vladimir Kozlov 10.00 20.00

2009 Jakks Pacific WWE Ruthless Aggression Series 40

NNO Chris Jericho 20.00 40.00
NNO Edge 17.50 35.00
NNO Matt Hardy 12.50 25.00
NNO Randy Orton 12.50 25.00
NNO R-Truth
NNO Undertaker 12.50 25.00

2009 Jakks Pacific WWE Ruthless Aggression Series 40.5

NNO Cody Rhodes 10.00 20.00
NNO Matt Hardy 10.00 20.00
NNO Ted DiBiase
NNO Triple H 12.50 25.00
NNO Undertaker 20.00 40.00
NNO Vladimir Kozlov 10.00 20.00

2009 Jakks Pacific WWE Ruthless Aggression Series 41

NNO The Brian Kendrick 20.00 40.00
NNO CM Punk 20.00 40.00
NNO Goldust 15.00 30.00
NNO Hornswoggle 25.00 50.00
NNO John Cena 25.00 50.00
NNO Rey Mysterio 20.00 40.00

2009 Jakks Pacific WWE Ruthless Aggression Series 42

NNO Christian 20.00 40.00
NNO CM Punk 20.00 40.00
NNO The Great Khali
NNO Jack Swagger
NNO Shawn Michaels 25.00 50.00
NNO Triple H 10.00 20.00

2009 Jakks Pacific WWE Ruthless Aggression Series 43

NNO Batista 15.00 30.00
NNO John Cena 20.00 40.00
NNO Randy Orton 20.00 40.00
NNO Rey Mysterio 25.00 50.00

NNO Triple H
NNO Undertaker

2009 Jakks Pacific WWE Ruthless Aggression Series 44

NNO Edge 15.00 30.00
NNO John Cena 12.50 25.00
NNO Kane 15.00 30.00
NNO Matt Hardy
NNO MVP
NNO Rey Mysterio

1998 Jakks Pacific WWF Shotgun Saturday Night Series 1

NNO Animal 7.50 15.00
NNO Hawk 7.50 15.00
NNO Henry Godwinn 6.00 12.00
NNO Phineas Godwinn 6.00 12.00
NNO Rocky Maivia 12.50 25.00
NNO Savio Vega 10.00 20.00
NNO Steve Austin 12.50 25.00
NNO Undertaker 7.50 15.00
NNO Stone Cold Steve Austin/Kane
Shawn Michaels/Rocky Maivia

1998 Jakks Pacific WWF Shotgun Saturday Night Series 2

NNO B.A. Billy Gunn 7.50 15.00
NNO Jeff Jarrett 6.00 12.00
NNO Jesse James 7.50 15.00
NNO Kane 10.00 20.00
NNO Sable 7.50 15.00
NNO Shawn Michaels 7.50 15.00

1999 Jakks Pacific WWF Shotgun Saturday Night Series 3

NNO Droz 5.00 10.00
NNO Edge 7.50 15.00
NNO Kurgann 6.00 12.00
NNO Road Dogg Jesse James 6.00 12.00
NNO Stone Cold Steve Austin 10.00 20.00
NNO Triple H 7.50 15.00

1999 Jakks Pacific WWF Shotgun Saturday Night Series 4

NNO Al Snow 6.00 12.00
NNO Gangrel 6.00 12.00
NNO Godfather 6.00 12.00
NNO Hardcore Holly 5.00 10.00
NNO Rock 7.50 15.00
NNO Test

2001 Jakks Pacific WWF Signature Jams Series 1

NNO Billy Gunn 7.50 15.00
NNO Chris Jericho 12.50 25.00
NNO Jeff Hardy 15.00 30.00
NNO Kurt Angle 7.50 15.00
NNO The Rock 12.50 25.00
NNO Triple H 7.50 15.00

2001 Jakks Pacific WWF Signature Jams Series 2

NNO Chris Benoit
NNO D-Von Dudley 7.50 15.00
NNO Kane
NNO Matt Hardy 12.50 25.00
NNO Stone Cold Steve Austin
NNO Undertaker

2002 Jakks Pacific WWF Signature Jams Series 3

NNO Kane
NNO Matt Hardy
NNO Stone Cold Steve Austin
NNO Undertaker

2002 Jakks Pacific WWF Signature Jams Slam Grooves

NNO Billy Gunn
NNO Jeff Hardy
NNO Stone Cold Steve Austin
NNO Undertaker

1997 Jakks Pacific WWF Signature Series 1

NNO Goldust 7.50 15.00
NNO HHH 6.00 12.00
NNO Mankind 10.00 20.00
NNO Road Warrior Animal 7.50 15.00
NNO Road Warrior Hawk 7.50 15.00
NNO Steve Austin 7.50 15.00

1998 Jakks Pacific WWF Signature Series 2

NNO B.A. Billy Gunn 5.00 10.00
NNO Dude Love 10.00 20.00
NNO Kane 10.00 20.00
NNO Road Dogg 5.00 10.00
NNO Shawn Michaels 7.50 15.00
NNO Undertaker 7.50 15.00

1998 Jakks Pacific WWF Signature Series 3

NNO Edge 6.00 12.00
NNO HHH 7.50 15.00
NNO Jacqueline 10.00 20.00
NNO The Rock 10.00 20.00
NNO Stone Cold Steve Austin 7.50 15.00
NNO Undertaker 12.50 25.00

1999 Jakks Pacific WWF Signature Series 4

NNO Big Show 10.00 20.00
NNO Edge 7.50 15.00
NNO Ken Shamrock 7.50 15.00
NNO Rock 10.00 20.00
NNO Stone Cold Steve Austin 7.50 15.00
NNO X-Pac 6.00 12.00

1999 Jakks Pacific WWF Signature Series 5

NNO Al Snow 7.50 15.00
NNO Big Bossman 6.00 12.00
NNO Billy Gunn 6.00 12.00
NNO Kane 10.00 20.00
NNO Road Dogg 6.00 12.00
NNO Stone Cold Steve Austin 10.00 20.00

1999 Jakks Pacific WWF Signature Series 6

NNO Hardcore Holly 5.00 10.00
NNO HHH 7.50 15.00
NNO Mankind 7.50 15.00
NNO Stone Cold Steve Austin 10.00 20.00
NNO Undertaker 7.50 15.00
NNO Vince McMahon 7.50 15.00

1998 Jakks Pacific WWF Slammers Series 1

NNO Bret Hart 7.50 15.00
NNO Faarooq 6.00 12.00
NNO Goldust 6.00 12.00
NNO Mankind 6.00 12.00
NNO Steve Austin 7.50 15.00
NNO Undertaker 7.50 15.00

1998 Jakks Pacific WWF Slammers Series 2

NNO Brian Pillman 6.00 12.00
NNO Dude Love 7.50 15.00
NNO Kane 7.50 15.00
NNO Patriot 6.00 12.00
NNO Shawn Michaels 7.50 15.00
NNO Taka 6.00 12.00

2002 Jakks Pacific WWE SmackDown Draft

1 The Rock/26,250* 10.00 20.00
2 Kurt Angle/25,000* 12.50 25.00
3 Chris Benoit/23,750* 10.00 20.00
4 Hollywood Hogan/22,500* 15.00 30.00
6 Edge/18,750* 10.00 20.00
7 Rikishi/17,500*
8 D-Von Dudley/16,250* 12.50 25.00
9 Mark Henry
10 Maven/15,000*
11 Billy Kidman
12 Tajiri/13,750* 15.00 30.00
13 Chris Jericho/11,250* 15.00 30.00
14 Ivory/11,250* 15.00 30.00
15 Albert/8,750* 20.00 40.00
16 The Hurricane/7,500* 25.00 50.00
17 Al Snow/6,250* 12.50 25.00
18 Lance Storm/5,000* 25.00 50.00
19 DDP/3,750* 30.00 75.00
20 Torrie Wilson
5A Billy/11,250* 15.00 30.00
5B Chuck/11,250* 15.00 30.00

2002 Jakks Pacific WWF Snappin' Bashers

NNO Chris Benoit 12.50 25.00
NNO Chris Jericho
NNO Jeff Hardy 15.00 30.00
NNO The Rock
NNO Stone Cold Steve Austin 7.50 15.00
NNO Undertaker

1997 Jakks Pacific WWF Special Edition Series 1

NNO Ahmed Johnson 6.00 12.00
NNO British Bulldog 6.00 12.00
NNO Rocky Maivia 10.00 20.00
NNO Sunny 7.50 15.00
NNO Undertaker 7.50 15.00
NNO Vader 12.50 25.00
NNO Yokozuna/18000* 15.00 30.00

1998 Jakks Pacific WWF Special Edition Series 2

NNO Faarooq 6.00 12.00
NNO Goldust 6.00 12.00
NNO HHH 7.50 15.00
NNO Sable 10.00 20.00
NNO Savio Vega 6.00 12.00
NNO Stone Cold Steve Austin 7.50 15.00

1998 Jakks Pacific WWF Special Edition Series 3

NNO Animal 10.00 20.00
NNO Dan Severn 12.50 25.00
NNO Hawk 10.00 20.00
NNO Hunter Hearst-Helmsley 7.50 15.00
NNO Marvelous Marc Mero 7.50 15.00
NNO Shamrock 6.00 12.00

1999 Jakks Pacific WWF Special Edition Series 4

NNO B.A. Billy Gunn 7.50 15.00
NNO Chyna 10.00 20.00
NNO Mankind 12.50 25.00
NNO Road Dogg 7.50 15.00
NNO Stone Cold Steve Austin 10.00 20.00
NNO Undertaker

1999 Jakks Pacific WWF Special Edition Series 5

NNO Al Snow 6.00 12.00
NNO Edge 7.50 15.00
NNO Mark Henry
NNO Shamrock
NNO Val Venis 6.00 12.00
NNO X-Pac

1999 Jakks Pacific WWF Special Edition Series 6

NNO Double J 7.50 15.00
NNO Hardcore Holly 6.00 12.00
NNO HHH 7.50 15.00
NNO Stone Cold Steve Austin 10.00 20.00
NNO Test
NNO The Rock 10.00 20.00

1997 Jakks Pacific WWF S.T.O.M.P. Series 1

NNO Ahmed Johnson 7.50 15.00
NNO Brian Pillman 5.00 10.00
NNO Crush 6.00 12.00
NNO Ken Shamrock 7.50 15.00
NNO Stone Cold Steve Austin 10.00 20.00
NNO Undertaker 7.50 15.00

1998 Jakks Pacific WWF S.T.O.M.P. Series 2

NNO Chyna 10.00 20.00
NNO Headbanger Mosh 7.50 15.00
NNO Headbanger Thrash 7.50 15.00
NNO Owen Hart 10.00 20.00
NNO Rocky Maivia 12.50 25.00
NNO Stone Cold Steve Austin 10.00 20.00

1998 Jakks Pacific WWF S.T.O.M.P. Series 3

NNO Animal 7.50 15.00
NNO Hawk 7.50 15.00
NNO Kane 7.50 15.00
NNO Marc Mero 15.00 30.00
NNO Sable 10.00 20.00
NNO Undertaker 10.00 20.00

2000 Jakks Pacific WWF S.T.O.M.P. Series 4

NNO B.A. Billy Gunn
NNO Chyna
NNO Road Dogg Jesse James
NNO Stone Cold Steve Austin

NNO Triple H
NNO X-Pac

1997 Jakks Pacific WWF Stretchin'

NNO Bret Hit Man Hart	12.50	25.00
NNO Shawn Michaels		
NNO Sycho Sid	10.00	20.00
NNO Undertaker	12.50	25.00

2001 Jakks Pacific WWF Stunt Action Superstars Series 1

NNO Jeff Hardy	12.50	25.00
NNO Kurt Angle	10.00	20.00
NNO Rikishi	7.50	15.00
NNO Stephanie McMahon	15.00	30.00
NNO Triple H	10.00	20.00
NNO X-Pac	7.50	15.00

2005 Jakks Pacific WWE SummerSlam Limited Edition

NNO Chris Benoit
NNO Chris Jericho
NNO Kane
NNO Matt Hardy
NNO Stone Cold Steve Austin
NNO Test
NNO The Rock
NNO X-Pac

1999 Jakks Pacific WWF Sunday Night Heat

NNO B.A. Billy Gunn	7.50	15.00
NNO Road Dogg		
NNO The Rock		
NNO Sable	7.50	15.00
NNO Stone Cold Steve Austin		
NNO Undertaker		

2016-17 Jakks Pacific WWE Superstar Buddies

NNO AJ Styles
NNO John Cena
NNO The Rock

1997 Jakks Pacific WWF Superstars Best of 1997

NNO Bret Hart		
NNO British Bulldog	7.50	15.00
NNO Owen Hart	10.00	20.00

1997 Jakks Pacific WWF Superstars Best of 1997 Tag Teams

NNO Godwinns	12.50	25.00
NNO Headbangers	15.00	30.00
NNO Legion of Doom		
NNO New Blackjacks	10.00	20.00

1998 Jakks Pacific WWF Superstars Best of 1998 Series 1

NNO 8-Ball	6.00	12.00
NNO Blackjack Bradshaw	10.00	20.00
NNO Brian Christopher	6.00	12.00
NNO Chyna	12.50	25.00
NNO Shawn Michaels	10.00	20.00
NNO Skull	6.00	12.00
NNO Stone Cold Steve Austin	12.50	25.00
NNO Vader	6.00	12.00

1998 Jakks Pacific WWF Superstars Best of 1998 Series 2

NNO Dan Severn	5.00	10.00
NNO Dude Love	6.00	12.00
NNO HHH	7.50	15.00
NNO Jeff Jarrett	6.00	12.00
NNO Ken Shamrock	6.00	12.00
NNO Mark Henry	6.00	12.00
NNO Stone Cold Steve Austin	10.00	20.00
NNO Undertaker	7.50	15.00

1998 Jakks Pacific WWF Superstars Best of 1998 Tag Teams

NNO Headbangers
NNO LOD 2000
NNO New Age Outlaws

1996 Jakks Pacific WWF Superstars Series 1

NNO Bret Hart	20.00	40.00
NNO Diesel	15.00	30.00
NNO Goldust	15.00	30.00
NNO Razor Ramon	20.00	40.00
NNO Shawn Michaels	12.50	25.00
NNO Undertaker	15.00	30.00

1996 Jakks Pacific WWF Superstars Series 2

NNO Bret Hart	12.50	25.00
NNO Owen Hart	20.00	40.00
NNO Shawn Michaels	15.00	30.00
NNO Ultimate Warrior	20.00	40.00
NNO Undertaker GITD	25.00	50.00
NNO Vader	10.00	20.00

1997 Jakks Pacific WWF Superstars Series 3

NNO Ahmed Johnson	10.00	20.00
NNO Bret Hart	12.50	25.00
NNO British Bulldog	7.50	15.00
NNO Mankind	10.00	20.00
NNO Shawn Michaels	10.00	20.00
NNO Sycho Sid	7.50	15.00

1997 Jakks Pacific WWF Superstars Series 4

NNO Faarooq	5.00	10.00
NNO Hunter Hearst Helmsley	6.00	12.00
NNO Jerry Lawler	7.50	15.00
NNO Justin Hawk Bradshaw	12.50	25.00
NNO Stone Cold Steve Austin	7.50	15.00
NNO Vader	7.50	15.00

1997 Jakks Pacific WWF Superstars Series 5

NNO Flash Funk	10.00	20.00
NNO Ken Shamrock	6.00	12.00
NNO Rocky Maivia	12.50	20.00
NNO Savio Vega	7.50	15.00
NNO Stone Cold Steve Austin	12.50	25.00
NNO Sycho Sid	6.00	12.00

1998 Jakks Pacific WWF Superstars Series 6

NNO Jeff Jarrett	10.00	20.00
NNO Marc Mero	6.00	12.00
NNO Mark Henry	7.50	15.00
NNO Owen Hart	12.50	25.00
NNO Steve Blackman	12.50	25.00
NNO Triple H	7.50	15.00

1998 Jakks Pacific WWF Superstars Series 7

NNO Dr. Death Steve Williams	12.50	25.00
NNO Edge	7.50	15.00
NNO Steve Austin	7.50	15.00
NNO Undertaker	7.50	15.00
NNO Val Venis	7.50	15.00
NNO X-Pac	6.00	12.00

1999 Jakks Pacific WWF Superstars Series 8

NNO Big Boss Man	6.00	12.00
NNO Kane	7.50	15.00
NNO Ken Shamrock		
NNO The Rock	7.50	15.00
NNO Shane McMahon	7.50	15.00
NNO Shawn Michaels	7.50	15.00

1999 Jakks Pacific WWF Superstars Series 9

NNO Bob Holly	6.00	12.00
NNO Christian	6.00	12.00
NNO Gangrel	10.00	20.00
NNO Paul Wight	7.50	15.00
NNO Undertaker	7.50	15.00
NNO Vince McMahon	7.50	15.00

2006 Jakks Pacific WWE Superstars Series 1

NNO Hulk Hogan
NNO The Rock
NNO Ric Flair
NNO Roddy Piper
Black Wrist Tape
NNO Roddy Piper
White Wrist Tape
NNO Stone Cold Steve Austin

2007 Jakks Pacific WWE Superstars Series 2

NNO Bret Hit Man Hart
NNO British Bulldog
NNO Kevin Nash
NNO Mr. Perfect
NNO Shawn Michaels

2007 Jakks Pacific WWE Superstars Series 3

NNO Jake The Snake Roberts
NNO Lex Luger
NNO Ravishing Rick Rude
NNO Scott Hall
NNO Undertaker

2008 Jakks Pacific WWE Superstars Series 4

NNO Brutus The Barber Beefcake
NNO Honky Tonk Man
NNO Iron Sheik
NNO Ted DiBiase
NNO Shawn Michaels

2008 Jakks Pacific WWE Superstars Series 5

NNO Buff Bagwell
NNO Diamond Dallas Page
NNO Jim The Anvil Neidhart
NNO Superfly Jimmy Snuka

2009 Jakks Pacific WWE Superstars Series 6

NNO Eddie Guerrero
NNO Hillbilly Jim
NNO Hunter Hearst Helmsley
NNO Kane
NNO Sgt. Slaughter

2009 Jakks Pacific WWE Superstars Series 7

NNO Bret Hit Man Hart
NNO Shawn Michaels
NNO El Matador
NNO The Rock
NNO Undertaker

2009 Jakks Pacific WWE Superstars Series 8

NNO Big John Studd
NNO Chainsaw Charlie
NNO Davey Boy Smith
NNO Dynamite Kid
NNO Stone Cold Steve Austin

2003 Jakks Pacific WWE Superstars Uncovered

NNO Hulk Hogan	20.00	40.00
NNO Kurt Angle	12.50	25.00
NNO Rob Van Dam	12.50	25.00
NNO The Rock	30.00	60.00
NNO Triple H	10.00	20.00
NNO Undertaker	15.00	30.00

2004 Jakks Pacific WWE Talkin' Pounders

NNO The Hurricane
NNO John Cena
NNO Randy Orton
NNO Rey Mysterio

1997 Jakks Pacific WWF Talking Undertaker 14-Inch

NNO Undertaker	25.00	50.00

1997 Jakks Pacific WWF Thumb Wrestlers

NNO Bulldog vs. Shamrock	10.00	20.00
NNO HHH vs. Mankind	10.00	20.00
NNO Steve Austin vs. Owen Hart	12.50	25.00
NNO Undertaker vs. HBK	15.00	30.00

1999 Jakks Pacific WWF Titan Tron Live Series 1

NNO Kane	7.50	15.00
NNO Mankind	7.50	15.00
NNO Road Dogg	6.00	12.00
NNO Rock	10.00	20.00
NNO Stone Cold Steve Austin	15.00	30.00
NNO Undertaker	15.00	30.00

2000 Jakks Pacific WWF Titan Tron Live Series 2

NNO Big Show	6.00	12.00
NNO Kane	17.50	35.00
NNO Ken Shamrock	7.50	15.00

NNO	The Rock	12.50	25.00
NNO	Stone Cold Steve Austin	7.50	15.00
NNO	X-Pac	6.00	12.00

2000 Jakks Pacific WWF Titan Tron Live Series 3

NNO	Big Boss Man	7.50	15.00
NNO	Chris Jericho	7.50	15.00
NNO	Chyna	12.50	25.00
NNO	The Rock	7.50	15.00
NNO	Stone Cold Steve Austin	10.00	20.00
NNO	Test	6.00	12.00

2000 Jakks Pacific WWF Titan Tron Live Series 4

NNO	Big Show		
NNO	Cactus Jack	10.00	20.00
NNO	Road Dogg		
NNO	The Rock		
NNO	Triple H		
NNO	X-Pac		

2000 Jakks Pacific WWF Titan Tron Live Series 5

NNO	Chris Jericho	6.00	15.00
NNO	Kurt Angle	6.00	15.00
NNO	The Rock	10.00	20.00
NNO	Stone Cold Steve Austin	10.00	20.00
NNO	Test	6.00	12.00
NNO	Undertaker	10.00	20.00

2000 Jakks Pacific WWF Titan Tron Live Series 6

NNO Big Show
NNO Edge
NNO Jeff Hardy
NNO Rock
NNO Tazz
NNO Triple H

2000 Jakks Pacific WWF Titan Tron Live Series 7

NNO Chris Jericho
NNO Kane
NNO Kurt Angle
NNO Stephanie McMahon
NNO Triple H
NNO Undertaker

2000 Jakks Pacific WWF Titan Tron Live Series 8

NNO Bubba Ray Dudley
NNO Jeff Hardy
NNO Matt Hardy
NNO Rikishi
NNO Road Dogg
NNO The Rock

2001 Jakks Pacific WWF Titan Tron Live Series 9

NNO Chyna
NNO Kurt Angle
NNO Mick Foley
NNO Rikishi
NNO The Rock
NNO Triple H

2001 Jakks Pacific WWF Titan Tron Live Series 10

NNO	Billy Gunn	7.50	15.00
NNO	Kane	7.50	15.00
NNO	Matt Hardy	7.50	15.00
NNO	Rikishi	7.50	15.00
NNO	Stone Cold Steve Austin	10.00	20.00
NNO	Triple H	10.00	20.00

2001 Jakks Pacific WWF Titan Tron Live Series 11

NNO	Jeff Hardy	7.50	15.00
NNO	Kurt Angle	7.50	15.00
NNO	Rikishi	7.50	15.00
NNO	Stephanie McMahon	10.00	20.00
NNO	Stone Cold Steve Austin	10.00	20.00
NNO	Triple H	10.00	20.00

2001 Jakks Pacific WWF Titan Tron Live Series 12

NNO	Big Show	6.00	12.00
NNO	Chris Jericho	7.50	15.00
NNO	Kurt Angle	6.00	12.00
NNO	Rock	10.00	20.00
NNO	Stone Cold Steve Austin	10.00	20.00
NNO	Undertaker	12.50	25.00

2001 Jakks Pacific WWF Titan Tron Live Series 13

NNO	Chris Jericho	6.00	12.00
NNO	Lita	7.50	15.00
NNO	Rock	10.00	20.00
NNO	Stone Cold Steve Austin	12.50	25.00
NNO	Triple H	7.50	15.00
NNO	Undertaker	12.50	25.00

2000 Jakks Pacific WWF ToyFare Exclusives

NNO	Big Show	12.50	25.00
NNO	Debra	15.00	30.00
NNO	The Rock	20.00	40.00

2002 Jakks Pacific WWE Trash Talkin' Champions

NNO	Chris Jericho	20.00	40.00
NNO	Kurt Angle	10.00	20.00

2005 Jakks Pacific WWE Treacherous Trios Series 1

NNO	Kurt Angle/Eddie Guerrero/Big Show		
NNO	Triple H/Ric Flair/Batista	12.50	25.00
NNO	Undertaker/JBL/Heidenreich	15.00	30.00

2005 Jakks Pacific WWE Treacherous Trios Series 2

NNO	Mark Jindrak/Booker T/Kurt Angle	15.00	30.00
NNO	Orlando Jordan/Danny Basham/Doug Basham	12.50	25.00
NNO	Trish Stratus/Tyson Tomko/Christian	15.00	30.00

2005 Jakks Pacific WWE Treacherous Trios Series 3

NNO	Edge/Lita/Matt Hardy	30.00	60.00
NNO	Randy Orton/Undertaker Cowboy Bob Orton Jr.	25.00	50.00
NNO	Rey Mysterio/Chris Benoit/Batista	25.00	50.00

2006 Jakks Pacific WWE Treacherous Trios Series 4

NNO Chris Benoit/Booker T/Randy Orton
NNO Melina/Johnny Nitro/Joey Mercury
NNO Kurt Angle/Daivari/Mark Henry

2007 Jakks Pacific WWE Treacherous Trios Series 5

NNO Randy Orton/Edge/Carlito
NNO Rey Mysterio/Booker T/Chavo
NNO Shawn Michaels/HHH/Coachman

2007 Jakks Pacific WWE Treacherous Trios Series 6

NNO Batista/Long/Undertaker
NNO Brian Kendrick/Yang/London
NNO Umaga/Cena/Armando Estrada

2008 Jakks Pacific WWE Treacherous Trios Series 7

NNO	Elijah Burke/CM Punk/Tommy Dreamer	25.00	50.00
NNO	Great Khali/Batista/Undertaker		
NNO	Randy Orton/John Cena/Jonathan Coachman		

2008 Jakks Pacific WWE Treacherous Trios Series 8

NNO	Curt Hawkins/Edge/Zack Ryder		
NNO	Deuce/Cherry/Domino	30.00	75.00
NNO	Triple H/John Cena/Orton	15.00	30.00

2009 Jakks Pacific WWE Treacherous Trios Series 9

NNO	Finlay/JBL/Hornswoggle		
NNO	JTG/John Cena/Shad	20.00	40.00
NNO	Miz/Matt Hardy/Morrison	25.00	50.00

2009 Jakks Pacific WWE Treacherous Trios Series 10

NNO Big Show/Undertaker/Khali
NNO Chris Jericho/Cena/CM Punk
NNO Matt Hardy/Edge/Jeff Hardy

2002 Jakks Pacific WWE Unchained Fury Series 1

NNO	Booker T	10.00	20.00
NNO	Hurricane Helms	12.50	25.00
NNO	Lance Storm	10.00	20.00
NNO	Ric Flair	12.50	25.00

2002 Jakks Pacific WWE Unchained Fury Series 1 2-Packs

NNO	Booker T/Steve Austin	20.00	40.00
NNO	Ric Flair/Vince McMahon	25.00	50.00
NNO	Rob Van Dam/Chris Jericho		

2002 Jakks Pacific WWE Unchained Fury Series 2

NNO	Booker T	10.00	20.00
NNO	Kevin Nash	15.00	30.00
NNO	Kurt Angle	10.00	20.00
NNO	Rhyno	12.50	25.00
NNO	Rob Van Dam	15.00	30.00
NNO	Tajiri	10.00	20.00

2002 Jakks Pacific WWE Unchained Fury Series 2 2-Packs

NNO	Christian/DDP	12.50	25.00
NNO	Chuck Palumbo/Billy Gunn	15.00	30.00
NNO	Kurt Angle/Edge	15.00	30.00

2003 Jakks Pacific WWE Unlimited Series 1

NNO	Chris Jericho	12.50	25.00
NNO	Edge	12.50	25.00
NNO	Hulk Hogan	15.00	30.00
NNO	Kurt Angle	10.00	20.00
NNO	Rob Van Dam	7.50	15.00
NNO	The Rock	12.50	25.00

2003 Jakks Pacific WWE Unlimited Series 2

NNO	Batista	15.00	30.00
NNO	Billy Kidman	10.00	20.00
NNO	Booker T	12.50	25.00
NNO	Brock Lesnar	15.00	30.00
NNO	Eddie Guerrero	12.50	25.00
NNO	Triple H	10.00	20.00

2003 Jakks Pacific WWE Unlimited Series 3

NNO	Booker T	12.50	25.00
NNO	Brock Lesnar	20.00	40.00
NNO	Chris Benoit	10.00	20.00
NNO	Chris Jericho	10.00	20.00
NNO	Hulk Hogan	15.00	30.00
NNO	The Rock	15.00	30.00

2003 Jakks Pacific WWE Unlimited Series 4

NNO	Chris Benoit		
NNO	Kurt Angle		
NNO	Rob Van Dam	10.00	20.00
NNO	The Rock	15.00	30.00
NNO	Triple H	12.50	25.00

2006 Jakks Pacific WWE Unmatched Fury Series 1

NNO Batista
NNO Hulk Hogan
NNO John Cena
NNO Rey Mysterio

2007 Jakks Pacific WWE Unmatched Fury Series 2

NNO	Rob Van Dam	20.00	40.00
NNO	Shawn Michaels	30.00	60.00
NNO	Triple H	12.50	25.00
NNO	Undertaker	20.00	40.00
NNO	Undertaker GITD 100* NYC TF	300.00	500.00

2007 Jakks Pacific WWE Unmatched Fury Series 3

NNO	Carlito	15.00	30.00
NNO	Jeff Hardy	20.00	40.00
NNO	John Cena	15.00	30.00
NNO	Sabu	15.00	30.00

2007 Jakks Pacific WWE Unmatched Fury Series 4

NNO	Ken Kennedy	12.50	25.00
NNO	Mr.Perfect	20.00	40.00
NNO	Ric Flair	15.00	30.00
NNO	Umaga	12.50	25.00

2007 Jakks Pacific WWE Unmatched Fury Series 5

NNO	Bobby Lashley	25.00	50.00
NNO	Mick Foley	15.00	30.00

NNO The Rock 20.00 40.00
NNO Undertaker

2007 Jakks Pacific WWE Unmatched Fury Series 6

NNO Eddie Guerrero 15.00 30.00
NNO Kane 12.50 25.00
NNO Randy Orton 25.00 50.00
NNO Rowdy Roddy Piper 30.00 60.00

2008 Jakks Pacific WWE Unmatched Fury Series 7

NNO British Bulldog
NNO Edge
NNO Ravishing Rick Rude
NNO Undertaker

2008 Jakks Pacific WWE Unmatched Fury Series 8

NNO Boogeyman
NNO Iron Sheik
NNO Matt Hardy
NNO Shawn Michaels

2008 Jakks Pacific WWE Unmatched Fury Series 9

NNO Bret Hitman Hart 30.00 60.00
NNO Finlay 12.50 25.00
NNO Hornswoggle 20.00 50.00
NNO Hornswoggle LE 200.00 350.00
(Green/Gold/500*
NNO Undertaker

2008 Jakks Pacific WWE Unmatched Fury Series 10

NNO Great Khali
NNO Junk Yard Dog
NNO MVP
NNO Ultimate Warrior

2008 Jakks Pacific WWE Unmatched Fury Series 11

NNO Chris Jericho
NNO CM Punk
NNO Honkytonk Man
NNO Ted DiBiase

2008 Jakks Pacific WWE Unmatched Fury Series 12

NNO Big Show
NNO JBL
NNO Razor Ramon
NNO Undertaker

2009 Jakks Pacific WWE Unmatched Fury Series 14

NNO Bret Hitman Hart 30.00 60.00
NNO Hornswoggle 20.00 40.00
NNO John Cena 15.00 30.00
NNO Rey Mysterio 20.00 40.00

2009 Jakks Pacific WWE Unmatched Fury Series 15

NNO CM Punk 60.00 120.00
NNO Eddie Guerrero 25.00 50.00
NNO Rowdy Roddy Piper 30.00 60.00
NNO Stone Cold Steve Austin 20.00 40.00

2003 Jakks Pacific WWE Unrelenting

NNO Booker T 7.50 15.00
NNO Chris Jericho 10.00 20.00
NNO Edge
NNO Jeff Hardy
NNO Rob Van Dam
NNO Triple H

2008 Jakks Pacific WWE Vinyl Aggression Exclusive

NNO Bret Hart RSC 20.00 40.00

2009 Jakks Pacific WWE Vinyl Aggression Exclusive

NNO Jesse Ventura/100* NYC TF

2008 Jakks Pacific WWE Vinyl Aggression Series 1

NNO Carlito
NNO ECW Stylized
NNO Hornswoggle
NNO John Cena
NNO Mankind
NNO Umaga
NNO Undertaker

2008 Jakks Pacific WWE Vinyl Aggression Series 2

NNO Batista
NNO Chris Jericho
NNO CM Punk
NNO DX Stylized
NNO Finlay
NNO Honkytonk Man
NNO Mr. Kennedy
NNO MVP
NNO Rey Mysterio
NNO Rock
NNO Shawn Michaels
NNO Tommy Dreamer
NNO Triple H Stylized

2008 Jakks Pacific WWE Vinyl Aggression Series 3

NNO Batista
NNO Chris Jericho
NNO Shawn Michaels
NNO Rock
NNO Tommy Dreamer
NNO Triple H

2008 Jakks Pacific WWE Vinyl Aggression Series 4

NNO Edge
NNO Jimmy Wang Yang
NNO Miz
NNO Randy Orton
NNO Santino
NNO Ted DiBiase

2008 Jakks Pacific WWE Vinyl Aggression Series 5

NNO Big Show
NNO DX Stylized
NNO Jake Roberts
NNO Kane
NNO Kofi Kingston
NNO Matt Hardy

2008 Jakks Pacific WWE Vinyl Aggression Series 6

NNO Festus
NNO Jesse
NNO John Morrison
NNO JTG
NNO Rowdy Roddy Piper
NNO Shad

2008 Jakks Pacific WWE Vinyl Aggression Series 7

NNO Beth Phoenix
NNO Boogeyman
NNO Great Khali
NNO Kane/Classic Mask
NNO Ricky Ortiz
NNO Triple H

1999 Jakks Pacific WWF White's Exclusives

NNO Sable
NNO Undertaker

1998 Jakks Pacific WWF WrestleMania XIV

NNO Headbanger Mosh 6.00 12.00
NNO Headbanger Thrasher 6.00 12.00
NNO HHH 10.00 20.00
NNO Rocky Maivia 7.50 15.00
NNO Shawn Michaels 10.00 20.00
NNO Stone Cold Steve Austin 7.50 15.00

2001 Jakks Pacific WWF WrestleMania X-7

NNO Chris Jericho 7.50 15.00
NNO Chyna 10.00 20.00
NNO Eddie Guerrero 7.50 15.00
NNO Edge 7.50 15.00
NNO Kane 10.00 20.00
NNO Stone Cold Steve Austin 12.50 25.00

2002 Jakks Pacific WWE WrestleMania X-8

NNO Billy Gunn 7.50 15.00
NNO Chuck Palumbo 7.50 15.00
NNO Diamond Dallas Page 7.50 15.00
NNO HHH 15.00 30.00
NNO Maven 7.50 15.00
NNO Rob Van Dam 12.50 25.00

2002 Jakks Pacific WWE WrestleMania X-8 2-Packs

NNO Booker T/Edge 15.00 30.00
NNO Kurt Angle/Kane 12.50 25.00
NNO The Rock vs. Hollywood Hogan 30.00 60.00
NNO Undertaker vs. Ric Flair 30.00 75.00

2004 Jakks Pacific WWE WrestleMania 19 Winners

NNO Chris Benoit
NNO Chris Jericho
NNO Kane
NNO Kurt Angle
NNO The Rock

2004 Jakks Pacific WWE WrestleMania 19 Winners 2-Packs

NNO D-Von and Bubba Ray Dudley
NNO La Resistance
Conway/Dupree
NNO Team Angle
Benjamin/Haas

2004 Jakks Pacific WWE WrestleMania 20 Series 1

NNO Edge
NNO Hardcore Holly
NNO Rob Van Dam
NNO Shane McMahon
NNO Stone Cold Steve Austin
NNO Triple H

2004 Jakks Pacific WWE WrestleMania 20 Series 3

NNO Booker T
NNO Chris Benoit
NNO Chris Jericho
NNO Kane
NNO Kurt Angle
NNO The Rock

2004 Jakks Pacific WWE WrestleMania 20 Series 3 2-Packs

NNO Bubba Ray & D-Von
NNO Rob Conway & Rene Dupree
NNO Shelton Benjamin & Charlie Haas

2004 Jakks Pacific WWE WrestleMania 20 Mask and Figure Sets Series 1

NNO Hurricane
NNO Kane
NNO Mankind
NNO Rey Mysterio

2004 Jakks Pacific WWE WrestleMania 20 Mask and Figure Sets Series 2

NNO Rey Mysterio
NNO Rosey
NNO Ultimo Dragon

2004 Jakks Pacific WWE WrestleMania 20 Playset

NNO Stage Entrance and Stunt Ring

2004 Jakks Pacific WWE WrestleMania 20 Times Square Limited Edition

NNO Ric Flair/600*
NNO Triple H/600*

2004 Jakks Pacific WWE WrestleMania 20 Series 2

NNO Chavo Guerrero
NNO Chris Benoit
NNO Christian
NNO Eddie Guerrero
NNO John Cena
NNO Undertaker

2004 Jakks Pacific WWE WrestleMania 20 Series 2 2-Packs

NNO Booker T/Rob Van Dam
NNO Ric Flair/Randy Orton
NNO Rikishi/Scotty 2 Hotty

2004 Jakks Pacific WWE WrestleMania 20 Series 1 2-Packs

NNO Brock Lesnar/Kurt Angle
NNO Edge/Christian
NNO Steve Austin/HBK

2005 Jakks Pacific WWE WrestleMania 21 Series 1

NNO Eddie Guerrero 12.50 25.00
NNO Rey Mysterio
NNO Triple H
NNO Victoria

2005 Jakks Pacific WWE WrestleMania 21 Series 1 2-Packs

NNO Chris Jericho vs. Shawn Michaels
NNO John Cena vs. Big Show
NNO Kane vs. Kurt Angle

2005 Jakks Pacific WWE WrestleMania 21 Series 2

NNO Batista
NNO Booker T
NNO Charlie Haas
NNO Chris Benoit
NNO Eddie Guerrero 12.50 25.00
NNO Lita

2005 Jakks Pacific WWE WrestleMania 21 Series 2 2-Packs

NNO Maven/Eugene
NNO Rey Mysterio/Rene Dupree
NNO Rob Conway/William Regal

2005 Jakks Pacific WWE WrestleMania 21 Series 3

NNO Booker T
NNO Carlito
NNO Edge
NNO Randy Orton
NNO Stone Cold Steve Austin
NNO Undertaker

2005 Jakks Pacific WWE WrestleMania 21 Series 3 2-Packs

NNO John Cena/John Bradshaw Layfield
NNO Kurt Angle/Shawn Michaels
NNO Triple H/Batista

2005 Jakks Pacific WWE WrestleMania 21 Gear and Figure Sets Series 1

NNO Edge 10.00 20.00
NNO Hurricane
NNO JBL
NNO Kurt Angle
NNO Rey Mysterio 12.50 25.00
NNO Undertaker

2005 Jakks Pacific WWE WrestleMania 21 Gear and Figure Sets Series 2

NNO John Cena
NNO Rey Mysterio 12.50 25.00
NNO Undertaker 10.00 20.00

2005 Jakks Pacific WWE WrestleMania 21 Gear and Figure Sets Series 3

NNO Edge 10.00 20.00
NNO JBL
NNO Kurt Angle

2005 Jakks Pacific WWE WrestleMania 21 Gear and Figure Sets Series 4

NNO Hurricane
NNO John Cena
NNO Rey Mysterio 12.50 25.00

2005 Jakks Pacific WWE WrestleMania 21 Gear and Figure Sets 2-Packs

NNO Rey Mysterio/Rey Mysterio
NNO Rosey/Hurricane

2002 Jakks Pacific WWE Wrestling's Most Wanted

NNO Rock n' Roll Rivals
Edge/Y2J
NNO Ultimate Hardcore Match
RVD/Hardcore Holly
NNO Iron Man Match
HHH/Chris Benoit

2020-21 Jazwares AEW Exclusives

NNO Britt Baker Lights Out 25.00 50.00
NNO Chris Jericho Bubbly 30.00 75.00
NNO Cody & Dustin Rhodes Blood Brothers 30.00 75.00
NNO Darby Allin Coffin Drop 30.00 60.00
NNO Jurassic Express 50.00 100.00
NNO Jurassic Express (Package Variant)75.00 150.00
NNO Kenny Omega & Jon Moxley Death Match 40.00 80.00

2022 Jazwares AEW Exclusives

NNO Brodie Lee & Neg.1 RSC 20.00 40.00
NNO CM Punk 1st Dance RSC 30.00 60.00
NNO Jim Ross RSC 25.00 50.00
NNO Owen Hart KOH RSC 30.00 75.00
NNO Tony Schiavone RSC 20.00 40.00

2023 Jazwares AEW Exclusives

NNO Excalibur RSC 20.00 40.00
NNO Thunder Rosa B&G RSC 30.00 75.00
NNO Hook FTW RSC 20.00 40.00
NNO Danhausen VNVE RSC 30.00 75.00
NNO Wheeler Yuta FIC RSC 25.00 50.00
NNO Sting SDCC/1,000* 125.00 250.00
NNO MJF/CM Punk DCM RSC 75.00 150.00

2021 Jazwares AEW Unmatched Series 1

1 Kenny Omega 30.00 60.00
2 Darby Allin 30.00 75.00
3 Miro 30.00 75.00
4 Britt Baker DMD 30.00 75.00
5 Dustin Rhodes 25.00 50.00
6 Britt Baker DMD/3,000* R 60.00 125.00
7 Darby Allin/5,000* CH 75.00 150.00
8 Cody (LJN style) 25.00 50.00

2021 Jazwares AEW Unmatched Series 2

9 Sting 20.00 40.00
10 Santana 10.00 20.00
11 Ortiz 10.00 20.00
12 Wardlow 20.00 40.00
13 Tay Conti 15.00 30.00
14 MJF 15.00 30.00
15 MJF/3,000* R 60.00 125.00
16 Sting/5,000* CH 75.00 150.00

2022 Jazwares AEW Unmatched Series 3

17 Mr. Brodie Lee 20.00 40.00
18 Stu Grayson 12.50 25.00
19 Evil Uno 12.50 25.00
20 John Silver 15.00 30.00
21 Anna Jay 15.00 30.00
22 Mr. Brodie Lee/5,000* CH 60.00 125.00
23 Anna Jay/3,000 R 50.00 100.00

2022 Jazwares AEW Unmatched Series 4

24 Corazon de Leon Chris Jericho 12.50 25.00
25 CM Punk 15.00 30.00
26 Hangman Adam Page 12.50 25.00
27 Cody Rhodes 15.00 30.00
28 Jade Cargill 15.00 30.00
29 MJF 12.50 25.00
30 CM Punk/5,000* CH 75.00 150.00
31 Cody Rhodes/3,000* R 75.00 150.00

2022 Jazwares AEW Unmatched Series 5

33 Darby Allin LJN 30.00 60.00
34 Sammy Guevara 15.00 30.00
35 Shawn Spears 15.00 30.00
36 Kenny Omega 15.00 30.00
37 Bryan Danielson 25.00 50.00
38 Red Velvet 20.00 40.00
39 Bryan Danielson/5,000* CH 50.00 100.00
40 Shawn Spears/3,000* R 100.00 200.00

2023 Jazwares AEW Unmatched Series 6

41 Owen Hart 15.00 30.00
42 Santana 12.50 25.00
43 Ortiz 15.00 30.00
44 Ruby Soho 20.00 40.00
45 Malakai Black 40.00 80.00
46 Brodie Lee 12.50 25.00
47 Owen Hart/5,000* CH 30.00 75.00
48 Brodie Lee/3,000* R 30.00 60.00

2023 Jazwares AEW Unmatched Series 7

51 CM Punk LJN 25.00 50.00
52 Thunder Rosa 15.00 30.00
53 HOOK 12.50 25.00
54 Rey Fenix 25.00 50.00
55 Penta El Zero 20.00 40.00
56 PAC 20.00 40.00
57 HOOK/5,000* CH 40.00 80.00
58 Thunder Rosa/3,000* R 50.00 100.00

2024 Jazwares AEW Unmatched Series 8

59 CM Punk 30.00 75.00
60 Malakai Black 20.00 40.00
61 Brody King 30.00 60.00
62 Buddy Matthews 30.00 60.00
63 Penta Oscuro 30.00 60.00
64 CM Punk/5,000 CH 150.00 300.00
65 Brody King/3,000* R 200.00 400.00

2020-21 Jazwares AEW Unrivaled Collection Playsets

NNO Action Ring 30.00 75.00
NNO Action Ring w/Cody UK 75.00 150.00
NNO Authentic Scale Ring (w Aubrey Edwards) 75.00 150.00
NNO Authentic Scale Ring (w Kenny Omega) 100.00 200.00

2020 Jazwares AEW Unrivaled Collection Series 1

1 Cody Rhodes 20.00 40.00
2 Kenny Omega 30.00 75.00
3 Matt Jackson 20.00 40.00
4 Nick Jackson 25.00 50.00
5 Brandi Rhodes 50.00 100.00
6 Chris Jericho 20.00 40.00
8 Chris Jericho/1000* CH 300.00 600.00
7 Cody Rhodes/500* R 1500.00 3000.00

2020 Jazwares AEW Unrivaled Collection Series 2

10 Jon Moxley 20.00 40.00
11 Hangman Adam Page 12.50 25.00
12 MJF 25.00 50.00
13 Rey Fenix 15.00 30.00
14 Pentagon Jr. 30.00 60.00
15 Dustin Rhodes 10.00 20.00
16 MJF/1,000* CH 200.00 400.00
17 Jon Moxley/500* R 150.00 300.00

2021 Jazwares AEW Unrivaled Collection Series 3

19 PAC 25.00 50.00
20 RIHO 20.00 40.00
21 Orange Cassidy 25.00 50.00
22 Darby Allin 30.00 60.00
23 Matt Jackson 20.00 40.00
24 Nick Jackson 20.00 40.00
25 RIHO/1,000* CH 100.00 200.00
26 Darby Allin/500* R 300.00 600.00

2021 Jazwares AEW Unrivaled Collection Series 4

31 Matt Hardy 25.00 50.00
28 Kenny Omega 30.00 60.00
29 Cody 25.00 50.00
30 Sammy Guevara 30.00 75.00
32 Santana 30.00 60.00
33 Ortiz 20.00 40.00
34 Cody/1,000* CH 200.00 400.00
35 Matt Hardy/500* R 200.00 400.00

2021 Jazwares AEW Unrivaled Collection Series 5

37 Jon Moxley 30.00 75.00
38 Scorpio Sky 25.00 50.00
39 Kazarian 25.00 50.00
40 Hangman Adam Page 25.00 50.00
41 Luchasaurus/black tights 30.00 75.00
42 Jungle Boy/black tights 30.00 60.00
43 Hangman Adam Page w chaps/3,000* R 125.00 250.00
44 Jon Moxley Paradigm Shift/5,000* CH 100.00 200.00

2021 Jazwares AEW Unrivaled Collection Series 6

45 Chris Jericho	25.00	50.00
46 Jake Hager	25.00	50.00
47 MJF	20.00	40.00
48 Hikaru Shida	20.00	40.00
49 Pentagon Jr.	30.00	75.00
50 Rey Fenix	20.00	40.00
51 Chris Jericho/5,000* CH	75.00	150.00
52 Jake Hager/3,000* R	200.00	400.00

2021 Jazwares AEW Unrivaled Collection Series 7

53 Lance Archer	10.00	20.00
54 Dax Harwood	15.00	30.00
55 Cash Wheeler	15.00	30.00
57 Nick Jackson	20.00	40.00
58 Nyla Rose	10.00	20.00
59 Nyla Rose w/orange scarf/5,000* CH	40.00	80.00
60 Lance Archer w/silver tights/3,000* R	50.00	100.00
56 Matt Jackson	20.00	40.00

2021 Jazwares AEW Unrivaled Collection Series 8

63 Chris Jericho	15.00	30.00
64 Jon Moxley	15.00	30.00
65 Trent?	12.50	25.00
66 Chuck Taylor	10.00	20.00
67 Orange Cassidy	15.00	30.00
68 Kris Statlander	20.00	40.00
69 Jon Moxley/5,000* CH	60.00	125.00
70 Chris Jericho/3,000* R	50.00	100.00

2022 Jazwares AEW Unrivaled Collection Series 9

73 Eddie Kingston	15.00	30.00
74 Brian Cage	10.00	20.00
75 Ricky Starks		
76 Christian Cage	12.50	25.00
77 Thunder Rosa		
78 Powerhouse Hobbs	10.00	20.00
79 Thunder Rosa/5,000* CH	40.00	80.00
80 Ricky Starks/3,000* R	60.00	120.00

2022 Jazwares AEW Unrivaled Collection Series 10

81 Wardlow	12.50	25.00
82 Jake Hager	12.50	25.00
83 Britt Baker	15.00	30.00
84 Taz	15.00	30.00
85 Miro	12.50	25.00
86 Andrade El Idolo	17.50	35.00
87 Britt Baker/5,000* CH	60.00	120.00
88 Taz/3,000* R	50.00	100.00

2023 Jazwares AEW Unrivaled Collection Series 11

94 Penelope Ford	25.00	50.00
95 Adam Cole	15.00	30.00
96 Kip Sabian	12.50	25.00
97 Jungle Boy	12.50	25.00
98 Chris Jericho	15.00	30.00
99 Darby Allin	20.00	40.00
100 Penelope Ford/5,000* CH	150.00	300.00
101 Jungle Boy/3,000 R		

2023 Jazwares AEW Unrivaled Collection Series 12

104 Dax Harwood	10.00	20.00
105 Cash Wheeler	10.00	20.00
106 Jon Moxley	17.50	35.00
107 Isiah Kassidy	15.00	30.00
108 Marq Quen	15.00	30.00
109 Jamie Hayter	20.00	40.00
110 Jon Moxley/5,000 CH	30.00	60.00
111 Jamie Hayter/3,000 R	40.00	80.00

2024 Jazwares AEW Unrivaled Collection Series 13

116 Sting	20.00	40.00
117 Darby Allin	15.00	30.00
118 Danhausen	20.00	40.00
119 The Butcher	15.00	30.00
120 The Blade	15.00	30.00
121 Wardlow	12.50	25.00
122 The Bunny/5,000* CH	75.00	150.00
123 Danhausen/3,000* R	75.00	150.00

2024 Jazwares AEW Unrivaled Collection Series 14

125 Keith Lee		
126 Swerve Strickland		
127 Anthony Bowen		
128 Ricky Starks		
129 Max Caster		
130 Toni Storm		
131 Billy Gunn/5,000* CH		
132 Keith Lee/3,000* R		

2022 Jazwares AEW Unrivaled Playsets

NNO Auth.Scale Ring w/Sting		

2022 Jazwares AEW Unrivaled Supreme Collection Series 1

NNO Britt Baker	30.00	60.00
NNO Cody Rhodes	30.00	60.00

2022 Jazwares AEW Unrivaled Supreme Collection Series 2

NNO Kenny Omega	60.00	125.00
NNO Malakai Black	75.00	150.00

1990 JusToys WCW Bend-Ems

NNO Arn Anderson	20.00	40.00
NNO Barry Windham	20.00	40.00
NNO Brian Pillman	15.00	30.00
NNO Butch Reed	15.00	30.00
NNO Lex Luger	15.00	30.00
NNO Ric Flair	30.00	60.00
NNO Rick Steiner	12.50	25.00
NNO Ron Simmons	15.00	30.00
NNO Scott Steiner	20.00	40.00
NNO Sid Vicious	15.00	30.00
NNO Sting	25.00	50.00
NNO Tom Zenk	30.00	75.00

1990 JusToys WCW Bend-Ems Challenge 2-Pack

NNO The Steiner Brothers		

2001 JusToys WWF Bend-Ems Gear

NNO Chris Jericho		
NNO Jeff Hardy	20.00	40.00
NNO Kane	25.00	50.00
NNO Matt Hardy	20.00	40.00
NNO Road Dogg	15.00	30.00
NNO Rock (black & white)	12.50	25.00
NNO Rock (blue & yellow)	15.00	30.00
NNO Steve Austin	12.50	25.00
NNO Triple H	20.00	40.00

1998 JusToys WWF Bend-Ems Playsets

NNO Super Slam Wrestling Ring (w/Austin & Michaels)		
NNO Super Slam Wrestling Ring (w/Paul Bearer)	30.00	60.00

1994 JusToys WWF Bend-Ems Series I

NNO Bret Hitman Hart	12.50	25.00
NNO Diesel	7.50	15.00
NNO Doink	7.50	15.00
NNO Lex Luger	10.00	20.00
NNO Razor Ramon	10.00	20.00

1995 JusToys WWF Bend-Ems Series II

NNO 1-2-3 Kid	6.00	12.00
NNO British Bulldog	7.50	15.00
NNO Mabel	6.00	12.00
NNO Undertaker	7.50	15.00

1996 JusToys WWF Bend-Ems Series III

NNO Ahmed Johnson	5.00	10.00
NNO Goldust	6.00	12.00
NNO Shawn Michaels	7.50	15.00
NNO Yokozuna	6.00	12.00

1996 JusToys WWF Bend-Ems Series IV

NNO Sunny	7.50	15.00
NNO Sycho Sid	6.00	12.00
NNO Vader	6.00	12.00
NNO Wildman Marc Mero	5.00	10.00

1997 JusToys WWF Bend-Ems Series V

NNO Faarooq	6.00	12.00
NNO Mankind	10.00	20.00
NNO Rocky Maivia	12.50	25.00
NNO Stone Cold Steve Austin	6.00	12.00

1997 JusToys WWF Bend-Ems Series VI

NNO Animal	6.00	12.00
NNO Hawk	6.00	12.00
NNO Hunter Hearts Helmsley	5.00	10.00
NNO Undertaker	10.00	20.00

1997 JusToys WWF Bend-Ems Series VII

NNO Crush	7.50	15.00
NNO Ken Shamrock	7.50	15.00
NNO Owen Hart	12.50	25.00
NNO The Patriot	10.00	20.00

1998 JusToys WWF Bend-Ems Series IX

NNO Brian Christopher	6.00	12.00
NNO Cactus Jack	7.50	15.00
NNO Sable	10.00	20.00
NNO X-Pac	6.00	12.00

1998 JusToys WWF Bend-Ems Series VIII

NNO Chyna	7.50	15.00
NNO Jeff Jarrett	6.00	12.00
NNO Kane	7.50	15.00
NNO Taka	5.00	10.00

1998 JusToys WWF Bend-Ems Series X

NNO B.A. Billy Gunn	6.00	12.00
NNO Edge	7.50	15.00
NNO Road Dogg	6.00	12.00
NNO Steve Blackman	5.00	10.00

1999 JusToys WWF Bend-Ems Series XI

NNO Al Snow	6.00	12.00
NNO Godfather	7.50	15.00
NNO Mr. McMahon	7.50	15.00
NNO Val Venis	5.00	10.00

1999 JusToys WWF Bend-Ems Series XII

NNO Big Boss Man	5.00	10.00
NNO Mankind	7.50	15.00
NNO Paul Wight	5.00	10.00
NNO Steve Austin	10.00	20.00
NNO Undertaker	7.50	15.00

1999 JusToys WWF Bend-Ems Series XIII

NNO Droz	5.00	10.00
NNO D'Lo Brown	5.00	10.00
NNO Hardcore Holly	5.00	10.00
NNO Shane McMahon	6.00	12.00
NNO Steve Austin	7.50	15.00

2000 JusToys WWF Bend-Ems Series XIV

NNO Chris Jericho	6.00	12.00
NNO Jeff Hardy	6.00	12.00
NNO Matt Hardy	5.00	10.00
NNO The Rock	7.50	15.00

2001 JusToys WWF Bend-Ems Series XV

NNO Tazz		
NNO Grandmaster Sexay		
NNO Rikishi		
NNO The Rock/Repack		
NNO Scotty 2 Hotty		

1994 Kelian AAA Wrestling Figures

NNO Blue Panther		
NNO Cien Caras	30.00	60.00
NNO Fuerza Guerrera		
NNO Heavy Metal	50.00	100.00
NNO Hijo Del Santo	60.00	120.00
NNO Konnan		
NNO La Parka	60.00	120.00
NNO Mascara Sagrada		
NNO Octagon		
NNO Perro Aguayo	40.00	80.00
NNO Psicosis		
NNO Rey Misterio		

1994 Kelian AAA Wrestling Figures (loose)

NNO Blue Panther		
NNO Cien Caras	20.00	40.00
NNO Fuerza Guerrera		
NNO Heavy Metal		
NNO Hijo Del Santo		

NNO	Konnan		
NNO	La Parka		
NNO	Mascara Sagrada		
NNO	Octagon	12.50	25.00
NNO	Perro Aguayo		
NNO	Psicosis	30.00	75.00
NNO	Rey Misterio	25.00	60.00

2019 Kidrobot Collectible Vinyl Mini Series WWE

NNO	AJ Styles	6.00	12.00
NNO	Alexa Bliss	7.50	15.00
NNO	Andre the Giant	4.00	8.00
NNO	Charlotte Flair	6.00	12.00
NNO	John Cena	7.50	15.00
NNO	Ric Flair	6.00	12.00
NNO	Roman Reigns	5.00	10.00
NNO	Ronda Rousey	5.00	10.00
NNO	Sasha Banks	7.50	15.00
NNO	Shawn Michaels	5.00	10.00
NNO	The Rock	7.50	15.00
NNO	Triple H Mystery CH		
NNO	Ultimate Warrior	20.00	40.00
NNO	Undertaker	7.50	15.00

1985 LJN WWF Wrestling Superstars 16-Inch

NNO	Hulk Hogan	225.00	450.00
NNO	Rowdy Roddy Piper	175.00	350.00

1985 LJN WWF Wrestling Superstars 16-Inch (loose)

NNO	Hulk Hogan	60.00	120.00
NNO	Rowdy Roddy Piper	75.00	150.00

1985 LJN WWF Wrestling Superstars Bendies

NNO	Andre the Giant	50.00	100.00
NNO	Big John Studd	30.00	75.00
NNO	Bobby Heenan	50.00	100.00
NNO	Brutus Beefcake	20.00	40.00
NNO	Captain Lou Albano	50.00	100.00
NNO	Corporal Kirchner	20.00	40.00
NNO	George Steele	30.00	75.00
NNO	Hillbilly Jim	30.00	75.00
NNO	Hulk Hogan/Blue Knee Pads	25.00	50.00
NNO	Hulk Hogan/Red Knee Pads	25.00	50.00
NNO	Iron Sheik	25.00	60.00
NNO	Jesse Ventura	30.00	60.00
NNO	Junk Yard Dog	30.00	75.00
NNO	King Kong Bundy	20.00	40.00
NNO	Mr. Wonderful	25.00	60.00
NNO	Nikolai Volkoff	25.00	60.00
NNO	Randy Macho Man Savage	75.00	150.00
NNO	Ricky The Dragon Steamboat	30.00	75.00
NNO	Rowdy Roddy Piper	50.00	100.00

1985 LJN WWF Wrestling Superstars Bendies (loose)

NNO	Andre the Giant	10.00	20.00
NNO	Big John Studd	10.00	20.00
NNO	Bobby Heenan	10.00	20.00
NNO	Brutus Beefcake	7.50	15.00
NNO	Captain Lou Albano	12.50	25.00
NNO	Corporal Kirchner	6.00	12.00
NNO	George Steele	7.50	15.00
NNO	Hillbilly Jim	6.00	12.00
NNO	Hulk Hogan/Blue Knee Pads	10.00	20.00
NNO	Hulk Hogan/Red Knee Pads	10.00	20.00
NNO	Iron Sheik	6.00	12.00
NNO	Jesse Ventura	7.50	15.00
NNO	Junk Yard Dog	7.50	15.00
NNO	King Kong Bundy	5.00	10.00
NNO	Mr. Wonderful	7.50	15.00
NNO	Nikolai Volkoff	6.00	12.00
NNO	Randy Macho Man Savage	20.00	40.00
NNO	Ricky The Dragon Steamboat	15.00	30.00
NNO	Rowdy Roddy Piper	15.00	30.00

1985 LJN WWF Wrestling Superstars Bendies Playset

NNO	Cage Match Challenge w/Hogan Blue Knee Pads	150.00	300.00

1985 LJN WWF Wrestling Superstars Bendies Playset (loose)

NNO	Cage Match Challenge	50.00	100.00

1985 LJN WWF Wrestling Superstars Bendies Tag Teams

NNO	Hulk Hogan/Junk Yard Dog		
NNO	Iron Sheik/Nikolai Volkoff	25.00	50.00
NNO	George Steele/Captain Lou Albano	25.00	50.00
NNO	King Kong Bundy/Big John Studd	50.00	100.00
NNO	Randy Savage/Jesse Ventura	50.00	100.00
NNO	Ricky Steamboat/Corporal Kirchner	60.00	120.00

1989 LJN WWF Wrestling Superstars Black Card Re-Release

NNO	Adrian Adonis		
NNO	Bam Bam Bigelow	50.00	100.00
NNO	Big John Studd		
NNO	Bret Hitman Hart		
NNO	Brutus The Barber Beefcake		
NNO	Demolition Ax		
NNO	Elizabeth/Gold Skirt	750.00	1500.00
NNO	Elizabeth/Purple Skirt		
NNO	Hacksaw Jim Duggan	350.00	500.00
NNO	Honky Tonk Man	450.00	900.00
NNO	Hulk Hogan/Red Shirt		
NNO	Hulk Hogan/White Shirt	1000.00	2000.00
NNO	Jake The Snake Roberts	150.00	300.00
NNO	Randy Macho Man Savage		
NNO	Ted DiBiase		

1984 LJN WWF Wrestling Superstars Series 1

NNO	Andre the Giant/Long Hair	250.00	500.00
NNO	Big John Studd	125.00	250.00
NNO	Hillbilly Jim	150.00	300.00
NNO	Hulk Hogan	350.00	700.00
NNO	Iron Sheik	200.00	400.00
NNO	Jimmy Snuka	125.00	250.00
NNO	Junk Yard Dog/Red Chain	125.00	250.00
NNO	Junk Yard Dog/Silver Chain	150.00	300.00
NNO	Nikolai Volkoff	125.00	250.00
NNO	Rowdy Roddy Piper/Brown Boots		
NNO	Rowdy Roddy Piiper/Red Boots	125.00	250.00

1984 LJN WWF Wrestling Superstars Series 1 (loose)

NNO	Andre the Giant/Long Hair	25.00	50.00
NNO	Big John Studd	15.00	40.00
NNO	Hillbilly Jim	15.00	40.00
NNO	Hulk Hogan	30.00	60.00
NNO	Iron Sheik	15.00	30.00
NNO	Jimmy Snuka	15.00	40.00
NNO	Junk Yard Dog/Red Chain	25.00	50.00
NNO	Junk Yard Dog/Silver Chain	15.00	30.00
NNO	Nikolai Volkoff	15.00	30.00
NNO	Rowdy Roddy Piper/Brown Boots		
NNO	Rowdy Roddy Piper/Red Boots	30.00	60.00

1985 LJN WWF Wrestling Superstars Series 2

NNO	Andre the Giant/Short Hair	300.00	600.00
NNO	Brutus Beefcake	200.00	400.00
NNO	George Steele	100.00	200.00
NNO	Greg Valentine/Dk. Blonde Hair		
NNO	Greg Valentine/Lt. Blonde Hair	100.00	200.00
NNO	King Kong Bundy	100.00	200.00
NNO	Mr. Wonderful	150.00	300.00

1985 LJN WWF Wrestling Superstars Series 2 (loose)

NNO	Andre the Giant/Short Hair	50.00	100.00
NNO	Brutus Beefcake	15.00	30.00
NNO	George Steele	15.00	30.00
NNO	Greg Valentine/Dk Blond Hair	12.50	25.00
NNO	Greg Valentine/Lt. Blonde Hair	10.00	20.00
NNO	King Kong Bundy	20.00	40.00
NNO	Mr. Wonderful	15.00	30.00

1986 LJN WWF Wrestling Superstars Series 3

NNO	Bobby Heenan/No Scrolls		
NNO	Bobby Heenan/Scrolls	75.00	150.00
NNO	Bruno Sammartino	60.00	120.00
NNO	Captain Lou Albano/Red Lapel	50.00	100.00
NNO	Captain Lou Albano/White Lapel	75.00	150.00
NNO	Classy Freddie Blassie	60.00	120.00
NNO	Corporal Kirchner/Beard		
NNO	Corporal Kirchner/No Stubble	60.00	120.00
NNO	Corporal Kirchner/Stubble		
NNO	Don Muraco	100.00	200.00
NNO	Jesse Ventura	125.00	250.00
NNO	Jimmy Hart/Hearts on Megaphone	60.00	120.00
NNO	Jimmy Hart/No Hearts on Megaphone	60.00	120.00
NNO	Randy Savage	300.00	500.00
NNO	Ricky Steamboat	100.00	200.00
NNO	SD Jones/Hawaiian Shirt	75.00	150.00
NNO	SD Jones/Red Shirt	60.00	120.00
NNO	Terry Funk	125.00	250.00
NNO	Tito Santana	100.00	200.00

1986 LJN WWF Wrestling Superstars Series 3 (loose)

NNO	Bobby Heenan/No Scrolls	30.00	60.00
NNO	Bobby Heenan/Scrolls	20.00	50.00
NNO	Bruno Sammartino	20.00	40.00
NNO	Captain Lou Albano/Red Lapel	12.50	25.00
NNO	Captain Lou Albano/White Lapel	15.00	30.00
NNO	Classy Freddie Blassie	30.00	60.00
NNO	Corporal Kirchner/Beard		
NNO	Corporal Kirchner/No Stubble	15.00	30.00
NNO	Corporal Kirchner/Stubble	15.00	30.00
NNO	Don Muraco	20.00	40.00
NNO	Jesse Ventura	20.00	40.00
NNO	Jimmy Hart/Hearts on Megaphone	20.00	40.00
NNO	Jimmy Hart/No Hearts on Megaphone	10.00	20.00
NNO	Randy Savage	30.00	60.00
NNO	Ricky Steamboat	15.00	30.00
NNO	SD Jones/Hawaiian Shirt	20.00	40.00
NNO	SD Jones/Red Shirt	12.50	25.00
NNO	Terry Funk	30.00	75.00
NNO	Tito Santana	20.00	40.00

1987 LJN WWF Wrestling Superstars Series 4

NNO	Adrian Adonis	75.00	150.00
NNO	Billy Jack Haynes	200.00	350.00
NNO	Bret Hart/Pink Tights	300.00	600.00
NNO	Bret Hart/Purple Tights		
NNO	Brian Blair/Non-Tan	75.00	150.00
NNO	Brian Blair/Tan	125.00	250.00
NNO	Cowboy Bob Orton	100.00	200.00
NNO	Elizabeth/Gold Skirt	125.00	250.00
NNO	Elizabeth/Purple Skirt	1200.00	1800.00
NNO	Hercules Hernandez	100.00	200.00
NNO	Jake the Snake Roberts	200.00	400.00
NNO	Jim Brunzell/Non-Tan	125.00	250.00
NNO	Jim Brunzell/Tan	150.00	300.00
NNO	Jim Neidhart/Pink Tights	300.00	600.00
NNO	Jim Neidhart/Purple Tights		
NNO	Kamala	150.00	300.00
NNO	King Harley Race	300.00	500.00
NNO	Koko B. Ware	200.00	350.00
NNO	Mean Gene Okerlund	100.00	200.00
NNO	Mr. Fuji	125.00	250.00
NNO	Outback Jack	100.00	200.00
NNO	Ted Arcidi	150.00	300.00

1987 LJN WWF Wrestling Superstars Series 4 (loose)

NNO	Adrian Adonis	25.00	50.00
NNO	Billy Jack Haynes	50.00	100.00
NNO	Bret Hart/Pink Tights	50.00	100.00
NNO	Bret Hart/Purple Tights		
NNO	Brian Blair/Non-Tan	20.00	40.00
NNO	Brian Blair/Tan		
NNO	Cowboy Bob Orton	30.00	60.00
NNO	Elizabeth/Gold Skirt	50.00	100.00
NNO	Elizabeth/Purple Skirt	200.00	350.00
NNO	Hercules Hernandez	20.00	40.00
NNO	Jake the Snake Roberts	50.00	100.00
NNO	Jim Brunzell/Non-Tan	15.00	30.00
NNO	Jim Brunzell/Tan		
NNO	Jim Neidhart/Pink Tights	30.00	75.00
NNO	Jim Neidhart/Purple Tights		
NNO	Kamala	30.00	60.00
NNO	King Harley Race	60.00	120.00
NNO	Koko B. Ware	30.00	75.00
NNO	Mean Gene Okerlund	20.00	40.00
NNO	Mr. Fuji	30.00	60.00
NNO	Outback Jack	30.00	75.00
NNO	Ted Arcidi	20.00	40.00

1988 LJN WWF Wrestling Superstars Series 5

NNO	Ax	300.00	600.00
NNO	Bam Bam Bigelow	200.00	400.00
NNO	Hacksaw Jim Duggan	300.00	450.00
NNO	Honky Tonk Man	300.00	500.00
NNO	Hulk Hogan/Red Shirt		
NNO	Hulk Hogan/White Shirt		
NNO	Johnny V	90.00	175.00
NNO	Ken Patera	150.00	300.00
NNO	One Man Gang	200.00	400.00
NNO	Referee/Blue Shirt	200.00	400.00
NNO	Referee/White Shirt	400.00	750.00
NNO	Rick Martel	300.00	600.00
NNO	Slick	150.00	300.00
NNO	Ted DiBiase	300.00	500.00
NNO	Tito Santana/White Trunks	200.00	350.00
NNO	Vince McMahon	150.00	300.00

1988 LJN WWF Wrestling Superstars Series 5 (loose)

NNO	Ax	50.00	100.00
NNO	Bam Bam Bigelow	50.00	100.00

NNO Hacksaw Jim Duggan 100.00 200.00
NNO Honky Tonk Man 50.00 100.00
NNO Hulk Hogan/Red Shirt 125.00 250.00
NNO Hulk Hogan/White Shirt 125.00 250.00
NNO Johnny V 20.00 40.00
NNO Ken Patera 30.00 60.00
NNO One Man Gang 30.00 75.00
NNO Referee/Blue Shirt 50.00 100.00
NNO Referee/White Shirt 60.00 120.00
NNO Rick Martel 30.00 60.00
NNO Slick 30.00 75.00
NNO Ted DiBiase 60.00 120.00
NNO Tito Santana 25.00 50.00
NNO Vince McMahon 60.00 120.00

1989 LJN WWF Wrestling Superstars Series 6

NNO Andre the Giant 3000.00 6000.00
NNO Big Boss Man 1250.00 2500.00
NNO Haku 500.00 1000.00
NNO Rick Rude 500.00 1000.00
NNO Ultimate Warrior 3000.00 6000.00
NNO Warlord 1500.00 3000.00

1984 LJN WWF Wrestling Superstars Accessories

NNO Hulkamania Barbell Workout Set
NNO Hulkamania Deluxe Workout Set300.00 600.00

1986 LJN WWF Wrestling Superstars Stretch Wrestlers

NNO George The Animal Steele 125.00 250.00
NNO Hulk Hogan 300.00 600.00
NNO Junkyard Dog 125.00 250.00
NNO King Kong Bundy 125.00 250.00
NNO Macho Man Randy Savage 250.00 400.00
NNO Mr. Wonderful Paul Orndorff 75.00 150.00
NNO Ricky The Dragon Steamboat 150.00 300.00
NNO Rowdy Roddy Piper 250.00 500.00

1985 LJN WWF Wrestling Superstars Tag Teams

NNO British Bulldogs 400.00 800.00
NNO Greg Valentine & Brutus Beefcake200.00 400.00
NNO Hart Foundation 1000.00 1500.00
NNO Hillbilly Jim & Hulk Hogan 250.00 500.00
NNO Iron Sheik & Nikolai Volkoff 150.00 300.00
NNO Killer Bees 200.00 400.00
NNO Strike Force 300.00 500.00

1986 LJN WWF Wrestling Superstars Thumb Wrestlers

NNO Hillbilly Jim/Big John Studd 75.00 150.00
NNO Hillbilly Jim/Macho Man Randy Savage 15.00 30.00
NNO Hillbilly Jim/Nikolai Volkoff 12.50 25.00
NNO Hillbilly Jim/Rowdy Roddy Piper30.00 60.00
NNO Hillbilly Jim/The Iron Sheik 30.00 75.00
NNO Hulk Hogan/Big John Studd 25.00 50.00
NNO Hulk Hogan/Jake The Snake Roberts30.00 75.00
NNO Hulk Hogan/King Kong Bundy 20.00 40.00
NNO Hulk Hogan/Macho Man Randy Savage 25.00 50.00
NNO Hulk Hogan/Nikolai Volkoff 30.00 75.00
NNO Hulk Hogan/Rowdy Roddy Piper 60.00 120.00
NNO Hulk Hogan/The Iron Sheik 20.00 40.00
NNO Junkyard Dog/Big John Studd 15.00 30.00
NNO Junkyard Dog/Nikolai Volkoff 30.00 75.00
NNO Junkyard Dog/Rowdy Roddy Piper100.00 200.00
NNO Junkyard Dog/The Iron Sheik 15.00 30.00
NNO Mr. Wonderful Paul Orndorff/Big John Studd 30.00 75.00
NNO Mr. Wonderful Paul Orndorff/King Kong Bundy 15.00 30.00
NNO Mr. Wonderful Paul Orndorff/Rowdy Roddy Piper 50.00 100.00
NNO Ricky The Dragon Steamboat/Jake The Snake Roberts 30.00 75.00
NNO Ricky The Dragon Steamboat Macho Man Randy Savage 25.00 50.00
NNO Ricky The Dragon Steamboat Nikolai Volkoff 12.50 25.00
NNO Ricky The Dragon Steamboat Rowdy Roddy Piper 15.00 30.00

1986 LJN WWF Wrestling Superstars Thumb Wrestlers (loose)

NNO Big John Studd 5.00 10.00
NNO Hillbilly Jim 5.00 10.00
NNO Hulk Hogan 7.50 15.00
NNO Iron Sheik 3.00 8.00
NNO Jake The Snake Roberts 5.00 10.00
NNO Junkyard Dog 3.00 8.00
NNO King Kong Bundy 6.00 12.00
NNO Macho Man Randy Savage 7.50 15.00
NNO Mr. Wonderful Paul Orndorff 3.00 8.00
NNO Nikolai Volkoff 3.00 8.00
NNO Ricky The Dragon Steamboat 5.00 10.00
NNO Rowdy Roddy Piper 6.00 12.00

2018 The Loyal Subjects Action Vinyls WWE

NNO AJ Styles
NNO Brock Lesnar 10.00 20.00
NNO Demon King Finn Balor 12.50 25.00
NNO Demon King Finn Balor Black and White
NNO Finn Balor/Blue Trunks 30.00 75.00
NNO John Cena 7.50 15.00
NNO Macho Man Randy Savage/Gold/2*
NNO Macho Man Randy Savage 12.50 25.00
NNO Macho Man Randy Savage American Flag 30.00 75.00
NNO Referee
NNO Referee/GITD
NNO Roman Reigns 10.00 20.00
NNO Sasha Banks CH 40.00 80.00
NNO Shinsuke Nakamura 7.50 15.00
NNO Shinsuke Nakamura/Black Pants 15.00 30.00
NNO Sting 15.00 30.00
NNO Undertaker 12.50 25.00
NNO RAW Ring/Bottom Left 10.00 20.00
NNO RAW Ring/Bottom Right 10.00 20.00
NNO RAW Ring/Top Left 10.00 20.00
NNO RAW Ring/Top Right 10.00 20.00

2018 The Loyal Subjects Action Vinyls WWE SDCC Exclusives

NNO AJ Styles vs. Shinsuke Nakamura20.00 40.00
NNO Brock Lesnar vs. Roman Reigns 12.50 25.00
NNO John Cena vs. Undertaker 30.00 75.00

2020 Major Wrestling Figure Podcast Ringside Collectibles Exclusives

NNO Zack Ryder/Curt Hawkins/500
NNO Zack Ryder/Curt Hawkins (NY Mets colors)/250

2015 Mattel Create A WWE Superstar Series 1

NNO Bray Wyatt 10.00 20.00
NNO Hulk Hogan 20.00 40.00
NNO John Cena 12.50 25.00
NNO The Rock 15.00 30.00

2015 Mattel Create A WWE Superstar Series 1 Sets

NNO Gladiator Set 10.00 20.00
NNO Lucha Set 10.00 20.00
NNO Rocker Set 10.00 20.00

2015 Mattel Create A WWE Superstar Series 2

NNO Kane 12.50 25.00
NNO Randy Orton 10.00 20.00
NNO Sheamus 10.00 20.00
NNO Stone Cold Steve Austin

2015 Mattel Create A WWE Superstar Series 2 Sets

NNO Samurai Set
NNO Special Ops Set 20.00 40.00
NNO Zombie Set 15.00 30.00

2015 Mattel Create A WWE Superstar Series 3

NNO Goldust 25.00 50.00
NNO John Cena 15.00 30.00
NNO Rusev
NNO Triple H
NNO Ultimate Warrior 12.50 25.00

2015 Mattel Create A WWE Superstar Series 3 Sets

NNO Enforcer Set 10.00 20.00
NNO Hip Hop Set 10.00 20.00
NNO Vigilante Set 15.00 30.00

2015 Mattel Create A WWE Superstar Series Playset

NNO Ring Builder 30.00 75.00

2019 Mattel Masters of the WWE Universe

NNO Finn Balor 20.00 40.00
NNO Sting 30.00 60.00
NNO Triple H 20.00 40.00
NNO Ultimate Warrior 15.00 30.00

2019 Mattel Masters of the WWE Universe Playsets

NNO Grayskull Mania (w/John Cena & Terror Claws Triple H) 25.00 50.00
NNO Grayskull Ring 20.00 40.00

2020 Mattel Masters of the WWE Universe Wave 2

NNO Macho Man 20.00 40.00
NNO John Cena 15.00 30.00
NNO Roman Reigns 20.00 40.00
NNO Rey Mysterio 25.00 50.00

2020 Mattel Masters of the WWE Universe Wave 3

NNO Braun Strowman 25.00 50.00
NNO The New Day 30.00 75.00
NNO The Rock 30.00 75.00
NNO Undertaker 50.00 100.00

2020 Mattel Masters of the WWE Universe Wave 4

NNO The Fiend Bray Wyatt 30.00 60.00
NNO Jake "The Snake" Roberts 25.00 50.00
NNO Mr. T 45.00 90.00
NNO Seth Rollins 25.00 50.00

2020 Mattel Masters of the WWE Universe Wave 5

NNO Becky Lynch 15.00 30.00
NNO Macho Man Randy Savage 20.00 40.00
NNO Ricky "The Dragon" Steamboat 15.00 30.00
NNO Rowdy Roddy Piper 15.00 30.00

2020 Mattel Masters of the WWE Universe Wave 6

NNO Goldberg 12.50 25.00
NNO Kane 12.50 25.00
NNO Stephanie McMahon 10.00 20.00
NNO Ultimate Warrior 12.50 25.00

2021 Mattel Masters of the WWE Universe Wave 7

NNO Bret "Hit Man" Hart 20.00 40.00
NNO Andre the Giant 30.00 75.00
NNO Junkyard Dog 20.00 40.00
NNO Sgt. Slaughter 20.00 40.00

2021 Mattel Masters of the WWE Universe Wave 8

NNO Chyna 20.00 40.00
NNO Rey Mysterio 20.00 40.00
NNO Stone Cold Steve Austin 15.00 30.00

2016 Mattel WWE 3-Count Crushers

NNO John Cena
NNO The Rock
NNO Roman Reigns
NNO Seth Rollins

2010 Mattel WWE Battle Packs Series 1

NNO Santino/Beth Phoenix 15.00 30.00
NNO Shawn Michaels vs. {Chris Jericho 20.00 40.00
NNO Ted DiBiase/Cody Rhodes 30.00 75.00

2010 Mattel WWE Battle Packs Series 2

NNO Carlito/Primo 12.50 25.00
NNO Finlay/Hornswoggle 20.00 40.00
NNO John Morrison/The Miz 15.00 30.00

2010 Mattel WWE Battle Packs Series 3

NNO Edge/Big Show
NNO Rey Mysterio/Evan Bourne 25.00 50.00
NNO Shad/JTG 30.00 60.00

2010 Mattel WWE Battle Packs Series 4

NNO Chavo vs. Hornswoggle 7.50 15.00
NNO Christian/Tommy Dreamer 40.00 80.00
NNO Hart Dynasty 20.00 40.00

2010 Mattel WWE Battle Packs Series 5

NNO Carlito/Primo 20.00 40.00
NNO D-Generation X 25.00 50.00
NNO Ricky Steamboat vs. Y2J 15.00 30.00

2010 Mattel WWE Battle Packs Series 6

Item	Low	High
NNO Mark Henry & MVP		
NNO Undertaker vs. Batista		
NNO Vladimir Kozlov & Ezekiel Jackson	7.50	15.00

2010 Mattel WWE Battle Packs Series 7

Item	Low	High
NNO CM Punk & Luke Gallows	20.00	40.00
NNO Dolph Ziggler vs. John Morrison		
NNO The Miz & Big Show		

2011 Mattel WWE Battle Packs Series 8

Item	Low	High
NNO John Cena vs. Randy Orton		
NNO Matt Hardy/Great Khali		
NNO Ted DiBiase/Cody Rhodes		

2011 Mattel WWE Battle Packs Series 9

Item	Low	High
NNO Christian/Heath Slater	7.50	15.00
NNO Hart Dynasty	15.00	30.00
NNO Sheamus/Triple H	12.50	25.00

2011 Mattel WWE Battle Packs Series 10

Item	Low	High
NNO Darren Young/Justin Gabriel	15.00	30.00
NNO David Otunga/Michael Tarver	15.00	30.00
NNO Randy Orton vs. Edge	40.00	80.00

2011 Mattel WWE Battle Packs Series 11

Item	Low	High
NNO Drew McIntyre/Cody Rhodes	75.00	150.00
NNO Jimmy Uso/Jey Uso	25.00	50.00
NNO Undertaker/Kane	30.00	75.00

2011 Mattel WWE Battle Packs Series 13

Item	Low	High
NNO John Cena vs. R-Truth	15.00	30.00
NNO The Miz vs. Alex Riley	20.00	40.00
NNO Rey Mysterio vs. Cody Rhodes	30.00	60.00

2012 Mattel WWE Battle Packs Series 14

Item	Low	High
NNO Heath Slater/Justin Gabriel	12.50	25.00
NNO Macho Man Randy Savage vs. CM Punk	25.00	50.00
NNO Randy Orton vs. Mason Ryan	12.50	25.00

2012 Mattel WWE Battle Packs Series 15

Item	Low	High
NNO Brie Bella/Nikki Bella	30.00	60.00
NNO Sin Cara vs. Daniel Bryan	25.00	50.00
NNO The Rock vs. John Cena	12.50	25.00

2012 Mattel WWE Battle Packs Series 16

Item	Low	High
NNO Alberto Del Rio vs. Big Show		
NNO David Otunga/Michael McGillicutty	12.50	25.00
NNO Randy Orton vs. Christian	15.00	30.00

2012 Mattel WWE Battle Packs Series 17

Item	Low	High
NNO John Cena vs. CM Punk	15.00	30.00
NNO Mark Henry vs. Trent Barreta	15.00	30.00
NNO Rey Mysterio vs. The Miz	25.00	50.00

2012 Mattel WWE Battle Packs Series 18

Item	Low	High
NNO CM Punk vs. Triple H	20.00	40.00
NNO Randy Orton vs. Wade Barrett		
NNO Zack Ryder vs. Dolph Ziggler	15.00	30.00

2012 Mattel WWE Battle Packs Series 19

Item	Low	High
NNO Daniel Bryan vs. Big Show	15.00	30.00
NNO Epico/Primo	25.00	50.00
NNO John Cena vs. Kane		

2013 Mattel WWE Battle Packs Series 20

Item	Low	High
NNO Brock Lesnar vs. Triple H	15.00	30.00
NNO Brodus Clay vs. Curt Hawkins	10.00	20.00
NNO Kofi Kingston/R-Truth	15.00	30.00

2013 Mattel WWE Battle Packs Series 21

Item	Low	High
NNO Darren Young/Titus O'Neil	12.50	25.00
NNO Kane vs. Daniel Bryan	20.00	40.00
NNO Sheamus vs. Randy Orton	15.00	30.00

2013 Mattel WWE Battle Packs Series 22

Item	Low	High
NNO Dolph Ziggler/Vickie Guerrero	12.50	25.00
NNO Ryback vs. Jinder Mahal	12.50	25.00
NNO Sin Cara/Rey Mysterio	7.50	15.00

2013 Mattel WWE Battle Packs Series 23

Item	Low	High
NNO CM Punk vs. Mr. McMahon	20.00	40.00
NNO Rey Mysterio vs. Kofi Kingston	15.00	30.00
NNO Sin Cara vs. Cody Rhodes	15.00	30.00

2013 Mattel WWE Battle Packs Series 24

Item	Low	High
NNO Naomi/Cameron	20.00	40.00
NNO The Rock vs. John Cena	17.50	35.00
NNO Seth Rollins/Roman Reigns	15.00	30.00

2013 Mattel WWE Battle Packs Series 25

Item	Low	High
NNO Brock Lesnar/Paul Heyman	15.00	30.00
NNO CM Punk vs. Undertaker	25.00	50.00
NNO Mark Henry vs. Ryback	20.00	40.00

2014 Mattel WWE Battle Packs Series 26

Item	Low	High
NNO Nikki Bella/Brie Bella	20.00	40.00
NNO Seth Rollins/Dean Ambrose	15.00	30.00
NNO Triple H vs. Curtis Axel	12.50	25.00

2014 Mattel WWE Battle Packs Series 27

Item	Low	High
NNO Big Show/Mark Henry	12.50	25.00
NNO Brodus Clay/Tensai	10.00	20.00
NNO Daniel Bryan/Randy Orton	12.50	25.00

2014 Mattel WWE Battle Packs Series 28

Item	Low	High
NNO Big E/AJ Lee	20.00	40.00
NNO Jimmy Uso/Jey Uso	10.00	20.00
NNO Luke Harper/Erick Rowan	15.00	30.00

2014 Mattel WWE Battle Packs Series 29

Item	Low	High
NNO CM Punk vs. Ryback	25.00	50.00
NNO Goldust/Cody Rhodes	20.00	40.00
NNO Los Matadores	12.50	25.00

2014 Mattel WWE Battle Packs Series 30

Item	Low	High
NNO Brock Lesnar vs. Undertaker	15.00	30.00
NNO Jake Roberts/Dean Ambrose	15.00	30.00
NNO Xavier Woods/R-Truth	12.50	25.00

2014 Mattel WWE Battle Packs Series 31

Item	Low	High
NNO John Cena/Ultimate Warrior	12.50	25.00
NNO Luke Harper/Erick Rowan	12.50	30.00
NNO Sin Cara/Alberto Del Rio	10.00	20.00

2015 Mattel WWE Battle Packs Series 32

Item	Low	High
NNO Daniel Bryan/Triple H	15.00	30.00
NNO Jimmy Uso/Jey Uso	20.00	40.00
NNO Road Dogg/Billy Gunn	15.00	30.00

2015 Mattel WWE Battle Packs Series 33

Item	Low	High
NNO Andre the Giant/Big Show	25.00	50.00
NNO Rey Mysterio/RVD	15.00	30.00
NNO Shawn Michaels/Undertaker	7.50	15.00

2015 Mattel WWE Battle Packs Series 34

Item	Low	High
NNO Animal/Hawk	30.00	75.00
NNO Hornswoggle/El Torito	30.00	60.00
NNO Lana/Rusev	15.00	30.00

2015 Mattel WWE Battle Packs Series 35

Item	Low	High
NNO Kane/Roman Reigns	12.50	25.00
NNO Ryback/Curtis Axel	15.00	30.00
NNO Zeb Colter/Jack Swagger	12.50	25.00

2015 Mattel WWE Battle Packs Series 36

Item	Low	High
NNO Big E/Kofi Kingston	15.00	30.00
NNO Dean Ambrose/Seth Rollins	10.00	20.00
NNO Kevin Nash/Scott Hall	15.00	30.00

2015 Mattel WWE Battle Packs Series 37

Item	Low	High
NNO Jamie Noble/Joey Mercury	12.50	25.00
NNO Jey Uso/Jimmy Uso	12.50	25.00
NNO Konnor/Viktor	10.00	20.00

2015 Mattel WWE Battle Packs Series 38

Item	Low	High
NNO Adam Rose/Bunny	10.00	20.00
NNO Bray Wyatt/Undertaker	15.00	30.00
NNO Nikki Bella/Brie Bella	20.00	40.00

2016 Mattel WWE Battle Packs Series 39

Item	Low	High
NNO Darren Young/Titus O'Neill	10.00	20.00
NNO John Cena/Kevin Owens	7.50	15.00
NNO Tyson Kidd/Cesaro	7.50	15.00

2016 Mattel WWE Battle Packs Series 40

Item	Low	High
NNO Bushwhackers	10.00	20.00
NNO Enzo Amore/Big Cass	15.00	30.00
NNO Steve Austin/Mr. McMahon	15.00	30.00

2016 Mattel WWE Battle Packs Series 41

Item	Low	High
NNO Bubba Ray/Devon Dudley	15.00	30.00
NNO Charlotte/Ric Flair	12.50	25.00
NNO Simon Gotch/Aiden English		

2016 Mattel WWE Battle Packs Series 42

Item	Low	High
NNO Edge/Christian	10.00	20.00
NNO Sin Cara/Kalisto	15.00	30.00
NNO Triple H/Stephanie	12.50	25.00

2016 Mattel WWE Battle Packs Series 43A

Item	Low	High
NNO Big E/Kofi Kingston	15.00	30.00
NNO Nikki Bella/Brie Bella	20.00	40.00
NNO Undertaker/Kane	12.50	25.00

2016 Mattel WWE Battle Packs Series 43B

Item	Low	High
NNO Dean Ambrose/Brock Lesnar	12.50	25.00
NNO Finn Balor/Samoa Joe	20.00	40.00
NNO John Cena/Seth Rollins	10.00	20.00
NNO Roman Reigns/Sheamus	12.50	25.00

2016 Mattel WWE Battle Packs Series 44

Item	Low	High
NNO American Alpha	10.00	20.00
NNO Sami Zayn/Kevin Owens	12.50	25.00
NNO The Usos	15.00	30.00

2017 Mattel WWE Battle Packs Series 45

Item	Low	High
NNO AJ Styles/Roman Reigns	15.00	30.00
NNO Enzo Amore/Big Cass	20.00	40.00
NNO Scott Dawson/Dash Wilder	15.00	30.00
NNO Triple H/Road Dogg	15.00	30.00

2017 Mattel WWE Battle Packs Series 46

Item	Low	High
NNO Dean Ambrose/Shane McMahon	15.00	30.00
NNO Karl Anderson/Luke Gallows	25.00	50.00
NNO The Miz & Maryse	15.00	30.00
NNO The New Day (Kingston/Woods)	15.00	30.00

2017 Mattel WWE Battle Packs Series 47

Item	Low	High
NNO Bray Wyatt/Luke Harper	12.50	25.00
NNO The Hart Foundation	12.50	25.00
NNO Roman Reigns vs. Rusev	12.50	25.00
NNO Sasha Banks vs. Charlotte Flair	15.00	30.00

2017 Mattel WWE Battle Packs Series 48

Item	Low	High
NNO American Alpha	12.50	25.00
NNO Hype Bros.	10.00	20.00
NNO Shawn Michaels/Diesel	12.50	25.00

2017 Mattel WWE Battle Packs Series 49

Item	Low	High
NNO Daniel Bryan/The Miz	12.50	25.00
NNO Sheamus/Cesaro	12.50	25.00
NNO Stephanie McMahon/Mick Foley	10.00	20.00

2017 Mattel WWE Battle Packs Series 50

NNO	Konnor/Viktor	10.00	20.00
NNO	Luke Gallows/Karl Anderson	20.00	40.00
NNO	Randy Orton/Bray Wyatt	12.50	25.00

2017 Mattel WWE Battle Packs Series 51

NNO	Big E/Xavier Woods	12.50	25.00
NNO	The Miz/Maryse	10.00	20.00
NNO	Scott Dawson/Dash Wilder	15.00	30.00

2018 Mattel WWE Battle Packs Series 52

NNO	Jey Uso/Jimmy Uso	30.00	60.00
NNO	Roman Reigns/Brock Lesnar	12.50	25.00
NNO	Sheamus/Cesaro	15.00	30.00

2018 Mattel WWE Battle Packs Series 53

NNO	Carmella/James Ellsworth	12.50	25.00
NNO	Matt Hardy/Jeff Hardy	25.00	50.00
NNO	S. Nakamura/D. Ziggler	12.50	25.00

2018 Mattel WWE Battle Packs Series 54

NNO	B. Strowman/R. Reigns	15.00	30.00
NNO	Bray Wyatt/Finn Balor	12.50	25.00
NNO	Nia Jax/Alexa Bliss	25.00	50.00
NNO	Tyler Breeze/Fandango	10.00	20.00

2018 Mattel WWE Battle Packs Series 55

NNO	Big Show/Big Cass	17.50	35.00
NNO	Charlotte Flair/Becky Lynch	20.00	40.00
NNO	Seth Rollins/Dean Ambrose	15.00	30.00

2018 Mattel WWE Battle Packs Series 56

NNO Miztourage
NNO Roman Reigns vs. John Cena
NNO Kurt Angle/Jason Jordan

2019 Mattel WWE Battle Packs Series 57

NNO Braun Strowman vs. Kane
NNO Sunil &Samir Singh
NNO Finn Balor vs. Shinsuke Nakamura

2019 Mattel WWE Battle Packs Series 58

NNO Kevin Owens/Sami Zayn
NNO S. Benjamin/C. Gable
NNO Triple H/HBK

2019 Mattel WWE Battle Packs Series 59

NNO The Hardy Boyz
NNO Jinder Mahal vs. AJ Styles
NNO The Shield (Ambrose/Rollins)

2019 Mattel WWE Battle Packs Series 60

NNO The Bar (Cesaro/Sheamus)
NNO Goldberg vs. Stone Cold Steve Austin
NNO Sasha Banks vs. Alexa Bliss

2019 Mattel WWE Battle Packs Series 61

NNO AJ Styles/Daniel Bryan
NNO The Iiconics (Billie Kay/Peyton Royce)
NNO Jimmy and Jey Uso

2019 Mattel WWE Battle Packs Series 62

NNO Akam & Rezar
NNO Andrade/Zelina Vega
NNO Rey Mysterio/Shinsuke Nakamura

2019 Mattel WWE Battle Packs Series 63

NNO Bobby Lashley vs. Finn Balor
NNO The New Day (Big E/Xavier Woods)
NNO Seth Rollins vs. Brock Lesnar

2020 Mattel WWE Battle Packs Series 64

NNO	Daniel Bryan vs. AJ Styles	15.00	30.00
NNO	Lita & Trish Stratus	30.00	75.00
NNO	The Usos	60.00	120.00

2020 Mattel WWE Battle Packs Series 65

NNO	Ali & Kevin Owens	20.00	40.00
NNO	The Hardy Boyz	25.00	50.00
NNO	Ricochet & Velveteen	20.00	40.00

2020 Mattel WWE Battle Packs Series 66

NNO	Seth Rollins & Becky Lynch	25.00	50.00
NNO	Roman Reigns & Undertaker	30.00	60.00
NNO	Shane McMahon & Drew McIntyre	15.00	30.00

2016 Mattel WWE Battle Packs SummerSlam Heritage

NNO	John Cena/Brock Lesnar	12.50	25.00
NNO	Roman Reigns/Dean Ambrose	10.00	20.00

2017 Mattel WWE Battle Packs SummerSlam Heritage

NNO	Brock Lesnar/Randy Orton	15.00	30.00
NNO	Ultimate Warrior/Honkytonk Man	15.00	30.00

2016 Mattel WWE Battle Packs Then Now Forever

NNO	Dean Ambrose/Brian Pillman	10.00	20.00
NNO	John Cena/Steve Austin	15.00	30.00
NNO	Ultimate Warrior/Sting	12.50	25.00

2010 Mattel WWE Battle Packs WrestleMania 26

NNO	John Cena/Batista		
NNO	The Miz/Big Show	20.00	40.00
NNO	R-Truth/John Morrison		

2014 Mattel WWE Battle Packs WrestleMania 30 Heritage

NNO	Batista vs. Brock Lesnar	15.00	30.00
NNO	Sheamus vs. Ultimate Warrior	12.50	25.00

2015 Mattel WWE Battle Packs WrestleMania 31 Heritage

NNO	Daniel Bryan vs. Rey Mysterio	20.00	40.00
NNO	Triple H vs. Roman Reigns	20.00	40.00

2016 Mattel WWE Battle Packs WrestleMania 32 Heritage

NNO	Bret Hart & Steve Austin	15.00	30.00
NNO	Ric Flair & The Rock	12.50	25.00

2016 Mattel WWE Battle Packs WrestleMania 33 Heritage

NNO	Andre the Giant/Ted DiBiase	10.00	20.00
NNO	The Rock/John Cena	12.50	25.00

2018 Mattel WWE Battle Packs WrestleMania 34 Heritage

NNO	Sting/Triple H	10.00	20.00
NNO	John Cena/Nikki Bella	15.00	30.00
NNO	Roman Reigns/Undertaker	12.50	25.00

2018 Mattel WWE Battle Packs WrestleMania 35 Heritage

NNO	AJ Styles vs. Shinsuke Nakamura	15.00	30.00
NNO	Jeff Hardy vs. Edge	15.00	30.00
NNO	The Miz vs. Seth Rollins	12.50	25.00

2020 Mattel WWE Beast Mode

NNO	AJ Styles	7.50	15.00
NNO	Becky Lynch	7.50	15.00
NNO	Braun Strowman	5.00	10.00
NNO	Daniel Bryan	6.00	12.00
NNO	Finn Balor	7.50	15.00
NNO	The Rock	5.00	10.00
NNO	Roman Reigns	10.00	20.00
NNO	Triple H	7.50	15.00

2021 Mattel WWE Beast Mode

NNO Becky Lynch
NNO Big E
NNO Bray Wyatt
NNO Kofi Kingston
NNO Seth Rollins
NNO The Rock
NNO Undertaker
NNO Xavier Woods

2022 Mattel WWE Bend 'N Bash Series 1

NNO	John Cena	15.00	30.00
NNO	Rey Mysterio	15.00	30.00
NNO	The Rock	20.00	40.00
NNO	Roman Reigns	15.00	30.00

2022 Mattel WWE Bend 'N Bash Series 2

NNO	Bobby Lashley	12.50	25.00
NNO	Drew McIntyre	12.50	25.00
NNO	Kofi Kingston		
NNO	Undertaker	12.50	25.00

2010 Mattel WWE Best of 2010

NNO	Batista	12.50	25.00
NNO	Evan Bourne	7.50	15.00
NNO	Hornswoggle	20.00	40.00
NNO	John Cena	10.00	20.00
NNO	Mark Henry	7.50	15.00
NNO	Rey Mysterio	12.50	25.00

2011 Mattel WWE Best of 2011

NNO	Big Show	12.50	25.00
NNO	John Cena	6.00	12.00
NNO	Kofi Kingston		
NNO	Randy Orton	7.50	15.00
NNO	Rey Mysterio	25.00	50.00
NNO	Santino Marella	7.50	15.00

2012 Mattel WWE Best of 2012

NNO	Alberto Del Rio		
NNO	Brodus Clay		
NNO	Daniel Bryan	15.00	30.00
NNO	Great Khali	40.00	80.00
NNO	Rey Mysterio	12.50	25.00
NNO	Sin Cara	25.00	50.00

2013 Mattel WWE Best of 2013

NNO Brock Lesnar
NNO Great Khali
NNO Kaitlyn
NNO Rey Mysterio
NNO Tensai
NNO Undertaker

2014 Mattel WWE Best of 2014

NNO	Cesaro	7.50	15.00
NNO	El Torito	12.50	25.00
NNO	John Cena	10.00	20.00
NNO	Roman Reigns	20.00	40.00
NNO	Sin Cara	25.00	50.00
NNO	Undertaker	10.00	20.00

2012 Mattel WWE Best of PPV Series 1

NNO	Christian		
NNO	John Cena		
NNO	Mark Henry		
NNO	Rey Mysterio	30.00	75.00

2012 Mattel WWE Best of PPV Series 2

NNO John Cena
NNO The Rock
NNO Sheamus
NNO Triple H

2013 Mattel WWE Best of PPV Series 3

NNO Alberto Del Rio
NNO John Cena
NNO Mark Henry
NNO Rey Mysterio

2013 Mattel WWE Best of PPV Series 4

NNO	Alberto Del Rio	7.50	15.00
NNO	Sheamus	7.50	15.00
NNO	The Rock	12.50	25.00
NNO	Undertaker	10.00	20.00

2014 Mattel WWE Best of PPV Series 5

NNO Damien Sandow
NNO Daniel Bryan
NNO Dolph Zziggler
NNO Kofi Kingston

2016 Mattel WWE Best of PPV

NNO	Chris Jericho	10.00	20.00
NNO	Neville		
NNO	Rusev		
NNO	Undertaker		

2023 Mattel WWE Best of Ultimate Edition Series 1

NNO Bret Hart
NNO Triple H

2023 Mattel WWE Best of Ultimate Edition Series 2

NNO Stone Cold Steve Austin
NNO Ultimate Warrior

2024 Mattel WWE Best of Ultimate Edition Series 3

NNO Charlotte Flair
NNO Hulk Hogan

2015 Mattel WWE Big Reveal 12-Inch

NNO Rey Mysterio
NNO Triple H
NNO Ultimate Warrior
NNO Undertaker

2012 Mattel WWE Brawlin' Buddies

NNO John Cena
NNO Randy Orton
NNO Rey Mysterio
NNO Sheamus

2013 Mattel WWE Brawlin' Buddies

NNO John Cena
NNO Kofi Kingston
NNO Rey Mysterio
NNO Zack Ryder

2012 Mattel WWE Brawlin' Buddies 2-Pack

NNO Rey Mysterio/John Cena
(Toys R Us Exclusive)

2013 Mattel WWE Brawlin' Buddies Championship Buddies

NNO Brodus Clay
NNO John Cena
NNO The Rock
NNO Sheamus

2023 Mattel WWE Defining Moments Exclusives 4-Pack Box

NNO HBK/Hit Man/Cody/Mankind 150.00 300.00

2014 Mattel WWE Dollar Store Series 1

NNO CM Punk
NNO John Cena
NNO Kane
NNO Randy Orton
NNO Rey Mysterio
NNO Sheamus

2014 Mattel WWE Dollar Store Series 2

NNO Alberto Del Rio
NNO Big Show
NNO Brodus Clay
NNO Daniel Bryan
NNO John Cena
NNO Undertaker

2017 Mattel WWE Dollar Store

NNO Brock Lesnar
NNO John Cena
NNO Roman Reigns
NNO Undertaker

2019 Mattel WWE Dollar Store

NNO AJ Styles
NNO Finn Balor
NNO John Cena
NNO The Rock
NNO Roman Reigns

2019 Mattel WWE Dollar Store 5-Pack

NNO Cena/Rock/Styles/Balor/Reigns

2020 Mattel WWE Elite Collection 2-Packs

NNO Bret "Hit Man" Hart & Goldberg 30.00 75.00
NNO Brood Hardy Boyz 50.00 100.00
(Ringside Exclusive)
NNO Chyna & Triple H 30.00 75.00
NNO Mr. T & "Rowdy" Roddy Piper 60.00 120.00

2021 Mattel WWE Elite Collection 2-Packs

NNO Jeff Hardy vs. Triple H 25.00 50.00
NNO The Rock & Mankind
(Rock 'N' Sock Connection) 50.00 100.00

2010 Mattel WWE Elite Collection Best of 2010

NNO John Cena 20.00 40.00
NNO Kane 50.00 100.00
NNO Randy Orton 50.00 90.00
NNO Rey Mysterio 60.00 120.00
NNO Triple H 25.00 50.00
NNO Undertaker 30.00 60.00

2011 Mattel WWE Elite Collection Best of 2011

NNO John Cena 25.00 50.00
NNO John Morrison 60.00 120.00
NNO Randy Orton 20.00 40.00
NNO Rey Mysterio 30.00 75.00
NNO Sheamus

2018 Mattel WWE Elite Collection Best of Attitude Era

NNO Chris Jericho 10.00 20.00
NNO The Rock 20.00 40.00
NNO Stone Cold Steve Austin 20.00 40.00
NNO Triple H 12.50 25.00

2012 Mattel WWE Elite Collection Best of PPV Series 1

NNO Bret Hart
NNO Daniel Bryan
NNO John Cena
NNO Triple H

2012 Mattel WWE Elite Collection Best of PPV Series 2

NNO Big Show
NNO CM Punk
NNO The Miz
NNO Shawn Michaels
NNO Undertaker EXCL

2013 Mattel WWE Elite Collection Best of PPV Series 3

NNO Christian 60.00 120.00
NNO John Cena 25.00 50.00
NNO Sheamus 15.00 30.00
NNO Sin Cara 30.00 75.00

2013 Mattel WWE Elite Collection Best of PPV Series 4

NNO Brock Lesnar 15.00 30.00
NNO CM Punk 30.00 60.00
NNO Daniel Bryan 15.00 30.00
NNO John Cena 12.50 25.00

2014 Mattel WWE Elite Collection Best of PPV Series 5

NNO Alberto Del Rio 20.00 40.00
NNO CM Punk 30.00 60.00
NNO Curtis Axel 25.00 50.00
NNO Paul Bearer 15.00 30.00
NNO Randy Orton 17.50 35.00

2014 Mattel WWE Elite Collection Best of PPV Series 6

NNO Bray Wyatt 12.50 25.00
NNO Daniel Bryan 20.00 40.00
NNO John Cena 12.50 25.00
NNO Undertaker 20.00 40.00

2017 Mattel WWE Elite Collection Booty-O's 3-Pack

NNO The New Day 25.00 50.00

2011 Mattel WWE Elite Collection Defining Moments Series 1

NNO Macho Man Randy Savage 50.00 100.00
NNO Shawn Michaels 75.00 150.00

2011 Mattel WWE Elite Collection Defining Moments Series 2

NNO The Rock 100.00 200.00
NNO Ultimate Warrior 60.00 120.00

2011 Mattel WWE Elite Collection Defining Moments Series 3

NNO Ricky Steamboat 40.00 80.00
NNO Triple H 125.00 250.00

2011 Mattel WWE Elite Collection Defining Moments Series 4

NNO Stone Cold Steve Austin 40.00 80.00
NNO Undertaker 100.00 200.00

2011 Mattel WWE Elite Collection Defining Moments Series 5

NNO Bret Hart 100.00 200.00
NNO John Cena 30.00 60.00

2014 Mattel WWE Elite Collection Defining Moments Series 6

NNO Hulk Hogan 30.00 75.00
NNO Ric Flair 40.00 80.00

2015 Mattel WWE Elite Collection Defining Moments Series 7

NNO Hulk Hogan
NNO Razor Ramon
NNO Sting
NNO Undertaker

2016 Mattel WWE Elite Collection Defining Moments Series 8

NNO John Cena
NNO Ric Flair/Retirement
NNO Stone Cold Steve Austin
NNO Sting/Surfer Gear
NNO Ultimate Warrior

2017 Mattel WWE Elite Collection Defining Moments Series 9

NNO Chris Jericho 15.00 30.00
NNO Macho Man Randy Savage 20.00 40.00
NNO Shinsuke Nakamura 20.00 40.00

2018 Mattel WWE Elite Collection Entrance Greats

NNO Bobby Roode 20.00 40.00
NNO Elias
NNO Finn Balor
NNO Goldberg 25.00 50.00
NNO Jeff Hardy 30.00 60.00
NNO Kurt Angle

2010 Mattel WWE Elite Collection Entrance Greats Series 1

NNO Rey Mysterio 50.00 100.00
NNO Shawn Michaels 25.00 50.00
NNO Triple H 20.00 40.00

2010 Mattel WWE Elite Collection Entrance Greats Series 2

NNO Chris Jericho 30.00 60.00
NNO Ted DiBiase 20.00 40.00
NNO Rowdy Roddy Piper 25.00 50.00

2010 Mattel WWE Elite Collection Entrance Greats Series 3

NNO The Rock 30.00 75.00
NNO Undertaker 50.00 100.00

2018 Mattel WWE Elite Collection Epic Moments

NNO Festival of Friendship 30.00 75.00
Chris Jericho/Kevin Owens
NNO Milk-O-Mania 25.00 50.00
Kurt Angle/Stone Cold Steve Austin/Stephanie McMahon
NNO Shield Reunion 50.00 100.00
Seth Rollins/Roman Reigns/Dean Ambrose
NNO Team Xtreme 30.00 60.00
Matt & Jeff Hardy
NNO Undisputed Era 60.00 120.00
Adam Cole/Bobby Fish/Kyle O'Reilly

2010 Mattel WWE Elite Collection Exclusives

NNO Rey Mysterio Flash RSC 150.00 300.00

2011 Mattel WWE Elite Collection Exclusives

NNO Bret Hart P&B Attack RSC 150.00 300.00
NNO CM Punk Straight Edge RSC 200.00 350.00
NNO Macho King RSC 150.00 300.00
NNO Undertaker SDCC 75.00 150.00
NNO Vince McMahon MA 60.00 120.00

2012 Mattel WWE Elite Collection Exclusives

NNO Macho Man nWo RSC 75.00 150.00
NNO Steve Austin Rattlesnake RSC
NNO Triple H COO MA 20.00 40.00

2013 Mattel WWE Elite Collection Exclusives

NNO Brock Lesnar Pain RSC 30.00 75.00

NNO Cactus Jack Bang RSC 30.00 60.00
NNO Undertaker 21-0 TRU

2014 Mattel WWE Elite Collection Exclusives

NNO CM Punk ECW 60.00 120.00
{Flashback RSC
NNO Edge Rated R RSC 100.00 200.00
NNO Kane Hardcore RSC 125.00 250.00
NNO Kane Unmasked RSC
NNO The Rock IC Champ RSC 25.00 50.00
NNO Mankind AMZ 25.00 50.00
NNO Rocky Maivia TAR 30.00 75.00
NNO Brock Lesnar 21-1 TRU 25.00 50.00

2015 Mattel WWE Elite Collection Exclusives

NNO Hulk Hogan American RSC 60.00 120.00
NNO John Cena TRU 50.00 100.00
NNO Scott Hall nWo RSC 50.00 100.00
NNO Seth Rollins TRU 30.00 60.00
NNO Shawn Michaels DX SE WG 30.00 60.00
NNO Shawn Michaels SS RSC 50.00 100.00
NNO Triple H DX SE WG 30.00 60.00
NNO Virgil Convention Sign 30.00 60.00

2016 Mattel WWE Elite Collection Exclusives

NNO Chris Jericho WM XIX RSC 25.00 50.00
NNO Finn Balor Balor Club RSC 30.00 75.00
NNO Kevin Nash nWo RSC 75.00 150.00
NNO Nation of Domination KM OL 60.00 120.00
NNO Sting nWo Wolfpac RSC 60.00 120.00
NNO Brock Lesnar/ 25.00 50.00
WWE 2K17 GS
NNO Shockmaster SDCC 60.00 120.00

2017 Mattel WWE Elite Collection Exclusives

NNO AJ Styles WRMS 25.00 50.00
NNO Andre the Giant AMZ 30.00 75.00
NNO Becky Lynch WG 20.00 40.00
NNO Bret Hit Man Hart KOTR RSC 60.00 120.00
NNO Chris Jericho List GS 30.00 75.00
NNO Hardy Boyz WWE SZ
NNO Isaac Yankem DDS TRU 60.00 120.00
NNO Macho Man Wolfpack RSC 75.00 150.00
NNO Maryse WG 20.00 40.00
NNO Samoa Joe GS 20.00 40.00
NNO Sasha Banks Title WG 25.00 50.00
NNO Shano Mac RSC 30.00 75.00

2018 Mattel WWE Elite Collection Exclusives

NNO AJ Styles TRU 25.00 50.00
NNO The Brian Kendrick RSC 20.00 40.00
NNO Hardy Boyz Brood RSC 50.00 100.00
NNO Kurt Angle Shield RSC 15.00 30.00
NNO Matt Hardy ECW RSC 25.00 50.00
NNO Pete Dunne 30.00 75.00
NNO The Shark SDCC 20.00 40.00

2019 Mattel WWE Elite Collection Exclusives

NNO Alexa Bliss WG 25.00 50.00
NNO Alexander Wolfe TAR 20.00 40.00
NNO Andrade Cien Almas
(NXT TakeOver) RSC 30.00 60.00
NNO Bob Backlund WM 20.00 40.00
NNO Gorilla Monsoon WM 60.00 120.00
NNO Kassius Ohno TAR 75.00 150.00
NNO Liv Morgan TAR 60.00 120.00
NNO Macho Man Randy
Savage (Slim Jim) SDCC 75.00 150.00
NNO Paige TAR 50.00 100.00
NNO Pat Patterson WM 20.00 40.00
NNO Red Rooster TAR 50.00 100.00
NNO Rock (SmackDown Live) WM 20.00 40.00
NNO Sensational Sherri WG 20.00 40.00
NNO Sonya Deville TAR 30.00 60.00
NNO Tyler Bate (UK Champion) 25.00 50.00
NNO Undertaker as Kane
(Deadman's Revenge) RSC 30.00 60.00

2020 Mattel WWE Elite Collection Exclusives

NNO Finn Balor/AJ Styles 30.00 75.00
NNO Rey Mysterio/Samoa Joe
(WrestleMania Moment) 60.00 120.00

2021 Mattel WWE Elite Collection Exclusives

NNO Bray Wyatt Firefly Funhouse RSC30.00 75.00
NNO Cactus Jack ECW RSC 25.00 50.00
NNO John Cena nWo RSC 30.00 60.00
NNO Ultimate Warrior
WrestleMania 12 RSC 20.00 40.00
NNO Undertaker Tag Champ RSC
NNO Walter RSC 25.00 50.00

2022 Mattel WWE Elite Collection Exclusives

NNO Cameron Grimes (To the Moon) 25.00 50.00
(Ringside Collectibles Exclusive)
NNO Mega Powers
(Hogan & Savage) 2-Pack 50.00 100.00
(Ringside Collectibles Exclusive)
NNO Tommaso Ciampa (Blackheart) 40.00 80.00
(Ringside Collectibles Exclusive)
NNO Wolfpac Hulk Hogan 30.00 75.00
(Ringside Collectibles Exclusive)

2018 Mattel WWE Elite Collection Fan Central

NNO Carmella 25.00 50.00

2019 Mattel WWE Elite Collection Fan Central

NNO Akira Tozawa 20.00 40.00
NNO Big Show 25.00 50.00
NNO Bobby The Brain Heenan 20.00 40.00
NNO Daniel Bryan 15.00 30.00
NNO Mark Henry 25.00 50.00
NNO Mojo Rawley 15.00 30.00
NNO Triple H 15.00 30.00

2018 Mattel WWE Elite Collection Flashback Series 1

NNO Mean Gene Okerlund 30.00 75.00
NNO Syxx 25.00 50.00
NNO Ultimate Warrior 25.00 50.00
NNO Yokozuna 20.00 40.00

2018 Mattel WWE Elite Collection Flashback Series 2

NNO Alundra Blayze 15.00 30.00
NNO Razor Ramon 15.00 30.00
NNO Shawn Michaels 20.00 40.00

2019 Mattel WWE Elite Collection Ghostbusters

NNO John Cena 12.50 25.00
NNO The Rock 15.00 30.00
NNO Shawn Michaels 12.50 25.00
NNO Stone Cold Steve Austin 12.50 25.00
NNO Undertaker 15.00 30.00

2022 Mattel WWE Elite Collection Greatest Hits Series 1

NNO Bam Bam Bigelow 20.00 40.00
NNO Jake The Snake Roberts 25.00 50.00
NNO Rey Mysterio 20.00 40.00
NNO Rikishi 30.00 75.00
NNO The Rock 20.00 40.00
NNO Undertaker 20.00 40.00

2023 Mattel WWE Elite Collection Greatest Hits Series 2

NNO Batista 15.00 30.00
NNO Diamond Dallas Page 12.50 25.00
NNO King Harley Race 15.00 30.00
NNO Seth Rollins 15.00 30.00
NNO Shawn Michaels 12.50 25.00
NNO Undertaker 12.50 25.00

2024 Mattel WWE Elite Collection Greatest Hits Series 3

NNO Brutus Beefcake
NNO Earthquake 20.00 40.00
NNO Rock/Scorpion King 20.00 40.00
NNO Roddy Piper/John Nada 25.00 50.00
NNO R-Truth 20.00 40.00
NNO Seth Rollins/Shield 15.00 30.00
NNO Typhoon 20.00 40.00

2018 Mattel WWE Elite Collection Hall of Champions Series 3

NNO Billy Gunn 15.00 30.00
NNO Paul Bearer 25.00 50.00
NNO Road Dogg 15.00 30.00
NNO Ultimate Warrior 25.00 50.00

2016 Mattel WWE Elite Collection Hall of Fame 2-Packs

NNO Papa Shango/Ultimate Warrior 25.00 50.00
NNO Wild Samoans 20.00 40.00

2017 Mattel WWE Elite Collection Hall of Fame 4-Pack

NNO Eddie Guerrero/Kevin Nash/ 25.00 50.00
Scott Hall/Larry Zybysko

2015 Mattel WWE Elite Collection Hall of Fame Four Horsemen 4-Pack

NNO Ric Flair/Arn Anderson/Barry
Windham/Tully Blanchard 30.00 75.00

2015 Mattel WWE Elite Collection Hall of Fame Series 1

NNO Sgt. Slaughter 20.00 40.00
NNO Stone Cold Steve Austin 25.00 50.00
NNO Trish Stratus 25.00 50.00
NNO Ultimate Warrior 20.00 40.00

2015 Mattel WWE Elite Collection Hall of Fame Series 2

NNO Eddie Guerrero 15.00 30.00
NNO Hulk Hogan 25.00 50.00
NNO Tito Santana 10.00 20.00
NNO Yokozuna 20.00 40.00

2016 Mattel WWE Elite Collection Hall of Fame Series 3

NNO Jimmy Hart 20.00 40.00
NNO Macho Man Randy Savage 25.00 50.00
NNO Ted DiBiase 17.50 35.00

2016 Mattel WWE Elite Collection Hall of Fame Series 4

NNO Edge 25.00 50.00
NNO Jerry Lawler 15.00 30.00
NNO King Booker 20.00 40.00
NNO Sting 20.00 40.00

2017 Mattel WWE Elite Collection Hall of Fame Series 5

NNO Diesel 17.50 35.00
NNO George The Animal Steele
NNO Jake Roberts 12.50 25.00
NNO Roddy Piper 12.50 25.00

2010 Mattel WWE Elite Collection Legends Hall of Fame Series

NNO Am. Dream Dusty Rhodes 25.00 50.00
NNO Jimmy Superfly Snuka 25.00 50.00
NNO Ricky Steamboat 30.00 75.00
NNO Sgt. Slaughter
NNO Stone Cold Steve Austin 50.00 100.00
NNO Terry Funk 25.00 50.00

2010 Mattel WWE Elite Collection Legends Series 1

NNO Am. Dream Dusty Rhodes 30.00 75.00
NNO Ricky Steamboat 30.00 75.00
NNO Road Warrior Animal 50.00 100.00
NNO Road Warrior Hawk 50.00 100.00
NNO Sgt. Slaughter 25.00 50.00
NNO Stone Cold Steve Austin 40.00 80.00

2010 Mattel WWE Elite Collection Legends Series 1 2-Packs

NNO Bushwhackers 30.00 75.00
NNO Iron Sheik/Nikolai Volkoff 50.00 100.00
NNO Rowdy Roddy Piper
Cowboy Bob Orton 50.00 100.00

2010 Mattel WWE Elite Collection Legends Series 2

NNO Iron Sheik 30.00 60.00
NNO Jake The Snake Roberts 30.00 60.00
NNO Jimmy Superfly Snuka 50.00 100.00
NNO Kamala 20.00 40.00
NNO Ravishing Rick Rude 30.00 75.00
NNO Terry Funk 20.00 40.00

2010 Mattel WWE Elite Collection Legends Series 2 2-Packs

NNO Kerry and Kevin Von Erich
NNO Marty Jannetty/HBK

2010 Mattel WWE Elite Collection Legends Series 3

NNO Brian Pillman 60.00 120.00
NNO British Bulldog 30.00 75.00
NNO Hacksaw Jim Duggan 50.00 100.00
NNO Mr. Perfect 30.00 75.00
NNO The Rock 25.00 50.00

NNO Vader/Black Mask 75.00 150.00
NNO Vader/Red Mask 50.00 100.00

2011 Mattel WWE Elite Collection Legends Series 4

NNO Ax 60.00 120.00
NNO George The Animal Steele 30.00 60.00
NNO Hillbilly Jim 30.00 75.00
NNO Paul Orndorff 75.00 150.00
NNO Smash 60.00 120.00
NNO Ultimate Warrior 30.00 60.00

2011 Mattel WWE Elite Collection Legends Series 5

NNO Akeem 100.00 200.00
NNO Bam Bam Bigelow 30.00 60.00
NNO Macho Man Randy Savage 30.00 75.00
NNO Rick Martel 100.00 200.00

2011 Mattel WWE Elite Collection Legends Series 6

NNO Eddie Guerrero 75.00 150.00
NNO Kerry Von Erich 100.00 200.00
NNO Kevin Von Erich 125.00 250.00
NNO Texas Tornado 75.00 150.00
NNO Ultimate Warrior 30.00 75.00

2015 Mattel WWE Elite Collection Network Spotlight

NNO The Ringmaster Steve Austin 15.00 30.00
NNO Big Boss Man 20.00 40.00
NNO Hunter Hearst Helmsley 15.00 30.00

2016 Mattel WWE Elite Collection Network Spotlight

NNO Bayley 17.50 35.00
NNO Roman Reigns 20.00 40.00
NNO Shawn Michaels 25.00 50.00

2017 Mattel WWE Elite Collection Network Spotlight

NNO Dean Ambrose 17.50 35.00
NNO Finn Balor 20.00 40.00
NNO TJ Perkins 25.00 50.00
NNO Undertaker 25.00 50.00
NNO Vince McMahon 15.00 30.00

2019 Mattel WWE Elite Collection Network Spotlight

NNO Asuka 20.00 40.00
NNO Diesel 17.50 35.00
NNO Jinder Mahal 15.00 30.00
NNO Rey Mysterio 25.00 50.00

2020 Mattel WWE Elite Collection Network Spotlight

NNO Kurt Angle 25.00 50.00
NNO Matt Hardy 20.00 40.00
NNO Ricochet 20.00 40.00
NNO Wendi Richter 12.50 25.00

2017 Mattel WWE Elite Collection NXT Series 1

NNO Austin Aries 20.00 40.00
NNO No Way Jose 30.00 60.00
NNO Seth Rollins 20.00 40.00

2017 Mattel WWE Elite Collection NXT Series 2

NNO Asuka 25.00 50.00
NNO Dash Wilder 17.50 35.00
NNO Scott Dawson 17.50 35.00
NNO Shinsuke Nakamura 15.00 30.00

2018 Mattel WWE Elite Collection NXT Series 3

NNO Alexander Rusev 15.00 30.00
NNO Bobby Roode 20.00 40.00
NNO Ember Moon 20.00 40.00
NNO Roman Reigns 20.00 40.00

2021 Mattel WWE Elite Collection Royal Rumble 2021

NNO Stone Cold Steve Austin 20.00 40.00
NNO Titus O'Neil 15.00 30.00
NNO Ultimate Warrior 30.00 60.00
NNO Umaga 20.00 40.00

2022 Mattel WWE Elite Collection Royal Rumble 2023

NNO Brie Bella 15.00 30.00
NNO Damian Priest 15.00 30.00
NNO Rey Mysterio (red pants) 20.00 40.00
NNO Vader 25.00 50.00

2024 Mattel WWE Elite Collection Royal Rumble 2024

NNO Batista 20.00 40.00
NNO Beth Phoenix 15.00 30.00
NNO Brock Lesnar 20.00 40.00
NNO Ridge Holland 20.00 40.00

2010 Mattel WWE Elite Collection Series 1

NNO CM Punk 75.00 150.00
NNO Edge 30.00 75.00
NNO MVP
NNO Rey Mysterio 75.00 150.00
NNO Undertaker 50.00 100.00

2010 Mattel WWE Elite Collection Series 2

NNO Batista
NNO Matt Hardy
NNO R-Truth 30.00 75.00
NNO Randy Orton 60.00 120.00
NNO Ted Dibiase 40.00 80.00
NNO Triple H 30.00 75.00
NNO Triple H (bottle pack)

2010 Mattel WWE Elite Collection Series 3

NNO Christian 60.00 120.00
NNO Cody Rhodes 30.00 60.00
NNO John Cena 40.00 80.00
NNO The Miz 25.00 50.00
NNO Santino Marella
NNO Shawn Michaels 60.00 120.00

2010 Mattel WWE Elite Collection Series 4

NNO Big Show 25.00 50.00
NNO Chris Jericho/Blue Gear 40.00 80.00
NNO Chris Jericho/Purple Gear 50.00 100.00
NNO Finlay
NNO John Morrison/Bright Red Robe
NNO John Morrison/Dk Red Robe 125.00 250.00
NNO Kane 60.00 120.00
NNO Kofi Kingston

2010 Mattel WWE Elite Collection Series 5

NNO Chavo Guerrero 25.00 50.00
NNO Dolph Ziggler 20.00 40.00
NNO Jack Swagger/No Singlet 20.00 40.00
NNO Jack Swagger/Singlet 30.00 60.00
NNO Mark Henry 20.00 40.00
NNO Rey Mysterio 75.00 150.00
NNO Vladimir Kozlov/Jacket Sleeves
NNO Vladimir Kozlov/No Jacket Sleeves

2010 Mattel WWE Elite Collection Series 6

NNO Batista 50.00 100.00
NNO CM Punk 60.00 120.00
NNO Goldust 30.00 75.00
NNO JTG 45.00 90.00
NNO Matt Hardy 50.00 100.00
NNO Shad 45.00 90.00

2011 Mattel WWE Elite Collection Series 7

NNO David Hart Smith 25.00 50.00
NNO Hornswoggle 60.00 120.00
NNO John Cena 30.00 75.00
NNO Shawn Michaels 75.00 150.00
NNO Triple H 30.00 75.00
NNO Tyson Kidd 25.00 50.00

2011 Mattel WWE Elite Collection Series 8

NNO Drew McIntyre 30.00 60.00
NNO Edge 30.00 75.00
NNO Evan Bourne 50.00 100.00
NNO Sheamus 25.00 50.00
NNO Undertaker 30.00 60.00
NNO William Regal 40.00 80.00

2011 Mattel WWE Elite Collection Series 9

NNO Kofi Kingston
NNO Luke Gallows 25.00 50.00
NNO The Miz 30.00 75.00
NNO MVP 60.00 120.00
NNO Randy Orton 25.00 50.00
NNO Zack Ryder 25.00 50.00

2011 Mattel WWE Elite Collection Series 10

NNO Big Show 30.00 75.00
NNO John Morrison 50.00 100.00
NNO Kane 50.00 100.00
NNO R-Truth 25.00 50.00
NNO Ted Dibiase 30.00 60.00
NNO Yoshi Tatsu 30.00 75.00

2011 Mattel WWE Elite Collection Series 11

NNO Christian 30.00 60.00
NNO CM Punk 50.00 100.00
NNO John Cena
NNO The Miz 40.00 80.00
NNO Rey Mysterio 60.00 120.00
NNO Wade Barrett 40.00 80.00

2011 Mattel WWE Elite Collection Series 12

NNO Alberto Del Rio 15.00 30.00
NNO Daniel Bryan 20.00 40.00
NNO Justin Gabriel 30.00 60.00
NNO Kane FB 50.00 100.00
NNO Papa Shango FB 25.00 50.00
NNO Randy Orton 20.00 40.00

2012 Mattel WWE Elite Collection Series 13

NNO Big Show 25.00 50.00
NNO Cody Rhodes 45.00 90.00
NNO Dolph Ziggler 20.00 40.00
NNO Edge FB 30.00 75.00
NNO Rey Mysterio 75.00 150.00
NNO Sheamus 20.00 40.00

2012 Mattel WWE Elite Collection Series 14

NNO Alberto Del Rio 20.00 40.00
NNO Big Boss Man FB 30.00 75.00
NNO John Cena 30.00 75.00
NNO King Booker FB 25.00 50.00
NNO The Rock 20.00 40.00
NNO Undertaker 30.00 60.00

2012 Mattel WWE Elite Collection Series 15

NNO Evan Bourne 30.00 75.00
NNO Mark Henry 25.00 50.00
NNO R-Truth 30.00 75.00
NNO Rey Mysterio
NNO Sin Cara 30.00 60.00
NNO Yokozuna FB 20.00 40.00

2012 Mattel WWE Elite Collection Series 16

NNO CM Punk 50.00 100.00
NNO Diesel FB 30.00 60.00
NNO Ezekiel Jackson 30.00 75.00
NNO Heath Slater 20.00 40.00
NNO Kevin Nash FB 60.00 120.00
NNO Randy Orton 15.00 30.00
NNO The Rock 30.00 60.00

2012 Mattel WWE Elite Collection Series 17

NNO John Cena 20.00 40.00
NNO Kelly Kelly 30.00 60.00
NNO Kofi Kingston 20.00 40.00
NNO Mankind FB 30.00 75.00
NNO Sheamus 15.00 30.00
NNO Zack Ryder 30.00 60.00

2012 Mattel WWE Elite Collection Series 18

NNO Brodus Clay 10.00 20.00
NNO Jerry Lawler FB 15.00 30.00
NNO Rey Mysterio 50.00 100.00
NNO Sin Cara 75.00 150.00
NNO Undertaker FB 30.00 75.00
NNO Wade Barrett 15.00 30.00

2013 Mattel WWE Elite Collection Series 19

NNO Brock Lesnar 20.00 40.00
NNO Daniel Bryan 20.00 40.00
NNO Dolph Ziggler 15.00 30.00
NNO Kane 30.00 60.00
NNO Miss Elizabeth FB 20.00 40.00
NNO Shawn Michaels 20.00 40.00

2013 Mattel WWE Elite Collection Series 20

NNO	Chris Jericho	20.00	40.00
NNO	Christian FB	30.00	60.00
NNO	CM Punk	50.00	100.00
NNO	Cody Rhodes	20.00	40.00
NNO	John Cena	25.00	50.00
NNO	Santino Morella	30.00	75.00

2013 Mattel WWE Elite Collection Series 21

NNO	AJ Lee	25.00	50.00
NNO	Alberto Del Rio	15.00	30.00
NNO	Honky Tonk Man FB	25.00	50.00
NNO	Randy Orton	17.50	35.00
NNO	Rey Mysterio	60.00	120.00
NNO	Ryback	15.00	30.00

2013 Mattel WWE Elite Collection Series 22

NNO	Big Show	25.00	50.00
NNO	Damien Sandow	12.50	25.00
NNO	The Giant FB	50.00	100.00
NNO	Kane	20.00	40.00
NNO	The Rock	30.00	60.00
NNO	Tensai	15.00	30.00

2013 Mattel WWE Elite Collection Series 23

NNO	Antonio Cesaro	15.00	30.00
NNO	JBL FB	25.00	50.00
NNO	John Cena	20.00	40.00
NNO	Macho Man Randy Savage	25.00	50.00
NNO	Triple H FB	15.00	30.00
NNO	Undertaker FB	20.00	40.00

2013 Mattel WWE Elite Collection Series 24

NNO	Dolph Ziggler	20.00	40.00
NNO	The Miz	12.50	25.00
NNO	Rey Mysterio	30.00	75.00
NNO	Ryback	15.00	30.00
NNO	Trish Stratus FB	30.00	75.00
NNO	Wade Barrett	15.00	30.00

2013 Mattel WWE Elite Collection Series 25

NNO	Brodus Clay	12.50	25.00
NNO	Bruno Sammartino FB	30.00	60.00
NNO	Dean Ambrose	20.00	40.00
NNO	Seth Rollins	20.00	40.00
NNO	Sheamus	15.00	30.00
NNO	Sin Cara	25.00	50.00

2014 Mattel WWE Elite Collection Series 26

NNO	Big E Langston	12.50	25.00
NNO	Jack Swagger	25.00	50.00
NNO	Mark Henry	20.00	40.00
NNO	Road Dogg FB	25.00	50.00
NNO	Roman Reigns	20.00	40.00
NNO	Ultimate Warrior FB	15.00	30.00

2014 Mattel WWE Elite Collection Series 27

NNO	Billy Gunn FB	25.00	50.00
NNO	Fandango	12.50	25.00
NNO	Kofi Kingston	12.50	25.00
NNO	Rikishi FB/Gear on Side	25.00	50.00
NNO	Rikishi FB/Wearing Gear	20.00	40.00
NNO	Rob Van Dam	30.00	75.00
NNO	Undertaker	20.00	40.00

2014 Mattel WWE Elite Collection Series 28

NNO	Big Show	20.00	40.00
NNO	Bray Wyatt	20.00	40.00
NNO	Daniel Bryan	20.00	40.00
NNO	Demolition Crush FB	20.00	50.00
NNO	John Cena	20.00	40.00
NNO	Triple H	15.00	30.00

2014 Mattel WWE Elite Collection Series 29

NNO	Andre the Giant FB	30.00	60.00
NNO	CM Punk	30.00	75.00
NNO	Damien Sandow	15.00	30.00
NNO	Erick Rowan	20.00	40.00
NNO	Goldust	15.00	30.00
NNO	Luke Harper	20.00	40.00

2014 Mattel WWE Elite Collection Series 30

NNO	Batista	20.00	40.00
NNO	Brock Lesnar	15.00	30.00
NNO	Lex Luger FB	20.00	40.00
NNO	Road Warrior Animal FB	60.00	120.00
NNO	Road Warrior Hawk FB	60.00	120.00
NNO	Ryback	15.00	30.00

2014 Mattel WWE Elite Collection Series 31

NNO	Dean Ambrose	25.00	50.00
NNO	Jey Uso	15.00	30.00
NNO	Jimmy Uso	15.00	30.00
NNO	Kane	30.00	75.00
NNO	The Rock FB	25.00	50.00
NNO	Vader FB	50.00	100.00

2014 Mattel WWE Elite Collection Series 32

NNO	Big E Langston	12.50	25.00
NNO	Cody Rhodes	25.00	50.00
NNO	Daniel Bryan	17.50	35.00
NNO	Mark Henry	20.00	40.00
NNO	Rey Mysterio FB	50.00	100.00
NNO	Sin Cara	40.00	80.00

2015 Mattel WWE Elite Collection Series 33

NNO	Batista	25.00	50.00
NNO	Cesaro	12.50	25.00
NNO	Junkyard Dog FB	15.00	30.00
NNO	Roman Reigns	15.00	30.00
NNO	Seth Rollins	12.50	25.00
NNO	X-Pac FB	20.00	40.00

2015 Mattel WWE Elite Collection Series 34

NNO	Bad News Barrett	12.50	25.00
NNO	Doink the Clown FB	20.00	40.00
NNO	Hulk Hogan	25.00	50.00
NNO	John Cena	20.00	40.00
NNO	Paige	25.00	50.00
NNO	Rusev	12.50	25.00

2015 Mattel WWE Elite Collection Series 35

NNO	Diego	10.00	20.00
NNO	Earthquake FB	17.50	35.00
NNO	Fernando	15.00	30.00
NNO	Luke Harper	20.00	40.00
NNO	Randy Orton	15.00	30.00
NNO	Triple H	12.50	25.00

2015 Mattel WWE Elite Collection Series 36

NNO	Bo Dallas	12.50	25.00
NNO	Bray Wyatt	12.50	25.00
NNO	Dean Ambrose	15.00	30.00
NNO	DDP FB	25.00	50.00
NNO	Goldust	17.50	35.00
NNO	Stardust	20.00	40.00

2015 Mattel WWE Elite Collection Series 37

NNO	Brock Lesnar	15.00	30.00
NNO	Dean Malenko FB	17.50	35.00
NNO	John Cena	15.00	30.00
NNO	The Miz	12.50	25.00
NNO	Seth Rollins	25.00	50.00
NNO	Stephanie McMahon	12.50	25.00

2015 Mattel WWE Elite Collection Series 38

NNO	Adam Rose	10.00	20.00
NNO	Bradshaw FB	15.00	30.00
NNO	Daniel Bryan	30.00	60.00
NNO	Faarooq FB	15.00	30.00
NNO	Macho Man Randy Savage FB	15.00	30.00
NNO	Roman Reigns	20.00	40.00

2015 Mattel WWE Elite Collection Series 39

NNO	British Bulldog FB	15.00	30.00
NNO	Damien Mizdow	10.00	20.00
NNO	Dolph Ziggler	25.00	50.00
NNO	Godfather FB	15.00	30.00
NNO	Sting	20.00	40.00
NNO	Sycho Sid FB	12.50	25.00

2016 Mattel WWE Elite Collection Series 40

NNO	Irwin R. Schyster FB	10.00	20.00
NNO	John Cena	25.00	50.00
NNO	Ravishing Rick Rude FB	15.00	30.00
NNO	Sami Zayn	10.00	20.00
NNO	Tyson Kidd	12.50	25.00
NNO	Umaga FB	12.50	25.00

2016 Mattel WWE Elite Collection Series 41

NNO	123 Kid FB	15.00	30.00
NNO	Dean Ambrose	15.00	30.00
NNO	Finn Balor	15.00	30.00
NNO	Lita FB	12.50	25.00
NNO	Ryback	15.00	30.00
NNO	Terry Funk FB	20.00	40.00

2016 Mattel WWE Elite Collection Series 42

NNO	Kalisto	20.00	40.00
NNO	Nasty Boy Brian Knobbs FB	12.50	25.00
NNO	Nasty Boy Jerry Sags FB	12.50	25.00
NNO	Neville	10.00	20.00
NNO	Triple H	12.50	25.00
NNO	Xavier Woods	10.00	20.00

2016 Mattel WWE Elite Collection Series 43

NNO	Alberto Del Rio	7.50	15.00
NNO	Bret Hart FB	25.00	50.00
NNO	Jim Neidhart FB	12.50	25.00
NNO	Kevin Owens	10.00	20.00
NNO	Kofi Kingston	10.00	20.00
NNO	Samoa Joe	10.00	20.00

2016 Mattel WWE Elite Collection Series 44

NNO	Big E	10.00	20.00
NNO	Braun Strowman	20.00	40.00
NNO	Randy Savage FB	15.00	30.00
NNO	Sasha Banks	15.00	30.00
NNO	Sin Cara	30.00	75.00
NNO	Tugboat FB	10.00	20.00

2016 Mattel WWE Elite Collection Series 45

NNO	Bubba Ray Dudley	25.00	50.00
NNO	D-Von Dudley	25.00	50.00
NNO	Lord Steven Regal FB	12.50	25.00
NNO	Narcissist Lex Luger FB	10.00	20.00
NNO	Roman Reigns	15.00	30.00
NNO	Seth Rollins	20.00	40.00

2016 Mattel WWE Elite Collection Series 46

NNO	Booker T FB	15.00	30.00
NNO	Finn Balor	12.50	25.00
NNO	John Cena	12.50	25.00
NNO	Rusev	10.00	20.00
NNO	Sheamus	10.00	20.00
NNO	Stevie Ray FB	12.50	25.00

2016 Mattel WWE Elite Collection Series 47A

NNO	AJ Styles	15.00	30.00
NNO	Asuka	20.00	40.00
NNO	Big Boss Man FB	12.50	25.00
NNO	Cesaro	15.00	30.00
NNO	Kevin Owens	10.00	20.00
NNO	Tatanka FB	12.50	25.00

2016 Mattel WWE Elite Collection Series 47B

NNO	Brian Pillman FB		
NNO	Demon Kane		
NNO	Goldust FB		
NNO	Konnor		
NNO	The Rock FB		
NNO	Viktor		

2017 Mattel WWE Elite Collection Series 48

NNO	Boogeyman FB	25.00	50.00
NNO	Cactus Jack FB	25.00	50.00
NNO	Dean Ambrose	20.00	40.00
NNO	Dolph Ziggler	20.00	40.00
NNO	Erick Rowan	15.00	30.00
NNO	Kalisto	25.00	50.00

2017 Mattel WWE Elite Collection Series 49

NNO	Apollo Crews	15.00	30.00
NNO	Becky Lynch	12.50	25.00
NNO	Big Cass	10.00	20.00
NNO	Brutus Beefcake FB	10.00	20.00

NNO	Enzo Amore	10.00	20.00
NNO	Randy Orton FB	20.00	40.00

2017 Mattel WWE Elite Collection Series 50

NNO	Baron Corbin	7.50	15.00
NNO	John Cena	12.50	25.00
NNO	Rhyno	10.00	20.00
NNO	Shane McMahon	15.00	30.00
NNO	Stephanie McMahon	15.00	30.00
NNO	Warlord FB	12.50	25.00

2017 Mattel WWE Elite Collection Series 51

NNO	AJ Styles	12.50	25.00
NNO	Berzerker FB	7.50	15.00
NNO	Mankind FB	12.50	25.00
NNO	Roman Reigns	12.50	25.00
NNO	Sami Zayn	7.50	15.00
NNO	Scott Hall FB	12.50	25.00

2017 Mattel WWE Elite Collection Series 52

NNO	Braun Strowman	20.00	40.00
NNO	D'Lo Brown FB	12.50	25.00
NNO	Ken Shamrock FB	12.50	25.00
NNO	Kofi Kingston	10.00	20.00
NNO	Seth Rollins	12.50	25.00
NNO	Xavier Woods	7.50	15.00

2017 Mattel WWE Elite Collection Series 53

NNO	Alexa Bliss	15.00	30.00
NNO	Big E	10.00	20.00
NNO	Chris Jericho	10.00	20.00
NNO	Heath Slater	12.50	25.00
NNO	Kevin Owens	10.00	20.00
NNO	The Miz	10.00	20.00

2017 Mattel WWE Elite Collection Series 54

NNO	Bray Wyatt	15.00	30.00
NNO	Charlotte Flair	15.00	30.00
NNO	Jey Uso	12.50	25.00
NNO	Jimmy Uso	12.50	25.00
NNO	John Cena	15.00	30.00
NNO	Rich Swann	15.00	30.00

2017 Mattel WWE Elite Collection Series 55

NNO	Big Cass	10.00	20.00
NNO	Brock Lesnar	25.00	50.00
NNO	Enzo Amore	30.00	60.00
NNO	James Ellsworth	15.00	30.00
NNO	Neville FB	25.00	50.00
NNO	Undertaker	25.00	50.00

2017 Mattel WWE Elite Collection Series 56

NNO	AJ Styles	15.00	30.00
NNO	Jack Gallagher	10.00	20.00
NNO	Karl Anderson	15.00	30.00
NNO	Luke Gallows	15.00	30.00
NNO	Roman Reigns	20.00	40.00
NNO	Samoa Joe	10.00	20.00

2017 Mattel WWE Elite Collection Series 57

NNO	Baron Corbin	10.00	20.00
NNO	Jeff Hardy	30.00	75.00
NNO	Scotty 2 Hotty	12.50	25.00
NNO	Seth Rollins	15.00	30.00
NNO	Shinsuke Nakamura	15.00	30.00
NNO	Tye Dillinger	15.00	30.00

2017 Mattel WWE Elite Collection Series 58

NNO	Braun Strowman	15.00	30.00
NNO	Cesaro	12.50	25.00
NNO	Dean Ambrose	12.50	25.00
NNO	Matt Hardy	25.00	50.00
NNO	Mickie James	17.50	35.00
NNO	Sheamus	12.50	25.00

2017 Mattel WWE Elite Collection Series 59

NNO	Chad Gable	15.00	30.00
NNO	Finn Balor	15.00	30.00
NNO	Jason Jordan	15.00	30.00
NNO	Kurt Angle	12.50	25.00
NNO	The Miz	12.50	25.00
NNO	Zack Ryder	10.00	20.00

2017 Mattel WWE Elite Collection Series 60

NNO	Andre/Giant Machine	20.00	40.00
NNO	Elias	20.00	40.00
NNO	John Cena	15.00	30.00
NNO	Kofi Kingston	12.50	25.00
NNO	Triple H	20.00	40.00
NNO	Xavier Woods	12.50	25.00

2018 Mattel WWE Elite Collection Series 61

NNO	AJ Styles	15.00	30.00
NNO	Big E	12.50	25.00
NNO	Fandango	12.50	25.00
NNO	Kevin Owens	12.50	25.00
NNO	Shane McMahon	15.00	30.00
NNO	Tyler Breeze	12.50	25.00

2018 Mattel WWE Elite Collection Series 62

NNO	Roman Reigns	17.50	35.00
NNO	Braun Strowman	20.00	40.00
NNO	Dude Love	15.00	30.00
NNO	Akam	12.50	25.00
NNO	Rezar	12.50	25.00
NNO	Sting/Surfer Gear	17.50	35.00

2018 Mattel WWE Elite Collection Series 63

NNO	Dean Ambrose	12.50	25.00
NNO	Dusty Rhodes	17.50	35.00
NNO	Kane	12.50	25.00
NNO	Sami Zayn	12.50	25.00
NNO	Shelton Benjamin	20.00	40.00
NNO	Shelton Benjamin Gold Tights CH		
NNO	Shinsuke Nakamura	12.50	25.00

2018 Mattel WWE Elite Collection Series 64

NNO	Curt Hawkins	25.00	50.00
NNO	Curt Hawkins Black Gear CH		
NNO	Jey Uso	15.00	30.00
NNO	Jimmy Uso	15.00	30.00
NNO	John Cena	20.00	40.00
NNO	Samoa Joe	20.00	40.00
NNO	Seth Rollins	25.00	50.00

2018 Mattel WWE Elite Collection Series 65

NNO	Aiden English		
NNO	Aiden English Black Scarf CH		
NNO	Eric Young	17.50	35.00
NNO	Nia Jax	15.00	30.00
NNO	Roman Reigns	15.00	30.00
NNO	Ronda Rousey	20.00	40.00
NNO	Rusev		

2018 Mattel WWE Elite Collection Series 66

NNO	AJ Styles	20.00	40.00
NNO	Erick Rowan	15.00	30.00
NNO	Kevin Owens	10.00	20.00
NNO	Kevin Owens (KO Mania) (CHASE)		
NNO	Kurt Angle	15.00	30.00
NNO	Luke Harper	15.00	30.00
NNO	Nikki Cross	25.00	50.00

2019 Mattel WWE Elite Collection Series 67

NNO	Cedric Alexander FP	12.50	25.00
NNO	Jeff Hardy	12.50	25.00
NNO	Jeff Hardy USA Face Paint CH		
NNO	Randy Orton	10.00	20.00
NNO	Rey Mysterio	15.00	30.00
NNO	Shayna Baszler FP	15.00	30.00
NNO	Velveteen Dream FP	12.50	25.00

2019 Mattel WWE Elite Collection Series 68

NNO	Braun Strowman	12.50	25.00
NNO	Brie Bella	12.50	25.00
NNO	Daniel Bryan	12.50	25.00
NNO	King Mabel FP	10.00	20.00
NNO	King Mabel FP Lightning CH		
NNO	Roman Reigns	12.50	25.00
NNO	Undertaker	20.00	40.00

2019 Mattel WWE Elite Collection Series 69

NNO	Bobby Lashley	10.00	20.00
NNO	Miz	10.00	20.00
NNO	Mustafa Ali	12.50	25.00
NNO	Mustafa Ali (orange pants) (CHASE)		
NNO	Rey Mysterio	12.50	25.00
NNO	Ricochet	15.00	30.00
NNO	Tommaso Ciampa	12.50	25.00

2019 Mattel WWE Elite Collection Series 70

NNO	Demon Finn Balor	15.00	30.00
NNO	Dolph Ziggler	12.50	25.00
NNO	Dolph Ziggler Pink CH	25.00	50.00
NNO	EC3	10.00	20.00
NNO	Johnny Gargano	15.00	30.00
NNO	Seth Rollins/Shield Fatigues	15.00	30.00
NNO	Vince McMahon	15.00	30.00

2019 Mattel WWE Elite Collection Series 71

NNO	Adam Cole		
NNO	Big Show		
NNO	Drew McIntyre		
NNO	Jeff Hardy		
NNO	John Cena		
NNO	Nikki Bella		
NNO	Nikki Bella Red Gear CH		

2019 Mattel WWE Elite Collection Series 72

NNO	Batista		
NNO	Becky Lynch		
NNO	Buddy Murphy		
NNO	Buddy Murphy Black Shorts CH		
NNO	Rey Mysterio		
NNO	Roderick Strong		
NNO	Velveteen Dream		

2019 Mattel WWE Elite Collection Series 73

NNO	Aleister Black		
NNO	Daniel Bryan		
NNO	Elias		
NNO	Gran Metalik		
NNO	Gran Metalik Black Shirt CH		
NNO	Kairi Sane		
NNO	Triple H		

2019 Mattel WWE Elite Collection Series 74

NNO	AJ Styles		
NNO	Andrade		
NNO	Finn Balor		
NNO	Goldberg		
NNO	Lince Dorado		
NNO	Lince Dorado Gold CH		
NNO	Natalya		

2020 Mattel WWE Elite Collection Series 75

NNO	Hurricane	20.00	40.00
NNO	Hurricane White Boots CH	30.00	60.00
NNO	Jeff Hardy	15.00	30.00
NNO	Kalisto	30.00	60.00
NNO	Mandy Rose	20.00	40.00
NNO	Pete Dunne	20.00	40.00
NNO	Seth Rollins	20.00	40.00

2020 Mattel WWE Elite Collection Series 76

NNO	Braun Strowman	20.00	40.00
NNO	Christian Black Shirt CH	20.00	40.00
NNO	Christian White Shirt	20.00	40.00
NNO	John Cena	25.00	50.00
NNO	Lacey Evans	20.00	40.00
NNO	Tucker	15.00	30.00

2020 Mattel WWE Elite Collection Series 77

NNO	AJ Styles	20.00	40.00
NNO	Classy Freddie Blassie RSC	30.00	60.00
NNO	The Fiend Bray Wyatt	25.00	50.00
NNO	Miss Elizabeth	20.00	40.00
NNO	Ravishing Rick Rude Ult. Warrior Tights	20.00	40.00
NNO	Ravishing Rick Rude Yellow Tights CH	30.00	60.00
NNO	Ronda Rousey	15.00	30.00
NNO	Viscera	20.00	40.00

2020 Mattel WWE Elite Collection Series 78

NNO	Drake Maverick	15.00	30.00
NNO	Kofi Kingston	20.00	40.00
NNO	Matt Riddle	25.00	50.00

NNO Naomi	15.00	30.00
NNO Naomi Glow CH	20.00	40.00
NNO Randy Orton	25.00	50.00
NNO R-Truth	15.00	30.00
NNO Superstar Billy Graham TAR	20.00	40.00

2020 Mattel WWE Elite Collection Series 79

NNO Big E	15.00	30.00
NNO Bobby Fish	20.00	40.00
NNO Bobby Fish Black Gear CH	25.00	50.00
NNO Daniel Bryan	15.00	30.00
NNO Io Shirai	20.00	40.00
NNO Roman Reigns	15.00	30.00
NNO Xavier Woods	15.00	30.00

2020 Mattel WWE Elite Collection Series 80

NNO Bayley	25.00	50.00
NNO Erik	15.00	30.00
NNO Ivar	15.00	30.00
NNO Kevin Owens	20.00	40.00
NNO Kyle O'Reilly	20.00	40.00
NNO Kyle O'Reilly Black Gear CH	25.00	50.00
NNO Ricochet	15.00	30.00
NNO Rocky Johnson TAR	20.00	40.00

2020 Mattel WWE Elite Collection Series 81

NNO Angelo Dawkins	15.00	30.00
NNO Bianca Belair	30.00	60.00
NNO Mae Young WM	25.00	50.00
NNO Montez Ford	15.00	30.00
NNO The Rock	20.00	40.00
NNO Shinsuke Nakamura	20.00	40.00
NNO S.Nakamura Black CH	25.00	50.00
NNO Stunning Steve Austin	25.00	50.00

2021 Mattel WWE Elite Collection Series 82

NNO Alexa Bliss	20.00	40.00
NNO Finn Balor	15.00	30.00
NNO Jerry The King Lawler	15.00	30.00
NNO John Morrison	15.00	30.00
NNO Keith Lee	15.00	30.00
NNO Keith Lee White Gear CH	20.00	40.00
NNO Rob Gronkowski	40.00	80.00

2021 Mattel WWE Elite Collection Series 83

NNO Drew McIntyre	15.00	30.00
NNO Dusty Rhodes	15.00	30.00
NNO Edge	20.00	40.00
NNO Edge Black Gear CH	20.00	40.00
NNO King Baron Corbin	15.00	30.00
NNO Michael PS Hayes TAR	20.00	40.00
NNO Sasha Banks	20.00	40.00

2021 Mattel WWE Elite Collection Series 84

NNO Angel Garza	15.00	30.00
NNO Jeff Hardy	15.00	30.00
NNO Jeff Hardy CH	20.00	40.00
NNO Murphy	15.00	30.00
NNO Rhea Ripley	15.00	30.00
NNO Roman Reigns	25.00	50.00
NNO Sheamus	15.00	30.00

2021 Mattel WWE Elite Collection Series 85

NNO Aleister Black	15.00	30.00
NNO Aleister Black CH	30.00	60.00
NNO Becky Lynch	15.00	30.00
NNO Bray Wyatt	20.00	40.00
NNO Karrion Kross	25.00	50.00
NNO Liv Morgan	20.00	40.00
NNO Undertaker	25.00	50.00

2021 Mattel WWE Elite Collection Series 86

NNO Carmella	20.00	40.00
NNO The Fiend Bray Wyatt	25.00	50.00
NNO The Miz	20.00	40.00
NNO Seth Rollins	20.00	40.00
NNO Sid Justice	20.00	40.00
NNO Triple H Purple	15.00	30.00
NNO Triple H Red CH	20.00	40.00

2021 Mattel WWE Elite Collection Series 87

NNO Apollo Crews (blue trunks)	15.00	30.00
NNO Apollo Crews (white trunks) (CHASE)	20.00	40.00
NNO Asuka	15.00	30.00
NNO Braun Strowman	15.00	30.00
NNO Candice LeRae	15.00	30.00
NNO Otis	12.50	25.00
NNO Santos Escobar	12.50	25.00

2021 Mattel WWE Elite Collection Series 88

NNO Kushida	12.50	25.00
NNO Matt Riddle	25.00	50.00
NNO MVP	20.00	40.00
NNO Rey Mysterio	20.00	40.00
NNO Trish Stratus	15.00	30.00
NNO Trish Stratus (Canadian gear) (CHASE)	25.00	50.00

2021 Mattel WWE Elite Collection Series 89

NNO Bobby Lashley	15.00	30.00
NNO Damian Priest	20.00	40.00
NNO Dominik Mysterio	30.00	60.00
NNO Drew McIntyre	15.00	30.00
NNO Nia Jax	12.50	25.00
NNO Nia Jax (purple gear) (CHASE)	15.00	30.00
NNO Sgt. Slaughter	20.00	40.00

2021 Mattel WWE Elite Collection Series 90

NNO Big Bossman	15.00	30.00
NNO Big Bossman (black gear) (CHASE)	25.00	50.00
NNO Bronson Reed	12.50	25.00
NNO Jey Uso	17.50	35.00
NNO Mustafa Ali	15.00	30.00
NNO Randy Orton	15.00	30.00

2022 Mattel WWE Elite Collection Series 91

NNO Austin Theory	20.00	40.00
NNO Bianca Belair	12.50	25.00
NNO Hulk Hogan	15.00	30.00
NNO Kevin Owens	15.00	30.00
NNO Rob Van Dam	12.50	25.00
NNO Rob Van Dam (CHASE)		
NNO Sami Zayn	20.00	40.00

2022 Mattel WWE Elite Collection Series 92

NNO Adam Cole	10.00	20.00
NNO Adam Cole (camo trunks) (CHASE)	20.00	40.00
NNO Burnt Fiend	15.00	30.00
NNO Charlotte Flair	12.50	25.00
NNO Rey Mysterio	12.50	25.00
NNO Ric Flair	12.50	25.00
NNO Scarlett	15.00	30.00

2022 Mattel WWE Elite Collection Series 93

NNO Cesaro	12.50	25.00
NNO Karrion Kross	12.50	25.00
NNO Raquel Gonzalez	12.50	25.00
NNO Ricky Steamboat (white gear)	12.50	25.00
NNO Ricky Steamboat (yellow year) (CHASE)	20.00	40.00
NNO Seth Rollins	15.00	30.00
NNO T-Bar	12.50	25.00

2022 Mattel WWE Elite Collection Series 94

NNO Bret Hart (black tights) (CHASE)	25.00	50.00
NNO Bret Hart (pink tights)	12.50	25.00
NNO British Bulldog	20.00	40.00
NNO Edge	15.00	30.00
NNO Mace	12.50	25.00
NNO Nash Carter	15.00	30.00
NNO Stephanie McMahon	15.00	30.00
NNO Wes Lee	12.50	25.00

2022 Mattel WWE Elite Collection Series 95

NNO Big E	12.50	25.00
NNO Bobby Lashley	15.00	30.00
NNO Eddie Guerrero (black gear) (CHASE)	25.00	50.00
NNO Eddie Guerrero (green gear)	15.00	30.00
NNO Jimmy Uso	30.00	60.00
NNO John Cena	20.00	40.00
NNO Shotzi	20.00	40.00

2022 Mattel WWE Elite Collection Series 96

NNO Brock Lesnar	15.00	30.00
NNO Doudrop (blue gear)	12.50	25.00
NNO Doudrop (metallic green) (CHASE)	20.00	40.00
NNO Hulk Hogan	12.50	25.00
NNO Ilja Dragunov	12.50	25.00
NNO Kofi Kingston	15.00	30.00
NNO Shinsuke Nakamura	12.50	25.00

2022 Mattel WWE Elite Collection Series 97

NNO Alexa Bliss	20.00	40.00
NNO Chainsaw Charlie	15.00	30.00
NNO Omos	12.50	25.00
NNO Ronda Rousey	10.00	20.00
NNO Sheamus	12.50	25.00
NNO Xavier Woods (red He-Man gear) (CHASE)	20.00	40.00
NNO Xavier Woods (white gear)	12.50	25.00

2022 Mattel WWE Elite Collection Series 98

NNO Big E	12.50	25.00
NNO Demon Finn Balor	20.00	40.00
NNO Faarooq	25.00	50.00
NNO Mandy Rose	20.00	40.00
NNO Randy Orton	12.50	25.00
NNO Rick Boogs (grey tights)	15.00	30.00
NNO Rick Boogs (red tights) (CHASE)	20.00	40.00

2023 Mattel WWE Elite Collection Series 99

NNO Boogeyman	15.00	30.00
NNO Boogeyman/Red Head CH	25.00	50.00
NNO Brock Lesnar	15.00	30.00
NNO Happy Corbin	12.50	25.00
NNO Matt Riddle	17.50	35.00
NNO Queen Zelina	15.00	30.00
NNO Seth Rollins	20.00	40.00

2023 Mattel WWE Elite Collection Series 100

NNO Andre the Giant	15.00	30.00
NNO Becky Lynch	15.00	30.00
NNO John Cena	20.00	40.00
NNO Rey Mysterio	12.50	25.00
NNO Stunning Steve Austin	15.00	30.00
NNO The Rock	15.00	30.00

2023 Mattel WWE Elite Collection Series 101

NNO Cody Rhodes	25.00	50.00
NNO Johnny Knoxville	25.00	50.00
NNO Kevin Owens as Stone Cold	15.00	30.00
NNO Mr. America	20.00	40.00
NNO Ricochet	30.00	60.00
NNO Sonya Deville	10.00	20.00

2023 Mattel WWE Elite Collection Series 102

NNO Austin Theory	15.00	30.00
NNO Austin Theory/Black Gear CH	20.00	40.00
NNO Commissioner Mick Foley	15.00	30.00
NNO Edge	20.00	40.00
NNO Gunther	30.00	60.00
NNO Rhea Ripley	20.00	40.00
NNO Sami Zayn	15.00	30.00

2023 Mattel WWE Elite Collection Series 103

NNO Angelo Dawkins	15.00	30.00
NNO Bobby Lashley	15.00	30.00
NNO Liv Morgan	20.00	40.00
NNO Montez Ford	15.00	30.00
NNO Roman Reigns	15.00	30.00
NNO Stardust	15.00	30.00
NNO Stardust/Blue Gear CH	25.00	50.00

2023 Mattel WWE Elite Collection Series 104

NNO AJ Styles	15.00	30.00
NNO Bron Breakker/Pink Gear	15.00	30.00
NNO Bron Breakker/Yellow Gear CH	20.00	40.00
NNO Dakota Kai	15.00	30.00
NNO Drew McIntyre	15.00	30.00
NNO Rick Steiner	15.00	30.00
NNO Solo Sikoa	25.00	50.00

2024 Mattel WWE Elite Collection Series 105

NNO	Braun Strowman	20.00	40.00
NNO	Carmelo Hayes	17.50	35.00
NNO	Carmelo Hayes/Red Gear CH	25.00	50.00
NNO	Dominik Mysterio	15.00	30.00
NNO	IYO SKY	15.00	30.00
NNO	Johnny Gargano	17.50	35.00
NNO	Scott Steiner	15.00	30.00

2024 Mattel WWE Elite Collection Series 106

NNO	Chad Gable	15.00	30.00
NNO	Jey Uso	20.00	40.00
NNO	Jimmy Uso	15.00	30.00
NNO	Paul Bearer/Black Suit	20.00	40.00
NNO	Paul Bearer/Blue Suit CH	30.00	75.00
NNO	Roxanne Perez	15.00	30.00
NNO	Sami Zayn	15.00	30.00

2024 Mattel WWE Elite Collection Series 107

NNO	Cora Jade	15.00	30.00
NNO	Finn Balor	25.00	50.00
NNO	Grayson Waller	20.00	40.00
NNO	Grayson Waller/Black Gear CH		
NNO	Otis	15.00	30.00
NNO	Solo Sikoa	25.00	50.00
NNO	Undertaker	17.50	35.00

2024 Mattel WWE Elite Collection Series 108

NNO	Brock Lesnar		
NNO	Bronson Reed		
NNO	Chelsea Green		
NNO	Chelsea Green/Red Gear CH		
NNO	LA Knight		
NNO	Omos		
NNO	T.Gordy/Executioner		

2018 Mattel WWE Elite Collection SummerSlam 2018

NNO	Dean Ambrose	20.00	40.00
NNO	Edge	12.50	25.00
NNO	Matt Hardy	10.00	20.00
NNO	Seth Rollins	15.00	30.00

2022 Mattel WWE Elite Collection SummerSlam 2022

NNO	Randy Orton	20.00	40.00
NNO	Rey Mysterio	20.00	40.00
NNO	Sensational Sherri	15.00	30.00
NNO	Shawn Michaels	15.00	30.00

2023 Mattel WWE Elite Collection SummerSlam 2023

NNO	Dolph Ziggler	25.00	50.00
NNO	Hulk Hogan	20.00	40.00
NNO	Jey Uso	17.50	35.00
NNO	Zeus	15.00	30.00

2019 Mattel WWE Elite Collection Survivor Series

NNO	Alicia Fox		
NNO	Don Muraco		
NNO	Jeff Hardy		
NNO	Shinsuke Nakamura		

2021 Mattel WWE Elite Collection Survivor Series 2021

NNO	Bayley	20.00	40.00
NNO	Bret "Hit Man" Hart	25.00	50.00
NNO	Hulk Hogan	25.00	50.00
NNO	Keith Lee	20.00	40.00

2022 Mattel WWE Elite Collection Survivor Series 2022

NNO	AJ Styles	20.00	40.00
NNO	Becky Lynch	15.00	30.00
NNO	Drew McIntyre	15.00	30.00
NNO	Ultimate Warrior	20.00	40.00

2017 Mattel WWE Elite Collection Then Now Forever 3-Packs

NNO	Lex Luger/Randy Savage/Sting	30.00	60.00
NNO	The Shield - Seth Rollins Dean Ambrose/Roman Reigns	75.00	150.00

2016 Mattel WWE Elite Collection Then Now Forever Series 1

NNO	Bam Bam Bigelow FB	25.00	50.00
NNO	Rusev	15.00	30.00
NNO	The Rock FB	20.00	40.00
NNO	Tyler Breeze	15.00	30.00

2017 Mattel WWE Elite Collection Then Now Forever Series 2

NNO	Earthquake FB	15.00	30.00
NNO	Macho Man Randy Savage FB	17.50	35.00
NNO	Sami Zayn	7.50	15.00
NNO	Typhoon FB	15.00	30.00

2017 Mattel WWE Elite Collection Then Now Forever Series 3

NNO	Chad Gable	12.50	25.00
NNO	Jason Jordan	10.00	20.00
NNO	Miss Elizabeth	15.00	30.00
NNO	Seth Rollins	12.50	25.00

2020 Mattel WWE Elite Collection Top Picks 2020

NNO	Braun Strowman	20.00	40.00
NNO	Ricochet	20.00	40.00
NNO	Roman Reigns	20.00	40.00
NNO	Seth Rollins	20.00	40.00

2021 Mattel WWE Elite Collection Top Picks 2021

NNO	Drew McIntyre	15.00	30.00
NNO	The Fiend Bray Wyatt	20.00	40.00
NNO	Kofi Kingston	12.50	25.00
NNO	Roman Reigns	12.50	25.00

2021 Mattel WWE Elite Collection Top Picks 2022

NNO	Drew McIntyre	15.00	30.00
NNO	John Cena	17.50	35.00
NNO	Rey Mysterio	25.00	50.00
NNO	Roman Reigns	15.00	30.00

2021 Mattel WWE Elite Collection Top Picks 2023

NNO	Rey Mysterio		
NNO	The Rock		
NNO	Undertaker		

2022 Mattel WWE Elite Collection Top Picks 2023 Wave 2

NNO	Rey Mysterio	15.00	30.00
NNO	Roman Reigns	15.00	30.00
NNO	Seth Rollins	12.50	25.00

2023 Mattel WWE Elite Collection Top Picks 2023 Wave 3

NNO	Bobby Lashley	12.50	25.00
NNO	John Cena	15.00	30.00
NNO	Ronda Rousey	12.50	25.00

2023 Mattel WWE Elite Collection Top Picks 2023 Wave 4

NNO	Jimmy Uso	15.00	30.00
NNO	The Rock	17.50	35.00
NNO	Roman Reigns	15.00	30.00

2023 Mattel WWE Elite Collection Top Picks 2023 Wave 5

NNO	Cody Rhodes	20.00	40.00
NNO	Matt Riddle	15.00	30.00
NNO	Rey Mysterio	15.00	30.00

2024 Mattel WWE Elite Collection Top Picks 2024 Wave 1

NNO	John Cena		
NNO	Roman Reigns		
NNO	Seth Rollins		

2024 Mattel WWE Elite Collection Top Picks 2024 Wave 2

NNO	Cody Rhodes		
NNO	Logan Paul		
NNO	Sheamus		

2018 Mattel WWE Elite Collection Top Talent 2018

NNO	AJ Styles	20.00	40.00
NNO	Braun Strowman	15.00	30.00
NNO	Finn Balor	15.00	30.00
NNO	Seth Rollins	15.00	30.00

2019 Mattel WWE Elite Collection Top Talent 2019

NNO	AJ Styles	15.00	30.00
NNO	Braun Strowman	12.50	25.00
NNO	Finn Balor	12.50	25.00
NNO	Seth Rollins	10.00	20.00

2021 Mattel WWE Elite Collection Top Talent 2022

NNO	Goldberg	8.00	20.00
NNO	Jeff Hardy	12.00	30.00
NNO	Roman Reigns	12.00	30.00

2022 Mattel WWE Elite Collection Top Talent 2023

NNO	Drew McIntyre		
NNO	John Cena		
NNO	Randy Orton		
NNO	Rey Mysterio (gray)		

2017 Mattel WWE Elite Collection Women's Division

NNO	Alexa Bliss	20.00	40.00
NNO	Becky Lynch	20.00	40.00
NNO	Maryse	15.00	30.00
NNO	Sasha Banks	17.50	35.00

2010 Mattel WWE Elite Collection WrestleMania 26

NNO	Jack Swagger	25.00	50.00
NNO	Rey Mysterio	30.00	60.00
NNO	Triple H		
NNO	Undertaker	30.00	60.00

2011 Mattel WWE Elite Collection WrestleMania 27

NNO	Kofi Kingston	17.50	35.00
NNO	The Miz	20.00	40.00
NNO	The Rock	30.00	75.00
NNO	Stone Cold Steve Austin	30.00	60.00
NNO	Undertaker	30.00	75.00

2014 Mattel WWE Elite Collection WrestleMania 30 Heritage

NNO	Bret Hart	25.00	50.00
NNO	Shawn Michaels	30.00	60.00

2015 Mattel WWE Elite Collection WrestleMania 31 Heritage

NNO	Kane	30.00	75.00
NNO	Undertaker	25.00	50.00

2016 Mattel WWE Elite Collection WrestleMania 32 Heritage

NNO	Brock Lesnar	20.00	40.00
NNO	Undertaker	20.00	40.00

2017 Mattel WWE Elite Collection WrestleMania 33 Heritage

NNO	Shawn Michaels	25.00	50.00
NNO	Triple H	15.00	30.00

2018 Mattel WWE Elite Collection WrestleMania 34 Heritage

NNO	Brutus Beefcake FB	7.50	15.00
NNO	John Cena	12.50	25.00
NNO	Kevin Owens	10.00	20.00
NNO	Randy Orton	20.00	40.00

2018 Mattel WWE Elite Collection WrestleMania 35 Heritage

NNO	Sasha Banks	15.00	30.00
NNO	Scott Hall	15.00	30.00
NNO	Triple H	12.50	25.00
NNO	Undertaker	17.50	35.00

2020 Mattel WWE Elite Collection WrestleMania 36 Heritage

NNO	Booker T	20.00	40.00
NNO	Kofi Kingston	15.00	30.00
NNO	Mick Foley	20.00	40.00
NNO	Woken Matt Hardy	12.50	25.00

2021 Mattel WWE Elite Collection WrestleMania 37 Heritage

NNO	Chyna	12.50	25.00
NNO	Edge	20.00	40.00
NNO	Goldberg	15.00	30.00
NNO	Shawn Michaels	30.00	60.00

2021 Mattel WWE Elite Collection WrestleMania 37 Heritage (loose)

NNO	Paul Ellering w/Rocco (Build-A-Figure)		

2021 Mattel WWE Elite Collection WrestleMania 38 Heritage

NNO	AJ Styles	15.00	30.00
NNO	Bret "Hit Man" Hart	15.00	30.00
NNO	Shawn Michaels	12.50	25.00
NNO	Stone Cold Steve Austin	15.00	30.00

2021 Mattel WWE Elite Collection WrestleMania 38 Heritage (loose)

NNO Vince McMahon (Build-A-Figure)

2022 Mattel WWE Elite Collection WrestleMania 39

NNO	Dusty Rhodes	20.00	40.00
NNO	Hollywood Hulk Hogan	25.00	50.00
NNO	Macho King Randy Savage	25.00	50.00
NNO	The Rock	30.00	60.00

2024 Mattel WWE Elite Collection WrestleMania 40

NNO John Cena
NNO Pat McAfee
NNO The Rock
NNO Trish Stratus

2011 Mattel WWE Elite Collection WWE All-Stars 2-Packs

NNO	Jake The Snake Roberts vs. Randy Orton	60.00	120.00
NNO	Macho Man Randy Savage vs. John Morrison	50.00	100.00
NNO	Stone Cold Steve Austin vs. CM Punk	125.00	250.00

2012 Mattel WWE Fan Central

NNO Big Show
NNO John Cena
NNO Kane
NNO Kofi Kingston

2014 Mattel WWE Fan Central

NNO	Daniel Bryan	30.00	60.00
NNO	The Rock		

2014-15 Mattel WWE Fan Central

NNO	Dean Ambrose	12.50	25.00
NNO	John Cena	10.00	20.00
NNO	Randy Orton	10.00	20.00

2015 Mattel WWE Fan Central

NNO Bad News Barrett
NNO Daniel Bryan
NNO Ultimate Warrior

2016 Mattel WWE Fan Central

NNO	Finn Balor	10.00	20.00
NNO	John Cena	7.50	15.00
NNO	Ryback	7.50	15.00
NNO	Triple H	6.00	12.00

2018 Mattel WWE Fan Central

NNO	Finn Balor	12.50	25.00
NNO	Kevin Nash	15.00	30.00
NNO	Randy Orton	10.00	20.00
NNO	Rusev	7.50	15.00

2018 Mattel WWE Flashback Series 1

NNO	Cowboy Bob Orton	7.50	15.00
NNO	Million Dollar Man	7.50	15.00
NNO	Ravishing Rick Rude	7.50	15.00
NNO	Sgt. Slaughter	10.00	20.00

2018 Mattel WWE Flashback Series 2

NNO	Booker T	12.50	25.00
NNO	Lex Luger	10.00	20.00
NNO	Ric Flair	12.50	25.00
NNO	Sting	15.00	30.00

2010-11 Mattel WWE Flex Force

NNO Batista
NNO Big Show
NNO Big Show (card variant)
NNO Chris Jericho
NNO CM Punk (back flippin')
NNO CM Punk (hook throwin' w/belt) (Toys R Us Exclusive)
NNO CM Punk (hook throwin')
NNO CM Punk (super jumpin')
NNO Edge
NNO Evan Bourne (back flippin')
NNO Evan Bourne (flip kickin')
NNO Jack Swagger
NNO John Cena (body slammin')
NNO John Cena (fist poundin' w/belt) (Toys R Us Exclusive)
NNO John Cena (fist poundin')
NNO John Cena (hook throwin')
NNO John Cena (hook throwin') (card variant)
NNO John Morrison (flip kickin')
NNO John Morrison (super jumpin')
NNO Kane
NNO Kofi Kingston
NNO Matt Hardy
NNO Matt Hardy (w/belt) (Toys R Us Exclusive)
NNO Miz (back flippin')
NNO Miz (hook throwin')
NNO Randy Orton (fist poundin')
NNO Randy Orton (flip kickin')
NNO Randy Orton (hook throwin')
NNO Rey Mysterio (fist poundin')
NNO Rey Mysterio (flip kickin' green)
NNO Rey Mysterio (flip kickin' red)
NNO Rey Mysterio (flip kickin' yellow w/belt) (Toys R Us Exclusive)
NNO Rey Mysterio (flip kickin' yellow)
NNO Rey Mysterio (super jumpin')
NNO R-Truth
NNO Shawn Michaels (flip kickin')
NNO Shawn Michaels (hook throwin')
NNO Sheamus
NNO Triple H
NNO Undertaker (fist poundin' w/belt) (Toys R Us Exclusive)
NNO Undertaker (fist poundin')
NNO Undertaker (fist poundin') (card variant)

2011-12 Mattel WWE Flex Force

NNO Alberto Del Rio
NNO Big Show
NNO Christian
NNO Evan Bourne
NNO John Cena (body slammin')
NNO John Cena (hook throwin')
NNO Kofi Kingston
NNO Randy Orton (flip kickin')
NNO Randy Orton (scissor kickin')
NNO Rey Mysterio (super jumpin')
NNO Rey Mysterio (swing kickin')
NNO The Rock
NNO Sheamus
NNO Sin Cara
NNO Wade Barrett

2010 Mattel WWE Flex Force Big Talkin'

NNO CM Punk
NNO MVP
NNO Randy Orton
NNO Triple H

2011 Mattel WWE Flex Force Champions Series 1

NNO John Cena vs. Sheamus
NNO The Miz vs. R-Truth
NNO Randy Orton vs. Rey Mysterio

2012 Mattel WWE Flex Force Champions Series 2

NNO Alberto Del Rio vs. Rey Mysterio
NNO John Cena vs. Undertaker
NNO Randy Orton vs. Kane
NNO Sheamus vs. Kofi Kingston

2010 Mattel WWE Flex Force Deluxe

NNO CM Punk
NNO John Cena
NNO Matt Hardy
NNO Rey Mysterio
NNO Undertaker

2010 Mattel WWE Flex Force DVD Heroes

NNO CM Punk
NNO John Cena
NNO John Morrison
NNO Rey Mysterio

2011-12 Mattel WWE Flex Force Lightning

NNO Big Show
NNO Evan Bourne
NNO John Cena (fist poundin')
NNO John Cena (hook throwin')
NNO Kane
NNO Kofi Kingston
NNO The Miz
NNO Randy Orton
NNO Rey Mysterio (blue)
NNO Rey Mysterio (red)
NNO Sheamus
NNO Sin Cara

2010 Mattel WWE Flex Force Playsets

NNO Breakdown Brawl Ring
NNO Breakdown Brawl Ring (w/Big Show) (Walmart Exclusive)
NNO Colossal Crashdown Arena
NNO Launchin' Entrance Ring

2011 Mattel WWE Flex Force Playsets

NNO High Flyin' Fury
NNO Money in the Bank Ring

2012 Mattel WWE Flex Force Playsets

NNO Tornado Takedown Ring

2010 Mattel WWE Flex Force Smash Scenes

NNO CM Punk
NNO John Cena (body slammin')
NNO John Cena (fist poundin')
NNO Matt Hardy
NNO Randy Orton
NNO Rey Mysterio

2018 Mattel WWE Flextremes

NNO Finn Balor
NNO John Cena
NNO The Rock
NNO Roman Reigns

2018 Mattel WWE Flextremes 4-Pack

NNO	Cena/Rock/Balor/Reigns	15.00	30.00

2011 Mattel WWE Heritage Series

NNO CM Punk
NNO John Cena
NNO Kane
NNO Melina
NNO Randy Orton
NNO Triple H

2011-12 Mattel WWE Legends Mattyshop Exclusives

NNO	Andre the Giant	125.00	250.00
NNO	Arn Anderson	100.00	200.00
NNO	Diamond Dallas Page	60.00	120.00
NNO	King Kong Bundy	125.00	250.00
NNO	The Rockers (Jannetty/Michaels)	200.00	350.00
NNO	Tully Blanchard	100.00	200.00

2017 Mattel WWE Make-A-Wish Foundation

NNO	John Cena	15.00	30.00

2015 Mattel WWE Mighty Minis Series 1

NNO	Bret Hart (blue)		
NNO	Bret Hart (pink)		
NNO	Daniel Bryan	2.50	5.00
NNO	Dolph Ziggler	2.00	4.00
NNO	John Cena	3.00	6.00
NNO	Roman Reigns	2.00	4.00
NNO	Rusev	2.50	5.00
NNO	Seth Rollins	2.00	4.00
NNO	Ted DiBiase	2.00	4.00
NNO	Undertaker	3.00	6.00

2015 Mattel WWE Mighty Minis Series 2

NNO	Brock Lesnar		
NNO	Dean Ambrose		
NNO	Goldust		
NNO	John Cena		
NNO	Kane	2.00	4.00
NNO	The Rock	4.00	8.00
NNO	Stone Cold Steve Austin		
NNO	Triple H		
NNO	Ultimate Warrior (orange)		
NNO	Ultimate Warrior (white)		

2016 Mattel WWE Mighty Minis SDCC Exclusive

NNO	Dean Ambrose	5.00	10.00

2017 Mattel WWE Monsters

NNO	Asuka as The Phantom	7.50	15.00
NNO	Braun Strowman as Frankenstein	12.50	25.00
NNO	Chris Jericho as The Mummy	7.50	15.00
NNO	Jake Roberts as The Creature	12.50	25.00
NNO	Roman Reigns as The Werewolf	10.00	20.00
NNO	Undertaker as The Vampire	12.50	25.00

2018 Mattel WWE M.U.S.C.L.E. SDCC Exclusives

NNO Andre the Giant
NNO Hacksaw Jim Duggan
NNO Iron Sheik
NNO Jake The Snake Roberts
NNO Junkyard Dog
NNO Macho Man Randy Savage
NNO Mean Gene Okerlund
NNO Million Dollar Man
NNO Ric Flair
NNO Rowdy Roddy Piper
NNO Sgt. Slaughter
NNO Ultimate Warrior

2018 Mattel WWE M.U.S.C.L.E. SDCC Exclusives 3-Pack

NNO	WWE Figurines	3.00	6.00

2016 Mattel WWE Mutants

NNO	Bray Wyatt	6.00	12.00
NNO	Brock Lesnar	20.00	40.00
NNO	Finn Balor	12.50	25.00
NNO	John Cena	7.50	15.00
NNO	Stardust	6.00	12.00
NNO	Sting	7.50	15.00

2017 Mattel WWE Network Spotlight

NNO	Big Cass	6.00	12.00
NNO	Brock Lesnar	7.50	15.00
NNO	Enzo Amore	12.50	25.00
NNO	Sting Surfer Gear FB	10.00	20.00

2017 Mattel WWE NXT Series 1

NNO	Andrade Cien Almas	15.00	30.00
NNO	Hideo Itami	7.50	15.00
NNO	Kevin Owens	6.00	12.00
NNO	Sami Zayn	6.00	12.00
NNO	Samoa Joe	7.50	15.00
NNO	Tye Dillinger	6.00	12.00

2017 Mattel WWE NXT Series 2

NNO	Akam	12.50	25.00
NNO	Bobby Roode	10.00	20.00
NNO	Eva Marie	20.00	40.00
NNO	Johnny Gargano		
NNO	Rezar	12.50	25.00
NNO	Tommaso Ciampa		

2017 Mattel WWE NXT Series 3

NNO	Johnny Gargano	15.00	30.00
NNO	Tommaso Ciampa	15.00	30.00

2018 Mattel WWE NXT Series 4

NNO Billie Kay
NNO Paige
NNO Roderick Strong
NNO Triple H
NNO Xavier Woods

2012 Mattel WWE Power Slammers

NNO	Brodus Clay	10.00	20.00
NNO	John Cena		
NNO	Kofi Kingston		
NNO	Rey Mysterio	12.50	25.00
NNO	Sheamus		
NNO	The Miz		
NNO	Zack Ryder		

2010 Mattel WWE PPV Series 1

NNO Batista
NNO Edge
NNO John Cena
NNO Randy Orton
NNO Steve Austin
NNO Undertaker

2010 Mattel WWE PPV Series 2

NNO John Cena
NNO John Morrison
NNO Kofi Kingston
NNO The Miz
NNO Rey Mysterio
NNO Undertaker

2010 Mattel WWE PPV Series 3

NNO Beth Phoenix
NNO Chris Jericho
NNO CM Punk
NNO Cody Rhodes
NNO Edge
NNO Triple H

2010 Mattel WWE PPV Series 4

NNO Batista
NNO Chris Jericho
NNO Drew McIntyre
NNO John Cena
NNO Rey Mysterio
NNO Undertaker

2010 Mattel WWE PPV Series 5

NNO Big Show
NNO CM Punk
NNO Jack Swagger
NNO John Cena
NNO Rey Mysterio
NNO R-Truth

2010 Mattel WWE PPV Series 6

NNO Christian
NNO John Cena
NNO Randy Orton
NNO Rey Mysterio
NNO Sheamus
NNO Undertaker

2011 Mattel WWE PPV Series 7

NNO CM Punk
NNO John Cena
NNO Kane
NNO Melina
NNO Randy Orton
NNO Triple H

2011 Mattel WWE PPV Series 8

NNO	Edge		
NNO	John Cena	20.00	40.00
NNO	John Morrison		
NNO	Rey Mysterio		
NNO	Sheamus		
NNO	Wade Barrett		

2011 Mattel WWE PPV Series 9

NNO	Edge	15.00	30.00
NNO	Great Khali	20.00	40.00
NNO	John Cena		
NNO	Randy Orton		
NNO	Rey Mysterio		
NNO	Triple H		

2011 Mattel WWE PPV Series 10

NNO Alberto Del Rio
NNO Christian
NNO John Cena
NNO Rey Mysterio
NNO R-Truth
NNO Sheamus

2011 Mattel WWE PPV Series 11

NNO Big Show
NNO Chris Masters
NNO Evan Bourne
NNO John Cena
NNO The Rock
NNO Sheamus

2023 Mattel WWE Retro DX 2-Packs

NNO Chyna/Triple H
NNO Billy Gunn/Road Dogg

2023 Mattel WWE Retro NWO 2-Packs

NNO	nWo 2-Pack Box Set	30.00	60.00
NNO	Hollywood Hogan & Syxx	15.00	30.00
NNO	Scott Hall & Kevin Nash	15.00	30.00

2016 Mattel WWE Retro Series 1

NNO	Brock Lesnar	15.00	30.00
NNO	John Cena	20.00	40.00
NNO	Kevin Owens	20.00	40.00
NNO	Roman Reigns	75.00	150.00
NNO	Ultimate Warrior	15.00	30.00
NNO	Undertaker	25.00	50.00

2017 Mattel WWE Retro Series 2

NNO	Kane	20.00	40.00
NNO	Mankind	20.00	40.00
NNO	The Rock	12.50	25.00
NNO	Sting	15.00	30.00
NNO	Stone Cold Steve Austin	15.00	30.00
NNO	Triple H	15.00	30.00

2017 Mattel WWE Retro Series 3

NNO	AJ Styles	6.00	12.00
NNO	Dean Ambrose	7.50	15.00
NNO	Goldberg	6.00	12.00
NNO	Seth Rollins	10.00	20.00

2017 Mattel WWE Retro Series 4

NNO	Finn Balor	15.00	30.00
NNO	Kevin Owens	10.00	20.00
NNO	Ric Flair	30.00	60.00
NNO	Sami Zayn	7.50	15.00

2017 Mattel WWE Retro Series 5

NNO	Big E	7.50	15.00
NNO	Kofi Kingston	10.00	20.00
NNO	Macho Man Randy Savage	12.50	25.00
NNO	Macho Man/Arms Down	12.50	25.00
NNO	Xavier Woods	6.00	12.00

2018 Mattel WWE Retro Series 6

NNO	Bray Wyatt	7.50	15.00
NNO	Daniel Bryan	10.00	20.00
NNO	Shinsuke Nakamura	7.50	15.00
NNO	Sting/Wolfpac	12.50	25.00

2018 Mattel WWE Retro Series 7

NNO	Chris Jericho	7.50	15.00
NNO	Kurt Angle	7.50	15.00
NNO	Shawn Michaels	10.00	20.00
NNO	Sheamus	7.50	15.00

2019 Mattel WWE Retro Series 8

NNO	Braun Strowman	7.50	15.00
NNO	Iron Sheik	7.50	15.00
NNO	Jeff Hardy	7.50	15.00
NNO	Zack Ryder	7.50	15.00

2019 Mattel WWE Retro Series 9

NNO	Goldust	7.50	15.00
NNO	Macho Man Randy Savage	12.50	25.00
NNO	Randy Orton	7.50	15.00
NNO	Samoa Joe	12.50	25.00

2019 Mattel WWE Retro Series 10

NNO	Diesel	10.00	20.00
NNO	Elias	7.50	15.00
NNO	Junkyard Dog	15.00	30.00
NNO	Matt Hardy	6.00	12.00

2018 Mattel WWE Retro Series Playset

NNO Collectible Retro Ring

2018-19 Mattel WWE Retrofest

NNO	Hacksaw Jim Duggan	10.00	20.00
NNO	Honky Tonk Man	10.00	20.00
NNO	Macho Man Randy Savage	12.50	25.00
NNO	Mr. Perfect	15.00	30.00
NNO	Ric Flair	10.00	20.00
NNO	Shawn Michaels	12.50	25.00

2010 Mattel WWE Series 1

NNO Batista
NNO Batista w/Title Belt/1000
NNO Big Show
NNO Big Show w/Title Belt/1000
NNO Evan Bourne
NNO Evan Bourne w/Title Belt/1000
NNO John Cena
NNO John Cena w/Title Belt/1000
NNO Kofi Kingston
NNO Kofi Kingston w/Title Belt/1000
NNO Triple H
NNO Triple H w/Title Belt/1000

2010 Mattel WWE Series 2

NNO	CM Punk		
NNO	CM Punk w/Title Belt/1000		
NNO	Jack Swagger		
NNO	Jack Swagger w/Title Belt/1000		
NNO	Kane		
NNO	Kane w/Title Belt/1000		
NNO	Mark Henry	10.00	20.00
NNO	Mark Henry w/Title Belt/1000		
NNO	Rey Mysterio/Dk Blue		
NNO	Rey Mysterio/Dk Blue w/Title Belt/1000		
NNO	Rey Mysterio/Lt Blue	25.00	50.00
NNO	Rey Mysterio/Lt Blue w/Title Belt/1000		
NNO	Vladimir Kozlov		
NNO	Vladimir Kozlov w/Title Belt/1000		

2010 Mattel WWE Series 3

NNO	Chris Jericho	10.00	20.00
NNO	Chris Jericho w/Title Belt/1000		
NNO	Chris Jericho Alt Head		
NNO	Chris Jericho Alt Head w/Title Belt/1000		
NNO	Great Khali		
NNO	Great Khali w/Title Belt/1000		
NNO	Mickie James	12.50	25.00
NNO	Mickie James w/Title Belt/1000		
NNO	Randy Orton		
NNO	Randy Orton w/Title Belt/1000		
NNO	Shelton Benjamin		
NNO	Shelton Benjamin w/Title Belt/1000		
NNO	Undertaker		
NNO	Undertaker w/Title Belt/1000		

2010 Mattel WWE Series 4

NNO	Dolph Ziggler	12.50	25.00
NNO	Dolph Ziggler w/Title Belt/1000		
NNO	Goldust	12.50	25.00
NNO	Goldust w/Title Belt/1000		
NNO	Matt Hardy	12.50	25.00
NNO	Matt Hardy w/Title Belt/1000		
NNO	MVP	15.00	30.00
NNO	MVP w/Title Belt/1000		
NNO	Shawn Michaels	17.50	35.00
NNO	Shawn Michaels w/Title Belt/1000		
NNO	William Regal	10.00	20.00
NNO	William Regal w/Title Belt/1000		

2010 Mattel WWE Series 5

NNO	Batista	12.50	25.00
NNO	Hurricane	12.50	25.00
NNO	Hurricane w/Title Belt/1000		
NNO	John Cena	10.00	20.00
NNO	Melina	20.00	40.00
NNO	Melina w/Title Belt/1000		
NNO	Mike Knox	25.00	50.00
NNO	Mike Knox w/Title Belt/1000		
NNO	R-Truth		
NNO	R-Truth w/Title Belt/1000		

2010 Mattel WWE Series 6

NNO	Big Show	10.00	20.00
NNO	Drew McIntyre	15.00	30.00
NNO	Edge		
NNO	Kelly Kelly	20.00	40.00
NNO	The Miz		
NNO	Ted DiBiase	12.50	25.00

2010 Mattel WWE Series 7

NNO	Kofi Kingston		
NNO	Michelle McCool	25.00	50.00
NNO	Rey Mysterio	25.00	50.00
NNO	Sheamus		
NNO	Undertaker		
NNO	Yoshi Tatsu	12.50	25.00
NNO	Yoshi Tatsu w/Title Belt/1000		
NNO	Sheamus w/Title Belt/1000		
NNO	Michelle McCool w/Title Belt/1000		

2011 Mattel WWE Series 8

NNO	Chris Masters	15.00	30.00
NNO	Christian	10.00	20.00
NNO	Finlay	12.50	25.00
NNO	Kane	12.50	25.00
NNO	Kofi Kingston	15.00	30.00
NNO	Maryse	30.00	60.00

2011 Mattel WWE Series 9

NNO	Evan Bourne	7.50	15.00
NNO	Jack Swagger	6.00	12.00
NNO	JTG	10.00	20.00
NNO	Mark Henry		
NNO	Natalya	20.00	40.00
NNO	Rey Mysterio		

2011 Mattel WWE Series 10

NNO	Dolph Ziggler	10.00	20.00
NNO	John Cena	12.50	25.00
NNO	Kofi Kingston	10.00	20.00
NNO	Triple H		
NNO	Wade Barrett	7.50	15.00
NNO	Zack Ryder	10.00	20.00

2011 Mattel WWE Series 11

NNO	Big Show	12.50	25.00
NNO	Daniel Bryan	7.50	15.00
NNO	Eve	12.50	25.00
NNO	Sheamus	6.00	12.00
NNO	Skip Sheffield	12.50	25.00

2011 Mattel WWE Series 12

NNO	Alberto Del Rio	7.50	15.00
NNO	Evan Bourne	7.50	15.00
NNO	John Morrison		
NNO	Randy Orton	7.50	15.00
NNO	Rey Mysterio		
NNO	Wade Barrett	7.50	15.00

2012 Mattel WWE Series 13

1	Rey Mysterio		
2	Vickie Guerrero	15.00	30.00
3	John Morrison		
4	R-Truth	15.00	30.00
5	Ezekiel Jackson		
6	Undertaker		

2012 Mattel WWE Series 14

7	Bret Hit Man Hart		
8	Shawn Michaels		
9	Goldust		
10	Rey Mysterio		
11	John Morrison		
12	Alberto Del Rio		

2012 Mattel WWE Series 15

13	Layla	30.00	75.00
14	Kofi Kingston	15.00	30.00
15	John Cena	7.50	15.00
16	Wade Barrett	20.00	40.00
17	Brodus Clay		
18	Kane		

2012 Mattel WWE Series 16

19	Ultimate Warrior	15.00	30.00
20	John Cena	10.00	20.00
21	Eddie Guerrero	17.50	35.00
22	Triple H		
23	Undertaker		
24	Jack Swagger	7.50	15.00

2012 Mattel WWE Series 17

25	Rey Mysterio	15.00	30.00
26	Dolph Ziggler	10.00	20.00
27	Zack Ryder	10.00	20.00
28	The Miz	7.50	15.00
29	Alex Riley	7.50	15.00
30	Mark Henry	10.00	20.00

2012 Mattel WWE Series 18

31	Kelly Kelly	12.50	25.00
32	Sin Cara		
33	Hunico	15.00	30.00
34	CM Punk	10.00	20.00
35	John Cena	7.50	15.00
36	Cody Rhodes		

2012 Mattel WWE Series 19

37	Hornswoggle		
38	Evan Bourne	10.00	20.00
39	Kofi Kingston	7.50	15.00
40	Justin Gabriel	6.00	12.00
41	Jinder Mahal	7.50	15.00
42	Randy Orton	7.50	15.00

2012 Mattel WWE Series 20

43	Natalya		
44	Rey Mysterio		
45	Yoshi Tatsu	7.50	15.00
46	John Cena	7.50	15.00
47	Sheamus	10.00	20.00
48	Wade Barrett		

2012 Mattel WWE Series 21

49	Beth Phoenix	25.00	50.00
50	R-Truth		
51	The Miz		
52	Mason Ryan		
53	Jack Swagger		
54	Big Show		

2012 Mattel WWE Series 22

55	Booker T	12.50	25.00
56	Mark Henry		
57	Chris Jericho	6.00	12.00
58	Christian	10.00	20.00
59	John Cena	7.50	15.00
60	Zack Ryder	7.50	15.00

2012 Mattel WWE Series 23

61	Rey Mysterio	15.00	30.00
62	Alicia Fox	15.00	30.00
63	Hunico	10.00	20.00
64	Santino Marella	7.50	15.00
65	Triple H		
66	Kane		

2013 Mattel WWE Series 24

1	John Cena		
2	CM Punk		
3	Zack Ryder	15.00	30.00
4	Drew McIntyre	15.00	30.00
5	Sheamus		
6	AJ	20.00	40.00

2013 Mattel WWE Series 25

7	Big Show		
8	Brock Lesnar		
9	Randy Orton		
10	The Miz	12.50	25.00
11	Eve	20.00	40.00
12	David Otunga	10.00	20.00

2013 Mattel WWE Series 26

13	Macho Man Randy Savage	12.50	25.00
14	Shawn Michaels	12.50	25.00
15	Undertaker	10.00	20.00
16	Kane	25.00	50.00
17	Mark Henry		
18	Daniel Bryan	10.00	20.00

2013 Mattel WWE Series 27

19	Cody Rhodes		
20	Kofi Kingston		
21	Wade Barrett		
22	Ryback	12.50	25.00
23	Brodus Clay		
24	Antonio Cesaro	10.00	20.00

2013 Mattel WWE Series 28

25	Rey Mysterio		
26	R-Truth	10.00	20.00
27	Heath Slater	10.00	20.00
28	Sin Cara	20.00	50.00
29	Tensai	7.50	15.00
30	Damien Sandow	7.50	15.00

2013 Mattel WWE Series 29

31	Ultimate Warrior		
32	Eddie Guerrero	15.00	30.00
33	Stone Cold Steve Austin		
34	Big Show		
35	John Cena	7.50	15.00
36	CM Punk		

2013 Mattel WWE Series 30

37	The Miz		
38	Hornswoggle	30.00	60.00
39	Santino Marella		
40	Sheamus	10.00	20.00
41	Daniel Bryan	10.00	20.00
42	AJ Lee	20.00	40.00

2013 Mattel WWE Series 31

43	Kane		
44	R-Truth	10.00	20.00
45	Zack Ryder		
46	Rosa Mendes	10.00	20.00
47	Wade Barrett	7.50	15.00
48	Alberto Del Rio	7.50	15.00

2013 Mattel WWE Series 32

49	Chris Jericho	10.00	20.00
50	The Rock	12.50	25.00
51	Randy Orton	12.50	25.00
52	John Cena	7.50	15.00
53	Ryback		
54	Antonio Cesaro	7.50	15.00

2013 Mattel WWE Series 33

55	Big Show		
56	Dolph Ziggler	10.00	20.00
57	Great Khali		
58	CM Punk	12.50	25.00
59	Tamina Snuka	10.00	20.00
60	Dean Ambrose		

2013 Mattel WWE Series 34

61	John Cena	7.50	15.00
62	The Miz		
63	Rey Mysterio		
64	Sin Cara	20.00	40.00
65	Ricardo Rodriguez	12.50	25.00
66	Brodus Clay	7.50	15.00

2014 Mattel WWE Series 35

1	Kane		
2	Damien Sandow	7.50	15.00
3	Daniel Bryan	17.50	35.00
4	Triple H		
5	Cody Rhodes	7.50	15.00
6	Jinder Mahal	10.00	20.00

2014 Mattel WWE Series 36

7 CM Punk 15.00 30.00
8 Big E Langston 7.50 15.00
9 Christian
10 Jack Swagger
11 Fandango
12 Kaitlyn 12.50 25.00

2014 Mattel WWE Series 37

13 Mr. Perfect
14 Batista
15 Roman Reigns
16 Ryback
17 Zeb Colter
18 Randy Orton

2014 Mattel WWE Series 38

19 Chris Jericho
20 Dolph Ziggler 7.50 15.00
21 Vickie Guerrero 10.00 20.00
22 Sheamus
23 The Miz
24 Kofi Kingston 7.50 15.00

2014 Mattel WWE Series 39

25 Bray Wyatt 7.50 15.00
26 Rob Van Dam 12.50 25.00
27 Justin Gabriel 10.00 20.00
28 John Cena
29 Christian
30 Heath Slater 10.00 20.00

2014 Mattel WWE Series 40

31 CM Punk 17.50 35.00
32 Alberto Del Rio 7.50 15.00
33 Rey Mysterio
34 The Great Khali
35 Zack Ryder 7.50 15.00
36 Edge 12.50 25.00

2014 Mattel WWE Series 41

37 Daniel Bryan 10.00 20.00
38 Santino Marella
39 Cesaro
40 Drew McIntyre
41 Bray Wyatt
42 Fandango

2014 Mattel WWE Series 42

43 Natalya 12.50 25.00
44 Batista
45 El Torito 10.00 20.00
46 Big Show
47 Roman Reigns 10.00 20.00
48 Sin Cara

2014 Mattel WWE Series 43

49 Mark Henry
50 Eva Marie 10.00 20.00
51 Rob Van Dam 17.50 35.00
52 John Cena 7.50 15.00
54 Dolph Ziggler 7.50 15.00
55 Rey Mysterio

2014 Mattel WWE Series 44

53 Kane 20.00 40.00
56 Big E
57 Randy Orton
58 Seth Rollins 10.00 20.00
59 Titus O'Neil
60 Goldust 10.00 20.00

2015 Mattel WWE Series 45

1 Triple H 6.00 12.00
2 Chris Jericho 10.00 20.00
3 Mankind 10.00 20.00
4 The Miz 7.50 15.00
5 Ricky The Dragon Steamboat 10.00 20.00
6 Daniel Bryan 15.00 30.00

2015 Mattel WWE Series 46

8 Big Show 12.50 25.00
9 Kofi Kingston 10.00 20.00
10 Bad News Barrett 7.50 15.00
11 Jerry The King Lawler 20.00 40.00
12 Batista 17.50 35.00

2015 Mattel WWE Series 47

13 Alicia Fox 7.50 15.00
14 Rusev 6.00 12.00
15 Brock Lesnar 10.00 20.00
16 Kane 20.00 40.00
17 Christian 10.00 20.00
18 Cesaro 10.00 20.00

2015 Mattel WWE Series 48

19 Ric Flair 10.00 20.00
20 Hulk Hogan 12.50 25.00
21 Brie Bella 10.00 20.00
22 John Cena 7.50 15.00
23 Booker T 15.00 30.00
24 Randy Orton

2015 Mattel WWE Series 49

25 Ryback
26 Bray Wyatt 7.50 15.00
27 Roman Reigns 10.00 20.00
28 Bret Hart 12.50 25.00
29 Bo Dallas 7.50 15.00
30A Emma FP 12.50 25.00
30B Emma FP/Legs Variant

2015 Mattel WWE Series 50

31 Daniel Bryan 10.00 20.00
32 Adam Rose 6.00 12.00
33 Seth Rollins 7.50 15.00
34 Goldust 10.00 20.00
35 Summer Rae FP 15.00 30.00
36 Sami Zayn FP 6.00 12.00

2015 Mattel WWE Series 51

37 Dolph Ziggler 7.50 15.00
38 Dean Ambrose 10.00 20.00
39 Stardust 25.00 50.00
40 Stephanie McMahon 10.00 20.00
41 Stone Cold Steve Austin FB 12.50 25.00
42 Heath Slater 7.50 15.00

2015 Mattel WWE Series 52

43 John Cena
44 Chris Jericho 6.00 12.00
45 The Miz 7.50 15.00
46 Nikki Bella 7.50 15.00
47 Mark Henry
48 Adrian Neville FP 10.00 20.00

2015 Mattel WWE Series 53

49 Brock Lesnar 7.50 15.00
50 The Rock 10.00 20.00
51 Triple H 7.50 15.00
52 Damien Mizdow 6.00 12.00
53 AJ Lee 30.00 75.00
54 Tyler Breeze FP 6.00 12.00

2015 Mattel WWE Series 54

55 Roman Reigns 10.00 20.00
56 The Rock 10.00 20.00
57 Rusev 6.00 12.00
58 Big Show 12.50 25.00
59 Dolph Ziggler 7.50 15.00
60 Tyson Kidd 6.00 12.00

2015 Mattel WWE Series 55

60 Sting FB 10.00 20.00
61 John Cena 7.50 15.00
62 El Torito 20.00 40.00
63 Kane 7.50 15.00
64 Randy Orton 10.00 20.00
65 Bray Wyatt 10.00 20.00
66 Undertaker 12.50 25.00
67 Charlotte FP 15.00 30.00

2015 Mattel WWE Series 56

NNO Dean Ambrose 7.50 15.00
NNO Dean Ambrose/WWE Title
NNO Hideo Itami FP 6.00 12.00
NNO John Cena 10.00 20.00
NNO John Cena/WWE Title 15.00 30.00
NNO Naomi 7.50 15.00
NNO Naomi/WWE Title 12.50 25.00
NNO Ultimate Warrior FB 12.50 25.00
NNO Ultimate Warrior FB/WWE Title
NNO Xavier Woods 6.00 12.00
NNO Xavier Woods/WWE Title

2015 Mattel WWE Series 57

NNO Big Show
NNO Big Show/WWE Title 15.00 30.00
NNO Daniel Bryan 7.50 15.00
NNO Daniel Bryan/WWE Title 12.50 25.00
NNO Erick Rowan 6.00 12.00
NNO Erick Rowan/WWE Title 10.00 20.00
NNO Finn Balor FP 10.00 20.00
NNO Paige 12.50 25.00
NNO Paige/WWE Title 20.00 40.00
NNO Ryback 6.00 12.00
NNO Ryback/WWE Title

2015 Mattel WWE Series 58

NNO Bad News Barrett 7.50 15.00
NNO Bad News Barrett/WWE Title
NNO Bayley 10.00 20.00
NNO Bayley/WWE Title
NNO Edge FB 7.50 15.00
NNO Edge FB/WWE Title
NNO Fandango 6.00 12.00
NNO Fandango/WWE Title
NNO Kevin Owens 7.50 15.00
NNO Kevin Owens/WWE Title
NNO Lana 7.50 15.00
NNO Lana/WWE Title 15.00 30.00
NNO Paul Orndorff FB 7.50 15.00
NNO Paul Orndorff FB/WWE Title
NNO Stardust 10.00 20.00
NNO Stardust/WWE Title
NNO Undertaker 12.50 25.00
NNO Undertaker/WWE Title 20.00 40.00

2016 Mattel WWE Series 59

NNO Bray Wyatt 7.50 15.00
NNO Bray Wyatt/WWE Title
NNO Eva Marie 10.00 20.00
NNO Eva Marie/WWE Title 12.50 25.00
NNO Honky Tonk Man FB 6.00 12.00
NNO Honky Tonk Man FB/WWE Title
NNO Iron Sheik FB 10.00 20.00
NNO Iron Sheik FB/WWE Title
NNO R-Truth 12.50 25.00
NNO R-Truth/WWE Title
NNO Sasha Banks FP 10.00 20.00
NNO Sasha Banks FP/WWE Title
NNO Sheamus 6.00 12.00
NNO Sheamus/WWE Title 7.50 15.00
NNO Triple H 6.00 12.00
NNO Triple H/WWE Title

2016 Mattel WWE Series 60

NNO Brock Lesnar 7.50 15.00
NNO Brock Lesnar/WWE Title
NNO John Cena 10.00 20.00
NNO John Cena/WWE Title
NNO Kalisto FP 12.50 25.00
NNO Kalisto FP/WWE Title
NNO Kofi Kingston 7.50 15.00
NNO Kofi Kingston/WWE Title
NNO Luke Harper 6.00 12.00
NNO Luke Harper/WWE Title
NNO Randy Orton 7.50 15.00
NNO Randy Orton/WWE Title
NNO Renee Young 7.50 15.00
NNO Renee Young/WWE Title 10.00 20.00
NNO Seth Rollins 7.50 15.00
NNO Seth Rollins/WWE Title

2016 Mattel WWE Series 61

NNO Big E 7.50 15.00
NNO Dean Ambrose 6.00 12.00
NNO Dolph Ziggler 7.50 15.00
NNO Finn Balor 10.00 20.00
NNO John Cena 7.50 15.00
NNO Natalya 10.00 20.00
NNO Neville 6.00 12.00
NNO Sami Zayn 6.00 12.00
NNO Zack Ryder 7.50 15.00

2016 Mattel WWE Series 62

NNO Becky Lynch FP 20.00 40.00
NNO The Miz 7.50 15.00
NNO Roman Reigns 10.00 20.00
NNO Sin Cara 20.00 40.00
NNO Sting FB 15.00 30.00

2016 Mattel WWE Series 63

NNO Alberto Del Rio 10.00 20.00
NNO Baron Corbin FP 7.50 15.00
NNO Paul Heyman 12.50 25.00
NNO Rusev 10.00 20.00
NNO Ryback 10.00 20.00
NNO Seth Rollins 7.50 15.00
NNO Sid Justice FB 10.00 20.00
NNO Undertaker 12.50 25.00

2016 Mattel WWE Series 64

NNO Apollo Crews FP 10.00 20.00
NNO Braun Strowman 15.00 30.00
NNO Brock Lesnar 12.50 25.00
NNO Dolph Ziggler 7.50 15.00
NNO John Cena 7.50 15.00
NNO Lana 10.00 20.00
NNO Xavier Woods 6.00 12.00

2016 Mattel WWE Series 65

NNO	Emma	10.00	20.00
NNO	Kane	10.00	20.00
NNO	Kevin Owens	7.50	15.00
NNO	The Rock	12.50	25.00
NNO	Roman Reigns	7.50	15.00
NNO	Samoa Joe	7.50	15.00
NNO	Sheamus	7.50	15.00

2016 Mattel WWE Series 66

NNO	Alberto Del Rio	7.50	15.00
NNO	Big Show		
NNO	Daniel Bryan	12.50	25.00
NNO	Dean Ambrose	7.50	15.00
NNO	Paige	15.00	30.00
NNO	Roman Reigns	12.50	25.00
NNO	Tyler Breeze	6.00	12.00

2016 Mattel WWE Series 67

NNO	Cesaro	6.00	12.00
NNO	Cesaro/Slammy		
NNO	Goldust	10.00	20.00
NNO	Goldust/Slammy	12.50	25.00
NNO	JBL	7.50	15.00
NNO	JBL/Slammy		
NNO	John Cena	7.50	15.00
NNO	John Cena/Slammy	12.50	25.00
NNO	Luke Harper	7.50	15.00
NNO	Luke Harper/Slammy	7.50	15.00
NNO	Naomi	10.00	20.00
NNO	Naomi/Slammy	7.50	15.00
NNO	Randy Orton	7.50	15.00
NNO	Randy Orton/Slammy	12.50	25.00
NNO	Xavier Woods	7.50	15.00
NNO	Xavier Woods/Slammy		

2016 Mattel WWE Series 68A

NNO	Bo Dallas	7.50	15.00
NNO	Bo Dallas/Slammy	7.50	15.00
NNO	Dana Brooke	12.50	25.00
NNO	Dana Brooke/Slammy	7.50	15.00
NNO	DDP FB	10.00	20.00
NNO	Diamond Dallas Page/Slammy	7.50	15.00
NNO	Finn Balor	7.50	15.00
NNO	Finn Balor/Slammy	7.50	15.00
NNO	Kalisto	15.00	30.00
NNO	Kalisto/Slammy	12.50	25.00
NNO	Neville	6.00	12.00
NNO	Neville/Slammy	6.00	12.00

2016 Mattel WWE Series 68B

NNO	AJ Styles	6.00	12.00
NNO	AJ Styles/Slammy	6.00	12.00
NNO	Alexa Bliss FP	20.00	40.00
NNO	Alexa Bliss FP/Slammy	12.50	25.00
NNO	Chris Jericho	7.50	15.00
NNO	Chris Jericho/Slammy	7.50	15.00
NNO	The Rock	10.00	20.00
NNO	The Rock/Slammy	15.00	30.00
NNO	Seth Rollins	7.50	15.00
NNO	Seth Rollins/Slammy	7.50	15.00
NNO	Sting FB	7.50	15.00
NNO	Sting FB/Slammy		

2016 Mattel WWE Series 69

NNO	Bray Wyatt	7.50	15.00
NNO	Bray Wyatt/Slammy	10.00	20.00
NNO	John Cena	6.00	12.00
NNO	John Cena/Slammy	7.50	15.00
NNO	Sami Zayn	6.00	12.00
NNO	Sami Zayn/Slammy	6.00	12.00
NNO	Sgt. Slaughter FB	6.00	12.00
NNO	Sgt. Slaughter FB/Slammy	10.00	20.00
NNO	Tamina	7.50	15.00
NNO	Tamina/Slammy	7.50	15.00
NNO	Triple H	7.50	15.00
NNO	Triple H/Slammy	7.50	15.00

2017 Mattel WWE Series 70

NNO	Apollo Crews	7.50	15.00
NNO	Brie Bella	10.00	20.00
NNO	Carmella FP	12.50	25.00
NNO	Ric Flair	7.50	15.00
NNO	The Rock FB	12.50	25.00
NNO	Roman Reigns	10.00	20.00
NNO	Samoa Joe	12.50	25.00
NNO	Ultimate Warrior	15.00	30.00

2017 Mattel WWE Series 71

NNO	Austin Aries FP	6.00	12.00
NNO	Baron Corbin	6.00	12.00
NNO	Charlotte Flair	10.00	20.00
NNO	Finn Balor	12.50	25.00
NNO	John Cena	7.50	15.00
NNO	Seth Rollins	7.50	15.00
NNO	Undertaker	20.00	40.00

2017 Mattel WWE Series 72

NNO	Dean Ambrose	10.00	20.00
NNO	Dolph Ziggler	7.50	15.00
NNO	Nia Jax FP	7.50	15.00
NNO	Sheamus	10.00	20.00
NNO	Shinsuke Nakamura	7.50	15.00
NNO	Zack Ryder	10.00	20.00

2017 Mattel WWE Series 73

NNO	AJ Styles	10.00	20.00
NNO	Big E	10.00	20.00
NNO	Cesaro	7.50	15.00
NNO	Kevin Owens	10.00	20.00
NNO	Seth Rollins	7.50	15.00
NNO	Triple H	6.00	12.00

2017 Mattel WWE Series 74

NNO	Bayley	10.00	20.00
NNO	John Cena	7.50	15.00
NNO	Kane	20.00	40.00
NNO	Neville	7.50	15.00
NNO	Roman Reigns	7.50	15.00
NNO	Samoa Joe	10.00	20.00

2017 Mattel WWE Series 75

NNO	Braun Strowman	12.50	25.00
NNO	Brock Lesnar	10.00	20.00
NNO	Chris Jericho	6.00	12.00
NNO	Finn Balor	6.00	12.00
NNO	Lana	7.50	15.00
NNO	Randy Orton	15.00	30.00

2017 Mattel WWE Series 76

NNO	AJ Styles	6.00	12.00
NNO	Dolph Ziggler	7.50	15.00
NNO	John Cena	7.50	15.00
NNO	Macho King Randy Savage FB	10.00	20.00
NNO	The Rock FB	12.50	25.00
NNO	Sami Zayn	6.00	12.00

2017 Mattel WWE Series 77

NNO	Corey Graves	6.00	12.00
NNO	Dean Ambrose	6.00	12.00
NNO	Finn Balor	10.00	20.00
NNO	Roman Reigns	10.00	20.00
NNO	Seth Rollins	12.50	25.00

2017 Mattel WWE Series 78

NNO	AJ Styles	10.00	20.00
NNO	AJ Styles/Case	7.50	15.00
NNO	Braun Strowman	20.00	40.00
NNO	Braun Strowman/Case		
NNO	Kevin Owens	7.50	15.00
NNO	Kevin Owens/Case		
NNO	Natalya	10.00	20.00
NNO	Natalya/Case	7.50	15.00
NNO	The Rock FB	12.50	25.00
NNO	The Rock FB/Case	12.50	25.00
NNO	Shane McMahon	10.00	20.00
NNO	Shane McMahon/Case	10.00	20.00

2017 Mattel WWE Series 79

NNO	Baron Corbin	7.50	15.00
NNO	Baron Corbin/Case	7.50	15.00
NNO	Neville	7.50	15.00
NNO	Neville/Case		
NNO	Nia Jax	7.50	15.00
NNO	Nia Jax/Case	7.50	15.00
NNO	Samoa Joe	7.50	15.00
NNO	Samoa Joe/Case	10.00	20.00
NNO	Stone Cold Steve Austin	10.00	20.00
NNO	Steve Austin/Case	15.00	30.00
NNO	TJ Perkins	10.00	20.00
NNO	TJ Perkins/Case		

2017 Mattel WWE Series 80

NNO	Brock Lesnar	7.50	15.00
NNO	Chris Jericho	7.50	15.00
NNO	Chris Jericho/Case	7.50	15.00
NNO	Rich Swann	6.00	12.00
NNO	Rich Swann/Case	6.00	12.00
NNO	Roman Reigns	7.50	15.00
NNO	Roman Reigns/Case	10.00	20.00
NNO	Sasha Banks	10.00	20.00
NNO	Sasha Banks/Case	12.50	25.00

2017 Mattel WWE Series 81

NNO	Dana Brooke	7.50	15.00
NNO	Dana Brooke/Case	7.50	15.00
NNO	Kofi Kingston	7.50	15.00
NNO	Kofi Kingston/Case	7.50	15.00
NNO	Rhyno	10.00	20.00
NNO	Rhyno/Case	10.00	20.00
NNO	Sami Zayn	7.50	15.00
NNO	Sami Zayn/Case	7.50	15.00
NNO	Seth Rollins	7.50	15.00
NNO	Seth Rollins/Case	7.50	15.00

2017 Mattel WWE Series 82

NNO	AJ Styles	10.00	20.00
NNO	AJ Styles/Case	10.00	20.00
NNO	Becky Lynch	15.00	30.00
NNO	Becky Lynch/Case	10.00	20.00
NNO	John Cena	6.00	12.00
NNO	John Cena/Case	6.00	12.00
NNO	Luke Harper	7.50	15.00
NNO	Luke Harper/Case	7.50	15.00
NNO	Shinsuke Nakamura	7.50	15.00
NNO	Shinsuke Nakaura/Case		

2017 Mattel WWE Series 83

NNO	Alicia Fox	7.50	15.00
NNO	Alicia Fox/Case	7.50	15.00
NNO	Kurt Angle	7.50	15.00
NNO	Kurt Angle/Case	7.50	15.00
NNO	Randy Orton	12.50	25.00
NNO	Randy Orton/Case	10.00	20.00
NNO	Triple H	7.50	15.00
NNO	Triple H/Case	7.50	15.00
NNO	Tye Dillinger	6.00	12.00
NNO	Tye Dillinger/Case	7.50	15.00

2017 Mattel WWE Series 84

NNO	Dean Ambrose	7.50	15.00
NNO	Dean Ambrose/Case	7.50	15.00
NNO	Finn Balor	7.50	15.00
NNO	Finn Balor/Case	10.00	20.00
NNO	Kevin Owens	10.00	20.00
NNO	Kevin Owens/Case		
NNO	Naomi	7.50	15.00
NNO	Naomi/Case		
NNO	Rusev	7.50	15.00
NNO	Rusev/Case		

2017 Mattel WWE Series 85

NNO	AJ Styles	10.00	20.00
NNO	AJ Styles/Case	10.00	20.00
NNO	Alexa Bliss	10.00	30.00
NNO	Alexa Bliss/Case		
NNO	Bobby Roode	12.50	25.00
NNO	Bobby Roode/Case		
NNO	John Cena	7.50	15.00
NNO	John Cena/Case	7.50	15.00
NNO	Seth Rollins	10.00	20.00
NNO	Seth Rollins/Case	10.00	20.00

2018 Mattel WWE Series 86

NNO	Akira Tozawa	6.00	12.00
NNO	Charlotte Flair	7.50	15.00
NNO	Dolph Ziggler	12.50	25.00
NNO	The Rock	15.00	30.00
NNO	Roman Reigns	12.50	25.00

2018 Mattel WWE Series 87

NNO	AJ Styles	10.00	20.00
NNO	Bayley	7.50	15.00
NNO	Dean Ambrose	10.00	20.00
NNO	Jason Jordan	6.00	12.00
NNO	The Miz	7.50	15.00

2018 Mattel WWE Series 88

NNO	Baron Corbin	7.50	15.00
NNO	Chad Gable	6.00	12.00
NNO	Elias	7.50	15.00
NNO	John Cena	7.50	15.00
NNO	Sasha Banks	10.00	20.00

2018 Mattel WWE Series 89

NNO	Carmella	10.00	20.00
NNO	Cesaro	6.00	12.00
NNO	Kalisto	12.50	25.00
NNO	Kurt Angle	7.50	15.00
NNO	Sheamus	10.00	20.00

2018 Mattel WWE Series 90

NNO	Aiden English	6.00	12.00
NNO	Kane	12.50	25.00
NNO	The Miz	7.50	15.00
NNO	Roman Reigns	7.50	15.00
NNO	Roman Reigns/Shield Shirt	10.00	20.00
NNO	Ronda Rousey	15.00	30.00

2018 Mattel WWE Series 91

NNO	Alexa Bliss	10.00	20.00
NNO	Dean Ambrose	7.50	15.00
NNO	Dean Ambrose/Shield Shirt		

NNO Drew Gulak	10.00	20.00
NNO Finn Balor	7.50	15.00
NNO Shinsuke Nakamura	7.50	15.00

2018 Mattel WWE Series 92

NNO Jeff Hardy	10.00	20.00
NNO John Cena	7.50	15.00
NNO Mandy Rose	15.00	30.00
NNO Samoa Joe	12.50	25.00
NNO Seth Rollins	6.00	12.00
NNO Seth Rollins/Shield Shirt		

2019 Mattel WWE Series 93

NNO Bayley	7.50	15.00
NNO Jinder Mahal	6.00	12.00
NNO Macho Man Randy Savage	7.50	15.00
NNO Macho Man/White Lightning CH	12.50	25.00
NNO Triple H	6.00	12.00
NNO Undertaker	7.50	15.00

2019 Mattel WWE Series 94

NNO Big E	6.00	12.00
NNO Kofi Kingston	10.00	20.00
NNO Matt Hardy	6.00	12.00
NNO Matt Hardy Mower of Lawn CH	12.50	25.00
NNO Randy Orton		
NNO Xavier Woods	6.00	12.00

2019 Mattel WWE Series 95

NNO AJ Styles		
NNO Bray Wyatt	7.50	15.00
NNO Kurt Angle	7.50	15.00
NNO Rusev	6.00	12.00
NNO Sonya Deville	6.00	12.00
NNO Sonya Deville Black Attire CH	10.00	20.00

2019 Mattel WWE Series 96

NNO Bobby Roode		
NNO Daniel Bryan	7.50	15.00
NNO Kevin Owens	6.00	12.00
NNO Sami Zayn	6.00	12.00
NNO Sami Zayn Arabic CH		
NNO Sasha Banks	10.00	20.00

2019 Mattel WWE Series 97

NNO AJ Styles	7.50	15.00
NNO Bret Hitman Hart	7.50	15.00
NNO Jeff Hardy	7.50	15.00
NNO Miz White Trunks	6.00	12.00
NNO Miz Black Trunks CH	10.00	20.00
NNO Razor Ramon	7.50	15.00

2019 Mattel WWE Series 98

NNO Finn Balor	10.00	20.00
NNO Elias	6.00	12.00
NNO Ruby Riott	10.00	20.00
NNO Tony Nese White Tights FP	7.50	15.00
NNO Tony Nese Gray Tights FP CH	12.50	25.00
NNO Ultimate Warrior	7.50	15.00

2019 Mattel WWE Series 99

NNO Ariya Daivari White Tights CH	6.00	12.00
NNO Ariya Daivari Black Tights CH	7.50	15.00
NNO Becky Lynch	10.00	20.00
NNO Drew McIntyre	10.00	20.00
NNO Rey Mysterio	7.50	15.00
NNO Shinsuke Nakamura	10.00	20.00

2019 Mattel WWE Series 100

NNO John Cena	10.00	20.00
NNO The Rock	10.00	20.00
NNO Stone Cold Steve Austin	12.50	25.00
NNO Shawn Michaels	10.00	20.00
NNO Shawn Michaels Red & White CH	20.00	40.00
NNO Undertaker	12.50	25.00

2019 Mattel WWE Series 101

NNO AJ Styles		
NNO Bobby Lashley		
NNO Ali		
NNO Ali Green Tights CH		
NNO Ronda Rousey		
NNO Sarah Logan		

2019 Mattel WWE Series 102

NNO Constable Baron Corbin		
NNO Drake Maverick		
NNO Drake Maverick (black gear) (CHASE)		
NNO Jeff Hardy		
NNO The Miz		
NNO Seth Rollins		

2019 Mattel WWE Series 103

NNO AJ Styles		
NNO Becky Lynch		
NNO Becky Lynch Orange Shirt CH		
NNO Brock Lesnar		
NNO Kofi Kingston		
NNO Matt Riddle		

2019 Mattel WWE Series 104

NNO Alexa Bliss		
NNO Daniel Bryan		
NNO Keith Lee		
NNO Keith Lee Black Tights CH		
NNO Randy Orton		
NNO Rey Mysterio		

2019 Mattel WWE Series 105

NNO John Cena		
NNO Lars Sullivan		
NNO Paige GM		
NNO Roman Reigns		
NNO Ronda Rousey		
NNO Ronda Rousey (CHASE)		

2020 Mattel WWE Series 106

NNO Carmella	15.00	30.00
NNO Carmella Orange/Purple CH	15.00	30.00
NNO Finn Balor	7.50	15.00
NNO Johnny Gargano	10.00	20.00
NNO R-Truth	10.00	20.00
NNO Triple H	7.50	15.00

2020 Mattel WWE Series 107

NNO Bianca Belair	10.00	20.00
NNO Braun Strowman	12.50	25.00
NNO EC3	12.50	25.00
NNO The Rock	15.00	30.00
NNO Shinsuke Nakamura Black Gear	7.50	15.00
NNO Shinsuke Nakamura Blue Gear CH	12.50	25.00

2020 Mattel WWE Series 108

NNO AJ Styles Red/Gray	15.00	30.00
NNO AJ Styles White/Gold CH	25.00	50.00
NNO Aleister Black	12.50	25.00
NNO Angelo Dawkins		
NNO Montez Ford	7.50	15.00
NNO Roman Reigns	15.00	30.00

2020 Mattel WWE Series 109

NNO Becky Lynch	10.00	20.00
NNO Lana Blue Gear CH	12.50	25.00
NNO Lana Red Gear	7.50	15.00
NNO Ricochet	10.00	20.00
NNO Seth Rollins	7.50	15.00
NNO Undertaker	12.50	25.00

2020 Mattel WWE Series 110

NNO Finn Balor	7.50	15.00
NNO John Cena	10.00	20.00
NNO Kofi Kingston	7.50	15.00
NNO Liv Morgan	15.00	30.00
NNO Mike Kanellis Barbed Wire Tights	7.50	15.00
NNO Mike Kanellis Name on Tights CH	12.50	25.00

2020 Mattel WWE Series 111

NNO Bray Wyatt	12.50	25.00
NNO Erick Rowan	7.50	15.00
NNO Jeff Hardy	10.00	20.00
NNO Kevin Owens	12.50	25.00
NNO Nikki Cross	10.00	20.00
NNO Nikki Cross Gray Pants CH	12.50	25.00

2020 Mattel WWE Series 112

NNO Adam Cole	10.00	20.00
NNO Bobby Lashley	10.00	20.00
NNO Bobby Lashley Red CH	12.50	25.00
NNO Braun Strowman	12.50	25.00
NNO Sasha Banks	20.00	40.00
NNO Seth Rollins	10.00	20.00

2020 Mattel WWE Series 113

NNO Buddy Murphy	15.00	30.00
NNO Drew McIntyre	15.00	30.00
NNO Edge	12.50	25.00
NNO Edge Silver Boots CH	15.00	30.00
NNO John Cena	12.50	25.00
NNO Mia Yim	15.00	30.00

2020 Mattel WWE Series 114

NNO The Fiend Bray Wyatt	20.00	40.00
NNO Kofi Kingston	7.50	15.00
NNO Rhea Ripley	15.00	30.00
NNO Ricochet	10.00	20.00
NNO Ricochet (yellow gear) (CHASE)	12.50	25.00
NNO Shorty G	7.50	15.00

2021 Mattel WWE Series 115

NNO Becky Lynch	12.50	25.00
NNO Big E	6.00	12.00
NNO Braun Strowman	10.00	20.00
NNO Humberto Carrillo	7.50	15.00
NNO Humberto Carrillo Blue/White CH	12.50	25.00
NNO Tegan Nox	10.00	20.00

2021 Mattel WWE Series 116

NNO Dakota Kai	15.00	30.00
NNO Kevin Owens	12.50	25.00
NNO Roderick Strong	10.00	20.00
NNO Roderick Strong Black Gear CH	12.50	25.00
NNO Seth Rollins	12.50	25.00
NNO Sheamus	7.50	15.00

2021 Mattel WWE Series 117

NNO Otis	10.00	20.00
NNO Roman Reigns	10.00	20.00
NNO Toni Storm	20.00	40.00
NNO Toni Storm Red Gear CH	25.00	50.00
NNO Tucker		
NNO Undertaker	15.00	30.00

2021 Mattel WWE Series 118

NNO Austin Theory	7.50	15.00
NNO Austin Theory Red Tights CH	10.00	20.00
NNO Erik	10.00	20.00
NNO Finn Balor	7.50	15.00
NNO Ivar	7.50	15.00
NNO Jeff Hardy	7.50	15.00

2021 Mattel WWE Series 119

NNO Dominik Dijakovic	7.50	15.00
NNO John Cena	12.50	25.00
NNO Lacey Evans Red CH	12.50	25.00
NNO Lacey Evans Yellow	6.00	12.00
NNO Randy Orton	12.50	25.00
NNO Triple H	7.50	15.00

2021 Mattel WWE Series 120

NNO Edge	10.00	20.00
NNO Karrion Kross	10.00	20.00
NNO Pete Dunne	12.50	25.00
NNO Scarlett (trunks and top)) (CHASE)	15.00	30.00
NNO Scarlett (body suit)	12.50	25.00
NNO Shawn Michaels	7.50	15.00

2021 Mattel WWE Series 121

NNO Apollo Crews (black trunks) (CHASE)	12.50	25.00
NNO Apollo Crews (gray trunks)	7.50	15.00
NNO Bayley	6.00	12.00
NNO Kane	12.50	25.00
NNO Rey Mysterio	10.00	20.00
NNO Roman Reigns	7.50	15.00

2021 Mattel WWE Series 122

NNO Charlotte Flair	10.00	20.00
NNO Drew McIntyre	7.50	15.00
NNO Chelsea Green (black gear) (CHASE)	15.00	30.00
NNO Chelsea Green (purple gear)	12.50	25.00
NNO Damian Priest	7.50	15.00

2021 Mattel WWE Series 123

NNO Bobby Lashley	12.50	25.00
NNO Braun Strowman	7.50	15.00
NNO Dexter Lumis	10.00	20.00
NNO Jake Atlas	7.50	15.00
NNO Jake Atlas (white gear) (CHASE)	12.50	25.00
NNO Otis	6.00	12.00

2021 Mattel WWE Series 124

NNO Angel Garza	7.50	15.00
NNO Angel Garza (green gear) (CHASE)	12.50	25.00
NNO Io Shirai	10.00	20.00
NNO Kyle O'Reilly	10.00	20.00
NNO Rey Mysterio	10.00	20.00
NNO Seth Rollins	7.50	15.00

2021 Mattel WWE Series 125

NNO Elias	6.00	12.00
NNO Ember Moon	12.50	25.00
NNO Isaiah Swerve Scott	10.00	20.00
NNO Isaiah Swerve Scott (red shorts) (CHASE)	15.00	30.00
NNO Jeff Hardy	12.50	25.00
NNO The Rock	12.50	25.00

2021 Mattel WWE Series 126

NNO	Bobby Fish	15.00	30.00
NNO	Drew McIntyre		
NNO	Macho Man Randy Savage	12.50	25.00
NNO	Mandy Rose	15.00	30.00
NNO	Mandy Rose (pink gear) (CHASE)	20.00	40.00
NNO	Seth Rollins	10.00	20.00

2021 Mattel WWE Series 127

NNO	Joaquin Wilde	10.00	20.00
NNO	Joaquin Wilde (no face paint) (CHASE)	15.00	30.00
NNO	Keith Lee	12.50	25.00
NNO	Rey Mysterio		
NNO	Santos Escobar	7.50	15.00
NNO	Shayna Baszler	12.50	25.00

2021 Mattel WWE Series 128

NNO	Big E	10.00	20.00
NNO	Edge	7.50	15.00
NNO	MVP	7.50	15.00
NNO	Raul Mendoza	10.00	20.00
NNO	Raul Mendoza (w/face paint) (CHASE)	12.50	25.00
NNO	Sasha Banks	15.00	30.00

2022 Mattel WWE Series 129

NNO	Carmella	10.00	20.00
NNO	Dominik Mysterio	30.00	60.00
NNO	The Miz	10.00	20.00
NNO	Noam Dar	12.50	25.00
NNO	Roman Reigns	12.50	25.00

2022 Mattel WWE Series 130

NNO	AJ Styles	15.00	30.00
NNO	Gran Metalik	10.00	20.00
NNO	John Cena	7.50	15.00
NNO	Johnny Gargano (black & red gear) (CHASE)	12.50	25.00
NNO	Johnny Gargano (The Way)	10.00	20.00
NNO	Omos	10.00	20.00

2022 Mattel WWE Series 131

NNO	Bianca Belair	10.00	20.00
NNO	Candice LeRae (purple gear) (CHASE)	20.00	40.00
NNO	Candice LeRae (The Way)	7.50	15.00
NNO	Happy Corbin	6.00	12.00
NNO	Lince Dorado	12.50	25.00
NNO	Randy Orton	6.00	12.00

2022 Mattel WWE Series 132

NNO	Bobby Lashley	7.50	15.00
NNO	Kushida	15.00	30.00
NNO	Matt Riddle	15.00	30.00
NNO	Rey Mysterio	7.50	15.00
NNO	Tamina (blue highlights)	10.00	20.00
NNO	Tamina (green highlights) (CHASE)	12.50	25.00

2022 Mattel WWE Series 133

NNO	Cedric Alexander (black & gold gear)	7.50	15.00
NNO	Cedric Alexander (red & yellow gear) (CHASE)	12.50	25.00
NNO	Finn Balor	10.00	20.00
NNO	Natalya	12.50	25.00
NNO	Roman Reigns	10.00	20.00
NNO	Stone Cold Steve Austin	10.00	20.00

2022 Mattel WWE Series 134

NNO	Becky Lynch	10.00	20.00
NNO	Indi Hartwell	15.00	30.00
NNO	Sami Zayn	12.50	25.00
NNO	Seth Rollins	10.00	20.00
NNO	Shelton Benjamin (black & white) (CHASE)	15.00	30.00
NNO	Shelton Benjamin (gold standard)	10.00	20.00

2022 Mattel WWE Series 135

NNO	Brock Lesnar	12.50	25.00
NNO	Bron Breakker	25.00	50.00
NNO	Damian Priest	12.50	25.00
NNO	Nikki A.S.H.	10.00	20.00
NNO	Reggie (orange pants)	7.50	15.00
NNO	Reggie (white pants) (CHASE)		

2022 Mattel WWE Series 136

NNO	Cody Rhodes	20.00	40.00
NNO	Dolph Ziggler (pink tights)	10.00	20.00
NNO	Dolph Ziggler (blue tights) (CHASE)	10.00	20.00
NNO	Goldberg	12.50	25.00
NNO	Robert Roode	7.50	15.00
NNO	Xia Li	30.00	75.00

2023 Mattel WWE Series 137

NNO	Aliyah FP	12.50	25.00
NNO	Austin Theory	12.50	25.00
NNO	Commander Azeez	10.00	20.00
NNO	Roman Reigns	10.00	20.00
NNO	Seth Rollins	10.00	20.00
NNO	Seth Rollins/Patterned Tights CH	12.50	25.00

2023 Mattel WWE Series 138

NNO	Drew McIntyre	12.50	25.00
NNO	Edge	12.50	25.00
NNO	Gigi Dolin FP	17.50	35.00
NNO	Jacy Jayne FP	15.00	30.00
NNO	S.Nakamura/Black Pants	10.00	20.00
NNO	S.Nakamura/White Pants CH	15.00	30.00

2023 Mattel WWE Series 139

NNO	Hulk Hogan	10.00	20.00
NNO	John Cena	12.50	25.00
NNO	Liv Morgan	15.00	30.00
NNO	Matt Riddle	10.00	20.00
NNO	Pat McAfee	10.00	20.00
NNO	Pat McAfee/For the Brand CH	15.00	30.00

2023 Mattel WWE Series 140

NNO	Cody Rhodes	12.50	25.00
NNO	Randy Orton	12.50	25.00
NNO	Rey Mysterio	10.00	20.00
NNO	Ronda Rousey		
NNO	Tommaso Ciampa	10.00	20.00
NNO	Tommaso Ciampa/Trunks CH	15.00	30.00

2024 Mattel WWE Series 141

NNO	Bianca Belair	12.50	25.00
NNO	Brock Lesnar	10.00	20.00
NNO	LA Knight	12.50	25.00
NNO	LA Knight/Yellow Trunks CH	17.50	35.00
NNO	The Rock	12.50	25.00
NNO	Seth Rollins	10.00	20.00

2024 Mattel WWE Series 142

NNO	Charlotte	12.50	25.00
NNO	Honky Tonk Man	12.50	25.00
NNO	Honky Tonk Man/Blue Pants CH	17.50	35.00
NNO	Hulk Hogan	10.00	20.00
NNO	Top Dolla	7.50	15.00
NNO	Undertaker	12.50	25.00

2024 Mattel WWE Series 143

NNO	Ashante Adonis	10.00	20.00
NNO	Becky Lynch	12.50	25.00
NNO	Cody Rhodes	17.50	35.00
NNO	John Cena	15.00	30.00
NNO	Mr. T	12.50	25.00
NNO	Mr. T/Black Socks CH		

2024 Mattel WWE Series 144

NNO	B-Fab	30.00	60.00
NNO	Dominik Mysterio	12.50	25.00
NNO	Karrion Kross	10.00	20.00
NNO	Rey Mysterio	7.50	15.00
NNO	Ultimate Warrior	10.00	20.00
NNO	Ultimate Warrior/Yellow Trunks CH	20.00	40.00

2024 Mattel WWE Series 145

NNO	Gunther
NNO	Kane
NNO	Ludwig Kaiser
NNO	Ludwig Kaiser/Red Trunks CH
NNO	Sami Zayn
NNO	Tiffany Stratton

2024 Mattel WWE Series 146

NNO	Bret Hart
NNO	Bret Hart/Black & Pink CH
NNO	Giovanni Vinci
NNO	Kevin Owens
NNO	Roman Reigns
NNO	Shayna Baszler

2020 Mattel WWE Showdown 2-Packs Series 1

NNO	Roman Reigns vs. Finn Balor	15.00	30.00
NNO	Sasha Banks vs. Alexa Bliss	25.00	50.00
NNO	Undertaker vs. Jeff Hardy	20.00	40.00

2020 Mattel WWE Showdown 2-Packs Series 2

NNO	Bobby Lashley vs. King Booker	20.00	40.00
NNO	Randy Orton vs. John Cena	25.00	50.00
NNO	The Rock vs. Triple H	20.00	40.00

2020 Mattel WWE Showdown 2-Packs Series 3

NNO	The Fiend Bray Wyatt vs. Daniel Bryan
NNO	The Giant vs. Ric Flair
NNO	Kane vs. Edge

2021 Mattel WWE Showdown 2-Packs Series 4

NNO	Drew McIntyre vs. Seth Rollins	15.00	30.00
NNO	John Morrison vs. Kofi Kingston	15.00	30.00
NNO	Riddle vs. AJ Styles	20.00	40.00

2021 Mattel WWE Showdown 2-Packs Series 5

NNO	Mankind vs. Stone Cold Steve Austin	15.00	30.00
NNO	British Bulldog vs. Big Boss Man	17.50	35.00
NNO	Chyna vs. Trish Stratus	15.00	30.00

2021 Mattel WWE Showdown 2-Packs Series 6

NNO	Angelo Dawkins & Montez Ford	20.00	40.00
NNO	Shawn Michaels & John Cena	17.50	35.00
NNO	The Usos	30.00	75.00

2021 Mattel WWE Showdown 2-Packs Series 7

NNO	Cesaro vs. Roman Reigns	20.00	40.00
NNO	Kane vs. "Stone Cold" Steve Austin	15.00	30.00
NNO	Rhea Ripley vs. Charlotte Flair	12.50	25.00

2021 Mattel WWE Showdown 2-Packs Series 8

NNO	Bret "Hit Man" Hart vs. Undertaker	25.00	50.00
NNO	Goldberg vs. Drew McIntyre	15.00	30.00
NNO	Street Profits	15.00	30.00

2022 Mattel WWE Showdown 2-Packs Series 9

NNO	Bayley vs. Sasha Banks	20.00	40.00
NNO	The Rock vs. John Cena	25.00	50.00
NNO	Sheamus vs. Ricochet	15.00	30.00

2022 Mattel WWE Showdown 2-Packs Series 10

NNO	The Miz vs. Bobby Lashley	15.00	30.00
NNO	Omos & AJ Styles	12.50	25.00

2022 Mattel WWE Showdown 2-Packs Series 11

NNO	Becky Lynch vs. Bianca Belair	30.00	60.00
NNO	Roman Reigns vs. John Cena	15.00	30.00
NNO	The Usos	30.00	60.00

2023 Mattel WWE Showdown 2-Packs Series 12

NNO	Bobby Lashley/Big E	15.00	30.00
NNO	Charlotte Flair/Alexa Bliss	12.50	25.00
NNO	RKBro	15.00	30.00

2023 Mattel WWE Showdown 2-Packs Series 13

NNO	Gunther vs. Ricochet	25.00	50.00
NNO	New Day	20.00	40.00
NNO	Undertaker vs. Batista	17.50	35.00

2023 Mattel WWE Showdown 2-Packs Series 14

NNO	Cody Rhodes & Austin Theory	30.00	60.00
NNO	Rock & Mankind	20.00	40.00
NNO	Street Profits	17.50	35.00

2010 Mattel WWE Signature Series

NNO	Chris Jericho		
NNO	Dave Batista	12.50	25.00
NNO	John Cena	10.00	20.00
NNO	Shawn Michaels		

2011 Mattel WWE Signature Series

NNO	Edge		
NNO	Edge/Black		
NNO	John Cena	7.50	15.00
NNO	Randy Orton	10.00	20.00
NNO	Rey Mysterio	7.50	15.00
NNO	Triple H		
NNO	Undertaker		

2012 Mattel WWE Signature Series

NNO	Big Show
NNO	CM Punk
NNO	John Cena/Dk Shorts
NNO	John Cena/

Green Wristbands
NNO John Cena/Lt Shorts
NNO Kane
NNO Randy Orton
NNO Rey Mysterio/Gray
NNO Rey Mysterio
Red and White
NNO Rey Mysterio/Red
NNO Sheamus
NNO Sin Cara
NNO The Miz
NNO The Rock

2015 Mattel WWE Signature Series

NNO Bray Wyatt 7.50 15.00
NNO Daniel Bryan 15.00 30.00
NNO Dave Batista 7.50 15.00
NNO Dean Ambrose 7.50 15.00
NNO Hulk Hogan 15.00 30.00
NNO John Cena 7.50 15.00

2013 Mattel WWE Slam City Series 1

NNO Alberto Del Rio
NNO Big Show 15.00 30.00
NNO Brock Lesnar
NNO John Cena 7.50 15.00
NNO Kane 20.00 40.00
NNO Rey Mysterio 15.00 30.00

2018 Mattel WWE Sound Slammers Playset

NNO Destruction Zone 50.00 100.00

2018 Mattel WWE Sound Slammers Series 1

NNO Dean Ambrose 12.50 25.00
NNO John Cena 20.00 40.00
NNO Kevin Owens 12.50 25.00
NNO Roman Reigns 12.50 25.00
NNO Seth Rollins 12.50 25.00

2018 Mattel WWE Sound Slammers Series 2

NNO AJ Styles 10.00 20.00
NNO Bobby Roode 10.00 20.00
NNO Finn Balor 20.00 40.00
NNO Kurt Angle 10.00 20.00
NNO The Miz 10.00 20.00

2018 Mattel WWE SummerSlam Heritage

NNO John Cena 6.00 12.00
NNO Kurt Angle 6.00 12.00
NNO Ric Flair 7.50 15.00
NNO Roman Reigns 7.50 15.00
NNO Shane McMahon 7.50 15.00
NNO Shinsuke Nakamura 12.50 25.00

2014 Mattel WWE SummerSlam Heritage

NNO CM Punk 15.00 30.00
NNO Ted DiBiase 12.50 25.00
NNO Rey Mysterio
NNO Shawn Michaels 12.50 25.00
NNO Triple H 10.00 20.00
NNO Undertaker 12.50 25.00

2016 Mattel WWE SummerSlam Heritage

NNO British Bulldog FB 6.00 12.00
NNO Dave Batista FB 6.00 12.00
NNO Jim Duggan FB 7.50 15.00
NNO Undertaker FB 12.50 25.00

2017 Mattel WWE SummerSlam Heritage

NNO Dusty Rhodes FB 7.50 15.00
NNO Nikki Bella 12.50 25.00
NNO The Rock FB 10.00 20.00
NNO Seth Rollins 7.50 15.00

2013 Mattel WWE Super Strikers

NNO Alberto Del Rio
NNO Big Show 7.50 15.00
NNO Brock Lesnar
NNO CM Punk 10.00 20.00
NNO Daniel Bryan 12.50 25.00
NNO Dolph Ziggler
NNO John Cena
NNO Kofi Kingston 7.50 15.00
NNO The Miz
NNO Randy Orton 10.00 20.00
NNO The Rock
NNO Roman Reigns 15.00 30.00
NNO Ryback
NNO Sheamus 10.00 20.00
NNO Undertaker 12.50 25.00

2012 Mattel WWE Superstar Entrances Series 1

NNO CM Punk 20.00 40.00
NNO Dolph Ziggler
NNO John Cena 12.50 25.00
NNO The Miz 7.50 15.00
NNO R-Truth 7.50 15.00
NNO Randy Orton 12.50 25.00
NNO Triple H 10.00 20.00

2013 Mattel WWE Superstar Entrances Series 2

NNO Daniel Bryan 15.00 30.00
NNO John Cena 10.00 20.00
NNO Ryback
NNO Santino Marella
NNO The Rock 10.00 20.00
NNO Zack Ryder

2014 Mattel WWE Superstar Entrances Series 3

NNO Brock Lesnar 10.00 20.00
NNO CM Punk 20.00 40.00
NNO Cody Rhodes 15.00 30.00
NNO John Cena 10.00 20.00
NNO Macho Man Randy Savage 15.00 30.00
NNO Sheamus 10.00 20.00
NNO The Rock 10.00 20.00

2014 Mattel WWE Superstar Entrances Series 4

NNO AJ Lee 30.00 60.00
NNO Daniel Bryan 15.00 30.00
NNO Dolph Ziggler
NNO John Cena 10.00 20.00
NNO Rob Van Dam 15.00 30.00
NNO The Rock 7.50 15.00

2015 Mattel WWE Superstar Entrances Series 5

NNO Daniel Bryan 15.00 30.00
NNO John Cena 10.00 20.00
NNO Randy Orton 10.00 20.00
NNO Rowdy Roddy Piper 15.00 30.00
NNO Triple H 7.50 15.00

2015 Mattel WWE Superstar Entrances Series 6

NNO Bo Dallas 7.50 15.00
NNO Hulk Hogan 20.00 40.00
NNO John Cena 10.00 20.00
NNO Kofi Kingston 7.50 15.00
NNO Wade Barrett 6.00 12.00

2011 Mattel WWE Superstar Matchups Series 4

NNO Rey Mysterio/
Blue and White
NNO Rey Mysterio/Black and Blue
NNO Sin Cara

2017 Mattel WWE Superstars Dolls 12-Inch

NNO Alicia Fox
NNO Asuka
NNO Bayley
NNO Becky Lynch 15.00 30.00
NNO Carmella
NNO Charlotte Flair 12.50 25.00
NNO Eva Marie 10.00 20.00
NNO Lana
NNO Natalya

2017 Mattel WWE Superstars Dolls 12-Inch Fashions

NNO Alexa Bliss
NNO Bayley
NNO Becky Lynch
NNO Brie Bella 12.50 25.00
NNO Natalya 12.50 25.00
NNO Nikki Bella 15.00 30.00
NNO Sasha Banks 12.50 25.00

2017 Mattel WWE Superstars Dolls 12-Inch Multi-Packs

NNO Charlotte Flair/Sasha Banks SDCC
NNO Natalya/Becky Lynch/Sasha Banks/Bellas

2017 Mattel WWE Superstars Dolls Action Figures Playset

NNO Ultimate Entrance Playset (w/Nikki Bella)

2017 Mattel WWE Superstars Dolls Action Figures Series 1

NNO Brie Bella
NNO Charlotte Flair
NNO Nikki Bella

2017 Mattel WWE Superstars Dolls Action Figures Series 2

NNO Alexa Bliss
NNO Brie Bella
NNO Natalya
NNO Nikki Bella

2017 Mattel WWE Superstars Dolls Action Figures Ultimate Fan Packs

NNO Bayley
NNO Charlotte Flair
NNO Sasha Banks

2022 Mattel WWE Superstars Series 1

NNO Bray Wyatt
NNO Hollywood Hogan
NNO Honky Tonk Man
NNO Ric Flair

2022 Mattel WWE Superstars Series 2

NNO Kevin Nash
NNO Scott Hall
NNO Shawn Michaels
NNO Ultimate Warrior

2022 Mattel WWE Superstars Series 3

NNO Mankind
NNO Million Dollar Man
NNO Papa Shango
NNO Undertaker

2022 Mattel WWE Superstars Series 4

NNO Macho Man
NNO Mr. T
NNO The Rock
NNO Typhoon

2023 Mattel WWE Superstars Series 5

NNO Earthquake 15.00 30.00
NNO Macho Man 17.50 35.00
NNO Ravishing Rick Rude 17.50 35.00
NNO The Rock 25.00 50.00

2023 Mattel WWE Superstars Series 6

NNO Bam Bam Bigelow 25.00 50.00
NNO Hulk Hogan 30.00 60.00
NNO Mr. Perfect 20.00 40.00
NNO Rowdy Roddy Piper 17.50 35.00

2023 Mattel WWE Superstars Series 7

NNO Captain Lou Albano 20.00 40.00
NNO Hulk Hogan 25.00 50.00
NNO Hulk Hogan/Blue Tights CH 30.00 75.00
NNO Rowdy Roddy Piper 20.00 40.00
NNO Vader 20.00 40.00

2023 Mattel WWE Superstars Series 8

NNO Andre the Giant 50.00 100.00
NNO Doink the Clown 40.00 80.00
NNO Hulk Hogan 25.00 50.00
NNO Hulk Hogan/Blue Tights CH 40.00 80.00

2017 Mattel WWE Surf's Up 2 WaveMania Action Figure DVD Combo

NNO Batista
NNO Big Show
NNO Bray Wyatt
NNO Daniel Bryan
NNO Dean Ambrose (black shirt)
NNO Dean Ambrose (white shirt)
NNO Dolph Ziggler
NNO El Torito
NNO Goldust

NNO John Cena (black shorts)
NNO John Cena (blue shorts)
NNO John Cena (green shorts)
NNO John Cena (tan shorts/blue armband)
NNO John Cena (tan shorts/red armband)
NNO Justin Gabriel
NNO Kane
NNO Mankind
NNO Miz
NNO Randy Orton
NNO Rey Mysterio
NNO Ric Flair
NNO Ricky "The Dragon" Steamboat
NNO Roman Reigns
NNO Rusev
NNO Ryback
NNO Santino Marella
NNO Seth Rollins
NNO Titus O'Neill
NNO Triple H

2013 Mattel WWE Survivor Series 2013

NNO CM Punk
NNO Ryback

2019 Mattel WWE Tag Team Buddies Plush Dolls 14"

NNO Bayley
NNO Becky Lynch
NNO Sasha Banks

2016 Mattel WWE Teenage Mutant Ninja Turtles Ninja Superstars Series 1

NNO Donatello as Undertaker 15.00 30.00
NNO Leonardo as John Cena 10.00 20.00
NNO Michelangelo as Macho Man Randy Savage12.50 25.00
NNO Raphael as Sting 12.50 25.00

2017 Mattel WWE Teenage Mutant Ninja Turtles Ninja Superstars Series 2

NNO Donatello as Ultimate Warrior 12.50 25.00
NNO Leonardo as Finn Balor 10.00 20.00
NNO Michelangelo as Rowdy Roddy Piper7.50 15.00
NNO Raphael as The Rock 15.00 30.00

2016 Mattel WWE Then Now Forever Series 1

NNO Chris Jericho 6.00 12.00
NNO Seth Rollins 10.00 20.00
NNO Sin Cara 40.00 80.00
NNO Undertaker 15.00 30.00

2017 Mattel WWE Then Now Forever Series 2

NNO Neville 6.00 12.00
NNO Sheamus 10.00 20.00
NNO Stone Cold Steve Austin FB 10.00 20.00
NNO Ultimate Warrior FB 12.50 25.00

2017 Mattel WWE Then Now Forever Series 3

NNO Bray Wyatt 7.50 15.00
NNO Kevin Owens 6.00 12.00
NNO Seth Rollins 10.00 20.00
NNO Triple H 12.50 25.00
NNO X-Pac 12.50 25.00

2013 Mattel WWE TLC 2013

NNO Alberto Del Rio
NNO Kofi Kingston
NNO Mark Henry
NNO Sheamus

2020 Mattel WWE Top Picks 2020

NNO John Cena 15.00 30.00
NNO Kofi Kingston 15.00 30.00
NNO The Rock 20.00 40.00
NNO Roman Reigns 12.50 25.00

2021 Mattel WWE Top Picks 2021

NNO Braun Strowman
NNO John Cena
NNO The Rock
NNO Roman Reigns

2021 Mattel WWE Top Picks 2022

NNO Drew McIntyre 6.00 12.00
NNO The Fiend Bray Wyatt 6.00 12.00
NNO John Cena 12.50 25.00
NNO The Rock 12.00 30.00

2022 Mattel WWE Top Picks 2023

NNO Bray Wyatt
NNO Roman Reigns
NNO Undertaker

2022 Mattel WWE Top Picks 2023 Wave 2

NNO John Cena
NNO Randy Orton
NNO Rey Mysterio

2023 Mattel WWE Top Picks 2023 Wave 3

NNO AJ Styles
NNO Brock Lesnar
NNO The Rock

2023 Mattel WWE Top Picks 2023 Wave 4

NNO Cody Rhodes
NNO Matt Riddle
NNO Roman Reigns

2024 Mattel WWE Top Picks 2024 Wave 2

NNO The Rock
NNO Seth Rollins
NNO Undertaker

2018 Mattel WWE Top Talent 2018

NNO AJ Styles 15.00 20.00
NNO John Cena 7.50 15.00
NNO Roman Reigns 7.50 15.00
NNO Seth Rollins 6.00 12.00

2019 Mattel WWE Top Talent 2019

NNO AJ Styles
NNO Jeff Hardy 7.50 15.00
NNO John Cena 12.50 25.00
NNO Seth Rollins 7.50 15.00

2020 Mattel WWE Top Talent 2020

NNO AJ Styles
NNO Braun Strowman 15.00 30.00
NNO Finn Balor
NNO John Cena 12.50 25.00

2021 Mattel WWE Top Talent 2022

NNO John Cena
NNO The Rock
NNO Roman Reigns

2022 Mattel WWE Top Talent 2023

NNO Brock Lesnar
NNO Rock
NNO Seth Rollins

2017 Mattel WWE Tough Talkers Series 1

NNO Bray Wyatt 15.00 30.00
NNO Dean Ambrose 12.50 25.00
NNO John Cena 15.00 30.00
NNO Kevin Owens 10.00 20.00
NNO Roman Reigns 12.50 25.00
NNO Seth Rollins 12.50 25.00

2017 Mattel WWE Tough Talkers Series 2

NNO Big E 7.50 15.00
NNO Brock Lesnar 12.50 25.00
NNO Dean Ambrose 12.50 25.00
NNO John Cena 20.00 40.00
NNO Kofi Kingston 10.00 20.00
NNO Xavier Woods 10.00 20.00

2017 Mattel WWE Tough Talkers 2-Packs Series 1

NNO The Rock/Stone Cold Steve Austin25.00 50.00
NNO Undertaker/Brock Lesnar 25.00 50.00

2017 Mattel WWE Tough Talkers 2-Packs Series 2

NNO AJ Styles/Seth Rollins 20.00 40.00
NNO Triple H/Roman Reigns 17.50 35.00

2017 Mattel WWE Tough Talkers Hall of Fame Series

NNO Macho Man Randy Savage 12.50 25.00
NNO Ric Flair 12.50 25.00
NNO Rowdy Roddy Piper 12.50 25.00

2017 Mattel WWE Tough Talkers Total Tag Team

NNO AJ Styles 15.00 30.00
NNO Randy Orton 12.50 25.00
NNO Sting 12.50 25.00
NNO Xavier Woods 10.00 20.00

2017 Mattel WWE Tough Talkers Total Tag Team 2-Packs

NNO Big E/Kofi Kingston 17.50 35.00
NNO Kevin Owens & Chris Jericho 15.00 30.00

2012 Mattel WWE Tribute to the Troops

NNO Big Show/Brown Hat
NNO Big Show/Green Hat
NNO John Cena 12.50 25.00
NNO Randy Orton/Brown Vest 10.00 20.00
NNO Randy Orton/Green Vest 10.00 20.00
NNO Rey Mysterio 20.00 40.00

2010 Mattel WWE Triple Threat 3-Packs

NNO Evan Bourne/Swagger/Kozlov
NNO John Cena/Batista/Y2J
NNO Kane/John Cena/Big Show
NNO Kane/Triple H/Great Khali
NNO Sheamus/John Cena/Triple H

2018 Mattel WWE True Moves 12-Inch

NNO AJ Styles 12.50 25.00
NNO Kane 10.00 20.00
NNO Randy Orton 10.00 20.00
NNO Kevin Owens 12.50 25.00
NNO Kurt Angle 10.00 20.00
NNO Kalisto 15.00 30.00
NNO Seth Rollins 12.50 25.00

2023 Mattel WWE Ultimate Edition Exclusives

NNO Jey Uso 30.00 60.00
NNO Jimmy Uso 30.00 60.00
NNO Usos 2-Pack 60.00 125.00

2021 Mattel WWE Ultimate Edition SDCC Exclusive

NNO Sgt. Slaughter 75.00 150.00

2019 Mattel WWE Ultimate Edition Series 1

NNO Ultimate Warrior 20.00 40.00
NNO Ronda Rousey 25.00 50.00

2019 Mattel WWE Ultimate Edition Series 2

NNO Bret "Hitman" Hart 25.00 50.00
NNO Shinsuke Nakamura 20.00 40.00

2019 Mattel WWE Ultimate Edition Series 3

NNO Finn Balor
NNO Triple H

2020 Mattel WWE Ultimate Edition Series 4

NNO Brock Lesnar 30.00 60.00
NNO Shawn Michaels 60.00 120.00

2020 Mattel WWE Ultimate Edition Series 5

NNO Becky Lynch 30.00 60.00
NNO John Cena 40.00 80.00

2020 Mattel WWE Ultimate Edition Series 6

NNO Charlotte Flair 30.00 60.00
NNO The Rock 60.00 120.00
(Amazon Exclusive)

2020 Mattel WWE Ultimate Edition Series 7

NNO The Fiend Bray Wyatt 30.00 75.00
NNO Hollywood Hulk Hogan 50.00 100.00

2021 Mattel WWE Ultimate Edition Series 8

NNO Edge 25.00 50.00
NNO Macho Man Randy Savage 25.00 50.00

2021 Mattel WWE Ultimate Edition Series 9

NNO Stone Cold Steve Austin 30.00 60.00
NNO Ric Flair 30.00 75.00

2021 Mattel WWE Ultimate Edition Series 10

NNO John Cena 20.00 40.00
NNO The Rock 25.00 50.00

2021 Mattel WWE Ultimate Edition Series 11

NNO Kane 30.00 60.00
NNO Undertaker 30.00 60.00

2022 Mattel WWE Ultimate Edition Series 12

NNO Alexa Bliss 20.00 40.00
NNO The Fiend Bray Wyatt 25.00 50.00

2022 Mattel WWE Ultimate Edition Series 13

NNO Hulk Hogan 25.00 50.00
NNO Mr. T 20.00 40.00

2022 Mattel WWE Ultimate Edition Series 14

NNO Jeff Hardy 20.00 40.00
NNO Roman Reigns 20.00 40.00

2022 Mattel WWE Ultimate Edition Series 15

NNO Brock Lesnar 30.00 60.00
NNO Ultimate Warrior 25.00 50.00

2023 Mattel WWE Ultimate Edition Series 16

NNO AJ Styles 25.00 50.00
NNO Razor Ramon 25.00 50.00
NNO Razor Ramon/Purple Gear CH 30.00 75.00

2023 Mattel WWE Ultimate Edition Series 17

NNO Andre the Giant 40.00 80.00
NNO Seth Rollins 25.00 60.00

2023 Mattel WWE Ultimate Edition Series 18

NNO Randy Orton 25.00 50.00

2024 Mattel WWE Ultimate Edition Series 19

NNO Bianca Belair
NNO Bobby Lashley
NNO Kurt Angle

2024 Mattel WWE Ultimate Edition Series 20

NNO Asuka
NNO Roman Reigns
NNO Undertaker

2017 Mattel WWE Undertaker 5-Pack

NNO 1990/1994/1998/2014/2016 30.00 75.00

2019 Mattel WWE Wrekkin' Playsets

NNO Entrance Stage Playset 40.00 80.00
NNO Performance Center Playset 30.00 75.00
NNO Slam Mobile (w/Braun Strowman)20.00 40.00

2019 Mattel WWE Wrekkin' Series 1

NNO AJ Styles 10.00 20.00
NNO John Cena 12.50 25.00
NNO Seth Rollins 10.00 20.00
NNO Undertaker 15.00 30.00

2019 Mattel WWE Wrekkin' Series 2

NNO Miz
NNO Woken Matt Hardy

2019 Mattel WWE Wrekkin' Series 3

NNO Daniel Bryan
NNO Rey Mysterio

2020 Mattel WWE Wrekkin' Playsets

NNO Collision Cage 60.00 120.00
NNO Slambulance 50.00 100.00
NNO Slamcycle (w/Drew McIntyre) 30.00 60.00
NNO Slamcycle (w/Undertaker) 30.00 60.00

2020 Mattel WWE Wrekkin' Series 4

NNO Elias 20.00 40.00
NNO Roman Reigns 25.00 50.00

2010 Mattel WWE WrestleMania 26

NNO Chris Jericho
NNO Christian 15.00 30.00
NNO Drew McIntyre 12.50 25.00
NNO Kane
NNO Matt Hardy
NNO Shawn Michaels
NNO Shelton Benjamin

2011 Mattel WWE WrestleMania 27

NNO Alberto Del Rio 6.00 12.00
NNO Christian 20.00 40.00
NNO John Cena 12.50 25.00
NNO John Morrison 10.00 20.00
NNO Randy Orton 10.00 20.00
NNO Triple H 12.50 25.00

2021 Mattel WWE WrestleMania 37 Celebration

NNO Andre the Giant 20.00 40.00
NNO Macho Man Randy Savage 20.00 40.00

2014 Mattel WWE WrestleMania 30 Heritage

NNO Brock Lesnar
NNO John Cena 12.50 25.00
NNO The Rock 12.50 25.00
NNO Undertaker 10.00 20.00

2015 Mattel WWE WrestleMania 31 Heritage

NNO Hulk Hogan 15.00 30.00
NNO John Cena
NNO The Rock 12.50 25.00
NNO Shawn Michaels 10.00 20.00

2016 Mattel WWE WrestleMania 32 Heritage

NNO Cesaro 6.00 12.00
NNO Eddie Guerrero 10.00 20.00
NNO Razor Ramon 17.50 35.00
NNO Roman Reigns 7.50 15.00

2017 Mattel WWE WrestleMania 33 Heritage

NNO Chris Jericho 12.50 25.00
NNO Roman Reigns 15.00 30.00
NNO Stone Cold Steve Austin 10.00 20.00
NNO Undertaker 15.00 30.00

2018 Mattel WWE WrestleMania 34 Heritage

NNO AJ Styles 7.50 15.00
NNO Bayley 7.50 15.00
NNO Big Show 20.00 40.00
NNO Dean Ambrose 7.50 15.00
NNO Mojo Rawley 6.00 12.00
NNO Seth Rollins 7.50 15.00

2018 Mattel WWE WrestleMania 35 Heritage

NNO Charlotte Flair 12.50 25.00
NNO Elias 7.50 15.00
NNO John Cena
NNO Kevin Nash 10.00 20.00
NNO Matt Hardy 7.50 15.00
NNO Trish Stratus 12.50 25.00

2020 Mattel WWE WrestleMania 36 Heritage

NNO Batista 20.00 40.00
NNO Becky Lynch 12.50 25.00
NNO The Rock 15.00 30.00
NNO Seth Rollins 10.00 20.00
NNO Shane McMahon 15.00 30.00
NNO Stephanie McMahon 12.50 25.00

2021 Mattel WWE WrestleMania 37 Heritage

NNO Andrade 6.00 12.00
NNO Drew McIntyre 12.50 25.00
NNO The Fiend Bray Wyatt 12.50 25.00
NNO Ricochet 6.00 12.00

2021 Mattel WWE WrestleMania 38 Heritage

NNO Bianca Belair 15.00 30.00
NNO Hulk Hogan 12.50 25.00
NNO Seth Rollins 10.00 20.00
NNO Sheamus 10.00 20.00

2022 Mattel WWE WrestleMania 39 Heritage

NNO Andre the Giant 25.00 50.00
NNO Bianca Belair 15.00 30.00
NNO Kane 12.50 25.00
NNO Undertaker 12.50 25.00

2016 Mattel WWE Zombies Series 1

NNO Bray Wyatt 7.50 15.00
NNO Dean Ambrose 15.00 30.00
NNO John Cena 15.00 30.00
NNO Paige 7.50 15.00
NNO The Rock 12.50 25.00
NNO Roman Reigns 12.50 25.00
NNO Triple H 7.50 15.00
NNO Undertaker 12.50 25.00

2017 Mattel WWE Zombies Series 2

NNO Stone Cold Steve Austin 12.50 25.00
NNO AJ Styles 7.50 15.00
NNO Brock Lesnar 7.50 15.00
NNO Kevin Owens 6.00 12.00
NNO Sasha Banks 12.50 25.00
NNO Seth Rollins 7.50 15.00

2018 Mattel WWE Zombies Series 3

NNO Charlotte Flair 10.00 20.00
NNO Finn Balor 12.50 25.00
NNO Jeff Hardy 10.00 20.00
NNO Kane 20.00 40.00
NNO Matt Hardy 10.00 20.00
NNO Shinsuke Nakamura 10.00 20.00

1990 Multi Toys WWF Power Grip Squirts

NNO Big Boss Man
NNO Hulk Hogan
NNO Jake The Snake Roberts
NNO Macho King Randy Savage
NNO Ted DiBiase
NNO Ultimate Warrior

1990 Multi Toys WWF Power Grip Squirts Tag Teams

NNO Bushwhackers
NNO Legion of Doom
NNO The Rockers

1990 Multi Toys WWF Squirt Heads

NNO Big Boss Man
NNO Hulk Hogan
NNO Jake The Snake Roberts
NNO Macho King Randy Savage
NNO Ted DiBiase
NNO Ultimate Warrior

2017 Ooshies WWE Series 1

NNO Asuka R
NNO Booker T Black Trunks R
NNO Booker T R
NNO Bray Wyatt C
NNO Brie Bella R
NNO Brock Lesnar C
NNO Cesaro C
NNO Charlotte Flair R
NNO Dean Ambrose C
NNO Dolph Ziggler C
NNO Finn Balor (hologram) LE
NNO Finn Balor R
NNO Jey Uso R
NNO Jimmy Uso R
NNO John Cena C
NNO John Cena Never Give Up R
NNO Junkyard Dog R
NNO Kalisto (golden) LE
NNO Kalisto R
NNO Kane R
NNO Kevin Owens C
NNO Kofi Kingston Green Tights R
NNO Kofi Kingston R
NNO Macho Man Randy Savage (glow-in-the-dark) R
NNO Macho Man Randy Savage C
NNO The Miz C
NNO Nikki Bella R
NNO Randy Orton (glow-in-the-dark) R
NNO Randy Orton C
NNO The Rock (glow-in-the-dark) R
NNO The Rock C
NNO Roman Reigns C
NNO Seth Rollins C
NNO Sheamus C
NNO Sting R
NNO Sting Wolfpack LE
NNO Stone Cold Steve Austin C
NNO Ultimate Warrior (glow-in-the-dark) R
NNO Ultimate Warrior C
NNO Undertaker R

1991 Original San Francisco Toymakers CMLL Luchadores

NNO Atlantis 25.00 50.00
NNO Lizmark 30.00 75.00
NNO Pierroth
NNO Rayo de Jalisco
NNO Ultimo Dragon 50.00 100.00
NNO Vampiro Canadiense 60.00 120.00

1999-00 Original San Francisco Toymakers ECW Wrestling Accessories

NNO Hardcore Grapple Gear
NNO Wrestling Ring Gift Set (w/Rob Van Dam & Sabu) (Toys R Us Exclusive)

1999-00 Original San Francisco Toymakers ECW Wrestling Series 1

NNO Chris Candido 25.00 50.00
NNO Justin Credible 15.00 30.00
NNO Rob Van Dam 30.00 60.00
NNO Sabu 20.00 40.00
NNO Shane Douglas 15.00 30.00
NNO Taz 25.00 50.00

1999-00 Original San Francisco Toymakers ECW Wrestling Series 2

NNO Buh Buh Ray Dudley 20.00 40.00
NNO D-Von Dudley 20.00 40.00
NNO Lance Storm 15.00 30.00
NNO New Jack 30.00 75.00
NNO Tommy Dreamer 15.00 30.00

1999-00 Original San Francisco Toymakers ECW Wrestling Series 3

NNO Justin Credible
NNO New Jack
NNO Taz

1999-00 Original San Francisco Toymakers ECW Wrestling Series 4

NNO Axl Rotten 20.00 40.00
NNO Balls Mahoney 20.00 40.00
NNO Jerry Lynn 30.00 75.00
NNO Raven 25.00 50.00
NNO Rhino 30.00 60.00
NNO Rob Van Dam 30.00 60.00
NNO Taz 20.00 40.00
NNO Yoshihiro Tajiri 30.00 60.00

1999-00 Original San Francisco Toymakers ECW Wrestling Series 5

NNO Justin Credible 15.00 30.00
NNO Little Guido
NNO Mike Awesome 60.00 120.00
NNO Nova 25.00 50.00
NNO Sabu 30.00 60.00
NNO Sandman 30.00 75.00
NNO Steve Corino
NNO Super Crazy

1999-00 Original San Francisco Toymakers ECW Wrestling Series 6

NNO Balls Mahoney 25.00 50.00
NNO Chris Candido 30.00 60.00
NNO Lance Storm 20.00 40.00
NNO New Jack 30.00 75.00
NNO Raven 30.00 75.00
NNO Rhino 50.00 100.00
NNO Rob Van Dam 30.00 60.00
NNO Tommy Dreamer 20.00 40.00

1998 Original San Francisco Toymakers WCW

NNO Bret Hart 10.00 20.00
NNO Chris Benoit 12.50 25.00
NNO Diamond Dallas Page 20.00 40.00
NNO Goldberg 15.00 30.00
NNO Raven 7.50 15.00
NNO Rey Mysterio 12.50 25.00
NNO Ric Flair 10.00 20.00
NNO Sting 10.00 20.00

1998 Original San Francisco Toymakers WCW 12-Inch

NNO Bill Goldberg 20.00 40.00
NNO Hollywood Hulk Hogan 15.00 30.00
NNO Macho Man Randy Savage 20.00 40.00
NNO Sting/Black & White 15.00 30.00
NNO Sting/Red & Black 12.50 25.00

1998 Original San Francisco Toymakers WCW 4.5-Inch

NNO Goldberg 7.50 15.00
NNO Ric Flair 7.50 15.00
NNO Rick Steiner 6.00 12.00
NNO Sting 7.50 15.00

1997-98 Original San Francisco Toymakers WCW Boxed Sets

NNO Clash of the Champions 25.00 50.00
Lex Luger/Scott Hall
NNO Fall Brawl 10.00 20.00
Sting/Giant
NNO Fearsome Foursome 20.00 40.00
Goldberg/Flair/DDP/Chris Benoit
NNO Halloween Havoc 20.00 40.00
Giant/Savage
NNO Live on Forever 30.00 75.00
Hogan/Bagwell/Giant/Scott Steiner
NNO No Retreat No Surrender 25.00 50.00
Nash/Sting/Savage/Luger
NNO Starrcade 20.00 40.00
Hogan/Sting
NNO We Are the Champions 25.00 50.00
Goldberg/Giant/Hall/Hart
NNO World War 3 12.50 25.00
Page/Nash

1997 Original San Francisco Toymakers WCW Fly Buddies

NNO Giant 10.00 20.00
NNO Hollywood Hulk Hogan 15.00 30.00
NNO Sting 10.00 20.00

1998 Original San Francisco Toymakers WCW nWo 4.5-Inch

NNO Giant 5.00 10.00
NNO Hollywood Hogan 6.00 12.00
NNO Kevin Nash 5.00 10.00
NNO Lex Luger 3.00 8.00
NNO Macho Man Randy Savage 5.00 10.00
NNO Scott Hall 5.00 10.00
NNO Scott Steiner 3.00 8.00

1998 Original San Francisco Toymakers WCW nWo Series

NNO Curt Henning UER 6.00 12.00
NNO The Giant 6.00 12.00
NNO Hollywood Hogan 7.50 15.00
NNO Kevin Nash 6.00 12.00
NNO Lex Luger 5.00 10.00
NNO Macho Man Randy Savage 7.50 15.00
NNO Marcus Bagwell 3.00 8.00
NNO Scott Hall 6.00 12.00
NNO Scott Steiner 5.00 10.00
NNO Sting 6.00 12.00

1995 Original San Francisco Toymakers WCW Playsets

NNO Wrestling Ring & Cage 25.00 50.00

1998 Original San Francisco Toymakers WCW Playsets

NNO Battle Royal Wrestling Ring & Cage
Hogan/Nash/Savage/Sting/Rick Steiner/Luger
NNO Thunder Wrestling Ring & Cage 30.00 60.00
Nash/Giant/Luger/Sting
NNO Wrestling Ring & Cage w/Action Sounds 20.00 40.00
NNO Wrestling Ring & Cage w/Giant/Luger30.0075.00
NNO Wrestling Ring & Cage w/Sting KMART
NNO Wrestling Ring & Cage 20.00 40.00
Hogan/Rick Steiner/Savage/Sting

1995 Original San Francisco Toymakers WCW Series 1

1 Brian Knobbs 12.50 25.00
2 Hulk Hogan 30.00 75.00
3 Jerry Sags 10.00 20.00
4 Jimmy Hart ERR/Dk. Skin 150.00 300.00
5 Jimmy Hart/Lt. Skin 12.50 25.00
6 Johnny B. Badd 20.00 40.00
7 Kevin Sullivan 12.50 25.00
8 Ric Flair/Blue Tights 15.00 30.00
9 Ric Flair/Purple Tights 15.00 30.00
10 Sting 25.00 50.00
11 Vader 20.00 40.00

1995 Original San Francisco Toymakers WCW Series 1 (loose)

NNO Brian Knobbs
NNO Hulk Hogan
NNO Jerry Sags
NNO Jimmy Hart
NNO Johnny B. Badd
NNO Kevin Sullivan
NNO Ric Flair/Blue Tights
NNO Ric Flair/Purple Tights
NNO Sting
NNO Vader

1996 Original San Francisco Toymakers WCW Series 2

NNO Hulk Hogan 20.00 40.00
NNO Jimmy Hart 12.50 25.00
NNO Johnny B. Badd 15.00 30.00
NNO Kevin Sullivan 10.00 20.00
NNO Macho Man Randy Savage 50.00 100.00
NNO Ric Flair/Green Tights 15.00 30.00
NNO Ric Flair/Purple Tights 15.00 30.00
NNO Sting 20.00 40.00
NNO Vader 25.00 50.00

1996 Original San Francisco Toymakers WCW Series 3

NNO Alex Wright 12.50 25.00
NNO Big Bubba Rogers 10.00 20.00
NNO Booker T 7.50 15.00
NNO Craig Pittman 7.50 15.00
NNO Giant 12.50 25.00
NNO Hulk Hogan 15.00 30.00
NNO Macho Man Randy Savage 15.00 30.00
NNO Ric Flair 12.50 25.00
NNO Stevie Ray 10.00 20.00
NNO Sting 15.00 30.00

1998 Original San Francisco Toymakers WCW Special Edition

NNO Sting/Diamond Dallas Page
NNO Diamond Dallas Page
NNO nWo Wolfpack Sting
NNO Sting/nWo Wolfpack Sting
NNO Sting 15.00 30.00

1995 Original San Francisco Toymakers WCW Tag Teams Series 1

NNO Harlem Heat 25.00 50.00
NNO Hulk Hogan/Sting 60.00 120.00
NNO Nasty Boys/Black 15.00 30.00
NNO Nasty Boys/Green 75.00 150.00

1995 Original San Francisco Toymakers WCW Tag Teams Series 1 (loose)

NNO Booker T
NNO Brian Knobbs/Black
NNO Brian Knobbs/Green
NNO Hulk Hogan
NNO Jerry Sags/Black
NNO Jerry Sags/Green
NNO Stevie Ray
NNO Sting

1996 Original San Francisco Toymakers WCW Tag Teams Series 2

NNO Harlem Heat 30.00 60.00
NNO Hulk Hogan/Sting 75.00 150.00
NNO Nasty Boys 25.00 50.00

1996 Original San Francisco Toymakers WCW Tag Teams Series 3

NNO Blue Bloods 25.00 50.00
NNO Harlem Heat 20.00 40.00
NNO Hollywood Hogan/Macho Man 20.00 40.00

1997 Original San Francisco Toymakers WCW Vibrating Action Figures

NNO Chris Benoit 7.50 15.00
NNO Giant 7.50 15.00
NNO Hollywood Hulk Hogan 12.50 25.00
NNO Lex Luger 6.00 12.00
NNO Scott Hall 7.50 15.00
NNO Sting 10.00 20.00
NNO Taskmaster Kevin Sullivan 6.00 12.00

1999 Planet Toys WWF Head Crushers

NNO Mankind
NNO The Rock
NNO Stone Cold Steve Austin

2010 Playmates Lucha Libre Masked Warriors

NNO Charly Malice
NNO Lizmark Jr.
NNO Marco Corleone
NNO Super Nova

NNO Sydistiko
NNO Tinieblas Jr.

2010 Playmates Lucha Libre Masked Warriors Accessories

NNO Hexalateral Wrestling Ring

2010 Playmates Lucha Libre Masked Warriors Combo Packs

NNO Super Nova
NNO Tinieblas Jr.

2010 Playmates Lucha Libre Masked Warriors Masks

NNO Super Nova
NNO Tinieblas Jr.

2021 Pro Wrestling Tees Micro Brawlers AEW Wave 1

NNO Brodie Lee 20.00 40.00
NNO Chris Jericho 25.00 50.00
NNO Darby Allin 20.00 40.00
NNO Dr. Britt Baker, DMD 30.00 60.00
NNO Hikaru Shida 25.00 50.00
NNO Jon Moxley 25.00 50.00
NNO Orange Cassidy 30.00 75.00

2021-22 Pro Wrestling Tees Micro Brawlers AEW Crate Exclusive

NNO Sting 30.00 75.00
NNO Nyla Rose 15.00 30.00

2021-22 Pro Wrestling Tees Micro Brawlers AEW Limited Edition

NNO Christian Cage 25.00 50.00
NNO Sting (retro blue and orange)
NNO Sting (retro black and green chase)

2017 Pro Wrestling Tees Micro Brawlers Crate Exclusives

NNO Villain Marty Scurll 15.00 30.00
NNO Big Van Vader 20.00 40.00
NNO CM Punk 30.00 75.00
NNO Colt Cabana 15.00 30.00
NNO Joey Ryan 12.50 25.00
NNO Kenny Omega 20.00 40.00
NNO Matt Jackson
NNO Nick Jackson
NNO Penta El Zero M 30.00 60.00
NNO Taz 75.00 150.00

2018 Pro Wrestling Tees Micro Brawlers Crate Exclusives

NNO American Nightmare Cody 15.00 30.00
NNO Andre the Giant 25.00 50.00
NNO Bad Boy Tama Tonga 12.50 25.00
NNO Candice LeRae 10.00 20.00
NNO Eddie Guerrero 20.00 40.00
NNO Hangman Adam Page 25.00 50.00
NNO Kazuchika Okada 20.00 40.00
NNO Papa Shango 15.00 30.00
NNO Road Warrior Animal 30.00 60.00
NNO Road Warrior Hawk 25.00 50.00
NNO Tetsuya Naito 20.00 40.00
NNO ZSJ Zack Sabre Jr. 10.00 20.00

2019 Pro Wrestling Tees Micro Brawlers Crate Exclusives

NNO Bruiser Brody 20.00 40.00
NNO Brutus "The Barber" Beefcake 10.00 20.00
NNO Demolition Ax 15.00 30.00
NNO Demolition Smash 20.00 40.00
NNO Jeff Cobb 7.50 15.00
NNO Jim Ross 12.50 25.00
NNO Kota Ibushi 12.50 25.00
NNO Macho Man Randy Savage 30.00 60.00
NNO MJF 12.50 25.00
NNO Raven 20.00 40.00
NNO Rey Fenix 15.00 30.00
NNO Warrior 25.00 50.00

2020 Pro Wrestling Tees Micro Brawlers Crate Exclusives

NNO The Boogeyman 10.00 20.00
NNO Bret "The Hitman" Hart 20.00 40.00
NNO Brian Meyers
NNO Chris Hero 7.50 15.00
NNO El Generico 12.50 25.00
NNO Hacksaw Jim Duggan 10.00 20.00
NNO Honky Tonk Man 10.00 20.00
NNO Kamala 10.00 20.00
NNO Koko B. Ware 15.00 30.00
NNO Matt Cardona 15.00 30.00
NNO Tatanka 7.50 15.00
NNO Tommy Dreamer 15.00 30.00

2021 Pro Wrestling Tees Micro Brawlers Crate Exclusives

NNO Jake "The Snake" Roberts 15.00 30.00
(blue and yellow tights)
NNO Jake "The Snake" Roberts
(black and yellow tights chase)
NNO Owen Hart 12.50 25.00
(blue tights)
NNO Owen Hart
(red tights chase)
NNO Kevin Nash (Super Shredder) 15.00 30.00
(black tights)
NNO Kevin Nash (Super Shredder) 15.00 30.00
(purple tights chase)
NNO Tanga Loa 15.00 30.00
(camo tights)
NNO Tanga Loa 30.00 75.00
(black camo tights chase)
NNO Iron Sheik
(red and black boots)
NNO Iron Sheik
(yellow boots chase)
NNO Bully Ray 15.00 30.00
(black and white attire)
NNO Bully Ray 25.00 50.00
(black and red attire chase)
NNO Flyin' Brian Pillman 10.00 20.00
(tiger print tights)
NNO Flyin' Brian Pillman 30.00 60.00
(blue tights chase)
NNO Lex Luger 12.50 25.00
(red white and blue tights)
NNO Lex Luger 30.00 75.00
(red white and blue tights chase)
NNO Adam Bomb 12.50 25.00
(red and yellow tights)
NNO Adam Bomb 50.00 100.00
(orange and yellow tights chase)
NNO Shane Helms 15.00 30.00
(brown hair)
NNO Shane Helms 50.00 100.00
(green hair chase)
NNO Virgil 10.00 20.00
NNO Virgil 30.00 60.00
(chase)
NNO Glacier 15.00 30.00
(blue and white)
NNO Glacier 30.00 75.00
(light blue and white chase)

2020-21 Pro Wrestling Tees Micro Brawlers Limited Edition

NNO Big Van Vader
NNO Brian Knobs/350* 20.00 40.00
NNO Dragon Lee 20.00 40.00
(Online Exclusive)
NNO Dynamite Kid 25.00 50.00
NNO Francine/300* 50.00 100.00
NNO Frank the Clown/300* 20.00 40.00
NNO Iron Sheik/150* 75.00 150.00
NNO Jerry Sags/350* 20.00 40.00
NNO Jonathan Gresham 15.00 30.00
NNO Josh Mathews
NNO Kevin Nash/350* 30.00 75.00
NNO Kurt Angle/150* 100.00 200.00
NNO Loose Cannon Brian Pillman 20.00 40.00
(Online Exclusive)
NNO Luna Vachon 25.00 50.00
NNO Macho Man (black & white) 20.00 40.00
(Online Exclusive)
NNO Macho Man (classic orange) 15.00 30.00
(Online Exclusive)
NNO Macho Man (classic pink) 12.50 25.00
(Online Exclusive)
NNO Macho Man (lime green) 10.00 20.00
(Online Exclusive)
NNO Macho Man (Mega Powers) 20.00 40.00
(Online Exclusive)
NNO Macho Man (USA Edition) 25.00 50.00
(Online Exclusive)
NNO New Jack 20.00 40.00
(Online Exclusive)
NNO Owen Hart (Japanese Tour) 20.00 40.00
(Online Exclusive)
NNO Owen Hart/150* 100.00 200.00
NNO Psychosis 20.00 40.00
(Online Exclusive)
NNO Rob Van Dam (green tights) 125.00 250.00
(Online Exclusive chase)
NNO Rob Van Dam 30.00 60.00
(Online Exclusive)
NNO Sabu 20.00 40.00
(Online Exclusive)
NNO Sandman 20.00 40.00
(Online Exclusive)
NNO Sommarhausen 30.00 60.00
(Online Exclusive)
NNO Terry Funk

2022 Pro Wrestling Tees Micro Brawlers Limited Edition

NNO Andre the Giant
NNO British Bulldog

2021 Pro Wrestling Tees Micro Brawlers MLW Exclusives

NNO Alexander Hammerstone 30.00 60.00
NNO LA Park 60.00 120.00
NNO Richard Holliday 30.00 60.00

2020-21 Pro Wrestling Tees Micro Brawlers ROH Exclusives

NNO Angelina Love 20.00 40.00
NNO Danhausen 30.00 75.00
NNO Jonathan Gresham
NNO Session Moth Martina 10.00 20.00
NNO Shane Taylor 15.00 30.00

2021 Pro Wrestling Tees Micro Brawlers Staff Edition Exclusives

NNO Barracuda Mailbox Bomber/150*75.00 150.00
NNO Marvelous Matt Knicks/150* 20.00 40.00

2022 Pro Wrestling Tees Micro Brawlers Talk 'N Shop-a-Mania

NNO Sex Ferguson
NNO Chico El Luchador
NNO Chad 2 Badd

2018 Pro Wrestling Tees Micro Brawlers Wave 1

NNO British Bulldog
NNO Brooklyn Brawler
NNO Burnard the Business Bear 30.00 60.00
NNO Cheeseburger
NNO Chris Hero 7.50 15.00
NNO Cody 12.50 25.00
NNO Dalton Castle
NNO Jay Lethal
NNO Jay White 20.00 40.00
NNO Kenny Omega 25.00 50.00
NNO Ricky The Dragon Steamboat
NNO Rosemary
NNO Rowdy Roddy Piper 300.00 500.00
NNO Sami Callihan
NNO Swoggle
NNO Tenille Dashwood
NNO Vickie Guerrero 15.00 30.00
NNO Villain Marty Scurll 17.50 35.00

2018 Pro Wrestling Tees Micro Brawlers Wave 1 Limited Edition Tag Team 2-Packs

NNO The Briscoes
NNO The Young Bucks

2019 Pro Wrestling Tees Micro Brawlers Wave 2

NNO Brandi Rhodes
NNO Bushi
NNO Christopher Daniels
NNO Evil Uno 10.00 20.00
NNO Flip Gordon
NNO Frankie Kazarian 17.50 35.00
NNO Hiromu Takahashi 20.00 40.00
NNO Joey Ryan 15.00 30.00
NNO Sanada 20.00 40.00
NNO Scorpio Sky
NNO Tetsuya Naito 15.00 30.00

2019 Pro Wrestling Tees Micro Brawlers Wave 3

NNO Blue Meanie
NNO Brian Cage
NNO Colt Cabana 12.50 25.00
NNO Fat Ass Masa 50.00 100.00
NNO Hiroshi Tanahashi/250* 25.00 50.00
NNO Hot Mess Chelsea Green 30.00 60.00
NNO Johnny Gimmick Name 25.00 50.00
NNO King Kong Bundy
NNO Mandy Leon 30.00 75.00
NNO Villain Marty Scurll

2019 Pro Wrestling Tees Micro Brawlers Wave 4

NNO Bandido 15.00 30.00
NNO Big Poppa Pump Scott Steiner 30.00 75.00
NNO Bone Soldier Taiji Ishimori
NNO Flamboyant Juice Robinson 25.00 50.00
NNO Penta El Zero M
NNO Rush 7.50 15.00
NNO Tomohiro Ishii

2019 Pro Wrestling Tees Micro Brawlers Wave 4 Limited Edition Multi-Packs

NNO The Kingdom 3-Pack 30.00 75.00
NNO The Road Warriors 2-Pack

2020 Pro Wrestling Tees Micro Brawlers Wave 5

NNO Crown Jewel Chase Owens
NNO Dustin Rhodes
NNO Kazuchika Okada 20.00 40.00
NNO Terry Funk 25.00 50.00
NNO The Enforcer Arn Anderson
NNO Underboss Bad Luck Fale 20.00 40.00

2020 Pro Wrestling Tees Micro Brawlers Wave 6

NNO Brody King 20.00 40.00
NNO Ian Riccaboni 15.00 30.00
NNO PCO
NNO Rhino 25.00 50.00
NNO Taya Valkyrie
NNO Undeniable Tessa B 20.00 40.00

1985 Remco AWA Wrestling Accessories and Playsets

NNO Battle Royal Playset (w/7 figures)400.00 600.00
NNO Battle Royal Playset 2 (w/7 figures)500.00800.00
NNO Championship Belt Figure Holder200.00 400.00
NNO Regular Ring Playset 125.00 200.00
NNO Steel Cage Match 300.00 600.00

1986 Remco AWA Wrestling Mini-Mashers

NNO Animal
NNO Barbarian
NNO Boris Zhukov
NNO Curt Henning
NNO Hawk
NNO Larry Zbyszko
NNO Marty Jannetty
NNO Nick Bockwinkel
NNO Ric Flair
NNO Scott Hall
NNO Shawn Michaels
NNO Stan Hansen

1986 Remco AWA Wrestling Mini-Mashers Green

NNO Animal
NNO Barbarian
NNO Boris Zhukov
NNO Curt Henning
NNO Hawk
NNO Larry Zbyszko
NNO Marty Jannetty
NNO Nick Bockwinkel
NNO Ric Flair
NNO Scott Hall
NNO Shawn Michaels
NNO Stan Hansen

1986 Remco AWA Wrestling Mini-Mashers Packs

NNO 4-Pack 25.00 50.00
NNO 8-Pack 50.00 100.00
NNO 12-Pack 60.00 120.00

1986 Remco AWA Wrestling Mini-Mashers Purple

NNO Animal
NNO Barbarian
NNO Boris Zhukov
NNO Curt Henning
NNO Hawk
NNO Larry Zbyszko
NNO Marty Jannetty
NNO Nick Bockwinkel
NNO Ric Flair
NNO Scott Hall
NNO Shawn Michaels
NNO Stan Hansen

1986 Remco AWA Wrestling Mini-Mashers Red

NNO Animal
NNO Barbarian
NNO Boris Zhukov
NNO Curt Henning
NNO Hawk
NNO Larry Zbyszko
NNO Marty Jannetty
NNO Nick Bockwinkel
NNO Ric Flair
NNO Scott Hall
NNO Shawn Michaels
NNO Stan Hansen

1985 Remco AWA Wrestling Series 1

NNO Fabulous Ones 100.00 200.00
Steve Keirn/Stan Lane
NNO High Flyers 100.00 200.00
Greg Gagne/Jim Brunzell
NNO Ric Flair/Larry Zbyszko 125.00 250.00
NNO Rick Martel/Baron von Raschke w/AWA Ring 125.00 250.00
NNO Rick Martel/Baron von Raschke w/AWA Sticker 75.00 150.00
NNO Road Warriors 200.00 400.00
Animal/Hawk No Belts
NNO Road Warriors 150.00 300.00
Animal/Hawk w/Belts

1985 Remco AWA Wrestling Series 1 (loose)

NNO Animal 6.00 12.00
NNO Baron Von Raschke 7.50 15.00
NNO Greg Gagne 7.50 15.00
NNO Hawk 6.00 12.00
NNO Jim Brunzell 6.00 12.00
NNO Larry Zbyszko 6.00 12.00
NNO Ric Flair 15.00 30.00
NNO Rick Martel 12.50 25.00
NNO Stan Lane 6.00 15.00
NNO Steve Keirn 6.00 12.00

1985 Remco AWA Wrestling Series 2

NNO Fabulous Freebirds 100.00 200.00
Buddy Roberts/Terry Gordy/Michael Hayes
NNO Gagne's Raiders 125.00 250.00
Greg Gagne/Curt Henning
NNO Jimmy Garvin/Precious/Steve Regal75.00 150.00
NNO Long Riders 100.00 200.00
Wild Bill Irwin/Scott Hog Irwin
NNO Road Warriors 150.00 300.00
Animal/Hawk/Paul Ellering

1985 Remco AWA Wrestling Series 2 (loose)

NNO Animal 10.00 20.00
NNO Buddy Roberts 12.50 25.00
NNO Curt Henning 10.00 20.00
NNO Greg Gagne 6.00 12.00
NNO Hawk 10.00 20.00
NNO Jimmy Garvin 10.00 20.00
NNO Michael Hayes 12.50 25.00
NNO Paul Ellering 12.50 25.00
NNO Precious 10.00 20.00
NNO Scott Hog Irwin 7.50 15.00
NNO Steve Regal 6.00 12.00
NNO Terry Gordy 12.50 25.00
NNO Wild Bill Irwin 7.50 15.00

1985 Remco AWA Wrestling Series 2 Fight to the Finish 2-Pack

NNO Steve Regal vs. Curt Hennig (w/VHS Tape) 50.00 100.00

1985 Remco AWA Wrestling Series 3

NNO Nick Bockwinkel vs. Larry Zbyszko150.00 300.00
NNO Scott Hall vs. Gorgeous Jimmy Garvin 150.00 300.00
NNO Stan Hansen vs. Jerry Blackwell100.00 200.00
NNO Carlos Colon vs. Abdullah the Butcher 150.00 300.00

1985 Remco AWA Wrestling Series 3 (loose)

NNO Abdullah the Butcher 20.00 40.00
NNO Carlos Colon 7.50 15.00
NNO Gorgeous Jimmy Garvin 5.00 10.00
NNO Jerry Blackwell 10.00 20.00
NNO Larry Zbyszko 15.00 30.00
NNO Nick Bockwinkel 20.00 40.00
NNO Referee Curley Brown 12.50 25.00
NNO Referee Nasty Ned 15.00 30.00
NNO Scott Hall 30.00 75.00
NNO Stan Hansen 20.00 40.00

1986 Remco AWA Wrestling Series 4

NNO Boris Zhukov 300.00 600.00
NNO Buddy Rose 250.00 500.00
NNO Doug Somers 200.00 400.00
NNO Marty Jannetty 400.00 800.00
NNO Nick Bockwinkel
NNO Nord the Barbarian 250.00 500.00
NNO Paul Ellering
NNO Referee Dick Woehrle 200.00 350.00
NNO Ric Flair 500.00 1000.00
NNO Shawn Michaels 750.00 1500.00
NNO Sheik Adnan Al-Kaissie 200.00 400.00

1986 Remco AWA Wrestling Series 4 (loose)

NNO Boris Zhukov 125.00 250.00
NNO Buddy Rose 125.00 250.00
NNO Doug Somers 100.00 200.00
NNO Marty Jannetty 150.00 300.00
NNO Nord the Barbarian 150.00 300.00
NNO Referee Dick Woehrle 60.00 120.00
NNO Shawn Michaels 250.00 400.00
NNO Sheik Adnan Al-Kaissie 250.00 500.00

1985 Remco AWA Wrestling Thumbsters

NNO Greg Gagne vs. Hawk 30.00 75.00
NNO Ric Flair vs. Larry Zbyszko 50.00 100.00
NNO Rick Martel vs. Animal 30.00 75.00

1985 Remco AWA Wrestling Thumbsters (loose)

NNO Animal 7.50 15.00
NNO Greg Gagne 5.00 10.00
NNO Hawk 7.50 15.00
NNO Larry Zbyszko 5.00 10.00
NNO Ric Flair 10.00 20.00
NNO Rick Martel 7.50 15.00

1998 Ringside Supplies WWF Squirt Heads Cellophane Package

NNO The Rock
NNO Stone Cold Steve Austin
NNO Undertaker

1998 Ringside Supplies WWF Squirt Heads Mesh Package

NNO The Rock
NNO Stone Cold Steve Austin
NNO Undertaker

2017 S.H. Figuarts WWE

NNO Kane 30.00 75.00
NNO The Rock 30.00 60.00
NNO Stone Cold Steve Austin 20.00 40.00
NNO Triple H 12.50 25.00
NNO Undertaker 30.00 75.00
NNO Vince McMahon

1990 Spectra Star WWF Rad Rollers Collection

NNO Hogan/Roberts/Savage
Big Boss Man/DiBiase/Warrior

1990 Spectra Star WWF Rad Rollers Collection (loose)

NNO Big Boss Man
NNO Hulk Hogan
NNO Jake The Snake Roberts
NNO Macho King Randy Savage
NNO Ted DiBiase
NNO Ultimate Warrior

1990 Spectra Star WWF Superstars Radical Flying Discs

NNO Ultimate Warrior (green)
NNO Ultimate Warrior (pink)

1991 Spectra Star WWF Superstars Radical Flying Discs

NNO Hulk Hogan

2019 Super 7 ReAction Wrestling Figures

NNO Andre the Giant (singlet)
NNO Andre the Giant (w/vest)

2021 Super 7 Ultimate Wrestling Figures

NNO Brian Meyers

NNO Doc Gallows
NNO Karl Anderson
NNO Matt Cardona

2017 TeenyMates WWE Collector Sets

NNO WWE Hall of Fame Inductees
NNO WWE Superstars (w/Andre the Giant GITD)

2016 TeenyMates WWE Series 1

NNO Big Show C
NNO Bray Wyatt C
NNO Bret Hart C
NNO Brie Bella C
NNO Brock Lesnar C
NNO Daniel Bryan C
NNO Dean Ambrose C
NNO Dolph Ziggler C
NNO Goldust C
NNO Jey Uso C
NNO Jimmy Uso C
NNO John Cena (crystal clear) R
NNO John Cena C
NNO Kane C
NNO Kofi Kingston C
NNO Macho Man Randy Savage (orange) C
NNO Macho Man Randy Savage (glow-in-the-dark) R (Collector Tin Exclusive)
NNO Macho Man Randy Savage (purple) R
NNO Nikki Bella C
NNO Randy Orton C
NNO The Rock C
NNO The Rock (metallic gold) UR
NNO Roman Reigns C
NNO Seth Rollins C
NNO Sheamus C
NNO Sin Cara C
NNO Stardust C
NNO Sting C
NNO Stone Cold Steve Austin C
NNO Triple H C
NNO Ultimate Warrior C
NNO Undertaker (glow-in-the-dark) R
NNO Undertaker C

2017 TeenyMates WWE Series 2

NNO AJ Styles C
NNO Andre the Giant C
NNO Andre the Giant (glow-in-the-dark) R (Collector's Set Exclusive)
NNO Becky Lynch C
NNO Big E C
NNO Bray Wyatt C
NNO Brock Lesnar C
NNO Chris Jericho C
NNO Dean Ambrose C
NNO Finn Balor C
NNO Finn Balor (glow-in-the-dark) R
NNO Jake the Snake Roberts C
NNO John Cena (ice blue) R
NNO John Cena C
NNO Kane C
NNO Kevin Owens C
NNO Kofi Kingston C
NNO Macho Man Randy Savage C
NNO Mankind C
NNO Ric Flair (blue robe) UR
NNO Ric Flair (pink robe) C
NNO The Rock C
NNO Roman Reigns C
NNO Rowdy Roddy Piper C
NNO Sasha Banks C
NNO Seth Rollins C
NNO Sgt. Slaughter R
NNO Shawn Michaels C
NNO Sting C
NNO Triple H C
NNO Ultimate Warrior C
NNO Ultimate Warrior (metallic gold) UR
NNO Xavier Woods C

2019 Tomy WWE Blitz Brawlers

NNO AJ Styles
NNO John Cena

1990 Tonka WWF Wrestling Buddies

NNO Big Boss Man 100.00 200.00
NNO Hulk Hogan 250.00 500.00
NNO Jake "The Snake" Roberts 325.00 650.00
NNO Macho King Randy Savage 150.00 300.00
NNO Ted DiBiase 400.00 800.00
NNO Ultimate Warrior 250.00 500.00

1990 Tonka WWF Wrestling Buddies (loose)

NNO Animal (Legion of Doom)
NNO Big Boss Man
NNO Hawk (Legion of Doom)
NNO Hulk Hogan
NNO Jake "The Snake" Roberts
NNO Macho King Randy Savage
NNO Ted DiBiase
NNO Ultimate Warrior

1990 Tonka WWF Wrestling Buddies Tag Team

NNO Legion of Doom

2005 Toy Biz Best of TNA Series 1

NNO AJ Styles
NNO Elix Skipper
NNO Jeff Hardy
NNO Ron Killings

2006 Toy Biz Best of TNA Series 2

NNO AJ Styles
NNO Chris Sabin
NNO Jeff Hardy
NNO Monty Brown
NNO Raven
NNO Ron Killings

2005 Toy Biz TNA Wrestling 2-Packs Series 1

NNO BG James/Konnan 15.00 30.00
NNO Elix Skipper/C. Daniels 12.50 25.00
NNO James Storm/Chris Harris 30.00 75.00

2006 Toy Biz TNA Wrestling 2-Packs Series 2

NNO AJ Styles vs. Samoa Joe 20.00 40.00
NNO Jeff Hardy vs. Abyss 50.00 100.00
NNO Jeff Jarrett vs. Monty Brown 20.00 40.00

2006 Toy Biz TNA Wrestling 2-Packs Series 3

NNO BG James/Kip James 20.00 40.00
NNO Raven vs. Sabu 30.00 75.00
NNO Sting vs. Jeff Jarrett 25.00 50.00

2007 Toy Biz TNA Wrestling 2-Packs Series 4

NNO Christian Cage/Rhyno 20.00 40.00
NNO Christopher Daniels 15.00 30.00
Homicide
NNO Kevin Nash/Chris Sabin 20.00 40.00

2007 TNA Wrestling Bashin' Brawlers Series 1

NNO Samoa Joe 12.50 25.00
NNO Sting 15.00 30.00

2007 TNA Wrestling Bashin' Brawlers Series 2

NNO Christian Cage 10.00 20.00
NNO Kevin Nash 10.00 20.00

2007 Toy Biz TNA Wrestling Collector's Edition 12-Inch Series 1

NNO AJ Styles 30.00 60.00
NNO Sting 30.00 75.00

2007 Toy Biz TNA Wrestling Collector's Edition 12-Inch Series 2

NNO Christopher Daniels 15.00 30.00
NNO Kurt Angle 25.00 50.00

2006 Toy Biz TNA Wrestling Masked Fury

NNO Abyss 20.00 40.00
NNO Shark Boy 20.00 40.00
NNO Sting 25.00 50.00

2005 Toy Biz TNA Wrestling Playsets

NNO 6-Sided Wrestling Ring 75.00 150.00
w/AJ Styles

2006 Toy Biz TNA Wrestling Playsets

NNO Lockdown Six Sides of Steel
w/Christian Cage
NNO Champion X Ring
w/AJ Styles
NNO Championship Belt
w/AJ Styles & Jeff Jarrett#{Blue Package
NNO Championship Belt
w/AJ Styles & Jeff Jarrett#{Red Package

2007 Toy Biz TNA Wrestling Playsets

NNO Ultimate X Ring 50.00 100.00
w/Christopher Daniels

2005 Toy Biz TNA Wrestling Series 1

NNO Abyss 15.00 30.00
NNO AJ Styles 20.00 40.00
NNO Jeff Jarrett 12.50 25.00
NNO Raven 12.50 25.00

2005 Toy Biz TNA Wrestling Series 2

NNO Christopher Daniels 12.50 25.00
NNO Jeff Hardy 20.00 40.00
NNO Ron The Truth Killings 15.00 30.00
NNO Shark Boy 12.50 25.00

2005 Toy Biz TNA Wrestling Series 3

NNO AJ Styles 15.00 30.00
NNO Alpha Male Monty Brown 20.00 40.00
NNO Chris Sabin 20.00 40.00
NNO Raven/Straight Jacket 12.50 25.00

2006 Toy Biz TNA Wrestling Series 4

NNO Kevin Nash
NNO Petey Williams 12.50 25.00
NNO Rhino 20.00 40.00
NNO Wildcat Chris Harris 7.50 15.00
Mustache
NNO Wildcat Chris Harris
No Mustache

2006 Toy Biz TNA Wrestling Series 5

NNO James Cowboy Storm 10.00 20.00
NNO Kip James 10.00 20.00
NNO Kip James/Black Trunks
NNO Lance Hoyt 15.00 30.00
NNO Lance Hoyt/White Pants
NNO Samoa Joe 12.50 25.00
NNO Samoa Joe
Blue and Black Trunks
NNO Sting 15.00 30.00

2007 Toy Biz TNA Wrestling Series 6

NNO Alex Shelley 10.00 20.00
NNO Alex Shelley
Green on Shorts
NNO Christian Cage 12.50 25.00
NNO Jay Lethal 12.50 25.00
NNO Jay Lethal/Green Gear
NNO Sonjay Dutt 7.50 15.00
NNO Sonjay Dutt/Green Gear

2007 Toy Biz TNA Wrestling Series 7

NNO Brother Devon 10.00 20.00
NNO Matt Bentley 10.00 20.00
NNO Robert Roode 12.50 25.00
NNO Robert Roode/Team Canada
NNO Scott Steiner 15.00 30.00
NNO Scott Steiner/Black Pants

2007 Toy Biz TNA Wrestling Series 8

NNO Chase Stevens 15.00 30.00
NNO Chase Stevens
Headband and Jacket
NNO Eric Young 12.50 25.00
NNO Eric Young/Team Canada 20.00 40.00
NNO James Mitchell CH 20.00 40.00
NNO Kurt Angle 10.00 20.00
NNO Senshi 20.00 40.00
NNO Senshi/Black Pants 25.00 50.00

2000 Toy Biz WCW Bash at the Beach

NNO Bret Hitman Hart
NNO Diamond Dallas Page
NNO Goldberg 10.00 20.00
NNO Lex Luger 6.00 12.00
NNO Sting

1998 Toy Biz WCW Bashin' Brawlers

NNO Big Poppa Pump Scott Steiner
NNO Diamond Dallas Page 30.00 75.00
NNO Goldberg 60.00 120.00
NNO Hollywood Hogan 75.00 150.00

NNO Kevin Nash
NNO Macho Man Randy Savage 50.00 100.00
NNO Sting 60.00 120.00
NNO Sting (Wolfpac)

2000 Toy Biz WCW Battle Arms

NNO Sting 12.50 25.00
NNO Goldberg 15.00 30.00
NNO Bret Hitman Hart 12.50 25.00

1999 Toy Biz WCW Bend 'N Flex

NNO Booker T 7.50 15.00
NNO Bret Hart 6.00 12.00
NNO Diamond Dallas Page 6.00 12.00
NNO Goldberg 10.00 20.00
NNO Kevin Nash 12.50 25.00
NNO Scott Hall 7.50 15.00
NNO Scott Steiner 6.00 12.00
NNO Sting 7.50 15.00

1999 Toy Biz WCW Bend 'N Flex 6-Pack

NNO Sting/Goldberg/DDP 25.00 50.00
Hall/Steiner/Nash

1999 Toy Biz WCW Boxed Sets

NNO Heavyweight Champions 30.00 75.00
Hogan/Goldberg/Sting
NNO IV Horsemen 15.00 30.00
Flair/Benoit/Malenko/Mongo
NNO Red & Black Attack 30.00 60.00
Hogan/Bischoff/Nash

1999 Toy Biz WCW Brawlin' Bikers

NNO DDP
NNO Goldberg 7.50 15.00
NNO Hulk Hogan 20.00 40.00
NNO Sting 10.00 20.00

2001 Toy Biz WCW Bruisers

NNO Bam Bam Bigelow 7.50 15.00
NNO DDP 12.50 25.00
NNO Disco Inferno 10.00 20.00
NNO Goldberg 20.00 40.00
NNO Kevin Nash 10.00 20.00
NNO Kidman 10.00 20.00
NNO Randy Macho Man Savage 12.50 25.00
NNO Raven 7.50 15.00
NNO Rey Mysterio Jr. 15.00 30.00
NNO Stevie Ray 10.00 20.00
NNO Sting 15.00 30.00
NNO Wrath 7.50 15.00

1999 Toy Biz WCW Collector's Edition 8-Inch Figures

NNO Hollywood Hogan TAR
NNO Kevin Nash TAR
NNO Sting KB

2000 Toy Biz WCW Grip 'N Flip Series 2

NNO Kevin Nash vs. Konnan 10.00 20.00
NNO Scott Steiner vs. Rick Steiner 7.50 15.00
NNO Sting vs. Buff Bagwell 7.50 15.00

2000 Toy Biz WCW Gross-Out Wrestlers

NNO Goldberg 30.00 75.00
NNO Sid Vicious 25.00 50.00
NNO Sting 50.00 100.00

1999 Toy Biz WCW Head Ringers

NNO Bret Hart
NNO Buff Bagwell
NNO Diamond Dallas Page
NNO Goldberg
NNO Hulk Hogan
NNO Kevin Nash
NNO Konnan
NNO Sting

1999 Toy Biz WCW Head Ringers (loose)

NNO Bret Hart
NNO Buff Bagwell
NNO Diamond Dallas Page
NNO Goldberg
NNO Hulk Hogan
NNO Kevin Nash
NNO Konnan
NNO Sting

2000 Toy Biz WCW Main Event 2-Packs

NNO Goldberg/Sid Vicious
NNO Hulk Hogan/Ric Flair 40.00 80.00
NNO Sting/The Total Package 30.00 60.00

2000 Toy Biz WCW Nitro Active Wrestlers

NNO Buff Bagwell/Black Pants
NNO Buff Bagwell/Red Pants
NNO Goldberg
NNO Jeff Jarrett
NNO Kevin Nash

1999 Toy Biz WCW Playset

NNO Electronic Monday Nitro Arena 125.00 250.00

2000 Toy Biz WCW Power Slam

NNO Buff Bagwell 7.50 15.00
NNO Dennis Rodman/Blue Hair 10.00 20.00
NNO Dennis Rodman/Green Hair
NNO Dennis Rodman/Orange Hair 15.00 30.00
NNO Goldberg 25.00 50.00
NNO Hak 15.00 30.00
NNO Hollywood Hogan 12.50 25.00
NNO Hulk Hogan 12.50 25.00
NNO Kanyon 6.00 12.00
NNO Kevin Nash 10.00 20.00
NNO Rowdy Roddy Piper 10.00 20.00
NNO Sid Vicious 7.50 15.00
NNO Sting 7.50 15.00

1999 Toy Biz WCW Ring Announcers

NNO Mean Gene 30.00 60.00
{w/Nash & Goldberg
NNO Michael Buffer 15.00 30.00
{w/Scott Steiner & DDP

2001 Toy Biz WCW Ring Fighters

NNO Booker T/Dk Tights 12.50 25.00
NNO Booker T/White Tights 10.00 20.00
NNO Bret Hart 7.50 15.00
NNO Chris Benoit/Red Tights 7.50 15.00
NNO Chris Benoit/Blue Tights 10.00 20.00
NNO Goldberg 10.00 20.00
NNO Scott Steiner/Black Tights
NNO Scott Steiner/White Tights 10.00 20.00
NNO Sting 12.50 25.00

1999 Toy Biz WCW Ring Masters

NNO Bret Hart 10.00 20.00
NNO Chris Jericho 10.00 20.00
NNO Goldberg 15.00 30.00
NNO Hulk Hogan 12.50 25.00
NNO Lex Luger 7.50 15.00
NNO Rick Steiner 10.00 20.00

2000 Toy Biz WCW Road Rebels

NNO Goldberg
NNO Hulk Hogan
NNO Sting

1999 Toy Biz WCW Road Wild Wrestlers

NNO Goldberg 25.00 50.00
NNO Hollywood Hogan 30.00 60.00
NNO Kevin Nash 15.00 30.00
NNO Sting 20.00 40.00

1999 Toy Biz WCW Rumble 'N Roar

NNO Goldberg 25.00 50.00
NNO Sting 30.00 60.00

1999 Toy Biz WCW Slam 'N Crunch

NNO Buff Bagwell 10.00 20.00
NNO Goldberg 15.00 30.00
NNO Kevin Nash 10.00 20.00
NNO Konnan 15.00 30.00
NNO Saturn
NNO Sting 12.50 25.00

2001 Toy Biz WCW Slam Force

NNO Bret Hart 20.00 40.00
NNO Goldberg
NNO Hollywood Hogan
NNO Kevin Nash 12.50 25.00
NNO Lex Luger

1999 Toy Biz WCW Smash 'N Slam

NNO DDP/No Vest 12.50 25.00
NNO DDP/Vest 6.00 12.00
NNO Giant w/Luchadore 10.00 20.00
NNO Goldberg KB
NNO Goldberg w/Blue 10.00 20.00
{Masked Lucha
NNO Goldberg w/Red 15.00 30.00
Masked Lucha
NNO Hollywood Hogan/ 10.00 20.00
No Tank Top
NNO Hollywood Hogan/ 12.50 25.00
Tank Top
NNO Kevin Nash w/Referee/ 7.50 15.00
No Red Pants
NNO Kevin Nash w/Referee/ 7.50 15.00
Red Pants
NNO Lex Luger/No Shirt 6.00 12.00
NNO Lex Luger/Shirt 12.50 25.00
NNO Macho Man/Black and Red 15.00 30.00
NNO Macho Man/Black and White 10.00 20.00
NNO Scott Hall/Black and Red 12.50 25.00
NNO Scott Hall/Black and White 12.50 25.00
NNO Sting/Black and Red 10.00 20.00
NNO Sting/Black and White 15.00 30.00

1999 Toy Biz WCW Smash 'N Slam 2-Packs

NNO The Giant/Kevin Nash
NNO Macho Man/Miss Elizabeth
NNO Sting/Hulk Hogan 15.00 30.00

2001 Toy Biz WCW Target Exclusives

NNO Hollywood Hogan 20.00 40.00
NNO Kevin Nash 12.50 25.00

2000 Toy Biz WCW Thunder Slam

NNO Bagwell/Jarrett/Vampiro
NNO Goldberg/Bam Bam Bigelow 10.00 20.00
NNO Scott Hall/KevinNash 20.00 40.00
NNO Sting/Bret Hart 10.00 20.00

2001 Toy Biz WCW TNT

NNO Goldberg 17.50 35.00
NNO Jeff Jarrett 12.50 25.00
NNO Scott Steiner 15.00 30.00
NNO Vampiro 12.50 25.00

2000 Toy Biz WCW Tuff Talkin' Wrestlers

NNO Scott Steiner 15.00 30.00
NNO Buff Bagwell 15.00 30.00
NNO Macho Man Randy Savage 25.00 50.00
NNO Konnan 12.50 25.00

2000 Toy Biz WCW Tuff Talkin' Wrestlers 2-Packs

NNO Goldberg/Kevin Nash 30.00 75.00
NNO Sting/Diamond Dallas Page 30.00 60.00

2000 Toy Biz WCW Unleashed

NNO Franchise (Shane Douglas) 15.00 30.00
NNO Kidman 15.00 30.00
NNO Mike Awesome 10.00 20.00
NNO Vampiro 12.50 25.00

2000 Toy Biz WCW Whiplashers

NNO Kidman vs. Rey Mysterio
NNO Scott Steiner vs. Buff Bagwell
NNO Sting vs. Goldberg

2000 Toy Biz WCW Window Crashers

NNO Goldberg
NNO Hulk Hogan
NNO Kevin Nash
NNO Sting

2019 Zag Toys Domez WWE

NNO Andre the Giant
NNO Jake The Snake Roberts
NNO Macho Man Randy Savage
NNO Ric Flair
NNO Rowdy Roddy Piper
NNO Sting
NNO Stone Cold Steve Austin
NNO Undertaker
NNO Undertaker Clear CH

2000 Hot Wheels Monster Jam WCW Monday Nitro 1:64

NNO Goldberg
NNO Grave Digger
NNO Nitro
NNO Sting